GOLF DIGEST'S PLACES *to* PLAY

3RD EDITION

Fodor's Travel Publications, Inc.

New York . Toronto . London . Sydney . Auckland

Fodor's   **GOLF DIGEST**

Copyright © 1998 The New York Times Company
Magazine Group, Inc.

All rights reserved under International and Pan-American Copyright Conventions. Published in the United States by Fodor's Travel Publications, Inc., a subsidiary of Random House, Inc., New York, and simultaneously in Canada by Random House of Canada Limited, Toronto. Distributed by Random House, Inc., New York.

ISBN 0-679-03402-1
Third Edition

The essay "Taking Your Act on the Road,"
by Guy Yocom, adapted from GOLF DIGEST 1990, copyright ©
1990, 1998 Golf Digest/Tennis, Inc.

Special Sales
Fodor's Travel Publications are available at special discounts for bulk purchases for sales promotions or premiums. Special editions, including personalized covers, excerpts of existing guides, and corporate imprints, can be created in large quantities for special needs. For more information, contact your local bookseller or write to Special Markets, Fodor's Travel Publications, 201 East 50th Street, New York, NY 10022. Inquiries from Canada should be directed to your local Canadian bookseller or sent to Random House of Canada, Ltd., Marketing Department, 2775 Matheson Blvd. East, Mississauga, Ontario L4W 4P7. Inquiries from the United Kingdom should be sent to Fodor's Travel Publications, 20 Vauxhall Bridge Road, London SW1V 2SA, England.

PRINTED IN THE
UNITED STATES OF AMERICA
10 9 8 7 6 5 4 3 2 1

Cover design by Lyndell Brookhouse-Gil.
Cover photographs by Jim Moriarty, taken at Coeur d'Alene Resort Golf Course on Lake Coeur d'Alene, Idaho.

Contents

Welcome to Golf Digest's Places to Play

We are currently in the midst of an astonishing boom in golf course construction. More than 400 courses are opening their doors for business in North America every year, and the growth of the game shows no sign of abating. There are new courses on mountain tops, across searing deserts, amid tropical jungles, alongside oceans, and downtown in a city near you. Never has there been such a choice of great places to go and play golf.

Faced with so many options, how do you decide which course deserves your money? There's nothing worse than paying out a hefty green fee only to be confronted by a boring layout in bad condition, where the staff is rude and the sandwiches in the clubhouse are stale.

As with all good decisions, the key is in having the right information, and that's where *Places to Play* steps in. The goal of *Places to Play* is simple: to provide you with the most comprehensive information on public-access golf courses in North America. No one else has attempted to rate all of the best courses on a national basis. And the courses are rated neither by the editors of GOLF DIGEST, nor by a panel of "experts," but by the most knowledgeable people in the game: the golfers.

The methodology: We began *Places to Play* in 1963. In this edition, some 18,000 GOLF DIGEST subscribers filled out a course ballot, sharing their opinions and experiences on more than 5,000 courses in the U.S., Canada, Mexico and the Caribbean.

The subscribers were asked to rate each course they had played within the previous year on three criteria: the overall golf experience, the value for money, and the standard of service at the facility. In addition, subscribers were invited to write comments on their experiences at each of the courses they rated—both the good and the bad.

All the numbers and comments were fed into a massive database. The figures for the overall golf experience were averaged out and used to determine each course's star rating, from one to five. The top-50 point scorers in value for money were designated "Great Value" courses; the next 150 scorers were designated as "Good Value." Similarly, the scores for service were used to determine the "Great Service" and "Good Service" facilities.

A team of 12 editors spent countless long evenings editing the comments for each individual course—great care was taken to use comments that were fair, accurate, and representative of the sample. Meanwhile, all the 5,000-plus courses were contacted for their latest, up-to-date information, such as their name, address, and green fee. All of the new information was fed into the database. Finally, the whole book was fact-checked and edited.

The cast: *Places to Play* was compiled by GOLF DIGEST staff including: John Barton, Bob Carney, Nick DiDio, Peter Farricker, Lisa Furlong, Byrute Johnson, Mike Johnson, Mary Jane McGirr, Yaminah McKessey, Mike O'Malley, Alan Pittman, Ginnie Preuss, Sue Sawyer, Cliff Schrock, Topsy Siderowf, Scott Smith, Mike Stachura, Lisa Sweet, Joan Sweet, Jerry Tarde, Bill Walsh, Ed Weathers, Ron Whitten, Melissa Yow and Hunki Yun.

It was a long but rewarding task, one that has made *Places to Play* as essential to golf as your favorite putter.

—**John Barton**
Senior Editor, GOLF DIGEST

Taking Your Act on the Road

**How to plan your next group golf vacation:
Take along a chief, a bookie, an accountant and a chef**

By Guy Yocom
Senior Editor, GOLF DIGEST

When Hinedog, a shrewd but companionable golf buddy from Virginia, phoned me about the possibility of going on a golf vacation, the first thing I did was try to change the subject. I'd never taken a conventional golf vacation, but I'd observed many of them in my line of work and was dead sure I wanted no part of one. My reasoning was simple: I like to play golf, and a typical four-day "golf vacation" consists of three 7 a.m. tee times followed by afternoons trudging through shopping malls with the wife, taking the kids to an amusement park, or visiting the "World's Largest Rattlesnake Farm."

"Thank you, no," I said. "How's the family?" Hinedog insisted on giving me the whole pitch. "Seven of us are in for Myrtle Beach," he said. "You're the eighth. No immediate family is invited. We're talking straight golf, nights on the town, poker games, whatever else comes to mind."

I told him to keep talking.

"Great courses, great restaurants, total, unadulterated fun," he said. "There's just one catch."

"What's that?"

"You're putting it together."

I laughed and agreed to do it. It sounded like a novel idea and besides, after six months in the freezing, miserable Northeast, I was very close to being handcuffed to a radiator inside the nearest psychiatric ward. So I went to work arranging things and within a couple of weeks a quorum of eight of us, from all parts of the country, were on jets bound for that superb golf destination, Myrtle Beach, S.C. There followed five days of therapeutic bliss, from which I returned to home and work a new man, stress-free and rejuvenated.

It's doubtful our trip would have been so successful had we not drawn on the experience of all eight fellows who attended. Hinedog, Czaplicki, the Colonel and Scooter travel a lot in their lines of work. Mack, Whiff and Ernie do not, but have taken golf trips before. Between their knowledge and information gathered through reading and talking to people who had taken similar expeditions, several "rules" emerged that, when followed, guaranteed a smooth, snafu-free trip.

Rule No. 1: Everyone has a role

Planning every detail for eight people is too much for one person to handle. That person might be able to do it, but he or she probably won't have an enjoyable trip. The answer is to delegate the important tasks to different members of your party. Here's how we broke it down:

The Chief. Because I had agreed to "put the trip together," I was charged with negotiating dates that were agreeable to everyone. After that was established (the phone bill was considerable), I arranged flight plans for three of us, housing accommodations for all and six starting times for the five-day trip.

That took some doing, because I didn't set things up as far in advance as I should have. You really need to plan at least a month to six weeks ahead. Plane fares are cheaper that way and it's easier to find convenient, affordable places to stay. You get better starting times, too. By planning well ahead of time, everyone has time to get their affairs in order before they leave.

By giving the trip time to incubate, you solve all kinds of problems before they can occur. For instance, the Colonel recently had a hip replacement, making it impossible for him to walk for very long. I wasn't aware of it and therefore didn't phone ahead to make sure he could drive his cart down the middle of the fairway on every course. Luckily, every course accommodated him. But what if they'd said no? I would have ruined his trip.

The Chief should arrange an approximate arrival time for everyone. The first person there should get the rental car (you'll need two cars if there are five players or more), check in at the lodging site, then act as a shuttle service for all those who arrive later. The person getting in last picks up the second rental car. When you search for lodging, try to find a place that is centrally located. Assess the drive time from the home base to each of the courses. That helps you set up a precise yet reasonable itinerary.

The Accountant. Every experienced group-golf traveler I talked to learned, through trial and error, how to handle finances for eight people. Strangely enough, they all subscribed to the same general system.

It works like this: Every time you spend money on something determined to be for the "common good," you keep a receipt and write your name on it. By common good I mean all accommodations, rental cars, gas, food, liquor and tipping. The night before we departed for home, everyone got together and submitted their receipts. The Accountant added them up, then divided by eight. After you get the average cost per person, each person deducts the total of his receipts from his share of the bill. That's what he owes. It's fast, simple and fair.

A lesson here. Don't be a cheapskate. One fellow told me that on an earlier trip, a companion mentioned on closing night that since he didn't drink beer, he shouldn't have to contribute for that portion of the tab. "He may have taken a golf trip after that," my friend said, "but he didn't take it with us."

The Bookie. Because my pals have a certain zest for the wager, it was important that we establish lively formats for each day's play. Scooter is a master at this. He thought up games that were equitable and kept everyone involved.

The stakes can vary, of course. In our case, each player put $50 into a pool, for a total of $400. We disbursed $100 each day, $75 to the winning individual and $25 for second. On days we played two-man team formats, the winners split the $100.

The first day, we played "Chicago," a format in which you take a fixed number, 37, from which you deduct your handicap. If you're a 12-handicapper, for instance, your quota becomes 25 points. Playing at scratch, you are awarded one point for a bogey, two for a par, four for a birdie, and six for an eagle. Whoever scores the most points over their quota wins.

We agreed that because we were making the trip in wintertime, nobody was likely to play well. So after every round we adjusted handicaps. How to do this? We took the Course Rating, which for the first round at beautiful and difficult Pawleys Plantation was 72.5 from the blue tees. We figured that Hinedog, a nervy 15, would shoot 88 if he was on his game. We took what he actually shot (99), halved the 11-stroke difference between his 99 and his projected 88, added it to his 15 and thus gave him 21 wallops the next day. The U.S. Golf Association might not endorse this method, but it worked well for us.

Next day we played a blind-partner format, in which we drew two-man teams at the end of the day and matched cards to determine the best net score for each hole. The third day was again a better-ball format, except this time we paired the high handicapper (after the daily adjustment) with the low handicapper, the second-best player with the second-worst player, and so on. The final day was individual, straight gross and net.

We agreed that on our next trip, we're going to include a scramble, probably on the first day. This will serve as a good warm-up, and it promotes sociability.

The Chef. If, like us, you prefer to stay in a house or condominium rather than a cramped, expensive hotel, you'll need someone who can cook. Since Hinedog happens to make the best barbecued chicken and ribs on the planet, we all agreed that he would cook at least twice.

Arrange ahead of time for the first or second person arriving to do a little shopping. Nothing fancy, just sandwich fixings, cereal, snacks, soda, milk, juice and beer. This will keep your stomach in abeyance between big meals. Actually, you'll probably only want to have one or two sit-down dinners. Leave the complicated stuff to the chef; Hinedog was nastily condescending when I came back from the store with the wrong type of pepper. Also, the cook shouldn't have to handle post-dinner cleanup. Be a demon for volunteering.

The Photographer. About the second day, someone mused how nice it would be if one of us were appointed "crew photographer" to document the trip. Enter the Colonel, who produced a snazzy 35-millimeter camera that he used liberally every day and night. When he got home he prepared a scrapbook for each of us that was a great touch. Naturally, everyone shares the cost for this.

The Chauffeur. To avoid stress-inducing discombobulation, someone should get directions in advance to golf courses, restaurants and other points of interest. The Chauffeur also might want to order from the chamber of commerce a brochure or two explaining other things to do in the area. The Chauffeur should drive the lead automobile on the way out to the course each morning, but, in the interest of equity, leave the drive home to someone else. As a corollary to this, make sure you appoint two designated drivers for your nights out on the town.

Rule No. 2: Compatibility counts

Age doesn't matter much. Neither does golf ability, really, so long as the handicaps are within a 10-stroke ballpark. What *does* matter is social flexibility—a desire and willingness to fit in with everyone else.

If you all enjoy poker, pizza, and a few beers, except for one guy, you've got a problem. You can work around him, but a certain tension is sure to arise. In our case, one fellow told an off-color joke the first night and everyone roared except one guy. He cleared his throat and said that certain subjects were not meant to be laughed about. The Committee understood his point of view but didn't endorse it. The verdict: Either he loosens up by next year or he's a goner.

Golf is great because it joins people of different minds and tastes. But it never occurred to me that the Colonel was retired Air Force while Hinedog had joined the National Guard to avoid getting drafted during the Vietnam War. Thankfully, the subject of national defense never came up.

Like I said, golf ability doesn't really matter. But I do recommend that everyone approach the game on the same level of seriousness. One of our guys once putted out using his putter as a pool cue. Noting that he was the only one who laughed, he didn't do it again.

Rule No. 3: Don't be a baby
Can we talk? We may be adults, but long plane flights, late nights and indifferent golf scores can make whiners out of the best of us. It doesn't take much—maybe a chilly morning shower due to the guy showering before you accidentally using up all the hot water—to make one sulky and petulant. One must bravely see these things through.

We made a little pact our first night in. If someone threw a club, complained about the group's predilection for watching "The Simpsons," or whined about anything else, he would be warned verbally: "Don't be a baby." The next warning would be: "Get a bib." For a third offense, he would have to actually wear a bib at dinner one night.

Who was the baby on our trip? It was me. It was I. Last fall I bent my putter and consequently couldn't make a four-footer this trip. I whined, I was warned, and I had to wear a bib.

Rule No. 4: Pace yourselves
From the moment everyone committed to make the trip, I was imbued with Golf Fever. Couldn't wait to make a total golf orgy out of the trip. As the Chief, I arranged for us to play six rounds in four days. Two afternoons off seemed more than plenty.

Boy, was I wrong. As I've explained, we were coming out of the dead of winter. After the first day (36 holes), everyone was tired but happy. After the second day (18 holes), I had a blister on my thumb, the Colonel's bad hip was giving him trouble and Ernie had entered a somnambulistic, sloe-eyed funk. We had planned 36 more holes the third day, with the first tee time at 7:15 a.m. I'm ashamed to tell you, we had to cancel the morning round and play the afternoon 18 only. After the final day (18 holes), we were absolutely pooped.

Eighteen holes per day is plenty. The consequences of getting overgolfed are serious. It's hard to describe the tranquil beauty of Pawleys Plantation, the charm of the Heritage Club, the brilliant design of Tidewater, the challenging back nine at Buck Creek and the treeless expanse of Scottish-style Legends, but I dare say we could have enjoyed them more had we been fully rested.

A final word about pacing. Night life is an integral part of any vacation, but I strongly suggest moderating your alcohol intake. Hangovers are no fun in any circumstances and particularly hellish on the golf course.

Few pursuits are as enjoyable as a well-organized golf trip. So exhilarating was ours, in fact, that stories about it inspired a similar sojourn from some other fellows at my club. I was invited to accompany one exceptionally fun group.

"Out of the question," I said. "I've promised my wife a vacation for the fall already."

"Yeah, you probably wouldn't care for Pinehurst anyway."

Ten minutes later I was at my wife's feet. "Honey, have I told you how beautiful Vermont is around Christmastime?"

America's 100 Greatest Golf Courses, 1997–98

As ranked by GOLF DIGEST in its biennial ranking. *Courses marked with an asterisk are public-access facilities and appear in this book.

FIRST 10

1. **Pine Valley G.C.,** Pine Valley, N.J.
2. **Augusta National G.C.,** Augusta, Ga.
3. **Cypress Point Club,** Pebble Beach, Calif.
4. ***Pebble Beach G. Links,** Pebble Beach, Calif.
5. **Shinnecock Hills G.C.,** Southampton, N.Y.
6. **Winged Foot G.C. (West),** Mamaroneck, N.Y
7. **Oakmont C.C.,** Oakmont, Pa.
8. **Merion G.C. (East),** Ardmore, Pa.
9. ***Pinehurst Resort & C.C. (No. 2),** Pinehurst, N.C.
10. **Oakland Hills C.C. (South),** Bloomfield Hills, Mich.

SECOND 10

11. **The Olympic Club (Lake),** San Francisco
12. **Seminole G.C.,** North Palm Beach, Fla.
13. **The Country Club (Clyde/Squirrel),** Brookline, Mass.
14. **National Golf Links,** Southampton, N.Y.
15. **Shadow Creek G.C.,** North Las Vegas, Nev.
16. **Medinah C.C. (No. 3),** Medinah, Ill.
17. **Prairie Dunes C.C.,** Hutchinson, Kan.
18. **Crystal Downs C.C.,** Frankfort, Mich.
19. **San Francisco G.C.,** San Francisco
20. **Wade Hampton G.C.,** Cashiers, N.C.

THIRD 10

21. **Muirfield Village G.C.,** Dublin, Ohio
22. **Oak Hill C.C. (East),** Rochester, N.Y.
23. **Qauker Ridge G.C.,** Scarsdale, N.Y
24. **Southern Hills C.C.,** Tulsa, Okla.
25. **Garden City G.C.,** Garden City, N.Y
26. **The Golf Club,** New Albany, Ohio
27. ***Spyglass Hill G. Cse.,** Pebble Beach, Calif.
28. **Baltusrol G.C. (Lower),** Springfield, N.J.
29. **Peachtree G.C.,** Atlanta
30. **Riviera C.C.,** Pacific Palisades, Calif.

FOURTH 10

31. **Cherry Hills C.C.,** Englewood, Colo.
32. **Scioto C.C.,** Columbus, Ohio
33. **Inverness Club,** Toledo, Ohio
34. **Maidstone Club,** East Hampton, N.Y.
35. **Chicago G.C.,** Wheaton, Ill.
36. **Winged Foot G.C. (East),** Mamaroneck, N.Y.
37. **The Honors Course,** Chattanooga, Tenn.
38. **Los Angeles C.C. (North),** Los Angeles
39. **Plainfield C.C.,** Plainfield, N.J.
40. **Baltimore C.C. (East),** Timonium, Md.

FIFTH 10

41. ***Kiawah Island Resort (Ocean),** Kiawah Island, S.C.
42. ***The Homestead Resort (Cascades),** Hot Springs, Va.
43. **Somerset Hills C.C.,** Bernardsville, N.J.
44. **Castle Pines G.C.,** Castle Rock, Colo.
45. **Kittansett Club,** Marion, Mass.
46. **Interlachen C.C.,** Edina, Minn.
47. **Colonial C.C.,** Fort Worth

48. **Forest Highlands G.C.,** Flagstaff, Ariz.
49. **Laurel Valley G.C.,** Ligonier, Pa.
50. ***Blackwolf Run Golf Club (River),** Kohler, Wis.

SIXTH 10
51. **Long Cove Club,** Hilton Head Island, S.C.
52. **Wannamoisett C.C.,** Rumford, R.I.
53. ***TPC at Sawgrass (Stadium),** Ponte Vedra Beach, Fla.
54. ***Cog Hill G. & C.C. (No. 4),** Lemont, Ill.
55. **Shoal Creek,** Shoal Creek, Ala.
56. **Point O'Woods G. & C.C.,** Benton Harbor, Mich.
57. **Desert Forest G.C.,** Carefree, Ariz.
58. **Butler National G.C.,** Oak Brook, Ill.
59. **Black Diamond (Quarry),** Lecanto, Fla.
60. ***Harbour Town G. Links,** Hilton Head Island, S.C.

SEVENTH 10
61. **Valhalla G.C.,** Louisville, Ky.
62. **Olympia Fields C.C. (North),** Olympia Fields, Ill.
63. **Canterbury G.C.,** Shaker Heights, Ohio
64. **Hazeltine National G.C.,** Chaska, Minn.
65. **Atlantic G.C.,** Bridgehampton, N.Y.
66. ***Princeville Resort (Prince),** Princeville Resort, Kauai, Hawaii
67. **Bellerive C.C.,** Creve Coeur, Mo.
68. **Oak Tree G.C.,** Edmond, Okla.
69. **Congressional C.C. (Blue),** Bethesda, Md.
70. **Camargo Club,** Indian Hill, Ohio

EIGHTH 10
71. **Double Eagle Club,** Galena, Ohio
72. **Haig Point Club (Calibogue),** Daufuskie Island, S.C.
73. **Milwaukee C.C.,** Milwaukee
74. **Jupiter Hills C. (Hills),** Tequesta, Fla.
75. **Stanwich Club,** Greenwich, Conn.
76. **Crooked Stick G.C.,** Carmel, Ind.
77. **Saucon Valley C.C. (Grace),** Bethlehem, Pa.
78. **Eugene C.C.,** Eugene, Ore.
79. **Salem C.C.,** Peabody, Mass.
80. **NCR C.C. (South),** Kettering, Ohio

NINTH 10
81. ***Pumpkin Ridge G.C. (Ghost Creek),** Cornelius, Ore.
82. **Wilmington C.C. (South),** Greenville, Del.
83. ***Pasatiempo G.C.,** Santa Cruz, Calif.
84. **Greenville C.C. (Chanticleer),** Greenville, S.C.
85. **Valley C. of Montecito,** Santa Barbara, Calif.
86. **C.C. of North Carolina (Dogwood),** Pinehurst
87. **Sycamore Hills G.C.,** Fort Wayne, Ind.
88. **Aronimink G.C.,** Newtown Square, Pa.
89. **Old Waverly G.C.,** West Point, Miss.
90. **Pine Tree G.C.,** Boynton Beach, Fla.

TENTH 10
91. ***Troon North G.C. (Monument),** Scottsdale, Ariz.
92. **Robert Trent Jones G.C.,** Gainesville, Va.
93. **Troon G. & C.C.,** Scottsdale, Ariz.
94. **East Lake G.C.,** Atlanta
95. **Sahalee C.C. (South/North),** Redmond, Wash.
96. **Old Warson C.C.,** Ladue, Mo.
97. ***Arnold Palmer's Bay Hill C. & Lodge,** Orlando
98. ***Mauna Kea Beach G.Cse.,** Kohala Coast, Hawaii
99. ***The Links at Spanish Bay,** Pebble Beach, Calif.
100. ***Bethpage State Park G.Cses. (Black),** Farmingdale, N.Y.

★★★★★
The Five-Star Courses

These are the 10 sublime courses that received the highest Places to Play rating from GOLF DIGEST subscribers: the maximum five stars.

Blackwolf Run Golf Club (River Course), Kohler, Wis.
Cabo del Sol, Los Cabos, Mexico
Casa de Campo Resort & Country Club (Teeth of the Dog), Dom. Rep.
The Homestead Resort (Cascades Course), Hot Springs, Va.
Karsten Creek Golf Course, Stillwater, Okla.
The Links at Crowbush Cove, Prince Edward Island, Canada
Pebble Beach Golf Links, Pebble Beach, Calif.
Pinehurst Country Club (No. 2 Course), Pinehurst, N.C.
Princeville Resort (The Prince Course), Kauai, Hawaii
Spyglass Hill Golf Course, Pebble Beach, Calif.

The Great-Value Courses

The top 50 golf courses in North America in terms of value for money, as rated by GOLF DIGEST subscribers.

UNITED STATES
Alabama
Grand National Golf Club (Short Course)
Arizona
Silver Creek Golf Club
California
Fall River Valley Golf & Country Club
Colorado
Hollydot Golf Course
Walking Stick Golf Course
Florida
Fort Walton Beach Golf Club (Oaks Course)
Hawaii
Waiehu Golf Course
Wailua Golf Course
Illinois
Park Hills Golf Club (East Course)
Park Hills Golf Club (West Course)
Iowa
Muscatine Municipal Golf Course
Kansas
Buffalo Dunes Golf Course
Kentucky
Gibson Bay Golf Course
Massachusetts
Chicopee Golf Club
Michigan
Binder Park Golf Course
Cascades Golf Course
Hickory Knoll Golf Course
L.E. Kaufman Golf Club

Marysville Golf Course
Milham Park Municipal Golf Club
Oak Crest Golf Course
New Hampshire
Bretwood Golf Course (South Course)
New Jersey
Flanders Valley Golf Course (White/Blue Course)
New Mexico
Pinon Hills Golf Course
New York
Bethpage State Park Golf Courses (Black Course)
Montauk Downs State Park Golf Course
Saratoga Spa Golf Course
North Dakota
The Links of North Dakota at Red Mike Resort
Oklahoma
Boiling Springs Golf Club
Oregon
Tokatee Golf Club
Pennsylvania
Stoughton Acres Golf Club
South Carolina
Cheraw State Park Golf Course
Texas
Painted Dunes Desert Golf Course
Underwood Golf Complex (Sunset Course)
Utah
Birch Creek Golf Club
Moab Golf Club
Valley View Golf Course
Wasatch State Park Golf Club
Washington
Gold Mountain Golf Complex (Olympic Course)
Hangman Valley Golf Course
Indian Canyon Golf Course
Wisconsin
Brighton Dale Golf Club (White Birch Course)
Brown County Golf Course

CANADA
Alberta
Kananaskis Country Golf Club (Mt. Kidd Course)
Kananaskis Country Golf Club (Mt. Lorette Course)
Manitoba
Hecla Golf Course at Gull Harbor Resort
Nova Scotia
Highlands Links Golf Course
Ontario
Renfrew Golf Club
Prince Edward Island
The Links at Crowbush Cove
Saskatchewan
Waskesiu Golf Course

The Good-Value Courses

The next 150 golf courses (Nos. 51 to 200) in terms of value for money, as rated by GOLF DIGEST subscribers.

UNITED STATES

Alabama
Cambrian Ridge Golf Club
Grand National Golf Club (Lake Course)
Grand National Golf Club (Links Course)
Highland Oaks Golf Club

Arizona
Emerald Canyon Golf Course
Papago Golf Course

Arkansas
Glenwood Country Club

California
Bennett Valley Golf Course
Oak Valley Golf Club
Pacific Grove Municipal Golf Links
Poppy Hills Golf Course
Poppy Ridge Golf Course
The SCGA Members' Club at Rancho California
San Juan Oaks Golf Club
Torrey Pines Golf Course (North Course)
Torrey Pines Golf Course (South Course)

Colorado
Battlement Mesa Golf Club
Hillcrest Golf Club

Florida
Golf Club of Jacksonville
PGA Golf Club at The Reserve (North Course)
PGA Golf Club at The Reserve (South Course)
World Woods Golf Club (Pine Barrens Course)
World Woods Golf Club (Rolling Oaks Course)

Georgia
Chicopee Woods Golf Course
Hard Labor Creek State Park Golf Course
Pine Bluff Golf & Country Club
University of Georgia Golf Club
Wallace Adams Golf Course

Idaho
Blackfoot Municipal Golf Course
Pinecrest Municipal Golf Course
Ridgecrest Golf Club
Scotch Pines Golf Course

Illinois
Bon Vivant Country Club
The Bourne Golf Club
Hawthorn Ridge Golf Club
Heritage Bluffs Golf Club
Jackson Park Golf Course
Laurel Greens Public Golfers Club
Lick Creek Golf Course

Orchard Valley Golf Club
Pontiac Elks Country Club
Prairie Vista Golf Course
Sandy Hollow Golf Course

Indiana
Rock Hollow Golf Club

Iowa
Jester Park Golf Course
The Meadows Golf Club
Valley Oaks Golf Club

Kansas
Custer Hill Golf Club
Mariah Hills Golf Course
Quail Ridge Golf Course
Rolling Meadows Golf Course
Village Greens Golf Club

Kentucky
Kearney Hill Golf Links
Lassing Pointe Golf Club
Tates Creek Golf Course
Western Hills Golf Course

Louisiana
Mallard Cove Golf Course

Maryland
Eagle's Landing Golf Club
Mount Pleasant Golf Club

Massachusetts
Larry Gannon Golf Club

Michigan
Bay County Golf Course
County Highlands Golf Club
Gaylord Country Club
George Young Recreational Complex
Grand View Golf Course
Groesbeck Municipal Golf Course
Hills Heart of the Lakes Golf Club
Huron Breeze Golf & Country Club
Lakewood Shores Resort (Serradella Course)
Springfield Oaks Golf Course
Treetops Sylvan Resort (Tradition Course)
White Pine National Golf Club

Minnesota
Braemar Golf Course
Bunker Hills Golf Course
Eagle Ridge Golf Course
Little Crow Country Club
Ortonville Municipal Golf Course
The Preserve Golf Club at Grand View Lodge

Mississippi
Mississippi State University Golf Course

Missouri
Bent Creek Golf Course
Eagle Lake Golf Club
Shirkey Golf Club

Nevada
Toana Vista Golf Course
New Hampshire
Bretwood Golf Course (North Course)
New Jersey
Flanders Valley Golf Course (Red/Gold Course)
New York
Bethpage State Park Golf Courses (Blue Course)
Bethpage State Park Golf Courses (Green Course)
Bethpage State Park Golf Courses (Red Course)
Green Lakes State Park Golf Club
Mark Twain Golf Club
Soaring Eagles Golf Club
North Carolina
Cypress Landing Golf Club
Oak Hollow Golf Course
North Dakota
Edgewood Golf Course
Souris Valley Golf Club
Ohio
Forest Hills Golf Center
J.E. Good Park Golf Club
Jaycee Public Golf Course
Mohican Hills Golf Club
River Greens Golf Course
Oklahoma
Cedar Creek Golf Course
Oregon
Eagle Point Golf Course
Elkhorn Valley Golf Club
Meadow Lakes Golf Course
Oregon Golf Association Members Course at Tukwila
Pennsylvania
Bucknell Golf Club
North Hills Golf Club
Pilgrim's Oak Golf Course
South Carolina
Buck Creek Golf Club
Foxboro Golf Club
LinRick Golf Course
South Dakota
Southern Hills Golf Course
Tennessee
Graysburg Hills Golf Course
Heatherhurst Golf Club
Roan Valley Golf Estates
Texas
Cedar Creek Golf Course
Evergreen Point Golf Club
Lady Bird Johnson Municipal Golf Course
Rayburn Country Club & Resort
San Saba Municipal Golf Course
Squaw Valley Golf Course
Sugartree Golf Club

Utah
Bountiful Ridge Golf Course
Hobble Creek Golf Club
Logan River Golf Course
Wingpointe Golf Course
Vermont
St. Johnsbury Country Club
Virginia
Newport News Golf Club at Deer Run (Cardinal Course)
Newport News Golf Club at Deer Run (Deer Run Course)
Woodlands Golf Course
Washington
The Creek at Qualchan Golf Course
Lake Padden Golf Course
Lipoma Firs Golf Course
MeadowWood Golf Course
Riverside Country Club
Wisconsin
Brighton Dale Golf Club (Blue Spruce Course)
Naga-Waukee Golf Course
Nemadji Golf Course (East/West Course)
New Richmond Golf Club
Northwood Golf Course

CANADA
Alberta
Barrhead Golf Club
Paradise Canyon Golf & Country Club
British Columbia
Castlegar Golf Club
Fairview Mountain Golf Club
Golden Golf & Country Club
Manitoba
Clear Lake Golf Course
Falcon Lake Golf Course
Quebec
Le Club de Golf Carling Lake

MEXICO
Baja Norte
Bajamar Ocean Front Golf Resort

THE ISLANDS
Dominican Republic
Casa de Campo Resort & Country Club (Teeth of the Dog)

The Great-Service Facilities

The top 50 golf facilities in North America in terms of service, as rated by GOLF DIGEST subscribers.

UNITED STATES
Alabama
Cambrian Ridge Golf Club
Grand National Golf Club
Highland Oaks Golf Club
Oxmoor Valley Golf Club
Silver Lakes Golf Club
Arizona
The Boulders Club
Grayhawk Golf Club
The Raven Golf Club at Sabino Springs
The Raven Golf Club at South Mountain
Troon North Golf Club
California
Ojai Valley Inn
Colorado
The Broadmoor Golf Club
Florida
Doral Golf Resort & Spa
Grand Cypress Golf Club
Saddlebrook Resort
St. Lucie West Country Club
Sawgrass Country Club
Tournament Players Club at Sawgrass
Turnberry Isle Resort & Club
Walt Disney World Resort
Georgia
Chateau Elan Resort
Sea Island Golf Club
Hawaii
The Experience at Koele
Hapuna Golf Course
Kapalua Golf Club
Mauna Lani Resort
Wailea Golf Club
Idaho
Coeur d'Alene Resort Golf Course
Iowa
The Meadows Golf Club
Michigan
Bay Harbor Golf Club
Minnesota
Madden's on Gull Lake
Nevada
Tournament Players Club at the Canyons
North Carolina
Pinehurst Resort & Country Club
South Carolina
Pine Lakes International Country Club

Wachesaw Plantation East
Texas
BridleWood Golf Club
Four Seasons Resort & Club
La Cantera Golf Club
Rayburn Country Club & Resort
Virginia
The Homestead Resort
Raspberry Falls Golf & Hunt Club
West Virginia
The Greenbrier
Wisconsin
Blackwolf Run Golf Club
Bristlecone Pines Golf Club
Nemadji Golf Course

CANADA
Alberta
Kananaskis Country Golf Club
British Columbia
Big Sky Golf & Country Club
Manitoba
The Links at Quarry Oaks
Quebec
Le Chateau Montebello

THE ISLANDS
Nevis
Four Seasons Resort Nevis

The Good-Service Facilities

The next 150 facilities (Nos. 51 to 200) in terms of service, as rated by GOLF DIGEST subscribers.

UNITED STATES
Alabama
Hampton Cove Golf Club
Magnolia Grove Golf Club
The Peninsula Golf Club
Rock Creek Golf Club
TimberCreek Golf Club
Arizona
Gainey Ranch Golf Club
The Golf Club at Vistoso
Legend Trail Golf Club
Omni Tucson National Golf Resort & Spa
Ventana Canyon Golf & Racquet Club
Arkansas
Glenwood Country Club
California
Coyote Hills Golf Course
The Links at Spanish Bay
Pebble Beach Golf Links

San Juan Oaks Golf Club
Spyglass Hill Golf Course
Steele Canyon Golf Club
Twelve Bridges Golf Club
Colorado
Keystone Ranch Golf Course
Pagosa Springs Golf Club
Florida
Amelia Island Plantation
Arnold Palmer's Bay Hill Club & Lodge
Dodger Pines Country Club
Emerald Bay Golf Course
Falcon's Fire Golf Club
Innisbrook Hilton Resort
Lost Lake Golf Club
Marcus Pointe Golf Club
Marriott at Sawgrass Resort
Mission Inn Golf & Tennis Resort
The Moors Golf Club
PGA Golf Club at the Reserve
Pelican's Nest Golf Club
Ponte Vedra Inn & Club
Sandridge Golf Club
Tiger Point Golf & Country Club
World Woods Golf Club
Georgia
Osprey Cove Golf Club
Reynolds Plantation
St. Simons Island Club
White Columns Golf Club
Hawaii
The Challenge at Manele
Grand Waikapu Resort, Golf & Spa
Kauai Lagoons
Makena Resort Golf Course
Poipu Bay Resort Golf Club
Princeville Resort
Illinois
Cantigny Golf
Eagle Ridge Inn & Resort
Mill Creek Golf Club
Orchard Valley Golf Club
Park Hills Golf Club
Pinnacle Country Club
Prairie Landing Golf Club
Seven Bridges Golf Club
Indiana
Covered Bridge Golf Club
Rock Hollow Golf Club
Winchester Golf Club
Kansas
Quail Ridge Golf Course
Massachusetts
Farm Neck Golf Club

Kings Way Golf Club
Michigan
Boyne Highlands Resort
Boyne Mountain Resort
Crystal Mountain Resort
Garland Golf Resort
Grand Hotel Golf Club
Grand Traverse Resort
Lakewood Shores Resort
Little Traverse Bay Golf Club
Oak Crest Golf Course
The Orchards Golf Club
St. Ives Golf Club
Shanty Creek
Sugarbush Golf Club
Treetops Sylvan Resort
West Branch Country Club
White Pine National Golf Club
Minnesota
The Pines at Grand View Lodge
Mississippi
The Bridges Golf Resort at Casino Magic
Missouri
Millwood Golf & Racquet Club
Nevada
Edgewood Tahoe Golf Course
New Hampshire
The Balsams Grand Resort Hotel
New Jersey
Blue Heron Pines Golf Club
Marriott's Seaview Resort
New York
Greystone Golf Club
North Carolina
Grandover Resort & Conference Center
Pine Needles Lodge & Golf Club
Waynesville Country Club Inn
North Dakota
The Links of North Dakota at Red Mike Resort
Ohio
Eaglesticks Golf Course
Quail Hollow Resort & Country Club
Shaker Run Golf Club
The Vineyard Golf Course
Oregon
Pumpkin Ridge Golf Club
Sunriver Lodge & Resort
Pennsylvania
Chestnut Ridge Golf Club
Country Club at Woodloch Springs
Country Club of Hershey
Hartefeld National Golf Club
Nemacolin Woodlands Resort & Spa
Pilgrim's Oak Golf Course

Stoughton Acres Golf Club
South Carolina
Buck Creek Golf Club
Caledonia Golf & Fish Club
The Club at Seabrook Island
Glen Dornoch Waterway Golf Links
Heather Glen Golf Links
Hilton Head National Golf Club
Kiawah Island Resort
Ocean Creek Golf Course
Ocean Point Golf Links
Palmetto Dunes Resort
Wild Wing Plantation
Tennessee
Egwani Farms Golf Course
Graysburg Hills Golf Course
Heatherhurst Golf Club
Legends Club of Tennessee
Texas
Barton Creek Resort & Country Club
Hill Country Golf Club
The Quarry Golf Club
The Woodlands Resort & Country Club
Vermont
Green Mountain National Golf Course
Virginia
Golden Horseshoe Golf Club
Kingsmill Resort & Club
The Legends of Stonehouse
The Tides Inn
Tides Lodge
Washington
McCormick Woods Golf Course
Semiahmoo Golf & Country Club
Wisconsin
The Bog Golf Club
Geneva National Golf Club
The Springs Golf Club Resort
Trappers Turn Golf Club
University Ridge Golf Course

CANADA
Alberta
Banff Springs Golf Course
Heritage Pointe Golf & Country Club
Wolf Creek Golf Resort
British Columbia
Chateau Whistler Golf Club
Harvest Golf Club
Westwood Plateau Golf & Country Club
Ontario
Angus Glen Golf Club
Lionhead Golf & Country Club

Prince Edward Island
The Links at Crowbush Cove
Quebec
Le Club de Golf Carling Lake
Tremblant Golf Resort

THE ISLANDS
Aruba
Tierra Del Sol Country Club
Dominican Republic
Casa de Campo Resort & Country Club
Jamaica
The Tryall Club, Resort & Villas
Puerto Rico
The Golf Club at El Conquistador
Turks & Caicos
Provo Golf Club

How to Use This Guide

ANYWHERE GOLF RESORT
★★★ **ANYWHERE GOLF COURSE**
PU-100 Anywhere Drive, Centerville, 10001, Nice County, (212)000-9999,
25 miles S of Nowhere.
Opened: 1920. **Holes:** 18. **Par:** 70/71. **Yards:** 6,500/5,500. **Course rating:**
72.5/71.5. **Slope:** 145/135. **Architect:** AW Tillinghast. **Green fee:** $75/$125.
Credit cards: MC,VISA. **Reduced fees:** Low season, resort guests.
Caddies: Yes. **Golf carts:** Included in Green Fee. **Discount golf packages:**
Yes. **Season:** April-Oct. **High:** April-Oct. **On site lodging:** Yes. **Rental clubs:**
Yes. **Walking policy:** Walking at certain times. **Metal spikes allowed:** Yes.
Range: Yes (grass). **To obtain tee times:** Call.
Notes: Ranked 5th in 1997 Best in State. 1990 Anywhere Golf Classic.
Subscriber comments: Like St. Andrews and Pebble Beach, play it at least
once in your life...Too expensive...Older course, needs renovating.
Special Notes: Formerly known as Somewhere Golf Club.

Explanation

ANYWHERE GOLF RESORT—The name of the resort or facility.
★★★—The star rating; a rating of the golf experience according to GOLF
DIGEST subscribers. See ratings chart below.
ANYWHERE GOLF COURSE—The name of the course at Anywhere Golf
Resort (generally only appears when there is more than one course at the
facility).
PU—Public course. **R:** Resort. **PM:** Municipal. **SP:** Semi-private.
100 Anywhere Drive, Centerville, 10001, Nice County—The address,
zip code and county.
(212)000-9999—The phone number of the facility. Please note that all phone
numbers were accurate at the time of going to press, but numbers and area
codes are subject to change.
25 miles S of Nowhere—Approximate directions.
Opened—The year the course first opened.
Holes—The number of holes.
Par—The figures shown represent the par from the back/front tees.
Yards—The yardage from the back/front tees.
Course rating—The USGA course rating from the back/front tees.
Slope—The USGA Slope rating from the back/front tees.
Architect—The architect of the golf course.
Green fee—Fees listed represent the lowest/highest fee for an 18-hole round
of golf. Please note that all fees are subject to change.
Credit cards—Credit cards accepted at the facility. MC: MasterCard, V: Visa,
AMEX: American Express, DISC: Discover.
Reduced fees—Times and/or situations when discount fees may be
available. Call ahead for details.
Caddies—Whether caddies are available at the course.
Golf carts—Price of renting golf carts at the course. Prices may be per
person or per cart, based on the policy at the facility.
Discount golf packages—Whether packages are available.
Season—Months of the year when the course is open for play.
High—When the course is likely to be busiest and the rates typically higher.
On site lodging—Whether lodging is available at the facility.

Rental clubs—Whether clubs are available for hire at the course.
Walking policy—Unrestricted walking: Walking is allowed at any time. Walking at certain times: Carts may be mandatory at certain (usually busy) times. Mandatory cart: Walking is never an option.
Metal spikes allowed—Whether metal spikes are allowed on the golf course (many clubs now have a spikeless shoe policy).
Range—Whether the facility has a driving range.
To obtain tee times—Procedure established by the course to secure a tee time.
Notes—Relevant additional information, including GOLF DIGEST rankings.
Subscriber comments—A representative sample of comments made by GOLF DIGEST subscribers in response to an April 1997 issue survey. These comments come from subscribers' impressions of the course based on their playing experiences between April 1, 1996, and April 30, 1997, and may not be indicative of current conditions. In general, comments are not shown for courses with two stars or less.
Special Notes—Final additional information.
N/A—This means that the information was not supplied by the facility and is not available.

Ratings

★ Basic golf.

★★ Good, but not great.

★★★ Very good. Tell a friend it's worth getting off the highway to play.

★★★★ Outstanding. Plan your next vacation around it.

★★★★★ Golf at its absolute best. Pay any price to play at least once in your life.

½ The equivalent of one-half star.

Please note that a number of courses do not have a star rating. A course that did not receive a minimum of 10 ballots—either because it is very new, has only recently turned public, or simply was not visited by a sufficient number of GOLF DIGEST subscribers—remains unrated.

Part I

The United States

★★½ALPINE BAY GOLF & COUNTRY CLUB

R-9855 Renfore Rd., Alpine, 35014, Talladega County, (205)268-2920, (800)925-0827, 40 miles SE of Birmingham.

Opened: 1972. **Holes:** 18. **Par:** 72/72. **Yards:** 6,518/5,518. **Course rating:** 70.9/69.8. **Slope:** 129/120. **Architect:** Robert Trent Jones. **Green fee:** $12/$20. **Credit cards:** All major. **Reduced fees:** Weekdays, resort guests, twilight. **Caddies:** No. **Golf carts:** $10. **Discount golf packages:** Yes. **Season:** Year-round. **High:** May-Sept. **On site lodging:** Yes. **Rental clubs:** Yes. **Walking policy:** Walking at certain times. **Metal spikes allowed:** Yes. **Range:** Yes (grass). **To obtain tee times:** Call anytime.

Subscriber comments: A good course to play, not too hard...Striving to improve...Very enjoyable...Nice layout...Interesting course, hilly, good doglegs....RT Jones layout being rebuilt.

★★★½AUBURN LINKS AT MILL CREEK

PU-826 Shell-Toomer Pkwy., Auburn, 36830, Lee County, (334)887-5151, 4 miles NW of Auburn-Opelika.

Opened: 1991. **Holes:** 18. **Par:** 72/72. **Yards:** 7,145/5,320. **Course rating:** 72.5/68.5. **Slope:** 129/118. **Architect:** Ward Northrup. **Green fee:** $30/$37. **Credit cards:** MC,VISA. **Reduced fees:** Low season, resort guests, seniors, juniors. **Caddies:** No. **Golf carts:** Included in Green Fee. **Discount golf packages:** Yes. **Season:** Year-round. **High:** June-Oct. **On site lodging:** No. **Rental clubs:** Yes. **Walking policy:** Walking at certain times. **Metal spikes allowed:** Yes. **Range:** Yes (grass). **To obtain tee times:** Call 7 days in advance.

Subscriber comments: Nice layout—adequate challenge. Well maintained...Par 5 No.12 is breathtaking...Quick greens...Nice fairways and greens...Great layout, great mix of easy, difficult holes...Good fair course...Very demanding off tee, with large greens...The beautiful greens and very tight fairways got my attention. A fun course to play...Pretty course, open, right off Interstate 85.

★★★½AZALEA CITY GOLF CLUB

PU-1000 Gaillard Dr., Mobile, 36608, Mobile County, (334)342-4221, 10 miles W of Mobile.

Opened: 1957. **Holes:** 18. **Par:** 72/72. **Yards:** 6,765/6,491. **Course rating:** 70.9/69.8. **Slope:** 124/121. **Architect:** R.B Harris. **Green fee:** $10/$15. **Credit cards:** MC,VISA,AMEX. **Reduced fees:** Twilight. **Caddies:** No. **Golf carts:** $10. **Discount golf packages:** No. **Season:** Year-round **High:** March-Oct. **On site lodging:** No. **Rental clubs:** Yes. **Walking policy:** Unrestricted walking. **Metal spikes allowed:** Yes. **Range:** Yes (grass). **To obtain tee times:** Call golf shop up to 14 days in advance for weekday tee times and the Wednesday prior to the weekend call at 8:00 a.m.

Subscriber comments: Excellent conditions for public course...Good for long drives off the tee. Greens test your skill with wedge. Also designed for the player that prefers to chip and run to green...Well maintained muny course wide fairways...Pleasure to play—slow round...Wonderful, great shape.

★½BAY OAKS GOLF CLUB

PU-P.O. Box 651, Bayou La Batre, 36509, Mobile County, (334)824-2429, (334)824-4133, 10 miles S of Mobile.

Opened: 1963. **Holes:** 18. **Par:** 72/72. **Yards:** 6,208/5,422. **Course rating:** N/A. **Slope:** 124/122. **Architect:** Boots Lange. **Green fee:** $11/$13. **Credit cards:** MC,VISA. **Reduced fees:** Weekdays. **Caddies:** No. **Golf carts:** $12. **Discount golf packages:** No. **Season:** Year-round. **High:** Nov.-March. **On site lodging:** No. **Rental clubs:** No. **Walking policy:** N/A. **Metal spikes allowed:** Yes. **Range:** Yes (grass). **To obtain tee times:** N/A.

★★★½BENT BROOK GOLF COURSE

PU-7900 Dickey Springs St., Bessemer, 35023, Jefferson County, (205)424-2368, 10 miles S of Birmingham.

Opened: 1988. **Holes:** 27. **Architect:** Ward Northrup. **Green fee:** $22/$32. **Credit cards:** All major. **Reduced fees:** Weekdays. **Caddies:** No. **Golf carts:** $11. **Discount golf packages:** No. **Season:** Year-round. **High:** N/A. **On site lodging:** No. **Rental clubs:** Yes. **Walking policy:** Walking at certain times. **Metal spikes allowed:** Yes. **Range:** Yes (grass). **To obtain tee times:** Call 3 days in advance.

BROOK/GRAVEYARD
Par: 71/71. **Yards:** 7,053/5,364. **Course rating:** 71.7. **Slope:** 121.
WINDMILL/BROOK
Par: 71/71. **Yards:** 6,934/5,333. **Course rating:** 69.6/70.3. **Slope:** 117/120.
WINDMILL/GRAVEYARD
Par: 70/70. **Yards:** 6,847/5,321. **Course rating:** 69.2/70.6. **Slope:** 116/123.
Subscriber comments: Three different courses. Each with its own different degree of difficulty. Always a challenge...Always in very good shape...Good public course—very open...Best public course in Alabama, but don't play it if it has rained in the last few days...Graveyard is hardest...Open, user friendly...Nice clubhouse.

★★CAHABA VALLEY GOLF & COUNTRY CLUB
7905 Roper Rd., Trussville, 35173, Jefferson County, (205)655-2095.
Call club for further information.

★★★★CAMBRIAN RIDGE GOLF CLUB
PU-101 Sunbelt Pkwy., Greenville, 36037, Butler County, (334)382-9787, (800)949-4444, 40 miles S of Montgomery.
Opened: 1993. **Holes:** 27. **Architect:** Robert Trent Jones. **Green fee:** $44/$44. **Credit cards:** All major. **Reduced fees:** Weekdays, low season, twilight, seniors, juniors. **Caddies:** No. **Golf carts:** $15. **Discount golf packages:** Yes. **Season:** Year-round. **High:** March-May; Sept.-Nov. **On site lodging:** No. **Rental clubs:** Yes. **Walking policy:** Unrestricted walking. **Metal spikes allowed:** Yes. **Range:** Yes (grass/mats). **To obtain tee times:** Call 1-800-949-4444.

CANYON/LOBLOLLY
Par: 71/71. **Yards:** 7,297/4,772. **Course rating:** 74.6/67.8. **Slope:** 140/126.
CANYON/SHERLING
Par: 72/72. **Yards:** 7,424/4,857. **Course rating:** 75.4/68.1. **Slope:** 142/127.
LOBLOLLY/SHERLING
Par: 71/36. **Yards:** 7,232/4,435. **Course rating:** 73.9/67.0. **Slope:** 133/119.
Notes: Ranked 8th in 1997 Best in State.
Subscriber comments: Most beautiful course I have ever played....Great course, for the young with good legs...Canyon real target golf test!...Staff was like family...Great scenery—severe greens...Beautiful, hilly, difficult, fair...Tough, but good...Very difficult for average golfer, outstanding beauty...Huge undulating greens put premium on iron play and putting. Wonderful clubhouse...Awesome!
Special Notes: Part of the Robert Trent Jones Golf Trail. Complex also includes Short Course, a 9-hole par-3 layout.

★CHRISWOOD GOLF COURSE
511 Wellington Rd., Athens, 35611, Limestone County, (205)232-9759.
Call club for further information.

★★½CITRONELLE MUNICIPAL GOLF COURSE
PM-Lakeview Dr., Citronelle, 36522, Mobile County, (334)866-7881.
Call club for further information.
Subscriber comments: Fun course...Great course for players who enjoy the hill country. Fast elevated greens. Will test your putting skills...Course keeps you thinking...Front nine wide open, back short and tight...Good public course. Great price, new greens...Great snack bar—best food in Alabama...Woodsy, rolling hills, good-value municipal.

★★COLONIAL GOLF CLUB
PU-102 Leesburg St., Huntsville, 35759, Madison County, (205)828-0431.
Call club for further information.

★★★½CRAFT FARMS COTTON CREEK CLUB
3840 Cotton Creek Blvd., Gulf Shores, 36542, Baldwin County, (334)968-7766, 40 miles E of Mobile.
Opened: 1987. **Holes:** 27. **Architect:** Arnold Palmer/Ed Seay. **Green fee:** $48/$53. **Credit cards:** MC,VISA,AMEX. **Reduced fees:** Weekdays, low season. **Caddies:** No.

Golf carts: Included in Green Fee. **Discount golf packages:** Yes. **Season:** Year-round. **High:** March-Oct. **On site lodging:** Yes. **Rental clubs:** Yes. **Walking policy:** Mandatory cart. **Metal spikes allowed:** Yes. **Range:** Yes (grass/mats). **To obtain tee times:** Call pro shop up to two months in advance.

EAST/NORTH
Par: 72/72. **Yards:** 7,028/5,175. **Course rating:** 73.9/70.9. **Slope:** 132/122.
EAST/WEST
Par: 72/72. **Yards:** 6,971/5,172. **Course rating:** 73.0/69.9. **Slope:** 127/117.
NORTH/WEST
Par: 72/72. **Yards:** 6,975/5,172. **Course rating:** 73.2/69.6. **Slope:** 131/117.

Subscriber comments: North course more links type; more trees on East and West...Very organized, nice clubhouse...Challenging course...Beautiful—fair to all handicaps—plush...Great shape, nice people...Some interesting par 5s with water...Arnold Palmer design, demands accuracy!...Fall golf package very good value...Good track, not difficult but still challenging.

★★★½CRAFT FARMS THE WOODLANDS COURSE

PU-19995 Oak Rd. W., Gulf Shores, 36542, Baldwin County, (334)968-4133, (800)327-2657, 30 miles W of Pensacola, FL.

Opened: 1994. **Holes:** 18. **Par:** 72/72. **Yards:** 6,484/5,145. **Course rating:** 70.8. **Slope:** 123. **Architect:** Larry Nelson. **Green fee:** $40/$48. **Credit cards:** MC,VISA,AMEX. **Reduced fees:** Weekdays, low season, twilight, juniors. **Caddies:** No. **Golf carts:** Included in Green Fee. **Discount golf packages:** Yes. **Season:** Year-round. **High:** April-Aug. **On site lodging:** Yes. **Rental clubs:** Yes. **Walking policy:** Walking at certain times. **Metal spikes allowed:** Yes. **Range:** Yes (grass). **To obtain tee times:** Call up to two months in advance.

Subscriber comments: Great new course for average golfer...New facility, good greens...Shorter course than scorecard shows...We were treated very nicely...Tight fairways, shotmaker's course...Lots of water, fair course, lots of fun...Challenging course—carries over water and marsh...

★★½CULLMAN GOLF COURSE

PU-2321 County Rd. 490, Hanceville, 35077, Cullman County, (205)739-2386, 50 miles N of Birmingham.

Opened: 1950. **Holes:** 18. **Par:** 72/72. **Yards:** 6,361/4,495. **Course rating:** 69.8/67.7. **Slope:** 120/115. **Architect:** Curtis Davis. **Green fee:** $15. **Credit cards:** None. **Reduced fees:** Twilight. **Caddies:** No. **Golf carts:** $10. **Discount golf packages:** No. **Season:** Year-round. **High:** May-Aug. **On site lodging:** No. **Rental clubs:** No. **Walking policy:** Unrestricted walking. **Metal spikes allowed:** Yes. **Range:** Yes (grass). **To obtain tee times:** Reservations taken for weekends and holidays only. Call after 8 a.m. on Wednesday.

Subscriber comments: Good local course...Beautiful greens, tight fairways...Good layout...Well maintained for amount of traffic...Hazards come into play on blind tee shots.

★★★CYPRESS LAKES GOLF & COUNTRY CLUB

R-1311 E. 6th St., Muscle Shoals, 35661, Colbert County, (205)381-1232, 50 miles W of Huntsville.

Opened: 1991. **Holes:** 18. **Par:** 71/71. **Yards:** 6,562/5,100. **Course rating:** 71.8/69.3. **Slope:** 126/128. **Architect:** Gary Roger Baird. **Green fee:** $23/$28. **Credit cards:** MC,VISA,AMEX. **Reduced fees:** Weekdays, low season, juniors. **Caddies:** No. **Golf carts:** $13. **Discount golf packages:** Yes. **Season:** Year-round. **High:** March-Oct. **On site lodging:** No. **Rental clubs:** Yes. **Walking policy:** Walking at certain times. **Metal spikes allowed:** No. **Range:** Yes (grass). **To obtain tee times:** Call pro shop.

Subscriber comments: Short course, excellent greens, little sand...Have made a lot of improvements recently...Very good greens, short but challenging...Big improvements made, still a ways to go...Short but demanding.
Special Notes: Formerly The Oaks Golf Club.

★★★DEER RUN GOLF COURSE

PM-1175 County Rd. 100, Moulton, 35650, Lawrence County, (205)974-7384, 24 miles SW of Decater.

Opened: 1981. **Holes:** 18. **Par:** 72. **Yards:** 6,745. **Course rating:** 70.9. **Slope:** 119. **Architect:** Earl Stone. **Green fee:** $14/$17. **Credit cards:** N/A. **Reduced fees:** N/A.

Caddies: No. **Golf carts:** $16. **Discount golf packages:** No. **Season:** Year-round. **High:** April-Oct. **On site lodging:** No. **Rental clubs:** Yes. **Walking policy:** Unrestricted walking. **Metal spikes allowed:** Yes. **Range:** Yes (grass). **To obtain tee times:** N/A. **Subscriber comments:** Good design—well manicured—tests player's ability...Facilities were good...Good bent-grass greens...Very scenic, challenging in places...Very fast greens...Back nine plays into the Bankhead Forest. Scenery is very nice...Very good for small town golf course...Country style...Excellent test from blues.

★½DON A. HAWKINS GOLF COURSE
PM-8920 Robuck Rd., Birmingham, 35206, Jefferson County, (205)836-7318. Call club for further information.

★★★EAGLE POINT GOLF CLUB
PU-4500 Eagle Point Dr., Birmingham, 35242, Shelby County, (205)991-9070, 18 miles SE of Birmingham.
Opened: 1990. **Holes:** 18. **Par:** 71/70. **Yards:** 6,470/4,691. **Course rating:** 70.2/61.9. **Slope:** 127/108. **Architect:** Earl Stone. **Green fee:** $22/$32. **Credit cards:** All major. **Reduced fees:** Seniors. **Caddies:** No. **Golf carts:** $11. **Discount golf packages:** No. **Season:** Year-round. **High:** April-Sept. **On site lodging:** No. **Rental clubs:** Yes. **Walking policy:** Unrestricted walking. **Metal spikes allowed:** Yes. **Range:** Yes (grass). **To obtain tee times:** Call up to five days in advance.
Subscriber comments: New greens, fairways tight...First 4 holes are too close...Hit it straight—score well. Good public course...Enjoyable to play. Fair to average golfer...Short but pleasant...After first three or four holes, great layout...Nice atmosphere...Good solid course for all levels of skill.

★★FRANK HOUSE MUNICIPAL GOLF CLUB
PU-801 Golf Course Rd., Bessemer, 35020, Jefferson County, (205)424-9540, 15 miles S of Birmingham.
Opened: 1972. **Holes:** 18. **Par:** 72/75. **Yards:** 6,320/5,034. **Course rating:** 69.0/63.3. **Slope:** 119/107. **Architect:** Earl Stone. **Green fee:** $12/$15. **Credit cards:** All major. **Reduced fees:** Weekdays, low season, resort guests, twilight, seniors. **Caddies:** No. **Golf carts:** $10. **Discount golf packages:** No. **Season:** Year-round. **High:** May-Aug. **On site lodging:** No. **Rental clubs:** Yes. **Walking policy:** Walking at certain times. **Metal spikes allowed:** Yes. **Range:** No. **To obtain tee times:** First come, first served.

★★★GLENLAKES GOLF CLUB
9530 Clubhouse Dr., Foley, 36535, Baldwin County, (334)955-1221, (800)264-8333, 50 miles SE of Mobile.
Opened: 1987. **Holes:** 18. **Par:** 72/72. **Yards:** 6,938/5,384. **Course rating:** 72.2/70.5. **Slope:** 123/114. **Architect:** Robert von Hagge/Bruce Devlin. **Green fee:** $23/$37. **Credit cards:** All major. **Reduced fees:** Weekdays, low season, resort guests, twilight, juniors. **Caddies:** No. **Golf carts:** $11. **Discount golf packages:** Yes. **Season:** Year-round. **High:** Jan.-March. **On site lodging:** No. **Rental clubs:** Yes. **Walking policy:** Mandatory cart.

★★★½GOOSE POND COLONY GOLF COURSE
R-417 Ed Hembree Dr., Scottsboro, 35769, Jackson County, (205)574-5353, (800)268-2884, 40 miles E of Huntsville.
Opened: 1968. **Holes:** 18. **Par:** 72/72. **Yards:** 6,860/5,370. **Course rating:** 71.7/70.0. **Slope:** 125/115. **Architect:** George Cobb. **Green fee:** $14/$21. **Credit cards:** MC,VISA,DISC. **Reduced fees:** Weekdays, resort guests, seniors, juniors. **Caddies:** No. **Golf carts:** $9. **Discount golf packages:** Yes. **Season:** Year-round. **High:** April-Aug. **On site lodging:** Yes. **Rental clubs:** Yes. **Walking policy:** Walking at certain times. **Metal spikes allowed:** Yes. **Range:** Yes (grass). **To obtain tee times:** Call Monday for weekend three days in advance.
Subscriber comments: Finest public course in that part of state...Long and challenging...Hidden jewel, great fairways, scenic wildlife...Great layout—challenge but fair...Very nice facility...Good for high handicappers...Beautiful layout—inexpensive cabins on water across street from pro shop...A dream layout. Great view of little mountain!

ALABAMA

GRAND NATIONAL GOLF CLUB
PU-3000 Sunbelt Pkwy., Opelika, 36801, Lee County, (205)749-9042, (800)949-4444, 55 miles E of Montgomery.
Opened: 1992. **Architect:** Robert Trent Jones. **Credit cards:** All major. **Caddies:** No. **Discount golf packages:** Yes. **Season:** Year-round. **High:** March-Oct. **On site lodging:** No. **Rental clubs:** Yes.
Walking policy: Unrestricted walking. **Metal spikes allowed:** Yes. **Range:** Yes (grass).
To obtain tee times: Call golf shop.

★★★★LAKE COURSE
Holes: 18. **Par:** 72/72. **Yards:** 7,149/4,910. **Course rating:** 74.9/68.7. **Slope:** 138/117. **Green fee:** $39/$49. **Reduced fees:** Low season, juniors. **Golf carts:** $15.
Notes: Ranked 4th in 1997 Best in State.
Subscriber comments: Great golf, excellent service, beautiful settings...Top-notch layout with tough finishing hole...Spectacular scenery, almost a distraction...Very beautiful and difficult. A player's course...Best, most playable on the Trail...Monster. Phenomenal experience...Outstanding layout and condition...Challenging, well laid out, beautiful surroundings, don't play from the tips.

★★★★LINKS COURSE
Holes: 18. **Par:** 72/72. **Yards:** 7,311/4,843. **Course rating:** 74.9/69.6. **Slope:** 141/113. **Green fee:** $39/$49. **Reduced fees:** Low season, juniors. **Golf carts:** $15.
Notes: Ranked 5th in 1997 Best in State.
Subscriber comments: Move up one set of tees on this one. Tough...Best of Trent Jones I've played...Outstanding course, very tough but enjoyable...18 tough finishing hole. Big undulating greens...Very fun but very difficult...Add 10-15 strokes to your handicap...I love this place! Can't get enough of it...Best of a wonderful Trail...Terrific amenities.

★★★★SHORT COURSE
Holes: 18. **Par:** 54/54. **Yards:** 3,328/1,715. **Course rating:** N/A. **Slope:** N/A. **Green fee:** $15/$15. **Reduced fees:** Juniors. **Golf carts:** $10.
Subscriber comments: Best par 3 layout—no expense spared. Highly recommended...A dozen signature holes...Great variety of short holes...Beautiful par-3 course for a workout on your irons...Short, fun, great to play after playing Lake and Links ...Beautiful par-3 track, great practice, use most clubs...Great fun, yet challenging.
Special Notes: Part of the Robert Trent Jones Golf Trail.

★★½GULF SHORES GOLF CLUB
520 Clubhouse Dr., Gulf Shores, 36547, Baldwin County, (334)968-7366, 20 miles W of Pensacola, FL.
Opened: 1964. **Holes:** 18. **Par:** 72/72. **Yards:** 6,570/5,522. **Course rating:** 72.1/72.0. **Slope:** 122/121. **Architect:** Earl Stone. **Green fee:** $32/$37. **Credit cards:** MC,VISA. **Reduced fees:** Juniors. **Caddies:** No. **Golf carts:** Included in Green Fee. **Discount golf packages:** No. **Season:** Year-round. **High:** Jan.-Aug. **On site lodging:** No. **Rental clubs:** Yes. **Walking policy:** Mandatory cart. **Metal spikes allowed:** Yes. **Range:** Yes (grass). **To obtain tee times:** Call pro shop five days in advance.
Subscriber comments: Excellent golf, staff, service, food...Tough par 3s...Nice course, big greens, good shape...Short course, great layout...New larger greens, very tight on certain holes...Short, good for walking...Older course, walks easily, not too crowded.

★★★GULF STATE PARK GOLF COURSE
PU-20115 State Hwy. 135, Gulf Shores, 36542, Baldwin County, (334)948-4653, 50 miles W of Mobile.
Opened: 1974. **Holes:** 18. **Par:** 72/72. **Yards:** 6,563/5,310. **Course rating:** 72.5/70.4. **Slope:** N/A. **Architect:** Earl Stone. **Green fee:** $20/$22. **Credit cards:** MC,VISA,AMEX. **Reduced fees:** Resort guests, seniors. **Caddies:** No. **Golf carts:** $13. **Discount golf packages:** Yes. **Season:** Year-round. **High:** Feb.-April/June-Aug. **On site lodging:** Yes. **Rental clubs:** Yes. **Walking policy:** Unrestricted walking. **Metal spikes allowed:** Yes. **Range:** Yes (grass). **To obtain tee times:** Call day before for weekdays, for weekends, call from Wednesday on.
Subscriber comments: The most relaxing round you'll ever play...Watch for

gators...Good condition for amount of play...Fun, always slow, meet nice people...Very good course, stays busy, good for everyone...Heaven for seniors...Scenic. Good for weekend golfer. Slow.

★★★½ GUNTER'S LANDING GOLF COURSE

1000 Gunter's Landing Rd., Gunterville, 35976, Marshall County, (205)582-3586, (800)833-6663, 35 miles SE of Huntsville.

Opened: 1992. **Holes:** 18. **Par:** 72/72. **Yards:** 6,863/5,274. **Course rating:** 73.3/70.0. **Slope:** 144/113. **Architect:** Jim Kennamer. **Green fee:** $30/$34. **Credit cards:** All major. **Reduced fees:** Low season. **Caddies:** No. **Golf carts:** Included in Green Fee. **Discount golf packages:** Yes. **Season:** Year-round. **High:** March-Sept. **On site lodging:** No. **Rental clubs:** No. **Walking policy:** Walking at certain times. **Metal spikes allowed:** Yes. **Range:** Yes (grass). **To obtain tee times:** Call seven days in advance for weekdays; Thursday prior for weekends.

Subscriber comments: Beautiful setting, narrow fairways, great greens...One of prettiest courses in North Alabama...Challenging—hilly lies...This course will get better every year...Some spectacular views. Super nice greens...Undulating greens are tough...Beautiful course, well manicured, landscaped...Fabulous course and great people...Great layout...Beautiful; intimidating.

HAMPTON COVE GOLF CLUB

PU-450 Old Hwy. 431 S., Huntsville, 35763, Madison County, (205)551-1818, (800)949-4444, 5 miles SE of Huntsville.
Architect: Robert Trent Jones. **Caddies:** No. **On site lodging:** No.
Metal spikes allowed: Yes.

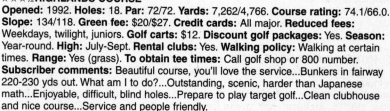

★★★½ HIGHLANDS COURSE

Opened: 1992. **Holes:** 18. **Par:** 72/72. **Yards:** 7,262/4,766. **Course rating:** 74.1/66.0. **Slope:** 134/118. **Green fee:** $20/$27. **Credit cards:** All major. **Reduced fees:** Weekdays, twilight, juniors. **Golf carts:** $12. **Discount golf packages:** Yes. **Season:** Year-round. **High:** July-Sept. **Rental clubs:** Yes. **Walking policy:** Walking at certain times. **Range:** Yes (grass). **To obtain tee times:** Call golf shop or 800 number.

Subscriber comments: Beautiful course, you'll love the service...Bunkers in fairway 220-230 yds out. What am I to do?...Outstanding, scenic, harder than Japanese math...Enjoyable, difficult, blind holes...Prepare to play target golf...Clean clubhouse and nice course...Service and people friendly.

★★★½ RIVER COURSE

Opened: 1993. **Holes:** 18. **Par:** 72/72. **Yards:** 7,507/5,283. **Course rating:** 75.6/67.0. **Slope:** 135/118. **Green fee:** $20/$27. **Credit cards:** All major. **Reduced fees:** Weekdays, twilight, juniors. **Golf carts:** $12. **Discount golf packages:** Yes. **Season:** Year-round. **High:** July-Sept. **Rental clubs:** Yes. **Walking policy:** Unrestricted walking. **Range:** Yes (grass). **To obtain tee times:** Tee times required. Call golf shop or 800 number.

Subscriber comments: Severe undulations make greens tough to two-putt...Be honest on tee selection, very very long...Look out for snakes in summer!...Water in play on 15 holes...Very fair test of golf; course is a little unusual, no sand...Take some extra balls. Great course. Staff excellent.

★★★★ SHORT COURSE

Holes: 18. **Par:** 54/54. **Yards:** 3,140/1,829. **Green fee:** $13. **Reduced fees:** Weekdays, low season, twilight, juniors.

Subscriber comments: Fun for golfers of any level...Excellent test of your short game...Great practice for iron play, very enjoyable...Short, wet, good for your iron play...Not your typical par 3 course: 200-yard. par 3s on water. Worth the time to play. Only $10 extra after playing 18...Mean and long...Great short course.

Special Notes: Part of the Robert Trent Jones Golf Trail.

★★★★½ HIGHLAND OAKS GOLF CLUB

PU-704 Royal Pkwy., Dothan, 36301, Houston County, (334)712-2820, (800)949-4444, 193 miles SE of Birmingham.
Opened: 1993. **Holes:** 27. **Architect:** Robert Trent Jones. **Green fee:** $20/$27. **Credit cards:** All major. **Reduced fees:** Weekdays, low season, twilight, seniors, juniors. **Caddies:** No. **Golf carts:** $15. **Discount

golf packages: Yes. **Season:** Year-round. **High:** March-Oct. **On site lodging:** No. **Rental clubs:** Yes. **Walking policy:** Unrestricted walking. **Metal spikes allowed:** Yes. **Range:** Yes (grass). **To obtain tee times:** Call seven days in advance.

HIGHLANDS/MAGNOLIA
Par: 72/72. **Yards:** 7,591/6,025. **Course rating:** 76.0/67.6. **Slope:** 135/118.
HIGHLANDS/MARSHWOOD
Par: 72/72. **Yards:** 7,704/5,085. **Course rating:** 76.9/68.3. **Slope:** 138/120.
MARSHWOOD/MAGNOLIA
Par: 72/72. **Yards:** 7,511/6,002. **Course rating:** 75.7/67.3. **Slope:** 133/116.
Subscriber comments: One of the best kept secrets of Trent Jones Trail...Probably the best Trail course for the average Joe...Tough course. Excellent facilities...Fantastic golf course, top of my list...Blind shots. Placement critical...Great service—course is beautiful...Championship caliber, could host a PGA event.
Special Notes: Part of the Robert Trent Jones Golf Trail. Complex also includes Short Course, a 9-hole par-3 layout.

★★HUNTSVILLE MUNICIPAL GOLF COURSE
PU-2151 Airport Rd., Huntsville, 35801, Madison County, (205)883-3647.
Opened: 1986. **Holes:** 18. **Par:** 72/72. **Yards:** 6,408/4,909. **Course rating:** 70.2/63.4. **Slope:** 122/109. **Architect:** Ron Kirby/Denis Griffiths. **Green fee:** $14/$14. **Credit cards:** None. **Reduced fees:** N/A. **Caddies:** No. **Golf carts:** $14. **Discount golf packages:** No. **Season:** Year-round. **High:** April-Oct. **On site lodging:** No. **Rental clubs:** No. **Walking policy:** Unrestricted walking. **Metal spikes allowed:** Yes. **Range:** Yes. **To obtain tee times:** N/A.
Subscriber comments: Well-kept short course. Fun to play...Good variety of different kinds of holes...Short but fair test...Average golf...Slow play...10 and 18 are strong holes.

★★★INDIAN PINES GOLF CLUB
PU-900 Country Club Lane, Auburn, 36830, Lee County, (334)821-0880, 50 miles W of Montgomery.
Opened: 1976. **Holes:** 18. **Par:** 71/71. **Yards:** 6,213/4,751. **Course rating:** 68.8/62.1. **Slope:** 119/105. **Architect:** N/A. **Green fee:** $11/$13. **Credit cards:** MC,VISA. **Reduced fees:** N/A. **Caddies:** No. **Golf carts:** $9. **Discount golf packages:** No. **Season:** Year-round. **High:** N/A. **On site lodging:** No. **Rental clubs:** Yes. **Walking policy:** Unrestricted walking. **Metal spikes allowed:** Yes. **Range:** Yes (grass/mats). **To obtain tee times:** Call up to 1 week in advance.
Subscriber comments: Fun for any ability player...Nice staff...Short fun course—very busy...Great public course, fairways could be better...Good little course for the money, no frills, tricky greens...In decent shape for a municipal course and the amount of play it gets. Impressed with the condition that the greens are kept. Good course for low and high handicappers.

★★ISLE DAUPHINE GOLF CLUB
PU-100 Orleans Dr., P.O. Box 39, Dauphin Island, 36528, Mobile County, (334)861-2433, 30 miles S of Mobile.
Opened: 1958. **Holes:** 18. **Par:** 72/72. **Yards:** 6,620/5,619. **Course rating:** 70.8/72.6. **Slope:** 123/122. **Architect:** Charles Maddox. **Green fee:** $12/$13. **Credit cards:** MC,VISA. **Reduced fees:** Weekdays, twilight, juniors. **Caddies:** No. **Golf carts:** $11. **Discount golf packages:** No. **Season:** Year-round. **High:** Feb.-May. **On site lodging:** No. **Rental clubs:** Yes. **Walking policy:** Unrestricted walking. **Metal spikes allowed:** Yes. **Range:** No. **To obtain tee times:** Call up to 1 week in advance.

★★½JOE WHEELER STATE PARK GOLF COURSE
R-Rte. 4, Box 369A, Rogersville, 35652, Lauderdale County, (205)247-9308, (800)252-7275, 20 miles E of Florence.
Opened: 1974. **Holes:** 18. **Par:** 72/72. **Yards:** 7,251/6,055. **Course rating:** 73.1/67.7. **Slope:** 120/109. **Architect:** Earl Stone. **Green fee:** $15. **Credit cards:** MC,VISA,AMEX. **Reduced fees:** Resort guests, seniors. **Caddies:** No. **Golf carts:** $18. **Discount golf packages:** Yes. **Season:** Year-round. **High:** March-Oct. **On site lodging:** Yes. **Rental clubs:** Yes. **Walking policy:** Unrestricted walking. **Metal spikes**

allowed: Yes. **Range:** Yes (grass). **To obtain tee times:** March to October tee times required for weekends and holidays taken Monday before play.
Subscriber comments: Wide fairways, challenging par 3s, long...Long. Blind shots. ..Very hilly course...Great course. Very demanding and long...Very good winter greens, scenic, challenging...Endurance needed...Par-5 13th and par-3 14th worth the price of admission...Beautiful course on banks of the Tennessee River.

★★★★ KIVA DUNES GOLF CLUB
PU-815 Plantation Dr., Gulf Shores, 36542, Baldwin County, (334)540-7000, 45 miles W of Pensacola, FL.
Opened: 1995. **Holes:** 18. **Par:** 72/72. **Yards:** 7,092/4,994. **Course rating:** 73.9/68.5.
Slope: 132/115. **Architect:** Jerry Pate. **Green fee:** $55/$75. **Credit cards:** All major.
Reduced fees: Low season. **Caddies:** No. **Golf carts:** Included in Green Fee.
Discount golf packages: Yes. **Season:** Year-round. **High:** Feb.-Oct. **On site lodging:** No (will be available 8/98). **Rental clubs:** Yes. **Walking policy:** Unrestricted walking.
Metal spikes allowed: Yes. **Range:** Yes (grass). **To obtain tee times:** Guests may call up to 60 days in advance.
Notes: Ranked 2nd in 1995 Best New Public Courses; ranked 3rd in 1997 Best in State.
Subscriber comments: Excellent facilities and grounds...Never seen so much sand...Outstanding design in great environment...Good golf but very punishing if you miss fairways...Beautiful, windy beach course...Play and play again/never get bored/stunning...Better be hitting your driver. Much trouble off the tee...Top notch course, always a wind, play 5+ hours on weekend.

★★★½ LAGOON PARK GOLF COURSE
PM-2855 Lagoon Park Dr., Montgomery, 36109, Montgomery County, (334)271-7000.
Opened: 1978. **Holes:** 18. **Par:** 72/72. **Yards:** 6,773/5,342. **Course rating:** 71.1/69.6.
Slope: 124/113. **Architect:** Charles M. Graves. **Green fee:** $15/$20. **Credit cards:** MC,VISA,DISC. **Reduced fees:** Weekdays, low season. **Caddies:** No. **Golf carts:** $10.
Discount golf packages: Yes. **Season:** Year-round. **High:** April-Oct. **On site lodging:** No. **Rental clubs:** Yes. **Walking policy:** Unrestricted walking. **Metal spikes allowed:** Yes. **Range:** Yes (grass). **To obtain tee times:** Call Thursday a.m. for weekend tee times. No reserved times during week.
Subscriber comments: Would recommend to anyone...Good course from back tees...Short but quality course...Crowned fairways are hard...Narrow fairways. Challenging course...A really good public course...Easy layout but tight...Great walking course, but usually crowded...A very good municipal course, better than many resort courses...Long par 4s. Easy walk...Fast greens, good service.

★★★ LAKE GUNTERSVILLE GOLF CLUB
PU-7966 Alabama Hwy. 227, Guntersville, 35976, Marshall County, (205)582-0379, 40 miles S of Huntsville.
Opened: 1974. **Holes:** 18. **Par:** 72/72. **Yards:** 6,785/5,776. **Course rating:** 71.2/70.3.
Slope: 128/124. **Architect:** Earl Stone. **Green fee:** $15/$15. **Credit cards:** MC,VISA,AMEX. **Reduced fees:** Seniors. **Caddies:** No. **Golf carts:** $20. **Discount golf packages:** Yes. **Season:** Year-round. **High:** July-Aug. **On site lodging:** Yes.
Rental clubs: Yes. **Walking policy:** Unrestricted walking. **Metal spikes allowed:** Yes.
Range: Yes (grass). **To obtain tee times:** Call Wednesday prior to weekend. Tee times for weekends and holidays only.
Subscriber comments: No water. Good amenities...On top of a mountain. Good driving range...Very hilly—lot of blind shots—fun to play...Good condition, nice people, fun...Beautiful course state owned and run...Grip and rip, tough to walk, not much trouble...Interesting course, plenty of hills and trees...Must hit to centers of greens. Don't be short...Beautiful place for a golf vacation!

★★ LAKEPOINT RESORT GOLF COURSE
R-Hwy. 431, Eufaula, 36027, Barbour County, (334)687-6677, (800)544-5253, 50 miles S of Columbus, GA.
Opened: 1971. **Holes:** 18. **Par:** 72/72. **Yards:** 6,752/5,363. **Course rating:** 73.6/69.2.
Slope: 123. **Architect:** Thomas Nicol. **Green fee:** $13. **Credit cards:** MC,VISA,AMEX.
Reduced fees: Seniors. **Caddies:** No. **Golf carts:** $9. **Discount golf packages:** Yes.
Season: Year-round. **High:** March-June. **On site lodging:** Yes. **Rental clubs:** Yes.

Walking policy: Unrestricted walking. **Metal spikes allowed:** Yes. **Range:** Yes. **To obtain tee times:** Call for weekends tee times only.

★★½ THE LINKSMAN GOLF CLUB

PU-3700 St. Andrews Dr., Mobile, 36693, Mobile County, (334)661-0018, 50 miles W of Pensacola, FL.
Opened: 1987. **Holes:** 18. **Par:** 72/72. **Yards:** 6,275/5,416. **Course rating:** 70.1/71.0.
Slope: 123/121. **Architect:** N/A. **Green fee:** $18/$18. **Credit cards:** All major.
Reduced fees: Weekdays, resort guests, twilight, seniors, juniors. **Caddies:** No. **Golf carts:** $11. **Discount golf packages:** Yes. **Season:** Year-round. **High:** March-June. **On site lodging:** No. **Rental clubs:** Yes. **Walking policy:** Unrestricted walking. **Metal spikes allowed:** Yes. **Range:** Yes (grass). **To obtain tee times:** Call golf shop.
Subscriber comments: Fun course if you hit it straight. Lots of water...14 holes with water, tough and fun...Very good staff...Have done a lot to improve...Great course and facilities, good friendly staff...Short, water all over, leave driver in bag mostly.

MAGNOLIA GROVE GOLF CLUB

PU-7000 Lamplighter Dr., Semmes, 36575, Mobile County, (334)645-0075, (800)949-4444, 22 miles E of Mobile.
Opened: 1992. **Architect:** Robert Trent Jones. **Credit cards:** All major.
Caddies: No. **Discount golf packages:** Yes. **Season:** Year-round. **On site lodging:** No. **Walking policy:** Unrestricted walking. **Metal spikes allowed:** Yes. **Range:** Yes (grass). **To obtain tee times:** Call pro shop up to 7 days in advance. Over 7 days call 1-800-949-4444.

(Good Service)

★★★★ CROSSINGS COURSE

Holes: 18. **Par:** 72/72. **Yards:** 7,150/5,184. **Course rating:** 74.6/70.4. **Slope:** 134/131.
Green fee: $34/$44. **Reduced fees:** Weekdays, low season, twilight, seniors, juniors.
Golf carts: $15. **High:** Feb.-April, Sept.-Nov. **Rental clubs:** Yes.
Notes: 1998 Nike Tour Championship.
Subscriber comments: Can be tough...Short game better be good...Outstanding lay-out...Real challenge. Great people...Great layout. Tough greens...Must hit landing areas to play effectively. Has large undulating greens that are well protected by bunkers...Tough finishing holes...Robert Trent Jones design, tough and beautiful greens have swales that can be unfair with pin placements.

★★★★ FALLS COURSE

Holes: 18. **Par:** 72/72. **Yards:** 7,240/5,253. **Course rating:** 75.1/71.0. **Slope:** 137/126.
Green fee: $34/$44. **Reduced fees:** Weekdays, low season, twilight, seniors, juniors.
Golf carts: $15. **High:** Feb.-April, Sept.-Nov. **Rental clubs:** Yes.
Notes: Ranked 6th in 1997 Best in State.
Subscriber comments: Less tough of the two...Outstanding facilities and grounds...Beautiful course, great layout, challenging...Very long, tough course, but fair, large greens...Difficult greens (much undulation) Enjoyed it!...Very good course, well groomed...Teaches you to be humble...Facilities, pro shop outstanding, immaculate grounds...Lots of fun. Tight opening holes.

★★★★ SHORT COURSE

Holes: 18. **Par:** 54/54. **Yards:** 3,140/1,829. **Course rating:** N/A. **Slope:** N/A. **Green fee:** $15/$15. **Reduced fees:** Weekdays, juniors. **Golf carts:** $10. **High:** April-Oct.
Rental clubs: No.
Subscriber comments: Favorite course in Mobile County is the par 3 (Short Course)...Awe-inspiring par 3, very fun and challenging...Good test, variety of par 3s all lengths, many tees...Great for sharpening up on iron play...Beautiful, greens slick, mounds all over, best par 3 you'll ever play...Beautiful and a great test as well!...Beautiful, yet difficult greens...Par is good score...For a par 3 course it's a 10.
Special Notes: Part of the Robert Trent Jones Golf Trail.

MARRIOTT'S LAKEWOOD GOLF CLUB

R-Marriott's Grand Hotel, Scenic Hwy. 98, Point Clear, 36564, Baldwin County, (334)990-6312, (800)544-9933, 30 miles SE of Mobile.
Opened: 1947. **Green fee:** $69/$69. **Credit cards:** All major. **Reduced fees:** Twilight, juniors. **Caddies:** No. **Golf carts:** Included in Green Fee. **Discount golf packages:** Yes. **Season:** Year-round. **High:** Feb.-May, Oct.-Dec. **On site lodging:** Yes. **Rental clubs:** Yes. **Walking policy:** Mandatory cart. **Metal spikes allowed:** Yes. **Range:** Yes (grass). **To obtain tee times:** Must be a member or a guest of hotel or member.

★★½ AZALEA COURSE
Holes: 18. **Par:** 72/72. **Yards:** 6,770/5,307. **Course rating:** 72.5/71.3. **Slope:** 128/118. **Architect:** Perry Maxwell/Ron Garl.
Subscriber comments: Fun little 18...Very traditional, tight...Improved greens, enjoyable service at hotel...A real class place...Small, personal—good service...Neat course with lots of old trees and stuff...Classic style and kept up well...Fun to play.

★★★ DOGWOOD COURSE
Holes: 18. **Par:** 71/72. **Yards:** 6,676/5,532. **Course rating:** 72.1/72.6. **Slope:** 124/122. **Architect:** Perry Maxwell/Joe Lee.
Subscriber comments: Old style course—difficult...Nice, pretty course at fabulous resort...A real class place...Fair course, excellent service...Good old course needs updating to compete in area...Bring your game with you—it can eat you up!...Real nice, long course...Service is a plus...Good basic golf.

★★ MCFARLAND PARK GOLF COURSE
PM-James M. Spain Dr., Florence, 35630, Lauderdale County, (205)760-6428, 120 miles NW of Birmingham.
Opened: 1972. **Holes:** 18. **Par:** 72/72. **Yards:** 6,660/5,741. **Course rating:** 71.9/72.9. **Slope:** 113/106. **Architect:** Earl Stone. **Green fee:** $6/$11. **Credit cards:** MC,VISA. **Reduced fees:** Low season, seniors, juniors. **Caddies:** No. **Golf carts:** $16. **Discount golf packages:** No. **Season:** Year-round. **High:** May-Oct. **On site lodging:** No. **Rental clubs:** Yes. **Walking policy:** Unrestricted walking. **Metal spikes allowed:** Yes. **Range:** Yes (grass). **To obtain tee times:** Call Tuesday before upcoming weekend and holidays.

★★½ THE MEADOWS GOLF COURSE
PU-1 Plantation Dr., Harpersville, 35078, Shelby County, (205)672-7529, 20 miles E of Birmingham.
Opened: 1995. **Holes:** 18. **Par:** 72/72. **Yards:** 6,823/5,275. **Course rating:** 71.6/70.1. **Slope:** 122/119. **Architect:** Steve Plumer. **Green fee:** $25/$30. **Credit cards:** All major. **Reduced fees:** Twilight, seniors, juniors. **Caddies:** No. **Golf carts:** Included in Green Fee. **Discount golf packages:** No. **Season:** Year-round. **High:** N/A. **On site lodging:** No. **Rental clubs:** Yes. **Walking policy:** Walking at certain times. **Metal spikes allowed:** Yes. **Range:** Yes (grass). **To obtain tee times:** Call 5 days in advance; walk-ons during the week.
Subscriber comments: Short but quality course—good condition always, open and fair...Good young course...New course, grass still growing. Good course...Challenging course with lots of rough...Will mature, still has some rough spots...Good mix of holes. Very few trees, pretty flat with mounding...Good layout. May deserve higher rating after course matures.

MONTEVALLO GOLF CLUB
SP-1481 Shelby County Hwy 204, Montevallo, 35115, Shelby County, (205)665-8057, 30 miles S of Birmingham.
Opened: 1956. **Holes:** 18. **Par:** 70. **Yards:** 6,000. **Course rating:** 66.0. **Slope:** 109. **Architect:** N/A. **Green fee:** $10/$16. **Credit cards:** MC,VISA. **Reduced fees:** Twilight, seniors, juniors. **Caddies:** No. **Golf carts:** $9. **Discount golf packages:** No. **Season:** Year-round. **High:** N/A. **On site lodging:** No. **Rental clubs:** Yes. **Walking policy:** Unrestricted walking. **Metal spikes allowed:** Yes. **Range:** Yes (grass). **To obtain tee times:** N/A.

★★½ MOUNTAIN VIEW GOLF CLUB
PU-3200 Mountain View Dr., Graysville, 35073, Jefferson County, (205)674-8362, 17 miles W of Birmingham.
Opened: 1991. **Holes:** 27. **Architect:** James Thursby. **Green fee:** $25/$30. **Credit cards:** MC,VISA,DISC. **Reduced fees:** Twilight, juniors. **Caddies:** No. **Golf carts:** Included in Green Fee. **Discount golf packages:** No. **Season:** Year-round. **High:** March-Oct. **On site lodging:** No. **Rental clubs:** No. **Walking policy:** Mandatory cart. **Metal spikes allowed:** Yes. **Range:** No. **To obtain tee times:** Call 3 days in advance for weekends.
RED/BLUE
Par: 71/71. **Yards:** 6,070/4,816. **Course rating:** 69.3/69.4. **Slope:** 114/120.

RED/WHITE
Holes: 27. **Par:** 71/71. **Yards:** 5,800/4,702. **Course rating:** 67.5/67.5. **Slope:** 111/116.
WHITE/BLUE
Holes: 27. **Par:** 70/70. **Yards:** 5,890/4,718. **Course rating:** 68.4/68.5. **Slope:** 114/123.
Subscriber comments: Very easy on the game and eyes...Hit fairways or else. Short course. Fair for average players. Low numbers for good players...Good course. Fun to play, many level changes...Good course, short—target golf...Very scenic...Lots of fun for short knockers.

★★★ OAK MOUNTAIN STATE PARK GOLF COURSE
PU-Findley Dr., Pelham, 35124, Shelby County, (205)620-2522, 15 miles S of Birmingham.
Opened: 1974. **Holes:** 18. **Par:** 72/72. **Yards:** 6,748/5,540. **Course rating:** 71.5.
Slope: 127/124. **Architect:** Earl Stone. **Green fee:** $12/$18. **Credit cards:**
MC,VISA,AMEX. **Reduced fees:** Seniors. **Caddies:** No. **Golf carts:** $18. **Discount golf packages:** Yes. **Season:** Year-round. **High:** May-Sept. **On site lodging:** Yes.
Rental clubs: No. **Walking policy:** Unrestricted walking. **Metal spikes allowed:** Yes.
Range: Yes (grass). **To obtain tee times:** Call Mondays for upcoming Saturday, Tuesday for Sunday, Wednesday for Monday, etc.
Subscriber comments: Great public course, always crowded...Nice course for the public. Was in decent shape...Good course for all. Be prepared for slow play...State park, beautiful mountain setting, wildlife (deer)...Short, nice layout for a muny...Could be better with work...Nice facilities, excellent course...Enjoyable, good practice area...Fairways suprisingly plush. Greens sometimes dry out in summer.

★★★ OLYMPIA SPA GOLF RESORT
Hwy. 231 S., Dothan, 36302, Houston County, (334)677-3326.
Opened: 1968. **Holes:** 18. **Par:** 72/72. **Yards:** 7,242/5,470. **Course rating:** 74.5/71.1.
Slope: 123/113. **Architect:** Bob Simmons. **Green fee:** $12/$18. **Credit cards:** All major. **Reduced fees:** Twilight. **Caddies:** No. **Golf carts:** $10. **Discount golf packages:** Yes. **Season:** Year-round. **High:** March-June. **On site lodging:** Yes. **Rental clubs:** Yes. **Walking policy:** Walking at certain times. **Metal spikes allowed:** Yes.
Range: Yes (grass). **To obtain tee times:** Call golf shop.
Subscriber comments: With proper maintenance, the US Open could be played here...Long course, no fairway bunkers, few water holes, old facilities, motel...Friendly staff...Best 19th hole in SE Alabama...Improvements being made.

OXMOOR VALLEY GOLF CLUB
PU-100 Sunbelt Pkwy., Birmingham, 35211, Jefferson County, (205)942-1177, (800)949-4444.
Opened: 1992. **Architect:** Robert Trent Jones. **Credit cards:** All major.
Caddies: No. **Discount golf packages:** Yes. **Season:** Year-round. **High:** April-Nov. **On site lodging:** No. **Rental clubs:** Yes. **Walking policy:** Unrestricted walking. **Metal spikes allowed:** Yes. **Range:** Yes (grass). **To obtain tee times:** Call course up to 7 days in advance. May reserve tee times up to 120 days in advance by calling toll free reservations number.

(GREAT SERVICE)

★★★½ RIDGE COURSE
Holes: 18. **Par:** 72/72. **Yards:** 7,055/4,869. **Course rating:** 73.5/69.1. **Slope:** 140/122.
Green fee: $39/$49. **Reduced fees:** Weekdays, low season, juniors. **Golf carts:** $15.
Subscriber comments: Best RTJ layout on the "Trail"...Great service, brute course from the blue tees!...Keeps the pressure on at every tee box...Hilly; lots of blind shorts...Scenic, well conditioned...Pretty tough for higher handicaps, plateau fairways...All clubs in bag will be used here!...Very difficult. Beautiful views. Great test for all levels...Fun. You play from hilltop to hilltop...Breathtaking views...Only for 10 handicap or better, greens tough to hold and putt...Roller coaster ride!...Staff excellent and friendly. Great clubhouse and view.

★★★★ SHORT COURSE
Holes: 18. **Par:** 54/54. **Yards:** 3,154/1,990. **Green fee:** $15/$15. **Reduced fees:** Juniors.
Subscriber comments: Can use most of the clubs in your bag—not your average par 3...Very enjoyable; challenging...Short course exposes all weaknessess of your game...Game better be on or this par 3 will give you fits...Excellent test of the iron game, multiple tee options...Great par 3 course; most fun I've ever had playing golf...It

might be par 3s, but a tremendous shotmaker's course...Great practice course.

★★★½ VALLEY COURSE

Holes: 18. **Par:** 72/72. **Yards:** 7,240/4,866. **Course rating:** 73.9/69.4. **Slope:** 135/122. **Green fee:** $39/$49. **Reduced fees:** Weekdays, low season, juniors. **Golf carts:** $15.
Subscriber comments: Par-4 15th is a killer...Beautiful bent-grass greens, extremely challenging...Beautiful course, everyone must try once...Tough track. Good greens. Bring your "A" game...More fun than Ridge course, plenty of challenges...Good mixture of tough and easy holes.
Special Notes: Part of the Robert Trent Jones Golf Trail.

★★★★ THE PENINSULA GOLF CLUB

PU-20 Peninsula Blvd., Gulf Shores, 36542, Baldwin County, (334)968-8009, 50 miles S of Mobile.
Opened: 1995. **Holes:** 18. **Par:** 72/72. **Yards:** 7,026/5,072. **Course rating:** 73.4/72.1. **Slope:** 126/119. **Architect:** Earl Stone. **Green fee:** $45/$68. **Credit cards:** All major. **Reduced fees:** Twilight. **Caddies:** No. **Golf carts:** Included in Green Fee. **Discount golf packages:** No. **Season:** Year-round. **High:** Feb.-May. **On site lodging:** No. **Rental clubs:** Yes. **Walking policy:** Walking at certain times. **Metal spikes allowed:** Yes. **Range:** Yes (grass). **To obtain tee times:** Call up to 30 days in advance.
Subscriber comments: Great layout, challenge from any tee...Excellent new course...Must have all shots...A beautiful course with enough water to challenge your accuracy. Great elevated greens to chip to...Beautiful, a must for all golfers; the picturesque par-3 17th is a treat.

★★★ POINT MALLARD GOLF COURSE

PU-1800 Point Mallard Dr., Decatur, 35601, Morgan County, (205)351-7776, 20 miles SW of Huntsville.
Opened: 1970. **Holes:** 18. **Par:** 72/73. **Yards:** 7,113/5,437. **Course rating:** 73.7. **Slope:** 125. **Architect:** Charles M. Graves. **Green fee:** $10/$15. **Credit cards:** MC,VISA. **Reduced fees:** Weekdays, low season, seniors, juniors. **Caddies:** No. **Golf carts:** $16. **Discount golf packages:** Yes. **Season:** Year-round. **High:** April-Sept. **On site lodging:** No. **Rental clubs:** Yes. **Walking policy:** Unrestricted walking. **Metal spikes allowed:** Yes. **Range:** Yes (grass). **To obtain tee times:** Call Thursday for Saturday tee times.
Subscriber comments: Good for average golfer...Flat, longish, pretty...Plays long on par 5s—good shape...Very long but fair...Long, tight, beautiful, play at least once...Good scenery, used every club...Long but nice...Collects water easily, otherwise solid.

★★ QUAIL CREEK GOLF COURSE

PM-19841 Quail Creek Dr., Fairhope, 36532, Baldwin County, (334)990-0240, (800)317-9530, 20 miles SE of Mobile.
Opened: 1988. **Holes:** 18. **Par:** 72/72. **Yards:** 6,426/5,305. **Course rating:** 70.1/69.6. **Slope:** 112/114. **Architect:** City Committee. **Green fee:** $20/$20. **Credit cards:** All major. **Reduced fees:** Twilight. **Caddies:** No. **Golf carts:** $10. **Discount golf packages:** No. **Season:** Year-round. **High:** Jan.-April. **On site lodging:** No. **Rental clubs:** Yes. **Walking policy:** Unrestricted walking. **Metal spikes allowed:** Yes. **Range:** Yes (grass). **To obtain tee times:** May call three days in advance.

★★½ RIVER RUN GOLF COURSE

PU-P.O. Box 240873, Montgomery, 36124, Montgomery County, (334)271-2448, 3 miles E of Montgomery.
Opened: 1989. **Holes:** 18. **Par:** 72/72. **Yards:** 6,585/5,079. **Course rating:** 69.4/68.6. **Slope:** 114/109. **Architect:** Cam Hardigree. **Green fee:** $15/$20. **Credit cards:** All major. **Reduced fees:** Weekdays, twilight, juniors. **Caddies:** No. **Golf carts:** $11. **Discount golf packages:** Yes. **Season:** Year-round. **High:** March-Oct. **On site lodging:** No. **Rental clubs:** Yes. **Walking policy:** Unrestricted walking. **Metal spikes allowed:** Yes. **Range:** Yes (grass). **To obtain tee times:** Call 2 days in advance for weekends, 7 days for weekdays.
Subscriber comments: Short par 4s...A great course for the average golfer...Good sporty course...Fun to play. Very easy to walk. Staff all very nice and pleasant. Good Bermuda greens...Fun course, wide open, worth a look...Great place to take high handicappers.

★★★RIVER'S EDGE GOLF CLUB

PU-634 River's Edge Trail, Cordova, 35550, Walker County, (205)648-8866, 26 miles W of Birmingham.
Opened: 1996. **Holes:** 18. **Par:** 72. **Yards:** 6,526. **Course rating:** 71.4. **Slope:** 125. **Architect:** Steve Hyche. **Green fee:** N/A. **Credit cards:** MC,VISA. **Reduced fees:** Weekdays, seniors. **Caddies:** No. **Golf carts:** Included in Green Fee. **Discount golf packages:** No. **Season:** Year-round. **High:** N/A. **On site lodging:** No. **Rental clubs:** No. **Walking policy:** Mandatory cart. **Metal spikes allowed:** Yes. **Range:** No. **To obtain tee times:** N/A.
Subscriber comments: Be in the fairway or there's trouble, lots of hills and water...Excellent course—very challenging and scenic...Tremendous elevation change; new and tough for all players.

★★★★ROCK CREEK GOLF CLUB

PU-140 Clubhouse Dr., Fairhope, 36532, Baldwin County, (334)928-4223, 10 miles E of Mobile.
Opened: 1993. **Holes:** 18. **Par:** 72/72. **Yards:** 6,920/5,135. **Course rating:** 72.2/68.4. **Slope:** 129/117. **Architect:** Earl Stone. **Green fee:** $59/$59. **Credit cards:** All major. **Reduced fees:** Twilight, juniors.
Caddies: No. **Golf carts:** Included in Green Fee. **Discount golf packages:** Yes.
Season: Year-round. **High:** Spring/Fall. **On site lodging:** No. **Rental clubs:** Yes.
Walking policy: Mandatory cart. **Metal spikes allowed:** Yes. **Range:** Yes (grass). **To obtain tee times:** Call golf shop.
Subscriber comments: Short but fun to play, rolling hills...Challenging but enjoyable course. Good course to play every day...Always excellent shape, good scoring course...Back tees add about eight strokes to score...A beautiful golf course with hills and woodlands to test your accuracy. Great putting greens...Average player can score—good pro shop and restaurant.

★★★★SILVER LAKES GOLF CLUB

PU-1 Sunbelt Pkwy., Glencoe, 35905, Calhoun County, (205)892-3268, 15 miles N of Anniston.
Opened: 1993. **Holes:** 27. **Architect:** Robert Trent Jones. **Green fee:** $29/$39. **Credit cards:** All major. **Reduced fees:** Weekdays, low season, twilight, seniors, juniors. **Caddies:** No. **Golf carts:** $15. **Discount golf packages:** Yes. **Season:** Year-round. **High:** March-May, Sept.-Nov. **On site lodging:** No. **Rental clubs:** Yes. **Walking policy:** Unrestricted walking. **Metal spikes allowed:** Yes. **Range:** Yes (grass). **To obtain tee times:** Call golf shop 7 a.m. till dark.
HEARTBREAKER/BACKBREAKER
Par: 72/72. **Yards:** 7,674/4,907. **Course rating:** 76.7/68.8. **Slope:** 131/120.
MINDBREAKER/BACKBREAKER
Par: 72/72. **Yards:** 7,425/4,681. **Course rating:** 75.2/67.5. **Slope:** 127/119.
MINDBREAKER/HEARTBREAKER
Par: 72/72. **Yards:** 7,407/4,860. **Course rating:** 75.5/68.3. **Slope:** 132/122.
Subscriber comments: Beautiful course but too tough for the amateur...Typical Trail layout—punishing bunkers, strategy a plus...Truly outstanding golf, great management and service...Elevation changes, undulating greens...Long and tricky...Excellent course. Outstanding staff...The par 5s would even bring a Tiger down...Difficult terrain, every green a fortress...Too difficult for tourist golfers.
Special Notes: Part of the Robert Trent Jones Golf Trail. Complex also includes Short Course, a 9-hole par-3 layout.

STILLWATERS RESORT GOLF COURSE

R-1816 Still Waters Dr., Dadeville, 36853, Tallapoosa County, (205)825-1353, (888)797-3767, 55 miles NE of Montgomery.
Credit cards: All major. **Reduced fees:** Weekdays, twilight, juniors. **Caddies:** No. **Golf carts:** $12. **Discount golf packages:** Yes. **Season:** Year-round. **High:** March-Oct. **On site lodging:** Yes. **Rental clubs:** Yes. **Walking policy:** Unrestricted walking. **Metal spikes allowed:** Yes. **Range:** Yes (grass). **To obtain tee times:** Call golf shop.
★★★½ THE LEGEND COURSE
Opened: 1972. **Holes:** 18. **Par:** 72/72. **Yards:** 6,407/5,287. **Course rating:** 69.9/71.5. **Slope:** 124/125. **Architect:** George Cobb. **Green fee:** $23/$28.

Subscriber comments: Resort course. Hilly and short but challenging...Neat course on lake. Challenging and fun. Well kept...Fun, fair...Great course and fun to play...Friendly staff...Challenging layout, great resort, beautiful clubhouse...Is unbelievably beautiful in the spring...Nice track, very pretty lake layout...Tight fairways! You better be good off the tee. Doesn't play long, requires making shots from various lies.

THE TRADITION COURSE

Opened: 1997. **Holes:** 18. **Par:** 72/72. **Yards:** 6,906/5,048. **Course rating:** 73.5/69.5. **Slope:** 139/126. **Architect:** Kurt Sandness. **Green fee:** $30/$35.
Notes: Ranked 8th in 1997 Best New Affordable Public Courses.

★★STONEY MOUNTAIN GOLF COURSE

PU-5200 Georgia Mtn. Rd., Guntersville, 35976, Marshall County, (205)582-2598, 25 miles S of Huntsville.
Opened: N/A. **Holes:** 18. **Par:** 72/72. **Yards:** 5,931/4,711. **Course rating:** 67.6/66.2. **Slope:** 118/117. **Architect:** N/A. **Green fee:** $16/$22. **Credit cards:** VISA. **Reduced fees:** Weekdays, seniors. **Caddies:** No. **Golf carts:** N/A. **Discount golf packages:** No. **Season:** Year-round. **High:** April-Dec. **On site lodging:** No. **Rental clubs:** Yes. **Walking policy:** Walking at certain times. **Metal spikes allowed:** Yes. **Range:** No. **To obtain tee times:** Call pro shop.

★★★TANNEHILL NATIONAL GOLF COURSE

12863 Tannehill Pkwy., McCalla, 35111, Tuscaloosa County, (205)477-4653, (888)218-7888, 15 miles W of Birmingham.
Opened: 1996. **Holes:** 18. **Par:** 72/72. **Yards:** 6,630/5,440. **Course rating:** 71.1/70.5. **Slope:** 121/119. **Architect:** Steve Plumer. **Green fee:** $21/$30. **Credit cards:** All major. **Reduced fees:** Weekdays. **Caddies:** No. **Golf carts:** $12. **Discount golf packages:** No. **Season:** Year-round. **High:** N/A. **On site lodging:** No. **Rental clubs:** Yes. **Walking policy:** Walking at certain times. **Metal spikes allowed:** Yes. **Range:** Yes (grass). **To obtain tee times:** N/A.
Subscriber comments: A beautiful rolling course with wide fairways, several lakes and swift streams...New course...Wide open course that allows everyone to enjoy the day...New but improving fast...A fair test for mid-high handicappers...Tougher than it looks. Good practice area, staff eager to serve.

★★TIMBER RIDGE GOLF CLUB

PU-101 Ironaton Rd., Talladega, 35160, Talladega County, (205)362-0346.
Opened: 1989. **Holes:** 18. **Par:** 71/71. **Yards:** 6,700/5,346. **Course rating:** 70.4/70.9. **Slope:** 126/122. **Architect:** Charlie Carter. **Green fee:** $14/$21. **Credit cards:** MC,VISA,AMEX. **Reduced fees:** Weekdays, twilight, seniors, juniors. **Caddies:** No. **Golf carts:** Included in Green Fee. **Discount golf packages:** No. **Season:** Year-round. **High:** June-Aug. **On site lodging:** No. **Rental clubs:** Yes. **Walking policy:** Unrestricted walking. **Metal spikes allowed:** Yes. **Range:** Yes (grass). **To obtain tee times:** Call two days in advance.

★★★½TIMBERCREEK GOLF CLUB

PU-9650 TimberCreek Blvd., Daphne, 36527, Baldwin County, (334)621-9900, 10 miles E of Mobile.
Opened: 1993. **Holes:** 27. **Architect:** Earl Stone. **Green fee:** $29/$34. **Credit cards:** MC,VISA,AMEX. **Reduced fees:** Weekdays, resort guests, twilight, juniors. **Caddies:** No. **Golf carts:** $15. **Discount golf packages:** Yes. **Season:** Year-round. **High:** N/A. **On site lodging:** No. **Rental clubs:** Yes. **Walking policy:** Walking at certain times. **Metal spikes allowed:** Yes. **Range:** Yes (grass). **To obtain tee times:** Call golf shop.
DOGWOOD/MAGNOLIA
Par: 72/72. **Yards:** 7,062/4,885. **Course rating:** 73.8/66.7. **Slope:** 144/106.
DOGWOOD/PINES
Par: 72/72. **Yards:** 6,928/4,911. **Course rating:** 72.9/66.7. **Slope:** 137/105.
MAGNOLIA/PINES
Par: 72/72. **Yards:** 7,090/4,990. **Course rating:** 74.3/67.8. **Slope:** 143/107.
Subscriber comments: Tricky and tough...Very nice, not much water or sand...Great course. Tough from back tees...A fun course to play whether you are a beginner or a pro. Beautiful fairways. Great putting greens...Excellent facilities, outstanding practice areas...Some very challenging holes, lots of marsh.

★★ TWIN LAKES GOLF COURSE
PU-211 Golfview Dr., Arab, 35016, Marshall County, (205)586-3269, (800)213-3938, 15 miles S of Huntsville.
Opened: 1963. **Holes:** 18. **Par:** 72/72. **Yards:** 6,691/5,609. **Course rating:** N/A. **Slope:** N/A. **Architect:** N/A. **Green fee:** $13/$13. **Credit cards:** MC,VISA. **Reduced fees:** Weekdays. **Caddies:** No. **Golf carts:** $10. **Discount golf packages:** No. **Season:** Year-round. **High:** N/A. **On site lodging:** No. **Rental clubs:** Yes. **Walking policy:** Unrestricted walking. **Metal spikes allowed:** Yes. **Range:** No. **To obtain tee times:** Call up to 7 days in advance for weekends.

★★½ UNIVERSITY OF ALABAMA HARRY PRITCHETT GOLF COURSE
PU-University of Alabama, Tuscaloosa, 35487, Tuscaloosa County, (205)348-7041.
Opened: N/A. **Holes:** 18. **Par:** 71/71. **Yards:** 6,180/5,047. **Course rating:** 69.7/67.2. **Slope:** 126/121. **Architect:** Harold Williams/Thomas Nicol. **Green fee:** $15/$17. **Credit cards:** MC,VISA,DISC. **Reduced fees:** Weekdays, seniors, juniors. **Caddies:** No. **Golf carts:** N/A. **Discount golf packages:** No. **Season:** Year-round. **High:** May, Aug., Sept. **On site lodging:** No. **Rental clubs:** Yes. **Walking policy:** Unrestricted walking. **Metal spikes allowed:** Yes. **Range:** Yes (grass). **To obtain tee times:** N/A.
Subscriber comments: Tight, fast greens. Friendly staff.

★★ WILLOW OAKS GOLF CLUB
Willow Oaks Dr., Ozark, 36360, Dale County, (205)774-7388.
Call club for further information.

★★½ANCHORAGE GOLF COURSE
PU-3651 O'Malley Rd., Anchorage, 99516, Anchorage County, (907)522-3363.
Opened: 1987. **Holes:** 18. **Par:** 72/72. **Yards:** 6,616/4,848. **Course rating:** 72.1/68.2.
Slope: 130/119. **Architect:** Bill Newcomb. **Green fee:** $26/$26. **Credit cards:** All
major. **Reduced fees:** Resort guests, seniors, juniors. **Caddies:** No. **Golf carts:** $12.
Discount golf packages: No. **Season:** May-Oct. **High:** June-Aug. **On site lodging:**
No. **Rental clubs:** Yes. **Walking policy:** Walking at certain times. **Metal spikes
allowed:** Yes. **Range:** Yes (grass). **To obtain tee times:** Residents call 5 days in
advance, nonresidents 3 days in advance.
Notes: Ranked 4th in 1997 Best in State.
Subscriber comments: Tight fairways, good layout...Very hilly...Challenging.

BIRCH RIDGE GOLF CLUB
PU-P.O. Box 828, Soldotna, 99669, Kenai Peninsula Borough County, (907)262-5270, 2
miles NE of Soldotna.
Opened: 1973. **Holes:** 9. **Par:** 70/69. **Yards:** 5,900/4,873. **Course rating:** 68.8/67.8.
Slope: 120/115. **Architect:** Thomas R. Smith. **Green fee:** $12/$19. **Credit cards:**
MC,VISA,AMEX. **Reduced fees:** Weekdays, resort guests, seniors, juniors. **Caddies:**
No. **Golf carts:** $20. **Discount golf packages:** Yes. **Season:** May-Sept. **High:** June-
Aug. **On site lodging:** Yes. **Rental clubs:** Yes. **Walking policy:** Unrestricted walking.
Metal spikes allowed: Yes. **Range:** Yes (grass/mats). **To obtain tee times:** Tee times
required on weekends and holidays, call golf shop.

CHENA BEND GOLF CLUB
PU-Bldg. 2092 Gaffney Rd., Fort Wainwright, 99703, Fairbanks County, (907)353-6223.
Opened: 1996. **Holes:** 18. **Par:** 72/72. **Yards:** 7,012/5,516. **Course rating:** 73.6/71.6.
Slope: 128/117. **Architect:** Jerry Matthews. **Green fee:** $11/$28. **Credit cards:**
MC,VISA. **Reduced fees:** Low season, twilight, seniors, juniors. **Caddies:** No. **Golf
carts:** $16. **Discount golf packages:** No. **Season:** May-Sept. **High:** June-July. **On site
lodging:** No. **Rental clubs:** Yes. **Walking policy:** Unrestricted walking. **Metal spikes
allowed:** Yes. **Range:** Yes (grass/mats). **To obtain tee times:** Authorized military may
call up to 5 days in advance; all others up to 2 days in advance.
Notes: Ranked 2nd in 1997 Best in State.

★★½EAGLEGLEN GOLF COURSE
PU-23-100 Elmendorf A.F.B., Anchorage, 99506, Anchorage County, (907)552-3821, 2
miles N of Anchorage.
Opened: 1973. **Holes:** 18. **Par:** 72/72. **Yards:** 6,689/5,457. **Course rating:** 71.6/70.4.
Slope: 128/123. **Architect:** Robert Trent Jones. **Green fee:** $24/$32. **Credit cards:**
MC,VISA. **Reduced fees:** Low season, twilight. **Caddies:** No. **Golf carts:** $21.
Discount golf packages: No. **Season:** May-Oct. **High:** June-Aug. **On site lodging:**
No. **Rental clubs:** Yes. **Walking policy:** Unrestricted walking. **Metal spikes allowed:**
Yes. **Range:** Yes (mats). **To obtain tee times:** Either call reservation system or call day
of play.
Notes: Ranked 1st in 1997 Best in State.
Subscriber comments: Best course in Alaska...Air Force course, military given prefer-
ence...The best the weather will allow...Very pleasurable...Well maintained, except for
geese.

FAIRBANKS GOLF & COUNTRY CLUB
PU-1735 Farmers Loop, Fairbanks, 99709, Fairbanks County, (907)479-6555.
Opened: 1946. **Holes:** 9. **Par:** 72/72. **Yards:** 6,264/5,186. **Course rating:** 69.8/69.9.
Slope: 120/115. **Architect:** N/A. **Green fee:** $28/$28. **Credit cards:** MC,VISA,DISC.
Reduced fees: Seniors, juniors. **Caddies:** No. **Golf carts:** $17. **Discount golf pack-
ages:** No. **Season:** May-Sept. **High:** June-Aug. **On site lodging:** No. **Rental clubs:**
Yes. **Walking policy:** Unrestricted walking. **Metal spikes allowed:** Yes. **Range:** Yes
(grass). **To obtain tee times:** Call golf shop.

★★½KENAI GOLF CLUB
PU-1420 Lawton Dr., Kenai, 99611, Kenai County, (907)283-7500, 180 miles S of
Anchorage.
Opened: 1986. **Holes:** 18. **Par:** 72/72. **Yards:** 6,641/5,644. **Course rating:** 73.2/74.4.

Slope: 135/133. **Architect:** N/A. **Green fee:** $15/$19. **Credit cards:** MC,VISA. **Reduced fees:** Seniors, juniors. **Caddies:** No. **Golf carts:** $15. **Discount golf packages:** No. **Season:** May-Sept. **High:** June-Aug. **On site lodging:** No. **Rental clubs:** Yes. **Walking policy:** Unrestricted walking. **Metal spikes allowed:** Yes. **Range:** Yes (mats). **To obtain tee times:** Call golf shop.

★★½MOOSE RUN GOLF COURSE

PU-P.O. Box 5130, Fort Richardson, 99505, Anchorage County, (907)428-0056, 1 mile from Anchorage.
Opened: N/A. **Holes:** 18. **Par:** 72/72. **Yards:** 6,499/5,382. **Course rating:** N/A. **Slope:** 119/120. **Architect:** U.S. Army. **Green fee:** N/A. **Credit cards:** MC,VISA. **Reduced fees:** Twilight. **Caddies:** No. **Golf carts:** N/A. **Discount golf packages:** No. **Season:** May-Oct. **High:** July-Aug. **On site lodging:** No. **Rental clubs:** No. **Walking policy:** Unrestricted walking. **Metal spikes allowed:** Yes. **Range:** Yes. **To obtain tee times:** N/A.
Notes: Ranked 3rd in 1997 Best in State.
Subscriber comments: Army course, civilians secondary.

NORTH STAR GOLF COURSE

330 Golf Club Dr., Fairbanks, 99712, Fairbanks County, (907)457-4653, 4 miles N of Fairbanks.
Opened: 1993. **Holes:** 18. **Par:** 72/72. **Yards:** 6,852/5,995. **Course rating:** N/A. **Slope:** N/A. **Architect:** Jack Stallings. **Green fee:** $20/$24. **Credit cards:** MC,VISA. **Reduced fees:** Weekdays, resort guests, juniors. **Caddies:** No. **Golf carts:** $14. **Discount golf packages:** No. **Season:** May-Oct. **High:** June-Sept. **On site lodging:** No. **Rental clubs:** Yes. **Walking policy:** Walking at certain times. **Metal spikes allowed:** Yes. **Range:** Yes (grass/mats). **To obtain tee times:** Call 24 hours in advance.

★½PALMER GOLF COURSE

PU-1000 Lepak Ave., Palmer, 99645, Matanuska County, (907)745-4653, 42 miles N of Anchorage.
Opened: 1990. **Holes:** 18. **Par:** 72/73. **Yards:** 7,125/5,895. **Course rating:** 74.5/74.6. **Slope:** 132/127. **Architect:** Illiad Group. **Green fee:** $20/$22. **Credit cards:** MC,VISA. **Reduced fees:** Seniors, juniors. **Caddies:** No. **Golf carts:** $18. **Discount golf packages:** Yes. **Season:** May-Sep. **High:** May-July. **On site lodging:** No. **Rental clubs:** Yes. **Walking policy:** Unrestricted walking. **Metal spikes allowed:** Yes. **Range:** Yes (grass). **To obtain tee times:** Call pro shop.

★★½SETTLERS BAY GOLF CLUB

PU-Mile 8 Knik Rd., Wasilla, 99654, Matanuska County, (907)376-5466, 50 miles NE of Anchorage.
Opened: 1977. **Holes:** 18. **Par:** 72/72. **Yards:** 6,596/5,461. **Course rating:** 71.4/70.8. **Slope:** 129/123. **Architect:** N/A. **Green fee:** $22/$29. **Credit cards:** MC,VISA,DISC. **Reduced fees:** Twilight, seniors, juniors. **Caddies:** No. **Golf carts:** $22. **Discount golf packages:** Yes. **Season:** April-Oct. **High:** June-Aug. **On site lodging:** No. **Rental clubs:** Yes. **Walking policy:** Unrestricted walking. **Metal spikes allowed:** Yes. **Range:** Yes (grass/mats). **To obtain tee times:** Call golf shop up to 7 days in advance.

SLEEPY HOLLOW GOLF CLUB

PU-Mile 2 Carney Rd., Wasilla, 99654, Matanuska County, (907)376-5948, 7 miles N of Wasilla.
Opened: 1989. **Holes:** 9. **Par:** 27/27. **Yards:** 1,304/1,215. **Course rating:** N/A. **Slope:** N/A. **Architect:** Carney Bros.. **Green fee:** $16/$18. **Credit cards:** N/A. **Reduced fees:** Weekdays. **Caddies:** No. **Golf carts:** $18. **Discount golf packages:** No. **Season:** May-Sept. **High:** June-July. **On site lodging:** No. **Rental clubs:** Yes. **Walking policy:** Unrestricted walking. **Metal spikes allowed:** Yes. **Range:** Yes (mats). **To obtain tee times:** First come, first served.

ARIZONA

★★★THE ASU KARSTEN GOLF COURSE
PU-1125 E. Rio Salado Pkwy., Tempe, 85281, Maricopa County, (602)921-8070, 5 miles SE of Phoenix.
Opened: 1989. **Holes:** 18. **Par:** 72/72. **Yards:** 7,057/4,765. **Course rating:** 74.3/63.4. **Slope:** 133/110. **Architect:** Pete Dye/Perry Dye. **Green fee:** $30/$84. **Credit cards:** MC,VISA,AMEX. **Reduced fees:** Weekdays, low season, juniors. **Caddies:** No. **Golf carts:** Included in Green Fee. **Discount golf packages:** No. **Season:** Year-round. **High:** Jan.-April. **On site lodging:** No. **Rental clubs:** Yes. **Walking policy:** Mandatory cart. **Metal spikes allowed:** Yes. **Range:** Yes (grass). **To obtain tee times:** Call golf shop up to 5 days in advance.
Subscriber comments: Great course and facility...16, 17, 18 murderous finishing holes...Uneven lies and views of power lines...Fun from regular tees, pain and suffering from championship tees...Extreme slopes...Nice course, ugly surroundings...Variety of holes...Dead elephants buried on front nine...Good test of golf...Challenging golf, last four holes are spectacular.

★★AHWATUKEE COUNTRY CLUB
12432 S. 48th St., Phoenix, 85044, Maricopa County, (602)893-1161.
Opened: 1971. **Holes:** 18. **Par:** 72/72. **Yards:** 6,713/5,506. **Course rating:** 71.5/70.3. **Slope:** 124/118. **Architect:** Johnny Bulla. **Green fee:** $20/$65. **Credit cards:** MC,VISA. **Reduced fees:** Weekdays, low season, twilight. **Caddies:** No. **Golf carts:** Included in Green Fee. **Discount golf packages:** No. **Season:** Year-round. **High:** Jan.-March. **On site lodging:** No. **Rental clubs:** Yes. **Walking policy:** Mandatory cart. **Metal spikes allowed:** Yes. **Range:** Yes (grass). **To obtain tee times:** Call golf shop up to seven days in advance.

ANTELOPE HILLS GOLF COURSES
PU-1 Perkins Dr., Prescott, 86301, Yavapai County, (520)776-7888, 90 miles N of Phoenix.
Credit cards: MC,VISA. **Reduced fees:** Low season, twilight, juniors. **Caddies:** No. **Discount golf packages:** Yes. **Season:** Year-round. **High:** April-Oct. **On site lodging:** No. **Rental clubs:** Yes. **Walking policy:** Unrestricted walking. **Metal spikes allowed:** Yes. **Range:** Yes (grass).
★★★NORTH COURSE
Opened: 1956. **Holes:** 18. **Par:** 72/74. **Yards:** 6,778/6,097. **Course rating:** 71.4/74.3. **Slope:** 131/126. **Architect:** Lawrence Hughes. **Green fee:** $25/$36. **Golf carts:** N/A. **To obtain tee times:** Call seven days in advance.
Subscriber comments: Nice course for the money...Old-style, tree-lined...Interesting, diverse holes...Fantastic public course, few humdrum holes...Nice parkland-style course, will play it again...Fine setting, mature trees...Very fair and enjoyable course...Classic old layout, small traditional greens...Course is very secluded, peaceful.
★★★SOUTH COURSE
Opened: 1992. **Holes:** 18. **Par:** 72/72. **Yards:** 7,014/5,560. **Course rating:** 71.3/71.0. **Slope:** 124/113. **Architect:** Gary Panks. **Green fee:** $22/$32. **Golf carts:** $10. **To obtain tee times:** Call three days in advance.
Subscriber comments: Very fair and enjoyable course...Wide open, windswept...Too new, not enough trees yet...Newer of the two courses, great potential...Newer links-style course, large greens.

★★½APACHE CREEK GOLF CLUB
PU-3401 S. Ironwood Dr., Apache Junction, 85220, Pinal County, (602)982-2677, 20 miles E of Phoenix.
Opened: 1994. **Holes:** 18. **Par:** 72/72. **Yards:** 6,591/5,516. **Course rating:** 71.0/65.4. **Slope:** 123/110. **Architect:** N/A. **Green fee:** $10/$55. **Credit cards:** MC,VISA. **Reduced fees:** Twilight, juniors. **Caddies:** No. **Golf carts:** Included in Green Fee. **Discount golf packages:** No. **Season:** Year-round. **High:** Oct.-April. **On site lodging:** No. **Rental clubs:** Yes. **Walking policy:** Unrestricted walking. **Metal spikes allowed:** Yes. **Range:** Yes (grass). **To obtain tee times:** Call 3 days in advance.
Subscriber comments: Improving each year...Very good desert course...Great practice facility...Target golf, windy and cool...Enjoyable, affordable desert course...Great layout on flat land.

ARIZONA BILTMORE COUNTRY CLUB

24th St. and Missouri, Phoenix, 85016, Maricopa County, (602)955-9655.
Green fee: $65/$115. **Credit cards:** MC,VISA,AMEX. **Reduced fees:** Low season.
Caddies: No. **Golf carts:** Included in Green Fee. **Discount golf packages:** Yes.
Season: Year-round. **High:** Jan.-May. **On site lodging:** Yes. **Rental clubs:** Yes.
Walking policy: Mandatory cart. **Metal spikes allowed:** Yes. **Range:** Yes (grass). **To obtain tee times:** May call five days in advance.

★★★ADOBE COURSE

Opened: 1928. **Holes:** 18. **Par:** 72/73. **Yards:** 6,800/6,101. **Course rating:** 71.5/74.3.
Slope: 121/123. **Architect:** William P. Bell.
Subscriber comments: The grand dame in Phoenix...Typical old-style flat course.
Challenging but somewhat boring. Hotel is fabulous...Flat, not too interesting...Nice old course...Great esthetics, old-style course...Nothing spectacular...Traditional older course.

★★★LINKS COURSE

Opened: 1978. **Holes:** 18. **Par:** 71/71. **Yards:** 6,300/4,747. **Course rating:** 69.3/68.0.
Slope: 122/107. **Architect:** Bill Johnston.
Subscriber comments: Fun with great terrain changes. A couple of funky but acceptable holes...Beautiful course...Interesting terrain, requires all the shots...Easier but more fun than Adobe...Good first course to start vacation...Short but tricky...Great back nine...OK but some quirky holes.

★★★THE ARIZONA GOLF RESORT & CONFERENCE CENTER

R-425 S. Power Rd., Mesa, 85206, Maricopa County, (602)832-1661, (800)458-8330,
25 miles SE of Phoenix.
Opened: 1961. **Holes:** 18. **Par:** 71/71. **Yards:** 6,574/6,195. **Course rating:** 71.2/68.6.
Slope: 123/117. **Architect:** Arthur Jack Snyder. **Green fee:** $25/$75. **Credit cards:** All major. **Reduced fees:** Weekdays, low season, resort guests, twilight. **Caddies:** No.
Golf carts: Included in Green Fee. **Discount golf packages:** Yes. **Season:** Year-round.
High: Jan.-March. **On site lodging:** Yes. **Rental clubs:** Yes. **Walking policy:**
Mandatory cart. **Metal spikes allowed:** Yes. **Range:** Yes (grass). **To obtain tee times:**
Call golf shop up to 30 days in advance with credit card.
Subscriber comments: Very nice layout, flat, lots of trees...Friendly, courteous, great food...Hard and long par 3s...Great par 3s...Difficult from tips.

★★ARTHUR PACK DESERT GOLF CLUB

PU-9101 N. Thornydale Rd., Tucson, 85742, Pima County, (520)744-3322.
Opened: 1975. **Holes:** 18. **Par:** 72/72. **Yards:** 6,900/5,100. **Course rating:** 71.6/67.6.
Slope: 118/108. **Architect:** Dave Bennett/Lee Trevino. **Green fee:** $12/$20. **Credit cards:** MC,VISA. **Reduced fees:** Low season, seniors, juniors. **Caddies:** No. **Golf carts:** $16. **Discount golf packages:** No. **Season:** Year-round. **High:** Nov.-May. **On site lodging:** No. **Rental clubs:** Yes. **Walking policy:** Unrestricted walking. **Metal spikes allowed:** Yes. **Range:** Yes (grass/mats). **To obtain tee times:** May call up to 7 days in advance.

THE BOULDERS CLUB

R-34631 N. Tom Darlington Dr., Carefree, 85377, Maricopa County,
(602)488-9028, 33 miles N of Phoenix.
Opened: 1984. **Architect:** Jay Morrish. **Green fee:** $72/$195. **Credit cards:** MC,VISA,AMEX,Diners Club. **Reduced fees:** Low season.
Caddies: No. **Golf carts:** Included in Green Fee. **Discount golf packages:** Yes. **Season:** Year-round. **High:** Feb.-May. **On site lodging:** Yes. **Rental clubs:** Yes. **Walking policy:** Walking at certain times. **Metal spikes allowed:** No. **Range:** Yes (grass). **To obtain tee times:** Tee time may be held up to 1 year in advance with confirmed hotel reservation.

(GREAT SERVICE)

★★★★NORTH COURSE

Holes: 18. **Par:** 17/72. **Yards:** 6,717/4,893. **Course rating:** 72.3/68.2. **Slope:** 135/111.
Notes: Ranked 19th in 1997 Best in State.
Subscriber comments: Outstanding, beautiful, great golf...Beautiful, unusual terrain.
Target golf at its best...Great layout around a rocky mountain. Quite an experience...Dramatic setting and skies...Has no equal in the world...Great course, fun, challenging but pricey...First class resort and course...Great layout, superb service,

worth the cost...Total excellence...Scenery outstanding...Great practice facility.

★★★★½SOUTH COURSE
Holes: 18. **Par:** 71/71. **Yards:** 6,589/4,715. **Course rating:** 71.4/68.1. **Slope:** 137/114.
Notes: Ranked 20th in 1997 Best in State.
Subscriber comments: Target golf, dramatic...Both North and South courses are the best...Very friendly...Excellent....Fabulous course, fabulous money...Long killer par 3s...Desert golf doesn't get any better...A must play course while in Phoenix...Requires proficency with all clubs...This is heaven on earth. South prettier than North.

★★★½CANOA HILLS GOLF COURSE
1401 W. Calle Urbano, Green Valley, 85614, Pima County, (520)648-1880, 25 miles S of Tucson.
Opened: 1984. **Holes:** 18. **Par:** 72/72. **Yards:** 6,610/5,158. **Course rating:** 70.8/68.5. **Slope:** 126/116. **Architect:** Dave Bennett. **Green fee:** $21/$52. **Credit cards:** All major. **Reduced fees:** Low season, twilight, juniors. **Caddies:** No. **Golf carts:** Included in Green Fee. **Discount golf packages:** No. **Season:** Year-round. **High:** Jan.-April. **On site lodging:** No. **Rental clubs:** Yes. **Walking policy:** Mandatory cart. **Metal spikes allowed:** Yes. **Range:** Yes (grass). **To obtain tee times:** Call 2 days in advance.
Subscriber comments: Fun course...Long, but not hard...Outstanding views, must control drives...Trees make this a handsome course; tough...Beautiful scenery, mountain ranges...Best greens in southern Arizona, hold ball very well.

★★CASA GRANDE MUNICIPAL GOLF COURSE
PM-2121 N. Thornton Rd., Casa Grande, 85222, Pinal County, (520)836-9216, 35 miles S of Phoenix.
Opened: 1978. **Holes:** 18. **Par:** 72/72. **Yards:** 6,316/5,038. **Course rating:** 68.8/66.5. **Slope:** 115/100. **Architect:** Gary Panks/Jack Snyder. **Green fee:** $15/$15. **Credit cards:** MC,VISA. **Reduced fees:** Weekdays, low season, twilight, seniors, juniors. **Caddies:** No. **Golf carts:** $8. **Discount golf packages:** No. **Season:** Year-round. **High:** Nov.-March. **On site lodging:** No. **Rental clubs:** Yes. **Walking policy:** Unrestricted walking. **Metal spikes allowed:** Yes. **Range:** Yes (grass). **To obtain tee times:** Call three days in advance.

★★½CAVE CREEK GOLF CLUB
PU-15202 N. 19th Ave., Phoenix, 85023, Maricopa County, (602)866-8076.
Opened: 1984. **Holes:** 18. **Par:** 72/72. **Yards:** 6,876/5,614. **Course rating:** 71.1/70.0. **Slope:** 122/112. **Architect:** Jack Snyder. **Green fee:** $19/$28. **Credit cards:** All major. **Reduced fees:** Low season, twilight, seniors, juniors. **Caddies:** No. **Golf carts:** $15. **Discount golf packages:** No. **Season:** Year-round. **High:** Nov.-April. **On site lodging:** No. **Rental clubs:** Yes. **Walking policy:** Unrestricted walking. **Metal spikes allowed:** Yes. **Range:** Yes (grass). **To obtain tee times:** Call 2 days in advance.
Subscriber comments: Good municipal course...Great par 3s...Easy course to score on...Roller-coaster muny...Has four to five great holes, as good as anywhere...Some great holes, but still muny course built on garbage dump.

★★★½CLUB WEST GOLF CLUB
PU-16400 S. 14th Ave., Phoenix, 85045, Maricopa County, (602)460-4400, 7 miles W of Phoenix.
Opened: 1993. **Holes:** 18. **Par:** 72/72. **Yards:** 7,057/4,985. **Course rating:** 73.1/63.5. **Slope:** 129/104. **Architect:** Brian Whitcomb. **Green fee:** $49/$105. **Credit cards:** All major,Diners Club. **Reduced fees:** Low season, twilight, seniors. **Caddies:** No. **Golf carts:** Included in Green Fee. **Discount golf packages:** No. **Season:** Year-round. **High:** Jan.-April. **On site lodging:** No. **Rental clubs:** Yes. **Walking policy:** Mandatory cart. **Metal spikes allowed:** Yes. **Range:** Yes (grass). **To obtain tee times:** Call 7 days in advance with credit card number.
Subscriber comments: Nifty little course...Solid desert course, beautiful setting...Good bar/restaurant...Scariest par 3 hole I ever saw!...Nice variance in holes...Pleasant track, forgiving, great views...Nice course with great views...Very interesting finishing holes, wide open...Average course. Nothing special...Beautiful scenery...Fun course, not too tough...Beautiful, challenging, varied terrain.

★★½ CONCHO VALLEY COUNTRY CLUB

HC-30, Box 900, Concho, 85924, Apache County, (520)337-4644, 28 miles NE of Show Low.
Opened: 1975. **Holes:** 18. **Par:** 72/72. **Yards:** 6,656/5,559. **Course rating:** 69.1/70.0.
Slope: 119/128. **Architect:** Arthur Jack Snyder. **Green fee:** $12/$21. **Credit cards:** None. **Reduced fees:** Low season, resort guests, twilight, seniors, juniors. **Caddies:** No. **Golf carts:** $10. **Discount golf packages:** Yes. **Season:** Year-round. **High:** May-Sept. **On site lodging:** Yes. **Rental clubs:** Yes. **Walking policy:** Unrestricted walking.
Metal spikes allowed: Yes. **Range:** Yes (grass/mats). **To obtain tee times:** Call 7 days in advance.
Subscriber comments: A hidden jewel...Enjoyable except for snakes!...Links-style course. Challenging.

★★★ COYOTE LAKES GOLF CLUB

PU-18800 N. Coyote Lakes Pkwy., Surprise, 85374, Maricopa County, (602)566-2323, 8 miles NW of Phoenix.
Opened: 1993. **Holes:** 18. **Par:** 71/71. **Yards:** 6,159/4,708. **Course rating:** 68.9/68.0.
Slope: 114/107. **Architect:** Arthur Jack Snyder/Forrest Richardson. **Green fee:** $16/$63. **Credit cards:** MC,VISA. **Reduced fees:** Weekdays, low season, twilight, juniors. **Caddies:** No. **Golf carts:** Included in Green Fee. **Discount golf packages:** No.
Season: Year-round. **High:** Jan.-April. **On site lodging:** No. **Rental clubs:** Yes.
Walking policy: Mandatory cart. **Metal spikes allowed:** Yes. **Range:** Yes (grass/mats).
To obtain tee times: Call 7 days in advance.
Subscriber comments: Fun course...Short course but must think to score...Dandy little course in an old river bed...Build your ego here, short holes...Best bang for a buck!...Laid out up and down a ravine...Very challenging layout for a shorter course.

★★★ DESERT HILLS GOLF COURSE

PM-1245 Desert Hills Dr., Yuma, 85364, Yuma County, (520)344-4653, 175 miles SW of Phoenix.
Opened: 1973. **Holes:** 18. **Par:** 72/74. **Yards:** 6,800/5,726. **Course rating:** 71.1/72.4.
Slope: 117/122. **Architect:** N/A. **Green fee:** $8/$16. **Credit cards:** None. **Reduced fees:** Low season, juniors. **Caddies:** No. **Golf carts:** $9. **Discount golf packages:** No.
Season: Year-round. **High:** Dec.-April. **On site lodging:** No. **Rental clubs:** Yes.
Walking policy: Unrestricted walking. **Metal spikes allowed:** Yes. **Range:** Yes (grass).
To obtain tee times: Call computerized reservation up to 48 hours in advance. You need a nine digit number to make reservations (such as social security number).
Subscriber comments: Some interesting holes...Nice muny course...Very playable.

★★★½ DESERT SPRINGS GOLF CLUB

PU-19900 N Remington Dr, Surprise, 85374, Maricopa County, (602)546-7400, 18 miles NW of Phoenix.
Opened: 1996. **Holes:** 18. **Par:** 72/72. **Yards:** 7,006/5,250. **Course rating:** 73.4/69.6.
Slope: 131/119. **Architect:** Billy Casper/Greg Nash. **Green fee:** $19/$65. **Credit cards:** MC,VISA. **Reduced fees:** Weekdays, low season, twilight, seniors, juniors. **Caddies:** No. **Golf carts:** Included in Green Fee. **Discount golf packages:** No.
Season: Year-round. **High:** Nov.-April. **On site lodging:** No. **Rental clubs:** Yes.
Walking policy: Mandatory cart. **Metal spikes allowed:** Yes. **Range:** Yes (grass). **To obtain tee times:** Call 7 days in advance.
Subscriber comments: Love this course...Nothing too tricky here...New course. Going to be great...Fun course, somewhat flat...Very playable, gives you a chance.

★★½ DOBSON RANCH GOLF CLUB

PU-2155 S. Dobson Rd., Mesa, 85202, Maricopa County, (602)644-2270, 15 miles SE of Phoenix.
Opened: 1973. **Holes:** 18. **Par:** 72/72. **Yards:** 6,593/5,598. **Course rating:** 71.0/71.3.
Slope: 117/116. **Architect:** Red Lawrence. **Green fee:** $12/$21. **Credit cards:** MC,VISA,AMEX. **Reduced fees:** Low season, twilight, juniors. **Caddies:** No. **Golf carts:** $17. **Discount golf packages:** No. **Season:** Year-round. **High:** Nov.-April. **On site lodging:** No. **Rental clubs:** Yes. **Walking policy:** Unrestricted walking. **Metal spikes allowed:** Yes. **Range:** Yes (grass). **To obtain tee times:** Call 4 days in advance.

Subscriber comments: Great muny golf...Too busy but pleasant...Mature trees, open...Nice public course...Great playability...Challenging course for most golfers. Great value...Not anything memorable.

★★★EAGLE'S NEST COUNTRY CLUB AT PEBBLE CREEK

3639 Clubhouse Dr., Goodyear, 85338, Maricopa County, (602)935-6750, (800)795-4663, 15 miles SW of Phoenix.
Opened: 1991. **Holes:** 18. **Par:** 72/72. **Yards:** 6,860/5,030. **Course rating:** 72.6/68.0.
Slope: 127/111. **Architect:** Keith Foster. **Green fee:** $21/$51. **Credit cards:** MC,VISA.
Reduced fees: Low season, twilight. **Caddies:** No. **Golf carts:** $9. **Discount golf packages:** No. **Season:** Year-round. **High:** Jan.-March. **On site lodging:** No. **Rental clubs:** Yes. **Walking policy:** Unrestricted walking. **Metal spikes allowed:** Yes. **Range:** Yes (grass). **To obtain tee times:** Call 2 days in advance.
Subscriber comments: Long, wide open...Will be great when it gets older...Nice design...A pleasure.

★★★ELDEN HILLS GOLF CLUB

PU-2380 N. Oakmont Dr., Flagstaff, 86004, Coconino County, (520)527-7999.
Opened: 1960. **Holes:** 18. **Par:** 71/71. **Yards:** 6,029/5,280. **Course rating:** 66.6/70.5.
Slope: 115/120. **Architect:** Bob Baldock. **Green fee:** $25. **Credit cards:** MC,VISA,AMEX. **Reduced fees:** Weekdays, low season, twilight, juniors. **Caddies:** No. Golf carts: $13. **Discount golf packages:** No. **Season:** March-Nov. **High:** May-Sept. **On site lodging:** No. **Rental clubs:** Yes. **Walking policy:** Unrestricted walking. **Metal spikes allowed:** Yes. **Range:** Yes (grass). **To obtain tee times:** May call up to 7 days in advance.
Subscriber comments: Very pretty area; requires long drives...Playing at 7,000 feet with lots of wind was a challenge...A very pleasant surprise...Great forest golf...Enjoy the beautiful walk.

★★★ELEPHANT ROCKS GOLF CLUB

PU-2200 Country Club Rd., Williams, 86046, Coconino County, (520)635-4935, 30 miles W of Flagstaff.
Opened: 1990. **Holes:** 9. **Par:** 70/72. **Yards:** 5,937/5,309. **Course rating:** 67.6/67.3.
Slope: 123/126. **Architect:** Gary Panks. **Green fee:** $20/$33. **Credit cards:** MC,VISA,DISC. **Reduced fees:** Weekdays, juniors. **Caddies:** No. **Golf carts:** $16.
Discount golf packages: No. **Season:** April-Oct. **High:** May-Sept. **On site lodging:** No. **Rental clubs:** Yes. **Walking policy:** Walking at certain times. **Metal spikes allowed:** Yes. **Range:** Yes (grass). **To obtain tee times:** Call 7 days in advance.
Subscriber comments: Gorgeous, lots of tall ponderosas...Best nine in Arizona, spectacular views.

★★½ELOY-TOHONO MUNICIPAL GOLF COURSE

PM-1505 S. Toltect Rd., Eloy, 85231, Pinal County, (602)466-7734, 47 miles SE of Tucson.
Opened: 1992. **Holes:** 18. **Par:** 72/72. **Yards:** 7,100/5,363. **Course rating:** 72.3/69.8.
Slope: 117/112. **Architect:** Forrest Richardson. **Green fee:** $24/$24. **Credit cards:** MC,VISA. **Reduced fees:** Low season, juniors. **Caddies:** No. **Golf carts:** $7. **Discount golf packages:** Yes. **Season:** Year-round. **High:** Oct.-April. **On site lodging:** No. **Rental clubs:** Yes. **Walking policy:** Unrestricted walking. **Metal spikes allowed:** Yes. **Range:** Yes (grass). **To obtain tee times:** Call seven days in advance.
Subscriber comments: Still maturing links course, locals love it...Wide open, not very interesting...Excellent layout...Very long but wide open...Pretty barren...Fun undulating greens. A great bargain...No trees, flat course...Worth the drive for the golf and value.

★★★★EMERALD CANYON GOLF COURSE

PU-72 Emerald Canyon Dr., Parker, 85344, La Paz County, (520)667-3366, 150 miles NW of Phoenix.
Opened: 1989. **Holes:** 18. **Par:** 72/71. **Yards:** 6,657/4,754. **Course rating:** 71.5/66.2. **Slope:** 131/119. **Architect:** William Phillips. **Green fee:** $18/$40. **Credit cards:** MC,VISA. **Reduced fees:** Weekdays, low season, twilight, juniors. **Caddies:** No. **Golf carts:** Included in Green Fee. **Discount golf packages:** Yes. **Season:** Year-round. **High:** Nov.-March. **On site lodging:** No. **Rental clubs:**

GOOD VALUE

Yes. **Walking policy:** Mandatory cart. **Metal spikes allowed:** Yes. **Range:** Yes (grass).
To obtain tee times: Call up to 7 days in advance.
Subscriber comments: Extremely beautiful desert mountain golf course...Some spectacular holes...Super challenge. Hills and ravines...Tricked up course...Challenging, narrow, a jewel in the desert...Some real thread-the-needle shots in the canyons...A little known hidden jewel...Amazing place, a must if you can get there...Real different, interesting and fun.

★★ENCANTO GOLF COURSE
PU-2705 N. 15th Ave., Phoenix, 85007, Maricopa County, (602)253-3963.
Opened: 1937. **Holes:** 27. **Par:** 70/72. **Yards:** 6,386/5,731. **Course rating:** 69.0/70.5.
Slope: 111/111. **Architect:** William P. Bell. **Green fee:** $10/$25. **Credit cards:**
MC,VISA. **Reduced fees:** Low season, twilight, seniors, juniors. **Caddies:** No. **Golf carts:** $18. **Discount golf packages:** No. **Season:** Year-round. **High:** Feb.-April. **On site lodging:** No. **Rental clubs:** Yes. **Walking policy:** Unrestricted walking. **Metal spikes allowed:** Yes. **Range:** Yes (grass). **To obtain tee times:** Call two days in advance.
Special Notes: Complex also includes a 9-hole par-3 course.

★½ESTRELLA MOUNTAIN GOLF COURSE
PU-15205 W. Vineyard Dr., Goodyear, 85338, Maricopa County, (602)932-3714, 15 miles SE of Phoenix.
Opened: 1962. **Holes:** 18. **Par:** 71/73. **Yards:** 6,767/5,383. **Course rating:** 71.2/71.2.
Slope: 121/116. **Architect:** Red Lawrence. **Green fee:** $10/$25. **Credit cards:**
MC,VISA. **Reduced fees:** Low season, twilight, seniors, juniors. **Caddies:** No. **Golf carts:** $18. **Discount golf packages:** No. **Season:** Year-round. **High:** Dec.-April. **On site lodging:** No. **Rental clubs:** Yes. **Walking policy:** Unrestricted walking. **Metal spikes allowed:** Yes. **Range:** Yes (grass/mats). **To obtain tee times:** Call 7 days in advance.

★★½THE 500 CLUB
PU-4707 W. Pinnacle Peak Rd., Glendale, 85310, Maricopa County, (602)492-9500, 20 miles W of Phoenix.
Opened: 1989. **Holes:** 18. **Par:** 72/73. **Yards:** 6,649/5,557. **Course rating:** 71.0/69.8.
Slope: 121/112. **Architect:** Brian Whitcomb. **Green fee:** $25/$55. **Credit cards:** All major. **Reduced fees:** Weekdays, low season, twilight, juniors. **Caddies:** No. **Golf carts:** $10. **Discount golf packages:** No. **Season:** Year-round. **High:** Jan.-March. **On site lodging:** No. **Rental clubs:** Yes. **Walking policy:** Unrestricted walking. **Metal spikes allowed:** Yes. **Range:** Yes (grass). **To obtain tee times:** Call up to three days in advance.
Subscriber comments: Course looks easy, but you can get into trouble...Fun public course, open and short...Challenging layout with spectacular views...Short but some good golf shots required...Good mountain holes...Nice desert scenery; short, fairly straight holes...A couple of challenging holes...Inexpensive desert golf, simple layout.

★★★½THE FOOTHILLS GOLF CLUB
PU-2201 E. Clubhouse Dr., Phoenix, 85048, Maricopa County, (602)460-4653, (800)493-1161.
Opened: 1987. **Holes:** 18. **Par:** 72/72. **Yards:** 6,968/5,441. **Course rating:** 73.2/70.1.
Slope: 132/114. **Architect:** Tom Weiskopf/Jay Morrish. **Green fee:** $35/$99. **Credit cards:** MC,VISA,AMEX. **Reduced fees:** Weekdays, low season, twilight, juniors.
Caddies: No. **Golf carts:** Included in Green Fee. **Discount golf packages:** No.
Season: Year-round. **High:** Jan.-March. **On site lodging:** No. **Rental clubs:** Yes.
Walking policy: Mandatory cart. **Metal spikes allowed:** Yes. **Range:** Yes (grass). **To obtain tee times:** Call up to 7 days in advance.
Subscriber comments: Above-average course...User-friendly, wide open fairways...Desert course. Big greens...Short par 5s...Fair test, good desert golf at good price...Some nice holes, 15 great holes...Enjoyable course...Nice setting, beautiful scenery...Fun to play.

★★FOUNTAIN HILLS GOLF CLUB
PU-10440 Indian Wells Dr., Fountain Hills, 85268, Maricopa County, (602)837-1173, 14 miles E of Scottsdale.

Opened: 1971. **Holes:** 18. **Par:** 71/71. **Yards:** 6,087/5,035. **Course rating:** 68.9/68.9. **Slope:** 119/112. **Architect:** John Allen. **Green fee:** $30/$75. **Credit cards:** All major. **Reduced fees:** Low season, twilight, juniors. **Caddies:** No. **Golf carts:** Included in Green Fee. **Discount golf packages:** No. **Season:** Year-round. **High:** Jan.-April. **On site lodging:** No. **Rental clubs:** Yes. **Walking policy:** Walking at certain times. **Metal spikes allowed:** Yes. **Range:** Yes (grass). **To obtain tee times:** Call up to 3 days in advance.

Subscriber comments: Very tight course...Fun but not difficult...OK course. Very hilly in canyon...Nice course, fun to play...Some wonderful views...Variety of holes...Accuracy a must on this short course...Visually appealing...Too hilly...Interesting elevation changes.

★★½FRANCISCO GRANDE RESORT & GOLF CLUB
R-26000 Gila Bend Hwy., Casa Grande, 85222, Pinal County, (602)836-6444, (800)237-4238, 45 miles S of Phoenix.
Opened: 1961. **Holes:** 18. **Par:** 72/72. **Yards:** 7,594/5,554. **Course rating:** 74.9/69.9. **Slope:** 126/112. **Architect:** Ralph Plummer. **Green fee:** $20/$75. **Credit cards:** MC,VISA,AMEX,Diners Club. **Reduced fees:** Low season, twilight, juniors. **Caddies:** No. **Golf carts:** $15. **Discount golf packages:** Yes. **Season:** Year-round. **High:** Nov.-April. **On site lodging:** Yes. **Rental clubs:** Yes. **Walking policy:** Mandatory cart. **Metal spikes allowed:** Yes. **Range:** Yes (grass). **To obtain tee times:** Call up to 5 days in advance, or with hotel room reservations.

Subscriber comments: Longest course in Arizona, play it from the tips!...Great old golf course...Long and mature, excellent...Has been improved last couple of years...Long, fairly uninteresting.

★★★FRED ENKE GOLF COURSE
PM-8251 E. Irvington Rd., Tucson, 85730, Pima County, (520)296-8607.
Opened: 1982. **Holes:** 18. **Par:** 72/72. **Yards:** 6,807/4,700. **Course rating:** 73.3/68.8. **Slope:** 137/111. **Architect:** Brad Benz/Michael Poellot. **Green fee:** $10/$26. **Credit cards:** MC,VISA,DISC. **Reduced fees:** Low season, twilight, seniors, juniors. **Caddies:** No. **Golf carts:** $16. **Discount golf packages:** No. **Season:** Year-round. **High:** Dec.-April. **On site lodging:** No. **Rental clubs:** Yes. **Walking policy:** Unrestricted walking. **Metal spikes allowed:** Yes. **Range:** Yes (grass). **To obtain tee times:** Call 6 days in advnace.

Subscriber comments: Tough short desert course...Target golf...Unfair, gimmicky...Desert muny...Accuracy is important...Some demanding holes.

★★★½GAINEY RANCH GOLF CLUB
R-7600 Gainey Club Dr., Scottsdale, 85258, Maricopa County, (602)483-2582.
Opened: 1984. **Holes:** 27. **Architect:** Brad Benz/Michael Poellot. **Green fee:** $70/$105. **Credit cards:** Must charge to hotel room. **Reduced fees:** Low season. **Caddies:** No. **Golf carts:** Included in Green Fee. **Discount golf packages:** No. **Season:** Year-round. **High:** Jan.-April. **On site lodging:** Yes. **Rental clubs:** Yes. **Walking policy:** Mandatory cart. **Metal spikes allowed:** Yes. **Range:** Yes (grass). **To obtain tee times:** Hotel guests make tee times with hotel golf coordinator.

DUNES/ARROYO
Par: 72/72. **Yards:** 6,662/5,151. **Course rating:** 70.7/68.5. **Slope:** 124/113.
DUNES/LAKES
Par: 72/72. **Yards:** 6,614/4,993. **Course rating:** 71.1/67.9. **Slope:** 126/115.
LAKES/ARROYO
Par: 72/72. **Yards:** 6,800/5,312. **Course rating:** 71.9/70.4. **Slope:** 128/116.

Subscriber comments: Excellent variety, outstanding service...9th hole Lakes with waterfall is outstanding...Some great holes...Expensive, but worth it...User friendly. Good challenge from back tees...Good courses from all tees...Playable...Beautiful lay-out...7, 8, 9 on Dunes great holes from back tees...Variety of shots, rolling terrain...Fun course, facilities good...9th on Lakes best finishing hole in Arizona...Challenging.

GOLD CANYON GOLF RESORT
R-6100 S. Kings Ranch Rd., Gold Canyon, 85219, Pinal County, (602)982-9449, (800)624-6445, 35 miles SE of Phoenix. **Green fee:** $29/$125. **Credit cards:** All

major,Diners Club. **Caddies:** No. **Golf carts:** Included in Green Fee. **Discount golf packages:** Yes. **Season:** Year-round. **High:** Jan.-March. **On site lodging:** Yes. **Rental clubs:** Yes. **Walking policy:** Mandatory cart. **Metal spikes allowed:** Yes. **Range:** Yes (grass/mats). **To obtain tee times:** Call and reserve up to 7 days in advance with a credit card. Call 8-60 days for $5 fee per player.

MOUNTAIN COURSE
Opened: 1997. **Holes:** 18. **Par:** 70/70. **Yards:** 6,584/4,921. **Course rating:** 70.9/67.4. **Slope:** 138/110. **Architect:** Ken Kavanaugh. **Reduced fees:** Weekdays, low season, twilight.

★★★½RESORT COURSE
Opened: 1982. **Holes:** 18. **Par:** 71/72. **Yards:** 6,398/4,876. **Course rating:** 69.8/67.5. **Slope:** 125/109. **Architect:** Greg Nash/Ken Kavanaugh. **Reduced fees:** Weekdays, low season, resort guests, twilight.
Subscriber comments: Beautiful setting, loved the course...Very interesting course...Back nine just beautiful...You'll need a camera. Beautiful...Super views, great golf...Spectacular, desert mountain course, an adventure!...Watch out for rattlers...Heaven in the canyons...New back nine impressive, views...Scenic gem!

★★★½THE GOLF CLUB AT EAGLE MOUNTAIN
PU-14915 E. Eagle Mtn. Pkwy., Fountain Hills, 85268, Maricopa County, (602)816-1234, 10 miles E of Scottsdale.
Opened: 1996. **Holes:** 18. **Par:** 71/71. **Yards:** 6,755/5,065. **Course rating:** 71.7/67.9. **Slope:** 139/118. **Architect:** Scott Miller. **Green fee:** $55/$130. **Credit cards:** MC,VISA,AMEX. **Reduced fees:** Weekdays, low season, twilight, juniors. **Caddies:** No. **Golf carts:** Included in Green Fee. **Discount golf packages:** No. **Season:** Year-round. **High:** Jan.-April. **On site lodging:** No. **Rental clubs:** Yes. **Walking policy:** Mandatory cart. **Metal spikes allowed:** Yes. **Range:** Yes (grass). **To obtain tee times:** Call golf shop.
Subscriber comments: Keep an eye on this up-and-comer. Beautiful layout...Terrain dictates valley fairways...Spectacular views and golf holes...Grip it, rip it first hole...Picturesque...More playable than it looks.

★★★★THE GOLF CLUB AT VISTOSO
PU-955 W. Vistoso Highlands Dr., Tucson, 85737, Pima County, (520)797-9900, 12 miles NW of Tucson.
Opened: 1995. **Holes:** 18. **Par:** 72/72. **Yards:** 6,905/5,165. **Course rating:** 72.1/65.4. **Slope:** 145/111. **Architect:** Tom Weiskopf. **Green fee:** $45/$120. **Credit cards:** All major. **Reduced fees:** Weekdays, low season, twilight. **Caddies:** No. **Golf carts:** Included in Green Fee. **Discount golf packages:** No. **Season:** Year-round. **High:** Jan.-April. **On site lodging:** No. **Rental clubs:** Yes. **Walking policy:** Mandatory cart. **Metal spikes allowed:** Yes. **Range:** Yes (grass). **To obtain tee times:** Call up to 7 days in advance.
Notes: Golf Digest School site. Ranked 14th in 1997 Best in State.
Subscriber comments: Long carries off tee...A real sleeper, fun to play, nice and subtle...Interesting layout. Some simplistic holes...Best kept secret in Tucson...Great desert style course...Very nice new course...Best new course in Arizona, mountain views and very playable...Play it before the houses take over.

GRAYHAWK GOLF CLUB
PU- 19600 N. Pima Rd., Scottsdale, 85255, Maricopa County, (602)502-1800.
Credit cards: MC,VISA,AMEX. **Reduced fees:** Low season. **Caddies:** No. **Golf carts:** Included in Green Fee. **Discount golf packages:** No. **On site lodging:** No. **Rental clubs:** Yes. **Walking policy:** Unrestricted walking. **Metal spikes allowed:** Yes. **Range:** Yes (grass).
★★★★RAPTOR COURSE
Opened: 1995. **Holes:** 18. **Par:** 71. **Yards:** 7,025. **Course rating:** N/A. **Slope:** N/A. **Architect:** Tom Fazio. **Green fee:** $95/$175. **Season:** Nov.-Sept. **High:** Nov.-May. **To obtain tee times:** Call pro shop up to 30 days in advance.
Notes: Ranked 18th in 1997 Best in State.
Subscriber comments: Fabulous desert course...A true golf experience, great track...Overrated, but better than Talon...Talon course much better...Great test of target

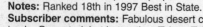

golf...Too many bunkers...A great experience...Great clubhouse...Another outstanding desert course.

★★★★TALON COURSE
Opened: 1994. **Holes:** 18. **Par:** 72/72. **Yards:** 7,000/5,200. **Course rating:** 74.3/70.0. **Slope:** 141/121. **Architect:** David Graham/Gary Panks. **Green fee:** $125/$125. **Season:** Year-round. **High:** Jan.-May. **To obtain tee times:** Call 30 days in advance. **Notes:** Ranked 12th in 1997 Best in State.
Subscriber comments: Very nice course, challenging...Greens are too severe...Greens are outstanding...Nice landscaping...Best of the two courses, very playable, walking a plus...Nice course but no real remarkable holes...Both great challenging courses.

★★★HAPPY TRAILS RESORT
17200 W. Bell Rd., Surprise, 85374, Maricopa County, (602)584-6000, 20 miles NW of Phoenix.
Opened: 1983. **Holes:** 18. **Par:** 72/72. **Yards:** 6,646/5,146. **Course rating:** 72.1/68.7. **Slope:** 124/113. **Architect:** Greg Nash/Ken Kavanaugh. **Green fee:** $20/$50. **Credit cards:** All major. **Reduced fees:** Weekdays, low season, resort guests, twilight, juniors. **Caddies:** No. **Golf carts:** Included in Green Fee. **Discount golf packages:** No. **Season:** Year-round. **High:** Nov.-April. **On site lodging:** No. **Rental clubs:** Yes. **Walking policy:** Mandatory cart. **Metal spikes allowed:** Yes. **Range:** Yes (grass/mats). **To obtain tee times:** Call 3 days in advance during season. Call 7 days in advance during summer.
Subscriber comments: A fun course...Excellent bent grass greens...Front nine not very scenic. Back nine is better...Don't tell anyone about this course...Beware of the par 3s, long and difficult...Short but challenging.

★★½HAVEN GOLF CLUB
PU-110 N. Abrego, Green Valley, 85614, Pima County, (520)625-4281.
Call club for further information.
Subscriber comments: User-friendly course...Best secret around...Flat, not much trouble, hackers' heaven...Fairly wide open, good greens...Easy walk...Great course for beginners, very forgiving...Good track, challenging, but fair...Good mountain views...Mediocre layout.

HERITAGE HIGHLANDS GOLF & COUNTRY CLUB
4949 W. Heritage Club Blvd., Marana, 85742, (520)579-7000, 10 miles NW of Tucson.
Opened: 1997. **Holes:** 18. **Par:** 72/72. **Yards:** 6,904/4,901. **Course rating:** 72.1/67.7. **Slope:** 134/121. **Architect:** Arthur Hills. **Green fee:** $55/$85. **Credit cards:** MC,VISA,AMEX. **Reduced fees:** Weekdays, low season, twilight. **Caddies:** No. **Golf carts:** Included in Green Fee. **Discount golf packages:** No. **Season:** Year-round. **High:** Dec.-April. **On site lodging:** No. **Rental clubs:** Yes. **Walking policy:** Mandatory cart. **Metal spikes allowed:** No. **Range:** Yes (grass). **To obtain tee times:** Call up to 7 days in advance.

★★★½HILLCREST GOLF CLUB
PU-20002 Star Ridge Rd., Sun City West, 85375, Maricopa County, (602)584-1500, 10 miles W of Phoenix.
Opened: N/A. **Holes:** 18. **Par:** 72/72. **Yards:** 6,960/5,880. **Course rating:** N/A. **Slope:** 127/119. **Architect:** Jeff Hardin/Greg Nash. **Green fee:** $25/$65. **Credit cards:** All major. **Reduced fees:** Weekdays, low season, twilight. **Caddies:** No. **Golf carts:** Included in Green Fee. **Discount golf packages:** No. **Season:** Year-round. **High:** Nov.-May. **On site lodging:** No. **Rental clubs:** Yes. **Walking policy:** Mandatory cart. **Metal spikes allowed:** Yes. **Range:** Yes (grass). **To obtain tee times:** Call up to 7 days in advance.
1985-1988 Senior PGA Tour Arizona Roundup; 1981-1983 LPGA Tour.
Subscriber comments: Excellent design...Nice test of golf...Classic design with large greens...Great traditional course, lots of trees and water, good par 5s...Very good vacation course...All around good course, deceptively challenging...Everything huge! Lakes, bunkers, fairways. Great par 5s...Very nice/scenic layout.

★★½KEN MCDONALD GOLF CLUB
PU-800 Divot Dr., Tempe, 85283, Maricopa County, (602)350-5256, 4 miles SE of Phoenix.
Opened: 1974. **Holes:** 18. **Par:** 72/73. **Yards:** 6,743/5,872. **Course rating:** 70.8/70.8.
Slope: 115/112. **Architect:** Jack Snyder. **Green fee:** $17. **Credit cards:** MC,VISA.
Reduced fees: Twilight. **Caddies:** Yes. **Golf carts:** $8. **Discount golf packages:** No.
Season: Year-round. **High:** Nov.-April. **On site lodging:** No. **Rental clubs:** Yes.
Walking policy: Unrestricted walking. **Metal spikes allowed:** Yes. **Range:** Yes (grass).
To obtain tee times: Call up to two days in advance.
Subscriber comments: Nice public course, can challenge you...Flat course, fairly easy...Traditional muny, nice mix of holes...A walk in the park...Another city course...#18 tough by any standard.
Special Notes: Reduced fees for twilight play in summer only.

★★★½KIERLAND GOLF CLUB
PU-15636 N. Clubgate Dr., Scottsdale, 85254, Maricopa County, (602)922-9283, 20 miles NE of Phoenix.
Opened: 1996. **Holes:** 27. **Architect:** Scott Miller. **Green fee:** $40/$125. **Credit cards:** MC,VISA,AMEX. **Reduced fees:** Weekdays, low season, twilight, juniors. **Caddies:** No.
Golf carts: Included in Green Fee. **Discount golf packages:** No. **Season:** Year-round.
High: Jan.-April. **On site lodging:** No. **Rental clubs:** No. **Walking policy:** Unrestricted walking. **Metal spikes allowed:** Yes. **Range:** Yes (grass). **To obtain tee times:** Guest may call golf shop up to 30 days in advance.
IRONWOOD/ACACIA
Par: 72/72. **Yards:** 6,974/4,985. **Course rating:** 72.9/69.2. **Slope:** 130/116.
IRONWOOD/MESQUITE
Par: 72/72. **Yards:** 7,017/5,017. **Course rating:** 73.3/69.4. **Slope:** 133/120.
MESQUITE/ACACIA
Par: 72/72. **Yards:** 6,913/4,898. **Course rating:** 72.6/69.0. **Slope:** 133/115.
Subscriber comments: Good layout...Ego booster, can be tamed...Another fine design...Good challenge, tough rough, rolling greens...Reward for good shots. Misery for bad...Excellent use of land...Challenging and creative layout...Sculpted fairways return errant shots back into play.
Notes: Golf Digest School site.

★★★KOKOPELLI GOLF RESORT
PU-1800 W. Guadalupe, Gilbert, 85233, Maricopa County, (602)926-3589, (800)468-7918, 10 miles SE of Phoenix.
Opened: 1993. **Holes:** 18. **Par:** 72/72. **Yards:** 6,716/4,992. **Course rating:** 72.2/68.8.
Slope: 132/120. **Architect:** William Phillips. **Green fee:** $40/$100. **Credit cards:** MC,VISA,AMEX. **Reduced fees:** Weekdays, low season, resort guests, twilight.
Caddies: No. **Golf carts:** Included in Green Fee. **Discount golf packages:** Yes.
Season: Year-round. **High:** Jan.-April. **On site lodging:** No. **Rental clubs:** Yes.
Walking policy: Mandatory cart. **Metal spikes allowed:** Yes. **Range:** Yes (grass). **To obtain tee times:** Call seven days in advance.
Subscriber comments: From tips is challenging, use all the clubs...Average layout...Small greens...Overall great place to play...Getting better as the course ages...Homes along most holes...Nice layout, first four holes tough...Not much on scenery but excellent golf...Fun...Many moguls...Too hilly, punished even good drives.

★★★LA PALOMA COUNTRY CLUB
R-3660 E. Sunrise Dr., Tucson, 85718, Pima County, (520)299-1500, (800)222-1249.
Opened: 1984. **Holes:** 27. **Architect:** Jack Nicklaus. **Green fee:** $75/$135. **Credit cards:** All major. **Reduced fees:** Low season, resort guests. **Caddies:** No. **Golf carts:** Included in Green Fee. **Discount golf packages:** Yes. **Season:** Year-round. **High:** Jan.-May. **On site lodging:** Yes. **Rental clubs:** Yes. **Walking policy:** Mandatory cart. **Metal spikes allowed:** Yes. **Range:** Yes (grass/mats). **To obtain tee times:** Resort guests up to 60 days in advance.
CANYON/HILL
Par: 72/72. **Yards:** 6,997/5,057. **Course rating:** 74.8/67.4. **Slope:** 151/114.
RIDGE/CANYON
Par: 72/72. **Yards:** 7,088/5,075. **Course rating:** 75.2/67.9. **Slope:** 152/121.

RIDGE/HILL
Par: 72/72. **Yards:** 7,017/4,878. **Course rating:** 74.2/66.9. **Slope:** 150/110.
Subscriber comments: Great resort...Very beautiful, very tough...Tough, maybe too much so...Difficult but fun...Nicklaus' revenge...A good challenge...Back tees, long carries over desert...Hard but fair...Beautiful views...Tough layout, difficult to score...A few great holes...Hit 'em straight when you play here or take lots of balls.

★★★LAKE POWELL NATIONAL GOLF CLUB
PU-400 Clubhouse Dr., Page, 86040, Coconina County, (520)645-2023, 270 miles N of Phoenix.
Opened: 1995. **Holes:** 18. **Par:** 72/72. **Yards:** 7,064/5,097. **Course rating:** 73.4/68.0.
Slope: 139/122. **Architect:** Bill Phillips. **Green fee:** $35/$60. **Credit cards:** MC,VISA.
Reduced fees: Low season, resort guests, juniors. **Caddies:** No. **Golf carts:** Included in Green Fee. **Discount golf packages:** No. **Season:** Year-round. **High:** May-Sept. **On site lodging:** Yes. **Rental clubs:** Yes. **Walking policy:** Mandatory cart. **Metal spikes allowed:** Yes. **Range:** Yes (grass). **To obtain tee times:** Up to 7 days in advance.
Subscriber comments: Great views...Windy open layout...Wonderful, challenging course. Will improve as it matures...Wonderful experience. Tough to score.

★★★LAS SENDAS GOLF CLUB
PU-7555 E. Eagle Crest Dr., Mesa, 85207, Maricopa County, (602)396-4000, 14 miles E of Phoenix.
Opened: 1995. **Holes:** 18. **Par:** 71/71. **Yards:** 6,836/5,100. **Course rating:** 73.8/69.9.
Slope: 149/126. **Architect:** Robert Trent Jones Jr. **Green fee:** $45/$135. **Credit cards:** All major. **Reduced fees:** Low season. **Caddies:** No. **Golf carts:** Included in Green Fee. **Discount golf packages:** No. **Season:** Year-round. **High:** Jan.-April. **On site lodging:** No. **Rental clubs:** Yes. **Walking policy:** Unrestricted walking. **Metal spikes allowed:** Yes. **Range:** Yes (grass). **To obtain tee times:** Call 7 days in advance. Call 8-30 days in advance for $15 fee p/player.
Notes: Ranked 16th in 1997 Best in State.
Subscriber comments: Beautiful view of the valley...Got to be on your game here, really hard but fun...This was a treat, must play...Will be a top 10 in Arizona...Back nine great, beautiful scenery...Some goofy holes...Great golf, great views...Greens much too undulating...Requires ability with all clubs...Very challenging.

★★★THE LEGEND GOLF RESORT AT ARROWHEAD
PU-21027 N. 67th Ave., Glendale, 85308, Maricopa County, (602)561-1902, (800)468-7918, 15 miles SW of Phoenix.
Opened: 1989. **Holes:** 18. **Par:** 72/72. **Yards:** 7,005/5,233. **Course rating:** 73.0/71.2.
Slope: 129/119. **Architect:** Arnold Palmer/Ed Seay. **Green fee:** $25/$85. **Credit cards:** MC,VISA,AMEX. **Reduced fees:** Weekdays, low season, twilight, juniors. **Caddies:** No. **Golf carts:** Included in Green Fee. **Discount golf packages:** Yes. **Season:** Year-round. **High:** Jan.-April. **On site lodging:** No. **Rental clubs:** Yes. **Walking policy:** Mandatory cart. **Metal spikes allowed:** Yes. **Range:** Yes (grass). **To obtain tee times:** Call 7 days in advance.
Subscriber comments: Good course...Course is lined with houses throughout...Good mountain holes...Very good Palmer/Seay design, challenging around greens...Not a flat putt anywhere...Great layout, par 5 across water...Testy Palmer layout in the foothills.

★★★LEGEND TRAIL GOLF CLUB
PU-9462 Legendary Trail, Scottsdale, 85262, Maricopa County, (602)488-7434.
Opened: 1995. **Holes:** 18. **Par:** 72/72. **Yards:** 6,820/5,000. **Course rating:** 72.3/68.2. **Slope:** 135/122. **Architect:** Rees Jones. **Green fee:** $45/$125. **Credit cards:** MC,VISA,AMEX. **Reduced fees:** Low season, juniors. **Caddies:** No. **Golf carts:** Included in Green Fee. **Discount golf packages:** No. **Season:** Year-round. **High:** Jan.-March. **On site lodging:** No. **Rental clubs:** Yes. **Walking policy:** Unrestricted walking. **Metal spikes allowed:** Yes. **Range:** Yes (grass). **To obtain tee times:** Call.
Notes: Ranked 15th in 1997 Best in State.
Subscriber comments: Playable course...If you can't get on Troon North, this is Plan B...Lush...Beautiful challenge...Challenging picturesque Rees Jones design...Great desert links...Fun course...Well kept secret.

★★½ THE LINKS AT QUEEN CREEK

PU-445 E. Ocotillo Rd., Queen Creek, 85242, (602)987-1910, 12 miles E of Mesa.
Opened: 1993. **Holes:** 18. **Par:** 70/71. **Yards:** 6,100/5,000. **Course rating:** N/A. **Slope:** 100/92. **Architect:** Sam West. **Green fee:** $18/$38. **Credit cards:** MC,VISA. **Reduced fees:** N/A. **Caddies:** No. **Golf carts:** Included in Green Fee. **Discount golf packages:** No. **Season:** Nov.-May. **High:** Dec.-March. **On site lodging:** No. **Rental clubs:** Yes. **Walking policy:** Unrestricted walking. **Metal spikes allowed:** Yes. **Range:** Yes (grass/mats). **To obtain tee times:** Call up to 6 days in advance.
Subscriber comments: Nice small course...Nice course, easier than most, fun...Great short course...Friendly.

LONDON BRIDGE GOLF CLUB

PU-2400 Clubhouse Dr., Lake Havasu City, 86405, Mohave County, (602)855-2719, 180 miles NE of Phoenix. **Architect:** Jack Snyder. **Credit cards:** MC,VISA. **Caddies:** No. **Discount golf packages:** Yes. **Season:** Year-round. **High:** Jan.-April. **On site lodging:** No. **Rental clubs:** Yes. **Metal spikes allowed:** Yes. **Range:** Yes (grass). **To obtain tee times:** Call.

★★½ LONDON BRIDGE COURSE

Opened: 1969. **Holes:** 18. **Par:** 71/72. **Yards:** 6,618/5,756. **Course rating:** 70.4/73.5. **Slope:** 122/133. **Green fee:** $35/$50. **Reduced fees:** Low season, twilight, seniors, juniors. **Golf carts:** Included in Green Fee. **Walking policy:** Mandatory cart.
Subscriber comments: Decent golf with nice views of Lake Havasu.

★★ STONEBRIDGE COURSE

Opened: 1979. **Holes:** 18. **Par:** 71/71. **Yards:** 6,166/5,045. **Course rating:** 68.8/68.6. **Slope:** 114/118. **Green fee:** $30/$35. **Reduced fees:** Weekdays, low season, resort guests, twilight, seniors. **Golf carts:** $23. **Walking policy:** Unrestricted walking.

★★★★ LOS CABALLEROS GOLF CLUB

R-1551 S. Vulture Mine Rd., Wickenburg, 85390, Maricopa County, (520)684-2704, 50 miles NW of Phoenix.
Opened: 1979. **Holes:** 18. **Par:** 72/72. **Yards:** 6,962/5,690. **Course rating:** 73.4/71.2. **Slope:** 136/124. **Architect:** Greg Nash/Jeff Hardin. **Green fee:** $50/$105. **Credit cards:** MC,VISA. **Reduced fees:** Low season, resort guests. **Caddies:** No. **Golf carts:** Included in Green Fee. **Discount golf packages:** Yes. **Season:** Year-round. **High:** Feb.-April. **On site lodging:** Yes. **Rental clubs:** Yes. **Walking policy:** Mandatory cart. **Metal spikes allowed:** Yes. **Range:** Yes (grass). **To obtain tee times:** Call 2 days in advance.
Subscriber comments: Beautiful desert course but out of the way...Hidden gem. Worth the two-hour drive from Phoenix...Three cars in lot on Saturday a.m...Perfect! Spectacular views!Still unknown and quiet but the fairest test in the desert...Desert views...Well worth the drive...Great golf experience.......Best kept secret in Arizona...Excellent course; beautiful setting.

MARRIOTT'S CAMELBACK GOLF CLUB

R-7847 N. Mockingbird Lane, Scottsdale, 85253, Maricopa County, (602)596-7050, (800)242-2635, 5 miles E of Phoenix.
Architect: Red Lawrence. **Green fee:** $35/$115. **Credit cards:** All major. **Reduced fees:** Weekdays, low season, resort guests, twilight. **Caddies:** No. **Golf carts:** Included in Green Fee. **Discount golf packages:** Yes. **Season:** Year-round. **High:** Jan.-April. **On site lodging:** Yes. **Rental clubs:** Yes. **Walking policy:** Mandatory cart. **Metal spikes allowed:** Yes. **Range:** Yes (grass). **To obtain tee times:** Call up to 30 days in advance. Marriott guests may call up to 45 days in advance.

★★½ INDIAN BEND COURSE

Opened: 1980. **Holes:** 18. **Par:** 72/72. **Yards:** 7,014/5,917. **Course rating:** 72.6/72.0. **Slope:** 122/118.
Subscriber comments: Very good...Older course...For average players...Overrated.

★★ PADRE COURSE

Opened: 1971. **Holes:** 18. **Par:** 71/73. **Yards:** 6,559/5,626. **Course rating:** 71.0/72.0. **Slope:** 125/124.

★★½MARYVALE GOLF CLUB

PU-5902 W. Indian School Rd., Phoenix, 85033, Maricopa County, (602)846-4022.
Opened: 1961. **Holes:** 18. **Par:** 72/72. **Yards:** 6,539/5,656. **Course rating:** 69.8/70.2.
Slope: 115/113. **Architect:** William F. Bell. **Green fee:** $6/$25. **Credit cards:** None.
Reduced fees: Weekdays, low season, twilight, seniors, juniors. **Caddies:** No. **Golf carts:** N/A. **Discount golf packages:** No. **Season:** Year-round. **High:** Nov.-April. **On site lodging:** No. **Rental clubs:** Yes. **Walking policy:** Unrestricted walking. **Metal spikes allowed:** Yes. **Range:** Yes (grass). **To obtain tee times:** Call two days in advance. Three tee times per hour are reserved for walk-on play.
Subscriber comments: A fun muny track...Simple layout, good for quick round to tune-up...Park-like course, lots of good doglegs...Flat, plain...City course, reasonable...Nice old course. Pretty flat...Fun ego-building muny.

MCCORMICK RANCH GOLF CLUB

R-7505 E. McCormick Pkwy., Scottsdale, 85258, Maricopa County, (602)948-0260.
Opened: 1972. **Architect:** Desmond Muirhead. **Green fee:** $37/$97. **Credit cards:** MC,VISA,AMEX. **Reduced fees:** Weekdays, low season, resort guests, twilight.
Caddies: No. **Golf carts:** Included in Green Fee. **Discount golf packages:** Yes.
Season: Year-round. **High:** Jan.-June. **On site lodging:** Yes. **Rental clubs:** Yes.
Walking policy: Mandatory cart. **Metal spikes allowed:** Yes. **Range:** Yes (grass/mats).
To obtain tee times: Call 7 days in advance. Call up to 30 days in advance when staying at any Scottsdale/Phoenix hotel.

★★★PALM COURSE

Holes: 18. **Par:** 72/72. **Yards:** 7,044/5,057. **Course rating:** 74.4/69.9. **Slope:** 137/117.
Notes: 1990-1996 National Junior College Championships.
Subscriber comments: Beautiful layout. Enjoyed playing all 36 holes...Wide fairways, lots of palms and water...Short, but not easy...A Phoenix/Scottsdale tradition...Fair course even from tips...Mature landscaping...Tourist golf on wide, wide fairways.

★★★PINE COURSE

Holes: 18. **Par:** 72/72. **Yards:** 7,187/5,333. **Course rating:** 74.4/69.9. **Slope:** 135/117.
Subscriber comments: Great course...Upscale but fun...An average resort layout...Course was OK, good par 4s...Nothing memorable, but convenient location...Good food, course nice.

MOUNT GRAHAM MUNICIPAL GOLF COURSE

PM-Golf Course Rd., Safford, 85546, Graham County, (520)348-3140, 120 miles NE of Tucson.
Opened: N/A. **Holes:** 18. **Par:** 72/73. **Yards:** 6,354/5,691. **Course rating:** 69.5/70.6.
Slope: 116/117. **Architect:** N/A. **Green fee:** $13. **Credit cards:** None. **Reduced fees:** Twilight, juniors. **Caddies:** No. **Golf carts:** $15. **Discount golf packages:** No. **Season:** Year-round. **High:** N/A. **On site lodging:** No. **Rental clubs:** Yes. **Walking policy:** Unrestricted walking. **Metal spikes allowed:** Yes. **Range:** Yes (grass/mats). **To obtain tee times:** Walk on.

MOUNTAIN BROOK GOLF CLUB

PU-5783 S. Mountain Brook Dr., Gold Canyon, 85219, (602)671-1000.
Opened: 1996. **Holes:** 18. **Par:** 71/71. **Yards:** 6,600/5,277. **Course rating:** 69.9/66.2.
Slope: 124/103. **Architect:** N/A. **Green fee:** $20/$65. **Credit cards:** None. **Reduced fees:** N/A. **Caddies:** No. **Golf carts:** Included in Green Fee. **Discount golf packages:** No. **Season:** Year-round. **High:** Nov.-March. **On site lodging:** No. **Rental clubs:** No.
Walking policy: Mandatory cart. **Metal spikes allowed:** Yes. **Range:** Yes (grass). **To obtain tee times:** Call golf shop up to 6 days in advance.

★★★MOUNTAIN SHADOWS

PU-5641 E Lincoln Dr, Scottsdale, 85253, Maricopa County, (602)951-5427.
Opened: 1959. **Holes:** 18. **Par:** 56/56. **Yards:** 3,083/2,650. **Course rating:** 56.9/55.4.
Slope: 92/89. **Architect:** Jack Snyder. **Green fee:** $30/$70. **Credit cards:** All major.
Reduced fees: N/A. **Caddies:** No. **Golf carts:** Included in Green Fee. **Discount golf packages:** No. **Season:** Year-round. **High:** Jan.-April. **On site lodging:** Yes. **Rental clubs:** Yes. **Walking policy:** Mandatory cart. **Metal spikes allowed:** Yes. **Range:** Yes (grass). **To obtain tee times:** N/A.
Subscriber comments: Overall very good facility...Good executive course...Great way

to start the season...Great for short game...Short course, don't need a driver...May be small but it's mighty.
Special Notes: Spikeless encouraged.

MOUNTAIN VIEW GOLF CLUB

PU-5740 W. Baseline, Phoenix, 85339, Maricopa County, (602)237-4567.
Opened: 1993. **Architect:** Dan Pohl. **Credit cards:** MC,VISA,AMEX. **Reduced fees:** Weekdays, low season, twilight, seniors. **Caddies:** No. **Golf carts:** $10. **Discount golf packages:** No. **Season:** Year-round. **High:** Nov.-Feb. **On site lodging:** No. **Rental clubs:** Yes. **Walking policy:** Unrestricted walking. **Metal spikes allowed:** Yes. **Range:** Yes (grass). **To obtain tee times:** N/A.

★★EAST COURSE
Holes: 18. **Par:** 72/72. **Yards:** 6,811/6,238. **Course rating:** 71.7/72.3. **Slope:** 119/114.
Green fee: $10/$92.

★★WEST COURSE
Holes: 18. **Par:** 71/71. **Yards:** 6,646/5,770. **Course rating:** 70.9/71.6. **Slope:** 121/116.
Green fee: $10/$42.
Subscriber comments: Very enjoyable links-style design...Wide open course, no trees...Lots of variety.
Special Notes: Formerly Pohlcat Mountain View Golf Club.

★★★OAKCREEK COUNTRY CLUB

690 Bell Rock Blvd., Sedona, 86351, Yavapai County, (520)284-1660, 100 miles N of Phoenix.
Opened: 1958. **Holes:** 18. **Par:** 72/72. **Yards:** 6,854/5,555. **Course rating:** 71.9/71.0.
Slope: 129/128. **Architect:** Robert Trent Jones. **Green fee:** $65. **Credit cards:** MC,VISA,DISC. **Reduced fees:** Twilight, juniors. **Caddies:** Yes. **Golf carts:** Included in Green Fee. **Discount golf packages:** No. **Season:** Year-round. **High:** March-May, Sept.-Nov. **On site lodging:** No. **Rental clubs:** Yes. **Walking policy:** Walking at certain times. **Metal spikes allowed:** Yes. **Range:** Yes (grass/mats). **To obtain tee times:** Call 6 days in advance.
Subscriber comments: Beautiful scenery...Good front, so-so back...A great Robert Trent Jones course!...Incredible scenery, fun course...Gotta play when visiting Sedona, bring camera...Old mature golf course.

★★★OCOTILLO GOLF CLUB

R-3751 S. Clubhouse Dr., Chandler, 85248, Maricopa County, (602)220-9000, 15 miles SE of Phoenix.
Opened: 1986. **Holes:** 27. **Architect:** Ted Robinson. **Green fee:** $35/$115. **Credit cards:** All major. **Reduced fees:** Low season, twilight. **Caddies:** No. **Golf carts:** Included in Green Fee. **Discount golf packages:** No. **Season:** Year-round. **High:** Jan.-April. **On site lodging:** No. **Rental clubs:** Yes. **Walking policy:** Mandatory cart. **Metal spikes allowed:** Yes. **Range:** Yes (grass/mats). **To obtain tee times:** Call 2 days in advance in season and 7 days in advance off season. Premium fees for advanced tee times outside these restrictions.
BLUE/GOLD
Par: 72/72. **Yards:** 6,729/5,128. **Course rating:** 71.3/71.3. **Slope:** 131/128.
BLUE/WHITE
Par: 71/71. **Yards:** 6,533/5,134. **Course rating:** 70.8/71.0. **Slope:** 128/127.
WHITE/GOLD
Par: 71/71. **Yards:** 6,612/5,124. **Course rating:** 71.4/68.4. **Slope:** 128/122.
Subscriber comments: Lots of water, flowers, geese...Challenging, makes you think about club selection...Bring A-game or extra sleeve of "floaters"...One of the best in Southwest...Water, water, more water...Awesome new clubhouse...Water on all three nines, target golf at its best, White nine is my favorite.

★★★OMNI TUCSON NATIONAL GOLF RESORT & SPA

R-2727 W. Club Dr., Tucson, 85741, Pima County, (520)575-7540, (800)528-4856, 20 miles NW of Tucson.
Opened: 1962. **Holes:** 27. **Architect:** R.B. Harris/Robert von Hagge/Bruce Devlin. **Green fee:** $70/$150. **Credit cards:** All major,Diners Club. **Reduced fees:** Low season, resort guests, twilight, juniors. **Caddies:** No. **Golf carts:** Included in Green Fee. **Discount golf pack-

GOOD SERVICE

ages: No. **Season:** Year-round. **High:** Oct.-May. **On site lodging:** Yes. **Rental clubs:** Yes. **Walking policy:** Mandatory cart. **Metal spikes allowed:** Yes. **Range:** Yes (grass/mats). **To obtain tee times:** Call 2 days in advance. Resort guests 30 days in advance.

GOLD/GREEN
Par: 73/73. **Yards:** 6,860/5,542. **Course rating:** 74.7/71.0. **Slope:** 135/118.
ORANGE/GOLD
Par: 73/73. **Yards:** 7,108/5,647. **Course rating:** 74.8/72.4. **Slope:** 136/123.
ORANGE/GREEN
Par: 72/72. **Yards:** 6,692/5,371. **Course rating:** 74.6/70.3. **Slope:** 134/117.
Notes: PGA Tour Tucson Chrysler Classic.
Subscriber comments: Midwest-type course...Good resort course...Traditional course in a great setting...PGA Tour stop; killed me week before tournament...All facilities great...The Green course very hilly...Not a real desert course...Very green...Good traditional desert course...Great history and tradition.

★★★ ORANGE TREE GOLF CLUB
R-10601 N. 56th St., Scottsdale, 85254, Maricopa County, (602)948-3730, (800)228-0386.
Opened: 1957. **Holes:** 18. **Par:** 72/72. **Yards:** 6,762/5,632. **Course rating:** 71.3/71.8. **Slope:** 122/116. **Architect:** Johnny Bulla. **Green fee:** $29/$98. **Credit cards:** All major,Diners Club. **Reduced fees:** Twilight. **Caddies:** No. **Golf carts:** Included in Green Fee. **Discount golf packages:** Yes. **Season:** Year-round. **High:** Jan.-April. **On site lodging:** Yes. **Rental clubs:** Yes. **Walking policy:** Mandatory cart. **Metal spikes allowed:** Yes. **Range:** Yes (grass). **To obtain tee times:** Call 7 days in advance.
Subscriber comments: Above average course...A good to very good traditional course...Relaxing to play, can score well...Nice park-like layout...Very flat, large greens...Generally OK...Some good holes...Old tree-lined course...Ordinary...Traditional.

★★½ PAINTED MOUNTAIN GOLF CLUB
PU-6210 E. McKellips Rd., Mesa, 85215, Maricopa County, (602)832-0156, 20 miles E of Phoenix.
Opened: N/A. **Holes:** 18. **Par:** 70/70. **Yards:** 6,021/4,651. **Course rating:** 67.2/64.3. **Slope:** 104/97. **Architect:** Milt Coggins. **Green fee:** $16/$38. **Credit cards:** MC,VISA. **Reduced fees:** Weekdays, low season, twilight, juniors. **Caddies:** No. **Golf carts:** $10. **Discount golf packages:** No. **Season:** Year-round. **High:** Jan.-April. **On site lodging:** No. **Rental clubs:** Yes. **Walking policy:** Unrestricted walking. **Metal spikes allowed:** Yes. **Range:** No. **To obtain tee times:** N/A.
Subscriber comments: Good flat course...Houses too close...Short course from blue tees but fun...Gets better every year...Good mix of holes.
Special Notes: Formerly Camelot Golf Club.

★★★½ PALM VALLEY GOLF CLUB
2211 N. Litchfield Rd., Goodyear, 85338, Maricopa County, (602)935-2500, 15 miles W of Phoenix.
Opened: 1993. **Holes:** 18. **Par:** 72/72. **Yards:** 7,015/5,300. **Course rating:** 72.8/68.7. **Slope:** 130/109. **Architect:** Arthur Hills. **Green fee:** $19/$64. **Credit cards:** MC,VISA,AMEX. **Reduced fees:** Weekdays, low season, twilight, juniors. **Caddies:** No. **Golf carts:** $12. **Discount golf packages:** No. **Season:** Year-round. **High:** Jan.-March. **On site lodging:** No. **Rental clubs:** Yes. **Walking policy:** Unrestricted walking. **Metal spikes allowed:** Yes. **Range:** Yes (grass). **To obtain tee times:** Call up to 4 days in advance.
Subscriber comments: Nice layout...Good use of terrain, a solid challenge...Young course. Very little shade. Windy...Fun, wonderful desert course, lots of variety...Wide open...Fine rolling course, built into housing development...Interesting holes...Worth the drive! Best kept secret in Phoenix area...Great bang for buck..Very nice, nice area.

★★★½ PAPAGO GOLF COURSE
PU-5595 E. Moreland St., Phoenix, 85008, Maricopa County, (602)275-8428.
Opened: 1963. **Holes:** 18. **Par:** 72/72. **Yards:** 7,068/5,937. **Course rating:** 73.3/72.4. **Slope:** 132/119. **Architect:** William F. Bell. **Green fee:** $12/$28. **Credit cards:** None. **Reduced fees:** Low season, twi-

light, seniors, juniors. **Caddies:** No. **Golf carts:** $17. **Discount golf packages:** No. **Season:** Year-round. **High:** Jan.-May. **On site lodging:** No. **Rental clubs:** Yes. **Walking policy:** Unrestricted walking. **Metal spikes allowed:** Yes. **Range:** Yes (grass/mats). **To obtain tee times:** Call 2 days in advance beginning at 6:30 a.m.
Notes: 1972 National Publinks Championship.
Subscriber comments: My favorite muny, great track...Great municipal course...Best value in Phoenix area...Best muny in the state...Awesome course. Long and difficult layout...One of the best true munys anywhere...Last four holes are killers...Great traditional layout...Super test of golf.

★★PAVILION LAKES GOLF CLUB
PU-8870 E. Indian Bend Rd., Scottsdale, 85250, Maricopa County, (602)948-3370.
Opened: 1992. **Holes:** 18. **Par:** 71/71. **Yards:** 6,489/5,135. **Course rating:** 70.1/68.2.
Slope: 120/110. **Architect:** N/A. **Green fee:** $16/$59. **Credit cards:** MC,VISA,AMEX.
Reduced fees: Weekdays, low season, twilight, juniors. **Caddies:** No. **Golf carts:** N/A.
Discount golf packages: No. **Season:** Year-round. **High:** Jan.-April. **On site lodging:** No. **Rental clubs:** Yes. **Walking policy:** Walking at certain times. **Metal spikes allowed:** Yes. **Range:** Yes (grass). **To obtain tee times:** Call up to 7 days in advance.

★★PAYSON GOLF COURSE
PU-1504 W. Country Club Dr., Payson, 85541, Gila County, (520)474-2273, 85 miles NE of Phoenix.
Opened: 1976. **Holes:** 18. **Par:** 71/71. **Yards:** 5,854/5,094. **Course rating:** 66.9/66.7.
Slope: 114/113. **Architect:** Frank Hughes/Russ Zakarisen. **Green fee:** $20/$28. **Credit cards:** None. **Reduced fees:** Weekdays, low season, juniors. **Caddies:** No. **Golf carts:** $22. **Discount golf packages:** No. **Season:** Year-round. **High:** April-Oct. **On site lodging:** No. **Rental clubs:** Yes. **Walking policy:** Unrestricted walking. **Metal spikes allowed:** Yes. **Range:** Yes (grass/mats). **To obtain tee times:** Call up to 7 days in advance.

★★★½THE PHOENICIAN GOLF CLUB
R-6000 E. Camelback Rd., Scottsdale, 85251, Maricopa County, (602)423-2449, (800)888-8234.
Opened: 1988. **Holes:** 27. **Architect:** Homer Flint. **Green fee:** $80/$150. **Credit cards:** All major,TCB. **Reduced fees:** Low season, resort guests. **Caddies:** No. **Golf carts:** Included in Green Fee. **Discount golf packages:** Yes. **Season:** Year-round. **High:** Oct.-May. **On site lodging:** Yes. **Rental clubs:** Yes. **Walking policy:** Mandatory cart. **Metal spikes allowed:** Yes. **Range:** Yes (grass). **To obtain tee times:** Call up to 30 days in advance.
DESERT/CANYON
Par: 70/70. **Yards:** 6,068/4,777. **Course rating:** 69.4/67.7. **Slope:** 131/114.
OASIS/CANYON
Par: 70/70. **Yards:** 6,258/4,871. **Course rating:** 70.1/69.1. **Slope:** 130/111.
OASIS/DESERT
Par: 70/70. **Yards:** 6,310/5,024. **Course rating:** 70.3/69.7. **Slope:** 130/113.
Subscriber comments: Class operation...Just a beautiful oasis in the desert...The new mountain holes are great...Pricey, but incredibly manicured with excellent hole variety...Best resort in Arizona...Very interesting holes with views...Excellent new holes...Beautiful course, new nine (1996) is a partial desert, partial green layout...Fun course, great resort...Beautiful landscaping.

★★★THE POINTE HILTON RESORT AT SOUTH MOUNTAIN
R-7777 S. Pointe Pkwy., Phoenix, 85044, Maricopa County, (602)431-6480, (800)876-4683.
Opened: 1988. **Holes:** 18. **Par:** 70/70. **Yards:** 6,003/4,550. **Course rating:** 68.1/66.2.
Slope: 117/107. **Architect:** Forrest Richardson. **Green fee:** $32/$125. **Credit cards:** All major,Diners Club. **Reduced fees:** Weekdays, low season, resort guests, twilight, juniors. **Caddies:** No. **Golf carts:** Included in Green Fee. **Discount golf packages:** Yes. **Season:** Year-round. **High:** Jan.-April. **On site lodging:** Yes. **Rental clubs:** Yes. **Walking policy:** Mandatory cart. **Metal spikes allowed:** Yes **Range:** No. **To obtain tee times:** Call golf shop 7 days in advance. For resort guests, call 30 days in advance.
Subscriber comments: Not many flat lies, fun course...Front nine is good; 15, 16 and 17 are too Mickey Mouse...Back nine fabulous...Challenging, up and down desert,

beautiful spot...Nice, shorter course...Target golf, bring the 2-iron...Gimmicky, tricked-up layout...Outstanding target golf, great views...Great variety...Front and back two different courses...Great mix of desert and water...Ultimate desert mountain target golf.

★★★★ THE POINTE HILTON RESORT AT TAPATIO CLIFFS
R-11111 N. 7th St., Phoenix, 85020, Maricopa County, (602)866-6356.
Opened: 1989. **Holes:** 18. **Par:** 72/72. **Yards:** 6,700/5,000. **Course rating:** 71.2/68.4.
Slope: 135/128. **Architect:** Bill Johnston. **Green fee:** $43/$130. **Credit cards:** All major,Diners Club, Carte Blanche. **Reduced fees:** Weekdays, low season, twilight.
Caddies: No. **Golf carts:** Included in Green Fee. **Discount golf packages:** No.
Season: Year-round. **High:** Nov.-May. **On site lodging:** Yes. **Rental clubs:** Yes.
Walking policy: Mandatory cart. **Metal spikes allowed:** Yes. **Range:** Yes (grass). **To obtain tee times:** Resort guests call 30 days in advance. Golf packages may reserve up to 60 days in advance.
Notes: 1989 Senior PGA Tour Arizona Classic.
Subscriber comments: In the mountains. Long and fun...Great use of terrain...Nice course but must hit fairways or it's over...Some really interesting holes...Excellent course with varied elevation changes...Some spectacular holes...Scenic, fun...Great breakfast...Spectacular mountain views...Some good holes.

★★★ PRESCOTT COUNTRY CLUB
1030 Prescott C.C. Blvd., Dewey, 86327, Yavapai County, (520)772-8984.
Call club for further information.
Subscriber comments: Very nice small course...Beautiful mountain course...Rolling hills, great par 3s, memorable holes...Nice layout, fun to play...Beautiful setting...Laid-back, easy going atmosphere.

★★½ PUEBLO DEL SOL COUNTRY CLUB
2770 St. Andrews Dr., Sierra Vista, 85635, Cochisa County, (520)378-6444, 70 miles SE of Tucson.
Opened: 1975. **Holes:** 18. **Par:** 72/74. **Yards:** 7,074/5,896. **Course rating:** 73.2/73.8.
Slope: 128/131. **Architect:** Tenneco Engineers. **Green fee:** $15/$30. **Credit cards:** MC,VISA,DISC. **Reduced fees:** Weekdays, low season, twilight, seniors, juniors.
Caddies: No. **Golf carts:** $20. **Discount golf packages:** No. **Season:** Year-round.
High: Feb.-March/June-Oct. **On site lodging:** No. **Rental clubs:** Yes. **Walking policy:** Unrestricted walking. **Metal spikes allowed:** Yes. **Range:** Yes (grass/mats). **To obtain tee times:** Call 7 days in advance.
Subscriber comments: Some tricky holes...Fastest greens in the west...Now has a pool and tennis courts.

★★ PUEBLO EL MIRAGE COUNTRY CLUB
R-11201 N. El Mirage Rd., El Mirage, 85335, Maricopa County, (602)583-0425, 10 miles W of Phoenix.
Opened: 1985. **Holes:** 18. **Par:** 72/72. **Yards:** 6,596/5,826. **Course rating:** 71.1/71.0.
Slope: 125/117. **Architect:** Ken Killian/Fuzzy Zoeller. **Green fee:** $12/$39. **Credit cards:** MC,VISA. **Reduced fees:** Weekdays, low season, resort guests, twilight.
Caddies: No. **Golf carts:** Included in Green Fee. **Discount golf packages:** Yes.
Season: Year-round. **High:** Nov.-March. **On site lodging:** Yes. **Rental clubs:** Yes.
Walking policy: Walking at certain times. **Metal spikes allowed:** Yes. **Range:** Yes (grass). **To obtain tee times:** Call golf shop 7 days in advance.

★★★ RANCHO MANANA GOLF CLUB
R-5734 E. Rancho Manana Blvd., Cave Creek, 85331, Maricopa County, (602)488-0398, 20 miles N of Phoenix.
Opened: 1988. **Holes:** 18. **Par:** 71/71. **Yards:** 6,378/5,910. **Course rating:** 67.8/68.8.
Slope: 125/114. **Architect:** Bill Johnston. **Green fee:** $20/$105. **Credit cards:** All major. **Reduced fees:** Weekdays, low season, twilight. **Caddies:** No. **Golf carts:** Included in Green Fee. **Discount golf packages:** Yes. **Season:** Year-round. **High:** Jan.-April. **On site lodging:** No. **Rental clubs:** Yes. **Walking policy:** Mandatory cart. **Metal spikes allowed:** Yes. **Range:** Yes (grass). **To obtain tee times:** Call up to 7 days in advance.
Subscriber comments: Tight course, lots of shots over washes, off mountains...Another course immersed in beautiful desert setting...Playable and pret-

ty...You'll use all your clubs!...Some gimmicky holes, nice scenery...Has been wonderfully improved...Fun to play...Fun, challenging course...Too many goofy holes...Hidden gem, views outstanding...Very scenic...Improving, great views, fun.

RANDOLPH PARK GOLF COURSE

PU-600 S. Alvernon, Tucson, 85711, Pima County, (520)325-2811.
Architect: William P. Bell. **Credit cards:** MC,VISA,DISC. **Reduced fees:** Low season, twilight, seniors, juniors. **Caddies:** No. **Golf carts:** $14. **Season:** Year-round. **High:** Oct.-May. **On site lodging:** No. **Rental clubs:** Yes. **Walking policy:** Unrestricted walking. **Metal spikes allowed:** Yes. **Range:** Yes (grass). **To obtain tee times:** Call Monday-Friday between 8 a.m. and 4 p.m.

★★★ **NORTH COURSE**
Opened: 1925. **Holes:** 18. **Par:** 72/73. **Yards:** 6,902/5,972. **Course rating:** 72.5/73.7. **Slope:** 128/124. **Green fee:** $15/$22. **Discount golf packages:** No.
Subscriber comments: Best muny in Tucson...Better than some of the expensive resort courses...Flat but fairly challenging...Very good course...A nice city course. Nice use of trees as hazards...Good test of shotmaking...Tucson version of Papago...Easy walk...Nice variety of holes...Hosts LPGA event.

★★★ **DELL URICH MUNICIPAL GOLF COURSE**
Opened: 1964. **Holes:** 18. **Par:** 70/72. **Yards:** 6,229/5,568. **Course rating:** 68.1/69.6. **Slope:** 101/108. **Green fee:** $13/$20. **Discount golf packages:** Yes.
Subscriber comments: Better now that it's been redesigned...Will be good in 2-3 years...Very good test...Another great muny value...Enjoyable desert course...Recently redone and much improved...Really nice makeover of old course, great par 4s from tips...Short, challenging, and fun...Needs time...Easy walk...When it matures, it will be a good one.
Special notes: Formerly Randolph Park Golf Club South Course.

★★★★ **THE RAVEN GOLF CLUB AT SABINO SPRINGS**
PU-9777 E. Sabino Greens Dr., Tucson, 85749, Pima County, (520)749-3636.
Opened: 1996. **Holes:** 18. **Par:** 71/71. **Yards:** 6,776/4,733. **Course rating:** 73.2/66.6. **Slope:** 144/112. **Architect:** Robert Trent Jones Jr. **Green fee:** $55/$125. **Credit cards:** All major,Diners Club. **Reduced fees:** Twilight. **Caddies:** No. **Golf carts:** Included in Green Fee. **Discount golf packages:** No. **Season:** Year-round. **High:** Jan.-April. **On site lodging:** No. **Rental clubs:** Yes. **Walking policy:** Unrestricted walking. **Metal spikes allowed:** Yes. **Range:** Yes (grass). **To obtain tee times:** Call up to 30 days in advance.
Notes: Ranked 11th in 1997 Best in State; 7th in 1996 Best New Upscale Courses.
Subscriber comments: Best golf in southern Arizona...Great golf experience. Unbelievable views...Excellent combination of desert and mountain golf...Great golf. Spectacular views...Great views and finishing hole...Fantastic, my desert course dream...Tough course from tips.

★★★★ **THE RAVEN GOLF CLUB AT SOUTH MOUNTAIN**
PU-3636 E. Baseline Rd., Phoenix, 85040, Maricopa County, (602)243-3636.
Opened: 1995. **Holes:** 18. **Par:** 72/72. **Yards:** 7,078/5,759. **Course rating:** 73.9/72.9. **Slope:** 133/124. **Architect:** David Graham/Gary Panks. **Green fee:** $65/$125. **Credit cards:** All major,Diners Club. **Reduced fees:** Low season, twilight, juniors. **Caddies:** No. **Golf carts:** Included in Green Fee. **Discount golf packages:** No. **Season:** Year-round. **High:** Oct.-April. **On site lodging:** No. **Rental clubs:** Yes. **Walking policy:** Unrestricted walking. **Metal spikes allowed:** Yes. **Range:** Yes (grass). **To obtain tee times:** Reservations accepted 7-10 days in advance with credit card. 48-hour cancellation policy.
Notes: Ranked 17th in 1997 Best in State.
Subscriber comments: Great new golf course...One of the best around. You can't tell you're in the middle of the desert...Pine trees in Arizona?...Great course and great service...When pines mature this course will be one of a kind, the mountain look in a desert city...Close to the airport...Excellent practice area, nice clubhouse...Super pampering...Excellent golfing experience.

★★★½ RED MOUNTAIN RANCH COUNTRY CLUB
6425 E. Teton, Mesa, 85215, Maricopa County, (602)985-0285, 15 miles E of Phoenix.
Opened: 1987. **Holes:** 18. **Par:** 72/72. **Yards:** 6,797/4,982. **Course rating:** 73.3/69.4.
Slope: 144/120. **Architect:** Pete Dye/Perry Dye. **Green fee:** $29/$125. **Credit cards:**
MC,VISA,AMEX. **Reduced fees:** Weekdays, low season, twilight. **Caddies:** No. **Golf
carts:** Included in Green Fee. **Discount golf packages:** No. **Season:** Year-round.
High: Jan.-April. **On site lodging:** No. **Rental clubs:** Yes. **Walking policy:** Mandatory
cart. **Metal spikes allowed:** Yes. **Range:** Yes (grass). **To obtain tee times:** Call 30
days prior after 7:30 a.m. with credit card.
Subscriber comments: Very tight course...Dramatic views, strange bounces...Difficult,
many changes in elevation...Need L-wedge...Beautiful desert course...Play the tees
where you belong...Long irons are your best friend on this course...Very tough, penaliz-
ing layout.

★★★½ RIO RICO RESORT & COUNTRY CLUB
R-1069 Camino Caralampi, Rio Rico, 85648, Santa Cruz County, (520)281-8567,
(800)288-4746, 50 miles S of Tucson.
Opened: 1972. **Holes:** 18. **Par:** 72/72. **Yards:** 7,119/5,649. **Course rating:** 72.9/70.4.
Slope: 128/126. **Architect:** Robert Trent Jones. **Green fee:** $30/$75. **Credit cards:** All
major. **Reduced fees:** Weekdays, low season, resort guests, twilight. **Caddies:** No.
Golf carts: Included in Green Fee. **Discount golf packages:** No. **Season:** Year-round.
High: Jan.-April. **On site lodging:** Yes. **Rental clubs:** Yes. **Walking policy:** Mandatory
cart. **Metal spikes allowed:** Yes. **Range:** Yes (grass). **To obtain tee times:** Call
(520)288-4746 for times.
Subscriber comments: Good day trip...Front up and down. Back rather easy...Very
mature...Fun, weaves along river, pleasant...A bit out of the way...Pleasant
course...Average...Great track, beautiful setting, well designed...Robert Trent Jones
classic!

★★★½ SAN IGNACIO GOLF CLUB
PU-4201 S. Camino Del Sol, Green Valley, 85614, Pima County, (520)648-3468, 25
miles S of Tucson.
Opened: 1989. **Holes:** 18. **Par:** 71/72. **Yards:** 6,704/5,200. **Course rating:** 71.4/68.7.
Slope: 129/116. **Architect:** Arthur Hills. **Green fee:** $22/$73. **Credit cards:** MC,VISA.
Reduced fees: Low season, twilight. **Caddies:** No. **Golf carts:** $11. **Discount golf
packages:** No. **Season:** Year-round. **High:** Jan.-April. **On site lodging:** No. **Rental
clubs:** Yes. **Walking policy:** Mandatory cart. **Metal spikes allowed:** Yes. **Range:** Yes
(grass). **To obtain tee times:** Call five days in advance.
Subscriber comments: Very nice place to play golf...Long thick rough, tricky...Tight, no
grip and rip here...13th hole is great...Couple of unfair holes, front nine
fun...Challenging, nice ambiance...Outstanding par 3s, a wonderful scenic layout.

★★★ SANTA RITA GOLF CLUB
PU-16461 Houghton Rd., Corna De Tucson, 85641, Pima County, (520)762-5620, 12
miles SE of Tucson.
Opened: 1962. **Holes:** 18. **Par:** 72/72. **Yards:** 6,523/5,539. **Course rating:** 70.9/69.7.
Slope: 125/117. **Architect:** Red Lawrence. **Green fee:** $15/$49. **Credit cards:** All
major. **Reduced fees:** Weekdays, low season, twilight, seniors, juniors. **Caddies:** No.
Golf carts: $8. **Discount golf packages:** Yes. **Season:** Year-round. **High:** Jan.-April.
On site lodging: No. **Rental clubs:** Yes. **Walking policy:** Unrestricted walking. **Metal
spikes allowed:** Yes. **Range:** Yes (grass/mats). **To obtain tee times:** Call up to 7 days
in advance.
Subscriber comments: Mountain course, views, challenging...Better than in recent
years...Long course. Always windy...Great scenery...Open fairways, straightforward
holes...Easy walk...Wide fairways, but don't miss them!

★★★ SCOTTSDALE COUNTRY CLUB
7702 E. Shea Blvd., Scottsdale, 85260, Maricopa County, (602)948-6000.
Opened: 1986. **Holes:** 27. **Architect:** Arnold Palmer/Ed Seay. **Credit cards:**
MC,VISA,AMEX. **Reduced fees:** Weekdays, low season, twilight. **Caddies:** No. **Golf
carts:** Included in Green Fee. **Discount golf packages:** No. **Season:** Year-round.
High: Jan.-April. **On site lodging:** No. **Rental clubs:** Yes. **Walking policy:** Mandatory

cart. **Metal spikes allowed:** Yes. **Green fee:** $25/$85. **Range:** Yes (grass/mats). **To obtain tee times:** Public, 5 days in advance.
NORTH/EAST
Par: 71/71. **Yards:** 6,292/5,339. **Course rating:** 69.7/69.4. **Slope:** 119/108.
NORTH/SOUTH
Holes: 27. **Par:** 70/70. **Yards:** 6,085/4,800. **Course rating:** 68.8/69.0. **Slope:** 118/111.
SOUTH/EAST
Holes: 27. **Par:** 71/71. **Yards:** 6,335/5,241. **Course rating:** 69.6/68.8. **Slope:** 118/109.
Subscriber comments: Narrow course, homes...Good value for area...Too short...Very nice holes...East course challenging, fun...Good value, OK course...Don't be fooled by the classy name...Fun course...Tight with lots of trees.

★★★★ SEDONA GOLF RESORT
R-35 Ridge Trail Dr., Sedona, 86351, Yavapai County, (520)284-9355, 100 miles N of Phoenix.
Opened: 1988. **Holes:** 18. **Par:** 71/71. **Yards:** 6,642/5,030. **Course rating:** 70.3/67.0. **Slope:** 129/109. **Architect:** Gary Panks. **Green fee:** $75/$85. **Credit cards:** MC,VISA,AMEX. **Reduced fees:** Twilight. **Caddies:** No. **Golf carts:** Included in Green Fee. **Discount golf packages:** Yes. **Season:** Year-round. **High:** March-Nov. **On site lodging:** Yes. **Rental clubs:** Yes. **Walking policy:** Unrestricted walking. **Metal spikes allowed:** Yes. **Range:** Yes (grass). **To obtain tee times:** Call up to 14 days in advance with credit card.
Notes: Ranked 13th in 1997 Best in State.
Subscriber comments: Fantastic view...A must in Arizona...Views are worth trip...Very good course in beautiful scenery. Bring your camera...Large greens, tough to putt...I got engaged there...Red rock views are God's masterpiece...Great diversity of holes...Must be golf heaven...Scenic, breathtaking...Average layout.

SHADOW MOUNTAIN GOLF CLUB
1105 Irene St., Pearce, 85625, Cochise County, (520)826-3412, 70 miles SE of Tucson.
Opened: N/A. **Holes:** 18. **Par:** 72/72. **Yards:** 6,632/5,980. **Course rating:** 71.8/72.3. **Slope:** 127/125. **Architect:** N/A. **Green fee:** $10/$16. **Credit cards:** MC,VISA. **Reduced fees:** Low season, twilight, juniors. **Caddies:** No. **Golf carts:** $16. **Discount golf packages:** No. **Season:** Year-round. **High:** Jan.-May. **On site lodging:** No. **Rental clubs:** Yes. **Walking policy:** Unrestricted walking. **Metal spikes allowed:** Yes. **Range:** No. **To obtain tee times:** Call 1 day in advance.

SHERATON EL CONQUISTADOR COUNTRY CLUB
R-10555 N. La Canada, Tucson, 85737, Pima County, (520)544-1800.
Opened: 1984. **Architect:** Greg Nash/Jeff Hardin. **Green fee:** $40/$105. **Credit cards:** All major. **Reduced fees:** Low season, resort guests. **Caddies:** No. **Golf carts:** Included in Green Fee. **Discount golf packages:** Yes. **Season:** Year-round. **High:** Feb.-April. **On site lodging:** Yes. **Rental clubs:** Yes. **Walking policy:** Mandatory cart. **Metal spikes allowed:** Yes. **Range:** Yes (grass). **To obtain tee times:** N/A.
★★★ SUNRISE COURSE
Holes: 18. **Par:** 72/72. **Yards:** 6,819/5,255. **Course rating:** 71.7/69.4. **Slope:** 123/116.
Subscriber comments: Great desert course...Narrow. Fairly interesting...Beautiful resort course...Several good holes...Tough par 3s lined by many homes...Nice test of golf...Requires all clubs in bag.
★★★ SUNSET COURSE
Holes: 18. **Par:** 72/72. **Yards:** 6,763/5,323. **Course rating:** 71.2/69.5. **Slope:** 123/114.
Subscriber comments: Better of the two courses...Always good...Good resort course, several good holes...Very interesting course.

★★★ SHERATON SAN MARCOS COUNTRY CLUB
100 N. Dakota St., Chandler, 85224, Maricopa County, (602)963-3358.
Opened: 1923. **Holes:** 18. **Par:** 72/73. **Yards:** 6,551/5,431. **Course rating:** 70.0/69.4. **Slope:** 117/112. **Architect:** Harry Collis. **Green fee:** $30/$75. **Credit cards:** All major. **Reduced fees:** Weekdays, low season, twilight, juniors. **Caddies:** No. **Golf carts:** Included in Green Fee. **Discount golf packages:** Yes. **Season:** Year-round. **High:** Jan.-April. **On site lodging:** Yes. **Rental clubs:** Yes. **Walking policy:** Walking at certain times. **Metal spikes allowed:** Yes. **Range:** Yes (grass). **To obtain tee times:** Call 7 days in advance.

Subscriber comments: One of Arizona's oldest, wide open. Historic...Old course with dignity...Not bad for a flat course, very mature, large trees...Not too challenging...Nice layout, a lot of trees...Old fashioned midwestern layout in the desert.

★★★½ SILVER CREEK GOLF CLUB

PU-2051 Silver Lake Blvd., Show Low, 85901, Navajo County, (520)537-2744, (800)909-5981, 12 miles NE of Show Low.
Opened: 1985. **Holes:** 18. **Par:** 71/71. **Yards:** 6,813/5,193. **Course rating:** 71.5/68.0. **Slope:** 131/120. **Architect:** Gary Panks. **Green fee:** $17/$38. **Credit cards:** MC,VISA,DISC. **Reduced fees:** Weekdays, low season, twilight, seniors, juniors. **Caddies:** No. **Golf carts:** $24. **Discount golf packages:** Yes. **Season:** Year-round. **High:** June-Sept. **On site lodging:** Yes. **Rental clubs:** Yes. **Walking policy:** Unrestricted walking. **Metal spikes allowed:** Yes. **Range:** Yes (grass). **To obtain tee times:** Call 3 days in advance.
Subscriber comments: A pretty course and tough...Jewel in the mountains...A true test...#15 hardest hole I have played...Great links layout, #9 a tough par...Worth the effort to get there...Keeps your mind sharp...Really out of the way, but a gem!

GREAT VALUE

★★½ SILVERBELL GOLF COURSE

PM-3600 N. Silverbell, Tucson, 85745, Pima County, (520)743-7284.
Opened: 1978. **Holes:** 18. **Par:** 72/73. **Yards:** 6,824/5,800. **Course rating:** 71.2/71.5. **Slope:** 123/118. **Architect:** Jack Snyder. **Green fee:** $10/$26. **Credit cards:** All major. **Reduced fees:** Low season, twilight, seniors, juniors. **Caddies:** No. **Golf carts:** $8. **Discount golf packages:** No. **Season:** Year-round. **High:** Oct.-April. **On site lodging:** No. **Rental clubs:** Yes. **Walking policy:** Unrestricted walking. **Metal spikes allowed:** Yes. **Range:** Yes (grass/mats). **To obtain tee times:** Call up to 7 days in advance.
Subscriber comments: City course, lots of water...Nice public course for the money...Showing improvement...Good back nine...Not too tough...Interesting variety of holes.

★★★½ STARR PASS GOLF CLUB

3645 W. Starr Pass Blvd., Tucson, 85745, Pima County, (520)670-0400, 4 miles W of Tucson.
Opened: 1986. **Holes:** 18. **Par:** 71/71. **Yards:** 6,910/5,071. **Course rating:** 74.6/70.7. **Slope:** 139/121. **Architect:** Robert Cupp. **Green fee:** $48/$95. **Credit cards:** MC,VISA,AMEX. **Reduced fees:** Low season, resort guests, twilight. **Caddies:** No. **Golf carts:** Included in Green Fee. **Discount golf packages:** Yes. **Season:** Year-round. **High:** Jan.-May. **On site lodging:** Yes. **Rental clubs:** Yes. **Walking policy:** Mandatory cart. **Metal spikes allowed:** Yes. **Range:** Yes (grass). **To obtain tee times:** Call up to 30 days in advance.
Subscriber comments: Another classic desert beauty!...Challenging, fun course. Great city views...Greens are very small...Tight fairways...The best public golf in Tucson. Don't build any more houses...Some very difficult holes, great views...Pleasurable, interesting course...A thinking person's course...Few exceptional holes, pleasant course.

★★★ STONECREEK, THE GOLF CLUB

4435 E. Paradise Village Pkwy. S., Paradise Valley, 85032, Maricopa County, (602)953-9111.
Opened: 1989. **Holes:** 18. **Par:** 71/71. **Yards:** 6,839/5,098. **Course rating:** 72.6/68.4. **Slope:** 134/118. **Architect:** Arthur Hills. **Green fee:** $20/$125. **Credit cards:** MC,VISA,AMEX. **Reduced fees:** Weekdays, low season, resort guests, twilight, juniors. **Caddies:** No. **Golf carts:** Included in Green Fee. **Discount golf packages:** Yes. **Season:** Year-round. **High:** Jan.-April. **On site lodging:** No. **Rental clubs:** Yes. **Walking policy:** Mandatory cart. **Metal spikes allowed:** Yes. **Range:** Yes (grass). **To obtain tee times:** Call 3 days in advance or up to 1 year through a local hotel.
Subscriber comments: Great links course...Nice design...Elevated greens...Lots of trouble everywhere; pretty...Have installed "kids" tees...Challenging course...Many holes tricked up...Challenging par 3s, fun...Treeless, interesting...Nice links-style layout.

★★★½ SUN CITY VISTOSO GOLF CLUB

1495 E. Rancho Vistoso Blvd., Tucson, 85737, Pima County, (520)825-3110.
Opened: 1987. **Holes:** 18. **Par:** 72/72. **Yards:** 6,723/5,109. **Course rating:** 71.8/68.3.

Slope: 137/114. **Architect:** Greg Nash. **Green fee:** $35/$35. **Credit cards:** MC,VISA. **Reduced fees:** N/A. **Caddies:** No. **Golf carts:** $13. **Discount golf packages:** No. **Season:** Year-round. **High:** Nov.-April. **On site lodging:** No. **Rental clubs:** Yes. **Walking policy:** Mandatory cart. **Metal spikes allowed:** Yes. **Range:** Yes (grass). **To obtain tee times:** Call one week in advance.
Subscriber comments: Difficult desert course with variety of challenging holes...Very well designed. Good risk/reward...A great desert layout.

★★★½ SUNRIDGE CANYON GOLF CLUB
PU-13100 N. SunRidge Dr., Fountain Hills, 85268, Maricopa County, (602)837-5100, (800)562-5178, 1 mile E of Scottsdale.
Opened: 1995. **Holes:** 18. **Par:** 71/71. **Yards:** 6,823/5,141. **Course rating:** 73.4/70.1. **Slope:** 140/125. **Architect:** Keith Foster. **Green fee:** $65/$145. **Credit cards:** MC,VISA,AMEX. **Reduced fees:** Low season, juniors. **Caddies:** No. **Golf carts:** Included in Green Fee. **Discount golf packages:** No. **Season:** Year-round. **High:** Nov.-April. **On site lodging:** No. **Rental clubs:** Yes. **Walking policy:** Mandatory cart. **Metal spikes allowed:** Yes. **Range:** Yes (grass). **To obtain tee times:** Call golf shop up to 30 days in advance.
Subscriber comments: Great panoramic views...Real potential...Two reachable par 4s...Comfortable in summer, course on northeast side of mountain...Absolute jewel...Good course, but nothing special...Very tough course if you can't keep your ball in fairway...Tough last three holes.

★★★½ SUPERSTITION SPRINGS GOLF CLUB
R-6542 E. Baseline Rd., Mesa, 85206, Maricopa County, (602)985-5622, (800)468-7918, 20 miles E of Phoenix.
Opened: 1986. **Holes:** 18. **Par:** 72/72. **Yards:** 7,005/5,328. **Course rating:** 74.1/70.9. **Slope:** 135/120. **Architect:** Greg Nash. **Green fee:** $30/$125. **Credit cards:** MC,VISA,AMEX. **Reduced fees:** Weekdays, low season, resort guests, twilight. **Caddies:** No. **Golf carts:** Included in Green Fee. **Discount golf packages:** Yes. **Season:** Year-round. **High:** Oct.-April. **On site lodging:** No. **Rental clubs:** Yes. **Walking policy:** Mandatory cart. **Metal spikes allowed:** Yes. **Range:** Yes (grass/mats). **To obtain tee times:** Accepted up to 7 days in advance. Tee time accepted eight to 60 days in advance for surcharge fee of $7.
Subscriber comments: Keeps getting better with age...Great finishing hole...Every hole is different...9th and 18th great holes, nice veranda on clubhouse...Tricky, trouble everywhere...Excellent test of your entire game...Great fun, some tough holes.

TALKING STICK GOLF CLUB
PU-9998 East Indian Bend Rd., Scottsdale, 85256, Maricopa County, (602)860-2221, 2 miles E of Scottsdale.
Opened: 1998. **Architect:** Ben Crenshaw/Bill Coore. **Green fee:** $40/$90. **Credit cards:** MC,VISA,AMEX. **Reduced fees:** Weekdays, low season, juniors. **Caddies:** No. **Golf carts:** Included in Green Fee. **Discount golf packages:** No. **Season:** Year-round. **High:** Nov.-April. **On site lodging:** No. **Rental clubs:** Yes. **Walking policy:** Unrestricted walking. **Metal spikes allowed:** Yes. **Range:** Yes (grass). **To obtain tee times:** Call golf shop up to 30 days in advance. Groups of 16 or more may call up to 6 months in advance.
Notes: Golf Digest School site.
NORTH COURSE
Holes: 18. **Par:** 70/70. **Yards:** 7,121/5,530. **Course rating:** 73.8/70.0. **Slope:** 125/116.
SOUTH COURSE
Holes: 18. **Par:** 71/71. **Yards:** 6,918/5,328. **Course rating:** N/A. **Slope:** N/A

★★★½ TATUM RANCH GOLF CLUB
PU-29888 N. Tatum Ranch Dr., Cave Creek, 85331, Maricopa County, (602)585-4909, (800)468-7918, 25 miles N of Phoenix.
Opened: 1987. **Holes:** 18. **Par:** 72/72. **Yards:** 6,870/5,609. **Course rating:** 73.4/71.5. **Slope:** 128/116. **Architect:** Robert Cupp. **Green fee:** $30/$125. **Credit cards:** MC,VISA,AMEX. **Reduced fees:** Weekdays, low season, resort guests, twilight, juniors. **Caddies:** No. **Golf carts:** Included in Green Fee. **Discount golf packages:** No. **Season:** Year-round. **High:** Nov.-April. **On site lodging:** No. **Rental clubs:** Yes. **Walking policy:** Mandatory cart. **Metal spikes allowed:** Yes. **Range:** Yes (grass). **To**

obtain tee times: Call 7 days in advance for no charge. Call up to 60 days in advance with a surcharge.

Subscriber comments: Good overall experience...Perfect desert golf, good track...Great desert experience. Hot air balloons made great scenery...Some brutal holes...Not too much trouble out there...Nice resort layout...All around pretty fair...Nice layout for housing development...Well worth the drive.

★★★½TONTO VERDE GOLF CLUB

18401 El Circulo Dr., Rio Verde, 85263, Maricopa County, (602)471-2710, 20 miles NE of Scottsdale.

Opened: 1994. **Holes:** 18. **Par:** 72/72. **Yards:** 6,736/5,376. **Course rating:** 71.1/70.8. **Slope:** 132/124. **Architect:** David Graham/Gary Panks International. **Green fee:** $35/$125. **Credit cards:** All major. **Reduced fees:** Low season, resort guests. **Caddies:** No. **Golf carts:** $10. **Discount golf packages:** Yes. **Season:** Year-round. **High:** Dec.-April. **On site lodging:** Yes. **Rental clubs:** Yes. **Walking policy:** Walking at certain times. **Metal spikes allowed:** Yes. **Range:** Yes (grass). **To obtain tee times:** Tee time must be made no sooner than 4 days in advance. Saturday tee time may be booked on Tuesday.

Subscriber comments: Great views, great clubhouse, great course...Narrow with fairways sloped toward desert edges. Tough test...Beautiful location, worth the drive...What desert golf should be...Hidden gem in North Scottsdale...A good experience...Beautiful views of mountains.

★★½TORRES BLANCAS GOLF CLUB

PU-3233 S. Abrego, Green Valley, 85614, Pima County, (520)625-5200, 20 miles S of Tucson.

Opened: 1996. **Holes:** 18. **Par:** N/A. **Yards:** N/A. **Course rating:** N/A. **Slope:** N/A. **Architect:** Lee Trevino. **Green fee:** $19/$59. **Credit cards:** MC,VISA. **Reduced fees:** Low season, resort guests, twilight, seniors. **Caddies:** No. **Golf carts:** Included in Green Fee. **Discount golf packages:** No. **Season:** Year-round. **High:** Jan.-April. **On site lodging:** No. **Rental clubs:** Yes. **Walking policy:** Mandatory cart. **Metal spikes allowed:** Yes. **Range:** Yes (grass). **To obtain tee times:** Call golf shop or make reservations through Best Western at (520)625-2250.

Subscriber comments: I'll be great when it matures...New course, fun, rather easy...Improving...Too many funky holes...Has potential...Not bad for a new course...Too short...Slick greens...Good views.

TOURNAMENT PLAYERS CLUB OF SCOTTSDALE

R-17020 N. Hayden Rd., Scottsdale, 85255, Maricopa County, (602)585-3939. **Architect:** Tom Weiskopf/Jay Morrish. **Credit cards:** MC,VISA,AMEX. **Caddies:** No. **Discount golf packages:** No. **Season:** Year-round. **On site lodging:** Yes. **Rental clubs:** Yes. **Metal spikes allowed:** Yes. **Range:** Yes (grass/mats).

★★½DESERT COURSE

Opened: 1987. **Holes:** 18. **Par:** 71/71. **Yards:** 6,552/4,715. **Course rating:** 71.4/66.3. **Slope:** 112/109. **Green fee:** $31/$41. **Reduced fees:** Low season, twilight, seniors, juniors. **Golf carts:** N/A. **High:** Oct.-April. **Walking policy:** Unrestricted walking. **To obtain tee times:** Call up to 7 days in advance.

Subscriber comments: Nice course but watch out for the snakes...Nice to be able to walk...Good test from tips...Some tough holes...Fun...More fun than the Stadium Course...This is the short course...A must play, warm-up course.

★★★½STADIUM COURSE

Opened: 1986. **Holes:** 18. **Par:** 71/71. **Yards:** 6,992/5,567. **Course rating:** 73.9/71.6. **Slope:** 131/122. **Green fee:** $62/$149. **Reduced fees:** Low season, twilight. **Golf carts:** $16. **High:** Jan.-April. **Walking policy:** Mandatory cart. **To obtain tee times:** Call 90 days in advance.

Notes: 1987-present, Phoenix Open.

Subscriber comments: Great golf course with excellent facilities...Overrated TPC course...Starts slow but ends fantastic...Long, dull...Course was simple, nothing spectacular...Gotta love 15th...Very good course, non-desert like, very long...Great course, interesting holes, a joy to play.

★★TRINI ALVAREZ EL RIO MUNICIPAL GOLF COURSE
PM-1400 W. Speedway Blvd., Tucson, 85745, Pima County, (520)623-6783.
Opened: 1929. **Holes:** 18. **Par:** 70/73. **Yards:** 6,418/5,624. **Course rating:** 69.6/72.2.
Slope: 110/115. **Architect:** William P. Bell. **Green fee:** $10/$20. **Credit cards:**
MC,VISA. **Reduced fees:** Weekdays, low season, twilight, seniors, juniors. **Caddies:**
No. **Golf carts:** $7. **Discount golf packages:** Yes. **Season:** Year-round. **High:** Oct.-
March. **On site lodging:** No. **Rental clubs:** Yes. **Walking policy:** Unrestricted walking.
Metal spikes allowed: Yes. **Range:** Yes (grass). **To obtain tee times:** Call central
reservation system.

TROON NORTH GOLF CLUB
10320 E. Dynamite Blvd., Scottsdale, 85255, Maricopa County, (602)585-
5300.
Green fee: $75/$175. **Credit cards:** MC,VISA,AMEX. **Reduced fees:**
Low season, juniors. **Caddies:** No. **Golf carts:** Included in Green Fee.
Discount golf packages: No. **Season:** Year-round. **High:** Nov.-May. **On
site lodging:** No. **Walking policy:** Unrestricted walking. **Metal spikes allowed:** Yes.
Range: Yes (grass).

(GREAT SERVICE)

★★★★½MONUMENT COURSE
Opened: 1990. **Holes:** 18. **Par:** 72/72. **Yards:** 7,008/5,050. **Course rating:** 73.1/69.0.
Slope: 146/116. **Architect:** Tom Weiskopf/Jay Morrish. **Rental clubs:** Yes. **To obtain
tee times:** Call 5 days in advance of play.
Notes: Golf Digest School site. Ranked 91st in 1997-98 America's 100 Greatest; 3rd in
1997 Best in State.
Subscriber comments: Best course in Arizona, fantastic condition, great shot values...Best desert course...A must play, forget about the price...Nearly a religious experience!...Sell your children to get there. It's worth it!...Back nine is a masterpiece, every
hole is memorable and great in its own right...A beauty and a beast...Outstanding golf
experience. One of the best.
Special Notes: Spikeless encouraged.

★★★★½PINNACLE COURSE
Opened: 1996. **Holes:** 18. **Par:** 72/72. **Yards:** 7,044/4,980. **Course rating:** 73.4/68.5.
Slope: 147/116. **Architect:** Tom Weiskopf. **Rental clubs:** No. **To obtain tee times:** Call
up to 5 days in advance.
Notes: Golf Digest School site. Ranked 8th in 1997 Best in State.
Subscriber comments: Best I have played, everyone should play...True test of
golf...Perfection. If you thought Monument Course was difficult try the Pinnacle...This
younger sister is gorgeous...Outstanding views, pristine shape, great staff, pricey...None
better...Wonderful!...Tougher than Monument, narrow!...Better than original course now
with no home building going on, very quiet and peaceful.
Special Notes: Spikeless encouraged.

★★★TUBAC GOLF RESORT
R-1 Otera Rd., Tubac, 85646, Santa Cruz County, (520)398-2021.
Opened: 1960. **Holes:** 18. **Par:** 71/71. **Yards:** 6,839/5,475. **Course rating:** 72.4/70.5.
Slope: 128/120. **Architect:** Red Lawrence. **Green fee:** $29/$70. **Credit cards:**
MC,VISA,AMEX. **Reduced fees:** Resort guests, twilight. **Caddies:** No. **Golf carts:**
Included in Green Fee. **Discount golf packages:** No. **Season:** Year-round. **High:** Jan.-
April. **On site lodging:** Yes. **Rental clubs:** Yes. **Walking policy:** Unrestricted walking.
Metal spikes allowed: Yes. **Range:** Yes (grass). **To obtain tee times:** Call up to 7
days in advance. Resort guests may make tee times with room reservation.
Subscriber comments: Where part of "Tin Cup" was shot...Good course; quick
rounds...Nice resort course. Jekyll and Hyde nines...Challenging, friendly, courteous,
great food...Sporty little resort course...Great scenery...Beautiful course and surroundings...Nice relaxing place to stay...Great back nine makes up for average front...Good
mix of holes.

★★★VALLE VISTA COUNTRY CLUB
PU-9686 Concho Dr, Kingman, 86401, Mohave County, (520)757-8744.
Call club for further information.
Subscriber comments: Wonderful atmosphere and pretty desert setting...Nondescript,
short, windy...Very good layout, very fun..Greens nicely contoured.

VENTANA CANYON GOLF & RACQUET CLUB

R-6200 N. Clubhouse Lane, Tucson, 85715, Pima County, (520)577-4061, (800)828-5701.

Architect: Tom Fazio. **Green fee:** $75/$150. **Credit cards:** MC,VISA,AMEX. **Reduced fees:** Low season, resort guests, twilight. **Caddies:** No. **Golf carts:** Included in Green Fee. **Discount golf packages:** No. **Season:** Year-round. **High:** Oct.-May. **On site lodging:** Yes. **Rental clubs:** Yes. **Walking policy:** Mandatory cart. **Metal spikes allowed:** No. **Range:** Yes (grass). **To obtain tee times:** Call 7 days in advance.

(GOOD SERVICE)

★★★½**CANYON COURSE**

Opened: 1987. **Holes:** 18. **Par:** 72/72. **Yards:** 6,819/4,919. **Course rating:** 72.7/68.3. **Slope:** 141/114.

Subscriber comments: Beautiful and challanging...Loved it...Very difficult desert course...Long, challenging, good shots rewarded...Far easier than rating/Slope...Difficult but fun! Great views, great course...Fazio layout with a few weird holes-good golf though!

★★★★**MOUNTAIN COURSE**

Opened: 1984. **Holes:** 18. **Par:** 72/72. **Yards:** 6,926/4,789. **Course rating:** 74.2/68.3. **Slope:** 146/117.

Subscriber comments: A must stop...Expensive, but a memorable mountain golf experience...Beautiful scenery, enjoyable holes...Thoroughly enjoyable golf...Incredible course from 1 to 18...The par 3 3rd hole is outstanding...Classic desert layout with beautiful scenery; 3rd hole alone worth price of admission!...Unbelievable scenery, was followed by a bobcat for six holes.

★★★**THE VISTAS CLUB**

PU-18823 N. Country Club Pkwy., Peoria, 85382, Maricopa County, (602)566-1633, 5 miles W of Phoenix.

Opened: 1990. **Holes:** 18. **Par:** 72/72. **Yards:** 6,544/5,225. **Course rating:** 70.3/68.2. **Slope:** 121/109. **Architect:** N/A. **Green fee:** $35/$74. **Credit cards:** MC,VISA. **Reduced fees:** Low season. **Caddies:** No. **Golf carts:** Included in Green Fee. **Discount golf packages:** No. **Season:** Year-round. **High:** Dec.-April. **On site lodging:** No. **Rental clubs:** Yes. **Walking policy:** Unrestricted walking. **Metal spikes allowed:** Yes. **Range:** Yes (grass). **To obtain tee times:** Call up to 3 days in advance. **Subscriber comments:** Well kept course that gets a lot of play...Fairly new.

★★★**WESTBROOK VILLAGE GOLF CLUB**

19260 N. Westbrook Pkwy., Peoria, 85345, Maricopa County, (602)933-0174. Call club for further information.

Subscriber comments: I like this one...Two of the best finishing holes.

★★½**WESTERN SKIES GOLF CLUB**

PU-1245 E. Warner Rd., Gilbert, 85234, Maricopa County, (602)545-8542, (800)437-0446, 20 miles E of Phoenix.

Opened: 1992. **Holes:** 18. **Par:** 72/72. **Yards:** 6,673/5,639. **Course rating:** 70.0/68.6. **Slope:** 120/116. **Architect:** Brian Whitcomb. **Green fee:** $20/$60. **Credit cards:** MC,VISA,AMEX. **Reduced fees:** N/A. **Caddies:** No. **Golf carts:** Included in Green Fee. **Discount golf packages:** No. **Season:** Year-round. **High:** Jan.-March. **On site lodging:** No. **Rental clubs:** Yes. **Walking policy:** Unrestricted walking. **Metal spikes allowed:** Yes. **Range:** Yes (grass). **To obtain tee times:** Call up to 7 days in advance. **Subscriber comments:** Wide open fairways, good test...Challenging, fun...Great little layout...Good basic golf...Lots of room, good, playable holes...Flat layout, enjoyable to play...Great muny course...Long and challenging...Fun layout.

THE WIGWAM GOLF & COUNTRY CLUB

R-451 N. Litchfield Rd., Litchfield Park, 85340, Maricopa County, (602)272-4653, (800)909-4224, 20 miles W of Phoenix.

Green fee: $28/$95. **Credit cards:** All major. **Reduced fees:** Low season, resort guests. **Caddies:** Yes. **Golf carts:** Included in Green Fee. **Discount golf packages:** Yes. **Season:** Year-round. **High:** Jan.-May. **On site lodging:** Yes. **Rental clubs:** Yes. **Walking policy:** Mandatory cart. **Metal spikes allowed:** Yes. **To obtain tee times:** Call 5 days in advance. Hotel guests can book up to 6 months in advance.

ARIZONA

★★★BLUE COURSE

Opened: 1961. **Holes:** 18. **Par:** 70/70. **Yards:** 6,130/5,235. **Course rating:** 67.9/69.3. **Slope:** 115/115. **Architect:** Robert Trent Jones. **Range:** Yes (grass).

Subscriber comments: Short enough to manage...Flat course...One of my top 10...Too many raised greens...Mature resort course...Good test of golf...Short yardage, shotmaker's course...Fun to play, large greens...Three toughest finishing holes anywhere...Have to hit the ball straight, lots of trees.

★★★½GOLD COURSE

Opened: 1961. **Holes:** 18. **Par:** 72/72. **Yards:** 7,021/5,737. **Course rating:** 73.6/72.8. **Slope:** 129/126. **Architect:** Robert Trent Jones. **Range:** Yes (grass).

Subscriber comments: All around great place...Long drive from Phoenix and Scottsdale, worth it, great course...Solid traditional design, tough to putt on huge greens...Great deal in the summer...Fabulous RT Jones course, a must play...A classic...A treat...A monster, beautiful but not fun, you have to grind...Old course, flat, good for resort golf...Most challenging, but not that interesting...Can be very tough!

★★★RED COURSE

Opened: 1974. **Holes:** 18. **Par:** 72/72. **Yards:** 6,867/5,821. **Course rating:** 71.8/72.4. **Slope:** 118/118. **Architect:** Red Lawrence. **Range:** Yes (grass/mats).

Subscriber comments: Course overrated. Food excellent...First nine easy...Best of the three...Plainer than other two Wigwams, except for three holes...Really fun forgiving course. Pretty...Traditional layout...Challenging course...Most interesting of three at Wigwam...Great test from back tees.

ARKANSAS

★★½BEN GEREN REGIONAL PARK GOLF COURSE
PU-7200 S. Zero, Fort Smith, 72903, Sebastian County, (501)646-5301.
Opened: 1972. **Holes:** 27. **Architect:** Marvin Ferguson/Jeff Brauer. **Green fee:** $12/$14. **Credit cards:** None. **Reduced fees:** Weekdays, twilight, seniors, juniors. **Caddies:** No. **Golf carts:** $21. **Discount golf packages:** No. **Season:** Year-round. **High:** April-Oct. **On site lodging:** No. **Rental clubs:** Yes. **Walking policy:** Unrestricted walking. **Metal spikes allowed:** Yes. **Range:** Yes (grass/mats). **To obtain tee times:** One day in advance.
MAGNOLIA/WILLOW
Par: 72/73. **Yards:** 6,782/5,023. **Course rating:** 71.7/67.7. **Slope:** 120/109.
SILO HILL/MAGNOLIA
Par: 72/74. **Yards:** 6,840/5,347. **Course rating:** N/A. **Slope:** N/A.
SILO HILL/WILLOW
Par: 72/73. **Yards:** 6,812/5,126. **Course rating:** N/A. **Slope:** N/A.
Subscriber comments: Nice, considering county-funded...Excellent conditions for the price...Wide open...Worth playing...Excellent greens...Very busy, well maintained...A swamp in wet weather.

BURNS PARK GOLF COURSE
PM-30 Championship Dr., North Little Rock, 72115, Pulaski County, (501)758-5800.
Green fee: $8/$10. **Reduced fees:** Twilight, seniors, juniors. **Caddies:** No. **Golf carts:** $18. **Discount golf packages:** No. **Season:** Year-round. **High:** N/A. **On site lodging:** No. **Walking policy:** Unrestricted walking. **Metal spikes allowed:** Yes. **Range:** Yes (grass/mats). **To obtain tee times:** Call up to 7 days in advance.
★★½CHAMPIONSHIP COURSE
Opened: 1964. **Holes:** 18. **Par:** 71/71. **Yards:** 6,350/5,189. **Course rating:** 69.5/67.8. **Slope:** 106/97. **Architect:** Joe Finger/Steve Ralston. **Credit cards:** None. **Rental clubs:** Yes.
Notes: Hosted Arkansas Open for 23 consecutive years.
Subscriber comments: Nice course, easy to walk...Older public course, busy, nice layout, fun...Great youth program...Good combination of tough and easy holes...Very clean, good greens, scenic.
★★½TOURNAMENT COURSE
Opened: 1995. **Holes:** 18. **Par:** 70/70. **Yards:** 5,725/5,400. **Course rating:** 65.1/70.8. **Slope:** 102/104. **Architect:** Steve Ralston. **Credit cards:** N/A. **Rental clubs:** No.
Subscriber comments: Challenging. Not long, but demanding...The new nine has some great shots, but course needs time to mature...Good open course for duffers.

CEDAR GLADE GOLF COURSE
R-900 Fourth St, Horseshoe Bend, 72512, Izard County, (870)670-4653, (800)585-2442, 90 miles NW of Jonesboro.
Opened: N/A. **Holes:** 18. **Par:** N/A. **Yards:** N/A. **Course rating:** N/A. **Slope:** N/A. **Architect:** N/A. **Green fee:** $10/$16. **Credit cards:** All major. **Reduced fees:** Resort guests. **Caddies:** No. **Golf carts:** $12. **Discount golf packages:** No. **Season:** Year-round. **High:** May-Sept. **On site lodging:** Yes. **Rental clubs:** Yes. **Walking policy:** Unrestricted walking. **Metal spikes allowed:** Yes. **Range:** No. **To obtain tee times:** Call golf shop.
Notes: 18 hole par-3 course.

★★★CHEROKEE VILLAGE GOLF CLUB (SOUTH COURSE)
R-Laguna Dr., Cherokee Village, 72529, Sharp County, (870)257-2555, 145 miles N of Little Rock.
Opened: 1972. **Holes:** 18. **Par:** 72/72. **Yards:** 7,058/5,270. **Course rating:** 73.5/70.4. **Slope:** 128/116. **Architect:** Edmund Ault. **Green fee:** $15/$25. **Credit cards:** MC,VISA. **Reduced fees:** N/A. **Caddies:** No. **Golf carts:** $10. **Discount golf packages:** No. **Season:** Year-round. **High:** May-Sept. **On site lodging:** No. **Rental clubs:** Yes. **Walking policy:** Walking at certain times. **Metal spikes allowed:** Yes. **Range:** Yes (grass). **To obtain tee times:** First come, first served.
Subscriber comments: Fun to play. Secluded, hilly...Good layout and design...Uncrowded. A gem in the hills...Beautiful setting; good par 4s...Beautiful, long, hilly...Very challenging from back tees.
Special Notes: Complex also includes private North Course.

★★THE CREEKS PUBLIC LINKS
PU-P.O. Box 190, Cave Springs, 72718, Benton County, (501)248-1000, 10 miles N of Fayetteville.
Opened: 1990. **Holes:** 18. **Par:** 71/71. **Yards:** 6,009/5,031. **Course rating:** 67.5/64.2. **Slope:** 111/104. **Architect:** Reed & Hughes. **Green fee:** $15/$18. **Credit cards:** MC,VISA,AMEX. **Reduced fees:** Weekdays, twilight, seniors, juniors. **Caddies:** No. **Golf carts:** $18. **Discount golf packages:** Yes. **Season:** Year-round. **High:** April-July. **On site lodging:** No. **Rental clubs:** Yes. **Walking policy:** Unrestricted walking. **Metal spikes allowed:** Yes. **Range:** Yes (grass). **To obtain tee times:** Call anytime in advance.

★★½DAWN HILL GOLF & RACQUET CLUB
R-R.R. No.1 Dawn Hill Rd., Siloam Springs, 72761, Benton County, (501)524-4838, (800)423-3786, 35 miles NW of Fayetteville.
Opened: 1966. **Holes:** 18. **Par:** 72/73. **Yards:** 6,852/5,330. **Course rating:** 71.3/69.1. **Slope:** 114/110. **Architect:** Ralph Jones. **Green fee:** $20/$22. **Credit cards:** All major. **Reduced fees:** Twilight. **Caddies:** No. **Golf carts:** $10. **Discount golf packages:** Yes. **Season:** Year-round. **High:** May-Oct. **On site lodging:** Yes. **Rental clubs:** Yes. **Walking policy:** Walking at certain times. **Metal spikes allowed:** Yes. **Range:** Yes (grass). **To obtain tee times:** Call anytime in advance.
Subscriber comments: Quality course, you'll use every club in bag...Well-maintained, good mix of difficulty...Good layout, tough when windy.

★★½DEGRAY LAKE RESORT STATE PARK GOLF COURSE
PU-Route 3, Box 490, Bismarck, 71929, Hot Spring County, (501)865-2807, (800)737-8355, 25 miles S of Hot Springs.
Opened: 1977. **Holes:** 18. **Par:** 72/72. **Yards:** 6,930/5,731. **Course rating:** 60.7/67.0. **Slope:** 134/123. **Architect:** N/A. **Green fee:** $10/$13. **Credit cards:** All major. **Reduced fees:** Weekdays, twilight, seniors. **Caddies:** No. **Golf carts:** $13. **Discount golf packages:** Yes. **Season:** Year-round. **High:** April-Sept. **On site lodging:** No. **Rental clubs:** Yes. **Walking policy:** Unrestricted walking. **Metal spikes allowed:** Yes. **Range:** Yes (grass). **To obtain tee times:** Call anytime.
Subscriber comments: Nice layout...Front nine open, back nine tight...Could be a great course with more upkeep and landscaping...Good resort course close to lake...Rolling hillside course, tight back nine...Some difficult holes...Very challenging...Scenic views.

★★½DIAMOND HILLS GOLF COURSE
Rte. 7 N. Diamond Blvd., Diamond City, 72630, Boone County, (870)422-7613, 35 miles SE of Branson, MO.
Opened: 1971. **Holes:** 18. **Par:** 69/72. **Yards:** 6,311/5,491. **Course rating:** 69.7/71.1. **Slope:** 125/115. **Architect:** Maury Bell. **Green fee:** $17/$17. **Credit cards:** N/A. **Reduced fees:** N/A. **Caddies:** No. **Golf carts:** $17. **Discount golf packages:** No. **Season:** Year-round. **High:** May-Sept. **On site lodging:** No. **Rental clubs:** Yes. **Walking policy:** Unrestricted walking. **Metal spikes allowed:** Yes. **Range:** Yes (grass). **To obtain tee times:** Tee times not required.

★★FOXWOOD COUNTRY CLUB
SP-701 Foxwood Dr, Jacksonville, 72076, Pulaski County, (501)982-1254, 15 miles N of Little Rock.
Opened: 1975. **Holes:** 18. **Par:** 72/72. **Yards:** 6,413/5,225. **Course rating:** 69.8/69.2. **Slope:** 110/111. **Architect:** N/A. **Green fee:** $10/$17. **Credit cards:** All major. **Reduced fees:** Seniors, juniors. **Caddies:** No. **Golf carts:** $16. **Discount golf packages:** Yes. **Season:** Year-round. **High:** April-Oct. **On site lodging:** No. **Rental clubs:** Yes. **Walking policy:** Walking at certain times. **Metal spikes allowed:** Yes. **Range:** Yes (grass). **To obtain tee times:** Call for weekend times.

★★★★GLENWOOD COUNTRY CLUB
PU-Hwy 70 E, Glenwood, 71943, Pike County, (870)356-4422, (800)833-3110, 32 miles W of Hot Springs.
Opened: 1994. **Holes:** 18. **Par:** 72/72. **Yards:** 6,550/5,076. **Course rating:** 70.8/64.1. **Slope:** 128/114. **Architect:** Bobby McGee. **Green fee:**

$18/$25. **Credit cards:** All major. **Reduced fees:** Weekdays, low season, twilight, seniors. **Caddies:** No. **Golf carts:** $19. **Discount golf pack ages:** No. **Season:** Year-round. **High:** April-Sept. **On site lodging:** No. **Rental clubs:** Yes. **Walking policy:** Unrestricted walking. **Metal spikes allowed:** Yes. **Range:** Yes (grass). **To obtain tee times:** N/A.

Subscriber comments: Good mix of tight and open fairways...Pretty course, good shape...Six holes require blind shots...Greens and fairways best in state...Good challenge...Wonderful to play and look at...Hard to get to, but worth the drive...Hilly. Great greens. Tight front nine...Great landscaping and rockwork...Great course for a small town.

★★½HARRISON COUNTRY CLUB
Hwy 62-65 N., Harrison, 72601, Boone County, (870)741-4947.
Opened: N/A. **Holes:** 18. **Par:** 70/72. **Yards:** 6,066/5,049. **Course rating:** 69.3/69.7. **Slope:** 121/122. **Architect:** N/A. **Green fee:** $17/$23. **Credit cards:** N/A. **Reduced fees:** N/A. **Caddies:** No. **Golf carts:** $8. **Discount golf packages:** No. **Season:** Year-round. **High:** March-Oct. **On site lodging:** No. **Rental clubs:** Yes. **Walking policy:** Unrestricted walking. **Metal spikes allowed:** No. **Range:** Yes (grass/mats). **To obtain tee times:** N/A.
Subscriber comments: Short...Outstanding bent-grass greens...Greens severely sloped, a 13 on Stimpmeter...Short course made better with new bunkers...Worth the trip.

★★½HINDMAN PARK GOLF COURSE
PM-60 Brookview Dr., Little Rock, 72209, Pulaski County, (501)565-6450.
Opened: N/A. **Holes:** 18. **Par:** 72/72. **Yards:** 6,393/4,349. **Course rating:** 68.9. **Slope:** 109. **Architect:** Dave Bennett/Leon Howard. **Green fee:** $8/$10. **Credit cards:** DISC. **Reduced fees:** Low season, twilight, seniors, juniors. **Caddies:** No. **Golf carts:** $17. **Discount golf packages:** No. **Season:** Year-round. **High:** May-Aug. **On site lodging:** No. **Rental clubs:** Yes. **Walking policy:** Unrestricted walking. **Metal spikes allowed:** Yes. **Range:** Yes (grass). **To obtain tee times:** Tee time reservations may be made one week in advance of playing date. Saturday, Sunday, Monday and Tuesday: Tee time reservation must be made in person at the golf course. Wednesday, Thursday and Friday: Tee time reservations may be made in person or by telephoning the Golf Pro Shop.
Subscriber comments: Good older muny...Lots of trees, hills, water, not much sand...Good public course, friendly personnel...Nice layout...Best muny in central Arkansas...Good layout, hilly, tight fairways, very challenging...Needs care...Gets better on back side; front side rough.
Special Notes: Complex includes 18-hole par-65 War Memorial Golf Course.

HOT SPRINGS COUNTRY CLUB
R-101 Country Club Dr., Hot Springs, 71901, Garland County, (501)624-2661, 60 miles W of Little Rock.
Credit cards: MC,VISA. **Reduced fees:** Resort guests. **Caddies:** No. **Golf carts:** Included in Green Fee. **Discount golf packages:** Yes. **Season:** Year-round. **High:** March-Oct. **On site lodging:** No. **Rental clubs:** Yes. **Walking policy:** Unrestricted walking. **Metal spikes allowed:** No. **To obtain tee times:** Call two days in advance.
★★★½ARLINGTON COURSE
Opened: 1932. **Holes:** 18. **Par:** 72/74. **Yards:** 6,646/6,206. **Course rating:** 72.0/75.6. **Slope:** 127/137. **Architect:** Bill Diddel. **Green fee:** $90/$90. **Range:** Yes (grass).
Notes: Ranked 9th in 1997 Best in State.
Subscriber comments: Classic course...Great layout with some long par 4s on back nine...Ben Crenshaw remodeled, now very challenging...Very nice after redesign...Beautiful layout, long.
★★★MAJESTIC COURSE
Opened: 1908. **Holes:** 18. **Par:** 72/72. **Yards:** 6,715/5,541. **Course rating:** 72.7/70.9. **Slope:** 131/121. **Architect:** Willie Park Jr.. **Green fee:** $60/$60. **Range:** Yes (grass/mats).

Subscriber comments: Stepsister to the Arlington course...Plain Jane...Beautiful restaurant...A nice challenge with long par 3s...Beautiful course, very traditional...Good course, well kept, great value...Still a challenge.
Special Notes: Complex also includes 9-hole par-33 Pineview Course.

LIL' BIT A HEAVEN GOLF CLUB
PU-Rte 1, Box 140, Magazine, 72943, Logan County, (501)969-2203, 50 miles E of Ft. Smith.
Opened: 1992. **Holes:** 18. **Par:** 72/78. **Yards:** 6,308/5,836. **Course rating:** N/A. **Slope:** N/A. **Architect:** Jack Fleck. **Green fee:** $9/$12. **Credit cards:** None. **Reduced fees:** Weekdays, seniors, juniors. **Caddies:** No. **Golf carts:** $14. **Discount golf packages:** Yes. **Season:** Year-round. **High:** April-Nov. **On site lodging:** No. **Rental clubs:** Yes. **Walking policy:** Unrestricted walking. **Metal spikes allowed:** Yes. **Range:** Yes (grass). **To obtain tee times:** Call one day in advance.

★★½LONGHILLS GOLF CLUB
PU-327 Hwy. 5 N., Benton, 72018, Saline County, (501)316-3000, 9 miles SW of Little Rock.
Opened: 1955. **Holes:** 18. **Par:** 72/73. **Yards:** 6,539/5,350. **Course rating:** 69.9/69.5. **Slope:** 110/110. **Architect:** William T. Martin. **Green fee:** $12/$16. **Credit cards:** MC,VISA. **Reduced fees:** Juniors. **Caddies:** No. **Golf carts:** $16. **Discount golf packages:** No. **Season:** Year-round. **High:** April-Sept. **On site lodging:** No. **Rental clubs:** Yes. **Walking policy:** Unrestricted walking. **Metal spikes allowed:** No. **Range:** Yes (grass). **To obtain tee times:** Call anytime for weekdays. For weekends and holidays call Wednesday beginning at 8 a.m.
Subscriber comments: No bunkers...Easy; needs work...Tight, very challenging...Greens are very smooth...Always enjoyable.

★★★★MOUNTAIN RANCH GOLF CLUB
R-820 Lost Creek Pkwy., Fairfield Bay, 72088, Van Buren County, (501)884-3400, (800)726-2418, 84 miles N of Little Rock.
Opened: 1983. **Holes:** 18. **Par:** 72/72. **Yards:** 6,780/5,325. **Course rating:** 71.8/69.8. **Slope:** 129/121. **Architect:** Edmund B. Ault. **Green fee:** $15/$35. **Credit cards:** MC,VISA. **Reduced fees:** Weekdays, low season, resort guests, twilight. **Caddies:** No. **Golf carts:** $10. **Discount golf packages:** Yes. **Season:** Year-round. **High:** May-Oct. **On site lodging:** Yes. **Rental clubs:** Yes. **Walking policy:** Walking at certain times. **Metal spikes allowed:** Yes. **Range:** Yes (grass/mats). **To obtain tee times:** Call up to two weeks in adavance.
Subscriber comments: Secluded, quiet getaway...Wide open...Beautiful setting...Back nine especially challenging...Best public course in Arkansas, always in good shape...A fun course for all skills...Beautiful scenery, very hilly, great golf...Best and most scenic course in Arkansas...Very hard course.

★★★½PRAIRIE CREEK COUNTRY CLUB
Hwy. 12 E., Rogers, 72757, Benton County, (501)925-2414, 100 miles E of Tulsa, OK.
Opened: 1968. **Holes:** 18. **Par:** 72/77. **Yards:** 6,707/5,921. **Course rating:** 73.4/76.3. **Slope:** 130/127. **Architect:** Joe Sanders. **Green fee:** $10/$16. **Credit cards:** None. **Reduced fees:** Weekdays, resort guests, twilight. **Caddies:** No. **Golf carts:** $9. **Discount golf packages:** Yes. **Season:** Year-round. **High:** April-Sept. **On site lodging:** No. **Rental clubs:** Yes. **Walking policy:** Unrestricted walking. **Metal spikes allowed:** Yes. **Range:** Yes (grass). **To obtain tee times:** First come, first served.
Subscriber comments: One of the toughest courses you'll want to play...Best public course in the state...Consistently immaculate...Most challenging public course in Arkansas...Hilly course...Stay out of the many ravines...Tight and challenging...Lots of trees; good greens; pretty surroundings...Two different nines, top nine is virtually on top of the hill, bottom nine has spring-fed creek in middle of course.

★★★QUAPAW GOLF LINKS
PU-110 St. Hwy. 391 N., North Little Rock, 72117, Pulaski County, (501)945-0945.
Opened: 1993. **Holes:** 18. **Par:** 72/72. **Yards:** 6,972/5,118. **Course rating:** 72.4/70.3. **Slope:** 119/120. **Architect:** Steve Holden. **Green fee:** $12/$20. **Credit cards:** MC,VISA. **Reduced fees:** Weekdays, low season, twilight, seniors, juniors. **Caddies:** No. **Golf carts:** $16. **Discount golf packages:** Yes. **Season:** Year-round. **High:** March-

Oct. **On site lodging:** No. **Rental clubs:** Yes. **Walking policy:** Unrestricted walking. **Metal spikes allowed:** Yes. **Range:** Yes (grass/mats). **To obtain tee times:** Call five days in advance.
Subscriber comments: Great links-style course, can play long...Wonderful greens, great practice facility...Look out for No. 10 and No. 15...Good bent-grass greens...Flat and uneventful; needs more trees...Five sets of different tees, very challenging...Links course in Arkansas River marshland...No trees, but a lot of water.

★RAZORBACK PARK GOLF COURSE
PU-2514 W. Lori Dr., Fayetteville, 72704, Washington County, (501)443-5862.
Opened: 1959. **Holes:** 18. **Par:** 71/71. **Yards:** 6,167/5,255. **Course rating:** 66.9/71.5. **Slope:** 108/110. **Architect:** E.H. Sonneman/David Taylor. **Green fee:** $11/$11. **Credit cards:** MC,VISA,DISC. **Reduced fees:** N/A. **Caddies:** No. **Golf carts:** N/A. **Discount golf packages:** No. **Season:** Year-round. **High:** May-Sept. **On site lodging:** No. **Rental clubs:** Yes. **Walking policy:** Unrestricted walking. **Metal spikes allowed:** Yes. **Range:** No. **To obtain tee times:** None required.

★★REBSAMEN PARK GOLF COURSE
PM-Rebsamen Park Rd., Little Rock, 72202, Pulaski County, (501)666-7965.
Opened: 1956. **Holes:** 27. **Par:** 71/71. **Yards:** 6,271/5,651. **Course rating:** 67.9/68.8. **Slope:** 100/106. **Architect:** Herman Hackbarth. **Green fee:** $8/$11. **Credit cards:** N/A. **Reduced fees:** N/A. **Caddies:** No. **Golf carts:** $16. **Discount golf packages:** No. **Season:** Year-round. **High:** May-Aug. **On site lodging:** No. **Rental clubs:** No. **Walking policy:** Unrestricted walking. **Metal spikes allowed:** Yes. **Range:** No. **To obtain tee times:** In person at golf shop.

★★½THE RED APPLE INN & COUNTRY CLUB
R-325 Club Rd., Heber Springs, 72543, Cleburne County, (501)362-3131, (800)255-8900, 65 miles N of Little Rock.
Opened: 1984. **Holes:** 18. **Par:** 71/71. **Yards:** 6,402/5,137. **Course rating:** 71.5/65.5. **Slope:** 128/117. **Architect:** Gary Panks. **Green fee:** $25/$25. **Credit cards:** All major. **Reduced fees:** N/A. **Caddies:** No. **Golf carts:** $18. **Discount golf packages:** No. **Season:** Year-round. **High:** April-Nov. **On site lodging:** Yes. **Rental clubs:** Yes. **Walking policy:** Walking at certain times. **Metal spikes allowed:** Yes. **Range:** Yes (grass/mats). **To obtain tee times:** Call 24 hours in advance.
Subscriber comments: Excellent service and accommodations...Interesting layout; good-irons-player haven...No.2 hole a must-play...Nice course on Greers Ferry Lake...Very tight, wooded...Good course and condition...Nice elevation, excellent views.

★★½SOUTH HAVEN GOLF CLUB
PU-Route 10, Box 201, Texarkana, 71854, Miller County, (870)774-5771.
Opened: 1931. **Holes:** 18. **Par:** 71/71. **Yards:** 6,227/4,951. **Course rating:** 69.3/69.8. **Slope:** 123/117. **Architect:** Jeff Miers. **Green fee:** $10/$12. **Credit cards:** None. **Reduced fees:** Seniors, juniors. **Caddies:** No. **Golf carts:** $16. **Discount golf packages:** No. **Season:** Year-round. **High:** April-Sept. **On site lodging:** No. **Rental clubs:** Yes. **Walking policy:** Unrestricted walking. **Metal spikes allowed:** Yes. **Range:** Yes (grass/mats). **To obtain tee times:** Call for weekdays only.
Subscriber comments: Superior course for the heavy use...The front and back nines like playing two courses the same day...Very nice, economical place to play.

★★TWIN LAKES GOLF CLUB
70 Elkway, Mountain Home, 72653, Baxter County, (870)425-2028, 120 miles SE of Springfield, MO.
Opened: 1959. **Holes:** 18. **Par:** 70/70. **Yards:** 5,910/5,018. **Course rating:** 67.2/69.1. **Slope:** 110/106. **Architect:** Cecil B. Hollingsworth. **Green fee:** $20/$20. **Credit cards:** VISA. **Reduced fees:** Low season. **Caddies:** No. **Golf carts:** $20. **Discount golf packages:** No. **Season:** Year-round. **High:** N/A. **On site lodging:** No. **Rental clubs:** Yes. **Walking policy:** Unrestricted walking. **Metal spikes allowed:** Yes. **Range:** No. **To obtain tee times:** First come, first served.

★½VACHE GRASSE COUNTRY CLUB
Country Club Rd., Greenwood, 72936, Sebastian County, (501)996-4191, 15 miles SW of Ft. Smith.

ARKANSAS

Opened: 1968. **Holes:** 18. **Par:** 72/72. **Yards:** 6,502/4,966. **Course rating:** 70.5/67.4. **Slope:** 114/113. **Architect:** William T. Martin. **Green fee:** $10/$13. **Credit cards:** None. **Reduced fees:** Twilight. **Caddies:** No. **Golf carts:** $16. **Discount golf packages:** No. **Season:** Year-round. **High:** May-Sept. **On site lodging:** No. **Rental clubs:** No. **Walking policy:** Unrestricted walking. **Metal spikes allowed:** No. **Range:** Yes (grass). **To obtain tee times:** Tee times taken only in the summer by calling one day in advance.

★★WAR MEMORIAL GOLF COURSE
5511 W Markham, Little Rock, 72205, Pulaski County, (501)663-0854.
Call club for further information.

★★½ADOBE CREEK GOLF CLUB

PU-1901 Frates Rd., Petaluma, 94954, Sonoma County, (707)765-3000, 35 miles N of San Francisco.
Opened: 1990. **Holes:** 18. **Par:** 72/72. **Yards:** 6,825/5,027. **Course rating:** 73.8/69.4. **Slope:** 131/120. **Architect:** Robert Trent Jones Jr. **Green fee:** $10/$55. **Credit cards:** MC,VISA. **Reduced fees:** Weekdays, twilight, seniors, juniors. **Caddies:** No. **Golf carts:** $10. **Discount golf packages:** No. **Season:** Year-round. **High:** May-Oct. **On site lodging:** No. **Rental clubs:** Yes. **Walking policy:** Unrestricted walking. **Metal spikes allowed:** No. **Range:** Yes (grass/mats). **To obtain tee times:** Call up to 7 days in advance.
Subscriber comments: Challenging, very entertaining links-style course...Six-hour weekend rounds...Lots of sand.

★★ALHAMBRA MUNICIPAL GOLF COURSE

PM-630 S. Almansor St., Alhambra, 91801, Los Angeles County, (818)570-5059, 8 miles E of Los Angeles.
Opened: 1952. **Holes:** 18. **Par:** 70/71. **Yards:** 5,214/4,501. **Course rating:** 64.5/64.7. **Slope:** 107/105. **Architect:** William P. Bell. **Green fee:** $18/$22. **Credit cards:** MC,VISA,AMEX. **Reduced fees:** Twilight, seniors, juniors. **Caddies:** No. **Golf carts:** $10. **Discount golf packages:** No. **Season:** Year-round. **High:** N/A. **On site lodging:** No. **Rental clubs:** Yes. **Walking policy:** Unrestricted walking. **Metal spikes allowed:** Yes. **Range:** Yes (mats). **To obtain tee times:** Call up to 7 days in advance at 5:30 a.m.

★★★½THE ALISAL RANCH GOLF COURSE

R-1054 Alisal Rd., Solvang, 93463, Santa Barbara County, (805)688-4215, 40 miles N of Santa Barbara.
Opened: 1955. **Holes:** 18. **Par:** 72/73. **Yards:** 6,472/5,767. **Course rating:** 71.0/74.4. **Slope:** 124/130. **Architect:** William F. Bell. **Green fee:** $60/$60. **Credit cards:** All major. **Reduced fees:** N/A. **Caddies:** No. **Golf carts:** $24. **Discount golf packages:** Yes. **Season:** Year-round. **High:** May-Oct. **On site lodging:** Yes. **Rental clubs:** Yes. **Walking policy:** Unrestricted walking. **Metal spikes allowed:** Yes. **Range:** Yes (grass/mats). **To obtain tee times:** Weekdays, 7 days in advance. Weekend, Thursday prior to weekend.
Subscriber comments: Nice track, very scenic, worth the trip...Interesting, tight, challenging layout...Great resort...Deer on course a real treat...Tight front nine opens up on back...Coastal winds can make course extremely tough...Attractive, challenging.

★★★ALTA SIERRA GOLF & COUNTRY CLUB

11897 Tammy Way, Grass Valley, 95949, Nevada County, (916)273-2010, 50 miles NE of Sacramento.
Opened: 1964. **Holes:** 18. **Par:** 72/72. **Yards:** 6,537/5,984. **Course rating:** 71.2/74.6. **Slope:** 128/128. **Architect:** Bob Baldock. **Green fee:** $35/$40. **Credit cards:** MC,VISA. **Reduced fees:** Weekdays, juniors. **Caddies:** No. **Golf carts:** $10. **Discount golf packages:** No. **Season:** Year-round. **High:** April-June. **On site lodging:** Yes. **Rental clubs:** Yes. **Walking policy:** Unrestricted walking. **Metal spikes allowed:** Yes. **Range:** Yes (grass/mats). **To obtain tee times:** Call on 1st of the month to book for upcoming month.
Subscriber comments: Great design, no adjacent fairways...Mountain course, lots of trees...Excellent condition; beautiful scenery...Great mountain course, above the fog, below the snow...Hilly to very hilly...Very scenic course...Beautiful, relaxing, challenging, well kept.

★★½ANAHEIM HILLS GOLF COURSE

PU-6501 Nohl Ranch Rd., Anaheim, 92807, Orange County, (714)998-3041, 25 miles S of Los Angeles.
Opened: 1972. **Holes:** 18. **Par:** 71/72. **Yards:** 6,245/5,361. **Course rating:** 69.6/70.0. **Slope:** 117/115. **Architect:** Richard Bigler. **Green fee:** $30/$36. **Credit cards:** MC,VISA. **Reduced fees:** Twilight, seniors, juniors. **Caddies:** No. **Golf carts:** Included in Green Fee. **Discount golf packages:** No. **Season:** Year-round. **High:** N/A. **On site lodging:** No. **Rental clubs:** Yes. **Walking policy:** Mandatory cart. **Metal spikes allowed:** Yes. **Range:** Yes (mats). **To obtain tee times:** Call up to 7 days in advance.
Subscriber comments: Mountain-goat course...Fore! Some dangerous tee

shots...Don't try to walk...Beautiful design...Too hilly, too many blind shots...More doglegs than a kennel...Great rolling hills.
Special Notes: Juniors may walk course.

★★½ANCIL HOFFMAN GOLF COURSE

PU-6700 Tarshes Dr., Carmichael, 95608, Sacramento County, (916)482-5660, 12 miles SW of Sacramento.
Opened: 1965. **Holes:** 18. **Par:** 72/73. **Yards:** 6,794/5,954. **Course rating:** 72.5/73.4. **Slope:** 123/123. **Architect:** William F. Bell. **Green fee:** $18/$25. **Credit cards:** MC,VISA. **Reduced fees:** Weekdays, twilight, seniors, juniors. **Caddies:** No. **Golf carts:** $19. **Discount golf packages:** Yes. **Season:** Year-round. **High:** N/A. **On site lodging:** No. **Rental clubs:** Yes. **Walking policy:** Unrestricted walking. **Metal spikes allowed:** Yes. **Range:** Yes (grass/mats). **To obtain tee times:** Call up to 7 days in advance. Monday morning, tee times taken for the following Saturday, Sunday and Monday.
Subscriber comments: Still a decent layout...Tough track, fun for the shotmaker...Great public course, narrow with trees...Course needs updating...Mature oak surroundings.

★★★APTOS SEASCAPE GOLF COURSE

PU-610 Clubhouse Dr., Aptos, 95003, Santa Cruz County, (408)688-3213, 20 miles NE of San Jose.
Opened: 1926. **Holes:** 18. **Par:** 72/72. **Yards:** 6,116/5,576. **Course rating:** 69.8/72.6. **Slope:** 126/127. **Architect:** N/A. **Green fee:** $16/$60. **Credit cards:** MC,VISA,AMEX. **Reduced fees:** Weekdays, low season, resort guests, twilight, seniors, juniors. **Caddies:** No. **Golf carts:** $28. **Discount golf packages:** No. **Season:** Year-round. **High:** April-Oct. **On site lodging:** No. **Rental clubs:** Yes. **Walking policy:** Unrestricted walking. **Metal spikes allowed:** Yes. **Range:** Yes (mats). **To obtain tee times:** Call up to 7 days in advance for weekdays. One month advance reservation for an additional $5.00 per player.
Subscriber comments: Extremely well laid out...Beautiful course...Good risk/reward...Like fog? Play here...Pretty setting...Watch approach on No.9—you might buy a window...Poor man's Pasatiempo...Good layout, hilly, tight...Rarely get a level lie...Busy place...Beautiful setting in pine-covered hills...Nice course—always slow!

★★★AVILA BEACH RESORT GOLF COURSE

PU-P.O. Box 2140, Avila Beach, 93424, San Luis Obispo County, (805)595-4000, 8 miles S of San Luis Obispo.
Opened: 1969. **Holes:** 18. **Par:** 71/71. **Yards:** 6,443/5,116. **Course rating:** 70.9/69.9. **Slope:** 122/126. **Architect:** Desmond Muirhead. **Green fee:** $25/$35. **Credit cards:** MC,VISA. **Reduced fees:** Twilight, seniors, juniors. **Caddies:** No. **Golf carts:** $12. **Discount golf packages:** Yes. **Season:** Year-round. **High:** April-Oct. **On site lodging:** No. **Rental clubs:** Yes. **Walking policy:** Unrestricted walking. **Metal spikes allowed:** Yes. **Range:** Yes (grass). **To obtain tee times:** Call up to 7 days in advance.
Subscriber comments: Great views, good variety...Front and back nine completely different......Neat ocean course...Front nine is fantastic! Nice views of bay...Well-kept secret...Terrific setting on beach...Pleasant ocean atmosphere...Beautiful back nine...Mountain-style front nine, beachfront back nine...Great layout, beautiful holes along river...Challenging coastal course...Foggy and misty...Great water holes.

★½AZUSA GREENS GOLF COURSE

PU-919 W. Sierra Madre Blvd., Azusa, 91702, Los Angeles County, (818)969-1727, 12 miles E of Pasadena.
Opened: 1963. **Holes:** 18. **Par:** 70/72. **Yards:** 6,266/5,637. **Course rating:** 69.1/70.9. **Slope:** 112/115. **Architect:** Bob Baldock. **Green fee:** $14/$33. **Credit cards:** MC,VISA,AMEX. **Reduced fees:** Weekdays, twilight, seniors, juniors. **Caddies:** No. **Golf carts:** Included in Green Fee. **Discount golf packages:** No. **Season:** Year-round. **High:** N/A. **On site lodging:** No. **Rental clubs:** Yes. **Walking policy:** Mandatory cart. **Metal spikes allowed:** Yes. **Range:** Yes (grass/mats). **To obtain tee times:** Call up to 7 days in advance.

CALIFORNIA

★★BALBOA PARK GOLF CLUB
PU-2600 Golf Course Dr., San Diego, 92102, San Diego County, (619)239-1632.
Opened: 1915. **Holes:** 18. **Par:** 72/72. **Yards:** 6,267/5,369. **Course rating:** 69.8/71.4. **Slope:** 119/119. **Architect:** William P. Bell. **Green fee:** $17/$34. **Credit cards:** MC,VISA. **Reduced fees:** Twilight. **Caddies:** No. **Golf carts:** $22. **Discount golf packages:** No. **Season:** Year-round. **High:** Summer. **On site lodging:** No. **Rental clubs:** Yes. **Walking policy:** Unrestricted walking. **Metal spikes allowed:** Yes. **Range:** Yes (mats). **To obtain tee times:** Call or walk on.
Subscriber comments: Narrow, lots of trouble off fairways...Old city course: Cheap for residents, not worth it for tourists...Renovations have helped...The place to play when you can't get on anywhere else.

★★½BARTLEY W. CAVANAUGH GOLF COURSE
PU-8301 Freeport Blvd., Sacramento, 95832, Sacramento County, (916)665-2020.
Opened: 1995. **Holes:** 18. **Par:** 71/71. **Yards:** 6,265/4,723. **Course rating:** 69.0/66.3. **Slope:** 114/107. **Architect:** Perry Dye. **Green fee:** $12/$23. **Credit cards:** None. **Reduced fees:** Weekdays, twilight, seniors, juniors. **Caddies:** No. **Golf carts:** $10. **Discount golf packages:** No. **Season:** Year-round. **High:** May-Sept. **On site lodging:** No. **Rental clubs:** Yes. **Walking policy:** Unrestricted walking. **Metal spikes allowed:** Yes. **Range:** No. **To obtain tee times:** Call up to 7 days in advance.
Subscriber comments: Short, tight city-owned layout...Clubhouse looks like Taj Mahal—course doesn't match...Bring a hardhat! Links course, too many parallel holes...18 holes on nine holes' worth of land.

BAYONET GOLF COURSE
PU-1 McClure Way, Seaside, 93955, Monterey County, (408)899-7271, 8 miles S of Pebble Beach.
Credit cards: MC,VISA,AMEX. **Reduced fees:** Weekdays, low season, twilight, seniors, juniors. **Golf carts:** $10. **Discount golf packages:** No. **Season:** Year-round. **High:** March-Nov. **On site lodging:** No. **Rental clubs:** Yes. **Walking policy:** Walking at certain times. **Metal spikes allowed:** Yes. **Range:** Yes (grass/mats). **To obtain tee times:** Call up to 30 days in advance.

★★★½BAYONET COURSE
Opened: 1954. **Holes:** 18. **Par:** 72/72. **Yards:** 7,003/5,680. **Course rating:** 74.0/73.7. **Slope:** 138/134. **Architect:** General Bob McClure. **Green fee:** $35/$65. **Caddies:** No.
Subscriber comments: Very tight and difficult course, Q-school toughness..."Combat Corner" (11-15) will eat your lunch...Old-style course, treelined fairways...Satanically tight and tough, must hit fairways...If USGA got a hold of it, winning score at the Open would be 301...Best course in Monterey...In transition to civilian management.

★★★BLACKHORSE COURSE
Opened: 1954. **Holes:** 18. **Par:** 72/72. **Yards:** 6,396/5,613. **Course rating:** 69.8/72.5. **Slope:** 128/124. **Architect:** N/A. **Green fee:** $25/$50. **Caddies:** Yes.
Subscriber comments: Some tricky holes...More forgiving than Bayonet...Narrow, tree-lined fairways, small greens, shorter course...Lots of ball eating trees, greens good...Will humble the best; good, but play Bayonet.
Special Notes: Formerly Fort Ord Golf Course.

★★BEAU PRE GOLF CLUB
1777 Norton Rd., McKinleyville, 95519, Humboldt County, (707)839-2342, (800)931-6690, 10 miles N of Eureka.
Opened: 1967. **Holes:** 18. **Par:** 71/72. **Yards:** 5,910/4,976. **Course rating:** 68.1/67.6. **Slope:** 118/112. **Architect:** Don Harling. **Green fee:** $17/$25. **Credit cards:** MC,VISA. **Reduced fees:** Weekdays, twilight, juniors. **Caddies:** No. **Golf carts:** $17. **Discount golf packages:** Yes. **Season:** Year-round. **High:** May-Sept. **On site lodging:** No. **Rental clubs:** Yes. **Walking policy:** Unrestricted walking. **Metal spikes allowed:** Yes. **Range:** Yes (grass/mats). **To obtain tee times:** Call golf shop.

★★½BENNETT VALLEY GOLF COURSE
PU-3330 Yulupa Ave., Santa Rosa, 95405, Sonoma County, (707)528-3673, 50 miles N of San Francisco.
Opened: 1969. **Holes:** 18. **Par:** 72/75. **Yards:** 6,600/5,958. **Course rating:** 70.6/72.5. **Slope:** 112/123. **Architect:** Ben

Harmon. **Green fee:** $8/$18. **Credit cards:** None. **Reduced fees:** Weekdays, twilight, seniors, juniors. **Caddies:** No. **Golf carts:** $20. **Discount golf packages:** No. **Season:** Year-round. **High:** May-Sept. **On site lodging:** No. **Rental clubs:** Yes. **Walking policy:** Unrestricted walking. **Metal spikes allowed:** Yes. **Range:** Yes (grass/mats). **To obtain tee times:** Call up to 7 days in advance.
Subscriber comments: Nice muny, not difficult, very affordable...For a heavily played public course, fairways and greens are excellent...Mature course with great variety of shots required...In the process of replacing greens with more challenging ones, good move...Great public course.

★★ BETHEL ISLAND GOLF COURSE
PM-3303 Gateway Rd., Bethel Island, 94511, Contra Costa County, (510)684-2654, 25 miles SE of Stockton.
Opened: 1960. **Holes:** 18. **Par:** 72/74. **Yards:** 6,632/5,813. **Course rating:** 70.8/72.2. **Slope:** 118/117. **Architect:** Ted Robinson. **Green fee:** $12/$22. **Credit cards:** All major. **Reduced fees:** Weekdays, low season, twilight, seniors. **Caddies:** No. **Golf carts:** $20. **Discount golf packages:** Yes. **Season:** Year-round. **High:** April-Oct. **On site lodging:** No. **Rental clubs:** Yes. **Walking policy:** Unrestricted walking. **Metal spikes allowed:** Yes. **Range:** Yes (grass). **To obtain tee times:** Call up to 7 days in advance.

★★½ BIDWELL PARK GOLF COURSE
PU-3199 Golf Course Road, Chico, 95973, Butte County, (916)891-8417, 90 miles N of Sacramento.
Opened: 1930. **Holes:** 18. **Par:** 70/71. **Yards:** 6,157/5,855. **Course rating:** 68.6/73.1. **Slope:** 115/123. **Architect:** City of Chico. **Green fee:** $14/$18. **Credit cards:** None. **Reduced fees:** Twilight, seniors, juniors. **Caddies:** No. **Golf carts:** $18. **Discount golf packages:** No. **Season:** Year-round. **High:** June-July. **On site lodging:** No. **Rental clubs:** Yes. **Walking policy:** Unrestricted walking. **Metal spikes allowed:** Yes. **Range:** No. **To obtain tee times:** Call two days in advance.
Subscriber comments: Very good for muny course...Challenging...Much improved since realigned...One of the best munys in California...Set in historical park...A few interesting holes.

★★ BING MALONEY GOLF COURSE
PU-6801 Freeport Blvd., Sacramento, 95822, Sacramento County, (916)428-9401, 40 miles E of Stockton.
Opened: 1952. **Holes:** 18. **Par:** 72/73. **Yards:** 6,558/5,972. **Course rating:** 70.3/72.6. **Slope:** 113/119. **Architect:** Mike McDonagh. **Green fee:** $17/$20. **Credit cards:** None. **Reduced fees:** Weekdays, low season, twilight, seniors, juniors. **Caddies:** No. **Golf carts:** $21. **Discount golf packages:** No. **Season:** Year-round. **High:** March-Aug. **On site lodging:** No. **Rental clubs:** Yes. **Walking policy:** Unrestricted walking. **Metal spikes allowed:** Yes. **Range:** Yes (mats). **To obtain tee times:** Call up to 7 days in advance or Tuesday prior to weekend.

★★★ BLACK LAKE GOLF RESORT
R-1490 Golf Course Lane, Nipomo, 93444, San Luis Obispo County, (805)343-1214, (800)423-0981, 10 miles N of Santa Maria.
Opened: 1964. **Holes:** 27. **Architect:** Ted Robinson. **Green fee:** $40/$55. **Credit cards:** MC,VISA,AMEX. **Reduced fees:** Weekdays, low season, resort guests, twilight. **Caddies:** No. **Golf carts:** $12. **Discount golf packages:** Yes. **Season:** Year-round. **High:** May-Sept. **On site lodging:** Yes. **Rental clubs:** Yes. **Walking policy:** Walking at certain times. **Metal spikes allowed:** Yes. **Range:** Yes (grass/mats). **To obtain tee times:** Resort guests tee times are set when reservation is made. Nonguests call 7 days in advance.
CANYON/OAKS
Par: 71/71. **Yards:** 6,034/5,047. **Course rating:** 69.3/70.5. **Slope:** 121/120.
LAKES/CANYON
Par: 72/72. **Yards:** 6,401/5,628. **Course rating:** 70.9/72.9. **Slope:** 123/126.
LAKES/OAKS
Par: 71/71. **Yards:** 6,185/5,161. **Course rating:** 69.7/70.8. **Slope:** 121/124.
Subscriber comments: Beautiful, new back nine terrific...Very nice resort...Good golf, great stay-and-play packages...Narrow fairways, great condition...Excellent course...The

new Oaks nine is short and narrow...A real variety of holes; long, straight, hilly, beautiful lakes...Lakes No.1 par 3 looks like a postcard...Scenic course...Lovely peaceful location, fun to play...Nice getaway...Super course, location.

★½BLUE SKIES COUNTRY CLUB
PU-55100 Martinez Trail, Yucca Valley, 92284, San Bernardino County, (760)365-0111, (800)877-1412, 19 miles N of Palm Springs.
Opened: 1957. **Holes:** 18. **Par:** 71/73. **Yards:** 6,400/5,757. **Course rating:** 69.8/71.6. **Slope:** 115/119. **Architect:** William F. Bell. **Green fee:** $6/$19. **Credit cards:** MC,VISA. **Reduced fees:** Weekdays, low season, resort guests, twilight, seniors, juniors. **Caddies:** No. **Golf carts:** $12. **Discount golf packages:** Yes. **Season:** Year-round. **High:** Oct. **On site lodging:** No. **Rental clubs:** No. **Walking policy:** Unrestricted walking. **Metal spikes allowed:** Yes. **Range:** Yes. **To obtain tee times:** Call up to 7 days in advance.

BLYTHE GOLF CLUB
PU-4708 Wells Rd., Blythe, 92225, Riverside County, (760)922-7272, 4 miles N of Blythe.
Opened: 1968. **Holes:** 18. **Par:** 72/73. **Yards:** 6,567/5,684. **Course rating:** 70.7/70.6. **Slope:** 109/110. **Architect:** William F. Bell. **Green fee:** $18. **Credit cards:** None. **Reduced fees:** N/A. **Caddies:** No. **Golf carts:** $20. **Discount golf packages:** No. **Season:** Year-round. **High:** Dec.-April. **On site lodging:** No. **Rental clubs:** Yes. **Walking policy:** Unrestricted walking. **Metal spikes allowed:** Yes. **Range:** Yes (grass/mats). **To obtain tee times:** Taken January thru April one day in advance starting at 7 a.m.

★★★½BODEGA HARBOUR GOLF LINKS
R-21301 Heron Dr., Bodega Bay, 94923, Sonoma County, (707)875-3538, 20 miles W of Santa Rosa.
Opened: 1976. **Holes:** 18. **Par:** 70/71. **Yards:** 6,265/4,749. **Course rating:** 71.9/67.7. **Slope:** 130/120. **Architect:** Robert Trent Jones Jr. **Green fee:** $35/$80. **Credit cards:** MC,VISA,AMEX. **Reduced fees:** Weekdays, low season, resort guests, twilight, juniors. **Caddies:** Yes. **Golf carts:** $15. **Discount golf packages:** Yes. **Season:** Year-round. **High:** April-Oct. **On site lodging:** Yes. **Rental clubs:** Yes. **Walking policy:** Walking at certain times. **Metal spikes allowed:** Yes. **Range:** Yes (mats). **To obtain tee times:** Call up to 90 days in advance.
Subscriber comments: Most extreme nines in golf...Prettier than Pebble Beach...16, 17, 18 are killers!...Very difficult, great views of ocean...High winds in p.m...Lots of summer fog...Good Trent Jones Jr. course...Most beautiful ocean course north of Pebble Beach...Great back nine.

★★½BOULDER CREEK GOLF & COUNTRY CLUB
R-16901 Big Basin Hwy., Boulder Creek, 95006, Santa Cruz County, (408)338-2121, 15 miles N of Santa Cruz.
Opened: 1962. **Holes:** 18. **Par:** 65/67. **Yards:** 4,396/4,027. **Course rating:** 61.5/63.3. **Slope:** 98/98. **Architect:** Jack Fleming. **Green fee:** $14/$35. **Credit cards:** All major. **Reduced fees:** Weekdays, low season, resort guests, twilight, seniors, juniors. **Caddies:** No. **Golf carts:** $18. **Discount golf packages:** Yes. **Season:** Year-round. **High:** April-Oct. **On site lodging:** Yes. **Rental clubs:** Yes. **Walking policy:** Unrestricted walking. **Metal spikes allowed:** Yes. **Range:** No. **To obtain tee times:** Call golf shop up to 7 days in advance. Resort guests can book tee times when reserving condo/villa.
Subscriber comments: Executive layout...Narrow and short...Great setting in redwoods...Tight fairways, good condition...10 par 3s...Leave your driver in the trunk...Ping pong in the redwood forest...Short but challenging.

★★★BOUNDARY OAKS COUNTRY CLUB
PU-3800 Valley Vista Rd., Walnut Creek, 94598, Contra Costa County, (510)934-6212. Call club for further information.
Subscriber comments: Beautiful course, great greens...One of the best munys in Northern California...Much improved...Hilly, treelined, hard fairways and greens...Tough and fair, bring all clubs...Great variation in elevation and shots to hole...Nice layout, some tough holes.

BROOKSIDE GOLF CLUB
PU-1133 N. Rosemont Ave., Pasadena, 91103, Los Angeles County, (818)796-8151, 7 miles NE of Los Angeles.
Architect: William P. Bell. **Green fee:** $16/$35. **Credit cards:** MC,VISA,AMEX.
Reduced fees: Weekdays, twilight, seniors, juniors. **Caddies:** No. **Golf carts:** $11.
Discount golf packages: No. **Season:** Year-round. **High:** April-Oct. **On site lodging:** No. **Rental clubs:** Yes. **Metal spikes allowed:** Yes. **To obtain tee times:** Call up to 7 days ahead for weekdays, Mondays after 9:30 a.m. for Saturday and Tuesdays after 9:30 for Sunday.
★★★C.W. KOINER COURSE
Opened: 1928. **Holes:** 18. **Par:** 72/75. **Yards:** 7,037/6,104. **Course rating:** 74.5/74.7.
Slope: 134/128. **Walking policy:** Walking at certain times. **Range:** Yes (grass/mats).
Notes: 1968 Los Angeles Open.
Subscriber comments: Historic "old style" course, lots of fun...Long par 4s always in good shape...Better of the two courses...Flat layout...Playing around Rose Bowl is great...Overrated, beat up...Pretty nice for a parking lot (Rose Bowl)...Great course, long from blue tees...Crowded at times.
★★½E.O. NAY COURSE
Opened: 1952. **Holes:** 18. **Par:** 70/71. **Yards:** 6,046/5,377. **Course rating:** 68.4/70.5.
Slope: 115/117. **Walking policy:** Unrestricted walking. **Range:** Yes (mats).
Subscriber comments: Short and open, greens bumpy...Overrated...Very penal rough, good par 5s, otherwise easy...Shouldn't allow cars to park on during football and soccer season...Not much character...Too crowded.

★★½CALIMESA COUNTRY CLUB
PU-1300 S3rd St, Calimesa, 92320, Riverside County, (909)795-2488, 8 miles E of Redlands.
Opened: 1965. **Holes:** 18. **Par:** 70/72. **Yards:** 5,970/5,293. **Course rating:** 67.3/69.6.
Slope: 114/112. **Architect:** N/A. **Green fee:** $9/$22. **Credit cards:** MC,VISA,AMEX.
Reduced fees: Weekdays, twilight. **Caddies:** No. **Golf carts:** $10. **Discount golf packages:** No. **Season:** Year-round. **High:** N/A. **On site lodging:** No. **Rental clubs:** No. **Walking policy:** Unrestricted walking. **Metal spikes allowed:** Yes. **Range:** No. **To obtain tee times:** Call up to 7 days in advance.
Subscriber comments: Slow play ruined beautiful course...A course of doglegs, not too interesting...Playable, challenging...Scruffy course, nice price...Short, tricky layout.

★★½CAMARILLO SPRINGS GOLF COURSE
PU-791 Camarillo Springs Rd., Camarillo, 93012, Ventura County, (805)484-1075, 54 miles N of Los Angeles.
Opened: 1972. **Holes:** 18. **Par:** 72/72. **Yards:** 6,375/5,297. **Course rating:** 70.2/70.2.
Slope: 115/116. **Architect:** Ted Robinson. **Green fee:** $22/$60. **Credit cards:** MC,VISA. **Reduced fees:** Weekdays, resort guests, twilight, seniors, juniors. **Caddies:** No. **Golf carts:** Included in Green Fee. **Discount golf packages:** Yes. **Season:** Year-round. **High:** May-Aug. **On site lodging:** No. **Rental clubs:** Yes. **Walking policy:** Mandatory cart. **Metal spikes allowed:** Yes. **Range:** Yes. **To obtain tee times:** Call seven days in advance.

★★★CANYON LAKES COUNTRY CLUB
PU-640 Bollinger Canyon Way, San Ramon, 94583, Contra Costa County, (510)735-6511, 30 miles E of San Francisco.
Opened: 1987. **Holes:** 18. **Par:** 71/71. **Yards:** 6,731/5,234. **Course rating:** 70.9/69.9.
Slope: 124/121. **Architect:** Ted Robinson. **Green fee:** $60/$75. **Credit cards:** MC,VISA. **Reduced fees:** N/A. **Caddies:** No. **Golf carts:** Included in Green Fee. **Discount golf packages:** No. **Season:** Year-round. **High:** Feb.-Oct. **On site lodging:** No. **Rental clubs:** Yes. **Walking policy:** Mandatory cart. **Metal spikes allowed:** Yes. **Range:** No. **To obtain tee times:** Call up to 7 days in advance.
Subscriber comments: Short, good greens...Overpriced...Tough and interesting course...Carts a must. Lots of hills...Course fit into housing development...Great condition. Fun for anyone...Last two holes are killers...Good course to play in the fall...Gated-community golf course.

★★CANYON SOUTH GOLF COURSE
PU-1097 Murray Canyon Dr., Palm Springs, 92264, Riverside County, (760)327-2019, 100 miles E of Los Angeles.
Opened: 1963. **Holes:** 18. **Par:** 71/71. **Yards:** 6,536/5,685. **Course rating:** 69.8/72.0. **Slope:** 119/117. **Architect:** William F. Bell. **Green fee:** $25/$60. **Credit cards:** MC,VISA,AMEX. **Reduced fees:** Weekdays, low season, twilight. **Caddies:** No. **Golf carts:** Included in Green Fee. **Discount golf packages:** No. **Season:** Nov.-Sept. **High:** Jan.-March. **On site lodging:** No. **Rental clubs:** Yes. **Walking policy:** Mandatory cart. **Metal spikes allowed:** Yes. **Range:** Yes (grass). **To obtain tee times:** We take tee times up to one week in advance.

★★★½CARLTON OAKS COUNTRY CLUB
PU-9200 Inwood Dr., Santee, 92071, San Diego County, (619)448-8500, (800)831-6757, 20 miles NE of San Diego.
Opened: 1990. **Holes:** 18. **Par:** 72/72. **Yards:** 7,088/4,548. **Course rating:** 74.6/62.1. **Slope:** 137/114. **Architect:** Perry Dye. **Green fee:** $65/$75. **Credit cards:** MC,VISA,AMEX. **Reduced fees:** Resort guests, twilight. **Caddies:** No. **Golf carts:** Included in Green Fee. **Discount golf packages:** Yes. **Season:** Year-round. **High:** N/A. **On site lodging:** Yes. **Rental clubs:** Yes. **Walking policy:** Walking at certain times. **Metal spikes allowed:** Yes. **Range:** Yes (grass/mats). **To obtain tee times:** Call up to 7 days in advance.
Subscriber comments: Nice golf course...Nice course but play in winter; grass brown in summer...Well designed, with all the Dye trademarks: Waste areas, railroad ties, blind shots...A good test of skill with interesting course design...Lovely gem, quiet and dangerous...Helps to have a long drive...Gets hot in the summer.

★★★CARMEL MOUNTAIN RANCH COUNTRY CLUB
PU-14050 Carmel Ridge Rd., San Diego, 92128, San Diego County, (619)487-9224, 15 miles N of San Diego.
Opened: 1986. **Holes:** 18. **Par:** 72/72. **Yards:** 6,728/5,372. **Course rating:** 71.9/71.0. **Slope:** 131/122. **Architect:** Ron Fream. **Green fee:** $60/$70. **Credit cards:** MC,VISA,AMEX. **Reduced fees:** Twilight, seniors, juniors. **Caddies:** No. **Golf carts:** Included in Green Fee. **Discount golf packages:** No. **Season:** Year-round. **High:** N/A. **On site lodging:** No. **Rental clubs:** Yes. **Walking policy:** Mandatory cart. **Metal spikes allowed:** Yes. **Range:** Yes (mats). **To obtain tee times:** Call up to 7 days in advance.
Subscriber comments: Blues only for the brave...Usually in excellent shape; very challenging...Condos left, condos right...Hilly and spread out among homes...Good test but you need a guide to find next tee...Good condition but will be better with maturing...Beautiful—good mixture of difficulty.

★★★½CARMEL VALLEY RANCH GOLF CLUB
R-1 Old Ranch Rd., Carmel, 93923, Monterey County, (408)626-2510, (800)422-7635.
Opened: 1981. **Holes:** 18. **Par:** 70/70. **Yards:** 6,515/5,088. **Course rating:** 70.1/69.6. **Slope:** 124/135. **Architect:** Pete Dye. **Green fee:** $135/$175. **Credit cards:** MC,VISA,AMEX,Diners Club. **Reduced fees:** Resort guests, juniors. **Caddies:** No. **Golf carts:** Included in Green Fee. **Discount golf packages:** Yes. **Season:** Year-round. **High:** April-Nov. **On site lodging:** Yes. **Rental clubs:** Yes. **Walking policy:** Mandatory cart. **Metal spikes allowed:** No. **Range:** Yes (grass). **To obtain tee times:** Resort guests anytime with resort reservation. Public, call golf shop.
Subscriber comments: Fun resort course, great area....Great conditions, great views, great greens...Very tight track. Accuracy needed...Front nine fun, back nine a bear...Redesign a big improvement...Tricked up back nine.

★★½CASTLE CREEK COUNTRY CLUB
8797 Circle R Dr., Escondido, 92026, San Diego County, (760)749-2422, (800)619-2465, 30 miles N of San Diego.
Opened: 1956. **Holes:** 18. **Par:** 72/72. **Yards:** 6,396/4,800. **Course rating:** 70.8/67.4. **Slope:** 124/108. **Architect:** Jack Daray Sr.. **Green fee:** $22/$40. **Credit cards:** All major. **Reduced fees:** Weekdays, low season, twilight. **Caddies:** No. **Golf carts:** $10. **Discount golf packages:** Yes. **Season:** Year-round. **High:** Jan.-April. **On site lodging:** No. **Rental clubs:** Yes. **Walking policy:** Unrestricted walking. **Metal spikes allowed:**

Yes. **Range:** No. **To obtain tee times:** Call 7 days in advance.
Subscriber comments: Well-maintained course, some great holes...Tough back nine, holes 10, 11, 12 very narrow...Sporty, fun, improving conditions, good for walkers...Scenic valley layout...Good test with risk/reward holes.

★★★½CASTLE OAKS GOLF CLUB
PU-1000 Castle Oaks Dr., Ione, 95640, Amador County, (209)274-0167, 30 miles SE of Sacramento.
Opened: 1994. **Holes:** 18. **Par:** 71/71. **Yards:** 6,739/4,953. **Course rating:** 72.3/67.3.
Slope: 129/114. **Architect:** Bradford Benz. **Green fee:** $16/$34. **Credit cards:** MC,VISA. **Reduced fees:** Weekdays, twilight, seniors, juniors. **Caddies:** No. **Golf carts:** $10. **Discount golf packages:** No. **Season:** Year-round. **High:** Sping-Fall. **On site lodging:** No. **Rental clubs:** Yes. **Walking policy:** Walking at certain times. **Metal spikes allowed:** Yes. **Range:** Yes (grass). **To obtain tee times:** Call up to 7 days in advance.
Subscriber comments: Great course, love the 1st and 18th holes...Best-kept secret in the valley...Best two finishing holes...Hidden gem...Best public course in Sacramento area...Oak trees, marshes, very nice setting...Excellent, arguably six signature holes...Beautiful foothills course...Great risk/reward 18th...Country club shape

★★★CHALK MOUNTAIN GOLF CLUB
PU-10000 El Bordo Ave., Atascadero, 93422, San Luis Obispo County, (805)466-8848.
Call club for further information.
Subscriber comments: Interesting short holes...Fun to play, lots of placement tee shots...Tougher than it looks..."Heart attack" hill is something else...Good views...Short, but challenging due to tightness and elevations...Play with someone who knows course.

THE CHARDONNAY GOLF CLUB
PU-2555 Jameson Canyon Rd. Hwy. 12, Napa, 94558, Napa County, (707)257-1900, (800)788-0136, 38 miles NE of San Francisco.
Architect: Algie Pulley. **Credit cards:** MC,VISA,AMEX,JCB. **Caddies:** No. **Golf carts:** Included in Green Fee. **Season:** Year-round. **High:** April-Oct. **On site lodging:** No.
Rental clubs: Yes. **Walking policy:** Mandatory cart. **Metal spikes allowed:** Yes.
Range: Yes (grass). **To obtain tee times:** Call up to 14 days in advance.
★★★½CLUB SHAKESPEARE
Opened: 1992. **Holes:** 18. **Par:** 72/72. **Yards:** 7,001/5,448. **Course rating:** 74.5/70.9.
Slope: 137/125. **Green fee:** $110/$110. **Reduced fees:** N/A. **Discount golf packages:** No.
Subscriber comments: Memorable course in the Wine Country...Extremely diverse holes. Great condition...Fun course, demands great tee shots...Beautiful course among the vineyards...Back nine tough but spectacular...A cut above sister track...Island green a treat...Excellent condition...Pretty, pretty long.
★★★VINEYARDS COURSE
Opened: 1987. **Holes:** 18. **Par:** 71/71. **Yards:** 6,811/5,200. **Course rating:** 73.7/70.1.
Slope: 133/126. **Green fee:** $45/$80. **Reduced fees:** Weekdays, low season, twilight.
Discount golf packages: Yes.
Subscriber comments: Vineyards provide a great setting...One of the most intriguing layouts in Northern California...The views are fantastic and the golf challenging, the greens come in all shapes and sizes...Beautiful in fall...Windy, but fun to play...Home of the ball-eating grape vines...Nearly as good as her twin.

★★½CHERRY ISLAND GOLF COURSE
PU-2360 Elverta Rd., Elverta, 95626, Sacramento County, (916)991-7293, 10 miles N of Sacramento.
Opened: 1990. **Holes:** 18. **Par:** 72/72. **Yards:** 6,562/5,163. **Course rating:** 71.1/70.0.
Slope: 124/117. **Architect:** Robert Muir Graves. **Green fee:** $17/$23. **Credit cards:** None. **Reduced fees:** Weekdays, low season, twilight, seniors, juniors. **Caddies:** No.
Golf carts: $22. **Discount golf packages:** No. **Season:** Year-round. **High:** April-Nov.
On site lodging: No. **Rental clubs:** Yes. **Walking policy:** Unrestricted walking. **Metal spikes allowed:** Yes. **Range:** Yes (grass/mats). **To obtain tee times:** Call up to 7 days in advance starting at 6:30 a.m. Call on Monday for weekend times.
Subscriber comments: Funny layout...Some contrived holes...It grows on you...A real premium on ability to place shots...Course spoiled by too many trick holes.

★★CHESTER WASHINGTON GOLF COURSE
PU-1930 W. 120th St., Los Angeles, 90047, Los Angeles County, (213)756-6975.
Holes: 18. **Par:** 70/70. **Yards:** 6,348/5,646. **Slope:** 107/115. **Season:** Year-round. **High:** June-Aug. Call club for further information.

★★CHIMNEY ROCK GOLF COURSE
PU-5320 Silverado Trail, Napa, 94558, Napa County, (707)255-3363, 62 miles NE of San Francisco.
Opened: 1965. **Holes:** 9. **Par:** 72/72. **Yards:** 6,824/5,866. **Course rating:** 71.5/73.0.
Slope: 115/122. **Architect:** N/A. **Green fee:** $18/$22. **Credit cards:** MC,VISA.
Reduced fees: N/A. **Caddies:** No. **Golf carts:** $20. **Discount golf packages:** No.
Season: Year-round. **High:** June-Aug. **On site lodging:** No. **Rental clubs:** No. **Walking policy:** Unrestricted walking. **Metal spikes allowed:** Yes. **Range:** No. **To obtain tee times:** Call up to 14 days in advance.

★★CHINA LAKE GOLF CLUB
411 Midway, China Lake, 93555, Kern County, (760)939-2990.
Call club for further information.

CHUCK CORICA GOLF COMPLEX
PM-No.1 Clubhouse Memorial Rd., Alameda, 94501, Alameda County, (510)522-4321, 5 miles W of Oakland.
Green fee: $14/$25. **Credit cards:** MC,VISA. **Reduced fees:** Weekdays, twilight, seniors, juniors. **Caddies:** No. **Golf carts:** $22. **Discount golf packages:** No. **Season:** Year-round. **High:** May-Oct. **On site lodging:** No. **Rental clubs:** Yes. **Walking policy:** Unrestricted walking. **Metal spikes allowed:** Yes. **Range:** Yes (mats). **To obtain tee times:** Call up to 7 days in advance.
★★½EARL FRY COURSE
Opened: 1927. **Holes:** 18. **Par:** 71/72. **Yards:** 6,141/5,560. **Course rating:** 69.2/71.0.
Slope: 119/114. **Architect:** William Lock/Desmond Muirhead.
★★JACK CLARK SOUTH COURSE
Opened: N/A. **Holes:** 18. **Par:** 71/71. **Yards:** 6,559/5,473. **Course rating:** 70.8/70.0.
Slope: 119/110. **Architect:** William P. Bell/Robert Muir Graves.

★★CHULA VISTA MUNICIPAL GOLF COURSE
PM-4475 Bonita Rd., Bonita, 91902, San Diego County, (619)479-4141, (800)833-8463, 10 miles S of San Diego.
Opened: N/A. **Holes:** 18. **Par:** 73/74. **Yards:** 6,759/5,776. **Course rating:** 72.3/72.7.
Slope: 128/124. **Architect:** Harry Rainville. **Green fee:** $18/$26. **Credit cards:** MC,VISA. **Reduced fees:** Weekdays, twilight, seniors, juniors. **Caddies:** No. **Golf carts:** $11. **Discount golf packages:** No. **Season:** Year-round. **High:** July-Sept. **On site lodging:** No. **Rental clubs:** Yes. **Walking policy:** Unrestricted walking. **Metal spikes allowed:** Yes. **Range:** Yes (grass/mats). **To obtain tee times:** Call 5 days in advance. Call 8 to 30 days in advance for $1 surcharge.

★★CITY OF SAN MATEO GOLF COURSE
PM-1700 Coyote Point Dr., San Mateo, 94401, San Mateo County, (415)347-1461, 18 miles S of San Francisco.
Opened: 1933. **Holes:** 18. **Par:** 70/72. **Yards:** 5,853/5,451. **Course rating:** 67.0/69.8.
Slope: 104/115. **Architect:** WPA. **Green fee:** $21/$26. **Credit cards:** None. **Reduced fees:** Weekdays, twilight, juniors. **Caddies:** No. **Golf carts:** $21. **Discount golf packages:** No. **Season:** Year-round. **High:** June-Aug. **On site lodging:** No. **Rental clubs:** Yes. **Walking policy:** Unrestricted walking. **Metal spikes allowed:** Yes. **Range:** No. **To obtain tee times:** Call 7 days in advance.

★★COLTON GOLF CLUB
PU-1901 W. Valley Blvd., Colton, 92324, San Bernardino County, (909)877-1712.
Call club for further information.

★½CORDOVA GOLF COURSE
9425 Jackson Rd, Sacramento, 95826, Sacramento County, (916)362-1196, 9 miles E of Sacramento.

Opened: 1960. **Holes:** 18. **Par:** 63/66. **Yards:** 4,755/4,728. **Course rating:** 61.2/64.9. **Slope:** 90/96. **Architect:** N/A. **Green fee:** $8/$10. **Credit cards:** N/A. **Reduced fees:** Weekdays, seniors, juniors. **Caddies:** No. **Golf carts:** $15. **Discount golf packages:** No. **Season:** Year-round. **High:** N/A. **On site lodging:** No. **Rental clubs:** Yes. **Walking policy:** Unrestricted walking. **Metal spikes allowed:** Yes. **Range:** Yes (grass/mats). **To obtain tee times:** Call Monday after 10 a.m. for weekend and holiday. Call Friday after 10 a.m. for next weekday.

★★★CORONADO GOLF COURSE

PM-2000 Visalia Row, Coronado, 92118, San Diego County, (619)435-3121, 2 miles S of San Diego.
Opened: 1957. **Holes:** 18. **Par:** 72/72. **Yards:** 6,633/5,784. **Course rating:** 71.8/73.7. **Slope:** 124/126. **Architect:** Jack Daray Sr. **Green fee:** $20/$20. **Credit cards:** MC,VISA. **Reduced fees:** Twilight, juniors. **Caddies:** No. **Golf carts:** $10. **Discount golf packages:** No. **Season:** Year-round. **High:** All. **On site lodging:** No. **Rental clubs:** Yes. **Walking policy:** Walking at certain times. **Metal spikes allowed:** Yes. **Range:** Yes. **To obtain tee times:** Call 2 days in advance at 7 a.m. Up to 14 days in advance you may buy a time for 11 a.m. or later for $30. Fee must be paid at least 3 days in advance.
Subscriber comments: Always good weather conditions...Great course for walking, beautiful bay view...Pool-table flat... Beautiful scenery of San Diego Harbor..."Never a bad day at Coronado"...A gem, don't miss it...Great course right in the middle of the city. I can see why the President likes it...Love the ocean holes.

COSTA MESA COUNTRY CLUB

PM-1701 Golf Course Dr., Costa Mesa, 92626, Orange County, (714)540-7500, 25 miles S of Los Angeles.
Opened: N/A. **Architect:** William F. Bell. **Credit cards:** None. **Reduced fees:** Twilight, seniors, juniors. **Caddies:** No. **Golf carts:** $22. **Discount golf packages:** No. **Season:** Year-round. **High:** Year-round. **On site lodging:** No. **Rental clubs:** Yes. **Walking policy:** Unrestricted walking. **Metal spikes allowed:** Yes. **Range:** Yes (grass/mats). **To obtain tee times:** Call up to 7 days in advance or Monday for Saturday, Sunday, Monday.

★★LOS LAGOS COURSE

Holes: 18. **Par:** 72/72. **Yards:** 6,542/5,925. **Course rating:** 70.7/73.3. **Slope:** 116/118. **Green fee:** $18/$24.

★★MESA LINDA COURSE

Holes: 18. **Par:** 70/70. **Yards:** 5,486/4,591. **Course rating:** 66.0/65.6. **Slope:** 104/103. **Green fee:** $17/$22.

★★★COYOTE HILLS GOLF COURSE

PU-1440 E. Bastachury Rd., Fullerton, 92635, Orange County, (714)672-6800, 5 miles N of Anaheim.
Opened: 1996. **Holes:** 18. **Par:** 70/70. **Yards:** 6,510/4,437. **Course rating:** 71.1/64.2. **Slope:** 128/108. **Architect:** Cal Olson/Payne Stewart. **Green fee:** $60/$85. **Credit cards:** MC,VISA,AMEX. **Reduced fees:** Twilight, juniors. **Caddies:** No. **Golf carts:** Included in Green Fee. **Discount golf packages:** No. **Season:** Year-round. **High:** Year-round. **On site lodging:** No. **Rental clubs:** Yes. **Walking policy:** Walking at certain times. **Metal spikes allowed:** Yes. **Range:** Yes (grass/mats). **To obtain tee times:** Call golf shop.
Subscriber comments: Payne Stewart's "jewel"...Challenging course...Bikini wax on greens...Excellent layout...Better be straight...Beautiful new course...Overpriced, gimmicky, plays around oil derricks...Fantastic views and elevation changes, great layout...Two very different nines, score on the front...Environmentally safe areas give you free drops...Short but testy, great new course.

★★½CREEKSIDE GOLF COURSE

PU-701 Lincoln Ave., Modesto, 95354, Stanislaus County, (209)571-5123, 25 miles S of Stockton.
Opened: 1992. **Holes:** 18. **Par:** 72/72. **Yards:** 6,610/5,496. **Course rating:** 70.3/69.5. **Slope:** 115/108. **Architect:** Halsey/Daray. **Green fee:** $8/$20. **Credit cards:** None. **Reduced fees:** Weekdays, twilight, seniors, juniors. **Caddies:** No. **Golf carts:** $20. **Discount golf packages:** No. **Season:** Year-round. **High:** May-Sept. **On site lodging:**

No. **Rental clubs:** Yes. **Walking policy:** Unrestricted walking. **Metal spikes allowed:** Yes. **Range:** Yes (grass). **To obtain tee times:** Call up to 7 days in advance beginning at 7 a.m.
Subscriber comments: Still young, not too many big trees, pretty flat...Interesting, well kept. Very nice course...Good young muny...Too flat...In good shape, pretty wide open...Rock-hard ground...Hot in summer, not enough water fountains...Maturing nicely.

★★½CRYSTAL SPRINGS GOLF CLUB
6650 Golf Course Dr., Burlingame, 94010, San Mateo County, (415)342-0603, 20 miles S of San Francisco.
Opened: 1920. **Holes:** 18. **Par:** 72/72. **Yards:** 6,683/5,920. **Course rating:** 72.1/74.0.
Slope: 125/130. **Architect:** Herbert Fowler. **Green fee:** $40/$60. **Credit cards:** MC,VISA,AMEX. **Reduced fees:** Weekdays, twilight, juniors. **Caddies:** No. **Golf carts:** $12. **Discount golf packages:** No. **Season:** Year-round. **High:** March-Oct. **On site lodging:** No. **Rental clubs:** Yes. **Walking policy:** Walking at certain times. **Metal spikes allowed:** Yes. **Range:** Yes (mats). **To obtain tee times:** Call up to 7 days in advance for weekdays. For weekends, call Monday before.
Subscriber comments: Built along a reservoir, has fantastic views...Golf on the San Andreas fault...Hilly course, never a flat lie...The deer enjoy it...Very hilly, beautiful vistas of San Francisco...A little work and this could be the best value in Bay Area.

★★★CYPRESS GOLF CLUB
PU-4921 Katella Ave., Los Alamitos, 90720, Orange County, (714)527-1800, 22 miles S of Los Angeles.
Opened: 1992. **Holes:** 18. **Par:** 71/71. **Yards:** 6,510/4,569. **Course rating:** 72.6/66.5.
Slope: 140/117. **Architect:** Perry Dye. **Green fee:** $50/$100. **Credit cards:** All major,JCB. **Reduced fees:** Weekdays, twilight, seniors. **Caddies:** No. **Golf carts:** Included in Green Fee. **Discount golf packages:** Yes. **Season:** Year-round. **High:** April-Oct. **On site lodging:** No. **Rental clubs:** Yes. **Walking policy:** Unrestricted walking. **Metal spikes allowed:** No. **Range:** Yes (grass/mats). **To obtain tee times:** Call up to 7 days in advance.
Subscriber comments: A real challenge...Next to a horse racetrack...Tight fairways, many mounds, lots of water...Overpriced, can't stand the horse smell...Stadium-type course...Redesign by Perry Dye improved course a lot...Nine lakes on 13 holes...Biggest claim to fame: Tiger Woods played here.

★★DAD MILLER GOLF COURSE
PM-430 N. Gilbert St., Anaheim, 92801, Orange County, (714)774-8055, 20 miles E of Los Angeles.
Opened: N/A. **Holes:** 18. **Par:** 71/71. **Yards:** 6,025/5,362. **Course rating:** 68.0/70.2.
Slope: 108/116. **Architect:** Dick Miller/Wayne Friday. **Green fee:** $18/$24. **Credit cards:** MC,VISA. **Reduced fees:** Weekdays, seniors. **Caddies:** No. **Golf carts:** $22. **Discount golf packages:** No. **Season:** Year-round. **High:** Year-round. **On site lodging:** No. **Rental clubs:** Yes. **Walking policy:** Unrestricted walking. **Metal spikes allowed:** Yes. **Range:** Yes (grass/mats). **To obtain tee times:** Call tee times phone up to 10 p.m., or call golf shop between 6 a.m. and 6 p.m. up to 8 days in advance.

★★½DAVIS GOLF COURSE
PU-24439 Fairway Dr., Davis, 95616, Yolo County, (916)756-4010, 12 miles W of Sacramento.
Opened: 1964. **Holes:** 18. **Par:** 66/66. **Yards:** 4,895/4,422. **Course rating:** 62.3/63.9.
Slope: 97/95. **Architect:** Bob Baldock. **Green fee:** $7/$14. **Credit cards:** MC,VISA. **Reduced fees:** Weekdays, twilight, seniors, juniors. **Caddies:** No. **Golf carts:** $17. **Discount golf packages:** No. **Season:** Year-round. **High:** N/A. **On site lodging:** No. **Rental clubs:** Yes. **Walking policy:** Unrestricted walking. **Metal spikes allowed:** Yes. **Range:** Yes (mats). **To obtain tee times:** Call golf shop up to 7 days in advance.

★★½DEBELL GOLF CLUB
PU-1500 Walnut Ave., Burbank, 91504, Los Angeles County, (818)845-0022, 3 miles N of Los Angeles.
Opened: 1958. **Holes:** 18. **Par:** 71/73. **Yards:** 5,610/5,412. **Course rating:** 67.4/72.9.
Slope: 108/126. **Architect:** William F. Bell/William H. Johnson. **Green fee:** $15/$19.
Credit cards: None. **Reduced fees:** Weekdays, low season, twilight, seniors, juniors.

Caddies: No. Golf carts: $20. Discount golf packages: No. Season: Year-round. High: Year-round. On site lodging: No. Rental clubs: Yes. Walking policy: Unrestricted walking. Metal spikes allowed: Yes. Range: Yes (mats). To obtain tee times: Call pro shop up to 5 days in advance.

Subscriber comments: Hilly, sporty, interesting...Many doglegs, leave driver in the garage...Very narrow, lots of thick woods...Mountain course, narrow fairways, slow greens......Tough opening hole...Lots of ups and downs for a tight canyon course.

★★★DELAVEAGA GOLF CLUB

PM-401 Upper Park Rd., Santa Cruz, 95065, Santa Cruz County, (408)423-7214, 25 miles S of San Jose.

Opened: 1970. Holes: 18. Par: 72/72. Yards: 6,010/5,331. Course rating: 70.4/70.6. Slope: 133/125. Architect: Bert Stamps. Green fee: $27/$37. Credit cards: All major. Reduced fees: Weekdays, twilight. Caddies: No. Golf carts: $15. Discount golf packages: No. Season: Year-round. High: July-Sept. On site lodging: No. Rental clubs: Yes. Walking policy: Unrestricted walking. Metal spikes allowed: Yes. Range: Yes (mats). To obtain tee times: Call up to 7 days in advance.

Subscriber comments: Great short course, excellent value, beautiful layout...Must hit it straight or end up in canyon...A classic...If you can't get on Pasatiempo, try this track...Great scenery...Trees everywhere...Very tight, the big dog slept most of the day...Nice location...Tight, hit it straight and score, well kept.

★★★DESERT DUNES GOLF CLUB

PU-19300 Palm Dr., Desert Hot Springs, 92240, Riverside County, (760)251-5367, (800)766-2767, 5 miles N of Palm Springs.

Opened: 1989. Holes: 18. Par: 72/72. Yards: 6,876/5,359. Course rating: 73.8/70.7. Slope: 142/122. Architect: Robert Trent Jones Jr. Green fee: $30/$120. Credit cards: MC,VISA,AMEX. Reduced fees: Weekdays, low season, resort guests, twilight, seniors, juniors. Caddies: No. Golf carts: Included in Green Fee. Discount golf packages: Yes. Season: Year-round. High: Jan.-May. On site lodging: No. Rental clubs: Yes. Walking policy: Unrestricted walking. Metal spikes allowed: Yes. Range: Yes (grass/mats). To obtain tee times: Call up to 7 days in advance.

Subscriber comments: Very challenging with wind...Good shape with tons of trees...Excellent summer treatment...Play early to avoid winds...Best in the valley, beautiful, terrific greens...No houses, no condos, pleasant change...The only Scottish Links in the desert...Keep your drives straight, may have rattlesnakes! High-desert links golf.

★★★½DESERT FALLS COUNTRY CLUB

1111 Desert Falls Pkwy., Palm Desert, 92211, Riverside County, (760)341-4020.

Opened: 1984. Holes: 18. Par: 72/72. Yards: 7,017/5,313. Course rating: 75.0/71.7. Slope: 145/124. Architect: Ron Fream. Green fee: $30/$130. Credit cards: MC,VISA. Reduced fees: Low season, twilight. Caddies: No. Golf carts: Included in Green Fee. Discount golf packages: No. Season: Year-round, except Oct.. High: Nov.-April. On site lodging: Yes. Rental clubs: Yes. Walking policy: Mandatory cart. Metal spikes allowed: Yes. Range: Yes (grass). To obtain tee times: Call three days in advance with credit card.

Subscriber comments: Except for 18, a truly great layout...Large greens...Big, mean sand traps...One of the best in the Coachella Valley...Outstanding course...Absolutely beautiful, challenging...Wow—in my top 10...Great course, great clubhouse...Great value, especially off-season...Fun layout.

★★★DESERT PRINCESS COUNTRY CLUB & RESORT

R-28-555 Landau Blvd., Cathedral City, 92234, Riverside County, (760)322-2280, (800)637-0577, 2 miles SE of Palm Springs.

Opened: 1984. Holes: 27. Architect: Davis Rainville. Green fee: $45/$115. Credit cards: MC,VISA,AMEX. Reduced fees: Weekdays, low season, resort guests, twilight. Caddies: No. Golf carts: Included in Green Fee. Discount golf packages: Yes. Season: Year-round. High: Nov.-May. On site lodging: Yes. Rental clubs: Yes. Walking policy: Mandatory cart. Metal spikes allowed: Yes. Range: Yes (grass). To obtain tee times: Resort guests call up to 30 days in advance.

CIELO/LAGOS

Par: 72/72. Yards: 6,587/5,217. Course rating: 71.2/69.8. Slope: 121/119.

CALIFORNIA

VISTA/CIELO
Par: 72/72. **Yards:** 6,764/5,273. **Course rating:** 72.5/70.3. **Slope:** 126/118.
VISTA/LAGOS
Par: 72/72. **Yards:** 6,667/5,298. **Course rating:** 71.8/69.9. **Slope:** 123/117.
Subscriber comments: Long, windy, true test to par...Fast greens, beautifully maintained...Distinct nines, good condition, fun golf...Flat but good golf...Lots of water and condos...Great scenery, variety of holes...Classy...Houses, pools etc. too close to fairways...Greens fast...Can get windy, wonderful condition.

DESERT WILLOW GOLF RESORT
PU-38-500 Portola Ave., Palm Desert, 92260, Riverside County, (760)346-7060, 130 miles E of Los Angeles.
Opened: 1997. **Holes:** 18. **Par:** 72/72. **Yards:** 7,056/5,079. **Course rating:** 73.9/69.0.
Slope: 131/120. **Architect:** Michael Hurdzan/Dana Fry/John Cook. **Green fee:** $35/$120. **Credit cards:** All major. **Reduced fees:** Weekdays, low season, twilight, juniors. **Caddies:** No. **Golf carts:** Included in Green Fee. **Discount golf packages:** No. **Season:** Year-round. **High:** Jan.-April. **On site lodging:** No. **Rental clubs:** Yes. **Walking policy:** Mandatory cart. **Metal spikes allowed:** Yes. **Range:** Yes (grass). **To obtain tee times:** Call golf shop up to 7 days in advance.

★★½DIABLO CREEK GOLF COURSE
PU-4050 Port Chicago Hwy., Concord, 94520, Contra Costa County, (510)686-6262, 40 miles NE of San Francisco.
Opened: 1962. **Holes:** 18. **Par:** 71/72. **Yards:** 6,866/5,872. **Course rating:** 72.2/72.5.
Slope: 122/119. **Architect:** Robert Muir Graves. **Green fee:** $17/$23. **Credit cards:** MC,VISA. **Reduced fees:** Weekdays, twilight, seniors, juniors. **Caddies:** No. **Golf carts:** $11. **Discount golf packages:** Yes. **Season:** Year-round. **High:** N/A. **On site lodging:** No. **Rental clubs:** Yes. **Walking policy:** Unrestricted walking. **Metal spikes allowed:** Yes. **Range:** Yes (mats). **To obtain tee times:** Call Mondays at noon to get available tee times.
Subscriber comments: Good value, nice layout...Flat, wide fairways; large, slow greens...Gets huge amount of play, not always in A-1 shape...Rattlesnakes!...Long and flat, tough when wind blows...Solid muny layout.

★★DIAMOND BAR GOLF CLUB
PU-22751 E. Golden Springs Dr., Diamond Bar, 91765, Los Angeles County, (909)861-8282, 25 miles E of Los Angeles.
Opened: 1964. **Holes:** 18. **Par:** 72/73. **Yards:** 6,810/6,009. **Course rating:** 72.8/73.9.
Slope: 125/122. **Architect:** William F. Bell. **Green fee:** $13/$23. **Credit cards:** All major,ATM. **Reduced fees:** Weekdays, twilight, seniors, juniors. **Caddies:** No. **Golf carts:** $11. **Discount golf packages:** No. **Season:** Year-round. **High:** N/A. **On site lodging:** No. **Rental clubs:** Yes. **Walking policy:** Unrestricted walking. **Metal spikes allowed:** Yes. **Range:** Yes (mats). **To obtain tee times:** Call golf shop up to 7 days in advance.

★★½DOUBLETREE CARMEL HIGHLAND RESORT
R-14455 Penasquitos Dr., San Diego, 92129, San Diego County, (619)672-9100, (800)622-9223, 20 miles N of San Diego.
Opened: 1967. **Holes:** 18. **Par:** 72/72. **Yards:** 6,428/5,361. **Course rating:** 70.7/71.9.
Slope: 123/125. **Architect:** Jack Daray. **Green fee:** $32/$52. **Credit cards:** MC,VISA,AMEX. **Reduced fees:** Weekdays, low season, resort guests, twilight, seniors, juniors. **Caddies:** No. **Golf carts:** Included in Green Fee. **Discount golf packages:** Yes. **Season:** Year-round. **High:** Jan.-April. **On site lodging:** Yes. **Rental clubs:** Yes. **Walking policy:** Walking at certain times. **Metal spikes allowed:** Yes. **Range:** Yes. **To obtain tee times:** Call up to 7 days in advance. Golf packages 30 days in advance.
Subscriber comments: Good course if you're a billy goat...A hidden treasure in San Diego...Quirky design...Good resort course. Short, but in good shape...Nice, tight layout, driving premium...Very hilly, hard greens...Nice facilities, but sidehill golf...Beautiful, very well maintained...Excellent short-game practice facility...Good conditions, strange layout.

★★★DRY CREEK RANCH GOLF COURSE
PU-809 Crystal Way, Galt, 95632, Sacramento County, (209)745-4653, 20 miles S of Sacramento.
Opened: 1962. **Holes:** 18. **Par:** 72/74. **Yards:** 6,773/5,952. **Course rating:** 72.7/73.9. **Slope:** 129/134. **Architect:** Jack Fleming. **Green fee:** $18/$28. **Credit cards:** MC,VISA. **Reduced fees:** Weekdays, low season, twilight. **Caddies:** No. **Golf carts:** $20. **Discount golf packages:** No. **Season:** Year-round. **High:** April-Sept. **On site lodging:** No. **Rental clubs:** Yes. **Walking policy:** Unrestricted walking. **Metal spikes allowed:** Yes. **Range:** Yes (grass/mats). **To obtain tee times:** Call up to 14 days in advance.
Subscriber comments: May be best public course in San Joaquin Valley...Good test of golf, rewarding and enjoyable...Toughest muny in Sacramento area...Memorable 18th hole...Great course in middle of nowhere...Mother of slow play lives here...Wide fairways, but lots of trouble (trees, traps)...Very challenging course.

★★DRYDEN PARK GOLF COURSE
PU-920 Sunset Ave., Modesto, 95351, Stanislaus County, (209)577-5359, 40 miles S of Stockton.
Opened: 1953. **Holes:** 18. **Par:** 72/74. **Yards:** 6,574/6,048. **Course rating:** 69.8/72.5. **Slope:** 119/115. **Architect:** William F. Bell/William P. Bell. **Green fee:** $16/$20. **Credit cards:** MC,VISA. **Reduced fees:** Weekdays, twilight, seniors, juniors. **Caddies:** No. **Golf carts:** $20. **Discount golf packages:** Yes. **Season:** Year-round. **High:** May-Sept. **On site lodging:** No. **Rental clubs:** Yes. **Walking policy:** Unrestricted walking. **Metal spikes allowed:** Yes. **Range:** Yes (grass/mats). **To obtain tee times:** Call tee times phone up to 7 days in advance beginning at 7 a.m.

★★★EAGLE CREST GOLF CLUB
PU-1656 Cloverdale Rd., Escondido, 92027, San Diego County, (760)737-9762, 20 miles NE of San Diego.
Opened: 1993. **Holes:** 18. **Par:** 72/72. **Yards:** 6,417/4,941. **Course rating:** 71.6/69.9. **Slope:** 136/123. **Architect:** David Rainville. **Green fee:** $43/$65. **Credit cards:** MC,VISA,AMEX. **Reduced fees:** Twilight, seniors, juniors. **Caddies:** No. **Golf carts:** Included in Green Fee. **Discount golf packages:** No. **Season:** Year-round. **High:** Jan.-April. **On site lodging:** No. **Rental clubs:** Yes. **Walking policy:** Walking at certain times. **Metal spikes allowed:** Yes. **Range:** Yes (grass). **To obtain tee times:** Call 7 days in advance.
Subscriber comments: Short, picturesque...A gem! But tight...Miss tree in middle of No.1 fairway...Natural wild setting...Better stay in the fairway...Very sporty course bounded by protected areas, pretty vistas...Will get better with age...Very tight, requires good iron shots...Lots of trouble, nice setting...Excellent greens, very challenging.

★★★EASTLAKE COUNTRY CLUB
PU-2375 Clubhouse Dr., Chula Vista, 91915, San Diego County, (619)482-5757, 20 miles SE of San Diego.
Opened: 1991. **Holes:** 18. **Par:** 72/72. **Yards:** 6,606/5,118. **Course rating:** 70.7/68.8. **Slope:** 116/114. **Architect:** Ted Robinson. **Green fee:** $25/$61. **Credit cards:** MC,VISA,AMEX. **Reduced fees:** Weekdays, twilight, seniors, juniors. **Caddies:** No. **Golf carts:** Included in Green Fee. **Discount golf packages:** No. **Season:** Year-round. **High:** Jan.-June. **On site lodging:** No. **Rental clubs:** Yes. **Walking policy:** Unrestricted walking. **Metal spikes allowed:** No. **Range:** Yes (grass/mats). **To obtain tee times:** Call up to 7 days in advance.
Subscriber comments: Not long and not very hard, but fun to play...Fair golf course inside housing development...Computer yardage in cart, cool...Lots of tee boxes for different skill levels...The water holes can get you...Interesting design, hilly, rolling fairways...Excellent range...Very good course, pleasant experience.

★★½EL DORADO PARK GOLF CLUB
PM-2400 Studebaker Rd., Long Beach, 90815, Los Angeles County, (562)430-5411.
Opened: 1960. **Holes:** 18. **Par:** 72/73. **Yards:** 6,401/5,918. **Course rating:** 70.6/74.3. **Slope:** 121/126. **Architect:** Ted Robinson. **Green fee:** $15/$23. **Credit cards:** MC,VISA,AMEX. **Reduced fees:** N/A. **Caddies:** No. **Golf carts:** $21. **Discount golf packages:** No. **Season:** Year-round. **High:** Year-round. **On site lodging:** No. **Rental**

clubs: Yes. **Walking policy:** Unrestricted walking. **Metal spikes allowed:** Yes. **Range:** Yes (grass/mats). **To obtain tee times:** Call up to 3 days in advance after 1 p.m. **Subscriber comments:** Nice layout...Trees line every hole. Water in play...Best in Long Beach...Holes 8, 9, and 10 are tough...Some narrow fairways...Greens are inconsistent...A good test of golf...Good mature course, fun to play...Difficult from back tees.

EL PRADO GOLF COURSE
PU-6555 Pine Ave., Chino, 91710, San Bernardino County, (909)597-1751, 30 miles E of Los Angeles.
Opened: 1976. **Architect:** Harry Rainville/David Rainville. **Green fee:** $10/$25. **Credit cards:** None. **Reduced fees:** Weekdays, low season, twilight, seniors, juniors. **Caddies:** No. **Golf carts:** $23. **Discount golf packages:** No. **Season:** Year-round. **High:** Year-round. **On site lodging:** No. **Rental clubs:** Yes. **Walking policy:** Unrestricted walking. **Metal spikes allowed:** Yes. **Range:** Yes (grass). **To obtain tee times:** Weekdays call 7 days in advance. Call Monday for upcoming weekend.

★★½BUTTERFIELD STAGE COURSE
Holes: 18. **Par:** 72/73. **Yards:** 6,508/5,503. **Course rating:** 70.6/72.0. **Slope:** 116/118.
Subscriber comments: Great round if you can handle the smell from nearby dairy farms...Literally a cow pasture, bring fly swatter...Very hard when windy...Excellent greens, not much character...OK golf...Wide open.

★★★CHINO CREEK
Holes: 18. **Par:** 72/73. **Yards:** 6,671/5,596. **Course rating:** 71.5/72.1. **Slope:** 119/121.
Subscriber comments: Nice course, lots of bugs...Consistently best public-course greens in area...Smell of cow pastures pretty strong on hot days...Best of the two courses here...Fast greens. Stay below the hole. You better like cows because they surround both courses...Gets dry in summer.

★★EL RANCHO VERDE COUNTRY CLUB
PU-Country Club Dr., Rialto, 92377, San Bernardino County, (909)875-5346, 5 miles W of San Bernardino.
Opened: N/A. **Holes:** 18. **Par:** 72/72. **Yards:** 6,800/5,589. **Course rating:** N/A. **Slope:** 124/118. **Architect:** Harry Rainville/David Rainville. **Green fee:** $10/$27. **Credit cards:** MC, VISA. **Reduced fees:** Weekdays, low season, twilight, seniors, juniors. **Caddies:** No. **Golf carts:** $10. **Discount golf packages:** No. **Season:** Year-round. **High:** Year-round. **On site lodging:** No. **Rental clubs:** Yes. **Walking policy:** Unrestricted walking. **Metal spikes allowed:** Yes. **Range:** Yes (grass/mats). **To obtain tee times:** Call up to 7 days in advance.

★★★EL RIVINO COUNTRY CLUB
PU-5530 El Rivino Rd. , P.O. Box 3369, Riverside, 92519, Riverside County, (909)684-8905, 3 miles SW of San Bernardino.
Opened: N/A. **Holes:** 18. **Par:** 73/73. **Yards:** 6,466/5,863. **Course rating:** N/A. **Slope:** 111/113. **Architect:** Joseph Calwell. **Green fee:** N/A. **Credit cards:** MC, VISA. **Reduced fees:** Weekdays, twilight. **Caddies:** No. **Golf carts:** N/A. **Discount golf packages:** No. **Season:** Year-round. **High:** Year-round. **On site lodging:** No. **Rental clubs:** No. **Walking policy:** N/A. **Metal spikes allowed:** Yes. **Range:** No. **To obtain tee times:** N/A.
Subscriber comments: Par-6 1st hole is unusual...Nice course, lots of water...Tight parallel fairways...Confidence builder...Worth a weekend outing with friends...Augusta of the Inland Empire. Must see, must play...Excellent...No driving range, no snack shop, only vending machines...Very good shape, lacks imagination, wide open.

★★★ELKINS RANCH GOLF COURSE
PU-1386 Chambersburg Rd., Fillmore, 93015, Ventura County, (805)524-1440, 20 miles NW of Valencia.
Opened: 1959. **Holes:** 18. **Par:** 71/73. **Yards:** 6,302/5,650. **Course rating:** 69.9/72.6. **Slope:** 117/122. **Architect:** William H. Tucker Jr./Bob Schipper. **Green fee:** $23/$29. **Credit cards:** MC, VISA. **Reduced fees:** Weekdays, twilight, seniors, juniors. **Caddies:** No. **Golf carts:** $11. **Discount golf packages:** No. **Season:** Year-round. **High:** April-Oct. **On site lodging:** No. **Rental clubs:** Yes. **Walking policy:** Unrestricted walking. **Metal spikes allowed:** Yes. **Range:** Yes (grass/mats). **To obtain tee times:** Call up to 10 days in advance.
Subscriber comments: Tremendous course, great cheeseburgers! Great elevated tee

shots...Pretty setting among orange groves and hills...A lot of character, lots of trees, some blind holes, water...17th hole the best...Great course if you can find it. Worth the trip...Beautiful setting and scenery...Makes you think tee to green...Tough par 4s.

EMERALD ISLE
PU-660 S El Camino Real, Oceanside, 92054, San Diego County, (760)721-4700, 25 miles N of San Diego.
Opened: 1987. **Holes:** 18. **Par:** 56. **Yards:** 2,780. **Course rating:** 55.6. **Slope:** N/A. **Architect:** N/A. **Green fee:** $14/$18. **Credit cards:** MC,VISA,AMEX. **Reduced fees:** N/A. **Caddies:** No. **Golf carts:** $18. **Discount golf packages:** No. **Season:** Year-round. **High:** July-Aug. **On site lodging:** No. **Rental clubs:** Yes. **Walking policy:** Unrestricted walking. **Metal spikes allowed:** Yes. **Range:** Yes (grass). **To obtain tee times:** Call or walk in for same day tee times.

★★★½EMPIRE LAKES GOLF COURSE
PU-11015 Sixth St., Rancho Cucamonga, 91730, San Bernardino County, (909)481-6663, 1 mile N of Ontario.
Opened: 1996. **Holes:** 18. **Par:** 72/72. **Yards:** 6,923/5,200. **Course rating:** 73.0/70.5. **Slope:** 127/125. **Architect:** Arnold Palmer/Ed Seay. **Green fee:** $50/$70. **Credit cards:** MC,VISA,AMEX,Diners Club. **Reduced fees:** Twilight, seniors, juniors. **Caddies:** No. **Golf carts:** N/A. **Discount golf packages:** No. **Season:** Year-round. **High:** Year-round. **On site lodging:** No. **Rental clubs:** Yes. **Walking policy:** Unrestricted walking. **Metal spikes allowed:** No. **Range:** Yes (grass). **To obtain tee times:** Call up to 7 days in advance.
Subscriber comments: Surprising find in Rancho Cucamonga...Tee off before noon to avoid strong winds later...Links, tight but fun course...Good target golf...What Palmer team did on flat land is great...Each set of tees gives you a different course...One of the most difficult in California.

★★★★FALL RIVER VALLEY GOLF & COUNTRY CLUB
PU-42889 State Hwy., 299 E., Fall River Mills, 96028, Shasta County, (916)336-5555, 70 miles NE of Redding.
Opened: 1978. **Holes:** 18. **Par:** 72/72. **Yards:** 7,365/6,200. **Course rating:** 74.1/74.6. **Slope:** 129/127. **Architect:** Clark Glasson. **Green fee:** $11/$24. **Credit cards:** None. **Reduced fees:** Weekdays, twilight, seniors, juniors. **Caddies:** No. **Golf carts:** $22. **Discount golf packages:** No. **Season:** March-Nov. **High:** May-Sept. **On site lodging:** No. **Rental clubs:** Yes. **Walking policy:** Unrestricted walking. **Metal spikes allowed:** Yes. **Range:** Yes (grass/mats). **To obtain tee times:** Call up to 14 days in advance.
Subscriber comments: Getaway treat. Well worth the trip...Beautiful setting, excellent layout, thinking man's course...Remote location. Never crowded. Beautiful views of Mt. Shasta...Northern California's finest...Favors long irons and fairway woods, with plenty of opportunities to slam away with driver...660-yard double dogleg par 5...Greens perfect...Best in state for the money.

(GREAT VALUE)

★★½FALLBROOK GOLF CLUB
PU-2757 Gird Rd., Fallbrook, 92028, San Diego County, (760)728-8334, 40 miles N of San Diego.
Opened: 1961. **Holes:** 18. **Par:** 72/72. **Yards:** 6,223/5,597. **Course rating:** 69.9/73.8. **Slope:** 119/130. **Architect:** Harry Rainville. **Green fee:** $9/$28. **Credit cards:** MC,VISA,DISC. **Reduced fees:** Weekdays, twilight, juniors. **Caddies:** No. **Golf carts:** $18. **Discount golf packages:** Yes. **Season:** Year-round. **High:** Year-round. **On site lodging:** No. **Rental clubs:** No. **Walking policy:** Unrestricted walking. **Metal spikes allowed:** Yes. **Range:** Yes (grass/mats). **To obtain tee times:** Call up to 10 days in advance.
Subscriber comments: Shotmaking course, fun to play...Good walking course...Open front nine, tight back nine...Well kept, country setting...Pretty, but not much to it...Keep driver in your bag on most holes...Course very scenic, but not in good condition...Nice short course...Wide fairways, large mature trees...Has some long tough holes.

★★½FIG GARDEN GOLF CLUB
7700 N. Van Ness Blvd., Fresno, 93711, Fresno County, (209)439-2928.
Opened: 1958. **Holes:** 18. **Par:** 72/72. **Yards:** 6,621/5,605. **Course rating:** 70.6/71.9.

Slope: 113/120. **Architect:** Nick Lombardo. **Green fee:** $40. **Credit cards:** MC,VISA,AMEX. **Reduced fees:** Weekdays, twilight, juniors. **Caddies:** No. **Golf carts:** $24. **Discount golf packages:** No. **Season:** Year-round. **High:** Year-round. **On site lodging:** No. **Rental clubs:** Yes. **Walking policy:** Unrestricted walking. **Metal spikes allowed:** Yes. **Range:** Yes. **To obtain tee times:** Call golf shop.
Subscriber comments: Narrow fairways, many trees, flat course, new 7th hole is nice...Nicest public course in Fresno...Fast fairways and greens...Crowded due to popularity with locals...Well maintained public track...Old, traditional course, good-sized trees.

★★★½FOUNTAINGROVE RESORT & COUNTRY CLUB

1525 Fountaingrove Pkwy., Santa Rosa, 95403, Sonoma County, (707)579-4653, 50 miles N of San Francisco.
Opened: 1985. **Holes:** 18. **Par:** 72/72. **Yards:** 6,797/5,644. **Course rating:** 72.8/72.1. **Slope:** 132/128. **Architect:** Ted Robinson. **Green fee:** $45/$70. **Credit cards:** MC,VISA,AMEX. **Reduced fees:** Weekdays, twilight. **Caddies:** No. **Golf carts:** Included in Green Fee. **Discount golf packages:** Yes. **Season:** Year-round. **High:** May-Oct. **On site lodging:** No. **Rental clubs:** Yes. **Walking policy:** Mandatory cart. **Metal spikes allowed:** Yes. **Range:** Yes (grass). **To obtain tee times:** Call up to 7 days in advance.
Subscriber comments: Beautiful layout...Beautiful vistas...10th, 17th holes are breathtaking...North Bay's best-kept secret...Toughest back nine in Bay Area—lots of OB...Every hole is different...Public course with a "private club" mentality...Beautifully maintained and pleasure to play...Hilly, many blind first and second shots...Very tough back nine...Must keep the ball straight.

★★★★ FOUR SEASONS RESORT AVIARA

R-7447 Batiquitos Dr., Carlsbad, 92009, San Diego County, (760)929-0077, 30 miles N of San Diego.
Opened: 1991. **Holes:** 18. **Par:** 72/72. **Yards:** 7,007/5,007. **Course rating:** 74.2/69.1. **Slope:** 137/119. **Architect:** Arnold Palmer/Ed Seay. **Green fee:** $135/$135. **Credit cards:** MC,VISA,AMEX,Diners Club, JCB. **Reduced fees:** Resort guests. **Caddies:** No. **Golf carts:** Included in Green Fee. **Discount golf packages:** Yes. **Season:** Year-round. **High:** April-Aug. **On site lodging:** Yes. **Rental clubs:** Yes. **Walking policy:** Mandatory cart. **Metal spikes allowed:** No. **Range:** Yes (grass/mats). **To obtain tee times:** Call up to 6 days in advance.
Subscriber comments: Beautiful view of lagoon...Great elevation changes...Great teaching academy...One great hole after another...Magnificent scenery, great test of golf...Some of the prettiest par 3s I've seen...Like Pebble, starts easy, then builds...Gorgeous wildflowers...Too pretty for golf—should be a garden...Pricey, play it at least once...Gives Augusta in April a challenge.

★★½FRANKLIN CANYON GOLF COURSE

PU-Highway 4, Hercules, 94547, Contra Costa County, (510)799-6191, 22 miles E of San Francisco.
Opened: 1968. **Holes:** 18. **Par:** 72/72. **Yards:** 6,776/5,516. **Course rating:** 70.9/71.2. **Slope:** 118/123. **Architect:** Robert Muir Graves. **Green fee:** $22/$47. **Credit cards:** MC,VISA,AMEX. **Reduced fees:** Weekdays, low season, twilight, seniors, juniors. **Caddies:** No. **Golf carts:** $12. **Discount golf packages:** Yes. **Season:** Year-round. **High:** N/A. **On site lodging:** No. **Rental clubs:** Yes. **Walking policy:** Unrestricted walking. **Metal spikes allowed:** Yes. **Range:** Yes (mats). **To obtain tee times:** Call golf shop up to 7 days in advance.
Subscriber comments: Course in good condition for high volume of play...Holes are fun and creative...Fairly easy layout, it's the everpresent wind that makes it tough...Nice elevation changes...242-yard par-3 11th nice...Challenging hill play...Best muny in East Bay area.

★★FRESNO WEST GOLF & COUNTRY CLUB

PU-23986 W. Whitesbridge Rd., Kerman, 93630, Fresno County, (209)846-8655, 23 miles W of Fresno.
Opened: 1966. **Holes:** 18. **Par:** 72/73. **Yards:** 6,959/6,000. **Course rating:** 72.6/74.1. **Slope:** 118/118. **Architect:** Bob Baldock. **Green fee:** $13/$16. **Credit cards:** MC,VISA. **Reduced fees:** Weekdays, low season, twilight, seniors, juniors. **Caddies:** No. **Golf**

carts: $20. **Discount golf packages:** No. **Season:** Year-round. **High:** N/A. **On site lodging:** No. **Rental clubs:** Yes. **Walking policy:** Unrestricted walking. **Metal spikes allowed:** Yes. **Range:** Yes (grass). **To obtain tee times:** Call 7 days in advance.

★½FURNACE CREEK GOLF COURSE
R-Hwy. 190, Death Valley, 92328, Inyo County, (760)786-2301, 140 miles NW of Las Vegas.
Opened: 1937. **Holes:** 18. **Par:** 70/71. **Yards:** 6,093/5,238. **Course rating:** 67.7/69.2. **Slope:** 103/111. **Architect:** William P. Bell/Perry Dye. **Green fee:** $30. **Credit cards:** All major. **Reduced fees:** Low season, resort guests, twilight. **Caddies:** No. **Golf carts:** $20. **Discount golf packages:** Yes. **Season:** Year-round. **High:** Oct.-May. **On site lodging:** Yes. **Rental clubs:** Yes. **Walking policy:** Unrestricted walking. **Metal spikes allowed:** Yes. **Range:** Yes (grass/mats). **To obtain tee times:** Call anytime.

★★★GOLD HILLS COUNTRY CLUB
SP-1950 Gold Hill Dr, Redding, 96003, Shasta County, (916)246-7867.
Opened: 1978. **Holes:** 18. **Par:** 72/72. **Yards:** 6,514/5,530. **Course rating:** 71.0/72.4. **Slope:** 130/127. **Architect:** N/A. **Green fee:** $18/$23. **Credit cards:** MC,VISA,DISC. **Reduced fees:** Seniors, juniors. **Caddies:** No. **Golf carts:** $10. **Discount golf packages:** No. **Season:** Year-round. **High:** March-June. **On site lodging:** Yes. **Rental clubs:** Yes. **Walking policy:** Unrestricted walking. **Metal spikes allowed:** No. **Range:** Yes (grass/mats). **To obtain tee times:** Call up to 7 days in advance.
Subscriber comments: Interesting holes, high enjoyment...Very challenging; lakes, trees and fast greens...Traditional layout...Relatively short course on paper, plays tough...Fun hot-weather course...Old course, tall trees, narrow, some hills, not long.

★★★½THE GOLF CLUB AT WHITEHAWK RANCH
R-1137 Hwy. 89, Clio, 96106, Plumas County, (916)836-0394, (800)332-4295, 60 miles W of Reno.
Opened: 1996. **Holes:** 18. **Par:** 71/71. **Yards:** 6,950/4,816. **Course rating:** 73.0/68.0. **Slope:** 134/110. **Architect:** Dick Bailey. **Green fee:** $60/$80. **Credit cards:** MC,VISA,AMEX. **Reduced fees:** Low season, resort guests, twilight, juniors. **Caddies:** No. **Golf carts:** Included in Green Fee. **Discount golf packages:** No. **Season:** May-Oct. **High:** June-Sept. **On site lodging:** Yes. **Rental clubs:** Yes. **Walking policy:** Unrestricted walking. **Metal spikes allowed:** Yes. **Range:** Yes (grass). **To obtain tee times:** Call golf shop. Credit Card required to guarantee time.
Subscriber comments: Good layout, scenic, plays fast...A challenge from each set of tees...Great for a new course...Starts great...A wonderful new mountain course to play...Scenery is tops...Very picturesque, interesting design.

GOLF RESORT AT INDIAN WELLS
44-500 Indian Wells Lane, Indian Wells, 92210, Riverside County, (760)346-4653, 19 miles E of Palm Springs.
Opened: 1986. **Architect:** Ted Robinson. **Green fee:** $40/$120. **Credit cards:** MC,VISA,AMEX,Diners Club. **Reduced fees:** Weekdays, low season, resort guests, twilight. **Caddies:** No. **Golf carts:** Included in Green Fee. **Discount golf packages:** Yes. **Season:** Year-round. **High:** Jan.-May. **On site lodging:** Yes. **Rental clubs:** Yes. **Walking policy:** Mandatory cart. **Metal spikes allowed:** Yes. **Range:** Yes (grass/mats). **To obtain tee times:** Stay at one of four participating hotels or call 3 days in advance. **Notes:** 1993 Senior PGA Gulfstream Invitational.
★★★½EAST COURSE
Holes: 18. **Par:** 72/72. **Yards:** 6,157/5,408. **Course rating:** 71.7/69.5. **Slope:** 122/117.
Subscriber comments: Great summer course, too expensive at other times...Not enough trouble for errant tee shot...Wide open, fun to play...Lush, manicured, moderately difficult...Excellent variety of holes for a desert course...Water comes into play a lot...Too many convention golfers...This place is awesome, even at 108 degrees.
★★★½WEST COURSE
Holes: 18. **Par:** 72/72. **Yards:** 6,500/5,408. **Course rating:** 70.7/69.0. **Slope:** 120/115.
Subscriber comments: Great variety of terrain and trouble...Slow-playing resort course...Beautiful conditioned course, a pleasure at a price...West is best...Very good layout...Fun course if no wind.

CALIFORNIA

★★★GRAEAGLE MEADOWS GOLF COURSE
R-Highway 89, Graeagle, 96103, Plumas County, (916)836-2323, 58 miles N of Reno.
Opened: 1967. **Holes:** 18. **Par:** 72/72. **Yards:** 6,680/5,640. **Course rating:** 70.7/71.3.
Slope: 119/127. **Architect:** Ellis Van Gorder. **Green fee:** $38. **Credit cards:** MC,VISA.
Reduced fees: Weekdays, twilight. **Caddies:** No. **Golf carts:** $24. **Discount golf packages:** Yes. **Season:** April-Nov. **High:** July-Aug. **On site lodging:** Yes. **Rental clubs:** Yes. **Walking policy:** Unrestricted walking. **Metal spikes allowed:** Yes. **Range:** Yes (grass). **To obtain tee times:** Call after February 1st for times during season.
Subscriber comments: Good course in the Sierras...Average course in beautiful location...Views galore...Good high-altitude test...Dogleg left 1st hole; look for "Chief"...Turtle-back greens are unpredictable...Fun resort course.

GREEN RIVER GOLF COURSE
PU-5215 Green River Rd., Corona, 91720, Riverside County, (909)737-7393, 25 miles S of San Bernardino.
Opened: 1965. **Green fee:** $23/$30. **Credit cards:** All major. **Reduced fees:** Twilight, juniors. **Caddies:** No. **Golf carts:** $11. **Discount golf packages:** No. **Season:** Year-round. **High:** N/A. **On site lodging:** No. **Rental clubs:** Yes. **Walking policy:** Unrestricted walking. **Metal spikes allowed:** Yes. **Range:** Yes (grass). **To obtain tee times:** Call 7 days in advance for weekday tee times. Call Monday for upcoming weekend.
★★½ORANGE COURSE
Holes: 18. **Par:** 71/72. **Yards:** 6,416/5,744. **Course rating:** 70.4/73.2. **Slope:** 119/120.
Architect: Harry Rainville.
Subscriber comments: Nice variety of holes...Too many fivesomes...Nice mountain views...Very narrow fairways, target golf...Nice new clubhouse...Windy every afternoon...Too many trees.
★★½RIVERSIDE COURSE
Holes: 18. **Par:** 71/71. **Yards:** 6,275/5,467. **Course rating:** 70.6/71.0. **Slope:** 122/115.
Architect: Harry Rainville/Cary Bickler.
Subscriber comments: Windy and slow...Good course, interesting layout...Lots of trees, fun to play, a good test...Nice old course for the money...Some great holes.

★★GREEN TREE GOLF CLUB
PU-999 Leisure Town Rd., Vacaville, 95687, Solano County, (707)448-1420, 30 miles W of Sacramento.
Opened: 1962. **Holes:** 18. **Par:** 71/71. **Yards:** 6,301/5,261. **Course rating:** 70.2/69.9.
Slope: 119/118. **Architect:** N/A. **Green fee:** $11/$22. **Reduced fees:** Twilight, seniors, juniors. **Credit cards:** MC,VISA. **Caddies:** No. **Golf carts:** $10. **Discount golf packages:** No. **Season:** Year-round. **High:** March-Nov. **On site lodging:** No. **Rental clubs:** Yes. **Walking policy:** Unrestricted walking. **Metal spikes allowed:** Yes. **Range:** Yes (mats). **To obtain tee times:** Call up to 7 days in advance.
EXECUTIVE COURSE
Holes: 9. **Par:** 29. **Yards:** 3,104. **Course rating:** 28.2. **Slope:** 80. **Green fee:** $8/$11.
Reduced fees: Seniors, juniors. **Golf carts:** N/A.

★★★GREEN TREE GOLF COURSE
14414 Green Tree Blvd., Victorville, 92392, San Bernardino County, (760)245-4860, 25 miles N of San Bernardino.
Opened: 1965. **Holes:** 18. **Par:** 72/72. **Yards:** 6,640/5,878. **Course rating:** 71.3/72.5.
Slope: 123/124. **Architect:** William F. Bell. **Green fee:** $17/$20. **Credit cards:** MC,VISA. **Reduced fees:** Weekdays, low season, resort guests, twilight, seniors, juniors. **Caddies:** No. **Golf carts:** $10. **Discount golf packages:** Yes. **Season:** Year-round. **High:** May-Sept. **On site lodging:** Yes. **Rental clubs:** Yes. **Walking policy:** Walking at certain times. **Metal spikes allowed:** Yes. **Range:** No. **To obtain tee times:** Call up to 14 days in advance.
Subscriber comments: Nice course. Difficult in places...Winds through housing tracts. Long walks from greens to tees...Mature course with trees...Tight fairways, nice greens.

★★★½GREENHORN CREEK GOLF CLUB
676 McCauley Ranch Rd., Angels Camp, 95222, (209)736-8110, (800)736-6203, 50 miles E of Stockton.

Opened: 1996. **Holes:** 18. **Par:** 72/72. **Yards:** 6,870/5,214. **Course rating:** 72.7/70.1. **Slope:** 130/119. **Architect:** Donald Boos/Patty Sheehan/Dick Lotz. **Green fee:** $27/$45. **Credit cards:** MC,VISA,AMEX. **Reduced fees:** Weekdays, resort guests, twilight, juniors. **Caddies:** No. **Golf carts:** $11. **Discount golf packages:** No. **Season:** Year-round. **High:** May-Oct. **On site lodging:** No. **Rental clubs:** Yes. **Walking policy:** Unrestricted walking. **Metal spikes allowed:** No. **Range:** Yes (grass/mats). **To obtain tee times:** Call up to 7 days in advance.

Subscriber comments: Best public course in Gold Country...Beautiful lodge...Just a youngster, potential ahead...Rolling fairways bordered by many oak trees, with many greens overlooking creeks and ponds...Computerized carts...Lots of local history...Fast greens, well manicured...Good par 3s...Worth the drive.

GRIFFITH PARK

PM-4730 Crystal Springs Dr., Los Angeles, 90027, Los Angeles County, (213)664-2255.

Architect: George C. Thomas Jr. **Green fee:** $10/$21. **Credit cards:** None. **Reduced fees:** Weekdays, twilight, seniors, juniors. **Caddies:** No. **Golf carts:** $10. **Discount golf packages:** No. **Season:** Year-round. **High:** March-Sept. **On site lodging:** No. **Rental clubs:** Yes. **Walking policy:** Unrestricted walking. **Metal spikes allowed:** Yes. **Range:** Yes (mats). **To obtain tee times:** Must have a City of L.A. reservation card to make tee times over the phone. To obtain a card, pick up application at any City course, fill out, pay fee, receive card. You can always come to the course and put your name on the waiting list with the starter.

★★½**HARDING COURSE**
Opened: 1924. **Holes:** 18. **Par:** 72/73. **Yards:** 6,536/6,028. **Course rating:** 70.4/72.5. **Slope:** 115/121.

Subscriber comments: Beautiful trees for LA...Very busy, well-maintained for number of people who play...Old established course...For public course, best shot in LA...Steep hills, tight fairways, short par 4s...Very natural, old-style...Heavily played muny, slow on weekends...Typical city course, fair condition, slow play.

★★★**WILSON COURSE**
Opened: 1923. **Holes:** 18. **Par:** 72/73. **Yards:** 6,942/6,330. **Course rating:** 72.7/74.6. **Slope:** 117/128.

Subscriber comments: Wilson longer and better than Harding, lots of trees, great character, wide fairways...More challenging than Harding; good layout...Great muny for the money...That's the 1st tee in the "I am Tiger Woods" commercial...Hardest of city courses...Some long holes, tight fairways for tee shots.

HAGGIN OAKS GOLF COURSE

PU-3645 Fulton Ave., Sacramento, 95821, Sacramento County, (916)481-4507.

Credit cards: None. **Reduced fees:** Weekdays, low season, twilight, seniors, juniors. **Caddies:** No. **Golf carts:** $10. **Discount golf packages:** No. **Season:** Year-round. **On site lodging:** No. **Rental clubs:** Yes. **Walking policy:** Unrestricted walking. **Metal spikes allowed:** Yes. **Range:** Yes (mats). **To obtain tee times:** Call up to 7 days in advance for weekdays and previous Tuesday after 6:30 a.m. for weekends and holidays.

★★**ALISTER MACKENZIE COURSE**
Opened: 1932. **Holes:** 18. **Par:** 72/72. **Yards:** 6,683/5,747. **Course rating:** 70.6/72.5. **Slope:** 112/124. **Architect:** Alister Mackenzie. **Green fee:** $10/$20. **High:** April-Oct. **Notes:** 1992 Women's Amateur.

★★½**ARCADE CREEK COURSE**
Opened: N/A. **Holes:** 18. **Par:** 72/72. **Yards:** 6,903/5,832. **Course rating:** 71.4/71.7. **Slope:** 115/111. **Architect:** Michael J. McDonagh. **Green fee:** $12/$19. **High:** April-Sept.

Special Notes: Usually played as two separate 9-hole courses, but may be played as 18-hole course.

★★★½**HALF MOON BAY GOLF CLUB**
PU-2000 Fairway Dr., Half Moon Bay, 94019, San Mateo County, (415)726-4438, 20 miles S of San Francisco.
Opened: 1973. **Holes:** 18. **Par:** 72/72. **Yards:** 7,131/5,769. **Course rating:** 75.0/73.3. **Slope:** 135/128. **Architect:** Francis Duane/Arnold Palmer. **Green fee:** $85/$105. **Credit cards:** MC,VISA. **Reduced fees:** Weekdays, resort guests, twilight. **Caddies:** No. **Golf**

carts: Included in Green Fee. **Discount golf packages:** Yes. **Season:** Year-round. **High:** N/A. **On site lodging:** Yes. **Rental clubs:** Yes. **Walking policy:** Mandatory cart. **Metal spikes allowed:** Yes. **Range:** No. **To obtain tee times:** Call 7 days in advance. **Subscriber comments:** Only two holes with ocean views...Nice course, great finishing hole...Poor man's Pebble Beach...18th hole is breathtaking...Pebble Beach comparisons are exaggerated...Great location and layout...Foggy in a.m., windy in p.m...Great last two holes...Beautiful but windy...Too many houses, overrated and highly overpriced...Tough set of par 3s.

★★½HANSEN DAM GOLF COURSE

PU-10400 Glen Oaks Blvd., Pacoima, 91331, Los Angeles County, (818)896-0050, 15 miles N of Los Angeles.
Opened: 1977. **Holes:** 18. **Par:** 72/75. **Yards:** 6,715/6,090. **Course rating:** 70.8/73.8. **Slope:** 115/123. **Architect:** Ray Goates. **Green fee:** $15/$20. **Credit cards:** None. **Reduced fees:** Weekdays, twilight, seniors, juniors. **Caddies:** No. **Golf carts:** $20. **Discount golf packages:** No. **Season:** Year-round. **High:** N/A. **On site lodging:** No. **Rental clubs:** Yes. **Walking policy:** Unrestricted walking. **Metal spikes allowed:** Yes. **Range:** Yes (mats). **To obtain tee times:** Advance reservations require an L.A. city reservation card. Daily, first come first served.
Subscriber comments: Wide fairways, very forgiving, long par 4s...No.9 longest par 4 on earth...Nice public track...Putts break away from dam...Back nine a little boring...Hot, dry, smoggy, flat...Very reachable par-4 No.11...One of the better LA muny courses.

★★HARDING PARK GOLF CLUB

PM-Harding Park Rd. at Skyline Blvd., San Francisco, 94132, San Francisco County, (415)664-4690.
Opened: 1925. **Holes:** 18. **Par:** 72/73. **Yards:** 6,743/6,205. **Course rating:** 72.1/74.1. **Slope:** 124/120. **Architect:** Willie Watson. **Green fee:** $26/$31. **Credit cards:** MC,VISA,ATM. **Reduced fees:** Weekdays, twilight, seniors, juniors. **Caddies:** No. **Golf carts:** $22. **Discount golf packages:** No. **Season:** Year-round. **High:** April-Nov. **On site lodging:** No. **Rental clubs:** Yes. **Walking policy:** Unrestricted walking. **Metal spikes allowed:** Yes. **Range:** Yes. **To obtain tee times:** Call 6 days in advance. **Special Notes:** Also has 9-hole executive course.

HERITAGE PALMS GOLF CLUB

44291 Heritage Palms Dr. S., Indio, 92201, (760)772-7334, 15 miles E of Palm Springs.
Opened: 1996. **Holes:** 18. **Par:** 72/72. **Yards:** 6,727/4,885. **Course rating:** 71.4/66.6. **Slope:** 119/107. **Architect:** Arthur Hills. **Green fee:** $40/$100. **Credit cards:** All major. **Reduced fees:** Low season, twilight. **Caddies:** No. **Golf carts:** N/A. **Discount golf packages:** No. **Season:** Year-round. **High:** Jan.-April. **On site lodging:** No. **Rental clubs:** Yes. **Walking policy:** Mandatory cart. **Metal spikes allowed:** Yes. **Range:** Yes (grass). **To obtain tee times:** Call 7 days in advance. Groups of 8 or more may secure tee time with credit card up to 90 days in advance.

★★★½HESPERIA GOLF & COUNTRY CLUB

17970 Bangor Ave., Hesperia, 92345, San Bernardino County, (760)244-9301, 30 miles N of San Bernardino.
Opened: 1955. **Holes:** 18. **Par:** 72/72. **Yards:** 6,996/6,136. **Course rating:** 74.6/73.9. **Slope:** 133/124. **Architect:** William F. Bell. **Green fee:** $15/$20. **Credit cards:** MC,VISA. **Reduced fees:** Weekdays, seniors, juniors. **Caddies:** No. **Golf carts:** $20. **Discount golf packages:** Yes. **Season:** Year-round. **High:** Spring/Fall. **On site lodging:** No. **Rental clubs:** Yes. **Walking policy:** Unrestricted walking. **Metal spikes allowed:** Yes. **Range:** Yes (grass/mats). **To obtain tee times:** Call up to 14 days ahead.
Subscriber comments: Old-style layout, simple and nice...Best-kept secret in High Desert...Perfect greens, great layout, 10th hole toughest I've ever played...Long and difficult with lots of trees...Outstanding value and a great course...Tough in the wind, tight driving holes...Who knew?

★★★½HIDDEN VALLEY GOLF CLUB

PU-10 Clubhouse Dr., Norco, 91760, Riverside County, (909)737-1010, 10 miles W of Riverside.
Opened: 1997. **Holes:** 18. **Par:** 72/71. **Yards:** 6,721/4,649. **Course rating:** 73.3/66.6.

Slope: 140/116. **Architect:** Casey O'Callaghan. **Green fee:** $35/$75. **Credit cards:** MC,VISA. **Reduced fees:** N/A. **Caddies:** No. **Golf carts:** N/A. **Discount golf packages:** No. **Season:** Year-round. **High:** Oct.-May. **On site lodging:** No. **Rental clubs:** Yes. **Walking policy:** Mandatory cart. **Metal spikes allowed:** Yes. **Range:** Yes (grass). **To obtain tee times:** Call up to 14 days in advance.
Subscriber comments: Very hilly...New course, needs to mature...Good layout...Awesome...Many hidden targets, not well defined...A public-course jewel in Inland Empire.

★★½HIDDEN VALLEY LAKE GOLF & COUNTRY CLUB
PU-19210 Hartman Rd., Middletown, 95461, Lake County, (707)987-3035, 40 miles E of Santa Rosa.
Opened: 1970. **Holes:** 18. **Par:** 72/74. **Yards:** 6,667/5,546. **Course rating:** 72.5/71.5. **Slope:** 124/124. **Architect:** William F. Bell. **Green fee:** $18/$28. **Credit cards:** MC,VISA. **Reduced fees:** Twilight, seniors, juniors. **Caddies:** No. **Golf carts:** $12. **Discount golf packages:** No. **Season:** Year-round. **High:** N/A. **On site lodging:** No. **Rental clubs:** Yes. **Walking policy:** Walking at certain times. **Metal spikes allowed:** Yes. **Range:** Yes (grass). **To obtain tee times:** Call up to 7 days in advance.
Subscriber comments: Each hole completely different...Good challenge, flat, hills, mountains, lakes...Hilly, and very hot in the summer...Challenging back nine in the hills...15th tee has great view...Nice course...Good solid course, front and back have nicely varied character.

★★★HIDDENBROOKE COUNTRY CLUB
PU-2708 Overlook Dr., Vallejo, 94591, Solano County, (707)557-8181, 40 miles NE of San Francisco.
Opened: 1995. **Holes:** 18. **Par:** 72/72. **Yards:** 6,638/4,557. **Course rating:** 72.8/66.4. **Slope:** 137/117. **Architect:** Arnold Palmer/Ed Seay. **Green fee:** $65/$85. **Credit cards:** All major. **Reduced fees:** N/A. **Caddies:** No. **Golf carts:** Included in Green Fee. **Discount golf packages:** No. **Season:** Year-round. **High:** N/A. **On site lodging:** No. **Rental clubs:** Yes. **Walking policy:** Unrestricted walking. **Metal spikes allowed:** Yes. **Range:** Yes (grass/mats). **To obtain tee times:** Non-members call 4 days in advance.
Subscriber comments: Arnie did good...Beautiful and challenging...Magnificent golf in beautiful wetlands setting...Play it quick, before it goes private...Too much water...Score on front, then pray on back...May be best course north of Golden Gate Bridge...Best new course in area...Exceptionally challenging course.

★★★HORSE THIEF COUNTRY CLUB
R-28930 Horse Thief Dr. , Stallion Spring, Tehachapi, 93561, Kern County, (805)822-5581, 50 miles E of Bakersfield.
Opened: 1972. **Holes:** 18. **Par:** 72/72. **Yards:** 6,678/5,677. **Course rating:** 72.1/72.1. **Slope:** 124/124. **Architect:** Bob Baldock. **Green fee:** $30/$30. **Credit cards:** All major. **Reduced fees:** Weekdays, twilight, seniors, juniors. **Caddies:** No. **Golf carts:** N/A. **Discount golf packages:** Yes. **Season:** Year-round. **High:** May-Sept. **On site lodging:** Yes. **Rental clubs:** Yes. **Walking policy:** Unrestricted walking. **Metal spikes allowed:** Yes. **Range:** Yes. **To obtain tee times:** Resort guests may make tee time up to one year in advance at time of room reservation. Nonguests call up to ten days in advance.
Subscriber comments: Super stay-and-play package...Fun and scenic...Back nine has large boulders and water...Beautiful hideaway...Looks like a tour layout...Very tight, interesting elevation changes...Lots of big oak trees and big rocks, well maintained...small greens, pretty course, but windy conditions.

★★★HUNTER RANCH GOLF COURSE
PU-4041 Hwy. 46 E., Paso Robles, 93446, San Luis Obispo County, (805)237-7444, 25 miles NE of San Luis Obispo.
Opened: 1994. **Holes:** 18. **Par:** 72/72. **Yards:** 6,741/5,639. **Course rating:** 72.2/72.8. **Slope:** 128/132. **Architect:** Ken Hunter Jr./Mike McGinnis. **Green fee:** $25/$55. **Credit cards:** MC,VISA. **Reduced fees:** Twilight, juniors. **Caddies:** No. **Golf carts:** $24. **Discount golf packages:** No. **Season:** Year-round. **High:** May-Oct. **On site lodging:** No. **Rental clubs:** Yes. **Walking policy:** Unrestricted walking. **Metal spikes allowed:** Yes. **Range:** Yes (grass). **To obtain tee times:** Call 7 days in advance.
Subscriber comments: Beautiful, hilly course, challenging...Best-kept secret in California...Great course with fantastic practice facility...Avoid summer play, really

hot...Nice setting in oaks...The rolling hills are very pleasing to the eyes...If you're in the area find time to play it...Best course on the Central Coast.

★★½IMPERIAL GOLF CLUB

PU-2200 E. Imperial Hwy., Brea, 92621, Orange County, (714)529-3923, 50 miles SE of Los Angeles.

Opened: N/A. **Holes:** 18. **Par:** 71/71. **Yards:** 6,211/5,474. **Course rating:** 69.3/71.0. **Slope:** 118/114. **Architect:** Harry Rainville/David Rainville. **Green fee:** $20/$26. **Credit cards:** MC,VISA. **Reduced fees:** N/A. **Caddies:** No. **Golf carts:** $10. **Discount golf packages:** No. **Season:** Year-round. **High:** Year-round. **On site lodging:** No. **Rental clubs:** No. **Walking policy:** Unrestricted walking. **Metal spikes allowed:** Yes. **Range:** Yes. **To obtain tee times:** N/A.

Subscriber comments: Easy, but fun to play...Good course for 15-plus handicappers...Good condition, lots of variety...No. 8 a good signature hole...Watch for nesting hawks on No.1.

★★½INDIAN HILLS GOLF CLUB

PU-5700 Clubhouse Dr., Riverside, 92509, Riverside County, (909)360-2090, (800)600-2090.

Opened: 1964. **Holes:** 18. **Par:** 70/72. **Yards:** 6,104/5,562. **Course rating:** 70.0/70.7. **Slope:** 126/118. **Architect:** William F. Bell. **Green fee:** $27/$40. **Credit cards:** MC,VISA. **Reduced fees:** Weekdays, low season, twilight, seniors, juniors. **Caddies:** No. **Golf carts:** Included in Green Fee. **Discount golf packages:** Yes. **Season:** Year-round. **High:** Nov.-June. **On site lodging:** No. **Rental clubs:** Yes. **Walking policy:** Mandatory cart. **Metal spikes allowed:** Yes. **Range:** No. **To obtain tee times:** Call golf shop.

Subscriber comments: Various elevations of tees and greens makes for some interesting holes...Nice course in the mountains, winds through housing tracts...Few level lies...Plays tougher than rating...No parallel fairways. 16th hole has 100-foot drop.

★★½INDIAN SPRINGS COUNTRY CLUB

PU-46-080 Jefferson St., La Quinta, 92253, Riverside County, (760)775-3360, 6 miles S of Palm Desert.

Opened: 1960. **Holes:** 18. **Par:** 71/72. **Yards:** 6,369/5,717. **Course rating:** 69.8/72.4. **Slope:** 112/117. **Architect:** Doc Gurly/Hogie Carmichael. **Green fee:** $15/$40. **Credit cards:** MC,VISA,DISC. **Reduced fees:** N/A. **Caddies:** No. **Golf carts:** N/A. **Discount golf packages:** Yes. **Season:** Year-round. **High:** Nov.-May. **On site lodging:** No. **Rental clubs:** Yes. **Walking policy:** Unrestricted walking. **Metal spikes allowed:** Yes. **Range:** Yes (grass). **To obtain tee times:** Call up to seven days in advance.

Subscriber comments: Lots of improvements of late...Adequate conditions...Best value in Palm Springs area...Long distances between holes...Old and easy design, in good shape, good value...Not very interesting.

★★½INDIAN VALLEY GOLF CLUB

PU-3035 Novato Blvd., Novato, 94948, Marin County, (415)897-1118, 22 miles N of San Francisco.

Opened: 1958. **Holes:** 18. **Par:** 72/72. **Yards:** 6,253/5,238. **Course rating:** 69.2/70.9. **Slope:** 119/128. **Architect:** Robert Nyberg. **Green fee:** $12/$40. **Credit cards:** MC,VISA,AMEX. **Reduced fees:** Weekdays, twilight, seniors, juniors. **Caddies:** No. **Golf carts:** $22. **Discount golf packages:** No. **Season:** Year-round. **High:** May-Sept. **On site lodging:** No. **Rental clubs:** Yes. **Walking policy:** Walking at certain times. **Metal spikes allowed:** Yes. **Range:** Yes (mats). **To obtain tee times:** Call up to 7 days in advance.

Subscriber comments: Short, hilly course with a few interesting holes...Scenic but simple...You don't want to walk, can be very windy...Hills and slopes pose a real test...Croutons for range balls...You'll enjoy wildlife...Elevator ride to 14th tee.

◀INDUSTRY HILLS SHERATON RESORT & CONFERENCE CENTER

R-One Industry Hills Pkwy., City of Industry, 91744, Los Angeles County, (818)810-4653, 25 miles E of Los Angeles.

Architect: William F. Bell. **Green fee:** $45/$60. **Caddies:** No. **Golf carts:** Included in Green Fee. **Discount golf packages:** Yes. **Season:** Year-round. **High:** April-July. **On site lodging:** Yes. **Rental clubs:** Yes. **Walking policy:** Mandatory cart. **Range:** Yes (mats). **To obtain tee times:** Call 3 days in advance.

★★★½BABE DIDRIKSON ZAHARIAS COURSE
Opened: 1980. **Holes:** 18. **Par:** 71/71. **Yards:** 6,600/5,363. **Course rating:** 72.5/72.4. **Slope:** 134/133. **Credit cards:** All major. **Reduced fees:** Weekdays, low season, twilight, seniors. **Metal spikes allowed:** Yes.
Subscriber comments: Awesome facility...Like playing golf in the Guggenheim...Accurate drives a must...Hit fairways, you'll score. Miss 'em, and you won't...Great challenge...Shorter of the two, but brutally tough. The greens are a nightmare, big and fast...Thinker's course.

★★★½EISENHOWER COURSE
Opened: 1979. **Holes:** 18. **Par:** 72/73. **Yards:** 6,735/5,589. **Course rating:** 72.9/73.1. **Slope:** 136/135. **Credit cards:** All major,Diners Club. **Reduced fees:** Weekdays, low season, twilight, seniors, juniors. **Metal spikes allowed:** No.
Subscriber comments: Very difficult. Beautiful layout on onetime landfill. A challenge...Keep it in the fairway, or else hit a provisional...Has been cleared out a lot, but rough is still brutal...Very difficult for average golfer...From tips all you can handle...Great course in a smog-infested locale.

★★½JURUPA HILLS COUNTRY CLUB
PU-6161 Moraga Ave., Riverside, 92509, Riverside County, (909)685-7214, 5 miles W of Riverside.
Opened: 1960. **Holes:** 18. **Par:** 70/71. **Yards:** 6,022/5,773. **Course rating:** 69.5/73.4. **Slope:** 122/123. **Architect:** William F. Bell. **Green fee:** $23/$40. **Credit cards:** MC,VISA. **Reduced fees:** Weekdays, low season, twilight, seniors, juniors. **Caddies:** No. **Golf carts:** Included in Green Fee. **Discount golf packages:** Yes. **Season:** Year-round. **High:** Year-round. **On site lodging:** No. **Rental clubs:** Yes. **Walking policy:** Walking at certain times. **Metal spikes allowed:** Yes. **Range:** Yes (grass/mats). **To obtain tee times:** Call golf club.
Subscriber comments: Difficult greens...Impressive layout for area...Short, tight course...Dreadfully slow...Best-kept greens in Inland Empire...Course a little short and too easy.

★★½KERN RIVER GOLF COURSE
PU-Rudal Rd., Bakersfield, 93386, Kern County, (805)872-5128.
Opened: 1920. **Holes:** 18. **Par:** 70/73. **Yards:** 6,458/5,971. **Course rating:** 70.5/72.3. **Slope:** 117/116. **Architect:** William P. Bell. **Green fee:** $9/$12. **Credit cards:** MC,VISA. **Reduced fees:** Weekdays, twilight, seniors, juniors. **Caddies:** No. **Golf carts:** $8. **Discount golf packages:** No. **Season:** Year-round. **High:** N/A. **On site lodging:** No. **Rental clubs:** Yes. **Walking policy:** Unrestricted walking. **Metal spikes allowed:** Yes. **Range:** Yes (grass). **To obtain tee times:** Call Wednesday at 7 a.m. for weekends. Call 24 hours in advance for weekdays.
Subscriber comments: Everything average...Semi-long, lots of mature trees, nice layout...Best public course in Bakersfield...Good walking course, noise from Lake Ming can be deafening...Some tough holes for public course.

★★★½LA CONTENTA GOLF CLUB
1653 Hwy. 26, Valley Springs, 95252, Calaveras County, (209)772-1081, (800)446-5321, 30 miles NE of Stockton.
Opened: 1972. **Holes:** 18. **Par:** 71/72. **Yards:** 6,425/5,120. **Course rating:** 70.2/70.8. **Slope:** 125/120. **Architect:** Richard Bigler. **Green fee:** $20/$34. **Credit cards:** MC,VISA,DISC. **Reduced fees:** Weekdays, resort guests, twilight, seniors, juniors. **Caddies:** No. **Golf carts:** $11. **Discount golf packages:** Yes. **Season:** Year-round. **High:** March-Oct. **On site lodging:** Yes. **Rental clubs:** Yes. **Walking policy:** Unrestricted walking. **Metal spikes allowed:** Yes. **Range:** No. **To obtain tee times:** Call golf shop up to 14 days in advance.
Subscriber comments: Lots of hills and blind shots...Like playing golf in the Andes, only steeper...This one is worth the drive...Nice setting in foothills...Elevation sensation. You're usually hitting up or down...Neon-green grass, good variety...Fun to play...Excellent in all aspects.

LA COSTA RESORT & SPA
R-Costa Del Mar Rd., Carlsbad, 92009, San Diego County, (760)438-9111, 30 miles N of San Diego.

Opened: 1964. **Architect:** Dick Wilson. **Green fee:** $110/$185. **Credit cards:** All major,Diners Club. **Reduced fees:** Weekdays, resort guests, twilight. **Caddies:** Yes. **Golf carts:** Included in Green Fee. **Discount golf packages:** Yes. **Season:** Year-round. **High:** Year-round. **On site lodging:** Yes. **Rental clubs:** Yes. **Walking policy:** Mandatory cart. **Metal spikes allowed:** Yes. **Range:** Yes (grass/mats). **To obtain tee times:** Call golf reservations at extension 25.

★★★½NORTH COURSE

Holes: 18. **Par:** 72/73. **Yards:** 6,987/5,939. **Course rating:** 74.8/74.0. **Slope:** 137/127. **Subscriber comments:** Great holes not seen on TV....Treat yourself...Good variety of holes, great greens...Beautiful, interesting course and facility...Two outstanding resort courses, long, testing...Original 18 is great but is now divided up...Overrated for reputation.

★★★½SOUTH COURSE

Holes: 18. **Par:** 72/74. **Yards:** 6,894/5,612. **Course rating:** 74.4/72.1. **Slope:** 138/123. **Subscriber comments:** Memorable course...Great golf, but "longest mile" finishing holes a bit boring...Tough near tournament time...Tough approach spots, well bunkered...Beautiful, interesting course...Very expensive...Very good...Overrated resort. **Notes:** PGA Tour Mercedes Championship, 1969-present.

★★½LA MIRADA GOLF COURSE

PM-15501 E. Alicante Rd., La Mirada, 90638, Los Angeles County, (562)943-7123, 20 miles SE of Los Angeles.
Opened: 1962. **Holes:** 18. **Par:** 70/71. **Yards:** 6,056/5,652. **Course rating:** 68.6/71.6. **Slope:** 114/117. **Architect:** N/A. **Green fee:** $19/$23. **Credit cards:** MC,VISA,AMEX. **Reduced fees:** Weekdays, twilight, seniors, juniors. **Caddies:** No. **Golf carts:** $22. **Discount golf packages:** No. **Season:** Year-round. **High:** Year-round. **On site lodging:** No. **Rental clubs:** Yes. **Walking policy:** Unrestricted walking. **Metal spikes allowed:** Yes. **Range:** Yes (grass/mats). **To obtain tee times:** Call 7 days in advance.
Subscriber comments: Good condition, hilly, fun to play...Requires some accurate shots...Good weekday course, too crowded on weekends......Vanilla...Too short, hilly, hard to walk...fivesomes allowed, five-plus hours to play.

★★★★LA PURISIMA GOLF COURSE

PU-3455 State Hwy. 246, Lompoc, 93436, Santa Barbara County, (805)735-8395, 40 miles N of Santa Barbara.
Opened: 1986. **Holes:** 18. **Par:** 72/72. **Yards:** 7,105/5,762. **Course rating:** 74.9/74.3. **Slope:** 143/131. **Architect:** Robert Muir Graves. **Green fee:** $45/$55. **Credit cards:** MC,VISA. **Reduced fees:** Twilight, juniors. **Caddies:** No. **Golf carts:** $24. **Discount golf packages:** No. **Season:** Year-round. **High:** May-Oct. **On site lodging:** No. **Rental clubs:** Yes. **Walking policy:** Unrestricted walking. **Metal spikes allowed:** Yes. **Range:** Yes (grass/mats). **To obtain tee times:** Call 7 days in advance.
Notes: Ranked 61st in 1996 America's Top 75 Affordable Courses. 1996 PGA Tour Final Qualifying School.
Subscriber comments: Tough but great; spectacular vistas...Watch for afternoon wind...Tight back nine...Nice setting with rolling hills...Good enough for Q-school final...Outstanding golf course, use every club...Worth stopping if traveling between LA and SF...Middle of nowhere but worth the drive.

LA QUINTA RESORT & CLUB

R-50-200 Vista Bonita, La Quinta, 92253, Riverside County, (760)564-7686, (800)742-9378, 15 miles E of Palm Springs.
Opened: 1981. **Architect:** Pete Dye. **Reduced fees:** Weekdays, low season, resort guests, twilight. **Caddies:** No. **Golf carts:** Included in Green Fee. **Discount golf packages:** Yes. **Season:** Year-round. **High:** Nov.-April. **On site lodging:** Yes. **Rental clubs:** Yes. **Walking policy:** Mandatory cart. **Metal spikes allowed:** Yes. **Range:** Yes (grass).

★★★½DUNES COURSE

Holes: 18. **Par:** 72/72. **Yards:** 6,747/5,005. **Course rating:** 73.1/68.0. **Slope:** 137/114. **Green fee:** $60/$160. **Credit cards:** MC,VISA,AMEX,JCB, Diners. **To obtain tee times:** Hotel guests may make tee times up to one year in advance. Non guests call 30 days in advance.
Notes: 1996 NCAA Women's National Championship.
Subscriber comments: Beautifully laid out and fun to play, expecially back nine...Tough desert course...Fairways thin, greens hard, otherwise great...Great

scenery...Very nice facilities, spend a week or weekend.

★★★★MOUNTAIN COURSE
Holes: 18. **Par:** 72/72. **Yards:** 6,758/5,010. **Course rating:** 74.1/68.4. **Slope:** 140/120.
Green fee: $60/$210. **Credit cards:** MC,VISA,AMEX,Diners Club. **To obtain tee times:** Hotel Guests may make tee times up to 1 yr in advance. Outside guests 3 days in advance. Call 760-564-5729 for all advance tee times.
Notes: Ranked 27th in 1997 Best in State. 1985 World Cup; 1989 Senior Skins Game; PGA Club Pro Championships.
Subscriber comments: Incredible par 3 16th...Beautiful scenery...Spectacular back nine, great facilities...Two nines are radically different...Can be a survival test...One of top courses in Greater Palm Springs...Very tough, every green like hitting to an aircraft carrier...Best Pete Dye track on West Coast.

★★★LAGUNA SECA GOLF CLUB
PU-10520 York Rd., Monterey, 93940, Monterey County, (408)373-3701.
Opened: 1970. **Holes:** 18. **Par:** 71/72. **Yards:** 6,157/5,204. **Course rating:** 70.4/70.8.
Slope: 123/121. **Architect:** Robert Trent Jones. **Green fee:** $55. **Credit cards:** MC,VISA,AMEX. **Reduced fees:** Twilight. **Caddies:** No. **Golf carts:** $28. **Discount golf packages:** Yes. **Season:** Year-round. **High:** April-Oct. **On site lodging:** No. **Rental clubs:** Yes. **Walking policy:** Unrestricted walking. **Metal spikes allowed:** Yes. **Range:** No. **To obtain tee times:** Call 30 days in advance for weekdays and 7 days in advance for weekends.
Subscriber comments: Short but challenging...Very hilly, accuracy needed...Look out for the 15th hole...Hard walking track...Old-time course, rewards good shots...Lots of bunkers around greens...A few treacherous holes...Best scenery.

★★½LAKE CHABOT GOLF COURSE
PM-11450 Golf Links Rd., Oakland, 94605, Alameda County, (510)351-5812, 10 miles E of Oakland.
Opened: 1927. **Holes:** 18. **Par:** 72/71. **Yards:** 5,982/5,268. **Course rating:** 68.6/68.5.
Slope: 115/116. **Architect:** William Lock. **Green fee:** $10/$23. **Credit cards:** None.
Reduced fees: Weekdays, twilight, seniors, juniors. **Caddies:** No. **Golf carts:** $22.
Discount golf packages: No. **Season:** Year-round. **High:** N/A. **On site lodging:** No.
Rental clubs: Yes. **Walking policy:** Unrestricted walking. **Metal spikes allowed:** Yes.
Range: No. **To obtain tee times:** Call up to 7 days in advance.
Subscriber comments: Very hilly course with many challenging lies...660-yard par 6 18th hole...Majestic fairways...Must be a billy goat to walk...Very few bunkers, but hilly, small greens...Pace is slow.

★★LAKE DON PEDRO GOLF CLUB
Ranchito Hernandez, La Grange, 95329, Tuolumne County, (209)852-2242.
Call club for further information.

LAKE SHASTINA GOLF RESORT
R-5925 Country Club Dr., Weed, 96094, Siskiyou County, (916)938-3205, (800)358-4653, 7 miles N of Weed.
Architect: Robert Trent Jones. **Credit cards:** MC,VISA,AMEX. **Caddies:** No. **Golf carts:** $15. **Season:** Year-round. **On site lodging:** Yes. **Rental clubs:** Yes. **Walking policy:** Unrestricted walking. **Metal spikes allowed:** Yes. **Range:** Yes (Mats).

★★★CHAMPIONSHIP COURSE
Opened: 1973. **Holes:** 18. **Par:** 72/72. **Yards:** 6,969/5,530. **Course rating:** 72.6.
Slope: 126/117. **Green fee:** $22/$45. **Reduced fees:** Low season, resort guests, twilight, juniors. **Discount golf packages:** Yes. **High:** May-Sept. **To obtain tee times:** Call golf shop up to 30 days in advance.
Subscriber comments: A giant course, breathtaking views...Nice course off beaten path...Average resort course; good scenery...Nice layout, water adds challenge...Good golf with beautiful Mt. Shasta backdrop...Mosquitos and deer everywhere...Great layout, awesome views.

★★SCOTTISH LINKS
5925 Country Club Dr, Weed, 96094, Siskiyou County, (916)938-3201.
Opened: N/A. **Holes:** 18. **Par:** 72/72. **Yards:** 6,969/5,530. **Course rating:** 72.6/70.2.
Slope: 126/117. **Green fee:** $29/$45. **Reduced fees:** N/A. **Discount golf packages:**

No. **High:** June-Sept. **To obtain tee times:** N/A.
Subscriber comments: Nice change of pace from championship course...Scottish feel, with sagebrush...Not memorably great...no shade.

★★★LAKE TAHOE GOLF COURSE
PU-2500 Emerald Bay Rd. Hwy. 50, South Lake Tahoe, 96150, El Dorado County, (916)577-0788, 60 miles SW of Reno.
Opened: 1960. **Holes:** 18. **Par:** 71/72. **Yards:** 6,685/5,654. **Course rating:** 70.9/70.1.
Slope: 120/115. **Architect:** William F. Bell. **Green fee:** $42/$60. **Credit cards:**
MC,VISA,AMEX. **Reduced fees:** Low season, twilight, juniors. **Caddies:** No. **Golf carts:** Included in Green Fee. **Discount golf packages:** Yes. **Season:** May-Oct. **High:** June-Sept. **On site lodging:** No. **Rental clubs:** Yes. **Walking policy:** Walking at certain times. **Metal spikes allowed:** Yes. **Range:** Yes (grass). **To obtain tee times:** Reservations available 60 days in advance with $5.00 reservation fee.
Subscriber comments: Most beautiful setting ...5,000-foot elevation...Beautiful course in meadow...Lots of trees...Water on 10 holes...Not too hard, not too easy...Very scenic with small spring running through it.

★★★LAKEWOOD COUNTRY CLUB
PU-3101 E. Carson St., Lakewood, 90712, Los Angeles County, (562)421-3741.
Opened: 1935. **Holes:** 18. **Par:** 72/73. **Yards:** 7,045/5,920. **Course rating:** 72.9/74.1.
Slope: 113/121. **Architect:** William P. Bell. **Green fee:** $19/$23. **Credit cards:**
MC,VISA,AMEX. **Reduced fees:** Weekdays, twilight, seniors, juniors. **Caddies:** No.
Golf carts: $22. **Discount golf packages:** No. **Season:** Year-round. **High:** April-Oct.
On site lodging: No. **Rental clubs:** Yes. **Walking policy:** Unrestricted walking. **Metal spikes allowed:** Yes. **Range:** Yes (mats). **To obtain tee times:** 7 days in advance by phone or in person.
Subscriber comments: Long enough to challenge the big hitters...Hogan won here...As good as its reputation...Wow! Celebrities, great layout...Should be lovely when they get the lakes fixed...Good old course. Slow play.

★★½LAS POSITAS GOLF COURSE
PM-917 Clubhouse Dr., Livermore, 94550, Alameda County, (510)455-7820, 1 miles W of Livermore.
Opened: 1965. **Holes:** 27. **Par:** 72/72. **Yards:** 6,725/5,270. **Course rating:** 72.0/70.1.
Slope: 126/120. **Architect:** Robert Muir Graves. **Green fee:** $24/$32. **Credit cards:**
MC,VISA. **Reduced fees:** Weekdays, low season, twilight, seniors, juniors. **Caddies:**
No. **Golf carts:** $11. **Discount golf packages:** No. **Season:** Year-round. **High:** April-June. **On site lodging:** No. **Rental clubs:** Yes. **Walking policy:** Unrestricted walking.
Metal spikes allowed: Yes. **Range:** Yes (grass/mats). **To obtain tee times:** Taken by computer up to 7 days in advance beginning at 5:00 a.m.
Subscriber comments: Great course since refurbishing...Just enough water to make it fun...Good 1st hole, hazards all around...A real sleeper...Can play long if windy...Easy course, pretty flat.
Special Notes: Also has 9-hole executive course.

★★½LAWRENCE WELK'S DESERT OASIS COUNTRY CLUB
34567 Cathedral Canyon Dr., Cathedral City, 92234, Riverside County, (760)328-6571, 10 miles SE of Palm Springs.
Opened: 1975. **Holes:** 27. **Architect:** David Rainville. **Green fee:** $35/$85. **Credit cards:** All major. **Reduced fees:** Weekdays, low season, twilight. **Caddies:** No. **Golf carts:** Included in Green Fee. **Discount golf packages:** Yes. **Season:** Year-round.
High: Jan.-April. **On site lodging:** No. **Rental clubs:** Yes. **Walking policy:** Mandatory cart. **Metal spikes allowed:** Yes. **Range:** Yes (grass). **To obtain tee times:** Call up to four days in advance.
LAKE VIEW/MOUNTAIN VIEW
Par: 72/72. **Yards:** 6,505/5,423. **Course rating:** 71.6/71.6. **Slope:** 128/127.
LAKE VIEW/RESORT
Par: 72/72. **Yards:** 6,366/5,183. **Course rating:** 70.3/70.1. **Slope:** 118/124.
MOUNTAIN VIEW/RESORT
Par: 72/72. **Yards:** 6,477/5,182. **Course rating:** 70.9/70.8. **Slope:** 119/124.
Subscriber comments: Nice mix of degrees of difficulty...Resort nine barren, not much

fun...Hidden water hazards...Varied courses...Lots of water...Great junior programs...Good vacation spot...Beautiful mature layout...Nothing special...Tight between houses...Good golf at a reasonable price...Lots of fun to play.

★★LEMOORE GOLF COURSE
PU-350 Iona Ave., Lemoore, 93245, Kings County, (209)924-9658, 30 miles S of Fresno.
Opened: 1930. **Holes:** 18. **Par:** 72/72. **Yards:** 6,431/5,126. **Course rating:** 69.8/67.9. **Slope:** 118/118. **Architect:** Bob Baldock/Bill Phillips. **Green fee:** $15/$17. **Credit cards:** MC,VISA. **Reduced fees:** N/A. **Caddies:** No. **Golf carts:** $18. **Discount golf packages:** No. **Season:** Year-round. **High:** N/A. **On site lodging:** No. **Rental clubs:** Yes. **Walking policy:** Unrestricted walking. **Metal spikes allowed:** Yes. **Range:** Yes (grass/mats). **To obtain tee times:** Call Tuesday for weekend times.

★★LINCOLN PARK GOLF COURSE
PU-34th Ave. and Clement St., San Francisco, 94121, San Francisco County, (415)221-9911.
Opened: 1916. **Holes:** 18. **Par:** 68/70. **Yards:** 5,149/4,984. **Course rating:** 64.4/67.4. **Slope:** 106/108. **Architect:** Jack Fleming. **Green fee:** $23/$27. **Credit cards:** None. **Reduced fees:** Weekdays, twilight, juniors. **Caddies:** No. **Golf carts:** $22. **Discount golf packages:** No. **Season:** Year-round. **High:** April-Nov. **On site lodging:** No. **Rental clubs:** Yes. **Walking policy:** Unrestricted walking. **Metal spikes allowed:** Yes. **Range:** No. **To obtain tee times:** Call 7 days in advance for weekdays; 3 days in advance for weekends.

★★★★THE LINKS AT SPANISH BAY
R-2700 17 Mile Dr., Pebble Beach, 93953, Monterey County, (408)647-7495, (800)654-9300, 2 miles S of Monterey.
Opened: 1987. **Holes:** 18. **Par:** 72/72. **Yards:** 6,820/5,309. **Course rating:** 74.8/70.6. **Slope:** 146/129. **Architect:** R.T. Jones Jr./T. Watson/S. Tatum. **Green fee:** $150/$165. **Credit cards:** All major,JCB. **Reduced fees:** Resort guests, twilight. **Caddies:** Yes. **Golf carts:** $25. **Discount golf packages:** Yes. **Season:** Year-round. **High:** Sept.-Nov. **On site lodging:** Yes. **Rental clubs:** Yes. **Walking policy:** Unrestricted walking. **Metal spikes allowed:** Yes. **Range:** No. **To obtain tee times:** Resort guest call 1 year in advance; outside play may reserve maximum of 60 days in advance.
Notes: Ranked 99th in 1997-98 America's 100 Greatest; 10th in 1997 Best in State.
Subscriber comments: A shotmaker's dream...A wonderful place in all respects...Blind and hilly, tee shots difficult...Very exposed to elements...Closest thing to Scotland in US...Great links course, great scenery...Finishing with bagpipes playing is wonderful...Lovely but expensive.

★★★LOCKEFORD SPRINGS GOLF COURSE
PU-16360 N. Hwy. 88, Lodi, 95240, San Joaquin County, (209)333-6275, 35 miles S of Sacramento.
Opened: 1995. **Holes:** 18. **Par:** 72/72. **Yards:** 6,861/5,951. **Course rating:** 72.8/74.0. **Slope:** 121/123. **Architect:** Jim Summers/Sandy Tatum. **Green fee:** $17/$27. **Credit cards:** MC,VISA. **Reduced fees:** Weekdays, twilight. **Caddies:** No. **Golf carts:** $10. **Discount golf packages:** No. **Season:** Year-round. **High:** N/A. **On site lodging:** No. **Rental clubs:** Yes. **Walking policy:** Unrestricted walking. **Metal spikes allowed:** Yes. **Range:** Yes (grass). **To obtain tee times:** Call 7 days in advance.
Subscriber comments: Links-style, lots of uneven lies...A sleeper with potential...Nice 18th hole...Exciting round of golf, long walk between some of the holes...An imitation St. Andrews...Very quick, undulating greens, lots of hazards, hidden water...Fairly new course, still developing.

★★LOS ANGELES ROYAL VISTA GOLF COURSE
20055 E. Colima Rd., Walnut, 91789, Los Angeles County, (909)595-7441, 22 miles E of Los Angeles.
Opened: 1963. **Holes:** 27. **Architect:** William F. Bell. **Green fee:** $21/$32. **Credit cards:** MC,VISA. **Reduced fees:** Weekdays, low season, resort guests, twilight, seniors, juniors. **Caddies:** No. **Golf carts:** Included in Green Fee. **Discount golf packages:** Yes. **Season:** Year-round. **High:** April-Sept. **On site lodging:** No. **Rental clubs:**

Yes. **Walking policy:** Walking at certain times. **Metal spikes allowed:** Yes. **Range:** Yes (mats). **To obtain tee times:** Call 7 days in advance.

NORTH/EAST

Par: 71/71. **Yards:** 6,381/5,545. **Course rating:** 69.0/71.3. **Slope:** 115/118.

NORTH/SOUTH

Par: 71/71. **Yards:** 6,071/5,316. **Course rating:** 67.6/69.8. **Slope:** 110/117.

SOUTH/EAST

Par: 72/72. **Yards:** 6,182/5,595. **Course rating:** 68.5/71.1. **Slope:** 112/117.

★★½**LOS ROBLES GOLF COURSE**

PU-299 S. Moorpark Rd., Thousand Oaks, 91360, Ventura County, (805)495-6421, 30 miles N of Los Angeles.

Opened: 1965. **Holes:** 18. **Par:** 69/69. **Yards:** 6,134/5,184. **Course rating:** 68.7/69.0. **Slope:** 116/115. **Architect:** William F. Bell. **Green fee:** $23/$27. **Credit cards:** MC,VISA. **Reduced fees:** Weekdays, twilight, seniors, juniors. **Caddies:** No. **Golf carts:** $20. **Discount golf packages:** Yes. **Season:** Year-round. **High:** N/A. **On site lodging:** No. **Rental clubs:** Yes. **Walking policy:** Unrestricted walking. **Metal spikes allowed:** Yes. **Range:** Yes (grass/mats). **To obtain tee times:** Residents call 8 days in advance; all others 7 days.

Subscriber comments: Interesting short course, but slowest play in Ventura County...Fun layout...Course works well with mountainous terrain...Great old layout among the oaks, nice greens...Big old oak trees.

LOS SERRANOS LAKES GOLF & COUNTRY CLUB

PU-15656 Yorba Ave., Chino Hills, 91709, San Bernardino County, (909)597-1711, 40 miles E of Los Angeles.

Opened: 1925. **Credit cards:** MC,VISA,DISC. **Reduced fees:** Weekdays, twilight, seniors. **Caddies:** No. **Golf carts:** $11. **Discount golf packages:** No. **Season:** Year-round. **High:** March-June. **On site lodging:** No. **Rental clubs:** Yes. **Walking policy:** Walking at certain times. **Metal spikes allowed:** Yes. **Range:** Yes (grass/mats). **To obtain tee times:** Call pro shop 7 days in advance.

★★★**NORTH COURSE**

Holes: 18. **Par:** 72/74. **Yards:** 6,440/5,949. **Course rating:** 71.3/73.9. **Slope:** 129/125. **Architect:** Harry Rainville. **Green fee:** $20/$34.

Subscriber comments: Nice course, excellent shape...No.6 is a killer...Picturesque elevated tees...More traditional than the South. Shorter, but just as challenging. Fast greens make the course...Old course, narrow with lots of traps...Easier than South course, but more interesting holes...Good public course.

★★★½**SOUTH COURSE**

Holes: 18. **Par:** 74/74. **Yards:** 7,036/5,957. **Course rating:** 74.0/73.9. **Slope:** 134/128. **Architect:** Bill Eaton. **Green fee:** $24/$34.

Subscriber comments: Great, long course. A real challenge...Afternoon wind a factor...Let the big dog eat! Long, fast, wide open with flat greens...Six par 5s...Some exciting holes...Lots of elevation changes...Good test.

★★★½**LOS VERDES GOLF COURSE**

PU-7000 W. Los Verdes Dr., Rancho Palos Verdes, 90275, Los Angeles County, (310)377-0338, 25 miles S of Los Angeles.

Opened: 1964. **Holes:** 18. **Par:** 71/72. **Yards:** 6,651/5,738. **Course rating:** 72.4/71.8. **Slope:** 122/118. **Architect:** William F. Bell. **Green fee:** $17/$21. **Credit cards:** MC,VISA. **Reduced fees:** Weekdays, twilight, seniors, juniors. **Caddies:** No. **Golf carts:** $10. **Discount golf packages:** No. **Season:** Year-round. **High:** June-Sept. **On site lodging:** No. **Rental clubs:** Yes. **Walking policy:** Unrestricted walking. **Metal spikes allowed:** Yes. **Range:** Yes (grass/mats). **To obtain tee times:** Call 7 days in advance, 6 a.m. on weekdays and 5 a.m. on weekends.

Subscriber comments: Great county course on cliffs overlooking ocean...On a clear day, absolutely beautiful...Spectacular setting...Worth it just for the view on No.15...Greens very much influenced by ocean...Back nine has spectacular views of Catalina Island...Pebble Beach for $27, but impossible to get tee time.

★★½**MACE MEADOWS GOLF & COUNTRY CLUB**

26570 Fairway Dr., Pioneer, 95666, Amador County, (209)295-7020.

Call club for further information.

Subscriber comments: Beautiful mountain course...Narrow and hilly, lots of trees on front nine, back nine open...A little gem in Mother Lode country.

★★½MADERA MUNICIPAL GOLF COURSE

PM-23200 Ave. 17, Madera, 93637, Madera County, (209)675-3504.
Opened: 1991. **Holes:** 18. **Par:** 72/72. **Yards:** 6,831/5,519. **Course rating:** 71.7/70.6. **Slope:** 121/112. **Architect:** Bob Putman. **Green fee:** $12/$17. **Credit cards:** MC,VISA,DISC. **Reduced fees:** N/A. **Caddies:** No. **Golf carts:** $19. **Discount golf packages:** No. **Season:** Year-round. **High:** N/A. **On site lodging:** No. **Rental clubs:** Yes. **Walking policy:** Unrestricted walking. **Metal spikes allowed:** Yes. **Range:** Yes (grass). **To obtain tee times:** Call up to 7 days in advance.
Subscriber comments: Great muny course, large undulating greens...Gets better as trees grow...Equal to Poppy Hills...Bermuda fairways, excellent greens...Great links-style layout...Becoming a very good course.

★★★½MALIBU COUNTRY CLUB

PU-901 Encinal Canyon Rd., Malibu, 90265, Los Angeles County, (818)889-6680, 30 miles NE of Los Angeles.
Opened: 1976. **Holes:** 18. **Par:** 72/72. **Yards:** 6,740/5,627. **Course rating:** 72.3/71.4. **Slope:** 130/120. **Architect:** William F. Bell. **Green fee:** $48/$68. **Credit cards:** MC,VISA,JCB. **Reduced fees:** Seniors. **Caddies:** No. **Golf carts:** Included in Green Fee. **Discount golf packages:** No. **Season:** Year-round. **High:** N/A. **On site lodging:** No. **Rental clubs:** Yes. **Walking policy:** Mandatory cart. **Metal spikes allowed:** Yes. **Range:** No. **To obtain tee times:** Call pro shop.
Subscriber comments: Great canyon course. Can always get on because of price...Shotmaker's challenge...Very hilly...Beautiful setting...Hidden value in mountain setting...Tight and technical, lots of celebrities.

MARRIOTT'S DESERT SPRINGS RESORT & SPA

R-74-855 Country Club Dr., Palm Desert, 92260, Riverside County, (760)341-1756, (800)331-3112, 85 miles E of Los Angeles.
Opened: 1987. **Architect:** Ted Robinson. **Green fee:** $65/$130. **Credit cards:** All major. **Reduced fees:** Weekdays, low season, resort guests, twilight. **Caddies:** No. **Golf carts:** Included in Green Fee. **Discount golf packages:** Yes. **Season:** Year-round. **High:** Oct.-May. **On site lodging:** Yes. **Rental clubs:** Yes. **Walking policy:** Mandatory cart. **Metal spikes allowed:** Yes. **Range:** Yes (grass). **To obtain tee times:** Hotel guest can call up to 60 days in advance. Nonguest may call 3 days in advance.
★★★½PALM COURSE
Holes: 18. **Par:** 72/72. **Yards:** 6,761/5,492. **Course rating:** 72.0/70.8. **Slope:** 124/116.
Subscriber comments: Beautiful course...Always in top shape...Palm much better than Valley...Immaculate...Almost perfect for a resort course...Greens and fairways in excellent condition...Great variety each hole...Beautiful scenery, plenty of water.
★★★½VALLEY COURSE
Holes: 18. **Par:** 72/72. **Yards:** 6,627/5,278. **Course rating:** 72:1/69.6. **Slope:** 124/110.
Subscriber comments: Beautiful surroundings...Just as fun as Palm course...Best resort in Palm Springs...Easier for the high handicapper than Palms...Great resort course, not a bad hole...Love the water...Great final holes.

★★½MARRIOTT'S RANCHO LAS PALMAS RESORT & COUNTRY CLUB

R-42000 Bob Hope Dr., Rancho Mirage, 92270, Riverside County, (760)862-4551, (760)568-2727, 5 miles W of Palm Springs.
Opened: 1978. **Holes:** 27. **Architect:** Ted Robinson. **Green fee:** $50/$109. **Credit cards:** All major. **Reduced fees:** Weekdays, low season, resort guests, twilight. **Caddies:** No. **Golf carts:** Included in Green Fee. **Discount golf packages:** Yes. **Season:** Year-round. **High:** Jan.-April. **On site lodging:** Yes. **Rental clubs:** Yes. **Walking policy:** Mandatory cart. **Metal spikes allowed:** Yes. **Range:** Yes (grass). **To obtain tee times:** Call up to 7 days in advance. Must be guest at the hotel.
NORTH/SOUTH
Par: 71/71. **Yards:** 6,019/5,421. **Course rating:** 67.2/69.7. **Slope:** 115/113.
NORTH/WEST
Par: 71/71. **Yards:** 6,113/5,308. **Course rating:** 67.8/66.9. **Slope:** 116/105.
SOUTH/WEST
Par: 70/70. **Yards:** 6,128/5,271. **Course rating:** 67.8/66.8. **Slope:** 115/110. **To obtain**

tee times: Call 7 days in advance. Must be guest at the hotel.
Subscriber comments: Very short, nice resort course...Boring...New hole additions on West are challenging...Enjoyable resort course...Short but tight...Generally good condition...Narrow fairways, small greens...Regular tees a must, not a place to gamble...Would recommend for novices...Irons off tees.

★★½MATHER GOLF COURSE
PU-4103 Eagles Nest Rd., Mather, 95655, Sacramento County, (916)364-4353, 7 miles E of Sacramento.
Opened: 1963. **Holes:** 18. **Par:** 72/74. **Yards:** 6,721/5,976. **Course rating:** 71.3/72.4. **Slope:** 121/119. **Architect:** Jack Fleming. **Green fee:** $17/$21. **Credit cards:** MC,VISA. **Reduced fees:** Weekdays, twilight, seniors, juniors. **Caddies:** No. **Golf carts:** $10. **Discount golf packages:** No. **Season:** Year-round. **High:** May-Aug. **On site lodging:** No. **Rental clubs:** Yes. **Walking policy:** Unrestricted walking. **Metal spikes allowed:** Yes. **Range:** No. **To obtain tee times:** Call up to 7 days in advance at 6:30 a.m for weekdays. For weekends, call on prior Monday morning at 6:30 a.m.
Subscriber comments: Old military course, now a good parkland muny...Great old trees. Great 10th hole...Tough three finishing holes...Need to play smart on short No.12...Longer course, wide open, tough in wind.

★★½MEADOW LAKE GOLF COURSE
10333 Meadow Glen Way, Escondido, 92026, San Diego County, (760)749-1620, 30 miles N of San Diego.
Opened: 1965. **Holes:** 18. **Par:** 72/74. **Yards:** 6,521/5,758. **Course rating:** 72.5/72.8. **Slope:** 131/123. **Architect:** Tom Sanderson. **Green fee:** $26/$38. **Credit cards:** MC,VISA,AMEX. **Reduced fees:** Weekdays, resort guests, twilight, seniors, juniors. **Caddies:** No. **Golf carts:** $12. **Discount golf packages:** No. **Season:** Year-round. **High:** N/A. **On site lodging:** No. **Rental clubs:** Yes. **Walking policy:** Walking at certain times. **Metal spikes allowed:** Yes. **Range:** Yes (grass). **To obtain tee times:** Call up to 7 days in advance.
Subscriber comments: Best finishing hole in the world...Too many blind shots...Hilly, no level lies...Tight layout with some weird holes...Very slow due to course design...Course is tougher than it looks...Par-4 9th is memorable, very difficult...Tough to walk.

★★½MEADOWOOD RESORT GOLF COURSE
900 Meadowood Lane, St. Helena, 94574, Napa County, (707)963-3646.
Call club for further information.
Subscriber comments: Pricey but good golf...Nine-hole course with outstanding resturant/hotel...Beautiful area.

★★★MENIFEE LAKES COUNTRY CLUB
29875 Menifee Lakes Dr., Menifee, 92584, Riverside County, (909)672-3090, 20 miles S of Riverside.
Opened: 1989. **Holes:** 27. **Architect:** Ted Robinson. **Green fee:** $22/$56. **Credit cards:** MC,VISA. **Reduced fees:** Weekdays, twilight, juniors. **Caddies:** No. **Golf carts:** Included in Green Fee. **Discount golf packages:** No. **Season:** Year-round. **High:** N/A. **On site lodging:** No. **Rental clubs:** Yes. **Walking policy:** Unrestricted walking. **Metal spikes allowed:** Yes. **Range:** Yes (grass). **To obtain tee times:** Call starter 6 days in advance for weekday tee times and Monday before for weekend.
FALLS/LAKES CSE
Par: 72/72. **Yards:** 6,500/5,500. **Course rating:** 70.7/72.4. **Slope:** 121/122.
LAKES/PALM CSE
Par: 72/72. **Yards:** 6,500/5,500. **Course rating:** 70.5/71.5. **Slope:** 120/120.
PALMS/FALLS CSE
Holes: 27. **Par:** 72/72. **Yards:** 6,500/5,500. **Course rating:** 71.1/70.7. **Slope:** 122/121.
Subscriber comments: Tough course, lots of undulation...Nice short course, much water...Don't hit it right! Summer winds and heat will tear you up...Needs maturing...Beautifully maintained, uncrowded.
Special Notes: No pullcarts.

CALIFORNIA

★★½MERCED HILLS GOLF CLUB
PU-5320 North Lake Rd., Merced, 95340, Merced County, (209)383-4943.
Opened: 1995. **Holes:** 18. **Par:** 72/72. **Yards:** 6,831/5,397. **Course rating:** 72.6/70.6.
Slope: 125/115. **Architect:** N/A. **Green fee:** $15/$20. **Credit cards:** MC,VISA.
Reduced fees: Weekdays, low season, twilight, seniors, juniors. **Caddies:** No. **Golf carts:** $15. **Discount golf packages:** No. **Season:** Year-round. **High:** May-Nov. **On site lodging:** No. **Rental clubs:** Yes. **Walking policy:** Unrestricted walking. **Metal spikes allowed:** Yes. **Range:** Yes (grass). **To obtain tee times:** Call golf shop.
Subscriber comments: Nice links course...Too dry and too much brush, but nice topography...Best greens in the valley...New course, will get better...Stay in the fairway...Fun in winter and spring, hot in summer.

★★★MESQUITE GOLF & COUNTRY CLUB
PU-2700 E. Mesquite Ave., Palm Springs, 92262, Riverside County, (760)323-1502, 120 miles E of Los Angeles.
Opened: N/A. **Holes:** 18. **Par:** 72/72. **Yards:** 6,328/5,244. **Course rating:** N/A. **Slope:** 117/118. **Architect:** Bert Stamps. **Green fee:** $45/$85. **Credit cards:** MC,VISA,AMEX.
Reduced fees: Weekdays, low season, twilight. **Caddies:** No. **Golf carts:** Included in Green Fee. **Discount golf packages:** No. **Season:** Year-round. **High:** Nov.-May. **On site lodging:** No. **Rental clubs:** Yes. **Walking policy:** Mandatory cart. **Metal spikes allowed:** Yes. **Range:** No. **To obtain tee times:** Call (760)325-4653 or (800)468-7918.
Subscriber comments: Nice views of mountains, lots of water...Lovely course and facility...Good condition...Has six par 5s, six par 4s, six par 3s...Good desert course...Flat course...Getting better with age, tough but gentle.

★★½MICKE GROVE GOLF LINKS
PU-11401 N. Micke Grove Rd., Lodi, 95240, San Joaquin County, (209)369-4410, 5 miles N of Stockton.
Opened: 1989. **Holes:** 18. **Par:** 72/72. **Yards:** 6,565/5,286. **Course rating:** 71.1/69.7.
Slope: 118/111. **Architect:** Garrett Gill/George B. Williams. **Green fee:** $17/$25. **Credit cards:** MC,VISA. **Reduced fees:** Weekdays, low season, twilight, seniors, juniors.
Caddies: No. **Golf carts:** $10. **Discount golf packages:** No. **Season:** Year-round.
High: March-Nov. **On site lodging:** No. **Rental clubs:** Yes. **Walking policy:** Unrestricted walking. **Metal spikes allowed:** Yes. **Range:** Yes (grass/mats). **To obtain tee times:** Call 7 days in advance.
Subscriber comments: Hard fairways, good roll, fairly easy course...Will be better when course matures...Links and lakes...Nice signature hole and finishing hole...Best links-type course in area...Flat, uninteresting, like a really big pitch-and-putt...Well conditioned.

★★½MILE SQUARE GOLF COURSE
PU-10401 Warner Ave., Fountain Valley, 92708, Orange County, (714)968-455-64410, (714)545-7106, 30 miles S of Los Angeles.
Opened: 1969. **Holes:** 18. **Par:** 72/72. **Yards:** 6,629/5,545. **Course rating:** 71.0/70.5.
Slope: 119/109. **Architect:** David Rainville. **Green fee:** $19/$25. **Credit cards:** None.
Reduced fees: Twilight. **Caddies:** Yes. **Golf carts:** $22. **Discount golf packages:** No.
Season: Year-round. **High:** March-Sept. **On site lodging:** No. **Rental clubs:** Yes.
Walking policy: Unrestricted walking. **Metal spikes allowed:** Yes. **Range:** Yes (mats).
To obtain tee times: Call 7 days in advance for weekdays; call Monday for Saturday, call Tuesday for Sunday.
Subscriber comments: Flat, wide fairways, well maintained muny...A good challenge at 6,700 yards...OK course if you like playing the same straight par 4 10 times...Nice course to walk...Flat, but fun, lots of trees.

★★★★MISSION HILLS NORTH GOLF COURSE
PU-70-705 Ramon Rd., Rancho Mirage, 92270, Riverside County, (760)770-9496, (800)358-2211, 5 miles E of Palm Springs.
Opened: 1991. **Holes:** 18. **Par:** 72/72. **Yards:** 7,062/4,907. **Course rating:** 73.9/68.0.
Slope: 134/118. **Architect:** Gary Player. **Green fee:** $55/$120. **Credit cards:** MC,VISA,AMEX. **Reduced fees:** Weekdays, low season, resort guests, twilight.
Caddies: No. **Golf carts:** Included in Green Fee. **Discount golf packages:** Yes.
Season: Year-round. **High:** Oct.-April. **On site lodging:** Yes. **Rental clubs:** Yes.

Walking policy: Mandatory cart. **Metal spikes allowed:** Yes. **Range:** Yes (grass). **To obtain tee times:** Public may call within 7 days. If staying at the Westin Mission Hills Resort Hotel, you may book tee times upon room confirmation.

Subscriber comments: One of best in desert area...Great finishing hole...Beautiful resort course...Great in a.m., strong winds in p.m....Great desert setting...Player's best in the west, each hole different...Great facilities, great layout, fabulous views, excellent greens...Excellent...Very playable...Designed for hookers and slicers...Front nine excellent, challenging...Beautiful course, good variety of holes.

★★★MISSION LAKES COUNTRY CLUB

8484 Clubhouse Blvd., Desert Hot Springs, 92240, Riverside County, (760)329-8061, 10 miles N of Palm Springs.

Opened: 1973. **Holes:** 18. **Par:** 71/72. **Yards:** 6,737/5,390. **Course rating:** 72.8/71.2. **Slope:** 131/122. **Architect:** Ted Robinson. **Green fee:** $30/$75. **Credit cards:** MC,VISA. **Reduced fees:** Weekdays, low season, resort guests, twilight, juniors. **Caddies:** No. **Golf carts:** Included in Green Fee. **Discount golf packages:** No. **Season:** Year-round. **High:** Jan.-May. **On site lodging:** Yes. **Rental clubs:** Yes. **Walking policy:** Mandatory cart. **Metal spikes allowed:** Yes. **Range:** Yes (grass). **To obtain tee times:** Call 3 days in advance.

Notes: Senior Tour Qualifier.

Subscriber comments: Great back nine, hard final four holes...Well-kept secret in the Palm Springs area...Beautiful, nice views, fairly open...Enhanced by mature trees...Well worth the drive...10, 11 and 12 are three of the best looking and challenging holes on any course.

★★★MONARCH BEACH GOLF LINKS

R-33033 Niguel Rd., Dana Point, 92629, Orange County, (714)240-8247, 60 miles N of San Diego.

Opened: 1984. **Holes:** 18. **Par:** 70/70. **Yards:** 6,340/5,046. **Course rating:** 69.2/68.5. **Slope:** 128/120. **Architect:** Robert Trent Jones Jr.. **Green fee:** $90/$135. **Credit cards:** MC,VISA,AMEX,Diners Club. **Reduced fees:** N/A. **Caddies:** No. **Golf carts:** Included in Green Fee. **Discount golf packages:** No. **Season:** Year-round. **High:** Year-round. **On site lodging:** No. **Rental clubs:** Yes. **Walking policy:** Unrestricted walking. **Metal spikes allowed:** Yes. **Range:** Yes (mats). **To obtain tee times:** Call 7 days in advance. Or 8 to 30 days in advance with additional $15 per player pre-book fee. Times are held with credit card which will be charged if 24 hour cancellation is not given.

Subscriber comments: Nice resort course...Must be least-played course in California, so overpriced...Putter's course...My California coastline favorite, requires smart shots...Tough with onshore wind.

★★½MONTEBELLO GOLF CLUB

PM-901 Via San Clemente, Montebello, 90640, Los Angeles County, (213)723-2971, 9 miles E of Los Angeles.

Opened: 1928. **Holes:** 18. **Par:** 71/72. **Yards:** 6,671/5,979. **Course rating:** 70.4/72.4. **Slope:** 114/117. **Architect:** William P. Bell. **Green fee:** $18/$21. **Credit cards:** None. **Reduced fees:** N/A. **Caddies:** No. **Golf carts:** $20. **Discount golf packages:** No. **Season:** Year-round. **High:** April-Oct. **On site lodging:** No. **Rental clubs:** No. **Walking policy:** Unrestricted walking. **Metal spikes allowed:** Yes. **Range:** Yes. **To obtain tee times:** Call seven days in advance.

Subscriber comments: Nice if you can get on...Tough front nine, long par 4s into wind...Very playable muny...Flat, open fairways...Fivesomes allowed, very crowded at times...Good muny course.

★★★½MORENO VALLEY RANCH GOLF CLUB

PU-28095 John F. Kennedy Dr., Moreno Valley, 92555, Riverside County, (909)924-4444, 15 miles E of Riverside.

Opened: 1988. **Holes:** 27. **Architect:** Pete Dye. **Green fee:** $28/$55. **Credit cards:** All major,Diners Club. **Reduced fees:** Weekdays, low season, twilight, seniors, juniors. **Caddies:** No. **Golf carts:** Included in Green Fee. **Discount golf packages:** Yes. **Season:** Year-round. **High:** Nov.-May. **On site lodging:** No. **Rental clubs:** Yes. **Walking policy:** Mandatory cart. **Metal spikes allowed:** Yes. **Range:** Yes (grass/mats). **To obtain tee times:** Call 7 days in advance.

LAKE/VALLEY
Par: 72/72. **Yards:** 6,898/5,196. **Course rating:** 74.1/70.1. **Slope:** 138/122.
MOUNTAIN/LAKE
Par: 72/72. **Yards:** 6,684/5,108. **Course rating:** 73.1/69.6. **Slope:** 139/121.
MOUNTAIN/VALLEY
Par: 72/72. **Yards:** 6,880/5,196. **Course rating:** 74.2/70.1. **Slope:** 140/122.
Subscriber comments: Should be on the big tour...Great course, fun to play...Beautiful target course...Great skills test—must have all the shots to score...All three nines are a challenge...Mountain/Valley combo best...Challenging Dye track, railroad-tie city...The wind plays a real role...Beautiful vistas...7th hole on Mountain is just plain evil...Smoggy in summer...Long drive from Los Angeles, but worth it.

★★MORGAN RUN RESORT & CLUB
PU-5690 Concha de Golf, Rancho Santa Fe, 92067, San Diego County, (619)756-2471, 20 miles N of San Diego.
Opened: N/A. **Holes:** 27. **Architect:** H. Rainville. **Green fee:** $35/$45. **Credit cards:** MC,VISA,AMEX. **Reduced fees:** Twilight. **Caddies:** No. **Golf carts:** $10. **Discount golf packages:** Yes. **Season:** Year-round. **High:** N/A. **On site lodging:** Yes. **Rental clubs:** Yes. **Walking policy:** Unrestricted walking. **Metal spikes allowed:** Yes. **Range:** Yes. **To obtain tee times:** Call seven days in advance.
EAST/NORTH
Par: 71/71. **Yards:** 6,141/5,860. **Course rating:** 68.8/70.2. **Slope:** 110/113.
EAST/SOUTH
Par: 72/72. **Yards:** 6,443/6,136. **Course rating:** 70.2/71.3. **Slope:** 112/117.
SOUTH/NORTH
Par: 71/71. **Yards:** 6,346/6,344. **Course rating:** 69.7/70.7. **Slope:** 112/115.

★★★MORRO BAY GOLF COURSE
PU-State Park Rd., Morro Bay, 93442, San Luis Obispo County, (805)772-4341, 15 miles N of San Luis Obispo.
Opened: 1929. **Holes:** 18. **Par:** 71/72. **Yards:** 6,360/5,055. **Course rating:** 70.4/69.5. **Slope:** 118/117. **Architect:** Russell Noyes. **Green fee:** $22/$28. **Credit cards:** MC,VISA,DISC. **Reduced fees:** Twilight, seniors, juniors. **Caddies:** No. **Golf carts:** $20. **Discount golf packages:** No. **Season:** Year-round. **High:** April-Aug. **On site lodging:** No. **Rental clubs:** Yes. **Walking policy:** Unrestricted walking. **Metal spikes allowed:** Yes. **Range:** Yes (grass/mats). **To obtain tee times:** N/A.
Subscriber comments: Ocean views make it great...Fun course...Adjacent to fine campground...Beautiful view of Morro Bay below...Breaks on greens very much influenced by ocean...Difficult but not a killer...Short course, feels like Monterey...Very hilly, mountain-style golf...Coastal winds can be tricky; sometimes foggy...Tee it up on No.8 and 13 and let it fly...Beautiful course, hard to get on.

★★★½MOUNT WOODSON COUNTRY CLUB
16422 N. Woodson Dr., Ramona, 92065, San Diego County, (760)788-3555, 25 miles NE of San Diego.
Opened: 1991. **Holes:** 18. **Par:** 70/70. **Yards:** 6,180/4,441. **Course rating:** 68.8/64.7. **Slope:** 130/108. **Architect:** Lee Schmidt/Brian Curley. **Green fee:** $28/$65. **Credit cards:** MC,VISA,AMEX. **Reduced fees:** Weekdays, twilight, juniors. **Caddies:** No. **Golf carts:** Included in Green Fee. **Discount golf packages:** Yes. **Season:** Year-round. **High:** N/A. **On site lodging:** No. **Rental clubs:** Yes. **Walking policy:** Mandatory cart. **Metal spikes allowed:** Yes. **Range:** Yes. **To obtain tee times:** Call 7 days in advance.
Subscriber comments: Beautiful setting and outstanding design...Very hilly and tough holes...Thinker's track...Target golf extraordinaire...Not long but very tough...Beautiful wooden bridge over canyon, riding in treetops...A lot of tricky holes...A ball eater...Favorite target course in San Diego...A unique course in stunning setting...Bring your camera; every tee a photo opportunity.

★★★MOUNTAIN MEADOWS GOLF CLUB
PU-1875 N. Fairplex Dr., Pomona, 91768, Los Angeles County, (909)623-3704, 20 miles E of Los Angeles.
Opened: 1977. **Holes:** 18. **Par:** 72/72. **Yards:** 6,509/5,637. **Course rating:** 71.5/71.5. **Slope:** 125/117. **Architect:** Ted Robinson. **Green fee:** $13/$21. **Credit cards:** MC,VISA. **Reduced fees:** Weekdays, low season, twilight, seniors, juniors. **Caddies:**

No. **Golf carts:** $10. **Discount golf packages:** No. **Season:** Year-round. **High:** May-Aug. **On site lodging:** No. **Rental clubs:** Yes. **Walking policy:** Unrestricted walking. **Metal spikes allowed:** Yes. **Range:** Yes (grass). **To obtain tee times:** Call one week in advance; weekdays at 6:00 a.m.; weekends and holidays at 5:00 a.m.
Subscriber comments: Long and hilly, lots of trees...Great opening drive...Back nine better than front...Elevation changes make it play longer than the yardage...Nos.13, 14 and 15 a great sequence of holes...Good except when smoggy...Good test, but crowded and slow...One of the best munys in LA County.

MOUNTAIN SHADOWS GOLF COURSE
PU-100 Golf Course Dr., Rohnert Park, 94928, Sonoma County, (707)584-7766, 7 miles S of Santa Rosa.
Credit cards: MC,VISA,AMEX. **Reduced fees:** Weekdays, low season, twilight, seniors, juniors. **Caddies:** No. **Golf carts:** $12. **Discount golf packages:** No. **Season:** Year-round. **High:** April-Oct. **On site lodging:** No. **Rental clubs:** Yes. **Metal spikes allowed:** Yes. **To obtain tee times:** Call 7 days in advance.
★★NORTH COURSE
Opened: 1974. **Holes:** 18. **Par:** 72/72. **Yards:** 7,035/5,503. **Course rating:** 72.1/70.5. **Slope:** 117. **Architect:** Gary Roger Baird. **Green fee:** $16/$35. **Walking policy:** Walking at certain times. **Range:** Yes.
★★SOUTH COURSE
Opened: 1963. **Holes:** 18. **Par:** 72/72. **Yards:** 6,720/5,805. **Course rating:** 70.1/71.4. **Slope:** 115/122. **Architect:** Bob Baldock. **Green fee:** $12/$30. **Walking policy:** Unrestricted walking. **Range:** Yes (mats).

★★★MOUNTAIN SPRINGS GOLF CLUB
PU-1000 Championship Dr., Sonora, 95370, Tuolumne County, (209)532-1000, 45 miles E of Stockton.
Opened: 1990. **Holes:** 18. **Par:** 72/71. **Yards:** 6,665/5,195. **Course rating:** 71.9/68.8. **Slope:** 128/112. **Architect:** Robert Muir Graves. **Green fee:** $10/$25. **Credit cards:** MC,VISA. **Reduced fees:** Twilight, seniors, juniors. **Caddies:** No. **Golf carts:** $10. **Discount golf packages:** Yes. **Season:** Year-round. **High:** April-Sept. **On site lodging:** No. **Rental clubs:** Yes. **Walking policy:** Unrestricted walking. **Metal spikes allowed:** Yes. **Range:** Yes (mats). **To obtain tee times:** Call up to 14 days in advance.
Subscriber comments: Challenging, pretty course...Many blind holes...OK course in the middle of nowhere...Hilly track, rough is hardpan...Too many blind holes, otherwise great...Great hotdogs...Good layout, beautiful in spring...Good, undulating greens.

★★MOUNTAIN VIEW COUNTRY CLUB
PU-2121 Mountain View Dr., Corona, 91720, Riverside County, (909)737-9798, 10 miles W of Riverside.
Opened: 1963. **Holes:** 18. **Par:** 72/73. **Yards:** 6,383/5,374. **Course rating:** 70.8/71.7. **Slope:** 124/120. **Architect:** N/A. **Green fee:** $29/$39. **Credit cards:** MC,VISA. **Reduced fees:** Weekdays, low season, resort guests, twilight, seniors, juniors. **Caddies:** No. **Golf carts:** Included in Green Fee. **Discount golf packages:** Yes. **Season:** Year-round. **High:** Oct.-June. **On site lodging:** No. **Rental clubs:** Yes. **Walking policy:** Walking at certain times. **Metal spikes allowed:** Yes. **Range:** Yes (grass/mats). **To obtain tee times:** Call 14 days in advance.

★★½NAPA MUNICIPAL GOLF CLUB
PM-2295 Streblow Dr., Napa, 94558, Napa County, (707)255-4333, 45 miles NW of San Francisco.
Opened: 1967. **Holes:** 18. **Par:** 72/73. **Yards:** 6,730/5,956. **Course rating:** 71.7/76.8. **Slope:** 127/137. **Architect:** Jack Fleming. **Green fee:** $14/$25. **Credit cards:** N/A. **Reduced fees:** Weekdays, low season, twilight, seniors, juniors. **Caddies:** No. **Golf carts:** $23. **Discount golf packages:** No. **Season:** Year-round. **High:** April-Nov. **On site lodging:** No. **Rental clubs:** Yes. **Walking policy:** Unrestricted walking. **Metal spikes allowed:** Yes. **Range:** Yes. **To obtain tee times:** Call 7 days in advance.
Subscriber comments: Water on 14 of 18 holes...Design and routing outstanding...Fun 19th hole...If you don't like water, stay away from this course...Needs work, but interesting and fun...Always challenging, bring plenty of balls.

CALIFORNIA

★★★NEEDLES MUNICIPAL GOLF COURSE
PM-144 Marina Dr., Needles, 92363, San Bernardino County, (760)326-3931, 100 miles S of Las Vegas.
Opened: 1962. **Holes:** 18. **Par:** 70/70. **Yards:** 6,550/5,850. **Course rating:** 71.4/71.1. **Slope:** 117/114. **Architect:** N/A. **Green fee:** $15/$18. **Credit cards:** MC,VISA. **Reduced fees:** Low season, seniors, juniors. **Caddies:** No. **Golf carts:** $10. **Discount golf packages:** No. **Season:** Year-round. **High:** Nov.-April. **On site lodging:** No. **Rental clubs:** Yes. **Walking policy:** Unrestricted walking. **Metal spikes allowed:** Yes. **Range:** Yes (grass). **To obtain tee times:** After 6:00 a.m. call 2 days in advance for weekdays; 1 day in advance for weekends.
Subscriber comments: Great for winter golf...Interesting...Windy, but excellent layout and scenic...Pretty course, on Colorado River...18 holes in four hours...Good for seniors...Flat, easy course.

★★★NORTHSTAR-AT-TAHOE RESORT GOLF COURSE
Hwy. 267 and Northstar Dr., Truckee, 96160, Nevada County, (916)562-2490, (800)466-6784, 40 miles W of Reno.
Opened: 1975. **Holes:** 18. **Par:** 72/72. **Yards:** 6,897/5,470. **Course rating:** 72.0/71.2. **Slope:** 137/134. **Architect:** Robert Muir Graves. **Green fee:** $45/$70. **Credit cards:** All major. **Reduced fees:** Low season, resort guests, twilight, seniors, juniors. **Caddies:** No. **Golf carts:** Included in Green Fee. **Discount golf packages:** Yes. **Season:** May-Oct. **High:** July-Aug. **On site lodging:** Yes. **Rental clubs:** Yes. **Walking policy:** Unrestricted walking. **Metal spikes allowed:** Yes. **Range:** Yes. **To obtain tee times:** Call 21 days in advance, unless hotel guest.
Subscriber comments: Great course...Front and back are like Jekyll and Hyde...Hard course, flat meadows to thick forest...Beautiful mountain setting...Water on 15 or 16 holes...Back nine excellent, front nine boring...Gorgeous walk through the woods...No.17 is unbelievable...Interesting track.

★★★OAK CREEK GOLF CLUB
PU-1 Golf Club Dr., Irvine, 92620, Orange County, (714)653-7300, 60 miles S of Los Angeles.
Opened: 1996. **Holes:** 18. **Par:** 71/71. **Yards:** 6,834/5,605. **Course rating:** 71.9/71.2. **Slope:** 127/121. **Architect:** Tom Fazio. **Green fee:** $80/$125. **Credit cards:** MC,VISA,AMEX,Diners Club. **Reduced fees:** Twilight, seniors, juniors. **Caddies:** No. **Golf carts:** Included in Green Fee. **Discount golf packages:** Yes. **Season:** Year-round. **High:** Year-round. **On site lodging:** No. **Rental clubs:** Yes. **Walking policy:** Mandatory cart. **Metal spikes allowed:** No. **Range:** Yes (grass). **To obtain tee times:** Call up to 6 days in advance beginning at 6:30 a.m. For additional $15 p/player tee times may be made 7-14 days in advance.
Subscriber comments: Course is excellent, but noisy with car, train and plane traffic...Great practice range...Doesn't look that tough, but ouch...Incredible layout for flat piece of land...Wide open course with tough greens...Many parallel holes...When it matures this will be awesome......User-friendly resort course.

★★★★OAK VALLEY GOLF CLUB
PU-37-600 14th St., Beaumont, 92223, Riverside County, (909)769-7200, 20 miles SE of San Bernadino.
Opened: 1991. **Holes:** 18. **Par:** 72/72. **Yards:** 7,003/5,494. **Course rating:** 73.9/71.1. **Slope:** 136/122. **Architect:** Lee Schmidt/Brian Curley. **Green fee:** $30/$50. **Credit cards:** MC,VISA,AMEX. **Reduced fees:** Weekdays, twilight. **Caddies:** No. **Golf carts:** Included in Green Fee. **Discount golf packages:** Yes. **Season:** Year-round. **High:** March-June. **On site lodging:** No. **Rental clubs:** Yes. **Walking policy:** Mandatory cart. **Metal spikes allowed:** Yes. **Range:** Yes (grass). **To obtain tee times:** Call 7 days in advance.
Subscriber comments: A great course, especially the front nine...Keep it straight, you'll have fun...Excellent desert course. Long and tough...A real find, and free range balls, too...What a course, neat par 3s, tough par 4s...Very challenging course with glass greens...Beware of wind...Lots of sand, water and jackrabbits.

★★★½OAKHURST COUNTRY CLUB
1001 Peacock Creek Dr., Clayton, 94517, Contra Costa County, (510)672-9737, 2 miles S of Concord.
Opened: 1990. **Holes:** 18. **Par:** 72/72. **Yards:** 6,739/5,285. **Course rating:** 73.1/70.3. **Slope:** 132/123. **Architect:** Ron Fream. **Green fee:** $50/$70. **Credit cards:** MC,VISA,DISC. **Reduced fees:** Twilight, seniors, juniors. **Caddies:** No. **Golf carts:** Included in Green Fee. **Discount golf packages:** No. **Season:** Year-round. **High:** N/A. **On site lodging:** No. **Rental clubs:** Yes. **Walking policy:** Mandatory cart. **Metal spikes allowed:** Yes. **Range:** Yes (grass). **To obtain tee times:** Call three days in advance.
Subscriber comments: Tough course, great finishing hole...Glorified condo golf...Very hilly with lots of trouble off fairways...Visually intimidating...Developing into good layout...Front nine is brutal...Lots of uphill and downhill lies...Great views...Innovative design given terrain...Would be better if walking allowed.

OAKMONT GOLF CLUB
PU-7025 Oakmont Dr., Santa Rosa, 95409, Sonoma County, 55 miles N of Santa Rosa.
Architect: Ted Robinson. **Credit cards:** MC,VISA. **Reduced fees:** Twilight. **Caddies:** No. **Golf carts:** $11. **Discount golf packages:** No. **Season:** Year-round. **High:** N/A. **On site lodging:** No. **Rental clubs:** Yes. **Walking policy:** Unrestricted walking. **Metal spikes allowed:** Yes. **Range:** Yes (grass/mats). **To obtain tee times:** Call 7 days in advance for weekends and holidays and 1 day ahead for weekdays.
EAST COURSE
(707)538-2454.
Opened: 1976. **Holes:** 18. **Par:** 63/63. **Yards:** 4,293/4,067. **Course rating:** 59.8/62.8. **Slope:** 94/102. **Green fee:** $22/$28.
★★★WEST COURSE
(707)539-0415.
Opened: 1963. **Holes:** 18. **Par:** 72/72. **Yards:** 6,379/5,573. **Course rating:** 70.5/71.9. **Slope:** 121/128. **Green fee:** $27/$35.
Subscriber comments: Wide open, a walk in the park...A few interesting holes with water and oak trees...Nice course hidden in retirement community...Short, fun to play...Tour-quality greens, always lush and green, quirky...Challenging layout with great scenery...Sneaky layout for a flat course.

★★OCEANSIDE MUNICIPAL GOLF COURSE
PM-825 Douglas Dr., Oceanside, 92054, San Diego County, (760)433-1360, 30 miles N of San Diego.
Opened: 1974. **Holes:** 18. **Par:** 72/72. **Yards:** 6,450/5,398. **Course rating:** 70.8/71.6. **Slope:** 118/121. **Architect:** Richard Bigler. **Green fee:** $17/$23. **Credit cards:** MC,VISA,AMEX. **Reduced fees:** Weekdays, twilight, seniors, juniors. **Caddies:** No. **Golf carts:** $19. **Discount golf packages:** No. **Season:** Year-round. **High:** Year-round. **On site lodging:** No. **Rental clubs:** Yes. **Walking policy:** Unrestricted walking. **Metal spikes allowed:** Yes. **Range:** Yes (grass). **To obtain tee times:** Call 8 days in advance.

★★★★OJAI VALLEY INN
R-Country Club Rd., Ojai, 93023, Ventura County, (805)646-2420, (800)422-6524, 60 miles N of Los Angeles.
Opened: 1923. **Holes:** 18. **Par:** 70/71. **Yards:** 6,235/5,225. **Course rating:** 70.2/70.2. **Slope:** 122/123. **Architect:** George Thomas/Jay Morrish. **Green fee:** $86/$105. **Credit cards:** All major. **Reduced fees:** Resort guests, twilight. **Caddies:** No. **Golf carts:** $15. **Discount golf packages:** Yes. **Season:** Year-round. **High:** March-Oct. **On site lodging:** Yes. **Rental clubs:** Yes. **Walking policy:** Unrestricted walking. **Metal spikes allowed:** Yes. **Range:** Yes (grass). **To obtain tee times:** Resort guests may make tee times 90 days in advance. All others 7 days in advance.
Notes: Senior PGA Tour events. 1997 NBC Golf Skills Challenge.
Subscriber comments: Scenic old beauty...Wonderful in every way...Two-union nines; first for power, second for touch...Excellent in all respects...The best service any

where...Beautiful scenery...In mint condition daily...Looks easy but extracts its pain...What golf in Shangri-la should be like...The best land, toughest back nine in the state...Best starter in all of golf...Old-style course, some great holes, wonderful service.

★★★OLD DEL MONTE GOLF COURSE

PM-1300 Sylvan Rd., Monterey, 93940, Monterey County, (408)373-2700, 60 miles S of San Jose.

Opened: 1897. **Holes:** 18. **Par:** 72/74. **Yards:** 6,339/5,526. **Course rating:** 71.3/71.1. **Slope:** 122/118. **Architect:** C. Maud. **Green fee:** $75. **Credit cards:** All major, JCB. **Reduced fees:** Resort guests, twilight, seniors, juniors. **Caddies:** Yes. **Golf carts:** $15. **Discount golf packages:** Yes. **Season:** Year-round. **High:** April-Oct. **On site lodging:** Yes. **Rental clubs:** Yes. **Walking policy:** Unrestricted walking. **Metal spikes allowed:** Yes. **Range:** No. **To obtain tee times:** Call up to 60 days in advance.

Subscriber comments: Great old California course...Not long, but fun...Great character...Tough, small greens...Superb condition always...Oldest course west of the Mississippi...Away from water, not a "Carmel" course full of snobs...Beautiful location...Old-style golf, very enjoyable.

★★½OLIVAS PARK GOLF COURSE

PM-3750 Olivas Park Dr., Ventura, 93001, Ventura County, (805)642-4303, 60 miles NW of Los Angeles.

Opened: 1964. **Holes:** 18. **Par:** 72/72. **Yards:** 6,760/5,501. **Course rating:** 72.6/72.4. **Slope:** 124/119. **Architect:** William F. Bell. **Green fee:** $16/$21. **Credit cards:** None. **Reduced fees:** Weekdays, twilight, seniors, juniors. **Caddies:** No. **Golf carts:** $20. **Discount golf packages:** No. **Season:** Year-round. **High:** May-Sept. **On site lodging:** No. **Rental clubs:** Yes. **Walking policy:** Unrestricted walking. **Metal spikes allowed:** Yes. **Range:** Yes (grass/mats). **To obtain tee times:** Call 7 days in advance.

Subscriber comments: Flat course, easy to walk...Pretty course near ocean, narrow streams cut some fairways...Always breezy, wide open...Best greens in 50 miles...Play in the morning; windy in p.m...Solid seaside muny...Interesting layout, tough with wind...Flat, but long...Grip it and rip it...Excellent practice area.

PGA WEST RESORT

R-56-150 PGA Blvd., La Quinta, 92253, Riverside County, (760)564-7170, 30 miles SE of Palm Springs.

Credit cards: MC, VISA, AMEX, Diners Club, JCB. **Reduced fees:** Weekdays, low season, resort guests, twilight. **Caddies:** No. **Golf carts:** Included in Green Fee. **Season:** Year-round. **High:** Jan.-April. **On site lodging:** Yes. **Rental clubs:** Yes. **Walking policy:** Mandatory cart. **Metal spikes allowed:** Yes. **Range:** Yes (grass/mats). **To obtain tee times:** Call golf shop.

★★★½JACK NICKLAUS TOURNAMENT COURSE

Opened: 1987. **Holes:** 18. **Par:** 72/72. **Yards:** 7,126/5,043. **Course rating:** 75.5/69.0. **Slope:** 138/116. **Architect:** Jack Nicklaus. **Green fee:** $45/$235. **Discount golf packages:** Yes.

Subscriber comments: Great course, everything was perfect except price...More playable and enjoyable than Stadium...Typical Nicklaus; target style, penalties everywhere...Mounds and more mounds...Elevated greens are tough...No.9 and 18 super holes...Challenging, great layout, great facility.

★★★★TPC STADIUM COURSE

Opened: 1986. **Holes:** 18. **Par:** 72/72. **Yards:** 7,261/5,087. **Course rating:** 77.3/70.3. **Slope:** 151/124. **Architect:** Pete Dye. **Green fee:** $55/$235. **Discount golf packages:** No.

Notes: Ranked 18th in 1997 Best in State.

Subscriber comments: Bring your "A" game or your snorkel and beach chair...Wow, it plays even harder than it looks...Even from the whites, it bites!...Only sadists need apply...Physically too much for high handicappers...Play at least once in your life...Very distinctive holes, very challenging...Lots of fun as long as you don't care about your score.

CALIFORNIA

★★★PACIFIC GROVE MUNICIPAL GOLF LINKS
PM-77 Asilomar Blvd., Pacific Grove, 93950, Monterey County, (408)648-3175, 17 miles W of Salinas.
Opened: 1932. **Holes:** 18. **Par:** 70/72. **Yards:** 5,732/5,305. **Course rating:** 67.5/70.5. **Slope:** 117/114. **Architect:** Jack Neville/Chandler Egan.
Green fee: $25/$30. **Credit cards:** None. **Reduced fees:** Twilight, juniors. **Caddies:** No. **Golf carts:** $25. **Discount golf packages:** No. **Season:** Year-round. **High:** N/A. **On site lodging:** No. **Rental clubs:** Yes. **Walking policy:** Unrestricted walking. **Metal spikes allowed:** Yes. **Range:** Yes (grass). **To obtain tee times:** Call 7 days in advance (each day for same day next week) beginning 7 a.m.
Subscriber comments: Poor man's Pebble Beach...Great ocean views, greens excellent...Play front nine to get to play back nine...Trees and deer...Very scenic back nine on sand dunes...Bring your ice plant wedge...As close to Scotland as you can get at a muny...Tight course, accuracy a must...Great value near Carmel...A classic gem.

★★½PAJARO VALLEY GOLF CLUB
PU-967 Salinas Rd., Watsonville, 95076, Santa Cruz County, (408)724-3851, 20 miles SE of Santa Cruz.
Opened: 1927. **Holes:** 18. **Par:** 72/72. **Yards:** 6,218/5,696. **Course rating:** 70.0/72.3. **Slope:** 122/123. **Architect:** Robert Muir Graves. **Green fee:** $27/$55. **Credit cards:** MC,VISA,AMEX. **Reduced fees:** Weekdays, twilight. **Caddies:** No. **Golf carts:** $28. **Discount golf packages:** Yes. **Season:** Year-round. **High:** April-Oct. **On site lodging:** No. **Rental clubs:** Yes. **Walking policy:** Unrestricted walking. **Metal spikes allowed:** Yes. **Range:** Yes (grass/mats). **To obtain tee times:** Call golf shop.
Subscriber comments: Great views...Tough 10th hole...Can be windy late in the afternoon...Charming, but can't buy a flat lie...A lovely course...Plays longer than yardage...Great layout...Lots of elevation changes, fun...Terrain somewhat hilly but can be walked.

★★★PALA MESA RESORT
R-2001 S. Hwy. 395, Fallbrook, 92028, San Diego County, (760)728-5881, (800)722-4700, 40 miles N of San Diego.
Opened: 1964. **Holes:** 18. **Par:** 72/73. **Yards:** 6,528/5,848. **Course rating:** 72.0/74.5. **Slope:** 131/128. **Architect:** Dick Rossen. **Green fee:** $35/$70. **Credit cards:** MC,VISA,AMEX. **Reduced fees:** Weekdays, low season, resort guests, twilight, juniors. **Caddies:** No. **Golf carts:** Included in Green Fee. **Discount golf packages:** Yes. **Season:** Year-round. **High:** Jan.-May. **On site lodging:** Yes. **Rental clubs:** Yes. **Walking policy:** Mandatory cart. **Metal spikes allowed:** Yes. **Range:** Yes (grass/mats). **To obtain tee times:** Call 7 days in advance.
Notes: Golf Digest School site.
Subscriber comments: Beautiful resort course, always in good shape...So narrow my foursome had to go single file...Lovely area. Good golf. Aging resort...Front and back nines very different...Fast, undulating greens...Wonderful course, gorgeous views...Real tight and tough, must be accurate off the tee...Nicely kept, tough but fair.

★★★PALM DESERT RESORT COUNTRY CLUB
77-333 Country Club Dr., Palm Desert, 92260, Riverside County, (760)345-2791.
Opened: 1980. **Holes:** 18. **Par:** 72/72. **Yards:** 6,585/5,670. **Course rating:** 70.8/71.8. **Slope:** 117/123. **Architect:** Joe Mulleneaux. **Green fee:** $60/$75. **Credit cards:** MC,VISA,AMEX. **Reduced fees:** Weekdays, low season, twilight. **Caddies:** No. **Golf carts:** Included in Green Fee. **Discount golf packages:** Yes. **Season:** Nov.-Sept. **High:** Nov.-April. **On site lodging:** Yes. **Rental clubs:** Yes. **Walking policy:** Mandatory cart. **Metal spikes allowed:** Yes. **Range:** Yes (grass). **To obtain tee times:** Call 5 days in advance.
Subscriber comments: Great variety...Tough back nine, great 18th...First-class resort...Fun layout...A fabulous off-season value...Good condo course...Nice course, fairways lined by homes...Very friendly...Moderate condition.

★★PALM SPRINGS COUNTRY CLUB
PU-2500 Whitewater Club Dr., Palm Springs, 92262, Riverside County, (760)323-2626.
Opened: N/A. **Holes:** 18. **Par:** 72/72. **Yards:** 6,396/4,991. **Course rating:** 68.9/71.4. **Slope:** 115/113. **Architect:** N/A. **Green fee:** $15/$50. **Credit cards:** MC,VISA,DISC.

Reduced fees: Weekdays, twilight, juniors. **Caddies:** No. **Golf carts:** Included in Green Fee. **Discount golf packages:** No. **Season:** Year-round. **High:** Jan.-April. **On site lodging:** No. **Rental clubs:** Yes. **Walking policy:** Mandatory cart. **Metal spikes allowed:** Yes. **Range:** Yes (grass). **To obtain tee times:** Call golf shop.

★★★½PALOS VERDES GOLF CLUB

3301 Via Campesina, Palos Verdes Estates, 90274, Los Angeles County, (310)375-2759, 20 miles S of Los Angeles.
Opened: 1924. **Holes:** 18. **Par:** 71/70. **Yards:** 6,116/5,506. **Course rating:** 70.4/68.9. **Slope:** 131/126. **Architect:** George C. Thomas Jr.. **Green fee:** $105/$105. **Credit cards:** MC,VISA,AMEX. **Reduced fees:** N/A. **Caddies:** No. **Golf carts:** Included in Green Fee. **Discount golf packages:** No. **Season:** Year-round. **High:** June-Aug. **On site lodging:** No. **Rental clubs:** No. **Walking policy:** Mandatory cart. **Metal spikes allowed:** No. **Range:** No. **To obtain tee times:** Call 7 days in advance.
Subscriber comments: Beautiful old course, play it at least once...Very scenic...Stop and look at the woodpeckers banging away...Fine location with good coastal views...Hilly, many ups and downs...Short, tight, old-fashioned course with small, guarded greens...Designed by the same architect who did Riviera, Bel-Air, Los Angeles CC, Ojai.

★★★½PARADISE VALLEY GOLF COURSE

PU-3950 Paradise Valley Dr., Fairfield, 94533, Solano County, (707)426-1600, 45 miles NE of San Francisco.
Opened: 1993. **Holes:** 18. **Par:** 72/72. **Yards:** 6,993/5,413. **Course rating:** 74.1/71.1. **Slope:** 135/119. **Architect:** Robert Muir Graves. **Green fee:** $18/$36. **Credit cards:** MC,VISA,AMEX. **Reduced fees:** Weekdays, low season, twilight. **Caddies:** No. **Golf carts:** $13. **Discount golf packages:** Yes. **Season:** Year-round. **High:** N/A. **On site lodging:** No. **Rental clubs:** Yes. **Walking policy:** Unrestricted walking. **Metal spikes allowed:** Yes. **Range:** Yes (grass/mats). **To obtain tee times:** Call 7 days in advance.
Subscriber comments: Great layout, classic 18th hole...Par 5 10th a "thinker"...Maturing into a nice track...Windy area...Lots of moguls, fast greens...Fun course to play...Best course in Solano County...Picturesque setting...Great sports bar...When the wind blows as tough as any.

★★★★½PASATIEMPO GOLF CLUB

18 Clubhouse Rd., Santa Cruz, 95060, Santa Cruz County, (408)459-9155, 30 miles S of San Jose.
Opened: 1929. **Holes:** 18. **Par:** 71/72. **Yards:** 6,483/5,647. **Course rating:** 72.7/73.6. **Slope:** 141/135. **Architect:** Alister Mackenzie. **Green fee:** $69/$115. **Credit cards:** MC,VISA,AMEX. **Reduced fees:** Twilight. **Caddies:** Yes. **Golf carts:** $34. **Discount golf packages:** No. **Season:** Year-round. **High:** May-Oct. **On site lodging:** No. **Rental clubs:** Yes. **Walking policy:** Unrestricted walking. **Metal spikes allowed:** Yes. **Range:** Yes (grass/mats). **To obtain tee times:** Call 7 days in advance for weekdays. Call on Monday after 10 a.m. for upcoming weekend.
Notes: Ranked 83rd in 1997-98 America's 100 Greatest; 8th in 1997 Best in State.
Subscriber comments: Difficult course that rewards great shots...Mackenzie masterpiece...Greatest golf course ever built...Great variety of holes...A classic...All-time toughest greens...No.1 handicap hole is best two-shotter in state...Great walking course...No.6 is most beautiful hole.

★★PEACOCK GAP GOLF & COUNTRY CLUB

333 Biscayne Dr., San Rafael, 94901, Marin County, (415)453-4940, 12 miles N of San Francisco.
Opened: 1960. **Holes:** 18. **Par:** 71/73. **Yards:** 6,354/5,629. **Course rating:** N/A. **Slope:** 121/126. **Architect:** William F. Bell. **Green fee:** $28/$47. **Credit cards:** MC,VISA. **Reduced fees:** Twilight. **Caddies:** No. **Golf carts:** $22. **Discount golf packages:** Yes. **Season:** Year-round. **High:** March-Oct. **On site lodging:** No. **Rental clubs:** Yes. **Walking policy:** Walking at certain times. **Metal spikes allowed:** Yes. **Range:** Yes (grass/mats). **To obtain tee times:** Call 7 days in advance for weekdays. Call Thursday after noon for weekends.

CALIFORNIA

★★★★★PEBBLE BEACH GOLF LINKS
R-17 Mile Dr., Pebble Beach, 93953, Monterey County, (408)624-3811, (800)654-9300, 45 miles S of San Jose.
Opened: 1919. **Holes:** 18. **Par:** 72/72. **Yards:** 6,799/5,197. **Course rating:** 74.4/71.9. **Slope:** 142/130. **Architect:** Jack Neville and Douglas Grant. **Green fee:** $225/$275. **Credit cards:** All major,Diners Club.
Reduced fees: N/A. **Caddies:** Yes. **Golf carts:** $25. **Discount golf packages:** Yes.
Season: Year-round. **High:** March-Nov. **On site lodging:** Yes. **Rental clubs:** Yes.
Walking policy: Unrestricted walking. **Metal spikes allowed:** Yes. **Range:** Yes (mats).
To obtain tee times: Call 1 day in advance.
Notes: Ranked 4th in 1997-98 America's 100 Greatest, 2nd in 1997 Best in State. 1972, 1982, 1992 U.S. Open; AT&T Pebble Beach National Pro-Am annually; 1977 PGA Championship.
Subscriber comments: The history makes you shake from nerves...Best true golf course...As good as it gets...Once before you die...Cheap at twice the price...Tremendous layout and beauty...A religious experience...Six-hour round...The most stunning course on the planet...It's Pebble, quit groaning about the price...Great course...Snobby...Still the finest golf on planet Earth.

PELICAN HILL GOLF CLUB
R-22651 Pelican Hill Rd., Newport Coast, 92657, Orange County, (714)759-5190, 40 miles N of Los Angeles.
Architect: Tom Fazio. **Green fee:** $135/$215. **Credit cards:** MC,VISA,AMEX,Diners Club, JCB. **Reduced fees:** Resort guests, twilight. **Caddies:** No. **Golf carts:** Included in Green Fee. **Discount golf packages:** Yes. **Season:** Year-round. **High:** Year-round.
On site lodging: No. **Rental clubs:** Yes. **Walking policy:** Mandatory cart. **Metal spikes allowed:** Yes. **To obtain tee times:** Call 6 days in advance with credit card beginning at 6:30 a.m. Noncancellable reservations may be made 14 days in advance.
★★★★OCEAN NORTH COURSE
Opened: 1993. **Holes:** 18. **Par:** 71/71. **Yards:** 6,856/5,800. **Course rating:** 73.6/73.0.
Slope: 136/125. **Range:** Yes (grass).
Notes: Ranked 20th in 1997 Best in State.
Subscriber comments: Easier than its sister, but great fun...Absolutely spectacular...Memorable ocean views...Hilly but in excellent condition, requires all shots and good course management...Target golf, with long carries over ravines...Worth the huge fee on a sunny day...Forget the South course, play this one! Better holes and better views, only drawback is nondescript 18th hole.
★★★★OCEAN SOUTH COURSE
Opened: 1991. **Holes:** 18. **Par:** 70/70. **Yards:** 6,634/5,409. **Course rating:** 72.1/72.5.
Slope: 130/124. **Range:** Yes (grass/mats).
Notes: Ranked 21st in 1997 Best in State.
Subscriber comments: Prettier and tougher than North course...Beautiful layout...Good test with wind...Canyons, canyons and more canyons...Beautiful course, fast greens...Worth every penny, breathtaking coastal views...High visual appeal...Tough, fair, but 90-yard par 3 detracts...Good finishing hole...Best in Southern California...Absolutely beautiful course and views.

★★★PINE MOUNTAIN LAKE COUNTRY CLUB
19228 Pine Mountain Dr., Groveland, 95321, Tuolumne County, (209)962-8620, 90 miles SE of Sacramento.
Opened: 1969. **Holes:** 18. **Par:** 70/72. **Yards:** 6,363/5,726. **Course rating:** 70.6/73.4.
Slope: 125/122. **Architect:** William F. Bell. **Green fee:** $16/$38. **Credit cards:** All major. **Reduced fees:** Twilight. **Caddies:** No. **Golf carts:** $26. **Discount golf packages:** No. **Season:** Year-round. **High:** May-Sept. **On site lodging:** No. **Rental clubs:** Yes. **Walking policy:** Walking at certain times. **Metal spikes allowed:** Yes. **Range:** Yes (grass/mats). **To obtain tee times:** Call up to 10 days in advance.
Subscriber comments: Nice mountain course...Beautiful 10th hole, view of Yosemite...Out of the way but a real great resort course...Tight, a lot of blind shots...Fun golf, interesting holes.

★★½PITTSBURG DELTA VIEW GOLF COURSE
PM-2242 Golf Club Rd., Pittsburg, 94565, Contra Costa County, (510)439-4040, 40 miles NE of San Francisco.
Opened: 1950. **Holes:** 18. **Par:** 71/72. **Yards:** 6,359/5,405. **Course rating:** 71.4/70.0. **Slope:** 130/124. **Architect:** Robert Muir Graves. **Green fee:** $13/$20. **Credit cards:** MC,VISA. **Reduced fees:** Twilight, seniors, juniors. **Caddies:** No. **Golf carts:** $19. **Discount golf packages:** No. **Season:** Year-round. **High:** Year-round. **On site lodging:** No. **Rental clubs:** Yes. **Walking policy:** Unrestricted walking. **Metal spikes allowed:** Yes. **Range:** Yes (grass/mats). **To obtain tee times:** Call golf shop one week in advance.
Subscriber comments: Play in the hills...8th hole, 250-foot drop to green...Good layout, a challenge all the way...A real sleeper, well-known to locals...Some interesting holes, many elevation changes...Don't walk; course goes way uphill...Excellent muny...Steep climbs to nice views...Great sleeper course.

★★★PLUMAS LAKE GOLF & COUNTRY CLUB
1551 Country Club Ave., Marysville, 95901, Yuba County, (916)742-3201.
Opened: 1926. **Holes:** 18. **Par:** 71/72. **Yards:** 6,437/5,759. **Course rating:** 70.5/70.3. **Slope:** 122/126. **Architect:** Jack Bosley/Bob Baldock. **Green fee:** $17/$22. **Credit cards:** None. **Reduced fees:** Twilight, seniors, juniors. **Caddies:** No. **Golf carts:** $18. **Discount golf packages:** No. **Season:** Year-round. **High:** April-Oct. **On site lodging:** No. **Rental clubs:** Yes. **Walking policy:** Unrestricted walking. **Metal spikes allowed:** Yes. **Range:** Yes (grass/mats). **To obtain tee times:** Call 7 days in advance.
Subscriber comments: Flat course. Fun to play...Old established course, easy to play, nice setting...Very tough back nine...Nice mix of holes...Fair course, walkable.

★★★PLUMAS PINES COUNTRY CLUB
PU-402 Poplar Valley Rd., Blairsden, 96103, Plumas County, (916)836-1420, 63 miles W of Reno.
Opened: N/A. **Holes:** 18. **Par:** 72/72. **Yards:** 6,504/5,106. **Course rating:** 71.6/68.5. **Slope:** 127/122. **Architect:** Homer Flint. **Green fee:** $25/$50. **Credit cards:** All major. **Reduced fees:** Weekdays, low season, twilight. **Caddies:** No. **Golf carts:** Included in Green Fee. **Discount golf packages:** Yes. **Season:** April-Oct. **High:** June-Sept. **On site lodging:** Yes. **Rental clubs:** Yes. **Walking policy:** Walking at certain times. **Metal spikes allowed:** Yes. **Range:** Yes (grass/mats). **To obtain tee times:** Call golf shop.
Subscriber comments: Enjoyable layout, not too demanding...Beautiful location...Short course in pretty mountain meadow...Spectacular greens, like putting on carpet...Very tight, treelined mountain course...Beautiful setting but too many condos...Target golf, keep ball in fairway...Beautifully maintained.

★★★★POPPY HILLS GOLF COURSE
PU-3200 Lopez Rd., Pebble Beach, 93953, Monterey County, (408)625-2154, 60 miles S of San Jose.
Opened: 1986. **Holes:** 18. **Par:** 72/72. **Yards:** 6,861/5,473. **Course rating:** 74.8/71.2. **Slope:** 143/131. **Architect:** Robert Trent Jones Jr. **Green fee:** $115/$130 (NCGA members: $45/$50). **Credit cards:** MC,VISA. **Reduced fees:** Juniors. **Caddies:** Yes. **Golf carts:** $30. **Discount golf packages:** No. **Season:** Year-round. **High:** May-Aug. **On site lodging:** No. **Rental clubs:** Yes. **Walking policy:** Unrestricted walking. **Metal spikes allowed:** No. **Range:** Yes (grass). **To obtain tee times:** Call up to 30 days in advance.
Notes: AT&T Pebble Beach National Pro Am.
Subscriber comments: Beautiful Peninsula course, no ocean, excellent golf...A good test on a hilly layout...Great course...Nice clubhouse, best grill in area...Tough...Home course for Northern California Golf Association, great deal for members...The devil designed the greens...Hilly and long...Beautiful forest setting.

★★★★POPPY RIDGE GOLF COURSE
PU-4280 Greenville Rd., Livermore, 94550, Alameda County, (510)447-6779, (510)456-8202, 10 miles E of Pleasanton.
Opened: 1996. **Holes:** 27. **Architect:** Rees Jones. **Green fee:** $35/$70. **Credit cards:** MC,VISA,AMEX. **Reduced fees:** Weekdays, twilight. **Caddies:** No. **Golf carts:** $24. **Discount golf packages:** No. **Season:** Year-round. **High:** April-Oct. **On site lodging:**

No. **Rental clubs:** Yes. **Walking policy:** Unrestricted walking. **Metal spikes allowed:** No. **Range:** Yes (grass). **To obtain tee times:** Call automated service any time at (510)455-2035.

CHARDONNAY/ZINFANDEL
Par: 72/72. **Yards:** 7,048/5,267. **Course rating:** 74.6/70.2. **Slope:** 139/120.

MERLOT/CHARDONNAY
Par: 72/72. **Yards:** 7,106/5,212. **Course rating:** 74.6/70.2. **Slope:** 139/120.

ZINFANDEL/MERLOT
Par: 72/72. **Yards:** 7,128/5,265. **Course rating:** 74.6/70.2. **Slope:** 139/120.

Subscriber comments: New but looks great...Wonderful vistas...Long, tough par 4s...Excellent course, play in a.m. before winds...Inland links gem...Slick, tiered greens...Needs some seasoning and some trees...Welcome addition to Bay Area golf...Plenty of trouble, bring your sand wedge.

(GOOD VALUE)

★★ PRESIDENTS CLUB AT INDIAN PALMS
R-48-630 Monroe St., Indio, 92201, Riverside County, (760)347-2326, (800)778-5288, 20 miles E of Palm Springs.
Opened: 1948. **Holes:** 27. **Par:** N/A. **Yards:** N/A. **Course rating:** N/A. **Slope:** N/A.
Architect: Jackie Cochran/Helen Detweiler. **Green fee:** $25/$65. **Credit cards:** MC,VISA,AMEX. **Reduced fees:** Low season, resort guests, twilight. **Caddies:** No.
Golf carts: Included in Green Fee. **Discount golf packages:** Yes. **Season:** Year-round.
High: Jan.-March. **On site lodging:** Yes. **Rental clubs:** Yes. **Walking policy:** Mandatory cart. **Metal spikes allowed:** Yes. **Range:** Yes (grass). **To obtain tee times:** Call up to 3 days in advance.

PRIMM VALLEY GOLF CLUB - LAKES COURSE
R-Sweetbay Dr., Nipton, San Bernardino County, (800)386-7867, (800)248-8453, 40 miles S of Las Vegas.
Opened: 1997. **Holes:** 18. **Par:** 71/71. **Yards:** 6,945/5,019. **Course rating:** 74.0.
Slope: 134. **Architect:** Tom Fazio. **Green fee:** $60/$185. **Credit cards:** All major.
Reduced fees: Weekdays, low season, resort guests, twilight. **Caddies:** No. **Golf carts:** Included in Green Fee. **Discount golf packages:** Yes. **Season:** Year-round.
High: Jan.-May, Oct.-Dec. **On site lodging:** Yes. **Rental clubs:** No. **Walking policy:** Unrestricted walking. **Metal spikes allowed:** No. **Range:** Yes (grass). **To obtain tee times:** Resort guests may book 14 days in advance. Outside guests 7 days in advance. Advanced tee times through Golf Packages.
Notes: Ranked 8th in 1997 Best New Upscale Courses.

★★★ QUAIL RANCH GOLF COURSE
15960 Gilman Springs Rd., Moreno Valley, 92555, Riverside County, (909)654-2727. Call club for further information.
Subscriber comments: Tough greens, three putts are common...Worth the drive...Narrow fairways, take extra balls...Sneaky long but nice...Beautiful 9th and 18th holes with waterfalls.

★★★½ RAMS HILL COUNTRY CLUB
R-1881 Rams Hill Rd., Borrego Springs, 92004, San Diego County, (760)767-5124, (800)292-2944, 70 miles E of San Diego.
Opened: 1983. **Holes:** 18. **Par:** 72/72. **Yards:** 6,866/5,694. **Course rating:** 74.0.
Slope: 133/119. **Architect:** Ted Robinson. **Green fee:** $50/$85. **Credit cards:** MC,VISA. **Reduced fees:** Low season, resort guests, twilight. **Caddies:** No. **Golf carts:** Included in Green Fee. **Discount golf packages:** Yes. **Season:** Nov.-Sept.
High: Nov.-April. **On site lodging:** Yes. **Rental clubs:** No. **Walking policy:** Mandatory cart. **Metal spikes allowed:** Yes. **Range:** Yes (grass/mats). **To obtain tee times:** Call golf shop up to 14 days in advance.

★★★½ THE RANCH COURSE AT DIABLO GRANDE
R-10001 Oak Flat Rd., Patterson, 95363, Stanislaus County, (209)892-4653, 75 miles S of Sacramento.
Opened: 1996. **Holes:** 18. **Par:** 72/71. **Yards:** 7,243/5,026. **Course rating:** 75.1/69.0.
Slope: 139/116. **Architect:** Denis Griffiths. **Green fee:** $40/$80. **Credit cards:** All

major. **Reduced fees:** Weekdays, twilight. **Caddies:** No. **Golf carts:** Included in Green Fee. **Discount golf packages:** No. **Season:** Year-round. **High:** N/A. **On site lodging:** No. **Rental clubs:** Yes. **Walking policy:** Unrestricted walking. **Metal spikes allowed:** Yes. **Range:** Yes (grass/mats). **To obtain tee times:** Call golf shop up to 7 days in advance.
Subscriber comments: Starts slow, but keeps getting better...Great new course...Demands accurate mid and long irons...Good layout, good pro shop, great restaurant...A diamond in the rough...One day may be considered among the country's greats...Out of the way...Quality design, great greens...Very challenging.
Special Notes: Walking is discouraged but not prohibited.

★★★RANCHO BERNARDO INN

R-17550 Bernardo Oaks Dr., San Diego, 92128, San Diego County, (619)675-8470, (800)662-6439.
Opened: 1962. **Holes:** 18. **Par:** 72/72. **Yards:** 6,458/5,448. **Course rating:** 70.6/71.2. **Slope:** 122/119. **Architect:** William F. Bell. **Green fee:** $65/$85. **Credit cards:** All major. **Reduced fees:** Weekdays, resort guests, twilight, juniors. **Caddies:** No. **Golf carts:** Included in Green Fee. **Discount golf packages:** Yes. **Season:** Year-round. **High:** Dec.-May. **On site lodging:** Yes. **Rental clubs:** Yes. **Walking policy:** Walking at certain times. **Metal spikes allowed:** Yes. **Range:** Yes (grass/mats). **To obtain tee times:** Hotel guest call anytime; outside guest, 7 days in advance.
Subscriber comments: Good resort course...Concrete-lined streams need softening...Wonderful course with very nice clubhouse...Neat old-style course, no gimmicks...Must stay for dinner...Great 18th...Well maintained...Plays long...Must be best hotel course in US.

RANCHO CANADA GOLF CLUB

PU-4860 Carmel Valley Rd., Carmel, 93923, Monterey County, (408)624-0111, (800)536-9459, 8 miles S of Monterey.
Architect: Robert Dean Putman. **Credit cards:** MC,VISA,AMEX,Diners Club. **Reduced fees:** Twilight. **Caddies:** No. **Golf carts:** $28. **Discount golf packages:** Yes. **Season:** Year-round. **High:** April-Oct. **On site lodging:** No. **Rental clubs:** Yes. **Walking policy:** Unrestricted walking. **Metal spikes allowed:** Yes. **Range:** Yes (grass/mats). **To obtain tee times:** Call golf shop any time.
★★★EAST COURSE
Opened: 1971. **Holes:** 18. **Par:** 71/72. **Yards:** 6,109/5,267. **Course rating:** 68.7/69.4. **Slope:** 120/114. **Green fee:** $30/$55.
Subscriber comments: Short, narrow, many trees...Unremarkable, but solid, tough golf, small greens...Shorter of two courses, some challenges...Need to knock down a few trees...Have to cross the river two times...Well kept, tight in spots, lots of good holes...Great location.
★★★WEST COURSE
Opened: 1970. **Holes:** 18. **Par:** 71/72. **Yards:** 6,349/5,568. **Course rating:** 70.4/71.9. **Slope:** 125/118. **Green fee:** $40/$70.
Subscriber comments: Sneaky tough. Better than East...Learn to work the ball or bring a chainsaw...Very good Monterey public golf...Challenging course...Picturesque, enjoyable to play...Views of valley and Carmel River are very nice...A notch above sister course...Best greens I've seen for a public course.

★★½RANCHO DEL RAY GOLF CLUB

PU-5250 Green Sands Ave., Atwater, 95301, Merced County, (209)358-7131, 30 miles S of Modesto.
Opened: N/A. **Holes:** 18. **Par:** 72/75. **Yards:** 6,712/5,845. **Course rating:** 71.8/73.6. **Slope:** 119/125. **Architect:** N/A. **Green fee:** $12/$22. **Credit cards:** All major,ATM Debit. **Reduced fees:** Weekdays, twilight. **Caddies:** No. **Golf carts:** $15. **Discount golf packages:** No. **Season:** Year-round. **High:** Spring-Fall. **On site lodging:** No. **Rental clubs:** Yes. **Walking policy:** Unrestricted walking. **Metal spikes allowed:** Yes. **Range:** Yes (grass). **To obtain tee times:** Tee times are taken on Monday for Tuesday-Monday.
Subscriber comments: Classic golf, long course, great...Significant improvement overall to course...Ownership just starting to spend money with increased competition.

★★½RANCHO MARIA GOLF CLUB

PU-1950 Casmalia Rd., Santa Maria, 93455, Santa Barbara County, (805)937-2019.
Opened: 1965. **Holes:** 18. **Par:** 72/73. **Yards:** 6,390/5,504. **Course rating:** 70.2/71.3.
Slope: 119/123. **Architect:** Bob Baldock. **Green fee:** $15/$25. **Credit cards:** MC,VISA.
Reduced fees: Weekdays, twilight, seniors, juniors. **Caddies:** No. **Golf carts:** $18.
Discount golf packages: No. **Season:** Year-round. **High:** Year-round. **On site lodging:**
No. **Rental clubs:** Yes. **Walking policy:** Unrestricted walking. **Metal spikes allowed:**
Yes. **Range:** Yes (grass). **To obtain tee times:** Call 2 days in advance for weekdays; 7
days in advance for weekends and holidays.
Subscriber comments: Nice wooded course. Gets windy in afternoon...Ocean views
great...Good mature layout...Fun course, could be in better shape.

RANCHO MURIETA COUNTRY CLUB

7000 Alameda Dr., Rancho Murieta, 95683, Sacramento County, (916)354-3440, 15
miles SE of Sacramento.
Opened: 1971. **Credit cards:** MC,VISA,AMEX. **Reduced fees:** Weekdays, low season,
juniors. **Caddies:** No. **Golf carts:** Included in Green Fee. **Discount golf packages:** No.
Season: Year-round. **High:** April-Oct. **Rental clubs:** Yes. **Walking policy:** Mandatory
cart. **Metal spikes allowed:** No. **Range:** Yes (grass/mats). **To obtain tee times:** Call 3
days in advance.
Notes: 1986-95 Raley's Senior Gold Rush.

★★★½NORTH COURSE

Holes: 18. **Par:** 72/72. **Yards:** 6,839/5,608. **Course rating:** 72.6/73.5. **Slope:** 136/135.
Architect: Bert Stamps/Arnold Palmer/Ed Seay. **Green fee:** $60/$85. **On site lodging:**
No.
Subscriber comments: Demanding course, tougher than the card suggests...Great
golf course, fast greens...Long and tough with fast greens. Bring your best game...Best
course within 150 miles...Requires different types of shots on each hole...Past home of
Senior PGA event...Wonderful setting, great holes.

★★★½SOUTH COURSE

Holes: 18. **Par:** 72/72. **Yards:** 6,894/5,583. **Course rating:** 72.9/71.8. **Slope:** 129/124.
Architect: Ted Robinson. **Green fee:** $50/$85. **On site lodging:** Yes.
Subscriber comments: Much easier than the North course...Challenging, too many
OBs...Wonderful setting, great holes...Solid.

★★★RANCHO PARK GOLF COURSE

PM-10460 W. Pico Blvd., Los Angeles, 90064, Los Angeles County, (310)839-4374.
Opened: 1949. **Holes:** 18. **Par:** 71/71. **Yards:** 6,585/5,928. **Course rating:** N/A. **Slope:**
124/122. **Architect:** William P. Bell/William H. Johnson. **Green fee:** $17/$23. **Credit
cards:** None. **Reduced fees:** Weekdays, twilight. **Caddies:** No. **Golf carts:** $20.
Discount golf packages: No. **Season:** Year-round. **High:** April-Oct. **On site lodging:**
No. **Rental clubs:** No. **Walking policy:** Unrestricted walking. **Metal spikes allowed:**
Yes. **Range:** Yes. **To obtain tee times:** Reservation card issued by city or walk in for
waiting list any time.
Notes: Los Angeles Open site 1956-72.
Subscriber comments: Best LA course...I can't believe it's smack in LA...Hilly, but a
good course...Great layout, harder than it looks...Played the LA Open here in the
1960s...Very slow play when you can get on...Golf balls from driving range ruin the 18th
hole...Saw OJ...Fun, cheap, crowded...Great course...Play early, play fast.

RANCHO SAN DIEGO GOLF CLUB

PU-3121 Willow Glen Dr., El Cajon, 92019, San Diego County, (619)442-9891.
Opened: 1963. **Architect:** O.W. Moorman/A.C. Sears. **Credit cards:** MC,VISA.
Caddies: No. **Golf carts:** $10. **Discount golf packages:** No. **Season:** Year-round.
High: March-Oct. **On site lodging:** No. **Rental clubs:** Yes. **Walking policy:**
Unrestricted walking. **Metal spikes allowed:** Yes. **Range:** Yes (grass/mats). **To obtain
tee times:** Call golf shop up to 14 days in advance.

★★½IVANHOE COURSE

Holes: 18. **Par:** 72/73. **Yards:** 7,011/5,624. **Course rating:** 72.6/72.0. **Slope:** 126/116.
Green fee: $11/$37. **Reduced fees:** Weekdays, twilight, seniors.
Subscriber comments: Basic golf. Better than working...Always good greens...Nice
course, fair condition, good to walk...Excellent course for all levels of golfer.

CALIFORNIA

★★½MONTE VISTA COURSE
Holes: 18. **Par:** 71/72. **Yards:** 6,248/5,540. **Course rating:** 69.7/75.7. **Slope:** 116/134.
Green fee: $11/$34. **Reduced fees:** Weekdays, twilight, seniors, juniors.
Subscriber comments: Not as good as sister course...Long walk, easy and flat...Killer 500-yard 1st...Shorter, little less challenging.

★★RANCHO SAN JOAQUIN GOLF CLUB
PU-1 Sandburg Way, Irvine, 92612, Orange County, (714)451-0840, 18 miles S of Los Angeles.
Opened: 1971. **Holes:** 18. **Par:** 72/72. **Yards:** 6,453/5,794. **Course rating:** 70.6/73.1.
Slope: 118/121. **Architect:** William F. Bell. **Green fee:** $13/$60. **Credit cards:**
MC,VISA,AMEX. **Reduced fees:** Weekdays, twilight, seniors, juniors. **Caddies:** No.
Golf carts: Included in Green Fee. **Discount golf packages:** No. **Season:** Year-round.
High: N/A. **On site lodging:** No. **Rental clubs:** Yes. **Walking policy:** Unrestricted walking. **Metal spikes allowed:** Yes. **Range:** Yes (grass/mats). **To obtain tee times:** Call golf shop.

★★★RANCHO SOLANO GOLF COURSE
PM-3250 Rancho Solano Pkwy., Fairfield, 94533, Solano County, (707)429-4653, 30 miles W of Sacramento.
Opened: 1991. **Holes:** 18. **Par:** 72/72. **Yards:** 6,705/5,206. **Course rating:** 72.1/69.6.
Slope: 128/117. **Architect:** Gary Roger Baird. **Green fee:** $18/$36. **Credit cards:** All major. **Reduced fees:** Weekdays, twilight, seniors, juniors. **Caddies:** No. **Golf carts:**
$13. **Discount golf packages:** Yes. **Season:** Year-round. **High:** June-Sept. **On site lodging:** No. **Rental clubs:** Yes. **Walking policy:** Unrestricted walking. **Metal spikes allowed:** Yes. **Range:** Yes (mats). **To obtain tee times:** Call 7 days in advance.
Subscriber comments: Very easy, open. Ego builder...Computerized golf carts are great...Too up and down, poor walking course...three-putt city, largest greens around...Excellent city-owned "resort"...If you can't putt, don't come...Beautiful newer foothills course...Plenty of water, good huge greens.

★★★RECREATION PARK GOLF COURSE
PU-5001 Deukmejian Dr., Long Beach, 90804, Los Angeles County, (562)494-5000, 15 miles S of Los Angeles.
Opened: 1924. **Holes:** 18. **Par:** 72/74. **Yards:** 6,317/5,793. **Course rating:** 69.0/72.6.
Slope: 112/120. **Architect:** William P. Bell. **Green fee:** $18/$23. **Credit cards:**
MC,VISA,AMEX. **Reduced fees:** Weekdays, twilight, seniors, juniors. **Caddies:** No.
Golf carts: $21. **Discount golf packages:** No. **Season:** Year-round. **High:** N/A. **On site lodging:** No. **Rental clubs:** Yes. **Walking policy:** Unrestricted walking. **Metal spikes allowed:** Yes. **Range:** Yes (mats). **To obtain tee times:** Must have reservation card ($10.00/year) to obtain tee times up to 6 days in advance. Without card call 1 day in advance after 12:30 p.m.
Subscriber comments: Public golf factory...Classic...Best of Long Beach courses...Hundreds of friendly rabbits on course...Old and pretty public course, good upkeep, but crowded...Has three of the toughest par 4s in a row anywhere...Average first six holes, then "wow"...Sporty layout, not very long.

★★★★REDHAWK GOLF CLUB
45100 Redhawk Pkwy., Temecula, 92592, Riverside County, (909)695-1424, (800)451-4295, 30 miles S of Riverside.
Opened: 1991. **Holes:** 18. **Par:** 72/72. **Yards:** 7,139/5,510. **Course rating:** 75.7/72.0.
Slope: 149/124. **Architect:** Ron Fream. **Green fee:** $45/$75. **Credit cards:**
MC,VISA,AMEX. **Reduced fees:** Twilight, juniors. **Caddies:** No. **Golf carts:** Included in Green Fee. **Discount golf packages:** No. **Season:** Year-round. **High:** Nov.-April. **On site lodging:** No. **Rental clubs:** Yes. **Walking policy:** Mandatory cart. **Metal spikes allowed:** Yes. **Range:** Yes (grass/mats). **To obtain tee times:** Available 7 days in advance.
Subscriber comments: Tough from the tips...Out of the way but worth it...Great golf course...Lots of variety, water, sand, change in elevation...What a finishing hole...Great golf adventure at reasonable price......Play it only if you're feeling masochistic...Great course, flowers everywhere, rock tunnels...Great par 3s.

CALIFORNIA

★★★½RESORT AT SQUAW CREEK
R-400 Squaw Creek Rd., Olympic Valley, 96146, Placer County, (916)581-6637, (800)327-3353, 45 miles W of Reno, NV.
Opened: 1992. **Holes:** 18. **Par:** 71/71. **Yards:** 6,931/5,097. **Course rating:** 72.9/68.9. **Slope:** 140/127. **Architect:** Robert Trent Jones Jr. **Green fee:** $110/$120. **Credit cards:** MC,VISA,AMEX. **Reduced fees:** Weekdays, low season, twilight. **Caddies:** No. **Golf carts:** Included in Green Fee. **Discount golf packages:** Yes. **Season:** May-Oct. **High:** N/A. **On site lodging:** Yes. **Rental clubs:** Yes. **Walking policy:** Walking at certain times. **Metal spikes allowed:** Yes. **Range:** Yes (mats). **To obtain tee times:** Call golf shop with credit card number to hold a tee time.
Subscriber comments: Great mountain vistas...Course is too tough, too many forced carries...Environmentally sensitive design, average player will need a dozen balls...Views and course outstanding...Plays through marshlands and woods...Just barely enough room for a course...Target golf, need accuracy.

RIDGEMARK GOLF & COUNTRY CLUB
R-3800 Airline Hwy., Hollister, 95023, San Benito County, (408)634-2222, (800)637-8151, 40 miles SE of San Jose.
Opened: 1972. **Architect:** Richard Bigler. **Credit cards:** All major,Diners Club. **Reduced fees:** Twilight. **Caddies:** No. **Golf carts:** Included in Green Fee. **Discount golf packages:** Yes. **Season:** Year-round. **High:** Year-round. **On site lodging:** Yes. **Rental clubs:** Yes. **Walking policy:** Mandatory cart. **Metal spikes allowed:** Yes. **Range:** Yes (grass/mats).
★★★DIABLO COURSE
Holes: 18. **Par:** 72/72. **Yards:** 6,603/5,475. **Course rating:** 72.5/71.7. **Slope:** 128/118. **Green fee:** $47/$59. **To obtain tee times:** Call 30 days in advance.
Subscriber comments: Fun, fun, fun...Better of the two...Very busy...Excellent facilities for small group tourney, good service...Can get breezy...Long for a senior, but fun to play...Fine destination.
★★★GABILAN COURSE
Holes: 36. **Par:** 72/72. **Yards:** 6,781/5,683. **Course rating:** 72.9/71.6. **Slope:** 129/118. **Green fee:** $40/$55. **To obtain tee times:** Call seven days in advance.
Subscriber comments: OK, not too exciting...Very nice but common layout...In great shape year-round...Loads of fun...Lots of good holes...Nice, affordable 36-hole resort.

★★★½RIO BRAVO COUNTRY CLUB
R-15200 Casa Club Dr., Bakersfield, 93306, Kern County, (805)871-4653, 120 miles N of Los Angeles.
Opened: 1975. **Holes:** 18. **Par:** 72/72. **Yards:** 6,993/5,704. **Course rating:** 73.1/70.4. **Slope:** 131/125. **Architect:** Robert Muir Graves. **Green fee:** $30/$50. **Credit cards:** MC,VISA,AMEX. **Reduced fees:** N/A. **Caddies:** No. **Golf carts:** $11. **Discount golf packages:** No. **Season:** Year-round. **High:** Spring, Fall. **On site lodging:** No. **Rental clubs:** No. **Walking policy:** Unrestricted walking. **Metal spikes allowed:** No. **Range:** Yes (grass/mats). **To obtain tee times:** Call up to 7 days in advance.
Subscriber comments: Excellent greens, probably best in Kern County...Tough course from back tees...Super-fast greens, course stays in great shape...The groundskeeper deserves a bonus...Best course in Bakersfield.

★★★RIO HONDO GOLF CLUB
PU-10627 Old River School Rd., Downey, 90241, Los Angeles County, (562)927-2329, 15 miles E of Los Angeles.
Opened: 1921. **Holes:** 18. **Par:** 71/71. **Yards:** 6,344/5,080. **Course rating:** 70.2/69.4. **Slope:** 119/117. **Architect:** John Duncan Dunn. **Green fee:** $30/$40. **Credit cards:** MC,VISA. **Reduced fees:** Twilight, seniors, juniors. **Caddies:** No. **Golf carts:** N/A. **Discount golf packages:** No. **Season:** Year-round. **High:** Year-round. **On site lodging:** No. **Rental clubs:** Yes. **Walking policy:** Unrestricted walking. **Metal spikes allowed:** No. **Range:** Yes (mats). **To obtain tee times:** Call 7 days in advance at 6 a.m.
Subscriber comments: Nicely rebuilt...Nice improvements and addition of water...Tight fairways. Stay straight...Short, but well kept...OK layout, doglegs in both directions...Tight with lots of trees...Excellent greens.

★★★RIVER COURSE AT THE ALISAL

PU-150 Alisal Rd., Solvang, 93463, Santa Barbara County, (805)688-6042, 35 miles NW of Santa Barbara.

Opened: 1992. **Holes:** 18. **Par:** 72/72. **Yards:** 6,830/5,815. **Course rating:** 73.1/73.4. **Slope:** 126/127. **Architect:** Halsey/Daray. **Green fee:** $40/$50. **Credit cards:** MC,VISA,AMEX. **Reduced fees:** Weekdays, resort guests, seniors, juniors. **Caddies:** No. **Golf carts:** $24. **Discount golf packages:** Yes. **Season:** Year-round. **High:** Jan-March, May, Oct. **On site lodging:** No. **Rental clubs:** Yes. **Walking policy:** Unrestricted walking. **Metal spikes allowed:** Yes. **Range:** Yes (grass/mats). **To obtain tee times:** Call or come in 7 days in advance.

Subscriber comments: Open fairways...Way too much money to play in a wind tunnel...Course a little tight in spots...Fun but tough, quiet, great views...Worth drive from LA...Plays short, when trees grow in will be more challenging...Great day trip...Pretty course.

★★★RIVER RIDGE GOLF CLUB

PU-2401 W. Vineyard Ave., Oxnard, 93030, Ventura County, (805)983-4653, 50 miles N of Los Angeles.

Opened: 1986. **Holes:** 18. **Par:** 72/72. **Yards:** 6,718/5,351. **Course rating:** 72.3/71.3. **Slope:** 121/124. **Architect:** William F. Bell. **Green fee:** $20/$25. **Credit cards:** MC,VISA,DISC. **Reduced fees:** Twilight, seniors, juniors. **Caddies:** No. **Golf carts:** $22. **Discount golf packages:** No. **Season:** Year-round. **High:** Year-round. **On site lodging:** Yes. **Rental clubs:** Yes. **Walking policy:** Unrestricted walking. **Metal spikes allowed:** No. **Range:** Yes (grass). **To obtain tee times:** Call 7 days in advance starting at 6 a.m. (usually sold out by 7 a.m.).

Subscriber comments: Has come a long way...Terrific track...Great improvement of first four holes...Built on a landfill...Very different, funky, but fun...Can be windy, near Pacific Ocean...Wide greens, no trees, too open...Great hotel course...Par 3 14th has an island green...Good back nine...Afternoon winds...Wide open and easy.

★½RIVER VIEW GOLF COURSE

PU-1800 West Santa Clara, Santa Ana, 92706, Orange County, (714)543-1115.

Opened: 1964. **Holes:** 18. **Par:** 70/70. **Yards:** 6,100/5,800. **Course rating:** 69.0/66.1. **Slope:** 106/103. **Architect:** Novel James. **Green fee:** $12/$17. **Credit cards:** MC,VISA. **Reduced fees:** Weekdays, low season, resort guests, twilight, seniors, juniors. **Caddies:** No. **Golf carts:** $18. **Discount golf packages:** Yes. **Season:** Year-round. **High:** March-Dec. **On site lodging:** No. **Rental clubs:** Yes. **Walking policy:** Walking at certain times. **Metal spikes allowed:** Yes. **Range:** Yes (grass/mats). **To obtain tee times:** Call within 10 days of desired time.

★★RIVERSIDE GOLF CLUB

PU-9770 Monterey Rd., Coyote, 95013, Santa Clara County, (408)463-0622, 8 miles S of San Jose.

Opened: 1957. **Holes:** 18. **Par:** 72/73. **Yards:** 6,881/5,942. **Course rating:** 72.2/72.5. **Slope:** 127/118. **Architect:** Pike Ross. **Green fee:** $25/$35. **Credit cards:** None. **Reduced fees:** Weekdays, low season, twilight, seniors, juniors. **Caddies:** No. **Golf carts:** $24. **Discount golf packages:** Yes. **Season:** Year-round. **High:** N/A. **On site lodging:** No. **Rental clubs:** Yes. **Walking policy:** Unrestricted walking. **Metal spikes allowed:** Yes. **Range:** Yes (grass). **To obtain tee times:** Call 7 days in advance.

★★½RIVERSIDE GOLF COURSE

PU-7672 N. Josephine, Fresno, 93711, Fresno County, (209)275-5900.

Opened: 1939. **Holes:** 18. **Par:** 72/75. **Yards:** 6,592/5,979. **Course rating:** 71.0/73.8. **Slope:** 122/125. **Architect:** Willaim P. Bell. **Green fee:** $8/$14. **Credit cards:** MC,VISA. **Reduced fees:** Weekdays, twilight, seniors, juniors. **Caddies:** No. **Golf carts:** $9. **Discount golf packages:** No. **Season:** Year-round. **High:** April-Oct. **On site lodging:** No. **Rental clubs:** Yes. **Walking policy:** Unrestricted walking. **Metal spikes allowed:** Yes. **Range:** Yes (grass). **To obtain tee times:** Call seven days in advance starting at 6:00 a.m.

Subscriber comments: Hard, some nice views of the river...Long course in very good shape...Challenging for a muny...No.10 a good 'un...Championship layout, long and strong...Best in Fresno.

★★ROSEVILLE DIAMOND OAKS MUNICIPAL GOLF COURSE

PM-349 Diamond Oaks Rd., Roseville, 95678, Placer County, (916)783-4947, 15 miles NE of Sacramento.
Opened: 1963. **Holes:** 18. **Par:** 72/73. **Yards:** 6,283/5,608. **Course rating:** 69.5/70.5. **Slope:** 115/112. **Architect:** Ted Robinson. **Green fee:** $10/$18. **Credit cards:** MC,VISA. **Reduced fees:** Weekdays, low season, twilight, seniors, juniors. **Caddies:** No. **Golf carts:** $19. **Discount golf packages:** No. **Season:** Year-round. **High:** April-Oct. **On site lodging:** No. **Rental clubs:** Yes. **Walking policy:** Unrestricted walking. **Metal spikes allowed:** Yes. **Range:** Yes (mats). **To obtain tee times:** Call 7 days in advance.

★★★½THE SCGA MEMBERS' CLUB AT RANCHO CALIFORNIA

PU-38275 Murrieta Hot Springs Rd., Murrieta, 92563, Riverside County, (909)677-7446, (800)752-9724, 45 miles N of San Diego.
Opened: 1972. **Holes:** 18. **Par:** 72/72. **Yards:** 7,059/5,355. **Course rating:** 73.9/70.5. **Slope:** 132/116. **Architect:** Robert Trent Jones. **Green fee:** $45/$55. **Credit cards:** MC,VISA. **Reduced fees:** Weekdays, twilight, juniors. **Caddies:** No. **Golf carts:** Included in Green Fee. **Discount golf packages:** No. **Season:** Year-round. **High:** Jan.-May. **On site lodging:** No. **Rental clubs:** Yes. **Walking policy:** Unrestricted walking. **Metal spikes allowed:** Yes. **Range:** Yes (grass). **To obtain tee times:** Members call 10 days in advance, nonmembers seven days.
Subscriber comments: Superbly conditioned, challenging Trent Jones course...Picture-perfect holes...Gets better every year...Fun course to play, hilly...Best greens I've ever seen...What a comeback...The SCGA has a true masterpiece on their hands...Long with wide fairways, well-bunkered landing areas and generous greens.

★★★★SADDLE CREEK GOLF CLUB

PU-3840 Little John Rd., Copperopolis, 95228, Calaveras County, (209)785-3700, (800)611-7722, 35 miles E of Stockton.
Opened: 1996. **Holes:** 18. **Par:** 72/72. **Yards:** 7,052/5,135. **Course rating:** 73.0/70.2. **Slope:** 134/122. **Architect:** Carter Morrish/Roy Bechtol. **Green fee:** $55/$62. **Credit cards:** MC,VISA. **Reduced fees:** Weekdays, low season, twilight. **Caddies:** No. **Golf carts:** $13. **Discount golf packages:** Yes. **Season:** Year-round. **High:** May-Sept. **On site lodging:** No. **Rental clubs:** Yes. **Walking policy:** Unrestricted walking. **Metal spikes allowed:** No. **Range:** Yes (grass). **To obtain tee times:** Call golf shop up to 14 days in advance.
Notes: Ranked 7th in 1997 Best New Upscale Public Courses.
Subscriber comments: Large undulating greens, beautiful views...Will be outstanding when it matures...Only fault is surrounding construction...Unbelievable, bring "A" game...Perfect, excellent greens...One of the best new courses in the Sierra foothills...Outstanding setting, great variey of holes.
Special Notes: No pullcarts.

★★½SALINAS FAIRWAYS GOLF COURSE

PU-45 Skyway Blvd., Salinas, 93905, Monterey County, (408)758-7300.
Call club for further information.
Subscriber comments: Difficult in the wind...Next to an airport, noisy...Excellent course for older people. Very walkable.

★★½SAN BERNARDINO GOLF CLUB

PU-1494 S. Waterman, San Bernardino, 92408, San Bernardino County, (909)885-2414, 45 miles W of Palm Springs.
Opened: 1967. **Holes:** 18. **Par:** 70/73. **Yards:** 5,779/5,218. **Course rating:** 67.5/69.9. **Slope:** 111/114. **Architect:** Dan Brown. **Green fee:** $8/$25. **Credit cards:** MC,VISA. **Reduced fees:** Weekdays, twilight, seniors, juniors. **Caddies:** No. **Golf carts:** $9. **Discount golf packages:** No. **Season:** Year-round. **High:** April-May/Sept.-Oct. **On site lodging:** No. **Rental clubs:** Yes. **Walking policy:** Unrestricted walking. **Metal spikes allowed:** Yes. **Range:** Yes (grass/mats). **To obtain tee times:** Call up to 7 days in advance.
Subscriber comments: Nice, clean, well-kept course...Straight drives a must, lots of trees...Good old course.

★★★SAN CLEMENTE MUNICIPAL GOLF CLUB

PM-150 E. Magdalena, San Clemente, 92672, Orange County, (714)361-8380, 60 miles N of San Diego.
Opened: 1929. **Holes:** 18. **Par:** 72/73. **Yards:** 6,447/5,722. **Course rating:** 70.2/73.0. **Slope:** 118/120. **Architect:** William P. Bell. **Green fee:** $20/$27. **Credit cards:** None. **Reduced fees:** Weekdays, twilight, seniors, juniors. **Caddies:** No. **Golf carts:** $20. **Discount golf packages:** No. **Season:** Year-round. **High:** June-Aug. **On site lodging:** No. **Rental clubs:** Yes. **Walking policy:** Unrestricted walking. **Metal spikes allowed:** Yes. **Range:** Yes (mats). **To obtain tee times:** Call 7 days in advance. 3 open times per hour for walk-ons.
Subscriber comments: Excellent ocean views, heavy play...Great local setting...Nice little muny.

★★★SAN DIMAS CANYON GOLF CLUB

PM-2100 Terrebonne Ave., San Dimas, 91773, Los Angeles County, (909)599-2313, 25 miles NE of Los Angeles.
Opened: 1962. **Holes:** 18. **Par:** 72/74. **Yards:** 6,309/5,539. **Course rating:** 70.3/73.9. **Slope:** 118/123. **Architect:** Jeff Brauer. **Green fee:** $20/$39. **Credit cards:** All major. **Reduced fees:** Weekdays, low season, twilight, seniors, juniors. **Caddies:** No. **Golf carts:** $12. **Discount golf packages:** Yes. **Season:** Year-round. **High:** April-Sept. **On site lodging:** No. **Rental clubs:** Yes. **Walking policy:** Walking at certain times. **Metal spikes allowed:** Yes. **Range:** Yes (mats). **To obtain tee times:** Call 7 days in advance starting at 6:30 a.m.
Subscriber comments: Short hilly course, straight shots a must...If you can putt here you're ready for Augusta...Back nine, water comes into play...Lots of trees and OB...Everything breaks away from mountains...Great canyon setting, deer, few houses...Quirky, but fun, excellent greens.

★★★SAN GERONIMO GOLF COURSE

PU-5800 Sir Francis Drake Blvd., San Geronimo, 94963, Marin County, (415)488-4030, (888)526-4653, 20 miles NW of San Francisco.
Opened: 1963. **Holes:** 18. **Par:** 72/72. **Yards:** 6,801/5,140. **Course rating:** 73.3/69.9. **Slope:** 130/125. **Architect:** A. Vernon Macan. **Green fee:** $25/$55. **Credit cards:** MC,VISA,AMEX. **Reduced fees:** Weekdays, twilight, seniors, juniors. **Caddies:** No. **Golf carts:** $10. **Discount golf packages:** No. **Season:** Year-round. **High:** March-Oct. **On site lodging:** No. **Rental clubs:** Yes. **Walking policy:** Unrestricted walking. **Metal spikes allowed:** Yes. **Range:** No. **To obtain tee times:** Call 7 days in advance.
Subscriber comments: Tough course...Nice layout, good greens...Very challenging, with completely different nines...Back nine harder than front...Nice course, beautiful scenery...Lots of golf for the price.

★★½SAN JOSE MUNICIPAL GOLF COURSE

PM-1560 Oakland Rd., San Jose, 95131, Santa Clara County, (408)441-4653.
Opened: 1968. **Holes:** 18. **Par:** 72/72. **Yards:** 6,602/5,594. **Course rating:** 70.1/69.7. **Slope:** 108/112. **Architect:** Robert Muir Graves. **Green fee:** $24/$32. **Credit cards:** None. **Reduced fees:** Weekdays, twilight, seniors, juniors. **Caddies:** No. **Golf carts:** N/A. **Discount golf packages:** No. **Season:** Year-round. **High:** Year-round. **On site lodging:** No. **Rental clubs:** Yes. **Walking policy:** Unrestricted walking. **Metal spikes allowed:** Yes. **Range:** Yes. **To obtain tee times:** Call or come in one week in advance for weekdays. Call Tuesday before 7 a.m. for weekend, alternating one reservation by phone and one in person.
Subscriber comments: Course gets tougher on back nine...Beware smoggy days...Flat, well-conditioned muny track...Best part is driving and practice area...Good course to improve your handicap.

★★½SAN JUAN HILLS COUNTRY CLUB

PU-32120 San Juan Creek Rd., San Juan Capistrano, 92675, Orange County, (714)493-1167, 60 miles S of Los Angeles.
Opened: 1966. **Holes:** 18. **Par:** 71/71. **Yards:** 6,295/5,402. **Course rating:** 69.5/71.4. **Slope:** 116/122. **Architect:** Harry Rainville. **Green fee:** $21/$33. **Credit cards:** MC,VISA. **Reduced fees:** Weekdays, twilight, seniors. **Caddies:** No. **Golf carts:** $10. **Discount golf packages:** No. **Season:** Year-round. **High:** May-Sept. **On site lodging:**

No. **Rental clubs:** Yes. **Walking policy:** Walking at certain times. **Metal spikes allowed:** Yes. **Range:** No. **To obtain tee times:** Call up to 10 days in advance. **Subscriber comments:** Decent...13th, 14th, 15th are three of the nicest holes in Southern California...Beautiful setting...Rolling hills, no surprises, interesting course...Fun course, 16th hole par-3 as good as there is in state.

★★★★SAN JUAN OAKS GOLF CLUB

PU-3825 Union Rd., Hollister, 95023, (408)636-6113, (800)453-8337, 45 miles S of San Jose.
Opened: 1996. **Holes:** 18. **Par:** 72/72. **Yards:** 7,133/4,770. **Course rating:** 74.8/67.1. **Slope:** 135/116. **Architect:** Fred Couples/Gene Bates. **Green fee:** $40/$60. **Credit cards:** MC,VISA,AMEX. **Reduced fees:** Weekdays, twilight, seniors, juniors. **Caddies:** No. **Golf carts:** $12. **Discount golf packages:** No. **Season:** Year-round. **High:** N/A. **On site lodging:** No. **Rental clubs:** Yes. **Walking policy:** Unrestricted walking. **Metal spikes allowed:** No. **Range:** Yes (grass). **To obtain tee times:** Call golf shop up to 30 days in advance.
Subscriber comments: This is a treasure, terrific...The real fun starts on No.12...Best value in the valley, will only get better...Thank you, Freddie...Back nine fantastic...My first no-smoking course...Great par 3s, what championship course should be...Very good course in rolling foothills.

★★★SAN LUIS REY DOWNS COUNTRY CLUB

R-31474 Golf Club Dr., Bonsall, 92003, San Diego County, (760)758-9699, 40 miles N of San Diego.
Opened: 1963. **Holes:** 18. **Par:** 72/72. **Yards:** 6,750/5,493. **Course rating:** 72.6/71.4. **Slope:** 128/124. **Architect:** William F. Bell. **Green fee:** $25/$50. **Credit cards:** MC,VISA,AMEX. **Reduced fees:** Twilight, juniors. **Caddies:** No. **Golf carts:** Included in Green Fee. **Discount golf packages:** Yes. **Season:** Year-round. **High:** Jan.-May. **On site lodging:** Yes. **Rental clubs:** Yes. **Walking policy:** Walking at certain times. **Metal spikes allowed:** Yes. **Range:** Yes (grass). **To obtain tee times:** Call 7 days in advance.
Subscriber comments: Great layout, back nine one of my favorites...Flat river valley course...Enough length and narrowness (trees) to pressure tee shots...Plays tougher in p.m. winds...A little-known and not heavily played course...10th tee very intimidating...Flat, narrow and tough.

★½SAN RAMON ROYAL VISTA GOLF CLUB

PU-9430 Fircrest Lane, San Ramon, 94583, Contra Costa County, (510)828-6100, 15 miles S of Walnut Creek.
Opened: 1960. **Holes:** 18. **Par:** 72/73. **Yards:** 6,560/5,770. **Course rating:** 70.9/72.7. **Slope:** 115/119. **Architect:** Clark Glasson. **Green fee:** $19/$35. **Credit cards:** MC,VISA. **Reduced fees:** Twilight, seniors, juniors. **Caddies:** No. **Golf carts:** $24. **Discount golf packages:** No. **Season:** Year-round. **High:** May-Sept. **On site lodging:** No. **Rental clubs:** Yes. **Walking policy:** Unrestricted walking. **Metal spikes allowed:** Yes. **Range:** Yes (mats). **To obtain tee times:** Call 7 days in advance.

★★★SAN VICENTE INN & GOLF CLUB

24157 San Vicente Rd., Ramona, 92065, San Diego County, (760)789-3477, 25 miles NE of San Diego.
Opened: 1972. **Holes:** 18. **Par:** 72/72. **Yards:** 6,610/5,543. **Course rating:** 71.5/72.8. **Slope:** 123/128. **Architect:** Ted Robinson. **Green fee:** $41/$53. **Credit cards:** MC,VISA,AMEX. **Reduced fees:** Weekdays, resort guests, twilight. **Caddies:** No. **Golf carts:** Included in Green Fee. **Discount golf packages:** Yes. **Season:** Year-round. **High:** Dec.-April. **On site lodging:** Yes. **Rental clubs:** Yes. **Walking policy:** Walking at certain times. **Metal spikes allowed:** No. **Range:** Yes (grass/mats). **To obtain tee times:** Call up to 5 days in advance.
Subscriber comments: Nice old-growth course...Great scenery, fun, good to walk...Beautiful oak trees...Great greens...Well laid out, well groomed...Fair for both men and women...Varied and interesting.

★★★★SANDPIPER GOLF COURSE
PU-7925 Hollister Ave., Goleta, 93117, Santa Barbara County, (805)968-1541, 100 miles N of Los Angeles.
Opened: 1972. **Holes:** 18. **Par:** 72/73. **Yards:** 7,068/5,725. **Course rating:** 74.5/73.3. **Slope:** 134/125. **Architect:** William F. Bell. **Green fee:** $68/$108. **Credit cards:** MC,VISA,AMEX. **Reduced fees:** Weekdays, low season, twilight, juniors. **Caddies:** Yes. **Golf carts:** $24. **Discount golf packages:** No. **Season:** Year-round. **High:** April-Oct. **On site lodging:** No. **Rental clubs:** Yes. **Walking policy:** Unrestricted walking. **Metal spikes allowed:** Yes. **Range:** Yes (grass). **To obtain tee times:** Call 7 days in advance.
Notes: Ranked 28th in 1997 Best in State. 1997 PGA Tour Qualifying School Final Stage.
Subscriber comments: Pebble Beach South, beautiful ocean views, very challenging...Tough, hilly, but fair challenge...Fabulous public course, great views, very long, trees and bunkers...Near perfect...A couple of holes away from greatness...Difficult when windy.

★★★SANTA ANITA GOLF COURSE
PM-405 S. Santa Anita Ave., Arcadia, 91006, Los Angeles County, (818)447-7156, 6 miles SE of Pasadena.
Opened: 1936. **Holes:** 18. **Par:** 71/74. **Yards:** 6,368/5,908. **Course rating:** 70.4/73.1. **Slope:** 122/121. **Architect:** L.A. County. **Green fee:** $19/$23. **Credit cards:** MC,VISA. **Reduced fees:** Twilight, seniors, juniors. **Caddies:** No. **Golf carts:** $20. **Discount golf packages:** No. **Season:** Year-round. **High:** N/A. **On site lodging:** No. **Rental clubs:** Yes. **Walking policy:** Unrestricted walking. **Metal spikes allowed:** Yes. **Range:** Yes (grass/mats). **To obtain tee times:** Call up to 7 days in advance beginning 6 a.m. weekdays, 5 a.m. weekends & holidays.
Subscriber comments: Rolling fairways, tough to get a flat lie, hard greens...LA County's best muny...Slowest round of golf...An excellent short old course...Too many mounds on the fairway...Many elevated greens...Fun course, great 18th hole...Surprisingly good.

★★SANTA BARBARA GOLF CLUB
PM-3500 McCaw Ave., Santa Barbara, 93105, Santa Barbara County, (805)687-7087, 90 miles N of Los Angeles.
Opened: 1958. **Holes:** 18. **Par:** 70/72. **Yards:** 6,014/5,541. **Course rating:** 67.6/71.9. **Slope:** 113/121. **Architect:** Lawrence Hughes. **Green fee:** $18/$20. **Credit cards:** None. **Reduced fees:** Weekdays, twilight, seniors, juniors. **Caddies:** No. **Golf carts:** $10. **Discount golf packages:** No. **Season:** Year-round. **High:** May-Sept. **On site lodging:** No. **Rental clubs:** Yes. **Walking policy:** Unrestricted walking. **Metal spikes allowed:** Yes. **Range:** Yes. **To obtain tee times:** Call Monday for Saturdays and call seven days in advance for Sunday and Monday.
Subscriber comments: Interesting layout...Short yet tough...Great condition considering amount of play...Don't need a driver much...Hilly, not a course to walk if you're out of shape...Good city course.

★★½SANTA CLARA GOLF & TENNIS CLUB
PU-5155 Stars and Stripes Dr., Santa Clara, 95054, Santa Clara County, (408)980-9515, 12 miles W of San Jose.
Opened: 1087. **Holes:** 18. **Par:** 72/72. **Yards:** 6,822/5,639. **Course rating:** 73.0/71.5. **Slope:** 126/115. **Architect:** Robert Muir Graves. **Green fee:** $14/$33. **Credit cards:** MC,VISA,AMEX. **Reduced fees:** Weekdays, resort guests, twilight, seniors, juniors. **Caddies:** No. **Golf carts:** $22. **Discount golf packages:** No. **Season:** Year-round. **High:** April-Sept. **On site lodging:** Yes. **Rental clubs:** Yes. **Walking policy:** Unrestricted walking. **Metal spikes allowed:** Yes. **Range:** Yes (mats). **To obtain tee times:** General public 7 days in advance. Santa Clara residents and Westin Hotel guests 8 days in advance.
Subscriber comments: Rebuilt greens in great shape...Rolling hills, some blind shots, brutal par-4 15th...Nice restaurant...Good layout, windy area...Accomplished a lot on old garbage dump...Best publinx in Silicon Valley.

CALIFORNIA

★★★SANTA TERESA GOLF CLUB
PU-260 Bernal Rd., San Jose, 95119, Santa Clara County, (408)225-2650.
Opened: 1963. **Holes:** 18. **Par:** 71/73. **Yards:** 6,742/6,032. **Course rating:** 71.1/73.5.
Slope: 121/125. **Architect:** George Santana. **Green fee:** $24/$34. **Credit cards:**
MC,VISA,DISC. **Reduced fees:** Weekdays, twilight, seniors, juniors. **Caddies:** No. **Golf carts:** N/A. **Discount golf packages:** No. **Season:** Year-round. **High:** April-Sept. **On site lodging:** No. **Rental clubs:** Yes. **Walking policy:** Unrestricted walking. **Metal spikes allowed:** Yes. **Range:** Yes. **To obtain tee times:** Call up to one week in advance.
Subscriber comments: A gem of a muny...Nice challenging course, good facilities...Great layout, back nine a tester from blues...Like playing two different nine-hole courses—flat front, hilly back...Six-hour rounds...Best public course in San Jose area.

★★SCHOLL CANYON GOLF COURSE
PU-3800 E Glen Oaks Blvd, Glendale, 91206, Los Angeles County, (818)243-4100.
Opened: 1994. **Holes:** 18. **Par:** 60/60. **Yards:** 3,039/2,400. **Course rating:** 56.8.
Slope: 81. **Architect:** George Williams. **Green fee:** $12/$16. **Credit cards:**
MC,VISA,AMEX. **Reduced fees:** Weekdays, twilight, seniors, juniors. **Caddies:** No.
Golf carts: $8. **Discount golf packages:** Yes. **Season:** Year-round. **High:** N/A. **On site lodging:** No. **Rental clubs:** Yes. **Walking policy:** Unrestricted walking. **Metal spikes allowed:** Yes. **Range:** Yes (grass/mats). **To obtain tee times:** Call golf shop up to 7 days in advance.

★★★THE SEA RANCH GOLF LINKS
PU-49300 Hwy. 1, The Sea Ranch, 95497, Sonoma County, (707)785-2468, (800)842-3270, 37 miles NW of Santa Rosa.
Opened: 1996. **Holes:** 18. **Par:** 72/72. **Yards:** 6,598/5,105. **Course rating:** 73.2/71.5.
Slope: 136/123. **Architect:** Robert Muir Graves. **Green fee:** $35/$50. **Credit cards:**
MC,VISA,AMEX. **Reduced fees:** Weekdays, twilight, juniors. **Caddies:** No. **Golf carts:** $12. **Discount golf packages:** No. **Season:** Year-round. **High:** July-Nov. **On site lodging:** Yes. **Rental clubs:** Yes. **Walking policy:** Unrestricted walking. **Metal spikes allowed:** Yes. **Range:** Yes (grass). **To obtain tee times:** Call golf shop up to 14 days in advance.
Subscriber comments: New back nine will develop into a great nine...Seaside course, nice layout...A real test...Great greens, bad fairways...Good links, tough to play in wind, but fun...Front nine scenic...Tough...Scenery great whether of ocean views or deer bedding down in sand bunkers...Very beautiful location.

★★SELMA VALLEY GOLF COURSE
PU-12389 E. Rose Ave., Selma, 93662, Fresno County, (209)896-2424, 20 miles S of Fresno.
Opened: 1963. **Holes:** 18. **Par:** 69/70. **Yards:** 5,370/5,170. **Course rating:** 64.7/69.6.
Slope: 107/118. **Architect:** Bob Baldock. **Green fee:** $12/$16. **Credit cards:** None.
Reduced fees: N/A. **Caddies:** No. **Golf carts:** $22. **Discount golf packages:** No.
Season: Year-round. **High:** N/A. **On site lodging:** No. **Rental clubs:** Yes. **Walking policy:** Unrestricted walking. **Metal spikes allowed:** Yes. **Range:** Yes (grass/mats). **To obtain tee times:** Call up to 7 days in advance.

SEPULVEDA GOLF COURSE
PU-16821 Burbank Blvd., Encino, 91436, Los Angeles County, (818)986-4560, 15 miles NW of Los Angeles.
Opened: 1960. **Architect:** William F. Bell/W.H. Johnson. **Green fee:** $17/$22. **Credit cards:** None. **Reduced fees:** Weekdays, twilight, seniors, juniors. **Caddies:** No. **Golf carts:** $11. **Discount golf packages:** No. **Season:** Year-round. **High:** April-Sept. **On site lodging:** No. **Rental clubs:** Yes. **Walking policy:** Unrestricted walking. **Metal spikes allowed:** Yes. **Range:** Yes (mats). **To obtain tee times:** N/A.
★★BALBOA COURSE
Holes: 18. **Par:** 70/72. **Yards:** 6,359/5,912. **Course rating:** 68.8/70.9. **Slope:** 107/115.
★★ENCINO COURSE
Holes: 18. **Par:** 72/75. **Yards:** 6,863/6,133. **Course rating:** 70.8/73.4. **Slope:** 112/119.

★★★SEVEN HILLS GOLF COURSE

PM-1537 S. Lyon St., Hemet, 92545, Riverside County, (909)925-4815.
Opened: N/A. **Holes:** 18. **Par:** 72/72. **Yards:** 6,600/5,500. **Course rating:** N/A. **Slope:** 118/115. **Architect:** Harry Rainville/David Rainville. **Green fee:** $13/$23. **Credit cards:** MC,VISA. **Reduced fees:** Weekdays, twilight. **Caddies:** No. **Golf carts:** $10. **Discount golf packages:** Yes. **Season:** Year-round. **High:** Jan.-April. **On site lodging:** No. **Rental clubs:** No. **Walking policy:** Unrestricted walking. **Metal spikes allowed:** Yes. **Range:** Yes (grass/mats). **To obtain tee times:** Call up to 7 days in advance beginning at 6 a.m.
Subscriber comments: Good mature course, usually good shape...Good challenge.

★★★SHANDIN HILLS GOLF CLUB

PU-3380 Little Mountain Dr., San Bernardino, 92407, San Bernardino County, (909)886-0669, 60 miles E of Los Angeles.
Opened: 1980. **Holes:** 18. **Par:** 72/72. **Yards:** 6,517/5,592. **Course rating:** 70.3/71.6. **Slope:** 120/122. **Architect:** Cary A. Bickler. **Green fee:** $9/$28. **Credit cards:** All major. **Reduced fees:** Weekdays, twilight, seniors, juniors. **Caddies:** No. **Golf carts:** $10. **Discount golf packages:** Yes. **Season:** Year-round. **High:** Oct. **On site lodging:** No. **Rental clubs:** Yes. **Walking policy:** Unrestricted walking. **Metal spikes allowed:** Yes. **Range:** Yes (grass/mats). **To obtain tee times:** Call 7 days in advance.
Subscriber comments: Tons of bunkers...Some tight fairways next to freeway...Nice layout...Good test. Need all of your shots......Only distraction is noise from freeway and railroads close by...A sleeper in the middle of nowhere.

★★SHARP PARK GOLF COURSE

PU-Highway 1, Pacifica, 94044, San Mateo County, (415)359-3380, 15 miles SW of San Francisco.
Opened: 1929. **Holes:** 18. **Par:** 72/74. **Yards:** 6,273/6,095. **Course rating:** 70.6/73.0. **Slope:** 119/120. **Architect:** Alister McKenzie. **Green fee:** $23/$27. **Credit cards:** None. **Reduced fees:** Weekdays, twilight, juniors. **Caddies:** No. **Golf carts:** $20. **Discount golf packages:** Yes. **Season:** Year-round. **High:** April-Oct. **On site lodging:** No. **Rental clubs:** Yes. **Walking policy:** Unrestricted walking. **Metal spikes allowed:** Yes. **Range:** No. **To obtain tee times:** Call 7 days in advance for weekdays and 4 days in advance for weekends.

★★★SHERWOOD FOREST GOLF CLUB

PU-79 N. Frankwood Ave., Sanger, 93657, Fresno County, (209)787-2611, 18 miles SE of Fresno.
Opened: 1968. **Holes:** 18. **Par:** 71/72. **Yards:** 6,345/5,605. **Course rating:** 69.2/71.4. **Slope:** 118/118. **Architect:** Bob Baldock. **Green fee:** $16/$19. **Credit cards:** MC,VISA. **Reduced fees:** Twilight, juniors. **Caddies:** No. **Golf carts:** $20. **Discount golf packages:** No. **Season:** Year-round. **High:** April-July. **On site lodging:** No. **Rental clubs:** Yes. **Walking policy:** Unrestricted walking. **Metal spikes allowed:** Yes. **Range:** Yes (grass). **To obtain tee times:** Call up to 7 days in advance.
Subscriber comments: Narrow, flat course. Hard greens, nice foothill views...Very scenic...Fun course along river...An old reliable...Challenging with low-hanging trees...Best course in Fresno area...A beautiful course, perfect for seniors.

★★SHORECLIFFS GOLF CLUB

PU-501 Avenida Vaquero, San Clemente, 92762, Orange County, (714)492-1177.
Opened: 1965. **Holes:** 18. **Par:** 71. **Yards:** N/A. **Course rating:** N/A. **Slope:** N/A. **Architect:** Joe Williams. **Green fee:** $30/$50. **Credit cards:** MC,VISA,AMEX. **Reduced fees:** Weekdays, twilight, seniors. **Caddies:** No. **Golf carts:** Included in Green Fee. **Discount golf packages:** No. **Season:** Year-round. **High:** May-Oct. **On site lodging:** No. **Rental clubs:** Yes. **Walking policy:** Mandatory cart. **Metal spikes allowed:** Yes. **Range:** Yes (mats). **To obtain tee times:** Call up to 7 days in advance. Tournaments 1 year in advance.

★★½SHORELINE GOLF LINKS AT MOUNTAIN VIEW

PM-2940 N. Shoreline Blvd., Mountain View, 94043-1347, Santa Clara County, (650)969-2041, 10 miles NW of San Jose.
Opened: 1982. **Holes:** 18. **Par:** 72/72. **Yards:** 6,695/5,398. **Course rating:** 72.4/71.7.

Slope: 125/120. **Architect:** Robert Trent Jones Jr. **Green fee:** $18/$42. **Credit cards:** MC,VISA,AMEX. **Reduced fees:** Weekdays, twilight, seniors, juniors. **Caddies:** No. **Golf carts:** $24. **Discount golf packages:** No. **Season:** Year-round. **High:** May-Sept. **On site lodging:** No. **Rental clubs:** Yes. **Walking policy:** Unrestricted walking. **Metal spikes allowed:** Yes. **Range:** Yes (grass/mats). **To obtain tee times:** Call 7 days in advance. Call Monday for weekend.

Subscriber comments: Fair muny, ducks and geese everywhere...Links course...Tough to play when wind is blowing...Bayside course, birds are part of the hazards...Love the course...Fun and challenging layout.

★★SIERRA VIEW PUBLIC GOLF COURSE
PU-12608 Ave. 264 at Rd. 124, Visalia, 93277, Tulare County, (209)732-2078, 40 miles S of Fresno.

Opened: 1957. **Holes:** 18. **Par:** 72/73. **Yards:** 6,388/5,886. **Course rating:** 68.9/71.6. **Slope:** 107/114. **Architect:** Robert Dean Putman. **Green fee:** $15/$18. **Credit cards:** MC,VISA. **Reduced fees:** Seniors, juniors. **Caddies:** No. **Golf carts:** $18. **Discount golf packages:** No. **Season:** Year-round. **High:** N/A. **On site lodging:** No. **Rental clubs:** Yes. **Walking policy:** Unrestricted walking. **Metal spikes allowed:** Yes. **Range:** Yes (grass/mats). **To obtain tee times:** Call golf shop.

SILVERADO COUNTRY CLUB & RESORT
R-1600 Atlas Peak Rd., Napa, 94558, Napa County, (707)257-5460, (800)532-0500, 50 miles NE of San Francisco.

Opened: 1955. **Architect:** Robert Trent Jones. **Green fee:** $60/$130. **Credit cards:** All major. **Reduced fees:** Low season, resort guests, twilight. **Caddies:** No. **Golf carts:** Included in Green Fee. **Discount golf packages:** Yes. **Season:** Year-round. **On site lodging:** Yes. **Rental clubs:** Yes. **Walking policy:** Mandatory cart. **Metal spikes allowed:** Yes. **Range:** Yes (grass/mats). **To obtain tee times:** May make tee time as far in advance as hotel room reservation.

★★★½NORTH COURSE

Holes: 18. **Par:** 72/72. **Yards:** 6,900/5,857. **Course rating:** 73.4/73.1. **Slope:** 131/128. **High:** March-Oct.

Subscriber comments: North better than South. Some great holes...Fun to play, beautiful setting...Resort course, Senior Tour stop...Wine Country must-play, don't miss food at turn...Wildlife on and around course adds to surroundings...Great way to spend the weekend...A classic course, beautiful location.

★★★½SOUTH COURSE

Holes: 18. **Par:** 72/72. **Yards:** 6,685/5,672. **Course rating:** 72.4/71.8. **Slope:** 129/123. **High:** March-Nov.

Subscriber comments: Beautiful course, complements North, more hills and more water...Lots of trees...Beautiful site...Great layout. Fair, but not easy...Great resort atmosphere...Great finishing hole...A classic course, beautiful location.

★★★SIMI HILLS GOLF CLUB
PM-5031 Alamo, Simi Valley, 93063, Ventura County, (805)522-0813.
Call club for further information.

Subscriber comments: Fun to play if you can get a tee time...Wide open, but still difficult for beginners...Very cool layout...Has character...Each hole a challenge, no "giveaways"...Lots of hills and sloping greens...Very good condition...Scenic course in hills, not long but makes you think...Fun to play.

SINGING HILLS COUNTRY CLUB
R-3007 Dehesa Rd., El Cajon, 92019, San Diego County, (619)442-3425, (800)457-5568, 17 miles E of San Diego.

Opened: 1956. **Architect:** Ted Robinson/Dave Fleming. **Green fee:** $30/$40. **Credit cards:** MC,VISA,AMEX. **Reduced fees:** Weekdays, twilight, juniors. **Caddies:** No. **Golf carts:** $20. **Discount golf packages:** Yes. **Season:** Year-round. **High:** N/A. **On site lodging:** Yes. **Rental clubs:** Yes. **Walking policy:** Unrestricted walking. **Metal spikes allowed:** Yes. **Range:** Yes (grass/mats). **To obtain tee times:** Weekday, 7 days prior; weekends, call prior Monday.

★★★½OAK GLEN COURSE

Holes: 18. **Par:** 72/72. **Yards:** 6,597/5,549. **Course rating:** 71.3/71.4. **Slope:** 122/124. **Notes:** 1973, 1989 USGA Boys Junior Championship.

CALIFORNIA

Subscriber comments: Treelined course, interesting...Very attractive...Superb walking course...Fun course, challenging at times...Crowded resort courses...Always nice...Great stay-and-play packages...Beautiful flowers, lovely setting...Top condition.

★★★½WILLOW GLEN COURSE
Holes: 18. **Par:** 72/72. **Yards:** 6,605/5,585. **Course rating:** 72.0/72.8. **Slope:** 124/122.
Subscriber comments: Good test of golf...Good facilities...Take a camera...Fairways and greens groomed like private course...Nice old course, big trees and lots of birds...Great course, fantastic landscaping...Well-run facilty...Good package deal...A tight but good test...Very pleasant surroundings, course in great shape, some huge greens.
Special Notes: Also has 18-hole par-54 Pine Glen Course. Non-metal spikes are recommended.

★★SKYLINKS GOLF CLUB
PM-4800 E. Wardlow Rd., Long Beach, 90808, Los Angeles County, (562)429-0030.
Opened: 1956. **Holes:** 18. **Par:** 72/74. **Yards:** 6,354/5,918. **Course rating:** 69.3/73.5.
Slope: 111/119. **Architect:** William F. Bell. **Green fee:** $15/$23. **Credit cards:**
MC,VISA,AMEX. **Reduced fees:** Twilight, seniors, juniors. **Caddies:** No. **Golf carts:**
$21. **Discount golf packages:** No. **Season:** Year-round. **High:** N/A. **On site lodging:**
No. **Rental clubs:** Yes. **Walking policy:** Unrestricted walking. **Metal spikes allowed:**
Yes. **Range:** Yes (grass/mats). **To obtain tee times:** Call 3 days in advance.

★★½SKYWEST GOLF COURSE
PM-1401 Golf Course Rd., Hayward, 94541, Alameda County, (510)278-6188, 22 miles SE of San Francisco.
Opened: 1965. **Holes:** 18. **Par:** 72/73. **Yards:** 6,930/6,171. **Course rating:** 72.9/74.3.
Slope: 121/123. **Architect:** Bob Baldock. **Green fee:** $19/$30. **Credit cards:** MC,VISA.
Reduced fees: Seniors, juniors. **Caddies:** No. **Golf carts:** $22. **Discount golf packages:** No. **Season:** Year-round. **High:** N/A. **On site lodging:** No. **Rental clubs:** Yes.
Walking policy: Unrestricted walking. **Metal spikes allowed:** Yes. **Range:** Yes (mats).
To obtain tee times: Call 8 days in advance beginning 9 p.m.
Subscriber comments: Tough, long, flat course, good greens...Well maintained public course...A lot of water fowl and what they leave behind...Nothing special here, flat, windy...The muny of muny courses...Working man's course...Plenty of airplanes overhead.

★★★½SOBOBA SPRINGS ROYAL VISTA GOLF COURSE
1020 Soboba Rd., San Jacinto, 92583, Riverside County, (909)654-9354, 25 miles W of Palm Springs.
Opened: 1967. **Holes:** 18. **Par:** 73/74. **Yards:** 6,829/5,762. **Course rating:** 73.5/73.2.
Slope: 135/131. **Architect:** Desmond Muirhead. **Green fee:** $32/$45. **Credit cards:**
MC,VISA. **Reduced fees:** Weekdays, low season, resort guests, twilight, juniors.
Caddies: No. **Golf carts:** Included in Green Fee. **Discount golf packages:** Yes.
Season: Year-round. **High:** Nov.-April. **On site lodging:** No. **Rental clubs:** Yes.
Walking policy: Mandatory cart. **Metal spikes allowed:** Yes. **Range:** Yes (grass). **To obtain tee times:** Call 7 days in advance.
Subscriber comments: Fun, challenging...Very good course; hot in summer...Nice big trees ...Has trees in the middle of the fairway...A great layout, will not be bored...Watch out for leaves in the fall...Well maintained...Nice old course, narrow but not long...Great greens, good layout...A classic course.

★★★½SONOMA GOLF CLUB
PU-17700 Arnold Dr., Sonoma, 95476, Sonoma County, (707)996-0300, (800)956-4653, 45 miles N of San Francisco.
Opened: 1991. **Holes:** 18. **Par:** 72/72. **Yards:** 7,069/5,871. **Course rating:** 74.9/73.8.
Slope: 135/130. **Architect:** Robert Muir Graves. **Green fee:** $45/$70. **Credit cards:**
MC,VISA,AMEX. **Reduced fees:** Weekdays, low season, twilight. **Caddies:** No. **Golf carts:** Included in Green Fee. **Discount golf packages:** Yes. **Season:** Year-round.
High: April-Oct. **On site lodging:** No. **Rental clubs:** Yes. **Walking policy:** Unrestricted walking. **Metal spikes allowed:** No. **Range:** Yes (grass/mats). **To obtain tee times:**
Call up to 14 days in advance.
Subscriber comments: Finest golf course in Northern California...Beautiful, long and open...Good variety of holes...Great course, great value, walkable...Fun in

wind...Beautiful course, a must-play...This is golf, bring "A" game...The place to play in Wine Country......Terrific old-style course. Great setting...Hidden gem in Sonoma. **Special Notes:** No pullcarts.

★★★SOULE PARK GOLF COURSE
PM-1033 E. Ojai Ave., Ojai, 93024, Ventura County, (805)646-5633, 16 miles NE of Ventura.
Opened: 1962. **Holes:** 18. **Par:** 72/72. **Yards:** 6,350/5,894. **Course rating:** 69.1/71.0.
Slope: 107/115. **Architect:** William F. Bell. **Green fee:** $19/$24. **Credit cards:** None.
Reduced fees: Weekdays, twilight, seniors, juniors. **Caddies:** No. **Golf carts:** $22.
Discount golf packages: No. **Season:** Year-round. **High:** N/A. **On site lodging:** Yes.
Rental clubs: Yes. **Walking policy:** Unrestricted walking. **Metal spikes allowed:** Yes.
Range: Yes (grass). **To obtain tee times:** Call 7 days in advance starting at 7 a.m.
Subscriber comments: Very interesting, scenic oak trees...Par-5 7th hole fantastic, rated hardest in Ventura County...Well-maintained...Great layout in beautiful valley...Park-like setting, hilly and lots of water...Tremendous location, lots of forced carries and large greens...First-rate public golf, scenic mountain views...Great weather year-round.

★★★SOUTHRIDGE GOLF CLUB
9413 S. Butte Rd., Sutter, 95982, Sutter County, (916)755-4653, 8 miles NW of Yuba City.
Opened: 1992. **Holes:** 18. **Par:** 72/72. **Yards:** 7,047/5,541. **Course rating:** 72.7/71.3.
Slope: 130/122. **Architect:** Cal Olson. **Green fee:** $19/$29. **Credit cards:**
MC,VISA,AMEX. **Reduced fees:** Weekdays, low season, twilight, seniors, juniors.
Caddies: No. **Golf carts:** $10. **Discount golf packages:** Yes. **Season:** Year-round.
High: March-June/Sept.-Nov. **On site lodging:** No. **Rental clubs:** Yes. **Walking policy:**
Walking at certain times. **Metal spikes allowed:** Yes. **Range:** Yes (grass). **To obtain tee times:** Call up to 7 days in advance.
Subscriber comments: Mountain-goat course in Gold Country...Flat front nine, hilly back nine...Nice layout...Needs trees, no shade...Beautiful scenery...Watch out for rattlesnakes...16th one of the all-time toughest par 5s...Built at the base of mountains...Frontside nice, backside a nightmare...Interesting layout, good variety.

★★SPRING VALLEY GOLF CLUB
PM-3441 E. Calaveras Blvd., Milpitas, 95036, Santa Clara County, (408)262-1722.
Call club for further information.

★★★★★SPYGLASS HILL GOLF COURSE
R-Spyglass Hill Rd. & Stevenson Dr., Pebble Beach, 93953, Monterey County, (408)625-8563, (800)654-9300.
Opened: 1966. **Holes:** 18. **Par:** 72/74. **Yards:** 6,855/5,642. **Course rating:** 75.9/73.7. **Slope:** 143/133. **Architect:** Robert Trent Jones. **Green fee:** $175/$200. **Credit cards:** All major,Diners Club, JCB. **Reduced fees:** Resort guests, twilight. **Caddies:** Yes. **Golf carts:** Included in green fee only if you are staying at the resort. Outside guests $25 per cart.
Discount golf packages: Yes. **Season:** Year-round. **High:** Aug.-Nov. **On site lodging:** No. **Rental clubs:** Yes. **Walking policy:** Unrestricted walking. **Metal spikes allowed:** Yes. **Range:** Yes (grass/mats). **To obtain tee times:** Call reservations up to 18 months in advance if you're staying at resort or 30 days in advance if you are not.
Notes: Ranked 27th in 1997-98 America's 100 Greatest; 5th in 1997 Best in State. AT&T Pebble Beach National Pro Am.
Subscriber comments: Best first five holes in golf...Once-in-a-lifetime golf...A wonderful walk in the park; use a caddie for an extra fine experience...Beats Pebble hands down...Great, tough course, with lots of deer to watch, too...Ocean views are incredible...Awesome course, refinements in '96 were great...Favorite course but can't afford it anymore...Some ordinary holes in the trees.

CALIFORNIA

★★★★STEELE CANYON GOLF CLUB
PU-3199 Stonefield Dr., Jamul, 91935, San Diego County, (619)441-6900, 20 miles E of San Diego.
Opened: 1991. **Holes:** 27. **Architect:** Gary Player. **Green fee:** $48/$65.
Credit cards: MC,VISA,AMEX. **Reduced fees:** Twilight, seniors, juniors.
Caddies: No. **Golf carts:** Included in Green Fee. **Discount golf packages:** No. **Season:** Year-round. **High:** Dec.-May. **On site lodging:** No. **Rental clubs:** No. **Walking policy:** Mandatory cart. **Metal spikes allowed:** Yes. **Range:** Yes (grass/mats). **To obtain tee times:** Call 7 days in advance.
CANYON/MEADOW
Par: 71/71. **Yards:** 6,672/4,813. **Course rating:** 72.2/67.9. **Slope:** 134/118.
CANYON/RANCH
Par: 71/71. **Yards:** 6,741/4,655. **Course rating:** 72.7/66.6. **Slope:** 135/112.
RANCH/MEADOW
Par: 72/72. **Yards:** 7,001/5,026. **Course rating:** 74.0/69.5. **Slope:** 137/124.
Subscriber comments: Tough nines, hilly, scenic...Must include the Ranch nine in any mix...Excellent course, gorgeous and classy...Remote location...Beautiful...Bring "A" game or lots of balls...Use all clubs for narrow, hilly course...Very tough for average golfer; greens invariably hard and difficult to hold...Interesting but quirky...Very dramatic...Great layout, great condition...Three distinctly different nines.

★★★★STEVINSON RANCH GOLF CLUB
PU-2700 N. Van Clief Rd., Stevinson, 95374, Merced County, (209)668-8200, 12 miles SW of Turlock.
Opened: 1995. **Holes:** 18. **Par:** 72/72. **Yards:** 7,205/5,461. **Course rating:** 74.3/71.9. **Slope:** 140/124. **Architect:** John Harbottle/George Kelley. **Green fee:** $35/$55. **Credit cards:** MC,VISA,AMEX. **Reduced fees:** Twilight. **Caddies:** Yes. **Golf carts:** $20.
Discount golf packages: Yes. **Season:** Year-round. **High:** Spring/Fall. **On site lodging:** No. **Rental clubs:** Yes. **Walking policy:** Unrestricted walking. **Metal spikes allowed:** No. **Range:** Yes (grass). **To obtain tee times:** Call 60 days in advance.
Notes: Ranked 25th in 1997 Best in State; 8th in 1996 Best New Upscale Courses.
Subscriber comments: Beautiful links-style course with wetlands...Greens and fairways are great...Good valley course...Lots of lateral hazards...Great unknown course...The best public course near Modesto...Fastest greens around...Miss fairway and reload...Terrific course...Top-notch in all respects...Wide variety of excellent holes...Nice, tricky layout in the San Joaquin Valley.

★★½SUMMIT POINTE GOLF CLUB
1500 Country Club Dr., Milpitas, 95035, Santa Clara County, (408)262-8813, (800)422-4653, 5 miles N of San Jose.
Opened: 1968. **Holes:** 18. **Par:** 72/72. **Yards:** 6,331/5,496. **Course rating:** 70.9/70.6. **Slope:** 125/121. **Architect:** Marvin Orgill. **Green fee:** $25/$70. **Credit cards:** MC,VISA,AMEX. **Reduced fees:** Twilight, seniors, juniors. **Caddies:** No. **Golf carts:** $15. **Discount golf packages:** Yes. **Season:** Year-round. **High:** March-Oct. **On site lodging:** No. **Rental clubs:** Yes. **Walking policy:** Walking at certain times. **Metal spikes allowed:** Yes. **Range:** Yes (mats). **To obtain tee times:** Call 7 days in advance or 60 days in advance with American Express Golf Card.
Subscriber comments: Hilly course, great views...Play back nine only, front is amusement park...Not long but hilly, tough lies, tricky greens with big breaks...Would not walk it...Back nine tough, tight, lots of water...Not a flat lie on the course.

★★★½SUN CITY PALM DESERT GOLF CLUB
R-38-180 Del Webb Blvd., Bermuda Dunes, 92211, Riverside County, (760)772-2200, 10 miles E of Palm Springs.
Opened: 1992. **Holes:** 18. **Par:** 72/72. **Yards:** 6,720/5,305. **Course rating:** 73.0/70.3. **Slope:** 131/118. **Architect:** Billy Casper/Greg Nash. **Green fee:** $30/$85. **Credit cards:** MC,VISA. **Reduced fees:** Weekdays, low season, twilight. **Caddies:** No. **Golf carts:** Included in Green Fee. **Discount golf packages:** No. **Season:** Year-round (closed Oct.). **High:** N/A. **On site lodging:** Yes. **Rental clubs:** Yes. **Walking policy:** Mandatory cart. **Metal spikes allowed:** Yes. **Range:** Yes (grass). **To obtain tee times:** Call 2 days in advance for weekdays or 7 days in advance for weekends.

Subscriber comments: Short but sweet...Good course...Beautiful scenery, very playable...One of the best in Palm Springs area...Wide open, some challenging holes...Get ready for the wind in p.m...Very nice.

★★★½SUN LAKES COUNTRY CLUB

850 S. Country Club Dr., Banning, 92220, Riverside County, (909)845-2135, 20 miles W of Palm Springs.
Opened: 1987. **Holes:** 18. **Par:** 72/72. **Yards:** 7,035/5,516. **Course rating:** 74.3/72.7.
Slope: 132/118. **Architect:** David Rainville. **Green fee:** $47. **Credit cards:** MC,VISA.
Reduced fees: Twilight, juniors. **Caddies:** No. **Golf carts:** Included in Green Fee.
Discount golf packages: No. **Season:** Year-round. **High:** April-Oct. **On site lodging:** No. **Rental clubs:** No. **Walking policy:** Mandatory cart. **Metal spikes allowed:** Yes.
Range: Yes (grass/mats). **To obtain tee times:** Call up to 4 days in advance.
Subscriber comments: Sometimes windy and smoggy...A good test, sandy for less-than-straight shooter...Tough course, lots of bunkers, some water, nice greens.

★★½SUNNYVALE GOLF COURSE

PM-605 Macara Lane, Sunnyvale, 94086, Santa Clara County, (408)738-3666, 5 miles N of San Jose.
Opened: 1968. **Holes:** 18. **Par:** 70/71. **Yards:** 6,249/5,305. **Course rating:** 69.7/70.2.
Slope: 119/120. **Architect:** David W. Kent. **Green fee:** $17/$32. **Credit cards:** None.
Reduced fees: Weekdays, twilight, seniors, juniors. **Caddies:** No. **Golf carts:** $23.
Discount golf packages: No. **Season:** Year-round. **High:** March-Sept. **On site lodging:** No. **Rental clubs:** Yes. **Walking policy:** Unrestricted walking. **Metal spikes allowed:** Yes. **Range:** No. **To obtain tee times:** Call 7 days in advance.
Subscriber comments: On short side...Last five holes are super...Best part of course is the play through orchards...All-around fun course...Always crowded...Lots of freeway noise...Flat course, but overall in good shape...Good muny, easy to walk, some good water holes.

SUNOL VALLEY GOLF COURSE

PU-6900 Mission Rd., Sunol, 94586, Alameda County, (510)862-0414, 5 miles N of Fremont.
Opened: 1968. **Architect:** Clark Glasson. **Green fee:** $14/$48. **Credit cards:** MC,VISA. **Reduced fees:** Twilight, juniors. **Caddies:** No. **Golf carts:** Included in Green Fee. **Discount golf packages:** No. **Season:** Year-round. **On site lodging:** No. **Rental clubs:** Yes. **Walking policy:** Walking at certain times. **Metal spikes allowed:** Yes. **Range:** No. **To obtain tee times:** Call 7 days in advance.

★★½CYPRESS COURSE

Holes: 18. **Par:** 72/72. **Yards:** 6,195/5,458. **Course rating:** 69.8/70.1. **Slope:** 120/115.
Subscriber comments: Easy course, great greens...Tight and short...Great bar...Front nine is best part, especially No.9...Some drivable par 4s...Shorter of two courses, a bit tight on some holes.

★★½PALM COURSE

Holes: 18. **Par:** 72/74. **Yards:** 6,843/5,997. **Course rating:** 72.4/74.4. **Slope:** 126/124.
Subscriber comments: Long course, great greens...As crowded as the highway next to it...Wind in late afternoon plays havoc on shots...Lots of trees, water, very busy...Well maintained.

★★SWENSON PARK GOLF CLUB

PU-6803 Alexandria Place, Stockton, 95207, San Joaquin County, (209)937-7360.
Opened: 1952. **Holes:** 18. **Par:** 72/74. **Yards:** 6,485/6,266. **Course rating:** 70.0/73.8.
Slope: 110/117. **Architect:** William P. Bell. **Green fee:** $7/$16. **Credit cards:** None.
Reduced fees: Weekdays, low season, twilight, seniors, juniors. **Caddies:** No. **Golf carts:** $20. **Discount golf packages:** Yes. **Season:** Year-round. **High:** N/A. **On site lodging:** No. **Rental clubs:** Yes. **Walking policy:** Unrestricted walking. **Metal spikes allowed:** Yes. **Range:** Yes (grass/mats). **To obtain tee times:** Call 7 days in advance.
Special Notes: Also 9-hole par-3 course.

★★½SYCAMORE CANYON GOLF CLUB

PU-500 Kenmar Lane, Arvin, 93203, Kern County, (805)854-3163, 25 miles SE of Bakersfield.
Opened: 1989. **Holes:** 18. **Par:** 72/73. **Yards:** 7,100/5,744. **Course rating:** 72.8/71.6.

CALIFORNIA

Slope: 125/120. **Architect:** Bob Putman. **Green fee:** $10/$13. **Credit cards:** MC,VISA. **Reduced fees:** Weekdays, twilight, seniors, juniors. **Caddies:** No. **Golf carts:** $8. **Discount golf packages:** No. **Season:** Year-round. **High:** Feb.-Oct. **On site lodging:** No. **Rental clubs:** Yes. **Walking policy:** Unrestricted walking. **Metal spikes allowed:** Yes. **Range:** Yes (grass). **To obtain tee times:** Call seven days in advance.
Subscriber comments: One of Kern County's best-kept secrets...A real challenge...Flat and long. Some tough water holes...Solid test of golf...Will be better when trees have grown.

★★½TABLE MOUNTAIN GOLF COURSE
PU-2700 Oro Dam Blvd. W., Oroville, 95965, Butte County, (916)533-3922, 70 miles N of Sacramento.
Opened: 1956. **Holes:** 18. **Par:** 72/68. **Yards:** 6,500/5,000. **Course rating:** 69.8/66.5. **Slope:** 116/104. **Architect:** Louis Bertolone. **Green fee:** $16/$20. **Credit cards:** MC,VISA. **Reduced fees:** Weekdays, twilight, seniors, juniors. **Caddies:** No. **Golf carts:** $18. **Discount golf packages:** Yes. **Season:** Year-round. **High:** May-Sept. **On site lodging:** No. **Rental clubs:** Yes. **Walking policy:** Unrestricted walking. **Metal spikes allowed:** Yes. **Range:** Yes (grass/mats). **To obtain tee times:** Call 7 days in advance.
Subscriber comments: Good muny course...Fun to play when there is no wind...Golf early, 110-plus temperatures in summer...Excellent greens.

★★★½TAHOE DONNER GOLF CLUB
12850 Northwoods Blvd., Truckee, 96161, Nevada County, (916)587-9440, 40 miles from Reno.
Opened: 1975. **Holes:** 18. **Par:** 72/74. **Yards:** 6,952/6,487. **Course rating:** 72.4/73.1. **Slope:** 130/138. **Architect:** Joseph B. Williams. **Green fee:** $27/$81. **Credit cards:** MC,VISA. **Reduced fees:** Low season, twilight. **Caddies:** No. **Golf carts:** $15. **Discount golf packages:** No. **Season:** May-Oct. **High:** July-Aug. **On site lodging:** No. **Rental clubs:** Yes. **Walking policy:** Mandatory cart. **Metal spikes allowed:** Yes. **Range:** Yes (grass/mats). **To obtain tee times:** Call 10 days in advance beginning 8:30 a.m.
Subscriber comments: Good course, great condition...Tight...Terrific challenge...Narrow fairways, lots of trees...Very demanding...Lots of fun...Terrific layout...Very scenic course...Hit it straight, tall rough and trees...Long and narrow through the woods.

TAHQUITZ CREEK RESORT
PU- 1885 Golf Club Dr., Palm Springs, 92264, Riverside County, (760)328-1005, (800)743-2211.
Credit cards: MC,VISA,AMEX. **Reduced fees:** Weekdays, low season, resort guests, twilight, seniors, juniors. **Caddies:** No. **Discount golf packages:** Yes. **Season:** Year-round. **On site lodging:** No. **Rental clubs:** Yes. **Metal spikes allowed:** Yes. **Range:** Yes (grass). **To obtain tee times:** Call up to 30 days in advance.
★★★LEGEND COURSE
Opened: 1960. **Holes:** 18. **Par:** 72/72. **Yards:** 6,660/6,077. **Course rating:** 71.0/74.0. **Slope:** 117/120. **Architect:** William F. Bell. **Green fee:** $18/$60. **Golf carts:** $10. **High:** Jan.-May. **Walking policy:** Walking at certain times.
Subscriber comments: New bunkers make this old-style course fun...Lots of challenges...Narrow fairways on back nine...Not bad for an old muny...Condoville, watch for cars...Good fun...Fairly easy...Mostly level and straight...Just a very average desert course...Great, well kept.
★★★½RESORT COURSE
Opened: 1995. **Holes:** 18. **Par:** 72/72. **Yards:** 6,705/5,206. **Course rating:** 71.4/70.0. **Slope:** 120/119. **Architect:** Ted Robinson. **Green fee:** $25/$90. **Golf carts:** Included in Green Fee. **High:** Nov.-March. **Walking policy:** Mandatory cart.
Subscriber comments: Good test. Fun...Play early to avoid strong afternoon wind...Love the scenery, driving range, and the 4th hole...One of the best in desert...Nice course, decent facilities...Rough very tough and a lot of water...Great public course, looks like a country club...Should be on shortlist of places to play.

★★★½TEMECULA CREEK INN

R-44501 Rainbow Canyon Rd., Temecula, 92592, Riverside County, (909)676-2405, (800)962-7335, 50 miles NE of San Diego.
Opened: 1970. **Holes:** 27. **Architect:** Dick Rossen/Ted Robinson. **Green fee:** $20/$75. **Credit cards:** All major. **Reduced fees:** Weekdays, low season, resort guests, twilight, juniors. **Caddies:** No. **Golf carts:** Included in Green Fee. **Discount golf packages:** Yes. **Season:** Year-round. **High:** Nov.-April. **On site lodging:** Yes. **Rental clubs:** Yes. **Walking policy:** Walking at certain times. **Metal spikes allowed:** No. **Range:** Yes (grass/mats). **To obtain tee times:** Call up to 7 days in advance.
CREEK/OAKS
Par: 72/72. **Yards:** 6,784/5,737. **Course rating:** 72.6/72.8. **Slope:** 125/123.
CREEK/STONEHOUSE
Par: 72/72. **Yards:** 6,605/5,686. **Course rating:** 71.8/71.9. **Slope:** 123/120.
OAKS/STONEHOUSE
Par: 72/72. **Yards:** 6,693/5,683. **Course rating:** 72.6/72.4. **Slope:** 130/125.
Subscriber comments: Easy to walk, very enjoyable, Oaks nine is great...Three nines are all quite different...Nice layout, tough greens...Interesting, well kept...Creek nine nothing to write home about...Narrow fairways, good challenge...Great golf getaway.

★★★TEMEKU HILLS GOLF & COUNTRY CLUB

PU-41687 Temeku Dr., Temecula, 92591, Riverside County, (909)693-1440, 65 miles N of San Diego.
Opened: 1995. **Holes:** 18. **Par:** 72/72. **Yards:** 6,522/5,139. **Course rating:** 70.3/70.5. **Slope:** 118/123. **Architect:** Ted Robinson. **Green fee:** $25/$49. **Credit cards:** All major. **Reduced fees:** Twilight. **Caddies:** No. **Golf carts:** Included in Green Fee. **Discount golf packages:** No. **Season:** Year-round. **High:** Oct.-April. **On site lodging:** No. **Rental clubs:** Yes. **Walking policy:** Walking at certain times. **Metal spikes allowed:** Yes. **Range:** Yes (grass/mats). **To obtain tee times:** Call 7 days in advance starting at 6 a.m.
Subscriber comments: Great new course...Tough, tough greens...Palm trees around greens are nice...In years to come will be a first-class golf residental community...Short challenging course...Every hole has unique characteristics...Sporty, interesting golf...Lots of ups and downs, blind shots, target shots.

★★½TIERRA DEL SOL GOLF CLUB

10300 N. Loop Dr., California City, 93505, Kern County, (760)373-2384.
Architect: Robert van Hagge/Bruce Devlin. **Caddies:** No. **Discount golf packages:** No. **On site lodging:** No. **Rental clubs:** No. **Metal spikes allowed:** Yes. **Range:** Yes. Call club for further information.
Subscriber comments: Considering location, course is on par...Lots of water and sand...All desert, links style.

★★★½TIJERAS CREEK GOLF CLUB

PU-29082 Tijeras Creek Rd., Rancho Santa Margarita, 92688, Orange County, (714)589-9793, 50 miles S of Los Angeles.
Opened: 1990. **Holes:** 18. **Par:** 72/72. **Yards:** 6,601/5,130. **Course rating:** 71.8/70.1. **Slope:** 125/115. **Architect:** Ted Robinson. **Green fee:** $85/$110. **Credit cards:** MC,VISA,AMEX,Diners Club. **Reduced fees:** Twilight, seniors, juniors. **Caddies:** No. **Golf carts:** Included in Green Fee. **Discount golf packages:** No. **Season:** Year-round. **High:** N/A. **On site lodging:** No. **Rental clubs:** Yes. **Walking policy:** Mandatory cart. **Metal spikes allowed:** Yes. **Range:** Yes (grass/mats). **To obtain tee times:** Call 7 days in advance.
Subscriber comments: Front nine open with water, back nine narrow and hard...Beautifully maintained; good variety...Watch for deer and hawks...Front nine is condo golf but the back nine is worth every cent.

★★½TILDEN PARK GOLF COURSE

PM-Grizzley Peak and Shasta Rd., Berkeley, 94708, Alameda County, (510)848-7373, 10 miles E of San Francisco.
Opened: 1936. **Holes:** 18. **Par:** 70/71. **Yards:** 6,300/5,400. **Course rating:** 69.9/69.2. **Slope:** 120/116. **Architect:** William P. Bell. **Green fee:** $18/$35. **Credit cards:** MC,VISA,AMEX. **Reduced fees:** Weekdays, twilight, seniors, juniors. **Caddies:** No.

Golf carts: $12. **Discount golf packages:** Yes. **Season:** Year-round. **High:** April-Oct. **On site lodging:** No. **Rental clubs:** Yes. **Walking policy:** Unrestricted walking. **Metal spikes allowed:** Yes. **Range:** Yes (mats). **To obtain tee times:** Call 7 days in advance. **Subscriber comments:** Classic parkland course, excellent par 3s...Picturesque...Short but challenging...Beautiful old course tucked in Berkeley hills...For agile goats...No.1 uphill par 4 is a killer...Six-hour rounds on weekends but still one of the best munys...Overplayed but fun...Very scenic, interesting course.

★★TONY LEMA GOLF COURSE
PU-13800 Neptune Dr., San Leandro, 94577, Alameda County, (510)895-2162, 5 miles S of Oakland.
Opened: N/A. **Holes:** 18. **Par:** 72/72. **Yards:** 6,660/5,718. **Course rating:** 72.0/67.6. **Slope:** 117/109. **Architect:** William F. Bell. **Green fee:** $12/$20. **Credit cards:** None. **Reduced fees:** Twilight, seniors, juniors. **Caddies:** No. **Golf carts:** $24. **Discount golf packages:** No. **Season:** Year-round. **High:** May-Nov. **On site lodging:** No. **Rental clubs:** Yes. **Walking policy:** Unrestricted walking. **Metal spikes allowed:** Yes. **Range:** Yes (grass). **To obtain tee times:** Call up to 7 days in advance starting at 6 a.m.

TORREY PINES GOLF COURSE
PU-11480 N. Torrey Pines Rd., La Jolla, 92037, San Diego County, (619)452-3226, (800)985-4653, 10 miles N of San Diego.
Opened: 1957. **Architect:** William F. Bell. **Green fee:** $45/$85. **Credit cards:** MC,VISA,AMEX. **Caddies:** No. **Golf carts:** $25. **Discount golf packages:** Yes. **Season:** Year-round. **High:** N/A. **On site lodging:** Yes. **Rental clubs:** Yes. **Walking policy:** Unrestricted walking. **Metal spikes allowed:** Yes. **Range:** Yes (grass/mats). **To obtain tee times:** You may call 4 to 8 weeks in advance.

★★★½NORTH COURSE
Holes: 18. **Par:** 72/74. **Yards:** 6,647/6,118. **Course rating:** 72.1/75.4. **Slope:** 129/134. **Reduced fees:** N/A.

GOOD VALUE

Subscriber comments: Long course, outstanding views...Playing PGA Tour course is exciting...Will never forget views...Just as good as Torrey South, just easier...Waited two hours as single...No.6 par 3 is breathtaking...An ocean beauty for any golfer...Crowded, but worth the wait...Probably the best muny in the country...Happiness is a tee time at Torrey...Great public golf in a glorious setting.

★★★★SOUTH COURSE
Holes: 18. **Par:** 72/76. **Yards:** 7,055/6,457. **Course rating:** 74.6/77.3. **Slope:** 136/139. **Reduced fees:** Twilight, seniors, juniors.
Notes: Ranked 16th in 1997 Best in State. PGA Tour Buick Invitational (annually); Junior World Championship (annually).

GOOD VALUE

Subscriber comments: Long, tough, windy, cool, but fabulous golf...Excellent ocean course, PGA plays here...Don't worry about your score, play for the scenery...Beautiful view of La Jolla...Most popular public course in the US....Ocean views awesome...Try not to get distracted by the whales...Nice well-kept course...Rough very high...Great course.

★★½TRACY GOLF & COUNTRY CLUB
35200 S. Chrisman Rd., Tracy, 95376, San Joaquin County, (209)835-9463.
Call club for further information.
Subscriber comments: Very small greens...Tougher than it looks...Can get real windy...Very flat, so fire away.

★★★½TUSTIN RANCH GOLF CLUB
PU-12442 Tustin Ranch Rd., Tustin, 92780, Orange County, (714)730-1611, 10 miles S of Anaheim.
Opened: 1989. **Holes:** 18. **Par:** 72/72. **Yards:** 6,736/5,204. **Course rating:** 72.4/70.3. **Slope:** 129/118. **Architect:** Ted Robinson. **Green fee:** $80/$115. **Credit cards:** MC,VISA,AMEX. **Reduced fees:** Twilight, seniors, juniors. **Caddies:** Yes. **Golf carts:** Included in Green Fee. **Discount golf packages:** No. **Season:** Year-round. **High:** June-Oct. **On site lodging:** No. **Rental clubs:** Yes. **Walking policy:** Unrestricted walking. **Metal spikes allowed:** No. **Range:** Yes (grass/mats). **To obtain tee times:** Call 7 days in advance.

Subscriber comments: Fun but tough, fair test of game...True greens...Beautifully maintained...No.18 is tricky...Wide fairways, with water, wildlife and hills...Nice resort course, big bucks...Two great par 5s...Challenging.

★★★★ TWELVE BRIDGES GOLF CLUB

PU-3070 Twelve Bridges Dr., Lincoln, 95648, Placer County, (916)645-7200, (888)893-5832, 25 miles E of Sacramento.
Opened: 1996. **Holes:** 18. **Par:** 72/72. **Yards:** 7,150/5,310. **Course rating:** 74.6/71.0. **Slope:** 139/123. **Architect:** Dick Phelps. **Green fee:** $25/$55. **Credit cards:** MC,VISA,AMEX. **Reduced fees:** N/A. **Caddies:** No. **Golf carts:** $15. **Discount golf packages:** No. **Season:** Year-round. **High:** Spring/Fall. **On site lodging:** No. **Rental clubs:** Yes. **Walking policy:** Unrestricted walking. **Metal spikes allowed:** No. **Range:** Yes (grass). **To obtain tee times:** Call 14 days in advance.
Notes: Ranked 10th in 1996 Best New Upscale Courses; 1997 Long's Drugs LPGA Challenge; 1996 Twelve Bridges LPGA Classic; 1996, 1997 AJGA.
Subscriber comments: Beautiful course...Great layout, super greens and fairways...No buildings, yet...Best in Sacramento area...Tough, tight, but playable...Outstanding...Incredible course and beautiful clubhouse...LPGA stop...Many tee boxes to suit varied handicaps...Long par 3s...Beautiful oak-tree setting, hit it straight...19th hole an A-plus.

(GOOD SERVICE)

★★½ TWIN OAKS GOLF COURSE

PU-1425 N. Twin Oaks Valley Rd., San Marcos, 92069, San Diego County, (760)591-4653, 3 miles W of Escondido.
Opened: 1993. **Holes:** 18. **Par:** 72/72. **Yards:** 6,535/5,423. **Course rating:** 71.2/71.6. **Slope:** 124/120. **Architect:** Ted Robinson. **Green fee:** $25/$65. **Credit cards:** All major,Diners Club. **Reduced fees:** Weekdays, low season, twilight, seniors, juniors. **Caddies:** No. **Golf carts:** Included in Green Fee. **Discount golf packages:** Yes. **Season:** Year-round. **High:** Dec.-April. **On site lodging:** No. **Rental clubs:** Yes. **Walking policy:** Mandatory cart. **Metal spikes allowed:** Yes. **Range:** Yes (grass/mats). **To obtain tee times:** Call up to 7 days in advance.
Subscriber comments: Great short course and challenging...Avoid after rain...Greens run true...Overpriced, needs to grow in...Beautiful area...Tough finishing hole...This course will be a monster in 10 years.

★★½ UPLAND HILLS COUNTRY CLUB

1231 E. 16th St., Upland, 91786, San Bernardino County, (909)946-4711, 20 miles NE of Los Angeles.
Opened: 1983. **Holes:** 18. **Par:** 70/70. **Yards:** 5,827/4,813. **Course rating:** 67.1/66.5. **Slope:** 111/106. **Architect:** H. Rainville. **Green fee:** $17/$31. **Credit cards:** All major. **Reduced fees:** N/A. **Caddies:** No. **Golf carts:** $11. **Discount golf packages:** No. **Season:** Year-round. **High:** N/A. **On site lodging:** No. **Rental clubs:** Yes. **Walking policy:** Walking at certain times. **Metal spikes allowed:** Yes. **Range:** No. **To obtain tee times:** Call 7 days in advance.
Subscriber comments: Not long, but you use all clubs...Accuracy is important, tight fairways...Miss fairway, hit condo...Beautiful course with a zillion trees...Fun course, but easy...Basic golf...Leave the driver at home.

★ VALLE GRANDE GOLF COURSE

PU-1119 Watts Dr., Bakersfield, 93307, Kern County, (805)832-2259, 7 miles E of Bakersfield.
Opened: 1952. **Holes:** 18. **Par:** 72/72. **Yards:** 6,240/5,531. **Course rating:** 69.8/68.9. **Slope:** 116/114. **Architect:** William P. Bell. **Green fee:** $11/$14. **Credit cards:** None. **Reduced fees:** Twilight, seniors, juniors. **Caddies:** No. **Golf carts:** $18. **Discount golf packages:** No. **Season:** Year-round. **High:** N/A. **On site lodging:** No. **Rental clubs:** No. **Walking policy:** Unrestricted walking. **Metal spikes allowed:** No. **Range:** Yes (grass/mats). **To obtain tee times:** Call 7 days in advance.

★★½ VAN BUSKIRK PARK GOLF COURSE

PM-1740 Houston Ave., Stockton, 95206, San Joaquin County, (209)937-7357, 3 miles S of Stockton.
Opened: 1961. **Holes:** 18. **Par:** 72/74. **Yards:** 6,928/5,927. **Course rating:** 72.2/72.2.

Slope: 118/113. **Architect:** Larry Norstrom. **Green fee:** $7/$16. **Credit cards:** None. **Reduced fees:** Twilight, seniors, juniors. **Caddies:** No. **Golf carts:** $20. **Discount golf packages:** No. **Season:** Year-round. **High:** N/A. **On site lodging:** No. **Rental clubs:** Yes. **Walking policy:** Unrestricted walking. **Metal spikes allowed:** Yes. **Range:** Yes (grass/mats). **To obtain tee times:** Call Monday for upcoming weekend.
Subscriber comments: Good, inexpensive test of golf...Long back nine, wide, lots of water...Big greens, hump in every green..."Radar" on carts...Great track for public course...Good and challenging course...Don't go OB on back nine...A punishment for slicers, right-side hazards...Delta winds influence play.

★★★THE VINEYARD AT ESCONDIDO
PU-925 San Pasqual Rd., Escondido, 92025, San Diego County, (760)735-9545, 15 miles N of San Diego.
Opened: 1993. **Holes:** 18. **Par:** 70/70. **Yards:** 6,531/5,073. **Course rating:** 70.3/70.3. **Slope:** 125/117. **Architect:** David Rainville. **Green fee:** $25/$40. **Credit cards:** MC,VISA,AMEX. **Reduced fees:** Weekdays, low season, twilight, seniors, juniors. **Caddies:** No. **Golf carts:** $10. **Discount golf packages:** No. **Season:** Year-round. **High:** N/A. **On site lodging:** No. **Rental clubs:** Yes. **Walking policy:** Walking at certain times. **Metal spikes allowed:** Yes. **Range:** Yes. **To obtain tee times:** Call seven days in advance.
Subscriber comments: Besides Torrey, my favorite golf course in area...Will be nice once the trees mature...Front nine flat with water, back nine up and down...Nice mix of target and rip-it holes...Very scenic...Back nine very scenic...Good facilities.

★★★WASCO VALLEY ROSE GOLF COURSE
PU-301 N. Leonard Ave., Wasco, 93280, Kern County, (805)758-8301, 19 miles N of Bakersfield.
Opened: 1991. **Holes:** 18. **Par:** 72/72. **Yards:** 6,862/5,356. **Course rating:** 72.5/70.5. **Slope:** 121/119. **Architect:** Bob Putman. **Green fee:** $11/$13. **Credit cards:** MC,VISA,AMEX. **Reduced fees:** Weekdays, low season, twilight, seniors, juniors. **Caddies:** No. **Golf carts:** $18. **Discount golf packages:** No. **Season:** Year-round. **High:** April-June/Oct. **On site lodging:** No. **Rental clubs:** Yes. **Walking policy:** Unrestricted walking. **Metal spikes allowed:** Yes. **Range:** Yes (grass). **To obtain tee times:** Call 7 days in advance.
Subscriber comments: Very open course...Excellent greens...Great newer course. Wait till trees get higher...In farm country...Improving with time...Flat, relatively young.

★★★WELK RESORT CENTER
PU-8860 Lawrence Welk Dr., Escondido, 92026, San Diego County, (760)749-3225, (800)932-9355, 35 miles N of San Diego.
Opened: 1964. **Holes:** 18. **Par:** 62/62. **Yards:** 4,002/3,099. **Course rating:** 59.1/57.7. **Slope:** 99/90. **Architect:** David Rainville. **Green fee:** $12/$23. **Credit cards:** All major. **Reduced fees:** Twilight. **Caddies:** No. **Golf carts:** $11. **Discount golf packages:** Yes. **Season:** Year-round. **High:** Jan.-April. **On site lodging:** Yes. **Rental clubs:** Yes. **Walking policy:** Walking at certain times. **Metal spikes allowed:** No. **Range:** No. **To obtain tee times:** Call golf shop.
Subscriber comments: Good for seniors and couples...Not a long course, but quite a few interesting holes...The best of the executives...Resort quality...A fun course. **Special Notes:** Also have a Par-3 course, Oaks.

★★★½THE WESTIN MISSION HILLS RESORT
R-71-501 Dinah Shore and Bob Hope Dr., Rancho Mirage, 92270, Riverside County, (760)328-3198, (800)358-2211, 10 miles E of Palm Springs.
Opened: 1987. **Holes:** 18. **Par:** 70/70. **Yards:** 6,987/4,841. **Course rating:** 73.7/67.4. **Slope:** 136/107. **Architect:** Pete Dye. **Green fee:** $55/$150. **Credit cards:** All major. **Reduced fees:** Low season, resort guests, twilight. **Caddies:** No. **Golf carts:** Included in Green Fee. **Discount golf packages:** Yes. **Season:** Year-round. **High:** Oct.-April. **On site lodging:** Yes. **Rental clubs:** Yes. **Walking policy:** Mandatory cart. **Metal spikes allowed:** Yes. **Range:** Yes. **To obtain tee times:** Call 30 days in advance for outside play and 90 days in advance for hotel guests.
Subscriber comments: Good resort course, with lots of variety...Perfect desert course. Water, palms, the works...Tough Dye course, but not tricked up...A mild hook or slice breaks a window...A real challenge, brutal 9th and 18th.

★★WHISPERING LAKES GOLF COURSE
PM-2525 Riverside Dr, Ontario, 91761, San Bernardino County, (909)923-3673, 15 miles W of San Bernardino.
Opened: 1960. **Holes:** 18. **Par:** 72/74. **Yards:** 6,700/6,000. **Course rating:** 71.4/72.8. **Slope:** 122/117. **Architect:** N/A. **Green fee:** $19/$23. **Credit cards:** MC,VISA. **Reduced fees:** Twilight, seniors, juniors. **Caddies:** No. **Golf carts:** $22. **Discount golf packages:** No. **Season:** Year-round. **High:** N/A. **On site lodging:** No. **Rental clubs:** Yes. **Walking policy:** Unrestricted walking. **Metal spikes allowed:** Yes. **Range:** Yes (grass). **To obtain tee times:** Call 7 days in advance for weekdays. Call Monday for upcoming weekend.

★★WHITTIER NARROWS GOLF COURSE
PU-8640 E. Rush St., Rosemead, 91770, Los Angeles County, (818)288-1044, 15 miles E of Los Angeles.
Opened: N/A. **Holes:** 27. **Par:** 72/74. **Yards:** 6,864/5,965. **Course rating:** 72.3. **Slope:** 121. **Architect:** William F. Bell. **Green fee:** $19/$23. **Credit cards:** MC,VISA. **Reduced fees:** Twilight, seniors, juniors. **Caddies:** No. **Golf carts:** $22. **Discount golf packages:** No. **Season:** Year-round. **High:** N/A. **On site lodging:** No. **Rental clubs:** Yes. **Walking policy:** Unrestricted walking. **Metal spikes allowed:** Yes. **Range:** Yes (grass/mats). **To obtain tee times:** Call up to 7 days in advance.
Special Notes: Also has a 9-hole executive course.

★★½WILLOW PARK GOLF CLUB
PU-17007 Redwood Rd., Castro Valley, 94546, Alameda County, (510)537-8989, 20 miles SE of Oakland.
Opened: 1967. **Holes:** 18. **Par:** 71/71. **Yards:** 6,227/5,193. **Course rating:** 67.4/69.2. **Slope:** 110/117. **Architect:** Bob Baldock. **Green fee:** $19/$26. **Credit cards:** MC,VISA. **Reduced fees:** N/A. **Caddies:** No. **Golf carts:** N/A. **Discount golf packages:** No. **Season:** Year-round. **High:** N/A. **On site lodging:** No. **Rental clubs:** No. **Walking policy:** Unrestricted walking. **Metal spikes allowed:** Yes. **Range:** Yes (mats). **To obtain tee times:** Call Monday for weekday at 7 a.m. and at 10 a.m. for weekend.
Subscriber comments: Woodsy, tight track...Fairways are all lined with trees...Fun, not long, picturesque...Beautiful canyon setting...Creek plays havoc.

★★★½WINDSOR GOLF CLUB
PU-6555 Skylane Blvd., Windsor, 95492, Sonoma County, (707)838-7888, 6 miles N of Santa Rosa.
Opened: 1989. **Holes:** 18. **Par:** 72/72. **Yards:** 6,650/5,116. **Course rating:** 72.3/69.3. **Slope:** 126/125. **Architect:** Ron Fream. **Green fee:** $22/$37. **Credit cards:** MC,VISA. **Reduced fees:** Weekdays, twilight, seniors, juniors. **Caddies:** No. **Golf carts:** $20. **Discount golf packages:** No. **Season:** Year-round. **High:** N/A. **On site lodging:** No. **Rental clubs:** Yes. **Walking policy:** Unrestricted walking. **Metal spikes allowed:** Yes. **Range:** Yes (grass/mats). **To obtain tee times:** Call seven days in advance at 6:30 a.m.
Subscriber comments: Loved the silo...Creek a hidden hazard...No two holes the same...Nike Tour has played here...The best all-around experience in Sonoma.

★★★WOODCREEK GOLF CLUB
PM-5880 Woodcreek Oaks Blvd., Roseville, 95747, Placer County, (916)771-4653, 15 miles E of Sacramento.
Opened: 1995. **Holes:** 18. **Par:** 72/70. **Yards:** 6,518/4,739. **Course rating:** 72.4/66.2. **Slope:** 128/112. **Architect:** Robert Muir Graves. **Green fee:** $23/$28. **Credit cards:** All major. **Reduced fees:** Weekdays, twilight, seniors, juniors. **Caddies:** No. **Golf carts:** $11. **Discount golf packages:** No. **Season:** Year-round. **High:** N/A. **On site lodging:** No. **Rental clubs:** Yes. **Walking policy:** Mandatory cart. **Metal spikes allowed:** Yes. **Range:** Yes (grass/mats). **To obtain tee times:** Call golf shop or automated service.
Subscriber comments: Tee areas far apart...All-around all-star location...Many pretty holes on back side...Tough No.5...Nice practice facility.

★★WOODLEY LAKES GOLF CLUB
6331 Woodley Ave., Van Nuys, 91406, Los Angeles County, (818)787-8163.
Call club for further information.

COLORADO

★★★ ADOBE CREEK NATIONAL GOLF COURSE
PU-876 18 1/2 Rd., Fruita, 81521, Mesa County, (970)858-0521, 9 miles W of Grand Junction.
Opened: 1992. **Holes:** 18. **Par:** 72/72. **Yards:** 6,997/4,980. **Course rating:** 71.2/55.1. **Slope:** 119/97. **Architect:** Ned Wilson. **Green fee:** $16/$22. **Credit cards:** None. **Reduced fees:** Weekdays, low season, twilight, seniors, juniors. **Caddies:** No. **Golf carts:** $16. **Discount golf packages:** No. **Season:** May-Dec. **High:** May-Sept. **On site lodging:** No. **Rental clubs:** Yes. **Walking policy:** Unrestricted walking. **Metal spikes allowed:** Yes. **Range:** Yes (grass). **To obtain tee times:** Call two days in advance.
Subscriber comments: Nice setting. Very playable...Good test...Back tees can make a big difference...More difficult in wind that often blows...Great tee boxes, play to handicap.

★★ APPLETREE GOLF COURSE
PU-10150 Rolling Ridge Rd., Colorado Springs, 80925, Pueblo County, (719)382-3649, (800)844-6531, 80 miles S of Denver.
Opened: 1972. **Holes:** 18. **Par:** 72/72. **Yards:** 6,407/5,003. **Course rating:** 68.6/66.9. **Slope:** 122/113. **Architect:** Lee Trevino/Dave Bennett. **Green fee:** $10/$20. **Credit cards:** MC,VISA. **Reduced fees:** Weekdays, low season, seniors, juniors. **Caddies:** No. **Golf carts:** $20. **Discount golf packages:** No. **Season:** Year-round. **High:** May-Sept. **On site lodging:** No. **Rental clubs:** Yes. **Walking policy:** Unrestricted walking. **Metal spikes allowed:** No. **Range:** Yes (grass). **To obtain tee times:** Call up to 7 days in advance.

★★ APPLEWOOD GOLF COURSE
PU-14001 W. 32nd Ave., Golden, 80401, Jefferson County, (303)279-3003, 13 miles W of Golden.
Opened: 1954. **Holes:** 18. **Par:** 71/72. **Yards:** 6,229/5,374. **Course rating:** 68.2/69.0. **Slope:** 122/118. **Architect:** Press Maxwell. **Green fee:** $20/$23. **Credit cards:** MC,VISA,AMEX. **Reduced fees:** Weekdays, twilight, seniors, juniors. **Caddies:** No. **Golf carts:** $9. **Discount golf packages:** Yes. **Season:** Year-round. **High:** April-Oct. **On site lodging:** No. **Rental clubs:** Yes. **Walking policy:** Unrestricted walking. **Metal spikes allowed:** No. **Range:** Yes (grass/mats). **To obtain tee times:** Call 6 days in advance.

★★★½ ARROWHEAD GOLF CLUB
PU-10850 W. Sundown Trail, Littleton, 80125, Arapahoe County, (303)973-9614, 25 miles S of Denver.
Opened: 1972. **Holes:** 18. **Par:** 70/72. **Yards:** 6,682/5,465. **Course rating:** 70.9/70.0. **Slope:** 134/123. **Architect:** Robert Trent Jones Jr.. **Green fee:** $45/$85. **Credit cards:** MC,VISA,AMEX. **Reduced fees:** Weekdays, low season, twilight, seniors. **Caddies:** No. **Golf carts:** Included in Green Fee. **Discount golf packages:** Yes. **Season:** March-Nov. **High:** June-Sept. **On site lodging:** No. **Rental clubs:** Yes. **Walking policy:** Mandatory cart. **Metal spikes allowed:** Yes. **Range:** Yes (grass/mats). **To obtain tee times:** Call 7 days in advance with credit card.
Subscriber comments: Incredible golf experience. Best around Denver...Unfortunately, beauty has too high a price...Wow, bring a camera...Par 3 cut into Red Rock Canyon is best I've seen...Deer, fox, black bear and if you're lucky, an eagle...Views are to die for...The beauty of this course offsets the high fees...The views are better than the golf...Great view.

★★★ ASPEN GOLF COURSE
PU-408 E. Cooper, Aspen, 81612, Pitkin County, (970)925-2145.
Opened: 1962. **Holes:** 18. **Par:** 71/72. **Yards:** 7,165/5,591. **Course rating:** 72.2/69.9. **Slope:** 125/116. **Architect:** Frank Hummel. **Green fee:** $35/$55. **Credit cards:** MC,VISA. **Reduced fees:** Low season, seniors, juniors. **Caddies:** No. **Golf carts:** $12. **Discount golf packages:** No. **Season:** April-Oct. **High:** July-Sept. **On site lodging:** No. **Rental clubs:** Yes. **Walking policy:** Unrestricted walking. **Metal spikes allowed:** Yes. **Range:** Yes (grass). **To obtain tee times:** Call three days in advance.
Subscriber comments: Long course, great views. Streams in fairways...Majestic view of Maroon Bell.

COLORADO

★★AURORA HILLS GOLF COURSE
PU-50 S. Peoria St., Aurora, 80012, Arapahoe County, (303)364-6111, 10 miles W of Denver.
Opened: 1968. **Holes:** 18. **Par:** 72/73. **Yards:** 6,735/5,919. **Course rating:** 70.0/71.3.
Slope: 115/109. **Architect:** Dick Phelps. **Green fee:** $13/$20. **Credit cards:**
MC,VISA,DISC. **Reduced fees:** Twilight, seniors, juniors. **Caddies:** No. **Golf carts:**
$20. **Discount golf packages:** No. **Season:** Year-round. **High:** May-Sept. **On site lodging:** No. **Rental clubs:** Yes. **Walking policy:** Unrestricted walking. **Metal spikes allowed:** Yes. **Range:** Yes (grass/mats). **To obtain tee times:** Call golf shop or tee times phone 4 days in advance.

★★★½BATTLEMENT MESA GOLF CLUB
PU-3930 N. Battlement Pkwy., Battlement Mesa, 81635, Garfield County, (970)285-7274, (888)285-7274, 42 miles W of Glenwood Springs.

Opened: 1987. **Holes:** 18. **Par:** 72/72. **Yards:** 7,309/5,386. **Course rating:** 73.9/69.9. **Slope:** 132/112. **Architect:** Finger/Dye/Spann. **Green fee:** $26/$30. **Credit cards:** All major. **Reduced fees:** Low season, seniors, juniors. **Caddies:** No. **Golf carts:** $12. **Discount golf packages:** Yes. **Season:** March-Nov. **High:** June-Aug. **On site lodging:** Yes. **Rental clubs:** Yes. **Walking policy:** Unrestricted walking. **Metal spikes allowed:** No. **Range:** Yes (grass). **To obtain tee times:** Call 3 days in advance or up to one year with lodging and golf package.
Subscriber comments: Challenging course with hidden greens...Gorgeous mountain setting with a fantastic layout...The vistas from this course are unbelievable...Worth the drive...One of the better courses in Colorado...Brutal from back tees...Really off the beaten path, but fun...Favors fade or straight ball...A hidden jewel...Multi tiered greens. Usually has wind.

★★★½BEAVER CREEK GOLF CLUB
R-P.O. Box 915, Avon, 81620, Boulder County, (970)845-5775.
Opened: 1982. **Holes:** 18. **Par:** 70/70. **Yards:** 6,752/5,200. **Course rating:** 69.2/70.2.
Slope: 133/121. **Architect:** Robert Trent. Jones Jr. **Green fee:** $100. **Credit cards:** All major. **Reduced fees:** Low season, resort guests. **Caddies:** No. **Golf carts:** Included in Green Fee. **Discount golf packages:** No. **Season:** May-Oct. **High:** May-June. **On site lodging:** Yes. **Rental clubs:** Yes. **Walking policy:** Mandatory cart. **Metal spikes allowed:** Yes. **Range:** Yes (grass). **To obtain tee times:** Call for information, depends on where you are staying.
Subscriber comments: Beauty, with narrow holes...Gorgeous mountain setting...First three holes great...Too many gimmicky holes...Enjoyed layout of course...Can't use driver very often, pricey...Lots of trees and water, like two seperate courses.

★★★BOOMERANG LINKS
PU-7309 West 4th St., Greeley, 80634, Weld County, (970)351-8934, (800)266-6371, 40 miles N of Denver.
Opened: 1991. **Holes:** 18. **Par:** 72/72. **Yards:** 7,214/5,285. **Course rating:** 72.6/68.5.
Slope: 131/113. **Architect:** William Neff. **Green fee:** $15/$18. **Credit cards:**
MC,VISA,DISC. **Reduced fees:** Weekdays, low season, twilight, seniors, juniors.
Caddies: No. **Golf carts:** N/A. **Discount golf packages:** No. **Season:** Year-round.
High: June-Sept. **On site lodging:** No. **Rental clubs:** Yes. **Walking policy:**
Unrestricted walking. **Metal spikes allowed:** Yes. **Range:** Yes (grass). **To obtain tee times:** Call Monday for the following seven days.
Subscriber comments: Links course. Hard from back tees...Good layout...Don't hit it right. Water on first four holes...Demanding front nine, challanging back nine, great course...A fun course, if you can control your slice...OB on left on back nine...Tough par 3s.

★★★★BRECKENRIDGE GOLF CLUB
PU-200 Clubhouse Dr., Breckenridge, 80424, Summit County, (970)453-9104, 80 miles SW of Denver.
Opened: 1985. **Holes:** 18. **Par:** 72/72. **Yards:** 7,279/5,066. **Course rating:** 73.1/67.7.
Slope: 146/118. **Architect:** Jack Nicklaus. **Green fee:** $45/$68. **Credit cards:**
MC,VISA,AMEX. **Reduced fees:** Low season, twilight. **Caddies:** No. **Golf carts:** $12.
Discount golf packages: Yes. **Season:** May-Oct. **High:** July-Sept. **On site lodging:**

No. **Rental clubs:** Yes. **Walking policy:** Walking at certain times. **Metal spikes allowed:** No. **Range:** Yes (grass). **To obtain tee times:** Call 4 days in advance. **Notes:** Ranked 12th in 1997 Best in State.
Subscriber comments: Pace of play consistently good...The best mountain course...Frost delay in June! Worth the wait...Beautiful setting...Challenging layout...Best Nicklaus course in state...Golf doesn't get better than #12...Windy and cool even in summer...Don't miss it...Tough from tips.

THE BROADMOOR GOLF CLUB
R-1 Pourtales Rd., Colorado Springs, 80906, El Paso County, (719)577-5790, (800)634-7711, 60 miles S of Denver.
Green fee: $120/$120. **Credit cards:** All major,Diners Club. **Reduced fees:** Twilight. **Caddies:** Yes. **Golf carts:** Included in Green Fee.
Discount golf packages: Yes. **Season:** Year-round. **On site lodging:** Yes. **Rental clubs:** Yes. **Walking policy:** Mandatory cart. **Range:** Yes (grass).
★★★★**EAST COURSE**
Opened: 1918. **Holes:** 18. **Par:** 72/72. **Yards:** 7,091/5,847. **Course rating:** 73.0/72.7. **Slope:** 129/139. **Architect:** Donald Ross/Robert Trent Jones. **High:** April-Oct. **Metal spikes allowed:** Yes. **To obtain tee times:** Confirm reservations in hotel. Call golf shop.
Notes: Ranked 15th in 1997 Best in State. 1995 U.S. Women's Open.
Subscriber comments: Great layout, tough greens, worth the drive...Traditional course...Terrific! Gorgeous setting...A trip back in time and a real treat...Some blind tee shots...It was the best golf vacation I've ever had...Greens very fast...Tough to shoot in 70s, easy to shoot in 80s.
★★★½**MOUNTAIN COURSE**
Opened: 1976. **Holes:** 18. **Par:** 72/71. **Yards:** 6,781/5,609. **Course rating:** 72.1/71.5. **Slope:** 135/126. **Architect:** Arnold Palmer/Ed Seay. **High:** May-Oct. **Metal spikes allowed:** Yes. **To obtain tee times:** Call golf shop.
Subscriber comments: Target golf, way too many blind shots.
★★★★**WEST COURSE**
Opened: 1918. **Holes:** 18. **Par:** 72/72. **Yards:** 7,340/5,375. **Course rating:** 73.0/70.5. **Slope:** 133/127. **Architect:** Donald Ross/Robert Trent Jones. **High:** April-Oct. **Metal spikes allowed:** No. **To obtain tee times:** Call golf shop.
Subscriber comments: Enjoyable course...Great classic course in a great setting. It doesn't get much better...Pamper yourself...This must be heaven!...Tougher than East. Foul balls have penalties.

★★★½BUFFALO RUN GOLF COURSE
PU-15700 E. 112th Ave., Commerce City, 80022, (303)289-1500, 35 miles NW of Denver.
Opened: 1996. **Holes:** 18. **Par:** 72/71. **Yards:** 7,411/5,227. **Course rating:** 73.5/68.1. **Slope:** 121/119. **Architect:** Keith Foster. **Green fee:** $21/$25. **Credit cards:** All major. **Reduced fees:** Seniors, juniors. **Caddies:** Yes. **Golf carts:** $10. **Discount golf packages:** No. **Season:** Year-round. **High:** May-Aug. **On site lodging:** No. **Rental clubs:** Yes. **Walking policy:** Unrestricted walking. **Metal spikes allowed:** No. **Range:** Yes (grass). **To obtain tee times:** Call 3 days in advance.
Notes: Ranked 6th in 1997 Best New Affordable Public Courses.
Subscriber comments: A stern test from the back tees...Excellent for all skill levels, great fun...Wide open, great clubhouse...Tough par 3s...Beautiful facilities in the middle of nowhere...A young course with lots of potential, needs to mature...Wide open, not a tree in sight...Tough bunkers and par 3 of 260 yards.

★★½CANTERBERRY GOLF COURSE
PU-11400 Canterberry Pkwy., Parker, 80134, Douglas County, (303)840-3100.
Opened: 1996. **Holes:** 18. **Par:** 72/72. **Yards:** 7,180/5,600. **Course rating:** 73.0/63.9. **Slope:** 138/104. **Architect:** Jeff Brauer. **Green fee:** $14/$30. **Credit cards:** MC,VISA,AMEX. **Reduced fees:** Weekdays, low season, twilight, seniors, juniors. **Caddies:** No. **Golf carts:** $10. **Discount golf packages:** Yes. **Season:** Year-round. **High:** March-Oct. **On site lodging:** No. **Rental clubs:** Yes. **Walking policy:** Walking at certain times. **Metal spikes allowed:** Yes. **Range:** Yes (grass). **To obtain tee times:** Call up to 3 days in advance after 8 a.m.
Notes: Ranked 9th in 1997 Best New Affordable Public Courses.

Subscriber comments: A great layout, but needs time to mature...Too far between greens and tees...The many different looks to this course make it worth it...Not for the timid or high handicappers...Isolated setting, tough par 3s...You'd better be straight and long...Tough in the wind ...Lots of fairway bunkers.

★★½CATTAILS GOLF CLUB

PU-6615 North River Rd., Alamosa, 81101, Alamosa County, (719)589-9515, (888)765-4653.

Opened: N/A. **Holes:** 18. **Par:** 72/73. **Yards:** 6,681/5,784. **Course rating:** 70.0/69.8. **Slope:** 129/120. **Architect:** Dick Phelps. **Green fee:** $16/$25. **Credit cards:** MC,VISA,DISC. **Reduced fees:** Juniors. **Caddies:** No. **Golf carts:** $18. **Discount golf packages:** Yes. **Season:** March-Nov. **High:** June-Aug. **On site lodging:** No. **Rental clubs:** Yes. **Walking policy:** Unrestricted walking. **Metal spikes allowed:** No. **Range:** Yes (grass/mats). **To obtain tee times:** Call golf shop.

Subscriber comments: Two completely different nines...Leave driver in bag on back nine, lovely course, good greens...Old front nine interesting, new back nine great.

★★CITY PARK GOLF CLUB

PU-2500 York, Denver, 80218, Denver County, (303)295-2095.

Opened: N/A. **Holes:** 18. **Par:** 72/74. **Yards:** 6,318/6,181. **Course rating:** 68.0/74.1. **Slope:** 111/116. **Architect:** Tom Bendelow. **Green fee:** $19/$20. **Credit cards:** MC,VISA. **Reduced fees:** N/A. **Caddies:** No. **Golf carts:** $20. **Discount golf packages:** No. **Season:** Year-round. **High:** April-Sept. **On site lodging:** No. **Rental clubs:** No. **Walking policy:** Unrestricted walking. **Metal spikes allowed:** No. **Range:** Yes (Mats). **To obtain tee times:** Call golf shop.

★★★½THE CLUB AT CORDILLERA (MOUNTAIN COURSE)

655 Club House Dr., Edwards, 81632, Eagle County, (970)926-5100, 100 miles W of Denver.

Opened: 1994. **Holes:** 18. **Par:** 72/72. **Yards:** 7,444/5,665. **Course rating:** 72.0/71.5. **Slope:** 145/138. **Architect:** Hale Irwin/Dick Phelps. **Green fee:** $150/$195. **Credit cards:** MC,VISA,AMEX. **Reduced fees:** N/A. **Caddies:** Yes. **Golf carts:** Included in Green Fee. **Discount golf packages:** No. **Season:** May-Oct. **High:** May-Oct. **On site lodging:** Yes. **Rental clubs:** Yes. **Walking policy:** Mandatory cart. **Metal spikes allowed:** Yes. **Range:** Yes (grass/mats). **To obtain tee times:** Call 24 hours in advance.

Notes: Ranked 20th in 1997 Best in State.

Special notes: Valley Course opened summer of 1997. Also has a par-3 course.

★★★COAL CREEK GOLF COURSE

PU-585 W. Dillon Rd., Louisville, 80027, Boulder County, (303)666-7888, 4 miles E of Boulder.

Opened: 1990. **Holes:** 18. **Par:** 72/72. **Yards:** 6,957/5,168. **Course rating:** 71.1/68.4. **Slope:** 130/114. **Architect:** Dick Phelps. **Green fee:** $21/$26. **Credit cards:** MC,VISA. **Reduced fees:** Weekdays, low season, twilight, seniors, juniors. **Caddies:** No. **Golf carts:** $18. **Discount golf packages:** No. **Season:** Year-round. **High:** April-Sept. **On site lodging:** No. **Rental clubs:** Yes. **Walking policy:** Unrestricted walking. **Metal spikes allowed:** Yes. **Range:** Yes (grass/mats). **To obtain tee times:** Call 3 days in advance beginning 8 a.m.

Subscriber comments: Short course, but fun. Nice people...Nice layout, tight, wandering creeks, houses are too close...More challenging than meets the eye...The blue tees present the best challenge...Elevated tee on 16 makes for long drives...Just a solid test.

★★½COLLINDALE GOLF CLUB

PU-1441 E. Horsetooth Road, Fort Collins, 80525, Larimer County, (970)221-6651, 60 miles N of Denver.

Opened: 1972. **Holes:** 18. **Par:** 71/73. **Yards:** 7,011/5,472. **Course rating:** 71.5/69.9. **Slope:** 126/113. **Architect:** Frank Hummel. **Green fee:** $15/$16. **Credit cards:** MC,VISA. **Reduced fees:** Weekdays, low season, twilight, seniors, juniors. **Caddies:** No. **Golf carts:** $16. **Discount golf packages:** No. **Season:** Year-round. **High:** May-Sept. **On site lodging:** No. **Rental clubs:** Yes. **Walking policy:** Unrestricted walking. **Metal spikes allowed:** No. **Range:** Yes (grass/mats). **To obtain tee times:** Call 3 days in advance.

Subscriber comments: Unbelievable greens, fast and true...Very long from the back tees, nice mature course...Getting better as trees grow...Flat, but challenging even from the white tees.

★★★CONQUISTADOR GOLF COURSE

2018 N. Delores Rd., Cortez, 81321, Montezuma County, (970)565-9208.
Call club for further information.
Subscriber comments: Very nice course, worth playing if in the area...Nice, flat, relaxing...Easy to walk, great layout, good people, fun.

★★★COPPER MOUNTAIN RESORT

R-104 Wheeler Circle, Copper Mountain, 80443, Summit County, (970)968-2882, (800)458-8386, 75 miles W of Denver.
Opened: 1976. **Holes:** 18. **Par:** 70/70. **Yards:** 6,094/4,374. **Course rating:** 67.6/63.8.
Slope: 124/100. **Architect:** Pete Dye/Perry Dye. **Green fee:** $55/$75. **Credit cards:** All major. **Reduced fees:** Low season, resort guests, twilight. **Caddies:** No. **Golf carts:** Included in Green Fee. **Discount golf packages:** Yes. **Season:** June-Oct. **High:** July-Aug. **On site lodging:** Yes. **Rental clubs:** Yes. **Walking policy:** Mandatory cart. **Metal spikes allowed:** Yes. **Range:** Yes (grass). **To obtain tee times:** Resort guests up to 60 days in advance, nonguests call 4 days in advance.
Notes: Highest 18-hole course in the United States.
Subscriber comments: Good mountain golf, greens are excellent...Toughest high altitude short course I've played...Breathtaking views...Golf holes are winter ski runs...Very tight and short front nine...Two courses in one. You need every club and have to place 'em...Classic Pete Dye design—fantastic setting...Some really great par 3s.

★★★★CRESTED BUTTE COUNTRY CLUB

385 Country Club Dr., Crested Butte, 81224, Gunnison County, (970)349-6131, (800)628-5496, 28 miles S of Gunnison.
Opened: 1983. **Holes:** 18. **Par:** 72/72. **Yards:** 7,208/5,702. **Course rating:** 72.6/72.4.
Slope: 129/123. **Architect:** Robert Trent Jones Jr.. **Green fee:** $55/$85. **Credit cards:** All major. **Reduced fees:** Low season, resort guests, twilight. **Caddies:** No. **Golf carts:** Included in Green Fee. **Discount golf packages:** Yes. **Season:** May-Oct. **High:** June-Sept. **On site lodging:** Yes. **Rental clubs:** Yes. **Walking policy:** Mandatory cart. **Metal spikes allowed:** No. **Range:** Yes (grass/mats). **To obtain tee times:** Call in advance.
Subscriber comments: Tough, sometimes unfair...Top notch...Beautiful vistas. Would probably get greater notice if it were not so isolated...Nice layout...Great eating places downtown...Both nines are unbelieveably different.

★★★½DALTON RANCH GOLF CLUB

589 C.R. 252, Durango, 81301, La Plata County, (970)247-8774, 210 miles NW of Albuquerque.
Opened: 1993. **Holes:** 18. **Par:** 72/72. **Yards:** 6,934/5,539. **Course rating:** 72.4/71.7.
Slope: 135/127. **Architect:** Ken Dye. **Green fee:** $25/$45. **Credit cards:** MC,VISA.
Reduced fees: Low season, resort guests, twilight. **Caddies:** No. **Golf carts:** $9.
Discount golf packages: Yes. **Season:** April-Oct. **High:** June-Sept. **On site lodging:** No. **Rental clubs:** Yes. **Walking policy:** Unrestricted walking. **Metal spikes allowed:** Yes. **Range:** Yes (grass). **To obtain tee times:** Call golf shop.
Subscriber comments: Beautiful setting (including narrow gauge railroad), landing areas hidden...Best 18th hole I've played in town...Super mountain/stream course...Bring lots of balls...13 of 18 holes could be postcards...Not for average player, difficult...Unusual challenge, very demanding, water everywhere.

★★★DOS RIOS GOLF CLUB

PU-501 Camino Del Rio, Gunnison, 81230, Gunnison County, (970)641-1482.
Call club for further information.
Subscriber comments: Back nine very good...Good away from home course...Great mountain course with very difficult holes...Bring your fishing pole...Nice place to enjoy life...Lots of water, deep rough.

★★EAGLE GOLF CLUB

PU-1200 Clubhouse Dr., Broomfield, 80020, Boulder County, (303)466-3322, 15 miles N of Denver.

Opened: 1968. **Holes:** 18. **Par:** 71/71. **Yards:** 6,609/5,745. **Course rating:** 69.7/65.8. **Slope:** 117/111. **Architect:** Dick Phelps. **Green fee:** $18/$38. **Credit cards:** MC,VISA,AMEX. **Reduced fees:** Weekdays, twilight, seniors, juniors. **Caddies:** No. **Golf carts:** $11. **Discount golf packages:** No. **Season:** Year-round. **High:** May-Sept. **On site lodging:** No. **Rental clubs:** Yes. **Walking policy:** Unrestricted walking. **Metal spikes allowed:** No. **Range:** Yes (Mats). **To obtain tee times:** Call up to 7 days in advance.

★★★EAGLE VAIL GOLF CLUB
PU-0431 Eagle Dr., Avon, 81620, Boulder County, (970)949-5267, 107 miles W of Denver.
Opened: 1975. **Holes:** 18. **Par:** 72/72. **Yards:** 6,819/4,856. **Course rating:** 71.3/67.4. **Slope:** 131/123. **Architect:** Bruce Devlin/Bob von Hagge. **Green fee:** $49/$80. **Credit cards:** MC,VISA,AMEX. **Reduced fees:** Low season, twilight. **Caddies:** No. **Golf carts:** Included in Green Fee. **Discount golf packages:** No. **Season:** May-Oct. **High:** June-Sept. **On site lodging:** No. **Rental clubs:** Yes. **Walking policy:** Mandatory cart. **Metal spikes allowed:** Yes. **Range:** Yes (grass/mats). **To obtain tee times:** Call 2 days in advance.
Subscriber comments: Fun, beautiful—true mountain course...Excellent course, many challenging holes...Tough, unforgiving course, I keep going back...Need every club in bag and what a view...A bit tricked up...Elevation changes fun, unique shots needed.

★★½EAGLES NEST GOLF CLUB
PU-305 Golden Eagle Rd., Silverthorne, 80498, Summit County, (970)468-0681, 67 miles W of Denver.
Opened: 1985. **Holes:** 18. **Par:** 72/72. **Yards:** 7,024/5,556. **Course rating:** 72.6/71.9. **Slope:** 141/126. **Architect:** Richard Phelps. **Green fee:** $25/$60. **Credit cards:** MC,VISA. **Reduced fees:** Weekdays, low season, twilight, juniors. **Caddies:** No. **Golf carts:** Included in Green Fee. **Discount golf packages:** Yes. **Season:** May-Oct. **High:** July-Sept. **On site lodging:** No. **Rental clubs:** Yes. **Walking policy:** Mandatory cart. **Metal spikes allowed:** Yes. **Range:** Yes (grass/mats). **To obtain tee times:** Call 7 days in advance.
Subscriber comments: Mountain course, season too short...Too many weird, tricked-up holes...Looks can be deceiving...Drive blind too often...Challenging...Beautiful scenery, rollercoaster golf...8th hole is a classic...Elevation changes tee to green are spectacular.

★★ENGLEWOOD GOLF COURSE
PM-2101 W. Oxford Ave., Englewood, 80110, Arapahoe County, (303)762-2670, 5 miles S of Denver.
Opened: 1977. **Holes:** 27. **Par:** 72/72. **Yards:** 6,836/5,967. **Course rating:** 71.0/72.2. **Slope:** 125/128. **Architect:** Dick Phelps. **Green fee:** $13/$20. **Credit cards:** MC,VISA. **Reduced fees:** Seniors, juniors. **Caddies:** No. **Golf carts:** $20. **Discount golf packages:** Yes. **Season:** Year-round. **High:** May-Oct. **On site lodging:** No. **Rental clubs:** Yes. **Walking policy:** Unrestricted walking. **Metal spikes allowed:** No. **Range:** Yes (grass/mats). **To obtain tee times:** Call up to 4 days in advance.

★★½ESTES PARK GOLF COURSE
PU-1080 South Saint Vrain Ave., Estes Park, 80517, Larimer County, (970)586-8146, 60 miles NW of Denver.
Opened: 1957. **Holes:** 18. **Par:** 71/72. **Yards:** 6,326/5,250. **Course rating:** 68.3/68.2. **Slope:** 118/125. **Architect:** Henry Hughes/Dick Phelps. **Green fee:** $20/$30. **Credit cards:** MC,VISA. **Reduced fees:** Low season, twilight. **Caddies:** No. **Golf carts:** $22. **Discount golf packages:** Yes. **Season:** April-Oct. **High:** June-Sept. **On site lodging:** No. **Rental clubs:** Yes. **Walking policy:** Unrestricted walking. **Metal spikes allowed:** Yes. **Range:** Yes (grass). **To obtain tee times:** Call 7 days in advance.
Subscriber comments: An excellent high altitude experience...Beautiful setting, some holes challenging...Short par 4s...OK golf, great 19th hole...Watch out for droppings!...Play in fall after tourists go home...Fun to play with the deer and elk.

★★½EVERGREEN GOLF COURSE
29614 Upper Bear Creek, Evergreen, 80439, Jefferson County, (303)674-6351. Call club for further information.

Subscriber comments: Tough greens, beautiful course...Short, but don't let that fool you, a fun course...Play it if you're in town...Tight on front nine, blind shots...Mountainside layout makes for tough course.

★★★★FAIRWAY PINES GOLF CLUB
PU-117 Ponderosa Dr., Ridgway, 81432, Ouray County, (970)626-5284, 25 miles S of Montrose.
Opened: 1993. **Holes:** 18. **Par:** 72/72. **Yards:** 6,826/5,291. **Course rating:** 71.6/72.2. **Slope:** 130/123. **Architect:** Byron Coker. **Green fee:** $30/$36. **Credit cards:** MC,VISA,DISC. **Reduced fees:** Twilight, juniors. **Caddies:** No. **Golf carts:** $11. **Discount golf packages:** Yes. **Season:** April-Oct. **High:** July-Sept. **On site lodging:** No. **Rental clubs:** Yes. **Walking policy:** Unrestricted walking. **Metal spikes allowed:** Yes. **Range:** Yes (grass/mats). **To obtain tee times:** Call 48 hours in advance.
Subscriber comments: Breathtaking views. Nice mountain course. Back nine needs to mature...Wonderful course...Placement...Worth the drive...Very beautiful, fun to play.

★★FLATIRONS GOLF COURSE
PU-5706 Araphahoe Rd., Boulder, 80303, Boulder County, (303)442-7851, 15 miles NW of Denver.
Opened: 1933. **Holes:** 18. **Par:** 70/71. **Yards:** 6,782/5,226. **Course rating:** 71.7/68.3. **Slope:** 126/119. **Architect:** Robert Bruce Harris. **Green fee:** $16/$21. **Credit cards:** MC,VISA. **Reduced fees:** N/A. **Caddies:** No. **Golf carts:** $20. **Discount golf packages:** No. **Season:** Year-round. **High:** March-Sept. **On site lodging:** No. **Rental clubs:** Yes. **Walking policy:** Unrestricted walking. **Metal spikes allowed:** No. **Range:** Yes (grass/mats). **To obtain tee times:** Call 1 day in advance for weekdays at 7 a.m. and 3 days in advance for weekends at 7 p.m.

★★½FOOTHILLS GOLF COURSE
PU-3901 South Carr St., Denver, 80235, Denver County, (303)989-3901.
Opened: 1971. **Holes:** 18. **Par:** 72/74. **Yards:** 6,908/6,028. **Course rating:** 71.1/72.9. **Slope:** 122/130. **Architect:** Dick Phelps. **Green fee:** $20. **Credit cards:** MC,VISA. **Reduced fees:** N/A. **Caddies:** No. **Golf carts:** $10. **Discount golf packages:** No. **Season:** Year-round. **High:** April-Oct. **On site lodging:** No. **Rental clubs:** Yes. **Walking policy:** Unrestricted walking. **Metal spikes allowed:** No. **Range:** Yes (grass/mats). **To obtain tee times:** Nonresidents call 2 days in advance.
Subscriber comments: Remarkable improvement in past four years. Fun golf...The view alone is worth any price...Only real challenge is trying to hit over pond on #6...Nice clubhouse.

★★FORT MORGAN GOLF CLUB
PU-17586 Colorado Rd. T.5, Fort Morgan, 80701, Morgan County, (970)867-5990, 70 miles NE of Denver.
Opened: N/A. **Holes:** 18. **Par:** 72/74. **Yards:** 6,575/5,457. **Course rating:** 69.9/65.8. **Slope:** 119/113. **Architect:** Henry B. Hughes. **Green fee:** $12/$18. **Credit cards:** MC,VISA. **Reduced fees:** N/A. **Caddies:** No. **Golf carts:** $20. **Discount golf packages:** No. **Season:** Year-round. **High:** April-Oct. **On site lodging:** No. **Rental clubs:** Yes. **Walking policy:** Unrestricted walking. **Metal spikes allowed:** No. **Range:** Yes (grass/mats). **To obtain tee times:** Call 7 days in advance for weekdays and 3 days in advance for weekends and holidays.

★★★★FOX HOLLOW AT LAKEWOOD GOLF COURSE
PU-13410 W. Morrison Rd., Lakewood, 80228, Jefferson County, (303)986-7888, 15 miles W of Denver.
Opened: 1993. **Holes:** 27. **Architect:** Denis Griffiths. **Green fee:** $30. **Credit cards:** MC,VISA. **Reduced fees:** Seniors, juniors. **Caddies:** Yes. **Golf carts:** $10. **Discount golf packages:** No. **Season:** Year-round. **High:** April-Oct. **On site lodging:** No. **Rental clubs:** Yes. **Walking policy:** Unrestricted walking. **Metal spikes allowed:** No. **Range:** Yes (grass/mats). **To obtain tee times:** Residents call 7 days in advance after 5 p.m. Nonresidents call 6 days in advance.
CANYON/LINKS
Par: 71/71. **Yards:** 7,030/4,802. **Course rating:** 72.3/67.5. **Slope:** 134/112.
CANYON/MEADOW
Par: 71/71. **Yards:** 6,808/4,439. **Course rating:** 71.2/65.3. **Slope:** 138/107.

MEADOW/LINKS
Par: 72/72. **Yards:** 6,888/4,801. **Course rating:** 71.1/66.6. **Slope:** 132/107.
Notes: Ranked 19th in 1997 Best in State.
Subscriber comments: Doesn't get much better than this for enjoyable golf...You can't beat the three layouts, but you can't pick and choose the two nines you will play on any set day...No private club could have service this good...Good variety of holes...Bring your long drive.

★★½GLENEAGLE GOLF CLUB
PU-345 Mission Hills Way, Colorado Springs, 80908, El Paso County, (719)488-0900, 5 miles N of Colorado Springs.
Opened: 1972. **Holes:** 18. **Par:** 72/72. **Yards:** 7,276/5,655. **Course rating:** 73.9/73.2. **Slope:** 128/120. **Architect:** Frank Hummel. **Green fee:** $17/$25. **Credit cards:** All major. **Reduced fees:** Low season, twilight, seniors, juniors. **Caddies:** No. **Golf carts:** $22. **Discount golf packages:** No. **Season:** Year-roundf. **High:** March-Oct. **On site lodging:** No. **Rental clubs:** Yes. **Walking policy:** Unrestricted walking. **Metal spikes allowed:** Yes. **Range:** Yes (grass). **To obtain tee times:** Call 3 days in advance. Call on Wednesday for weekend.
Subscriber comments: Houses on top of fairways, no margin for error...A good workout to walk this course...Challenging and enjoyable from the tips...Clubhouse doesn't have beer...Nice view of Pikes Peak and Air Force Academy...Good golf but course crosses to many public roads.

★★★½GRAND LAKE GOLF COURSE
PU-1415 County Rd. 48, Grand Lake, 80447, Grand County, (970)627-8008, 100 miles NW of Denver.
Opened: 1964. **Holes:** 18. **Par:** 72/74. **Yards:** 6,542/5,685. **Course rating:** 70.5/70.9. **Slope:** 131/123. **Architect:** Dick Phelps. **Green fee:** $45/$45. **Credit cards:** MC,VISA,DISC. **Reduced fees:** N/A. **Caddies:** No. **Golf carts:** $24. **Discount golf packages:** No. **Season:** May-Oct. **High:** July-Aug. **On site lodging:** No. **Rental clubs:** Yes. **Walking policy:** Unrestricted walking. **Metal spikes allowed:** Yes. **Range:** Yes (grass/mats). **To obtain tee times:** Call 2 days in advance for weekdays and Thursday 6:30 a.m. prior to weekend.
Subscriber comments: Better be straight or you're with the bears!...Beautiful setting for golf course...Cut out of the woods, very serene setting...Tight mountain course, back nine totally different than front nine...Likely to see deer or fox...One of my favorites...Great for the ego to hit a ball at 9,000 feet...Narrow landing areas.

★★★★GRANDOTE PEAKS GOLF CLUB
R-5540 Hwy. 12, La Veta, 81055, Huerfano County, (719)742-3391, (800)457-9986, 45 miles SW of Pueblo.
Opened: 1986. **Holes:** 18. **Par:** 72/72. **Yards:** 7,085/5,608. **Course rating:** 72.8/70.7. **Slope:** 133/117. **Architect:** Tom Weiskopf/Jay Morrish. **Green fee:** $40/$55. **Credit cards:** All major. **Reduced fees:** Weekdays, low season. **Caddies:** No. **Golf carts:** $20. **Discount golf packages:** Yes. **Season:** April-Oct. **High:** July-Sept. **On site lodging:** No. **Rental clubs:** Yes. **Walking policy:** Unrestricted walking. **Metal spikes allowed:** Yes. **Range:** Yes (grass). **To obtain tee times:** Call anytime.
Notes: Ranked 16th in 1997 Best in State.
Subscriber comments: Stay in fairway or goodbye ball...This course makes me want to play any Weiskopf course I find...Off the beaten path...Pleasant surprise, uncrowded, beautiful valley...Demanding...Great variety of holes...Course tough but fair—stay out of the gunge.

★★★GREAT SAND DUNES GOLF COURSE AT ZAPATA RANCH
R-5303 Hwy. 150, Mosca, 81146, Alamosa County, (719)378-2357, (800)284-9213, 30 miles NE of Alamosa.
Opened: 1990. **Holes:** 18. **Par:** 72/72. **Yards:** 7,006/5,327. **Course rating:** 71.2/67.8. **Slope:** 126/118. **Architect:** John Sanford/R.M. Phelps. **Green fee:** $35/$35. **Credit cards:** All major. **Reduced fees:** Twilight, seniors, juniors. **Caddies:** No. **Golf carts:** $20. **Discount golf packages:** Yes. **Season:** March-Oct. **High:** July-Sept. **On site lodging:** Yes. **Rental clubs:** Yes. **Walking policy:** Unrestricted walking. **Metal spikes allowed:** Yes. **Range:** Yes (grass). **To obtain tee times:** Call golf shop.
Subscriber comments: Wind and thin air...Very narrow...Hard to get to, but worth it...A

surprise! A gem in the middle of nowhere...Fun layout, easy walking, watch the buffalo.

★★★½HIGHLAND HILLS GOLF COURSE

PU-2200 Clubhouse Dr., Greeley, 80634, Weld County, (970)330-7327, 50 miles N of Denver.
Opened: 1961. **Holes:** 18. **Par:** 71/75. **Yards:** 6,700/6,002. **Course rating:** 71.4/72.8.
Slope: 128/120. **Architect:** Frank Hummel. **Green fee:** $16/$20. **Credit cards:**
MC,VISA,DISC. **Reduced fees:** Weekdays, low season, twilight, seniors, juniors.
Caddies: No. **Golf carts:** N/A. **Discount golf packages:** Yes. **Season:** Year-round.
High: May-Oct. **On site lodging:** No. **Rental clubs:** Yes. **Walking policy:** Unrestricted walking. **Metal spikes allowed:** Yes. **Range:** Yes (grass). **To obtain tee times:** Call seven days in advance.
Subscriber comments: Tight, good shape, makes you think...Lots of trees...Poor man's country club.

★★★½HILLCREST GOLF CLUB

2300 Rim Dr., Durango, 81301, La Plata County, (970)247-1499.
Opened: 1969. **Holes:** 18. **Par:** 71/71. **Yards:** 6,838/5,252. **Course rating:** 71.3/68.1. **Slope:** 127/111. **Architect:** Frank Hummel. **Green fee:** $17/$17. **Credit cards:** MC,VISA. **Reduced fees:** Twilight. **Caddies:** No. **Golf carts:** $16. **Discount golf packages:** No. **Season:** March-Nov.
High: June-Aug. **On site lodging:** No. **Rental clubs:** Yes. **Walking policy:** Unrestricted walking. **Metal spikes allowed:** Yes. **Range:** Yes (grass/mats). **To obtain tee times:** Call 7 days in advance.
Subscriber comments: Fast greens, great views of mountains, well maintained bunkers...99 percent of difficulty is deceiving greens...Beautiful setting above Durango...Used rolling terrain well...Enjoyable and fun course to play, good par 3s...Nice place to play.

★★★½HOLLYDOT GOLF COURSE

PU-North Park St., Colorado City, 81019, Pueblo County, (719)676-3340, 20 miles S of Pueblo.
Opened: 1989. **Holes:** 18. **Par:** 71/71. **Yards:** 7,003/5,224. **Course rating:** 71.9/67.0. **Slope:** 126/111. **Architect:** N/A. **Green fee:** $11/$16. **Credit cards:** None. **Reduced fees:** Weekdays, low season, juniors.
Caddies: No. **Golf carts:** $16. **Discount golf packages:** No. **Season:** Year-round. **High:** April-Oct. **On site lodging:** No. **Rental clubs:** No. **Walking policy:** Unrestricted walking. **Metal spikes allowed:** No. **Range:** Yes (grass). **To obtain tee times:** Call on Monday prior to weekend, or 7 days in advance for weekdays.
Subscriber comments: Spectacular scenery...Best weekend ever...Nice out of the way course...Lots of good holes...One of Colorado's hidden gems...Very soft greens.
Special Notes: Also has a 9-hole par-36 course.

★★★½HYLAND HILLS GOLF COURSE - GOLD COURSE

PU-9650 N. Sheridan Blvd., Westminster, 80030, Adams County, (303)428-6526, 10 miles N of Denver.
Opened: 1964. **Holes:** 18. **Par:** 72/73. **Yards:** 7,021/5,654. **Course rating:** 71.9/71.9. **Slope:** 132/120. **Architect:** Henry Hughes. **Green fee:** $16/$21. **Credit cards:** MC,VISA,AMEX. **Reduced fees:** N/A. **Caddies:** Yes. **Golf carts:** $20. **Discount golf packages:** No. **Season:** Year-round. **High:** June-Aug. **On site lodging:** No. **Rental clubs:** Yes. **Walking policy:** Unrestricted walking. **Metal spikes allowed:** Yes. **Range:** Yes (grass/mats). **To obtain tee times:** Call at 7 a.m. day before on weekdays. Call on Wednesday at 9 a.m. for Saturday play. Call Friday at 9 a.m. for Sunday play.
Notes: 1990 U.S. Women's Amateur Public Links.
Subscriber comments: Classic golf design...Good facilities and food...Water comes into play on 13 of 18 holes..."Trick" putting greens...Fun to play, fair and challenging...A good mix of tough and easy holes, nice fairways...Great track will use every club in bag.
Special Notes: Also has a 9-hole, par-37 Blue Course; 9-hole par-3 South Course and 7-hole par-3 North Course.

★★★½INDIAN PEAKS GOLF CLUB

PU-2300 Indian Peaks Trail, Lafayette, 80026, Boulder County, (303)666-4706, 10 miles SE of Boulder.

Opened: 1993. **Holes:** 18. **Par:** 72/72. **Yards:** 7,083/5,468. **Course rating:** 72.5/69.9. **Slope:** 134/116. **Architect:** Hale Irwin/Dick Phelps. **Green fee:** $30/$30. **Credit cards:** MC,VISA,DISC. **Reduced fees:** N/A. **Caddies:** No. **Golf carts:** $22. **Discount golf packages:** No. **Season:** Year-round. **High:** May-Sept. **On site lodging:** No. **Rental clubs:** Yes. **Walking policy:** Unrestricted walking. **Metal spikes allowed:** Yes. **Range:** Yes (grass/mats). **To obtain tee times:** Call 2 days in advance for weekdays. Call Monday for Saturday tee time and Tuesday for Sunday tee time.
Subscriber comments: Pleasure to play...Can't wait till the trees grow up...Winds exact a toll, a real challenge...Good job Hale, but #7 is too gimmicky...A good test of golf skills. Lots of sand...I like everything about this course...18th hole view Wow!

★★½ INDIAN TREE GOLF CLUB
PU-7555 Wadsworth Blvd., Arvada, 80003, Jefferson County, (303)403-2541, 10 miles NW of Denver.
Opened: 1971. **Holes:** 18. **Par:** 70/75. **Yards:** 6,742/5,850. **Course rating:** 69.6/71.4. **Slope:** 114/116. **Architect:** Dick Phelps. **Green fee:** $20/$20. **Credit cards:** MC,VISA. **Reduced fees:** N/A. **Caddies:** No. **Golf carts:** $18. **Discount golf packages:** No. **Season:** Year-round. **High:** May-Sept. **On site lodging:** No. **Rental clubs:** Yes. **Walking policy:** Unrestricted walking. **Metal spikes allowed:** Yes. **Range:** Yes (grass/mats). **To obtain tee times:** Call 24 hours in advance.
Subscriber comments: Great junior golf program, fast greens, little sand. Two water holes—par 3s...Great place to play with large open fairways...Some challenging holes...12th hole is a very good par 5...Beautiful, trees, geese, easy walking...Par-3 13th makes my best 18 list...Good course to get your game back on track.
Special Notes: Also 9-hole par-3 course.

★★★½ INVERNESS HOTEL & GOLF CLUB
R-200 Inverness Dr. W., Englewood, 80112, Arapahoe County, (303)397-7878, (800)346-4891, 3 miles S of Denver.
Opened: 1974. **Holes:** 18. **Par:** 70/70. **Yards:** 6,948/6,407. **Course rating:** 71.8/69.2. **Slope:** 136/129. **Architect:** Press Maxwell. **Green fee:** $59/$99. **Credit cards:** All major,. **Reduced fees:** Twilight. **Caddies:** No. **Golf carts:** Included in Green Fee. **Discount golf packages:** Yes. **Season:** Year-round. **High:** June-Aug. **On site lodging:** Yes. **Rental clubs:** Yes. **Walking policy:** Unrestricted walking. **Metal spikes allowed:** No. **Range:** Yes (grass). **To obtain tee times:** Call golf shop. You must be overnight guest at Inverness Hotel or member to play.
Subscriber comments: Tough from tips...Some great holes, very challenging...Classic design, tough greens...Nice large greens...Back nine will surprise you...Fine layout, greens tend to always be hard.

★★½ JOHN F. KENNEDY GOLF CLUB
PU-10500 E. Hampden Ave., Aurora, 80014, Arapahoe County, (303)755-0105, (800)661-1419.
Opened: 1963. **Holes:** 27. **Architect:** Henry Hughes/Dick Phelps. **Green fee:** $13/$18. **Credit cards:** None. **Reduced fees:** Seniors, juniors. **Caddies:** No. **Golf carts:** $22. **Discount golf packages:** No. **Season:** Year-round. **High:** April-Sept. **On site lodging:** No. **Rental clubs:** Yes. **Walking policy:** Unrestricted walking. **Metal spikes allowed:** No. **Range:** Yes (grass/mats). **To obtain tee times:** Central computer for advanced times (303)784-4000. Day of play call starter at (303)751-0311.
EAST/CREEK
Par: 71/71. **Yards:** 6,886/5,769. **Course rating:** 71.6. **Slope:** 131.
WEST/CREEK
Par: 74/71. **Yards:** 6,751/5,729. **Course rating:** 70.9. **Slope:** 124.
WEST/EAST
Par: 75/73. **Yards:** 7,035/6,456. **Course rating:** 71.7. **Slope:** 119.
Subscriber comments: New back nine along a creek bed is fun...Love the wide open layout. Can use the driver on 13 holes...Big hitter's course...Too many geese...Nice driving range and pro shop, get up early if you don't have a reservation...Good place to practice fairway irons.
Special Notes: Also has a par-3 course.

★★★½KEYSTONE RANCH GOLF COURSE

R-P.O. Box 38, Keystone, 80435, Summit County, (970)496-4250, (800)354-4386, 7 miles W of Silverthorne.
Opened: 1980. **Holes:** 18. **Par:** 72/72. **Yards:** 7,090/5,596. **Course rating:** 71.4/70.7. **Slope:** 130/129. **Architect:** Robert T. Jones Jr. **Green fee:** $89/$101. **Credit cards:** All major. **Reduced fees:** Low season, resort guests, twilight, juniors. **Caddies:** No. **Golf carts:** Included in Green Fee. **Discount golf packages:** Yes. **Season:** May-Oct. **High:** June-Sept. **On site lodging:** Yes. **Rental clubs:** Yes. **Walking policy:** Walking at certain times. **Metal spikes allowed:** Yes. **Range:** Yes (grass/mats). **To obtain tee times:** Call 7 days in advance.
Notes: Ranked 14th in 1997 Best in State.
Subscriber comments: The golf course is like a country club...Great view, windy, numerous transitional areas...Give your game an extra hour for the views...Excellent challenge...Very interesting holes...Impressive mountain setting...Great restaurant.
Special Notes: Spikeless encouraged.

★★½LAKE ARBOR GOLF COURSE

PU-8600 Wadsworth Blvd., Arvada, 80003, Jefferson County, (303)423-1643, 15 miles N of Denver.
Opened: 1971. **Holes:** 18. **Par:** 70/69. **Yards:** 5,865/4,965. **Course rating:** 66.7/71.1. **Slope:** 108/113. **Architect:** Clark Glasson. **Green fee:** $13/$17. **Credit cards:** MC,VISA. **Reduced fees:** N/A. **Caddies:** No. **Golf carts:** $17. **Discount golf packages:** No. **Season:** Year-round. **High:** April-Sept. **On site lodging:** No. **Rental clubs:** Yes. **Walking policy:** Unrestricted walking. **Metal spikes allowed:** No. **Range:** Yes (grass). **To obtain tee times:** For weekdays call 1 day in advance. For weekends start Wednesday. For major holidays call 2 days in advance.
Subscriber comments: Tricky, need to manage game...Tight!...No doubt the best greens. Spikeless course...Condos too close to fairway.

★★½LAKE VALLEY GOLF CLUB

4400 Lake Valley Dr., Longmont, 80503, Boulder County, (303)444-2114, 3 miles N of Boulder.
Opened: 1964. **Holes:** 18. **Par:** 70/70. **Yards:** 6,725/5,713. **Course rating:** 69.6/71.8. **Slope:** 121/119. **Architect:** Press Maxwell. **Green fee:** $20/$29. **Credit cards:** MC,VISA. **Reduced fees:** Weekdays, twilight, seniors, juniors. **Caddies:** No. **Golf carts:** $19. **Discount golf packages:** Yes. **Season:** Year-round. **High:** April-Aug. **On site lodging:** No. **Rental clubs:** Yes. **Walking policy:** Unrestricted walking. **Metal spikes allowed:** No. **Range:** Yes (grass). **To obtain tee times:** Call 3 days in advance.
Subscriber comments: Very easy, good for corporate outings...Good front nine, tough with wind...Great setting. Interesting variety...New tree plantings are finally making more challenging.

★★★★LEGACY RIDGE GOLF COURSE

PU-10801 Legacy Ridge Parkway, Westminster, 80030, Adams County, (303)438-8997x2210, 15 miles NW of Denver.
Opened: 1994. **Holes:** 18. **Par:** 72/72. **Yards:** 7,251/5,383. **Course rating:** 74.0/70.6. **Slope:** 134/122. **Architect:** Arthur Hills. **Green fee:** $20/$32. **Credit cards:** MC,VISA. **Reduced fees:** Weekdays, twilight, seniors, juniors. **Caddies:** No. **Golf carts:** $20. **Discount golf packages:** No. **Season:** Year-round. **High:** April-Oct. **On site lodging:** No. **Rental clubs:** Yes. **Walking policy:** Unrestricted walking. **Metal spikes allowed:** No. **Range:** Yes (grass/mats). **To obtain tee times:** Nonresidents call 1 day in advance starting at 5 p.m.
Subscriber comments: One of the best in Colorado...Excellent, beautiful course, challenging...Great layout, tough par 4s...Nasty rough! Bring your straight game..Huge, undulating greens...Beautiful setting through wetlands...Blind shots, great course once you learn it...Not easy to walk, carts on paths only...Outstanding test of golf, pick your tees carefully...Very unforgiving...Environmentally friendly.

★★½LONE TREE GOLF CLUB

PU-9808 Sunningdale Blvd., Littleton, 80124, Arapahoe County, (303)799-9940, 25 miles S of Denver.
Opened: 1983. **Holes:** 18. **Par:** 72/72. **Yards:** 7,012/5,340. **Course rating:** 72.1/70.6.

Slope: 127/120. **Architect:** Arnold Palmer/Ed Seay. **Green fee:** $32/$42. **Credit cards:** All major. **Reduced fees:** Seniors. **Caddies:** No. **Golf carts:** $10. **Discount golf packages:** Yes. **Season:** Year-round. **High:** April-Oct. **On site lodging:** Yes. **Rental clubs:** Yes. **Walking policy:** Unrestricted walking. **Metal spikes allowed:** No. **Range:** Yes (grass/mats). **To obtain tee times:** Nonresidents call 3 days in advance after noon. **Subscriber comments:** More you play it, better you like it...Decent layout, lots of houses...Deceptively tough.

★½MAD RUSSIAN GOLF COURSE

PU-24361 Highway 257, Milliken, 80543, Weld County, (970)587-5157.
Opened: 1987. **Holes:** 18. **Par:** 70/70. **Yards:** 5,464/4,250. **Course rating:** 65.2/64.1. **Slope:** 117/103. **Architect:** N/A. **Green fee:** $16/$20. **Credit cards:** MC,VISA. **Reduced fees:** Weekdays, low season, seniors. **Caddies:** No. **Golf carts:** $20. **Discount golf packages:** No. **Season:** Year-round. **High:** April-Oct. **On site lodging:** No. **Rental clubs:** No. **Walking policy:** Unrestricted walking. **Metal spikes allowed:** Yes. **Range:** Yes (grass). **To obtain tee times:** Call up to 7 days in advance.

★★★★MARIANA BUTTE GOLF COURSE

PU-701 Clubhouse Dr., Loveland, 80537, Larimer County, (970)667-8308, 45 miles N of Denver.
Opened: 1992. **Holes:** 18. **Par:** 72/72. **Yards:** 6,572/5,420. **Course rating:** 70.6/70.2. **Slope:** 130/121. **Architect:** Dick Phelps. **Green fee:** $18/$28. **Credit cards:** MC,VISA,AMEX. **Reduced fees:** Weekdays, low season, twilight. **Caddies:** No. **Golf carts:** $12. **Discount golf packages:** Yes. **Season:** Year-round. **High:** May-Sept. **On site lodging:** No. **Rental clubs:** Yes. **Walking policy:** Unrestricted walking. **Metal spikes allowed:** No. **Range:** Yes (grass/mats). **To obtain tee times:** Call pro shop. **Subscriber comments:** Challenging, but still fun...Always a fun experience for every level of golfer. Never pass up a chance to play it...Love it, hope new houses do not ruin scenery...Need all your shots...Back side par 3s are great...Nice elevation changes...Bring flyrod, great holes on Big Thompson.

★★★½MEADOW HILLS GOLF COURSE

PU-3609 S. Dawson St., Aurora, 80014, Arapahoe County, (303)690-2500, 6 miles E of Denver.
Opened: 1957. **Holes:** 18. **Par:** 70/72. **Yards:** 6,717/5,481. **Course rating:** 70.9/70.5. **Slope:** 133/117. **Architect:** Henry Hughes. **Green fee:** $15/$24. **Credit cards:** MC,VISA,DISC. **Reduced fees:** Weekdays, twilight, seniors, juniors. **Caddies:** Yes. **Golf carts:** $11. **Discount golf packages:** No. **Season:** Year-round. **High:** May-Sept. **On site lodging:** No. **Rental clubs:** Yes. **Walking policy:** Unrestricted walking. **Metal spikes allowed:** No. **Range:** Yes (grass/mats). **To obtain tee times:** Nonresidents may call 4 days in advance.
Subscriber comments: Fine old-style course, trees can get you...Beautiful mature course...Great finishing hole...Don't be left on 16—the houses cost a lot and the fence is hard to climb quickly...Accuracy off the tee a must...Narrow fairways on many holes, some tough par 4s...Good time.

★★★THE MEADOWS GOLF CLUB

PU-6937 S. Simms, Littleton, 80127, Arapahoe County, (303)972-8831, 15 miles SW of Denver.
Opened: 1984. **Holes:** 18. **Par:** 72/72. **Yards:** 6,995/5,416. **Course rating:** 71.6/71.1. **Slope:** 130/123. **Architect:** Dick Phelps. **Green fee:** $15/$23. **Credit cards:** MC,VISA. **Reduced fees:** Low season, seniors, juniors. **Caddies:** No. **Golf carts:** $20. **Discount golf packages:** No. **Season:** Year-round. **High:** May-Sept. **On site lodging:** No. **Rental clubs:** Yes. **Walking policy:** Unrestricted walking. **Metal spikes allowed:** Yes. **Range:** Yes (grass). **To obtain tee times:** Nonresidents may call two days in advance.
Subscriber comments: Good test of golf...If accurate on par 5s you have a chance to score well...Front nine is excellent, nice facilities...Number 18 is the toughest...Tough to play in the wind...A very good challenge!

MONTROSE GOLF COURSE

1350 Birch St., Montrose, 81401, Montrose County, (970)249-8551.
Opened: 1960. **Holes:** 18. **Par:** 70. **Yards:** 6,446. **Course rating:** 68.1. **Slope:** 123. **Architect:** N/A. **Green fee:** $16/$20. **Credit cards:** MC,VISA. **Reduced fees:** Twilight,

juniors. **Caddies:** No. **Golf carts:** $10. **Discount golf packages:** Yes. **Season:** Year-round. **High:** March-Oct. **On site lodging:** No. **Rental clubs:** Yes. **Walking policy:** Unrestricted walking. **Metal spikes allowed:** No. **Range:** Yes (grass/mats). **To obtain tee times:** Call 3 days in advance.

★★★THE OLDE COURSE AT LOVELAND
PU-2115 W. 29th St., Loveland, 80538, Larimer County, (303)667-5256, 45 miles N of Denver.
Opened: 1959. **Holes:** 18. **Par:** 72/71. **Yards:** 6,827/5,498. **Course rating:** 70.9/70.6. **Slope:** 125/124. **Architect:** Richard Phelps. **Green fee:** $18/$20. **Credit cards:** MC,VISA. **Reduced fees:** Weekdays, twilight, juniors. **Caddies:** No. **Golf carts:** $20. **Discount golf packages:** Yes. **Season:** Year-round. **High:** May-Sept. **On site lodging:** No. **Rental clubs:** Yes. **Walking policy:** Unrestricted walking. **Metal spikes allowed:** Yes. **Range:** Yes (grass/mats). **To obtain tee times:** Call golf shop.
Subscriber comments: Old fashioned treelined course...Good test of golf. Back nine tougher than front...Hit the ball straight...Island green, great hole #14.

★★OVERLAND PARK GOLF COURSE
PM-1801 S. Huron St., Denver, 80223, Denver County, (303)777-7331, 2 miles S of Denver.
Opened: 1895. **Holes:** 18. **Par:** 72/74. **Yards:** 6,312/6,126. **Course rating:** 69.2/72.7. **Slope:** 114/115. **Architect:** N/A. **Green fee:** $16/$21. **Credit cards:** None. **Reduced fees:** Weekdays, seniors, juniors. **Caddies:** No. **Golf carts:** $20. **Discount golf packages:** No. **Season:** Year-round. **High:** April-Nov. **On site lodging:** No. **Rental clubs:** Yes. **Walking policy:** Unrestricted walking. **Metal spikes allowed:** Yes. **Range:** Yes (grass/mats). **To obtain tee times:** N/A.

★★★½PAGOSA SPRINGS GOLF CLUB
R-One Pines Club Place, Pagosa Springs, 81157, Archuleta County, (970)731-4755, 55 miles E of Durango.
Opened: 1973. **Holes:** 27. **Architect:** Johnny Bulla. **Green fee:** $14/$35. **Credit cards:** All major. **Reduced fees:** Low season, twilight, juniors. **Caddies:** No. **Golf carts:** $12. **Discount golf packages:** Yes. **Season:** April-Oct. **High:** July-Aug. **On site lodging:** Yes. **Rental clubs:** Yes. **Walking policy:** Unrestricted walking. **Metal spikes allowed:** No. **Range:** Yes (grass/mats). **To obtain tee times:** Call 7 days in advance.
PINON/MEADOWS
Par: 72/72. **Yards:** 7,221/5,400. **Course rating:** 72.9/68.0. **Slope:** 125/110.
PINON/PONDEROSA
Par: 71/71. **Yards:** 6,670/5,320. **Course rating:** 69.4/67.4. **Slope:** 119/107.
PONDEROSA/MEADOWS
Par: 71/71. **Yards:** 6,913/5,074. **Course rating:** 70.9/66.2. **Slope:** 123/108.
Subscriber comments: Spectacular views...Makes you work for a good score...Fun course but tough, worth the visit...Stay and play all three. Every mix is a different look. Greens big for mountain course. Meadows is where you can let it hang out...Pinon/Ponderosa is best...Course nestled in Ponderosa Pines.

★★PARK HILL GOLF CLUB
PU-4141 E. 35th Ave., Denver, 80207, Denver County, (303)333-5411.
Opened: 1931. **Holes:** 18. **Par:** 71/72. **Yards:** 6,585/5,811. **Course rating:** 69.4/73.4. **Slope:** 120/124. **Architect:** N/A. **Green fee:** $19/$22. **Credit cards:** MC,VISA. **Reduced fees:** N/A. **Caddies:** No. **Golf carts:** $22. **Discount golf packages:** No. **Season:** Year-round. **High:** May-Aug. **On site lodging:** No. **Rental clubs:** Yes. **Walking policy:** Unrestricted walking. **Metal spikes allowed:** Yes. **Range:** Yes. **To obtain tee times:** Call up to six days in advance.

★★½PATTY JEWETT GOLF CLUB
PU-900 E. Espanola, Colorado Springs, 80907, El Paso County, (719)578-6826.
Opened: 1898. **Holes:** 18. **Par:** 72/75. **Yards:** 6,811/5,998. **Course rating:** 71.5/73.0. **Slope:** 124/124. **Architect:** Willy Campbell/Press Maxwell. **Green fee:** $17/$24. **Credit cards:** None. **Reduced fees:** N/A. **Caddies:** No. **Golf carts:** $20. **Discount golf packages:** No. **Season:** Year-round. **High:** May-Aug. **On site lodging:** No. **Rental clubs:** Yes. **Walking policy:** Unrestricted walking. **Metal spikes allowed:** No. **Range:** Yes

(Mats). **To obtain tee times:** Call 7 days in advance.
Subscriber comments: Crowded, not too difficult...Wide open, yet good test...Beautiful setting with views of Pikes Peak...Rather flat, play early in day to avoid storms...Busy, good diversity of holes.
Special Notes: Also a 9-hole course. Par: 35. Yards: 3,160/2,874.

★★★½PINE CREEK GOLF CLUB

PU-9850 Divot Trail, Colorado Springs, 80920, Pueblo County, (719)594-9999, 2 miles N of Colorado Springs.
Opened: 1988. **Holes:** 18. **Par:** 72/72. **Yards:** 7,194/5,314. **Course rating:** 72.6/69.0.
Slope: 139/113. **Architect:** Richard Phelps. **Green fee:** $22/$26. **Credit cards:** MC,VISA,DISC. **Reduced fees:** Weekdays, low season, twilight, seniors, juniors.
Caddies: No. **Golf carts:** $22. **Discount golf packages:** No. **Season:** Year-round.
High: April-Oct. **On site lodging:** No. **Rental clubs:** Yes. **Walking policy:** Unrestricted walking. **Metal spikes allowed:** No. **Range:** Yes (grass). **To obtain tee times:** Call up to 3 days in advance or 7 days in advance w/credit card for foursome using carts.
Subscriber comments: Too tight. Ball in fairway or it's lost...Serious rough, good workout to walk...Front side lulls you to sleep, look out on back!...Great gambling course on par 5s...Lots of fun...Challenging. Tough back nine...Difficult if you play the wrong tees.

★★★½PLUM CREEK GOLF & COUNTRY CLUB

331 Players Club Dr., Castle Rock, 80104, Douglas County, (303)688-2611, (800)488-2612.
Opened: 1985. **Holes:** 18. **Par:** 72/72. **Yards:** 6,700/4,875. **Course rating:** 70.1/68.3.
Slope: 131/118. **Architect:** Pete Dye. **Green fee:** $65/$77. **Credit cards:** All major.
Reduced fees: Weekdays, low season, twilight. **Caddies:** No. **Golf carts:** Included in Green Fee. **Discount golf packages:** No. **Season:** Year-round. **High:** June-Sept. **On site lodging:** No. **Rental clubs:** Yes. **Walking policy:** Mandatory cart. **Metal spikes allowed:** Yes. **Range:** Yes (grass). **To obtain tee times:** Call up to 3 days in advance.
Notes: Ranked 18th in 1997 Best in State.
Subscriber comments: 16, 17, 18 toughest finishing holes...Beautiful. Every hole is different...Too many blind shots...Good course to play on special occasions...Pete Dye hates slicers...This course is for long hitters.

★★★★POLE CREEK GOLF CLUB

PU-P.O. Box 3348, Winter Park, 80482, Grand County, (970)726-8847, 80 miles NW of Denver.
Opened: 1984. **Holes:** 18. **Par:** 72/72. **Yards:** 7,107/5,006. **Course rating:** 73.1/69.9.
Slope: 135/119. **Architect:** Ron Kirby/Denis Griffiths. **Green fee:** $35/$67. **Credit cards:** All major. **Reduced fees:** Weekdays, low season, twilight, juniors. **Caddies:** No.
Golf carts: $12. **Discount golf packages:** No. **Season:** May-Oct. **High:** June-Sept. **On site lodging:** No. **Rental clubs:** Yes. **Walking policy:** Unrestricted walking. **Metal spikes allowed:** Yes. **Range:** Yes (grass). **To obtain tee times:** Call up to 5 days in advance. More than 5 days in advance requires credit card and $5 per player reservation charge.
Notes: Ranked 11th in 1997 Best in State.
Subscriber comments: Best of the mountain courses...Play smart or bring extra sleeves...Great breakfast...Yardages very deceiving...Great golf course, spectacular views...Tough course! Ate me up!...A golf course that matches the scenery, magnifico!...Tough course if you spray the ball.

★★★½PTARMIGAN COUNTRY CLUB

5412 Vardon Way, Fort Collins, 80525, Larimer County, (970)226-6600, 45 miles N of Denver.
Opened: 1988. **Holes:** 18. **Par:** 72/72. **Yards:** 7,201/5,327. **Course rating:** 73.0/69.0.
Slope: 135/116. **Architect:** Jack Nicklaus. **Green fee:** $55/$65. **Credit cards:** MC,VISA,AMEX. **Reduced fees:** Juniors. **Caddies:** No. **Golf carts:** Included in Green Fee. **Discount golf packages:** No. **Season:** Year-round. **High:** May-Sept. **On site lodging:** No. **Rental clubs:** Yes. **Walking policy:** Walking at certain times. **Metal spikes allowed:** No. **Range:** Yes (grass). **To obtain tee times:** Call 2 days in advance.
Subscriber comments: Tough, you need to enjoy sand...This '80s classic Nicklaus is coming of age...Nice use of land...Great golf, tough test...Makes you think...Large greens...Back nine in spectacular scenery. Very enjoyable.

COLORADO

★★½PUEBLO CITY PARK GOLF COURSE
PU-3900 Thatcher Ave., Pueblo, 81005, Pueblo County, (719)561-4946, 40 miles S of Colorado Springs.
Opened: 1918. **Holes:** 18. **Par:** 70/73. **Yards:** 6,500/5,974. **Course rating:** 68.9/72.5.
Slope: 111/114. **Architect:** Tom Bendelow. **Green fee:** $17/$18. **Credit cards:** MC,VISA. **Reduced fees:** Seniors, juniors. **Caddies:** No. **Golf carts:** $9. **Discount golf packages:** No. **Season:** Year-round. **High:** May-Sept. **On site lodging:** No. **Rental clubs:** Yes. **Walking policy:** Unrestricted walking. **Metal spikes allowed:** No. **Range:** Yes. **To obtain tee times:** N/A.
Subscriber comments: Lot of trees...Flat terrain...As difficult as you make it...Nice finishing holes.
Special Notes: Also have a 9-hole course.

★★PUEBLO WEST GOLF COURSE
PU-251 S. McCulloch Blvd., Pueblo West, 81007, Pueblo County, (719)547-2280, 8 miles W of Pueblo.
Opened: 1972. **Holes:** 18. **Par:** 72/72. **Yards:** 7,368/5,688. **Course rating:** 73.3/71.4.
Slope: 125/117. **Architect:** Clyde B. Young. **Green fee:** $13/$16. **Credit cards:** MC,VISA. **Reduced fees:** Weekdays, seniors, juniors. **Caddies:** No. **Golf carts:** $8.
Discount golf packages: No. **Season:** Year-round. **High:** April-Sept. **On site lodging:** Yes. **Rental clubs:** Yes. **Walking policy:** Unrestricted walking. **Metal spikes allowed:** Yes. **Range:** Yes (grass). **To obtain tee times:** Call golf shop.

★★★½RACCOON CREEK GOLF CLUB
PU-7301 W. Bowles Ave., Littleton, 80123, Arapahoe County, (303)973-4653.
Opened: 1983. **Holes:** 18. **Par:** 72/72. **Yards:** 7,045/5,130. **Course rating:** 72.6/67.9.
Slope: 128/118. **Architect:** Dick Phelps/Brad Benz. **Green fee:** $28/$32. **Credit cards:** MC,VISA,DISC. **Reduced fees:** N/A. **Caddies:** No. **Golf carts:** $11. **Discount golf packages:** No. **Season:** Year-round. **High:** May-Sept. **On site lodging:** No. **Rental clubs:** Yes. **Walking policy:** Unrestricted walking. **Metal spikes allowed:** No. **Range:** Yes (grass). **To obtain tee times:** Call up to 4 days in advance.
Subscriber comments: 17th is excellent hole...Good driving holes...Need all your shots on this course...One of the better Denver area courses. No two holes are similar...Good place in winter...Nice course, can be a real bear on windy days...Very hilly, water everywhere, not good for beginner.

★★★RIFLE CREEK GOLF COURSE
3004 State Hwy.325, Rifle, 81650, Garfield County, (970)625-1093, (888)247-0370, 60 miles NE of Grand Junction.
Opened: 1960. **Holes:** 18. **Par:** 72/72. **Yards:** 6,241/5,131. **Course rating:** 69.3/68.5.
Slope: 123/109. **Architect:** Dick Phelps. **Green fee:** $12/$26. **Credit cards:** MC,VISA,DISC. **Reduced fees:** Low season, twilight, juniors. **Caddies:** No. **Golf carts:** $12. **Discount golf packages:** Yes. **Season:** March-Nov. **High:** June-Sept. **On site lodging:** No. **Rental clubs:** Yes. **Walking policy:** Unrestricted walking. **Metal spikes allowed:** No. **Range:** Yes (grass/mats). **To obtain tee times:** Call up to 7 days in advance.
Subscriber comments: Two completely different nines, one flat and one canyons. Great fun...Front nine very easy; back nine very difficult. Beautiful scenery...Neat golf the two nines are as diverse as it gets...Greens have too much slope...Fun little layout.

RIVERDALE GOLF CLUB
PU-13300 Riverdale Rd., Brighton, 80601, Adams County, (303)659-6700, 10 miles N of Denver. **Credit cards:** MC,VISA. **Reduced fees:** N/A. **Caddies:** No. **Golf carts:** $20.
Discount golf packages: No. **Season:** Year-round. **High:** May-Sept. **On site lodging:** No. **Rental clubs:** Yes. **Walking policy:** Unrestricted walking. **Metal spikes allowed:** Yes. **Range:** Yes (grass/mats).
★★★★DUNES COURSE
Opened: 1985. **Holes:** 18. **Par:** 72/72. **Yards:** 7,030/4,903. **Course rating:** 72.1/67.5.
Slope: 129/109. **Architect:** Pete Dye/Perry Dye. **Green fee:** $25/$27. **To obtain tee times:** Call 2 days in advance for weekday. Call Monday at 5:30 p.m. for Saturday and Tuesday at 5:30 p.m. for Sunday.
Notes: Ranked 17th in 1997 Best in State.

Subscriber comments: One of the best in the state...True Dye links type course, can eat your lunch...Excellent championship layout...Great test!...Fairways as smooth as greens. Awesome...Play the right tees...Best example of links course in Colorado...15th hole is great...Don't hit it in the rough, can't find the ball...Wonderful links style course in isolated setting, great in every way.

★★★KNOLLS COURSE

Opened: 1963. **Holes:** 18. **Par:** 71/73. **Yards:** 6,756/5,931. **Course rating:** 70.2/72.2. **Slope:** 118/117. **Architect:** Henry B. Hughes. **Green fee:** $14/$17. **To obtain tee times:** Call 2 days in advance for weekdays. Call Monday at 5:30 p.m. for Saturday and Tuesday at 5:30 p.m. for Sunday.

Subscriber comments: Good course for beginners...Elevated greens...Easy to walk, fun to play.

★★★★SHERATON STEAMBOAT GOLF CLUB

R-2000 Clubhouse Dr., Steamboat Springs, 80477, Routt County, (970)879-1391, (800)848-8878, 157 miles NW of Denver.

Opened: 1974. **Holes:** 18. **Par:** 72/72. **Yards:** 6,902/5,536. **Course rating:** 71.2/71.5. **Slope:** 133/127. **Architect:** Robert Trent Jones Jr.. **Green fee:** $62/$92. **Credit cards:** All major,All major. **Reduced fees:** Low season, resort guests, twilight, seniors. **Caddies:** No. **Golf carts:** $18. **Discount golf packages:** Yes. **Season:** May-Oct. **High:** June-Aug. **On site lodging:** Yes. **Rental clubs:** Yes. **Walking policy:** Walking at certain times. **Metal spikes allowed:** No. **Range:** Yes (grass/mats). **To obtain tee times:** Hotel guests up to one year in advance. Nonguests call 24 hours in advance.

Subscriber comments: Very challenging course.."Amen Corner West" at #5...Beautiful setting...Steamboat is awesome...Quiet course until you lose one in the water...Wild life galore, mountain course...Fun layout.

★★★½SNOWMASS CLUB GOLF COURSE

R-P.O. Box G-2, Snowmass Village, 81615, Pitkin County, (970)923-3148, (800)525-6200, 7 miles W of Aspen.

Opened: 1970. **Holes:** 18. **Par:** 71/71. **Yards:** 6,662/5,056. **Course rating:** 70.1/67.5. **Slope:** 134/127. **Architect:** Arnold Palmer/Ed Seay. **Green fee:** $55/$95. **Credit cards:** All major,Diners Club. **Reduced fees:** Low season, resort guests, twilight, juniors. **Caddies:** No. **Golf carts:** Included in Green Fee. **Discount golf packages:** Yes. **Season:** May-Oct. **High:** June-Sept. **On site lodging:** Yes. **Rental clubs:** Yes. **Walking policy:** Mandatory cart. **Metal spikes allowed:** Yes. **Range:** Yes (grass). **To obtain tee times:** Nonguests call 1 day in advance. Hotel guests may call up to 14 days in advance.

Subscriber comments: Best in the valley. Tough in the wind...Hard to read greens...A quality course, beautiful area...Fun mountain course...Inspiring views from the valley.

★★★½SONNENALP GOLF CLUB

R-1265 Berry Creek Rd., Edwards, 81632, Eagle County, (970)926-3533, 110 miles W of Denver.

Opened: 1981. **Holes:** 18. **Par:** 71/71. **Yards:** 7,059/5,293. **Course rating:** 72.3/70.0. **Slope:** 138/115. **Architect:** Bob Cupp/Jay Morrish. **Green fee:** $75/$110. **Credit cards:** MC,VISA. **Reduced fees:** Weekdays, low season, resort guests, twilight, juniors. **Caddies:** No. **Golf carts:** Included in Green Fee. **Discount golf packages:** Yes. **Season:** April-Oct. **High:** June-Sept. **On site lodging:** No. **Rental clubs:** Yes. **Walking policy:** Mandatory cart. **Metal spikes allowed:** Yes. **Range:** Yes (grass). **To obtain tee times:** Nonresort guest call day of play. Resort guests may reserve tee time upon making reservation.

Subscriber comments: Bring your Gold Card...My favorite mountain course...Once you played here you don't want to leave...Lots of homes and very few trees for a mountain course...Well designed, challenging...Fun open golf course...Best spring condition course in Colorado.

★★½SOUTH SUBURBAN GOLF COURSE

PU-7900 S. Colorado Blvd., Littleton, 80122, Arapahoe County, (303)770-5508, (303)770-5500, 9 miles S of Denver.

Opened: 1973. **Holes:** 18. **Par:** 72/72. **Yards:** 6,705/5,573. **Course rating:** 69.6/70.6. **Slope:** 120/120. **Architect:** Dick Phelps. **Green fee:** $17/$28. **Credit cards:** MC,VISA,DISC. **Reduced fees:** Seniors. **Caddies:** No. **Golf carts:** $10. **Discount golf**

packages: No. **Season:** Year-round. **High:** April-Oct. **On site lodging:** No. **Rental clubs:** Yes. **Walking policy:** Unrestricted walking. **Metal spikes allowed:** No. **Range:** Yes (grass/mats). **To obtain tee times:** Residents call 5 days in advance. Nonresidents call 3 days in advance.

Subscriber comments: Wide open, hard greens...Good test...Variety of holes...Average less than two putts a hole—apply for pro job...Stay below the hole. **Special Notes:** Also 9-hole par-3 course.

★★★SOUTHRIDGE GOLF CLUB
PU-5750 S. Lemay Ave., Fort Collins, 80525, Larimer County, (970)226-2828, 60 miles N of Denver.
Opened: 1984. **Holes:** 18. **Par:** 71/71. **Yards:** 6,363/5,508. **Course rating:** 69.1/69.3. **Slope:** 122/118. **Architect:** Frank Hummel. **Green fee:** $15/$18. **Credit cards:** MC,VISA. **Reduced fees:** Weekdays, low season, twilight, seniors, juniors. **Caddies:** No. **Golf carts:** $18. **Discount golf packages:** Yes. **Season:** Year-round. **High:** April-Sept. **On site lodging:** No. **Rental clubs:** Yes. **Walking policy:** Unrestricted walking. **Metal spikes allowed:** No. **Range:** Yes (grass/mats). **To obtain tee times:** Call up to 3 days in advance.
Subscriber comments: Blind shots, fun, friendly...Staff is always helpful and cordial...Easy when hitting straight...The back nine is tough...A course which will test shotmaking ability.

★★★★TAMARRON RESORT
R-P.O. Box 3131, Durango, 81301, La Plata County, (970)259-2000, (800)678-1000, 230 miles NW of Albuquerque.
Opened: 1975. **Holes:** 18. **Par:** 72/72. **Yards:** 6,885/5,330. **Course rating:** 73.0/71.9. **Slope:** 142/126. **Architect:** Arthur Hills. **Green fee:** $65/$105. **Credit cards:** All major. **Reduced fees:** Low season, resort guests, twilight, seniors, juniors. **Caddies:** No. **Golf carts:** Included in Green Fee. **Discount golf packages:** Yes. **Season:** May-Nov. **High:** June-Sept. **On site lodging:** Yes. **Rental clubs:** Yes. **Walking policy:** Mandatory cart. **Metal spikes allowed:** Yes. **Range:** Yes (grass/mats). **To obtain tee times:** Outside play call 1 day before. Resort guest 2 days in advance. Golf package in advance with room reservation.
Notes: Ranked 13th in 1997 Best in State.
Subscriber comments: Very tough, gorgeous...Greens too fast, play too slow, but what a view...Setting unmatched. Watch for marmots...Great mountain golf, front nine especially picturesque.

TELLURIDE SKI & GOLF CLUB
R-562 Mountain Village Boulevard, Telluride, 81435, San Miguel County, (970)728-6157, 180 miles S of Grand Junction.
Opened: 1992. **Holes:** 18. **Par:** 71/71. **Yards:** 6,739/5,724. **Course rating:** 71.0/72.4. **Slope:** 130/140. **Architect:** N/A. **Green fee:** $90/$110. **Credit cards:** MC,VISA,DISC. **Reduced fees:** Twilight. **Caddies:** No. **Golf carts:** Included in Green Fee. **Discount golf packages:** Yes. **Season:** May-Sept. **High:** July, Aug. **On site lodging:** Yes. **Rental clubs:** No. **Walking policy:** Mandatory cart. **Metal spikes allowed:** No. **Range:** Yes (grass). **To obtain tee times:** Members and guests at Peaks Hotel call up to 30 days in advance. Public may call 2 days in advance.

★★½THORNCREEK GOLF CLUB
PU-13555 N. Washington St., Thornton, 80241, Adams County, (303)450-7055, 18 miles N of Denver.
Opened: 1992. **Holes:** 18. **Par:** 72/72. **Yards:** 7,268/5,547. **Course rating:** 73.7/70.5. **Slope:** 136/120. **Architect:** Baxter Spann. **Green fee:** $28/$28. **Credit cards:** MC,VISA,AMEX. **Reduced fees:** Weekdays, twilight, seniors, juniors. **Caddies:** No. **Golf carts:** $12. **Discount golf packages:** No. **Season:** Year-round. **High:** May-Sept. **On site lodging:** No. **Rental clubs:** Yes. **Walking policy:** Unrestricted walking. **Metal spikes allowed:** No. **Range:** Yes (grass). **To obtain tee times:** May call up to 7 days in advance. Reservations may be made for $5 per player for times outside 7-day window.
Subscriber comments: Difficult from back tees...If you like to walk this is the one. Nice views...Tough back nine...Have to know course to score on it...Lots of blind tee shots, concrete cartpaths intruding into fairways.

COLORADO

★★★TIARA RADO GOLF COURSE
PM-2063 S. Broadway, Grand Junction, 81503, Mesa County, (970)245-8085, 4 miles W of Grand Junction.
Opened: 1972. **Holes:** 18. **Par:** 71/71. **Yards:** 6,182/4,967. **Course rating:** 68.4/66.9.
Slope: 115/113. **Architect:** N/A. **Green fee:** $15/$18. **Credit cards:** MC,VISA.
Reduced fees: Weekdays, juniors. **Caddies:** No. **Golf carts:** $17. **Discount golf packages:** No. **Season:** N/A. **High:** N/A. **On site lodging:** No. **Rental clubs:** Yes. **Walking policy:** Unrestricted walking. **Metal spikes allowed:** No. **Range:** Yes. **To obtain tee times:** Call 2 days in advance starting at 7 a.m.
Subscriber comments: Wonderful view of Colorado National monument...Flat, easy course, fun for family to play...No. 2 you can make eagle or triple bogey...Too many houses too close to course on front...Front nine more interesting than back nine.

★★TWIN PEAKS GOLF COURSE
PU-1200 Cornell Dr., Longmont, 80503, Boulder County, (303)772-1722, 35 miles N of Denver.
Opened: 1977. **Holes:** 18. **Par:** 70/71. **Yards:** 6,810/5,398. **Course rating:** 71.7/68.8.
Slope: 123/117. **Architect:** Frank Hummel. **Green fee:** $19. **Credit cards:** MC,VISA.
Reduced fees: Weekdays, seniors, juniors. **Caddies:** No. **Golf carts:** $20. **Discount golf packages:** No. **Season:** Year-round. **High:** May-Sept. **On site lodging:** No. **Rental clubs:** Yes. **Walking policy:** Unrestricted walking. **Metal spikes allowed:** No. **Range:** Yes (grass). **To obtain tee times:** Call or come in 2 days in advance.

★★★VAIL GOLF CLUB
PU-1778 Vail Valley Dr., Vail, 81657, Eagle County, (970)479-2260, 100 miles W of Denver.
Opened: 1968. **Holes:** 18. **Par:** 77/72. **Yards:** 7,100/5,291. **Course rating:** 70.8/69.5.
Slope: 121/114. **Architect:** Press Maxwell. **Green fee:** $45/$70. **Credit cards:** MC,VISA,AMEX. **Reduced fees:** Low season. **Caddies:** No. **Golf carts:** $15. **Discount golf packages:** No. **Season:** May-Oct. **High:** June-Sept. **On site lodging:** No. **Rental clubs:** Yes. **Walking policy:** Walking at certain times. **Metal spikes allowed:** Yes. **Range:** Yes (grass). **To obtain tee times:** Call 2 days in advance.
Subscriber comments: Flat, not a mountain course...Downhill on front nine and uphill back nine...Nice foothills design...Challenging course, mountain scenery and your ball goes farther. What more could a you want?

★★VALLEY HI GOLF COURSE
PU-610 S. Chelton Rd., Colorado Springs, 80910, El Paso County, (719)578-6926.
Opened: 1954. **Holes:** 18. **Par:** 71/73. **Yards:** 6,806/5,384. **Course rating:** 71.1/68.7.
Slope: 116/110. **Architect:** Henry B. Hughes. **Green fee:** $17/$24. **Credit cards:** MC,VISA. **Reduced fees:** Seniors, juniors. **Caddies:** No. **Golf carts:** $20. **Discount golf packages:** No. **Season:** Year-round. **High:** June-Aug. **On site lodging:** No. **Rental clubs:** Yes. **Walking policy:** Unrestricted walking. **Metal spikes allowed:** Yes. **Range:** Yes (grass). **To obtain tee times:** Call 7 days in advance.

★★★★WALKING STICK GOLF COURSE
PU-4301 Walking Stick Blvd., Pueblo, 81001, Pueblo County, (719)584-3400, 40 miles S of Colorado Springs.
Opened: 1991. **Holes:** 18. **Par:** 72/72. **Yards:** 7,147/5,181. **Course rating:** 72.6/69.0. **Slope:** 130/114. **Architect:** Arthur Hills. **Green fee:** $19/$21. **Credit cards:** MC,VISA,DISC. **Reduced fees:** Weekdays, twilight, seniors, juniors. **Caddies:** No. **Golf carts:** $18. **Discount golf packages:** No. **Season:** Year-round. **High:** May-Sept. **On site lodging:** No. **Rental clubs:** Yes. **Walking policy:** Unrestricted walking. **Metal spikes allowed:** No. **Range:** Yes (grass/mats). **To obtain tee times:** Call on Wednesday for Saturday or Sunday. Call after Saturday for any day during the week.
Subscriber comments: Don't miss this one if in southern Colorado...Enjoyable course...Winds make course tough...Beautiful desert-type setting, excellent layout, great value...Excellent par 4s from back tees...Greens are among the best, lots of undulation, good test of golf...Not one to walk on hot days! Long way from green to tee!...Rough is rough.

GREAT VALUE

★★½WELLSHIRE GOLF COURSE

PU-3333 S. Colorado Blvd., Denver, 80222, Denver County, (303)757-1352.
Opened: 1927. **Holes:** 18. **Par:** 71/73. **Yards:** 6,608/5,890. **Course rating:** 70.1/69.3.
Slope: 124/121. **Architect:** Donald Ross. **Green fee:** $16/$21. **Credit cards:** MC,VISA.
Reduced fees: Weekdays. **Caddies:** No. **Golf carts:** $22. **Discount golf packages:**
No. **Season:** Year-round. **High:** April-Sept. **On site lodging:** No. **Rental clubs:** Yes.
Walking policy: Unrestricted walking. **Metal spikes allowed:** Yes. **Range:** Yes (Mats).
To obtain tee times: Purchase reservation card $10 for all 5 Denver city courses. Call
5 days in advance at central number (303) 784-4000.
Subscriber comments: Old Donald Ross course looking better...Lightning fast
greens...Some excellent holes. Hogan won here in '48...Great restaurant...Par 5s are
all within eagle range...Very old course with huge trees.

★★★½WEST WOODS GOLF CLUB

PU-6655 Quaker St., Arvada, 80403, Jefferson County, (303)424-3334, 14 miles NW of
Denver.
Opened: 1994. **Holes:** 18. **Par:** 72/72. **Yards:** 7,035/5,197. **Course rating:** 72.1/69.5.
Slope: 135/112. **Architect:** Dick Phelps. **Green fee:** $22/$26. **Credit cards:** MC,VISA.
Reduced fees: Juniors. **Caddies:** No. **Golf carts:** $9. **Discount golf packages:** No.
Season: Year-round. **High:** April-Aug. **On site lodging:** No. **Rental clubs:** Yes.
Walking policy: Unrestricted walking. **Metal spikes allowed:** No. **Range:** Yes
(grass/mats). **To obtain tee times:** Call automated tee times phone 2 days in advance.
Subscriber comments: Nice mix of holes with elevation changes galore...Difficult to
walk, homes too close to course, long walk from green to next tee box...A good challenge and fun layout...Good test of golf...If not for the housing development it winds
through, it might be the perfect course.

★★½WILLIS CASE GOLF COURSE

PU-4999 Vrain St., Denver, 80212, Denver County, (303)455-9801.
Opened: 1929. **Holes:** 18. **Par:** 72/75. **Yards:** 6,364/6,144. **Course rating:** 68.7/72.8.
Slope: 112/115. **Architect:** N/A. **Green fee:** $14/$20. **Credit cards:** None. **Reduced
fees:** Weekdays. **Caddies:** No. **Golf carts:** $20. **Discount golf packages:** No.
Season: Year-round. **High:** June-Aug. **On site lodging:** No. **Rental clubs:** Yes.
Walking policy: Unrestricted walking. **Metal spikes allowed:** Yes. **Range:** No. **To
obtain tee times:** Annual reservation access card or walk on.
Subscriber comments: Great city course, excellent mountain views...Old course, yet
still a fun challenge and fair...Tough front nine...Food is outstanding!...No water but not
easy. Lots of fun...Very short back, can be good for ego...Hilly and rolling terrain.

★★★WOODLAND PARK FUJIKI GOLF & COUNTRY CLUB

100 Lucky Lady Dr., Woodland Park, 80863, Teller County, (719)687-7587.
Opened: 1995. **Holes:** 18. **Par:** 72/72. **Yards:** 6,827/5,233. **Course rating:** 71.5/69.6.
Slope: 129/126. **Architect:** John Harbottle. **Green fee:** $15/$28. **Credit cards:** All
major. **Reduced fees:** Weekdays, low season, seniors, juniors. **Caddies:** No. **Golf
carts:** $20. **Discount golf packages:** No. **Season:** Year-round. **High:** May-Sept. **On
site lodging:** No. **Rental clubs:** Yes. **Walking policy:** Unrestricted walking. **Metal
spikes allowed:** No. **Range:** Yes (grass/mats). **To obtain tee times:** Call 7 days in
advance.
Subscriber comments: Narrow fairways, serious rough...Very challenging...Beautiful
mountain course...Doesn't appear to be that tough, until you add it up.

★★★YAMPA VALLEY GOLF CLUB

PU-2194 Hwy. 394, Craig, 81625, Moffat County, (970)824-3673, 200 miles NW of
Denver.
Opened: 1968. **Holes:** 18. **Par:** 72/72. **Yards:** 6,514/5,242. **Course rating:** 69.9/67.9.
Slope: 126/120. **Architect:** William H. Neff. **Green fee:** $23. **Credit cards:** MC,VISA.
Reduced fees: Seniors, juniors. **Caddies:** No. **Golf carts:** $8. **Discount golf pack-
ages:** No. **Season:** April-Oct. **High:** June-Aug. **On site lodging:** No. **Rental clubs:** Yes.
Walking policy: Unrestricted walking. **Metal spikes allowed:** Yes. **Range:** Yes (grass).
To obtain tee times: Call 3 days in advance.
Subscriber comments: Look for the eagles nesting on the 15th hole...#3 is one of the
shortest and hardest par 4s in the state...Don't miss it...Out of way but worth the trip.

★½AIRWAYS GOLF CLUB

PU-1070 S. Grand St., West Suffield, 06093, Hartford County, (860)668-4973, 18 miles N of Hartford.
Opened: 1976. **Holes:** 18. **Par:** 71/72. **Yards:** 5,900/5,400. **Course rating:** 66.0/63.0. **Slope:** 105/105. **Architect:** N/A. **Green fee:** $19/$20. **Credit cards:** MC,VISA. **Reduced fees:** Weekdays, low season, seniors. **Caddies:** No. **Golf carts:** $20. **Discount golf packages:** Yes. **Season:** Year-round. **High:** April-Oct. **On site lodging:** No. **Rental clubs:** Yes. **Walking policy:** Unrestricted walking. **Metal spikes allowed:** Yes. **Range:** No. **To obtain tee times:** Call golf shop.

★½ALLING MEMORIAL GOLF COURSE

PU-35 Eastern St., New Haven, 06513, New Haven County, (203)946-8014.
Call club for further information.

★★BANNER RESORT & COUNTRY CLUB

PU-10 Banner Rd., Moodus, 06469, Middlesex County, (860)873-9075, 18 miles SE of Hartford.
Opened: 1958. **Holes:** 18. **Par:** 72/74. **Yards:** 6,100/5,600. **Course rating:** 68.9. **Slope:** 118. **Architect:** Frank Gamberdella. **Green fee:** $13/$22. **Credit cards:** None. **Reduced fees:** Weekdays, low season, seniors. **Caddies:** No. **Golf carts:** $20. **Discount golf packages:** No. **Season:** April-first snow. **High:** June-Aug. **On site lodging:** No. **Rental clubs:** Yes. **Walking policy:** Unrestricted walking. **Metal spikes allowed:** Yes. **Range:** Yes (grass). **To obtain tee times:** Call seven days in advance.

★★★BLACKLEDGE COUNTRY CLUB

PU-180 W. St., Hebron, 06248, Tolland County, (860)228-0250, 15 miles E of Hartford.
Opened: 1964. **Holes:** 27. **Architect:** Geoffrey Cornish. **Green fee:** $26/$28. **Credit cards:** MC,VISA. **Reduced fees:** Weekdays, low season, twilight, seniors, juniors. **Caddies:** No. **Golf carts:** $22. **Discount golf packages:** Yes. **Season:** March-Dec. **High:** June-Aug. **On site lodging:** No. **Rental clubs:** No. **Walking policy:** Unrestricted walking. **Metal spikes allowed:** Yes. **Range:** No. **To obtain tee times:** Call 7 days in advance for weekday. Call on Monday prior at 8 a.m. for weekend.
ANDERSON/GILEAD
Par: 72/72. **Yards:** 6,787/5,458. **Course rating:** 72.0/71.7. **Slope:** 128/123.
GILEAD/LINKS
Par: 72/72. **Yards:** 6,718/5,208. **Course rating:** 72.5/70.3. **Slope:** 131/122.
LINKS/ANDERSON
Par: 72/72. **Yards:** 6,701/5,158. **Course rating:** 72.3/70.2. **Slope:** 126/117.
Subscriber comments: A hidden gem...Tough test of golf skills...Course has character; a plus with 27 holes to play!...Great course to play in the fall, very pretty...One of the nicest courses in my area...Shown great improvement over last few years...Fast greens...Good playable courses for all handicaps...Tight, sloping fairways...Links course provides target golf challenge...Links nine requires too many "perfect" shots.

★★★BLUE FOX RUN GOLF CLUB

PU-65 Nod Rd., Avon, 06001, Hartford County, (860)678-1679, 10 miles NW of Hartford.
Opened: 1974. **Holes:** 18. **Par:** 71/71. **Yards:** 6,779/5,171. **Course rating:** 71.9/69.5. **Slope:** 125/116. **Architect:** Joe Brunoli. **Green fee:** $23/$29. **Credit cards:** None. **Reduced fees:** Weekdays, seniors, juniors. **Caddies:** No. **Golf carts:** $12. **Discount golf packages:** No. **Season:** April-Nov. **High:** May-Sept. **On site lodging:** No. **Rental clubs:** Yes. **Walking policy:** Unrestricted walking. **Metal spikes allowed:** No. **Range:** Yes (mats). **To obtain tee times:** Call up to 7 days in advance for weekday. Call at 7:30 a.m. on Tuesday for weekend and holiday.
Subscriber comments: Good challenge for low handicaps from back tees...Big greens, large sand traps...Spot it on the front; rip it on the back...Front nine through woods...Good challenge for a flat course...Back is varied, fun and difficult.
Special Notes: Formerly Bel Compo Golf Club.

★★BRUCE MEMORIAL GOLF COURSE

1300 King St., Greenwich, 06831, Fairfield County, (203)531-7261, 20 miles NE of New York City.
Opened: 1963. **Holes:** 18. **Par:** 71/73. **Yards:** 6,512/5,710. **Course rating:** 71.1/72.0.

Slope: 124/115. **Architect:** Robert Trent Jones. **Green fee:** $10/$15. **Credit cards:** None. **Reduced fees:** Weekdays, seniors, juniors. **Caddies:** No. **Golf carts:** $22. **Discount golf packages:** No. **Season:** April-Nov. **High:** June-Aug. **On site lodging:** No. **Rental clubs:** Yes. **Walking policy:** Unrestricted walking. **Metal spikes allowed:** Yes. **Range:** Yes (mats). **To obtain tee times:** No reserved tee time for weekdays. For weekends there is a lottery system held on Wednesday nights, or you can call on Friday after 11 a.m.

★★½CANDLEWOOD VALLEY COUNTRY CLUB

PU-401 Danbury Rd., New Milford, 06776, Litchfield County, (860)354-9359, 60 miles NE of New York City.
Opened: 1961. **Holes:** 18. **Par:** 72/72. **Yards:** 6,295/5,403. **Course rating:** 70.3/70.9. **Slope:** 120/126. **Architect:** Geoffrey Cornish/Stephen Kay. **Green fee:** $26/$30. **Credit cards:** MC,VISA. **Reduced fees:** Weekdays, twilight, seniors. **Caddies:** No. **Golf carts:** $22. **Discount golf packages:** No. **Season:** March-Dec. **High:** May-Sept. **On site lodging:** No. **Rental clubs:** Yes. **Walking policy:** Unrestricted walking. **Metal spikes allowed:** No. **Range:** Yes (mats). **To obtain tee times:** Threesomes and foursomes call up to 4 days in advance beginning at 7 a.m.
Subscriber comments: Flat, tight back nine...Two different worlds, front easy; back, killer...Overhead wires, ugly... Good new holes on back nine...Back unfair, only one par 3 and it's 210 yards...Tough to get tee time...Jekyll and Hyde: lullaby front, vicious back.

★★CANTON PUBLIC GOLF CLUB

PU-110 Rte. 44, Canton, 06019-0305, Hartford County, (860)693-8305, 12 miles W of Hartford.
Opened: 1932. **Holes:** 9. **Par:** 36/36. **Yards:** 3,068/2,569. **Course rating:** 68.2/67.0. **Slope:** 117/123. **Architect:** Jack Ross. **Green fee:** N/A. **Credit cards:** MC,VISA,AMEX. **Reduced fees:** Seniors, juniors. **Caddies:** No. **Golf carts:** N/A. **Discount golf packages:** No. **Season:** March-Dec. **High:** May-Sept. **On site lodging:** No. **Rental clubs:** Yes. **Walking policy:** Unrestricted walking. **Metal spikes allowed:** Yes. **Range:** No. **To obtain tee times:** Call 24 hours in advance for weekend and holiday.

★★★CEDAR KNOB GOLF CLUB

PU-Billings Rd., Somers, 06071, Tolland County, (860)749-3550, 11 miles SE of Springfield, MA.
Opened: 1963. **Holes:** 18. **Par:** 72/74. **Yards:** 6,734/5,784. **Course rating:** 72.3/73.9. **Slope:** 119/129. **Architect:** Geoffrey Cornish. **Green fee:** $20/$24. **Credit cards:** None. **Reduced fees:** Weekdays, low season, seniors. **Caddies:** No. **Golf carts:** $22. **Discount golf packages:** No. **Season:** Year-round. **High:** April-Sept. **On site lodging:** No. **Rental clubs:** Yes. **Walking policy:** Unrestricted walking. **Metal spikes allowed:** Yes. **Range:** No. **To obtain tee times:** Call 7 days in advance for weekdays. Call Wednesday after noon for weekend.
Subscriber comments: You need some local knowledge...#7 tough par 5...Good finishing holes over lake...Narrow fairways; long par 3s; great scenery...Premium on accuracy...Big greens, scenic, two 90-degree dogleg par 5s...The greens were tough to read...Gently rolling good course.

★★★½CRESTBROOK PARK GOLF CLUB

PU-834 Northfield Rd., Watertown, 06795, Litchfield County, (860)945-5249, 5 miles N of Waterbury.
Opened: 1970. **Holes:** 18. **Par:** 71/75. **Yards:** 6,906/5,718. **Course rating:** 73.2/73.8. **Slope:** 132/128. **Architect:** Cornish/Zikorus. **Green fee:** $12/$22. **Credit cards:** None. **Reduced fees:** Weekdays, seniors, juniors. **Caddies:** No. **Golf carts:** $21. **Discount golf packages:** No. **Season:** April-Dec. **High:** June-Aug. **On site lodging:** No. **Rental clubs:** Yes. **Walking policy:** Unrestricted walking. **Metal spikes allowed:** Yes. **Range:** Yes (grass). **To obtain tee times:** Call two days in advance for weekends and holidays.
Subscriber comments: Interesting course, a little of everything...Lightning greens, large undulations...Very hilly...Tough course, sidehill lies, fast greens...Two completely different nines...If you can play this course well, you can play anywhere...Big, tough brute from the back tees...Bring all your clubs.

D. FAIRCHILD-WHEELER GOLF COURSE

PU-2390 Easton Tpke., Fairfield, 06432, Fairfield County, (203)373-5911.
Opened: 1931. **Architect:** Robert White. **Green fee:** $16/$20. **Credit cards:** None.
Reduced fees: N/A. **Caddies:** No. **Golf carts:** $20. **Discount golf packages:** No.
Season: Year-round. **High:** May-Aug. **On site lodging:** No. **Rental clubs:** Yes. **Walking policy:** Unrestricted walking. **Metal spikes allowed:** Yes. **Range:** Yes (Mats). **To obtain tee times:** First come, first served.
★★**BLACK COURSE**
Holes: 18. **Par:** 71/73. **Yards:** 6,402/5,764. **Course rating:** 70.0/71.9. **Slope:** 124/114.
★½**RED COURSE**
Holes: 18. **Par:** 72/79. **Yards:** 6,775/6,382. **Course rating:** 71.0/78.0. **Slope:** 124/122.

★½E. GAYNOR BRENNAN MUNICIPAL GOLF COURSE

PM-451 Stillwater Rd., Stamford, 06902, Fairfield County, (203)324-4185, 1 mile S of Stamford.
Opened: 1931. **Holes:** 18. **Par:** 71/71. **Yards:** 6,107/5,736. **Course rating:** 69.8.
Slope: 122. **Architect:** Maurice McCarthy. **Green fee:** $11/$30. **Credit cards:** None.
Reduced fees: Juniors. **Caddies:** No. **Golf carts:** $22. **Discount golf packages:** No.
Season: April-Dec. **High:** May-Sept. **On site lodging:** No. **Rental clubs:** Yes. **Walking policy:** Unrestricted walking. **Metal spikes allowed:** Yes. **Range:** No. **To obtain tee times:** Call golf shop.

★★EAST HARTFORD GOLF COURSE

PU-130 Long Hill St., East Hartford, 06108, Hartford County, (860)528-5082, 3 miles E of Hartford.
Opened: 1930. **Holes:** 18. **Par:** 71/72. **Yards:** 6,076/5,072. **Course rating:** 68.6/68.1.
Slope: 114/112. **Architect:** Orrin Smith. **Green fee:** $21/$23. **Credit cards:** None.
Reduced fees: Seniors, juniors. **Caddies:** No. **Golf carts:** $10. **Discount golf packages:** No. **Season:** April-Dec. **High:** May-Aug. **On site lodging:** No. **Rental clubs:** No.
Walking policy: Unrestricted walking. **Metal spikes allowed:** Yes. **Range:** No. **To obtain tee times:** Call or come in 7 days in advance for weekends and holidays.

★★EAST MOUNTAIN GOLF CLUB

PM-171 E. Mountain Rd., Waterbury, 06706, New Haven County, (203)756-1676.
Opened: 1933. **Holes:** 18. **Par:** 67/67. **Yards:** 5,817/5,211. **Course rating:** 68.0/67.0.
Slope: 118/113. **Architect:** Wayne Stiles. **Green fee:** $13/$21. **Credit cards:** None.
Reduced fees: Low season. **Caddies:** No. **Golf carts:** $20. **Discount golf packages:** No. **Season:** April-Dec. **High:** June-Aug. **On site lodging:** No. **Rental clubs:** No.
Walking policy: Unrestricted walking. **Metal spikes allowed:** Yes. **Range:** No. **To obtain tee times:** Call or walk in starting at 6:30 a.m. Call 3 days in advance for weekend or holiday.

★★★ELMRIDGE GOLF COURSE

Elmridge Rd., Pawcatuck, 06379, New London County, (860)599-2248, 14 miles E of New London.
Opened: 1968. **Holes:** 27. **Architect:** Joe Rustici/Charlie Rustici. **Green fee:** $24/$28.
Credit cards: MC,VISA,AMEX. **Reduced fees:** Low season, twilight. **Caddies:** No.
Golf carts: $11. **Discount golf packages:** Yes. **Season:** March-Dec. **High:** May-Sept.
On site lodging: No. **Rental clubs:** Yes. **Walking policy:** Unrestricted walking. **Metal spikes allowed:** Yes. **Range:** Yes (grass). **To obtain tee times:** Call Friday for following Monday through Friday. Call Monday for following weekend and holiday.
BLUE/WHITE
Par: 72. **Yards:** 6,639. **Course rating:** N/A. **Slope:** N/A.
RED/BLUE
Holes: 27. **Par:** 71. **Yards:** 6,402. **Course rating:** N/A. **Slope:** N/A.
RED/WHITE
Holes: 27. **Par:** 72. **Yards:** 6,449. **Course rating:** N/A. **Slope:** N/A.
Subscriber comments: Great layout since modification...Plain and simple golf...Wonderful in autumn!...Good layout, back nine better than front...New holes, some good, some gimmicky...New greens are too hard, not receptive...Good food and drink...New holes are strange.

★★GOODWIN PARK GOLF COURSE
PU-25 Stonington St., Hartford, 06106, Hartford County, (860)956-3601.
Call club for further information.

★★½GRASSY HILL COUNTRY CLUB
PU-441 Clark Lane, Orange, 06477, New Haven County, (203)795-1422, 8 miles W of New Haven.
Opened: 1927. **Holes:** 18. **Par:** 70/71. **Yards:** 6,208/5,209. **Course rating:** 70.5/71.1. **Slope:** 122/118. **Architect:** N/A. **Green fee:** $20/$42. **Credit cards:** MC,VISA,AMEX. **Reduced fees:** Weekdays, seniors. **Caddies:** No. **Golf carts:** Included in Green Fee. **Discount golf packages:** Yes. **Season:** April-Nov. **High:** April-Oct. **On site lodging:** No. **Rental clubs:** Yes. **Walking policy:** Walking at certain times. **Metal spikes allowed:** Yes. **Range:** Yes (grass/mats). **To obtain tee times:** Call golf shop.
Subscriber comments: Some interesting holes...Tough front, 600-yard par 5, back easy...Wide fairways...Made vast all around improvements last three years...Quiet location with some nice views...Some difficult undulating greens...Great par 3s.

★★★H. SMITH RICHARDSON GOLF COURSE
PU-2425 Morehouse Hwy., Fairfield, 06430, Fairfield County, (203)255-7300, 50 miles NE of New York.
Opened: 1972. **Holes:** 18. **Par:** 72/72. **Yards:** 6,700/5,764. **Course rating:** 71.0/72.8. **Slope:** 127/129. **Architect:** Hal Purdy. **Green fee:** $12/$28. **Credit cards:** None. **Reduced fees:** Weekdays, twilight, seniors, juniors. **Caddies:** No. **Golf carts:** $10. **Discount golf packages:** Yes. **Season:** March-Dec. **High:** May-Oct. **On site lodging:** No. **Rental clubs:** Yes. **Walking policy:** Unrestricted walking. **Metal spikes allowed:** Yes. **Range:** Yes (grass/mats). **To obtain tee times:** Call golf shop.
Subscriber comments: Championship caliber course from blues...Fair, if you play well you can shoot a good round, but lots of trouble if you're not striking the ball well...Difficult to get weekend tee times...Not hard, but never play well here...Most underrated muny in Fairfield County.

★★★HUNTER GOLF CLUB
PU-685 Westfield Rd., Meriden, 06450, New Haven County, (203)634-3366, 12 miles S of Hartford.
Opened: N/A. **Holes:** 18. **Par:** 71/72. **Yards:** 6,604/5,569. **Course rating:** 71.9/72.7. **Slope:** 124/131. **Architect:** Robert Pride/Al Zikorus. **Green fee:** $17/$25. **Credit cards:** None. **Reduced fees:** Weekdays, seniors, juniors. **Caddies:** No. **Golf carts:** $22. **Discount golf packages:** No. **Season:** March-Dec. **High:** June-Aug. **On site lodging:** No. **Rental clubs:** Yes. **Walking policy:** Unrestricted walking. **Metal spikes allowed:** Yes. **Range:** Yes (grass). **To obtain tee times:** Lottery system drawn on Wednesday for weekend only.
Subscriber comments: Good challenge and very enjoyable...Fairways too close to each other...Very interesting back nine...Pretty setting, could be special...Best for long hitters...Very difficult and long for ladies...Great par 4s...Fun to play, tough walking.

★★KENEY GOLF COURSE
PU-280 Tower Ave., Hartford, 06120, Hartford County, (860)525-3656.
Opened: 1927. **Holes:** 18. **Par:** 70/70. **Yards:** 5,969/5,005. **Course rating:** 68.2/67.2. **Slope:** 118/107. **Architect:** Devereux Emmet/Geoffrey Cornish/William Robinson. **Green fee:** $11/$18. **Credit cards:** MC,VISA. **Reduced fees:** Weekdays, low season, twilight, seniors, juniors. **Caddies:** No. **Golf carts:** $19. **Discount golf packages:** No. **Season:** April-Nov. **High:** May-Sept. **On site lodging:** No. **Rental clubs:** Yes. **Walking policy:** Unrestricted walking. **Metal spikes allowed:** Yes. **Range:** No. **To obtain tee times:** Call seven days in advance.

★★½LAUREL VIEW GOLF COURSE
PU-310 W. Shepard Ave., Hamden, 06514, New Haven County, (203)287-2656.
Opened: 1969. **Holes:** 18. **Par:** 72/72. **Yards:** 6,899/5,558. **Course rating:** 72.7/71.8. **Slope:** 130/130. **Architect:** Geoffrey S. Cornish/William G. Robinson. **Green fee:** $9/$25. **Credit cards:** None. **Reduced fees:** N/A. **Caddies:** No. **Golf carts:** $20. **Discount golf packages:** No. **Season:** March-Dec. **High:** May-Aug. **On site lodging:** No. **Rental clubs:** No. **Walking policy:** Unrestricted walking. **Metal spikes allowed:**

Yes. **Range:** No. **To obtain tee times:** N/A.
Subscriber comments: Some very narrow holes for high handicappers...Challenging course, tight fairways...Use everything in bag. Tough to walk back nine. Big greens...Great hills...Long front nine.

★★½LONGSHORE CLUB PARK

260 Compo Rd. S., Westport, 06880, Fairfield County, (203)222-7535, 13 miles W of Bridgeport.
Opened: 1925. **Holes:** 18. **Par:** 69/73. **Yards:** 5,845/5,227. **Course rating:** 69.3/69.9.
Slope: 115/113. **Architect:** Orrin Smith. **Green fee:** $11/$13. **Credit cards:** None.
Reduced fees: Weekdays, seniors, juniors. **Caddies:** No. **Golf carts:** $22. **Discount golf packages:** No. **Season:** N/A. **High:** N/A. **On site lodging:** No. **Rental clubs:** No.
Walking policy: N/A. **Metal spikes allowed:** Yes. **Range:** Yes. **To obtain tee times:** Guests must be accompanied by a Westport resident.
Subscriber comments: Fair and challenging; every hole different...Course flat, water-views, links style...Good old short layout, fun to play...Tougher than it looks.

LYMAN ORCHARDS GOLF CLUB

Rte. 157, Middlefield, 06455, Middlesex County, (860)349-8055, 15 miles N of New Haven.
Green fee: $31/$44. **Credit cards:** MC, VISA. **Reduced fees:** Weekdays, low season, twilight, seniors, juniors. **Caddies:** No. **Golf carts:** $11. **Discount golf packages:** No.
Season: March-Nov. **High:** May-Oct. **On site lodging:** No. **Rental clubs:** Yes. **Metal spikes allowed:** Yes. **Range:** Yes (grass/mats). **To obtain tee times:** Call the automated teletee system 24 hours a day up to seven days in advance. Times open at 7 p.m.

★★★GARY PLAYER COURSE

Opened: 1994. **Holes:** 18. **Par:** 71/71. **Yards:** 6,660/4,667. **Course rating:** 73.0/67.8.
Slope: 135/116. **Architect:** Gary Player. **Walking policy:** Mandatory cart.
Subscriber comments: Too many doglegs!...Must place the ball. Very hilly...Tough the first time, many blind shots...Nice course, some holes are crazy...Severe dropoffs to greens!...I like it! High-tech...Target golf; tough greens...Great experience to challenge your skills...A trick course...Needs to mature...Each hole requires you to think...Loved the yardage books, first class.

★★★ROBERT TRENT JONES COURSE

Opened: 1969. **Holes:** 18. **Par:** 72/72. **Yards:** 7,011/5,812. **Course rating:** 73.5/73.5.
Slope: 129/122. **Architect:** Robert Trent Jones. **Walking policy:** Unrestricted walking.
Subscriber comments: Water, water, everywhere...Tough in wind...Very difficult for beginners...Wonderful layout good strong test...Open fairways...Easy from whites, need to play blues...Very fast greens, big but tough to putt...Satellite positioning system on each cart for distances...Great layout, use every shot in bag...Great scenic views from clubhouse...Tough finishing hole.

★★½MILLBROOK GOLF COURSE

PU-147 Pigeon Hill Rd., Windsor, 06095, Hartford County, (860)688-2575, 10 miles N of Hartford.
Opened: N/A. **Holes:** 18. **Par:** 71/73. **Yards:** 6,258/5,715. **Course rating:** 71.0/71.0.
Slope: 125/124. **Architect:** Geoffrey S. Cornish. **Green fee:** $22/$26. **Credit cards:** MC, VISA. **Reduced fees:** Seniors, juniors. **Caddies:** No. **Golf carts:** $10. **Discount golf packages:** Yes. **Season:** April-Nov. **High:** May-Oct. **On site lodging:** No. **Rental clubs:** Yes. **Walking policy:** Unrestricted walking. **Metal spikes allowed:** Yes. **Range:** No. **To obtain tee times:** Call golf shop.
Subscriber comments: Narrow fairways, many water hazards...Walking is a good workout...Short, but hilly in spots...9 and 18 great finishing holes...Have to be alert, lot of parallel fairways...A few steep hills for walkers, local knowledge helps...Tough course, must put ball in right place...Needs to add more difficult greens...Toughest starting hole I've ever seen.

★★★NORWICH GOLF COURSE

PU-685 New London Tpke., Norwich, 06360, New London County, (860)889-6973.
Opened: 1910. **Holes:** 18. **Par:** 71/71. **Yards:** 6,183/5,104. **Course rating:** 69.6/70.2.
Slope: 123/118. **Architect:** Donald Ross. **Green fee:** $20/$29. **Credit cards:** MC, VISA.
Reduced fees: Twilight. **Caddies:** No. **Golf carts:** $10. **Discount golf packages:** No.
Season: April-Dec. **High:** May-Aug. **On site lodging:** Yes. **Rental clubs:** Yes. **Walking

policy: Unrestricted walking. **Metal spikes allowed:** Yes. **Range:** Yes. **To obtain tee times:** Call same day beginning at 7 a.m. Weekends call Wednesday prior for Saturday tee times and Thursday for prior Sunday.
Subscriber comments: Longer course, placement a premium...Nice old Donald Ross course...Great old New England golf course...Variety of holes, no flat lies...Beautiful in autumn.

★★OAK HILLS GOLF CLUB

PM-165 Fillow St., Norwalk, 06850, Fairfield County, (203)853-8400, 53 miles NE of New York.
Opened: 1969. **Holes:** 18. **Par:** 71/72. **Yards:** 6,407/5,221. **Course rating:** 70.5/69.2.
Slope: 125/119. **Architect:** Alfred H. Tull. **Green fee:** $18/$34. **Credit cards:** None.
Reduced fees: Twilight. **Caddies:** No. **Golf carts:** $23. **Discount golf packages:** No.
Season: Year-round. **High:** April-Nov. **On site lodging:** No. **Rental clubs:** Yes.
Walking policy: Unrestricted walking. **Metal spikes allowed:** Yes. **Range:** No. **To obtain tee times:** Nonresidents must come in to club up to 7 days in advance for weekdays or Wednesday at 6:30 a.m. for weekend.

★★½ORANGE HILLS COUNTRY CLUB

PU-389 Racebrook Rd., Orange, 06477, New Haven County, (203)795-4161, 7 miles SW of New Haven.
Opened: 1940. **Holes:** 18. **Par:** 71/74. **Yards:** 6,389/5,729. **Course rating:** 71.2/71.5.
Slope: 121/120. **Architect:** Geoffrey Cornish. **Green fee:** $24/$34. **Credit cards:** MC,VISA. **Reduced fees:** N/A. **Caddies:** No. **Golf carts:** $25. **Discount golf packages:** No. **Season:** March-Nov. **High:** May-Oct. **On site lodging:** No. **Rental clubs:** No. **Walking policy:** Unrestricted walking. **Metal spikes allowed:** No. **Range:** No. **To obtain tee times:** Call Wednesday 6 p.m. for weekends.
Subscriber comments: Getting better each year...Great layout, challenging...Family golf course...Fun to play...Good layout in a pretty spot. Several very short, sharp dogleg par 4s on back nine...Back nine much better than front.

★★PATTON BROOK COUNTRY CLUB

201 Pattonwood Dr., Southington, 06489, Hartford County, (860)793-6000.
Call club for further information.

★★★PEQUABUCK GOLF CLUB

School St., Pequabuck, 06781, Litchfield County, (860)583-7307, 12 miles N of Waterbury.
Opened: 1902. **Holes:** 18. **Par:** 69/72. **Yards:** 6,015/5,388. **Course rating:** 69.1/71.0.
Slope: 122/117. **Architect:** Geoffrey S. Cornish/William G. Robinson. **Green fee:** $25/$34. **Credit cards:** None. **Reduced fees:** Weekdays. **Caddies:** No. **Golf carts:** $13. **Discount golf packages:** No. **Season:** April-Dec. **High:** May-Sept. **On site lodging:** No. **Rental clubs:** No. **Walking policy:** Unrestricted walking. **Metal spikes allowed:** No. **Range:** Yes (grass). **To obtain tee times:** None taken. Course open to public before 2 p.m. on weekdays and after 2 p.m. on weekends and holidays. No public play on Fridays.
Subscriber comments: Course short and tight. All shots required...Nos. 10 and 11 holes tough but really nice...Top track, a must play!...Narrow fairways, a true test...One of the best kept secrets...No water except for two holes.

★★PEQUOT GOLF CLUB

PU-127 Wheeler Rd., Stonington, 06378, New London County, (860)535-1898, 15 miles N of New London.
Opened: 1959. **Holes:** 18. **Par:** 70/70. **Yards:** 5,903/5,246. **Course rating:** 67.2/69.4.
Slope: 108/112. **Architect:** N/A. **Green fee:** $21/$26. **Credit cards:** MC,VISA.
Reduced fees: Seniors, juniors. **Caddies:** No. **Golf carts:** $24. **Discount golf packages:** Yes. **Season:** Feb.-Dec. **High:** June-Sept. **On site lodging:** No. **Rental clubs:** Yes. **Walking policy:** Unrestricted walking. **Metal spikes allowed:** Yes. **Range:** No. **To obtain tee times:** Call up to 7 days in advance.

★★★PILGRIM'S HARBOR COUNTRY CLUB

Harrison Rd., Wallingford, 06492, New Haven County, (203)269-6023..
Call club for further information.
Subscriber comments: Hard course for nine holes...Noisy because near I-91...Great layout, tough from blue tees...Still the best greens in the state!...Enjoyable nine holes.

★★★PINE VALLEY COUNTRY CLUB

PU-300 Welch Rd., Southington, 06489, Hartford County, (860)628-0879, 15 miles SW of Hartford.
Opened: 1960. **Holes:** 18. **Par:** 71/73. **Yards:** 6,325/5,482. **Course rating:** 70.6/72.0.
Slope: 123/122. **Architect:** Orrin Smith. **Green fee:** $25/$29. **Credit cards:** None.
Reduced fees: N/A. **Caddies:** No. **Golf carts:** $26. **Discount golf packages:** No.
Season: March-Dec. **High:** June-Aug. **On site lodging:** No. **Rental clubs:** No.
Walking policy: Unrestricted walking. **Metal spikes allowed:** Yes. **Range:** Yes (grass/mats). **To obtain tee times:** Call Wednesday 6 p.m. for Saturday or Sunday. For weekdays call 7 days in advance. Must have a foursome to obtain tee time.
Subscriber comments: Excellent greens...Tight course, nice layout...Rolling hills, large greens...Rough on high handicappers...Great doglegs on front, holes 12 through 14 are Amen Corner...Thinking person's course...Tight but fun to walk...Back nine more interesting than front...Underrated since it's not long, but you'd better be straight...Requires accuracy more than length.
Special Notes: Spikeless encouraged.

★★★PORTLAND GOLF COURSE

169 Bartlett St., Portland, 06480, Middlesex County, (860)342-2833, 20 miles S of Hartford.
Opened: 1974. **Holes:** 18. **Par:** 71/71. **Yards:** 6,213/5,039. **Course rating:** 70.8/68.6.
Slope: 124/118. **Architect:** Geoffrey Cornish/William Robinson. **Green fee:** $26/$31.
Credit cards: None. **Reduced fees:** Weekdays, seniors, juniors. **Caddies:** No. **Golf carts:** $12. **Discount golf packages:** Yes. **Season:** March-Dec. **High:** May-Oct. **On site lodging:** No. **Rental clubs:** Yes. **Walking policy:** Unrestricted walking. **Metal spikes allowed:** Yes. **Range:** Yes (grass/mats). **To obtain tee times:** Call Monday a.m. for weekend.
Subscriber comments: Fun course, short, a lot of blind tee shots...Fast greens, fun to play...Fun course...Best greens in the area, one of my favorites...Hilly with plenty of doglegs...Great track. Very playable. Fast pace of play.

★★RACEWAY GOLF CLUB

E. Thompson Rd., Thompson, 06277, Windham County, (860)923-9591.
Call club for further information.

★★★★RICHTER PARK GOLF CLUB

PU-100 Aunt Hack Rd., Danbury, 06811, Fairfield County, (203)792-2552, 60 miles NE of New York City.
Opened: 1971. **Holes:** 18. **Par:** 72/72. **Yards:** 6,740/5,627. **Course rating:** 73.0/72.8.
Slope: 130/122. **Architect:** Edward Ryder. **Green fee:** $27/$44. **Credit cards:** MC,VISA. **Reduced fees:** Twilight. **Caddies:** No. **Golf carts:** $23. **Discount golf packages:** No. **Season:** April-Nov. **High:** June-Aug. **On site lodging:** No. **Rental clubs:** Yes. **Walking policy:** Unrestricted walking. **Metal spikes allowed:** No. **Range:** No. **To obtain tee times:** Nonresidents call Thursday 9 a.m. for weekend.
Notes: Ranked 7th in 1997 Best in State.
Subscriber comments: Best in CT...Lots of water—ouch...Classic layout, must play!...It's a beauty...Redone greens different from others...Wonderful challenge. Fast greens...Getting a tee time if nonresident is a stroke of luck...Tough to get on, but worth it...Worth the one-hour drive from New York City...Hard to believe it's municipal...Play it in the fall. That way you can enjoy the view while struggling to score.

★★★RIDGEFIELD GOLF COURSE

PU-545 Ridgebury Rd., Ridgefield, 06877, Fairfield County, (203)748-7008, 1 mile E of Danbury.
Opened: 1974. **Holes:** 18. **Par:** 70/71. **Yards:** 6,380/5,295. **Course rating:** 70.0/70.7.
Slope: 122/120. **Architect:** George Fazio/Tom Fazio. **Green fee:** $8/$27. **Credit cards:**

None. **Reduced fees:** Twilight, seniors, juniors. **Caddies:** No. **Golf carts:** $22.
Discount golf packages: No. **Season:** April-Dec. **High:** June-Aug. **On site lodging:**
No. **Rental clubs:** Yes. **Walking policy:** Unrestricted walking. **Metal spikes allowed:**
Yes. **Range:** Yes (grass). **To obtain tee times:** Lottery for reservations Thursday a.m.
Telephone after 9 a.m. Thursday.
Subscriber comments: Front nine too easy. Back nine very good. Facilities
modest...Nice course with some beautiful scenery and wildlife...Front nine boring, back
nine interesting...Wide fairways, slow greens...Picturesque, fairly hilly, great par
3s...Great alternative when Richter is unavailable...Back nine very narrow and unforgiving. Must be straight off tee...Improves every year...Nice surprise.

★★★ROCKLEDGE COUNTRY CLUB

PU-289 S. Main St., West Hartford, 06107, Hartford County, (860)521-3156, 7 miles W
of Hartford.
Opened: 1949. **Holes:** 18. **Par:** 72/74. **Yards:** 6,366/5,608. **Course rating:** 71.3/71.5.
Slope: 121/118. **Architect:** Orrin Smith. **Green fee:** $16/$27. **Credit cards:** MC,VISA.
Reduced fees: Seniors. **Caddies:** No. **Golf carts:** $20. **Discount golf packages:** No.
Season: April-Dec. **High:** June-July. **On site lodging:** No. **Rental clubs:** Yes. **Walking
policy:** Unrestricted walking. **Metal spikes allowed:** Yes. **Range:** Yes (grass/mats). **To
obtain tee times:** Call 3 days in advance.
Subscriber comments: Excellent challenge for senior golfer...Short but fun...Well laid
out course, excellent greens...Good test, must stay in fairways...A local knowledge
course...Changing a few holes this year, adding some ponds, only going to make it better!

★★½SHENNECOSSETT MUNICIPAL GOLF COURSE

PM-93 Plant St., Groton, 06340, New London County, (860)445-0262, 2 miles E of New
London.
Opened: N/A. **Holes:** 18. **Par:** 72/76. **Yards:** 6,491/5,796. **Course rating:** 71.1/73.2.
Slope: 122/121. **Architect:** Donald Ross. **Green fee:** $22/$26. **Credit cards:** None.
Reduced fees: N/A. **Caddies:** No. **Golf carts:** N/A. **Discount golf packages:** No.
Season: Year-round. **High:** July-Aug. **On site lodging:** No. **Rental clubs:** No. **Walking
policy:** Unrestricted walking. **Metal spikes allowed:** Yes. **Range:** No. **To obtain tee
times:** Call Tuesday for Saturday tee time and Wednesday for Sunday tee time.
Subscriber comments: My wife's favorite—not mine!...Donald Ross original, lots of
bunkers...Nice to play an old course...Unique fairways, challenging greens...Links type,
fair test...Demanding par 3s...Playable most of winter...Very flat and open...Great seaside course...Lots of sand, little water.

★★★SIMSBURY FARMS GOLF CLUB

PM-100 Old Farms Rd., West Simsbury, 06092, Hartford County, (860)658-6246, 15
miles NW of Hartford.
Opened: 1972. **Holes:** 18. **Par:** 72/72. **Yards:** 6,421/5,439. **Course rating:** 71.1/70.1.
Slope: 124/117. **Architect:** Geoffrey Cornish/William Robinson. **Green fee:** $14/$26.
Credit cards: MC,VISA. **Reduced fees:** N/A. **Caddies:** No. **Golf carts:** $22. **Discount
golf packages:** No. **Season:** April-Nov. **High:** May-Sept. **On site lodging:** No. **Rental
clubs:** Yes. **Walking policy:** Unrestricted walking. **Metal spikes allowed:** Yes. **Range:**
Yes (mats). **To obtain tee times:** Call 2 days in advance at 10 a.m.
Subscriber comments: Quality golf...Scenic Geoffrey Cornish layout, good test from
tips...Can usually get tee time. Easy for a single. Some challenging par 3s...Nice variety
of holes, not real long...Fantastic hills and slopes...Wind and breaking putts challenge.

★★SKUNGAMAUG RIVER GOLF CLUB

PU-104 Folly Lane, Coventry, 06238, Tolland County, (860)742-9348, 20 miles E of
Hartford.
Opened: 1963. **Holes:** 18. **Par:** 70/71. **Yards:** 5,785/4,862. **Course rating:** 69.4/69.4.
Slope: 120/114. **Architect:** Joseph & John Motycka. **Green fee:** $22/$25. **Credit
cards:** MC,VISA. **Reduced fees:** N/A. **Caddies:** No. **Golf carts:** $20. **Discount golf
packages:** No. **Season:** March-Dec. **High:** June-Sept. **On site lodging:** No. **Rental
clubs:** Yes. **Walking policy:** Unrestricted walking. **Metal spikes allowed:** Yes. **Range:**
Yes (grass). **To obtain tee times:** Call golf shop up to 7 days in advance for weekday.
Call on Monday for upcoming weekend.

★★SOUTHINGTON COUNTRY CLUB
Savage St., Southington, 06489, Hartford County, (860)628-7032.
Call club for further information.

★★★½STANLEY GOLF CLUB
PU- 245 Hartford Rd., New Britain, 06052, Hartford County, (860)827-8144, 10 miles SW of Hartford.
Opened: 1930. **Holes:** 27. **Architect:** R.J. Ross/O. Smith/G.S. Cornish. **Green fee:** $19/$23. **Credit cards:** None. **Reduced fees:** Weekdays. **Golf carts:** $21. **Caddies:** No. **Discount golf packages:** No. **Season:** April-Dec. **High:** June-Sept. **On site lodging:** No. **Rental clubs:** Yes. **Walking policy:** Unrestricted walking. **Metal spikes allowed:** Yes. **Range:** No. **To obtain tee times:** Call seven days in advance.
BLUE/RED
Par: 73/73. **Yards:** 6,453/5,700. **Course rating:** 70.5/72.0. **Slope:** 120/122.
Subscriber comments: Good for average players...A favorite for seniors...Great track for public course...Red portion of course not very interesting...Restaurant has excellent food...Crowded muny...Wide fairways...Nice course, a little dry in summer.
Special notes: Other combinations include Red/White and White/Blue.

★★★STERLING FARMS GOLF CLUB
PU-1349 Newfield Ave., Stamford, 06905, Fairfield County, (203)329-7888.
Opened: 1969. **Holes:** 18. **Par:** 72/73. **Yards:** 6,410/5,600. **Course rating:** 71.7/72.6. **Slope:** 127/121. **Architect:** Geoffrey Cornish/William Robinson. **Green fee:** $12/$33. **Credit cards:** None. **Reduced fees:** Weekdays, low season, twilight, seniors, juniors. **Caddies:** No. **Golf carts:** $20. **Discount golf packages:** No. **Season:** Year-round. **High:** July-Aug. **On site lodging:** No. **Rental clubs:** Yes. **Walking policy:** Unrestricted walking. **Metal spikes allowed:** Yes. **Range:** Yes. **To obtain tee times:** Call three days in advance.
Subscriber comments: Some of the scenery is breathtaking...Very much improved, greens like carpet...Quite possibly the best muny course in CT...Great from tips, challenging layout...Nice course, too many tournaments, can't get out...Terribly short from the reds...Tougher back nine. #12 should be blown up, deceptively difficult...Can play it every day without getting bored.

★★★TALLWOOD COUNTRY CLUB
PU-91 N. St., Rte. 85, Hebron, 06248, Tolland County, (860)646-3437, 15 miles SE of Hartford.
Opened: 1970. **Holes:** 18. **Par:** 72/72. **Yards:** 6,366/5,430. **Course rating:** 70.2/70.8. **Slope:** 119/114. **Architect:** Mike Ovian. **Green fee:** $18/$22. **Credit cards:** None. **Reduced fees:** Low season, twilight, seniors, juniors. **Caddies:** No. **Golf carts:** $10. **Discount golf packages:** Yes. **Season:** March-Dec. **High:** May-Sept. **On site lodging:** No. **Rental clubs:** Yes. **Walking policy:** Unrestricted walking. **Metal spikes allowed:** Yes. **Range:** Yes (grass/mats). **To obtain tee times:** Call one week in advance for weekday and Monday a.m. for upcoming weekend.
Subscriber comments: Good track, fun to play, couple of par 4s that average player can't get to...Terrific greens, great layout...Some tough holes...Tight course...Front nine is dry, back nine has lots of water holes...Great course to play in the fall, very pretty...Great greens. Lots of trouble to get into...Nice challenge, bring your "A" game...Middle of nowhere keeps it quiet.

★★★TASHUA KNOLLS GOLF COURSE
PU-40 Tashua Knolls Lane, Trumbull, 06611, Fairfield County, (203)261-5989, 7 miles N of Bridgeport.
Opened: 1976. **Holes:** 18. **Par:** 72/72. **Yards:** 6,502/5,454. **Course rating:** 71.1/71.7. **Slope:** 118/124. **Architect:** Al Zikorus. **Green fee:** $24/$27. **Credit cards:** None. **Reduced fees:** Seniors, juniors. **Caddies:** No. **Golf carts:** $24. **Discount golf packages:** No. **Season:** March-Dec. **High:** May-Sept. **On site lodging:** No. **Rental clubs:** Yes. **Walking policy:** Unrestricted walking. **Metal spikes allowed:** Yes. **Range:** Yes (grass). **To obtain tee times:** Call golf shop.
Subscriber comments: A fun course...They must do something about the Canada Geese...Good mix of easy and tough holes, fantastic scenery in fall...Very pleasant surprise, a sleeper...Huge greens...Very pasturesque...Lots of hills. Long walk.

★★★½TIMBERLIN GOLF CLUB

PM-Ken Bates Dr., Kensington, 06037, Hartford County, (860)828-3228, 18 miles S of Hartford.

Opened: 1970. **Holes:** 18. **Par:** 72/72. **Yards:** 6,733/5,477. **Course rating:** 71.9/70.5. **Slope:** 127/109. **Architect:** Al Zikorus. **Green fee:** $12/$24. **Credit cards:** None. **Reduced fees:** N/A. **Caddies:** No. **Golf carts:** $20. **Discount golf packages:** No. **Season:** April-Nov. **High:** June-Sept. **On site lodging:** No. **Rental clubs:** Yes. **Walking policy:** Unrestricted walking. **Metal spikes allowed:** Yes. **Range:** Yes (grass/mats). **To obtain tee times:** Call 2 days in advance at 7 a.m.

Subscriber comments: Great layout, very easy to get out...One of the best in the area...Played once but loved it, I'll be there this year...Par 3 11th over water, one of several gems...Some very challenging holes...Favorite course, great layout and scenery...Good mix of holes varying in length.

TUNXIS PLANTATION COUNTRY CLUB

PU-87 Town Farm Rd., Farmington, 06032, Hartford County, (860)677-1367, 10 miles S of Hartford.

Opened: 1962. **Architect:** Al Zikorus. **Green fee:** $22/$29. **Credit cards:** MC,VISA,AMEX. **Reduced fees:** Seniors, juniors. **Caddies:** No. **Golf carts:** $25. **Discount golf packages:** No. **Season:** April-Nov. **High:** May-Aug. **On site lodging:** No. **Rental clubs:** Yes. **Walking policy:** Unrestricted walking. **Metal spikes allowed:** Yes. **Range:** Yes (grass/mats). **To obtain tee times:** Call Tuesday prior to weekend at 7:30 a.m.

★★★GREEN COURSE

Holes: 18. **Par:** 70/70. **Yards:** 6,354/4,883. **Course rating:** 70.0/71.0. **Slope:** 120/115.

Subscriber comments: Flat with many bunkers...Very enjoyable golf...New part of course needs to mature...Short, tight, layouts. A fun course, great for seniors...A little too easy, White course is tougher...Wide, easy walking, good combo of holes...Set in a beautiful valley...New 18 is good, but too flat...Pretty open, not much trouble...Easy to score here...Walker's dream.

★★★WHITE COURSE

Holes: 18. **Par:** 72/72. **Yards:** 6,638/5,744. **Course rating:** 72.2/71.5. **Slope:** 129/125.

Subscriber comments: Nice course, some good water holes...Modest challenge...A few too many back and forth holes...Nice course, but not memorable...New holes seem cramped and short...Water in play on five holes...Long holes good test...Nice layout plenty of scenery...White course is a good test of golf, especially the middle six holes, very tough!

★★★TWIN HILLS COUNTRY CLUB

PU-Rte. 31, Coventry, 06238, Tolland County, (860)742-9705, 10 miles E of Hartford.

Opened: 1971. **Holes:** 18. **Par:** 71/71. **Yards:** 6,257/5,249. **Course rating:** 68.7/69.5. **Slope:** 118/116. **Architect:** Mike McDermott/George McDermott. **Green fee:** $21/$23. **Credit cards:** None. **Reduced fees:** Seniors. **Caddies:** No. **Golf carts:** $20. **Discount golf packages:** No. **Season:** Year-round. **High:** May-Aug. **On site lodging:** No. **Rental clubs:** Yes. **Walking policy:** Unrestricted walking. **Metal spikes allowed:** Yes. **Range:** No. **To obtain tee times:** Call golf shop for weekend play.

Subscriber comments: Interesting layout, par 3s short, par 5s true 5s...You feel you're playing in your own backyard...All this course needs is a clubhouse...Nice simple course, use all irons, greens fast...Front/back nines feel like different courses...Another fun place...Really improved and getting better!

★★WESTERN HILLS GOLF CLUB

PU-Park Rd., Waterbury, 06708, New Haven County, (203)755-6828, 60 miles NE of New York.

Opened: 1961. **Holes:** 18. **Par:** 72/72. **Yards:** 6,427/5,393. **Course rating:** 69.6/69.6. **Slope:** 125/122. **Architect:** Al Zikorus. **Green fee:** $13/$21. **Credit cards:** None. **Reduced fees:** Weekdays, low season, seniors, juniors. **Caddies:** No. **Golf carts:** $20. **Discount golf packages:** No. **Season:** April-Dec. **High:** April-Aug. **On site lodging:** No. **Rental clubs:** Yes. **Walking policy:** Unrestricted walking. **Metal spikes allowed:** Yes. **Range:** No. **To obtain tee times:** Call (203)756-1211 Thur. for Sat.; Fri for Sun.; Times start at 7:00 a.m.

★★WESTWOODS GOLF CLUB
Rte. 177, Farmington, 06032, Hartford County, (860)677-9192.
Call club for further information.

★★★WHITNEY FARMS GOLF COURSE
PU-175 Shelton Rd., Monroe, 06468, Fairfield County, (203)268-0707, 20 miles N of Bridgeport.
Opened: 1981. **Holes:** 18. **Par:** 72/73. **Yards:** 6,628/5,832. **Course rating:** 72.4/72.9. **Slope:** 130/124. **Architect:** Hal Purdy. **Green fee:** $37/$42. **Credit cards:** MC,VISA,AMEX. **Reduced fees:** N/A. **Caddies:** No. **Golf carts:** Included in Green Fee. **Discount golf packages:** No. **Season:** March-Dec. **High:** June-Aug. **On site lodging:** No. **Rental clubs:** Yes. **Walking policy:** Mandatory carts. **Metal spikes allowed:** No. **Range:** Yes. **To obtain tee times:** Call 7 days in advance for weekday; Thursday before 8:00 a.m. for weekends. Outing reservations up to 1 year in advance.
Subscriber comments: Difficult course if you don't know it...Greens real tough and very challenging...Must be a straight hitter...Beautiful views. Challenging holes...#7 is excellent downhill par 3...Never boring. 18th green: 3 elephants buried in shallow graves...Good day of golf, tough test on greens...Lots of water and OB.

★★★½WILLIMANTIC COUNTRY CLUB
184 Club Rd., Windham, 06280, Windham County, (860)456-1971, 28 miles SE of Hartford.
Opened: 1922. **Holes:** 18. **Par:** 71/71. **Yards:** 6,278/5,106. **Course rating:** 70.5/68.5. **Slope:** 123/113. **Architect:** Designed by members. **Green fee:** $55. **Credit cards:** MC,VISA,AMEX. **Reduced fees:** N/A. **Caddies:** No. **Golf carts:** N/A. **Discount golf packages:** No. **Season:** April-Dec. **High:** Summer. **On site lodging:** No. **Rental clubs:** No. **Walking policy:** Walking at certain times. **Metal spikes allowed:** No. **Range:** No. **To obtain tee times:** N/A.
Subscriber comments: Great greens...Very enjoyable...Some great holes...Simple to play, fun course...Short but a very nice course...Not difficult from advanced tees...Narrow cut fairways with a lot of thick heavy rough.

★★★WOODHAVEN COUNTRY CLUB
PU-275 Miller Rd., Bethany, 06524, New Haven County, (203)393-3230, 5 miles N of New Haven.
Opened: 1968. **Holes:** 9. **Par:** 36/37. **Yards:** 3,387/2,859. **Course rating:** 72.7/73.0. **Slope:** 128/125. **Architect:** Al Zikorus. **Green fee:** N/A. **Credit cards:** MC,VISA. **Reduced fees:** Weekdays, low season, seniors. **Caddies:** No. **Golf carts:** $26. **Discount golf packages:** No. **Season:** Year-round. **High:** April-Nov. **On site lodging:** No. **Rental clubs:** Yes. **Walking policy:** Unrestricted walking. **Metal spikes allowed:** Yes. **Range:** Yes (mats). **To obtain tee times:** Call up to 7 days in advance.
Subscriber comments: Very pretty, nice setting...Easy to get tee time...Holes 7, 8 and 9 are inspiring...Hike into the woods to play the blue tee on the 4th, it's worth it...Excellent nine-holer, blues and whites keep it interesting if you go around twice...Large fast undulating greens.

★★★½YALE GOLF COURSE
SP-200 Conrad Dr., New Haven, 06515, New Haven County, (203)432-0895.
Opened: 1926. **Holes:** 18. **Par:** 70/70. **Yards:** 6,620/5,395. **Course rating:** 72.8/70.2. **Slope:** 139/123. **Architect:** C.B. Macdonald. **Green fee:** $80. **Credit cards:** MC,VISA. **Reduced fees:** N/A. **Caddies:** No. **Golf carts:** $30. **Discount golf packages:** No. **Season:** April-Nov. **High:** Summer. **On site lodging:** No. **Rental clubs:** Yes. **Walking policy:** Unrestricted walking. **Metal spikes allowed:** Yes. **Range:** Yes (grass). **To obtain tee times:** N/A.
Notes: Ranked 3rd in 1997 Best in State.
Subscriber comments: A treat, target golf at its best...True greens. Tough par 3s. Many blind shots. Workout when walking...exceptional bunkering...Very tough from all tees. High handicappers will be frustrated...Same era and layout design as Bethpage Black...A must for the avid golfer...Every hole is unique and very memorable...A must! See it to believe it...A part of golf history...Bring a ladder, steep deep bunkers.

DELAWARE

★★DEL CASTLE GOLF CLUB
PU-801 McKennans Church Rd., Wilmington, 19808, New Castle County, (302)995-1990, 20 miles S of Philadelphia.
Opened: 1972. **Holes:** 18. **Par:** 72/72. **Yards:** 6,628/5,396. **Course rating:** 70.4/70.9. **Slope:** 116/116. **Architect:** Edmund B. Ault. **Green fee:** $14/$23. **Credit cards:** None. **Reduced fees:** Low season, twilight, seniors, juniors. **Caddies:** No. **Golf carts:** $25. **Discount golf packages:** No. **Season:** Year-round. **High:** March-Nov. **On site lodging:** No. **Rental clubs:** Yes. **Walking policy:** Unrestricted walking. **Metal spikes allowed:** Yes. **Range:** Yes (grass/mats). **To obtain tee times:** Come in Monday to sign up foursome for upcoming weekend. Tee times are taken for weekend and holidays only. **Special Notes:** Spikeless shoes encouraged.

★★ED "PORKY" OLIVER GOLF COURSE
PU-800 N. DuPont Rd., Wilmington, 19807, New Castle County, (302)571-9041, 25 miles S of Philadelphia.
Opened: N/A. **Holes:** 18. **Par:** 69/71. **Yards:** 6,115/5,692. **Course rating:** 69.8/71.8. **Slope:** 118/121. **Architect:** Wilfrid Reid. **Green fee:** $15/$22. **Credit cards:** All major. **Reduced fees:** Weekdays, low season, twilight, seniors, juniors. **Caddies:** No. **Golf carts:** N/A. **Discount golf packages:** No. **Season:** Year-round. **High:** May-Sept. **On site lodging:** No. **Rental clubs:** Yes. **Walking policy:** Unrestricted walking. **Metal spikes allowed:** Yes. **Range:** Yes (grass). **To obtain tee times:** Must be in tee time reservation system.

★½OLD LANDING GOLF CLUB
P.O. Box 39, Rehoboth Beach, 19971, Sussex County, (302)227-3616.
Call club for further information.

★★RON JAWORSKI'S GARRISONS LAKE COUNTRY CLUB
PU-101 Fairways Circle, Smyrna, 19977, Kent County, (302)653-6349, 5 miles N of Dover.
Opened: 1963. **Holes:** 18. **Par:** 72/72. **Yards:** 7,028/5,460. **Course rating:** 73.1/71.6. **Slope:** 125/126. **Architect:** Edmund B. Ault. **Green fee:** $20/$35. **Credit cards:** All major. **Reduced fees:** Weekdays, low season, twilight, seniors. **Caddies:** No. **Golf carts:** Included in Green Fee. **Discount golf packages:** Yes. **Season:** Year-round. **High:** May-Sept. **On site lodging:** No. **Rental clubs:** Yes. **Walking policy:** Walking at certain times. **Metal spikes allowed:** Yes. **Range:** Yes (grass/mats). **To obtain tee times:** Call 7 days in advance.

★★★½THREE LITTLE BAKERS COUNTRY CLUB
3542 Foxcroft Dr., Wilmington, 19808, New Castle County, (302)737-1877, 65 miles N of Baltimore.
Opened: 1973. **Holes:** 18. **Par:** 71/72. **Yards:** 6,609/5,209. **Course rating:** 71.9/70.3. **Slope:** 130/120. **Architect:** Edmund B. Ault. **Green fee:** $21/$25. **Credit cards:** All major. **Reduced fees:** Weekdays, low season, twilight, seniors, juniors. **Caddies:** No. **Golf carts:** $11. **Discount golf packages:** No. **Season:** Year-round. **High:** April-Oct. **On site lodging:** No. **Rental clubs:** Yes. **Walking policy:** Walking at certain times. **Metal spikes allowed:** No. **Range:** No. **To obtain tee times:** Call Thursday a.m. for following weekend.
Subscriber comments: Good layout, fast greens, good test of skills...Very well-groomed. True greens. Tough test...Not for high handicaps or spray hitters...Some blind driving holes and shots to green...Great layout. Challenging...Each hole distinct, enjoyable. Tough walk!...By far best public course in Delaware.

DISTRICT OF COLUMBIA

★½EAST POTOMAC PARK GOLF COURSE
PU-Ohio Dr., Washington D.C., 20024, District of Columbia County, (202)554-7660.
Opened: 1920. **Holes:** 18. **Par:** 72/72. **Yards:** 6,303/5,761. **Course rating:** 68.5.
Slope: 109. **Architect:** Robert White/Walter Travis. **Green fee:** $10/$17. **Credit cards:** MC,VISA. **Reduced fees:** Weekdays, seniors. **Caddies:** No. **Golf carts:** $18. **Discount golf packages:** No. **Season:** Year-round. **High:** May-Sept. **On site lodging:** No. **Rental clubs:** Yes. **Walking policy:** Unrestricted walking. **Metal spikes allowed:** Yes. **Range:** Yes. **To obtain tee times:** First come, first served.

★★LANGSTON GOLF COURSE
PU-2600 Benning Rd. N.E., Washington D.C., 20001, District of Columbia County, (202)397-8638.
Opened: 1939. **Holes:** 18. **Par:** 72. **Yards:** 6,340. **Course rating:** 69.6. **Slope:** 112.
Architect: William Gordon. **Green fee:** $10/$17. **Credit cards:** None. **Reduced fees:** Weekdays. **Caddies:** No. **Golf carts:** $19. **Discount golf packages:** Yes. **Season:** Year-round. **High:** March-Oct. **On site lodging:** No. **Rental clubs:** Yes. **Walking policy:** Unrestricted walking. **Metal spikes allowed:** Yes. **Range:** Yes (grass). **To obtain tee times:** First come, first served.

★½ROCK CREEK PARK GOLF COURSE
PU-16th & Rittenhouse N.W., Washington D.C., 20011, District of Columbia County, (202)882-7332
Opened: 1923. **Holes:** 18. **Par:** 65/65. **Yards:** 4,715/4,715. **Course rating:** 62.5/65.5.
Slope: 112/102. **Architect:** William S. Flynn. **Green fee:** $10/$17. **Credit cards:** MC,VISA. **Reduced fees:** Weekdays, seniors. **Caddies:** No. **Golf carts:** $18. **Discount golf packages:** No. **Season:** Year-round. **High:** June-Aug. **On site lodging:** No. **Rental clubs:** Yes. **Walking policy:** Unrestricted walking. **Metal spikes allowed:** Yes. **Range:** Yes. **To obtain tee times:** First come, first served.

ADMIRAL LEHIGH GOLF RESORT

R- **Architect:** Mark Mahannah. **Green fee:** $11/$30. **Credit cards:** All major. **Reduced fees:** Low season, resort guests, twilight. **Caddies:** No. **Golf carts:** $18. **Discount golf packages:** Yes. **Season:** Year-round. **High:** Dec.-April. **Rental clubs:** Yes. **Walking policy:** Walking at certain times. **Metal spikes allowed:** Yes. **To obtain tee times:** Call 24 hours in advance.

★★½NORTH COURSE

225 E. Joel Blvd., Lehigh, 33972, Lee County, (941)369-2121, 13 miles E of Fort Myers.
Opened: 1958. **Holes:** 18. **Par:** 70/70. **Yards:** 5,870/4,703. **Course rating:** 70.0/67.3. **Slope:** 119/116. **On site lodging:** Yes. **Range:** Yes (mats).
Subscriber comments: Good rehab work...Not too difficult...Nice course to play.

★★½SOUTH COURSE AT MIRROR LAKES

670 Milwaukee Ave., Lehigh, 33936, Lee County, (941)369-1322, 12 miles E of Ft. Myers.
Opened: 1973. **Holes:** 18. **Par:** 73/73. **Yards:** 7,058/5,697. **Course rating:** 74.0/72.9. **Slope:** 123/125. **On site lodging:** No. **Range:** Yes (grass/mats).
Subscriber comments: Good course, well maintained...Had fun playing this course and will play it again...Nice course to play...Great experience...Basic golf. Enjoyable...Good test, many improvements.

AMELIA ISLAND PLANTATION

R-3000 1st Coast Hwy., Amelia Island, 32035, Nassau County, (904)277-5907, (800)874-6878, 35 miles NE of Jacksonville.
Caddies: No. **Golf carts:** Included in Green Fee. **Discount golf packages:** Yes. **Season:** Year-round. **High:** March-May. **On site lodging:** Yes. **Rental clubs:** Yes. **Walking policy:** Mandatory cart. **Range:** Yes (grass).

★★★½AMELIA LINKS

Opened: 1973. **Holes:** 27. **Architect:** Pete Dye. **Green fee:** $85/$95. **Credit cards:** MC,VISA,DISC. **Reduced fees:** Low season, resort guests, twilight, juniors. **Metal spikes allowed:** Yes. **To obtain tee times:** May be booked when reservation is made at Amelia Island Plantation.

OAKMARSH/OCEANSIDE
Par: 71/71. **Yards:** 6,140/4,676. **Course rating:** 69.3/68.0. **Slope:** 120/116.
OAKMARSH/OYSTERBAY
Par: 72/72. **Yards:** 6,502/5,041. **Course rating:** 70.7/69.7. **Slope:** 127/123.
OYSTERBAY/OCEANSIDE
Par: 71/71. **Yards:** 6,026/4,712. **Course rating:** 68.6/67.6. **Slope:** 117/115.
Notes: 1998 USGA Women's Mid-Amateur.
Subscriber comments: Well maintained...Met expectations...Beautiful live oaks and marshes...Enjoyed the experience...Too much target golf...Bring all your shots...Lots of water...Beautiful view...Nice layout...Liked holes along beach...Tricky...Short, but fun...Immaculate, but nothing really memorable...Scenic and fun as well as a challenge...Short, but fun...Beautiful course and ocean views.

★★★★LONG POINT GOLF CLUB

Opened: 1987. **Holes:** 18. **Par:** 72/72. **Yards:** 6,775/4,927. **Course rating:** 72.9/69.1. **Slope:** 129/121. **Architect:** Tom Fazio. **Green fee:** $120. **Credit cards:** Resort Charge Card. **Reduced fees:** Juniors. **High:** March-May. **Metal spikes allowed:** No. **To obtain tee times:** Call 1 day in advance. Resort guests of Amelia Island Plantation only.
Subscriber comments: Pretty...Narrow fairways...Breathtaking views on several holes...Every hole is an adventure...Severe marshes...Nice challenge...Ocean views worth the high cost...Wind will get you.

★★APOLLO BEACH GOLF & SEA CLUB

PU-801 Golf and Sea Blvd., Apollo Beach, 33572, Hillsborough County, (813)645-6212, 15 miles S of Tampa.
Opened: 1972. **Holes:** 18. **Par:** 72/72. **Yards:** 7,040/4,831. **Course rating:** 73.9/69.1. **Slope:** 130/115. **Architect:** Robert Trent Jones. **Green fee:** $25/$38. **Credit cards:** All major. **Reduced fees:** Low season, twilight, seniors, juniors. **Caddies:** No. **Golf carts:** Included in Green Fee. **Discount golf packages:** Yes. **Season:** Year-round. **High:** Nov.-March. **On site lodging:** No. **Rental clubs:** Yes. **Walking policy:** Mandatory cart. **Metal spikes allowed:** Yes. **Range:** Yes (grass). **To obtain tee times:** Call.

FLORIDA

★★★★½ARNOLD PALMER'S BAY HILL CLUB & LODGE
R-9000 Bay Hill Blvd., Orlando, 32819, Orange County, (407)876-2429x630.
Opened: 1961. **Holes:** 27. **Par:** 72/72. **Yards:** 7,207/5,235. **Course rating:** 75.1/72.7. **Slope:** 139/130. **Architect:** Dick Wilson. **Green fee:** $175. **Credit cards:** MC,VISA,AMEX. **Reduced fees:** Resort guests, juniors. **Caddies:** Yes. **Golf carts:** Included in Green Fee. **Discount golf packages:** No. **Season:** Year-round. **High:** Jan.-April. **On site lodging:** Yes. **Rental clubs:** Yes. **Walking policy:** Walking at certain times. Caddie is required when walking. **Metal spikes allowed:** Yes. **Range:** Yes (grass/mats). **To obtain tee times:** Tee times made through Lodge reservation.
Notes: Ranked 97th in 1997-98 America's 100 Greatest; 6th in 1997 Best in State. PGA Tour Bay Hill Invitational; USGA National Junior.
Subscriber comments: Great to play...Got to play next to Arnold Palmer...A real challenge...Tough track, but hey, it's Arnie's place...Must play smart.
Special Notes: Also has 9-hole, par-36 Charger Course.

★★½ARROWHEAD GOLF COURSE
PU-8201 S.W. 24th St., Fort Lauderdale, 33324, Broward County, (954)475-8200, 5 miles W of Fort Lauderdale.
Opened: 1976. **Holes:** 18. **Par:** 70/70. **Yards:** 6,311/4,838. **Course rating:** 70.8/68.7. **Slope:** 115/109. **Architect:** Bill Watts. **Green fee:** $15/$40. **Credit cards:** MC,VISA,AMEX. **Reduced fees:** Weekdays, low season, twilight. **Caddies:** No. **Golf carts:** Included in Green Fee. **Discount golf packages:** Yes. **Season:** Year-round. **High:** Jan.-March. **On site lodging:** No. **Rental clubs:** Yes. **Walking policy:** Mandatory cart. **Metal spikes allowed:** Yes. **Range:** Yes (grass/mats). **To obtain tee times:** Call 7 days in advance.
Subscriber comments: Could be nice. Needs work...Back nine good...Water comes into play on several holes...Flat.

★★★ATLANTIS COUNTRY CLUB & INN
R-190 Atlantis Blvd., Atlantis, 33462, Palm Beach County, (561)968-1300, 7 miles S of West Palm Beach.
Opened: 1972. **Holes:** 18. **Par:** 72/72. **Yards:** 6,537/5,258. **Course rating:** 71.5/70.9. **Slope:** 128/123. **Architect:** Robert Simmons. **Green fee:** $20/$60. **Credit cards:** MC,VISA,DISC. **Reduced fees:** Weekdays, low season, resort guests. **Caddies:** No. **Golf carts:** $15. **Discount golf packages:** Yes. **Season:** Year-round. **High:** Oct.-March. **On site lodging:** Yes. **Rental clubs:** Yes. **Walking policy:** Mandatory cart. **Metal spikes allowed:** Yes. **Range:** Yes (grass). **To obtain tee times:** Non-resort guests call 24 hours in advance. Members and Inn guests call 3 days in advance. Groups may book up to 1 year in advance.
Subscriber comments: Good layout...Very narrow fairways...Beautiful vistas...Fun course to play with great facilities...Not too tough...Excellent conditions...Long, challenging...Plays longer than yardage...Beautiful, well-maintained course.

★★BABE ZAHARIAS GOLF COURSE
PM-11412 Forest Hills Dr., Tampa, 33612, Hillsborough County, (813)631-4374, 20 miles W of St. Petersburg.
Opened: 1974. **Holes:** 18. **Par:** 70/71. **Yards:** 6,163/5,236. **Course rating:** 68.9/68.9. **Slope:** 121/118. **Architect:** Ron Garl. **Green fee:** $15/$32. **Credit cards:** MC,VISA,DISC. **Reduced fees:** Weekdays, low season, twilight, seniors, juniors, **Caddies:** No. **Golf carts:** Included in Green Fee. **Discount golf packages:** No. **Season:** Year-round. **High:** Dec.-May. **On site lodging:** No. **Rental clubs:** Yes. **Walking policy:** Unrestricted walking. **Metal spikes allowed:** Yes. **Range:** No. **To obtain tee times:** Call on Thursday for upcoming weekdays. Call on Monday for upcoming weekend.

★★★BARDMOOR NORTH GOLF CLUB
PU-8000 Cumberland Rd., Largo, 33777, Pinellas County, (813)392-1234, 15 miles W of Tampa.
Opened: 1970. **Holes:** 18. **Par:** 72/72. **Yards:** 7,000/5,550. **Course rating:** 74.4/71.8. **Slope:** 129/118. **Architect:** William Diddel. **Green fee:** $35/$65. **Credit cards:** All

major. **Reduced fees:** Weekdays, low season, twilight, juniors. **Caddies:** Yes. **Golf carts:** Included in Green Fee. **Discount golf packages:** Yes. **Season:** Year-round. **High:** Dec.-April. **On site lodging:** No. **Rental clubs:** Yes. **Walking policy:** Mandatory cart. **Metal spikes allowed:** Yes. **Range:** Yes (grass/mats). **To obtain tee times:** Call 4 days in advance.

Notes: 1977-1989 JCPenney Classic.

Subscriber comments: Bring your game...Needed left-handed putter and they got me one...When changes and remodeling are complete, it'll be a much better course...New greens and tees make a great layout even better.

★★½BAYMEADOWS GOLF CLUB

7981 Baymeadows Circle W., Jacksonville, 32256, Duval County, (904)731-5701.
Opened: 1969. **Holes:** 18. **Par:** 72/72. **Yards:** 7,002/5,309. **Course rating:** 73.7/72.2.
Slope: 130/130. **Architect:** Desmond Muirhead/Gene Sarazen. **Green fee:** $24/$35.
Credit cards: MC,VISA,AMEX. **Reduced fees:** Weekdays, low season, resort guests, twilight, seniors, juniors. **Caddies:** No. **Golf carts:** Included in Green Fee. **Discount golf packages:** No. **Season:** Year-round. **High:** Year-round. **On site lodging:** Yes. **Rental clubs:** Yes. **Walking policy:** Mandatory cart. **Metal spikes allowed:** Yes. **Range:** Yes (grass/mats). **To obtain tee times:** Call 7 days in advance.
Subscriber comments: Very good experience...Nice course...Tough course...Need to put money into it...Basic golf outing...Not much for your buck...Typical Florida course (sand and water).

★★BAYSHORE GOLF COURSE

PU-2301 Alton Rd., Miami Beach, 33140, Dade County, (305)532-3350.
Opened: N/A. **Holes:** 18. **Par:** 72/73. **Yards:** 6,903/5,538. **Course rating:** 73.0/71.6.
Slope: 127/120. **Architect:** Robert von Hagge/Bruce Devlin. **Green fee:** $30/$55.
Credit cards: MC,VISA,AMEX. **Reduced fees:** Weekdays, low season, twilight, juniors.
Caddies: No. **Golf carts:** Included in Green Fee. **Discount golf packages:** Yes.
Season: Year-round. **High:** Dec.-March. **On site lodging:** No. **Rental clubs:** Yes.
Walking policy: Mandatory cart. **Metal spikes allowed:** Yes. **Range:** Yes (mats). **To obtain tee times:** Call 7 days in advance.

★★★★BAYTREE NATIONAL GOLF LINKS

8207 National Dr., Melbourne, 32940, Brevard County, (407)259-9060, (800)955-1234, 50 miles SE of Orlando.
Opened: 1994. **Holes:** 18. **Par:** 72/72. **Yards:** 7,043/4,803. **Course rating:** 74.4/67.5.
Slope: 138/109. **Architect:** Gary Player. **Green fee:** $35/$85. **Credit cards:** MC,VISA,AMEX. **Reduced fees:** Low season, resort guests, twilight, juniors. **Caddies:** No. **Golf carts:** Included in Green Fee. **Discount golf packages:** Yes. **Season:** Year-round. **High:** Jan.-March. **On site lodging:** No. **Rental clubs:** Yes. **Walking policy:** Mandatory cart. **Metal spikes allowed:** Yes. **Range:** Yes (grass/mats). **To obtain tee times:** Call 6 days in advance.
Subscriber comments: Challenging but fun...Groomed...Fun to play...Houses still under construction...Played with six guys from Scotland. They loved it...Worth the cost...Great finishing hole...Very good course...Very pleasurable experience.

★★½BELLA VISTA GOLF & YACHT CLUB

P.O. Box 66, Hwy. 48, Howey-in-the-Hills, 34737, Lake County, (352)324-3233, (800)955-7001, 25 miles W of Orlando.
Opened: 1990. **Holes:** 18. **Par:** 71/71. **Yards:** 6,321/5,386. **Course rating:** 68.4/71.9.
Slope: 119/123. **Architect:** Lloyd Clifton. **Green fee:** $16/$38. **Credit cards:** MC,VISA.
Reduced fees: Weekdays, low season, resort guests, twilight, seniors, juniors.
Caddies: No. **Golf carts:** Included in Green Fee. **Discount golf packages:** Yes.
Season: Year-round. **High:** Sept.-April. **On site lodging:** Yes. **Rental clubs:** Yes.
Walking policy: Mandatory cart. **Metal spikes allowed:** Yes. **Range:** Yes (grass). **To obtain tee times:** Call 48 hours in advance.
Subscriber comments: Challenging, especially the par 3s...Good condition.

★★BELLEVIEW BILTMORE RESORT & GOLF CLUB

R-1501 Indian Rocks Rd., Belleair, 34616, Pinellas County, (813)581-5498, 20 miles W of Tampa.
Opened: 1926. **Holes:** 18. **Par:** 72/74. **Yards:** 6,695/5,703. **Course rating:** 70.7/72.1.

Slope: 118/119. **Architect:** Donald Ross. **Green fee:** $25/$60. **Credit cards:** All major. **Reduced fees:** Low season, resort guests, twilight, seniors. **Caddies:** No. **Golf carts:** Included in Green Fee. **Discount golf packages:** Yes. **Season:** Year-round. **High:** Jan.-April. **On site lodging:** No. **Rental clubs:** Yes. **Walking policy:** Walking at certain times. **Metal spikes allowed:** Yes. **Range:** Yes (grass). **To obtain tee times:** Hotel guests may make tee times with room reservation. Nonguests call 4 days in advance.

★★★THE BILTMORE GOLF COURSE
PU-1210 Anastasia Ave., Coral Gables, 33134, Dade County, (305)460-5364.
Opened: 1925. **Holes:** 18. **Par:** 71/74. **Yards:** 6,642/5,237. **Course rating:** 71.5/70.1. **Slope:** 119/115. **Architect:** Donald Ross. **Green fee:** $12/$44. **Credit cards:** MC,VISA,AMEX. **Reduced fees:** Low season, resort guests, twilight, juniors. **Caddies:** No. **Golf carts:** $15. **Discount golf packages:** Yes. **Season:** Year-round. **High:** Nov.-April. **On site lodging:** Yes. **Rental clubs:** Yes. **Walking policy:** Walking at certain times. **Metal spikes allowed:** No. **Range:** Yes (grass/mats). **To obtain tee times:** Call 48 hours in advance from a touch tone telephone. Same day reservation call starter at (305)460-5365.
Subscriber comments: Great hotel...Always enjoyable...Nice location...Good value...Great scramble layout for all skill levels.

★★★½BINKS FOREST GOLF COURSE
400 Binks Forest Dr., Wellington, 33414, Palm Beach County, (561)795-0595.
Opened: 1990. **Holes:** 18. **Par:** 72/72. **Yards:** 7,065/5,599. **Course rating:** 75.0/71.9. **Slope:** 138/127. **Architect:** Johnny Miller. **Green fee:** $27/$65. **Credit cards:** MC,VISA,AMEX. **Reduced fees:** Weekdays, low season, resort guests, twilight. **Caddies:** No. **Golf carts:** Included in Green Fee. **Discount golf packages:** Yes. **Season:** Year-round. **High:** Nov.-April. **On site lodging:** No. **Rental clubs:** Yes. **Walking policy:** Mandatory cart. **Metal spikes allowed:** Yes. **Range:** Yes (grass). **To obtain tee times:** Call one week in advance with credit card.
Subscriber comments: Uncrowded...Beautifully kept...Scenic layout. Well designed...Beautiful vistas...Great layout, though new housing is infringing and getting expensive...Some narrow fairways...Tight, challenging...A wonderful trip into the forest...Wow! What a course...Great finishing hole.

★★★½BLACK BEAR GOLF CLUB
PU-24505 Calusa Blvd., Eustis, 32736, Lake County, (352)357-4732, (800)423-2718, 40 miles N of Orlando.
Opened: 1995. **Holes:** 18. **Par:** 72/72. **Yards:** 7,002/5,044. **Course rating:** 74.7/70.5. **Slope:** 134/121. **Architect:** P.B. Dye. **Green fee:** $35/$65. **Credit cards:** MC,VISA,AMEX. **Reduced fees:** Weekdays, low season, twilight, juniors. **Caddies:** No. **Golf carts:** Included in Green Fee. **Discount golf packages:** No. **Season:** Year-round. **High:** Jan.-March. **On site lodging:** No. **Rental clubs:** Yes. **Walking policy:** Unrestricted walking. **Metal spikes allowed:** Yes. **Range:** Yes (grass). **To obtain tee times:** Call golf shop.
Subscriber comments: Will be a great course...Needs to mature...When wind blows, watch out...Tough bunkers...Not for everyone. Links course with some fantastic holes...Hard to tell direction of fairway on a couple of holes...Excellent practice facility...Must play again.

★★★BLOOMINGDALE GOLFER'S CLUB
4113 Great Golfers Place, Valrico, 33594, Hillsborough County, (813)685-4105, 15 miles SE of Tampa.
Opened: 1983. **Holes:** 18. **Par:** 72/73. **Yards:** 7,165/5,506. **Course rating:** 74.4/71.6. **Slope:** 137/129. **Architect:** Ron Garl. **Green fee:** $27/$43. **Credit cards:** MC,VISA,AMEX. **Reduced fees:** Weekdays, low season, twilight, seniors, juniors. **Caddies:** No. **Golf carts:** $14. **Discount golf packages:** Yes. **Season:** Year-round. **High:** Dec.-April. **On site lodging:** No. **Rental clubs:** Yes. **Walking policy:** Mandatory cart. **Metal spikes allowed:** No. **Range:** Yes (grass/mats). **To obtain tee times:** Call up to 7 days in advance.
Subscriber comments: Great course, out of the way. Greens are not as quick as advertised...Deserves its high rating. Very difficult course...A shotmaker's course. Thoroughly enjoyable...Excellent practice facility.

BLUEWATER BAY RESORT

R-1950 Bluewater Blvd., Niceville, 32578, Okaloosa County, (904)897-3241, (800)274-2128, 60 miles E of Pensacola.

Opened: 1981. **Architect:** Tom Fazio/Jerry Pate. **Green fee:** $30/$37. **Credit cards:** All major. **Reduced fees:** Low season, resort guests, juniors. **Caddies:** No. **Golf carts:** $12. **Discount golf packages:** Yes. **Season:** Year-round. **High:** Feb.-May. **On site lodging:** Yes. **Rental clubs:** Yes. **Walking policy:** Walking at certain times. **Metal spikes allowed:** Yes. **Range:** Yes (grass). **To obtain tee times:** Call anytime.

★★★BAY/LAKE COURSE

Holes: 18. **Par:** 72/72. **Yards:** 6,803/5,378. **Course rating:** 73.0/70.6. **Slope:** 140/124.
Subscriber comments: Course was in very good condition, enjoyable...Tight fairways...Good layout. Fair. Well manicured...Great! Enjoyable and challenging...Too tight in housing area...Easy to get to since new bridge opened...Will play again...Nice facility.

★★★MAGNOLIA/MARSH COURSE

Holes: 18. **Par:** 72/72. **Yards:** 6,669/5,048. **Course rating:** 72.2/68.4. **Slope:** 132/117.
Subscriber comments: Outstanding course, challenging...Very good condition, enjoyable...Terrific value...Good variety...Well manicured...Out of the way, but worth it...Super golf...Peaceful, well kept.

BOBBY JONES GOLF COMPLEX

PU-1000 Circus Blvd., Sarasota, 34232, Sarasota County, (941)955-8097, (800)955-3529.

Opened: 1927. **Architect:** Donald Ross. **Green fee:** $9/$18. **Credit cards:** MC,VISA. **Reduced fees:** Low season, twilight, juniors. **Caddies:** No. **Golf carts:** $10. **Discount golf packages:** No. **Season:** Year-round. **High:** Dec.-April. **On site lodging:** No. **Rental clubs:** Yes. **Walking policy:** Walking at certain times. **Metal spikes allowed:** Yes. **Range:** Yes (mats). **To obtain tee times:** Call automated computer system on touch-tone phone.

★★AMERICAN COURSE

Holes: 18. **Par:** 71/71. **Yards:** 6,009/4,453. **Course rating:** 68.4/65.1. **Slope:** 117/107.

★★BRITISH COURSE

Holes: 18. **Par:** 72/72. **Yards:** 6,468/5,695. **Course rating:** 70.0/71.8. **Slope:** 111/115.
Notes: 1940 PGA Senior Championship. LPGA tournaments in 1950s.
Special Notes: Also has 9-hole par-30 Colonel Gillespie Course.

BOCA RATON RESORT & CLUB

R-Palm Beach County, (561)395-3000.

Opened: N/A. **Green fee:** N/A. **Credit cards:** All major,. **Reduced fees:** Low season, twilight. **Caddies:** No. **Golf carts:** $19. **Discount golf packages:** Yes. **Season:** Year-round. **High:** Oct.-May. **On site lodging:** Yes. **Rental clubs:** No. **Walking policy:** N/A. **Metal spikes allowed:** Yes. **Range:** Yes (grass). **To obtain tee times:** Call club.

★★½COUNTRY CLUB COURSE

7751 Boca Club Blvd., Boca Raton, 33487.
Holes: 18. **Par:** 72/72. **Yards:** 6,564/5,565. **Course rating:** N/A. **Slope:** 126/124.
Architect: Joe Lee.

★★½RESORT COURSE

501 E. Camino Real, Boca Raton, 33432.
Holes: 18. **Par:** 71/71. **Yards:** 6,682/5,518. **Course rating:** N/A. **Slope:** 122/124.
Architect: William Flynn.
Subscriber comments: Typical upscale Florida resort course...Nice layout and flow...Fair course. Something for all levels.....Not challenging enough...Flat and wide fairways.

BONAVENTURE COUNTRY CLUB

R-200 Bonaventure Blvd., Weston, 33326, Broward County, (954)389-2100, 10 miles W of Fort Lauderdale.

Green fee: $45/$75. **Credit cards:** MC,VISA,AMEX. **Reduced fees:** Low season, resort guests, twilight. **Caddies:** No. **Golf carts:** Included in Green Fee. **Discount golf packages:** No. **Season:** Year-round. **High:** Nov.-April. **On site lodging:** Yes. **Walking policy:** Mandatory cart. **Range:** Yes (grass).

★★½EAST COURSE

Opened: 1971. **Holes:** 18. **Par:** 72/72. **Yards:** 7,011/5,345. **Course rating:** 74.2/71.6.

Slope: 132/122. **Architect:** Joe Lee. **Rental clubs:** No. **Metal spikes allowed:** Yes. **To obtain tee times:** Call 3 days in advance. Hotel guests call anytime in advance.
Subscriber comments: Loved the signature-hole waterfall...Great greens...Great, challenging course...Lots of water...Many tough holes...Tough when windy...New sand was welcome.

★★½**WEST COURSE**
Opened: N/A. **Holes:** 18. **Par:** 70/70. **Yards:** 6,189/4,993. **Course rating:** 70.0/69.0.
Slope: 118/114. **Architect:** Charles Mahannah. **Rental clubs:** Yes. **Metal spikes allowed:** No. **To obtain tee times:** Call up to 3 days in advance. Hotel guests may call anytime in advance.
Subscriber comments: Fun to play...Long par 5s for average golfer...Lots of water...Too crowded.

★½**BONIFAY COUNTRY CLUB**
State Rd. 177A, Bonifay, 32425, Holmes County, (904)547-4653, 40 miles N of Panama City.
Opened: 1963. **Holes:** 18. **Par:** 72/72. **Yards:** 6,850/5,405. **Course rating:** 73.1.
Slope: N/A. **Architect:** N/A. **Green fee:** $22. **Credit cards:** MC,VISA,DISC. **Reduced fees:** Weekdays, low season, twilight, juniors. **Caddies:** No. **Golf carts:** Included in Green Fee. **Discount golf packages:** No. **Season:** Year-round. **High:** Oct.-April. **On site lodging:** No. **Rental clubs:** Yes. **Walking policy:** Unrestricted walking. **Metal spikes allowed:** Yes. **Range:** Yes (grass). **To obtain tee times:** Call up to 7 days in advance.

★★½**BONITA SPRINGS GOLF CLUB**
10200 Maddox Lane, Bonita Springs, 33923, Lee County, (941)992-2800, 10 miles N of Naples.
Opened: 1977. **Holes:** 18. **Par:** 72/72. **Yards:** 6,761/5,306. **Course rating:** 71.2/70.1.
Slope: 129/121. **Architect:** William Maddox. **Green fee:** $15/$60. **Credit cards:** MC,VISA,DISC. **Reduced fees:** Low season, twilight. **Caddies:** No. **Golf carts:** Included in Green Fee. **Discount golf packages:** No. **Season:** Year-round. **High:** Jan.-March. **On site lodging:** No. **Rental clubs:** Yes. **Walking policy:** Walking at certain times. **Metal spikes allowed:** Yes. **Range:** No. **To obtain tee times:** Call up to 2 days in advance from 7 a.m. to 5 p.m.
Subscriber comments: Fairways are very narrow...Enjoyed the day and the course...Not bad. Nice layout...Just a fair course when one considers the cost of green fees. Does have some good holes...Too close to houses.

★★½**BOYNTON BEACH MUNICIPAL GOLF COURSE**
PM-8020 Jog Rd., Boynton Beach, 33437, Palm Beach County, (561)969-2201, 10 miles S of West Palm Beach.
Opened: 1984. **Holes:** 27. **Architect:** Von Hagge/Devlin/Charles Ankrom. **Green fee:** $13/$24. **Credit cards:** None. **Reduced fees:** Low season, juniors. **Caddies:** No. **Golf carts:** $12. **Discount golf packages:** No. **Season:** Year-round. **High:** Jan.-March. **On site lodging:** No. **Rental clubs:** Yes. **Walking policy:** Walking at certain times. **Metal spikes allowed:** Yes. **Range:** Yes (grass). **To obtain tee times:** Call 1 day in advance for weekdays and 2 days in advance for weekends and holidays.
RED/BLUE
Par: 65/65. **Yards:** 5,062/4,057. **Course rating:** 63.9/63.4. **Slope:** N/A.
RED/WHITE
Par: 71/71. **Yards:** 6,316/4,958. **Course rating:** 70.1/67.7. **Slope:** 129/127.
WHITE/BLUE
Par: 66/66. **Yards:** 5,290/4,175. **Course rating:** 65.0/63.9. **Slope:** 113.
Subscriber comments: Good maintenance and good service...Keep the rangers in the clubhouse (very distracting)...Great course, facilities, maintenance and service...Nice course. Fast play. Good complex...Too hard...Gets a lot of use...Good dollar value.

BRAMBLE RIDGE GOLF COURSE
PU-2505 Bramble Ridge Drive, Lakeland, 33813, Polk County, (941)667-1988, 2 miles SE of Lakeland.
Opened: 1991. **Holes:** 18. **Par:** 72/72. **Yards:** 5,925/4,833. **Course rating:** 68.1/67.8.
Slope: 125/119. **Architect:** Ed Holloway. **Green fee:** $14/$16. **Credit cards:** MC,VISA,DISC. **Reduced fees:** Low season, resort guests, twilight. **Caddies:** No. **Golf**

carts: N/A. **Discount golf packages:** No. **Season:** Year-round. **High:** Jan.-March. **On site lodging:** No. **Rental clubs:** Yes. **Walking policy:** Unrestricted walking. **Metal spikes allowed:** Yes. **Range:** Yes (grass). **To obtain tee times:** Call golf shop.

★★THE BREAKERS CLUB

R-1 S. County Rd., Palm Beach, 33480, Palm Beach County, (561)659-8407, 2 miles E of West Palm Beach.
Opened: 1897. **Holes:** 18. **Par:** 70/72. **Yards:** 6,017/5,582. **Course rating:** 69.3/72.6. **Slope:** 121/122. **Architect:** Alexander Findlay. **Green fee:** $85. **Credit cards:** All major,All major. **Reduced fees:** Resort guests, twilight, juniors. **Caddies:** Yes. **Golf carts:** Included in Green Fee. **Discount golf packages:** Yes. **Season:** Year-round. **High:** Dec.-April. **On site lodging:** Yes. **Rental clubs:** Yes. **Walking policy:** Walking at certain times. **Metal spikes allowed:** Yes. **Range:** Yes (grass/mats). **To obtain tee times:** Tee times obtained 30 days in advance.

★★★BREAKERS WEST COUNTRY CLUB

1550 Flagler Pkwy., West Palm Beach, 33411, Palm Beach County, (561)653-6320, 10 miles W of Palm Beach.
Opened: 1969. **Holes:** 18. **Par:** 71/71. **Yards:** 6,905/5,385. **Course rating:** 73.9/71.1. **Slope:** 135/123. **Architect:** Willard Byrd/Joe Lee. **Green fee:** $60/$105. **Credit cards:** MC,VISA,AMEX. **Reduced fees:** N/A. **Caddies:** No. **Golf carts:** Included in Green Fee. **Discount golf packages:** Yes. **Season:** Year-round. **High:** Nov.-April. **On site lodging:** No. **Rental clubs:** Yes. **Walking policy:** Mandatory cart. **Metal spikes allowed:** Yes. **Range:** Yes (grass). **To obtain tee times:** Must be staying at Breakers Hotel or member guest to play here.
Subscriber comments: Premier resort services at premium resort prices...Challenge from blue tees...Entertaining...Needs work. Great real estate...Lots of slow play.

★★CALIFORNIA CLUB

20898 San Simeon Way, North Miami, 33179, Dade County, (305)651-3590.
Opened: N/A. **Holes:** 18. **Par:** 72/72. **Yards:** 6,670/5,675. **Course rating:** 70.9/69.7. **Slope:** 125/117. **Architect:** N/A. **Green fee:** $22/$45. **Credit cards:** MC,VISA,AMEX. **Reduced fees:** Weekdays, low season, twilight. **Caddies:** No. **Golf carts:** Included in Green Fee. **Discount golf packages:** No. **Season:** Year-round. **High:** Dec.-April. **On site lodging:** No. **Rental clubs:** Yes. **Walking policy:** Mandatory cart. **Metal spikes allowed:** Yes. **Range:** Yes (grass/mats). **To obtain tee times:** Call golf shop up to 7 days in advance.

★★★CALUSA LAKES GOLF COURSE

1995 Calusa Lakes Blvd., Nokomis, 34275, Sarasota County, (941)484-8995, 5 miles S of Sarasota.
Opened: 1991. **Holes:** 18. **Par:** 72/72. **Yards:** 6,760/5,197. **Course rating:** N/A. **Slope:** 124/118. **Architect:** Ted McAnlis. **Green fee:** $27/$46. **Credit cards:** MC,VISA. **Reduced fees:** Low season, twilight. **Caddies:** No. **Golf carts:** Included in Green Fee. **Discount golf packages:** No. **Season:** Year-round. **High:** Jan.-April. **On site lodging:** No. **Rental clubs:** No. **Walking policy:** Walking at certain times. **Metal spikes allowed:** Yes. **Range:** Yes (grass/mats). **To obtain tee times:** Call 2 days in advance.
Subscriber comments: Nice greens...Good off-season bargain...Good challenge for all levels...Very playable, even from the tips.

★★★CAPE CORAL GOLF & TENNIS RESORT

R-4003 Palm Tree Blvd., Cape Coral, 33904, Lee County, (941)542-7879, (800)848-1475, 10 miles SE of Fort Myers.
Opened: 1963. **Holes:** 18. **Par:** 72/72. **Yards:** 6,707/5,152. **Course rating:** 72.0/71.2. **Slope:** 127/119. **Architect:** Dick Wilson. **Green fee:** $17/$60. **Credit cards:** All major. **Reduced fees:** Low season, resort guests, twilight, juniors. **Caddies:** No. **Golf carts:** Included in Green Fee. **Discount golf packages:** Yes. **Season:** Year-round. **High:** Jan.-March. **On site lodging:** Yes. **Rental clubs:** Yes. **Walking policy:** Mandatory cart. **Metal spikes allowed:** Yes. **Range:** Yes (grass/mats). **To obtain tee times:** Call 3 days in advance after 4 p.m.
Notes: 1972 NCAA Division I Golf Championship.
Subscriber comments: Terrifice resort course. Well bunkered...Lots of sand...Good vacation golf...Fun.

★★★CAPRI ISLES GOLF CLUB
849 Capri Isles Blvd., Venice, 34292, Sarasota County, (941)485-3371, 60 miles S of Tampa.
Opened: 1972. **Holes:** 18. **Par:** 72/72. **Yards:** 6,472/5,480. **Course rating:** 70.6/70.9. **Slope:** 122/116. **Architect:** Andy Anderson. **Green fee:** $41. **Credit cards:** MC,VISA. **Reduced fees:** Low season, twilight. **Caddies:** No. **Golf carts:** Included in Green Fee. **Discount golf packages:** No. **Season:** Year-round. **High:** Jan.-April. **On site lodging:** No. **Rental clubs:** Yes. **Walking policy:** Walking at certain times. **Metal spikes allowed:** Yes. **Range:** Yes (grass). **To obtain tee times:** Call up to 3 days ahead.
Subscriber comments: Good place to start a Florida golf vacation...Enjoyed course and services. Priced right...Short course. Lots of hazards, tight fairways.

★★★CELEBRATION GOLF CLUB
R-701 Golf Park Dr., Celebration, 34747, Osceola County, (407)566-4653, (888)275-2918, 15 miles S of Orlando.
Opened: 1996. **Holes:** 18. **Par:** 72/72. **Yards:** 6,786/5,724. **Course rating:** 72.7/68.0. **Slope:** 129/115. **Architect:** Robert Trent Jones/Robert Trent Jones Jr. **Green fee:** $55/$105. **Credit cards:** MC,VISA,AMEX. **Reduced fees:** Low season, twilight, juniors. **Caddies:** No. **Golf carts:** Included in Green Fee. **Discount golf packages:** No. **Season:** Year-round. **High:** Jan.-April. **On site lodging:** No. **Rental clubs:** Yes. **Walking policy:** Walking at certain times. **Metal spikes allowed:** Yes. **Range:** Yes (grass). **To obtain tee times:** Call up to 60 days in advance.
Subscriber comments: Should improve with age...Short. Needs good course management....Tougher than its length.

★★★½CHAMPIONS CLUB AT JULINGTON CREEK
1111 Durbin Creek Blvd., Jacksonville, 32259, St. Johns County, (904)287-4653, 15 miles S of Jacksonville.
Opened: 1992. **Holes:** 18. **Par:** 72/72. **Yards:** 6,872/4,994. **Course rating:** 72.8/68.6. **Slope:** 126/114. **Architect:** Bob Walker/Steve Melynk. **Green fee:** $30/$40. **Credit cards:** MC,VISA,DISC. **Reduced fees:** Weekdays, twilight, seniors, juniors. **Caddies:** No. **Golf carts:** Included in Green Fee. **Discount golf packages:** No. **Season:** Year-round. **High:** March-May/Oct.-Dec. **On site lodging:** No. **Rental clubs:** Yes. **Walking policy:** Mandatory cart. **Metal spikes allowed:** No. **Range:** Yes (grass). **To obtain tee times:** Call golf shop 5 days in advance for outside guest play.
Subscriber comments: Really liked this course...Good golf, slick greens...Good front nine. Back nine contrived...Keep ball in fairway (a lot of OB)...Excellent par 3s...Well maintained...Nice and secluded.

★★★½THE CHAMPIONS CLUB AT SUMMERFIELD
PU-3400 S.E. Summerfield Way, Stuart, 34997, Martin County, (561)283-1500, 25 miles N of West Palm Beach.
Opened: 1994. **Holes:** 18. **Par:** 72/72. **Yards:** 6,809/4,941. **Course rating:** 72.8/71.0. **Slope:** 131/120. **Architect:** Tom Fazio. **Green fee:** $20/$58. **Credit cards:** MC,VISA,DISC. **Reduced fees:** Weekdays, low season, resort guests, twilight, juniors. **Caddies:** No. **Golf carts:** Included in Green Fee. **Discount golf packages:** Yes. **Season:** Year-round. **High:** Nov.-April. **On site lodging:** No. **Rental clubs:** Yes. **Walking policy:** Mandatory cart. **Metal spikes allowed:** Yes. **Range:** Yes (grass). **To obtain tee times:** Call up to 7 days in advance.
Subscriber comments: Most enjoyable...Wonderful layout. Smart design. Playable...Forgiving, wide fairways. Great greens. Play there a lot...Beautiful, accessible, playable, quiet...Good track, good location...A Fazio gem you can afford...Scenic course, marred by distance between holes...Embedded in nature.

★★★½CHI CHI RODRIGUEZ GOLF CLUB
PU-3030 McMullen Booth Rd., Clearwater, 34621, Pinellas County, (813)726-8829, 15 miles W of Tampa.
Opened: 1989. **Holes:** 18. **Par:** 69/71. **Yards:** 5,454/3,929. **Course rating:** 67.6/64.0. **Slope:** 118/110. **Architect:** Denis Griffiths. **Green fee:** $22/$25. **Credit cards:** MC,VISA,DISC. **Reduced fees:** Twilight. **Caddies:** No. **Golf carts:** Included in Green Fee. **Discount golf packages:** Yes. **Season:** Year-round. **High:** Feb.-April. **On site lodging:** No. **Rental clubs:** Yes. **Walking policy:** Walking at certain times. **Metal**

spikes allowed: Yes. **Range:** No. **To obtain tee times:** Call 4 days in advance. **Subscriber comments:** Short, but hilly and tight...Needs some work on fairways...Club selection important...A bit narrow...A fun test if you're not the longest hitter.

★★★½CIMARRONE GOLF & COUNTRY CLUB

2690 Cimarrone Blvd., Jacksonville, 32259, Duval County, (904)287-2000, 22 miles S of Jacksonville.

Opened: 1989. **Holes:** 18. **Par:** 72/72. **Yards:** 6,891/4,707. **Course rating:** N/A. **Slope:** 128/119. **Architect:** David Postlethwait. **Green fee:** $29/$40. **Credit cards:** MC,VISA. **Reduced fees:** Weekdays, low season, twilight, juniors. **Caddies:** No. **Golf carts:** Included in Green Fee. **Discount golf packages:** Yes. **Season:** Year-round. **High:** Spring/Fall. **On site lodging:** No. **Rental clubs:** No. **Walking policy:** Mandatory cart. **Metal spikes allowed:** Yes. **Range:** Yes (grass). **To obtain tee times:** Call up to 4 days in advance.

Subscriber comments: Very nice...Difficult from back tee when wind blows...Quite a challenge with all the water...Upgraded facilities...More rolling and hilly than most Florida courses...Bring your ball retriever...Scenic and challenging...Wonderful greens...Beautiful clubhouse...Out of the way.

Special Notes: Only members may walk course.

CITRUS HILLS GOLF & COUNTRY CLUB

509 E. Hartford St., Hernando, 34442, Citrus County, (352)746-4425, 90 miles N of Tampa.

Green fee: $14/$35. **Credit cards:** All major. **Reduced fees:** Low season, twilight. **Caddies:** No. **Golf carts:** Included in Green Fee. **Discount golf packages:** Yes. **Season:** Year-round. **High:** Dec.-April. **On site lodging:** Yes. **Rental clubs:** No. **Metal spikes allowed:** Yes.

★★★½OAKS COURSE

Opened: 1985. **Holes:** 18. **Par:** 70/70. **Yards:** 6,323/4,647. **Course rating:** 71.0/67.0. **Slope:** 121/114. **Architect:** Mike Andrijiszyn. **Walking policy:** Mandatory cart. **Range:** Yes (grass/mats). **To obtain tee times:** Call 3 days in advance.

Subscriber comments: Challenging layout, excellent value and service...Tough challenge...Outstanding...Tight fairways...Relatively short.

★★★MEADOWS COURSE

Opened: 1983. **Holes:** 18. **Par:** 70/70. **Yards:** 5,885/4,585. **Course rating:** 68.5/66.9. **Slope:** 114/112. **Architect:** Phil Friel. **Walking policy:** Walking at certain times. **Range:** Yes (grass). **To obtain tee times:** Call up to 3 days in advance.

Subscriber comments: Nice greens...Just too open and easy...Easy but fun.

★★★CITRUS SPRINGS COUNTRY CLUB

8690 Golfview Dr., Citrus Springs, 32630, Citrus County, (352)489-5045, 4 miles S of Dunellon.

Opened: 1972. **Holes:** 18. **Par:** 72/72. **Yards:** 6,600/6,242. **Course rating:** 72.0/71.0. **Slope:** 126/118. **Architect:** N/A. **Green fee:** $28. **Credit cards:** MC,VISA. **Reduced fees:** Low season. **Caddies:** No. **Golf carts:** Included in Green Fee. **Discount golf packages:** No. **Season:** Year-round. **High:** Nov.-April. **On site lodging:** No. **Rental clubs:** Yes. **Walking policy:** Mandatory cart. **Metal spikes allowed:** Yes. **Range:** Yes (grass). **To obtain tee times:** Call up to 5 days in advance.

Subscriber comments: A real test...Could be longer...A very enjoyable resort course.

★★CLEARWATER COUNTRY CLUB

525 N. Betty Lane, Clearwater, 33755, Pinellas County, (813)443-5078, 20 miles W of Tampa.

Opened: 1922. **Holes:** 18. **Par:** 72/72. **Yards:** 6,231/5,202. **Course rating:** 69.4/69.7. **Slope:** 123/118. **Architect:** N/A. **Green fee:** $20/$50. **Credit cards:** None. **Reduced fees:** Weekdays, low season, twilight. **Caddies:** No. **Golf carts:** Included in Green Fee. **Discount golf packages:** No. **Season:** Year-round. **High:** Jan.-March. **On site lodging:** No. **Rental clubs:** Yes. **Walking policy:** Walking at certain times. **Metal spikes allowed:** Yes. **Range:** Yes (grass). **To obtain tee times:** Call golf shop 3 days in advance.

CLERBROOK RESORT
R-20005 U.S. Hwy. 27, Clermont, 34711, Lake County, (352)394-6165, 20 miles W of Orlando.
Opened: 1984. **Holes:** 18. **Par:** 67/67. **Yards:** 5,154/4,140. **Course rating:** 64.8/64.8. **Slope:** 108/105. **Architect:** Dean Refram. **Green fee:** $13/$25. **Credit cards:** MC,VISA,DISC. **Reduced fees:** Low season, resort guests, twilight, juniors. **Caddies:** No. **Golf carts:** $14. **Discount golf packages:** No. **Season:** Year-round. **High:** Nov.-March. **On site lodging:** Yes. **Rental clubs:** Yes. **Walking policy:** Walking at certain times. **Metal spikes allowed:** Yes. **Range:** Yes (grass/mats). **To obtain tee times:** Call up to 5 days in advance.

CLEVELAND HEIGHTS GOLF & COUNTRY CLUB
PM-2900 Buckingham Ave., Lakeland, 33803, Polk County, (941)682-3277, 45 miles E of Tampa.
Opened: 1925. **Architect:** N/A. **Green fee:** $21/$23. **Credit cards:** None. **Reduced fees:** N/A. **Caddies:** No. **Golf carts:** $12. **Discount golf packages:** No. **Season:** Year-round. **High:** Dec.-March. **On site lodging:** No. **Rental clubs:** No. **Walking policy:** Walking at certain times. **Metal spikes allowed:** Yes. **Range:** No. **To obtain tee times:** Call up to 3 days in advance.
A/B
Holes: 27. **Par:** 72/72. **Yards:** 6,378/5,389. **Course rating:** 70.3/70.1. **Slope:** 118/116.
A/C
Holes: 27. **Par:** 72/72. **Yards:** 6,517/5,546. **Course rating:** 71.0/71.5. **Slope:** 120/115.
B/C
Holes: 27. **Par:** 72/72. **Yards:** 6,459/5,455. **Course rating:** 70.3/70.8. **Slope:** 119/116.

CLEWISTON GOLF COURSE
PM-1200 San Luis Rd., Clewiston, 33440, Hendry County, (941)983-1448.
Opened: N/A. **Holes:** 18. **Par:** 72/72. **Yards:** 6,353/5,052. **Course rating:** 70.6/69.7. **Slope:** 120/116. **Architect:** N/A. **Green fee:** $3/$19. **Credit cards:** None. **Reduced fees:** N/A. **Caddies:** No. **Golf carts:** $21. **Discount golf packages:** No. **Season:** Year-round. **High:** N/A. **On site lodging:** No. **Rental clubs:** Yes. **Walking policy:** Unrestricted walking. **Metal spikes allowed:** Yes. **Range:** Yes. **To obtain tee times:** Call up to 3 days in advance.

THE CLUB AT EAGLEBROOKE
1300 Eaglebrooke Blvd., Lakeland, 33813, Polk County, (941)701-0101, 30 miles NE of Tampa.
Opened: 1997. **Holes:** 18. **Par:** 72/72. **Yards:** 7,005/4,981. **Course rating:** 74.0/69.0. **Slope:** 136/115. **Architect:** Ron Garl. **Green fee:** $36/$46. **Credit cards:** MC,VISA,AMEX. **Reduced fees:** Weekdays, low season, juniors. **Caddies:** No. **Golf carts:** $11. **Discount golf packages:** No. **Season:** Year-round. **High:** Nov.-April. **On site lodging:** No. **Rental clubs:** Yes. **Walking policy:** Walking at certain times. **Metal spikes allowed:** Yes. **Range:** Yes (grass). **To obtain tee times:** Call 2 days in advance.

★★★½THE CLUB AT EMERALD HILLS
4100 N. Hills Dr., Hollywood, 33021, Broward County, (954)961-4000, 5 miles S of Ft. Lauderdale.
Opened: 1969. **Holes:** 18. **Par:** 72/72. **Yards:** 7,003/5,032. **Course rating:** 74.1/70.1. **Slope:** 133/116. **Architect:** Bruce Devlin/Robert von Hagge/Chuck Ankrom. **Green fee:** $5/$70. **Credit cards:** MC,VISA,AMEX. **Reduced fees:** Weekdays, low season. **Caddies:** No. **Golf carts:** $25. **Discount golf packages:** No. **Season:** Year-round. **High:** Dec.-April. **On site lodging:** No. **Rental clubs:** Yes. **Walking policy:** Mandatory cart. **Metal spikes allowed:** No. **Range:** Yes (grass). **To obtain tee times:** Call up to 5 days in advance.
Subscriber comments: Lots of sand and water...Very challenging...Classy operation.

★★★½THE CLUB AT HIDDEN CREEK
3070 PGA Blvd., Navarre, 32566, Santa Rosa County, (904)939-4604, 20 miles E of Pensacola.
Opened: 1988. **Holes:** 18. **Par:** 72/72. **Yards:** 6,862/5,213. **Course rating:** 73.2/70.1.

Slope: 139/124. **Architect:** Ron Garl. **Green fee:** $25/$50. **Credit cards:**
MC,VISA,AMEX. **Reduced fees:** Weekdays, low season, twilight, juniors. **Caddies:** No.
Golf carts: Included in Green Fee. **Discount golf packages:** Yes. **Season:** Year-round.
High: Jan.-April. **On site lodging:** No. **Rental clubs:** Yes. **Walking policy:** Mandatory
cart. **Metal spikes allowed:** Yes. **Range:** Yes (grass). **To obtain tee times:** Call up to 7
days in advance.
Subscriber comments: Very challenging to average player...Tough from back tees.

★★★THE CLUB AT OAK FORD
PU-1552 Palm View Rd., Sarasota, 34240, Sarasota County, (941)371-3680, (888)881-
3673, 60 miles S of Tampa.
Opened: 1989. **Holes:** 27. **Architect:** Ron Garl. **Green fee:** $15/$45. **Credit cards:**
MC,VISA. **Reduced fees:** Low season. **Caddies:** No. **Golf carts:** Included in Green
Fee. **Discount golf packages:** Yes. **Season:** Year-round. **High:** Jan.-April. **On site
lodging:** No. **Rental clubs:** Yes. **Walking policy:** Mandatory cart. **Metal spikes
allowed:** Yes. **Range:** Yes (grass). **To obtain tee times:** Call up to 7 days in advance.
MYRTLE/LIVE OAK
Par: 72/72. **Yards:** 6,750/5,085. **Course rating:** 72.7/69.0. **Slope:** 131/118.
MYRTLE/PALMS
Par: 72/72. **Yards:** 6,750/5,085. **Course rating:** 72.7/69.0. **Slope:** 131/118.
PALMS/LIVE OAK
Par: 72/72. **Yards:** 6,750/5,085. **Course rating:** 72.7/69.0. **Slope:** 131/118.
Subscriber comments: Fun to play...Too short...Excellent setting...In wildlife pre-
serve...Good target golf...Out of the way.

★★★THE CLUB AT WINSTON TRAILS
6101 Winston Trails Blvd., Lake Worth, 33463, Palm Beach County, (561)439-3700, 15
miles S of West Palm Beach.
Opened: 1993. **Holes:** 18. **Par:** 72/72. **Yards:** 6,835/5,405. **Course rating:** 72.8/71.1.
Slope: 123/117. **Architect:** Joe Lee. **Green fee:** $30/$75. **Credit cards:**
MC,VISA,AMEX. **Reduced fees:** Weekdays, low season, twilight. **Caddies:** No. **Golf
carts:** Included in Green Fee. **Discount golf packages:** Yes. **Season:** Year-round.
High: March-Nov. **On site lodging:** No. **Rental clubs:** Yes. **Walking policy:** Mandatory
cart. **Metal spikes allowed:** Yes. **Range:** Yes (grass/mats). **To obtain tee times:** Call 2
days in advance.
Subscriber comments: Wide open. Good to build confidence in driver...Many holes
are similar...Will be much better in a few years.
Special Notes: Formerly Winston Trails Golf Club.

CLUB MED SANDPIPER
R-3500 S.E. Morningside Blvd., Port St. Lucie, 34952, St. Lucie County, (561)337-6638,
35 miles N of West Palm Beach.
Opened: 1961. **Architect:** Mark Mahannah. **Green fee:** $25/$45. **Credit cards:**
MC,VISA,AMEX. **Reduced fees:** Low season, juniors. **Caddies:** No. **Golf carts:**
Included in Green Fee. **Discount golf packages:** Yes. **Season:** Year-round. **High:**
Dec.-April. **On site lodging:** Yes. **Rental clubs:** Yes. **Walking policy:** Mandatory cart.
Metal spikes allowed: Yes. **Range:** Yes (grass). **To obtain tee times:** Call up to 24
hours in advance.
★★SAINTS COURSE
Holes: 18. **Par:** 72/72. **Yards:** 6,478/5,379. **Course rating:** 70.7/71.3. **Slope:** 120/119.
★★SINNERS COURSE
Holes: 18. **Par:** 72/72. **Yards:** 6,888/5,384. **Course rating:** 72.3/71.1. **Slope:** 123/116.

★★★COCOA BEACH GOLF COURSE
PM-5000 Tom Warriner Blvd., Cocoa Beach, 32931, Brevard County, (407)868-3351,
40 miles E of Orlando.
Opened: 1992. **Holes:** 27. **Architect:** Charles Ankrom. **Green fee:** $17/$27. **Credit
cards:** MC,VISA. **Reduced fees:** Weekdays, low season, twilight, juniors. **Caddies:** No.
Golf carts: $8. **Discount golf packages:** No. **Season:** Year-round. **High:** Dec.-April.
On site lodging: No. **Rental clubs:** Yes. **Walking policy:** Walking at certain times.
Metal spikes allowed: Yes. **Range:** Yes (grass). **To obtain tee times:** Call 4 days in
advance after 4 p.m.

DOLPHIN/LAKES
Par: 71/71. **Yards:** 6,393/4,985. **Course rating:** 70.1/68.0. **Slope:** 115/109.
RIVER/DOLPHIN
Par: 71/71. **Yards:** 6,363/4,903. **Course rating:** 69.9/67.5. **Slope:** 116/108.
RIVER/LAKES
Par: 72/72. **Yards:** 6,714/5,294. **Course rating:** 71.7/69.3. **Slope:** 119/113.
Subscriber comments: Great value in summertime...Nice course...Good, solid golf experience...Typical Florida muny...Very nice layout on river.

★★★½COLONY WEST COUNTRY CLUB
PU-6800 N.W. 88th Ave., Tamarac, 33321, Broward County, (954)726-8430, 10 miles W of Fort Lauderdale.
Opened: 1970. **Holes:** 18. **Par:** 71/71. **Yards:** 7,271/5,422. **Course rating:** 75.8/71.6. **Slope:** 138/127. **Architect:** Bruce Devlin/Robert von Hagge. **Green fee:** $35/$70. **Credit cards:** MC,VISA,AMEX. **Reduced fees:** Weekdays, low season, twilight. **Caddies:** No. **Golf carts:** Included in Green Fee. **Discount golf packages:** Yes. **Season:** Year-round. **High:** Dec.-April. **On site lodging:** No. **Rental clubs:** Yes. **Walking policy:** Mandatory cart. **Metal spikes allowed:** Yes. **Range:** No. **To obtain tee times:** Call golf shop.
Subscriber comments: A must play...You will come back...Not easy...Long and tough...I make sure to always leave time for this one...Bring your A game...Will play it again...Condos surround otherwise nice course.
Special Notes: Also 18-hole par-65 Glades Course.

★★CONTINENTAL COUNTRY CLUB
50 Continental Blvd., Wildwood, 34785, Sumter County, (352)748-3293, 5 miles W of Leesburg.
Opened: N/A. **Holes:** 18. **Par:** 72/73. **Yards:** 6,461/5,438. **Course rating:** 70.1/71.1. **Slope:** 123/122. **Architect:** Ron Garl. **Green fee:** $20/$35. **Credit cards:** MC,VISA,DISC. **Reduced fees:** Low season, twilight. **Caddies:** No. **Golf carts:** Included in Green Fee. **Discount golf packages:** No. **Season:** Year-round. **High:** Nov.-May. **On site lodging:** No. **Rental clubs:** Yes. **Walking policy:** Mandatory cart. **Metal spikes allowed:** Yes. **Range:** Yes (grass). **To obtain tee times:** Call up to 2 days in advance.

CONTINENTAL GOLF CLUB AT CORAL SPRINGS
9001 W. Sample Rd., Coral Springs, 33065, Broward County, (305)752-2140, 20 miles N of Ft. Lauderdale.
Opened: 1965. **Holes:** 18. **Par:** 69/70. **Yards:** 5,659/4,874. **Course rating:** 67.3/64.9. **Slope:** 120/114. **Architect:** Bill Watts/Edmund B. Ault. **Green fee:** $12/$26. **Credit cards:** MC,VISA,AMEX. **Reduced fees:** Low season. **Caddies:** No. **Golf carts:** Included in Green Fee. **Discount golf packages:** No. **Season:** Year-round. **High:** Nov.-April. **On site lodging:** No. **Rental clubs:** Yes. **Walking policy:** Mandatory cart. **Metal spikes allowed:** Yes. **Range:** No. **To obtain tee times:** Call two days in advance.

★★★½CORAL OAKS GOLF COURSE
PU-1800 N.W. 28th Ave., Cape Coral, 33993, Lee County, (941)283-4100, 12 miles NW of Ft. Myers.
Opened: 1988. **Holes:** 18. **Par:** 72/72. **Yards:** 6,623/4,803. **Course rating:** 71.7/68.9. **Slope:** 123/117. **Architect:** Arthur Hills. **Green fee:** $22/$27. **Credit cards:** All major. **Reduced fees:** Low season. **Caddies:** No. **Golf carts:** $14. **Discount golf packages:** Yes. **Season:** Year-round. **High:** Dec.-April. **On site lodging:** No. **Rental clubs:** Yes. **Walking policy:** Walking at certain times. **Metal spikes allowed:** Yes. **Range:** Yes (grass). **To obtain tee times:** Call 2 days in advance.
Subscriber comments: Solid muny...Mature...Nice layout.

COSTA DEL SOL GOLF & CC
100 Costa Del Sol Blvd, Miami, 33178, Dade County, (305)592-9210.
Opened: 1973. **Holes:** 18. **Par:** 72/72. **Yards:** 6,400/5,487. **Course rating:** 70.0/70.2. **Slope:** 118/115. **Architect:** Robert Cupp. **Green fee:** $16/$25. **Credit cards:** MC,VISA. **Reduced fees:** Weekdays, low season, twilight. **Caddies:** No. **Golf carts:** Included in Green Fee. **Discount golf packages:** No. **Season:** Year-round. **High:** Nov.-April. **On**

site lodging: No. **Rental clubs:** Yes. **Walking policy:** Mandatory cart. **Metal spikes allowed:** Yes. **Range:** Yes (grass). **To obtain tee times:** Call up to 7 days in advance.

★★★½THE COUNTRY CLUB AT SILVER SPRINGS SHORES

565 Silver Rd., Ocala, 34472, Marion County, (904)687-2828, 69 miles NW of Orlando.
Opened: 1969. **Holes:** 18. **Par:** 72/72. **Yards:** 6,857/5,188. **Course rating:** 73.7/70.2.
Slope: 131/120. **Architect:** Desmond Muirhead. **Green fee:** $16/$39. **Credit cards:** All major. **Reduced fees:** Low season, twilight. **Caddies:** No. **Golf carts:** Included in Green Fee. **Discount golf packages:** Yes. **Season:** Year-round. **High:** Dec.-April. **On site lodging:** No. **Rental clubs:** Yes. **Walking policy:** Mandatory cart. **Metal spikes allowed:** Yes. **Range:** Yes (grass). **To obtain tee times:** Call up to 7 days in advance.
Subscriber comments: Fun to play...Slow at times...Very pretty...Watch for water.

★★★COUNTRY CLUB OF MOUNT DORA

1900 Country Club Blvd., Mount Dora, 32757, Lake County, (352)735-2263, 90 miles S of Orlando.
Opened: 1991. **Holes:** 18. **Par:** 72/72. **Yards:** 6,571/5,002. **Course rating:** 72.1/71.0.
Slope: 125/120. **Architect:** Lloyd Clifton. **Green fee:** $22/$45. **Credit cards:** MC,VISA.
Reduced fees: Weekdays, low season, resort guests, twilight. **Caddies:** No. **Golf carts:** Included in Green Fee. **Discount golf packages:** Yes. **Season:** Year-round.
High: Jan.-March. **On site lodging:** No. **Rental clubs:** Yes. **Walking policy:** Mandatory cart. **Metal spikes allowed:** Yes. **Range:** Yes (grass/mats). **To obtain tee times:** Call 5 days in advance.
Subscriber comments: Nice course in residential setting...Enjoyed playing here.

★★★COUNTRY CLUB OF SEBRING

4800 Haw Branch Rd., Sebring, 33872, Highlands County, (941)382-3500, 90 miles S of Orlando.
Opened: 1984. **Holes:** 18. **Par:** 71/71. **Yards:** 6,722/4,938. **Course rating:** 72.0/67.7.
Slope: 124/112. **Architect:** Ron Garl. **Green fee:** $10/$40. **Credit cards:** All major.
Reduced fees: Twilight. **Caddies:** No. **Golf carts:** Included in Green Fee. **Discount golf packages:** No. **Season:** Year-round. **High:** Nov.-April. **On site lodging:** No.
Rental clubs: Yes. **Walking policy:** Mandatory cart. **Metal spikes allowed:** Yes.
Range: Yes (grass). **To obtain tee times:** Call 48 hours in advance Nov.-April. Call up to 7 days in advance May-Oct.
Subscriber comments: Interesting course. Lots of sand...A great little woodland course...Good contrast between two nines.

★★½THE COURSE AT WESTLAND

PU-7502 Plantation Bay Dr., Jacksonville, 32244, Duval County, (904)778-4653, 10 miles S of Jacksonville.
Opened: 1974. **Holes:** 18. **Par:** 71/71. **Yards:** 6,347/5,380. **Course rating:** 70.3/71.2.
Slope: 121/118. **Architect:** Lloyd Clifton. **Green fee:** $18/$35. **Credit cards:** All major,ATM Debit Cards. **Reduced fees:** Weekdays, low season, twilight, seniors, juniors. **Caddies:** No. **Golf carts:** Included in Green Fee. **Discount golf packages:** No.
Season: Year-round. **High:** Feb.-May. **On site lodging:** No. **Rental clubs:** Yes.
Walking policy: Mandatory cart. **Metal spikes allowed:** Yes. **Range:** Yes (grass). **To obtain tee times:** Call up to 30 days in advance.

★★★★CRANDON GOLF AT KEY BISCAYNE

PU-6700 Crandon Blvd., Key Biscayne, 33149, Dade County, (305)361-9129, 7 miles S of Miami.
Opened: 1972. **Holes:** 18. **Par:** 72/72. **Yards:** 7,107/5,722. **Course rating:** 75.2/73.1.
Slope: 139/129. **Architect:** Robert von Hagge/Bruce Devlin. **Green fee:** $45/$90.
Credit cards: MC,VISA,AMEX. **Reduced fees:** Weekdays, low season, twilight.
Caddies: No. **Golf carts:** Included in Green Fee. **Discount golf packages:** No.
Season: Year-round. **High:** Dec.-May. **On site lodging:** No. **Rental clubs:** Yes.
Walking policy: Walking at certain times. **Metal spikes allowed:** Yes. **Range:** Yes (grass). **To obtain tee times:** Call up to 5 days in advance.
Notes: Ranked 22nd in 1997 Best in State. PGA Senior Tour Royal Carribean Classic since 1987.

Subscriber comments: Spectacular layout, especially holes along the bay...A real pretty location...Great challenge: lots of wind, water and sand...Outstanding.
Special Notes: Formerly Links at Key Biscayne.

CREEKSIDE GOLF CLUB

PU-5555 Esperanto Dr., Pensacola, 32526, Escambia County, (904)944-7969, 60 miles E of Mobile.
Opened: 1972. **Holes:** 18. **Par:** 72/72. **Yards:** 6,107/4,741. **Course rating:** 69.6/66.8.
Slope: 119/113. **Architect:** N/A. **Green fee:** $15/$15. **Credit cards:** MC,VISA.
Reduced fees: Weekdays, twilight, seniors, juniors. **Caddies:** No. **Golf carts:** $10.
Discount golf packages: No. **Season:** Year-round. **High:** N/A. **On site lodging:** No.
Rental clubs: Yes. **Walking policy:** Walking at certain times. **Metal spikes allowed:** Yes. **Range:** No. **To obtain tee times:** Call 2 days in advance.

CRYSTAL LAKE COUNTRY CLUB

SP-3800 Crystal Lake Dr., Pompano Beach, 33064, Broward County, (954)942-1900, 5 miles N of Fort Lauderdale.
Architect: Rees Jones. **Credit cards:** MC,VISA,AMEX. **Reduced fees:** Low season, twilight. **Caddies:** No. **Golf carts:** Included in Green Fee. **Discount golf packages:** No. **Season:** Year-round. **High:** Nov.-April. **On site lodging:** No. **Rental clubs:** Yes. **Walking policy:** Mandatory cart. **Metal spikes allowed:** Yes. **To obtain tee times:** Call 2 days in advance.
★★½**SOUTH COURSE**
(305)943-2902.
Opened: 1963. **Holes:** 18. **Par:** 72/72. **Yards:** 6,610/5,458. **Course rating:** 71.7/71.5.
Slope: 120/121. **Green fee:** $28/$55. **Range:** Yes (Mats).
Subscriber comments: A little tight...Has come a long way in last five years.
★★½**TAM O'SHANTER NORTH COURSE**
(305)942-1900.
Opened: 1967. **Holes:** 18. **Par:** 70/72. **Yards:** 6,390/5,205. **Course rating:** 71.0/70.0.
Slope: 121/118. **Green fee:** $28/$48. **Range:** No.
Subscriber comments: Fun resort course.

★★½CYPRESS CREEK COUNTRY CLUB

9400 N. Military Trail, Boynton Beach, 33436, Palm Beach County, (561)727-4202, 10 miles S of West Palm Beach.
Opened: 1964. **Holes:** 18. **Par:** 72/72. **Yards:** 6,808/5,425. **Course rating:** 72.0/67.1.
Slope: 129/109. **Architect:** Robert von Hagge. **Green fee:** $20/$50. **Credit cards:** MC,VISA. **Reduced fees:** Weekdays, low season. **Caddies:** No. **Golf carts:** Included in Green Fee. **Discount golf packages:** Yes. **Season:** Year-round. **High:** Nov.-April. **On site lodging:** No. **Rental clubs:** Yes. **Walking policy:** Mandatory cart. **Metal spikes allowed:** Yes. **Range:** Yes (grass). **To obtain tee times:** Call 24 hours in advance at 7 a.m.

DAYTONA BEACH GOLF COURSE

PM-600 Wilder Blvd., Daytona Beach, 32114, Volusia County, (904)258-3119.
Green fee: $10/$12. **Credit cards:** MC,VISA. **Reduced fees:** Weekdays, low season, twilight. **Caddies:** No. **Golf carts:** $14. **Discount golf packages:** No. **Season:** Year-round. **High:** Nov.-May. **On site lodging:** No. **Rental clubs:** No. **Walking policy:** Unrestricted walking. **Metal spikes allowed:** Yes. **Range:** Yes (Mats). **To obtain tee times:** Call 2 days in advance.
★★½**NORTH COURSE**
Opened: 1965. **Holes:** 18. **Par:** 72/72. **Yards:** 6,338/4,938. **Course rating:** 71.0/69.1.
Slope: 111/111. **Architect:** Lloyd Clifton.
Subscriber comments: Fun golf...Flat, easy walking.
★★**SOUTH COURSE**
Opened: 1921. **Holes:** 18. **Par:** 71/71. **Yards:** 6,229/5,346. **Course rating:** 69.7/69.6.
Slope: 106/106. **Architect:** Donald Ross.

★★★½DEBARY GOLF & COUNTRY CLUB

300 Plantation Dr., DeBary, 32713, Volusia County, (407)668-2061, 15 miles N of Orlando.
Opened: 1990. **Holes:** 18. **Par:** 72/72. **Yards:** 6,776/5,060. **Course rating:** 72.3/68.8.

Slope: 128/122. **Architect:** Lloyd Clifton. **Green fee:** $19/$60. **Credit cards:** MC,VISA,AMEX. **Reduced fees:** Low season, twilight, juniors. **Caddies:** No. **Golf carts:** Included in Green Fee. **Discount golf packages:** Yes. **Season:** Year-round. **High:** Feb.-April. **On site lodging:** No. **Rental clubs:** Yes. **Walking policy:** Mandatory cart. **Metal spikes allowed:** Yes. **Range:** Yes (grass). **To obtain tee times:** Call up to 7 days in advance.
Subscriber comments: Tight but fair...Very good course...Lose the OB stakes.

★★½DEEP CREEK GOLF CLUB
1260 San Cristobal Ave., Port Charlotte, 33983, Charlotte County, (941)625-6911, 25 miles N of Fort Myers.
Opened: 1985. **Holes:** 18. **Par:** 70/70. **Yards:** 6,005/4,860. **Course rating:** 67.5/68.0. **Slope:** 112/110. **Architect:** Mark McCumber. **Green fee:** $16/$24. **Credit cards:** MC,VISA. **Reduced fees:** Weekdays, low season, twilight, seniors, juniors. **Caddies:** No. **Golf carts:** $10. **Discount golf packages:** No. **Season:** Year-round. **High:** Dec.-April. **On site lodging:** No. **Rental clubs:** Yes. **Walking policy:** Walking at certain times. **Metal spikes allowed:** Yes. **Range:** Yes (grass). **To obtain tee times:** Call up to 48 hours in advance.
Subscriber comments: Lots of water...Wind can make a big difference...Typical Florida course.

★★★½DEER CREEK GOLF CLUB
2801 Country Club Blvd., Deerfield Beach, 33442, Broward County, (954)421-5550, 6 miles N of Fort Lauderdale.
Opened: 1971. **Holes:** 18. **Par:** 72/72. **Yards:** 7,038/5,319. **Course rating:** 74.8/71.6. **Slope:** 133/120. **Architect:** Bill Watts/Arthur Hills. **Green fee:** $39/$110. **Credit cards:** MC,VISA,AMEX. **Reduced fees:** Weekdays, low season, resort guests, twilight, juniors. **Caddies:** No. **Golf carts:** Included in Green Fee. **Discount golf packages:** Yes. **Season:** Year-round. **High:** Dec.-April. **On site lodging:** No. **Rental clubs:** Yes. **Walking policy:** Unrestricted walking. **Metal spikes allowed:** Yes. **Range:** Yes (grass). **To obtain tee times:** Call 3 days in advance.
Subscriber comments: Enjoyable...Excellent experience. I keep coming back...One of the most enjoyable courses I play in South Florida.

★★★DEER ISLAND GOLF CLUB
17450 Deer Island Rd., Tavares, 32778, Lake County, (352)343-7550, (800)269-0006, 30 miles NW of Orlando.
Opened: 1994. **Holes:** 18. **Par:** 72/72. **Yards:** 6,676/5,298. **Course rating:** 73.1/71.0. **Slope:** 137/118. **Architect:** Joe Lee. **Green fee:** $25/$45. **Credit cards:** MC,VISA. **Reduced fees:** Weekdays, twilight, seniors. **Caddies:** No. **Golf carts:** Included in Green Fee. **Discount golf packages:** Yes. **Season:** Year-round. **High:** Oct.-March. **On site lodging:** No. **Rental clubs:** Yes. **Walking policy:** Mandatory cart. **Metal spikes allowed:** Yes. **Range:** Yes (grass). **To obtain tee times:** Call 7 days in advance.
Subscriber comments: Very watery and windy, a real challenge...Better-suited to low- to middle-handicappers.

★½DEERFIELD LAKES GOLF COURSE
PU-3825 Deerfield Country Club Rd., Callahan, 32011, Nassau County, (904)879-1210, 7 miles NW of Jacksonville.
Opened: 1970. **Holes:** 18. **Par:** 72/74. **Yards:** 6,700/5,266. **Course rating:** 70.2/69.0. **Slope:** 114/102. **Architect:** N/A. **Green fee:** $18/$26. **Credit cards:** MC,VISA,DISC. **Reduced fees:** Weekdays, seniors. **Caddies:** No. **Golf carts:** Included in Green Fee. **Discount golf packages:** No. **Season:** Year-round. **High:** Feb.-May. **On site lodging:** No. **Rental clubs:** Yes. **Walking policy:** Walking at certain times. **Metal spikes allowed:** Yes. **Range:** Yes (grass/mats). **To obtain tee times:** Call for weekends and holidays.

★★★DELRAY BEACH GOLF CLUB
PU-2200 Highland Ave., Delray Beach, 33445, Palm Beach County, (561)243-7380, 18 miles S of West Palm Beach.
Opened: 1923. **Holes:** 18. **Par:** 72/72. **Yards:** 6,907/5,189. **Course rating:** 73.0/69.8. **Slope:** 126/117. **Architect:** Donald Ross. **Green fee:** $18/$45. **Credit cards:** MC,VISA. **Reduced fees:** Low season, juniors. **Caddies:** No. **Golf carts:** Included in Green Fee.

Discount golf packages: No. **Season:** Year-round. **High:** Dec.-March. **On site lodging:** No. **Rental clubs:** Yes. **Walking policy:** Walking at certain times. **Metal spikes allowed:** Yes. **Range:** Yes (grass/mats). **To obtain tee times:** Call 2 days in advance at 6:30 a.m.
Subscriber comments: Classic Donald Ross bunkering...A good challenge from Ross...Good test of skills...Renovations are a tremendous improvement.

DELTONA HILLS GOLF & COUNTRY CLUB

1120 Elkcam Blvd., Deltona, 32725, Volusia County, (904)789-4911.
Opened: 1962. **Holes:** 18. **Par:** 72/73. **Yards:** 6,892/5,668. **Course rating:** 72.7/72.5.
Slope: 125/125. **Architect:** David Wallace. **Green fee:** $21/$44. **Credit cards:**
MC,VISA. **Reduced fees:** Weekdays, low season, resort guests, twilight, juniors.
Caddies: No. **Golf carts:** Included in Green Fee. **Discount golf packages:** No.
Season: Year-round. **High:** Jan.-April. **On site lodging:** No. **Rental clubs:** Yes.
Walking policy: Mandatory cart. **Metal spikes allowed:** Yes. **Range:** Yes (grass/mats).
To obtain tee times: Call 5 days in advance.
Special Notes: Only members only may walk course.

★★★½DIAMONDBACK GOLF CLUB

6501 S.R. 544 E., Haines City, 33844, Polk County, (941)421-0437.
Opened: 1995. **Holes:** 18. **Par:** 72/72. **Yards:** 6,805/5,061. **Course rating:** 73.3/70.3.
Slope: 138/122. **Architect:** Joe Lee. **Green fee:** $30/$90. **Credit cards:** All major.
Reduced fees: Weekdays, twilight, juniors. **Caddies:** No. **Golf carts:** Included in Green
Fee. **Discount golf packages:** Yes. **Season:** Year-round. **High:** Nov.-April. **On site
lodging:** No. **Rental clubs:** Yes. **Walking policy:** Mandatory cart. **Metal spikes
allowed:** Yes. **Range:** Yes (grass). **To obtain tee times:** Call 7 days in advance.
Subscriber comments: A real treat...Love the layout. Needs some maturing...Nice
track...Very challenging...Tight driving holes...Trees, trees and more trees. Fun to
play...Cut out of the woods...Full of surprises...Outstanding facility.

★½DIPLOMAT COUNTRY CLUB GOLF COURSE

PU-501 Diplomat Pkwy., Hallandale, 33009, Broward County, (954)457-2080, 15 miles
S of Fort Lauderdale.
Opened: 1957. **Holes:** 18. **Par:** 72/72. **Yards:** 6,700/5,400. **Course rating:** 70.6/69.3.
Slope: 115/110. **Architect:** Red Lawrence. **Green fee:** $12/$45. **Credit cards:**
MC,VISA. **Reduced fees:** Low season, resort guests, twilight. **Caddies:** No. **Golf
carts:** Included in Green Fee. **Discount golf packages:** No. **Season:** Year-round.
High: Dec.-March. **On site lodging:** No. **Rental clubs:** Yes. **Walking policy:**
Mandatory cart. **Metal spikes allowed:** Yes. **Range:** Yes (grass). **To obtain tee times:**
Call.

★★½DODGER PINES COUNTRY CLUB

4600 26th St., Vero Beach, 32966, Indian River County, (561)569-4400,
60 miles N of West Palm Beach.
Opened: 1971. **Holes:** 18. **Par:** 73/74. **Yards:** 6,692/5,776. **Course rating:** 71.2/72.3. **Slope:** 122/124. **Architect:** Marion Luke. **Green fee:**
$25/$45. **Credit cards:** MC,VISA,AMEX. **Reduced fees:** Low season,
twilight. **Caddies:** No. **Golf carts:** $12. **Discount golf packages:** No. **Season:** Year-round. **High:** Jan.-April. **On site lodging:** No. **Rental clubs:** Yes. **Walking policy:**
Walking at certain times. **Metal spikes allowed:** Yes. **Range:** Yes (grass/mats). **To
obtain tee times:** Call 2 days in advance.
Subscriber comments: Very playable.

★★★DON SHULA'S GOLF CLUB

R-7601 Miami Lakes Dr., Miami Lakes, 33014, Dade County, (305)820-8106.
Opened: 1963. **Holes:** 18. **Par:** 72/72. **Yards:** 7,055/5,287. **Course rating:** 72.3/70.1.
Slope: 121/117. **Architect:** Bill Watts. **Green fee:** $26/$80. **Credit cards:** All major.
Reduced fees: Weekdays, low season, resort guests, twilight. **Caddies:** No. **Golf
carts:** $18. **Discount golf packages:** Yes. **Season:** Year-round. **High:** Jan.-April. **On
site lodging:** Yes. **Rental clubs:** Yes. **Walking policy:** Walking at certain times. **Metal
spikes allowed:** Yes. **Range:** Yes (grass/mats). **To obtain tee times:** Call.
Subscriber comments: Enjoyable...Layout not bad.
Special Notes: Also has an 18-hole par-3 course.

FLORIDA

DORAL GOLF RESORT & SPA
R-4400 N.W. 87th Ave., Miami, 33178, Dade County, (305)592-2000x2105, (800)713-6725.
Opened: 1961. **Credit cards:** All major,Diners Club. **Reduced fees:** Weekdays, low season, resort guests, twilight, seniors, juniors. **Caddies:** Yes. **Golf carts:** Included in Green Fee. **Discount golf packages:** Yes. **Season:** Year-round. **High:** Oct.-April. **On site lodging:** Yes. **Rental clubs:** Yes. **Walking policy:** Walking at certain times. **Metal spikes allowed:** No. **Range:** Yes (grass/mats). **To obtain tee times:** Resort guests may make tee times with hotel reservation. Nonguests call 30 days in advance.

(GREAT SERVICE)

★★★★BLUE COURSE
Holes: 18. **Par:** 72/72. **Yards:** 7,125/5,392. **Course rating:** 74.5/73.0. **Slope:** 130/124. **Architect:** Dick Wilson. **Green fee:** $90/$220.
Notes: Ranked 11th in 1997 Best in State. 1962-present Doral-Ryder Open.
Subscriber comments: I can't wait to play the Blue Monster again. I now have a better respect for the pros. Learning center is awesome...Great after rehab by Ray Floyd...Golf factory...Fantastic but humbling golf experience...More sand than fairways. Tough as hell...Sand, sand, sand everywhere...Bury me there!

★★★½GOLD COURSE
Holes: 18. **Par:** 70/70. **Yards:** 6,602/5,179. **Course rating:** 73.3/71.4. **Slope:** 129/123. **Architect:** Robert von Hagge. **Green fee:** $75/$185.
Subscriber comments: Lots of water, and I found it all...One step below the Blue Monster...Almost as much fun as the Blue...Flat...Tough to stay dry.

★★★½RED COURSE
Holes: 18. **Par:** 70/70. **Yards:** 6,214/5,216. **Course rating:** 69.9/70.6. **Slope:** 118/118. **Architect:** Robert von Hagge. **Green fee:** $70/$160.
Subscriber comments: Had fun...Changes made in recent years continue to improve course...Short, short, short...Florida golf.

★★★WHITE COURSE
Holes: 18. **Par:** 72/72. **Yards:** 6,208/5,286. **Course rating:** 69.7/70.1. **Slope:** 117/116. **Architect:** Robert von Hagge. **Green fee:** $45/$110.
Subscriber comments: Easier than the others, but fun to play.

★★★DORAL PARK GOLF & COUNTRY CLUB
5001 N.W. 104th Ave., Miami, 33178, Dade County, (305)594-0954.
Opened: 1984. **Holes:** 18. **Par:** 71/71. **Yards:** 6,614/4,661. **Course rating:** 72.0/66.6. **Slope:** 129/113. **Architect:** Bruce Devlin/Robert von Hagge. **Green fee:** $53/$63. **Credit cards:** MC,VISA,AMEX. **Reduced fees:** Weekdays, low season, resort guests. **Caddies:** No. **Golf carts:** Included in Green Fee. **Discount golf packages:** No. **Season:** Year-round. **High:** Jan.-April. **On site lodging:** No. **Rental clubs:** Yes. **Walking policy:** Mandatory cart. **Metal spikes allowed:** Yes. **Range:** Yes. **To obtain tee times:** Call two days in advance.
Subscriber comments: Could play all day. Great for confidence...Challenging, nice course.

★★½DOUG FORD'S LACUNA GOLF CLUB
6400 Grand Lacuna Blvd., Lake Worth, 33467, Palm Beach County, (561)433-3006, 5 miles SW of West Palm Beach.
Opened: 1985. **Holes:** 18. **Par:** 71/71. **Yards:** 6,700/5,119. **Course rating:** N/A. **Slope:** 121/111. **Architect:** Joe Lee. **Green fee:** $17/$37. **Credit cards:** MC,VISA. **Reduced fees:** Low season. **Caddies:** No. **Golf carts:** Included in Green Fee. **Discount golf packages:** No. **Season:** Year-round. **High:** Nov.-May. **On site lodging:** No. **Rental clubs:** Yes. **Walking policy:** Mandatory cart. **Metal spikes allowed:** Yes. **Range:** Yes (grass). **To obtain tee times:** Call up to 4 days in advance.
Subscriber comments: Plenty of sand and water...Potential galore...Nice and challenging for average golfer.

★★★DUNEDIN COUNTRY CLUB
1050 Palm Blvd., Dunedin, 34698, Pinellas County, (813)733-7836, 20 miles NW of Tampa.
Opened: 1928. **Holes:** 18. **Par:** 72/73. **Yards:** 6,565/5,726. **Course rating:** 71.5/73.1. **Slope:** 125/120. **Architect:** Donald Ross. **Green fee:** $33/$41. **Credit cards:** None.

Reduced fees: Low season, twilight. **Caddies:** No. **Golf carts:** Included in Green Fee. **Discount golf packages:** No. **Season:** Year-round. **High:** Dec.-April. **On site lodging:** No. **Rental clubs:** Yes. **Walking policy:** Walking at certain times. **Metal spikes allowed:** Yes. **Range:** Yes (grass). **To obtain tee times:** Call 2 days in advance. **Notes:** Senior PGA Tour events in 1950s.

★★★THE DUNES GOLF CLUB AT SEVILLE
PU-18200 Seville Clubhouse Dr., Brooksville, 34614, Hernando County, (352)596-7888, (800)232-1363, 70 miles N of Tampa.
Opened: 1988. **Holes:** 18. **Par:** 72/72. **Yards:** 7,140/5,236. **Course rating:** 74.9/70.8. **Slope:** 138/126. **Architect:** Arthur Hills. **Green fee:** $15/$25. **Credit cards:** MC,VISA. **Reduced fees:** Weekdays, low season, twilight. **Caddies:** No. **Golf carts:** Included in Green Fee. **Discount golf packages:** Yes. **Season:** Year-round. **High:** Jan.-April. **On site lodging:** No. **Rental clubs:** Yes. **Walking policy:** Mandatory cart. **Metal spikes allowed:** Yes. **Range:** Yes (grass). **To obtain tee times:** Call golf shop.
Subscriber comments: Long, plenty of sand...Great sand craters...Unique layout, always fun to play...Challenging.

★★★½EAGLE HARBOR GOLF CLUB
2217 Eagle Harbor Pkwy., Orange Park, 32073, Clay County, (904)269-9300, 10 miles S of Jacksonville.
Opened: 1993. **Holes:** 18. **Par:** 72/72. **Yards:** 6,840/4,980. **Course rating:** 72.6/68.2. **Slope:** 133/121. **Architect:** Clyde Johnston. **Green fee:** $38/$46. **Credit cards:** MC,VISA. **Reduced fees:** Weekdays, twilight, juniors. **Caddies:** No. **Golf carts:** Included in Green Fee. **Discount golf packages:** Yes. **Season:** Year-round. **High:** April-June. **On site lodging:** No. **Rental clubs:** Yes. **Walking policy:** Walking at certain times. **Metal spikes allowed:** Yes. **Range:** Yes (grass). **To obtain tee times:** Call 4 days in advance.
Subscriber comments: Lots of nature. Nice new course...A pleasure to play for all handicaps...Nice, open course.

★★★THE EAGLES GOLF CLUB
16101 Nine Eagles Dr., Odessa, 33556, Hillsborough County, (813)920-6681, 10 miles N of Tampa.
Opened: 1973. **Holes:** 27. **Architect:** Rick Rollins/Gary Koch/Ron Garl. **Green fee:** $32/$45. **Credit cards:** MC,VISA. **Reduced fees:** Weekdays, low season, twilight. **Caddies:** No. **Golf carts:** Included in Green Fee. **Discount golf packages:** No. **Season:** Year-round. **High:** Jan.-April. **On site lodging:** No. **Rental clubs:** Yes. **Walking policy:** Walking at certain times. **Metal spikes allowed:** Yes. **Range:** Yes (grass). **To obtain tee times:** Call up to four days in advance.
FOREST/LAKES
Par: 72/73. **Yards:** 7,134/5,453. **Course rating:** 70.3/70.2. **Slope:** 130/114.
FOREST/OAKS
Par: 72/72. **Yards:** 7,068/5,429. **Course rating:** 70.3/70.0. **Slope:** 130/114.
LAKES/OAKS
Par: 72/73. **Yards:** 7,194/5,586. **Course rating:** 70.3/70.2. **Slope:** 130/114.
Subscriber comments: Nice, but too many homes...Challenging and interesting. Good mix...Plenty of water...Computer carts...Construction has changed atmosphere...Narrow...Nice course, not real difficult...Fun course for all ability levels...Plenty of trees...Challenging...State-of-the-art technology with carts.

EAST BAY GOLF CLUB
702 Country Club Dr., Largo, 33771, Pinellas County, (813)581-3333, 5 miles W of St. Petersburg.
Opened: 1979. **Holes:** 18. **Par:** 71/71. **Yards:** 6,462/5,193. **Course rating:** 71.2/70.7. **Slope:** 125/118. **Architect:** N/A. **Green fee:** $20/$38. **Credit cards:** MC,VISA. **Reduced fees:** Low season, twilight. **Caddies:** No. **Golf carts:** Included in Green Fee. **Discount golf packages:** No. **Season:** Year-round. **High:** Nov.-April. **On site lodging:** No. **Rental clubs:** No. **Walking policy:** Walking at certain times. **Metal spikes allowed:** No. **Range:** Yes (grass). **To obtain tee times:** Call up to 3 days in advance.

FLORIDA

★★★EASTWOOD GOLF CLUB
PU-13950 Golfway Blvd., Orlando, 32828, Orange County, (407)281-4653, 10 miles E of Orlando.
Opened: 1989. **Holes:** 18. **Par:** 72/72. **Yards:** 7,176/5,393. **Course rating:** 73.9/70.5.
Slope: 124/117. **Architect:** Lloyd Clifton. **Green fee:** $22/$66. **Credit cards:** All major.
Reduced fees: Weekdays, low season, twilight, seniors, juniors. **Caddies:** No. **Golf carts:** Included in Green Fee. **Discount golf packages:** Yes. **Season:** Year-round.
High: Jan.-April 15. **On site lodging:** No. **Rental clubs:** Yes. **Walking policy:** Mandatory cart. **Metal spikes allowed:** Yes. **Range:** Yes (grass). **To obtain tee times:** Call 7 days in advance.
Subscriber comments: Enjoyable...Typical muny...Very pretty...Somewhat of a links style...Big greens, wide fairways...Condo golf.

★★★½EASTWOOD GOLF COURSE
PU-4600 Bruce Herd Lane, Fort Myers, 33994, Lee County, (813)275-4848.
Opened: 1977. **Holes:** 18. **Par:** 72/72. **Yards:** 6,772/5,116. **Course rating:** 73.3/68.9.
Slope: 130/120. **Architect:** Robert von Hagge/Bruce Devlin. **Green fee:** $27/$50.
Credit cards: MC,VISA. **Reduced fees:** Weekdays, low season, twilight. **Caddies:** No.
Golf carts: Included in Green Fee. **Discount golf packages:** No. **Season:** Year-round.
High: Dec.-March. **On site lodging:** No. **Rental clubs:** Yes. **Walking policy:** Walking at certain times. **Metal spikes allowed:** Yes. **Range:** Yes (grass/mats). **To obtain tee times:** Call 1 day in advance at 8 a.m.
Subscriber comments: One of my favorite Florida courses at any price...Great course, good challenge...You use all the clubs in your bag...Just do it...A must play...This course has everything...No two holes alike...Lots of sand.

★★★½EKANA GOLF CLUB
2100 Ekana Dr., Oviedo, 32765, Seminole County, (407)366-1211, 10 miles NE of Orlando.
Opened: 1989. **Holes:** 18. **Par:** 72/72. **Yards:** 6,683/5,544. **Course rating:** 72.0/72.1.
Slope: 130/128. **Architect:** Joe Lee. **Green fee:** $22/$60. **Credit cards:** MC,VISA.
Reduced fees: Weekdays, low season, twilight. **Caddies:** No. **Golf carts:** Included in Green Fee. **Discount golf packages:** Yes. **Season:** Year-round. **High:** Jan.-April. **On site lodging:** No. **Rental clubs:** Yes. **Walking policy:** Mandatory cart. **Metal spikes allowed:** Yes. **Range:** Yes (grass). **To obtain tee times:** Call 7 days in advance.
Subscriber comments: Good layout...Play if you get the chance...Very playable...Would play again...Need cart between holes...Hit it straight or else it's in the water...Lots of wildlife...Good time.

★★★★EMERALD BAY GOLF COURSE
40001 Emerald Coast Pkwy., Destin, 32541, Okaloosa County, (904)837-5197, 15 miles E of Fort Walton Beach.
Opened: 1991. **Holes:** 18. **Par:** 72/72. **Yards:** 6,802/5,184. **Course rating:** 73.1/70.1. **Slope:** 135/122. **Architect:** Robert Cupp. **Green fee:** $40/$75. **Credit cards:** MC,VISA,AMEX. **Reduced fees:** Weekdays, low season, resort guests, juniors. **Caddies:** No. **Golf carts:** Included in Green Fee.
Discount golf packages: No. **Season:** Year-round. **High:** March-Nov. **On site lodging:** No. **Rental clubs:** Yes. **Walking policy:** Mandatory cart. **Metal spikes allowed:** Yes. **Range:** Yes (grass). **To obtain tee times:** Call two weeks in advance.
Subscriber comments: Pretty course. Lots of wind and water. Tough...Some very good holes. A couple of weak ones...Great tourist course...Good hole variety...Tight fairways...Small greens.

★★★★EMERALD DUNES GOLF COURSE
PU-2100 Emerald Dunes Dr., West Palm Beach, 33411, Palm Beach County, (561)684-4653, (888)560-4653, 3 miles W of West Palm Beach.
Opened: 1990. **Holes:** 18. **Par:** 72/72. **Yards:** 7,006/4,676. **Course rating:** 73.8/67.1.
Slope: 133/115. **Architect:** Tom Fazio. **Green fee:** $45/$135. **Credit cards:** All major,Diners Club. **Reduced fees:** Low season, twilight, seniors, juniors. **Caddies:** No.
Golf carts: Included in Green Fee. **Discount golf packages:** No. **Season:** Year-round.
High: Nov.-April. **On site lodging:** No. **Rental clubs:** Yes. **Walking policy:** Unrestricted walking. **Metal spikes allowed:** Yes. **Range:** Yes (grass). **To obtain tee

times: Call and secure with credit card.
Notes: Ranked 30th in 1997 Best in State.
Subscriber comments: Has to be one of the best publics in Florida. A must...Wish it was less expensive...Not for the high-handicapper...Expensive, but Fazio is worth it...Computers on carts giving yardage enhanced the fun...Memorable...Some long distances from greens to next tees.

★★★FAIRWINDS GOLF COURSE

PU-4400 Fairwinds Dr., Fort Pierce, 34946, St. Lucie County, (561)462-2722, (800)894-1781, 40 miles N of West Palm Beach.
Opened: 1991. **Holes:** 18. **Par:** 72/72. **Yards:** 6,783/5,392. **Course rating:** 71.1/68.5. **Slope:** 119/112. **Architect:** Jim Fazio. **Green fee:** $20/$38. **Credit cards:** MC,VISA. **Reduced fees:** Low season, juniors. **Caddies:** No. **Golf carts:** Included in Green Fee. **Discount golf packages:** No. **Season:** Year-round. **High:** Jan.-April. **On site lodging:** No. **Rental clubs:** Yes. **Walking policy:** Walking at certain times. **Metal spikes allowed:** Yes. **Range:** Yes (grass). **To obtain tee times:** Call 48 hours in advance.
Subscriber comments: Average course...18th a tough finisher...Busy muny...Wide open to lots of wind.

★★★★FALCON'S FIRE GOLF CLUB

PU-3200 Seralago Blvd., Kissimmee, 34746, Osceola County, (407)239-5445, 6 miles S of Orlando.
Opened: 1993. **Holes:** 18. **Par:** 72/72. **Yards:** 6,901/5,417. **Course rating:** 72.5/70.4. **Slope:** 125/118. **Architect:** Rees Jones. **Green fee:** $56/$95. **Credit cards:** MC,VISA,AMEX. **Reduced fees:** Low season, twilight, juniors. **Caddies:** No. **Golf carts:** Included in Green Fee. **Discount golf packages:** No. **Season:** Year-round. **High:** Jan.-April. **On site lodging:** No. **Rental clubs:** Yes. **Walking policy:** Mandatory cart. **Metal spikes allowed:** Yes. **Range:** Yes (grass). **To obtain tee times:** Call 7 days in advance, or 8-30 days in advance with extra fee. Groups may call up to 6 months in advance.
Notes: 1994-present Senior PGA Tour Qualifying School.
Subscriber comments: Fantastic golf, lots of sand...Fair course...Yardage computers in carts are a big help...Flat course...Great landscaping...All the amenities...Very plush...Expensive, but worth it...Wind can get you...Falcon nest at the 16th.

★★½FERNANDINA BEACH MUNICIPAL GOLF COURSE

PM-2800 Bill Melton Rd., Fernandina Beach, 32034, Nassau County, (904)277-7370, (800)646-5997, 35 miles NE of Jacksonville.
Opened: 1954. **Holes:** 27. **Architect:** Ed Mattson/Tommy Birdsong. **Green fee:** $14/$17. **Credit cards:** MC,VISA. **Reduced fees:** Weekdays, twilight, juniors. **Caddies:** No. **Golf carts:** $9. **Discount golf packages:** No. **Season:** Year-round. **High:** Year-round. **On site lodging:** No. **Rental clubs:** Yes. **Walking policy:** Walking at certain times. **Metal spikes allowed:** No. **Range:** Yes (grass). **To obtain tee times:** Call 5 days in advance.
NORTH/SOUTH
Par: 71/72. **Yards:** 6,412/5,156. **Course rating:** 69.7/69.0. **Slope:** 121/119.
NORTH/WEST
Par: 72/73. **Yards:** 6,803/5,720. **Course rating:** 71.5/71.5. **Slope:** 118/119.
WEST/SOUTH
Par: 73/74. **Yards:** 7,027/5,308. **Course rating:** 72.6/72.0. **Slope:** 123/120.
Subscriber comments: Nice to play...Don't make them like this anymore...Good walking courses...Alligators.

FONTAINEBLEAU GOLF COURSE

PU-9603 Fontainebleau Blvd., Miami, 33172, Dade County, (305)221-5181, 5 miles W of Miami. **Architect:** Mark Mahannah. **Green fee:** $20/$32. **Credit cards:** MC,VISA,AMEX,Diners Club. **Reduced fees:** Weekdays, low season, resort guests, twilight. **Caddies:** No. **Golf carts:** Included in Green Fee. **Discount golf packages:** Yes. **Season:** Year-round. **High:** Nov.-April. **On site lodging:** No. **Rental clubs:** Yes. **Walking policy:** Mandatory cart. **Metal spikes allowed:** Yes. **Range:** Yes (grass). **To obtain tee times:** Call up to 14 days in advance.

FLORIDA

★★EAST COURSE
Opened: 1969. **Holes:** 18. **Par:** 72/72. **Yards:** 7,035/5,586. **Course rating:** 73.3/71.5. **Slope:** 122/119.
★WEST COURSE
Opened: 1976. **Holes:** 18. **Par:** 72/72. **Yards:** 6,944/5,565. **Course rating:** 72.5/71.0. **Slope:** 120/118.

★★★FOREST LAKE GOLF CLUB OF OCOEE
PU-10521 Clarcona-Ocoee Rd., Ocoee, 34761, Orange County, (407)654-4653, 5 miles W of Orlando.
Opened: 1994. **Holes:** 18. **Par:** 72/72. **Yards:** 7,113/5,103. **Course rating:** 73.6/69.2. **Slope:** 127/113. **Architect:** Clifton/Ezell/Clifton. **Green fee:** $29/$50. **Credit cards:** MC,VISA. **Reduced fees:** Weekdays, low season, twilight, juniors. **Caddies:** No. **Golf carts:** Included in Green Fee. **Discount golf packages:** Yes. **Season:** Year-round. **High:** N/A. **On site lodging:** No. **Rental clubs:** Yes. **Walking policy:** Mandatory cart. **Metal spikes allowed:** Yes. **Range:** Yes (grass). **To obtain tee times:** Call 5 days in advance.
Subscriber comments: Good finishing holes...All natural...Fun par 3s...Out of the way.

★★½FOREST LAKES GOLF CLUB
2401 Beneva Rd., Sarasota, 34232, Sarasota County, (941)922-1312, 40 miles S of Tampa.
Opened: 1964. **Holes:** 18. **Par:** 71/71. **Yards:** 6,500/5,500. **Course rating:** 70.8/71.3. **Slope:** 124/117. **Architect:** Andy Anderson. **Green fee:** $16/$42. **Credit cards:** All major. **Reduced fees:** Weekdays, low season, resort guests, twilight, juniors. **Caddies:** No. **Golf carts:** Included in Green Fee. **Discount golf packages:** No. **Season:** Year-round. **High:** Jan.-May. **On site lodging:** No. **Rental clubs:** No. **Walking policy:** Walking at certain times. **Metal spikes allowed:** Yes. **Range:** Yes. **To obtain tee times:** Call golf shop up to 4 days in advance.
Subscriber comments: Nice, convenient course right in town.

★★★FORT MYERS COUNTRY CLUB
PU-3591 McGregor Blvd., Fort Myers, 33901, Lee County, (941)936-2457, 120 miles S of Tampa.
Opened: N/A. **Holes:** 18. **Par:** 71/71. **Yards:** 6,414/5,135. **Course rating:** N/A. **Slope:** 118/117. **Architect:** Donald Ross. **Green fee:** $12/$32. **Credit cards:** MC,VISA. **Reduced fees:** Weekdays, low season, twilight. **Caddies:** No. **Golf carts:** $15. **Discount golf packages:** No. **Season:** Year-round. **High:** Dec.-April. **On site lodging:** No. **Rental clubs:** Yes. **Walking policy:** Unrestricted walking. **Metal spikes allowed:** Yes. **Range:** Yes (grass). **To obtain tee times:** Call tee times phone 1 day in advance beginning at 8 a.m.
Subscriber comments: Fun for average golfer...Domed greens are a real challenge.

FORT WALTON BEACH GOLF CLUB
PM- Fort Walton Beach, 32547, Okaloosa County, (904)833-9530, 50 miles E of Pensacola.
Green fee: $15/$15. **Reduced fees:** Twilight. **Caddies:** No. **Golf carts:** $8. **Season:** Year-round. **High:** Jan.-Sept. **On site lodging:** No. **Rental clubs:** Yes. **Walking policy:** Unrestricted walking. **Metal spikes allowed:** Yes. **Range:** No. **To obtain tee times:** Outside 400 mile radius may call up to 60 days in advance.
★★★OAKS COURSE
1909 Lewis Turner Blvd.
Opened: 1993. **Holes:** 18. **Par:** 72/72. **Yards:** 6,409/5,366. **Course rating:** 70.2/67.8. **Slope:** 119/107. **Architect:** David Smith. **Credit cards:** None. **Discount golf packages:** Yes.
Subscriber comments: Good muny...New greens...Challenging.

★★½PINES COURSE
699 Country Club Dr.
Opened: 1961. **Holes:** 18. **Par:** 72/72. **Yards:** 6,802/5,320. **Course rating:** 69.9/69.1. **Slope:** 110/107. **Architect:** William Amick. **Credit cards:** MC,VISA. **Discount golf packages:** No.
Subscriber comments: Some fun holes.

★★★½FOX HOLLOW GOLF CLUB

PU-10050 Robert Trent Jones Pkwy., New Port Richey, 34655, Pasco County, (813)376-6333, (800)943-1902, 25 miles NW of Tampa.
Opened: 1994. **Holes:** 18. **Par:** 71/71. **Yards:** 7,138/4,454. **Course rating:** 75,1/65.7. **Slope:** 137/112. **Architect:** Robert Trent Jones/Roger Rulewich. **Green fee:** $33/$65. **Credit cards:** All major,Sandri Card. **Reduced fees:** Weekdays, low season, twilight, juniors. **Caddies:** No. **Golf carts:** Included in Green Fee. **Discount golf packages:** Yes. **Season:** Year-round. **High:** Jan.-March. **On site lodging:** No. **Rental clubs:** Yes. **Walking policy:** Unrestricted walking. **Metal spikes allowed:** Yes. **Range:** Yes (grass). **To obtain tee times:** Call up to 4 days in advance. Groups of 8 or more may call up to 1 year in advance.
Subscriber comments: Rolling hills. Not flat like Florida...Real challenge...Young course, but demanding when wind blows...Should be great when grown up...Needs time to mature...Good layout through woods...Makes you play all the shots...Variety of tees challenges all levels.

★★FOXFIRE GOLF CLUB

PU-7200 Proctor Rd., Sarasota, 34241, Sarasota County, (941)921-7757, 50 miles S of Tampa.
Opened: 1975. **Holes:** 27. **Architect:** Andy Anderson. **Green fee:** $16/$49. **Credit cards:** MC,VISA. **Reduced fees:** Low season, twilight, juniors. **Caddies:** No. **Golf carts:** Included in Green Fee. **Discount golf packages:** No. **Season:** Year-round. **High:** Jan.-March. **On site lodging:** No. **Rental clubs:** Yes. **Walking policy:** Unrestricted walking. **Metal spikes allowed:** Yes. **Range:** Yes (grass). **To obtain tee times:** Call up to 3 days in advance.
PALM/OAK
Par: 72/72. **Yards:** 6,280/5,024. **Course rating:** 70.0/67.7. **Slope:** N/A.
PINE/OAK
Par: 72/72. **Yards:** 6,101/4,941. **Course rating:** 69.8/67.6. **Slope:** N/A.
PINE/PALM
Par: 72/72. **Yards:** 6,213/4,983. **Course rating:** 69.8/67.5. **Slope:** 119/115.

★★FOXWOOD COUNTRY CLUB

4927 Antioch Rd., Crestview, 32536, Okaloosa County, (850)682-2012, 40 miles NE of Pensacola.
Opened: 1962. **Holes:** 18. **Par:** 72/72. **Yards:** 6,282/5,016. **Course rating:** 69.6/69.5. **Slope:** 119/119. **Architect:** Bill Amick/Earl Stone. **Green fee:** $12/$16. **Credit cards:** All major. **Reduced fees:** Weekdays, low season, twilight. **Caddies:** No. **Golf carts:** $14. **Discount golf packages:** No. **Season:** Year-round. **High:** Jan.-March. **On site lodging:** No. **Rental clubs:** Yes. **Walking policy:** Walking at certain times. **Metal spikes allowed:** Yes. **Range:** Yes (grass). **To obtain tee times:** Call anytime 7 days in advance.

★★GATEWAY GOLF & COUNTRY CLUB

11360 Championship Dr., Fort Myers, 33913, Lee County, (941)561-1010.
Opened: 1989. **Holes:** 18. **Par:** 72/72. **Yards:** 6,974/5,323. **Course rating:** 73.7/70.6. **Slope:** 130/120. **Architect:** Tom Fazio. **Green fee:** $35/$102. **Credit cards:** MC,VISA,AMEX. **Reduced fees:** Low season, twilight. **Caddies:** No. **Golf carts:** Included in Green Fee. **Discount golf packages:** No. **Season:** Year-round. **High:** Jan.-March. **On site lodging:** No. **Rental clubs:** Yes. **Walking policy:** Mandatory cart. **Metal spikes allowed:** Yes. **Range:** Yes (grass). **To obtain tee times:** Call 2 days in advance.
Subscriber comments: Good variety, good challenge...Very playable...Nice layout but a few bad holes.

★★½GATOR TRACE GOLF & COUNTRY CLUB

4302 Gator Trace Dr., Fort Pierce, 34982, St. Lucie County, (561)464-7442, 40 miles N of West Palm Beach.
Opened: 1986. **Holes:** 18. **Par:** 70/70. **Yards:** 6,092/4,573. **Course rating:** 68.9/67.1. **Slope:** 123/123. **Architect:** Arthur Hills. **Green fee:** $18/$37. **Credit cards:** MC,VISA,DISC. **Reduced fees:** N/A. **Caddies:** No. **Golf carts:** N/A. **Discount golf packages:** No. **Season:** Year-round. **High:** Dec.-May. **On site lodging:** No. **Rental**

clubs: Yes. **Walking policy:** Unrestricted walking. **Metal spikes allowed:** Yes. **Range:** No. **To obtain tee times:** N/A.
Subscriber comments: Narrow fairways. Not long, but you must be straight...Errant shots hit condos...Vacation golf...Not bad after a winter in the North...Bring extra balls.

★★★GOLDEN BEAR GOLF CLUB AT HAMMOCK CREEK
PU-2400 Golden Bear Way, Palm City, 34990, Martin County, (561)220-2599, 35 miles N of West Beach.
Opened: 1996. **Holes:** 18. **Par:** 72/72. **Yards:** 7,050/5,130. **Course rating:** 73.6/70.0.
Slope: 134/119. **Architect:** Jack Nicklaus/Jack Nicklaus Jr.. **Green fee:** $25/$50.
Credit cards: MC,VISA,DISC,Diners Club. **Reduced fees:** Weekdays, resort guests, twilight, juniors. **Caddies:** No. **Golf carts:** Included in Green Fee. **Discount golf packages:** No. **Season:** Year-round. **High:** Jan.-March. **On site lodging:** No. **Rental clubs:** Yes. **Walking policy:** Unrestricted walking. **Metal spikes allowed:** Yes. **Range:** Yes (grass). **To obtain tee times:** Call golf shop up to 7 days in advance with credit card.
Subscriber comments: Fair, playable, challenging...New course. Enjoyable. Could move up...Greens a joy to putt...Very open.

★★★½GOLDEN OCALA GOLF & COUNTRY CLUB
PU-7300 U.S. Hwy. 27 N.W., Ocala, 34482, Marion County, (352)622-2245, (800)251-7674, 85 miles N of Orlando.
Opened: 1986. **Holes:** 18. **Par:** 72/72. **Yards:** 6,735/5,595. **Course rating:** 72.2/72.2.
Slope: 132/124. **Architect:** Ron Garl. **Green fee:** $30/$59. **Credit cards:** MC,VISA.
Reduced fees: Weekdays, low season, twilight. **Caddies:** No. **Golf carts:** Included in Green Fee. **Discount golf packages:** Yes. **Season:** Year-round. **High:** Nov.-April. **On site lodging:** No. **Rental clubs:** Yes. **Walking policy:** Walking at certain times. **Metal spikes allowed:** Yes. **Range:** Yes (grass). **To obtain tee times:** Call up to 14 days in advance.
Subscriber comments: Love the replica holes...Felt like Faldo at Augusta...If you can't play the real ones, definitely try this one...A sleeper...Memorable experience.

★★★THE GOLF CLUB AT AMELIA ISLAND
R-4700 Amelia Island Pkwy., Amelia Island, 32034, Nassau County, (904)277-8015, (904)245-4224, 26 miles N of Jacksonville.
Opened: 1987. **Holes:** 18. **Par:** 72/72. **Yards:** 6,681/5,039. **Course rating:** 71.7/70.6.
Slope: 127/122. **Architect:** Mark McCumber. **Green fee:** $67/$96. **Credit cards:** MC,VISA,AMEX. **Reduced fees:** Twilight, juniors. **Caddies:** No. **Golf carts:** Included in Green Fee. **Discount golf packages:** Yes. **Season:** Year-round. **High:** March-Oct. **On site lodging:** Yes. **Rental clubs:** Yes. **Walking policy:** Mandatory cart. **Metal spikes allowed:** Yes. **Range:** Yes (grass). **To obtain tee times:** Guests must stay at Ritz-Carlton, Amelia Island 1-800-241-3333 or Summer Beach Resort 1-800-862-9297.
Notes: 1998 Senior PGA Tour Liberty Mutual Legions of Golf.
Subscriber comments: Very nice...Very playable resort course...Not too tough for average golfer...Lush.

THE GOLF CLUB AT CYPRESS CREEK
880 Cypress Village Blvd., Ruskin, 33573, Hillsborough County, (813)634-8888, 20 miles S of Tampa.
Opened: 1988. **Holes:** 18. **Par:** 72/72. **Yards:** 6,839/4. **Course rating:** 74.0/66.6.
Slope: 133/114. **Architect:** Steve Smyers. **Green fee:** $20/$34. **Credit cards:** MC,VISA. **Reduced fees:** Weekdays, low season, resort guests, twilight, seniors.
Caddies: No. **Golf carts:** Included in Green Fee. **Discount golf packages:** Yes.
Season: Year-round. **High:** Feb.-April. **On site lodging:** No. **Rental clubs:** Yes.
Walking policy: Mandatory cart. **Metal spikes allowed:** Yes. **Range:** Yes (grass). **To obtain tee times:** Call one week in advance.
Special Notes: Also has 18-hole executive Upper Creek Course.

★★★THE GOLF CLUB AT CYPRESS HEAD
PM-6231 Palm Vista St., Port Orange, 32124, Volusia County, (904)756-5449, 5 miles S of Daytona Beach.
Opened: 1992. **Holes:** 18. **Par:** 72/72. **Yards:** 6,814/4,909. **Course rating:** 72.4/68.3.
Slope: 133/116. **Architect:** Arthur Hills. **Green fee:** $30/$48. **Credit cards:** MC,VISA.
Reduced fees: Weekdays, low season, resort guests, twilight, juniors. **Caddies:** No.

Golf carts: Included in Green Fee. **Discount golf packages:** Yes. **Season:** Year-round. **High:** Jan.-April. **On site lodging:** No. **Rental clubs:** Yes. **Walking policy:** Walking at certain times. **Metal spikes allowed:** Yes. **Range:** Yes (grass). **To obtain tee times:** Call up to 3 days in advance.
Subscriber comments: Fair...A good test.

★★★½GOLF CLUB OF JACKSONVILLE

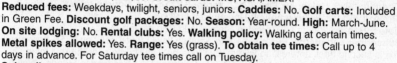

PM-10440 Tournament Lane, Jacksonville, 32222, Duval County, (904)779-0800.
Opened: 1989. **Holes:** 18. **Par:** 71/71. **Yards:** 6,620/5,021. **Course rating:** 70.7/68.0. **Slope:** 120/115. **Architect:** Bobby Weed/Mark McCumber. **Green fee:** $20/$39. **Credit cards:** MC,VISA,AMEX.
Reduced fees: Weekdays, twilight, seniors, juniors. **Caddies:** No. **Golf carts:** Included in Green Fee. **Discount golf packages:** No. **Season:** Year-round. **High:** March-June. **On site lodging:** No. **Rental clubs:** Yes. **Walking policy:** Walking at certain times. **Metal spikes allowed:** Yes. **Range:** Yes (grass). **To obtain tee times:** Call up to 4 days in advance. For Saturday tee times call on Tuesday.
Subscriber comments: Exceptional course...Beautiful layout...Large greens...Good challenge...Almost a great course...Interesting layout.

GOLF CLUB OF MIAMI

PM-6801 Miami Gardens Dr., Miami, 33015, Dade County, (305)829-4700, 10 miles NW of Miami.
Opened: 1940. **Architect:** Robert Trent Jones/Bobby Weed. **Green fee:** $20/$65.
Credit cards: All major. **Reduced fees:** Weekdays, low season, twilight. **Caddies:** No. **Golf carts:** Included in Green Fee. **Discount golf packages:** Yes. **Season:** Year-round. **High:** Feb.-Nov. **On site lodging:** No. **Rental clubs:** Yes. **Walking policy:** Mandatory cart. **Metal spikes allowed:** Yes. **To obtain tee times:** Call 3 days in advance.
★★★EAST COURSE
Holes: 18. **Par:** 70/70. **Yards:** 6,553/5,025. **Course rating:** 70.3/68.8. **Slope:** 124/117. **Range:** Yes (grass/mats).
Subscriber comments: Gets lots of play, but it is a very good facility...Better than average...A lot of water.
★★★WEST COURSE
Holes: 18. **Par:** 72/72. **Yards:** 7,017/5,298. **Course rating:** 73.5/70.1. **Slope:** 130/123. **Range:** Yes (grass).
Subscriber comments: Long and difficult, but you can score...Fun...From the tips it's a test...Challenging.
Special Notes: Arnold Palmer was first club pro here. Lee Trevino had first win here. Jack Nickalus made first professional check here.

GOLF CLUB OF QUINCY

Solomon Dairy Rd., Quincy, 32353, Gadsden County, (904)627-9631, 20 miles NW of Tallahassee.
Opened: 1968. **Holes:** 18. **Par:** 72/72. **Yards:** 6,742/5,398. **Course rating:** 71.2/70.3. **Slope:** 135/117. **Architect:** Joe Lee. **Green fee:** $11/$23. **Credit cards:** MC,VISA.
Reduced fees: Weekdays. **Caddies:** No. **Golf carts:** $11. **Discount golf packages:** No. **Season:** Year-round. **High:** April-May, Sept.-Oct. **On site lodging:** No. **Rental clubs:** Yes. **Walking policy:** Unrestricted walking. **Metal spikes allowed:** Yes. **Range:** Yes (grass/mats). **To obtain tee times:** Call.
Special Notes: Formerly Gadsden G & CC.

★★★GOLF HAMMOCK COUNTRY CLUB

2222 Golf Hammock Dr., Sebring, 33872, Highlands County, (941)382-2151, 90 miles S of Orlando.
Opened: 1976. **Holes:** 18. **Par:** 72/72. **Yards:** 6,431/5,352. **Course rating:** 71.0/70.2. **Slope:** 127/118. **Architect:** Ron Garl. **Green fee:** $14/$40. **Credit cards:** MC,VISA.
Reduced fees: Low season, resort guests, twilight, juniors. **Caddies:** No. **Golf carts:** Included in Green Fee. **Discount golf packages:** No. **Season:** Year-round. **High:** Oct.-April. **On site lodging:** No. **Rental clubs:** Yes. **Walking policy:** Mandatory cart. **Metal spikes allowed:** Yes. **Range:** Yes (grass). **To obtain tee times:** Call up to 48 hours in advance.
Subscriber comments: Ordinary...Open...Tough par 3s.

GRAND CYPRESS GOLF CLUB

R-One N. Jacaranda, Orlando, 32836, Orange County, (407)239-1904, (800)835-7377.

Architect: Jack Nicklaus. **Green fee:** $90/$179. **Credit cards:** All major,Diners Club, Carte Blanche. **Reduced fees:** Low season, twilight, juniors. **Caddies:** Yes. **Golf carts:** Included in Green Fee. **Discount golf packages:** Yes. **Season:** Year-round. **High:** Oct.-May. **On site lodging:** Yes. **Rental clubs:** Yes. **Metal spikes allowed:** Yes. **Range:** Yes (grass). **To obtain tee times:** Call starter. You must be a guest at the Villas of Grand Cypress or at the Hyatt Regency Grand Cypress to play golf. You may book up to 4 tee times up to 60 days in advance.

★★★★**NEW COURSE**
Opened: 1988. **Holes:** 18. **Par:** 72/72. **Yards:** 6,773/5,314. **Course rating:** 72.1/69.8. **Slope:** 126/117. **Walking policy:** Unrestricted walking.
Notes: Ranked 28th in 1997 Best in State. World Cup of Golf.
Subscriber comments: Fun course, like Scottish links...If you can't go to St. Andrews, this is second-best...Interesting layout...Fun idea but can't come near the real thing...I can hardly wait to play it again...Beautiful, but you can't put Scotland in Florida...Watch out for pot bunkers...Love those double greens.

★★★½**NORTH/EAST/SOUTH COURSES**
Opened: 1984. **Holes:** 27. **Walking policy:** Mandatory cart.
NORTH/EAST
Par: 72/72. **Yards:** 6,955/5,056. **Course rating:** 73.9/69.1. **Slope:** 130/130.
NORTH/SOUTH
Par: 72/72. **Yards:** 6,993/5,328. **Course rating:** 73.9/71.1. **Slope:** 130/130.
SOUTH/EAST
Par: 72/72. **Yards:** 6,906/5,126. **Course rating:** 74.4/70.2. **Slope:** 132/132.
Notes: LPGA Tournament of Champions; PGA Tour Skills Challenge and Shark Shootout.
Subscriber comments: Good quality...Nice course but not memorable...Lots of shots over water...Looking forward to playing again...Did not want to leave...Wonderful resort...Plush...Need to know the course or bring extra golf balls.

★★★**GRAND PALMS GOLF & COUNTRY CLUB RESORT**
R-110 Grand Palms Dr., Pembroke Pines, 33027, Broward County, (305)437-3334, (800)327-9246, 15 miles SW of Ft. Lauderdale.
Opened: 1987. **Holes:** 27. **Architect:** Ward Northrup. **Green fee:** $25/$70. **Credit cards:** MC,VISA,AMEX. **Reduced fees:** Weekdays, low season, resort guests, twilight. **Caddies:** No. **Golf carts:** Included in Green Fee. **Discount golf packages:** Yes. **Season:** Year-round. **High:** Dec.-April. **On site lodging:** Yes. **Rental clubs:** Yes. **Walking policy:** Mandatory cart. **Metal spikes allowed:** Yes. **Range:** Yes (grass/mats). **To obtain tee times:** Call up to 3 days in advance.
GRAND/ROYAL
Par: 72/72. **Yards:** 6,816/5,245. **Course rating:** 71.6/69.4. **Slope:** 127/119.
ROYAL/SABAL
Par: 73/73. **Yards:** 6,736/5,391. **Course rating:** 71.9/69.7. **Slope:** 128/120.
SABAL/GRAND
Par: 71/71. **Yards:** 6,653/5,198. **Course rating:** 71.5/69.5. **Slope:** 124/117.
Subscriber comments: Breezes make most shots tricky...Good greens...Great way to play 27...Very challenging...Nice course, some gimmicky holes...Swampy when wet...Trees are getting bigger.

GRENELEFE GOLF & TENNIS RESORT

R- 3200 State Rd. 546, Haines City, 33844, Polk County, (941)422-7511, (800)237-9549, 25 miles S of Orlando.
Credit cards: MC,VISA,AMEX. **Reduced fees:** Weekdays, low season, resort guests, twilight. **Caddies:** No. **Golf carts:** Included in Green Fee. **Discount golf packages:** Yes. **Season:** Year-round. **High:** Jan.-April. **On site lodging:** Yes. **Rental clubs:** Yes. **Walking policy:** Mandatory cart. **Metal spikes allowed:** Yes. **Range:** Yes (grass). **To obtain tee times:** Package guests may book starting times 90 days in advance.
Notes: PGA Tour Qualifying School.
★★★**EAST COURSE**
Opened: 1978. **Holes:** 18. **Par:** 72/72. **Yards:** 6,802/5,114. **Course rating:** 72.5/69.2.

Slope: 123/114. **Architect:** Arnold Palmer/Ed Seay. **Green fee:** $32/$100.
Subscriber comments: Thick rough...Tight course, small greens...Some interesting holes...Ample bunkers.

★★★½SOUTH COURSE
Opened: 1983. **Holes:** 18. **Par:** 71/71. **Yards:** 6,869/5,174. **Course rating:** 72.6/69.5.
Slope: 124/115. **Architect:** Ron Garl. **Green fee:** $32/$100.
Subscriber comments: Fair...Good playing conditions...Looking forward to playing again...Demanding, fair, pleasant...Sand and water make it a challenge.

★★★★WEST COURSE
Opened: 1971. **Holes:** 18. **Par:** 72/72. **Yards:** 7,325/5,398. **Course rating:** 75.0/70.9.
Slope: 130/118. **Architect:** Robert Trent Jones/David Wallace. **Green fee:** $32/$120.
Subscriber comments: Fair course for average golfer, good to seniors...Small, well-protected greens...Wonderful practice facilities...Villas/condos on fairways...Eager to return...Old Florida...A very good test of skills.

★★★GULF HARBOUR YACHT & COUNTRY CLUB
14700 Portsmouth Blvd. S.W., Fort Myers, 33908, Lee County, (941)433-4211.
Opened: 1984. **Holes:** 18. **Par:** 72/72. **Yards:** 6,708/5,248. **Course rating:** 72.5/70.1.
Slope: 130/121. **Architect:** Ron Garl. **Green fee:** $27/$90. **Credit cards:** All major.
Reduced fees: Low season, twilight. **Caddies:** No. **Golf carts:** Included in Green Fee.
Discount golf packages: No. **Season:** Year-round. **High:** Jan.-May. **On site lodging:** No. **Rental clubs:** Yes. **Walking policy:** Mandatory cart. **Metal spikes allowed:** Yes.
Range: Yes (grass). **To obtain tee times:** Call up to 2 days in advance.
Subscriber comments: Conditions OK...Lots of water...Decent.

★★★HABITAT GOLF COURSE
PU-3591 Fairgreen St., Valkaria, 32905, Brevard County, (407)952-6312, 16 miles S of Melbourne.
Opened: 1991. **Holes:** 18. **Par:** 72/72. **Yards:** 6,836/4,969. **Course rating:** 72.9/68.2.
Slope: 129/115. **Architect:** Charles Ankrom. **Green fee:** $13/$25. **Credit cards:** MC,VISA. **Reduced fees:** Weekdays, low season, resort guests, juniors. **Caddies:** No.
Golf carts: $9. **Discount golf packages:** Yes. **Season:** Year-round. **High:** Dec.-March.
On site lodging: No. **Rental clubs:** Yes. **Walking policy:** Walking at certain times.
Metal spikes allowed: Yes. **Range:** Yes (grass). **To obtain tee times:** Call up to 3 days in advance.
Subscriber comments: Impossible to walk. Ride to tee is longer than some holes...Course needs work and is getting it. Good layout. Good test for every level...Good, tough test.

★★★HAILE PLANTATION GOLF & COUNTRY CLUB
9905 S.W. 44th Ave., Gainesville, 32608, Alachua County, (352)335-0055, 120 miles N of Tampa.
Opened: 1993. **Holes:** 18. **Par:** 72/72. **Yards:** 6,526/4,807. **Course rating:** 71.5/67.7.
Slope: 124/109. **Architect:** Gary Player. **Green fee:** $33/$37. **Credit cards:** MC,VISA,AMEX. **Reduced fees:** Twilight. **Caddies:** No. **Golf carts:** Included in Green Fee. **Discount golf packages:** No. **Season:** Year-round. **High:** Nov.-April. **On site lodging:** No. **Rental clubs:** Yes. **Walking policy:** Mandatory cart. **Metal spikes allowed:** Yes. **Range:** Yes (mats). **To obtain tee times:** Call up to 3 days in advance.
Subscriber comments: Interesting layout: Six par 5s, six par 4s and six par 3s...OK. Short. Nothing great...Has retained natural setting.

★★★HALIFAX PLANTATION GOLF CLUB
4000 Old Dixie Hwy., Ormond Beach, 32174, Volusia County, (904)676-9600, 20 miles N of Daytona Beach.
Opened: 1993. **Holes:** 18. **Par:** 72/72. **Yards:** 7,128/4,971. **Course rating:** 73.9/67.6.
Slope: 129/113. **Architect:** Bill Amick. **Green fee:** $10/$35. **Credit cards:** MC,VISA,AMEX. **Reduced fees:** Weekdays, low season, resort guests, twilight.
Caddies: No. **Golf carts:** $14. **Discount golf packages:** Yes. **Season:** Year-round.
High: Nov.-April. **On site lodging:** No. **Rental clubs:** Yes. **Walking policy:** Walking at certain times. **Metal spikes allowed:** Yes. **Range:** Yes (grass). **To obtain tee times:** Call 2 days in advance.
Subscriber comments: Beautiful new course. Walkable...Will improve...Lots of bugs...Easy to score...Parkland course. Very few views.

FLORIDA

★½HALL OF FAME GOLF COURSE
2227 N Westshore Blvd., Tampa, 33607, Hillsborough County, (813)876-4913.
Call club for further information.

★½HARDER HALL COUNTRY CLUB
PU-3600 Golfview Dr., Sebring, 33872, Highlands County, (941)382-0500, 80 miles S of Orlando.
Opened: 1956. **Holes:** 18. **Par:** 72/72. **Yards:** 6,300/5,003. **Course rating:** 70.0/68.5. **Slope:** 116/114. **Architect:** Dick Wilson. **Green fee:** $13/$34. **Credit cards:** MC,VISA,DISC. **Reduced fees:** Low season, resort guests, twilight. **Caddies:** No. **Golf carts:** Included in Green Fee. **Discount golf packages:** No. **Season:** Year-round. **High:** Jan.-April. **On site lodging:** No. **Rental clubs:** Yes. **Walking policy:** Mandatory cart. **Metal spikes allowed:** Yes. **Range:** Yes (grass). **To obtain tee times:** Call 2 days in advance in season.

HERITAGE LINKS COUNTRY CLUB AT TURKEY CREEK
11400 Turkey Creek Blvd., Alachua, 32615, Alchua County, (904)462-4655, 5 miles NW of Gainesville.
Opened: 1977. **Holes:** 18. **Par:** 72/72. **Yards:** 6,570/5,580. **Course rating:** 71.2/71.8. **Slope:** 121/121. **Architect:** Wade Northrup. **Green fee:** $19/$28. **Credit cards:** All major. **Reduced fees:** Weekdays, low season, resort guests, twilight, juniors. **Caddies:** Yes. **Golf carts:** Included in Green Fee. **Discount golf packages:** No. **Season:** Year-round. **High:** Nov.-March. **On site lodging:** Yes. **Rental clubs:** Yes. **Walking policy:** Walking at certain times. **Metal spikes allowed:** Yes. **Range:** Yes (grass). **To obtain tee times:** Nonmembers call up to 3 days in advance.
Special Notes: This course is open to members only on weekends.

★½HILAMAN PARK MUNICIPAL GOLF COURSE
PM-2737 Blairstone Rd., Tallahassee, 32301, Leon County, (904)891-3935.
Opened: 1972. **Holes:** 18. **Par:** 72/72. **Yards:** 6,364/5,365. **Course rating:** 70.1/70.8. **Slope:** 121/116. **Architect:** Edward Lawrence Packard. **Green fee:** $11/$15. **Credit cards:** MC,VISA,DISC. **Reduced fees:** Weekdays, twilight, seniors, juniors. **Caddies:** No. **Golf carts:** $10. **Discount golf packages:** No. **Season:** Year-round. **High:** March-June. **On site lodging:** No. **Rental clubs:** Yes. **Walking policy:** Walking at certain times. **Metal spikes allowed:** Yes. **Range:** Yes (grass/mats). **To obtain tee times:** Call 7 days in advance.

★★★½HOMBRE GOLF CLUB
120 Coyote Pass, Panama City Beach, 32407, Bay County, (904)234-3673, 100 miles SE of Pensacola.
Opened: 1990. **Holes:** 18. **Par:** 72/74. **Yards:** 6,820/4,793. **Course rating:** 73.4/67.2. **Slope:** 136/118. **Architect:** Wes Burnham. **Green fee:** $60/$65. **Credit cards:** MC,VISA,DISC. **Reduced fees:** Weekdays, low season, resort guests, twilight, juniors. **Caddies:** No. **Golf carts:** Included in Green Fee. **Discount golf packages:** Yes. **Season:** Year-round. **High:** March-April/June-July. **On site lodging:** No. **Rental clubs:** Yes. **Walking policy:** Mandatory cart. **Metal spikes allowed:** Yes. **Range:** Yes (grass). **To obtain tee times:** Call up to 7 days in advance. Golf package tee times up to 6 months in advance.
Subscriber comments: Difficult course, fun to play...Stay away from the tips and its very playable...Heavy traffic on course in spring/summer months...Tough when the wind blows...Too crowded, but nice course...I play it every winter...Lots of water.

★★★½HUNTER'S CREEK GOLF CLUB
R-14401 Sports Club Way, Orlando, 32837, Orange County, (407)240-4653.
Opened: 1986. **Holes:** 18. **Par:** 72/72. **Yards:** 7,432/5,755. **Course rating:** 75.2/72.5. **Slope:** 127/120. **Architect:** Lloyd Clifton. **Green fee:** $35/$80. **Credit cards:** MC,VISA. **Reduced fees:** Weekdays, low season, twilight. **Caddies:** No. **Golf carts:** Included in Green Fee. **Discount golf packages:** No. **Season:** Year-round. **High:** Jan.-March. **On site lodging:** No. **Rental clubs:** Yes. **Walking policy:** Mandatory cart. **Metal spikes allowed:** Yes. **Range:** Yes (grass). **To obtain tee times:** Call 3 days in advance.
Subscriber comments: Good facilities...Too long except for low-handicappers...Back tees are very challenging...Challenging.

★★★½ HUNTINGTON HILLS GOLF & COUNTRY CLUB
2626 Duff Rd., Lakeland, 33809, Polk County, (941)859-3689, 33 miles E of Tampa.
Opened: 1992. **Holes:** 18. **Par:** 72/72. **Yards:** 6,631/5,011. **Course rating:** 72.5/68.7.
Slope: 122/115. **Architect:** Ron Garl. **Green fee:** $25/$35. **Credit cards:** All major,Diners Club. **Reduced fees:** Weekdays, low season, twilight. **Caddies:** No. **Golf carts:** Included in Green Fee. **Discount golf packages:** Yes. **Season:** Year-round.
High: Dec.-March. **On site lodging:** No. **Rental clubs:** Yes. **Walking policy:** Mandatory cart. **Metal spikes allowed:** Yes. **Range:** Yes (grass). **To obtain tee times:** Call three days in advance.
Subscriber comments: Nice elevations for South Florida...Greens tough to read...Imaginative layout.

★★½ HYDE PARK GOLF CLUB
PU-6439 Hyde Grove Ave., Jacksonville, 32210, Duval County, (904)786-5410, 5 miles W of Jacksonville.
Opened: 1925. **Holes:** 18. **Par:** 72/73. **Yards:** 6,500/5,500. **Course rating:** 70.3/71.0.
Slope: 120/122. **Architect:** Donald Ross. **Green fee:** $15/$18. **Credit cards:** MC,VISA.
Reduced fees: N/A. **Caddies:** No. **Golf carts:** $14. **Discount golf packages:** No.
Season: Year-round. **High:** N/A. **On site lodging:** No. **Rental clubs:** Yes. **Walking policy:** Walking at certain times. **Metal spikes allowed:** Yes. **Range:** Yes (grass). **To obtain tee times:** N/A.
Notes: 1947 PGA Jacksonville Open.
Subscriber comments: Old course with a lot of nostalgia...A must play for golf history buffs...Not one of Donald Ross' best...Could be great. A classic course...Big trees.

★★★ IMPERIAL LAKEWOODS GOLF CLUB
6807 Buffalo Rd., Palmetto, 34221, Manatee County, (941)747-4653, 20 miles S of Tampa.
Opened: 1987. **Holes:** 18. **Par:** 72/72. **Yards:** 6,658/5,270. **Course rating:** 71.5/69.7.
Slope: 123/117. **Architect:** Ted McAnlis. **Green fee:** $45. **Credit cards:** MC,VISA.
Reduced fees: Weekdays, low season, twilight, juniors. **Caddies:** No. **Golf carts:** Included in Green Fee. **Discount golf packages:** No. **Season:** Year-round. **High:** Nov.-April. **On site lodging:** No. **Rental clubs:** Yes. **Walking policy:** Unrestricted walking. **Metal spikes allowed:** Yes. **Range:** Yes (grass). **To obtain tee times:** Call or come in 2 days in advance.
Subscriber comments: Wide open...OK...Needs better drainage...Don't remember much...Can be very windy.

★★★ INDIAN BAYOU GOLF & COUNTRY CLUB
1 Country Club Dr. E., Destin, 32541, Okaloosa County, (850)837-6191, 30 miles W of Pensacola.
Opened: 1978. **Holes:** 27. **Architect:** Earl Stone. **Green fee:** $45/$50. **Credit cards:** MC,VISA,AMEX. **Reduced fees:** N/A. **Caddies:** No. **Golf carts:** Included in Green Fee.
Discount golf packages: No. **Season:** Year-round. **High:** Feb.-Aug. **On site lodging:** No. **Rental clubs:** Yes. **Walking policy:** Walking at certain times. **Metal spikes allowed:** Yes. **Range:** Yes (grass). **To obtain tee times:** Call up to 30 days in advance.
CHOCTAW/CREEK
Par: 72/71. **Yards:** 6,892/5,080. **Course rating:** 73.1/69.3. **Slope:** 129/113.
SEMINOLE/CHOCTAW
Par: 72/72. **Yards:** 6,958/5,455. **Course rating:** 73.3/71.2. **Slope:** 126/116.
SEMINOLE/CREEK
Par: 72/71. **Yards:** 7,016/5,081. **Course rating:** 73.7/69.2. **Slope:** 128/113.
Subscriber comments: Huge oaks, Spanish moss, beautiful...Flat course with some water...Nice course in a nice town...Friendly layout...I vacation in Destin each year to play here...Great lies in fairway...Solid course for vacationers...Big, soft greens...Hit straight, score well.

★★ INDIAN CREEK GOLF CLUB
PU-1800 Central Blvd., Jupiter, 33458, Palm Beach County, (561)747-6262.
Opened: 1982. **Holes:** 18. **Par:** 70/71. **Yards:** 6,265/5,150. **Course rating:** 69.9/69.5.
Slope: 117/118. **Architect:** Lamar Smith. **Green fee:** $26/$55. **Credit cards:** MC,VISA.
Reduced fees: Weekdays, low season, twilight. **Caddies:** No. **Golf carts:** Included in

Green Fee. **Discount golf packages:** No. **Season:** Year-round. **High:** Jan.-April. **On site lodging:** No. **Rental clubs:** Yes. **Walking policy:** Mandatory cart. **Metal spikes allowed:** Yes. **Range:** Yes (grass). **To obtain tee times:** Call up to 4 days in advance.

INDIAN LAKE ESTATES GOLF & COUNTRY CLUB
95 Red Grange Blvd., Indian Lake Estates, 33855, Polk County, (941)692-1514, 17 miles E of Lake Wales.
Opened: 1972. **Holes:** 18. **Par:** 72/72. **Yards:** 6,485/5,194. **Course rating:** 70.7/70.6.
Slope: 123/116. **Architect:** George W. Cobb. **Green fee:** $11/$30. **Credit cards:** MC,VISA. **Reduced fees:** Twilight. **Caddies:** No. **Golf carts:** Included in Green Fee.
Discount golf packages: No. **Season:** Year-round. **High:** Nov.-April. **On site lodging:** No. **Rental clubs:** Yes. **Walking policy:** Unrestricted walking. **Metal spikes allowed:** Yes. **Range:** Yes (grass). **To obtain tee times:** Call golf shop between 7 a.m. and 5 p.m. up to 7 days in advance. Groups of 12 or more may call anytime in advance for special rates.

★★★INDIGO LAKES GOLF CLUB
312 Indigo Dr., Daytona Beach, 32114, Volusia County, (904)254-3607, 1 mile E of Daytona Beach.
Opened: 1977. **Holes:** 18. **Par:** 72/72. **Yards:** 7,168/5,159. **Course rating:** 73.5/69.1.
Slope: 128/123. **Architect:** Lloyd Clifton. **Green fee:** $30/$55. **Credit cards:** MC,VISA,AMEX. **Reduced fees:** Weekdays, low season, twilight. **Caddies:** No. **Golf carts:** Included in Green Fee. **Discount golf packages:** Yes. **Season:** Year-round.
High: Jan.-May. **On site lodging:** Yes. **Rental clubs:** Yes. **Walking policy:** Mandatory cart. **Metal spikes allowed:** Yes. **Range:** Yes (grass/mats). **To obtain tee times:** Call up to 7 days in advance.
Notes: 1994 LPGA Sprint Championship.
Subscriber comments: Challenging...Long...Greens are small and fast...Delightful old-time course...Bring your sand wedge...Lots of water.
Special Notes: Formerly Holiday Inn Crowne Plaza Resort.

INNISBROOK HILTON RESORT
R-36750 Hwy. 19 N., Palm Harbor, 34684, Pinellas County, (813)942-2000, 25 miles NW of Tampa.
Credit cards: All major. **Reduced fees:** Low season, resort guests, juniors. **Caddies:** No. **Golf carts:** Included in Green Fee. **Discount golf packages:** Yes. **Season:** Year-round. **High:** Nov.-April. **On site lodging:** Yes. **Rental clubs:** Yes. **Walking policy:** Mandatory cart. **Metal spikes allowed:** Yes. **To obtain tee times:** Call.
★★★★½COPPERHEAD COURSE
Opened: 1972. **Holes:** 18. **Par:** 71/71. **Yards:** 7,087/5,506. **Course rating:** 74.4/72.0.
Slope: 140/128. **Architect:** Lawrence Packard/Roger Packard. **Green fee:** $18/$140.
Range: Yes (grass/mats).
Notes: Golf Digest School site. Ranked 23rd in 1997 Best in State. 1990-1998 JCPenney Classic.
Subscriber comments: A memorable course. Very long, just great...Great layout...A great resort...Would recommend to anyone...Scenic...Worth the price, once...Outstanding golf and service...Tough but rewarding...Treated like a king...It was everything I expected...Setup too hard for the average golfer.
★★★★ISLAND COURSE
Opened: 1970. **Holes:** 18. **Par:** 72/72. **Yards:** 6,999/5,795. **Course rating:** 73.2/74.1.
Slope: 133/130. **Architect:** Lawrence Packard. **Green fee:** $65/$120. **Range:** Yes (grass).
Notes: Golf Digest School site.
Subscriber comments: Still one of my favorite resorts...They really know how to take care of you...Lots of water. Can make you think twice...Hard to believe the hills and elevations in Florida.
★★★½SANDPIPER COURSE
Opened: 1971. **Holes:** 27. **Architect:** Lawrence Packard. **Green fee:** $55/$100.
Range: Yes (grass).
PALMETTO/PALMS
Par: 70/70. **Yards:** 5,969/4,733. **Course rating:** 68.7/66.9. **Slope:** 122/115.

PALMETTO/PINES
Par: 70/70. **Yards:** 6,245/5,001. **Course rating:** 69.8/68.4. **Slope:** 119/115.
PALMS/PINES
Par: 70/70. **Yards:** 6,200/4,926. **Course rating:** 69.8/68.1. **Slope:** 125/116.
Notes: Golf Digest School site.
Subscriber comments: Pretty short. Fairly tight...Great warm-up for the big courses.
Not enough variety...A little short...Short but sweet...Lots of water...Short.

★★★**INTERNATIONAL GOLF CLUB**
R-6351 International Golf Club Rd., Orlando, 32821, Orange County, (407)239-6909,
(800)371-1165.
Opened: 1986. **Holes:** 18. **Par:** 72/72. **Yards:** 6,776/5,077. **Course rating:** 71.7/68.5.
Slope: 117/109. **Architect:** Joe Lee. **Green fee:** $65/$65. **Credit cards:**
MC,VISA,AMEX. **Reduced fees:** Low season, twilight. **Caddies:** No. **Golf carts:**
Included in Green Fee. **Discount golf packages:** No. **Season:** Year-round. **High:** Jan.-
April. **On site lodging:** No. **Rental clubs:** Yes. **Walking policy:** Mandatory cart. **Metal
spikes allowed:** Yes. **Range:** Yes (grass). **To obtain tee times:** Call 1 day in advance.
Subscriber comments: OK for area and time of year...Good course for the
amateur...Acceptable backup course.

INTERNATIONAL LINKS MIAMI AT MELREESE GOLF COURSE
PU-1802 N.W. 37th Ave., Miami, 33125, Dade County, (305)633-4583.
Opened: 1997. **Holes:** 18. **Par:** 71/71. **Yards:** 7,173/5,534. **Course rating:** 73.5/71.2.
Slope: 132/118. **Architect:** Charles Mahannah. **Green fee:** $45/$75. **Credit cards:** All
major. **Reduced fees:** Weekdays, low season, twilight, juniors. **Caddies:** No. **Golf
carts:** Included in Green Fee. **Discount golf packages:** Yes. **Season:** Year-round.
High: Dec.-April. **On site lodging:** No. **Rental clubs:** Yes. **Walking policy:** Mandatory
cart. **Metal spikes allowed:** No. **Range:** Yes (grass/mats). **To obtain tee times:** Call 3
days in advance.
Special notes: Formerly Melreese Golf Course.

★★**IRONWOOD GOLF COURSE**
PU-2100 N.E. 39th Ave., Gainesville, 32609, Alachua County, (352)334-3120.
Opened: 1964. **Holes:** 18. **Par:** 72/72. **Yards:** 6,465/5,234. **Course rating:** 71.3/70.2.
Slope: 122/117. **Architect:** David G. Wallace. **Green fee:** $10/$13. **Credit cards:**
MC,VISA,DISC. **Reduced fees:** Weekdays, low season, twilight, seniors, juniors.
Caddies: Yes. **Golf carts:** $8. **Discount golf packages:** No. **Season:** Year-round.
High: Feb.-June. **On site lodging:** No. **Rental clubs:** Yes. **Walking policy:**
Unrestricted walking. **Metal spikes allowed:** Yes. **Range:** Yes (grass). **To obtain tee
times:** Call 2 days in advance.

JACARANDA GOLF CLUB
9200 W. Broward Blvd., Plantation, 33324, Broward County, (954)472-5836, 12 miles W
of Fort Lauderdale.
Opened: N/A. **Green fee:** $25/$93. **Credit cards:** MC,VISA,AMEX. **Reduced fees:**
Weekdays, low season, twilight. **Caddies:** No. **Golf carts:** Included in Green Fee.
Discount golf packages: Yes. **Season:** Year-round. **High:** Nov.-May. **On site lodging:**
No. **Rental clubs:** No. **Walking policy:** Walking at certain times. **Metal spikes
allowed:** Yes. **Range:** Yes (grass/mats). **To obtain tee times:** Call up to 7 days in
advance. Anytime in advance with credit card.
★★★½**EAST COURSE**
Holes: 18. **Par:** 72/72. **Yards:** 7,195/5,638. **Course rating:** 74.0/72.3. **Slope:** 130/124.
Architect: Mark Mahannah.
Subscriber comments: Beautiful in early spring...Long from the blues. Lots of 3-
woods!...One of my favorites.
★★★**WEST COURSE**
Holes: 18. **Par:** 72/72. **Yards:** 6,729/5,314. **Course rating:** 72.5/71.1. **Slope:** 132/118.
Architect: Mark Mahannah/Charles Mahannah.
Subscriber comments: Average course...Golf-cart gridlock.

★★½**JACARANDA WEST COUNTRY CLUB**
601 Jacaranda Blvd., Venice, 34293, Sarasota County, (941)493-2664, 20 miles S of
Sarasota.

Opened: 1974. **Holes:** 18. **Par:** 72/72. **Yards:** 6,602/5,321. **Course rating:** 71.9/70.7. **Slope:** 126/120. **Architect:** Mark Mahannah. **Green fee:** $23/$50. **Credit cards:** MC,VISA,DISC. **Reduced fees:** Low season, twilight, juniors. **Caddies:** No. **Golf carts:** Included in Green Fee. **Discount golf packages:** No. **Season:** Year-round. **High:** Jan.-April. **On site lodging:** No. **Rental clubs:** Yes. **Walking policy:** Mandatory cart. **Metal spikes allowed:** Yes. **Range:** Yes (grass/mats). **To obtain tee times:** Call 2 days in advance.
Subscriber comments: Fair layout and course.

★★JACKSONVILLE BEACH GOLF CLUB
PM-605 S. Penman Rd., Jacksonville, 32250, Duval County, (904)247-6184, 10 miles E of Jacksonville.
Opened: 1959. **Holes:** 18. **Par:** 72/72. **Yards:** 6,510/5,245. **Course rating:** 70.5/69.2. **Slope:** 119/114. **Architect:** Robert Walker. **Green fee:** $17/$19. **Credit cards:** MC,VISA. **Reduced fees:** Weekdays, low season, twilight, juniors. **Caddies:** No. **Golf carts:** N/A. **Discount golf packages:** No. **Season:** Year-round. **High:** Spring/Fall. **On site lodging:** No. **Rental clubs:** Yes. **Walking policy:** Walking at certain times. **Metal spikes allowed:** Yes. **Range:** Yes (grass/mats). **To obtain tee times:** Call Monday at 7 a.m. for next 7 days only.

★★★KEY WEST RESORT GOLF COURSE
PU-6450 E. College Rd., Key West, 33040, Monroe County, (305)294-5232.
Opened: N/A. **Holes:** 18. **Par:** 70/70. **Yards:** 6,526/5,183. **Course rating:** 71.2/70.1. **Slope:** 124/118. **Architect:** Rees Jones. **Green fee:** $42/$53. **Credit cards:** MC,VISA,AMEX. **Reduced fees:** Low season, twilight, juniors. **Caddies:** No. **Golf carts:** N/A. **Discount golf packages:** Yes. **Season:** Year-round. **High:** Nov.-April. **On site lodging:** No. **Rental clubs:** Yes. **Walking policy:** Walking at certain times. **Metal spikes allowed:** Yes. **Range:** Yes. **To obtain tee times:** Call up to 14 days in advance.
Subscriber comments: Different course from tips...Good potential. Must check back after repairs and completion of construction of nearby condos.

★★★KILLEARN COUNTRY CLUB & INN
R-100 Tyron Circle, Tallahassee, 32308, Leon County, (850)893-2144, (800)476-4101.
Opened: 1967. **Holes:** 27. **Architect:** William Amick. **Green fee:** $30/$35. **Credit cards:** All major. **Reduced fees:** Low season, resort guests, juniors. **Caddies:** No. **Golf carts:** $12. **Discount golf packages:** Yes. **Season:** Year-round. **High:** March-Aug. **On site lodging:** Yes. **Rental clubs:** Yes. **Walking policy:** Walking at certain times. **Metal spikes allowed:** Yes. **Range:** Yes (grass/mats). **To obtain tee times:** Call 7 days in advance.
EAST/NORTH
Par: 72/74. **Yards:** 6,760/5,524. **Course rating:** 73.1/72.6. **Slope:** 131/120.
SOUTH/EAST
Par: 72/74. **Yards:** 7,025/5,661. **Course rating:** 73.9/73.0. **Slope:** 133/123.
SOUTH/NORTH
Par: 72/74. **Yards:** 6,899/5,537. **Course rating:** 73.3/72.5. **Slope:** 132/121.
Notes: PGA Tour Tallahassee Open (18 years.); LPGA Tour Centel Classic (2 years.).
Subscriber comments: Relies on wind...16th, 17th and 18th make a great finish...Good facilities...Average course...Lakes come into play.

KINGS ISLAND GOLF CLUB
P-175 Kings Highway, Port Charlotte, 33981, Charlotte County, (941)629-7800, 2 miles E of Port Charlotte.
Opened: 1996. **Holes:** 18. **Par:** 63/63. **Yards:** 4,150/3,005. **Course rating:** 61.7/60.0. **Slope:** 108/100. **Architect:** N/A. **Green fee:** $16/$28. **Credit cards:** MC,VISA. **Reduced fees:** Low season, twilight. **Caddies:** No. **Golf carts:** Included in Green Fee. **Discount golf packages:** No. **Season:** Year-round. **High:** Nov.-April. **On site lodging:** No. **Rental clubs:** No. **Walking policy:** Mandatory cart. **Metal spikes allowed:** Yes. **Range:** Yes (grass). **To obtain tee times:** Call up to 3 days in advance.

★★★KISSIMMEE BAY COUNTRY CLUB
2801 Kissimmee Bay Blvd., Kissimmee, 34744, Osceola County, (407)348-4653, 10 miles S of Orlando.
Opened: 1990. **Holes:** 18. **Par:** 71/71. **Yards:** 6,846/5,171. **Course rating:** 70.1/71.0.

Slope: 125/122. **Architect:** Lloyd Clifton. **Green fee:** $35/$70. **Credit cards:** MC,VISA,DISC. **Reduced fees:** Weekdays, low season, twilight. **Caddies:** No. **Golf carts:** Included in Green Fee. **Discount golf packages:** Yes. **Season:** Year-round. **High:** Jan.-April. **On site lodging:** No. **Rental clubs:** Yes. **Walking policy:** Mandatory cart. **Metal spikes allowed:** Yes. **Range:** Yes (grass). **To obtain tee times:** Call 7 days in advance.
Subscriber comments: A lot of water...Tougher than it looks.

★★★KISSIMMEE GOLF CLUB

3103 Florida Coach Dr., Kissimmee, 34741, Osceola County, (407)847-2816, 15 miles S of Orlando.
Opened: 1970. **Holes:** 18. **Par:** 72/72. **Yards:** 6,537/5,083. **Course rating:** 71.4/68.6.
Slope: 119/109. **Architect:** Bill Bulmer/Gordon Lewis. **Green fee:** $30/$48. **Credit cards:** MC,VISA. **Reduced fees:** Low season, resort guests, twilight. **Caddies:** No.
Golf carts: Included in Green Fee. **Discount golf packages:** Yes. **Season:** Year-round. **High:** Dec.-April. **On site lodging:** No. **Rental clubs:** Yes. **Walking policy:** Walking at certain times. **Metal spikes allowed:** Yes. **Range:** Yes (grass). **To obtain tee times:** Call up to 4 days in advance.
Subscriber comments: Airport along first hole. Noisy...Some tight holes.

★★★★LPGA INTERNATIONAL

PU-300 Champions Dr., Daytona Beach, 32124, Volusia County, (904)274-3880, 40 miles NE of Orlando.
Opened: 1994. **Holes:** 18. **Par:** 72/72. **Yards:** 7,088/5,131. **Course rating:** 74.0/68.9.
Slope: 134/122. **Architect:** Rees Jones. **Green fee:** $25/$60. **Credit cards:** MC,VISA,AMEX. **Reduced fees:** Low season, twilight. **Caddies:** No. **Golf carts:** Included in Green Fee. **Discount golf packages:** No. **Season:** Year-round. **High:** Nov.-Dec. **On site lodging:** No. **Rental clubs:** Yes. **Walking policy:** Walking at certain times. **Metal spikes allowed:** Yes. **Range:** Yes (grass). **To obtain tee times:** Call seven days in advance.
Notes: Home of the LPGA Tour.
Subscriber comments: Great layout...Beautiful new course...Windy and open...Exceptional practice facility...Course still maturing...Worth the trip to Daytona...Very pretty...Lots of wildlife...Treated like a pro...Too much wind. Nothing to block wind...Need your A game.

★★LAKE WORTH GOLF CLUB

PM-1-7th Ave. N., Lake Worth, 33460, Palm Beach County, (561)582-9713, 7 miles S of Palm Beach.
Opened: 1926. **Holes:** 18. **Par:** 70/70. **Yards:** 6,113/5,413. **Course rating:** 68.6/69.6.
Slope: 116/113. **Architect:** William B. Langford/Theodore J. Moreau. **Green fee:** $10/$23. **Credit cards:** MC,VISA,Debit cards. **Reduced fees:** Low season, twilight, juniors. **Caddies:** No. **Golf carts:** $21. **Discount golf packages:** Yes. **Season:** Year-round. **High:** Jan.-March. **On site lodging:** No. **Rental clubs:** Yes. **Walking policy:** Unrestricted walking. **Metal spikes allowed:** Yes. **Range:** No. **To obtain tee times:** Call 1 day in advance at 9 a.m.

★★★LANSBROOK GOLF COURSE

4605 Village Center Dr., Palm Harbor, 34685, Pinellas County, (813)784-7333, 20 miles W of Tampa.
Opened: 1975. **Holes:** 18. **Par:** 72/72. **Yards:** 6,719/5,264. **Course rating:** 71.6/69.3.
Slope: 126/119. **Architect:** Lane Marshall. **Green fee:** $30/$45. **Credit cards:** MC,VISA,DISC. **Reduced fees:** Weekdays, low season, twilight. **Caddies:** No. **Golf carts:** Included in Green Fee. **Discount golf packages:** No. **Season:** Year-round. **High:** Dec.-April. **On site lodging:** No. **Rental clubs:** Yes. **Walking policy:** Mandatory cart. **Metal spikes allowed:** Yes. **Range:** Yes (grass/mats). **To obtain tee times:** Call 4 days in advance.
Subscriber comments: Better hit it straight. Water and woods...Narrow fairways.

LELY RESORT GOLF & COUNTRY CLUB

PU-8004 Lely Resort Blvd., Naples, 34113, Collier County, (941)793-2223, (800)388-4653, 30 miles S of Ft. Myers.
Credit cards: All major. **Reduced fees:** Low season, twilight. **Caddies:** No. **Golf carts:**

Included in Green Fee. **Discount golf packages:** No. **Season:** Year-round. **High:** Nov.-April. **On site lodging:** No. **Rental clubs:** Yes. **Walking policy:** Mandatory cart. **Metal spikes allowed:** Yes. **Range:** Yes (grass). **To obtain tee times:** Call up to 3 days in advance. Credit card required Nov.-April.

★★★½LELY FLAMINGO ISLAND CLUB
Opened: 1990. **Holes:** 18. **Par:** 72/72. **Yards:** 7,171/5,377. **Course rating:** 73.9/70.6. **Slope:** 135/126. **Architect:** Robert Trent Jones. **Green fee:** $35/$135.
Subscriber comments: Beautiful scenery. Great resort course...Too much wind, too much sand...Must play if you come to Southwest Florida...Bunkers are tough...Lots of water and wildlife.

LELY MUSTANG GOLF CLUB
Opened: 1997. **Holes:** 18. **Par:** 72/72. **Yards:** 7,217/5,197. **Course rating:** N/A. **Slope:** N/A. **Architect:** Charles Mahannah/Lee Trevino. **Green fee:** $43/$148.

LEMON BAY GOLF CLUB
9600 Eagle Preserve Dr., Englewood, 34224, Sarasota County, (941)697-3729, 28 miles S of Sarasota.
Opened: 1982. **Holes:** 18. **Par:** 71/71. **Yards:** 6,176/4,992. **Course rating:** 69.2/67.8. **Slope:** 119/114. **Architect:** Jim Petrides/Chip Powell. **Green fee:** $19/$44. **Credit cards:** MC,VISA. **Reduced fees:** Low season. **Caddies:** No. **Golf carts:** Included in Green Fee. **Discount golf packages:** No. **Season:** Year-round. **High:** Jan.-April. **On site lodging:** No. **Rental clubs:** Yes. **Walking policy:** Walking at certain times. **Metal spikes allowed:** Yes. **Range:** Yes (grass). **To obtain tee times:** Call 2 days in advance.

★★★½THE LINKS AT POLO TRACE
13481 Polo Trace Dr., Delray Beach, 33446, Palm Beach County, (407)495-5300, 30 miles S of West Palm Beach.
Opened: 1989. **Holes:** 18. **Par:** 72/72. **Yards:** 7,096/5,314. **Course rating:** 73.4/71.0. **Slope:** 134/124. **Architect:** Karl Litten/Joey Sindelar. **Green fee:** $30/$100. **Credit cards:** All major. **Reduced fees:** Weekdays, low season, resort guests, twilight, seniors, juniors. **Caddies:** No. **Golf carts:** Included in Green Fee. **Discount golf packages:** Yes. **Season:** Year-round. **High:** Dec.-April. **On site lodging:** No. **Rental clubs:** Yes. **Walking policy:** Mandatory cart. **Metal spikes allowed:** Yes. **Range:** Yes (grass/mats). **To obtain tee times:** Call golf shop.
Subscriber comments: Good, fair course...Lots of hills...Solid test...Wide-open fairways. Drive without fear...Worth the trip.
Special Notes: Spikeless encouraged.

★★★THE LINKS OF LAKE BERNADETTE
5430 Links Lane, Zephyrhills, 33541, Pasco County, (813)788-4653, 20 miles N of Tampa.
Opened: 1985. **Holes:** 18. **Par:** 71/71. **Yards:** 6,392/5,031. **Course rating:** 70.0/68.0. **Slope:** 117/118. **Architect:** Dean Refram. **Green fee:** $20/$35. **Credit cards:** MC,VISA,AMEX. **Reduced fees:** Weekdays, low season, twilight. **Caddies:** No. **Golf carts:** Included in Green Fee. **Discount golf packages:** No. **Season:** Year-round. **High:** Jan.-April. **On site lodging:** No. **Rental clubs:** Yes. **Walking policy:** Mandatory cart. **Metal spikes allowed:** Yes. **Range:** No. **To obtain tee times:** Call 3 days in advance.
Subscriber comments: Some good holes...Good layout for mid-handicapper.

★★½LOCHMOOR COUNTRY CLUB
3911 Orange Grove Blvd., North Fort Myers, 33903, Lee County, (941)995-0501, 5 miles N of Fort Myers.
Opened: 1972. **Holes:** 18. **Par:** 72/72. **Yards:** 6,908/5,152. **Course rating:** 73.1/69.1. **Slope:** 128/116. **Architect:** William F. Mitchell. **Green fee:** $14/$50. **Credit cards:** MC,VISA,AMEX. **Reduced fees:** Low season, twilight, juniors. **Caddies:** No. **Golf carts:** Included in Green Fee. **Discount golf packages:** No. **Season:** Year-round. **High:** Jan.-April. **On site lodging:** No. **Rental clubs:** Yes. **Walking policy:** Walking at certain times. **Metal spikes allowed:** Yes. **Range:** Yes (grass). **To obtain tee times:** Call up to 2 days in advance.
Subscriber comments: Open, but lots of wind...Wide fairways.

FLORIDA

★★★LONGBOAT KEY CLUB (ISLANDSIDE COURSE)
R-361 Gulf of Mexico Dr., Longboat Key, 34228, Sarasota County, (941)387-1632, 3 miles NW of Sarasota.
Opened: N/A. **Holes:** 18. **Par:** 72/72. **Yards:** 6,792/5,198. **Course rating:** N/A. **Slope:** 138/121. **Architect:** William F. Mitchell. **Green fee:** $65/$110. **Credit cards:** None. **Reduced fees:** Low season, twilight. **Caddies:** No. **Golf carts:** Included in Green Fee. **Discount golf packages:** Yes. **Season:** Year-round. **High:** Dec.-May. **On site lodging:** Yes. **Rental clubs:** Yes. **Walking policy:** Mandatory cart. **Metal spikes allowed:** Yes. **Range:** Yes (grass/mats). **To obtain tee times:** Must be a guest at the resort to play.
Subscriber comments: Nice, lots of trees...Challenging for average golfer...Lots of water.

LOST KEY GOLF CLUB
PU-625 Lost Key Dr., Perdido Key, 32507, Escambia County, (904)492-1300, (888)256-7853, 2 miles S of Pensacola.
Opened: 1997. **Holes:** 18. **Par:** 72/72. **Yards:** 6,810/4,825. **Course rating:** 74.3/69.6. **Slope:** 144/121. **Architect:** A. Palmer/E. Seay/H. Minchew/E. Wiltse. **Green fee:** $50/$65. **Credit cards:** MC,VISA,AMEX. **Reduced fees:** Twilight, juniors. **Caddies:** No. **Golf carts:** Included in Green Fee. **Discount golf packages:** No. **Season:** Year-round. **High:** June-Aug., Jan.-April. **On site lodging:** No. **Rental clubs:** Yes. **Walking policy:** Mandatory cart. **Metal spikes allowed:** Yes. **Range:** Yes (grass). **To obtain tee times:** Call golf shop.

★★★½LOST LAKE GOLF CLUB
8310 S.E. Fazio Dr., Hobe Sound, 33455, Martin County, (561)220-6666, 25 miles N of West Plam Beach.
Opened: 1992. **Holes:** 18. **Par:** 72/72. **Yards:** 6,850/5,106. **Course rating:** 73.4/69.5. **Slope:** 135/123. **Architect:** Jim Fazio. **Green fee:** $20/$45. **Credit cards:** MC,VISA. **Reduced fees:** Low season. **Caddies:** No. **Golf carts:** Included in Green Fee. **Discount golf packages:** No. **Season:** Year-round. **High:** Jan.-April. **On site lodging:** No. **Rental clubs:** Yes. **Walking policy:** Mandatory cart. **Metal spikes allowed:** Yes. **Range:** Yes (grass). **To obtain tee times:** Call one day in advance.
Subscriber comments: Challenging course...Wide fairways. Long course...Has private-course feel. Looks first-class...Holes all blend together...Decent course...Some interesting holes.

★★½MAGNOLIA VALLEY GOLF CLUB
7223 Massachusetts Ave., New Port Richey, 34653, Pasco County, (813)847-2342, 20 miles NW of Tampa.
Opened: N/A. **Holes:** 27. **Par:** 71/72. **Yards:** 6,106/4,869. **Course rating:** 69.1/67.2. **Slope:** 121/112. **Architect:** Phil Leckey. **Green fee:** $10/$25. **Credit cards:** MC,VISA,DISC. **Reduced fees:** Low season, twilight. **Caddies:** No. **Golf carts:** Included in Green Fee. **Discount golf packages:** No. **Season:** Year-round. **High:** Jan.-April. **On site lodging:** No. **Rental clubs:** Yes. **Walking policy:** Walking at certain times. **Metal spikes allowed:** Yes. **Range:** Yes (grass). **To obtain tee times:** Call golf shop up to 5 days in advance.
Subscriber comments: Watch out for the gators...Must be accurate off tee...Lots of water and doglegs.
Special Notes: Also has a 9-hole executive course.

★★½MANATEE COUNTY GOLF CLUB
PU-6415 53rd Ave. West, Bradenton, 34210, Manatee County, (941)792-6773, 40 miles S of Tampa.
Opened: 1977. **Holes:** 18. **Par:** 72/72. **Yards:** 6,747/5,619. **Course rating:** 71.6/71.6. **Slope:** 122/119. **Architect:** Lane Marshall. **Green fee:** $12/$22. **Credit cards:** MC,VISA. **Reduced fees:** Weekdays, low season, twilight. **Caddies:** No. **Golf carts:** N/A. **Discount golf packages:** No. **Season:** Year-round. **High:** Nov.-May. **On site lodging:** No. **Rental clubs:** Yes. **Walking policy:** Unrestricted walking. **Metal spikes allowed:** Yes. **Range:** Yes (grass). **To obtain tee times:** Call 2 days in advance.
Subscriber comments: Beside waste-treatment plant...Very good for public course, fun to play...Nice municipal course.

★★★ MANGROVE BAY GOLF COURSE

PU-875 62nd Ave. N.E., St. Petersburg, 33702, Pinellas County, (813)893-7800, 15 miles E of Tampa.
Opened: 1978. **Holes:** 18. **Par:** 72/72. **Yards:** 6,779/5,204. **Course rating:** 71.5/68.5. **Slope:** 120/112. **Architect:** Bill Amick. **Green fee:** $22/$33. **Credit cards:** MC,VISA,DISC,ATM Debit Card. **Reduced fees:** Twilight. **Caddies:** No. **Golf carts:** Included in Green Fee. **Discount golf packages:** No. **Season:** Year-round. **High:** Jan.-April. **On site lodging:** No. **Rental clubs:** Yes. **Walking policy:** Unrestricted walking. **Metal spikes allowed:** Yes. **Range:** Yes (grass). **To obtain tee times:** Call 7 days in advance.
Subscriber comments: Good little layout. Fun to play...Will go back...Lots of retirees...Busy muny.

★★ MARCO SHORES COUNTRY CLUB

PU-1450 Mainsail Dr., Naples, 34114, Collier County, (941)394-2581.
Opened: 1974. **Holes:** 18. **Par:** 72/72. **Yards:** 6,879/5,634. **Course rating:** 73.0/72.3. **Slope:** 125/121. **Architect:** Bruce Devlin/Robert von Hagge. **Green fee:** $23/$80. **Credit cards:** MC,VISA. **Reduced fees:** Low season, twilight, juniors. **Caddies:** No. **Golf carts:** Included in Green Fee. **Discount golf packages:** No. **Season:** Year-round. **High:** Jan.-April. **On site lodging:** No. **Rental clubs:** Yes. **Walking policy:** Mandatory cart. **Metal spikes allowed:** Yes. **Range:** Yes (grass/mats). **To obtain tee times:** Call or in person 4 days in advance.

★★★½ MARCUS POINTE GOLF CLUB

PU-2500 Oak Pointe Dr., Pensacola, 32505, Escambia County, (904)484-9770, (800)362-7287.

Opened: 1990. **Holes:** 18. **Par:** 72/72. **Yards:** 6,737/5,252. **Course rating:** 72.3/69.6. **Slope:** 129/119. **Architect:** Earl Stone. **Green fee:** $20/$30. **Credit cards:** MC,VISA. **Reduced fees:** Weekdays, low season, twilight, juniors. **Caddies:** No. **Golf carts:** $13. **Discount golf packages:** Yes. **Season:** Year-round. **High:** Feb.-May. **On site lodging:** No. **Rental clubs:** Yes. **Walking policy:** Walking at certain times. **Metal spikes allowed:** Yes. **Range:** Yes (grass). **To obtain tee times:** Call up to 3 days in advance.
Subscriber comments: Fun...Rolling hills...Very playable.

MARRIOTT AT SAWGRASS RESORT

R-Ponte Vedra Beach, 32082, St. Johns County
Architect: N/A. **Caddies:** No. **Discount golf packages:** Yes. **Season:** Year-round. **Metal spikes allowed:** Yes. **Range:** Yes (grass).

★★★★ MARSH LANDING GOLF CLUB

1000 TPC Blvd., (904)273-3720, 15 miles E of Jacksonville.
Opened: N/A. **Holes:** 18. **Par:** 72/72. **Yards:** 6,841/6,001. **Course rating:** N/A. **Slope:** 131/120. **Green fee:** N/A. **Credit cards:** All major. **Reduced fees:** Low season. **Golf carts:** N/A. **High:** March-May. **On site lodging:** Yes. **Rental clubs:** No. **Walking policy:** N/A. **To obtain tee times:** N/A.
Subscriber comments: Beautiful course...Very scenic through the marshes...Target golf.

★★½ OAK BRIDGE GOLF CLUB

254 Alta Mar Dr., (904)285-0204, 12 miles E of Jacksonville.
Opened: 1972. **Holes:** 18. **Par:** 70/70. **Yards:** 6,383/4,869. **Course rating:** 70.3/67.8. **Slope:** 126/116. **Green fee:** $25/$25. **Credit cards:** MC,VISA. **Reduced fees:** N/A. **Golf carts:** $14. **High:** Feb.-May. **On site lodging:** No. **Rental clubs:** Yes. **Walking policy:** Walking at certain times. **To obtain tee times:** May book tee times through travel agents when making resort reservations.
Subscriber comments: Six par 3s and lots of water...OK.

MARRIOTT'S BAY POINT RESORT

R-P.O. Box 27880, Panama City Beach, 32411, Bay County, (850)235-6950, 90 miles E of Pensacola.
Green fee: $50/$70. **Credit cards:** MC,VISA,AMEX,Diners Club. **Reduced fees:** Low season, resort guests, twilight, juniors. **Caddies:** No. **Golf carts:** Included in Green Fee. **Discount golf packages:** No. **Season:** Year-round. **High:** Feb.-May. **On site lodg-**

ing: Yes. **Rental clubs:** Yes. **Walking policy:** Mandatory cart. **Metal spikes allowed:**
Yes. **Range:** Yes (grass). **To obtain tee times:** Call for tee times (850)235-6909.

★★★½ CLUB MEADOWS COURSE
(850)235-6950.
Opened: 1973. **Holes:** 18. **Par:** 72/72. **Yards:** 6,913/4,999. **Course rating:** 73.3/68.0.
Slope: 126/118. **Architect:** Willard Byrd.
Subscriber comments: Enjoyable and relaxing layout...Would love to retire here...Very
open.

★★★★ LAGOON LEGEND
(850)235-6937.
Opened: 1986. **Holes:** 18. **Par:** 72/72. **Yards:** 6,885/4,942. **Course rating:** 75.3/69.8.
Slope: 152/127. **Architect:** Bruce Devlin/Robert von Hagge.
Subscriber comments: Tough! Tough! Tough! ...Very challenging, even on your greatest ball-striking day...Ridiculously hard. Give me a break...Awesome from the tips...Too
demanding for average player...Golf-ball graveyard...Highest Slope I've ever
played...Knocked me on my butt and dragged me through the swamp, but what fun!...A
high-handicapper in our group lost 21 balls in 16 holes...Many forced carries...It's unfair
on the first trip, but I'm going back.

★★★½ MARRIOTT'S GOLF CLUB AT MARCO
R-3433 Marriott Club Dr., Naples, 33937, Collier County, (941)793-6060.
Opened: 1991. **Holes:** 18. **Par:** 72/72. **Yards:** 6,898/5,416. **Course rating:** 73.1/70.9.
Slope: 137/122. **Architect:** Joe Lee. **Green fee:** $35/$115. **Credit cards:** All
major,Diners Club. **Reduced fees:** Juniors. **Caddies:** No. **Golf carts:** Included in Green
Fee. **Discount golf packages:** No. **Season:** Year-round. **High:** Nov.-April. **On site**
lodging: Yes. **Rental clubs:** Yes. **Walking policy:** Mandatory cart. **Metal spikes**
allowed: Yes. **Range:** Yes (grass). **To obtain tee times:** Call up to 2 days in advance.
Confirmed Marriott resort guests may call up to 30 days in advance.
Subscriber comments: Watch out for alligators...Lots of water...Great finishing
holes...Bring the insect repellent...Great course, lots of bugs...Abundant wildlife (alligators)...First class...What a view of the ocean.

MARSH CREEK COUNTRY CLUB
169 Marshside Dr., St. Augustine, 32084, St. Johns County, (904)461-1145.
Call club for futher information.

MARTIN COUNTY GOLF & COUNTRY CLUB
PU-2000 S.E. Saint Lucie Blvd., Stuart, 34996, Martin County, (561)287-3747, 40 miles
N of West Palm Beach.
Opened: 1925. **Architect:** Ron Garl. **Green fee:** $10/$22. **Credit cards:** None.
Reduced fees: Low season, juniors. **Caddies:** No. **Discount golf packages:** No.
Season: Year-round. **High:** Dec.-April. **On site lodging:** No. **Rental clubs:** Yes. **Metal**
spikes allowed: Yes. **Range:** Yes (grass). **To obtain tee times:** Call five days in
advance. Must call pro shop for PIN number.

★★★ BLUE/GOLD COURSE
Holes: 18. **Par:** 72/72. **Yards:** 5,900/5,236. **Course rating:** 67.5/69.1. **Slope:** 120/120.
Golf carts: $6. **Walking policy:** Mandatory cart.
Subscriber comments: The best thing about the course, besides being a great value
for the money, is the speed of play. Some of the locals I was paired with suggested
that they had to play fast, as they didn't have a lot of time left.

★★½ RED/WHITE COURSE
Holes: 18. **Par:** 72/73. **Yards:** 6,200/5,400. **Course rating:** 69.1/70.4. **Slope:** 116/120.
Golf carts: N/A. **Walking policy:** Walking at certain times.
Subscriber comments: Overcrowded muny with a decent layout...Very busy.

★★★½ MATANZAS WOODS GOLF CLUB
398 Lakeview Dr., Palm Coast, 32137, Flagler County, (904)446-6330, (800)874-2101,
30 miles N of Daytona Beach.
Opened: 1985. **Holes:** 18. **Par:** 72/72. **Yards:** 6,985/5,336. **Course rating:** 73.3/71.2.
Slope: 132/126. **Architect:** Arnold Palmer. **Green fee:** $39/$48. **Credit cards:**
MC,VISA. **Reduced fees:** Low season, resort guests, twilight, juniors. **Caddies:** No.
Golf carts: Included in Green Fee. **Discount golf packages:** Yes. **Season:** Year-round.
High: Jan.-April. **On site lodging:** No. **Rental clubs:** Yes. **Walking policy:** Mandatory

cart. **Metal spikes allowed:** Yes. **Range:** Yes (grass). **To obtain tee times:** Call up to five days in advance.
Subscriber comments: Enjoyable golf...Lots of water, including island green at 18th...Would enjoy playing it every day...Pretty and quiet.

★★MAYFAIR COUNTRY CLUB
PU-3536 Country Club Rd., Sanford, 32771, Seminole County, (407)322-2531, (800)279-5098, 15 miles N of Orlando.
Opened: 1920. **Holes:** 18. **Par:** 72/72. **Yards:** 6,375/5,223. **Course rating:** N/A. **Slope:** 119/115. **Architect:** N/A. **Green fee:** $25/$40. **Credit cards:** All major. **Reduced fees:** Weekdays, low season. **Caddies:** No. **Golf carts:** Included in Green Fee. **Discount golf packages:** Yes. **Season:** Year-round. **High:** Dec.-April. **On site lodging:** No. **Rental clubs:** Yes. **Walking policy:** Mandatory cart. **Metal spikes allowed:** Yes. **Range:** Yes (grass). **To obtain tee times:** Call (800)279-5098.
Notes: Former PGA Tour Mayfair Inn Open (1950s).

★★MEADOWBROOK GOLF CLUB
3200 N.W. 98th St., Gainesville, 32606, Alachua County, (352)332-0577, 60 miles SW of Jacksonville.
Opened: 1987. **Holes:** 18. **Par:** 72/72. **Yards:** 6,289/4,720. **Course rating:** 69.9/66.7. **Slope:** 119/117. **Architect:** Steven R. Smyers. **Green fee:** $7/$24. **Credit cards:** MC,VISA,DISC. **Reduced fees:** Weekdays, low season, twilight. **Caddies:** No. **Golf carts:** N/A. **Discount golf packages:** No. **Season:** Year-round. **High:** Jan.-April. **On site lodging:** No. **Rental clubs:** Yes. **Walking policy:** Walking at certain times. **Metal spikes allowed:** Yes. **Range:** Yes (grass). **To obtain tee times:** Call 1 day in advance.

★★★½METROWEST COUNTRY CLUB
2100 S. Hiawassee Rd., Orlando, 32835, Orange County, (407)299-1099, 10 miles SW of Orlando.
Opened: 1987. **Holes:** 18. **Par:** 72/72. **Yards:** 7,051/5,325. **Course rating:** 73.1/69.6. **Slope:** 126/117. **Architect:** Robert Trent Jones. **Green fee:** $40/$80. **Credit cards:** MC,VISA,AMEX. **Reduced fees:** Low season, twilight, juniors. **Caddies:** No. **Golf carts:** Included in Green Fee. **Discount golf packages:** Yes. **Season:** Year-round. **High:** Jan.-May. **On site lodging:** No. **Rental clubs:** Yes. **Walking policy:** Mandatory cart. **Metal spikes allowed:** Yes. **Range:** Yes (grass/mats). **To obtain tee times:** Call up to 7 days in advance.
Subscriber comments: Lets you swing for the fence...Not too difficult, but challenging...Wide open, forgiving...Beautiful landscaping...No real problems.

★★½MIAMI NATIONAL GOLF CLUB
6401 Kendale Lakes Dr., Miami, 33183, Dade County, (305)382-3935.
Opened: 1970. **Holes:** 27. **Architect:** Mark Mahannah. **Green fee:** $20/$45. **Credit cards:** MC,VISA,AMEX. **Reduced fees:** Weekdays, low season, twilight, juniors. **Caddies:** No. **Golf carts:** Included in Green Fee. **Discount golf packages:** No. **Season:** Year-round. **High:** Nov.-April. **On site lodging:** No. **Rental clubs:** Yes. **Walking policy:** Mandatory cart. **Metal spikes allowed:** Yes. **Range:** Yes (grass/mats). **To obtain tee times:** Call golf shop up to 7 days in advance. May call up to 60 days in advance with credit card and 48-hour cancellation policy.
Notes: 1971-1973 LPGA Tour site.
BARRACUDA/MARLIN
Par: 72/74. **Yards:** 6,719/5,445. **Course rating:** 73.6/70.1. **Slope:** 132/118.
DOLPHIN/BARRACUDA
Par: 72/73. **Yards:** 6,679/5,281. **Course rating:** 73.1/69.3. **Slope:** 130/119.
DOLPHIN/MARLIN
Par: 72/73. **Yards:** 6,678/5,364. **Course rating:** 72.9/69.6. **Slope:** 129/119.
Subscriber comments: Good test—lots of water...Average...Nice staff, well maintained, some tough holes...Fun course when we played.
Special Notes: Formerly Kendale Lakes Golf Course.

★★MIAMI SHORES COUNTRY CLUB
10000 Biscayne Blvd., Miami Shores, 33138, Dade County, (305)795-2366, 15 miles N of Miami.
Opened: 1938. **Holes:** 18. **Par:** 71/72. **Yards:** 6,400/5,400. **Course rating:** 70.6/71.3.

Slope: 121/126. **Architect:** Red Lawrence. **Green fee:** $30/$60. **Credit cards:** MC,VISA,AMEX. **Reduced fees:** Weekdays, low season, twilight. **Caddies:** No. **Golf carts:** Included in Green Fee. **Discount golf packages:** No. **Season:** Year-round. **High:** Dec.-April. **On site lodging:** No. **Rental clubs:** Yes. **Walking policy:** Mandatory cart. **Metal spikes allowed:** Yes. **Range:** Yes (grass/mats). **To obtain tee times:** Call up to 3 days in advance.

★★½MILL COVE GOLF CLUB
PU-1700 Monument Rd., Jacksonville, 32225, Duval County, (904)646-4653.
Opened: 1990. **Holes:** 18. **Par:** 71/71. **Yards:** 6,671/4,719. **Course rating:** 71.7/66.3.
Slope: 129/112. **Architect:** Arnold Palmer/Ed Seay. **Green fee:** $13/$22. **Credit cards:** MC,VISA,AMEX. **Reduced fees:** Weekdays, low season, twilight, seniors, juniors.
Caddies: No. **Golf carts:** $13. **Discount golf packages:** No. **Season:** Year-round.
High: Year-round. **On site lodging:** No. **Rental clubs:** Yes. **Walking policy:** Walking at certain times. **Metal spikes allowed:** Yes. **Range:** Yes (grass/mats). **To obtain tee times:** Call 5 days in advance.
Subscriber comments: Interesting layout...Heavy play...Short and tight...Plain...Hilly, unusual for Florida.

MISSION INN GOLF & TENNIS RESORT
10400 County Rd. 48, Howey-in-the-Hills, 34737, Lake County,
(352)324-3885, (800)874-9053, 30 miles NW of Orlando.
Credit cards: All major. **Reduced fees:** Weekdays, low season, twilight, seniors, juniors. **Caddies:** No. **Golf carts:** Included in Green Fee.
Discount golf packages: Yes. **Season:** Year-round. **High:** Feb.-April.
On site lodging: Yes. **Rental clubs:** Yes. **Walking policy:** Mandatory cart. **Metal spikes allowed:** Yes. **Range:** Yes (grass). **To obtain tee times:** Call.
★★★★EL CAMPEON COURSE
Opened: 1926. **Holes:** 18. **Par:** 72/73. **Yards:** 6,860/4,709. **Course rating:** 73.6/67.3.
Slope: 133/118. **Architect:** Charles Clark. **Green fee:** $48/$95.
Subscriber comments: Keep this place a secret...Excellent old design...Some excellent holes with terrific hills...Be aware of alligators...Lots of fun...Par 3s will get your attention...Great place.
★★★½LAS COLINAS COURSE
Opened: 1992. **Holes:** 18. **Par:** 72/72. **Yards:** 6,879/4,651. **Course rating:** 73.2/64.3.
Slope: 128/103. **Architect:** Gary Koch. **Green fee:** $40/$75.
Subscriber comments: Enjoyable resort...Young course with great potential.

MONASTERY GOLF & COUNTRY CLUB
1717 Monastery Rd., Orange City, 32763, Volusia County, (904)774-2714.
Opened: N/A. **Holes:** 18. **Par:** 72/72. **Yards:** 6,300/6,000. **Course rating:** N/A. **Slope:** 121/116. **Architect:** N/A. **Green fee:** N/A. **Credit cards:** MC,VISA. **Reduced fees:** Weekdays, low season. **Caddies:** No. **Golf carts:** Included in Green Fee. **Discount golf packages:** Yes. **Season:** Year-round. **High:** Nov-April. **On site lodging:** No. **Rental clubs:** No. **Walking policy:** N/A. **Metal spikes allowed:** Yes. **Range:** Yes (grass). **To obtain tee times:** N/A.

★★★★THE MOORS GOLF CLUB
PU-3220 Avalon Blvd., Milton, 32583, Santa Rosa County, (850)995-4653, (800)727-1010, 6 miles NE of Pensacola.
Opened: 1993. **Holes:** 18. **Par:** 70/70. **Yards:** 6,828/5,259. **Course rating:** 72.9/70.3. **Slope:** 126/117. **Architect:** John B. LaFoy. **Green fee:** $22/$33. **Credit cards:** All major. **Reduced fees:** Weekdays, resort guests, juniors. **Caddies:** No. **Golf carts:** $12. **Discount golf packages:** No. **Season:** Year-round. **High:** Spring/Fall. **On site lodging:** No. **Rental clubs:** Yes. **Walking policy:** Walking at certain times. **Metal spikes allowed:** Yes. **Range:** Yes (grass/mats). **To obtain tee times:** Call 3 days in advance.
Notes: PGA Senior Tour Emerald Coast Classic (annually).
Subscriber comments: Outstanding dunes course...Different...Best links-type course I've played...Stay home if it's very windy...Beautiful clubhouse...Tough but fair.

★★★ MOUNT DORA GOLF CLUB
1100 S. Highland, Mount Dora, 32757, Lake County, (352)383-3954, 20 miles N of Orlando.
Opened: 1945. **Holes:** 18. **Par:** 70/72. **Yards:** 5,719/5,238. **Course rating:** 67.9/69.2.
Slope: 114/113. **Architect:** N/A. **Green fee:** $18/$30. **Credit cards:** MC,VISA,DISC.
Reduced fees: Low season, twilight. **Caddies:** No. **Golf carts:** Included in Green Fee.
Discount golf packages: No. **Season:** Year-round. **High:** Jan.-April. **On site lodging:** No. **Rental clubs:** Yes. **Walking policy:** Unrestricted walking. **Metal spikes allowed:** Yes. **Range:** No. **To obtain tee times:** Call up to 3 days in advance.
Subscriber comments: Excellent drainage. Was able to play immediately after rain shower...Nothing special...Excellent older course...Nice course, kind of a strange layout...Private atmosphere.

MOUNT PLYMOUTH GOLF CLUB
24953 Pine Valley Dr., Mt. Plymouth, 32776, Lake County, (352)383-4821, 20 miles NW of Orlando.
Opened: 1926. **Holes:** 18. **Par:** 70/70. **Yards:** 6,457/5,269. **Course rating:** 70.4/70.7.
Slope: 111/114. **Architect:** N/A. **Green fee:** $3/$16. **Credit cards:** MC,VISA,DISC.
Reduced fees: N/A. **Caddies:** No. **Golf carts:** $11. **Discount golf packages:** No.
Season: Year-round. **High:** Jan.-April. **On site lodging:** No. **Rental clubs:** Yes.
Walking policy: Walking at certain times. **Metal spikes allowed:** Yes. **Range:** Yes (grass). **To obtain tee times:** Call up to 3 days in advance.

★★½ MYAKKA PINES GOLF CLUB - RED/WHITE/BLUE
2550 S. River Rd., Englewood, 34223, Sarasota County, (941)474-1745, 11 miles S of Venice.
Opened: 1977. **Holes:** 27. **Architect:** Lane Marshall. **Green fee:** $15/$28. **Credit cards:** MC,VISA,DISC. **Reduced fees:** Low season, twilight. **Caddies:** No. **Golf carts:** $28. **Discount golf packages:** No. **Season:** Year-round. **High:** Jan.-April. **On site lodging:** No. **Rental clubs:** Yes. **Walking policy:** Walking at certain times. **Metal spikes allowed:** Yes. **Range:** Yes (grass). **To obtain tee times:** Call 2 days in advance beginning at 9 a.m.
Subscriber comments: Good course for seniors...Too crowded.

★★★ NAPLES BEACH HOTEL & GOLF CLUB
851 Gulf Shore Blvd. N., Naples, 34102, Collier County, (941)435-2475, (800)237-7600.
Opened: 1930. **Holes:** 18. **Par:** 72/72. **Yards:** 6,500/5,300. **Course rating:** 71.2/70.1.
Slope: 129/120. **Architect:** Ron Garl. **Green fee:** $39/$110. **Credit cards:** All major,Diners Club, Carte Blanche. **Reduced fees:** Resort guests. **Caddies:** No. **Golf carts:** Included in Green Fee. **Discount golf packages:** Yes. **Season:** Year-round.
High: Jan.-April. **On site lodging:** Yes. **Rental clubs:** Yes. **Walking policy:** Mandatory cart. **Metal spikes allowed:** Yes. **Range:** Yes (grass/mats). **To obtain tee times:** Hotel guests 90 days in advance, nonguests call 3 days in advance.
Subscriber comments: Fair challenge...Traditional course...Tired...Fair challenge.

★★ NORMANDY SHORES GOLF COURSE
PU-2401 Biarritz Dr., Miami Beach, 33141, Dade County, (305)868-6502.
Opened: 1938. **Holes:** 18. **Par:** 71/73. **Yards:** 6,402/5,527. **Course rating:** 70.5/71.0.
Slope: 120/119. **Architect:** William S. Flynn/Howard Toomey. **Green fee:** $30/$55.
Credit cards: MC,VISA,AMEX. **Reduced fees:** Weekdays, low season, twilight, juniors.
Caddies: No. **Golf carts:** Included in Green Fee. **Discount golf packages:** Yes.
Season: Year-round. **High:** Nov.-April. **On site lodging:** No. **Rental clubs:** Yes.
Walking policy: Walking at certain times. **Metal spikes allowed:** Yes. **Range:** Yes (grass/mats). **To obtain tee times:** Call 7 days in advance.

★★½ NORTH PALM BEACH COUNTRY CLUB
PM-951 U.S. Hwy. 1, North Palm Beach, 33408, Palm Beach County, (561)626-4344, 5 miles N of West Palm Beach.
Opened: 1963. **Holes:** 18. **Par:** 11/72. **Yards:** 6,281/5,033. **Course rating:** 69.9/68.9.
Slope: 120/114. **Architect:** Mark McCumber. **Green fee:** $20/$50. **Credit cards:** MC,VISA. **Reduced fees:** Low season, juniors. **Caddies:** No. **Golf carts:** Included in Green Fee. **Discount golf packages:** No. **Season:** Year-round. **High:** Nov.-May. **On

site lodging: No. **Rental clubs:** Yes. **Walking policy:** Mandatory cart. **Metal spikes allowed:** Yes. **Range:** Yes (grass/mats). **To obtain tee times:** Call 1 day in advance at 8 a.m.
Subscriber comments: Too busy...Improved conditions.

★★½ NORTHDALE GOLF CLUB
4417 Northdale Blvd., Tampa, 33624, Hillsborough County, (813)962-0428.
Opened: 1978. **Holes:** 18. **Par:** 72/72. **Yards:** 6,767/5,383. **Course rating:** 71.8/71.0.
Slope: 122/121. **Architect:** Ron Garl. **Green fee:** $40. **Credit cards:** MC,VISA.
Reduced fees: Twilight, juniors. **Caddies:** No. **Golf carts:** Included in Green Fee.
Discount golf packages: No. **Season:** Year-round. **High:** Dec.-April. **On site lodging:** No. **Rental clubs:** Yes. **Walking policy:** Mandatory cart. **Metal spikes allowed:** Yes.
Range: No. **To obtain tee times:** Call up to 3 days in advance.
Subscriber comments: Average course...Needs work.

★★½ OAK HILLS GOLF CLUB
PU-10059 Northcliff Blvd., Spring Hill, 34608, Hernando County, (352)683-6830, 37 miles NW of Tampa.
Opened: 1982. **Holes:** 18. **Par:** 72/72. **Yards:** 6,774/5,468. **Course rating:** 72.2/71.1.
Slope: 123/119. **Architect:** Chuck Almony. **Green fee:** $18/$27. **Credit cards:** MC,VISA,DISC. **Reduced fees:** Weekdays, low season, twilight, seniors, juniors.
Caddies: No. **Golf carts:** Included in Green Fee. **Discount golf packages:** Yes.
Season: Year-round. **High:** Dec.-March. **On site lodging:** No. **Rental clubs:** Yes.
Walking policy: Walking at certain times. **Metal spikes allowed:** Yes. **Range:** Yes (grass). **To obtain tee times:** Call.
Subscriber comments: Treed fairways.

★★★ OKEEHEELEE GOLF COURSE
PM-1200 Country Club Way, West Palm Beach, 33413, Palm Beach County, (561)964-4653, 1 mile W of West Palm Beach.
Opened: 1995. **Holes:** 27. **Architect:** Roy Case. **Green fee:** $22/$49. **Credit cards:** MC,VISA. **Reduced fees:** N/A. **Caddies:** No. **Golf carts:** Included in Green Fee.
Discount golf packages: No. **Season:** Year-round. **High:** Dec.-April. **On site lodging:** No. **Rental clubs:** No. **Walking policy:** Walking at certain times. **Metal spikes allowed:** Yes. **Range:** Yes (grass). **To obtain tee times:** Call.
EAGLE/OSPREY (BLUE/WHITE)
Par: 72/72. **Yards:** 6,648/4,591. **Course rating:** 71.7/62.7. **Slope:** 130/103.
HERON/EAGLE (RED/BLUE)
Par: 72/72. **Yards:** 6,916/4,842. **Course rating:** 72.9/63.4. **Slope:** 128/103.
OSPREY/HERON (WHITE/RED)
Par: 72/72. **Yards:** 6,826/4,731. **Course rating:** 72.6/62.9. **Slope:** 130/102.
Subscriber comments: Water, water everywhere...Good practice facilities...Needs another year of growth...Too many holes are close together.

★★★ OLDE HICKORY GOLF & COUNTRY CLUB
14670 Olde Hickory Blvd., Fort Myers, 33912, Lee County, (941)768-3335.
Opened: 1992. **Holes:** 18. **Par:** 72/72. **Yards:** 6,601/4,456. **Course rating:** 71.9/65.8.
Slope: 127/113. **Architect:** Ron Garl. **Green fee:** $20/$30. **Credit cards:** None.
Reduced fees: N/A. **Caddies:** No. **Golf carts:** N/A. **Discount golf packages:** No.
Season: May 1-Oct. 31 open to public. **High:** N/A. **On site lodging:** No. **Rental clubs:** Yes. **Walking policy:** Mandatory cart. **Metal spikes allowed:** Yes. **Range:** Yes (grass).
To obtain tee times: Call 2 days in advance.
Subscriber comments: Wouldn't want to play every day, but worth playing...Really enjoyed this one...Very soggy in rainy season.

ORANGE BLOSSOM HILLS GOLF & COUNTRY CLUB
1100 Main St., Lady Lake, 32159, Lake County, (352)753-5200, 60 miles N of Orlando.
Opened: 1986. **Holes:** 18. **Par:** 72/72. **Yards:** 6,200/2,600. **Course rating:** 69.1/68.9.
Slope: 117/117. **Architect:** Lloyd Clifton. **Green fee:** $34. **Credit cards:** None.
Reduced fees: N/A. **Caddies:** No. **Golf carts:** $8. **Discount golf packages:** No.
Season: Year-round. **High:** Nov.-May. **On site lodging:** No. **Rental clubs:** No. **Walking policy:** Unrestricted walking. **Metal spikes allowed:** No. **Range:** No. **To obtain tee times:** Call golf shop.

★★★ORANGE LAKE COUNTRY CLUB

R-8505 W. Irlo Bronson Mem. Hwy., Kissimmee, 34747, Osceola County, (407)239-1050, 15 miles W of Orlando.
Opened: 1982. **Holes:** 27. **Par:** 72/72. **Yards:** 6,531/5,289. **Course rating:** 72.6/71.1.
Slope: 132/126. **Architect:** Joe Lee. **Green fee:** $40/$80. **Credit cards:**
MC,VISA,AMEX. **Reduced fees:** Weekdays, low season, resort guests, twilight, juniors.
Caddies: No. **Golf carts:** Included in Green Fee. **Discount golf packages:** Yes.
Season: Year-round. **High:** Jan.-April. **On site lodging:** Yes. **Rental clubs:** Yes.
Walking policy: Mandatory cart. **Metal spikes allowed:** Yes. **Range:** Yes (grass/mats).
To obtain tee times: Call.
Subscriber comments: Too many time-share units around course. Too tight...Too short...Well-placed bunkers.

★★½ORIOLE GOLF & TENNIS CLUB OF MARGATE

PU-8000 W. Margate Blvd., Margate, 33063, Broward County, (954)972-8140, 5 miles N of Fort Lauderdale.
Opened: 1972. **Holes:** 27. **Par:** 72/72. **Yards:** 6,418/4,875. **Course rating:** 70.9/67.7.
Slope: 120/112. **Architect:** Bill Dietsch. **Green fee:** $12/$32. **Credit cards:** MC,VISA.
Reduced fees: Low season, twilight. **Caddies:** No. **Golf carts:** Included in Green Fee.
Discount golf packages: No. **Season:** Year-round. **High:** Jan.-April. **On site lodging:**
No. **Rental clubs:** Yes. **Walking policy:** Mandatory cart. **Metal spikes allowed:** Yes.
Range: Yes (grass/mats). **To obtain tee times:** Call 2 days in advance.

★★★ORLANDO WORLD CENTER - MARRIOTT

R-8701 World Center Dr., Orlando, 32821, Orange County, (407)238-8660.
Opened: 1986. **Holes:** 18. **Par:** 71/71. **Yards:** 6,307/4,988. **Course rating:** 69.8/68.5.
Slope: 121/115. **Architect:** Joe Lee. **Green fee:** $50/$110. **Credit cards:** All major.
Reduced fees: Resort guests, twilight, juniors. **Caddies:** No. **Golf carts:** Included in
Green Fee. **Discount golf packages:** Yes. **Season:** Year-round. **High:** Jan.-April. **On
site lodging:** Yes. **Rental clubs:** Yes. **Walking policy:** Mandatory cart. **Metal spikes
allowed:** Yes. **Range:** Yes (grass). **To obtain tee times:** Call up to 7 days in advance.
Hotel guests may call up to 60 days in advance.
Subscriber comments: I'm a right-to-left player. Too many water hazards to the left...A lot of water...Expected more...Nothing memorable.

★★★OXBOW GOLF CLUB

R-1 Oxbow Dr., La Belle, 33935, Hendry County, (941)675-4411, (800)282-3375, 30 miles E of Fort Myers.
Opened: 1982. **Holes:** 18. **Par:** 72/72. **Yards:** 6,862/5,000. **Course rating:** 72.7/68.5.
Slope: 129/116. **Architect:** LeRoy Phillips. **Green fee:** $10/$45. **Credit cards:**
MC,VISA,AMEX. **Reduced fees:** Low season. **Caddies:** No. **Golf carts:** Included in
Green Fee. **Discount golf packages:** No. **Season:** Year-round. **High:** Nov.-May. **On
site lodging:** Yes. **Rental clubs:** Yes. **Walking policy:** Walking at certain times. **Metal
spikes allowed:** Yes. **Range:** Yes (grass). **To obtain tee times:** Call up to 3 days in
advance. Resort guests may reserve tee times with confirmed hotel reservations.
Subscriber comments: Challenging tee shots...Worth the drive.

OYSTER CREEK GOLF & COUNTRY CLUB

6500 Oriole Blvd., Englewood, 34224, Charlotte County, (941)475-0334, 10 miles S of Venice.
Opened: 1993. **Holes:** 18. **Par:** 60/60. **Yards:** 4,000/2,600. **Course rating:** 59.7/57.3.
Slope: 100/85. **Architect:** Ted McAnlis. **Green fee:** $16/$30. **Credit cards:** MC,VISA.
Reduced fees: Low season, twilight. **Caddies:** No. **Golf carts:** Included in Green Fee.
Discount golf packages: No. **Season:** Year-round. **High:** Nov.-April. **On site lodging:**
No. **Rental clubs:** No. **Walking policy:** Unrestricted walking. **Metal spikes allowed:**
Yes. **Range:** No. **To obtain tee times:** N/A.

PGA GOLF CLUB AT THE RESERVE

PU-1916 Perfect Dr., Port St. Lucie, 34986, St. Lucie County, (800)800-4653, (800)800-4653, 45 miles N of Palm Beach.
Opened: 1996. **Architect:** Tom Fazio. **Green fee:** $15/$64. **Credit
cards:** MC,VISA. **Reduced fees:** Low season, twilight, juniors. **Caddies:**

FLORIDA

No. **Golf carts:** Included in Green Fee. **Discount golf packages:** Yes. **Season:** Year-round. **High:** Jan.-March. **On site lodging:** No. **Rental clubs:** Yes. **Walking policy:** Unrestricted walking. **Metal spikes allowed:** Yes. **Range:** Yes (grass). **To obtain tee times:** Call up to 3 days in advance.

★★★★**NORTH COURSE**
Holes: 18. **Par:** 72/72. **Yards:** 7,026/4,993. **Course rating:** 73.8/68.8.
Slope: 133/114.
Notes: Ranked 7th in 1996 Best New Affordable Courses.
Subscriber comments: I'm afraid to say how nice it is because I don't want it to become crowded...Wonderful experience...Great rates in summer...No tipping allowed...Gorgeous...Not to be missed...Best deal in South Florida...Tough undulating greens.

★★★★**SOUTH COURSE**
Holes: 18. **Par:** 72/72. **Yards:** 7,087/4,933. **Course rating:** 74.5/68.7.
Slope: 141/119.
Notes: Ranked 13th in 1997 Best in State, 1st in 1996 Best New Affordable Courses.
Subscriber comments: Terrific...I've never enjoyed a golf experience as much...Course needs maturing, but it's fair...Monster bunkers...Very challenging...I could play this course the rest of my life...Tons of sand...Used every club in my bag.

PGA NATIONAL GOLF CLUB
R-1000 Ave. of the Champions, Palm Beach Gardens, 33418, Palm Beach County, (561)627-1800, (800)633-9150, 15 miles N of West Palm Beach.
Credit cards: MC,VISA,AMEX. **Reduced fees:** Low season. **Caddies:** No. **Golf carts:** $21. **Discount golf packages:** Yes. **Season:** Year-round. **High:** Jan.-April. **On site lodging:** Yes. **Rental clubs:** Yes. **Walking policy:** Mandatory cart. **Metal spikes allowed:** Yes. **To obtain tee times:** Registered resort guests may call up to 1 year in advance.

★★★½**CHAMPION COURSE**
Opened: 1981. **Holes:** 18. **Par:** 72/72. **Yards:** 7,022/5,377. **Course rating:** 74.7/71.1.
Slope: 142/123. **Architect:** Tom Fazio/Jack Nicklaus. **Green fee:** $166. **Range:** Yes (grass).
Notes: 1997 PGA Junior Championship; 1992 PGA Seniors Championship; 1987 PGA Championship; 1983 Ryder Cup.
Subscriber comments: Would go back to this resort in a heartbeat...I expected a lot nicer course...Great place...Tough...Good course, bad everything else...A lot of golf course...Jammed.

★★★½**ESTATE COURSE**
Opened: 1984. **Holes:** 18. **Par:** 72/72. **Yards:** 6,784/4,903. **Course rating:** 73.4/68.4.
Slope: 131/118. **Architect:** Karl Litten. **Green fee:** $99. **Range:** Yes (grass/mats).
Subscriber comments: Everything about this place was top of the shelf...A very fun course, semi-challenging...Ridiculous starting hole. Rest of course tough but fair.

★★★½**GENERAL COURSE**
Opened: 1984. **Holes:** 18. **Par:** 72/72. **Yards:** 6,768/5,324. **Course rating:** 73.0/71.0.
Slope: 130/122. **Architect:** Arnold Palmer/Ed Seay. **Green fee:** $99. **Range:** Yes (grass/mats).
Subscriber comments: Feels good to play there...Heavily played...Resort factory.

★★★½**HAIG COURSE**
Opened: 1980. **Holes:** 18. **Par:** 72/72. **Yards:** 6,806/5,645. **Course rating:** 73.0/72.5.
Slope: 130/121. **Architect:** Tom Fazio. **Green fee:** $99. **Range:** Yes (grass).
Subscriber comments: Well done...How do they keep it full with the competition around?.

★★★½**SQUIRE COURSE**
Opened: 1981. **Holes:** 18. **Par:** 72/72. **Yards:** 6,478/4,982. **Course rating:** 71.3/69.8.
Slope: 127/123. **Architect:** Tom Fazio. **Green fee:** $99. **Range:** Yes (grass).
Subscriber comments: This course was my favorite...Very similar holes...So much sand and water.

★★★½**PALISADES GOLF CLUB**
16510 Palisades Blvd., Clermont, 34711, Lake County, (352)394-0085, 20 miles W of Orlando.
Opened: 1991. **Holes:** 18. **Par:** 72/72. **Yards:** 6,988/5,528. **Course rating:** 73.8/72.1.

Slope: 127/122. **Architect:** Joe Lee. **Green fee:** $30/$55. **Credit cards:** MC,VISA. **Reduced fees:** Weekdays, low season, twilight, seniors, juniors. **Golf carts:** Included in Green Fee. **Discount golf packages:** Yes. **Season:** Year-round. **High:** Jan.-April. **On site lodging:** No. **Rental clubs:** Yes. **Walking policy:** Mandatory cart. **Metal spikes allowed:** Yes. **Range:** Yes (grass). **To obtain tee times:** Call up to 30 days in advance.
Subscriber comments: Real sleeper...One of my favorite courses in Florida...Clubhouse could be nicer, but course is worth it...Nicely kept secret...Some quirky holes.

PALM AIRE SPA RESORT & COUNTRY CLUB
R-3701 Oaks Clubhouse Dr., Pompano Beach, 33069, Broward County, (954)978-1737, 10 miles N of Fort Lauderdale.
Green fee: $20/$42. **Credit cards:** MC,VISA,AMEX. **Reduced fees:** N/A. **Caddies:** No. **Golf carts:** $15. **Discount golf packages:** Yes. **Season:** Year-round. **High:** May-Sept. **On site lodging:** Yes. **Rental clubs:** Yes. **Walking policy:** Mandatory cart. **Metal spikes allowed:** Yes. **Range:** Yes (grass). **To obtain tee times:** Members can come in and submit card five to seven days in advance.
CYPRESS COURSE
Opened: 1979. **Holes:** 18. **Par:** 72/72. **Yards:** 6,868/5,447. **Course rating:** 73.3/70.8. **Slope:** 128/118. **Architect:** George Fazio.
OAKS COURSE
Opened: 1973. **Holes:** 18. **Par:** 72/72. **Yards:** 6,747/5,402. **Course rating:** 72.2/70.4. **Slope:** 122/114. **Architect:** George Fazio.
★★★PALMS COURSE
2601 Palm Aire Dr. N., Pompano Beach, 33069, Broward County, (305)974-7699
Opened: 1962. **Holes:** 18. **Par:** 72/72. **Yards:** 6,932/5,434. **Course rating:** 73.7/70.9. **Slope:** 128/120. **Architect:** William Mitchell.
Subscriber comments: They put on great tournaments...Fun course.
★★½PINES COURSE
Opened: 1969. **Holes:** 18. **Par:** 72/72. **Yards:** 6,610/5,232. **Course rating:** 71.3/69.4. **Slope:** 122/115. **Architect:** Robert von Hagge.
Subscriber comments: Small greens.
Special Notes: Also has 18-hole par-3 Sabals Course.

★★½PALM BEACH GARDENS MUNICIPAL GOLF COURSE
PM-11401 Northlake Blvd., Palm Beach Gardens, 33418, Palm Beach County, (561)775-2556, 8 miles N of West Palm Beach.
Opened: 1991. **Holes:** 18. **Par:** 72/72. **Yards:** 6,375/4,663. **Course rating:** 71.1/66.5. **Slope:** 125/110. **Architect:** Roy Case. **Green fee:** $8/$27. **Credit cards:** MC,VISA. **Reduced fees:** Weekdays, low season, twilight, seniors, juniors. **Caddies:** No. **Golf carts:** N/A. **Discount golf packages:** Yes. **Season:** Year-round. **High:** Dec.-April. **On site lodging:** No. **Rental clubs:** Yes. **Walking policy:** Walking at certain times. **Metal spikes allowed:** Yes. **Range:** Yes (grass). **To obtain tee times:** Call up to three days in advance.
Subscriber comments: Busy...Marshy...Great setting. Lots of trouble...Tough new course...Too much water.

PALM BEACH POLO & COUNTRY CLUB
R-11830 Polo Club Rd., West Palm Beach, 33414, Palm Beach County, (561)798-7401.
Green fee: $75/$100. **Credit cards:** MC,VISA,AMEX. **Caddies:** No. **Golf carts:** $14. **Discount golf packages:** Yes. **Season:** Year-round. **High:** Dec.-April. **On site lodging:** Yes. **Rental clubs:** Yes. **Walking policy:** Mandatory cart. **Metal spikes allowed:** Yes. **Range:** Yes (grass). **To obtain tee times:** Must be a registered resort guest, guest of a member or member of another private club arranged through their golf pro.
★★★½CYPRESS COURSE
Opened: 1977. **Holes:** 18. **Par:** 72/72. **Yards:** 7,116/5,172. **Course rating:** 74.4/69.8. **Slope:** 138/121. **Architect:** P.B. Dye/Pete Dye. **Reduced fees:** Resort guests, twilight.
Subscriber comments: Great design...Fun, challenging.

FLORIDA

★★★ DUNES COURSE
Opened: 1984. **Holes:** 18. **Par:** 72/72. **Yards:** 7,050/5,516. **Course rating:** 73.6/71.4.
Slope: 132/122. **Architect:** Ron Garl/Jerry Pate. **Reduced fees:** Twilight.
Subscriber comments: Nice layout...Some of the best fairways and greens.
Special Notes: Also the 9-hole par-3 Olde Course.

★★★½ PALM COAST RESORT
R-53 E. Hampton Blvd., Palm Coast, 32164, Flagler County, (904)437-5807, (800)874-2101, 30 miles N of Daytona Beach.
Opened: 1990. **Holes:** 18. **Par:** 72/72. **Yards:** 6,591/5,386. **Course rating:** 71.6/69.3.
Slope: 130/117. **Architect:** Gary Player. **Green fee:** $18/$48. **Credit cards:** All major.
Reduced fees: Weekdays, low season, resort guests, twilight, juniors. **Caddies:** No.
Golf carts: $16. **Discount golf packages:** Yes. **Season:** Year-round. **High:** Jan.-April.
On site lodging: Yes. **Rental clubs:** Yes. **Walking policy:** Mandatory cart. **Metal spikes allowed:** Yes. **Range:** Yes (grass). **To obtain tee times:** Call up to 5 days in advance.
Subscriber comments: Fun course. Tight fairways...Flat greens...Nice change in area.

★★★ PALM HARBOR GOLF CLUB
Palm Harbor Pkwy., Palm Coast, 32137, Flagler County, (904)445-0845, (800)874-2101, 30 miles N of Daytona Beach.
Opened: 1973. **Holes:** 18. **Par:** 72/72. **Yards:** 6,572/5,346. **Course rating:** 71.8/71.2.
Slope: 127/128. **Architect:** William W. Amick. **Green fee:** $39/$48. **Credit cards:** MC,VISA. **Reduced fees:** Low season, resort guests, twilight, juniors. **Caddies:** No.
Golf carts: Included in Green Fee. **Discount golf packages:** Yes. **Season:** Year-round.
High: Jan.-May. **On site lodging:** No. **Rental clubs:** Yes. **Walking policy:** Mandatory cart. **Metal spikes allowed:** Yes. **Range:** Yes (grass). **To obtain tee times:** Call up to five days in advance.
Subscriber comments: Well-defined holes...Large greens...Boring...Fun.

★★★½ PALM RIVER COUNTRY CLUB
Palm River Blvd., Naples, 34110, Collier County, (941)597-6082, 6 miles N of Naples.
Opened: 1960. **Holes:** 18. **Par:** 72/72. **Yards:** 6,488/5,364. **Course rating:** 72.2/70.6.
Slope: 127/121. **Architect:** Ernie Smith. **Green fee:** $30/$70. **Credit cards:** All major.
Reduced fees: Low season, twilight. **Caddies:** No. **Golf carts:** Included in Green Fee.
Discount golf packages: No. **Season:** Year-round. **High:** Jan.-March. **On site lodging:** No. **Rental clubs:** Yes. **Walking policy:** Mandatory cart. **Metal spikes allowed:** Yes. **Range:** Yes (grass). **To obtain tee times:** Call up to 2 days in advance.
Subscriber comments: Water on many holes...Wide open...Range is lacking.

★★★½ PALMETTO GOLF COURSE
PM-9300 S.W. 152nd St., Miami, 33157, Dade County, (305)238-2922.
Opened: 1959. **Holes:** 18. **Par:** 70/73. **Yards:** 6,648/5,710. **Course rating:** 72.2/73.4.
Slope: 128/125. **Architect:** Dick Wilson. **Green fee:** $12/$25. **Credit cards:** MC,VISA,AMEX. **Reduced fees:** Weekdays, low season, twilight, juniors. **Caddies:** No.
Golf carts: $13. **Discount golf packages:** Yes. **Season:** Year-round. **High:** Jan.-March. **On site lodging:** No. **Rental clubs:** Yes. **Walking policy:** Unrestricted walking.
Metal spikes allowed: Yes. **Range:** Yes (Mats). **To obtain tee times:** Call golf shop up to 7 days in advance.
Subscriber comments: Very crowded...My favorite spot when wintering in Miami. Enjoy the people.

★★★ PELICAN BAY COUNTRY CLUB
550 Sea Duck Dr., Daytona Beach, 32119, Volusia County, (904)788-6496, 40 miles NE of Orlando.
Opened: 1985. **Holes:** 18. **Par:** 72/72. **Yards:** 6,630/5,278. **Course rating:** 71.9/70.8.
Slope: 123/127. **Architect:** Lloyd Clifton. **Green fee:** $15/$37. **Credit cards:** MC,VISA.
Reduced fees: Weekdays, low season, twilight. **Caddies:** No. **Golf carts:** Included in Green Fee. **Discount golf packages:** Yes. **Season:** Year-round. **High:** Dec.-April. **On site lodging:** No. **Rental clubs:** No. **Walking policy:** Mandatory cart. **Metal spikes allowed:** Yes. **Range:** No. **To obtain tee times:** Call up to 6 days in advance.
Subscriber comments: Condo course makes for a lot of out-of-bounds...Some very testy water holes.

★★★½PELICAN POINTE GOLF & COUNTRY CLUB
PU-575 Center Rd., Venice, 34292, Sarasota County, (941)496-4653, 15 miles S of Sarasota.
Opened: 1995. **Holes:** 18. **Par:** 72/72. **Yards:** 7,202/4,939. **Course rating:** 74.8/68.3. **Slope:** 145/113. **Architect:** Ted McAnlis. **Green fee:** $35/$60. **Credit cards:** All major. **Reduced fees:** N/A. **Caddies:** No. **Golf carts:** Included in Green Fee. **Discount golf packages:** No. **Season:** Year-round. **High:** Jan.-March. **On site lodging:** No. **Rental clubs:** Yes. **Walking policy:** Mandatory cart. **Metal spikes allowed:** Yes. **Range:** Yes (mats). **To obtain tee times:** N/A.
Subscriber comments: Wonderful course...Worth visiting again...Getting better every year...Fine course, except for holes bordering homesite construction...When construction is finished will be a good one...Water on many holes.

★★★★PELICAN'S NEST GOLF CLUB
PU-4450 Pelican's Nest Dr., Bonita Springs, 34134, Lee County, (941)947-4600, (800)952-6378, 15 miles S of Fort Myers.
Opened: 1985. **Holes:** 36. **Architect:** Tom Fazio. **Green fee:** $45/$135. **Credit cards:** MC,VISA,AMEX. **Reduced fees:** Low season, twilight, juniors. **Caddies:** No. **Golf carts:** Included in Green Fee. **Discount golf packages:** No. **Season:** Year-round. **High:** Jan.-March. **On site lodging:** No. **Rental clubs:** Yes. **Walking policy:** Mandatory cart. **Metal spikes allowed:** Yes. **Range:** Yes (grass). **To obtain tee times:** Call up to 30 days in advance.
GATOR/SEMINOLE
Par: 72/72. **Yards:** 7,064/5,226. **Course rating:** 74.7/69.6. **Slope:** 137/123.
HURRICANE/GATOR
Par: 72/72. **Yards:** 7,116/5,201. **Course rating:** 74.8/69.2. **Slope:** 140/122.
HURRICANE/SEMINOLE
Par: 72/72. **Yards:** 6,964/5,047. **Course rating:** 74.1/68.6. **Slope:** 136/120.
SEMINOLE/PANTHER
Par: 72/72. **Yards:** 6,975/5,149. **Course rating:** 74.2/69.1. **Slope:** 133/120.
Subscriber comments: Feels like a pro atmosphere...Water everywhere...Wow. Must play...Heavy green fee, but will play it again...Older, tighter holes are best/most challenging...You feel like a king...Still building homes around it (I hit one)...Wish I could afford to play it other than in the summer...Acceptable golf factory...Tougher than it looks...Lots of water, good bunkers.

★★½PERDIDO BAY GOLF RESORT
R-One Doug Ford Dr., Pensacola, 32507, Escambia County, (904)492-1223.
Opened: 1963. **Holes:** 18. **Par:** 72/72. **Yards:** 7,154/5,478. **Course rating:** 73.6/71.4. **Slope:** 125/121. **Architect:** Bill Amick. **Green fee:** $24/$43. **Credit cards:** MC,VISA,DISC. **Reduced fees:** Resort guests, twilight, juniors. **Caddies:** No. **Golf carts:** Included in Green Fee. **Discount golf packages:** Yes. **Season:** Year-round. **High:** Jan.-April. **On site lodging:** Yes. **Rental clubs:** Yes. **Walking policy:** Mandatory cart. **Metal spikes allowed:** Yes. **Range:** Yes (grass). **To obtain tee times:** Call. Credit card required if more than 7 days in advance.
Notes: 1978-1987 PGA Tour Pensacola Open.
Subscriber comments: Creeks border nearly every fairway. Keep it straight...Pretty course...Older, dated course...Plenty of water challenges...Some tough driving holes.

★★½PINE LAKES COUNTRY CLUB
400 Pine Lakes Pkwy., Palm Coast, 32164, Flagler County, (904)445-0852, (800)874-2101, 30 miles N of Daytona Beach.
Opened: 1980. **Holes:** 18. **Par:** 72/72. **Yards:** 7,074/5,166. **Course rating:** 73.5/71.4. **Slope:** 126/124. **Architect:** Arnold Palmer/Ed Seay. **Green fee:** $39/$48. **Credit cards:** All major. **Reduced fees:** Low season, resort guests, twilight, juniors. **Caddies:** No. **Golf carts:** Included in Green Fee. **Discount golf packages:** Yes. **Season:** Year-round. **High:** Jan.-April. **On site lodging:** No. **Rental clubs:** Yes. **Walking policy:** Mandatory cart. **Metal spikes allowed:** Yes. **Range:** Yes (grass/mats). **To obtain tee times:** Call up to 5 days in advance.
Subscriber comments: For winter golf, good...Sand, water, undulating greens. Wide open...Pretty course...Shot placement/club selection very important.

★★PINE LAKES GOLF CLUB
PU-153 Northside Dr. S., Jacksonville, 32218, Duval County, (904)757-0318, 15 miles N of Jacksonville.
Opened: 1986. **Holes:** 18. **Par:** 72/72. **Yards:** 6,631/5,192. **Course rating:** 71.1/69.8. **Slope:** 127/118. **Architect:** N/A. **Green fee:** $13/$30. **Credit cards:** All major. **Reduced fees:** Weekdays, low season, twilight, seniors, juniors. **Caddies:** No. **Golf carts:** Included in Green Fee. **Discount golf packages:** Yes. **Season:** Year-round. **High:** Jan.-April. **On site lodging:** No. **Rental clubs:** Yes. **Walking policy:** Walking at certain times. **Metal spikes allowed:** Yes. **Range:** Yes (grass). **To obtain tee times:** Call golf shop.

PLANT CITY GOLF CLUB
3102 Coronet Rd., Plant City, 33566, Hillsborough County, (813)752-1524, 20 miles E of Tampa.
Opened: 1932. **Holes:** 18. **Par:** 72/72. **Yards:** 6,479/4,929. **Course rating:** 70.4/67.3. **Slope:** 118/109. **Architect:** Built by members. **Green fee:** $18/$25. **Credit cards:** MC,VISA,DISC. **Reduced fees:** Weekdays, low season, twilight, juniors. **Caddies:** No. **Golf carts:** Included in Green Fee. **Discount golf packages:** No. **Season:** Year-round. **High:** Nov.-April. **On site lodging:** No. **Rental clubs:** Yes. **Walking policy:** Walking at certain times. **Metal spikes allowed:** Yes. **Range:** Yes (grass). **To obtain tee times:** Call two days in advance.

PLANTATION GOLF & COUNTRY CLUB
500 Rockley Blvd., Venice, 34293, Sarasota County, (941)493-2000, 15 miles S of Sarasota.
Architect: Ron Garl. **Green fee:** $31/$52. **Credit cards:** MC,VISA,DISC. **Reduced fees:** Low season, resort guests. **Caddies:** No. **Golf carts:** $11. **Discount golf packages:** No. **Season:** Year-round. **High:** Oct.-April. **On site lodging:** Yes. **Rental clubs:** Yes. **Walking policy:** Walking at certain times. **Metal spikes allowed:** Yes. **Range:** Yes (grass). **To obtain tee times:** Public may call two days in advance. Resort guests call three days in advance.
★★★½BOBCAT COURSE
Opened: 1981. **Holes:** 18. **Par:** 72/72. **Yards:** 6,840/5,023. **Course rating:** 73.0/70.6. **Slope:** 130/121.
Subscriber comments: Some holes get your attention...Lots of trouble...Treated like a king.
★★★½PANTHER COURSE
Opened: 1985. **Holes:** 18. **Par:** 72/72. **Yards:** 6,311/4,751. **Course rating:** 70.7/68.0. **Slope:** 124/117.
Subscriber comments: Water and woods...Shorter and prettier than its counterpart.

★★★PLANTATION INN & GOLF RESORT
R-9301 W. Fort Island Trail, Crystal River, 34429, Citrus County, (352)795-7211, (800)632-6262, 80 miles N of Orlando.
Opened: 1956. **Holes:** 18. **Par:** 72/72. **Yards:** 6,502/5,395. **Course rating:** 71.6/71.1. **Slope:** 126/117. **Architect:** Mark Mahannah. **Green fee:** $15/$32. **Credit cards:** MC,VISA,AMEX. **Reduced fees:** Weekdays, low season, resort guests, twilight, juniors. **Caddies:** No. **Golf carts:** Included in Green Fee. **Discount golf packages:** Yes. **Season:** Year-round. **High:** Feb.-April. **On site lodging:** Yes. **Rental clubs:** Yes. **Walking policy:** Walking at certain times. **Metal spikes allowed:** Yes. **Range:** Yes (grass). **To obtain tee times:** Call two days in advance.
Subscriber comments: Wildlife was a plus to an average course...Gator on fifth hole...A lot of water for me.
Special Notes: Resort also has 9-hole par-34 Lagoons Course.

★★★POINCIANA GOLF & RACQUET RESORT
R-500 E. Cypress Pkwy., Kissimmee, 34759, Osceola County, (407)933-5300, (800)331-7743, 14 miles S of Orlando.
Opened: 1973. **Holes:** 18. **Par:** 72/72. **Yards:** 6,700/4,938. **Course rating:** 72.2/68.4. **Slope:** 125/118. **Architect:** Bruce Devlin/Robert von Hagge. **Green fee:** $40/$65. **Credit cards:** MC,VISA,AMEX. **Reduced fees:** Low season, resort guests, twilight, juniors. **Caddies:** No. **Golf carts:** Included in Green Fee. **Discount golf packages:**

Yes. **Season:** Year-round. **High:** Jan.-April. **On site lodging:** Yes. **Rental clubs:** Yes. **Walking policy:** Mandatory cart. **Metal spikes allowed:** Yes. **Range:** Yes (grass). **To obtain tee times:** Call 7 days in advance.
Subscriber comments: Not as much water for Florida...A couple of poor holes, otherwise nice...Good test.

POMPANO BEACH GOLF COURSE
PM-1101 N. Federal Hwy., Pompano Beach, 33062, Broward County, (954)781-0426, 7 miles N of Ft. Lauderdale.
Green fee: $20/$36. **Credit cards:** None. **Reduced fees:** Low season, twilight, juniors. **Caddies:** No. **Golf carts:** Included in Green Fee. **Discount golf packages:** No. **Season:** Year-round. **High:** Jan.-April. **On site lodging:** No. **Rental clubs:** Yes. **Walking policy:** Unrestricted walking. **Metal spikes allowed:** Yes. **Range:** Yes (grass). **To obtain tee times:** First come, first served.
★★½**PALMS COURSE**
Opened: 1954. **Holes:** 18. **Par:** 71/72. **Yards:** 6,366/5,397. **Course rating:** 69.4/70.2. **Slope:** 113/114. **Architect:** Red Lawrence.
Subscriber comments: Very busy...Wonderful to walk in Florida. Great walking course...Easy to walk.
★★½**PINES COURSE**
Opened: 1967. **Holes:** 18. **Par:** 72/74. **Yards:** 6,886/5,748. **Course rating:** 72.2/72.5. **Slope:** 123/120. **Architect:** Robert von Hagge.
Subscriber comments: Can let out the shaft...Very busy...Plays slow.

PONTE VEDRA INN & CLUB
R-200 Ponte Vedra Blvd., Ponte Vedra Beach, 32082, St. Johns County, (904)285-1111, (800)234-7842, 20 miles SE of Jacksonville.
Credit cards: All major,Diners Club. **Reduced fees:** N/A. **Caddies:** No. **Golf carts:** Included in Green Fee. **Discount golf packages:** Yes. **Season:** Year-round. **High:** March-May. **On site lodging:** Yes. **Rental clubs:** Yes. **Walking policy:** Walking at certain times. **Metal spikes allowed:** Yes. **Range:** Yes (grass). **To obtain tee times:** May call as soon as Inn reservation is made. Must be hotel guest to play.
★★★**LAGOON COURSE**
Opened: 1962. **Holes:** 18. **Par:** 70/70. **Yards:** 5,574/4,641. **Course rating:** 66.2/66.9. **Slope:** 110/113. **Architect:** Robert Trent Jones. **Green fee:** $85.
Subscriber comments: Can score on this course...Fewer stressful shots...Water and sand...Ocean breeze.
★★★½**OCEAN COURSE**
Opened: 1928. **Holes:** 18. **Par:** 72/72. **Yards:** 6,573/5,237. **Course rating:** 71.3/69.6. **Slope:** 120/119. **Architect:** Herbert Strong. **Green fee:** $90.
Subscriber comments: Lots of history, fun to play...Challenging with wind. Tame otherwise...Fine old course...Pretty...Very playable.

PRESIDENTIAL COUNTRY CLUB
19650 N.E. 18th Ave., North Miami Beach, 33179, Dade County, (305)933-5266. Call club for further information.

QUAIL HEIGHTS COUNTRY CLUB
Route 18, Box 707, Lake City, 32025, Columbia County, (904)752-3339, 45 miles N of Gainesville.
Opened: 1972. **Holes:** 27. **Architect:** N/A. **Green fee:** $18/$26. **Credit cards:** MC,VISA. **Reduced fees:** Weekdays, low season, resort guests, juniors. **Caddies:** No. **Golf carts:** N/A. **Discount golf packages:** Yes. **Season:** Year-round. **High:** N/A. **On site lodging:** Yes. **Rental clubs:** Yes. **Walking policy:** Walking at certain times. **Metal spikes allowed:** No. **Range:** Yes (grass). **To obtain tee times:** Call in advance.
CREEKS/PONDS
Par: 72/72. **Yards:** 6,672/5,144. **Course rating:** 71.6/68.9. **Slope:** 127/113.
DUNES/CREEKS
Par: 72/72. **Yards:** 6,731/5,141. **Course rating:** 72.6/69.9. **Slope:** 130/117.
PONDS/DUNES
Par: 72/72. **Yards:** 6,819/5,257. **Course rating:** 72.8/70.0. **Slope:** 135/117.

★★½QUALITY INN & SUITES GOLF RESORT

R-4100 Golden Gate Pkwy., Naples, 33999, Collier County, (941)455-9498, (800)277-0017, 6 miles E of Naples.
Opened: 1964. **Holes:** 18. **Par:** 72/72. **Yards:** 6,570/5,374. **Course rating:** 70.8/70.3. **Slope:** 125/123. **Architect:** Dick Wilson/Joe Lee. **Green fee:** $14/$48. **Credit cards:** All major. **Reduced fees:** Low season, resort guests, twilight, juniors. **Caddies:** No. **Golf carts:** $17. **Discount golf packages:** Yes. **Season:** Year-round. **High:** Nov.-April. **On site lodging:** Yes. **Rental clubs:** Yes. **Walking policy:** Walking at certain times. **Metal spikes allowed:** Yes. **Range:** Yes (grass). **To obtain tee times:** Public call 2 days in advance. Hotel guests, at time of reservation.
Notes: LPGA Greater Naples Classic.
Subscriber comments: I keep coming back...Mature Florida course actually has trees...Enjoyable and challenging.
Special Notes: Formerly Golden Gate Country Club.

★★★RADISSON PONCE DE LEON GOLF & CONFERENCE RESORT

R-4000 U.S. Highway 1 N., St. Augustine, 32095, St. Johns County, (904)829-5314, (888)829-5314, 25 miles S of Jacksonville.
Opened: 1916. **Holes:** 18. **Par:** 72/72. **Yards:** 6,823/5,308. **Course rating:** 72.9/70.7. **Slope:** 131/125. **Architect:** Donald Ross. **Green fee:** $25/$80. **Credit cards:** MC,VISA,AMEX. **Reduced fees:** Weekdays, low season, resort guests, twilight, juniors. **Caddies:** No. **Golf carts:** Included in Green Fee. **Discount golf packages:** Yes. **Season:** Year-round. **High:** Feb.-May/Oct.-Nov. **On site lodging:** Yes. **Rental clubs:** Yes. **Walking policy:** Mandatory cart. **Metal spikes allowed:** Yes. **Range:** Yes (grass). **To obtain tee times:** Book tee times with hotel reservations up to 1 year in advance. Others call 5 days in advance; with priority card, 2 days in advance.
Subscriber comments: Challenging...Scenic...Great course by Mr. Ross...Busy...Nice practice area.

★★★RAINTREE GOLF RESORT

R-1600 S. Hiatus Rd., Pembroke Pines, 33025, Broward County, (954)432-4400, (800)346-5332, 8 miles SW of Ft. Lauderdale.
Opened: 1985. **Holes:** 18. **Par:** 72/72. **Yards:** 6,461/5,382. **Course rating:** 70.8/70.2. **Slope:** 126/122. **Architect:** Charles M. Mahannah. **Green fee:** $27/$55. **Credit cards:** All major. **Reduced fees:** Weekdays, low season, resort guests, twilight, seniors, juniors. **Caddies:** No. **Golf carts:** Included in Green Fee. **Discount golf packages:** Yes. **Season:** Year-round. **High:** Nov.-April. **On site lodging:** Yes. **Rental clubs:** Yes. **Walking policy:** Mandatory cart. **Metal spikes allowed:** Yes. **Range:** Yes (mats). **To obtain tee times:** Call 3 days in advance.
Subscriber comments: Six par 3s, six par 4s and six par 5s...Lots of water...Enjoyable, but slow.

★★★RAVINES GOLF & COUNTRY CLUB

2932 Ravines Rd., Middleburg, 32068, Clay County, (904)282-7888.
Opened: 1979. **Holes:** 18. **Par:** 72/70. **Yards:** 6,733/4,817. **Course rating:** 72.4/67.4. **Slope:** 133/120. **Architect:** Mark McCumber/Ron Garl. **Green fee:** $25/$50. **Credit cards:** All major. **Reduced fees:** N/A. **Caddies:** No. **Golf carts:** Included in Green Fee. **Discount golf packages:** Yes. **Season:** Year-round. **High:** March-May. **On site lodging:** Yes. **Rental clubs:** Yes. **Walking policy:** Mandatory cart. **Metal spikes allowed:** Yes. **Range:** Yes (grass). **To obtain tee times:** Call 7 days in advance.
Subscriber comments: Great use of natural terrain...Well laid out, local ravines well placed, very fair...Seems like you are in the Carolinas...Better be on your game...A little bit of a hilly course for Florida...Great scenery.

REDLAND GOLF & COUNTRY CLUB

PU-24451 S.W. 177th Ave., Homestead, 33030, Dade County, (305)247-8503.
Opened: 1946. **Holes:** 18. **Par:** 72/72. **Yards:** 6,613/5,639. **Course rating:** 72.6/73.0. **Slope:** 123/123. **Architect:** Red Lawrence. **Green fee:** $22/$40. **Credit cards:** MC,VISA. **Reduced fees:** Low season. **Caddies:** No. **Golf carts:** Included in Green Fee. **Discount golf packages:** No. **Season:** Year-round. **High:** Nov.-April. **On site lodging:** No. **Rental clubs:** Yes. **Walking policy:** Mandatory cart. **Metal spikes allowed:** Yes. **Range:** Yes (grass). **To obtain tee times:** Call one week in advance.

FLORIDA

★★★**REMINGTON GOLF CLUB**
PU-2995 Remington Blvd., Kissimmee, 34741, Osceola County, (407)344-4004, 12 miles SE of Orlando.
Opened: 1996. **Holes:** 18. **Par:** 72/72. **Yards:** 7,111/5,178. **Course rating:** 73.9/69.8. **Slope:** 134/118. **Architect:** Lloyd Clifton/George Clifton/Ken Ezell. **Green fee:** $24/$60. **Credit cards:** MC,VISA. **Reduced fees:** Weekdays, low season, resort guests, twilight, seniors, juniors. **Caddies:** No. **Golf carts:** Included in Green Fee. **Discount golf packages:** No. **Season:** Year-round. **High:** Nov.-March. **On site lodging:** No. **Rental clubs:** Yes. **Walking policy:** Unrestricted walking. **Metal spikes allowed:** Yes. **Range:** Yes (grass). **To obtain tee times:** N/A.
Subscriber comments: For a new course, it is excellent...Flat Florida course...Will be even better in three years...Should improve with age...Enjoyed layout.

RENAISSANCE VINOY RESORT
R-600 Snell Isle Blvd. N.E., St. Petersburg, 33704, Pinellas County, (813)896-8000.
Opened: 1992. **Holes:** 18. **Par:** 70/71. **Yards:** 6,267/4,818. **Course rating:** 70.2/67.3. **Slope:** 118/111. **Architect:** Ron Garl. **Green fee:** $95. **Credit cards:** All major,Diners Club. **Reduced fees:** Twilight. **Caddies:** Yes. **Golf carts:** Included in Green Fee. **Discount golf packages:** Yes. **Season:** Year-round. **High:** Jan.-April. **On site lodging:** Yes. **Rental clubs:** Yes. **Walking policy:** Walking at certain times. **Metal spikes allowed:** Yes. **Range:** Yes (grass/mats). **To obtain tee times:** Unlimited time frame for resort guests.

★★★**RIDGEWOOD LAKES GOLF CLUB**
200 Eagle Ridge Dr., Davenport, 33837, Polk County, (941)424-8688, (800)684-8800, 35 miles SW of Orlando.
Opened: 1993. **Holes:** 18. **Par:** 72/72. **Yards:** 7,016/5,217. **Course rating:** 73.7/69.9. **Slope:** 129/116. **Architect:** Ted McAnlis. **Green fee:** $15/$65. **Credit cards:** MC,VISA. **Reduced fees:** Low season, resort guests, twilight, seniors. **Caddies:** No. **Golf carts:** Included in Green Fee. **Discount golf packages:** Yes. **Season:** Year-round. **High:** Nov.-April. **On site lodging:** No. **Rental clubs:** Yes. **Walking policy:** Mandatory cart. **Metal spikes allowed:** Yes. **Range:** Yes (grass). **To obtain tee times:** Call up to 7 days in advance.
Subscriber comments: Lots of good holes...Good vacation course...Tough...Lots of water.

★★★**RIVER BEND GOLF CLUB**
730 Airport Rd., Ormond Beach, 32174, Volusia County, (904)673-6000, (800)334-8841, 3 miles N of Daytona Beach.
Opened: 1990. **Holes:** 18. **Par:** 72/72. **Yards:** 6,821/5,112. **Course rating:** 72.3/69.6. **Slope:** 126/120. **Architect:** Lloyd Clifton. **Green fee:** $28/$40. **Credit cards:** MC,VISA,AMEX. **Reduced fees:** Weekdays, low season, twilight, juniors. **Caddies:** No. **Golf carts:** Included in Green Fee. **Discount golf packages:** Yes. **Season:** Year-round. **High:** Jan.-April. **On site lodging:** No. **Rental clubs:** Yes. **Walking policy:** Mandatory cart. **Metal spikes allowed:** Yes. **Range:** Yes (grass). **To obtain tee times:** Call up to 4 days in advance.
Subscriber comments: Tight, woods...Very scenic...Nice clubhouse...Manatees in creek.

★★★**THE RIVER CLUB**
6600 River Club Blvd., Bradenton, 34202, Manatee County, (941)751-4211, 45 miles S of Tampa.
Opened: N/A. **Holes:** 18. **Par:** 72/72. **Yards:** 7,026/5,252. **Course rating:** 74.5/70.4. **Slope:** 135/121. **Architect:** Ron Garl. **Green fee:** $22/$60. **Credit cards:** All major. **Reduced fees:** Weekdays, low season, resort guests, twilight. **Caddies:** No. **Golf carts:** Included in Green Fee. **Discount golf packages:** Yes. **Season:** Year-round. **High:** Jan.-April. **On site lodging:** No. **Rental clubs:** Yes. **Walking policy:** Walking at certain times. **Metal spikes allowed:** Yes. **Range:** Yes (grass). **To obtain tee times:** Call 2 days in advance.
Subscriber comments: Challenging but very playable from back tees...Good course, very good layout...Par 3s are demanding...Wide-open fairways...Hills and mounds a decent challenge for everyone.

★★★½RIVER HILLS COUNTRY CLUB
3943 New River Hills Pkwy., Valrico, 33594, Hillsborough County, (813)653-3323, 20 miles W of Tampa.
Opened: 1989. **Holes:** 18. **Par:** 72/72. **Yards:** 7,004/5,236. **Course rating:** 74.0/70.4. **Slope:** 132/124. **Architect:** Joe Lee. **Green fee:** $21/$40. **Credit cards:** MC,VISA. **Reduced fees:** Low season, twilight. **Caddies:** No. **Golf carts:** $16. **Discount golf packages:** Yes. **Season:** Year-round. **High:** Jan.-April. **On site lodging:** No. **Rental clubs:** Yes. **Walking policy:** Mandatory cart. **Metal spikes allowed:** Yes. **Range:** Yes (grass). **To obtain tee times:** Call 2 days in advance.
Subscriber comments: A little monotonous, but nice...Excellent course, tough, nice...Enjoyable day.

★★★RIVER RUN GOLF LINKS
PU-1801 27th St. E., Bradenton, 34208, Manatee County, (941)747-6331, 30 miles S of St. Petersburg.
Opened: 1987. **Holes:** 18. **Par:** 70/70. **Yards:** 5,900/4,811. **Course rating:** 67.9/66.5. **Slope:** 115/110. **Architect:** Ward Northrup. **Green fee:** $8/$17. **Credit cards:** None. **Reduced fees:** Weekdays, low season, twilight. **Caddies:** No. **Golf carts:** $9. **Discount golf packages:** No. **Season:** Year-round. **High:** Jan.-April. **On site lodging:** No. **Rental clubs:** Yes. **Walking policy:** Unrestricted walking. **Metal spikes allowed:** Yes. **Range:** No. **To obtain tee times:** Call 2 days in advance.
Subscriber comments: Right beside Pittsburgh Pirates spring-training camp...Not long but very tight.

★★★★RIVERWOOD GOLF CLUB
4100 Riverwood Dr., Port Charlotte, 33953, Charlotte County, (941)764-6661, 45 miles S of Sarasota.
Opened: 1993. **Holes:** 18. **Par:** 72/72. **Yards:** 6,938/4,695. **Course rating:** 73.2/66.8. **Slope:** 131/112. **Architect:** Gene Bates. **Green fee:** $50/$85. **Credit cards:** MC,VISA. **Reduced fees:** Low season, resort guests, twilight. **Caddies:** No. **Golf carts:** Included in Green Fee. **Discount golf packages:** Yes. **Season:** Year-round. **High:** Nov.-April. **On site lodging:** Yes. **Rental clubs:** Yes. **Walking policy:** Mandatory cart. **Metal spikes allowed:** Yes. **Range:** Yes (grass). **To obtain tee times:** Call 3 days in advance.
Subscriber comments: One of best in Southwest Florida...Good test...Tough but fair layout....Long and narrow...Pretty...Beautiful scenery.

★★RIVIERA COUNTRY CLUB
500 Calle Grande, Ormond Beach, 32174, Volusia County, (904)677-2464, 4 miles N of Daytona Beach.
Opened: 1935. **Holes:** 18. **Par:** 71/72. **Yards:** 6,302/5,207. **Course rating:** 68.0/69.9. **Slope:** 113/122. **Architect:** Dave Wallace. **Green fee:** $18/$30. **Credit cards:** MC,VISA. **Reduced fees:** Low season, resort guests, twilight. **Caddies:** No. **Golf carts:** Included in Green Fee. **Discount golf packages:** Yes. **Season:** Year-round. **High:** Jan.-March. **On site lodging:** No. **Rental clubs:** Yes. **Walking policy:** Mandatory cart. **Metal spikes allowed:** Yes. **Range:** Yes (grass/mats). **To obtain tee times:** First come, first served. Call ahead to insure course availability.

★★ROCKY POINT GOLF COURSE
PU-4151 Dana Shores Dr., Tampa, 33634, Hillsborough County, (813)673-4316.
Opened: 1900. **Holes:** 18. **Par:** 71/71. **Yards:** 6,398/4,910. **Course rating:** 71.1/65.7. **Slope:** 122/111. **Architect:** Ron Garl. **Green fee:** $15/$32. **Credit cards:** MC,VISA,DISC. **Reduced fees:** Low season. **Caddies:** No. **Golf carts:** Included in Green Fee. **Discount golf packages:** No. **Season:** Year-round. **High:** Year-round. **On site lodging:** No. **Rental clubs:** Yes. **Walking policy:** Unrestricted walking. **Metal spikes allowed:** Yes. **Range:** No. **To obtain tee times:** Call Thursday a.m. for the following week.

★★½ROGERS PARK GOLF COURSE
PU-7910 N. 30th St., Tampa, 33610, Hillsborough County, (813)673-4396.
Opened: 1950. **Holes:** 18. **Par:** 72/72. **Yards:** 6,850/5,900. **Course rating:** 71.0/67.0. **Slope:** 122/114. **Architect:** Ron Garl. **Green fee:** $20/$35. **Credit cards:** MC,VISA. **Reduced fees:** Weekdays, low season, twilight, juniors. **Caddies:** No. **Golf carts:** $24.

Discount golf packages: No. **Season:** Year-round. **High:** Jan.-April. **On site lodging:** No. **Rental clubs:** Yes. **Walking policy:** Unrestricted walking. **Metal spikes allowed:** Yes. **Range:** Yes (grass). **To obtain tee times:** Call 7 days in advance.
Subscriber comments: Great course for first round after a layoff...Fun and easy little muny.

★★½ROLLING GREEN GOLF CLUB
4501 N. Tuttle Ave., Sarasota, 34234, Sarasota County, (941)355-7621.
Opened: 1968. **Holes:** 18. **Par:** 72/72. **Yards:** 6,343/5,010. **Course rating:** 69.7/67.9. **Slope:** 119/110. **Architect:** R. Albert Anderson. **Green fee:** $10/$32. **Credit cards:** MC,VISA. **Reduced fees:** Low season, seniors. **Caddies:** No. **Golf carts:** $12.
Discount golf packages: No. **Season:** Year-round. **High:** Nov.-April. **On site lodging:** No. **Rental clubs:** Yes. **Walking policy:** Walking at certain times. **Metal spikes allowed:** Yes. **Range:** Yes (grass). **To obtain tee times:** Call 3 days in advance.
Subscriber comments: Fair layout...Large crowds (they handle them well)...Not too difficult...Blah course.

★★★ROLLING HILLS HOTEL & GOLF RESORT
R-3501 W. Rolling Hills Circle, Fort Lauderdale, 33328, Broward County, (954)475-3010.
Opened: 1953. **Holes:** 18. **Par:** 72/72. **Yards:** 6,905/5,630. **Course rating:** 72.7/71.7. **Slope:** 124/121. **Architect:** William Mitchell. **Green fee:** $25/$60. **Credit cards:** All major. **Reduced fees:** Weekdays, low season, resort guests, twilight. **Caddies:** No. **Golf carts:** Included in Green Fee. **Discount golf packages:** Yes. **Season:** Year-round. **High:** Jan.-April. **On site lodging:** Yes. **Rental clubs:** Yes. **Walking policy:** Mandatory cart. **Metal spikes allowed:** Yes. **Range:** Yes (grass/mats). **To obtain tee times:** Call 3 days in advance.
Subscriber comments: Reminds one of a northern course...Nice to not see a lot of palm trees and ponds for a change...Heavily played...One of my favorites.

★★★½ROSEDALE GOLF & COUNTRY CLUB
5100 87th St. E., Bradenton, 34202, Manatee County, (941)756-0004, 30 miles S of Tampa.
Opened: 1993. **Holes:** 18. **Par:** 72/72. **Yards:** 6,779/5,169. **Course rating:** 72.6/69.7. **Slope:** 130/120. **Architect:** Ted McAnlis. **Green fee:** $20/$56. **Credit cards:** MC,VISA. **Reduced fees:** Low season, resort guests, twilight. **Caddies:** No. **Golf carts:** Included in Green Fee. **Discount golf packages:** Yes. **Season:** Year-round. **High:** Oct.-May. **On site lodging:** No. **Rental clubs:** Yes. **Walking policy:** Walking at certain times. **Metal spikes allowed:** Yes. **Range:** Yes (grass). **To obtain tee times:** Call up to 3 days in advance.
Subscriber comments: Tight. Good test...Enjoyable...Great practice facility...Excellent...One of the toughest 18th holes I've played.

★★ROSEMONT GOLF & COUNTRY CLUB
4224 Clubhouse Rd., Orlando, 32808, Orange County, (407)298-1230.
Opened: 1970. **Holes:** 18. **Par:** 72/72. **Yards:** 6,803/5,488. **Course rating:** 72.3/70.3. **Slope:** 130/114. **Architect:** Lloyd Clifton. **Green fee:** $15/$38. **Credit cards:** All major. **Reduced fees:** Weekdays, low season, twilight. **Caddies:** No. **Golf carts:** Included in Green Fee. **Discount golf packages:** No. **Season:** Year-round. **High:** Nov.-Dec. **On site lodging:** No. **Rental clubs:** Yes. **Walking policy:** Mandatory cart. **Metal spikes allowed:** Yes. **Range:** Yes (grass/mats). **To obtain tee times:** Call golf shop.

ROTONDA GOLF & COUNTRY CLUB
PU-**Architect:** N/A. **Credit cards:** MC,VISA. **Reduced fees:** Low season, resort guests, twilight. **Caddies:** No. **Golf carts:** Included in Green Fee. **Season:** Year-round. **High:** Nov.-April. **On site lodging:** No. **Rental clubs:** No. **Walking policy:** Walking at certain times. **Metal spikes allowed:** Yes. **To obtain tee times:** Call up to 3 days in advance.
HILLS COURSE
100 Rotonda Circle, Rotonda, 33947, Charlotte County, (941)697-2414, 10 miles N of Port Charlotte.
Opened: 1972. **Holes:** 18. **Par:** 72/72. **Yards:** 6,304/5,075. **Course rating:** 70.3/69.3. **Slope:** 126/121. **Green fee:** $20/$40. **Discount golf packages:** No. **Range:** Yes (grass).

LINKS COURSE
13 Ann Underwood Dr., Cape Haze, 33947, Charlotte County, (941)697-8877, 10 miles N of Port Charlotte.
Opened: 1990. **Holes:** 18. **Par:** 63/63. **Yards:** 4,197/3,190. **Course rating:** 61.2/59.1.
Slope: 108/94. **Green fee:** $20/$30. **Discount golf packages:** No. **Range:** No.
PALMS COURSE
100 Rotonda Circle, Rotonda, 33947, Charlotte County, (941)697-8118, 10 miles N of Port Charlotte.
Opened: 1989. **Holes:** 18. **Par:** 72/72. **Yards:** 6,511/4,700. **Course rating:** 71.0/67.5.
Slope: 127/115. **Green fee:** $32/$49. **Discount golf packages:** Yes. **Range:** Yes (grass).

★★★ROYAL OAK GOLF CLUB
2150 Country Club Dr., Titusville, 32780, Brevard County, (407)268-1550, (800)884-2150, 45 miles E of Orlando.
Opened: 1964. **Holes:** 18. **Par:** 71/72. **Yards:** 6,709/5,471. **Course rating:** 72.3/71.5.
Slope: 126/128. **Architect:** Dick Wilson. **Green fee:** $15/$45. **Credit cards:**
MC,VISA,AMEX. **Reduced fees:** Weekdays, low season, resort guests, twilight, juniors.
Caddies: No. **Golf carts:** Included in Green Fee. **Discount golf packages:** Yes.
Season: Year-round. **High:** Jan.-April. **On site lodging:** Yes. **Rental clubs:** Yes.
Walking policy: Walking at certain times. **Metal spikes allowed:** Yes. **Range:** Yes
(grass). **To obtain tee times:** Call up to 7 days in advance.
Subscriber comments: Would play again...Has potential...Good challenge.

★★★½ROYAL TEE COUNTRY CLUB
11460 Royal Tee Circle, Cape Coral, 33991, Lee County, (941)283-5522, 15 miles W of Fort Myers.
Opened: 1985. **Holes:** 27. **Architect:** Gordon Lewis. **Green fee:** $15/$49. **Credit cards:** MC,VISA,DISC. **Reduced fees:** Low season, twilight, seniors. **Caddies:** No.
Golf carts: Included in Green Fee. **Discount golf packages:** Yes. **Season:** Year-round.
High: Jan.-April. **On site lodging:** No. **Rental clubs:** Yes. **Walking policy:** Walking at certain times. **Metal spikes allowed:** Yes. **Range:** Yes (grass). **To obtain tee times:**
Call up to 3 days in advance.
PRINCE/KING
Par: 72/72. **Yards:** 6,736/4,685. **Course rating:** 71.5/67.0. **Slope:** 126/114.
PRINCE/QUEEN
Par: 72/72. **Yards:** 6,606/4,670. **Course rating:** 71.3/66.4. **Slope:** 126/114.
QUEEN/KING
Par: 72/72. **Yards:** 6,574/4,631. **Course rating:** 71.4/66.2. **Slope:** 128/110.
Subscriber comments: Fun, not too hard, women's tees way up...Good parking and clubhouse...Not a long course, but challenging.

★★★SABAL POINT COUNTRY CLUB
2662 Sabal Club Way, Longwood, 32779, Seminole County, (407)869-4622.
Opened: 1981. **Holes:** 18. **Par:** 72/72. **Yards:** 6,603/5,278. **Course rating:** 71.6/70.0.
Slope: 129/119. **Architect:** Wade Northrup. **Green fee:** $25/$55. **Credit cards:**
MC,VISA,AMEX. **Reduced fees:** Weekdays, low season, twilight, juniors. **Caddies:** No.
Golf carts: Included in Green Fee. **Discount golf packages:** No. **Season:** Year-round.
High: Jan.-April. **On site lodging:** No. **Rental clubs:** Yes. **Walking policy:** Mandatory cart. **Metal spikes allowed:** Yes. **Range:** Yes (grass). **To obtain tee times:** Call two days in advance.
Subscriber comments: Very tight. Condos are too close...Worth a look...Mature course.

SADDLEBROOK RESORT
R-5700 Saddlebrook Way, Wesley Chapel, 33543, Pasco County,
(813)973-1111, (800)729-8383, 30 miles N of Tampa.
Credit cards: All major. **Reduced fees:** Low season, resort guests.
Caddies: No. **Golf carts:** Included in Green Fee. **Discount golf pack-**
ages: Yes. **Season:** Year-round. **High:** Nov.-April. **On site lodging:** Yes.
Rental clubs: Yes. **Walking policy:** Mandatory cart. **Metal spikes allowed:** Yes.
Range: Yes (grass). **To obtain tee times:** Call 48 hours in advance. Resort guests may reserve tee times 60 days in advance.

★★★★**PALMER COURSE**
Opened: 1986. **Holes:** 18. **Par:** 71/71. **Yards:** 6,469/5,212. **Course rating:** 71.0/70.2.
Slope: 126/121. **Architect:** Arnold Palmer/Ed Seay. **Green fee:** $35/$95.
Subscriber comments: Great resort course...Biggest gators I ever
saw...Challenging...Great landscaping.

★★★½**SADDLEBROOK COURSE**
Opened: 1976. **Holes:** 18. **Par:** 70/70. **Yards:** 6,603/5,183. **Course rating:** 72.0/70.8.
Slope: 124/124. **Architect:** Dean Refram. **Green fee:** $40/$115.
Subscriber comments: Great finishing hole...Very good...Very challenging and enjoy-
able.

★½**ST. AUGUSTINE SHORES GOLF CLUB**
PU-707 Shores Blvd., St. Augustine, 32086, St. Johns County, (904)794-4653, 50 miles
S of Jacksonville.
Opened: 1974. **Holes:** 18. **Par:** 70/70. **Yards:** 5,736/4,355. **Course rating:** 64.6/64.2.
Slope: 102/106. **Architect:** Chuck Almony. **Green fee:** $24/$28. **Credit cards:**
MC,VISA. **Reduced fees:** Low season, twilight, juniors. **Caddies:** No. **Golf carts:**
Included in Green Fee. **Discount golf packages:** No. **Season:** Year-round. **High:** Jan.-
April. **On site lodging:** No. **Rental clubs:** Yes. **Walking policy:** Walking at certain
times. **Metal spikes allowed:** Yes. **Range:** Yes (grass/mats). **To obtain tee times:** Call
up to 5 days in advance.

★★★**ST. JOHNS COUNTY GOLF CLUB**
PU-4900 Cypress Links Blvd., Elkton, 32033, St. Johns County, (904)825-4900, 30
miles S of Jacksonville.
Opened: 1989. **Holes:** 18. **Par:** 72/72. **Yards:** 6,926/5,173. **Course rating:** 72.9/68.8.
Slope: 130/117. **Architect:** Robert Walker. **Green fee:** $16/$19. **Credit cards:**
MC,VISA. **Reduced fees:** Low season, twilight. **Caddies:** No. **Golf carts:** $10.
Discount golf packages: No. **Season:** Year-round. **High:** Jan.-April. **On site lodging:**
No. **Rental clubs:** Yes. **Walking policy:** Walking at certain times. **Metal spikes
allowed:** Yes. **Range:** Yes (grass). **To obtain tee times:** Call up to 7 days in advance.
Subscriber comments: Not great, but OK for high-play public course...Worth the wait.

★★★★**ST. LUCIE WEST COUNTRY CLUB**
951 S.W. Country Club Dr., Port St. Lucie, 34986, St. Lucie County,
(561)340-1911, (800)800-4653, 45 miles N of West Palm Beach.
Opened: 1987. **Holes:** 18. **Par:** 72/72. **Yards:** 6,906/5,035. **Course rating:** 74.0/69.8. **Slope:** 134/121. **Architect:** Jim Fazio. **Green fee:**
$15/$59. **Credit cards:** MC,VISA. **Reduced fees:** Low season, twilight,
juniors. **Caddies:** No. **Golf carts:** Included in Green Fee. **Discount golf packages:** No.
Season: Year-round. **High:** Jan.-March. **On site lodging:** No. **Rental clubs:** Yes.
Walking policy: Walking at certain times. **Metal spikes allowed:** Yes. **Range:** Yes
(grass). **To obtain tee times:** Call 3 days in advance.
Subscriber comments: Tremendous challenge...Very fair...Lots of water...Tight fairways...Vacation golf...Excellent facilities.

(GREAT SERVICE)

SANDESTIN RESORT
R-9300 Hwy. 98 W., Destin, 32541, Okaloosa County, 20 miles E of Fort Walton Beach.
Caddies: No. **Golf carts:** Included in Green Fee. **Discount golf packages:** Yes.
Season: Year-round. **High:** Feb.-Oct. **On site lodging:** Yes. **Rental clubs:** Yes. **Metal
spikes allowed:** Yes. **Range:** Yes (grass).

★★★½**BAYTOWNE GOLF COURSE**
(904)267-8155.
Opened: 1985. **Holes:** 27. **Architect:** Tom Jackson. **Green fee:** $68/$86. **Credit cards:**
All major. **Reduced fees:** Low season, resort guests, twilight, juniors. **Walking policy:**
Mandatory cart. **To obtain tee times:** Call 2 days in advance.
DUNES/HARBOR
Par: 72/72. **Yards:** 6,890/4,862. **Course rating:** 73.4/68.5. **Slope:** 127/114.
TROON/DUNES
Par: 72/72. **Yards:** 7,185/5,158. **Course rating:** 74.6/69.1. **Slope:** 128/115.
TROON/HARBOR
Par: 72/72. **Yards:** 6,891/4,884. **Course rating:** 73.9/68.2. **Slope:** 127/113.
Subscriber comments: You won't be disappointed...Lots of water...Some narrow load-

FLORIDA

ing areas...We spend a week every year at Sandestin and enjoy it...Enjoyable...Good, but too many holes that look alike...Fun...Tight and tough...Very enjoyable.

★★★★BURNT PINES GOLF COURSE
(904)267-6500.
Opened: 1994. **Holes:** 18. **Par:** 72/72. **Yards:** 7,046/5,950. **Course rating:** 74.1/68.7. **Slope:** 135/124. **Architect:** Rees Jones. **Green fee:** $88/$116. **Credit cards:** All major. **Reduced fees:** Resort guests, juniors. **Walking policy:** Unrestricted walking. **To obtain tee times:** Must be a guest at the resort to play. Call golf shop.
Notes: Ranked 19th in 1997 Best in State; 3rd in 1995 Best New Resort Courses.
Subscriber comments: Everyone should play here once...Will be a gem when it matures...If played from the correct tees, can be a good test, yet fair...Natural setting makes the course...Would recommend it to anyone...Expensive, but don't we all deserve a treat?

★★★½LINKS COURSE
(904)267-8144.
Opened: 1977. **Holes:** 18. **Par:** 72/72. **Yards:** 6,710/4,969. **Course rating:** 72.8/69.2. **Slope:** 124/115. **Architect:** Tom Jackson. **Green fee:** $68/$86. **Credit cards:** MC,VISA,DISC. **Reduced fees:** Low season, resort guests, twilight, juniors. **Walking policy:** Unrestricted walking. **To obtain tee times:** Call 2 days in advance.
Subscriber comments: Enjoyable...Lots of wind and water...Narrow landing areas...Too many out-of-bounds...Quiet, almost private each round.

★★½SANDPIPER GOLF & COUNTRY CLUB
6001 Sandpipers Dr., Lakeland, 33809, Polk County, (941)859-5461.
Opened: 1987. **Holes:** 18. **Par:** 70/70. **Yards:** 6,442/5,024. **Course rating:** 70.4/67.7. **Slope:** 120/109. **Architect:** Steve Smyers. **Green fee:** $12/$29. **Credit cards:** MC,VISA. **Reduced fees:** Weekdays, low season, twilight. **Caddies:** No. **Golf carts:** Included in Green Fee. **Discount golf packages:** Yes. **Season:** Year-round. **High:** Jan.-March. **On site lodging:** No. **Rental clubs:** Yes. **Walking policy:** Mandatory cart. **Metal spikes allowed:** Yes. **Range:** No. **To obtain tee times:** Call a minimum of 2 days in advance and a maximum of 4 days in advance.
Subscriber comments: Fun course, but very short...Nice environment.

SANDRIDGE GOLF CLUB
PU-5300 73rd St., Vero Beach, 32967, Indian River County, (561)770-5000, 70 miles N of West Palm Beach.
Architect: Ron Garl. **Credit cards:** MC,VISA,DISC. **Reduced fees:** Weekdays, low season, twilight, juniors. **Caddies:** No. **Golf carts:** Included in Green Fee. **Discount golf packages:** Yes. **Season:** Year-round. **High:** Jan.-March. **On site lodging:** No. **Rental clubs:** Yes. **Walking policy:** Walking at certain times. **Metal spikes allowed:** Yes. **Range:** Yes (grass). **To obtain tee times:** Call golf shop.

★★★½DUNES COURSE
Opened: 1987. **Holes:** 18. **Par:** 72/72. **Yards:** 6,900/4,922. **Course rating:** 72.2/68.8. **Slope:** 123/109. **Green fee:** $12/$34.
Subscriber comments: Tight fairways, very fast greens, excellent facilities...Sand city...Tougher than it looks...Nice...Scenic.

★★★½LAKES COURSE
Opened: 1992. **Holes:** 18. **Par:** 72/72. **Yards:** 6,200/4,625. **Course rating:** 69.3/66.6. **Slope:** 120/109. **Green fee:** $18/$34.
Subscriber comments: Rather short but demanding...Loads of wildlife...Tough, sloping fairways...Tough to stay out of water...Gets lots of play.

★★½SANTA ROSA GOLF & BEACH CLUB
334 Golf Club Dr., Santa Rosa Beach, 32459, Walton County, (904)267-2229.
Opened: 1969. **Holes:** 18. **Par:** 72/72. **Yards:** 6,474/4,988. **Course rating:** 71.8/68.8. **Slope:** 128/115. **Architect:** Tom Jackson. **Green fee:** $34/$44. **Credit cards:** MC,VISA,AMEX,Diners Club. **Reduced fees:** Low season, twilight, juniors. **Caddies:** No. **Golf carts:** $15. **Discount golf packages:** No. **Season:** Year-round. **High:** April-Sept. **On site lodging:** No. **Rental clubs:** Yes. **Walking policy:** Walking at certain times. **Metal spikes allowed:** Yes. **Range:** Yes (grass). **To obtain tee times:** Call 3 days in advance.
Subscriber comments: Off the beaten path...Tough: tight fairways, trees, water...Hilly for Florida.

★★½SARASOTA GOLF CLUB
7280 N. Leewynn Dr., Sarasota, 34240, Sarasota County, (941)371-2431.
Opened: 1950. **Holes:** 18. **Par:** 72/72. **Yards:** 7,066/5,004. **Course rating:** 73.0/67.4.
Slope: 122/108. **Architect:** Wayne Tredway. **Green fee:** $22/$40. **Credit cards:**
MC,VISA. **Reduced fees:** Low season, resort guests, twilight, seniors, juniors.
Caddies: No. **Golf carts:** Included in Green Fee. **Discount golf packages:** Yes.
Season: Year-round. **High:** Jan.-April. **On site lodging:** No. **Rental clubs:** Yes.
Walking policy: Walking at certain times. **Metal spikes allowed:** Yes. **Range:** Yes
(grass). **To obtain tee times:** Call 3 days in advance.
Subscriber comments: Not too tough...Wide fairways.

★★★SAVANNAHS AT SYKES CREEK GOLF CLUB
PU-3915 Savannahs Trail, Merritt Island, 32953, Brevard County, (407)455-1375, 40
miles E of Orlando.
Opened: 1990. **Holes:** 18. **Par:** 72/72. **Yards:** 6,636/4,795. **Course rating:** 70.6/65.9.
Slope: 118/108. **Architect:** Gordon Lewis. **Green fee:** $15/$19. **Credit cards:**
MC,VISA. **Reduced fees:** Low season, twilight, juniors. **Caddies:** No. **Golf carts:** $9.
Discount golf packages: No. **Season:** Year-round. **High:** Oct.-April. **On site lodging:**
No. **Rental clubs:** Yes. **Walking policy:** Walking at certain times. **Metal spikes**
allowed: Yes. **Range:** Yes. **To obtain tee times:** Call (407)455-1377.
Subscriber comments: Good golf...Too long between some holes to walk.

★★★★½SAWGRASS COUNTRY CLUB
10034 Golf Club Dr., Ponte Vedra Beach, 32082, St. Johns County,
(904)273-3720, (800)457-4653, 15 miles S of Jacksonville.
Opened: 1972. **Holes:** 27. **Par:** 72/72. **Yards:** 7,109/5,715. **Course rat-**
ing: 74.2/69.6. **Slope:** 139/118. **Architect:** Ed Seay. **Green fee:**
$80/$140. **Credit cards:** N/A. **Reduced fees:** N/A. **Caddies:** No. **Golf**
carts: N/A. **Discount golf packages:** No. **Season:** Year-round. **High:** Feb.-May/Oct.-
Nov. **On site lodging:** No. **Rental clubs:** No. **Walking policy:** Walking at certain times.
Metal spikes allowed: Yes. **Range:** No. **To obtain tee times:** Nonmembers must be
staying at Marriott at Sawgrass to play. Call the Marriott at (800)457-4653 ext. 4 with
hotel room confirmation.
Subscriber comments: It broke me, but I'll be back...A really fine facility...Beautiful
course...Very tough and tight in the wind...Everyone should play here...My favorite
course...Lots of sand.

★★SCENIC HILLS COUNTRY CLUB
PU-8891 Burning Tree Rd., Pensacola, 32514, Escambia County, (904)476-0611.
Opened: N/A. **Holes:** 18. **Par:** 71/71. **Yards:** 6,689/5,187. **Course rating:** N/A. **Slope:**
135/116. **Architect:** Chic Adams/Jerry Pate. **Green fee:** N/A. **Credit cards:**
MC,VISA,AMEX. **Reduced fees:** Weekdays, low season, resort guests, twilight.
Caddies: No. **Golf carts:** Included in Green Fee. **Discount golf packages:** Yes.
Season: Year-round. **High:** Feb.-April. **On site lodging:** No. **Rental clubs:** No.
Walking policy: N/A. **Metal spikes allowed:** Yes. **Range:** Yes. **To obtain tee times:**
N/A.

★★½SCHALAMAR CREEK GOLF & COUNTRY CLUB
4500 U.S. Hwy. 92 E., Lakeland, 33801, Polk County, (941)666-1623, 30 miles E of
Tampa.
Opened: 1987. **Holes:** 18. **Par:** 72/72. **Yards:** 6,399/4,363. **Course rating:** 70.9/64.8.
Slope: 124/106. **Architect:** Ron Garl. **Green fee:** $8/$21. **Credit cards:** MC,VISA.
Reduced fees: Weekdays, low season, twilight. **Caddies:** No. **Golf carts:** $16.
Discount golf packages: No. **Season:** Year-round. **High:** Jan.-April. **On site lodging:**
No. **Rental clubs:** Yes. **Walking policy:** Walking at certain times. **Metal spikes**
allowed: Yes. **Range:** Yes (grass). **To obtain tee times:** Call two days in advance.
Subscriber comments: Tight...Excellent golf.

★★½SEASCAPE RESORT
R-100 Seascape Dr., Destin, 32541, Okaloosa County, (904)654-7888, (800)874-9106,
45 miles E of Pensacola.
Opened: 1969. **Holes:** 18. **Par:** 71/71. **Yards:** 6,480/5,014. **Course rating:** 71.5/70.3.

Slope: 120/113. **Architect:** Joe Lee. **Green fee:** $37/$55. **Credit cards:** All major. **Reduced fees:** Low season, resort guests, juniors. **Caddies:** No. **Golf carts:** Included in Green Fee. **Discount golf packages:** Yes. **Season:** Year-round. **High:** March-Oct. **On site lodging:** Yes. **Rental clubs:** Yes. **Walking policy:** Walking at certain times. **Metal spikes allowed:** Yes. **Range:** Yes (grass). **To obtain tee times:** Call up to 2 days in advance.
Subscriber comments: Nice, average vacation course...Short.

★★SEBASTIAN MUNICIPAL GOLF COURSE
PM-101 E. Airport Dr., Sebastian, 32958, Indian River County, (561)589-6801, 75 miles SE of Orlando.
Opened: 1981. **Holes:** 18. **Par:** 72/72. **Yards:** 6,717/4,579. **Course rating:** 71.0/64.6. **Slope:** 112/101. **Architect:** Charles Ankrom. **Green fee:** $14/$31. **Credit cards:** MC,VISA. **Reduced fees:** Low season, twilight, juniors. **Caddies:** No. **Golf carts:** Included in Green Fee. **Discount golf packages:** Yes. **Season:** Year-round. **High:** Nov.-April. **On site lodging:** No. **Rental clubs:** Yes. **Walking policy:** Walking at certain times. **Metal spikes allowed:** Yes. **Range:** Yes (grass). **To obtain tee times:** Call.

★★½SEMINOLE GOLF CLUB
PU-2550 Pottsdamer St., Tallahassee, 32304, Leon County, (850)644-2582.
Opened: 1962. **Holes:** 18. **Par:** 72/72. **Yards:** 7,033/5,930. **Course rating:** 73.4/73.0. **Slope:** 121/111. **Architect:** R.A. Anderson. **Green fee:** $12/$17. **Credit cards:** MC,VISA,DISC. **Reduced fees:** Weekdays, resort guests, twilight, juniors. **Caddies:** No. **Golf carts:** $10. **Discount golf packages:** No. **Season:** Year-round. **High:** N/A. **On site lodging:** No. **Rental clubs:** Yes. **Walking policy:** Walking at certain times. **Metal spikes allowed:** Yes. **Range:** Yes (grass/mats). **To obtain tee times:** Call on Monday for weekend tee times only.
Subscriber comments: I like the hills and trees...Open.

★★★SEVEN HILLS GOLFERS CLUB
10599 Fairchild Rd., Spring Hill, 34608, Hernando County, (352)688-8888.
Opened: 1989. **Holes:** 18. **Par:** 72/72. **Yards:** 6,715/4,902. **Course rating:** 70.5/66.5. **Slope:** 126/109. **Architect:** Denis Griffiths. **Green fee:** $16/$30. **Credit cards:** None. **Reduced fees:** Weekdays, low season, twilight. **Caddies:** No. **Golf carts:** Included in Green Fee. **Discount golf packages:** No. **Season:** Year-round. **High:** Dec.-April. **On site lodging:** No. **Rental clubs:** Yes. **Walking policy:** Mandatory cart. **Metal spikes allowed:** Yes. **Range:** Yes (grass). **To obtain tee times:** Call up to 7 days in advance.
Subscriber comments: Lots of water...Wide open...Heavily played...Rolling fairways...Woods...Lots of bunkers.

★★★½SEVEN SPRINGS GOLF & COUNTRY CLUB
PU-3535 Trophy Blvd., New Port Richey, 34655, Pasco County, (813)376-0035.
Opened: N/A. **Holes:** 18. **Par:** 72/72. **Yards:** 6,566/5,250. **Course rating:** N/A. **Slope:** 128/125. **Architect:** Ron Garl. **Green fee:** $31/$45. **Credit cards:** MC,VISA. **Reduced fees:** Low season, twilight. **Caddies:** No. **Golf carts:** Included in Green Fee. **Discount golf packages:** No. **Season:** Year-round. **High:** Jan.-April. **On site lodging:** No. **Rental clubs:** Yes. **Walking policy:** Mandatory cart. **Metal spikes allowed:** Yes. **Range:** Yes (grass). **To obtain tee times:** Call up to 2 days in advance.
Subscriber comments: Fairly tight...OK layout...Not very memorable.
Special notes: Also has an 18-hole par-64 executive course.

★★★SHALIMAR POINTE GOLF & COUNTRY CLUB
302 Country Club Rd., Shalimar, 32579, Okaloosa County, (904)651-1416, (800)964-2833, 45 miles E of Pensacola.
Opened: 1968. **Holes:** 18. **Par:** 72/72. **Yards:** 6,765/5,427. **Course rating:** 72.9/70.7. **Slope:** 125/115. **Architect:** Joe Finger/Ken Dye. **Green fee:** $21/$49. **Credit cards:** MC,VISA,AMEX. **Reduced fees:** Weekdays, low season, resort guests, twilight. **Caddies:** No. **Golf carts:** Included in Green Fee. **Discount golf packages:** Yes. **Season:** Year-round. **High:** Jan.-April. **On site lodging:** No. **Rental clubs:** Yes. **Walking policy:** Mandatory cart. **Metal spikes allowed:** Yes. **Range:** Yes (grass). **To obtain tee times:** Call up to 5 days in advance.
Subscriber comments: Playable...Many waste areas...Better than I deserve...Too much sand...Scenic.

★★★SHERMAN HILLS GOLF CLUB
PU-31200 Eagle Falls Dr., Brooksville, 34602, Hernando County, (352)544-0990, 45 miles N of Tampa.
Opened: 1993. **Holes:** 18. **Par:** 72/72. **Yards:** 6,778/4,959. **Course rating:** 72.1/68.2. **Slope:** 118/110. **Architect:** Ted McAnlis. **Green fee:** $15/$30. **Credit cards:** MC,VISA. **Reduced fees:** Weekdays, low season, twilight, juniors. **Caddies:** No. **Golf carts:** Included in Green Fee. **Discount golf packages:** Yes. **Season:** Year-round. **High:** Oct.-April. **On site lodging:** No. **Rental clubs:** Yes. **Walking policy:** Mandatory cart. **Metal spikes allowed:** Yes. **Range:** Yes (grass/mats). **To obtain tee times:** Call up to 7 days in advance.
Subscriber comments: Very playable...Needs some trees...No shade...Play it frequently despite the long drive.

★★★SHOAL RIVER COUNTRY CLUB
1100 Shoal River Dr., Crestview, 32539, Okaloosa County, (904)689-1010, 25 miles N of Fort Walton Beach.
Opened: 1986. **Holes:** 18. **Par:** 72/72. **Yards:** 6,782/5,183. **Course rating:** 73.5/70.3. **Slope:** 136/124. **Architect:** Dave Bennett. **Green fee:** $18/$18. **Credit cards:** All major. **Reduced fees:** Weekdays, low season, twilight, juniors. **Caddies:** No. **Golf carts:** $15. **Discount golf packages:** Yes. **Season:** Year-round. **High:** Feb.-March. **On site lodging:** No. **Rental clubs:** Yes. **Walking policy:** Walking at certain times. **Metal spikes allowed:** Yes. **Range:** Yes (grass). **To obtain tee times:** Call up to 3 days in advance.
Subscriber comments: Always on my list of courses to play when I'm in the area.

★★½SIGNAL HILL GOLF & COUNTRY CLUB
PU-9615 N. Thomas Dr., Panama City Beach, 32407, Bay County, (904)234-5051, 10 miles W of Panama City.
Opened: 1962. **Holes:** 18. **Par:** 71/71. **Yards:** 5,617/4,790. **Course rating:** 63.6/63.0. **Slope:** 101/103. **Architect:** John Henry Sherman. **Green fee:** $20/$35. **Credit cards:** MC,VISA,DISC. **Reduced fees:** Low season. **Caddies:** No. **Golf carts:** N/A. **Discount golf packages:** No. **Season:** Year-round. **High:** April-Sept. **On site lodging:** No. **Rental clubs:** Yes. **Walking policy:** Unrestricted walking. **Metal spikes allowed:** Yes. **Range:** No. **To obtain tee times:** Call or come in up to 7 days in advance.
Subscriber comments: Short, easy course...Easy to walk...Wide open.

★★½SILVER OAKS GOLF & COUNTRY CLUB
36841 Clubhouse Dr., Zephyrhills, 33541, Pasco County, (813)788-1225, (800)853-4653, 20 miles NE of Tampa.
Opened: 1988. **Holes:** 18. **Par:** 72/72. **Yards:** 6,702/5,147. **Course rating:** 72.5/68.8. **Slope:** 126/109. **Architect:** Bob Simmons. **Green fee:** $10/$35. **Credit cards:** MC,VISA. **Reduced fees:** Weekdays, low season, resort guests, twilight, seniors, juniors. **Caddies:** No. **Golf carts:** Included in Green Fee. **Discount golf packages:** Yes. **Season:** Year-round. **High:** Dec-May. **On site lodging:** No. **Rental clubs:** Yes. **Walking policy:** Mandatory cart. **Metal spikes allowed:** Yes. **Range:** Yes (grass). **To obtain tee times:** Call, fax or come in person to make tee time.

★★★★SOUTHERN DUNES GOLF & COUNTRY CLUB
2888 Southern Dunes Blvd., Haines City, 33844, Polk County, (941)421-4653, (800)632-6400, 20 miles SW of Orlando.
Opened: 1993. **Holes:** 18. **Par:** 72/72. **Yards:** 7,200/5,200. **Course rating:** 74.7/72.4. **Slope:** 135/126. **Architect:** Steve Smyers. **Green fee:** $27/$47. **Credit cards:** MC,VISA,DISC. **Reduced fees:** Weekdays, low season, twilight, juniors. **Caddies:** No. **Golf carts:** Included in Green Fee. **Discount golf packages:** Yes. **Season:** Year-round. **High:** Oct.-April. **On site lodging:** Yes. **Rental clubs:** Yes. **Walking policy:** Mandatory cart. **Metal spikes allowed:** Yes. **Range:** Yes (grass). **To obtain tee times:** Call up to 7 days in advance April 15-Oct. 15; and 30 days in advance Oct.15-April 15.
Subscriber comments: Am I in Scotland?...Incredible dunes...Should be called Sudden Doom...Recommend it highly...Holy Sand Trap...Lots of large, deep bunkers...Spectacular...Rolling fairways...Beautiful landscaping...Keep it on the fairway...Nice change from typical Florida swamps...Pace of play strongly enforced...One of the hardest courses I have ever played.

★★½SOUTHWINDS GOLF COURSE
PM-19557 Lyons Rd., Boca Raton, Palm Beach County, (561)483-1305, 5 miles W of Boca Raton.
Opened: 1955. **Holes:** 18. **Par:** 70/71. **Yards:** 5,559/4,402. **Course rating:** 67.7/65.7. **Slope:** 120/112. **Architect:** N/A. **Green fee:** $22/$45. **Credit cards:** MC,VISA. **Reduced fees:** Low season, twilight, juniors. **Caddies:** No. **Golf carts:** Included in Green Fee. **Discount golf packages:** No. **Season:** Year-round. **High:** Jan.-April. **On site lodging:** No. **Rental clubs:** Yes. **Walking policy:** Walking at certain times. **Metal spikes allowed:** Yes. **Range:** Yes (grass/mats). **To obtain tee times:** Call up to 4 days in advance.
Subscriber comments: Very enjoyable...Played it five days in a row while visiting my sister and will do it again next year.

★★SPRING HILL GOLF CLUB
12079 Coronado Dr., Spring Hill, 34609, Hernando County, (352)683-2261, 35 miles N of Tampa.
Opened: 1975. **Holes:** 18. **Par:** 72/73. **Yards:** 6,917/5,588. **Course rating:** 73.0/71.8. **Slope:** 133/127. **Architect:** David Wallace. **Green fee:** $17/$25. **Credit cards:** None. **Reduced fees:** Weekdays, low season, twilight. **Caddies:** No. **Golf carts:** Included in Green Fee. **Discount golf packages:** No. **Season:** Year-round. **High:** Dec.-March. **On site lodging:** No. **Rental clubs:** Yes. **Walking policy:** Walking at certain times. **Metal spikes allowed:** Yes. **Range:** Yes (grass). **To obtain tee times:** Call up to 7 days in advance.

★★★SPRING LAKE GOLF & TENNIS RESORT
R-100 Clubhouse Lane, Sebring, 33870, Highlands County, (941)655-1276, (800)635-7277, 65 miles S of Orlando.
Opened: 1977. **Holes:** 27. **Architect:** Frank Duane. **Green fee:** $17/$36. **Credit cards:** All major. **Reduced fees:** Resort guests, twilight. **Caddies:** No. **Golf carts:** Included in Green Fee. **Discount golf packages:** Yes. **Season:** Year-round. **High:** Jan.-March. **On site lodging:** Yes. **Rental clubs:** Yes. **Walking policy:** Mandatory cart. **Metal spikes allowed:** Yes. **Range:** Yes (grass/mats). **To obtain tee times:** Call 2 days in advance.
EAGLE/HAWK
Par: 72/72. **Yards:** 6,578/5,000. **Course rating:** 71.8/68.8. **Slope:** 126/116.
HAWK/OSPREY
Par: 71/71. **Yards:** 6,496/4,939. **Course rating:** 71.3/68.4. **Slope:** 122/113.
OSPREY/EAGLE
Par: 71/71. **Yards:** 6,272/4,973. **Course rating:** 70.1/68.2. **Slope:** 121/113.
Subscriber comments: Less crowded than Orlando area...Watch out for gators...Has potential, but need lots of work...Lots of sand...Good practice facility.
Special Notes: Also has an executive 9-hole course.

★★★SPRUCE CREEK COUNTRY CLUB
1900 Country Club Dr., Daytona Beach, 32124, Volusia County, (904)756-6114, 45 miles NE of Orlando.
Opened: 1971. **Holes:** 18. **Par:** 72/72. **Yards:** 6,751/5,157. **Course rating:** 72.2/70.3. **Slope:** 125/121. **Architect:** Bill Amick. **Green fee:** $16/$48. **Credit cards:** MC,VISA. **Reduced fees:** Weekdays, low season, resort guests, twilight, juniors. **Caddies:** No. **Golf carts:** Included in Green Fee. **Discount golf packages:** No. **Season:** Year-round. **High:** Jan.-April. **On site lodging:** No. **Rental clubs:** Yes. **Walking policy:** Mandatory cart. **Metal spikes allowed:** Yes. **Range:** Yes (grass). **To obtain tee times:** Call 3 days in advance.

★★★½SUGAR MILL COUNTRY CLUB
100 Clubhouse Circle, New Smyrna Beach, 32168, Volusia County, (904)426-5210, 10 miles S of Daytona Beach.
Opened: 1970. **Holes:** 27. **Architect:** Joe Lee. **Green fee:** $35/$65. **Credit cards:** MC,VISA. **Reduced fees:** Low season. **Caddies:** No. **Golf carts:** Included in Green Fee. **Discount golf packages:** No. **Season:** Year-round. **High:** Jan.-April. **On site lodging:** No. **Rental clubs:** Yes. **Walking policy:** Mandatory cart. **Metal spikes allowed:** No. **Range:** Yes (grass/mats). **To obtain tee times:** Call up to 2 days in advance.

RED/BLUE
Par: 72/72. **Yards:** 6,695/5,404. **Course rating:** 72.1/71.7. **Slope:** 126/125.
WHITE/BLUE
Holes: 27. **Par:** 72/72. **Yards:** 6,749/5,478. **Course rating:** 72.4/71.8. **Slope:** 127/123.
WHITE/RED
Holes: 27. **Par:** 72/72. **Yards:** 6,766/5,428. **Course rating:** 72.1/71.5. **Slope:** 125/124.
Subscriber comments: OK, but nothing unusual...Nice...Challenge...Enjoyed...Treated like a member.

★★★ SUMMERFIELD GOLF CLUB
13050 Summerfield Blvd., Riverview, 33569, Hillsborough County, (813)671-3311, 15 miles SE of Tampa.
Opened: 1986. **Holes:** 18. **Par:** 71/71. **Yards:** 6,883/5,139. **Course rating:** 73.0/69.6. **Slope:** 125/114. **Architect:** Ron Garl. **Green fee:** $18/$34. **Credit cards:** All major. **Reduced fees:** Low season, twilight. **Caddies:** No. **Golf carts:** Included in Green Fee. **Discount golf packages:** Yes. **Season:** Year-round. **High:** Jan.-April. **On site lodging:** No. **Rental clubs:** Yes. **Walking policy:** Mandatory cart. **Metal spikes allowed:** Yes. **Range:** Yes (grass). **To obtain tee times:** Call.
Subscriber comments: Typical Central Florida course.

SUNNYBREEZE GOLF COURSE
8135 S.W. Sunnybreeze Rd., Arcadia, 34266, De Soto County, (941)625-0424, 45 miles N of Fort Myers.
Opened: 1971. **Holes:** 18. **Par:** 70/71. **Yards:** 6,261/4,793. **Course rating:** 68.7/67.0. **Slope:** 124/117. **Architect:** Andy Anderson/Bill Baker. **Green fee:** $10/$30. **Credit cards:** MC,VISA,DISC. **Reduced fees:** Weekdays, low season. **Caddies:** No. **Golf carts:** $12. **Discount golf packages:** Yes. **Season:** Year-round. **High:** Dec.-April. **On site lodging:** No. **Rental clubs:** Yes. **Walking policy:** Unrestricted walking. **Metal spikes allowed:** Yes. **Range:** Yes (grass/mats). **To obtain tee times:** Call up to 7 days in advance.
Special Notes: Also has a 9-hole par-35 course.

★½ SUNRISE COUNTRY CLUB
7400 N.W. 24th Place, Sunrise, 33313, Broward County, (954)742-4333, 7 miles W of Fort Lauderdale.
Opened: 1959. **Holes:** 18. **Par:** 72/72. **Yards:** 6,624/5,317. **Course rating:** 71.8/69.8. **Slope:** 126/119. **Architect:** Bill Watts. **Green fee:** $25/$45. **Credit cards:** MC,VISA,AMEX. **Reduced fees:** Twilight. **Caddies:** No. **Golf carts:** Included in Green Fee. **Discount golf packages:** No. **Season:** Year-round. **High:** Dec.-April. **On site lodging:** No. **Rental clubs:** Yes. **Walking policy:** Mandatory cart. **Metal spikes allowed:** Yes. **Range:** Yes (grass). **To obtain tee times:** Call 7 days in advance.

★★ SUNRISE GOLF CLUB
5710 Draw Lane, Sarasota, 34238, Sarasota County, (941)924-1402.
Opened: 1970. **Holes:** 18. **Par:** 72/72. **Yards:** 6,455/5,271. **Course rating:** 70.6/69.3. **Slope:** 122/117. **Architect:** Andy Anderson. **Green fee:** $15/$40. **Credit cards:** MC,VISA. **Reduced fees:** Low season, twilight, juniors. **Caddies:** No. **Golf carts:** Included in Green Fee. **Discount golf packages:** Yes. **Season:** Year-round. **High:** Feb.-April. **On site lodging:** No. **Rental clubs:** Yes. **Walking policy:** Walking at certain times. **Metal spikes allowed:** Yes. **Range:** Yes (grass). **To obtain tee times:** Call three days in advance.

★★ TANGLEWOOD GOLF & COUNTRY CLUB
PU-5916 Tanglewood Dr., Milton, 32570, Santa Rosa County, (904)623-6176, 10 miles SE of Pensacola.
Opened: 1964. **Holes:** 18. **Par:** 72/72. **Yards:** 6,455/5,295. **Course rating:** 70.0/69.9. **Slope:** 115/118. **Architect:** N/A. **Green fee:** $17/$20. **Credit cards:** MC,VISA. **Reduced fees:** Low season, seniors. **Caddies:** No. **Golf carts:** $10. **Discount golf packages:** No. **Season:** Year-round. **High:** April-Nov. **On site lodging:** No. **Rental clubs:** Yes. **Walking policy:** Unrestricted walking. **Metal spikes allowed:** Yes. **Range:** Yes (grass). **To obtain tee times:** Call anytime.

★★TARPON SPRINGS GOLF CLUB
PU-1310 Pinellas Ave., S. (Alt. 19), Tarpon Springs, 34689, Pinellas County, (813)937-6906, 25 miles NW of Tampa.
Opened: 1927. **Holes:** 18. **Par:** 72/72. **Yards:** 6,099/5,338. **Course rating:** 68.9/71.5. **Slope:** 112/110. **Architect:** John Van Kleek/Wayne Stiles. **Green fee:** $20/$25. **Credit cards:** None. **Reduced fees:** Low season, twilight. **Caddies:** No. **Golf carts:** N/A. **Discount golf packages:** No. **Season:** Year-round. **High:** Jan.-April. **On site lodging:** No. **Rental clubs:** Yes. **Walking policy:** Walking at certain times. **Metal spikes allowed:** Yes. **Range:** Yes (grass). **To obtain tee times:** Call 2 days in advance.

★★★TARPON WOODS GOLF & COUNTRY CLUB
1100 Tarpon Woods Blvd., Palm Harbor, 34685, Pinellas County, (813)784-2273.
Opened: 1975. **Holes:** 18. **Par:** 72/72. **Yards:** 6,466/5,205. **Course rating:** 71.2/69.5. **Slope:** 128/115. **Architect:** Lane Marshall. **Green fee:** $32/$46. **Credit cards:** MC,VISA,AMEX. **Reduced fees:** Weekdays, low season, twilight. **Caddies:** No. **Golf carts:** Included in Green Fee. **Discount golf packages:** Yes. **Season:** Year-round. **High:** Jan.-May. **On site lodging:** No. **Rental clubs:** Yes. **Walking policy:** Walking at certain times. **Metal spikes allowed:** Yes. **Range:** Yes (grass). **To obtain tee times:** Call in advance.
Subscriber comments: Osprey nests, nice stations...Holds water...Liked the course and the alligators...Lots of woods and hidden water.

★★★TATUM RIDGE GOLF LINKS
421 N. Tatum Rd., Sarasota, 34240, Sarasota County, (941)378-4211, 55 miles S of Tampa.
Opened: 1989. **Holes:** 18. **Par:** 72/72. **Yards:** 6,757/5,149. **Course rating:** 71.9/68.9. **Slope:** 124/114. **Architect:** Ted McAnlis. **Green fee:** $18/$42. **Credit cards:** MC,VISA. **Reduced fees:** Low season, seniors. **Caddies:** No. **Golf carts:** Included in Green Fee. **Discount golf packages:** No. **Season:** Year-round. **High:** Nov.-May. **On site lodging:** No. **Rental clubs:** Yes. **Walking policy:** Mandatory cart. **Metal spikes allowed:** Yes. **Range:** Yes (grass). **To obtain tee times:** Call 4 days in advance.
Subscriber comments: Middle of pack...Lots of water...Wide open.

TIERRA DEL SOL GOLF CLUB
1100 Main St., Lady Lake, 32159, Lake County, (352)750-4600, 45 miles N of Orlando.
Opened: 1996. **Holes:** 18. **Par:** 72/71. **Yards:** 6,835/5,486. **Course rating:** 72.8/71.7. **Slope:** 124/120. **Architect:** N/A. **Green fee:** $36/$23. **Credit cards:** MC,VISA. **Reduced fees:** N/A. **Caddies:** No. **Golf carts:** Included in Green Fee. **Discount golf packages:** No. **Season:** Year-round. **High:** Nov.-April. **On site lodging:** No. **Rental clubs:** Yes. **Walking policy:** Unrestricted walking. **Metal spikes allowed:** Yes. **Range:** Yes (grass/mats). **To obtain tee times:** Call 2 days in advance.

TIGER POINT GOLF & COUNTRY CLUB
1255 Country Club Rd., Gulf Breeze, 32561, Santa Rosa County, (904)932-1333, (888)218-8463, 15 miles SE of Pensacola.
Credit cards: MC,VISA,AMEX. **Reduced fees:** Weekdays, low season, twilight. **Caddies:** No. **Golf carts:** Included in Green Fee. **Discount golf packages:** Yes. **Season:** Year-round. **High:** Feb.-April/Oct.-Nov. **On site lodging:** No. **Rental clubs:** Yes. **Walking policy:** Mandatory cart. **Metal spikes allowed:** Yes. **Range:** Yes (grass).

(GOOD SERVICE)

★★★½EAST COURSE
Opened: 1979. **Holes:** 18. **Par:** 72/72. **Yards:** 7,033/5,217. **Course rating:** 73.8/70.2. **Slope:** 132/125. **Architect:** Bill Amick/Ron Garl/Jerry Pate. **Green fee:** $37/$48. **To obtain tee times:** Call up to 7 days in advance between 7 a.m. and 6 p.m.
Notes: 1988 PGA Pensacola Open.
Subscriber comments: A lot of fun...Tough: Lots of water, wind...Plenty of bunkers (white powder).

★★★½WEST COURSE
Opened: 1965. **Holes:** 18. **Par:** 71/72. **Yards:** 6,737/5,314. **Course rating:** 72.2/70.2. **Slope:** 119/121. **Architect:** Bill Amick. **Green fee:** $30/$38. **To obtain tee times:** Call up to 7 days in advance.
Subscriber comments: Challenging when the wind blows...Slow play...Could be great.

★★★½ TIMACUAN GOLF & COUNTRY CLUB
550 Timacuan Blvd., Lake Mary, 32746, Seminole County, (407)321-0010, (888)955-1234, 15 miles NE of Orlando.
Opened: 1987. **Holes:** 18. **Par:** 71/71. **Yards:** 6,915/4,576. **Course rating:** 73.2/66.8. **Slope:** 133/118. **Architect:** Ron Garl/Bobby Weed. **Green fee:** $30/$89. **Credit cards:** MC,VISA,AMEX. **Reduced fees:** Weekdays, low season, resort guests, twilight. **Caddies:** No. **Golf carts:** Included in Green Fee. **Discount golf packages:** Yes. **Season:** Year-round. **High:** Jan.-April. **On site lodging:** No. **Rental clubs:** Yes. **Walking policy:** Mandatory cart. **Metal spikes allowed:** Yes. **Range:** Yes (grass/mats). **To obtain tee times:** Call 5 days in advance.
Subscriber comments: Fun...Take plenty of balls...Excellent practice facility.

★★½ TOMOKA OAKS GOLF & COUNTRY CLUB
20 Tomoka Oaks Blvd., Ormond Beach, 32174, Volusia County, (904)677-7117, 5 miles N of Daytona Beach.
Opened: 1962. **Holes:** 18. **Par:** 72/72. **Yards:** 6,745/5,385. **Course rating:** 72.0/71.4. **Slope:** 124/121. **Architect:** J. Porter Gibson. **Green fee:** $25/$32. **Credit cards:** All major. **Reduced fees:** Low season, twilight. **Caddies:** No. **Golf carts:** Included in Green Fee. **Discount golf packages:** Yes. **Season:** Year-round. **High:** Jan.-April. **On site lodging:** No. **Rental clubs:** Yes. **Walking policy:** Mandatory cart. **Metal spikes allowed:** Yes. **Range:** Yes (grass). **To obtain tee times:** Call golf shop 1 day in advance.
Subscriber comments: Many trees...Mature course...Heavily played...OK.

★★★½ TOURNAMENT PLAYERS CLUB AT HERON BAY
PU-11801 Heron Bay Blvd., Coral Springs, 33076, Broward County, (954)796-2000, 20 miles NW of Fort Lauderdale.
Opened: 1996. **Holes:** 18. **Par:** 72/72. **Yards:** 7,268/4,961. **Course rating:** 74.9/68.7. **Slope:** 133/113. **Architect:** Mark McCumber/Mike Beebe. **Green fee:** $52/$94. **Credit cards:** MC,VISA,AMEX,Diners Club. **Reduced fees:** Weekdays, low season, twilight, juniors. **Caddies:** No. **Golf carts:** Included in Green Fee. **Discount golf packages:** No. **Season:** Year-round. **High:** Dec.-April. **On site lodging:** No. **Rental clubs:** Yes. **Walking policy:** Unrestricted walking. **Metal spikes allowed:** Yes. **Range:** Yes (grass). **To obtain tee times:** Call golf shop up to 7 days in advance.
Notes: PGA Tour Honda Classic since 1996.
Subscriber comments: New course, will improve with maturity...Flat...Wind and sand are obstacles...Too many bunkers for a 17-handicapper...Lots of sand, but fair...Would you like some fairway with your bunkers?...Beautiful clubhouse...Great finishing hole...Some intimidating holes.

TOURNAMENT PLAYERS CLUB AT SAWGRASS
R-110 TPC Blvd., Ponte Vedra Beach, 32082, St. Johns County, (904)273-3235, 15 miles SE of Jacksonville.
Reduced fees: Low season, juniors. **Caddies:** No. **Discount golf packages:** No. **Season:** Year-round. **On site lodging:** Yes. **Rental clubs:** Yes. **Walking policy:** Unrestricted walking. **Metal spikes allowed:** Yes. **To obtain tee times:** Guests of Marriott call golf reservations at (800)457-4653.

GREAT SERVICE

★★★★½ STADIUM COURSE
Opened: 1980. **Holes:** 18. **Par:** 72/72. **Yards:** 6,857/5,034. **Course rating:** 74.0/64.7. **Slope:** 135/123. **Architect:** Pete Dye. **Green fee:** $90/$160. **Credit cards:** MC,VISA,AMEX,Resort Charge Sawgrass Marriot. **Golf carts:** Included in Green Fee. **High:** March-April. **Range:** Yes (grass).
Notes: Ranked 53rd in 1997-98 America's 100 Greatest; 2nd in 1997 Best in State; The Players Championship (annually); U.S. Amateur.
Subscriber comments: Everyone should play it at least once...One of the best...Good luck if the wind is blowing...Concentration fogged by the ambience...Too tough for high handicappers...Leave your ego at the bag drop...Visually intimidating...Landing areas the size of toilet bowls...You'll never forget No. 17...Variety of tees makes it fair...Everything I expected...Truly amazing...Too tough for me, but fun to play.

★★★★ VALLEY COURSE
Opened: 1987. **Holes:** 18. **Par:** 72/72. **Yards:** 6,864/5,126. **Course rating:** 72.6/63.8. **Slope:** 129/117. **Architect:** Pete Dye/Bobby Weed. **Green fee:** $60/$95. **Credit cards:**

MC,VISA,AMEX,Resort Charge. **Golf carts:** N/A. **High:** March-May. **Range:** Yes (grass/mats).
Notes: Senior Players Championship.
Subscriber comments: Feel like a pro for a day...Easier to score than at Stadium Course...Less contrived than Stadium...Nice warm-up for the Stadium...Lush...Real challenge.

★★★★TOURNAMENT PLAYERS CLUB OF TAMPA BAY
5100 Terrain de Golf Dr., Lutz, 33549, Hillsborough County, (813)949-0091, 15 miles NW of Tampa.
Opened: 1991. **Holes:** 18. **Par:** 71/71. **Yards:** 6,898/5,036. **Course rating:** 73.4/69.1.
Slope: 130/119. **Architect:** Bobby Weed. **Green fee:** $45/$89. **Credit cards:**
MC,VISA,AMEX,Diners Club. **Reduced fees:** Weekdays, low season, twilight, juniors.
Caddies: No. **Golf carts:** Included in Green Fee. **Discount golf packages:** No.
Season: Year-round. **High:** Jan.-April. **On site lodging:** No. **Rental clubs:** Yes.
Walking policy: Mandatory cart. **Metal spikes allowed:** Yes. **Range:** Yes (grass). **To obtain tee times:** Call 7 days in advance.
Notes: Senior PGA Tour GTE Classic.
Subscriber comments: Bury me here, this is heaven...Plush fairways...Tough from tips. Requires much imagination...Excellent test...Lots of water...Excellent practice facility...Always fun to play where the pros play.

TURNBERRY ISLE RESORT & CLUB
R-19999 W. Country Club Dr., Aventura, 33180, Dade County, (305)933-6929, (800)327-7208, 10 miles S of Fort Lauderdale.
Opened: 1971. **Architect:** Robert Trent Jones Sr.. **Green fee:** $45/$90.
Credit cards: MC,VISA,AMEX. **Reduced fees:** Low season. **Caddies:**
No. **Golf carts:** $19. **Discount golf packages:** Yes. **Season:** Year-round.
High: Nov.-April. **On site lodging:** Yes. **Rental clubs:** Yes. **Walking policy:** Mandatory cart. **Metal spikes allowed:** Yes. **Range:** Yes (grass/mats). **To obtain tee times:**
Reserve tee times when making hotel reservations.

(GREAT SERVICE)

★★★½NORTH COURSE
Holes: 18. **Par:** 70/70. **Yards:** 6,348/4,991. **Course rating:** 70.3/67.9. **Slope:** 127/107.
Subscriber comments: Excellent.
★★★★SOUTH COURSE
Holes: 18. **Par:** 72/72. **Yards:** 7,003/5,581. **Course rating:** 73.7/71.3. **Slope:** 136/116.
Subscriber comments: Cleverly designed...Excellent resort course.

★★★½TURNBULL BAY GOLF COURSE
New Smyrna Beach, Volusia County, (904)427-5176.
Call club for further information.
Subscriber comments: Love the course...Nice visual variety...Natural beauty...Needs time.

★★★TURTLE CREEK GOLF CLUB
PU-1278 Admiralty Blvd., Rockledge, 32955, Brevard County, (407)632-2520, 35 miles SE of Orlando.
Opened: 1970. **Holes:** 18. **Par:** 72/72. **Yards:** 6,709/4,880. **Course rating:** 70.1/68.8.
Slope: 129/113. **Architect:** Bob Renaud. **Green fee:** $20/$43. **Credit cards:**
MC,VISA,AMEX. **Reduced fees:** Weekdays, low season, twilight, juniors. **Caddies:** No.
Golf carts: Included in Green Fee. **Discount golf packages:** Yes. **Season:** Year-round.
High: Jan.-April. **On site lodging:** No. **Rental clubs:** Yes. **Walking policy:** Walking at certain times. **Metal spikes allowed:** Yes. **Range:** Yes (grass/mats). **To obtain tee times:** Call up to 7 days in advance.
Subscriber comments: Nice variety of shots...Classy atmosphere...Tight. Water hazards plentiful.

★★TWISTED OAKS GOLF CLUB
PU-4545 Forest Ridge Blvd., Beverly Hills, 34465, Citrus County, (352)746-6257.
Call club for further information.

FLORIDA

★★★UNIVERSITY COUNTRY CLUB
9400 S.W. 130th Ave., Miami, 33186, Dade County, (305)386-5533, (305)386-5559, 5 miles SW of Miami.
Opened: 1968. **Holes:** 18. **Par:** 72/72. **Yards:** 7,172/5,476. **Course rating:** 74.3/70.9. **Slope:** 123/118. **Architect:** Mark Mahannah. **Green fee:** $23/$55. **Credit cards:** MC,VISA,AMEX. **Reduced fees:** Weekdays, low season, resort guests, twilight. **Caddies:** No. **Golf carts:** Included in Green Fee. **Discount golf packages:** No. **Season:** Year-round. **High:** Nov.-April. **On site lodging:** Yes. **Rental clubs:** Yes. **Walking policy:** Mandatory cart. **Metal spikes allowed:** No. **Range:** Yes (grass/mats). **To obtain tee times:** Call up to 5 days in advance.
Subscriber comments: New owners show promise...Much improved...Long, open course.

★★½UNIVERSITY OF SOUTH FLORIDA GOLF COURSE
PU-13801 46th St., Tampa, 33612, Hillsborough County, (813)632-6893.
Opened: 1967. **Holes:** 18. **Par:** 71/71. **Yards:** 6,876/5,353. **Course rating:** 74.2/70.9. **Slope:** 132/115. **Architect:** William Mitchell. **Green fee:** $14/$32. **Credit cards:** MC,VISA. **Reduced fees:** Weekdays, low season, twilight, seniors, juniors. **Caddies:** No. **Golf carts:** $12. **Discount golf packages:** No. **Season:** Year-round. **High:** Nov.-April. **On site lodging:** No. **Rental clubs:** Yes. **Walking policy:** Unrestricted walking. **Metal spikes allowed:** Yes. **Range:** Yes (grass/mats). **To obtain tee times:** Call. **Subscriber comments:** Most greens elevated...Challenging...Keep it straight...Very busy.

★★★★UNIVERSITY PARK COUNTRY CLUB
7671 Park Blvd., University Park, 34201, Manatee County, (941)359-9999, 45 miles S of Tampa.
Opened: 1991. **Holes:** 27. **Architect:** Ron Garl. **Green fee:** $50/$85. **Credit cards:** MC,VISA,DISC. **Reduced fees:** Weekdays, low season, twilight. **Caddies:** No. **Golf carts:** Included in Green Fee. **Discount golf packages:** No. **Season:** Year-round. **High:** Nov.-April. **On site lodging:** No. **Rental clubs:** Yes. **Walking policy:** Walking at certain times. **Metal spikes allowed:** Yes. **Range:** Yes (grass/mats). **To obtain tee times:** Call 3 days in advance.
COURSE 1 & 19
Par: 72/72. **Yards:** 7,247/5,576. **Course rating:** 74.4/71.8. **Slope:** 132/122.
COURSE 1 & 10
Par: 72/72. **Yards:** 7,001/5,511. **Course rating:** 73.6/71.6. **Slope:** 138/126.
COURSE 10 & 19
Par: 72/72. **Yards:** 7,152/5,695. **Course rating:** 74.0/72.4. **Slope:** 134/124.
Subscriber comments: Very pretty...Some great holes, some without much character...A lot of fun.

VENTURA COUNTRY CLUB
3201 Woodgate Blvd., Orlando, 32822, Orange County, (407)277-2640, 75 miles E of Tampa.
Opened: 1980. **Holes:** 18. **Par:** 70/70. **Yards:** 5,467/4,392. **Course rating:** 66.6/65.1. **Slope:** 113/109. **Architect:** Mark Mahannah. **Green fee:** $25/$40. **Credit cards:** MC,VISA. **Reduced fees:** Low season, resort guests, twilight. **Caddies:** No. **Golf carts:** Included in Green Fee. **Discount golf packages:** No. **Season:** Year-round. **High:** Jan.-April. **On site lodging:** Yes. **Rental clubs:** Yes. **Walking policy:** Mandatory cart. **Metal spikes allowed:** Yes. **Range:** Yes (grass). **To obtain tee times:** Call golf shop 2 days in advance.

★★★½VIERA EAST GOLF CLUB
PU-2300 Clubhouse Dr., Viera, 32955, Brevard County, (407)639-6500, (888)843-7232, 5 miles N of Melbourne.
Opened: 1994. **Holes:** 18. **Par:** 72/72. **Yards:** 6,720/5,428. **Course rating:** 72.1/71.0. **Slope:** 129/122. **Architect:** Joe Lee. **Green fee:** $20/$25. **Credit cards:** MC,VISA,AMEX. **Reduced fees:** Low season, resort guests, twilight, juniors. **Caddies:** Yes. **Golf carts:** $12. **Discount golf packages:** No. **Season:** Year-round. **High:** Dec.-April. **On site lodging:** Yes. **Rental clubs:** Yes. **Walking policy:** Walking at certain

times. **Metal spikes allowed:** Yes. **Range:** Yes (grass). **To obtain tee times:** Call 3 days in advance starting at 7 a.m.
Subscriber comments: Typical Florida golf: sand, water and wind.

★★½THE VILLAGE GOLF CLUB
PU-122 Country Club Dr., Royal Palm Beach, 33411, Palm Beach County, (561)793-1400.
Opened: N/A. **Holes:** 18. **Par:** 72/72. **Yards:** 6,883/5,455. **Course rating:** 73.3/71.7.
Slope: 134/126. **Architect:** N/A. **Green fee:** $24/$50. **Credit cards:** All major.
Reduced fees: N/A. **Caddies:** No. **Golf carts:** Included in Green Fee. **Discount golf packages:** No. **Season:** Year-round. **High:** Nov.-April. **On site lodging:** No. **Rental clubs:** Yes. **Walking policy:** Mandatory cart. **Metal spikes allowed:** Yes. **Range:** Yes (grass). **To obtain tee times:** Call golf shop.
Subscriber comments: Trees, water and trouble...Back tees for single-digits only.

THE VILLAGES
1200 Morse Blvd., Lady Lake, 32159, Sumter County, (352)753-5155, 50 miles NW of Orlando.
Opened: 1990. **Holes:** 18. **Par:** 72/72. **Yards:** 6,417/5,224. **Course rating:** 70.4/69.6.
Slope: 122/114. **Architect:** Clifton/Ezell/Clifton. **Green fee:** $20/$36. **Credit cards:** MC,VISA,AMEX. **Reduced fees:** Low season, resort guests, twilight. **Caddies:** No.
Golf carts: Included in Green Fee. **Discount golf packages:** Yes. **Season:** Year-round.
High: Nov.-April. **On site lodging:** Yes. **Rental clubs:** Yes. **Walking policy:** Unrestricted walking. **Metal spikes allowed:** Yes. **Range:** Yes (grass/mats). **To obtain tee times:** Nonresidents may call starter up to 3 days in advance.

WALDEN LAKES GOLF & COUNTRY CLUB
2001 Club House Dr., Plant City, 33566, Hillsborough County, (813)754-8575, (888)218-8463, 20 miles E of Tampa.
Opened: 1977. **Architect:** Ron Garl/Bob Cupp/Jay Morrish. **Green fee:** $25/$50.
Credit cards: MC,VISA,AMEX. **Reduced fees:** Weekdays, low season, twilight.
Caddies: No. **Golf carts:** Included in Green Fee. **Discount golf packages:** No.
Season: Year-round. **High:** Nov.-April. **On site lodging:** Yes. **Rental clubs:** Yes.
Walking policy: Mandatory cart. **Metal spikes allowed:** Yes. **Range:** Yes (grass). **To obtain tee times:** Call golf shop anytime.
★★★½HILLS COURSE
Holes: 18. **Par:** 72/72. **Yards:** 6,610/4,800. **Course rating:** 71.5/68.6. **Slope:** 131/120.
Subscriber comments: OK...You can score reasonably well...Wooded, flat.
LAKES COURSE
Holes: 18. **Par:** 72/72. **Yards:** 6,588/5,016. **Course rating:** 71.9/69.0. **Slope:** 131/123.

WALT DISNEY WORLD RESORT
R- Lake Buena Vista, 32830, Orange County, (407)939-4653, 20 miles SW of Orlando Airport.
Credit cards: MC,VISA,AMEX,The Disney Card. **Caddies:** No. **Season:** Year-round. **High:** Jan.-April. **On site lodging:** Yes. **Rental clubs:** Yes.
Metal spikes allowed: Yes. **To obtain tee times:** Resort guests with confirmed reservation may call 60 days in advance. Nonguests call 30 days in advance with credit card.
Notes: PGA Tour Walt Disney World/Oldsmobile Golf Classic; LPGA Tour HealthSouth Inaugural.
★★★★EAGLE PINES GOLF COURSE
3451 Golf View Dr.
Opened: 1992. **Holes:** 18. **Par:** 72/72. **Yards:** 6,772/4,838. **Course rating:** 72.3/68.0.
Slope: 131/111. **Architect:** Pete Dye. **Green fee:** $90/$150. **Reduced fees:** Low season, resort guests, twilight. **Golf carts:** Included in Green Fee. **Discount golf packages:** Yes. **Walking policy:** Mandatory cart. **Range:** Yes (grass/mats).
Subscriber comments: Tough course...Beautiful...No complaints, except the cost...Generous fairways and multiple tees make this a pleasure for all levels...Lots of sand.
★★★½LAKE BUENA VISTA GOLF COURSE
One Club Lake Dr.
Opened: 1972. **Holes:** 18. **Par:** 72/73. **Yards:** 6,819/5,194. **Course rating:** 72.7/69.4.

Slope: 128/120. **Architect:** Joe Lee. **Green fee:** $90/$130. **Reduced fees:** Low season, resort guests, twilight. **Golf carts:** Included in Green Fee. **Discount golf packages:** Yes. **Walking policy:** Walking at certain times. **Range:** Yes (grass).
Subscriber comments: Playable...Lots of water...Wide open...Easy for a PGA Tour course...Can't wait to go back...Wife appreciated length from forward tees.

MAGNOLIA GOLF COURSE
1950 W. Magnolia Dr.
Opened: 1971. **Holes:** 18. **Par:** 72/72. **Yards:** 7,190/5,232. **Course rating:** 73.9/70.5. **Slope:** 133/123. **Architect:** Joe Lee. **Green fee:** $90/$130. **Reduced fees:** Low season, resort guests, twilight. **Golf carts:** Included in Green Fee. **Discount golf packages:** Yes. **Walking policy:** Mandatory cart. **Range:** Yes (grass/mats).

★★★½OAK TRAIL GOLF COURSE
1950 W. Magnolia Palm Dr.
Opened: 1971. **Holes:** 9. **Par:** 36/36. **Yards:** 2,913/2,532. **Course rating:** N/A. **Slope:** N/A. **Architect:** Ron Garl. **Green fee:** $32. **Reduced fees:** Juniors. **Golf carts:** N/A. **Discount golf packages:** No. **Walking policy:** Unrestricted walking. **Range:** Yes (grass/mats).
Subscriber comments: Excellent resort course...Good challenge...Lots of water...Long...My favorite in Florida.

★★★★½OSPREY RIDGE GOLF COURSE
3451 Golf View Dr.
Opened: 1992. **Holes:** 18. **Par:** 72/72. **Yards:** 7,101/5,402. **Course rating:** 73.9/70.5. **Slope:** 135/122. **Architect:** Tom Fazio. **Green fee:** $90/$150. **Reduced fees:** Low season, resort guests, twilight. **Golf carts:** Included in Green Fee. **Discount golf packages:** Yes. **Walking policy:** Mandatory cart. **Range:** Yes (grass).
Subscriber comments: At Disney, I like this one best...Great resort course...Mickey shows his teeth!...Super treat...Beautiful setting...Some very tough holes...Lots of bunkers...Manageable from tee matching your ability...Breathtaking! 16, 17 and 18...Great variety.

★★★½PALM GOLF COURSE
1950 W. Magnolia Dr.
Opened: 1971. **Holes:** 18. **Par:** 72/72. **Yards:** 6,957/5,311. **Course rating:** 73.0/70.4. **Slope:** 133/124. **Architect:** Joe Lee. **Green fee:** $90/$130. **Reduced fees:** Low season, resort guests, twilight. **Golf carts:** Included in Green Fee. **Discount golf packages:** Yes. **Walking policy:** Mandatory cart. **Range:** Yes (grass/mats).
Subscriber comments: Good test...Older Disney course...Friendly course...Lots of water...Less scenic.

★★★WATERFORD GOLF CLUB
1454 Gleneagles Dr., Venice, 34292, Sarasota County, (941)484-6621, 15 miles S of Sarasota.
Opened: 1989. **Holes:** 27. **Architect:** Ted McAnlis. **Green fee:** $27/$46. **Credit cards:** MC,VISA. **Reduced fees:** Low season, resort guests, twilight. **Caddies:** No. **Golf carts:** Included in Green Fee. **Discount golf packages:** Yes. **Season:** Year-round. **High:** Jan.-April. **On site lodging:** No. **Rental clubs:** No. **Walking policy:** Walking at certain times. **Metal spikes allowed:** Yes. **Range:** Yes (grass/mats). **To obtain tee times:** Call 2 days in advance.

GLENEAGLES/SAWGRASS
Par: 72/72. **Yards:** 6,498/4,998. **Course rating:** 71.5/69.9. **Slope:** 125/118.

GLENEAGLES/TURNBERRY
Par: 72/72. **Yards:** 6,504/5,168. **Course rating:** 71.9/69.6. **Slope:** 127/118.

TURNBERRY/SAWGRASS
Par: 72/72. **Yards:** 6,670/5,124. **Course rating:** 71.9/69.7. **Slope:** 126/119.
Subscriber comments: Challenging...Rangers kept it moving.

WEDGEFIELD GOLF & COUNTRY CLUB
20550 Maxim Pkwy., Orlando, 32833, Orange County, (407)568-2116.
Opened: N/A. **Holes:** 18. **Par:** 72/72. **Yards:** 6,537/5,226. **Course rating:** 71.8/70.7. **Slope:** 123/122. **Architect:** N/A. **Green fee:** $15/$38. **Credit cards:** MC,VISA. **Reduced fees:** N/A. **Caddies:** No. **Golf carts:** Included in Green Fee. **Discount golf packages:** No. **Season:** Year-round. **High:** Nov.-May. **On site lodging:** No. **Rental clubs:** Yes. **Walking policy:** Unrestricted walking. **Metal spikes allowed:** Yes. **Range:** Yes (grass). **To obtain tee times:** Call up to 7 days in advance.

★★WEDGEWOOD GOLF & COUNTRY CLUB
401 Carpenter's Way, Lakeland, 33809, Polk County, (941)858-4451, 25 miles E of Tampa.
Opened: 1984. **Holes:** 18. **Par:** 70/70. **Yards:** 6,402/4,885. **Course rating:** 69.1/68.1. **Slope:** 115/113. **Architect:** Ron Garl. **Green fee:** $16/$24. **Credit cards:** MC,VISA. **Reduced fees:** Weekdays, low season, twilight. **Caddies:** No. **Golf carts:** Included in Green Fee. **Discount golf packages:** No. **Season:** Year-round. **High:** Nov.-May. **On site lodging:** No. **Rental clubs:** No. **Walking policy:** Mandatory cart. **Metal spikes allowed:** Yes. **Range:** Yes (grass). **To obtain tee times:** Call three days in advance.

★★★WEKIVA GOLF CLUB
PU-200 Hunt Club Blvd., Longwood, 32779, Seminole County, (407)862-5113. Call club for further information.

WEST MEADOWS GOLF CLUB
PU-11400 W. Meadows Dr., Jacksonville, 32221, Duval County, (904)781-4834, 12 miles W of Downtown Jacksonville.
Opened: 1968. **Holes:** 18. **Par:** 72/72. **Yards:** 6,350/6,000. **Course rating:** 70.0. **Slope:** 108. **Architect:** Sam Caruso. **Green fee:** $14/$22. **Credit cards:** N/A. **Reduced fees:** Weekdays, twilight, seniors. **Caddies:** No. **Golf carts:** Included in Green Fee. **Discount golf packages:** No. **Season:** Year-round. **High:** Oct.-May. **On site lodging:** No. **Rental clubs:** Yes. **Walking policy:** Walking at certain times. **Metal spikes allowed:** Yes. **Range:** Yes (grass). **To obtain tee times:** Open play.

★★½WEST PALM BEACH MUNICIPAL COUNTRY CLUB
PM-7001 Parker Ave., West Palm Beach, 33405, Palm Beach County, (561)582-2019.
Opened: 1947. **Holes:** 18. **Par:** 72/72. **Yards:** 6,800/5,871. **Course rating:** 71.0/72.8. **Slope:** 121/121. **Architect:** Dick Wilson. **Green fee:** $14/$36. **Credit cards:** MC,VISA,DISC. **Reduced fees:** Low season, twilight, juniors. **Caddies:** No. **Golf carts:** $12. **Discount golf packages:** No. **Season:** Year-round. **High:** Dec.-April. **On site lodging:** No. **Rental clubs:** Yes. **Walking policy:** Walking at certain times. **Metal spikes allowed:** Yes. **Range:** Yes (grass). **To obtain tee times:** Lottery system. One person per foursome enters names evening before day of play at 7 p.m. As slips are drawn golfer gets choice of available times. Other: call starter after lottery or day of play to secure a time. Saturday and Sunday double crossover lottery. Wednesday evening for Saturday and Thursday for Sunday at 7:30 p.m.

★★★½WESTCHASE GOLF CLUB
PU-10217 Radcliffe Dr., Tampa, 33626, Hillsborough County, (813)854-2331.
Opened: 1992. **Holes:** 18. **Par:** 72/72. **Yards:** 6,710/5,205. **Course rating:** 71.8/69.1. **Slope:** 130/121. **Architect:** Clifton/Ezell/Clifton. **Green fee:** $37/$55. **Credit cards:** All major. **Reduced fees:** Weekdays, low season, twilight, juniors. **Caddies:** No. **Golf carts:** Included in Green Fee. **Discount golf packages:** No. **Season:** Year-round. **High:** Jan.-April. **On site lodging:** No. **Rental clubs:** Yes. **Walking policy:** Mandatory cart. **Metal spikes allowed:** Yes. **Range:** Yes (grass/mats). **To obtain tee times:** Call up to 3 days in advance.
Subscriber comments: Challenging...Tight...Difficult carries and waste areas...Pretty...Beautiful clubhouse...Expect to lose a few balls...Tough from back tees...New clubhouse completes package...Makes you play all the shots.

★★★WESTCHESTER GOLF & COUNTRY CLUB
12250 Westchester Club Dr., Boynton Beach, 33437, Palm Beach County, (561)734-6300, 12 miles S of West Palm Beach.
Opened: 1988. **Holes:** 27. **Architect:** Karl Litten. **Green fee:** $18/$55. **Credit cards:** MC,VISA,AMEX. **Reduced fees:** Weekdays, low season, resort guests. **Caddies:** No. **Golf carts:** Included in Green Fee. **Discount golf packages:** Yes. **Season:** Year-round. **High:** Nov.-April. **On site lodging:** No. **Rental clubs:** Yes. **Walking policy:** Mandatory cart. **Metal spikes allowed:** Yes. **Range:** Yes (grass). **To obtain tee times:** Call 2 days in advance.
BLUE/GOLD
Par: 72/72. **Yards:** 6,735/4,728. **Course rating:** 72.8/69.7. **Slope:** 137/121.

GOLD/RED
Par: 72/72. **Yards:** 6,657/4,808. **Course rating:** 72.3/70.0. **Slope:** 134/120.
RED/BLUE
Par: 72/72. **Yards:** 6,772/4,758. **Course rating:** 72.9/70.3. **Slope:** 136/119.
Subscriber comments: Challenging...Beautiful...Lots of water...For first-time player it's difficult to find holes while crossing streets...Distance between holes. Houses get in the way.

WESTMINSTER GOLF CLUB
PU-2199 Berkley Way, Lehigh, 33971, (941)368-1110, 3 miles E of Fort Myers.
Opened: 1996. **Holes:** 18. **Par:** 72/72. **Yards:** 6,930/5,280. **Course rating:** 73.4/70.5.
Slope: 133/120. **Architect:** Ted McAnlis. **Green fee:** $25/$50. **Credit cards:** MC,VISA.
Reduced fees: Low season. **Caddies:** No. **Golf carts:** Included in Green Fee.
Discount golf packages: Yes. **Season:** Year-round. **High:** Dec.-April. **On site lodging:** No. **Rental clubs:** Yes. **Walking policy:** Mandatory cart. **Metal spikes allowed:** Yes.
Range: Yes (grass). **To obtain tee times:** Call 2 days in advance.

WHISPERING OAKS COUNTRY CLUB
34450 Whispering Oaks Blvd., Ridge Manor, 33525, Hernando County, (352)583-4233.
Opened: N/A. **Holes:** 18. **Par:** 72/72. **Yards:** 6,313/6,055. **Course rating:** N/A. **Slope:** 123/118. **Architect:** N/A. **Green fee:** $25. **Credit cards:** MC,VISA. **Reduced fees:** Low season, twilight. **Caddies:** No. **Golf carts:** Included in Green Fee. **Discount golf packages:** Yes. **Season:** Year-round. **High:** Nov-April. **On site lodging:** No. **Rental clubs:** No. **Walking policy:** Mandatory cart. **Metal spikes allowed:** Yes. **Range:** Yes (grass).
To obtain tee times: Call up to 7 days in advance.

WILLOW BROOK GOLF COURSE
4200 S.R. 544 E., Winter Haven, 33881, Polk County, (941)291-5898.
Call club for further information.

★★★½WINDSOR PARKE GOLF CLUB
4747 Hodges Blvd., Jacksonville, 32224, Duval County, (904)223-4653, 12 miles E of Jacksonville.
Opened: 1991. **Holes:** 18. **Par:** 72/72. **Yards:** 6,740/5,206. **Course rating:** 71.9/69.4.
Slope: 133/123. **Architect:** Arthur Hills. **Green fee:** $47/$55. **Credit cards:** All major.
Reduced fees: Weekdays, twilight, seniors, juniors. **Caddies:** No. **Golf carts:** Included in Green Fee. **Discount golf packages:** Yes. **Season:** Year-round. **High:** March-May.
On site lodging: No. **Rental clubs:** Yes. **Walking policy:** Walking at certain times.
Metal spikes allowed: No. **Range:** Yes (grass). **To obtain tee times:** Call 5 days in advance.
Subscriber comments: Class!...My favorite course: long, challenging, beautiful...Tough but fair...Still needs maturing...Challenging...Demanding par 3s...Lost a lot of balls here...Driving range makes 10th hole very exciting...They treat women equally with men (morning tee times).

WORLD WOODS GOLF CLUB
R-17590 Ponce De Leon Blvd., Brooksville, 34614, Hernando County, (352)796-5500, 60 miles N of Tampa.
Opened: 1993. **Architect:** Tom Fazio. **Green fee:** $50/$75. **Credit cards:** All major. **Reduced fees:** Weekdays, low season. **Caddies:** No.
Golf carts: Included in Green Fee. **Discount golf packages:** Yes.
Season: Year-round. **High:** Jan.-April. **On site lodging:** No. **Rental clubs:** Yes.
Walking policy: Unrestricted walking. **Metal spikes allowed:** Yes. **Range:** Yes (grass).
To obtain tee times: Call up to 30 days in advance with credit card.

(GOOD SERVICE)

★★★★½PINE BARRENS COURSE
Holes: 18. **Par:** 71/71. **Yards:** 6,902/5,301. **Course rating:** 73.7/70.9.
Slope: 140/132.
Notes: Ranked 8th in 1997 Best in State.

(GOOD VALUE)

Subscriber comments: The closest to playing Pine Valley that many of us will ever get...One of the best overall golf experiences around...One of the top 10 courses I have played...Best practice facilities I have ever seen...One of the finest courses in Florida, public or private...One of the best in the country...True golf test.

FLORIDA

★★★★ROLLING OAKS COURSE
Holes: 18. **Par:** 72/72. **Yards:** 6,985/5,245. **Course rating:** 73.5/70.7.
Slope: 136/128.
Notes: Ranked 26th in 1997 Best in State.
Subscriber comments: Great deal for the serious golfer...Beautiful setting...Tour conditions...Would play there forever...Now I know what golf should really be...Golfer's delight...Can't wait to go back...Wooded, rolling, interesting.

★★½ZELLWOOD STATION COUNTRY CLUB
2126 Spillman Dr., Zellwood, 32798, Orange County, (407)886-3303, 20 miles N of Orlando.
Opened: 1977. **Holes:** 18. **Par:** 72/74. **Yards:** 6,400/5,377. **Course rating:** 70.5/71.1.
Slope: 122/122. **Architect:** William Maddox. **Green fee:** $22/$30. **Credit cards:** None.
Reduced fees: Low season, twilight. **Caddies:** No. **Golf carts:** Included in Green Fee.
Discount golf packages: No. **Season:** Year-round. **High:** Nov.-April. **On site lodging:** No. **Rental clubs:** Yes. **Walking policy:** Mandatory cart. **Metal spikes allowed:** Yes.
Range: Yes. **To obtain tee times:** Call 2 days in advance.
Subscriber comments: A hidden jewel.

GEORGIA

★★BACON PARK GOLF COURSE
PU-Shorty Cooper Dr., Savannah, 31406, Chatham County, (912)354-2625, 35 miles S of Hilton Head, SC.
Opened: 1927. **Holes:** 27. **Architect:** Donald Ross/Ron Kirby/Denis Griffiths. **Green fee:** $12/$14. **Credit cards:** MC,VISA. **Reduced fees:** Weekdays, low season, twilight, seniors, juniors. **Caddies:** No. **Golf carts:** N/A. **Discount golf packages:** No. **Season:** Year-round. **High:** June-Aug. **On site lodging:** No. **Rental clubs:** Yes. **Walking policy:** Walking at certain times. **Metal spikes allowed:** Yes. **Range:** Yes (grass). **To obtain tee times:** Call up to 30 days in advance.
CYPRESS/LIVE OAK
Par: 72/72. **Yards:** 6,679/5,160. **Course rating:** 70.5/68.3. **Slope:** 119/116.
CYPRESS/MAGNOLIA
Par: 72/72. **Yards:** 6,573/4,943. **Course rating:** 69.9/66.9. **Slope:** 118/114.
MAGNOLIA/LIVE OAK
Par: 72/72. **Yards:** 6,740/5,309. **Course rating:** 70.7/69.4. **Slope:** 120/118.

★★★BARRINGTON HALL GOLF CLUB
7100 Zebulon Rd., Macon, 31210, Monroe County, (912)757-8358, 65 miles S of Atlanta.
Opened: 1992. **Holes:** 18. **Par:** 72/72. **Yards:** 7,062/5,012. **Course rating:** 73.8/69.3. **Slope:** 138/118. **Architect:** Tom Clark. **Green fee:** $19/$29. **Credit cards:** MC,VISA. **Reduced fees:** Weekdays. **Caddies:** No. **Golf carts:** $10. **Discount golf packages:** Yes. **Season:** Year-round. **High:** April-May. **On site lodging:** No. **Rental clubs:** Yes. **Walking policy:** Walking at certain times. **Metal spikes allowed:** Yes. **Range:** Yes (grass). **To obtain tee times:** Call golf shop.
Subscriber comments: Narrow fairways...Need to hit driver straight and long.

★★BEAVER KREEK GOLF CLUB
Rte. 4, Box 167, Hwy. 221 N., Douglas, 31533, Coffee County, (912)384-8230, 60 miles NE of Valdosta.
Opened: 1988. **Holes:** 18. **Par:** 72/72. **Yards:** 6,543/5,424. **Course rating:** 71.1. **Slope:** 119. **Architect:** Kirby Holton. **Green fee:** $24/$24. **Credit cards:** MC,VISA. **Reduced fees:** N/A. **Caddies:** No. **Golf carts:** $16. **Discount golf packages:** Yes. **Season:** Year-round. **High:** April-Oct. **On site lodging:** No. **Rental clubs:** Yes. **Walking policy:** Walking at certain times. **Metal spikes allowed:** Yes. **Range:** Yes (grass). **To obtain tee times:** Call pro shop.

★★½BELLE MEADE COUNTRY CLUB
2660 Twin Pine Rd. N.W., Thomson, 30824, McDuffie County, (706)595-4511, 35 miles W of Augusta.
Opened: 1968. **Holes:** 18. **Par:** 72/73. **Yards:** 6,403/5,362. **Course rating:** 69.9/68.6. **Slope:** 120/113. **Architect:** Boone A. Knox, Pete Knox. **Green fee:** $18/$26. **Credit cards:** MC,VISA. **Reduced fees:** Weekdays. **Caddies:** No. **Golf carts:** $9. **Discount golf packages:** No. **Season:** Year-round. **High:** May-Aug. **On site lodging:** No. **Rental clubs:** Yes. **Walking policy:** Walking at certain times. **Metal spikes allowed:** Yes. **Range:** Yes (grass). **To obtain tee times:** Call pro shop.

★★½BIG CANOE GOLF CLUB
R-586 Big Canoe, Big Canoe, 30143, Pickens County, (706)268-3323, 50 miles N of Atlanta.
Opened: 1972. **Holes:** 27. **Architect:** Joe Lee. **Green fee:** $29/$54. **Credit cards:** All major. **Reduced fees:** Weekdays, low season, twilight. **Caddies:** No. **Golf carts:** $14. **Discount golf packages:** No. **Season:** Year-round. **High:** April-Oct. **On site lodging:** Yes. **Rental clubs:** Yes. **Walking policy:** Mandatory cart. **Metal spikes allowed:** Yes. **Range:** Yes (grass/mats). **To obtain tee times:** Must be an overnight guest on Big Canoe property or guest of member. Call 2 days in advance.
CHEROKEE/CREEK
Par: 72/72. **Yards:** 6,247/4,818. **Course rating:** 70.4/68.1. **Slope:** 134/117.
CHOCTAW/CHEROKEE
Par: 72/73. **Yards:** 6,371/4,933. **Course rating:** 71.0/68.6. **Slope:** 136/119.
CHOCTAW/CREEK
Par: 72/72. **Yards:** 6,276/5,159. **Course rating:** 70.2/70.1. **Slope:** 132/123.

Subscriber comments: Great mountain views for miles...Challenging layout...Good golf...Average conditions...Good course...Fun to play.
Special Notes: Formerly Sconti Golf Club.

★★★BLACK CREEK GOLF CLUB
PU-Bill Futch Rd., Ellabell, 31308, Bryan County, (912)858-4653, 30 miles W of Savannah.
Opened: 1994. **Holes:** 18. **Par:** 72/72. **Yards:** 6,287/4,551. **Course rating:** 70.4/66.0. **Slope:** 130/109. **Architect:** Jim Bevins. **Green fee:** $30/$36. **Credit cards:** MC,VISA. **Reduced fees:** Seniors, juniors. **Caddies:** No. **Golf carts:** $8. **Discount golf packages:** Yes. **Season:** Year-round. **High:** April-Sept. **On site lodging:** No. **Rental clubs:** No. **Walking policy:** Unrestricted walking. **Metal spikes allowed:** Yes. **Range:** Yes (grass). **To obtain tee times:** Call 7 days in advance.
Subscriber comments: Interesting back nine with bridges crossing marsh swamps...Fairways and greens are nicely maintained...Knowledgeable pro-shop staff...Short but tight track...Keep driver in the bag.

★★BOBBY JONES GOLF CLUB
PM-384 Woodward Way, Atlanta, 30305, Fulton County, (404)355-1009.
Opened: 1932. **Holes:** 18. **Par:** 71/71. **Yards:** 6,155/4,661. **Course rating:** 69.0/67.6. **Slope:** 119/114. **Architect:** John Van Kleek/Garrett Gill/George B. Williams. **Green fee:** $19/$33. **Credit cards:** MC,VISA. **Reduced fees:** Weekdays, twilight, seniors, juniors. **Caddies:** No. **Golf carts:** $10. **Discount golf packages:** No. **Season:** Year-round. **High:** May-Sept. **On site lodging:** No. **Rental clubs:** Yes. **Walking policy:** Mandatory cart. **Metal spikes allowed:** Yes. **Range:** No. **To obtain tee times:** Call pro shop.

★★BOWDEN GOLF COURSE
3111 Millerfield Rd., Macon, 31201, Bibb County, (912)742-1610.
Call club for further information.

★★★½BRASSTOWN VALLEY GOLF CLUB
PU-6321 U.S. Hwy. 76, Young Harris, 30582, Towns County, (706)379-4613, (800)201-3205, 90 miles N of Atlanta.
Opened: 1995. **Holes:** 18. **Par:** 72/72. **Yards:** 7,100/5,028. **Course rating:** 73.9/69.2. **Slope:** 139/116. **Architect:** Denis Griffiths. **Green fee:** $45/$55. **Credit cards:** All major. **Reduced fees:** Twilight, juniors. **Caddies:** No. **Golf carts:** Included in Green Fee. **Discount golf packages:** Yes. **Season:** Year-round. **High:** April-Nov. **On site lodging:** Yes. **Rental clubs:** Yes. **Walking policy:** Mandatory cart. **Metal spikes allowed:** Yes. **Range:** Yes (grass/mats). **To obtain tee times:** N/A.
Notes: Ranked 16th in 1997 Best in State.
Subscriber comments: A beautiful course but too many blind shots into greens...A difficult test...Friendly service...Fast, large greens...Hilly terrain...Nice views of mountains...Buy a yardage guide...A hidden gem.

★★★BRICKYARD PLANTATION GOLF CLUB
1619 U.S. 280 E., Americus, 31709, Sumter County, (912)874-1234.
Opened: 1979. **Holes:** 27. **Architect:** W.N. Clark. **Green fee:** $15/$15. **Credit cards:** All major. **Reduced fees:** N/A. **Caddies:** No. **Golf carts:** $10. **Discount golf packages:** No. **Season:** Year-round. **High:** May-Aug. **On site lodging:** No. **Rental clubs:** No. **Walking policy:** Unrestricted walking. **Metal spikes allowed:** Yes. **Range:** Yes (grass). **To obtain tee times:** Call golf shop.
DITCHES/MOUNDS
Par: 72/72. **Yards:** 6,700/5,300. **Course rating:** 70.5/69.9. **Slope:** 129/114.
DITCHES/WATERS
Par: 72/72. **Yards:** 6,300/5,100. **Course rating:** 70.0/70.6. **Slope:** 128/120.
WATERS/MOUNDS
Par: 72/72. **Yards:** 6,400/5,100. **Course rating:** 67.7/69.8. **Slope:** 124/116.
Subscriber comments: Staff is helpful and friendly...Nice links-style design.

★★BROWNS MILL GOLF COURSE
PM-480 Cleveland Ave., Atlanta, 30354, Fulton County, (404)366-3573.
Opened: 1969. **Holes:** 18. **Par:** 72/72. **Yards:** 6,539/5,545. **Course rating:** 71.0/71.4. **Slope:** 123/118. **Architect:** George W. Cobb. **Green fee:** $19/$22. **Credit cards:**

MC,VISA. **Reduced fees:** Weekdays, twilight, seniors, juniors. **Caddies:** No. **Golf carts:** $11. **Discount golf packages:** No. **Season:** Year-round. **High:** March-Oct. **On site lodging:** No. **Rental clubs:** Yes. **Walking policy:** Unrestricted walking. **Metal spikes allowed:** Yes. **Range:** Yes (grass). **To obtain tee times:** Call pro shop.

BULL CREEK GOLF COURSE

PU-7333 Lynch Rd., Midland, 31820, Muscogee County, (706)561-1614
Opened: 1972. **Architect:** Joe Lee/Ward Northrup. **Green fee:** $13/$17. **Credit cards:** MC,VISA. **Reduced fees:** Weekdays, seniors, juniors. **Caddies:** No. **Golf carts:** $11. **Discount golf packages:** Yes. **Season:** Year-round. **High:** April-Aug. **On site lodging:** No. **Rental clubs:** Yes. **Walking policy:** Unrestricted walking. **Metal spikes allowed:** Yes. **Range:** Yes (grass). **To obtain tee times:** Call pro shop.

★★★½EAST COURSE

Holes: 18. **Par:** 72/74. **Yards:** 6,705/5,430. **Course rating:** 71.2/69.8. **Slope:** 124/114.
Subscriber comments: Nice challenge...Hilly layout and heavily wooded...Conditions are good.

★★★½WEST COURSE

Holes: 18. **Par:** 72/74. **Yards:** 6,921/5,385. **Course rating:** 72.5/69.9. **Slope:** 130/121.
Subscriber comments: Hit every club in the bag from tips...Several interesting holes...A nice public course...Good conditions.

CALLAWAY GARDENS RESORT

R- U.S. Highway 27, Pine Mountain, 31822, Harris County, (706)663-2281.
Credit cards: All major. **Reduced fees:** Low season, twilight. **Caddies:** No. **Golf carts:** Included in Green Fee. **Discount golf packages:** Yes. **Season:** Year-round. **High:** March-Nov. **On site lodging:** Yes. **Rental clubs:** Yes. **Metal spikes allowed:** Yes. **Range:** Yes (grass). **To obtain tee times:** Resort guests can make tee times when room reservations are guaranteed. Nonguests call 800 number 48 hours in advance or pro shop day of play.

★★★GARDENS VIEW COURSE

Opened: 1964. **Holes:** 18. **Par:** 72/72. **Yards:** 6,392/5,848. **Course rating:** 70.7/72.7.
Slope: 121/123. **Architect:** Joe Lee. **Green fee:** $55/$70. **Walking policy:** Walking at certain times.
Subscriber comments: Nice setting...Excellent accommodations...Well-maintained...Good food, good golf...Wide open layout...Great greens, forgiving, a lot of fun...A solid golf course.

★★★½LAKE VIEW COURSE

Opened: 1952. **Holes:** 18. **Par:** 70/71. **Yards:** 6,006/5,452. **Course rating:** 69.4/70.3.
Slope: 115/122. **Architect:** J.B. McGovern. **Green fee:** $55/$70. **Walking policy:** Walking at certain times.
Subscriber comments: Beautiful views and landscaping...Fine layout...Easiest of three courses...Friendly staff.

★★★MOUNTAIN VIEW COURSE

Opened: 1968. **Holes:** 18. **Par:** 72/74. **Yards:** 7,057/5,848. **Course rating:** 74.1/73.2.
Slope: 138/122. **Architect:** Dick Wilson/Joe Lee. **Green fee:** $70/$90. **Walking policy:** Mandatory cart.
Notes: Ranked 17th in 1997 Best in State.
Subscriber comments: Several interesting holes...Well-designed...Stern test, but fun...Most difficult of three courses...Good conditions...Tough par 5s...Miss a shot and it will cost you...Tough bunkers.
Special Notes: Also 9-hole Sky View Course.

★★½CENTENNIAL GOLF CLUB

PU-5225 Woodstock Rd., Acworth, 30102, Cobb County, (770)975-1000.
Opened: 1990. **Holes:** 18. **Par:** 72/72. **Yards:** 6,850/5,095. **Course rating:** 73.1/69.5.
Slope: 134/122. **Architect:** Larry Nelson/Jeff Brauer. **Green fee:** $40/$50. **Credit cards:** All major. **Reduced fees:** Twilight, seniors, juniors. **Caddies:** No. **Golf carts:** Included in Green Fee. **Discount golf packages:** No. **Season:** Year-round. **High:** April-Oct. **On site lodging:** No. **Rental clubs:** Yes. **Walking policy:** Unrestricted walking. **Metal spikes allowed:** Yes. **Range:** Yes (grass). **To obtain tee times:** Call seven days in advance.
Subscriber comments: A few holes with blind shots...Tough from the tips...The 18th is a nice finishing hole...Difficult test for short hitters...Back nine better.

GEORGIA

★★★THE CHAMPIONS CLUB AT APALACHEE
1008 Dacula Rd., Dacula, 30211, Gwinnett County, (770)822-9220.
Call club for further information.
Subscriber comments: A tight, tough course...Friendly staff...Hilly fairways...The 8th is a great short hole...Course needs to mature...Several interesting holes.

★★★THE CHAMPIONS CLUB OF ATLANTA
15135 Hopewell Rd., Alpharetta, 30201, Fulton County, (770)343-9700, 20 miles N of Atlanta.
Opened: 1991. **Holes:** 18. **Par:** 72/72. **Yards:** 6,725/4,470. **Course rating:** 72.9/65.2. **Slope:** 131/108. **Architect:** D.J. DeVictor//Steve Melnyk. **Green fee:** $49/$65. **Credit cards:** MC,VISA,AMEX. **Reduced fees:** Twilight, seniors, juniors. **Caddies:** No. **Golf carts:** Included in Green Fee. **Discount golf packages:** No. **Season:** Year-round. **High:** March-Dec. **On site lodging:** No. **Rental clubs:** Yes. **Walking policy:** Mandatory cart. **Metal spikes allowed:** No. **Range:** Yes (grass). **To obtain tee times:** Call up to three days in advance.
Subscriber comments: A short, tight course with small undulating greens...Houses too close to some fairways...Free range balls...Several interesting holes...Nice elevation changes...Helpful staff...Only four long holes.

★★★THE CHAMPIONS CLUB OF GWINNETT
3254 Clubside View Court, Snellville, 30278, Gwinnett County, (770)978-7755, 25 miles E of Atlanta.
Opened: 1993. **Holes:** 18. **Par:** 72/72. **Yards:** 6,305/4,861. **Course rating:** 70.4/68.3. **Slope:** 128/118. **Architect:** Steve Melnyk. **Green fee:** $40/$50. **Credit cards:** MC,VISA. **Reduced fees:** Twilight, seniors, juniors. **Caddies:** No. **Golf carts:** Included in Green Fee. **Discount golf packages:** No. **Season:** Year-round. **High:** N/A. **On site lodging:** No. **Rental clubs:** No. **Walking policy:** N/A. **Metal spikes allowed:** Yes. **Range:** Yes (grass/mats). **To obtain tee times:** Call golf shop up to 7 days in advance.
Subscriber comments: Short, tight course...A lot of fun...The 9th is a difficult hole...Well-maintained...Beautiful lake...Consistent greens.

CHATEAU ELAN RESORT
R- **Architect:** Denis Griffiths. **Credit cards:** MC,VISA,AMEX. **Caddies:** No. **Golf carts:** Included in Green Fee. **Season:** Year-round. **High:** April/Oct. **On site lodging:** Yes. **Rental clubs:** Yes. **Metal spikes allowed:** Yes. **Range:** Yes (grass).

★★★½CHATEAU ELAN COURSE
6060 Golf Club Dr., Braselton, 30517, Barrow County, (770)271-6050, (800)233-9463, 45 miles NE of Atlanta.
Opened: 1989. **Holes:** 18. **Par:** 71/71. **Yards:** 7,030/5,092. **Course rating:** 73.5/70.8. **Slope:** 136/124. **Green fee:** $50/$70. **Reduced fees:** Weekdays, low season, resort guests, twilight. **Discount golf packages:** Yes. **Walking policy:** Walking at certain times. **To obtain tee times:** Call up to seven days in advance. Weekend tee times guaranteed with credit card.
Notes: Golf Digest School site.
Subscriber comments: Good service...A challenging track in good condition...Well-designed...Long par 3s from tips...The new Woodlands course is a great addition.
Special Notes: Also 9 hole par-3 walking course.

★★★★½LEGENDS COURSE
5473 Legends Dr., Braselton, 30517, Gwinnett County, (770)932-8653, (800)233-9463, 45 miles NE of Atlanta.
Opened: 1993. **Holes:** 18. **Par:** 72/72. **Yards:** 6,781/5,467. **Course rating:** 73.3/72.1. **Slope:** 133/126. **Green fee:** $125/$125. **Reduced fees:** N/A. **Discount golf packages:** No. **Walking policy:** Mandatory cart. **To obtain tee times:** Call up to 30 days in advance. Must be a property guest to book a tee time.
Notes: Golf Digest School site. Gene Sarazen World Open Championship 1994-97.
Subscriber comments: Great layout...Always in good shape...A must play...Best greens around...A true test but fun...Tough approach shots...Be sure to play sister course...Plays difficult even from the white tees.

GEORGIA

WOODLANDS COURSE
6060 Golf Club Dr., Braselton, 30517, Barrow County, (770)271-6050, (800)233-9463, 45 miles NE of Atlanta.
Opened: 1996. **Holes:** 18. **Par:** 72/72. **Yards:** 6,738/4,850. **Course rating:** 72.6/68.5. **Slope:** 128/123. **Green fee:** $50/$70. **Reduced fees:** Weekdays, low season, resort guests, twilight. **Discount golf packages:** Yes. **Walking policy:** Walking at certain times. **To obtain tee times:** Call up to seven days in advance. Weekend tee times guaranteed with credit card.
Notes: Golf Digest School site.

★★★CHATTAHOOCHEE GOLF CLUB
PU-301 Tommy Aaron Dr., Gainesville, 30506, Hall County, (770)532-0066, 50 miles N of Atlanta.
Opened: 1955. **Holes:** 18. **Par:** 72/72. **Yards:** 6,700/5,000. **Course rating:** 72.6/67.4. **Slope:** 127/113. **Architect:** Robert Trent Jones. **Green fee:** $14/$29. **Credit cards:** MC,VISA,AMEX. **Reduced fees:** Twilight, seniors, juniors. **Caddies:** No. **Golf carts:** $10. **Discount golf packages:** No. **Season:** Year-round. **High:** April-Sept. **On site lodging:** No. **Rental clubs:** Yes. **Walking policy:** Walking at certain times. **Metal spikes allowed:** Yes. **Range:** Yes (grass). **To obtain tee times:** Call three days in advance.
Subscriber comments: Traditional...Short but narrow...Nice views...Several right to left shots required..Friendly pro-shop staff...Large greens...Walk it.

★★★★CHEROKEE RUN GOLF CLUB
PU-90,000 Centennial Olympic Pkwy., Conyers, 30208, Rockdale County, (770)785-7904, 20 miles E of Atlanta.
Opened: 1995. **Holes:** 18. **Par:** 72/72. **Yards:** 7,016/4,948. **Course rating:** 74.9/70.0. **Slope:** 142/123. **Architect:** Arnold Palmer/Ed Seay. **Green fee:** $39/$55. **Credit cards:** All major. **Reduced fees:** Weekdays, twilight. **Caddies:** No. **Golf carts:** Included in Green Fee. **Discount golf packages:** Yes. **Season:** Year-round. **High:** March-Nov. **On site lodging:** No. **Rental clubs:** Yes. **Walking policy:** Walking at certain times. **Metal spikes allowed:** Yes. **Range:** Yes (grass). **To obtain tee times:** Call 7 days in advance.
Notes: Ranked 15th in 1997 Best in State.
Subscriber comments: A fun course with a few tricks...Friendly staff...Bent-grass greens in great condition...Hold your breath on 18...A difficult, hilly test of golf...Needs to mature...Not Arnie's best, but good enough to play again.

★★★½CHICOPEE WOODS GOLF COURSE
PU-2515 Atlanta Hwy., Gainesville, 30504, Hall County, (770)534-7322, 30 miles NE of Atlanta.
Opened: 1991. **Holes:** 18. **Par:** 72/72. **Yards:** 7,040/5,001. **Course rating:** 74.0/69.0. **Slope:** 135/117. **Architect:** Denis Griffiths. **Green fee:** $28/$28. **Credit cards:** MC,VISA,AMEX. **Reduced fees:** Twilight. **Caddies:** No. **Golf carts:** $10. **Discount golf packages:** No. **Season:** Year-round. **High:** April-Sept. **On site lodging:** No. **Rental clubs:** Yes. **Walking policy:** Unrestricted walking. **Metal spikes allowed:** Yes. **Range:** Yes (grass). **To obtain tee times:** Call three days in advance at 9 a.m.
Subscriber comments: Well-maintained course...Enjoyable layout...Nice pro shop with friendly personnel...Better be long and straight from the tips...Excellent twilight rates...Must think before each shot...Walk it.

★★CITY CLUB MARIETTA
PU-510 Powder Spring St., Marietta, 30064, Cobb County, (770)528-0799, 15 miles N of Atlanta.
Opened: 1991. **Holes:** 18. **Par:** 71/71. **Yards:** 5,721/4,715. **Course rating:** 67.3/67.5. **Slope:** 118/115. **Architect:** Mike Young. **Green fee:** $37/$46. **Credit cards:** MC,VISA,AMEX. **Reduced fees:** Weekdays, twilight, seniors, juniors. **Caddies:** No. **Golf carts:** Included in Green Fee. **Discount golf packages:** Yes. **Season:** Year-round. **High:** April-Aug. **On site lodging:** Yes. **Rental clubs:** Yes. **Walking policy:** Unrestricted walking. **Metal spikes allowed:** Yes. **Range:** Yes (grass). **To obtain tee times:** Call seven days in advance.

★★★★COBBLESTONE GOLF COURSE

PU-4200 Nance Rd., Acworth, 30101, Cobb County, (770)917-5151, 20 miles N of Atlanta.

Opened: 1993. **Holes:** 18. **Par:** 71/71. **Yards:** 6,759/5,400. **Course rating:** 73.1/71.5. **Slope:** 140/129. **Architect:** Ken Dye. **Green fee:** $34/$49. **Credit cards:** MC,VISA. **Reduced fees:** Weekdays, low season, twilight, seniors, juniors. **Caddies:** No. **Golf carts:** $10. **Discount golf packages:** No. **Season:** Year-round. **High:** March-Oct. **On site lodging:** No. **Rental clubs:** Yes. **Walking policy:** Walking at certain times. **Metal spikes allowed:** Yes. **Range:** Yes (grass). **To obtain tee times:** Call four days in advance at 7:30 a.m.

Subscriber comments: A challenging but fair golf course...Tight layout, too difficult from the tips...Rough is a killer...Bring all your clubs...Beautiful scenery around lake...Lots of trouble, water in play on seven holes...Fun course, but demanding. **Special Notes:** Formerly The Boulders Course at Lake Acworth.

★★★COVINGTON PLANTATION GOLF CLUB

10400 Covington Bypass SE, Covington, 30209, Newton County, (770)385-0064, 30 miles E of Atlanta.

Opened: 1996. **Holes:** 18. **Par:** 72/72. **Yards:** 6,906/4,803. **Course rating:** N/A. **Slope:** N/A. **Architect:** Desmond Muirhead. **Green fee:** $45/$55. **Credit cards:** MC,VISA,AMEX. **Reduced fees:** Twilight, seniors. **Caddies:** No. **Golf carts:** Included in Green Fee. **Discount golf packages:** No. **Season:** Year-round. **High:** March-May; Sept.-Nov. **On site lodging:** No. **Rental clubs:** Yes. **Walking policy:** Walking at certain times. **Metal spikes allowed:** Yes. **Range:** Yes (grass/mats). **To obtain tee times:** Call golf shop.

Subscriber comments: Challenging layout...Nice greens...Toughest par 3s in Georgia.

★★★½CROOKED CREEK GOLF CLUB

3430 Highway 9, Alpharetta, 30201, Fulton County, (770)475-2300, 20 miles N of Atlanta.

Opened: 1996. **Holes:** 18. **Par:** 72/72. **Yards:** 7,007/5,056. **Course rating:** 73.2/68.2. **Slope:** 137/111. **Architect:** Michael Riley. **Green fee:** $55/$66. **Credit cards:** MC,VISA,AMEX. **Reduced fees:** Twilight, juniors. **Caddies:** No. **Golf carts:** Included in Green Fee. **Discount golf packages:** No. **Season:** Year-round. **High:** May-Sept. **On site lodging:** No. **Rental clubs:** No. **Walking policy:** Mandatory cart. **Metal spikes allowed:** No. **Range:** Yes (grass). **To obtain tee times:** Call 5 days in advance for weekdays; call Thursday after 2 p.m. for weekends.

Subscriber comments: Great greens...Beautiful layout...Elevation changes require dramatic carries...Bring extra balls, your long stick and accuracy.

★★★EAGLE WATCH GOLF CLUB

3055 Eagle Watch Dr., Woodstock, 30189, Cherokee County, (770)591-1000, 25 miles N of Atlanta.

Opened: 1989. **Holes:** 18. **Par:** 72/72. **Yards:** 6,900/5,243. **Course rating:** 72.6/68.9. **Slope:** 136/126. **Architect:** Arnold Palmer/Ed Seay. **Green fee:** $40/$65. **Credit cards:** MC,VISA,AMEX. **Reduced fees:** Weekdays, twilight, seniors, juniors. **Caddies:** No. **Golf carts:** Included in Green Fee. **Discount golf packages:** No. **Season:** Year-round. **High:** June-Aug. **On site lodging:** No. **Rental clubs:** Yes. **Walking policy:** Mandatory cart. **Metal spikes allowed:** Yes. **Range:** Yes (grass). **To obtain tee times:** Call 7 days in advance.

Subscriber comments: Nice course but tough slopes...A good test from the tips...Excellent course, service...Lots of doglegs...The 18th is a great par 5...Course grows on you...Wide open, nice track.

★★★½EMERALD POINT GOLF CLUB AT LAKE LANIER ISLANDS

R-7000 Holiday Rd., Buford, 30518, Hall County, (770)945-8787, (800)768-5253, 35 miles NE of Atlanta.

Opened: 1989. **Holes:** 18. **Par:** 72/72. **Yards:** 6,341/4,935. **Course rating:** 70.1/68.3. **Slope:** 124/117. **Architect:** Joe Lee. **Green fee:** $20/$52. **Credit cards:** All major,Diners Club. **Reduced fees:** Weekdays, low season, twilight, seniors. **Caddies:** No. **Golf carts:** $15. **Discount golf packages:** Yes. **Season:** Year-round. **High:** April-Sept. **On site lodging:** Yes. **Rental clubs:** Yes. **Walking policy:** Mandatory cart. **Metal spikes allowed: Yes. Range: Yes (grass). To obtain tee times: Call 7 days in advance.

Subscriber comments: Great target golf...Beautiful and challenging...Some tough carries over water...Lake views on 13 holes...Solid par 5s...Some very interesting holes and great scenery.

Special notes: Formerly Lake Lanier Islands Hilton Resort.

★★★½FIELDS FERRY GOLF CLUB

PU-581 Fields Ferry Dr., Calhoun, 30701, Gordon County, (706)625-5666, 50 miles N of Atlanta.

Opened: 1992. Holes: 18. Par: 72/72. Yards: 6,824/5,355. Course rating: 71.8/70.5. Slope: 123/120. Architect: Arthur Davis. Green fee: $13/$25. Credit cards: MC,VISA. Reduced fees: Weekdays, low season, twilight, seniors, juniors. Caddies: No. Golf carts: $10. Discount golf packages: No. Season: Year-round. High: April-Oct. On site lodging: No. Rental clubs: Yes. Walking policy: Unrestricted walking. Metal spikes allowed: Yes. Range: Yes (grass/mats). To obtain tee times: Call 3 days in advance.

Subscriber comments: Best value around...Fun course to play...Beautiful links-style design...A real delight to play...The three finishing holes are as good as you'll find.

★★★½THE FIELDS GOLF CLUB

257 S. Smith Rd., LaGrange, 30240, Troup County, (706)845-7425, 30 miles N of Columbus.

Opened: 1990. Holes: 18. Par: 72/72. Yards: 6,650/5,000. Course rating: 71.4/67.4. Slope: 128/113. Architect: Butch Gill. Green fee: $11/$19. Credit cards: MC,VISA. Reduced fees: Weekdays, low season, twilight, seniors. Caddies: No. Golf carts: $9. Discount golf packages: Yes. Season: Year-round. High: March-Oct. On site lodging: No. Rental clubs: Yes. Walking policy: Walking at certain times. Metal spikes allowed: Yes. Range: Yes (grass/mats). To obtain tee times: Call monday a.m. prior to weekend.

Subscriber comments: Open and good for high handicapper...Great layout, very playable...You will use all of your clubs...Nice public course.

★★½FIELDSTONE COUNTRY CLUB

2720 Salem Rd. SE, Conyers, 30208, Rockdale County, (770)483-4372.
Call club for further information.

FOLKSTON GOLF CLUB

PU-202 Country Club Rd., Folkston, 31537, Charlton County, (912)496-7155, 35 miles N of Jacksonville.

Opened: 1958. Holes: 18. Par: 72/73. Yards: 6,033/4,776. Course rating: 67.9/66.4. Slope: 116/109. Architect: Ed Mattson. Green fee: $9/$13. Credit cards: MC,VISA. Reduced fees: Seniors. Caddies: No. Golf carts: $12. Discount golf packages: No. Season: Year-round. High: Jan.-April. On site lodging: No. Rental clubs: Yes. Walking policy: Walking at certain times. Metal spikes allowed: No. Range: Yes (grass). To obtain tee times: N/A.

★★★FOREST HILLS GOLF CLUB

PM-1500 Comfort Rd., Augusta, 30909, Richmond County, (706)733-0001, 140 miles W of Atlanta.

Opened: 1926. Holes: 18. Par: 72/72. Yards: 6,875/4,875. Course rating: 72.2/68.3. Slope: 126/116. Architect: Donald Ross. Green fee: $15/$22. Credit cards: All major. Reduced fees: Juniors. Caddies: No. Golf carts: $12. Discount golf packages: No. Season: Year-round. High: March-Nov. On site lodging: No. Rental clubs: Yes. Walking policy: Unrestricted walking. Metal spikes allowed: Yes. Range: Yes (grass). To obtain tee times: Call up to 7 days in advance.

Subscriber comments: One of the better public courses in area...Fun, traditional layout...Friendly staff...Straightforward course, easy to keep ball in play.

FORSYTH COUNTRY CLUB

PU-400 Country Club Dr., Forsyth, 31029, Monroe County, (912)994-5328, 20 miles N of Macon.

Opened: 1936. Holes: 18. Par: 72/72. Yards: 6,051/4,521. Course rating: 68.1/65.4.

Slope: 112/107. **Architect:** WPA. **Green fee:** $9/$11. **Credit cards:** None. **Reduced fees:** N/A. **Caddies:** No. **Golf carts:** $20. **Discount golf packages:** No. **Season:** Year-round. **High:** N/A. **On site lodging:** No. **Rental clubs:** Yes. **Walking policy:** Walking at certain times. **Metal spikes allowed:** Yes. **Range:** Yes (grass). **To obtain tee times:** No tee times.

★★FOX CREEK GOLF CLUB

PU-1501 Windy Hill Rd, Smyrna, 30080, Cobb County, (770)435-1000, 10 miles N of Atlanta.
Opened: 1985. **Holes:** 18. **Par:** 61/61. **Yards:** 3,879/2,973. **Course rating:** N/A. **Slope:** N/A. **Architect:** John LaFoy. **Green fee:** $22/$36. **Credit cards:** MC,VISA,AMEX,Diners Club, JCB. **Reduced fees:** Twilight, seniors, juniors. **Caddies:** No. **Golf carts:** Included in Green Fee. **Discount golf packages:** No. **Season:** Year-round. **High:** Spring/Fall. **On site lodging:** No. **Rental clubs:** Yes. **Walking policy:** Unrestricted walking. **Metal spikes allowed:** Yes. **Range:** Yes (grass/mats). **To obtain tee times:** Call up to 7 days in advance.
Special Notes: 7 holes are par 4, rest are par 3.

★★½FOXFIRE GOLF CLUB

1916 Foxfire Dr., Vidalia, 30474, Montgomery County, (912)538-8670, 75 miles W of Savannah.
Opened: 1992. **Holes:** 18. **Par:** 72/71. **Yards:** 6,118/4,757. **Course rating:** 69.3/67.5. **Slope:** 125/116. **Architect:** Jim Bivins. **Green fee:** $21/$25. **Credit cards:** MC,VISA. **Reduced fees:** Weekdays, seniors, juniors. **Caddies:** No. **Golf carts:** Included in Green Fee. **Discount golf packages:** Yes. **Season:** Year-round. **High:** March-Sept. **On site lodging:** No. **Rental clubs:** Yes. **Walking policy:** Walking at certain times. **Metal spikes allowed:** Yes. **Range:** Yes (grass). **To obtain tee times:** Call one day in advance.

★★½FRANCIS LAKE GOLF CLUB

PU-5366 Golf Dr., Lake Park, 31636, Lowndes County, (912)559-7961, 12 miles S of Valdosta.
Opened: 1973. **Holes:** 18. **Par:** 72/72. **Yards:** 6,458/5,709. **Course rating:** 71.4/70.1. **Slope:** 124/117. **Architect:** Williard C. Byrd. **Green fee:** $18/$22. **Credit cards:** MC,VISA. **Reduced fees:** Weekdays, resort guests, twilight, juniors. **Caddies:** No. **Golf carts:** Included in Green Fee. **Discount golf packages:** Yes. **Season:** Year-round. **High:** Jan.-March. **On site lodging:** No. **Rental clubs:** Yes. **Walking policy:** Walking at certain times. **Metal spikes allowed:** Yes. **Range:** Yes (mats). **To obtain tee times:** Call in advance.

★★★½GEORGIA NATIONAL GOLF CLUB

PU-1715 Lake Dow Rd., McDonough, 30252, Henry County, (770)914-9994, 30 miles S of Atlanta.
Opened: 1994. **Holes:** 18. **Par:** 71/71. **Yards:** 6,874/5,005. **Course rating:** 73.3/68.6. **Slope:** 132/117. **Architect:** Denis Griffiths. **Green fee:** $26/$47. **Credit cards:** All major. **Reduced fees:** Weekdays, resort guests, seniors, juniors. **Caddies:** No. **Golf carts:** Included in Green Fee. **Discount golf packages:** No. **Season:** Year-round. **High:** April-Sept. **On site lodging:** No. **Rental clubs:** Yes. **Walking policy:** Walking at certain times. **Metal spikes allowed:** Yes. **Range:** Yes (grass). **To obtain tee times:** Call 5 days in advance.
Subscriber comments: A challenging course but a lot of fun...Needs improvement...A memorable experience...Rolling and beautiful terrain...Not much trouble.

★★★½GEORGIA VETERANS STATE PARK GOLF COURSE

PM-2315 Hwy. 280 W., Cordele, 31015, Crisp County, (912)276-2377, 45 miles S of Macon.
Opened: 1990. **Holes:** 18. **Par:** 72/72. **Yards:** 7,088/5,171. **Course rating:** 72.1/73.5. **Slope:** 130/124. **Architect:** Denis Griffiths. **Green fee:** $15/$20. **Credit cards:** All major. **Reduced fees:** Weekdays, twilight, seniors, juniors. **Caddies:** No. **Golf carts:** $16. **Discount golf packages:** Yes. **Season:** Year-round. **High:** April-Sept. **On site lodging:** Yes. **Rental clubs:** Yes. **Walking policy:** Unrestricted walking. **Metal spikes allowed:** Yes. **Range:** Yes (grass). **To obtain tee times:** Tee times accepted daily.

Subscriber comments: Large greens in good condition...Rolling, Scottish-like fairways...Nice clubhouse and staff...Long and tough...Well-designed...Good value...Great state park golf.

★★★½GOLD CREEK GOLF CLUB

PU-1 Gold Creek Dr., Dawsonville, 30534, Dawson County, (770)844-1327.
Call club for further information.
Subscriber comments: Great new course...Fastest greens this side of Augusta National...Dramatic elevation changes...Hard for the average golfer...Too many blind shots and uphill holes...Superb conditions...Good course design.

★★★THE GOLF CLUB AT BRADSHAW FARM

PU-3030 Bradshaw Club Dr., Woodstock, 30188, Cherokee County, (770)592-2222, 30 miles N of Atlanta.
Opened: 1995. **Holes:** 18. **Par:** 72/72. **Yards:** 6,838/4,972. **Course rating:** 72.7/68.4. **Slope:** 134/116. **Architect:** Grant Wencel. **Green fee:** $25/$65. **Credit cards:** MC,VISA,AMEX. **Reduced fees:** N/A. **Caddies:** No. **Golf carts:** Included in Green Fee. **Discount golf packages:** No. **Season:** Year-round. **High:** March-Nov. **On site lodging:** No. **Rental clubs:** No. **Walking policy:** Mandatory cart. **Metal spikes allowed:** Yes. **Range:** Yes (grass). **To obtain tee times:** Call up to 7 days in advance.
Subscriber comments: Very hilly...Challenging layout...Needs time...Spectacular views on front nine...Great layout, huge greens...Good track, getting better.

★★★GOSHEN PLANTATION COUNTRY CLUB

1601 Goshen Clubhouse Dr., Augusta, 30906, Richmond County, (706)793-1168.
Opened: 1970. **Holes:** 18. **Par:** 72/72. **Yards:** 6,902/5,688. **Course rating:** 72.6/70.9. **Slope:** 130/125. **Architect:** Ellis Maples. **Green fee:** $27/$32. **Credit cards:** MC,VISA. **Reduced fees:** Weekdays, low season, twilight, seniors, juniors. **Caddies:** No. **Golf carts:** Included in Green Fee. **Discount golf packages:** No. **Season:** Year-round. **High:** March-Oct. **On site lodging:** No. **Rental clubs:** Yes. **Walking policy:** Walking at certain times. **Metal spikes allowed:** Yes. **Range:** Yes (grass). **To obtain tee times:** Call two days in advance. Members, seven days in advance.
Subscriber comments: Staff always helpful, great snack bar...New management company has made improvements...Very large and fast greens...Designed for a good iron player.

★★★½HAMILTON MILL GOLF CLUB

PU-1995 Hamilton Mill Pkwy., Dacula, 30211, Gwinnett County, (770)945-4653, 10 miles SE of Buford.
Opened: 1995. **Holes:** 18. **Par:** 72/72. **Yards:** 6,810/4,744. **Course rating:** 73.7/68.4. **Slope:** 137/116. **Architect:** Gene Bates/Fred Couples. **Green fee:** $42/$64. **Credit cards:** MC,VISA,AMEX. **Reduced fees:** Juniors. **Caddies:** No. **Golf carts:** Included in Green Fee. **Discount golf packages:** No. **Season:** Year-round. **High:** May-Sept. **On site lodging:** No. **Rental clubs:** Yes. **Walking policy:** Mandatory cart. **Metal spikes allowed:** Yes. **Range:** Yes (grass). **To obtain tee times:** Call up to 5 days in advance.
Subscriber comments: Great tough track, good practice area...Numerous doglegs and layups...Nice clubhouse amenities...Very hilly layout, good greens.

★★★½HAMPTON CLUB

R-100 Tabbystone, St. Simons Island, 31522, Glynn County, (912)634-0255, 70 miles N of Jacksonville, FL.
Opened: 1989. **Holes:** 18. **Par:** 72/72. **Yards:** 6,400/5,233. **Course rating:** 71.4/71.0. **Slope:** 130/123. **Architect:** Joe Lee. **Green fee:** $58. **Credit cards:** All major. **Reduced fees:** Resort guests, juniors. **Caddies:** No. **Golf carts:** $17. **Discount golf packages:** Yes. **Season:** Year-round. **High:** March-April. **On site lodging:** No. **Rental clubs:** Yes. **Walking policy:** Mandatory cart. **Metal spikes allowed:** Yes. **Range:** Yes (grass). **To obtain tee times:** Call 2 days in advance.
Subscriber comments: An entertaining track...Watch out for the bugs in May...Great test of golf...Beautiful marsh views with live oaks and Spanish moss.

★★★HARBOR CLUB

One Club Dr., Greensboro, 30642, Greene County, (706)453-4414, (800)505-4653, 70 miles SE of Atlanta.

Opened: 1991. **Holes:** 18. **Par:** 72/72. **Yards:** 7,014/5,207. **Course rating:** 73.7/70.2. **Slope:** 135/123. **Architect:** Tom Weiskopf/Jay Morrish. **Green fee:** $28/$57. **Credit cards:** MC,VISA, AMEX. **Reduced fees:** Weekdays, low season, resort guests, seniors, juniors. **Caddies:** No. **Golf carts:** $12. **Discount golf packages:** Yes. **Season:** Year-round. **High:** March-Oct. **On site lodging:** Yes. **Rental clubs:** Yes. **Walking policy:** Walking at certain times. **Metal spikes allowed:** Yes. **Range:** Yes (grass). **To obtain tee times:** Call 7 days in advance.

Subscriber comments: First-class operation...An outstanding course in a beautiful setting...Playable for all skill levels...Fair but testing.

★★★ HARD LABOR CREEK STATE PARK GOLF COURSE

PU-Knox Chapel Rd., Rutledge, 30663, Morgan County, (706)557-3006, 45 miles E of Atlanta.

Opened: 1967. **Holes:** 18. **Par:** 72/75. **Yards:** 6,437/4,854. **Course rating:** 71.5/68.6. **Slope:** 129/123. **Architect:** O.C. Jones. **Green fee:** $18/$22. **Credit cards:** All major. **Reduced fees:** Twilight, seniors, juniors. **Caddies:** No. **Golf carts:** $10. **Discount golf packages:** Yes. **Season:** Year-round. **High:** April-Oct. **On site lodging:** Yes. **Rental clubs:** Yes. **Walking policy:** Unrestricted walking. **Metal spikes allowed:** Yes. **Range:** Yes (grass). **To obtain tee times:** Call up to 14 days in advance.

Subscriber comments: Well-designed course...Good deal on golf...Look out for the deer...A tight, hilly layout in a wooded setting...Nice views...Glad I played it.

★★½ HENDERSON GOLF CLUB

PU-1 A1 Henderson Dr., Savannah, 31419, Chatham County, (912)920-4653, 16 miles S of Savannah.

Opened: 1995. **Holes:** 18. **Par:** 71/71. **Yards:** 6,650/4,788. **Course rating:** 72.4/67.7. **Slope:** 136/115. **Architect:** Mike Young. **Green fee:** $30/$40. **Credit cards:** MC,VISA,AMEX. **Reduced fees:** Weekdays, twilight, seniors, juniors. **Caddies:** No. **Golf carts:** Included in Green Fee. **Discount golf packages:** Yes. **Season:** Year-round. **High:** March-Oct. **On site lodging:** No. **Rental clubs:** Yes. **Walking policy:** Walking at certain times. **Metal spikes allowed:** Yes. **Range:** Yes (grass). **To obtain tee times:** Call 10 days in advance.

Subscriber comments: Good place to play...Nicely designed...Interesting front nine...A few difficult holes.

★★★½ THE HERITAGE GOLF CLUB

PU-4445 Britt Rd., Norcross, 30093, Gwinnett County, (770)493-4653. Call club for further information.

Subscriber comments: Toughest Slope rating around...Too difficult for average golfer...Target golf...Nice new course, fun to play...Watch out for the 18th.

★★★ HIGHLAND GOLF CLUB

2271 Flat Shoals Rd., Conyers, 30208, Rockdale County, (770)483-4235, 20 miles E of Atlanta.

Opened: 1961. **Holes:** 18. **Par:** 72/72. **Yards:** 6,817/5,383. **Course rating:** 72.7/71.0. **Slope:** 128/118. **Architect:** Neil Edwards. **Green fee:** $34/$44. **Credit cards:** MC,VISA. **Reduced fees:** Seniors, juniors. **Caddies:** No. **Golf carts:** Included in Green Fee. **Discount golf packages:** Yes. **Season:** Year-round. **High:** April-Nov. **On site lodging:** No. **Rental clubs:** Yes. **Walking policy:** Mandatory cart. **Metal spikes allowed:** No. **Range:** Yes (grass/mats). **To obtain tee times:** Call up to 5 days in advance.

Subscriber comments: Good track for short hitters...Management has improved service and attitude...Picturesque with lots of wildlife...Putted with deer on the green...Wide open, hard to lose a ball...Fairways too close together.

★★★ HOUSTON LAKE COUNTRY CLUB

2323 Highway 127, Perry, 31069, Houston County, (912)987-3243, 20 miles S of Macon.

Opened: 1966. **Holes:** 18. **Par:** 72/72. **Yards:** 6,800/5,100. **Course rating:** 71.8/70.0. **Slope:** 132/122. **Architect:** O. C. Jones. **Green fee:** $20/$30. **Credit cards:** MC,VISA,AMEX. **Reduced fees:** Juniors. **Caddies:** No. **Golf carts:** Included in Green Fee. **Discount golf packages:** Yes. **Season:** Year-round. **High:** N/A. **On site lodging:**

No. **Rental clubs:** Yes. **Walking policy:** Unrestricted walking. **Metal spikes allowed:** Yes. **Range:** Yes (grass/mats). **To obtain tee times:** Call golf shop.
Subscriber comments: Great place to play...Greens are always nice...New lake should be finished by '98...The 18th is a solid finishing hole...Relatively flat course...Challenging test.

★★★INNSBRUCK RESORT & GOLF CLUB
Bahn Innsbruck, Helen, 30545, White County, (706)878-2100, (800)642-2709, 65 miles NE of Atlanta.
Opened: 1987. **Holes:** 18. **Par:** 72/72. **Yards:** 6,748/5,174. **Course rating:** 72.4.
Slope: 136/118. **Architect:** Bill Watts. **Green fee:** $30/$40. **Credit cards:** MC,VISA,AMEX. **Reduced fees:** Low season, resort guests, twilight, seniors, juniors.
Caddies: No. **Golf carts:** Included in Green Fee. **Discount golf packages:** Yes.
Season: Year-round. **High:** April-Oct. **On site lodging:** Yes. **Rental clubs:** Yes.
Walking policy: Mandatory cart. **Metal spikes allowed:** Yes. **Range:** Yes (grass). **To obtain tee times:** Resort guests may call any time.
Subscriber comments: Nicely designed course...Fast greens, a lot of slope in fairways...Tough test but fair...Fun and creative holes...The 15th is a great par 3...Deer and wild turkeys roam the fairways.

★★INTERNATIONAL CITY MUNICIPAL GOLF COURSE
PM-100 Sandy Run Lane, Warner Robins, 31088, Houston County, (912)922-3892, 15 miles S of Macon.
Opened: 1957. **Holes:** 18. **Par:** 70/70. **Yards:** 5,900/4,900. **Course rating:** 66.4/64.4.
Slope: 112/106. **Architect:** Lew Burnette/Arnie Smith. **Green fee:** $5/$13. **Credit cards:** N/A. **Reduced fees:** Weekdays, seniors, juniors. **Caddies:** No. **Golf carts:** $7.
Discount golf packages: No. **Season:** Year-round. **High:** June-Aug. **On site lodging:** No. **Rental clubs:** Yes. **Walking policy:** Unrestricted walking. **Metal spikes allowed:** Yes. **Range:** Yes (grass). **To obtain tee times:** Reservations accepted for holiday and weekends only. Must have three or four players in group.

JEKYLL ISLAND GOLF RESORT
R-322 Captain Wylly Rd., Jekyll Island, 31527, Glynn County, (912)635-2368, 70 miles N of Jacksonville, FL.
Architect: Dick Wilson/Joe Lee. **Credit cards:** All major. **Reduced fees:** Twilight, juniors. **Caddies:** No. **Discount golf packages:** Yes. **Season:** Year-round. **High:** Feb.-April. **On site lodging:** No. **Rental clubs:** Yes. **Metal spikes allowed:** Yes.
★★★INDIAN MOUND COURSE
Opened: 1975. **Holes:** 18. **Par:** 72/72. **Yards:** 6,596/5,345. **Course rating:** 74.3/70.0.
Slope: 127/122. **Green fee:** $26/$26. **Golf carts:** $13. **Walking policy:** Unrestricted walking. **Range:** Yes (grass). **To obtain tee times:** May call anytime up to 1 year in advance.
Subscriber comments: Great place to play 'til you drop...54 holes with no waiting...Open and long...Well-managed and maintained...Excellent golf for golf vacation...Treated like longtime friends...Watch for alligators (saw four).
★★★½OLEANDER COURSE
Opened: 1964. **Holes:** 18. **Par:** 72/72. **Yards:** 6,679/5,654. **Course rating:** 72.8/72.6.
Slope: 128/124. **Green fee:** $26/$26. **Golf carts:** $13. **Walking policy:** Unrestricted walking. **Range:** Yes (grass). **To obtain tee times:** May call anytime up to 1 year.
Subscriber comments: A lovely weekend of golf at a reasonable rate...Best of Jekyll's courses...Island views...Wildlife everywhere...Fun to play...Exceptional condition...Bring bug spray...Good courses no matter what your skill.
★★★½PINE LAKES COURSE
Opened: 1968. **Holes:** 18. **Par:** 72/72. **Yards:** 6,802/5,742. **Course rating:** 72.2/71.9.
Slope: 130/124. **Green fee:** $26/$26. **Golf carts:** $13. **Walking policy:** Walking at certain times. **Range:** Yes (grass). **To obtain tee times:** May call anytime up to 1 year in advance.
Subscriber comments: Play moved very well...Good golf course but most difficult of Jekyll Island tracks...Tight layout...Friendly pro-shop staff...Long course for women.
OCEANSIDE COURSE
Beachview Dr., Jekyll Island, 31527, Glynn County, (912)635-2170, 70 miles N of Jacksonville, FL.
Opened: 1898. **Architect:** Walter Travis. **Holes:** 9. **Par:** 36/36. **Yards:** 3,298/2,570. **Golf**

carts: $14. **Walking policy:** Unrestricted walking. **Range:** No. **To obtain tee times:** May call anytime up to 1 year in advance.

★★★½ JONES CREEK GOLF CLUB
PU-4101 Hammond's Ferry Rd., Evans, 30809, Columbia County, (706)860-4228, 5 miles NW of Augusta.
Opened: 1986. **Holes:** 18. **Par:** 72/72. **Yards:** 7,008/5,430. **Course rating:** 73.8/72.4. **Slope:** 137/130. **Architect:** Rees Jones. **Green fee:** $21/$31. **Credit cards:** MC,VISA,AMEX. **Reduced fees:** Seniors, juniors. **Caddies:** No. **Golf carts:** $11. **Discount golf packages:** No. **Season:** Year-round. **High:** April-Aug. **On site lodging:** No. **Rental clubs:** Yes. **Walking policy:** Walking at certain times. **Metal spikes allowed:** Yes. **Range:** Yes (grass). **To obtain tee times:** Call on Friday for following week and weekend.
Subscriber comments: Nice layout, good greens...Expensive, but a nice place to play...Tight, tough and long...Beats me every time, but I love it...Hard on a hacker...It'll make you sweat...Errant balls lost easily.

★½ LAKE ARROWHEAD COUNTRY CLUB
L.A. Station 20, Waleska, 30183, Cherokee County, (770)479-5505, 55 miles NW of Atlanta.
Opened: 1975. **Holes:** 18. **Par:** 72/71. **Yards:** 6,400/4,468. **Course rating:** 71.2/66.3. **Slope:** 135/117. **Architect:** N/A. **Green fee:** $31/$39. **Credit cards:** All major,Diners Club. **Reduced fees:** Weekdays, resort guests, juniors. **Caddies:** No. **Golf carts:** Included in Green Fee. **Discount golf packages:** Yes. **Season:** Year-round. **High:** May-Aug. **On site lodging:** Yes. **Rental clubs:** Yes. **Walking policy:** Mandatory cart. **Metal spikes allowed:** Yes. **Range:** Yes (grass). **To obtain tee times:** Resort guests may reserve tee times at time of reservation; all others call two days in advance.

★★★½ LAKE BLACKSHEAR GOLF & COUNTRY CLUB
PU-2078 Antioch Church Rd., Cordele, 31015, Crisp County, (912)535-4653, 24 miles NE of Albany.
Opened: 1995. **Holes:** 18. **Par:** 72/72. **Yards:** 6,930/5,372. **Course rating:** 71.6/70.0. **Slope:** 129/120. **Architect:** Don McMillan/Ray Jensen/Don Marbury. **Green fee:** $15. **Credit cards:** MC,VISA. **Reduced fees:** N/A. **Caddies:** No. **Golf carts:** $9. **Discount golf packages:** No. **Season:** Year-round. **High:** Spring/Fall. **On site lodging:** No. **Rental clubs:** Yes. **Walking policy:** Walking at certain times. **Metal spikes allowed:** Yes. **Range:** Yes (grass). **To obtain tee times:** Call (912)535-4653.
Subscriber comments: Young course, will improve with age...Enjoyable for average golfer...Nice links-style layout.

★★½ LAKESIDE COUNTRY CLUB
PU-3600 Old Fairburn Rd., Atlanta, 30331, Fulton County, (404)344-3629, 10 miles W of Atlanta.
Opened: 1962. **Holes:** 18. **Par:** 71/71. **Yards:** 6,522/5,279. **Course rating:** 71.4/70.7. **Slope:** 127/121. **Architect:** George Cobb. **Green fee:** $20/$45. **Credit cards:** MC,VISA. **Reduced fees:** Weekdays, low season, twilight, seniors. **Caddies:** No. **Golf carts:** Included in Green Fee. **Discount golf packages:** Yes. **Season:** Year-round. **High:** March-May. **On site lodging:** No. **Rental clubs:** Yes. **Walking policy:** Mandatory cart. **Metal spikes allowed:** Yes. **Range:** Yes (grass/mats). **To obtain tee times:** Call up to 14 days in advance.
Subscriber comments: Traditional layout, narrow and short...Tight, tree-lined back nine...Fun course, nice people...Must fade or draw tee shot on several holes.

LAKEVIEW GOLF CLUB
510 Golf Club Rd., Blackshear, 31516, Pierce County, (912)449-4411, 100 miles NE of Savannah.
Opened: 1971. **Holes:** 18. **Par:** 72/72. **Yards:** 6,505/4,928. **Course rating:** 69.7/69.5. **Slope:** 113/113. **Architect:** N/A. **Green fee:** $15/$15. **Credit cards:** None. **Reduced fees:** N/A. **Caddies:** No. **Golf carts:** $8. **Discount golf packages:** No. **Season:** Year-round. **High:** July-Sept. **On site lodging:** No. **Rental clubs:** Yes. **Walking policy:** Unrestricted walking. **Metal spikes allowed:** Yes. **Range:** Yes (grass/mats). **To obtain tee times:** First come, first served.

★★★½LANDINGS GOLF CLUB
309 Statham's Way, Warner Robins, 31088, Houston County, (912)923-5222, 15 miles SE of Macon.
Opened: 1987. **Holes:** 27. **Architect:** Tom Clark. **Green fee:** $16/$23. **Credit cards:** MC,VISA,AMEX. **Reduced fees:** Weekdays. **Caddies:** No. **Golf carts:** $10. **Discount golf packages:** Yes. **Season:** Year-round. **High:** March-Dec. **On site lodging:** No. **Rental clubs:** Yes. **Walking policy:** Unrestricted walking. **Metal spikes allowed:** Yes. **Range:** Yes (grass). **To obtain tee times:** Members call 9 days in advance. Non members call 5 days in advance.
BLUFF/CREEK
Par: 72/73. **Yards:** 6,671/5,157. **Course rating:** 71.9/70.6. **Slope:** 130/118.
TRESTLE/BLUFF
Par: 72/74. **Yards:** 6,998/5,481. **Course rating:** 73.1/72.0. **Slope:** 133/119.
TRESTLE/CREEK
Par: 72/73. **Yards:** 6,819/5,174. **Course rating:** 72.6/71.8. **Slope:** 131/121.
Subscriber comments: All nines equal in play...Excellent practice area...A good course...The 14th is a killer...A nice pro shop...A bit pricey...Long layout...Good layout, well-kept greens...A good test of golf...Enjoyable course.

★★★LANE CREEK GOLF CLUB
PU-1201 Club Dr., Bishop, 30621, Oconee County, (706)769-6699, (800)842-6699, 8 miles S of Athens.
Opened: 1992. **Holes:** 18. **Par:** 72/72. **Yards:** 6,725/5,195. **Course rating:** 72.6/68.4. **Slope:** 134/115. **Architect:** Mike Young. **Green fee:** $27/$39. **Credit cards:** MC,VISA. **Reduced fees:** Weekdays, twilight, seniors, juniors. **Caddies:** No. **Golf carts:** Included in Green Fee. **Discount golf packages:** No. **Season:** Year-round. **High:** N/A. **On site lodging:** No. **Rental clubs:** Yes. **Walking policy:** Walking at certain times. **Metal spikes allowed:** Yes. **Range:** Yes (grass/mats). **To obtain tee times:** Call up to 7 days in advance.
Subscriber comments: Short but interesting golf course...Requires some thinking...Friendly staff...Course enjoyable for middle handicap player...Tough to find but worth the trip...Outstanding potential.

★★★LAURA WALKER GOLF COURSE
PU-5500 Laura Walker Rd., Waycross, 31503, Ware County, (912)285-6154, 68 miles N of Jacksonville.
Opened: 1996. **Holes:** 18. **Par:** 72/72. **Yards:** 6,719/5,536. **Course rating:** 71.9/66.6. **Slope:** 122/106. **Architect:** Steve Burns. **Green fee:** $17/$20. **Credit cards:** All major. **Reduced fees:** Weekdays, seniors, juniors. **Caddies:** No. **Golf carts:** $9. **Discount golf packages:** No. **Season:** Year-round. **High:** N/A. **On site lodging:** No. **Rental clubs:** Yes. **Walking policy:** Unrestricted walking. **Metal spikes allowed:** Yes. **Range:** Yes (grass). **To obtain tee times:** Call (915)285-6155.
Subscriber comments: Very enjoyable new course...Bring bug spray...Beautiful layout...A few years from maturity.

★★½THE LINKS GOLF CLUB
PM-340 Hewell Rd., Jonesboro, 30238, Fayette County, (770)461-5100, 3 miles E of Jonesboro.
Opened: 1991. **Holes:** 18. **Par:** 70/70. **Yards:** 6,376/4,398. **Course rating:** 69.4/64.7. **Slope:** 118/111. **Architect:** N/A. **Green fee:** $16/$21. **Credit cards:** MC,VISA. **Reduced fees:** Twilight, seniors. **Caddies:** No. **Golf carts:** $11. **Discount golf packages:** No. **Season:** April-Oct. **High:** N/A. **On site lodging:** No. **Rental clubs:** Yes. **Walking policy:** Walking at certain times. **Metal spikes allowed:** Yes. **Range:** Yes (grass). **To obtain tee times:** Call golf shop.
Subscriber comments: Greens have improved...Fun course to play, some good holes. **Special Notes:** Also have a 9-hole par-3 called The Wee Links.

★★LITTLE FISHING CREEK GOLF CLUB
PM-Highway 22 W., Milledgeville, 31061, Baldwin County, (912)445-0796, 35 miles E of Macon.
Opened: 1981. **Holes:** 18. **Par:** 72/73. **Yards:** 6,718/5,509. **Course rating:** 72.4/73.6. **Slope:** 121/121. **Architect:** N/A. **Green fee:** $7/$12. **Credit cards:** All major. **Reduced**

fees: Twilight, seniors, juniors. **Caddies:** No. **Golf carts:** $8. **Discount golf packages:** No. **Season:** Year-round. **High:** March-June. **On site lodging:** No. **Rental clubs:** Yes. **Walking policy:** Unrestricted walking. **Metal spikes allowed:** Yes. **Range:** Yes (grass). **To obtain tee times:** N/A.

★★½LITTLE MOUNTAIN GOLF COURSE
PU-1850 Little Mountain Rd., Ellenwood, 30049, Henry County, (770)981-7921, 15 miles SE of Atlanta.
Opened: 1969. **Holes:** 18. **Par:** 72/72. **Yards:** 5,771/4,832. **Course rating:** N/A. **Slope:** N/A. **Architect:** N/A. **Green fee:** $14/$20. **Credit cards:** N/A. **Reduced fees:** Twilight, seniors. **Caddies:** No. **Golf carts:** $20. **Discount golf packages:** No. **Season:** Year-round. **High:** April-Sept. **On site lodging:** No. **Rental clubs:** Yes. **Walking policy:** Unrestricted walking. **Metal spikes allowed:** Yes. **Range:** Yes (mats). **To obtain tee times:** Call golf shop.
Subscriber comments: Nice layout and friendly staff...Making effort to improve course...Short track, well-maintained, easy walking...I hope it stays a secret.

MAPLE CREEK GOLF COURSE
PU-1735 Cashtown Rd., Bremen, 30110, Haralson County, (770)537-4172, 40 miles W of Atlanta.
Opened: 1993. **Holes:** 18. **Par:** 70/70. **Yards:** 5,404/4,454. **Course rating:** 65.6/65.3. **Slope:** 114/112. **Architect:** N/A. **Green fee:** $10/$17. **Credit cards:** None. **Reduced fees:** Weekdays, low season, twilight, seniors. **Caddies:** No. **Golf carts:** $8. **Discount golf packages:** No. **Season:** Year-round. **High:** March-Oct. **On site lodging:** No. **Rental clubs:** Yes. **Walking policy:** Unrestricted walking. **Metal spikes allowed:** Yes. **Range:** No. **To obtain tee times:** N/A.

★★★MAPLE RIDGE GOLF CLUB
4700 Maple Ridge Trail, Columbus, 31909, Muscogee County, (706)569-0966.
Opened: 1993. **Holes:** 18. **Par:** 71/71. **Yards:** 6,652/5,030. **Course rating:** 72.2/68.9. **Slope:** 132/127. **Architect:** Mike Young. **Green fee:** $15/$22. **Credit cards:** MC,VISA,AMEX. **Reduced fees:** Weekdays, low season, twilight, seniors, juniors. **Caddies:** No. **Golf carts:** $13. **Discount golf packages:** No. **Season:** Year-round. **High:** April-July. **On site lodging:** No. **Rental clubs:** Yes. **Walking policy:** Unrestricted walking. **Metal spikes allowed:** Yes. **Range:** Yes (grass). **To obtain tee times:** Call or come in up to 7 days in advance for weekdays, or 2 days in advance for weekends and holidays.
Subscriber comments: A hilly, tight layout...Tough first hole...Greens severely sloped...Lots of houses on front, back nine winds through woods...Good staff, nice course.

★★★METROPOLITAN GOLF CLUB
300 Fairington Pkwy., Lithonia, 30038, De Kalb County, (770)981-7696, 10 miles SE of Atlanta.
Opened: 1967. **Holes:** 18. **Par:** 72/72. **Yards:** 6,030/5,966. **Course rating:** 74.2/74.8. **Slope:** 138/131. **Architect:** Robert Trent Jones. **Green fee:** $32/$43. **Credit cards:** MC,VISA,AMEX. **Reduced fees:** Weekdays, twilight. **Caddies:** No. **Golf carts:** Included in Green Fee. **Discount golf packages:** No. **Season:** Year-round. **High:** April-Sept. **On site lodging:** No. **Rental clubs:** Yes. **Walking policy:** Walking at certain times. **Metal spikes allowed:** Yes. **Range:** Yes (grass). **To obtain tee times:** Call five days in advance.
Subscriber comments: A good hard course...A little rough around the edges...Fast greens...Long layout demands smart course management...No gimmicks...Interesting layout.

★★½MYSTERY VALLEY GOLF COURSE
PU-6094 Shadowrock Dr., Lithonia, 30058, De Kalb County, (770)469-6913, 20 miles S of Atlanta.
Opened: 1965. **Holes:** 18. **Par:** 72/75. **Yards:** 6,705/5,928. **Course rating:** 71.5/67.9. **Slope:** 124/115. **Architect:** Dick Wilson/Joe Lee. **Green fee:** $16/$20. **Credit cards:** None. **Reduced fees:** Weekdays, seniors, juniors. **Caddies:** No. **Golf carts:** $10. **Discount golf packages:** No. **Season:** Year-round. **High:** March-Sept. **On site lodging:** No. **Rental clubs:** Yes. **Walking policy:** Unrestricted walking. **Metal spikes**

allowed: Yes. **Range:** Yes (grass). **To obtain tee times:** Call 1 day in advance for weekdays and 7 days in advance for weekends.
Subscriber comments: Nice variety of holes...Good use of sand traps and water...Heavily played...Hilly.

★★½NOB NORTH GOLF COURSE
PU-298 Nob N. Dr., Cohutta, 30710, Whitfield County, (706)694-8505, 15 miles S of Chattanooga, TN.
Opened: 1978. **Holes:** 18. **Par:** 72/72. **Yards:** 6,573/5,448. **Course rating:** 71.7/71.7.
Slope: 128/126. **Architect:** Ron Kirby. **Green fee:** $20/$20. **Credit cards:** MC,VISA,DISC. **Reduced fees:** Seniors, juniors. **Caddies:** No. **Golf carts:** $9.
Discount golf packages: No. **Season:** Year-round. **High:** March-Nov. **On site lodging:** No. **Rental clubs:** Yes. **Walking policy:** Unrestricted walking. **Metal spikes allowed:** Yes. **Range:** Yes (grass). **To obtain tee times:** Call 5 days in advance.
Subscriber comments: Good service...Tough track from the tips, nice greens...US Open rough during summer...Best value in the area...Well-designed layout...Must think about each shot.

★★NORTH FULTON GOLF COURSE
PM-216 W. Wieuca Rd., Atlanta, 30342, Fulton County, (404)255-0723.
Opened: 1935. **Holes:** 18. **Par:** 71/71. **Yards:** 6,570/5,120. **Course rating:** 71.8/69.5.
Slope: 126/118. **Architect:** H. Chandler Egan. **Green fee:** $14/$16. **Credit cards:** MC,VISA. **Reduced fees:** Weekdays, low season, twilight, seniors, juniors. **Caddies:** No. **Golf carts:** N/A. **Discount golf packages:** Yes. **Season:** Year-round. **High:** July.
On site lodging: No. **Rental clubs:** Yes. **Walking policy:** Unrestricted walking. **Metal spikes allowed:** Yes. **Range:** No. **To obtain tee times:** Call up to four days in advance.

★★½OAK GROVE ISLAND GOLF CLUB
100 Clipper Bay, Brunswick, 31523, Glynn County, (912)280-9525, 60 miles S of Savannah.
Opened: 1993. **Holes:** 18. **Par:** 72/72. **Yards:** 6,910/4,855. **Course rating:** 73.2/67.6.
Slope: 132/116. **Architect:** Mike Young. **Green fee:** $6/$20. **Credit cards:** All major.
Reduced fees: Weekdays, resort guests, twilight, seniors, juniors. **Caddies:** No. **Golf carts:** $11. **Discount golf packages:** Yes. **Season:** Year-round. **High:** April-Oct. **On site lodging:** No. **Rental clubs:** Yes. **Walking policy:** Mandatory cart. **Metal spikes allowed:** Yes. **Range:** Yes (grass). **To obtain tee times:** Public may call up to 14 days in advance.

★★★THE OAKS GOLF COURSE
11240 Brown Bridge Rd., Covington, 30209, Newton County, (770)786-3801, 30 miles E of Atlanta.
Opened: 1990. **Holes:** 18. **Par:** 70/70. **Yards:** 6,437/4,600. **Course rating:** 70.2/64.5.
Slope: 121/107. **Architect:** Michael Hirsch/Richard M. Schulz. **Green fee:** $25/$41.
Credit cards: All major. **Reduced fees:** Weekdays, low season, resort guests, twilight, seniors, juniors. **Caddies:** No. **Golf carts:** Included in Green Fee. **Discount golf packages:** Yes. **Season:** Year-round. **High:** April-Oct. **On site lodging:** No. **Rental clubs:** Yes. **Walking policy:** Walking at certain times. **Metal spikes allowed:** No. **Range:** Yes (grass). **To obtain tee times:** Call.
Subscriber comments: The 11th is a great par 3...Fast greens...Short layout, forces you to think...A fun little course.

★★★OLDE ATLANTA GOLF CLUB
5750 Olde Atlanta Pkwy., Suwanee, 30174, Forsyth County, (770)497-0097.
Opened: 1993. **Holes:** 18. **Par:** 71/71. **Yards:** 6,800/5,147. **Course rating:** 73.1/69.3.
Slope: 132/120. **Architect:** Arthur Hills. **Green fee:** $47/$58. **Credit cards:** MC,VISA, AMEX. **Reduced fees:** Twilight, seniors. **Caddies:** No. **Golf carts:** Included in Green Fee. **Discount golf packages:** No. **Season:** Year-round. **High:** April-Sept. **On site lodging:** No. **Rental clubs:** Yes. **Walking policy:** Walking at certain times. **Metal spikes allowed:** Yes. **Range:** Yes (grass/mats). **To obtain tee times:** Call 7 days in advance.
Subscriber comments: Play it from the tips...Good finishing hole...Friendly service...Some long carries to fairways.

★★★½ORCHARD HILLS GOLF CLUB

PU-600 E. Hwy. 16, Newnan, 30263, Coweta County, (770)251-5683, 33 miles SW of Atlanta.

Opened: 1990. **Holes:** 27. **Architect:** Don Cottle Jr.. **Green fee:** $39/$49. **Credit cards:** All major. **Reduced fees:** Weekdays, low season, twilight, seniors, juniors. **Caddies:** No. **Golf carts:** Included in Green Fee. **Discount golf packages:** Yes. **Season:** Year-round. **High:** April-May. **On site lodging:** No. **Rental clubs:** Yes. **Walking policy:** Walking at certain times. **Metal spikes allowed:** Yes. **Range:** Yes (grass). **To obtain tee times:** Call 7 days in advance.

LOGO/ROCK GARDEN
Par: 72/72. **Yards:** 7,002/5,052. **Course rating:** 73.4/68.4. **Slope:** 134/118.
ORCHARD/LOGO
Par: 72/72. **Yards:** 7,012/5,153. **Course rating:** 73.4/68.9. **Slope:** 131/116.
ROCK GARDEN/ORCHARD COURSE
Par: 72/72. **Yards:** 7,014/5,245. **Course rating:** 72.8/68.4. **Slope:** 132/118.

Subscriber comments: Good service...Wide open fun course...Nice links design, no trees...Slick greens...Plays extremely tough when wind blows...Best deal in town...Love the par 3s...Don't miss the fairway or you're in trouble.

★★★★OSPREY COVE GOLF CLUB

123 Osprey Dr., St. Marys, 31558, Camden County, (912)882-5575, (800)352-5575, 35 miles N of Jacksonville, FL.

Opened: 1990. **Holes:** 18. **Par:** 72/72. **Yards:** 6,791/5,263. **Course rating:** 73.0/71.1. **Slope:** 130/120. **Architect:** Mark McCumber. **Green fee:** $30/$35. **Credit cards:** MC,VISA,AMEX. **Reduced fees:** Juniors. **Caddies:** No. **Golf carts:** $12. **Discount golf packages:** Yes. **Season:** Year-round. **High:** Feb.-July. **On site lodging:** No. **Rental clubs:** Yes. **Walking policy:** Walking at certain times. **Metal spikes allowed:** Yes. **Range:** Yes (grass). **To obtain tee times:** Call up to one week in advance.

Subscriber comments: Excellent golf course but a bit pricey...Long distances between greens and tee boxes...A must play...Outstanding challenge...Immaculate conditions...Professional service...Can you drive it safely on 18?...Several difficult carries...A scenic beauty on East Coast...Some target golf over marsh.

★★★½PINE BLUFF GOLF & COUNTRY CLUB

PU-Hwy. 341 S., Eastman, 31023, Dodge County, (912)374-0991, 50 miles S of Macon.

Opened: 1994. **Holes:** 18. **Par:** 72/72. **Yards:** 6,499/5,065. **Course rating:** 70.6/69.1. **Slope:** 125/119. **Architect:** Tim Moore. **Green fee:** $8/$12. **Credit cards:** MC,VISA. **Reduced fees:** Twilight, seniors, juniors. **Caddies:** No. **Golf carts:** $8. **Discount golf packages:** No. **Season:** Year-round. **High:** March-May. **On site lodging:** No. **Rental clubs:** Yes. **Walking policy:** Walking at certain times. **Metal spikes allowed:** Yes. **Range:** Yes (grass). **To obtain tee times:** Call golf shop.

Subscriber comments: Relatively new, getting better...Not too crowded...Surprisingly good...Open front, tight back...Super friendly staff...Best kept secret in area.

★★★½PORT ARMOR RESORT & COUNTRY CLUB

R-One Port Armor Pkwy., Greensboro, 30642, Greene County, (706)453-4564, (800)804-7678, 50 miles E of Atlanta.

Opened: 1986. **Holes:** 18. **Par:** 72/72. **Yards:** 6,926/5,177. **Course rating:** 74.0/72.8. **Slope:** 140/131. **Architect:** Bob Cupp. **Green fee:** $50/$70. **Credit cards:** MC,VISA, AMEX. **Reduced fees:** Low season, resort guests. **Caddies:** No. **Golf carts:** Included in Green Fee. **Discount golf packages:** Yes. **Season:** Year-round. **High:** April-Oct. **On site lodging:** Yes. **Rental clubs:** Yes. **Walking policy:** Mandatory cart. **Metal spikes allowed:** Yes. **Range:** Yes (grass). **To obtain tee times:** Call golf shop.

Subscriber comments: Challenging, quality layout...Less crowded than Atlanta area...Memorable holes, good condition...Tough lakeside track, particularly the 10th hole...Professional service.

★★★½RENAISSANCE PINEISLE RESORT

R-9000 Holiday Rd., Lake Lanier Islands, 30518, Hall County, (770)945-8921, (800)468-3571, 45 miles NE of Atlanta.
Opened: 1973. **Holes:** 18. **Par:** 72/72. **Yards:** 6,527/5,297. **Course rating:** 71.6/70.6. **Slope:** 132/127. **Architect:** Arthur Davis/Ron Kirby. **Green fee:** $49/$59. **Credit cards:** All major. **Reduced fees:** Low season, twilight. **Caddies:** No. **Golf carts:** Included in Green Fee. **Discount golf packages:** Yes. **Season:** Year-round. **High:** April-Oct. **On site lodging:** Yes. **Rental clubs:** Yes. **Walking policy:** Walking at certain times. **Metal spikes allowed:** Yes. **Range:** Yes (grass/mats). **To obtain tee times:** Hotel guests may make tee times with confirmed reservation of room. Others call 7 days in advance.
Notes: Nestle LPGA World Championship.
Subscriber comments: Fun back nine...Beautiful layout, great views of lake...Recently remodeled...Hidden gem...Extremely tight, good test of skills...Lots of water...Several interesting holes.
Special Notes: Formerly Stouffer PineIsle Resort.

REYNOLDS PLANTATION

R-**Credit cards:** All major. **Reduced fees:** Weekdays. **Caddies:** No. **Golf carts:** $18. **Discount golf packages:** Yes. **Season:** Year-round. **On site lodging:** Yes. **Rental clubs:** Yes. **Walking policy:** Walking at certain times. **Metal spikes allowed:** No. **To obtain tee times:** Overnight guests may obtain tee times through reservations at (800)852-5885.

★★★★½GREAT WATERS COURSE

130 Wood Crest Dr. N.E., Eatonton, 31024, Putnam County, (706)485-0235, 70 miles N of Macon.
Opened: 1992. **Holes:** 18. **Par:** 72/72. **Yards:** 7,058/5,057. **Course rating:** 73.8/69.2. **Slope:** 135/114. **Architect:** Jack Nicklaus. **Green fee:** $75/$85. **High:** April-Oct. **Range:** Yes (grass).
Notes: Ranked 7th in 1997 Best in State. 1996, 1997 Andersen Consulting World Championship Regional Finals.
Subscriber comments: Great scenic layout...One of the best I've played...As good as it gets...One of Jack's best...Go for it on 18...Beautiful water holes...A must play...A miniature Augusta National.

NATIONAL COURSE

100 Linger Longer Rd., Greensboro, 30642, Greene County, (706)467-3159, 75 miles E of Atlanta.
Opened: 1997. **Holes:** 18. **Par:** 72/72. **Yards:** 7,015/5,292. **Course rating:** 72.7/69.5. **Slope:** 127/116. **Architect:** Tom Fazio. **Green fee:** $75/$85. **High:** April-Aug. **Range:** Yes (grass/mats).

★★★½PLANTATION COURSE

100 Linger Longer Rd., Greensboro, 30642, Greene County, (706)467-3159, 75 miles E of Atlanta.
Opened: 1987. **Holes:** 18. **Par:** 72/72. **Yards:** 6,698/5,162. **Course rating:** 71.7/69.1. **Slope:** 128/117. **Architect:** Bob Cupp/Fuzzy Zoeller/Hubert Green. **Green fee:** $65/$75. **High:** April-Aug. **Range:** Yes (mats).
Subscriber comments: As tough as it gets from the blues...Nice course.

★★★½RIVER'S EDGE GOLF COURSE

PU-40 Southern Golf Court, Fayetteville, 30215, Fayette County, (770)460-1098, 19 miles S of Atlanta.
Opened: 1990. **Holes:** 18. **Par:** 71/71. **Yards:** 6,810/5,641. **Course rating:** 72.9/69.9. **Slope:** 135/121. **Architect:** Bobby Weed. **Green fee:** $35/$49. **Credit cards:** MC,VISA,AMEX. **Reduced fees:** Weekdays, twilight, seniors, juniors. **Caddies:** No. **Golf carts:** Included in Green Fee. **Discount golf packages:** Yes. **Season:** Year-round. **High:** March-Oct. **On site lodging:** No. **Rental clubs:** Yes. **Walking policy:** Mandatory cart. **Metal spikes allowed:** Yes. **Range:** Yes (grass). **To obtain tee times:** Call 7 days in advance.
Notes: Public Links 1996.
Subscriber comments: Management runs a tight ship...Sloping, multilayer greens are tough...Narrow front nine...Watch out for the second hole...Good twilight rates.
Special Notes: Formerly Champions Club at River's Edge.

★★½RIVERPINES GOLF CLUB

PU-4775 Old Alabama Rd., Alpharetta, 30202, Fulton County, (770)442-5960, 20 miles NE of Atlanta.

Opened: 1993. **Holes:** 18. **Par:** 70/70. **Yards:** 6,511/4,279. **Course rating:** 71.3/64.7. **Slope:** 126/107. **Architect:** Dennis Griffiths. **Green fee:** $47/$53. **Credit cards:** MC,VISA,AMEX. **Reduced fees:** Twilight, juniors. **Caddies:** No. **Golf carts:** Included in Green Fee. **Discount golf packages:** Yes. **Season:** Year-round. **High:** April-Sept. **On site lodging:** No. **Rental clubs:** Yes. **Walking policy:** Walking at certain times. **Metal spikes allowed:** Yes. **Range:** Yes (grass/mats). **To obtain tee times:** Call on Monday to book for active week.

★★★½ROYAL LAKES GOLF & COUNTRY CLUB

4700 Royal Lakes Dr., Flowery Branch, 30542, Hall County, (770)535-8800, 35 miles NE of Atlanta.

Opened: 1989. **Holes:** 18. **Par:** 72/72. **Yards:** 6,871/5,325. **Course rating:** 72.0/70.4. **Slope:** 131/125. **Architect:** Arthur Davis. **Green fee:** $40/$47. **Credit cards:** MC,VISA,AMEX. **Reduced fees:** Weekdays, twilight, seniors, juniors. **Caddies:** No. **Golf carts:** Included in Green Fee. **Discount golf packages:** No. **Season:** Year-round. **High:** March-Sept. **On site lodging:** No. **Rental clubs:** Yes. **Walking policy:** Walking at certain times. **Metal spikes allowed:** Yes. **Range:** Yes (grass). **To obtain tee times:** Tee times required. Call 4 days in advance.

Subscriber comments: Wonderful scenery...Nice layout...Terrific greens, extremely quick...You must use every shot...Plenty of trouble...Rolling terrain, some target golf...Several memorable holes.

★★ROYAL OAKS GOLF CLUB

256 Summit Ridge Dr., Cartersville, 30120, Bartow County, (770)382-3999, 40 miles N of Atlanta.

Opened: 1978. **Holes:** 18. **Par:** 71/75. **Yards:** 6,409/4,890. **Course rating:** 70.0/71.0. **Slope:** 124/121. **Architect:** Kirby/Davis/Bingaman. **Green fee:** $27/$32. **Credit cards:** MC,VISA. **Reduced fees:** Weekdays, low season, twilight, seniors, juniors. **Caddies:** No. **Golf carts:** $10. **Discount golf packages:** Yes. **Season:** Year-round. **High:** April-Oct. **On site lodging:** No. **Rental clubs:** Yes. **Walking policy:** Walking at certain times. **Metal spikes allowed:** Yes. **Range:** Yes (grass/mats). **To obtain tee times:** Call 7 days in advance.

★★★½ST. MARLO COUNTRY CLUB

PU-7755 St. Marlo Country Club Pkwy., Duluth, 30136, Forsyth County, (770)495-7725, 25 miles N of Atlanta.

Opened: 1995. **Holes:** 18. **Par:** 72/72. **Yards:** 6,900/5,300. **Course rating:** 73.6/70.3. **Slope:** 137/121. **Architect:** Denis Griffiths. **Green fee:** $58/$70. **Credit cards:** MC,VISA,AMEX. **Reduced fees:** Weekdays, juniors. **Caddies:** No. **Golf carts:** Included in Green Fee. **Discount golf packages:** No. **Season:** Year-round. **High:** April-Oct. **On site lodging:** No. **Rental clubs:** Yes. **Walking policy:** Unrestricted walking. **Metal spikes allowed:** Yes. **Range:** Yes (grass/mats). **To obtain tee times:** Call 4 days in advance.

Notes: Ranked 10th in 1995 Best New Public Courses.

Subscriber comments: Greens in good shape...Several interesting holes...Condo front nine, solid back...Terrific par 3s, all signature holes...Plush conditions...A good test of golf...The 18th is a great finishing hole...Needs clubhouse.

★★★★ST. SIMONS ISLAND CLUB

PU-100 Kings Way, St. Simons Island, 31522, Glynn County, (912)638-5130, 4 miles E of Brunswick.

Opened: 1974. **Holes:** 18. **Par:** 72/72. **Yards:** 6,490/5,361. **Course rating:** 71.8/70.0. **Slope:** 133/124. **Architect:** Joe Lee. **Green fee:** $85. **Credit cards:** MC,VISA. **Reduced fees:** Low season, resort guests, juniors. **Caddies:** Yes. **Golf carts:** Included in Green Fee. **Discount golf packages:** No. **Season:** Year-round. **High:** March-April. **On site lodging:** No. **Rental clubs:** Yes. **Walking policy:** Walking at certain times. **Metal spikes allowed:** Yes. **Range:** Yes (grass/mats). **To obtain tee times:** Call starter or golf shop.

Subscriber comments: First class golf experience...Tight fairways...Quality condi-

tions...A very challenging course...Magnificent views...A bit pricey...A good resort course...One of my favorites.
Special Notes: Site of Golf Digest Schools.

SEA ISLAND GOLF CLUB
R-100 Retreat Ave., St. Simons Island, 31522, Glynn County, (912)638-5118, (800)732-4752, 50 miles N of Jacksonville, FL.
Green fee: $90/$125. **Caddies:** Yes. **Golf carts:** Included in Green Fee. **Discount golf packages:** Yes. **Season:** Year-round. **Walking policy:** Walking at certain times. **Metal spikes allowed:** Yes. **Range:** Yes (grass/mats). **To obtain tee times:** Call.

(GREAT SERVICE)

★★★½ RETREAT/MARSHSIDE
Opened: 1959. **Holes:** 18. **Architect:** Dick Wilson/Joe Lee. **Par:** 72/74. **Yards:** 6,550/5,331. **Course rating:** 69.5/71.2. **Slope:** 127/122. **Credit cards:** MC,VISA,Sea Island Card. **Reduced fees:** Low season, resort guests, twilight, juniors. **High:** N/A. **On site lodging:** Yes. **Rental clubs:** Yes.
Notes: Golf Digest School site.
Subscriber comments: Good course, service...A difficult test of golf...Seaside nine is the best...Stay at the Cloister.

★★★★ SEASIDE/PLANTATION
Opened: 1927. **Holes:** 18. **Par:** 72/74. **Yards:** 6,900/5,244. **Course rating:** 73.2/70.1. **Slope:** 134/121. **Architect:** Walter Travis/C.H. Alison/H.S. Colt/Rees Jones. **Credit cards:** MC,VISA,Sea Island Card. **Reduced fees:** Low season, resort guests, twilight, juniors. **High:** N/A. **On site lodging:** Yes. **Rental clubs:** Yes.
Notes: Golf Digest School site. Ranked 14th in 1997 Best in State.
Subscriber comments: Nice course, good service...Fun to play, beautiful backdrop...Incredible golf course...Take a caddie...Exceptional amenities...Best combination of four nines.

★★½ SEA PALMS RESORT
R-5445 Frederica Rd., St. Simons Island, 31522, Glynn County, (912)638-9041, (800)841-6268, 65 miles N of Jacksonvill, FL.
Opened: 1966. **Holes:** 27. **Architect:** George Cobb/Tom Jackson. **Green fee:** $35/$45. **Credit cards:** MC,VISA,AMEX. **Reduced fees:** Weekdays, low season, resort guests, twilight, juniors. **Caddies:** No. **Golf carts:** $16. **Discount golf packages:** Yes. **Season:** Year-round. **High:** Feb.-May. **On site lodging:** Yes. **Rental clubs:** Yes. **Walking policy:** Mandatory cart. **Metal spikes allowed:** Yes. **Range:** Yes (grass/mats). **To obtain tee times:** Call 7 days in advance. Hotel guest may call 30 days in advance.
GREAT OAKS/SEA PALMS
Par: 72/72. **Yards:** 6,350/5,113. **Course rating:** 71.1/69.3. **Slope:** 126/124.
TALL PINES/GREAT OAKS
Par: 72/72. **Yards:** 6,658/5,328. **Course rating:** 71.3/70.9. **Slope:** 128/119.
TALL PINES/SEA PALMS
Par: 72/72. **Yards:** 6,198/5,249. **Course rating:** 69.7/70.4. **Slope:** 124/125.
Subscriber comments: Nice course...Wind and water make it tough...Average conditions...Watch for OB stakes...Nice resort course...Friendly staff....Difficult in the wind.

★★★½ SHERATON SAVANNAH RESORT & COUNTRY CLUB
R-612 Wilmington Island Rd., Savannah, 31410, Chatham County, (912)897-1612.
Opened: 1927. **Holes:** 18. **Par:** 72/72. **Yards:** 6,876/5,328. **Course rating:** 73.5/70.6. **Slope:** 137/128. **Architect:** Donald Ross. **Green fee:** $30/$48. **Credit cards:** MC,VISA,AMEX. **Reduced fees:** Weekdays, low season, resort guests, twilight, seniors, juniors. **Caddies:** Yes. **Golf carts:** Included in Green Fee. **Discount golf packages:** Yes. **Season:** Year-round. **High:** March-Oct. **On site lodging:** No. **Rental clubs:** Yes. **Walking policy:** Walking at certain times. **Metal spikes allowed:** Yes. **Range:** Yes (grass/mats). **To obtain tee times:** Call up to 10 months in advance.
Subscriber comments: Simple, straightforward layout...Hope it stays a secret...Good conditions...Challenging...Lots of fun...Plenty of sand and water.

★★★ SKY VALLEY GOLF & SKI RESORT
R-One Sky Valley, Sky Valley, 30537, Rabun County, (706)746-5303, (800)437-2416, 100 miles N of Atlanta.
Opened: 1971. **Holes:** 18. **Par:** 72/72. **Yards:** 6,452/5,017. **Course rating:** 71.7/69.0.

Slope: 128/118. **Architect:** Bill Watts. **Green fee:** $25/$40. **Credit cards:** All major.
Reduced fees: Weekdays, low season, resort guests, twilight, seniors. **Caddies:** No.
Golf carts: Included in Green Fee. **Discount golf packages:** No. **Season:** Year-round.
High: April-Oct. **On site lodging:** Yes. **Rental clubs:** Yes. **Walking policy:** Walking at
certain times. **Metal spikes allowed:** Yes. **Range:** Yes (grass). **To obtain tee times:**
Call up to 20 days in advance.
Subscriber comments: Beautiful fall course...Fun layout for average player...A good
mix of hill and valley holes.

★★★½SOUTHBRIDGE GOLF CLUB
415 Southbridge Blvd., Savannah, 31405, Chatham County, (912)651-5455.
Opened: 1988. **Holes:** 18. **Par:** 72/72. **Yards:** 6,990/5,181. **Course rating:** 73.4/69.2.
Slope: 136/118. **Architect:** Rees Jones. **Green fee:** $30/$36. **Credit cards:** All major.
Reduced fees: Weekdays, low season, seniors. **Caddies:** No. **Golf carts:** Included in
Green Fee. **Discount golf packages:** No. **Season:** Year-round. **High:** April-May. **On
site lodging:** No. **Rental clubs:** Yes. **Walking policy:** Mandatory cart. **Metal spikes
allowed:** Yes. **Range:** Yes (grass). **To obtain tee times:** Call two weeks in advance.
Subscriber comments: Not a straight putt on the course...Tough layout...Wonderful, I
could play it every day...Professional staff...Longer than it looks...Lots of play.

★★★½SOUTHERNESS GOLF CLUB
4871 Flat Bridge Rd., Stockbridge, 30281, Rockdale County, (770)808-6000, 20 miles
E of Atlanta.
Opened: 1991. **Holes:** 18. **Par:** 72/72. **Yards:** 6,766/4,956. **Course rating:** 72.2/69.0.
Slope: 127/119. **Architect:** Clyde Johnston. **Green fee:** $25/$33. **Credit cards:**
MC,VISA,AMEX. **Reduced fees:** Twilight, seniors. **Caddies:** No. **Golf carts:** $12.
Discount golf packages: No. **Season:** Year-round. **High:** April-Sept. **On site lodging:**
No. **Rental clubs:** Yes. **Walking policy:** Mandatory cart. **Metal spikes allowed:** No.
Range: Yes (grass/mats). **To obtain tee times:** Call 5 days in advance.
Subscriber comments: Excellent links-style layout...Friendly service...Average condi-
tions...Nice views, fun place to play...Drive 'em straight...The 3rd is a great hole, but the
last three are the best...Challenging.

★½SPRINGBROOK PUBLIC GOLF CLUB
PM-585 Camp Perrin Rd., Lawrenceville, 30243, Gwinnett County, (770)822-5400, 35
miles NE of Atlanta.
Opened: 1963. **Holes:** 18. **Par:** 71/72. **Yards:** 6,000/4,738. **Course rating:** 68.0/67.1.
Slope: 120/113. **Architect:** Perrin Walker. **Green fee:** $34/$38. **Credit cards:**
MC,VISA. **Reduced fees:** Weekdays, twilight, seniors, juniors. **Caddies:** No. **Golf
carts:** Included in Green Fee. **Discount golf packages:** No. **Season:** Year-round.
High: April-Nov. **On site lodging:** No. **Rental clubs:** Yes. **Walking policy:** Walking at
certain times. **Metal spikes allowed:** Yes. **Range:** Yes (grass). **To obtain tee times:**
Call on Wednesday for weekends.

★★★STONE CREEK GOLF CLUB
R-4300 Coleman Rd., Valdosta, 31602, Lowndes County, (770)247-2527.
Opened: 1987. **Holes:** 18. Call club for further information.
Subscriber comments: Good shape for new course...A sleeper...Nice layout...Hard to
walk...Excellent in all respects.

STONE MOUNTAIN PARK GOLF COURSE
R-P.O. Box 778, Stone Mountain, 30086, De Kalb County, (770)498-5715, 12 miles E of
Atlanta. **Green fee:** $45. **Credit cards:** All major,Diners Club. **Reduced fees:** N/A.
Caddies: No. **Golf carts:** Included in Green Fee. **Discount golf packages:** Yes.
Season: Year-round. **High:** April-Oct. **On site lodging:** Yes. **Rental clubs:** Yes.
Walking policy: Mandatory cart. **Metal spikes allowed:** Yes. **Range:** Yes (grass/mats).
★★★LAKEMONT/WOODMONT COURSE
Opened: 1987. **Holes:** 18. **Par:** 72/72. **Yards:** 6,595/5,231. **Course rating:** 71.6/69.4.
Slope: 130/120. **Architect:** John LaFoy. **To obtain tee times:** Call Tuesday for follow-
ing weekend and holidays starting at 7:30 a.m. For weekdays call 7 days in advance.
Subscriber comments: One of the best public courses in Atlanta...Traditional
design...Mountain golf with a few blind approaches and tee shots...Scenic...Receives
lots of play...The first hole is a difficult start.

★★★STONEMONT COURSE
Opened: 1971. **Holes:** 18. **Par:** 72/72. **Yards:** 6,683/5,020. **Course rating:** 72.6/69.1. **Slope:** 133/121. **Architect:** Robert Trent Jones. **To obtain tee times:** Call on Tuesday for upcoming weekend starting at 7:30 a.m. Call 7 days in advance for weekdays. **Subscriber comments:** A nice overall experience...Great test...Beautiful in spring.

★★★½STONEBRIDGE GOLF CLUB
PM-585 Stonebridge Dr., Rome, 30165, Floyd County, (706)236-5046, (800)336-5046, 50 miles N of Atlanta.
Opened: 1994. **Holes:** 18. **Par:** 72/72. **Yards:** 6,816/5,130. **Course rating:** 72.8/64.6. **Slope:** 123/109. **Architect:** Arthur Davis. **Green fee:** $29/$37. **Credit cards:** MC,VISA,AMEX. **Reduced fees:** Weekdays, twilight, seniors, juniors. **Caddies:** No. **Golf carts:** Included in Green Fee. **Discount golf packages:** Yes. **Season:** Year-round. **High:** March-Sept. **On site lodging:** No. **Rental clubs:** Yes. **Walking policy:** Unrestricted walking. **Metal spikes allowed:** No. **Range:** Yes (grass/mats). **To obtain tee times:** Call up to 7 days in advance.
Notes: Ranked 19th in 1997 Best in State.
Subscriber comments: Management has made improvements...Plenty of pine trees.

★★SUGAR HILL GOLF CLUB
PU-6094 Suwanee Dam Rd., Sugar Hill, 30518, Gwinnett County, (770)271-0519, 35 miles NE of Atlanta.
Opened: 1992. **Holes:** 18. **Par:** 72/72. **Yards:** 6,423/4,207. **Course rating:** 70.7/65.3. **Slope:** 127/112. **Architect:** William Byrd. **Green fee:** $33/$43. **Credit cards:** MC,VISA. **Reduced fees:** Low season, twilight, seniors, juniors. **Caddies:** No. **Golf carts:** Included in Green Fee. **Discount golf packages:** No. **Season:** Year-round. **High:** April-Oct. **On site lodging:** No. **Rental clubs:** Yes. **Walking policy:** Walking at certain times. **Metal spikes allowed:** Yes. **Range:** Yes (grass/mats). **To obtain tee times:** Tee times taken 2 days in advance.
Special Notes: Spikeless encouraged.

★★★TOWNE LAKE HILLS GOLF CLUB
PU-1003 Towne Lake Hills E., Woodstock, 30188, Cherokee County, (770)592-9969, 25 miles N of Atlanta.
Opened: 1994. **Holes:** 18. **Par:** 72/72. **Yards:** 6,757/4,984. **Course rating:** 72.3/69.0. **Slope:** 133/116. **Architect:** Arthur Hills. **Green fee:** $39/$49. **Credit cards:** MC,VISA. **Reduced fees:** Low season, twilight. **Caddies:** No. **Golf carts:** Included in Green Fee. **Discount golf packages:** Yes. **Season:** Year-round. **High:** May-Oct. **On site lodging:** No. **Rental clubs:** Yes. **Walking policy:** Unrestricted walking. **Metal spikes allowed:** Yes. **Range:** Yes (grass). **To obtain tee times:** Call 4 days in advance.
Subscriber comments: Great new track...The 18th is the hardest par 5 I've played...A difficult test...Narrow fairways...Errant shots will find water...Greens won't hold.

★★★½UNIVERSITY OF GEORGIA GOLF CLUB
PU-2600 Riverbend Rd., Athens, 30605, Clarke County, (706)369-5739, (800)936-4833, 60 miles E of Atlanta.

Opened: 1968. **Holes:** 18. **Par:** 72/73. **Yards:** 6,890/5,713. **Course rating:** 73.4/74.0. **Slope:** 133/128. **Architect:** Robert Trent Jones/John LaFoy. **Green fee:** $10/$20. **Credit cards:** MC,VISA. **Reduced fees:** Weekdays, twilight. **Caddies:** No. **Golf carts:** $9. **Discount golf packages:** No. **Season:** Year-round. **High:** March-June. **On site lodging:** No. **Rental clubs:** Yes. **Walking policy:** Unrestricted walking. **Metal spikes allowed:** Yes. **Range:** Yes (grass). **To obtain tee times:** Call one day in advance for weekdays and Thursday after 1 p.m. for weekend.
Subscriber comments: Extremely testy from the tips...The 12th and 13th holes are tough par 5s...Design requires a variety of shots...Some tight and open holes.

★★★WALLACE ADAMS GOLF COURSE
PU-Hwy. 441 N., McRae, 31055, Telfair County, (912)868-6651, 75 miles SE of Macon.
Opened: 1965. **Holes:** 18. **Par:** 72/72. **Yards:** 6,625/5,001. **Course rating:** 70.8/69.1. **Slope:** 128/120. **Architect:** O. C. Jones. **Green fee:** $15/$20. **Credit cards:** MC,VISA. **Reduced fees:** Weekdays, resort

guests, seniors. **Caddies:** Yes. **Golf carts:** $14. **Discount golf packages:** Yes.
Season: Year-round. **High:** Spring/Fall. **On site lodging:** Yes. **Rental clubs:** Yes.
Walking policy: Unrestricted walking. **Metal spikes allowed:** Yes. **Range:** Yes (grass).
To obtain tee times: First come, first served.
Subscriber comments: A good mix of tough and easy holes...Staff folksy and friendly.

WESLYN HILLS
PU-1591 Springlake Smyrna Rd., Chatsworth, 30705, Murray County, (706)695-9300.
Call club for further information.

★★★★½WHITE COLUMNS GOLF CLUB
PU-300 White Columns Dr., Alpharetta, 30201, Fulton County, (770)343-
9025, 25 miles N of Atlanta.
Opened: 1994. **Holes:** 18. **Par:** 72/72. **Yards:** 7,053/6,015. **Course rating:** 73.6/69.0. **Slope:** 137/116. **Architect:** Tom Fazio. **Green fee:**
$70/$95. **Credit cards:** MC,VISA,AMEX. **Reduced fees:** N/A. **Caddies:**
No. **Golf carts:** Included in Green Fee. **Discount golf packages:** No. **Season:** Year-
round. **High:** March-Oct. **On site lodging:** No. **Rental clubs:** Yes. **Walking policy:**
Unrestricted walking. **Metal spikes allowed:** No. **Range:** Yes (grass). **To obtain tee
times:** Call golf shop.
Notes: Ranked 8th in 1997 Best in State; 6th in 1995 Best New Public Courses.
Subscriber comments: Beautiful golf course...Friendly service...You'll want to play this
one again...Hilly and tough to walk...Good conditions.

★★½WHITEPATH GOLF CLUB
PU-Rte 4, Box 281-C, Ellijay, 30540, Gilmer County, (706)276-3080.
Call club for further information.
Subscriber comments: Not an ordinary hole on the course...Some 100-yard drops.

★★★½WHITEWATER COUNTRY CLUB
175 Birkdale Dr., Fayetteville, 30214, Fayette County, (770)461-6545, 30 miles S of
Atlanta.
Opened: 1988. **Holes:** 18. **Par:** 72/72. **Yards:** 6,739/4,909. **Course rating:** 72.3/68.2.
Slope: 133/123. **Architect:** Arnold Palmer/Ed Seay. **Green fee:** $32/$42. **Credit cards:**
MC,VISA,AMEX. **Reduced fees:** Weekdays, low season, twilight, seniors, juniors.
Caddies: No. **Golf carts:** $12. **Discount golf packages:** Yes. **Season:** Year-round.
High: March-Oct. **On site lodging:** No. **Rental clubs:** Yes. **Walking policy:** Mandatory
cart. **Metal spikes allowed:** Yes. **Range:** Yes (grass). **To obtain tee times:** Call 3 days
in advance.
Subscriber comments: Lacks character...Good conditions...Will use all your
clubs...Requires some thought to score well...Tough but fun to play...Too many houses.

★★½WILLOWPEG GOLF CLUB
1 Clubhouse Dr., Rincon, 31326, Effingham County, (912)826-2092, 20 miles N of
Savannah.
Opened: 1988. **Holes:** 18. **Par:** 72/72. **Yards:** 6,800/5,250. **Course rating:** 72.4/69.1.
Slope: 127/123. **Architect:** Ward Northrup. **Green fee:** $18/$32. **Credit cards:**
MC,VISA,DISC. **Reduced fees:** Weekdays, low season, twilight, seniors, juniors.
Caddies: No. **Golf carts:** Included in Green Fee. **Discount golf packages:** Yes.
Season: Year-round. **High:** N/A. **On site lodging:** No. **Rental clubs:** Yes. **Walking pol-
icy:** Walking at certain times. **Metal spikes allowed:** Yes. **Range:** Yes (grass). **To
obtain tee times:** Call up to 7 days in advance.

★★★½WINDSTONE GOLF CLUB
9230 Windstone Dr., Ringgold, 30736, Catoosa County, (423)894-1231, 6 miles S of
Chattanooga.
Opened: 1990. **Holes:** 18. **Par:** 72/72. **Yards:** 6,626/4,956. **Course rating:** 71.7/66.8.
Slope: 127/108. **Architect:** Jeff Brauer. **Green fee:** $16/$23. **Credit cards:** All major.
Reduced fees: Low season, seniors. **Caddies:** No. **Golf carts:** $11. **Discount golf
packages:** No. **Season:** Year-round. **High:** April-Oct. **On site lodging:** No. **Rental
clubs:** Yes. **Walking policy:** Unrestricted walking. **Metal spikes allowed:** Yes. **Range:**
Yes (grass). **To obtain tee times:** Call 2 days in advance.
Subscriber comments: Several challenging holes...Straight game a must...Super staff.

★★ALA WAI GOLF COURSE
PM-404 Kapahulu Ave., Honolulu, 96815, Oahu County, (808)732-5274.
Opened: 1931. **Holes:** 18. **Par:** 70/70. **Yards:** 6,208/5,095. **Course rating:** 67.2/67.2.
Slope: 116/109. **Architect:** Donald MacKay/B.Baldock/R. Nelson. **Green fee:** $5/$40.
Credit cards: None. **Reduced fees:** Weekdays, seniors, juniors. **Caddies:** No. **Golf carts:** $14. **Discount golf packages:** No. **Season:** Year-round. **High:** April-Sept. **On site lodging:** No. **Rental clubs:** Yes. **Walking policy:** Unrestricted walking. **Metal spikes allowed:** Yes. **Range:** Yes. **To obtain tee times:** Call 7 days in advance at 6:30 a.m.
Notes: 1960 National Public Links Championship.

★★★★THE CHALLENGE AT MANELE
R-P.O. Box L, Lanai City, 96763, Lanai County, (808)565-2222.
Opened: 1993. **Holes:** 18. **Par:** 72/72. **Yards:** 7,039/5,024. **Course rating:** N/A. **Slope:** N/A. **Architect:** Jack Nicklaus. **Green fee:** $100/$150.
Credit cards: MC,VISA,AMEX. **Reduced fees:** Resort guests. **Caddies:** No. **Golf carts:** Included in Green Fee. **Discount golf packages:** Yes.
Season: Year-round. **High:** Nov.-Feb. **On site lodging:** Yes. **Rental clubs:** Yes.
Walking policy: Mandatory cart. **Metal spikes allowed:** Yes. **Range:** Yes (grass/mats).
To obtain tee times: Call golf shop.
Notes: Ranked 5th in 1997 Best in State.
Subscriber comments: Spectacular ocean views, excellent service, new clubhouse...Outstanding views, great course...Unforgetable experience...Take boat from Maui to Lanai and play Challenge...Great scenery, will play again.

DISCOVERY HARBOUR GOLF & COUNTRY CLUB
Naalehu, Hawaii County, (808)929-7353.
Call club for further information
Special Notes: Southernmost course in the US.

★★★½THE EXPERIENCE AT KOELE
R-730 Lanai Ave., Lanai City, 96763, Lanai County, (808)565-4653.
Opened: 1991. **Holes:** 18. **Par:** 72/72. **Yards:** 7,014/5,425. **Course rating:** 73.3/66.0. **Slope:** 141/123. **Architect:** Ted Robinson/Greg Norman. **Green fee:** $150. **Credit cards:** All major,JCB. **Reduced fees:** Twilight, juniors. **Caddies:** No. **Golf carts:** Included in Green Fee. **Discount golf packages:** Yes. **Season:** Year-round. **High:** Dec.-May. **On site lodging:** Yes. **Rental clubs:** Yes. **Walking policy:** Mandatory cart. **Metal spikes allowed:** Yes. **Range:** Yes (grass). **To obtain tee times:** Call 30 days in advance.
Notes: Ranked 15th in 1997 Best in State.
Subscriber comments: Great front nine, excellent service...Front nine outstanding, #8 greatest signature hole ever...Need guide, blind shots...Lovely highland course, doesn't look like Hawaii...Front nine more scenic, difficult and fun...Back nine on flat land.

★★★½GRAND WAIKAPU RESORT, GOLF & SPA
R-2500 Honoapiilani Hwy., Wailuku, 96793, Maui County, (808)244-7888, 4 miles S of Wailuku.
Opened: 1991. **Holes:** 18. **Par:** 72/72. **Yards:** 7,105/5,425. **Course rating:** 74.7/68.6. **Slope:** 139/126. **Architect:** Ted Robinson. **Green fee:** $45/$100. **Credit cards:** MC,VISA,AMEX,Diners Club/JCB.
Reduced fees: Resort guests. **Caddies:** Yes. **Golf carts:** Included in Green Fee.
Discount golf packages: No. **Season:** Year-round. **High:** Jan.-April. **On site lodging:** No. **Rental clubs:** Yes. **Walking policy:** Mandatory cart. **Metal spikes allowed:** Yes.
Range: Yes (grass). **To obtain tee times:** Call up to 1 year in advance.
Subscriber comments: The most beautiful course I have ever seen...Incredible clubhouse, winds are deadly...Good place to work on your wind game...Simply wonderful.

★★★★HAPUNA GOLF COURSE
R-62-100 Kauna'oa Dr., Kamuela, 96743, Hawaii County, (808)880-3000, 34 miles S of Kailua-Kona.
Opened: 1992. **Holes:** 18. **Par:** 72/72. **Yards:** 6,875/5,067. **Course rating:** 72.1/63.9. **Slope:** 134/117. **Architect:** Arnold Palmer/Ed Seay.
Green fee: $80/$130. **Credit cards:** MC,VISA,AMEX,JCB, Carte

Blanche. **Reduced fees:** Resort guests, juniors. **Caddies:** No. **Golf carts:** $20.
Discount golf packages: Yes. **Season:** Year-round. **High:** Nov.-April. **On site lodging:** Yes. **Rental clubs:** Yes. **Walking policy:** Mandatory cart. **Metal spikes allowed:** Yes.
Range: Yes (grass). **To obtain tee times:** Guests may call 4 days in advance. Off-property guests 2 days in advance.
Notes: Ranked 11th in 1997 Best in State.
Subscriber comments: Beautiful views, outstanding course...Enjoyed it better the second time...Ball leaves fairway too easily...Great layout, thank you Arnie...Fun golf course if hitting straight...Wild and relaxing...Requires too much local knowledge.

HAWAII KAI GOLF COURSE

PU-8902 Kalanianaole Hwy., Honolulu, 96825, Oahu County, (808)395-2358, 10 miles E of Waikiki. **Credit cards:** MC,VISA,AMEX,JCB. **Caddies:** No. **Golf carts:** Included in Green Fee. **Discount golf packages:** No. **Season:** Year-round. **High:** Year-round. **On site lodging:** No. **Rental clubs:** Yes. **Metal spikes allowed:** Yes. **Range:** Yes (grass). **To obtain tee times:** Call or Fax request.

★★★CHAMPIONSHIP COURSE

Opened: 1973. **Holes:** 18. **Par:** 72/72. **Yards:** 6,614/5,591. **Course rating:** 71.4/72.7.
Slope: 127/124. **Architect:** William F. Bell. **Green fee:** $80/$100. **Reduced fees:** Weekdays, twilight. **Walking policy:** Mandatory cart.
Subscriber comments: Very windy...A very nice experience.

EXECUTIVE COURSE

Opened: 1950. **Holes:** 18. **Par:** 55/55. **Yards:** 2,386/2,094. **Course rating:** N/A. **Slope:** N/A. **Architect:** Robert Trent Jones. **Green fee:** $28/$33. **Reduced fees:** Weekdays, twilight, juniors. **Walking policy:** Unrestricted walking.

★★½HAWAII PRINCE GOLF CLUB

R-91-1200 Fort Weaver Rd., Ewa Beach, 96706, Oahu County, (808)944-4567, 20 miles W of Honolulu.
Opened: 1992. **Holes:** 27. **Architect:** Arnold Palmer/Ed Seay. **Green fee:** $50/$135.
Credit cards: MC,VISA,AMEX,Diners Club, JCB. **Reduced fees:** Weekdays, resort guests, twilight, seniors, juniors. **Caddies:** No. **Golf carts:** Included in Green Fee.
Discount golf packages: Yes. **Season:** Year-round. **High:** Dec.-Feb. **On site lodging:** No. **Rental clubs:** Yes. **Walking policy:** Mandatory cart. **Metal spikes allowed:** Yes.
Range: Yes (grass). **To obtain tee times:** N/A.

A/B
Par: 72/72. **Yards:** 7,117/5,275. **Course rating:** 74.2/70.4. **Slope:** 131/120.
A/C
Par: 72/72. **Yards:** 7,166/5,300. **Course rating:** 74.4/69.9. **Slope:** 134/118.
B/C
Par: 72/72. **Yards:** 7,255/5,205. **Course rating:** 75.0/69.5. **Slope:** 132/117.

HILO MUNICIPAL GOLF COURSE

PM-340 Haihai St., Hilo, 96720, Hawaii County, (808)959-9601, 3 miles S of Hilo.
Opened: 1950. **Holes:** 18. **Par:** 71/71. **Yards:** 6,325/5,034. **Course rating:** 70.4/69.1.
Slope: 121/114. **Architect:** Willard Wilkinson. **Green fee:** $20/$25. **Credit cards:** N/A.
Reduced fees: Weekdays. **Caddies:** No. **Golf carts:** $14. **Discount golf packages:** No. **Season:** Year-round. **High:** N/A. **On site lodging:** No. **Rental clubs:** No. **Walking policy:** Unrestricted walking. **Metal spikes allowed:** Yes. **Range:** Yes (mats). **To obtain tee times:** Call starter at (808)959-7711.

★★★★½HUALALAI GOLF CLUB

R-Mile Marker 87, Queen Kaahumanu Hwy., Kailua Kona, 96745, Hawaii County, (808)325-8480, 15 miles N of Kona.
Opened: 1996. **Holes:** 18. **Par:** 72/72. **Yards:** 7,117/5,374. **Course rating:** 75.7/70.4.
Slope: 131/118. **Architect:** Jack Nicklaus. **Green fee:** $110. **Credit cards:** All major,JCB. **Reduced fees:** Juniors. **Caddies:** Yes. **Golf carts:** Included in Green Fee.
Discount golf packages: Yes. **Season:** Year-round. **High:** Oct.-May. **On site lodging:** Yes. **Rental clubs:** Yes. **Walking policy:** Unrestricted walking. **Metal spikes allowed:** Yes. **Range:** Yes (grass). **To obtain tee times:** Play is limited to guests of Four Seasons Hualalai and homeowners. More than 7 days in advance call hotel reservations at (808)325-8108. Within 7 days call golf shop at (808)325-8480.

Notes: Senior Tour: 1997 Mastercard Championship.
Subscriber comments: A lot of fun...Lots of fun and very fair...Outstanding practice facilty and lodging and food...Good Nicklaus resort course, but there are better.

KAANAPALI GOLF COURSES

R-Kaanapali Resort, Lahaina, 96761, Maui County, (808)661-3691, (800)665-4742, 5 miles N of Historic Lahaina Town.
Credit cards: MC,VISA,AMEX,JCB. **Reduced fees:** Low season, resort guests, twilight. **Caddies:** No. **Golf carts:** Included in Green Fee. **Discount golf packages:** Yes. **Season:** Year-round. **High:** Dec.-April. **On site lodging:** Yes. **Rental clubs:** Yes. **Walking policy:** Mandatory cart. **Metal spikes allowed:** Yes. **Range:** Yes (grass/mats). **To obtain tee times:** Resort guests call 4 days in advance. Nonguests call 2 days in advance.

★★★½NORTH COURSE

Opened: 1963. **Holes:** 18. **Par:** 71/72. **Yards:** 6,994/5,417. **Course rating:** 72.8/71.1. **Slope:** 134/123. **Architect:** Robert Trent Jones. **Green fee:** $100/$120. **Credit cards:** MC,VISA,AMEX,JCB. **Reduced fees:** Low season, resort guests, twilight. **Caddies:** No. **Golf carts:** Included in Green Fee. **Discount golf packages:** Yes. **Season:** Year-round. **High:** Dec.-April. **On site lodging:** Yes. **Rental clubs:** Yes. **Walking policy:** Mandatory cart. **Metal spikes allowed:** Yes. **Range:** Yes (grass/mats). **To obtain tee times:** Resort guests call 4 days in advance. Nonguests 2 days in advance.
Notes: 1964 Canada Cup; 1982-85 The Women's Kemper; 1996, 1997 Senior PGA Tour Kaanapali Classic.
Subscriber comments: Learn to hit a low draw...One of Maui's best...Incredible scenery...Somewhat flat but enjoyable...Tourist trap!...Mature course.

★★★SOUTH COURSE

Opened: 1976. **Holes:** 18. **Par:** 71/71. **Yards:** 6,555/5,485. **Course rating:** 70.7/69.8. **Slope:** 127/120. **Architect:** Jack Snyder. **Green fee:** $100/$120.
Subscriber comments: Great course, lot of fun...Fantastic view, world class golf course...Enjoyed playing both courses...View was awesome, course was great.

★★★½KALUAKOI GOLF COURSE

R-P.O. Box 26, Maunaloa, 96770, Molokai County, (808)552-2739, (800)435-7208, 20 miles E of Kaunakakai.
Opened: 1977. **Holes:** 18. **Par:** 72/72. **Yards:** 6,600/5,461. **Course rating:** 72.3/71.4. **Slope:** 129/119. **Architect:** Ted Robinson. **Green fee:** $55/$75. **Credit cards:** All major,JCB, Diners Club. **Reduced fees:** Low season, resort guests, twilight, juniors. **Caddies:** No. **Golf carts:** Included in Green Fee. **Discount golf packages:** Yes. **Season:** Year-round. **High:** Dec.-March. **On site lodging:** Yes. **Rental clubs:** Yes. **Walking policy:** Mandatory cart. **Metal spikes allowed:** Yes. **Range:** Yes (grass). **To obtain tee times:** Call 30 days in advance. Groups of 16 and over may call up to 1 year in advance.
Subscriber comments: Five holes on ocean front...Hidden on Molokai, exceptional scenery, great challenge...Tough if windy, but fair and fun.

★★★KANEOHE KLIPPER GOLF CLUB

Kaneohe Marines Corps Air Station, Kanehoe Bay, 96863, Oahu County, (808)254-2107, 15 miles N of Waikiki.
Opened: 1948. **Holes:** 18. **Par:** 72/71. **Yards:** 6,739/5,575. **Course rating:** 70.9/76.3. **Slope:** 128/133. **Architect:** William P. Bell. **Green fee:** $8/$35. **Credit cards:** N/A. **Reduced fees:** N/A. **Caddies:** No. **Golf carts:** N/A. **Discount golf packages:** No. **Season:** Year-round. **High:** May-June. **On site lodging:** No. **Rental clubs:** No. **Walking policy:** Unrestricted walking. **Metal spikes allowed:** Yes. **Range:** Yes. **To obtain tee times:** Active duty MCBH may call 6 days in advance. Active duty other may call 4 days in advance. Retired military may call 3 days in advance.
Subscriber comments: Nice enough, not championship caliber...Challenging, great back nine...Beautiful course on Oahu. Holes 13, 14, 15 run right along the ocean.

KAPALUA GOLF CLUB

R- 300 Kapalua Dr., Kapalua, 96761, Maui County, 8 miles N of Lahaina. **Credit cards:** All major,Diners Club, JCB. **Reduced fees:** Resort guests, twilight, juniors. **Caddies:** Yes. **Golf carts:** Included in Green Fee. **Discount golf packages:** Yes. **Season:** Year-round. **High:** Dec.-March. **On site lodging:** Yes. **Rental clubs:** Yes. **Walking policy:** Walking at certain times. **Metal spikes allowed:** Yes.

★★★★THE BAY COURSE

(808)669-8820.

Opened: 1975. **Holes:** 18. **Par:** 72/72. **Yards:** 6,600/5,124. **Course rating:** 71.7/69.6. **Slope:** 138/121. **Architect:** Frank Duane/Arnold Palmer. **Green fee:** $85/$130. **Range:** Yes (grass). **To obtain tee times:** Resort guests may reserve tee time 7 days in advance. Nonguests call 4 days in advance.

Notes: Ranked 13th in 1997 Best in State. 1981-1997 PGA Tour Lincoln Mercury Kapalua International; The World Cup; The Nissan Cup.

Subscriber comments: First class golf!...Best ocean views in Maui...Beautiful and forgiving layout...Gorgeous vistas...Playable for any handicap...Great par 3 over ocean...Whale watching and golf at the same time, terrific...Paradise.

★★★★½THE PLANTATION COURSE

(808)669-8877.

Opened: 1991. **Holes:** 18. **Par:** 73/73. **Yards:** 7,263/5,627. **Course rating:** 75.2/73.2. **Slope:** 142/129. **Architect:** Bill Coore/Ben Crenshaw. **Green fee:** $90/$140. **Range:** Yes (grass). **To obtain tee times:** Resort guests may reserve up to 7 days in advance. Nonguests call 4 days in advance.

Notes: Ranked 4th in 1997 Best in State. 1981-1997 PGA Tour Lincoln Mercury Kapalua International;.

Subscriber comments: Challenging and beautiful. Putts break to ocean...Hell during trade winds...Great course, wonderful views...A true test...Bring your knockdown shots!...The expansive fairways and green complexes were reminiscent of Augusta.

★★★½THE VILLAGE COURSE

(808)669-8835.

Opened: 1980. **Holes:** 18. **Par:** 71/71. **Yards:** 6,632/5,134. **Course rating:** 73.3/70.9. **Slope:** 139/122. **Architect:** Arnold Palmer/Ed Seay. **Green fee:** $85/$130. **Range:** No. **To obtain tee times:** Resort guests call 7 days in advance. Nonguests call 4 days in advance.

Subscriber comments: Beautiful course, average in challenge...A great course that doesn't get the attention of the other two Kapalua courses...Inland course, some views pleasant, not memorable...Beautiful, lots of fun...Very hilly...No houses, condos!

KAUAI LAGOONS

R-3351 Hoolaulea Way, Lihue, 96766, Kauai County, (808)241-6000, (800)634-6400. **Opened:** 1988. **Architect:** Jack Nicklaus. **Credit cards:** MC,VISA,AMEX,Diners Club. **Caddies:** No. **Golf carts:** Included in Green Fee. **Discount golf packages:** Yes. **Season:** Year-round. **High:** Jan.-March/Aug. **On site lodging:** Yes. **Rental clubs:** Yes. **Metal spikes allowed:** Yes. **Range:** Yes (grass). **To obtain tee times:** Call up to 30 days in advance.

★★★★½KIELE COURSE

Holes: 18. **Par:** 72/72. **Yards:** 7,070/5,417. **Course rating:** 73.7/66.5. **Slope:** 137/123. **Green fee:** $145. **Reduced fees:** Resort guests, juniors. **Walking policy:** Mandatory cart.

Notes: Ranked 7th in 1997 Best in State. 1991 PGA Tour Grand Slam of Golf.

Subscriber comments: Beautiful test, great resort...Beautiful course on ocean. Some tough holes but playable...Ocean views, wild animals a plus, every hole a beautiful painting...Jack outdid himself!...Strong layout. Wonderful views, a veritable garden.

★★★½LAGOONS COURSE

Holes: 18. **Par:** 72/72. **Yards:** 6,942/5,607. **Course rating:** 72.8/67.0. **Slope:** 135/116. **Green fee:** $59/$100. **Reduced fees:** Resort guests, twilight, juniors. **Walking policy:** Walking at certain times.

Subscriber comments: Great fun, a few buried elephants on greens...Very playable...Nice, very pretty and scenic holes, but not the challenge of sister course...Not as good as Kiele course...Every hole is different.

★★½KIAHUNA GOLF CLUB
R-2545 Kiahuna Plantation Dr., Poipu, 96756, Kauai County, (808)742-9595, 15 miles S of Lihue.
Opened: 1983. **Holes:** 18. **Par:** 70/70. **Yards:** 6,353/5,631. **Course rating:** 69.7/71.4. **Slope:** 128/119. **Architect:** Robert Trent Jones Jr.. **Green fee:** $37/$60. **Credit cards:** All major. **Reduced fees:** Weekdays, low season, resort guests, twilight. **Caddies:** No. **Golf carts:** Included in Green Fee. **Discount golf packages:** No. **Season:** Year-round. **High:** Nov.-March. **On site lodging:** No. **Rental clubs:** Yes. **Walking policy:** Mandatory cart. **Metal spikes allowed:** Yes. **Range:** Yes (grass). **To obtain tee times:** Call 1 day in advance.
Subscriber comments: Located next to sugar cane...Tight, short course...OK.

★★★½KO OLINA GOLF CLUB
R-92-1220 Aliinui Dr., Kapolei, 96707, Oahu County, (808)676-5300, 20 miles W of Honolulu.
Opened: 1990. **Holes:** 18. **Par:** 72/72. **Yards:** 6,867/5,392. **Course rating:** 72.8/71.3. **Slope:** 137/125. **Architect:** Ted Robinson. **Green fee:** $95/$145. **Credit cards:** All major,Diners Club, JCB. **Reduced fees:** Resort guests, twilight. **Caddies:** No. **Golf carts:** Included in Green Fee. **Discount golf packages:** Yes. **Season:** Year-round. **High:** Dec.-Feb. **On site lodging:** Yes. **Rental clubs:** Yes. **Walking policy:** Walking at certain times. **Metal spikes allowed:** Yes. **Range:** Yes (grass/mats). **To obtain tee times:** Call up to 7 days in advance.
Notes: 1990-1995 LPGA Tour Hawaiian Open; 1992 Sr. PGA Tour Ko Olina Senior Invitational.
Subscriber comments: Beautiful resort course...Strong winds...Good variety.

KONA SURF RESORT & COUNTRY CLUB
R-78-7000 Alii Dr., Kailua Kona, 96740, Hawaii County, (808)322-2595.
Green fee: $70/$125. **Reduced fees:** Resort guests, twilight. **Caddies:** No. **Golf carts:** Included in Green Fee. **Discount golf packages:** Yes. **Season:** Year-round. **High:** Jan.-March. **On site lodging:** Yes. **Rental clubs:** Yes. **Walking policy:** Mandatory cart. **Metal spikes allowed:** Yes. **Range:** Yes (grass/mats). **To obtain tee times:** Call up to 7 days in advance.
★★★½MOUNTAIN COURSE
Opened: 1985. **Holes:** 18. **Par:** 72/72. **Yards:** 6,471/4,906. **Course rating:** 71.5/69.2. **Slope:** 133/125. **Architect:** William F. Bell/Robin Nelson/Rodney Wright. **Credit cards:** MC,VISA,AMEX,Diners Club, JCB.
Subscriber comments: Extreme challenge, beautiful scenery...Great ocean views from every hole...Underrated for beauty and test of play...Many tough sidehill lies; challenging...Superb setting and course.
★★★½OCEAN COURSE
Opened: 1968. **Holes:** 18. **Par:** 72/73. **Yards:** 6,579/5,499. **Course rating:** 71.6/71.9. **Slope:** 129/127. **Architect:** William F. Bell. **Credit cards:** MC,VISA,AMEX.
Subscriber comments: Tough greens, big breaks...Great vistas...Scenic...Surfside holes are beautiful...Very fun and picturesque, #17 lots of fun!...Superb setting.

★★★★KOOLAU GOLF COURSE
PU-45-550 Kionaole, Kaneohe, 96744, Oahu County, (808)236-4653, (800)556-6528, 13 miles N of Honolulu.
Opened: 1992. **Holes:** 18. **Par:** 72/72. **Yards:** 7,310/5,119. **Course rating:** 76.4/72.9. **Slope:** 162/134. **Architect:** Dick Nugent. **Green fee:** $90/$90. **Credit cards:** MC,VISA,AMEX. **Reduced fees:** Weekdays, low season, twilight. **Caddies:** No. **Golf carts:** Included in Green Fee. **Discount golf packages:** Yes. **Season:** Year-round. **High:** N/A. **On site lodging:** No. **Rental clubs:** Yes. **Walking policy:** Unrestricted walking. **Metal spikes allowed:** Yes. **Range:** Yes (grass). **To obtain tee times:** Call 60 days in advance.
Notes: Ranked 3rd in 1997 Best in State.
Subscriber comments: Hardest course in Hawaii...Challenging, probably too much "carry" golf for many...Toughest in the nation, picturesque, great...Brutal, but fun, 18th could take all day...Keep track of lost balls.
Special Notes: Highest Slope rating in the country.

★★★½THE LINKS AT KUILIMA

R-57-049 Kuilima Dr., Kahuku, 96731, Oahu County, (808)293-8574, 38 miles N of Honolulu.

Opened: 1992. **Holes:** 18. **Par:** 72/72. **Yards:** 7,199/4,851. **Course rating:** 75.0/64.3. **Slope:** 141/121. **Architect:** Arnold Palmer/Ed Seay. **Green fee:** $75/$125. **Credit cards:** All major,JCB. **Reduced fees:** Resort guests. **Caddies:** No. **Golf carts:** Included in Green Fee. **Discount golf packages:** Yes. **Season:** Year-round. **High:** Dec.-March. **On site lodging:** Yes. **Rental clubs:** Yes. **Walking policy:** Mandatory cart. **Metal spikes allowed:** Yes. **Range:** Yes (grass). **To obtain tee times:** Call or fax golf shop or hotel up to 30 days in advance, or up to 6 months in advance if staying at the Turtle Bay Hilton.

Subscriber comments: Golf in paradise...Straightforward but challenging...Challenging golf, will improve with age...Beautiful golf course.

★★★MAKAHA VALLEY COUNTRY CLUB

PU-84-627 Makaha Valley Rd., Waianae, 96792, Oahu County, (808)695-7111, 40 miles NW of Honolulu.

Opened: 1969. **Holes:** 18. **Par:** 71/71. **Yards:** 6,369/5,720. **Course rating:** 69.2/72.7. **Slope:** 133/120. **Architect:** William F. Bell. **Green fee:** $55/$95. **Credit cards:** MC,VISA,AMEX,Diners Club. **Reduced fees:** N/A. **Caddies:** No. **Golf carts:** Included in Green Fee. **Discount golf packages:** No. **Season:** Year-round. **High:** Dec.-March. **On site lodging:** No. **Rental clubs:** Yes. **Walking policy:** Mandatory cart. **Metal spikes allowed:** Yes. **Range:** Yes (grass). **To obtain tee times:** Call for tee time.

Subscriber comments: Play from tips...Nice layout, good golf.

★★★½MAKALEI HAWAII COUNTRY CLUB

PU-72-3890 Hawaii Belt Rd., Kailua-Kona, 96740, Hawaii County, (808)325-6625, (800)606-9606, 5 miles N of Kailua-Kona.

Opened: 1992. **Holes:** 18. **Par:** 72/72. **Yards:** 7,091/5,242. **Course rating:** 73.5/64.9. **Slope:** 143/125. **Architect:** Dick Nugent. **Green fee:** $110/$110. **Credit cards:** MC,VISA,AMEX,Diners Club, JCB. **Reduced fees:** Weekdays, low season, resort guests, twilight, seniors, juniors. **Caddies:** No. **Golf carts:** Included in Green Fee. **Discount golf packages:** Yes. **Season:** Year-round. **High:** Dec.-March. **On site lodging:** No. **Rental clubs:** Yes. **Walking policy:** Mandatory cart. **Metal spikes allowed:** Yes. **Range:** Yes (grass). **To obtain tee times:** Call up to 7 days in advance.

Subscriber comments: Spectacular scenery, course is at 2,000 feet above Kona...Tough golf course particularly in the wind...Spectacular course, cool climate...Hilly, a place to cool off...Different, a pleasant change.

MAKENA RESORT GOLF COURSE

R-5415 Makena Alanui, Kihei, 96753, Maui County, (808)879-3344, (800)321-6284, 6 miles S of Kihei.

Opened: 1993. **Architect:** Robert Trent Jones Jr.. **Green fee:** $85/$120. **Credit cards:** MC,VISA,AMEX,Diners Club, Carte Blanche. **Reduced fees:** Low season, resort guests, twilight, juniors. **Caddies:** Yes. **Golf carts:** Included in Green Fee. **Discount golf packages:** Yes. **Season:** Year-round. **High:** Oct.-April/Aug. **On site lodging:** Yes. **Rental clubs:** Yes. **Walking policy:** Walking at certain times. **Metal spikes allowed:** Yes. **Range:** Yes (grass/mats). **To obtain tee times:** Guests of Makena Resort & Maui Prince Hotel may call up to 1 year in advance. Nonguests may call up to 5 days in advance.

★★★★NORTH COURSE

Holes: 18. **Par:** 72/72. **Yards:** 6,914/5,303. **Course rating:** 72.1/70.9. **Slope:** 139/128. **Notes:** Ranked 10th in 1997 Best in State.

Subscriber comments: Must play course on Maui...Beautiful with great vistas...Both courses are great...Michael Jordan was playing ahead of us...As good or better than Kapalua; tough to putt...Golf heaven on earth.

★★★½SOUTH COURSE

Holes: 18. **Par:** 72/72. **Yards:** 7,017/5,529. **Course rating:** 72.6/71.1. **Slope:** 138/130. **Notes:** Ranked 14th in 1997 Best in State.

Subscriber comments: Very pretty course...Very playable fun course, nice views...Great views of Maui coast...Not as good as North...Ask about Makena's 36-hole special...Excellent in all areas.

★★★★½MAUNA KEA BEACH GOLF COURSE
R-62-100 Mauna Kea Beach Dr., Kamuela, 96743, Hawaii County, (808)882-5400, 34 miles S of Kailua-Kona.
Opened: 1965. **Holes:** 18. **Par:** 72/72. **Yards:** 7,114/5,277. **Course rating:** 73.6/70.2. **Slope:** 143/124. **Architect:** Robert Trent Jones. **Green fee:** $90/$150. **Credit cards:** MC,VISA,AMEX,JCB, Carte Blanche. **Reduced fees:** Resort guests, twilight, juniors. **Caddies:** No. **Golf carts:** Included in Green Fee. **Discount golf packages:** Yes. **Season:** Year-round. **High:** Nov.-April. **On site lodging:** Yes. **Rental clubs:** Yes. **Walking policy:** Walking at certain times. **Metal spikes allowed:** Yes. **Range:** Yes (grass/mats). **To obtain tee times:** Guests call up to 4 days in advance. Off-property guests call 2 days in advance.
Notes: Ranked 98th in 1997-98 America's 100 Greatest; 2nd in 1997 Best in State.
Subscriber comments: Great classic course...Course has character...Excellent golf course, great vistas, awesome par 3s...The best all-around in the isles...Don't play back tees, too difficult...As good as ever...Hard to score while taking photos.

MAUNA LANI RESORT
R-68-1310 Mauna Lani Dr., Suite 103, Kohala Coast, 96743, Hawaii County, (808)885-6655, 30 miles N of Kailua-Kona.
Opened: 1981. **Caddies:** No. **Golf carts:** Included in Green Fee. **Discount golf packages:** Yes. **Season:** Year-round. **On site lodging:** Yes. **Walking policy:** Mandatory cart. **Metal spikes allowed:** Yes. **Range:** Yes (grass).

★★★★NORTH COURSE
Holes: 18. **Par:** 72/72. **Yards:** 6,993/5,474. **Course rating:** 73.2/71.4. **Slope:** 136/124. **Architect:** Nelson/Wright/Haworth. **Green fee:** $85/$160. **Credit cards:** MC,VISA,AMEX,Diners Club. **Reduced fees:** Low season, twilight. **High:** Nov.-April. **Rental clubs:** Yes. **To obtain tee times:** Resort guests call up to 14 days in advance. Off-property guests call up to 3 days in advance.
Notes: Ranked 9th in 1997 Best in State.
Subscriber comments: Volcanic rock adds to the beauty and play...Just like I pictured it...Very enjoyable if the wind doesn't blow...Not as dramatic as South course...Lots of lava...Some tricky, challenging holes from the tips...Great fun to play, glad most tourists want to play South course...Very pretty, we were in paradise.

★★★★½SOUTH COURSE
Holes: 18. **Par:** 72/72. **Yards:** 7,029/5,331. **Course rating:** N/A. **Slope:** 133/122. **Architect:** Nelson, Wright/Haworth. **Green fee:** $90/$170. **Credit cards:** MC,VISA,AMEX,. **Reduced fees:** N/A. **High:** Dec.-March. **Rental clubs:** No. **To obtain tee times:** Resort guests may call up to 14 days in advance. Off-property guests may call up to 3 days in advance.
Notes: Ranked 12th in 1997 Best in State. Senior PGA Tour Skins Game.
Subscriber comments: Beautiful setting with the black lava, the green grass and the ocean...Easy to lose balls...Just like on TV...Great course...Exceptional golf and exceptional setting...Beautiful seaside course...Great par 3s!...Absolutely the best.

★★½MILILANI GOLF CLUB
95-176 Kuahelani Ave., Mililani, 96789, Oahu County, (808)623-2222, 12 miles NW of Honolulu.
Opened: 1967. **Holes:** 18. **Par:** 72/72. **Yards:** 6,455/5,985. **Course rating:** 69.3/73.6. **Slope:** 121/127. **Architect:** Bob Baldock. **Green fee:** $84/$92. **Credit cards:** MC,VISA,AMEX,Diners Club. **Reduced fees:** Weekdays, twilight, seniors. **Caddies:** No. **Golf carts:** Included in Green Fee. **Discount golf packages:** Yes. **Season:** Year-round. **High:** Jan.-Feb./June. **On site lodging:** No. **Rental clubs:** Yes. **Walking policy:** Mandatory cart. **Metal spikes allowed:** Yes. **Range:** Yes (Mats). **To obtain tee times:** Call up to 30 days in advance.

★★★½NEW EWA BEACH GOLF CLUB
91-050 Fort Weaver Rd., Ewa Beach, 96706, Oahu County, (808)689-8351, 18 miles W of Honolulu.
Opened: 1992. **Holes:** 18. **Par:** 72/72. **Yards:** 6,541/5,230. **Course rating:** 71.3/70.5. **Slope:** 125/121. **Architect:** Robin Nelson/Rodney Wright. **Green fee:** $60/$150. **Credit cards:** MC,VISA,AMEX. **Reduced fees:** Twilight, seniors, juniors. **Caddies:** No. **Golf**

carts: Included in Green Fee. **Discount golf packages:** No. **Season:** Year-round.
High: Aug./Winter. **On site lodging:** No. **Rental clubs:** Yes. **Walking policy:**
Mandatory cart. **Metal spikes allowed:** Yes. **Range:** No. **To obtain tee times:** Call 7
days in advance. Special tournament and club rate available.
Subscriber comments: Will be good...Tough and interesting, especially with the wind.

★★★OLOMANA GOLF LINKS

41-1801 Kalanianaole Hwy., Waimanalo, 96795, Oahu County, (808)259-7926.
Opened: 1967. **Holes:** 18. **Par:** 72/73. **Yards:** 6,326/5,456. **Course rating:** 70.3/72.4.
Slope: 129/128. **Architect:** Bob Baldock/Robert L. Baldock. **Green fee:** $90. **Credit
cards:** All major,JCB. **Reduced fees:** Weekdays, twilight, seniors. **Caddies:** No. **Golf
carts:** Included in Green Fee. **Discount golf packages:** Yes. **Season:** Year-round.
High: July-Aug. **On site lodging:** No. **Rental clubs:** Yes. **Walking policy:** Walking at
certain times. **Metal spikes allowed:** Yes. **Range:** Yes (Mats). **To obtain tee times:**
Call 30 days in advance.

★★½PALI MUNICIPAL GOLF COURSE

PM-45-050 Kamehameha Hwy., Kaneohe, 96744, Oahu County, (808)266-7612, 5
miles W of Honolulu.
Opened: 1954. **Holes:** 18. **Par:** 72/74. **Yards:** 6,500/6,050. **Course rating:** 78.8/70.4.
Slope: 126/127. **Architect:** Willard Wilkinson. **Green fee:** $20/$40. **Credit cards:**
MC,VISA. **Reduced fees:** Twilight, seniors, juniors. **Caddies:** No. **Golf carts:** Included
in Green Fee. **Discount golf packages:** No. **Season:** Year-round. **High:** June-Aug. **On
site lodging:** No. **Rental clubs:** No. **Walking policy:** Unrestricted walking. **Metal
spikes allowed:** Yes. **Range:** Yes (grass). **To obtain tee times:** Call automated tee
time system at (808)296-2000 up to 7 days in advance.
Subscriber comments: Great site...Very windy, greens poor...Tough municipal
course...Wonderful old course.

★★★PEARL COUNTRY CLUB

PU-98-535 Kaonohi St., Aiea, 96701, Oahu County, (808)487-3802, 10 miles W of
Honolulu.
Opened: 1967. **Holes:** 18. **Par:** 72/72. **Yards:** 6,787/5,536. **Course rating:** 72.0/72.1.
Slope: 135/130. **Architect:** Akiro Sato. **Green fee:** $47/$120. **Credit cards:**
MC,VISA,AMEX,Diners Club, JCB. **Reduced fees:** Twilight. **Caddies:** No. **Golf carts:**
Included in Green Fee. **Discount golf packages:** No. **Season:** Year-round. **High:** Year-
round. **On site lodging:** No. **Rental clubs:** Yes. **Walking policy:** Mandatory cart. **Metal
spikes allowed:** Yes. **Range:** Yes. **To obtain tee times:** Call in advance.

★★★★POIPU BAY RESORT GOLF CLUB

R-2250 Ainako St., Koloa, 96756, Kauai County, (808)742-8711,
(800)858-6300, 16 miles SW of Lihue.
Opened: 1990. **Holes:** 18. **Par:** 72/72. **Yards:** 6,959/5,241. **Course rating:** 73.4/70.9. **Slope:** 132/121. **Architect:** Robert Trent Jones Jr..
Green fee: $80/$135. **Credit cards:** MC,VISA,AMEX,Diners Club, JCB.
Reduced fees: Resort guests, twilight, juniors. **Caddies:** No. **Golf carts:** Included in
Green Fee. **Discount golf packages:** Yes. **Season:** Year-round. **High:** Jan.-May. **On
site lodging:** Yes. **Rental clubs:** Yes. **Walking policy:** Mandatory cart. **Metal spikes
allowed:** Yes. **Range:** Yes (grass/mats). **To obtain tee times:** Call up to 2 days in
advance.
Notes: Ranked 8th in 1997 Best in State. 1994-Present MasterCard PGA Grand Slam.
Subscriber comments: Great ocean views...Very scenic last three holes, on the
water...Tough, tough, tough, strong winds, great views...Spectacular scenery...Watched
whales off 16th green...Routing is inspired, cliff holes are unforgettable.
Special Notes: Green fee includes range balls, bag tag, towel, water, tees and marker.

PRINCEVILLE RESORT

R- **Architect:** Robert Trent Jones Jr.. **Caddies:** No. **Golf carts:** Included
in Green Fee. **Discount golf packages:** Yes. **Season:** Year-round. **High:**
Nov.-March. **On site lodging:** Yes. **Rental clubs:** Yes. **Metal spikes
allowed:** Yes. **Range:** Yes (grass/mats).

★★★½ MAKAI GOLF CLUB

1 Lei O Papa Rd., Princeville, 96722, Kauai County, (808)826-3580, (800)826-4400, 30 miles N of Lihue.

Opened: 1973. **Holes:** 27. **Green fee:** $95/$115. **Credit cards:** MC,VISA,AMEX,Diners Club. **Reduced fees:** Resort guests, twilight, juniors. **Walking policy:** Mandatory cart. **To obtain tee times:** Call up to 30 days in advance.

LAKES/WOODS
Par: 72/72. **Yards:** 6,901/5,631. **Course rating:** 72.3/69.8. **Slope:** 129/114.

OCEAN/LAKES
Par: 72/72. **Yards:** 6,886/5,516. **Course rating:** 72.7/70.0. **Slope:** 134/114.

OCEAN/WOODS
Par: 72/72. **Yards:** 6,875/5,631. **Course rating:** 72.7/70.6. **Slope:** 133/115.

Notes: Ranked 6th in 1997 Best in State. 1990 Itoman LPGA World Match Play Championship; 1986-1989 Women's Kemper Open; 1978 26th World Cup International Trophy Golf Championship.

Subscriber comments: Mature, beautiful, user-friendly...OK...A good challenge...Great for average golfers...#7 on Ocean, great view...Mix of ordinary and challenging holes...Some spectacular ocean holes...Incredible views.

★★★★★ PRINCE COURSE

5-3900 Kuhio Hwy., Princeville, 96722, Kauai County, (808)826-5000, (800)826-4400, 30 miles N of Lihue.

Opened: 1991. **Holes:** 18. **Par:** 72/72. **Yards:** 7,309/5,338. **Course rating:** 75.6/70.0. **Slope:** 144/127. **Green fee:** $120/$150. **Credit cards:** MC,VISA,AMEX,Diners Club, JCB. **Reduced fees:** Weekdays, resort guests, twilight, juniors. **Walking policy:** Mandatory cart. **To obtain tee times:** Call 30 days in advance.

Notes: Ranked 66th in 1997-98 America's 100 Greatest; 1st in 1997 Best in State.

Subscriber comments: Excellent, unparalleled beauty...A magnificent experience but very difficult...Outstanding, natural course design...I've played all over the world and this is my favorite course...Fabulous golf, tough from the tips...The ultimate experience. Spectacular views...Venerable test of golf in a tropical paradise.

★★★ PUKALANI COUNTRY CLUB

PU-360 Pukalani St., Pukalani, 96768, Maui County, (808)572-1314.

Opened: 1981. **Holes:** 18. **Par:** 72/74. **Yards:** 6,945/5,574. **Course rating:** 72.8/71.1. **Slope:** 121/118. **Architect:** Bob Baldock. **Green fee:** $35/$55. **Credit cards:** MC,VISA,AMEX. **Reduced fees:** Low season, twilight. **Caddies:** No. **Golf carts:** Included in Green Fee. **Discount golf packages:** No. **Season:** Year-round. **High:** Jan.-March. **On site lodging:** No. **Rental clubs:** Yes. **Walking policy:** Mandatory cart. **Metal spikes allowed:** Yes. **Range:** Yes (grass). **To obtain tee times:** Call anytime.

Subscriber comments: Good course, low price for Hawaii...Awesome upcountry views...Hillside site, fantastic views.

★★★ ROYAL KUNIA COUNTRY CLUB

460 Ena Rd. Suite 301, Honolulu, 96815, Oahu County, (808)949-1088. Call club for further information.

★★½ SEAMOUNTAIN GOLF COURSE

R-Off Hwy. 11, Punaluu, 96777, Hawaii County, (808)928-6222, 56 miles S of Hilo.

Opened: 1973. **Holes:** 18. **Par:** 72/72. **Yards:** 6,492/5,663. **Course rating:** 72.5/70.9. **Slope:** 135/116. **Architect:** Arthur Jack Snyder. **Green fee:** $25/$40. **Credit cards:** MC,VISA. **Reduced fees:** Resort guests, juniors. **Caddies:** No. **Golf carts:** Included in Green Fee. **Discount golf packages:** Yes. **Season:** Year-round. **High:** Jan.-March. **On site lodging:** Yes. **Rental clubs:** Yes. **Walking policy:** Mandatory cart. **Metal spikes allowed:** Yes. **Range:** Yes (grass). **To obtain tee times:** Call for reservations any time.

Subscriber comments: Nice layout...Quiet setting, reasonable challenge...Quiet, out of the way, great potential...Beautiful area...Spartan.

★★½ SHERATON MAKAHA GOLF CLUB

R-84-626 Makaha Valley Rd., Waianae, 96792, Oahu County, (808)695-9544, (800)757-8060, 40 miles W of Honolulu.

Opened: 1969. **Holes:** 18. **Par:** 72/72. **Yards:** 7,077/5,856. **Course rating:** 73.2/73.9. **Slope:** 139/129. **Architect:** William F. Bell. **Green fee:** $90/$160. **Credit cards:** All major,Diners Club, JCB. **Reduced fees:** Weekdays, resort guests, twilight. **Caddies:**

No. **Golf carts:** Included in Green Fee. **Discount golf packages:** No. **Season:** Year-round. **High:** Jan.-March. **On site lodging:** No. **Rental clubs:** Yes. **Walking policy:** Mandatory cart. **Metal spikes allowed:** Yes. **Range:** Yes (Mats). **To obtain tee times:** Call golf shop.
Subscriber comments: Great views, good test, reasonable...A scenic delight with some of the holes up against the water and others near the mountains.

★★★ SILVERSWORD GOLF CLUB
PU-1345 Piilani Hwy., Kihei, 96753, Maui County, (808)874-0777, 12 miles N of Kahului.
Opened: 1987. **Holes:** 18. **Par:** 71/71. **Yards:** 6,801/5,265. **Course rating:** 72.0/70.0. **Slope:** 124/118. **Architect:** W.J. Newis. **Green fee:** $59/$70. **Credit cards:** MC,VISA,AMEX,JCB. **Reduced fees:** Low season, twilight. **Caddies:** No. **Golf carts:** Included in Green Fee. **Discount golf packages:** No. **Season:** Year-round. **High:** Jan.-March. **On site lodging:** No. **Rental clubs:** Yes. **Walking policy:** Mandatory cart. **Metal spikes allowed:** Yes. **Range:** Yes (grass). **To obtain tee times:** Call up to 30 days in advance.
Subscriber comments: Beautiful views of ocean...Hard and flat. Wide open, can spray shots...Fair at best...Tougher that it looks, fun to play...Excellent local course for the money...Nice semi links-style course...Stay out of the lava.

★★½ VOLCANO GOLF & COUNTRY CLUB
PU-P.O. Box 46, Volcano Nat'l Park, 96718, Hawaii County, (808)967-7331, 32 miles S of Hilo.
Opened: N/A. **Holes:** 18. **Par:** 72/72. **Yards:** 6,250/5,449. **Course rating:** N/A. **Slope:** 128/117. **Architect:** Arthur Jack Snyder. **Green fee:** N/A. **Credit cards:** MC,VISA,AMEX,. **Reduced fees:** N/A. **Caddies:** No. **Golf carts:** Included in Green Fee. **Discount golf packages:** No. **Season:** Year-round. **High:** July-Sept. **On site lodging:** No. **Rental clubs:** No. **Walking policy:** N/A. **Metal spikes allowed:** Yes. **Range:** Yes (grass). **To obtain tee times:** N/A.

★★★ WAIEHU GOLF COURSE
PU-P.O. Box 507, Wailuku, 96793, Maui County, (808)244-5934.
Opened: N/A. **Holes:** 18. **Par:** 72/71. **Yards:** 6,330/5,511. **Course rating:** 69.8/70.6. **Slope:** 111/115. **Architect:** Arthur Jack Snyder. **Green fee:** $25/$30. **Credit cards:** None. **Reduced fees:** N/A. **Caddies:** No. **Golf carts:** $15. **Discount golf packages:** No. **Season:** Year-round. **High:** Nov.-March. **On site lodging:** No. **Rental clubs:** Yes. **Walking policy:** Unrestricted walking. **Metal spikes allowed:** Yes. **Range:** Yes. **To obtain tee times:** Call 2 days in advance.
Subscriber comments: Cheapest golf on Maui...My must play, love the local flavor...Good muny course...Casual...On the ocean, great views...What an experience, golf with the locals.

GREAT VALUE

★★★ WAIKELE GOLF CLUB
94-200 Paioa Place, Waipahu, 96797, Oahu County, (808)676-9000, 15 miles W of Honolulu.
Opened: 1993. **Holes:** 18. **Par:** 72/72. **Yards:** 6,663/5,226. **Course rating:** 71.7/65.6. **Slope:** 126/113. **Architect:** Ted Robinson. **Green fee:** $100/$105. **Credit cards:** All major,JCB. **Reduced fees:** Weekdays, twilight. **Caddies:** No. **Golf carts:** Included in Green Fee. **Discount golf packages:** No. **Season:** Year-round. **High:** Jan.-Feb. **On site lodging:** No. **Rental clubs:** Yes. **Walking policy:** Mandatory cart. **Metal spikes allowed:** Yes. **Range:** Yes (grass). **To obtain tee times:** Call golf shop.

WAIKOLOA BEACH RESORT
R- **Green fee:** $120. **Credit cards:** All major,JCB. **Reduced fees:** Resort guests, twilight. **Caddies:** No. **Golf carts:** Included in Green Fee. **Discount golf packages:** Yes. **Season:** Year-round. **High:** Dec.-March. **On site lodging:** Yes. **Rental clubs:** Yes. **Walking policy:** Mandatory cart. **Metal spikes allowed:** Yes. **To obtain tee times:** Call or fax 30 days in advance with major credit card to guarantee.
★★★½ BEACH GOLF COURSE
1020 Keana Place, Waikoloa, 96738, Hawaii County, (808)886-6060, (800)552-1422, 23 miles S of Kailua-Kona.

HAWAII

Opened: 1981. **Holes:** 18. **Par:** 72/72. **Yards:** 6,566/5,094. **Course rating:** 71.5/69.4. **Slope:** 133/119. **Architect:** Robert Trent Jones Jr.. **Range:** Yes (grass/mats).
Subscriber comments: Pretty course, back side tougher and better...Beautiful course, green grass, black lava, blue sky...Holes on beach are beautiful...Although Kings course gets better press, Beach is more fun.

★★★½KINGS GOLF COURSE
600 Waikoloa Beach Dr., Waikoloa, 96738, Hawaii County, (808)886-7888, (800)552-1422, 23 miles S of Kailua-Kona.
Opened: 1990. **Holes:** 18. **Par:** 72/72. **Yards:** 7,074/5,459. **Course rating:** 73.9/71.0. **Slope:** 133/121. **Architect:** Tom Weiskopf/Jay Morrish. **Range:** Yes (grass).
Subscriber comments: Bring your sand wedge...Beautiful course...A good course and great scenery...Course can be real tough when the ocean winds blow...Good test for players of every caliber...Fair course...Worthwhile resort course...Lots of lava.

★★★WAIKOLOA VILLAGE GOLF CLUB
R-68-1792 Melia St., Waikoloa, 96738, Hawaii County, (808)883-9621, 18 miles N of Kailua-Kona Airport.
Opened: 1972. **Holes:** 18. **Par:** 72/72. **Yards:** 6,791/5,479. **Course rating:** 71.8/72.1. **Slope:** 130/119. **Architect:** Robert Trent Jones Jr. **Green fee:** $40/$70. **Credit cards:** MC,VISA,AMEX,JCB. **Reduced fees:** Twilight, juniors. **Caddies:** No. **Golf carts:** Included in Green Fee. **Discount golf packages:** Yes. **Season:** Year-round. **High:** Dec.-Feb. **On site lodging:** Yes. **Rental clubs:** Yes. **Walking policy:** Walking at certain times. **Metal spikes allowed:** Yes. **Range:** Yes (grass/mats). **To obtain tee times:** Call 3 days in advance. Reservations taken 30 days in advance with a 50 percent prepay. Groups of 12 or more call 1 year in advance.
Subscriber comments: Underrated. Good basic course...Wind makes it long and difficult...Nice course...Very fair test of golf.

WAILEA GOLF CLUB
R-**Credit cards:** All major,JCB. **Caddies:** No. **Golf carts:** Included in Green Fee. **Discount golf packages:** Yes. **Season:** Year-round. **High:** Dec.-April. **On site lodging:** Yes. **Rental clubs:** Yes. **Walking policy:** Mandatory cart. **Metal spikes allowed:** Yes. **Range:** Yes (grass/mats). **To obtain tee times:** Call 30 days in advance.

★★★½BLUE COURSE
120 Kaukahi St., Wailea, 96753, Maui County, (808)875-5111, (800)332-1614, 17 miles S of Kahului.
Opened: 1972. **Holes:** 18. **Par:** 72/72. **Yards:** 6,758/5,291. **Course rating:** 71.6/72.0. **Slope:** 130/117. **Architect:** Arthur Jack Snyder. **Green fee:** $80/$125. **Reduced fees:** Low season, resort guests, twilight, juniors.
Notes: 1990-1992 LPGA Women's Kemper Open.
Subscriber comments: Wide open course, a pleasure to play...Three fair courses...Nothing memorable but enjoyable...Resort golf at its best, breathtaking views...Some interesting holes.

★★★★EMERALD COURSE
100 Wailea Golf Club Dr., Wailea, 96753, Maui County, (808)875-7450, (800)332-1614, 17 miles S of Kahului.
Opened: 1994. **Holes:** 18. **Par:** 72/72. **Yards:** 6,825/5,256. **Course rating:** 71.7/69.6. **Slope:** 130/115. **Architect:** Robert Trent Jones Jr.. **Green fee:** $80/$125. **Reduced fees:** Low season, resort guests.
Notes: Ranked 2nd in 1995 Best New Resort Courses.
Subscriber comments: Spectacular views on every hole...Great views. Challenging greens...Like playing in a flower garden...Where is the rough? Take your wife, have fun...You won't catch me without my camera at this course...Golf at its best...Easy but gorgeous views...Play before wind arrives.

★★★★GOLD COURSE
100 Wailea Golf Club Dr., Wailea, 96753, Maui County, (808)875-7450, (800)332-1614, 17 miles S of Kahului.
Opened: 1994. **Holes:** 18. **Par:** 72/72. **Yards:** 7,070/5,317. **Course rating:** 73.0/70.3. **Slope:** 139/121. **Architect:** Robert Trent Jones Jr. **Green fee:** $85/$130. **Reduced fees:** Low season, resort guests.
Subscriber comments: Bunkers, bunkers and more bunkers...High handicappers should play the whites, they will have more fun...Great course layout and

views...Excellent and challenging holes...Most memorable moment was pausing prior to hitting on a par 3 so I could watch whales out at sea.

★★★½WAILUA GOLF COURSE

PM-3-5350 Kuhio Hwy., Lihue, 96766, Kauai County, (808)245-8092, 3 miles S of Lihue.

Opened: 1963. **Holes:** 18. **Par:** 36/36. **Yards:** 6,981/5,974. **Course rating:** 73.0/73.1. **Slope:** 136/122. **Architect:** Toyo Shirai. **Green fee:** $25/$35. **Credit cards:** None. **Reduced fees:** Twilight, seniors. **Caddies:** No. **Golf carts:** $14. **Discount golf packages:** No. **Season:** Year-round. **High:** Jan.-April. **On site lodging:** No. **Rental clubs:** Yes. **Walking policy:** Unrestricted walking. **Metal spikes allowed:** Yes. **Range:** Yes (grass/mats). **To obtain tee times:** Call 7 days in advance, minimum two players.

Notes: 1975, 1985, 1996 USGA Amateur Public Links Championship.

Subscriber comments: Fun for all, wonderful challenge...A gem in Hawaii...Beautiful long course, 1st, 2nd holes along seashore...Has to be the best value in Hawaii...Some beautiful holes...Tough par 3s, especially 17th...Fun, fun, fun...Best golf for best price...A sound course, good value...Strong layout, lovely ocean views.

(GREAT VALUE)

★★★½WAIMEA COUNTRY CLUB

Mamalohoa Hwy., Kamuela, 96743, Hawaii County, (808)885-8777, 51 miles N of Hilo.

Opened: 1994. **Holes:** 18. **Par:** 72/72. **Yards:** 6,661/5,673. **Course rating:** 71.1/68.5. **Slope:** 130/126. **Architect:** John Sanford. **Green fee:** $60/$60. **Credit cards:** MC,VISA,AMEX. **Reduced fees:** Twilight, seniors, juniors. **Caddies:** No. **Golf carts:** Included in Green Fee. **Discount golf packages:** No. **Season:** Year-round. **High:** N/A. **On site lodging:** No. **Rental clubs:** Yes. **Walking policy:** Unrestricted walking. **Metal spikes allowed:** Yes. **Range:** Yes. **To obtain tee times:** Call up to 7 days in advance.

Subscriber comments: Good layout. Wonderful setting...Fun course...If no rain, excellent value...Great scenery, peaceful, relaxing!...A very enjoyable experience.

★★★WEST LOCH GOLF COURSE

PM-91-1126 Okupe St., Ewa Beach, 96706, Oahu County, (808)671-2292, 15 miles W of Honolulu.

Opened: 1990. **Holes:** 18. **Par:** 72/72. **Yards:** 6,479/5,296. **Course rating:** 70.3/68.6. **Slope:** 123/117. **Architect:** Robin Nelson/Rodney Wright. **Green fee:** $14/$18. **Credit cards:** None. **Reduced fees:** Twilight, seniors, juniors. **Caddies:** No. **Golf carts:** Included in Green Fee. **Discount golf packages:** No. **Season:** Year-round. **High:** April-Sept. **On site lodging:** No. **Rental clubs:** Yes. **Walking policy:** Mandatory cart. **Metal spikes allowed:** Yes. **Range:** Yes (grass/mats). **To obtain tee times:** Call 7 days in advance.

★★★ AVONDALE GOLF CLUB
10745 Avondale Loop Rd., Hayden Lake, 83835, Kootenai County, (208)772-5963, 35 miles E of Spokane, WA.
Opened: N/A. **Holes:** 18. **Par:** 72/74. **Yards:** 6,525/4,719. **Course rating:** 71.1/73.2. **Slope:** 118/123. **Architect:** Mel "Curley" Hueston. **Green fee:** $20/$20. **Credit cards:** MC,VISA,DISC. **Reduced fees:** Low season, twilight, juniors. **Caddies:** No. **Golf carts:** $21. **Discount golf packages:** No. **Season:** March-Oct. **High:** June-Aug. **On site lodging:** No. **Rental clubs:** Yes. **Walking policy:** Walking at certain times. **Metal spikes allowed:** Yes. **Range:** Yes (grass). **To obtain tee times:** Call pro shop seven days in advance.
Subscriber comments: New design changes, very well done...There's a lot of hidden beauty, play it twice...Best I have played...Idaho's golf is a good buy and lots of fun...Treelined, pretty setting...Nice course, fairly tough pin placements.

★★★ BLACKFOOT MUNICIPAL GOLF COURSE
PM-3115 Teeples Dr., Blackfoot, 83221, Bingham County, (208)785-9960, 19 miles N of Pocatello.
Opened: 1959. **Holes:** 18. **Par:** 72/78. **Yards:** 6,899/6,385. **Course rating:** 71.0/75.0. **Slope:** 123/124. **Architect:** George Von Elm. **Green fee:** $12/$12. **Credit cards:** MC,VISA. **Reduced fees:** Weekdays, low season. **Caddies:** No. **Golf carts:** $15. **Discount golf packages:** No. **Season:** March-Nov. **High:** May-Oct. **On site lodging:** No. **Rental clubs:** Yes. **Walking policy:** Unrestricted walking. **Metal spikes allowed:** Yes. **Range:** No. **To obtain tee times:** Call two days in advance.
Subscriber comments: Tough front nine...Fairly long, several holes seem repetitive...Wonderful small-town course, greens and courses always in excellent shape, pro and help are all friendly and accommodating...Enjoyable experience all around.

★★½ BRYDEN CANYON PUBLIC GOLF CLUB
PU-445 O'Connor Rd., Lewiston, 83501, Nez Perce County, (208)746-0863, 100 miles SW of Spokane.
Opened: 1975. **Holes:** 18. **Par:** 71/71. **Yards:** 6,103/5,380. **Course rating:** 67.4/69.9. **Slope:** 106/111. **Architect:** N/A. **Green fee:** $11/$11. **Credit cards:** MC,VISA. **Reduced fees:** N/A. **Caddies:** No. **Golf carts:** $11. **Discount golf packages:** Yes. **Season:** Year-round. **High:** Feb.-Sept. **On site lodging:** No. **Rental clubs:** Yes. **Walking policy:** Unrestricted walking. **Metal spikes allowed:** Yes. **Range:** Yes (grass). **To obtain tee times:** Call up to seven days in advance.

★★★ CANYON SPRINGS GOLF COURSE
PU-Canyon Springs Rd., Twin Falls, 83301, Twin Falls County, (208)734-7609, 110 miles SE of Boise.
Opened: 1975. **Holes:** 18. **Par:** 72/74. **Yards:** 6,452/5,190. **Course rating:** 68.7/68.3. **Slope:** 112/111. **Architect:** N/A. **Green fee:** $20. **Credit cards:** MC,VISA. **Reduced fees:** N/A. **Caddies:** No. **Golf carts:** $20. **Discount golf packages:** No. **Season:** Feb.-Dec. **High:** May-Sept. **On site lodging:** No. **Rental clubs:** Yes. **Walking policy:** Unrestricted walking. **Metal spikes allowed:** No. **Range:** Yes (grass). **To obtain tee times:** Call up to 3 days in advance.
Subscriber comments: Nice setting and good variety of holes...Very scenic...This course gets lots of play, still fun...Good facilities, course needs a little TLC...Neat setting in Snake River Canyon...Good variety...Play inside Snake River Canyon, waterfalls and great views, better when course greens up...Some very tight, tough, short par 4s.

★★½ CENTENNIAL GOLF CLUB
PU-Box 52, Centennial Dr., Nampa, 83653, Canyon County, (208)467-3011. Call club for further information.

★★★ CLEAR LAKE COUNTRY CLUB
403 Clear Lake Lane, Buhl, 83316, Twin Falls County, (208)543-4849, 90 miles E of Boise.
Opened: 1987. **Holes:** 18. **Par:** 72/73. **Yards:** 5,905/5,378. **Course rating:** 68.2/69.4. **Slope:** 112/113. **Architect:** Dutch Kuse. **Green fee:** $15/$20. **Credit cards:** MC,VISA. **Reduced fees:** Weekdays, juniors. **Caddies:** No. **Golf carts:** N/A. **Discount golf packages:** No. **Season:** Year-round. **High:** May-Oct. **On site lodging:** No. **Rental clubs:**

Yes. **Walking policy:** Unrestricted walking. **Metal spikes allowed:** Yes. **Range:** Yes (grass). **To obtain tee times:** Call four days in advance.
Subscriber comments: Tough course, target golf...Exceptional value, bring your fly rod...Beware of OBs, scenic Snake River, water fowl...Good most of the year.....Nice little layout...Pretty setting, short course...Everything slopes toward river.

★★★★ COEUR D'ALENE RESORT GOLF COURSE
R-900 Floating Green Dr., Coeur d'Alene, 83814, Kootenai County, (208)667-4653, (800)688-5253, 32 miles E of Spokane, WA.
Opened: 1991. **Holes:** 18. **Par:** 71/71. **Yards:** 6,309/5,490. **Course rating:** 69.9/70.3. **Slope:** 121/118. **Architect:** Scott Miller. **Green fee:** $75/$180. **Credit cards:** All major. **Reduced fees:** Low season, resort guests. **Caddies:** Yes. **Golf carts:** Included in Green Fee. **Discount golf packages:** Yes. **Season:** April-Oct. **High:** June-Sept. **On site lodging:** Yes. **Rental clubs:** Yes. **Walking policy:** Walking at certain times. **Metal spikes allowed:** No. **Range:** Yes (grass). **To obtain tee times:** Guests may call up to 1 year in advance.
Notes: Ranked 1st in 1997 Best in State.
Subscriber comments: Once in a lifetime...Forecaddies are great...You're treated like royalty. Fairways like greens...Played better courses but total purchase is great...Meticulous grooming, go spring or fall for good deals...Staff attitude great...A birdie on the island helps!...Most beautiful Northwest Idaho golf course.

GREAT SERVICE

★★★ EAGLE HILLS GOLF COURSE
PU-605 N. Edgewood Lane, Eagle, 83616, Ada County, (208)939-0402, 4 miles NW of Boise.
Opened: 1968. **Holes:** 18. **Par:** 72/72. **Yards:** 6,485/5,305. **Course rating:** 70.5/70.2. **Slope:** 118/114. **Architect:** C. Edward Trout. **Green fee:** $14/$22. **Credit cards:** MC,VISA. **Reduced fees:** Weekdays, low season, twilight, seniors, juniors. **Caddies:** No. **Golf carts:** $9. **Discount golf packages:** Yes. **Season:** Year-round. **High:** March-Oct. **On site lodging:** No. **Rental clubs:** Yes. **Walking policy:** Unrestricted walking. **Metal spikes allowed:** Yes. **Range:** Yes (grass/mats). **To obtain tee times:** Call 7 days in advance.
Subscriber comments: A fun little course, well kept...Wild shots break windows...Several very good improvements in last two years...Back nine the best.

★★★½ ELKHORN RESORT
R-Elkhorn Rd., Sun Valley, 83354, Blaine County, (208)622-3300, (800)355-4676, 150 miles E of Boise.
Opened: 1975. **Holes:** 18. **Par:** 72/72. **Yards:** 7,101/5,424. **Course rating:** 72.2/69.3. **Slope:** 127/125. **Architect:** Robert Trent Jones/R.T. Jones Jr. **Green fee:** $96. **Credit cards:** All major. **Reduced fees:** Low season, resort guests. **Caddies:** No. **Golf carts:** Included in Green Fee. **Discount golf packages:** Yes. **Season:** May-Oct. **High:** June-Aug. **On site lodging:** Yes. **Rental clubs:** Yes. **Walking policy:** Mandatory cart. **Metal spikes allowed:** No. **Range:** Yes (grass/mats). **To obtain tee times:** Public may call 2 days in advance or 30 days in advance with a credit card.
Notes: Ranked 3rd in 1997 Best in State.
Subscriber comments: Big golf course from tips. Front nine tougher than back. One of best in state...A must play...A great Robert Trent Jones layout...Fun, long course...Many tough holes in scenic setting...Best course in Idaho!...639-yard par 5.

★★★½ HIDDEN LAKES GOLF RESORT
R-8838 Lower Pack River Rd., Sandpoint, 83864, Bonner County, (208)263-1642, 86 miles NE of Spokane, WA.
Opened: 1986. **Holes:** 18. **Par:** 71/71. **Yards:** 6,655/5,078. **Course rating:** 71.7/69.1. **Slope:** 128/119. **Architect:** Jim Krause. **Green fee:** $25/$29. **Credit cards:** MC,VISA. **Reduced fees:** Low season, resort guests, twilight, seniors, juniors. **Caddies:** No. **Golf carts:** $11. **Discount golf packages:** Yes. **Season:** April-Oct. **High:** April-Oct. **On site lodging:** No. **Rental clubs:** Yes. **Walking policy:** Unrestricted walking. **Metal spikes allowed:** Yes. **Range:** Yes (grass/mats). **To obtain tee times:** Nonmembers may call 7 days in advance, or any time with credit card.
Subscriber comments: Great place for a golf vacation...True to its name...Lots of water, take extra balls...Loved the moose...Beautiful mountain course.

★★★HIGHLAND GOLF COURSE
PU-201 Vonelm Rd., Pocatello, 83201, Bannock County, (208)237-9922.
Opened: 1963. **Holes:** 18. **Par:** 72/76. **Yards:** 6,512/6,100. **Course rating:** 67.5/73.0.
Slope: 114/117. **Architect:** Babe Hiskey. **Green fee:** $12/$13. **Credit cards:** None.
Reduced fees: Seniors, juniors. **Caddies:** No. **Golf carts:** $16. **Discount golf packages:** No. **Season:** March-Oct. **High:** May-Sept. **On site lodging:** No. **Rental clubs:** Yes. **Walking policy:** Unrestricted walking. **Metal spikes allowed:** Yes. **Range:** Yes (grass). **To obtain tee times:** Call Thursday for upcoming weekend.
Subscriber comments: Steep fairways, seniors need a cart; small range...The greens run toward the city, very interesting...Don't try to putt from above the hole...Great course...Nice people...Rolling fairways provide challenge.

★★★THE HIGHLANDS GOLF & COUNTRY CLUB
PU-N. 701 Inverness Dr., Post Falls, 83854, Kootenai County, (208)773-3673, (800)797-7339, 30 miles E of Spokane.
Opened: 1991. **Holes:** 18. **Par:** 72/73. **Yards:** 6,369/5,115. **Course rating:** 70.7/69.5.
Slope: 125/121. **Architect:** N/A. **Green fee:** $21/$25. **Credit cards:** All major.
Reduced fees: Weekdays, low season, seniors, juniors. **Caddies:** No. **Golf carts:** $22.
Discount golf packages: Yes. **Season:** March-Oct. **High:** June-Aug. **On site lodging:** No. **Rental clubs:** Yes. **Walking policy:** Walking at certain times. **Metal spikes allowed:** Yes. **Range:** Yes (grass/mats). **To obtain tee times:** Call 7 days in advance.
Subscriber comments: Water holes, surprising layout...Requires a lot of well placed shots...Excellent restaurant and lounge...Tough but fair...Clubhouse staff excellent...Nice course, a must in Spokane area...This course keeps getting better!

★★★JEROME COUNTRY CLUB
6 mi. S of Town, Jerome, 83338, Jerome County, (208)324-5281, 5 miles NW of Twin Falls.
Opened: 1930. **Holes:** 18. **Par:** 72/73. **Yards:** 6,429/5,644. **Course rating:** 68.8/71.2.
Slope: 106/114. **Architect:** Ed Hunnicutt. **Green fee:** $30. **Credit cards:** None.
Reduced fees: N/A. **Caddies:** No. **Golf carts:** $18. **Discount golf packages:** No.
Season: March-Dec. **High:** May-Sept. **On site lodging:** No. **Rental clubs:** Yes.
Walking policy: Unrestricted walking. **Metal spikes allowed:** Yes. **Range:** Yes (grass).
To obtain tee times: Call up to 3 days in advance.
Subscriber comments: Have replaced bad front nine holes to make it better...Windy... Back nine more interesting...Good track, many tournaments...Well manicured, relaxed atmosphere...Flat front nine, challenging back nine, good layout.

★★★MCCALL MUNICIPAL GOLF COURSE
PM-off Fairway Dr., McCall, 83638, Valley County, (208)634-7200.
Call club for further information.
Subscriber comments: Beautiful setting, Short but tight. Hit it straight...Newest nine is so different from previous 18...Potential...27 holes of mountain golf...Limited good weather...Course design needs work...Very busy place in the summer.

★★★½PINECREST MUNICIPAL GOLF COURSE
PM-701 E. Elva St., Idaho Falls, 83401, Bonneville County, (208)529-1485, 180 miles N of Salt Lake City.
Opened: 1934. **Holes:** 18. **Par:** 70/75. **Yards:** 6,394/6,123. **Course rating:** 69.0/73.2. **Slope:** 110/122. **Architect:** W. H. Tucker. **Green fee:** $12/$13. **Credit cards:** MC,VISA,DISC. **Reduced fees:** N/A. **Caddies:** No. **Golf carts:** $14. **Discount golf packages:** No. **Season:** March-Nov. **High:** May-Sept. **On site lodging:** No. **Rental clubs:** Yes. **Walking policy:** Unrestricted walking. **Metal spikes allowed:** No. **Range:** No. **To obtain tee times:** Call 1 day in advance starting at 6:30 a.m.

GOOD VALUE

Subscriber comments: Stately course, requires control...Really good for small-town course...Don't tell people about it please!...Wonderful...Long and tight, mature trees.

★★★PURPLE SAGE GOLF COURSE
PU-15192 Purple Sage Rd., Caldwell, 83605, Canyon County, (208)459-2223, 25 miles W of Boise.
Opened: 1963. **Holes:** 18. **Par:** 71/71. **Yards:** 6,747/5,343. **Course rating:** 70.7/68.9.

Slope: 117/111. **Architect:** A. Vernon Macan. **Green fee:** $12/$14. **Credit cards:** None. **Reduced fees:** Weekdays. **Caddies:** No. **Golf carts:** $16. **Discount golf packages:** No. **Season:** March-Dec. **High:** May-Aug. **On site lodging:** No. **Rental clubs:** Yes. **Walking policy:** Unrestricted walking. **Metal spikes allowed:** No. **Range:** Yes (grass). **To obtain tee times:** Call one day in advance, or on Thursday for coming weekend.
Subscriber comments: Mature course in good shape...Back tees difficult, small greens, narrow fairways...Lush due to new sprinkler system, plays long.

★★★½QUAIL HOLLOW GOLF CLUB
4520 N. 36th St., Boise, 83703, Ada County, (208)344-7807.
Opened: 1982. **Holes:** 18. **Par:** 70/70. **Yards:** 6,444/4,530. **Course rating:** 70.7/68.0. **Slope:** 128/129. **Architect:** von Hagge & Devlin. **Green fee:** $18/$22. **Credit cards:** MC,VISA. **Reduced fees:** Weekdays, low season, seniors, juniors. **Caddies:** No. **Golf carts:** $9. **Discount golf packages:** No. **Season:** Year-round. **High:** March-Oct. **On site lodging:** No. **Rental clubs:** Yes. **Walking policy:** Unrestricted walking. **Metal spikes allowed:** No. **Range:** Yes (grass). **To obtain tee times:** Call 5 days in advance.
Subscriber comments: Nice layout...A very tough track...Fun course, hilly, elevated tees, nice greens, perfect sand...A fine target golf course. Greens can be a little tricky...Some very interesting holes, needs to mature.

★★★★RIDGECREST GOLF CLUB
PU-3730 Ridgecrest Dr., Nampa, 83687, Canyon County, (208)888-3730, 15 miles W of Boise.
Opened: 1996. **Holes:** 18. **Par:** 72/72. **Yards:** 6,836/5,193. **Course rating:** N/A. **Slope:** N/A. **Architect:** John Harbottle. **Green fee:** $16/$19.
Credit cards: MC,VISA. **Reduced fees:** Weekdays, low season, twilight, juniors. **Caddies:** No. **Golf carts:** $18. **Discount golf packages:** No. **Season:** Year-round. **High:** April-Sept. **On site lodging:** No. **Rental clubs:** Yes. **Walking policy:** Unrestricted walking. **Metal spikes allowed:** Yes. **Range:** Yes (grass). **To obtain tee times:** Call 2 days in advance.
Notes: Ranked 4th in 1997 Best New Affordable Public Courses.
Subscriber comments: New great layout. It could be Idaho's best when this course matures...Excellent links layout...Great front nine. Back is quirky...Challenging new course in surprisingly good condition, difficult rough and waste bunkers.
Special notes: Also has a 9-hole par-3 course.

★★★RIVERSIDE GOLF COURSE
PU-3500 S. Bannock Hwy., Pocatello, 83204, Bannock County, (208)232-9515.
Opened: 1963. **Holes:** 18. **Par:** 72/75. **Yards:** 6,397/5,710. **Course rating:** 69.7/72.2. **Slope:** 114/119. **Architect:** Babe Hiskey. **Green fee:** $12/$13. **Credit cards:** None. **Reduced fees:** N/A. **Caddies:** No. **Golf carts:** $16. **Discount golf packages:** No. **Season:** March-Oct. **High:** May-Aug. **On site lodging:** No. **Rental clubs:** Yes. **Walking policy:** Unrestricted walking. **Metal spikes allowed:** Yes. **Range:** Yes (grass). **To obtain tee times:** Call Thursday for upcoming weekend.
Subscriber comments: Tight course...Nice old course, laidback play...Treelined fairways provide shade on hot days...Love the elevated greens on front nine.

★★★SAGE LAKES MUNICIPAL GOLF
100 E. 65N, Idaho Falls, 83401, Bonneville County, (208)528-5535.
Call club for further information.
Subscriber comments: Grass bunkers, lots of water; putting green, chipping green, driving range, cafe; walkable...Newer course. Longest tee boxes I've ever seen. Courteous, friendly staff...Open, no trees...Will improve with maturity.

★★★SAND CREEK GOLF CLUB
PU-5200 S. Hackman Rd., Idaho Falls, 83403, Bonneville County, (208)529-1115.
Opened: 1978. **Holes:** 18. **Par:** 72/73. **Yards:** 6,805/5,770. **Course rating:** 70.5/72.2. **Slope:** 115/116. **Architect:** William F. Bell. **Green fee:** $11/$12. **Credit cards:** MC,VISA. **Reduced fees:** Seniors, juniors. **Caddies:** No. **Golf carts:** $14. **Discount golf packages:** No. **Season:** March-Nov. **High:** June-Aug. **On site lodging:** No. **Rental clubs:** Yes. **Walking policy:** Unrestricted walking. **Metal spikes allowed:** Yes. **Range:** Yes. **To obtain tee times:** Call one day in advance.

Subscriber comments: Easy walk...Friendly, accommodating staff. Excellent mainte-nance. Scenic sand dunes located on course...A confidence builder, makes me feel like a 6-handicap...Fun course, well managed, easy walk, not difficult.

★★★½SCOTCH PINES GOLF COURSE

PU-10610 Scotch Pines Rd., Payette, 83661, Payette County, (208)642-1829, (888)260-6071, 58 miles NW of Boise.
Opened: 1960. **Holes:** 18. **Par:** 72/72. **Yards:** 6,454/5,586. **Course rat-ing:** 69.4/71.8. **Slope:** 110/116. **Architect:** Cliff Masingill/Scott Masingill. **Green fee:** $13/$15. **Credit cards:** MC,VISA,AMEX. **Reduced fees:** Twilight. **Caddies:** No. **Golf carts:** $8. **Discount golf packages:** No. **Season:** Feb.-Nov. **High:** May-Aug. **On site lodging:** No. **Rental clubs:** Yes. **Walking policy:** Unrestricted walking. **Metal spikes allowed:** Yes. **Range:** Yes (grass). **To obtain tee times:** Call two days in advance.
Subscriber comments: Best course in the Treasure Valley...Pleasant...Scotch Pines is one of the true hidden values of the Northwest. Front nine narrow, back nine open...Best kept secret in Northwest...Great course for such a small community.

★★★½SHADOW VALLEY GOLF CLUB

PU-Rt. 1, Highway 55, Boise, 83703, Ada County, (208)939-6699, (800)936-7035, 10 miles NW of Boise.
Opened: 1973. **Holes:** 18. **Par:** 72/72. **Yards:** 6,433/5,394. **Course rating:** 69.2/71.8. **Slope:** 117/117. **Architect:** Ed Trout. **Green fee:** $18/$24. **Credit cards:** All major. **Reduced fees:** Seniors, juniors. **Caddies:** No. **Golf carts:** $18. **Discount golf pack-ages:** No. **Season:** Year-round. **High:** April-Sept. **On site lodging:** No. **Rental clubs:** Yes. **Walking policy:** Unrestricted walking. **Metal spikes allowed:** No. **Range:** Yes (grass). **To obtain tee times:** Call up to 5 days in advance. Credit card is required for Sat., Sun. and holiday tee times before 1 p.m.
Subscriber comments: Great layout, mature course, hills...Subtle greens, pace of play policy in effect...Course maintenance is excellent...Several wonderful driving holes, challenging greens...Great track, serious golf...Great front nine, every hole different.

★★½STONERIDGE GOLF CLUB & RESORT

R-1 Blanchard Rd., Blanchard, 83804, Bonner County, (208)437-4682, 35 miles NE of Spokane.
Opened: 1971. **Holes:** 18. **Par:** 72/72. **Yards:** 6,522/5,678. **Course rating:** 71.4/72.4. **Slope:** 127/126. **Architect:** Jim Krause. **Green fee:** $20. **Credit cards:** MC,VISA. **Reduced fees:** Resort guests, twilight, seniors, juniors. **Caddies:** No. **Golf carts:** $22. **Discount golf packages:** Yes. **Season:** April-Oct. **High:** May-Sept. **On site lodging:** Yes. **Rental clubs:** Yes. **Walking policy:** Unrestricted walking. **Metal spikes allowed:** Yes. **Range:** Yes (grass). **To obtain tee times:** Call seven days in advance for week-ends and holidays; 48 hours for weekdays.

★★★★SUN VALLEY RESORT GOLF COURSE

R-Sun Valley Rd., Sun Valley, 83353, Blaine County, (208)622-2251, (800)786-8259.
Opened: 1938. **Holes:** 18. **Par:** 72/73. **Yards:** 6,565/5,241. **Course rating:** 71.1/70.4. **Slope:** 128/125. **Architect:** William P. Bell/Robert Trent Jones Jr. **Green fee:** $49/$83. **Credit cards:** All major. **Reduced fees:** Low season, resort guests. **Caddies:** No. **Golf carts:** Included in Green Fee. **Discount golf packages:** Yes. **Season:** April-Oct. **High:** June-Sept. **On site lodging:** Yes. **Rental clubs:** Yes. **Walking policy:** Walking at cer-tain times. **Metal spikes allowed:** Yes. **Range:** Yes (grass). **To obtain tee times:** Hotel guests anytime. Public may call 48 hours in advance. All tee times reserved with credit card.
Notes: Golf Digest School site. Ranked 2nd in 1997 Best in State.
Subscriber comments: Tight but very picturesque. Maybe best in state. Very balanced nines. Better players need to play tips. Some holes simply majestic...Scenic course. Fun to play...Beautiful setting with aspen, pines and big houses, best driving range.

★★★TETON LAKES GOLF COURSE
2000 W. Hibbard Pkwy., Rexburg, 83440, Madison County, (208)359-3036.
Call club for further information.
Subscriber comments: Easy front nine, back nine is a real tester. Water everywhere...
Nice pro shop, excellent pro...Lots of new trees, home of big wind, No. 18 can play into
wind forever...Great staff...Lots of water on back nine.

★½TWIN FALLS MUNICIPAL GOLF COURSE
PU-Grandview Dr., Twin Falls, 83301, Twin Falls County, (208)733-3326.
Opened: N/A. **Holes:** 18. **Par:** 68/72. **Yards:** 5,234/4,961. **Course rating:** 64.0/68.0.
Slope: 106/105. **Architect:** N/A. **Green fee:** $18. **Credit cards:** MC,VISA. **Reduced
fees:** Weekdays, low season, twilight, seniors, juniors. **Caddies:** No. **Golf carts:** $20.
Discount golf packages: No. **Season:** March-Nov. **High:** Feb.-Nov. **On site lodging:**
No. **Rental clubs:** Yes. **Walking policy:** Unrestricted walking. **Metal spikes allowed:**
Yes. **Range:** Yes (grass). **To obtain tee times:** Call up to 7 days in advance.
Special Notes: Fivesomes must take 3 carts.

★★★TWIN LAKES VILLAGE GOLF COURSE
W. 5500 Village Blvd., Rathdrum, 83858, Kootenai County, (208)687-1311, (888)836-
7949, 15 miles N of Coeur d'Alene.
Opened: 1975. **Holes:** 18. **Par:** 72/72. **Yards:** 6,277/5,363. **Course rating:** 70.0/70.5.
Slope: 121/118. **Architect:** William Robinson. **Green fee:** $17/$25. **Credit cards:**
MC,VISA. **Reduced fees:** Weekdays, low season, twilight, seniors, juniors. **Caddies:**
No. **Golf carts:** $22. **Discount golf packages:** No. **Season:** April-Oct. **High:** June-Aug.
On site lodging: Yes. **Rental clubs:** Yes. **Walking policy:** Unrestricted walking. **Metal
spikes allowed:** No. **Range:** Yes (grass). **To obtain tee times:** Call 7 days in advance.
Subscriber comments: Beautiful location...Great course, undiscovered...Front nine
easy, back nine challenging...Harder than it looks. It's still developing...Lots of water,
trees and sand...Beautiful setting...Houses can keep your ball in play.

★★★UNIVERSITY OF IDAHO GOLF COURSE
PU-1215 Nez Perce, Moscow, 83843, Latah County, (208)885-6171, 85 miles S of
Spokane.
Opened: 1933. **Holes:** 18. **Par:** 72/72. **Yards:** 6,639/5,770. **Course rating:** 72.0/73.0.
Slope: 130/130. **Architect:** Francis L. James. **Green fee:** $10/$18. **Credit cards:**
MC,VISA,DISC. **Reduced fees:** Weekdays, twilight, seniors, juniors. **Caddies:** No. **Golf
carts:** $20. **Discount golf packages:** Yes. **Season:** March-Oct. **High:** May-Aug. **On
site lodging:** No. **Rental clubs:** Yes. **Walking policy:** Unrestricted walking. **Metal
spikes allowed:** Yes. **Range:** Yes (grass). **To obtain tee times:** Call up to 7 days in
advance.
Subscriber comments: A lot of elevated tees and greens with great views of the
rolling hills of the Palouse...Good course for a university...Tough and quirky...Many good
holes, no flat lies...Great course design...Tough course especially in the wind.

★★WARM SPRINGS GOLF COURSE
PU-2495 Warm Springs Ave., Boise, 83712, Ada County, (208)343-5661.
Opened: N/A. **Holes:** 18. **Par:** 72/72. **Yards:** 6,719/5,660. **Course rating:** N/A. **Slope:**
113/113. **Architect:** N/A. **Green fee:** $15/$17. **Credit cards:** All major. **Reduced fees:**
Weekdays, twilight. **Caddies:** No. **Golf carts:** $9. **Discount golf packages:** No.
Season: Year-round. **High:** May-Sept. **On site lodging:** No. **Rental clubs:** No. **Walking
policy:** Unrestricted walking. **Metal spikes allowed:** Yes. **Range:** Yes (grass/mats). **To
obtain tee times:** Call up to 5 days in advance.

★★★½ALDEEN GOLF CLUB
PU-1900 Reid Farm Rd., Rockford, 61107, Winnebago County, (815)282-4653, (888)425-3336, 90 miles W of Chicago.
Opened: 1991. **Holes:** 18. **Par:** 72/72. **Yards:** 7,058/5,038. **Course rating:** 73.6/69.1. **Slope:** 126/115. **Architect:** Dick Nugent. **Green fee:** $35/$39. **Credit cards:** MC,VISA,DISC. **Reduced fees:** Weekdays, twilight. **Caddies:** No. **Golf carts:** $24. **Discount golf packages:** No. **Season:** April-Oct. **High:** June-Aug. **On site lodging:** No. **Rental clubs:** Yes. **Walking policy:** Unrestricted walking. **Metal spikes allowed:** Yes. **Range:** Yes (grass). **To obtain tee times:** Call with credit card to reserve up to 7 days in advance.
Subscriber comments: One of the best in Illinois; great course...Great fairways, layout a little constricted, greens good...Water hazards on half the holes, including island green par 3...Fast greens—good pin placements for challenging putts.

★★★★ANNBRIAR GOLF COURSE
PU-1524 Birdie Lane, Waterloo, 62298, Monroe County, (618)939-4653, 25 miles SE of St. Louis.
Opened: 1993. **Holes:** 18. **Par:** 72/72. **Yards:** 6,841/4,792. **Course rating:** 72.3/66.4. **Slope:** 141/110. **Architect:** Michael Hurdzan. **Green fee:** $48/$58. **Credit cards:** MC,VISA,AMEX. **Reduced fees:** Low season. **Caddies:** No. **Golf carts:** Included in Green Fee. **Discount golf packages:** No. **Season:** Year-round. **High:** April-Oct. **On site lodging:** No. **Rental clubs:** Yes. **Walking policy:** Mandatory cart. **Metal spikes allowed:** Yes. **Range:** Yes (grass). **To obtain tee times:** Call up to 7 days in advance. Call (618)939-4653 from Ill. or (314)367-4653 from Mo.
Subscriber comments: Best course in St. Louis Metro Area...Very well groomed, excellent greens...Challenging and fun—pleasing to the eye, beautiful course...Good layout; overrated, but good...Overpriced somewhat—but still good...Nice clubhouse...Great back nine, bring your camera...Wish you could walk.

★½ANTIOCH GOLF CLUB
PU-40150 N. Rte. 59, Antioch, 60021, Lake County, (847)395-3004, 60 miles NW of Chicago.
Opened: 1925. **Holes:** 18. **Par:** 71/72. **Yards:** 6,321/5,556. **Course rating:** 68.2/72.4. **Slope:** 114/112. **Architect:** Mike Hurdzan/Dave Esler. **Green fee:** $17/$23. **Credit cards:** MC,VISA,AMEX. **Reduced fees:** Weekdays, low season, twilight, seniors, juniors. **Caddies:** No. **Golf carts:** $24. **Discount golf packages:** Yes. **Season:** Year-round. **High:** May-Sept. **On site lodging:** No. **Rental clubs:** Yes. **Walking policy:** Unrestricted walking. **Metal spikes allowed:** Yes. **Range:** Yes. **To obtain tee times:** Call up to 7 days in advance (credit card required).

★★★ARBORETUM GOLF CLUB
PU-401 Half Day Rd., Buffalo Grove, 60089, Lake County, (847)913-1112, 45 miles NE of Chicago.
Opened: 1990. **Holes:** 18. **Par:** 72/72. **Yards:** 6,477/5,039. **Course rating:** 71.1/68.7. **Slope:** 132/118. **Architect:** Dick Nugent. **Green fee:** $29/$40. **Credit cards:** All major. **Reduced fees:** Weekdays, low season, twilight. **Caddies:** No. **Golf carts:** N/A. **Discount golf packages:** Yes. **Season:** March-Dec. **High:** June-Aug. **On site lodging:** No. **Rental clubs:** Yes. **Walking policy:** Walking at certain times. **Metal spikes allowed:** Yes. **Range:** No. **To obtain tee times:** Nonresidents call 5 days in advance with credit card.
Subscriber comments: Pray for no wind on front nine...Just not enough land available, nothing special...Nice clubhouse...High quality muny. Target golf...Good condition, great twilight value...Fairways too tight for average golfer, small greens...Sporty layout.

★★ARROWHEAD GOLF CLUB
PU-26 W. 151 Butterfield Rd., Wheaton, 60187, Du Page County, (630)653-5800, 35 miles NW of Chicago.
Opened: 1924. **Holes:** 27. **Architect:** Stan Pelchar/David Gill. **Green fee:** $22/$25. **Credit cards:** MC,VISA. **Reduced fees:** Weekdays, twilight, seniors, juniors. **Caddies:** No. **Golf carts:** $10. **Discount golf packages:** No. **Season:** April-Dec. **High:** May-Oct. **On site lodging:** No. **Rental clubs:** Yes. **Walking policy:** Unrestricted walking. **Metal spikes allowed:** Yes. **Range:** Yes. **To obtain tee times:** Call up to seven days in advance for weekdays, Monday before for weekends.

EAST/SOUTH
Par: 71/74. **Yards:** 6,310/5,669. **Course rating:** 69.1/71.3. **Slope:** 114/116.
EAST/WEST
Par: 71/72. **Yards:** 6,107/5,506. **Course rating:** 69.1/71.3. **Slope:** 114/116.
WEST/SOUTH
Par: 70/74. **Yards:** 6,217/5,807. **Course rating:** 69.1/71.3. **Slope:** 114/116.

★★★½BALMORAL WOODS COUNTRY CLUB
PU-26732 S. Balmoral Woods Dr., Crete, 60417, Will County, (708)672-7448, 40 miles
S of Chicago.
Opened: 1976. **Holes:** 18. **Par:** 72/72. **Yards:** 6,683/5,282. **Course rating:** 72.6/71.8.
Slope: 131/117. **Architect:** Don Mortell. **Green fee:** $27/$45. **Credit cards:** All major.
Reduced fees: Weekdays, low season, twilight, seniors. **Caddies:** No. **Golf carts:**
Included in Green Fee. **Discount golf packages:** Yes. **Season:** March-Nov. **High:**
June-Aug. **On site lodging:** No. **Rental clubs:** Yes. **Walking policy:** Unrestricted walk-
ing. **Metal spikes allowed:** Yes. **Range:** Yes (grass). **To obtain tee times:** Call up to 7
days in advance. Credit card required to reserve weekend tee time.
Subscriber comments: Has some great holes...High handicappers stay home, poor
man's country club...Lots of trees, a challenge...Good hotdogs...Accuracy a must—
modern, comfortable clubhouse...Middle holes beautiful; bring a high draw.

★★½BARTLETT HILLS GOLF COURSE
PM-800 W. Oneida, Bartlett, 60103, Cook County, (630)837-2741, 25 miles NW of
Chicago.
Opened: 1924. **Holes:** 18. **Par:** 71/71. **Yards:** 6,482/5,488. **Course rating:** 71.2/71.8.
Slope: 124/121. **Architect:** Charles Maddox/Bob Lohman. **Green fee:** $16/$29. **Credit
cards:** MC,VISA. **Reduced fees:** Weekdays, low season, twilight, seniors, juniors.
Caddies: No. **Golf carts:** $12. **Discount golf packages:** No. **Season:** Year-round.
High: April-Sept. **On site lodging:** No. **Rental clubs:** Yes. **Walking policy:**
Unrestricted walking. **Metal spikes allowed:** Yes. **Range:** Yes (grass/mats). **To obtain
tee times:** Call up to 7 days in advance.

★★★BELK PARK GOLF CLUB
PU-880 Belk Park Rd., Wood River, 62095, Madison County, (618)251-3115, 10 miles
E of St. Louis, MO.
Opened: 1970. **Holes:** 18. **Par:** 72/73. **Yards:** 6,761/5,726. **Course rating:** 71.5/70.8.
Slope: 121/118. **Architect:** E.L. Packard. **Green fee:** $21/$25. **Credit cards:** MC,VISA.
Reduced fees: Low season, twilight, juniors. **Caddies:** No. **Golf carts:** $10. **Discount
golf packages:** No. **Season:** Year-round. **High:** May-Sept. **On site lodging:** No. **Rental
clubs:** Yes. **Walking policy:** Walking at certain times. **Metal spikes allowed:** Yes.
Range: Yes (grass). **To obtain tee times:** Call up to 7 days in advance.
Subscriber comments: Great value...Very good course—nice people...Good challenge, irons only on driving range...Fairways look like rough...Great course except fairways, grass always too long...What public golf should be.

★★★½BIG RUN GOLF CLUB
PU-17211 W. 135th St., Lockport, 60441, Will County, (815)838-1057, 35 miles SW of
Chicago.
Opened: 1930. **Holes:** 18. **Par:** 72/74. **Yards:** 7,010/5,975. **Course rating:** 73.9/74.8.
Slope: 139/132. **Architect:** Muhlenford/Sneed/Didier/Killian/Nugent. **Green fee:**
$34/$39. **Credit cards:** MC,VISA. **Reduced fees:** Low season, twilight, juniors.
Caddies: No. **Golf carts:** $13. **Discount golf packages:** No. **Season:** April-Nov. **High:**
June-Aug. **On site lodging:** No. **Rental clubs:** Yes. **Walking policy:** Walking at certain
times. **Metal spikes allowed:** Yes. **Range:** No. **To obtain tee times:** Call 7 days in
advance at 7 a.m.
Subscriber comments: Nice place, plays long...Family run...Fun to play a hilly course
in Illinois...Trees overhang fairway, tees, greens; trim back to make it better...Longest
9th hole ever played, more than 600 yards...No.18 is called "Cardiac Hill"

★★BITTERSWEET GOLF CLUB
PU-875 Almond St., Gurnee, 60031, Lake County, (847)855-9031, 40 miles N of
Chicago.
Opened: 1996. **Holes:** 18. **Par:** 72/72. **Yards:** 6,754/5,027. **Course rating:** 72.8/69.6.

Slope: 130/115. **Architect:** Jack Porter/Harry Vignocchi. **Green fee:** $45. **Credit cards:** All major. **Reduced fees:** Twilight, seniors. **Caddies:** No. **Golf carts:** $14. **Discount golf packages:** No. **Season:** April-Nov. **High:** May-Oct. **On site lodging:** No. **Rental clubs:** Yes. **Walking policy:** Walking at certain times. **Metal spikes allowed:** Yes. **Range:** Yes (grass/mats). **To obtain tee times:** Nonresidents may reserve 7 days in advance with credit card. Residents may reserve 8 days in advance.

★★★BLACKBERRY OAKS GOLF COURSE
PU-2245 Kennedy Rd., Bristol, 60512, Kendall County, (630)553-7170, 40 miles SW of Chicago.
Opened: 1993. **Holes:** 18. **Par:** 72/72. **Yards:** 6,258/5,230. **Course rating:** 69.8/70.1. **Slope:** 121/119. **Architect:** David Gill. **Green fee:** $19/$27. **Credit cards:** All major. **Reduced fees:** Twilight, seniors, juniors. **Caddies:** No. **Golf carts:** $13. **Discount golf packages:** No. **Season:** April-Nov. **High:** May-Sept. **On site lodging:** No. **Rental clubs:** Yes. **Walking policy:** Unrestricted walking. **Metal spikes allowed:** Yes. **Range:** Yes (grass). **To obtain tee times:** Call up to 7 days in advance.
Subscriber comments: Not enough trees...Best chicken wings around...Super staff...Needs another 500 yards to become a real test...People, manager, pro and owner were so friendly, you feel accepted right away.

★★BLACKHAWK GOLF CLUB
PU-5n748 Burr Rd., St. Charles, 60175, Kane County, (630)443-3500, 40 miles W of Chicago.
Opened: 1974. **Holes:** 18. **Par:** 72/72. **Yards:** 6,640/5,111. **Course rating:** 72.5/70.9. **Slope:** 128/120. **Architect:** Charles Maddox. **Green fee:** $24/$45. **Credit cards:** All major. **Reduced fees:** Weekdays, low season, twilight, seniors. **Caddies:** No. **Golf carts:** $10. **Discount golf packages:** No. **Season:** Year-round. **High:** May-Aug. **On site lodging:** No. **Rental clubs:** Yes. **Walking policy:** Walking at certain times. **Metal spikes allowed:** Yes. **Range:** Yes (grass). **To obtain tee times:** Call up to 7 days in advance. Tee times may be made further in advance with credit card.
Special Notes: Formerly The Burr Hill Club.

★★BLOOMINGDALE GOLF CLUB
PM-5 N 181 Glen Ellyn Rd., Bloomingdale, 60108, Du Page County, (630)529-6232, 20 miles W of Chicago.
Opened: 1934. **Holes:** 18. **Par:** 72/72. **Yards:** 6,240/5,871. **Course rating:** 69.6/69.6. **Slope:** 108/108. **Architect:** Bob Lohmann. **Green fee:** $10/$29. **Credit cards:** MC,VISA. **Reduced fees:** Weekdays, low season, twilight, seniors, juniors. **Caddies:** No. **Golf carts:** $19. **Discount golf packages:** No. **Season:** March-Nov. **High:** June-Aug. **On site lodging:** No. **Rental clubs:** Yes. **Walking policy:** Walking at certain times. **Metal spikes allowed:** Yes. **Range:** No. **To obtain tee times:** Call up to 7 days in advance.
Special Notes: Formerly Glendale Country Club.

★★★BON VIVANT COUNTRY CLUB
PU-Career Center Rd., Bourbonnais, 60914, Kankakee County, (815)935-0403, (800)248-7775, 2 miles N of Kankakee.
Opened: 1980. **Holes:** 18. **Par:** 72/75. **Yards:** 7,498/5,979. **Course rating:** 76.2/74.7. **Slope:** 128/123. **Architect:** N/A. **Green fee:** $14/$22. **Credit cards:** MC,VISA,AMEX. **Reduced fees:** N/A. **Caddies:** No. **Golf carts:** $18. **Discount golf packages:** No. **Season:** April-Nov. **High:** May-Sept. **On site lodging:** No. **Rental clubs:** Yes. **Walking policy:** Unrestricted walking. **Metal spikes allowed:** Yes. **Range:** Yes (grass). **To obtain tee times:** Call 7 days in advance.
Subscriber comments: Long, but playable...Course too long for average golfer...Not very tough yet, but wait till those trees grow...Great course, great price...Nice facilities...Good length, difficult...Bit of a drive from Chicago, area's best value.

GOOD VALUE

★★★½BONNIE BROOK GOLF CLUB
PU-2800 N. Lewis Ave., Waukegan, 60087, Lake County, (847)360-4730, 25 miles N of Chicago.
Opened: 1927. **Holes:** 18. **Par:** 72/73. **Yards:** 6,701/5,559. **Course rating:** 72.4/72.2. **Slope:** 126/124. **Architect:** Jim Foulis. **Green fee:** $18/$30. **Credit cards:** MC,VISA. **Reduced fees:** Twilight, seniors. **Caddies:** No. **Golf carts:** $24. **Discount golf pack-

ages: No. **Season:** April-Nov. **High:** May-Sept. **On site lodging:** No. **Rental clubs:** Yes. **Walking policy:** Unrestricted walking. **Metal spikes allowed:** Yes. **Range:** Yes (grass/mats). **To obtain tee times:** Weekend tee times only. Call 3 days in advance. **Subscriber comments:** Best course in the world...A test of all clubs, very challenging...Good municipal course...Good conditions, inexpensive, fair, challenging...Old course. Great tradition, fair...Very popular, makes it hard to get times.

★★BONNIE DUNDEE GOLF CLUB

PU-270 Kennedy Dr., Carpentersville, 60110, Kane County, (847)426-5511, 25 miles NW of Chicago.
Opened: 1924. **Holes:** 18. **Par:** 69/75. **Yards:** 6,176/6,024. **Course rating:** 68.1/72.5. **Slope:** 113/113. **Architect:** C. D. Wagstaff. **Green fee:** $13/$25. **Credit cards:** MC,VISA,DISC. **Reduced fees:** Weekdays, twilight, seniors, juniors. **Caddies:** No. **Golf carts:** $13. **Discount golf packages:** No. **Season:** April-Nov. **High:** N/A. **On site lodging:** No. **Rental clubs:** Yes. **Walking policy:** Unrestricted walking. **Metal spikes allowed:** Yes. **Range:** No. **To obtain tee times:** Call 7 days in advance.

★★★½THE BOURNE GOLF CLUB

Norway, La Salle County, (815)496-2301.
Call club for further information.
Subscriber comments: Very scenic, hilly, must ride...This is a course with an attitude!...Unique fun...Tight fairways, good facility...A picturesque course in NW Illinois...Every golfer should play at least once!.

★★BRAE LOCH COUNTRY CLUB

PM-33600 N. Route 45, Grayslake, 60030, Lake County, (847)223-5542, 55 miles from Chicago.
Opened: 1931. **Holes:** 18. **Par:** 68/68. **Yards:** 5,644/5,268. **Course rating:** 67.5/67.5. **Slope:** 114/116. **Architect:** N/A. **Green fee:** $24/$28. **Credit cards:** MC,VISA. **Reduced fees:** Twilight. **Caddies:** No. **Golf carts:** $24. **Discount golf packages:** No. **Season:** Year-round. **High:** June-Aug. **On site lodging:** No. **Rental clubs:** Yes. **Walking policy:** Unrestricted walking. **Metal spikes allowed:** Yes. **Range:** No. **To obtain tee times:** Call on Monday for upcoming weekend.

★★★BROKEN ARROW GOLF CLUB

PU-16325 W. Broken Arrow Dr., Lockport, 60441, Will County, (815)836-8858, 30 miles SW of Chicago.
Opened: 1996. **Holes:** 27. **Architect:** Bob Lohmann. **Green fee:** $27/$36. **Credit cards:** MC,VISA. **Reduced fees:** Weekdays, low season, twilight, seniors, juniors. **Caddies:** No. **Golf carts:** $13. **Discount golf packages:** Yes. **Season:** Year-round. **High:** May-Aug. **On site lodging:** No. **Rental clubs:** Yes. **Walking policy:** Unrestricted walking. **Metal spikes allowed:** Yes. **Range:** Yes (grass/mats). **To obtain tee times:** Call up to 14 days in advance.
EAST/NORTH COURSE
Par: 72/72. **Yards:** 6,865/5,163. **Course rating:** 74.1/70.3. **Slope:** 131/121.
NORTH/SOUTH COURSE
Par: 72/72. **Yards:** 6,897/5,178. **Course rating:** 73.9/70.5. **Slope:** 131/121.
SOUTH/EAST
Par: 72/72. **Yards:** 6,756/5,125. **Course rating:** 73.6/70.4. **Slope:** 129/121.
Subscriber comments: One of the best courses, undiscovered, challenging, great price for juniors...New course, a lot of holes look alike...Treat you well; course needs to mature...Outstanding layout in otherwise nothing piece of land...Very hard on windy days...Lots of water...Open with little trees, not too challenging...Will be a great course once the back nine grows in...Great track, excellent staff...Two-pin concept is fun. Easy to get a tee time.

★★BUFFALO GROVE GOLF CLUB

PU-48 Raupp Blvd., Buffalo Grove, 60089, Lake County, (847)459-5520, 40 miles NW of Chicago.
Opened: 1965. **Holes:** 18. **Par:** 72/75. **Yards:** 6,892/6,003. **Course rating:** 71.5/73.5. **Slope:** 120/122. **Architect:** Dick Nugent. **Green fee:** $13/$27. **Credit cards:** All major. **Reduced fees:** Low season, twilight, seniors, juniors. **Caddies:** No. **Golf carts:** $25. **Discount golf packages:** Yes. **Season:** Year-round. **High:** May-Oct. **On site lodging:**

No. **Rental clubs:** Yes. **Walking policy:** Unrestricted walking. **Metal spikes allowed:** No. **Range:** Yes (grass). **To obtain tee times:** Call on Monday for upcoming Friday, weekend or holiday. First come first served Monday.-Thursday.

★★½BUNKER LINKS MUNICIPAL GOLF COURSE

PU-3500 Lincoln Park Dr., Galesburg, 61401, Knox County, (309)344-1818, 42 miles NW of Peoria.
Opened: 1922. **Holes:** 18. **Par:** 71/73. **Yards:** 5,934/5,354. **Course rating:** 67.4/69.4. **Slope:** 106/108. **Architect:** D.C. Bunker. **Green fee:** $8/$9. **Credit cards:** None. **Reduced fees:** Twilight. **Caddies:** No. **Golf carts:** $9. **Discount golf packages:** No. **Season:** March-Nov. **High:** April-Sept. **On site lodging:** No. **Rental clubs:** No. **Walking policy:** Unrestricted walking. **Metal spikes allowed:** Yes. **Range:** Yes (grass). **To obtain tee times:** Call up to one week in advance for weekends only.
Subscriber comments: Fun short course, lots of traffic...Tough course if you play a slice...Fun, interesting design, good variety of holes...Short and tight...Flat greens, easy course, pricey for course...Basic golf...Old course but nice, good outing.

★★BUNN GOLF COURSE

PU-2500 S. 11th, Springfield, 62703, Sangamon County, (217)522-2633.
Opened: 1901. **Holes:** 18. **Par:** 72/73. **Yards:** 6,104/5,355. **Course rating:** 68.7/68.4. **Slope:** 118/119. **Architect:** Edward Lawrence Packard. **Green fee:** $9/$13. **Credit cards:** MC,VISA. **Reduced fees:** Seniors, juniors. **Caddies:** No. **Golf carts:** $9. **Discount golf packages:** No. **Season:** March-Nov. **High:** June-July. **On site lodging:** No. **Rental clubs:** Yes. **Walking policy:** Unrestricted walking. **Metal spikes allowed:** Yes. **Range:** No. **To obtain tee times:** In person 7 days in advance with nominal fee.

★★★★CANTIGNY GOLF

PU-27 W. 270 Mack Rd., Wheaton, 60187, Du Page County, (630)668-3323, 40 miles W of Chicago.
Opened: 1989. **Holes:** 27. **Architect:** Roger Packard. **Green fee:** $65. **Credit cards:** All major. **Reduced fees:** Seniors, juniors. **Caddies:** Yes. **Golf carts:** $15. **Discount golf packages:** No. **Season:** April-Oct. **High:** June-Aug. **On site lodging:** No. **Rental clubs:** Yes. **Walking policy:** Unrestricted walking. **Metal spikes allowed:** No. **Range:** Yes (grass/mats). **To obtain tee times:** Call up to 7 days in advance.
LAKESIDE/HILLSIDE
Par: 72/72. **Yards:** 6,625/5,165. **Course rating:** 71.1/64.3. **Slope:** 126/108.
WOODSIDE/HILLSIDE
Par: 72/72. **Yards:** 6,760/5,214. **Course rating:** 72.2/64.9. **Slope:** 125/105.
WOODSIDE/LAKESIDE
Par: 72/72. **Yards:** 6,709/5,421. **Course rating:** 72.4/65.7. **Slope:** 130/114.
Subscriber comments: Great design, tough par 3s from tips...Challenging but not tough layout, fairly priced...Facilities great, personnel very courteous and accommodating...Sunday brunch a winner!...My favorite; I played it the morning of my wedding.

★★CARDINAL GOLF COURSE

PU-Town of Effingham, Effingham, 62401, Effingham County, (217)868-2860.
Opened: 1963. **Holes:** 18. **Par:** 72. **Yards:** 5,980. **Course rating:** N/A. **Slope:** N/A. **Architect:** N/A. **Green fee:** $16. **Credit cards:** None. **Reduced fees:** N/A. **Caddies:** No. **Golf carts:** $16. **Discount golf packages:** No. **Season:** April-Oct. **High:** N/A. **On site lodging:** No. **Rental clubs:** Yes. **Walking policy:** Unrestricted walking. **Metal spikes allowed:** Yes. **Range:** No. **To obtain tee times:** First come, first served.

★★★CARILLON GOLF CLUB

PU-21200 S. Carillon, Plainfield, 60544, Will County, (815)886-2132, 30 miles S of Chicago.
Opened: 1990. **Holes:** 18. **Par:** 71/71. **Yards:** 6,607/5,194. **Course rating:** 71.1/68.4. **Slope:** 121/108. **Architect:** Greg Martin. **Green fee:** $32/$42. **Credit cards:** MC,VISA,DISC. **Reduced fees:** Weekdays, low season, twilight, seniors, juniors. **Caddies:** No. **Golf carts:** $12. **Discount golf packages:** Yes. **Season:** March-Nov. **High:** June-Sept. **On site lodging:** No. **Rental clubs:** Yes. **Walking policy:** Unrestricted walking. **Metal spikes allowed:** Yes. **Range:** Yes (grass). **To obtain tee times:** Call 7 days in advance.

Subscriber comments: Very nice shorter course, good bargain for fee...Course interesting and challenging...Great links type course getting better and better...18th is "different"...New nine in '97...Nice fairways and green. Hard on windy days.
Special Notes: Also has a 9-hole par-35 course.

★★CARRIAGE GREENS COUNTRY CLUB
PU-8700 Carriage Greens Dr., Darien, 60559, Du Page County, (630)985-3730, 25 miles SW of Chicago.
Opened: 1969. **Holes:** 18. **Par:** 70/72. **Yards:** 6,451/6,009. **Course rating:** 70.9/73.5. **Slope:** 121/123. **Architect:** N/A. **Green fee:** $28/$43. **Credit cards:** MC,VISA,AMEX. **Reduced fees:** N/A. **Caddies:** No. **Golf carts:** Included in Green Fee. **Discount golf packages:** Yes. **Season:** March-Nov. **High:** June-Aug. **On site lodging:** No. **Rental clubs:** Yes. **Walking policy:** Walking at certain times. **Metal spikes allowed:** Yes. **Range:** No. **To obtain tee times:** Call 7 days in advance.

★★½CARY COUNTRY CLUB
2400 Grove Lane, Cary, 60013, McHenry County, (847)639-3161, 40 miles NW of Chicago.
Opened: 1923. **Holes:** 18. **Par:** 72/77. **Yards:** 6,135/5,595. **Course rating:** 68.7/70.8. **Slope:** 114/118. **Architect:** N/A. **Green fee:** $23/$27. **Credit cards:** All major. **Reduced fees:** Weekdays, twilight, seniors. **Caddies:** No. **Golf carts:** $26. **Discount golf packages:** No. **Season:** April-Oct. **High:** June-Aug. **On site lodging:** No. **Rental clubs:** Yes. **Walking policy:** Unrestricted walking. **Metal spikes allowed:** Yes. **Range:** No. **To obtain tee times:** Call up to 7 days in advance.
Special Notes: 9-hole play only on weekdays.

★★★★CHALET HILLS GOLF CLUB
PU-943 W. Rawson Bridge Rd., Cary, 60013, McHenry County, (847)639-0666, 40 miles NW of Chicago.
Opened: 1995. **Holes:** 18. **Par:** 73/73. **Yards:** 6,877/4,934. **Course rating:** 73.4/68.1. **Slope:** 131/114. **Architect:** Ken Killian. **Green fee:** $28/$46. **Credit cards:** MC,VISA,DISC. **Reduced fees:** Weekdays, twilight, seniors, juniors. **Caddies:** No. **Golf carts:** $12. **Discount golf packages:** No. **Season:** April-Oct. **High:** May-Sept. **On site lodging:** No. **Rental clubs:** Yes. **Walking policy:** Walking at certain times. **Metal spikes allowed:** No. **Range:** Yes (mats). **To obtain tee times:** Call golf shop.
Subscriber comments: Good value for money...A position course versus raw distance...Scenic beauty yet challenging...Course improved over past few years...Still trying to figure out where the landing areas are...Great course, not so good clubhouse...Bring two sleeves of balls when you play No.13; very narrow.

★★½CHAPEL HILL COUNTRY CLUB
PU-2500 Chapel Hill Rd, McHenry, 60005, McHenry County, (815)385-3337.
Opened: 1928. **Holes:** 18. **Par:** 70/72. **Yards:** 6,021/5,359. **Course rating:** 68.7/70.4. **Slope:** 117/117. **Architect:** N/A. **Green fee:** $18/$25. **Credit cards:** All major. **Reduced fees:** Twilight, seniors, juniors. **Caddies:** No. **Golf carts:** $12. **Discount golf packages:** No. **Season:** Year-round. **High:** May-Sept. **On site lodging:** No. **Rental clubs:** Yes. **Walking policy:** Walking at certain times. **Metal spikes allowed:** Yes. **Range:** Yes (grass). **To obtain tee times:** Call up to 7 days in advance.
Subscriber comments: Short, but course was in excellent condition...For price...Nothing special about the course...Another fine course, keep up the good work.

★★CHERRY HILLS GOLF CLUB
191 St & Flossmoor Rd., Flossmoor, 60422, Cook County, (708)799-5600.
Call club for further information.

★★CHEVY CHASE GOLF CLUB
PU-1000 N. Milwaukee Ave., Wheeling, 60090, Cook County, (847)537-0082.
Opened: 1923. **Holes:** 18. **Par:** 72/72. **Yards:** 6,608/5,215. **Course rating:** 71.7/69.3. **Slope:** 126/119. **Architect:** Tom Bendelow. **Green fee:** $17/$28. **Credit cards:** MC,VISA,DISC. **Reduced fees:** Low season, twilight, seniors, juniors. **Caddies:** No. **Golf carts:** $23. **Discount golf packages:** No. **Season:** Year-round. **High:** April-Oct. **On site lodging:** No. **Rental clubs:** Yes. **Walking policy:** Unrestricted walking. **Metal spikes allowed:** Yes. **Range:** No. **To obtain tee times:** Call 7 days in advance.

★½CHICK EVANS GOLF COURSE
PU-6145 Golf Rd., Morton Grove, 60053, Cook County, (847)965-5353.
Opened: 1940. **Holes:** 18. **Par:** 73/71. **Yards:** 5,680/5,680. **Course rating:** 67.5/63.0.
Slope: N/A. **Architect:** N/A. **Green fee:** $16/$19. **Credit cards:** MC,VISA. **Reduced fees:** Weekdays, twilight, seniors, juniors. **Caddies:** No. **Golf carts:** $20. **Discount golf packages:** No. **Season:** March-Dec. **High:** June-Aug. **On site lodging:** No. **Rental clubs:** Yes. **Walking policy:** Unrestricted walking. **Metal spikes allowed:** Yes. **Range:** Yes (grass). **To obtain tee times:** Call seven days in advance.

★★½CINDER RIDGE GOLF LINKS
PU-24801 Lakepoint Dr., Wilmington, 60481, Will County, (815)476-4000, 55 miles S of Chicago.
Opened: 1995. **Holes:** 18. **Par:** 72/72. **Yards:** 6,803/5,644. **Course rating:** 72.9/73.2.
Slope: 130/126. **Architect:** George Kappos. **Green fee:** $40. **Credit cards:** All major.
Reduced fees: Weekdays, twilight, seniors, juniors. **Caddies:** No. **Golf carts:** Included in Green Fee. **Discount golf packages:** No. **Season:** Year-round. **High:** May-Sept. **On site lodging:** No. **Rental clubs:** Yes. **Walking policy:** Unrestricted walking. **Metal spikes allowed:** Yes. **Range:** Yes (grass/mats). **To obtain tee times:** Call up to 7 days in advance with a credit card. Yearly times may be purchased with 3 weeks deposit in advance.
Subscriber comments: Coal cinder traps! Good value...Nice layout, needs to mature...Interesting layout, friendly staff...Once matured, will be a winner.

★★½CLINTON HILL COUNTRY CLUB
PU-3700 Old Collinsville Rd., Belleville, 62201, St. Clair County, (618)277-3700.
Opened: 1969. **Holes:** 18. **Par:** 71/71. **Yards:** 6,700/5,176. **Course rating:** 70.6/68.4.
Slope: 129/119. **Architect:** N/A. **Green fee:** $11/$19. **Credit cards:** MC,VISA,DISC.
Reduced fees: Low season, seniors. **Caddies:** No. **Golf carts:** $10. **Discount golf packages:** No. **Season:** Year-round. **High:** N/A. **On site lodging:** No. **Rental clubs:** No. **Walking policy:** Walking at certain times. **Metal spikes allowed:** No. **Range:** Yes (grass/mats). **To obtain tee times:** N/A.
Subscriber comments: Course condition good for southern Illinois...Some good greens...Ho-hum...Good entry/mid-level course.

COG HILL GOLF CLUB
PU-12294 Archer Ave., Lemont, 60439, Cook County, (630)257-5872, 32 miles SW of Chicago.
Credit cards: MC,VISA,DISC. **Caddies:** Yes. **Discount golf packages:** No. **High:** April-Oct. **On site lodging:** No. **Rental clubs:** Yes. **Walking policy:** Unrestricted walking. **Metal spikes allowed:** Yes. **Range:** Yes (grass/mats).

★★★COURSE NO. 1
Opened: 1928. **Holes:** 18. **Par:** 71/72. **Yards:** 6,329/5,594. **Course rating:** 69.9/71.3.
Slope: 117/118. **Architect:** David McIntosh/Bert Coghill. **Green fee:** $8/$32. **Reduced fees:** Weekdays, low season, twilight, juniors. **Golf carts:** $27. **Season:** Year-round. **To obtain tee times:** Call 6 days in advance.
Subscriber comments: No.1 least challenging of Cog Hill's four courses...Wide open, no rough...Easy course with very little trouble...Always in good condition. Fun courses; good facilities; Joe Jemsek always says hello...Good quality at reasonable cost.

★★★½COURSE NO. 2
Opened: 1930. **Holes:** 18. **Par:** 72/72. **Yards:** 6,268/5,564. **Course rating:** 69.4/72.3.
Slope: 120/120. **Architect:** Bert Coghill. **Green fee:** $20/$41. **Reduced fees:** Weekdays, low season, twilight, juniors. **Golf carts:** $27. **Season:** Year-round. **To obtain tee times:** Call 90 days in advance with prepayment or 6 days in advance without.
Subscriber comments: Huge complex, good clubhouse...Challenging, crowded, too much on weekends, need all types of shots...Great course, would play anytime!...As good as No.4 at half the price...No.2 a better course for the average golfer than No.4.

★★★COURSE NO. 3
Opened: 1969. **Holes:** 18. **Par:** 72/71. **Yards:** 6,437/5,321. **Course rating:** 70.1/69.9.
Slope: 117/114. **Architect:** Dick Wilson. **Green fee:** $8/$32. **Reduced fees:** Weekdays, low season, twilight, juniors. **Golf carts:** $27. **Season:** Year-round. **To obtain tee times:** Call 6 days in advance.

Subscriber comments: Short course...Good for money, busy, tight, accuracy a key...Five-hour round normal...Always get a fair round...Easy course with little trouble...The weakest course at Cog...Very playable...Boring compared to Nos. 2 and 4.

★★★★½COURSE NO. 4

Opened: 1964. **Holes:** 18. **Par:** 72/72. **Yards:** 6,930/5,874. **Course rating:** 75.6/76.7. **Slope:** 142/134. **Architect:** Dick Wilson. **Green fee:** $95. **Reduced fees:** Weekdays, twilight, juniors. **Golf carts:** Included in Green Fee. **Season:** April-Oct. **To obtain tee times:** Call up to 90 days in advance with pre-pay on credit card.

Notes: Ranked 54th in America's 100 Greatest; 3rd in 1997 Best in State. Motorola Western Open; 1997 US Amateur; 1989, 1970 USGA Amateur Public Links Championship; 1987 USGA Women's Amateur Public Links Championship.

Subscriber comments: "Dubsdread" a true top 100 course. Great challenge. Excellent practice facilities, pros and golf shops...Pricey but worth every penny for this U.S. Open-style course...No.4 is terrific!...All I thought it would be!...Simply the best by far—enough said...Wow, absolutely perfect—play it right after the Western Open. Bring your sand game...Golf factory. Good courses...Better than advertised.

★★COLONIAL GOLF COURSE

Old Route 51 S., Sandoval, 62882, Marion County, (618)247-3307.
Call club for further information.

★★COLUMBIA GOLF CLUB

PU-125 AA Rd., Columbia, 62236, Monroe County, (618)286-4455, 15 miles N of St. Louis, MO.

Opened: 1972. **Holes:** 18. **Par:** 71/72. **Yards:** 6,275/5,000. **Course rating:** 69.4/68.4. **Slope:** N/A. **Architect:** Al Linkogel. **Green fee:** $12/$21. **Credit cards:** None. **Reduced fees:** Weekdays, low season, seniors. **Caddies:** No. **Golf carts:** $10. **Discount golf packages:** No. **Season:** Year-round. **High:** April-Oct. **On site lodging:** No. **Rental clubs:** No. **Walking policy:** Unrestricted walking. **Metal spikes allowed:** Yes. **Range:** No. **To obtain tee times:** Call golf shop.

se marginal...New greens are great...Good prices. Interested management.

★½COUNTRY LAKES VILLAGE GOLF CLUB

1601 Fairway Dr., Naperville, 60563, Du Page County, (630)420-1060.
Call club for further information.

COUNTRYSIDE GOLF COURSE

PM-20800 W. Hawley St., Mundelein, 60060, Lake County, (847)566-5544, 30 miles N of Chicago.

Opened: 1927. **Architect:** Bob Lohmann. **Green fee:** $15/$31. **Credit cards:** None. **Reduced fees:** Weekdays, low season, twilight, seniors, juniors. **Caddies:** No. **Golf carts:** $25. **Discount golf packages:** Yes. **Season:** Year-round. **High:** May-Sept. **On site lodging:** No. **Rental clubs:** Yes. **Walking policy:** Unrestricted walking. **Metal spikes allowed:** Yes. **Range:** Yes (grass/mats). **To obtain tee times:** Call on Monday for upcoming weekend or holiday.

★★½EAST COURSE

Holes: 18. **Par:** 72/72. **Yards:** 6,757/5,050. **Course rating:** 71.5/68.3. **Slope:** 123/114.
Subscriber comments: Average...New, needs maturing...Great forest-preserve course...Outstanding golf for the price...Nice challenging course.

★★½WEST COURSE

Holes: 18. **Par:** 72/72. **Yards:** 6,178/5,111. **Course rating:** 69.4/68.8. **Slope:** 114/112.
Subscriber comments: Easy, short, but interesting, good bargain...Good for average Sunday golfer...Spend the day...Decent challenge, fair maintenance...Nice inexpensive public course.

★★½CRAB ORCHARD GOLF CLUB

901 W. Grand Ave., Carterville, 62918, Williamson County, (618)985-2321, 100 miles SE of St. Louis.

Opened: 1959. **Holes:** 18. **Par:** 70/71. **Yards:** 6,420/5,058. **Course rating:** 71.0/68.4. **Slope:** 129/114. **Architect:** Roy Glenn. **Green fee:** $20. **Credit cards:** MC,VISA,DISC. **Reduced fees:** Seniors. **Caddies:** No. **Golf carts:** $9. **Discount golf packages:** No. **Season:** Year-round. **High:** April-Oct. **On site lodging:** No. **Rental clubs:** Yes. **Walking policy:** Unrestricted walking. **Metal spikes allowed:** No. **Range:** Yes (grass). **To**

obtain tee times: Call. Must have threesome or foursome to reserve tee time.
Subscriber comments: Heavy weekend and special events play...First few holes not hard. Try to get you off to a nice start...Nice little public course...Good challenging course...Course has improved tremendously each year.

★★½CRYSTAL WOODS GOLF CLUB
5915 S. Route 47, Woodstock, 60098, McHenry County, (815)338-3111, 3 miles S of Woodstock.
Opened: 1957. **Holes:** 18. **Par:** 72/73. **Yards:** 6,403/5,488. **Course rating:** 70.3/70.5.
Slope: 117/114. **Architect:** William Langford. **Green fee:** $24/$42. **Credit cards:** All major. **Reduced fees:** Twilight, seniors. **Caddies:** No. **Golf carts:** Included in Green Fee. **Discount golf packages:** No. **Season:** April-Nov. **High:** June-Sept. **On site lodging:** No. **Rental clubs:** No. **Walking policy:** Walking at certain times. **Metal spikes allowed:** Yes. **Range:** Yes (grass). **To obtain tee times:** Call up to 7 days in advance.
Subscriber comments: Facilities OK, course attractive and a challenge...Owners are exceptional! I can play several home courses but this is the best for me...Pleasant surprise after not playing it for 10 years. Decent test of golf.

★★½DEER CREEK GOLF CLUB
PU-26201 S. Western Ave., University Park, 60466, Will County, (708)672-6667, 30 miles S of Chicago.
Opened: 1972. **Holes:** 18. **Par:** 72/72. **Yards:** 6,755/5,835. **Course rating:** 72.4/73.2.
Slope: 124/120. **Architect:** Edward Lawrence Packard. **Green fee:** $19/$25. **Credit cards:** All major. **Reduced fees:** Weekdays, twilight, seniors, juniors. **Caddies:** No.
Golf carts: $10. **Discount golf packages:** No. **Season:** Year-round. **High:** May-Sept.
On site lodging: No. **Rental clubs:** Yes. **Walking policy:** Unrestricted walking. **Metal spikes allowed:** Yes. **Range:** Yes (grass/mats). **To obtain tee times:** Call anytime.
Subscriber comments: Good food service...Very forgiving...Good course to use every club...Enjoyable day...Very plain...Acceptable public course...Nice range and putting green...A thinker's course...Slow.

★★½DEERFIELD PARK GOLF CLUB
PU-1201 Saunders Rd., Riverwoods, 60015, Lake County, (847)945-8333, 6 miles W of Highland Park.
Opened: N/A. **Holes:** 18. **Par:** 72/74. **Yards:** 6,756/5,635. **Course rating:** 71.8/71.9.
Slope: 125/121. **Architect:** Edward Lawrence Packard. **Green fee:** $26/$32. **Credit cards:** MC,VISA,DISC. **Reduced fees:** Weekdays, twilight. **Golf carts:** $24. **Discount golf packages:** Yes. **Season:** April-Dec. **High:** June-Sept. **On site lodging:** No. **Rental clubs:** Yes. **Walking policy:** Unrestricted walking. **Metal spikes allowed:** Yes. **Range:** No. **To obtain tee times:** Call 2 days in advance.
Subscriber comments: Nice layout...Members treated better than "walk-on"...Fair conditions, good for price, interesting holes...Good solid golf holes, but too close to expressway, noisy...Can't wait to play it again...Big and good greens.

★★½DEERPATH PARK GOLF COURSE
PU-500 W. Deerpath, Lake Forest, 60045, Lake County, (847)615-4290, 25 miles N of Chicago.
Opened: 1927. **Holes:** 18. **Par:** 70/72. **Yards:** 6,105/5,542. **Course rating:** 68.7/72.1.
Slope: 124/122. **Architect:** Alex Pirie. **Green fee:** $23/$31. **Credit cards:** MC,VISA.
Reduced fees: Seniors, juniors. **Caddies:** No. **Golf carts:** $23. **Discount golf packages:** No. **Season:** April-Dec. **High:** June-Aug. **On site lodging:** No. **Rental clubs:** Yes. **Walking policy:** Unrestricted walking. **Metal spikes allowed:** Yes. **Range:** Yes (grass/mats). **To obtain tee times:** Call 1 day in advance.
Subscriber comments: Good track, good golf...Fair...OK, overpriced for what you get...Well maintained. Moderate challenge...Play here regularly—a little gem.

★★½DOWNERS GROVE GOLF COURSE
PM-2420 Haddow, Downers Grove, 60515, Du Page County, (630)963-1306, 25 miles W of Chicago.
Opened: 1892. **Holes:** 9. **Par:** 38/35. **Yards:** 3,230/2,629. **Course rating:** 70.5/69.4.
Slope: 122/115. **Architect:** C.B. Macdonald/David Gill/Steven Halberg. **Green fee:** $20/$28. **Credit cards:** MC,VISA. **Reduced fees:** Seniors, juniors. **Caddies:** No. **Golf carts:** $24. **Discount golf packages:** No. **Season:** March-Nov. **High:** June-Aug. **On**

site lodging: No. **Rental clubs:** Yes. **Walking policy:** Unrestricted walking. **Metal spikes allowed:** Yes. **Range:** Yes (grass/mats). **To obtain tee times:** Call 5 days in advance for weekends and holidays.
Subscriber comments: New clubhouse...Great layout...Nice variety...Extremely crowded...Nine holes only...Fun to play, rolling fairways.

★★½DWIGHT COUNTRY CLUB

RR 2, Golf Rd., Dwight, 60420, Livingston County, (815)584-1399.
Call club for further information.

EAGLE RIDGE INN & RESORT

R- **Credit cards:** All major,Diners Club. **Reduced fees:** Resort guests, twilight. **Caddies:** No. **Golf carts:** $28. **Discount golf packages:** Yes. **On site lodging:** Yes. **Rental clubs:** Yes. **Range:** Yes (grass). **To obtain tee times:** Nonguests call up to 7 days in advance.

★★★★THE GENERAL COURSE

P.O. Box 777, Galena, 61036, Jo Daviess County, (815)777-4525, (800)892-2269, 30 miles SE of Dubuque.
Opened: 1997. **Holes:** 18. **Par:** 72/72. **Yards:** 6,820/5,335. **Course rating:** 73.8/66.7. **Slope:** 137/119. **Architect:** Roger Packard/Andy North. **Green fee:** $97/$117. **Season:** May-Oct. **High:** N/A. **Walking policy:** Mandatory cart. **Metal spikes allowed:** No.
Notes: Ranked 6th in 1997 Best New Upscale Public Courses.
Subscriber comments: Great course, very expensive...Scenic, challenging holes...Best courses in Midwest...Top of the line course, kind of course where you feel you are all alone. Beautiful...A lot of money to play golf—maybe I'm spoiled...First-class course with good service...It's a perfect course but really hurts the wallet.

★★★★NORTH COURSE

400 Eagle Ridge Dr., Galena, 61036, Jo Daviess County, (815)777-2500, (800)892-2269, 20 miles SE of Dubuque, IA.
Opened: 1977. **Holes:** 18. **Par:** 72/72. **Yards:** 6,836/5,578. **Course rating:** 73.4/72.3. **Slope:** 134/127. **Architect:** Larry Packard/Roger Packard. **Green fee:** $77/$97. **Season:** April-Nov. **High:** May-Oct. **Walking policy:** Walking at certain times. **Metal spikes allowed:** Yes.
Subscriber comments: Grand, panoramic views...Great course, very expensive...Beautiful views...Great scenery, hills...Very difficult to score; magnificent...Weekend stay is good with golf...Ultimate golf...Difficult courses for average women golfers...Hard to believe there's a golf resort like this in corn country.

★★★★SOUTH COURSE

10 Clubhouse Dr., Galena, 61036, Jo Daviess County, (815)777-2280, (800)892-2269, 12 miles SE of Dubuque, IA.
Opened: 1984. **Holes:** 18. **Par:** 72/72. **Yards:** 6,762/5,609. **Course rating:** 72.9/72.4. **Slope:** 133/128. **Architect:** Roger Packard. **Green fee:** $77/$97. **Season:** April-Nov. **High:** May-Oct. **Walking policy:** Walking at certain times. **Metal spikes allowed:** Yes.
Notes: Ranked 20th in 1997 Best in State.
Subscriber comments: Great course, very expensive...Playable, but fairway slopes cause unfair penalties...Charge way too much to play there compared to other courses just as nice in area...Great overnight facilities...Nice contrast from the North.
Special Notes: Also has 9-hole par-34 East Course. Spikeless encouraged.

★★½EDGEBROOK COUNTRY CLUB

2100 Sudyam Rd., Sandwich, 60548, De Kalb County, (815)786-3058, 35 miles SW of Aurora.
Opened: 1968. **Holes:** 18. **Par:** 72/73. **Yards:** 6,500/5,134. **Course rating:** 69.1/69.5. **Slope:** 123/114. **Architect:** Ken Killian/Dick Nugent. **Green fee:** $20/$22. **Credit cards:** MC,VISA,DISC. **Reduced fees:** Low season, twilight, juniors. **Caddies:** No. **Golf carts:** $24. **Discount golf packages:** No. **Season:** Year-round. **High:** April-Dec. **On site lodging:** No. **Rental clubs:** Yes. **Walking policy:** Unrestricted walking. **Metal spikes allowed:** Yes. **Range:** Yes (grass/mats). **To obtain tee times:** Call at least 5 days in advance.
Subscriber comments: Long course; nice people...Good value...Variety of holes, good challenges, strong par 3s...Small elevated greens...Challenging wooded course.

★½EDGEBROOK GOLF CLUB
6100 North Central Ave., Chicago, 60646, Cook County, (773)763-8320.
Call club for further information.

★★★EDGEWOOD GOLF COURSE - GOLD/RED/WHITE
RR 3, Auburn, 62615, Sangamon County, (217)438-3221.
Call club for further information.
Subscriber comments: Affordable, love the layout...Lots of water holes...Working man's golf club...Above average course in all aspects...Very nice golf course, several tough holes...Wide open front nine, wooded back nine; very deceiving.

★★★EL PASO GOLF CLUB
RR 1 Box 63A, El Paso, 61738, Woodford County, (309)527-5225, 10 miles N of Bloomington.
Opened: 1924. **Holes:** 18. **Par:** 71/71. **Yards:** 6,052/5,064. **Course rating:** 70.1/69.9. **Slope:** 122/121. **Architect:** James Spear. **Green fee:** $18. **Credit cards:** MC,VISA. **Reduced fees:** N/A. **Caddies:** No. **Golf carts:** $16. **Discount golf packages:** No. **Season:** March-Nov. **High:** June-Aug. **On site lodging:** No. **Rental clubs:** No. **Walking policy:** Unrestricted walking. **Metal spikes allowed:** Yes. **Range:** No. **To obtain tee times:** Call golf shop. Sundays and holidays members only play.
Subscriber comments: Fun, hilly, water. Nice par 3s...Need to advertise...Great value, back nine as good as there is...Hooters Tour stop; great condition...Front nine short and forgettable; back much nicer.

★★ELLIOTT GOLF COURSE
PU-888 S. Lyford Rd., Rockford, 61108, Winnebago County, (815)332-5130, 2 miles E of Rockford.
Opened: 1968. **Holes:** 18. **Par:** 72/76. **Yards:** 6,393/6,253. **Course rating:** 69.4/74.1. **Slope:** 107/107. **Architect:** Edward Lawrence Packard. **Green fee:** $12/$21. **Credit cards:** MC,VISA. **Reduced fees:** Twilight. **Caddies:** No. **Golf carts:** $20. **Discount golf packages:** No. **Season:** April-Oct. **High:** May-Aug. **On site lodging:** No. **Rental clubs:** Yes. **Walking policy:** Unrestricted walking. **Metal spikes allowed:** Yes. **Range:** Yes. **To obtain tee times:** Call or come in 7 days in advance.
Special Notes: Also 9-hole par-3 course.

★★½EMERALD HILL COUNTRY CLUB
16802 Prairie Ville Rd., Sterling, 61081, Whiteside County, (815)622-6204.
Call club for further information.
Subscriber comments: Not very challenging, very average...Getting better each year...Tight course, tall trees, pretty layout...Cozy little course.

★★EVERGREEN GOLF & COUNTRY CLUB
9140 South Western Ave., Chicago, 60620, Cook County, (773)238-6680.
Call club for further information.

★½FAIRLAKES GOLF COURSE
PU-RR 1, Box 122, Secor, 61771, Woodford County, (309)744-2222, 10 miles N of Bloomington.
Opened: 1989. **Holes:** 18. **Par:** 67/69. **Yards:** 5,400/4,274. **Course rating:** 64.1/64.8. **Slope:** 102/103. **Architect:** Harold Sparks. **Green fee:** $11/$14. **Credit cards:** MC,VISA. **Reduced fees:** Weekdays, seniors. **Caddies:** No. **Golf carts:** $18. **Discount golf packages:** No. **Season:** March-Oct. **High:** June-Aug. **On site lodging:** No. **Rental clubs:** Yes. **Walking policy:** Unrestricted walking. **Metal spikes allowed:** Yes. **Range:** Yes (grass/mats). **To obtain tee times:** Call up to 7 days in advance, at least 2 days in advance.

★★FARIES PARK GOLF COURSE
PU-1 Faries Park, Decatur, 62521, Macon County, (217)422-2211.
Opened: 1961. **Holes:** 18. **Par:** 72/75. **Yards:** 6,708/5,763. **Course rating:** 70.8/73.0. **Slope:** 117/113. **Architect:** Edward Lawrence Packard. **Green fee:** $11/$16. **Credit cards:** MC,VISA. **Reduced fees:** N/A. **Caddies:** No. **Golf carts:** $16. **Discount golf packages:** No. **Season:** March-Nov. **High:** June-Aug. **On site lodging:** No. **Rental

clubs: Yes. **Walking policy:** Unrestricted walking. **Metal spikes allowed:** Yes. **Range:** Yes (grass/mats). **To obtain tee times:** Call on Mondays at 6:30 a.m. for upcoming weekend. Call 7 days in advance for weekdays.
Subscriber comments: People very friendly, nice greens...Front nine hilly, back is flat...An above-average muny course. Lack of facilities...Long par 5s...Good golf challenge, nice old course.

★★½FOSS PARK GOLF CLUB

3124 Argonne Dr., North Chicago, 60064, Lake County, (847)689-1633.
Call club for further information.
Subscriber comments: Nice course for average player...Sporty track...Beautiful course; hidden trees...Course has matured, is a fun place...Good greens.

★★FOUR WINDS GOLF CLUB

PU-Route 176, Mundelein, 60060, Lake County, (847)566-8502, 40 miles N of Chicago.
Opened: 1963. **Holes:** 18. **Par:** 71/71. **Yards:** 6,527/4,855. **Course rating:** 71.5/68.5.
Slope: 122/114. **Architect:** Herman Schwinge. **Green fee:** $29/$52. **Credit cards:** All major. **Reduced fees:** Weekdays, twilight, seniors, juniors. **Caddies:** No. **Golf carts:** Included in Green Fee. **Discount golf packages:** No. **Season:** March-Oct. **High:** June-Aug. **On site lodging:** No. **Rental clubs:** Yes. **Walking policy:** Unrestricted walking. **Metal spikes allowed:** Yes. **Range:** Yes (grass). **To obtain tee times:** Call up to 10 days in advance. Credit card required to guarantee weekend tee times.

★★★FOX BEND GOLF COURSE

PU-Route 34, Oswego, 60543, Kendall County, (630)554-3939, 6 miles S of Aurora.
Opened: 1967. **Holes:** 18. **Par:** 72/72. **Yards:** 6,800/5,400. **Course rating:** 72.1/70.1.
Slope: 124/116. **Architect:** Brent Wadsworth/Paul Loague. **Green fee:** $26/$36. **Credit cards:** MC,VISA,AMEX. **Reduced fees:** Weekdays, low season, twilight, seniors, juniors. **Caddies:** No. **Golf carts:** $13. **Discount golf packages:** No. **Season:** March-Dec. **High:** May-Sept. **On site lodging:** No. **Rental clubs:** Yes. **Walking policy:** Unrestricted walking. **Metal spikes allowed:** No. **Range:** Yes (grass/mats). **To obtain tee times:** Call 7 days in advance.
Subscriber comments: They keep pace without being rude...Good greens and nice fairways, well kept...Treat you good, too much cost for non-residents...Has everything. Excellent golf shop and restaurant...Very enjoyable. Somewhat crowded.

★★★½FOX CREEK GOLF CLUB

PU-6555 Fox Creek Dr., Edwardsville, 62025, Madison County, (618)692-9400, (800)692-9401, 20 miles NE of St. Louis, MO.
Opened: 1992. **Holes:** 18. **Par:** 72/72. **Yards:** 7,027/5,185. **Course rating:** 74.9/72.1.
Slope: 144/132. **Architect:** Gary Kern. **Green fee:** $25/$35. **Credit cards:** MC,VISA.
Reduced fees: Weekdays, low season, twilight, seniors. **Caddies:** No. **Golf carts:** Included in Green Fee. **Discount golf packages:** Yes. **Season:** Year-round. **High:** May-Sept. **On site lodging:** No. **Rental clubs:** Yes. **Walking policy:** Mandatory cart. **Metal spikes allowed:** Yes. **Range:** Yes (grass). **To obtain tee times:** Call four days in advance.
Subscriber comments: Back nine tough; inexpensive...Tough but enjoyable. Gets better all the time...Tough course/long carries/good service, price and food...Toughest course I've ever played, low handicapper won't even play it.

★★★½FOX LAKE COUNTRY CLUB

PU-7220 N. State Park Rd., Fox Lake, 60020, Lake County, (847)587-6411, 35 miles N of Chicago.
Opened: 1920. **Holes:** 18. **Par:** 72/73. **Yards:** 6,347/5,852. **Course rating:** 71.2/73.2.
Slope: 129/120. **Architect:** N/A. **Green fee:** $40/$50. **Credit cards:** MC,VISA.
Reduced fees: N/A. **Caddies:** No. **Golf carts:** Included in Green Fee. **Discount golf packages:** No. **Season:** April-Oct. **High:** N/A. **On site lodging:** No. **Rental clubs:** Yes.
Walking policy: Mandatory cart. **Metal spikes allowed:** Yes. **Range:** Yes (grass). **To obtain tee times:** Call anytime.
Subscriber comments: Very lovely, sporty course...Not a flat lie on the course; very hilly...Even with many parallel fairways, good challenging holes...Good old-style course, tough greens...Never got tired of it.

★★½ FOX RUN GOLF LINKS
PU-333 Plum Grove Rd., Elk Grove Village, 60007, Cook County, (847)228-3544, 20 miles NW of Chicago.
Opened: 1984. **Holes:** 18. **Par:** 70/70. **Yards:** 6,287/5,288. **Course rating:** 70.5/70.2. **Slope:** 117/114. **Architect:** William Newcomb. **Green fee:** $12/$29. **Credit cards:** MC,VISA,AMEX. **Reduced fees:** Weekdays, twilight, seniors, juniors. **Caddies:** No. **Golf carts:** $13. **Discount golf packages:** Yes. **Season:** April-Nov. **High:** June-Aug. **On site lodging:** No. **Rental clubs:** Yes. **Walking policy:** Unrestricted walking. **Metal spikes allowed:** Yes. **Range:** Yes (grass/mats). **To obtain tee times:** Call up to 7 days in advance.
Subscriber comments: Nice muny course, all should be like this...Leave driver in the bag...Must keep pace, very strict.
Special Notes: Spikeless shoes encouraged.

★★ FOX VALLEY GOLF CLUB
PM-Route 25, N. Aurora, 60542, Kane County, (630)879-1030, 3 miles N of Aurora.
Opened: 1930. **Holes:** 18. **Par:** 72/72. **Yards:** 5,927/5,279. **Course rating:** 68.5/70.4. **Slope:** 118/117. **Architect:** N/A. **Green fee:** $17/$22. **Credit cards:** MC,VISA. **Reduced fees:** N/A. **Caddies:** No. **Golf carts:** $21. **Discount golf packages:** No. **Season:** March-Nov. **High:** N/A. **On site lodging:** No. **Rental clubs:** No. **Walking policy:** Unrestricted walking. **Metal spikes allowed:** Yes. **Range:** No. **To obtain tee times:** N/A.

★½ FRESH MEADOWS GOLF COURSE
PU-2144 S. Wolf Rd., Hillside, 60162, Cook County, (708)449-3434.
Opened: N/A. **Holes:** 18. **Par:** 70/70. **Yards:** 6,178/5,693. **Course rating:** N/A. **Slope:** 113/110. **Architect:** N/A. **Green fee:** $27/$32. **Credit cards:** MC,VISA,AMEX. **Reduced fees:** Weekdays, low season, twilight, seniors. **Caddies:** No. **Golf carts:** $13. **Discount golf packages:** No. **Season:** Year-round. **High:** May-Sept. **On site lodging:** No. **Rental clubs:** Yes. **Walking policy:** Walking at certain times. **Metal spikes allowed:** Yes. **Range:** Yes (grass/mats). **To obtain tee times:** Call up to 8 days in advance.

GAMBIT GOLF CLUB
PU-1550 St. Rte. 146 E., Vienna, 62995, (618)658-6022, (800)942-6248, 27 miles N of Paducah, KY.
Opened: 1996. **Holes:** 18. **Par:** 71/72. **Yards:** 6,546/4,725. **Course rating:** 72.4/66.1. **Slope:** 137/102. **Architect:** Richard Osborne. **Green fee:** $32/$42. **Credit cards:** MC,VISA,AMEX. **Reduced fees:** Twilight, seniors, juniors. **Caddies:** No. **Golf carts:** Included in Green Fee. **Discount golf packages:** No. **Season:** Feb.-Nov. **High:** March-Sept. **On site lodging:** No. **Rental clubs:** No. **Walking policy:** Unrestricted walking. **Metal spikes allowed:** Yes. **Range:** Yes (grass). **To obtain tee times:** Call up to 7 days in advance.

★★★½ GEORGE W. DUNNE NATIONAL GOLF COURSE
PU-16300 S. Central, Oak Forest, 60452, Cook County, (708)614-2600, 25 miles SW of Chicago.
Opened: 1982. **Holes:** 18. **Par:** 72/72. **Yards:** 7,170/5,535. **Course rating:** 75.1/71.4. **Slope:** 135/121. **Architect:** Killian & Nugent. **Green fee:** $30/$40. **Credit cards:** MC,VISA,DISC. **Reduced fees:** Weekdays, twilight, seniors, juniors. **Caddies:** No. **Golf carts:** Included in Green Fee. **Discount golf packages:** No. **Season:** March-Dec. **High:** May-Aug. **On site lodging:** No. **Rental clubs:** Yes. **Walking policy:** Unrestricted walking. **Metal spikes allowed:** Yes. **Range:** Yes (grass). **To obtain tee times:** Call (708)366-9466 up to 7 days in advance, 24 hours a day.
Subscriber comments: Could be a world-class course...Overrated...Great value...Great track...Used to be a fabulous course. Still a great layout, with several good risk-reward holes...Bring the whole game here, all shots required.

★★★ GIBSON WOODS GOLF COURSE
PU-1321 N. 11th St., Monmouth, 61462, Warren County, (309)734-9968, 16 miles W of Galesburg.
Opened: 1966. **Holes:** 18. **Par:** 71/75. **Yards:** 6,362/5,885. **Course rating:** 70.9/73.9.

Slope: 119/119. **Architect:** Homer Fieldhouse. **Green fee:** $12/$13. **Credit cards:** None. **Reduced fees:** Weekdays, low season, twilight. **Caddies:** No. **Golf carts:** $18. **Discount golf packages:** No. **Season:** March-Nov. **High:** June-Aug. **On site lodging:** No. **Rental clubs:** Yes. **Walking policy:** Unrestricted walking. **Metal spikes allowed:** Yes. **Range:** Yes (grass/mats). **To obtain tee times:** First come, first served. **Subscriber comments:** Old course, full of trees...Tough, tough and hilly, hilly...They don't take tee times ever, but the longest wait I've ever had is 45 minutes. Service is always very friendly...Very good challenge.

★★½GLENCOE GOLF CLUB
621 Westley Rd., Glencoe, 60022, Cook County, (847)835-0981.
Call club for further information.
Subscriber comments: Sporty and short; tough greens...Nice course...Good, old tree-lined muny...Difficult to get tee times...Old course, slow play...Nice little neighborhood course...Challenging, has rolling hills in a flat land...Back-to-back par-5 finish.

★★GLENDALE LAKES GOLF COURSE
PU-1550 President St., Glendale Heights, 60139, Du Page County, (630)260-0018, 30 miles E of Chicago.
Opened: 1987. **Holes:** 18. **Par:** 71/71. **Yards:** 6,143/5,390. **Course rating:** 62.1/71.1. **Slope:** 121/124. **Architect:** Dick Nugent. **Green fee:** $16/$30. **Credit cards:** All major,Diners Club. **Reduced fees:** Weekdays, low season, twilight, seniors, juniors. **Caddies:** No. **Golf carts:** $14. **Discount golf packages:** Yes. **Season:** March-Nov. **High:** June-Aug. **On site lodging:** No. **Rental clubs:** Yes. **Walking policy:** Walking at certain times. **Metal spikes allowed:** Yes. **Range:** No. **To obtain tee times:** Call 7 days in advance.

GLENEAGLES GOLF CLUB
PU-13070 McNulty Rd., Lemont, 60439, Cook County, (630)257-5466, 25 miles SW of Chicago.
Opened: 1924. **Architect:** Charles Maddox/Frank P. Macdonald. **Green fee:** $23/$30. **Credit cards:** None. **Reduced fees:** Low season, twilight, seniors. **Caddies:** No. **Golf carts:** $13. **Discount golf packages:** No. **Season:** March-Dec. **High:** June-Aug. **On site lodging:** No. **Rental clubs:** Yes. **Walking policy:** Unrestricted walking. **Metal spikes allowed:** Yes. **Range:** Yes (grass/mats). **To obtain tee times:** Call golf shop.
★★½RED COURSE
Holes: 18. **Par:** 70/74. **Yards:** 6,090/6,090. **Course rating:** 67.6/71.3. **Slope:** 112/111.
Subscriber comments: Nice short course, good condition, fair price for Chicago area...When crowded, very very slow...Postage stamp greens, very nostalgic.
★★★WHITE COURSE
Holes: 18. **Par:** 70/75. **Yards:** 6,250/6,080. **Course rating:** 70.1/72.3. **Slope:** 120/114.
Subscriber comments: Very tight course...Excellent layout...Great shape, jam in too many players, six-hour round...Decent challenge; reasonably priced...Short, hilly and treelined, small rolling greens are the significant feature of this course.

★★½GLENVIEW PARK GOLF CLUB
800 Shermer Rd., Glenview, 60025, Cook County, (847)724-0250.
Call club for further information.
Subscriber comments: Overpriced...Nice muny, good management...Need to be straight...Shows what a traditional "muny" course can become with excellent maintenance...A little expensive...Sleeper course, friendly people...The course is easy and short for the money.

★★★GLENWOODIE COUNTRY CLUB
PU-193rd and State, Glenwood, 60425, Cook County, (708)758-1212, 25 miles S of Chicago.
Opened: 1923. **Holes:** 18. **Par:** 72/72. **Yards:** 6,715/5,176. **Course rating:** 71.8/68.4. **Slope:** 120/108. **Architect:** Harry Collis. **Green fee:** $8/$25. **Credit cards:** MC,VISA,DISC. **Reduced fees:** Weekdays, low season, twilight, seniors, juniors. **Caddies:** No. **Golf carts:** N/A. **Discount golf packages:** No. **Season:** Year-round. **High:** April-Sept. **On site lodging:** No. **Rental clubs:** Yes. **Walking policy:** Unrestricted walking. **Metal spikes allowed:** Yes. **Range:** Yes (grass). **To obtain tee times:** Call.

Subscriber comments: Old time good course...Average muny. A couple of real good holes...Nice back nine. Too much play...Nice blend of easy and difficult holes.

★★★GOLF CLUB OF ILLINOIS
PU-1575 Edgewood Rd., Algonquin, 60102, McHenry County, (847)658-4400, 35 miles NW of Chicago.
Opened: 1987. **Holes:** 18. **Par:** 71/71. **Yards:** 7,011/4,896. **Course rating:** 74.6/68.6. **Slope:** 133/115. **Architect:** Dick Nugent. **Green fee:** $33/$43. **Credit cards:** All major. **Reduced fees:** Weekdays, low season, twilight, seniors, juniors. **Caddies:** No. **Golf carts:** $13. **Discount golf packages:** Yes. **Season:** March-Nov. **High:** May-Sept. **On site lodging:** No. **Rental clubs:** Yes. **Walking policy:** Walking at certain times. **Metal spikes allowed:** Yes. **Range:** Yes (grass/mats). **To obtain tee times:** Call 7 days in advance with credit card.
Subscriber comments: Great links style without the ocean; best greens in the state...Country setting...Needed help with "blind" holes.
Special Notes: Spikeless encouraged.

★★GOLFMOHR GOLF COURSE
16724 Hubbard Rd., East Moline, 61244, Rock Island County, (309)496-2434.
Opened: 1965. **Holes:** 18. **Par:** 72/72. **Yards:** 6,659/5,402. **Course rating:** 71.2/70.0. **Slope:** N/A. **Architect:** Ted Lockie. **Green fee:** $9/$15. **Credit cards:** None. **Reduced fees:** Weekdays, twilight, seniors, juniors. **Caddies:** No. **Golf carts:** $18. **Discount golf packages:** No. **Season:** March-Oct. **High:** June-Aug. **On site lodging:** No. **Rental clubs:** Yes. **Walking policy:** Unrestricted walking. **Metal spikes allowed:** Yes. **Range:** Yes (mats). **To obtain tee times:** Call up to 7 days in advance.

★½GRAND MARAIS GOLF COURSE
PU-5802 Lake Dr., East St. Louis, 62205, St. Clair County, (618)398-9999, (888)398-9002, 7 miles E of St. Louis, MO.
Opened: 1936. **Holes:** 18. **Par:** 72/72. **Yards:** 6,600/5,324. **Course rating:** 71.7/68.1. **Slope:** 126/120. **Architect:** Joseph A. Roseman. **Green fee:** $16/$20. **Credit cards:** MC,VISA. **Reduced fees:** Weekdays, low season, seniors, juniors. **Caddies:** Yes. **Golf carts:** $20. **Discount golf packages:** No. **Season:** Year-round. **High:** May-Oct. **On site lodging:** No. **Rental clubs:** Yes. **Walking policy:** Unrestricted walking. **Metal spikes allowed:** Yes. **Range:** Yes (grass/mats). **To obtain tee times:** Call 7 days in advance.

★★GREEN ACRES GOLF COURSE
Route 148 S., Herrin, 62933, Williamson County, (618)942-6816.
Call club for further information.

GREEN GARDEN COUNTRY CLUB
PU-9511 W. Monee Manhattan Rd., Frankfort, 60423, Will County, (815)469-3350, 30 miles S of Chicago.
Architect: Tom Walsh. **Green fee:** $13/$30. **Credit cards:** All major. **Reduced fees:** Weekdays, low season, twilight, seniors, juniors. **Caddies:** No. **Golf carts:** $11. **Discount golf packages:** No. **Season:** Year-round. **High:** May-Sept. **On site lodging:** No. **Rental clubs:** Yes. **Walking policy:** Walking at certain times. **Metal spikes allowed:** Yes. **Range:** Yes (grass/mats). **To obtain tee times:** Call up to 7 days in advance.
★★½BLUE COURSE
Opened: 1972. **Holes:** 18. **Par:** 72/73. **Yards:** 6,665/5,652. **Course rating:** 70.1/69.5. **Slope:** 112/110.
Subscriber comments: Very pricey for the course...Food is excellent; outstanding clubhouse...Both courses in very good condition.
★★★GOLD COURSE
Opened: 1992. **Holes:** 18. **Par:** 72/72. **Yards:** 6,519/5,442. **Course rating:** 70.2/70.2. **Slope:** 115/116.
Subscriber comments: Good course. Preference over Blue Course...A super head golf pro...Young course, affordable green fee...Yearly improvements. Great courses!

★★★GREENVIEW COUNTRY CLUB
2801 Putter Lane, Centralia, 62801, Marion County, (618)532-7395.
Call club for further information.

Subscriber comments: Two distinct nines...Nice layout; Tom Wargo's course (enough said?)...Good mix of holes, good layout...Excellent condition...Only complaint is hard bunkers...A must play in southwest Illinois.

HARBORSIDE INTERNATIONAL GOLF CENTER

PU-11001 S. Doty Ave. E., Chicago, 60628, Cook County, (312)782-7837, 12 miles S of Chicago.
Opened: 1995. **Architect:** Dick Nugent/Tim Nugent. **Green fee:** $65/$75. **Credit cards:** MC,VISA,AMEX. **Reduced fees:** Twilight. **Caddies:** No. **Golf carts:** Included in Green Fee. **Discount golf packages:** No. **Season:** April-Nov. **High:** May-Aug. **On site lodging:** No. **Rental clubs:** Yes. **Walking policy:** Unrestricted walking. **Metal spikes allowed:** Yes. **Range:** Yes (grass/mats). **To obtain tee times:** Foursomes call up to 14 days in advance. Groups of less than 4 players call up to 2 days in advance.
★★★**PORT COURSE**
Holes: 18. **Par:** 72/72. **Yards:** 7,164/5,164. **Course rating:** 75.1/70.8. **Slope:** 136/122.
Notes: 1997 Golf Digest's Environmental Leaders in Golf Award.
Subscriber comments: Rough can get unplayable. Unique setting with challenging golf...Very, very windy; great course; spectacular views...Interesting place/location...Lots of blind shots...Enjoyed all 100 shots...Every garbage dump should be used this way...Felt like I was in Scotland...Two terrific courses, great layout!
STARBOARD COURSE
Holes: 18. **Par:** 72/72. **Yards:** 7,152/5,106. **Course rating:** 75.2/70.4. **Slope:** 137/122.

★★½HARRISON PARK GOLF COURSE

W. Voorhees, Danville, 61832, Vermillion County, (217)431-2266.
Call club for further information.
Subscriber comments: Fine course...Good value...Course weakened by changes when driving range was added...Park district course.

★★★½HAWTHORN RIDGE GOLF CLUB

PU-621 State Hwy. 94, Aledo, 61231, Mercer County, (309)582-5641.
Opened: 1977. **Holes:** 18. **Par:** 72/72. **Yards:** 6,701/5,674. **Course rating:** 71.4/71.6. **Slope:** N/A. **Architect:** William James Spear. **Green fee:** $9/$15. **Credit cards:** None. **Reduced fees:** Weekdays, twilight, seniors, juniors. **Caddies:** No. **Golf carts:** $19. **Discount golf packages:** No. **Season:** March-Oct. **High:** June-Aug. **On site lodging:** No. **Rental clubs:** Yes. **Walking policy:** Unrestricted walking. **Metal spikes allowed:** Yes. **Range:** Yes (grass). **To obtain tee times:** Call up to 7 days in advance.
Subscriber comments: One of the best values in the Midwest...Good test...Could be maintained better...Lots of bunkers, some very tight holes...Great young course. Super greens...Long holes for amateurs; narrow fairways.

★★★★HERITAGE BLUFFS GOLF CLUB

PU-24355 W. Bluff Rd., Channahon, 60410, Will County, (815)467-7888, 45 miles S of Chicago.
Opened: 1993. **Holes:** 18. **Par:** 72/72. **Yards:** 7,106/4,967. **Course rating:** 73.9/68.4. **Slope:** 132/112. **Architect:** Dick Nugent. **Green fee:** $29/$36. **Credit cards:** MC,VISA. **Reduced fees:** Weekdays, twilight, seniors, juniors. **Caddies:** No. **Golf carts:** $12. **Discount golf packages:** No. **Season:** April-Oct. **High:** May-Sept. **On site lodging:** No. **Rental clubs:** Yes. **Walking policy:** Unrestricted walking. **Metal spikes allowed:** Yes. **Range:** Yes (grass/mats). **To obtain tee times:** Call 7 days in advance with credit card.
Subscriber comments: Nice people, awesome course...Scenic and demanding. Tops for value...Hilly...Superb course...Best value-package around Chicago...Some outstanding holes...Just a nice place to play...Carved through trees, no ugly holes.

★★HICKORY HILLS COUNTRY CLUB

PU-8201 West 95th St., Hickory Hills, 60457, Cook County, (708)598-6460, 20 miles SW of Chicago.
Opened: 1930. **Holes:** 27. **Par:** 71/71. **Yards:** 6,018/5,928. **Course rating:** 67.9/67.9. **Slope:** 116/116. **Architect:** N/A. **Green fee:** $25/$30. **Credit cards:** MC,VISA,AMEX. **Reduced fees:** Weekdays, low season, twilight, seniors. **Caddies:** No. **Golf carts:** $13. **Discount golf packages:** No. **Season:** Year-round. **High:** N/A. **On site lodging:** No.

Rental clubs: Yes. Walking policy: Walking at certain times. Metal spikes allowed: Yes. Range: Yes (mats). To obtain tee times: Call up to 7 days in advance.

★★★½HICKORY POINT GOLF CLUB
PU-R.R. 11 Weaver Rd., Decatur, 62826, Macon County, (217)421-7444.
Opened: 1970. Holes: 18. Par: 72/73. Yards: 6,855/5,896. Course rating: 71.4.
Slope: 121. Architect: Edward L. Packard. Green fee: $12/$15. Credit cards: MC,VISA. Reduced fees: Twilight, seniors, juniors. Caddies: No. Golf carts: N/A. Discount golf packages: No. Season: March-Nov. High: June-Aug. On site lodging: No. Rental clubs: Yes. Walking policy: Unrestricted walking. Metal spikes allowed: Yes. Range: Yes (grass). To obtain tee times: Weekdays, call up to seven days in advance. Weekend and holidays call the Monday prior to starting at 6:30 a.m.
Subscriber comments: Good price and well-kept course...Basically flat, poor sand...Hills...Long and open. Good practice facilities...Very nice course and challenging on windy days...Nice course with some "bump and runs".

★★★★HICKORY RIDGE GOLF CENTER
PU-2727 West Glenn Rd., Carbondale, 62902, Jackson County, (618)529-4386, 100 miles SE of St. Louis.
Opened: 1993. Holes: 18. Par: 72/72. Yards: 6,863/5,506. Course rating: 73.3/71.6.
Slope: 137/134. Architect: William James Spear. Green fee: $15/$18. Credit cards: MC,VISA. Reduced fees: Twilight, seniors, juniors. Caddies: No. Golf carts: $9. Discount golf packages: Yes. Season: Year-round. High: April-Sept. On site lodging: No. Rental clubs: Yes. Walking policy: Unrestricted walking. Metal spikes allowed: Yes. Range: Yes (grass). To obtain tee times: Call one week in advance.
Subscriber comments: Course still being refined...Noisy neighborhood, good greens...Great layout, tough, challenging, inexpensive...Could be one of the greats in time...Great layout requiring variety of shots...Course architecture is good...Long and challenging course, very well kept...Best track in southern Illinois.

★★½HIGHLAND PARK COUNTRY CLUB
PU-1201 Park Ave. West, Highland Park, 60035, Lake County, (847)433-9015, 20 miles N of Chicago.
Opened: 1966. Holes: 18. Par: 70/70. Yards: 6,522/5,353. Course rating: 72.1/71.8.
Slope: 130/122. Architect: Ted Lockie. Green fee: $40/$51. Credit cards: MC,VISA. Reduced fees: Weekdays, low season, twilight. Caddies: No. Golf carts: $14. Discount golf packages: No. Season: April-Nov. High: May-Sept. On site lodging: No. Rental clubs: Yes. Walking policy: Walking at certain times. Metal spikes allowed: Yes. Range: Yes (grass). To obtain tee times: Call seven days in advance.
Subscriber comments: Recent changes have made course very good...Tight fairways fun to play...Former private course...Service excellent.

★★½HIGHLAND PARK GOLF COURSE
PU-1613 S. Main, Bloomington, 61701, McLean County, (309)823-4200, 120 miles SW of Chicago.
Opened: N/A. Holes: 18. Par: 70/70. Yards: 5,725/5,530. Course rating: N/A. Slope: 115/111. Architect: N/A. Green fee: $11. Credit cards: MC,VISA. Reduced fees: Twilight. Caddies: No. Golf carts: $14. Discount golf packages: No. Season: Year-round. High: N/A. On site lodging: No. Rental clubs: Yes. Walking policy: Unrestricted walking. Metal spikes allowed: Yes. Range: No. To obtain tee times: Call golf shop.
Subscriber comments: Hidden hazards, relatively short, but sporty, fun course...Too short, mature trees, very tight...Bring your straight ball...Typical municipal course, nothing flashy but enjoyable...Moderate hills...Nice old mature course.

★★★HIGHLAND SPRINGS GOLF COURSE
PM-9500 35th. St. W., Rock Island, 61201, Rock Island County, (309)787-5814, 5 miles S of Davenport, IA.
Opened: 1968. Holes: 18. Par: 72/72. Yards: 6,884/5,875. Course rating: 73.0/69.0.
Slope: 118/118. Architect: William James Spear. Green fee: $11/$13. Credit cards: None. Reduced fees: Weekdays, twilight, seniors, juniors. Caddies: No. Golf carts: $17. Discount golf packages: No. Season: April-Oct. High: May-Aug. On site lodging: No. Rental clubs: Yes. Walking policy: Unrestricted walking. Metal spikes

allowed: Yes. **Range:** Yes (grass). **To obtain tee times:** Call 1 day in advance for weekends and holidays only.
Subscriber comments: Good golf, cheap...Could be great...Huge greens; fast and undulating greens...Lots of hazards...Interesting layout, lots of play...Fun course at a fair price...Long course with lots of opportunities.

★★½HIGHLAND WOODS GOLF COURSE
PU-2775 N. Ela Rd., Hoffman Estates, 60172, Cook County, (847)202-0340, 20 miles W of Chicago.
Opened: 1975. **Holes:** 18. **Par:** 72/72. **Yards:** 6,995/5,895. **Course rating:** 72.5/72.0.
Slope: 129/125. **Architect:** William James Spear. **Green fee:** $21/$25. **Credit cards:** MC,VISA. **Reduced fees:** Weekdays, twilight. **Caddies:** No. **Golf carts:** $20. **Discount golf packages:** No. **Season:** March-Dec. **High:** May-Sept. **On site lodging:** No. **Rental clubs:** No. **Walking policy:** Unrestricted walking. **Metal spikes allowed:** Yes. **Range:** No. **To obtain tee times:** Automated call in system.
Subscriber comments: A little rough around edges...A boom-boomer's paradise...County forest-preserve course...Nice layout...Challenging near greens.

★★½HILLDALE GOLF CLUB
PU-1625 Ardwick Dr., Hoffman Estates, 60195, Cook County, (847)310-1100, 40 miles NW of Chicago.
Opened: 1971. **Holes:** 18. **Par:** 71/72. **Yards:** 6,432/5,409. **Course rating:** 71.3/72.1.
Slope: 130/125. **Architect:** Robert Trent Jones. **Green fee:** $35/$48. **Credit cards:** All major. **Reduced fees:** Weekdays, low season, twilight, seniors. **Caddies:** No. **Golf carts:** Included in Green Fee. **Discount golf packages:** Yes. **Season:** April-Nov. **High:** June-Aug. **On site lodging:** No. **Rental clubs:** Yes. **Walking policy:** Walking at certain times. **Metal spikes allowed:** Yes. **Range:** Yes (grass). **To obtain tee times:** Call up to 7 days in advance.

★★HUGHES CREEK GOLF CLUB
PU-1749 Spring Valley Dr., Elburn, 60119, Kane County, (630)365-9200, 30 miles SW of Chicago.
Opened: 1993. **Holes:** 18. **Par:** 72/72. **Yards:** 6,506/5,561. **Course rating:** 70.9/71.7.
Slope: 117/115. **Architect:** Gordon Cunningham. **Green fee:** $14/$22. **Credit cards:** MC,VISA. **Reduced fees:** Weekdays, low season, twilight, seniors, juniors. **Caddies:** No. **Golf carts:** $12. **Discount golf packages:** No. **Season:** April-Nov. **High:** June-Aug. **On site lodging:** No. **Rental clubs:** Yes. **Walking policy:** Unrestricted walking. **Metal spikes allowed:** Yes. **Range:** Yes. **To obtain tee times:** Call one week in advance.

★★★ILLINOIS STATE UNIVERSITY GOLF COURSE
PU-W. Gregory St., Normal, 61761, McLean County, (309)438-8065, 100 miles SW of Chicago.
Opened: 1964. **Holes:** 18. **Par:** 71/73. **Yards:** 6,533/5,581. **Course rating:** 71.1/71.8.
Slope: 120/119. **Architect:** Robert Bruce Harris. **Green fee:** $14. **Credit cards:** MC,VISA,DISC. **Reduced fees:** Twilight, seniors, juniors. **Caddies:** No. **Golf carts:** $16. **Discount golf packages:** No. **Season:** March-Dec. **High:** May-Aug. **On site lodging:** No. **Rental clubs:** Yes. **Walking policy:** Unrestricted walking. **Metal spikes allowed:** Yes. **Range:** No. **To obtain tee times:** Reservation in person date of play Monday through Friday.
Subscriber comments: Outstanding for students...Good shot/good reward...Nice surprise...Lots of sand and long course...A great university course. One can learn all they can about golf here. Interesting short par 4s.

★★½INDIAN BLUFF GOLF COURSE
PU-6200 78th Ave., Milan, 61264, Rock Island County, (309)799-3868, 185 miles W of Chicago.
Opened: N/A. **Holes:** 18. **Par:** 70/71. **Yards:** 5,516/4,510. **Course rating:** 66.7/67.1.
Slope: 111/108. **Architect:** N/A. **Green fee:** $13/$14. **Credit cards:** MC,VISA,DISC. **Reduced fees:** Twilight, seniors, juniors. **Caddies:** No. **Golf carts:** $9. **Discount golf packages:** No. **Season:** April-Nov. **High:** May-Aug. **On site lodging:** No. **Rental clubs:** Yes. **Walking policy:** Unrestricted walking. **Metal spikes allowed:** Yes. **Range:** No. **To obtain tee times:** Call golf shop.

ILLINOIS

Subscriber comments: Hilly, old design, lots of trouble...Greens and fairways good; food service limited...Never seen so many ravines.

★½ INDIAN BOUNDARY GOLF COURSE
PM-8600 W. Forest Preserve Dr, Chicago, 60634, Cook County, (773)625-2013.
Opened: N/A. **Holes:** 18. **Par:** 70/70. **Yards:** 5,838/5,621. **Course rating:** N/A. **Slope:** N/A. **Architect:** N/A. **Green fee:** $19. **Credit cards:** MC,VISA. **Reduced fees:** Weekdays, twilight, seniors, juniors. **Caddies:** No. **Golf carts:** $20. **Discount golf packages:** No. **Season:** Year-round. **High:** April-Aug. **On site lodging:** No. **Rental clubs:** No. **Walking policy:** Unrestricted walking. **Metal spikes allowed:** Yes. **Range:** No. **To obtain tee times:** Call automated tee times phone (708)366-9466 up to 7 days in advance.

★★½ INDIAN HILLS GOLF COURSE
RT 2 Indian Trail Dr., Mt. Vernon, 62864, Jefferson County, (618)244-4905.
Call club for further information.
Subscriber comments: Great layout. Reasonable rates and great staff. Pro a gem...Not really good test of golf...Turtle-back greens make the challenge...Good beginner's course...Good natural layout.

INDIAN LAKES RESORT
R-250 Schick Rd., Bloomingdale, 60108, Du Page County, (630)529-0200, 15 miles W of Chicago.
Opened: 1965. **Architect:** Robert Bruce Harris. **Green fee:** $37/$54. **Credit cards:** All major. **Reduced fees:** Weekdays, low season, resort guests, twilight. **Caddies:** No. **Golf carts:** Included in Green Fee. **Discount golf packages:** No. **Season:** March-Dec. **High:** May-Sept. **On site lodging:** Yes. **Rental clubs:** Yes. **Walking policy:** Walking at certain times. **Metal spikes allowed:** Yes. **Range:** Yes (mats). **To obtain tee times:** Call up to 14 days in advance.
★★½ EAST COURSE
Holes: 36. **Par:** 72/72. **Yards:** 6,890/5,031. **Course rating:** 72.4/70.5. **Slope:** 120/117.
Subscriber comments: No real memorable holes on the entire 18...Twilight rates a good value...Both courses are challenging, nice grounds and people.
Special Notes: Formerly Indian Lakes Country Club Iroquois Course.
★★½ WEST COURSE
Holes: 36. **Par:** 72/72. **Yards:** 6,901/5,088. **Course rating:** 72.1/71.1. **Slope:** 123/120.
Subscriber comments: Too many geese...Six-hour rounds...Rocky sand traps...Course much improved from 1995...Challenging...Courses are overplayed...A little pricey, but a nice course.
Special Notes: Formerly Indian Lakes Country Club Sioux Course.

★½ INDIAN VALLEY COUNTRY CLUB
RT 83 & 45, Mundelein, 60060, Lake County, (847)566-1313.
Call club for further information.

★★★ INGERSOLL MEMORIAL GOLF CLUB
PU-101 Daisyfield Rd., Rockford, 61102, Winnebago County, (815)987-8834, 70 miles W of Chicago.
Opened: 1922. **Holes:** 18. **Par:** 71/74. **Yards:** 5,991/5,140. **Course rating:** 68.2/73.3. **Slope:** 108/108. **Architect:** Thomas M. Bendelow. **Green fee:** $12/$21. **Credit cards:** MC,VISA. **Reduced fees:** Twilight. **Caddies:** No. **Golf carts:** $20. **Discount golf packages:** No. **Season:** April-Oct. **High:** April-Oct. **On site lodging:** No. **Rental clubs:** Yes. **Walking policy:** Unrestricted walking. **Metal spikes allowed:** Yes. **Range:** Yes. **To obtain tee times:** Call seven days in advance.
Subscriber comments: Good condition, short, tight course, small greens a plus...Flat course, but beautiful nature...Must keep ball in play; can shoot 70 or 90...Leave the driver at home...Beautiful trees...Above average course.

★★★ THE INN AT EAGLE CREEK
R-P.O. Box 230, Findlay, 62534, Shelby County, (217)756-3456, (800)876-3245, 35 miles S of Decatur.
Opened: 1989. **Holes:** 18. **Par:** 72/72. **Yards:** 6,908/4,978. **Course rating:** 73.5/69.1. **Slope:** 132/115. **Architect:** Ken Killian. **Green fee:** $28/$48. **Credit cards:** All

major,Diners Club. **Reduced fees:** Weekdays, low season, resort guests, twilight, seniors, juniors. **Caddies:** No. **Golf carts:** Included in Green Fee. **Discount golf packages:** Yes. **Season:** Year-round. **High:** May-Oct. **On site lodging:** Yes. **Rental clubs:** Yes. **Walking policy:** Mandatory cart. **Metal spikes allowed:** Yes. **Range:** Yes (grass). **To obtain tee times:** Call in advance with credit card to guarantee.
Subscriber comments: Difficult, picturesque, nice resort...Tricky, scenic course lots of doglegs...Playing back tees eliminates trouble areas...Inexpensive resort facility, just great...Lots of doglegs.

★★½ INWOOD GOLF COURSE
PU-3000 W. Jefferson, Joliet, 60435, Will County, (815)741-7265, 40 miles SW of Chicago.
Opened: 1931. **Holes:** 18. **Par:** 71/71. **Yards:** 6,078/5,559. **Course rating:** 69.4/71.4. **Slope:** 117/121. **Architect:** Edward Lawrence Packard. **Green fee:** $12/$24. **Credit cards:** MC,VISA,DISC. **Reduced fees:** Weekdays, twilight, seniors, juniors. **Caddies:** No. **Golf carts:** $18. **Discount golf packages:** Yes. **Season:** April-Oct. **High:** June-Aug. **On site lodging:** No. **Rental clubs:** Yes. **Walking policy:** Unrestricted walking. **Metal spikes allowed:** Yes. **Range:** Yes (grass). **To obtain tee times:** Call 24 hours in advance for weekday and Monday for upcoming weekend.
Subscriber comments: Slow play...Decent course, not much character though...Open fairways.

★★½ IRONWOOD GOLF COURSE
PU-1901 N. Towanda Ave., Normal, 61761, McLean County, (309)454-9620, 100 miles S of Chicago.
Opened: 1990. **Holes:** 18. **Par:** 72/72. **Yards:** 6,960/5,385. **Course rating:** 72.4/69.8. **Slope:** 126/113. **Architect:** Roger Packard. **Green fee:** $9/$16. **Credit cards:** MC,VISA. **Reduced fees:** Weekdays, low season, twilight, seniors, juniors. **Caddies:** No. **Golf carts:** $10. **Discount golf packages:** Yes. **Season:** March-Nov. **High:** May-July. **On site lodging:** No. **Rental clubs:** Yes. **Walking policy:** Unrestricted walking. **Metal spikes allowed:** Yes. **Range:** Yes (grass/mats). **To obtain tee times:** Call 7 days in advance.
Subscriber comments: Layout lacks character...Flat; front nine is open, back nine has houses...Tough to walk...Windy links course...Good range.

★★ JACKSON PARK GOLF COURSE
6400 S. Hayes Dr., Chicago, 60637, Cook County, (773)493-1455.
Call club for further information.
Subscriber comments: Great buy, especially for beginners...A fun course, challenging and reasonable...You never leave the course mad...One of oldest courses in Chicago...Slow play on weekends.

★★★½ KANKAKEE ELKS COUNTRY CLUB
2283 Bittersweet Dr., St. Anne, 60964, Kankakee County, (815)937-9547.
Call club for further information.
Subscriber comments: Weekend duffers type of course...Super fairways; elevated greens...Great shape, bring your lob wedge...Great greens, fairways. Every hole has a different look...They make you feel at home!

★★★ KELLOGG GOLF COURSE
PU-7716 N. Radnor Rd., Peoria, 61614, Peoria County, (309)691-0293.
Opened: 1974. **Holes:** 18. **Par:** 72/72. **Yards:** 6,735/5,675. **Course rating:** 70.9/71.5. **Slope:** 117/120. **Architect:** Larry Packard/Roger Packard. **Green fee:** $10/$13. **Credit cards:** MC,VISA. **Reduced fees:** Weekdays, twilight, juniors. **Caddies:** No. **Golf carts:** $10. **Discount golf packages:** No. **Season:** March-Nov. **High:** June-Aug. **On site lodging:** No. **Rental clubs:** Yes. **Walking policy:** Unrestricted walking. **Metal spikes allowed:** Yes. **Range:** Yes (grass). **To obtain tee times:** One week in advance in person. Phone reservations taken only on day of play.
Subscriber comments: Long holes, fast greens, wide open...Can be windy and tough...Nice course, well maintained...Open links course. Windy when no wind!...The course makes you think about your shots.
Special Notes: Also 9-hole executive course.

★★★★½ KEMPER LAKES GOLF COURSE

PU-Old McHenry Rd., Long Grove, 60049, Lake County, (847)320-3450, 25 miles NW of Chicago.

Opened: 1979. **Holes:** 18. **Par:** 72/72. **Yards:** 7,217/5,638. **Course rating:** 75.7/67.9. **Slope:** 140/125. **Architect:** Nugent/Killian. **Green fee:** $100. **Credit cards:** MC,VISA. **Reduced fees:** N/A. **Caddies:** No. **Golf carts:** Included in Green Fee. **Discount golf packages:** No. **Season:** April-Nov. **High:** June-Aug. **On site lodging:** No. **Rental clubs:** Yes. **Walking policy:** Unrestricted walking. **Metal spikes allowed:** Yes. **Range:** Yes (grass). **To obtain tee times:** Call 14 days in advance.

Notes: Ranked 13th in 1997 Best in State. 1989 PGA Championship.

Subscriber comments: Expensive but worth it...18th hole a great finish, especially after a par 3...A good test of golf but overpriced/overrated experience...Excellent condition...Excellent and demanding...Must play!....Love to play the courses the pros play...Get some rangers out there to speed up play. Lengthy five- to six-hour rounds...Second best to Cog Hill No.4.

★★★ KLEIN CREEK GOLF CLUB

PU-1 N. 333 Pleasant Hill Rd., Winfield, 60190, Du Page County, (630)690-0101, 18 miles W of Chicago.

Opened: 1994. **Holes:** 18. **Par:** 72/72. **Yards:** 6,673/4,509. **Course rating:** 71.9/66.2. **Slope:** 127/110. **Architect:** Dick Nugent. **Green fee:** $58/$68. **Credit cards:** MC,VISA,AMEX,Diners Club. **Reduced fees:** Weekdays, low season, twilight. **Caddies:** No. **Golf carts:** Included in Green Fee. **Discount golf packages:** No. **Season:** April-Nov. **High:** June-Sept. **On site lodging:** No. **Rental clubs:** Yes. **Walking policy:** Unrestricted walking. **Metal spikes allowed:** No. **Range:** Yes. **To obtain tee times:** Call up to 14 days in advance with credit card.

Subscriber comments: Nice, newer course...Too difficult for average golfer...Best new course I played last year...Nice layout, well kept, decent parking, good challenge...Be at your best from start to finish...Good layout with limited practice facilities.

KOKOPELLI GOLF CLUB

1401 Champions Dr., Marion, 62959, Williamson County, (618)997-5656, 100 miles SE of St. Louis.

Opened: 1997. **Holes:** 18. **Par:** 72/72. **Yards:** 7,150/5,375. **Course rating:** 75.2. **Slope:** 139. **Architect:** Steve Smyers. **Green fee:** $13/$25. **Credit cards:** MC,VISA,DISC. **Reduced fees:** N/A. **Caddies:** No. **Golf carts:** $9. **Discount golf packages:** No. **Season:** Year-round. **High:** April-Nov. **On site lodging:** No. **Rental clubs:** No. **Walking policy:** Unrestricted walking. **Metal spikes allowed:** No. **Range:** Yes (grass). **To obtain tee times:** Call up to 5 days in advance.

LACOMA GOLF COURSE

PU-8080 Timmerman Rd., East Dubuque, 61025, Jo Daviess County, (815)747-3874, 1 miles E of Dubuque.

Opened: 1967. **Architect:** Gordon Cunningham. **Credit cards:** MC,VISA,DISC. **Reduced fees:** N/A. **Caddies:** No. **Golf carts:** $18. **Discount golf packages:** No. **Season:** March-First snow. **High:** May-Sept. **On site lodging:** No. **Rental clubs:** Yes. **Walking policy:** Unrestricted walking. **Metal spikes allowed:** Yes. **To obtain tee times:** Call 7 days in advance.

★★★ BLUE COURSE

Holes: 18. **Par:** 71/71. **Yards:** 6,705/5,784. **Course rating:** 71.8/70.0. **Slope:** 123/117. **Green fee:** $12/$16. **Range:** Yes (grass/mats).

Subscriber comments: My favorite course in northern Illinois...A personal favorite. Lots of fun...Good challenge, beautiful fairways...Open front nine, tight back nine...Several blind holes...Some unusual holes on back nine...Fairly mundane with a couple of interesting holes.

★★½ RED/GOLD COURSE

Holes: 18. **Par:** 69/69. **Yards:** 5,552/4,895. **Course rating:** 63.5/63.8. **Slope:** 105/102. **Green fee:** $12/$13. **Range:** Yes (grass).

Subscriber comments: Short courses, nice greens, scenery...Short, but pretty much trouble free...Red course is too short...Nice course, interesting, good layout...Great value for the money, wide open front, target golf on back.

Special Notes: Also 9-hole par-3 course.

ILLINOIS

★★★ LAKE BLUFF GOLF CLUB
PU-Green Bay Rd. & Washington St., Lake Bluff, 60044, Lake County, (847)234-6771.
Opened: 1969. **Holes:** 18. **Par:** 72/72. **Yards:** 6,457/5,585. **Course rating:** N/A. **Slope:** 119/117. **Architect:** N/A. **Green fee:** $17/$32. **Credit cards:** MC,VISA. **Reduced fees:** Weekdays, low season, twilight. **Caddies:** No. **Golf carts:** $25. **Discount golf packages:** No. **Season:** April-Nov. **High:** May-Sept. **On site lodging:** No. **Rental clubs:** Yes. **Walking policy:** Unrestricted walking. **Metal spikes allowed:** Yes. **Range:** Yes (grass/mats). **To obtain tee times:** Call up to 7 days in advance or come in up to 6 days in advance.
Subscriber comments: Low price, good course...Well kept, inexpensive, great value. Most bang for the buck...Senior season pass, great greens/fairways...Play is slow...Well manicured, great staff, easy to get times...Fantastic greens! Good layout...Easy flat course with very difficult greens...Restaurant staff excellent.

★★★ LAKE OF THE WOODS GOLF CLUB
PU-405 N. Lake of the Woods Rd., Mahomet, 61853, Champaign County, (217)586-2183, 8 miles W of Champaign.
Opened: 1954. **Holes:** 18. **Par:** 72/72. **Yards:** 6,520/5,187. **Course rating:** 70.8/69.1. **Slope:** 118/112. **Architect:** Robert Bruce Harris. **Green fee:** $14/$16. **Credit cards:** MC,VISA. **Reduced fees:** Seniors, juniors. **Caddies:** No. **Golf carts:** $8. **Discount golf packages:** No. **Season:** March-Dec. **High:** June-Aug. **On site lodging:** No. **Rental clubs:** Yes. **Walking policy:** Unrestricted walking. **Metal spikes allowed:** Yes. **Range:** Yes (grass/mats). **To obtain tee times:** Call 7 days in advance.
Subscriber comments: Starts with two difficult holes. a long par 4 with narrow fairway. and a 200-yard carry over a lake...Beautiful. My favorite...Challenging course...Nice terrain...Facilities good...Has wonderful little par-3 course next to big course; holes range from 70 to 120 yards...Swimming and rec area part of complex.
Special Notes: Also 9-hole par-3 course.

★★★½ LAKE SHORE GOLF COURSE
PM-316 N. Shumway, Taylorsville, 62568, Christian County, (217)824-5521, 26 miles E of Springfield.
Opened: 1969. **Holes:** 18. **Par:** 72/74. **Yards:** 6,778/5,581. **Course rating:** 72.0/74.0. **Slope:** 117/114. **Architect:** William James Spear. **Green fee:** $20. **Credit cards:** MC,VISA,DISC. **Reduced fees:** Low season, twilight, seniors, juniors. **Caddies:** No. **Golf carts:** $18. **Discount golf packages:** No. **Season:** March-Dec. **High:** May-Aug. **On site lodging:** No. **Rental clubs:** Yes. **Walking policy:** Unrestricted walking. **Metal spikes allowed:** No. **Range:** Yes (grass). **To obtain tee times:** Call up to 7 days in advance for weekdays. Call on Monday for upcoming weekend.
Subscriber comments: Very windy all year...Some very nice holes and very challenging...Accuracy course, pretty in woods. Fun to play...Great value. Four good, interesting par 5s...Very nice, wooded layout, lots of doglegs...Nice view of lake...Not bad for a small town...Wonderful scenic golf course.

★½ LAKE VIEW COUNTRY CLUB
23319 Hazel Rd., Sterling, 61081, Whiteside County, (815)626-2886.
Call club for further information.

★★½ LAUREL GREENS PUBLIC GOLFERS CLUB
PU-1133 Hwy. 150 E, Knoxville, 61448, Knox County, (309)289-4146, 6 miles E of Galesburg.
Opened: 1971. **Holes:** 27. **Par:** 72/72. **Yards:** 6,703/5,089. **Course rating:** N/A. **Slope:** N/A. **Architect:** N/A. **Green fee:** $10/$11. **Credit cards:** None. **Reduced fees:** N/A. **Caddies:** No. **Golf carts:** $8. **Discount golf packages:** No. **Season:** April-Dec. **High:** June-Aug. **On site lodging:** No. **Rental clubs:** No. **Walking policy:** Unrestricted walking. **Metal spikes allowed:** Yes. **Range:** No. **To obtain tee times:** Call up to 7 days in advance.
Subscriber comments: 27 holes; very beautiful course...Back nine very beautiful, almost peaceful...Mostly flat course except for beautiful creek valley holes...Very long and through the woods and over the hills.
Special Notes: Formerly Laurel Green Golf Course.

LAWRENCE COUNTY COUNTRY CLUB

US #50, Lawrenceville, 62439, Lawrence County, (618)943-2011, 150 miles E of St. Louis.
Opened: 1915. **Holes:** 9. **Par:** 72. **Yards:** 6,252/5,388. **Course rating:** 68.9. **Slope:** 113. **Architect:** N/A. **Green fee:** $15. **Credit cards:** None. **Reduced fees:** N/A. **Caddies:** No. **Golf carts:** $18. **Discount golf packages:** No. **Season:** March-Nov. **High:** May-Sept. **On site lodging:** No. **Rental clubs:** No. **Walking policy:** Unrestricted walking. **Metal spikes allowed:** Yes. **Range:** No. **To obtain tee times:** Call 1 day in advance for weekdays. Members only play weekends.

★★★½ THE LEDGES GOLF CLUB

PU-7111 McCurry Rd., Roscoe, 61073, Winnebago County, (815)389-0979, 10 miles N of Rockford.
Opened: N/A. **Holes:** 18. **Par:** 72/72. **Yards:** 6,740/5,881. **Course rating:** 72.5/74.1. **Slope:** 129/129. **Architect:** Edward Lawrence Packard. **Green fee:** $14/$24. **Credit cards:** None. **Reduced fees:** Weekdays, low season, twilight, seniors, juniors. **Caddies:** No. **Golf carts:** $22. **Discount golf packages:** No. **Season:** April-Oct. **High:** May-Aug. **On site lodging:** No. **Rental clubs:** Yes. **Walking policy:** Unrestricted walking. **Metal spikes allowed:** Yes. **Range:** Yes (grass/mats). **To obtain tee times:** Call anytime.
Subscriber comments: Excellent public course, best bet for your money in the area. Has everything, woods, water, sand, doglegs, narrow and wide holes and good changes in terrain...Each hole distinct...Former private club. Very interesting layout.

★★ LEGACY GOLF CLUB

PU-3500 Cargill Rd., Granite City, 62040, Madison County, (618)931-4653, 12 miles SW of St. Louis, MO.
Opened: 1990. **Holes:** 18. **Par:** 71/71. **Yards:** 6,300/5,600. **Course rating:** 70.4/69.4. **Slope:** 114/110. **Architect:** Jerry Loomis. **Green fee:** $14/$21. **Credit cards:** MC. **Reduced fees:** Weekdays, low season, twilight, seniors, juniors. **Caddies:** No. **Golf carts:** $10. **Discount golf packages:** Yes. **Season:** Year-round. **High:** April-Oct. **On site lodging:** No. **Rental clubs:** Yes. **Walking policy:** Unrestricted walking. **Metal spikes allowed:** Yes. **Range:** Yes (grass/mats). **To obtain tee times:** Call 7 days in advance.

★★½ LEO DONOVAN GOLF COURSE

PU-5805 Knoxville Ave., Peoria, 61614, Peoria County, (309)691-8361.
Opened: 1929. **Holes:** 18. **Par:** 72/72. **Yards:** 6,735/5,675. **Course rating:** 70.9/71.5. **Slope:** 117/120. **Architect:** N/A. **Green fee:** $4/$12. **Credit cards:** MC,VISA. **Reduced fees:** Weekdays, twilight, juniors. **Caddies:** No. **Golf carts:** N/A. **Discount golf packages:** No. **Season:** March-Nov. **High:** April-Aug. **On site lodging:** No. **Rental clubs:** Yes. **Walking policy:** Unrestricted walking. **Metal spikes allowed:** Yes. **Range:** No. **To obtain tee times:** In person up to seven days in advance. By telephone, day of play.
Subscriber comments: Very playable for all levels; stay out of the pines...Old course; lots of flowers, slow greens...Tough course...Nice public course, nothing spectacular.

★★★½ LICK CREEK GOLF COURSE

PM-2210 N. Pkwy. Dr., Pekin, 61554, Tazewell County, (309)346-0077, 12 miles S of Peoria.
Opened: 1976. **Holes:** 18. **Par:** 72/72. **Yards:** 6,909/5,729. **Course rating:** 72.8/72.9. **Slope:** 128/125. **Architect:** Edward Lawrence Packard. **Green fee:** $9/$18. **Credit cards:** MC,VISA. **Reduced fees:** Weekdays, twilight, seniors, juniors. **Caddies:** No. **Golf carts:** $15. **Discount golf packages:** No. **Season:** April-Nov. **High:** June-Sept. **On site lodging:** No. **Rental clubs:** Yes. **Walking policy:** Unrestricted walking. **Metal spikes allowed:** No. **Range:** Yes (grass). **To obtain tee times:** Call 7 days in advance.
Subscriber comments: There's no more consistently hard demanding muny course anywhere than this; big-time challenge...Extremely difficult from back tees but well worth the frustration...Heavy rough and rolling greens can be brutal...Hilly and treed; No. 6 is the toughest hole I've ever played...Has its own "Amen Corner".

★★½ LINCOLN GREENS GOLF COURSE
PU-700 E. Lake Dr., Springfield, 62707, Sangamon County, (217)786-4000, 90 miles N of St. Louis.
Opened: 1957. **Holes:** 18. **Par:** 72/72. **Yards:** 6,582/5,625. **Course rating:** 70.3/70.9. **Slope:** 112/114. **Architect:** Robert Bruce Harris. **Green fee:** $7/$22. **Credit cards:** MC,VISA. **Reduced fees:** Weekdays, twilight, seniors, juniors. **Caddies:** No. **Golf carts:** $18. **Discount golf packages:** Yes. **Season:** March-Dec. **High:** June-Aug. **On site lodging:** No. **Rental clubs:** Yes. **Walking policy:** Unrestricted walking. **Metal spikes allowed:** Yes. **Range:** Yes (grass). **To obtain tee times:** Call up to 7 days in advance. $2 charge per tee time—no refund unless it rains or cancel 1 day prior to tee time.
Subscriber comments: Very nice municipal...Good facility; top five in Springfield...Flat layout and some different holes...Pretty good test and fun to play...The best local value and upkeep; very slow on weekends...Nice wide open course, fairly long.

★★½ LINCOLN OAKS GOLF COURSE
PU-390 Richton Rd., Crete, 60417, Will County, (708)672-9401, 25 miles S of Chicago.
Opened: 1927. **Holes:** 18. **Par:** 71/73. **Yards:** 6,087/4,699. **Course rating:** 68.1/65.8. **Slope:** 112/105. **Architect:** Tom Bendelow. **Green fee:** $10/$25. **Credit cards:** MC,VISA. **Reduced fees:** Weekdays, low season, twilight, seniors, juniors. **Caddies:** No. **Golf carts:** $12. **Discount golf packages:** No. **Season:** Year-round. **High:** June-Aug. **On site lodging:** No. **Rental clubs:** Yes. **Walking policy:** Unrestricted walking. **Metal spikes allowed:** Yes. **Range:** Yes (grass). **To obtain tee times:** Call up to 7 days in advance.
Subscriber comments: Short, but nicely kept and has its tough holes...Easy course, but dry...Medium challenge...Very small greens; course is in a scenic and quiet residential area...Narrow fairways...Good value...Play your straight clubs! Friendly service.

★★★ THE LINKS GOLF COURSE
PM-Nichols Park, Jacksonville, 62650, Morgan County, (217)479-4663, 30 miles SW of Springfield.
Opened: 1979. **Holes:** 18. **Par:** 72/72. **Yards:** 6,836/5,310. **Course rating:** 71.3/69.0. **Slope:** 116/108. **Architect:** David Gill. **Green fee:** $13/$16. **Credit cards:** None. **Reduced fees:** Weekdays, seniors, juniors. **Caddies:** No. **Golf carts:** $10. **Discount golf packages:** No. **Season:** March-Nov. **High:** May-Sept. **On site lodging:** No. **Rental clubs:** Yes. **Walking policy:** Unrestricted walking. **Metal spikes allowed:** Yes. **Range:** Yes (grass). **To obtain tee times:** Call 7 days in advance.
Subscriber comments: Good layout...Good greens; wide open; always windy!..Large, great greens, lookout for the 18th...One of the best courses around...Long hitter's course...Well-trapped links course...Cooperative staff.
Special Notes: Also 9-hole course.

★½ LOCUST HILLS GOLF CLUB
PU-1015 Belleville St., Lebanon, 62254, St. Clair County, (618)537-4590, 22 miles E of St. Louis, MO.
Opened: 1967. **Holes:** 18. **Par:** 71/71. **Yards:** 5,662/4,276. **Course rating:** 68.2/71.0. **Slope:** 109/113. **Architect:** N/A. **Green fee:** $11/$17. **Credit cards:** None. **Reduced fees:** Weekdays, low season, twilight, seniors, juniors. **Caddies:** No. **Golf carts:** $18. **Discount golf packages:** No. **Season:** Feb.-Dec. **High:** April-Sept. **On site lodging:** No. **Rental clubs:** No. **Walking policy:** Unrestricted walking. **Metal spikes allowed:** Yes. **Range:** No. **To obtain tee times:** Call up to 7 days in advance.

★★½ LONGWOOD COUNTRY CLUB
3503 E. Steger Rd., Crete, 60417, Will County, (708)758-1811, 40 miles S of Chicago.
Opened: 1957. **Holes:** 18. **Par:** 70/72. **Yards:** 3,244/2,785. **Course rating:** 70.5/72.1. **Slope:** 121/120. **Architect:** N/A. **Green fee:** $15/$28. **Credit cards:** MC,VISA,AMEX. **Reduced fees:** Weekdays, twilight, seniors, juniors. **Caddies:** No. **Golf carts:** $12. **Discount golf packages:** No. **Season:** Year-round. **High:** N/A. **On site lodging:** No. **Rental clubs:** Yes. **Walking policy:** Unrestricted walking. **Metal spikes allowed:** Yes. **Range:** Yes (grass). **To obtain tee times:** Call up to 7 days in advance.
Subscriber comments: Wide fairways, small to medium greens...Much better since watered fairways...Risk-reward opportunities.

★★★ LOST NATION GOLF CLUB
PU-6931 S. Lost Nation Rd., Dixon, 61021, Ogle County, (815)652-4212, 90 miles W of Chicago.
Opened: 1965. **Holes:** 18. **Par:** 71/72. **Yards:** 6,235/5,626. **Course rating:** 69.5/72.0. **Slope:** 114/114. **Architect:** N/A. **Green fee:** $15/$18. **Credit cards:** None. **Reduced fees:** Twilight. **Caddies:** No. **Golf carts:** $21. **Discount golf packages:** No. **Season:** March-Dec. **High:** May-Sept. **On site lodging:** No. **Rental clubs:** Yes. **Walking policy:** Unrestricted walking. **Metal spikes allowed:** Yes. **Range:** No. **To obtain tee times:** Call up to 14 days in advance.
Subscriber comments: Worth looking for...Fun course, pleasant employees...Short course, good greens...Rather wide-open layout...Big greens; watered fairways...Front nine wide open. Back nine tight and lots of trees. Par 3s are tough...Too pricey for area, yet easy to get on to play...Very picturesque...Always open early...Open nearly all winter...Beautiful rural setting; lots of wildlife...Just a great place to spend the day...Good value.

★★½ MACKTOWN GOLF COURSE
2221 Freeport Rd., Rockton, 61072, Winnebago County, (815)624-9931.
Call club for further information.
Subscriber comments: Short, small greens too slow...Lots of trees, relaxing, straightforward course. Good 9th and 10th holes. I liked the elevated tees on the par 3s...Ego builder; good for seniors, women and beginners...Great service...Mature course; can score if straight...Great breakfast from snack bar...Not many obstacles...Good county course...Accuracy a must.

★★ MADISON PARK GOLF COURSE
PM-2735 W. Martin Luther King Dr., Peoria, 61604, Peoria County, (309)673-7161.
Opened: 1909. **Holes:** 18. **Par:** 69/69. **Yards:** 5,476/5,120. **Course rating:** 64.5/67.7. **Slope:** 96/100. **Architect:** N/A. **Green fee:** $12/$13. **Credit cards:** MC,VISA. **Reduced fees:** Weekdays, twilight, juniors. **Caddies:** No. **Golf carts:** $15. **Discount golf packages:** No. **Season:** March-Dec. **High:** June-Sept. **On site lodging:** No. **Rental clubs:** No. **Walking policy:** Unrestricted walking. **Metal spikes allowed:** Yes. **Range:** No. **To obtain tee times:** Call up to 7 days in advance.

★★½ MANTENO GOLF CLUB
Village Hall 269 N. Main St., Manteno, 60950, Kankakee County, (815)468-8827.
Call club for further information.
Subscriber comments: Back nine in better shape...Basic, flat course. Compared to other better courses in the area, it's a bit expensive...Well-kept driving range, greens are relatively flat.

★★½ MAPLE MEADOWS GOLF COURSE
271 South Addison Rd., Wood Dale, 60191, Du Page County, (630)616-8424.
Call club for further information.
Subscriber comments: Always enjoyed the course...Pretty, short, cut out of forest...Key to a decent round is stay out of the creek...Big mature trees.

★★★ MARENGO RIDGE GOLF CLUB
PU-9508 Harmony Hill Rd., Marengo, 60152, McHenry County, (815)923-2332, 35 miles NW of Chicago.
Opened: 1965. **Holes:** 18. **Par:** 72/73. **Yards:** 6,636/5,659. **Course rating:** 71.4/72.2. **Slope:** 122/120. **Architect:** William James Spear. **Green fee:** $19/$24. **Credit cards:** MC,VISA,DISC. **Reduced fees:** Weekdays, low season, twilight, seniors, juniors. **Caddies:** No. **Golf carts:** N/A. **Discount golf packages:** Yes. **Season:** March-Dec. **High:** May-Sept. **On site lodging:** No. **Rental clubs:** Yes. **Walking policy:** Unrestricted walking. **Metal spikes allowed:** Yes. **Range:** Yes (grass). **To obtain tee times:** Call 7 days in advance.
Subscriber comments: Fun, reasonable challenge...A hidden gem out in the country...Senior discounts...Two totally different nines; front old trees, back new and open with difficult greens...Nice clubhouse...Great spot in countryside.

★★½ MARRIOTT'S LINCOLNSHIRE RESORT

R-Ten Marriott Dr., Lincolnshire, 60069, Lake County, (847)634-5935, 30 miles N of Chicago.
Opened: 1975. **Holes:** 18. **Par:** 70/69. **Yards:** 6,313/4,892. **Course rating:** 71.1/68.9. **Slope:** 129/117. **Architect:** Tom Fazio/George Fazio. **Green fee:** $37/$56. **Credit cards:** All major. **Reduced fees:** Weekdays, low season, twilight. **Caddies:** No. **Golf carts:** Included in Green Fee. **Discount golf packages:** Yes. **Season:** April-Oct. **High:** May-Sept. **On site lodging:** Yes. **Rental clubs:** Yes. **Walking policy:** Walking at certain times. **Metal spikes allowed:** Yes. **Range:** No. **To obtain tee times:** Call up to 7 days in advance. Resort guests may reserve tee times with room confirmation up to 90 days in advance.
Subscriber comments: A couple of good par 3s...Short, tight, sporty and a good challenge...Resort...Terrific short course...Course quality declines as prices go up...Always treated well...Several par 4s under 350 yards...Back nine very good.

★½ THE MEADOWS GOLF CLUB OF BLUE ISLAND

PU-2802 W. 123rd St., Blue Island, 60406, Cook County, (708)385-1994.
Opened: 1994. **Holes:** 18. **Par:** 71/71. **Yards:** 6,550/4,830. **Course rating:** N/A. **Slope:** N/A. **Architect:** Porter Gibson. **Green fee:** $12/$10. **Credit cards:** MC,VISA. **Reduced fees:** Weekdays, low season, twilight, seniors, juniors. **Caddies:** No. **Golf carts:** $10. **Discount golf packages:** No. **Season:** March-Dec. **High:** May-Sept. **On site lodging:** No. **Rental clubs:** No. **Walking policy:** Unrestricted walking. **Metal spikes allowed:** Yes. **Range:** Yes (grass/mats). **To obtain tee times:** Call pro shop.

★★★ MEADOWVIEW GOLF COURSE

PU-6489 Meadowview Lane, Mattoon, 61938, Coles County, (217)258-7888, 50 miles S of Champaign.
Opened: 1991. **Holes:** 18. **Par:** 72/72. **Yards:** 6,907/5,559. **Course rating:** 72.6/71.3. **Slope:** 121/117. **Architect:** William James Spears. **Green fee:** $17/$19. **Credit cards:** MC,VISA,DISC. **Reduced fees:** Weekdays, low season, twilight, seniors, juniors. **Caddies:** No. **Golf carts:** $10. **Discount golf packages:** No. **Season:** Feb.-Dec. **High:** June-Aug. **On site lodging:** No. **Rental clubs:** Yes. **Walking policy:** Unrestricted walking. **Metal spikes allowed:** Yes. **Range:** Yes (grass). **To obtain tee times:** Call up to 7 days in advance (217)258-PUTT.
Subscriber comments: Water, interesting...New management making many improvements...Fairways are a little tight...Clubhouse has been upgraded.

★★★½ MIDLANE COUNTRY CLUB

PU-14565 W. Yorkhouse Rd., Wadsworth, 60083, Lake County, (847)623-46530, 50 miles N of Chicago.
Opened: 1964. **Holes:** 18. **Par:** 72/73. **Yards:** 7,073/5,635. **Course rating:** 74.4/72.7. **Slope:** 132/124. **Architect:** Robert Bruce Harris. **Green fee:** $35/$56. **Credit cards:** All major. **Reduced fees:** Weekdays, low season, twilight, seniors. **Caddies:** No. **Golf carts:** N/A. **Discount golf packages:** No. **Season:** March-Nov. **High:** June-Sept. **On site lodging:** No. **Rental clubs:** Yes. **Walking policy:** Walking at certain times. **Metal spikes allowed:** Yes. **Range:** Yes (grass). **To obtain tee times:** Call seven days in advance.
Subscriber comments: The newest nine holes are worth the trip to north Chicago...Very enjoyable...Outings galore! Had to play same nine two different times...Private club caliber. Beautiful clubhouse...Favorite of Chicago Bear players.
Special Notes: Also has 9-hole course.

★★★½ MILL CREEK GOLF CLUB

PU-39 W. 525 Herrington, Geneva, 60134, Kane County, (630)208-7272.
Opened: 1996. **Holes:** 18. **Par:** 73/73. **Yards:** 7,600/4,700. **Course rating:** N/A. **Slope:** N/A. **Architect:** Roy Case. **Green fee:** $55/$65. **Credit cards:** All major,Diners Club. **Reduced fees:** Low season, twilight. **Caddies:** No. **Golf carts:** Included in Green Fee. **Discount golf packages:** No. **Season:** April-Nov. **High:** May-Oct. **On site lodging:** No. **Rental clubs:** Yes. **Walking policy:** Unrestricted walking. **Metal spikes allowed:** Yes. **Range:** Yes (grass). **To obtain tee times:** Call up to 14 days in advance.

Subscriber comments: New course, maturing...No rollups, need good shots to greens...Excellent new course. Will only get better!...Nice golf community. Will play again...Great condition, a lot of fun. Staff excellent.

★★★ MINNE MONESSE GOLF CLUB

15944 E. Six Mi Grove Rd., Grant Park, 60940, Kankakee County, (815)465-6653, (800)339-3126, 20 miles NE of Kankakee.
Opened: 1926. **Holes:** 9. **Par:** 72/72. **Yards:** 6,500/5,100. **Course rating:** 69.3. **Slope:** 119. **Architect:** Ted Lockie. **Green fee:** $20/$33. **Credit cards:** All major. **Reduced fees:** Weekdays, low season, twilight, seniors, juniors. **Caddies:** No. **Golf carts:** Included in Green Fee. **Discount golf packages:** Yes. **Season:** March-Dec. **High:** June-Aug. **On site lodging:** No. **Rental clubs:** Yes. **Walking policy:** Unrestricted walking. **Metal spikes allowed:** Yes. **Range:** Yes (grass). **To obtain tee times:** Call.
Subscriber comments: Short course fun for men and women; best little couple's course on south side of Chicago...Good service...Nice course...Friendly staff makes you feel welcome...Clubhouse is big; food OK.

★★½ MOUNT CARMEL MUNICIPAL GOLF CLUB

RR #3 Park Rd., Mt. Carmel, 62863, Wabash County, (618)262-5771.
Call club for further information.
Subscriber comments: Great challenge, pace of play good...No.15 is as tough a par 3 as any I've seen...Well respected and gaining maturity.

★★½ MOUNT PROSPECT GOLF CLUB

PM-600 See Gwum Ave., Mt. Prospect, 60056, Cook County, (847)632-9334, 6 miles NW of Chicago.
Opened: 1927. **Holes:** 18. **Par:** 71/73. **Yards:** 6,200/5,355. **Course rating:** 70.3/70.8. **Slope:** 128/123. **Architect:** N/A. **Green fee:** $32/$42. **Credit cards:** MC,VISA,DISC. **Reduced fees:** Twilight. **Caddies:** No. **Golf carts:** $24. **Discount golf packages:** No. **Season:** March-Nov. **High:** Summer. **On site lodging:** No. **Rental clubs:** Yes. **Walking policy:** Unrestricted walking. **Metal spikes allowed:** Yes. **Range:** Yes (grass/mats). **To obtain tee times:** Call up to 5 days in advance.
Subscriber comments: Lots of play, not real long. Water on 12 holes...Short but tight...Too much money for a so-so course...One of Chicago's converted private clubs. Short, but difficult. Everyone works to make it enjoyable...Fees out of kilter for area. Residents get a break...Good park district course, too busy...Sneaky tough, but a little expensive...A course that's well cared for.

★★★ NAPERBROOK GOLF COURSE

PU-22204 111th St., Plainfield, 60544, Will County, (630)378-4215, 24 miles SW of Chicago.
Opened: 1990. **Holes:** 18. **Par:** 72/72. **Yards:** 6,755/5,381. **Course rating:** 71.2/69.5. **Slope:** 120/112. **Architect:** Roger Packard. **Green fee:** $12/$38. **Credit cards:** MC,VISA. **Reduced fees:** Weekdays, low season, twilight, seniors, juniors. **Caddies:** No. **Golf carts:** $12. **Discount golf packages:** No. **Season:** March-Dec. **High:** June-Aug. **On site lodging:** No. **Rental clubs:** Yes. **Walking policy:** Unrestricted walking. **Metal spikes allowed:** Yes. **Range:** Yes (grass). **To obtain tee times:** Call 7 days in advance starting at 5 p.m.
Subscriber comments: Solid service; great greens...Good value...Links-style course...Makes you think, bring your better game, worth a visit...Nice condition for public links...Water on both sides of green on par 5 No.7 make approach hard...Good par 5s...Too many holes that look alike.

★★ NELSON PARK GOLF COURSE

PU-200 Nelson Blvd, Decatur, 62521, Macon County, (217)422-7241, 45 miles E of Springfield.
Opened: 1920. **Holes:** 18. **Par:** 65/65. **Yards:** 4,793/4,378. **Course rating:** 63.2/63.2. **Slope:** 101/101. **Architect:** N/A. **Green fee:** $9/$14. **Credit cards:** MC,VISA. **Reduced fees:** Weekdays, low season, twilight, seniors, juniors. **Caddies:** No. **Golf carts:** $16. **Discount golf packages:** No. **Season:** Year-round. **High:** May-Sept. **On site lodging:** No. **Rental clubs:** Yes. **Walking policy:** Unrestricted walking. **Metal spikes allowed:** Yes. **Range:** No. **To obtain tee times:** Call on Monday starting at 6:30 a.m. for upcoming weekend. Call up to 7 days in advance for weekdays.

★★★ NETTLE CREEK GOLF CLUB
PU-5355 Saratoga Rd., Morris, 60450, Grundy County, (815)941-4300, 50 miles SW of Chicago.
Opened: 1993. **Holes:** 18. **Par:** 71/71. **Yards:** 6,489/5,800. **Course rating:** 70.4. **Slope:** 117. **Architect:** Buzz Didier. **Green fee:** $30/$40. **Credit cards:** MC,VISA. **Reduced fees:** Twilight, seniors, juniors. **Caddies:** No. **Golf carts:** Included in Green Fee. **Discount golf packages:** No. **Season:** March-Nov. **High:** June-Aug. **On site lodging:** No. **Rental clubs:** No. **Walking policy:** Walking at certain times. **Metal spikes allowed:** Yes. **Range:** No. **To obtain tee times:** Call up to 7 days in advance.
Subscriber comments: The nicest people and a well-kept course...Good course...Can play in rain, course holds water well...Great test...Very nice but not worth the price...Highly recommended...A forgiving course...Basic but getting better...Courteous staff, good service...The more it matures, the better it gets.

★★★ NEWMAN GOLF COURSE
PM-2021 W. Nebraska, Peoria, 61604, Peoria County, (309)674-1663.
Opened: 1934. **Holes:** 18. **Par:** 71/74. **Yards:** 6,838/5,933. **Course rating:** 71.8/74.2. **Slope:** 119/120. **Architect:** N/A. **Green fee:** $5/$13. **Credit cards:** MC,VISA. **Reduced fees:** Weekdays, twilight, juniors. **Caddies:** No. **Golf carts:** N/A. **Discount golf packages:** No. **Season:** March-Nov. **High:** April-Aug. **On site lodging:** No. **Rental clubs:** Yes. **Walking policy:** Unrestricted walking. **Metal spikes allowed:** Yes. **Range:** No. **To obtain tee times:** Come in up to 7 days or call day of play.
Subscriber comments: Could be great course; fast, but small greens...One of best around...You play the front nine and think there's not much to this. Back nine is very challenging; bogey golf is great, lots of trees...Great pure golf in the Peoria area.

★★ NORDIC HILLS RESORT
Nordic Rd., Itasca, 60743, Du Page County, (630)773-3510, 20 miles W of Chicago.
Opened: N/A. **Holes:** 18. **Par:** 71/71. **Yards:** 5,910/5,331. **Course rating:** N/A. **Slope:** 105/113. **Architect:** Charles Maddox/Frank P. MacDonald. **Green fee:** N/A. **Credit cards:** All major,. **Reduced fees:** Weekdays, low season, twilight. **Caddies:** No. **Golf carts:** N/A. **Discount golf packages:** No. **Season:** April-Nov. **High:** June-Aug. **On site lodging:** Yes. **Rental clubs:** No. **Walking policy:** N/A. **Metal spikes allowed:** Yes. **Range:** No. **To obtain tee times:** N/A.

★★ OAK BROOK GOLF CLUB
PU-9157 Fruit Rd., Edwardsville, 62025, Madison County, (618)656-5600, 30 miles N of St. Louis, MO.
Opened: 1972. **Holes:** 18. **Par:** 71/71. **Yards:** 6,250/5,214. **Course rating:** 68.2. **Slope:** 113. **Architect:** Larry Suhre. **Green fee:** $14/$16. **Credit cards:** None. **Reduced fees:** Seniors, juniors. **Caddies:** No. **Golf carts:** $18. **Discount golf packages:** No. **Season:** Year-round. **High:** April-Sept. **On site lodging:** No. **Rental clubs:** No. **Walking policy:** Unrestricted walking. **Metal spikes allowed:** Yes. **Range:** Yes (grass). **To obtain tee times:** Call up to 7 days in advance.

★★½ OAK BROOK GOLF COURSE
PU-2606 York Rd., Oak Brook, 60523, Du Page County, (630)990-3032, 15 miles W of Chicago.
Opened: 1980. **Holes:** 18. **Par:** 72/72. **Yards:** 6,541/5,341. **Course rating:** 71.2/70.9. **Slope:** 121/120. **Architect:** Roger Packard. **Green fee:** $32/$36. **Credit cards:** MC,VISA,AMEX. **Reduced fees:** Twilight. **Caddies:** No. **Golf carts:** $12. **Discount golf packages:** No. **Season:** March-Dec. **High:** April-Sept. **On site lodging:** No. **Rental clubs:** Yes. **Walking policy:** Unrestricted walking. **Metal spikes allowed:** Yes. **Range:** Yes (grass). **To obtain tee times:** Call 7 days in advance.
Notes: 1991 LPGA Chicago Sun Times Shootout. 1987 Western Open Co-host.
Subscriber comments: Keep the driver in the bag on several holes...Greens are sneaky quick; good value; fair service...Lots of doglegs...Typical muny track, everything just OK..Fast, hilly greens.

★★½ OAK BROOK HILLS HOTEL & RESORT
R-3500 Midwest Rd., Oak Brook, 60522, Du Page County, (630)850-5530, (800)445-3315, 20 miles W of Chicago.

Opened: 1987. **Holes:** 18. **Par:** 70/69. **Yards:** 6,372/5,152. **Course rating:** 70.4/69.2. **Slope:** 122/114. **Architect:** Dick Nugent. **Green fee:** $50/$66. **Credit cards:** All major. **Reduced fees:** Low season, twilight, seniors, juniors. **Caddies:** No. **Golf carts:** Included in Green Fee. **Discount golf packages:** No. **Season:** March-Nov. **High:** N/A. **On site lodging:** Yes. **Rental clubs:** No. **Walking policy:** Walking at certain times. **Metal spikes allowed:** Yes. **Range:** Yes (grass/mats). **To obtain tee times:** Hotel guests may reserve up to 21 days in advance. Nonguests may call up to 7 days in advance.
Subscriber comments: Holes too close together...Facilities great. Course kept in good condition...Tight layout, people friendly.

★★★ THE OAK CLUB OF GENOA

PU-11770 Ellwood Greens Rd., Genoa, 60135, De Kalb County, (815)784-5678, 50 miles W of Chicago.
Opened: 1973. **Holes:** 18. **Par:** 72/72. **Yards:** 7,032/5,556. **Course rating:** 74.1/72.5. **Slope:** 135/127. **Architect:** Charles Maddox. **Green fee:** $19/$29. **Credit cards:** All major. **Reduced fees:** Weekdays, low season, twilight, seniors. **Caddies:** No. **Golf carts:** Included in Green Fee. **Discount golf packages:** No. **Season:** March-Dec. **High:** May-Sept. **On site lodging:** No. **Rental clubs:** Yes. **Walking policy:** Walking at certain times. **Metal spikes allowed:** Yes. **Range:** Yes (grass/mats). **To obtain tee times:** Call 7 days in advance.
Subscriber comments: Bring all clubs...Great value for $...The course nobody knows about. Lots of trees. Fast greens; water. Excellent course for the money...A relaxing day in the country...Long par 3s...Hidden gem, make the effort to find it...Always a pleasant round...Some of the most scenic holes in northeast Illinois.

OAK GLEN GOLF COURSE

Stoy Rd., Robinson, 62454, Crawford County, (618)592-3030, 50 miles E of Effingham.
Opened: 1963. **Holes:** 18. **Par:** 71/71. **Yards:** 6,086/5,220. **Course rating:** 67.7/67.8. **Slope:** 112/108. **Architect:** N/A. **Green fee:** $10/$15. **Credit cards:** MC,VISA. **Reduced fees:** Weekdays, twilight. **Caddies:** No. **Golf carts:** $15. **Discount golf packages:** No. **Season:** March-Nov. **High:** May-Aug. **On site lodging:** No. **Rental clubs:** No. **Walking policy:** Unrestricted walking. **Metal spikes allowed:** Yes. **Range:** Yes (grass/mats). **To obtain tee times:** No tee times reserved.

★★★ OAK MEADOWS GOLF CLUB

PU-900 N. Wood Dale Rd., Addison, 60101, Du Page County, (630)595-0071, 8 miles NW of Elmhurst.
Opened: 1925. **Holes:** 18. **Par:** 71/73. **Yards:** 6,871/5,954. **Course rating:** 72.1/73.8. **Slope:** 126/128. **Architect:** N/A. **Green fee:** $28/$30. **Credit cards:** MC,VISA. **Reduced fees:** Twilight. **Caddies:** No. **Golf carts:** $26. **Discount golf packages:** No. **Season:** April-Nov. **High:** June-Sept. **On site lodging:** No. **Rental clubs:** Yes. **Walking policy:** Walking at certain times. **Metal spikes allowed:** Yes. **Range:** Yes (grass). **To obtain tee times:** Call 7 days in advance.
Subscriber comments: Great old layout...Made a mistake putting cartpaths in play...Nice variety of holes. One of the best closing holes in the area...Lots of trees...Was much better when private...Good challenging place to practice...Great golf for the money...Beautiful old, oak trees.

★★½ OAK SPRINGS GOLF COURSE

6740 E. 3500 South Rd., St. Anne, 60964, Kankakee County, (815)937-1648.
Call club for further information.
Subscriber comments: Good food, nice showers...Lots of trees...Hidden treasure, worth the drive from Chicago...Excellent course to play and test your golf...Drive, wedge, drive, wedge.

★★★½ OAK TERRACE GOLF COURSE

100 Beyers Lake Rd, Pana, 62557, Shelby County, (217)539-4477.
Call club for further information.
Subscriber comments: Nice course, open...New course with excellent service and is well manicured..Jekyll and Hyde, front nine not strong, back nine beautiful...Surprisingly good course in the middle of nowhere...You'll need every club in the bag.

★½ THE OAKS GOLF COURSE

PU-851 Dave Stockton Dr., Springfield, 62707-3116, Sangamon County, (217)528-6600.
Opened: 1926. **Holes:** 18. **Par:** 70/70. **Yards:** 6,054/4,665. **Course rating:** 68.4/66.0.
Slope: 112/112. **Architect:** N/A. **Green fee:** $9/$16. **Credit cards:** MC,VISA. **Reduced fees:** Weekdays, low season, twilight, seniors, juniors. **Caddies:** No. **Golf carts:** $18.
Discount golf packages: No. **Season:** Year-round. **High:** June-Sept. **On site lodging:** No. **Rental clubs:** Yes. **Walking policy:** Unrestricted walking. **Metal spikes allowed:** Yes. **Range:** No. **To obtain tee times:** Call up to 7 days in advance.

★★★ ODYSSEY GOLF COURSE

PU-19110 S. Ridgeland, Tinley Park, 60477, Cook County, (708)429-7400, 20 miles SW of Chicago.
Opened: 1992. **Holes:** 18. **Par:** 72/72. **Yards:** 7,095/5,554. **Course rating:** 73.1/69.3.
Slope: 131/116. **Architect:** Harry Bowers/Curtis Strange. **Green fee:** $16/$60. **Credit cards:** MC,VISA. **Reduced fees:** Weekdays, low season, twilight. **Caddies:** No. **Golf carts:** Included in Green Fee. **Discount golf packages:** No. **Season:** April-Nov. **High:** June-Aug. **On site lodging:** No. **Rental clubs:** No. **Walking policy:** Walking at certain times. **Metal spikes allowed:** Yes. **Range:** Yes (grass/mats). **To obtain tee times:** Call up to 14 days in advance.
Subscriber comments: 18 is a great finishing hole...Fairly priced, good challenge...One of Chicagoland's best public courses and will get better with age...Many water hazards, but landing areas are generous.

★★★ OLD OAK COUNTRY CLUB

PU-14200 S. Parker Rd., Lockport, 60441, Will County, (708)301-3344, 19 miles SW of Chicago.
Opened: 1926. **Holes:** 18. **Par:** 71/72. **Yards:** 6,535/5,274. **Course rating:** 70.1.
Slope: 124. **Architect:** N/A. **Green fee:** $20/$27. **Credit cards:** All major. **Reduced fees:** Weekdays, low season, twilight, seniors, juniors. **Caddies:** No. **Golf carts:** $15.
Discount golf packages: No. **Season:** April-Dec. **High:** June-Sept. **On site lodging:** No. **Rental clubs:** Yes. **Walking policy:** Unrestricted walking. **Metal spikes allowed:** Yes. **Range:** No. **To obtain tee times:** Call up to 7 days in advance.
Subscriber comments: Excellent course, modest fee, tough with lots of water and trees...Second green must have been 12 on Stimpmeter...Great old course...Recent improvements make this the course to play in the southwest suburbs.

★★★ OLD ORCHARD COUNTRY CLUB

PU-700 W. Rand Rd., Mt. Prospect, 60056, Cook County, (847)255-2025.
Opened: N/A. **Holes:** 18. **Par:** 70/70. **Yards:** 6,022/5,719. **Course rating:** N/A. **Slope:** 131/127. **Architect:** Leonard Macomber. **Green fee:** $36/$48. **Credit cards:** All major,Diners Club. **Reduced fees:** Weekdays, twilight. **Caddies:** No. **Golf carts:** Included in Green Fee. **Discount golf packages:** No. **Season:** April-Nov. **High:** June-July. **On site lodging:** No. **Rental clubs:** Yes. **Walking policy:** Walking at certain times. **Metal spikes allowed:** Yes. **Range:** No. **To obtain tee times:** Call up to 7 days in advance.
Subscriber comments: Short but in good shape...Overpriced...Best fairways and greens in Chicago...Challenging...Good condition...Fast, consistent greens; tight layout, real target golf...Way too slow...Easy to get tee times...Price increased to take out the cheap golfers. Improvements great...Narrow fairways; 17th as tough as it gets!

★★ ORCHARD HILLS COUNTRY CLUB

PU-38342 N. Green Bay Rd., Waukegan, 60087, Lake County, (847)336-5118, 40 miles N of Chicago.
Opened: 1930. **Holes:** 18. **Par:** 71/71. **Yards:** 6,366/6,043. **Course rating:** 68.8/68.8.
Slope: 104/104. **Architect:** Robert Bruce Harris. **Green fee:** $25/$27. **Credit cards:** MC,VISA,DISC. **Reduced fees:** Weekdays, low season, twilight. **Caddies:** No. **Golf carts:** $12. **Discount golf packages:** Yes. **Season:** March-Jan. **High:** May-Sept. **On site lodging:** No. **Rental clubs:** Yes. **Walking policy:** Walking at certain times. **Metal spikes allowed:** Yes. **Range:** Yes (grass/mats). **To obtain tee times:** Call up to 7 days in advance.

ILLINOIS

★★★★ ORCHARD VALLEY GOLF CLUB

PU-2411 W. Illinois Ave., Aurora, 60506, Kane County, (847)907-0500, 35 miles W of Chicago.
Opened: 1993. **Holes:** 18. **Par:** 72/72. **Yards:** 6,745/5,162. **Course rating:** 72.2/70.1. **Slope:** 132/118. **Architect:** Ken Kavanaugh. **Green fee:** $38/$45. **Credit cards:** MC,VISA,AMEX. **Reduced fees:** Twilight, seniors, juniors. **Caddies:** No. **Golf carts:** $13. **Discount golf packages:** No. **Season:** April-Oct. **High:** June-Sept. **On site lodging:** No. **Rental clubs:** Yes. **Walking policy:** Unrestricted walking. **Metal spikes allowed:** Yes. **Range:** Yes (grass/mats). **To obtain tee times:** Call 7 days in advance with credit card. Club has a twenty-four hour cancellation policy.
Subscriber comments: Multiple tees, water, have fun your way...Believe it or not, it's a muny...Best value and challenge in the area...Has it all—conditioning, beauty, diversity, challenge...Doesn't seem difficult, but check your score...Too expensive...Lots of water and fun, great condition, great value...Most players walk.

★★★ THE ORCHARDS GOLF CLUB

PU-1499 Golf Course Dr., Belleville, 62221, St. Clair County, (618)233-8921, (800)452-0358, 20 miles SE of St. Louis.
Opened: 1991. **Holes:** 18. **Par:** 71/71. **Yards:** 6,405/5,001. **Course rating:** 69.0/70.1. **Slope:** 121/120. **Architect:** Bob Goalby. **Green fee:** $16/$30. **Credit cards:** MC,VISA. **Reduced fees:** Weekdays, low season, twilight, seniors, juniors. **Caddies:** No. **Golf carts:** $10. **Discount golf packages:** No. **Season:** Year-round. **High:** April-Oct. **On site lodging:** No. **Rental clubs:** Yes. **Walking policy:** Walking at certain times. **Metal spikes allowed:** Yes. **Range:** Yes (grass). **To obtain tee times:** Call up to seven days.
Subscriber comments: Good mix of wide open holes and holes with trees...Excellent shape...Slow play is obvious problem...Best value in area...Strong par 3s...Unwalkable. Long distance green to next tee...Midwest feel, variety.

★★½ PALATINE HILLS GOLF COURSE

PU-512 W. Northwest Hwy., Palatine, 60067, Cook County, (847)359-4020, 25 miles NW of Chicago.
Opened: 1965. **Holes:** 18. **Par:** 72/72. **Yards:** 6,800/5,975. **Course rating:** 71.6/73.2. **Slope:** 120/119. **Architect:** Edward L. Packard. **Green fee:** $26/$31. **Credit cards:** MC,VISA. **Reduced fees:** Weekdays, low season, twilight. **Caddies:** No. **Golf carts:** $12. **Discount golf packages:** Yes. **Season:** April-Nov. **High:** June-Aug. **On site lodging:** No. **Rental clubs:** Yes. **Walking policy:** Unrestricted walking. **Metal spikes allowed:** Yes. **Range:** Yes (grass/mats). **To obtain tee times:** Call 2 days in advance for weekdays and 7 days in advance for weekend tee times.
Subscriber comments: Above average park district course...Best value in northwest suburbs...Well maintained...Short course with some challenging holes...No-nonsense track, no hidden features or obstacles...Old standby...Value fair...Just OK...Can hit it anywhere and still be OK.

PALOS COUNTRY CLUB

13100 S.W. Hwy., Palos Park, 60464, Cook County, (708)448-6550.
Opened: 1929. **Holes:** 27. **Architect:** Charles Maddox/Frank P. MacDonald. **Green fee:** $25/$30. **Credit cards:** MC,VISA. **Reduced fees:** Low season, twilight, seniors. **Caddies:** No. **Golf carts:** $26. **Discount golf packages:** No. **Season:** Year-round. **High:** March-Oct. **On site lodging:** No. **Rental clubs:** Yes. **Walking policy:** Walking at certain times. **Metal spikes allowed:** Yes. **Range:** Yes (grass/mats). **To obtain tee times:** N/A.
★★ RED/WHITE
Par: 70/70. **Yards:** 6,076/5,280. **Course rating:** 69.5/69.9. **Slope:** 113/114.
★★ WHITE/BLUE
Par: 72/72. **Yards:** 6,533/5,773. **Course rating:** 70.6/72.4. **Slope:** 116/114.

PARK HILLS GOLF CLUB

PU-3240 W. Stephenson Rd., Freeport, 61032, Stephenson County, (815)235-3611, 100 miles W of Chicago.
Architect: C.D. Wagstaff. **Green fee:** $12/$20. **Credit cards:** MC,VISA. **Reduced fees:** Weekdays, juniors. **Caddies:** No. **Golf carts:** $10. **Discount golf packages:** No. **Season:** April-Nov. **High:** June-Aug. **On site lodging:** No. **Rental clubs:** Yes. **Walking policy:** Unrestricted walking. **Metal spikes allowed:** Yes. **Range:** Yes (grass). **To obtain tee times:** Call 7 days in advance.

★★★½ **EAST COURSE**
Opened: 1953. **Holes:** 18. **Par:** 72/72. **Yards:** 6,477/5,401. **Course rating:** 69.9/69.8. **Slope:** 116/115.
Subscriber comments: Great public course, well maintained...Fairly easy; pleasant staff...Country club atmosphere, Excellent course, never hard to get on either course...Mature trees; creek on six holes...Open layout...Very scenic, tough but fair...Best public course greens around...More open than West Course but plenty of length on most holes.

★★★½ **WEST COURSE**
Opened: 1964. **Holes:** 18. **Par:** 72/73. **Yards:** 6,622/5,940. **Course rating:** 71.3/76.2. **Slope:** 121/127.
Subscriber comments: Above average; well maintained...Tough but fair...Pleasant staff...Challenging, especially back nine...Both interesting layouts with plenty of challenging holes, good greens, outstanding conditioning, friendly staff, fast to walk...Back-to-back par 5s...Scenic, variety of holes...Outstanding value.

★★ PARKVIEW GOLF COURSE

PM-2202 Broadway, Pekin, 61554, Tazewell County, (309)346-8494, 12 miles S of Peoria.
Opened: N/A. **Holes:** 18. **Par:** 70/76. **Yards:** 6,002/5,376. **Course rating:** 65.4/63.6. **Slope:** 102/100. **Architect:** N/A. **Green fee:** $9/$12. **Credit cards:** MC,VISA. **Reduced fees:** Weekdays, twilight, seniors, juniors. **Caddies:** No. **Golf carts:** $15. **Discount golf packages:** No. **Season:** Year-round. **High:** May-Sept. **On site lodging:** No. **Rental clubs:** Yes. **Walking policy:** Unrestricted walking. **Metal spikes allowed:** No. **Range:** No. **To obtain tee times:** N/A.
Special Notes: $2 charge for wearing metal spikes.

★★ PHEASANT RUN RESORT GOLF COURSE

4051 East Main St., St. Charles, 60174, Kane County, (630)584-4914.
Opened: N/A. **Holes:** 18. **Par:** 71/71. **Yards:** 6,315/5,452. **Course rating:** N/A. **Slope:** 124/121. **Architect:** N/A. **Green fee:** $25/$49. **Credit cards:** All major,. **Reduced fees:** Weekdays, low season, twilight. **Caddies:** No. **Golf carts:** Included in Green Fee. **Discount golf packages:** Yes. **Season:** Year-round. **High:** April-Dec. **On site lodging:** Yes. **Rental clubs:** No. **Walking policy:** Unrestricted walking. **Metal spikes allowed:** Yes. **Range:** No. **To obtain tee times:** Call up to 7 days in advance.

★★ PHILLIPS PARK GOLF COURSE

PU-901 Moses Dr., Aurora, 60507, Kane County, (630)898-7352, 40 miles W of Chicago.
Opened: 1930. **Holes:** 18. **Par:** 71. **Yards:** 5,634. **Course rating:** 66.8. **Slope:** 109. **Architect:** N/A. **Green fee:** $15/$20. **Credit cards:** MC,VISA. **Reduced fees:** Twilight. **Caddies:** No. **Golf carts:** $21. **Discount golf packages:** No. **Season:** March-Nov. **High:** June-Sept. **On site lodging:** No. **Rental clubs:** No. **Walking policy:** Unrestricted walking. **Metal spikes allowed:** Yes. **Range:** No. **To obtain tee times:** N/A.

★★½ PINE LAKES GOLF CLUB

25130 Schuck Rd., Washington, 61571, Tazewell County, (309)745-9344.
Call club for further information.
Subscriber comments: Have made some improvements, getting better...Best greens in the area...Improving conditions. Well-kept fairways...A lot of work done by new owners. Nice course...Start interesting...Has some really good holes, but not enough.

★★★★ PINE MEADOW GOLF CLUB
PU-1 Pine Meadow Lane, Mundelein, 60060, Lake County, (847)566-4653, 30 miles N of Chicago.
Opened: 1985. **Holes:** 18. **Par:** 72/72. **Yards:** 7,141/5,412. **Course rating:** 74.4/70.9.
Slope: 131/121. **Architect:** Joe Lee/Rocky Roquemore. **Green fee:** $59/$59. **Credit cards:** MC,VISA,DISC,Diners Club. **Reduced fees:** Twilight, juniors. **Caddies:** Yes. **Golf carts:** $27. **Discount golf packages:** No. **Season:** Year-round. **High:** April-Nov. **On site lodging:** No. **Rental clubs:** Yes. **Walking policy:** Unrestricted walking. **Metal spikes allowed:** Yes. **Range:** Yes (grass/mats). **To obtain tee times:** Call up to 120 days in advance. Green fee must be pre-paid from May 15th to Oct. 1st.
Notes: Golf Digest School site. Ranked 15th in 1997 Best in State.
Subscriber comments: Fair test for all players...Excellent layout with water presenting challenge...Best course in the area! Great practice facility, too...Great course, great staff...Lived up to its reputation as one of the best in Illinois...Best hotdogs...Front nine traditional with new back nine...Heaven...Can get crowded and slow.

★★★ PINECREST GOLF & COUNTRY CLUB
PU-11220 Algonquin Rd., Huntley, 60142, McHenry County, (847)669-3111, 50 miles NW of Chicago.
Opened: 1972. **Holes:** 18. **Par:** 72/72. **Yards:** 6,636/5,061. **Course rating:** 71.4/68.9.
Slope: 119/112. **Architect:** Ted Lockie. **Green fee:** $25/$31. **Credit cards:** MC,VISA,DISC. **Reduced fees:** Twilight, seniors, juniors. **Caddies:** No. **Golf carts:** $13. **Discount golf packages:** No. **Season:** March-Dec. **High:** June-Aug. **On site lodging:** No. **Rental clubs:** Yes. **Walking policy:** Walking at certain times. **Metal spikes allowed:** Yes. **Range:** Yes (grass). **To obtain tee times:** Call 7 days in advance.
Subscriber comments: Intense play; bent fairways hold up...A well-kept course, friendly service, excellent equipment display...Impeccable condition, short but fun...Great service...Fun short course. Efficient management. Friendly people...Great pricing...Treats you exceptionally well. Great course for women.

★★★½ PINNACLE COUNTRY CLUB
11928 Knoxville Rd., Milan, 61264, Rock Island County, (309)787-5446. Call club for further information.
Subscriber comments: Really a gem...Well managed, a great municipal course...Super course.

★★★★ PIPER GLEN GOLF CLUB
PU-7112 Piper Glen Dr., Springfield, 62707, Sangamon County, (217)483-6537, 100 miles N of St. Louis.
Opened: 1996. **Holes:** 18. **Par:** 72/72. **Yards:** 6,985/5,138. **Course rating:** 73.6/70.3.
Slope: 133/123. **Architect:** Bob Lohmann. **Green fee:** $25/$25. **Credit cards:** All major. **Reduced fees:** Seniors, juniors. **Caddies:** No. **Golf carts:** $10. **Discount golf packages:** No. **Season:** March-Dec. **High:** May-Sept. **On site lodging:** No. **Rental clubs:** No. **Walking policy:** Unrestricted walking. **Metal spikes allowed:** No. **Range:** Yes (grass). **To obtain tee times:** Call golf shop up to 7 days in advance.
Subscriber comments: New course that will become a "Great One"...Facilities will improve...Will be outstanding course...Good layout. Tight course, good conditions...Challenging. A good round can go down the tubes at any time...A year away from being best course in central Illinois...Best course in town.

★★★½ PLUM TREE NATIONAL GOLF CLUB
PU-19511 Lembcke Rd., Harvard, 60033, McHenry County, (815)943-7474, (800)851-3578, 35 miles NW of Chicago.
Opened: 1969. **Holes:** 18. **Par:** 72/72. **Yards:** 6,648/5,954. **Course rating:** 71.8/74.9.
Slope: 126/132. **Architect:** Joe Lee. **Green fee:** $40/$55. **Credit cards:** All major. **Reduced fees:** Weekdays, low season, twilight, seniors, juniors. **Caddies:** No. **Golf carts:** Included in Green Fee. **Discount golf packages:** No. **Season:** April-Dec. **High:** June-Aug. **On site lodging:** No. **Rental clubs:** Yes. **Walking policy:** Walking at certain times. **Metal spikes allowed:** Yes. **Range:** Yes (grass). **To obtain tee times:** Call 7 days in advance.

ILLINOIS

Subscriber comments: A driver's course, good variety, scenic...Good course; well worth the 90-minute ride from Chicago...Solid traditional course, provides options...I can't believe it's never crowded...Out of the way, but nice.

★★★½PONTIAC ELKS COUNTRY CLUB

Rte. 116W, Pontiac, 61764, Livingston County, (815)842-1249, 100 miles S of Chicago.
Opened: 1975. **Holes:** 18. **Par:** 72/72. **Yards:** 6,804/5,507. **Course rating:** 72.2/70.6. **Slope:** 122/113. **Architect:** N/A. **Green fee:** $16/$19.
Credit cards: N/A. **Reduced fees:** N/A. **Caddies:** No. **Golf carts:** $10.
Discount golf packages: No. **Season:** March-Nov. **High:** June-Aug. **On site lodging:** No. **Rental clubs:** No. **Walking policy:** Unrestricted walking. **Metal spikes allowed:** Yes. **Range:** Yes (grass). **To obtain tee times:** Call golf shop.

Subscriber comments: Keep this a secret...First hole grabs your attention, good challenge, great value...Staff is most accommodating...Lots of water...As close to a championship course as there is in the area. Long and lots of sand and large rolling greens...Great putting greens...Well worth money...Please do not tell the folks from Chicago...Good every day layout for small town...Well maintained...Nice clubhouse.

★★½POPLAR CREEK COUNTRY CLUB

PU-1400 Poplar Creek Dr., Hoffman Estates, 60194, Cook County, (847)781-3681, 30 miles NW of Chicago.
Opened: 1971. **Holes:** 18. **Par:** 70/70. **Yards:** 6,108/5,386. **Course rating:** 69.6/69.9.
Slope: 124/118. **Architect:** Dick Nugent/Ken Killian. **Green fee:** $12/$29. **Credit cards:** MC,VISA. **Reduced fees:** Twilight, seniors, juniors. **Caddies:** No. **Golf carts:** N/A.
Discount golf packages: No. **Season:** March-Nov. **High:** June-Aug. **On site lodging:** No. **Rental clubs:** Yes. **Walking policy:** Walking at certain times. **Metal spikes allowed:** Yes. **Range:** Yes (grass/mats). **To obtain tee times:** Call 7 days in advance.
Subscriber comments: What you see is what you get...Call ahead to check for course condition...Tight course, great iron course...Course condition varies throughout season.

★★½POTTAWATOMIE PARK GOLF COURSE

PM-845 N. 2nd Ave., St. Charles, 60174, Kane County, (630)584-8356.
Opened: 1939. **Holes:** 9. **Par:** 35/37. **Yards:** 3,005/2,546. **Course rating:** 68.2/69.2.
Slope: 116/113. **Architect:** Robert Trent Jones. **Green fee:** N/A. **Credit cards:** MC,VISA. **Reduced fees:** N/A. **Caddies:** No. **Golf carts:** $24. **Discount golf packages:** No. **Season:** March-Dec. **High:** June-Aug. **On site lodging:** No. **Rental clubs:** Yes. **Walking policy:** Unrestricted walking. **Metal spikes allowed:** Yes. **Range:** Yes. **To obtain tee times:** Call 1 day in advance for weekday. Call on Wednesday at noon for weekend.
Subscriber comments: Heavily played RT Jones course...Short, but no snap...Picturesque..Always like second shot on 3rd hole to island green...Old classic.

★★★½PRAIRIE ISLE GOLF CLUB

2216 Rte. 176, Prairie Grove, 60012, McHenry County, (815)356-0202, 50 miles NW of Chicago.
Opened: 1994. **Holes:** 18. **Par:** 72/73. **Yards:** 6,469/5,468. **Course rating:** 70.7/71.3.
Slope: 124/117. **Architect:** Gordon Cunningham. **Green fee:** $25/$48. **Credit cards:** All major. **Reduced fees:** Weekdays, low season, twilight, seniors, juniors. **Caddies:** No. **Golf carts:** $12. **Discount golf packages:** No. **Season:** Year-round. **High:** July-Aug. **On site lodging:** No. **Rental clubs:** Yes. **Walking policy:** Walking at certain times. **Metal spikes allowed:** Yes. **Range:** Yes. **To obtain tee times:** Call up to 14 days in advance.
Subscriber comments: Nice course, but expensive...Too many close tee-off times...New course and well maintained...One of the excellent new courses in northern suburbs...Many feels of different golfing on one course.

★★★★PRAIRIE LANDING GOLF CLUB

PU-2325 Longest Dr., West Chicago, 60165, Du Page County, (630)208-7600, 30 miles W of Chicago.
Opened: 1994. **Holes:** 18. **Par:** 72/72. **Yards:** 6,862/4,859. **Course rating:** 73.8/69.3. **Slope:** 131/119. **Architect:** Robert Trent Jones,Jr.. **Green fee:** $50/$78. **Credit cards:** All major,Diners Club. **Reduced**

fees: Low season, twilight, juniors. **Caddies:** No. **Golf carts:** Included in Green Fee. **Discount golf packages:** No. **Season:** April-Nov. **High:** May-Sept. **On site lodging:** No. **Rental clubs:** Yes. **Walking policy:** Unrestricted walking. **Metal spikes allowed:** Yes. **Range:** Yes (grass/mats). **To obtain tee times:** Call up to 14 days in advance. **Subscriber comments:** Challenging from any set of tees...A little toward the upper cost, but great...Best value on early bird specials...A great layout, fun to play...A true test...Excellent amenities. A little pricey...Best new course played in two years...The wind howls through links. Try this one on a windy day!...Noise from airport distracting...Expensive, but wonderful golf course.

★★★★PRAIRIE VISTA GOLF COURSE
PM-504 Sale Barn Rd., Bloomington, 61704, McLean County, (309)434-2217, 140 miles S of Chicago.
Opened: 1991. **Holes:** 18. **Par:** 72/71. **Yards:** 6,748/5,224. **Course rating:** 71.8/68.9. **Slope:** 128/114. **Architect:** Roger B. Packard. **Green fee:** $17/$20. **Credit cards:** MC,VISA. **Reduced fees:** Twilight, seniors, juniors. **Caddies:** Yes. **Golf carts:** $18. **Discount golf packages:** No. **Season:** March-Nov. **High:** May-Aug. **On site lodging:** No. **Rental clubs:** Yes. **Walking policy:** Unrestricted walking. **Metal spikes allowed:** No. **Range:** Yes (grass/mats). **To obtain tee times:** Call up to 7 days in advance.
Subscriber comments: Excellent course, great shape...Must play. Best value...Top-notch golf in a great golf town...Always windy...Great course...Beautiful course, best public course in area...Another great test with great value...Young course is only going to get better...Easy to walk...Must be able to hit straight; very narrow fairways.

(GOOD VALUE seal)

★★★½PRAIRIEVIEW GOLF COURSE
PU-7993 N. River Rd., Byron, 61010, Ogle County, (815)234-4653, 12 miles SW of Rockford.
Opened: 1992. **Holes:** 18. **Par:** 72/72. **Yards:** 6,893/5,658. **Course rating:** 72.3/71.6. **Slope:** 123/117. **Architect:** William James Spear. **Green fee:** $20/$25. **Credit cards:** MC,VISA. **Reduced fees:** Weekdays, twilight, seniors, juniors. **Caddies:** No. **Golf carts:** $24. **Discount golf packages:** No. **Season:** April-Oct. **High:** June-Aug. **On site lodging:** No. **Rental clubs:** Yes. **Walking policy:** Unrestricted walking. **Metal spikes allowed:** Yes. **Range:** Yes (grass/mats). **To obtain tee times:** Call up to 7 days in advance.
Subscriber comments: Great greens and fairways...Good layout...Bentgrass...Too wide open front nine, back nine better...Exceptional small-town course; challenging...Best course for the money anywhere.

★½PRESTBURY COUNTRY CLUB
Golfview & Hankes, Sugar Grove, 60554, Kane County, (630)466-4177.
Call club for further information.

★★★QUAIL MEADOWS GOLF COURSE
PU-2215 Centennial Dr., Washington, 61571, Tazewell County, (309)694-3139.
Opened: 1972. **Holes:** 18. **Par:** 72/72. **Yards:** 6,647/5,492. **Course rating:** 71.3/71.6. **Slope:** 121/117. **Architect:** N/A. **Green fee:** $13. **Credit cards:** MC,VISA,DISC. **Reduced fees:** Twilight, seniors, juniors. **Caddies:** No. **Golf carts:** $16. **Discount golf packages:** No. **Season:** Year-round. **High:** May-Sept. **On site lodging:** No. **Rental clubs:** Yes. **Walking policy:** Unrestricted walking. **Metal spikes allowed:** Yes. **Range:** Yes (grass). **To obtain tee times:** Call up to 7 days in advance.
Subscriber comments: Best and most reasonably priced course in this area...Good value for money...Course is in good shape...A few boring holes, need more trees.

★★★½THE RAIL GOLF CLUB
PU-R.R. No. 5-124 N., Springfield, 62707, Sangamon County, (217)525-0365, 100 miles N of St. Louis.
Opened: 1970. **Holes:** 18. **Par:** 72/72. **Yards:** 6,583/5,406. **Course rating:** 71.1/70.6. **Slope:** 120/116. **Architect:** Robert Trent Jones. **Green fee:** $28. **Credit cards:** MC,VISA,AMEX. **Reduced fees:** Twilight, seniors, juniors. **Caddies:** No. **Golf carts:** $12. **Discount golf packages:** No. **Season:** March-Dec. **High:** May-Sept. **On site lodging:** No. **Rental clubs:** Yes. **Walking policy:** Unrestricted walking. **Metal spikes allowed:** Yes. **Range:** Yes (grass). **To obtain tee times:** Call up to 10 days in advance.

Notes: LPGA State Farm Rail Classic.
Subscriber comments: Beautiful course...Open course...Nice, challenging; great staff...Nice traditional layout, good use of flat land...Site of LPGA State Farm Rail Classic on Labor Day weekend; length acceptable for women...Course is getting tighter with age...No wonder the LPGA comes here! Good challenge...Nothing spectacular but always a joy to play.

★★★RAILSIDE GOLF CLUB
PU-120 W. 19th St., Gibson City, 60936, Ford County, (217)784-5000, 25 miles E of Bloomington.
Opened: 1993. **Holes:** 18. **Par:** 72/72. **Yards:** 6,801/5,367. **Course rating:** 71.8/70.2. **Slope:** 122/115. **Architect:** Paul Loague. **Green fee:** $9/$18. **Credit cards:** All major. **Reduced fees:** Weekdays, low season, twilight, seniors, juniors. **Caddies:** No. **Golf carts:** $9. **Discount golf packages:** Yes. **Season:** Year-round. **High:** May-Sept. **On site lodging:** No. **Rental clubs:** Yes. **Walking policy:** Unrestricted walking. **Metal spikes allowed:** Yes. **Range:** Yes (grass). **To obtain tee times:** Call up to 5 days in advance.
Subscriber comments: Staff and service is very good...Nice course. Wind can be mean...Wide open. Premium on putting, not much risk taking required...Great for flat central Illinois, and will get tough...Very young course, well done...Kind of wide open, but will definitely challenge you. Undulating greens. Bent-grass fairways wind around a lot and are too narrow...Young course with some challenges.

★★★RANDALL OAKS GOLF CLUB
PU-37 W. 361 Binnie Rd., Dundee, 60118, Kane County, (847)428-5661, 35 miles NW of Chicago.
Opened: 1966. **Holes:** 18. **Par:** 71/71. **Yards:** 6,160/5,379. **Course rating:** 67.7/70.3. **Slope:** 113/110. **Architect:** William James Spear. **Green fee:** $15/$26. **Credit cards:** MC,VISA,DISC. **Reduced fees:** Weekdays, twilight, seniors, juniors. **Caddies:** No. **Golf carts:** $12. **Discount golf packages:** No. **Season:** April-Nov. **High:** June-Aug. **On site lodging:** No. **Rental clubs:** Yes. **Walking policy:** Unrestricted walking. **Metal spikes allowed:** Yes. **Range:** Yes (grass). **To obtain tee times:** Call 7 days in advance.
Subscriber comments: Good value for a family outing...Deserves award for "most improved"...Tranquil...Nice park district course; lots of doglegs...Keeps improving...Outstanding price...Rapidly improving...Excellent course for average player...Short but well maintained. Best greens.

★★RED HAWK COUNTRY CLUB
Route 154, Tamaroa, 62888, Perry County, (618)357-9704.
Opened: 1921. **Holes:** 18. **Par:** 70/71. **Yards:** 5,904/4,494. **Course rating:** N/A. **Slope:** N/A. **Architect:** N/A. **Green fee:** $15/$20. **Credit cards:** N/A. **Reduced fees:** Low season. **Caddies:** Yes. **Golf carts:** $10. **Discount golf packages:** Yes. **Season:** Year-round. **High:** May-Oct. **On site lodging:** No. **Rental clubs:** Yes. **Walking policy:** Unrestricted walking. **Metal spikes allowed:** No. **Range:** Yes (grass). **To obtain tee times:** Call.
Special Notes: Formerly Perry County Country Club.

★★★REDTAIL GOLF CLUB
PU-7900 Redtail Dr., Lakewood, 60014, McHenry County, (815)477-0055.
Opened: 1991. **Holes:** 18. **Par:** 72/72. **Yards:** 6,902/5,455. **Course rating:** 72.1/70.3. **Slope:** 123/116. **Architect:** Roger Packard. **Green fee:** $36/$47. **Credit cards:** MC,VISA,AMEX. **Reduced fees:** Weekdays, low season, twilight, seniors. **Caddies:** No. **Golf carts:** $11. **Discount golf packages:** Yes. **Season:** April-Nov. **High:** June-Sept. **On site lodging:** No. **Rental clubs:** Yes. **Walking policy:** Walking at certain times. **Metal spikes allowed:** Yes. **Range:** Yes (grass/mats). **To obtain tee times:** Call up to 7 days in advance. Must reserve with credit card for weekend.
Subscriber comments: Enjoyable course for outing...Hitting its stride, great greens, very windy, I'll be back!...Too much distance between green and next tee...Wide open, need cart. Enjoyable...Sleeper course; will be one fine track in the future...Deceptively hard test for average golfer.
Special Notes: Formerly Lakewood Golf Club.

REND LAKE GOLF COURSE

PU-12476 Golf Course Dr., Whittington, 62897, Franklin County, (618)629-2353, 90 miles SE of St. Louis.

Opened: 1975. **Holes:** 27. **Architect:** Edward Lawrence Packard. **Green fee:** $22/$26. **Credit cards:** MC,VISA,AMEX. **Reduced fees:** Weekdays, twilight, seniors. **Caddies:** No. **Golf carts:** $10. **Discount golf packages:** Yes. **Season:** March-Nov. **High:** May-Oct. **On site lodging:** Yes. **Rental clubs:** Yes. **Walking policy:** Walking at certain times. **Metal spikes allowed:** Yes. **Range:** Yes (grass/mats). **To obtain tee times:** Call golf shop.

★★★½EAST/SOUTH
Par: 72/72. **Yards:** 6,861/5,830. **Course rating:** 72.2/72.5. **Slope:** 130/116.
EAST/WEST
Par: 72/72. **Yards:** 6,812/5,849. **Course rating:** 71.8/72.6. **Slope:** 131/116.
Subscriber comments: Course acceptable in mid-summer...Best courses in southern Illinois...Excellent all around...Great course; great value...Fantastic 27 holes...Fun to play...Great place to spend a weekend...Very good mix of different type holes...Has hotel and food/bar facilities.

★★RENWOOD COUNTRY CLUB

PM-1413 Hainesville Rd., Round Lake Beach, 60073, Lake County, (847)546-8242, 50 miles N of Chicago.

Opened: N/A. **Holes:** 18. **Par:** 72/72. **Yards:** 6,004/5,584. **Course rating:** 68.6/71.5. **Slope:** 116/118. **Architect:** N/A. **Green fee:** $9/$27. **Credit cards:** MC,VISA,DISC. **Reduced fees:** Weekdays, low season, twilight, seniors, juniors. **Caddies:** No. **Golf carts:** $12. **Discount golf packages:** No. **Season:** April-Nov. **High:** May-Sept. **On site lodging:** No. **Rental clubs:** Yes. **Walking policy:** Unrestricted walking. **Metal spikes allowed:** Yes. **Range:** Yes (mats). **To obtain tee times:** Call up to 5 days in advance with credit card to guarantee.

★★★RIVER OAKS GOLF COURSE

1 Park Ave., Calumet City, 60409, Cook County, (708)730-1878.
Call club for further information.
Subscriber comments: Fun little course...Tough and narrow, lots of water...Average course, low green fees. Usually in good shape despite a drainage problem...$6 green fee for senior with activity card...Former private club.

★★½ROLLING HILLS GOLF COURSE

PU-5801 Pierce Lane, Godfrey, 62035, Madison County, (618)466-8363, 15 miles SW of St. Louis.

Opened: 1964. **Holes:** 18. **Par:** 71/71. **Yards:** 5,687/4,814. **Course rating:** 66.1/66.5. **Slope:** 100/101. **Architect:** N/A. **Green fee:** $14/$16. **Credit cards:** MC,VISA. **Reduced fees:** Low season, twilight, seniors, juniors. **Caddies:** No. **Golf carts:** $10. **Discount golf packages:** No. **Season:** Year-round. **High:** April-Sept. **On site lodging:** No. **Rental clubs:** Yes. **Walking policy:** Unrestricted walking. **Metal spikes allowed:** Yes. **Range:** Yes (grass/mats). **To obtain tee times:** Call up to 7 days in advance between 6 a.m. and 6 p.m. in season.
Subscriber comments: Good course for beginners...Easy course. Great value and management...Good course, value...Very short; great for seniors and high handicappers...New nine still maturing, fair course...Old part OK, new part forgettable...Play here most, "fits budget".

★★★½RUFFLED FEATHERS GOLF CLUB

1 Pete Dye Dr., Lemont, 60439, Cook County, (630)257-1000, 20 miles SW of Chicago.
Opened: 1992. **Holes:** 18. **Par:** 72/72. **Yards:** 6,878/5,273. **Course rating:** 73.1/65.7. **Slope:** 134/110. **Architect:** Pete Dye/P. B. Dye. **Green fee:** $50/$85. **Credit cards:** MC,VISA,AMEX. **Reduced fees:** Weekdays, low season, twilight. **Caddies:** No. **Golf carts:** Included in Green Fee. **Discount golf packages:** No. **Season:** March-Nov. **High:** April-Oct. **On site lodging:** No. **Rental clubs:** Yes. **Walking policy:** Unrestricted walking. **Metal spikes allowed:** Yes. **Range:** Yes (grass/mats). **To obtain tee times:** Tee times per foursomes only - 7 days in advance. Golf events (12 or more players) call any time.
Subscriber comments: Some solid golf holes. Great condition. Somewhat

unknown...A classic Dye design! Several memorable holes, great greens...Worth playing...One of my favorites. Little high in cost...Some of the best holes in Chicagoland...A miniature Blackwolf Run.

ST. ANDREWS GOLF & COUNTRY CLUB
PU-3N441 Rte. 59, West Chicago, 60185, Du Page County, (630)231-3100, 30 miles W of Chicago.
Opened: 1926. **Green fee:** $24/$32. **Credit cards:** MC,VISA,DISC. **Reduced fees:** Weekdays, low season, twilight, juniors. **Caddies:** No. **Golf carts:** $27. **Discount golf packages:** No. **Season:** Year-round. **High:** May-Sept. **On site lodging:** No. **Rental clubs:** Yes. **Walking policy:** Unrestricted walking. **Metal spikes allowed:** Yes. **Range:** Yes (grass/mats). **To obtain tee times:** For weekdays call 6 days before day desired; for weekends call the Monday before the weekend. During season players may obtain a guaranteed foursome time for a fee of $114 (on the weekends before 1:00).
★★½**LAKEWOOD COURSE**
Holes: 18. **Par:** 72/72. **Yards:** 6,666/5,353. **Course rating:** 71.1/69.4. **Slope:** 121/114. **Architect:** Ed Dearie Jr..
Subscriber comments: Probably one of the best courses for value...Good for average players. Best practice facility available....Good value, can get slow in the afternoon...Two of the best value tracks around...Overplayed; too many outings.
★★★**ST. ANDREWS COURSE**
Holes: 18. **Par:** 71/71. **Yards:** 6,759/5,138. **Course rating:** 71.2/68.2. **Slope:** 118/110. **Architect:** John McGregor.
Subscriber comments: No.18 is a good finishing hole, otherwise average layout...Tough old course, Very nice clubhouse...Lots of outings; good practice area...Fun for all abilities...Lots of doglegs.

THE SANCTUARY GOLF COURSE
PU-485 N. Marley Rd., New Lenox, 60451, Will County, (815)462-4653, 35 miles S of Chicago.
Opened: 1996. **Holes:** 18. **Par:** 72/72. **Yards:** 6,701/5,120. **Course rating:** 70.6/67.6. **Slope:** 118/111. **Architect:** Steve Halberg. **Green fee:** $25/$33. **Credit cards:** MC,VISA,DISC. **Reduced fees:** Low season, twilight, seniors, juniors. **Caddies:** No. **Golf carts:** $12. **Discount golf packages:** No. **Season:** March-Nov. **High:** June-Sept. **On site lodging:** No. **Rental clubs:** Yes. **Walking policy:** Unrestricted walking. **Metal spikes allowed:** Yes. **Range:** Yes (grass/mats). **To obtain tee times:** Call 7 days in advance.
Subscriber comments: New course that's still settling in...One day it will be great.

★★★**SANDY HOLLOW GOLF COURSE**
PU-2500 Sandy Hollow Rd., Rockford, 61109, Winnebago County, (815)987-8836, 70 miles NW of Chicago.
Opened: 1930. **Holes:** 18. **Par:** 71/76. **Yards:** 6,228/5,883. **Course rating:** 69.4/72.8. **Slope:** 113/113. **Architect:** Charles Dudley Wagstaff. **Green fee:** $12/$21. **Credit cards:** MC,VISA,DISC. **Reduced fees:** Twilight. **Caddies:** No. **Golf carts:** $20. **Discount golf packages:** No. **Season:** April-Oct. **High:** June-Aug. **On site lodging:** No. **Rental clubs:** Yes. **Walking policy:** Unrestricted walking. **Metal spikes allowed:** Yes. **Range:** No. **To obtain tee times:** Call one week in advance.

(GOOD VALUE)

Subscriber comments: Average public course; named Sandy Hollow for 50-plus traps, mostly greenside...Great price for the buck...Good balance of length and narrow fairways...Nice small course for beginners...Estheically appealing, challenging...An old course, but challenging.

★★**SAUKIE MUNICIPAL GOLF COURSE**
PM-3101 38th St., Rock Island, 61201, Rock Island County, (309)788-2267.
Opened: 1926. **Holes:** 18. **Par:** 66/66. **Yards:** 5,002/4,456. **Course rating:** N/A. **Slope:** N/A. **Architect:** N/A. **Green fee:** $11/$12. **Credit cards:** None. **Reduced fees:** Twilight, seniors, juniors. **Caddies:** No. **Golf carts:** $17. **Discount golf packages:** No. **Season:** Year-round. **High:** May-Aug. **On site lodging:** No. **Rental clubs:** Yes. **Walking policy:** Unrestricted walking. **Metal spikes allowed:** Yes. **Range:** No. **To obtain tee times:** N/A.

★★★SCHAUMBURG GOLF CLUB
PU-401 N. Roselle Rd., Schaumburg, 60194, Cook County, (847)885-9000.
Opened: 1926. **Holes:** 27. **Par:** 71/71. **Yards:** 6,522/4,885. **Course rating:** 70.6/67.2.
Slope: 117/114. **Architect:** Robert Lohmann. **Green fee:** $23/$26. **Credit cards:**
MC,VISA. **Reduced fees:** Weekdays, twilight, seniors, juniors. **Caddies:** No. **Golf
carts:** $13. **Discount golf packages:** No. **Season:** April-Dec. **High:** June-Aug. **On site
lodging:** No. **Rental clubs:** Yes. **Walking policy:** Unrestricted walking. **Metal spikes
allowed:** Yes. **Range:** Yes (grass). **To obtain tee times:** Call one week in advance.
Subscriber comments: Great 27 holes...A great value for residents...They've come a
long way babe, great remake...Great improvements since 1996...Short...Redid course
and clubhouse...Great improvement in past three years...Resident rates are exceptional...New look to an old course.

★★★SCOVILL GOLF CLUB
PU-3909 West Main St., Decatur, 62522, Macon County, (217)429-6243, 120 miles N
of St. Louis.
Opened: 1925. **Holes:** 18. **Par:** 71/71. **Yards:** 5,900/4,303. **Course rating:** 67.8/64.8.
Slope: 119/108. **Architect:** Dick Nugent. **Green fee:** $12/$15. **Credit cards:** MC,VISA.
Reduced fees: N/A. **Caddies:** No. **Golf carts:** $16. **Discount golf packages:** No.
Season: Year-round. **High:** May-Aug. **On site lodging:** No. **Rental clubs:** Yes. **Walking
policy:** Unrestricted walking. **Metal spikes allowed:** Yes. **Range:** Yes (grass/mats). **To
obtain tee times:** Call up to 7 days in advance during the week. Call on Monday for
upcoming weekend or holiday.
Subscriber comments: Hilly but not dangerous, need accuracy...Short, hilly and beautiful. Large greens; easy par 5...Course short. Tried to make a championship course
without the real estate...Not very long, but hills make it interesting. Different...Good public course...Lots of character and great price.

★★★½SENICA OAK RIDGE GOLF CLUB
658 E. Rte. 6, La Salle, 61301, La Salle County, (815)223-7273, 90 miles SW of
Chicago.
Opened: 1994. **Holes:** 18. **Par:** 72/72. **Yards:** 6,900/5,825. **Course rating:** 72.6/73.0.
Slope: 117/117. **Architect:** William James Spear. **Green fee:** $30/$36. **Credit cards:**
MC,VISA,DISC. **Reduced fees:** Weekdays, low season, seniors. **Caddies:** No. **Golf
carts:** $18. **Discount golf packages:** No. **Season:** Year-round. **High:** June-Sept. **On
site lodging:** No. **Rental clubs:** Yes. **Walking policy:** Walking at certain times. **Metal
spikes allowed:** Yes. **Range:** Yes (grass/mats). **To obtain tee times:** Call anytime.
Subscriber comments: Newer course needs time to mature...Course almost resort-
like...Best value for bentgrass this part of state...A very nice course, well managed,
friendly staff...Good test of all your game...Good lunches.

★★½SETTLER'S HILL GOLF COURSE
919 E. Fabyan Pkwy., Batavia, 60510, Kane County, (630)232-1636.
Call club for further information.
Subscriber comments: Built around landfill, fun for the money. Couple of weak and
tough holes...If ball is off fairway it is gone...Interesting and affordable...Conditions
improving with age...Fun course, try it at least once.

★★★½SEVEN BRIDGES GOLF CLUB
PU-One Mulligan Dr., Woodridge, 60517, Du Page County, (630)964-
7777, 25 miles W of Chicago.
Opened: 1991. **Holes:** 18. **Par:** 72/72. **Yards:** 7,118/5,277. **Course rating:** 74.6/70.4. **Slope:** 135/121. **Architect:** Dick Nugent. **Green fee:**
$45/$83. **Credit cards:** MC,VISA,AMEX,Diners Club. **Reduced fees:**
Low season, twilight. **Caddies:** Yes. **Golf carts:** Included in Green Fee. **Discount golf
packages:** No. **Season:** April-Nov. **High:** May-Oct. **On site lodging:** No. **Rental clubs:**
Yes. **Walking policy:** Unrestricted walking. **Metal spikes allowed:** Yes. **Range:** Yes
(grass/mats). **To obtain tee times:** Call 14 days in advance.
Subscriber comments: Mostly great golf. Back nine water can be too severe...Course
is "tricked up," which detracts from otherwise good layout, not natural...One of the finest
courses in the Chicago area...Well worth the cost...10, 11, and 12 are unplayable
holes...Probably the toughest back nine in Chicago.

★★½SHADY LAWN GOLF COURSE
615 Dixie Hwy., Beecher, 60401, Will County, (708)946-2800, 30 miles S of Chicago.
Opened: 1927. **Holes:** 27. **Par:** 72/72. **Yards:** 6,340/5,541. **Course rating:** N/A. **Slope:** N/A. **Architect:** R. Albert Anderson. **Green fee:** $14/$26. **Credit cards:** MC,VISA. **Reduced fees:** Weekdays, low season, twilight, seniors, juniors. **Caddies:** No. **Golf carts:** $12. **Discount golf packages:** Yes. **Season:** Year-round. **High:** June-Sept. **On site lodging:** No. **Rental clubs:** Yes. **Walking policy:** Unrestricted walking. **Metal spikes allowed:** Yes. **Range:** No. **To obtain tee times:** Call anytime.
Subscriber comments: Economical, short and forgiving; no challenge...Nice variety of holes...Friendly atmosphere...Pretty good golf for the money...Nice course for an outing...Walkable, pretty ordinary...Economical golf, nice people, fair course.

SILVER LAKE COUNTRY CLUB
PU-147th St. and 82nd Ave., Orland Park, 60462, Cook County, (708)349-6940, (800)525-3465, 22 miles SW of Chicago.
Green fee: $27/$33. **Credit cards:** All major. **Reduced fees:** Weekdays, low season, twilight, seniors, juniors. **Caddies:** No. **Golf carts:** $13. **Discount golf packages:** No. **Season:** March-Jan. **High:** April-Oct. **On site lodging:** No. **Rental clubs:** Yes. **Walking policy:** Unrestricted walking. **Metal spikes allowed:** Yes. **Range:** No. **To obtain tee times:** Tee time may be made by phone (708-833-8463) up to 14 days in advance.
★★★NORTH COURSE
Opened: 1927. **Holes:** 18. **Par:** 72/77. **Yards:** 6,826/5,659. **Course rating:** 71.9/71.5. **Slope:** 116/116. **Architect:** Leonard Macomber.
Subscriber comments: Toughest rough ever played...Fine layout...Full golf shop, good 18th par-3 hole...Old established course in excellent condition. Very popular. Play during the week...Nice front nine, nondescript back nine...Fair food...Nothing outstanding.
★★★SOUTH COURSE
Opened: 1929. **Holes:** 18. **Par:** 70/72. **Yards:** 5,948/5,138. **Course rating:** 67.9/69.3. **Slope:** 108/109. **Architect:** Raymond Didier.
Subscriber comments: South Course challenging, well kept...Greens are very challenging...Enjoyable to play...Well kept...Average course...Oak trees everywhere, nice greens...Great golf shop, fair food...Nothing outstanding...You need to use all of your clubs, very good course...Mature trees, well rounded.
Special Notes: Also has a 9-hole par-29 course called Rolling Hills.

★★★SILVER RIDGE GOLF COURSE
3069 N. Hill Rd., Oregon, 61061, Ogle County, (815)734-4440, 2 miles N of Oregon.
Opened: N/A. **Holes:** 18. **Par:** 72/72. **Yards:** 6,614/5,181. **Course rating:** 71.2/72.0. **Slope:** 116/106. **Architect:** N/A. **Green fee:** $19/$23. **Credit cards:** MC,VISA,DISC. **Reduced fees:** Twilight, seniors, juniors. **Caddies:** No. **Golf carts:** $11. **Discount golf packages:** No. **Season:** March-Nov. **High:** May-Sept. **On site lodging:** No. **Rental clubs:** Yes. **Walking policy:** Walking at certain times. **Metal spikes allowed:** Yes. **Range:** Yes (grass). **To obtain tee times:** Call golf shop up to 7 days in advance.
Subscriber comments: Variety: valleys, hills, woods. Will mature...Good greens and fairways in spite of weather woes...A good new course...My second favorite course in northern Illinois...What a gem, very challenging, great greens.

★★½SNAG CREEK GOLF COURSE
PU-RR 1, Washburn, 61570, Woodford County, (309)248-7300, 25 miles NE of Peoria.
Opened: 1965. **Holes:** 18. **Par:** 72/73. **Yards:** 6,300/5,635. **Course rating:** 69.9. **Slope:** N/A. **Architect:** N/A. **Green fee:** $8/$12. **Credit cards:** None. **Reduced fees:** N/A. **Caddies:** No. **Golf carts:** $14. **Discount golf packages:** No. **Season:** March-Oct. **High:** May-Aug. **On site lodging:** No. **Rental clubs:** No. **Walking policy:** Unrestricted walking. **Metal spikes allowed:** Yes. **Range:** No. **To obtain tee times:** Call up to 7 days in advance.
Subscriber comments: Hate to rate it so good; afraid it might get crowded...Just OK...Good for having been a prior cornfield...If you don't respect this unassuming course, it will bite you!...Middle of nowhere, average greens but lots of fun holes.

★★½SOUTH SHORE GOLF COURSE
PU-1727 N. River South Rd., Momence, 60954, Kankakee County, (815)472-4407, 7 miles E of Kankakee.

Opened: 1927. **Holes:** 18. **Par:** 72/72. **Yards:** 6,174/5,439. **Course rating:** 68.6/70.2. **Slope:** 117/115. **Architect:** N/A. **Green fee:** $10/$20. **Credit cards:** MC,VISA. **Reduced fees:** Weekdays, twilight, seniors. **Caddies:** No. **Golf carts:** $22. **Discount golf packages:** No. **Season:** Year-round. **High:** April-Nov. **On site lodging:** No. **Rental clubs:** No. **Walking policy:** Unrestricted walking. **Metal spikes allowed:** Yes. **Range:** Yes (grass). **To obtain tee times:** Call golf shop.

Subscriber comments: Small and hard-to-hold greens...Well-run operation, but not an outstanding golf experience...A quiet course along Kankakee River.

★★½SPARTAN MEADOWS GOLF CLUB
PU-1969 Spartan, Elgin, 60123, Kane County, (847)931-5950, 40 miles W of Chicago.
Opened: 1971. **Holes:** 18. **Par:** 72/72. **Yards:** 6,853/5,353. **Course rating:** 72.7/70.3. **Slope:** 123/116. **Architect:** Edward Lawrence Packard/Greg Bayor. **Green fee:** $19/$28. **Credit cards:** MC,VISA,DISC. **Reduced fees:** Weekdays, low season, twilight, seniors, juniors. **Caddies:** No. **Golf carts:** $24. **Discount golf packages:** Yes. **Season:** April-Nov. **High:** May-Sept. **On site lodging:** No. **Rental clubs:** Yes. **Walking policy:** Unrestricted walking. **Metal spikes allowed:** Yes. **Range:** No. **To obtain tee times:** Call 7 days in advance.

Subscriber comments: Very typical average public course...Flat and unspectacular...Could be nice with some fairway contouring, which is planned...New minor changes add some difficulty.

★★★★SPENCER T. OLIN COMMUNITY GOLF COURSE
PU-4701 College Ave., Alton, 62002, Madison County, (618)465-3111, 25 miles NE of St. Louis.
Opened: 1989. **Holes:** 18. **Par:** 72/72. **Yards:** 6,941/5,049. **Course rating:** 73.8/68.5. **Slope:** 135/117. **Architect:** Arnold Palmer/Ed Seay. **Green fee:** $28/$52. **Credit cards:** MC,VISA,AMEX. **Reduced fees:** Weekdays, low season, resort guests, twilight, juniors. **Caddies:** No. **Golf carts:** Included in Green Fee. **Discount golf packages:** Yes. **Season:** Year-round. **High:** April-Oct. **On site lodging:** No. **Rental clubs:** Yes. **Walking policy:** Walking at certain times. **Metal spikes allowed:** Yes. **Range:** Yes (grass). **To obtain tee times:** Call up to 7 days in advance with credit card to guarantee. Foursomes only accepted for weekends/holidays.
Notes: 1996 Amateur Public Links Championship.

Subscriber comments: Beautiful...Great course; value right, management excellent...Great condition, good challenge, super-fast greens...Woods, hills—has it all...Outstanding, period...One of the King's best, awesome layout...Have "golf assisters" instead of marshals that travel the course and give you golf tips if asked.

★★★SPORTSMAN'S COUNTRY CLUB
PM-3535 Dundee Rd., Northbrook, 60062, Cook County, (847)291-2351, 2 miles N of Deerfield.
Opened: 1931. **Holes:** 27. **Par:** 70/72. **Yards:** 6,354/5,470. **Course rating:** 70.7/71.9. **Slope:** 124/122. **Architect:** Edward B. Dearie Jr.. **Green fee:** $28. **Credit cards:** MC,VISA. **Reduced fees:** N/A. **Caddies:** No. **Golf carts:** $31. **Discount golf packages:** No. **Season:** March-Nov. **High:** June-Aug. **On site lodging:** No. **Rental clubs:** Yes. **Walking policy:** Unrestricted walking. **Metal spikes allowed:** Yes. **Range:** Yes. **To obtain tee times:** Call 2 days in advance.

Subscriber comments: Very busy, but worth it...Well kept. Interesting but not difficult...Improving year to year, better upkeep, decent challenge...Superintendent does great job with number of rounds played...Easy to score on.

★★½SPRING CREEK GOLF COURSE
PU-RR 1, Spring Valley, 61362, Bureau County, (815)894-2137, 60 miles N of Peoria.
Opened: 1964. **Holes:** 18. **Par:** 72/73. **Yards:** 6,465/5,196. **Course rating:** 71.6/70.9. **Slope:** 125/120. **Architect:** N/A. **Green fee:** $14/$17. **Credit cards:** None. **Reduced fees:** N/A. **Caddies:** No. **Golf carts:** $20. **Discount golf packages:** No. **Season:** April-Nov. **High:** May-Aug. **On site lodging:** No. **Rental clubs:** Yes. **Walking policy:** Unrestricted walking. **Metal spikes allowed:** Yes. **Range:** No. **To obtain tee times:** Tee times not required. First come, first served. Outings of more than 20 players require reservations.

Subscriber comments: Good variation...Wonderful course...Two different nines, short and curvy, and long and straight...Lots of potential, more money needed to be spent.

★★★SPRINGBROOK GOLF COURSE
PU-2220 83rd St., Naperville, 60564, Du Page County, (630)420-4215, 28 miles SW of Chicago.
Opened: 1974. **Holes:** 18. **Par:** 72/73. **Yards:** 6,896/5,850. **Course rating:** 72.6/72.7. **Slope:** 124/125. **Architect:** Edward Lawrence Packard. **Green fee:** $20/$38. **Credit cards:** MC,VISA. **Reduced fees:** Weekdays, low season, twilight, seniors, juniors. **Caddies:** No. **Golf carts:** $12. **Discount golf packages:** No. **Season:** March-Dec. **High:** May-Aug. **On site lodging:** No. **Rental clubs:** Yes. **Walking policy:** Unrestricted walking. **Metal spikes allowed:** Yes. **Range:** Yes (grass). **To obtain tee times:** Call up to 7 days in advance after 5 p.m.
Subscriber comments: Nice course. Very friendly staff and other players...Great layout and facilities; great value...A well-kept course, some tough holes...Need to be long and aggressive, tough greens...An excellent muny course...Nice layout good greens...Well bunkered, straightforward course. I've played Springbrook since high school and have always enjoyed it.

★★★½STEEPLE CHASE GOLF CLUB
PU-200 N. La Vista Dr., Mundelein, 60060, Lake County, (847)949-8900, 35 miles NW of Chicago.
Opened: 1993. **Holes:** 18. **Par:** 72/72. **Yards:** 6,827/4,831. **Course rating:** 73.1/68.1. **Slope:** 129/113. **Architect:** Ken Killian. **Green fee:** $40. **Credit cards:** All major. **Reduced fees:** Weekdays, twilight, seniors, juniors. **Caddies:** No. **Golf carts:** $13. **Discount golf packages:** No. **Season:** April-Nov. **High:** May-Sept. **On site lodging:** No. **Rental clubs:** Yes. **Walking policy:** Walking at certain times. **Metal spikes allowed:** Yes. **Range:** No. **To obtain tee times:** Call 7 days in advance at 6 a.m.; foursomes only, credit card required.
Subscriber comments: A lot of golf for price...Nice course, excellent greens...Open course that can be scored on with good second shots. Water on several holes...Rolling terrain provides a fun...Very nice clubhouse...Scenic course with tough driving holes...Will be great once all the new trees mature...Fast greens, great shape.

★★★★STONEWOLF GOLF CLUB
PU-1195 Stonewolf Trail, Fairview Heights, 62208, St. Claire County, (618)624-4653, (888)709-4653, 12 miles E of St. Louis.
Opened: 1996. **Holes:** 18. **Par:** 71/72. **Yards:** 6,943/4,849. **Course rating:** 74.0/67.2. **Slope:** 141/126. **Architect:** Jack Nicklaus. **Green fee:** $40/$65. **Credit cards:** All major. **Reduced fees:** Weekdays, twilight, seniors. **Caddies:** No. **Golf carts:** Included in Green Fee. **Discount golf packages:** No. **Season:** Year-round. **High:** June-Sept. **On site lodging:** No. **Rental clubs:** Yes. **Walking policy:** Unrestricted walking. **Metal spikes allowed:** No. **Range:** Yes (grass). **To obtain tee times:** Call golf shop.
Notes: Ranked 2nd in 1997 Best New Upscale Public Courses.
Subscriber comments: New, terrific shape...Great course...Too expensive to play often...Will be best public course in St. Louis area!...Owners are great golf enthusiats...May be best course around...Typical Nicklaus but its great if you have the shots.

★★STORYBROOK COUNTRY CLUB
2124 W Storybrook Rd., Hanover, 61041, Jo Daviess County, (815)591-2210, 40 miles E of Dubuque, IA.
Opened: 1965. **Holes:** 9. **Par:** 72/75. **Yards:** 6,194/5,501. **Course rating:** N/A. **Slope:** N/A. **Architect:** N/A. **Green fee:** $14/$16. **Credit cards:** MC,VISA. **Reduced fees:** N/A. **Caddies:** No. **Golf carts:** $18. **Discount golf packages:** No. **Season:** Year-round. **High:** June-Aug. **On site lodging:** No. **Rental clubs:** Yes. **Walking policy:** Unrestricted walking. **Metal spikes allowed:** Yes. **Range:** Yes (grass). **To obtain tee times:** Tee times not required.

★★★SUNSET VALLEY GOLF CLUB
PU-1390 Sunset Rd., Highland Park, 60035, Lake County, (847)432-7140, 20 miles N of Chicago.
Opened: 1922. **Holes:** 18. **Par:** 72/72. **Yards:** 6,458/5,465. **Course rating:** 70.5/71.6. **Slope:** 121/119. **Architect:** N/A. **Green fee:** N/A. **Credit cards:** MC,VISA. **Reduced fees:** Weekdays, low season, twilight, seniors, juniors. **Caddies:** No. **Golf carts:** $12. **Discount golf packages:** No. **Season:** March-Nov. **High:** March-Aug. **On site lodg-

ing: No. **Rental clubs:** Yes. **Walking policy:** Unrestricted walking. **Metal spikes allowed:** Yes. **Range:** No. **To obtain tee times:** Tee times can be reserved for three or four people one week in advance. This can be done over the phone. Times are held with a credit card number.

Subscriber comments: Pretty straight course...Old wooded course. Not bad...Excellent condition for very busy municipal course...Very impressed, can't wait to play again...Every year they do something to improve.

SYCAMORE COMMUNITY GOLF COURSE
Rte. #64, Sycamore, 60178, De Kalb County, (815)895-3884.
Call club for further information.

★★SYCAMORE HILLS GOLF CLUB
928 Clinton Rd., Paris, 61944, Edgar County, (217)465-4031, 30 miles W of Terre Haute, IN.
Opened: 1927. **Holes:** 18. **Par:** 72/72. **Yards:** 6,589/5,222. **Course rating:** 72.2/70.6.
Slope: 124/117. **Architect:** N/A. **Green fee:** $15/$20. **Credit cards:** MC,VISA,DISC.
Reduced fees: Weekdays, low season. **Caddies:** No. **Golf carts:** $10. **Discount golf packages:** No. **Season:** April-Nov. **High:** June-Aug. **On site lodging:** No. **Rental clubs:** No. **Walking policy:** Unrestricted walking. **Metal spikes allowed:** Yes. **Range:** Yes (grass). **To obtain tee times:** Call anytime for availability.

★★TAMARACK COUNTRY CLUB
PU-800 Tamarack Lane, O'Fallon, 62269, St. Clair County, (618)632-6666, 20 miles E of St. Louis, MO.
Opened: 1965. **Holes:** 18. **Par:** 71/74. **Yards:** 6,282/5,120. **Course rating:** 68.2/67.7.
Slope: 106/104. **Architect:** Pete Dye. **Green fee:** $15/$18. **Credit cards:** MC,VISA.
Reduced fees: N/A. **Caddies:** No. **Golf carts:** $10. **Discount golf packages:** No.
Season: Year-round. **High:** April-Sept. **On site lodging:** No. **Rental clubs:** Yes.
Walking policy: Unrestricted walking. **Metal spikes allowed:** Yes. **Range:** Yes (grass).
To obtain tee times: Call 7 days in advance.

★★★TAMARACK GOLF CLUB
24032 Royal Worlington Dr., Naperville, 60564, Will County, (630)904-4004, 20 miles SW of Chicago.
Opened: 1989. **Holes:** 18. **Par:** 70/70. **Yards:** 6,955/5,016. **Course rating:** 74.2/68.8.
Slope: 131/114. **Architect:** David Gill. **Green fee:** $30/$49. **Credit cards:** MC,VISA,AMEX. **Reduced fees:** Weekdays, low season, twilight, seniors. **Caddies:** No. **Golf carts:** Included in Green Fee. **Discount golf packages:** No. **Season:** March-Nov. **High:** June-Sept. **On site lodging:** No. **Rental clubs:** Yes. **Walking policy:** Mandatory cart. **Metal spikes allowed:** Yes. **Range:** No. **To obtain tee times:** Call seven days in advance; credit card number needed to reserve tee-time. Foursomes only on weekends.

Subscriber comments: Nice, fair price...A great value! Lot of variety in layout, true greens...Long, troublesome from back tees...Too many blind shots; local knowledge required...Fairways slope to water...Tough holes, can't go to sleep.

★½THUNDERBIRD COUNTRY CLUB
1010 E. Northwest Hwy., Barrington, 60010, Cook County, (847)381-6500, 15 miles NW of Chicago.
Opened: 1958. **Holes:** 18. **Par:** 71/72. **Yards:** 6,169/5,155. **Course rating:** 69.6/70.3.
Slope: 115/117. **Architect:** N/A. **Green fee:** $20/$27. **Credit cards:** MC,VISA.
Reduced fees: Low season, seniors. **Caddies:** No. **Golf carts:** $12. **Discount golf packages:** No. **Season:** Year-round. **High:** May-Sept. **On site lodging:** No. **Rental clubs:** Yes. **Walking policy:** Unrestricted walking. **Metal spikes allowed:** Yes. **Range:** Yes (grass). **To obtain tee times:** Call Monday at 8:00 a.m. for times Tuesday thru Sunday. Call Sunday at 3:00 p.m. for times on Monday.

★★★TIMBER TRAILS COUNTRY CLUB
PU-11350 Plainfield Rd., La Grange, 60525, Cook County, (708)246-0275, 20 miles W of Chicago.
Opened: 1934. **Holes:** 18. **Par:** 71/73. **Yards:** 6,197/5,581. **Course rating:** 68.7/71.1.
Slope: 113/116. **Architect:** Robert Bruce Harris. **Green fee:** $26/$33. **Credit cards:**

MC,VISA. **Reduced fees:** Low season, twilight, seniors. **Caddies:** No. **Golf carts:** $30. **Discount golf packages:** No. **Season:** March-Dec. **High:** May-Oct. **On site lodging:** No. **Rental clubs:** Yes. **Walking policy:** Unrestricted walking. **Metal spikes allowed:** Yes. **Range:** No. **To obtain tee times:** Reservations accepted for foursomes, three-somes, twosomes up to 7 days in advance with credit card for gurarantee.
Subscriber comments: It does have trees!...Clubhouse is 1930s...Too short...Very traditional...Too crowded, too many first-time golfers...Bent fairways...Average, average, average...Great scenery...More trees than Sherwood Forest. Leaf rule should always apply...Great challenge...One of area's most underrated.

★½TRIPLE LAKES GOLF COURSE
6942 Triple Lakes Rd., Millstadt, 62260, St. Clair County, (618)476-9985.
Call club for further information.

★★½TUCKAWAY GOLF COURSE
27641 Stony Island, Crete, 60417, Will County, (708)946-2259, 25 miles S of Chicago.
Opened: 1961. **Holes:** 18. **Par:** 72/74. **Yards:** 6,245/5,581. **Course rating:** 68.7/72.2.
Slope: 110/116. **Architect:** John Ellis. **Green fee:** $30/$37. **Credit cards:** MC,VISA.
Reduced fees: Low season, twilight, seniors, juniors. **Caddies:** No. **Golf carts:** Included in Green Fee. **Discount golf packages:** No. **Season:** March-Dec. **High:** June-Sept. **On site lodging:** No. **Rental clubs:** Yes. **Walking policy:** Unrestricted walking. **Metal spikes allowed:** Yes. **Range:** Yes (grass). **To obtain tee times:** Call 7 days in advance.
Subscriber comments: Greens tough to hit from 150 yards...Long and open, but small greens make it interesting...OK for a change of pace. Nothing exciting.

UNIVERSITY OF ILLINOIS GOLF CLUB
PU-800 Hartwell Dr., Savoy, 61874, Champaign County, (217)359-5613, 120 miles S of Chicago.
Architect: C.W. Wagstaff. **Credit cards:** MC,VISA,DISC. **Reduced fees:** Low season, twilight, seniors. **Caddies:** No. **Golf carts:** $17. **Discount golf packages:** No. **On site lodging:** No. **Rental clubs:** Yes. **Walking policy:** Unrestricted walking. **Metal spikes allowed:** Yes. **Range:** Yes (grass). **To obtain tee times:** Phone golf shop seven days in advance.
★★★ORANGE COURSE
Opened: 1950. **Holes:** 18. **Par:** 72/76. **Yards:** 6,817/5,721. **Course rating:** 72.1/72.2.
Slope: 120/121. **Green fee:** $11/$14. **Season:** March-Nov. **High:** June-Aug.
Subscriber comments: The U of I keeps these in good shape...Disapppointing...Don't shoot right or left on second shots...Small, steep greens...Excellent college course...It was good enough for Steve Stricker.
★★½BLUE COURSE
Opened: 1966. **Holes:** 18. **Par:** 73/74. **Yards:** 6,579/6,129. **Course rating:** 70.4/74.1.
Slope: 114/118. **Green fee:** $9/$12. **Season:** Year-round. **High:** June-Aug.
Subscriber comments: Nice course...Improving with age...Good course to learn the game...Boring courses, always crowded and slow...Nice, must play Orange and Blue.

★★½URBAN HILLS COUNTRY CLUB
PU-23520 Crawford Ave., Richton Park, 60471, Will County, (708)747-0306, 20 miles S of Chicago.
Opened: 1967. **Holes:** 18. **Par:** 71/71. **Yards:** 6,650/5,266. **Course rating:** 71.1/69.1.
Slope: 114/110. **Architect:** Larry Packard. **Green fee:** $11/$24. **Credit cards:** MC,VISA. **Reduced fees:** Weekdays, low season, twilight, seniors, juniors. **Caddies:** No. **Golf carts:** $23. **Discount golf packages:** No. **Season:** Year-round. **High:** April-Oct. **On site lodging:** No. **Rental clubs:** Yes. **Walking policy:** Unrestricted walking. **Metal spikes allowed:** Yes. **Range:** No. **To obtain tee times:** Call 7 days in advance.
Subscriber comments: Good course to work out the kinks...Very flat course, few trees, always windy...16th hole is over 600 yards...Pretty forgiving but some wicked doglegs...Best winter golf value in Chicagoland.

★★½VILLA OLIVIA COUNTRY CLUB
PU-Rte. 20 and Naperville Rd., Bartlett, 60103, Du Page County, (630)289-1000.
Opened: N/A. **Holes:** 18. **Par:** 73/73. **Yards:** 6,165/5,546. **Course rating:** N/A. **Slope:** 122/122. **Architect:** Dick Nugent. **Green fee:** N/A. **Credit cards:** MC,VISA,DISC.

Reduced fees: Weekdays, twilight. **Caddies:** No. **Golf carts:** N/A. **Discount golf packages:** No. **Season:** March-Nov. **High:** May-Oct. **On site lodging:** No. **Rental clubs:** No. **Walking policy:** N/A. **Metal spikes allowed:** Yes. **Range:** Yes (grass). **To obtain tee times:** N/A.

Subscriber comments: Fun course, varied, 10th to 13th holes play on the ski slopes of the resort...Much improved each year...Great mix of holes, great dining...Nine hilly, nine flat...Hilly layout, reasonable cost...Good track for mid to high handicappers...Nice to play...Ski winter/golf summer.

★★VILLAGE GREEN COUNTRY CLUB

PU-2501 N. Midlothian Rd., Mundelein, 60060, Lake County, (847)566-7373, 25 miles NW of Chicago.

Opened: 1963. **Holes:** 18. **Par:** 70/70. **Yards:** 6,235/5,600. **Course rating:** 69.2/69.2. **Slope:** 115/118. **Architect:** William B. Langford. **Green fee:** $17/$24. **Credit cards:** MC,VISA. **Reduced fees:** Weekdays, low season, twilight, seniors, juniors. **Caddies:** No. **Golf carts:** $25. **Discount golf packages:** Yes. **Season:** April-Oct. **High:** June-Aug. **On site lodging:** No. **Rental clubs:** Yes. **Walking policy:** Walking at certain times. **Metal spikes allowed:** Yes. **Range:** No. **To obtain tee times:** Call 7 days in advance.

★★½VILLAGE GREENS OF WOODRIDGE

PU-1575 W. 75th St., Woodridge, 60517, Du Page County, (630)985-3610, 25 miles W of Chicago.

Opened: 1959. **Holes:** 18. **Par:** 72/73. **Yards:** 6,650/5,847. **Course rating:** 71.2/72.2. **Slope:** 121/119. **Architect:** Robert Bruce Harris. **Green fee:** $26/$29. **Credit cards:** MC,VISA. **Reduced fees:** Weekdays, low season, twilight, seniors, juniors. **Caddies:** No. **Golf carts:** $12. **Discount golf packages:** No. **Season:** March-Nov. **High:** May-Sept. **On site lodging:** No. **Rental clubs:** Yes. **Walking policy:** Unrestricted walking. **Metal spikes allowed:** Yes. **Range:** Yes (grass). **To obtain tee times:** Non-residents call five days in advance. Credit card required for weekends and holidays.

Subscriber comments: Well-furbished golf shop, lots of water...Has improved, needs to continue...Challenging...Average muny...Overpriced for non-residents...One of my favorites...Middle of the road...Playable course...Well-rounded course design.

★★★½VILLAGE LINKS OF GLEN ELLYN

PM-485 Winchell Way, Glen Ellyn, 60137, Du Page County, (630)469-8180, 20 miles W of Chicago.

Opened: 1967. **Holes:** 18. **Par:** 71/73. **Yards:** 6,933/5,753. **Course rating:** 73.5/73.3. **Slope:** 130/127. **Architect:** David Gill. **Green fee:** $42/$46. **Credit cards:** All major. **Reduced fees:** Weekdays, low season, seniors, juniors. **Caddies:** Yes. **Golf carts:** $28. **Discount golf packages:** No. **Season:** Year-round. **High:** May-Aug. **On site lodging:** No. **Rental clubs:** Yes. **Walking policy:** Unrestricted walking. **Metal spikes allowed:** Yes. **Range:** Yes (grass/mats). **To obtain tee times:** Call or come in 7 days in advance.

Subscriber comments: Always in great shape...Great course...A bit overpriced for non-resident...Great overall facility. Lots of water...Great tournament course, especially from blues...The ultimate chess match on a golf course...One of the original upscale public tracks...Don't tell anyone in Chicago, it's our secret.

Special Notes: Also has a 9-hole par-36 course.

★★★½WEDGEWOOD GOLF COURSE

PU-Rte.59 and Caton Farm Rd., Joliet, 60544, Will County, (815)741-7270, 40 miles SW of Chicago.

Opened: 1970. **Holes:** 18. **Par:** 72/72. **Yards:** 6,836/5,792. **Course rating:** 72.0/72.4. **Slope:** 119/123. **Architect:** Edward Lawrence Packard. **Green fee:** $13/$26. **Credit cards:** MC,VISA,DISC. **Reduced fees:** Weekdays, twilight, seniors, juniors. **Caddies:** No. **Golf carts:** $20. **Discount golf packages:** Yes. **Season:** April-Oct. **High:** June-Aug. **On site lodging:** No. **Rental clubs:** Yes. **Walking policy:** Unrestricted walking. **Metal spikes allowed:** Yes. **Range:** Yes (grass/mats). **To obtain tee times:** Call 1 day in advance for weekday. Call Monday for upcoming weekend.

Subscriber comments: Flat, simple course with a couple of challenging holes...Above average muny. Very long...Excellent greens...A good layout. A little work on it would make it very good...Fair, tough holes from back tees. Nothing too tricky.

★½WESTGATE VALLEY GOLF CLUB

PU-13100 S. Ridgeland Ave., Palos Heights, 60463, Cook County, (708)385-1810, 20 miles S of Chicago.
Opened: 1929. **Holes:** 18. **Par:** 71/81. **Yards:** 6,399/6,048. **Course rating:** 67.3/74.0. **Slope:** 105. **Architect:** Tom Walsh. **Green fee:** $20/$24. **Credit cards:** None. **Reduced fees:** Low season, twilight, seniors. **Caddies:** No. **Golf carts:** $12. **Discount golf packages:** No. **Season:** Year-round. **High:** July-Sept. **On site lodging:** No. **Rental clubs:** Yes. **Walking policy:** Unrestricted walking. **Metal spikes allowed:** Yes. **Range:** Yes (mats). **To obtain tee times:** Call 7 days in advance.
Special Notes: Also has 18-hole par-67 East Course.

★★★WESTVIEW GOLF COURSE

PU-S. 36th St., Quincy, 62301, Adams County, (217)223-7499.
Opened: 1946. **Holes:** 18. **Par:** 71/71. **Yards:** 6,400/5,898. **Course rating:** 70.1/70.2. **Slope:** 116/114. **Architect:** Scotty Glasgow. **Green fee:** $11/$20. **Credit cards:** MC,VISA,DISC. **Reduced fees:** Low season, twilight. **Caddies:** No. **Golf carts:** $9. **Discount golf packages:** No. **Season:** Jan.-Dec. **High:** May-Aug. **On site lodging:** No. **Rental clubs:** Yes. **Walking policy:** Unrestricted walking. **Metal spikes allowed:** Yes. **Range:** No. **To obtain tee times:** Tee time to be offered on an alternating reserved and open basis throughout the day. Call or come in 6 days in advance. More than 6 days in advance $2.00 per reservation fee.
Subscriber comments: Fast greens, crowded...Tough greens, keep it out of trees and rough...My home course. Best public course in 100-mile radius...Nice layout...Fun to play...A lot of nice holes...Every town should have one like this.
Special Notes: Also has 9-hole par-35 South Course.

WHITE PINES GOLF CLUB

PM-500 W. Jefferson St., Bensenville, 60102, Du Page County, (630)766-0304, 10 miles W of Chicago.
Opened: 1930. **Architect:** Jack Daray. **Green fee:** $28/$29. **Credit cards:** MC,VISA,DISC. **Reduced fees:** Weekdays, low season, twilight. **Caddies:** No. **Golf carts:** $25. **Discount golf packages:** No. **Season:** Year-round. **High:** May-Oct. **On site lodging:** No. **Rental clubs:** Yes. **Walking policy:** Unrestricted walking. **Metal spikes allowed:** Yes. **Range:** Yes (grass/mats). **To obtain tee times:** Call 6 days in advance.
★★½EAST COURSE
Holes: 18. **Par:** 70/73. **Yards:** 6,371/5,331. **Course rating:** 70.6/70.6. **Slope:** 123/118.
Subscriber comments: Both courses (East and West) perfect for high and low handicappers...Nice little course to work on shots...A good, local golf course.
★★½WEST COURSE
Holes: 18. **Par:** 72/74. **Yards:** 6,601/5,998. **Course rating:** 71.5/73.4. **Slope:** 119/121.
Subscriber comments: Course requires accuracy. Many young trees...Difficult with narrow fairways, lots of trees and small greens...Both back nines better than both front nines...West is a lot more mature than East.

★★★WILLOW POND GOLF COURSE

PU-808 Golf Course Rd., Rantoul, 61868, Champaign County, (217)893-9000, 15 miles N of Champaign.
Opened: 1956. **Holes:** 18. **Par:** 72/72. **Yards:** 6,799/6,550. **Course rating:** 71.8/71.9. **Slope:** 115/114. **Architect:** Edward Lawrence Packard/Brent H. Wadsworth. **Green fee:** $14/$16. **Credit cards:** MC,VISA. **Reduced fees:** Twilight, seniors, juniors. **Caddies:** No. **Golf carts:** $16. **Discount golf packages:** No. **Season:** March-Nov. **High:** June-Aug. **On site lodging:** No. **Rental clubs:** Yes. **Walking policy:** Unrestricted walking. **Metal spikes allowed:** Yes. **Range:** Yes (grass/mats). **To obtain tee times:** Reservations taken for weekends only. Call on Tuesday.
Subscriber comments: Slick greens; better hope wind is not too strong...Open, flat, lighter play, fairly easy...Average golf course...Good condition, just not real interesting...Interesting course, though a little flat.

★★½WILMETTE GOLF COURSE

PU-3900 Fairway Dr., Wilmette, 60091, Cook County, (847)256-9646, 10 miles N of Chicago.
Opened: 1922. **Holes:** 18. **Par:** 70/70. **Yards:** 6,093/5,760. **Course rating:** 69.5/73.1.

Slope: 122/127. **Architect:** Joseph A. Roseman. **Green fee:** $26/$29. **Credit cards:** MC,VISA,DISC. **Reduced fees:** Weekdays, twilight, juniors. **Caddies:** No. **Golf carts:** $24. **Discount golf packages:** No. **Season:** April-Nov. **High:** June-Sept. **On site lodging:** No. **Rental clubs:** Yes. **Walking policy:** Unrestricted walking. **Metal spikes allowed:** Yes. **Range:** Yes (grass). **To obtain tee times:** Call one day before at 10 a.m. for weekdays and six days prior to weekend and holidays.
Subscriber comments: Short; good course to learn golf...Not long or too challenging, but worth the trip...Will improve in time...Difficult greens.

★★½WINNETKA GOLF CLUB
PU-1300 Oak St., Winnetka, 60093, Cook County, (847)501-2050, 12 miles N of Chicago.
Opened: 1917. **Holes:** 18. **Par:** 71/72. **Yards:** 6,485/5,857. **Course rating:** 70.9/73:3. **Slope:** 125/124. **Architect:** W.H. Langford. **Green fee:** $37/$40. **Credit cards:** MC,VISA. **Reduced fees:** Weekdays, low season, twilight. **Caddies:** No. **Golf carts:** $25. **Discount golf packages:** No. **Season:** April-Dec. **High:** May-Aug. **On site lodging:** No. **Rental clubs:** Yes. **Walking policy:** Unrestricted walking. **Metal spikes allowed:** Yes. **Range:** Yes. **To obtain tee times:** Call 7 days in advance.
Subscriber comments: Expensive for a public course...Tight fairways...Plays harder than rating and slope. Tight. Improving each year...Decent muny given price charged...Considerable water...Well run and maintained.

★★★WOLF CREEK GOLF CLUB
PU-off Old #66, Pontiac, 61764, Livingston County, (815)842-9008, 35 miles N of Bloomington.
Opened: 1973. **Holes:** 18. **Par:** 72/72. **Yards:** 6,674/5,470. **Course rating:** 70.1/72.8. **Slope:** 119/121. **Architect:** N/A. **Green fee:** $16. **Credit cards:** None. **Reduced fees:** N/A. **Caddies:** No. **Golf carts:** $16. **Discount golf packages:** No. **Season:** March-Nov. **High:** June-Aug. **On site lodging:** No. **Rental clubs:** Yes. **Walking policy:** Unrestricted walking. **Metal spikes allowed:** Yes. **Range:** Yes (grass). **To obtain tee times:** Call up to 7 days in advance.
Subscriber comments: Great course in the middle of nowhere north of Pontiac...Great food, great golf, what more do you need...Very friendly place...Flat course...Country setting...One of central Illinois' best-kept secrets.

★★½WOODBINE GOLF COURSE
PU-14240 W. 151st St., Lockport, 60441, Will County, (708)301-1252, 30 miles SW of Chicago.
Opened: 1988. **Holes:** 18. **Par:** 70/70. **Yards:** 6,020/5,618. **Course rating:** 68.1/71.3. **Slope:** 108/113. **Architect:** Gordon Cunningham. **Green fee:** $24/$32. **Credit cards:** MC,VISA,AMEX. **Reduced fees:** Weekdays, low season, twilight, seniors, juniors. **Caddies:** No. **Golf carts:** $12. **Discount golf packages:** No. **Season:** March-Nov. **High:** May-Sept. **On site lodging:** No. **Rental clubs:** Yes. **Walking policy:** Unrestricted walking. **Metal spikes allowed:** Yes. **Range:** No. **To obtain tee times:** Call 7 days in advance.
Subscriber comments: Easy layout with excellent conditions...Staff is always friendly..

★★½WOODRUFF GOLF COURSE
PU-Geiger Rd., Joliet, 60432, Will County, (815)741-7272, 40 miles SW of Chicago.
Opened: 1921. **Holes:** 18. **Par:** 68/68. **Yards:** 5,424/5,059. **Course rating:** 64.9/67.8. **Slope:** 99/105. **Architect:** Edward Lawrence Packard. **Green fee:** $12/$24. **Credit cards:** MC,VISA,DISC. **Reduced fees:** Weekdays, twilight, seniors, juniors. **Caddies:** No. **Golf carts:** $18. **Discount golf packages:** Yes. **Season:** April-Oct. **High:** June-Aug. **On site lodging:** No. **Rental clubs:** Yes. **Walking policy:** Unrestricted walking. **Metal spikes allowed:** Yes. **Range:** No. **To obtain tee times:** Call 24 hours in advance for weekdays and call Monday for upcoming weekend.

★★★½AUTUMN RIDGE GOLF CLUB

11420 Old Auburn Rd., Fort Wayne, 46845, Allen County, (219)637-8727.
Opened: 1993. **Holes:** 18. **Par:** 72/72. **Yards:** 7,103/5,273. **Course rating:** 73.9/70.1.
Slope: 134/122. **Architect:** Ernie Schrock. **Green fee:** $24/$29. **Credit cards:**
MC,VISA,AMEX. **Reduced fees:** Weekdays, low season, twilight, seniors. **Caddies:**
No. **Golf carts:** $11. **Discount golf packages:** No. **Season:** March-Dec. **High:** May-
Sept. **On site lodging:** No. **Rental clubs:** Yes. **Walking policy:** Walking at certain
times. **Metal spikes allowed:** Yes. **Range:** Yes (grass). **To obtain tee times:** Call 7
days in advance.
Subscriber comments: A real test, but not unfair...Well run, very friendly service...Very
good clubhouse, home construction on course makes it loud...Keeps you on your
toes...Beautiful course with lots of water. Super fast greens...Lots of trees...Good solid
golf course...Too long between holes...Awesome course and service.

★★★★BEAR SLIDE GOLF CLUB

6770 E. 231st St., Cicero, 46034, Hamilton County, (317)984-3837, (800)252-8337, 20
miles N of Indianapolis.
Opened: 1993. **Holes:** 18. **Par:** 71/71. **Yards:** 7,041/4,831. **Course rating:** 74.6/69.5.
Slope: 136/117. **Architect:** Dean Refram. **Green fee:** $32/$42. **Credit cards:**
MC,VISA. **Reduced fees:** N/A. **Caddies:** Yes. **Golf carts:** $13. **Discount golf pack-
ages:** No. **Season:** March-Dec. **High:** May-Oct. **On site lodging:** No. **Rental clubs:**
Yes. **Walking policy:** Unrestricted walking. **Metal spikes allowed:** Yes. **Range:** Yes
(grass/mats). **To obtain tee times:** Call 7 days in advance.
Notes: Ranked 7th in 1997 Best in State.
Subscriber comments: Two different nines...Best assortment of holes in one
course...Links style, sand traps aplenty...Several blind tee shots and approaches...Back
side very tough...Plays well from any tee box...No map of holes, playing first time is difficult...Very windy makes tough play...You need all your clubs...Real Scottish look.

★★½BLACK SQUIRREL GOLF CLUB

PU-Hwy. 119 S., Goshen, 46526, Elkhart County, (219)533-1828, 19 miles SE of South
Bend.
Opened: 1989. **Holes:** 18. **Par:** 72/72. **Yards:** 6,483/5,018. **Course rating:** 69.8/67.8.
Slope: 115/110. **Architect:** Larimer Development. **Green fee:** $15/$22. **Credit cards:**
MC,VISA. **Reduced fees:** Weekdays, low season, juniors. **Golf carts:**
$10. **Discount golf packages:** No. **Season:** March-Nov. **High:** June-Aug. **On site
lodging:** No. **Rental clubs:** Yes. **Walking policy:** Unrestricted walking. **Metal spikes
allowed:** No. **Range:** No. **To obtain tee times:** Call up to 7 days in advance.
Subscriber comments: Average course...Heavily bunkered greens, hard to hold
approach shots...Good layout and variety...Many tight fairways.
Special Notes: Formerly Larimer Green.

★★★★BLACKTHORN GOLF CLUB

PU-6100 Nimtz Pkwy., South Bend, 46628, St. Joseph County, (219)232-4653, 90
miles E of Chicago.
Opened: 1994. **Holes:** 18. **Par:** 72/72. **Yards:** 7,106/5,036. **Course rating:** 75.2/71.0.
Slope: 135/120. **Architect:** Michael Hurdzan. **Green fee:** $24/$47. **Credit cards:**
MC,VISA,AMEX. **Reduced fees:** Weekdays, low season, twilight, juniors. **Caddies:** No.
Golf carts: $12. **Discount golf packages:** No. **Season:** March-Dec. **High:** May-Sept.
On site lodging: No. **Rental clubs:** Yes. **Walking policy:** Unrestricted walking. **Metal
spikes allowed:** Yes. **Range:** Yes (grass). **To obtain tee times:** Call up to 7 days in
advance.
Notes: Ranked 8th in 1997 Best in State; 4th in 1995 Best New Public Courses.
Subscriber comments: A real gem!...Most holes are distinctive...Outstanding test...A
treat to play, tall heather-like grass is reminiscent of Scottish courses...Practice facility
top notch...Some holes have smallest greens...Heavy play, beautiful layout...Golf at its
purest. Truly amazing!...Challenging but not impossible...Didn't like tree in fairway at
#4...Next best thing to a private country club...Great grill.
Special Notes: Also has a 19th practice hole.

★★BRIAR LEAF GOLF CLUB

PU-3233 N. State Rd. 39, La Porte, 46350, La Porte County, (219)326-1992, 60 miles E
of Chicago.

Opened: 1973. **Holes:** 18. **Par:** 72/72. **Yards:** 6,438/5,362. **Course rating:** 71.6/67.5. **Slope:** 126/116. **Architect:** N/A. **Green fee:** $12/$24. **Credit cards:** All major. **Reduced fees:** Weekdays, low season, twilight, seniors, juniors. **Caddies:** No. **Golf carts:** $12. **Discount golf packages:** No. **Season:** Year-round. **High:** April-Oct. **On site lodging:** No. **Rental clubs:** Yes. **Walking policy:** Unrestricted walking. **Metal spikes allowed:** Yes. **Range:** Yes (grass). **To obtain tee times:** Call golf shop.

★★★★BRICKYARD CROSSING GOLF CLUB
R-4400 W. 16th St., Indianapolis, 46222, Marion County, (317)484-6572.
Opened: 1993. **Holes:** 18. **Par:** 72/72. **Yards:** 6,994/5,038. **Course rating:** 74.5/68.3. **Slope:** 137/116. **Architect:** Pete Dye. **Green fee:** $80/$80. **Credit cards:** MC,VISA,AMEX. **Reduced fees:** N/A. **Caddies:** No. **Golf carts:** Included in Green Fee. **Discount golf packages:** No. **Season:** April-Oct. **High:** May-Aug. **On site lodging:** Yes. **Rental clubs:** Yes. **Walking policy:** Walking at certain times. **Metal spikes allowed:** Yes. **Range:** Yes (grass). **To obtain tee times:** Call up to 14 days in advance.
Notes: Ranked 4th in 1997 Best in State. Senior PGA Tour Comfort Classic.
Subscriber comments: Best in state, tough to score well...A must play!...Excellent course in a very unique setting...Good finishing holes...Tricky but typical Pete Dye revamp...Many blind shots to greens...The four holes inside the Indy 500 race track are a novelty...Generous fairways, undulating greens.

★½BROADMOOR COUNTRY CLUB
PU-4300 W. 81st St., Merrillville, 46410, Lake County, (219)769-5444.
Call club for further information.

★★★BROOK HILL GOLF CLUB
PU-11175 Fairway Lane, Brookville, 47012, Franklin County, (765)647-4522, (800)708-4522, 35 miles NW of Cincinnati.
Opened: 1975. **Holes:** 18. **Par:** 71/71. **Yards:** 6,361/4,776. **Course rating:** 70.2/67.9. **Slope:** 125/125. **Architect:** N/A. **Green fee:** $16/$19. **Credit cards:** MC,VISA,DISC. **Reduced fees:** Weekdays, low season, twilight, seniors. **Caddies:** No. **Golf carts:** $11. **Discount golf packages:** No. **Season:** Year-round. **High:** May-Oct. **On site lodging:** No. **Rental clubs:** Yes. **Walking policy:** Unrestricted walking. **Metal spikes allowed:** Yes. **Range:** Yes (grass). **To obtain tee times:** Call golf shop.
Subscriber comments: Fine public course...Great weekday value...Friendly...New nine has some good holes.

★★½BROOKSHIRE GOLF CLUB
12120 Brookshire Pkwy., Carmel, 46033, Hamilton County, (317)846-7431, 15 miles N of Indianapolis.
Opened: 1971. **Holes:** 18. **Par:** 72/75. **Yards:** 6,651/5,635. **Course rating:** 71.8/74.4. **Slope:** 123/129. **Architect:** William H. Diddel. **Green fee:** $32/$38. **Credit cards:** MC,VISA,AMEX. **Reduced fees:** Weekdays, twilight, juniors. **Caddies:** No. **Golf carts:** Included in Green Fee. **Discount golf packages:** No. **Season:** Year-round. **High:** May-Oct. **On site lodging:** No. **Rental clubs:** Yes. **Walking policy:** Mandatory cart. **Metal spikes allowed:** Yes. **Range:** Yes (grass). **To obtain tee times:** Call up to 3 days in advance.
Subscriber comments: Beautiful creek through course...Fairways too close...People go out of their way to take care of you...Lots of trees, hills. Very challenging.

★★★BROOKWOOD GOLF CLUB
PU-10304 Bluffton Rd., Fort Wayne, 46809, Allen County, (219)747-3136.
Opened: 1925. **Holes:** 18. **Par:** 72/73. **Yards:** 6,700/6,250. **Course rating:** 70.3/67.9. **Slope:** 123/111. **Architect:** N/A. **Green fee:** $15. **Credit cards:** MC,VISA,DISC. **Reduced fees:** N/A. **Caddies:** No. **Golf carts:** $18. **Discount golf packages:** No. **Season:** March-Dec. **High:** April-Sept. **On site lodging:** No. **Rental clubs:** Yes. **Walking policy:** Unrestricted walking. **Metal spikes allowed:** Yes. **Range:** Yes (grass). **To obtain tee times:** Call ahead.
Subscriber comments: Four difficult par 3s...Great public course...Old style...Too many outings...Watch for low-flying planes...Good for the ego, very enjoyable.

★★★CHESTNUT HILL GOLF CLUB

PU-11502 Illinois Rd., Fort Wayne, 46804, Allen County, (219)625-4146.
Opened: 1995. **Holes:** 18. **Par:** 72. **Yards:** 6,996. **Course rating:** N/A. **Slope:** N/A.
Architect: Clyde Johnston/Fuzzy Zoeller. **Green fee:** $29/$29. **Credit cards:**
MC,VISA,AMEX. **Reduced fees:** N/A. **Caddies:** No. **Golf carts:** $10. **Discount golf packages:** No. **Season:** March-Nov. **High:** May-Sept. **On site lodging:** No. **Rental clubs:** Yes. **Walking policy:** Unrestricted walking. **Metal spikes allowed:** Yes. **Range:** Yes (grass). **To obtain tee times:** Call up to 7 days in advance for weekdays. Call on Tuesday for upcoming weekend.
Subscriber comments: Very impressive for new course...Needs signs to give yardage to ponds and valleys off the tee...Generous fairways...Front nine wide open target style, back nine links.

★★★CHRISTMAS LAKE GOLF CLUB

PU-1 Country Club Dr., Santa Claus, 47579, Spencer County, (812)544-2571, (800)927-2571, 45 miles E of Evansville.
Opened: 1968. **Holes:** 18. **Par:** 72/72. **Yards:** 7,191/5,135. **Course rating:** 74.4/69.2.
Slope: 134/117. **Architect:** Edmund Ault. **Green fee:** $24/$44. **Credit cards:**
MC,VISA,DISC. **Reduced fees:** Weekdays, low season, twilight. **Caddies:** No. **Golf carts:** Included in Green Fee. **Discount golf packages:** Yes. **Season:** Jan.-Dec. **High:** April-Oct. **On site lodging:** No. **Rental clubs:** Yes. **Walking policy:** Walking at certain times. **Metal spikes allowed:** Yes. **Range:** Yes (grass). **To obtain tee times:** Call 14 days in advance.
Subscriber comments: Tricky greens...Long back nine, easy front nine...Good layout.

★★★COFFIN GOLF CLUB

PU-2401 Cold Springs Rd., Indianapolis, 46222, Marion County, (317)327-7845, 2 miles NW of downtown Indianapolis.
Opened: 1995. **Holes:** 18. **Par:** 72/72. **Yards:** 6,789/5,135. **Course rating:** 73.7/70.3.
Slope: 129/114. **Architect:** Tim Liddy. **Green fee:** $20/$22. **Credit cards:** MC,VISA.
Reduced fees: Weekdays, low season, twilight, seniors, juniors. **Caddies:** No. **Golf carts:** $15. **Discount golf packages:** No. **Season:** March-Dec. **High:** N/A. **On site lodging:** No. **Rental clubs:** Yes. **Walking policy:** Unrestricted walking. **Metal spikes allowed:** Yes. **Range:** No. **To obtain tee times:** Call up to 7 days in advance.
Subscriber comments: View from #5 tee is one of the best in Indiana...Long and demanding. Shotmaker's course. Tight 18th hole...Fun to play!...Short course, but still tough, tight greens...River in play on five holes...Two scenic bluff holes.

★★½COOL LAKE GOLF CLUB

520 E. 750 N., Lebanon, 46052, Boone County, (765)325-9271, 35 miles NW of Indianapolis.
Opened: 1968. **Holes:** 18. **Par:** 70/72. **Yards:** 6,000/4,827. **Course rating:** 66.0/71.0.
Slope: 100/102. **Architect:** G&J Design Inc.. **Green fee:** $14/$18. **Credit cards:**
MC,VISA. **Reduced fees:** N/A. **Caddies:** No. **Golf carts:** N/A. **Discount golf packages:** No. **Season:** March-Dec. **High:** May-Sept. **On site lodging:** No. **Rental clubs:** No. **Walking policy:** Walking at certain times. **Metal spikes allowed:** Yes. **Range:** Yes (grass). **To obtain tee times:** Call anytime in advance.
Subscriber comments: Great little course, nice people...New back nine better than front...Great greens, some good holes.

★★★★COVERED BRIDGE GOLF CLUB

12510 Covered Bridge Rd., Sellersburg, 47172, Clark County, (812)246-8880, 12 miles N of Louisville, KY.
Opened: 1994. **Holes:** 18. **Par:** 72/72. **Yards:** 6,832/5,943. **Course rating:** 73.0/74.7. **Slope:** 128/126. **Architect:** Clyde Johnston/Fuzzy Zoeller. **Green fee:** $50/$60. **Credit cards:** All major. **Reduced fees:** Weekdays, low season. **Caddies:** No. **Golf carts:** Included in Green Fee. **Discount golf packages:** No. **Season:** Year-round. **High:** April-Oct. **On site lodging:** No. **Rental clubs:** Yes. **Walking policy:** Mandatory cart. **Metal spikes allowed:** Yes. **Range:** Yes (grass). **To obtain tee times:** Public may call up to 10 days in advance with a credit card to guarantee.
Subscriber comments: Fuzzy's place is great!...Beautiful course; fantastic greens;

very challenging...Four sets of tees make it hard as you like...Not all 'tricked' up... Lunch on veranda is tops, overlooking 9th and 18th simply beautiful...If you can't putt these greens, you can't putt...Excellent par 3s.

★★★CURTIS CREEK COUNTRY CLUB
Rte. 3, Rensselaer, 47978, Jasper County, (219)866-7729, 95 miles S of Chicago.
Opened: 1924. **Holes:** 18. **Par:** 72/72. **Yards:** 6,118/5,029. **Course rating:** 70.6/70.2.
Slope: 117/106. **Architect:** Leonard Macomber. **Green fee:** $22/$22. **Credit cards:** MC,VISA. **Reduced fees:** N/A. **Caddies:** No. **Golf carts:** $10. **Discount golf packages:** No. **Season:** March-Nov. **High:** May-Sept. **On site lodging:** No. **Rental clubs:** Yes. **Walking policy:** Walking at certain times. **Metal spikes allowed:** No. **Range:** Yes (grass). **To obtain tee times:** Public may play on Monday and Friday only. Call golf shop for availability.
Subscriber comments: Short but good test...Nice out of the way course. Good greens.

★★½DEER CREEK GOLF CLUB
PU-State Rd. #39, Clayton, 46118, Hendricks County, (317)539-2013, 18 miles W of Indianapolis.
Opened: 1991. **Holes:** 18. **Par:** 71/72. **Yards:** 6,510/5,033. **Course rating:** 71.2/68.8.
Slope: 128/120. **Architect:** N/A. **Green fee:** $18/$25. **Credit cards:** MC,VISA.
Reduced fees: N/A. **Caddies:** No. **Golf carts:** $11. **Discount golf packages:** No.
Season: March-Dec. **High:** May-Oct. **On site lodging:** No. **Rental clubs:** No. **Walking policy:** Walking at certain times. **Metal spikes allowed:** Yes. **Range:** Yes (grass/mats). **To obtain tee times:** N/A.
Subscriber comments: Nice course...Hilly with lots of water...Some tees too close to adjoining fairways...Many hazards at landing areas take driver out of your hands.

★★½DYKEMAN PARK GOLF COURSE
PM-Eberts Rd., Logansport, 46947, Cass County, (219)753-0222, 50 miles N of Indianapolis.
Opened: N/A. **Holes:** 18. **Par:** 70/73. **Yards:** 6,185/5,347. **Course rating:** 69.4/69.8.
Slope: 118/102. **Architect:** William B. Langford/Theodore J. Moreau. **Green fee:** $14/$16. **Credit cards:** None. **Reduced fees:** Twilight, seniors, juniors. **Caddies:** No.
Golf carts: $20. **Discount golf packages:** Yes. **Season:** March-Nov. **High:** April-Aug.
On site lodging: No. **Rental clubs:** Yes. **Walking policy:** Unrestricted walking. **Metal spikes allowed:** Yes. **Range:** Yes (grass). **To obtain tee times:** Call 2 days in advance.
Subscriber comments: A good muny course...Lots of fun, some unique holes.

★★★EAGLE CREEK GOLF CLUB
PM-8802 W. 56th St., Indianapolis, 46234, Marion County, (317)297-3366, 12 miles NW of Indianapolis.
Opened: 1974. **Holes:** 18. **Par:** 72/72. **Yards:** 7,159/5,800. **Course rating:** 74.6/68.2.
Slope: 139/116. **Architect:** Pete Dye. **Green fee:** $20/$22. **Credit cards:** MC,VISA.
Reduced fees: Weekdays, low season, twilight, seniors, juniors. **Caddies:** No. **Golf carts:** $17. **Discount golf packages:** No. **Season:** Feb.-Dec. **High:** June-Aug. **On site lodging:** No. **Rental clubs:** Yes. **Walking policy:** Unrestricted walking. **Metal spikes allowed:** Yes. **Range:** Yes (grass/mats). **To obtain tee times:** Call 7 days in advance for weekdays. Call on Monday for upcoming weekend.
Subscriber comments: The course always plays tough for me...They keep making improvements every year...Beautiful woods and lakes. Great elevation changes...The most demanding back nine you can imagine...A long, long walk, lots of hills...Great finishing hole...Early Pete Dye, too many blind shots.
Special Notes: Also has 9-hole par 36 West Course.

★★★EAGLE POINTE GOLF & TENNIS RESORT
R-2250 E. Pointe Rd., Bloomington, 47401, Monroe County, (812)824-4040, (800)860-8604, 65 miles S of Indianapolis.
Opened: 1973. **Holes:** 18. **Par:** 71/71. **Yards:** 6,604/5,186. **Course rating:** 73.0/71.2.
Slope: 140/126. **Architect:** Robert Simmons. **Green fee:** $31/$49. **Credit cards:** All major. **Reduced fees:** Weekdays, low season, twilight. **Caddies:** No. **Golf carts:** Included in Green Fee. **Discount golf packages:** Yes. **Season:** Year-round. **High:** May-Sept. **On site lodging:** Yes. **Rental clubs:** Yes. **Walking policy:** Mandatory cart. **Metal

spikes allowed: Yes. **Range:** Yes (grass/mats). **To obtain tee times:** Call anytime in advance.
Subscriber comments: Don't miss the Monday night Italian buffet!...Condos everywhere, good test from blues...Very narrow fairways...Scenic, almost to distraction.
Special Notes: Formerly The Pointe Golf & Tennis Resort.

★★★ELBEL PARK GOLF COURSE
PM-26595 Auten Rd., South Bend, 46628, St. Joseph County, (219)271-9180.
Opened: 1963. **Holes:** 18. **Par:** 72/73. **Yards:** 6,700/5,750. **Course rating:** 70.7/71.4.
Slope: 113/114. **Architect:** William J. Spear. **Green fee:** $11/$18. **Credit cards:**
MC,VISA. **Reduced fees:** Weekdays, low season, twilight, seniors, juniors. **Caddies:**
No. **Golf carts:** $10. **Discount golf packages:** No. **Season:** March-Dec. **High:** June-Aug. **On site lodging:** No. **Rental clubs:** Yes. **Walking policy:** Unrestricted walking.
Metal spikes allowed: Yes. **Range:** Yes (grass/mats). **To obtain tee times:** Call up to 7 days in advance.
Subscriber comments: Fine layout...Dogleg capital of the world...Huge greens. Fun layout...Nice city course, improving water problems...Lush, fast greens but true lines...Difficult to get good tee time...Beautiful country setting wrapped around a wetlands area.

★★★ERSKINE PARK GOLF CLUB
PU-4200 Miami St., South Bend, 46614, St. Joseph County, (219)291-3216.
Opened: 1925. **Holes:** 18. **Par:** 70/74. **Yards:** 6,104/5,536. **Course rating:** 68.5/70.9.
Slope: 120/120. **Architect:** William H. Diddel. **Green fee:** $10/$21. **Credit cards:**
MC,VISA. **Reduced fees:** Twilight, seniors, juniors. **Caddies:** No. **Golf carts:** $10.
Discount golf packages: Yes. **Season:** March-Nov. **High:** April-Sept. **On site lodging:**
No. **Rental clubs:** Yes. **Walking policy:** Unrestricted walking. **Metal spikes allowed:**
Yes. **Range:** No. **To obtain tee times:** Call 7 days in advance.
Subscriber comments: Tree-lined city course...Greens too close to adjacent tees...Improvements to facilities in last couple years make it great value...Great old style course, little water, up and down through oaks...Par 3s are signature holes...Plays tough when wet...Good par 5s.

★★ETNA ACRES GOLF COURSE
9803 W. 600 S., Andrews, 46702, Huntington County, (219)468-2906, 16 miles N of Marion.
Opened: 1960. **Holes:** 18. **Par:** 72/72. **Yards:** 6,096/5,142. **Course rating:** 68.6/68.9.
Slope: 109/108. **Architect:** Gene Kaufman. **Green fee:** $12/$14. **Credit cards:** None.
Reduced fees: Weekdays, low season, seniors, juniors. **Caddies:** No. **Golf carts:** $8.
Discount golf packages: Yes. **Season:** March-Nov. **High:** June-Aug. **On site lodging:**
No. **Rental clubs:** Yes. **Walking policy:** Unrestricted walking. **Metal spikes allowed:**
Yes. **Range:** Yes (grass/mats). **To obtain tee times:** Call pro shop.

★★½FAIRVIEW GOLF COURSE
PU-7102 S. Calhoun St., Fort Wayne, 46807, Allen County, (219)745-7093.
Opened: 1927. **Holes:** 18. **Par:** 72/72. **Yards:** 6,620/5,125. **Course rating:** 70.8/71.1.
Slope: 119/108. **Architect:** Donald Ross. **Green fee:** $10/$10. **Credit cards:** MC,VISA.
Reduced fees: N/A. **Caddies:** No. **Golf carts:** $17. **Discount golf packages:** No.
Season: March-Oct. **High:** May-Sept. **On site lodging:** No. **Rental clubs:** Yes.
Walking policy: Unrestricted walking. **Metal spikes allowed:** Yes. **Range:** Yes (grass).
To obtain tee times: Weekend tee times only. Call Tuesday prior to weekend.
Subscriber comments: Excellent value. Interesting holes. Don't miss...Some very tough holes...More difficult than it looks.

★★FENDRICH GOLF COURSE
PU-1900 Diamond Ave., Evansville, 47711, Vanderburgh County, (812)435-6070.
Opened: 1945. **Holes:** 18. **Par:** 70/70. **Yards:** 5,791/5,232. **Course rating:** 67.1/69.2.
Slope: 106/109. **Architect:** William Diddel. **Green fee:** $10/$10. **Credit cards:** None.
Reduced fees: N/A. **Caddies:** No. **Golf carts:** $18. **Discount golf packages:** No.
Season: Year-round. **High:** April-Sept. **On site lodging:** No. **Rental clubs:** Yes.
Walking policy: Unrestricted walking. **Metal spikes allowed:** Yes. **Range:** Yes (grass).
To obtain tee times: Call seven days in advance.

★★½FOREST PARK GOLF COURSE
PM-P.O. Box 42, Brazil, 47834, Clay County, (812)442-5681, 15 miles NE of Terre Haute.
Opened: 1935. **Holes:** 18. **Par:** 71/73. **Yards:** 6,012/5,647. **Course rating:** 68.0/69.8. **Slope:** 110/112. **Architect:** Pete Dye. **Green fee:** N/A. **Credit cards:** None. **Reduced fees:** Low season, twilight. **Caddies:** No. **Golf carts:** N/A. **Discount golf packages:** No. **Season:** Year-round. **High:** March-Nov. **On site lodging:** No. **Rental clubs:** No. **Walking policy:** Unrestricted walking. **Metal spikes allowed:** Yes. **Range:** No. **To obtain tee times:** Tee times are not taken in advance.
Subscriber comments: Good small town course. Nice greens...Short course, easy to score.

★★½FOREST PARK GOLF COURSE
PM-1155 Sheffield Dr., Valparaiso, 46383, Porter County, (219)462-4411, 60 miles W of South Bend.
Opened: 1973. **Holes:** 18. **Par:** 70/72. **Yards:** 5,731/5,339. **Course rating:** 67.4/70.7. **Slope:** 114/111. **Architect:** N/A. **Green fee:** $15/$20. **Credit cards:** None. **Reduced fees:** Twilight, juniors. **Caddies:** No. **Golf carts:** $20. **Discount golf packages:** No. **Season:** April-Dec. **High:** June-Sept. **On site lodging:** No. **Rental clubs:** Yes. **Walking policy:** Unrestricted walking. **Metal spikes allowed:** Yes. **Range:** No. **To obtain tee times:** Call up to 7 days in advance in season.
Subscriber comments: Fantastic municipal course...Back nine pretty challenging...Dogleg holes. Needs a restaurant facility...Easy par 5s tough par 3s.

★★★FOX PRAIRIE GOLF CLUB
PM-8465 E. 196th St., Noblesville, 46060, Hamilton County, (317)776-6357.
Opened: 1970. **Holes:** 18. **Par:** 72/75. **Yards:** 6,946/5,533. **Course rating:** 72.6/71.4. **Slope:** 118/114. **Architect:** Bill Newcomb. **Green fee:** $19/$24. **Credit cards:** MC,VISA. **Reduced fees:** Weekdays, twilight. **Caddies:** No. **Golf carts:** $11. **Discount golf packages:** Yes. **Season:** Year-round. **High:** April-Oct. **On site lodging:** No. **Rental clubs:** Yes. **Walking policy:** Unrestricted walking. **Metal spikes allowed:** Yes. **Range:** Yes (grass). **To obtain tee times:** Call on Monday to reserve for upcoming week and weekend.
Subscriber comments: Hitting the 430-yard uphill #11 in regulation: Wow!...Unique course for an area with many flat courses...Toughest back to back par 4s in area, 10-11-12...Long course with big greens and hard, fast fairways...Two or three unique holes.

★★FOX RIDGE COUNTRY CLUB
PU-Hillcrest Extension Rd., Vincennes, 47591, Knox County, (812)886-5929, 50 miles S of Terre Haute, IN.
Opened: 1987. **Holes:** 18. **Par:** 72/72. **Yards:** 6,578/5,412. **Course rating:** 72.0/71.0. **Slope:** 131/124. **Architect:** N/A. **Green fee:** $25/$30. **Credit cards:** All major. **Reduced fees:** Weekdays. **Caddies:** No. **Golf carts:** Included in Green Fee. **Discount golf packages:** No. **Season:** Year-round. **High:** April-Oct. **On site lodging:** No. **Rental clubs:** Yes. **Walking policy:** Walking at certain times. **Metal spikes allowed:** Yes. **Range:** Yes (grass). **To obtain tee times:** Call on Monday for upcoming weekend. First come, first served on weekdays.

FRENCH LICK SPRINGS RESORT
R- Hwy. 56, French Lick, 47432, Orange County, (812)936-9300, (800)457-4042, 60 miles NW of Louisville, KY.
Caddies: No. **Golf carts:** $12. **Discount golf packages:** Yes. **Season:** March-Nov. **High:** May-Oct. **On site lodging:** Yes. **Rental clubs:** Yes. **Metal spikes allowed:** Yes.
★★★½COUNTRY CLUB COURSE
Opened: 1920. **Holes:** 18. **Par:** 70/71. **Yards:** 6,650/5,927. **Course rating:** 71.6/70.3. **Slope:** 119/116. **Architect:** Donald Ross. **Green fee:** $35/$47. **Credit cards:** All major,Hotel Chg. **Reduced fees:** Low season, resort guests, twilight. **Walking policy:** Mandatory cart. **Range:** No. **To obtain tee times:** Call golf shop. Preference given to hotel guests.
Subscriber comments: Outstanding Donald Ross course...Fast undulating greens...Lots of hills and sidehill lies...Good test...Must position ball well...Classic old course...Deceptively long...Forces you to play all you clubs.

★★VALLEY COURSE
Opened: 1905. **Holes:** 18. **Par:** 70/71. **Yards:** 6,001/5,627. **Course rating:** 67.6/66.0. **Slope:** 110/106. **Architect:** Tom Bendelow. **Green fee:** $18/$18. **Credit cards:** All major,Hotel Chg. if guest. **Reduced fees:** Low season, resort guests. **Walking policy:** Walking at certain times. **Range:** Yes (grass/mats). **To obtain tee times:** Call golf shop.

★★½GENEVA HILLS GOLF CLUB
PU-13446 S. Geneva Rd., Clinton, 47842, Vermillion County, (765)832-8384, 15 miles N of Terre Haute.
Opened: 1970. **Holes:** 18. **Par:** 72/72. **Yards:** 6,768/4,785. **Course rating:** 70.2/67.3. **Slope:** 118/115. **Architect:** R. D. Shaw. **Green fee:** $15/$17. **Credit cards:** MC,VISA. **Reduced fees:** Weekdays, low season, twilight, seniors, juniors. **Caddies:** No. **Golf carts:** $11. **Discount golf packages:** No. **Season:** Year-round. **High:** April-Oct. **On site lodging:** No. **Rental clubs:** Yes. **Walking policy:** Unrestricted walking. **Metal spikes allowed:** Yes. **Range:** Yes (grass). **To obtain tee times:** Call up to 5 days in advance.
Subscriber comments: Nice layout. Greens a little slow...Improvements constantly being made...Watch the 12th green, don't think driver all the time.

★★★½GOLF CLUB OF INDIANA
PU-I 65 at Zionsville Exit 130, Lebanon, 46052, Boone County, (317)769-6388, 16 miles NW of Indianapolis.
Opened: 1974. **Holes:** 18. **Par:** 72/72. **Yards:** 7,084/5,498. **Course rating:** 73.2/72.7. **Slope:** 140/122. **Architect:** Charles Maddox. **Green fee:** $32/$42. **Credit cards:** MC,VISA. **Reduced fees:** Low season, twilight. **Caddies:** No. **Golf carts:** $5. **Discount golf packages:** No. **Season:** Feb.-Dec. **High:** May-Sept. **On site lodging:** No. **Rental clubs:** Yes. **Walking policy:** Unrestricted walking. **Metal spikes allowed:** Yes. **Range:** Yes (grass). **To obtain tee times:** Call golf shop.
Subscriber comments: Great layout for flatland, huge greens...Best ryegrass fairways around...A fair test...Great course for business outings!...Pray the wind doesn't blow.

★★★½GRAND OAK GOLF CLUB
370 Grand Oak Dr., West Harrison, 47060, Dearborn County, (812)637-3943, 25 miles W of Cincinnati, OH.
Opened: 1989. **Holes:** 18. **Par:** 71/71. **Yards:** 6,363/4,842. **Course rating:** 70.3/69.4. **Slope:** 127/121. **Architect:** Michael Hurdzan. **Green fee:** $21/$26. **Credit cards:** MC,VISA. **Reduced fees:** Low season, seniors, juniors. **Caddies:** No. **Golf carts:** $11. **Discount golf packages:** No. **Season:** Feb.-Dec. **High:** April-Oct. **On site lodging:** No. **Rental clubs:** Yes. **Walking policy:** Unrestricted walking. **Metal spikes allowed:** Yes. **Range:** Yes (grass/mats). **To obtain tee times:** Call up to 7 days in advance.
Subscriber comments: A lot of hills...Trouble if you can't hit straight...Fun course... Nice country setting...Difficult first time around...Some trick holes...Course rewards conservative player...Great fall colors course...Exceptional beauty, terrain unbelievable.

★★½GREEN ACRES GOLF CLUB
PU-1300 Green Acres Dr., Kokomo, 40601-9546, Howard County, (765)883-5771, 9 miles W of Kokomo.
Opened: 1968. **Holes:** 18. **Par:** 72/72. **Yards:** 6,767/5,248. **Course rating:** 72.8/72.7. **Slope:** 129/118. **Architect:** Bob Simmons. **Green fee:** $17/$20. **Credit cards:** All major. **Reduced fees:** Low season, seniors, juniors. **Caddies:** No. **Golf carts:** $10. **Discount golf packages:** No. **Season:** March-Dec. **High:** May-Oct. **On site lodging:** No. **Rental clubs:** Yes. **Walking policy:** Unrestricted walking. **Metal spikes allowed:** Yes. **Range:** Yes (grass). **To obtain tee times:** Call anytime.
Subscriber comments: Interesting layout, beautiful setting...Either too wet or too dry...Variety of holes...Good layout with creek.

★★★GREENFIELD COUNTRY CLUB
145 S. Morristown Pike, Greenfield, 46140, Hancock County, (317)462-2706, 15 miles E of Indianapolis.
Opened: 1927. **Holes:** 18. **Par:** 72/73. **Yards:** 6,773/5,501. **Course rating:** 71.2/73.5. **Slope:** 119/120. **Architect:** Gary Kern. **Green fee:** $18/$23. **Credit cards:** MC,VISA. **Reduced fees:** Weekdays. **Caddies:** No. **Golf carts:** $12. **Discount golf packages:** No. **Season:** March-Nov. **High:** May-Sept. **On site lodging:** No. **Rental clubs:** No.

Walking policy: Unrestricted walking. **Metal spikes allowed:** Yes. **Range:** Yes (grass).
To obtain tee times: Call 7 days in advance.
Subscriber comments: Use all your clubs.

★★★½HANGING TREE GOLF CLUB

2302 W. 161st St., Westfield, 46074, Hamilton County, (317)896-2474, 20 miles N of
Indianapolis.
Opened: 1990. **Holes:** 18. **Par:** 71/71. **Yards:** 6,519/5,151. **Course rating:** 72.6/70.6.
Slope: 130/122. **Architect:** Gary Kern. **Green fee:** $30/$46. **Credit cards:**
MC,VISA,DISC. **Reduced fees:** Weekdays, low season, twilight. **Caddies:** No. **Golf
carts:** Included in Green Fee. **Discount golf packages:** No. **Season:** Year-round.
High: April-Nov. **On site lodging:** No. **Rental clubs:** Yes. **Walking policy:** Mandatory
cart. **Metal spikes allowed:** Yes. **Range:** Yes (grass/mats). **To obtain tee times:** Call
anytime in advance.
Subscriber comments: Bring plenty of balls for water holes...Tight course, narrow fairways, lots of traps, rolling greens...Tough course on a windy day...An average putter's
nightmare...Creek is always in play.

HARRISON HILLS GOLF & COUNTRY CLUB

PU- 413 E. New St., Attica, 47918, Fountain County, (765)762-1135, 25 miles SW of
Lafayette.
Opened: 1924. **Holes:** 18. **Par:** 72/72. **Yards:** 6,820/5,223. **Course rating:** 72.6/69.7.
Slope: 130/120. **Architect:** William Langford/Tim Liddy. **Green fee:** $20/$25. **Credit
cards:** MC,VISA. **Reduced fees:** Weekdays, low season. **Caddies:** No. **Golf carts:**
$10. **Discount golf packages:** No. **Season:** March-Nov. **High:** May-Sept. **On site
lodging:** No. **Rental clubs:** No. **Walking policy:** Walking at certain times. **Metal
spikes allowed:** No. **Range:** Yes (grass). **To obtain tee times:** Call up to 7 days in
advance.

★★½HART GOLF COURSE

PU-2500 E. 550 N., Marion, 46952, Grant County, (765)662-8236, 4 miles N of Marion.
Opened: 1966. **Holes:** 18. **Par:** 72/72. **Yards:** 6,535/5,060. **Course rating:** 69.5/67.6.
Slope: 108/106. **Architect:** H. Lamboley. **Green fee:** $15/$17. **Credit cards:** MC,VISA.
Reduced fees: Seniors. **Caddies:** No. **Golf carts:** $10. **Discount golf packages:** No.
Season: March-Dec. **High:** May-Sept. **On site lodging:** No. **Rental clubs:** Yes.
Walking policy: Unrestricted walking. **Metal spikes allowed:** Yes. **Range:** No. **To
obtain tee times:** Call golf shop.
Subscriber comments: Pleasure to play...Friendly course for average golfer...
Conditions improving every year.
Special Notes: Spikeless shoes encouraged.

★★½HELFRICH GOLF COURSE

PM-1550 Mesker Park Dr., Evansville, 47720, Vanderburgh County, (812)435-6075.
Opened: 1923. **Holes:** 18. **Par:** 71/74. **Yards:** 6,306/5,506. **Course rating:** 69.8/71.4.
Slope: 124/117. **Architect:** Tom Bendelow. **Green fee:** $12/$12. **Credit cards:**
MC,VISA,DISC. **Reduced fees:** N/A. **Caddies:** No. **Golf carts:** $18. **Discount golf
packages:** No. **Season:** Year-round. **High:** April-Oct. **On site lodging:** No. **Rental
clubs:** Yes. **Walking policy:** Unrestricted walking. **Metal spikes allowed:** Yes. **Range:**
No. **To obtain tee times:** Call 7 days in advance.
Subscriber comments: Great elevation changes...Small greens...New clubhouse big
improvement...Tough old course with lots of play.

★★★HIDDEN CREEK GOLF CLUB

PU-4975 Utica Sellersburg Rd., Sellersburg, 47172, Clark County, (812)246-2556,
(800)822-2556, 4 miles N of Louisville, KY.
Opened: 1992. **Holes:** 18. **Par:** 71/71. **Yards:** 6,756/5,245. **Course rating:** 73.0/70.6.
Slope: 133/123. **Architect:** David Pfaff. **Green fee:** $19/$22. **Credit cards:** All major.
Reduced fees: Low season, twilight, seniors, juniors. **Caddies:** No. **Golf carts:** $10.
Discount golf packages: Yes. **Season:** Year-round. **High:** March-Oct. **On site lodging:** No. **Rental clubs:** Yes. **Walking policy:** Unrestricted walking. **Metal spikes
allowed:** Yes. **Range:** Yes (grass/mats). **To obtain tee times:** Call 4 days in advance
for Monday through Thursday and weekend tee times available after 11 a.m. Call 1 day
prior for weekend tee times available before 11 a.m.

Subscriber comments: Fun to play...Good test of golf...Interesting layout. Tricky around water...#15 and #16 are very, very tough...Narrow fairways...Must be accurate and putt well...Back nine will get you if you stray.

★★★HONEYWELL GOLF COURSE
PU-3360 W. Division Rd., Wabash, 46992, Wabash County, (219)563-8663, 45 miles SW of Fort Wayne.
Opened: 1980. **Holes:** 18. **Par:** 71/71. **Yards:** 6,430/5,650. **Course rating:** 69.4/70.4. **Slope:** 121/118. **Architect:** Arthur Hills. **Green fee:** $16/$18. **Credit cards:** MC,VISA. **Reduced fees:** Weekdays, low season. **Caddies:** No. **Golf carts:** $11. **Discount golf packages:** No. **Season:** Mar-Nov. **High:** June-Sept. **On site lodging:** No. **Rental clubs:** Yes. **Walking policy:** Unrestricted walking. **Metal spikes allowed:** Yes. **Range:** Yes (grass). **To obtain tee times:** Call in advance.
Subscriber comments: Very short holes on back nine, very tight...Fast greens. Back nine challenging...Nice old style course.

★★★½HULMAN LINKS GOLF COURSE
PM-990 N. Chamberlain St., Terre Haute, 47803, Vigo County, (812)877-2096, 75 miles SW of Indianapolis.
Opened: 1978. **Holes:** 18. **Par:** 72/72. **Yards:** 7,225/5,775. **Course rating:** 74.9/68.7. **Slope:** 144/127. **Architect:** David Gill. **Green fee:** $18/$22. **Credit cards:** All major. **Reduced fees:** Low season. **Caddies:** No. **Golf carts:** $11. **Discount golf packages:** No. **Season:** March-Dec. **High:** May-Sept. **On site lodging:** No. **Rental clubs:** Yes. **Walking policy:** Unrestricted walking. **Metal spikes allowed:** Yes. **Range:** Yes (grass). **To obtain tee times:** Call anytime for weekday play. Call on Wednesday for following weekend.
Notes: Ranked 10th in 1997 Best in State.
Subscriber comments: Challenging...Excellent course...Great shots needed, beautiful course...Long, tight course...Lots of sand and water.

★★½INDIANA UNIVERSITY GOLF CLUB
PU-State Rd. 46 Bypass, Bloomington, 47401, Monroe County, (812)855-7543, 45 miles S of Indianapolis.
Opened: 1959. **Holes:** 18. **Par:** 71/72. **Yards:** 6,891/5,661. **Course rating:** 72.4/73.1. **Slope:** 129/123. **Architect:** Jim Soutar. **Green fee:** $17/$18. **Credit cards:** None. **Reduced fees:** N/A. **Caddies:** No. **Golf carts:** $10. **Discount golf packages:** Yes. **Season:** March-Dec. **High:** April-Oct. **On site lodging:** No. **Rental clubs:** Yes. **Walking policy:** Walking at certain times. **Metal spikes allowed:** Yes. **Range:** Yes (grass/mats). **To obtain tee times:** Call 7 days in advance.
Subscriber comments: Every hole is different...Tight and tough...Very challenging from back tees, greens fast...Hoosier forests.
Special Notes: Also has 9-hole par-3 course.

★★IRONHORSE GOLF CLUB
PU-20 Cedar Island, Logansport, 46947, Cass County, (219)722-1110, 5 miles E of Logansport.
Opened: 1904. **Holes:** 18. **Par:** 71/72. **Yards:** 6,100/5,400. **Course rating:** 67.8/64.8. **Slope:** 109/103. **Architect:** Robert A. Simmons. **Green fee:** $10/$13. **Credit cards:** MC,VISA. **Reduced fees:** N/A. **Caddies:** No. **Golf carts:** $10. **Discount golf packages:** No. **Season:** March-Dec. **High:** May-Sept. **On site lodging:** No. **Rental clubs:** Yes. **Walking policy:** Walking at certain times. **Metal spikes allowed:** Yes. **Range:** Yes (grass/mats). **To obtain tee times:** Call golf shop.

★★★IRONWOOD GOLF CLUB
10955 Fall Rd., Fishers, 46038, Hamilton County, (317)842-0551, 5 miles NE of Indianapolis.
Opened: N/A. **Holes:** 27. **Par:** 72/72. **Yards:** 6,901/5,104. **Course rating:** 73.9/70.0. **Slope:** 132/119. **Architect:** Built by owners. **Green fee:** $25/$30. **Credit cards:** N/A. **Reduced fees:** N/A. **Caddies:** No. **Golf carts:** $12. **Discount golf packages:** No. **Season:** Year-round. **High:** April-Oct. **On site lodging:** No. **Rental clubs:** No. **Walking policy:** Walking at certain times. **Metal spikes allowed:** No. **Range:** No. **To obtain tee times:** Call up to 7 days in advance.

Subscriber comments: Hazards not always visible, tough on first time...I try to play this one every year. Very challenging...Long walk between holes...Not forgiving...Good holes, but some rather short...Tough course, water and more water.

★★★JASPER MUNICIPAL GOLF COURSE
PM-17th and Jackson, Jasper, 47546, Dubois County, (812)482-4600.
Call club for further information.
Subscriber comments: Small greens, back nine narrow and long...Wonderful experience...This is a real sleeper...Many blind shots.

★★★½JUDAY CREEK GOLF COURSE
PU-14770 Lindy Dr., Granger, 46530, St. Joseph County, (219)277-4653, 5 miles NE of South Bend.
Opened: 1989. **Holes:** 18. **Par:** 72/72. **Yards:** 6,940/5,000. **Course rating:** 73.3/67.1. **Slope:** 133/116. **Architect:** Ken Killian. **Green fee:** $21/$26. **Credit cards:** MC,VISA,AMEX. **Reduced fees:** Twilight, seniors, juniors. **Caddies:** No. **Golf carts:** $11. **Discount golf packages:** No. **Season:** March-Oct. **High:** June-Aug. **On site lodging:** No. **Rental clubs:** Yes. **Walking policy:** Walking at certain times. **Metal spikes allowed:** Yes. **Range:** Yes (grass/mats). **To obtain tee times:** Call anytime.
Subscriber comments: Challenging course, tough layout...Excellent course for all skill levels...Flat with lots of water. Nothing to block wind...Good test...Some homes too close to course.

★★★LAFAYETTE MUNICIPAL GOLF CLUB
PM-800 Golf View Dr., Lafayette, 47902, Tippecanoe County, (765)476-4588, 68 miles N of Indianapolis.
Opened: 1972. **Holes:** 18. **Par:** 72/75. **Yards:** 7,018/5,241. **Course rating:** 73.0/71.7. **Slope:** 129/115. **Architect:** Bob Simmons. **Green fee:** $10/$12. **Credit cards:** MC,VISA. **Reduced fees:** Twilight. **Caddies:** No. **Golf carts:** $10. **Discount golf packages:** No. **Season:** Year-round. **High:** June-Aug. **On site lodging:** No. **Rental clubs:** No. **Walking policy:** Unrestricted walking. **Metal spikes allowed:** Yes. **Range:** No. **To obtain tee times:** Call Monday after 8 a.m. for upcoming weekend. First come, first served on weekdays.
Subscriber comments: All greens are elevated, always crowded, fun to play...Nicer in spring and early summer.

★★LAKE HILLS GOLF CLUB
PU-10001 W. 85th Ave., St. John, 46373, Lake County, (219)365-8601, (888)274-4557, 35 miles SE of Chicago.
Opened: 1925. **Holes:** 27. **Architect:** Charles Maddox/Frank P. MacDonald. **Green fee:** $18/$40. **Credit cards:** All major. **Reduced fees:** Weekdays, low season, twilight, seniors, juniors. **Caddies:** No. **Golf carts:** Included in Green Fee. **Discount golf packages:** No. **Season:** April-Nov. **High:** June-Sept. **On site lodging:** No. **Rental clubs:** Yes. **Walking policy:** Unrestricted walking. **Metal spikes allowed:** No. **Range:** No. **To obtain tee times:** Call (888)274-4557.
CLUB COURSE
Par: 71/72. **Yards:** 5,888/4,648. **Course rating:** 68.1/66.1. **Slope:** 110/105.
COUNTRY COURSE
Par: 71/72. **Yards:** 5,889/4,471. **Course rating:** 68.0/65.4. **Slope:** 109/102.
PLAYERS COURSE
Par: 70/70. **Yards:** 6,194/4,504. **Course rating:** 70.1/65.8. **Slope:** 124/111.

★★½LAKE JAMES GOLF CLUB
PU-1445 W. 275 N., Angola, 46703, Steuben County, (219)833-3967, 45 miles N of Fort Wayne.
Opened: N/A. **Holes:** 18. **Par:** 72/73. **Yards:** 6,651/5,311. **Course rating:** 72.6/69.3. **Slope:** 134/124. **Architect:** Robert Beard. **Green fee:** $16/$20. **Credit cards:** MC,VISA,DISC. **Reduced fees:** Weekdays, seniors, juniors. **Caddies:** No. **Golf carts:** $10. **Discount golf packages:** No. **Season:** March-Oct. **High:** June-Aug. **On site lodging:** No. **Rental clubs:** Yes. **Walking policy:** Unrestricted walking. **Metal spikes allowed:** Yes. **Range:** No. **To obtain tee times:** Call golf shop.
Subscriber comments: Beautiful course...Very hilly, challenging...Interesting back nine...Course gets tougher as you go...A joy to play.

★★½LAUREL LAKES GOLF COURSE
PU-2460 E. State Rd. 26 E., Hartford City, 47348, Blackford County, (765)348-4876.
Call club for further information.
Subscriber comments: Beautiful setting. Nice course...Easy, builds confidence.

★★★½THE LEGENDS OF INDIANA GOLF COURSE
PU-2313 N. Hurricane Rd., Franklin, 46131, Johnson County, (317)736-8186, 12 miles
S of Indianapolis.
Opened: 1991. **Holes:** 27. **Architect:** Jim Fazio. **Green fee:** $35/$35. **Credit cards:**
MC,VISA. **Reduced fees:** Twilight. **Caddies:** No. **Golf carts:** $10. **Discount golf packages:** Yes. **Season:** March-Dec. **High:** May-Oct. **On site lodging:** No. **Rental clubs:**
Yes. **Walking policy:** Walking at certain times. **Metal spikes allowed:** Yes. **Range:** Yes
(grass). **To obtain tee times:** Call 14 days in advance.
CREEK/MIDDLE
Par: 72/72. **Yards:** 7,029/5,287. **Course rating:** 74.0/70.3. **Slope:** 132/120.
CREEK/ROAD
Par: 72/72. **Yards:** 7,177/5,399. **Course rating:** 74.8/71.0. **Slope:** 134/120.
MIDDLE/ROAD
Par: 72/72. **Yards:** 7,044/5,244. **Course rating:** 74.0/71.1. **Slope:** 132/121.
Subscriber comments: Challenge when the wind is blowing...Lots of variety...Rewards
accuracy...Going to be wonderful when it matures...Tough par 4s...Flat but tough from
the blues...Not many trees...Fair test...Exceptional in every way...Best greens around.

★★½LIBERTY COUNTRY CLUB
1391 U.S. 27 N., Liberty, 47353, Union County, (765)458-5664, 35 miles N of
Cincinnati, OH.
Opened: 1927. **Holes:** 18. **Par:** 70/71. **Yards:** 6,203/4,544. **Course rating:** 70.5/69.3.
Slope: 120/115. **Architect:** Nipper Campbell. **Green fee:** $16/$18. **Credit cards:** None.
Reduced fees: Twilight. **Caddies:** No. **Golf carts:** $11. **Discount golf packages:** No.
Season: Year-round. **High:** June-Aug. **On site lodging:** No. **Rental clubs:** No. **Walking
policy:** Unrestricted walking. **Metal spikes allowed:** Yes. **Range:** Yes (grass/mats). **To
obtain tee times:** Call 3 days in advance.
Subscriber comments: Relaxed place to play...Beautiful, both hilly and flat holes.

LIMBERLOST GOLF CLUB
3204 E. Rd 900 N, Rome City, 46784, Noble County, (219)854-4878, 32 miles NW of
Fort Wayne.
Opened: 1927. **Holes:** 18. **Par:** 70/70. **Yards:** 5,770/4,973. **Course rating:** 64.9/69.3.
Slope: 101/109. **Architect:** N/A. **Green fee:** $12/$15. **Credit cards:** MC,VISA,AMEX.
Reduced fees: N/A. **Caddies:** No. **Golf carts:** $17. **Discount golf packages:** No.
Season: March-Nov. **High:** May-Sept. **On site lodging:** No. **Rental clubs:** No.
Walking policy: Unrestricted walking. **Metal spikes allowed:** Yes. **Range:** No. **To
obtain tee times:** First come, first served. Call golf shop for outings.

★★½THE LINKS GOLF CLUB
PU-11425 N. Shelby 700 W., New Palestine, 46163, Shelby County, (317)861-4466, 15
miles SE of Indianapolis.
Opened: 1972. **Holes:** 18. **Par:** 72/72. **Yards:** 7,054/5,018. **Course rating:** 73.3/68.4.
Slope: 122/100. **Architect:** Charles Maddox. **Green fee:** $20/$38. **Credit cards:**
MC,VISA. **Reduced fees:** Weekdays, low season, twilight. **Caddies:** No. **Golf carts:**
$5. **Discount golf packages:** No. **Season:** Year-round. **High:** May-Sept. **On site lodging:** No. **Rental clubs:** Yes. **Walking policy:** Walking at certain times. **Metal spikes
allowed:** Yes. **Range:** Yes (grass/mats). **To obtain tee times:** Call 7 days in advance.
Subscriber comments: Cut through cornfields but nice to play...Too easy...Links feel
with huge greens.

★½MAPLEWOOD GOLF CLUB
4261 E. County Rd. 700 S., Muncie, 47302, Delaware County, (765)284-8007, 7 miles
S of Muncie.
Opened: 1961. **Holes:** 18. **Par:** 72/76. **Yards:** 6,013/5,759. **Course rating:** 68.5/68.5.
Slope: 115/115. **Architect:** N/A. **Green fee:** $10/$14. **Credit cards:** MC,VISA,DISC.
Reduced fees: Weekdays, low season. **Caddies:** No. **Golf carts:** $10. **Discount golf

packages: No. **Season:** April-Oct. **High:** June-Sept. **On site lodging:** No. **Rental clubs:** Yes. **Walking policy:** Unrestricted walking. **Metal spikes allowed:** Yes. **Range:** Yes (grass). **To obtain tee times:** Call after Tuesday for weekend play.

★★½MAXWELTON GOLF CLUB

5721 E. Elkhart County Line Rd., Syracuse, 46567, Kosciusko County, (219)457-3504, 45 miles SE of South Bend.
Opened: 1930. **Holes:** 18. **Par:** 72/72. **Yards:** 6,490/5,992. **Course rating:** 70.1/73.4. **Slope:** 124/128. **Architect:** William B. Langford. **Green fee:** $18/$20. **Credit cards:** All major. **Reduced fees:** N/A. **Caddies:** No. **Golf carts:** $10. **Discount golf packages:** No. **Season:** March-Nov. **High:** May-Sept. **On site lodging:** No. **Rental clubs:** Yes. **Walking policy:** Unrestricted walking. **Metal spikes allowed:** No. **Range:** No. **To obtain tee times:** Call anytime.
Subscriber comments: Very hilly, lot of blind shots, hard course to walk...Challenging greens...Borders a pretty lake...Good test of golf.

★★MICHIGAN CITY MUNICIPAL COURSE

PM-400 E. Michigan Blvd., Michigan City, 46360, La Porte County, (219)873-1516, 55 miles SE of Chicago.
Opened: 1930. **Holes:** 18. **Par:** 72/74. **Yards:** 6,169/5,363. **Course rating:** 67.6/68.6. **Slope:** 113/113. **Architect:** N/A. **Green fee:** $13/$17. **Credit cards:** None. **Reduced fees:** Low season, twilight, seniors, juniors. **Caddies:** No. **Golf carts:** $20. **Discount golf packages:** No. **Season:** April-Nov. **High:** June-Aug. **On site lodging:** No. **Rental clubs:** Yes. **Walking policy:** Unrestricted walking. **Metal spikes allowed:** Yes. **Range:** No. **To obtain tee times:** Call 7 days in advance.

OAK GROVE COUNTRY CLUB

PU-State Rd. 55 S., Oxford, 47971, Benton County, (765)385-2713, 15 miles NW of Lafayette.
Opened: 1928. **Holes:** 18. **Par:** 71/73. **Yards:** 6,050/5,410. **Course rating:** 69.2/68.4. **Slope:** 113/113. **Architect:** William H. Diddel. **Green fee:** $9/$13. **Credit cards:** None. **Reduced fees:** Weekdays, low season, juniors. **Caddies:** No. **Golf carts:** $8. **Discount golf packages:** No. **Season:** Year-round. **High:** June-Aug. **On site lodging:** No. **Rental clubs:** Yes. **Walking policy:** Unrestricted walking. **Metal spikes allowed:** Yes. **Range:** No. **To obtain tee times:** Call golf shop.

★½OAK KNOLL GOLF COURSE

PU-11200 Whitcomb St., Crown Point, 46307, Lake County, (219)663-3349.
Call club for further information.

★★½OTIS PARK GOLF CLUB

PM-607 Tunnelton Rd., Bedford, 47421, Lawrence County, (812)279-9092, 75 miles S of Indianapolis.
Opened: 1920. **Holes:** 18. **Par:** 72/72. **Yards:** 6,308/5,184. **Course rating:** 70.0/68.1. **Slope:** 128/124. **Architect:** N/A. **Green fee:** $14/$17. **Credit cards:** None. **Reduced fees:** N/A. **Caddies:** No. **Golf carts:** $20. **Discount golf packages:** No. **Season:** Jan.-Dec. **High:** May-Oct. **On site lodging:** Yes. **Rental clubs:** Yes. **Walking policy:** Unrestricted walking. **Metal spikes allowed:** Yes. **Range:** Yes (grass). **To obtain tee times:** Call anytime.
Subscriber comments: No flat lies...Interesting challenge...Scenery great.

★★★★OTTER CREEK GOLF CLUB

PU-11522 E. 50 N., Columbus, 47201, Bartholomew County, (812)579-5227, 35 miles S of Indianapolis.
Opened: 1964. **Holes:** 18. **Par:** 72/72. **Yards:** 7,258/5,690. **Course rating:** 74.2/72.1. **Slope:** 137/116. **Architect:** Robert Trent Jones. **Green fee:** $50/$73. **Credit cards:** All major. **Reduced fees:** Weekdays, low season. **Caddies:** No. **Golf carts:** Included in Green Fee. **Discount golf packages:** Yes. **Season:** March-Nov. **High:** May-Sept. **On site lodging:** No. **Rental clubs:** Yes. **Walking policy:** Unrestricted walking. **Metal spikes allowed:** Yes. **Range:** Yes (grass/mats). **To obtain tee times:** Call anytime in advance with credit card to guarantee reservation.
Notes: Ranked 3rd in 1997 Best in State. 1991 USGA Public Links.
Subscriber comments: Lots of play...Long course, tight in spots. Quick greens...

Strategy in playing holes a must...Everyone treated as special guest...Use every club in your bag...New links nine is a blast, great design...Closest thing to a US Open-style course public can play and walk...Tough for high handicapper...New nine adds a nice change to the original layout...Old 18 is classic golf. Bring your sand wedge.
Special Notes: Also has a 9-hole Rees Jones designed course.

★★★PALMIRA GOLF & COUNTRY CLUB
12111 W. 109th St., St. John, 46373, Lake County, (219)365-4331, 40 miles SE of Chicago.
Opened: 1972. **Holes:** 18. **Par:** 71/73. **Yards:** 6,922/5,725. **Course rating:** 72.7/74.6.
Slope: 122/117. **Architect:** Bob Lohmann/Al Humphrey. **Green fee:** $15/$27. **Credit cards:** MC,VISA. **Reduced fees:** Weekdays, low season, twilight, seniors, juniors.
Caddies: No. **Golf carts:** $25. **Discount golf packages:** No. **Season:** Year-round.
High: May-Sept. **On site lodging:** No. **Rental clubs:** Yes. **Walking policy:** Unrestricted walking. **Metal spikes allowed:** No. **Range:** Yes (grass). **To obtain tee times:** Call golf shop.
Subscriber comments: Tiger woods couldn't reach #17 in two...Needs clubhouse... Greens crowned, hard, small...Lots of improvements...700+ yard par 5.

PEBBLE BROOK GOLF & COUNTRY CLUB
PU-3110 Westfield Rd., Noblesville, 46060, Hamilton County, (317)896-5596, 30 miles N of Indianapolis.
Green fee: $26/$31. **Credit cards:** MC,VISA. **Reduced fees:** Weekdays, twilight.
Caddies: No. **Golf carts:** $12. **Discount golf packages:** No. **Season:** March-Dec.
High: May-Sept. **On site lodging:** No. **Rental clubs:** Yes. **Walking policy:** Walking at certain times. **Metal spikes allowed:** Yes. **Range:** Yes (grass).
★★★NORTH COURSE
Opened: 1989. **Holes:** 18. **Par:** 70/70. **Yards:** 6,392/5,806. **Course rating:** 70.5/74.1.
Slope: 118/115. **Architect:** Gary Kern/Ron Kern. **To obtain tee times:** Call on Tuesday for upcoming weekend. Call on Sunday for upcoming weekday.
Subscriber comments: Links course fun and good test...Challenging. Small greens. Tight fairways...The charcoal grill odor at the turn is unforgettable.
★★★SOUTH COURSE
Opened: 1974. **Holes:** 18. **Par:** 72/72. **Yards:** 6,557/5,261. **Course rating:** 70.5/71.9.
Slope: 121/115. **Architect:** James Dugan. **To obtain tee times:** Call on Tuesday for upcoming weekend. Call on Sunday for following weekday.
Subscriber comments: Old course with some very good holes, great place for 36-hole outings.

★★★½PHEASANT VALLEY GOLF CLUB
3838 W. 141st Ave., Crown Point, 46307, Lake County, (219)663-5000, 30 miles SE of Chicago.
Opened: 1967. **Holes:** 18. **Par:** 72/73. **Yards:** 6,869/6,166. **Course rating:** 72.3/72.6.
Slope: 126. **Architect:** R. Albert Anderson. **Green fee:** $17/$25. **Credit cards:** All major. **Reduced fees:** Weekdays, low season, twilight, seniors, juniors. **Caddies:** No.
Golf carts: $28. **Discount golf packages:** No. **Season:** April-Dec. **High:** May-Oct. **On site lodging:** No. **Rental clubs:** Yes. **Walking policy:** Unrestricted walking. **Metal spikes allowed:** Yes. **Range:** No. **To obtain tee times:** Call 7 days in advance.
Subscriber comments: Blind shots...Tough course, great clubhouse...
Bring your "A" game...Classic course, lots of trees...Premium on accuracy...Very good test of golf...A 90-degree dogleg!...Scenic holes, need every club in the bag and all the shots.

★★★½THE PLAYERS CLUB AT WOODLAND TRAILS
PU-6610 W. River Rd., Yorktown, 46224, Delaware County, (765)759-8536, 40 miles NE of Indianapolis.
Opened: 1991. **Holes:** 18. **Par:** 72/72. **Yards:** 6,884/5,482. **Course rating:** 72.8/71.2.
Slope: 122/115. **Architect:** N/A. **Green fee:** $14/$22. **Credit cards:** MC,VISA.
Reduced fees: Twilight, seniors, juniors. **Caddies:** No. **Golf carts:** $11. **Discount golf packages:** Yes. **Season:** Year-round. **High:** May-Sept. **On site lodging:** No. **Rental clubs:** Yes. **Walking policy:** Walking at certain times. **Metal spikes allowed:** Yes.
Range: Yes (grass). **To obtain tee times:** Call 7 days in advance.
Subscriber comments: Fun to play, real test from the championship tees...Back nine

much tougher, difficult greens...Tight course, mounded fairways, some water in play, good greens...Would pay more, don't tell them that...Very enjoyable to play...Long green to tee...Excellent from any tees.

PLUM CREEK COUNTRY CLUB

PU- 12401 Lynnwood Blvd., Carmel, 46033, Hamilton County, (317)573-9900, 4 miles N of Indianapolis.

Opened: 1997. **Holes:** 18. **Par:** 72/72. **Yards:** 6,766/5,209. **Course rating:** 72.5/69.6. **Slope:** 127/117. **Architect:** N/A. **Green fee:** $26/$30. **Credit cards:** MC,VISA. **Reduced fees:** N/A. **Caddies:** No. **Golf carts:** $15. **Discount golf packages:** No. **Season:** March-Dec. **High:** May-Sept. **On site lodging:** No. **Rental clubs:** Yes. **Walking policy:** Walking at certain times. **Metal spikes allowed:** No. **Range:** Yes (grass). **To obtain tee times:** Call up to 7 days in advance.

★★PLYMOUTH ROCK GOLF COURSE

PU-12641 7B Rd., Plymouth, 46563, Marshall County, (219)936-4405, 25 miles S of South Bend.

Opened: 1960. **Holes:** 18. **Par:** 72/74. **Yards:** 6,533/5,068. **Course rating:** 70.0/68.2. **Slope:** 115/108. **Architect:** Robert Beard. **Green fee:** $6/$12. **Credit cards:** None. **Reduced fees:** Weekdays, low season, twilight, seniors, juniors. **Caddies:** No. **Golf carts:** $10. **Discount golf packages:** No. **Season:** Year-round. **High:** May-Sept. **On site lodging:** No. **Rental clubs:** Yes. **Walking policy:** Unrestricted walking. **Metal spikes allowed:** Yes. **Range:** Yes (grass/mats). **To obtain tee times:** Call in advance in summer.

★★POND VIEW GOLF COURSE

PU-850 South 300 E., Star City, 46985, Pulaski County, (219)595-7431, (800)972-9636, 75 miles N of Indianapolis.

Opened: N/A. **Holes:** 18. **Par:** 70/72. **Yards:** 6,270/5,115. **Course rating:** N/A. **Slope:** 121/121. **Architect:** N/A. **Green fee:** $11/$14. **Credit cards:** MC,VISA,DISC. **Reduced fees:** N/A. **Caddies:** No. **Golf carts:** $12. **Discount golf packages:** No. **Season:** March-Nov. **High:** July-Aug. **On site lodging:** No. **Rental clubs:** Yes. **Walking policy:** Unrestricted walking. **Metal spikes allowed:** Yes. **Range:** Yes (grass). **To obtain tee times:** N/A.

★★½POND-A-RIVER GOLF CLUB

PU-26025 River Rd., Woodburn, 46797, Allen County, (219)632-5481, 25 miles E of Fort Wayne.

Opened: N/A. **Holes:** 18. **Par:** 68/68. **Yards:** 4,729/3,962. **Course rating:** 65.0/67.8. **Slope:** 90/90. **Architect:** N/A. **Green fee:** $14/$14. **Credit cards:** None. **Reduced fees:** Juniors. **Caddies:** No. **Golf carts:** $8. **Discount golf packages:** No. **Season:** April-Nov. **High:** June-Aug. **On site lodging:** No. **Rental clubs:** Yes. **Walking policy:** Unrestricted walking. **Metal spikes allowed:** Yes. **Range:** No. **To obtain tee times:** Call golf shop up to 14 days in advance for weekends.

Subscriber comments: Back nine very hilly.

★★½PORTLAND COUNTRY CLUB

Route 1 County Rd. 120, Portland, 47371, Jay County, (219)726-4646.
Call club for further information.

Subscriber comments: Good place to play, not too crowded.

PRAIRIE VIEW GOLF CLUB

PU-7000 Longest Dr., Carmel, 46033, Hamilton County, (317)816-3100, (888)646-4653, 10 miles N of Indianapolis.

Opened: 1997. **Holes:** 18. **Par:** 72/72. **Yards:** 7,073/5,203. **Course rating:** 74.3/70.2. **Slope:** 134/118. **Architect:** N/A. **Green fee:** $60/$70. **Credit cards:** All major. **Reduced fees:** Weekdays, juniors. **Caddies:** No. **Golf carts:** Included in Green Fee. **Discount golf packages:** No. **Season:** March-Dec. **High:** April-Oct. **On site lodging:** No. **Rental clubs:** Yes. **Walking policy:** Unrestricted walking. **Metal spikes allowed:** No. **Range:** Yes (grass). **To obtain tee times:** Call up to 14 days in advance. Groups of 4 or more players must deposit for guarantee.

★★★ PURDUE UNIVERSITY GOLF COURSE
PU-1202 Cherry Lane, West Lafayette, 47907, Tippecanoe County, (765)494-3139, 60 miles NW of Indianapolis.
Opened: 1934. **Holes:** 18. **Par:** 71/72. **Yards:** 6,428/5,382. **Course rating:** 70.5. **Slope:** 122. **Architect:** William H. Diddel. **Green fee:** $10/$13. **Credit cards:** All major. **Reduced fees:** Weekdays, low season, twilight, seniors, juniors. **Caddies:** No. **Golf carts:** $11. **Discount golf packages:** No. **Season:** March-Nov. **High:** May-Oct. **On site lodging:** Yes. **Rental clubs:** Yes. **Walking policy:** Unrestricted walking. **Metal spikes allowed:** Yes. **Range:** Yes (grass/mats). **To obtain tee times:** Call on Monday for the week.
Subscriber comments: Interesting terrain...Fun to play. Nice mature trees...Good course, challenging, it's too bad they park cars on it during home football games...Many blind shots...Classic old course. Great scenery.

★★ RABER GOLF COURSE
PU-19396 St. Rd. No.120, Bristol, 46507, Elkhart County, (219)848-4020.
Holes: 27. **Architect:** Bill Daniel.
Call club for further information.

★★ RIVERBEND GOLF COURSE
PU-7207 St. Joe Rd., Fort Wayne, 46835, Allen County, (219)485-2732.
Opened: 1974. **Holes:** 18. **Par:** 72/72. **Yards:** 6,702/5,633. **Course rating:** 72.5/72.5. **Slope:** 127/124. **Architect:** Ernie Schrock. **Green fee:** $15/$20. **Credit cards:** MC,VISA. **Reduced fees:** Weekdays, low season, twilight, seniors, juniors. **Caddies:** No. **Golf carts:** $10. **Discount golf packages:** No. **Season:** March-Nov. **High:** May-Sept. **On site lodging:** No. **Rental clubs:** Yes. **Walking policy:** Unrestricted walking. **Metal spikes allowed:** Yes. **Range:** Yes (grass/mats). **To obtain tee times:** Call golf shop.

★★½ RIVERSIDE GOLF COURSE
PU-3502 White River Pkwy., Indianapolis, 46222, Marion County, (317)327-7300.
Opened: 1935. **Holes:** 18. **Par:** 70/71. **Yards:** 6,260/5,385. **Course rating:** 67.9/69.7. **Slope:** 100/100. **Architect:** William H. Diddel. **Green fee:** $10/$15. **Credit cards:** MC,VISA. **Reduced fees:** Weekdays, low season, twilight, seniors, juniors. **Caddies:** No. **Golf carts:** $12. **Discount golf packages:** No. **Season:** Year-round. **High:** May-Sept. **On site lodging:** No. **Rental clubs:** Yes. **Walking policy:** Unrestricted walking. **Metal spikes allowed:** Yes. **Range:** Yes (grass/mats). **To obtain tee times:** Call 7 days in advance for weekdays. Call Monday at 7 a.m. for upcoming weekend.
Subscriber comments: Beware of errant shots...Lots of play on course...Short, wide open, great for beginners...Confidence building course.

★★★★½ ROCK HOLLOW GOLF CLUB
PU-County Rd. 250 W., Peru, 46970, Miami County, (765)473-6100, 15 miles N of Kokomo.
Opened: 1994. **Holes:** 18. **Par:** 72/72. **Yards:** 6,944/4,967. **Course rating:** 74.0/64.8. **Slope:** 132/112. **Architect:** Tim Liddy. **Green fee:** $20/$29. **Credit cards:** MC,VISA. **Reduced fees:** Weekdays. **Caddies:** No. **Golf carts:** $10. **Discount golf packages:** No. **Season:** March-Oct. **High:** June-Sept. **On site lodging:** No. **Rental clubs:** Yes. **Walking policy:** Unrestricted walking. **Metal spikes allowed:** No. **Range:** Yes (grass/mats). **To obtain tee times:** Call up to 14 weeks in advance.
Notes: Ranked 6th in 1997 Best in State; 8th in 1995 Best New Public Courses.
Subscriber comments: Best course for the $ in the state...A must play...Tough course, love the layout...Course built in a rock quarry. Every golfer should play here once!...So much fun you don't want to quit...Truly unique setting...Rewards good shotmaking. Play tees that match your ability...First five holes take my breath away!...Sssh! I'd love to keep this beauty a secret!

★★★ ROYAL HYLANDS GOLF CLUB
PU-7629 S. Greensboro Pike, Knightstown, 46148, Henry County, (317)345-2123, 23 miles E of Indianapolis.

Opened: 1982. **Holes:** 18. **Par:** 71/71. **Yards:** 6,500/4,800. **Course rating:** 71.9/68.8.
Slope: 130/122. **Architect:** Gary Kern. **Green fee:** $20/$25. **Credit cards:** MC,VISA.
Reduced fees: Weekdays, low season, juniors. **Caddies:** No. **Golf carts:** $11.
Discount golf packages: Yes. **Season:** March-Dec. **High:** May-Oct. **On site lodging:**
Yes. **Rental clubs:** Yes. **Walking policy:** Unrestricted walking. **Metal spikes allowed:**
Yes. **Range:** Yes (grass). **To obtain tee times:** Call golf shop.
Subscriber comments: #10 outstanding par 4...Great greens, great service, worth the
drive...Nearby bed & breakfast makes for a great two-day golf getaway...Links in the
farmlands...Watch out for heather grass...A hidden gem in the middle of nowhere.

★★½SADDLEBROOK GOLF CLUB
5516 Arabian Rd., Indianapolis, 46208, Marion County, (317)290-0539.
Call club for further information.
Subscriber comments: Narrow fairways through housing...Short but has a lot of
teeth...Stay out of the heather.

★★½SALT CREEK GOLF CLUB
PU-Hwy. 46 E. and Salt Creek Rd., Nashville, 47448, Brown County, (812)988-7888, 45
miles N of Indianapolis.
Opened: 1992. **Holes:** 18. **Par:** 72/72. **Yards:** 6,407/5,001. **Course rating:** 71.2/68.8.
Slope: 132/122. **Architect:** Duane Dammeyer. **Green fee:** $33/$33. **Credit cards:**
MC,VISA,DISC. **Reduced fees:** N/A. **Caddies:** No. **Golf carts:** $12. **Discount golf
packages:** Yes. **Season:** March-Nov. **High:** May-Aug. **On site lodging:** No. **Rental
clubs:** Yes. **Walking policy:** Walking at certain times. **Metal spikes allowed:** Yes.
Range: Yes (grass). **To obtain tee times:** Call pro shop.
Subscriber comments: Too many layup holes...A wooded course; fun to play...
Beautiful scenery...Good food and clubhouse...If it isn't trees, it's water.

★★★SANDY PINES GOLF COURSE
U.S. 231 and County Rd. 1100 N., De Motte, 46310, Jasper County, (219)987-3611, 60
miles S of Chicago.
Opened: 1974. **Holes:** 18. **Par:** 72/72. **Yards:** 6,500/4,935. **Course rating:** 71.0/71.4.
Slope: 120. **Architect:** William James Spear. **Green fee:** $15/$20. **Credit cards:** None.
Reduced fees: Low season, twilight, seniors, juniors. **Caddies:** No. **Golf carts:** $10.
Discount golf packages: No. **Season:** April-Nov. **High:** June-Aug. **On site lodging:**
No. **Rental clubs:** No. **Walking policy:** Unrestricted walking. **Metal spikes allowed:**
Yes. **Range:** No. **To obtain tee times:** Call 7 days in advance.
Subscriber comments: Another nice track, but off the path...Nice country setting. Tight
fairways...Not allowed to ride on fairways with carts except at 90 degrees...Need at
least two rounds to learn course...If you can find it, play it.

★★SARAH SHANK GOLF COURSE
PM-2901 S. Keystone, Indianapolis, 46203, Marion County, (317)784-0631.
Opened: 1940. **Holes:** 18. **Par:** 72/72. **Yards:** 6,491/5,352. **Course rating:** 68.9/70.8.
Slope: 106/115. **Architect:** City of Indianapolis. **Green fee:** $12/$13. **Credit cards:**
MC,VISA. **Reduced fees:** Weekdays, low season, twilight, seniors, juniors. **Caddies:**
No. **Golf carts:** $20. **Discount golf packages:** No. **Season:** Year-round. **High:** March-
Sept. **On site lodging:** No. **Rental clubs:** Yes. **Walking policy:** Unrestricted walking.
Metal spikes allowed: Yes. **Range:** No. **To obtain tee times:** Call seven days in
advance.

★★½SCHERWOOD GOLF COURSE
PU-600 E. Joliet St., Schererville, 46375-0567, Lake County, (219)865-2554.
Opened: 1967. **Holes:** 18. **Par:** 72/72. **Yards:** 6,710/5,053. **Course rating:** 72.0/67.3.
Slope: 127/108. **Architect:** Ted Locke. **Green fee:** $17/$24. **Credit cards:**
MC,VISA,AMEX. **Reduced fees:** Weekdays, low season, twilight, seniors, juniors.
Caddies: No. **Golf carts:** $21. **Discount golf packages:** Yes. **Season:** April-Dec.
High: May-Sept. **On site lodging:** No. **Rental clubs:** Yes. **Walking policy:** Unrestricted
walking. **Metal spikes allowed:** Yes. **Range:** Yes (grass/mats). **To obtain tee times:**
Call anytime.
Subscriber comments: Gets too much play. Good food...Wide, flat fairways are good
for an ailing game. Nice clubhouse.
Special Notes: Also has 18-hole executive course.

★★★SHADOWOOD GOLF COURSE
PU-333 N. Sandy Creek Dr, Seymour, 47274, Jackson County, (812)522-8164, 62 miles S of Indianapolis.
Opened: 1994. **Holes:** 18. **Par:** 72/73. **Yards:** 6,713/5,416. **Course rating:** 71.8/70.8. **Slope:** 127/118. **Architect:** N/A. **Green fee:** $16/$28. **Credit cards:** MC,VISA. **Reduced fees:** Weekdays. **Caddies:** No. **Golf carts:** $11. **Discount golf packages:** No. **Season:** Year-round. **High:** April-Oct. **On site lodging:** No. **Rental clubs:** Yes. **Walking policy:** Unrestricted walking. **Metal spikes allowed:** Yes. **Range:** Yes (grass/mats). **To obtain tee times:** N/A.
Subscriber comments: A lot of improvements...Nice greens, decent layout, tough but not overbearing.

★★½SHADY HILLS GOLF COURSE
PU-1520 W. Chapel Pike, Marion, 46952, Grant County, (765)668-8256, 50 miles N of Indianapolis.
Opened: 1957. **Holes:** 18. **Par:** 71/72. **Yards:** 6,513/5,595. **Course rating:** 71.6/71.6. **Slope:** 123/110. **Architect:** William H. Diddel. **Green fee:** $15/$17. **Credit cards:** MC,VISA. **Reduced fees:** Seniors, juniors. **Caddies:** No. **Golf carts:** $10. **Discount golf packages:** No. **Season:** March-Nov. **High:** June-Aug. **On site lodging:** Yes. **Rental clubs:** Yes. **Walking policy:** Unrestricted walking. **Metal spikes allowed:** Yes. **Range:** Yes (grass/mats). **To obtain tee times:** Call anytime.
Subscriber comments: Good public course layout. Friendly staff...Cart paths all the way around, good for short hitter.

★★½SMOCK GOLF COURSE
PU-3910 E. County Line Rd., Indianapolis, 46237, Marion County, (317)888-0036.
Opened: 1976. **Holes:** 18. **Par:** 72/72. **Yards:** 7,055/6,230. **Course rating:** 73.7/75.7. **Slope:** 125/127. **Architect:** Bob Simmons. **Green fee:** $14/$15. **Credit cards:** MC,VISA. **Reduced fees:** Twilight, seniors, juniors. **Caddies:** No. **Golf carts:** $13. **Discount golf packages:** No. **Season:** Year-round. **High:** May-Sept. **On site lodging:** No. **Rental clubs:** Yes. **Walking policy:** Unrestricted walking. **Metal spikes allowed:** Yes. **Range:** No. **To obtain tee times:** Call pro shop up to 7 days in advance.
Subscriber comments: Very open. Long tough par 5s. Good bunker layout...Heavy play...Plays a lot tougher than it looks, a nice surprise.

★★½SOUTH GROVE GOLF COURSE
PM-1800 W. 18th St., Indianapolis, 46202, Marion County, (317)327-7350.
Opened: 1902. **Holes:** 18. **Par:** 70/74. **Yards:** 6,259/5,126. **Course rating:** 69.3/74.5. **Slope:** 108/108. **Architect:** N/A. **Green fee:** $10/$15. **Credit cards:** MC,VISA,DISC. **Reduced fees:** Twilight, seniors, juniors. **Caddies:** No. **Golf carts:** $12. **Discount golf packages:** No. **Season:** Year-round. **High:** May-Aug. **On site lodging:** No. **Rental clubs:** Yes. **Walking policy:** Unrestricted walking. **Metal spikes allowed:** Yes. **Range:** No. **To obtain tee times:** Call 7 days in advance for weekdays. Call on Monday at 7 a.m. for upcoming weekend.
Subscriber comments: Very nice greens. Lacks bunkers...Short, challenging, lots of fun to play.

★★½SOUTH SHORE GOLF CLUB
PU-10601 State Rd. 13, Syracuse, 46567, Kosciusko County, (219)457-5711, (219)457-2832.
Call club for further information.
Subscriber comments: Shorter, good for ladies...Small greens...Lots of old pine trees lining fairways.

★★★SUGAR RIDGE GOLF CLUB
PU-21010 State Line Rd., Lawrenceburg, 47025, Dearborn County, (812)537-9300, 22 miles W of Cincinnati, OH.
Opened: 1996. **Holes:** 18. **Par:** 72/72. **Yards:** 7,000/4,812. **Course rating:** 72.7/66.9. **Slope:** 127/109. **Architect:** Brian Huntley. **Green fee:** $32/$39. **Credit cards:** MC,VISA,AMEX. **Reduced fees:** Weekdays, low season, twilight, seniors, juniors. **Caddies:** No. **Golf carts:** Included in Green Fee. **Discount golf packages:** Yes. **Season:** Year-round. **High:** April-Oct. **On site lodging:** No. **Rental clubs:** Yes. **Walking**

policy: Unrestricted walking. **Metal spikes allowed:** Yes. **Range:** Yes (grass). **To obtain tee times:** Call up to 14 days in advance.

Subscriber comments: Very hilly...Outstanding views...Tough for high handicappers...Should be nicer with age...Several blind shots...Twists, turns, rises and falls...Par 5s are gimmicky. Greens won't hold, nor can you bump and run...Don't walk it, you could die out there on a hot day...Bring all the sticks...Best new course around...Love it.

★★★½SULTAN'S RUN GOLF COURSE

PU-1490 N. Meridian Rd., Jasper, 47546, Dubois County, (812)482-1009, (888)684-3287, 60 miles W of Louisville, KY.

Opened: 1992. **Holes:** 18. **Par:** 72/72. **Yards:** 6,859/4,911. **Course rating:** 72.9/68.0. **Slope:** 132/118. **Architect:** Tom Jones/Allen Sternberg/Tim Liddy. **Green fee:** $31/$39. **Credit cards:** MC,VISA,DISC. **Reduced fees:** Weekdays, low season, twilight, juniors. **Caddies:** No. **Golf carts:** $11. **Discount golf packages:** Yes. **Season:** Year-round. **High:** April-Oct. **On site lodging:** No. **Rental clubs:** Yes. **Walking policy:** Unrestricted walking. **Metal spikes allowed:** Yes. **Range:** Yes (grass/mats). **To obtain tee times:** Call up to 30 days in advance. Groups of 16 or more and golf package guests may call up to 6 months in advance.

Subscriber comments: One of the best challenges ever...Breathtaking, each hole is unique, no two alike. #18 is arguably the most beautiful finishing hole in the state...Long way from anywhere...The waterfall just takes your breath away...There is so much privacy even when course is full...Really good par 4s.

Special Notes: Spikeless encouraged.

★★½SUMMERTREE GOLF CLUB

PU-2323 E. 101st St., Crown Point, 46307, Lake County, (219)663-0800, 35 miles SE of Chicago.

Opened: 1975. **Holes:** 18. **Par:** 71/72. **Yards:** 6,586/5,654. **Course rating:** 71.9/72.3. **Slope:** 124/117. **Architect:** Bruce Matthews/Jerry Matthews. **Green fee:** $15/$21. **Credit cards:** MC,VISA. **Reduced fees:** Low season, seniors. **Caddies:** No. **Golf carts:** $21. **Discount golf packages:** No. **Season:** Year-round. **High:** April-Oct. **On site lodging:** No. **Rental clubs:** Yes. **Walking policy:** Unrestricted walking. **Metal spikes allowed:** Yes. **Range:** Yes (grass). **To obtain tee times:** Call one week in advance.

Subscriber comments: #5 long par 3...Has potential...Nice layout, good test...Good course worth the money...Nice people.

SWAN LAKE GOLF CLUB

PU-5203 Plymouth LaPorte Trail, Plymouth, 46563, Marshall County, (219)936-9798, 30 miles SW of South Bend.

Opened: 1967. **Architect:** Al Humphrey. **Green fee:** $11/$15. **Credit cards:** All major. **Reduced fees:** Weekdays, twilight, seniors. **Caddies:** No. **Golf carts:** $12. **Discount golf packages:** No. **Season:** March-Oct. **High:** April-June. **On site lodging:** Yes. **Rental clubs:** Yes. **Walking policy:** Unrestricted walking. **Metal spikes allowed:** Yes. **Range:** Yes (grass/mats).

★★★EAST COURSE

Holes: 18. **Par:** 72/72. **Yards:** 6,854/5,289. **Course rating:** 72.1/69.4. **Slope:** 120/109. **To obtain tee times:** Call golf shop.

Subscriber comments: Must use all shots...Lots of water, fun to play...Large greens. No bar...Some nice holes...Must be accurate with drive! Bring extra balls...Good test.

★★★WEST COURSE

Holes: 18. **Par:** 72/72. **Yards:** 6,507/5,545. **Course rating:** 70.5/71.7. **Slope:** 117/106. **To obtain tee times:** Call.

Subscriber comments: Thinking man's course...Excellent facilities...Play early spring or late fall, summer golf school...Large greens. No bar...Wonderful people!...Very easy to lose balls in rough.

★★TAMEKA WOODS GOLF CLUB

PU-State Rd. 135 and County Rd. 450W, Trafalgar, 46181, Johnson County, (317)878-4331, 24 miles S of Indianpolis.

Opened: 1991. **Holes:** 18. **Par:** 72/72. **Yards:** 6,526/5,341. **Course rating:** 69.1/68.3. **Slope:** 106/105. **Architect:** James A. Hague III. **Green fee:** $14/$16. **Credit cards:** VISA. **Reduced fees:** Weekdays, twilight. **Caddies:** No. **Golf carts:** $10. **Discount golf**

packages: No. **Season:** Year-round. **High:** June-Aug. **On site lodging:** No. **Rental clubs:** Yes. **Walking policy:** Unrestricted walking. **Metal spikes allowed:** Yes. **Range:** No. **To obtain tee times:** Call 7 days in advance.

★★TIPTON MUNICIPAL GOLF COURSE
PM-Golf Course Rd., Tipton, 46072, Tipton County, (765)675-6627.
Call club for further information.

★★TRI COUNTY GOLF CLUB
PU-8170 N. CR 400 W., Middletown, 47356, Henry County, (765)533-4107, 40 miles N of Indianapolis.
Opened: 1964. **Holes:** 18. **Par:** 72/73. **Yards:** 6,706/5,456. **Course rating:** 76.1/70.3. **Slope:** 110/97. **Architect:** Robert Beard. **Green fee:** $21/$26. **Credit cards:** N/A. **Reduced fees:** Seniors. **Caddies:** No. **Golf carts:** Included in Green Fee. **Discount golf packages:** No. **Season:** Year-round. **High:** May-Sept. **On site lodging:** No. **Rental clubs:** Yes. **Walking policy:** Unrestricted walking. **Metal spikes allowed:** Yes. **Range:** Yes (grass). **To obtain tee times:** Call or come in.

★½TRI-WAY GOLF CLUB
PU-12939-4A Rd., Plymouth, 46563, Marshall County, (219)936-9517, 16 miles S of South Bend.
Opened: 1966. **Holes:** 18. **Par:** 71/71. **Yards:** 6,175/5,386. **Course rating:** 69.9/68.6. **Slope:** 110/110. **Architect:** Al Humphrey/Don Kinney/Dana Kinney. **Green fee:** $10/$12. **Credit cards:** None. **Reduced fees:** Weekdays, low season. **Caddies:** No. **Golf carts:** $16. **Discount golf packages:** Yes. **Season:** April-Oct. **High:** June-Aug. **On site lodging:** No. **Rental clubs:** Yes. **Walking policy:** Unrestricted walking. **Metal spikes allowed:** Yes. **Range:** No. **To obtain tee times:** Call.

★★TURKEY CREEK COUNTRY CLUB
PU-6400 Harrison St., Merrillville, 46410, Lake County, (219)980-5170.
Call club for further information.

★★★TURKEY RUN GOLF COURSE
PU-R.R. 1, Waveland, 47989, Montgomery County, (317)435-2048.
Call club for further information.
Subscriber comments: Nice course, small greens, very much worth the drive...Fun to play, some tough holes...Greens putt true.

★★½VALLE VISTA GOLF CLUB
PU-755 E. Main St., Greenwood, 46143, Johnson County, (317)888-5313, 10 miles S of Indianapolis.
Opened: 1971. **Holes:** 18. **Par:** 70/74. **Yards:** 6,306/5,680. **Course rating:** 70.3/72.4. **Slope:** 127/124. **Architect:** Bob Simmons. **Green fee:** $19/$25. **Credit cards:** All major. **Reduced fees:** Weekdays, low season, twilight, seniors, juniors. **Caddies:** No. **Golf carts:** $11. **Discount golf packages:** No. **Season:** Year-round. **High:** May-Sept. **On site lodging:** No. **Rental clubs:** Yes. **Walking policy:** Unrestricted walking. **Metal spikes allowed:** Yes. **Range:** No. **To obtain tee times:** Call 7 days in advance.
Subscriber comments: Leave your driver at home...Greens are tough but fair...Too much OB...Great clubhouse and service...A challenge...Homes come into play.

★★½VALLEY VIEW GOLF CLUB
PU-3748 Lawrence Banet Rd., Floyd Knobs, 47119, Floyd County, (812)923-7291, 5 miles W of Louisville.
Opened: 1962. **Holes:** 18. **Par:** 71/76. **Yards:** 6,523/5,488. **Course rating:** 71.0/71.0. **Slope:** 125/122. **Architect:** N/A. **Green fee:** $16/$18. **Credit cards:** MC,VISA. **Reduced fees:** Weekdays, twilight, seniors. **Caddies:** No. **Golf carts:** $10. **Discount golf packages:** No. **Season:** Year-round. **High:** April-Sept. **On site lodging:** No. **Rental clubs:** Yes. **Walking policy:** Unrestricted walking. **Metal spikes allowed:** Yes. **Range:** No. **To obtain tee times:** Call one to two days in advance.
Subscriber comments: Nice variety in types of holes and elevations...Easy course...Has several signature holes...Basic golf...Tough greens to putt.

★★★VALLEY VIEW GOLF COURSE
6950 W. County Rd. 850 N., Middletown, 47356, Henry County, (765)354-2698, 7 miles E of Anderson.
Opened: 1964. **Holes:** 18. **Par:** 72/72. **Yards:** 6,421/5,281. **Course rating:** 70.3/69.9.
Slope: 114/109. **Architect:** E.V. Ratliff. **Green fee:** $14/$17. **Credit cards:** None.
Reduced fees: Seniors. **Caddies:** No. **Golf carts:** $11. **Discount golf packages:** No.
Season: March-Nov. **High:** May-Sept. **On site lodging:** No. **Rental clubs:** No.
Walking policy: Unrestricted walking. **Metal spikes allowed:** Yes. **Range:** No. **To obtain tee times:** Call for weekends and holidays only.
Subscriber comments: Very hilly. Fun course. Fast greens, good pace...Great course with lovely scenery...Creeks and lakes in play.

★★★WABASH VALLEY GOLF CLUB
PU-207 N. Dr., Geneva, 46740, Adams County, (219)368-7388, 32 miles S of Fort Wayne.
Opened: 1963. **Holes:** 18. **Par:** 71/71. **Yards:** 6,375/5,018. **Course rating:** 70.5/69.8.
Slope: 117/106. **Architect:** Henry Culp/Gary Kern. **Green fee:** $14/$18. **Credit cards:** MC,VISA. **Reduced fees:** Weekdays, low season. **Caddies:** No. **Golf carts:** $11.
Discount golf packages: No. **Season:** March-Nov. **High:** June-Aug. **On site lodging:** No. **Rental clubs:** Yes. **Walking policy:** Unrestricted walking. **Metal spikes allowed:** Yes. **Range:** Yes (grass). **To obtain tee times:** Call up to 7 days in advance.
Subscriber comments: One of Indiana's best...Pretty course, fun to play...Quiet wooded course, a little bit of everything...Some tough holes, some trick holes.

★★½WALNUT CREEK GOLF COURSE
PU-7453 E. 400 S., Marion, 46953, Grant County, (765)998-7651, (800)998-7651, 25 miles S of Fort Wayne.
Opened: 1970. **Holes:** 18. **Par:** 72/72. **Yards:** 6,880/5,154. **Course rating:** 72.1/68.5.
Slope: 121/109. **Architect:** Randy Ballinger. **Green fee:** $15/$20. **Credit cards:** MC,VISA. **Reduced fees:** Weekdays. **Caddies:** No. **Golf carts:** $12. **Discount golf packages:** Yes. **Season:** March-Dec. **High:** June-Aug. **On site lodging:** No. **Rental clubs:** Yes. **Walking policy:** Unrestricted walking. **Metal spikes allowed:** Yes. **Range:** Yes (grass/mats). **To obtain tee times:** Call at least 1 day in advance. Packages may be reserved up to 6 months in advance.
Subscriber comments: Very scenic. Fun to play. One of the best...Worth taking time to play. Well-kept secret...Rolling wooded fairways. Well trapped with water...Some long carries over creek beds.
Special notes: New nine in December 1997; another nine due to open May 1998.

★★★½WESTCHASE GOLF CLUB
4 Hollaway Blvd., Brownsburg, 46112, Hendricks County, (317)892-7888, 10 miles W of Indianapolis.
Opened: 1996. **Holes:** 18. **Par:** 71/71. **Yards:** 6,700/4,869. **Course rating:** 70.8/68.2.
Slope: 129/112. **Architect:** Ron Kern. **Green fee:** $30/$35. **Credit cards:** MC,VISA,AMEX. **Reduced fees:** Weekdays, low season, twilight, juniors. **Caddies:** No. **Golf carts:** $10. **Discount golf packages:** No. **Season:** Year-round. **High:** May-Oct. **On site lodging:** No. **Rental clubs:** Yes. **Walking policy:** Unrestricted walking. **Metal spikes allowed:** Yes. **Range:** Yes (grass). **To obtain tee times:** Call.
Subscriber comments: Very enjoyable...Will get better with age...Great new course!...Makes you want to keep playing...Great strategic bunkering...Pleasant surprise, back nine beautiful.

★½WICKER MEMORIAL PARK GOLF COURSE
PU-Indianapolis Blvd. and Ridge Rd., Highland, 46322, Lake County, (219)838-9809, 1 mile N of Hammond.
Opened: 1930. **Holes:** 18. **Par:** 72/73. **Yards:** 6,515/5,301. **Course rating:** 70.8/69.3.
Slope: 106/107. **Architect:** Tom Bendelow. **Green fee:** $12/$16. **Credit cards:** None.
Reduced fees: Weekdays, low season, twilight, seniors, juniors. **Caddies:** No. **Golf carts:** $11. **Discount golf packages:** Yes. **Season:** Year-round. **High:** May-Sept. **On site lodging:** No. **Rental clubs:** Yes. **Walking policy:** Unrestricted walking. **Metal spikes allowed:** Yes. **Range:** Yes (grass). **To obtain tee times:** Call in advance.

★★WILLIAM S. REA GOLF CLUB
PU-3500 S. 7th St., Terre Haute, 47802, Vigo County, (812)232-0709, 70 miles W of Indianapolis.
Opened: N/A. **Holes:** 18. **Par:** 72/72. **Yards:** 6,482/5,353. **Course rating:** 70.2/71.7. **Slope:** 110/110. **Architect:** Rea family. **Green fee:** $10/$12. **Credit cards:** MC,VISA. **Reduced fees:** Low season, juniors. **Caddies:** No. **Golf carts:** $11. **Discount golf packages:** No. **Season:** March-Dec. **High:** May-Aug. **On site lodging:** No. **Rental clubs:** Yes. **Walking policy:** Unrestricted walking. **Metal spikes allowed:** Yes. **Range:** Yes (grass). **To obtain tee times:** Call on Wednesday for upcoming weekend.
Special Notes: Formerly Rea Park Golf Course.

★★WILLIAM SAHM GOLF COURSE
PU-6800 E. 91st. St., Indianapolis, 46250, Marion County, (317)842-5076.
Opened: 1963. **Holes:** 18. **Par:** 70/70. **Yards:** 6,347/5,459. **Course rating:** 69.2/69.2. **Slope:** 105/104. **Architect:** Pete Dye. **Green fee:** $15/$16. **Credit cards:** MC,VISA. **Reduced fees:** Twilight, seniors, juniors. **Caddies:** No. **Golf carts:** $11. **Discount golf packages:** No. **Season:** Year-round. **High:** April-Oct. **On site lodging:** No. **Rental clubs:** Yes. **Walking policy:** Unrestricted walking. **Metal spikes allowed:** Yes. **Range:** Yes (grass/mats). **To obtain tee times:** Call 7 days in advance.

★★★WINCHESTER GOLF CLUB
PU-Simpson Dr., Winchester, 47394, Randolph County, (765)584-5151, 20 miles E of Muncie.
Opened: 1937. **Holes:** 18. **Par:** 72/74. **Yards:** 6,540/5,023. **Course rating:** 70.4/67.6. **Slope:** 115/106. **Architect:** William Diddel/Tim Liddy. **Green fee:** $9/$18. **Credit cards:** None. **Reduced fees:** Weekdays, low season. **Caddies:** No. **Golf carts:** $12. **Discount golf packages:** No. **Season:** Year-round. **High:** April-Oct. **On site lodging:** No. **Rental clubs:** Yes. **Walking policy:** Unrestricted walking. **Metal spikes allowed:** Yes. **Range:** Yes (grass). **To obtain tee times:** Call up to 14 days in advance.
Subscriber comments: Very interesting...Most par 5s very short...Most consistent greens I've ever played...Becoming too popular.

★★½WOODED VIEW GOLF CLUB
PU-2404 Greentree N., Clarksville, 47129, Clark County, (812)283-9274, 5 miles S of Louisville, KY.
Opened: 1978. **Holes:** 18. **Par:** 71/73. **Yards:** 6,385/5,059. **Course rating:** 70.4/69.6. **Slope:** 125/110. **Architect:** N/A. **Green fee:** $12/$17. **Credit cards:** None. **Reduced fees:** Weekdays, low season, seniors, juniors. **Caddies:** No. **Golf carts:** $9. **Discount golf packages:** No. **Season:** Year-round. **High:** March-Oct. **On site lodging:** No. **Rental clubs:** Yes. **Walking policy:** Unrestricted walking. **Metal spikes allowed:** Yes. **Range:** Yes (grass). **To obtain tee times:** Call 3 days in advance.
Subscriber comments: Fun course...Called "The Bowling Alley"; narrow fairways... Gotta hit 'em straight...Beautiful setting...Just as it is named.

★★★ZOLLNER GOLF COURSE
PU-300 W. Park St., Angola, 46703, Steuben County, (219)665-4269, 30 miles N of Fort Wayne.
Opened: 1971. **Holes:** 18. **Par:** 72/73. **Yards:** 6,628/5,259. **Course rating:** 71.1/69.4. **Slope:** 124/117. **Architect:** Robert Beard. **Green fee:** $15/$18. **Credit cards:** MC,VISA. **Reduced fees:** Weekdays, low season, twilight, seniors, juniors. **Caddies:** No. **Golf carts:** $11. **Discount golf packages:** Yes. **Season:** March-Dec. **High:** May-Sept. **On site lodging:** No. **Rental clubs:** Yes. **Walking policy:** Unrestricted walking. **Metal spikes allowed:** Yes. **Range:** Yes (grass). **To obtain tee times:** Call one week in advance.
Subscriber comments: Nice hill holes...Hard to get on...Greens tough to read...Great layout...Nice elevation changes...Par 3 11th has tree impossible to circumvent...Several short par 4s...A gem of a course.

IOWA

★★½A.H. BLANK GOLF COURSE
PU-808 County Line Rd., Des Moines, 50315, Polk County, (515)285-0864.
Opened: 1971. **Holes:** 18. **Par:** 72/72. **Yards:** 6,815/5,617. **Course rating:** 72.0.
Slope: 119/115. **Architect:** Edward Lawrence Packard. **Green fee:** $14/$17. **Credit cards:** MC, VISA. **Reduced fees:** Low season, twilight, seniors, juniors. **Caddies:** No.
Golf carts: $20. **Discount golf packages:** No. **Season:** March-Oct. **High:** May-Aug.
On site lodging: No. **Rental clubs:** Yes. **Walking policy:** Unrestricted walking. **Metal spikes allowed:** Yes. **Range:** Yes (grass/mats). **To obtain tee times:** Call 7 days in advance.
Subscriber comments: Fences run along left side for most of course...Can't get into much trouble...Improved conditioning with watered fairways.

★½AIRPORT NATIONAL GOLF
PU-3001 Wright Bros Blvd. E., Cedar Rapids, 52404, Linn County, (319)848-4500.
Opened: 1994. **Holes:** 18. **Par:** 63. **Yards:** 4,500. **Course rating:** 58.5. **Slope:** 80.
Architect: N/A. **Green fee:** $5/$12. **Credit cards:** MC, VISA. **Reduced fees:** Seniors, juniors. **Caddies:** No. **Golf carts:** $20. **Discount golf packages:** No. **Season:** March-Dec. **High:** May-Aug. **On site lodging:** No. **Rental clubs:** Yes. **Walking policy:** Unrestricted walking. **Metal spikes allowed:** Yes. **Range:** Yes (grass/mats). **To obtain tee times:** N/A.

★★★★AMANA COLONIES GOLF COURSE
PU-451 27th Ave., Amana, 52203, Iowa County, (319)622-6222, (800)383-3636, 20 miles S of Cedar Rapids.
Opened: 1989. **Holes:** 18. **Par:** 72/72. **Yards:** 6,824/5,228. **Course rating:** 73.3/69.7.
Slope: 136/115. **Architect:** Jim Spear. **Green fee:** $44/$49. **Credit cards:**
MC, VISA, AMEX. **Reduced fees:** Weekdays, low season, twilight. **Caddies:** No. **Golf carts:** Included in Green Fee. **Discount golf packages:** No. **Season:** March-Nov.
High: June-Sept. **On site lodging:** Yes. **Rental clubs:** Yes. **Walking policy:** Walking at certain times. **Metal spikes allowed:** Yes. **Range:** Yes (grass). **To obtain tee times:** Call up to 30 days in advance with credit card for guarantee.
Subscriber comments: A jewel among Iowa's courses...Natural beauty...Carved out of forest...Lots of trouble...Challenging but fair...Fun to play...Wildlife abounds...Each hole isolated...Very scenic holes through wooded hills...Leaves are a problem in fall...Bring a camera, especially in fall...Lots of hills...Two-sleeve course if wild off the tee.

AMERICAN LEGION COUNTRY CLUB
1800 S. Elm St., Shenandoah, 51601, Page County, (712)246-3308, 60 miles SE of Omaha, NE.
Opened: 1956. **Holes:** 18. **Par:** 70/72. **Yards:** 5,803/5,261. **Course rating:** 66.6/69.1.
Slope: 102/113. **Architect:** Chic Adams. **Green fee:** $14/$18. **Credit cards:** MC, VISA.
Reduced fees: N/A. **Caddies:** No. **Golf carts:** $18. **Discount golf packages:** Yes.
Season: April-Oct. **High:** June-Aug. **On site lodging:** No. **Rental clubs:** Yes. **Walking policy:** Unrestricted walking. **Metal spikes allowed:** No. **Range:** No. **To obtain tee times:** Call golf shop.

★★★BEAVER RUN GOLF COURSE
PU-11200 N.W. Towner Dr., Grimes, 50111, Polk County, (515)986-3221, 10 miles NE of Des Moines.
Opened: 1991. **Holes:** 18. **Par:** 72/72. **Yards:** 6,685/5,245. **Course rating:** 71.8/70.4.
Slope: 121/122. **Architect:** Jerry Raible. **Green fee:** $20. **Credit cards:**
MC, VISA, AMEX. **Reduced fees:** Weekdays, seniors, juniors. **Caddies:** No. **Golf carts:** $10. **Discount golf packages:** No. **Season:** March-Nov. **High:** May-Aug. **On site lodging:** No. **Rental clubs:** Yes. **Walking policy:** Walking at certain times. **Metal spikes allowed:** Yes. **Range:** Yes (grass/mats). **To obtain tee times:** Call or come in 7 days in advance.
Subscriber comments: Newer course...Pine trees will be tough in 10 years...Very enjoyable, great variety of holes...Beautiful bent-grass fairways...Two nines completely different...Tough course if windy...Playable for a wide variety of players.

★★★★BOS LANDEN GOLF RESORT
R-2411 Bos Landen Dr., Pella, 50219, Marion County, (515)628-4625, (800)916-7888, 35 miles SE of Des Moines.

Opened: 1994. Holes: 18. Par: 72/72. Yards: 6,932/5,155. Course rating: 73.5/70.9. Slope: 136/122. Architect: Dick Phelps. Green fee: $20/$35. Credit cards: MC,VISA,AMEX. Reduced fees: Weekdays, low season, resort guests, twilight, seniors, juniors. Caddies: No. Golf carts: $10. Discount golf packages: Yes. Season: April-Nov. High: April-Oct. On site lodging: Yes. Rental clubs: Yes. Walking policy: Unrestricted walking. Metal spikes allowed: Yes. Range: Yes (grass). To obtain tee times: Resort guests may call up to 60 days in advance. Public may call up to 30 days in advance.
Notes: Ranked 4th in 1997 Best in State.
Subscriber comments: Natural beauty...Lots of trouble...Wonderful design...Calls for every shot in the bag...Many nice hills...Getting better every year...Don't know you're in Iowa...Need to be a straight hitter...Lots of variety in the layout...Tough on hackers.

★★★ BRIARWOOD GOLF COURSE
PU-3405 N.E. Trilein Dr., Ankeny, 50021, Polk County, (515)964-4653, 15 miles N of Des Moines.
Opened: 1995. Holes: 18. Par: N/A. Yards: N/A. Course rating: N/A. Slope: N/A. Architect: Gordon Cunningham. Green fee: $19/$23. Credit cards: N/A. Reduced fees: Weekdays, twilight. Caddies: No. Golf carts: $10. Discount golf packages: No. Season: March-Nov. High: April-Oct. On site lodging: No. Rental clubs: Yes. Walking policy: Walking at certain times. Metal spikes allowed: Yes. Range: Yes (grass). To obtain tee times: Call up to 7 days in advance.
Subscriber comments: New course, but will be outstanding later...Beautiful views...Need more trees...Wide open...Residential course...Tough in the wind...Fun to play...Will be better in five years...Some large, undulating greens.

★★½ BRIGGS WOODS GOLF COURSE
PU-2501 Briggs Woods Trail, Webster City, 50595, Hamilton County, (515)832-9572, 17 miles E of Fort Dodge.
Opened: 1971. Holes: 18. Par: 72/71. Yards: 6,502/5,267. Course rating: 72.0/70.0. Slope: 128/118. Architect: Jerry Raible. Green fee: $11/$15. Credit cards: MC,VISA. Reduced fees: Weekdays, low season, twilight, juniors. Caddies: No. Golf carts: $16. Discount golf packages: Yes. Season: April-Oct. High: April-Sept. On site lodging: No. Rental clubs: Yes. Walking policy: Unrestricted walking. Metal spikes allowed: Yes. Range: Yes (grass). To obtain tee times: Call 3 days in advance.
Subscriber comments: Back nine is a challenge. A lot of trees. Very tough and tight...Typical "rural" Iowa course...Back nine is more fun to play...Could be tremendous.

★★★½ BROOKS GOLF CLUB
R-P.O. Box 379, Okoboji, 51355, Dickinson County, (712)332-5011, (800)204-0507, 90 miles E of Sioux Falls, SD.
Opened: 1932. Holes: 18. Par: 70/71. Yards: 6,406/5,176. Course rating: 69.5/68.5. Slope: 117/114. Architect: Warren Dickenson. Green fee: $35/$45. Credit cards: All major. Reduced fees: Low season, twilight. Caddies: No. Golf carts: Included in Green Fee. Discount golf packages: Yes. Season: May-Oct. High: June-Aug. On site lodging: Yes. Rental clubs: Yes. Walking policy: Mandatory cart. Metal spikes allowed: Yes. Range: Yes (grass). To obtain tee times: Call golf shop.
Subscriber comments: A flat track , but very cheap...Excellent landscaping...Pretty course...Lots of flowers...Easy to score on.

★★★ BROWN DEER GOLF CLUB
1900 Country Club Dr., Coralville, 52241, Johnson County, (319)337-8508, 111 miles E of Des Moines.
Opened: 1992. Holes: 9. Par: 35/36. Yards: 3,192/2,694. Course rating: 36.7/35.6. Slope: 132/118. Architect: N/A. Green fee: $14/$18. Credit cards: MC,VISA. Reduced fees: Resort guests, twilight, seniors, juniors. Caddies: No. Golf carts: $10. Discount golf packages: No. Season: April-Nov. High: N/A. On site lodging: No. Rental clubs: Yes. Walking policy: Unrestricted walking. Metal spikes allowed: Yes. Range: Yes (mats). To obtain tee times: Call golf shop.
Subscriber comments: Tight, demanding course...Leave your driver in the bag...Lots of water...Will eat up your ball supply...Very difficult for average golfer...Still young...Scenic.

★★½BUNKER HILL GOLF COURSE
PU-2200 Bunker Hill Rd., Dubuque, 52001, Dubuque County, (319)589-4261.
Opened: N/A. **Holes:** 18. **Par:** 69/69. **Yards:** 5,316/4,318. **Course rating:** 65.7/64.1.
Slope: 111/113. **Architect:** Gordon Cunningham. **Green fee:** $12/$14. **Credit cards:** MC,VISA. **Reduced fees:** Weekdays, low season, twilight, seniors, juniors. **Caddies:** No. **Golf carts:** $9. **Discount golf packages:** No. **Season:** March-Nov. **High:** May-Sept. **On site lodging:** No. **Rental clubs:** Yes. **Walking policy:** Unrestricted walking. **Metal spikes allowed:** Yes. **Range:** No. **To obtain tee times:** Call 7 days in advance.
Subscriber comments: Short, hilly terrain...Very scenic course in the bluffs along the Mississippi...Golf amid rock formations...Lots of variety...Challenging for a short course.

★★½BYRNES PARK GOLF COURSE
PU-100 Fletcher Ave., Waterloo, 50701, Black Hawk County, (319)234-9271, 50 miles NW of Cedar Rapids.
Opened: 1908. **Holes:** 18. **Par:** 72/72. **Yards:** 6,268/5,325. **Course rating:** 68.2/68.6.
Slope: 113/102. **Architect:** N/A. **Green fee:** $10. **Credit cards:** None. **Reduced fees:** Seniors, juniors. **Caddies:** No. **Golf carts:** $20. **Discount golf packages:** Yes.
Season: April-Nov. **High:** May-Aug. **On site lodging:** No. **Rental clubs:** Yes. **Walking policy:** Unrestricted walking. **Metal spikes allowed:** Yes. **Range:** Yes (grass/mats). **To obtain tee times:** Call golf shop.
Subscriber comments: Hardly any trouble...Play to boost your confidence...Fairly short...Decent muny...Best played in early summer before it dries...Easy walking.

★★½DODGE PARK GOLF COMPLEX
4041 W. Broadway, Council Bluffs, 51501, Pottawattamie County, (712)322-9970.
Call club for further information.
Subscriber comments: On the river...Tight fairways...Fairly short.

★★½DUCK CREEK GOLF CLUB
PU-Locust and Marlow, Davenport, 52803, Scott County, (319)326-7824.
Opened: 1930. **Holes:** 18. **Par:** 70/74. **Yards:** 5,900/5,500. **Course rating:** 67.9/72.0.
Slope: 115/120. **Architect:** William B. Langford. **Green fee:** $11/$11. **Credit cards:** None. **Reduced fees:** Seniors, juniors. **Caddies:** No. **Golf carts:** $16. **Discount golf packages:** No. **Season:** April-Nov. **High:** April-Sept. **On site lodging:** No. **Rental clubs:** Yes. **Walking policy:** Unrestricted walking. **Metal spikes allowed:** Yes. **Range:** No. **To obtain tee times:** Call one day in advance.
Subscriber comments: Rolls nicely around Duck Creek...Many large hardwoods... Easy to putt,..Very forgiving...Trees line most fairways...Straight drivers score well.

★★EDMUNDSON GOLF COURSE
PU-1608 Edmundson Dr., Oskaloosa, 52577, Mahaska County, (515)673-5120, 60 miles SE of Des Moines.
Opened: N/A. **Holes:** 18. **Par:** 70/70. **Yards:** 6,024/4,701. **Course rating:** 68.3/68.0.
Slope: 114. **Architect:** C.C. (Nick) Carter. **Green fee:** $10/$11. **Credit cards:** None. **Reduced fees:** N/A. **Caddies:** No. **Golf carts:** $16. **Discount golf packages:** No. **Season:** April-Oct. **High:** May-July. **On site lodging:** No. **Rental clubs:** Yes. **Walking policy:** Unrestricted walking. **Metal spikes allowed:** Yes. **Range:** Yes (grass). **To obtain tee times:** Call on Thursday for upcoming weekend.

★★★ELLIS PARK MUNICIPAL GOLF COURSE
PM-1401 Zika Ave. N.W., Cedar Rapids, 52405, Linn County, (319)398-5180.
Opened: 1920. **Holes:** 18. **Par:** 72/72. **Yards:** 6,648/5,210. **Course rating:** 72.0/70.8.
Slope: 124/111. **Architect:** William B. Langford. **Green fee:** $10/$12. **Credit cards:** MC,VISA. **Reduced fees:** Weekdays, twilight, seniors, juniors. **Caddies:** No. **Golf carts:** $20. **Discount golf packages:** No. **Season:** April-Nov. **High:** June-Aug. **On site lodging:** No. **Rental clubs:** Yes. **Walking policy:** Unrestricted walking. **Metal spikes allowed:** Yes. **Range:** No. **To obtain tee times:** Call Monday through Saturday 9 a.m. to 3 p.m. up to 10 days in advance.
Subscriber comments: Contrasting nines...Front nine is open...Tight, hilly, heavily wooded back nine...Need to be accurate...Women-friendly course...Lovely trees and rolling hills...Challenging.

★★★EMEIS GOLF CLUB
PU-4500 W. Central Park, Davenport, 52804, Scott County, (319)326-7825.
Opened: 1961. **Holes:** 18. **Par:** 72/74. **Yards:** 6,500/5,549. **Course rating:** 71.9/74.0.
Slope: 120/115. **Architect:** C. D. Wagstaff. **Green fee:** $11/$11. **Credit cards:** None.
Reduced fees: Seniors, juniors. **Caddies:** No. **Golf carts:** $8. **Discount golf packages:** No. **Season:** April-Oct. **High:** May-Aug. **On site lodging:** No. **Rental clubs:** Yes.
Walking policy: Walking at certain times. **Metal spikes allowed:** Yes. **Range:** No. **To obtain tee times:** Call or come in one day in advance. A $2.00 nonrefundable fee required up to one week in advance.
Subscriber comments: Long and fair...Tough...Hilly...Above average for a muny...Fun to play...All levels of players enjoy this course...Will go back...Challenging but not brutal...Not bad for the money...Great vistas...Open fairways, so grip it and rip it.

★★★EMERALD HILLS GOLF CLUB
808 S. Hwy. 71, Arnolds Park, 51331, Dickinson County, (712)332-7100, 103 miles SW of Sioux City.
Opened: 1972. **Holes:** 18. **Par:** 72/72. **Yards:** 6,600/5,956. **Course rating:** 70.6/72.2.
Slope: 118/121. **Architect:** Leo Johnson. **Green fee:** $25/$30. **Credit cards:** MC,VISA.
Reduced fees: Weekdays, low season, twilight, juniors. **Caddies:** No. **Golf carts:** $10.
Discount golf packages: Yes. **Season:** April-Oct. **High:** May-Sept. **On site lodging:** No. **Rental clubs:** Yes. **Walking policy:** Unrestricted walking. **Metal spikes allowed:** Yes. **Range:** Yes (grass). **To obtain tee times:** Call anytime.
Subscriber comments: Fun course...Good challenge...Very nice vacation golf setting...Mature course...Very friendly staff...Good condition...Great atmosphere...Very friendly staff...You get to use every club in your bag.

★★★½FINKBINE GOLF COURSE
PU-1362 W. Melrose Ave., Iowa City, 52240, Johnson County, (319)335-9556, 110 miles E of Des Moines.
Opened: 1955. **Holes:** 18. **Par:** 72/72. **Yards:** 7,030/5,645. **Course rating:** 73.9/73.1.
Slope: 132/123. **Architect:** Robert Bruce Harris. **Green fee:** $21/$25. **Credit cards:** MC,VISA. **Reduced fees:** Twilight. **Caddies:** No. **Golf carts:** $22. **Discount golf packages:** No. **Season:** April-Nov. **High:** June-Aug. **On site lodging:** No. **Rental clubs:** Yes. **Walking policy:** Unrestricted walking. **Metal spikes allowed:** Yes. **Range:** Yes (grass/mats). **To obtain tee times:** Call 7 days in advance.
Notes: 1991-93 Nike Hawkeye Open.
Subscriber comments: Long, challenging layout highlighted by the island-green 13th...Hillside tram from 13th green to 14th tee...Good test of your skills...Beautiful, mature University of Iowa course...Home of former Amana VIP pro-am...New bunkers make course tougher...Keeps you coming back...Nice, traditional layout.

★★FLINT HILLS MUNICIPAL GOLF CLUB
PM-Highway 61, Burlington, 52601, Des Moines County, (319)752-2018.
Opened: 1943. **Holes:** 18. **Par:** 71/71. **Yards:** 5,648/4,952. **Course rating:** 66.7.
Slope: 110. **Architect:** N/A. **Green fee:** $9/$11. **Credit cards:** MC,VISA. **Reduced fees:** Weekdays, twilight, seniors, juniors. **Caddies:** No. **Golf carts:** $16. **Discount golf packages:** No. **Season:** April-Nov. **High:** N/A. **On site lodging:** No. **Rental clubs:** Yes.
Walking policy: Unrestricted walking. **Metal spikes allowed:** Yes. **Range:** No. **To obtain tee times:** Call on Wednesday for upcoming weekend.

FOX RUN GOLF COURSE
PU-3001 MacIneery Dr., Council Bluffs, 51501, Pottawattamie County, (712)366-4653, 1 mile E of Omaha.
Opened: 1985. **Holes:** 18. **Par:** 71/71. **Yards:** 6,500/4,968. **Course rating:** 70.3/69.2.
Slope: 117/115. **Architect:** N/A. **Green fee:** $15/$18. **Credit cards:** MC,VISA.
Reduced fees: Seniors, juniors. **Caddies:** No. **Golf carts:** $10. **Discount golf packages:** No. **Season:** Year-round. **High:** April-Sept. **On site lodging:** No. **Rental clubs:** Yes. **Walking policy:** Walking at certain times. **Metal spikes allowed:** No. **Range:** Yes. **To obtain tee times:** Call up to 7 days in advance.
Subscriber comments: Very flat and long.
Special Notes: Formerly The Links Golf Course.

★★★GATES PARK GOLF COURSE
PU-820 E. Donald St., Waterloo, 50701, Black Hawk County, (319)291-4485, 115 miles NE of Des Moines.
Opened: 1953. **Holes:** 18. **Par:** 72/72. **Yards:** 6,833/5,635. **Course rating:** 70.0/69.5. **Slope:** 104/104. **Architect:** Robert Bruce Harris. **Green fee:** $10/$10. **Credit cards:** None. **Reduced fees:** Seniors, juniors. **Caddies:** No. **Golf carts:** $16. **Discount golf packages:** No. **Season:** April-Dec. **High:** June-Aug. **On site lodging:** No. **Rental clubs:** Yes. **Walking policy:** Unrestricted walking. **Metal spikes allowed:** Yes. **Range:** Yes. **To obtain tee times:** Call Tuesday after 8 a.m. for upcoming weekend.
Subscriber comments: Nice old-style course...Challenges all levels of players...Very enjoyable to play...Very good test for very little money...Adding water to fairways would make this a supurb track...Great back nine...Well-developed trees.

★★★½GLYNNS CREEK GOLF COURSE
PU-19251 290th St., Long Grove, 52756, Scott County, (319)285-6444, 10 miles N of Davenport.
Opened: 1992. **Holes:** 18. **Par:** 72/72. **Yards:** 7,036/5,435. **Course rating:** 73.5/70.4. **Slope:** 131/124. **Architect:** Dick Watson. **Green fee:** $15/$18. **Credit cards:** MC,VISA. **Reduced fees:** Weekdays, low season, twilight, seniors, juniors. **Caddies:** No. **Golf carts:** $10. **Discount golf packages:** No. **Season:** April-Oct. **High:** June-Aug. **On site lodging:** No. **Rental clubs:** Yes. **Walking policy:** Walking at certain times. **Metal spikes allowed:** Yes. **Range:** Yes (grass). **To obtain tee times:** Call up to 30 days in advance.
Subscriber comments: Great young course with variety...Challenging...Native prairie rough...Environmentally friendly...Lots of wildlife...Deer, turkeys, birds a plus...Nice practice facilities...Good value...Combination of woods and links layout...A nice find...A good course, still developing.

★★GRANDVIEW GOLF COURSE
PU-2401 East 29th. St., Des Moines, 50317, Polk County, (515)262-8414.
Opened: N/A. **Holes:** 18. **Par:** 70/71. **Yards:** 5,422/5,191. **Course rating:** 65.5. **Slope:** 106. **Architect:** N/A. **Green fee:** $13/$15. **Credit cards:** MC,VISA. **Reduced fees:** Twilight, seniors. **Caddies:** No. **Golf carts:** $9. **Discount golf packages:** No. **Season:** April-Nov. **High:** June-Aug. **On site lodging:** No. **Rental clubs:** Yes. **Walking policy:** Unrestricted walking. **Metal spikes allowed:** Yes. **Range:** No. **To obtain tee times:** Call on Sunday for Monday tee time and Monday for the rest of that week.

★★½GREEN VALLEY GOLF COURSE
4300 Donner Ave., Sioux City, 51106, Woodbury County, (712)252-2025.
Call club for further information.
Subscriber comments: Good course for high handicapper...Good test for little money...Average muny...Good day of golf...Fun course...Tough in the wind.

★½HIDDEN HILLS GOLF COURSE
I-80 & Middle Rd., Bettendorf, 52722, Scott County, (319)332-5616.
Call club for further information.

★★½HIGHLAND PARK GOLF COURSE
PM-944 17th St., N.E., Mason City, 50401, Cerro Gordo County, (515)423-9693, 110 miles N of Des Moines.
Opened: 1920. **Holes:** 18. **Par:** 72/72. **Yards:** 6,022/5,633. **Course rating:** 70.9. **Slope:** 110. **Architect:** N/A. **Green fee:** $8/$15. **Credit cards:** None. **Reduced fees:** Twilight. **Caddies:** No. **Golf carts:** $18. **Discount golf packages:** No. **Season:** April-Oct. **High:** N/A. **On site lodging:** No. **Rental clubs:** Yes. **Walking policy:** Unrestricted walking. **Metal spikes allowed:** Yes. **Range:** No. **To obtain tee times:** Call up to 2 days in advance.
Subscriber comments: Very good facilities...Front nine is a spray hitter's nightmare, back nine opens up...Tough the first time you play it...Good but not outstanding.

★★★½JESTER PARK GOLF COURSE
PU-R.R. No.1, Granger, 50109, Polk County, (515)999-2903, 10 miles NW of Des Moines.
Opened: 1970. **Holes:** 18. **Par:** 72/73. **Yards:** 6,801/6,062. **Course rating:** 72.7. **Slope:** 125. **Architect:** Richard Phelps. **Green fee:** $15/$17. **Credit cards:** MC,VISA. **Reduced fees:** Low season, twilight, seniors, juniors. **Caddies:** No. **Golf carts:** $20. **Discount golf packages:** No. **Season:** March-Oct. **High:** June-Aug. **On site lodging:** No. **Rental clubs:** Yes. **Walking policy:** Unrestricted walking. **Metal spikes allowed:** Yes. **Range:** Yes (grass/mats). **To obtain tee times:** Call 7 days in advance.
Subscriber comments: Great test of your skills, great variety of holes...Some outstanding golf holes...Lot of fun to play...Good course, great value...Good for the long players...Length needed on doglegs...Lots of water...Worth getting off the freeway.
Special Notes: Also has 9-hole par-3 course.

★★★½LAKE PANORAMA NATIONAL GOLF COURSE
R-5019 Clover Ridge Rd., Panora, 50216, Guthrie County, (515)755-2024, (800)766-7013, 45 miles W of Des Moines.
Opened: 1970. **Holes:** 18. **Par:** 72/72. **Yards:** 7,015/5,765. **Course rating:** 73.2/73.2. **Slope:** 131/121. **Architect:** Richard Watson. **Green fee:** $30/$35. **Credit cards:** All major. **Reduced fees:** Low season. **Caddies:** No. **Golf carts:** Included in Green Fee. **Discount golf packages:** Yes. **Season:** April-Nov. **High:** June-Aug. **On site lodging:** Yes. **Rental clubs:** Yes. **Walking policy:** Walking at certain times. **Metal spikes allowed:** Yes. **Range:** Yes (grass/mats). **To obtain tee times:** Call 7 days in advance. Outings with 40+ players may book up to a year in advance.
Subscriber comments: Some very challenging holes...Felt more could have been done with available terrain...Overrated...Greens are excellent...Fair track...Small lake resort area...Too long and difficult for average or high handicap players, a bit too wide open for low handicappers.

★★½LAKESIDE MUNICIPAL GOLF COURSE
PU-R.R. No.2, Fort Dodge, 50501, Webster County, (515)576-6741.
Opened: 1976. **Holes:** 18. **Par:** 72/72. **Yards:** 6,436/5,540. **Course rating:** 70.1/69.8. **Slope:** 114/109. **Architect:** City Engineers. **Green fee:** $10/$11. **Credit cards:** MC,VISA. **Reduced fees:** N/A. **Caddies:** No. **Golf carts:** $14. **Discount golf packages:** No. **Season:** April-Oct. **High:** June-Aug. **On site lodging:** No. **Rental clubs:** Yes. **Walking policy:** Unrestricted walking. **Metal spikes allowed:** Yes. **Range:** Yes (grass). **To obtain tee times:** Call 48 hours in advance.
Subscriber comments: Good mix of holes...Tough to read greens...Too many forced carries on back nine...You get what you pay for.

LANDSMEER GOLF CLUB
PU-902 7th St. N.E., Orange City, 51041, Sioux County, (712)737-3429, 40 miles NE of Sioux City.
Opened: 1995. **Holes:** 18. **Par:** 71/71. **Yards:** 6,370/5,252. **Course rating:** 70.6. **Slope:** 120. **Architect:** Don Sechrest. **Green fee:** $15/$17. **Credit cards:** MC,VISA,AMEX. **Reduced fees:** N/A. **Caddies:** No. **Golf carts:** $8. **Discount golf packages:** No. **Season:** April-Nov. **High:** May-Aug. **On site lodging:** No. **Rental clubs:** Yes. **Walking policy:** Unrestricted walking. **Metal spikes allowed:** Yes. **Range:** Yes (grass/mats). **To obtain tee times:** Call up to 5 days in advance.

★★½LE MARS MUNICIPAL GOLF COURSE
PM-935 Park Lane SE, Le Mars, 51031, Plymouth County, (712)546-6849, 25 miles N of Sioux City.
Opened: N/A. **Holes:** 18. **Par:** 71. **Yards:** 6,232. **Course rating:** 68.8. **Slope:** 124. **Architect:** N/A. **Green fee:** $13/$15. **Credit cards:** N/A. **Reduced fees:** N/A. **Caddies:** No. **Golf carts:** $15. **Discount golf packages:** No. **Season:** April-Oct. **High:** N/A. **On site lodging:** No. **Rental clubs:** No. **Walking policy:** Unrestricted walking. **Metal spikes allowed:** Yes. **Range:** Yes (grass). **To obtain tee times:** Call up to 3 days in advance.
Subscriber comments: Newest holes still rough...Fairways need work...Good value.

★★★½THE MEADOWS GOLF CLUB

PU-15730 Asbury Rd., Dubuque, 52001, Dubuque County, (319)583-7385, 180 miles W of Chicago.
Opened: 1996. **Holes:** 18. **Par:** 72/72. **Yards:** 6,667/5,199. **Course rating:** 72.6/68.7. **Slope:** 132/114. **Architect:** Bob Lohmann. **Green fee:** $18/$21. **Credit cards:** MC,VISA. **Reduced fees:** Weekdays. **Caddies:** No. **Golf carts:** $10. **Discount golf packages:** No. **Season:** March-Nov. **High:** June-Aug. **On site lodging:** No. **Rental clubs:** Yes. **Walking policy:** Unrestricted walking. **Metal spikes allowed:** Yes. **Range:** No. **To obtain tee times:** Call up to 7 days in advance.
Subscriber comments: Great new course, super facilities...It will just get better and better...Beautiful clubhouse...Very nice people...Can use all of your clubs...Bent-grass fairways...Great potential, can't wait to play again...New course should be very good in couple of years...Some tough holes.

★★★½MUSCATINE MUNICIPAL GOLF COURSE

PM-1820 Hwy. 38 N., Muscatine, 52761, Muscatine County, (319)263-4735, 20 miles S of Davenport.
Opened: 1969. **Holes:** 18. **Par:** 72/72. **Yards:** 6,471/5,471. **Course rating:** 69.7/72.5. **Slope:** 117/108. **Architect:** N/A. **Green fee:** $8/$8. **Credit cards:** None. **Reduced fees:** Seniors, juniors. **Caddies:** No. **Golf carts:** $8. **Discount golf packages:** No. **Season:** March-Nov. **High:** May-Jun. **On site lodging:** No. **Rental clubs:** Yes. **Walking policy:** Unrestricted walking. **Metal spikes allowed:** Yes. **Range:** Yes (grass). **To obtain tee times:** Call or come in seven days in advance.
Subscriber comments: Nicely maintained...Surprised a municipal course was that nice...Fantastic value...New clubhouse...Wonderful greens...Fun to play for average golfer...Need a lot of different shots...New layout improves flow...I wish I could play it more often.

★★OAKLAND ACRES GOLF CLUB

PU-Highway 6, Grinnell, 50112, Poweshiek County, (515)236-7111, 60 miles E of Des Moines.
Opened: N/A. **Holes:** 18. **Par:** 69/71. **Yards:** 5,878/5,410. **Course rating:** 69.0. **Slope:** 114. **Architect:** N/A. **Green fee:** $12/$14. **Credit cards:** MC,VISA,DISC. **Reduced fees:** Weekdays, seniors, juniors. **Caddies:** No. **Golf carts:** $16. **Discount golf packages:** No. **Season:** April-Oct. **High:** June-Aug. **On site lodging:** No. **Rental clubs:** No. **Walking policy:** Unrestricted walking. **Metal spikes allowed:** Yes. **Range:** Yes (grass). **To obtain tee times:** First come, first served.

★★★OKOBOJI VIEW GOLF COURSE

PU-1665 Hwy. 86, Spirit Lake, 51360, Dickinson County, (712)337-3372, 74 miles SE of Sioux Falls.
Opened: 1962. **Holes:** 18. **Par:** 70/73. **Yards:** 6,051/5,441. **Course rating:** 68.5/70.1. **Slope:** 113/113. **Architect:** E.G. McCoy. **Green fee:** $26/$32. **Credit cards:** All major. **Reduced fees:** Low season, twilight. **Caddies:** No. **Golf carts:** $10. **Discount golf packages:** Yes. **Season:** April-Oct. **High:** June-Aug. **On site lodging:** No. **Rental clubs:** Yes. **Walking policy:** Unrestricted walking. **Metal spikes allowed:** Yes. **Range:** Yes (grass). **To obtain tee times:** Call 1 day in advance.
Subscriber comments: Nice course for big hitters...Resort area. Not a difficult course...Above average...Interesting course.

★★½OTTER CREEK GOLF CLUB

PU-1410 N.E. 36th, Ankeny, 50021, Polk County, (515)965-6464.
Opened: 1981. **Holes:** 18. **Par:** 71/73. **Yards:** 6,473/5,889. **Course rating:** 71.0/73.1. **Slope:** 117/119. **Architect:** Don Rippel. **Green fee:** $16/$16. **Credit cards:** MC,VISA. **Reduced fees:** Weekdays, twilight. **Caddies:** No. **Golf carts:** $19. **Discount golf packages:** No. **Season:** April-Oct. **High:** April-Oct. **On site lodging:** No. **Rental clubs:** Yes. **Walking policy:** Unrestricted walking. **Metal spikes allowed:** Yes. **Range:** Yes (grass). **To obtain tee times:** Call up to 30 days in advance.
Subscriber comments: Nice course. Well maintained...Always score my best rounds there...Friendly staff...Still needs work, but it's better than it was.

★★★OTTUMWA MUNICIPAL GOLF COURSE

PM-4101 Angle Rd., Ottumwa, 52501, Wapello County, (515)683-0646, 90 miles SE of Des Moines.

Opened: 1931. **Holes:** 18. **Par:** 70/70. **Yards:** 6,335/4,954. **Course rating:** 70.4/66.7. **Slope:** 118/102. **Architect:** Tom Bendelow/Chic Adams. **Green fee:** $8/$12. **Credit cards:** None. **Reduced fees:** N/A. **Caddies:** No. **Golf carts:** $18. **Discount golf packages:** No. **Season:** March-Nov. **High:** June-Aug. **On site lodging:** No. **Rental clubs:** Yes. **Walking policy:** Unrestricted walking. **Metal spikes allowed:** Yes. **Range:** Yes (grass). **To obtain tee times:** Call up to 7 days in advance.

Subscriber comments: A good muny course, wide fairways, not too much trouble but no pushover...Price is very reasonable...Short but fun city course...A creek winds through course.

★★★PALMER HILLS MUNICIPAL GOLF COURSE

PM-2999 Middle Rd., Bettendorf, 52722, Scott County, (319)332-8296, 3 miles E of Davenport.

Opened: 1975. **Holes:** 18. **Par:** 71/71. **Yards:** 6,535/5,923. **Course rating:** 71.5/74.0. **Slope:** 124/130. **Architect:** William James Spear. **Green fee:** $12/$12. **Credit cards:** MC,VISA. **Reduced fees:** Weekdays, twilight, seniors, juniors. **Caddies:** No. **Golf carts:** $16. **Discount golf packages:** No. **Season:** April-Dec. **High:** April-Sept. **On site lodging:** No. **Rental clubs:** Yes. **Walking policy:** Unrestricted walking. **Metal spikes allowed:** Yes. **Range:** Yes. **To obtain tee times:** Call anytime.

Subscriber comments: Test of your skills...Variety of holes...Very hilly...Lots of trouble...Will go back...Some quirky holes...Position is everything...Some blind shots...Good course for all.

★★★PHEASANT RIDGE MUNICIPAL GOLF COURSE

PM-3205 W. 12th St., Cedar Falls, 50613, Black Hawk County, (319)266-8266, 5 miles W of Waterloo.

Opened: 1972. **Holes:** 18. **Par:** 72/70. **Yards:** 6,730/5,179. **Course rating:** 72.5/68.4. **Slope:** 122/101. **Architect:** Donald Brauer. **Green fee:** $10/$10. **Credit cards:** None. **Reduced fees:** Low season, seniors, juniors. **Caddies:** No. **Golf carts:** $20. **Discount golf packages:** No. **Season:** April-Nov. **High:** April-Sept. **On site lodging:** No. **Rental clubs:** Yes. **Walking policy:** Unrestricted walking. **Metal spikes allowed:** Yes. **Range:** Yes (grass). **To obtain tee times:** Call up to one week in advance.

Subscriber comments: Windy...Wide-open fairways, can really let it fly...Not much tree growth...Bunkers make it interesting.

★★★½PLEASANT VALLEY GOLF COURSE

PU-4390 S.E. Sand Rd., Iowa City, 52240, Johnson County, (319)337-7209, 100 miles E of Des Moines.

Opened: 1987. **Holes:** 18. **Par:** 72/72. **Yards:** 6,472/4,754. **Course rating:** 71.0. **Slope:** 119. **Architect:** William James Spear. **Green fee:** $16/$20. **Credit cards:** All major. **Reduced fees:** Weekdays, twilight, seniors, juniors. **Caddies:** No. **Golf carts:** $10. **Discount golf packages:** No. **Season:** April-Oct. **High:** June-July. **On site lodging:** No. **Rental clubs:** Yes. **Walking policy:** Unrestricted walking. **Metal spikes allowed:** Yes. **Range:** Yes (grass/mats). **To obtain tee times:** Call up to 7 days in advance.

Subscriber comments: Good mix of water, bunkers and rough...Very challenging course...Lots of undulating greens...You will enjoy it...Florida-style water and sand...Good for walking...Fun, fun, fun...Very enjoyable for the average golfer.

★★★RED CARPET GOLF CLUB

1409 Newell St., Waterloo, 50703, Black Hawk County, (319)235-1242.

Opened: 1920. **Holes:** 18. **Par:** 72/73. **Yards:** 6,557/5,754. **Course rating:** 70.8/72.1. **Slope:** 119. **Architect:** N/A. **Green fee:** $11/$12. **Credit cards:** None. **Reduced fees:** N/A. **Caddies:** No. **Golf carts:** $18. **Discount golf packages:** No. **Season:** March-Nov. **High:** May-Sept. **On site lodging:** No. **Rental clubs:** No. **Walking policy:** Unrestricted walking. **Metal spikes allowed:** Yes. **Range:** No. **To obtain tee times:** Call ahead. May call as early as Tuesday for upcoming weekend.

Subscriber comments: Old country club...Fun course...Acceptable.

★★★RIVER VALLEY GOLF COURSE
PU-2267 Valley View Trail, Adel, 50003, Dallas County, (515)993-4029, 15 miles W of Des Moines.
Opened: 1995. **Holes:** 18. **Par:** 72/72. **Yards:** 6,635/5,482. **Course rating:** 71.1/67.4. **Slope:** 121/114. **Architect:** N/A. **Green fee:** $10/$18. **Credit cards:** All major. **Reduced fees:** Weekdays, low season, twilight, juniors. **Caddies:** No. **Golf carts:** $20. **Discount golf packages:** No. **Season:** Feb.-Dec. **High:** April-Oct. **On site lodging:** No. **Rental clubs:** Yes. **Walking policy:** Walking at certain times. **Metal spikes allowed:** Yes. **Range:** Yes (grass). **To obtain tee times:** Call golf shop.
Subscriber comments: Young course coming into its own...Log clubhouse...Will mature nicely...A few fun holes, mostly wide open...Will improve with age.

★★ST. ANDREWS GOLF CLUB
1866 Blairs Ferry Rd. N.E., Cedar Rapids, 52402, Linn County, (319)393-9915. Call club for further information.

★★★SHEAFFER MEMORIAL GOLF PARK
PU-1760 308th Ave., Fort Madison, 52627, Lee County, (319)528-6214, 15 miles SW of Burlington.
Opened: 1962. **Holes:** 18. **Par:** 72/73. **Yards:** 6,303/5,441. **Course rating:** 69.9/69.9. **Slope:** 118/113. **Architect:** C.D. Wagstaff. **Green fee:** $11/$13. **Credit cards:** None. **Reduced fees:** Weekdays, twilight, seniors, juniors. **Caddies:** No. **Golf carts:** $16. **Discount golf packages:** No. **Season:** March-Nov. **High:** June-Aug. **On site lodging:** No. **Rental clubs:** Yes. **Walking policy:** Unrestricted walking. **Metal spikes allowed:** Yes. **Range:** Yes (grass/mats). **To obtain tee times:** Call anytime. Tee times needed on weekends and holidays only.
Subscriber comments: Challenging front nine, open back nine...Somewhat flat...Fun.

SHORELINE GOLF COURSE
PU-210 Locust St., Carter Lake, 51510, Douglas County, (712)347-5173, 3 miles W of Omaha, NE.
Opened: 1991. **Holes:** 18. **Par:** 72/72. **Yards:** 7,000/5,439. **Course rating:** 71.9/66.0. **Slope:** 124/107. **Architect:** Pat Wyss. **Green fee:** $13/$16. **Credit cards:** MC,VISA. **Reduced fees:** Weekdays, low season, seniors, juniors. **Caddies:** No. **Golf carts:** $17. **Discount golf packages:** Yes. **Season:** Year-round. **High:** April-Oct. **On site lodging:** No. **Rental clubs:** Yes. **Walking policy:** Unrestricted walking. **Metal spikes allowed:** Yes. **Range:** Yes (grass). **To obtain tee times:** Call 7 days in advance.

★★★SOUTH HILLS GOLF COURSE
PU-1101 Campbell, Waterloo, 50701, Black Hawk County, (319)291-4268.
Opened: 1972. **Holes:** 18. **Par:** 72/72. **Yards:** 6,698/5,818. **Course rating:** 71.4. **Slope:** 108. **Architect:** City of Waterloo. **Green fee:** $10/$10. **Credit cards:** None. **Reduced fees:** Seniors, juniors. **Caddies:** No. **Golf carts:** $16. **Discount golf packages:** No. **Season:** April-Dec. **High:** June-Aug. **On site lodging:** No. **Rental clubs:** Yes. **Walking policy:** Unrestricted walking. **Metal spikes allowed:** Yes. **Range:** Yes. **To obtain tee times:** Call Tuesday after 8 a.m. for upcoming weekend.
Subscriber comments: Fun, hilly course, can be a real challenge in the wind...Very open course...The price is right...Tough for seniors to walk those hills.

★★★½SPENCER GOLF & COUNTRY CLUB
2200 W. 18th St., Spencer, 51301, Clay County, (712)262-2028, 100 miles NE of Sioux City.
Opened: 1966. **Holes:** 18. **Par:** 72/73. **Yards:** 6,888/5,760. **Course rating:** 73.0/74.5. **Slope:** 127/124. **Architect:** David A. Gill. **Green fee:** $27/$27. **Credit cards:** MC,VISA. **Reduced fees:** N/A. **Caddies:** No. **Golf carts:** $11. **Discount golf packages:** No. **Season:** March-Oct. **High:** June-Sept. **On site lodging:** No. **Rental clubs:** Yes. **Walking policy:** Unrestricted walking. **Metal spikes allowed:** Yes. **Range:** Yes (grass). **To obtain tee times:** Call up to one month in advance.
Subscriber comments: Great fairways and greens...Excellent course...A nice, fair test...Well kept...Outstanding course...Very fair course...Great course, but relatively pricey.

★★½SQUAW CREEK GOLF COURSE
PU-5101 Golf Course Rd., Marion, 52302, Linn County, (319)398-5182, (800)373-8433, 2 miles N of Cedar Rapids.
Opened: N/A. **Holes:** 18. **Par:** 72/72. **Yards:** 6,629/5,574. **Course rating:** N/A. **Slope:** 111/109. **Architect:** Herman Thompson. **Green fee:** $7/$12. **Credit cards:** MC,VISA. **Reduced fees:** Twilight, seniors, juniors. **Caddies:** No. **Golf carts:** $20. **Discount golf packages:** No. **Season:** April-Nov. **High:** June-Sept. **On site lodging:** No. **Rental clubs:** No. **Walking policy:** Unrestricted walking. **Metal spikes allowed:** Yes. **Range:** Yes (grass). **To obtain tee times:** Call up to 10 days.
Subscriber comments: Could be a lot of fun...Good course for every skill level...Super golf shop with great value...Golf shop well stocked...Very dry, but excellent value.

★★TERRACE HILLS GOLF COURSE
PU-8700 NE 46th. Ave., Altoona, 50009, Polk County, (515)967-2932.
Opened: 1964. **Holes:** 18. **Par:** 71. **Yards:** 6,300. **Course rating:** 68.8. **Slope:** 116. **Architect:** N/A. **Green fee:** N/A. **Credit cards:** N/A. **Reduced fees:** N/A. **Caddies:** No. **Golf carts:** N/A. **Discount golf packages:** No. **Season:** March-Nov. **High:** N/A. **On site lodging:** No. **Rental clubs:** Yes. **Walking policy:** Unrestricted walking. **Metal spikes allowed:** Yes. **Range:** Yes (grass). **To obtain tee times:** N/A.

★★★TIMBERLINE GOLF COURSE
PU-19804 E. Pleasant Grove Rd., Peosta, 52068, Dubuque County, (319)876-3422, 20 miles SW of Dubuque.
Opened: 1959. **Holes:** 18. **Par:** 72/73. **Yards:** 6,545/5,318. **Course rating:** 71.4/73.5. **Slope:** 119/113. **Architect:** N/A. **Green fee:** $12/$15. **Credit cards:** MC,VISA. **Reduced fees:** Seniors, juniors. **Caddies:** No. **Golf carts:** $10. **Discount golf packages:** No. **Season:** April-Oct. **High:** June-Aug. **On site lodging:** No. **Rental clubs:** No. **Walking policy:** Unrestricted walking. **Metal spikes allowed:** Yes. **Range:** No. **To obtain tee times:** Call 1 day in advance.
Subscriber comments: Lots of timber...Hilly, wooded layout...Play smart golf. Lots of doglegs bark, bark, bark...Straight driver needed...Pleasant country setting.

★★½TOAD VALLEY PUBLIC GOLF COURSE
PU-237 NE 80th St., Runnells, 50237-2028, Polk County, (515)967-9575, 5 miles E of Des Moines.
Opened: 1973. **Holes:** 18. **Par:** 71/71. **Yards:** 6,170/5,295. **Course rating:** 69.1/71.2. **Slope:** 114/114. **Architect:** N/A. **Green fee:** $16/$18. **Credit cards:** MC,VISA,DISC. **Reduced fees:** Low season, seniors. **Caddies:** No. **Golf carts:** $20. **Discount golf packages:** No. **Season:** Year-round. **High:** April-Sept. **On site lodging:** No. **Rental clubs:** Yes. **Walking policy:** Unrestricted walking. **Metal spikes allowed:** Yes. **Range:** Yes (grass). **To obtain tee times:** Call up to 21 days in advance.
Subscriber comments: Lack of bunkers...Short course, but very relaxing...Great for beginners...A good course for medium- and high-handicap players.

★★TWIN PINES GOLF COURSE
3800 42nd St NE, Cedar Rapids, 52402, Linn County, (319)398-5183.
Call club for further information.

★★★½VALLEY OAKS GOLF CLUB
3330 Harts Mill Rd., Clinton, 52732, Clinton County, (319)242-7221, 40 miles NE of Davenport.
Opened: 1966. **Holes:** 18. **Par:** 72/73. **Yards:** 6,855/5,325. **Course rating:** 72.5/70.3. **Slope:** 124/121. **Architect:** Robert Bruce Harris. **Green fee:** $15/$18. **Credit cards:** MC,VISA. **Reduced fees:** Weekdays, juniors. **Caddies:** No. **Golf carts:** $10. **Discount golf packages:** No. **Season:** April-Oct. **High:** April-Oct. **On site lodging:** No. **Rental clubs:** Yes. **Walking policy:** Unrestricted walking. **Metal spikes allowed:** Yes. **Range:** Yes (grass/mats). **To obtain tee times:** Call up to 7 days in advance.
Subscriber comments: Nice course...Has some very nice holes...Nice course, kept well...Challenging...Scenic...It's got every challenge you want in golf...Good and long...Had lots of fun and challenges...Big trees...Beautiful oaks.

GOOD VALUE

★★★½VEENKER MEMORIAL GOLF COURSE

PU-Stange Rd., Ames, 50011, Story County, (515)294-6727, 30 miles N of Des Moines.
Opened: 1938. **Holes:** 18. **Par:** 72/73. **Yards:** 6,543/5,357. **Course rating:** 71.3/70.6. **Slope:** 124/120. **Architect:** Perry Maxwell. **Green fee:** $17/$20. **Credit cards:** MC,VISA. **Reduced fees:** Weekdays, juniors. **Caddies:** No. **Golf carts:** $18. **Discount golf packages:** No. **Season:** March-Nov. **High:** June-Aug. **On site lodging:** No. **Rental clubs:** Yes. **Walking policy:** Unrestricted walking. **Metal spikes allowed:** Yes. **Range:** Yes (grass). **To obtain tee times:** Call up to 7 days in advance.
Subscriber comments: Great college course...Very challenging...Narrow...Several hilly, blind shots...Tough...Tight back nine...Need all the shots...Very enjoyable...Lots of trees...Exciting course...Wonderful when in good condition.

★★★½WAVELAND GOLF COURSE

PU-4908 University Ave., Des Moines, 50311, Polk County, (515)271-8725.
Opened: 1894. **Holes:** 18. **Par:** 72/71. **Yards:** 6,419/5,295. **Course rating:** 71.4/69.4. **Slope:** 126/116. **Architect:** Warren Dickinson. **Green fee:** $14/$17. **Credit cards:** MC,VISA,DISC. **Reduced fees:** Low season, twilight, seniors, juniors. **Caddies:** No. **Golf carts:** $20. **Discount golf packages:** Yes. **Season:** March-Nov. **High:** May-Aug. **On site lodging:** No. **Rental clubs:** Yes. **Walking policy:** Unrestricted walking. **Metal spikes allowed:** Yes. **Range:** No. **To obtain tee times:** Call Sunday for Monday tee times and Monday for the rest of the week.
Subscriber comments: Classic old muny...Very hilly...Gets a lot of play...Could be great...Great place to play team matches...Large oak trees and rolling hills...Tough one to walk...Name says it: Like large ocean waves...A shrine to its regulars...City needs to understand it has a gem.
Special Notes: Spikeless shoes encouraged.

★★★WAVERLY GOLF COURSE

Hwy 218S Fairgrounds, Waverly, 50677, Bremer County, (319)352-1530.
Opened: N/A. **Holes:** 18. **Par:** 70/72. **Yards:** 5,881/5,440. **Course rating:** 69.2/69.5. **Slope:** 115/105. **Architect:** N/A. **Green fee:** $10/$13. **Credit cards:** MC,VISA. **Reduced fees:** N/A. **Caddies:** No. **Golf carts:** $20. **Discount golf packages:** No. **Season:** April-Nov. **High:** June-Aug. **On site lodging:** No. **Rental clubs:** No. **Walking policy:** Unrestricted walking. **Metal spikes allowed:** No. **Range:** No. **To obtain tee times:** Call up to 7 days in advance.
Subscriber comments: Nice small-town course...Not too long...Short but enjoyable.

★★½WESTWOOD GOLF CLUB

PU-3387 Hwy. F 48 W., Newton, 50208, Jasper County, (515)792-3087.
Opened: 1927. **Holes:** 18. **Par:** 71/71. **Yards:** 6,245/5,645. **Course rating:** 68.3/74.5. **Slope:** 116. **Architect:** Dave Gill. **Green fee:** $12/$15. **Credit cards:** None. **Reduced fees:** Juniors. **Caddies:** No. **Golf carts:** $18. **Discount golf packages:** No. **Season:** April-Oct. **High:** June-Aug. **On site lodging:** No. **Rental clubs:** Yes. **Walking policy:** Unrestricted walking. **Metal spikes allowed:** Yes. **Range:** Yes (grass). **To obtain tee times:** Call 7 days in advance.
Subscriber comments: Will be better after reconstruction...Two distinct nines.

WILLOW CREEK GOLF COURSE

PU-140 Army Post Rd., West Des Moines, 50265, Polk County, (515)285-4558.
Opened: 1961. **Green fee:** $17/$20. **Reduced fees:** N/A. **Caddies:** No. **Golf carts:** $20. **Discount golf packages:** No. **Season:** April-Oct. **High:** June-Sept. **On site lodging:** No. **Rental clubs:** Yes. **Walking policy:** Unrestricted walking. **Metal spikes allowed:** Yes. **Range:** Yes (grass/mats). **To obtain tee times:** Call golf shop.
★★BLUE/WHITE COURSE
Holes: 18. **Par:** 68/69. **Yards:** 5,385/4,625. **Course rating:** 65.4/67.4. **Slope:** N/A. **Architect:** N/A. **Credit cards:** N/A.
★★½RED COURSE
Holes: 18. **Par:** 71/74. **Yards:** 6,465/5,758. **Course rating:** 70.2/71.4. **Slope:** 116/112. **Architect:** Dick Phelps. **Credit cards:** MC,VISA,DISC.
Subscriber comments: Nice, but heavily used...Fun layout for an unplanned day...Like two different courses with new holes.

KANSAS

★★★½ALVAMAR GOLF CLUB
1800 Crossgate Dr., Lawrence, 66047, Douglas County, (913)842-1907, 25 miles SW of Kansas City.
Opened: 1968. **Holes:** 18. **Par:** 72/72. **Yards:** 7,096/5,489. **Course rating:** 75.0. **Slope:** 135. **Architect:** Bob Dunning. **Green fee:** $15/$30. **Credit cards:** MC,VISA,DISC. **Reduced fees:** Weekdays, low season, resort guests, twilight, seniors, juniors. **Caddies:** No. **Golf carts:** $12. **Discount golf packages:** Yes. **Season:** Year-round. **High:** May-Sept. **On site lodging:** No. **Rental clubs:** Yes. **Walking policy:** Unrestricted walking. **Metal spikes allowed:** Yes. **Range:** Yes (grass). **To obtain tee times:** Call seven days in advance.
Subscriber comments: Long when wind is blowing...A great course...Big, fast greens...Very challenging. A test for all...Some difficult holes, tight but fair...Always enjoyable, very good fairways...Simply a great test of golf...One of the best courses I have played...You'll use every club in your bag.

★★ARTHUR B. SIM PARK GOLF COURSE
PU-2020 W. Murdock, Wichita, 67203, Sedgwick County, (316)337-9100.
Opened: 1920. **Holes:** 18. **Par:** 71/71. **Yards:** 6,330/5,048. **Course rating:** 70.5/67.9. **Slope:** 119/103. **Architect:** N/A. **Green fee:** $13/$13. **Credit cards:** None. **Reduced fees:** Twilight. **Caddies:** No. **Golf carts:** $16. **Discount golf packages:** No. **Season:** Year-round. **High:** April-Sept. **On site lodging:** No. **Rental clubs:** Yes. **Walking policy:** Unrestricted walking. **Metal spikes allowed:** Yes. **Range:** No. **To obtain tee times:** Call golf shop.

★★BRAEBURN GOLF CLUB AT WICHITA STATE UNIVERSITY
4201 E. 21st, Wichita, 67208, Sedgwick County, (316)978-4653.
Opened: 1924. **Holes:** 18. **Par:** 70/71. **Yards:** 6,320/5,301. **Course rating:** 71.6/71.4. **Slope:** 129/121. **Architect:** N/A. **Green fee:** $13/$13. **Credit cards:** MC,VISA. **Reduced fees:** Weekdays, low season, twilight, seniors, juniors. **Caddies:** No. **Golf carts:** $17. **Discount golf packages:** No. **Season:** Year-round. **High:** March-Oct. **On site lodging:** No. **Rental clubs:** Yes. **Walking policy:** Unrestricted walking. **Metal spikes allowed:** Yes. **Range:** Yes (grass/mats). **To obtain tee times:** Call Sunday at 3 p.m. for following week.

★★★BUFFALO DUNES GOLF COURSE
PM-S. Star Rte., Garden City, 67846, Finney County, (316)276-1210, 180 miles NW of Wichita.
Opened: 1976. **Holes:** 18. **Par:** 72/72. **Yards:** 6,767/5,598. **Course rating:** 72.5/72.0. **Slope:** 124/114. **Architect:** Frank Hummel. **Green fee:** $11/$14. **Credit cards:** None. **Reduced fees:** Twilight. **Caddies:** No. **Golf carts:** $18. **Discount golf packages:** No. **Season:** Year-round. **High:** April-Oct. **On site lodging:** No. **Rental clubs:** Yes. **Walking policy:** Unrestricted walking. **Metal spikes allowed:** No. **Range:** Yes (grass/mats). **To obtain tee times:** Call Mondays at 5 p.m. for following week.
Subscriber comments: Lots of wind, fun!...Narrow fairways, nasty rough, fun though...Best in Kansas...A diamond in the rough, worth the trip, easy to walk...Watch out for rattlesnakes...Built to be a challenge with a prevailing south wind.

★★CAREY PARK GOLF CLUB
PU-P.O. Box 1212, Hutchinson, 67504, Reno County, (316)694-2698, 40 miles W of Wichita.
Opened: 1930. **Holes:** 18. **Par:** 71/71. **Yards:** 6,410/5,101. **Course rating:** 69.9/69.2. **Slope:** 115/108. **Architect:** Bob Blake. **Green fee:** $9/$13. **Credit cards:** None. **Reduced fees:** Weekdays. **Caddies:** No. **Golf carts:** $16. **Discount golf packages:** No. **Season:** Year-round. **High:** N/A. **On site lodging:** No. **Rental clubs:** No. **Walking policy:** Unrestricted walking. **Metal spikes allowed:** Yes. **Range:** Yes. **To obtain tee times:** Call up to 5 days in advance.

★★★CUSTER HILL GOLF CLUB

PU-Normandy Dr., Fort Riley, 66442, Geary County, (913)239-5412, 4 miles N of Junction City.
Opened: 1957. **Holes:** 18. **Par:** 72/72. **Yards:** 7,072/5,323. **Course rating:** 74.2. **Slope:** 127. **Architect:** Robert Trent Jones. **Green fee:** $12/$15. **Credit cards:** All major. **Reduced fees:** Twilight. **Caddies:** No. **Golf carts:** $18. **Discount golf packages:** No. **Season:** Jan.-Mid-Dec. **High:** April-June. **On site lodging:** No. **Rental clubs:** No. **Walking policy:** Unrestricted walking. **Metal spikes allowed:** No. **Range:** Yes (Mats). **To obtain tee times:** Call (913)784-6000 for weekend tee times.
Subscriber comments: Good soft fairways, tough fast greens, nice and long, good pro shop on military base, so there is no tax!...Hidden treasure, classic front nine, very hilly...Small greens...Wide fairways...Greens like tilted dinner plates...From the tips it's a monster. Love it!
Special Notes: Military course.

(GOOD VALUE)

★★★★DEER CREEK GOLF CLUB

7000 W. 133rd St., Overland Park, 66209, Johnson County, (913)681-3100, 15 miles S of Kansas City.
Opened: 1989. **Holes:** 18. **Par:** 72/72. **Yards:** 6,870/5,120. **Course rating:** 74.5/68.5. **Slope:** 137/113. **Architect:** Robert Trent Jones Jr. **Green fee:** $39/$47. **Credit cards:** MC,VISA,DISC. **Reduced fees:** Weekdays, low season, twilight. **Caddies:** No. **Golf carts:** N/A. **Discount golf packages:** No. **Season:** Year-round. **High:** March-Nov. **On site lodging:** No. **Rental clubs:** Yes. **Walking policy:** Unrestricted walking. **Metal spikes allowed:** Yes. **Range:** Yes (grass). **To obtain tee times:** Call 24 hours in advance.
Subscriber comments: Good design, tough test...Very good restaurant...Very pretty course for Kansas, narrow with trees...Hard course with few level lies...Need every club in the bag!...Interesting layout. Some strange holes...Want to play it again...Long and tight...Lots of trees, lots of water, lots of balls...Lots of character.

★★★½DUB'S DREAD GOLF CLUB

PU-12601 Hollingsworth Rd., Kansas City, 66109, Wyandotte County, (913)721-1333.
Opened: 1965. **Holes:** 18. **Par:** 72/72. **Yards:** 6,987/5,454. **Course rating:** 73.6/70.4. **Slope:** 131/121. **Architect:** Bob Dunning. **Green fee:** $20/$27. **Credit cards:** MC,VISA,AMEX. **Reduced fees:** Twilight, seniors, juniors. **Caddies:** No. **Golf carts:** $12. **Discount golf packages:** No. **Season:** Year-round. **High:** April-Oct. **On site lodging:** No. **Rental clubs:** Yes. **Walking policy:** Unrestricted walking. **Metal spikes allowed:** Yes. **Range:** Yes (grass). **To obtain tee times:** Call or come in up to three days in advance. Credit card required for weekend and holidays.
Subscriber comments: Long and narrow...Soft greens, tons of trees and water...Will use all your clubs...Well done...Greens as good as you will see...New golf cart paths have ruined it...Par 3s are an adventure from the tips...A mere stone's throw from original 8,000-yard monster, but still a test...Too many dogleg holes...Reachable par 5s...Beautiful layout, some tough driving holes.

★★½EMPORIA MUNICIPAL GOLF CLUB

PM-1133 S. Hwy. 99, Emporia, 66801, Lyon County, (316)342-7666.
Opened: 1971. **Holes:** 18. **Par:** 71/71. **Yards:** 6,500/5,900. **Course rating:** 71.4/69.4. **Slope:** 118/106. **Architect:** Bob Dunning. **Green fee:** $10/$12. **Credit cards:** N/A. **Reduced fees:** Twilight, seniors, juniors. **Caddies:** No. **Golf carts:** $16. **Discount golf packages:** No. **Season:** Year-round. **High:** May-Sept. **On site lodging:** No. **Rental clubs:** Yes. **Walking policy:** Unrestricted walking. **Metal spikes allowed:** No. **Range:** Yes (grass). **To obtain tee times:** Call on Wednesday for upcoming weekend.
Subscriber comments: Never crowded, favorite course...Super greens...Worth the drive, just a really nice course...Short course with a little of everything.

★★★HERITAGE PARK GOLF COURSE

PU-16445 Lackman Rd., Olathe, 66062, Johnson County, (913)829-4653, 12 miles SE of Kansas City.
Opened: 1990. **Holes:** 18. **Par:** 71/71. **Yards:** 6,876/5,797. **Course rating:** 72.6/72.3. **Slope:** 131/121. **Architect:** Don Sechrest. **Green fee:** $18/$22. **Credit cards:**

MC,VISA. **Reduced fees:** Weekdays, low season, twilight, seniors, juniors. **Caddies:** No. **Golf carts:** $22. **Discount golf packages:** No. **Season:** Year-round. **High:** March-Oct. **On site lodging:** No. **Rental clubs:** Yes. **Walking policy:** Unrestricted walking. **Metal spikes allowed:** Yes. **Range:** Yes (grass). **To obtain tee times:** Call 2 days in advance.

Subscriber comments: Very challenging course, several tough par 3s...Well-contoured greens. Unusual routing...Long distance between some greens and tees...Looks good, plays difficult...Best to play when there is no wind...Used every club.

★★½HESSTON MUNICIPAL GOLF PARK

PM-520 Golf Course Dr., Hesston, 67062, Harvey County, (316)327-2331, 35 miles N of Wichita.

Opened: 1976. **Holes:** 18. **Par:** 71/71. **Yards:** 6,526/5,475. **Course rating:** 71.4/66.7. **Slope:** 125/118. **Architect:** Frank Hummel. **Green fee:** $9/$11. **Credit cards:** MC,VISA,DISC. **Reduced fees:** Seniors. **Caddies:** No. **Golf carts:** $9. **Discount golf packages:** No. **Season:** Year-round. **High:** May-Sept. **On site lodging:** No. **Rental clubs:** Yes. **Walking policy:** Unrestricted walking. **Metal spikes allowed:** Yes. **Range:** Yes (grass/mats). **To obtain tee times:** Call golf shop.

Subscriber comments: Front nine is wide open but back nine requires placing the ball...Beautiful greens...Great driving range...Don't play on windy days...Dry county.

★★½HIDDEN LAKES GOLF COURSE

PU-6020 S. Greenwich Rd., Derby, 67037, Sedgwick County, (316)788-2855, 6 miles SE of Wichita.

Opened: 1960. **Holes:** 18. **Par:** 72/71. **Yards:** 6,523/5,426. **Course rating:** 70.9/70.2. **Slope:** 123/120. **Architect:** Floyd Farley. **Green fee:** $9/$15. **Credit cards:** All major. **Reduced fees:** Weekdays, twilight, seniors, juniors. **Caddies:** No. **Golf carts:** $17. **Discount golf packages:** No. **Season:** Year-round. **High:** March-Oct. **On site lodging:** No. **Rental clubs:** Yes. **Walking policy:** Unrestricted walking. **Metal spikes allowed:** Yes. **Range:** Yes (grass). **To obtain tee times:** Call 7 days in advance.

Subscriber comments: Plenty of water to contend with...Some very good challenges.

★★★★IRONHORSE GOLF CLUB

PU-15400 Mission Rd., Leawood, 66224, Johnson County, (913)685-4653, 15 miles S of Kansas City.

Opened: 1995. **Holes:** 18. **Par:** 72/72. **Yards:** 6,889/4,745. **Course rating:** 73.8/67.5. **Slope:** 140/119. **Architect:** Michael Hurdzan. **Green fee:** $29/$35. **Credit cards:** MC,VISA,AMEX. **Reduced fees:** Twilight, seniors, juniors. **Caddies:** No. **Golf carts:** $13. **Discount golf packages:** No. **Season:** Year-round. **High:** April-Oct. **On site lodging:** No. **Rental clubs:** Yes. **Walking policy:** Unrestricted walking. **Metal spikes allowed:** No. **Range:** Yes. **To obtain tee times:** Call up to 3 days in advance.

Notes: Ranked 3rd in 1996 Best New Affordable Courses.

Subscriber comments: Great design...Great practice facilities. Perhaps best layout around KC...This place is a winner...Young course with jungle-like rough...Will be great once it matures...Very long and fun...Really enjoyed the elevated tee boxes.

★★½L.W. CLAPP GOLF COURSE

PM-4611 E. Harry, Wichita, 67218, Sedgwick County, (316)688-9341.

Opened: 1923. **Holes:** 18. **Par:** 70/70. **Yards:** 6,087/4,965. **Course rating:** 70.0/69.7. **Slope:** 120/110. **Architect:** N/A. **Green fee:** $13/$13. **Credit cards:** MC,VISA,AMEX. **Reduced fees:** Weekdays, twilight, seniors, juniors. **Caddies:** No. **Golf carts:** $9. **Discount golf packages:** No. **Season:** Year-round. **High:** May-Aug. **On site lodging:** No. **Rental clubs:** Yes. **Walking policy:** Unrestricted walking. **Metal spikes allowed:** Yes. **Range:** No. **To obtain tee times:** Call on Sunday at 3 p.m. for following week.

Subscriber comments: Meandering stream keeps me in trouble...Fairways too close to each other...Short but tight and a lot of creeks...Fun to play.

★★★LAKE SHAWNEE GOLF COURSE

PU-4141 S.E. East Edge Rd., Topeka, 66609, Shawnee County, (913)267-2295.

Opened: 1970. **Holes:** 18. **Par:** 69/69. **Yards:** 6,013/5,459. **Course rating:** 68.3/70.8. **Slope:** 107/113. **Architect:** Larry Flatt. **Green fee:** $9/$18. **Credit cards:** None. **Reduced fees:** Weekdays, seniors, juniors. **Caddies:** Yes. **Golf carts:** $10. **Discount golf packages:** No. **Season:** Year-round. **High:** May-Sept. **On site lodging:** No. **Rental**

clubs: Yes. **Walking policy:** Unrestricted walking. **Metal spikes allowed:** Yes. **Range:** Yes (grass/mats). **To obtain tee times:** Call 4 days in advance.
Subscriber comments: Nice hills, great pro shop, very slow play, plays short...Beautiful views of Lake Shawnee...Enjoyable course...Nice mix of holes.

★★★½MACDONALD GOLF COURSE
PU-840 N. Yale, Wichita, 67208, Sedgwick County, (316)688-9391.
Opened: 1996. **Holes:** 18. **Par:** 71/71. **Yards:** 6,837/6,347. **Course rating:** N/A. **Slope:** 119/115. **Architect:** N/A. **Green fee:** $9/$14. **Credit cards:** None. **Reduced fees:** Twilight. **Caddies:** No. **Golf carts:** $17. **Discount golf packages:** No. **Season:** Year-round. **High:** June-Aug. **On site lodging:** No. **Rental clubs:** Yes. **Walking policy:** Unrestricted walking. **Metal spikes allowed:** Yes. **Range:** No. **To obtain tee times:** Call on Sunday starting at 3 p.m. for following week.
Subscriber comments: Long and lots of trouble...Great layout, good challenge, tough course for most...A lot of big trees...A great layout recently revamped.

★★★MARIAH HILLS GOLF COURSE
PU-1800 Matt Down Lane, Dodge City, 67801, Ford County, (316)225-8182, 150 miles W of Wichita.
Opened: 1975. **Holes:** 18. **Par:** 71/73. **Yards:** 6,868/5,559. **Course rating:** 72.4/71.5. **Slope:** 118/112. **Architect:** Frank Hummel. **Green fee:** $9/$13. **Credit cards:** None. **Reduced fees:** Twilight, juniors. **Caddies:** No. **Golf carts:** $15. **Discount golf packages:** No. **Season:** Year-round. **High:** April-Oct. **On site lodging:** No. **Rental clubs:** Yes. **Walking policy:** Unrestricted walking. **Metal spikes allowed:** No. **Range:** Yes (grass). **To obtain tee times:** Call Thursday before weekend.
Subscriber comments: Long, usually windy...Huge fairways, great greens...Fairly flat terrain, good test...Wonderful surprise.

★★★OVERLAND PARK GOLF CLUB
PU-12501 Quivira Rd., Overland Park, 66213, Johnson County, (913)897-3809, 9 miles S of Kansas City.
Opened: 1970. **Holes:** 27. **Architect:** Floyd Farley/Craig Schreiner. **Green fee:** $15/$15. **Credit cards:** MC,VISA,DISC. **Reduced fees:** Twilight, seniors, juniors. **Caddies:** No. **Golf carts:** $11. **Discount golf packages:** No. **Season:** Year-round. **High:** April-Sept. **On site lodging:** No. **Rental clubs:** Yes. **Walking policy:** Walking at certain times. **Metal spikes allowed:** Yes. **Range:** Yes (grass/mats). **To obtain tee times:** Call 7 days in advance.
NORTH/WEST
Par: 70/70. **Yards:** 6,455/5,038. **Course rating:** 69.7/67.7. **Slope:** 119/108.
SOUTH/NORTH
Par: 70/71. **Yards:** 6,446/5,143. **Course rating:** 69.9/68.2. **Slope:** 113/105.
SOUTH/WEST
Par: 70/71. **Yards:** 6,367/5,067. **Course rating:** 69.9/67.9. **Slope:** 115/111.
Subscriber comments: A real treat!...Nice course...West is best...West is newer, wide open...Well run, but too many players...Don't play if you're short on time...You have to call early to get tee time...Challenging...South/North not much excitement...Removed a few bunkers to speed play, bad move...Never get tired of playing it...Very crowded.
Special Notes: Also has 9-hole executive course.

★★PAINTED HILLS GOLF COURSE
PU-7101 Parallel Pkwy., Kansas City, 66112, Wyandotte County, (913)334-1111, 6 miles W of Kansas City, MO.
Opened: 1927. **Holes:** 18. **Par:** 70/70. **Yards:** 5,914/4,698. **Course rating:** 67.7/63.5. **Slope:** 119/107. **Architect:** James Dalgleish/Jeff Brauer. **Green fee:** $16/$18. **Credit cards:** MC,VISA. **Reduced fees:** Weekdays, twilight, seniors, juniors. **Caddies:** No. **Golf carts:** $20. **Discount golf packages:** No. **Season:** Year-round. **High:** April-Sept. **On site lodging:** No. **Rental clubs:** Yes. **Walking policy:** Unrestricted walking. **Metal spikes allowed:** Yes. **Range:** No. **To obtain tee times:** Call up to 2 days in advance.
Special Notes: Formerly Victory Hills.

KANSAS

★★★PAWNEE PRAIRIE GOLF COURSE
PU-1931 S. Tyler Rd., Wichita, 67209, Sedgwick County, (316)721-7474.
Opened: 1970. **Holes:** 18. **Par:** 72/72. **Yards:** 7,361/5,928. **Course rating:** 74.8/73.3.
Slope: 123/119. **Architect:** Bob Dunning. **Green fee:** $12/$12. **Credit cards:** None.
Reduced fees: Twilight, seniors, juniors. **Caddies:** No. **Golf carts:** $17. **Discount golf packages:** No. **Season:** Year-round. **High:** May-Sept. **On site lodging:** No. **Rental clubs:** Yes. **Walking policy:** Unrestricted walking. **Metal spikes allowed:** Yes. **Range:** Yes (grass/mats). **To obtain tee times:** Call 7 days in advance starting Sunday 3:30 p.m.
Subscriber comments: Very long and always windy...Enjoyable to play...Nice greens, good water hazards.

★★★½QUAIL RIDGE GOLF COURSE
PU-3805 Quail Ridge Dr., Winfield, 67156, Cowley County, (316)221-5645, 35 miles SE of Wichita.
Opened: 1992. **Holes:** 18. **Par:** 72/72. **Yards:** 6,826/5,328. **Course rating:** 73.0/71.4. **Slope:** 125/130. **Architect:** Jerry Slack. **Green fee:** $13/$16. **Credit cards:** MC,VISA,DISC. **Reduced fees:** Weekdays, resort guests, seniors, juniors. **Caddies:** No. **Golf carts:** $9. **Discount golf packages:** Yes. **Season:** Year-round. **High:** April-Oct. **On site lodging:** Yes. **Rental clubs:** Yes. **Walking policy:** Unrestricted walking. **Metal spikes allowed:** No. **Range:** Yes (grass). **To obtain tee times:** Call up to 7 days in advance for weekdays. Call on Monday starting 8 a.m. for following weekend.

Subscriber comments: Links style. Wide open...A very nice, challenging layout...A good balance of tough holes, will get better with time...Entire course is beautiful...Fun, worth every penny...New course, one of a few courses you look forward to playing again and again...Reminds me of a small Augusta.

★★★½ROLLING MEADOWS GOLF COURSE
PM-7550 Old Milford Rd., Milford, 66514, Geary County, (913)238-4303, 60 miles W of Topeka.
Opened: 1981. **Holes:** 18. **Par:** 72/72. **Yards:** 6,879/5,515. **Course rating:** 74.0/70.7. **Slope:** 134/116. **Architect:** Richard Watson. **Green fee:** $11/$13. **Credit cards:** All major. **Reduced fees:** Weekdays, twilight.
Caddies: No. **Golf carts:** $8. **Discount golf packages:** Yes. **Season:** Year-round. **High:** April-Oct. **On site lodging:** No. **Rental clubs:** Yes. **Walking policy:** Unrestricted walking. **Metal spikes allowed:** No. **Range:** Yes (grass/mats). **To obtain tee times:** Call Wednesday a.m. for following weekend.
Subscriber comments: Every hole has its own life. Very nice...Enjoy it more each time I play it...Best-kept secret in Kansas...Better play it smart, or bring balls...Beautiful in fall...Water comes into play often and the course design is both fun and challenging. I would recommend this course as a must stop and play for the vacation traveler...Some tough holes...Awesome course for scoring. Three of the par 5s are reachable in two with drives of 230 or better. Par 4s short with very easy putting greens...If you need a confidence builder, play here.

★★½ST. ANDREWS GOLF COURSE
PU-11099 W. 135th St., Overland Park, 66221, Johnson County, (913)897-3804, 10 miles S of Kansas City.
Opened: 1962. **Holes:** 18. **Par:** 70/70. **Yards:** 6,205/4,713. **Course rating:** 69.5/67.7. **Slope:** 109/108. **Architect:** Jess Nash/John Nash. **Green fee:** $11/$13. **Credit cards:** MC,VISA. **Reduced fees:** Twilight, seniors, juniors. **Caddies:** No. **Golf carts:** $11. **Discount golf packages:** No. **Season:** Year-round. **High:** June-July. **On site lodging:** No. **Rental clubs:** Yes. **Walking policy:** Unrestricted walking. **Metal spikes allowed:** Yes. **Range:** Yes (grass). **To obtain tee times:** Call three days in advance.
Subscriber comments: Doing a lot of work, should be great...Fairly flat, a few tough holes. Building new clubhouse...Fun basic golf...Easy to walk, crowded at times.

★★★SALINA MUNICIPAL GOLF CLUB
PM-2500 E. Crawford St., Salina, 67401, Saline County, (913)826-7450.
Opened: 1969. **Holes:** 18. **Par:** 70/72. **Yards:** 6,500/5,398. **Course rating:** 72.1/71.3.

Slope: 117/116. **Architect:** Floyd Farley. **Green fee:** $9/$11. **Credit cards:** MC,VISA. **Reduced fees:** Twilight, juniors. **Caddies:** No. **Golf carts:** $9. **Discount golf packages:** No. **Season:** Year-round. **High:** April-Oct. **On site lodging:** No. **Rental clubs:** Yes. **Walking policy:** Unrestricted walking. **Metal spikes allowed:** No. **Range:** Yes (grass). **To obtain tee times:** Call up to 5 days in advance.
Subscriber comments: Good layout, good fast greens...Kansas wind makes it tough...Fun, wide open...Some challenging hills...Bring your long irons. Too long for women and me...Long ball hitter's delight. Wind and length=challenge...Makes you play well to score.

★★½STAGG HILL GOLF CLUB
4441 Ft. Riley Blvd., Manhattan, 66502, Riley County, (913)539-1041, 130 miles W of Kansas City.
Opened: 1968. **Holes:** 18. **Par:** 72/72. **Yards:** 6,697/5,642. **Course rating:** 73.1/72.1. **Slope:** 131/117. **Architect:** Richard Morse/Ray Weisenberger. **Green fee:** $14/$15. **Credit cards:** All major. **Reduced fees:** Low season, twilight, juniors. **Caddies:** No. **Golf carts:** $18. **Discount golf packages:** No. **Season:** Year-round. **High:** April-Oct. **On site lodging:** No. **Rental clubs:** Yes. **Walking policy:** Unrestricted walking. **Metal spikes allowed:** Yes. **Range:** Yes (mats). **To obtain tee times:** Members call Wednesday for weekend tee times. Nonmembers call on Thursday.
Subscriber comments: Great layout, lots of trees, thinking man's course...Easy to walk...Narrow fairways...Very challenging course, ancient cottonwoods line every hole.

★★★½SUNFLOWER HILLS GOLF CLUB
PU-122 Riverview, Bonner Springs, 66012, Wyandotte County, (913)721-2727.
Opened: 1977. **Holes:** 18. **Par:** 72/73. **Yards:** 7,001/5,850. **Course rating:** 73.3/72.6. **Slope:** 124/124. **Architect:** Roger Packard. **Green fee:** $13/$19. **Credit cards:** MC,VISA. **Reduced fees:** Weekdays, twilight, seniors, juniors. **Caddies:** No. **Golf carts:** $22. **Discount golf packages:** No. **Season:** Year-round. **High:** April-Sept. **On site lodging:** No. **Rental clubs:** Yes. **Walking policy:** Unrestricted walking. **Metal spikes allowed:** Yes. **Range:** Yes (grass/mats). **To obtain tee times:** Call 4 days in advance.
Subscriber comments: Can be long if played to the hilt...An excellent course. Fun to play...A nice test with variation...Very fair course to play. Lots of fun...Can't wait to play again...Somewhat hilly...Very tough course to score...Interesting design...If it's windy, you're in for a long day.

★★★½TERRADYNE RESORT HOTEL & COUNTRY CLUB
R-1400 Terradyne, Andover, 67002, Butler County, (316)733-5851, (800)892-4613, 10 miles E of Wichita.
Opened: 1987. **Holes:** 18. **Par:** 71/71. **Yards:** 6,704/5,048. **Course rating:** 74.3/70.2. **Slope:** 139/121. **Architect:** Don Sechrest. **Green fee:** $25/$75. **Credit cards:** MC,VISA,AMEX. **Reduced fees:** Resort guests. **Caddies:** No. **Golf carts:** $10. **Discount golf packages:** Yes. **Season:** Year-round. **High:** April-Oct. **On site lodging:** Yes. **Rental clubs:** Yes. **Walking policy:** Unrestricted walking. **Metal spikes allowed:** No. **Range:** Yes (grass). **To obtain tee times:** Resort guests call 7 days in advance.
Subscriber comments: Links style, huge greens...Test for better players...Tough in wind...Better hit it straight here. If you didn't know better you might think you were in Scotland...Tall rough too punishing...If you're in the area, play it...Hit the fairways and you'll enjoy the course.

★★½TOMAHAWK HILLS GOLF CLUB
PU-17501 Midland Dr., Shawnee, 66218, Johnson County, (913)631-8000, 5 miles S of Kansas City.
Opened: 1911. **Holes:** 18. **Par:** 70/71. **Yards:** 6,003/5,643. **Course rating:** 69.1/71.1. **Slope:** 118/117. **Architect:** Bill Leonard. **Green fee:** $15/$19. **Credit cards:** MC,VISA. **Reduced fees:** Weekdays, low season, twilight, seniors, juniors. **Caddies:** No. **Golf carts:** $22. **Discount golf packages:** No. **Season:** Year-round. **High:** April-Oct. **On site lodging:** No. **Rental clubs:** Yes. **Walking policy:** Unrestricted walking. **Metal spikes allowed:** Yes. **Range:** Yes (grass/mats). **To obtain tee times:** Call 2 days in advance.
Subscriber comments: Hilly...Holes #9 and #18 are unique. Hit off a cliff to green... Course is tougher if you walk, lots of hills...Fun to play.

★★½TOPEKA PUBLIC GOLF CLUB
PM-2533 S.W. Urish Rd., Topeka, 66614, Shawnee County, (913)272-0511.
Opened: 1954. **Holes:** 18. **Par:** 71/71. **Yards:** 6,335/5,468. **Course rating:** 70.0/70.1.
Slope: 114/114. **Architect:** William Leonard/L.J. "Dutch" McLellan. **Green fee:** $12/$12.
Credit cards: MC,VISA. **Reduced fees:** Seniors, juniors. **Caddies:** No. **Golf carts:**
$10. **Discount golf packages:** Yes. **Season:** Year-round. **High:** May-Sept. **On site
lodging:** No. **Rental clubs:** Yes. **Walking policy:** Unrestricted walking. **Metal spikes
allowed:** Yes. **Range:** Yes (grass). **To obtain tee times:** Call Tuesday after 7 a.m. for
weekends and holidays only.
Subscriber comments: Very nice course, some real challenges...Sometimes slow...
Wide fairways...Rather plain, but still a fun round, no surprises.

★★★½TURKEY CREEK GOLF COURSE
PU-1000 Fox Run, McPherson, 67460, McPherson County, (316)241-8530.
Opened: 1990. **Holes:** 18. **Par:** 70/69. **Yards:** 6,241/4,723. **Course rating:** 71.3/66.7.
Slope: 125/112. **Architect:** Phil Smith. **Green fee:** $12/$14. **Credit cards:** MC,VISA.
Reduced fees: Weekdays. **Caddies:** No. **Golf carts:** $18. **Discount golf packages:**
Yes. **Season:** Year-round. **High:** April-Sept. **On site lodging:** No. **Rental clubs:** Yes.
Walking policy: Unrestricted walking. **Metal spikes allowed:** No. **Range:** Yes (grass).
To obtain tee times: Call 7 days in advance for weekdays. Call on Wednesday for
upcoming weekend or holiday.
Subscriber comments: Better play smart...Need to hit it down the middle...Tough and
fun...Bring extra balls...Excellent greens. Fun to play...Good for women...Tough greens;
challenging makes you think and use course management... Lots of water...Rough is
tough...Great course, check it out...A nice course, worth playing, but not after it rains.

★★★VILLAGE GREENS GOLF CLUB
Box 1, Ozawkie, 66070, Jefferson County, (913)876-2255.
Call club for further information.
Subscriber comments: Great charm and personality...Nicely laid out. A
course a person can go after without getting into much trouble...Mom
and Pop course that is great fun...Unexpected but pleasant
surprise...Watch out for the wind!...Good greens. Fun to play.

★★½WELLINGTON GOLF CLUB
PM-1500 W. Harvey, Wellington, 67152, Sumner County, (316)326-7904.
Opened: 1919. **Holes:** 18. **Par:** 70/70. **Yards:** 6,201/5,384. **Course rating:** 70.5/70.9.
Slope: 135/113. **Architect:** Built by members. **Green fee:** $10/$12. **Credit cards:**
MC,VISA. **Reduced fees:** Weekdays, twilight. **Caddies:** No. **Golf carts:** $15. **Discount
golf packages:** No. **Season:** Year-round. **High:** April-Sept. **On site lodging:** No.
Rental clubs: Yes. **Walking policy:** Unrestricted walking. **Metal spikes allowed:** No.
Range: Yes (grass/mats). **To obtain tee times:** Call up to 7 days in advance.
Subscriber comments: Very fast greens...Small-town golf course with big-time
look...Will bring you to your knees...Small undulating greens...Floods in places.

★★½WESTERN HILLS GOLF CLUB
8533 S.W. 21st. St., Topeka, 66615, Shawnee County, (913)478-4000.
Opened: 1967. **Holes:** 18. **Par:** 70/70. **Yards:** 6,089/4,728. **Course rating:** 69.2/66.1.
Slope: 121/110. **Architect:** Maury Bell. **Green fee:** $12/$14. **Credit cards:** All major.
Reduced fees: N/A. **Caddies:** No. **Golf carts:** $10. **Discount golf packages:** No.
Season: Year-round. **High:** April-Sept. **On site lodging:** No. **Rental clubs:** Yes.
Walking policy: Unrestricted walking. **Metal spikes allowed:** Yes. **Range:** No. **To
obtain tee times:** Call Wednesday for weekend tee time.
Subscriber comments: Very tight...Back nine the better...Stay in fairway...Great
greens, long from blues...Nice clubhouse for a drink, food...Good par 5s, a fair course.

★★★½WILLOW BEND GOLF CLUB
8001 E. Mulberry, Wichita, 67226, Sedgwick County, (316)636-4653.
Call club for further information.
Subscriber comments: Good course with challenging holes, needs more H2O...Good
variety. Two short par 4s are brilliant holes...Great use of water to direct play, layups and
go-for-its...Let the wind blow and watch out...A nice play to play...Fun for all levels.

★★½A.J. JOLLY GOLF COURSE
5350 South U.S. 27, Alexandria, 41001, Campbell County, (606)635-2106.
Call club for further information.
Subscriber comments: Always in very good shape...Carved out of hilly terrain...Fun...
Fair layout, scenic location...No.10 is intimidating...Lots of water, scenic.

★★½BARREN RIVER STATE PARK GOLF COURSE
PU-1149 State Park Rd., Lucas, 42156, Barren County, (502)646-4653, 30 miles SE of
Bowling Green.
Opened: 1957. **Holes:** 18. **Par:** 72/72. **Yards:** 6,440/4,919. **Course rating:** 69.1/66.6.
Slope: 118/106. **Architect:** Edward Lawrence Packard. **Green fee:** $16/$16. **Credit
cards:** All major. **Reduced fees:** Twilight. **Caddies:** No. **Golf carts:** $9. **Discount golf
packages:** Yes. **Season:** Year-round. **High:** April-Sept. **On site lodging:** Yes. **Rental
clubs:** Yes. **Walking policy:** Unrestricted walking. **Metal spikes allowed:** Yes. **Range:**
Yes. **To obtain tee times:** Call anytime.
Subscriber comments: Beautiful and fun...Tight...Great views, very well kept...Deer
and other wild critters everywhere...Hilly, treelined, challenging...Scenic.

★★BOB-O-LINK GOLF COURSE
PU-1014 Mary Elizabeth, Lawrenceburg, 40849, Anderson County, (502)839-4029, 35
miles SW of Lexington.
Opened: 1968. **Holes:** 18. **Par:** 71/71. **Yards:** 6,430/4,889. **Course rating:** 69.7/67.5.
Slope: 109/105. **Architect:** Harold England/Jack Ridge. **Green fee:** $14/$16. **Credit
cards:** MC,VISA,DISC. **Reduced fees:** Weekdays, low season, juniors. **Caddies:** Yes.
Golf carts: $10. **Discount golf packages:** No. **Season:** Year-round. **High:** April-Oct.
On site lodging: No. **Rental clubs:** Yes. **Walking policy:** Walking at certain times.
Metal spikes allowed: Yes. **Range:** Yes (grass). **To obtain tee times:** Call golf shop.
Subscriber comments: Very average golf course...Water in play on nine holes...Basic
golf...Rough needs work...Average, small-town course...Generally in decent shape.

★★★BOONE LINKS
PU-19 Clubhouse Dr., Florence, 41042, Boone County, (606)371-7550, 10 miles S of
Cincinnati.
Opened: 1980. **Holes:** 27. **Architect:** Robert von Hagge/Michael Hurdzan. **Green fee:**
$20. **Credit cards:** MC,VISA. **Reduced fees:** Seniors, juniors. **Caddies:** No. **Golf
carts:** $10. **Discount golf packages:** No. **Season:** Feb-Dec. **High:** May-Aug. **On site
lodging:** No. **Rental clubs:** Yes. **Walking policy:** Unrestricted walking. **Metal spikes
allowed:** Yes. **Range:** No. **To obtain tee times:** Call 7 days in advance at 7:30 a.m.
BROOKVIEW/LAKEVIEW
Par: 72/72. **Yards:** 6,634/5,648. **Course rating:** 72.1/71.1. **Slope:** 128/123.
BROOKVIEW/RIDGEVIEW
Par: 70/70. **Yards:** 5,950/4,725. **Course rating:** 68.4/69.2. **Slope:** 118/122.
RIDGEVIEW/LAKEVIEW
Par: 70/70. **Yards:** 6,110/4,749. **Course rating:** 69.2/66.8. **Slope:** 122/113.
Subscriber comments: Long, wide open...Short nine perfect for kids...Watch out for
low flying airplanes, take earplugs...Good course, always in great shape...27-hole lay-
out, barely had room for 18...Rolling hills, well manicured...A lot of uphill blind
shots...Scenic, fun to play.

★★½BRIGHT LEAF GOLF RESORT
R-200 Adams Lane, 1742 Danville Rd., Harrodsburg, 40330, Mercer County, (606)734-
4231, (800)469-6038, 29 miles SW of Lexington.
Opened: 1966. **Holes:** 18. **Par:** 72/77. **Yards:** 6,474/5,800. **Course rating:** 69.8/66.1.
Slope: 118/109. **Architect:** Buck Blankenship. **Green fee:** $15/$17. **Credit cards:**
MC,VISA. **Reduced fees:** Weekdays, low season, twilight. **Caddies:** No. **Golf carts:**
$20. **Discount golf packages:** No. **Season:** March-Oct. **High:** March-Oct. **On site
lodging:** Yes. **Rental clubs:** Yes. **Walking policy:** Unrestricted walking. **Metal spikes
allowed:** Yes. **Range:** No. **To obtain tee times:** Call 7 days in advance.
Subscriber comments: Heavy play...Wide open...Nice lighted par 3 course on premis-
es...A grand spot...Better in the spring...Great for groups, good restaurant on site.
Special Notes: Also 9-hole course.

★★CABIN BROOK GOLF CLUB
PU-2260 Lexington Rd., Versailles, 40383, Woodford County, (606)873-8404, 7 miles W of Lexington.
Opened: 1965. **Holes:** 18. **Par:** 72/72. **Yards:** 7,017/5,233. **Course rating:** 72.4/68.3. **Slope:** 117/108. **Architect:** Danny McQueen. **Green fee:** $12/$14. **Credit cards:** MC,VISA. **Reduced fees:** N/A. **Caddies:** No. **Golf carts:** $8. **Discount golf packages:** No. **Season:** Year-round. **High:** May-Sept. **On site lodging:** No. **Rental clubs:** Yes. **Walking policy:** Walking at certain times. **Metal spikes allowed:** Yes. **Range:** Yes (grass). **To obtain tee times:** Call 7 days in advance.

★★CHARLIE VETTINER GOLF COURSE
PM-10207 Mary Dell Lane, Jeffersontown, 40299, Jefferson County, (502)267-9958, 25 miles SE of Louisville.
Opened: 1967. **Holes:** 18. **Par:** 72/73. **Yards:** 6,914/5,388. **Course rating:** 72.3/70.0. **Slope:** 123/116. **Architect:** Jack Kidwell/Michael Hurdzan. **Green fee:** $7/$7. **Credit cards:** None. **Reduced fees:** Twilight, seniors. **Caddies:** No. **Golf carts:** $9. **Discount golf packages:** No. **Season:** Year-round. **High:** April-Sept. **On site lodging:** No. **Rental clubs:** Yes. **Walking policy:** Unrestricted walking. **Metal spikes allowed:** Yes. **Range:** No. **To obtain tee times:** Call two days in advance.

★★CONNEMARA GOLF LINKS
PU-2327 Lexington Rd., Nicholasville, 40356, Jessamine County, (606)885-4331, 7 miles S of Lexington.
Opened: 1992. **Holes:** 18. **Par:** 71/71. **Yards:** 6,533/4,956. **Course rating:** 71.1/69.5. **Slope:** 115/111. **Architect:** Jack Ridge. **Green fee:** $14/$18. **Credit cards:** All major. **Reduced fees:** Weekdays, low season, twilight, seniors, juniors. **Caddies:** No. **Golf carts:** $9. **Discount golf packages:** No. **Season:** Year-round. **High:** April-Sept. **On site lodging:** No. **Rental clubs:** Yes. **Walking policy:** Walking at certain times. **Metal spikes allowed:** Yes. **Range:** Yes (grass/mats). **To obtain tee times:** Call 5 days in advance. Tee times will be accepted further in advance for long-distance travelers.

★★★★CROOKED CREEK GOLF CLUB
781 Crooked Creek Dr., London, 40744, Laurel County, (606)877-1993, 66 miles S of Lexington.
Opened: 1993. **Holes:** 18. **Par:** 72/72. **Yards:** 7,007/5,087. **Course rating:** 73.4/71.3. **Slope:** 134/122. **Architect:** Brian M. Silva. **Green fee:** $20/$28. **Credit cards:** MC,VISA. **Reduced fees:** Weekdays, low season, twilight, juniors. **Caddies:** No. **Golf carts:** $91. **Discount golf packages:** No. **Season:** Year-round. **High:** March-Oct. **On site lodging:** No. **Rental clubs:** Yes. **Walking policy:** Unrestricted walking. **Metal spikes allowed:** Yes. **Range:** Yes (grass). **To obtain tee times:** Call up to 14 days in advance.
Subscriber comments: Very scenic...Very good course, tight, keep ball in play...Awesome, great imagination...Very challenging, good layout...Excellent course when it matures...Good variety of holes and shots, lots of character...A beautiful course...Interesting par 3s...Deep rough...Tight course, lots of trees, nicest in the area.

★★DEVOU PARK GOLF COURSE
PM-1344 Audubon Rd., Covington, 41011, Kenton County, (606)431-8030, 2 miles S of Cincinnati, OH.
Opened: 1928. **Holes:** 18. **Par:** 70/70. **Yards:** 6,091/5,065. **Course rating:** 65.8/66.7. **Slope:** 112/110. **Architect:** N/A. **Green fee:** $9/$18. **Credit cards:** MC,VISA. **Reduced fees:** N/A. **Caddies:** No. **Golf carts:** $10. **Discount golf packages:** No. **Season:** Year-round. **High:** May-Sept. **On site lodging:** No. **Rental clubs:** Yes. **Walking policy:** Unrestricted walking. **Metal spikes allowed:** Yes. **Range:** No. **To obtain tee times:** Call up to 7 days in advance.

★★★DOE VALLEY GOLF CLUB
1 Doe Valley Pkwy., Brandenburg, 40108, Meade County, (502)422-3397, 30 miles SW of Louisville.
Opened: 1972. **Holes:** 18. **Par:** 71/72. **Yards:** 6,471/5,519. **Course rating:** 69.8/70.3. **Slope:** 119/118. **Architect:** Dick Watson. **Green fee:** $13/$32. **Credit cards:** MC,VISA,AMEX. **Reduced fees:** Twilight, seniors. **Caddies:** No. **Golf carts:** $12.

Discount golf packages: Yes. Season: Year-round. High: April-Sept. On site lodging: No. Rental clubs: Yes. Walking policy: Walking at certain times. Metal spikes allowed: Yes. Range: No. To obtain tee times: Call seven days in advance.
Subscriber comments: Very good course with potential if maintained...Tough back nine...Large pond on 18th hole...Very hilly with woods and wildlife...A beautiful and scenic course with about five challenging holes...Great country setting...Heavy wooded, narrow fairways...Could be made into terrific course.

★★★½EAGLE TRACE GOLF COURSE
1000 Ramey Ridge Rd., Morehead, 40351, Rowan County, (606)783-9973, 60 miles W of Lexington.
Opened: 1995. Holes: 18. Par: 72/72. Yards: 6,902/5,247. Course rating: 73.8/70.8. Slope: 139/127. Architect: David Pfaff. Green fee: $20/$24. Credit cards: All major. Reduced fees: Low season, twilight, seniors, juniors. Caddies: No. Golf carts: $9. Discount golf packages: No. Season: Year-round. High: April-Sept. On site lodging: No. Rental clubs: Yes. Walking policy: Unrestricted walking. Metal spikes allowed: Yes. Range: Yes (grass/mats). To obtain tee times: Call 8 days in advance.
Subscriber comments: Great place to play...Outstanding course...Potential to be one of state's best...Very challenging, makes you think...Great new course, too many dogleg lefts for slicers...Very tight, must place every shot...Beautiful golf course, tight fairways, lots of trees...Nice new course in an area starved for decent courses.

★★★EAGLE'S NEST COUNTRY CLUB
Hwy. 39 N., Somerset, 42501, Pulaski County, (606)679-7754, 70 miles S of Lexington.
Opened: 1979. Holes: 18. Par: 71/72. Yards: 6,404/5,010. Course rating: 69.8/67.9. Slope: 123/117. Architect: Ben Wihry. Green fee: $21/$21. Credit cards: MC,VISA. Reduced fees: N/A. Caddies: No. Golf carts: $10. Discount golf packages: No. Season: Feb.-Dec. High: May-Oct. On site lodging: No. Rental clubs: Yes. Walking policy: Unrestricted walking. Metal spikes allowed: Yes. Range: Yes (grass). To obtain tee times: Call in advance. If you live in the county you must be a member of the course to play.
Subscriber comments: Good greens...No.1 and No.10 too gimmicky...Plays through neighborhood...Some interesting holes over ravines...Challenging, tight fairways, hilly.

FAIRWAY GOLF COURSE
PU-4940 Hwy. 227 N, Wheatley, 40359, Owen County, (502)463-2338, (888)289-1417, 50 miles N of Louisville.
Opened: 1960. Holes: 18. Par: 70/70. Yards: 5,900/5,400. Course rating: 66.0/68.6. Slope: 100/101. Architect: Harold England. Green fee: $22/$24. Credit cards: MC,VISA,AMEX. Reduced fees: Low season, juniors. Caddies: No. Golf carts: Included in Green Fee. Discount golf packages: No. Season: Year-round. High: April-Oct. On site lodging: No. Rental clubs: No. Walking policy: Unrestricted walking. Metal spikes allowed: Yes. Range: Yes (grass). To obtain tee times: Call up to 14 days in advance.

★★★½FRANCES E. MILLER GOLF COURSE
PU-2814 Pottertown Rd., Murray, 42071, Calloway County, (502)762-2238, 50 miles SE of Paducah.
Opened: 1983. Holes: 18. Par: 71/71. Yards: 6,592/5,058. Course rating: 71.6/68.9. Slope: 125/117. Architect: Jack Kidwell/Michael Hurdzan. Green fee: $7/$15. Credit cards: MC,VISA. Reduced fees: Twilight, seniors, juniors. Caddies: No. Golf carts: $17. Discount golf packages: No. Season: Year-round. High: May-Aug. On site lodging: No. Rental clubs: Yes. Walking policy: Walking at certain times. Metal spikes allowed: Yes. Range: Yes (grass). To obtain tee times: Call golf shop.
Subscriber comments: Nice hilly layout, some tight holes...Great greens...Fine, challenging course, varied nines...Rough means "rough"...Good layout, built for Murray State University.

★★GENERAL BURNSIDE STATE PARK GOLF COURSE
PU-P.O. Box 488, Burnside, 42519, Pulaski County, (606)561-4104, 71 miles S of Lexington.
Opened: 1958. Holes: 18. Par: 71/71. Yards: 5,905/5,905. Course rating: 67.5/71.6. Slope: N/A. Architect: N/A. Green fee: $14/$14. Credit cards: All major. Reduced

KENTUCKY

fees: Twilight, seniors. **Caddies:** No. **Golf carts:** $9. **Discount golf packages:** No. **Season:** Year-round. **High:** April-Sept. **On site lodging:** No. **Rental clubs:** Yes. **Walking policy:** Unrestricted walking. **Metal spikes allowed:** Yes. **Range:** No. **To obtain tee times:** Call anytime.

★★★½GIBSON BAY GOLF COURSE
PU-2000 Gibson Bay Dr., Richmond, 40475, Madison County, (606)623-0225, 20 miles S of Lexington.
Opened: 1993. **Holes:** 18. **Par:** 72/72. **Yards:** 7,113/5,069. **Course rating:** 74.1/69.1. **Slope:** 128/115. **Architect:** Michael Hurdzan. **Green fee:** $10/$14. **Credit cards:** MC,VISA. **Reduced fees:** Weekdays, twilight, seniors, juniors. **Caddies:** No. **Golf carts:** $8. **Discount golf packages:** No. **Season:** Year-round. **High:** N/A. **On site lodging:** No. **Rental clubs:** Yes. **Walking policy:** Unrestricted walking. **Metal spikes allowed:** Yes. **Range:** Yes (grass/mats). **To obtain tee times:** Call 7 days in advance.
Subscriber comments: Great course...Central Kentucky's best...Long, nice fairways... Incredible layout...Needs trees...The greens are small but the fairways are wide...Lots of elevation changes...Great challenge, diversity...Open, rolling...Finding ball in cut rough very difficult...Yardage could be better marked...Good test, well maintained.

(GREAT VALUE)

THE GOLF COURSES AT KENTON COUNTY
PU-3908 Richardson Rd., Independence, 41051, Kenton County, (606)371-3200.
Credit cards: MC,VISA. **Caddies:** No. **Discount golf packages:** No. **On site lodging:** No. **Rental clubs:** Yes. **Metal spikes allowed:** Yes. **Range:** Yes (grass/mats). **To obtain tee times:** Call or come in up to 9 days in advance for weekends and 7 days in advance for weekdays.

★★★½FOX RUN COURSE
Opened: 1992. **Holes:** 18. **Par:** 72/72. **Yards:** 7,055/4,707. **Course rating:** 74.8/68.1. **Slope:** 143/123. **Architect:** Arthur Hills. **Green fee:** $36. **Reduced fees:** N/A. **Golf carts:** Included in Green Fee. **Season:** April-Oct. **High:** May-Aug. **Walking policy:** Mandatory cart.
Notes: Ranked 9th in 1997 Best in State.
Subscriber comments: Great place, what a challenge...Never a level lie, too tricky for weekenders...Tough from the tips...No.17 and 18 too gimmicky...Slow-play rules enforced...No adjoining fairways...Target layout, will punish...Play only if you think you're great...Challenging and scenic...Tough Arthur Hills layout, No.18 one tough par 5...Hilly but enjoyable to play.

★★½PIONEER COURSE
Opened: 1968. **Holes:** 18. **Par:** 70/71. **Yards:** 6,059/5,336. **Course rating:** 67.9/69.5. **Slope:** 114/115. **Architect:** Taylor Boyd. **Green fee:** $8/$16. **Reduced fees:** Weekdays, seniors, juniors. **Golf carts:** $11. **Season:** Year-round. **High:** May-Aug. **Walking policy:** Unrestricted walking.
Subscriber comments: Short but tough in spots...Monster 16th hole...Least challenging of the three courses...Nice for beginners...Short, even from blues, No.16 great..

★★★WILLOWS COURSE
Opened: 1976. **Holes:** 18. **Par:** 72/72. **Yards:** 6,791/5,669. **Course rating:** 72.5/74.0. **Slope:** 130/129. **Architect:** Jack Kidwell/Michael Hurdzan. **Green fee:** $14/$19. **Reduced fees:** Seniors, juniors. **Golf carts:** $10. **Season:** March-Nov. **High:** May-Sept. **Walking policy:** Unrestricted walking.
Subscriber comments: Nice course, lot of play, good scores can be shot here...Medium length, good course, always in good shape...Back nine is a good test...Nice veranda overlooks 18th...Rolling fairways...Back nine is my favorite in area.

★★★HARTLAND MUNICIPAL GOLF COURSE
PU-1031 Wilkinson Trace, Bowling Green, 42103, Warren County, (502)843-5559, (800)786-7263, 45 miles N of Nashville, TN.
Opened: 1989. **Holes:** 18. **Par:** 71/72. **Yards:** 6,512/5,044. **Course rating:** 69.9/68.3. **Slope:** 119/113. **Architect:** Kevin Tucker. **Green fee:** $12/$15. **Credit cards:** MC,VISA,AMEX. **Reduced fees:** Weekdays, low season, twilight, seniors, juniors. **Caddies:** No. **Golf carts:** $9. **Discount golf packages:** No. **Season:** Year-round. **High:** July-Aug. **On site lodging:** No. **Rental clubs:** Yes. **Walking policy:** Walking at certain times. **Metal spikes allowed:** Yes. **Range:** No. **To obtain tee times:** Call 7 days in advance.

Subscriber comments: Flat course...OK...Good use of traps and ponds.

HOUSTON OAKS GOLF COURSE
4285 Lexington Rd., Paris, 40361, Bourbon County, (606)987-5600, 12 miles E of Lexington.
Opened: 1996. Holes: 18. Par: 72/73. Yards: 6,842/5,079. Course rating: 73.9/69.3.
Slope: 127/114. Architect: Jack Ridge. Green fee: $16/$19. Credit cards:
MC,VISA,AMEX. Reduced fees: N/A. Caddies: No. Golf carts: $9. Discount golf
packages: No. Season: Year-round. High: May-Sept. On site lodging: No. Rental
clubs: Yes. Walking policy: Unrestricted walking. Metal spikes allowed: No. Range:
Yes (grass). To obtain tee times: Call up to 7 days in advance.

★★½INDIAN SPRINGS GOLF CLUB
3408 Indian Lake Dr., Louisville, 40241, Jefferson County, (502)426-7111, 8 miles NE
of Downtown Louisville.
Opened: 1994. Holes: 18. Par: 72/72. Yards: 6,799/5,253. Course rating: 71.4/68.4.
Slope: 133/122. Architect: N/A. Green fee: $22/$28. Credit cards: MC,VISA.
Reduced fees: Low season, twilight, juniors. Caddies: No. Golf carts: $5. Discount
golf packages: No. Season: Year-round. High: May-Sept. On site lodging: No. Rental
clubs: Yes. Walking policy: Unrestricted walking. Metal spikes allowed: Yes. Range:
Yes (grass). To obtain tee times: Call up to 3 days in advance.
Subscriber comments: Good, fair design; good greens...Houses too close...Ruination
of good farmland...Very scenic par 3s...Difficult back-to-back par 5s (9 and 10).

★★IROQUOIS GOLF COURSE
PU-1501 Rundill Rd., Louisville, 40214, Jefferson County, (502)363-9520.
Opened: 1947. Holes: 18. Par: 71/73. Yards: 6,138/5,004. Course rating: 67.3/70.2.
Slope: 106/112. Architect: Robert Bruce Harris. Green fee: $5/$9. Credit cards:
None. Reduced fees: Twilight, seniors, juniors. Caddies: No. Golf carts: $10.
Discount golf packages: No. Season: Year-round. High: April-Nov. On site lodging:
No. Rental clubs: Yes. Walking policy: Unrestricted walking. Metal spikes allowed:
No. Range: No. To obtain tee times: Call 2 days in advance.

★★JUNIPER HILLS GOLF COURSE
PU-800 Louisville Rd., Frankfort, 40601, Franklin County, (502)875-8559, 35 miles W of
Louisville.
Opened: 1956. Holes: 18. Par: 70/74. Yards: 6,200/5,904. Course rating: 68.7/67.7.
Slope: 111/106. Architect: Buck Blankenship. Green fee: $10/$10. Credit cards:
None. Reduced fees: Twilight. Caddies: No. Golf carts: $10. Discount golf pack-
ages: No. Season: Year-round. High: April-Oct. On site lodging: No. Rental clubs:
Yes. Walking policy: Unrestricted walking. Metal spikes allowed: Yes. Range: No. To
obtain tee times: Call 7 days in advance.

★★★★KEARNEY HILL GOLF LINKS
PM-3403 Kearney Rd., Lexington, 40511, Fayette County, (606)253-
1981.

(GOOD VALUE)

Opened: 1989. Holes: 18. Par: 72/72. Yards: 6,987/5,362. Course rating: 73.5/70.1. Slope: 128/118. Architect: P.B. Dye & Pete Dye. Green
fee: $20/$20. Credit cards: MC,VISA. Reduced fees: Twilight, seniors,
juniors. Caddies: No. Golf carts: N/A. Discount golf packages: No. Season: Year-
round. High: April-Oct. On site lodging: No. Rental clubs: Yes. Walking policy:
Unrestricted walking. Metal spikes allowed: Yes. Range: Yes (grass). To obtain tee
times: Call up to seven days in advance for threesomes or foursomes.
Notes: Ranked 10th in 1997 Best in State.
Subscriber comments: Senior Tour stop...Beautiful track...Good greens, nice fairways,
hard to get on...My favorite links-style course in area...Be prepared for wind and three-
putts...Better to walk than ride. Carts must stay on path...Simply superb...Challenging
four finishing holes...If you can't putt, forget it...Better conditioned than my country
club...Wide open and long...Some great holes on bargain Dye layout.

★★★KENTUCKY DAM VILLAGE STATE RESORT PARK GOLF COURSE
R-Highway 641, Gilbertsville, 42044, Marshall County, (502)362-8658, (800)295-1877,
20 miles E of Paducah.

Opened: 1952. **Holes:** 18. **Par:** 72/72. **Yards:** 6,704/5,094. **Course rating:** 73.0/70.0. **Slope:** 135/124. **Architect:** Perry Maxwell/Press Maxwell. **Green fee:** $16/$16. **Credit cards:** All major. **Reduced fees:** Twilight. **Caddies:** No. **Golf carts:** N/A. **Discount golf packages:** Yes. **Season:** Year-round. **High:** March-Oct. **On site lodging:** Yes. **Rental clubs:** Yes. **Walking policy:** Unrestricted walking. **Metal spikes allowed:** Yes. **Range:** Yes (grass). **To obtain tee times:** Call golf shop.
Subscriber comments: Good condition...Lots of traffic...Good layout, heavily played...Tight treelined fairways, beautiful in fall...Challenging state-park course, excellent greens...Nice course for a state park...The village's other treat, besides fishing.

★★LA GRANGE WOODS COUNTRY CLUB
2820 S. Hwy. 53, La Grange, 40031, Oldham County, (502)222-7927.
Opened: 1970. **Holes:** 18. **Par:** 71/71. **Yards:** 6,104/4,577. **Course rating:** 68.9/65.8. **Slope:** 115/106. **Architect:** Buck Blankenship/Rick Crawford. **Green fee:** $12/$16. **Credit cards:** MC,VISA. **Reduced fees:** Weekdays, seniors. **Caddies:** No. **Golf carts:** N/A. **Discount golf packages:** Yes. **Season:** Year-round. **High:** March-Oct. **On site lodging:** No. **Rental clubs:** Yes. **Walking policy:** Walking at certain times. **Metal spikes allowed:** Yes. **Range:** Yes. **To obtain tee times:** Call seven days in advance.

★★★LAKE BARKLEY STATE PARK
PU-Hwy. 68 W., Cadiz, 42211, Trigg County, (502)924-9076, (800)295-1878, 80 miles NE of Nashville.
Opened: 1972. **Holes:** 18. **Par:** 72/73. **Yards:** 6,751/5,191. **Course rating:** 72.7/70.2. **Slope:** 131/121. **Architect:** Edward Lawrence Packard. **Green fee:** $16/$16. **Credit cards:** All major. **Reduced fees:** Twilight. **Caddies:** No. **Golf carts:** $18. **Discount golf packages:** No. **Season:** Year-round. **High:** May-Oct. **On site lodging:** Yes. **Rental clubs:** Yes. **Walking policy:** Unrestricted walking. **Metal spikes allowed:** Yes. **Range:** Yes (grass/mats). **To obtain tee times:** Call up to one year in advance.
Subscriber comments: Beautiful setting...Nice greens and scenic trees...18 is a tough finishing hole...Nice, roomy course...Very nice state-park course...Good layout, fun to play...Long course with undulating greens.

★★½LAKESIDE GOLF CLUB
PU-3725 Richmond Rd., Lexington, 40509, Fayette County, (606)263-5315.
Opened: 1970. **Holes:** 18. **Par:** 72/72. **Yards:** 6,844/5,269. **Course rating:** 72.2/69.6. **Slope:** 123/116. **Architect:** Bob Carr. **Green fee:** $10/$10. **Credit cards:** MC,VISA. **Reduced fees:** Twilight, seniors, juniors. **Caddies:** No. **Golf carts:** $7. **Discount golf packages:** No. **Season:** Year-round. **High:** April-Sept. **On site lodging:** No. **Rental clubs:** Yes. **Walking policy:** Unrestricted walking. **Metal spikes allowed:** Yes. **Range:** Yes (grass). **To obtain tee times:** Threesomes and foursomes may call up to 7 days in advance.
Subscriber comments: Heavily played...Boring...Must be the most popular course in state...Very challenging, tough 615-yard finisher...Lots of traffic...Good fairways.

★★★★LASSING POINTE GOLF CLUB
PU-2266 Double Eagle Dr., Union, 41091, Boone County, (606)384-2266, 12 miles S of Cincinnati.
Opened: 1994. **Holes:** 18. **Par:** 71/71. **Yards:** 6,724/5,153. **Course rating:** 72.2/69.5. **Slope:** 132/122. **Architect:** Michael Hurdzan. **Green fee:** $26. **Credit cards:** MC,VISA. **Reduced fees:** Seniors, juniors. **Caddies:** No. **Golf carts:** $10. **Discount golf packages:** No. **Season:** April-Oct. **High:** May-Sept. **On site lodging:** No. **Rental clubs:** Yes. **Walking policy:** Unrestricted walking. **Metal spikes allowed:** Yes. **Range:** Yes (grass/mats). **To obtain tee times:** Call 7 days in advance for weekdays.

GOOD VALUE

Notes: Ranked 5th in 1997 Best in State.
Subscriber comments: Great course for all levels...One of the best in Kentucky...Challenging, love the 18th green...Over the river and through the woods...Great condition, four tees to choose from. Fair and fun...Wonderful course, both layout and conditioning...Worth the drive from anywhere in the Cincinnati metro area...Great golf course...Beautifully landscaped and designed course...Excellent practice facility...Worth a special trip...Like the double fairways...Nice course, tough greens...Great public course, good layout, good variety...Thoroughly enjoyable, back nine a killer from the tips.

★★★LINCOLN HOMESTEAD STATE PARK
PU-5079 Lincoln Park Rd., Springfield, 40069, Washington County, (606)336-7461, 50 miles SW of Louisville.
Opened: 1958. **Holes:** 18. **Par:** 71/73. **Yards:** 6,359/5,472. **Course rating:** 70.0/71.0.
Slope: 119/118. **Architect:** Buck Blankenship. **Green fee:** $16. **Credit cards:** All major.
Reduced fees: Weekdays, low season, twilight. **Caddies:** No. **Golf carts:** $9.
Discount golf packages: Yes. **Season:** Year-round. **High:** April-Oct. **On site lodging:** No. **Rental clubs:** Yes. **Walking policy:** Walking at certain times. **Metal spikes allowed:** Yes. **Range:** No. **To obtain tee times:** Call or come in person.
Subscriber comments: Good state-park course, never crowded, three-hour rounds...Long par 3s, tough course...Good rural course, enjoy the country setting...Good variety, open, hilly, narrow fairways, some blind shots...Excellent greens.

★★LONG RUN GOLF CLUB
PU-1605 Flatrock Rd., Anchorage, 40245, Jefferson County, (502)245-0702.
Opened: 1965. **Holes:** 18. **Par:** 72/73. **Yards:** 6,839/5,562. **Course rating:** 71.5/17.4.
Slope: 111/113. **Architect:** Benjamin Wihry. **Green fee:** $18/$9. **Credit cards:** None.
Reduced fees: Weekdays, low season, twilight, seniors, juniors. **Caddies:** No. **Golf carts:** $20. **Discount golf packages:** No. **Season:** Year-round. **High:** May-Aug. **On site lodging:** No. **Rental clubs:** Yes. **Walking policy:** N/A. **Metal spikes allowed:** Yes. **Range:** Yes (grass). **To obtain tee times:** Call up to 2 days in advance.

★★★MARRIOTT'S GRIFFIN GATE RESORT GOLF CLUB
R-1720 Newtown Pike, Lexington, 40511, Fayette County, (606)288-6193, (606)231-5100.
Opened: 1981. **Holes:** 18. **Par:** 72/72. **Yards:** 6,801/4,979. **Course rating:** 73.3/69.3.
Slope: 132/119. **Architect:** Rees Jones. **Green fee:** $32/$62. **Credit cards:** All major.
Reduced fees: Weekdays, low season, twilight. **Caddies:** No. **Golf carts:** Included in Green Fee. **Discount golf packages:** Yes. **Season:** Year-round. **High:** April-Oct. **On site lodging:** Yes. **Rental clubs:** Yes. **Walking policy:** Mandatory cart. **Metal spikes allowed:** Yes. **Range:** No. **To obtain tee times:** Hotel guests may make reservations up to 60 days in advance. Outside guests up to 7 days in advance.
Notes: 1983-89 Bank One Senior Classic.
Subscriber comments: Short and tight. Bring your "A" wedge game...Nice resort course that is always fun to play...Ruined by building houses next to course...One of Lexington's finest...Extremely overrated...A course you can score on...Good tourist course...Too much water for average golfer...Short, well maintained, good greens.

★★★½MAYWOOD GOLF CLUB
PU-130 Maywood Ave., Bardstown, 40004, Nelson County, (502)348-6600, (800)791-8633, 34 miles S of Louisville.
Opened: 1995. **Holes:** 18. **Par:** 72/72. **Yards:** 6,965/4,711. **Course rating:** 72.2/66.5.
Slope: 121/107. **Architect:** David Pfaff. **Green fee:** $19/$22. **Credit cards:** All major.
Reduced fees: Twilight. **Caddies:** No. **Golf carts:** $10. **Discount golf packages:** Yes.
Season: Year-round. **High:** March-Nov. **On site lodging:** No. **Rental clubs:** Yes.
Walking policy: Unrestricted walking. **Metal spikes allowed:** Yes. **Range:** Yes (grass).
To obtain tee times: Call up to 14 days in advance.
Subscriber comments: Best par 3s in Kentucky...Lots of homes on fairways, some blind shots...Good variety of long and short holes...Four sets of tees, well maintained...Excellent links course, kept in very good shape...A great driving course, young course with a lot of promise...Very enjoyable layout.

★★★½MY OLD KENTUCKY HOME STATE PARK GOLF CLUB
PU-Hwy. 49, Bardstown, 40004, Nelson County, (502)349-6542.
Opened: 1938. **Holes:** 18. **Par:** 70/71. **Yards:** 6,065/5,239. **Course rating:** 69.5/70.2.
Slope: 119/118. **Architect:** H.H. Rudy. **Green fee:** $16/$16. **Credit cards:** All major.
Reduced fees: Weekdays, twilight. **Caddies:** No. **Golf carts:** $9. **Discount golf packages:** No. **Season:** Year-round. **High:** April-Sept. **On site lodging:** No. **Rental clubs:** Yes. **Walking policy:** Unrestricted walking. **Metal spikes allowed:** Yes. **Range:** Yes (grass). **To obtain tee times:** Call up to 7 days in advance.
Subscriber comments: Love the bells ringing "My Old Kentucky Home"...New back nine very good, need to redo front...Fun course, good variety of holes.

★★★½NEVEL MEADE GOLF COURSE
PU-3123 Nevel Meade Dr., Prospect, 40059, Oldham County, (502)228-9522, 10 miles N of Louisville.
Opened: 1991. **Holes:** 18. **Par:** 72/72. **Yards:** 6,956/5,616. **Course rating:** 72.2/70.4. **Slope:** 122/117. **Architect:** Steve Smyers. **Green fee:** $17/$22. **Credit cards:** MC,VISA. **Reduced fees:** Low season, twilight, juniors. **Caddies:** No. **Golf carts:** $10. **Discount golf packages:** No. **Season:** Year-round. **High:** March-Nov. **On site lodging:** No. **Rental clubs:** Yes. **Walking policy:** Unrestricted walking. **Metal spikes allowed:** Yes. **Range:** Yes (grass). **To obtain tee times:** Call 4 days in advance for weekdays and Wednesday morning for weekend tee times.
Subscriber comments: Great links course...Very nicely maintained...A nice Scottish links course in the middle of Bluegrass country...My favorite course in area.

★★OLD BRIDGE GOLF CLUB
1 Old Bridge Rd., Danville, 40422, Boyle County, (606)236-6051, (800)783-7153, 20 miles SW of Lexington.
Opened: 1990. **Holes:** 18. **Par:** 72/72. **Yards:** 6,400/4,600. **Course rating:** 68.0/64.9. **Slope:** 117/104. **Architect:** Benjamin Wihry. **Green fee:** $14/$20. **Credit cards:** MC,VISA. **Reduced fees:** Low season. **Caddies:** No. **Golf carts:** $20. **Discount golf packages:** Yes. **Season:** Year-round. **High:** N/A. **On site lodging:** No. **Rental clubs:** Yes. **Walking policy:** Unrestricted walking. **Metal spikes allowed:** Yes. **Range:** Yes (grass/mats). **To obtain tee times:** Call in advance anytime.

★½PARK MAMMOTH GOLF CLUB
Hwy. U.S. 31W., Park City, 42160, Barren County, (502)749-4101, 19 miles E of Bowling Green.
Opened: 1962. **Holes:** 18. **Par:** 70/74. **Yards:** 6,073/5,299. **Course rating:** 68.0/72.0. **Slope:** 114/107. **Architect:** Buck Blankenship. **Green fee:** $10/$10. **Credit cards:** MC,VISA,AMEX. **Reduced fees:** N/A. **Caddies:** No. **Golf carts:** $8. **Discount golf packages:** Yes. **Season:** Year-round. **High:** April-June. **On site lodging:** No. **Rental clubs:** No. **Walking policy:** Unrestricted walking. **Metal spikes allowed:** Yes. **Range:** No. **To obtain tee times:** Call 48 hours in advance.

★★PAXTON PARK GOLF CLUB
PM-841 Berger Rd., Paducah, 42002, McCracken County, (502)444-9514, 140 miles W of Nashville, TN.
Opened: 1940. **Holes:** 18. **Par:** 71/76. **Yards:** 6,880/5,799. **Course rating:** 71.1/70.6. **Slope:** 119/116. **Architect:** N/A. **Green fee:** $9/$12. **Credit cards:** N/A. **Reduced fees:** Twilight. **Caddies:** No. **Golf carts:** $16. **Discount golf packages:** No. **Season:** Year-round. **High:** May-Sept. **On site lodging:** No. **Rental clubs:** Yes. **Walking policy:** Unrestricted walking. **Metal spikes allowed:** Yes. **Range:** Yes (grass). **To obtain tee times:** Call up to 2 days in advance.

★★½PINE VALLEY COUNTRY CLUB & RESORT
R-805 Pine Valley Dr., Elizabethtown, 42701, Hardin County, (502)737-8300, (800)844-1904, 35 miles S of Louisville.
Opened: 1968. **Holes:** 18. **Par:** 72/73. **Yards:** 6,648/5,357. **Course rating:** 71.3/69.6. **Slope:** 119/114. **Architect:** Bill Amick. **Green fee:** $12/$18. **Credit cards:** MC,VISA,DISC. **Reduced fees:** Weekdays, low season, resort guests, twilight, seniors, juniors. **Caddies:** No. **Golf carts:** $10. **Discount golf packages:** Yes. **Season:** Year-round. **High:** April-Oct. **On site lodging:** Yes. **Rental clubs:** Yes. **Walking policy:** Walking at certain times. **Metal spikes allowed:** Yes. **Range:** Yes (grass/mats). **To obtain tee times:** Call.
Subscriber comments: Good variety of holes...Water, hills, sand, need to keep it straight...Some very tough holes...Very tight course, good challenge.

★★★½PLAYERS CLUB OF LEXINGTON
4850 Leestown Rd., Lexington, 40511, Fayette County, (606)255-1011, 5 miles W of Lexington.
Opened: 1991. **Holes:** 27. **Architect:** Danny McQueen. **Green fee:** $21/$24. **Credit cards:** MC,VISA. **Reduced fees:** Weekdays, low season, twilight, seniors. **Caddies:** No. **Golf carts:** $9. **Discount golf packages:** No. **Season:** Year-round. **High:** April-Oct.

On site lodging: No. **Rental clubs:** Yes. **Walking policy:** Walking at certain times. **Metal spikes allowed:** No. **Range:** Yes (grass). **To obtain tee times:** Out-of-state guests may call up to 21 days in advance. Local guests may call up to 7 days in advance for weekday play and Monday for upcoming weekend.
CREEK/ISLAND
Par: 72/72. **Yards:** 6,889/4,976. **Course rating:** 72.3/69.4. **Slope:** 129/119.
ISLAND/LAKE
Par: 72/72. **Yards:** 6,818/4,850. **Course rating:** 72.1/68.1. **Slope:** 128/116.
LAKE/CREEK
Par: 72/72. **Yards:** 6,987/5,022. **Course rating:** 72.6/69.4. **Slope:** 129/119.
Subscriber comments: Outstanding...27 holes of great golf, soon to be 36...When trees mature, will be great...No.8 island green tough to hit...Fun holes, lots of options.

★★★QUAIL CHASE GOLF CLUB
PU-7000 Cooper Chapel Rd., Louisville, 40229, Jefferson County, (502)239-2110.
Opened: 1988. **Holes:** 27. **Architect:** David Pfaff. **Green fee:** $17/$22. **Credit cards:** MC,VISA,AMEX. **Reduced fees:** Weekdays, low season, twilight, seniors, juniors. **Caddies:** No. **Golf carts:** $10. **Discount golf packages:** Yes. **Season:** Year-round. **High:** May-Aug. **On site lodging:** No. **Rental clubs:** Yes. **Walking policy:** Unrestricted walking. **Metal spikes allowed:** No. **Range:** Yes (grass/mats). **To obtain tee times:** Call 2 days in advance. Out-of-town players may call up to 1 year in advance.
EAST/SOUTH
Par: 72/72. **Yards:** 6,728/5,361. **Course rating:** 71.7/77.6. **Slope:** 127/136.
SOUTH/WEST
Par: 72/72. **Yards:** 6,493/5,117. **Course rating:** 70.5/76.3. **Slope:** 124/133.
WEST/EAST
Par: 72/72. **Yards:** 6,715/5,122. **Course rating:** 72.0/77.9. **Slope:** 133/141.
Subscriber comments: Short course, good service, fun layout...No.1 hole on East is magnificent...All three nines are a challenge...Narrow fairways. Some blind shots.

★★★SENECA GOLF COURSE
PM-2300 Seneca Park Rd., Louisville, 40206, Jefferson County, (502)458-9298.
Opened: 1935. **Holes:** 18. **Par:** 72/73. **Yards:** 7,034/5,469. **Course rating:** 73.7/71.5. **Slope:** 130/122. **Architect:** Alex McKay/Michael Hurdzan. **Green fee:** $8/$9. **Credit cards:** None. **Reduced fees:** Weekdays, twilight, seniors, juniors. **Caddies:** No. **Golf carts:** $20. **Discount golf packages:** No. **Season:** Year-round. **High:** April-Sept. **On site lodging:** No. **Rental clubs:** Yes. **Walking policy:** Unrestricted walking. **Metal spikes allowed:** Yes. **Range:** Yes (grass/mats). **To obtain tee times:** Call 2 days in advance for weekday play. Sign in at golf shop on Tuesday or call in on Thursday for weekends.
Subscriber comments: Great for a muny; long and challenging...Hills and valleys...Next to river, fog early...Best golf course in city park system.

★★SHAWNEE GOLF COURSE
PU-460 Northwestern Pkwy., Louisville, 40212, Jefferson County, (502)776-9389.
Opened: 1933. **Holes:** 18. **Par:** 70/70. **Yards:** 6,072/5,476. **Course rating:** 65.1/68.5. **Slope:** 100/105. **Architect:** Alex McKay. **Green fee:** $8/$8. **Credit cards:** None. **Reduced fees:** Twilight. **Caddies:** No. **Golf carts:** N/A. **Discount golf packages:** No. **Season:** Year-round. **High:** May-Oct. **On site lodging:** No. **Rental clubs:** Yes. **Walking policy:** Unrestricted walking. **Metal spikes allowed:** Yes. **Range:** Yes (grass). **To obtain tee times:** Call two days in advance.

★★SOUTHWIND GOLF COURSE
2480 New Boonesboro Rd., Winchester, 40391, Clark County, (606)744-0375, 15 miles E of Lexington.
Opened: 1992. **Holes:** 18. **Par:** 71/71. **Yards:** 6,265/4,700. **Course rating:** 67.1/70.0. **Slope:** 113/102. **Architect:** Dan McQueen/Ken Arnold. **Green fee:** $11/$13. **Credit cards:** None. **Reduced fees:** Weekdays, low season, twilight, seniors. **Caddies:** No. **Golf carts:** $8. **Discount golf packages:** Yes. **Season:** Feb.-Dec. **High:** May-Sept. **On site lodging:** No. **Rental clubs:** Yes. **Walking policy:** Walking at certain times. **Metal spikes allowed:** Yes. **Range:** Yes (grass/mats). **To obtain tee times:** Call for weekend and holiday tee times only.

★★½TANGLEWOOD GOLF COURSE

PU-245 Tanglewood Dr., Taylorsville, 40071, Spencer County, (502)477-2468, 25 miles SE of Louisville.
Opened: 1984. **Holes:** 18. **Par:** 72/72. **Yards:** 6,626/5,275. **Course rating:** 70.2/68.8. **Slope:** 121/115. **Architect:** Buck Blankenship. **Green fee:** $12/$16. **Credit cards:** MC,VISA. **Reduced fees:** Weekdays, low season, resort guests, twilight, seniors, juniors. **Caddies:** No. **Golf carts:** $11. **Discount golf packages:** Yes. **Season:** Year-round. **High:** May-Sept. **On site lodging:** Yes. **Rental clubs:** Yes. **Walking policy:** Walking at certain times. **Metal spikes allowed:** No. **Range:** Yes (grass/mats). **To obtain tee times:** Call 3 days in advance.
Subscriber comments: Very busy, but good...Beautiful, good degree of difficulty.

★★½TATES CREEK GOLF COURSE

PU-1400 Gainesway Dr., Lexington, 40502, Fayette County, (606)272-3428, 75 miles S of Cincinnati.
Opened: 1957. **Holes:** 18. **Par:** 72/73. **Yards:** 6,240/5,260. **Course rating:** 69.5/69.3. **Slope:** 120/117. **Architect:** Buck Blankenship. **Green fee:** $10/$10. **Credit cards:** MC,VISA. **Reduced fees:** Twilight, seniors, juniors. **Caddies:** No. **Golf carts:** $14. **Discount golf packages:** No. **Season:** Year-round. **High:** April-Oct. **On site lodging:** No. **Rental clubs:** Yes. **Walking policy:** Unrestricted walking. **Metal spikes allowed:** Yes. **Range:** No. **To obtain tee times:** Call 7 days in advance. Must be at least 3 players in group to reserve tee time.
Subscriber comments: Short, tight, plenty of mature trees...Places value on shotmaking...Good senior's course...Tight back side best.

★★★WEISSINGER HILLS GOLF COURSE

PU-2240 Mt. Eden Rd., Shelbyville, 40065, Shelby County, (502)633-7332, 15 miles E of Louisville.
Opened: 1990. **Holes:** 18. **Par:** 72/73. **Yards:** 6,534/5,165. **Course rating:** 70.8/69.0. **Slope:** 118/112. **Architect:** Jack Ridge. **Green fee:** $12/$17. **Credit cards:** MC,VISA. **Reduced fees:** Weekdays, low season, twilight, seniors, juniors. **Caddies:** No. **Golf carts:** $9. **Discount golf packages:** Yes. **Season:** Year-round. **High:** April-Sept. **On site lodging:** No. **Rental clubs:** Yes. **Walking policy:** Walking at certain times. **Metal spikes allowed:** Yes. **Range:** Yes (grass/mats). **To obtain tee times:** Call 7 days in advance.
Subscriber comments: Big greens, neat clubhouse......Short par 5s...Fun course.

★★★½WESTERN HILLS GOLF COURSE

PU-2160 Russellville Rd., Hopkinsville, 42240, Christian County, (502)885-6023, 60 miles N of Nashville.
Opened: 1985. **Holes:** 18. **Par:** 72/72. **Yards:** 6,907/3,921. **Course rating:** 73.8/64.0. **Slope:** 134/109. **Architect:** Earl Stone. **Green fee:** $12/$15. **Credit cards:** MC,VISA. **Reduced fees:** Weekdays, seniors, juniors. **Caddies:** No. **Golf carts:** $16. **Discount golf packages:** No. **Season:** Year-round. **High:** May-Sept. **On site lodging:** No. **Rental clubs:** No. **Walking policy:** Walking at certain times. **Metal spikes allowed:** Yes. **Range:** Yes (grass/mats). **To obtain tee times:** Call up to 7 days in advance.
Subscriber comments: Worth the trip...Very hilly, interesting course...Fast greens...Tees for everyone, good condition...Tough with wind...Best in western Kentucky.

★★★WOODSON BEND RESORT

R-14 Woodson Bend, Bronston, 42518, Wayne County, (606)561-5316, 60 miles S of Lexington.
Opened: 1973. **Holes:** 18. **Par:** 72/75. **Yards:** 6,189/5,155. **Course rating:** 69.2/72.0. **Slope:** 117/113. **Architect:** Dave Bennett/Lee Trevino. **Green fee:** $18/$23. **Credit cards:** MC,VISA. **Reduced fees:** Low season, juniors. **Caddies:** No. **Golf carts:** Included in Green Fee. **Discount golf packages:** Yes. **Season:** Feb.-Dec. **High:** May-Sept. **On site lodging:** Yes. **Rental clubs:** Yes. **Walking policy:** Mandatory cart. **Metal spikes allowed:** Yes. **Range:** Yes (grass/mats). **To obtain tee times:** Call 7 days in advance.
Subscriber comments: Scenic...Too many blind approach shots too greens...Trees and condos line most fairways...Nice course, tight if played from back tees.

★★ALPINE MEADOWS GOLF CLUB
PU-5730 Meadowlake, Keithville, 71047, Caddo County, (318)925-9547, 5 miles SW of Shreveport.
Opened: 1962. **Holes:** 18. **Par:** 72/72. **Yards:** 6,473/5,345. **Course rating:** 70.5/69.1. **Slope:** 113/108. **Architect:** N/A. **Green fee:** $10/$12. **Credit cards:** All major.
Reduced fees: Twilight, seniors, juniors. **Caddies:** No. **Golf carts:** $16. **Discount golf packages:** No. **Season:** Jan.-Dec. **High:** May-Aug. **On site lodging:** No. **Rental clubs:** Yes. **Walking policy:** Unrestricted walking. **Metal spikes allowed:** Yes. **Range:** Yes. **To obtain tee times:** Call anytime between 7 a.m. and 6 p.m.

BAYOU OAKS GOLF COURSES
PM-1040 Filmore, New Orleans, 70124, Orleans County, (504)483-9396.
Opened: 1936. **Architect:** N/A. **Credit cards:** None. **Reduced fees:** Twilight, seniors, juniors. **Caddies:** No. **Golf carts:** $18. **Discount golf packages:** No. **Season:** Year-round. **High:** April-June/Sept.-Oct. **On site lodging:** No. **Rental clubs:** Yes. **Walking policy:** Unrestricted walking. **Metal spikes allowed:** Yes. **Range:** Yes (grass/mats).
★★½CHAMPIONSHIP COURSE
Holes: 18. **Par:** 72/72. **Yards:** 7,061/6,013. **Course rating:** 71.5/73.3. **Slope:** 116/118. **Green fee:** $12/$17. **To obtain tee times:** Call 1 day in advance for weekends and holidays. Weekdays, first come, first served.
Subscriber comments: Flat, open, well maintained...No.3 a classic par 5...Very long, must pump-up the driver...Take a lunch...Old layout, fair greens, busy.
★★LAKESIDE COURSE
Holes: 18. **Par:** 70/70. **Yards:** 6,054/5,872. **Course rating:** 68.5/70.5. **Slope:** 110/103. **Green fee:** $9/$14. **To obtain tee times:** Call 1 day in advance for weekends and holidays. Weekdays first come, first served.
★★WISNER COURSE
Holes: 18. **Par:** 72/72. **Yards:** 6,465/5,707. **Course rating:** 70.5/71.8. **Slope:** 111/116. **Green fee:** $9/$14. **To obtain tee times:** Call 1 day in advance for weekends and holidays. Weekdays, first come, first served.
Special Notes: Also has 18-hole par-68 Little Course.

★★★BELLE TERRE COUNTRY CLUB
111 Fairway Dr., La Place, 70068, St. John the Baptist County, (504)652-5000, 30 miles W of New Orleans.
Opened: 1977. **Holes:** 18. **Par:** 72/72. **Yards:** 6,840/5,510. **Course rating:** 72.2/71.6. **Slope:** 130/113. **Architect:** David Pfaff. **Green fee:** $35/$45. **Credit cards:** MC,VISA,AMEX. **Reduced fees:** Weekdays. **Caddies:** No. **Golf carts:** Included in Green Fee. **Discount golf packages:** No. **Season:** Year-round. **High:** April-Oct. **On site lodging:** No. **Rental clubs:** Yes. **Walking policy:** Mandatory cart. **Metal spikes allowed:** Yes. **Range:** Yes (grass). **To obtain tee times:** Nonmembers call 4 days in advance.
Subscriber comments: Great undulating greens...Wind, water but open...Tight fairways...Nice course for a subdivision layout...A few long holes...Tough course, kept in good shape year-round...Holes 4, 5, and 6 give the true Louisiana "Bayou" look.

★½BRECHTEL GOLF COURSE
PM-3700 Behrman Place, New Orleans, 70114, Orleans County, (504)362-4761.
Opened: 1965. **Holes:** 18. **Par:** 70/70. **Yards:** 6,065/5,556. **Course rating:** 66.0. **Slope:** 97. **Architect:** R.W. LaConte/T. McAnlis. **Green fee:** $7/$10. **Credit cards:** None. **Reduced fees:** Twilight, seniors, juniors. **Caddies:** No. **Golf carts:** $14. **Discount golf packages:** No. **Season:** Year-round. **High:** April-Oct. **On site lodging:** No. **Rental clubs:** Yes. **Walking policy:** Unrestricted walking. **Metal spikes allowed:** Yes. **Range:** Yes (grass/mats). **To obtain tee times:** First come, first served.

★★½CHENNAULT PARK GOLF COURSE
PM-8475 Millhaven Rd., Monroe, 71203, Quachita County, (318)329-2454.
Holes: 18. **Par:** 72/72. **Yards:** 7,044/5,783. **Slope:** 118/109. **Architect:** Winnie Cole. Call club for further information.
Subscriber comments: North Louisiana's best-kept secret...A 620-yard par 5 and 458-yard par 4 are tough finishers...Good course to learn on...In flight pattern of airport.

LOUISIANA

★★★★**THE CLUB AND LODGE AT THE BLUFFS ON THOMPSON CREEK**
R-Hwy. 965 at Freeland Rd., The Bluffs, 70775, West Feliciana County, (504)634-5551, (888)634-3410, 25 miles NW of Baton Rouge.
Opened: 1989. **Holes:** 18. **Par:** 72/72. **Yards:** 7,143/4,813. **Course rating:** 74.6/69.0. **Slope:** 143/123. **Architect:** Arnold Palmer/Ed Seay. **Green fee:** $40/$70. **Credit cards:** All major. **Reduced fees:** Weekdays, low season, resort guests, twilight. **Caddies:** No. **Golf carts:** $12. **Discount golf packages:** Yes. **Season:** Year-round. **High:** March-June/Sept.-Nov. **On site lodging:** Yes. **Rental clubs:** Yes. **Walking policy:** Walking at certain times. **Metal spikes allowed:** Yes. **Range:** Yes (grass). **To obtain tee times:** Lodge guests may arrange tee times when room reservations are made.
Notes: Ranked 2nd in 1997 Best in State.
Subscriber comments: Awesome...Long, very tight, good greens...Hidden gem, must play if in state...Grueling hills whether you walk or ride...No.18 a beast into wind...Nice layout, tough course...Beautiful scenery...9th hole (split fairway) most challenging par 5 around...Best course in Louisiana...Tight fairways, No.17 very scenic...Bring lots of ammo, Thompson Creek eats balls...Need more like it.

★★★½**EASTOVER COUNTRY CLUB**
5889 Eastover Rd., New Orleans, 70128, Orleans County, (504)245-7347, 15 miles E of New Orleans.
Opened: N/A. **Holes:** 19. **Par:** 72/72. **Yards:** 6,825/5,470. **Course rating:** 72.5/72.2. **Slope:** 129/123. **Architect:** Joe Lee/Rocky Roquemore. **Green fee:** $88/$88. **Credit cards:** All major. **Reduced fees:** N/A. **Caddies:** No. **Golf carts:** N/A. **Discount golf packages:** No. **Season:** Year-round. **High:** N/A. **On site lodging:** No. **Rental clubs:** No. **Walking policy:** Unrestricted walking. **Metal spikes allowed:** Yes. **Range:** Yes (grass). **To obtain tee times:** Call in advance.
Subscriber comments: Short, but testy...Shape depends on weather and season...Beautiful layout, nice variety of holes...Best in New Orleans...Excellent shape, great food and service, rough is thick...Water, wind, open...No.16 a classic par 5...Great course, fast greens, beautiful area...A real pleasure to play.

★★½**EMERALD HILLS GOLF RESORT**
R-P.O. Box 460, Florien, 71429, Sabine County, (318)586-4661, (800)533-5031, 75 miles NW of Alexandria.
Opened: N/A. **Holes:** 18. **Par:** 72/72. **Yards:** 6,550/6,300. **Course rating:** N/A. **Slope:** 120/118. **Architect:** N/A. **Green fee:** $10/$17. **Credit cards:** All major. **Reduced fees:** Weekdays, low season. **Caddies:** No. **Golf carts:** $20. **Discount golf packages:** Yes. **Season:** Year-round. **High:** April-Sept. **On site lodging:** Yes. **Rental clubs:** Yes. **Walking policy:** Mandatory cart. **Metal spikes allowed:** Yes. **Range:** Yes (grass/mats). **To obtain tee times:** Call.
Subscriber comments: Tight—leave driver at home. Great greens...Lots of trees...Gnats are terrible...Some doglegs, several uphill greens, tough sand.
Special Notes: Formerly Toro Hills Lodge.

★½**HOWELL PARK GOLF COURSE**
PU-5511 Winbourne Ave., Baton Rouge, 70805, East Baton Rouge County, (504)357-9292.
Opened: 1956. **Holes:** 18. **Par:** 70/70. **Yards:** 5,779/4,577. **Course rating:** 67.6. **Slope:** N/A. **Architect:** N/A. **Green fee:** $5/$5. **Credit cards:** MC,VISA. **Reduced fees:** Twilight, juniors. **Caddies:** No. **Golf carts:** $14. **Discount golf packages:** No. **Season:** Year-round. **High:** March-Sept. **On site lodging:** No. **Rental clubs:** Yes. **Walking policy:** Unrestricted walking. **Metal spikes allowed:** Yes. **Range:** No. **To obtain tee times:** Call in for weekends only.

★★★**HUNTINGTON PARK GOLF COURSE**
PU-8300 Pines Rd., Shreveport, 71129, Caddo County, (318)673-7765.
Opened: 1969. **Holes:** 18. **Par:** 72/74. **Yards:** 7,294/6,171. **Course rating:** 73.3/74.7. **Slope:** N/A. **Architect:** Tommy Moore. **Green fee:** $10/$13. **Credit cards:** MC,VISA. **Reduced fees:** Weekdays, twilight, seniors, juniors. **Caddies:** No. **Golf carts:** $8. **Discount golf packages:** No. **Season:** Year-round. **High:** May-Sept. **On site lodging:** No. **Rental clubs:** Yes. **Walking policy:** Unrestricted walking. **Metal spikes allowed:** Yes. **Range:** Yes (grass). **To obtain tee times:** Call or come in on Thursday at 7 a.m.

for upcoming weekend. Weekdays, first come, first served.
Subscriber comments: Good public course...No.10 is a bear...Great course, wide fairways...No.18 hardest hole, must carry water on second shot for any chance of par...Big receptive greens...Best of city courses.

★★★LES VIEUX CHENES GOLF CLUB
PU-Rt. 2C, Box 15 GC, Youngsville, 70592, Lafayette County, (318)837-1159, 9 miles S of Lafayette.
Opened: 1977. **Holes:** 18. **Par:** 72/74. **Yards:** 6,900/5,600. **Course rating:** 70.1/69.1.
Slope: 119/113. **Architect:** Dr. Marvin Ferguson. **Green fee:** $8/$8. **Credit cards:**
MC,VISA,AMEX. **Reduced fees:** Twilight, seniors, juniors. **Caddies:** No. **Golf carts:**
$13. **Discount golf packages:** No. **Season:** Year-round. **High:** June-Sept. **On site lodging:** No. **Rental clubs:** No. **Walking policy:** Unrestricted walking. **Metal spikes allowed:** Yes. **Range:** Yes (grass). **To obtain tee times:** Call two days in advance.
Subscriber comments: Good course, well taken care of...Fairways are wide, very little rough...Very crowded year-round...Occasional challenges keep you from relaxing.

★★★MALLARD COVE GOLF COURSE
PM-Chennault Air Base, Lake Charles, 70601, Calcasieu County,
(318)491-1204, 125 miles W of Baton Rouge.
Opened: 1976. **Holes:** 18. **Par:** 72/72. **Yards:** 6,903/5,294. **Course rating:** 72.4/70.1. **Slope:** 125/117. **Architect:** A. James Wall. **Green fee:**
$10/$13. **Credit cards:** MC,VISA,DISC. **Reduced fees:** Weekdays, twilight, seniors, juniors. **Caddies:** No. **Golf carts:** $8. **Discount golf packages:** No.
Season: Year-round. **High:** April-Oct. **On site lodging:** No. **Rental clubs:** Yes. **Walking policy:** Unrestricted walking. **Metal spikes allowed:** Yes. **Range:** Yes (grass/mats). **To obtain tee times:** Call or come in up to 2 days in advance.
Subscriber comments: The best holes will challenge you...Very long from back tees...Excellent greens, nice fairways...Best public course in the area.

GOOD VALUE

★★★½OAK HARBOR GOLF CLUB
201 Oak Harbor Blvd., Slidell, 70458, St. Tammany County, (504)646-0110, 25 miles NE of New Orleans.
Opened: 1991. **Holes:** 18. **Par:** 72/72. **Yards:** 6,896/5,305. **Course rating:** 72.7/70.0.
Slope: 132/118. **Architect:** Lee Schmidt. **Green fee:** $40/$48. **Credit cards:** All major.
Reduced fees: Twilight, juniors. **Caddies:** No. **Golf carts:** Included in Green Fee.
Discount golf packages: Yes. **Season:** Year-round. **High:** April-July. **On site lodging:**
No. **Rental clubs:** Yes. **Walking policy:** Mandatory cart. **Metal spikes allowed:** Yes.
Range: Yes (grass). **To obtain tee times:** Call 7 days in advance.
Subscriber comments: A very good links-style course...Wind makes extremely difficult...This course is beginning to be great...Real challenge...Tough from blue tees, lots of water, good greens...Needs decent clubhouse...Lots of water, lots of trouble...Challenging course with many uneven lies...One of the top-three layouts in the state.

★★PINE SHADOWS GOLF CENTER
PU-750 Goodman Rd, Lake Charles, 70601, Calcasieu County, (318)433-8681.
Call club for further information.

★★PINEWOOD COUNTRY CLUB
405 Country Club Blvd, Slidell, 70458, St. Tammany County, (504)643-6893, 20 miles N of New Orleans.
Opened: 1963. **Holes:** 18. **Par:** 71/72. **Yards:** 6,300/5,300. **Course rating:** 68.5/70.2.
Slope: 121/117. **Architect:** Bill Bergin. **Green fee:** $27/$30. **Credit cards:** MC,VISA.
Reduced fees: N/A. **Caddies:** No. **Golf carts:** Included in Green Fee. **Discount golf packages:** No. **Season:** Year-round. **High:** N/A. **On site lodging:** No. **Rental clubs:**
No. **Walking policy:** Mandatory cart. **Metal spikes allowed:** Yes. **Range:** Yes (grass).
To obtain tee times: Call up to 2 days in advance.

★★QUERBES PARK GOLF COURSE
PU-3500 Beverly Place, Shreveport, 71104, Caddo County, (318)673-7773.
Opened: 1922. **Holes:** 18. **Par:** 71/71. **Yards:** 6,207/5,360. **Course rating:** 69.0/70.0.
Slope: 118/110. **Architect:** N/A. **Green fee:** $6/$13. **Credit cards:** MC,VISA. **Reduced**

fees: Weekdays, twilight, seniors, juniors. **Caddies:** No. **Golf carts:** $16. **Discount golf packages:** No. **Season:** Year-round. **High:** May-Oct. **On site lodging:** No. **Rental clubs:** Yes. **Walking policy:** Unrestricted walking. **Metal spikes allowed:** Yes. **Range:** Yes (grass/mats). **To obtain tee times:** Call golf shop.

★★★½SANTA MARIA GOLF COURSE

PU-19301 Old Perkins Rd., Baton Rouge, 70810, East Baton Rouge County, (504)752-9667.

Opened: 1986. **Holes:** 18. **Par:** 72/72. **Yards:** 7,051/5,267. **Course rating:** 72.9/69.6. **Slope:** 129/120. **Architect:** Robert Trent Jones. **Green fee:** $18/$22. **Credit cards:** MC,VISA. **Reduced fees:** Twilight, seniors, juniors. **Caddies:** No. **Golf carts:** $8. **Discount golf packages:** No. **Season:** Year-round. **High:** April-Oct. **On site lodging:** No. **Rental clubs:** No. **Walking policy:** Unrestricted walking. **Metal spikes allowed:** Yes. **Range:** Yes (grass). **To obtain tee times:** Call up to 6 days in advance.
Subscriber comments: Small greens, good layout, but needs work...Could be one of the top-three courses in state...Best buy in the South...Country club course at public course price...Traps are only problem...No.18 a quality par 5...RT Jones' typical long, deep greens...Best in Baton Rouge, would be better if not owned by city.

★★WEBB MEMORIAL GOLF COURSE

PU-1352 Country Club Dr., Baton Rouge, 70806, East Baton Rouge County, (504)383-4919.

Opened: 1932. **Holes:** 18. **Par:** 72/72. **Yards:** 6,412/5,442. **Course rating:** 70.1/70.3. **Slope:** 120. **Architect:** E.E. Evans/Al Michael. **Green fee:** $6/$6. **Credit cards:** MC,VISA. **Reduced fees:** Twilight, juniors. **Caddies:** No. **Golf carts:** $14. **Discount golf packages:** No. **Season:** Year-round. **High:** May-Aug. **On site lodging:** No. **Rental clubs:** Yes. **Walking policy:** Unrestricted walking. **Metal spikes allowed:** Yes. **Range:** No. **To obtain tee times:** Call up to 2 days in advance.

★★★½AROOSTOOK VALLEY COUNTRY CLUB
Russell Rd., Fort Fairfield, 04742, Aroostook County, (207)476-8083, 15 miles NE of Presque Isle.
Opened: 1927. **Holes:** 18. **Par:** 72/72. **Yards:** 6,304/5,393. **Course rating:** 69.8/70.0. **Slope:** 117/108. **Architect:** Howard Watson. **Green fee:** $22/$22. **Credit cards:** MC,VISA. **Reduced fees:** Low season. **Caddies:** No. **Golf carts:** $22. **Discount golf packages:** No. **Season:** May-Oct. **High:** July-Aug. **On site lodging:** No. **Rental clubs:** Yes. **Walking policy:** Unrestricted walking. **Metal spikes allowed:** Yes. **Range:** Yes (grass/mats). **To obtain tee times:** Call 2 days in advance.
Subscriber comments: Great golf experience—a must play course...Has everything, elevation changes, woods, nice views, fun to play in two countries (U.S. and Canada), not too hard, but can eat you alive if not careful...Great par 5 holes.
Special Notes: The course extends into New Brunswick.

★★★BANGOR MUNICIPAL GOLF COURSE
PM-278 Webster Ave., Bangor, 04401, Penobscot County, (207)941-0232.
Opened: 1964. **Holes:** 27. **Par:** 71/71. **Yards:** 6,345/5,173. **Course rating:** 67.9/69.1. **Slope:** 112/111. **Architect:** Geoffrey Cornish. **Green fee:** $19/$20. **Credit cards:** MC,VISA. **Reduced fees:** Weekdays, twilight. **Caddies:** No. **Golf carts:** $18. **Discount golf packages:** No. **Season:** April-Nov. **High:** June-Aug. **On site lodging:** No. **Rental clubs:** Yes. **Walking policy:** Unrestricted walking. **Metal spikes allowed:** Yes. **Range:** Yes (grass/mats). **To obtain tee times:** Call up to 7 days in advance on the 9-hole course. No tee times taken on the 18.
Notes: 1978 USGA National Public Links Championship.
Subscriber comments: Enjoyable place to play...New nine is a great challenge...Jet flight path to nearby airport a distraction...Wide fairways—blind tee shots...Front nine wide open, back nine tighter, large greens.
Special Notes: Also 9-hole par-36 course.

★★½BAR HARBOR GOLF CLUB
Rte. 3, Trenton, 04605, Hancock County, (207)667-7505.
Architect: Phil Wogan. **Caddies:** No. **Discount golf packages:** No. **On site lodging:** No. **Rental clubs:** No. **Metal spikes allowed:** Yes. **Range:** Yes.
Call club for further information.
Subscriber comments: Beautiful scenery...Links style...Great long course on tidal, Jordon River...Wide open but watch out for deceptive distance...Too many blind shots...One of my favorite courses.

★★½BATH COUNTRY CLUB
East Brunswick Rd., Bath, 04530, Sagadahoc County, (207)442-8411, 30 miles N of Portland.
Opened: 1932. **Holes:** 18. **Par:** 70/70. **Yards:** 6,216/4,708. **Course rating:** 70.2/67.0. **Slope:** 128/115. **Architect:** N/A. **Green fee:** $18/$25. **Credit cards:** All major. **Reduced fees:** Low season, twilight. **Caddies:** No. **Golf carts:** $10. **Discount golf packages:** No. **Season:** April-Nov. **High:** June-Aug. **On site lodging:** No. **Rental clubs:** Yes. **Walking policy:** Unrestricted walking. **Metal spikes allowed:** Yes. **Range:** No. **To obtain tee times:** Call up to 7 days in advance.
Subscriber comments: Underrated, good course...An interesting design with a number of blind shots...Some very unique holes.

★★½THE BETHEL INN & COUNTRY CLUB
R-Broad St., Bethel, 04217, Oxford County, (207)824-6276, (800)654-0125, 70 miles NW of Portland.
Opened: 1915. **Holes:** 18. **Par:** 72/72. **Yards:** 6,663/5,280. **Course rating:** 72.3/71.4. **Slope:** 133/129. **Architect:** Geoffrey Cornish. **Green fee:** $26/$33. **Credit cards:** All major. **Reduced fees:** Weekdays, low season, resort guests, twilight. **Caddies:** No. **Golf carts:** $24. **Discount golf packages:** Yes. **Season:** May-Oct. **High:** July-Aug. **On site lodging:** Yes. **Rental clubs:** Yes. **Walking policy:** Unrestricted walking. **Metal spikes allowed:** Yes. **Range:** Yes (grass/mats). **To obtain tee times:** Call up to 2 days in advance.
Subscriber comments: New holes have modern expansive tees while old holes have

small tee boxes...Excellent restaurant for dinner...Old course, pleasant challenge, on the upswing...Very scenic, many changes in terrain...Package deal good value with stay, good meals.

★★★BIDDEFORD SACO COUNTRY CLUB
101 Old Orchard Rd., Saco, 04072, York County, (207)282-5883, 13 miles S of Portland.
Opened: 1921. **Holes:** 18. **Par:** 71/72. **Yards:** 6,192/5,053. **Course rating:** 69.6/69.2. **Slope:** 123/110. **Architect:** Donald Ross. **Green fee:** $25/$35. **Credit cards:** MC,VISA. **Reduced fees:** Twilight. **Caddies:** No. **Golf carts:** $22. **Discount golf packages:** No. **Season:** April-Nov. **High:** June-Aug. **On site lodging:** No. **Rental clubs:** Yes. **Walking policy:** Unrestricted walking. **Metal spikes allowed:** Yes. **Range:** Yes (grass/mats). **To obtain tee times:** Call 3 days in advance.
Subscriber comments: Great greens...Fairly easy front nine is a good warm up for difficult back...The back nine is outstanding...Continues to improve yearly...Front nine flat and open, back nine tight and mounded...Sleepy, small town feel...Two very different nines, tough in wind.

★★★BRUNSWICK GOLF CLUB
River Rd., Brunswick, 04011, Cumberland County, (207)725-8224, 20 miles N of Portland.
Opened: N/A. **Holes:** 18. **Par:** 72/74. **Yards:** 6,609/5,772. **Course rating:** 69.3/71.6. **Slope:** 126/123. **Architect:** Stiles and Van Kleek/Cornish and Robinson. **Green fee:** $30/$30. **Credit cards:** N/A. **Reduced fees:** N/A. **Caddies:** No. **Golf carts:** $24. **Discount golf packages:** No. **Season:** April-Nov. **High:** July-Aug. **On site lodging:** No. **Rental clubs:** Yes. **Walking policy:** Unrestricted walking. **Metal spikes allowed:** Yes. **Range:** Yes. **To obtain tee times:** Call up to 3 days in advance for weekend tee times.
Subscriber comments: Always enjoyable...One of the best in the state...Good variety of holes, 9 is very unusual...Challenging par 3s.

★★★CAPE ARUNDEL GOLF CLUB
Old River Rd., Kennebunkport, 04046, York County, (207)967-3494, 20 miles S of Portland.
Opened: 1897. **Holes:** 18. **Par:** 69/70. **Yards:** 5,869/5,134. **Course rating:** 67.0/68.6. **Slope:** 117/106. **Architect:** Walter Travis. **Green fee:** $35/$35. **Credit cards:** None. **Reduced fees:** N/A. **Caddies:** Yes. **Golf carts:** $20. **Discount golf packages:** No. **Season:** April-Oct. **High:** July-Sept. **On site lodging:** No. **Rental clubs:** Yes. **Walking policy:** Unrestricted walking. **Metal spikes allowed:** Yes. **Range:** No. **To obtain tee times:** Call 1 day in advance.
Subscriber comments: Short but great fun...Unique British style layout...Nice course, southern Maine...Short course. George Bush country...Missed President Bush by a day...Crosses road three times. Tidal rivers in play...Play it to say that you've played it.

★★DUTCH ELM GOLF CLUB
PU-5 Brimstone Rd., Arundel, 04046, York County, (207)282-9850, 20 miles S of Portland.
Opened: 1965. **Holes:** 18. **Par:** 72/73. **Yards:** 6,230/5,384. **Course rating:** 71.0/70.1. **Slope:** 125/115. **Architect:** Lucian Bourque. **Green fee:** $20/$25. **Credit cards:** MC,VISA. **Reduced fees:** Weekdays, low season, resort guests, twilight, seniors. **Caddies:** No. **Golf carts:** N/A. **Discount golf packages:** Yes. **Season:** April-Nov. **High:** July-Aug. **On site lodging:** No. **Rental clubs:** Yes. **Walking policy:** Unrestricted walking. **Metal spikes allowed:** Yes. **Range:** Yes (grass/mats). **To obtain tee times:** Call.
Special Notes: Spikeless encouraged.

★★½FAIRLAWN GOLF & COUNTRY CLUB
434 Empire Rd., Poland, 04274, Androscoggin County, (207)998-4277, 25 miles N of Portland.
Opened: 1963. **Holes:** 18. **Par:** 72/72. **Yards:** 6,300/5,379. **Course rating:** 69.4/69.9. **Slope:** 118/112. **Architect:** Chick Adams. **Green fee:** $15/$17. **Credit cards:** None. **Reduced fees:** Weekdays. **Caddies:** No. **Golf carts:** $12. **Discount golf packages:** No. **Season:** May-First Snow. **High:** July-Aug. **On site lodging:** No. **Rental clubs:** Yes.

Walking policy: Unrestricted walking. **Metal spikes allowed:** Yes. **Range:** Yes (grass).
To obtain tee times: No tee times taken. First come, first served.
Subscriber comments: All types of shots needed...Would play again...Low price draws a tremendous crowd...Good walking course, you earn your score.

★★GORHAM GOLF CLUB
134 McClellan Rd., Gorham, 04038, Cumberland County, (207)839-3490, 10 miles S of Portland.
Opened: 1960. **Holes:** 9. **Par:** 71/73. **Yards:** 6,552/5,868. **Course rating:** 70.8/71.4.
Slope: 116/124. **Architect:** Jim McDonald Sr.. **Green fee:** $22/$25. **Credit cards:**
None. **Reduced fees:** N/A. **Caddies:** No. **Golf carts:** $20. **Discount golf packages:**
No. **Season:** April-Nov. **High:** June-Aug. **On site lodging:** No. **Rental clubs:** No.
Walking policy: Unrestricted walking. **Metal spikes allowed:** Yes. **Range:** Yes
(grass/mats). **To obtain tee times:** Call Thursday a.m. for upcoming weekend.

★★HERMON MEADOW GOLF CLUB
PU-RR8, Box 6160, Bangor, 04401, Penobscot County, (207)848-3241, 3 miles W of Bangor.
Opened: 1964. **Holes:** 18. **Par:** 72/73. **Yards:** 6,329/5,395. **Course rating:** 69.4/70.9.
Slope: 117/120. **Architect:** N/A. **Green fee:** $18/$20. **Credit cards:** MC,VISA,AMEX.
Reduced fees: Weekdays. **Caddies:** No. **Golf carts:** $9. **Discount golf packages:** No.
Season: April-Dec. **High:** July-Aug. **On site lodging:** No. **Rental clubs:** Yes. **Walking policy:** Unrestricted walking. **Metal spikes allowed:** Yes. **Range:** Yes (grass/mats). **To obtain tee times:** First come, first served.

★★★½KEBO VALLEY GOLF COURSE
PU-Eagle Lake Rd., Bar Harbor, 04609, Hancock County, (207)288-3000, 42 miles SE of Bangor.
Opened: 1888. **Holes:** 18. **Par:** 70/72. **Yards:** 6,131/5,440. **Course rating:** 69.0/68.0.
Slope: 130/121. **Architect:** Herbert Leeds/A.E. Liscombe. **Green fee:** $25/$50. **Credit cards:** MC,VISA,AMEX. **Reduced fees:** Low season. **Caddies:** No. **Golf carts:** $30.
Discount golf packages: No. **Season:** April-Nov. **High:** July-Aug. **On site lodging:**
No. **Rental clubs:** Yes. **Walking policy:** Unrestricted walking. **Metal spikes allowed:**
Yes. **Range:** No. **To obtain tee times:** Call 2 days in advance.
Subscriber comments: Very old, very pretty...Maybe the state's best...Classic...Great scenic views...Designed for tourist play...Mountain views from valley fairways...A must play...17th hole is unique and historic...Know your distances here, blind shots...Best vacation spot. Would be my summer retreat.
Special Notes: Spikeless shoes strongly encouraged.

★★★KENNEBEC HEIGHTS GOLF CLUB
PU-Green Meadow Dr., Farmingdale, 04344, Kennebec County, (207)582-2000, 3 miles S of Augusta.
Opened: 1964. **Holes:** 18. **Par:** 70/70. **Yards:** 6,003/4,820. **Course rating:** 69.0/67.7.
Slope: 129/119. **Architect:** Brian Silva. **Green fee:** $20/$24. **Credit cards:** MC,VISA.
Reduced fees: Weekdays, low season. **Caddies:** No. **Golf carts:** $10. **Discount golf packages:** Yes. **Season:** April-Oct. **High:** June-Aug. **On site lodging:** No. **Rental clubs:** Yes. **Walking policy:** Unrestricted walking. **Metal spikes allowed:** Yes. **Range:**
Yes (Mats). **To obtain tee times:** Nonmembers may call up to 3 days in advance.
Subscriber comments: Second nine much tougher than first nine...The back nine is great!...Front open, back nine, beautiful, tough.
Special Notes: Spikeless shoes strongly recommended.

★★½MINGO SPRINGS GOLF COURSE
PU-Proctor Rd. and Rte. 4, Rangeley, 04970, Franklin County, (207)864-5021, 120 miles N of Portland.
Opened: 1925. **Holes:** 18. **Par:** 70/70. **Yards:** 6,014/5,158. **Course rating:** 66.3/67.4.
Slope: 109/110. **Architect:** Skip Wogan. **Green fee:** $26/$26. **Credit cards:** None.
Reduced fees: N/A. **Caddies:** No. **Golf carts:** $26. **Discount golf packages:** No.
Season: May-Oct. **High:** July-Sept. **On site lodging:** No. **Rental clubs:** Yes. **Walking policy:** Unrestricted walking. **Metal spikes allowed:** Yes. **Range:** Yes (grass). **To obtain tee times:** No tee times taken.
Subscriber comments: Challenging layout...Confidence builder...Breathtaking scenery.

★★★NATANIS GOLF CLUB
PU-Webber Pond Rd., Vassalboro, 04989, Kennebec County, (207)622-3561.
Architect: Paul Browne/Philip Wogan. **Caddies:** No. **Discount golf packages:** No. **On site lodging:** No. **Rental clubs:** No. **Metal spikes allowed:** Yes. **Range:** No.
Call club for further information.
Subscriber comments: Very long par 5, 605 yds; short par 4s; out of the way...Beautiful new clubhouse...Love it...27-hole facility with nine really good holes...Newest nine is fun...Something for everybody, very fair course.

★★★★PENOBSCOT VALLEY COUNTRY CLUB
366 Main St., Orono, 04473, Penobscot County, (207)866-2423, 5 miles N of Bangor.
Opened: 1923. **Holes:** 18. **Par:** 72/74. **Yards:** 6,450/5,856. **Course rating:** 70.3/73.2.
Slope: 123/126. **Architect:** Donald Ross. **Green fee:** $45/$45. **Credit cards:** MC,VISA.
Reduced fees: N/A. **Caddies:** No. **Golf carts:** $26. **Discount golf packages:** No.
Season: April-Oct. **High:** June-Aug. **On site lodging:** No. **Rental clubs:** Yes. **Walking policy:** Unrestricted walking. **Metal spikes allowed:** Yes. **Range:** Yes (grass). **To obtain tee times:** Call seven days in advance.
Notes: Ranked 4th in 1997 Best in State.
Subscriber comments: High rough and small fast greens equal great challenge...An old great course...Classic design...Great Donald Ross layout.

★★★½POINT SEBAGO GOLF & BEACH RV RESORT
PU-Rt. 302, Casco, 04015, Cumberland County, (207)655-2747.
Opened: 1996. **Holes:** 18. **Par:** 72/72. **Yards:** 7,002/4,866. **Course rating:** 73.7/68.4.
Slope: 135/117. **Architect:** Phil Wogan and George Sargent. **Green fee:** $38/$44.
Credit cards: MC,VISA,DISC. **Reduced fees:** Low season, resort guests. **Caddies:** No. **Golf carts:** Included in Green Fee. **Discount golf packages:** No. **Season:** May-Oct. **High:** July-Aug. **On site lodging:** Yes. **Rental clubs:** Yes. **Walking policy:** Mandatory cart. **Metal spikes allowed:** Yes. **Range:** Yes (grass/mats). **To obtain tee times:** Call golf shop up to 7 days in advance.
Notes: Ranked 5th in 1997 Best in State, 4thin 1996 Best New Affordable Courses..
Subscriber comments: Loon and eagle tees are tough...Some great holes but impossible to walk...Definitely in top 5 in state...Tests your shotmaking skills...Needs clubhouse...Needs to mature...Very playable and challenging.

★★½POLAND SPRING COUNTRY CLUB
R-Rte. 26, Poland Spring, 04274, Androscoggin County, (207)998-6002, 20 miles NW of Portland.
Opened: 1896. **Holes:** 18. **Par:** 71/74. **Yards:** 6,200/5,393. **Course rating:** 68.2/71.6.
Slope: 119/117. **Architect:** A.H. Fenn/Donald Ross. **Green fee:** $20/$20. **Credit cards:** All major. **Reduced fees:** Resort guests. **Caddies:** Yes. **Golf carts:** $20. **Discount golf packages:** Yes. **Season:** May-Oct. **High:** June-Sept. **On site lodging:** Yes. **Rental clubs:** Yes. **Walking policy:** Unrestricted walking. **Metal spikes allowed:** No. **Range:** Yes (grass). **To obtain tee times:** Call up to 1 year in advance.
Subscriber comments: Postcard views...4th hole one of the most beautiful...Good short challange...Tricky greens...Donald Ross design...Nos. 11-14 holes are as challenging as they come...Moral booster...Some very demanding holes.

★★½PRESQUE ISLE COUNTRY CLUB
35 Parkhurst Siding Rd. (Rte. 205), Presque Isle, 04769, Aroostook County, (207)764-0430.
Opened: 1958. **Holes:** 18. **Par:** 72/72. **Yards:** 6,730/5,600. **Course rating:** 71.4/72.5.
Slope: 122/119. **Architect:** Ben Gray/Geoffrey Cornish. **Green fee:** $20/$20. **Credit cards:** MC,VISA. **Reduced fees:** Low season. **Caddies:** No. **Golf carts:** $20.
Discount golf packages: Yes. **Season:** May-Oct. **High:** June-Aug. **On site lodging:** No. **Rental clubs:** Yes. **Walking policy:** Unrestricted walking. **Metal spikes allowed:** Yes. **Range:** Yes (grass). **To obtain tee times:** First come, first served.

★½PROSPECT HILL GOLF COURSE
694 S. Main St., Auburn, 04210, Androscoggin County, (207)782-9220, 5 miles W of Lewiston.
Opened: 1957. **Holes:** 18. **Par:** 71/73. **Yards:** 5,846/5,227. **Course rating:** 66.9/68.7.

Slope: 111/119. **Architect:** Arthur David Chapman. **Green fee:** $16/$16. **Credit cards:** MC,VISA,DISC. **Reduced fees:** Weekdays, twilight. **Caddies:** No. **Golf carts:** $18. **Discount golf packages:** No. **Season:** April-Nov. **High:** April-Nov. **On site lodging:** No. **Rental clubs:** No. **Walking policy:** Unrestricted walking. **Metal spikes allowed:** Yes. **Range:** No. **To obtain tee times:** No tee times given.

★★½RIVERSIDE MUNICIPAL GOLF COURSE

PU-1158 Riverside St., Portland, 04103, Cumberland County, (207)797-3524.
Opened: 1935. **Holes:** 18. **Par:** 72/72. **Yards:** 6,450/5,640. **Course rating:** 69.5/70.7. **Slope:** 115/112. **Architect:** Wayne Stiles. **Green fee:** $15/$18. **Credit cards:** MC,VISA. **Reduced fees:** Seniors, juniors. **Caddies:** No. **Golf carts:** $18. **Discount golf packages:** No. **Season:** April-Nov. **High:** July-Aug. **On site lodging:** No. **Rental clubs:** Yes. **Walking policy:** Unrestricted walking. **Metal spikes allowed:** Yes. **Range:** Yes (grass). **To obtain tee times:** Call Wednesday prior to weekend of play.
Subscriber comments: Have taken some of challenge out...Varied holes...Better than average muny...Good greens, good use of hill...Lots of up and down.

★★★ROCKLAND GOLF CLUB

606 Old County Rd., Rockland, 04841, Knox County, (207)594-9322, 45 miles E of Augusta.
Opened: 1932. **Holes:** 18. **Par:** 70/73. **Yards:** 6,121/5,583. **Course rating:** 68.6/71.8. **Slope:** 114/119. **Architect:** Wayne Stiles/Roger Sorrent. **Green fee:** $25/$30. **Credit cards:** MC,VISA. **Reduced fees:** Twilight, juniors. **Caddies:** No. **Golf carts:** $22. **Discount golf packages:** No. **Season:** April-Oct. **High:** June-Sept. **On site lodging:** No. **Rental clubs:** Yes. **Walking policy:** Unrestricted walking. **Metal spikes allowed:** Yes. **Range:** No. **To obtain tee times:** Call 2 days in advance.
Subscriber comments: Excellent greens...Too many open parallel holes!...Good putters score best...Par-3 8th another great challenge...Back nine fantastic views.

★★★½SABLE OAKS GOLF CLUB

PU-505 Country Club Dr., South Portland, 04106, Cumberland County, (207)775-6257.
Opened: 1989. **Holes:** 18. **Par:** 70/72. **Yards:** 6,359/4,786. **Course rating:** 71.8. **Slope:** 134/121. **Architect:** Geoffrey Cornish and Brian Silva. **Green fee:** $23/$29. **Credit cards:** MC,VISA. **Reduced fees:** Twilight. **Caddies:** Yes. **Golf carts:** $22. **Discount golf packages:** No. **Season:** April-Dec. **High:** April-Sept. **On site lodging:** No. **Rental clubs:** No. **Walking policy:** Unrestricted walking. **Metal spikes allowed:** Yes. **Range:** No. **To obtain tee times:** Call seven days in advance.
Subscriber comments: Very difficult (narrow)...Much improved greens...Tough to walk. Tough to play. No room for error...Worth the trip...4th hole drive is impossible...Some blind shots. Trouble off tees...Requires good course management...Punishes the long ball...Bring plenty of ammo...You remember the unfair holes, not the seven good ones...Love the forced carries...Leave driver in the trunk.

★★★★SAMOSET RESORT GOLF CLUB

R-220 Warrenton St., Rockport, 04856, Knox County, (207)594-1431, (800)341-1650, 80 miles NE of Portland.
Opened: 1978. **Holes:** 18. **Par:** 70/72. **Yards:** 6,548/5,360. **Course rating:** 70.8/70.1. **Slope:** 129/120. **Architect:** Robert Elder. **Green fee:** $55/$100. **Credit cards:** All major. **Reduced fees:** Low season, resort guests. **Caddies:** No. **Golf carts:** Included in Green Fee. **Discount golf packages:** Yes. **Season:** April-Nov. **High:** June-Sept. **On site lodging:** Yes. **Rental clubs:** Yes. **Walking policy:** Unrestricted walking. **Metal spikes allowed:** No. **Range:** Yes (grass/mats). **To obtain tee times:** Hotel guests may reserve tee times with room confirmation as early as April 1. Members may reserve up to 7 days in advance. Others may reserve up to 2 days in advance.
Notes: Ranked 2nd in 1997 Best in State.
Subscriber comments: Nice summer resort course...A lot of fun, plays short...Fast greens—ocean views...Can't wait to go back!...Absolutely stunning. Well worth the hike!...The Pebble Beach of the East!...#1 on my list...Enjoyable if not windy.

★★★★½SUGARLOAF GOLF CLUB

R-R.R. No.1, P.O. Box 5000, Carrabassett Valley, 04947, Franklin County, (207)237-2000, (800)843-5623, 100 miles N of Portland.
Opened: 1986. **Holes:** 18. **Par:** 72/72. **Yards:** 6,451/5,376. **Course rating:** 70.0/73.7.

Slope: 141/136. **Architect:** Robert Trent Jones Jr. **Green fee:** $45/$69. **Credit cards:** MC,VISA,AMEX. **Reduced fees:** Low season, resort guests, twilight, juniors. **Caddies:** No. **Golf carts:** $16. **Discount golf packages:** Yes. **Season:** May-Oct. **High:** Aug.-Sept. **On site lodging:** Yes. **Rental clubs:** Yes. **Walking policy:** Unrestricted walking. **Metal spikes allowed:** Yes. **Range:** Yes (grass/mats). **To obtain tee times:** Call 14 days in advance. Guests may make tee times with room reservations at (800)843-5623. **Notes:** Ranked 1st in 1997 Best in State.

Subscriber comments: Beautiful course surrounded by birches...The fox may help you look for ball on the 9th...Frustrating but gorgeous...Worth the long drive...Don't be distracted by the mountain views...Be prepared, the moose are everywhere.

★★★VA JO WA GOLF COURSE

R-142A Walker Rd., Island Falls, 04747, Aroostook County, (207)463-2128, 85 miles NE of Bangor.

Opened: 1964. **Holes:** 18. **Par:** 72/72. **Yards:** 6,223/5,065. **Course rating:** 70.4/69.6. **Slope:** 125/119. **Architect:** Vaughan Walker and Warren Walker. **Green fee:** $18/$20. **Credit cards:** MC,VISA,DISC. **Reduced fees:** Weekdays, low season, resort guests, twilight, juniors. **Caddies:** No. **Golf carts:** $12. **Discount golf packages:** Yes. **Season:** May-Oct. **High:** July-Sept. **On site lodging:** Yes. **Rental clubs:** Yes. **Walking policy:** Unrestricted walking. **Metal spikes allowed:** Yes. **Range:** Yes (grass). **To obtain tee times:** Call 1 day in advance.

Subscriber comments: Good variety of holes...Front nine in a valley, bordering a lake, back nine in mountains—scenic—a good test.

★★★VAL HALLA GOLF & RECREATION CENTER

PM-1 Val Halla Rd., Cumberland, 04021, Cumberland County, (207)829-2225, 10 miles N of Portland.

Opened: 1965. **Holes:** 18. **Par:** 72/72. **Yards:** 6,574/5,437. **Course rating:** 71.1/70.4. **Slope:** 126/116. **Architect:** Phil Wogan. **Green fee:** $21/$27. **Credit cards:** MC,VISA. **Reduced fees:** Weekdays, seniors, juniors. **Caddies:** No. **Golf carts:** $28. **Discount golf packages:** Yes. **Season:** April-Nov. **High:** June-Sept. **On site lodging:** No. **Rental clubs:** Yes. **Walking policy:** Unrestricted walking. **Metal spikes allowed:** Yes. **Range:** Yes (grass/mats). **To obtain tee times:** Call 7 days in advance.

Subscriber comments: Good par 3s...Back nine better than front nine...Tougher than it appears. Some tricky holes...Lots of variety and fun to play...Best finishing holes in the state 15-18...Getting better with age—like me...Need trees to separate fairways...Earn your pars here...Got to like the 2nd hole.

★★★½WATERVILLE COUNTRY CLUB

Country Club Rd., Oakland, 04963, Kennebec County, (207)465-9861, 5 miles W of Waterville.

Opened: 1916. **Holes:** 18. **Par:** 70/73. **Yards:** 6,412/5,466. **Course rating:** 69.6/71.4. **Slope:** 124/121. **Architect:** Orrin Smith/Geoffrey S. Cornish. **Green fee:** $38/$38. **Credit cards:** None. **Reduced fees:** N/A. **Caddies:** No. **Golf carts:** $22. **Discount golf packages:** No. **Season:** April-Nov. **High:** May-Sept. **On site lodging:** No. **Rental clubs:** Yes. **Walking policy:** Unrestricted walking. **Metal spikes allowed:** No. **Range:** Yes (grass/mats). **To obtain tee times:** Call.

Subscriber comments: Outstanding layout, needs ranger...Challenging par 3s...Great old style course...You'll need a full bag of clubs here...A hidden gem...Narrow, hilly beauty.

★★WILLOWDALE GOLF CLUB

PU-52 Willowdale Rd., Scarborough, 04074, Cumberland County, (207)883-9351, 9 miles S of Portland.

Opened: 1924. **Holes:** 18. **Par:** 70/70. **Yards:** 5,980/5,344. **Course rating:** 68.7/73.7. **Slope:** 110/112. **Architect:** Skip Wogan/Fred Nanney. **Green fee:** $23/$23. **Credit cards:** MC,VISA,DISC. **Reduced fees:** Twilight. **Caddies:** No. **Golf carts:** $20. **Discount golf packages:** No. **Season:** April-Oct. **High:** July-Aug. **On site lodging:** No. **Rental clubs:** Yes. **Walking policy:** Unrestricted walking. **Metal spikes allowed:** Yes. **Range:** No. **To obtain tee times:** Call Wednesday for following weekend.

Subscriber comments: Few hazards, back nine more interesting...Very basic golf, good for beginners...Easy and wide open confidence builder...Mosquitoes always there...Front nine fairways quite close together.

MARYLAND

★★★THE BAY CLUB
R-9122 Libertytown Rd., Berlin, 21811, Worcester County, (800)229-2582, 7 miles W of Ocean City.
Opened: 1989. **Holes:** 18. **Par:** 72/72. **Yards:** 6,958/5,609. **Course rating:** 73.1/71.3.
Slope: 126/118. **Architect:** Russell Roberts. **Green fee:** $20/$55. **Credit cards:**
MC,VISA,AMEX. **Reduced fees:** Weekdays, low season, resort guests, twilight.
Caddies: No. **Golf carts:** Included in Green Fee. **Discount golf packages:** Yes.
Season: Year-round. **High:** April-Oct. **On site lodging:** No. **Rental clubs:** Yes. **Walking policy:** Unrestricted walking. **Metal spikes allowed:** Yes. **Range:** Yes (grass/mats). **To obtain tee times:** Call up to 1 year in advance.
Subscriber comments: Nice design and well maintained...Interesting par 3s...The 18th is a good finishing hole...Friendly and knowledgeable pro staff...Straightforward track with lots of water...New 18 holes being built.

★★½BAY HILLS GOLF CLUB
545 Bay Hills Dr., Arnold, 21012, Anne Arundel County, (410)974-0669, 30 miles S of Baltimore.
Opened: 1969. **Holes:** 18. **Par:** 70/70. **Yards:** 6,423/5,029. **Course rating:** 70.8/69.2.
Slope: 118/121. **Architect:** Ed Ault. **Green fee:** $30/$37. **Credit cards:** None.
Reduced fees: Twilight. **Caddies:** No. **Golf carts:** Included in Green Fee. **Discount golf packages:** No. **Season:** Year-round. **High:** April-Oct. **On site lodging:** No. **Rental clubs:** Yes. **Walking policy:** Mandatory cart. **Metal spikes allowed:** No. **Range:** No.
To obtain tee times: Call up to 3 days in advance.
Subscriber comments: Short, tight course, generally in good shape...A local favorite...Course management has made recent improvements...Some fun holes...Congenial staff...Good layout for average golfer.

THE BEACH CLUB GOLF LINKS
9715 Deer Park Dr., Berlin, 21811, Worcester County, (410)641-4653, (800)435-9223, 7 miles W of Ocean City.
Opened: 1991. **Architect:** Brian Ault. **Green fee:** $25/$60. **Credit cards:** All major.
Reduced fees: Low season, twilight. **Caddies:** No. **Golf carts:** Included in Green Fee.
Discount golf packages: Yes. **Season:** Year-round. **High:** April-Oct. **On site lodging:**
No. **Rental clubs:** Yes. **Walking policy:** Walking at certain times. **Metal spikes allowed:** No. **Range:** Yes (Mats). **To obtain tee times:** Call anytime with credit card to confirm.
★★★½INNER LINKS COURSE
Holes: 18. **Par:** 72/72. **Yards:** 7,020/5,167. **Course rating:** 73.0/69.0. **Slope:** 128/117.
Subscriber comments: Nice practice facility...36 holes offer a variety of challenges...Course is well maintained...Layout will improve with age...New links-style track boasts plenty of water...A fun beach course...Older layout is nice, new track is too short...Narrow fairways and fast greens...Keep it straight off the tee.
OUTER LINKS COURSE
Holes: 18. **Par:** 72/72. **Yards:** 6,548/5,022. **Course rating:** 71.7/68.6. **Slope:** 134/119.

★★★BEAVER CREEK COUNTRY CLUB
9535 Mapleville Rd., Hagerstown, 21740, Washington County, (301)733-5152, 60 miles NW of Baltimore.
Opened: 1956. **Holes:** 18. **Par:** 72/73. **Yards:** 6,878/5,636. **Course rating:** 71.6/71.4.
Slope: 117/124. **Architect:** Reuben Hines. **Green fee:** $30/$35. **Credit cards:** None.
Reduced fees: Weekdays, low season, twilight, seniors, juniors. **Caddies:** No. **Golf carts:** $10. **Discount golf packages:** No. **Season:** Jan.-Dec. **High:** May-Oct. **On site lodging:** No. **Rental clubs:** Yes. **Walking policy:** Walking at certain times. **Metal spikes allowed:** Yes. **Range:** Yes (grass/mats). **To obtain tee times:** Call 7 days in advance.
Subscriber comments: Long track features small greens and steep hills...Appears tight from tees but opens up...A nice golf course, nothing fancy...Friendly pro shop staff...Country setting...Could use better care.

★★★½BLACK ROCK GOLF COURSE
PU-20025 Mt. Aetna Rd., Hagerstown, 21742, Washington County, (301)791-3040, 70 miles NW of Baltimore.

Opened: 1989. **Holes:** 18. **Par:** 72/74. **Yards:** 6,646/5,179. **Course rating:** 70.7/64.7. **Slope:** 124/112. **Architect:** Robert L. Elder. **Green fee:** $13/$25. **Credit cards:** MC,VISA. **Reduced fees:** Twilight, seniors, juniors. **Caddies:** No. **Golf carts:** $11. **Discount golf packages:** Yes. **Season:** Year-round. **High:** May-Sept. **On site lodging:** No. **Rental clubs:** Yes. **Walking policy:** Walking at certain times. **Metal spikes allowed:** Yes. **Range:** Yes (grass/mats). **To obtain tee times:** Call 7 days in advance for weekday tee times. Call Monday at 7:30 a.m. for upcoming weekend.
Subscriber comments: Challenging layout...Nice greens...Converted dairy farm, but kept in good shape...President Clinton has been spotted playing a round...Nice all-around course...Some good holes.

★★BRANTWOOD GOLF CLUB
1190 Augustine Herman Hwy., Elkton, 21921, Cecil County, (410)398-8849, 15 miles S of Wilmington, DE.
Opened: 1962. **Holes:** 18. **Par:** 70/72. **Yards:** 6,101/5,237. **Course rating:** 67.6/70.5. **Slope:** 118/114. **Architect:** Wallace William. **Green fee:** $22/$27. **Credit cards:** None. **Reduced fees:** Twilight, seniors, juniors. **Caddies:** No. **Golf carts:** $12. **Discount golf packages:** No. **Season:** Year-round. **High:** April-Oct. **On site lodging:** No. **Rental clubs:** Yes. **Walking policy:** Walking at certain times. **Metal spikes allowed:** Yes. **Range:** Yes (grass/mats). **To obtain tee times:** First come, first served on weekdays. Call 7 days in advance for weekends and holidays.

★★★BRETON BAY GOLF & COUNTRY CLUB
21935 Society Hill Rd., Leonardtown, 20650, St. Mary's County, (301)475-2300, 7 miles N of Leonardtown.
Opened: 1974. **Holes:** 18. **Par:** 72/73. **Yards:** 6,933/5,457. **Course rating:** 73.0/70.0. **Slope:** 126/117. **Architect:** J. Porter Gibson. **Green fee:** $21/$21. **Credit cards:** MC,VISA. **Reduced fees:** Juniors. **Caddies:** No. **Golf carts:** $12. **Discount golf packages:** No. **Season:** March-Dec. **High:** May-Aug. **On site lodging:** No. **Rental clubs:** Yes. **Walking policy:** Walking at certain times. **Metal spikes allowed:** No. **Range:** Yes (grass/mats). **To obtain tee times:** Call on Thursday for weekend play.
Subscriber comments: First hole features great view of Potomac...Starts easy, but gets progressively harder...Water in play on three of last four holes...Fairways have improved with conversion to Bermuda.

★★½CAMBRIDGE COUNTRY CLUB
Horns Point Rd., Cambridge, 21613, Dorchester County, (410)228-4808, 40 miles NW of Salisbury.
Opened: 1925. **Holes:** 18. **Par:** 72/73. **Yards:** 6,387/5,416. **Course rating:** 69.3/71.0. **Slope:** 113/118. **Architect:** Russell Roberts. **Green fee:** $35/$35. **Credit cards:** MC,VISA. **Reduced fees:** Resort guests. **Caddies:** No. **Golf carts:** N/A. **Discount golf packages:** Yes. **Season:** Year-round. **High:** May-Oct. **On site lodging:** No. **Rental clubs:** Yes. **Walking policy:** Unrestricted walking. **Metal spikes allowed:** Yes. **Range:** Yes (grass). **To obtain tee times:** Only members and guests of members can play on the weekends. No tee time required for weekdays.
Subscriber comments: Golf professional and staff are accommodating...Great view from the clubhouse...Open layout...The eighth hole plays short but extremely difficult...A bit pricey.

★★CARROLL PARK GOLF COURSE
PU-2100 Washington Blvd., Baltimore, 21230, Baltimore County, (410)685-8344, 3 miles SW of Baltimore.
Opened: 1923. **Holes:** 12. **Par:** 44/43. **Yards:** 3,214/2,862. **Course rating:** N/A. **Slope:** N/A. **Architect:** N/A. **Green fee:** $8. **Credit cards:** MC,VISA. **Reduced fees:** Weekdays, twilight, seniors, juniors. **Caddies:** No. **Golf carts:** $15. **Discount golf packages:** No. **Season:** Year-round. **High:** March-Oct. **On site lodging:** No. **Rental clubs:** Yes. **Walking policy:** Unrestricted walking. **Metal spikes allowed:** Yes. **Range:** Yes (grass/mats). **To obtain tee times:** Call golf shop.

★★★CHANTILLY MANOR COUNTRY CLUB
128 Karen Dr., Rising Sun, 21911, Cecil County, (410)658-4343, 18 miles S of Wilmington, DE.
Opened: 1967. **Holes:** 18. **Par:** 71/72. **Yards:** 6,593/5,323. **Course rating:** 72.3/65.8.

Slope: 130/115. **Architect:** N/A. **Green fee:** $40/$48. **Credit cards:** MC,VISA. **Reduced fees:** Weekdays, twilight, seniors, juniors. **Caddies:** No. **Golf carts:** Included in Green Fee. **Discount golf packages:** No. **Season:** Year-round. **High:** April-Oct. **On site lodging:** No. **Rental clubs:** No. **Walking policy:** Unrestricted walking. **Metal spikes allowed:** No. **Range:** Yes (grass). **To obtain tee times:** Call up to 7 days in advance.

Subscriber comments: A lot of potential...Large, fast greens...Terrific layout features plenty of water, native grasses, shaped mounds and sculptured bunkers...The 14th is a great hole...Too many blind shots.

★★½CHESAPEAKE BAY GOLF CLUB

PU-1500 Chesapeake Club Dr, North East, 21901, Cecil County, (410)287-0200.
Opened: 1994. **Holes:** 18. **Par:** 70/70. **Yards:** 6,434/4,811. **Course rating:** 71.2/70.1. **Slope:** 132/110. **Architect:** N/A. **Green fee:** $35/$50. **Credit cards:** MC,VISA,DISC. **Reduced fees:** Weekdays, low season, resort guests, twilight, seniors, juniors. **Caddies:** No. **Golf carts:** Included in Green Fee. **Discount golf packages:** Yes. **Season:** Year-round. **High:** March-Nov. **On site lodging:** No. **Rental clubs:** Yes. **Walking policy:** Unrestricted walking. **Metal spikes allowed:** No. **Range:** Yes (grass/mats). **To obtain tee times:** Call up to 7 days in advance.

Subscriber comments: A difficult test from the tips...Treelined narrow fairways, target golf...Short layout but a long walk...Relatively new course will improve with age...Management has added a clubhouse.

★★½CLUSTERED SPIRES GOLF COURSE

PU-8415 Gas House Pike, Frederick, 21701, Frederick County, (301)624-1295.
Opened: 1991. **Holes:** 18. **Par:** 72/72. **Yards:** 6,769/5,230. **Course rating:** 70.5/70.0. **Slope:** 115/124. **Architect:** Brian T. Ault. **Green fee:** $18/$25. **Credit cards:** MC,VISA. **Reduced fees:** Weekdays, low season, twilight, seniors, juniors. **Caddies:** No. **Golf carts:** $12. **Discount golf packages:** No. **Season:** Year-round. **High:** April-Oct. **On site lodging:** No. **Rental clubs:** Yes. **Walking policy:** Unrestricted walking. **Metal spikes allowed:** Yes. **Range:** Yes (grass). **To obtain tee times:** Call up to 5 days in advance.

Subscriber comments: Nice practice facility (grass range)...Challenging course for average player...Good test from the tips...Relatively flat layout with hit and miss conditions...Weekend rates a bit expensive.

★★DIAMOND RIDGE GOLF COURSE

PM-2309 Ridge Rd., Woodlawn, 21244, Baltimore County, (410)887-1349, 10 miles W of Baltimore.
Opened: 1968. **Holes:** 18. **Par:** 70/72. **Yards:** 6,550/5,833. **Course rating:** 71.0/73.2. **Slope:** 120/123. **Architect:** Ed Ault. **Green fee:** $15/$17. **Credit cards:** None. **Reduced fees:** Twilight, seniors, juniors. **Caddies:** No. **Golf carts:** $18. **Discount golf packages:** No. **Season:** Year-round. **High:** April-Oct. **On site lodging:** No. **Rental clubs:** Yes. **Walking policy:** Unrestricted walking. **Metal spikes allowed:** Yes. **Range:** Yes (grass). **To obtain tee times:** Call anytime.

★★★★EAGLE'S LANDING GOLF CLUB

PU-12367 Eagle's Nest Rd., Berlin, 21811, Worcester County, (410)213-7277, 3 miles S of Ocean City.
Opened: 1991. **Holes:** 18. **Par:** 72/72. **Yards:** 7,003/4,896. **Course rating:** 74.3/69.3. **Slope:** 126/115. **Architect:** Michael Hurdzan. **Green fee:** $16/$23. **Credit cards:** MC,VISA,AMEX. **Reduced fees:** Weekdays, low season, twilight. **Caddies:** No. **Golf carts:** $14. **Discount golf packages:** Yes. **Season:** Year-round. **High:** April-Oct. **On site lodging:** No. **Rental clubs:** Yes. **Walking policy:** Unrestricted walking. **Metal spikes allowed:** Yes. **Range:** No. **To obtain tee times:** Call up to 1 year in advance.

Notes: Ranked 7th in 1997 Best in State.

Subscriber comments: Outstanding layout in excellent condition...Beautiful scenic course...A good variety of holes...Fair, smart play can keep you out of trouble...Difficult test in the wind...Terrific use of wetlands...Some memorable bayside holes...Requires course management to score...Plenty of wildlife...Great blend of golf and nature...Bring bug spray...The 17th and 18th are top-notch finishing holes...Tough getting tee time...The beast of the east.

MARYLAND

★★★THE EASTON CLUB
PU-28449 Clubhouse Dr., Easton, 21601, Talbot County, (410)820-9017, (800)277-9800, 45 miles SE of Baltimore.
Opened: 1995. **Holes:** 18. **Par:** 72/72. **Yards:** 6,703/5,230. **Course rating:** 72.1/70.2.
Slope: 122/119. **Architect:** Robert Rauch. **Green fee:** $22/$28. **Credit cards:** MC,VISA,DISC. **Reduced fees:** Juniors. **Caddies:** No. **Golf carts:** $12. **Discount golf packages:** No. **Season:** Year-round. **High:** April-Oct. **On site lodging:** No. **Rental clubs:** Yes. **Walking policy:** Walking at certain times. **Metal spikes allowed:** Yes. **Range:** Yes (grass/mats). **To obtain tee times:** Call 14 days in advance.
Subscriber comments: New course needs to mature...Attractive layout with good par 3s...Solid course, excellent value and service...Watch for geese...Great menu at pub...Construction of surrounding condos is a distraction.

★★½EISENHOWER GOLF COURSE
PM-1576 General Hwy., Crownsville, 21032, Anne Arundel County, (410)222-7922, 27 miles S of Baltimore.
Opened: 1970. **Holes:** 18. **Par:** 71/71. **Yards:** 6,693/4,853. **Course rating:** 71.3/66.9.
Slope: 122/96. **Architect:** Eddie Ault. **Green fee:** $15/$15. **Credit cards:** None.
Reduced fees: Twilight, seniors, juniors. **Caddies:** No. **Golf carts:** $22. **Discount golf packages:** No. **Season:** Year-round. **High:** May-Oct. **On site lodging:** No. **Rental clubs:** Yes. **Walking policy:** Unrestricted walking. **Metal spikes allowed:** Yes. **Range:** Yes. **To obtain tee times:** Call seven days in advance.
Subscriber comments: Great layout, but overplayed...A good test of golf...Requires accuracy off the tee.

★★★½ENTERPRISE GOLF COURSE
PU-2802 Enterprise Rd., Mitchellville, 20721, Prince George's County, (301)249-2040, 2 miles E of Washington DC.
Opened: 1976. **Holes:** 18. **Par:** 72/72. **Yards:** 6,586/5,157. **Course rating:** 71.7/69.6.
Slope: 128/114. **Architect:** Dunovan & Assoc.. **Green fee:** $14/$30. **Credit cards:** MC,VISA. **Reduced fees:** Weekdays, low season, twilight, seniors, juniors. **Caddies:** No. **Golf carts:** $23. **Discount golf packages:** No. **Season:** Year-round. **High:** March-Oct. **On site lodging:** No. **Rental clubs:** Yes. **Walking policy:** Walking at certain times. **Metal spikes allowed:** Yes. **Range:** Yes. **To obtain tee times:** First come, first served.
Subscriber comments: Good course but difficult getting tee time...First come, first serve...Beautiful setting...Well maintained despite heavy play...A good variety of holes...Expect a five-hour round.

★★FALLS ROAD GOLF CLUB
PU-10800 Falls Rd., Potomac, 20854, Montgomery County, (301)299-5156, 20 miles SE of Washington, DC.
Opened: 1955. **Holes:** 18. **Par:** 71/75. **Yards:** 6,257/5,476. **Course rating:** 67.7/59.3.
Slope: 120/111. **Architect:** Edward Ault. **Green fee:** $15/$24. **Credit cards:** None.
Reduced fees: Seniors, juniors. **Caddies:** No. **Golf carts:** $20. **Discount golf packages:** No. **Season:** Year-round. **High:** April-Nov. **On site lodging:** No. **Rental clubs:** Yes. **Walking policy:** Unrestricted walking. **Metal spikes allowed:** Yes. **Range:** Yes. **To obtain tee times:** Call one week in advance for weekends only.

★★FOREST PARK GOLF CLUB
PU-2900 Hillsdale Rd., Baltimore, 20331, Baltimore County, (410)448-4653.
Opened: N/A. **Holes:** 18. **Par:** 71/71. **Yards:** 6,127/4,824. **Course rating:** 68.2/66.0.
Slope: 116/100. **Architect:** Alex (Nipper) Campbell. **Green fee:** $10. **Credit cards:** MC,VISA. **Reduced fees:** Weekdays, twilight, seniors, juniors. **Caddies:** No. **Golf carts:** N/A. **Discount golf packages:** No. **Season:** Year-round. **High:** April-Oct. **On site lodging:** No. **Rental clubs:** Yes. **Walking policy:** Unrestricted walking. **Metal spikes allowed:** Yes. **Range:** No. **To obtain tee times:** Call golf shop.

★★½GLENN DALE GOLF CLUB
PU-11501 Old Prospect Hill Rd., Glenn Dale, 20769, Prince George's County, (301)464-0904, 15 miles NE of Washington, DC.
Opened: 1955. **Holes:** 18. **Par:** 70/70. **Yards:** 6,282/4,809. **Course rating:** 70.0/67.2.
Slope: 115/107. **Architect:** George W. Cobb. **Green fee:** $22/$27. **Credit cards:**

MC,VISA. **Reduced fees:** Low season, twilight, seniors, juniors. **Caddies:** No. **Golf carts:** $20. **Discount golf packages:** No. **Season:** Year-round. **High:** April-Oct. **On site lodging:** No. **Rental clubs:** Yes. **Walking policy:** Walking at certain times. **Metal spikes allowed:** Yes. **Range:** Yes (Mats). **To obtain tee times:** Call 1 day in advance for weekday. Call on Monday at 11 a.m. for weekend or holiday.

Subscriber comments: On the short side but a nice layout...Well-maintained course for amount of play...A good mix of challenging holes...A fun track to play...Small, fast greens...Congenial staff.

★★★★THE GOLF CLUB AT WISP

R-296 Marsh Hill Rd., P.O. Box 629, McHenry, 21541, Garrett County, (301)387-4911, 90 miles SE of Pittsburgh, PA.

Opened: 1973. **Holes:** 18. **Par:** 72/72. **Yards:** 6,911/5,166. **Course rating:** 73.0/72.0. **Slope:** 137/128. **Architect:** Dominic Palombo. **Green fee:** $45/$55. **Credit cards:** All major. **Reduced fees:** Low season, resort guests, twilight. **Caddies:** No. **Golf carts:** Included in Green Fee. **Discount golf packages:** Yes. **Season:** April-Oct. **High:** July-Sept. **On site lodging:** Yes. **Rental clubs:** Yes. **Walking policy:** Walking at certain times. **Metal spikes allowed:** No. **Range:** Yes. **To obtain tee times:** Call.

Subscriber comments: Fun on a mountain...Scenic views...One of the toughest courses I've played...How can you go uphill for three holes and down in one hole?...Hit 'em straight or bring extra balls...Course is in wonderful shape...One par 4 has two carries over water.

★★★GREAT HOPE GOLF COURSE

PU-8380 Crisfield Hwy., Westover, 21872, Somerset County, (410)651-5900, (800)537-8009, 10 miles S of Salisbury.

Opened: 1995. **Holes:** 18. **Par:** 72/72. **Yards:** 7,047/5,204. **Course rating:** 72.8/68.5. **Slope:** 125/112. **Architect:** Michael Hurdzan. **Green fee:** $18/$26. **Credit cards:** MC,VISA. **Reduced fees:** Weekdays, low season, resort guests, twilight, juniors. **Caddies:** No. **Golf carts:** $11. **Discount golf packages:** Yes. **Season:** Year-round. **High:** April-Oct. **On site lodging:** No. **Rental clubs:** Yes. **Walking policy:** Unrestricted walking. **Metal spikes allowed:** Yes. **Range:** Yes (grass). **To obtain tee times:** Call golf shop.

Subscriber comments: A nice new course...Greens are in great condition...A fair test of golf...Hard to judge distance.

★★★GREEN HILL YACHT & COUNTRY CLUB

5473 White Haven Rd., Quantico, 21856, Wicomico County, (410)749-1605, (888)465-3855, 25 miles W of Ocean City.

Opened: 1927. **Holes:** 18. **Par:** 72/72. **Yards:** 6,800/5,600. **Course rating:** 72.2/72.0. **Slope:** 126/126. **Architect:** Alfred H. Tull. **Green fee:** $38/$57. **Credit cards:** MC,VISA,AMEX. **Reduced fees:** Weekdays, low season. **Caddies:** No. **Golf carts:** Included in Green Fee. **Discount golf packages:** Yes. **Season:** Year-round. **High:** Summer. **On site lodging:** No. **Rental clubs:** Yes. **Walking policy:** Mandatory cart. **Metal spikes allowed:** No. **Range:** Yes (grass). **To obtain tee times:** Call golf shop. Members take priority.

Subscriber comments: Nice track with some interesting holes...Course recently changed management...Has potential to be outstanding golf course...Congenial staff.

★★★HARBOURTOWNE GOLF RESORT & COUNTRY CLUB

R-Rt. 33 at Martingham Dr., St. Michaels, 21663, Talbot County, (410)745-5183, (800)446-9066, 75 miles SE of Washington, DC.

Opened: 1971. **Holes:** 18. **Par:** 70/71. **Yards:** 6,320/5,036. **Course rating:** 69.5/68.5. **Slope:** 120/113. **Architect:** Pete Dye and Roy Dye. **Green fee:** $38. **Credit cards:** All major. **Reduced fees:** Low season, resort guests. **Caddies:** No. **Golf carts:** $12. **Discount golf packages:** Yes. **Season:** Year-round. **High:** April-Oct. **On site lodging:** Yes. **Rental clubs:** Yes. **Walking policy:** Mandatory cart. **Metal spikes allowed:** Yes. **Range:** Yes (grass). **To obtain tee times:** Call.

Subscriber comments: Well-maintained course with nice views...Some difficult, narrow holes...Relatively flat but interesting layout...Keep it straight on the back...The rough is tough...Not for beginners.

★★★½HOG NECK GOLF COURSE

PM-10142 Old Cordova Rd., Easton, 21601, Talbot County, (410)822-6079, 50 miles SE of Baltimore.
Opened: 1976. **Holes:** 18. **Par:** 72/72. **Yards:** 7,000/5,500. **Course rating:** 73.8/71.3. **Slope:** 131/125. **Architect:** Lindsay Ervin. **Green fee:** $37. **Credit cards:** MC,VISA. **Reduced fees:** Weekdays, low season, twilight, juniors. **Caddies:** No. **Golf carts:** $12. **Discount golf packages:** No. **Season:** Feb.-Dec. **High:** April-Oct. **On site lodging:** No. **Rental clubs:** Yes. **Walking policy:** Unrestricted walking. **Metal spikes allowed:** Yes. **Range:** Yes (Mats). **To obtain tee times:** Call on Saturday for upcoming week. **Notes:** Ranked 9th in 1997 Best in State.
Subscriber comments: Outstanding test of golf...Front nine is open with water, back nine is tight and lined with trees...Well-maintained...Service with a smile...World-class back nine...Long and tight...Distances are measured in meters...Boasts excellent nine-hole executive course.

★★½LAYTONSVILLE GOLF COURSE

PU-7130 Dorsey Rd., Laytonsville, 20882, Montgomery County, (301)948-5288, (301)977-7736, 18 miles N of Washington, DC.
Opened: 1973. **Holes:** 18. **Par:** 70/73. **Yards:** 6,311/5,439. **Course rating:** 69.8/71.4. **Slope:** 117/113. **Architect:** Robert L. Elder. **Green fee:** $20/$25. **Credit cards:** MC,VISA. **Reduced fees:** Seniors, juniors. **Caddies:** No. **Golf carts:** $22. **Discount golf packages:** No. **Season:** Year-round. **High:** April-Sept. **On site lodging:** No. **Rental clubs:** Yes. **Walking policy:** Unrestricted walking. **Metal spikes allowed:** No. **Range:** Yes (grass/mats). **To obtain tee times:** Call on Monday at 7 a.m. for weekends and holidays only.
Subscriber comments: Nice course for average player...Features strong par 4s on front side...Friendly pro-shop staff...Conditions are good...Open and fun...A solid back nine...Typically crowded.

★★★THE LINKS AT CHALLEDON

PU-6166 Challedon Circle, Mount Airy, 21771, (301)829-3000, 18 miles W of Baltimore.
Opened: 1996. **Holes:** 18. **Par:** 72/72. **Yards:** 6,730/5,355. **Course rating:** 71.3/70.7. **Slope:** 124/122. **Architect:** N/A. **Green fee:** $55. **Credit cards:** MC,VISA,AMEX. **Reduced fees:** Weekdays, low season, twilight, seniors, juniors. **Caddies:** No. **Golf carts:** Included in Green Fee. **Discount golf packages:** No. **Season:** Year-round. **High:** March-Oct. **On site lodging:** No. **Rental clubs:** Yes. **Walking policy:** Walking at certain times. **Metal spikes allowed:** No. **Range:** Yes (grass/mats). **To obtain tee times:** Call up to 5 days in advance.
Subscriber comments: New course will improve as it matures...Great service and amenities...Watch for OB stakes on almost every hole...Scenic layout...Greens and fairways are well-groomed...The fourth hole is a terrific par 4.

★★MAPLE RUN GOLF COURSE

PU-13610-A Moser Rd., Thurmont, 21788, Frederick County, (301)271-7870.
Opened: 1992. **Holes:** 18. **Par:** 72/72. **Yards:** 6,553/4,822. **Course rating:** 71.2/66.1. **Slope:** 128/114. **Architect:** Russell and Joe Moser. **Green fee:** $15/$19. **Credit cards:** MC,VISA,DISC. **Reduced fees:** Weekdays, low season, twilight, seniors. **Caddies:** No. **Golf carts:** $10. **Discount golf packages:** Yes. **Season:** Year-round. **High:** April-Oct. **On site lodging:** No. **Rental clubs:** Yes. **Walking policy:** Unrestricted walking. **Metal spikes allowed:** Yes. **Range:** Yes (Mats). **To obtain tee times:** Call golf shop.

★★½MARLBOROUGH COUNTRY CLUB

4750 John Rodgers Blvd., Upper Marlboro, 20772, Prince George's County, (301)952-1350, 20 miles E of Washington, DC.
Opened: 1974. **Holes:** 18. **Par:** 71/71. **Yards:** 6,119/5,130. **Course rating:** 69.5/69.5. **Slope:** 127/120. **Architect:** Algie Pulley. **Green fee:** $19/$27. **Credit cards:** MC,VISA,AMEX. **Reduced fees:** Weekdays, low season, twilight. **Caddies:** No. **Golf carts:** $11. **Discount golf packages:** Yes. **Season:** Year-round. **High:** April-Oct. **On site lodging:** No. **Rental clubs:** Yes. **Walking policy:** Walking at certain times **Metal spikes allowed:** Yes. **Range:** Yes (Mats). **To obtain tee times:** Call 7 days in advance.

Subscriber comments: Tight layout...Back nine is tougher...Plenty of woods and water...Homes are too close to fairways...Watch for geese.

★★★MOUNT PLEASANT GOLF CLUB

PU-6001 Hillen Rd., Baltimore, 21239, Baltimore County, (410)254-5100.
Opened: 1933. **Holes:** 18. **Par:** 71/73. **Yards:** 6,728/5,294. **Course rating:** 71.8/69.4. **Slope:** 119/118. **Architect:** Gus Hook. **Green fee:** $11/$12. **Credit cards:** MC,VISA. **Reduced fees:** Weekdays, twilight, seniors, juniors. **Caddies:** No. **Golf carts:** $18. **Discount golf packages:** No. **Season:** Year-round. **High:** June-Aug. **On site lodging:** No. **Rental clubs:** Yes. **Walking policy:** Unrestricted walking. **Metal spikes allowed:** Yes. **Range:** No. **To obtain tee times:** Lottery times for weekends. Call up to 14 days in advance for weekdays.
Notes: 1950-58, 1962 Eastern Open; 1939 U.S. Publinx.
Subscriber comments: A nice, rolling layout that's well-maintained despite heavy play...Short on amenities...Good value...Tough to get tee times...Moving white tees up to increase pace of play took away some of the challenge...Still tough from the tips.

(GOOD VALUE)

★★½NASSAWANGO COUNTRY CLUB

3940 Nassawango Rd., Snow Hill, 21863, Worcester County, (410)632-3144, 18 miles SE of Salisbury.
Opened: 1970. **Holes:** 18. **Par:** 72/73. **Yards:** 6,644/5,760. **Course rating:** 70.2/72.1. **Slope:** 125/125. **Architect:** Russell Roberts. **Green fee:** $27. **Credit cards:** MC,VISA. **Reduced fees:** Low season. **Caddies:** No. **Golf carts:** $12. **Discount golf packages:** Yes. **Season:** Year-round. **High:** May-Oct. **On site lodging:** No. **Rental clubs:** Yes. **Walking policy:** Mandatory cart. **Metal spikes allowed:** Yes. **Range:** No. **To obtain tee times:** Call.
Subscriber comments: Course sets up left to right...Average conditions but fun to play...A good value...Nice greens...Play it in the fall...Friendly staff.

★★½NEEDWOOD GOLF COURSE

PU-6724 Needwood Rd., Derwood, 20855, Worcester County, (301)948-1075, 22 miles N of Washington, DC.
Opened: 1969. **Holes:** 18. **Par:** 70/72. **Yards:** 6,254/5,112. **Course rating:** 69.1/69.2. **Slope:** 113/105. **Architect:** Lindsay Ervin. **Green fee:** $18/$23. **Credit cards:** MC,VISA. **Reduced fees:** Seniors, juniors. **Caddies:** No. **Golf carts:** $22. **Discount golf packages:** No. **Season:** Year-round. **High:** May-Sept. **On site lodging:** No. **Rental clubs:** Yes. **Walking policy:** Unrestricted walking. **Metal spikes allowed:** Yes. **Range:** Yes. **To obtain tee times:** Weekday, first come, first served; weekend, reservations optional.
Subscriber comments: Challenging course...Relatively short, hilly layout with three really nice holes...Geese a problem...Good beginners' track...Lots of water...Also features fun executive nine-hole course...The 18th is a solid finishing hole.

★★½NORTHWEST PARK GOLF COURSE

PU-15701 Layhill Rd., Wheaton, 20906, Montgomery County, (301)598-6100, 15 miles N of Washington, DC.
Opened: 1964. **Holes:** 27. **Par:** 72/74. **Yards:** 7,185/6,325. **Course rating:** 74.0/74.5. **Slope:** 122/126. **Architect:** Edmund B. Ault/Russell Roberts. **Green fee:** $17/$25. **Credit cards:** MC,VISA. **Reduced fees:** Weekdays, seniors, juniors. **Caddies:** No. **Golf carts:** $12. **Discount golf packages:** No. **Season:** Year-round. **High:** June-Aug. **On site lodging:** No. **Rental clubs:** Yes. **Walking policy:** Unrestricted walking. **Metal spikes allowed:** Yes. **Range:** Yes (Mats). **To obtain tee times:** Call up to 6 days in advance for weekdays. Call on Monday a.m. for upcoming weekend.
Subscriber comments: Long and tough...Good conditions considering amount of play...Grip it and rip it on No. 2, a 460-yard par 4...New irrigation system...Nice driving range...Wide-open layout but not much trouble.

★★★NUTTERS CROSSING GOLF CLUB

30287 S. Hampton Bridge Rd., Salisbury, 21801, Wicomico County, (410)860-4653.
Opened: 1991. **Holes:** 18. **Par:** 70/70. **Yards:** 6,033/4,800. **Course rating:** 67.1/66.5. **Slope:** 115/110. **Architect:** Ault and Clark. **Green fee:** $30/$30. **Credit cards:** MC,VISA. **Reduced fees:** Twilight. **Caddies:** No. **Golf carts:** Included in Green Fee.

Discount golf packages: No. **Season:** Year-round. **High:** April-Oct. **On site lodging:** No. **Rental clubs:** Yes. **Walking policy:** Unrestricted walking. **Metal spikes allowed:** Yes. **Range:** Yes (grass). **To obtain tee times:** Call anytime during the week. **Subscriber comments:** Short layout, not too difficult for good player...Friendly pro-shop staff...Good conditions...Watch for hidden water...An attractive, well-designed course...Nice setting near eastern shore.

OCEAN CITY GOLF & YACHT CLUB

R-11401 Country Club Dr., Berlin, 21811, Worcester County, (410)641-1779, (800)442-3570, 150 miles SE of Washington, DC. **Green fee:** $13/$29. **Credit cards:** MC,VISA. **Reduced fees:** Weekdays, low season. **Caddies:** No. **Golf carts:** $11. **Discount golf packages:** Yes. **Season:** Year-round. **High:** April-Oct. **On site lodging:** No. **Rental clubs:** Yes. **Walking policy:** Walking at certain times. **Metal spikes allowed:** Yes. **Range:** Yes (grass). **To obtain tee times:** Call. Credit card needed to guarantee tee time.

★★★BAYSIDE COURSE

Opened: N/A. **Holes:** 18. **Par:** 72/72. **Yards:** 6,526/5,396. **Course rating:** 71.7/71.3. **Slope:** 121/119. **Architect:** Russell Roberts/Lester George. **Subscriber comments:** Tight but fair layout...Keep it straight, and you can score...Pleasant clubhouse and staff...Bring bug spray...Bayside track boasts better views...Expect a five-hour round.

★★★SEASIDE COURSE

Opened: 1959. **Holes:** 18. **Par:** 73/75. **Yards:** 6,520/5,848. **Course rating:** 70.9/73.1. **Slope:** 115/119. **Architect:** William Gordon, David Gordon and Russell Roberts. **Subscriber comments:** Seaside track easier and more wide open than Bayside...Both courses kept in good condition...Nice views of Chesapeake Bay...Friendly staff.

★★PATUXENT GREENS COUNTRY CLUB

14415 Greenview Dr., Laurel, 20708, Prince George's County, (301)776-5533, 15 miles N of Washington, DC. **Opened:** 1970. **Holes:** 18. **Par:** 71/71. **Yards:** 6,482/5,456. **Course rating:** 71.0/71.8. **Slope:** 126/119. **Architect:** George Cobb/Buddy Loving. **Green fee:** $38/$44. **Credit cards:** MC,VISA,AMEX. **Reduced fees:** Weekdays, low season, twilight. **Caddies:** No. **Golf carts:** Included in Green Fee. **Discount golf packages:** No. **Season:** Year-round. **High:** March-Oct. **On site lodging:** No. **Rental clubs:** Yes. **Walking policy:** Walking at certain times. **Metal spikes allowed:** No. **Range:** No. **To obtain tee times:** Call 4 days in advance.

★★★PINE RIDGE GOLF COURSE

PU-2101 Dulaney Valley Rd., Lutherville, 21093, Baltimore County, (410)252-1408, 15 miles N of Baltimore. **Opened:** 1958. **Holes:** 18. **Par:** 72/72. **Yards:** 6,724/5,679. **Course rating:** 71.9/71.3. **Slope:** 123/119. **Architect:** Gus Hook. **Green fee:** $11/$12. **Credit cards:** MC,VISA. **Reduced fees:** Weekdays, twilight, seniors, juniors. **Caddies:** No. **Golf carts:** $18. **Discount golf packages:** No. **Season:** Year-round. **High:** June-Aug. **On site lodging:** No. **Rental clubs:** Yes. **Walking policy:** Walking at certain times. **Metal spikes allowed:** Yes. **Range:** Yes (Mats). **To obtain tee times:** Call up to 14 days in advance. Weekday tee times cost $2 in person, $5 over the phone with a credit card. Weekend a.m. tee times are sold in a lottery, weekend p.m. times cost $5. **Subscriber comments:** Fair conditions...Inexpensive to walk...Scenic layout, best to play in spring or fall...The 8th par 3 is a gem...Expect a five-hour round...Dogleg heaven.

★★POOLESVILLE GOLF COURSE

PU-16601 W. Willard Rd., Poolesville, 20837, Montgomery County, (301)428-8143, 25 miles NW of Washington, DC. **Opened:** 1959. **Holes:** 18. **Par:** 71/73. **Yards:** 6,811/5,521. **Course rating:** 72.3/71.4. **Slope:** 123/118. **Architect:** Edmund B. Ault and Al Jamison. **Green fee:** $14/$31. **Credit cards:** MC,VISA. **Reduced fees:** Seniors, juniors. **Caddies:** No. **Golf carts:** $24. **Discount golf packages:** No. **Season:** Year-round. **High:** June-Oct. **On site lodging:** No. **Rental clubs:** Yes. **Walking policy:** Unrestricted walking. **Metal spikes allowed:** Yes. **Range:** Yes (grass/mats). **To obtain tee times:** Call or come in 7 days in advance for weekends and holidays.

QUEENSTOWN HARBOR GOLF LINKS

PU-310 Links Lane, Queenstown, 21658, Queen Anne's County, (410)827-6611, (800)827-5257, 45 miles SE of Baltimore.
Opened: 1991. **Architect:** Lindsay Ervin. **Green fee:** $50/$60. **Credit cards:** MC,VISA,AMEX. **Reduced fees:** Weekdays, twilight, juniors. **Caddies:** No. **Golf carts:** Included in Green Fee. **Discount golf packages:** No. **Season:** Year-round. **High:** April-Oct. **On site lodging:** No. **Rental clubs:** Yes. **Walking policy:** Unrestricted walking. **Metal spikes allowed:** Yes. **Range:** Yes (grass/mats). **To obtain tee times:** Call 7 days in advance after 12 p.m.

★★★★**LAKES COURSE**

Holes: 18. **Par:** 71/71. **Yards:** 6,537/4,576. **Course rating:** 71.0/66.6. **Slope:** 124/111.
Subscriber comments: Nice course but expensive...Nice place...Shorter, tighter than big brother! Always good shape...I could play here everyday...Love this course! Twilight in summer, play til dark, unwalkable!...Great course, too expensive, long rounds...Same as River but a little easier...One of the best in Maryland...A pleasure to play, worth the travel from Pennsylvania...Big rival of Hog Neck...No. 15 awesome!...The more natural, picturesque, and playable of both courses.

★★★★**RIVER COURSE**

Holes: 18. **Par:** 72/72. **Yards:** 7,110/5,026. **Course rating:** 74.2/69.0. **Slope:** 138/123.
Notes: Ranked 5th in 1997 Best in State.
Subscriber comments: Excellent conditions...Bring your "A" game for 7,000+ yards of wind and water...The 18th is a great finishing hole...Beautiful scenery...The best track in Maryland...A fun all-around experience...Pace of play is slow because of amount of traffic...Demands accuracy...River track is better than Lakes layout, but not by much...The 16th is a top-notch par 3.

★★★**REDGATE MUNICIPAL GOLF COURSE**

PM-14500 Avery Rd., Rockville, 20853, Montgomery County, (301)309-3055, 8 miles N of Washington, DC.
Opened: 1974. **Holes:** 18. **Par:** 71/71. **Yards:** 6,432/5,271. **Course rating:** 71.7/70.2. **Slope:** 131/121. **Architect:** Thurman Donovan. **Green fee:** $22/$25. **Credit cards:** None. **Reduced fees:** Seniors, juniors. **Caddies:** No. **Golf carts:** $22. **Discount golf packages:** No. **Season:** Year-round. **High:** April-Nov. **On site lodging:** No. **Rental clubs:** Yes. **Walking policy:** Unrestricted walking. **Metal spikes allowed:** No. **Range:** Yes (grass/mats). **To obtain tee times:** Tee times for weekends only. Call Monday 7:30 a.m. for upcoming weekend.
Subscriber comments: Challenging course, particularly last five holes...A diversity of shots required...Tight layout, extremely hilly...The 16th is hardest hole in Montgomery County...Too many blind shots and no level lies...Well-designed other than a couple quirky holes...Numerous creek crossings.

★★★**RIVER DOWNS GOLFERS' CLUB**

1900 River Downs Dr., Finksburg, 21048, Carroll County, (410)526-2000, (800)518-7337, 30 miles NW of Baltimore.
Opened: 1995. **Holes:** 18. **Par:** 72/72. **Yards:** 6,873/5,003. **Course rating:** 72.6/70.4. **Slope:** 129/122. **Architect:** Arthur Hills. **Green fee:** $39/$55. **Credit cards:** MC,VISA,DISC. **Reduced fees:** Weekdays, low season, twilight, seniors, juniors. **Caddies:** No. **Golf carts:** Included in Green Fee. **Discount golf packages:** No. **Season:** Year-round. **High:** April-Oct. **On site lodging:** No. **Rental clubs:** Yes. **Walking policy:** Mandatory cart. **Metal spikes allowed:** Yes. **Range:** Yes (grass). **To obtain tee times:** Call up to 7 days in advance.
Subscriber comments: Challenging new course, a bit tricky in spots...Position is key...Good conditions...Extremely hilly, not for walking...Keep driver in the bag...Watch for small stones in fairways, built on quarry.

★★★½**RIVER RUN GOLF CLUB**

PU-11605 Masters Lane, Berlin, 21811, Worcester County, (410)641-7200, (800)733-7786, 110 miles SE of Washington, DC.
Opened: 1991. **Holes:** 18. **Par:** 71/71. **Yards:** 6,705/5,002. **Course rating:** 70.4/73.1. **Slope:** 128/117. **Architect:** Gary Player. **Green fee:** $8/$36. **Credit cards:** All major. **Reduced fees:** Weekdays, low season, resort guests, twilight, juniors. **Caddies:** No. **Golf carts:** $12. **Discount golf packages:** Yes. **Season:** Year-round. **High:** April-Oct.

On site lodging: Yes. **Rental clubs:** Yes. **Walking policy:** Walking at certain times. **Metal spikes allowed:** No. **Range:** Yes (grass). **To obtain tee times:** Call (800)733-7786 with credit card to confirm.

Subscriber comments: Well-designed layout in good condition...A bit pricey but reasonable evening rates...Demands good iron play...A difficult but fair test of golf...Tight openings to greens...Congenial staff...Tight back nine with plenty of trees.

★★½ROCKY POINT GOLF CLUB
PU-1935 Back River Neck Rd., Essex, 21221, Baltimore County, (410)391-2906, (888)246-5384, 9 miles E of Baltimore.

Opened: 1971. **Holes:** 18. **Par:** 72/74. **Yards:** 6,753/5,750. **Course rating:** 72.3/73.1. **Slope:** 122/121. **Architect:** Russell Roberts. **Green fee:** $15/$17. **Credit cards:** MC,VISA,AMEX,ATM Debit cards. **Reduced fees:** Weekdays, twilight, seniors, juniors. **Caddies:** No. **Golf carts:** $22. **Discount golf packages:** No. **Season:** Year-round. **High:** April-Sept. **On site lodging:** No. **Rental clubs:** Yes. **Walking policy:** Unrestricted walking. **Metal spikes allowed:** No. **Range:** Yes (grass/mats). **To obtain tee times:** Call up to 7 days in advance.

Subscriber comments: Relatively short layout with a few tight holes...Great walking rate...Good for average golfer with wide-open fairways and large greens...Five-hour rounds are the norm.

RUM POINTE SEASIDE GOLF LINKS
R-7000 Rum Pointe Lane, Berlin, 21811, Worcester County, (410)629-1414, (888)809-4653, 7 miles S of Ocean City.

Opened: 1997. **Holes:** 18. **Par:** 72/72. **Yards:** 7,020/5,080. **Course rating:** 72.6/70.3. **Slope:** 122/120. **Architect:** Pete Dye and P.B. Dye. **Green fee:** $25/$57. **Credit cards:** MC,VISA. **Reduced fees:** Weekdays, low season, resort guests, twilight, juniors. **Caddies:** No. **Golf carts:** $12. **Discount golf packages:** Yes. **Season:** Year-round. **High:** April-Oct. **On site lodging:** Yes. **Rental clubs:** Yes. **Walking policy:** Unrestricted walking. **Metal spikes allowed:** No. **Range:** Yes (grass). **To obtain tee times:** Call golf shop.

★★★½SOUTH RIVER GOLF LINKS
PU-3451 Solomon's Island Rd., Edgewater, 21037, Anne Arundel County, (410)798-5865, (800)767-4837, 4 miles S of Annapolis.

Opened: 1996. **Holes:** 18. **Par:** 72/72. **Yards:** 6,723/4,935. **Course rating:** 71.8/66.9. **Slope:** 133/115. **Architect:** Brian Ault. **Green fee:** $30/$60. **Credit cards:** MC,VISA,AMEX. **Reduced fees:** Twilight, juniors. **Caddies:** No. **Golf carts:** Included in Green Fee. **Discount golf packages:** No. **Season:** Year-round. **High:** May-Sept. **On site lodging:** No. **Rental clubs:** Yes. **Walking policy:** Unrestricted walking. **Metal spikes allowed:** Yes. **Range:** Yes (Mats). **To obtain tee times:** Call up to 7 days in advance after noon.

Subscriber comments: A good and fair test of golf...A new layout that needs time to mature...Will be a must play in a couple of years...A good variety of holes...Reasonable twilight rates...Nice clubhouse.

★★½SOUTHVIEW GOLF COURSE
PU-15800 Sharperville Rd., Waldorf, 20601, Charles County, (301)372-1305.

Opened: 1995. **Holes:** 18. **Architect:** Tom Clark. **Caddies:** No. **Discount golf packages:** No. **On site lodging:** No. **Rental clubs:** No. **Metal spikes allowed:** Yes. **Range:** No.

Call club for further information.

Subscriber comments: Needs time to grow in...Terrific greens and tee boxes...Plenty of water...Keep it straight.

★★★★SWAN POINT GOLF YACHT & COUNTRY CLUB
11550 Swan Point Blvd., Issue, 20645, Charles County, (301)259-0047, (800)706-3488, 50 miles SE of Washington, DC.

Opened: 1989. **Holes:** 18. **Par:** 72/72. **Yards:** 6,761/5,009. **Course rating:** 72.5/69.3. **Slope:** 126/116. **Architect:** Arthur Davis/Bob Cupp. **Green fee:** $37/$60. **Credit cards:** MC,VISA. **Reduced fees:** Weekdays, low season, twilight, seniors, juniors. **Caddies:** No. **Golf carts:** Included in Green Fee. **Discount golf packages:** Yes. **Season:** March-Dec. **High:** June-Sept. **On site lodging:** No. **Rental clubs:** Yes. **Walking policy:**

Walking at certain times. **Metal spikes allowed:** Yes. **Range:** Yes (grass/mats). **To obtain tee times:** Call up to 7 days in advance with credit card.
Subscriber comments: Wonderful course...Abundant wildlife...Good variety of holes.

★★½TANTALLON COUNTRY CLUB

Fort Washington, Prince George's County, (301)292-0003.
Call club for further information.
Subscriber comments: Some fun holes...Has made improvements...Tight layout.

★★★THE TIMBERS OF TROY

PU-6100 Marshalee Dr., Elkridge, 21227, Howard County, (410)313-4653, 10 miles S of Baltimore.
Opened: 1996. **Holes:** 18. **Par:** 72/72. **Yards:** 6,652/4,926. **Course rating:** 72.1.
Slope: 134. **Architect:** Brian Ault/Ken Killian. **Green fee:** $23/$37. **Credit cards:**
MC,VISA,AMEX. **Reduced fees:** Low season, twilight. **Caddies:** No. **Golf carts:** $12.
Discount golf packages: No. **Season:** Feb.-Dec. **High:** May-Sept. **On site lodging:**
No. **Rental clubs:** Yes. **Walking policy:** Unrestricted walking. **Metal spikes allowed:**
Yes. **Range:** Yes (grass/mats). **To obtain tee times:** Call up to 7 days in advance.
Subscriber comments: Young course with a lot of potential...Good conditions...A nice variety of holes...A bit pricey.

★½TROTTERS GLEN GOLF COURSE

PU-16501 Batchellors Forest Rd., Olney, 20832, Montgomery County, (301)570-4951, 15 miles NW of Washington, DC.
Opened: 1993. **Holes:** 18. **Par:** 72/72. **Yards:** 6,220/4,983. **Course rating:** 69.3/68.2.
Slope: 113/111. **Architect:** Ault, Clark and Assoc. **Green fee:** $18/$23. **Credit cards:**
MC,VISA,AMEX. **Reduced fees:** Weekdays, low season, twilight, seniors, juniors.
Caddies: No. **Golf carts:** $11. **Discount golf packages:** No. **Season:** Year-round.
High: June-Aug. **On site lodging:** Yes. **Rental clubs:** Yes. **Walking policy:**
Unrestricted walking. **Metal spikes allowed:** Yes. **Range:** Yes (grass/mats). **To obtain tee times:** Call Monday 8 a.m. for current week and upcoming weekend.

TURF VALLEY HOTEL & COUNTRY CLUB

R-2700 Turf Valley Rd., Ellicott City, 21042, Howard County, (410)465-1504, (800)666-8873, 20 miles W of Baltimore.
Green fee: $30/$50. **Credit cards:** All major. **Reduced fees:** Weekdays, low season, resort guests, twilight. **Caddies:** No. **Golf carts:** $11. **Discount golf packages:** Yes.
Season: Year-round. **High:** April-Oct. **On site lodging:** Yes. **Rental clubs:** Yes.
Walking policy: Walking at certain times. **Metal spikes allowed:** Yes. **Range:** Yes
(grass). **To obtain tee times:** In person, seven days in advance. By phone, six days in advance.

★★½SOUTH COURSE
Opened: 1963. **Holes:** 18. **Par:** 70/72. **Yards:** 6,323/5,572. **Course rating:** 69.2/72.8.
Slope: 113/126. **Architect:** Edmund B. Ault.
Subscriber comments: Well-designed course...U.S. Open rough makes it difficult...Conditions could be better...A fair course to all players.

★★½EAST COURSE
Opened: 1959. **Holes:** 18. **Par:** 71/71. **Yards:** 6,592/5,564. **Course rating:** 72.0/71.6.
Slope: 128/131. **Architect:** Edmund B. Ault and Al Jamison.
Subscriber comments: Challenging layout with plenty of hills and trees...Some tough par 4s...Keep it straight.

★★½NORTH COURSE
Opened: 1959. **Holes:** 18. **Par:** 71/71. **Yards:** 6,633/5,600. **Course rating:** 69.5/71.8.
Slope: 117/124. **Architect:** Edmund B. Ault and Al Jamison.
Subscriber comments: Best of the three tracks...Tough hills, a lot of wetlands...Good shape...Tight layout...Sweeping fairways with fast greens...First hole over water.

★★½TWIN SHIELDS GOLF CLUB

PU-2425 Roarty Rd., Dunkirk, 20754, Calvert County, (410)257-7800, 15 miles E of Washington, DC.
Opened: 1969. **Holes:** 18. **Par:** 70/70. **Yards:** 6,321/5,305. **Course rating:** 68.2/67.0.
Slope: 118/113. **Architect:** Roy Shields and Ray Shields. **Green fee:** $25/$30. **Credit cards:** None. **Reduced fees:** Twilight, seniors, juniors. **Caddies:** No. **Golf carts:** $25.

Discount golf packages: No. **Season:** Year-round. **High:** April-Oct. **On site lodging:** No. **Rental clubs:** No. **Walking policy:** Walking at certain times. **Metal spikes allowed:** Yes. **Range:** Yes (grass/mats). **To obtain tee times:** Call 3 days in advance. **Subscriber comments:** Beautiful grassy layout...Fun par 3s...Nice people.

★★★UNIVERSITY OF MARYLAND GOLF COURSE
University Blvd., College Park, 20740, Prince George's County, (301)403-4299, 5 miles E of Washington, DC.
Opened: 1956. **Holes:** 18. **Par:** 71/72. **Yards:** 6,654/5,563. **Course rating:** 71.7/71.1. **Slope:** 120/117. **Architect:** George W. Cobb. **Green fee:** $22/$26. **Credit cards:** MC,VISA. **Reduced fees:** Weekdays, low season, twilight, seniors, juniors. **Caddies:** No. **Golf carts:** $12. **Discount golf packages:** No. **Season:** Year-round. **High:** April-Oct. **On site lodging:** No. **Rental clubs:** No. **Walking policy:** Walking at certain times. **Metal spikes allowed:** No. **Range:** Yes (grass/mats). **To obtain tee times:** Call 6 days in advance.
Subscriber comments: Nice layout...Good everyday course...Each hole is different.

★★★WAKEFIELD VALLEY GOLF & CONFERENCE CENTER
1000 Fenby Farm Rd., Westminster, 21158, Carroll County, (410)876-6662, 30 miles NW of Baltimore.
Opened: 1978. **Holes:** 27. **Par:** 72/73. **Yards:** 6,933/5,549. **Course rating:** 74.4/73.3. **Slope:** 139/132. **Architect:** Wayne Weller/Russell Roberts. **Green fee:** $32/$39. **Credit cards:** MC,VISA,DISC. **Reduced fees:** Low season, twilight, seniors, juniors. **Caddies:** No. **Golf carts:** Included in Green Fee. **Discount golf packages:** No. **Season:** March-Dec. **High:** June-Sept. **On site lodging:** No. **Rental clubs:** Yes. **Walking policy:** Walking at certain times. **Metal spikes allowed:** Yes. **Range:** Yes (grass/mats). **To obtain tee times:** Call or come in up to 14 days in advance.
Subscriber comments: Challenging 27-hole layout...A good variety of holes...Undulating, slick greens...Good prices in the pro shop...Demands accuracy off the tee...Beautiful country setting...Excellent snack bar...A lot of risk-reward shots.

★★★WHITE PLAINS REGIONAL PARK GOLF CLUB
St. Charles Pkwy., White Plains, 20695, Charles County, (301)843-2947.
Architect: J. Porter Gibson. **Caddies:** No. **Discount golf packages:** No. **On site lodging:** No. **Rental clubs:** No. **Metal spikes allowed:** Yes. **Range:** No.
Call club for further information.
Subscriber comments: Short but challenging...Proper placement on rolling terrain is imperative...Service with a smile...Good greens...The second hole is the hardest short par 4 I've played...Several doglegs...Tight, treelined fairways.

★★½WICOMICO SHORES MUNICIPAL GOLF COURSE
PM-Rt. 234, 20621 Aviation Yacht & CC Rd., Chaptico, 20621, St. Mary's County, (301)934-8191, 45 miles SE of Washington, DC.
Opened: 1962. **Holes:** 18. **Par:** 72/72. **Yards:** 6,482/5,460. **Course rating:** 70.7/68.3. **Slope:** 120/120. **Architect:** Edmund B. Ault. **Green fee:** $15/$19. **Credit cards:** None. **Reduced fees:** Weekdays, twilight, seniors, juniors. **Caddies:** No. **Golf carts:** $12. **Discount golf packages:** Yes. **Season:** Year-round. **High:** May-Sept. **On site lodging:** No. **Rental clubs:** Yes. **Walking policy:** Unrestricted walking. **Metal spikes allowed:** Yes. **Range:** Yes (grass/mats). **To obtain tee times:** Call Monday for upcoming weekend or holiday.
Subscriber comments: Spectacular view from clubhouse...Narrow fairways, small greens...Most putts break toward the river...New irrigation system has improved conditions...Fun layout.

★WORTHINGTON VALLEY COUNTRY CLUB
12425 Greenspring Ave., Owings Mills, 21117, Baltimore County, (410)356-8355, 12 miles N of Baltimore.
Opened: 1954. **Holes:** 18. **Par:** N/A. **Yards:** N/A. **Course rating:** N/A. **Slope:** N/A. **Architect:** N/A. **Green fee:** $15/$20. **Credit cards:** N/A. **Reduced fees:** N/A. **Caddies:** No. **Golf carts:** $20. **Discount golf packages:** No. **Season:** March-Dec. **High:** April-Oct. **On site lodging:** No. **Rental clubs:** No. **Walking policy:** Unrestricted walking. **Metal spikes allowed:** Yes. **Range:** Yes. **To obtain tee times:** Call anytime.
Subscriber comments: Track has promise, but needs a commitment to maintenance.

★★★½ATLANTIC COUNTRY CLUB

PU-450 Little Sandy Pond Rd., Plymouth, 02360, Plymouth County, (508)888-6644, 50 miles S of Boston.
Opened: 1994. **Holes:** 18. **Par:** 72/72. **Yards:** 6,728/4,918. **Course rating:** 71.5/67.4.
Slope: 130/113. **Architect:** Geoffrey Cornish, Brian Silva and Mark Mungeam. **Green fee:** $30/$35. **Credit cards:** MC,VISA. **Reduced fees:** Weekdays, low season, twilight.
Caddies: No. **Golf carts:** $13. **Discount golf packages:** No. **Season:** March-Dec.
High: June-Aug. **On site lodging:** No. **Rental clubs:** Yes. **Walking policy:** Unrestricted walking. **Metal spikes allowed:** Yes. **Range:** Yes (grass/mats). **To obtain tee times:** Call two days in advance.
Subscriber comments: Very hilly & windy. Excellent variety of holes...Improves with every visit...Used to be a well kept secret—no more...Good test...Beautiful fairways, good greens, fair price...Good chance to use all clubs...Too busy...Future star...Good new course, limited clubhouse...Exceptionally challenging from the back.

★★★BALLYMEADE COUNTRY CLUB

125 Falmouth Woods Rd., North Falmouth, 02556, Barnstable County, (508)540-4005, 58 miles S of Boston.
Opened: 1988. **Holes:** 18. **Par:** 72/72. **Yards:** 6,928/5,001. **Course rating:** 74.3/68.9.
Slope: 139/119. **Architect:** Jim Fazio. **Green fee:** $40/$75. **Credit cards:** All major.
Reduced fees: Weekdays, low season, twilight. **Caddies:** No. **Golf carts:** Included in Green Fee. **Discount golf packages:** No. **Season:** Year-round. **High:** June-Aug. **On site lodging:** No. **Rental clubs:** Yes. **Walking policy:** Mandatory cart. **Metal spikes allowed:** No. **Range:** Yes (grass). **To obtain tee times:** Call seven days in advance.
Subscriber comments: Beautiful course. Excellent clubhouse. Great practice facilities...Good winter course...Demanding tee to green...Slow playing on weekends...Hard to play in wind—all carry to greens...Tough if you are not straight off of tee box...Big greens...Very narrow. Some blind shots.

★★★BASS RIVER GOLF COURSE

PU-Highbank Rd., South Yarmouth, 02664, Barnstable County, (508)398-9079, 70 miles S of Boston.
Opened: 1902. **Holes:** 18. **Par:** 72/72. **Yards:** 6,129/5,343. **Course rating:** 79.3/69.3.
Slope: 122/111. **Architect:** P. Sheppard/Donald Ross. **Green fee:** $19/$37. **Credit cards:** MC,VISA. **Reduced fees:** Low season, twilight. **Caddies:** No. **Golf carts:** $22.
Discount golf packages: No. **Season:** Year-round. **High:** May-Sept. **On site lodging:** No. **Rental clubs:** Yes. **Walking policy:** Unrestricted walking. **Metal spikes allowed:** Yes. **Range:** No. **To obtain tee times:** Call four days in advance.
Subscriber comments: Nice old Ross layout. Short with small greens...Good for beginners and advanced players...One of oldest courses on Cape, enjoyable...Cordial atmosphere...6th best par 3 on the Cape, best view from clubhouse too!

★★½BAY POINTE COUNTRY CLUB

Onset Ave., Onset, 02558, Plymouth County, (508)759-8802.
Caddies: No. **Discount golf packages:** No. **On site lodging:** No. **Rental clubs:** No.
Metal spikes allowed: Yes. **Range:** No.
Call club for further information.
Subscriber comments: Very hilly, always a slanted lie or blind shot...Must have good accuracy with irons...Narrow fairways...Island hole #16...Starts with a long par 3.

★★★BAYBERRY HILLS GOLF COURSE

PM-W. Yarmouth Rd., West Yarmouth, 02673, Barnstable County, (508)394-5597,.
Opened: 1987. **Holes:** 18. **Par:** 72/72. **Yards:** 7,172/5,275. **Course rating:** 73.5/69.2.
Slope: 132/111. **Architect:** Brian Silva and Geoffrey S. Cornish. **Green fee:** $19/$37.
Credit cards: MC,VISA. **Reduced fees:** Low season, twilight. **Caddies:** No. **Golf carts:** $22. **Discount golf packages:** No. **Season:** April-Nov. **High:** May-Oct. **On site lodging:** No. **Rental clubs:** Yes. **Walking policy:** Unrestricted walking. **Metal spikes allowed:** Yes. **Range:** Yes (grass). **To obtain tee times:** Call four days in advance; earlier reservations require prepayment.
Subscriber comments: A Silva course, natural terrain, interesting holes...Good for all skill levels, fun to play...Conditions improve every year...Generous fairways...V-E-R-Y busy...A must play on the Cape...f you can't hit it straight, you can pick cranberries... Wide fairways, forgiving course...Good course to use all of your clubs.

★★★BLISSFUL MEADOWS GOLF CLUB
801 Chockalog Rd., Uxbridge, 01569, Worcester County, (508)278-6113, 20 miles SE of Worcester.
Opened: 1992. **Holes:** 18. **Par:** 72/72. **Yards:** 6,656/5,072. **Course rating:** N/A. **Slope:** N/A. **Architect:** Geoffrey Cornish and Brian Silva. **Green fee:** $18/$22. **Credit cards:** MC,VISA,AMEX. **Reduced fees:** Low season, twilight, seniors. **Caddies:** No. **Golf carts:** $10. **Discount golf packages:** No. **Season:** April-Nov. **High:** May-Oct. **On site lodging:** No. **Rental clubs:** No. **Walking policy:** Unrestricted walking. **Metal spikes allowed:** Yes. **Range:** Yes (grass). **To obtain tee times:** Call up to two days in advance.
Subscriber comments: Small course, wide open, slow on weekends...Love the back 9...Fun place to play—demands straightness off the tee...Short, lots of irons off the tee...Nice course but sadistic pin placements on very fast greens...Visually peaceful...Many scoring opportunities...Good par 3s...Front nine narrow, back nine let it rip.

★★★½BLUE ROCK GOLF COURSE
PU-48 Todd Rd., South Yarmouth, Barnstable County, (508)398-9295, (800)237-8887, 70 miles SE of Boston.
Opened: 1962. **Holes:** 18. **Par:** 54/54. **Yards:** 3,000/2,200. **Course rating:** 56.4/55.8. **Slope:** 83/80. **Architect:** Geoffrey Cornish. **Green fee:** $24/$29. **Credit cards:** MC,VISA. **Reduced fees:** Twilight. **Caddies:** No. **Golf carts:** N/A. **Discount golf packages:** No. **Season:** Year-round. **High:** June-Sept. **On site lodging:** Yes. **Rental clubs:** Yes. **Walking policy:** Unrestricted walking. **Metal spikes allowed:** Yes. **Range:** Yes (grass). **To obtain tee times:** Call 7 days in advance with credit card confirmation.
Subscriber comments: Could be the best par-3 course anywhere...Very narrow, great for beginner...Quiet and scenic. Starts easy buts gets tough...Great water holes...Awesome! Fun, fun, fun.

★★BRADFORD COUNTRY CLUB
PU-201 Chadwick Rd., Bradford, 01835, Essex County, (508)372-8587, 25 miles N of Boston.
Opened: 1990. **Holes:** 18. **Par:** 70/70. **Yards:** 6,511/4,939. **Course rating:** 72.8/67.8. **Slope:** 141/129. **Architect:** Geoffrey Cornish and Brian Silva. **Green fee:** $23/$31. **Credit cards:** MC,VISA,AMEX. **Reduced fees:** Weekdays, low season, twilight, seniors, juniors. **Caddies:** No. **Golf carts:** $12. **Discount golf packages:** Yes. **Season:** April-Dec. **High:** May-Sept. **On site lodging:** No. **Rental clubs:** Yes. **Walking policy:** Unrestricted walking. **Metal spikes allowed:** Yes. **Range:** No. **To obtain tee times:** Call up to five days in advance.

★★BROOKMEADOW COUNTRY CLUB
PU-100 Everendon Rd., Canton, 02021, Norfolk County, (617)828-4444, 20 miles SW of Boston.
Opened: 1967. **Holes:** 18. **Par:** 72/72. **Yards:** 6,660/5,690. **Course rating:** 71.6/71.2. **Slope:** 123/114. **Architect:** Samuel Mitchell. **Green fee:** $20/$25. **Credit cards:** MC,VISA,DISC. **Reduced fees:** Low season, twilight, seniors, juniors. **Caddies:** No. **Golf carts:** $26. **Discount golf packages:** No. **Season:** Year-round. **High:** April-Oct. **On site lodging:** No. **Rental clubs:** Yes. **Walking policy:** Unrestricted walking. **Metal spikes allowed:** Yes. **Range:** Yes (grass/mats). **To obtain tee times:** Call five days in advance.

BROOKSHIRE INN & GOLF CLUB
PU-205 W. Church, Williamstown, 48895, Berkshire County, (517)655-4694.
Call club for further information.

★★★CAPE COD COUNTRY CLUB
PU-Theater Rd., North Falmouth, 02556, Barnstable County, (508)563-9842, 50 miles S of Boston.
Opened: 1929. **Holes:** 18. **Par:** 71/72. **Yards:** 6,404/5,348. **Course rating:** 71.0/70.6. **Slope:** 122/119. **Architect:** Devereux Emmett and Alfred H. Tull. **Green fee:** $30/$38. **Credit cards:** MC,VISA. **Reduced fees:** Weekdays, low season, twilight, juniors. **Caddies:** No. **Golf carts:** $24. **Discount golf packages:** Yes. **Season:** Year-round. **High:** March-Oct. **On site lodging:** No. **Rental clubs:** Yes. **Walking policy:**

Unrestricted walking. **Metal spikes allowed:** Yes. **Range:** No. **To obtain tee times:** Call Friday for following Friday, Saturday and Sunday. One week in advance for week-days.

Subscriber comments: Good course. Quite hilly...Crowded...Pretty easy...My favorite on all Cape Cod!...Fun to play...Worth the trip...Very nice greens, par 5s too short...Old fashioned delight. 14th a great hole...Good variety...Plays like a Donald Ross course. Small greens...A challenge for every golfer...Nice course but too many elevated greens.

★★★½CAPTAINS GOLF COURSE

PM-1000 Freeman's Way, Brewster, 02631, Barnstable County, (508)896-1716, 100 miles SE of Boston.
Opened: 1985. **Holes:** 18. **Par:** 72/72. **Yards:** 6,794/5,388. **Course rating:** 72.7/70.5. **Slope:** 130/117. **Architect:** G. Cornish and Brian Silva. **Green fee:** $25/$40. **Credit cards:** MC,VISA. **Reduced fees:** Low season, twilight. **Caddies:** No. **Golf carts:** $24. **Discount golf packages:** No. **Season:** March-Dec. **High:** May-Oct. **On site lodging:** No. **Rental clubs:** Yes. **Walking policy:** Unrestricted walking. **Metal spikes allowed:** Yes. **Range:** Yes (grass/mats). **To obtain tee times:** Call two days prior at 6 p.m. on automated system or pre paid by calling throughout the year with payment by check at least 2 weeks prior to play date.
Subscriber comments: Playable for all levels...Good layout...Great folks, a pleasure to visit...Good food...Getting on as a single is easy...A joy to play...Excellent test...Stay out of trees and you'll score...Nice practice area including bunker...Top notch...Feels like private course; only one water hole.

★½CHEQUESSETT YACHT & COUNTRY CLUB

Chequessett Neck Rd., Wellfleet, 02667, Barnstable County, (508)349-3704.
Call club for further information.

★★★½CHICOPEE GOLF CLUB

PU-1290 Burnett Rd., Chicopee, 01020, Hampden County, (413)594-9295.
Opened: 1964. **Holes:** 18. **Par:** 72/72. **Yards:** 7,010/5,284. **Course rating:** 73.0/72.5. **Slope:** 126/115. **Architect:** Geoffrey S. Cornish. **Green fee:** $14/$15. **Credit cards:** N/A. **Reduced fees:** N/A. **Caddies:** No. **Golf carts:** $14. **Discount golf packages:** No. **Season:** April-Nov. **High:** May-Aug. **On site lodging:** No. **Rental clubs:** No. **Walking policy:** Unrestricted walking. **Metal spikes allowed:** Yes. **Range:** No. **To obtain tee times:** Call golf shop.
Subscriber comments: Tough from back tees, good test...Challenging for the low handicappers and pleasant to play for those who have a high handicap...Hate the boundary nets...Many tough driving holes...Great layout...Tough first hole...Holes that require strategy and variety of shots...Breaking 80 is a challenge.

GREAT VALUE

★★½COLONIAL COUNTRY CLUB

PU-1 Audubon Rd., Wakefield, 01880, Middlesex County, (617)245-9300, 12 miles N of Boston.
Opened: 1929. **Holes:** 18. **Par:** 70/72. **Yards:** 6,565/5,280. **Course rating:** 72.8/69.5. **Slope:** 130/109. **Architect:** Bob Mitchell. **Green fee:** $42/$52. **Credit cards:** All major,Diners Club. **Reduced fees:** Low season, twilight, seniors, juniors. **Caddies:** No. **Golf carts:** Included in Green Fee. **Discount golf packages:** Yes. **Season:** April-Dec. **High:** May-Oct. **On site lodging:** Yes. **Rental clubs:** Yes. **Walking policy:** Mandatory cart. **Metal spikes allowed:** Yes. **Range:** Yes (grass/mats). **To obtain tee times:** Hotel guests 21 days in advance. Public, seven days in advance.
Subscriber comments: Back nine makes you work...Wet and windy. Nice greens. Flat...Difficult to get tee times...Pretty back nine in the spring...Too many geese.

★★★½CRANBERRY VALLEY GOLF COURSE

PU-183 Oak St., Harwich, 02645, Barnstable County, (508)430-7560, 85 miles S of Boston.
Opened: 1974. **Holes:** 18. **Par:** 72/72. **Yards:** 6,745/5,518. **Course rating:** 71.9/71.3. **Slope:** 129/115. **Architect:** Cornish and Robinson. **Green fee:** $35/$45. **Credit cards:** None. **Reduced fees:** Weekdays, low season, twilight. **Caddies:** No. **Golf carts:** $20. **Discount golf packages:** No. **Season:** Year-round. **High:** March-Nov. **On site lodging:** No. **Rental clubs:** Yes. **Walking policy:** Unrestricted walking. **Metal spikes allowed:**

Yes. **Range:** Yes (grass/mats). **To obtain tee times:** Prepayment by check or cash starting March 1st or two days in advance with no pre-payment, starting at 8 a.m. **Subscriber comments:** Each hole isolated. Enjoyable for all levels...Tough to get tee times in summer...Great if you can get on...Real challenge...Long par 3s; does get wet...Love the layout...Very large, heavily contoured greens...Beautiful tall trees...Need better clubhouse...Terrific design for both short and long hitters...A pleasant surprise...Hard but fair...Heaven on Cape Cod.

★★CRANWELL RESORT & GOLF CLUB

R-55 Lee Rd, Lenox, 01240, Berkshire County, (413)637-1364, (800)272-6935. **Opened:** 1926. **Holes:** 18. **Par:** 70/73. **Yards:** 6,173/5,248. **Course rating:** 70.0/72.4. **Slope:** 125/129. **Architect:** Stiles and Van Kleek. **Green fee:** $39/$75. **Credit cards:** All major. **Reduced fees:** Weekdays, low season, resort guests, twilight. **Caddies:** Yes. **Golf carts:** Included in Green Fee. **Discount golf packages:** Yes. **Season:** April-Nov. **High:** June-Sept. **On site lodging:** Yes. **Rental clubs:** Yes. **Walking policy:** Unrestricted walking. **Metal spikes allowed:** Yes. **Range:** Yes (grass). **To obtain tee times:** Call golf shop.

★★★★½CRUMPIN-FOX CLUB

Parmenter Rd., Bernardston, 01337, Franklin County, (413)648-9101, 30 miles N of Springfield.
Opened: 1978. **Holes:** 18. **Par:** 72/72. **Yards:** 7,007/5,432. **Course rating:** 73.8/71.5. **Slope:** 141/131. **Architect:** Roger Rulewich. **Green fee:** $59/$59. **Credit cards:** All major. **Reduced fees:** Resort guests, juniors. **Caddies:** Yes. **Golf carts:** $14. **Discount golf packages:** Yes. **Season:** April-Nov. **High:** June-Oct. **On site lodging:** Yes. **Rental clubs:** Yes. **Walking policy:** Unrestricted walking. **Metal spikes allowed:** No. **Range:** Yes (grass). **To obtain tee times:** Call three days in advance for public. Members or golf and dinner packages may book as far in advance as desired.
Subscriber comments: Some great golf holes, too penal for mid to high handicaps... Beautiful, you must think...On a windy day, too tough...One of the toughest tracks in Massachusetts...Excellent restaurant deal...Lots of elevated greens...A masterpiece... Each hole is a picture...Play with fall foliage...Keeps you honest...8th, a par 5 everyone should experience...You will come back again...One of the best, wish it were closer.

★★CRYSTAL SPRINGS GOLF CLUB

PU-940 N. Broadway, Haverhill, 01830, Essex County, (508)374-9621, 35 miles NE of Boston.
Opened: 1961. **Holes:** 18. **Par:** 72/73. **Yards:** 6,706/5,596. **Course rating:** 72.0/71.1. **Slope:** 116/112. **Architect:** Geoffrey S. Cornish. **Green fee:** $17/$20. **Credit cards:** N/A. **Reduced fees:** N/A. **Caddies:** No. **Golf carts:** $20. **Discount golf packages:** No. **Season:** N/A. **High:** N/A. **On site lodging:** No. **Rental clubs:** No. **Walking policy:** Unrestricted walking. **Metal spikes allowed:** Yes. **Range:** Yes (grass/mats). **To obtain tee times:** N/A.

★★D.W. FIELD GOLF CLUB

PM-331 Oak St., Brockton, 02401, Plymouth County, (508)580-7855.
Opened: 1926. **Holes:** 18. **Par:** 70/70. **Yards:** 5,972/5,415. **Course rating:** 68.4/70.1. **Slope:** 127/111. **Architect:** Wayne Stiles and John Van Kleek. **Green fee:** $17/$21. **Credit cards:** None. **Reduced fees:** Low season, twilight, juniors. **Caddies:** No. **Golf carts:** $22. **Discount golf packages:** No. **Season:** Year-round. **High:** June-Aug. **On site lodging:** No. **Rental clubs:** Yes. **Walking policy:** Unrestricted walking. **Metal spikes allowed:** Yes. **Range:** No. **To obtain tee times:** First come, first served.

★★★DENNIS HIGHLANDS GOLF COURSE

PM-825 Old Bass River Rd., Dennis, 02638, Barnstable County, (508)385-8347, 80 miles S of Boston.
Opened: 1984. **Holes:** 18. **Par:** 71/71. **Yards:** 6,464/4,927. **Course rating:** 70.4/67.4. **Slope:** 118/112. **Architect:** Jack Kidwell and Michael Hurdzan. **Green fee:** $35/$40. **Credit cards:** MC,VISA. **Reduced fees:** Weekdays, low season, twilight. **Caddies:** No. **Golf carts:** $22. **Discount golf packages:** No. **Season:** Year-round. **High:** April-Nov. **On site lodging:** No. **Rental clubs:** Yes. **Walking policy:** Unrestricted walking. **Metal spikes allowed:** Yes. **Range:** Yes (grass). **To obtain tee times:** Call four days in advance or guarantee with prepayment (no refunds) anytime in advance.

Subscriber comments: Fair layout with challenging greens...Open fairways, undulating greens, must be able to putt...Busy in summer...A few of the best holes on Cape...Good degree of difficulty—fun to play...Toughest greens I ever played...Huge 3-putt greens, multi-tiered...You can stray and still make green in two...A confidence builder...Very hilly for Cape course...Makes you use all of your clubs and has a great finishing hole.

★★★DENNIS PINES GOLF COURSE
PU-Golf Course Rd., Dennis, 02641, Barnstable County, (508)385-9826, 80 miles S of Boston.
Opened: 1964. **Holes:** 18. **Par:** 72/73. **Yards:** 7,029/5,798. **Course rating:** 71.9/73.2. **Slope:** 127/128. **Architect:** Henry Mitchell. **Green fee:** $20/$40. **Credit cards:** MC,VISA. **Reduced fees:** Weekdays, low season, twilight. **Caddies:** No. **Golf carts:** $21. **Discount golf packages:** No. **Season:** Year-round. **High:** April-Nov. **On site lodging:** No. **Rental clubs:** Yes. **Walking policy:** Unrestricted walking. **Metal spikes allowed:** Yes. **Range:** Yes (Mats). **To obtain tee times:** Call four days in advance or guarantee with prepayment (no refund) anytime in advance.
Subscriber comments: Tight fairways. Plays long tip to tip...Average but good, worth the price...Great layout. A great challenge...Very enjoyable course...Very scenic, guarded fairways lined with tallpines...An oldie but goodie. Showing some wear...You must be long and straight...Course management is key.

★★½FALMOUTH COUNTRY CLUB
630 Carriage Shop Rd., East Falmouth, 02536, Barnstable County, (508)548-3211. Call club for further information.
Subscriber comments: Forgiving for ordinary golfers...Wide open fairways... Nice greens...I don't see people burning it up...Not too much variety...Wind is main hazard.

★★½FAR CORNER GOLF CLUB
PU-Main St. and Barker Rd., West Boxford, 01885, Essex County, (508)352-8300. **Architect:** Geoffrey S. Cornish and William G. Robinson. **Caddies:** No. **Discount golf packages:** No. **On site lodging:** No. **Rental clubs:** No. **Metal spikes allowed:** Yes. Call club for further information.
Subscriber comments: Some tough holes, hilly, but enjoyable...A lot of league play... Great par 3s...Hard to find...Lot of blind shots, need course knowledge...Excellent test

★★★★½FARM NECK GOLF CLUB
Farm Neck Way, Oak Bluffs, 02557, Dukes County, (508)693-3057, 90 miles S of Boston.
Opened: 1969. **Holes:** 18. **Par:** 72/72. **Yards:** 6,777/5,019. **Course rating:** 72.1/68.3. **Slope:** 129/120. **Architect:** Cornish and Robinson. **Green fee:** $35/$75. **Credit cards:** MC,VISA,AMEX. **Reduced fees:** Low season, twilight. **Caddies:** No. **Golf carts:** $24. **Discount golf packages:** No. **Season:** April-Dec. **High:** July-Aug. **On site lodging:** No. **Rental clubs:** Yes. **Walking policy:** Walking at certain times. **Metal spikes allowed:** No. **Range:** Yes (grass/mats). **To obtain tee times:** Call two days in advance.
Subscriber comments: Beautiful ocean holes, crowded, slow rounds in summer...Gorgeous from 1st tee to 18th green ...Well worth the trouble getting a tee time...Simply the best...Clinton never broke 80 here!...Good enough for the President, good enough for me...Wonderful island setting...Left to right course...Worth a special trip to Martha's Vineyard...Very enjoyable for all golfers.

★★FRANCONIA GOLF COURSE
PM-619 Dwight Rd., Springfield, 01108, Hampden County, (413)734-9334. **Architect:** Wayne Stiles and John Van Kleek. **Caddies:** No. **Discount golf packages:** No. **On site lodging:** No. **Rental clubs:** No. **Metal spikes allowed:** Yes. **Range:** No. Call club for further information.

★★½GARDNER MUNICIPAL GOLF COURSE
PM-152 Eaton St., Gardner, 01440, Worcester County, (508)632-9703, 20 miles N of Worcester.
Opened: 1936. **Holes:** 18. **Par:** 71/75. **Yards:** 6,106/5,653. **Course rating:** 68.9/72.2. **Slope:** 124/123. **Architect:** Samuel Mitchell. **Green fee:** $15/$25. **Credit cards:** None. **Reduced fees:** Weekdays, twilight. **Caddies:** No. **Golf carts:** $11. **Discount golf**

packages: No. **Season:** April-First snow. **High:** June-Sept. **On site lodging:** No. **Rental clubs:** Yes. **Walking policy:** Unrestricted walking. **Metal spikes allowed:** Yes. **Range:** Yes (grass/mats). **To obtain tee times:** Call two days in advance. Thursday for Saturday and Friday for Sunday.
Subscriber comments: Front side short, back nine great...Diamond in the rough... Tight fairways...Nice greens.

★★★ GEORGE WRIGHT GOLF COURSE
PU-420 W. St., Hyde Park, 02136, Suffolk County, (617)361-8313, 5 miles S of Boston.
Opened: N/A. **Holes:** 18. **Par:** 70/70. **Yards:** 6,400/5,500. **Course rating:** 69.5/70.3.
Slope: 126/115. **Architect:** Donald Ross. **Green fee:** $18/$21. **Credit cards:** MC,VISA.
Reduced fees: Seniors, juniors. **Caddies:** No. **Golf carts:** $22. **Discount golf packages:** Yes. **Season:** Year-round. **High:** June-Aug. **On site lodging:** No. **Rental clubs:** Yes. **Walking policy:** Unrestricted walking. **Metal spikes allowed:** Yes. **Range:** No. **To obtain tee times:** Call on Thursday for upcoming weekend.
Subscriber comments: Heavy play...Great old-style course...Being restored...Lots of hills and blind shots...You'll find this course challenging...Shows its age. Nice layout... Too many company outings...9th and 10th holes require your best golf...A gem, relaxed atmosphere...No target golf here...Billy goat has problems walking back nine. Nice greens.

★★ GREEN HARBOR GOLF CLUB
PU-624 Webster St., Marshfield, 02050, Plymouth County, (617)834-7303, 30 miles S of Boston.
Opened: 1971. **Holes:** 18. **Par:** 71/71. **Yards:** 6,211/5,355. **Course rating:** 69.1/69.3.
Slope: 115/109. **Architect:** Manuel Francis. **Green fee:** $27/$30. **Credit cards:** None.
Reduced fees: Twilight. **Caddies:** No. **Golf carts:** N/A. **Discount golf packages:** No.
Season: March-Dec. **High:** March-Dec. **On site lodging:** No. **Rental clubs:** Yes.
Walking policy: Unrestricted walking. **Metal spikes allowed:** Yes. **Range:** No. **To obtain tee times:** Two days prior at 6 a.m. for 18 holes; day of play at 6 a.m. for 9 holes.

★★½ HAMPDEN COUNTRY CLUB
128 Wilbraham Rd., Hampden, 01036, Hampden County, (413)566-8010.
Call club for further information.
Subscriber comments: Enjoyable...Beautiful veiws...Super course, something for everyone...Extreme elevation changes...Target golf; don't need driver a lot...Long course on side of mountain, very good layout, must putt well to score...Real test of golf...Tough four finishing holes.

★★ HEATHER HILL COUNTRY CLUB
PU-149 W. Bacon St., Plainville, 02762, Norfolk County, (508)695-0309.
Call club for further information.

★★★½ HICKORY RIDGE COUNTRY CLUB
191 W. Pomeroy Lane, Amherst, 01002, Hampshire County, (413)253-9320.
Opened: 1970. **Holes:** 18. **Par:** 72/72. **Yards:** 6,794/5,340. **Course rating:** 72.5/70.3.
Slope: 129/114. **Architect:** Geoffrey Cornish and William Robinson. **Green fee:** $32/$43. **Credit cards:** MC,VISA,AMEX. **Reduced fees:** Weekdays, juniors. **Caddies:** No. **Golf carts:** $25. **Discount golf packages:** No. **Season:** April-Nov. **High:** May-Sept. **On site lodging:** No. **Rental clubs:** Yes. **Walking policy:** Unrestricted walking. **Metal spikes allowed:** Yes. **Range:** Yes (grass). **To obtain tee times:** Outside play: 24 hours in advance.
Subscriber comments: Good food...Some challenging holes, especially the par 3s...Like a private country club, great golf...Nice mix of holes.

★★½ HIGHLAND GOLF LINKS
PU-Highland Light Rd. P.O. Box 162, North Truro, 02652, Barnstable County, (508)487-9201, 45 miles N of Hyannis.
Opened: 1892. **Holes:** 9. **Par:** 70/74. **Yards:** 5,299/4,782. **Course rating:** 65.0/67.4.
Slope: 103/107. **Architect:** Isiah Small. **Green fee:** $25/$30. **Credit cards:** MC,VISA.
Reduced fees: Low season. **Caddies:** No. **Golf carts:** $21. **Discount golf packages:** Yes. **Season:** April-Oct. **High:** June-Sept. **On site lodging:** No. **Rental clubs:** Yes.

Walking policy: Unrestricted walking. **Metal spikes allowed:** Yes. **Range:** No. **To obtain tee times:** Call 48 hours in advance.

Subscriber comments: Unique oceanside links...Scenery....Wind makes it a better challenge... Golf nuts are allowed to play at 5:30 a.m. and pay at the end of the round.

★★★HOLLY RIDGE GOLF CLUB

PU-Country Club Rd., South Sandwich, 02563, (508)428-5577.
Opened: 1966. **Holes:** 18. **Par:** 54/54. **Yards:** 2,952/2,194. **Course rating:** N/A. **Slope:** N/A. **Architect:** Geoffrey Cornish and William Robinson. **Green fee:** $12/$21. **Credit cards:** MC,VISA,AMEX. **Reduced fees:** Weekdays, low season, twilight, seniors, juniors. **Caddies:** No. **Golf carts:** $8. **Discount golf packages:** No. **Season:** Year-round. **High:** June-Aug. **On site lodging:** No. **Rental clubs:** Yes. **Walking policy:** Unrestricted walking. **Metal spikes allowed:** Yes. **Range:** Yes (Mats). **To obtain tee times:** Call up to 7 days in advance.

Subscriber comments: Good iron play needed, tough...Great beginner track...Good par-3 layout...Fun, challenging...Pleasant but very slow greens...Good lunch restaurant.

★★★HYANNIS GOLF CLUB AT IYANOUGH HILLS

Rte. 132, Hyannis, 02601, Barnstable County, (508)362-2606, 3 miles N of Hyannis.
Opened: 1976. **Holes:** 18. **Par:** 71/72. **Yards:** 6,711/5,149. **Course rating:** 69.4/69.0. **Slope:** 121/125. **Architect:** Geoffrey Cornish and William Robinson. **Green fee:** $32/$45. **Credit cards:** All major. **Reduced fees:** Weekdays, low season, twilight, seniors. **Caddies:** No. **Golf carts:** $14. **Discount golf packages:** Yes. **Season:** Year-round. **High:** June-Sept. **On site lodging:** No. **Rental clubs:** Yes. **Walking policy:** Unrestricted walking. **Metal spikes allowed:** Yes. **Range:** Yes (grass/mats). **To obtain tee times:** Call golf shop.

Subscriber comments: Have made many good changes...Good package deals...Nice greens, tough to walk...Great winter course, not a level lie to be found...Tough course to score...Best greens on the Cape, in January or July...Good attention to detail...Tricky, thinking man's course...A lot of elevated greens. Very difficult when windy.

JUNIPER HILL GOLF COURSE

PU-202 Brigham St., Northborough, 01532, Worcester County, (508)393-2444, 15 miles E of Worcester.
Opened: 1931. **Architect:** Homer Darling/Philip Wogan. **Green fee:** $25/$30. **Credit cards:** MC,VISA. **Reduced fees:** Seniors, juniors. **Caddies:** No. **Golf carts:** $24. **Discount golf packages:** No. **Season:** April-Dec. **High:** May-Sept. **On site lodging:** No. **Rental clubs:** Yes. **Walking policy:** Walking at certain times. **Metal spikes allowed:** No. **Range:** Yes (grass). **To obtain tee times:** Call one week in advance.

LAKESIDE COURSE

Holes: 18. **Par:** 71/71. **Yards:** 6,140/4,707. **Course rating:** 69.9/65.3. **Slope:** 127/102.

★★★RIVERSIDE COURSE

Holes: 18. **Par:** 71/71. **Yards:** 6,306/5,373. **Course rating:** 70.4/70.2. **Slope:** 123/117.

Subscriber comments: Sow on weekends...Both great courses...Great fairways and greens...Interesting holes...Lack of practice area surprising for 36-hole facility... Outstanding par 5s and par 3s...Lots of wildlife, very scenic...Lakeside course fun and quirky. Riverside 10th the best par 5 I've played...Prefer Lakeside course...Worth the trip...Riverside course more forgiving than narrower Lakeside

★★★½KINGS WAY GOLF CLUB

Rte. 6-A, Yarmouth Port, 02675, Essex County, (508)362-8870.
Opened: 1988. **Holes:** 18. **Par:** 59/59. **Yards:** 3,953/2,937. **Course rating:** 60.5/55.8. **Slope:** 95/85. **Architect:** N/A. **Green fee:** $45/$45. **Credit cards:** MC,VISA. **Reduced fees:** Low season, twilight. **Caddies:** No. **Golf carts:** Included in Green Fee. **Discount golf packages:** No. **Season:** April-Nov. **High:** July-Sept. **On site lodging:** No. **Rental clubs:** No. **Walking policy:** Walking at certain times. **Metal spikes allowed:** Yes. **Range:** No. **To obtain tee times:** N/A.

(GOOD SERVICE)

Subscriber comments: Fantastic executive course, tough par 4s...Very interesting...Excellent greens and facility but no pratice range, too bad it is not regulation...Good to tune the irons...Exceeds expectations for an executive course...Scenic, challenging and fun.

★★★ LAKEVILLE COUNTRY CLUB

PU-44 Clear Pond Rd., Lakeville, 02347, Plymouth County, (508)947-6630, 50 miles S of Boston.

Opened: 1970. **Holes:** 18. **Par:** 72/72. **Yards:** 6,274/5,297. **Course rating:** 70.1/68.5. **Slope:** 123/118. **Architect:** N/A. **Green fee:** $25/$30. **Credit cards:** MC,VISA,DISC. **Reduced fees:** N/A. **Caddies:** No. **Golf carts:** $20. **Discount golf packages:** No. **Season:** Year-round. **High:** May-Sept. **On site lodging:** No. **Rental clubs:** No. **Walking policy:** Unrestricted walking. **Metal spikes allowed:** Yes. **Range:** No. **To obtain tee times:** Tee times can be made one week ahead with a major credit card. Foursomes only on weekends and holidays during the morning.

Subscriber comments: Island greens back to back...Nice variety, some narrow fairways...Fun course, couple holes too close together...Last three holes are devil's triangle...Nice layout...Challenging for all levels...Excellent greens...Too many par 3s...Pleasant surprise...Tight course—requires accuracy... Bring driver. Good winter golf...

★★★½ LARRY GANNON GOLF CLUB

PM-42 Great Woods Rd., Lynn, 01904, Essex County, (781)592-8238, 10 miles S of Boston.

Opened: 1932. **Holes:** 18. **Par:** 70/71. **Yards:** 6,106/5,215. **Course rating:** 67.9/68.8. **Slope:** 113/115. **Architect:** Wayne Stiles. **Green fee:** $20/$23. **Credit cards:** N/A. **Reduced fees:** N/A. **Caddies:** No. **Golf carts:** N/A. **Discount golf packages:** No. **Season:** March-Nov. **High:** June-Oct. **On site lodging:** No. **Rental clubs:** Yes. **Walking policy:** Unrestricted walking. **Metal spikes allowed:** Yes. **Range:** Yes. **To obtain tee times:** First come, first served except for weekends.

Subscriber comments: Challenging course...A lot of blind shots. 4th hole is tough...Very hilly, scenic, love 18th hole...Do not spray off the tee!...Extremely fast greens...Tremendous views—blind par 3s...Great view of Boston's skyline from 6th.

★★★ LITTLE HARBOR COUNTRY CLUB

PU-Little Harbor Rd., Wareham, 02571, Plymouth County, (508)295-2617, (800)649-2617, 15 miles NE of New Bedford.

Opened: 1963. **Holes:** 18. **Par:** 56/56. **Yards:** 3,038/2,692. **Course rating:** 54.4/51.9. **Slope:** 79/72. **Architect:** N/A. **Green fee:** $14/$18. **Credit cards:** MC,VISA. **Reduced fees:** Weekdays, low season, twilight, seniors, juniors. **Caddies:** No. **Golf carts:** $18. **Discount golf packages:** No. **Season:** Year-round. **High:** N/A. **On site lodging:** No. **Rental clubs:** No. **Walking policy:** Unrestricted walking. **Metal spikes allowed:** Yes. **Range:** No. **To obtain tee times:** Call up to 3 days in advance.

Subscriber comments: Great, longer than usual executive course, fun...Limited food...A very good executive par 3, excellent greens.

★★★½ MAPLEGATE COUNTRY CLUB

PU-160 Maple St., Bellingham, 02019, Norfolk County, (508)966-4040, 25 miles SW of Boston.

Opened: 1990. **Holes:** 18. **Par:** 72/72. **Yards:** 6,815/4,852. **Course rating:** 74.2/70.2. **Slope:** 133/124. **Architect:** Phil Wogan. **Green fee:** $22/$39. **Credit cards:** MC,VISA. **Reduced fees:** Weekdays, low season, twilight, juniors. **Caddies:** No. **Golf carts:** $13. **Discount golf packages:** No. **Season:** April-Dec. **High:** May-Sept. **On site lodging:** No. **Rental clubs:** Yes. **Walking policy:** Walking at certain times. **Metal spikes allowed:** Yes. **Range:** Yes (grass/mats). **To obtain tee times:** Call six days in advance for foursomes; previous day after 4 p.m. for all others.

Subscriber comments: Has it all...Play it from the tips...Still maturing, good par 4s...Pace of play is very good...Tight fairways, keep it straight. Creeks on some fairways...Nice variety of holes...Thinking man's course...Tougher from the whites than blues...Very scenic, beautiful par-3 8th hole with a waterfall...Challenging layout for all.

★★★ NEW ENGLAND COUNTRY CLUB

PU-180 Paine St., Bellingham, 02019, Norfolk County, (508)883-2300, 35 miles S of Boston.

Opened: 1990. **Holes:** 18. **Par:** 71/71. **Yards:** 6,378/4,908. **Course rating:** 71.1/68.7. **Slope:** 129/121. **Architect:** Hale Irwin and Gary Kern. **Green fee:** $25/$54. **Credit cards:** MC,VISA. **Reduced fees:** Weekdays, low season, twilight. **Caddies:** No. **Golf**

GOOD VALUE

carts: Included in Green Fee. **Discount golf packages:** Yes. **Season:** April-Nov. **High:** June-Sept. **On site lodging:** No. **Rental clubs:** Yes. **Walking policy:** Walking at certain times. **Metal spikes allowed:** Yes. **Range:** Yes (grass). **To obtain tee times:** Call pro shop up to five days in advance.

Subscriber comments: Target golf, penalized on good shots...Premium on course management...Lots of marsh. Not easy...Fun...Front and back nines very different...A lot of blind tee shots, with impossible landing areas...Not much on amenities, but scenic and fun course...12th hole makes you hit 3-iron off tee, then a 3-wood over marsh...

NEW SEABURY COUNTRY CLUB

R-P.O. Box 549, Mashpee, 02649, Barnstable County, (508)477-9110, 70 miles S of Boston.

Opened: 1964. **Architect:** William Mitchell. **Green fee:** $30/$60. **Credit cards:** MC,VISA,AMEX. **Reduced fees:** Low season, twilight. **Caddies:** No. **Golf carts:** $15. **Discount golf packages:** Yes. **Season:** Year-round. **High:** July-Aug. **On site lodging:** Yes. **Rental clubs:** Yes. **Walking policy:** Walking at certain times. **Metal spikes allowed:** Yes. **Range:** Yes.

★★★★BLUE COURSE

Holes: 18. **Par:** 72/72. **Yards:** 7,200/5,764. **Course rating:** 75.3/73.8. **Slope:** 130/128. **To obtain tee times:** Guests of the resort may make tee times one day in advance. **Notes:** Ranked 7th in 1997 Best in State.

Subscriber comments: Front nine is outstanding...Great first four holes! Tough on windy days...Best on Cape. True championship test...Good blend of holes...This is a good challenge for low handicaps...Pebble Beach East! Great course with beautiful ocean views...Ocean holes make course memorable...Two different nines, seaside and wooded...Great 19th hole...Difficult front nine with the wind blowing...Vacation stop for sure...Great finishing holes...Does not get any better.

★★★½GREEN COURSE

Holes: 18. **Par:** 70/68. **Yards:** 5,939/5,105. **Course rating:** 67.0/66.3. **Slope:** 117/110. **To obtain tee times:** Resort guests may call one day in advance.

Subscriber comments: Small, protected, greens...Not as easy a course to play as some people think...Fun for all handicaps...Not on a level with Blue, yet enjoyable round...Some tough par 4s...Considerably easier than the Blue course...Nice ocean view, beautiful area for fall golf...More fun than the Blue course.

★★NEWTON COMMONWEALTH GOLF COURSE

PU-212 Kenrick St, Newton, 02158, Middlesex County, (617)630-1971, 5 miles W of Boston.

Opened: 1897. **Holes:** 18. **Par:** 70/70. **Yards:** 5,313/4,466. **Course rating:** 67.0/69.4. **Slope:** 125/118. **Architect:** Donald Ross. **Green fee:** $21/$28. **Credit cards:** MC,VISA. **Reduced fees:** Weekdays, twilight, seniors, juniors. **Caddies:** No. **Golf carts:** $23. **Discount golf packages:** No. **Season:** N/A. **High:** N/A. **On site lodging:** No. **Rental clubs:** Yes. **Walking policy:** Unrestricted walking. **Metal spikes allowed:** No. **Range:** No. **To obtain tee times:** Call up to 4 days in advance.

★½NORWOOD COUNTRY CLUB

PU-400 Providence Hwy., Norwood, 02062, Norfolk County, (617)769-5880, 20 miles S of Boston.

Opened: 1975. **Holes:** 18. **Par:** 71/71. **Yards:** 6,009/4,997. **Course rating:** 67.1/68.7. **Slope:** 112/108. **Architect:** Samuel Mitchell. **Green fee:** $16/$20. **Credit cards:** None. **Reduced fees:** Weekdays, twilight, seniors, juniors. **Caddies:** No. **Golf carts:** $11. **Discount golf packages:** No. **Season:** Year-round. **High:** June-Sept. **On site lodging:** No. **Rental clubs:** Yes. **Walking policy:** Unrestricted walking. **Metal spikes allowed:** Yes. **Range:** Yes. **To obtain tee times:** Call one week in advance for weekends and holidays only.

★★★½OAK RIDGE GOLF CLUB

PU-850 S. Westfield St., Feeding Hills, 01030, Hampden County, (413)789-7307, 10 miles NW of Springfield.

Opened: 1974. **Holes:** 18. **Par:** 70/70. **Yards:** 6,819/5,307. **Course rating:** 71.2/70.0. **Slope:** 124/124. **Architect:** George Fazio and Tom Fazio. **Green fee:** $22/$33. **Credit cards:** None. **Reduced fees:** Weekdays, seniors, juniors. **Caddies:** No. **Golf carts:** $12. **Discount golf packages:** No. **Season:** March-Dec. **High:** June-Sept. **On site

lodging: No. **Rental clubs:** Yes. **Walking policy:** Unrestricted walking. **Metal spikes allowed:** Yes. **Range:** No. **To obtain tee times:** Call one week in advance for weekday and Wednesdays for weekend play.
Subscriber comments: Great course, excellent condition, could play often!...Super layout. Difficult to putt. Service outstanding. Enjoyable all around...Excellent golf variety...Watch out for the par 5 12th...Provides fair test of golf skills...Great place for an outing...Suitable to all levels of skill.

★★★½OCEAN EDGE GOLF CLUB
R-832 Villages Dr., Brewster, 02631, Barnstable County, (508)896-5911, 90 miles S of Boston.
Opened: 1986. **Holes:** 18. **Par:** 72/72. **Yards:** 6,665/5,098. **Course rating:** 71.9/73.2.
Slope: 129/129. **Architect:** Geoffrey S. Cornish and Brian M. Silva. **Green fee:** $36/$54. **Credit cards:** MC,VISA,AMEX. **Reduced fees:** Weekdays, low season, resort guests, juniors. **Caddies:** No. **Golf carts:** $14. **Discount golf packages:** Yes. **Season:** March-Dec. **High:** June-Sept. **On site lodging:** Yes. **Rental clubs:** Yes. **Walking policy:** Walking at certain times. **Metal spikes allowed:** Yes. **Range:** Yes (grass). **To obtain tee times:** Hotel guests may make tee times at time of room reservation.
Subscriber comments: Very tough; not for high handicapper...8th hardest par 5 in New England...Always a pleasure to play here...Great pin placements...Some interesting holes...Love this place, firm, fast greens...Great vacation golf, course is challenging...Slow play because of heavy traffic.

★★★OLDE BARNSTABLE FAIRGROUNDS GOLF COURSE
PU-Rte. 149, Marstons Mills, 02648, Barnstable County, (508)420-1141, 90 miles SE of Boston.
Opened: 1992. **Holes:** 18. **Par:** 71/71. **Yards:** 6,503/5,162. **Course rating:** 70.7/69.2.
Slope: 123/118. **Architect:** Geoffrey S. Cornish, Brian M. Silva and Mark Mungeam.
Green fee: $20/$35. **Credit cards:** MC,VISA. **Reduced fees:** Weekdays, twilight.
Caddies: No. **Golf carts:** $21. **Discount golf packages:** No. **Season:** Year-round.
High: April-Nov. **On site lodging:** No. **Rental clubs:** Yes. **Walking policy:** Unrestricted walking. **Metal spikes allowed:** Yes. **Range:** Yes (Mats). **To obtain tee times:** Call 48 hours in advance at 10 a.m. Prepaid reservations by mail with no restrictions.
Subscriber comments: Most enjoyable for all handicaps...A nice course, fair for ladies...A fun course to play year round...If pins are near edges, good luck! Great restaurant...Layout through woods, greens fast...Easy walking. Easy scoring...Need to drive well to score, won't be disappointed.

★★½PEMBROKE COUNTRY CLUB
W. Elm St., Pembroke, 02359, Plymouth County, (617)826-5191, 30 miles S of Boston.
Opened: 1972. **Holes:** 18. **Par:** 71/75. **Yards:** 6,532/5,887. **Course rating:** 71.1/73.4.
Slope: 124/120. **Architect:** Phil Wogan. **Green fee:** $15/$35. **Credit cards:** MC,VISA.
Reduced fees: N/A. **Caddies:** No. **Golf carts:** $26. **Discount golf packages:** No.
Season: Year-round. **High:** June-Sept. **On site lodging:** No. **Rental clubs:** Yes.
Walking policy: Unrestricted walking. **Metal spikes allowed:** Yes. **Range:** Yes (grass/mats). **To obtain tee times:** Call Thursday morning for weekend play; anytime for weekdays.
Subscriber comments: Challenging...Greens good...Tough back nine...Good clubhouse...Some long Par 4s and 3s...Fairly narrow with water on seven holes.

★★PONKAPOAG GOLF CLUB
PU-2167 Washington St., Canton, 02021, Norfolk County, (617)575-1001, 10 miles S of Boston.
Opened: 1933. **Holes:** 36. **Par:** 72/74. **Yards:** 6,728/5,523. **Course rating:** 72.0/70.8.
Slope: 126/115. **Architect:** Donald Ross. **Green fee:** $5/$14. **Credit cards:** MC,VISA,AMEX. **Reduced fees:** Weekdays, twilight, seniors, juniors. **Caddies:** No.
Golf carts: $24. **Discount golf packages:** Yes. **Season:** April-Dec. **High:** May-Aug. **On site lodging:** No. **Rental clubs:** Yes. **Walking policy:** Unrestricted walking. **Metal spikes allowed:** Yes. **Range:** Yes (grass/mats). **To obtain tee times:** First come, first serve.

★★★½POQUOY BROOK GOLF CLUB

PU-20 Leonard St., Lakeville, 02347, Plymouth County, (508)947-5261, 45 miles SE of Boston.

Opened: 1962. **Holes:** 18. **Par:** 72/73. **Yards:** 6,762/5,415. **Course rating:** 72.4/71.0. **Slope:** 128/114. **Architect:** Geoffrey S. Cornish. **Green fee:** $32/$35. **Credit cards:** All major,Debit Card. **Reduced fees:** Weekdays, low season, twilight. **Caddies:** No. **Golf carts:** $14. **Discount golf packages:** No. **Season:** Year-round. **High:** May-Oct. **On site lodging:** No. **Rental clubs:** Yes. **Walking policy:** Unrestricted walking. **Metal spikes allowed:** No. **Range:** Yes (grass). **To obtain tee times:** Call up to 7 days in advance for weekdays; 2 days in advance for weekends.

Subscriber comments: Country club conditions...Always a great place to play...Wide open course, easy to score well...Bar has deck overlooking 18th green...Thinking man's course...Fun to play...Hard to beat for visual beauty and value...Very nice place with plenty of variety...Be sure to have bug spray handy...Nice touches everywhere.

★★★QUASHNET VALLEY COUNTRY CLUB

309 Old Barnstable Rd., Mashpee, 02649, Barnstable County, (508)477-4412, (800)433-8633, 55 miles S of Boston.

Opened: 1974. **Holes:** 18. **Par:** 72/72. **Yards:** 6,602/5,094. **Course rating:** 71.7/70.3. **Slope:** 132/119. **Architect:** Geoffrey S. Cornish and William Robinson. **Green fee:** $30/$47. **Credit cards:** MC,VISA. **Reduced fees:** Weekdays, low season, twilight. **Caddies:** No. **Golf carts:** $12. **Discount golf packages:** No. **Season:** Year-round. **High:** April-Oct. **On site lodging:** No. **Rental clubs:** Yes. **Walking policy:** Walking at certain times. **Metal spikes allowed:** Yes. **Range:** Yes (grass). **To obtain tee times:** Call one week in advance.

Subscriber comments: Good nature walk. Interesting holes...Gotten better in the last few years...Target golf...Beautiful layout...Long and hard. Complete practice facilities... Big greens, challenging course...Keep it in the fairway...Great scenery through the wetlands...Interesting second shots; suckers beware...No room for error, lots of water.,

★★★REHOBOTH COUNTRY CLUB

PU-155 Perryville Rd., Rehoboth, 02769, Bristol County, (508)252-6259, 15 miles E of Providence.

Opened: 1966. **Holes:** 18. **Par:** 72/75. **Yards:** 6,950/5,450. **Course rating:** 72.5/70.4. **Slope:** 125/115. **Architect:** Geoffrey Cornish and William Robinson. **Green fee:** $20/$25. **Credit cards:** None. **Reduced fees:** Twilight, seniors, juniors. **Caddies:** No. **Golf carts:** $10. **Discount golf packages:** No. **Season:** Year-round. **High:** May-Sept. **On site lodging:** No. **Rental clubs:** No. **Walking policy:** Unrestricted walking. **Metal spikes allowed:** Yes. **Range:** No. **To obtain tee times:** Tee times taken three days in advance for weekends only.

Subscriber comments: Beautiful country setting. Don't miss this one...Use every club in bag...4 is a killer...Very long, lots of water...Nice course, fun to play...Tough course for a beginner...Much easier if you draw the ball...Nice course, flat and narrow, pitched greens, five ponds.

★★½RIDDER GOLF CLUB

PU-300 Oak St., Rte. 14, Whitman, 02382, Plymouth County, (781)447-9003, 20 miles S of Boston.

Opened: 1961. **Holes:** 18. **Par:** 70/70. **Yards:** 5,847/5,400. **Course rating:** 67.6/67.6. **Slope:** 109/109. **Architect:** Henry Hohman/Geoffrey S. Cornish. **Green fee:** $26/$28. **Credit cards:** None. **Reduced fees:** Weekdays, low season, juniors. **Caddies:** No. **Golf carts:** $21. **Discount golf packages:** No. **Season:** Year-round. **High:** May-Sept. **On site lodging:** No. **Rental clubs:** Yes. **Walking policy:** Unrestricted walking. **Metal spikes allowed:** No. **Range:** Yes (grass). **To obtain tee times:** Call up to 48 hours in advance.

Subscriber comments: Wide open, simple layout, sometimes slow...Very easy front nine, a good confidence builder...Hard to lose a ball...Short, but a lot of fun.

★★½ROUND HILL COUNTRY CLUB

Round Hill Rd., East Sandwich, 02537, Barnstable County, (508)888-3384, 50 miles S of Boston.

Opened: 1972. **Holes:** 18. **Par:** 71/70. **Yards:** 6,157/4,842. **Course rating:** 70.4/68.1.

Slope: 124/115. **Architect:** Richard Cross. **Green fee:** $17/$40. **Credit cards:** MC,VISA. **Reduced fees:** Weekdays, low season, twilight, seniors. **Caddies:** No. **Golf carts:** $24. **Discount golf packages:** No. **Season:** Year-round. **High:** June-Sept. **On site lodging:** No. **Rental clubs:** Yes. **Walking policy:** Walking at certain times. **Metal spikes allowed:** Yes. **Range:** Yes (grass). **To obtain tee times:** Call up to 7 days in advance.

Subscriber comments: Many great holes, a few stupid ones...Great 19th-hole views... 17th almost unfair...Extremely hilly, very narrow fairways...Watch out for the groundhogs.

★★½SADDLE HILL COUNTRY CLUB
PU-204 Saddle Hill Rd., Hopkinton, 01748, Middlesex County, (508)435-4630, 26 miles W of Boston.
Opened: 1963. **Holes:** 18. **Par:** 72/72. **Yards:** 6,900/5,619. **Course rating:** 72.8/70.3. **Slope:** 124/108. **Architect:** William F. Mitchell. **Green fee:** $22/$28. **Credit cards:** MC,VISA. **Reduced fees:** Seniors. **Caddies:** No. **Golf carts:** $11. **Discount golf packages:** No. **Season:** March-Dec. **High:** N/A. **On site lodging:** No. **Rental clubs:** Yes. **Walking policy:** Unrestricted walking. **Metal spikes allowed:** Yes. **Range:** Yes (Mats). **To obtain tee times:** Call up to 7 days in advance for weekdays; Wednesday prior for weekends.
Subscriber comments: Great par 3s, wide fairways, yet challenging...Nice greens, nice layout, not too long...Tough from the tips...Wide open front, back more challenging.

★★½SAGAMORE SPRING GOLF CLUB
PU-1287 Main St., Lynnfield, 01940, Essex County, (781)334-3151, 15 miles N of Boston.
Opened: 1929. **Holes:** 18. **Par:** 70/70. **Yards:** 5,936/4,784. **Course rating:** 68.6/66.5. **Slope:** 119/112. **Architect:** Richard Luff. **Green fee:** $28/$34. **Credit cards:** None. **Reduced fees:** Weekdays, low season, seniors. **Caddies:** No. **Golf carts:** $22. **Discount golf packages:** No. **Season:** March-Dec. **High:** June-Sept. **On site lodging:** No. **Rental clubs:** Yes. **Walking policy:** Unrestricted walking. **Metal spikes allowed:** Yes. **Range:** Yes (Mats). **To obtain tee times:** Call four days in advance between 9 a.m. - 5 p.m.
Subscriber comments: Back nine better than the front...Tends to be busy...Fun course with some decision making...Ends with back-to-back par 3s, nice atmosphere...Busy

★★ST. ANNE COUNTRY CLUB
PU-781 Shoemaker Ln, Feeding Hills, Hampden County, (413)786-2088.
Call club for further information.

★★½SANDY BURR COUNTRY CLUB
PU-103 Cochituate Rd., Wayland, 01778, Middlesex County, (508)358-7211.
Architect: Donald Ross. **Caddies:** No. **Discount golf packages:** No. **On site lodging:** No. **Rental clubs:** No.**Metal spikes allowed:** Yes. **Range:** No.
Call club for further information.
Subscriber comments: Each hole is unique...Crowded on weekends...Back nine more challenging than front...Nice course for all abilities...Play in the fall.

★★★★SHAKER HILLS GOLF CLUB
PU-Shaker Rd., Harvard, 01451, Middlesex County, (508)772-2227, 35 miles NW of Boston.
Opened: 1991. **Holes:** 18. **Par:** 71/71. **Yards:** 6,850/5,001. **Course rating:** 72.3/67.9. **Slope:** 135/116. **Architect:** Brian M. Silva. **Green fee:** $45/$50. **Credit cards:** MC,VISA. **Reduced fees:** Twilight. **Caddies:** Yes. **Golf carts:** Included in Green Fee. **Discount golf packages:** No. **Season:** April-Nov. **High:** June-Sept. **On site lodging:** No. **Rental clubs:** Yes. **Walking policy:** Unrestricted walking. **Metal spikes allowed:** Yes. **Range:** Yes (grass). **To obtain tee times:** Call automated 24-hour tee time reservations.
Subscriber comments: The best! Scenic, tough, fun...Awesome golf course, great service...Bring your best game. Play smart...Tough landing areas, two-digit handicaps stay away...Private conditions and easy tee times...I always look forward to playing here...Variety of shots required...Fast play is strongly advised...A New England course carved out of woods, old rock walls...Top notch, must be long and straight...As good as you'll find...Breathtaking track!...Secluded locale...Every hole could be signature hole.

★★★SOUTH SHORE COUNTRY CLUB
274 S. St., Hingham, 02043, Plymouth County, (617)749-6947, 25 miles SE of Boston.
Opened: N/A. **Holes:** 18. **Par:** 72/72. **Yards:** 6,444/5,064. **Course rating:** 71.0/69.3.
Slope: 128/116. **Architect:** Wayne Stiles. **Green fee:** $22/$33. **Credit cards:** MC,VISA.
Reduced fees: Twilight, seniors, juniors. **Caddies:** No. **Golf carts:** $21. **Discount golf packages:** No. **Season:** April-Dec. **High:** June-Sept. **On site lodging:** No. **Rental clubs:** Yes. **Walking policy:** Unrestricted walking. **Metal spikes allowed:** Yes. **Range:** Yes (Mats). **To obtain tee times:** Call up to 1 day in advance.
Subscriber comments: Good solid track...Improving each year...Hilly New England layout—plenty of wind near the ocean...Good food...Best challenge in the area...Not too many flat lies.

★★★SQUIRREL RUN GOLF & COUNTRY CLUB
PU-Rte. 44, Carver Rd., Plymouth, 02360, Plymouth County, (508)746-5001, 40 miles S of Boston.
Opened: 1991. **Holes:** 18. **Par:** N/A. **Yards:** N/A. **Course rating:** N/A. **Slope:** N/A.
Architect: Ray Richard. **Green fee:** $19/$22. **Credit cards:** MC,VISA. **Reduced fees:** Seniors, juniors. **Caddies:** No. **Golf carts:** N/A. **Discount golf packages:** No. **Season:** Year-round. **High:** July-Aug. **On site lodging:** No. **Rental clubs:** Yes. **Walking policy:** N/A. **Metal spikes allowed:** No. **Range:** Yes (grass/mats). **To obtain tee times:** N/A.
Subscriber comments: Good par 3 to improve short game...Treacherous greens and traps—what fun! You can't wait to play it again!...Very enjoyable executive course...Superb, fantastic greens.

STOW ACRES COUNTRY CLUB
PU-58 Randall Rd., Stow, 01775, Middlesex County, (508)568-1100, 25 miles NW of Boston. **Architect:** Geoffrey S. Cornish. **Green fee:** $30/$40. **Credit cards:** None.
Reduced fees: Weekdays, low season, twilight, seniors, juniors. **Caddies:** No. **Golf carts:** $26. **Discount golf packages:** No. **Season:** March-Dec. **High:** April-Nov. **On site lodging:** No. **Rental clubs:** Yes. **Walking policy:** Unrestricted walking. **Metal spikes allowed:** No. **Range:** Yes (Mats). **To obtain tee times:** Call six days in advance.
★★★½NORTH COURSE
Opened: 1965. **Holes:** 18. **Par:** 72/72. **Yards:** 6,950/6,011. **Course rating:** 72.8/70.6.
Slope: 130/120.
Notes: 1995 USGA Amateur Public Links Championship.
Subscriber comments: Need all clubs; short game important!...Very crowded...Old course, very good, play every year...Large greens; cut out of woods...Outstanding but slow...Great test of shotmaking...Tougher than South...Good for outings...A lot of fun...Good challenge for all levels...No target golf here. Intelligent play and club selection are the key...Makes you work for your score...Love to play course.
★★★SOUTH COURSE
Opened: 1965. **Holes:** 18. **Par:** 72/72. **Yards:** 6,520/5,642. **Course rating:** 71.8/69.7.
Slope: 120/116.
Subscriber comments: Well worth the trip, not for duffers, very busy...Variety in layout...Great design, very hilly...Tall trees abound...Almost as good as the North, not as many memorable holes...South more forgiving.

★★½SWANSEA COUNTRY CLUB
PU-299 Market St., Swansea, 02777, Bristol County, (508)379-9886, 10 miles E of Providence, RI.
Opened: 1963. **Holes:** 18. **Par:** 72/72. **Yards:** 6,840/5,239. **Course rating:** 72.7/69.9.
Slope: 121/109. **Architect:** Geoffrey S. Cornish. **Green fee:** $23/$28. **Credit cards:** None. **Reduced fees:** Weekdays, low season, twilight, seniors, juniors. **Caddies:** No. **Golf carts:** $21. **Discount golf packages:** No. **Season:** Year-round. **High:** April-Sept. **On site lodging:** No. **Rental clubs:** Yes. **Walking policy:** Unrestricted walking. **Metal spikes allowed:** No. **Range:** Yes (grass). **To obtain tee times:** Call five days in advance.
Subscriber comments: Tough greens, big pro shop...Nice layout, good greens...Flat and straight...A bit damp in low places...Par-3 6th over water—beautiful as you'll play.

★★★★½TACONIC GOLF CLUB

Meacham St., Williamstown, 01267, Berkshire County, (413)458-3997, 35 miles E of Albany, NY.

Opened: 1896. **Holes:** 18. **Par:** 71/71. **Yards:** 6,614/5,202. **Course rating:** 70.5/69.9. **Slope:** 127/123. **Architect:** Wayne E. Stiles and John R. Van Kleek. **Green fee:** $80/$80. **Credit cards:** MC,VISA. **Reduced fees:** N/A. **Caddies:** No. **Golf carts:** Included in Green Fee. **Discount golf packages:** No. **Season:** April-Nov. **High:** July-Sept. **On site lodging:** No. **Rental clubs:** Yes. **Walking policy:** Mandatory cart. **Metal spikes allowed:** Yes. **Range:** Yes (grass). **To obtain tee times:** Call up to one week in advance.

Subscriber comments: A little known treasure...Beautiful, great golf holes...Tradition oozes, must play in fall...My favorite course in New England...Very enjoyable...Good course for beginners...One of the best...Unforgettable course well worth trip across the state from Boston...Holes are demanding either through distance or layout.

★★★★TARA FERNCROFT COUNTRY CLUB

R-50 Ferncroft Rd., Danvers, 01923, Essex County, (508)777-5614, 15 miles N of Boston.

Opened: 1970. **Holes:** 18. **Par:** 72/73. **Yards:** 6,601/5,543. **Course rating:** 73.2/71.4. **Slope:** 132/118. **Architect:** Robert Trent Jones. **Green fee:** $75/$75. **Credit cards:** All major. **Reduced fees:** N/A. **Caddies:** No. **Golf carts:** Included in Green Fee. **Discount golf packages:** Yes. **Season:** April-Dec. **High:** May-Oct. **On site lodging:** Yes. **Rental clubs:** Yes. **Walking policy:** Mandatory cart. **Metal spikes allowed:** No. **Range:** Yes (grass). **To obtain tee times:** Hotel guests call two days prior to play.

Notes: LPGA Boston Five Classic 1980-1990.

Subscriber comments: Always in top condition and difficult...Excellent fairways and greens...Front open, back tight great track, must play...Nice challenge, but you can score...Lots of water and bunkers...Golf as it should be, except for the cart path rules...Challenging and fun...12th a picturesque par 3...A must when in the area.

Special Notes: Also has a 9-hole par-3 course.

★★★TARA HYANNIS GOLF COURSE

R-W. End Circle, Hyannis, 02601, Barnstable County, (508)775-7775, (800)843-8272, 75 miles S of Boston.

Opened: 1965. **Holes:** 18. **Par:** 54/54. **Yards:** 2,361/2,239. **Course rating:** N/A. **Slope:** N/A. **Architect:** Geoffrey Cornish and William Robinson. **Green fee:** $15/$25. **Credit cards:** All major. **Reduced fees:** Weekdays, low season, twilight, seniors, juniors. **Caddies:** No. **Golf carts:** $19. **Discount golf packages:** No. **Season:** Year-round. **High:** June-Sept. **On site lodging:** No. **Rental clubs:** Yes. **Walking policy:** Unrestricted walking. **Metal spikes allowed:** Yes. **Range:** Yes (grass). **To obtain tee times:** Call golf shop.

Subscriber comments: Must be accurate with irons...Most holes are very secluded...Challenge with winds. Front nine very short...Good restaurant...Use all your clubs on this par 3 course, interesting greens...Lack of room makes for out of bounds on several holes.

★★★½TRULL BROOK GOLF COURSE

PU-170 River Rd., Tewksbury, 01876, Middlesex County, (978)851-6731, 28 miles NW of Boston.

Opened: 1963. **Holes:** 18. **Par:** 72/72. **Yards:** 6,350/5,385. **Course rating:** 68.4/70.2. **Slope:** 118/118. **Architect:** Geoffrey S. Cornish. **Green fee:** $33/$37. **Credit cards:** MC,VISA. **Reduced fees:** Weekdays, low season, twilight, seniors, juniors. **Caddies:** No. **Golf carts:** $24. **Discount golf packages:** No. **Season:** March-Nov. **High:** June-Aug. **On site lodging:** No. **Rental clubs:** Yes. **Walking policy:** Unrestricted walking. **Metal spikes allowed:** Yes. **Range:** No. **To obtain tee times:** Call up to seven days in advance.

Subscriber comments: No flat greens. Beautiful and hilly layout...Nice course, great shape, a little slow but very enjoyable...Target golf...Many unique holes...Runs along Merrimack River...Quirky layout, but I liked it...Can bottle up...Very pretty New England course...Rewards long hitters.

★★★½WACHUSETT COUNTRY CLUB
187 Prospect St., West Boylston, 01583, Worcester County, (508)835-2264, 7 miles N of Worcester.
Opened: 1928. **Holes:** 18. **Par:** 72/72. **Yards:** 6,608/6,216. **Course rating:** 71.7/70.0. **Slope:** 124/120. **Architect:** Donald Ross. **Green fee:** $20/$35. **Credit cards:** MC,VISA,AMEX. **Reduced fees:** Low season, twilight. **Caddies:** No. **Golf carts:** $12. **Discount golf packages:** No. **Season:** April-Nov. **High:** May-Oct. **On site lodging:** No. **Rental clubs:** Yes. **Walking policy:** Unrestricted walking. **Metal spikes allowed:** Yes. **Range:** Yes (grass). **To obtain tee times:** Call.
Subscriber comments: Challenging holes...Hidden gem...Many recent changes have made this a very good test...Great greens...Some outstanding holes...Tough par 3s...Wonderful par 5s...Long par 4s...Donald Ross at its best!...Wide open, bring driver.

★★★½WAHCONAH COUNTRY CLUB
15 Orchard Rd., Dalton, 01226, Berkshire County, (413)684-1333, 4 miles N of Pittsfield.
Opened: 1930. **Holes:** 18. **Par:** 71/73. **Yards:** 6,567/5,567. **Course rating:** 71.9/72.5. **Slope:** 126/123. **Architect:** W. Stiles/G.S. Cornish and R. Armacost. **Green fee:** $50/$60. **Credit cards:** MC,VISA. **Reduced fees:** N/A. **Caddies:** No. **Golf carts:** $24. **Discount golf packages:** No. **Season:** April-Nov. **High:** April-Nov. **On site lodging:** No. **Rental clubs:** No. **Walking policy:** Unrestricted walking. **Metal spikes allowed:** Yes. **Range:** Yes (grass). **To obtain tee times:** Call eight days in advance.
Subscriber comments: Terrific views. Fairways and greens great condition...Fun course...Scenic, nice layout, challenging rolling countryside...Layout is challenging, greens tough...Best track I played last season.

★★½WAUBEEKA GOLF LINKS
PU-137 New Ashford Rd., Williamstown, 01267, Berkshire County, (413)458-8355, 12 miles N of Pittsfield.
Opened: 1966. **Holes:** 18. **Par:** 72/72. **Yards:** 6,394/5,023. **Course rating:** 70.9/71.2. **Slope:** 127/111. **Architect:** Rowland Armacost. **Green fee:** $20/$25. **Credit cards:** All major. **Reduced fees:** Juniors. **Caddies:** No. **Golf carts:** $20. **Discount golf packages:** No. **Season:** April-Nov. **High:** July-Aug. **On site lodging:** No. **Rental clubs:** Yes. **Walking policy:** Unrestricted walking. **Metal spikes allowed:** Yes. **Range:** Yes (grass). **To obtain tee times:** Call in advance.
Subscriber comments: Interesting course, beautiful setting...Play in late summer/early fall...Best views in the area...Good layout. Front nine hilly, back nine flat.

★★½WESTMINSTER COUNTRY CLUB
51 Ellis Rd., Westminster, 01473, Worcester County, (978)874-5938, 22 miles N of Worcester.
Opened: 1957. **Holes:** 18. **Par:** 71/71. **Yards:** 6,491/5,453. **Course rating:** 70.9/70.0. **Slope:** 133/115. **Architect:** Manny Francis. **Green fee:** $22/$28. **Credit cards:** All major. **Reduced fees:** Twilight. **Caddies:** No. **Golf carts:** $22. **Discount golf packages:** No. **Season:** April-Nov. **High:** May-Sept. **On site lodging:** No. **Rental clubs:** Yes. **Walking policy:** Unrestricted walking. **Metal spikes allowed:** Yes. **Range:** No. **To obtain tee times:** Call one day in advance for weekdays and on Friday for weekend times.
Subscriber comments: Terrific course. Very challenging, fast greens...Tough if you miss greens...Firm fairways, hilly backside, flat front...Seems to improve each year.

★★½WESTOVER GOLF COURSE
PU-South St., Granby, 01033, Hampshire County, (413)547-8610, 10 miles NE of Springfield.
Opened: 1957. **Holes:** 18. **Par:** 72/72. **Yards:** 7,025/5,980. **Course rating:** 73.9/72.0. **Slope:** 131/118. **Architect:** Al Zikorus. **Green fee:** $14/$16. **Credit cards:** None. **Reduced fees:** Twilight, seniors, juniors. **Caddies:** No. **Golf carts:** $16. **Discount golf packages:** No. **Season:** April-Dec. **High:** June-Sept. **On site lodging:** No. **Rental clubs:** Yes. **Walking policy:** Unrestricted walking. **Metal spikes allowed:** Yes. **Range:** Yes (grass). **To obtain tee times:** Call or come in 48 hours in advance.
Subscriber comments: The first 9 holes are long with sand traps. The back 9 demands accuracy or you'll spend time in the woods...Tough course from white tees.

★★★A-GA-MING GOLF CLUB
PU-McLachlan Rd., Kewadin, 49648, Antrim County, (616)264-5081, (800)678-0122, 9 miles N of Elk Rapids.
Opened: 1986. **Holes:** 18. **Par:** 72/72. **Yards:** 6,663/5,125. **Course rating:** 73.2/69.2. **Slope:** 133/124. **Architect:** "Chick" Harbert. **Green fee:** $45. **Credit cards:** All major. **Reduced fees:** Low season, resort guests, twilight, juniors. **Caddies:** No. **Golf carts:** Included in Green Fee. **Discount golf packages:** Yes. **Season:** April-Oct. **High:** July-Sept. **On site lodging:** Yes. **Rental clubs:** Yes. **Walking policy:** Walking at certain times. **Metal spikes allowed:** Yes. **Range:** Yes (grass/mats). **To obtain tee times:** Call in advance.
Subscriber comments: Enjoyable, with great views of Torch Lake. Very hilly, very hard walking—cart a must...Some quirky holes...Classic construction style. Narrower fairways, tighter holes, a shotmakers' course...Two thumbs up...Very scenic!...Course was in great condition, the view from 16 tee is spectacular...Fun for many levels.

★★★ALPENA GOLF CLUB
PU-1135 Golf Course Rd., Alpena, 49707, Alpena County, (517)354-5052.
Opened: 1934. **Holes:** 18. **Par:** 71/71. **Yards:** 6,407/5,048. **Course rating:** 70.5/69.0. **Slope:** 120/113. **Architect:** Warner Bowen. **Green fee:** $22/$24. **Credit cards:** MC,VISA. **Reduced fees:** Resort guests, seniors, juniors. **Caddies:** No. **Golf carts:** $20. **Discount golf packages:** Yes. **Season:** April-Oct. **High:** July-Aug. **On site lodging:** No. **Rental clubs:** Yes. **Walking policy:** Unrestricted walking. **Metal spikes allowed:** Yes. **Range:** Yes (grass). **To obtain tee times:** Call.
Subscriber comments: Staff helpful, prices acceptable...Back nine very good, front nine needs redo...Nice staff...Front nine drab...A good course for the buck...Super mix of old/new styles in front/back.

★★★ANTRIM DELLS GOLF CLUB
PU-12352 Antrim Drive, Ellsworth, 49729, Antrim County, (616)599-2679, 35 miles NE of Traverse City.
Opened: 1973. **Holes:** 18. **Par:** 72/72. **Yards:** 6,606/5,493. **Course rating:** N/A. **Slope:** 125/121. **Architect:** Bruce Matthews and Jerry Matthews. **Green fee:** $27/$45. **Credit cards:** MC,VISA. **Reduced fees:** Weekdays, low season, twilight, juniors. **Caddies:** No. **Golf carts:** Included in Green Fee. **Discount golf packages:** Yes. **Season:** April-Oct. **High:** July-Aug. **On site lodging:** No. **Rental clubs:** Yes. **Walking policy:** Mandatory cart. **Metal spikes allowed:** Yes. **Range:** Yes (grass/mats). **To obtain tee times:** Call in advance.
Subscriber comments: Pretty decent golf. Well taken care of, some good deals for spring and fall. Staff super...Always able to get out...Very scenic, hilly, fairly open...Fun and tough from back tees, front tougher than back...Back nine a lot better than front...Good value, easy access to tee times...Golfer friendly.

★★½BALD MOUNTAIN GOLF COURSE
PU-3350 Kern Rd., Lake Orion, 48360, Oakland County, (248)373-1110, 25 miles N of Detroit.
Opened: 1929. **Holes:** 18. **Par:** 71/72. **Yards:** 6,624/5,775. **Course rating:** 71.2/72.9. **Slope:** 120/120. **Architect:** Wilfrid Reid. **Green fee:** $22/$27. **Credit cards:** All major. **Reduced fees:** Low season, twilight. **Caddies:** No. **Golf carts:** $22. **Discount golf packages:** No. **Season:** April-Nov. **High:** May-Sept. **On site lodging:** No. **Rental clubs:** No. **Walking policy:** Unrestricted walking. **Metal spikes allowed:** Yes. **Range:** Yes (grass). **To obtain tee times:** Call 3 days in advance for weekdays and 7 days in advance for weekends and holidays.
Subscriber comments: Fairly short but challenging layout!...Open with nice elevation...Good greens, not so good fairways...Range closes early...Good for knocking the ball around...Very hilly, tough to walk...Back nine, great par 3s..."Big Cat" Williams' old track...Look out if it's windy. Often swampy, don't play after rain.
Special Notes: Also 9-hole executive course.

MICHIGAN

★★★BAY COUNTY GOLF COURSE
PU-584 Hampton Rd., Essexville, 48732, Bay County, (517)892-2161,
6 miles NE of Bay City.
Opened: 1966. **Holes:** 18. **Par:** 72/74. **Yards:** 6,557/5,706. **Course rating:** 71.3/72.4. **Slope:** 113/114. **Architect:** Moranci. **Green fee:** $13/$14.
Credit cards: MC,VISA. **Reduced fees:** Weekdays, seniors, juniors.
Caddies: No. **Golf carts:** $18. **Discount golf packages:** No. **Season:**
March-Dec. **High:** May-Aug. **On site lodging:** No. **Rental clubs:** Yes. **Walking policy:**
Unrestricted walking. **Metal spikes allowed:** Yes. **Range:** Yes (grass/mats). **To obtain tee times:** Call up to 7 days in advance.
Subscriber comments: Muny that is in club shape, great condition...Don't like out-of-bounds inside course...Good service, excellent greens...Best maintained course in Bay County...Great, well kept fairways and greens...Immaculate conditions and very inexpensive—great value...Needs more trouble...Crowded, but a bargain.

BAY HARBOR GOLF CLUB
5800 Coastal Ridge, Bay Harbor, 49770, Emmet County, (616)439-4028,
10 miles N of Petoskey.
Opened: 1996. **Holes:** 27. **Par:** 72. **Yards:** 6,800. **Course rating:** N/A.
Slope: N/A. **Architect:** Arthur Hills. **Green fee:** $160. **Credit cards:** All
major. **Reduced fees:** Low season, resort guests, twilight. **Caddies:** No.
Golf carts: Included in Green Fee. **Discount golf packages:** No. **Season:** May-Oct.
High: July-Aug. **On site lodging:** Yes. **Rental clubs:** Yes. **Walking policy:** Mandatory
cart. **Metal spikes allowed:** No. **Range:** Yes (grass). **To obtain tee times:** Call up to
30 days in advance.
Notes: NAIA National Collegiate Tournament.
Subscriber comments: Are you kidding me? Is this heaven?...Magnificant
setting...Hypnotizing beauty...The layout and condition are among the best ever...Pay
any price to play this—awe inspiring!...Most beautiful views in America...200 feet above
Little Traverse Bay, what more to say?

★★★BAY VALLEY GOLF CLUB
R-2470 Old Bridge Rd., Bay City, 48706, Bay County, (517)686-5400, (800)292-5028, 5
miles S of Bay City.
Opened: 1973. **Holes:** 18. **Par:** 71/71. **Yards:** 6,610/5,151. **Course rating:** 71.3/68.5.
Slope: 125/114. **Architect:** Desmond Muirhead. **Green fee:** $46/$54. **Credit cards:** All
major. **Reduced fees:** Weekdays, low season. **Caddies:** No. **Golf carts:** Included in
Green Fee. **Discount golf packages:** No. **Season:** April-Oct. **High:** June-Sept. **On site
lodging:** Yes. **Rental clubs:** Yes. **Walking policy:** Mandatory cart. **Metal spikes
allowed:** Yes. **Range:** Yes (grass). **To obtain tee times:** Call in advance.
Subscriber comments: A little "pricey" but a nice track...Early season and late season
good golf values...Challenging resort course. Excellent staff...A top course in area, challenging for all levels...Lots of water hazards.

★★BEAVER CREEK LINKS
850 Stoney Creek Rd., Oakland Township, 48363, Oakland County, (248)693-7170, 5
miles N of Rochester.
Opened: N/A. **Holes:** 27. **Par:** 72/72. **Yards:** 6,415/5,047. **Course rating:** 69.5/67.8.
Slope: 129/116. **Architect:** N/A. **Green fee:** $30/$40. **Credit cards:** None. **Reduced
fees:** N/A. **Caddies:** No. **Golf carts:** Included in Green Fee. **Discount golf packages:**
No. **Season:** Year-round weather permitting. **High:** May-Oct. **On site lodging:** No.
Rental clubs: Yes. **Walking policy:** Mandatory cart. **Metal spikes allowed:** Yes.
Range: No. **To obtain tee times:** Call up to 7 days in advance in peak season.

★★★BEDFORD HILLS GOLF CLUB
PU-6400 Jackman Rd., Temperance, 48182, Monroe County, (313)847-5004, 1 mile N
of Toledo, OH.
Opened: 1993. **Holes:** 27. **Par:** 72/72. **Yards:** 6,231/4,876. **Course rating:** 68.1/65.1.
Slope: 113/107. **Architect:** N/A. **Green fee:** $18/$24. **Credit cards:** MC,VISA.
Reduced fees: Seniors, juniors. **Caddies:** No. **Golf carts:** $11. **Discount golf packages:** No. **Season:** April-Oct. **High:** June-Sept. **On site lodging:** No. **Rental clubs:**
No. **Walking policy:** Unrestricted walking. **Metal spikes allowed:** No. **Range:** Yes

(mats). **To obtain tee times:** Call up to 7 days in advance.
Subscriber comments: Well manicured...Another pro layout, fast greens, good fairways, must play...Good condition, wide area between fairways...Like golfing on a lush carpet...Nice condition, tight, slow...Good shape, good value...Large, very well maintained greens...Too narrow at spots.

★★BEDFORD VALLEY GOLF COURSE
PU-23161 Waubascon Rd., Battle Creek, 49017, Calhoun County, (616)965-3384, 10 miles N of Battle Creek.
Opened: 1966. **Holes:** 18. **Par:** 71/72. **Yards:** 6,876/5,104. **Course rating:** 73.8/70.0.
Slope: 135/119. **Architect:** Bill Mitchell. **Green fee:** $28/$37. **Credit cards:** MC,VISA.
Reduced fees: Weekdays, low season, resort guests, twilight, juniors. **Caddies:** No.
Golf carts: $12. **Discount golf packages:** Yes. **Season:** April-Nov. **High:** May-Aug. **On site lodging:** No. **Rental clubs:** Yes. **Walking policy:** Walking at certain times. **Metal spikes allowed:** Yes. **Range:** Yes (grass). **To obtain tee times:** Call.
Subscriber comments: Classic course. Black tees are a handful...Underrated course, tough but fair...Great sand traps, greens, fairways in fabulous condition...Excellent condition must play...Have a tendency to overbook...One of the better courses in Battle Creek area...Old style, you'll use all your clubs. Maybe worthy of national attention...Mature trees, bunkers good test...Largest sand traps and greens I've seen.

★★BEECH HOLLOW GOLF COURSE
PU-7494 Hospital Rd., Freeland, 48623, Freeland County, (517)695-5427, 5 miles NW of Sabinaw.
Opened: 1969. **Holes:** 18. **Par:** 72. **Yards:** 5,700. **Course rating:** 66.0. **Slope:** 112.
Architect: N/A. **Green fee:** $13/$17. **Credit cards:** MC,VISA,DISC. **Reduced fees:** Weekdays, low season, seniors. **Caddies:** No. **Golf carts:** $20. **Discount golf packages:** No. **Season:** March-Nov. **High:** May-Aug. **On site lodging:** No. **Rental clubs:** No. **Walking policy:** Unrestricted walking. **Metal spikes allowed:** Yes. **Range:** No. **To obtain tee times:** Call.

★★★BELLE RIVER GOLF & COUNTRY CLUB
PU-12564 Belle River Rd., Memphis, 48041, St. Clair County, (810)392-2121, 25 miles W of Fort Huron, MI.
Opened: 1981. **Holes:** 18. **Par:** 72/72. **Yards:** 6,556/5,159. **Course rating:** 71.4/67.7.
Slope: 118/111. **Architect:** N/A. **Green fee:** $15/$18. **Credit cards:** MC,VISA.
Reduced fees: Seniors, juniors. **Caddies:** No. **Golf carts:** N/A. **Discount golf packages:** No. **Season:** April-Nov. **High:** May-July. **On site lodging:** No. **Rental clubs:** Yes.
Walking policy: Unrestricted walking. **Metal spikes allowed:** Yes. **Range:** Yes (grass).
To obtain tee times: Call golf shop.
Subscriber comments: This course has incredible potential! But often neglected—too bad...Good course to play. Price very fair...Great greens, fantastic value, needs more sand.

★★BELLO WOODS GOLF CLUB
PU-23650-23 Mile Rd., Macomb, 48042, Macomb County, (810)949-1200.
Opened: 1986. **Holes:** 27. **Architect:** N/A. **Green fee:** $15/$21. **Credit cards:** MC,VISA. **Reduced fees:** Weekdays, low season, seniors, juniors. **Caddies:** No. **Golf carts:** $20. **Discount golf packages:** No. **Season:** April-Nov. **High:** July-Sept. **On site lodging:** No. **Rental clubs:** Yes. **Walking policy:** Unrestricted walking. **Metal spikes allowed:** Yes. **Range:** No. **To obtain tee times:** Call up to 30 days in advance for weekends. Call up to 7 days in advance for weekdays.
RED/GOLD
Par: 72/72. **Yards:** 6,201/5,830.
RED/WHITE
Par: 72/72. **Yards:** 6,320/6,020.
WHITE/GOLD
Par: 72/72. **Yards:** 6,197/5,830.

★★★½BELVEDERE GOLF CLUB
P.O. Box 218, Charlevoix, 49720, Charlevoix County, (616)547-2611, 40 miles NE of Traverse City.
Opened: 1927. **Holes:** 18. **Par:** 72/74. **Yards:** 6,715/5,629. **Course rating:** 72.1/72.9.

Slope: 124/124. **Architect:** William Watson. **Green fee:** $30/$55. **Credit cards:** MC,VISA. **Reduced fees:** Weekdays, low season, resort guests, twilight. **Caddies:** Yes. **Golf carts:** $11. **Discount golf packages:** Yes. **Season:** April-Oct. **High:** July-Aug. **On site lodging:** No. **Rental clubs:** No. **Walking policy:** Unrestricted walking. **Metal spikes allowed:** Yes. **Range:** Yes (grass). **To obtain tee times:** Call.

Subscriber comments: An old style course, beautiful views, golfers' track...Small greens make second shots count...Beautiful layout, unknown gem...Traditional old course, no tricks...Favorite course in America...Always in good shape...Country club quality...Plush fairways...A step back in time. A traditionalist's delight...Great greens, classic layout...Very forgiving fairways, nice old course.

★★BENT PINE GOLF CLUB

PU-2480 Duck Lake Rd., Whitehall, 49442, Muskegon County, (616)766-2045, 8 miles NW of Muskegon.

Opened: N/A. **Holes:** 18. **Par:** 71/72. **Yards:** 6,007/5,429. **Course rating:** N/A. **Slope:** N/A. **Architect:** Oiler Family. **Green fee:** $9/$15. **Credit cards:** None. **Reduced fees:** Weekdays, low season, seniors, juniors. **Caddies:** No. **Golf carts:** $8. **Discount golf packages:** No. **Season:** March-Nov. **High:** May-Sept. **On site lodging:** No. **Rental clubs:** Yes. **Walking policy:** Unrestricted walking. **Metal spikes allowed:** Yes. **Range:** No. **To obtain tee times:** Call.

★★★½BINDER PARK GOLF COURSE

PU-6723 B Dr. S., Battle Creek, 49014, Calhoun County, (616)966-3459.
Opened: 1962. **Holes:** 18. **Par:** 72/75. **Yards:** 6,328/4,965. **Course rating:** 69.9/68.4. **Slope:** 114/109. **Architect:** Charles Darl Scott. **Green fee:** $14/$15. **Credit cards:** MC,VISA,DISC. **Reduced fees:** Weekdays, seniors, juniors. **Caddies:** No. **Golf carts:** $20. **Discount golf packages:** Yes. **Season:** April-Oct. **High:** June-Aug. **On site lodging:** No. **Rental clubs:** Yes. **Walking policy:** Unrestricted walking. **Metal spikes allowed:** Yes. **Range:** No. **To obtain tee times:** Call.

GREAT VALUE

Subscriber comments: Outstanding muny. Great shape for the play it gets...Best muny in area...Unbelievable value on well maintained course...Jewel of Battle Creek but a little short...Very nice course, affordable, great service...Challenging county course...Rolling terrain, wooded. Not rangered so you may get some slow play.

★★★BLACK BEAR GOLF RESORT

PU-1500 W. Alexander Rd., Vanderbilt, 49795, Ostego County, (517)983-4505, (800)923-2711, 8 miles·N of Gaylord.

Opened: 1996. **Holes:** 18. **Par:** 72/72. **Yards:** 6,500/4,400. **Course rating:** N/A. **Slope:** N/A. **Architect:** Mark Sauger. **Green fee:** $25/$59. **Credit cards:** MC,VISA,DISC. **Reduced fees:** Twilight. **Caddies:** No. **Golf carts:** Included in Green Fee. **Discount golf packages:** No. **Season:** May-Oct. **High:** June-Aug. **On site lodging:** No. **Rental clubs:** Yes. **Walking policy:** Mandatory cart. **Metal spikes allowed:** Yes. **Range:** Yes (grass). **To obtain tee times:** Call anytime.

Subscriber comments: New facility...Not typical Northern Michigan layout...Too many blind holes, and too much unplayable...Challenging 19-hole course (practice par 3 before first hole). Not a level spot on any green...Will be great!...Close to I-75...Course will improve with age, but has several weak holes...Hilly, interesting and challenging, some greens too severe.

BLACK FOREST & WILDERNESS VALLEY GOLF RESORT

R-7519 Mancelona Rd., Gaylord, 49735, Otsego County, (616)585-7090, 15 miles SW of Gaylord.

Credit cards: All major. **Reduced fees:** Weekdays, low season, resort guests, twilight, seniors, juniors. **Caddies:** No. **Discount golf packages:** Yes. **Season:** April-Oct. **High:** July-Aug. **On site lodging:** Yes. **Rental clubs:** Yes. **Walking policy:** Unrestricted walking. **Metal spikes allowed:** Yes. **Range:** Yes (grass/mats). **To obtain tee times:** Call golf shop.

★★★VALLEY COURSE

Opened: 1971. **Holes:** 18. **Par:** 71/71. **Yards:** 6,485/4,889. **Course rating:** 70.6/67.8. **Slope:** 126/115. **Architect:** Al Watrous. **Green fee:** $15/$23. **Golf carts:** $16.

Subscriber comments: Easier than the Black Forest by far...Good course for 10 to 30 handicap...Old resort course minus tricks...An ego builder...Walking is restricted...Almost every hole is a dogleg...Price is good, needs better fairway grooming...Very nice...Inexpensive test in land of high price.

★★★★BLACK FOREST COURSE

Opened: 1992. **Holes:** 18. **Par:** 73/74. **Yards:** 7,044/5,282. **Course rating:** 75.3/71.8. **Slope:** 145/131. **Architect:** Tom Doak. **Green fee:** $20/$35. **Golf carts:** $25. **Notes:** Ranked 13th in 1997 Best in State.

Subscriber comments: The best time had getting beat up by a course. Slope should be 200. Perfect name...One of the more difficult courses...Unbelievably beautiful...Some holes unfair from back tees...Best course in state...One of the best courses I've played for the price...One of toughest in upper Michigan...Black Forest very challenging, Valley Course forgiving...Best when fall colors come...Incredible closing holes.

★½BLOSSOM TRAILS GOLF COURSE

1565 E. Britain Ave., Benton Harbor, 49022, Berrien County, (616)925-4951, 90 miles E of Chicago.
Opened: 1959. **Holes:** 18. **Par:** 70/70. **Yards:** 5,980/4,957. **Course rating:** 68.3. **Slope:** 121/118. **Architect:** Bruce Mathews. **Green fee:** $16/$18. **Credit cards:** MC,VISA,DISC. **Reduced fees:** Weekdays, low season. **Caddies:** No. **Golf carts:** $9. **Discount golf packages:** No. **Season:** March-Nov. **High:** May-Aug. **On site lodging:** No. **Rental clubs:** Yes. **Walking policy:** Unrestricted walking. **Metal spikes allowed:** Yes. **Range:** Yes (grass). **To obtain tee times:** Call.
Special Notes: Also 9-hole par 3 course.

★★BOGIE LAKE GOLF CLUB

PU-11231 Bogie Lake Rd., White Lake, 48386, Oakland County, (248)363-4449, 10 miles W of Pontiac.
Opened: N/A. **Holes:** 18. **Par:** 71. **Yards:** 6,120. **Course rating:** 68.9. **Slope:** 122. **Architect:** N/A. **Green fee:** $19/$22. **Credit cards:** None. **Reduced fees:** Weekdays, low season, twilight, seniors, juniors. **Caddies:** No. **Golf carts:** $21. **Discount golf packages:** Yes. **Season:** Year-round. **High:** June-Aug. **On site lodging:** No. **Rental clubs:** Yes. **Walking policy:** Unrestricted walking. **Metal spikes allowed:** Yes. **Range:** Yes (grass/mats). **To obtain tee times:** Call.

BOYNE HIGHLANDS RESORT

R-600 Highland Dr., Harbor Springs, 49740, Emmet County, (616)526-3028, (616)526-3029, (800)462-6963, 6 miles NW of Petoskey.
Credit cards: All major. **Reduced fees:** Low season, resort guests, twilight. **Caddies:** No. **Golf carts:** Included in Green Fee. **Discount golf packages:** Yes. **High:** June-Aug. **On site lodging:** Yes. **Rental clubs:** Yes. **Range:** Yes (grass). **To obtain tee times:** Call anytime.

★★★★DONALD ROSS MEMORIAL COURSE

Opened: 1985. **Holes:** 18. **Par:** 72/72. **Yards:** 6,814/4,929. **Course rating:** 73.4/68.5. **Slope:** 132/119. **Architect:** Newcomb, E. Kircher, Flick and S. Kircher. **Green fee:** $45/$99. **Season:** May-Oct. **Walking policy:** Mandatory cart. **Metal spikes allowed:** Yes.

Subscriber comments: The way golf should be...Great condition, great layout...Absolutely beautiful setting, any golfer would love this course, immaculate, unbelievable value...Golf doesn't get better than this...A must for every Ross fan. The Pinehurst holes were exact duplicates of the original...A real adventure...Fine tribute to Mr. Ross...Heaven in the real world, enjoyed it even in the rain...Like playing many courses on one layout.

★★★★HEATHER COURSE

Opened: 1968. **Holes:** 18. **Par:** 72/72. **Yards:** 7,210/5,245. **Course rating:** 74.0/67.8. **Slope:** 131/111. **Architect:** Robert Trent Jones. **Green fee:** $51/$110. **Season:** May-Oct. **Walking policy:** Walking at certain times. **Metal spikes allowed:** No. **Notes:** Ranked 23rd in 1997 Best in State.

Subscriber comments: If you care about golf history, play this one...Rewards good shots...Changed shoes from metal to Softspikes at no charge...The way I think golf should be...Excellent in every way, condition, service, playability, scenery...I could play it every day...Heather Course is best I've played...Very playable Trent Jones design...All around best resort for golf...Worth every penny...Beautiful setting...Too costly...Should rename it Heaven. Nice greens.

MICHIGAN

★★★½MOOR COURSE
Opened: 1972. **Holes:** 18. **Par:** 72/72. **Yards:** 7,127/5,459. **Course rating:** 74.0/70.0.
Slope: 131/118. **Architect:** William Newcomb. **Green fee:** $36/$70. **Season:** May-Dec.
Walking policy: Mandatory cart. **Metal spikes allowed:** Yes.
Subscriber comments: Moor is tough but so much fun you don't care...An average
course amongst some real gems...Needs more maturity. Great layout. Has two or three
of the best holes I've played...Great condition...Wide open...Too many doglegs...Nothing
special compared to the gems. Good 1st day course...Moor Course wetter, more difficult for women...A tough underrated course.

BOYNE MOUNTAIN RESORT
R-Deer Lake Rd., Boyne Falls, 49713, Charlevoix County, (616)549-
6029, (800)462-6963, 18 miles S of Petoskey. **Green fee:** $21/$80.
Credit cards: All major,Diners Club. **Reduced fees:** Low season,
resort guests, twilight. **Caddies:** No. **Golf carts:** Included in Green
Fee. **Discount golf packages:** Yes. **Season:** April-Oct. **High:** June-
Aug. **On site lodging:** Yes. **Rental clubs:** Yes. **Walking policy:** Mandatory cart. **Metal
spikes allowed:** Yes. **Range:** Yes (grass/mats). **To obtain tee times:** Call 800 number
up to 30 days in advance.

(badge: GOOD SERVICE)

★★★★ALPINE COURSE
Opened: N/A. **Holes:** 18. **Par:** 72/72. **Yards:** 7,017/4,986. **Course rating:** 73.6/68.4.
Slope: 129/114. **Architect:** Bill Newcomb.
Subscriber comments: Bring your best putter...Course is well-maintained, prices
good...Front nine has spectacular views, greens are difficult to read,course is in excellent condition...One mile drive through woods to 1st tee was great!...Scatter my ashes
in the traps...Rock solid course with many nice holes but not many good holes...I like to
watch the deer run onto the fairways.

★★★½MONUMENT COURSE
Opened: 1986. **Holes:** 18. **Par:** 72/72. **Yards:** 7,086/4,909. **Course rating:** 75.0/68.9.
Slope: 139/122. **Architect:** Bill Newcomb.
Subscriber comments: Even with a bad day, I thoroughly enjoyed it...Breathtaking
beauty...Love the isolation of first nine...Ranks with the Ross and Heather. A beautiful
mountain experience...Tough 1st hole, especially for right-to-left player. Great finishing
hole...Not a fair course for average golfer...Good test...I love this course, brutally
tough!...Lots of elevation changes...GPS in carts.

★★½BRAE BURN GOLF COURSE
PU-10860 W 5 Mile Rd., Plymouth, 48170, Wayne County, (313)453-1900, (800)714-
6700, 20 miles W of Detroit.
Opened: 1923. **Holes:** 18. **Par:** 70/71. **Yards:** 6,320/5,072. **Course rating:** 70.0/70.6.
Slope: 120/119. **Architect:** N/A. **Green fee:** $17/$38. **Credit cards:** MC,VISA.
Reduced fees: Weekdays, low season, twilight, seniors, juniors. **Caddies:** No. **Golf
carts:** Included in Green Fee. **Discount golf packages:** No. **Season:** April-Nov. **High:**
April-Sept. **On site lodging:** No. **Rental clubs:** Yes. **Walking policy:** Walking at certain
times. **Metal spikes allowed:** Yes. **Range:** Yes (grass/mats). **To obtain tee times:** Call
up to 7 days in advance. Outings may be booked 1 year in advance.
Subscriber comments: Could be excellent course...Good holiday deals...Bit expensive
for course conditions...Can play easy or hard...OK for price, a little short...Good bargain.

★★★BRAESIDE GOLF COURSE
5460 Eleven Mile Rd., Rockford, 49341, Kent County, (616)866-1402.
Call club for further information.
Subscriber comments: Fast greens, tight fairways, not long and a little rustic...Great
value. Five putts are not uncommon...Unbelievably fast greens/can be unfair at
times...Fast greens, scenic layout, fairly long par 4s, lots of trees, water, condition is
usually good...Fastest greens in west Mich...Fun course if you're in the area.

★★½BRAMBLEWOOD GOLF COURSE
PU-2154 Bramblewood Rd., Holly, 48442, Oakland County, (248)634-3481, 20 miles W
of Pontiac.
Opened: 1965. **Holes:** 18. **Par:** 70/72. **Yards:** 6,005/5,052. **Course rating:** 70.0/74.0.
Slope: 113/113. **Architect:** N/A. **Green fee:** $15/$21. **Credit cards:** MC,VISA.

Reduced fees: Weekdays, low season, seniors, juniors. **Caddies:** No. **Golf carts:** $10. **Discount golf packages:** No. **Season:** April-Oct. **High:** June-Aug. **On site lodging:** No. **Rental clubs:** Yes. **Walking policy:** Walking at certain times. **Metal spikes allowed:** Yes. **Range:** No. **To obtain tee times:** Call golf shop.

Subscriber comments: Can always get tee times...Short, inexpensive...Back nine is most impressive!...Rugged course...Tight back nine...The course plays better with a 3 wood...Challenging back nine, front nine open. Tricky to find...Interesting layout—doglegs, elevations.

★★½ BRANSON BAY GOLF COURSE

PU-215 Branson Bay Dr., Mason, 48854, Ingham County, (517)663-4144.
Opened: 1968. **Holes:** 18. **Par:** 72/73. **Yards:** 6,497/5,145. **Course rating:** 71.5/69.5. **Slope:** 124/116. **Architect:** N/A. **Green fee:** $12/$19. **Credit cards:** MC,VISA. **Reduced fees:** Low season, twilight. **Caddies:** No. **Golf carts:** $20. **Discount golf packages:** No. **Season:** March-Nov. **High:** June-Aug. **On site lodging:** No. **Rental clubs:** Yes. **Walking policy:** Unrestricted walking. **Metal spikes allowed:** Yes. **Range:** Yes (grass). **To obtain tee times:** Call in advance.

Subscriber comments: Good greens, tight fairways...Gets better on the back...Back nine all blind holes...Beginner's course...Front nine wide open easy to score on. Back tough hidden greens...Beautiful back nine.

★★½ BRIAR DOWNS GOLF COURSE

PU-5441 E. M-115, Mesick, 49668, Wexford County, (616)885-1220, 26 miles S of Traverse City.
Opened: 1989. **Holes:** 18. **Par:** 71/71. **Yards:** 5,759/4,481. **Course rating:** N/A. **Slope:** N/A. **Architect:** Orman Bishop. **Green fee:** $14/$28. **Credit cards:** MC,VISA. **Reduced fees:** Weekdays, low season, twilight, seniors, juniors. **Caddies:** No. **Golf carts:** $9. **Discount golf packages:** No. **Season:** April-Oct. **High:** June-Aug. **On site lodging:** No. **Rental clubs:** Yes. **Walking policy:** Unrestricted walking. **Metal spikes allowed:** Yes. **Range:** No. **To obtain tee times:** Call. Reservations not necessary.

Subscriber comments: Average course with some interesting holes. Lots of geese frolicking in the fall...Priced right...Links style course...Position type course...Needs time to mature...Very undulating, lots of trouble (hazards)...Short course, right club from tee is important.

BRIAR HILL GOLF COURSE

PU-950 W. 40th St., Fremont, 49412, Newaygo County, (616)924-2070, 40 miles NW of Grand Rapids.
Opened: 1928. **Holes:** 18. **Par:** 72/71. **Yards:** 6,134/4,624. **Course rating:** 67.5/65.8. **Slope:** 113/104. **Architect:** William Wuthenow/Forrest Lewis. **Green fee:** $16/$17. **Credit cards:** N/A. **Reduced fees:** Weekdays, low season, resort guests, twilight, seniors. **Caddies:** No. **Golf carts:** N/A. **Discount golf packages:** No. **Season:** March-Dec. **High:** June-Aug. **On site lodging:** No. **Rental clubs:** Yes. **Walking policy:** Unrestricted walking. **Metal spikes allowed:** Yes. **Range:** Yes (grass/mats). **To obtain tee times:** Call. No restrictions.

★★½ BRIARWOOD

PU-2900 92nd St., Caledonia, 49316, Kent County, (616)698-8720.
Opened: 1963. **Holes:** 27. **Architect:** N/A. **Green fee:** $10/$19. **Credit cards:** MC,VISA,AMEX. **Reduced fees:** Weekdays, low season, seniors, juniors. **Caddies:** No. **Golf carts:** $21. **Discount golf packages:** No. **Season:** March-Nov. **High:** April-Sept. **On site lodging:** No. **Rental clubs:** Yes. **Walking policy:** Unrestricted walking. **Metal spikes allowed:** Yes. **Range:** Yes (grass). **To obtain tee times:** Call anytime.

EAST/BACK
Par: 72/78. **Yards:** 6,250/5,716.
FRONT/BACK
Par: 72/76. **Yards:** 6,020/5,350.
FRONT/EAST
Par: 72/76. **Yards:** 6,140/5,645.

Subscriber comments: All holes provide a nice challenge—lots of hills. Enjoyable 27 holes, nice mixture...The new nine is a real test...Good course for hackers and outings...Overplayed, needs TLC...Built on clay, not kept up for what they charge...Well kept...Refreshing design, nice condition.

MICHIGAN

★★½BRIGADOON GOLF CLUB
PU-12559 Bagley Ave., Grant, 49327, Newaygo County, (616)834-8200, (800)839-8206, 30 miles N of Grand Rapids.
Opened: 1989. **Holes:** 27. **Par:** 72/72. **Yards:** 6,115/4,825. **Course rating:** 70.9/68.6.
Slope: 135/124. **Architect:** Grant McKinley. **Green fee:** $25/$31. **Credit cards:**
MC,VISA. **Reduced fees:** Weekdays, low season, seniors. **Caddies:** No. **Golf carts:**
Included in Green Fee. **Discount golf packages:** Yes. **Season:** April-Nov. **High:** May-Aug. **On site lodging:** No. **Rental clubs:** Yes. **Walking policy:** Walking at certain
times. **Metal spikes allowed:** Yes. **Range:** Yes (grass/mats). **To obtain tee times:** Call.
Subscriber comments: Locally known as "bringadozen"...Beautiful setting...Tough,
must play shots perfect...Course maintenance fair at best...Too tricky...Way too much
water...Blind greens surrounded by water.

★★BROADMOOR COUNTRY CLUB
PU-7725 Kraft Ave. SE, Caledonia, 49316, Kent County, (616)891-8000, 8 miles SE of
Grand Rapids.
Opened: 1964. **Holes:** 18. **Par:** 72/74. **Yards:** 6,400/5,800. **Course rating:** N/A. **Slope:**
N/A. **Architect:** N/A. **Green fee:** $10/$19. **Credit cards:** MC,VISA,AMEX. **Reduced
fees:** Weekdays, low season, seniors, juniors. **Caddies:** No. **Golf carts:** $21. **Discount
golf packages:** No. **Season:** March-Nov. **High:** April-Sept. **On site lodging:** No.
Rental clubs: Yes. **Walking policy:** Unrestricted walking. **Metal spikes allowed:** Yes.
Range: Yes (grass). **To obtain tee times:** N/A.

★★★BROOKWOOD GOLF COURSE
6045 Davison Rd, Burton, 48509, Genesee County, (810)742-4930, 5 miles E of Flint.
Opened: N/A. **Holes:** 18. **Par:** 72/72. **Yards:** 6,972/5,977. **Course rating:** 72.9/78.7.
Slope: 123/122. **Architect:** N/A. **Green fee:** $16/$26. **Credit cards:** MC,VISA.
Reduced fees: N/A. **Caddies:** No. **Golf carts:** $22. **Discount golf packages:** No.
Season: April-Nov. **High:** June-Aug. **On site lodging:** No. **Rental clubs:** Yes. **Walking
policy:** Unrestricted walking. **Metal spikes allowed:** Yes. **Range:** Yes (grass). **To
obtain tee times:** Call up to 7 days in advance.
Subscriber comments: Some great par 4s...A couple of outstanding holes, nice lay-out, good maintenance...Very average...Don't play after rain. Course gets
soaked...Course OK but a little pricey...Well maintained, very playable...Club choices
are crucial to good scoring...Attentive staff. Rangers keep it moving.

★★BURNING OAK COUNTRY CLUB
PU-4345 Redwood Dr., Roscommon, 48653, Roscommon County, (517)821-9821, 62
miles SE of Traverse City.
Opened: 1962. **Holes:** 18. **Par:** 72/72. **Yards:** 6,240/5,256. **Course rating:** 69.7/70.0.
Slope: 117/115. **Architect:** N/A. **Green fee:** $18/$18. **Credit cards:** MC,VISA,DISC.
Reduced fees: N/A. **Caddies:** No. **Golf carts:** $9. **Discount golf packages:** No.
Season: April-Oct. **High:** June-Aug. **On site lodging:** No. **Rental clubs:** Yes. **Walking
policy:** Unrestricted walking. **Metal spikes allowed:** Yes. **Range:** Yes (grass/mats). **To
obtain tee times:** Call.

★★½BURR OAK GOLF CLUB
PU-3491 N. Parma Rd., Parma, 49269, Jackson County, (517)531-4741, 5 miles W of
Jackson.
Opened: 1965. **Holes:** 18. **Par:** 72/72. **Yards:** 5,906/5,011. **Course rating:** 69.7.
Slope: N/A. **Architect:** N/A. **Green fee:** $10/$13. **Credit cards:** None. **Reduced fees:**
Twilight, seniors, juniors. **Caddies:** No. **Golf carts:** $8. **Discount golf packages:** Yes.
Season: April-Oct. **High:** May-Aug. **On site lodging:** No. **Rental clubs:** Yes. **Walking
policy:** Unrestricted walking. **Metal spikes allowed:** Yes. **Range:** Yes (grass). **To
obtain tee times:** Call anytime.
Subscriber comments: Greens good overall, excellent...Family course, great rates,
excellent greens to putt...Great par 3s...Well-kept course.

BUTTERNUT BROOK GOLF COURSE
PU-2200 Island Hwy., Charlotte, 48813, Eaton County, (517)543-0570, 12 miles SW of
Lansing.
Opened: 1970. **Holes:** 18. **Par:** 71/71. **Yards:** 6,289/5,307. **Course rating:** 70.3/69.2.

Slope: N/A. **Architect:** Delbert Palmer. **Green fee:** $10/$13. **Credit cards:** None. **Reduced fees:** Weekdays, seniors. **Caddies:** No. **Golf carts:** $18. **Discount golf packages:** No. **Season:** April-Oct. **High:** May-Aug. **On site lodging:** No. **Rental clubs:** Yes. **Walking policy:** Unrestricted walking. **Metal spikes allowed:** Yes. **Range:** Yes (grass). **To obtain tee times:** First come, first served.

★★BYRON HILLS GOLF CLUB
PU-7330 Burlingame Rd., Byron Center, 49315, Kent County, (616)878-1522, 10 miles S of Grand Rapids.
Opened: 1963. **Holes:** 18. **Par:** 71/75. **Yards:** 5,622/5,041. **Course rating:** 67.3/70.1. **Slope:** 110/112. **Architect:** Fred Ellis. **Green fee:** $13/$20. **Credit cards:** MC,VISA. **Reduced fees:** Weekdays, low season, seniors, juniors. **Caddies:** No. **Golf carts:** $20. **Discount golf packages:** No. **Season:** March-Dec. **High:** May-Sept. **On site lodging:** No. **Rental clubs:** Yes. **Walking policy:** Unrestricted walking. **Metal spikes allowed:** Yes. **Range:** No. **To obtain tee times:** Call up to 30 days in advance for weekends and holidays.

★★★CABERFAE PEAKS SKI & GOLF RESORT
PU-Caberfae Rd., Cadillac, 49601, Wexford County, (616)862-3000, 12 miles W of Cadillac.
Opened: 1995. **Holes:** 9. **Par:** 36/36. **Yards:** 3,248/2,250. **Course rating:** N/A. **Slope:** N/A. **Architect:** Harry Bowers. **Green fee:** $18/$24. **Credit cards:** MC,VISA,DISC. **Reduced fees:** Weekdays, low season, resort guests, twilight. **Caddies:** No. **Golf carts:** $14. **Discount golf packages:** Yes. **Season:** May-Nov. **High:** July-Aug. **On site lodging:** Yes. **Rental clubs:** Yes. **Walking policy:** Unrestricted walking. **Metal spikes allowed:** Yes. **Range:** Yes (grass). **To obtain tee times:** Call or walk-in.
Subscriber comments: Played off-season, but very beautiful...Very good value...Very pretty, very difficult (trees, swamps)...Carved through a Northern Michigan pine forest.

★★★½CANDLESTONE GOLF CLUB
R-8100 N. Storey, Belding, 48809, Ionia County, (616)794-1580, 20 miles NE of Grand Rapids.
Opened: 1975. **Holes:** 18. **Par:** 72/74. **Yards:** 6,692/5,547. **Course rating:** 72.8/73.1. **Slope:** 129/126. **Architect:** Bruce Matthews and Jerry Matthews. **Green fee:** $23/$27. **Credit cards:** All major. **Reduced fees:** Weekdays, low season, resort guests, twilight, seniors. **Caddies:** No. **Golf carts:** $12. **Discount golf packages:** Yes. **Season:** March-Oct. **High:** May-Sept. **On site lodging:** Yes. **Rental clubs:** Yes. **Walking policy:** Unrestricted walking. **Metal spikes allowed:** Yes. **Range:** Yes (grass/mats). **To obtain tee times:** Call 7 days in advance.
Subscriber comments: Tight, good greens...Many scenic holes. Gets very busy on weekends...Good public course...Very nice but some tough holes...Needs better grooming most of the year...Best finishing holes in western Michigan...Super course for the cost...Greens and fairways like country club quality...Good weekly specials.

★★½CARLETON GLEN GOLF CLUB
13470 Grafton Rd., Carleton, 48117, Monroe County, (313)654-6201, 19 miles SW of Detroit.
Opened: 1961. **Holes:** 18. **Par:** 71/71. **Yards:** 6,496/5,602. **Course rating:** 70.5/73.0. **Slope:** 120/112. **Architect:** Robert G. Milosch. **Green fee:** $20/$22. **Credit cards:** MC,VISA. **Reduced fees:** Low season, seniors, juniors. **Caddies:** No. **Golf carts:** N/A. **Discount golf packages:** No. **Season:** April-Nov. **High:** May-Sept. **On site lodging:** No. **Rental clubs:** No. **Walking policy:** Unrestricted walking. **Metal spikes allowed:** Yes. **Range:** Yes (grass). **To obtain tee times:** Call seven days in advance. Send money for earlier times.
Subscriber comments: Course is flat and straight but playable...Could be better maintained...Fairways not that great...I would give this course a C+...Nice greens. Good mixture of different holes...Very easy to get tee times...Course was in very good shape for spring.

★★★½CASCADES GOLF COURSE
PU-1992 Warren Ave., Jackson, 49203, Jackson County, (517)788-4323, 37 miles E of Battle Creek.
Opened: 1929. **Holes:** 18. **Par:** 72/73. **Yards:** 6,614/5,282. **Course rating:** 71.8/70.5. **Slope:** 122/117. **Architect:** Tom Bendelow. **Green fee:** $13/$17. **Credit cards:** None. **Reduced fees:** Weekdays, low season, twilight, seniors, juniors. **Caddies:** No. **Golf carts:** N/A. **Discount golf packages:** No. **Season:** March-Oct. **High:** July-Sept. **On site lodging:** No. **Rental clubs:** Yes. **Walking policy:** Walking at certain times. **Metal spikes allowed:** Yes. **Range:** Yes (grass). **To obtain tee times:** Call one week in advance.
Subscriber comments: Best long public course in area...Well maintained fairways and greens...An excellent value, wonderful test...Best course in Jackson County...Very tight fairways, heavily wooded...Top notch public, long, tough course.

(GREAT VALUE)

★★★CATTAILS GOLF CLUB
PU-57737 W. 9 Mile Rd., South Lyon, 48178, Oakland County, (248)486-8777, 35 miles W of Detroit.
Opened: 1991. **Holes:** 18. **Par:** 72/72. **Yards:** 6,436/4,987. **Course rating:** 71.8/70.3. **Slope:** 132/117. **Architect:** Reggie Sauger. **Green fee:** $28/$38. **Credit cards:** MC,VISA. **Reduced fees:** Weekdays, low season, twilight, seniors. **Caddies:** No. **Golf carts:** $12. **Discount golf packages:** Yes. **Season:** April-Nov. **High:** June-Aug. **On site lodging:** No. **Rental clubs:** Yes. **Walking policy:** Walking at certain times. **Metal spikes allowed:** Yes. **Range:** Yes (grass/mats). **To obtain tee times:** Call 7 days in advance.
Subscriber comments: Great course. Can't believe it's public...Need more info on distances to hazards...Thinkers' course, keep the big dog leashed on 10...Front nine squeezed in; back nine nicely wooded and separated...Good operation, great challenge...New and getting better. Too tough for high-handicappers.

★★★CEDAR CHASE GOLF CLUB
PU-7551 17 Mile Rd. N.E., Cedar Springs, 49319, Kent County, (616)696-2308, 20 miles N of Grand Rapids.
Opened: 1993. **Holes:** 18. **Par:** 72/72. **Yards:** 7,066/5,115. **Course rating:** 74.6/70.1. **Slope:** 135/122. **Architect:** Bruce Matthews III. **Green fee:** $25/$29. **Credit cards:** All major. **Reduced fees:** Weekdays, low season, seniors, juniors. **Caddies:** No. **Golf carts:** $11. **Discount golf packages:** No. **Season:** April-Nov. **High:** June-Aug. **On site lodging:** No. **Rental clubs:** No. **Walking policy:** Unrestricted walking. **Metal spikes allowed:** Yes. **Range:** No. **To obtain tee times:** Call up to 14 days in advance.
Subscriber comments: In excellent shape for a newer course...As this course matures, it will become a definite 5...Nice layout needs to mature..Long from the tips...Course will be fantastic when mature...Needs work but could be outstanding given time...Upscale wannabe.

★★½CEDAR CREEK GOLF COURSE
14000 Renton Rd., Battle Creek, 49017, Calhoun County, (616)965-6423.
Call club for further information.
Subscriber comments: Short track. Little trouble...Grounds flood easy with little rain, fairways soft...Front nine the best...Course has made improvements yearly for the past eight years...Nice course, nice price, great people.

★★CEDAR GLEN GOLF CLUB
36860 25 Mile Rd., New Baltimore, 48047, Macomb County, (810)725-8156.
Architect: Jerry Matthews. **Caddies:** No. **Discount golf packages:** No. **On site lodging:** No. **Rental clubs:** No. **Metal spikes allowed:** Yes. **Range:** No.
Call club for further information.

★★★CENTENNIAL ACRES GOLF COURSE
PU-12485 Dow Rd., Sunfield, 48890, Eaton County, (517)566-8055, 15 miles W of Lansing.
Opened: 1979. **Holes:** 18. **Par:** 72/72. **Yards:** 6,581/4,932. **Course rating:** 72.8/69.0. **Slope:** 126/113. **Architect:** Warner Bowen. **Green fee:** $13/$21. **Credit cards:** MC,VISA,DISC. **Reduced fees:** Low season, seniors, juniors. **Caddies:** No. **Golf carts:**

$10. **Discount golf packages:** Yes. **Season:** April-Nov. **High:** June-Aug. **On site lodging:** No. **Rental clubs:** Yes. **Walking policy:** Unrestricted walking. **Metal spikes allowed:** Yes. **Range:** No. **To obtain tee times:** Call.
Subscriber comments: Good for outings, but out of the way...Very helpful staff; super clubhouse...Wonderful atmosphere, beautiful course...Very good greens, lots of trouble...Puts a premium on good driving...Nice challenge...Real sleeper. Don't play in August because it's mosquito city.

★½CENTER VIEW GOLF COURSE
564 N. Adrian Hwy., Adrian, 49221, Lenawee County, (517)263-8081.
Call club for further information.

★★★½CHARLEVOIX COUNTRY CLUB
9600 Clubhouse Dr., Charlevoix, 49720, Charlevoix County, (616)547-1922, (800)618-9796, 40 miles N of Traverse City.
Opened: 1994. **Holes:** 18. **Par:** 72/72. **Yards:** 6,520/5,084. **Course rating:** 70.6/68.4.
Slope: 127/115. **Architect:** Jerry Matthews. **Green fee:** $39/$60. **Credit cards:**
MC,VISA,AMEX. **Reduced fees:** Weekdays, low season, resort guests, twilight.
Caddies: No. **Golf carts:** Included in Green Fee. **Discount golf packages:** Yes.
Season: May-Oct. **High:** June-Aug. **On site lodging:** No. **Rental clubs:** Yes. **Walking policy:** Mandatory cart. **Metal spikes allowed:** Yes. **Range:** Yes (grass). **To obtain tee times:** Call.
Subscriber comments: Fun to play, pretty flat...Country club quality...Beautiful course: Northern Michigan and Scottish mix...Great service. Back nine toughest nine holes around...Tough when wind blows...Course in excellent condition but pace of play slow.

★★½CHASE HAMMOND GOLF COURSE
PM-2454 N. Putnam Rd., Muskegon, 49445, Muskegon County, (616)766-3035, 40 miles NW of Grand Rapids.
Opened: 1970. **Holes:** 18. **Par:** 72/72. **Yards:** 6,307/5,135. **Course rating:** 71.2/71.1.
Slope: 133/123. **Architect:** Mark DeVries. **Green fee:** $16/$20. **Credit cards:**
MC,VISA. **Reduced fees:** Weekdays, low season, twilight, seniors, juniors. **Caddies:**
No. **Golf carts:** $10. **Discount golf packages:** No. **Season:** March-Nov. **High:** June-Aug. **On site lodging:** No. **Rental clubs:** Yes. **Walking policy:** Unrestricted walking.
Metal spikes allowed: Yes. **Range:** Yes (grass). **To obtain tee times:** Call up to 7 days in advance.
Subscriber comments: Great course but not maintained...Great layout for muny...Needs total improvement in all areas...Good potential, new management should make it better...Used to be one of the best in the area, but has gone down a little...Under new management, should climb back up charts...Tight fairways, hardest par 5 in area...A shorter Grand Haven.

★★½CHEBOYGAN GOLF & COUNTRY CLUB
1431 Old Mackinaw Rd., Cheboygan, 49721, Cheboygan County, (616)627-4264, 12 miles SE of Mackinaw City.
Opened: 1922. **Holes:** 18. **Par:** 70/71. **Yards:** 6,003/4,653. **Course rating:** 67.4/67.7.
Slope: 120/113. **Architect:** Bill Newcomb. **Green fee:** $16/$23. **Credit cards:** All major. **Reduced fees:** Low season, twilight, seniors, juniors. **Caddies:** No. **Golf carts:** $12. **Discount golf packages:** No. **Season:** April-Oct. **High:** June-Aug. **On site lodging:** No. **Rental clubs:** Yes. **Walking policy:** Unrestricted walking. **Metal spikes allowed:** Yes. **Range:** Yes (grass). **To obtain tee times:** Call 1 day in advance.
Subscriber comments: Nice for the money. User friendly course & staff...Very hilly. Great bargain...With wind off lake, conditions are tough...Nice place. Overpriced however...Great greens.

★★★½CHERRY CREEK GOLF CLUB
PU-52000 Cherry Creek Dr., Shelby Township, 48316, Macomb County, (810)254-7700, 16 miles NW of Detroit.
Opened: 1995. **Holes:** 18. **Par:** 72/72. **Yards:** 6,784/5,012. **Course rating:** 72.7/67.1.
Slope: 139/114. **Architect:** Lanny Wadkins and Mike Bylen. **Green fee:** $35/$55.
Credit cards: MC,VISA. **Reduced fees:** Low season, seniors, juniors. **Caddies:** No.
Golf carts: Included in Green Fee. **Discount golf packages:** No. **Season:** April-Dec.
High: All. **On site lodging:** No. **Rental clubs:** Yes. **Walking policy:** Walking at certain

times. **Metal spikes allowed:** Yes. **Range:** Yes (grass/mats). **To obtain tee times:** Call up to 7 days in advance.
Subscriber comments: Course new but good condition. Great practice facility...Best course in the metro area, even as new as it is...As maturity grows so does the course...Thought I was at a northern Michigan course—yet near Detroit...A superb course...Hard to get on.

★★★CHESHIRE HILLS GOLF COURSE
PU-3829 - 102nd Ave., Allegan, 49010, Allegan County, (616)673-2882.
Opened: 1972. **Holes:** 27. **Architect:** Herb Johnson. **Green fee:** $16/$18. **Credit cards:** MC,VISA,DISC. **Reduced fees:** Seniors, juniors. **Caddies:** No. **Golf carts:** $8.
Discount golf packages: No. **Season:** April-Oct. **High:** June-Aug. **On site lodging:** No. **Rental clubs:** Yes. **Walking policy:** Unrestricted walking. **Metal spikes allowed:** Yes. **Range:** Yes (grass/mats). **To obtain tee times:** Call ahead.
BLUE BIRD/RED FOX
Par: 70/70. **Yards:** 6,112/4,564. **Course rating:** 68.8/64.7. **Slope:** 114/103.
RED FOX/WHITETAIL
Par: 70/70. **Yards:** 6,026/4,490. **Course rating:** 68.8/64.7. **Slope:** 114/103.
BLUE BIRD/WHITETAIL
Par: 70/70. **Yards:** 5,904/4,482. **Course rating:** 68.8/64.7. **Slope:** 114/103.
Subscriber comments: No tee times taken...Timing is everything...27 holes, well maintained...Must place your ball well...Good course, adequate facilities...27 holes and still crowded.

★★★½CHESTNUT VALLEY GOLF COURSE
1875 Clubhouse Dr., Harbor Springs, 49740, Emmet County, (616)526-9100, (800)992-1225, 10 miles N of Petoskey.
Opened: 1994. **Holes:** 18. **Par:** 72/72. **Yards:** 6,406/5,166. **Course rating:** 71.8/72.1.
Slope: 125/116. **Architect:** Larry Mancour. **Green fee:** $40/$62. **Credit cards:** MC,VISA,DISC. **Reduced fees:** Weekdays, low season, resort guests, twilight.
Caddies: No. **Golf carts:** Included in Green Fee. **Discount golf packages:** Yes.
Season: May-Nov. **High:** June-Sept. **On site lodging:** No. **Rental clubs:** Yes. **Walking policy:** Walking at certain times. **Metal spikes allowed:** Yes. **Range:** Yes (grass). **To obtain tee times:** Call golf shop.
Subscriber comments: Should be great in a few more years...Not a killer for northern Michigan...A great undiscovered course...Interesting, hilly track. Super-friendly employees...A reasonably priced "up north" course...Watch for bugs in summer.
Special Notes: Spikeless shoes encouraged.

★½CHISHOLM HILLS COUNTRY CLUB
2395 S. Washington Rd., Lansing, 48911, Ingham County, (517)694-0169.
Call club for further information.
Subscriber comments: Just a tiny neighborhood course...Small greens but very fast. Not a very long course...Open early spring and late fall...OK for average weekend golfers.

★★½CHOCOLAY DOWNS GOLF COURSE
PU-125 Chocolay Downs Golf Dr., Marquette, 49855, Marquette County, (906)249-3111, 7 miles E of Marquette.
Opened: 1992. **Holes:** 18. **Par:** 72/72. **Yards:** 6,375/4,878. **Course rating:** N/A. **Slope:** N/A. **Architect:** Jerry Matthews. **Green fee:** $20/$20. **Credit cards:** MC,VISA.
Reduced fees: Low season, seniors. **Caddies:** No. **Golf carts:** $18. **Discount golf packages:** Yes. **Season:** April-Nov. **High:** June-Aug. **On site lodging:** No. **Rental clubs:** Yes. **Walking policy:** Unrestricted walking. **Metal spikes allowed:** Yes. **Range:** Yes (grass/mats). **To obtain tee times:** Call golf shop.

★★CLARK LAKE GOLF CLUB
PU-5535 Wesch Rd. P.O. Box 519, Brooklyn, 49230, Jackson County, (517)592-6259, 17 miles S of Jackson.
Opened: 1919. **Holes:** 18. **Par:** 73/73. **Yards:** 6,632/5,511. **Course rating:** N/A. **Slope:** N/A. **Architect:** N/A. **Green fee:** $9/$14. **Credit cards:** N/A. **Reduced fees:** Weekdays, seniors. **Caddies:** No. **Golf carts:** $24. **Discount golf packages:** No. **Season:** Year-round. **High:** May-Oct. **On site lodging:** No. **Rental clubs:** Yes. **Walking policy:**

Unrestricted walking. **Metal spikes allowed:** Yes. **Range:** Yes (grass). **To obtain tee times:** First come, first served.
Special Notes: Also a 9-hole par 35 course.

★★CLARKSTON CREEK GOLF CLUB

6060 Maybee Rd., Clarkston, 48346, Oakland County, (248)625-3731, 35 miles N of Detroit.
Opened: 1969. **Holes:** 18. **Par:** 71. **Yards:** 6,300. **Course rating:** 69.5. **Slope:** 126.
Architect: N/A. **Green fee:** $19/$28. **Credit cards:** MC,VISA,AMEX. **Reduced fees:** Weekdays, low season, twilight, seniors, juniors. **Caddies:** No. **Golf carts:** $22.
Discount golf packages: No. **Season:** March-Nov. **High:** May-Sept. **On site lodging:** No. **Rental clubs:** Yes. **Walking policy:** Unrestricted walking. **Metal spikes allowed:** Yes. **Range:** Yes (grass). **To obtain tee times:** Call up to 7 days in advance.

★★★CLEARBROOK GOLF CLUB

6494 Clearbrook Dr., Saugatuck, 49453, Allegan County, (616)857-2000, 25 miles SW of Grand Rapids.
Opened: 1920. **Holes:** 18. **Par:** 72/74. **Yards:** 6,453/5,153. **Course rating:** 72.8/70.0. **Slope:** 132/127. **Architect:** Charles Darl Scott. **Green fee:** $27/$32. **Credit cards:** All major. **Reduced fees:** Low season, juniors. **Caddies:** No. **Golf carts:** $11. **Discount golf packages:** Yes. **Season:** April-Oct. **High:** June-Aug. **On site lodging:** No. **Rental clubs:** Yes. **Walking policy:** Unrestricted walking. **Metal spikes allowed:** No. **Range:** Yes (grass/mats). **To obtain tee times:** Call up to 6 days in advance.
Subscriber comments: Old course with character...Everyone should play this once or twice. Nice layout...Very challenging, great condition, wonderful food/service...Memorable signature hole...Back nine is the test...This course gets lots of play and still looks very good.

★★★½CONCORD HILLS GOLF COURSE

PU-7331 Pulaski Rd., Concord, 49237, Jackson County, (517)524-8337, 12 miles SW of Jackson.
Opened: 1976. **Holes:** 18. **Par:** 72/72. **Yards:** 6,422/5,104. **Course rating:** 71.5/71.0. **Slope:** 125/125. **Architect:** William Newcomb. **Green fee:** $16/$19. **Credit cards:** MC,VISA. **Reduced fees:** Weekdays, low season, resort guests, twilight, seniors, juniors. **Caddies:** No. **Golf carts:** $9. **Discount golf packages:** Yes. **Season:** April-Nov. **High:** June-Sept. **On site lodging:** No. **Rental clubs:** Yes. **Walking policy:** Unrestricted walking. **Metal spikes allowed:** Yes. **Range:** Yes (grass). **To obtain tee times:** Call up to 7 days in advance. Groups or hotel guests may call up to 1 year in advance with deposit or credit card.
Subscriber comments: Hidden gem, play all day...Hardest tee positions I've ever played...Great variety, tees suffer from overuse...Easy front, tough back. Hilly course with great character, great service...Elevated tees and greens, beautiful, a challenge...Tough greens to two putt.

★★★½COUNTY HIGHLANDS GOLF CLUB

Hwy. 31S., Bear Lake, 49614, Manistee County, (616)864-3817, 40 miles S of Traverse City.
Opened: 1966. **Holes:** 18. **Par:** 72/72. **Yards:** 6,527/5,188. **Course rating:** 71.0/70.1. **Slope:** 121/121. **Architect:** N/A. **Green fee:** $30/$34. **Credit cards:** MC,VISA,DISC. **Reduced fees:** Twilight, juniors. **Caddies:** No. **Golf carts:** N/A. **Discount golf packages:** No. **Season:** April-Oct. **High:** June-Aug. **On site lodging:** No. **Rental clubs:** Yes. **Walking policy:** Unrestricted walking. **Metal spikes allowed:** Yes. **Range:** No. **To obtain tee times:** Call.
Subscriber comments: Gets better every year—needs some traps...Excellent value for local favorite...Nice layout; kept in good condition; challenging yet forgiving...A real sleeper with excellent water holes...A well-kept secret...Long and tight.
Special Notes: Spikeless shoes strongly encouraged.

★★½COYOTE GOLF CLUB

PU-28700 Milford Rd., New Hudson, 48165, Oakland County, (248)486-1228, 30 miles NW of Detroit.
Opened: 1996. **Holes:** 18. **Par:** 72/72. **Yards:** 7,201/4,923. **Course rating:** 73.8/68.4. **Slope:** 130/114. **Architect:** Scott Thacker. **Green fee:** $15/$37. **Credit cards:**

MC,VISA. **Reduced fees:** Weekdays, low season, twilight, seniors, juniors. **Caddies:** No. **Golf carts:** $11. **Discount golf packages:** No. **Season:** March-Nov. **High:** N/A. **On site lodging:** No. **Rental clubs:** Yes. **Walking policy:** Walking at certain times. **Metal spikes allowed:** Yes. **Range:** Yes (grass/mats). **To obtain tee times:** Call up to 14 days in advance.

Subscriber comments: New course. Will be super!...Good value during week, over-priced on weekend...Long, lots of trouble to shoot over...Front and back nines quite differenct...Long course...Needs time to grow.

★★½CRACKLEWOOD GOLF CLUB
18215 24 Mile Macomb Township, Mt. Clemens, 48858, Macomb County, (810)781-0808.
Architect: Jerry Matthews. **Caddies:** No. **Discount golf packages:** No. **On site lodging:** No. **Rental clubs:** No. **Metal spikes allowed:** Yes. **Range:** Yes.
Call club for further information.
Subscriber comments: Fun course through the woods, good condition reasonably priced...Very average, doesn't inspire you to return...Always overbooked...What a sleeper...Greens are fast...Excellent, reasonably priced course...Excellent test, needs TLC...Name is very appropriate, it's tight.

★★CRESTVIEW GOLF CLUB
900 W D Ave., Kalamazoo, 49001, Kalamazoo County, (616)349-1111.
Call club for further information.

★½CROOKED CREEK GOLF CLUB
9387 Gratiot Rd., Saginaw, 48609, Saginaw County, (517)781-0050.
Architect: Donald Bray. **Caddies:** No. **Discount golf packages:** No. **On site lodging:** No. **Rental clubs:** No. **Metal spikes allowed:** Yes. **Range:** No.
Call club for further information.

★★★½CROOKED TREE GOLF CLUB
PU-600 Crooked Tree Dr., Petoskey, 49770, Emmet County, (616)439-4030, 100 miles NE of Grand Rapids.
Opened: 1995. **Holes:** 18. **Par:** 71/71. **Yards:** 6,584/4,713. **Course rating:** 72.8/68.0. **Slope:** 140/121. **Architect:** Harry Bowers. **Green fee:** $45/$75. **Credit cards:** All major. **Reduced fees:** Weekdays, low season, resort guests, twilight. **Caddies:** No. **Golf carts:** Included in Green Fee. **Discount golf packages:** No. **Season:** April-Nov. **High:** June-Aug. **On site lodging:** No. **Rental clubs:** Yes. **Walking policy:** Walking at certain times. **Metal spikes allowed:** Yes. **Range:** Yes (grass/mats). **To obtain tee times:** Call with credit card to reserve.
Subscriber comments: Intimidating greens...Best new value up north...Pricey but good course...Going to be a must play...Some fantastic views of Little Traverse Bay. A very fun golf course...You get a outstanding yardage guide...Some unfair greens.

★★CRYSTAL LAKE GOLF CLUB
R-Hwy. 31, Beulah, 49617, Benzie County, (616)882-4061, 30 miles W of Traverse City.
Opened: 1970. **Holes:** 18. **Par:** 70/72. **Yards:** 6,400/5,500. **Course rating:** 70.4/69.6. **Slope:** 118/113. **Architect:** Bruce Matthews/Jerry Matthews. **Green fee:** $18/$25. **Credit cards:** MC,VISA. **Reduced fees:** Low season, twilight, seniors, juniors. **Caddies:** No. **Golf carts:** N/A. **Discount golf packages:** No. **Season:** May-Oct. **High:** July-Aug. **On site lodging:** No. **Rental clubs:** No. **Walking policy:** N/A. **Metal spikes allowed:** Yes. **Range:** Yes (grass). **To obtain tee times:** Call golf shop.
Subscriber comments: Flat and uninteresting...Average layout beautiful views...Never crowded...Nice family course, well maintained...Friendly people, good golf value. Flat course with short rough, inconsistent greens, good condition...Great greens, great views...Staff very courteous.
Special Notes: Spikeless shoes encouraged.

MICHIGAN

CRYSTAL MOUNTAIN RESORT

R-12500 Crystal Mountain Dr., Thompsonville, 49683, Benzie County, (616)378-2000, (800)968-7686, 30 miles S of Traverse City.
Opened: 1977. **Architect:** William Newcomb. **Credit cards:** All major. **Caddies:** No. **Discount golf packages:** Yes. **Season:** April-Oct. **High:** June-Aug. **On site lodging:** Yes. **Rental clubs:** Yes. **Metal spikes allowed:** Yes. **To obtain tee times:** Call 800 number.

★★★½**BETSIE VALLEY COURSE**

Holes: 18. **Par:** 71/71. **Yards:** 6,345/4,947. **Course rating:** 70.5/68.0. **Slope:** 128/115. **Green fee:** $40/$40. **Reduced fees:** Weekdays, low season, resort guests, twilight. **Golf carts:** $12. **Walking policy:** Unrestricted walking. **Range:** Yes (grass/mats).
Subscriber comments: Picturesque views, long distance between holes...Designed for faders; great condition...Best of their layout...Terrific example of working with the land...Fun course to play...Unbelievable views...Very scenic courses...Challenging but playable.

★★★½**MOUNTAIN RIDGE COURSE**

Holes: 18. **Par:** 72/72. **Yards:** 7,015/5,105. **Course rating:** 73.0/70.0. **Slope:** 134/121. **Green fee:** $31/$65. **Reduced fees:** Weekdays, low season, resort guests, twilight, juniors. **Golf carts:** Included in Green Fee. **Walking policy:** Mandatory cart. **Range:** Yes (grass/mats).
Subscriber comments: Interesting layout...Unbelievable warm-up area...Fun to play and very beautiful...Green fees a little steep; courses offer variety of terrain and well maintained...Very picturesque course, well maintained not difficult.

★★**CURRIE MUNICIPAL GOLF COURSE**

PU-1006 Currie Pkwy., Midland, 48640, Midland County, (517)839-9600.
Opened: 1954. **Holes:** 18. **Par:** 72/72. **Yards:** 6,523/5,244. **Course rating:** 71.0/69.2. **Slope:** 118/109. **Architect:** Gill Currie. **Green fee:** $14/$14. **Credit cards:** None. **Reduced fees:** Twilight, seniors, juniors. **Caddies:** No. **Golf carts:** $12. **Discount golf packages:** No. **Season:** April-Oct. **High:** May-Sept. **On site lodging:** No. **Rental clubs:** Yes. **Walking policy:** Unrestricted walking. **Metal spikes allowed:** No. **Range:** Yes (grass/mats). **To obtain tee times:** Call 3 days in advance.
Special Notes: Also 9-hole West Course.

★★½**DAMA FARMS GOLF COURSE**

PU-410 E. Marr Rd., Howell, 48843, Livingston County, (517)546-4635, 45 miles W of Detroit.
Opened: 1969. **Holes:** 18. **Par:** 72/72. **Yards:** 6,500/5,700. **Course rating:** 69.6/66.1. **Slope:** 119/109. **Architect:** N/A. **Green fee:** $15/$21. **Credit cards:** MC,VISA,DISC. **Reduced fees:** Weekdays, low season, twilight, seniors, juniors. **Caddies:** No. **Golf carts:** $18. **Discount golf packages:** No. **Season:** April-Nov. **High:** May-Oct. **On site lodging:** No. **Rental clubs:** Yes. **Walking policy:** Unrestricted walking. **Metal spikes allowed:** Yes. **Range:** Yes (grass). **To obtain tee times:** Call golf shop.
Subscriber comments: Nice course, very nice people...Easy to walk...Rough on some holes, others too easy, good shape...Several challenging holes, well taken care of...Needs work, but getting better.

★★½**DE MOR HILLS GOLF COURSE**

10275 Ranger Hwy., Morenci, 49256, Lenawee County, (517)458-6679.
Call club for further information.
Subscriber comments: Very few hazards. Long driver's dream...Short par 4s, long par 3s...Fun to play, small greens...Course, fairly easy, great price, excellent service...18 holes and a steak under $15...Nice course. They run some good golf, dinner specials.

★★½**DEARBORN HILLS GOLF CLUB**

PU-1300 S. Telegraph Rd., Dearborn, 48124, Wayne County, (313)563-4653.
Opened: 1992. **Holes:** 18. **Par:** 60/60. **Yards:** 4,495/3,217. **Course rating:** 61.2/57.7. **Slope:** 100/92. **Architect:** Warner Bowen. **Green fee:** $12/$22. **Credit cards:** MC,VISA,DISC. **Reduced fees:** Twilight, seniors, juniors. **Caddies:** No. **Golf carts:** $20. **Discount golf packages:** No. **Season:** March-Nov. **High:** N/A. **On site lodging:** No. **Rental clubs:** Yes. **Walking policy:** Unrestricted walking. **Metal spikes allowed:** Yes. **Range:** No. **To obtain tee times:** Call golf shop.

Subscriber comments: Short course, but beautiful...Par 60, water on every hole...Challenging course, lot of fun...No water or sand around greens...Play the back tees and you have a good course...Very short, great place to work on your irons...Short course with 12 par 3s...Good value.

★★★DEER RUN GOLF CLUB
13955 Cascade Rd., Lowell, 49331, Kent County, (616)897-8481.
Call club for further information.
Subscriber comments: This is a great place to play golf, out of town but worth the drive...Long; good conditon; fun to play...Too flat to be outstanding...Long, tough when wind blows...Needs more care and watering...Second best outing venue in the area...Great backyard secret, a test always.

DEME ACRES GOLF COURSE
PU-17655 Albain Rd., Petersburg, 49270, Monroe County, (313)279-1151, 15 miles N of Toledo, OH.
Opened: 1962. **Holes:** 18. **Par:** 70/70. **Yards:** 5,735/5,200. **Course rating:** N/A. **Slope:** N/A. **Architect:** N/A. **Green fee:** $12/$16. **Credit cards:** None. **Reduced fees:** Weekdays, twilight, seniors, juniors. **Caddies:** No. **Golf carts:** $9. **Discount golf packages:** No. **Season:** April-Oct. **High:** July-Aug. **On site lodging:** No. **Rental clubs:** Yes. **Walking policy:** Unrestricted walking. **Metal spikes allowed:** Yes. **Range:** No. **To obtain tee times:** Tee times not required.

★★★DEVIL'S RIDGE GOLF CLUB
PU-3700 Metamora Rd., Oxford, 48371, Oakland County, (248)969-0100, 11 miles N of Pontiac.
Opened: 1995. **Holes:** 18. **Par:** 72/72. **Yards:** 6,722/4,130. **Course rating:** 72.2/64.4. **Slope:** 123/100. **Architect:** Patrick Conroy. **Green fee:** $37/$50. **Credit cards:** All major. **Reduced fees:** Weekdays, low season, twilight, seniors. **Caddies:** No. **Golf carts:** Included in Green Fee. **Discount golf packages:** No. **Season:** April-Nov. **High:** April-Nov. **On site lodging:** No. **Rental clubs:** Yes. **Walking policy:** Mandatory cart. **Metal spikes allowed:** Yes. **Range:** Yes (grass/mats). **To obtain tee times:** Call 7 days in advance.
Subscriber comments: Elevated tees, lot of trees, blind shots but firm and fair...Too many tricked up holes...Couldn't walk it if you were half burro..Must take carts (no walking)...Weak on service, tricky course...Tough landing areas, a great challenge..Tricked up, well maintained, however...Challenging, lots of elevation changes...Difficult, but fun...Course in good condition.

★★THE DUNES GOLF CLUB
PU-6489 W. Empire Hwy., Empire, 49630, Leelanau County, (616)326-5390, 18 miles W of Traverse City.
Opened: 1984. **Holes:** 18. **Par:** 72/72. **Yards:** 5,868/5,041. **Course rating:** 67.3/68.1. **Slope:** 112/114. **Architect:** N/A. **Green fee:** $16/$16. **Credit cards:** None. **Reduced fees:** Low season, twilight. **Caddies:** No. **Golf carts:** N/A. **Discount golf packages:** No. **Season:** April-Oct. **High:** July-Aug. **On site lodging:** No. **Rental clubs:** Yes. **Walking policy:** Walking at certain times. **Metal spikes allowed:** Yes. **Range:** No. **To obtain tee times:** Call golf shop.

★★★½DUNHAM HILLS GOLF & COUNTRY CLUB
PU-13561 Dunham Rd., Hartland, 48353, Livingston County, (248)887-9170, 23 miles W of Pontiac.
Opened: 1968. **Holes:** 18. **Par:** 71/74. **Yards:** 6,820/5,310. **Course rating:** 71.8/70.8. **Slope:** 133/121. **Architect:** Built by owners. **Green fee:** $40/$48. **Credit cards:** MC,VISA. **Reduced fees:** Weekdays, twilight, seniors, juniors. **Caddies:** No. **Golf carts:** Included in Green Fee. **Discount golf packages:** No. **Season:** March-Nov. **High:** May-Sept. **On site lodging:** No. **Rental clubs:** No. **Walking policy:** Walking at certain times. **Metal spikes allowed:** Yes. **Range:** Yes (grass/mats). **To obtain tee times:** Call.
Subscriber comments: Championship course. A real test...Not a flat lie to be found on entire course...Classic layout, challenging and great shape/value...Tough layout, need "A" game...Well maintained course...Mature, well manicured and challenging.

★★★½DUNMAGLAS GOLF CLUB

PU-09031 Boyne City Rd., Charlevoix, 49720, Charlevoix County, (616)547-1022, (888)847-0909, 50 miles NE of Traverse City.

Opened: 1992. **Holes:** 18. **Par:** 72/74. **Yards:** 6,897/5,334. **Course rating:** 74.0/70.9. **Slope:** 142/127. **Architect:** Larry Mancour. **Green fee:** $50/$85. **Credit cards:** All major. **Reduced fees:** Low season, twilight. **Caddies:** No. **Golf carts:** Included in Green Fee. **Discount golf packages:** Yes. **Season:** May-Oct. **High:** July-Aug. **On site lodging:** No. **Rental clubs:** Yes. **Walking policy:** Mandatory cart. **Metal spikes allowed:** Yes. **Range:** Yes (grass). **To obtain tee times:** Call anytime in advance with credit card to confirm.

Notes: Ranked 5th in 1997 Best in State.

Subscriber comments: Nicest course I've ever played in Michigan. Some of the holes are just breathtaking...Without question, most challenging in Michigan...Don't expect to score well...Difficult course, expect to shoot a high score...Beautiful and uncrowded...Best course in Michigan...Most difficult course I've played...Perhaps the most scenic course in Michigan...Unique, must be played at least once.

★★DUTCH HOLLOW GOLF CLUB

8500 Lansing Rd., Durand, 48429, Shiawassee County, (517)288-3960.
Call club for further information.

★★★½EAGLE CREST GOLF CLUB

R-1275 Huron St., Ypsilanti, 48197, Washtenaw County, (313)487-2441, 30 miles SW of Detroit.

Opened: 1989. **Holes:** 18. **Par:** 72/72. **Yards:** 6,750/5,185. **Course rating:** 73.6/69.7. **Slope:** 138/124. **Architect:** Karl V. Litten. **Green fee:** $40/$55. **Credit cards:** MC,VISA,AMEX. **Reduced fees:** Weekdays, low season, twilight, seniors, juniors. **Caddies:** No. **Golf carts:** Included in Green Fee. **Discount golf packages:** Yes. **Season:** March-Nov. **High:** June-Aug. **On site lodging:** Yes. **Rental clubs:** Yes. **Walking policy:** Walking at certain times. **Metal spikes allowed:** Yes. **Range:** Yes (grass/mats). **To obtain tee times:** Call up to 14 days in advance.

Subscriber comments: Great match play course...Nice views of Ford Lake, two very different nines...Great views on lake, great signature hole...Lots of water, challenges...Many tees to challenge any handicap...Back nine is one of the best in SE Michigan.

★★★½EAGLE GLEN GOLF COURSE

PU-1251 Club House Dr., Farwell, 48622, Clare County, (517)588-4424.

Opened: 1992. **Holes:** 18. **Par:** 72/72. **Yards:** 6,602/5,119. **Course rating:** 71.1/69.2. **Slope:** 123/116. **Architect:** Jerry Matthews. **Green fee:** $21/$28. **Credit cards:** MC,VISA,DISC. **Reduced fees:** Weekdays, low season, resort guests, seniors, juniors. **Caddies:** No. **Golf carts:** $9. **Discount golf packages:** Yes. **Season:** April-Oct. **High:** June-Oct. **On site lodging:** No. **Rental clubs:** Yes. **Walking policy:** Walking at certain times. **Metal spikes allowed:** Yes. **Range:** Yes (grass). **To obtain tee times:** Call anytime.

Subscriber comments: Hitting over wild grown areas was exciting...Well laid out, almost a links style...Very fair, playable course...Tough rough, nice greens, nice layout...What a jewel. Fantastic condition. Great layout...Course looks wide open, but rough is killer.

★★½EASTERN HILLS GOLF CLUB

6075 East G Ave., Kalamazoo, 49004, Kalamazoo County, (616)385-8175.
Call club for further information.

Subscriber comments: Great value, carts are not mandatory...Easy course fairways open...Rapidly improving course, slowish greens...Can't do much about the course, but you can't beat the price or the people.

★★EL DORADO COUNTRY CLUB

PU-2869 Pontiac Trail, Walled Lake, 48390, Oakland County, (248)624-1736, 40 miles NW of Detroit.

Opened: 1967. **Holes:** 18. **Par:** 70/74. **Yards:** 5,753/4,846. **Course rating:** 68.3/68.0. **Slope:** 122/116. **Architect:** Walter R. Lorang Sr.. **Green fee:** $22/$25. **Credit cards:**

MC,VISA. **Reduced fees:** Weekdays, low season, twilight, seniors, juniors. **Caddies:** No. **Golf carts:** $12. **Discount golf packages:** No. **Season:** April-Oct. **High:** June-Aug. **On site lodging:** No. **Rental clubs:** Yes. **Walking policy:** Walking at certain times. **Metal spikes allowed:** Yes. **Range:** Yes (grass). **To obtain tee times:** Call golf shop.

★★★ EL DORADO GOLF COURSE
PU-3750 Howell Rd., Mason, 48854, Ingham County, (517)676-2854, 15 miles S of Lansing.
Opened: 1968. **Holes:** 27. **Architect:** Bruce Matthews/Jerry Matthews. **Green fee:** $22/$25. **Credit cards:** MC,VISA,DISC. **Reduced fees:** Weekdays, low season, twilight, seniors, juniors. **Caddies:** No. **Golf carts:** $12. **Discount golf packages:** No. **Season:** March-Nov. **High:** N/A. **On site lodging:** No. **Rental clubs:** No. **Walking policy:** Unrestricted walking. **Metal spikes allowed:** No. **Range:** Yes (grass). **To obtain tee times:** Call up to 7 days in advance.
RED/WHITE COURSE
Par: 71/71. **Yards:** 6,400/5,393.
BLUE/WHITE COURSE
Par: 71/71. **Yards:** 6,536/6,536.
RED/BLUE COURSE
Par: 72/72. **Yards:** 6,712/5,498.
Subscriber comments: New nine needs time. Will be nice 27 hole course...Well maintained, great practice facilities, good people...Original 18 better...Outstanding grooming; very playable...Plush fairways and fast greens...Best 18 of 27 would be strong...Favorite course in Capital area, offers something for all levels.

★★★ ELDORADO
PU-1 Automotive Ave., Cadillac, 49601, Wexford County, (616)779-9977, (888)374-8318, 75 miles N of Grand Rapids.
Opened: 1996. **Holes:** 18. **Par:** 72/72. **Yards:** 7,070/5,050. **Course rating:** 73.0/68.2. **Slope:** 132/125. **Architect:** Bob Meyer. **Green fee:** $30/$35. **Credit cards:** MC,VISA. **Reduced fees:** Weekdays. **Caddies:** No. **Golf carts:** $10. **Discount golf packages:** No. **Season:** April-Oct. **High:** June-Aug. **On site lodging:** No. **Rental clubs:** Yes. **Walking policy:** Unrestricted walking. **Metal spikes allowed:** Yes. **Range:** Yes (grass). **To obtain tee times:** Call golf shop.
Notes: Golf Digest School site.
Subscriber comments: Will be great when greens mature...Challenging yet playable...Should not be opened so early...Needs time to mature...Impossible for women, far too many forced carries...Five tee boxes, no ridiculous holes.

★★★★ ELK RIDGE GOLF CLUB
PU-9400 Rouse Rd., Atlanta, 49709, Montgomery County, (517)785-2275, (800)626-4355, 30 miles E of Gaylord.
Opened: 1991. **Holes:** 18. **Par:** 72/72. **Yards:** 7,072/5,261. **Course rating:** 74.7/72.3. **Slope:** 143/130. **Architect:** Jerry Matthews. **Green fee:** $50/$65. **Credit cards:** All major. **Reduced fees:** Weekdays, low season, seniors, juniors. **Caddies:** No. **Golf carts:** Included in Green Fee. **Discount golf packages:** Yes. **Season:** May-Oct. **High:** June-Aug. **On site lodging:** No. **Rental clubs:** Yes. **Walking policy:** Walking at certain times. **Metal spikes allowed:** Yes. **Range:** Yes (grass). **To obtain tee times:** Call golf shop anytime with credit card.
Notes: Ranked 17th in 1997 Best in State.
Subscriber comments: Beautiful, scenic course. Loved pig-shaped bunker at #10...Great course in the middle of nowhere...Best course in Michigan. Extremely well kept, scenic...This is a great golf course...By far, the best public course I've played...Watch out for elk and deer on the driving range...Needs lodging...Tough, tight and expensive...Didn't like double dogleg par 5s, too many layups...Beautiful views...Super conditions, top 10 in Michigan.

★★★ ELLA SHARP PARK GOLF COURSE
PU-3225 4th St., Jackson, 49203, Jackson County, (517)788-4066, 35 miles S of Lansing.
Opened: 1923. **Holes:** 18. **Par:** 71/71. **Yards:** 5,751/5,168. **Course rating:** 67.4/69.1. **Slope:** 113/114. **Architect:** Tom Bendelow. **Green fee:** $12/$13. **Credit cards:** None. **Reduced fees:** Weekdays, low season, twilight, seniors, juniors. **Caddies:** No. **Golf**

carts: $14. **Discount golf packages:** No. **Season:** March-Dec. **High:** June-Aug. **On site lodging:** No. **Rental clubs:** Yes. **Walking policy:** Unrestricted walking. **Metal spikes allowed:** Yes. **Range:** Yes (Mats). **To obtain tee times:** Call golf shop.
Subscriber comments: Nice layout, good shape for as much play it has...Short course. Treelined. Excellent conditions...Best price for golf around. Very tight, relatively short. Good condition...Solid course, reasonable priced, excellent service...Needs bar...Fun course for all levels of players, bargain prices.

★★★ ELMBROOK GOLF COURSE
PU-420 Hammond Rd., Traverse City, 49684, Grand Traverse County, (616)946-9180.
Opened: 1966. **Holes:** 18. **Par:** 72/72. **Yards:** 6,131/5,194. **Course rating:** 68.4/68.5.
Slope: 114/112. **Architect:** Jerry Matthews. **Green fee:** $26/$28. **Credit cards:** MC,VISA,DISC. **Reduced fees:** Low season, resort guests. **Caddies:** No. **Golf carts:** $14. **Discount golf packages:** Yes. **Season:** April-Nov. **High:** June-Aug. **On site lodging:** No. **Rental clubs:** Yes. **Walking policy:** Unrestricted walking. **Metal spikes allowed:** Yes. **Range:** Yes (grass/mats). **To obtain tee times:** Call golf shop in advance.
Subscriber comments: Well groomed course...Close to town, pretty views of bay...New super has helped with redesigning holes...Wonderful panoramic views...Inexpensive for area, good value...Recent change in course maintenance has improved the course...Greens could use better upkeep...Mushroom cap greens.

★★★ THE EMERALD AT MAPLE CREEK GOLF COURSE
PU-8103 N. U.S. 27, St. Johns, 48879, Clinton County, (517)224-6287, (800)924-5993, 25 miles N of Lansing.
Opened: 1996. **Holes:** 18. **Par:** 71. **Yards:** 6,644. **Course rating:** 70.9. **Slope:** 123.
Architect: Jerry Matthews. **Green fee:** $28/$33. **Credit cards:** MC,VISA. **Reduced fees:** Weekdays, low season, twilight, seniors, juniors. **Caddies:** No. **Golf carts:** $24.
Discount golf packages: Yes. **Season:** April-Oct. **High:** May-Sept. **On site lodging:** No. **Rental clubs:** Yes. **Walking policy:** Unrestricted walking. **Metal spikes allowed:** No. **Range:** Yes (grass). **To obtain tee times:** Call golf shop.
Subscriber comments: Five good holes...Greens were perfect. Needs to mature...Beautiful rework of old course...Two old holes are out of place.

★★ ENGLISH HILLS GOLF COURSE
1200 Four Mile Rd., Grand Rapids, 49504, Kent County, (616)784-3420.
Architect: Mark DeVries. **Caddies:** No. **Discount golf packages:** No. **On site lodging:** No. **Rental clubs:** No. **Metal spikes allowed:** Yes. **Range:** No.
Call club for further information.

★★★ FAULKWOOD SHORES GOLF CLUB
PU-300 S. Hughes Rd., Howell, 48843, Livingston County, (517)546-4180, 20 miles W of Detroit.
Opened: 1967. **Holes:** 18. **Par:** 72/72. **Yards:** 6,828/5,341. **Course rating:** 74.3/71.8.
Slope: 140/128. **Architect:** Ralph. Banfield. **Green fee:** $24/$37. **Credit cards:** MC,VISA. **Reduced fees:** Weekdays, low season, twilight, seniors, juniors. **Caddies:** No. **Golf carts:** Included in Green Fee. **Discount golf packages:** No. **Season:** April-Nov. **High:** June-Sept. **On site lodging:** No. **Rental clubs:** Yes. **Walking policy:** Walking at certain times. **Metal spikes allowed:** Yes. **Range:** Yes (grass/mats). **To obtain tee times:** Call 7 days in advance for weekdays and call Monday for upcoming weekend.
Subscriber comments: Difficult, great value...Not flashy but a very good course...Long tough course, fair greens, fair price. Very cheap for the quality of course...Don't leave any clubs at home. You will need full set to play this course. Some very difficult holes for the average player...Excellent greens, good old time golf...Located in the boonies. But worth the drive.

★★½ FELLOWS CREEK GOLF CLUB
PU-2936 Lotz Rd., Canton, 48188, Washtenaw County, (313)728-1300, 20 miles W of Detroit.
Opened: 1961. **Holes:** 27. **Architect:** Bruce Matthews/Jerry Matthews. **Green fee:** $19/$22. **Credit cards:** MC,VISA. **Reduced fees:** Weekdays, low season, twilight, seniors, juniors. **Caddies:** No. **Golf carts:** $11. **Discount golf packages:** No. **Season:**

April-Dec. **High:** June-Aug. **On site lodging:** No. **Rental clubs:** No. **Walking policy:** Unrestricted walking. **Metal spikes allowed:** Yes. **Range:** No. **To obtain tee times:** Call during the week for a weekend time.

EAST/SOUTH
Par: 72/72. **Yards:** 6,489/5,276. **Course rating:** 71.0/70.0. **Slope:** 118.

EAST/WEST
Par: 72/72. **Yards:** 6,399/5,290. **Course rating:** 70.9/69.9. **Slope:** N/A.

SOUTH/WEST
Par: 72/72. **Yards:** 6,430/5,346. **Course rating:** 70.9/69.9. **Slope:** N/A.

Subscriber comments: The course is getting better maintained...Fun course for the money...Nice altitude changes...Plain Jane, nothing special...Seemed to play long...Short but a challenge...Decent clubhouse, some interesting holes, overpriced...Beautiful fairways and bunkers...West nine is tight and challenging...Not real memorable but good for the price...Greens well kept.

★★½FENTON FARMS GOLF CLUB

PU-12312 Torrey Rd., Fenton, 48430, Genesee County, (810)629-1212, 10 miles S of Flint.

Opened: 1920. **Holes:** 18. **Par:** 72/70. **Yards:** 6,596/5,196. **Course rating:** 71.7/69.8. **Slope:** 125/117. **Architect:** N/A. **Green fee:** $16/$20. **Credit cards:** MC,VISA. **Reduced fees:** Weekdays, low season, twilight, seniors, juniors. **Caddies:** No. **Golf carts:** $12. **Discount golf packages:** No. **Season:** April-Nov. **High:** May-Sept. **On site lodging:** No. **Rental clubs:** Yes. **Walking policy:** Unrestricted walking. **Metal spikes allowed:** Yes. **Range:** Yes (grass). **To obtain tee times:** Call up to 7 days in advance.
Subscriber comments: A links-style course that's tough yet fun to play. Would recommend it to anyone...Heavy play. Mediocre course...Fair condition...Firm fairways and greens...Great value with coupon books!...Overpriced for what it presents...Golf course is improving every year...Backups common on many tees.

★★FERN HILL GOLF & COUNTRY CLUB

PU-17600 Clinton River Rd., Clinton Township, 48044, Macomb County, (810)286-4700, 20 miles SW of Detroit.

Opened: 1972. **Holes:** 18. **Par:** 70/73. **Yards:** 6,018/4,962. **Course rating:** 67.6/65.7. **Slope:** 115/108. **Architect:** Fred Severini III. **Green fee:** $10/$17. **Credit cards:** MC,VISA. **Reduced fees:** Low season, twilight, seniors. **Caddies:** No. **Golf carts:** $18. **Discount golf packages:** Yes. **Season:** April-Nov. **High:** June-Sept. **On site lodging:** No. **Rental clubs:** No. **Walking policy:** Unrestricted walking. **Metal spikes allowed:** Yes. **Range:** No. **To obtain tee times:** Call golf shop.

★★½FIREFLY GOLF LINKS

PU-7795 S. Clare Ave., Clare, 48617, Clare County, (517)386-3510, 45 miles NW of Saginaw.

Opened: 1932. **Holes:** 18. **Par:** 72/72. **Yards:** 5,761/4,523. **Course rating:** 67.9/65.6. **Slope:** 124/113. **Architect:** Darrell & Fran Loar. **Green fee:** $19/$23. **Credit cards:** MC,VISA,DISC. **Reduced fees:** Weekdays, low season, seniors. **Caddies:** No. **Golf carts:** $9. **Discount golf packages:** Yes. **Season:** April-Oct. **High:** June-Aug. **On site lodging:** No. **Rental clubs:** Yes. **Walking policy:** Unrestricted walking. **Metal spikes allowed:** Yes. **Range:** No. **To obtain tee times:** Call golf shop.
Subscriber comments: Short course, good service, small greens a lot of trees...Needs work but good value...Gets better every time I play it...Short but tough greens...Very enjoyable local course.

FOREST AKERS GOLF COURSE AT MSU

PU-Mich. St. Univ. Harrison Rd., East Lansing, 48823, Ingham County, (517)355-1635, 3 miles E of Lansing. **Credit cards:** MC,VISA. **Reduced fees:** N/A. **Caddies:** No. **Golf carts:** $24. **Season:** March-Oct. **High:** May-Sept. **On site lodging:** No. **Rental clubs:** Yes. **Walking policy:** Unrestricted walking. **Metal spikes allowed:** Yes. **Range:** Yes (grass/mats). **To obtain tee times:** Call up to 7 days in advance.

★★★EAST COURSE

Opened: 1972. **Holes:** 18. **Par:** 72/73. **Yards:** 6,510/5,380. **Course rating:** 71.4/70.4. **Slope:** 118/115. **Architect:** M.S.U. Campus Planning. **Green fee:** $18/$20. **Discount golf packages:** Yes.
Subscriber comments: Lots of fun to play...Great student rate bargain...Difficult to get

good tee time...OK when West is busy...Good course, easy layout, condition questionable...Not the West, but in great shape...Mediocre course with a mediocre price.

★★★★WEST COURSE
Opened: 1958. **Holes:** 18. **Par:** 72/72. **Yards:** 7,003/5,251. **Course rating:** 74.4/70.0. **Slope:** 139/119. **Architect:** Arthur Hills. **Green fee:** $30/$34. **Discount golf packages:** No.
Subscriber comments: A strong test of your game in a Big 10 atmosphere. Course always in great shape...Overrated. The old West course was better...Pure golf, great track...First rate university course...Still the strongest public course in the area...Difficult to get good tee time...Awesome course condition, good for low handicappers.

★★★★THE FORTRESS
R-950 Flint St., Box 304, Frankenmuth, 48734, Saginaw County, (517)652-0400, (800)863-7999, 15 miles SE of Saginaw.
Opened: 1992. **Holes:** 18. **Par:** 72/72. **Yards:** 6,813/4,837. **Course rating:** 73.6/68.8. **Slope:** 138/124. **Architect:** Dick Nugent. **Green fee:** $39/$65. **Credit cards:** All major. **Reduced fees:** Weekdays, low season, resort guests, twilight, seniors, juniors. **Caddies:** No. **Golf carts:** Included in Green Fee. **Discount golf packages:** Yes. **Season:** April-Oct. **High:** June-Sept. **On site lodging:** No. **Rental clubs:** Yes. **Walking policy:** Walking at certain times. **Metal spikes allowed:** No. **Range:** Yes (grass). **To obtain tee times:** Call with credit card to reserve. 48 hour cancellation policy.
Subscriber comments: Course in excellent shape, staff very accommodating...A reason to go to Frankenmuth besides chicken...Worth a yearly visit, very quick greens...Very tough from back tees, 11th is exciting, water both sides...Hard to score. Overly punishes...Best in this part of Michigan. Last five holes tough but fair...Very windy...No hesitation to enforce pace of play...Great yardage markings and pin sheets.

★★½FOX CREEK GOLF COURSE
PU-36000 Seven Mile, Livonia, 48152, Wayne County, (248)471-3400.
Opened: 1987. **Holes:** 18. **Par:** 71/71. **Yards:** 6,612/5,231. **Course rating:** 71.4/69.8. **Slope:** 123/117. **Architect:** Mike DeVries. **Green fee:** $20/$22. **Credit cards:** MC,VISA. **Reduced fees:** Twilight, seniors, juniors. **Caddies:** No. **Golf carts:** $24. **Discount golf packages:** No. **Season:** Year-round weather permitting. **High:** April-Nov. **On site lodging:** No. **Rental clubs:** Yes. **Walking policy:** Unrestricted walking. **Metal spikes allowed:** No. **Range:** No. **To obtain tee times:** Call up to 2 days in advance.
Subscriber comments: Challenging but very playable. Good value...Bent-grass fairways and some tight driving holes. Small pro shop with attached upscale restaurant...Great municipal course...Holds water, needs upkeep around greens...Front side short and tight, back side long and open...Good course to play with the guys after work.

FOX HILLS GOLF & CONFERENCE CENTER
PU-8768 N. Territorial Rd., Plymouth, 48170, Wayne County, (313)453-7272, 25 miles W of Detroit.
Caddies: No. **Discount golf packages:** Yes. **On site lodging:** No. **Rental clubs:** Yes. **Metal spikes allowed:** Yes. **Range:** Yes (grass). **To obtain tee times:** Call.
★★★½GOLDEN FOX COURSE
Opened: 1989. **Holes:** 18. **Par:** 72/72. **Yards:** 6,783/5,040. **Course rating:** 73.0/69.7. **Slope:** 136/122. **Architect:** Arthur Hills. **Green fee:** $50/$55. **Credit cards:** All major. **Reduced fees:** Weekdays, low season, twilight, seniors. **Golf carts:** Included in Green Fee. **Season:** April-Nov. **High:** May-Sept. **Walking policy:** Mandatory cart.
Subscriber comments: Very fair but challenging-well run...Good mix of water, sand and trees. Excellent facilities...May be best public course in Detroit area...Demanding & beautiful. Bring your wallet. This is what golf should be...Cart carries laser rangefinder.
★★½HILLS/WOODLANDS/LAKES
Opened: 1921. **Holes:** 27. **Par:** 70/73 (H/W); 71/75.(L/H); 71/72.(W/L). **Yards:** 6,398/5,588 (H/W); 6,784/6,028 (L/H); 6,514/5,548 (W/L). **Course rating:** 67.4/70.0 (H/W); 69.4/72.6 (L/H); 67.8/69.9 (W/L). **Slope:** 104/100 (H/W); 112/108 (L/H); 112/107 (W/L). **Architect:** Jim Lipe. **Green fee:** $22/$26. **Credit cards:** All major. **Reduced fees:** Weekdays, low season, twilight, seniors, juniors. **Golf carts:** $25. **Season:** Year-round weather permitting. **High:** April-Oct. **Walking policy:** Unrestricted walking.
Subscriber comments: Woodlands is best nine. Reasonably kept up...Could use

a face lift...Greens well maintained, not challenging...Nice courses, could be cut shorter in fairways...Short, undemanding...Easy to get on...Tends to be overcrowded but overall nice course..."Golden Fox" getting all the care!

★★★½ FOX RUN COUNTRY CLUB

PU-5825 W. Four Mile Rd., Grayling, 49738, Crawford County, (517)348-4343, (800)436-9786, 40 miles E of Traverse City.
Opened: 1990. **Holes:** 18. **Par:** 72/72. **Yards:** 6,293/4,829. **Course rating:** 71.0/69.7. **Slope:** 128/119. **Architect:** J. John Gorney. **Green fee:** $26/$26. **Credit cards:** MC,VISA. **Reduced fees:** Low season, twilight. **Caddies:** No. **Golf carts:** $16. **Discount golf packages:** No. **Season:** April-Oct. **High:** June-Sept. **On site lodging:** No. **Rental clubs:** Yes. **Walking policy:** Walking at certain times. **Metal spikes allowed:** Yes. **Range:** Yes (grass). **To obtain tee times:** Call. Credit card required to reserve more than 1 tee time.
Subscriber comments: Excellent; great fairways and greens; short...Traditional track...Fun course, manicured, fun staff...Nice greens, good fairways...Another excellent value for the money...Very attractive "Northern style" at a reasonable price.

★★ FRUITPORT GOLF CLUB

PU-6330 S. Harvey, Muskegon, 49444, Muskegon County, (616)798-3355, 4 miles N of Grand Haven.
Opened: 1971. **Holes:** 18. **Par:** 71. **Yards:** 5,725. **Course rating:** 68.9. **Slope:** N/A. **Architect:** Dennis Snider. **Green fee:** $17/$19. **Credit cards:** None. **Reduced fees:** Weekdays, low season, seniors. **Caddies:** No. **Golf carts:** $19. **Discount golf packages:** No. **Season:** March-Nov. **High:** N/A. **On site lodging:** No. **Rental clubs:** Yes. **Walking policy:** Unrestricted walking. **Metal spikes allowed:** Yes. **Range:** Yes (grass). **To obtain tee times:** Call.

GARLAND GOLF RESORT

R-HCR-1 Box 364M, Lewiston, 49756, Oscoda County, (517)786-2211, (800)968-0042, 30 miles E of Gaylord.
Architect: Ron Otto. **Credit cards:** All major,Diners Club. **Reduced fees:** Weekdays, low season, resort guests, twilight, juniors. **Caddies:** No. **Season:** April-Oct. **High:** June-Aug. **On site lodging:** Yes. **Rental clubs:** Yes. **Walking policy:** Mandatory cart. **Metal spikes allowed:** Yes. **Range:** Yes (grass/mats).

(GOOD SERVICE)

★★★½ FOUNTAINS COURSE

Opened: 1995. **Holes:** 18. **Par:** 72/72. **Yards:** 6,760/4,617. **Course rating:** 73.0/74.1. **Slope:** 130/128. **Green fee:** $85/$90. **Golf carts:** N/A. **Discount golf packages:** No. **To obtain tee times:** Call in advance.
Subscriber comments: Outstanding track. Great greens. A real test from tips...Water everywhere; saw a bald eagle...Stay at Garland and play all courses, they treat you like a king...Nice golf resort, service is a 10...Service above excellent, greens outstanding and the best food and lodging. The prices are expensive but you get what you pay for...Should be in Michigan top 10 when matures.

★★★★ MONARCH COURSE

Opened: N/A. **Holes:** 18. **Par:** 72/72. **Yards:** 7,188/4,904. **Course rating:** 75.6/69.5. **Slope:** 140/123. **Green fee:** $70/$75. **Golf carts:** Included in Green Fee. **Discount golf packages:** Yes. **To obtain tee times:** Call anytime in advance.
Subscriber comments: Super resort...Very long course, difficult for mid-high handicappers...Best golf value around, service at a premium...Worth the cost...Gorgeous views...Best golf in the state...Great shape, visually pleasing, a bit costly...The crown jewel of Garland...You get to hit all of your shots.

★★★½ REFLECTIONS COURSE

Opened: 1990. **Holes:** 18. **Par:** 72/72. **Yards:** 6,407/4,778. **Course rating:** 70.4/66.9. **Slope:** 120/110. **Green fee:** $50/$70. **Golf carts:** Included in Green Fee. **Discount golf packages:** Yes. **To obtain tee times:** Call anytime in advance.
Subscriber comments: Large amount of water in play...After first three holes it's very good...Watch for bald eagle on 4th... Long from the back tees...Tricky and tight...Greens need some attention...Somewhat boring after Monarch...Pricey, but beautiful course...Only Blackwolf Run offers better in Midwest, maybe.

★★★★ SWAMPFIRE COURSE

Opened: N/A. **Holes:** 18. **Par:** 72/72. **Yards:** 6,854/4,791. **Course rating:** 73.9/68.4.

Slope: 138/121. **Green fee:** $70/$75. **Golf carts:** Included in Green Fee. **Discount golf packages:** Yes. **To obtain tee times:** Call.
Subscriber comments: Small distance around greens to deep rough/woods...Tough track, bring a sleeve or two...My personal favorite of the four courses at Garland...Take some extra balls for the water...Lots of carries over water ...Medium length, water on every hole, lots of undulations...Hazards poorly placed from red tees...Water, water everwhere...Very difficult for the average golfer...Take a camera and a calculator.

★★★½ GAYLORD COUNTRY CLUB

P.O. Box 207, Gaylord, 49735, Otsego County, (616)546-3376.
Architect: Wilfried Reid. **Caddies:** No. **Discount golf packages:** No.
On site lodging: No. **Rental clubs:** No. **Metal spikes allowed:** Yes.
Range: Yes.
Call club for further information.

(GOOD VALUE)

Subscriber comments: Underrated! Great value for area...Beautiful greens and fairways; terrific value...Reasonably priced...Good greens, scenic views...An often overlooked gem in land of plenty...Excellent challenge and fair, good value...Another established course not used as much so you can relax...First nine links; second woods and water...Best greens in the North...Plush from tee to green.

★★★ GENESEE VALLEY MEADOWS

PU-5499 Miller Rd., Swartz Creek, 48473, Genesee County, (810)732-1401, 5 miles W of Flint.
Opened: 1965. **Holes:** 18. **Par:** 72/72. **Yards:** 6,867/6,490. **Course rating:** 72.3/72.3.
Slope: 133/122. **Architect:** D Sincerbaugh. **Green fee:** $19/$23. **Credit cards:** N/A.
Reduced fees: Weekdays, low season, twilight, seniors, juniors. **Caddies:** No. **Golf carts:** $24. **Discount golf packages:** No. **Season:** April-Nov. **High:** June-Aug. **On site lodging:** No. **Rental clubs:** Yes. **Walking policy:** Walking at certain times. **Metal spikes allowed:** Yes. **Range:** No. **To obtain tee times:** Call golf shop.
Subscriber comments: Always a good experience here...Great greens!...Wide open and well taken care of...Very pleasant people. Well maintained...Good solid course, strong bunkers...Excellent shape for a public course...Water can come into play on 12 holes...Looks open and easy. Not so. Deceiving greens.

★★★½ GEORGE YOUNG RECREATIONAL COMPLEX

PU-Young Lane, Hwy. 424, Gaastra, 49927, Iron County, (906)265-3401, 125 miles N of Green Bay, WI.
Opened: 1993. **Holes:** 18. **Par:** 72/72. **Yards:** 6,076/5,338. **Course rating:** 74.3/71.2. **Slope:** 130/120. **Architect:** N/A. **Green fee:** $20. **Credit cards:** None. **Reduced fees:** N/A. **Caddies:** No. **Golf carts:** $19.

(GOOD VALUE)

Discount golf packages: No. **Season:** May-Oct. **High:** July-Aug. **On site lodging:** No. **Rental clubs:** No. **Walking policy:** Unrestricted walking. **Metal spikes allowed:** No. **Range:** No. **To obtain tee times:** Call golf shop 7 days in advance.
Subscriber comments: A gem off the beaten track...Too good to believe...Greens are a little slow...For $20 you can golf all day...Beautiful panoramic views, a bargain, test from tips...Could have developed course better...Pretty course, hilly and narrow back nine, nice greens.

★★★ GIANT OAKS GOLF COURSE

PU-1024 Valetta Dr., Temperance, 48182, Monroe County, (313)847-6733, 5 miles N of Toledo, OH.
Opened: 1969. **Holes:** 27. **Par:** 72/72. **Yards:** 6,415/4,994. **Course rating:** 71.1/68.0.
Slope: 124/111. **Architect:** Arthur Hills. **Green fee:** $19/$23. **Credit cards:** None.
Reduced fees: N/A. **Caddies:** No. **Golf carts:** N/A. **Discount golf packages:** No.
Season: March-Dec. weather permitting. **High:** N/A. **On site lodging:** No. **Rental clubs:** No. **Walking policy:** Unrestricted walking. **Metal spikes allowed:** Yes. **Range:** No. **To obtain tee times:** Call up to 7 days in advance.
Subscriber comments: Nice course, good price, very good service...Well kept course...Facilities excellent...Big greens, well manicured.

★★★½ GLACIER CLUB

8000 Glacier Club Dr., Washington, 48094, Macomb County, (810)786-0800, 27 miles N of Detroit.

Opened: 1994. **Holes:** 18. **Par:** 72/72. **Yards:** 7,018/4,937. **Course rating:** 74.1/68.5. **Slope:** 134/116. **Architect:** William Newcomb. **Green fee:** $35/$55. **Credit cards:** MC,VISA,AMEX. **Reduced fees:** Weekdays, twilight, seniors, juniors. **Caddies:** No. **Golf carts:** Included in Green Fee. **Discount golf packages:** No. **Season:** April-Dec. **High:** May-Sept. **On site lodging:** No. **Rental clubs:** Yes. **Walking policy:** Mandatory cart. **Metal spikes allowed:** Yes. **Range:** Yes (grass/mats). **To obtain tee times:** Call 7 days in advance.
Notes: 1997 U.S. Amateur Quallifying.
Subscriber comments: Great spring rate, always windy, tee times available...Needs to mature...Play it before it turns private...Resort type setting...Very upscale...Building houses too close to course...Outstanding greens...Great finishing holes...Quick play as a single, service carts on course...Fun for all levels...Every effort was made to make ladies welcome.

★★★GLADSTONE GOLF COURSE
Days River, Gladstone, 49837, Delta County, (906)428-9646.
Call club for further information.
Subscriber comments: Outstanding value. Beautiful northern course...Don't try to walk this one...Excellent condition for being so far north...The course crosses a river six times. Wide fairways with woods on either side...Narrow in places.

★★GLADWIN HEIGHTS GOLF COURSE
PU-3551 W. M-61, Gladwin, 48624, Gladwin County, (517)426-9941, 30 miles NE of Midland.
Opened: 1959. **Holes:** 18. **Par:** 71/72. **Yards:** 6,007/5,226. **Course rating:** 68.7/69.7. **Slope:** 110/112. **Architect:** N/A. **Green fee:** $13/$14. **Credit cards:** None. **Reduced fees:** Twilight, seniors. **Caddies:** No. **Golf carts:** $14. **Discount golf packages:** No. **Season:** April-Oct. **High:** July-Aug. **On site lodging:** No. **Rental clubs:** Yes. **Walking policy:** Unrestricted walking. **Metal spikes allowed:** Yes. **Range:** Yes (grass). **To obtain tee times:** First come, first served. Call ahead to see if tee times are available due to league play.

★★GLEN OAKS GOLF & COUNTRY CLUB
PM-30500 W-13 Mile Rd., Farmington Hills, 48024, Oakland County, (248)851-8356, 20 miles N of Detroit.
Opened: N/A. **Holes:** 18. **Par:** 70/70. **Yards:** 6,090/5,088. **Course rating:** 67.6/66.5. **Slope:** 114/110. **Architect:** N/A. **Green fee:** $23/$26. **Credit cards:** MC,VISA. **Reduced fees:** Weekdays, twilight, seniors, juniors. **Caddies:** No. **Golf carts:** $20. **Discount golf packages:** No. **Season:** April-Nov. **High:** May-Aug. **On site lodging:** No. **Rental clubs:** No. **Walking policy:** Unrestricted walking. **Metal spikes allowed:** No. **Range:** No. **To obtain tee times:** Call golf shop.

★★GLENBRIER GOLF COURSE
PU-Box 500, 4178 W. Locke Rd., Perry, 48872, Shiawassee County, (517)625-3800, 15 miles NE of Lansing.
Opened: 1972. **Holes:** 18. **Par:** 72/72. **Yards:** 6,310/5,245. **Course rating:** 68.4/69.4. **Slope:** 120/115. **Architect:** Bob Fink. **Green fee:** $15/$16. **Credit cards:** MC,VISA. **Reduced fees:** Weekdays, low season, twilight, seniors, juniors. **Caddies:** No. **Golf carts:** $20. **Discount golf packages:** Yes. **Season:** April-Nov. **High:** May-Aug. **On site lodging:** No. **Rental clubs:** Yes. **Walking policy:** Unrestricted walking. **Metal spikes allowed:** Yes. **Range:** Yes (grass/mats). **To obtain tee times:** Call golf shop.

★★★GLENEAGLE GOLF CLUB
PU-6150 14th Ave., Hudsonville, 49426, Ottawa County, (616)457-3680, 5 miles SW of Grand Rapids.
Opened: 1960. **Holes:** 18. **Par:** 72/72. **Yards:** 6,764/5,376. **Course rating:** 69.4/68.8. **Slope:** 125/124. **Architect:** N/A. **Green fee:** $29/$26. **Credit cards:** MC,VISA. **Reduced fees:** Low season, seniors, juniors. **Caddies:** No. **Golf carts:** $26. **Discount golf packages:** No. **Season:** April-Nov. **High:** June-Aug. **On site lodging:** No. **Rental clubs:** No. **Walking policy:** Walking at certain times. **Metal spikes allowed:** Yes. **Range:** Yes (grass/mats). **To obtain tee times:** Call at least 7 days in advance.
Subscriber comments: Some new, very challenging holes...Much improvement. Condos too close to fairways on several holes...Too tight for average

golfer...Reconstruction is making this course a good one...Rebuilt greens, very good...Improving every year.
Special Notes: Formerly Fairway Golf Club.

★★GLENHURST GOLF COURSE
PU-25345 W. 6 Mile Rd., Redford, 48240, Wayne County, (313)592-8758, 18 miles W of Detroit.
Opened: 1932. **Holes:** 18. **Par:** 70/72. **Yards:** 5,508/4,978. **Course rating:** 65.5/70.6. **Slope:** 107/115. **Architect:** Mr. McClane. **Green fee:** $11/$22. **Credit cards:** None. **Reduced fees:** Weekdays, low season, twilight, seniors, juniors. **Caddies:** No. **Golf carts:** $20. **Discount golf packages:** No. **Season:** March-Jan. **High:** June-Aug. **On site lodging:** No. **Rental clubs:** Yes. **Walking policy:** Unrestricted walking. **Metal spikes allowed:** Yes. **Range:** No. **To obtain tee times:** Tee times for weekends and holidays only. Reservations taken 7 days in advance.

GOGEBIC COUNTRY CLUB
PU-Country Club Rd., Ironwood, 49938, Gogebic County, (906)932-2515.
Opened: 1922. **Holes:** 18. **Par:** 71/72. **Yards:** 5,752/5,132. **Course rating:** 66.5/68.5. **Slope:** 109/111. **Architect:** N/A. **Green fee:** $17/$17. **Credit cards:** MC,VISA. **Reduced fees:** Twilight, juniors. **Caddies:** No. **Golf carts:** $18. **Discount golf packages:** No. **Season:** May-Oct. **High:** June-Aug. **On site lodging:** No. **Rental clubs:** Yes. **Walking policy:** Unrestricted walking. **Metal spikes allowed:** Yes. **Range:** No. **To obtain tee times:** Call up to 14 days in advance.

THE GOLF CLUB AT THORNAPPLE POINTE
R-4747 Champions Circle S.E., Grand Rapids, 49512, Kent County, (616)554-4747.
Opened: 1997. **Holes:** 18. **Par:** 72/72. **Yards:** 6,821/4,878. **Course rating:** N/A. **Slope:** N/A. **Architect:** William Newcomb. **Green fee:** $45/$60. **Credit cards:** MC,VISA,AMEX. **Reduced fees:** Weekdays, twilight. **Caddies:** No. **Golf carts:** Included in Green Fee. **Discount golf packages:** No. **Season:** April-Nov. **High:** June-Sept. **On site lodging:** No. **Rental clubs:** Yes. **Walking policy:** Unrestricted walking. **Metal spikes allowed:** No. **Range:** Yes (grass/mats). **To obtain tee times:** Call up to 30 days in advance.

★★½GOODRICH COUNTRY CLUB
PU-10080 Hegel Rd., Goodrich, 48438, Genesee County, (810)636-2493, 7 miles S of Davison.
Opened: 1970. **Holes:** 18. **Par:** 70/71. **Yards:** 5,497/4,365. **Course rating:** 66.4/65.0. **Slope:** 104/100. **Architect:** N/A. **Green fee:** $18/$22. **Credit cards:** MC,VISA. **Reduced fees:** Weekdays, low season, seniors, juniors. **Caddies:** No. **Golf carts:** $24. **Discount golf packages:** No. **Season:** April-Oct. **High:** June-Aug. **On site lodging:** No. **Rental clubs:** Yes. **Walking policy:** Walking at certain times. **Metal spikes allowed:** No. **Range:** No. **To obtain tee times:** Call in advance for weekends and holidays.
Subscriber comments: Hard greens to putt on...Has small greens, hard to score well...Short, well maintained.

GRACEWIL COUNTRY CLUB
PU-2597 Four Mile Rd. N.W., Grand Rapids, 49504, Kent County, (616)784-2455.
Opened: 1929. **Architect:** J. Morris Wilson. **Green fee:** $14/$17. **Credit cards:** MC,VISA. **Reduced fees:** Weekdays, low season, twilight, seniors, juniors. **Caddies:** No. **Golf carts:** $18. **Discount golf packages:** No. **Season:** March-Nov. **High:** June-Aug. **On site lodging:** No. **Rental clubs:** Yes. **Walking policy:** Unrestricted walking. **Metal spikes allowed:** Yes. **Range:** No. **To obtain tee times:** Call up to ten days in advance. Tee times taken on weekends only until 4 p.m.
★½EAST COURSE
Holes: 18. **Par:** 72/72. **Yards:** 6,180/5,025. **Course rating:** 69.9/71.3. **Slope:** N/A.
★½WEST COURSE
Holes: 18. **Par:** 72/72. **Yards:** 6,070/4,840. **Course rating:** 69.7/71.0. **Slope:** N/A.

★★½GRACEWIL PINES GOLF CLUB
PU-5400 Trailer Park Dr., Jackson, 49201, Jackson County, (517)764-4200, 20 miles N of Lansing.
Opened: 1984. **Holes:** 18. **Par:** 72/72. **Yards:** 6,170/4,405. **Course rating:** N/A. **Slope:**

N/A. **Architect:** Morris Wilson. **Green fee:** $10/$13. **Credit cards:** VISA. **Reduced fees:** Weekdays, low season, twilight, seniors, juniors. **Caddies:** No. **Golf carts:** $18. **Discount golf packages:** Yes. **Season:** March-Nov. **High:** May-Aug. **On site lodging:** No. **Rental clubs:** Yes. **Walking policy:** Unrestricted walking. **Metal spikes allowed:** Yes. **Range:** No. **To obtain tee times:** Call golf shop.

Subscriber comments: Fun course to play and very cheap...Tight, lots of trees...Has the potential to be great...Don't believe what others say, it's a challenge...Priced right...Staff is very welcoming, plenty of golf cars and always a tee time...Nice course, but very busy.

GRAND BLANC GOLF & COUNTRY CLUB
PU-5270 Perry Rd., Grand Blanc, 48439, Genesee County, (810)694-5960, 7 miles S of Flint.
Caddies: No. **Discount golf packages:** No. **On site lodging:** No.
★★NORTH COURSE
Opened: 1997. **Holes:** 18. **Par:** 72/72. **Yards:** 7,023/5,471. **Course rating:** 73.5/71.0. **Slope:** 122/118. **Architect:** Ron Lenard/Joe Roeski. **Green fee:** $20/$23. **Credit cards:** MC,VISA. **Reduced fees:** Twilight, seniors, juniors. **Golf carts:** $20. **Season:** Year-round weather permitting. **High:** May-Sept. **Rental clubs:** Yes. **Walking policy:** Walking at certain times. **Metal spikes allowed:** Yes. **Range:** Yes (grass). **To obtain tee times:** Call up to 7 days in advance.
★★SOUTH COURSE
Opened: 1970. **Holes:** 18. **Par:** 72/74. **Yards:** 6,545/5,774. **Course rating:** 71.0/72.8. **Slope:** 122/120. **Architect:** Bruce and Jerry Matthews. **Green fee:** $20/$23. **Credit cards:** MC,VISA. **Reduced fees:** Twilight, seniors, juniors. **Golf carts:** $20. **Season:** Year-round weather permitting. **High:** May-Sept. **Rental clubs:** Yes. **Walking policy:** Unrestricted walking. **Metal spikes allowed:** No. **Range:** Yes (grass). **To obtain tee times:** Call up to 7 days in advance.

★★★½GRAND HAVEN GOLF CLUB
17000 Lincoln St., Grand Haven, 49417, Ottawa County, (616)842-4040, (888)657-8821, 28 miles E of Grand Rapids.
Opened: 1965. **Holes:** 18. **Par:** 72/72. **Yards:** 6,725/5,256. **Course rating:** 73.3/70.6. **Slope:** 134/122. **Architect:** W. Bruce Matthews and Jerry Matthews. **Green fee:** $24/$34. **Credit cards:** MC,VISA. **Reduced fees:** Weekdays, low season, twilight, seniors, juniors. **Caddies:** No. **Golf carts:** $11. **Discount golf packages:** No. **Season:** March-Nov. **High:** June-Aug. **On site lodging:** No. **Rental clubs:** Yes. **Walking policy:** Unrestricted walking. **Metal spikes allowed:** Yes. **Range:** Yes (grass/mats). **To obtain tee times:** Call anytime in advance for weekdays. Call up to 7 days in advance for weekend.

Subscriber comments: Many scenic holes...Very tight. Always a challenge...A little overpriced...A hidden gem, fun to play, not crowded on weekends...A once a year course, no rough...Great greens, so so fairways...Sometimes overlooked because of all the new courses. But this is just a beautiful old golf course, a must play.

★★½GRAND HOTEL GOLF CLUB
R-Mackinac Island, Mackinac Island, 49757, Mackinac County, (906)847-3331, 250 miles N of Detroit.
Opened: 1911. **Holes:** 18. **Par:** 67/67. **Yards:** 5,415/4,212. **Course rating:** 65.7. **Slope:** 110/106. **Architect:** Jerry Matthews. **Green fee:** $75/$75. **Credit cards:** MC,VISA,AMEX. **Reduced fees:** N/A. **Caddies:** No. **Golf carts:** Included in Green Fee. **Discount golf packages:** No. **Season:** May-Oct. **High:** June-Aug. **On site lodging:** No. **Rental clubs:** No. **Walking policy:** Unrestricted walking. **Metal spikes allowed:** Yes. **Range:** No. **To obtain tee times:** Call.

Subscriber comments: Beautiful in summer. "Does it get better?"...Pricey due to location...Kind of a neat atmosphere...Great course to spend a fall afternoon...Magnificent views and excellent golf...Need to install watering in fairways. Prices are grand, the golf good...Part of Grand Hotel...The view is the highlight, short holes...New back nine is very good test...Some unfair holes from blue tees (1 and 3).

★½GRAND ISLAND GOLF RANCH
PU-6266 W. River Dr., Belmont, 49306, Kent County, (616)363-1262, 10 miles SW of Grand Rapids.

Opened: 1965. **Holes:** 18. **Par:** 72/73. **Yards:** 6,266/5,522. **Course rating:** 71.9/71.4. **Slope:** 124/119. **Architect:** Floyd Brunsink/Jerry Brunsink. **Green fee:** $17/$18. **Credit cards:** MC,VISA,DISC. **Reduced fees:** Low season, seniors, juniors. **Caddies:** No. **Golf carts:** $18. **Discount golf packages:** Yes. **Season:** March-Dec. **High:** May-Sept. **On site lodging:** No. **Rental clubs:** Yes. **Walking policy:** Unrestricted walking. **Metal spikes allowed:** Yes. **Range:** Yes (grass/mats). **To obtain tee times:** Call 7 days in advance.

★★GRAND LEDGE COUNTRY CLUB
5811 St Joe Rd., Grand Ledge, 48837, Eaton County, (517)627-2495.
Opened: 1958. **Holes:** 18. **Par:** N/A. **Yards:** N/A. **Course rating:** 70.2/66.5. **Slope:** 116/111. **Architect:** Steve Lipkowitz. **Green fee:** $19/$21. **Credit cards:** MC,VISA. **Reduced fees:** Low season. **Caddies:** No. **Golf carts:** $20. **Discount golf packages:** No. **Season:** April-Nov. **High:** June-Aug. **On site lodging:** No. **Rental clubs:** Yes. **Walking policy:** N/A. **Metal spikes allowed:** Yes. **Range:** Yes (grass). **To obtain tee times:** Call up to 3 days in advance.

★★GRAND RAPIDS GOLF CLUB
PU-4300 Leonard N.E., Grand Rapids, 49525, Kent County, (616)949-2820, (800)709-1100, 5 miles E of Grand Rapids.
Opened: 1969. **Holes:** 27. **Architect:** N/A. **Green fee:** $18/$20. **Credit cards:** MC,VISA. **Reduced fees:** Weekdays, low season, twilight, seniors, juniors. **Caddies:** No. **Golf carts:** $20. **Discount golf packages:** No. **Season:** March-Nov. **High:** May-Aug. **On site lodging:** No. **Rental clubs:** Yes. **Walking policy:** Unrestricted walking. **Range:** Yes (grass/mats). **To obtain tee times:** Call golf shop.
RED/BLUE
Par: 70/71. **Yards:** 5,887/4,582. **Course rating:** 68.5/66.2. **Slope:** 107/103. **Metal spikes allowed:** No.
RED/WHITE
Par: 72/73. **Yards:** 6,127/4,926. **Course rating:** 70.3/68.9. **Slope:** 116/112. **Metal spikes allowed:** Yes.
WHITE/BLUE
Par: 72/72. **Yards:** 6,194/4,854. **Course rating:** 69.8/67.9. **Slope:** 116/110. **Metal spikes allowed:** Yes.

GRAND TRAVERSE RESORT
R-6300 U.S. 31 N., Acme, 49610, Grand Traverse County, (616)938-1620, (800)748-0303, 6 miles NE of Traverse City.
Credit cards: All major,Diners Club, JCB. **Reduced fees:** Weekdays, low season, resort guests, twilight. **Caddies:** No. **Golf carts:** Included in Green Fee. **Discount golf packages:** Yes. **Season:** April-Oct. **High:** June-Aug. **On site lodging:** Yes. **Rental clubs:** Yes. **Walking policy:** Mandatory cart. **Metal spikes allowed:** Yes. **Range:** Yes (grass).

(GOOD SERVICE)

★★★½SPRUCE RUN COURSE
Opened: 1979. **Holes:** 18. **Par:** 71/72. **Yards:** 6,579/4,973. **Course rating:** 73.7/69.2. **Slope:** 137/116. **Architect:** William Newcomb. **Green fee:** $42/$87. **To obtain tee times:** Hotel guests may reserve tee times with room confirmation. Public may call 7 days in advance.
Subscriber comments: Well maintained resort course...Tough but very playable...Great for all abilities and genders...Very playable alternative to the Bear...One of best courses in area, I play it every week...Nice course not as high priced as the Bear...Always in mint condition...Very playable, great condition.

★★★★THE BEAR
Opened: 1985. **Holes:** 18. **Par:** 72/72. **Yards:** 7,065/5,281. **Course rating:** 75.8/72.0. **Slope:** 149/131. **Architect:** Jack Nicklaus. **Green fee:** $62/$113. **To obtain tee times:** Hotel guests may reserve tee times with room reservation. Public may call 7 days in advance.
Notes: Ranked 21st in 1997 Best in State.
Subscriber comments: Tough, tough, but a lot of fun on a very well maintained course, super condition. Staff a delight...Best in the north...Earlier Jack design...Best course in Michigan! Better than some of the best private clubs...Don't play on a windy day, need lots of balls...First class, expensive and very tough on a 12 handicapper but worth it...Not for the weak at heart...I liked the "Fast Play Incentive" discounts.

MICHIGAN

★★★½GRAND VIEW GOLF COURSE
PU-5464 S. 68th Ave., New Era, 49446, Oceana County, (616)861-6616, 20 miles N of Muskegon.
Opened: 1993. **Holes:** 18. **Par:** 71/71. **Yards:** 6,258/4,737. **Course rating:** 69.5/66.7. **Slope:** 120/130. **Architect:** David Goerbig. **Green fee:** $15/$17. **Credit cards:** MC,VISA,DISC. **Reduced fees:** Weekdays, seniors. **Caddies:** No. **Golf carts:** $18. **Discount golf packages:** No. **Season:** April-Oct. **High:** June-Aug. **On site lodging:** No. **Rental clubs:** Yes. **Walking policy:** Unrestricted walking. **Metal spikes allowed:** Yes. **Range:** Yes (grass). **To obtain tee times:** Call ahead. Tee times recommended.
Subscriber comments: Great course for the money...The name fits "Grand view"...Best value for the dollar...A must play...Great course with much variety...One of the best buys in Michigan...Always in excellent condition...Fun course, affordable, challenging, extremely well maintained...A real sleeper.

★★★GRANDVIEW GOLF CLUB
PU-3003 Hagni Rd., Kalkaska, 49646, Kalkaska County, (616)258-3244, 30 miles E of Traverse City.
Opened: 1993. **Holes:** 18. **Par:** 71/71. **Yards:** 6,528/4,864. **Course rating:** 72.2/68.4. **Slope:** 133/122. **Architect:** N/A. **Green fee:** $15/$30. **Credit cards:** MC,VISA. **Reduced fees:** Weekdays, low season, twilight, seniors, juniors. **Caddies:** No. **Golf carts:** $12. **Discount golf packages:** No. **Season:** May-Oct. **High:** June-Aug. **On site lodging:** No. **Rental clubs:** Yes. **Walking policy:** Unrestricted walking. **Metal spikes allowed:** Yes. **Range:** Yes (grass/mats). **To obtain tee times:** Call.
Subscriber comments: God made Grandview. It's gorgeous!...Great golf for the price...First four holes quirky, rest of course two thumbs up...Great fun, great shape, a challenge...Not difficult but interesting...Best kept secret in northern Michigan...Going to be great...Fantastic value.

★★½GRAYLING COUNTRY CLUB
Business I-75 S., Grayling, 49738, Crawford County, (517)348-5618, 25 miles S of Gaylord.
Opened: 1923. **Holes:** 18. **Par:** 70/70. **Yards:** 5,800/4,609. **Course rating:** 67.0/66.0. **Slope:** 115/110. **Architect:** N/A. **Green fee:** $10/$20. **Credit cards:** All major. **Reduced fees:** Low season, seniors, juniors. **Caddies:** No. **Golf carts:** $12. **Discount golf packages:** No. **Season:** April-Oct. **High:** June-Aug. **On site lodging:** No. **Rental clubs:** Yes. **Walking policy:** Unrestricted walking. **Metal spikes allowed:** Yes. **Range:** Yes (grass). **To obtain tee times:** Call in advance.
Subscriber comments: I loved the 95-yard par 3...Nice course, nice people...Mostly open, forgiving...The best hole is the 18th hole...Scenery is fantastic. Well maintained course...Everyone feels welcome at Grayling...Cheap fun!

★★GREEN ACRES GOLF COURSE
PU-7323 Dixie Hwy, Bridgeport, 48722, Saginaw County, (517)777-3510, 6 miles S of Saginaw.
Opened: 1957. **Holes:** 18. **Par:** 72/72. **Yards:** 6,400/6,100. **Course rating:** 72.0/69.1. **Slope:** 113/115. **Architect:** N/A. **Green fee:** N/A. **Credit cards:** MC,VISA. **Reduced fees:** N/A. **Caddies:** No. **Golf carts:** $20. **Discount golf packages:** No. **Season:** April-Nov. **High:** June-Aug. **On site lodging:** No. **Rental clubs:** Yes. **Walking policy:** Unrestricted walking. **Metal spikes allowed:** Yes. **Range:** Yes (grass). **To obtain tee times:** Call.

★★½GREEN HILLS GOLF CLUB
PU-1699 N M-13, Pinconning, 48650, Bay County, (517)697-3011, 10 miles N of Bay City.
Opened: 1971. **Holes:** 18. **Par:** 71. **Yards:** 6,000. **Course rating:** 67.1. **Slope:** 112. **Architect:** N/A. **Green fee:** $18/$20. **Credit cards:** MC,VISA,DISC. **Reduced fees:** Seniors. **Caddies:** No. **Golf carts:** $20. **Discount golf packages:** No. **Season:** March-Nov. **High:** June-Sept. **On site lodging:** No. **Rental clubs:** Yes. **Walking policy:** Unrestricted walking. **Metal spikes allowed:** Yes. **Range:** No. **To obtain tee times:** Call up to 4 days in advance for weekends during summer.
Subscriber comments: Always in good shape. Nice little course...Family business for

years, treat golfers well...Decent course, good greens...Easy course...Decent average course...Course is short but decent, service is poor...Easy scoring course...Always working to improve...Needs better management...Pricey for what you get, near 600-yard par 5...Nice course to have a scramble, good dining.

★★GREEN MEADOWS GOLF COURSE
PU-1555 Strasburg Rd., Monroe, 48161, Monroe County, (313)242-5566, 35 miles S of Detroit.
Opened: 1973. **Holes:** 18. **Par:** 70/70. **Yards:** 6,448/5,310. **Course rating:** 69.2/68.6. **Slope:** 107/105. **Architect:** N/A. **Green fee:** $18/$22. **Credit cards:** MC,VISA,DISC. **Reduced fees:** Seniors, juniors. **Caddies:** No. **Golf carts:** $10. **Discount golf packages:** No. **Season:** Year-round. **High:** June-Sept. **On site lodging:** No. **Rental clubs:** No. **Walking policy:** Unrestricted walking. **Metal spikes allowed:** Yes. **Range:** No. **To obtain tee times:** Call up to 7 days in advance for weekends & holidays.

★★½GREEN OAKS GOLF COURSE
PM-1775 Clark Rd., Ypsilanti, 48241, Washtenaw County, (313)485-0881, 8 miles E of Ann Arbor.
Opened: 1970. **Holes:** 18. **Par:** 71/71. **Yards:** 6,500/6,000. **Course rating:** 69.5/70.1. **Slope:** 121/123. **Architect:** N/A. **Green fee:** $10/$21. **Credit cards:** MC,VISA. **Reduced fees:** Weekdays, resort guests. **Caddies:** No. **Golf carts:** $20. **Discount golf packages:** No. **Season:** March-Dec. **High:** July. **On site lodging:** No. **Rental clubs:** No. **Walking policy:** Unrestricted walking. **Metal spikes allowed:** Yes. **Range:** No. **To obtain tee times:** Call up to 7 days in advance.
Subscriber comments: A very average course...Course OK, management very accommodating...Best course in area to play after rain, great run off...Nice public course...One of my favorites...Good service...Always playable. Dry when others are unplayable...Fair test, back nine more demanding...Easy to get on; can help your score...Well maintained muny, good value.

GREEN VALLEY GOLF CLUB
PU-25379 W. Fawn River Rd., Rt. 4, Sturgis, 49091, St. Joseph County, (616)651-6331.
Opened: 1970. **Holes:** 9. **Par:** 68/71. **Yards:** 5,355/5,053. **Course rating:** 66.5/67.5. **Slope:** N/A. **Architect:** N/A. **Green fee:** N/A. **Credit cards:** N/A. **Reduced fees:** N/A. **Caddies:** No. **Golf carts:** $18. **Discount golf packages:** No. **Season:** March-Oct. **High:** June-Aug. **On site lodging:** No. **Rental clubs:** No. **Walking policy:** Unrestricted walking. **Metal spikes allowed:** Yes. **Range:** No. **To obtain tee times:** Call.

★★★GREEN VALLEY GOLF COURSE
PU-5751 Brooklyn Rd., Jackson, 49201, Jackson County, (517)764-0270, 10 miles E of Jackson.
Opened: 1959. **Holes:** 18. **Par:** 70/70. **Yards:** 6,035/5,000. **Course rating:** 70.3. **Slope:** N/A. **Architect:** N/A. **Green fee:** $14/$16. **Credit cards:** MC,VISA,DISC. **Reduced fees:** Low season, seniors, juniors. **Caddies:** No. **Golf carts:** $20. **Discount golf packages:** No. **Season:** April-Oct. **High:** June-Aug. **On site lodging:** No. **Rental clubs:** Yes. **Walking policy:** Unrestricted walking. **Metal spikes allowed:** Yes. **Range:** Yes (grass/mats). **To obtain tee times:** Call golf shop.
Subscriber comments: Front open and short, back long, tight...Lots of sand makes holes fun...The best hole is the 10th hole...Some easy holes, one great hole...Good value. Challenging holes...Well kept, closes too early...Good cheap golf.

★★GREENBRIAR GOLF COURSE
9350 N Lapeer Rd., Mayville, 48744, Tuscola County, (517)843-6575.
Call club for further information.

★★GREENBRIER GOLF COURSE
14820 Wellwood Rd., Brooklyn, 49230, Jackson County, (313)646-6657.
Call club for further information.

★★★½GREYSTONE GOLF CLUB
PU-67500 Mound Rd., Romeo, 48095, Macomb County, (810)752-7030, 15 miles NE of Troy.
Opened: 1992. **Holes:** 18. **Par:** 72/71. **Yards:** 6,861/4,816. **Course rating:** 73.6/68.5.

Slope: 132/113. **Architect:** Jerry Matthews. **Green fee:** $45/$50. **Credit cards:** All major. **Reduced fees:** Low season, twilight, seniors, juniors. **Caddies:** No. **Golf carts:** Included in Green Fee. **Discount golf packages:** No. **Season:** April-Nov. **High:** June-Aug. **On site lodging:** No. **Rental clubs:** Yes. **Walking policy:** Mandatory cart. **Metal spikes allowed:** Yes. **Range:** Yes (grass/mats). **To obtain tee times:** Call for tee times 7 days in advance. More than 7 days a deposit is required.

Subscriber comments: A real test, especially 16, 17 & 18...Service was wonderful but course is overrated as far as conditions are concerned...Best three finishing holes in Michigan...Always in good shape...Fast greens, great layout...Very tough. This course makes you use all your clubs...Always enjoyable, great layout, expensive but worth it...Can be a bit slow at times.

★★★GROESBECK MUNICIPAL GOLF COURSE

PM-1600 Ormond Ave., Lansing, 48906, Ingham County, (517)483-4232.
Opened: 1927. **Holes:** 18. **Par:** 72/72. **Yards:** 6,710/4,600. **Course rating:** N/A. **Slope:** N/A. **Architect:** Jack Darcy. **Green fee:** $18/$22. **Credit cards:** None. **Reduced fees:** Twilight, seniors, juniors. **Caddies:** No. **Golf carts:** $20. **Discount golf packages:** No. **Season:** April-Nov. **High:** N/A. **On site lodging:** No. **Rental clubs:** Yes. **Walking policy:** Unrestricted walking. **Metal spikes allowed:** Yes. **Range:** No. **To obtain tee times:** Call up to 7 days in advance.

(GOOD VALUE)

Subscriber comments: For the money-best around...City owned, well maintained...Being reworked during 1997...The best golf value in Lansing area...Excellent course for a muny. Comparable with the best...Nice, fair older muny. Tough to locate...Best city course west of Detroit, nothing compares for value.

GULL LAKE VIEW GOLF CLUB

PU-7417 N. 38th St., Augusta, 49012, Kalamazoo County, (616)731-4148, 15 miles NE of Kalamazoo.
Opened: 1963. **Architect:** Darl Scott. **Green fee:** $28/$32. **Credit cards:** MC,VISA. **Reduced fees:** Weekdays, low season, resort guests, twilight, juniors. **Caddies:** No. **Golf carts:** $24. **Discount golf packages:** Yes. **Season:** April-Nov. **High:** May-Aug. **On site lodging:** Yes. **Rental clubs:** Yes. **Walking policy:** Walking at certain times. **Metal spikes allowed:** Yes. **Range:** No. **To obtain tee times:** Call golf shop.

★★★½EAST COURSE

Holes: 18. **Par:** 70/70. **Yards:** 6,002/4,918. **Course rating:** 69.4/68.5. **Slope:** 124/118.
Subscriber comments: Good course for shotmaking. (Take the driver out of bag)...Short, scoreable, but bring your straight game...Gorgeous!...Real value...Very sporty short course...Some good par 4s...Best course layout in the area...Play green tees to enjoy views...Very hilly, must ride...Best value golf resort in lower Michigan.

★★★½WEST COURSE

Holes: 18. **Par:** 71/72. **Yards:** 6,300/5,218. **Course rating:** 70.6/69.0. **Slope:** 123/114.
Subscriber comments: A very fun course to play...Good resort style. Back is more interesting...Excellent shape for the amount of play...One of the best complexes in this country...Challenging and well maintained.

HAMPSHIRE COUNTRY CLUB

29592 Pokagon Hwy., Dowagiac, 49047, Cass County, (616)782-7476, 18 miles N of South Bend, IN.
Opened: 1962. **Architect:** Edward Packard. **Green fee:** $16/$18. **Credit cards:** MC,VISA. **Reduced fees:** Weekdays, twilight, juniors. **Caddies:** No. **Golf carts:** $20. **Discount golf packages:** Yes. **Season:** April-Nov. **High:** June-Aug. **On site lodging:** No. **Rental clubs:** Yes. **Walking policy:** Unrestricted walking. **Metal spikes allowed:** Yes. **Range:** No. **To obtain tee times:** Call up to 7 days in advance.

★★★ HAMPSHIRE COUNTRY CLUB

Holes: 18. **Par:** 72/75. **Yards:** 7,030/6,185. **Course rating:** 72.6/73.0. **Slope:** 120.
Subscriber comments: Long!...Excellent course...Far superior to new 18...Worth going out of your way to play...Recently expanded to 36 holes, great value...Original 18 strong, wooded course, good value...Quality golf at bargain prices...Excellent back nine on original course...Very good course for the money.

DOGWOOD TRAIL

Holes: 18. **Par:** 72. **Yards:** 6,795. **Course rating:** 71.8. **Slope:** 122.

★★★HARBOR POINT GOLF COURSE
M-119 Lower Shore Dr., Harbor Springs, 49740, Emmet County, (616)526-2951.
Call club for further information.
Subscriber comments: Delightful course to play, plenty of room...A fun, walkable old style layout. Great for couples golf...Spectacular views, fast greens...A fun place, lots of history...Old course, postage-stamp greens. Great views.

HARTLAND GLEN GOLF & COUNTRY CLUB
PU-12400 Highland Rd., Hartland, 48353, Livingston County, (248)887-3777, 25 miles N of Ann Arbor.
Architect: G. Duke/K. Sustic/R. Boyt. **Green fee:** $16/$25. **Credit cards:** None.
Reduced fees: Weekdays, low season, twilight, seniors, juniors. **Caddies:** No. **Golf carts:** $10. **Discount golf packages:** No. **Season:** April-Oct. **High:** June-Aug. **On site lodging:** No. **Rental clubs:** Yes. **Walking policy:** Unrestricted walking. **Metal spikes allowed:** Yes. **To obtain tee times:** Call 7 days in advance.
★★NORTH COURSE
Opened: 1972. **Holes:** 18. **Par:** 72/72. **Yards:** 6,280/5,109. **Course rating:** 67.6/67.8.
Slope: 107/105. **Range:** Yes (grass/mats).
★★SOUTH COURSE
Opened: 1992. **Holes:** 18. **Par:** 71/71. **Yards:** 6,175/4,661. **Course rating:** N/A. **Slope:** N/A. **Range:** Yes (grass).

★★★HASTINGS COUNTRY CLUB
1550 N Broadway, Hastings, 49058, Barry County, (616)945-2756, 20 miles N of Battle Creek.
Opened: 1921. **Holes:** 18. **Par:** 72/73. **Yards:** 6,331/6,201. **Course rating:** 71.0/71.5.
Slope: 121/118. **Architect:** N/A. **Green fee:** $25/$25. **Credit cards:** MC,VISA.
Reduced fees: N/A. **Caddies:** No. **Golf carts:** $20. **Discount golf packages:** No.
Season: April-Oct. **High:** May-Aug. **On site lodging:** No. **Rental clubs:** Yes. **Walking policy:** Unrestricted walking. **Metal spikes allowed:** Yes. **Range:** Yes (grass). **To obtain tee times:** Call golf shop.
Subscriber comments: Poor maintenance but nice layout with potential...Good buy...Fun course; needs watering and better upkeep.

★★★HAWK HOLLOW GOLF CLUB - EAST/NORTH/WEST
PU-1501 Chandler Rd., Bath, 48808, Clinton County, (517)641-4295, (888)411-4295.
Opened: 1996. **Holes:** 27. **Architect:** Jerry Matthews. **Caddies:** No. **Discount golf packages:** No. **On site lodging:** No. **Rental clubs:** No. **Metal spikes allowed:** Yes.
Range: No.
Call club for further information.
Subscriber comments: Par 3s are killers...Probably the best mid-Michigan course...One of the finest new courses in Michigan...Remarkable greens for new course...Gorgeous. Best course I ever played...Expensive...Feels like Myrtle Beach...Tight, but not long...Still new. Will be an excellent course with maturity.

★★★HAWKSHEAD GOLF LINKS
PU-6959 105th Ave., South Haven, 49090, Allegan County, (616)639-2121, 25 miles S of Holland.
Opened: 1997. **Holes:** 18. **Par:** 72/72. **Yards:** 7,050/5,085. **Course rating:** N/A. **Slope:** N/A. **Architect:** Arthur Hills. **Green fee:** $23/$44. **Credit cards:** All major. **Reduced fees:** Weekdays, low season, resort guests, twilight. **Caddies:** No. **Golf carts:** $12.
Discount golf packages: Yes. **Season:** April-Oct. **High:** June-Sept. **On site lodging:** Yes. **Rental clubs:** Yes. **Walking policy:** Unrestricted walking. **Metal spikes allowed:** Yes. **Range:** Yes (grass). **To obtain tee times:** Call up to 6 days in advance.
Subscriber comments: New course, fairways need to mature but excellent layout...Excellent practice facilities...A must play from the blues. Unexpected links course...Good now should be great soon. Several holes have huge sandy waste areas.

★★★HEATHER HIGHLANDS GOLF CLUB
PU-11450 E. Holly Rd., Holly, 48442, Oakland County, (248)634-6800, 50 miles NW of Detroit.
Opened: 1966. **Holes:** 18. **Par:** 72/72. **Yards:** 6,845/5,764. **Course rating:** 72.6/73.4.

Slope: 124/122. **Architect:** Robert Bruce Harris. **Green fee:** $20/$28. **Credit cards:** MC,VISA. **Reduced fees:** Low season. **Caddies:** No. **Golf carts:** $20. **Discount golf packages:** Yes. **Season:** April-Nov. **High:** May-Sept. **On site lodging:** No. **Rental clubs:** Yes. **Walking policy:** Walking at certain times. **Metal spikes allowed:** Yes. **Range:** Yes (grass/mats). **To obtain tee times:** Call 6 days in advance.
Subscriber comments: Best public course in the area...Good value...Best greens around...Great golf, fast pace, and fantastic shape...Tight, great greens. Excellent golf course...Outstanding for outings...Better than it looks from the clubhouse...Good course conditions, a little higher priced...Best public course in Michigan for the money.
Special Notes: Also 9-hole par-31 course.

★★★HEATHER HILLS GOLF COURSE

PU-3100 McKail Rd., Romeo, 48065, Macomb County, (810)798-3971, 17 miles N of Rochester.
Opened: 1980. **Holes:** 18. **Par:** 71/71. **Yards:** 6,282/5,029. **Course rating:** 69.7/68.5.
Slope: 118/114. **Architect:** N/A. **Green fee:** $20/$24. **Credit cards:** MC,VISA,DISC.
Reduced fees: Low season, twilight, seniors, juniors. **Caddies:** No. **Golf carts:** $20.
Discount golf packages: Yes. **Season:** April-Oct. **High:** June-Sept. **On site lodging:** No. **Rental clubs:** No. **Walking policy:** Unrestricted walking. **Metal spikes allowed:** Yes. **Range:** Yes (grass). **To obtain tee times:** Call golf shop up to 7 days in advance.
Subscriber comments: A hidden gem...Great layout and value...Nice elevation change, tight fairways, U.S. Open rough, no traps...Needs sand and better greens...Fun for hackers...Difficult to walk...Excellent course,not well known...Very rural setting, blast away type course with rolling terrain...Moderately priced.

★★★½HERITAGE GLEN GOLF CLUB

PU-29795 Heritage Lane, Paw Paw, 49079, Van Buren County, (616)657-2552, 10 miles SW of Kalamazoo.
Opened: 1994. **Holes:** 18. **Par:** 72/72. **Yards:** 6,598/4,946. **Course rating:** 70.1/68.4.
Slope: N/A. **Architect:** Jerry Matthews. **Green fee:** $22/$26. **Credit cards:** MC,VISA.
Reduced fees: Weekdays, low season, twilight, seniors, juniors. **Caddies:** No. **Golf carts:** $13. **Discount golf packages:** Yes. **Season:** April-Nov. **High:** May-Sept. **On site lodging:** No. **Rental clubs:** Yes. **Walking policy:** Unrestricted walking. **Metal spikes allowed:** Yes. **Range:** Yes (grass). **To obtain tee times:** Call anytime.
Subscriber comments: My favorite Michigan course for the money...Don't be lulled to sleep by easy early holes...A new course that already has character. Good layout with variety and challenge from the tips...A real gem...Brace yourself for the monster par 5s...Play it in the fall...Beautiful facilities...Best course in southwest Michigan.

★★★HICKORY HILLS GOLF CLUB - RED/WHITE/BLUE

2540 Parview Dr., Jackson, 49201, Jackson County, (517)750-3636.
Holes: 27. **Caddies:** No. **Discount golf packages:** No. **On site lodging:** No. **Rental clubs:** No. **Metal spikes allowed:** Yes. **Range:** No.
Call club for further information.
Subscriber comments: Could be in better shape, nice terrain...Very busy which makes it hard to play...Absolutely beautiful course!...Best deal in Jackson county...27 holes, good selection...Very nice and challenging course, great staff...Challenging. Right amount of sand and water...Can be marshy in spots.

★½HICKORY HOLLOW GOLF COURSE

PU-49001 North Ave., Macomb, 48043, Macomb County, (810)949-9033, 21 miles N of Detroit.
Opened: 1963. **Holes:** 18. **Par:** 73/73. **Yards:** 6,384/5,220. **Course rating:** 70.1/68.9.
Slope: 116/116. **Architect:** N/A. **Green fee:** $18/$21. **Credit cards:** MC,VISA.
Reduced fees: Seniors. **Caddies:** No. **Golf carts:** $11. **Discount golf packages:** No.
Season: March-Nov. **High:** June-Aug. **On site lodging:** No. **Rental clubs:** Yes.
Walking policy: Unrestricted walking. **Metal spikes allowed:** Yes. **Range:** No. **To obtain tee times:** Call up to 7 days in advance.

★★HICKORY KNOLL GOLF COURSE

7945 Old Channel Trail, Montague, 48042, Muskegon County, (616)894-5535.
Call club for further information.
Subscriber comments: Good for beginners but very crowded...Inexpensive...Probably the best value for the money in the county...No frills, inexpensive golf on decent course...A real bargain, but play is heavy and slow.

HIDDEN VALLEY COLLECTION OF GREAT GOLF

R- **Credit cards:** All major. **Caddies:** No. **Golf carts:** Included in Green Fee. **Discount golf packages:** Yes. **High:** June-Sept. **Metal spikes allowed:** Yes. **Range:** Yes (grass).

★★★½THE LOON

4400 Championship Dr., Gaylord, 49735, Otsego County, (517)732-4454, (888)875-2954, 55 miles NE of Traverse City.
Opened: 1994. **Holes:** 18. **Par:** 71/71. **Yards:** 6,701/5,123. **Course rating:** 72.7/71.1. **Slope:** 128/121. **Architect:** Mike Husby. **Green fee:** $35/$75. **Reduced fees:** Low season, resort guests, twilight. **Season:** April-Sept. **On site lodging:** No. **Rental clubs:** Yes. **Walking policy:** Walking at certain times. **To obtain tee times:** Call 7 days in advance.
Subscriber comments: Good course but overpriced for the area...The stay and play packages are an excellent value...Good test of game...A strategic golf course, need to have accurate tee shots, needs time to mature...Need to have course guide to play...Good condition...Unique/tough layout worth 200-mile trip...Getting overpriced.

★★★THE CLASSIC

P.O. Box 556, Gaylord, 49735, Otsego County, (517)732-4653, (888)875-2954, 60 miles NE of Traverse City.
Opened: 1958. **Holes:** 18. **Par:** 71/71. **Yards:** 6,305/5,591. **Course rating:** N/A. **Slope:** 121/113. **Architect:** William H. Diddel. **Green fee:** $25/$59. **Reduced fees:** Weekdays, low season, resort guests, twilight. **Season:** April-Oct. **On site lodging:** Yes. **Rental clubs:** No. **Walking policy:** Unrestricted walking. **To obtain tee times:** Call up to 7 days in advance.
Subscriber comments: I had to hit driver on some of the par 3s...Beautiful vistas and challenging holes...Good facilities. Group of three courses...Very playable...Nice golf package...Greens and fairways are excellent...Good course, with a lot of sand but not very long...Good buy especially for twilight play...Pleasant resort course.

★★★½THE LAKE

1535 Opal Lake Rd., Gaylord, 49375, Otsego County, (517)732-4653, (888)875-2954, 45 miles NE of Traverse City.
Opened: N/A. **Holes:** 18. **Par:** 71/71. **Yards:** 6,310/4,952. **Course rating:** 71.0/68.5. **Slope:** 136/122. **Architect:** Jerry Matthews. **Green fee:** $59. **Credit cards:** MC,VISA. **Reduced fees:** Weekdays, low season, resort guests, twilight. **Season:** April-Oct. **On site lodging:** Yes. **Rental clubs:** No. **Walking policy:** Unrestricted walking. **To obtain tee times:** Call up to 7 days in advance.
Subscriber comments: Beautiful northern course, elevated tees, excellent conditions...The stay and play packages are an excellent value...Better value than most in Gaylord...Just like the name, plenty of water, but not enough to frustrate your game...Tough, especially first four holes...Terrific routing provides for scenic privacy.
Special Notes: Formerly Michaywe Hills Golf Club.

★★★½HIGH POINTE GOLF CLUB

PU-5555 Arnold Rd., Williamsburg, 49690, Grand Traverse County, (616)267-9900, (800)753-7888, 10 miles NE of Traverse City.
Opened: 1989. **Holes:** 18. **Par:** 71/72. **Yards:** 6,849/5,101. **Course rating:** 72.9/69.6. **Slope:** 135/121. **Architect:** Tom Doak. **Green fee:** $27/$50. **Credit cards:** All major. **Reduced fees:** Weekdays, low season, resort guests, twilight, juniors. **Caddies:** No. **Golf carts:** $15. **Discount golf packages:** Yes. **Season:** April-Oct. **High:** June-Aug. **On site lodging:** No. **Rental clubs:** Yes. **Walking policy:** Unrestricted walking. **Metal spikes allowed:** Yes. **Range:** Yes (grass). **To obtain tee times:** Call. Credit card may be required for advanced tee times and groups.
Subscriber comments: Like two courses, front links, back target...Best twilight value in Michigan...I drive past "The Bear" to get to this beauty...Greens need

improvement...Underrated by those who don't like natural golf...Twice as good as any course in the area. Great value.

★★HIGHLAND GOLF CLUB
3011 U.S. 2-41, Escanaba, 49829, Delta County, (906)466-7457, 90 miles N of Green Bay, WI.
Opened: 1930. **Holes:** 18. **Par:** 71/72. **Yards:** 6,237/5,499. **Course rating:** 69.3/71.0.
Slope: 117/115. **Architect:** Merrill Maissack, Reinhold Bittnor. **Green fee:** $11/$20.
Credit cards: MC,VISA. **Reduced fees:** N/A. **Caddies:** No. **Golf carts:** $20. **Discount golf packages:** No. **Season:** April-Oct. **High:** June-Aug. **On site lodging:** No. **Rental clubs:** Yes. **Walking policy:** Unrestricted walking. **Metal spikes allowed:** No. **Range:** No. **To obtain tee times:** Call 3 days in advance.

★★HIGHLAND HILLS GOLF COURSE
450 E Alward Rd., De Witt, 48820, Clinton County, (517)669-9873.
Call club for further information.

★★HILLS HEART OF THE LAKES GOLF CLUB
500 Case Rd., Brooklyn, 49230, Jackson County, (517)592-2110.
Call club for further information.
Subscriber comments: Best course in area, it's short but the back nine has an interesting and tough layout...Course is short but immaculate...Well-maintained: easy front, tight back...Back nine is very challenging; beautifully; maintained...Solid course, excellent value, superb service.

(GOOD VALUE)

★★HILLTOP GOLF COURSE
PM-47000 Powell Rd., Plymouth, 48170, Wayne County, (313)453-9800, 15 miles W of Ann Arbor.
Opened: N/A. **Holes:** 18. **Par:** 70/75. **Yards:** 5,998/4,761. **Course rating:** 69.7/73.0.
Slope: 120/115. **Architect:** N/A. **Green fee:** $24/$27. **Credit cards:** MC,VISA,AMEX.
Reduced fees: Weekdays, low season, twilight, seniors, juniors. **Caddies:** No. **Golf carts:** $23. **Discount golf packages:** Yes. **Season:** Year-round weather permitting. **High:** April-Sept. **On site lodging:** No. **Rental clubs:** Yes. **Walking policy:** Unrestricted walking. **Metal spikes allowed:** Yes. **Range:** No. **To obtain tee times:** Call up to 8 days in advance.
Subscriber comments: Nice relaxing course...Greens, when cut, can be like glass...Greens you will never forget—faaast...Slick greens...A shooting gallery. Mediocre facilities...New management has provided new improvements...Fun course, tough fast greens, leave your putter cover on.

★★HUDSON MILLS METRO PARK GOLF COURSE
PU-4800 Dexter-Pickney Rd., Dexter, 48130, Washtenaw County, (313)426-0466, (800)477-3191, 12 miles N of Ann Arbor.
Opened: 1991. **Holes:** 18. **Par:** 71/71. **Yards:** 6,560/5,411. **Course rating:** 70.6/70.2.
Slope: 116/113. **Architect:** Sue Nyquist. **Green fee:** $18/$20. **Credit cards:** None.
Reduced fees: Weekdays, low season, seniors, juniors. **Caddies:** No. **Golf carts:** $20.
Discount golf packages: No. **Season:** March-Nov. **High:** May-Sept. **On site lodging:** No. **Rental clubs:** Yes. **Walking policy:** Unrestricted walking. **Metal spikes allowed:** Yes. **Range:** No. **To obtain tee times:** Call 7 days in advance.
Subscriber comments: Metro park course, always in great condition, and great greens...Good public course...Excellent conditions...A well conditioned course...Wide fairways, few hazards...Harder than appears-good test for all...Great value.
Special Notes: Spikeless shoes encouraged.

★★★HUNTER'S RIDGE GOLF CLUB
PU-8101 Byron Rd., Howell, 48843, Livingston County, (517)545-4653, 35 miles E of Lansing.
Opened: 1996. **Holes:** 18. **Par:** 71/71. **Yards:** 6,530/4,624. **Course rating:** 71.9.
Slope: 134/122. **Architect:** Jerry Matthews. **Green fee:** $18/$28. **Credit cards:** MC,VISA,DISC. **Reduced fees:** Weekdays, low season, twilight, seniors, juniors.
Caddies: No. **Golf carts:** $10. **Discount golf packages:** No. **Season:** April-Oct. **High:** June-Aug. **On site lodging:** No. **Rental clubs:** Yes. **Walking policy:** Walking at certain times. **Metal spikes allowed:** No. **Range:** Yes (grass). **To obtain tee times:** Call.

Subscriber comments: Nice links layout. Great use of old dairy farm...Good shot placement course...Tricky, must play more than once to know shot positioning...Remote location, not crowded, very scenic...Pleasant surprise...New course, hard to get to, but worth it!...Best new course in the area, superior condition.

★★★½HURON BREEZE GOLF & COUNTRY CLUB
PU-5200 Huron Breeze Dr., Au Gres, 48703, Arenac County, (517)876-6868, 50 miles N of Saginaw.
Opened: 1991. **Holes:** 18. **Par:** 72/72. **Yards:** 6,806/5,075. **Course rating:** 73.1/69.4. **Slope:** 133/123. **Architect:** William Newcomb. **Green fee:** $14/$24. **Credit cards:** MC,VISA. **Reduced fees:** Weekdays, low season, twilight, seniors, juniors. **Caddies:** No. **Golf carts:** $10. **Discount golf packages:** Yes. **Season:** April-Oct. **High:** June-Sept. **On site lodging:** No. **Rental clubs:** Yes. **Walking policy:** Unrestricted walking. **Metal spikes allowed:** Yes. **Range:** Yes (grass). **To obtain tee times:** Call in advance, no restrictions.
Subscriber comments: Tight: fairways edged by woods on most holes; a joy to walk; scorable from middle tees, scary from the tips...Good test of golf skills...One of the best values in Michigan...Nature at its finest...Excellent fairways and greens...Great course for medium handicapper.
Special Notes: Spikeless shoes encouraged.

★½HURON HILLS GOLF COURSE
3465 E. Huron River Dr., Ann Arbor, 48104, Washtenaw County, (313)971-6840.
Architect: Tom Bendelow. **Caddies:** No. **Discount golf packages:** No. **On site lodging:** No. **Rental clubs:** No. **Metal spikes allowed:** Yes. **Range:** No.
Call club for further information.

★★★HURON MEADOWS GOLF COURSE
PM-8765 Hammel Rd., Brighton, 48116, Livingston County, (313)685-1561, (800)477-3193, 4 miles S of Brighton.
Opened: 1982. **Holes:** 18. **Par:** 72/71. **Yards:** 6,603/5,344. **Course rating:** 71.2/69.9. **Slope:** 122/116. **Architect:** N/A. **Green fee:** $18/$18. **Credit cards:** MC,VISA. **Reduced fees:** Seniors, juniors. **Caddies:** No. **Golf carts:** N/A. **Discount golf packages:** No. **Season:** March-Nov. **High:** June-Aug. **On site lodging:** No. **Rental clubs:** Yes. **Walking policy:** Unrestricted walking. **Metal spikes allowed:** Yes. **Range:** Yes (grass/mats). **To obtain tee times:** Call up to 7 days in advance.
Subscriber comments: Good golf for the money...Very well maintained muny, challenging and fun...Wide open, large greens. Fun to play...Always well kept fairways, greens, traps...Very playable, forgiving...Wide fairways, recent improvements, beautiful natural areas.

★★IDLE WYLD COUNTRY CLUB
PM-35780 Five Mile Rd., Livonia, 48154, Wayne County, (248)464-6325, 20 miles NW of Detroit.
Opened: N/A. **Holes:** 18. **Par:** 70/71. **Yards:** 5,817/5,022. **Course rating:** 68.0/69.2. **Slope:** 115/118. **Architect:** N/A. **Green fee:** $16/$22. **Credit cards:** MC,VISA. **Reduced fees:** Weekdays, twilight. **Caddies:** No. **Golf carts:** $24. **Discount golf packages:** No. **Season:** April-Nov. **High:** June-Aug. **On site lodging:** No. **Rental clubs:** No. **Walking policy:** Unrestricted walking. **Metal spikes allowed:** Yes. **Range:** No. **To obtain tee times:** Tee times required for weekends only. Residents may call on Wednesday after 9 a.m. Non-residents may call Thursday after 9 a.m.
Special Notes: Spikeless shoes encouraged.

★★INDIAN LAKE HILLS GOLF COURSE
PU-55321 Brush Lake Rd., Eau Claire, 49111, Cass County, (616)782-2540, 90 miles E of Chicago.
Opened: 1924. **Holes:** 27. **Architect:** N/A. **Green fee:** $15/$20. **Credit cards:** MC,VISA. **Reduced fees:** Weekdays, low season, twilight. **Caddies:** No. **Golf carts:** $22. **Season:** March-Oct. **High:** June-Aug. **On site lodging:** No. **Walking policy:** Walking at certain times. **Metal spikes allowed:** Yes. **Range:** Yes (grass). **Discount golf packages:** Yes. **Rental clubs:** Yes. **To obtain tee times:** Call up to 7 days in advance.

GOOD VALUE

EAST/NORTH
Par: 71. **Yards:** 6,201/5,156. **Course rating:** 67.5. **Slope:** 112.
WEST/EAST
Par: 71. **Yards:** 6,043/5,170. **Course rating:** 67.0. **Slope:** 111.
WEST/NORTH
Par: 72/73. **Yards:** 6,532/5,450. **Course rating:** 68.5. **Slope:** 113.
Subscriber comments: Good all around, great for the average golfer, not long not short...Not especially challenging...North is outstanding. East is short and uninteresting...Nice course, scenic lake view...Lack of marshalling with many backups...Play through orchard, interesting...Easy 18, good for family...North side very pretty and challenging.

★★★INDIAN RIVER GOLF CLUB
6460 Chippewa Beach Rd., Indian River, 49749, Cheboygan County, (616)238-7011, 20 miles N of Gaylord.
Opened: 1921. **Holes:** 18. **Par:** 72/72. **Yards:** 6,718/5,277. **Course rating:** 72.4/71.3. **Slope:** 124/119. **Architect:** Warner Bowen & Sons. **Green fee:** $20/$35. **Credit cards:** MC,VISA,DISC. **Reduced fees:** Weekdays, low season, twilight, juniors. **Caddies:** No. **Golf carts:** $15. **Discount golf packages:** Yes. **Season:** May-Oct. **High:** July-Aug. **On site lodging:** No. **Rental clubs:** No. **Walking policy:** Unrestricted walking. **Metal spikes allowed:** No. **Range:** No. **To obtain tee times:** Call anytime.
Subscriber comments: Front—blah; back will be very good...Best kept secret in northern Michigan...Fast greens...The course had wide fairways and was heavily wooded...Not very challenging...Well maintained nice course, a great value for northern Michigan.

★★½INDIAN RUN GOLF CLUB
6359 E. RS Ave., Scotts, 49088, Kalamazoo County, (616)327-1327, 6 miles SE of Kalamazoo.
Opened: 1966. **Holes:** 18. **Par:** 72/72. **Yards:** 6,808/5,028. **Course rating:** 72.1/68.8. **Slope:** 126/115. **Architect:** Charles Darl Scott. **Green fee:** $17/$20. **Credit cards:** MC,VISA,DISC. **Reduced fees:** Weekdays, low season, seniors, juniors. **Caddies:** No. **Golf carts:** $12. **Discount golf packages:** Yes. **Season:** April-Oct. **High:** May-Sept. **On site lodging:** No. **Rental clubs:** Yes. **Walking policy:** Unrestricted walking. **Metal spikes allowed:** Yes. **Range:** Yes (grass). **To obtain tee times:** Call.
Subscriber comments: Excellent value, great shape...Long course, few hazards...Fabulous course for beginners...Good conditions, good greens...Winds through housing area, nicely laid out.

★★★INDIAN SPRINGS METRO PARK GOLF COURSE
PU-5200 Indian Trail, White Lake, 48386, Oakland County, (248)625-7870, (800)477-3192, 8 miles W of Pontiac.
Opened: 1989. **Holes:** 18. **Par:** 71/71. **Yards:** 6,688/6,474. **Course rating:** 71.0/70.1. **Slope:** 120/114. **Architect:** Sue Nyquist. **Green fee:** $17/$19. **Credit cards:** MC,VISA. **Reduced fees:** N/A. **Caddies:** No. **Golf carts:** N/A. **Discount golf packages:** No. **Season:** March-Nov. **High:** March-Nov. **On site lodging:** No. **Rental clubs:** Yes. **Walking policy:** Unrestricted walking. **Metal spikes allowed:** No. **Range:** Yes (grass). **To obtain tee times:** Call up to 7 days in advance.
Subscriber comments: Great greens and fairways...Excellent course...Very long. Good challenge...Better than average course...Blind holes and some difficult greens make some holes more difficult than neccessary...Outstanding maintenance and greens...Longest of metro-park courses...The price is right.

★½INDIAN TRAILS GOLF COURSE
PU-2776 Kalamazoo Ave. S.E., Grand Rapids, 49507, Kent County, (616)245-2021.
Opened: 1921. **Holes:** 18. **Par:** 68/72. **Yards:** 5,100/4,785. **Course rating:** 66.8/71.6. **Slope:** N/A. **Architect:** Jeffrey John Gorney. **Green fee:** $13. **Credit cards:** None. **Reduced fees:** Weekdays, low season, seniors, juniors. **Caddies:** No. **Golf carts:** N/A. **Discount golf packages:** Yes. **Season:** April-Oct. **High:** June-July. **On site lodging:** No. **Rental clubs:** Yes. **Walking policy:** Unrestricted walking. **Metal spikes allowed:** Yes. **Range:** No. **To obtain tee times:** No tee times required.

★★¼INTERLOCHEN GOLF & CC

PU-P.O. Box 155, Interlochen, 49643, Grand Traverse County, (616)275-7311, 13 miles SW of Traverse City.
Opened: 1965. **Holes:** 18. **Par:** 71/72. **Yards:** 6,400/5,136. **Course rating:** 70.2/69.2. **Slope:** 130/117. **Architect:** N/A. **Green fee:** $15/$22. **Credit cards:** MC,VISA. **Reduced fees:** Twilight, seniors, juniors. **Caddies:** No. **Golf carts:** $20. **Discount golf packages:** Yes. **Season:** April-Oct. **High:** July-Aug. **On site lodging:** No. **Rental clubs:** Yes. **Walking policy:** Unrestricted walking. **Metal spikes allowed:** Yes. **Range:** Yes (grass). **To obtain tee times:** Call up to 30 days in advance.
Subscriber comments: Good solid golfing test at reasonable cost...Fun course to play...Lots of play...Tight. Good value. Great condition. Liked it...Old course, needs tune-up...Doglegs right and left predominate...Scenic short course...Offers different types of holes that suit the average player.

★★¼IRONWOOD GOLF CLUB

PU-6902 (M-59) Highland Rd., Howell, 48843, Livingston County, (517)546-3211, 31 miles SE of Lansing.
Opened: 1972. **Holes:** 18. **Par:** 72/72. **Yards:** 6,083/5,172. **Course rating:** 68.3/67.7. **Slope:** 116/117. **Architect:** David Pardon. **Green fee:** $18/$25. **Credit cards:** All major. **Reduced fees:** Weekdays, low season, twilight, seniors, juniors. **Caddies:** No. **Golf carts:** $20. **Discount golf packages:** No. **Season:** March-Nov. **High:** June-Sept. **On site lodging:** No. **Rental clubs:** Yes. **Walking policy:** Unrestricted walking. **Metal spikes allowed:** Yes. **Range:** No. **To obtain tee times:** Call golf shop.
Subscriber comments: Friendly, clean, upkeep good...Inexpensive, challenging...Crowned greens...Design is outstanding, reasonably priced...Very entertaining. Good test for all levels.

★★IRONWOOD GOLF COURSE

3750 64th St. S.W., Byron Center, 49315, Kent County, (616)538-4000, 10 miles S of Grand Rapids.
Opened: 1004. **Holes:** 19. **Par:** 71/71. **Yards:** 5,405/4,870. **Course rating:** N/A. **Slope:** N/A. **Architect:** George Woolferd. **Green fee:** $10/$18. **Credit cards:** None. **Reduced fees:** Weekdays, low season, seniors, juniors. **Golf carts:** $18. **High:** May-Aug. **To obtain tee times:** Call.

★★★KATKE GOLF COURSE AT FSU

PU-1003 Perry St., Big Rapids, 49307, Mecosta County, (616)592-2213, 50 miles N of Grand Rapids.
Opened: 1974. **Holes:** 18. **Par:** 72/72. **Yards:** 6,729/5,344. **Course rating:** 72.5/70.8. **Slope:** 124/119. **Architect:** Robert Beard. **Green fee:** $18/$20. **Credit cards:** MC,VISA,DISC. **Reduced fees:** Weekdays, low season, resort guests, seniors, juniors. **Caddies:** No. **Golf carts:** $10. **Discount golf packages:** Yes. **Season:** April-Nov. **High:** May-Sept. **On site lodging:** Yes. **Rental clubs:** Yes. **Walking policy:** Unrestricted walking. **Metal spikes allowed:** Yes. **Range:** Yes (grass/mats). **To obtain tee times:** Call up to 14 days in advance.
Subscriber comments: Great layout. Best greens I played all year...Beautifully landscaped; convient range...Straight golf, no tricks or gimmicks...Windy always...Gets better every season...Course operated and maintained by Ferris State Professional Golf Course Management students...Good value.

★★½KEARSLEY LAKE GOLF COURSE

PM-4266 E. Pierson Rd., Flint, 48506, Genesee County, (810)736-0930.
Opened: N/A. **Holes:** 18. **Par:** 72/72. **Yards:** 6,594/5,766. **Course rating:** 70.6/70.1. **Slope:** 113/112. **Architect:** N/A. **Green fee:** $18/$20. **Credit cards:** MC,VISA. **Reduced fees:** Low season, twilight, seniors, juniors. **Caddies:** No. **Golf carts:** $20. **Discount golf packages:** No. **Season:** April-Sept. **High:** N/A. **On site lodging:** No. **Rental clubs:** No. **Walking policy:** Unrestricted walking. **Metal spikes allowed:** No. **Range:** No. **To obtain tee times:** Call on Monday for upcoming weekend or 5 days in advance for weekdays.
Subscriber comments: Nice straight ahead course...Great value...Lots of water, nice challenges front and back...Lots of birdie holes...Nice city course with plenty of trouble spots...Good track, but golf course maintenence not priority.

★★★KENSINGTON METRO PARK GOLF CLUB

PU-2240 W. Buno Rd., Milford, 48380, Oakland County, (248)685-9332, 25 miles NW of Detroit.
Opened: 1961. **Holes:** 18. **Par:** 71/71. **Yards:** 6,378/5,206. **Course rating:** 70.8/69.8.
Slope: 115/112. **Architect:** H.A. Lemley. **Green fee:** $17/$19. **Credit cards:** None.
Reduced fees: Weekdays, seniors, juniors. **Caddies:** No. **Golf carts:** $20. **Discount golf packages:** No. **Season:** March-Nov. **High:** May-Sept. **On site lodging:** No.
Rental clubs: No. **Walking policy:** Unrestricted walking. **Metal spikes allowed:** No.
Range: Yes. **To obtain tee times:** Call up to 7 days in advance.
Subscriber comments: Good park course, deceptively long, good design mix...Not the toughest but a delight to play...Busy course. Hard to get on...Good course for amount of play...Popular and challenging muny...Slow play and nice setting...Simple layout in an urban setting...Deer herds in morning hours common...Easy to walk-on.

★★★½KIMBERLEY OAKS GOLF CLUB

1100 W. Walnut St., St. Charles, 48655, Saginaw County, (517)865-8261.
Opened: 1967. **Holes:** 18. **Par:** 72/74. **Yards:** 6,663/5,156. **Course rating:** 72.7/69.9.
Slope: 134/117. **Architect:** N/A. **Green fee:** $18/$24. **Credit cards:** MC,VISA.
Reduced fees: Low season, twilight, seniors, juniors. **Caddies:** No. **Golf carts:** $22.
Discount golf packages: No. **Season:** April-Oct. **High:** June-Sept. **On site lodging:**
No. **Rental clubs:** No. **Walking policy:** Unrestricted walking. **Metal spikes allowed:**
Yes. **Range:** Yes (grass). **To obtain tee times:** Call up to 14 days in advance.
Subscriber comments: One of Saginaw's finest, good test from the back, nice clubhouse...Very demanding, lots of trouble...Great value, course was in great shape, best grass for range and tees...Lots of water. Tougher than it looks. Fun!...Weekend coupons for cheap great golf...Many improvements over last five years...Great rates, great specials, super condition.

★★★KINCHELOE MEMORIAL GOLF COURSE

50 Woodside Rd., Kincheloe, 49788, Chippewa County, (906)495-5706.
Call club for further information.
Subscriber comments: Flat and long. Fairly wide open...Tee positions critical on most holes...Not fancy, but good golf, long.

★★★★L.E. KAUFMAN GOLF CLUB

PM-4807 Clyde Park S.W., Wyoming, 49509, Kent County, (616)538-5050, 8 miles S of Grand Rapids.
Opened: 1965. **Holes:** 18. **Par:** 72/72. **Yards:** 6,812/5,202. **Course rating:** 72.0/69.7. **Slope:** 125/117. **Architect:** Bruce Matthews.
Green fee: $19/$19. **Credit cards:** MC,VISA. **Reduced fees:**
Seniors, juniors. **Caddies:** No. **Golf carts:** $20. **Discount golf packages:** No. **Season:** March-Nov. **High:** June-Aug. **On site lodging:** No. **Rental clubs:**
Yes. **Walking policy:** Unrestricted walking. **Metal spikes allowed:** Yes. **Range:** Yes
(grass/mats). **To obtain tee times:** Call up to 7 days in advance.
Subscriber comments: Best kept secret in westen Michigan...Great greens and overall shape. You'll use all clubs...Best public course for the money in the area, but busy...Best value in the state...Country club for muny price...Always in great shape, super value...Course always in great shape.

★★LAKE CORA HILLS GOLF COURSE

PU-Red Arrow Hwy., Paw Paw, 49079, Van Buren County, (616)657-4074.
Opened: N/A. **Holes:** 18. **Par:** 72/72. **Yards:** 6,300/5,702. **Course rating:** 69.9/70.9.
Slope: 121/120. **Architect:** Al Humphrey. **Green fee:** $14/$14. **Credit cards:** MC,VISA.
Reduced fees: N/A. **Caddies:** No. **Golf carts:** $20. **Discount golf packages:** No.
Season: Year-round. **High:** N/A. **On site lodging:** No. **Rental clubs:** Yes. **Walking policy:** Unrestricted walking. **Metal spikes allowed:** Yes. **Range:** No. **To obtain tee times:** Call ahead for weekends.

★★★½LAKE DOSTER GOLF CLUB

136 Country Club Blvd., Plainwell, 49080, Allegan County, (616)685-5308, 40 miles S of Grand Rapids.
Opened: 1969. **Holes:** 18. **Par:** 72/72. **Yards:** 6,570/5,530. **Course rating:** 72.7/72.8.

Slope: 134/128. **Architect:** Charles Darl Scott. **Green fee:** $24/$27. **Credit cards:** MC,VISA,DISC. **Reduced fees:** N/A. **Caddies:** No. **Golf carts:** $10. **Discount golf packages:** Yes. **Season:** April-Oct. **High:** June-Aug. **On site lodging:** No. **Rental clubs:** Yes. **Walking policy:** Walking at certain times. **Metal spikes allowed:** Yes. **Range:** Yes (grass). **To obtain tee times:** Call anytime.
Subscriber comments: Worth the money...Out of way, but worth the drive...Tough greens...Many difficult tight holes...Underrated...Needs loving care...Add two clubs to reach the greens...Fantastic course I will play once a year till I die.

★★★½LAKE MICHIGAN HILLS GOLF CLUB
2520 Kerlikowske Rd., Benton Harbor, 49022, Berrien County, (616)849-2722, (800)247-3437, 90 miles N of Chicago.
Opened: 1967. **Holes:** 18. **Par:** 72/72. **Yards:** 6,911/5,250. **Course rating:** 73.9/70.8. **Slope:** 135/124. **Architect:** Charles Maddox Sr.. **Green fee:** $20/$35. **Credit cards:** MC,VISA,AMEX. **Reduced fees:** N/A. **Caddies:** No. **Golf carts:** $24. **Discount golf packages:** No. **Season:** April-Nov. **High:** June-Aug. **On site lodging:** No. **Rental clubs:** No. **Walking policy:** Walking at certain times. **Metal spikes allowed:** No. **Range:** Yes (grass). **To obtain tee times:** Call up to 7 days in advance.
Subscriber comments: One of the best...Beautiful, challenging, tough greens...Very beautiful and well kept...Length requires good long iron play...Worth playing at least once. Scenic, but expensive...Great Bloody Marys...Definitely worth playing...Super course to play, many bunkers...Demanding but fair.

★★½LAKELAND HILLS GOLF COURSE
PU-5119 Page Ave., Jackson, 49201, Jackson County, (517)764-5292, 50 miles W of Detroit.
Opened: 1969. **Holes:** 18. **Par:** 72/72. **Yards:** 6,199/5,090. **Course rating:** 68.9/68.4. **Slope:** 110/109. **Architect:** N/A. **Green fee:** $12/$16. **Credit cards:** MC,VISA. **Reduced fees:** Resort guests, twilight, seniors, juniors. **Caddies:** No. **Golf carts:** $18. **Discount golf packages:** Yes. **Season:** March-Dec. **High:** April-Sept. **On site lodging:** No. **Rental clubs:** Yes. **Walking policy:** Unrestricted walking. **Metal spikes allowed:** Yes. **Range:** No. **To obtain tee times:** Call 7 days in advance.
Subscriber comments: Wide open, great shape...Two years from a real good track...Almost a links style...Cheap twilight rates. Wide open and flat...Fast greens. Very inexpensive.

LAKES OF TAYLOR GOLF CLUB
PM-25505 Northline Rd., Taylor, 48180, Wayne County, (313)295-7790, 10 miles SW of Detroit.
Opened: 1996. **Holes:** 18. **Par:** 72/72. **Yards:** 7,028/5,119. **Course rating:** 73.4/69.4. **Slope:** 136/121. **Architect:** Arthur Hills and Steve Forrest. **Green fee:** $23/$35. **Credit cards:** MC,VISA,AMEX. **Reduced fees:** Low season, twilight, seniors, juniors. **Caddies:** No. **Golf carts:** $24. **Discount golf packages:** No. **Season:** March-Nov. **High:** June-Sept. **On site lodging:** No. **Rental clubs:** No. **Walking policy:** Unrestricted walking. **Metal spikes allowed:** Yes. **Range:** Yes (grass/mats). **To obtain tee times:** Call golf shop.

★★★½LAKES OF THE NORTH DEER RUN
R-8151 Pineview, Mancelona, 49659, Antrim County, (616)585-6806, (800)851-4653, 15 miles W of Gaylord.
Opened: N/A. **Holes:** 18. **Par:** 72/74. **Yards:** 6,996/5,465. **Course rating:** N/A. **Slope:** 130. **Architect:** Jerry Matthews/William Newcomb. **Green fee:** $22/$25. **Credit cards:** MC,VISA,AMEX. **Reduced fees:** Low season, twilight. **Caddies:** No. **Golf carts:** $15. **Discount golf packages:** Yes. **Season:** May-Oct. **High:** June-Aug. **On site lodging:** No. **Rental clubs:** Yes. **Walking policy:** Unrestricted walking. **Metal spikes allowed:** Yes. **Range:** Yes (grass). **To obtain tee times:** Call golf shop.
Subscriber comments: Bit of a secret/very nice layout...Long; great condition; greens hold well...Great layout from back tees...Good mature course, plays longer than yardage...Clean, fun, not crowded...Front flat, back better, not too hard...Nice course for the 90-100 golfer...Newer back nine enhanced course a lot!...Wait until 2:00 twilight for value...Back nine scenic. Off the beaten track...Great place to go alone.

★★½LAKESIDE LINKS
5369 W. Chauves Rd., Ludington, 49431, Mason County, (616)843-3660.
Call club for further information.
Subscriber comments: Lotta golf for the money, but basic...Busy in the summer...Great public course, best around south east Detroit...Some spectacular holes with water and elevation changes...A sleeper...A little short but challenging.

LAKEVIEW HILLS COUNTRY CLUB & RESORT
R-6560 Peck Rd. (M-90), Lexington, 48450, Sanilac County, (810)359-8901, 20 miles N of Port Huron.
Credit cards: MC,VISA,AMEX. **Caddies:** No. **Discount golf packages:** Yes. **Season:** April-Oct. **High:** July-Sept. **On site lodging:** Yes. **Rental clubs:** Yes. **To obtain tee times:** Call.
★★★NORTH COURSE
Opened: 1991. **Holes:** 18. **Par:** 72/74. **Yards:** 6,852/4,995. **Course rating:** 73.5/71.8. **Slope:** 139/131. **Architect:** Jeffery John Gorney. **Green fee:** $42/$48. **Reduced fees:** Weekdays, low season, seniors. **Golf carts:** Included in Green Fee. **Walking policy:** Mandatory cart. **Metal spikes allowed:** No. **Range:** Yes (grass/mats).
Subscriber comments: Pricey...A couple of gimmicky holes...Target golf...More difficult of two courses, tight fairways...Tough course with long roughs...Good course for all skill levels, well maintained.
★★★SOUTH COURSE
Opened: 1928. **Holes:** 18. **Par:** 72/74. **Yards:** 6,290/4,707. **Course rating:** 70.1/67.6. **Slope:** 119/116. **Architect:** Walter Hagen. **Green fee:** $24/$27. **Reduced fees:** Weekdays, low season, twilight, seniors, juniors. **Golf carts:** $12. **Walking policy:** Unrestricted walking. **Metal spikes allowed:** Yes. **Range:** Yes (grass).
Subscriber comments: Half the price of the North Course, very nice challenging greens and worth the ride...Traditional course...Variety and challenge...Open rolling terrain, both tees are well groomed...Nice for a relaxing day of golf.

LAKEWOOD SHORES RESORT
R-7751 Cedar Lake Rd., Oscoda, 48750, Iosco County, (517)739-2073, (800)882-2493, 80 miles NE of Saginaw.
Credit cards: MC,VISA. **Reduced fees:** Weekdays, low season, resort guests, twilight, juniors. **Caddies:** No. **Discount golf packages:** Yes. **Season:** April-Oct. **High:** June-Sept. **On site lodging:** Yes. **Rental clubs:** Yes. **Walking policy:** Unrestricted walking. **Metal spikes allowed:** Yes. **Range:** Yes (grass). **To obtain tee times:** Call anytime in advance.
★★★½SERRADELLA COURSE
Opened: 1969. **Holes:** 18. **Par:** 72/74. **Yards:** 6,806/5,295. **Course rating:** 72.9/70.9. **Slope:** 120/115. **Architect:** Bruce Matthews and Jerry Matthews. **Green fee:** $23/$30. **Golf carts:** $11.
Subscriber comments: More traditional course of two in fine shape...Keep this one secret...Great resort course. Long and flat large greens well kept...Good challenge for average golfer...Classic Northern Michigan course, nice alteranative to Gailes...Good strong course, not up to Gailes standard, but still a very good experience.
★★★★½THE GAILES COURSE
Opened: 1992. **Holes:** 18. **Par:** 72/73. **Yards:** 6,954/5,246. **Course rating:** 74.6/72.0. **Slope:** 137/132. **Architect:** Kevin Aldridge. **Green fee:** $30/$50. **Golf carts:** $12.
Notes: Ranked 6th in 1997 Best in State.
Subscriber comments: Special. A unique layout...Spectacular layout, automatic lost-ball rough, murderously fast undulating greens; 10 strokes harder than your home course unless you putt like Crenshaw; too hard for 20+ handicapper...Murder! Low handicappers only! Impossible roughs...Great layout, great condition. Good deal...The kind of course you want to replay immediately..
Special Notes: Also The Wee Links Course, which is a pitch and putt.

★★★LAPEER COUNTRY CLUB
PU-3786 Hunt Rd., Lapeer, 48446, Lapeer County, (810)664-2442, 2 miles W of Lapeer.
Opened: N/A. **Holes:** 18. **Par:** 72/73. **Yards:** 6,082/5,120. **Course rating:** N/A. **Slope:**

122/120. **Architect:** N/A. **Green fee:** $16/$17. **Credit cards:** None. **Reduced fees:** Seniors, juniors. **Caddies:** No. **Golf carts:** N/A. **Discount golf packages:** No. **Season:** March-Nov. **High:** April-Sept. **On site lodging:** No. **Rental clubs:** No. **Walking policy:** Unrestricted walking. **Metal spikes allowed:** Yes. **Range:** No. **To obtain tee times:** Call in advance.
Subscriber comments: Never disappointed...Well maintained. Interesting holes...Short hilly front...Could be great...Very hilly, fast greens, a bit overcrowded...Outstanding service, very comfortable...Wonderful conditions—too good to be true.

★½LEDGE MEADOWS GOLF COURSE
1801 Grand Ledge Hwy, Grand Ledge, 48837, Eaton County, (517)627-7492.
Call club for further information.

★★★LESLIE PARK GOLF COURSE
PU-2120 Traver Rd., Ann Arbor, 48105, Washtenaw County, (313)994-1163.
Opened: 1968. **Holes:** 9. **Par:** 72/72. **Yards:** 6,591/4,985. **Course rating:** 71.9/68.6. **Slope:** 127/115. **Architect:** Edward Lawrence Packard. **Green fee:** $20/$23. **Credit cards:** MC,VISA. **Reduced fees:** Weekdays, twilight. **Caddies:** No. **Golf carts:** $24. **Discount golf packages:** No. **Season:** March-Nov. **High:** June-Aug. **On site lodging:** No. **Rental clubs:** Yes. **Walking policy:** Unrestricted walking. **Metal spikes allowed:** Yes. **Range:** Yes. **To obtain tee times:** Call golf shop.
Subscriber comments: Very challenging public course...Enjoyable and well maintained...Renovations made excellent public course even better...Always famous for fast greens...Good value for price. Greens much less penal since makeover...Great value under $25...Don't suggest walking unless in excellent shape...No level putts.

★½LILAC GOLF CLUB
PU-9090 Armstrong Rd., Newport, 48166, Monroe County, (313)586-9902, 20 miles S of Detroit.
Opened: 1959. **Holes:** 18. **Par:** 72/72. **Yards:** 7,050/5,900. **Course rating:** 72.4/69.9. **Slope:** 125/118. **Architect:** Al Lilac/Sam Lilac. **Green fee:** $17/$20. **Credit cards:** None. **Reduced fees:** Weekdays, twilight, seniors, juniors. **Caddies:** No. **Golf carts:** $20. **Discount golf packages:** No. **Season:** March-Nov. **High:** June-Aug. **On site lodging:** No. **Rental clubs:** No. **Walking policy:** Unrestricted walking. **Metal spikes allowed:** Yes. **Range:** Yes (grass). **To obtain tee times:** Call.

★LINCOLN COUNTRY CLUB
3485 Lake Michigan Dr., Grand Rapids, 49504, Kent County, (616)453-6348.
Call club for further information.

★★½LINCOLN GOLF CLUB
4907 N. Whitehall Rd., Muskegon, 49445, Muskegon County, (616)766-2226, 9 miles N of Muskegon.
Opened: N/A. **Holes:** N/A. **Par:** 72/76. **Yards:** 6,100/5,500. **Course rating:** N/A. **Slope:** 116. **Architect:** Jerry Matthews. **Green fee:** $12/$22. **Credit cards:** MC,VISA. **Reduced fees:** Seniors. **Caddies:** No. **Golf carts:** $18. **Discount golf packages:** No. **Season:** April-Oct. **High:** N/A. **On site lodging:** No. **Rental clubs:** No. **Walking policy:** N/A. **Metal spikes allowed:** No. **Range:** Yes (grass). **To obtain tee times:** Call golf shop.
Subscriber comments: Nice clubhouse, great atmosphere, quick greens...Excellent facilities and layout, great staff...A very inexpensive links style course. What a value!...Fair with good conditions...Overpriced for the course.

★★★LINCOLN HILLS GOLF CLUB
1527 N. Lakeshore Dr., Ludington, 49431, Mason County, (616)843-4666.
Opened: 1921. **Holes:** 18. **Par:** 70. **Yards:** 6,100. **Course rating:** 68.7. **Slope:** 117. **Architect:** Bruce Matthews/Jerry Matthews. **Green fee:** $30/$40. **Credit cards:** MC,VISA. **Reduced fees:** N/A. **Caddies:** No. **Golf carts:** $24. **Discount golf packages:** No. **Season:** April-Nov. **High:** June-Aug. **On site lodging:** No. **Rental clubs:** No. **Walking policy:** Unrestricted walking. **Metal spikes allowed:** Yes. **Range:** Yes (grass). **To obtain tee times:** No tee times for non-members. Call for walk-on availability.
Subscriber comments: Great lakeside course nobody knows about...A nice track for a resort town...Great challenge for low cost...Nice, no frills golf course.

★★★THE LINKS AT PINEWOOD
PU-8600 P.G.A. Dr., Walled Lake, 48390, Oakland County, (248)669-9802.
Opened: 1985. **Holes:** 18. **Par:** 70/70. **Yards:** 6,572/5,559. **Course rating:** 72.0/72.3.
Slope: 125/124. **Architect:** Ernest Fuller. **Green fee:** $40/$45. **Credit cards:**
MC,VISA,AMEX. **Reduced fees:** Weekdays, low season, twilight. **Caddies:** No. **Golf carts:** Included in Green Fee. **Discount golf packages:** No. **Season:** March-Dec.
High: May-Sept. **On site lodging:** No. **Rental clubs:** Yes. **Walking policy:** Walking at certain times. **Metal spikes allowed:** Yes. **Range:** Yes (grass/mats). **To obtain tee times:** Call up to 6 days in advance.
Subscriber comments: Cart paths only, long walks...You better be straight, great track, hard fast greens...Outstanding clubhouse and food...Very accommodating, with public locker room, range, great staff...Beaten up by outings...Flat course with elevated hard greens.

★★★THE LINKS OF NOVI
PU-50395 Ten Mile Rd., Novi, 48374, Oakland County, (248)380-9595.
Opened: 1991. **Holes:** 27. **Architect:** Jerry Matthews. **Green fee:** $31/$36. **Credit cards:** MC,VISA. **Reduced fees:** Twilight, seniors, juniors. **Caddies:** No. **Golf carts:** $12. **Discount golf packages:** No. **Season:** April-Dec. **High:** June-Aug. **On site lodging:** No. **Rental clubs:** Yes. **Walking policy:** Walking at certain times. **Metal spikes allowed:** Yes. **Range:** Yes (grass/mats). **To obtain tee times:** Call 6 days in advance for weekdays. Call Monday for the upcoming weekend.
EAST/SOUTH
Par: 69/72. **Yards:** 6,014/4,646. **Course rating:** 67.9/66.8. **Slope:** 118/115.
EAST/WEST
Par: 71/74. **Yards:** 6,497/5,122. **Course rating:** 71.2/70.4. **Slope:** 127/126.
SOUTH/WEST
Par: 70/74. **Yards:** 6,093/4,862. **Course rating:** 68.3/68.0. **Slope:** 119/121.
Subscriber comments: Great condition of fairways and greens. West is most picturesque...Feels like you're in Carolinas...East nine features narrow fairways and undulating greens, especially 3 and 4...Beautiful in fall...Some holes impossible off the tee with any wind...Nice Scottish layout...Mosquitos as big as airplanes.

★★★★LITTLE TRAVERSE BAY GOLF CLUB
PU-995 Hideaway Valley Rd., Harbor Springs, 49740, Emmet County, (616)526-6200, 80 miles NE of Traverse City.
Opened: 1991. **Holes:** 18. **Par:** 72/72. **Yards:** 6,895/5,061. **Course rating:** 73.9/69.3. **Slope:** 136/119. **Architect:** Jeff Gorney. **Green fee:** $50/$78. **Credit cards:** MC,VISA. **Reduced fees:** Weekdays, low season, juniors. **Caddies:** No. **Golf carts:** Included in Green Fee. **Discount golf packages:** No. **Season:** May-Oct. **High:** June-Sept. **On site lodging:** No. **Rental clubs:** Yes. **Walking policy:** Mandatory cart. **Metal spikes allowed:** Yes. **Range:** Yes (grass/mats). **To obtain tee times:** Call golf shop with credit card. Cancellations can be made 2 days prior to play.
Subscriber comments: Most beautiful view from 1st tee...Best food, best views,best golf. WOW!...Friendly, helpful pro. Fantastic view. Lots of elevation changes...Nothing flat on course...Immaculate...A few quirky holes, but what an experience...Good couples course...A little more variety would make it a 5...Pricey but worth it.

★★LUM INTERNATIONAL GOLF CLUB
PU-5191 Lum Rd., Lum, 48412, Lapeer County, (810)724-0851, 30 miles E of Flint.
Opened: 1979. **Holes:** 27. **Architect:** N/A. **Green fee:** $16/$19. **Credit cards:** All major. **Reduced fees:** Weekdays, low season, twilight, seniors, juniors. **Caddies:** No. **Golf carts:** $20. **Discount golf packages:** No. **Season:** March-Nov. **High:** May-Sept. **On site lodging:** No. **Rental clubs:** Yes. **Walking policy:** Unrestricted walking. **Metal spikes allowed:** Yes. **Range:** Yes (grass). **To obtain tee times:** Call golf shop.
RED/GOLD
Par: 71/71. **Yards:** 6,695/5,239.
RED/WHITE
Par: 72/72. **Yards:** 6,629/5,201.
WHITE/GOLD
Holes: 27. **Par:** 71/71. **Yards:** 6,274/5,082.

★★★★THE MAJESTIC AT LAKE WALDEN
PU-9600 Crouse Rd., Hartland, 48353, Livingston County, (810)632-5235, (800)762-3280, 45 miles W of Detroit.
Opened: 1994. **Holes:** 27. **Architect:** Jerry Matthews. **Green fee:** $55/$60. **Credit cards:** All major. **Reduced fees:** Weekdays, low season, twilight, juniors. **Caddies:** No. **Golf carts:** Included in Green Fee. **Discount golf packages:** No. **Season:** April-Nov. **High:** June-Aug. **On site lodging:** No. **Rental clubs:** Yes. **Walking policy:** Mandatory cart. **Metal spikes allowed:** Yes. **Range:** Yes (grass). **To obtain tee times:** Call up to 7 days in advance.
FIRST/SECOND
Par: 72/72. **Yards:** 7,035/5,045. **Course rating:** 73.8/68.7. **Slope:** 136/111.
FIRST/THIRD
Holes: 27. **Par:** 72/72. **Yards:** 6,914/5,001. **Course rating:** 71.4/67.9. **Slope:** 134/111.
SECOND/THIRD
Holes: 27. **Par:** 72/72. **Yards:** 6,930/4,916. **Course rating:** 72.0/67.6. **Slope:** 137/111.
Subscriber comments: Beautiful blend of treelined and prairie holes...May be best in Southern Michigan. Boat ride to start at 10th hole is dumb...Frustrating par 3s...Could be outstanding with age...Northern Michigan golf in SE Michigan...Beautiful course, best in Detroit metro area...Course goes around the lake, great views.

MANISTEE GOLF & COUNTRY CLUB
500 Cherry St., Manistee, 49660, Manistee County, (616)723-2509, 60 miles S of Traverse City.
Opened: 1901. **Holes:** 18. **Par:** 70/71. **Yards:** 5,614/5,094. **Course rating:** 67.9/70.9. **Slope:** 115/118. **Architect:** N/A. **Green fee:** $40/$40. **Credit cards:** MC,VISA. **Reduced fees:** N/A. **Caddies:** No. **Golf carts:** Included in Green Fee. **Discount golf packages:** No. **Season:** April-Oct. **High:** N/A. **On site lodging:** No. **Rental clubs:** Yes. **Walking policy:** Walking at certain times. **Metal spikes allowed:** Yes. **Range:** Yes (grass). **To obtain tee times:** Call up to 2 days in advance.

MAPLE GROVE GOLF COURSE
PU-6360 Secor Rd., Lambertville, 48144, Monroe County, (313)854-6777, 1 mile N of Toledo, OH.
Opened: 1980. **Holes:** 18. **Par:** 69/71. **Yards:** 5,403/4,850. **Course rating:** N/A. **Slope:** N/A. **Architect:** N/A. **Green fee:** $14/$14. **Credit cards:** All major. **Reduced fees:** Low season. **Caddies:** No. **Golf carts:** $16. **Discount golf packages:** No. **Season:** Year-round. **High:** May-Sept. **On site lodging:** No. **Rental clubs:** Yes. **Walking policy:** Unrestricted walking. **Metal spikes allowed:** Yes. **Range:** Yes (grass/mats). **To obtain tee times:** First come, first served.

★★MAPLE HILL GOLF COURSE
PU-5555 Ivanrest Ave., Grandville, 49418, Kent County, (616)538-0290, 3 miles SW of Grand Rapids.
Opened: 1967. **Holes:** 18. **Par:** 68/70. **Yards:** 4,724/3,760. **Course rating:** N/A. **Slope:** N/A. **Architect:** N/A. **Green fee:** $11/$17. **Credit cards:** None. **Reduced fees:** Seniors, juniors. **Caddies:** No. **Golf carts:** $18. **Discount golf packages:** No. **Season:** Year-round. **High:** May-Sept. **On site lodging:** No. **Rental clubs:** Yes. **Walking policy:** Unrestricted walking. **Metal spikes allowed:** Yes. **Range:** Yes (grass). **To obtain tee times:** Call in advance.

MAPLE LANE GOLF COURSE
33203 Maple Lane Dr., Sterling Heights, 48312, Macomb County, (810)754-3020.
Call club for further information.
★½EAST COURSE
★★NORTH COURSE
★½WEST COURSE

★★★MAPLE LEAF GOLF COURSE
PU-158 N. Mackinaw Rd., Linwood, 48634, Bay County, (517)697-3531, 10 miles N of Bay City.
Opened: 1963. **Holes:** 27. **Architect:** Robert W. Bills and Donald L. Childs. **Green fee:** $17/$19. **Credit cards:** MC,VISA,DISC. **Reduced fees:** Weekdays, low season,

seniors, juniors. **Caddies:** No. **Golf carts:** $18. **Discount golf packages:** No. **Season:** April-Nov. **High:** June-Aug. **On site lodging:** No. **Rental clubs:** Yes. **Walking policy:** Unrestricted walking. **Metal spikes allowed:** Yes. **Range:** Yes (grass/mats). **To obtain tee times:** Call up to 7 days in advance.

EAST/NORTH
Par: 71/73. **Yards:** 5,762/4,466. **Course rating:** 67.6/66.2. **Slope:** 116/113.
EAST/WEST
Par: 70/72. **Yards:** 5,697/4,752. **Course rating:** 66.4/66.7. **Slope:** 109/109.
NORTH/WEST
Par: 71/73. **Yards:** 5,997/4,794. **Course rating:** 68.3/67.5. **Slope:** 114/114.
Subscriber comments: A great course off the beaten path...Play on weekdays if you can, always crowded...Water on North a challenge...Real good golf. Makes you work. Good value...Built for short hitters, North is a jewel...North nine is remarkably different from the other two...Maybe best value in state for the golf...West has flat but diverse look...Lots of sand, water and woods...Great value...A good little course that is getting a lot better...A little overpriced...West course open and flat.

★★½**MARION OAKS GOLF CLUB**
PU-2255 Pinckney Rd., Howell, 48843, Livingston County, (517)548-0050, 30 miles E of Lansing.
Opened: 1990. **Holes:** 18. **Par:** 70/70. **Yards:** 6,691/4,851. **Course rating:** 71.3/67.1. **Slope:** 128/110. **Architect:** Frank Godwin. **Green fee:** $22/$34. **Credit cards:** MC,VISA,AMEX. **Reduced fees:** Weekdays, twilight, seniors, juniors. **Caddies:** No. **Golf carts:** Included in Green Fee. **Discount golf packages:** No. **Season:** April-Nov. **High:** June-Sept. **On site lodging:** No. **Rental clubs:** Yes. **Walking policy:** Unrestricted walking. **Metal spikes allowed:** No. **Range:** Yes (grass). **To obtain tee times:** Call up to 7 days in advance.
Subscriber comments: Very economical. You get what you pay for...Fun Sunday course...Several strong holes...Too many hidden spots...Well kept course, nice wooded fairways...Free drop from wildflowers if you find your ball...Take a lot of balls for front, score on back...Play in spring before bloomed wildflowers hide stray balls.

★★★**MARQUETTE GOLF & COUNTRY CLUB**
Grove St, Marquette, 49855, Marquette County, (906)225-0721.
Call club for further information.
Subscriber comments: Some holes have view of Lake Superior. Tough winters show...Suffers from hard winters...Picturesque...Long with fun elevated holes on the back side...Back nine is the best nine.

★★½**MARQUETTE TRAILS COUNTRY CLUB**
Big Star Lake Rd., Baldwin, 49304, Lake County, (616)898-2450.
Call club for further information.
Subscriber comments: Huge greens...Great scenery, lot of different trees to play around. Well groomed...Fun course/some challenging driving holes.

★★★½**MARSH RIDGE RESORT**
R-4815 Old 27 S., Gaylord, 49735, Otsego County, (517)731-1563, (800)968-2633, 55 miles NE of Traverse City.
Opened: 1992. **Holes:** 18. **Par:** 71/71. **Yards:** 6,100/5,088. **Course rating:** 69.7/65.7. **Slope:** 126/117. **Architect:** Mike Husby. **Green fee:** $37/$60. **Credit cards:** All major. **Reduced fees:** Weekdays, low season, resort guests, twilight, juniors. **Caddies:** No. **Golf carts:** Included in Green Fee. **Discount golf packages:** Yes. **Season:** April-Oct. **High:** June-Sept. **On site lodging:** Yes. **Rental clubs:** Yes. **Walking policy:** Mandatory cart. **Metal spikes allowed:** Yes. **Range:** Yes (grass). **To obtain tee times:** Call anytime in advance.
Subscriber comments: Excellent condition. Very challenging. Very scenic...Short but tricky. Lots of doglegs...My favorite golf course in Gaylord...Hidden treasure...Lots of carries...Short but narrow...Spoil yourself...Good value...Good place to take the wife...Easy to find off I-75...Shot makers' course, short and tight...Short but testing with several dramatic carries over the marshes.

MICHIGAN

★★★½MARYSVILLE GOLF COURSE
PM-2080 River Rd., Marysville, 48040, St. Clair County, (810)364-4653, 55 miles N of Detroit.
Opened: 1954. **Holes:** 18. **Par:** 72/72. **Yards:** 6,542/5,311. **Course rating:** 71.4/70.5. **Slope:** 119/115. **Architect:** N/A. **Green fee:** $12/$21. **Credit cards:** MC,VISA,DISC. **Reduced fees:** Weekdays, low season, seniors, juniors. **Caddies:** No. **Golf carts:** $18. **Discount golf packages:** No. **Season:** March-Nov. **High:** June-Sept. **On site lodging:** No. **Rental clubs:** No. **Walking policy:** Unrestricted walking. **Metal spikes allowed:** Yes. **Range:** Yes (grass). **To obtain tee times:** Call at noon on Tuesdays for the next 7 days.
Subscriber comments: Well manicured, great prices, excellent experience...Best maintained muny in SE Michigan; layout has traditional character to it; subtle, hard-to-read greens; no bad holes; can't beat the price...The best public course for the money in eastern Michigan...Greens perfect.

★★★½MARYWOOD GOLF CLUB
PU-21310 N. Ave., Battle Creek, 49017, Calhoun County, (616)968-1168, 90 miles W of Detroit.
Opened: 1926. **Holes:** 18. **Par:** 72/72. **Yards:** 6,631/5,233. **Course rating:** 73.0/71.6. **Slope:** 132/126. **Architect:** Maurice McCarthy. **Green fee:** $22/$42. **Credit cards:** MC,VISA,DISC. **Reduced fees:** Weekdays, low season, twilight, seniors. **Caddies:** No. **Golf carts:** $12. **Discount golf packages:** Yes. **Season:** April-Nov. **High:** June-Sept. **On site lodging:** No. **Rental clubs:** Yes. **Walking policy:** Walking at certain times. **Metal spikes allowed:** Yes. **Range:** Yes (grass/mats). **To obtain tee times:** Call anytime.
Subscriber comments: Fairways and greens very plush, rough is thinned out...Grounds are great, price is slightly over budget, very challenging...Great value if you catch a two-for-one coupon...Another private gone public—thank you...Fast greens...Fairly long, but a must when in the area.

★½MASON HILLS GOLF COURSE
2602 Tomlinson Rd., Mason, 48854, Eaton County, (517)676-5366, 10 miles SE of Lansing.
Opened: 1926. **Holes:** 18. **Par:** 72/72. **Yards:** 6,348/5,550. **Course rating:** N/A. **Slope:** N/A. **Architect:** Henry Chisholm. **Green fee:** $7/$15. **Credit cards:** None. **Reduced fees:** Weekdays, low season, twilight, seniors, juniors. **Caddies:** No. **Golf carts:** $18. **Discount golf packages:** Yes. **Season:** March-Oct. **High:** May-Aug. **On site lodging:** No. **Rental clubs:** Yes. **Walking policy:** Unrestricted walking. **Metal spikes allowed:** Yes. **Range:** Yes (grass). **To obtain tee times:** Call.

★★★½MATHESON GREENS GOLF COURSE
PU-Matheson Rd., Northport, 49670, Leelanau County, (616)386-5171, (800)443-6883, 25 miles N of Traverse City.
Opened: 1991. **Holes:** 18. **Par:** 72/72. **Yards:** 6,609/4,716. **Course rating:** 72.1/67.2. **Slope:** 132/116. **Architect:** Steve White and Gary Pulsipher. **Green fee:** $30/$45. **Credit cards:** All major. **Reduced fees:** Low season, twilight, juniors. **Caddies:** No. **Golf carts:** Included in Green Fee. **Discount golf packages:** Yes. **Season:** April-Oct. **High:** July-Aug. **On site lodging:** No. **Rental clubs:** Yes. **Walking policy:** Walking at certain times. **Metal spikes allowed:** Yes. **Range:** Yes (Mats). **To obtain tee times:** Call anytime in advance.
Subscriber comments: Terrific course all around. Good service...A little out of the way, but worth the trip...Great condition; pretty views; well managed; friendly...Affordable for the Traverse City area...Nine open holes, nine tight holes, great greens.

★★★MCGUIRE'S RESORT
R-7880 Mackinaw Trail, Cadillac, 49601, Wexford County, (616)775-9949, (800)632-7302, 90 miles N of Grand Rapids.
Opened: 1959. **Holes:** 18. **Par:** 71/71. **Yards:** 6,443/5,107. **Course rating:** 71.3/69.6. **Slope:** 124/118. **Architect:** Bruce Matthews. **Green fee:** $32/$52. **Credit cards:** All major. **Reduced fees:** Resort guests, twilight. **Caddies:** No. **Golf carts:** Included in Green Fee. **Discount golf packages:** Yes. **Season:** April-Oct. **High:** May-Sept. **On site lodging:** Yes. **Rental clubs:** No. **Walking policy:** Mandatory cart. **Metal spikes**

allowed: Yes. **Range:** Yes (grass). **To obtain tee times:** Call in advance.
Subscriber comments: Don't let the secret out...Front nine excellent back nine so so...Excellent, a little pricey but it's worth it!...Good all around resort...Very fast greens. Good fairways...Wonderful golf resort. A good value all around...Play each year with 12 friends, we really enjoy it.
Special Notes: Also has 9-hole par-36 Norway Course.

MEADOW LANE GOLF COURSE
3356 44th St., S.E., Grand Rapids, 49508, Kent County, (616)698-8034.
Call club for further information.

★★★½THE MEADOWS GOLF CLUB
PU-4645 W. Campus Dr., Allendale, 49401, Ottawa County, (616)895-1000, 15 miles W of Grand Rapids.
Opened: 1994. **Holes:** 18. **Par:** 71/72. **Yards:** 7,034/4,777. **Course rating:** 74.5/67.4. **Slope:** 133/117. **Architect:** Michael Hurdzan. **Green fee:** $25/$36. **Credit cards:** All major. **Reduced fees:** Weekdays, low season, juniors. **Caddies:** No. **Golf carts:** $12. **Discount golf packages:** No. **Season:** April-Oct. **High:** June-Sept. **On site lodging:** No. **Rental clubs:** Yes. **Walking policy:** Unrestricted walking. **Metal spikes allowed:** Yes. **Range:** Yes (grass/mats). **To obtain tee times:** Call up to 10 days in advance. Multiple tee times require credit card guarantee.
Subscriber comments: Long, great condition. Country club amenities...Relatively low price for a beautiful course...On campus of Grand Valley State Univ., excellent facilities...Great restaurant...1st a little unfair...Beautiful links style course...Practice facility great...Treated like royalty by staff.

MECEOLA COUNTRY CLUB
218 N Warren, Big Rapids, 49307, Mecosta County, (616)796-9004, 50 miles N of Grand Rapid.
Opened: 1919. **Holes:** 18. **Par:** 72/74. **Yards:** 6,504/5,890. **Course rating:** 70.7/69.9. **Slope:** 117/121. **Architect:** Jeff Gorney. **Green fee:** $12/$20. **Credit cards:** MC,VISA. **Reduced fees:** Weekdays, seniors. **Caddies:** No. **Golf carts:** $24. **Discount golf packages:** No. **Season:** April-Oct. **High:** May-Aug. **On site lodging:** No. **Rental clubs:** No. **Walking policy:** Unrestricted walking. **Metal spikes allowed:** Yes. **Range:** Yes (grass). **To obtain tee times:** Call in advance.

★★★½MICHAYWE HILLS RESORT - PINE COURSE
R-1535 Opal Lake Rd., Gaylord, 49735, Otsego County, (517)939-8911, (800)322-6636, 5 miles NE of Traverse City.
Opened: 1972. **Holes:** 18. **Par:** 72/73. **Yards:** 6,835/5,901. **Course rating:** 73.6/74.4. **Slope:** 129/126. **Architect:** Robert W. Bills and Donald L. Childs. **Green fee:** $40/$42. **Credit cards:** MC,VISA. **Reduced fees:** Weekdays, low season, resort guests, twilight, juniors. **Caddies:** No. **Golf carts:** $10. **Discount golf packages:** Yes. **Season:** April-Oct. **High:** June-Aug. **On site lodging:** Yes. **Rental clubs:** Yes. **Walking policy:** Walking at certain times. **Metal spikes allowed:** Yes. **Range:** Yes (grass). **To obtain tee times:** Call anytime. Credit card necessary to hold tee time.
Subscriber comments: Nice, classic parks course...Looks simple but can be tough...Blue sky, green pine trees,deep sand...Very enjoyable round of golf. A good value...Excellent greens, nice layout...Great traditional golf course amidst Michigan pines.

★½MIDDLE CHANNEL GOLF & COUNTRY CLUB
PU-2306 Golf Course Rd., Harsens Island, 48028, St. Clair County, (810)748-9922, 25 miles NE of Mt. Clemens.
Opened: 1923. **Holes:** 18. **Par:** 70. **Yards:** 6,140. **Course rating:** N/A. **Slope:** N/A. **Architect:** N/A. **Green fee:** $16/$19. **Credit cards:** MC,VISA. **Reduced fees:** Weekdays, low season, twilight, seniors, juniors. **Caddies:** No. **Golf carts:** $18. **Discount golf packages:** No. **Season:** April-Oct. **High:** June-Aug. **On site lodging:** No. **Rental clubs:** Yes. **Walking policy:** Unrestricted walking. **Metal spikes allowed:** Yes. **Range:** No. **To obtain tee times:** Call anytime.

★★★½MILHAM PARK MUNICIPAL GOLF CLUB

PM-4200 Lovers Lane, Kalamazoo, 49001, Kalamazoo County, (616)344-7639.

Opened: 1931. **Holes:** 18. **Par:** 73/72. **Yards:** 6,578/5,582. **Course rating:** 71.3/71.8. **Slope:** 120/120. **Architect:** David Millar. **Green fee:** $15/$17. **Credit cards:** All major. **Reduced fees:** Seniors, juniors. **Caddies:** No. **Golf carts:** $20. **Discount golf packages:** No. **Season:** March-Dec. **High:** June-Aug. **On site lodging:** No. **Rental clubs:** Yes. **Walking policy:** Unrestricted walking. **Metal spikes allowed:** Yes. **Range:** Yes (grass/mats). **To obtain tee times:** Call 3 days in advance for weekends and holidays only.

Subscriber comments: Great "walk only" course...One of the best public courses I've ever played...Greatest asset: no carts unless physically necessary...You won't find a better groomed course with a super dollar value. Country club greens and fairways...The model for all munys to follow...Bargain for seniors...Excellent condition.

★★½MISSAUKEE GOLF CLUB

5300 S Morey Rd, Lake City, 49651, Missaukee County, (616)825-2756, 11 miles E of Cadillac.

Opened: 1970. **Holes:** 18. **Par:** 71/71. **Yards:** 5,755/4,968. **Course rating:** 67.0/68.0. **Slope:** 110/110. **Architect:** N/A. **Green fee:** $17/$20. **Credit cards:** MC,VISA,AMEX. **Reduced fees:** N/A. **Caddies:** No. **Golf carts:** $17. **Discount golf packages:** No. **Season:** April-Oct. **High:** July-Aug. **On site lodging:** No. **Rental clubs:** No. **Walking policy:** Unrestricted walking. **Metal spikes allowed:** Yes. **Range:** Yes (Mats). **To obtain tee times:** Call up to 14 days in advance.

Subscriber comments: Playable for all...Fun course to play, lots of challenge...Good course for average player. Wide fairways. Good size greens...Nice "small town" course...Good course for starting players...Nice fun, fair course, great value.

★★★½MISTWOOD GOLF COURSE

PU-7568 Sweet Lake Rd., Lake Ann, 49650, Benzie County, (616)275-5500, 18 miles SW of Traverse City.

Opened: 1993. **Holes:** 27. **Par:** 71/71. **Yards:** 6,715/5,070. **Course rating:** 72.4/69.6. **Slope:** 130/120. **Architect:** Jerry Matthews. **Green fee:** $30/$33. **Credit cards:** All major. **Reduced fees:** Weekdays, low season, resort guests, twilight, seniors, juniors. **Caddies:** No. **Golf carts:** $12. **Discount golf packages:** No. **Season:** April-Nov. **High:** June-Aug. **On site lodging:** No. **Rental clubs:** Yes. **Walking policy:** Unrestricted walking. **Metal spikes allowed:** Yes. **Range:** Yes (grass). **To obtain tee times:** Call anytime.

Subscriber comments: Nice course but pricey. Treated well...Fairways like greens...Front nine especially scenic...New nine rivals some of the best resort courses in northern Michigan...Championship course that's very affordable. Great condition. Fast greens...Hard but enjoyable...Fairly new, nice staff...Great value. A fun and challenging course. Good variety.

★★½MORRISON LAKE COUNTRY CLUB

PU-6425 West Portland Rd., Saranac, 48881, Ionia County, (616)642-9528, 28 miles E of Grand Rapids.

Opened: 1927. **Holes:** 18. **Par:** 70/72. **Yards:** 5,368/5,100. **Course rating:** 65.7/66.4. **Slope:** 102/103. **Architect:** N/A. **Green fee:** $10/$13. **Credit cards:** None. **Reduced fees:** Weekdays, twilight, seniors, juniors. **Caddies:** No. **Golf carts:** $18. **Discount golf packages:** No. **Season:** March-Sept. **High:** April-Sept. **On site lodging:** No. **Rental clubs:** Yes. **Walking policy:** Unrestricted walking. **Metal spikes allowed:** Yes. **Range:** No. **To obtain tee times:** Call anytime.

Subscriber comments: Very nice course to play, not overly long, fun...New watering system...Good value, short, hilly, no trees...Short, fun, decent shape...Early specials.

★★MULBERRY FORE GOLF COURSE

PU-955 N Main St. (M-66), Nashville, 49073, Barry County, (517)852-0760, (800)450-0760, 20 miles N of Battle Creek.

Opened: 1979. **Holes:** 18. **Par:** 72/75. **Yards:** 6,000/5,460. **Course rating:** N/A. **Slope:** N/A. **Architect:** N/A. **Green fee:** $14/$14. **Credit cards:** MC,VISA. **Reduced fees:** Weekdays, low season, twilight, seniors, juniors. **Caddies:** No. **Golf carts:** $19.

Discount golf packages: Yes. **Season:** March-Nov. **High:** May-Sept. **On site lodging:** No. **Rental clubs:** Yes. **Walking policy:** Unrestricted walking. **Metal spikes allowed:** Yes. **Range:** Yes. **To obtain tee times:** Call 800 number anytime.

★MULBERRY HILLS GOLF COURSE
PU-3530 Noble Rd., Oxford, 48370, Oakland County, (248)628-2808, 40 miles N of Detroit.
Opened: 1962. **Holes:** 18. **Par:** 71/71. **Yards:** 6,497/4,781. **Course rating:** N/A. **Slope:** N/A. **Architect:** N/A. **Green fee:** $16/$20. **Credit cards:** MC,VISA. **Reduced fees:** Weekdays, low season, twilight, seniors, juniors. **Caddies:** No. **Golf carts:** $10. **Discount golf packages:** No. **Season:** April-Nov. **High:** May-Sept. **On site lodging:** No. **Rental clubs:** No. **Walking policy:** Unrestricted walking. **Metal spikes allowed:** Yes. **Range:** Yes (grass/mats). **To obtain tee times:** Call.

★★½MULLENHURST GOLF COURSE
9810 Mullen Rd., Delton, 49046, Barry County, (616)623-8383.
Call club for further information.
Subscriber comments: Nice medium distance course, clean...Short but interesting...Best public course in the area...Very good value...Not an every day course in an out of the way location...Not enough hazards.

★★★MYSTIC CREEK GOLF CLUB
PU-1 Champions Circle, Milford, 48380, Oakland County, (248)684-3333, 45 miles NW of Detroit.
Opened: 1996. **Holes:** 27. **Architect:** Pat Conroy and Jim Dewling. **Green fee:** $35/$48. **Credit cards:** All major. **Reduced fees:** Twilight. **Caddies:** No. **Golf carts:** Included in Green Fee. **Discount golf packages:** No. **Season:** March-Nov. **High:** May-Oct. **On site lodging:** No. **Rental clubs:** Yes. **Walking policy:** Walking at certain times. **Metal spikes allowed:** No. **Range:** Yes (mats). **To obtain tee times:** Call golf shop.
LAKES/WOODS
Par: 72/72. **Yards:** 6,802/5,000. **Course rating:** 72.2/66.7. **Slope:** 130/114.
MEADOWS/LAKES
Par: 72/72. **Yards:** 6,700/5,000. **Course rating:** 71.1/65.4. **Slope:** 131/109.
MEADOWS/WOODS
Par: 72/72. **Yards:** 6,700/5,000. **Course rating:** 71.5/66.3. **Slope:** 130/116.
Subscriber comments: Needs to mature...Some postage stamp landing areas...Lakes course needs more time to fill in...Outstanding in every aspect, total enjoyment...Real tough course, lots of hazards...Picturesque driving range...Good golf, good test, fair price, lots of fun.

★★★½THE NATURAL AT BEAVER CREEK RESORT
R-5004 W. Otsego Lake Dr., Gaylord, 49735, Otsego County, (517)732-1785, (517)732-1785, 50 miles NE of Traverse City.
Opened: 1992. **Holes:** 18. **Par:** 71/71. **Yards:** 6,350/4,830. **Course rating:** 69.5/69.0. **Slope:** 129/117. **Architect:** Jerry Matthews. **Green fee:** $40/$55. **Credit cards:** MC,VISA,DISC. **Reduced fees:** Weekdays, low season, resort guests, twilight. **Caddies:** No. **Golf carts:** Included in Green Fee. **Discount golf packages:** Yes. **Season:** May-Oct. **High:** June-Aug. **On site lodging:** Yes. **Rental clubs:** Yes. **Walking policy:** Walking at certain times. **Metal spikes allowed:** Yes. **Range:** Yes (grass/mats). **To obtain tee times:** Call.
Subscriber comments: My wife loved this course: short with forced carries...8 and 18 are terrific...They've done an outstanding job...440-yard par 4 with last 175 yards over swamp. Turns a 2-handicapper into a 15...Beautiful in fall, tight course, bring lots of balls.

★★½NORTH KENT GOLF COURSE
11029 Stout Ave. N.E., Rockford, 49341, Kent County, (616)866-2659.
Call club for further information.
Subscriber comments: Country course with great greens...Well kept up course/always making improvements...Wide open, let it rip...Don't underestimate it...Excellent greens fun to play...Nice way to spend a day, nice course, worth the money...Seasonal specials.

MICHIGAN

NORTH SHORE GOLF CLUB
N. 2315 Hwy. M-35, Menominee, 49858, Menominee County, (906)863-8421, 6 miles N of Menominee.
Opened: 1928. **Holes:** 18. **Par:** 72/72. **Yards:** 6,428/5,367. **Course rating:** 69.9/72.3. **Slope:** 120/122. **Architect:** N/A. **Green fee:** $18/$20. **Credit cards:** MC,VISA. **Reduced fees:** Weekdays. **Caddies:** Yes. **Golf carts:** $18. **Discount golf packages:** No. **Season:** April-Nov. **High:** N/A. **On site lodging:** No. **Rental clubs:** No. **Walking policy:** Unrestricted walking. **Metal spikes allowed:** No. **Range:** No. **To obtain tee times:** N/A.

★★NORTH STAR GOLF & COUNTRY CLUB
4550 South Bagley Rd., Ithaca, 48847, Gratiot County, (517)875-3841.
Call club for further information.

★★NORTHBROOK GOLF CLUB
PU-21690 27 Mile Rd., Ray Township, 48096, Macomb County, (810)749-3415.
Opened: 1965. **Holes:** 18. **Par:** 72/72. **Yards:** 6,352/4,949. **Course rating:** 70.3/68.5. **Slope:** 121/114. **Architect:** N/A. **Green fee:** $10/$24. **Credit cards:** MC,VISA,DISC. **Reduced fees:** Seniors, juniors. **Caddies:** No. **Golf carts:** $24. **Discount golf packages:** No. **Season:** April-Nov. **High:** May-Sept. **On site lodging:** No. **Rental clubs:** No. **Walking policy:** Unrestricted walking. **Metal spikes allowed:** Yes. **Range:** No. **To obtain tee times:** Call up to 1 day in advance.

★★NORTHWOOD GOLF COURSE
PU-2888 Comstock Ave., Fremont, 49412, Newaygo County, (616)924-3380, 40 miles NW of Grand Rapids.
Opened: 1968. **Holes:** 18. **Par:** 71/71. **Yards:** 6,313/5,608. **Course rating:** 69.7/66.1. **Slope:** 115/111. **Architect:** N/A. **Green fee:** $16/$16. **Credit cards:** MC,VISA. **Reduced fees:** Seniors. **Caddies:** No. **Golf carts:** $18. **Discount golf packages:** No. **Season:** April-Oct. **High:** July-Aug. **On site lodging:** No. **Rental clubs:** Yes. **Walking policy:** Unrestricted walking. **Metal spikes allowed:** Yes. **Range:** Yes (Mats). **To obtain tee times:** Call anytime.

★★★½OAK CREST GOLF COURSE
PM-Highway U.S. 8, Norway, 49870, Dickinson County, (906)563-5891.
Opened: 1929. **Holes:** 18. **Par:** 72/74. **Yards:** 6,158/5,430. **Course rating:** 69.2/71.0. **Slope:** 120/121. **Architect:** N/A. **Green fee:** $22/$22. **Credit cards:** None. **Reduced fees:** N/A. **Caddies:** No. **Golf carts:** $22. **Discount golf packages:** No. **Season:** N/A. **High:** June-Aug. **On site lodging:** No. **Rental clubs:** No. **Walking policy:** N/A. **Metal spikes allowed:** No. **Range:** No. **To obtain tee times:** Call up to 7 days in advance.
Subscriber comments: Tough greens but not a real long course...Membership of 1,200 golfers. A scenic beauty which is unimaginable. The greens are tough to putt only because of their undulation...Not long, so most golfers (if they can hit the ball) will have fun playing this course...Challenging par 3s.

★★★OAK LANE GOLF COURSE
PU-800 N. Main St., Webberville, 48892, Ingham County, (517)521-3900, 20 miles E of Lansing.
Opened: 1967. **Holes:** 18. **Par:** 70/71. **Yards:** 5,714/5,115. **Course rating:** 67.3/69.1. **Slope:** 107/115. **Architect:** Harley Hodges. **Green fee:** $16/$19. **Credit cards:** MC,VISA. **Reduced fees:** Twilight, seniors, juniors. **Caddies:** No. **Golf carts:** $10. **Discount golf packages:** No. **Season:** April-Oct. **High:** June-Aug. **On site lodging:** No. **Rental clubs:** Yes. **Walking policy:** Unrestricted walking. **Metal spikes allowed:** Yes. **Range:** No. **To obtain tee times:** Call or come in up to 14 days in advance.
Subscriber comments: Great golf at great price...Long, but nice play...Fairways in great shape...Good for group golf outing...Baffling greens.

★★★½OAK POINTE
5341 Brighton Rd., Brighton, 48116, Livingston County, (810)227-1381.
Call club for further information.
Subscriber comments: Almost too tough, bring your best drives...Very enjoyable.
Good staff and facilities...Course needs to be beefed up a little...Tough for seniors...Too
tough for most, great course...Great layout, great shape, bring every club.

★★OAK RIDGE GOLF CLUB
513 W. Pontaluna Rd., Muskegon, 49444, Muskegon County, (616)798-4591.
Call club for further information.

OAK RIDGE GOLF CLUB
35035 26 Mile Rd., New Haven, 48048, Macomb County, (810)749-5151, 20 miles NE
of Detroit.
MARSH OAKS AT OAK RIDGE
Opened: 1996. **Holes:** 18. **Par:** 72/72. **Yards:** 6,706/4,916. **Course rating:** N/A. **Slope:**
N/A. **Architect:** Bruce Matthews. **Green fee:** $40/$48. **Credit cards:** All major.
Reduced fees: Weekdays, low season, twilight, seniors, juniors. **Golf carts:** Included in
Green Fee. **Discount golf packages:** Yes. **Season:** April-Nov. **High:** April-Sept. **Rental
clubs:** Yes. **Walking policy:** Mandatory cart. **Range:** Yes (grass). **To obtain tee times:**
Call up to 14 days in advance.
★★★OLD OAKS AT OAK RIDGE
Opened: 1966. **Holes:** 18. **Par:** 71/71. **Yards:** 6,563/5,427. **Course rating:** 71.0/72.6.
Slope: 117/119. **Architect:** Bruce Matthews. **Green fee:** $21/$24. **Credit cards:** All
major. **Reduced fees:** Weekdays, low season, twilight, seniors, juniors. **Golf carts:**
$12. **Discount golf packages:** Yes. **Season:** April-Nov. **High:** April-Sept. **Rental clubs:**
Yes. **Walking policy:** Unrestricted walking. **Range:** Yes (grass/mats). **To obtain tee
times:** Call up to 14 days in advance.
Subscriber comments: Nice layout, good greens...Long and flat...Much
improved...Moderate price, greens and fairways OK...Green fees fair...Nice course for
the money, good for high handicappers.

★★½OAKLAND HILLS GOLF CLUB
PU-11619 H Dr. N., Battle Creek, 49017, Calhoun County, (616)965-0809, 6 miles E of
Battle Creek.
Opened: 1973. **Holes:** 18. **Par:** 72/72. **Yards:** 6,327/5,517. **Course rating:** 71.5/73.3.
Slope: N/A. **Architect:** George V. Nickolaou. **Green fee:** $14/$14. **Credit cards:** None.
Reduced fees: N/A. **Caddies:** No. **Golf carts:** $18. **Discount golf packages:** No.
Season: March-Nov. **High:** May-Aug. **On site lodging:** No. **Rental clubs:** No. **Walking
policy:** Unrestricted walking. **Metal spikes allowed:** Yes. **Range:** No. **To obtain tee
times:** Call golf shop.
Subscriber comments: Popular blue-collar course with impressive greens...Can be
seen from expressway, worth afternoon stop...Very well groomed greens...Good value,
easy to get tee times on short notice...Excellent value.

★★½THE OAKS COUNTRY CLUB
3711 Niles Rd., St. Joseph, 49085, Berrien County, (616)429-8411.
Call club for further information.
Subscriber comments: Fast greens...Hard and fast but fair. Very busy...Well maintained, friendly staff...Back nine a bit classier...Good course for the cost...Wide open
front nine, tighter back nine...Easy to get on, nice challenge, straightforward test of
golf...Great back nine.

★★★OCEANA COUNTRY CLUB
PU-3333 W. Weaver Rd., Shelby, 49455, Oceana County, (616)861-4211, 25 miles N of
Muskegon.
Opened: 1962. **Holes:** 18. **Par:** 73/71. **Yards:** 6,172/5,403. **Course rating:** 70.0/71.8.
Slope: 120/123. **Architect:** Designed by members. **Green fee:** $13/$17. **Credit cards:**
MC,VISA. **Reduced fees:** Weekdays, low season, juniors. **Caddies:** No. **Golf carts:** $9.
Discount golf packages: No. **Season:** April-Oct. **High:** June-Aug. **On site lodging:**
No. **Rental clubs:** Yes. **Walking policy:** Unrestricted walking. **Metal spikes allowed:**
Yes. **Range:** Yes (mats). **To obtain tee times:** Call anytime.

Subscriber comments: Long par 5s and par 4s on back nine...Exceptional greens...Old course; too many power lines; basic layout...Excellent value for quality of course...Bargain for seniors...Tough greens...Quaint course, usually in good shape.

★★★½ OLD CHANNEL TRAIL GOLF CLUB
PU-8325 N. Old Channel Trail, Montague, 49437, Muskegon County, (616)894-5076, 20 miles NW of Muskegon.
Opened: 1927. **Holes:** 27. **Par:** 72/74. **Yards:** 6,605/5,115. **Course rating:** 69.5/71.2. **Slope:** 123/118. **Architect:** R.B. Harris/Bruce Matthews/Jerry Matthews. **Green fee:** $17/$21. **Credit cards:** MC, VISA. **Reduced fees:** Weekdays, low season, twilight, seniors. **Caddies:** No. **Golf carts:** $18. **Discount golf packages:** Yes. **Season:** April-Oct. **High:** July-Aug. **On site lodging:** No. **Rental clubs:** Yes. **Walking policy:** Walking at certain times. **Metal spikes allowed:** Yes. **Range:** Yes (grass). **To obtain tee times:** Call.
Subscriber comments: All three nines different...Course in great shape...New nine is exceptional...Bring your clubs and picnic basket...Each nine built on different terrain on Lake Michigan...New nine allows wide variety and easy access...An outstanding public course.

★★ OLDE MILL GOLF CLUB
6101 West XY Ave., Schoolcraft, 49087, Kalamazoo County, (616)679-5625, 13 miles S of Kalamazoo.
Opened: N/A. **Holes:** 18. **Par:** 72. **Yards:** 6,195. **Course rating:** 69.2. **Slope:** 117. **Architect:** N/A. **Green fee:** $18/$20. **Credit cards:** MC, VISA. **Reduced fees:** N/A. **Caddies:** No. **Golf carts:** $20. **Discount golf packages:** No. **Season:** March-Nov. **High:** June-Sept. **On site lodging:** No. **Rental clubs:** Yes. **Walking policy:** Unrestricted walking. **Metal spikes allowed:** Yes. **Range:** Yes (grass). **To obtain tee times:** Call up to 7 days in advance.

★★★ ORCHARD HILLS GOLF COURSE
PU-714 125th Ave., Shelbyville, 49344, Allegan County, (616)672-7096, 20 miles S of Grand Rapids.
Opened: 1955. **Holes:** 18. **Par:** 72/74. **Yards:** 5,800/5,200. **Course rating:** 67.6/68.3. **Slope:** 110/110. **Architect:** Art Young. **Green fee:** $13/$18. **Credit cards:** All major. **Reduced fees:** Weekdays, low season, seniors, juniors. **Caddies:** No. **Golf carts:** N/A. **Discount golf packages:** No. **Season:** April-Oct. **High:** May-Aug. **On site lodging:** No. **Rental clubs:** Yes. **Walking policy:** Unrestricted walking. **Metal spikes allowed:** Yes. **Range:** Yes (grass). **To obtain tee times:** Call in advance.
Subscriber comments: The best course in southeast Michigan...A fun course to play. Not too hard...Best public course in the area...Being redesigned and getting better.

★★★★ THE ORCHARDS GOLF CLUB
PU-62900 Campground Rd., Washington, 48094, Macomb County, (810)786-7200, 30 miles N of Detroit.
Opened: 1993. **Holes:** 18. **Par:** 72/72. **Yards:** 7,026/5,158. **Course rating:** 74.5/70.3. **Slope:** 136/123. **Architect:** Robert Trent Jones Jr.. **Green fee:** $35/$65. **Credit cards:** All major. **Reduced fees:** Low season, twilight. **Caddies:** No. **Golf carts:** Included in Green Fee. **Discount golf packages:** No. **Season:** April-Oct. **High:** May-Sept. **On site lodging:** No. **Rental clubs:** Yes. **Walking policy:** Unrestricted walking. **Metal spikes allowed:** Yes. **Range:** Yes (grass). **To obtain tee times:** Call 30 days in advance.
Notes: Ranked 16th in 1997 Best in State.
Subscriber comments: Great from back tees...Should be a tour stop...Nice clubhouse...Top notch service with superb facilities...Great condition...Nice option to walk...As tough as you want to make it...Best public course in Michigan...Nine tight holes, nine open holes...Great par 5s.

(GOOD SERVICE)

★★½ OXFORD HILLS GOLF CLUB
PU-300 E. Drahner Rd., Oxford, 48371, Oakland County, (248)628-2518, 8 miles N of Pontiac.
Opened: 1964. **Holes:** 18. **Par:** 72/72. **Yards:** 6,522/5,312. **Course rating:** 71.4/70.5. **Slope:** 120/116. **Architect:** John Hubbard. **Green fee:** $20/$24. **Credit cards:** MC, VISA, AMEX. **Reduced fees:** Weekdays, low season, seniors, juniors. **Caddies:** No.

Golf carts: $11. **Discount golf packages:** No. **Season:** April-Nov. **High:** June-Aug. **On site lodging:** No. **Rental clubs:** Yes. **Walking policy:** Unrestricted walking. **Metal spikes allowed:** Yes. **Range:** No. **To obtain tee times:** Call in advance.
Subscriber comments: Better than average...Short front, long back...Fun, good mix of holes...Gets lots of play. Good condition...Don't walk the back nine...Great back nine, No. 11 is a 480-yard par 4...Fair challenge with fast greens...Two long par 5s. Nice all around course.

★★PALMER PARK GOLF COURSE

Woodward At 7 Mile Rd., Detroit, 48203, Wayne County, (313)883-2525.
Call club for further information.

PARK SHORE GOLF COURSE

PU-610 Park Shore Dr., Cassopolis, 49031, Cass County, (616)445-2834.
Opened: 1928. **Holes:** 18. **Par:** 68/70. **Yards:** 4,981/4,981. **Course rating:** 62.8/63.4. **Slope:** 97/90. **Architect:** N/A. **Green fee:** $10/$14. **Credit cards:** None. **Reduced fees:** Twilight. **Caddies:** No. **Golf carts:** $18. **Discount golf packages:** No. **Season:** April-Oct. **High:** June-Aug. **On site lodging:** No. **Rental clubs:** No. **Walking policy:** Unrestricted walking. **Metal spikes allowed:** Yes. **Range:** No. **To obtain tee times:** Call.

PARTRIDGE CREEK GOLF CLUB

PU-43843 Romeo Plank Rd., Clinton Township, 48038, Macomb County, (810)228-3030, 30 miles NW of Mt. Clemens.
Credit cards: MC,VISA,AMEX. **Caddies:** No. **Discount golf packages:** No. **On site lodging:** No. **Rental clubs:** Yes. **Walking policy:** Unrestricted walking. **Range:** Yes (grass). **To obtain tee times:** Call up to 7 days in advance.
★½NORTH/WEST/SOUTH COURSE
Opened: 1960. **Holes:** 27. **Par:** 72/72. **Yards:** 6,439/5,220 (N/W); 6,455/5,165 (N/S); 6,706/5,225 (S/W). **Course rating:** 70.0/69.0. **Slope:** 114/114. **Architect:** Kenny Nieman. **Green fee:** $17/$19. **Reduced fees:** Twilight, seniors, juniors. **Golf carts:** $22. **Season:** March-Nov. **High:** May-Aug. **Metal spikes allowed:** Yes.
THE HAWK
Opened: 1996. **Holes:** 18. **Par:** 72/72. **Yards:** 7,024/5,366. **Course rating:** 73.6/70.6. **Slope:** 132/126. **Architect:** Jerry Matthews. **Green fee:** $45/$50. **Reduced fees:** Low season, twilight, seniors, juniors. **Golf carts:** Included in Green Fee. **Season:** March-Nov. **High:** N/A. **Metal spikes allowed:** No.

★★½PAW PAW LAKE GOLF COURSE

PU-4548 Forest Beach Rd., Watervliet, 49098, Berrien County, (616)463-3831, 10 miles NE of Benton Harbor.
Opened: 1928. **Holes:** 18. **Par:** 70/73. **Yards:** 6,105/5,064. **Course rating:** 68.5. **Slope:** N/A. **Architect:** N/A. **Green fee:** $18/$20. **Credit cards:** None. **Reduced fees:** Weekdays, low season, twilight. **Caddies:** No. **Golf carts:** $10. **Discount golf packages:** No. **Season:** April-Nov. **High:** June-Aug. **On site lodging:** No. **Rental clubs:** Yes. **Walking policy:** Unrestricted walking. **Metal spikes allowed:** Yes. **Range:** Yes (grass). **To obtain tee times:** Call golf shop.
Subscriber comments: Nice course with few services. Lots of water...Short, scenic course on lake, drains poorly...Average, pretty dry, gets lots of play...Somewhat pricey for a mediocre course...Short little course. Good to tune up the irons.

★★PEBBLE CREEK GOLF COURSE

24095 Currie Rd., South Lyon, 48178, Oakland County, (248)437-5411.
Architect: Don Herford. **Caddies:** No. **Discount golf packages:** No. **On site lodging:** No. **Rental clubs:** No. **Metal spikes allowed:** Yes. **Range:** No.
Call club for further information.

★★PEBBLEWOOD COUNTRY CLUB

PU-9794 Jericho Rd., Bridgman, 49106, Berrien County, (616)465-5611, 35 miles NW of South Bend, IN.
Opened: 1923. **Holes:** 18. **Par:** 68/70. **Yards:** 5,421/4,636. **Course rating:** 65.6/65.6. **Slope:** 106/106. **Architect:** N/A. **Green fee:** $18/$20. **Credit cards:** All major. **Reduced fees:** N/A. **Caddies:** No. **Golf carts:** $18. **Discount golf packages:** No.

MICHIGAN

Season: March-Nov. **High:** June-Aug. **On site lodging:** No. **Rental clubs:** Yes. **Walking policy:** Unrestricted walking. **Metal spikes allowed:** Yes. **Range:** No. **To obtain tee times:** Call golf shop.

★★★PHEASANT RUN GOLF COURSE

PU-46500 Summit Pkwy., Canton, 48188, Wayne County, (313)397-6460, 15 miles W of Detroit.
Opened: 1995. **Holes:** 18. **Par:** 72/72. **Yards:** 7,001/5,143. **Course rating:** 73.4/68.9. **Slope:** 138/117. **Architect:** Arthur Hills and Steve Forrest. **Green fee:** $30/$52. **Credit cards:** MC,VISA. **Reduced fees:** Twilight. **Caddies:** No. **Golf carts:** Included in Green Fee. **Discount golf packages:** No. **Season:** April-Nov. **High:** May-Sept. **On site lodging:** No. **Rental clubs:** Yes. **Walking policy:** Mandatory cart. **Metal spikes allowed:** No. **Range:** Yes (grass/mats). **To obtain tee times:** Call up to 14 days in advance.
Subscriber comments: New city course, good condition...Twilight bargain. Excellent links style course...Homes a little too close for comfort...Bring lots of club to play from championship tees...Great condition. Very playable for all handicaps...Great challenge from the tips...Typical subdivision golf course.

★★★½PIERCE LAKE GOLF COURSE

PM-2960 Washtenaw Ave., Chelsea, 48107, Washtenaw County, (313)475-5858, 15 miles W of Ann Arbor.
Opened: 1996. **Holes:** 18. **Par:** 72/72. **Yards:** 6,853/4,753. **Course rating:** 72.5/67.4. **Slope:** 135/109. **Architect:** Harry Bowers. **Green fee:** $20/$24. **Credit cards:** MC,VISA. **Reduced fees:** N/A. **Caddies:** No. **Golf carts:** $10. **Discount golf packages:** No. **Season:** N/A. **High:** N/A. **On site lodging:** No. **Rental clubs:** Yes. **Walking policy:** Unrestricted walking. **Metal spikes allowed:** No. **Range:** No. **To obtain tee times:** Call up to 7 days in advance.
Subscriber comments: Nice new course, needs another year...18 is the toughest par 3 in state...Varied and challenging holes...Great course for the money...Beautifully set in wooded, protected, marshland. Challenging carries, great layout...Highway noise...Great $20 course.

★★★PINE HILL GOLF CLUB

PU-3459 U.S. 31 N., Brutus, 49716, Emmet County, (616)529-6574, 12 miles N of Petoskey.
Opened: 1991. **Holes:** 18. **Par:** 71/72. **Yards:** 6,007/5,059. **Course rating:** 71.0/72.0. **Slope:** 113/113. **Architect:** Larry Holbert. **Green fee:** $20/$30. **Credit cards:** MC,VISA. **Reduced fees:** Low season, twilight, seniors, juniors. **Caddies:** No. **Golf carts:** $20. **Discount golf packages:** Yes. **Season:** April-Oct. **High:** June-Aug. **On site lodging:** No. **Rental clubs:** Yes. **Walking policy:** Unrestricted walking. **Metal spikes allowed:** Yes. **Range:** Yes (grass). **To obtain tee times:** Not required.
Subscriber comments: Greens were good...Not well marked (I aimed for a couple wrong greens)...Difficult back nine, easy front. Lots of water...Not for those who spray it around. Narrow is operative word.
Special Notes: Also has an 18-hole par-54 executive course.

★★★½PINE KNOB GOLF CLUB

PU-5580 Waldon Rd., Clarkston, 48346, Oakland County, (248)625-4430, 9 miles NW of Pontiac.
Opened: 1972. **Holes:** 18. **Par:** 72/70. **Yards:** 6,647/5,227. **Course rating:** 71.4/69.9. **Slope:** 123/120. **Architect:** Leo Bishop. **Green fee:** $39/$47. **Credit cards:** All major. **Reduced fees:** N/A. **Caddies:** No. **Golf carts:** Included in Green Fee. **Discount golf packages:** No. **Season:** April-Oct. **High:** June-Sept. **On site lodging:** No. **Rental clubs:** Yes. **Walking policy:** Mandatory cart. **Metal spikes allowed:** Yes. **Range:** Yes. **To obtain tee times:** Call seven days in advance.
Subscriber comments: Condition of course improving yearly...Good resort type course. Great food selection at the turn...Much better layout and service than expected...Huge greens, well kept fairways, beautiful layout...Has the flavor of a northern Michigan course...If you hit a fade this is your course...Great view of downtown Detroit from high hill.

★★PINE LAKE GOLF COURSE

PU-1018 Haslett Rd., Haslett, 48840, Ingham County, (517)339-8281, 10 miles E of Lansing.
Opened: 1954. **Holes:** 18. **Par:** 71/71. **Yards:** 6,155/4,677. **Course rating:** 69.9/67.0. **Slope:** 122/113. **Architect:** N/A. **Green fee:** $16/$18. **Credit cards:** MC,VISA. **Reduced fees:** Weekdays, low season, twilight, seniors, juniors. **Caddies:** No. **Golf carts:** $11. **Discount golf packages:** Yes. **Season:** March-Dec. **High:** June-Aug. **On site lodging:** No. **Rental clubs:** Yes. **Walking policy:** Unrestricted walking. **Metal spikes allowed:** Yes. **Range:** No. **To obtain tee times:** Call golf shop.

★★★PINE RIVER GOLF CLUB

PU-2244 Pine River Rd., Standish, 48658, Arenac County, (517)846-6819, 30 miles N of Bay City.
Opened: 1966. **Holes:** 18. **Par:** 71/74. **Yards:** 6,250/5,156. **Course rating:** 70.8/70.7. **Slope:** 126/126. **Architect:** Bruce Matthews and Jerry Matthews. **Green fee:** $18/$22. **Credit cards:** MC,VISA,DISC. **Reduced fees:** Weekdays, seniors, juniors. **Caddies:** No. **Golf carts:** $10. **Discount golf packages:** No. **Season:** April-Oct. **High:** June-Aug. **On site lodging:** No. **Rental clubs:** No. **Walking policy:** Unrestricted walking. **Metal spikes allowed:** Yes. **Range:** Yes (grass). **To obtain tee times:** Call golf shop.
Subscriber comments: Old front, new back...Back nine is great...Course has possibilities, but needs more care...Tough, tight back nine...Excellent challenge...Great course for average golfer...New nine is terrific. Old needs upgrade. Still a great value...Take the driver out on the front, put it in the trunk on the back.

★★★PINE TRACE GOLF CLUB

PU-3600 Pine Trace Blvd., Rochester Hills, 48309, Oakland County, (248)852-7100, 30 miles N of Detroit.
Opened: 1989. **Holes:** 18. **Par:** 72/72. **Yards:** 6,610/4,974. **Course rating:** 72.8/69.9. **Slope:** 139/125. **Architect:** Arthur Hills. **Green fee:** $45/$55. **Credit cards:** MC,VISA. **Reduced fees:** Low season, seniors, juniors. **Caddies:** No. **Golf carts:** Included in Green Fee. **Discount golf packages:** No. **Season:** March-Nov. **High:** May-Sept. **On site lodging:** No. **Rental clubs:** No. **Walking policy:** Walking at certain times. **Metal spikes allowed:** Yes. **Range:** Yes. **To obtain tee times:** Tee times can be reserved up to 7 days in advance.
Subscriber comments: Excellent course, difficult holes...Many challenging holes, must use every shot you have...Target golf, bent greens and fairways...Excellent condition, one of southeastern Michigan's best...Heavily used, pressure to play faster...Rangers are a bit pushy.

★★★PINE VALLEY GOLF CLUB

PU-16801 31 Mile Rd., Ray, 48096, Macomb County, (810)752-9633, 12 miles NW of Mt. Clemens.
Opened: 1968. **Holes:** 27. **Architect:** Donald McKinley. **Green fee:** $18/$23. **Credit cards:** MC,VISA. **Reduced fees:** Weekdays, low season, twilight, seniors. **Caddies:** No. **Golf carts:** $20. **Discount golf packages:** No. **Season:** March-Nov. **High:** May-Sept. **On site lodging:** No. **Rental clubs:** Yes. **Walking policy:** Walking at certain times. **Metal spikes allowed:** Yes. **Range:** Yes (grass/mats). **To obtain tee times:** Call 7 days in advance.
BLUE/GOLD
Par: 72/70. **Yards:** 6,373/4,971. **Course rating:** 68.3/64.5. **Slope:** 114/100.
RED/BLUE
Par: 72/72. **Yards:** 6,259/5,417. **Course rating:** 69.5/65.6. **Slope:** 118/106.
RED/GOLD
Par: 72/70. **Yards:** 6,490/5,208. **Course rating:** 69.0/64.7. **Slope:** 110/103.
Subscriber comments: A step above your usual public course...Pine trees make it good for fall play...A hidden secret...Beautiful, scenic...Pure muny...Front nine challenging, back nine boring...Good elevation changes...Par 5s very reachable, basic golf...Good northern suburban course, well kept, good value...Very good shape...Good course for a challenge...Pretty course and forgiving confidence booster.

MICHIGAN

★★★PINE VIEW GOLF CLUB
PU-5820 Stoney Creek Rd., Ypsilanti, 48197, Washtenaw County, (313)481-0500, (800)214-5963, 3 miles S of Ypsilanti.
Opened: 1990. **Holes:** 18. **Par:** 72/72. **Yards:** 6,533/5,267. **Course rating:** 71.3/70.7. **Slope:** 124/119. **Architect:** Harley Hodges and Greg Hodges. **Green fee:** $13/$32. **Credit cards:** MC,VISA. **Reduced fees:** Weekdays, low season, twilight, seniors, juniors. **Caddies:** No. **Golf carts:** $12. **Discount golf packages:** Yes. **Season:** March-Dec. **High:** April-Sept. **On site lodging:** No. **Rental clubs:** Yes. **Walking policy:** Unrestricted walking. **Metal spikes allowed:** Yes. **Range:** Yes (grass/mats). **To obtain tee times:** Call 7 days in advance. Groups of 20 or more tee times can be made 1 year in advance.
Subscriber comments: Fairly easy course, very relaxing...Good but not great...Perfect for league play, great greens...A pleasant surprise...Great location; picturesque; good price for the area...Back nine tight...Front and back very different; front is open, back has narrow fairways...Short but demanding...Would play it daily.
Special Notes: Also has 9-hole par-30 executive course.

★★★½PINECROFT GOLF CLUB
PU-8260 Henry Rd., Beulah, 49617, Benzie County, (616)882-9100, 30 miles SW of Traverse City.
Opened: 1992. **Holes:** 18. **Par:** 72/72. **Yards:** 6,447/4,975. **Course rating:** 70.8/69.6. **Slope:** 121/124. **Architect:** L. Stone/A. Normal/J. Cole/C. Carlson. **Green fee:** $15/$29. **Credit cards:** MC,VISA. **Reduced fees:** Low season, twilight. **Caddies:** No. **Golf carts:** $10. **Discount golf packages:** No. **Season:** April-Oct. **High:** June-Aug. **On site lodging:** No. **Rental clubs:** Yes. **Walking policy:** Unrestricted walking. **Metal spikes allowed:** Yes. **Range:** Yes (grass). **To obtain tee times:** Call golf shop.
Subscriber comments: A sleeper...Great views; fun course...Very courteous staff, nice track. Beautiful views of Crystal Lake...One of the best values in Michigan...Can't be beat for the money...Fairway grass cut too high...Off the stimpmeter greens...Too expensive for quality of course.

★★★THE PINES AT LAKE ISABELLA GOLF CLUB
PU-7231 Clubhouse Dr., Weidman, 48893, Isabella County, (517)644-2300, (800)741-3435, 10 miles W of Mt. Pleasant.
Opened: 1969. **Holes:** 18. **Par:** 72/72. **Yards:** 6,856/5,529. **Course rating:** 72.5/72.7. **Slope:** 128/125. **Architect:** N/A. **Green fee:** $20/$25. **Credit cards:** MC,VISA,DISC. **Reduced fees:** Weekdays, low season, seniors. **Caddies:** No. **Golf carts:** $12. **Discount golf packages:** Yes. **Season:** April-Oct. **High:** N/A. **On site lodging:** No. **Rental clubs:** Yes. **Metal spikes allowed:** Yes. **Range:** Yes (grass). **Walking policy:** Unrestricted walking. **To obtain tee times:** Call anytime.
Subscriber comments: One of the best courses in mid-Michigan...Course lives up to its name...Pines make flat course interesting...Great for outings...Usually windy...Delightful.

★★THE PINES GOLF COURSE
5050 Byron Center Ave., Wyoming, 49509, Kent County, (616)538-8380, 12 miles S of Grand Rapid.
Opened: 1968. **Holes:** 18. **Par:** 70/72. **Yards:** 5,542/5,124. **Course rating:** 67.3. **Slope:** N/A. **Green fee:** $12/$18. **Reduced fees:** Weekdays, low season, seniors, juniors. **Golf carts:** $20. **Season:** March-Nov. **High:** May-Aug. **Walking policy:** Mandatory cart. **To obtain tee times:** Call up to 7 days in advance.

★½PIPESTONE CREEK GOLF COURSE
PU-6768 Naomi Rd., Eau Claire, 49111, Berrien County, (616)944-1611, 10 miles E of Benton Harbor.
Opened: 1957. **Holes:** 18. **Par:** 67/68. **Yards:** 4,402/4,188. **Course rating:** N/A. **Slope:** N/A. **Architect:** N/A. **Green fee:** $15/$17. **Credit cards:** MC,VISA. **Reduced fees:** Low season. **Caddies:** No. **Golf carts:** $18. **Discount golf packages:** No. **Season:** March-Oct. **High:** June-Sept. **On site lodging:** No. **Rental clubs:** Yes. **Walking policy:** Unrestricted walking. **Metal spikes allowed:** Yes. **Range:** No. **To obtain tee times:** Call golf shop.

★★PLEASANT HILLS GOLF CLUB

PU-4452 E. Millbrook Rd., Mt. Pleasant, 48858, Isabella County, (517)772-0487, 50 miles NW of Saginaw.
Opened: 1964. **Holes:** 18. **Par:** 72/72. **Yards:** 6,012/4,607. **Course rating:** 68.2/65.9. **Slope:** 110/107. **Architect:** Richard Krauss. **Green fee:** $16/$18. **Credit cards:** MC,VISA,DISC. **Reduced fees:** Weekdays, low season, twilight, seniors, juniors. **Caddies:** No. **Golf carts:** $20. **Discount golf packages:** No. **Season:** March-Dec. **High:** June-Aug. **On site lodging:** No. **Rental clubs:** Yes. **Walking policy:** Unrestricted walking. **Metal spikes allowed:** Yes. **Range:** No. **To obtain tee times:** Call 1 day in advance.

★★½PLUM BROOK GOLF CLUB

PU-13390 Plum Brook Dr., Sterling Heights, 48312, Macomb County, (810)264-9411, 10 miles N of Detroit.
Opened: 1927. **Holes:** 18. **Par:** 71/71. **Yards:** 6,300/5,500. **Course rating:** 67.5/68.1. **Slope:** 109/110. **Architect:** N/A. **Green fee:** $19/$23. **Credit cards:** MC,VISA. **Reduced fees:** Twilight. **Caddies:** No. **Golf carts:** $20. **Discount golf packages:** No. **Season:** March-Dec. **High:** May-Sept. **On site lodging:** No. **Rental clubs:** No. **Walking policy:** Unrestricted walking. **Metal spikes allowed:** No. **Range:** No. **To obtain tee times:** Call.
Subscriber comments: Course always in good shape. Playable for all...Fairly flat. Nice course for a quick 18...Excellent condition for a league course...Crowded...Open late in season...Friendly service. Very well kept...Nice for a twilight with my wife...Since 1927, a nice course to walk, a friendly little well kept neighborhood course.

★★★½POHLCAT GOLF COURSE

R-6595 E. Airport Rd., Mt. Pleasant, 48858, Isabella County, (517)773-4221, (800)292-8891, 60 miles N of Lansing.
Opened: 1991. **Holes:** 18. **Par:** 72/72. **Yards:** 6,810/5,140. **Course rating:** 74.2/70.8. **Slope:** 139/124. **Architect:** Dan Pohl. **Green fee:** $25/$65. **Credit cards:** All major. **Reduced fees:** Weekdays, low season, resort guests, twilight, seniors, juniors. **Caddies:** No. **Golf carts:** Included in Green Fee. **Discount golf packages:** Yes. **Season:** April-Nov. **High:** July-Sept. **On site lodging:** Yes. **Rental clubs:** Yes. **Walking policy:** Walking at certain times. **Metal spikes allowed:** No. **Range:** Yes (grass/mats). **To obtain tee times:** Call 800 number after Feb. 1 for anytime.
Subscriber comments: Short resort style course, very playable...Good mix of tough/easy holes...Good vacation course...Great condition...Nice layout, room to hit the ball...Tough from back tees...Perfect fairways, great variety...Casino close by...Typical resort course, nicely maintained, but nothing fancy...A bit expensive for this area.

★★½PONTIAC COUNTRY CLUB

4335 Elizabeth Lake Rd, Waterford, 48328, Oakland County, (248)682-6333, 3 miles W of Pontiac.
Opened: 1914. **Holes:** 18. **Par:** 72/74. **Yards:** 6,366/5,552. **Course rating:** 70.4/71.6. **Slope:** 125. **Architect:** N/A. **Green fee:** $20/$30. **Credit cards:** MC,VISA,DISC. **Reduced fees:** N/A. **Caddies:** No. **Golf carts:** $22. **Discount golf packages:** No. **Season:** April-Nov. **High:** May-Sept. **On site lodging:** No. **Rental clubs:** Yes. **Walking policy:** Unrestricted walking. **Metal spikes allowed:** Yes. **Range:** Yes (grass). **To obtain tee times:** Call up to 7 days in advance.
Subscriber comments: Many holes have water...Great old course!...Improved condtions and layout...Lots of play but in good shape...Always fun to play, accommodating...Excellent shape, a little pricey...Walking allowed...Best public course greens around. Not very long but challenging...Short with small undulating greens.

★★½PONTIAC MUNICIPAL GOLF COURSE

PU-800 Golf Dr., Pontiac, 48341, Oakland County, (248)858-8990.
Call club for further information.
Subscriber comments: Redesigned, tough!...A redesigned first year course—will get better...Short, simple course...Good routing on redesign.

★★½PORTAGE LAKE GOLF COURSE
PU-Michigan Tech. Univ., U.S. 41, Houghton, 49931, Houghton County, (906)487-2641, 200 miles N of Green Bay, WI.
Opened: 1902. **Holes:** 18. **Par:** 72/72. **Yards:** 6,266/5,297. **Course rating:** 69.2/69.8. **Slope:** 115/113. **Architect:** N/A. **Green fee:** $22/$22. **Credit cards:** MC,VISA,DISC. **Reduced fees:** N/A. **Caddies:** No. **Golf carts:** $20. **Discount golf packages:** No. **Season:** May-Oct. **High:** July-Aug. **On site lodging:** No. **Rental clubs:** Yes. **Walking policy:** Unrestricted walking. **Metal spikes allowed:** No. **Range:** Yes. **To obtain tee times:** Call up to 2 days in advance.
Subscriber comments: Good, tough greens...Two different nines, one built using horses...Front nine has a modern layout, back nine is short—take in the view on the second shot on the par-5 17th.

PORTLAND COUNTRY CLUB
PU-Divine Hwy, Portland, 48875, Ionia County, (517)647-4521, 17 miles W of Lansing.
Opened: 1927. **Holes:** 18. **Par:** 70/70. **Yards:** 5,568/4,542. **Course rating:** 67.1/70.0. **Slope:** 115/118. **Architect:** Charles Lockwood/Bob Waara. **Green fee:** $15/$15. **Credit cards:** None. **Reduced fees:** Low season, twilight, seniors, juniors. **Caddies:** No. **Golf carts:** $18. **Discount golf packages:** No. **Season:** March-Nov. **High:** May-Sept. **On site lodging:** No. **Rental clubs:** Yes. **Walking policy:** Unrestricted walking. **Metal spikes allowed:** Yes. **Range:** No. **To obtain tee times:** Call up to 7 days in advance.

★★PRAIRIE CREEK GOLF COURSE
PU-800 E. Webb Dr., De Witt, 48820, Clinton County, (517)669-1958, 12 miles N of Lansing.
Opened: 1979. **Holes:** 18. **Par:** 72/72. **Yards:** 6,165/5,171. **Course rating:** N/A. **Slope:** N/A. **Architect:** N/A. **Green fee:** $9/$15. **Credit cards:** None. **Reduced fees:** Weekdays, low season, twilight, seniors, juniors. **Caddies:** No. **Golf carts:** $10. **Discount golf packages:** Yes. **Season:** March-Oct. **High:** June-Aug. **On site lodging:** No. **Rental clubs:** Yes. **Walking policy:** Unrestricted walking. **Metal spikes allowed:** Yes. **Range:** No. **To obtain tee times:** Call golf shop for weekends.

★★PRAIRIEWOOD GOLF COURSE
PU-315 Prairiewood Dr., Otsego, 49078, Allegan County, (616)694-6633, 14 miles N of Kalamazoo.
Opened: 1990. **Holes:** 18. **Par:** 72/72. **Yards:** 6,519/4,705. **Course rating:** 70.4/66.2. **Slope:** 114/106. **Architect:** Warner Bowen/Duane Kuiper. **Green fee:** $15/$18. **Credit cards:** MC,VISA. **Reduced fees:** Weekdays, low season, seniors, juniors. **Caddies:** No. **Golf carts:** $10. **Discount golf packages:** No. **Season:** April-Nov. **High:** June-Aug. **On site lodging:** No. **Rental clubs:** Yes. **Walking policy:** Unrestricted walking. **Metal spikes allowed:** Yes. **Range:** Yes (grass/mats). **To obtain tee times:** Call.

★★★THE QUEST GOLF CLUB
PU-116 Questview Dr., Houghton Lake, 48629, Roscommon County, (517)422-4516, 115 miles N of Lansing.
Opened: 1994. **Holes:** 18. **Par:** 72/72. **Yards:** 6,773/5,027. **Course rating:** 72.0/73.0. **Slope:** 130/118. **Architect:** Ken Green and John Sanford. **Green fee:** $48/$58. **Credit cards:** MC,VISA. **Reduced fees:** Weekdays, low season. **Caddies:** No. **Golf carts:** Included in Green Fee. **Discount golf packages:** Yes. **Season:** April-Oct. **High:** May-Oct. **On site lodging:** No. **Rental clubs:** Yes. **Walking policy:** Walking at certain times. **Metal spikes allowed:** Yes. **Range:** Yes (grass). **To obtain tee times:** Call golf shop. Groups of nine or more are required to send a deposit or provide a credit card number.
Subscriber comments: Beautiful but overpriced...Beautiful views of lake...Good northern resort golf, bad view of back of Kmart...Too expensive...People are outstanding and course will be very soon...Course in very good condition...Great northern Michigan value...Needs to mature.

★★½RACKHAM GOLF CLUB
PU-10100 W. Ten Mile Rd., Huntington Woods, 48070, Oakland County, (248)543-4040, 15 miles N of Detroit.
Opened: 1924. **Holes:** 18. **Par:** 71/72. **Yards:** 6,555/5,413. **Course rating:** 71.1/70.7. **Slope:** 118/115. **Architect:** Donald Ross. **Green fee:** $20/$26. **Credit cards:**

MC,VISA,AMEX. **Reduced fees:** Weekdays, low season, twilight, seniors, juniors. **Caddies:** No. **Golf carts:** $20. **Discount golf packages:** Yes. **Season:** Year-round. **High:** May-Sept. **On site lodging:** No. **Rental clubs:** Yes. **Walking policy:** Unrestricted walking. **Metal spikes allowed:** No. **Range:** No. **To obtain tee times:** Call with credit card to guarantee.

Subscriber comments: Being brought back to life...Partial Donald Ross design. Decent track...Great course for the money...Well maintained, good prices, great par 4s...Recovering from years of abuse, but needs time...Slow play from 11am to 3pm on weekends...Built in 1920s...Detroit public course that's largely improved in last two years...Open all winter.

RAISIN RIVER COUNTRY CLUB

PU-1500 N. Dixie Hwy., Monroe, 48162, Monroe County, (313)289-3700, (800)321-9564, 25 miles S of Detroit.
Architect: Charles Maddox. **Credit cards:** None. **Caddies:** No. **Golf carts:** $10. **Discount golf packages:** Yes. **Season:** March-Nov. **High:** May-Sept. **On site lodging:** Yes. **Rental clubs:** Yes. **Walking policy:** Unrestricted walking. **Metal spikes allowed:** Yes. **Range:** Yes (grass/mats).

★★★**EAST COURSE**
Opened: 1974. **Holes:** 18. **Par:** 71/71. **Yards:** 6,930/5,606. **Course rating:** 72.9/70.1. **Slope:** 122/111. **Green fee:** $17/$17. **Reduced fees:** Low season, resort guests, seniors, juniors. **To obtain tee times:** Call 8 days in advance for weekend and holidays only. Tee times not required for weekdays.
Subscriber comments: Much better than the West Course...Best greens around...Too flat by today's standards...Fairly priced, very solid service...Large greens (easy to 4-putt) with water hazards on tight holes...Slow...Huge greens, mostly open, well kept.

★★½**WEST COURSE**
Opened: 1964. **Holes:** 18. **Par:** 70/74. **Yards:** 6,106/5,749. **Course rating:** 66.9/70.6. **Slope:** 114/120. **Green fee:** $15/$15. **Reduced fees:** Resort guests, seniors, juniors. **To obtain tee times:** Call 8 days in advance for weekends and holidays only. Tee times not required for weekday play.
Subscriber comments: Uninspired layout...Flat terrain, large greens...Challenging, but not overbearing...Play the East Course...Good greens, good value, a little short...Short, manicured, fun course.

★★½RAISIN VALLEY GOLF CLUB

PU-4057 Comfort Rd., Tecumseh, 49286, Lenawee County, (517)423-2050, 35 miles N of Toledo, OH.
Opened: 1969. **Holes:** 18. **Par:** 71/71. **Yards:** 5,650/4,630. **Course rating:** 67.5/69.0. **Slope:** N/A. **Architect:** William Porter. **Green fee:** $10/$18. **Credit cards:** MC,VISA. **Reduced fees:** Weekdays, low season, seniors, juniors. **Caddies:** No. **Golf carts:** $18. **Discount golf packages:** No. **Season:** April-Nov. **High:** N/A. **On site lodging:** No. **Rental clubs:** Yes. **Walking policy:** Unrestricted walking. **Metal spikes allowed:** Yes. **Range:** No. **To obtain tee times:** Call 7 days in advance.
Subscriber comments: Well maintained...Wide variety of holes, short but challenging...Easy course. Great value, very good service...Ordinary...Well cared for...Good shape, easy short, cheap golf.
Special Notes: Spikeless shoes preferred.

★★RAMMLER GOLF CLUB

PU-38180 Utica Rd., Sterling Heights, 48312, Macomb County, (810)978-1411, 8 miles N of Detroit.
Opened: 1922. **Holes:** 27. **Par:** 71/71. **Yards:** 6,305/4,951. **Course rating:** 69.5/73.1. **Slope:** 113/119. **Architect:** N/A. **Green fee:** $20/$23. **Credit cards:** None. **Reduced fees:** Seniors. **Caddies:** No. **Golf carts:** $22. **Discount golf packages:** No. **Season:** April-Nov. **High:** June-Aug. **On site lodging:** No. **Rental clubs:** Yes. **Walking policy:** Unrestricted walking. **Metal spikes allowed:** Yes. **Range:** No. **To obtain tee times:** Call.

★★★½RATTLE RUN GOLF COURSE

PU-7163 St. Clair Highway, St. Clair, 48054, St. Clair County, (810)329-2070, 23 miles N of Detroit.
Opened: 1977. **Holes:** 18. **Par:** 72/75. **Yards:** 6,891/5,085. **Course rating:** 73.6/70.4.

Slope: 140/124. **Architect:** Lou Powers. **Green fee:** $35/$45. **Credit cards:** All major. **Reduced fees:** Low season, twilight, seniors, juniors. **Caddies:** No. **Golf carts:** Included in Green Fee. **Discount golf packages:** Yes. **Season:** April-Nov. **High:** May-Sept. **On site lodging:** No. **Rental clubs:** Yes. **Walking policy:** Walking at certain times. **Metal spikes allowed:** Yes. **Range:** Yes (grass). **To obtain tee times:** Call up to 14 days in advance.

Subscriber comments: A tough, true test of golf. Little pricey for area, but what a course...Recent improvements have made course better...This place is a gem...Should be in championship form this year or next...Best challenge in the state...Under 4 hour rounds on weekends...Suburban course with "up north" feel.

RAVENNA GOLF COURSE

PU-11566 Hts Ravenna Rd., Ravenna, 49451, Muskegon County, (616)853-6736, 10 miles E of Muskegon.

Opened: 1981. **Holes:** 18. **Par:** 37/35. **Yards:** 3,181/2,956. **Course rating:** N/A. **Slope:** N/A. **Architect:** N/A. **Green fee:** $7/$12. **Credit cards:** None. **Reduced fees:** Weekdays, seniors. **Caddies:** No. **Golf carts:** Included in Green Fee. **Discount golf packages:** No. **Season:** March-Oct. **High:** May-Aug. **On site lodging:** No. **Rental clubs:** No. **Walking policy:** Unrestricted walking. **Metal spikes allowed:** Yes. **Range:** No. **To obtain tee times:** Call anytime.

★★½REDDEMAN FARMS GOLF CLUB

PU-555 S. Dancer Rd., Chelsea, 48118, Washtenaw County, (313)475-3020, 8 miles W of Ann Arbor.

Opened: 1991. **Holes:** 18. **Par:** 72/72. **Yards:** 6,513/5,034. **Course rating:** 71.6/68.9. **Slope:** 122/120. **Architect:** Bob Louhouse and Howard Smith. **Green fee:** $22/$27. **Credit cards:** MC,VISA,DISC. **Reduced fees:** Weekdays, low season, twilight, seniors, juniors. **Caddies:** No. **Golf carts:** $10. **Discount golf packages:** No. **Season:** April-Nov. **High:** June-Sept. **On site lodging:** No. **Rental clubs:** Yes. **Walking policy:** Unrestricted walking. **Metal spikes allowed:** No. **Range:** Yes (grass). **To obtain tee times:** Call anytime.

Subscriber comments: Good course for average player...Nice husband and wife course...Excellent food...Good layout, good shape...Good public course, nice bar and grill...Terrific clubhouse and restaurant...Good layout, crowned greens...Good course to walk.

★★★RICHMOND FOREST GOLF CLUB

PU-33300 32 Mile Rd., Lenox, 48050, (810)727-4742, 30 miles N of Detroit.

Opened: 1994. **Holes:** 18. **Par:** 72/72. **Yards:** 6,542/5,288. **Course rating:** N/A. **Slope:** N/A. **Architect:** W. Bruce Matthews III. **Green fee:** $20/$22. **Credit cards:** MC,VISA. **Reduced fees:** Weekdays, low season, twilight, seniors, juniors. **Caddies:** No. **Golf carts:** $10. **Discount golf packages:** No. **Season:** March-Nov. **High:** June-Aug. **On site lodging:** No. **Rental clubs:** Yes. **Walking policy:** Unrestricted walking. **Metal spikes allowed:** Yes. **Range:** Yes (grass). **To obtain tee times:** Call or come in up to seven days in advance.

Subscriber comments: New course, nice layout, needs grooming...Deceiving...Open on most holes, fun to play...Great walking course...Fun course for anyone to play...Moderately priced...Maturing slowly.

★★RIDGEVIEW GOLF COURSE

10360 W. Main, Kalamazoo, 49009, Kalamazoo County, (616)375-8821.
Call club for further information.

RIVER BEND GOLF COURSE

PU-1370 W. State Rd., Hastings, 49058, Barry County, (616)945-3238, 18 miles S of Grand Rapids.

Opened: 1962. **Holes:** 27. **Architect:** N/A. **Green fee:** $15/$15. **Credit cards:** None. **Reduced fees:** N/A. **Caddies:** No. **Golf carts:** $25. **Discount golf packages:** No. **Season:** April-Oct. **High:** June-Aug. **On site lodging:** No. **Rental clubs:** No. **Walking policy:** Unrestricted walking. **Metal spikes allowed:** Yes. **Range:** No. **To obtain tee times:** Call golf shop.

RED/BLUE
Par: 72/72. **Yards:** 5,912/5,457.

RED/WHITE
Par: 72/72. **Yards:** 6,075/5,755.
WHITE/BLUE
Par: 72/72. **Yards:** 5,947/5,472.

★★½RIVERVIEW HIGHLANDS GOLF CLUB
PM-15015 Sibley Rd., Riverview, 48192, Wayne County, (313)479-2266, 20 miles S of Detroit.
Opened: 1973. **Holes:** 27. **Architect:** W.K. Newcomb/Arthur Hills. **Green fee:** $19/$19.
Credit cards: All major. **Reduced fees:** Weekdays, low season, twilight, seniors, juniors. **Caddies:** No. **Golf carts:** $22. **Discount golf packages:** Yes. **Season:** March-Dec. **High:** May-Sept. **On site lodging:** No. **Rental clubs:** Yes. **Walking policy:** Unrestricted walking. **Metal spikes allowed:** Yes. **Range:** No. **To obtain tee times:** Call.
GOLD/BLUE
Par: 72/72. **Yards:** 6,667/5,293. **Course rating:** 71.4/70.1. **Slope:** 119/118.
RED/BLUE
Par: 72/72. **Yards:** 6,485/5,224. **Course rating:** 70.8/70.1. **Slope:** 119/118.
RED/GOLD
Par: 72/70. **Yards:** 6,732/5,173. **Course rating:** 69.2/69.0. **Slope:** 115/112.
Subscriber comments: You can't go wrong...Course gets a little too much play, Red is the most challenging nine...Gold nine is fine, Blue nine bring your "A" game...Gold is open and Blue means water (need to hit straight)...Too crowded...Course excellent. Facilities fair...Acceptable local course...Too many geese...Red has treelined holes and combined with Blue is challenging...Red is tight, Gold is open.

★★★½RIVERWOOD RESORT
R-1313 E. Broomfield Rd., Mt. Pleasant, 48858, Isabella County, (517)772-5726, (800)882-5211, 45 miles N of Lansing.
Opened: 1932. **Holes:** 27. **Architect:** Jerry Matthews/Richard Figg. **Green fee:** $17/$21. **Credit cards:** MC,VISA,DISC. **Reduced fees:** Low season, resort guests, twilight, seniors. **Caddies:** No. **Golf carts:** $10. **Discount golf packages:** Yes. **Season:** March-Oct. **High:** June-Aug. **On site lodging:** Yes. **Rental clubs:** Yes. **Walking policy:** Walking at certain times. **Metal spikes allowed:** Yes. **Range:** Yes (grass). **To obtain tee times:** Call two months in advance.
RED/BLUE
Par: 72/72. **Yards:** 6,182/4,462. **Course rating:** 70.3/66.6. **Slope:** 121/106.
RED/WHITE
Par: 72/72. **Yards:** 6,600/4,952. **Course rating:** 72.0/69.4. **Slope:** 125/116.
WHITE/BLUE
Par: 72/72. **Yards:** 6,100/4,667. **Course rating:** 70.3/66.4. **Slope:** 116/109.
Subscriber comments: Very nice relaxing place...Very tight and long...Red is tough to drive with tight fairways...Great value...Some positive improvements lately...Blue course not up to level of Red course...Great fun, a challenge, well kept. Good value with good service...Very tight and long...Red and White together is a challenge.

★★ROCHESTER HILLS GOLF & COUNTRY CLUB
PU-655 Michelson Rd., Rochester, 48073, Oakland County, (248)852-4800, 30 miles N of Detroit.
Opened: 1905. **Holes:** 18. **Par:** 72/72. **Yards:** 6,800/5,747. **Course rating:** 70.8/72.5. **Slope:** 121/123. **Architect:** Thomas Bendelow. **Green fee:** $23/$28. **Credit cards:** All major. **Reduced fees:** N/A. **Caddies:** No. **Golf carts:** $11. **Discount golf packages:** No. **Season:** March-Dec. **High:** May-Sept. **On site lodging:** No. **Rental clubs:** No. **Walking policy:** Walking at certain times. **Metal spikes allowed:** Yes. **Range:** No. **To obtain tee times:** Call up to 5 days in advance.

★★★★THE ROCK AT DRUMMOND ISLAND
R-26 Maxton Rd.d, Drummond Island, 49726, Chippewa County, (906)493-1006, (800)999-6343, 60 miles SE of Sault Ste. Marie.
Opened: 1989. **Holes:** 18. **Par:** 71/71. **Yards:** 6,837/4,992. **Course rating:** 74.9/70.9. **Slope:** 142/130. **Architect:** Harry Bowers. **Green fee:** $30/$65. **Credit cards:** All major. **Reduced fees:** Weekdays, low season, resort guests, twilight, juniors. **Caddies:** No. **Golf carts:** Included in Green Fee. **Discount golf packages:** Yes. **Season:** May-

Oct. **High:** June-Aug. **On site lodging:** Yes. **Rental clubs:** Yes. **Walking policy:** Mandatory cart. **Metal spikes allowed:** Yes. **Range:** Yes (grass/mats). **To obtain tee times:** Call golf shop between 9 a.m. and 5 p.m.

Subscriber comments: Most wildlife I've ever seen on a golf course...Tough to get to, must take ferry...Beautiful setting, remote fairways...The best of all worlds...Very secluded setting. Nice accommodations...Midweek prices unbeatable...Great getaway...Lots of critters, not people...Remote, but worth the visit.

★★½ROGELL GOLF COURSE

PM-18601 Berg Rd., Detroit, 48219, Wayne County, (313)935-5331.
Opened: 1905. **Holes:** 18. **Par:** 70/70. **Yards:** 6,075/4,985. **Course rating:** 70.2/68.3. **Slope:** 129/117. **Architect:** Donald Ross. **Green fee:** $18/$12. **Credit cards:** None. **Reduced fees:** Weekdays, seniors, juniors. **Caddies:** No. **Golf carts:** $22. **Discount golf packages:** No. **Season:** March-Dec. **High:** May-Oct. **On site lodging:** No. **Rental clubs:** Yes. **Walking policy:** Unrestricted walking. **Metal spikes allowed:** Yes. **Range:** No. **To obtain tee times:** Call up to 7 days in advance.

Subscriber comments: Too many blind shots to greens...Real value...Old, be aware of the trees, almost unfair...Hilly and a lot of trees and water...Hard to believe there's hills like this in Detroit...Can play very tough. Unusual holes...Many elevation changes. Walking great for cardio health.

★★½ROGUE RIVER GOLF COURSE

PU-12994 Paine Ave. N.W., Sparta, 49345, Kent County, (616)887-7182, (888)779-4653, 15 miles N of Grand Rapids.
Opened: 1962. **Holes:** 18. **Par:** N/A. **Yards:** N/A. **Course rating:** N/A. **Slope:** N/A. **Architect:** Warner Bowen. **Green fee:** $18/$19. **Credit cards:** MC,VISA. **Reduced fees:** N/A. **Caddies:** No. **Golf carts:** $10. **Discount golf packages:** No. **Season:** April-Nov. **High:** May-Sept. **On site lodging:** No. **Rental clubs:** Yes. **Walking policy:** Unrestricted walking. **Metal spikes allowed:** Yes. **Range:** No. **To obtain tee times:** Call golf shop.

Subscriber comments: Fine greens but tees and fairways could be improved...Short course, great greens...Good to boost your ego. Maintenance exceptional...Challenging, good balance of par 3, 4, and 5s. Some nice over water shots...Fun short course, good for kids and less serious golfer...Lots of water.

★★ROLLING HILLS GOLF CLUB

PU-3274 Davison Rd., Lapeer, 48446, Lapeer County, (810)664-2281, 20 miles E of Flint.
Opened: 1968. **Holes:** 18. **Par:** 71/72. **Yards:** 6,060/5,184. **Course rating:** 69.3/69.8. **Slope:** 113/112. **Architect:** Reitz & Turdales. **Green fee:** $12/$18. **Credit cards:** MC,VISA. **Reduced fees:** Weekdays, low season, twilight, seniors, juniors. **Caddies:** No. **Golf carts:** $30. **Discount golf packages:** No. **Season:** April-Oct. **High:** June-Aug. **On site lodging:** No. **Rental clubs:** Yes. **Walking policy:** Unrestricted walking. **Metal spikes allowed:** Yes. **Range:** Yes (grass). **To obtain tee times:** Call. Tee times not always required.

★★ROLLING HILLS GOLF COURSE

PU-3100 Baldwin Dr., Hudsonville, 49426, Ottawa County, (616)669-9768, 15 miles SW of Grand Rapids.
Opened: N/A. **Holes:** 18. **Par:** 70/71. **Yards:** 5,832/4,693. **Course rating:** 67.0/65.7. **Slope:** 106/102. **Architect:** N/A. **Green fee:** $17/$18. **Credit cards:** MC,VISA. **Reduced fees:** N/A. **Caddies:** No. **Golf carts:** $20. **Discount golf packages:** No. **Season:** April-Nov. **High:** June-Aug. **On site lodging:** No. **Rental clubs:** Yes. **Walking policy:** Unrestricted walking. **Metal spikes allowed:** Yes. **Range:** Yes (grass). **To obtain tee times:** Call.

★★ROLLING MEADOWS GOLF COURSE

6484 Sutton Rd., Whitmore Lake, 48189, Washtenaw County, (313)662-5144.
Call club for further information.

★★½ROMEO GOLF & COUNTRY CLUB

14600 - 32 Mile Rd., Washington, 48095, Macomb County, (810)752-9673.
Call club for further information.

Subscriber comments: Excellent senior rates, trying hard to keep in shape...Not the most challenging, but inexpensive...They try not to overbook...Nice greens...Good for public course...Leave the driver in the trunk...Short course, fair condition.

★★★ROUGE PARK GOLF CLUB

11701 Burt Rd., Detroit, 48228, Wayne County, (313)837-5900.
Call club for further information.
Subscriber comments: Popular course with very high prices...2nd hole is best par 4 in state, rates with private clubs...The greatest city course in any city, wow...Great return from years of abuse...Seems almost in the middle of Detroit but the scenery and difficulty of the course are unbelievable...Very beautiful and open all year round...Very affordable.

★★★ROYAL SCOT GOLF COURSE

PU-4722 W. Grand River, Lansing, 48906, Clinton County, (517)321-4653.
Opened: 1962. **Holes:** 18. **Par:** 71/71. **Yards:** 6,568/4,700. **Course rating:** 71.7/66.8.
Slope: 123/117. **Architect:** Jim Holmes. **Green fee:** $17/$26. **Credit cards:** All major,Diners Club. **Reduced fees:** Weekdays, low season, resort guests, twilight, seniors, juniors. **Caddies:** No. **Golf carts:** $22. **Discount golf packages:** Yes. **Season:** Year-round. **High:** May-Aug. **On site lodging:** No. **Rental clubs:** Yes. **Walking policy:** Unrestricted walking. **Metal spikes allowed:** Yes. **Range:** Yes (grass/mats). **To obtain tee times:** Call.
Subscriber comments: Next to airport...Plush fairways. Fast greens. Kinda pricey...Fun course at a fair price...Tough par 3s, good course...Every hole if different, a great variety of golf holes...Best greens in Lansing...Ridiculously long distance between tees, maybe 100 yards or more...Good all around course, sand traps need a little work.

★★½RUSH LAKE HILLS GOLF CLUB

PU-3199 Rush Lake Rd., Pinckney, 48169, Livingston County, (313)878-9790, 20 miles N of Ann Arbor.
Opened: 1960. **Holes:** 18. **Par:** N/A. **Yards:** N/A. **Course rating:** N/A. **Slope:** N/A.
Architect: N/A. **Green fee:** $9/$21. **Credit cards:** MC,VISA,DISC. **Reduced fees:** Low season, twilight, seniors, juniors. **Caddies:** No. **Golf carts:** $20. **Discount golf packages:** No. **Season:** April-Oct. **High:** May-Aug. **On site lodging:** No. **Rental clubs:** No. **Walking policy:** Unrestricted walking. **Metal spikes allowed:** Yes. **Range:** No. **To obtain tee times:** Call up to 7 days in advance.
Subscriber comments: Not much difficulty, little food available...Needs new clubhouse...I had a 227-yard hole in one...Greens too small...Greens are like an upside down soup bowl...Pleasant employees...Needs work...Basic golf not bad for the price.

★★★ST. CLAIR SHORES COUNTRY CLUB

22185 Masonic Boulevard, St. Clair Shores, 48082, Macomb County, (810)294-2000.
Call club for further information.
Subscriber comments: No surprise but a very well kept semi-public course...Short course with character in good shape...Play early on weekend, otherwise very slow...Open year round, great shape considering amount of play...Playable for all levels.

★★★★½ST. IVES GOLF CLUB

PU-9900 St. Ives Dr., Stanwood, 49346, Mecosta County, (616)972-8410, (800)972-4837, 30 miles W of Mount Pleasant.
Opened: 1996. **Holes:** 18. **Par:** 72/72. **Yards:** 6,702/5,707. **Course rating:** 74.1/68.7. **Slope:** 141/127. **Architect:** Jerry Matthews. **Green fee:** $27/$50. **Credit cards:** All major. **Reduced fees:** Weekdays, low season, twilight, juniors. **Caddies:** No. **Golf carts:** $12. **Discount golf packages:** No. **Season:** April-Nov. **High:** June-Sept. **On site lodging:** Yes. **Rental clubs:** Yes. **Walking policy:** Unrestricted walking. **Metal spikes allowed:** No. **Range:** Yes (grass). **To obtain tee times:** Call.
Notes: Ranked 5th in 1997 Best New Affordable Public Courses.
Subscriber comments: Nos. 1 and 18 very difficult...Very nice layout after questionable 1st hole...Pricey, but a great new course...Beautiful views...Has to be the best new course in Michigan...Fairways immaculate, no unfair holes, greens fast and true...14 and 18 great, tough holes...Course and clubhouse are breathtaking.

MICHIGAN

★★½SAINT JOE VALLEY GOLF CLUB
PU-24953 M 86, Sturgis, 49091, St. Joseph County, (616)467-6275.
Opened: 1962. **Holes:** 18. **Par:** 68/71. **Yards:** 5,225/4,616. **Course rating:** 64.6/65.7.
Slope: 109/108. **Architect:** N/A. **Green fee:** $14/$17. **Credit cards:** MC,VISA.
Reduced fees: Seniors, juniors. **Caddies:** No. **Golf carts:** $10. **Discount golf packages:** No. **Season:** April-Oct. **High:** N/A. **On site lodging:** No. **Rental clubs:** Yes.
Walking policy: N/A. **Metal spikes allowed:** Yes. **Range:** No. **To obtain tee times:**
Call.
Subscriber comments: Great little course, well maintained, good staff...Nice flat
course...Short but has a challenging back nine. Front nine flat...Short, but fun for all
family members.

★★½ST. JOHN'S GOLF CLUB
PU-14380 Sheldon Rd, Plymouth, 48170, Wayne County, (313)453-1047, 10 miles W of
Detroit.
Opened: N/A. **Holes:** 18. **Par:** N/A. **Yards:** N/A. **Course rating:** N/A. **Slope:** N/A.
Architect: N/A. **Green fee:** $25/$30. **Credit cards:** MC,VISA,AMEX. **Reduced fees:**
Weekdays, low season, resort guests, twilight, seniors, juniors. **Caddies:** No. **Golf
carts:** $10. **Discount golf packages:** No. **Season:** March-Nov. **High:** June-Aug. **On
site lodging:** No. **Rental clubs:** Yes. **Walking policy:** N/A. **Metal spikes allowed:** Yes.
Range: Yes (grass/mats). **To obtain tee times:** Call up to 7 days in advance.
Subscriber comments: Beautiful course, very fun to play, great staff...Fun and challenging, lots of hills...New management, seems to be improving...Typical muny...Nice
parkland style; easy to play...Very good shape. Play moves very well.

★★★SALEM HILLS GOLF CLUB
PU-8810 W. Six Mile Rd., Northville, 48167, Washentaw County, (248)437-2152, 25
miles NW of Detroit.
Opened: 1961. **Holes:** 18. **Par:** 72/76. **Yards:** 6,966/5,874. **Course rating:** 72.9/73.4.
Slope: 121/119. **Architect:** Bruce Matthews/Jerry Matthews. **Green fee:** $19/$38.
Credit cards: MC,VISA. **Reduced fees:** Twilight, seniors, juniors. **Caddies:** No. **Golf
carts:** $23. **Discount golf packages:** No. **Season:** April-Nov. **High:** May-Sept. **On site
lodging:** No. **Rental clubs:** Yes. **Walking policy:** Walking at certain times. **Metal
spikes allowed:** Yes. **Range:** Yes (grass). **To obtain tee times:** Call 7 days in advance
with credit card to guarantee.
Subscriber comments: Best public course near Detroit, excellent condition...Straight
ahead golf, no gimmicks, solid...Long, large greens...Price is a bit high, good condition
throughout year...Lots of play is hard on course...Have begun much needed improvements.

★★SALT RIVER COUNTRY CLUB
33633 23 Mile Rd., New Baltimore, 48047, Macomb County, (810)725-0311.
Call club for further information.

★★½SANDY RIDGE GOLF COURSE
PU-2750 W. Lauria Rd., Midland, 48642, Midland County, (517)631-6010, 100 miles
NW of Detroit.
Opened: 1966. **Holes:** 18. **Par:** 72/72. **Yards:** 6,385/5,304. **Course rating:** 70.4/70.2.
Slope: 118/115. **Architect:** Bruce Matthews and Jerry Matthews. **Green fee:** $17/$20.
Credit cards: MC,VISA,DISC. **Reduced fees:** Seniors, juniors. **Caddies:** No. **Golf
carts:** $12. **Discount golf packages:** Yes. **Season:** April-Oct. **High:** June-Aug. **On site
lodging:** No. **Rental clubs:** Yes. **Walking policy:** Unrestricted walking. **Metal spikes
allowed:** Yes. **Range:** Yes (grass/mats). **To obtain tee times:** Call up to 3 days in
advance.
Subscriber comments: Small greens toughen this course...Challenging par
4s...Elevated tees and greens, many doglegs...Grounds need help...A few challenging
holes, especially #8...Fast greens, friendly...Flat, need to add a little undulation.

SASKATOON GOLF CLUB
PU-9038 92nd St., Alto, 49302, Kent County, (616)891-9229, 12 miles SE of Grand
Rapids.
Opened: 1970. **Architect:** Mark DeVries. **Green fee:** $18/$20. **Credit cards:**

MC,VISA,DISC. **Reduced fees:** Seniors. **Caddies:** No. **Golf carts:** $9. **Discount golf packages:** No. **Season:** March-Dec. **High:** May-July. **On site lodging:** No. **Rental clubs:** Yes. **Walking policy:** Unrestricted walking. **Metal spikes allowed:** Yes. **Range:** Yes (grass/mats). **To obtain tee times:** Call 14 days in advance for weekdays and 7 days in advance for weekends.

★★★BLUE/WHITE COURSE
Holes: 18. **Par:** 73/73. **Yards:** 6,750/6,125. **Course rating:** 70.7/71.7. **Slope:** 123/122.
Subscriber comments: Four separate nines...Course winds through pine trees, lakes. Is in nice shape, gets lots of play...Best kept secret near Grand Rapids...Blue/White course is a good combo: links and regular...When I play this course I think I'm back at Pinehurst...Very good practice area...Blue is a tight course, White is long.

★★★RED/GOLD COURSE
Holes: 18. **Par:** 71/70. **Yards:** N/A/5,300. **Course rating:** 68.8/67.7. **Slope:** 117/114.
Subscriber comments: A little rough around the edges...Gold is a 5...What a tee shot on 2nd!...Busy play in spring or on weekdays...Gold is best...Personal favorite as a local course.

SAUGANASH COUNTRY CLUB
61270 Lutz Rd., Three Rivers, 49093, St. Joseph County, (616)278-7825.
Call club for further information.

★★SAULT STE. MARIE COUNTRY CLUB
1520 Riverside Dr., Sault Ste. Marie, 49783, Chippewa County, (906)632-7812.
Opened: 1903. **Holes:** 18. **Par:** 71/72. **Yards:** 6,295/5,100. **Course rating:** 70.6/70.0.
Slope: 125/119. **Architect:** Jerry Matthews. **Green fee:** $18/$22. **Credit cards:** MC,VISA. **Reduced fees:** Low season. **Caddies:** No. **Golf carts:** $16. **Discount golf packages:** No. **Season:** April-Oct. **High:** June-Aug. **On site lodging:** No. **Rental clubs:** Yes. **Walking policy:** Unrestricted walking. **Metal spikes allowed:** Yes. **Range:** Yes (grass). **To obtain tee times:** Call up to three days in advance.

★★★SCENIC COUNTRY CLUB
8364 Filion Rd., Pigeon, 48755, Huron County, (517)453-3350.
Call club for further information.
Subscriber comments: Should be great this year...Not much style, but will give you some fun...Complete renovation.

★★½SCOTT LAKE COUNTRY CLUB
911 Hayes Rd. N.E., Comstock Park, 49321, Kent County, (616)784-1355, 10 miles S of Grand Rapids.
Opened: 1962. **Holes:** 18. **Par:** 72/72. **Yards:** 6,333/4,794. **Course rating:** 70.8/67.6.
Slope: 122/110. **Architect:** Bruce Matthews. **Green fee:** $16/$20. **Credit cards:** All major. **Reduced fees:** Weekdays, low season, seniors, juniors. **Caddies:** No. **Golf carts:** $10. **Discount golf packages:** No. **Season:** April-Nov. **High:** May-Sept. **On site lodging:** No. **Rental clubs:** Yes. **Walking policy:** Unrestricted walking. **Metal spikes allowed:** Yes. **Range:** Yes (grass/mats). **To obtain tee times:** Call 7 days in advance.
Subscriber comments: Challenging...Fine greens, hilly layout...Friday scramble is best game in town...Very playable, nice elevation changes and views...A few too many blind shots.

★★★SHADOW RIDGE GOLF CLUB
PU-1191 Kelsey Hwy., Ionia, Ionia County, (616)527-1180.
Opened: 1916. **Holes:** 9. **Par:** 35/35. **Yards:** 2,989/2,350. **Course rating:** 70.3/70.8.
Slope: 123/122. **Architect:** Donald Ross. **Green fee:** $11/$13. **Credit cards:** MC,VISA.
Reduced fees: Low season, twilight, seniors, juniors. **Caddies:** No. **Golf carts:** $18.
Discount golf packages: No. **Season:** April-Oct. **High:** June-Aug. **On site lodging:** No. **Rental clubs:** Yes. **Walking policy:** Unrestricted walking. **Metal spikes allowed:** Yes. **Range:** No. **To obtain tee times:** Call golf shop.
Subscriber comments: Nine holes...Excellent fairways, tough to score on...Toughest par 3s around...A Donald Ross design...Built on top of a mountain, beautiful.

★SHADY HOLLOW GOLF COURSE
34777 Smith Rd. At Wayne, Romulus, 48174, Wayne County, (313)721-0430.
Call club for further information.

SHANTY CREEK

R-One Shanty Creek Rd., Bellaire, 49615, Antrim County, (616)533-8621, (800)678-4111, 35 miles NE of Traverse City.
Credit cards: All major. **Reduced fees:** Low season, resort guests, twilight, seniors. **Caddies:** No. **Golf carts:** Included in Green Fee.
Discount golf packages: Yes. **Season:** April-Oct. **High:** June-Aug.
On site lodging: Yes. **Rental clubs:** Yes. **Walking policy:** Unrestricted walking. **Metal spikes allowed:** Yes. **To obtain tee times:** Hotel Guests may reserve tee time with room reservations. Non-guests may call up to 30 days in advance for weekdays and 14 days in advance for weekends.

★★★½SCHUSS MOUNTAIN GOLF CLUB

Opened: 1972. **Holes:** 18. **Par:** 72/72. **Yards:** 6,922/5,423. **Course rating:** 73.4/71.2. **Slope:** 127/126. **Architect:** Warner Bowen/Bill Newcombe. **Green fee:** $43/$70. **Range:** Yes (grass/mats).
Subscriber comments: Good sister to Legend...One of the best values in northern Michigan...Better than Shanty Creek...Management putting love into course...Best of two resort courses...Holes never see another...Still one of most beautiful courses in the state...Well kept, breathtaking views. Must play...Not too penal...#1 in my book...Great condition...Each hole unique.

★★★SHANTY CREEK GOLF CLUB

Opened: 1965. **Holes:** 18. **Par:** 71/71. **Yards:** 6,276/4,545. **Course rating:** 71.7/70.7. **Slope:** 120/116. **Architect:** Bill Diddle. **Green fee:** $33/$50. **Range:** Yes (grass).
Subscriber comments: Very playable, can score well, good accommodations...Underrated, great greens, toughest par 3s at Shanty...Fastest greens at the resort...Challenging but reasonable for the average golfer...Service, rooms and food excellent...Lots of blind tee shots.

★★★★½THE LEGEND GOLF CLUB

Opened: 1985. **Holes:** 18. **Par:** 72/72. **Yards:** 6,764/5,801. **Course rating:** 73.6/69.4. **Slope:** 137/121. **Architect:** Arnold Palmer and Ed Seay. **Green fee:** $55/$110. **Range:** Yes (grass/mats).
Notes: Ranked 12th in 1997 Best in State.
Subscriber comments: The best golfing in Michigan, period...Excellent course, difficult for average golfer...High priced...Play this course at least once in your life....Accuracy required. Try to reach #7 in two...Bring a camera...Each hole isolated...Must play at any price, view is worth it...Fairways and greens are tops. Service is excellent...Prettiest course in state...Outstanding in every respect. Worth the money...A masterpiece by "The King".

★★½SHENANDOAH GOLF & COUNTRY CLUB

PU-5600 Walnut Lake Rd., West Bloomfield, 48033, Oakland County, (248)682-4300, 15 miles NW of Detroit.
Opened: 1967. **Holes:** 18. **Par:** 72/72. **Yards:** 6,620/6,409. **Course rating:** 72.9/70.8. **Slope:** 129/124. **Architect:** Bruce Matthews and Jerry Matthews. **Green fee:** $45/$50. **Credit cards:** MC,VISA. **Reduced fees:** Twilight, seniors, juniors. **Caddies:** No. **Golf carts:** Included in Green Fee. **Discount golf packages:** No. **Season:** March-Dec. **High:** June-Aug. **On site lodging:** No. **Rental clubs:** Yes. **Walking policy:** Mandatory cart. **Metal spikes allowed:** Yes. **Range:** Yes (grass/mats). **To obtain tee times:** Call.
Subscriber comments: Could be a must play...Country club like course...Back nine is beautiful...Challenging course, but a bit pricey...Front nice, back always wet, nice range...Takes long time to dry out after heavy rains...No walking.

★★★½SNOW SNAKE SKI & GOLF CLUB

R-3407 E. Mannsiding Rd., Harrison, 48625, Clare County, (517)539-6583, 25 miles N of Mt. Pleasant.
Opened: 1994. **Holes:** 18. **Par:** 71/71. **Yards:** 6,025/4,447. **Course rating:** 69.7/65.8. **Slope:** 130/117. **Architect:** Jeff Gorney. **Green fee:** $25/$38. **Credit cards:** MC,VISA,DISC. **Reduced fees:** Low season, twilight, seniors. **Caddies:** No. **Golf carts:** Included in Green Fee. **Discount golf packages:** No. **Season:** May-Oct. **High:** June-Aug. **On site lodging:** No. **Rental clubs:** Yes. **Walking policy:** N/A **Metal spikes allowed:** Yes. **Range:** Yes (grass/mats). **To obtain tee times:** Call.
Subscriber comments: Very tricky, keep driver in bag...Have two favorite elevated holes...Must be accurate...Unexpectedly hilly course for mid Michigan...

Short holes, lots of trouble...Becoming a popular course...Can't hold greens, like an upside down saucer, short...Needs a bit more maturity.

★★SOUTH HAVEN COUNTRY CLUB
Blue Star Hwy., South Haven, 49090, Allegan County, (616)637-3896.
Call club for further information.

★½SOUTHMOOR COUNTRY CLUB
PU-G-4312 S. Dort Highway, Burton, 48529, Genesee County, (810)743-4080, 5 miles S of Flint.
Opened: 1963. **Holes:** 18. **Par:** 69/69. **Yards:** 5,205/4,810. **Course rating:** 67.0/67.0. **Slope:** 109/109. **Architect:** N/A. **Green fee:** $15/$16. **Credit cards:** MC,VISA,AMEX. **Reduced fees:** Weekdays, low season, twilight, seniors, juniors. **Caddies:** Yes. **Golf carts:** $20. **Discount golf packages:** No. **Season:** April-Dec. **High:** May-Aug. **On site lodging:** No. **Rental clubs:** No. **Walking policy:** N/A. **Metal spikes allowed:** Yes. **Range:** Yes (grass/mats). **To obtain tee times:** First come, first served.

★★★SPRING VALLEY GOLF COURSE
PU-18396 W. U.S. 10, Hersey, 49639, Osceola County, (616)832-5041, 70 miles N of Grand Rapids.
Opened: 1962. **Holes:** 18. **Par:** 72/74. **Yards:** 6,439/5,273. **Course rating:** N/A. **Slope:** N/A. **Architect:** Donald Semeyn. **Green fee:** $16/$23. **Credit cards:** MC,VISA. **Reduced fees:** Weekdays, low season, seniors. **Caddies:** No. **Golf carts:** $16. **Discount golf packages:** No. **Season:** April-Oct. **High:** June-Aug. **On site lodging:** No. **Rental clubs:** Yes. **Walking policy:** Unrestricted walking. **Metal spikes allowed:** Yes. **Range:** Yes (grass). **To obtain tee times:** Call golf shop.
Subscriber comments: You're treated as if you're family...A few unusual holes...Golfer friendly, no sand, homey clubhouse.

SPRINGBROOK GOLF COURSE
PU-Springvale Rd., Walloon Lake, 49796, Charlevoix County, (616)535-2413, 13 miles SE of Petoskey.
Opened: 1970. **Holes:** 18. **Par:** 72/72. **Yards:** 6,260/5,980. **Course rating:** 67.3/69.5. **Slope:** 113/114. **Architect:** N/A. **Green fee:** $10/$25. **Credit cards:** All major. **Reduced fees:** Weekdays, low season, twilight, seniors, juniors. **Caddies:** No. **Golf carts:** $11. **Discount golf packages:** Yes. **Season:** March-Oct. **High:** June-Aug. **On site lodging:** No. **Rental clubs:** Yes. **Walking policy:** Unrestricted walking. **Metal spikes allowed:** Yes. **Range:** No. **To obtain tee times:** Call golf shop.

★★★SPRINGFIELD OAKS GOLF COURSE
PM-12450 Andersonville Rd., Davisburg, 48350, Oakland County, (248)625-2540, 15 miles NW of Pontiac.
Opened: N/A. **Holes:** 18. **Par:** 71/71. **Yards:** 6,033/4,911. **Course rating:** 68.4/68.1. **Slope:** 118/114. **Architect:** Mark DeVries. **Green fee:** $12/$20. **Credit cards:** MC,VISA. **Reduced fees:** Weekdays, low season, twilight, seniors, juniors. **Caddies:** No. **Golf carts:** $10. **Discount golf packages:** No. **Season:** March-Nov. **High:** June-Aug. **On site lodging:** No. **Rental clubs:** Yes. **Walking policy:** Unrestricted walking. **Metal spikes allowed:** Yes. **Range:** No. **To obtain tee times:** Call 7 days in advance for weekdays. Call on Wednesday evening starting at 6:00 p.m. in person or 6:15 p.m. by phone for upcoming weekend.
Subscriber comments: Tough county course. Kept in great shape...Fantastic facilities, private club ambiance...Seeing foxes trotting down the fairway adds to the day...Fun routing with good elevation changes...Great county course. Such a deal.

★★★STATES GOLF COURSE
20 East West Ave., Vicksburg, 49097, Kalamazoo County, (616)649-1931.
Call club for further information.
Subscriber comments: Excellent greens...Best value in western Michigan...Flat, few hazards, very enjoyable experience.

★★★STONEBRIDGE GOLF CLUB
PU-5315 Stonebridge Dr. S., Ann Arbor, 48108, Washtenaw County, (313)429-8383, 30 miles W of Detroit.

Opened: 1991. **Holes:** 18. **Par:** 72/72. **Yards:** 6,932/5,075. **Course rating:** 73.6/68.6. **Slope:** 136/122. **Architect:** Arthur Hills. **Green fee:** $30/$40. **Credit cards:** MC,VISA,AMEX. **Reduced fees:** Low season, twilight, seniors, juniors. **Caddies:** No. **Golf carts:** $12. **Discount golf packages:** Yes. **Season:** March-Dec. **High:** June-Aug. **On site lodging:** No. **Rental clubs:** Yes. **Walking policy:** Walking at certain times. **Metal spikes allowed:** Yes. **Range:** Yes (grass). **To obtain tee times:** Call up to 5 days in advance.

Subscriber comments: Good layout, some target golf, tee times available...Good luck finding this course...Overpriced. Brings me to my knees every time!...Killer course in wind...Signature hole is very difficult...Play with coupon...Housing development annoying...Great set of par 3s...Getting built up with houses...Postage stamp greens.

STONEHEDGE GOLF COURSE
PU-15503 E. M-89, Augusta, 49012, Kalamazoo County, (616)731-2300, 20 miles NE of Kalamazoo.
Opened: 1988. **Architect:** Charles Scott. **Green fee:** $28/$32. **Credit cards:** MC,VISA. **Reduced fees:** Weekdays, low season, resort guests, juniors. **Caddies:** No. **Golf carts:** $12. **Discount golf packages:** Yes. **Season:** April-Nov. **High:** May-Aug. **On site lodging:** No. **Rental clubs:** Yes. **Walking policy:** Walking at certain times. **Metal spikes allowed:** Yes. **Range:** Yes (grass). **To obtain tee times:** Call golf shop.
NORTH COURSE
Holes: 18. **Par:** 72/72. **Yards:** 6,673/5,785. **Course rating:** 72.2/72.1. **Slope:** 127/114.
★★★★SOUTH COURSE
Holes: 18. **Par:** 72/72. **Yards:** 6,656/5,191. **Course rating:** 72.4/70.3. **Slope:** 133/120.
Subscriber comments: Condition tops...I'd play it every day if I could...Has British look...Upper peninsula flavor...This course has it all...Love it, but slow on weekends...Pricey for area...North course is best...Tough upscale course...Couldn't ask for a better course to play.

★★½STONY CREEK GOLF COURSE
PU-5140 Main Pkwy., Shelby Township, 48316, Macomb County, (810)781-9166, 5 miles NE of Rochester.
Opened: 1979. **Holes:** 18. **Par:** 72/72. **Yards:** 6,900/5,023. **Course rating:** 73.1/74.1. **Slope:** 124/124. **Architect:** N/A. **Green fee:** $19/$23. **Credit cards:** MC,VISA,DISC. **Reduced fees:** N/A. **Caddies:** No. **Golf carts:** N/A. **Discount golf packages:** No. **Season:** April-Nov. **High:** June-Aug. **On site lodging:** No. **Rental clubs:** No. **Walking policy:** Unrestricted walking. **Metal spikes allowed:** Yes. **Range:** Yes. **To obtain tee times:** Call up to 3 days in advance.
Subscriber comments: Three of the best finishing holes in metro Detroit...Has lots of potential...Hard to get tee times...Could be much better with work...Allows walkers...Another metro park, the most challenging of the five.

★★½SUGAR LOAF RESORT GOLF CLUB
PU-4500 Sugarloaf Mt. Rd., Cedar, 49621, Leelanau County, (616)228-1880, (800)952-6390, 18 miles NW of Traverse City.
Opened: 1870. **Holes:** 18. **Par:** 72/74. **Yards:** 6,813/5,134. **Course rating:** 73.3/70.5. **Slope:** 125/117. **Architect:** C.D. Wagstaff. **Green fee:** $35/$45. **Credit cards:** All major,Diners Club. **Reduced fees:** Weekdays, twilight. **Caddies:** No. **Golf carts:** Included in Green Fee. **Discount golf packages:** Yes. **Season:** May-Oct. **High:** July-Aug. **On site lodging:** Yes. **Rental clubs:** Yes. **Walking policy:** Walking at certain times. **Metal spikes allowed:** Yes. **Range:** Yes (grass/mats). **To obtain tee times:** Call golf shop.
Subscriber comments: No. 17 a monstrous par 5 with uphill green and rock pile in middle of fairway...Fun and challenging...Comparable to Pine Knob but it's up north...Not great for northern Michigan but the price is right.

★★★½SUGAR SPRINGS COUNTRY CLUB
1930 Sugar River Blvd., Gladwin, 48624, Gladwin County, (517)426-4111, 11 miles N of Gladwin.
Opened: 1972. **Holes:** 18. **Par:** 72/74. **Yards:** 6,737/5,636. **Course rating:** 72.6/72.5. **Slope:** 124/121. **Architect:** N/A. **Green fee:** $23/$23. **Credit cards:** None. **Reduced fees:** N/A. **Caddies:** No. **Golf carts:** $10. **Discount golf packages:** No. **Season:** April-Oct. **High:** N/A. **On site lodging:** No. **Rental clubs:** No. **Walking policy:** Unrestricted

walking. **Metal spikes allowed:** Yes. **Range:** Yes (grass). **To obtain tee times:** Call. **Subscriber comments:** Nice course, tough and easy holes, fair...Pretty setting...Good all around course and facilities...Staff was very nice, fairways needed help...Three very high tees with rolling hills.

★★★½SUGARBUSH GOLF CLUB

PU-1 Sugarbush Dr., Davison, 48423, Genesee County, (810)653-3326, (800)924-3888, 8 miles E of Flint.
Opened: 1995. **Holes:** 18. **Par:** 72/72. **Yards:** 7,285/5,035. **Course rating:** N/A. **Slope:** N/A. **Architect:** Larry Mancour and David Mancour. **Green fee:** $38/$48. **Credit cards:** MC,VISA,AMEX. **Reduced fees:** Weekdays, low season, twilight, seniors, juniors. **Caddies:** No. **Golf carts:** Included in Green Fee. **Discount golf packages:** Yes. **Season:** April-Nov. **High:** June-Aug. **On site lodging:** No. **Rental clubs:** Yes. **Walking policy:** Unrestricted walking. **Metal spikes allowed:** Yes. **Range:** Yes (grass/mats). **To obtain tee times:** Call 14 days in advance. **Subscriber comments:** Very nice newer course...Range included, great layout...One of toughest layouts in mid-Michigan...Long and difficult...#1 for the money...Pick the right tees...Good test for middle handicap.

★SUNNYBROOK GOLF CLUB

7191-17 Mile Rd., Sterling Heights, 48078, Macomb County, (810)977-9759.
Call club for further information.

★★SWAN VALLEY GOLF COURSE

9499 Geddes Rd., Saginaw, 48603, Saginaw County, (517)781-4945.
Call club for further information.

★★⅓SWARTZ CREEK GOLF COURSE

PM-1902 Hammerberg Rd., Flint, 48503, Genesee County, (810)766-7043, 45 miles N of Detroit.
Opened: 1926. **Holes:** 27. **Par:** 72/72. **Yards:** 6,662/5,798. **Course rating:** 72.1/73.0. **Slope:** 121/123. **Architect:** Frederick A. Ellis. **Green fee:** $18/$20. **Credit cards:** MC,VISA. **Reduced fees:** Low season, twilight, seniors, juniors. **Caddies:** No. **Golf carts:** $18. **Discount golf packages:** No. **Season:** Year-round. **High:** April-Oct. **On site lodging:** No. **Rental clubs:** Yes. **Walking policy:** Unrestricted walking. **Metal spikes allowed:** Yes. **Range:** No. **To obtain tee times:** Call on Monday for upcoming weekend.
Subscriber comments: Good city course, nice for practice...Winding creek drives through the course...Hard to get on at prime time...Good practice course after work. Upkeep improves every year...Great value, good greens, public country club...Best of Flint munys.
Special Notes: Spikeless shoes preferred.

★★★SYCAMORE HILLS GOLF CLUB

PU-48787 North Ave., Macomb, 48042, Macomb County, (810)598-9500, 20 miles N of Detroit.
Opened: 1990. **Holes:** 27. **Architect:** Jerry Matthews. **Green fee:** $16/$34. **Credit cards:** MC,VISA. **Reduced fees:** Weekdays, low season, twilight, seniors, juniors. **Caddies:** No. **Golf carts:** $11. **Discount golf packages:** Yes. **Season:** April-Oct. **High:** May-Sept. **On site lodging:** No. **Rental clubs:** Yes. **Walking policy:** Walking at certain times. **Metal spikes allowed:** Yes. **Range:** Yes (grass/mats). **To obtain tee times:** Call up to 21 days in advance.
NORTH/WEST
Par: 72/72. **Yards:** 6,305/5,070. **Course rating:** 70.3/68.3. **Slope:** 123/119.
SOUTH/NORTH
Par: 72/72. **Yards:** 6,267/4,934. **Course rating:** 70.2/67.2. **Slope:** 132/121.
SOUTH/WEST
Par: 72/72. **Yards:** 6,336/5,119. **Course rating:** 70.7/68.5. **Slope:** 130/120.
Subscriber comments: A little expensive. All else is very nice...Too wet to play in spring, some forced carries...Three nines...Great shape, but need to make it harder...Great condition, good challenge...27 holes on 18-hole land...The South is the toughest of the three nines...Lots of water holes for a Michigan course.

★★SYLVAN GLEN GOLF COURSE
5725 Rochester Rd., Troy, 48084, Oakland County, (248)879-0040.
Call club for further information.

★★★THE TAMARACKS
PU-8900 N. Clare Ave., Harrison, 48625, Clare County, (517)539-5441, (888)838-1162, 30 miles N of Mt. Pleasant.
Opened: 1984. **Holes:** 18. **Par:** 70/70. **Yards:** 5,760/4,370. **Course rating:** N/A. **Slope:** N/A. **Architect:** N/A. **Green fee:** $17/$20. **Credit cards:** All major. **Reduced fees:** Low season, twilight, seniors. **Caddies:** No. **Golf carts:** $12. **Discount golf packages:** No. **Season:** April-Nov. **High:** N/A. **On site lodging:** Yes. **Rental clubs:** Yes. **Walking policy:** Unrestricted walking. **Metal spikes allowed:** Yes. **Range:** No. **To obtain tee times:** Call or stop in.
Subscriber comments: Water hazards make for interesting play...Well kept secret...Fair but tough, great staff...Sloped fairways...More challenging each year...Beautiful, challenging, managed well in a very small town...Family owned and placed in God's country.

★★★TANGLEWOOD GOLF CLUB
PU-53503 W. Ten Mile Rd., South Lyon, 48178, Oakland County, (248)486-3355, 25 miles NW of Detroit.
Opened: 1991. **Holes:** 27. **Architect:** Bill Newcomb. **Credit cards:** MC,VISA,AMEX. **Reduced fees:** Low season, twilight, seniors, juniors. **Caddies:** No. **Golf carts:** $10. **Discount golf packages:** Yes. **Season:** March-Nov. **High:** May-Aug. **On site lodging:** Yes. **Rental clubs:** Yes. **Walking policy:** Walking at certain times. **Metal spikes allowed:** Yes. **Range:** Yes (grass/mats). **To obtain tee times:** Call golf shop.
NORTH/SOUTH
Par: 72/72. **Yards:** 7,077/5,011. **Course rating:** 73.6/72.9. **Slope:** 129/119. **Green fee:** $30/$40.
NORTH/WEST
Par: 72/72. **Yards:** 6,922/4,896. **Course rating:** 73.0/72.1. **Slope:** 128/118. **Green fee:** $30/$40.
SOUTH/WEST
Par: 72/72. **Yards:** 7,117/5,031. **Course rating:** 76.4/75.6. **Slope:** 138/128. **Green fee:** $30/$45.
Subscriber comments: North course has blind first tee shot, no warning...Very much like a country club...Busy...Will mature from good to very good...Getting pricey, nice layout, heavily played...Each nine is different...South/West is the best...Clubhouse is new...Very good condition, great people to be around, good rates.

★★TAWAS CREEK GOLF CLUB
1022 Monument Rd., Tawas City, 48763, Iosco County, (517)362-6262, (888)829-2727, 80 miles NE of Saginaw.
Opened: N/A. **Holes:** 18. **Par:** 72/73. **Yards:** 6,527/5,006. **Course rating:** 71.9/69.3. **Slope:** 126/123. **Architect:** N/A. **Green fee:** $14/$20. **Credit cards:** MC,VISA. **Reduced fees:** N/A. **Caddies:** No. **Golf carts:** $10. **Discount golf packages:** No. **Season:** April-Oct. **High:** July-Aug. **On site lodging:** No. **Rental clubs:** Yes. **Walking policy:** Unrestricted walking. **Metal spikes allowed:** Yes. **Range:** No. **To obtain tee times:** Call up to 7 days in advance.

★★½TAYLOR MEADOWS GOLF CLUB
PU-25360 Ecorse Rd., Taylor, 48180, Wayne County, (313)295-0506.
Opened: 1989. **Holes:** 18. **Par:** 71/71. **Yards:** 6,049/5,160. **Course rating:** 67.8/67.6. **Slope:** 114/111. **Architect:** Arthur Hills. **Green fee:** $12/$26. **Credit cards:** MC,VISA. **Reduced fees:** Weekdays, low season, twilight, seniors, juniors. **Caddies:** No. **Golf carts:** $24. **Discount golf packages:** No. **Season:** March-Dec. **High:** May-Oct. **On site lodging:** No. **Rental clubs:** Yes. **Walking policy:** Unrestricted walking. **Metal spikes allowed:** Yes. **Range:** Yes. **To obtain tee times:** Call 2 days in advance for weekdays. Call Thursday at noon for weekends.
Subscriber comments: Average layout, good condition...Long rough steals balls...Nice course for the money...Great little course, overplayed...Outstanding service at outings...Short rolling course, hit 'em straight and you'll be rewarded.

★★★TERRACE BLUFF GOLF COURSE
7527 Lake Bluff 19.4 Rd., Gladstone, 49837, Delta County, (906)428-2343.
Opened: 1972. **Holes:** 18. **Par:** 72/72. **Yards:** 7,001/5,900. **Course rating:** 69.5/71.5.
Slope: 119/117. **Architect:** N/A. **Green fee:** $22/$22. **Credit cards:** MC,VISA.
Reduced fees: N/A. **Caddies:** No. **Golf carts:** $20. **Discount golf packages:** No.
Season: April-Oct. **High:** June-Aug. **On site lodging:** No. **Rental clubs:** Yes. **Walking policy:** N/A. **Metal spikes allowed:** Yes. **Range:** Yes (grass). **To obtain tee times:** Call up to 2 days in advance.
Subscriber comments: Gorgeous course, scenic...A nice layout...Course can play tough with wind...Flat, lots of trees, greens usually good. Fun to play.

★★★½THORNAPPLE CREEK GOLF CLUB
PU-6415 W. F Ave., Kalamazoo, 49009, Kalamazoo County, (616)344-0040, 5 miles N of Kalamazoo.
Opened: 1979. **Holes:** 18. **Par:** 72/72. **Yards:** 6,960/4,948. **Course rating:** 73.7/68.9.
Slope: 137/121. **Architect:** Mike Shields. **Green fee:** $18/$24. **Credit cards:** MC,VISA,DISC. **Reduced fees:** Weekdays, low season. **Caddies:** No. **Golf carts:** $20.
Discount golf packages: Yes. **Season:** April-Nov. **High:** June-Aug. **On site lodging:** No. **Rental clubs:** Yes. **Walking policy:** Unrestricted walking. **Metal spikes allowed:** Yes. **Range:** Yes (grass). **To obtain tee times:** Call in advance one week. Groups of 12 or larger can book any day or time but need to put down deposit.
Subscriber comments: Could use some TLC but still tops...Recommend it highly...Tough greens...Course yields little roll...Watch your three-putts...A monster from back tees...Heavily wooded, very secluded, natural beauty...Several greens crowned...Hard to find, worth the effort. Back nine a workout for walkers.

★THORNE HILLS GOLF COURSE
PU-12915 Sumpter Rd., Carleton, 48117, Monroe County, (313)587-2332, 9 miles S of Belleville.
Opened: 1981. **Holes:** 18. **Par:** 72/72. **Yards:** 5,827/5,205. **Course rating:** N/A. **Slope:** N/A. **Architect:** Daniel G. Thorne. **Green fee:** $13/$15. **Credit cards:** N/A. **Reduced fees:** Weekdays, low season, seniors. **Caddies:** No. **Golf carts:** $13. **Discount golf packages:** No. **Season:** N/A. **High:** N/A. **On site lodging:** No. **Rental clubs:** No.
Walking policy: Unrestricted walking. **Metal spikes allowed:** Yes. **Range:** No. **To obtain tee times:** Call golf shop.

★★★★THOROUGHBRED GOLF CLUB AT DOUBLE JJ RESORT
R-6886 Water Rd., Rothbury, 49452, Oceana County, (616)893-4653, 20 miles N of Muskegon.
Opened: 1993. **Holes:** 18. **Par:** 72/72. **Yards:** 6,900/4,851. **Course rating:** 74.4/69.5.
Slope: 147/126. **Architect:** Arthur Hills. **Green fee:** $45/$69. **Credit cards:** All major.
Reduced fees: Weekdays, low season, resort guests, twilight. **Caddies:** No. **Golf carts:** Included in Green Fee. **Discount golf packages:** Yes. **Season:** April-Nov. **High:** June-Sept. **On site lodging:** Yes. **Rental clubs:** Yes. **Walking policy:** Unrestricted walking. **Metal spikes allowed:** Yes. **Range:** Yes (grass). **To obtain tee times:** Call up to 7 days in advance. Tee times may be made for entire year with deposit.
Notes: Ranked 8th in 1997 Best in State.
Subscriber comments: Tough track: have to be long and straight...It's the Augusta National of Michigan. Fast greens, unbelievable clubhouse and the most beautiful course I've ever played...Many signature holes, must think on every shot...Visually outstanding. 2nd toughest par 4 I ever played...Great vacation spot.

★★★THUNDER BAY GOLF RESORT
R-27800 M-32 E., Hillman, 49746, Montmorency County, (517)742-4875, (800)729-9375, 22 miles W of Alpena.
Opened: 1971. **Holes:** 18. **Par:** 73/75. **Yards:** 6,466/5,584. **Course rating:** 72.1/72.1.
Slope: 129/124. **Architect:** Jack Matthias. **Green fee:** $16/$22. **Credit cards:** All major,Diners Club, Amoco. **Reduced fees:** Weekdays, low season, resort guests, twilight, seniors, juniors. **Caddies:** No. **Golf carts:** $12. **Discount golf packages:** Yes.
Season: April-Nov. **High:** June-Sept. **On site lodging:** Yes. **Rental clubs:** Yes.
Walking policy: Walking at certain times. **Metal spikes allowed:** Yes. **Range:** Yes (grass). **To obtain tee times:** Call.

Subscriber comments: Very wooded, challenging, beautiful...Excellent fall course, very colorful...Course places a premium on accuracy...Nice course, nice people, great prices...Sneaks up on you...Three par 5s on the back nine...Good food, great staff...Terrific golf packages.

★★★½TIMBER RIDGE GOLF COURSE
PU-16339 Park Lake Rd., East Lansing, 48823, Ingham County, (517)339-8000, (800)874-3432, 5 miles E of Lansing.
Opened: 1989. **Holes:** 18. **Par:** 72/72. **Yards:** 6,497/5,048. **Course rating:** 72.4/70.9. **Slope:** 140/129. **Architect:** Jerry Matthews. **Green fee:** $40. **Credit cards:** MC,VISA,DISC. **Reduced fees:** Weekdays, low season, twilight, seniors. **Caddies:** No. **Golf carts:** $12. **Discount golf packages:** Yes. **Season:** March-Nov. **High:** May-Sept. **On site lodging:** No. **Rental clubs:** Yes. **Walking policy:** Unrestricted walking. **Metal spikes allowed:** Yes. **Range:** Yes (grass/mats). **To obtain tee times:** Call 7 days prior for a foursome. Groups of eight or more may book further in advance.
Subscriber comments: Too tight for length, beveled fairways don't hold...Very tight course. Bring extra balls...The aristocrat of this area...Great course...Very hilly for mid-Michigan...A 10 for character...One of the most beautiful courses anywhere...Dollar for dollar there's nothing better...A few blind shots, need to know layout...Championship quality, tree trouble everywhere...Nice, no homes or roads.

★★★THE TIMBERS GOLF CLUB
R-900 Timbers Trail, Tuscola, 48769, Tuscola County, (517)871-4884, (888)617-1479.
Opened: 1996. **Holes:** 18. **Par:** 18/18. **Yards:** 6,674/4,886. **Course rating:** N/A. **Slope:** N/A. **Architect:** Lorrie Viola. **Green fee:** $14/$21. **Credit cards:** MC,VISA,AMEX. **Reduced fees:** Weekdays, low season, resort guests, twilight, seniors, juniors. **Caddies:** No. **Golf carts:** $16. **Discount golf packages:** No. **Season:** March-Nov. **High:** June-Aug. **On site lodging:** No. **Rental clubs:** Yes. **Walking policy:** N/A. **Metal spikes allowed:** Yes. **Range:** Yes (grass/mats). **To obtain tee times:** Call.

★★★TOMAC WOODS GOLF COURSE
PU-14827 26 1/2 Mile Rd., Albion, 49224, Calhoun County, (517)629-8241, 20 miles E of Battle Creek.
Opened: 1964. **Holes:** 18. **Par:** 72/72. **Yards:** 6,290/5,800. **Course rating:** 69.8/76.0. **Slope:** N/A. **Architect:** Robert Beard. **Green fee:** $12/$14. **Credit cards:** MC,VISA,DISC. **Reduced fees:** Weekdays, low season, twilight, seniors, juniors. **Caddies:** No. **Golf carts:** $9. **Discount golf packages:** Yes. **Season:** April-Oct. **High:** June-Aug. **On site lodging:** No. **Rental clubs:** Yes. **Walking policy:** Unrestricted walking. **Metal spikes allowed:** Yes. **Range:** Yes (grass/mats). **To obtain tee times:** Call anytime.
Subscriber comments: Greens too fast, but overall very nice...Old, fun course, not long...Great course.

TREETOPS SYLVAN RESORT
R-3962 Wilkinson Rd., Gaylord, 49735, Otsego County, (517)732-6711, (888)873-3867, 50 miles NW of Traverse City.
Credit cards: MC,VISA,AMEX. **Reduced fees:** Low season, resort guests, twilight. **Discount golf packages:** Yes. **Season:** April-Oct. **High:** June-Sept. **On site lodging:** Yes. **Metal spikes allowed:** Yes. **Range:** Yes (grass).

(GOOD SERVICE)

★★★★RICK SMITH SIGNATURE
Opened: 1993. **Holes:** 18. **Par:** 70/70. **Yards:** 6,653/4,604. **Course rating:** 72.8/67.0. **Slope:** 140/123. **Architect:** Rick Smith. **Green fee:** $74/$74. **Caddies:** No. **Golf carts:** Included in Green Fee. **Rental clubs:** Yes. **Walking policy:** Mandatory cart. **To obtain tee times:** Call with credit card to guarantee.
Notes: Ranked 24th in 1997 Best in State.
Subscriber comments: Scores are secondary to the views...Probably the best golf value in state...Elk are everywhere...Treetops' best...Easy for any level of play...Great course and service, slightly overpriced...3, 4 and 11 great holes...Just as good as Fazio...Greens too fast and tricky for resort course...Great value with package...Saw an eagle, many deer, a fox and elk...Many tees see 25 miles...Huge two-tiered greens.

★★★★ROBERT TRENT JONES MASTERPIECE
Opened: 1987. **Holes:** 18. **Par:** 71/71. **Yards:** 7,060/4,972. **Course rating:** 75.8/70.2.

Slope: 146/124. **Architect:** Robert Trent Jones. **Green fee:** $74/$74. **Caddies:** No. **Golf carts:** Included in Green Fee. **Rental clubs:** Yes. **Walking policy:** Mandatory cart. **To obtain tee times:** Call.

Notes: Ranked 19th in 1997 Best in State.

Subscriber comments: Beautiful layout! Good facilities...No flat lies. Too unfair, too expensive...Highly overated, good shots, bad rewards...Jones, Jones, Jones!...Tough course from back tees...A classic...Enjoy the surroundings because the course is tough...If I could only play one course in Michigan, this is it...Great challenge for long hitters...Absolutely loved it...Fairest of Treetops courses...Way too hard for a resort, great clubhouse...Gorgeous panoramic views, spectacular in the fall.

★★★★TOM FAZIO PREMIER

Opened: 1992. **Holes:** 18. **Par:** 72/72. **Yards:** 6,832/5,039. **Course rating:** 73.2/70.1. **Slope:** 135/123. **Architect:** Tom Fazio. **Green fee:** $84/$84. **Caddies:** No. **Golf carts:** Included in Green Fee. **Rental clubs:** No. **Walking policy:** Mandatory cart. **To obtain tee times:** Call with credit card to guarantee.

Notes: Ranked 22nd in 1997 Best in State.

Subscriber comments: Extremely challenging, yet very pleasurable...Very playable, unlike other courses...Beautiful course, very fair to all levels, great views...Loved wide driving areas. Three elevated 4-pars. Two "death drop" par 3s I didn't like...A must stop on anyone's list...Greens can be nightmare...Wonderful, beautiful setting, food good, great facilities, gift shop too pricey.

★★★★½TRADITION COURSE

Opened: 1997. **Holes:** 18. **Par:** 72/72. **Yards:** 6,467/4,907. **Course rating:** N/A. **Slope:** N/A. **Architect:** Rick Smith. **Green fee:** $52/$52. **Caddies:** Yes. **Golf carts:** N/A. **Rental clubs:** Yes. **Walking policy:** Unrestricted walking. **To obtain tee times:** Call with credit card to guarantee.

Subscriber comments: My favorite resort...Very nice. Loved the only walking rule...Magnificent views. Unbelievable layout. All expensive but worth it...No complaints, love this course...Awful tough for the average golfer...What looked like terror was fun, excellent conditions...Rick Smith design, fun to play...Bring the "A" game.

Special Notes: Walking only course.

TURTLE CREEK GOLF CLUB

PU-9044 R Drive S., Burlington, 49029, Calhoun County, (517)765-2232, 10 miles SE of Battle Creek.

Opened: 1970. **Holes:** 27. **Par:** 72/72. **Yards:** 5,905/4,972. **Course rating:** 69.0/68.0. **Slope:** 109/109. **Architect:** N/A. **Green fee:** $9/$12. **Credit cards:** MC,VISA. **Reduced fees:** Weekdays, low season, twilight, seniors. **Caddies:** No. **Golf carts:** $16. **Discount golf packages:** No. **Season:** March-Nov. **High:** June-Aug. **On site lodging:** No. **Rental clubs:** Yes. **Walking policy:** Unrestricted walking. **Metal spikes allowed:** Yes. **Range:** No. **To obtain tee times:** Call for weekends and holidays.

★★★TWIN BIRCH GOLF COURSE

PU-1030 Highway 612 N.E., Kalkaska, 49646, Kalkaska County, (616)258-9691, (800)968-9699, 17 miles E of Traverse City.

Opened: N/A. **Holes:** 18. **Par:** 72/70. **Yards:** 6,133/4,969. **Course rating:** 69.5/68.6. **Slope:** 115/111. **Architect:** N/A. **Green fee:** $27/$27. **Credit cards:** MC,VISA. **Reduced fees:** Seniors, juniors. **Caddies:** No. **Golf carts:** $24. **Discount golf packages:** No. **Season:** April-Oct. **High:** N/A. **On site lodging:** No. **Rental clubs:** Yes. **Walking policy:** Unrestricted walking. **Metal spikes allowed:** Yes. **Range:** Yes (grass). **To obtain tee times:** Call.

Subscriber comments: Pretty fair test, great course to walk. Maintenance fair...Lots of blind shots...Good course for quick round of golf...Lots of trees but fair, fun course...Real sleeper, good conditions...Just plain fun, always good condition...Fairly flat, flat greens.

★★TWIN BROOKS GOLF CLUB

1005 McKeighan Rd., Chesaning, 48616, Saginaw County, (517)845-6403. Call club for further information.

TWIN LAKES GOLF CLUB
455 Twin Lakes Dr., Oakland, 48363, Oakland County, (248)650-4960, 35 miles N of Detroit.
Opened: 1996. **Holes:** 18. **Par:** 71/71. **Yards:** 6,745/4,701. **Course rating:** 71.0/65.9. **Slope:** 122/109. **Architect:** Roy Hearn and Jerry Matthews. **Green fee:** $50/$55. **Credit cards:** All major. **Reduced fees:** Twilight. **Caddies:** No. **Golf carts:** Included in Green Fee. **Discount golf packages:** No. **Season:** April-Nov. **High:** June-Aug. **On site lodging:** No. **Rental clubs:** Yes. **Walking policy:** Unrestricted walking. **Metal spikes allowed:** Yes. **Range:** Yes (grass). **To obtain tee times:** Call up to 30 days in advance. **Special Notes:** No pullcarts.

★½TWIN OAKS GOLF COURSE
6710 W. Freeland, Freeland, 48623, Bay County, (517)695-9746.
Call club for further information.

★★½TYLER CREEK RECREATION AREA
PU-13495 92nd St., Alto, 49302, Kent County, (616)868-6751.
Opened: N/A. **Holes:** 18. **Par:** 70. **Yards:** 6,200. **Course rating:** 69.5. **Slope:** 117. **Architect:** N/A. **Green fee:** $10/$17. **Credit cards:** MC,VISA. **Reduced fees:** Weekdays, resort guests, seniors, juniors. **Caddies:** No. **Golf carts:** $10. **Discount golf packages:** Yes. **Season:** March-Nov. **High:** June-Aug. **On site lodging:** Yes. **Rental clubs:** Yes. **Walking policy:** Unrestricted walking. **Metal spikes allowed:** Yes. **Range:** No. **To obtain tee times:** Call or come in up to 7 days in advance. **Subscriber comments:** Fun to play; needs permanent ground crew; friendly...Tiny greens; needs sand traps...11th hole is beautiful...Good place for beginners.

★★★TYRONE HILLS GOLF COURSE
PU-8449 U.S. Highway 23, Fenton, 48430, Livingston County, (810)629-5011.
Opened: 1965. **Holes:** 18. **Par:** 72/72. **Yards:** 6,400/5,200. **Course rating:** 70.3/69.1. **Slope:** 123/118. **Architect:** N/A. **Green fee:** $16/$22. **Credit cards:** N/A. **Reduced fees:** Twilight, seniors, juniors. **Caddies:** No. **Golf carts:** $11. **Discount golf packages:** No. **Season:** April-Nov. **High:** June-Aug. **On site lodging:** No. **Rental clubs:** No. **Walking policy:** Unrestricted walking. **Metal spikes allowed:** Yes. **Range:** No. **To obtain tee times:** Call up to 7 days in advance. **Subscriber comments:** Well maintained, fun to play...Inexpensive, fairways a little long, greens are too elevated...Overplayed and needs care...Always work you in...Friendly, clubhouse staff is excellent, great service...Beautiful course to walk...Presents a little bit of everything.

★★★VALLEY VIEW FARM GOLF COURSE
1435 S. Thomas Rd., Saginaw, 48603, Saginaw County, (517)781-1248.
Call club for further information.
Subscriber comments: Always in good shape...Best greens in mid-Michigan...Does not take tee times...Short course but interesting, excellent condition...First come first served...A well kept public course for the price...Lots of room off the tee, fast undulating greens.

★★★VASSAR GOLF & COUNTRY CLUB
3509 Kirk Rd., Vassar, 48768, Tuscola County, (517)823-7221, 17 miles E of Saginaw.
Opened: 1963. **Holes:** 18. **Par:** 72/72. **Yards:** 6,439/5,482. **Course rating:** 71.1/72.1. **Slope:** 126/125. **Architect:** William Newcomb. **Green fee:** $18/$29. **Credit cards:** MC,VISA. **Reduced fees:** N/A. **Caddies:** No. **Golf carts:** $10. **Discount golf packages:** No. **Season:** April-Oct. **High:** June-Sept. **On site lodging:** No. **Rental clubs:** No. **Walking policy:** Unrestricted walking. **Metal spikes allowed:** Yes. **Range:** No. **To obtain tee times:** Call golf shop. **Subscriber comments:** Good course...Laid back, country-boy atmosphere, OK...Usually play on way up north. Nice...Medium speed greens, front tough, back easy...Hidden gem in boondocks. Always a pleasant experience...Easy course to walk...Flat greens! Flat course! Good for outings!...Not a good value for weekend wonderer...Greens are always great.

★★★VERONA HILLS GOLF CLUB
3175 Sand Beach Rd., Bad Axe, 48413, Huron County, (517)269-8132.
Opened: 1924. **Holes:** 18. **Par:** 71/72. **Yards:** 6,466/5,140. **Course rating:** 71.8/70.6.
Slope: 129/125. **Architect:** N/A. **Green fee:** $36. **Credit cards:** MC,VISA. **Reduced fees:** N/A. **Caddies:** No. **Golf carts:** $14. **Discount golf packages:** No. **Season:** April-Nov. **High:** N/A. **On site lodging:** No. **Rental clubs:** No. **Walking policy:** N/A. **Metal spikes allowed:** Yes. **Range:** Yes (grass). **To obtain tee times:** Call.
Subscriber comments: Overpriced for the area it is in...Nice layout. Very challenging. Tough to walk. Michigan's thumb area's finest.

★★½VIENNA GREENS GOLF COURSE
1184 E. Tobias, Clio, 48420, Genesee County, (810)686-1443.
Call club for further information.
Subscriber comments: Good course for the money...Not a hard course.

★★★WALLINWOOD SPRINGS GOLF CLUB
8152 Weatherwax, Jenison, 49428, Ottawa County, (616)457-9920, 15 miles SW of Grand Rapids.
Opened: 1992. **Holes:** 18. **Par:** 72/72. **Yards:** 6,751/5,067. **Course rating:** 72.4/69.1.
Slope: 128/115. **Architect:** Jerry Matthews. **Green fee:** $24/$27. **Credit cards:** MC,VISA,DISC. **Reduced fees:** Weekdays. **Caddies:** No. **Golf carts:** $11. **Discount golf packages:** Yes. **Season:** April-Nov. **High:** June-Aug. **On site lodging:** No. **Rental clubs:** Yes. **Walking policy:** Walking at certain times. **Metal spikes allowed:** Yes. **Range:** No. **To obtain tee times:** Call.
Subscriber comments: Front nine open and fun, back nine a little wet especially when the river floods...The back nine has water on every hole and is a dream to play...Can be a nightmare in the wind...Will be great challenge when it matures.

WARREN VALLEY GOLF COURSE
PU-26116 W. Warren, Dearborn Heights, 48127, Wayne County, (313)561-1040, 10 miles SW of Detroit.
Opened: 1927. **Architect:** Donald Ross. **Green fee:** $15/$19. **Credit cards:** MC,VISA.
Reduced fees: Weekdays, low season, twilight, seniors, juniors. **Caddies:** Yes. **Golf carts:** $20. **Discount golf packages:** No. **High:** May-Oct. **On site lodging:** No. **Rental clubs:** No. **Walking policy:** Unrestricted walking. **Metal spikes allowed:** Yes. **Range:** No. **To obtain tee times:** Call one week in advance.
★★½EAST COURSE
Holes: 18. **Par:** 72/72. **Yards:** 6,189/5,328. **Course rating:** 69.1/70.0. **Slope:** 114/113.
Season: March-Oct.
Subscriber comments: Very hilly, you have to hit the ball straight...Could be great course if kept up better...Good price, courteous...Great new clubhouse. Average course...Urban course, well kept.
★★WEST COURSE
Holes: 18. **Par:** 71/71. **Yards:** 6,066/5,150. **Course rating:** 68.5/69.2. **Slope:** 115/114.
Season: March-Nov.

★★★WASHAKIE GOLF CLUB
PU-3461 Burnside Rd., North Branch, 48461, Lapeer County, (810)688-3235, 30 miles NE of Flint.
Opened: 1986. **Holes:** 18. **Par:** 72/72. **Yards:** 5,805/5,152. **Course rating:** N/A. **Slope:** N/A. **Architect:** Brian Ferrier. **Green fee:** $17/$19. **Credit cards:** None. **Reduced fees:** Seniors. **Caddies:** No. **Golf carts:** $20. **Discount golf packages:** No. **Season:** April-Nov. **High:** May-Aug. **On site lodging:** Yes. **Rental clubs:** Yes. **Walking policy:** Unrestricted walking. **Metal spikes allowed:** No. **Range:** No. **To obtain tee times:** First come, first served.
Subscriber comments: Short, well maintained...High traffic, good novice course...Easy to play, ego builder...Good course to warm up on...What a layout, with campground...Good mix of water, woods and hills.

★★★½WAWASHKAMO GOLF CLUB
British Landing Rd., Mackinac Island, 49757, Mackinac County, (906)847-3871.
Opened: 1898. **Holes:** 9. **Par:** 36/36. **Yards:** 2,999/2,380. **Course rating:** 68.0. **Slope:**

115. Architect: Alex Smith. **Green fee:** N/A. **Credit cards:** N/A. **Reduced fees:** N/A. **Caddies:** No. **Golf carts:** N/A. **Discount golf packages:** No. **Season:** May-Sept. **High:** July-Aug. **On site lodging:** No. **Rental clubs:** Yes. **Walking policy:** Unrestricted walking. **Metal spikes allowed:** Yes. **Range:** No. **To obtain tee times:** N/A.
Subscriber comments: Links course, one of the oldest in Michigan...Historic and fun...Course built within historic battlefields...Use the hickory sticks/gutta percha balls...Top of the island near the airport, very out of the way.
Special Notes: Course is on an island with no cars.

★★★WAWONOWIN COUNTRY CLUB
3432 County Rd. #478, Champion, 49814, Marquette County, (906)485-5660.
Call club for further information.
Subscriber comments: Basic family golf...Beautiful course, play it in July and August...Back nine outstanding...Several fun holes, worth the drive.

WESBURN GOLF COURSE
5617 S. Huron River Dr., South Rockwood, 48179, Monroe County, (313)379-3555.
Call club for further information.

★★★WEST BRANCH COUNTRY CLUB
198 Fairview, West Branch, 48661, Ogemaw County, (517)345-2501, 60 miles N of Saginaw.
Opened: 1930. **Holes:** 18. **Par:** 72/73. **Yards:** 6,402/5,436. **Course rating:** 70.5/71.4. **Slope:** 122/119. **Architect:** William Newcomb.
Green fee: $24/$30. **Credit cards:** MC,VISA. **Reduced fees:** Low season, twilight, seniors. **Caddies:** No. **Golf carts:** $14. **Discount golf packages:** Yes. **Season:** April-Oct. **High:** May-Sept. **On site lodging:** No. **Rental clubs:** Yes. **Walking policy:** Unrestricted walking. **Metal spikes allowed:** Yes. **Range:** Yes (grass/mats). **To obtain tee times:** Call golf shop up to 14 days in advance.
Subscriber comments: Small town course...Tough greens, excellent dining facilities...Open front, tight back, fast and true greens...Traditional layout...Love this whole facility and the people...Nice course for the money.

★★WEST OTTAWA GOLF CLUB
PU-6045 136th Ave., Holland, 49424, Ottawa County, (616)399-1678, 7 miles N of Holland.
Opened: 1965. **Holes:** 27. **Par:** 70/67. **Yards:** 6,250/5,700. **Course rating:** 68.5/66.0. **Slope:** N/A. **Architect:** Bruce Matthews. **Green fee:** $16/$18. **Credit cards:** MC,VISA. **Reduced fees:** Weekdays, low season, seniors, juniors. **Caddies:** No. **Golf carts:** $19. **Discount golf packages:** No. **Season:** March-Nov. **High:** July-Aug. **On site lodging:** No. **Rental clubs:** Yes. **Walking policy:** Unrestricted walking. **Metal spikes allowed:** Yes. **Range:** Yes (grass/mats). **To obtain tee times:** Call golf shop.

★½WESTBROOKE GOLF COURSE
26817 Beck Rd., Novi, 48734, Oakland County, (248)349-2723.
Call club for further information.

★★½WESTERN GREENS GOLF COURSE
PU-2475 Johnson Rd., Marne, 49435, Ottawa County, (616)677-3677, 12 miles W of Grand Rapids.
Opened: 1966. **Holes:** 18. **Par:** 71/73. **Yards:** 6,460/5,552. **Course rating:** N/A. **Slope:** N/A. **Architect:** N/A. **Green fee:** $17/$18. **Credit cards:** MC,VISA. **Reduced fees:** N/A. **Caddies:** No. **Golf carts:** $18. **Discount golf packages:** No. **Season:** April-Nov. **High:** N/A. **On site lodging:** No. **Rental clubs:** Yes. **Walking policy:** Unrestricted walking. **Metal spikes allowed:** Yes. **Range:** Yes (grass). **To obtain tee times:** Call.
Subscriber comments: Nice operation, great for outings...Too much play

---

★★½WHIFFLE TREE HILL GOLF COURSE
PU-15730 Homer Rd., Concord, 49237, Jackson County, (517)524-6655, 15 miles W of Jackson.
Opened: 1969. **Holes:** 18. **Par:** 72/72. **Yards:** 6,370/4,990. **Course rating:** N/A. **Slope:** N/A. **Architect:** Arthur Young. **Green fee:** $8/$14. **Credit cards:** MC,VISA. **Reduced fees:** Weekdays, low season, twilight, seniors, juniors. **Caddies:** No. **Golf carts:** $9.

Discount golf packages: Yes. **Season:** April-Oct. **High:** May-Sept. **On site lodging:** No. **Rental clubs:** Yes. **Walking policy:** Unrestricted walking. **Metal spikes allowed:** Yes. **Range:** Yes (grass). **To obtain tee times:** Call golf shop.
Subscriber comments: Making some improvements, fairly open...Has improved, worth playing...Course is being reshaped and upgraded...Easy course, good value, good solid service...Good basic affordable golf...Best greens in the area.

★★★WHISPERING PINES GOLF CLUB
PU-2500 Whispering Pines Dr., Pinckney, 48169, Livingston County, (313)878-0009, 17 miles N of Ann Arbor.
Opened: 1992. **Holes:** 18. **Par:** 71/73. **Yards:** 6,440/4,813. **Course rating:** 69.8/67.3. **Slope:** 126/117. **Architect:** Donald Moon. **Green fee:** $30/$40. **Credit cards:** MC,VISA. **Reduced fees:** Weekdays, low season, twilight, seniors. **Caddies:** No. **Golf carts:** Included in Green Fee. **Discount golf packages:** No. **Season:** April-Oct. **High:** May-Sept. **On site lodging:** No. **Rental clubs:** No. **Walking policy:** Walking at certain times. **Metal spikes allowed:** No. **Range:** Yes (Mats). **To obtain tee times:** Call up to 14 days in advance.
Subscriber comments: Pure target, use irons only...Too hard, too damn tight...Hit it straight or bring lots of balls...I hate the sound of balls hitting tree trunks...90-degrees shot, very tricked-up course.

★★½WHISPERING WILLOWS GOLF COURSE
PM-20500 Newburg Rd., Livonia, 48152, Wayne County, (248)476-4493, 24 miles NW of Detroit.
Opened: 1968. **Holes:** 18. **Par:** 70/72. **Yards:** 6,056/5,424. **Course rating:** 67.5/69.4. **Slope:** 108/111. **Architect:** Mark DeVries. **Green fee:** $15/$21. **Credit cards:** MC,VISA. **Reduced fees:** Weekdays, seniors, juniors. **Caddies:** No. **Golf carts:** $24. **Discount golf packages:** No. **Season:** April-Nov. **High:** June-Aug. **On site lodging:** No. **Rental clubs:** Yes. **Walking policy:** Unrestricted walking. **Metal spikes allowed:** Yes. **Range:** Yes (grass). **To obtain tee times:** Call up to 3 days in advance from noon to 7 p.m. for weekdays. Nonresidents call on Thursday after 9 a.m. for weekend.
Subscriber comments: City course needs work...Short, cookie-cutter design, only a couple of memorable holes...Easy to get on, OK conditions.

★½WHITE BIRCH HILLS GOLF COURSE
PU-360 Ott Rd., Bay City, 48706, Bay County, (517)662-6523.
Opened: 1949. **Holes:** 18. **Par:** 70/70. **Yards:** 5,600/5,300. **Course rating:** N/A. **Slope:** N/A. **Architect:** N/A. **Green fee:** $15/$15. **Credit cards:** MC,VISA,DISC. **Reduced fees:** Seniors, juniors. **Caddies:** Yes. **Golf carts:** $20. **Discount golf packages:** No. **Season:** April-Oct. **High:** June-Aug. **On site lodging:** Yes. **Rental clubs:** No. **Walking policy:** Unrestricted walking. **Metal spikes allowed:** No. **Range:** Yes (grass). **To obtain tee times:** Call.

★★½WHITE DEER COUNTRY CLUB
PU-1309 Bright Angel Dr., Prudenville, 48651, Roscommon County, (517)366-5812, 70 miles NW of Saginaw.
Opened: 1965. **Holes:** 18. **Par:** 72/72. **Yards:** 6,311/5,290. **Course rating:** 68.8/69.9. **Slope:** 115/116. **Architect:** Glenn Gulder. **Green fee:** $16/$17. **Credit cards:** MC,VISA,DISC. **Reduced fees:** Low season, twilight, juniors. **Caddies:** No. **Golf carts:** $8. **Discount golf packages:** Yes. **Season:** April-Oct. **High:** July-Aug. **On site lodging:** No. **Rental clubs:** Yes. **Walking policy:** Unrestricted walking. **Metal spikes allowed:** Yes. **Range:** No. **To obtain tee times:** Call golf shop.
Subscriber comments: Best value in mid Michigan...Flat, easy to walk...Long par 3s over 200 yards...Small suburban type. Pretty and relaxing.

★★½WHITE LAKE OAKS GOLF COURSE
PM-991 Williams Lake Rd., White Lake, 48386, Oakland County, (248)698-2700, 5 miles W of Pontiac.
Opened: 1940. **Holes:** 18. **Par:** 70/71. **Yards:** 5,738/4,900. **Course rating:** 67.1/67.9. **Slope:** 111/114. **Architect:** N/A. **Green fee:** $12/$20. **Credit cards:** MC,VISA. **Reduced fees:** Weekdays, low season, twilight, seniors, juniors. **Caddies:** No. **Golf carts:** $20. **Discount golf packages:** No. **Season:** April-Nov. **High:** June-Aug. **On site lodging:** No. **Rental clubs:** Yes. **Walking policy:** Unrestricted walking. **Metal spikes**

allowed: No. **Range:** No. **To obtain tee times:** Call on Wednesday at 6:15 p.m. for upcoming weekend.
Subscriber comments: The best fairways I played last year...High marks for playability, mix of holes from easy to challenging...No range, short front, nice back, older crowd...Walking allowed...City run course.

★★★½WHITE PINE NATIONAL GOLF CLUB

PU-3450 N. Hubbard Lake Rd., P.O. Box 130, Spruce, 49747, Alcona County, (517)736-3279, 30 miles S of Alpena.
Opened: 1994. **Holes:** 18. **Par:** 72/72. **Yards:** 6,883/5,268. **Course rating:** 72.7/70.5. **Slope:** 127/124. **Architect:** Bruce Wolfrom and Clem Wolfrom. **Green fee:** $35/$45. **Credit cards:** MC,VISA,DISC. **Reduced fees:** Juniors. **Caddies:** No. **Golf carts:** Included in Green Fee. **Discount golf packages:** Yes. **Season:** April-Nov. **High:** May-Sept. **On site lodging:** No. **Rental clubs:** Yes. **Walking policy:** Walking at certain times.**Metal spikes allowed:** Yes. **Range:** Yes (grass). **To obtain tee times:** Call golf shop.

Subscriber comments: No water, but still challenging as you wind through pine forests...Excellent course with friendly driving holes...Very scenic, well kept, good service, no range, no halfway house...Not too well marked...My secret of the north, relatively new, unheard of gem...A real value...Built with the player in mind, walk anytime.

WHITEFORD VALLEY GOLF CLUB

PU-7980 Beck Rd, Ottawa Lake, 49267, Monroe County, (313)856-4545, 3 miles N of Toledo, OH.
Opened: 1995. **Green fee:** $11/$22. **Credit cards:** MC,VISA,DISC. **Caddies:** No. **Golf carts:** $20. **Season:** Year-round. **High:** April-Oct. **On site lodging:** No. **Rental clubs:** Yes. **Walking policy:** Unrestricted walking. **Metal spikes allowed:** Yes. **Range:** Yes (grass). **To obtain tee times:** Call up to 14 days in advance.

★EAST COURSE
Holes: 18. **Par:** 72/71. **Yards:** 6,631/5,176. **Course rating:** 70.8/68.2. **Slope:** 116/108.
Architect: Harley Hodges. **Reduced fees:** Low season, twilight, seniors, juniors.
Discount golf packages: No.

★★NORTH COURSE
Holes: 18. **Par:** 72/73. **Yards:** 6,808/5,677. **Course rating:** 71.8/71.4. **Slope:** 123/119.
Architect: Harley Hodges. **Reduced fees:** Low season, twilight, seniors, juniors.
Discount golf packages: Yes.

★★SOUTH COURSE
Holes: 18. **Par:** 72/72. **Yards:** 6,659/5,195. **Course rating:** 70.4/68.7. **Slope:** 116/109.
Architect: Harley Hodges. **Reduced fees:** N/A. **Discount golf packages:** No.

WEST COURSE
Holes: 18. **Par:** 72/71. **Yards:** 7,004/5,318. **Course rating:** 72.6/69.8. **Slope:** 122/109.
Architect: N/A. **Reduced fees:** Low season, twilight, seniors, juniors. **Discount golf packages:** No.

WHITTAKER WOODS GOLF CLUB

PU-12578 Wilson Rd., New Buffalo, 49117, Berrien County, (616)469-5070, 70 miles E of Chicago.
Opened: 1996. **Holes:** 18. **Par:** 72/72. **Yards:** 7,011/4,912. **Course rating:** 74.3/68.6. **Slope:** 144/121. **Architect:** Ken Killian. **Green fee:** $50/$55. **Credit cards:** All major. **Reduced fees:** Weekdays, twilight. **Caddies:** No. **Golf carts:** Included in Green Fee. **Discount golf packages:** No. **Season:** Year-round. **High:** June-Aug. **On site lodging:** No. **Rental clubs:** Yes. **Walking policy:** Mandatory cart. **Metal spikes allowed:** No. **Range:** Yes (grass). **To obtain tee times:** Call 7 days in advance.

★★½WILLOW BROOK PUBLIC GOLF CLUB

311 W. Maple, Byron, 48418, Shiawassee County, (810)266-4660.
Call club for further information.
Subscriber comments: Fades on front, draws on back...Very tight and demanding golf course...Enjoyable for money...Could be a very good course...Demanding layout in country setting. Must be versatile in shot making...Hard to find, worth the effort.

★★★½WILLOW METROPARK GOLF COURSE
PU-22900 Huron River Dr., New Boston, 48164, Wayne County, (313)753-4040, (800)234-6534, 4 miles S of Romulus.
Opened: 1979. **Holes:** 18. **Par:** 71/72. **Yards:** 6,378/5,278. **Course rating:** 71.0/70.9. **Slope:** 126/122. **Architect:** William Newcomb. **Green fee:** $18/$20. **Credit cards:** MC,VISA. **Reduced fees:** Weekdays, seniors, juniors. **Caddies:** No. **Golf carts:** $10. **Discount golf packages:** No. **Season:** April-Nov. **High:** May-Aug. **On site lodging:** No. **Rental clubs:** No. **Walking policy:** Unrestricted walking. **Metal spikes allowed:** Yes. **Range:** Yes (grass). **To obtain tee times:** Call up to 7 days in advance.
Subscriber comments: Best of metro courses, every type of hole, textbook layout that makes you use evey club...Tough to get tee time...Long, very challenging.

★★½WINDING BROOK GOLF CLUB
PU-8240 S. Genuine, Shepherd, 48883, Isabella County, (517)828-5688, 6 miles S of Mt. Pleasant.
Opened: 1970. **Holes:** 18. **Par:** 72/72. **Yards:** 6,614/5,015. **Course rating:** 72.6/69.2. **Slope:** 127/115. **Architect:** N/A. **Green fee:** $17/$19. **Credit cards:** MC,VISA,DISC. **Reduced fees:** Weekdays, low season, twilight, seniors, juniors. **Caddies:** No. **Golf carts:** $10. **Discount golf packages:** Yes. **Season:** March-Nov. **High:** June-Aug. **On site lodging:** No. **Rental clubs:** Yes. **Walking policy:** N/A. **Metal spikes allowed:** Yes. **Range:** Yes (grass). **To obtain tee times:** Call.
Subscriber comments: Much tougher from the back tees...Good long ball course...Good value, lots of tough holes...Course in fair condition...Plain Jane...Wide open, best holes are those crossing river and #18...Worth the drive from Mt Pleasant.
Special Notes: Formerly Valley View Golf Course.

★★½WINDING CREEK GOLF COURSE
PU-4514 Ottogan St., Holland, 49423, Allegan County, (616)396-4516, 20 miles SW of Grand Rapids.
Opened: 1968. **Holes:** 27. **Par:** 72/72. **Yards:** 6,665/5,027. **Course rating:** 71.9/69.0. **Slope:** 122/114. **Architect:** Bruce Matthews and Jerry Matthews. **Green fee:** $18/$19. **Credit cards:** MC,VISA. **Reduced fees:** Weekdays, low season, twilight, seniors, juniors. **Caddies:** No. **Golf carts:** $9. **Discount golf packages:** No. **Season:** April-Oct. **High:** May-Aug. **On site lodging:** No. **Rental clubs:** Yes. **Walking policy:** Unrestricted walking. **Metal spikes allowed:** Yes. **Range:** Yes (grass). **To obtain tee times:** Call or come in two days in advance.
Subscriber comments: Decent local course with variety of holes...Of three nines, Gold nine is the most interesting...The second hole on old back nine is terrible. Not fair...Creeks and woods everywhere, very tight...Getting too expensive and too trendy.

★★½WINTERS CREEK GOLF CLUB
13120 Northland Dr., Big Rapids, 49307, Mecosta County, (616)796-2613.
Call club for further information.
Subscriber comments: Much improved, new owner, high marks...Pretty, rolling terrain. Needs to improve fairway maintenance...Some nice elevation chages, but some holes too tight.

★★½WOLVERINE GOLF CLUB
PU-17201 25 Mile Rd., Macomb, 48042, Macomb County, (810)781-5544, 20 miles N of Detroit.
Opened: 1965. **Holes:** 45. **Architect:** Jerry Matthews. **Green fee:** $21/$29. **Credit cards:** All major. **Reduced fees:** Low season, twilight, seniors, juniors. **Caddies:** No. **Golf carts:** $13. **Discount golf packages:** No. **Season:** Year-round weather permitting. **High:** May-Sept. **On site lodging:** No. **Rental clubs:** No. **Walking policy:** Walking at certain times. **Metal spikes allowed:** Yes. **Range:** Yes (grass/mats). **To obtain tee times:** Call up to 14 days in advance.
BLUE/GREEN
Par: 72/72. **Yards:** 6,455/4,967. **Course rating:** 70.3/69.6. **Slope:** 120/116.
GREEN/WHITE
Par: 72/72. **Yards:** 6,521/5,044. **Course rating:** 70.2/68.9. **Slope:** 119/116.
RED/GOLD
Par: 72/72. **Yards:** 6,443/4,825. **Course rating:** 70.7/69.5. **Slope:** 122/119.

MICHIGAN

★★★WOODFIELD GOLF & COUNTRY CLUB

PU-1 Golfside Dr., Grand Blanc, 48439, Genesee County, (810)695-4653, 30 miles NW of Detroit.

Opened: 1994. **Holes:** 18. **Par:** 72/72. **Yards:** 6,780/5,071. **Course rating:** 73.3/68.3. **Slope:** 133/121. **Architect:** Raymond Floyd and Harry F. Bowers. **Green fee:** $30/$40. **Credit cards:** MC,VISA,AMEX. **Reduced fees:** Weekdays, low season, twilight, seniors, juniors. **Caddies:** No. **Golf carts:** Included in Green Fee. **Discount golf packages:** Yes. **Season:** April-Oct. **High:** June-Aug. **On site lodging:** No. **Rental clubs:** Yes. **Walking policy:** Unrestricted walking. **Metal spikes allowed:** Yes. **Range:** Yes (grass/mats). **To obtain tee times:** Call up to 30 days in advance.

Subscriber comments: New course, needs maturity...Very enjoyable, secluded, felt like only players on course...Good variety of hole layouts...Great track...Great greens...Lot of water on the course all around...Forced carries abound...Each year it improves...Demanding layout from all tees.

WOODLAND HILLS GOLF CLUB

PU-320 N. Gates Rd., Sandusky, 48471, Sanilac County, (810)648-2400, (800)648-2400, 65 miles E of Saginaw.

Opened: 1980. **Holes:** 18. **Par:** 71/71. **Yards:** 6,606/5,441. **Course rating:** 70.7/71.0. **Slope:** 121/117. **Architect:** Dick Blank. **Green fee:** $13/$17. **Credit cards:** MC,VISA. **Reduced fees:** Twilight, seniors. **Caddies:** No. **Golf carts:** $9. **Discount golf packages:** Yes. **Season:** April-Oct. **High:** May-Aug. **On site lodging:** No. **Rental clubs:** Yes. **Walking policy:** Walking at certain times. **Metal spikes allowed:** Yes. **Range:** Yes (grass). **To obtain tee times:** Call golf shop.

★★★WOODLAWN GOLF CLUB

PU-4634 Treat Highway, Adrian, 49221, Lenawee County, (517)263-3288, 25 miles NW of Toledo, OH.

Opened: 1954. **Holes:** 18. **Par:** 71/71. **Yards:** 6,080/4,686. **Course rating:** 69.0/66.0. **Slope:** 116/112. **Architect:** N/A. **Green fee:** $14/$20. **Credit cards:** None. **Reduced fees:** Low season, twilight, seniors, juniors. **Caddies:** No. **Golf carts:** $9. **Discount golf packages:** No. **Season:** April-Oct. **High:** May-Sept. **On site lodging:** No. **Rental clubs:** Yes. **Walking policy:** Unrestricted walking. **Metal spikes allowed:** Yes. **Range:** No. **To obtain tee times:** Call golf shop.

Subscriber comments: Tough course, can be tough to get on, service can be so so...Well laid out...Good condition. Too many golf leagues...Needs to mature.

★½AFTON ALPS GOLF COURSE

PU-6600 Peller Ave. S., Hastings, 55033, Washington County, (612)436-1320, (800)328-1328, 20 miles E of St. Paul.
Opened: 1989. **Holes:** 18. **Par:** 72/72. **Yards:** 5,528/4,866. **Course rating:** 67.0/68.4. **Slope:** 108/114. **Architect:** Paul Augustine. **Green fee:** $15/$18. **Credit cards:** MC,VISA. **Reduced fees:** Weekdays, seniors. **Caddies:** No. **Golf carts:** $18. **Discount golf packages:** No. **Season:** April-Oct. **High:** June-Aug. **On site lodging:** No. **Rental clubs:** Yes. **Walking policy:** Unrestricted walking. **Metal spikes allowed:** Yes. **Range:** No. **To obtain tee times:** Call golf shop.

★★½ALBANY GOLF COURSE

PM-500 Church Ave., Albany, 56307, Stearns County, (320)845-2505, 15 miles W of St. Cloud.
Opened: 1960. **Holes:** 18. **Par:** 72/74. **Yards:** 6,415/5,268. **Course rating:** 70.0/69.7. **Slope:** 122/117. **Architect:** Willie Kidd, Sr. **Green fee:** N/A. **Credit cards:** MC,VISA. **Reduced fees:** N/A. **Caddies:** No. **Golf carts:** $18. **Discount golf packages:** No. **Season:** April-Oct. **High:** May-Aug. **On site lodging:** No. **Rental clubs:** No. **Walking policy:** Unrestricted walking. **Metal spikes allowed:** Yes. **Range:** Yes (grass/mats). **To obtain tee times:** Call up to 3 days in advance.
Subscriber comments: Nice rural course...Very good value, wide open course...Decent course, good clubhouse.

★★★½ALBION RIDGES GOLF COURSE

PU-7771 20th St. NW, Annadale, 55302, Wright County, (320)963-5500, 40 miles W of Minneapolis.
Opened: 1991. **Holes:** 18. **Par:** 72/72. **Yards:** 6,502/6,109. **Course rating:** N/A. **Slope:** 118/122. **Architect:** Todd Severud. **Green fee:** $19/$22. **Credit cards:** N/A. **Reduced fees:** Weekdays, seniors, juniors. **Caddies:** No. **Golf carts:** $20. **Discount golf packages:** No. **Season:** April-Nov. **High:** N/A. **On site lodging:** No. **Rental clubs:** Yes. **Walking policy:** Unrestricted walking. **Metal spikes allowed:** Yes. **Range:** Yes (grass). **To obtain tee times:** N/A.
Subscriber comments: Great greens, fast and rolling...Fun course. Links type...New, clean, well kept...Friendly ma and pa operation...A nice course hidden in the country...Condition is always excellent...Wide open, hard to lose a ball.

★★★½ALEXANDRIA GOLF CLUB

C.R. 42, Alexandria, 56308, Douglas County, (320)763-3605.
Architect: Gerry Pirkl and Donald Brauer. **Caddies:** No. **Discount golf packages:** No. **On site lodging:** No. **Rental clubs:** No. **Metal spikes allowed:** Yes. **Range:** No. Call club for further information.
Subscriber comments: Busy!...Good classic track, small but fair greens. Back nine is tight...Excellent mature course. Well maintained...Tom Lehman's high school course...Great traditional golf course.

★★★½BAKER NATIONAL GOLF COURSE

PM-2935 Parkview Dr., Medina, 55340, Hennepin County, (612)473-0800, 20 miles W of Minneapolis.
Opened: 1990. **Holes:** 18. **Par:** 72/74. **Yards:** 6,762/5,395. **Course rating:** 74.2/72.7. **Slope:** 133/129. **Architect:** Michael Hurdzan. **Green fee:** $26/$26. **Credit cards:** MC,VISA,DISC. **Reduced fees:** Seniors, juniors. **Caddies:** No. **Golf carts:** $24. **Discount golf packages:** No. **Season:** April-Oct. **High:** June-Aug. **On site lodging:** No. **Rental clubs:** Yes. **Walking policy:** Unrestricted walking. **Metal spikes allowed:** No. **Range:** Yes (grass). **To obtain tee times:** Call three days in advance.
Subscriber comments: Beautiful setting...Mammoth driving range. Environmentally sound. Great scenery...Almost every hole a "signature".
Special Notes: Also has a 9-hole executive course.

★★★BALMORAL GOLF COURSE

Rte. 3 Box 119, Battle Lake, 56515, Otter Tail County, (218)864-5414.
Architect: Arnold Hemquist. **Caddies:** No. **Discount golf packages:** No. **On site lodging:** No. **Rental clubs:** No. **Metal spikes allowed:** Yes. **Range:** No. Call club for further information.

Subscriber comments: Great northern Minnesota course, carved out of the woods...Kept in excellent condition at all times...Challenging design makes you think...Very tight course, many trees...Pretty course.

★★½BELLWOOD OAKS GOLF COURSE
PU-13239 210th St., Hastings, 55033, Dakota County, (612)437-4141, 25 miles SE of St. Paul.
Opened: 1972. **Holes:** 18. **Par:** 73/74. **Yards:** 6,775/5,707. **Course rating:** 72.5/72.3. **Slope:** 123/126. **Architect:** Don Raskob. **Green fee:** $15/$21. **Credit cards:** None. **Reduced fees:** Weekdays, seniors. **Caddies:** No. **Golf carts:** $22. **Discount golf packages:** Yes. **Season:** April-Nov. **High:** May-Sept. **On site lodging:** No. **Rental clubs:** Yes. **Walking policy:** Unrestricted walking. **Metal spikes allowed:** Yes. **Range:** Yes (grass). **To obtain tee times:** Call five days in advance.
Subscriber comments: Gets better every year...Well maintained. Friendly service...Nice, quiet and not crowded always in good shape.

★★★½BEMIDJI TOWN & COUNTRY CLUB
R-Birchmont Dr. N.E., Bemidji, 56601, Beltrami County, (218)751-9215, 220 miles NW of Minneapolis/St. Paul.
Opened: 1920. **Holes:** 18. **Par:** 72/72. **Yards:** 6,535/5,058. **Course rating:** 71.8/69.1. **Slope:** 127/120. **Architect:** Joel Goldstrand. **Green fee:** $20/$30. **Credit cards:** All major. **Reduced fees:** Low season, resort guests, twilight. **Caddies:** No. **Golf carts:** $23. **Discount golf packages:** No. **Season:** April-Oct. **High:** June-Aug. **On site lodging:** No. **Rental clubs:** Yes. **Walking policy:** Unrestricted walking. **Metal spikes allowed:** Yes. **Range:** Yes (grass). **To obtain tee times:** Call golf shop.
Subscriber comments: Recent upgrades have made it better...Picturesque setting...Played in fall, beautiful...Wonderful pine-lined fairways...Some beautiful holes carved out of the Northwoods...Relaxing...Fair test for all abilities.

★★★½BLUEBERRY PINES GOLF CLUB
N. Highway 71, Menahga, 56464, Wadena County, (218)564-4653, (800)652-4940, 115 miles NE of Fargo, ND.
Opened: 1991. **Holes:** 18. **Par:** 72/72. **Yards:** 6,663/5,024. **Course rating:** 72.6/69.3. **Slope:** 132/123. **Architect:** Joel Goldstrand. **Green fee:** $18/$26. **Credit cards:** All major. **Reduced fees:** Twilight, seniors, juniors. **Caddies:** No. **Golf carts:** $22. **Discount golf packages:** No. **Season:** April-Oct. **High:** June-Aug. **On site lodging:** No. **Rental clubs:** Yes. **Walking policy:** Unrestricted walking. **Metal spikes allowed:** Yes. **Range:** Yes (grass). **To obtain tee times:** Call up to 6 days in advance.
Subscriber comments: Northern Minnesota golfing at its finest. Huge log cabin clubhouse...Great course, nice facilities, Treelined. Very tight fairways...Golf and nature in perfect harmony...Scenic...Tight and long layout...Testy greens, lots of breaks.

★★BLUFF CREEK GOLF COURSE
PU-1025 Creekwood, Chaska, 55318, Carver County, (612)445-5685, 3 miles S of Minneapolis.
Opened: 1972. **Holes:** 18. **Par:** 70/76. **Yards:** 6,359/5,093. **Course rating:** 69.9/68.3. **Slope:** 119/109. **Architect:** Gerry Pirkl and Donald G. Brauer. **Green fee:** $21/$26. **Credit cards:** None. **Reduced fees:** Weekdays, low season, twilight, seniors, juniors. **Caddies:** No. **Golf carts:** $26. **Discount golf packages:** No. **Season:** April-Nov. **High:** June-Aug. **On site lodging:** No. **Rental clubs:** Yes. **Walking policy:** Unrestricted walking. **Metal spikes allowed:** Yes. **Range:** Yes (grass). **To obtain tee times:** Weekday call up to 7 days in advance. Weekends/Holidays call up to 3 days in advance.

★★★BRAEMAR GOLF COURSE
PU-6364 John Harris Dr., Edina, 55439, Hennepin County, (612)941-2072, 8 miles SW of Minneapolis.
Opened: 1964. **Architect:** Don Brauer. **Credit cards:** All major. **Reduced fees:** Low season, juniors. **Caddies:** Yes. **Discount golf packages:** No. **Season:** April-Oct. **High:** May-Sept. **On site lodging:** No. **Rental clubs:** Yes. **Walking policy:** Unrestricted walking. **Range:** Yes (grass/mats). **To obtain tee times:** First come, first served.

MINNESOTA

CASTLE/HAYS
Holes: 27. **Par:** 71/73. **Yards:** 6,739/5,739. **Course rating:**
71.8/73.4. **Slope:** 124/129. **Green fee:** $20/$20. **Golf carts:** $23.
Metal spikes allowed: Yes.

(GOOD VALUE)

CLUNIE/CASTLE
Holes: 27. **Par:** 72/73. **Yards:** 6,692/5,679. **Course rating:**
73.0/73.8. **Slope:** 134/131. **Green fee:** $23/$23. **Metal spikes
allowed:** No.

HAYS/CLUNIE
Holes: 27. **Par:** 71/72. **Yards:** 6,377/5,400. **Course rating:** 71.6/72.0. **Slope:** 129/126.
Green fee: $23/$23. **Golf carts:** $22. **Metal spikes allowed:** No.
Subscriber comments: Traditional...Three very different, very enjoyable nines. Difficult
to get tee time...Good pro shop...New nine OK, old nines great.

BREEZY POINT RESORT
R-HCR 2 Box 70, County Rd. 11, Breezy Point, 56472, Crow Wing County, (218)562-
7177, (800)950-4960, 20 miles N of Brainerd.
 Credit cards: All major,Diners Club. **Reduced fees:** Weekdays, low season, twilight,
juniors. **Caddies:** No. **Golf carts:** $13. **Discount golf packages:** Yes. **Season:** April-
Oct. **High:** June-Sept. **On site lodging:** Yes. **Rental clubs:** Yes. **Walking policy:**
Unrestricted walking. **To obtain tee times:** Call up to 2 days in advance.
★★½TRADITIONAL COURSE
Opened: 1930. **Holes:** 18. **Par:** 68/72. **Yards:** 5,192/5,127. **Course rating:** 62.9/65.5.
Slope: 114/111. **Architect:** Bill Fawcett. **Green fee:** $27/$30. **Metal spikes allowed:**
Yes. **Range:** No.
Subscriber comments: Typical resort course...Short but very challenging...Well used
resort course...Front nine open, back nine will get you.
★★★WHITEBIRCH GOLF COURSE
Opened: 1981. **Holes:** 18. **Par:** 72/72. **Yards:** 6,704/4,711. **Course rating:** 71.8/72.8.
Slope: 124/123. **Architect:** Landecker/Hubbard. **Green fee:** $32/$37. **Metal spikes
allowed:** No. **Range:** Yes (grass).
Subscriber comments: Wide fairways,...Beautiful country...Another picturesque north-
ern Minnesota course...Spectacular clubhouse...Will be a great course when it matures.

★★★BROOKTREE MUNICIPAL GOLF COURSE
PM-1369 Cherry St., Owatonna, 55060, Steele County, (507)444-2467, 40 miles S of
Minneapolis/St. Paul.
Opened: 1957. **Holes:** 18. **Par:** 71/72. **Yards:** 6,648/5,534. **Course rating:** 71.9/71.3.
Slope: 121/121. **Architect:** Gerry Pirkl and Donald G. Brauer. **Green fee:** $14/$16.
Credit cards: None. **Reduced fees:** Weekdays. **Caddies:** No. **Golf carts:** $17.
Discount golf packages: No. **Season:** April-Oct. **High:** June-Aug. **On site lodging:**
No. **Rental clubs:** Yes. **Walking policy:** Unrestricted walking. **Metal spikes allowed:**
Yes. **Range:** No. **To obtain tee times:** Call three days in advance.
Subscriber comments: Fast greens...Two nines totally opposite, front flat.

★★½BROOKVIEW GOLF COURSE
PU-200 Brookview Pkwy., Golden Valley, 55426, Hennepin County, (612)512-2300, 5
miles SW of Minneapolis.
Opened: 1922. **Holes:** 18. **Par:** 72/72. **Yards:** 6,369/5,463. **Course rating:** 70.3/71.4.
Slope: 127/124. **Architect:** Garrett Gill. **Green fee:** $22/$22. **Credit cards:** MC,VISA.
Reduced fees: Twilight. **Caddies:** No. **Golf carts:** $21. **Discount golf packages:** No.
Season: April-Oct. **High:** June-Sept. **On site lodging:** No. **Rental clubs:** Yes. **Walking
policy:** Unrestricted walking. **Metal spikes allowed:** Yes. **Range:** Yes (grass/mats). **To
obtain tee times:** Call two days in advance. Patron card holders may call from three to
seven days in advance.
Subscriber comments: Good public course, very busy...Rather noisy by the freeway...Greens OK...A challenge...Busy metro area course.
Special Notes: Also has a 9-hole par-3 course.

★★★★BUNKER HILLS GOLF COURSE

PU-Highway 242 and Foley Blvd., Coon Rapids, 55448, Anoka County, (612)755-4141, 15 miles N of Minneapolis.
Opened: 1968. **Holes:** 27. **Architect:** David Gill/Joel Goldstrand. **Green fee:** $23/$29. **Credit cards:** None. **Reduced fees:** Seniors, juniors. **Caddies:** No. **Golf carts:** $24. **Discount golf packages:** No. **Season:** April-Nov. **High:** June-Aug. **On site lodging:** No. **Rental clubs:** Yes. **Walking policy:** Unrestricted walking. **Metal spikes allowed:** Yes. **Range:** Yes (grass/mats). **To obtain tee times:** Call three days in advance after 2 p.m.
EAST/WEST
Par: 72/73. **Yards:** 6,901/5,809. **Course rating:** 73.4/74.2. **Slope:** 133/128.
NORTH/EAST
Par: 72/72. **Yards:** 6,799/5,618. **Course rating:** 72.7/72.6. **Slope:** 130/126.
NORTH/WEST
Par: 72/73. **Yards:** 6,938/5,779. **Course rating:** 73.1/73.6. **Slope:** 135/130.
Subscriber comments: One of best public experiences I've had...Hats off to green-keeper...Great 27-hole layout, recommend all three combinations...The best public course in Minnesota...Fun to be able to play where Senior Tour visits...Outstanding mix of golf holes, a steal.
Special Notes: Senior Tour stop. Also has a 9-hole executive course. Discount for wearing softspikes.

GOOD VALUE

★★★½CANNON GOLF CLUB

8606 295th St. E., Cannon Falls, 55009, Dakota County, (507)263-3126, 25 miles SE of St. Paul.
Opened: 1927. **Holes:** 18. **Par:** 71/71. **Yards:** 6,099/5,011. **Course rating:** 69.5/70.1. **Slope:** 127/125. **Architect:** Joel Goldstrand. **Green fee:** $21/$25. **Credit cards:** MC,VISA. **Reduced fees:** Weekdays, twilight, seniors. **Caddies:** Yes. **Golf carts:** $25. **Discount golf packages:** No. **Season:** April-Oct. **High:** April-Oct. **On site lodging:** No. **Rental clubs:** Yes. **Walking policy:** Unrestricted walking. **Metal spikes allowed:** Yes. **Range:** Yes (grass). **To obtain tee times:** Call golf shop up to 7 days in advance.
Subscriber comments: Short course, but you better place your shots, not easy...Fast greens...Southern Minnesota silent surprise. A must play...Enjoy a hamburger at the turn...Excellent greens, great value...Tough course, lots of water.

★½CARRIAGE HILLS COUNTRY CLUB

PU-3535 Wescott Hills Dr., Eagan, 55123, Ramsey County, (612)452-7211.
Opened: 1965. **Holes:** 18. **Par:** 71/72. **Yards:** 5,800/4,920. **Course rating:** 67.5/68.4. **Slope:** 119/111. **Architect:** N/A. **Green fee:** $14/$24. **Credit cards:** MC,VISA. **Reduced fees:** Weekdays, twilight, seniors, juniors. **Caddies:** No. **Golf carts:** $18. **Discount golf packages:** No. **Season:** April-Oct. **High:** N/A. **On site lodging:** No. **Rental clubs:** Yes. **Walking policy:** Unrestricted walking. **Metal spikes allowed:** Yes. **Range:** No. **To obtain tee times:** Call up to 7 days in advance.

★★½CASTLE HIGHLANDS GOLF COURSE

RT 5 Box, Bemidji, 56601, Beltrami County, (218)586-2681.
Call club for further information.
Subscriber comments: Beautiful course in the woods. Fairly easy...Peaceful...Short, wooded, hit it straight and get low scores.

★★★CEDAR RIVER COUNTRY CLUB

PU-Hwy. 56 W., Adams, 55909, Mower County, (507)582-3595, 16 miles SE of Austin.
Opened: 1969. **Holes:** 18. **Par:** 72/74. **Yards:** 6,211/5,517. **Course rating:** 70.3/72.0. **Slope:** 124/124. **Architect:** John Queenland. **Green fee:** $18/$18. **Credit cards:** MC,VISA. **Reduced fees:** N/A. **Caddies:** No. **Golf carts:** $18. **Discount golf packages:** Yes. **Season:** March-Nov. **High:** June-Aug. **On site lodging:** No. **Rental clubs:** Yes. **Walking policy:** Unrestricted walking. **Metal spikes allowed:** Yes. **Range:** Yes (grass). **To obtain tee times:** Call golf shop.
Subscriber comments: Course is kept in very good shape...Lots of pines, tough but rewarding... Great value.

MINNESOTA

★★★CEDAR VALLEY GOLF COURSE
County Rd. 9, Winona, 55987, Winona County, (507)457-3129, 100 miles S of Minneapolis.
Opened: 1992. **Holes:** 27. **Par:** 72/72. **Yards:** 6,218/5,560. **Course rating:** 69.5/71.7. **Slope:** 119/122. **Architect:** N/A. **Green fee:** $20/$22. **Credit cards:** MC,VISA. **Reduced fees:** N/A. **Caddies:** No. **Golf carts:** $20. **Discount golf packages:** No. **Season:** April-Nov. **High:** June-Aug. **On site lodging:** No. **Rental clubs:** Yes. **Walking policy:** Unrestricted walking. **Metal spikes allowed:** Yes. **Range:** Yes (grass). **To obtain tee times:** Call up to 3 days in advance.
Subscriber comments: Friendly little place. Hate to share this hidden gem!...Beautiful setting. Very good greens...Outstanding appeal, valley golf, well routed...Excellent value, beautiful setting...Will beccome more challenging as matures.

★★★CHISAGO LAKES GOLF COURSE
PU-292nd St., Lindstrom, 55045, Chisago County, (612)257-1484, 35 miles NE of St. Paul.
Opened: 1972. **Holes:** 18. **Par:** 72/72. **Yards:** 6,529/5,714. **Course rating:** 71.2/72.7. **Slope:** 119/124. **Architect:** Donald Brauer/Joel Goldstrand. **Green fee:** $20/$22. **Credit cards:** MC,VISA. **Reduced fees:** N/A. **Caddies:** No. **Golf carts:** $20. **Discount golf packages:** No. **Season:** April-Oct. **High:** June-Aug. **On site lodging:** No. **Rental clubs:** Yes. **Walking policy:** Unrestricted walking. **Metal spikes allowed:** Yes. **Range:** Yes (grass). **To obtain tee times:** Call up to 7 days in advance for weekdays; Thursday for weekends.
Subscriber comments: Best kept secret...Tough starting holes...Needs new clubhouse, but otherwise a good rural course. Big greens...Beautiful course to walk, front nine good warmup for tougher back nine.

★★½CHOMONIX GOLF COURSE
PU-646 Sandpiper Dr., Lino Lakes, 55014, Anoka County, (612)482-8484, 22 miles N of Minneapolis.
Opened: 1970. **Holes:** 18. **Par:** 72/72. **Yards:** 6,596/5,455. **Course rating:** 72.2/72.3. **Slope:** 121/123. **Architect:** Don Herfort/Gerry Pirkl. **Green fee:** $18/$20. **Credit cards:** MC,VISA,DISC. **Reduced fees:** Weekdays, seniors, juniors. **Caddies:** No. **Golf carts:** $20. **Discount golf packages:** No. **Season:** April-Nov. **High:** June-Aug. **On site lodging:** No. **Rental clubs:** Yes. **Walking policy:** Unrestricted walking. **Metal spikes allowed:** Yes. **Range:** Yes (grass). **To obtain tee times:** Call four days in advance starting at 6 a.m.
Subscriber comments: Narrow fairways. Nice layout...Lots of trees and water. Recent work should decrease wetness...Friendly staff, watch out for mosquitos...Reworked low lying holes. Greatly improved.

★★½COLUMBIA GOLF COURSE
.PU-3300 Central Ave., Minneapolis, 55418, Hennepin County, (612)789-2627, 3 miles N of Minneapolis (downtown).
Opened: 1920. **Holes:** 18. **Par:** 71/71. **Yards:** 6,385/5,489. **Course rating:** 70.0/71.9. **Slope:** 121/123. **Architect:** Edward Lawrence Packard. **Green fee:** $20/$20. **Credit cards:** MC,VISA. **Reduced fees:** Twilight, seniors, juniors. **Caddies:** No. **Golf carts:** $22. **Discount golf packages:** No. **Season:** April-Nov. **High:** May-Sept. **On site lodging:** No. **Rental clubs:** Yes. **Walking policy:** Unrestricted walking. **Metal spikes allowed:** Yes. **Range:** Yes (grass/mats). **To obtain tee times:** Call up to 4 days in advance.
Subscriber comments: A pleasant walk...Old layout...Great from back tees...Hilly, mature...Easy...Neat layout, lots of potential.

★★COMO GOLF COURSE
PU-1431 N. Lexington Pkwy., St. Paul, 55103, Ramsey County, (612)488-9673.
Opened: 1988. **Holes:** 18. **Par:** 70/70. **Yards:** 5,814/5,068. **Course rating:** 68.6/70.4. **Slope:** 121/125. **Architect:** Don Herfort. **Green fee:** $21/$21. **Credit cards:** MC,VISA. **Reduced fees:** Low season, twilight, seniors, juniors. **Caddies:** No. **Golf carts:** $22. **Discount golf packages:** No. **Season:** April-Oct. **High:** June-Aug. **On site lodging:** No. **Rental clubs:** Yes. **Walking policy:** Unrestricted walking. **Metal spikes allowed:**

Yes. **Range:** No. **To obtain tee times:** Call one day in advance for weekdays, Monday-Friday. For weekends you must sign up in person the Thursday before. For holidays call the Thursday before at 7 a.m.

CROSSWOODS GOLF COURSE
PU-HC 83 Box 106, Crosslake, 56442, Crow Wing County, (218)692-4653, 23 miles N of Brainerd.
Opened: 1997. **Holes:** 18. **Par:** 67/67. **Yards:** 5,149/4,440. **Course rating:** N/A. **Slope:** N/A. **Architect:** Michael Stone. **Green fee:** $16/$20. **Credit cards:** MC,VISA. **Reduced fees:** Weekdays, twilight, seniors, juniors. **Caddies:** No. **Golf carts:** $20. **Discount golf packages:** No. **Season:** May-Oct. **High:** June-Aug. **On site lodging:** No. **Rental clubs:** Yes. **Walking policy:** Unrestricted walking. **Metal spikes allowed:** No. **Range:** Yes (grass/mats). **To obtain tee times:** Call golf shop.

★★★CUYUNA COUNTRY CLUB
20 Golf Course Rd., Deerwood, 56444, Crow Wing County, (218)534-3489, 90 miles NW of Minneapolis.
Opened: 1923. **Holes:** 18. **Par:** 72/74. **Yards:** 6,407/5,749. **Course rating:** 71.9/74.2. **Slope:** 132/138. **Architect:** Don Herfort. **Green fee:** $30/$35. **Credit cards:** MC,VISA,DISC. **Reduced fees:** Weekdays, low season, resort guests. **Caddies:** No. **Golf carts:** $20. **Discount golf packages:** Yes. **Season:** April-Oct. **High:** July-Aug. **On site lodging:** No. **Rental clubs:** Yes. **Walking policy:** Unrestricted walking. **Metal spikes allowed:** No. **Range:** Yes (grass). **To obtain tee times:** Call or come in three days in advance.
Subscriber comments: Beautiful and challenging, they treat you like royalty!...Great back nine...Newer holes are great, very hilly...Nice practice facilities...Front nine pleasant, back nine carved out of the dense woods by the devil...Great course.

★★½DAHLGREEN GOLF CLUB
PU-6940 Dahlgreen Rd., Chaska, 55318, Carver County, (612)448-7463, 20 miles SW of Minneapolis.
Opened: 1971. **Holes:** 18. **Par:** 72/72. **Yards:** 6,761/5,346. **Course rating:** 72.4/70.4. **Slope:** 132/124. **Architect:** Gerry Pirkl and Donald Brauer. **Green fee:** $22/$28. **Credit cards:** MC,VISA. **Reduced fees:** Weekdays, low season, seniors, juniors. **Caddies:** No. **Golf carts:** $24. **Discount golf packages:** Yes. **Season:** March-Nov. **High:** June-Aug. **On site lodging:** No. **Rental clubs:** Yes. **Walking policy:** Unrestricted walking. **Metal spikes allowed:** No. **Range:** Yes (grass). **To obtain tee times:** Call three days in advance for weekdays; Wednesday morning for weekends.
Subscriber comments: Nice resort course...Very peaceful country setting...Fun course, next to cow pasture...Good greens.

★★DAYTONA COUNTRY CLUB
PU-14730 Lawndale Lane, Dayton, 55327, Hennepin County, (612)427-6110, 20 miles NW of Minneapolis.
Opened: 1964. **Holes:** 18. **Par:** 72/73. **Yards:** 6,363/5,468. **Course rating:** 69.7/70.7. **Slope:** 118/112. **Architect:** Jerry McCann. **Green fee:** $16/$26. **Credit cards:** All major. **Reduced fees:** Weekdays, low season, seniors, juniors. **Caddies:** No. **Golf carts:** $23. **Discount golf packages:** No. **Season:** Year-round. **High:** April-Nov. **On site lodging:** No. **Rental clubs:** Yes. **Walking policy:** Unrestricted walking. **Metal spikes allowed:** Yes. **Range:** Yes (grass). **To obtain tee times:** Call or come in up to seven days in advance.

★★½DEER RUN GOLF CLUB
PU-8661 Deer Run Dr., Victoria, 55386, Carver County, (612)443-2351.
Opened: 1989. **Holes:** 18. **Par:** 71/71. **Yards:** 6,265/5,541. **Course rating:** 70.5/72.1. **Slope:** 122/121. **Architect:** Mike Schultz. **Green fee:** $21/$25. **Credit cards:** MC,VISA. **Reduced fees:** Twilight, seniors, juniors. **Caddies:** No. **Golf carts:** $21. **Discount golf packages:** No. **Season:** March-Nov. **High:** June-Aug. **On site lodging:** No. **Rental clubs:** No. **Walking policy:** Unrestricted walking. **Metal spikes allowed:** Yes. **Range:** Yes (grass). **To obtain tee times:** Call three days in advance.
Subscriber comments: Fun, rolling course. Needs to mature...Great potential...Good long course. Back nine old...Course gets a lot of play, gets rather worn...Nice, rural prairie course...Too many houses on course...Nice course, excellent service.

★★★DETROIT COUNTRY CLUB
R-Rte. 5, Detroit Lakes, 56501, Becker County, (218)847-5790, 47 miles E of Fargo, ND.
Opened: 1916. **Holes:** 18. **Par:** 71/71. **Yards:** 5,941/5,508. **Course rating:** 69.2/72.3. **Slope:** 122/129. **Architect:** Tom Bendelow/Don Herfort. **Green fee:** $23/$25. **Credit cards:** MC,VISA. **Reduced fees:** Weekdays. **Caddies:** Yes. **Golf carts:** $20. **Discount golf packages:** No. **Season:** May-Oct. **High:** June-Aug. **On site lodging:** No. **Rental clubs:** Yes. **Walking policy:** Unrestricted walking. **Metal spikes allowed:** Yes. **Range:** Yes (grass). **To obtain tee times:** Call one week in advance.
Subscriber comments: Good value, challenging course...Very well kept. Beautiful setting...Short and tight. Good variety of holes...Old style resort course, fun to play...Old course, short, wooded, fun...Fantastic food and beverage.
Special Notes: Also 18-hole executive Lakeview Course.

DOUBLE EAGLE GOLF CLUB
PM-County Road #3, Eagle Bend, 56446, Todd County, (218)738-5155, 30 miles NE of Alexandria.
Opened: 1982. **Holes:** 9. **Architect:** Joel Goldstrand. **Green fee:** $20/$20. **Credit cards:** MC,VISA. **Reduced fees:** N/A. **Caddies:** No. **Golf carts:** $19. **Discount golf packages:** No. **Season:** April-Oct. **High:** July-Aug. **On site lodging:** No. **Rental clubs:** Yes. **Walking policy:** Unrestricted walking. **Metal spikes allowed:** Yes. **Range:** Yes. **To obtain tee times:** Call golf shop.
★★★GOLD/GREEN COURSE
Par: 37/37. **Yards:** 3,500/2,920. **Course rating:** 37.1/36.4. **Slope:** 132/124.
Subscriber comments: Unique...Great course, well maintained and good people...Challenging, reversible, long nine-hole course.
Special Notes: First reversible course built in the USA. Play Gold course in one direction, then play Green course in reverse direction to make 18 holes.

★★★EAGLE CREEK
1000 26th. Ave. N.E., Willmar, 56201, Kandiyohi County, (612)235-1166, 80 miles W of Minneapolis.
Opened: 1930. **Holes:** 18. **Par:** 72/73. **Yards:** 6,342/5,271. **Course rating:** 70.8/70.9. **Slope:** 129/127. **Architect:** Albert Anderson. **Green fee:** $25/$28. **Credit cards:** MC,VISA. **Reduced fees:** Weekdays, low season. **Caddies:** No. **Golf carts:** $22. **Discount golf packages:** Yes. **Season:** April-Oct. **High:** May-Aug. **On site lodging:** No. **Rental clubs:** Yes. **Walking policy:** Unrestricted walking. **Metal spikes allowed:** No. **Range:** Yes (grass). **To obtain tee times:** Call up to 2 days in advance.
Subscriber comments: Fun, tight course, bring your "A" game...Championship layout. True test of golf...Great golf terrain...Every hole is a challenge.
Special Notes: Formerly Willmar Golf Club.

★★★½EAGLE RIDGE GOLF COURSE
PU-1 Green Way, Coleraine, 55722, Itasca County, (218)245-2217, 5 miles E of Grand Rapids.
Opened: 1996. **Holes:** 18. **Par:** 72/72. **Yards:** 6,772/5,220. **Course rating:** 71.8/69.2. **Slope:** 126/114. **Architect:** Garrett Gill. **Green fee:** $13/$20. **Credit cards:** MC,VISA,DISC. **Reduced fees:** Weekdays, low season, resort guests, juniors. **Caddies:** No. **Golf carts:** $20. **Discount golf packages:** No. **Season:** March-Oct. **High:** June-Aug. **On site lodging:** No. **Rental clubs:** Yes. **Walking policy:** Unrestricted walking. **Metal spikes allowed:** Yes. **Range:** Yes (grass/mats). **To obtain tee times:** Call up to 7 days in advance.
Subscriber comments: New course...Great views...Great new golf course carved through virgin woods...New course, give it time, will be one to play...Challenging.

★★½EASTWOOD GOLF CLUB
PM-3505 Eastwood Rd. S.E., Rochester, 55904, Olmsted County, (507)281-6173.
Opened: 1968. **Holes:** 18. **Par:** 70/70. **Yards:** 6,178/5,289. **Course rating:** 69.9/71.0. **Slope:** 120/121. **Architect:** Ray Keller. **Green fee:** $18/$18. **Credit cards:** N/A. **Reduced fees:** N/A. **Caddies:** No. **Golf carts:** $18. **Discount golf packages:** No. **Season:** April-Nov. **High:** May-Aug. **On site lodging:** No. **Rental clubs:** Yes. **Walking policy:** Unrestricted walking. **Metal spikes allowed:** Yes. **Range:** Yes (grass). **To**

obtain tee times: Call two days in advance.
Subscriber comments: Small greens and par 4s make it a challenge...Nice municipal course...Extremely busy; friendly service...Back nine better than front.

★★★★EDINBURGH USA GOLF CLUB
PU-8700 Edinbrook Crossing, Brooklyn Park, 55443, Hennepin County, (612)493-8098, 12 miles N of Minneapolis.
Opened: 1987. Holes: 18. Par: 72/72. Yards: 6,701/5,255. Course rating: 73.0/71.4. Slope: 133/128. Architect: Robert Trent Jones Jr. Green fee: $35/$35. Credit cards: MC,VISA,AMEX. Reduced fees: Twilight, seniors, juniors. Caddies: Yes. Golf carts: $24. Discount golf packages: No. Season: April-Oct. High: June-Aug. On site lodging: No. Rental clubs: Yes. Walking policy: Unrestricted walking. Metal spikes allowed: Yes. Range: Yes (grass). To obtain tee times: Call four days in advance of play at 2 p.m.
Notes: 1992 USGA Public Links Championship; 1990-96 LPGA Tour event.
Subscriber comments: Top of the line...Fantastic golf course in every aspect...Good design, good shape, tough greens...Tough but fair...Former LPGA site. Immaculate conditions, sugar sand...All the amenities...Demanding water holes....Tough course to score on...Great practice range.

★★½ELK RIVER COUNTRY CLUB
20015 Elk Lake Rd., Elk River, 55330, Sherburne County, (612)441-4111.
Architect: Willie Kidd. Caddies: No. Discount golf packages: No. On site lodging: No. Rental clubs: No. Metal spikes allowed: Yes. Range: No.
Call club for further information.
Subscriber comments: Nice course...Old type layout, nicely wooded...Fun, challenging, hilly...Good turf, small greens....Forgiving layout...One of my favorites...Nice course...Tight, small greens.

★★ELM CREEK GOLF LINKS OF PLYMOUTH
PU-18940 Highway 55, Plymouth, 55446, Hennepin County, (612)478-6716, 16 miles W of Minneapolis.
Opened: 1960. Holes: 18. Par: 70/71. Yards: 6,215/4,839. Course rating: 70.4/68.0. Slope: 132/117. Architect: Michael Klatte and Mark Klatte. Green fee: $21/$24. Credit cards: MC,VISA,AMEX. Reduced fees: N/A. Caddies: No. Golf carts: $22. Discount golf packages: No. Season: April-Oct. High: June-Aug. On site lodging: No. Rental clubs: No. Walking policy: Unrestricted walking. Metal spikes allowed: Yes. Range: No. To obtain tee times: Reservation system with credit card.

★★½ENGER PARK GOLF CLUB
PU-1801 W. Skyline Blvd., Duluth, 55806, St. Louis County, (218)723-3451.
Opened: 1927. Holes: 27. Par: 72/72. Yards: 6,434/5,247. Course rating: 70.9/65.3. Slope: 126/115. Architect: Dick Phelps. Green fee: $20/$20. Credit cards: MC,VISA. Reduced fees: Low season, twilight, seniors, juniors. Caddies: No. Golf carts: $18. Discount golf packages: No. Season: April-Nov. High: June-Aug. On site lodging: No. Rental clubs: Yes. Walking policy: Unrestricted walking. Metal spikes allowed: Yes. Range: Yes (grass). To obtain tee times: Call up to 7 days in advance.
Subscriber comments: Very enjoyable since they've expanded to 27 holes...Great view of Lake Superior...Good public course...Excellent views, hilly...Fairways very patchy, wide open...Wish they would have left it alone, some good holes.

★★FALCON RIDGE GOLF COURSE
PU-33942 Falcon Ave., Stacy, 55079, Chisago County, (612)462-5797.
Opened: 1993. Holes: 18. Par: 72/72. Yards: 5,787/5,070. Course rating: 67.7/69.6. Slope: 106/117. Architect: Lyle Kleven/Martin Johnson/Doug Lien. Green fee: $17/$20. Credit cards: MC,VISA,DISC. Reduced fees: Weekdays, seniors, juniors. Caddies: No. Golf carts: $20. Discount golf packages: No. Season: April-Oct. High: June-Aug. On site lodging: No. Rental clubs: Yes. Walking policy: Unrestricted walking. Metal spikes allowed: Yes. Range: Yes (grass). To obtain tee times: Call golf shop.
Special Notes: Also has a 9-hole executive course.

★★½FOUNTAIN VALLEY GOLF CLUB

PU-2830 220th St. W., Farmington, 55024, Dakota County, (612)463-2121, 30 miles S of Minneapolis.

Opened: 1977. **Holes:** 18. **Par:** 72/72. **Yards:** 6,540/5,980. **Course rating:** 71.5/73.4. **Slope:** 119/122. **Architect:** Ray Rahn. **Green fee:** $18/$23. **Credit cards:** MC,VISA. **Reduced fees:** Weekdays, seniors. **Caddies:** No. **Golf carts:** $12. **Discount golf packages:** No. **Season:** April-Oct. **High:** June-Aug. **On site lodging:** No. **Rental clubs:** Yes. **Walking policy:** Unrestricted walking. **Metal spikes allowed:** No. **Range:** Yes (grass). **To obtain tee times:** Call seven days in advance.
Subscriber comments: Wide open layout with several remarkable par 5s. Fun to play...Excellent greens...Generally wide open. Sparse fairways and good layout.

★★★FOX HOLLOW GOLF CLUB

4780 Palmgren Lane N.E., Rogers, 55374, Hennepin County, (612)428-4468, 30 miles W of Minneapolis.

Opened: 1989. **Holes:** 18. **Par:** 72/72. **Yards:** 6,726/5,161. **Course rating:** 72.7/70.8. **Slope:** 129/122. **Architect:** Joel Goldstrand. **Green fee:** $25/$30. **Credit cards:** MC,VISA,Diners Club. **Reduced fees:** Seniors, juniors. **Caddies:** No. **Golf carts:** N/A. **Discount golf packages:** No. **Season:** April-Nov. **High:** June-Aug. **On site lodging:** No. **Rental clubs:** Yes. **Walking policy:** Unrestricted walking. **Metal spikes allowed:** Yes. **Range:** Yes (grass). **To obtain tee times:** Call three days in advance at 7 a.m.
Subscriber comments: Excellent public course. Greens, great range, great grass...Water on 13 holes, requires carry to seven greens...Nice driving range.

★★★FRANCIS A. GROSS GOLF COURSE

PU-2201 St. Anthony Blvd., Minneapolis, 55418, Hennepin County, (612)789-2542.

Opened: 1925. **Holes:** 18. **Par:** 71/71. **Yards:** 6,575/5,400. **Course rating:** 70.8/73.2. **Slope:** 120/121. **Architect:** W.C. Clark. **Green fee:** $20/$20. **Credit cards:** MC,VISA. **Reduced fees:** Weekdays, twilight, seniors, juniors. **Caddies:** No. **Golf carts:** $22. **Discount golf packages:** Yes. **Season:** April-Nov. **High:** June-Aug. **On site lodging:** No. **Rental clubs:** Yes. **Walking policy:** Unrestricted walking. **Metal spikes allowed:** Yes. **Range:** Yes (grass). **To obtain tee times:** Call up to 4 days in advance.
Notes: 1964 USGA National Public Links Championship.
Subscriber comments: Mature course, keep it in the fairway...Fun course...A fine municipal course...Great urban golf value, but tough to get on...For all of the play it gets it is in good shape...Fair to every level of play.

★★★GLENCOE COUNTRY CLUB

1325 E 1st. St., Glencoe, 55336, McLeod County, (320)864-3023, (800)399-3023, 54 miles W of Minneapolis.

Opened: 1958. **Holes:** 18. **Par:** 71/71. **Yards:** 6,074/4,940. **Course rating:** 69.7/69.7. **Slope:** 117/117. **Architect:** N/A. **Green fee:** $18/$23. **Credit cards:** MC,VISA. **Reduced fees:** Seniors, juniors. **Caddies:** No. **Golf carts:** $20. **Discount golf packages:** No. **Season:** April-Oct. **High:** N/A. **On site lodging:** No. **Rental clubs:** Yes. **Walking policy:** Unrestricted walking. **Metal spikes allowed:** No. **Range:** Yes (grass). **To obtain tee times:** N/A.
Subscriber comments: The new back nine needs refinement...Some difficult par 5s...A true golf course...Unimaginative, but usually in good condition.

★★GOODRICH GOLF COURSE

PU-1820 N. Van Dyke, Maplewood, 55109, Ramsey County, (612)777-7355, 3 miles NE of St. Paul.

Opened: 1959. **Holes:** 18. **Par:** 70/72. **Yards:** 6,015/5,728. **Course rating:** 67.8/71.8. **Slope:** 105/111. **Architect:** Paul Coates. **Green fee:** $16/$20. **Credit cards:** None. **Reduced fees:** Weekdays, twilight, seniors, juniors. **Caddies:** No. **Golf carts:** $22. **Discount golf packages:** No. **Season:** April-Nov. **High:** June-Aug. **On site lodging:** No. **Rental clubs:** Yes. **Walking policy:** Unrestricted walking. **Metal spikes allowed:** Yes. **Range:** Yes (mats). **To obtain tee times:** Call four days in advance.

★★★½GRAND NATIONAL GOLF CLUB

PU-300 Lady Luck Dr., Hinckley, 55037, Pine County, (320)384-7427, 60 miles N of Minneapolis/St. Paul.

Opened: 1995. **Holes:** 18. **Par:** 72/72. **Yards:** 6,894/5,100. **Course rating:** 72.0/68.7. **Slope:** 123/117. **Architect:** Joel Goldstrand. **Green fee:** $25/$28. **Credit cards:** MC,VISA. **Reduced fees:** Resort guests, twilight, seniors. **Caddies:** No. **Golf carts:** $24. **Discount golf packages:** Yes. **Season:** April-Oct. **High:** May-Aug. **On site lodging:** Yes. **Rental clubs:** Yes. **Walking policy:** Unrestricted walking. **Metal spikes allowed:** Yes. **Range:** Yes (grass). **To obtain tee times:** Call seven days in advance. **Subscriber comments:** Excellent overall condition. Great greens, bent-grass landing areas. Several challenging par 4s...Dry and dusty...Excellent tees and greens, target fairways fun, tough when windy.

★★½GREEN LEA GOLF COURSE

PU-101 Richway Dr., Albert Lea, 56007, Freeborn County, (507)373-1061, 90 miles S of Minneapolis.
Opened: 1947. **Holes:** 18. **Par:** 73/77. **Yards:** 6,166/5,404. **Course rating:** 70.2/71.4. **Slope:** 122/126. **Architect:** N/A. **Green fee:** $17/$19. **Credit cards:** MC,VISA,DISC. **Reduced fees:** Weekdays, low season, twilight, seniors, juniors. **Caddies:** No. **Golf carts:** $9. **Discount golf packages:** Yes. **Season:** April-Oct. **High:** June-Aug. **On site lodging:** No. **Rental clubs:** Yes. **Walking policy:** Unrestricted walking. **Metal spikes allowed:** Yes. **Range:** No. **To obtain tee times:** Call 3 days in advance for weekends and holidays.
Subscriber comments: It's going to get better. They are working on it...Owner is putting a lot of money into it. Good layout...Short but very enjoyable and well maintained muny course...Good walking course...Very playable, fun course.

★★½GREENHAVEN COUNTRY CLUB

2800 Greenhaven Rd., Anoka, 55303, Anoka County, (612)427-3180.
Call club for further information.
Subscriber comments: Short but nice track...Friendly people and nice clubhouse but it is a short course...Lots of mature trees...Well maintained.

★★½GREENWOOD GOLF LINKS

PU-4520 E. Viking Blvd., Wyoming, 55092, Chisago County, (612)462-4653, 30 miles N of St. Paul.
Opened: 1986. **Holes:** 9. **Par:** 72/72. **Yards:** 5,518/4,791. **Course rating:** 67.2/67.3. **Slope:** 105/112. **Architect:** C.M. Johnson. **Green fee:** $17/$19. **Credit cards:** None. **Reduced fees:** Seniors, juniors. **Caddies:** No. **Golf carts:** $20. **Discount golf packages:** Yes. **Season:** April-Oct. **High:** May-Aug. **On site lodging:** Yes. **Rental clubs:** Yes. **Walking policy:** Unrestricted walking. **Metal spikes allowed:** Yes. **Range:** No. **To obtain tee times:** Call up to 2 days in advance.
Subscriber comments: A fun short course.

★HAMPTON HILLS GOLF COURSE

PU-5313 Juneau Lane, Plymouth, 55428, Hennepin County, (612)559-9800, 12 miles NW of Minneapolis.
Opened: 1966. **Holes:** 18. **Par:** 73/73. **Yards:** 6,135/5,554. **Course rating:** 68.2/68.8. **Slope:** 104/112. **Architect:** N/A. **Green fee:** $17/$20. **Credit cards:** N/A. **Reduced fees:** Low season, twilight, seniors, juniors. **Caddies:** No. **Golf carts:** $20. **Discount golf packages:** Yes. **Season:** N/A. **High:** N/A. **On site lodging:** No. **Rental clubs:** Yes. **Walking policy:** Unrestricted walking. **Metal spikes allowed:** Yes. **Range:** Yes (grass). **To obtain tee times:** Call on Monday for reservations for the week.

★★½HAWLEY GOLF & COUNTRY CLUB

PU-Highway 10, Hawley, 56549, Clay County, (218)483-4808, 22 miles E of Fargo, ND.
Opened: 1923. **Holes:** 18. **Par:** 70/71. **Yards:** 5,887/5,197. **Course rating:** 68.2/69.5. **Slope:** 115/115. **Architect:** N/A. **Green fee:** $16/$16. **Credit cards:** MC,VISA. **Reduced fees:** N/A. **Caddies:** No. **Golf carts:** $17. **Discount golf packages:** No. **Season:** April-Oct. **High:** June-Aug. **On site lodging:** No. **Rental clubs:** Yes. **Walking policy:** Unrestricted walking. **Metal spikes allowed:** Yes. **Range:** No. **To obtain tee times:** Call up to 7 days in advance for weekdays; Thursday for weekends and holidays.
Subscriber comments: Easier course, great value and treatment...Lots of hills and may want a golf cart...Good course for a short course...Very open layout.

★★★HEADWATERS COUNTRY CLUB

P.O. Box 9, Park Rapids, 56470, Hubbard County, (218)732-4832, 112 miles NW of St. Cloud.
Opened: 1969. **Holes:** 18. **Par:** 72/72. **Yards:** 6,455/5,362. **Course rating:** 70.9/71.0. **Slope:** 120/118. **Architect:** N/A. **Green fee:** $20/$25. **Credit cards:** MC,VISA. **Reduced fees:** Low season, twilight, juniors. **Caddies:** No. **Golf carts:** $23. **Discount golf packages:** No. **Season:** March-Nov. **High:** June-Aug. **On site lodging:** No. **Rental clubs:** Yes. **Walking policy:** Unrestricted walking. **Metal spikes allowed:** Yes. **Range:** Yes (grass). **To obtain tee times:** Local call two days in advance. Out of town, call anytime.
Subscriber comments: Fun resort course...Hidden northwoods gem...Very friendly....Some tight fairways...Loons fly over.... Beautiful in the fall...Beautiful back nine...Small greens...Beautiful setting in lake country...Favorite.

★★HIAWATHA GOLF COURSE

PU-4553 Longfellow Ave. S., Minneapolis, 55407, Hennepin County, (612)724-7715.
Opened: 1934. **Holes:** 18. **Par:** 73/74. **Yards:** 6,645/5,796. **Course rating:** 70.6/71.7. **Slope:** 114/123. **Architect:** N/A. **Green fee:** $20/$20. **Credit cards:** MC,VISA. **Reduced fees:** Weekdays, low season, twilight, seniors, juniors. **Caddies:** No. **Golf carts:** $22. **Discount golf packages:** Yes. **Season:** April-Nov. **High:** June-Aug. **On site lodging:** No. **Rental clubs:** Yes. **Walking policy:** Unrestricted walking. **Metal spikes allowed:** Yes. **Range:** Yes (grass). **To obtain tee times:** Call up to 4 days in advance.

★★★HIDDEN GREENS GOLF CLUB

PU-12977 200th St. E., Hastings, 55033, Dakota County, (612)437-3085, 24 miles SE of Minneapolis.
Opened: 1976. **Holes:** 18. **Par:** 72/72. **Yards:** 5,954/5,559. **Course rating:** 68.8/72.2. **Slope:** 118/127. **Architect:** Joel Goldstrand. **Green fee:** $17/$18. **Credit cards:** None. **Reduced fees:** Weekdays, seniors. **Caddies:** No. **Golf carts:** $18. **Discount golf packages:** No. **Season:** April-Nov. **High:** July-Aug. **On site lodging:** No. **Rental clubs:** Yes. **Walking policy:** Unrestricted walking. **Metal spikes allowed:** No. **Range:** Yes (grass). **To obtain tee times:** Call after 9 a.m. on Tuesday.
Subscriber comments: Older course, mature fairways and greens...An undiscovered gem. Excellent greens. Many holes carved through woods...Fun layout...Great setting. Well kept and friendly...Keep it straight or tree trouble.

★★HIGHLAND PARK GOLF COURSE

PU-1403 Montreal Ave., St. Paul, 55116, Ramsey County, (612)699-5825.
Opened: 1929. **Holes:** 18. **Par:** 72/73. **Yards:** 6,265/5,600. **Course rating:** 69.0/71.1. **Slope:** 111/118. **Architect:** G. Pirkl, D. Brauer and E. Perret. **Green fee:** $18. **Credit cards:** MC,VISA. **Reduced fees:** Low season, twilight, seniors, juniors. **Caddies:** No. **Golf carts:** $20. **Discount golf packages:** No. **Season:** April-Nov. **High:** May-Sept. **On site lodging:** No. **Rental clubs:** Yes. **Walking policy:** Unrestricted walking. **Metal spikes allowed:** Yes. **Range:** Yes (grass). **To obtain tee times:** For weekdays call 8 a.m. one day in advance. For weekends come in Wednesday in person 6 a.m. to 7 a.m. or call on Thursday after 7 a.m.

★★½HOLLYDALE GOLF COURSE

PU-4710 Holly Lane N., Plymouth, 55446, Hennepin County, (612)559-9847.
Opened: 1965. **Holes:** 18. **Par:** 71/73. **Yards:** 6,115/5,922. **Course rating:** 68.7/72.0. **Slope:** 108/120. **Architect:** N/A. **Green fee:** $19/$21. **Credit cards:** N/A. **Reduced fees:** Weekdays, seniors, juniors. **Caddies:** No. **Golf carts:** $22. **Discount golf packages:** No. **Season:** April-Nov. **High:** June-Aug. **On site lodging:** No. **Rental clubs:** Yes. **Walking policy:** Unrestricted walking. **Metal spikes allowed:** Yes. **Range:** Yes (grass). **To obtain tee times:** Call Tuesday after 7:30 a.m. for weekends and holidays.
Subscriber comments: Fairly open, confidence builder...Small greens, must chip and run...Very busy, fun course, in good condition despite heavy play...Long course but always good shape...Fair, open, easy to underrate.

★★★INVER WOOD GOLF COURSE

PU-1850 70th St. E., Inver Grove Heights, 55077, Dakota County, (612)457-3667, 8 miles S of St. Paul.

Opened: 1991. **Holes:** 18. **Par:** 72/72. **Yards:** 6,724/5,175. **Course rating:** 72.5/70.3. **Slope:** 135/124. **Architect:** Garrett Gill and George B. Williams. **Green fee:** $24/$24. **Credit cards:** MC,VISA. **Reduced fees:** Juniors. **Caddies:** No. **Golf carts:** $22. **Discount golf packages:** No. **Season:** April-Oct. **High:** May-Aug. **On site lodging:** No. **Rental clubs:** Yes. **Walking policy:** Unrestricted walking. **Metal spikes allowed:** Yes. **Range:** Yes (grass). **To obtain tee times:** Call or come in three days in advance. **Subscriber comments:** Good facility, best practice putting green I've seen...Needs conditioning...Great layout...Each hole is a different experience. Fun track, good value for your buck...Very hilly...Hard to walk.
Special Notes: Also has 9-hole course.

★★★ISLAND VIEW GOLF COURSE
PU-9150 Island View Rd., Waconia, 55387, Carver County, (612)442-6116, 20 miles W of Minneapolis.
Opened: 1957. **Holes:** 18. **Par:** 72/72. **Yards:** 6,552/5,382. **Course rating:** 70.7/70.1. **Slope:** 129/124. **Architect:** Willie Kidd. **Green fee:** $30/$35. **Credit cards:** MC,VISA,DISC. **Reduced fees:** N/A. **Caddies:** No. **Golf carts:** $24. **Discount golf packages:** No. **Season:** April-Oct. **High:** June-Aug. **On site lodging:** No. **Rental clubs:** Yes. **Walking policy:** Unrestricted walking. **Metal spikes allowed:** No. **Range:** Yes (grass). **To obtain tee times:** Call up to 2 days in advance.
Subscriber comments: Country club like course...Super course...Beautiful, mature course, peaceful...Challenging holes, hilly...Good shape, good bargain.

★★★½IZATY'S GOLF & YACHT CLUB
R-40005 85th Ave., Onamia, 56359, Mille Lacs County, (612)532-4575, (800)533-1728, 90 miles N of Minneapolis.
Opened: N/A. **Holes:** 18. **Par:** 72/72. **Yards:** 6,481/4,939. **Course rating:** 72.1/69.7. **Slope:** 132/127. **Architect:** Perry Dye. **Green fee:** $35/$55. **Credit cards:** All major,Diner's Club. **Reduced fees:** Weekdays, resort guests, twilight. **Caddies:** No. **Golf carts:** $28. **Discount golf packages:** Yes. **Season:** April-Oct. **High:** June-Sept. **On site lodging:** Yes. **Rental clubs:** Yes. **Walking policy:** Unrestricted walking. **Metal spikes allowed:** Yes. **Range:** Yes (grass/mats). **To obtain tee times:** Anytime for resort guests or members. Nonguests call four days in advance.
Subscriber comments: Facilities are wonderful...Excellent greens...Historically challenging and beautiful...Very tight fairways...Solid course...Leave your woods at home...Small but good pro shop...Good layout, difficult from tips...Irons get workout. Excellent dinner menu...Short, but keep it in play...Tough but fair.

★★★KELLER GOLF COURSE
PU-2166 Maplewood Dr., St. Paul, 55109, Ramsey County, (612)484-3011, 10 miles N of Minneapolis/St. Paul.
Opened: 1929. **Holes:** 18. **Par:** 72/73. **Yards:** 6,566/5,373. **Course rating:** 71.7/71.4. **Slope:** 127/124. **Architect:** Paul N. Coates. **Green fee:** $23/$23. **Credit cards:** None. **Reduced fees:** Low season, twilight, seniors, juniors. **Caddies:** No. **Golf carts:** $22. **Discount golf packages:** No. **Season:** March-Nov. **High:** May-Sept. **On site lodging:** No. **Rental clubs:** Yes. **Walking policy:** Unrestricted walking. **Metal spikes allowed:** Yes. **Range:** Yes (grass). **To obtain tee times:** Call four days in advance starting at 7 a.m.
Notes: St. Paul Open 1930-1968; National Public Links 1931; National PGA Championship 1932 and 1954; Western Open 1949; Patty Berg Golf Classic 1973-1980.
Subscriber comments: Wonderful course, if greens are kept up...Championship layout, well groomed...Hosted the PGA Championship twice...One of the great old public courses, a joy to play...Granddaddy of Minnesota golf.

★★★LAKESIDE GOLF CLUB
RR#3, Waseca, 56093, Waseca County, (507)835-2574.
Call club for further information.
Subscriber comments: Very nice course, kept in great shape...A changing course...Good course and getting better with improvements...This is a nice golf course, not too many big challenges.

MINNESOTA

★★LAKEVIEW GOLF OF ORONO
PU-710 North Shore Drive, W., Mound, 55364, Hennepin County, (612)472-3459.
Opened: 1956. **Holes:** 18. **Par:** 70/70. **Yards:** 5,424/4,894. **Course rating:** 65.8/67.1.
Slope: 108/109. **Architect:** Russ Wenkstern. **Green fee:** $14/$22. **Credit cards:**
MC,VISA,AMEX. **Reduced fees:** Twilight, seniors, juniors. **Caddies:** No. **Golf carts:**
$21. **Discount golf packages:** No. **Season:** April-Oct. **High:** June-Aug. **On site lodging:** No. **Rental clubs:** Yes. **Walking policy:** Unrestricted walking. **Metal spikes allowed:** Yes. **Range:** No. **To obtain tee times:** Call golf shop.

★★★LES BOLSTAD UNIV. OF MINNESOTA GOLF CLUB
2275 W. Larpenteur Ave., St. Paul, 55113, Ramsey County, (612)627-4000.
Opened: 1922. **Holes:** 18. **Par:** 71/75. **Yards:** 6,123/5,684. **Course rating:** 69.2/75.2.
Slope: 117/132. **Architect:** Seth Raynor. **Green fee:** $12/$22. **Credit cards:**
MC,VISA,DISC. **Reduced fees:** Weekdays, low season, twilight. **Caddies:** No. **Golf carts:** $18. **Discount golf packages:** No. **Season:** April-Oct. **High:** June-Aug. **On site lodging:** No. **Rental clubs:** Yes. **Walking policy:** Unrestricted walking. **Metal spikes allowed:** Yes. **Range:** Yes (grass). **To obtain tee times:** Call up to 5 days in advance.
Subscriber comments: Grand old course, small elevated greens....Great course and value if the greens are in shape...Fun, tight treelined course, price is right...Mature, nice balance...Have to play with your head.

★★★LESTER PARK GOLF CLUB
PU-1860 Lester River Rd., Duluth, 55804, St. Louis County, (218)525-1400.
Opened: 1931. **Holes:** 27. **Architect:** Dick Phelps. **Green fee:** $18/$18. **Credit cards:**
None. **Reduced fees:** Low season, twilight, seniors, juniors. **Caddies:** No. **Golf carts:** $18. **Discount golf packages:** No. **Season:** April-Nov. **High:** June-July. **On site lodging:** No. **Rental clubs:** Yes. **Walking policy:** Unrestricted walking. **Metal spikes allowed:** Yes. **Range:** Yes (grass). **To obtain tee times:** Call 72 hours in advance.
BACK/LAKE
Par: 72/73. **Yards:** 6,606/5,486. **Course rating:** 71.7/72.1. **Slope:** 126/125.
FRONT/BACK
Par: 72/74. **Yards:** 6,371/5,604. **Course rating:** 70.8/72.6. **Slope:** 118/122.
FRONT/LAKE
Par: 72/73. **Yards:** 6,599/5,504. **Course rating:** 71.7/72.7. **Slope:** 125/126.
Subscriber comments: Public course, better than some private ones...Difficult greens to read, lake effect...The course does not drain well...Lake nine calls for accurate shooting...Great layout and views.

★★★½THE LINKS AT NORTHFORK
PU-9333 153rd Ave., Ramsey, 55303, Anoka County, (612)241-0506.
Opened: 1992. **Holes:** 18. **Par:** 72/72. **Yards:** 6,989/5,242. **Course rating:** 73.7/70.5.
Slope: 127/117. **Architect:** Joel Goldstrand. **Green fee:** $27/$29. **Credit cards:**
MC,VISA,AMEX. **Reduced fees:** Weekdays, low season, twilight, seniors, juniors.
Caddies: No. **Golf carts:** $22. **Discount golf packages:** Yes. **Season:** April-Oct. **High:** June-Aug. **On site lodging:** No. **Rental clubs:** Yes. **Walking policy:** Unrestricted walking. **Metal spikes allowed:** Yes. **Range:** Yes (grass). **To obtain tee times:** Call three days in advance for an additional charge.
Subscriber comments: Awesome Scottish links-style course...Forgiving but challenging...Long and windy...Two different courses front to back...Neat, challenging course, housing development, clubhouse austere...Lookout if wind is blowing!

★★½LITCHFIELD GOLF COURSE
PM-W. Pleasure Dr., Litchfield, 55355, Meeker County, (320)693-6059, 70 miles W of Minneapolis.
Opened: 1974. **Holes:** 18. **Par:** 70/70. **Yards:** 6,350/5,011. **Course rating:** 69.8/69.4.
Slope: 123/121. **Architect:** N/A. **Green fee:** $14/$20. **Credit cards:** MC,VISA.
Reduced fees: Weekdays. **Caddies:** No. **Golf carts:** $16. **Discount golf packages:**
No. **Season:** April-Oct. **High:** June-Aug. **On site lodging:** No. **Rental clubs:** Yes.
Walking policy: Unrestricted walking. **Metal spikes allowed:** Yes. **Range:** No. **To obtain tee times:** Call up to 3 days in advance.
Subscriber comments: Not bad for a small town course...Great layout; great greens; long but fair...Short and flat.

MINNESOTA

★★★LITTLE CROW COUNTRY CLUB
Highway 23, Spicer, 56288, Kandiyohi County, (320)354-2296,
47 miles SW of St. Cloud.
Opened: 1969. **Holes:** 18. **Par:** 72/72. **Yards:** 6,765/5,757. **Course rating:** 72.3/73.1. **Slope:** 123/125. **Architect:** Don Herfort. **Green fee:** $15/$25. **Credit cards:** MC,VISA. **Reduced fees:** Weekdays, low season. **Caddies:** No. **Golf carts:** $10. **Discount golf packages:** No.
Season: April-Nov. **High:** June-Aug. **On site lodging:** No. **Rental clubs:** Yes. **Walking policy:** Unrestricted walking. **Metal spikes allowed:** No. **Range:** Yes (grass). **To obtain tee times:** Call one day in advance.
Subscriber comments: Good layout...Excellent value...A very nice golf club in a nice town...A good country course...Nice, short but challenging, super service.

★★½LITTLE FALLS COUNTRY CLUB
PU-1 Edgewater Dr., Little Falls, 56345, Morrison County, (320)632-3584, 30 miles N of St. Cloud.
Opened: 1982. **Holes:** 18. **Par:** 72/72. **Yards:** 6,051/5,713. **Course rating:** 69.0/72.0. **Slope:** 121/125. **Architect:** N/A. **Green fee:** $17/$18. **Credit cards:** All major. **Reduced fees:** Weekdays, low season, juniors. **Caddies:** No. **Golf carts:** $17. **Discount golf packages:** Yes. **Season:** April-Oct. **High:** June-Aug. **On site lodging:** No. **Rental clubs:** Yes. **Walking policy:** Unrestricted walking. **Metal spikes allowed:** Yes. **Range:** Yes (grass). **To obtain tee times:** Call up to one week in advance.
Subscriber comments: Challenging, small, fast greens, beautiful signature hole...I like the back nine along the river...Tight, heavily pined course with numerous doglegs...Great course.

★★LONE PINES COUNTRY CLUB
15451 Howard Lake Rd., Shakopee, 55379, Scott County, (612)445-3575.
Call club for further information.

MADDEN'S ON GULL LAKE
R-8001 Pine Beach Peninsula, Brainerd, 56401, Crow Wing County, (218)829-7118, 120 miles N of Minneapolis.
Green fee: $29/$31. **Credit cards:** MC,VISA. **Reduced fees:** Weekdays, resort guests, twilight. **Caddies:** No. **Golf carts:** $25. **Discount golf packages:** Yes. **Season:** April-Oct. **High:** July-Aug. **On site lodging:** Yes. **Rental clubs:** Yes. **Walking policy:** Unrestricted walking. **Metal spikes allowed:** No. **Range:** Yes (grass). **To obtain tee times:** Call up to 30 days in advance.

★★★★THE CLASSIC AT MADDEN'S RESORT
Opened: 1997. **Holes:** 18. **Par:** 72/72. **Yards:** 7,100/4,883. **Course rating:** 74.9/68.6. **Slope:** 139/119. **Architect:** Scott Hoffman. **Green fee:** $75/$90. **Golf carts:** Included in Green Fee. **Discount golf packages:** No.
Notes: Ranked 3rd in 1997 Best New Upscale Public Courses.
Subscriber comments: Great new course, outstanding challenge and beauty...The Northern Augusta National, enough said...Beautiful and playable.

★★★PINE BEACH EAST COURSE
Opened: 1926. **Holes:** 18. **Par:** 72/72. **Yards:** 5,956/5,352. **Course rating:** 67.9/70.9. **Slope:** 119/116. **Architect:** James Delgleish.
Subscriber comments: Great weekend getaway...Made for the long, straight hitter, narrow fairways...Always in great shape, many good improvements...Typical resort course, no rough.

★★★PINE BEACH WEST COURSE
Opened: 1950. **Holes:** 18. **Par:** 67/67. **Yards:** 5,049/4,662. **Course rating:** 64.0/66.7. **Slope:** 103/107. **Architect:** Paul Coates/Jim Madden.
Subscriber comments: Good companion to East Course...Extremely pleasant to play...Short, but excellent greens...Requires good shotmaking...Well maintained...Short par 67, pretty course, nice leisurely playing course.

MAJESTIC OAKS GOLF CLUB
PU-701 Bunker Lake Blvd., Ham Lake, 55304, Anoka County, (612)755-2142, 20 miles N of Minneapolis.

Credit cards: All major. **Reduced fees:** Weekdays, low season, twilight, seniors, juniors. **Caddies:** No. **Golf carts:** $22. **Discount golf packages:** No. **Season:** April-Oct. **On site lodging:** Yes. **Rental clubs:** Yes. **Walking policy:** Unrestricted walking. **Metal spikes allowed:** Yes. **Range:** Yes (grass). **To obtain tee times:** Call four days in advance for nonpatrons and one week in advance for patrons.

★★½GOLD COURSE
Opened: 1991. **Holes:** 18. **Par:** 72/72. **Yards:** 6,396/4,848. **Course rating:** 71.2/68.4. **Slope:** 123/120. **Architect:** Garrett Gill. **Green fee:** $19/$23. **High:** June-Aug.
Subscriber comments: New greenkeeper has really improved course condition...Lots of bunkers...Mature course, great greens...Course needs work...Shorter course, well maintained...Course can be challenging...Awesome locker room, large banquet room.

★★★PLATINUM COURSE
Opened: 1972. **Holes:** 18. **Par:** 72/72. **Yards:** 7,013/5,268. **Course rating:** 73.9/71.6. **Slope:** 129/126. **Architect:** Charles Maddox. **Green fee:** $21/$26. **High:** May-Sept.
Subscriber comments: Good test use all clubs in bag. Too much corporate use...Always a beverage cart close. Greens are fast...Nice clubhouse...Greens are big, fun to putt.
Special Notes: Also has 9-hole executive course.

★★½MANITOU RIDGE GOLF COURSE
PU-3200 N. McKnight Rd., White Bear Lake, 55110, Ramsey County, (612)777-2987, 15 miles N of St. Paul.
Opened: 1930. **Holes:** 18. **Par:** 71/71. **Yards:** 6,422/5,556. **Course rating:** 70.5/71.5. **Slope:** 120/119. **Architect:** Don Herfort. **Green fee:** $20/$20. **Credit cards:** MC,VISA. **Reduced fees:** Low season, twilight, seniors, juniors. **Caddies:** No. **Golf carts:** $22. **Discount golf packages:** No. **Season:** April-Oct. **High:** April-Oct. **On site lodging:** No. **Rental clubs:** Yes. **Walking policy:** Unrestricted walking. **Metal spikes allowed:** Yes. **Range:** Yes (grass). **To obtain tee times:** Call four days in advance.
Subscriber comments: Went from a cow pasture to challenging course...Getting better with redesigned holes. Great staff...Best golf shop/service in the state...Nice course, excellent value for seniors, very excellent service.

★★★MAPLE VALLEY GOLF & COUNTRY CLUB
8600 Maple Valley Rd. S.E., Rochester, 55904, Olmstead County, (507)285-9100, 8 miles S of Rochester.
Opened: 1964. **Holes:** 18. **Par:** 71/71. **Yards:** 6,270/5,330. **Course rating:** 68.9/68.5. **Slope:** 108/108. **Architect:** Wayne Idso. **Green fee:** $18/$18. **Credit cards:** MC,VISA. **Reduced fees:** N/A. **Caddies:** No. **Golf carts:** N/A. **Discount golf packages:** No. **Season:** March-Nov. **High:** July-Aug. **On site lodging:** No. **Rental clubs:** Yes. **Walking policy:** Unrestricted walking. **Metal spikes allowed:** Yes. **Range:** No. **To obtain tee times:** Call five days in advance.
Subscriber comments: Tough par 4s, good greens...Challenging layout could be outstanding with a little work...Great condition...In the fall the scenery is breathtaking...Small greens, good blend of holes...Water, trees, hills, sand.

★★★½MARSHALL GOLF CLUB
800 Country Club Dr., Marshall, 56258, Lyon County, (507)537-1622, 90 miles NE of Souix Falls, SD.
Opened: N/A. **Holes:** 18. **Par:** 72/72. **Yards:** 6,565/5,136. **Course rating:** 71.6/69.5. **Slope:** 123/120. **Architect:** J.W. Whitney. **Green fee:** $15/$25. **Credit cards:** MC,VISA. **Reduced fees:** N/A. **Caddies:** No. **Golf carts:** $22. **Discount golf packages:** Yes. **Season:** April-Oct. **High:** May-Sept. **On site lodging:** No. **Rental clubs:** Yes. **Walking policy:** Unrestricted walking. **Metal spikes allowed:** No. **Range:** Yes (grass). **To obtain tee times:** Call one week in advance.
Subscriber comments: Bent-grass fairways and greens...Great challenging course. Slick greens and tighter fairways make you think your way around the course...Good course management helps, ponds and stream.

MARSHALL HIGH SCHOOL GOLF CLUB
401 S. Saratoga, Marshall, 56258, Lyon County, (507)537-0551.
Call club for further information.

MINNESOTA

★★½MEADOWBROOK GOLF COURSE
PU-201 Meadowbrook Rd., Hopkins, 55343, Hennepin County, (612)929-2077, 3 miles W of Minneapolis.
Opened: 1926. **Holes:** 18. **Par:** 72/72. **Yards:** 6,593/5,610. **Course rating:** N/A. **Slope:** 113/122. **Architect:** James Foulis/K. Killian and D.Nugent. **Green fee:** $17/$17. **Credit cards:** VISA. **Reduced fees:** Low season, twilight, seniors, juniors. **Caddies:** No. **Golf carts:** N/A. **Discount golf packages:** No. **Season:** April-Nov. **High:** May-Aug. **On site lodging:** No. **Rental clubs:** Yes. **Walking policy:** Unrestricted walking. **Metal spikes allowed:** Yes. **Range:** No. **To obtain tee times:** For weekdays come in three days in advance. For weekends come in person the Tuesday before.
Subscriber comments: Good variety, some blind shots...Go for it on the 5th hole!...Course improvements have improvemed drainage and toughened the course...Challenging new water holes.

★★★½THE MEADOWS GOLF COURSE
PU-401 34th St. S., Moorhead, Clay County, (218)299-5244.
Opened: 1994. **Holes:** 18. **Par:** 72/72. **Yards:** 6,862/5,150. **Course rating:** 72.2/69.3. **Slope:** 125/114. **Architect:** Joel Goldstrand. **Green fee:** $16/$18. **Credit cards:** All major. **Reduced fees:** Seniors, juniors. **Caddies:** No. **Golf carts:** $20. **Discount golf packages:** No. **Season:** May-Oct. **High:** June-Aug. **On site lodging:** No. **Rental clubs:** Yes. **Walking policy:** Unrestricted walking. **Metal spikes allowed:** Yes. **Range:** Yes (grass). **To obtain tee times:** Call golf shop 1 day in advance.
Subscriber comments: A real links course, challenging, good value and treatment...Young course. Beautiful layout...Not one tree...Tough to play in the wind and it is windy a lot around here...Fun, fun, fun.

★★★MESABA COUNTRY CLUB
415 E. 51st St., Hibbing, 55746, St. Louis County, (218)263-4826, 70 miles NW of Duluth.
Opened: 1923. **Holes:** 18. **Par:** 72/74. **Yards:** 6,792/5,747. **Course rating:** 71.7/73.0. **Slope:** 131/129. **Architect:** Charles Erickson. **Green fee:** $24/$30. **Credit cards:** None. **Reduced fees:** Weekdays. **Caddies:** No. **Golf carts:** $18. **Discount golf packages:** No. **Season:** April-Oct. **High:** June-Aug. **On site lodging:** No. **Rental clubs:** Yes. **Walking policy:** Unrestricted walking. **Metal spikes allowed:** Yes. **Range:** Yes (grass/mats). **To obtain tee times:** Call golf shop.
Subscriber comments: Good shape, reasonable value, excellent hospitality...Pro is always willing to help and my game needs it...Fast greens, good layout...Postcard hole is No. 2, one of the toughest par 4s in state.

★★½MILLE LACS GOLF RESORT
R-18517 Captive Lake Rd., Garrison, 56450, Mille Lacs County, (612)692-4325, (800)435-8720, 95 miles N of Minneapolis.
Opened: 1964. **Holes:** 18. **Par:** 71/72. **Yards:** 6,290/5,106. **Course rating:** 69.7/68.7. **Slope:** 119/113. **Architect:** Fred Murphy. **Green fee:** $20/$29. **Credit cards:** MC,VISA,DISC. **Reduced fees:** Weekdays, low season, resort guests, twilight, juniors. **Caddies:** No. **Golf carts:** $24. **Discount golf packages:** Yes. **Season:** April-Oct. **High:** June-Aug. **On site lodging:** Yes. **Rental clubs:** Yes. **Walking policy:** Unrestricted walking. **Metal spikes allowed:** Yes. **Range:** Yes (grass). **To obtain tee times:** Call golf shop.
Subscriber comments: Working to be better...Good course, challenges you...Player friendly... Great greens...Friendly employees, very crowded...Fun course...We even got a free meal...Not a difficult course.

★★★MINNEWASKA GOLF CLUB
PU-Golf Course Rd., Glenwood, 56334, Pope County, (320)634-3680, 120 miles NW of Minneapolis.
Opened: 1923. **Holes:** 18. **Par:** 72/73. **Yards:** 6,457/5,398. **Course rating:** 70.7/71.7. **Slope:** 122/123. **Architect:** Joel Goldstrand. **Green fee:** $15/$20. **Credit cards:** MC,VISA. **Reduced fees:** Weekdays, low season, resort guests, juniors. **Caddies:** No. **Golf carts:** $20. **Discount golf packages:** Yes. **Season:** April-Oct. **High:** June-Sept. **On site lodging:** No. **Rental clubs:** Yes. **Walking policy:** Unrestricted walking. **Metal spikes allowed:** Yes. **Range:** Yes (grass/mats). **To obtain tee times:** Call golf shop.

MINNESOTA

Subscriber comments: Not busy, great views, has some interesting holes...Nice pro staff...Not bad for a country course, very playable...Not memorable...Great views and great course...New holes make fun course.

★★★MISSISSIPPI DUNES GOLF LINKS
10351 Grey Cloud Trail, Cottage Grove, 55016, Washington County, (612)768-7611, 15 miles SE of Minneapolis/St. Paul.
Opened: 1995. **Holes:** 18. **Par:** 72/72. **Yards:** 6,715/4,988. **Course rating:** 74.0/71.0. **Slope:** 135/121. **Architect:** N/A. **Green fee:** $26/$32. **Credit cards:** All major. **Reduced fees:** Weekdays, low season, twilight, seniors, juniors. **Caddies:** No. **Golf carts:** $13. **Discount golf packages:** No. **Season:** April-Nov. **High:** May-Sept. **On site lodging:** No. **Rental clubs:** Yes. **Walking policy:** Unrestricted walking. **Metal spikes allowed:** Yes. **Range:** Yes (grass). **To obtain tee times:** N/A.
Subscriber comments: Links style. Will be outstanding as it matures...Young new course, a future great!...Small clubhouse...Great challenge, only links-style around...You either love or hate it. Challenging greens.

★★★½MISSISSIPPI NATIONAL GOLF LINKS
PU-409 Golf Links Dr., Red Wing, 55066, Goodhue County, (612)388-1874, 50 miles SE of Minneapolis.
Opened: 1987. **Holes:** 27. **Architect:** Gordon Cunningham. **Green fee:** $23/$25. **Credit cards:** MC,VISA,DISC. **Reduced fees:** Weekdays. **Caddies:** No. **Golf carts:** $25. **Discount golf packages:** No. **Season:** April-Oct. **High:** July-Aug. **On site lodging:** No. **Rental clubs:** Yes. **Walking policy:** Unrestricted walking. **Metal spikes allowed:** Yes. **Range:** Yes (grass/mats). **To obtain tee times:** Call up to 7 days in advance.
LOWLANDS/HIGHLANDS
Par: 70/70. **Yards:** 6,035/5,028. **Course rating:** 70.0/70.1. **Slope:** 125/125.
LOWLANDS/MIDLANDS
Par: 71/72. **Yards:** 6,488/5,465. **Course rating:** 71.5/71.9. **Slope:** 128/126.
MIDLANDS/HIGHLANDS
Par: 71/72. **Yards:** 6,215/5,085. **Course rating:** 71.1/70.8. **Slope:** 130/127.
Subscriber comments: All very enjoyable. Interesting mix of holes. Walked 27 holes...Fun layout, especially Highlands...Real challenge, cart a must, hills...Tough combination of courses.

★★★MONTICELLO COUNTRY CLUB
PU-1201 Golf Course Rd., Monticello, 55362, Wright County, (612)295-4653, 30 miles NW of Minneapolis.
Opened: 1969. **Holes:** 18. **Par:** 71/72. **Yards:** 6,390/5,298. **Course rating:** 70.4/70.8. **Slope:** 118/119. **Architect:** Tim Murphy/Joel Goldstrand. **Green fee:** $16/$22. **Credit cards:** MC,VISA. **Reduced fees:** Weekdays, low season, seniors. **Caddies:** No. **Golf carts:** $22. **Discount golf packages:** No. **Season:** April-Oct. **High:** June-Aug. **On site lodging:** No. **Rental clubs:** Yes. **Walking policy:** Unrestricted walking. **Metal spikes allowed:** Yes. **Range:** Yes (grass). **To obtain tee times:** Call five days in advance.
Subscriber comments: Undiscovered jewel in North Metro area...Fun course, nice greens...Well kept, wide variety, easy to score...Fun golf course to play. Not too heavily played...Maturity and continued improvements increase course playability.

★★★MOUNT FRONTENAC GOLF COURSE
PU-Hwy. 61, Frontenac, 55026, Goodhue County, (612)388-5826, 9 miles SE of Red Wing.
Opened: 1985. **Holes:** 18. **Par:** 70/70. **Yards:** 6,050/4,832. **Course rating:** 69.2/67.7. **Slope:** 119/117. **Architect:** Gordon Emerson. **Green fee:** $14/$17. **Credit cards:** MC,VISA. **Reduced fees:** Weekdays, twilight, seniors. **Caddies:** No. **Golf carts:** $18. **Discount golf packages:** Yes. **Season:** April-Oct. **High:** June-Aug. **On site lodging:** No. **Rental clubs:** Yes. **Walking policy:** Unrestricted walking. **Metal spikes allowed:** Yes. **Range:** No. **To obtain tee times:** Call ten days in advance.
Subscriber comments: For Minnesota, some spectacular mountain views...Bald Eagle flew overhead...Fun to play, some tough holes...Overlooking Mississippi River. Friendly...Nice track, not very busy, beautiful scenery...Well kept secret, don't tell...A real joy to play...Nice people, nice course.

MINNESOTA

★★★NEW PRAGUE GOLF CLUB
PU-400 Lexington Ave.S., New Prague, 56071, Le Sueur County, (612)758-3126, 40 miles SW of Minneapolis.
Opened: 1929. **Holes:** 18. **Par:** 72/72. **Yards:** 6,335/5,032. **Course rating:** 69.5/68.3. **Slope:** 121/116. **Architect:** Don Herfort/Bob Pomije. **Green fee:** $23/$26. **Credit cards:** MC,VISA. **Reduced fees:** Weekdays, low season, seniors, juniors. **Caddies:** No. **Golf carts:** $26. **Discount golf packages:** No. **Season:** April-Oct. **High:** May-Aug. **On site lodging:** No. **Rental clubs:** No. **Walking policy:** Unrestricted walking. **Metal spikes allowed:** No. **Range:** Yes (grass/mats). **To obtain tee times:** Call four days in advance.
Subscriber comments: Good greens and service...Good solid golf...Fine condition, good layout and good greens...Great 19th hole...Well maintained course.

★★½NORTH LINKS GOLF COURSE
PU-Nicollet County Rd. 66, North Mankato, 56003, Nicollet County, (507)947-3355, 80 miles SW of Minneapolis.
Opened: 1993. **Holes:** 18. **Par:** 72/72. **Yards:** 6,073/4,659. **Course rating:** 69.5/66.9. **Slope:** 117/114. **Architect:** Pat Wyss. **Green fee:** $18/$20. **Credit cards:** MC,VISA. **Reduced fees:** Twilight, seniors, juniors. **Caddies:** No. **Golf carts:** $18. **Discount golf packages:** No. **Season:** April-Nov. **High:** June-Aug. **On site lodging:** No. **Rental clubs:** Yes. **Walking policy:** Unrestricted walking. **Metal spikes allowed:** Yes. **Range:** Yes (grass/mats). **To obtain tee times:** Call up to 7 days in advance.
Subscriber comments: Some very challenging terrain, scenic...Good greens...Very short...Squeezed into small area.

★★★NORTHERN HILLS GOLF COURSE
PU-4805 41st Ave. N.W., Rochester, 59901, Olmstead County, (507)281-6170, 65 miles S of Minneapolis.
Opened: 1976. **Holes:** 18. **Par:** 72/72. **Yards:** 6,315/5,456. **Course rating:** 70.4/71.6. **Slope:** 123/123. **Architect:** Clayton Westrum. **Green fee:** $18/$18. **Credit cards:** MC,VISA. **Reduced fees:** N/A. **Caddies:** No. **Golf carts:** $18. **Discount golf packages:** No. **Season:** April-Oct. **High:** May-Sept. **On site lodging:** No. **Rental clubs:** Yes. **Walking policy:** Unrestricted walking. **Metal spikes allowed:** Yes. **Range:** Yes (grass). **To obtain tee times:** Call two days in advance.
Subscriber comments: Fairly short course, nice fairways...Good course for the average golfer...If you can't score here, get more lessons...Nice municipal course. Lots of trouble, busy...Good greens...Could play it every day, in fact I do.

★★★NORTHFIELD GOLF CLUB
707 Prairie St., Northfield, 55057, Dakota County, (507)645-4026.
Opened: 1926. **Holes:** 18. **Par:** 69/71. **Yards:** 5,856/5,103. **Course rating:** 68.7/70.4. **Slope:** 128/126. **Architect:** Don Herfort. **Green fee:** $25/$35. **Credit cards:** MC,VISA. **Reduced fees:** N/A. **Caddies:** Yes. **Golf carts:** $20. **Discount golf packages:** No. **Season:** April-Oct. **High:** April-Sept. **On site lodging:** No. **Rental clubs:** Yes. **Walking policy:** Unrestricted walking. **Metal spikes allowed:** Yes. **Range:** No. **To obtain tee times:** Call or come in two days in advance.
Subscriber comments: Nice clubhouse with friendly people...Pretty setting...Excellent condition; short but fun...Sporting course...Great greens, narrow fairways...Seven short par 3s...Good prices and service...Unique challenging course, tricky greens.

★★★OAK GLEN GOLF CLUB
PU-1599 McKusick Rd., Stillwater, 55082, Washington County, (612)439-6963,.
Opened: 1982. **Holes:** 18. **Par:** 72/72. **Yards:** 6,550/5,626. **Course rating:** 72.4/73.4. **Slope:** 131/130. **Architect:** Don Herfort. **Green fee:** $21/$26. **Credit cards:** MC,VISA. **Reduced fees:** Twilight. **Caddies:** No. **Golf carts:** $10. **Discount golf packages:** No. **Season:** April-Nov. **High:** June-Aug. **On site lodging:** No. **Rental clubs:** Yes. **Walking policy:** Unrestricted walking. **Metal spikes allowed:** Yes. **Range:** Yes (grass). **To obtain tee times:** Call two days in advance.
Subscriber comments: Nicely groomed, condos/townhouses amuck!...Challenging little-known gem...Too many houses...Nice shape...Nice greens; good test of golf...Staff is excellent...Wide open, some good holes.
Special Notes: Also has 9-hole short course.

★★OAK SUMMIT GOLF COURSE
PU-2751 County Rd. 16 S.W., Rochester, 55902, Olmstead County, (507)252-1808.
Opened: 1992. **Holes:** 18. **Par:** 72/72. **Yards:** 6,364/5,535. **Course rating:** 69.4/70.4.
Slope: 113/115. **Architect:** Leon DeCook. **Green fee:** $13/$18. **Credit cards:**
MC,VISA. **Reduced fees:** Weekdays, seniors. **Caddies:** No. **Golf carts:** $16. **Discount golf packages:** No. **Season:** April-Nov. **High:** June-Aug. **On site lodging:** No. **Rental clubs:** Yes. **Walking policy:** Unrestricted walking. **Metal spikes allowed:** Yes. **Range:** No. **To obtain tee times:** Call up to three days in advance.

★★OAKS COUNTRY CLUB
Country Club Rd., Hayfield, 55940, Dodge County, (507)477-3233, 20 miles W of Rochester.
Opened: 1977. **Holes:** 18. **Par:** 72/72. **Yards:** 6,404/5,663. **Course rating:** 69.7/71.7.
Slope: 114/118. **Architect:** John Queenland. **Green fee:** $16/$17. **Credit cards:**
MC,VISA. **Reduced fees:** Low season. **Caddies:** No. **Golf carts:** $9. **Discount golf packages:** Yes. **Season:** April-Oct. **High:** June-Aug. **On site lodging:** No. **Rental clubs:** Yes. **Walking policy:** Unrestricted walking. **Metal spikes allowed:** No. **Range:** Yes (grass). **To obtain tee times:** Nonmembers contact pro shop five days in advance.
Subscriber comments: Normally in pretty good shape...Friendly staff...Challenge when windy, greens are tricky...Golf and steak dinner Wednesdays.

★★ONEKA RIDGE GOLF COURSE
PU-5610 120th St. N., White Bear Lake, 55110, Ramsey County, (612)429-2390, 15 miles N of St. Paul.
Opened: 1996. **Holes:** 18. **Par:** 72/72. **Yards:** 6,351/5,166. **Course rating:** 70.4/68.8.
Slope: 118/115. **Architect:** N/A. **Green fee:** $21/$24. **Credit cards:** N/A. **Reduced fees:** N/A. **Caddies:** No. **Golf carts:** $22. **Discount golf packages:** No. **Season:** March-Oct. **High:** June-July. **On site lodging:** No. **Rental clubs:** No. **Walking policy:** Unrestricted walking. **Metal spikes allowed:** Yes. **Range:** No. **To obtain tee times:** Call Monday for next week; Friday for next weekend.
Subscriber comments: New course, sporty and interesting...A challenge for the player who likes wind...Great service and facilities, very good value for a new course...Some blind shots...Good layout...New course, needs time...Great condition for new course.

★★★½ORTONVILLE MUNICIPAL GOLF COURSE
PM-R.R. 1, Ortonville, 56278, Big Stone County, (320)839-3606,
150 miles W of Minneapolis.
Opened: N/A. **Holes:** 18. **Par:** 72/72. **Yards:** 6,001/5,419. **Course rating:** 68.1/70.6. **Slope:** 111/115. **Architect:** Joel Goldstrand. **Green fee:** $15/$18. **Credit cards:** None. **Reduced fees:** Weekdays. **Caddies:** No. **Golf carts:** $18. **Discount golf packages:** No. **Season:** April-Oct. **High:** July-Aug. **On site lodging:** No. **Rental clubs:** Yes. **Walking policy:** Unrestricted walking. **Metal spikes allowed:** Yes. **Range:** Yes (grass). **To obtain tee times:** Call golf shop.
Subscriber comments: Great golf, good price, great food...A real gem of a rural course...Open course with wide fairways...Back nine is great...Huge greens.

★★★½PEBBLE CREEK COUNTRY CLUB
PU-14000 Club House Lane, Becker, 55308, Sherburne County, (612)261-4653, 17 miles NW of St. Cloud.
Opened: 1987. **Holes:** 27. **Par:** 72/72. **Yards:** 6,820/5,633. **Course rating:** 73.2/72.9.
Slope: 129/127. **Architect:** Don Herfort/Garrett Gill. **Green fee:** $24/$28. **Credit cards:**
MC,VISA. **Reduced fees:** Low season, twilight, seniors, juniors. **Caddies:** Yes. **Golf carts:** $12. **Discount golf packages:** No. **Season:** April-Nov. **High:** June-Sept. **On site lodging:** No. **Rental clubs:** Yes. **Walking policy:** Unrestricted walking. **Metal spikes allowed:** Yes. **Range:** Yes (grass). **To obtain tee times:** Call 3 days in advance.
Subscriber comments: One of the best public courses I've played...Best buy for an excellent quality course...From the blues, a great challenge...Worth the drive, nice layout, fair course.

★★★PEBBLE LAKE GOLF CLUB

PU-County 82 S., Fergus Falls, 56537, Otter Tail County, (218)736-7404, 175 miles NW of Minneapolis.
Opened: 1941. **Holes:** 18. **Par:** 72/74. **Yards:** 6,711/5,531. **Course rating:** 72.3/72.1.
Slope: 128/126. **Architect:** Paul Coates. **Green fee:** $22/$25. **Credit cards:** MC,VISA.
Reduced fees: Low season, twilight, juniors. **Caddies:** No. **Golf carts:** $19. **Discount golf packages:** No. **Season:** April-Oct. **High:** June-Aug. **On site lodging:** No. **Rental clubs:** Yes. **Walking policy:** Unrestricted walking. **Metal spikes allowed:** Yes. **Range:** Yes (grass). **To obtain tee times:** Call up to one week in advance.
Subscriber comments: Long, requires you to strike ball well...New holes are awesome...Change in elevation...Not too much trouble, fun course...Challenging greens, but fair...Very nice.

★★★½PERHAM LAKESIDE COUNTRY CLUB

PU-P.O. Box 313, Perham, 56573, Otter Tail County, (218)346-6070, 20 miles SE of Detroit Lakes.
Opened: 1938. **Holes:** 18. **Par:** 72/72. **Yards:** 6,575/5,312. **Course rating:** 72.5/71.1.
Slope: 128/122. **Architect:** Joel Goldstrand. **Green fee:** $23/$25. **Credit cards:** MC,VISA. **Reduced fees:** Weekdays, low season, twilight. **Caddies:** No. **Golf carts:** $20. **Discount golf packages:** No. **Season:** April-Nov. **High:** June-Aug. **On site lodging:** No. **Rental clubs:** Yes. **Walking policy:** Unrestricted walking. **Metal spikes allowed:** Yes. **Range:** Yes (grass/mats). **To obtain tee times:** Call up to one week in advance.
Subscriber comments: Interesting layout...Constantly busy...Very tough and beautiful...Unique layout...Good golf course, relaxing atmosphere.

★★★PEZHEKEE GOLF CLUB

R-2500 S. Lakeshore Dr., Glenwood, 56334, Pope County, (320)634-4501, (800)356-8654, 120 miles NW of Minneapolis/St. Paul.
Opened: 1967. **Holes:** 18. **Par:** 72/75. **Yards:** 6,454/5,465. **Course rating:** 70.8/71.5.
Slope: 119/122. **Architect:** Tim Murphy/Bill Peters. **Green fee:** $23/$28. **Credit cards:** MC,VISA. **Reduced fees:** Weekdays, low season, resort guests, twilight, juniors.
Caddies: No. **Golf carts:** $23. **Discount golf packages:** Yes. **Season:** May-Oct. **High:** June-Sept. **On site lodging:** Yes. **Rental clubs:** Yes. **Walking policy:** Unrestricted walking. **Metal spikes allowed:** Yes. **Range:** No. **To obtain tee times:** Call in advance or walk on.
Subscriber comments: Hard to walk, but has nice views...Great value...Beautiful scenery in fall overlooking Lake Minnewaska...Another outstanding public course...Flat lies rare.. Everyone should play it once.

PARK GOLF COURSE

PU-1615 Phalen Dr., St. Paul, 55106, Ramsey County, (612)778-0413.
Opened: 1920. **Holes:** 18. **Par:** 70/71. **Yards:** 6,101/5,439. **Course rating:** 68.7/70.7.
Slope: 121/121. **Architect:** Don Herfort. **Green fee:** $21/$21. **Credit cards:** MC,VISA.
Reduced fees: Twilight, seniors, juniors. **Caddies:** No. **Golf carts:** $22. **Discount golf packages:** No. **Season:** March-Nov. **High:** June-Aug. **On site lodging:** No. **Rental clubs:** Yes. **Walking policy:** Unrestricted walking. **Metal spikes allowed:** Yes. **Range:** Yes (grass). **To obtain tee times:** Call 1 day in advance for weekdays; Thursday at 6 a.m. for weekends.
Subscriber comments: Good public course...Very good shorter course...Heavily played...Well groomed and challenging...A good buy for average golfer...City course...Tight layout...Good for public course.

★★★½PHEASANT RUN GOLF CLUB

PU-10705 County Rd. 116, Rogers, 55374, Hennepin County, (612)428-8244, 20 miles NW of Minneapolis.
Opened: 1988. **Holes:** 18. **Par:** 71/72. **Yards:** 6,400/5,200. **Course rating:** 69.9/68.7.
Slope: 117/115. **Architect:** Lyle Johansen. **Green fee:** $14/$20. **Credit cards:** MC,VISA. **Reduced fees:** Weekdays, low season, twilight, seniors, juniors. **Caddies:** No. **Golf carts:** $20. **Discount golf packages:** No. **Season:** April-Nov. **High:** June-Sept. **On site lodging:** No. **Rental clubs:** Yes. **Walking policy:** Unrestricted walking. **Metal spikes allowed:** Yes. **Range:** Yes (grass/mats). **To obtain tee times:** Call

Tuesday for weekend times; Saturday for weekdays.
Subscriber comments: Nice after work course for a quick nine holes...Fun, not much trouble and can play in four hours...Even the ranger is friendly.

★★½PINE MEADOWS GOLF COURSE

PU-500 Golf Course Dr., Brainerd, 56401, Crow Wing County, (218)829-5733, (800)368-2048, 120 miles NW of Minneapolis/St. Paul.
Opened: N/A. **Holes:** 18. **Par:** 72/74. **Yards:** 6,200/5,538. **Course rating:** 70.7/72.7.
Slope: 129/133. **Architect:** N/A. **Green fee:** $23/$26. **Credit cards:** All major.
Reduced fees: Weekdays, low season, resort guests, twilight, seniors, juniors.
Caddies: No. **Golf carts:** $11. **Discount golf packages:** Yes. **Season:** April-Oct. **High:** June-Aug. **On site lodging:** No. **Rental clubs:** Yes. **Walking policy:** Unrestricted walking. **Metal spikes allowed:** Yes. **Range:** Yes (grass). **To obtain tee times:** Call golf shop up to four days in advance.
Subscriber comments: Nice local club...Fully stocked pro shop, good prices...Attempts to play with the big boys...Reasonably priced in resort area...Nice public course. Challenging...Good public course, plays tough.

★★★★THE PINES AT GRAND VIEW LODGE

R-S. 134 Nokomis, Nisswa, 56468, Crow Wing County, (218)963-0001, (800)432-3788, 120 miles NW of Minneapolis.
Opened: 1990. **Holes:** 27. **Architect:** Joel Goldstrand. **Green fee:** $39/$63. **Credit cards:** All major. **Reduced fees:** Weekdays, low season, resort guests, twilight. **Caddies:** No. **Golf carts:** $16. **Discount golf packages:** Yes. **Season:** April-Oct. **High:** June-Sept. **On site lodging:** Yes. **Rental clubs:** Yes. **Walking policy:** Unrestricted walking. **Range:** Yes (grass). **To obtain tee times:** Call golf shop.

GOOD SERVICE

LAKES/MARSH
Par: 72/72. **Yards:** 6,837/5,112. **Course rating:** 73.7/70.0. **Slope:** 134/128. **Metal spikes allowed:** No.
LAKES/WOODS
Par: 72/72. **Yards:** 6,874/5,134. **Course rating:** 74.2/70.6. **Slope:** 137/128. **Metal spikes allowed:** Yes.
WOODS/MARSH
Par: 72/72. **Yards:** 6,883/5,210. **Course rating:** 73.3/70.6. **Slope:** 132/125. **Metal spikes allowed:** No.
Subscriber comments: Great staff...Possibly the best resort golf in Minnesota...Breathtaking...Great clubhouse, narrow fairways, great greens...I saw two bald eagles fly over me...Carved through the trees, a great test of golf.

★★★½POKEGAMA GOLF CLUB

PU-3910 Golf Course Rd., Grand Rapids, 55744, Itasca County, (218)326-3444.
Opened: 1926. **Holes:** 18. **Par:** 71/72. **Yards:** 6,481/5,046. **Course rating:** 70.3/67.7.
Slope: 121/116. **Architect:** Donald Brauer. **Green fee:** $21/$26. **Credit cards:** MC,VISA. **Reduced fees:** Weekdays, resort guests, twilight, juniors. **Caddies:** No. **Golf carts:** $22. **Discount golf packages:** No. **Season:** April-Oct. **High:** June-Aug. **On site lodging:** No. **Rental clubs:** Yes. **Walking policy:** Unrestricted walking. **Metal spikes allowed:** Yes. **Range:** Yes (grass). **To obtain tee times:** Call one week in advance.
Subscriber comments: Old traditional course. Friendly staff...Wonderful. A hidden gem...Nice older course...One of Minnesota's finest layouts...Fun course, scenic...Good layout...Recent design changes have improved this gem in northern Minnesota.

★★½PRAIRIE VIEW GOLF COURSE

PU-Hwy. 266 N., Worthington, 56187, Nobles County, (507)372-8670, 50 miles E of Sioux Falls, SD.
Opened: 1983. **Holes:** 18. **Par:** 71/71. **Yards:** 6,366/5,103. **Course rating:** 69.9/68.3.
Slope: 112/113. **Architect:** Joel Goldstrand. **Green fee:** $17/$20. **Credit cards:** MC,VISA. **Reduced fees:** Weekdays, twilight. **Caddies:** No. **Golf carts:** $9. **Discount golf packages:** No. **Season:** April-Oct. **High:** June-Aug. **On site lodging:** No. **Rental clubs:** Yes. **Walking policy:** Unrestricted walking. **Metal spikes allowed:** No. **Range:** Yes (grass). **To obtain tee times:** Call Thursday for weekend times.
Subscriber comments: Good layout for a links-style course...Good public course. The wind really comes into play...Nos. 11 and 14 are difficult par 4s.

★★★★THE PRESERVE GOLF CLUB AT GRAND VIEW LODGE

R-C.R. 107, Pequot Lakes, 56472, Crow Wing County, (218)568-4944, 20 miles N of Brainerd.
Opened: 1996. **Holes:** 18. **Par:** 72/72. **Yards:** 6,601/4,816. **Course rating:** 71.6/68.8. **Slope:** 135/119. **Architect:** Dan Helbling and Mike Morley. **Green fee:** $43/$49. **Credit cards:** MC,VISA,AMEX. **Reduced fees:** Weekdays, resort guests, twilight. **Caddies:** No. **Golf carts:** $32.
Discount golf packages: Yes. **Season:** April-Oct. **High:** June-Sept. **On site lodging:** No. **Rental clubs:** Yes. **Walking policy:** Unrestricted walking. **Metal spikes allowed:** No. **Range:** Yes (grass). **To obtain tee times:** Call golf shop.
Subscriber comments: Great new course, fun to play, a real challenge...Great scenery, good golf holes...Going to be one of the best courses in the Midwest.

★★★PRESTWICK GOLF CLUB AT WEDGEWOOD

9555 Wedgewood Dr., Woodbury, 55125, Washington County, (612)731-4779, 10 miles E of St. Paul.
Opened: 1985. **Holes:** 18. **Par:** 72/72. **Yards:** 6,717/5,267. **Course rating:** 72.5/71.0. **Slope:** 127/121. **Architect:** Norb Anderson. **Green fee:** $30/$35. **Credit cards:** All major. **Reduced fees:** Weekdays, twilight, juniors. **Caddies:** No. **Golf carts:** $13.
Discount golf packages: No. **Season:** March-Nov. **High:** April-Sept. **On site lodging:** No. **Rental clubs:** Yes. **Walking policy:** Unrestricted walking. **Metal spikes allowed:** No. **Range:** Yes (grass). **To obtain tee times:** Credit card guarantee required with 24 hour cancellation policy.
Subscriber comments: Too many houses, would be great if left natural...Well conditioned like a country club...Nice layout. Great shape. Fun course to play...Keeps improving...Course has matured...Plays tough from blues...Sneaky difficult.

★★½PRINCETON GOLF CLUB

Golf Club Rd., Princeton, 55371, Mille Lacs County, (612)389-5109, (800)542-7601, 45 miles N of Minneapolis/St. Paul.
Opened: 1951. **Holes:** 18. **Par:** 71/71. **Yards:** 6,271/4,849. **Course rating:** 70.8/68.9. **Slope:** 126/115. **Architect:** Joe Goldstrand. **Green fee:** $19/$22. **Credit cards:** All major. **Reduced fees:** Weekdays, low season, twilight, seniors, juniors. **Caddies:** No. **Golf carts:** $22. **Discount golf packages:** Yes. **Season:** April-Oct. **High:** June-Aug. **On site lodging:** No. **Rental clubs:** Yes. **Walking policy:** Unrestricted walking. **Metal spikes allowed:** No. **Range:** Yes (grass). **To obtain tee times:** Call five days in advance.
Subscriber comments: Long walk between some holes...Challenging and scenic back nine...Great value, nice course...Long, well maintained, picturesque riverside setting.

★★★½PURPLE HAWK COUNTRY CLUB

N. Hwy. 65, Cambridge, 55008, Isanti County, (612)689-3800, 60 miles N of Minneapolis.
Opened: 1970. **Holes:** 18. **Par:** 72/74. **Yards:** 6,679/5,748. **Course rating:** 72.3/73.5. **Slope:** 132/131. **Architect:** Don Herfort. **Green fee:** $19/$26. **Credit cards:** MC,VISA,DISC. **Reduced fees:** Twilight, seniors, juniors. **Caddies:** No. **Golf carts:** $22. **Discount golf packages:** No. **Season:** April-Oct. **High:** June-Aug. **On site lodging:** No. **Rental clubs:** Yes. **Walking policy:** Unrestricted walking. **Metal spikes allowed:** Yes. **Range:** Yes (grass). **To obtain tee times:** Call up to 5 days in advance.
Subscriber comments: Best value in Central Minnesota...Excellent course front and back, keeps improving each year...Worth the drive from the Twin Cities...Great greens, good layout.

★½RAMSEY GOLF CLUB

PU-R.R. No.1, Box 83, Austin, 55912, Mower County, (507)433-9098, 95 miles S of Minneapolis/St. Paul.
Opened: 1940. **Holes:** 18. **Par:** 71/72. **Yards:** 5,987/5,426. **Course rating:** 67.6/70.1. **Slope:** 118/118. **Architect:** Jim Vacura. **Green fee:** $17/$17. **Credit cards:** None. **Reduced fees:** Low season. **Caddies:** No. **Golf carts:** $18. **Discount golf packages:** Yes. **Season:** April-Nov. **High:** May-Sept. **On site lodging:** No. **Rental clubs:** Yes. **Walking policy:** Unrestricted walking. **Metal spikes allowed:** Yes. **Range:** Yes (grass). **To obtain tee times:** First come, first served. Cart reservations are available.

★★RICH ACRES GOLF COURSE
PU-2201 E. 66th St., Richfield, 55423, Hennepin County, (612)861-9341, 10 miles SW of Minneapolis.
Opened: 1980. **Holes:** 18. **Par:** 71/73. **Yards:** 6,606/5,746. **Course rating:** 69.8/72.3. **Slope:** 115/121. **Architect:** Jerry Perkl. **Green fee:** $15/$22. **Credit cards:** MC,VISA,DISC. **Reduced fees:** Weekdays, low season, twilight, seniors, juniors. **Caddies:** No. **Golf carts:** $21. **Discount golf packages:** No. **Season:** April-Nov. **High:** April-Nov. **On site lodging:** No. **Rental clubs:** Yes. **Walking policy:** Unrestricted walking. **Metal spikes allowed:** Yes. **Range:** Yes (grass). **To obtain tee times:** Call (612)861-9345.

★★½RICH SPRING GOLF COURSE
17467 Fairway Circle, Cold Spring, 56320, Stearns County, (320)685-8810, 20 miles SW of St. Cloud.
Opened: 1962. **Holes:** 18. **Par:** 72/72. **Yards:** 6,542/5,347. **Course rating:** 69.7/70.0. **Slope:** 119/110. **Architect:** N/A. **Green fee:** $18/$21. **Credit cards:** MC,VISA,DISC. **Reduced fees:** Seniors. **Caddies:** No. **Golf carts:** $10. **Discount golf packages:** No. **Season:** April-Oct. **High:** May-Sept. **On site lodging:** No. **Rental clubs:** Yes. **Walking policy:** Unrestricted walking. **Metal spikes allowed:** Yes. **Range:** Yes (grass). **To obtain tee times:** Call up to three days in advance.
Subscriber comments: Outstanding course; very accommodating people...Never that crowded, very friendly staff...Interesting combination of terrain, rock, trees and water...Flat and rolling, country setting, small greens.

RICH VALLEY GOLF CLUB
PU-3855 145th St. E., Rosemount, 55068, Dakota County, (612)437-4653, 4 miles E of Rosemount.
Opened: 1988. **Holes:** 27. **Architect:** Ray Rahn. **Green fee:** $12/$17. **Credit cards:** N/A. **Reduced fees:** Seniors, juniors. **Caddies:** No. **Golf carts:** $17. **Discount golf packages:** No. **Season:** April-Oct. **High:** N/A. **On site lodging:** No. **Rental clubs:** Yes. **Walking policy:** Unrestricted walking. **Metal spikes allowed:** Yes. **Range:** Yes (grass). **To obtain tee times:** N/A.
RED/BLUE
Par: 69/70. **Yards:** 5,286/4,539. **Course rating:** 64.1/64.4. **Slope:** 100/101.
RED/WHITE
Par: 67/69. **Yards:** 5,289/4,680. **Course rating:** 63.7/65.1. **Slope:** 95/99.
WHITE/BLUE
Par: 68/69. **Yards:** 5,079/4,397. **Course rating:** 63.0/63.7. **Slope:** 98/98.

★★★½RIDGEWOOD GOLF COURSE
PU-County Rd. 7, Longville, 56655, Cass County, (218)363-2444.
Call club for further information.
Subscriber comments: Two different layouts...Front more mature than back nine...Excellent condition.

★★★RIVER OAKS MUNICIPAL GOLF CLUB
PM-11099 S. Highway 61, Cottage Grove, 55016, Washington County, (612)438-2121, 15 miles S of St. Paul.
Opened: 1991. **Holes:** 18. **Par:** 71/71. **Yards:** 6,433/5,224. **Course rating:** 71.4/74.9. **Slope:** 131/137. **Architect:** N/A. **Green fee:** $20/$23. **Credit cards:** MC,VISA. **Reduced fees:** Seniors, juniors. **Caddies:** No. **Golf carts:** $21. **Discount golf packages:** No. **Season:** April-Nov. **High:** May-Sept. **On site lodging:** No. **Rental clubs:** Yes. **Walking policy:** Unrestricted walking. **Metal spikes allowed:** Yes. **Range:** Yes (grass). **To obtain tee times:** Call Monday for weekends, Sunday for weekdays.
Subscriber comments: Views of Mississippi River, friendly staff...Long, fun to play...Nifty layout, nice practice range...Good challenge...Opens early in season, great views across valley...Excellent yardage markers, tough greens, very reasonable, beautiful course...Excellent staff.

★★½ROSE LAKE GOLF COURSE
PU-R.R. No.2, Fairmont, 56031, Martin County, (507)235-5274, 3 miles E of Fairmont.
Opened: 1957. **Holes:** 18. **Par:** 71/71. **Yards:** 6,196/5,276. **Course rating:** 69.6/70.3.

Slope: 121/120. **Architect:** Joel Goldstrand. **Green fee:** $18/$18. **Credit cards:** MC,VISA. **Reduced fees:** N/A. **Caddies:** No. **Golf carts:** $18. **Discount golf packages:** No. **Season:** April-Nov. **High:** June-Aug. **On site lodging:** No. **Rental clubs:** Yes. **Walking policy:** Unrestricted walking. **Metal spikes allowed:** No. **Range:** Yes (grass). **To obtain tee times:** Call up to 7 days in advance.
Subscriber comments: Tough course, back nine excellent...Water on 14 holes. Little sand, small greens...Good course designed around lake. Small pro shop.

★★½RUM RIVER HILLS GOLF CLUB
PU-16659 St. Francis Blvd., Anoka, 55303, Anoka County, (612)753-3339, 15 miles N of Minneapolis.
Opened: 1986. **Holes:** 18. **Par:** 71/71. **Yards:** 6,338/5,095. **Course rating:** 70.0/69.6.
Slope: 117/120. **Architect:** Joel Goldstrand. **Green fee:** $18/$25. **Credit cards:** MC,VISA,Diners Club. **Reduced fees:** Twilight, seniors, juniors. **Caddies:** No. **Golf carts:** $22. **Discount golf packages:** Yes. **Season:** March-Nov. **High:** June-Aug. **On site lodging:** No. **Rental clubs:** Yes. **Walking policy:** Unrestricted walking. **Metal spikes allowed:** Yes. **Range:** Yes (grass). **To obtain tee times:** Call three days in advance.
Subscriber comments: A little "sloppy" when it rains but they have improved drainage...Most of front quite flat, some water, some gimmick holes...Bring lots of balls...Not too difficult but lets you use all your clubs.
Special Notes: Spikeless encouraged.

★★★½RUSH CREEK GOLF CLUB
PU-7801 C.R. 101, Maple Grove, 55311, Hennepin County, (612)494-8844, 20 miles NW of Minneapolis.
Opened: 1996. **Holes:** 18. **Par:** 72/72. **Yards:** 6,874/5,317. **Course rating:** 72.5/70.7.
Slope: 133/123. **Architect:** Bob Cupp and John Fought. **Green fee:** $70/$70. **Credit cards:** MC,VISA,AMEX,Diners Club. **Reduced fees:** Twilight, juniors. **Caddies:** Yes. **Golf carts:** $10. **Discount golf packages:** No. **Season:** April-Oct. **High:** June-Aug. **On site lodging:** No. **Rental clubs:** Yes. **Walking policy:** Unrestricted walking. **Metal spikes allowed:** Yes. **Range:** Yes (grass/mats). **To obtain tee times:** Call up to 14 days in advance.
Notes: 1997 Edina Realty LPGA Classic; 1997 AJGA Event.
Subscriber comments: Nice clubhouse, great service, very nice course...You'll use an iron on several tees...Great practice range...Beautiful, tough from the tips.

★★★RUTTGER'S BAY LAKE LODGE
R-Rte. 2, Deerwood, 56401, Crow Wing County, (218)678-2885, (800)450-4545, 15 miles NE of Brainerd.
Opened: 1992. **Holes:** 18. **Par:** 72/72. **Yards:** 6,750/510. **Course rating:** 72.5/69.3.
Slope: 132/125. **Architect:** Joel Goldstrand. **Green fee:** $24/$40. **Credit cards:** All major. **Reduced fees:** Low season, resort guests, twilight. **Caddies:** Yes. **Golf carts:** $14. **Discount golf packages:** Yes. **Season:** April-Oct. **High:** May-Sept. **On site lodging:** Yes. **Rental clubs:** Yes. **Walking policy:** Unrestricted walking. **Metal spikes allowed:** Yes. **Range:** Yes (grass). **To obtain tee times:** Call 800 number anytime.
Subscriber comments: Some of best holes in Minnesota...A great resort course...Turf quality improving...A very tough course, best to keep the driver in the bag...Front nine spectacular...Challenging course...Blind tee shots.

★★ST. CHARLES GOLF CLUB
1920 Park Rd., St. Charles, 55972, Winona County, (507)932-5444, 20 miles E of Rochester.
Opened: 1991. **Holes:** 18. **Par:** 71/71. **Yards:** 6,347/5,877. **Course rating:** 69.3/72.6.
Slope: 111/116. **Architect:** Wayne Idso. **Green fee:** $18/$18. **Credit cards:** MC,VISA. **Reduced fees:** N/A. **Caddies:** No. **Golf carts:** $18. **Discount golf packages:** No. **Season:** March-Nov. **High:** July-Aug. **On site lodging:** No. **Rental clubs:** Yes. **Walking policy:** Unrestricted walking. **Metal spikes allowed:** Yes. **Range:** Yes (grass). **To obtain tee times:** Tee times taken seven days in advance.

SARTELL GOLF CLUB
801 Pinecone Rd. Box 363, Sartell, 56377, Stearns County, (320)259-0551.
Opened: N/A. **Holes:** 18. **Par:** 72/72. **Yards:** 6,303/5,321. **Course rating:** 68.3/69.9.

Slope: 113/115. **Architect:** N/A. **Green fee:** $15/$17. **Credit cards:** N/A. **Reduced fees:** Seniors, juniors. **Caddies:** No. **Golf carts:** $17. **Discount golf packages:** No. **Season:** March-Nov. **High:** May-July. **On site lodging:** No. **Rental clubs:** Yes. **Walking policy:** Unrestricted walking. **Metal spikes allowed:** No. **Range:** Yes (grass/mats). **To obtain tee times:** Call golf shop.

★★½SAWMILL GOLF CLUB

11177 McKusick Rd., Grant, 55082, Washington County, (612)439-7862, 15 miles NE of St. Paul.

Opened: 1983. **Holes:** 18. **Par:** 70/71. **Yards:** 6,300/5,300. **Course rating:** 70.2/69.5. **Slope:** 125/122. **Architect:** Dan Pohl/John McCarthy/Pat Rooney. **Green fee:** $22/$28. **Credit cards:** MC,VISA,AMEX. **Reduced fees:** Twilight, seniors, juniors. **Caddies:** No. **Golf carts:** $24. **Discount golf packages:** No. **Season:** April-Nov. **High:** May-Sept. **On site lodging:** No. **Rental clubs:** Yes. **Walking policy:** Unrestricted walking. **Metal spikes allowed:** No. **Range:** Yes (grass). **To obtain tee times:** Call three days in advance.

Subscriber comments: Course has improved 200%, especially greens...Unique, an adventure to play. A walk in the wild...Nice scenery...Beautiful layout...Fun course for beginners...Improving, picturesque course...Some good holes.

★★SHAMROCK GOLF COURSE

PU-19625 Larkin Rd., Corcoran, 55340, Hennepin County, (612)478-9977, 15 miles NW of Minneapolis.

Opened: 1974. **Holes:** 18. **Par:** N/A. **Yards:** N/A. **Course rating:** N/A. **Slope:** N/A. **Architect:** N/A. **Green fee:** $13/$21. **Credit cards:** N/A. **Reduced fees:** N/A. **Caddies:** No. **Golf carts:** $22. **Discount golf packages:** No. **Season:** April-Oct. **High:** June-Aug. **On site lodging:** No. **Rental clubs:** No. **Walking policy:** Unrestricted walking. **Metal spikes allowed:** Yes. **Range:** No. **To obtain tee times:** Call Tuesday morning at 7 a.m.

★★SHORELAND GOLF & TENNIS CLUB

Lake Emily/County 21, St. Peter, 56082, Nicollet County, (507)931-3470. Call club for further information.

SILVER SPRINGS GOLF COURSE

PU-P.O. Box 246, Monticello, 55362, Wright County, (612)295-2951, 30 miles W of Minneapolis.

Architect: Al Joyner. **Green fee:** $19/$23. **Credit cards:** MC,VISA,AMEX. **Reduced fees:** Weekdays, twilight, seniors, juniors. **Caddies:** No. **Golf carts:** $24. **Discount golf packages:** No. **Season:** March-Oct. **High:** May-Sept. **On site lodging:** No. **Rental clubs:** Yes. **Walking policy:** Unrestricted walking. **Metal spikes allowed:** Yes. **Range:** Yes (grass). **To obtain tee times:** Call up to 7 days in advance.

★★½GOLD COURSE

Opened: 1984. **Holes:** 18. **Par:** 72/72. **Yards:** 6,750/5,959. **Course rating:** 69.8/72.6. **Slope:** 115/121.

Subscriber comments: Large, flat, sticky greens...Narrow fairways, water, best bang for buck in Minnesota...Challenging tee shots.

★★SILVER COURSE

Opened: 1974. **Holes:** 18. **Par:** 72/72. **Yards:** 6,956/6,176. **Course rating:** 70.5/73.9. **Slope:** 115/126.

★★★SOUTHERN HILLS GOLF CLUB

PU-18950 Chippendale Ave., Farmington, 55024, Dakota County, (612)463-4653, 20 miles S of Minneapolis.

Opened: 1989. **Holes:** 18. **Par:** 71/71. **Yards:** 6,314/4,970. **Course rating:** 70.4/68.3. **Slope:** 123/116. **Architect:** Joel Goldstrand. **Green fee:** $16/$20. **Credit cards:** MC,VISA. **Reduced fees:** Weekdays, low season, twilight, seniors, juniors. **Caddies:** No. **Golf carts:** $19. **Discount golf packages:** No. **Season:** April-Oct. **High:** June-Aug. **On site lodging:** No. **Rental clubs:** Yes. **Walking policy:** Unrestricted walking. **Metal spikes allowed:** Yes. **Range:** Yes (grass). **To obtain tee times:** Public may call one week in advance.

Subscriber comments: Fun course...Good greens...Course condition improving...Links-style course has real charm...Great people!...Revamped links-style course, challenging...A little maturity will make this a great course.

★★★½STONEBROOKE GOLF CLUB
2693 County Rd. 79, Shakopee, 55379, Scott County, (612)496-3171, (800)263-3189, 20 miles SW of Minneapolis.
Opened: 1989. **Holes:** 18. **Par:** 71/71. **Yards:** 6,604/5,033. **Course rating:** 71.7/69.3. **Slope:** 133/118. **Architect:** T.L. Haugen. **Green fee:** $29/$39. **Credit cards:** MC,VISA. **Reduced fees:** Twilight. **Caddies:** No. **Golf carts:** $24. **Discount golf packages:** No. **Season:** April-Oct. **High:** June-July. **On site lodging:** No. **Rental clubs:** Yes. **Walking policy:** Unrestricted walking. **Metal spikes allowed:** Yes. **Range:** Yes (grass/mats). **To obtain tee times:** Call three days in advance.
Subscriber comments: Scenic course with flowers, trees, creeks and wetlands. Shotmaker's course tests skills with different types of lies...Large greens...You board a ferry on #8 to cross lake between tee and landing area...Might not be for everyone, especially really high handicappers...A few oddball holes.
Special Notes: Also has a 9-hole par-30 executive course.

★★½SUGARBROOKE GOLF CLUB
R-Ruttger's Sugar Lake Lodge P.O. Box 847, Grand Rapids, 55744, Itasca County, (218)327-1853, 80 miles W of Duluth.
Opened: 1994. **Holes:** 18. **Par:** 71. **Yards:** 6,545. **Course rating:** N/A. **Slope:** N/A. **Architect:** Joel Goldstrand. **Green fee:** N/A. **Credit cards:** N/A. **Reduced fees:** N/A. **Caddies:** No. **Golf carts:** N/A. **Discount golf packages:** No. **Season:** April-Nov. **High:** N/A. **On site lodging:** Yes. **Rental clubs:** No. **Walking policy:** Unrestricted walking. **Metal spikes allowed:** Yes. **Range:** Yes (grass). **To obtain tee times:** N/A.
Subscriber comments: Will mature into a very good course...Unique back nine not good for walking...Nice layout...Part of Sugar Lake Lodge, it's worth a visit...Tight and hazardous but not difficult.

★★SUNDANCE GOLF CLUB
PU-15240 113th Ave. N., Maple Grove, 55369, Hennepin County, (612)420-4700, 15 miles NW of Minneapolis.
Opened: 1970. **Holes:** 18. **Par:** 72/72. **Yards:** 6,446/5,548. **Course rating:** 70.7/71.6. **Slope:** 127/126. **Architect:** N/A. **Green fee:** $12/$24. **Credit cards:** All major. **Reduced fees:** Weekdays, seniors, juniors. **Caddies:** No. **Golf carts:** N/A. **Discount golf packages:** No. **Season:** April-Nov. **High:** May-July. **On site lodging:** No. **Rental clubs:** Yes. **Walking policy:** Unrestricted walking. **Metal spikes allowed:** Yes. **Range:** Yes (grass). **To obtain tee times:** Call up to 7 days in advance for weekdays, Tuesday for weekends.

★★★★SUPERIOR NATIONAL GOLF COURSE
PU-P.O. Box 177, Lutsen, 55612, Cook County, (218)663-7195, 90 miles NE of Duluth.
Opened: 1992. **Holes:** 18. **Par:** 72/72. **Yards:** 6,323/5,174. **Course rating:** 70.9/70.4. **Slope:** 130/123. **Architect:** Don Herfort. **Green fee:** $31/$39. **Credit cards:** MC,VISA. **Reduced fees:** Weekdays, low season, resort guests, twilight, juniors. **Caddies:** No. **Golf carts:** $28. **Discount golf packages:** Yes. **Season:** May-Oct. **High:** June-Sept. **On site lodging:** No. **Rental clubs:** Yes. **Walking policy:** Unrestricted walking. **Metal spikes allowed:** No. **Range:** Yes (grass). **To obtain tee times:** Call golf shop. Must guarantee with credit card.
Subscriber comments: Great facility, putts roll towards Lake Superior...Great golf experience..No.17 a fantastic par 3 with 100-foot drop...Outstanding scenery...Saw a bear!...Excellent course...A true beauty...A couple of breathtaking holes.

★★THEODORE WIRTH GOLF COURSE
PU-1300 Theodore Wirth Pkwy., Golden Valley, 55422, Hennepin County, (612)522-4584, 3 miles W of Minneapolis.
Opened: 1916. **Holes:** 18. **Par:** 72/72. **Yards:** 6,585/5,552. **Course rating:** 72.7/72.6. **Slope:** 132/124. **Architect:** Garrett Gill. **Green fee:** $16/$20. **Credit cards:** MC,VISA. **Reduced fees:** Weekdays, low season, twilight, seniors, juniors. **Caddies:** No. **Golf carts:** $22. **Discount golf packages:** No. **Season:** April-Nov. **High:** June-Aug. **On site lodging:** No. **Rental clubs:** Yes. **Walking policy:** Unrestricted walking. **Metal spikes allowed:** Yes. **Range:** No. **To obtain tee times:** Call 4 days in advance.

★★★ TIANNA COUNTRY CLUB
P.O. Box 177, Walker, 56484, Cass County, (218)547-1712, 60 miles N of Brainerd.
Opened: 1925. **Holes:** 18. **Par:** 72/74. **Yards:** 6,550/5,681. **Course rating:** 70.7/73.5.
Slope: 127/127. **Architect:** Ernie Tardiff. **Green fee:** $20/$25. **Credit cards:** All major.
Reduced fees: Twilight. **Caddies:** No. **Golf carts:** $25. **Discount golf packages:** No.
Season: May-Oct. **High:** June-Aug. **On site lodging:** No. **Rental clubs:** Yes. **Walking policy:** Unrestricted walking. **Metal spikes allowed:** Yes. **Range:** Yes (grass). **To obtain tee times:** Call golf shop.
Subscriber comments: Look for deer and black bear...Nice layout but too many severe sidehills...Friendly staff...The elevations from tee to green are incredible...Great northern course...Gold tees super...Hilly, pretty, good greens...Too many blind shots...Northwoods gem, everyone always has a great time, get fishing tips from staff.
Special Notes: Spikeless encouraged.

★★ TIMBER CREEK GOLF COURSE
9750 County Rd. #24, Watertown, 55388, Carver County, (612)955-3490, 20 miles W of Minneapolis.
Opened: 1986. **Holes:** 18. **Par:** 72/72. **Yards:** 6,500/5,100. **Course rating:** 71.7/72.0.
Slope: 130/127. **Architect:** N/A. **Green fee:** $18/$24. **Credit cards:** MC,VISA.
Reduced fees: N/A. **Caddies:** No. **Golf carts:** $20. **Discount golf packages:** No.
Season: April-Oct. **High:** May-Sept. **On site lodging:** No. **Rental clubs:** Yes. **Walking policy:** Unrestricted walking. **Metal spikes allowed:** No. **Range:** Yes (grass). **To obtain tee times:** N/A.

TIPSINAH MOUNDS GOLF COURSE
County Rd. #24 / Township Rd. 52, Elbow Lake, 56531, Grant County, (218)685-4271, (800)660-8642, 75 miles SE of Fargo, N.D.
Opened: 1982. **Holes:** 9. **Par:** 34/34. **Yards:** 2,957/2,297. **Course rating:** 33.9/32.9.
Slope: 108/105. **Architect:** Joel Goldstrand. **Green fee:** $17/$17. **Credit cards:** MC,VISA. **Reduced fees:** Weekdays, juniors. **Caddies:** No. **Golf carts:** $17. **Discount golf packages:** Yes. **Season:** April-Oct. **High:** June-Aug. **On site lodging:** No. **Rental clubs:** Yes. **Walking policy:** Unrestricted walking. **Metal spikes allowed:** Yes. **Range:** Yes (grass). **To obtain tee times:** Call golf shop.
Special Notes: Spikeless encouraged.

★★★ VALLEY GOLF ASSOCIATION
1800 21st St. N.W., East Grand Forks, 56721, Polk County, (218)773-1207, 5 miles NE of Grand Forks, ND.
Opened: 1971. **Holes:** 18. **Par:** 72/72. **Yards:** 6,210/5,261. **Course rating:** 69.6/69.2.
Slope: 118/112. **Architect:** N/A. **Green fee:** $12/$12. **Credit cards:** MC,VISA.
Reduced fees: Twilight, seniors, juniors. **Caddies:** No. **Golf carts:** $16. **Discount golf packages:** No. **Season:** April-Oct. **High:** May-Aug. **On site lodging:** No. **Rental clubs:** Yes. **Walking policy:** Unrestricted walking. **Metal spikes allowed:** Yes. **Range:** No. **To obtain tee times:** First come, first served. Tee times for members only.
Subscriber comments: Difficult greens, heavily wooded...Several difficult par 5s...Nice course...Don't miss these greens.

★★ VALLEY HIGH COUNTRY CLUB
PU-Rte 2, Box 234, Houston, 55943, Houston County, (507)896-3239, 15 miles E of La Crosse, WI.
Opened: 1970. **Holes:** 18. **Par:** 71/75. **Yards:** 6,168/5,319. **Course rating:** 68.3/70.6.
Slope: 111/116. **Architect:** N/A. **Green fee:** $17/$17. **Credit cards:** N/A. **Reduced fees:** N/A. **Caddies:** No. **Golf carts:** $17. **Discount golf packages:** No. **Season:** April-Oct. **High:** N/A. **On site lodging:** No. **Rental clubs:** Yes. **Walking policy:** Unrestricted walking. **Metal spikes allowed:** Yes. **Range:** Yes (grass). **To obtain tee times:** Call golf shop.

★★½ VALLEY VIEW GOLF CLUB
PU-23795 Laredo Ave., Belle Plane, 56011, Scott County, (612)873-4653, 30 miles SW of Minneapolis.
Opened: 1992. **Holes:** 18. **Par:** 70/71. **Yards:** 6,309/4,921. **Course rating:** 70.1/68.4.
Slope: 121/113. **Architect:** S & H Golf, Inc. **Green fee:** $22/$25. **Credit cards:**

MC,VISA. **Reduced fees:** Weekdays, low season, twilight, seniors, juniors. **Caddies:** No. **Golf carts:** $22. **Discount golf packages:** Yes. **Season:** April-Oct. **High:** June-Aug. **On site lodging:** No. **Rental clubs:** Yes. **Walking policy:** Unrestricted walking. **Metal spikes allowed:** Yes. **Range:** Yes (grass/mats). **To obtain tee times:** Call up to 3 days in advance with credit card guarantee.
Subscriber comments: Nice course, open and windy...Hilly...Beautiful bent-grass fairways, excellent golf for the price...Some water comes into play...Another nice, new Minnesota course...Good variety, fast greens.

★★★VALLEYWOOD GOLF COURSE
PM-4851 West 125th St., Apple Valley, 55124, Dakota County, (612)953-2323, 10 miles S of Minneapolis.
Opened: 1973. **Holes:** 18. **Par:** 71/72. **Yards:** 6,421/5,144. **Course rating:** 70.6/71.5. **Slope:** 123/122. **Architect:** N/A. **Green fee:** $22/$27. **Credit cards:** MC,VISA,DISC. **Reduced fees:** Seniors, juniors. **Caddies:** No. **Golf carts:** $24. **Discount golf packages:** No. **Season:** May-Oct. **High:** July. **On site lodging:** No. **Rental clubs:** Yes. **Walking policy:** Unrestricted walking. **Metal spikes allowed:** Yes. **Range:** Yes (grass/mats). **To obtain tee times:** Call up to 5 days in advance.
Subscriber comments: Best golf for the money for 20 miles...Nice layout with woods and hills...Use all clubs, challenging...Very good greens. Too expensive for conditions...Doglegs.

★½VIKING MEADOWS GOLF COURSE
PU-1788 Viking Blvd., Cedar, 55011, Anoka County, (612)434-4205, 20 miles N of Minneapolis.
Opened: 1989. **Holes:** 18. **Par:** 72/73. **Yards:** 6,364/5,534. **Course rating:** 70.6/71.4. **Slope:** 124/121. **Architect:** N/A. **Green fee:** $16/$21. **Credit cards:** MC,VISA. **Reduced fees:** Weekdays, seniors, juniors. **Caddies:** No. **Golf carts:** $21. **Discount golf packages:** No. **Season:** April-Nov. **High:** July-Aug. **On site lodging:** No. **Rental clubs:** Yes. **Walking policy:** Unrestricted walking. **Metal spikes allowed:** Yes. **Range:** Yes (grass). **To obtain tee times:** Call up to 7 days in advance for weekdays; Tuesday for weekends.

★★★VIRGINIA GOLF COURSE
PU-9th. St. N., Virginia, 55792, St. Louis County, (218)741-4366, 59 miles N of Duluth.
Opened: 1930. **Holes:** 18. **Par:** 71/74. **Yards:** 6,181/5,460. **Course rating:** 69.5/70.9. **Slope:** 118/129. **Architect:** Hugh Vincent Feehan. **Green fee:** $21/$21. **Credit cards:** MC,VISA. **Reduced fees:** Twilight. **Caddies:** No. **Golf carts:** $21. **Discount golf packages:** No. **Season:** May-Oct. **High:** July-Aug. **On site lodging:** No. **Rental clubs:** Yes. **Walking policy:** Unrestricted walking. **Metal spikes allowed:** Yes. **Range:** No. **To obtain tee times:** Call up to 2 days in advance.
Subscriber comments: Good shape, excellent hospitality...Recent improvements make it fun...A nice layout and a great setting. A hidden gem in northern Minnesota...Recently redone...Wide open course. Easy to score well.

★★★WAPICADA GOLF CLUB
SR 23 4498 15th St. NE, Sauk Rapids, 56379, Stearns County, (320)251-7804, 4 miles E of St. Cloud.
Opened: 1957. **Holes:** 18. **Par:** 72/73. **Yards:** 6,269/5,497. **Course rating:** 70.1/71.6. **Slope:** 124/126. **Architect:** N/A. **Green fee:** $21/$21. **Credit cards:** MC,VISA. **Reduced fees:** Twilight. **Caddies:** No. **Golf carts:** $21. **Discount golf packages:** No. **Season:** N/A. **High:** N/A. **On site lodging:** No. **Rental clubs:** No. **Walking policy:** Unrestricted walking. **Metal spikes allowed:** Yes. **Range:** Yes (grass). **To obtain tee times:** Call up to 2 days in advance.
Subscriber comments: Back nine most challenging...Cream of the crop...Variety of easy to hard holes...Good shape, easy play, inexpensive...Good public golf course and value...Nice course...Not overly long, can be wet.

WARROAD ESTATES GOLF COURSE
PU-201 Birch Dr. N., Warroad, 56763, Roseau County, (218)386-2025, 126 miles E of Grand Forks, ND.
Opened: 1976. **Holes:** 9. **Par:** 72/73. **Yards:** 6,942/5,455. **Course rating:** 74.3/72.0. **Slope:** 128/121. **Architect:** N/A. **Green fee:** $13/$17. **Credit cards:** MC,VISA.

Reduced fees: Weekdays, twilight, seniors, juniors. Caddies: No. Golf carts: $18.
Discount golf packages: No. Season: April-Oct. High: June-Aug. On site lodging:
No. Rental clubs: Yes. Walking policy: Unrestricted walking. Metal spikes allowed:
Yes. Range: No. To obtain tee times: Call golf shop.

★★★½ WENDIGO GOLF COURSE
PU-750 Golf Crest Dr., Grand Rapids, 55744, Itasca County, (218)327-2211, 180 miles
N of Minneapolis.
Opened: 1995. Holes: 18. Par: 72/72. Yards: 6,756/5,151. Course rating: 72.0/70.0.
Slope: 132/127. Architect: Joel Goldstrand. Green fee: $20/$22. Credit cards:
MC,VISA. Reduced fees: Twilight. Caddies: No. Golf carts: $22. Discount golf packages: Yes. Season: April-Oct. High: June-Aug. On site lodging: No. Rental clubs:
Yes. Walking policy: Unrestricted walking. Metal spikes allowed: Yes. Range: Yes
(grass/mats). To obtain tee times: Call up to 7 days in advance.
Subscriber comments: My favorite new course. Great variety...Most scenic course in
Minnesota...New course, lots of potential, beautiful building clubhouse...Once the
greens mature, will be a great golf course...Many blind shots.

★★★½ WHITEFISH GOLF CLUB
Rte. 1, Pequot Lakes, 56472, Crow Wing County, (218)543-4900, 36 miles N of
Brainerd.
Opened: 1966. Holes: 18. Par: 72/72. Yards: 6,407/5,682. Course rating: 70.7/72.6.
Slope: 128/124. Architect: Don Herfort. Green fee: $20/$30. Credit cards: MC,VISA.
Reduced fees: Weekdays, low season, resort guests, twilight. Caddies: No. Golf
carts: $22. Discount golf packages: No. Season: April-Oct. High: June-Aug. On site
lodging: No. Rental clubs: Yes. Walking policy: Unrestricted walking. Metal spikes
allowed: Yes. Range: Yes (grass). To obtain tee times: Call golf shop.
Subscriber comments: Outstanding course...Sporty, slow greens...Little gem. Scenic
back nine. Very tight...Vastly underrated. Great back nine...Narrow fairways challenge
you on every shot...Keeps improving...Trees require accurate drives.

★★★★ WILDFLOWER AT FAIR HILLS
PU-CR 20, Detroit Lakes, 56501, Becker County, (218)439-3357, (800)323-2849, 45
miles E of Fargo, ND.
Opened: 1993. Holes: 18. Par: 72/72. Yards: 6,965/5,250. Course rating: 74.2/71.6.
Slope: 139/121. Architect: Joel Goldstrand. Green fee: $12/$30. Credit cards: All
major. Reduced fees: Weekdays, low season, resort guests, twilight, seniors, juniors.
Caddies: No. Golf carts: $26. Discount golf packages: Yes. Season: May-First
Snow. High: June-Aug. On site lodging: Yes. Rental clubs: Yes. Walking policy:
Unrestricted walking. Metal spikes allowed: Yes. Range: Yes (grass). To obtain tee
times: Call one week in advance.
Notes: Maxfli Jr. Regional.
Subscriber comments: Challenging in the wind but fun...Prairie links...The most beautiful course I have ever played, fairways are lined with wildflowers...Catch the flowers
blooming in August.

★★★★½ THE WILDS GOLF CLUB
PU-14819 Wilds Pkwy. N.W., Prior Lake, 55372, Scott County, (612)445-4455, 30 miles
SW of Minneapolis.
Opened: 1995. Holes: 18. Par: 72/72. Yards: 7,025/5,095. Course rating: 74.7/70.2.
Slope: 140/126. Architect: Tom Weiskopf and Jay Morrish. Green fee: $50/$89. Credit
cards: N/A. Reduced fees: Weekdays, resort guests, seniors, juniors. Caddies: Yes.
Golf carts: Included in Green Fee. Discount golf packages: No. Season: April-Oct.
High: June-Aug. On site lodging: No. Rental clubs: Yes. Walking policy: Unrestricted
walking. Metal spikes allowed: Yes. Range: No. To obtain tee times: Foursomes may
call up to 14 days in advance; twosomes and threesomes 5 days in advance.
Notes: Golf Digest School site. Ranked 7th in 1997 Best in State; 4th in 1996 Best
New Upscale Courses.
Subscriber comments: Plush fairways and greens...Good course, not worth the
price...Great service. Lots of tough par 4s. Great shape...Lush fairways, excellent
greens...Playable but challenging...Great practice area, service fantastic, the ground
crew blew leaves off the green between groups.

MINNESOTA

★★★★WILLINGER'S GOLF CLUB
PU-6900 Canby Trail, Northfield, 55057, Dakota County, (612)440-7000, 40 miles S of Minneapolis.
Opened: 1992. **Holes:** 18. **Par:** 72/72. **Yards:** 6,711/5,166. **Course rating:** 73.3/71.6.
Slope: 140/130. **Architect:** George Williams and Garrett Gill. **Green fee:** $29/$34.
Credit cards: MC,VISA. **Reduced fees:** Twilight, seniors, juniors. **Caddies:** No. **Golf carts:** $25. **Discount golf packages:** No. **Season:** April-Oct. **High:** June-Aug. **On site lodging:** No. **Rental clubs:** Yes. **Walking policy:** Unrestricted walking. **Metal spikes allowed:** Yes. **Range:** Yes (grass). **To obtain tee times:** Call four days in advance for weekend times; seven days in advance for weekday times.
Subscriber comments: Favorite in Minnesota; brawny...Great course, hilly, oaks, water, everything...Interesting layout...This gem is worth the drive...A real jewel, marsh front, wooded back.

★★½WILLOW CREEK GOLF CLUB
1700 S.W. 48th St., Rochester, 55902, Olmstead County, (507)285-0305, 65 miles S of Minneapolis.
Opened: 1974. **Holes:** 18. **Par:** 70/70. **Yards:** 6,053/5,293. **Course rating:** 69.1/70.5.
Slope: 117/121. **Architect:** William James Spear. **Green fee:** $16/$16. **Credit cards:** MC,VISA. **Reduced fees:** N/A. **Caddies:** No. **Golf carts:** $9. **Discount golf packages:** No. **Season:** March-Nov. **High:** June-Aug. **On site lodging:** No. **Rental clubs:** Yes. **Walking policy:** Unrestricted walking. **Metal spikes allowed:** Yes. **Range:** Yes (grass). **To obtain tee times:** Call seven days in advance.
Subscriber comments: Easy short course for high handicapper...Hilly...Best greens in SE Minnesota...Nice course...Streams running through.

★★½BAY POINTE RESORT & GOLF CLUB

800 Bay Pointe Dr., Brandon, 39042, Rankin County, (601)829-1862.
Opened: 1987. **Holes:** 18. **Par:** 72/72. **Yards:** 6,600/4,668. **Course rating:** 70.6/66.3.
Slope: 123/108. **Architect:** Marvin Ferguson. **Green fee:** $15/$20. **Credit cards:**
None. **Reduced fees:** Twilight. **Caddies:** No. **Golf carts:** $10. **Discount golf packages:** No. **Season:** Year-round. **High:** March-Oct. **On site lodging:** Yes. **Rental clubs:**
No. **Walking policy:** Walking at certain times. **Metal spikes allowed:** Yes. **Range:** Yes
(grass). **To obtain tee times:** Call for weekends.
Subscriber comments: Course is set up for faders and slicers; hookers put driver
away...Tight course...Course is challenging...Lots of pine trees. Nice scenery.

★★★½BIG OAKS GOLF CLUB

PU-3481 Big Oaks Blvd., Saltillo, 38866, Lee County, (601)844-8002, 2 miles NE of
Tupelo.
Opened: 1996. **Holes:** 18. **Par:** 72/72. **Yards:** 6,784/5,098. **Course rating:** 73.1/69.1.
Slope: 124/114. **Architect:** Tracy May. **Green fee:** $18/$23. **Credit cards:** All major.
Reduced fees: Low season, twilight, juniors. **Caddies:** No. **Golf carts:** $10. **Discount
golf packages:** Yes. **Season:** Year-round. **High:** April-Oct. **On site lodging:** No. **Rental
clubs:** Yes. **Walking policy:** N/A. **Metal spikes allowed:** Yes. **Range:** Yes (grass). **To
obtain tee times:** Call up to 14 days in advance.
Subscriber comments: Rough is long and hard to avoid...Interesting; must play
shots...Great greens...Will be great in another year or so. Pro is more than helpful...Fair
for both high and low handicappers...Use every club in your bag!

★½BLACKJACK BAY GOLF LINKS

15312 Dismuke Dr., Biloxi, 39532, Harrison County, (601)392-0400, 50 miles W of
Mobile, AL..
Opened: 1992. **Holes:** 18. **Par:** 72/72. **Yards:** 6,202/5,577. **Course rating:** 65.0/66.0.
Slope: 113/113. **Architect:** Chuck Gregory. **Green fee:** $22/$22. **Credit cards:**
MC,VISA. **Reduced fees:** N/A. **Caddies:** No. **Golf carts:** $10. **Discount golf packages:** Yes. **Season:** Year-round. **High:** Feb.-April. **On site lodging:** No. **Rental clubs:**
Yes. **Walking policy:** Unrestricted walking. **Metal spikes allowed:** Yes. **Range:** No. **To
obtain tee times:** Call two days in advance.
Special notes: Formerly Southwind Country Club.

★★★THE BRIDGES GOLF RESORT AT CASINO MAGIC

R-711 Casino Magic Dr., Bay St. Louis, 39520, Hancock County,
(800)562-4425, (800)562-4425, 45 miles E of New Orleans, LA.
Opened: 1997. **Holes:** 18. **Par:** 72/72. **Yards:** 6,841/5,108. **Course rating:** 73.5/70.1. **Slope:** 138/126. **Architect:** Arnold Palmer and Ed Seay.
Green fee: $75/$75. **Credit cards:** MC,VISA,AMEX. **Reduced fees:**
N/A. **Caddies:** No. **Golf carts:** Included in Green Fee. **Discount golf packages:** No.
Season: Year-round. **High:** Feb.-April. **On site lodging:** Yes. **Rental clubs:** No.
Walking policy: Mandatory cart. **Metal spikes allowed:** Yes. **Range:** Yes (grass). **To
obtain tee times:** Call.
Subscriber comments: Played second week open, great layout...Will be one heck of a
golf course—real good design...Tough course, challenging to mid/high handicappers.

BROADWATER RESORT

R- **Credit cards:** All major. **Caddies:** No. **Golf carts:** Included in Green Fee. **Discount
golf packages:** Yes. **Season:** Year-round. **High:** Feb.-May. **Rental clubs:** Yes. **Metal
spikes allowed:** Yes. **To obtain tee times:** Call golf shop.
★★½SUN COURSE
200 Beauvoir Rd., Biloxi, 39531, Harrison County, (601)385-4081, (800)647-3964, 3
miles E of Gulfport.
Opened: 1968. **Holes:** 18. **Par:** 72/72. **Yards:** 7,140/5,398. **Course rating:** 74.1/70.4.
Slope: 134/120. **Architect:** Earl Stone. **Green fee:** $44/$44. **Reduced fees:** Resort
guests, twilight. **On site lodging:** Yes. **Walking policy:** Mandatory cart. **Range:** Yes
(grass).
Subscriber comments: Long, water, sand, trees, fast greens...Fun course...Wide open
course...Casino money has refurbished an old run-down course...Nice open course
with a good facilities...Straightforward course...Big greens.

MISSISSIPPI

★★SEA COURSE
2000 Beach Dr., Gulfport, 39532, Harrison County, (601)896-3536, 69 miles E of New Orleans.
Opened: 1908. **Holes:** 18. **Par:** 71/71. **Yards:** 6,200/5,400. **Course rating:** 70.4/70.4. **Slope:** 124/124. **Architect:** N/A. **Green fee:** $25/$44. **Reduced fees:** Twilight, juniors. **On site lodging:** No. **Walking policy:** Walking at certain times. **Range:** No.
Notes: 1940-1945 PGA Tour host; Gulfport Open.
Subscriber comments: Under new ownership. Making changes for the better...Nice course, sand and trees, small greens...Nice vacation course.

★★★CHEROKEE VALLEY GOLF CLUB
PU-6635 Crumpler Rd., Olive Branch, 38654, De Soto County, (601)893-4444, 7 miles S of Memphis, TN.
Opened: 1996. **Holes:** 18. **Par:** 72/72. **Yards:** 6,751/5,358. **Course rating:** 72.0/69.5. **Slope:** 124/112. **Architect:** Don Cottle Jr.. **Green fee:** $32/$46. **Credit cards:** MC,VISA,AMEX. **Reduced fees:** Weekdays, low season, twilight, seniors, juniors. **Caddies:** No. **Golf carts:** Included in Green Fee. **Discount golf packages:** No. **Season:** Year-round. **High:** April-Oct. **On site lodging:** No. **Rental clubs:** Yes. **Walking policy:** Walking at certain times. **Metal spikes allowed:** Yes. **Range:** Yes (grass/mats). **To obtain tee times:** Call up to 5 days in advance at (601)893-4444 or (901)525-4653.
Subscriber comments: Great layout, great bent-grass greens, new course, maturing well...Course needs to mature....A real fun course, well bunkered, good greens.

DIAMONDHEAD COUNTRY CLUB
R-7600 Country Club Circle, Diamondhead, 39525, Hancock County, (601)255-3910, (800)346-8741, 20 miles W of Gulfport.
Reduced fees: Low season, resort guests, juniors. **Green fee:** $28/$45. **Credit cards:** MC,VISA,DISC. **Caddies:** No. **Golf carts:** $15. **Discount golf packages:** Yes. **Season:** Year-round. **High:** Feb.-May. **On site lodging:** Yes. **Rental clubs:** Yes. **Walking policy:** Mandatory cart. **Metal spikes allowed:** Yes. **Range:** Yes (grass/mats). **To obtain tee times:** Advanced tee times only available through golf packages. Call (800)221-2423 or (800)345-7915 for package information. Packages also available through hotels and motels along the coast.

★★★½CARDINAL COURSE
Opened: 1972. **Holes:** 18. **Par:** 72/72. **Yards:** 6,831/5,065. **Course rating:** 72.7/68.9. **Slope:** 132/117. **Architect:** Bill Atkins. .
Subscriber comments: Loved the course...Fun...Tight driving. Good test. Not long...Well kept...Nike Tour course, beautiful area, hard to get tee time...Good course.

★★★PINE COURSE
Opened: 1977. **Holes:** 18. **Par:** 72/72. **Yards:** 6,817/5,313. **Course rating:** 73.6/71.1. **Slope:** 133/118. **Architect:** Earl Stone.
Subscriber comments: Old classic, wide fairways, doglegs...Accuracy, not length is important...Great, great course...Good course, had some bad spots—but enjoyable.

★★½DOGWOOD HILLS GOLF CLUB
17476 Dogwood Hills Dr., Biloxi, 39532, Harrison County, (601)392-9805, 12 miles N of Biloxi.
Opened: 1993. **Holes:** 18. **Par:** 72/72. **Yards:** 6,076/4,687. **Course rating:** 69.0/68.7. **Slope:** 118/115. **Architect:** Brent Williams. **Green fee:** $14/$15. **Credit cards:** MC,VISA. **Reduced fees:** Low season, juniors. **Caddies:** No. **Golf carts:** $10. **Discount golf packages:** Yes. **Season:** Year-round. **High:** Dec.-March. **On site lodging:** No. **Rental clubs:** Yes. **Walking policy:** Walking at certain times. **Metal spikes allowed:** Yes. **Range:** Yes (grass). **To obtain tee times:** Call golf shop.
Subscriber comments: Will be one of the nicer public courses...Hilly for the area. Good layout...Nice tight course...Good course for starters.

★★½EAGLE RIDGE GOLF COURSE
PU-Hwy. 18 S., Raymond, 39154, Hinds County, (601)857-5993, 10 miles SW of Jackson.
Opened: 1955. **Holes:** 18. **Par:** 72/72. **Yards:** 6,500/5,135. **Course rating:** 68.5. **Slope:** 113. **Architect:** Hinds Community College. **Green fee:** $9/$12. **Credit cards:** MC,VISA. **Reduced fees:** Weekdays, seniors. **Caddies:** No. **Golf carts:** $18. **Discount golf packages:** No. **Season:** Year-round. **High:** March-Aug. **On site lodging:** No.

Rental clubs: Yes. **Walking policy:** Unrestricted walking. **Metal spikes allowed:** Yes. **Range:** Yes (grass/mats). **To obtain tee times:** Call Thursday for upcoming weekend. **Subscriber comments:** Good layout, small greens are like hilltops...Best groomed university-type course...Fairly short, no sand, major improvements in recent years.

★★½EDGEWATER BAY GOLF COURSE
2674 Pass Rd., Biloxi, 39531, Harrison County, (601)388-9670, 75 miles E of New Orleans, LA.
Opened: 1927. **Holes:** 18. **Par:** 71/71. **Yards:** 6,200/5,114. **Course rating:** 70.0/69.8. **Slope:** 125/121. **Architect:** N/A. **Green fee:** $15/$25. **Credit cards:** MC,VISA. **Reduced fees:** Weekdays, low season, twilight. **Caddies:** No. **Golf carts:** $12. **Discount golf packages:** Yes. **Season:** Year-round. **High:** Jan.-March. **On site lodging:** Yes. **Rental clubs:** Yes. **Walking policy:** Walking at certain times. **Metal spikes allowed:** Yes. **Range:** No. **To obtain tee times:** Call golf shop.
Subscriber comments: Good course, sand, water, trees, small greens...Close but nice...Good course for all handicaps...Basic golf, greens OK.

★★GRAND OAKS RESORT
R-Corner of Lyles Dr. and Hwy. 7, Oxford, 38655, Lafayette County, (601)236-3008, (800)541-3881, 60 miles S of Memphis, TN.
Opened: 1994. **Holes:** 18. **Par:** 70/70. **Yards:** 6,210/5,490. **Course rating:** 69.7/67.6. **Slope:** 121/117. **Architect:** Greg Clark. **Green fee:** $32/$32. **Credit cards:** All major. **Reduced fees:** Weekdays, low season, twilight, seniors, juniors. **Caddies:** No. **Golf carts:** Included in Green Fee. **Discount golf packages:** Yes. **Season:** Year-round. **High:** March-Oct. **On site lodging:** Yes. **Rental clubs:** Yes. **Walking policy:** Walking at certain times. **Metal spikes allowed:** Yes. **Range:** Yes (grass). **To obtain tee times:** Call up to 30 days in advance.

GREENVILLE MUNICIPAL GOLF COURSE
Airbase Rd., Greenville, 38703, Washington County, (601)332-4079.
Call club for further information.

★★HOLIDAY GOLF CLUB
11300 Goodman Rd., Olive Branch, 38654, De Soto County, (901)525-2402, 2 miles S of Memphis, TN.
Opened: 1975. **Holes:** 18. **Par:** 72/72. **Yards:** 6,498/5,114. **Course rating:** 70.8/68.8. **Slope:** 116/109. **Architect:** Bill Munguia. **Green fee:** $19/$21. **Credit cards:** MC,VISA. **Reduced fees:** Resort guests, seniors, juniors. **Caddies:** No. **Golf carts:** $9. **Discount golf packages:** Yes. **Season:** Year-round. **High:** May-Sept. **On site lodging:** Yes. **Rental clubs:** Yes. **Walking policy:** Walking at certain times. **Metal spikes allowed:** Yes. **Range:** Yes (grass/mats). **To obtain tee times:** Call 5 days in advance.

★★★★KIRKWOOD NATIONAL GOLF CLUB
785 Hwy. 4 West, Holly Springs, 38635, Marshall County, (601)252-4888, (800)461-4653, 40 miles SE of Memphis.
Opened: 1994. **Holes:** 18. **Par:** 72/72. **Yards:** 7,129/4,898. **Course rating:** 73.6/68.2. **Slope:** 135/116. **Architect:** Ed Connor and Harris Gholson. **Green fee:** $25/$42. **Credit cards:** MC,VISA,AMEX. **Reduced fees:** Weekdays, low season, twilight, seniors, juniors. **Caddies:** No. **Golf carts:** Included in Green Fee. **Discount golf packages:** Yes. **Season:** Year-round. **High:** June-Aug. **On site lodging:** Yes. **Rental clubs:** Yes. **Walking policy:** Walking at certain times. **Metal spikes allowed:** Yes. **Range:** Yes (grass/mats). **To obtain tee times:** Call up to 7 days in advance.
Notes: Ranked 4th in 1997 Best in State; 5th in 1995 Best New Public Courses.
Subscriber comments: Best layout in state, combines links and country club...The most beautiful greens that I have ever seen...Terrific, don't miss on trip to Memphis...Very long and difficult. Scenic 18th green...Great variety of holes. Memorable holes.

★★★½MISSISSIPPI NATIONAL GOLF CLUB
PU-900 Hickory Hill Dr., Gautier, 39553, Jackson County, (601)497-2372, (800)477-4044, 15 miles E of Biloxi.
Opened: 1965. **Holes:** 18. **Par:** 72/72. **Yards:** 7,003/5,229. **Course rating:** 73.1/69.6. **Slope:** 128/113. **Architect:** Earl Stone. **Green fee:** $20/$60. **Credit cards:** MC,VISA.

Reduced fees: Weekdays, low season, resort guests. **Caddies:** No. **Golf carts:** $10. **Discount golf packages:** Yes. **Season:** Year-round. **High:** Feb.-April. **On site lodging:** Yes. **Rental clubs:** Yes. **Walking policy:** Walking at certain times. **Metal spikes allowed:** Yes. **Range:** Yes (grass/mats). **To obtain tee times:** Call up to 7 days in advance. ·

Subscriber comments: Friendly staff. Well-kept greens and fairways...Enjoyable layout—water on many holes. Good pro shop and clubhouse...Tour quality—on Nike circuit, plays like it...Quality course, good variety...Wide open, small elevated greens, good challenge.

Special Notes: Formerly known as Hickory Hill C.C.

★★★½MISSISSIPPI STATE UNIVERSITY GOLF COURSE

PU-1520 Old Hwy. 82E., Starkville, 39759, Oktibbeha County, (601)325-3028, 120 miles NE of Jackson.

Opened: 1989. **Holes:** 18. **Par:** 72/72. **Yards:** 6,926/5,443. **Course rating:** 73.5/71.8. **Slope:** 130/121. **Architect:** Brian Ault. **Green fee:** $12/$17. **Credit cards:** All major. **Reduced fees:** Weekdays, juniors. **Caddies:** No. **Golf carts:** $10. **Discount golf packages:** No. **Season:** Year-round. **High:** March-Sept. **On site lodging:** No. **Rental clubs:** Yes. **Walking policy:** Unrestricted walking. **Metal spikes allowed:** Yes. **Range:** Yes (grass/mats). **To obtain tee times:** Call on Wednesday for following week.

Subscriber comments: Very good layout, course in good shape usually...Small hard greens...Best course in the area...Great improvements in last five years.

★★½NATCHEZ TRACE GOLF CLUB

Beech Springs Rd., Saltillo, 38866, Lee County, (601)869-2166, 5 miles N of Tupelo.

Opened: 1964. **Holes:** 18. **Par:** 72/72. **Yards:** 6,669/4,731. **Course rating:** 72.1/62.5. **Slope:** 125/113. **Architect:** John Frazier. **Green fee:** $15/$24. **Credit cards:** MC,VISA. **Reduced fees:** Weekdays, twilight. **Caddies:** No. **Golf carts:** $18. **Discount golf packages:** No. **Season:** Year-round. **High:** April-Sept. **On site lodging:** No. **Rental clubs:** No. **Walking policy:** Unrestricted walking. **Metal spikes allowed:** Yes. **Range:** Yes (grass). **To obtain tee times:** First come, first served on weekdays. Members only on weekends.

★★½OLE MISS GOLF CLUB

PU-U of MS, College Hill Rd. #147 CR 1056, Oxford, 38655, Lafayette County, (601)234-4816, 70 miles S of Memphis, TN.

Opened: 1965. **Holes:** 18. **Par:** 72/72. **Yards:** 6,682/5,276. **Course rating:** 72.8/70.9. **Slope:** 129/120. **Architect:** Sonny Guy. **Green fee:** $12/$14. **Credit cards:** MC,VISA. **Reduced fees:** Seniors, juniors. **Caddies:** No. **Golf carts:** $18. **Discount golf packages:** No. **Season:** Year-round. **High:** May-Aug. **On site lodging:** No. **Rental clubs:** Yes. **Walking policy:** Unrestricted walking. **Metal spikes allowed:** Yes. **Range:** Yes (grass/mats). **To obtain tee times:** Call in advance.

Subscriber comments: Course improving year to year. Greens usually need a little work...Good college course, needs watering in summer.

★★PASS CHRISTIAN ISLES GOLF CLUB

150 Country Club Dr., Pass Christian, 39571, Harrison County, (601)452-3830, 16 miles W of Gulfport.

Opened: 1951. **Holes:** 18. **Par:** 72/72. **Yards:** 6,438/5,428. **Course rating:** 69.7/71.6. **Slope:** 124/120. **Architect:** Tom Bendelow. **Green fee:** $24/$24. **Credit cards:** MC,VISA,AMEX. **Reduced fees:** N/A. **Caddies:** No. **Golf carts:** $12. **Discount golf packages:** Yes. **Season:** Year-round. **High:** Feb.-April. **On site lodging:** No. **Rental clubs:** Yes. **Walking policy:** Walking at certain times. **Metal spikes allowed:** Yes. **Range:** No. **To obtain tee times:** Call in advance.

★★★PINE BURR COUNTRY CLUB

SP-800 Pine Burr Dr, Wiggins, 39577, Stone County, (601)928-4911. Call club for further information.

Subscriber comments: Beautiful lush greens, various challenges, uphills, downhills, tight, open. A definite must-play again...Tight course, sand, water, hilly, good layout...Dogwoods and pines...Nice course with lots of water and wildlife...Love the greens, hate the trees.

★★PINE ISLAND GOLF CLUB

2021 Beachview Dr., Ocean Springs, 39564, Jackson County, (601)875-1674.
Opened: 1973. **Holes:** 18. **Par:** 71/71. **Yards:** 6,369/4,915. **Course rating:** 70.9/67.8.
Slope: 129/109. **Architect:** Pete Dye. **Green fee:** $14/$30. **Credit cards:** .
MC,VISA,AMEX. **Reduced fees:** Weekdays, low season, resort guests, twilight.
Caddies: No. **Golf carts:** $12. **Discount golf packages:** Yes. **Season:** Year-round.
High: Feb.-April. **On site lodging:** No. **Rental clubs:** Yes. **Walking policy:** Walking at
certain times. **Metal spikes allowed:** Yes. **Range:** Yes (grass). **To obtain tee times:**
Call golf shop.

★★★PLANTATION GOLF CLUB

9425 Plantation Rd., Olive Branch, 38654, De Soto County, (601)895-3530.
Opened: 1990. **Holes:** 18. **Par:** 72/72. **Yards:** 6,773/5,055. **Course rating:** 72.0/64.4.
Slope: 122/109. **Architect:** William Heathers. **Green fee:** $32/$42. **Credit cards:**
MC,VISA. **Reduced fees:** Weekdays, low season, twilight, seniors, juniors. **Caddies:**
No. **Golf carts:** Included in Green Fee. **Discount golf packages:** No. **Season:** Year-
round. **High:** April-Oct. **On site lodging:** No. **Rental clubs:** Yes. **Walking policy:**
Walking at certain times. **Metal spikes allowed:** Yes. **Range:** Yes (grass/mats). **To
obtain tee times:** Call 5 days in advance.
Notes: 1997 Bubba Conlee National Junior.
Subscriber comments: Great fairways, fairly challenging, houses are close...Zoysia
fairways, many holes with water...Great finishing hole.

QUAIL HOLLOW GOLF COURSE

1102 Percy Quin Dr., McComb, 39648, Pike County, (601)684-2903.
Opened: 1997. **Holes:** 18. **Par:** 72. **Yards:** 6,754. **Course rating:** 71.9. **Slope:** 118.
Architect: Arthur Hills. **Green fee:** $35/$35. **Credit cards:** N/A. **Reduced fees:** N/A.
Caddies: N/A. **Golf carts:** Included in Green Fee. **Discount golf packages:** N/A.
Season: Year-round. **High:** April-Sept. **On site lodging:** Yes. **Rental clubs:** N/A.
Walking policy: Unrestricted walking. **Metal spikes allowed:** Yes. **Range:** Yes (grass).
To obtain tee times: Call golf shop.
Notes: Ranked 10th in 1997 Best New Affordable Public Courses.

★★ST. ANDREWS GOLF CLUB

2 Golfing Green Dr., Ocean Springs, 39564, Jackson County, (601)875-7730, 40 miles
W of Mobile, AL.
Opened: 1968. **Holes:** 18. **Par:** 72/72. **Yards:** 6,540/4,960. **Course rating:** 69.7/67.8.
Slope: 119/111. **Architect:** N/A. **Green fee:** $17/$30. **Credit cards:** MC,VISA,AMEX.
Reduced fees: Weekdays, low season, resort guests. **Caddies:** No. **Golf carts:** $11.
Discount golf packages: Yes. **Season:** Year-round. **High:** Feb.-March. **On site lodg-
ing:** Yes. **Rental clubs:** Yes. **Walking policy:** Walking at certain times. **Metal spikes
allowed:** Yes. **Range:** Yes (grass). **To obtain tee times:** Call golf shop.

★½SONNY GUY MUNICIPAL GOLF COURSE

PM-3200 Woodrow Wilson Dr., Jackson, 39209, Hinds County, (601)960-1905.
Opened: 1949. **Holes:** 18. **Par:** 72/72. **Yards:** 6,935/5,217. **Course rating:** 71.9/69.0.
Slope: 117/104. **Architect:** Sonny Guy. **Green fee:** $6/$8. **Credit cards:** MC,VISA.
Reduced fees: Weekdays, twilight, seniors, juniors. **Caddies:** No. **Golf carts:** $14.
Discount golf packages: Yes. **Season:** Year-round. **High:** March-July. **On site lodg-
ing:** No. **Rental clubs:** Yes. **Walking policy:** Unrestricted walking. **Metal spikes
allowed:** Yes. **Range:** No. **To obtain tee times:** Call one day in advance.

★★★SUNKIST COUNTRY CLUB

R-2381 Sunkist Country Club Rd., Biloxi, 39532, Harrison County, (601)388-3961, 86
miles E of New Orleans, LA.
Opened: 1954. **Holes:** 18. **Par:** 72/72. **Yards:** 6,000/5,300. **Course rating:** 69.0/71.0.
Slope: 117/121. **Architect:** Roland "Robby" Robertson. **Green fee:** $20/$37. **Credit
cards:** MC,VISA,DISC. **Reduced fees:** Weekdays, low season, resort guests, twilight.
Caddies: No. **Golf carts:** Included in Green Fee. **Discount golf packages:** No.
Season: Year-round. **High:** Feb.-April. **On site lodging:** No. **Rental clubs:** No.
Walking policy: Mandatory cart. **Metal spikes allowed:** Yes. **Range:** Yes (grass/mats).
To obtain tee times: Call anytime in advance.

★★★★TIMBERTON GOLF CLUB
PU-22 Clubhouse Dr., Hattiesburg, 39401, Forest County, (601)584-4653, (800)848-3222, 90 miles N of New Orleans, LA.
Opened: 1991. **Holes:** 27. **Par:** 72/72. **Yards:** 7,028/5,439. **Course rating:** 73.1/71.4. **Slope:** 131/128. **Architect:** Mark McCumber/J.R. Carpenter and Ron Hickman. **Green fee:** $45/$45. **Credit cards:** MC,VISA. **Reduced fees:** Twilight. **Caddies:** No. **Golf carts:** Included in Green Fee. **Discount golf packages:** Yes. **Season:** Year-round. **High:** March-April. **On site lodging:** Yes. **Rental clubs:** Yes. **Walking policy:** Mandatory cart. **Metal spikes allowed:** Yes. **Range:** Yes (grass/mats). **To obtain tee times:** Call up to 60 days in advance with credit card to guarantee.
Notes: Ranked 5th in 1997 Best in State.
Subscriber comments: Great course, very well manicured and challenging, very beautiful...Tops in Mississippi. Excellent condition. Several great holes.

★★TRAMARK GOLF COURSE
PU-P.O. Box 6631, Gulfport, 39506, Harrison County, (601)863-7808, 65 miles E of New Orleans.
Opened: 1967. **Holes:** 18. **Par:** 72/72. **Yards:** 6,350/5,800. **Course rating:** 68.5/69.5. **Slope:** 116/109. **Architect:** Floyd Trehern. **Green fee:** $12/$12. **Credit cards:** MC,VISA. **Reduced fees:** Juniors. **Caddies:** No. **Golf carts:** $16. **Discount golf packages:** Yes. **Season:** Year-round. **High:** Feb.-April. **On site lodging:** No. **Rental clubs:** Yes. **Walking policy:** Unrestricted walking. **Metal spikes allowed:** Yes. **Range:** Yes (grass). **To obtain tee times:** Call anytime.

★★½USM'S VAN HOOK GOLF COURSE
PU-One Golf Course Rd., Hattiesburg, 39402, Forest County, (601)264-1872, 60 miles N of Biloxi.
Opened: 1957. **Holes:** 18. **Par:** 72/73. **Yards:** 6,660/5,226. **Course rating:** 69.0/70.0. **Slope:** N/A. **Architect:** Sonny Guy. **Green fee:** $7/$13. **Credit cards:** MC,VISA,AMEX. **Reduced fees:** Weekdays, low season, twilight, seniors, juniors. **Caddies:** No. **Golf carts:** $20. **Discount golf packages:** Yes. **Season:** Year-round. **High:** May-Dec. **On site lodging:** No. **Rental clubs:** Yes. **Walking policy:** Unrestricted walking. **Metal spikes allowed:** Yes. **Range:** Yes (grass/mats). **To obtain tee times:** Call 1 day in advance.
Subscriber comments: Getting better. Still a practice course...Older layout, well developed...Hilly. Very little sand. Some water...New construction on #18. Good track, lots of play...Good course for the amount of play it gets.

★★½WEDGEWOOD GOLF COURSE
5206 Tournament Dr., Olive Branch, 38654, De Soto County, (601)521-8275.
Opened: 1990. **Holes:** 18. **Par:** 72/72. **Yards:** 6,863/5,627. **Course rating:** 72.8/69.1. **Slope:** 127/118. **Architect:** John Floyd. **Green fee:** $23/$23. **Credit cards:** MC,VISA. **Reduced fees:** Weekdays, low season, resort guests, twilight, seniors, juniors. **Caddies:** No. **Golf carts:** $10. **Discount golf packages:** Yes. **Season:** Year-round. **High:** May-Sept. **On site lodging:** Yes. **Rental clubs:** Yes. **Walking policy:** Walking at certain times. **Metal spikes allowed:** Yes. **Range:** Yes (grass). **To obtain tee times:** Call seven days in advance.
Subscriber comments: Tough, but fair...Very tight, big greens always in good shape...Good course, too many ditches.

★★★½WINDANCE COUNTRY CLUB
19385 Champion Circle, Gulfport, 39505, Harrison County, (601)832-4871.
Opened: 1986. **Holes:** 18. **Par:** 72/72. **Yards:** 6,678/5,179. **Course rating:** 73.1/70.1. **Slope:** 129/120. **Architect:** Mark McCumber. **Green fee:** $55. **Credit cards:** MC,VISA,AMEX. **Reduced fees:** N/A. **Caddies:** Yes. **Golf carts:** $15. **Discount golf packages:** Yes. **Season:** Year-round. **High:** Feb.-April. **On site lodging:** No. **Rental clubs:** Yes. **Walking policy:** Mandatory cart. **Metal spikes allowed:** Yes. **Range:** Yes (grass). **To obtain tee times:** Call with a credit card to guarantee. There is a 24-hour cancellation policy. Packages are available through most hotels in the area.
Notes: 1990-91 Ben Hogan Tour; 1992-95 Nike Tour; Mississippi Gulf Coast Classic.
Subscriber comments: Very difficult but good, challenging course...Excellent test from the tips, very good condition...Excellent course and service...Good golf.

★★BELTON MUNICIPAL GOLF COURSE

PU-4200 Bong Ave., Belton, 64012, Cass County, (816)331-6777, 25 miles S of Kansas City.

Opened: 1965. **Holes:** 18. **Par:** 72/73. **Yards:** 6,855/5,500. **Course rating:** 73.1/71.0. **Slope:** 134/119. **Architect:** Bob Baldock. **Green fee:** $12/$14. **Credit cards:** None. **Reduced fees:** Seniors, juniors. **Caddies:** No. **Golf carts:** $21. **Discount golf packages:** No. **Season:** Year-round. **High:** May-Sept. **On site lodging:** No. **Rental clubs:** Yes. **Walking policy:** Unrestricted walking. **Metal spikes allowed:** Yes. **Range:** Yes (grass/mats). **To obtain tee times:** Call Wednesday prior to weekend.

★★★½BENT CREEK GOLF COURSE

PU-1 Bent Creek Dr., Jackson, 63755, Cape Girardeau County, (573)243-6060, 90 miles S of St. Louis.

Opened: 1990. **Holes:** 18. **Par:** 72/72. **Yards:** 6,958/5,148. **Course rating:** 72.5/69.8. **Slope:** 136/112. **Architect:** Gary Kern. **Green fee:** $16/$25. **Credit cards:** All major. **Reduced fees:** Weekdays, low season, twilight, seniors, juniors. **Caddies:** No. **Golf carts:** $12. **Discount golf packages:** Yes. **Season:** Year-round. **High:** May-Sept. **On site lodging:** No. **Rental clubs:** Yes. **Walking policy:** Walking at certain times. **Metal spikes allowed:** Yes. **Range:** Yes (grass/mats). **To obtain tee times:** Call up to 7 days in advance. **Subscriber comments:** Fast, true greens. Use every club in the bag...Good golf environment...One of my favorites...Tough Par 3s...Best course in area...A fabulous course built to flow with great terrain...Lots of traps...Real bang for your buck.

(GOOD VALUE)

★★★BENT OAK GOLF CLUB

1300 S.E. 30th, Oak Grove, 64075, Jackson County, (816)690-3028, 20 miles E of Kansas City.

Opened: 1980. **Holes:** 18. **Par:** 72/73. **Yards:** 6,855/5,500. **Course rating:** 73.1/71.0. **Slope:** 134/119. **Architect:** Bob Simmons. **Green fee:** $16/$19. **Credit cards:** MC,VISA,DISC. **Reduced fees:** Weekdays, low season, twilight, seniors, juniors. **Caddies:** No. **Golf carts:** $24. **Discount golf packages:** Yes. **Season:** Year-round. **High:** May-Sept. **On site lodging:** No. **Rental clubs:** Yes. **Walking policy:** Unrestricted walking. **Metal spikes allowed:** Yes. **Range:** Yes (grass). **To obtain tee times:** Call up to 7 days in advance.

Notes: 1996 Senior Series.

Subscriber comments: Need length and shots...Fun golf...Has improved over last few years...This is a hidden gem. Long, tough, tight, beautiful...Tough back nine...Needs better drainage but they're trying...Long par 4s...Super place to play.

★★½BILL & PAYNE STEWART GOLF COURSE

PU-1825 E. Norton, Springfield, 65803, Greene County, (417)833-9962.

Opened: 1947. **Holes:** 18. **Par:** 70/72. **Yards:** 6,043/5,693. **Course rating:** 68.4/71.3. **Slope:** 113/117. **Architect:** Perry Maxwell. **Green fee:** $11/$14. **Credit cards:** MC,VISA. **Reduced fees:** Weekdays, seniors, juniors. **Caddies:** No. **Golf carts:** $9. **Discount golf packages:** No. **Season:** Year-round. **High:** March-Oct. **On site lodging:** No. **Rental clubs:** Yes. **Walking policy:** Unrestricted walking. **Metal spikes allowed:** Yes. **Range:** Yes (grass). **To obtain tee times:** Call golf shop. **Subscriber comments:** Wide and open fairways, excellent staff...Few traps, no water...Gets a lot for play...A fun track that can be tough with pin placements. **Special Notes:** Also has 9-hole par-3 Oscar Blom Course.

BOOTHEEL GOLF CLUB

PU-1218 N. Ingram, Sikeston, 63801, Scott County, (573)472-6111, (888)472-6111, 150 miles S of St. Louis.

Opened: 1996. **Holes:** 18. **Par:** 72/72. **Yards:** 6,880/5,825. **Course rating:** 73.0. **Slope:** 123. **Architect:** David Pfaff. **Green fee:** $17/$20. **Credit cards:** MC,VISA,AMEX. **Reduced fees:** Weekdays, low season, seniors. **Caddies:** No. **Golf carts:** $10. **Discount golf packages:** No. **Season:** Year-round. **High:** April-Nov. **On site lodging:** No. **Rental clubs:** Yes. **Walking policy:** Unrestricted walking. **Metal spikes allowed:** Yes. **Range:** Yes (grass/mats). **To obtain tee times:** Call up to 14 days in advance. Out-of-town guests may call up to 30 days in advance.

★★½CARTHAGE MUNICIPAL GOLF COURSE

PM-2000 Oak St., Carthage, 64836, Jasper County, (417)358-8724, 10 miles NE of Joplin.
Opened: 1937. **Holes:** 18. **Par:** 71/73. **Yards:** 6,402/5,469. **Course rating:** 69.4/70.5. **Slope:** 124/115. **Architect:** Tom Bendelow/Don Sechrest. **Green fee:** $9/$11. **Credit cards:** None. **Reduced fees:** Weekdays, twilight, juniors. **Caddies:** No. **Golf carts:** $18. **Discount golf packages:** No. **Season:** Year-round. **High:** April-Aug. **On site lodging:** No. **Rental clubs:** Yes. **Walking policy:** Unrestricted walking. **Metal spikes allowed:** No. **Range:** No. **To obtain tee times:** Call or come in 7 days in advance.
Subscriber comments: Very nice muny course...Lots of trees...Front and back are very different...Challenging but fun.

★★★CASSVILLE GOLF CLUB

Hwy. 112 S., Cassville, 65625, Barry County, (417)847-2399, 55 miles SW of Springfield.
Opened: 1966. **Holes:** 18. **Par:** 72/72. **Yards:** 6,620/5,802. **Course rating:** 71.3/79.9. **Slope:** 118/117. **Architect:** Ken Sisney. **Green fee:** $17/$20. **Credit cards:** None. **Reduced fees:** N/A. **Caddies:** No. **Golf carts:** $10. **Discount golf packages:** No. **Season:** Year-round. **High:** April-Oct. **On site lodging:** No. **Rental clubs:** Yes. **Walking policy:** Unrestricted walking. **Metal spikes allowed:** No. **Range:** Yes (grass/mats). **To obtain tee times:** Call up to 14 days in advance.
Subscriber comments: Good course in the middle of nowhere...Nice small town course...Has some of the finest greens with great character...Wide fairways.

★½CHAPEL WOODS GOLF COURSE

PU-800 Woods Chapel Rd., Lees Summit, 64064, Jackson County, (816)795-8870, 15 miles SE of Kansas City.
Opened: 1959. **Holes:** 18. **Par:** 72/72. **Yards:** 6,326/5,916. **Course rating:** 69.5/72.9. **Slope:** 117/117. **Architect:** Ray Bondurant. **Green fee:** $13/$16. **Credit cards:** None. **Reduced fees:** N/A. **Caddies:** No. **Golf carts:** $22. **Discount golf packages:** No. **Season:** Year-round. **High:** April-Sept. **On site lodging:** No. **Rental clubs:** Yes. **Walking policy:** Unrestricted walking. **Metal spikes allowed:** Yes. **Range:** No. **To obtain tee times:** First come, first served.

★★½CHERRY HILLS GOLF CLUB

PU-16700 Manchester Rd., St. Louis, 63040, St. Louis County, (314)458-4113, 12 miles W of St. Louis.
Opened: 1964. **Holes:** 18. **Par:** 71/72. **Yards:** 6,450/5,491. **Course rating:** 71.1/72.6. **Slope:** 132/120. **Architect:** Art Linkogel/Gary Kern. **Green fee:** $30/$50. **Credit cards:** MC,VISA. **Reduced fees:** Low season, twilight, seniors. **Caddies:** No. **Golf carts:** Included in Green Fee. **Discount golf packages:** No. **Season:** Year-round. **High:** May-Aug. **On site lodging:** No. **Rental clubs:** Yes. **Walking policy:** Unrestricted walking. **Metal spikes allowed:** Yes. **Range:** Yes (grass/mats). **To obtain tee times:** Call up to 7 days in advance. Weekend tee times require a credit card to reserve.
Subscriber comments: Formerly private. Nice layout...Attentive marshalls...Traditional layout...Challenging but a little short...Very few flat lies.

★★½CLAYCREST GOLF CLUB

925 N. Lightburne, Liberty, 64068, Clay County, (816)781-6522, 15 miles NE of Kansas City.
Opened: 1967. **Holes:** 18. **Par:** 72/72. **Yards:** 6,457/5,375. **Course rating:** 69.5/68.2. **Slope:** 115/109. **Architect:** Chet Mendenhall. **Green fee:** $14/$16. **Credit cards:** MC,VISA. **Reduced fees:** Seniors. **Caddies:** No. **Golf carts:** $24. **Discount golf packages:** No. **Season:** Year-round. **High:** April-Nov. **On site lodging:** No. **Rental clubs:** Yes. **Walking policy:** Unrestricted walking. **Metal spikes allowed:** Yes. **Range:** Yes. **To obtain tee times:** Call 7 a.m. Wednesday prior to weekend.
Subscriber comments: Lot of blind shots but fun...Seems like it's all uphill...Tricky greens...Many doglegs.

★★CRACKERNECK GOLF COURSE

PU-18800 E. 40 Hwy., Independence, 64055, Jackson County, (816)795-7771, 13 miles E of Kansas City.

Opened: 1964. **Holes:** 18. **Par:** 72/74. **Yards:** 6,246/5,175. **Course rating:** 69.1/68.8.
Slope: 115/108. **Architect:** Charles Maddox and William Maddox. **Green fee:** $15/$18.
Credit cards: MC,VISA. **Reduced fees:** Weekdays, low season, twilight, seniors.
Caddies: No. **Golf carts:** $22. **Discount golf packages:** No. **Season:** Year-round.
High: June-Aug. **On site lodging:** No. **Rental clubs:** Yes. **Walking policy:** Unrestricted
walking. **Metal spikes allowed:** No. **Range:** Yes (Mats). **To obtain tee times:** Tee
times are not required.

★★★CRYSTAL HIGHLANDS GOLF CLUB

PU-3030 U.S. Highway 61, Crystal City, 63028, Jefferson County, (314)931-3880, 30
miles S of St. Louis.
Opened: 1988. **Holes:** 18. **Par:** 72/72. **Yards:** 6,480/4,946. **Course rating:** 71.6/68.0.
Slope: 135/109. **Architect:** Michael Hurdzan. **Green fee:** $20/$29. **Credit cards:**
MC,VISA,DISC. **Reduced fees:** Weekdays, low season, twilight, seniors, juniors.
Caddies: No. **Golf carts:** $10. **Discount golf packages:** No. **Season:** Year-round.
High: April-Oct. **On site lodging:** No. **Rental clubs:** Yes. **Walking policy:** Walking at
certain times. **Metal spikes allowed:** Yes. **Range:** Yes (grass). **To obtain tee times:**
Call 5 days in advance.
Subscriber comments: Tough undulated greens, slick...Many blind holes...Good lay-
out. Interesting short par 4s...Very good finishing holes 16-17-18...Holes make use of
hilly terrain...Beautiful setting, lots of fun...A good test of golf.

★★DOGWOOD HILLS GOLF CLUB

R-1252 State Hwy. KK, Osage Beach, 65065, Camden County, (573)348-1735, 160
miles SW of St. Louis.
Opened: 1962. **Holes:** 18. **Par:** 70/71. **Yards:** 6,073/4,641. **Course rating:** 68.5/65.2.
Slope: 116/95. **Architect:** Herman Hackbarth. **Green fee:** $37/$45. **Credit cards:** All
major. **Reduced fees:** Weekdays, low season, resort guests, twilight, seniors, juniors.
Caddies: No. **Golf carts:** Included in Green Fee. **Discount golf packages:** Yes.
Season: Year-round. **High:** March-Oct. **On site lodging:** Yes. **Rental clubs:** Yes.
Walking policy: Walking at certain times. **Metal spikes allowed:** Yes. **Range:** Yes
(grass/mats). **To obtain tee times:** Call 14 days in advance.

★★★½EAGLE KNOLL GOLF CLUB

PU-5757 E. Eagle Knoll Dr., Hartsburg, 65039, Boone County, (573)761-4653,
(800)909-0564, 10 miles N of Jefferson City.
Opened: 1996. **Holes:** 18. **Par:** 72/72. **Yards:** 6,920/5,323. **Course rating:** 73.8.
Slope: 141. **Architect:** Gary Kern. **Green fee:** $24/$35. **Credit cards:** MC,VISA,DISC.
Reduced fees: Weekdays, twilight, seniors, juniors. **Caddies:** No. **Golf carts:** Included
in Green Fee. **Discount golf packages:** No. **Season:** Year-round. **High:** April-Sept. **On
site lodging:** No. **Rental clubs:** Yes. **Walking policy:** Unrestricted walking. **Metal
spikes allowed:** Yes. **Range:** Yes (grass/mats). **To obtain tee times:** Call up to 7 days
in advance.
Notes: Ranked tied for 8th in 1996 Best New Affordable Courses.
Subscriber comments: Long, narrow fairways, picturesque...Fantastic new course,
must play it...Challenging and fun to play...Awesome par 3s...Very tough and unforgiving course.

★★★½EAGLE LAKE GOLF CLUB

4215 Hunt Rd., Farmington, 63640, St. Francois County, (573)756-6660,
70 miles S of St. Louis.
Opened: 1993. **Holes:** 18. **Par:** 72/72. **Yards:** 7,093/5,648. **Course rat-
ing:** 73.9. **Slope:** 130. **Architect:** Gary Kern. **Green fee:** $20/$30.
Credit cards: All major. **Reduced fees:** Low season, twilight, seniors.
Caddies: No. **Golf carts:** $12. **Discount golf packages:** Yes. **Season:**
Year-round. **High:** April-Oct. **On site lodging:** No. **Rental clubs:** Yes. **Walking policy:**
Walking at certain times. **Metal spikes allowed:** Yes. **Range:** Yes (grass/mats). **To
obtain tee times:** Call 7 days in advance.
Subscriber comments: Challenging greens...Wide open but lots of
mounds...Outstanding, period...Links style, bring your A game. Always windy...No two
holes are similar...A must in Missouri!...Worth the drive from St. Louis.

★★½EAGLE SPRINGS GOLF COURSE
PU-2575 Redman Rd., St. Louis, 63136, St. Louis County, (314)355-7277.
Opened: 1989. **Holes:** 18. **Par:** 72/72. **Yards:** 6,563/5,533. **Course rating:** 71.4/72.3.
Slope: 122/121. **Architect:** David Gill. **Green fee:** $19/$28. **Credit cards:** MC,VISA.
Reduced fees: Weekdays, low season, seniors, juniors. **Caddies:** No. **Golf carts:** $10.
Discount golf packages: No. **Season:** Year-round. **High:** May-Sept. **On site lodging:**
No. **Rental clubs:** Yes. **Walking policy:** Unrestricted walking. **Metal spikes allowed:**
Yes. **Range:** Yes (grass). **To obtain tee times:** Call golf shop.
Subscriber comments: Nice place to play...Very tight-long par 5s...Lots of play...Good
layout...A fun course...The ball rolls forever...Gets better every year.
Special Notes: Also has 9-hole par-3 course.

★★★EXCELSIOR SPRINGS GOLF CLUB
PU-1201 E. Golf Hill Dr., Excelsior Springs, 64024, Ray County, (816)630-3731, 28
miles NE of Kansas City.
Opened: 1915. **Holes:** 18. **Par:** 72/72. **Yards:** 6,700/5,200. **Course rating:** 72.0/65.8.
Slope: 120/107. **Architect:** Tom Bendelow. **Green fee:** $16/$19. **Credit cards:** None.
Reduced fees: Weekdays, twilight. **Caddies:** No. **Golf carts:** $10. **Discount golf
packages:** No. **Season:** Feb.-Dec. **High:** May-Sept. **On site lodging:** No. **Rental
clubs:** No. **Walking policy:** Unrestricted walking. **Metal spikes allowed:** Yes. **Range:**
No. **To obtain tee times:** Call on Monday for upcoming weekend or holiday.
Subscriber comments: Nice small town course, down home feel...Making improvements...Middle of nowhere, short attractive layout, no amenities...Fine layout, tough to
score...Beautiful old course, some very challenging holes...Lots of hills...Old style
design.

★★½FAIRVIEW GOLF COURSE
PM-33rd and Pacific Sts., St. Joseph, 64507, Buchanan County, (816)271-5350.
Opened: N/A. **Holes:** 18. **Par:** 72/73. **Yards:** 6,312/5,490. **Course rating:** 69.5/72.0.
Slope: 116/120. **Architect:** N/A. **Green fee:** $14. **Credit cards:** MC,VISA. **Reduced
fees:** Twilight, seniors, juniors. **Caddies:** No. **Golf carts:** $20. **Discount golf pack-
ages:** No. **Season:** Year-round. **High:** April-Oct. **On site lodging:** No. **Rental clubs:**
No. **Walking policy:** Unrestricted walking. **Metal spikes allowed:** Yes. **Range:** Yes
(Mats). **To obtain tee times:** Call 1 day in advance for weekdays. Call on Thursday for
upcoming weekend.
Subscriber comments: Nice old course. Hard to get on...Lots of trees.

★★½THE FALLS GOLF CLUB
PU-1170 Turtle Creek Dr., O'Fallon, 63366, St. Charles County, (314)240-4653, 17
miles W of St. Louis.
Opened: 1995. **Holes:** 18. **Par:** 71/71. **Yards:** 6,394/4,933. **Course rating:** 70.6/67.2.
Slope: 126/107. **Architect:** John Allen. **Green fee:** $21/$41. **Credit cards:** None.
Reduced fees: N/A. **Caddies:** No. **Golf carts:** Included in Green Fee. **Discount golf
packages:** No. **Season:** Year-round. **High:** May-Oct. **On site lodging:** No. **Rental
clubs:** No. **Walking policy:** Walking at certain times. **Metal spikes allowed:** Yes.
Range: No. **To obtain tee times:** Call up to 7 days in advance.
Subscriber comments: Exceptional muny...Nice water holes...Good variety in
layout...It needs to mature...Nice clubhouse...Large greens...Relatively tight.

★★FOREST PARK GOLF COURSE
PM-5591 Grand Dr., St. Louis, 63112, St. Louis County, (314)367-1337.
Opened: 1912. **Holes:** 18. **Par:** 71/74. **Yards:** 6,024/5,528. **Course rating:** 67.8/67.8.
Slope: 113/113. **Architect:** Robert Foulis. **Green fee:** $13/$31. **Credit cards:**
MC,VISA,AMEX. **Reduced fees:** Low season, twilight, seniors. **Caddies:** No. **Golf
carts:** Included in Green Fee. **Discount golf packages:** No. **Season:** Year-round.
High: May-Sept. **On site lodging:** No. **Rental clubs:** Yes. **Walking policy:** Unrestricted
walking. **Metal spikes allowed:** Yes. **Range:** No. **To obtain tee times:** Call anytime in
advance with credit card to confirm.

★★½FRANK E. PETERS MUNICIPAL GOLF COURSE
PU-Route 3, Box 261-A, Nevada, 64772, Vernon County, (417)448-2750, 100 miles S
of Kansas City.

Opened: 1978. **Holes:** 18. **Par:** 72/72. **Yards:** 6,512/5,159. **Course rating:** 70.1/68.2. **Slope:** 109/110. **Architect:** Jim Lewis. **Green fee:** $7/$11. **Credit cards:** MC,VISA. **Reduced fees:** Weekdays, twilight. **Caddies:** No. **Golf carts:** N/A. **Discount golf packages:** No. **Season:** Year-round. **High:** April-Sept. **On site lodging:** No. **Rental clubs:** Yes. **Walking policy:** Unrestricted walking. **Metal spikes allowed:** Yes. **Range:** Yes (grass/mats). **To obtain tee times:** First come, first served.
Subscriber comments: Small town course, fun.

★★½GUSTIN GOLF CLUB
PU-Stadium Blvd., Columbia, 65211, Boone County, (573)882-6016.
Opened: N/A. **Holes:** 18. **Par:** 70/70. **Yards:** 6,400/5,565. **Course rating:** 69.7/71.3. **Slope:** 123/116. **Architect:** Floyd Farley. **Green fee:** $12/$15. **Credit cards:** MC,VISA,DISC,ATM Debit Cards. **Reduced fees:** Low season, twilight, juniors. **Caddies:** No. **Golf carts:** $22. **Discount golf packages:** No. **Season:** Year-round. **High:** March-Oct. **On site lodging:** No. **Rental clubs:** Yes. **Walking policy:** Unrestricted walking. **Metal spikes allowed:** Yes. **Range:** Yes (grass/mats). **To obtain tee times:** Call up to 7 days in advance.
Subscriber comments: Good scenic layout in the bluffs and hills of central Missouri...Closed too often for tournaments. New clubhouse is great.

★★★HAWK RIDGE GOLF CLUB
PU-18 Hawk Ridge Dr., Lake St. Louis, 63367, St. Charles County, (314)561-2828.
Opened: 1995. **Holes:** 18. **Par:** 72/72. **Yards:** 6,619/4,890. **Course rating:** 70.8/67.2. **Slope:** 127/105. **Architect:** Larry Flatt. **Green fee:** $23/$30. **Credit cards:** MC,VISA. **Reduced fees:** Weekdays, twilight, juniors. **Caddies:** No. **Golf carts:** $11. **Discount golf packages:** Yes. **Season:** Year-round. **High:** April-Oct. **On site lodging:** No. **Rental clubs:** Yes. **Walking policy:** Walking at certain times. **Metal spikes allowed:** Yes. **Range:** Yes (grass). **To obtain tee times:** Call one week in advance.
Subscriber comments: Best kept secret in St. Louis...A real golf course. No houses. Good layout...Needs more trees...Use every club in the bag...It's rather short for women...Several blind-shot holes...Still maturing.

★★HIDDEN VALLEY GOLF LINKS
PU-Rte. 1, Clever, 65631, Stone County, (417)743-2860, 18 miles SW of Springfield.
Opened: 1975. **Holes:** 18. **Par:** 73/75. **Yards:** 6,611/5,889. **Course rating:** 71.9. **Slope:** 118. **Architect:** Mario Alfonzo. **Green fee:** $12/$16. **Credit cards:** MC,VISA. **Reduced fees:** Seniors. **Caddies:** No. **Golf carts:** $18. **Discount golf packages:** No. **Season:** Year-round. **High:** May-Sept. **On site lodging:** No. **Rental clubs:** Yes. **Walking policy:** Unrestricted walking. **Metal spikes allowed:** Yes. **Range:** No. **To obtain tee times:** Call Monday for upcoming weekend.

★★½HODGE PARK GOLF COURSE
PU-7000 N.E. Barry Rd., Kansas City, 64156, Clay County, (816)781-4152.
Opened: 1975. **Holes:** 18. **Par:** 71/71. **Yards:** 6,223/5,293. **Course rating:** 69.5/69.4. **Slope:** 117/115. **Architect:** Larry Runyon and Michael H. Malyn. **Green fee:** $15/$17. **Credit cards:** MC,VISA. **Reduced fees:** Twilight, seniors, juniors. **Caddies:** No. **Golf carts:** $22. **Discount golf packages:** No. **Season:** Year-round. **High:** April-Oct. **On site lodging:** No. **Rental clubs:** Yes. **Walking policy:** Unrestricted walking. **Metal spikes allowed:** No. **Range:** Yes (Mats). **To obtain tee times:** Call 1 day in advance.
Subscriber comments: Good blue-collar course. Gets a lot of play...Quiet location...Fun to play...Hard to get tee time...Easy to score, good ego builder...Short par 4s...Good for average golfer.

★★½HONEY CREEK GOLF CLUB
PU-R.R. 1, Aurora, 65605, Lawrence County, (417)678-3353.
Opened: 1932. **Holes:** 18. **Par:** 71/79. **Yards:** 6,732/5,972. **Course rating:** 71.9. **Slope:** 118. **Architect:** Horton Smith/Mark Welch. **Green fee:** $12/$15. **Credit cards:** MC,VISA,DISC. **Reduced fees:** N/A. **Caddies:** No. **Golf carts:** $18. **Discount golf packages:** No. **Season:** Year-round. **High:** April-Oct. **On site lodging:** No. **Rental clubs:** Yes. **Walking policy:** Unrestricted walking. **Metal spikes allowed:** No. **Range:** Yes (grass). **To obtain tee times:** Call Wednesday for weekends.
Subscriber comments: Very friendly staff, some interesting and tough holes...Course for long hitters, super greens...Probably the most challenging course in the area.

★★HORTON SMITH GOLF COURSE
PU-2409 S. Scenic, Springfield, 65807, Greene County, (417)891-1639.
Opened: 1962. **Holes:** 18. **Par:** 70/71. **Yards:** 6,317/5,199. **Course rating:** 69.5/68.5.
Slope: 103/101. **Architect:** Tom Talbot. **Green fee:** $8/$11. **Credit cards:** MC,VISA.
Reduced fees: Weekdays, seniors, juniors. **Caddies:** No. **Golf carts:** $8. **Discount golf packages:** No. **Season:** Year-round. **High:** May-Sept. **On site lodging:** No. **Rental clubs:** Yes. **Walking policy:** Unrestricted walking. **Metal spikes allowed:** Yes. **Range:** Yes (grass). **To obtain tee times:** Call golf shop.

★★★½INNSBROOK RESORT GOLF COURSE
R-1 Innsbrook Estates Dr., Wright City, 63390, Warren County, (314)928-6886,.
Opened: 1982. **Holes:** 18. **Par:** 70/70. **Yards:** 6,465/5,035. **Course rating:** 72.3/67.7.
Slope: 133/120. **Architect:** Jay Randolph and Mark Waltman. **Green fee:** N/A. **Credit cards:** N/A. **Reduced fees:** N/A. **Caddies:** No. **Golf carts:** N/A. **Discount golf packages:** No. **Season:** Year-round weather permitting. **High:** April-Oct. **On site lodging:** Yes. **Rental clubs:** Yes. **Walking policy:** Walking at certain times. **Metal spikes allowed:** No. **Range:** Yes (grass). **To obtain tee times:** N/A.
Subscriber comments: Very relaxed atmosphere...Beautiful...Color coded flags...I almost hate to let other people know about this one...Tough from the tips...Direction is important, not distance.

★★½KIRKSVILLE COUNTRY CLUB
S. Hwy. 63, Kirksville, 63501, Adair County, (816)665-5335, 85 miles N of Columbia.
Opened: 1921. **Holes:** 18. **Par:** 71/71. **Yards:** 6,418/5,802. **Course rating:** 70.9/71.6.
Slope: 118/114. **Architect:** N/A. **Green fee:** N/A. **Credit cards:** MC,VISA,DISC.
Reduced fees: N/A. **Caddies:** No. **Golf carts:** $17. **Discount golf packages:** No.
Season: March-Dec. **High:** June-Aug. **On site lodging:** No. **Rental clubs:** Yes.
Walking policy: Unrestricted walking. **Metal spikes allowed:** Yes. **Range:** Yes (grass/mats). **To obtain tee times:** Non-members first come, first served.
Subscriber comments: Best part is the fast greens...Good length, average difficulty.

★★L.A. NICKELL GOLF COURSE
PM-1800 Parkside Dr., Columbia, 65202, Boone County, (573)445-4213.
Opened: N/A. **Holes:** 18. **Par:** 70/70. **Yards:** 6,007/4,869. **Course rating:** 65.1/67.7.
Slope: 100/103. **Architect:** N/A. **Green fee:** $10/$12. **Credit cards:** MC,VISA,DISC.
Reduced fees: Twilight. **Caddies:** No. **Golf carts:** $18. **Discount golf packages:** No.
Season: Year-round. **High:** N/A. **On site lodging:** No. **Rental clubs:** Yes. **Walking policy:** Unrestricted walking. **Metal spikes allowed:** Yes. **Range:** Yes (Mats). **To obtain tee times:** Tee times required for weekends & holidays. Call on Wednesday for upcoming Saturday. Call on Thursday for upcoming Sunday or holiday.

★★★LAKE VALLEY GOLF CLUB
Lake Rd. 54-79, Camdenton, 65020, Camden County, (573)346-7213.
Opened: 1967. **Holes:** 18. **Par:** 72/74. **Yards:** 6,430/5,320. **Course rating:** 71.1/70.5.
Slope: 121/118. **Architect:** Floyd Farley. **Green fee:** $25/$46. **Credit cards:** MC,VISA.
Reduced fees: Low season, resort guests, twilight, juniors. **Caddies:** No. **Golf carts:** Included in Green Fee. **Discount golf packages:** Yes. **Season:** Year-round. **High:** April-Oct. **On site lodging:** No. **Rental clubs:** Yes. **Walking policy:** Walking at certain times. **Metal spikes allowed:** Yes. **Range:** Yes (grass/mats). **To obtain tee times:** Call 7 days in advance.
Subscriber comments: Fun imaginative design, six par 3s, six par 4s, six par 5s...The most friendly 18 holes around...A test when windy.

THE LODGE OF FOUR SEASONS
R- **Credit cards:** All major. **Caddies:** No. **Golf carts:** Included in Green Fee. **Discount golf packages:** Yes. **On site lodging:** Yes. **Rental clubs:** Yes. **Walking policy:** Mandatory cart.

★★★½ROBERT TRENT JONES COURSE
State Rd. HH at HK's Restaurant, Lake Ozark, 65049, Camden County, (573)365-8532, (800)843-5253, 150 miles SW of St. Louis. .
Opened: 1969. **Holes:** 18. **Par:** 71/71. **Yards:** 6,557/5,238. **Course rating:** 71.4/70.8.
Slope: 136/124. **Architect:** Robert Trent Jones Sr. **Green fee:** $65/$75. **Reduced fees:**

Weekdays, twilight. **Season:** April-Oct. **High:** May-Sept. **Metal spikes allowed:** Yes. **Range:** Yes (grass/mats). **To obtain tee times:** Call central reservations. **Notes:** 1994 National Club Pro Championship. **Subscriber comments:** Challenging course set in the Ozark Hills...Beautiful views...Excellent pro shop...Undulating greens...Fun to play...Championship course in beautiful setting...Tight, must stay in fairways.

★★★½SEASONS RIDGE COURSE

State Rd. HH and Duckhead Rd., Lake Ozark, 65049, Camden County, (573)365-8544, (800)843-5253, 150 miles SW of St. Louis. **Opened:** 1991. **Holes:** 18. **Par:** 72/72. **Yards:** 6,447/4,617. **Course rating:** 71.4/71.0. **Slope:** 130/118. **Architect:** Ken Kavanaugh. **Green fee:** $51/$68. **Reduced fees:** Weekdays, low season, resort guests, twilight. **Season:** Year-round. **High:** May-Oct. **Metal spikes allowed:** No. **Range:** Yes (grass). **To obtain tee times:** Call. **Subscriber comments:** Best course at the lake...Excellent design...Good test...Course with a lot of character...Playable for all levels of golfers...Great views and not too long, very enjoyable...Wilderness setting...Many blind shots...One of my favorites.

★★★LONGVIEW LAKE GOLF COURSE

PU-1100 View High Dr., Kansas City, 64134, Jackson County, (816)761-9445. **Opened:** 1986. **Holes:** 18. **Par:** 72/72. **Yards:** 6,835/5,534. **Course rating:** 71.9/70.8. **Slope:** 121/113. **Architect:** Benz & Poellet. **Green fee:** $12/$16. **Credit cards:** MC,VISA. **Reduced fees:** Weekdays, seniors, juniors. **Caddies:** No. **Golf carts:** $22. **Discount golf packages:** No. **Season:** Year-round. **High:** May-Aug. **On site lodging:** No. **Rental clubs:** Yes. **Walking policy:** Unrestricted walking. **Metal spikes allowed:** Yes. **Range:** Yes (grass). **To obtain tee times:** Call seven days in advance. **Subscriber comments:** Challenging course, well laid out...Greens heavily mounded...Good view of the lake...Spikeless policy has greatly improved greens...Long ball course...Back nine better than front. **Special Notes:** Also has 9-hole, par-3 course.

★★★½MARRIOTT'S TAN-TAR-A RESORT

R-State Rd. KK, Osage Beach, 65065, Camden County, (573)348-8521, (800)826-8272, 45 miles SW of Jefferson City. **Opened:** 1980. **Holes:** 18. **Par:** 71/70. **Yards:** 6,442/3,943. **Course rating:** 72.1/62.5. **Slope:** 143/103. **Architect:** Bruce Devlin and Robert Von Hagge. **Green fee:** $56/$68. **Credit cards:** All major. **Reduced fees:** Weekdays, low season, twilight. **Caddies:** No. **Golf carts:** Included in Green Fee. **Discount golf packages:** Yes. **Season:** Year-round. **High:** May-Oct. **On site lodging:** Yes. **Rental clubs:** Yes. **Walking policy:** Mandatory cart. **Metal spikes allowed:** Yes. **Range:** Yes (grass/mats). **To obtain tee times:** Members and hotel guests call up to 30 days in advance. Public call 14 days in advance. **Notes:** 1994 National PGA Club Professional Championship. **Subscriber comments:** Lush greens and fairways, great layout...Fun par 3 over a lake from the bluffs...Pretty course, we play every time we're on vacation...Lots of trees and character, good risk/reward...Incredible scenery...Not a level lie on the course. **Special Notes:** Also has 9-hole par-35 Hidden Lakes Course.

★★★★MILLWOOD GOLF & RACQUET CLUB

PU-3701 Millwood Dr., Springfield, 65809, Greene County, (417)889-4200.

Opened: 1996. **Holes:** 18. **Architect:** Greg Martin. **Caddies:** No. **Discount golf packages:** No. **On site lodging:** No. **Rental clubs:** No. **Metal spikes allowed:** Yes. **Range:** No. Call club for further information. **Subscriber comments:** Very hilly...Beautiful setting, great golf, solid finishing holes, strong par 4s...Grabs your attention from the first tee to the last putt...Blind holes make it interesting...Premium on accuracy.

★½MINOR PARK GOLF CLUB

11215 Holmes Rd., Kansas City, 64131, Jackson County, (816)942-4033. **Architect:** Larry W. Flatt. **Caddies:** No. **Discount golf packages:** No. **On site lodging:** No. **Rental clubs:** No. **Metal spikes allowed:** Yes. **Range:** Yes. Call club for further information.

MISSOURI

★★★★MISSOURI BLUFFS GOLF CLUB
PU-18 Research Park Circle, St. Charles, 63304, St. Charles County, (314)939-6494, 20 miles W of St. Louis.
Opened: 1994. **Holes:** 18. **Par:** 71/71. **Yards:** 7,047/5,197. **Course rating:** 74.4/69.2.
Slope: 140/115. **Architect:** Tom Fazio. **Green fee:** $85/$105. **Credit cards:**
MC,VISA,AMEX. **Reduced fees:** Twilight. **Caddies:** No. **Golf carts:** Included in Green Fee. **Discount golf packages:** No. **Season:** March-Nov. **High:** May-Oct. **On site lodging:** No. **Rental clubs:** Yes. **Walking policy:** Unrestricted walking. **Metal spikes allowed:** Yes. **Range:** Yes (grass). **To obtain tee times:** Call 4 days in advance.
Notes: Ranked 6th in 1997 Best in State; 3rd in 1995 Best New Public Courses. Nike Golf Classic.
Subscriber comments: Scenic holes, fast greens, excellent driving range...Sloped fairways make it easy to stripe it...Must play...Great par 3s...Not enough water holes...Awesome layout...Great golf, great service, but you really pay for it.

★★★½MOZINGO LAKE GOLF COURSE
PU-R.R. 3, Box 112A, Maryville, 64468, Nodaway County, (816)562-3864, (888)562-3864, 4 miles E of Maryville.
Opened: 1996. **Holes:** 18. **Par:** 72/72. **Yards:** 7,072/5,583. **Course rating:** 73.5/71.3.
Slope: 134/124. **Architect:** Don Sechrest. **Green fee:** $14/$17. **Credit cards:**
MC,VISA,DISC. **Reduced fees:** Weekdays, twilight. **Caddies:** No. **Golf carts:** $9.
Discount golf packages: No. **Season:** Year-round. **High:** May-Sept. **On site lodging:** No. **Rental clubs:** Yes. **Walking policy:** Unrestricted walking. **Metal spikes allowed:** Yes. **Range:** Yes (grass). **To obtain tee times:** Call.
Subscriber comments: New course, will be great in time...Lots of water.

★★NEW MELLE LAKES GOLF CLUB
PU-404 Foristel Rd., New Melle, 63365, St. Charles County, (314)398-4653.
Opened: 1993. **Holes:** 18. **Par:** 71/71. **Yards:** 6,348/4,905. **Course rating:** 69.8/68.6.
Slope: 126/120. **Architect:** Theodore Christener. **Green fee:** $29/$39. **Credit cards:**
All major. **Reduced fees:** Twilight, seniors, juniors. **Caddies:** No. **Golf carts:** Included in Green Fee. **Discount golf packages:** No. **Season:** Year-round. **High:** April-Oct. **On site lodging:** No. **Rental clubs:** Yes. **Walking policy:** Walking at certain times. **Metal spikes allowed:** Yes. **Range:** Yes (grass/mats). **To obtain tee times:** Call or come in 7 days in advance.

★★½NORMANDIE GOLF CLUB
PU-7605 St. Charles Rock Rd., St. Louis, 63133, St. Louis County, (314)862-4884.
Opened: 1901. **Holes:** 18. **Par:** 71/77. **Yards:** 6,534/5,943. **Course rating:** 71.1/73.1.
Slope: 120/133. **Architect:** Robert Foulis. **Green fee:** $19/$28. **Credit cards:**
MC,VISA,AMEX. **Reduced fees:** Weekdays, low season, twilight, seniors, juniors.
Caddies: No. **Golf carts:** $10. **Discount golf packages:** No. **Season:** Year-round.
High: April-Oct. **On site lodging:** No. **Rental clubs:** Yes. **Walking policy:** Unrestricted walking. **Metal spikes allowed:** Yes. **Range:** Yes (grass). **To obtain tee times:** Call anytime.
Subscriber comments: Oldest course in St Louis...Great old golf course, the way it should be...Blind shots galore.

★★★★NORTH PORT NATIONAL GOLF CLUB
R-Osage Hills Rd., Lake Ozark, 65049, Miller County, (573)346-7213, 175 miles SW of St. Louis.
Opened: 1992. **Holes:** 18. **Par:** 72/72. **Yards:** 7,150/5,252. **Course rating:** 75.6/70.5.
Slope: 145/122. **Architect:** Arnold Palmer and Ed Seay. **Green fee:** $50/$52. **Credit cards:** MC,VISA,AMEX. **Reduced fees:** Weekdays, low season, resort guests, twilight, seniors, juniors. **Caddies:** No. **Golf carts:** Included in Green Fee. **Discount golf packages:** Yes. **Season:** Year-round. **High:** April-Oct. **On site lodging:** Yes. **Rental clubs:** Yes. **Walking policy:** Mandatory cart. **Metal spikes allowed:** Yes. **Range:** Yes (grass). **To obtain tee times:** Call up to two weeks in advance.
Subscriber comments: Great hole after great hole...Best course at the lake. Could be a gem...Traditional layout despite lake resort...Another gem from the King...Long and tough, some par 4s are driver, 3 wood...Not for the meek! Requires target placement...Excellent food in clubhouse.

★★OLD FLEURISSANT GOLF CLUB
PU-50 Country Club Lane, Florissant, 63033, St. Louis County, (314)741-7444, 15 miles N of St. Louis.
Opened: 1964. **Holes:** 18. **Par:** 72/73. **Yards:** 6,493/5,593. **Course rating:** 69.9/71.0. **Slope:** 120/114. **Architect:** Homer Herpel. **Green fee:** $19/$26. **Credit cards:** MC,VISA,DISC. **Reduced fees:** Weekdays, twilight, seniors, juniors. **Caddies:** No. **Golf carts:** $10. **Discount golf packages:** No. **Season:** Year-round weather permitting. **High:** April-Oct. **On site lodging:** No. **Rental clubs:** Yes. **Walking policy:** Unrestricted walking. **Metal spikes allowed:** Yes. **Range:** Yes (grass). **To obtain tee times:** Call 7 days in advance.
Special Notes: Formerly Paddock Country Club.

PARADISE POINTE GOLF CLUB
PU-18212 Golf Course Rd., Smithville, 64089, Clay County, (816)532-4100, 25 miles N of Kansas City.
Green fee: $15/$20. **Reduced fees:** Weekdays, low season, seniors. **Caddies:** No. **Golf carts:** $11. **Discount golf packages:** No. **Season:** Year-round. **High:** May-Oct. **On site lodging:** No. **Rental clubs:** Yes. **Walking policy:** Unrestricted walking. **Metal spikes allowed:** Yes. **Range:** Yes (grass). **To obtain tee times:** Weekend tee times required. Call Tuesday for upcoming weekend.
★★★OUTLAW COURSE
Opened: 1994. **Holes:** 18. **Par:** 72/72. **Yards:** 6,988/5,322. **Course rating:** 73.8/67.0. **Slope:** 138/118. **Architect:** Craig Schriener. **Credit cards:** All major.
Subscriber comments: Links style along lake...Kansas City's best kept secret...Great views and use of lake...Long, tight and brutal...Spectacular scenery. All around fun course...Challenging greens...Many blind holes...A test, not for high handicap player.
★★★POSSE COURSE
Opened: 1982. **Holes:** 18. **Par:** 72/73. **Yards:** 6,663/5,600. **Course rating:** 71.8/70.0. **Slope:** 125/115. **Architect:** Tom Clark and Brian Ault. **Credit cards:** MC,VISA,AMEX.
Subscriber comments: Older course. Lots of trees and sand...Still maturing, great promise...A real test in the wind...Lots of fun...Great layout along Smithville Lake...Don't play on a windy day.

★½PARADISE VALLEY GOLF & COUNTRY CLUB
PU-Old Hillsboro Rd., Valley Park, 63088, St. Louis County, (314)225-5157, 19 miles W of St. Louis.
Opened: 1965. **Holes:** 18. **Par:** 70/72. **Yards:** 6,185/5,102. **Course rating:** 68.2/67.6. **Slope:** 112/101. **Architect:** James Cochran. **Green fee:** $31/$35. **Credit cards:** MC,VISA,AMEX. **Reduced fees:** Weekdays, low season, juniors. **Caddies:** No. **Golf carts:** Included in Green Fee. **Discount golf packages:** No. **Season:** Year-round. **High:** May-Sept. **On site lodging:** No. **Rental clubs:** Yes. **Walking policy:** Walking at certain times. **Metal spikes allowed:** Yes. **Range:** Yes (grass/mats). **To obtain tee times:** Call golf shop.

★★★POINTE ROYALE GOLF CLUB
1000 Pointe Royale Dr., Branson, 65616, Taney County, (417)334-4477.
Architect: Ault and Clark. **Caddies:** No. **Discount golf packages:** No. **On site lodging:** No. **Rental clubs:** No. **Metal spikes allowed:** Yes. **Range:** Yes.
Call club for further information.
Subscriber comments: Fun course, lots of blind spots...Condos and houses close to fairways...Short, tight fairways, small greens...Tough course, no level fairways...Saw Andy Williams on the tee box...12th is beautiful.

★★★½QUAIL CREEK GOLF CLUB
PU-6022 Wells Rd., St. Louis, 63128, St. Louis County, (314)487-1988.
Opened: N/A. **Holes:** 18. **Par:** 72/72. **Yards:** 6,984/5,244. **Course rating:** N/A. **Slope:** 141/109. **Architect:** Gary Kern and Hale Irwin. **Green fee:** N/A. **Credit cards:** MC,VISA,AMEX. **Reduced fees:** Weekdays, low season, twilight. **Caddies:** No. **Golf carts:** N/A. **Discount golf packages:** No. **Season:** Year-round. **High:** April-Oct. **On site lodging:** No. **Rental clubs:** No. **Walking policy:** N/A. **Metal spikes allowed:** Yes. **Range:** Yes. **To obtain tee times:** N/A.

MISSOURI

Subscriber comments: Beautiful...Long and demanding, fast greens...Outstanding course...Some very scenic holes...From golds, this course will challenge any golfer...Too many tricked up holes...Long par 4s.

★★RAINTREE COUNTRY CLUB
5925 Plantation Dr., Hillsboro, 63050, Jefferson County, (314)797-4020, 45 miles S of St. Louis.
Opened: 1980. **Holes:** 18. **Par:** 72/71. **Yards:** 6,125/4,959. **Course rating:** 73.1/69.4. **Slope:** 124/119. **Architect:** N/A. **Green fee:** $18/$22. **Credit cards:** All major. **Reduced fees:** Weekdays, low season. **Caddies:** No. **Golf carts:** $10. **Discount golf packages:** No. **Season:** Year-round. **High:** May-Sept. **On site lodging:** No. **Rental clubs:** Yes. **Walking policy:** Walking at certain times. **Metal spikes allowed:** Yes. **Range:** No. **To obtain tee times:** Call or come in up to 7 days in advance.

★★RIVER OAKS GOLF CLUB
PU-14204 St. Andrews Dr., Grandview, 64030, Jackson County, (816)966-8111, 20 miles SE of Kansas City.
Opened: 1973. **Holes:** 18. **Par:** 71/73. **Yards:** 6,354/5,036. **Course rating:** 70.2/69.9. **Slope:** 119/114. **Architect:** Larry Runyon and Michael H. Malyn. **Green fee:** $14/$17. **Credit cards:** MC,VISA,DISC. **Reduced fees:** Weekdays, twilight, seniors, juniors. **Caddies:** No. **Golf carts:** $23. **Discount golf packages:** No. **Season:** Year-round weather permitting. **High:** N/A. **On site lodging:** No. **Rental clubs:** Yes. **Walking policy:** Unrestricted walking. **Metal spikes allowed:** Yes. **Range:** No. **To obtain tee times:** Call up to 7 days in advance.

★★RIVER PARK GOLF CLUB
10306 N.W. 45 Hwy., Parkville, 64152, Platte County, (816)741-9520, 10 miles NW of Kansas City.
Opened: 1955. **Holes:** 18. **Par:** 71/70. **Yards:** 6,253/4,939. **Course rating:** 69.8/67.4. **Slope:** 119/112. **Architect:** Robert Steigler. **Green fee:** $30/$35. **Credit cards:** MC,VISA. **Reduced fees:** Juniors. **Caddies:** No. **Golf carts:** Included in Green Fee. **Discount golf packages:** No. **Season:** Year-round. **High:** May-Sept. **On site lodging:** No. **Rental clubs:** Yes. **Walking policy:** Mandatory cart. **Metal spikes allowed:** Yes. **Range:** Yes (grass/mats). **To obtain tee times:** Call Friday for upcoming weekend and holidays. Members have preference for tee times.

★½RIVERSIDE GOLF COURSE
PU-1210 Larkin Williams, Fenton, 63026, St. Louis County, (314)343-6333, 10 miles SW of St. Louis.
Opened: 1964. **Holes:** 18. **Par:** 69/70. **Yards:** 5,800/5,400. **Course rating:** 67.5/67.5. **Slope:** 99/99. **Architect:** Walter Wolfner/Jack Wolfner. **Green fee:** $19/$22. **Credit cards:** MC,VISA. **Reduced fees:** Weekdays, low season, twilight, seniors, juniors. **Caddies:** No. **Golf carts:** $20. **Discount golf packages:** No. **Season:** Year-round. **High:** April-Oct. **On site lodging:** No. **Rental clubs:** No. **Walking policy:** Unrestricted walking. **Metal spikes allowed:** Yes. **Range:** No. **To obtain tee times:** First come, first served.
Special Notes: Also has 9-hole par-3 course.

★½ROYAL MEADOWS GOLF COURSE
PU-10501 E. 47th, Kansas City, 64133, Jackson County, (816)353-1323.
Opened: 1930. **Holes:** 27. **Architect:** Charles Stayton. **Green fee:** $13/$16. **Credit cards:** MC,VISA. **Reduced fees:** Weekdays, low season, twilight, seniors, juniors. **Caddies:** No. **Golf carts:** N/A. **Discount golf packages:** No. **Season:** Year-round. **High:** March-Oct. **On site lodging:** No. **Rental clubs:** Yes. **Walking policy:** Unrestricted walking. **Metal spikes allowed:** Yes. **Range:** No. **To obtain tee times:** Call five days in advance.
WEST/EAST
Par: 73/70. **Yards:** 5,994/5,176. **Course rating:** 68.3/68.8. **Slope:** 110/113.
EAST/NORTH
WEST/NORTH

MISSOURI

★★½SCHIFFERDECKER GOLF COURSE
PU-506 Schifferdecker, Joplin, 64801, Jasper County, (417)624-3533.
Opened: 1920. **Holes:** 18. **Par:** 71/72. **Yards:** 6,123/5,251. **Course rating:** 68.7/69.7.
Slope: 108/117. **Architect:** Perk Latimere. **Green fee:** $8/$9. **Credit cards:** MC,VISA.
Reduced fees: Twilight, seniors, juniors. **Caddies:** No. **Golf carts:** $14. **Discount golf packages:** No. **Season:** Year-round. **High:** April-Sept. **On site lodging:** No. **Rental clubs:** Yes. **Walking policy:** Unrestricted walking. **Metal spikes allowed:** Yes. **Range:** No. **To obtain tee times:** Call on Tuesday prior to weekend.
Subscriber comments: Usually very crowded...Fun course...Wide open, let it rip, crowded...18th is a great finishing hole...Always windy.

★★★★SHIRKEY GOLF CLUB
901 Wollard Blvd., Richmond, 64085, Ray County, (816)470-2582, 38 miles NE of Independence.
Opened: 1969. **Holes:** 18. **Par:** 71/74. **Yards:** 6,907/5,516. **Course rating:** 71.3/73.1. **Slope:** 139/129. **Architect:** Chet Mendenhall. **Green fee:** $20/$25. **Credit cards:** MC,VISA,AMEX. **Reduced fees:** Weekdays, seniors. **Caddies:** No. **Golf carts:** $26. **Discount golf packages:** No. **Season:** Year-round. **High:** May-Oct. **On site lodging:** No. **Rental clubs:** Yes. **Walking policy:** Walking at certain times. **Metal spikes allowed:** Yes. **Range:** Yes (grass/mats). **To obtain tee times:** Call 7 days in advance for weekends.
Subscriber comments: A wonderful course...Very long but fair. Tough marshalls...Worth the trip...Doesn't appear difficult but it is...A good blend of hills, trees and water.

★★½SOUTHVIEW GOLF CLUB
PU-16001 S. 71 Hwy., Belton, 64012, Cass County, (816)331-4042, 5 miles S of Kansas City.
Opened: 1955. **Holes:** 18. **Par:** 72/73. **Yards:** 6,594/5,805. **Course rating:** 70.6/73.0. **Slope:** 115/113. **Architect:** Jess Nash. **Green fee:** $14/$17. **Credit cards:** MC,VISA. **Reduced fees:** Weekdays, seniors, juniors. **Caddies:** No. **Golf carts:** $11. **Discount golf packages:** No. **Season:** Year-round. **High:** May-Aug. **On site lodging:** No. **Rental clubs:** Yes. **Walking policy:** Unrestricted walking. **Metal spikes allowed:** Yes. **Range:** Yes (grass/mats). **To obtain tee times:** First come, first served.
Subscriber comments: Somewhat difficult...Nice walk...Smooth greens...Great fairways, small hard greens...Played my game, no doglegs left.
Special Notes: Also has 9-hole par-3 course.

★★★SUN VALLEY GOLF COURSE
PU-Rte. 2, Elsberry, 63343, Lincoln County, (573)898-2613, (800)737-4653, 55 miles N of St. Louis.
Opened: 1988. **Holes:** 18. **Par:** 70/70. **Yards:** 6,395/5,036. **Course rating:** 70.5/69.3. **Slope:** 134/109. **Architect:** Gary Kern. **Green fee:** $16/$21. **Credit cards:** MC,VISA. **Reduced fees:** Weekdays, low season, seniors, juniors. **Caddies:** No. **Golf carts:** $9. **Discount golf packages:** No. **Season:** Year-round. **High:** June-Sept. **On site lodging:** No. **Rental clubs:** Yes. **Walking policy:** Unrestricted walking. **Metal spikes allowed:** Yes. **Range:** Yes (grass/mats). **To obtain tee times:** Call or come in up to 7 days in advance.
Subscriber comments: A real sleeper...Beautiful scenery...Mix of long and short tough par 4s...Excellent layout for terrain and amount of land available...Tight back nine...Has potential to be great course...Long drive from civilization...Country course, nice people.

★★★SWOPE MEMORIAL GOLF COURSE
PU-6900 Swope Memorial Dr., Kansas City, 64132, Jackson County, (816)523-9081.
Opened: 1934. **Holes:** 18. **Par:** 72/72. **Yards:** 6,274/4,517. **Course rating:** 70.9/65.9. **Slope:** 128/107. **Architect:** A.W. Tillinghast. **Green fee:** $15/$17. **Credit cards:** MC,VISA. **Reduced fees:** Twilight, seniors, juniors. **Caddies:** No. **Golf carts:** $10. **Discount golf packages:** No. **Season:** Year-round. **High:** April-Oct. **On site lodging:** No. **Rental clubs:** Yes. **Walking policy:** Unrestricted walking. **Metal spikes allowed:** No. **Range:** No. **To obtain tee times:** Call 1 day in advance.

Subscriber comments: Classic old parkland course, new Zoysia fairways...Short, tight, hilly. Dead if not in fairway...Nice course for experienced golfer...Beautiful in fall...Challenging. Want to play again...Character that comes with age. Not too tough but interesting...Shotmaker's dream.

★★★½TAPAWINGO NATIONAL GOLF CLUB
PU-13001 Gary Player Dr., St. Louis, 63127, St. Louis County, (314)349-3100.
Opened: 1994. **Holes:** 18. **Par:** 72/72. **Yards:** 7,151/5,566. **Course rating:** 75.1/72.2.
Slope: 144/121. **Architect:** Gary Player. **Green fee:** $50/$60. **Credit cards:**
MC,VISA,AMEX. **Reduced fees:** Weekdays, low season, twilight, seniors, juniors.
Caddies: No. **Golf carts:** Included in Green Fee. **Discount golf packages:** No.
Season: Year-round. **High:** April-Oct. **On site lodging:** No. **Rental clubs:** Yes. **Walking policy:** Walking at certain times. **Metal spikes allowed:** No. **Range:** Yes (grass). **To obtain tee times:** Call up to 7 days in advance with a credit card to guarantee.
Notes: Ranked 10th in 1997 Best in State.
Subscriber comments: Challenging, need better distance markers...Scenic holes...Good test from the tips...One of the best in area...Thinking man's golf course...Two different nines...Great bunkers...Outstanding variety of woods and links holes...Great par 3s...Slow play is not tolerated...Beautiful in the fall...Don't go left.

★★★½THOUSAND HILLS GOLF CLUB
PU-245 S Wildwood Dr, Branson, 65616, Taney County, (417)334-4553.
Opened: 1995. **Holes:** 18. **Architect:** Mike Riley. **Caddies:** No. **Discount golf packages:** No. **On site lodging:** No. **Rental clubs:** No. **Metal spikes allowed:** Yes. **Range:** No.
Call club for further information.
Subscriber comments: Built on hills, no flat lies, but fun course...Nice fairways and greens...Fun but you'd better like par 3s...Toughest short course around, #3 best hole in Missouri...Lovely setting...Short, tight with blind holes...Too difficult a walk from cart paths to ball...Great target golf.

★½VALLEY HILLS GOLF CLUB
1600 R.D. Mize Rd., Grain Valley, 64029, Jackson County, (816)229-3032.
Call club for further information.

MONTANA

★★BIG SKY GOLF CLUB
PU-2160 Black Otter Rd. , Meadow Village, Big Sky, 59716, Gallatin County, (406)995-4706, 45 miles S of Bozeman.
Opened: 1974. **Holes:** 18. **Par:** 72/72. **Yards:** 6,748/5,374. **Course rating:** 69.0/67.4. **Slope:** 111/104. **Architect:** Frank Duane and Arnold Palmer. **Green fee:** $32/$32. **Credit cards:** All major. **Reduced fees:** Twilight, juniors. **Caddies:** No. **Golf carts:** $20. **Discount golf packages:** No. **Season:** May-Oct. **High:** June-Sept. **On site lodging:** No. **Rental clubs:** No. **Walking policy:** Unrestricted walking. **Metal spikes allowed:** Yes. **Range:** Yes (grass). **To obtain tee times:** Call seven days in advance.

★★½BILL ROBERTS MUNICIPAL GOLF COURSE
PU-220 Cole Ave., Helena, 59601, Lewis and Clark County, (406)442-2191.
Opened: 1950. **Holes:** 18. **Par:** 72/72. **Yards:** 6,782/4,700. **Course rating:** 70.5/65.1. **Slope:** 117/101. **Architect:** Robert Muir Graves. **Green fee:** $18/$19. **Credit cards:** None. **Reduced fees:** Low season, twilight, seniors, juniors. **Caddies:** No. **Golf carts:** $20. **Discount golf packages:** Yes. **Season:** March-Nov. **High:** April-Sept. **On site lodging:** No. **Rental clubs:** Yes. **Walking policy:** Unrestricted walking. **Metal spikes allowed:** Yes. **Range:** Yes (grass/mats). **To obtain tee times:** Call 2 days in advance. **Subscriber comments:** Good course, fairways good shape...New work has made fun course...Excellent improvements, good for all levels.

★★BRIDGER CREEK GOLF COURSE
PU-2710 McIlahattan Rd., Bozeman, 59715, Gallatin County, (406)586-2333.
Opened: 1996. **Holes:** 18. **Par:** 71/71. **Yards:** 6,417/4,855. **Course rating:** 68.9/66.4. **Slope:** 116/110. **Architect:** Mac Hunter, Mark Holiday and Dane Gamble. **Green fee:** N/A. **Credit cards:** MC,VISA. **Reduced fees:** Juniors. **Caddies:** No. **Golf carts:** $18. **Discount golf packages:** No. **Season:** April-Oct. **High:** June-Aug. **On site lodging:** No. **Rental clubs:** No. **Walking policy:** Unrestricted walking. **Metal spikes allowed:** Yes. **Range:** Yes (grass). **To obtain tee times:** Call up to 7 days in advance.

★★★½BUFFALO HILL GOLF COURSE
PU-1176 N. Main St., Kalispell, 59901, Flathead County, (406)756-4547, 200 miles E of Spokane, WA.
Opened: 1933. **Holes:** 27. **Par:** 72/74. **Yards:** 6,525/5,258. **Course rating:** 71.4/70.3. **Slope:** 131/125. **Architect:** Robert Muir Graves. **Green fee:** $22/$32. **Credit cards:** MC,VISA. **Reduced fees:** Low season, twilight. **Caddies:** No. **Golf carts:** $22. **Discount golf packages:** No. **Season:** April-Oct. **High:** May-Sept. **On site lodging:** No. **Rental clubs:** Yes. **Walking policy:** Unrestricted walking. **Metal spikes allowed:** Yes. **Range:** Yes (grass/mats). **To obtain tee times:** Call anytime in advance. **Notes:** Ranked 3rd in 1997 Best in State. **Subscriber comments:** Great public course!...Excellent mature track...Tough walk but worth it. Best I've played...Greens are very small...Not long, accuracy important, well maintained, charming old clubhouse. **Special Notes:** Also has a 9-hole course.

★★★½EAGLE BEND GOLF CLUB
279 Eagle Bend Dr., Bigfork, 59911, Flathead County, (406)837-7312, (800)255-5641, 15 miles SE of Kalispell.
Opened: 1988. **Holes:** 27. **Par:** 72/72. **Yards:** 6,802/5,398. **Course rating:** 71.7/69.9. **Slope:** 124/122. **Architect:** William Hull/Jack Nicklaus Jr. **Green fee:** $30/$47. **Credit cards:** All major. **Reduced fees:** Low season, twilight, juniors. **Caddies:** No. **Golf carts:** $13. **Discount golf packages:** Yes. **Season:** April-Oct. **High:** June-Aug. **On site lodging:** Yes. **Rental clubs:** Yes. **Walking policy:** Unrestricted walking. **Metal spikes allowed:** No. **Range:** Yes (grass/mats). **To obtain tee times:** Call (800)392-9795 (Flathead Valley Central Reservations) or club at 837-7300. **Notes:** 1994 USGA Public Links Championship. **Subscriber comments:** Beautiful course with views...Overrated...Very nice facility. Good service...Lots of challenge...Good views, nice variety, beautiful Montana setting and scenery.

★★½FAIRMONT HOT SPRINGS RESORT
R-1500 Fairmont Rd., Anaconda, 59711, Deer Lodge County, (406)797-3241, (800)332-3272, 20 miles NW of Butte.
Opened: 1974. **Holes:** 18. **Par:** 72/72. **Yards:** 6,741/5,921. **Course rating:** 68.5/70.7. **Slope:** 107/109. **Architect:** Lloyd Wilder. **Green fee:** $26/$26. **Credit cards:** All major. **Reduced fees:** Resort guests. **Caddies:** No. **Golf carts:** $22. **Discount golf packages:** No. **Season:** March-Oct. **High:** June-Aug. **On site lodging:** Yes. **Rental clubs:** Yes. **Walking policy:** Unrestricted walking. **Metal spikes allowed:** Yes. **Range:** Yes (grass). **To obtain tee times:** Call golf shop.
Subscriber comments: Excellent course...It's a very relaxed course with seldom someone in front of you or someone pushing you...Beautiful course...Long, long, par 5 (650 yards), tough par 3s.

★★GLACIER VIEW GOLF COURSE
PU-River Bend Rd., West Glacier, 59936, Flathead County, (406)888-5471, (800)843-5777, 15 miles E of Columbia Falls.
Opened: 1969. **Holes:** 18. **Par:** 69/69. **Yards:** 5,116/4,432. **Course rating:** N/A. **Slope:** N/A. **Architect:** Bob Baldock. **Green fee:** $20/$20. **Credit cards:** MC,VISA. **Reduced fees:** N/A. **Caddies:** No. **Golf carts:** $18. **Discount golf packages:** No. **Season:** April-Oct. **High:** June-Aug. **On site lodging:** No. **Rental clubs:** Yes. **Walking policy:** Unrestricted walking. **Metal spikes allowed:** Yes. **Range:** No. **To obtain tee times:** Call up to 7 days in advance or further in advance with credit card to guarantee.

★★½HAMILTON GOLF CLUB
PU-570 Country Club Lane, Hamilton, 59840, Ravalli County, (406)363-4251. Call club for further information.
Subscriber comments: Good location. Good public course...Fun place to play...Beautiful views. Back nine more fun...Like two different courses, new nine, old nine, beautiful scenery...Good condition, service friendly.

★★LAKE HILLS GOLF COURSE
1930 Clubhouse Way, Billings, 59105, Yellowstone County, (406)252-9244.
Opened: 1956. **Holes:** 18. **Par:** 72/74. **Yards:** 6,802/5,126. **Course rating:** 70.1/67.0. **Slope:** 112/104. **Architect:** George Schneiter Sr.. **Green fee:** $14/$17. **Credit cards:** MC,VISA,DISC. **Reduced fees:** Low season, seniors. **Caddies:** No. **Golf carts:** $8. **Discount golf packages:** No. **Season:** Year-round. **High:** May-Sept. **On site lodging:** No. **Rental clubs:** Yes. **Walking policy:** Unrestricted walking. **Metal spikes allowed:** Yes. **Range:** Yes (grass/mats). **To obtain tee times:** Call 2 days in advance. For weekend tee times call Thursday a.m.

★★★LARCHMONT GOLF COURSE
PU-3200 Old Fort Rd., Missoula, 59801, Missoula County, (406)721-4416.
Opened: 1982. **Holes:** 18. **Par:** 72/72. **Yards:** 7,114/5,936. **Course rating:** 72.7/72.9. **Slope:** 118/118. **Architect:** Randy Lilje. **Green fee:** $16/$18. **Credit cards:** All major. **Reduced fees:** Weekdays, seniors, juniors. **Caddies:** No. **Golf carts:** $20. **Discount golf packages:** No. **Season:** March-Oct. **High:** May-Aug. **On site lodging:** No. **Rental clubs:** Yes. **Walking policy:** Unrestricted walking. **Metal spikes allowed:** Yes. **Range:** Yes (grass). **To obtain tee times:** Call one day in advance.
Subscriber comments: Going to be excellent when it matures...Nice course for municipal...Long track with little trouble...Straightforward layout, no tricks, good course.

★★★MEADOW LAKE GOLF RESORT
R-490 St. Andrews Dr., Columbia Falls, 59912, Flathead County, (406)892-2111, (800)321-4653, 12 miles N of Kalispell.
Opened: 1984. **Holes:** 18. **Par:** 72/73. **Yards:** 6,714/5,344. **Course rating:** 70.9/69.8. **Slope:** 124/121. **Architect:** Richard Phelps. **Green fee:** $25/$36. **Credit cards:** All major. **Reduced fees:** Low season, resort guests, twilight. **Caddies:** No. **Golf carts:** $13. **Discount golf packages:** Yes. **Season:** April-Nov. **High:** June-Sept. **On site lodging:** Yes. **Rental clubs:** Yes. **Walking policy:** Unrestricted walking. **Metal spikes allowed:** Yes. **Range:** Yes (grass/mats). **To obtain tee times:** Call with credit card to guarantee.
Subscriber comments: A real sleeper. Superb golf...Resort course, tight, a little short,

can be very challenging...Better and better each time you play it. You have to think about where to place your shots. Excellent test...Beautiful area, resort is great...Most underrated course in Montana.

★★★MISSION MOUNTAIN COUNTRY CLUB
640 Stagecoach Trail, Ronan, 59864, Lake County, (406)676-4653, 60 miles N of Missoula.
Opened: 1988. **Holes:** 18. **Par:** 72/73. **Yards:** 6,528/5,125. **Course rating:** 69.7/67.5.
Slope: 114/108. **Architect:** Gary Roger Baird. **Green fee:** $24/$24. **Credit cards:** MC,VISA. **Reduced fees:** N/A. **Caddies:** No. **Golf carts:** $22. **Discount golf packages:** No. **Season:** March-Oct. **High:** June-Aug. **On site lodging:** No. **Rental clubs:** Yes. **Walking policy:** Unrestricted walking. **Metal spikes allowed:** No. **Range:** Yes (grass). **To obtain tee times:** Call 2 days in advance.
Subscriber comments: Best kept secret in Montana...Good greens, small-town welcome...Scenic and basic golf, a few great holes...Spectacular view...Walkable...Friendly efficient staff; excellent greens.

★★★½NORTHERN PINES GOLF CLUB
PU-3230 Hwy. 93 North, Kalispell, 59901, Flathead County, (406)751-1950, (800)255-5641, 2 miles N of Kalispell.
Opened: 1996. **Holes:** 18. **Par:** 72/72. **Yards:** 7,015/5,421. **Course rating:** 72.5/69.9.
Slope: 121/118. **Architect:** Andy North and Roger Packard. **Green fee:** $29/$38.
Credit cards: MC,VISA,AMEX. **Reduced fees:** Low season, twilight, juniors. **Caddies:** No. **Golf carts:** $13. **Discount golf packages:** No. **Season:** April-Oct. **High:** June-Aug.
On site lodging: No. **Rental clubs:** Yes. **Walking policy:** Unrestricted walking. **Metal spikes allowed:** No. **Range:** Yes (grass). **To obtain tee times:** Call golf shop or 800 number.
Notes: Ranked 7th in 1997 Best New Affordable Public Courses.
Subscriber comments: Very good new course...Very difficult to play...New course, needs maturity...Fabulous layout. Great when it matures.

★★PETER YEGEN JR. GOLF CLUB
PU-3400 Grand Ave., Billings, 59102, Yellowstone County, (406)656-8099.
Opened: 1993. **Holes:** 18. **Par:** 71/71. **Yards:** 6,617/4,994. **Course rating:** 69.7/67.0.
Slope: 112/109. **Architect:** Carl Thuesen. **Green fee:** $15/$16. **Credit cards:** MC,VISA,AMEX. **Reduced fees:** Weekdays. **Caddies:** No. **Golf carts:** $15. **Discount golf packages:** Yes. **Season:** Year-round. **High:** April-Oct. **On site lodging:** No. **Rental clubs:** Yes. **Walking policy:** Unrestricted walking. **Metal spikes allowed:** Yes. **Range:** Yes (grass/mats). **To obtain tee times:** Call 3 days in advance.

★★★POLSON COUNTRY CLUB
PU-111 Bayview Dr., Polson, 59860, Lake County, (406)883-2440, 60 miles N of Missoula.
Opened: 1936. **Holes:** 18. **Par:** 72/72. **Yards:** 6,756/5,215. **Course rating:** 70.9/68.4.
Slope: 119/114. **Architect:** Frank Hummel. **Green fee:** $22/$22. **Credit cards:** MC,VISA. **Reduced fees:** N/A. **Caddies:** No. **Golf carts:** $22. **Discount golf packages:** Yes. **Season:** March-Nov. **High:** June-Aug. **On site lodging:** No. **Rental clubs:** Yes. **Walking policy:** Unrestricted walking. **Metal spikes allowed:** Yes. **Range:** Yes (grass/mats). **To obtain tee times:** Call up to 2 days in advance.
Subscriber comments: Hometown service at resort. Front and back nines very different...Beautiful lakeside course...Back nine challenging, front nine growing.

★★R.O. SPECK MUNICIPAL GOLF COURSE
PM-29th and River Drive N., Great Falls, 59401, Cascade County, (406)761-1078.
Opened: N/A. **Holes:** 18. **Par:** 72/73. **Yards:** 6,830/5,817. **Course rating:** 69.6/71.4.
Slope: 111/115. **Architect:** N/A. **Green fee:** $16/$16. **Credit cards:** None. **Reduced fees:** Twilight, juniors. **Caddies:** No. **Golf carts:** $15. **Discount golf packages:** No. **Season:** March-Oct. **High:** April-Oct. **On site lodging:** No. **Rental clubs:** Yes. **Walking policy:** Unrestricted walking. **Metal spikes allowed:** Yes. **Range:** Yes (grass). **To obtain tee times:** Call two days in advance.

★★½ RED LODGE MOUNTAIN RESORT GOLF COURSE

PU-828 Upper Continental Dr., Red Lodge, 59068, Carbon County, (406)446-3344, (800)514-3088, 60 miles SW of Billings.
Opened: 1983. **Holes:** 18. **Par:** 72/72. **Yards:** 6,863/5,678. **Course rating:** 69.3/70.4. **Slope:** 115/115. **Architect:** Bob Baldock. **Green fee:** $20/$23. **Credit cards:** MC,VISA. **Reduced fees:** Weekdays, low season, twilight, juniors. **Caddies:** No. **Golf carts:** $18. **Discount golf packages:** No. **Season:** May-Oct. **High:** July-Aug. **On site lodging:** No. **Rental clubs:** Yes. **Walking policy:** Unrestricted walking. **Metal spikes allowed:** Yes. **Range:** Yes (grass). **To obtain tee times:** Call golf shop.
Subscriber comments: A real gem, out in the middle of nowhere...Course needs TLC...Love the view, challenging, nice people...Back nine creek eats balls...Liked the par 3s...Several unique holes, outstanding view of mountains.

★★★ VILLAGE GREENS GOLF CLUB

PU-500 Palmer Dr., Kalispell, 59901, Flathead County, (406)752-4666, 230 miles NE of Spokane, WA.
Opened: 1992. **Holes:** 18. **Par:** 70/70. **Yards:** 6,227/5,209. **Course rating:** 67.9/68.5. **Slope:** 111/111. **Architect:** William Robinson. **Green fee:** $24/$24. **Credit cards:** MC,VISA,DISC. **Reduced fees:** Twilight, juniors. **Caddies:** No. **Golf carts:** $20. **Discount golf packages:** No. **Season:** April-Oct. **High:** June-Aug. **On site lodging:** No. **Rental clubs:** Yes. **Walking policy:** Unrestricted walking. **Metal spikes allowed:** No. **Range:** Yes (grass). **To obtain tee times:** Call up to 3 days in advance.
Subscriber comments: Not an impressive course, but in good shape...Splendid surprise...Great greens, you can really turn loose the driver...Nice course, some small lakes, pretty wide open.

WHITEFISH LAKE GOLF CLUB

PU-Hwy. 93 N., Whitefish, 59937, Flathead County, (406)862-5960, 130 miles N of Missoula. **Architect:** John Steidel. **Green fee:** $29/$29. **Credit cards:** MC,VISA. **Reduced fees:** Resort guests, twilight. **Caddies:** No. **Golf carts:** $24. **Discount golf packages:** Yes. **Season:** April-Oct. **High:** June-Sept. **Rental clubs:** Yes. **Walking policy:** Unrestricted walking. **Range:** Yes (grass/mats). **To obtain tee times:** Call 2 days in advance starting at 7 a.m.

★★★½ NORTH COURSE

Opened: 1936. **Holes:** 18. **Par:** 72/72. **Yards:** 6,556/5,556. **Course rating:** 69.8/70.1. **Slope:** 118/115. **On site lodging:** No. **Metal spikes allowed:** Yes.
Notes: Ranked 2nd in 1997 Best in State.
Subscriber comments: Montana's best...Beautiful scenery...Exceptional public course...Great old course...Very courteous and helpful...Well maintained, fun place to play, charming clubhouse, excellent food...A fair test of golf in great surroundings.

★★★½ SOUTH COURSE

Opened: 1980. **Holes:** 18. **Par:** 71/72. **Yards:** 6,563/5,358. **Course rating:** 70.5/70.3. **Slope:** 122/120. **On site lodging:** Yes. **Metal spikes allowed:** No.
Subscriber comments: Long but forgiving. Beautiful scenery and wildlife...Montana's best...Great greens, ample landing areas...New holes may make you forget where you are...The better of the two courses, tight, must hit fairways, scenic views...Beautiful mountain setting...Houses and condos too close.

NEBRASKA

★★½APPLEWOOD GOLF COURSE
PU-6111 S. 99th St., Omaha, 68127, Douglas County, (402)444-4656.
Opened: 1971. **Holes:** 18. **Par:** 72/76. **Yards:** 6,916/6,014. **Course rating:** 72.4/74.6.
Slope: 121/126. **Architect:** Dave Bennett and Leon Howard. **Green fee:** $13/$14.
Credit cards: None. **Reduced fees:** Weekdays, seniors, juniors. **Caddies:** No. **Golf carts:** $8. **Discount golf packages:** No. **Season:** Year-round. **High:** May-Sept. **On site lodging:** No. **Rental clubs:** No. **Walking policy:** Unrestricted walking. **Metal spikes allowed:** Yes. **Range:** Yes (grass). **To obtain tee times:** Call 7 days in advance.
Subscriber comments: Grip it and rip it, great city course...A nice valley course. Challenging yet fair...Wide open, can be tough or easy. Priced right.

★★½ASHLAND COUNTRY CLUB
R2, Ashland, 68003, Saunders County, (402)944-3388, 25 miles W of Omaha.
Opened: 1967. **Holes:** 18. **Par:** 70/74. **Yards:** 6,337/5,606. **Course rating:** 70.0/69.8.
Slope: 112/112. **Architect:** Dick Watson. **Green fee:** $18/$20. **Credit cards:** None.
Reduced fees: N/A. **Caddies:** No. **Golf carts:** $18. **Discount golf packages:** No.
Season: March-Oct. **High:** June-Sept. **On site lodging:** No. **Rental clubs:** Yes.
Walking policy: Unrestricted walking. **Metal spikes allowed:** Yes. **Range:** No. **To obtain tee times:** Call seven days in advance.
Subscriber comments: Easy to play...Tough and fun.

★★BENSON PARK GOLF COURSE
PU-5333 N. 72nd St., Omaha, 68134, Douglas County, (402)444-4626.
Opened: 1964. **Holes:** 18. **Par:** 72/78. **Yards:** 6,814/6,085. **Course rating:** 72.1/73.4.
Slope: 120/121. **Architect:** Edward Lawrence Packard. **Green fee:** $12/$13. **Credit cards:** None. **Reduced fees:** Seniors, juniors. **Caddies:** No. **Golf carts:** $16. **Discount golf packages:** Yes. **Season:** March-Dec. **High:** May-Sept. **On site lodging:** No. **Rental clubs:** Yes. **Walking policy:** Unrestricted walking. **Metal spikes allowed:** Yes. **Range:** No. **To obtain tee times:** Call one week in advance.

COVINGTON LINKS GOLF COURSE
PU-497 Golf Rd., South Sioux City, 68776, Dakota County, (402)494-9841.
Opened: 1977. **Holes:** 18. **Par:** 71/71. **Yards:** 5,977/5,263. **Course rating:** N/A. **Slope:** N/A. **Architect:** Marty Johnson. **Green fee:** $11/$13. **Credit cards:** MC,VISA. **Reduced fees:** N/A. **Caddies:** No. **Golf carts:** $16. **Discount golf packages:** No. **Season:** March-Nov. **High:** June-Aug. **On site lodging:** No. **Rental clubs:** No. **Walking policy:** Unrestricted walking. **Metal spikes allowed:** Yes. **Range:** No. **To obtain tee times:** Tee times required. Call Thursday after 8 a.m. for upcoming weekend.

★★½CROOKED CREEK GOLF CLUB
PU-134th & O St., Lincoln, 68520, Lancaster County, (402)489-7899, 3 miles E of Lincoln.
Opened: 1995. **Holes:** 18. **Par:** 72/72. **Yards:** 6,720/5,024. **Course rating:** 70.8/68.2.
Slope: 113/109. **Architect:** Pat Wyss. **Green fee:** $15/$19. **Credit cards:** MC,VISA.
Reduced fees: Low season, seniors, juniors. **Caddies:** No. **Golf carts:** $10. **Discount golf packages:** No. **Season:** Year-round. **High:** April-Oct. **On site lodging:** No. **Rental clubs:** Yes. **Walking policy:** Unrestricted walking. **Metal spikes allowed:** No. **Range:** Yes (grass/mats). **To obtain tee times:** Call.
Subscriber comments: A bargain...Only a few years old, will get better...Great clubhouse...Diverse layout. Fun.

ELMWOOD PARK GOLF COURSE
PU-6232 Pacific St., Omaha, 68106, Douglas County, (402)444-4683.
Opened: 1934. **Holes:** 18. **Par:** 68/68. **Yards:** 5,000/4,300. **Course rating:** 64.0.
Slope: 101. **Architect:** N/A. **Green fee:** $12/$13. **Credit cards:** None. **Reduced fees:** N/A. **Caddies:** No. **Golf carts:** $8. **Discount golf packages:** No. **Season:** March-Dec.
High: May-Sept. **On site lodging:** No. **Rental clubs:** Yes. **Walking policy:** Unrestricted walking. **Metal spikes allowed:** No. **Range:** No. **To obtain tee times:** Call up to 7 days in advance.

★★★GRAND ISLAND MUNICIPAL GOLF COURSE
PM-2800 Shady Bend Rd., Grand Island, 68801, Hall County, (308)385-5340, 90 miles NE of Lincoln.
Opened: 1977. **Holes:** 18. **Par:** 72/72. **Yards:** 6,752/5,487. **Course rating:** 71.3/70.8. **Slope:** 118/112. **Architect:** Frank Hummel. **Green fee:** $8/$9. **Credit cards:** None. **Reduced fees:** Seniors, juniors. **Caddies:** No. **Golf carts:** $16. **Discount golf packages:** No. **Season:** Year-round. **High:** April-Sept. **On site lodging:** No. **Rental clubs:** Yes. **Walking policy:** Unrestricted walking. **Metal spikes allowed:** Yes. **Range:** Yes (grass/mats). **To obtain tee times:** Call 7 days in advance.
Subscriber comments: Course in good shape...Thick rough...One of the best muny courses in Nebraska, great value...Getting better as it matures...Short.

★★★HERITAGE HILLS GOLF COURSE
6000 Clubhouse Dr., McCook, 69001, Red Willow County, (308)345-5032, 240 miles SW of Lincoln.
Opened: 1981. **Holes:** 18. **Par:** 72/72. **Yards:** 6,715/5,475. **Course rating:** 72.7/71.1. **Slope:** 130/127. **Architect:** Phelps and Benz. **Green fee:** $20/$30. **Credit cards:** None. **Reduced fees:** Twilight, juniors. **Caddies:** No. **Golf carts:** $20. **Discount golf packages:** No. **Season:** Year-round. **High:** May-Sept. **On site lodging:** No. **Rental clubs:** Yes. **Walking policy:** Unrestricted walking. **Metal spikes allowed:** Yes. **Range:** Yes (grass). **To obtain tee times:** Call 7 days in advance.
Subscriber comments: What a jewel in the middle of nowhere...Best course in Nebraska for the price...Great golf and buy...Perhaps too many blind shots.

★★HIDDEN VALLEY GOLF COURSE
PU-10501 Pine Lake Rd., Lincoln, 68526, Lancaster County, (402)483-2532.
Opened: 1962. **Holes:** 18. **Par:** 71/75. **Yards:** 6,080/5,411. **Course rating:** 68.3/71.6. **Slope:** 110/114. **Architect:** C.J. Dietrich. **Green fee:** $11/$13. **Credit cards:** MC,VISA. **Reduced fees:** Weekdays, low season, seniors, juniors. **Caddies:** No. **Golf carts:** $20. **Discount golf packages:** Yes. **Season:** March-Dec. **High:** June-Aug. **On site lodging:** No. **Rental clubs:** Yes. **Walking policy:** Unrestricted walking. **Metal spikes allowed:** Yes. **Range:** Yes (grass/mats). **To obtain tee times:** Call 7 days in advance.
Special Notes: Also has 9-hole par-35 West Course.

★★★½HIGHLANDS GOLF COURSE
PU-5501 N.W. 12th St., Lincoln, 68521, Lancaster County, (402)441-6081.
Opened: 1993. **Holes:** 18. **Par:** 72/72. **Yards:** 7,021/5,280. **Course rating:** 72.5/69.4. **Slope:** 119/111. **Architect:** Jeff Brauer. **Green fee:** $12/$15. **Credit cards:** MC,VISA. **Reduced fees:** Twilight, seniors, juniors. **Caddies:** No. **Golf carts:** $10. **Discount golf packages:** No. **Season:** Year-round. **High:** April-Oct. **On site lodging:** No. **Rental clubs:** Yes. **Walking policy:** Unrestricted walking. **Metal spikes allowed:** No. **Range:** Yes (grass/mats). **To obtain tee times:** Call 7 days in advance.
Subscriber comments: Fun to play...Challenging links...Like the real highlands, no trees, lots of sand...Lush and beautiful...Wide open and long from gold markers.

HILLSIDE GOLF COURSE
PM-2616 Hillside Dr., Sidney, 69162, Cheyenne County, (308)254-2311, 170 miles NE of Denver, CO.
Opened: N/A. **Holes:** 18. **Par:** 72/73. **Yards:** 6,924/5,308. **Course rating:** 72.5/70.0. **Slope:** 121/110. **Architect:** N/A. **Green fee:** $15. **Credit cards:** All major. **Reduced fees:** Seniors, juniors. **Caddies:** No. **Golf carts:** $16. **Discount golf packages:** No. **Season:** March-Dec. **High:** May-Aug. **On site lodging:** No. **Rental clubs:** Yes. **Walking policy:** Unrestricted walking. **Metal spikes allowed:** Yes. **Range:** Yes (grass). **To obtain tee times:** Call up to 7 days in advance.

★★★HIMARK GOLF COURSE
PU-9001 Pioneers Blvd., Lincoln, 68520, Lancaster County, (402)488-7888.
Opened: 1993. **Holes:** 18. **Par:** 72/70. **Yards:** 6,700/4,900. **Course rating:** 72.6/68.8. **Slope:** 122/111. **Architect:** Larry Glatt/Lammle Brothers. **Green fee:** $11/$19. **Credit cards:** MC,VISA. **Reduced fees:** Weekdays, low season, twilight, seniors, juniors. **Caddies:** No. **Golf carts:** $10. **Discount golf packages:** No. **Season:** March-Nov. **High:** June-Aug. **On site lodging:** No. **Rental clubs:** Yes. **Walking policy:** Unrestricted

walking. **Metal spikes allowed:** No. **Range:** Yes (grass/mats). **To obtain tee times:** Call 5 days in advance.
Subscriber comments: A fun course...Course always in immaculate condition...Nice layout, wind can blow like hell...Immaculate conditions, great greens, friendly staff.

★★½HOLMES PARK GOLF COURSE
PU-3701 S. 70th St., Lincoln, 68506, Lancaster County, (402)441-8960.
Opened: 1964. **Holes:** 18. **Par:** 72/74. **Yards:** 6,805/6,054. **Course rating:** 72.2/73.8.
Slope: 120/126. **Architect:** Floyd Farley. **Green fee:** $11/$15. **Credit cards:** MC,VISA.
Reduced fees: Weekdays, seniors, juniors. **Caddies:** No. **Golf carts:** $20. **Discount golf packages:** Yes. **Season:** Jan.-Dec. **High:** May-June. **On site lodging:** No. **Rental clubs:** Yes. **Walking policy:** Unrestricted walking. **Metal spikes allowed:** No. **Range:** Yes (grass/mats). **To obtain tee times:** Call 7 days in advance.
Subscriber comments: Very playable...Challenging large greens, wide open. Lots of traffic...The best in Lincoln, not for the beginner...Great group running this course. Pro may join you for a few holes.

★★★½INDIAN CREEK GOLF COURSE
PU-20100 W. Maple Rd., Elkhorn, 68022, Douglas County, (402)289-0900, 5 miles W of Omaha.
Opened: 1992. **Holes:** 27. **Architect:** Frank Hummel/Mark Rathert. **Green fee:** $18/$25. **Credit cards:** MC,VISA. **Reduced fees:** Twilight, seniors. **Caddies:** No. **Golf carts:** $18. **Discount golf packages:** No. **Season:** March-Nov. **High:** June-July. **On site lodging:** No. **Rental clubs:** Yes. **Walking policy:** Unrestricted walking. **Metal spikes allowed:** Yes. **Range:** Yes (grass/mats). **To obtain tee times:** Call 7 days in advance.
BLACKBIRD/GRAYHAWK
Par: 72/72. **Yards:** 7,154/5,282. **Course rating:** 74.1/68.5. **Slope:** 128/113.
RED FEATHER/BLACKBIRD
Par: 72/72. **Yards:** 7,157/5,040. **Course rating:** 75.0/68.1. **Slope:** 131/112.
RED FEATHER/GRAYHAWK
Par: 72/72. **Yards:** 7,041/5,120. **Course rating:** 73.9/69.4. **Slope:** 131/115.
Subscriber comments: Good challenge, fun course...New nine very challenging...Strong, hilly course...Long with heavy winds, great shape.

★★★INDIAN TRAILS COUNTRY CLUB
Highway 275, Beemer, 68716, Cuming County, (402)528-3404, 30 miles S of Norfolk.
Opened: 1960. **Holes:** 18. **Par:** 71/73. **Yards:** 6,302/5,692. **Course rating:** 68.8/74.2.
Slope: 115/120. **Architect:** N/A. **Green fee:** $12/$16. **Credit cards:** MC,VISA.
Reduced fees: N/A. **Caddies:** No. **Golf carts:** $14. **Discount golf packages:** No.
Season: March-Nov. **High:** May-Aug. **On site lodging:** No. **Rental clubs:** No. **Walking policy:** N/A. **Metal spikes allowed:** Yes. **Range:** Yes (grass). **To obtain tee times:** Call up to 7 days in advance.
Subscriber comments: Great course, river views great...Windy.

INDIANHEAD GOLF CLUB
PU-4100 W. Husker Hwy., Grand Island, 68803, Hall County, (308)381-4653, 90 miles W of Lincoln.
Opened: 1990. **Holes:** 18. **Par:** 72/72. **Yards:** 6,597/5,664. **Course rating:** 70.9/71.9.
Slope: 122/117. **Architect:** N/A. **Green fee:** $9/$11. **Credit cards:** MC,VISA. **Reduced fees:** Weekdays, twilight, seniors, juniors. **Caddies:** No. **Golf carts:** $9. **Discount golf packages:** Yes. **Season:** Year-round. **High:** May-Sept. **On site lodging:** No. **Rental clubs:** Yes. **Walking policy:** Unrestricted walking. **Metal spikes allowed:** Yes. **Range:** Yes (grass/mats). **To obtain tee times:** Call 7 days in advance.

IRON EAGLE MUNICIPAL GOLF COURSE
PM-2401 Halligan Dr, North Platte, 69101, Lincoln County, (308)535-6730.
Opened: 1994. **Holes:** 18. **Par:** 72/72. **Yards:** 6,401/4,459. **Course rating:** 70.8/66.3.
Slope: 120/114. **Architect:** Pat Wyss. **Green fee:** $12/$15. **Credit cards:** MC,VISA.
Reduced fees: Seniors, juniors. **Caddies:** No. **Golf carts:** $8. **Discount golf packages:** No. **Season:** Year-round weather permitting. **High:** April-Sept. **On site lodging:** No. **Rental clubs:** Yes. **Walking policy:** Unrestricted walking. **Metal spikes allowed:** Yes. **Range:** Yes (grass/mats). **To obtain tee times:** Call 7 days in advance.

★★★THE KNOLLS GOLF COURSE
PU-11630 Sahler St., Omaha, 68164, Douglas County, (402)493-1740.
Opened: 1976. **Holes:** 18. **Par:** 71/71. **Yards:** 6,300/5,111. **Course rating:** 69.8/69.8.
Slope: 123. **Architect:** N/A. **Green fee:** $14/$20. **Credit cards:** MC,VISA,AMEX.
Reduced fees: Twilight, seniors, juniors. **Caddies:** No. **Golf carts:** $10. **Discount golf packages:** Yes. **Season:** Year-round. **High:** April-Oct. **On site lodging:** No. **Rental clubs:** Yes. **Walking policy:** Unrestricted walking. **Metal spikes allowed:** Yes. **Range:** No. **To obtain tee times:** Call or come in.
Subscriber comments: Front nine tight, back nine, watch the wind...Very friendly atmosphere...Nice course, have to play smart, quite a bit of trouble, good price, ranger keeps play moving...Always a great time.

LAKE MALONEY GOLF COURSE
608 Birdie Lane, North Platte, 69101, Lincoln County, (308)532-9998.
Opened: 1990. **Holes:** 18. **Par:** 72/72. **Yards:** 6,550/5,050. **Course rating:** 72.6/70.1.
Slope: 124/115. **Architect:** Bill Burns. **Green fee:** $8/$11. **Credit cards:** None.
Reduced fees: N/A. **Caddies:** No. **Golf carts:** $14. **Discount golf packages:** No.
Season: March-Nov. **High:** May-Aug. **On site lodging:** No. **Rental clubs:** Yes. **Walking policy:** Unrestricted walking. **Metal spikes allowed:** No. **Range:** Yes (grass/mats). **To obtain tee times:** Call golf shop. Tee times required for weekends.

LAKESIDE COUNTRY CLUB
PU-RR 2 Box 36A, Elwood, 68937, Gosper County, (308)785-2818.
Opened: 1961. **Holes:** 18. **Par:** 72/72. **Yards:** 6,200/5,200. **Course rating:** 70.0/67.2.
Slope: 128/128. **Architect:** N/A. **Green fee:** $10/$20. **Credit cards:** MC,VISA.
Reduced fees: N/A. **Caddies:** No. **Golf carts:** $20. **Discount golf packages:** No.
Season: Year-round weather permitting. **High:** May-Sept. **On site lodging:** No. **Rental clubs:** Yes. **Walking policy:** Unrestricted walking. **Metal spikes allowed:** No. **Range:** Yes (grass). **To obtain tee times:** Call up to 7 days in advance.

★★MAHONEY GOLF COURSE
PM-7900 Adams St., Lincoln, 68507, Lancaster County, (402)441-8969.
Opened: 1975. **Holes:** 18. **Par:** 70/72. **Yards:** 6,459/5,582. **Course rating:** 69.9/72.6.
Slope: 113/120. **Architect:** Floyd Farley. **Green fee:** $12/$15. **Credit cards:** All major.
Reduced fees: Twilight, seniors, juniors. **Caddies:** No. **Golf carts:** $10. **Discount golf packages:** No. **Season:** Year-round weather permitting. **High:** June-Aug. **On site lodging:** No. **Rental clubs:** Yes. **Walking policy:** Unrestricted walking. **Metal spikes allowed:** Yes. **Range:** Yes (grass/mats). **To obtain tee times:** Call 7 days in advance.

★★★½MEADOWLARK HILLS GOLF COURSE
PM-3300 30th Ave., Kearney, 68848, Buffalo County, (308)233-3265, 120 miles W of Lincoln.
Opened: 1994. **Holes:** 18. **Par:** 71/72. **Yards:** 6,485/4,967. **Course rating:** 70.4/68.2.
Slope: 119/112. **Architect:** David Gill. **Green fee:** $7/$17. **Credit cards:** MC,VISA.
Reduced fees: Weekdays, low season, twilight, seniors, juniors. **Caddies:** No. **Golf carts:** $9. **Discount golf packages:** No. **Season:** Year-round. **High:** May-Aug. **On site lodging:** No. **Rental clubs:** Yes. **Walking policy:** Unrestricted walking. **Metal spikes allowed:** No. **Range:** Yes (grass/mats). **To obtain tee times:** Call 6 days in advance.
Subscriber comments: Used every club in my bag...One of the best new courses in last three years...Good mix of open and tight holes...A challenging new course...Nice for area, but rather expensive for Nebraska.

★★½MIRACLE HILL GOLF & TENNIS CENTER
PU-1401 N.120th St., Omaha, 68154, Douglas County, (402)498-0220.
Opened: 1960. **Holes:** 18. **Par:** 70/70. **Yards:** 6,412/5,069. **Course rating:** 71.0/69.0.
Slope: 129/117. **Architect:** Floyd Farley. **Green fee:** $16/$24. **Credit cards:** MC,VISA.
Reduced fees: Twilight, seniors. **Caddies:** No. **Golf carts:** $19. **Discount golf packages:** No. **Season:** Year-round. **High:** May-Aug. **On site lodging:** No. **Rental clubs:** Yes. **Walking policy:** Unrestricted walking. **Metal spikes allowed:** Yes. **Range:** Yes (grass/mats). **To obtain tee times:** Call 7 days in advance.
Subscriber comments: A friendly course for a high-handicap golfer, no serious hazards...Tough. High rough...Priced right. Good service...Very playable older course.

NORTH PLATTE COUNTRY CLUB
1008 W. 18th St., North Platte, 69101, Lincoln County, (308)532-7550.
Opened: 1916. **Holes:** 18. **Par:** 70/72. **Yards:** 6,392/5,260. **Course rating:** 70.0/70.5.
Slope: 117/118. **Architect:** N/A. **Green fee:** $20/$35. **Credit cards:** None. **Reduced fees:** N/A. **Caddies:** No. **Golf carts:** $8. **Discount golf packages:** No. **Season:** March-Dec. **High:** May-Aug. **On site lodging:** No. **Rental clubs:** Yes. **Walking policy:** Unrestricted walking. **Metal spikes allowed:** No. **Range:** Yes (grass). **To obtain tee times:** Call up to 7 days in advance.

★★★THE PINES COUNTRY CLUB
7516 N. 286th St., Valley, 68064, Douglas County, (402)359-4311, 30 miles W of Omaha.
Opened: 1979. **Holes:** 18. **Par:** 72/72. **Yards:** 6,650/5,370. **Course rating:** 69.9/70.2.
Slope: 117/117. **Architect:** Bill Kubly. **Green fee:** $16/$24. **Credit cards:** MC,VISA.
Reduced fees: Weekdays, seniors, juniors. **Caddies:** No. **Golf carts:** $10. **Discount golf packages:** No. **Season:** March-Oct. **High:** May-Aug. **On site lodging:** No. **Rental clubs:** Yes. **Walking policy:** Unrestricted walking. **Metal spikes allowed:** No. **Range:** Yes (grass/mats). **To obtain tee times:** Call 7 days in advance for weekday. Call on Friday for upcoming weekend.
Subscriber comments: Trains are a bother...Nice fast greens...Good fun.

★★★½PIONEERS GOLF COURSE
PU-3403 W. Van Dorn, Lincoln, 68522, Lancaster County, (402)441-8966, 2 miles W of Lincoln.
Opened: 1930. **Holes:** 18. **Par:** 71/74. **Yards:** 6,478/5,771. **Course rating:** 69.2/73.2.
Slope: 110/114. **Architect:** W. H. Tucker. **Green fee:** $12/$15. **Credit cards:** MC,VISA.
Reduced fees: Weekdays, twilight, seniors, juniors. **Caddies:** No. **Golf carts:** $20.
Discount golf packages: No. **Season:** Year-round. **High:** June-Aug. **On site lodging:** No. **Rental clubs:** Yes. **Walking policy:** Unrestricted walking. **Metal spikes allowed:** No. **Range:** Yes (grass). **To obtain tee times:** Call up to 7 days in advance.
Subscriber comments: Bumpy, unpredictable greens. Old course, short and easy...Beautiful...Best value in area. Tall pine trees everywhere, great muny.

★★★QUAIL RUN GOLF COURSE
PU-327 S. 5th St., Columbus, 68601, Platte County, (402)564-1313, 80 miles SE of Omaha.
Opened: 1991. **Holes:** 18. **Par:** 72/72. **Yards:** 7,024/5,147. **Course rating:** 75.1/70.7.
Slope: 140/125. **Architect:** Frank Hummel. **Green fee:** $12/$16. **Credit cards:** None.
Reduced fees: Weekdays, twilight, seniors, juniors. **Caddies:** No. **Golf carts:** $17.
Discount golf packages: No. **Season:** April-Oct. **High:** June-Aug. **On site lodging:** No. **Rental clubs:** Yes. **Walking policy:** Unrestricted walking. **Metal spikes allowed:** Yes. **Range:** Yes (grass/mats). **To obtain tee times:** Call 3 days in advance.
Subscriber comments: Good golf course...Excellent course near the river...Half course open, other half tight, good value, well laid out.

QUARRY OAKS GOLF CLUB
PU-16600 Quarry Oaks Dr., Ashland, 68003-3820, Cass County, (402)944-6000, (888)944-6001, 25 miles W of Omaha.
Opened: 1997. **Holes:** 18. **Par:** 72/72. **Yards:** 7,051/5,378. **Course rating:** 73.2/70.0.
Slope: 135/131. **Architect:** John LaFoy. **Green fee:** $35/$45. **Credit cards:** MC,VISA,AMEX. **Reduced fees:** N/A. **Caddies:** No. **Golf carts:** $12. **Discount golf packages:** No. **Season:** March-Nov. **High:** May-Sept. **On site lodging:** No. **Rental clubs:** Yes. **Walking policy:** Unrestricted walking. **Metal spikes allowed:** No. **Range:** Yes (grass). **To obtain tee times:** Call up to 7 days in advance.
Notes: Ranked 1st Best New Affordable Public Course of 1997.

★★★RIVERVIEW GOLF CLUB
PU-West 20th St., Scottsbluff, 69361, Scotts Bluff County, (308)635-1555, 200 miles NE of Denver, CO.
Opened: N/A. **Holes:** 18. **Par:** 71/73. **Yards:** 6,000/5,400. **Course rating:** 68.0/70.0.
Slope: 118/119. **Architect:** N/A. **Green fee:** $12/$12. **Credit cards:** MC,VISA.
Reduced fees: N/A. **Caddies:** No. **Golf carts:** $13. **Discount golf packages:** No.

Season: March-Dec. **High:** May-Oct. **On site lodging:** No. **Rental clubs:** Yes. **Walking policy:** Unrestricted walking. **Metal spikes allowed:** Yes. **Range:** Yes (grass). **To obtain tee times:** Call or come in anytime.
Subscriber comments: Course in excellent shape, fun...Trees make course challenging...Lake driving range...Tough course, lots of water and trees.

SKYVIEW GOLF COURSE
PU-R.R. 2, Alliance, 69301, Box Butte County, (308)762-1446, 45 miles NE of Scottsbluff.
Opened: 1953. **Holes:** 18. **Par:** 70/72. **Yards:** 6,501/5,364. **Course rating:** 70.0/70.6. **Slope:** 112/115. **Architect:** Henry B. Hughes. **Green fee:** $13/$15. **Credit cards:** None. **Reduced fees:** Juniors. **Caddies:** No. **Golf carts:** $6. **Discount golf packages:** No. **Season:** March-Nov. **High:** June-Aug. **On site lodging:** No. **Rental clubs:** Yes. **Walking policy:** Unrestricted walking. **Metal spikes allowed:** No. **Range:** Yes (grass). **To obtain tee times:** Not necessary.

SOUTHERN HILLS GOLF COURSE
3005 S. Southern Hills Dr., Hastings, 68901, Adams County, (402)463-8006, 150 miles W of Omaha.
Opened: N/A. **Holes:** 18. **Par:** 72/72. **Yards:** 6,351/5,195. **Course rating:** 70.7/69.6. **Slope:** 127/116. **Architect:** N/A. **Green fee:** $13. **Credit cards:** None. **Reduced fees:** N/A. **Caddies:** No. **Golf carts:** $17. **Discount golf packages:** No. **Season:** Year-round weather permitting. **High:** N/A. **On site lodging:** No. **Rental clubs:** No. **Walking policy:** Unrestricted walking. **Metal spikes allowed:** No. **Range:** Yes (grass). **To obtain tee times:** Call 1 day in advance.

★★★TIBURON GOLF CLUB
10302 S. 168th St., Omaha, 68136, Sarpy County, (402)895-2688.
Opened: 1989. **Holes:** 27. **Par:** 72/72. **Yards:** 6,887/5,335. **Course rating:** 73.4/71.0. **Slope:** 131/126. **Architect:** Dave Bennett. **Green fee:** $20/$25. **Credit cards:** All major. **Reduced fees:** Weekdays, seniors, juniors. **Caddies:** No. **Golf carts:** $10. **Discount golf packages:** No. **Season:** March-Nov. **High:** June-Sept. **On site lodging:** No. **Rental clubs:** Yes. **Walking policy:** Unrestricted walking. **Metal spikes allowed:** Yes. **Range:** Yes (grass/mats). **To obtain tee times:** Call 7 days in advance for weekdays, and 5 days in advance for weekends.
Subscriber comments: 27 holes...Fun layout, fair...It is maturing...Regular golf course, open play...My favorite in Nebraska. Love the layout...Wind always there, but always fun...Could be better...Newest nine has several tough holes.

VALLEY VIEW GOLF COURSE
PU-Route 2, Box 44, Fremont, 68025, Saunders County, (402)721-7772.
Opened: 1960. **Holes:** 18. **Par:** 71/71. **Yards:** 5,295/4,982. **Course rating:** 64.6/67.9. **Slope:** 108/116. **Architect:** N/A. **Green fee:** $13/$14. **Credit cards:** None. **Reduced fees:** N/A. **Caddies:** No. **Golf carts:** $16. **Discount golf packages:** No. **Season:** April-Oct. **High:** N/A. **On site lodging:** No. **Rental clubs:** Yes. **Walking policy:** N/A. **Metal spikes allowed:** Yes. **Range:** Yes (grass/mats). **To obtain tee times:** Call.

WAYNE COUNTRY CLUB
PU-RR#2, Wayne, 68787, Wayne County, (402)375-1152, 100 miles N of Omaha.
Opened: N/A. **Holes:** 18. **Par:** 72. **Yards:** 6,315. **Course rating:** 70.1/71.4. **Slope:** 113/117. **Architect:** N/A. **Green fee:** $17/$20. **Credit cards:** None. **Reduced fees:** N/A. **Caddies:** No. **Golf carts:** N/A. **Discount golf packages:** No. **Season:** April-Oct. **High:** June-July. **On site lodging:** No. **Rental clubs:** No. **Walking policy:** Unrestricted walking. **Metal spikes allowed:** No. **Range:** No. **To obtain tee times:** N/A.

WILLOW LAKES GOLF COURSE
PU-Bldg. 9950 Offutt AFB, 25th St., Bellevue, 68113, Sarpy County, (402)292-1680, 10 miles S of Omaha.
Opened: 1962. **Holes:** 18. **Par:** 72/72. **Yards:** 6,850/5,504. **Course rating:** 72.8/71.5. **Slope:** 128/125. **Architect:** Robert Trent Jones. **Green fee:** $13/$22. **Credit cards:** MC,VISA. **Reduced fees:** Twilight, seniors. **Caddies:** No. **Golf carts:** $8. **Discount golf packages:** No. **Season:** March-Nov. **High:** May-Aug. **On site lodging:** No. **Rental clubs:** Yes. **Walking policy:** Unrestricted walking. **Metal spikes allowed:** Yes. **Range:**

Yes (Mats). **To obtain tee times:** Call on Tuesday for Saturday play. Call on Wednesday for Sunday play.

★★★½**WOODLAND HILLS GOLF COURSE**
PU-6000 Woodland Hills Dr., Eagle, 68347, Otoe County, (402)475-4653, 12 miles E of Lincoln.
Opened: 1991. **Holes:** 18. **Par:** 71/71. **Yards:** 6,592/4,945. **Course rating:** 72.6/70.3. **Slope:** 132/122. **Architect:** Jeffrey D. Brauer. **Green fee:** $10/$25. **Credit cards:** All major. **Reduced fees:** Weekdays, low season, resort guests, twilight, seniors, juniors. **Caddies:** Yes. **Golf carts:** $10. **Discount golf packages:** Yes. **Season:** Year-round. **High:** July-Aug. **On site lodging:** No. **Rental clubs:** Yes. **Walking policy:** Unrestricted walking. **Metal spikes allowed:** Yes. **Range:** Yes (grass/mats). **To obtain tee times:** Call up to 30 days in advance.
Subscriber comments: Best course in Nebraska...Great layout...Continues to improve...Some long walks from green to tee, but worth it...Unique for Nebraska, difficult but playable for 12-18 handicapper...Great course, natural setting, bent grass.

ANGEL PARK GOLF CLUB
PU-100 S. Rampart Blvd., Las Vegas, 89128, Clark County, (702)254-4653, (888)446-5358.
Opened: 1989. **Architect:** Arnold Palmer and Ed Seay/Bob Cupp. **Green fee:** $50/$90.
Credit cards: MC,VISA,AMEX. **Reduced fees:** Low season, twilight, juniors. **Caddies:**
No. **Golf carts:** Included in Green Fee. **Discount golf packages:** No. **Season:** Year-round. **High:** Feb.-June/Sept.-Nov. **On site lodging:** No. **Rental clubs:** Yes. **Walking policy:** Mandatory cart. **Metal spikes allowed:** Yes. **Range:** Yes (grass/mats). **To obtain tee times:** Call 60 days in advance.
★★★½**MOUNTAIN COURSE**
Holes: 18. **Par:** 71/72. **Yards:** 6,722/5,164. **Course rating:** 72.4/69.9. **Slope:** 128/119.
Subscriber comments: Both courses challenging, Palm Course prettier...Nice greens...12-hole par 3 course is the star of facility...Tight fairways, nice area...Fair course for scoring...Played it lots, never got tired of it...Great escape from casinos.
★★★**PALM COURSE**
Holes: 18. **Par:** 70/70. **Yards:** 6,530/4,570. **Course rating:** 72.6/67.6. **Slope:** 130/110.
Subscriber comments: Challenging, yet very playable...Worth golfing again and again...Nice fairways and greens.
Special Notes: Also an 18-hole putting course and Cloud 9, a 12-hole par-3 course made up of famous par 3s from around the world.

★★★½**THE BADLANDS GOLF CLUB**
PU-9115 Alta Dr., Las Vegas, 89128, Clark County, (702)242-4653.
Opened: 1995. **Holes:** 18. **Architect:** Johnny Miller and Fred Bliss. **Caddies:** No.
Discount golf packages: No. **On site lodging:** No. **Rental clubs:** No. **Metal spikes allowed:** Yes. **Range:** No.
Call club for further information.
Notes: Ranked 10th in 1997 Best in State.
Subscriber comments: Extremely tough target golf, nice layout...Silly course where you are treated like royalty!...Free sleeve of balls because you need it...Outstanding desert course, carts have distance computers...Desert canyons everywhere...Too difficult for high handicaps...Will improve with age.

★★½**BLACK MOUNTAIN GOLF & COUNTRY CLUB**
500 E. Greenway Rd., Henderson, 89015, Clark County, (702)565-7933.
Opened: N/A. **Holes:** 18. **Par:** 72/72. **Yards:** 6,541/5,478. **Course rating:** N/A. **Slope:** 123/125. **Architect:** Bob Baldock. **Green fee:** $52/$57. **Credit cards:** MC,VISA.
Reduced fees: Low season. **Caddies:** No. **Golf carts:** Included in Green Fee.
Discount golf packages: No. **Season:** Year-round. **High:** Jan.-May. **On site lodging:**
No. **Rental clubs:** Yes. **Walking policy:** Walking at certain times. **Metal spikes allowed:** No. **Range:** Yes (grass). **To obtain tee times:** Call 4 days in advance.
Subscriber comments: Great old course...Lots of wildlife, road-runners...Unpredictable winds may blow!

★★★**BOULDER CITY GOLF CLUB**
PM-1 Clubhouse Dr., Boulder City, 89005, Clark County, (702)293-9236, 20 miles S of Las Vegas.
Opened: 1972. **Holes:** 18. **Par:** 72/72. **Yards:** 6,561/5,566. **Course rating:** 70.2/70.7.
Slope: 110/113. **Architect:** Harry Rainville and David Rainville. **Green fee:** $23/$23.
Credit cards: MC,VISA. **Reduced fees:** Low season, twilight. **Caddies:** No. **Golf carts:** $9. **Discount golf packages:** No. **Season:** Year-round. **High:** Spring/Fall. **On site lodging:** No. **Rental clubs:** Yes. **Walking policy:** Unrestricted walking. **Metal spikes allowed:** Yes. **Range:** Yes (grass/mats). **To obtain tee times:** Call 7 days in advance weekdays. Call up to 9 days in advance for weekends.
Subscriber comments: Love it. Fun course...Great summer deals...Recently added lakes, makes course interesting.

★★★½**CALVADA VALLEY GOLF & COUNTRY CLUB**
Red Butte and Mt. Charleston Rd., Pahrump, 89041, Nye County, (702)727-4653, 63 miles NW of Las Vegas.
Opened: 1978. **Holes:** 18. **Par:** 71/73. **Yards:** 7,025/5,948. **Course rating:** 73.2/74.3.
Slope: 124/123. **Architect:** William F. Bell. **Green fee:** $42/$42. **Credit cards:**

MC,VISA. **Reduced fees:** Seniors, juniors. **Caddies:** No. **Golf carts:** Included in Green Fee. **Discount golf packages:** Yes. **Season:** Year-round. **High:** Feb.-May/Sept.-Nov. **On site lodging:** No. **Rental clubs:** Yes. **Walking policy:** Mandatory cart. **Metal spikes allowed:** Yes. **Range:** Yes (grass/mats). **To obtain tee times:** Call 3 days in advance starting at 7 a.m.

★★CRAIG RANCH GOLF COURSE
PU-628 W. Craig Rd., North Las Vegas, 89030, Clark County, (702)642-9700.
Opened: 1962. **Holes:** 18. **Par:** 70/70. **Yards:** 6,001/5,221. **Course rating:** 66.8/67.4. **Slope:** 105/101. **Architect:** John F. Stimson and John C. Stimson. **Green fee:** $15/$15. **Credit cards:** None. **Reduced fees:** N/A. **Caddies:** No. **Golf carts:** $8. **Discount golf packages:** No. **Season:** Year-round. **High:** March-May/Oct.-Nov. **On site lodging:** No. **Rental clubs:** Yes. **Walking policy:** Unrestricted walking. **Metal spikes allowed:** Yes. **Range:** Yes (grass). **To obtain tee times:** Call up to 7 days in advance.

★★★½DAYTON VALLEY COUNTRY CLUB
51 Palmer Dr., Dayton, 89403, Lyon County, (702)246-7888, 35 miles SE of Reno.
Opened: 1991. **Holes:** 18. **Par:** 72/72. **Yards:** 7,218/5,161. **Course rating:** 74.2/68.4. **Slope:** 143/121. **Architect:** Arnold Palmer and Ed Seay. **Green fee:** $25/$70. **Credit cards:** MC,VISA. **Reduced fees:** Weekdays, low season, twilight, juniors. **Caddies:** No. **Golf carts:** Included in Green Fee. **Discount golf packages:** No. **Season:** Year-round. **High:** May-Oct. **On site lodging:** No. **Rental clubs:** Yes. **Walking policy:** Unrestricted walking. **Metal spikes allowed:** Yes. **Range:** Yes (grass). **To obtain tee times:** Call 14 days in advance.
Notes: Ranked 7th in 1997 Best in State.
Subscriber comments: Made you feel welcome...Good layout, enjoyable place to play...Remote location but worth the drive, lots of wind...A challenge to your golf game...I'll go back...Different tees change difficulty...Palmer-designed course playing into the teeth of the "Washoe Zephyr"...A real challenge at 16-17-18...For players of all abilities...Lots of water, gets windy at midday.

★★★½DESERT INN GOLF CLUB
R-3145 Las Vegas Blvd. S., Las Vegas, 89109, Clark County, (702)733-4290, (800)634-6909.
Opened: 1952. **Holes:** 18. **Par:** 72/72. **Yards:** 7,066/5,791. **Course rating:** 73.9/72.7. **Slope:** 124/121. **Architect:** Lawrence Hughes. **Green fee:** $120/$215. **Credit cards:** All major. **Reduced fees:** Low season, resort guests. **Caddies:** No. **Golf carts:** Included in Green Fee. **Discount golf packages:** No. **Season:** Year-round. **High:** Feb.-May. **On site lodging:** Yes. **Rental clubs:** Yes. **Walking policy:** Mandatory cart. **Metal spikes allowed:** Yes. **Range:** Yes (grass). **To obtain tee times:** Call.
Notes: Ranked 9th in 1997 Best in State.
Subscriber comments: Must win lottery to play...What Las Vegas golf is all about, great course...For "high rollers" wanting to avoid crowd...Good greens, carts computerized, nice gimmick.

DESERT LAKES GOLF COURSE
PU-4000 Farm District Rd., Fernley, 89408, (702)575-4653, 35 miles E of Reno.
Opened: 1996. **Holes:** 18. **Par:** 71/71. **Yards:** 6,507/5,197. **Course rating:** 69.9/68.3. **Slope:** 124. **Architect:** N/A. **Green fee:** $20/$30. **Credit cards:** MC,VISA. **Reduced fees:** Weekdays, low season, twilight, seniors, juniors. **Caddies:** No. **Golf carts:** Included in Green Fee. **Discount golf packages:** No. **Season:** Year-round. **High:** N/A. **On site lodging:** No. **Rental clubs:** Yes. **Walking policy:** Unrestricted walking. **Metal spikes allowed:** Yes. **Range:** Yes (grass). **To obtain tee times:** Call 7 days in advance.

DESERT PINES GOLF CLUB
PU-3415 E. Bonanza, Las Vegas, 89101, Clark County, (702)388-4400.
Opened: 1996. **Holes:** 18. **Par:** 71/71. **Yards:** 6,810/5,873. **Course rating:** N/A. **Slope:** N/A. **Architect:** Perry Dye. **Green fee:** $70/$129. **Credit cards:** MC,VISA,AMEX. **Reduced fees:** Weekdays, low season, twilight, juniors. **Caddies:** No. **Golf carts:** Included in Green Fee. **Discount golf packages:** No. **Season:** Year-round. **High:** Sept.-May. **On site lodging:** No. **Rental clubs:** Yes. **Walking policy:** Mandatory cart. **Metal spikes allowed:** No. **Range:** Yes (mats). **To obtain tee times:** Call golf shop.

★★DESERT ROSE GOLF COURSE
PU-5483 Clubhouse Dr., Las Vegas, 89122, Clark County, (702)431-4653, 6 miles E of Las Vegas.
Opened: 1962. **Holes:** 18. **Par:** 71/71. **Yards:** 6,511/5,458. **Course rating:** 70.7/69.6.
Slope: 112/107. **Architect:** Dick Wilson/Jeff Brauer. **Green fee:** $51/$75. **Credit cards:** All major. **Reduced fees:** Low season, twilight, seniors, juniors. **Caddies:** No. **Golf carts:** Included in Green Fee. **Discount golf packages:** No. **Season:** Year-round.
High: Sept.-June. **On site lodging:** No. **Rental clubs:** Yes. **Walking policy:** Unrestricted walking. **Metal spikes allowed:** Yes. **Range:** Yes (grass/mats). **To obtain tee times:** Call 7 days in advance for weekdays, and 3 days in advance for weekend play.

EAGLE VALLEY GOLF CLUB
PM-3999 Centennial Park Dr., Carson City, 89706, Carson County, (702)887-2380, 30 miles S of Reno. **Architect:** Homer Flint. **Credit cards:** None. **Reduced fees:** Twilight. **Caddies:** No. **Discount golf packages:** No. **Season:** Year-round. **High:** May-Sept. **On site lodging:** No. **Rental clubs:** Yes. **Metal spikes allowed:** Yes. **To obtain tee times:** Call Friday at 3 p.m. for the following Monday through Sunday.

★★½EAST COURSE
Opened: 1987. **Holes:** 18. **Par:** 72/72. **Yards:** 6,658/5,980. **Course rating:** 68.7/72.5.
Slope: 117/127. **Green fee:** $21/$21. **Golf carts:** $18. **Walking policy:** Unrestricted walking. **Range:** Yes (grass/mats).
Subscriber comments: Wide open fairways...Sagebrush rough, but fairly open, good course...Okay if you can play with 30-35 mph winds...We call it ego valley, plays easy.

★★★WEST COURSE
Opened: 1987. **Holes:** 18. **Par:** 72/72. **Yards:** 6,851/5,293. **Course rating:** 73.5/68.8.
Slope: 131/117. **Green fee:** $26/$37. **Golf carts:** $18. **Walking policy:** Mandatory cart. **Range:** Yes (grass/mats).
Subscriber comments: Tough, fair, fun, don't miss it...Course is much too hard for senior women...Fun track...Nice desert course, some tricky holes...Sagebrush and rattlesnakes, target course...West course is superb.

★★★★½EDGEWOOD TAHOE GOLF COURSE
PU-U.S. Hwy. 50 and Lake Pky., Stateline, 89449, Douglas County, (702)588-3566, 50 miles SW of Reno.
Opened: 1968. **Holes:** 18. **Par:** 72/72. **Yards:** 7,491/5,749. **Course rating:** 75.1/71.5. **Slope:** 136/130. **Architect:** George Fazio. **Green fee:** $150/$150. **Credit cards:** MC,VISA,AMEX. **Reduced fees:** N/A.
Caddies: Yes. **Golf carts:** Included in Green Fee. **Discount golf packages:** No.
Season: May-Oct. **High:** July-Sept. **On site lodging:** No. **Rental clubs:** Yes. **Walking policy:** Unrestricted walking. **Metal spikes allowed:** Yes. **Range:** Yes (grass/mats). **To obtain tee times:** Call 90 days in advance. There is a $25 booking fee per player.
Notes: Ranked 2nd in 1997 Best in State. 1985 Senior Open; 1982 Public Links Championship.
Subscriber comments: Hard to score on this course...Play it in the morning before the wind...Long with large greens...Must play at least once...16th hole tee shot: bunker left and right, tree in center. Where are you supposed to hit it?...Great course and scenery is outstanding...Best golf course at Lake Tahoe by far...How is this not in the Top 100?

★★★EMERALD RIVER GOLF COURSE
PU-1155 W. Casino Dr., Laughlin, 89029, Clark County, (702)298-0061, 90 miles S of Las Vegas.
Opened: 1990. **Holes:** 18. **Par:** 72/72. **Yards:** 6,572/5,230. **Course rating:** 73.6/71.3.
Slope: 144/129. **Architect:** Tom Clark. **Green fee:** $40/$75. **Credit cards:** All major.
Reduced fees: Weekdays, low season, resort guests, twilight, seniors. **Caddies:** No.
Golf carts: Included in Green Fee. **Discount golf packages:** Yes. **Season:** Year-round.
High: Jan.-May/Oct.-Nov. **On site lodging:** No. **Rental clubs:** Yes. **Walking policy:** Mandatory cart. **Metal spikes allowed:** Yes. **Range:** Yes (grass). **To obtain tee times:** Call up to 30 days in advance.
Subscriber comments: A true test of golf from the tips and in the wind...Very demanding...Beautiful fairways parallelling Colorado River...Tough course. Bring your A game...Challenges you at every hole...Take a lot of balls, you'll need them.

EMPIRE RANCH GOLF COURSE
PU-1875 Fairway Dr., Carson City, Carson County, (702)885-2100, 3 miles E of Carson City.
Opened: 1997. **Holes:** 27. **Architect:** Cary Bickler. **Green fee:** $20/$35. **Credit cards:** MC,VISA. **Reduced fees:** Low season, twilight, seniors, juniors. **Caddies:** No. **Golf carts:** $10. **Discount golf packages:** No. **Season:** Year-round. **High:** April-Oct. **On site lodging:** No. **Rental clubs:** Yes. **Walking policy:** Walking at certain times. **Metal spikes allowed:** No. **Range:** Yes (grass). **To obtain tee times:** Call up to 7 days in advance.
BLUE/RED
Par: 72/72. **Yards:** 6,710/5,554. **Course rating:** 70.5/71.0. **Slope:** 127/128.
BLUE/YELLOW
Par: 72/72. **Yards:** 6,956/5,611. **Course rating:** 71.6/71.4. **Slope:** 129/129.
RED/YELLOW
Par: 72/72. **Yards:** 6,896/5,605. **Course rating:** 71.3/71.4. **Slope:** 128/129.

★★★½THE GOLF CLUB AT GENOA LAKES
PU-1 Genoa Lakes Dr., Genoa, 89411, Douglas County, (702)782-4653, 15 miles NE of So. Lake Tahoe.
Opened: 1993. **Holes:** 18. **Par:** 72/72. **Yards:** 7,263/5,008. **Course rating:** 73.5/67.6. **Slope:** 134/117. **Architect:** John Harbottle and Peter Jacobsen. **Green fee:** $40/$90. **Credit cards:** MC,VISA,AMEX. **Reduced fees:** Weekdays, low season, twilight, juniors. **Caddies:** No. **Golf carts:** Included in Green Fee. **Discount golf packages:** Yes. **Season:** Year-round. **High:** July-Sept. **On site lodging:** No. **Rental clubs:** Yes. **Walking policy:** Unrestricted walking. **Metal spikes allowed:** No. **Range:** Yes (grass). **To obtain tee times:** Call up to 30 days in advance.
Notes: Ranked 4th in 1997 Best in State.
Subscriber comments: Beautiful valley, great view of the mountains, loved the course...New clubhouse. Very long and windy...Some long carries...Great design....Lots of wildlife, my favorite...Quality course with a lot of trouble...Tough but fun.

★★★½INCLINE VILLAGE GOLF RESORT
R-955 Fairway Blvd., Incline Village, 89452, Washoe County, (702)832-1144, 30 miles SW of Reno.
Opened: 1964. **Holes:** 18. **Par:** 72/72. **Yards:** 6,915/5,350. **Course rating:** 72.6/70.5. **Slope:** 129/126. **Architect:** Robert Trent Jones. **Green fee:** $90/$115. **Credit cards:** MC,VISA. **Reduced fees:** Low season, twilight. **Caddies:** No. **Golf carts:** Included in Green Fee. **Discount golf packages:** No. **Season:** May-Oct. **High:** June-Sept. **On site lodging:** No. **Rental clubs:** Yes. **Walking policy:** Unrestricted walking. **Metal spikes allowed:** Yes. **Range:** Yes (mats). **To obtain tee times:** Call 14 days in advance.
Subscriber comments: Must play! Guests treated like pros...Great views. Beware of summer afternoon thunderstorms...Challenging course, but you can score...Creek meanders through course...Great vistas. Tough greens...Love playing here.
Special Notes: Also has 18-hole par-58 executive course.

★★½JACKPOT GOLF CLUB
R-P.O. Box 370, Jackpot, 89825, Elko County, (702)755-2260, 165 miles S of Boise, ID.
Opened: 1970. **Holes:** 18. **Par:** 72/72. **Yards:** 6,875/5,549. **Course rating:** 69.2/70.0. **Slope:** 107/109. **Architect:** Robert Muir Graves. **Green fee:** $15/$18. **Credit cards:** MC,VISA,DISC. **Reduced fees:** Weekdays, juniors. **Caddies:** No. **Golf carts:** $10. **Discount golf packages:** Yes. **Season:** March-Nov. **High:** May-Sept. **On site lodging:** No. **Rental clubs:** Yes. **Walking policy:** Walking at certain times. **Metal spikes allowed:** Yes. **Range:** Yes (grass). **To obtain tee times:** Call anytime in advance.
Subscriber comments: Hilly; lots of blind shots, doglegs, sand...Good challenging course for average golfer...Appears simple but one of the most challenging.

★★★½LAKERIDGE GOLF COURSE
PU-1200 Razorback Rd., Reno, 89509, Washoe County, (702)825-2200.
Opened: 1969. **Holes:** 18. **Par:** 71/71. **Yards:** 6,703/5,159. **Course rating:** 70.8/68.5. **Slope:** 127/117. **Architect:** Robert Trent Jones. **Green fee:** $41/$70. **Credit cards:** MC,VISA. **Reduced fees:** Low season, twilight. **Caddies:** No. **Golf carts:** Included in Green Fee. **Discount golf packages:** No. **Season:** March-Dec. **High:** April-Oct. **On

site lodging: No. **Rental clubs:** Yes. **Walking policy:** Walking at certain times. **Metal spikes allowed:** Yes. **Range:** Yes (Mats). **To obtain tee times:** Call 7 days in advance.

Subscriber comments: Good course, rewards good shots...Lots of personality...Great holes, fun, par 3 15th island green awesome...Good test, particularly in the wind...Play it every time I'm in town...Best view of Reno from signature hole.

★★½LAS VEGAS GOLF CLUB

PU-4300 W. Washington, Las Vegas, 89107, Clark County, (702)646-3003.
Opened: 1947. **Holes:** 18. **Par:** 72/72. **Yards:** 6,631/5,715. **Course rating:** 71.8/71.2. **Slope:** 117/113. **Architect:** William P. Bell. **Green fee:** $16/$16. **Credit cards:** MC,VISA,AMEX. **Reduced fees:** Twilight, seniors, juniors. **Caddies:** No. **Golf carts:** $18. **Discount golf packages:** No. **Season:** Year-round. **High:** Feb.-May. **On site lodging:** No. **Rental clubs:** Yes. **Walking policy:** Unrestricted walking. **Metal spikes allowed:** Yes. **Range:** Yes (grass/mats). **To obtain tee times:** Call up to 7 days in advance.

Subscriber comments: Easy access, good golf!...Fun course...Generous fairways, good maintenance. Fair greens...Safest bet in Las Vegas if there is such a thing.

★★★½LAS VEGAS HILTON COUNTRY CLUB

R-1911 E. Desert Inn Rd., Las Vegas, 89109, Clark County, (702)734-1796, (800)468-7918.
Opened: 1961. **Holes:** 18. **Par:** 71/71. **Yards:** 6,815/5,741. **Course rating:** 72.1/72.9. **Slope:** 130/127. **Architect:** Bert Stamps. **Green fee:** $100/$175. **Credit cards:** MC,VISA,AMEX. **Reduced fees:** Weekdays, low season, resort guests, twilight, juniors. **Caddies:** No. **Golf carts:** Included in Green Fee. **Discount golf packages:** No. **Season:** Year-round. **High:** Feb.-May. **On site lodging:** No. **Rental clubs:** Yes. **Walking policy:** Mandatory cart. **Metal spikes allowed:** No. **Range:** Yes (grass/mats). **To obtain tee times:** Call American Golf Corporations Resort time office up to 60 days in advance with credit card to guarantee.
Notes: 1994-96 Las Vegas Invitational.
Subscriber comments: Computerized cart is a plus...Great classic layout!
Special Notes: Formerly Sahara Country Club.

LAS VEGAS PAIUTE RESORT

PU-10325 Nu-Wav Kaiv Blvd., Las Vegas, 89124, Clark County, (702)658-1400, (800)711-2833.
Opened: 1995. **Architect:** Pete Dye and Brian Curley. **Credit cards:** All major. **Caddies:** No. **Golf carts:** Included in Green Fee. **Discount golf packages:** No. **Season:** Year-round. **High:** Spring/Fall. **On site lodging:** No. **Rental clubs:** Yes. **Walking policy:** Mandatory cart. **Metal spikes allowed:** Yes. **Range:** Yes (grass). **To obtain tee times:** Call up to 60 days in advance with credit card to guarantee.

★★★★NU-WAV KAIV COURSE

Holes: 18. **Par:** 72/72. **Yards:** 7,158/5,341. **Course rating:** 73.9/70.4. **Slope:** 125/117.
Green fee: $65/$110. **Reduced fees:** Weekdays, low season, twilight.
Notes: Ranked 8th in 1997 Best in State.
Subscriber comments: One of the best secrets in Vegas...Excellent layout, in the middle of nowhere...Very picturesque...They clean your clubs and take them to your car too...A jewel in the desert...Don't take the cover off your putter, fastest greens in the west...Tough even with open fairways due to wind.

TAV-AI KAIV COURSE

Holes: 18. **Par:** 72/72. **Yards:** 7,112/5,465. **Course rating:** 73.3/71.0. **Slope:** 130/123.
Green fee: $60/$110. **Reduced fees:** Low season, twilight.
Special Notes: Spikeless shoes preferred.

★★★THE LEGACY GOLF CLUB

PU-130 Par Excellence Dr., Henderson, 89014, Clark County, (702)897-2187, 10 miles SE of Las Vegas.
Opened: 1989. **Holes:** 18. **Par:** 72/72. **Yards:** 7,233/5,340. **Course rating:** 74.9/71.0. **Slope:** 136/120. **Architect:** Arthur Hills. **Green fee:** $125. **Credit cards:** MC,VISA,AMEX. **Reduced fees:** Twilight. **Caddies:** No. **Golf carts:** Included in Green Fee. **Discount golf packages:** No. **Season:** Year-round. **High:** Sept.-June. **On site lodging:** No. **Rental clubs:** Yes. **Walking policy:** Mandatory cart. **Metal spikes**

allowed: Yes. **Range:** Yes (grass/mats). **To obtain tee times:** Tee times can be made with a credit card to guarantee.
Subscriber comments: Great course, chipmunks will rob you blind though...Good practice facility...Long and tough layout...A bright new star...Long drive from strip...One of best I've ever played...Lots of water, nice fast greens.

THE LINKS AT MONTELAGO

R-1605 Lake Las Vegas Pkwy., Henderson, 89011, Clark County, (702)558-0022, 17 miles E of Las Vegas.
Opened: 1998. **Holes:** 18. **Par:** 72/72. **Yards:** 7,202/5,189. **Course rating:** N/A. **Slope:** N/A. **Architect:** N/A. **Green fee:** N/A. **Credit cards:** MC,VISA,AMEX. **Reduced fees:** N/A. **Caddies:** No. **Golf carts:** N/A. **Discount golf packages:** No. **Season:** Year-round. **High:** Oct.-May. **On site lodging:** Yes. **Rental clubs:** Yes. **Walking policy:** Walking at certain times. **Metal spikes allowed:** No. **Range:** Yes (grass). **To obtain tee times:** Call.
Special notes: Formerly Lake Las Vegas Resort.

★★★ NORTHGATE GOLF COURSE

PU-1111 Clubhouse Dr., Reno, 89523, Washoe County, (702)747-7577, 5 miles NW of Reno.
Opened: 1988. **Holes:** 18. **Par:** 72/72. **Yards:** 6,966/5,521. **Course rating:** 72.3/70.2. **Slope:** 131/127. **Architect:** Benz Poellot. **Green fee:** $29/$46. **Credit cards:** MC,VISA. **Reduced fees:** Weekdays, low season, resort guests, twilight. **Caddies:** No. **Golf carts:** Included in Green Fee. **Discount golf packages:** No. **Season:** Year-round. **High:** June-Sept. **On site lodging:** No. **Rental clubs:** Yes. **Walking policy:** Unrestricted walking. **Metal spikes allowed:** Yes. **Range:** Yes (grass/mats). **To obtain tee times:** Call 7 days in advance.
Subscriber comments: Hilly but fun...Sagebrush instead of heather. A great course...Target golf...Wind can be brutal...Great links golf, challenging.

OASIS RESORT HOTEL CASINO

R- **Credit cards:** All major. **Caddies:** No. **Golf carts:** Included in Green Fee. **Discount golf packages:** Yes. **Season:** Year-round. **High:** Jan.-May/Oct.-Nov. **On site lodging:** Yes. **Rental clubs:** Yes. **Walking policy:** Mandatory cart. **Metal spikes allowed:** Yes. **Range:** Yes (grass/mats).

★★★★ OASIS GOLF COURSE

851 Oasis Blvd., Mesquite, 89024, Clark County, (702)346-7820, (800)621-0187, 77 miles NE of Las Vegas.
Opened: 1995. **Holes:** 18. **Par:** 72. **Yards:** 6,982. **Course rating:** N/A. **Slope:** N/A. **Architect:** Arnold Palmer and Ed Seay. **Green fee:** $125/$125. **Reduced fees:** Low season, resort guests, twilight. **To obtain tee times:** Call up to 60 days in advance.
Notes: Ranked 6th in 1997 Best in State; 5th in 1995 Best New Resort Courses.
Subscriber comments: Good course. Lots of elevated tees...Great views and box canyon holes, awesome!...Greens like glass...Good desert course...Could play here every day...Arnie truly did a dandy!

★★★½ PALMS GOLF COURSE

2200 Hillside Dr., Mesquite, 89024, Clark County, (702)346-5232, (800)346-0187, 77 miles NE of Las Vegas.
Opened: 1989. **Holes:** 18. **Par:** 72/72. **Yards:** 7,008/6,284. **Course rating:** 74.9/70.4. **Slope:** 137/122. **Architect:** William Hull. **Green fee:** $65/$85. **Reduced fees:** Weekdays, low season, resort guests, twilight. **To obtain tee times:** Call up to 28 days in advance.
Subscriber comments: Big difference front to back...Back nine worth the trip...Loved it...Breathtaking canyon course, very unique.
Special Notes: Formerly Peppermill Palms Golf Club.

★★★ PAINTED DESERT GOLF CLUB

PU-5555 Painted Mirage Way, Las Vegas, 89129, Clark County, (702)645-2568.
Opened: 1987. **Holes:** 18. **Par:** 72/72. **Yards:** 6,840/5,711. **Course rating:** 73.7/72.7. **Slope:** 136/120. **Architect:** Jay Morrish. **Green fee:** $99/$117. **Credit cards:** MC,VISA,AMEX. **Reduced fees:** Weekdays, low season, resort guests, twilight, juniors. **Caddies:** No. **Golf carts:** Included in Green Fee. **Discount golf packages:** No. **Season:** Year-round. **High:** Sept.-June. **On site lodging:** No. **Rental clubs:** Yes.

Walking policy: Mandatory cart. **Metal spikes allowed:** Yes. **Range:** Yes (grass/mats). **To obtain tee times:** Call 7 days in advance.
Subscriber comments: Tough with long carries...Better not spray the ball...Tight driving course...In Vegas but feels like Arizona...Wind makes this course very tough.

★★★ROSEWOOD LAKES GOLF COURSE

PU-6800 Pembroke Dr., Reno, 89502, Washoe County, (702)857-2892.
Opened: 1991. **Holes:** 18. **Par:** 72/72. **Yards:** 6,693/5,082. **Course rating:** 71.1/68.2. **Slope:** 127/117. **Architect:** Bradford Benz. **Green fee:** $14/$22. **Credit cards:** MC,VISA. **Reduced fees:** Low season, twilight, seniors, juniors. **Caddies:** No. **Golf carts:** $22. **Discount golf packages:** No. **Season:** Year-round. **High:** April-Nov. **On site lodging:** No. **Rental clubs:** Yes. **Walking policy:** Unrestricted walking. **Metal spikes allowed:** Yes. **Range:** Yes (grass). **To obtain tee times:** Call 7 days in advance for weekdays and Monday prior for weekends.
Subscriber comments: Beautiful, great service...Surcharge to out-of-state players...Difficult to play first time...Target golf with lots of danger. Neat...Challenging, interesting holes...Bring extra balls.

★★★RUBY VIEW GOLF COURSE

PM-2100 Ruby View Dr., Elko, 89801, Elko County, (702)777-7277.
Opened: 1967. **Holes:** 18. **Par:** 72/72. **Yards:** 6,928/5,958. **Course rating:** 70.5/72.5. **Slope:** 118/123. **Architect:** Jack Snyder. **Green fee:** $18/$18. **Credit cards:** None. **Reduced fees:** Twilight. **Caddies:** No. **Golf carts:** $20. **Discount golf packages:** No. **Season:** March-Nov. **High:** June-Aug. **On site lodging:** No. **Rental clubs:** Yes. **Walking policy:** Unrestricted walking. **Metal spikes allowed:** No. **Range:** Yes (grass). **To obtain tee times:** Call 7 days in advance.
Subscriber comments: Good course, lush fairways...Outstanding for this country desert.

★★SIERRA SAGE GOLF COURSE

PM-6355 Silverlake Rd., Reno, 89506, Washoe County, (702)972-1564.
Opened: 1963. **Holes:** 18. **Par:** 71/72. **Yards:** 6,650/5,573. **Course rating:** 69.3/69.6. **Slope:** 120/113. **Architect:** N/A. **Green fee:** $17/$23. **Credit cards:** MC,VISA. **Reduced fees:** Weekdays, low season, twilight, seniors, juniors. **Caddies:** No. **Golf carts:** $20. **Discount golf packages:** No. **Season:** Year-round. **High:** May-Oct. **On site lodging:** No. **Rental clubs:** Yes. **Walking policy:** Unrestricted walking. **Metal spikes allowed:** Yes. **Range:** Yes (grass/mats). **To obtain tee times:** Call on Monday for upcoming weekend. Call on Tuesday at 7 a.m. for holidays. Call 7 days in advance.

SPRING CREEK GOLF COURSE

PU-431 E. Spring Creek Pkwy., Elko, 89801, Elko County, (702)753-6331.
Holes: 18. **Par:** 71/71. **Yards:** 6,258/5,658. **Slope:** 125/119. **Green fee:** $14/$16. **Credit cards:** MC,VISA. **Caddies:** No. **Discount golf packages:** Yes. **Season:** March-Nov. **High:** June-Aug. **On site lodging:** No. **Rental clubs:** No. **Metal spikes allowed:** No. **Range:** Yes (grass/mats). **To obtain tee times:** Call.
Call club for further information.

SUN CITY LAS VEGAS GOLF CLUB

Opened: 1989. **Architect:** Billy Casper/Greg Nash. **Green fee:** $35/$95. **Credit cards:** MC,VISA,AMEX. **Caddies:** No. **Golf carts:** Included in Green Fee. **Discount golf packages:** No. **Season:** Year-round. **High:** Oct.-May. **On site lodging:** No. **Rental clubs:** Yes. **Walking policy:** Mandatory cart. **Metal spikes allowed:** Yes. **Range:** Yes (grass/mats). **To obtain tee times:** Call 7 days in advance for weekends. Call up to 3 days in advance after 3 p.m. for weekdays.

HIGHLAND FALLS COURSE
10201 Sun City Blvd., Las Vegas, 89134, Clark County, (702)254-7010.
Holes: 18. **Par:** 72/72. **Yards:** 6,512/5,099. **Course rating:** 71.2/68.8. **Slope:** 126/110. **Reduced fees:** Weekdays, low season, twilight, juniors.

PALM VALLEY COURSE
9201-B Del Webb Blvd., Las Vegas, 89134, Clark County, (702)254-7010.
Holes: 18. **Par:** 72/72. **Yards:** 6,849/5,502. **Course rating:** 72.3/71.5. **Slope:** 127/124. **Reduced fees:** Weekdays, low season, juniors.

★★★½SUNRISE VISTA GOLF CLUB
PU-2841 Kinley Dr., Nellis AFB, 89191, Clark County, (702)652-2602, 12 miles N of Las Vegas.
Opened: 1962. **Architect:** Ted Robinson. **Green fee:** $35. **Credit cards:** MC,VISA. **Reduced fees:** N/A. **Caddies:** No. **Golf carts:** $16. **Discount golf packages:** No. **Season:** Year-round. **High:** Sept.-April. **On site lodging:** No. **Rental clubs:** Yes. **Walking policy:** Unrestricted walking. **Metal spikes allowed:** Yes. **Range:** Yes (grass/mats). **To obtain tee times:** Public call day of play. Military call up to 3 days in advance.
EAGLE/FALCON
Holes: 27. **Par:** 72/72. **Yards:** 7,200/5,380. **Course rating:** 73.8. **Slope:** 127.
PHANTOM/EAGLE
Holes: 27. **Par:** 72/72. **Yards:** 7,102/5,460. **Course rating:** 72.3/69.1. **Slope:** 119/109.
PHANTOM/FALCON
Holes: 27. **Par:** 72/72. **Yards:** 6,950/5,370. **Course rating:** 71.8. **Slope:** 119.
Subscriber comments: Who said the military couldn't get it right! They did!...New nine adds a lot, easy walk.

★★★½TOANA VISTA GOLF COURSE
PU-2319 Pueblo Blvd., Wendover, 89883, Elko County, (702)664-4300, (800)352-4330, 110 miles E of Elko.
Opened: 1986. **Holes:** 18. **Par:** 72/72. **Yards:** 6,911/5,220. **Course rating:** 72.6/71.0. **Slope:** 124/124. **Architect:** Homer Flint. **Green fee:** $30/$35. **Credit cards:** MC,VISA. **Reduced fees:** Juniors. **Caddies:** No. **Golf carts:** Included in Green Fee. **Discount golf packages:** Yes. **Season:** Feb.-Nov. **High:** April-Sept. **On site lodging:** No. **Rental clubs:** Yes. **Walking policy:** Mandatory cart. **Metal spikes allowed:** Yes. **Range:** Yes (grass/mats). **To obtain tee times:** Call 14 days in advance.
Subscriber comments: Narrow desert course...Tight fariways, undulating greens...Stop here! Play this one. You won't be sorry...Rattlesnakes!...A favorite, well kept, target golf.

(GOOD VALUE)

★★★★TOURNAMENT PLAYERS CLUB AT THE CANYONS
PU-9851 Canyon Run Dr., Las Vegas, 89134, Clark County, (702)256-2000.
Opened: 1996. **Holes:** 18. **Par:** 71/71. **Yards:** 7,063/5,039. **Course rating:** 73.0/67.0. **Slope:** 131/109. **Architect:** Bobby Weed. **Green fee:** $40/$110. **Credit cards:** MC,VISA,AMEX,Diners Club. **Reduced fees:** Low season, juniors. **Caddies:** No. **Golf carts:** $20. **Discount golf packages:** No. **Season:** Year-round. **High:** Sept.-May. **On site lodging:** No. **Rental clubs:** Yes. **Walking policy:** Walking at certain times. **Metal spikes allowed:** Yes. **Range:** Yes (grass). **To obtain tee times:** N/A.
Subscriber comments: Bring your "A" game to the back nine...Nice course, will be even better when it matures...Best ever, kicked my butt and I enjoyed it. Awesome!!...Played on a windy day. Should have stayed home...Tough layout makes you appreciate the pros.

(GREAT SERVICE)

★★WASHOE COUNTY GOLF CLUB
PM-2601 S. Arlington, Reno, 89509, Washoe County, (702)828-6640.
Opened: 1948. **Holes:** 18. **Par:** 72/74. **Yards:** 6,695/5,863. **Course rating:** 70.0/72.9. **Slope:** 119/122. **Architect:** WPA. **Green fee:** $15/$20. **Credit cards:** None. **Reduced fees:** Low season, twilight, seniors, juniors. **Caddies:** No. **Golf carts:** N/A. **Discount golf packages:** No. **Season:** Year-round. **High:** April-Oct. **On site lodging:** No. **Rental clubs:** Yes. **Walking policy:** Unrestricted walking. **Metal spikes allowed:** Yes. **Range:** Yes. **To obtain tee times:** Call one week in advance.

★★★WILD HORSE GOLF CLUB
R-2100 Warm Springs Rd., Henderson, 89014, Clark County, (702)434-9000, (800)468-7918, 8 miles SE of Las Vegas.
Opened: 1992. **Holes:** 18. **Par:** 72/72. **Yards:** 7,053/5,372. **Course rating:** 75.2/71.3. **Slope:** 135/125. **Architect:** Robert Cupp and Hubert Green. **Green fee:** $95/$110. **Credit cards:** MC,VISA,AMEX. **Reduced fees:** Low season, twilight, juniors. **Caddies:**

No. **Golf carts:** Included in Green Fee. **Discount golf packages:** No. **Season:** Year-round. **High:** Oct.-May. **On site lodging:** No. **Rental clubs:** Yes. **Walking policy:** Mandatory cart. **Metal spikes allowed:** Yes. **Range:** Yes (grass/mats). **To obtain tee times:** Call 800 number up to 60 days in advance. Golf shop will book 7 days in advance.
Subscriber comments: Tough greens...Seems wide open in comparison to desert courses in area...Dry, windy, very tough greens, hard to read...Tee-shot placement a key to good scoring here...Fun course.
Special Notes: Formerly Royal Kenfield Golf Club.

★★★WILDCREEK GOLF COURSE
PU-3500 Sullivan Lane, Sparks, 89431, Washoe County, (702)673-3100, 1 miles N of Reno.
Opened: 1978. **Holes:** 18. **Par:** 72/72. **Yards:** 6,932/5,472. **Course rating:** 73.0/70.5. **Slope:** 133/120. **Architect:** Benz/Phelps. **Green fee:** $28/$48. **Credit cards:** MC,VISA. **Reduced fees:** Low season, twilight. **Caddies:** No. **Golf carts:** Included in Green Fee. **Discount golf packages:** Yes. **Season:** Feb.-Dec. **High:** April-Oct. **On site lodging:** No. **Rental clubs:** Yes. **Walking policy:** Walking at certain times. **Metal spikes allowed:** Yes. **Range:** Yes (grass/mats). **To obtain tee times:** Call 7 days in advance.
Notes: 1983-85 Senior Tour event.
Subscriber comments: A good course, a good challenge...Short, but target golf...Beautiful views of Reno...Nice way to spend the day in Reno area...Nice layout. Variety of shots...Slanted fairways hard to hold.

★★★AMHERST COUNTRY CLUB

PU-76 Ponemah Rd., Amherst, 03031, Hillsborough County, (603)673-9908, 10 miles NW of Nashua.

Opened: 1965. **Holes:** 18. **Par:** 72/74. **Yards:** 6,520/5,532. **Course rating:** 71.0/74.2. **Slope:** 123/129. **Architect:** William F. Mitchell. **Green fee:** $22/$29. **Credit cards:** MC,VISA. **Reduced fees:** Weekdays, seniors. **Caddies:** No. **Golf carts:** $12. **Discount golf packages:** No. **Season:** March-Dec. **High:** May-Oct. **On site lodging:** No. **Rental clubs:** Yes. **Walking policy:** Unrestricted walking. **Metal spikes allowed:** Yes. **Range:** No. **To obtain tee times:** Call three days in advance.

Subscriber comments: Calls for creative shotmaking...Good pace of play...Flat and relatively easy...A great course on which to score well...Too many geese...Great bunkers, big soft greens.

★★★½THE BALSAMS GRAND RESORT HOTEL

R-Rte. 26, Dixville Notch, 03576, Coos County, (603)255-4961, 110 miles NE of Portland, Maine.

Opened: 1912. **Holes:** 18. **Par:** 72/72. **Yards:** 6,804/5,069. **Course rating:** 73.9/69.9. **Slope:** 136/115. **Architect:** Donald Ross. **Green fee:** $50/$60. **Credit cards:** All major. **Reduced fees:** Resort guests.

Caddies: No. **Golf carts:** $16. **Discount golf packages:** Yes. **Season:** May-Oct. **High:** July-Aug. **On site lodging:** Yes. **Rental clubs:** Yes. **Walking policy:** Unrestricted walking. **Metal spikes allowed:** Yes. **Range:** Yes (grass/mats). **To obtain tee times:** Hotel guests call up to 7 days in advance all others up to 3 days.

Notes: Ranked 1st in 1997 Best in State.

Subscriber comments: Spectacular course...Top-shelf people and service...Unfortunately too short a season, great food...Played in May, lots of black flies...Beautiful surroundings, service bounds on pampering...First-rate course...A classic Ross design...A long drive, but worth it...Bring a camera and play at peak foliage.

★★½BEAVER MEADOW GOLF CLUB

PU-1 Beaver Meadow Dr., Concord, 03301, Merrimack County, (603)228-8954.

Opened: 1896. **Holes:** 18. **Par:** 72/72. **Yards:** 6,356/5,519. **Course rating:** 70.0/71.8. **Slope:** 121/123. **Architect:** Geoffrey Cornish. **Green fee:** $15/$25. **Credit cards:** None. **Reduced fees:** Weekdays, low season, twilight, seniors, juniors. **Caddies:** No. **Golf carts:** N/A. **Discount golf packages:** No. **Season:** April-Nov. **High:** May-Sept. **On site lodging:** No. **Rental clubs:** Yes. **Walking policy:** Unrestricted walking. **Metal spikes allowed:** Yes. **Range:** Yes. **To obtain tee times:** Call two days in advance.

Subscriber comments: Back nine is really good...Use all of your arsenal...Great municipal course...Nice outdoor patio...What a view!...A fun track.

★★BETHLEHEM COUNTRY CLUB

PM-1901 Main St., Rte. 302, Bethlehem, 03574, Grafton County, (603)869-5745, 80 miles N of Manchester.

Opened: 1898. **Holes:** 18. **Par:** 70/70. **Yards:** 5,808/5,008. **Course rating:** 68.2/67.8. **Slope:** 114/109. **Architect:** Donald Ross. **Green fee:** $20/$24. **Credit cards:** MC,VISA. **Reduced fees:** Weekdays, resort guests, twilight, seniors, juniors. **Caddies:** No. **Golf carts:** $12. **Discount golf packages:** Yes. **Season:** May-Oct. **High:** July-Aug. **On site lodging:** No. **Rental clubs:** Yes. **Walking policy:** Unrestricted walking. **Metal spikes allowed:** Yes. **Range:** No. **To obtain tee times:** Call.

BRETWOOD GOLF COURSE

PU-E. Surry Rd., Keene, 03431, Cheshire County, (603)352-7626.

Opened: 1968. **Architect:** Geoffrey Cornish/Hugh Barrett. **Green fee:** $25/$32. **Credit cards:** MC,VISA,DISC. **Reduced fees:** Twilight. **Caddies:** No. **Golf carts:** $20. **Discount golf packages:** No. **Season:** April-Nov. **High:** June-Oct. **On site lodging:** No. **Rental clubs:** Yes. **Walking policy:** Unrestricted walking. **Metal spikes allowed:** Yes. **Range:** Yes (grass). **To obtain tee times:** Call Wednesday for upcoming weekend.

★★★★NORTH COURSE

Holes: 18. **Par:** 72/72. **Yards:** 6,974/5,140. **Course rating:** 73.9/71.5. **Slope:** 134/120.
Notes: Ranked 4th in 1997 Best in State.
Subscriber comments: Always look forward to playing this course...Nice course, need to speed up play...Solid...Play all 36 holes in one day...My favorite "away" course; 18 different holes, all challenging...Old holes nice, beautiful river...Water and quaint covered bridges provide motif.

★★★½SOUTH COURSE

Holes: 18. **Par:** 72/71. **Yards:** 6,952/4,990. **Course rating:** 73.0/70.0. **Slope:** 137/121.
Subscriber comments: Fine layout...Holes 15,16 and 17 are awesome!...Fair front nine, great back nine...7th hole is a beast...Beautiful, challenging course, (great milkshakes)...Consistent greens...Interesting finishing four, beautiful river.

★★★CAMPBELL'S SCOTTISH HIGHLANDS GOLF COURSE

PU-79 Brady Ave., Salem, 03079, Rockingham County, (603)894-4653, 30 miles N of Boston.
Opened: 1994. **Holes:** 18. **Par:** 71/71. **Yards:** 6,249/5,056. **Course rating:** 69.5/68.4. **Slope:** 120/114. **Architect:** George F. Sargent. **Green fee:** $24/$30. **Credit cards:** MC,VISA. **Reduced fees:** Weekdays, twilight, seniors. **Caddies:** No. **Golf carts:** $10. **Discount golf packages:** No. **Season:** April-Nov. **High:** June-Sept. **On site lodging:** No. **Rental clubs:** Yes. **Walking policy:** Unrestricted walking. **Metal spikes allowed:** No. **Range:** Yes (grass/mats). **To obtain tee times:** Call 3 days in advance.
Subscriber comments: Keeps getting better...Short, play the blues...Links style, unusual in this area...The good new kid in town...Excellent layout, multiple shot choices on holes...Playable par 4s...Great practice area.

★★CANDIA WOODS GOLF LINKS

PU-313 S. Rd., Candia, 03034, Rockingham County, (603)483-2307, (800)564-4344.
Opened: 1964. **Holes:** 18. **Par:** 71/73. **Yards:** 6,558/5,582. **Course rating:** 70.9/72.2. **Slope:** 121/130. **Architect:** Phil Wogan. **Green fee:** $25/$35. **Credit cards:** MC,VISA,DISC. **Reduced fees:** Weekdays, low season, twilight, seniors, juniors. **Caddies:** No. **Golf carts:** $12. **Discount golf packages:** No. **Season:** March-Dec. **High:** June-Sept. **On site lodging:** No. **Rental clubs:** Yes. **Walking policy:** Unrestricted walking. **Metal spikes allowed:** Yes. **Range:** Yes (grass/mats). **To obtain tee times:** Call 5 days in advance.

★★★COUNTRY CLUB OF NEW HAMPSHIRE

PU-Kearsarge Valley Rd., North Sutton, 03260, Merrimack County, (603)927-4246, 30 miles NW of Concord.
Opened: 1957. **Holes:** 18. **Par:** 72/72. **Yards:** 6,727/5,446. **Course rating:** 71.6/71.7. **Slope:** 125/127. **Architect:** William Mitchell. **Green fee:** $25/$32. **Credit cards:** MC,VISA,DISC. **Reduced fees:** Weekdays, twilight. **Caddies:** No. **Golf carts:** $11. **Discount golf packages:** Yes. **Season:** April-Nov. **High:** July-Sept. **On site lodging:** Yes. **Rental clubs:** Yes. **Walking policy:** Unrestricted walking. **Metal spikes allowed:** Yes. **Range:** Yes (grass). **To obtain tee times:** Call up to 7 days in advance. Motel guests and outings can book anytime.
Notes: Ranked 9th in 1997 Best in State.
Subscriber comments: Greens rolled true...A beautiful old classic course...Nice mountain views...Exceptional shotmaker's course...Some excellent par 4s...Great course and layout, watch out for the mosquitos though!...No nightlife within 50 miles.

★★DERRYFIELD COUNTRY CLUB

PU-625 Mammoth Rd., Manchester, 03104, Hillsborough County, (603)669-0235.
Opened: 1932. **Holes:** 18. **Par:** 70/74. **Yards:** 6,100/5,535. **Course rating:** 68.7/71.0. **Slope:** 113/125. **Architect:** Wayne Stiles and John Van Kleek. **Green fee:** $24/$24. **Credit cards:** None. **Reduced fees:** N/A. **Caddies:** Yes. **Golf carts:** $22. **Discount golf packages:** No. **Season:** April-Dec. **High:** June-Sept. **On site lodging:** No. **Rental clubs:** No. **Walking policy:** Unrestricted walking. **Metal spikes allowed:** Yes. **Range:** No. **To obtain tee times:** Call on Thursday for upcoming weekend and holiday. First come, first served on weekdays.

NEW HAMPSHIRE

★★★½EASTMAN GOLF LINKS
PU-Clubhouse Lane, Grantham, 03753, Sullivan County, (603)863-4500, 43 miles NW of Concord.
Opened: 1973. **Holes:** 18. **Par:** 71/73. **Yards:** 6,731/5,369. **Course rating:** 73.5/71.9. **Slope:** 137/128. **Architect:** Geoffrey Cornish. **Green fee:** $38/$38. **Credit cards:** MC,VISA. **Reduced fees:** N/A. **Caddies:** No. **Golf carts:** $15. **Discount golf packages:** No. **Season:** May-Nov. **High:** July-Sept. **On site lodging:** No. **Rental clubs:** Yes. **Walking policy:** Walking at certain times. **Metal spikes allowed:** No. **Range:** Yes (grass/mats). **To obtain tee times:** Call two days in advance.
Notes: Ranked 10th in 1997 Best in State.
Subscriber comments: Pleasant surprise..Lots of blind shots...Always a favorite. Plenty of character...Great track, solid all around, spectacular views...Tight course, many uneven lies...Accuracy is premium.

GREEN MEADOW GOLF CLUB
PU-59 Steele Rd., Hudson, 03051, Hillsborough County, (603)889-1555, 11 miles S of Manchester.
Opened: 1959. **Architect:** Philip Friel/David Friel. **Green fee:** $24/$30. **Credit cards:** MC,VISA,DISC. **Reduced fees:** Weekdays, low season, twilight, seniors, juniors. **Caddies:** Yes. **Golf carts:** $22. **Discount golf packages:** No. **Season:** March-Dec. **High:** April-Aug. **On site lodging:** No. **Rental clubs:** Yes. **Walking policy:** Unrestricted walking. **Metal spikes allowed:** Yes. **To obtain tee times:** Come in 7 days in advance, or call on Monday for upcoming weekend.
★★NORTH COURSE
Holes: 18. **Par:** 72/72. **Yards:** 6,495/5,102. **Course rating:** 67.6/68.3. **Slope:** 109/113. **Range:** Yes (grass).
★★SOUTH COURSE
Holes: 18. **Par:** 72/72. **Yards:** 6,598/5,173. **Course rating:** 70.0/71.2. **Slope:** 114/120. **Range:** Yes (grass/mats).

★★★HANOVER COUNTRY CLUB
PU-Rope Ferry Rd., Hanover, 03755, Grafton County, (603)646-2000, 10 miles N of Lebanon.
Opened: 1899. **Holes:** 18. **Par:** 69/73. **Yards:** 5,876/5,468. **Course rating:** 68.7/72.7. **Slope:** 118/127. **Architect:** Barton/Smith/Cornish/Robinson. **Green fee:** $31/$31. **Credit cards:** MC,VISA. **Reduced fees:** Twilight, juniors. **Caddies:** Yes. **Golf carts:** $14. **Discount golf packages:** Yes. **Season:** April-Nov. **High:** June-Sept. **On site lodging:** No. **Rental clubs:** Yes. **Walking policy:** Unrestricted walking. **Metal spikes allowed:** Yes. **Range:** Yes (grass). **To obtain tee times:** Call 5 days in advance.
Subscriber comments: Short but challenging. Very enjoyable...An excellent course demanding accuracy and all 14 clubs...Beautiful setting, very challenging back nine...If you don't take a cart, may the Lord be with you...Challenging mountain course...Good cross country skiing in winter.

★★½HOOPER GOLF CLUB
Prospect Hill, Walpole, 03608, Cheshire County, (603)756-4080, 16 miles N of Keene.
Opened: 1927. **Holes:** 9. **Par:** 72/72. **Yards:** 3,007/2,748. **Course rating:** 69.3/73.5. **Slope:** 122/132. **Architect:** Wayne Stiles/John Van Kleek. **Green fee:** $23. **Credit cards:** MC,VISA. **Reduced fees:** N/A. **Caddies:** No. **Golf carts:** $20. **Discount golf packages:** No. **Season:** April-Oct. **High:** July-Aug. **On site lodging:** Yes. **Rental clubs:** Yes. **Walking policy:** Unrestricted walking. **Metal spikes allowed:** No. **Range:** No. **To obtain tee times:** Tee times not required. Course is closed to public Thursday at 5 p.m. and Saturday & Sunday mornings until 10:30 a.m.
Subscriber comments: High and dry when wet in spring...Great greens, not too hard, not too easy...Nine-hole course with two sets of tees...Best golf in fall, scenic.

★★½JACK O'LANTERN RESORT
R-Rte. 3, Box A, Woodstock, 03292, Grafton County, (603)745-3636, 60 miles N of Manchester.
Opened: 1947. **Holes:** 18. **Par:** 70/70. **Yards:** 5,829/4,725. **Course rating:** 67.5/67.5. **Slope:** 113/113. **Architect:** Robert Keating. **Green fee:** $26/$32. **Credit cards:** All major. **Reduced fees:** Weekdays, resort guests, twilight. **Caddies:** No. **Golf carts:** $12.

Discount golf packages: Yes. **Season:** May-Oct. **High:** N/A. **On site lodging:** Yes. **Rental clubs:** Yes. **Walking policy:** Walking at certain times. **Metal spikes allowed:** Yes. **Range:** No. **To obtain tee times:** Call 24 hours in advance.
Subscriber comments: Very short with postage stamp greens...Wide open...Flat winding layout along river...Spectacular in the fall when leaves change...Very quiet and scenic...Nice for a weekend...Doglegs and more doglegs, difficult for first timers.

★★★JOHN H. CAIN GOLF CLUB

Unity Rd., Newport, 03773, Sullivan County, (603)863-7787, 35 miles NW of Concord.
Opened: 1920. **Holes:** 18. **Par:** 71/71. **Yards:** 6,415/4,738. **Course rating:** 71.4/63.8. **Slope:** 133/112. **Architect:** Phillip Wogan. **Green fee:** $20/$25. **Credit cards:** MC,VISA. **Reduced fees:** Weekdays, low season, twilight, seniors, juniors. **Caddies:** No. **Golf carts:** $11. **Discount golf packages:** Yes. **Season:** April-Nov. **High:** July-Sept. **On site lodging:** No. **Rental clubs:** Yes. **Walking policy:** Unrestricted walking. **Metal spikes allowed:** Yes. **Range:** Yes (grass/mats). **To obtain tee times:** Call 7 days in advance.
Subscriber comments: Great course, variety of holes, very scenic...Lots of water...Terrific old style course...Great challenge especially with "sucker" holes like 3 and 13, bring plenty of balls...Last three holes are a true test.

★★★½KEENE COUNTRY CLUB

755 W. Hill Rd., Keene, 03431, Cheshire County, (603)352-9722, 60 miles W of Manchester.
Opened: 1900. **Holes:** 18. **Par:** 72/75. **Yards:** 6,200/5,900. **Course rating:** 69.0/72.2. **Slope:** 121/130. **Architect:** Wayne Stiles. **Green fee:** $40. **Credit cards:** MC,VISA. **Reduced fees:** N/A. **Caddies:** No. **Golf carts:** $30. **Discount golf packages:** Yes. **Season:** April-Nov. **High:** May-Sept. **On site lodging:** No. **Rental clubs:** Yes. **Walking policy:** Unrestricted walking. **Metal spikes allowed:** Yes. **Range:** Yes (grass). **To obtain tee times:** Call ahead.
Subscriber comments: Wonderful classic layout...Two totally different nines, course can come up and bite you...A diamond in the rough!...Nice par 4s.

★★★½LACONIA COUNTRY CLUB

607 Elm St., Laconia, 03246, Belknap County, (603)524-1273.
Opened: 1926. **Holes:** 18. **Par:** 72/72. **Yards:** 6,483/5,552. **Course rating:** 71.7/72.1. **Slope:** 128/125. **Architect:** Wayne Stiles. **Green fee:** $60/$60. **Credit cards:** MC,VISA. **Reduced fees:** Low season, resort guests, juniors. **Caddies:** Yes. **Golf carts:** Included in Green Fee. **Discount golf packages:** No. **Season:** April-Nov. **High:** June-Sept. **On site lodging:** No. **Rental clubs:** Yes. **Walking policy:** Mandatory cart. **Metal spikes allowed:** Yes. **Range:** Yes (grass). **To obtain tee times:** Call Thursday for upcoming weekend.
Subscriber comments: Great greens, nice scenery...Lots of holes on a hillside. Nothing flat...Hard to score...Two very long par 3s separate the men from the boys...Very good course for seniors...Hilly front nine, tight challenging back.

★★½MAPLEWOOD COUNTRY CLUB

PU-Rte. 302, Bethlehem, 03574, Grafton County, (603)869-3335, 80 miles N of Concord.
Opened: 1907. **Holes:** 18. **Par:** 72/72. **Yards:** 6,100/5,200. **Course rating:** 67.5/68.4. **Slope:** 113/114. **Architect:** Donald Ross. **Green fee:** $22/$24. **Credit cards:** MC,VISA,DISC. **Reduced fees:** Weekdays, low season, twilight. **Caddies:** No. **Golf carts:** $12. **Discount golf packages:** Yes. **Season:** May-Oct. **High:** May-Sept. **On site lodging:** No. **Rental clubs:** Yes. **Walking policy:** Mandatory cart. **Metal spikes allowed:** Yes. **Range:** Yes (grass). **To obtain tee times:** Call anytime.
Subscriber comments: Greens can be fastest around...Course is picturesque and challenging ...Difficult course, tight fairways. Hole 16 par 6, 651 yards, awesome...Beautiful clubhouse.

★★★MOUNT WASHINGTON HOTEL & RESORT

R-Rte. 302, Bretton Woods, 03575, Carroll County, (603)278-4653, (800)258-1330, 90 miles N of Concord.
Opened: 1915. **Holes:** 18. **Par:** 71/71. **Yards:** 6,638/5,336. **Course rating:** 70.1/70.1. **Slope:** 123/118. **Architect:** Donald Ross. **Green fee:** $20/$30. **Credit cards:** All major.

Reduced fees: Resort guests. **Caddies:** No. **Golf carts:** $20. **Discount golf packages:** Yes. **Season:** May-Oct. **High:** July-Sept. **On site lodging:** Yes. **Rental clubs:** Yes. **Walking policy:** Walking at certain times. **Metal spikes allowed:** Yes. **Range:** No. **To obtain tee times:** Call anytime in advance.

Subscriber comments: They are adding water to improve several holes; great views of mountains...Good course, don't miss...Babe Ruth, Winston Churchill, Thomas Edison and me...Old fashioned course with lots of character.

Special Notes: Also has 9-hole par-35 Mount Pleasant Course.

★★★½ NORTH CONWAY COUNTRY CLUB

Norcross Circle, North Conway, 03860, Carroll County, (603)356-9391.

Opened: 1895. **Holes:** 18. **Par:** 71/71. **Yards:** 6,659/5,530. **Course rating:** 71.9/71.4. **Slope:** 126/120. **Architect:** Alex Findlay/Phil Wogan. **Green fee:** $28/$35. **Credit cards:** MC,VISA. **Reduced fees:** Low season, twilight, seniors, juniors. **Caddies:** No. **Golf carts:** $22. **Discount golf packages:** No. **Season:** May-Oct. **High:** June-Oct. **On site lodging:** No. **Rental clubs:** Yes. **Walking policy:** Unrestricted walking. **Metal spikes allowed:** Yes. **Range:** Yes (grass). **To obtain tee times:** Call three days in advance.

Subscriber comments: Fast greens...Great views, different front and back nine, nice spot...Needs better signing from hole to hole...Long par 4s, good challenge...Beautiful 1st tee, surrounded by mountains...Fun, not as easy as it looks.

★★★½ OVERLOOK COUNTRY CLUB

PU-5 Overlook Dr., Hollis, 03049, Hillsborough County, (603)465-2909, 60 miles N of Boston.

Opened: 1989. **Holes:** 18. **Par:** 71/72. **Yards:** 6,290/5,230. **Course rating:** 70.2/70.4. **Slope:** 128/126. **Architect:** David E. Friel. **Green fee:** $28/$37. **Credit cards:** MC,VISA,DISC. **Reduced fees:** Weekdays, twilight. **Caddies:** No. **Golf carts:** $22. **Discount golf packages:** No. **Season:** April-Dec. **High:** June-Aug. **On site lodging:** No. **Rental clubs:** Yes. **Walking policy:** Unrestricted walking. **Metal spikes allowed:** Yes. **Range:** No. **To obtain tee times:** Call 7 days in advance.

Subscriber comments: Shotmaker's course...Too many short doglegs...Beware of the bugs!...Challenging but fair, nice layout, slow...Par 5s test you. Nice greens...A little tricked up but enjoyable...You haven't played a challenging hole until you play the 3rd...Nice course that runs along Nashua River...Some tight holes, well bunkered.

★★★ PASSACONAWAY COUNTRY CLUB

PU-12 Midway Ave., Litchfield, 03052, Hillsborough County, (603)424-4653, 5 miles S of Manchester.

Opened: 1989. **Holes:** 18. **Par:** 71/72. **Yards:** 6,855/5,369. **Course rating:** 72.2/70.3. **Slope:** 126/118. **Architect:** Cornish and Silva. **Green fee:** $20/$35. **Credit cards:** MC,VISA. **Reduced fees:** Weekdays, low season, twilight, seniors, juniors. **Caddies:** No. **Golf carts:** $11. **Discount golf packages:** No. **Season:** April-Dec. **High:** May-Sept. **On site lodging:** No. **Rental clubs:** Yes. **Walking policy:** Unrestricted walking. **Metal spikes allowed:** Yes. **Range:** No. **To obtain tee times:** Call 7 days in advance for weekdays and 5 days in advance for weekends.

Subscriber comments: Harder than it looks...Plays long from back tees, rough can be severe...Nos. 12 and 13 are monsters...Holes close together—too close...Very open and very tough when windy...Tricky back nine...Superb course!

★★½ PEASE GOLF COURSE

PU-2 Country Club Rd., Portsmouth, 03801, Rockingham County, (603)433-1331.

Opened: 1960. **Holes:** 18. **Par:** 71/71. **Yards:** 6,328/5,324. **Course rating:** 70.8/69.9. **Slope:** 128/120. **Architect:** Al Zikorus. **Green fee:** $28. **Credit cards:** MC,VISA. **Reduced fees:** N/A. **Caddies:** No. **Golf carts:** $22. **Discount golf packages:** No. **Season:** April-Nov. **High:** June-Aug. **On site lodging:** No. **Rental clubs:** Yes. **Walking policy:** Unrestricted walking. **Metal spikes allowed:** Yes. **Range:** Yes (grass). **To obtain tee times:** Call 3 days in advance.

Subscriber comments: Improvements turning this into a great golf course...Old Air Force base, not tough...Watch out for the low-flying planes at Pease field!...Small greens...Lots of risk/reward holes.

★★★ PERRY HOLLOW GOLF & COUNTRY CLUB

PU-250 Perry Hollow Rd., Wolfeboro, 03899, Carroll County, (603)569-3055.
Opened: N/A. **Holes:** 18. **Par:** 71/71. **Yards:** 6,338/4,788. **Course rating:** 71.0/67.0.
Slope: 132/115. **Architect:** Geoffrey S. Cornish and Brian Silva. **Green fee:** $28/$28.
Credit cards: All major. **Reduced fees:** Low season, juniors. **Caddies:** No. **Golf carts:**
$24. **Discount golf packages:** No. **Season:** April-Nov. **High:** June-Sept. **On site lodging:** No. **Rental clubs:** Yes. **Walking policy:** Unrestricted walking. **Metal spikes
allowed:** No. **Range:** Yes (grass). **To obtain tee times:** Call up to 7 days in advance.
Subscriber comments: Worth the trip...Back nine still growing in...A well kept
secret...Superior 19th hole, the others ain't too bad either...Fancy clubhouse...The golf
is challenging up and down hills, in and out of woods...Putting green unbelievable.

★★½ PLAUSAWA VALLEY COUNTRY CLUB

42 Whittemore Rd., Pembroke, 03275, Merrimack County, (603)224-6267.
Opened: 1963. **Holes:** 18. **Par:** 72/73. **Yards:** 6,545/5,391. **Course rating:** 72.6/71.5.
Slope: 131/128. **Architect:** Geoffrey Cornish and Brian Silva. **Green fee:** $24/$27.
Credit cards: MC,VISA. **Reduced fees:** Weekdays, low season, resort guests, twilight,
seniors, juniors. **Caddies:** No. **Golf carts:** $24. **Discount golf packages:** Yes. **Season:**
April-Nov. **High:** July-Aug. **On site lodging:** No. **Rental clubs:** Yes. **Walking policy:**
Unrestricted walking. **Metal spikes allowed:** Yes. **Range:** Yes (grass). **To obtain tee
times:** Call seven days in advance.
Subscriber comments: Excellent course, tough to play...Somewhat lengthy with
wind...Front nine is old, back nine is championship...Given the amount of play, a good
bargain...10th hole is a fun tee shot...A pleasant surprise.

★★★½ PORTSMOUTH COUNTRY CLUB

1 Country Club Lane, Greenland, 03840, Rockingham County, (603)436-9719.
Opened: 1957. **Holes:** 18. **Par:** 72/78. **Yards:** 7,050/6,202. **Course rating:** 74.1/77.1.
Slope: 127/135. **Architect:** Robert Trent Jones. **Green fee:** $40/$40. **Credit cards:**
MC,VISA,DISC. **Reduced fees:** Twilight. **Caddies:** No. **Golf carts:** $20. **Discount golf
packages:** No. **Season:** April-Nov. **High:** June-Sept. **On site lodging:** No. **Rental
clubs:** Yes. **Walking policy:** Unrestricted walking. **Metal spikes allowed:** Yes. **Range:**
Yes (grass/mats). **To obtain tee times:** Call 1 day in advance.
Notes: Ranked 5th in 1997 Best in State.
Subscriber comments: Nice spot, long for men, impossibly long for
women...Views...Trent Jones at his sneakiest, hard to get on...When the wind blows,
watch out!...A lot of fun to play...Always enjoyable...Want to play again.

★★★ ROCHESTER COUNTRY CLUB

Church St., Gonic, 03839, Strafford County, (603)332-9892, 2 miles S of Rochester.
Opened: 1916. **Holes:** 18. **Par:** 72/73. **Yards:** 6,596/5,414. **Course rating:** 72.7/70.4.
Slope: 125/123. **Architect:** Phil Wogan. **Green fee:** $45/$45. **Credit cards:**
MC,VISA,AMEX. **Reduced fees:** N/A. **Caddies:** No. **Golf carts:** Included in Green Fee.
Discount golf packages: No. **Season:** April-Nov. **High:** June-Aug. **On site lodging:**
No. **Rental clubs:** Yes. **Walking policy:** Mandatory cart. **Metal spikes allowed:** Yes.
Range: No. **To obtain tee times:** First come, first served. Non-members must play
before 3 p.m. on weekdays, and after 2 p.m. on weekends.
Subscriber comments: Outstanding New England style course...Tricky par 3s, other
funny holes, improving conditions...Nice day of golf...A good golf course but not difficult,
holes are wide open and not much water or sand hazards to challenge shotmaking.

★★½ SAGAMORE-HAMPTON GOLF CLUB

PU-101 N. Rd., North Hampton, 03862, Rockingham County, (603)964-5341.
Opened: 1962. **Holes:** 18. **Par:** 71/71. **Yards:** 6,014/5,647. **Course rating:** 67.4/71.5.
Slope: 110/111. **Architect:** C.S. Luff. **Green fee:** $25/$26. **Credit cards:** None.
Reduced fees: Low season. **Caddies:** No. **Golf carts:** N/A. **Discount golf packages:**
No. **Season:** April-Dec. **High:** May-Sept. **On site lodging:** No. **Rental clubs:** Yes.
Walking policy: Unrestricted walking. **Metal spikes allowed:** Yes. **Range:** No. **To
obtain tee times:** Call 7 days in advance for weekends and holidays and 2 days in
advance for weekdays.
Subscriber comments: Tough greens to putt, decent test...Short but enjoyable to
play...Mostly flat and wide open...Walking only, the best way to play.

★★★★SHATTUCK GOLF COURSE
PU-28 Dublin Rd., Jaffrey, 03452, Cheshire County, (603)532-4300, 20 miles E of Keene.
Opened: 1991. **Holes:** 18. **Par:** 71/71. **Yards:** 6,701/4,632. **Course rating:** 74.1/73.1. **Slope:** 145/139. **Architect:** Brian Silva. **Green fee:** $35/$35. **Credit cards:** MC,VISA. **Reduced fees:** Weekdays, low season, twilight. **Caddies:** No. **Golf carts:** $12. **Discount golf packages:** Yes. **Season:** May-Oct. **High:** June-Sept. **On site lodging:** No. **Rental clubs:** No. **Walking policy:** Unrestricted walking. **Metal spikes allowed:** Yes. **Range:** Yes (grass/mats). **To obtain tee times:** Call 30 days in advance for weekdays. Call on Tuesday at 7 a.m. for upcoming weekend.
Notes: Ranked 2nd in 1997 Best in State.
Subscriber comments: Great challenge, great fun...Hardest course in New England...For straight hitters only...Very difficult if iron play is weak...Some gorgeous scenery...Bring an extra sleeve or two...Target golf in great natural setting...Nos. 12, 13, 14 Devil's Triangle...Only time I had fun shooting over 100...A monster!

★★★★SKY MEADOW COUNTRY CLUB
6 Mountain Laurels Dr., Nashua, 03062, Hillsborough County, (603)888-3000, 30 miles N of Boston.
Opened: 1986. **Holes:** 18. **Par:** 72/72. **Yards:** 6,590/5,127. **Course rating:** 73.3/71.2. **Slope:** 133/131. **Architect:** William W. Amick. **Green fee:** $53/$80. **Credit cards:** MC,VISA,AMEX. **Reduced fees:** N/A. **Caddies:** No. **Golf carts:** Included in Green Fee. **Discount golf packages:** No. **Season:** April-Nov. **High:** June-Sept. **On site lodging:** No. **Rental clubs:** Yes. **Walking policy:** Mandatory cart. **Metal spikes allowed:** Yes. **Range:** Yes. **To obtain tee times:** Guests may make reservations two days in advance.
Notes: Ranked 7th in 1997 Best in State.
Subscriber comments: Excellent layout, tough greens...#17 a toughie...Enjoyable from whites, impossible from back tees...One of New Hampshire's best...Worthy of a PGA event...Very pretty and hilly...Cut out of the woods, long, tough par 3s...Must experience the first par 3 with 100-foot drop from the tee to green...Breathtaking views.

★★★SOUHEGAN WOODS GOLF CLUB
PU-65 Thorton Ferry Rd., Amherst, 03031, Hillsborough County, (603)673-0200, 10 miles NW of Nashua.
Opened: 1992. **Holes:** 18. **Par:** 72/71. **Yards:** 6,497/5,423. **Course rating:** 70.4/65.6. **Slope:** 120/111. **Architect:** Phil Friel. **Green fee:** $27/$34. **Credit cards:** MC,VISA,DISC. **Reduced fees:** Weekdays, twilight. **Caddies:** No. **Golf carts:** $22. **Discount golf packages:** No. **Season:** April-Nov. **High:** May-Aug. **On site lodging:** No. **Rental clubs:** Yes. **Walking policy:** Unrestricted walking. **Metal spikes allowed:** Yes. **Range:** Yes (grass). **To obtain tee times:** Call up to 5 days before.
Subscriber comments: Huge sand traps everywhere, wide open...Great practice area...Some holes are too close together...Fairly long and very tight...Drive it straight...Outstanding in every measure...Back nine is good, front is boring.

★★½WAUKEWAN GOLF CLUB
PU-Waukewan Rd., Center Harbor, 03253, Belknap County, (603)279-6661, 50 miles N of Manchester.
Opened: 1961. **Holes:** 18. **Par:** 71/73. **Yards:** 5,735/5,010. **Course rating:** 67.1/68.7. **Slope:** 120/112. **Architect:** Melvyn D. Hale. **Green fee:** $20/$25. **Credit cards:** MC,VISA. **Reduced fees:** Low season. **Caddies:** No. **Golf carts:** $22. **Discount golf packages:** No. **Season:** May-Oct. **High:** June-Sept. **On site lodging:** No. **Rental clubs:** Yes. **Walking policy:** Unrestricted walking. **Metal spikes allowed:** Yes. **Range:** Yes (grass). **To obtain tee times:** Call up to 2 days in advance.
Subscriber comments: Back nine much better than front...Nice vacation course, some interesting angles...Lots of short par 4s...Beautiful mountain views.

★½WAUMBEK GOLF CLUB
PU-Route 2, Jefferson, 03583, Coos County, (603)586-7777, 115 miles N of Manchester.
Opened: 1895. **Holes:** 18. **Par:** 71/71. **Yards:** 6,128/4,772. **Course rating:** 69.9/69.9. **Slope:** 107/107. **Architect:** Willie Norton. **Green fee:** $20/$25. **Credit cards:** MC,VISA,DISC. **Reduced fees:** Weekdays, low season, resort guests, twilight, seniors,

juniors. **Caddies:** No. **Golf carts:** $20. **Discount golf packages:** Yes. **Season:** April-Nov. **High:** July-Sept. **On site lodging:** No. **Rental clubs:** Yes. **Walking policy:** Unrestricted walking. **Metal spikes allowed:** Yes. **Range:** No. **To obtain tee times:** Call anytime in advance.

★★½WENTWORTH RESORT GOLF COURSE
Rt. 16A, Jackson, 03846, Carroll County, (603)383-9641.
Call club for further information.
Subscriber comments: Beautiful mountain views...Short, can be difficult...Sporty, good for the ego. Great set of par 3s.

★★★WHITE MOUNTAIN COUNTRY CLUB
PU-Ashland Rd., Ashland, 03217, Grafton County, (603)536-2227, 300 miles N of Concord.
Opened: 1974. **Holes:** 18. **Par:** 71/73. **Yards:** 6,408/5,410. **Course rating:** 70.4/70.2. **Slope:** 125/118. **Architect:** Cornish and Robinson. **Green fee:** $12/$27. **Credit cards:** MC,VISA. **Reduced fees:** Weekdays, low season, twilight. **Caddies:** No. **Golf carts:** $11. **Discount golf packages:** No. **Season:** May-Oct. **High:** July-Sept. **On site lodging:** Yes. **Rental clubs:** Yes. **Walking policy:** Unrestricted walking. **Metal spikes allowed:** Yes. **Range:** Yes (grass). **To obtain tee times:** Call up to seven days in advance.
Subscriber comments: Most greens hold, fairways plush...Crosswinds you won't believe...Some forced carries...Nice mountain course...Wide open, fun to play and easy to score...Very flat course...Beautiful short par 4s.

★★★½WINDHAM GOLF & COUNTRY CLUB
PU-One Country Club Rd., Windham, 03087, Rockingham County, (603)434-2093, 20 miles N of Boston, MA.
Opened: 1995. **Holes:** 18. **Par:** 72/72. **Yards:** 6,442/5,127. **Course rating:** 71.3/69.0. **Slope:** 136/132. **Architect:** Dean Bowen. **Green fee:** $30/$35. **Credit cards:** MC,VISA. **Reduced fees:** N/A. **Caddies:** No. **Golf carts:** $12. **Discount golf packages:** No. **Season:** Year-round. **High:** May-Oct. **On site lodging:** No. **Rental clubs:** Yes. **Walking policy:** Unrestricted walking. **Metal spikes allowed:** Yes. **Range:** Yes (grass/mats). **To obtain tee times:** Call up to 5 days in advance.
Notes: Ranked 8th in 1997 Best in State.
Subscriber comments: Uphill walk to clubhouse...Extremely tight, any ball off fairway is lost in woods...Nice new course. Will test your ability to gamble...Makes you talk to yourself. Need every club...A pleasure to play.

NEW JERSEY

★★APPLE MOUNTAIN GOLF CLUB
PU-369 Hazen Oxford Rd., Rte. 624, Belvidere, 07823, Warren County, (908)453-3023, (800)752-9576, 80 miles W of New York City.
Opened: 1973. **Holes:** 18. **Par:** 71/71. **Yards:** 6,593/5,214. **Course rating:** 71.8/69.8. **Slope:** 121/123. **Architect:** Andrew Kiszonak. **Green fee:** $24/$49. **Credit cards:** MC,VISA,AMEX. **Reduced fees:** Weekdays, low season, twilight, seniors, juniors. **Caddies:** No. **Golf carts:** Included in Green Fee. **Discount golf packages:** Yes. **Season:** Year-round. **High:** June-Aug. **On site lodging:** No. **Rental clubs:** Yes. **Walking policy:** Walking at certain times. **Metal spikes allowed:** Yes. **Range:** No. **To obtain tee times:** Call.

★★ASH BROOK GOLF COURSE
PU-1210 Raritan Rd., Scotch Plains, 07076, Union County, (908)668-8503, 15 miles SW of Newark.
Opened: 1958. **Holes:** 18. **Par:** 72/72. **Yards:** 6,962/5,661. **Course rating:** 72.1/71.8. **Slope:** 117/119. **Architect:** Alfred H. Tull. **Green fee:** $8/$50. **Credit cards:** None. **Reduced fees:** Weekdays, seniors, juniors. **Caddies:** No. **Golf carts:** $22. **Discount golf packages:** No. **Season:** Year-round. **High:** March-Oct. **On site lodging:** No. **Rental clubs:** No. **Walking policy:** Unrestricted walking. **Metal spikes allowed:** No. **Range:** No. **To obtain tee times:** Call golf shop.

★★½AVALON COUNTRY CLUB
1510 Route 9 N., Cape May Court House, 08210, Cape May County, (609)465-4653, (800)643-4766, 30 miles S of Atlantic City.
Opened: 1971. **Holes:** 18. **Par:** 71/72. **Yards:** 6,325/4,924. **Course rating:** 70.3/70.7. **Slope:** 122/122. **Architect:** Bob Hendricks. **Green fee:** $20/$55. **Credit cards:** MC,VISA,AMEX. **Reduced fees:** Weekdays, low season, twilight, juniors. **Caddies:** No. **Golf carts:** Included in Green Fee. **Discount golf packages:** Yes. **Season:** Year-round. **High:** May-Sept. **On site lodging:** No. **Rental clubs:** Yes. **Walking policy:** Walking at certain times. **Metal spikes allowed:** Yes. **Range:** Yes (Mats). **To obtain tee times:** Call 14 days in advance.
Subscriber comments: Fine greens. No two holes alike. Friendly and helpful staff. Good pro shop and superb food...High demand in summer...Relatively flat, in good shape, fair to any handicap...Go midweek, no lines...Beautiful course, nicely wooded.

★★★BEAVER BROOK COUNTRY CLUB
Rte. #31 S. Country Club Rd., Clinton, 08809, Hunterdon County, (908)735-4022, (800)433-8567, 45 miles W of New York City.
Opened: 1964. **Holes:** 18. **Par:** 72/72. **Yards:** 6,546/5,283. **Course rating:** 71.7/71.7. **Slope:** 125/122. **Architect:** Alec Ternyei. **Green fee:** $22/$52. **Credit cards:** MC,VISA,AMEX. **Reduced fees:** Twilight. **Caddies:** No. **Golf carts:** $16. **Discount golf packages:** No. **Season:** March-Dec. **High:** June-Aug. **On site lodging:** No. **Rental clubs:** Yes. **Walking policy:** Walking at certain times. **Metal spikes allowed:** Yes. **Range:** Yes (grass). **To obtain tee times:** Call 7 days in advance.
Subscriber comments: Tough long course. Fast greens...Love the 15th hole...Challenging layout; very short par 3s...Great views, tough walk...Big greens, interesting...Lots of uphill approaches...Par 5s on first two and last two holes.

★★BECKETT GOLF CLUB
RD #2, P.O. Box 76A, Swedesboro, 08085, Gloucester County, (732)467-4700.
Call club for further information.

★★½BEY LEA GOLF CLUB
1536 N. Bay Ave., Toms River, 08753, Ocean County, (732)349-0566.
Architect: Hal Purdy. **Caddies:** No. **Discount golf packages:** No. **On site lodging:** No. **Rental clubs:** No. **Metal spikes allowed:** Yes. **Range:** No.
Call club for further information.
Subscriber comments: Great shape for all the play it gets...Big greens, great to score well, fun!...Course too wide open, not penalized for poor shots.

★★★BLACK BEAR GOLF & COUNTRY CLUB

PU-Hwy. 23, Franklin, 07416, Sussex County, (973)209-2226, 50 miles N of New York.
Opened: 1996. **Holes:** 18. **Par:** 72/72. **Yards:** 6,673/4,756. **Course rating:** 72.2/67.7.
Slope: 130/115. **Architect:** N/A. **Green fee:** $45/$60. **Credit cards:** MC,VISA,AMEX.
Reduced fees: Weekdays, low season, twilight, seniors, juniors. **Caddies:** No. **Golf carts:** Included in Green Fee. **Discount golf packages:** No. **Season:** March-Nov.
High: May-Oct. **On site lodging:** No. **Rental clubs:** Yes. **Walking policy:** Mandatory cart. **Metal spikes allowed:** No. **Range:** Yes (Mats). **To obtain tee times:** Call golf shop.
Subscriber comments: Easy course, good combination with Crystal Springs...Very fair layout...Picturesque mountain course...Great course but hate the mandatory carts...Nice layout. Will improve as it matures.

★★★★BLUE HERON PINES GOLF CLUB

PU-550 W. Country Club Dr., Cologne, Galloway Twsp., 08213, Atlantic County, (609)965-4653, (888)478-2746, 18 miles W of Atlantic City.
Opened: 1993. **Holes:** 18. **Par:** 72/72. **Yards:** 6,777/5,053. **Course rating:** 72.9/69.2. **Slope:** 132/119. **Architect:** Stephen Kay. **Green fee:** $49/$115. **Credit cards:** All major. **Reduced fees:** Weekdays, low season, twilight. **Caddies:** No. **Golf carts:** Included in Green Fee. **Discount golf packages:** No. **Season:** Year-round. **High:** May-Oct. **On site lodging:** No. **Rental clubs:** Yes. **Walking policy:** Unrestricted walking. **Metal spikes allowed:** No. **Range:** Yes (grass/mats). **To obtain tee times:** Call up to 5 days in advance.
Notes: Golf Digest School site.
Subscriber comments: Excellent layout, very good conditions, pricey...Golf at its finest! Worth every penny...One of Jersey's finest...Reminiscent of Pine Valley in spots...No.2 is a great par 3...Beautiful par-5 14th with huge waste bunker.

★★★½BOWLING GREEN GOLF CLUB

Schoolhouse Rd., Milton, 07438, Morris County, (973)697-2426, 45 miles NW of New York City.
Opened: 1966. **Holes:** 18. **Par:** 72/72. **Yards:** 6,689/4,966. **Course rating:** 72.9/69.4.
Slope: 131/122. **Architect:** Geoffrey Cornish. **Green fee:** $30/$48. **Credit cards:** MC,VISA,AMEX. **Reduced fees:** Weekdays, twilight. **Caddies:** No. **Golf carts:** $17.
Discount golf packages: No. **Season:** March-Dec. **High:** April-Sept. **On site lodging:** No. **Rental clubs:** No. **Walking policy:** Unrestricted walking. **Metal spikes allowed:** No. **Range:** Yes. **To obtain tee times:** Call 5 days in advance after 8 a.m.
Subscriber comments: Tight, tight, tight, keep the driver in your bag...Course is in outstanding condition. Great track...Long 18th is real challenge...Challenging par 3s, large, good greens...Carolina-like course, great front nine.

★★½BRIGANTINE GOLF LINKS

PU-Roosevelt Blvd. and N. Shore, Brigantine, 08203, Atlantic County, (609)266-1388, (800)698-1388, 4 miles N of Atlantic City.
Opened: 1926. **Holes:** 18. **Par:** 72/72. **Yards:** 6,520/6,233. **Course rating:** 71.3/69.5.
Slope: 123/120. **Architect:** Stiles and Van Kleek/Gill and Williams. **Green fee:** $35/$60.
Credit cards: MC,VISA,AMEX. **Reduced fees:** Weekdays, low season, resort guests, twilight. **Caddies:** Yes. **Golf carts:** Included in Green Fee. **Discount golf packages:** Yes. **Season:** Year-round. **High:** May-Sept. **On site lodging:** No. **Rental clubs:** Yes.
Walking policy: Walking at certain times. **Metal spikes allowed:** Yes. **Range:** No. **To obtain tee times:** Call up to 5 days in advance.
Subscriber comments: Nice little course...British Open-style is great, wind creates different course...Improving, affordable seaside layout, some nice bayfront scenes.

★★★BUENA VISTA COUNTRY CLUB

PU-Box 307, Rte. 40 & Country Club Lane, Buena, 08310, Atlantic County, (609)697-3733, 30 miles SE of Philadelphia.
Opened: 1957. **Holes:** 18. **Par:** 72/72. **Yards:** 6,869/5,651. **Course rating:** 73.5/72.2.
Slope: 131/128. **Architect:** William Gordon & Son. **Green fee:** $24/$32. **Credit cards:** None. **Reduced fees:** Weekdays, low season, twilight. **Caddies:** No. **Golf carts:** $24.
Discount golf packages: No. **Season:** Year-round. **High:** May-Oct. **On site lodging:** No. **Rental clubs:** Yes. **Walking policy:** Walking at certain times. **Metal spikes**

allowed: Yes. **Range:** Yes (grass). **To obtain tee times:** Call 6 days in advance. **Subscriber comments:** Fun golf course to play, real good shape...Tight, bunkered course, 10th hole toughest ever played...Good layout, about 150 bunkers.

★★½BUNKER HILL GOLF COURSE
PU-220 Bunker Hill Rd, Somerset, 08540, Mercer County, (908)359-6335, 8 miles S of New Brunswick.
Opened: 1972. **Holes:** 18. **Par:** 72/72. **Yards:** 6,200/5,766. **Course rating:** 67.9/72.6. **Slope:** 111/113. **Architect:** N/A. **Green fee:** $15/$18. **Credit cards:** MC,VISA. **Reduced fees:** Weekdays, low season, twilight, seniors, juniors. **Caddies:** No. **Golf carts:** $26. **Discount golf packages:** No. **Season:** Year-round. **High:** April-Sept. **On site lodging:** No. **Rental clubs:** Yes. **Walking policy:** Walking at certain times. **Metal spikes allowed:** Yes. **Range:** No. **To obtain tee times:** Call up to 7 days in advance.
Subscriber comments: Good test of all clubs...Very hilly, lots of water, slow...Picnic grove makes for excellent outings...A lot of elevation change...Short course for women, open all year...Interesting holes, especially Nos. 9 and 18, short and tight.

★★★½CAPE MAY NATIONAL GOLF CLUB
Rte. 9 & Florence Ave., Cape May, 08204, Cape May County, (609)884-1563, (800)227-3874, 35 miles S of Atlantic City.
Opened: 1991. **Holes:** 18. **Par:** 71/71. **Yards:** 6,920/4,696. **Course rating:** 72.9/68.8. **Slope:** 136/115. **Architect:** Karl Litten/Robert Mullock. **Green fee:** $35/$71. **Credit cards:** MC,VISA. **Reduced fees:** Weekdays, low season, twilight, juniors. **Caddies:** No. **Golf carts:** Included in Green Fee. **Discount golf packages:** Yes. **Season:** Year-round. **High:** May-Oct. **On site lodging:** No. **Rental clubs:** Yes. **Walking policy:** Unrestricted walking. **Metal spikes allowed:** No. **Range:** Yes (grass/mats). **To obtain tee times:** Call 7 days in advance.
Subscriber comments: Beautiful course. Upkeep outstanding...Tough greens, nice amount of water...Links style...Excellent design, very natural...Course very natural, no houses...Beautiful windy course...Great water holes and par 3s...Great 18th...Like playing in bird sanctuary, great character and great layout, natural beauty...Huge mature trees, great greens...Good hole variety...Large fast greens, sand dunes...Wind a big factor, many water hazards...Tough finishing holes.

★★½CEDAR CREEK GOLF COURSE
PU-Tilton Blvd., Bayville, 08721, Ocean County, (732)269-4460, 50 miles N of Atlantic City.
Opened: 1981. **Holes:** 18. **Par:** 72/72. **Yards:** 6,325/5,154. **Course rating:** 70.5/69.5. **Slope:** 120/118. **Architect:** Nicholas T. Psiahas. **Green fee:** $8/$26. **Credit cards:** None. **Reduced fees:** Weekdays, low season, twilight, seniors, juniors. **Caddies:** No. **Golf carts:** $26. **Discount golf packages:** No. **Season:** Year-round. **High:** May-Sept. **On site lodging:** No. **Rental clubs:** Yes. **Walking policy:** Unrestricted walking. **Metal spikes allowed:** Yes. **Range:** No. **To obtain tee times:** No tee times.
Subscriber comments: Good layout through the Pine Barrens...Very scenic. Nice layout in the pines...Front nine tight, treelined, back nine water and hills...Great muny! 230-yard par 3 uphill!...I like the last four holes.

★★CENTERTON GOLF CLUB
PU-Rte. #540-Almond Rd., Elmer, 08318, Salem County, (609)358-2220, 10 miles W of Vineland.
Opened: 1962. **Holes:** 18. **Par:** 71/71. **Yards:** 6,725/5,525. **Course rating:** 69.2/71.5. **Slope:** 120/120. **Architect:** Ed Carmen. **Green fee:** $12/$24. **Credit cards:** MC,VISA. **Reduced fees:** Weekdays, low season, twilight. **Caddies:** No. **Golf carts:** $26. **Discount golf packages:** Yes. **Season:** Year-round. **High:** May-Aug. **On site lodging:** No. **Rental clubs:** Yes. **Walking policy:** Walking at certain times. **Metal spikes allowed:** Yes. **Range:** Yes (grass/mats). **To obtain tee times:** Call 7 days in advance.

★★COHANZICK COUNTRY CLUB
PU-Bridgeton-Fairton Rd., Fairton, 08320, Cumberland County, (609)455-2127.
Opened: N/A. **Holes:** 18. **Par:** 71/71. **Yards:** 6,285/5,470. **Course rating:** 70.2/70.5. **Slope:** 123/120. **Architect:** Alex Findlay. **Green fee:** $13/$17. **Credit cards:** MC,VISA. **Reduced fees:** Weekdays, low season, twilight. **Caddies:** No. **Golf carts:** $22. **Discount golf packages:** No. **Season:** Year-round. **High:** May-Oct. **On site lodging:**

No. **Rental clubs:** Yes. **Walking policy:** Walking at certain times. **Metal spikes allowed:** Yes. **Range:** No. **To obtain tee times:** Call 5 days in advance. Tee times are required.

★★½CRANBURY GOLF CLUB
49 Southfield Rd., Cranbury, 08512, Mercer County, (609)799-0341, 6 miles SE of Princeton.
Opened: N/A. **Holes:** 18. **Par:** 70/71. **Yards:** 6,265/5,395. **Course rating:** 69.5/69.1.
Slope: 122/123. **Architect:** G. Wrenn. **Green fee:** $25/$35. **Credit cards:**
MC,VISA,AMEX. **Reduced fees:** Weekdays, low season, twilight, seniors, juniors.
Caddies: No. **Golf carts:** $13. **Discount golf packages:** No. **Season:** Year-round.
High: May-Sept. **On site lodging:** No. **Rental clubs:** Yes. **Walking policy:** Walking at certain times. **Metal spikes allowed:** Yes. **Range:** Yes (grass/mats). **To obtain tee times:** Call 7 days in advance.
Subscriber comments: Good course, short but interesting...Crowded, hacker's delight, spray it and play it...Tricky course for its length...Good walking course; short, but challenging...Central Jersey shorter layout with a couple good doglegs.

★★½CREAM RIDGE GOLF CLUB
181 Rte. 539, Cream Ridge, 08514, Monmouth County, (609)259-2849, 12 miles SE of Trenton.
Opened: 1958. **Holes:** 18. **Par:** 71/71. **Yards:** 6,630/5,101. **Course rating:** 72.3/72.3.
Slope: 119/119. **Architect:** Frank Miscoski. **Green fee:** $16/$30. **Credit cards:**
MC,VISA. **Reduced fees:** Weekdays, low season, twilight, seniors, juniors. **Caddies:**
No. **Golf carts:** $30. **Discount golf packages:** No. **Season:** Year-round. **High:** May-Sept. **On site lodging:** No. **Rental clubs:** No. **Walking policy:** Walking at certain times. **Metal spikes allowed:** No. **Range:** Yes (grass). **To obtain tee times:** Call 7 days in advance for weekends.
Subscriber comments: Some very challenging holes...Good walking course...Sporty course, fun...Mogul-mania, must hit it straight off the tee...Short but good test, tough 18th...Tough, hilly course...Good back nine.

★★★½CRYSTAL SPRINGS GOLF CLUB
123 Crystal Springs Rd., Hamburg, 07419, Sussex County, (973)827-1444, 56 miles NW of New York City.
Opened: 1991. **Holes:** 18. **Par:** 72/72. **Yards:** 6,857/5,131. **Course rating:** 74.1/70.5.
Slope: 137/123. **Architect:** Robert von Hagge. **Green fee:** $29/$80. **Credit cards:**
MC,VISA,AMEX. **Reduced fees:** Weekdays, low season, resort guests, twilight.
Caddies: No. **Golf carts:** Included in Green Fee. **Discount golf packages:** Yes.
Season: April-Nov. **High:** May-Sept. **On site lodging:** No. **Rental clubs:** Yes. **Walking policy:** Mandatory cart. **Metal spikes allowed:** Yes. **Range:** Yes (grass). **To obtain tee times:** Call 10 days in advance.
Subscriber comments: Beautiful rolling fairways and overall scenery...Nos. 10 and 11 are beautiful quarry holes...Keep it in the short grass...Challenging, scenic, some "one-of-a-kind" holes...Awesome links holes...Darth Vader design...10th hole worth the trip...A real test, bring a camera for the 10th.

★★★DARLINGTON GOLF COURSE
2777 Campgaw Rd., Mahwah, 07430, Bergen County, (201)327-8770.
Architect: Nicholas Psiahas. **Caddies:** No. **Discount golf packages:** No. **On site lodging:** No. **Rental clubs:** No. **Metal spikes allowed:** Yes. **Range:** No.
Call club for further information.
Subscriber comments: Well run muny...Lots of hills and blind shots...Heavy play, nice old course...Some nice challenging holes for a muny...Short par 5s...If you hit bad shots, you will be penalized.

★★★DEERWOOD GOLF CLUB
Woodland Rd., Westhampton, (609)265-1800.
Call club for further information.
Subscriber comments: A great surprise. Looks like a Myrtle Beach course...Front nine holes harder than back...Best course in Mt. Holly area...Not for high handicapper.

★½EAST ORANGE GOLF COURSE
440 Parsonage Hill Rd., Short Hills, 07078, Essex County, (973)379-7190, 10 miles W of Newark.
Opened: 1920. **Holes:** 18. **Par:** 72/73. **Yards:** 6,120/5,640. **Course rating:** 67.6/69.8. **Slope:** 100/105. **Architect:** Tom Bendelow. **Green fee:** $25/$30. **Credit cards:** None. **Reduced fees:** Weekdays, twilight, juniors. **Caddies:** No. **Golf carts:** $20. **Discount golf packages:** No. **Season:** April-Dec. **High:** May-Sept. **On site lodging:** No. **Rental clubs:** No. **Walking policy:** Unrestricted walking. **Metal spikes allowed:** Yes. **Range:** No. **To obtain tee times:** First come, first served after 11 a.m. weekends only.

★★EMERSON GOLF CLUB
PU-99 Palisade Ave., Emerson, 07630, Bergen County, (201)261-1100, 15 miles NE of New York City.
Opened: 1963. **Holes:** 18. **Par:** 71/71. **Yards:** 6,702/5,625. **Course rating:** 71.1/70.8. **Slope:** 118/117. **Architect:** N/A. **Green fee:** $69. **Credit cards:** MC,VISA,AMEX. **Reduced fees:** Weekdays, low season, twilight, juniors. **Caddies:** No. **Golf carts:** Included in Green Fee. **Discount golf packages:** No. **Season:** April-Jan. **High:** May-Sept. **On site lodging:** No. **Rental clubs:** Yes. **Walking policy:** Walking at certain times. **Metal spikes allowed:** Yes. **Range:** Yes (grass). **To obtain tee times:** Call up to 5 days in advance.

★★★FARMSTEAD GOLF & COUNTRY CLUB
PU-88 Lawrence Rd., Lafayette, 07848, Sussex County, (973)383-1666, 50 miles W of New York City.
Opened: 1963. **Holes:** 27. **Architect:** Byron Phoebus. **Green fee:** $21/$40. **Credit cards:** MC,VISA,AMEX. **Reduced fees:** Low season, twilight, seniors. **Caddies:** No. **Golf carts:** $26. **Discount golf packages:** No. **Season:** March-Dec. **High:** May-Oct. **On site lodging:** No. **Rental clubs:** Yes. **Metal spikes allowed:** Yes. **Range:** No. **To obtain tee times:** Call 7 days in advance. For weekends call after 10 a.m.
CLUBVIEW/LAKEVIEW
Par: 71/70. **Yards:** 6,680/4,910. **Course rating:** 71.3/67.0. **Slope:** 118/112. **Walking policy:** Walking at certain times.
CLUBVIEW/VALLEYVIEW
Par: 69/70. **Yards:** 6,221/4,822. **Course rating:** 69.3/67.3. **Slope:** 117/115. **Walking policy:** Mandatory cart.
LAKEVIEW/VALLEYVIEW
Par: 68/68. **Yards:** 6,161/4,636. **Course rating:** 68.9/65.6. **Slope:** 116/111. **Walking policy:** Walking at certain times.
Subscriber comments: Good value, 27 holes, all different...Par 3s are the toughest holes on the course...Doglegs keep it interesting...Nice water holes...True test of will for those nervous on water-lined holes...Par 3s great over water.

FLANDERS VALLEY GOLF COURSE
PU-Pleasant Hill Rd., Flanders, 07836, Morris County, (973)584-5382, 50 miles W of New York City.
Opened: 1963. **Architect:** Hal Purdy/Rees Jones. **Credit cards:** None. **Reduced fees:** Weekdays, twilight, seniors. **Caddies:** No. **Golf carts:** $25. **Discount golf packages:** No. **Season:** April-Nov. **High:** May-Aug. **On site lodging:** No. **Rental clubs:** Yes. **Walking policy:** Unrestricted walking. **Metal spikes allowed:** Yes. **Range:** No. **To obtain tee times:** Call golf shop.
★★★½RED/GOLD COURSE
Holes: 18. **Par:** 72/73. **Yards:** 6,770/5,540. **Course rating:** 72.6/72.0. **Slope:** 126/121. **Green fee:** $13/$60.
Notes: 1985 USGA Women's Public Links Championship; 1973 USGA Men's Public Links Championship.
Subscriber comments: Very hilly and narrow...A terrific facility, just a bit difficult to get a tee time...Red is flat and open, Gold goes up side of mountain and is carved through the trees. Tremendous views, especially in autumn. Love par-5 10th and par-3 15th...Very interesting layout.

★★★★WHITE/BLUE COURSE

Holes: 18. **Par:** 72/72. **Yards:** 6,765/5,534. **Course rating:** 72.7/72.6.
Slope: 126/122. **Green fee:** $11/$53.
Notes: 1985 USGA Women's Public Links Championship; 1973 USGA
Men's Public Links Championship.

GREAT VALUE

Subscriber comments: Good greens, challenging and interesting
holes...More challenging than Red/Gold, subtle design...Tremendous
county-run course...Have to be in good shape to walk back nine...Well-groomed interesting course...Position a key to scoring well. Better than many private
courses...Rough extremely penal for public course, tight.

★★½FRANCIS A. BYRNE GOLF CLUB

PU-1100 Pleasant Valley Way, West Orange, 07052, Essex County, (973)736-2306, 25
miles W of New York.
Opened: 1920. **Holes:** 18. **Par:** 70/72. **Yards:** 6,653/5,384. **Course rating:** 70.2/73.0.
Slope: 128/125. **Architect:** Charles H. Banks. **Green fee:** $22/$75. **Credit cards:**
None. **Reduced fees:** Seniors, juniors. **Caddies:** No. **Discount golf**
packages: No. **Season:** April-Dec. **High:** June-Aug. **On site lodging:** No. **Rental**
clubs: Yes. **Walking policy:** Walking at certain times. **Metal spikes allowed:** Yes.
Range: No. **To obtain tee times:** First come, first served.
Subscriber comments: Great for average golfer...Challenging, hilly, sharp doglegs,
long par-3 2nd hole...Beautiful, woodsy, great back nine from the blues...Very crowded...Nos. 4, 9 and 10 are interesting...Only one short par 5, so it's tough to score.

★½FREEWAY GOLF COURSE

PU-1858 Sicklerville Rd., Sicklerville, 08081, Camden County, (609)227-1115, 16 miles
SE of Philadelphia.
Opened: 1968. **Holes:** 18. **Par:** 72/72. **Yards:** 6,536/5,395. **Course rating:** 73.6/73.4.
Slope: 111/115. **Architect:** Horace Smith. **Green fee:** $10/$18. **Credit cards:** VISA.
Reduced fees: Weekdays, low season, twilight, seniors, juniors. **Caddies:** No. **Golf**
carts: Included in Green Fee. **Discount golf packages:** No. **Season:** Year-round.
High: April-June. **On site lodging:** No. **Rental clubs:** Yes. **Walking policy:** Walking at
certain times. **Metal spikes allowed:** Yes. **Range:** Yes (grass/mats). **To obtain tee**
times: Call or come in.

★★GALLOPING HILL GOLF COURSE

PU-P.O. Box 988, Union, 07083, Union County, (908)686-1556.
Opened: 1920. **Holes:** 18. **Par:** 73/76. **Yards:** 6,690/5,514. **Course rating:** 71.3.
Slope: 122. **Architect:** Willard Wilkinson. **Green fee:** $23/$27. **Credit cards:** None.
Reduced fees: Weekdays, twilight, seniors, juniors. **Caddies:** No. **Golf carts:** $22.
Discount golf packages: No. **Season:** Year-round. **High:** April-Oct. **On site lodging:**
No. **Rental clubs:** Yes. **Walking policy:** Unrestricted walking. **Metal spikes allowed:**
Yes. **Range:** No. **To obtain tee times:** First come, first served.

★½GAMBLER RIDGE GOLF CLUB

P.O. Box 109, Cream Ridge, 08514, Monmouth County, (609)758-3588.
Call club for further information.

★★½GOLDEN PHEASANT GOLF CLUB

141 Country Club Dr. & Eayrestown Rd., Medford, 08055, Burlington County, (609)267-
4276, 20 miles SE of Philadelphia.
Opened: 1963. **Holes:** 18. **Par:** 72/72. **Yards:** 6,273/5,105. **Course rating:** 68.1/68.4.
Slope: 119/114. **Architect:** Richard Kidder/Carmen N. Capri. **Green fee:** $12/$29.
Credit cards: MC,VISA. **Reduced fees:** Weekdays, twilight, seniors. **Caddies:** No.
Golf carts: $11. **Discount golf packages:** No. **Season:** Year-round. **High:** April-Oct.
On site lodging: No. **Rental clubs:** Yes. **Walking policy:** Walking at certain times.
Metal spikes allowed: Yes. **Range:** Yes (grass/mats). **To obtain tee times:** Call
Monday before weekend and holiday.
Subscriber comments: Many eye-appealing holes...Excellent condition...Tricky, use all
your clubs...Hilly, narrow...Hole No. 4 is difficult...Watch out for flying balls first four
holes...Well kept greens and overall good playing.

★★★½GREAT GORGE COUNTRY CLUB
PU-Rte. 517, McAfee, 07428, Sussex County, (973)827-5757, 50 miles NW of New York.
Opened: 1971. **Holes:** 27. **Architect:** George Fazio. **Green fee:** $49/$75. **Credit cards:** MC,VISA,AMEX,JCB. **Reduced fees:** Weekdays, low season, resort guests, twilight, seniors. **Caddies:** No. **Golf carts:** Included in Green Fee. **Discount golf packages:** Yes. **Season:** March-Nov. **High:** May-Oct. **On site lodging:** Yes. **Rental clubs:** Yes. **Walking policy:** Mandatory cart. **Metal spikes allowed:** Yes. **Range:** Yes (grass/mats). **To obtain tee times:** Call up to 30 days in advance.
LAKE/QUARRY
Par: 71/71. **Yards:** 6,819/5,390. **Course rating:** 73.3/71.5. **Slope:** 131/124.
LAKE/RAIL
Par: 72/72. **Yards:** 6,921/5,555. **Course rating:** 73.4/72.0. **Slope:** 128/123.
QUARRY/RAIL
Par: 71/71. **Yards:** 6,826/5,539. **Course rating:** 72.7/71.7. **Slope:** 126/121.
Subscriber comments: Beautiful scenic views...Quarry holes great...Good layout, lots of water...Well kept, great experience, even for not so good golfers...Rail has a few interesting holes, especially No.3...Great scenery bring camera.

★★★GREATE BAY RESORT & COUNTRY CLUB
901 Mays Landing Rd., Somers Point, 08244, Atlantic County, (609)927-0066, 8 miles from Atlantic City.
Opened: 1921. **Holes:** 18. **Par:** 71/71. **Yards:** 6,750/5,495. **Course rating:** N/A. **Slope:** 130/126. **Architect:** Willie Park Jr./Ron Garl/George Fazio. **Green fee:** $25/$88. **Credit cards:** MC,VISA,DISC. **Reduced fees:** Weekdays, low season, resort guests, twilight. **Caddies:** No. **Golf carts:** Included in Green Fee. **Discount golf packages:** Yes. **Season:** Year-round. **High:** May-Sept. **On site lodging:** Yes. **Rental clubs:** Yes. **Walking policy:** Mandatory cart. **Metal spikes allowed:** Yes. **Range:** Yes (grass/mats). **To obtain tee times:** Call 7 days in advance.
Notes: 1988-present, ShopRite LPGA Classic.
Subscriber comments: Pro-style greens...Great course, tough but fair, fabulous condition, plenty of sand...No.9 is a great hole...Good golf course, fine greens, tricky winds...Must be accurate, 13th my favorite...Short for the ladies.

★★GREEN KNOLL GOLF COURSE
PU-587 Garretson Rd., Bridgewater, 08807, Somerset County, (908)722-1301, 30 miles W of New York City.
Opened: 1960. **Holes:** 18. **Par:** 71/72. **Yards:** 6,443/5,324. **Course rating:** 70.5/71.1. **Slope:** 120/124. **Architect:** William F. Gordon. **Green fee:** $11/$39. **Credit cards:** MC,VISA. **Reduced fees:** Twilight, seniors, juniors. **Caddies:** No. **Golf carts:** $23. **Discount golf packages:** No. **Season:** Year-round. **High:** May-Sept. **On site lodging:** No. **Rental clubs:** Yes. **Walking policy:** Unrestricted walking. **Metal spikes allowed:** No. **Range:** No. **To obtain tee times:** Call for 24-hour access for a per reservation fee.

★★HANOVER COUNTRY CLUB
Larrison Rd., Wrightstown, 08562, Burlington County, (609)758-8301.
Call club for further information.

★★★★HARBOR PINES GOLF CLUB
PU-500 St. Andrews Dr., Egg Harbor Township, 08234, (609)927-0006, 15 miles SW of Atlantic City.
Opened: 1996. **Holes:** 18. **Par:** 72/72. **Yards:** 6,827/5,099. **Course rating:** 72.3/68.8. **Slope:** 129/118. **Architect:** Stephen Kay. **Green fee:** $55/$95. **Credit cards:** N/A. **Reduced fees:** Weekdays, low season, twilight, juniors. **Caddies:** No. **Golf carts:** Included in Green Fee. **Discount golf packages:** No. **Season:** Year-round. **High:** May-Sept. **On site lodging:** No. **Rental clubs:** Yes. **Walking policy:** Mandatory cart. **Metal spikes allowed:** No. **Range:** Yes (grass/mats). **To obtain tee times:** Call up to 8 days in advance with credit card to guarantee.
Subscriber comments: Very golfer-friendly...Another outstanding new course for New Jersey...Great new course, greens wonderful...Marvelous course, tremendous condition, superior service...Forgiving for all levels of golfers, five sets of tees.

★½HENDRICKS FIELD GOLF COURSE
Franklin Ave., Belleville, 07109, Essex County, (973)751-0178.
Architect: Tom Bendelow. **Caddies:** No. **Discount golf packages:** No. **On site lodging:** No. **Rental clubs:** No. **Metal spikes allowed:** Yes. **Range:** No.
Call club for further information.

★★½HIGH MOUNTAIN GOLF CLUB
845 Ewing Ave., Franklin Lakes, 07417, Bergen County, (201)891-4653, 15 miles W of New York.
Opened: 1967. **Holes:** 18. **Par:** 71/71. **Yards:** 6,347/5,426. **Course rating:** 69.5/70.0.
Slope: 118/117. **Architect:** Alec Ternyei. **Green fee:** $27/$34. **Credit cards:** None.
Reduced fees: Weekdays, twilight. **Caddies:** No. **Golf carts:** Included in Green Fee.
Discount golf packages: No. **Season:** April-Nov. **High:** May-Oct. **On site lodging:**
No. **Rental clubs:** Yes. **Walking policy:** Walking at certain times. **Metal spikes**
allowed: Yes. **Range:** Yes (grass). **To obtain tee times:** Call Monday of the week of play.
Subscriber comments: Intimidating 1st hole. Good test...Good condition, fair test, 575-yard par 5 memorable...Nice interesting layout, great thinking man's 18th hole...Front nine is short, back nine more challenging...Nice club, pretty good condition.

★★★HIGH POINT COUNTRY CLUB
P.O. Box 1154, Montague, 07827, Sussex County, (973)293-3282.
Architect: Gerald Roby. **Caddies:** No. **Discount golf packages:** No. **On site lodging:**
No. **Rental clubs:** No. **Metal spikes allowed:** Yes. **Range:** No.
Call club for further information.
Subscriber comments: Long ride from anywhere. Hard opening par 5 over water, great short par 3 with carry over water and driveable par 4 with water carry...Doglegs all over the place...14 holes have water, some very tight shots.

★½HILLSBOROUGH COUNTRY CLUB
146 Wertsville Rd., PO Box 365, Neshanic, 08853, Somerset County, (908)369-3322, 7 miles S of Flemington.
Opened: N/A. **Holes:** 18. **Par:** 70/73. **Yards:** 5,840/5,445. **Course rating:** 68.2/74.1.
Slope: 114/119. **Architect:** N/A. **Green fee:** $18/$34. **Credit cards:** None. **Reduced fees:** Weekdays, twilight, seniors, juniors. **Caddies:** No. **Golf carts:** $14. **Discount golf**
packages: No. **Season:** Year-round weather permitting. **High:** N/A. **On site lodging:**
No. **Rental clubs:** Yes. **Walking policy:** Walking at certain times. **Metal spikes**
allowed: Yes. **Range:** Yes (grass). **To obtain tee times:** Call in advance. Call on Monday for upcoming weekend.

★★★HOLLY HILLS GOLF CLUB
PU-374 Freisburg Rd., Alloway, 08001, Salem County, (609)455-5115, 25 miles E of Wilmington, DE.
Opened: 1970. **Holes:** 18. **Par:** 72/72. **Yards:** 6,376/5,056. **Course rating:** 70.8/68.0.
Slope: 120/114. **Architect:** Horace Smith. **Green fee:** $30/$40. **Credit cards:**
MC,VISA,AMEX. **Reduced fees:** Weekdays, low season, twilight, juniors. **Caddies:** No.
Golf carts: Included in Green Fee. **Discount golf packages:** Yes. **Season:** Year-round.
High: April-Oct. **On site lodging:** No. **Rental clubs:** Yes. **Walking policy:** Walking at certain times. **Metal spikes allowed:** Yes. **Range:** Yes (grass/mats). **To obtain tee**
times: Call 7 days in advance for weekend tee times only.
Subscriber comments: A fun course with great hill holes in a relatively flat area. A real challenge from the back tees...Long course requiring precise shots...Hidden hilly jewel in Jersey, near nowhere...Enjoyable course for all levels.

★★★★HOMINY HILL GOLF COURSE
PU-92 Mercer Rd., Colts Neck, 07722, Monmouth County, (732)462-9222, 50 miles N of Philadelphia.
Opened: 1964. **Holes:** 18. **Par:** 72/72. **Yards:** 7,056/5,794. **Course rating:** 74.4/73.9.
Slope: 132/128. **Architect:** Robert Trent Jones. **Green fee:** $18/$38. **Credit cards:**
None. **Reduced fees:** Weekdays, twilight, seniors, juniors. **Caddies:** No. **Golf carts:**
$28. **Discount golf packages:** No. **Season:** March-Dec. **High:** May-Oct. **On site lodging:** No. **Rental clubs:** Yes. **Walking policy:** Unrestricted walking. **Metal spikes**

allowed: No. **Range:** Yes (grass/mats). **To obtain tee times:** Call 7 days in advance. **Notes:** 1983 USGA Men's Public Links Amateur; 1995 USGA Women's Public Links Amateur.
Subscriber comments: One of best county courses in nation, Robert Trent Jones, a great test...Tough to get tee times. Beautiful layout...Remains of one country's best public courses...A big, beautiful, thoroughbred in the rolling countryside...Water at No. 11 is a magnet...Great course, lots of doglegs.

★★★★HOWELL PARK GOLF COURSE
PU-Yellow Brook and Preventorium Rd., Farmingdale, 07727, Monmouth County, (732)938-4771, 40 miles N of Philadelphia, PA.
Opened: 1972. **Holes:** 18. **Par:** 72/72. **Yards:** 6,916/5,725. **Course rating:** 73.0/72.5. **Slope:** 126/125. **Architect:** Frank Duane. **Green fee:** $20/$41. **Credit cards:** None. **Reduced fees:** Weekdays, twilight, seniors, juniors. **Caddies:** No. **Golf carts:** Included in Green Fee. **Discount golf packages:** No. **Season:** March-Dec. **High:** April-Oct. **On site lodging:** No. **Rental clubs:** Yes. **Walking policy:** Unrestricted walking. **Metal spikes allowed:** No. **Range:** Yes (grass). **To obtain tee times:** Call golf shop.
Subscriber comments: Excellent greens...Great value, not a weak hole, second only to Hominy Hill...Out-of-county player? Good luck trying to get tee time!...Too many doglegs, well maintained...Howell Park and Hominy Hill give Monmouth County two of the best in daily fee courses.

★★½JUMPING BROOK COUNTRY CLUB
210 Jumping Brook Rd., Neptune, 07753, Monmouth County, (732)922-6140, 50 miles S of New York City.
Opened: 1925. **Holes:** 18. **Par:** 72/72. **Yards:** 6,591/5,316. **Course rating:** 71.4/71.2. **Slope:** 122/118. **Architect:** Willard Wilkinson. **Green fee:** $33/$45. **Credit cards:** MC,VISA,AMEX. **Reduced fees:** Weekdays, twilight, seniors, juniors. **Caddies:** No. **Golf carts:** $17. **Discount golf packages:** No. **Season:** Year-round. **High:** May-Sept. **On site lodging:** No. **Rental clubs:** Yes. **Walking policy:** Walking at certain times. **Metal spikes allowed:** Yes. **Range:** Yes (grass). **To obtain tee times:** Call 3 days in advance or Wednesday for the upcoming weekend.
Subscriber comments: Very pleasant...One of the toughest front nines in state, 18th hole also great...Short course. Tricky...Great old layout, improvements with new owners...Difficult greens...Nice, forgiving course, pretty design.

KNOLL COUNTRY CLUB
★★EAST COURSE
1001 Parsippany Blvd., Parsippany, 07054, Morris County, (973)263-7115.
Architect: Hal Purdy.
Call club for further information.
★★★WEST COURSE
Knoll & Green Bank Rds., Parsippany, 07054, Morris County, (973)263-7111.
Architect: Charles Banks.
Call club for further information.
Subscriber comments: Good layout, good condition...Older Northeast club, beautiful old trees, good length, attractive course...Excellent layout and challenge...Small greens, terrific finishing hole...Nice facilities.

★★LAKEWOOD COUNTRY CLUB
PU-145 Country Club Dr., Lakewood, 08701, Ocean County, (732)364-8899, 40 miles S of New York City.
Opened: 1902. **Holes:** 18. **Par:** 72/74. **Yards:** 6,200/5,800. **Course rating:** 71.0/70.7. **Slope:** 117/116. **Architect:** Willie Dunn Jr. **Green fee:** $18/$24. **Credit cards:** MC,VISA,AMEX. **Reduced fees:** Weekdays, twilight. **Caddies:** No. **Golf carts:** $24. **Discount golf packages:** No. **Season:** Year-round. **High:** June-Aug. **On site lodging:** No. **Rental clubs:** Yes. **Walking policy:** Unrestricted walking. **Metal spikes allowed:** Yes. **Range:** Yes (mats). **To obtain tee times:** Call 1 day in advance for weekdays. Call 5 days in advance for weekends.

bscriber comments: Outstanding design and conditions...Best in area, good fair-
ys and maintenance...Long, usually crowded...Fabulous muny. Very open. A healthy
k...Needs more water and sand...When wind blows, the 6th is unreachable.

MINEBROOK GOLF CLUB

-500 Schooley's Mt. Rd., Hackettstown, 07840, Morris County, (908)979-0366, 45
es W of New York.
ened: 1919. **Holes:** 18. **Par:** 70/72. **Yards:** 6,100/5,645. **Course rating:** 69.7/72.6.
pe: 128/118. **Architect:** M. Coopman/J. Rocco. **Green fee:** $22/$35. **Credit cards:**
,VISA,AMEX. **Reduced fees:** Low season, twilight, seniors, juniors. **Caddies:** No.
lf carts: $13. **Discount golf packages:** No. **Season:** March-Nov. **High:** June-Sept.
site lodging: No. **Rental clubs:** Yes. **Walking policy:** Walking at certain times.
tal spikes allowed: No. **Range:** No. **To obtain tee times:** Call up to 7 days in
vance.
ecial Notes: Formerly Hidden Hills Golf Club.

MIRY RUN COUNTRY CLUB

6 B. Sharon Rd., Robbinsville, 08691, Mercer County, (609)259-1010, 45 miles E of
ladelphia, PA.
ened: 1961. **Holes:** 18. **Par:** 72/72. **Yards:** 6,893/5,562. **Course rating:** 71.7/70.7.
pe: 119/113. **Architect:** Fred Lambert. **Green fee:** $14/$22. **Credit cards:** None.
duced fees: Twilight. **Caddies:** No. **Golf carts:** $22. **Discount golf packages:** No.
ason: Year-round. **High:** May-Sept. **On site lodging:** No. **Rental clubs:** No. **Walking**
licy: Walking at certain times. **Metal spikes allowed:** Yes. **Range:** Yes (grass). **To**
tain tee times: Call up to 4 days in advance.

½MOUNTAIN VIEW GOLF COURSE

1-Bear Tavern Rd., West Trenton, 08650, Mercer County, (609)882-4093.
ened: 1952. **Holes:** 18. **Par:** 72/73. **Yards:** 6,775/5,500. **Course rating:** 72.0/70.8.
ope: 124/118. **Architect:** N/A. **Green fee:** $11/$26. **Credit cards:** None. **Reduced**
s: Twilight, seniors, juniors. **Caddies:** No. **Golf carts:** N/A. **Discount golf pack-**
es: No. **Season:** Year-round weather permitting. **High:** April-Aug. **On site lodging:**
. **Rental clubs:** No. **Walking policy:** Unrestricted walking. **Metal spikes allowed:**
s. **Range:** Yes (grass). **To obtain tee times:** First come, first served.
bscriber comments: Very good muny. Fairly hilly in parts...Not too crowded for a NJ
any...Grand old course when greens are firm...Very hilly; demanding, but open...Great
time golf, need local knowledge, tough.

OAK RIDGE GOLF COURSE

J-136 Oak Ridge Rd., Clark, 07066, Union County, (732)574-0139.
ened: N/A. **Holes:** 18. **Par:** 70/72. **Yards:** 6,388/5,275. **Course rating:** 70.0/69.7.
ope: 110/106. **Architect:** N/A. **Green fee:** $8/$28. **Credit cards:** None. **Reduced**
es: Seniors, juniors. **Caddies:** No. **Golf carts:** $22. **Discount golf packages:** No.
ason: Year-round. **High:** April-Oct. **On site lodging:** No. **Rental clubs:** Yes. **Walking**
licy: Unrestricted walking. **Metal spikes allowed:** No. **Range:** No. **To obtain tee**
mes: Call.

½OCEAN ACRES COUNTRY CLUB

5 Buccaneer Lane, Manahawkin, 08050, Ocean County, (609)597-9393, 12 miles W
Long Beach Island.
ened: 1967. **Holes:** 18. **Par:** 72/72. **Yards:** 6,548/5,412. **Course rating:** 70.5/70.7.
ope: 120/118. **Architect:** Hal Purdy/John Davies. **Green fee:** $15/$22. **Credit cards:**
C,VISA,AMEX. **Reduced fees:** Low season, twilight. **Caddies:** No. **Golf carts:** $20.
scount golf packages: No. **Season:** Year-round. **High:** June-Aug. **On site lodging:**
. **Rental clubs:** Yes. **Walking policy:** Walking at certain times. **Metal spikes**
lowed: Yes. **Range:** No. **To obtain tee times:** Call five days in advance for weekends
d holidays only.
bscriber comments: A real nice course for the average golfer...No.10, par 3 island
le, interesting holes, good restaurant...Average in all areas...Can get crowded in July
d August...Hike from 9th to 10th.

MARRIOTT'S SEAVIEW RESORT
R-401 S. New York Rd., Absecon, 08201, Atlantic County, (609)748-7680, 8 miles NW of Atlantic City. **Green fee:** $39/$99. **Credit cards:** All major,Diners Club. **Reduced fees:** Weekdays, low season, twilight, juniors. **Caddies:** No. **Discount golf packages:** Yes. **High:** May-Oct. **On site lodging:** Yes. **Rental clubs:** Yes. **Walking policy:** Walking at certain times. **Range:** Yes (grass).

★★★½ BAY COURSE
Opened: 1914. **Holes:** 18. **Par:** 71/72. **Yards:** 6,263/5,586. **Course rating:** 69
Slope: 113/115. **Architect:** Donald Ross. **Golf carts:** N/A. **Season:** Year-round
spikes allowed: No. **To obtain tee times:** Hotel guests call 30 days in advanc
Others call 3 days in advance Monday-Thursday.
Notes: 1998 LPGA ShopRite Classic; 1985-86 LPGA Atlantic City Classic; 194
Championship.
Subscriber comments: Absolutely enjoyable golf, great pro shop staff...Sceni
course...Good for women...Ross must have designed it on a windy day...One o
best in NJ...Along the bay, windy...Must bring bug spray...Grand old course in g
shape...Great practice area.

★★★½ PINES COURSE
Opened: 1929. **Holes:** 18. **Par:** 71/75. **Yards:** 6,885/5,837. **Course rating:** 73.
Slope: 132/128. **Architect:** Toomey and Flynn/Gordon. **Golf carts:** Included in
Fee. **Season:** April-Nov. **Metal spikes allowed:** Yes. **To obtain tee times:** Hot
call 30 days in advance. Others call 3 days in advance.
Notes: 1942 PGA Championship.
Subscriber comments: Public or private, a New Jersey top 5 layout...A beauti
out, wildlife, deep traps fast greens...Tougher golf with wind blowing...Fine golf
dining. Close to casinos...Great service before and after round...Very good cou
the crab cakes are the best!)...Fine old design...Great weekend getaway.

★★½ MAYS LANDING COUNTRY CLUB
PU-1855 Cates Rd., McKee City, 08232, Atlantic County, (609)641-4411, 13 mi
Atlantic City.
Opened: 1962. **Holes:** 18. **Par:** 72/71. **Yards:** 6,662/5,432. **Course rating:** 71.
Slope: 116/114. **Architect:** Hal Purdy. **Green fee:** $15/$40. **Credit cards:** MC,\
Reduced fees: Weekdays, low season, resort guests, twilight. **Caddies:** No. **G**
carts: $14. **Discount golf packages:** Yes. **Season:** Year-round. **High:** April-Oct
site lodging: No. **Rental clubs:** Yes. **Walking policy:** Walking at certain times.
spikes allowed: Yes. **Range:** Yes (grass). **To obtain tee times:** Call up to 7 day
advance.
Subscriber comments: Good for both high and low handicap golfer...Recently
improved in several areas. A real challenge...Better every year, good value comp
other courses in area.

★½ MEADOWS GOLF CLUB
79 Two Bridges Rd., Lincoln Park, 07035, Morris County, (973)696-7212, 22 mile
New York City.
Opened: 1960. **Holes:** 18. **Par:** 68/68. **Yards:** 6,100/4,600. **Course rating:** 68.5
Slope: 116/105. **Architect:** Frank Duane. **Green fee:** $22/$39. **Credit cards:** No
Reduced fees: Weekdays, twilight, seniors. **Caddies:** No. **Golf carts:** $28. Disc
golf packages: No. **Season:** Year-round. **High:** April-Oct. **On site lodging:** No.
clubs: Yes. **Walking policy:** Walking at certain times. **Metal spikes allowed:** Yes
Range: No. **To obtain tee times:** Call for weekend tee times only.

★★★½ MERCER OAKS GOLF CLUB
PM-County Parks Commission, 640 S. Broad St, Trenton, 08650, Mercer County,
(609)936-9603, 5 miles S of Princeton.
Opened: 1993. **Holes:** 18. **Par:** 72/72. **Yards:** 7,012/6,330. **Course rating:** 73.5/7
Slope: 126/120. **Architect:** Bill Love and Brian Ault. **Green fee:** $9/$34. **Credit ca**
None. **Reduced fees:** Weekdays, twilight, seniors, juniors. **Caddies:** No. **Golf car**
$23. **Discount golf packages:** No. **Season:** April-Dec. **High:** N/A. **On site lodgin**
No. **Rental clubs:** No. **Walking policy:** Unrestricted walking. **Metal spikes allowe**
Yes. **Range:** Yes (grass). **To obtain tee times:** Call.

★★★OCEAN COUNTY GOLF COURSE AT ATLANTIS
PU-Country Club Blvd., Tuckerton, 08087, Ocean County, (609)296-2444, 30 miles N of Atlantic City.
Opened: 1961. **Holes:** 18. **Par:** 72/72. **Yards:** 6,845/5,579. **Course rating:** 73.6/71.8. **Slope:** 134/124. **Architect:** George Fazio. **Green fee:** $10/$28. **Credit cards:** None. **Reduced fees:** Twilight, seniors, juniors. **Caddies:** No. **Golf carts:** $22. **Discount golf packages:** No. **Season:** Year-round. **High:** Aug. **On site lodging:** No. **Rental clubs:** Yes. **Walking policy:** Walking at certain times. **Metal spikes allowed:** Yes. **Range:** Yes. **To obtain tee times:** Call eight days in advance at 6 p.m. I.D. card required.
Subscriber comments: Long and narrow...Crowded in summer, great off-season...Hidden greatness, extremely tough...Keep out of woods...Buggy in summer-time...Toughest South Jersey course, play in fall.

★★½OLD ORCHARD COUNTRY CLUB
54 Monmouth Rd., Eatontown, 07724, Monmouth County, (732)542-7666, 40 miles S of New York City.
Opened: 1929. **Holes:** 18. **Par:** 72/72. **Yards:** 6,588/5,575. **Course rating:** 70.5/70.8. **Slope:** 116/115. **Architect:** N/A. **Green fee:** $15/$30. **Credit cards:** MC,VISA,AMEX. **Reduced fees:** Weekdays, low season, twilight, seniors. **Caddies:** No. **Golf carts:** $32. **Discount golf packages:** No. **Season:** Year-round. **High:** May-Sept. **On site lodging:** No. **Rental clubs:** Yes. **Walking policy:** Unrestricted walking. **Metal spikes allowed:** Yes. **Range:** Yes (grass). **To obtain tee times:** Call for current month.
Subscriber comments: Flat course. Easy to walk. Good chance to score...Short course, open, some challenge...Race track nearby, makes for a great day...7th hole, island par 5, reachable, great hole...Tough greens, easy walk.

★★OVERPECK COUNTY GOLF COURSE
PU-E Cedar Lane, Teaneck, 07666, Bergen County, (201)837-8395, 10 miles W of New York.
Opened: 1968. **Holes:** 18. **Par:** 72/72. **Yards:** 6,559/5,557. **Course rating:** 72.6/73.7. **Slope:** 124/127. **Architect:** Nicholas Psiahas. **Green fee:** $45/$45. **Credit cards:** None. **Reduced fees:** Weekdays, twilight, seniors, juniors. **Caddies:** No. **Golf carts:** $20. **Discount golf packages:** No. **Season:** March-Dec. **High:** June-Sept. **On site lodging:** No. **Rental clubs:** Yes. **Walking policy:** Unrestricted walking. **Metal spikes allowed:** Yes. **Range:** Yes (grass). **To obtain tee times:** Call golf shop.

★★½PARAMUS GOLF CLUB
PU-314 Paramus Rd., Paramus, 07652, Bergen County, (201)447-6067, 15 miles W of New York City.
Opened: 1976. **Holes:** 18. **Par:** 71/70. **Yards:** 6,212/5,241. **Course rating:** 69.1/72.0. **Slope:** 118/117. **Architect:** Stephen Kay. **Green fee:** $14/$32. **Credit cards:** None. **Reduced fees:** Weekdays, seniors. **Caddies:** No. **Golf carts:** $23. **Discount golf packages:** No. **Season:** Year-round. **High:** April-Nov. **On site lodging:** No. **Rental clubs:** Yes. **Walking policy:** Unrestricted walking. **Metal spikes allowed:** Yes. **Range:** No. **To obtain tee times:** Call.
Subscriber comments: Short and open...Loads of play, need to know starter, flat and short...Course in good condition for amount of play. Good finishing holes.

★★PASCACK BROOK GOLF & COUNTRY CLUB
PU-15 Rivervale Rd., River Vale, 07675, Bergen County, (201)664-5886, 15 miles NW of New York City.
Opened: 1962. **Holes:** 18. **Par:** 71/71. **Yards:** 5,991/5,117. **Course rating:** 69.0/69.3. **Slope:** 119/117. **Architect:** John Handwerg Jr. **Green fee:** $58. **Credit cards:** MC,VISA,AMEX. **Reduced fees:** Weekdays, low season, twilight, seniors, juniors. **Caddies:** No. **Golf carts:** Included in Green Fee. **Discount golf packages:** Yes. **Season:** Year-round weather permitting. **High:** May-Sept. **On site lodging:** No. **Rental clubs:** No. **Walking policy:** Walking at certain times. **Metal spikes allowed:** Yes. **Range:** No. **To obtain tee times:** Call up to 5 days in advance.

PASSAIC COUNTY GOLF COURSE

209 Totowa Rd., Wayne, 07470, Passaic County, (973)696-8185.
Architect: Alfred H. Tull. **Caddies:** No. **Discount golf packages:** No. **On site lodging:** No. **Rental clubs:** No. **Metal spikes allowed:** Yes. **Range:** No.
Call club for further information.
★½**BLUE COURSE**
Holes: 18.
★½**RED COURSE**
Holes: 18.

★★★PENNSAUKEN COUNTRY CLUB

3800 Haddonfield Rd., Pennsauken, 08109, Camden County, (609)662-4961, 4 miles N of Philadelphia, PA.
Opened: 1930. **Holes:** 18. **Par:** 70/70. **Yards:** 6,006/4,860. **Course rating:** 67.9/67.9.
Slope: 111/111. **Architect:** N/A. **Green fee:** $21/$28. **Credit cards:** N/A. **Reduced fees:** Twilight. **Caddies:** No. **Golf carts:** $12. **Discount golf packages:** No. **Season:** Year-round. **High:** May-July. **On site lodging:** No. **Rental clubs:** Yes. **Walking policy:** Walking at certain times. **Metal spikes allowed:** Yes. **Range:** No. **To obtain tee times:** Reserve for weekend or holiday beginning at daylight on Monday prior. Reserve weekdays beginning at daylight on Wednesday prior.
Subscriber comments: For an old, heavily played layout, it's almost always in great shape and good for the ego...Small, fast, firm greens. No.7 is tough.

★★½PINE BROOK GOLF CLUB

1 Covered Bridge Blvd., Englishtown, 07726, Monmouth County, (732)536-7272.
Architect: Hal Purdy. **Caddies:** No. **Discount golf packages:** No. **On site lodging:** No. **Rental clubs:** No. **Metal spikes allowed:** Yes. **Range:** No.
Call club for further information.
Subscriber comments: Toughest short course I've played...Good starter course...Basically a par-3 course, but has some of the toughest par 3s in the state, pin placements very tough...Short course but large rolling greens make it challenging.

★★PINELANDS GOLF CLUB

PU-887 S. Mays Landing Rd., Winslow, 08037, Camden County, (609)561-8900, 25 miles NW of Altantic City.
Opened: 1963. **Holes:** 18. **Par:** 71/71. **Yards:** 6,224/5,375. **Course rating:** 69.7/70.4.
Slope: 114/119. **Architect:** N/A. **Green fee:** $12/$24. **Credit cards:** MC,VISA.
Reduced fees: Weekdays, low season, twilight. **Caddies:** No. **Golf carts:** $24.
Discount golf packages: No. **Season:** Year-round. **High:** May-Nov. **On site lodging:** No. **Rental clubs:** Yes. **Walking policy:** Walking at certain times. **Metal spikes allowed:** Yes. **Range:** Yes (grass/mats). **To obtain tee times:** Call 5 days in advance for minimum of 3 players.

★★½PRINCETON GOLF CLUB

PM-Wheeler Way, Princeton, 08611, Mercer County, (609)452-9382, 2 miles S of Princeton.
Opened: N/A. **Holes:** 18. **Par:** 70/71. **Yards:** 5,845/5,005. **Course rating:** 68.6/69.9.
Slope: 113/113. **Architect:** William Gordon and David Gordon. **Green fee:** $11/$26.
Credit cards: None. **Reduced fees:** Twilight, seniors, juniors. **Caddies:** No. **Golf carts:** $23. **Discount golf packages:** No. **Season:** Year-round. **High:** April-Aug. **On site lodging:** No. **Rental clubs:** Yes. **Walking policy:** Unrestricted walking. **Metal spikes allowed:** Yes. **Range:** Yes (grass). **To obtain tee times:** First come, first served.
Subscriber comments: Short, accuracy a must...Nice layout...Challenging tight course that makes you hit accurate shots off tee...Our favorite. Excellent bargain...Short and narrow, good walking course.

★★★QUAIL BROOK GOLF COURSE

PU-625 New Brunswick Rd., Somerset, 08873, Somerset County, (908)231-1122, 30 miles W of New York City.
Opened: 1982. **Holes:** 18. **Par:** 71/72. **Yards:** 6,617/5,385. **Course rating:** 71.4/70.9.
Slope: 123/119. **Architect:** Edmund Ault. **Green fee:** $11/$39. **Credit cards:** MC,VISA.
Reduced fees: Twilight, seniors, juniors. **Caddies:** No. **Golf carts:** $23. **Discount golf**

packages: No. **Season:** Year-round. **High:** May-Sept. **On site lodging:** No. **Rental clubs:** Yes. **Walking policy:** Unrestricted walking. **Metal spikes allowed:** Yes. **Range:** Yes (mats). **To obtain tee times:** 24-hour access for tee time for a per reservation fee. **Subscriber comments:** Good track. Well bunkered and decent condition. Nos. 17 and 18 are two toughest in area...Par 3 11th beautiful from elevated tee.

★★½RAMBLEWOOD COUNTRY CLUB
PU-200 Country Club Pkwy., Mt. Laurel, 08054, Burlington County, (609)235-2118, 8 miles E of Philadelphia.
Opened: 1962. **Holes:** 27. **Architect:** Edmund Ault. **Green fee:** $28/$35. **Credit cards:** MC,VISA. **Reduced fees:** Weekdays, low season, twilight, seniors. **Caddies:** No. **Golf carts:** $15. **Discount golf packages:** Yes. **Season:** Year-round. **High:** April-Oct. **On site lodging:** No. **Rental clubs:** Yes. **Walking policy:** Walking at certain times. **Metal spikes allowed:** Yes. **Range:** No. **To obtain tee times:** Call 7 days in advance.
RED/BLUE
Par: 72/73. **Yards:** 6,723/5,499. **Course rating:** 72.1/71.4. **Slope:** 130/126.
RED/WHITE
Par: 72/74. **Yards:** 6,883/5,741. **Course rating:** 72.9/72.7. **Slope:** 130/128.
WHITE/BLUE
Par: 72/73. **Yards:** 6,624/5,308. **Course rating:** 71.1/70.1. **Slope:** 129/123.
Subscriber comments: Another great course, good conditions...Some tight fairways, long par 5s...Like the three different nines...Blue is more difficult...Wide open fairways fool big hitters.

★★½RANCOCAS GOLF CLUB
PU-Clubhouse Dr., Willingboro, 08046, Burlington County, (609)877-5344, 10 miles N of Philadelphia.
Opened: 1968. **Holes:** 18. **Par:** 71/72. **Yards:** 6,634/5,284. **Course rating:** 73.0/73.0. **Slope:** 130/127. **Architect:** Robert Trent Jones. **Green fee:** $20/$42. **Credit cards:** MC,VISA. **Reduced fees:** Weekdays, low season, twilight, seniors, juniors. **Caddies:** No. **Golf carts:** Included in Green Fee. **Discount golf packages:** Yes. **Season:** Year-round. **High:** April-Nov. **On site lodging:** No. **Rental clubs:** Yes. **Walking policy:** Walking at certain times. **Metal spikes allowed:** Yes. **Range:** Yes (mats). **To obtain tee times:** Call up to 7 days in advance.
Subscriber comments: Robert Trent Jones with two souls, open and woods...Good for all skill levels...Excellent design, difficult 9th...Challenging and scenic...Flat front, hilly back...Good challenge, flat, fairly long...Excellent No.11.

★★★½RIVER VALE COUNTRY CLUB
PU-660 Rivervale Rd., River Vale, 07675, Bergen County, (201)391-2300, 30 miles N of New York City.
Opened: 1928. **Holes:** 18. **Par:** 72/74. **Yards:** 6,470/5,293. **Course rating:** 71.4/70.7. **Slope:** 128/123. **Architect:** Orrin Smith. **Green fee:** $61/$87. **Credit cards:** MC,VISA,AMEX. **Reduced fees:** Low season, twilight. **Caddies:** No. **Golf carts:** Included in Green Fee. **Discount golf packages:** Yes. **Season:** March-Nov. **High:** June-Sept. **On site lodging:** No. **Rental clubs:** Yes. **Walking policy:** Mandatory cart. **Metal spikes allowed:** Yes. **Range:** Yes. **To obtain tee times:** Call up to 14 days in advance.
Subscriber comments: A gem...Short, good course...Good sushi...Great operation, treated us well...Short but interesting, rolling terrain...Great shotmaking holes.

★★ROCKLEIGH GOLF COURSE
15 Paris Ave., Rockleigh, 07647, Bergen County, (201)768-6353.
Architect: Alfred H. Tull. **Caddies:** No. **Discount golf packages:** No. **On site lodging:** No. **Rental clubs:** No. **Metal spikes allowed:** Yes. **Range:** No.
Call club for further information.

★½ROLLING GREENS GOLF CLUB
PU-214 Newton-Sparta Rd, Newton, 07860, Sussex County, (973)383-3082, 60 miles NW of New York City.
Opened: 1969. **Holes:** 18. **Par:** 65/67. **Yards:** 5,189/4,679. **Course rating:** 64.8/62.1. **Slope:** 110/98. **Architect:** Nicholas Psiahas. **Green fee:** $17/$23. **Credit cards:** MC,VISA,AMEX. **Reduced fees:** Weekdays, low season, twilight, seniors. **Caddies:**

No. **Golf carts:** $12. **Discount golf packages:** No. **Season:** Feb.-Dec. **High:** July-Sept. **On site lodging:** No. **Rental clubs:** Yes. **Walking policy:** Unrestricted walking. **Metal spikes allowed:** Yes. **Range:** No. **To obtain tee times:** Call up to 7 days in advance.

★★½RON JAWORSKI'S EAGLES' NEST COUNTRY CLUB
Woodbury-Glassboro Rd., Sewell, 08080, Gloucester County, (609)468-3542.
Opened: N/A. **Holes:** 18. **Par:** 71/71. **Yards:** 6,376/5,210. **Course rating:** 71.3/71.2. **Slope:** 130/125. **Architect:** W. F. Gordon and David Gordon. **Green fee:** $18/$25. **Credit cards:** MC,VISA,AMEX. **Reduced fees:** Weekdays, low season, twilight, seniors. **Caddies:** No. **Golf carts:** $10. **Discount golf packages:** No. **Season:** Year-round. **High:** April-Oct. **On site lodging:** No. **Rental clubs:** No. **Walking policy:** Walking at certain times. **Metal spikes allowed:** Yes. **Range:** No. **To obtain tee times:** Call anytime.
Subscriber comments: Fun course, staff makes you feel welcome...Back nine is tight...Not many doglegs. Long bunker-filled holes...Easy front, back nine is great. Good greens, narrow fairways, some hills...No.7 is an excellent hole.

★★★RUTGERS UNIVERSITY GOLF CLUB
PU-777 Hoes Lane, Piscataway, 08854, Middlesex County, (732)445-2631, (732)445-2631, 3 miles N of New Brunswick.
Opened: 1963. **Holes:** 18. **Par:** 72/71. **Yards:** 6,300/5,461. **Course rating:** 69.9/71.3. **Slope:** 115/116. **Architect:** Hal Purdy. **Green fee:** $21/$30. **Credit cards:** None. **Reduced fees:** Weekdays. **Caddies:** No. **Golf carts:** $27. **Discount golf packages:** No. **Season:** March-Dec. **High:** N/A. **On site lodging:** No. **Rental clubs:** No. **Walking policy:** Unrestricted walking. **Metal spikes allowed:** Yes. **Range:** No. **To obtain tee times:** Call Thursday at noon for following Monday-Friday. Come in up to 7 days in advance for weekend.
Subscriber comments: Made for the average golfer, always pleasant...Tough greens. Play from the blues or else it's a little short...Good course to learn and teach on...Tough to get a tee time...Stay on fairways or you are dead.

SAND BARRENS GOLF CLUB
PU-1765 Rte. 9 North, Swainton, 08210, (609)465-3555, (888)465-3122.
Opened: 1997. **Holes:** 18. **Par:** 72/72. **Yards:** 6,902/4,817. **Course rating:** 72.5/68.9. **Slope:** 134/119. **Architect:** Michael Hurdzan and Dana Fry. **Caddies:** No. **Discount golf packages:** No. **On site lodging:** No. **Rental clubs:** No. **Metal spikes allowed:** No. **Range:** No.
Call club for further information.

★★★SHARK RIVER GOLF COURSE
PU-320 Old Corlies Ave., Neptune, 07753, Monmouth County, (908)922-4141, 50 miles S of Newark.
Opened: 1973. **Holes:** 18. **Par:** 71/71. **Yards:** 6,176/5,532. **Course rating:** N/A. **Slope:** 112/116. **Architect:** Joseph "Scotty" Anson. **Green fee:** $29/$40. **Credit cards:** None. **Reduced fees:** Weekdays, twilight, seniors, juniors. **Caddies:** No. **Golf carts:** $27. **Discount golf packages:** No. **Season:** March-Dec. **High:** June-Sept. **On site lodging:** No. **Rental clubs:** Yes. **Walking policy:** Unrestricted walking. **Metal spikes allowed:** No. **Range:** No. **To obtain tee times:** Nonresidents are on first come, first served.
Subscriber comments: Well kept course with some challenging holes...Lots of trouble off fairways, No.9 is 586 yards long...Easy par 3s, tough par 5s...Good practice course...Tight...Good course, a lot of long par 4s.

★★½SPOOKY BROOK GOLF COURSE
PU-582 Elizabeth Ave., Somerset, 08873, Somerset County, (732)873-2242, 30 miles W of New York City.
Opened: 1970. **Holes:** 18. **Par:** 71/72. **Yards:** 6,612/5,376. **Course rating:** 71.0/70.8. **Slope:** 121/122. **Architect:** Edmund Ault. **Green fee:** $11/$39. **Credit cards:** MC,VISA. **Reduced fees:** Twilight, seniors, juniors. **Caddies:** No. **Golf carts:** $23. **Discount golf packages:** No. **Season:** Year-round. **High:** May-Sept. **On site lodging:** No. **Rental clubs:** Yes. **Walking policy:** Unrestricted walking. **Metal spikes allowed:** No. **Range:** Yes (grass/mats). **To obtain tee times:** 24-hour access number for a per reservation fee.

Subscriber comments: Fairly long, wide open...Good course for seniors and beginners...Wide fairways, slow play...Course in good condition and it's pretty...Blind shots...Easy to walk...Good value.

★★SPRING MEADOW GOLF COURSE
PU-4181 Atlantic Ave., Farmingdale, 07727, Monmouth County, (732)449-0806, 40 miles E of Trenton.
Opened: 1920. **Holes:** 18. **Par:** 72/76. **Yards:** 5,953/5,310. **Course rating:** 68.7/70.4. **Slope:** 118/120. **Architect:** Ron Faulseit. **Green fee:** $19/$22. **Credit cards:** None. **Reduced fees:** Weekdays, twilight, seniors. **Caddies:** No. **Golf carts:** $26. **Discount golf packages:** No. **Season:** Year-round. **High:** April-Oct. **On site lodging:** No. **Rental clubs:** Yes. **Walking policy:** Unrestricted walking. **Metal spikes allowed:** Yes. **Range:** Yes (grass/mats). **To obtain tee times:** First come, first served.

★★★½SUNSET VALLEY GOLF COURSE
PU-47 W. Sunset Rd., Pompton Plains, 07444, Morris County, (973)835-1515.
Opened: 1974. **Holes:** 18. **Par:** 70/70. **Yards:** 6,483/5,274. **Course rating:** 71.4/70.2. **Slope:** 129/122. **Architect:** Hal Purdy. **Green fee:** $13/$60. **Credit cards:** None. **Reduced fees:** Twilight, seniors. **Caddies:** No. **Golf carts:** $25. **Discount golf packages:** No. **Season:** April-Dec. **High:** May-Sept. **On site lodging:** No. **Rental clubs:** Yes. **Walking policy:** Unrestricted walking. **Metal spikes allowed:** Yes. **Range:** No. **To obtain tee times:** Call or come in person.
Subscriber comments: One of New Jersey's best public courses...Glass greens, tough putting...Beautiful course, crowded...Greens large, three-putts galore...No.16, 17 and 18 must be the three toughest holes in state...Nice changes in elevation, scenic...No.7 may be a little gimmicky.

TAMARACK GOLF COURSE
PU-97 Hardenburg Lane, East Brunswick, 08816, Middlesex County, (732)821-8881.
Opened: 1970. **Architect:** Hal Purdy. **Green fee:** $6/$57. **Credit cards:** None. **Reduced fees:** Seniors, juniors. **Caddies:** No. **Golf carts:** $26. **Discount golf packages:** No. **Season:** Year-round. **High:** March-Oct. **On site lodging:** No. **Rental clubs:** Yes. **Walking policy:** Unrestricted walking. **Metal spikes allowed:** Yes. **Range:** Yes. **To obtain tee times:** Call.
★★½BLUE/GOLD COURSE
Holes: 18. **Par:** 72/72. **Yards:** 7,025/5,810. **Course rating:** 73.3/72.5. **Slope:** 118/113.
Subscriber comments: Watch out for additional out-of-county fee...Very difficult but fair. More open than Red/White...Short and open.
★★½RED/WHITE COURSE
Holes: 18. **Par:** 72/72. **Yards:** 7,025/5,810. **Course rating:** 73.3/72.5. **Slope:** 118/113.
Subscriber comments: Best track of the two, good variety but needs work...Very nice shape. Very challenging: long and narrow...Better layout, loved No.6 White...Both are good designs, both have shown vast improvement in conditioning.

★★VALLEYBROOK GOLF CLUB
PU-1 Golfview, Blackwood, 08012, Camden County, (609)227-3171, 10 miles SE of Camden.
Opened: 1990. **Holes:** 18. **Par:** 72/72. **Yards:** 6,123/5,319. **Course rating:** 70.6/69.1. **Slope:** 125/120. **Architect:** N/A. **Green fee:** $12/$24. **Credit cards:** None. **Reduced fees:** Weekdays, twilight. **Caddies:** No. **Golf carts:** N/A. **Discount golf packages:** Yes. **Season:** Year-round. **High:** April-Oct. **On site lodging:** No. **Rental clubs:** Yes. **Walking policy:** Walking at certain times. **Metal spikes allowed:** Yes. **Range:** Yes (grass/mats). **To obtain tee times:** Call 7 days in advance.

★★WARRENBROOK GOLF COURSE
PU-500 Warrenville Rd., Warren, 07059, Somerset County, (908)754-8402, 30 miles W of New York City.
Opened: 1978. **Holes:** 18. **Par:** 71/70. **Yards:** 6,372/5,095. **Course rating:** 70.8/69.2. **Slope:** 124/117. **Architect:** Hal Purdy. **Green fee:** $11/$39. **Credit cards:** MC,VISA. **Reduced fees:** Twilight, seniors, juniors. **Caddies:** No. **Golf carts:** $23. **Discount golf packages:** No. **Season:** April-Nov. **High:** May-Sept. **On site lodging:** No. **Rental clubs:** Yes. **Walking policy:** Unrestricted walking. **Metal spikes allowed:** No. **Range:** No. **To obtain tee times:** 24-hour access number for a per reservation fee.

★★WEDGEWOOD COUNTRY CLUB

200 Hurffville Rd., Turnersville, 08012, Camden County, (609)227-5522.
Architect: Gary Wrenn. **Caddies:** No. **Discount golf packages:** No. **On site lodging:** No. **Rental clubs:** No. **Metal spikes allowed:** Yes. **Range:** No.
Call club for further information.

★★½WESTWOOD GOLF CLUB

PU-850 Kings Hwy., Woodbury, 08096, Gloucester County, (609)845-2000, 10 miles S of Philadelphia, PA.
Opened: 1961. **Holes:** 18. **Par:** 71/72. **Yards:** 5,968/5,182. **Course rating:** 68.2/69.1. **Slope:** 116/114. **Architect:** Horace W. Smith. **Green fee:** $19/$23. **Credit cards:** None. **Reduced fees:** N/A. **Caddies:** No. **Golf carts:** $24. **Discount golf packages:** No. **Season:** Year-round. **High:** April-Oct. **On site lodging:** No. **Rental clubs:** No. **Walking policy:** Mandatory cart. **Metal spikes allowed:** Yes. **Range:** No. **To obtain tee times:** Call on Monday for upcoming weekend.
Subscriber comments: Nice tune-up course...Beautiful course, get your money's worth. A great back nine...Slow play...Acceptable layout, not much trouble...Short course, need accuracy...11th green unfair, unreceptive to tee shots...I am a beginner and I like the price...Greens are always in nice shape.

★★½WILLOW BROOK COUNTRY CLUB

4310 Bridgeboro Rd., Moorestown, 08057, Burlington County, (609)461-0131, 10 miles SE of Cherry Hills.
Opened: 1967. **Holes:** 18. **Par:** 72/72. **Yards:** 6,457/5,028. **Course rating:** 71.2/68.3. **Slope:** 125/110. **Architect:** William Gordon. **Green fee:** $19/$28. **Credit cards:** MC,VISA,DISC. **Reduced fees:** Weekdays, low season, twilight, seniors. **Caddies:** No. **Golf carts:** $10. **Discount golf packages:** No. **Season:** Year-round. **High:** May-Sept. **On site lodging:** No. **Rental clubs:** Yes. **Walking policy:** Walking at certain times. **Metal spikes allowed:** Yes. **Range:** Yes (grass). **To obtain tee times:** Call Monday to Friday for weekend tee time and call anytime for weekday.
Subscriber comments: Great finishing hole, second shot over water...Not really difficult...Short, open, great finishing...Nice tune up course, No.3 is best hole...Flat, open but good value...Overpriced...Very nice fairways, great layout.

★★½WOODLAKE GOLF & COUNTRY CLUB

25 New Hampshire Ave., Lakewood, 08701, Ocean County, (732)370-1002, 45 miles S of Newark.
Opened: 1972. **Holes:** 18. **Par:** 72/74. **Yards:** 6,766/5,557. **Course rating:** 72.5/72.2. **Slope:** 126/120. **Architect:** Edward L. Packard. **Green fee:** $29/$50. **Credit cards:** MC,VISA,AMEX. **Reduced fees:** Weekdays, low season, twilight. **Caddies:** No. **Golf carts:** $17. **Discount golf packages:** Yes. **Season:** Year-round. **High:** May-Aug. **On site lodging:** No. **Rental clubs:** Yes. **Walking policy:** Mandatory cart. **Metal spikes allowed:** Yes. **Range:** Yes (grass/mats). **To obtain tee times:** Non-members call 3 days in advance.
Subscriber comments: Some great holes, too expensive, more of a target golf course...Some condos...Well kept, challenging...Flat, level, open and enough water to keep you interested...Challenging course, tough greens, immaculate traps.

★★½ANGEL FIRE COUNTRY CLUB

Drawer B, Angel Fire, 87710, Taos County, (505)377-3055, 150 miles NW of Albuquerque.

Opened: N/A. **Holes:** 18. **Par:** 72/72. **Yards:** 6,624/5,328. **Course rating:** N/A. **Slope:** 128/118. **Architect:** N/A. **Green fee:** N/A. **Credit cards:** All major. **Reduced fees:** Low season, resort guests. **Caddies:** No. **Golf carts:** $20. **Discount golf packages:** Yes. **Season:** May-Oct. **High:** June-Sept. **On site lodging:** Yes. **Rental clubs:** No. **Walking policy:** N/A. **Metal spikes allowed:** Yes. **Range:** Yes. **To obtain tee times:** N/A.

★★★ARROYO DEL OSO MUNICIPAL GOLF COURSE

PU-7001 Osuna Rd. N.E., Albuquerque, 87109, Bernalillo County, (505)884-7505.

Opened: 1966. **Holes:** 18. **Par:** 72/73. **Yards:** 6,892/5,998. **Course rating:** 72.3/72.3. **Slope:** 125/120. **Architect:** Arthur Jack Snyder. **Green fee:** $14/$14. **Credit cards:** MC,VISA,DISC. **Reduced fees:** Twilight, seniors, juniors. **Caddies:** No. **Golf carts:** $9. **Discount golf packages:** No. **Season:** Year-round. **High:** April-Nov. **On site lodging:** No. **Rental clubs:** Yes. **Walking policy:** Unrestricted walking. **Metal spikes allowed:** Yes. **Range:** Yes (grass/mats). **To obtain tee times:** Call in advance for weekends and holidays.

Subscriber comments: Interesting...Great to walk.

Special Notes: Also has 9-hole par-36 Dam Course.

DOS LAGOS GOLF CLUB

PU-232 Duffer Lane, Anthony, 88021, Dona Ana County, (505)882-2830, 20 miles N of El Paso.

Opened: 1963. **Holes:** 18. **Par:** 72/72. **Yards:** 6,424/5,658. **Course rating:** 70.4/70.6. **Slope:** 120/111. **Architect:** Sam Gillett. **Green fee:** $11/$15. **Credit cards:** None. **Reduced fees:** Twilight, juniors. **Caddies:** No. **Golf carts:** $16. **Discount golf packages:** No. **Season:** Year-round. **High:** May-Aug. **On site lodging:** No. **Rental clubs:** Yes. **Walking policy:** Unrestricted walking. **Metal spikes allowed:** Yes. **Range:** Yes (grass). **To obtain tee times:** Weekends and holidays call up to one week in advance. Weekdays, call prior day.

★★★★INN OF THE MOUNTAIN GODS GOLF COURSE

R-P.O. Box 269, Rte. 4, Mescalero, 88340, Otero County, (505)257-5141, (800)446-2963, 80 miles NE of Las Cruces.

Opened: 1975. **Holes:** 18. **Par:** 72/72. **Yards:** 6,834/5,478. **Course rating:** 72.1/70.2. **Slope:** 132/128. **Architect:** Theodore G. Robinson. **Green fee:** $35/$50. **Credit cards:** All major. **Reduced fees:** N/A. **Caddies:** No. **Golf carts:** $20. **Discount golf packages:** No. **Season:** March-Dec. **High:** May-Oct. **On site lodging:** Yes. **Rental clubs:** Yes. **Walking policy:** Mandatory cart. **Metal spikes allowed:** Yes. **Range:** Yes (grass/mats). **To obtain tee times:** Resort guests may call anytime. Nonguests call 14 days in advance.

Notes: Ranked 10th in 1997 Best in State.

Subscriber comments: Great par-3 finishing hole...Awesome mountain course...Fast greens, great scenery, commune with nature...Everybody should play this once in life!

★★LADERA GOLF COURSE

PM-3401 Ladera Dr. N.W., Albuquerque, 87120, Bernalillo County, (505)836-4449.

Opened: 1980. **Holes:** 18. **Par:** 72/72. **Yards:** 7,107/5,966. **Course rating:** 73.0/72.8. **Slope:** 123/116. **Architect:** Dick Phelps. **Green fee:** $10/$14. **Credit cards:** MC,VISA,AMEX. **Reduced fees:** Twilight, seniors, juniors. **Caddies:** No. **Golf carts:** $20. **Discount golf packages:** Yes. **Season:** Year-round. **High:** April-Sept. **On site lodging:** No. **Rental clubs:** Yes. **Walking policy:** Unrestricted walking. **Metal spikes allowed:** Yes. **Range:** Yes (grass/mats). **To obtain tee times:** Call or come in Wednesday at 7 a.m. for upcoming weekend or holiday. Foursomes may call up to 7 days in advance for weekdays.

Special Notes: Also has 9-hole executive course.

★★★½THE LINKS AT SIERRA BLANCA

PU-105 Sierra Blanca Dr., Ruidoso, 88345, Lincoln County, (505)258-5330, (800)854-6571, 170 miles NE of El Paso.

Opened: 1990. **Holes:** 18. **Par:** 72/72. **Yards:** 6,912/5,026. **Course rating:** 71.9/62.7.

Slope: 127/104. **Architect:** Jeff Brauer and Jim Colbert. **Green fee:** $26/$65. **Credit cards:** All major. **Reduced fees:** Weekdays, low season, twilight, seniors, juniors. **Caddies:** No. **Golf carts:** $11. **Discount golf packages:** No. **Season:** Year-round. **High:** June-Sept. **On site lodging:** No. **Rental clubs:** Yes. **Walking policy:** Walking at certain times. **Metal spikes allowed:** No. **Range:** Yes (grass). **To obtain tee times:** Call days in advance.
Notes: Ranked 6th in 1997 Best in State.
Subscriber comments: Only mountain/links course I've played...Great front nine.

THE LODGE GOLF CLUB

R-1 Corona Place, Cloudcroft, 88317, Otero County, (505)682-2098, (800)395-6343, 100 miles NE of El Paso.
Opened: 1899. **Holes:** 9. **Par:** 34/34. **Yards:** 2,471/2,036. **Course rating:** 63.0/65.0.
Slope: 97/103. **Architect:** N/A. **Green fee:** $18/$26. **Credit cards:** All major. **Reduced fees:** Weekdays, resort guests, twilight. **Caddies:** No. **Golf carts:** $10. **Discount golf packages:** Yes. **Season:** April-Nov. **High:** June-Aug. **On site lodging:** Yes. **Rental clubs:** Yes. **Walking policy:** Unrestricted walking. **Metal spikes allowed:** Yes. **Range:** Yes (grass/mats). **To obtain tee times:** Call with credit card to guarantee.

LOS ALAMOS GOLF CLUB

PU-4250 Diamond Dr., Los Alamos, 87544, Los Alamos County, (505)662-8139, 35 miles N of Santa Fe.
Opened: 1947. **Holes:** 18. **Par:** 72/72. **Yards:** 6,496/5,301. **Course rating:** 70.1/68.7.
Slope: 120/113. **Architect:** Bill Keith/William Tucker. **Green fee:** $17/$21. **Credit cards:** MC,VISA. **Reduced fees:** Weekdays. **Caddies:** No. **Golf carts:** $18. **Discount golf packages:** Yes. **Season:** March-Nov. **High:** June-Sept. **On site lodging:** No. **Rental clubs:** Yes. **Walking policy:** Unrestricted walking. **Metal spikes allowed:** Yes. **Range:** Yes (mats). **To obtain tee times:** Call 1 day in advance for weekdays. Call on Wednesday for upcoming weekend or holidays.

★★½LOS ALTOS GOLF COURSE

PM-9717 Copper N.E. St., Albuquerque, 87123, Bernalillo County, (505)298-1897.
Opened: 1960. **Holes:** 18. **Par:** 71/74. **Yards:** 6,459/5,895. **Course rating:** 69.9/71.9.
Slope: 110/113. **Architect:** Bob Baldock. **Green fee:** $13/$13. **Credit cards:** MC,VISA,DISC. **Reduced fees:** Weekdays, low season, twilight, seniors, juniors. **Caddies:** No. **Golf carts:** N/A. **Discount golf packages:** No. **Season:** Year-round. **High:** May-Aug. **On site lodging:** No. **Rental clubs:** Yes. **Walking policy:** Unrestricted walking. **Metal spikes allowed:** No. **Range:** Yes (grass/mats). **To obtain tee times:** Call Wednesday for upcoming weekend.
Subscriber comments: Fun to play, very fair, nice greens.
Special Notes: Also has a 9-hole course.

★★½NEW MEXICO STATE UNIVERSITY GOLF COURSE

PU-P.O. Box 30001, Dept. 3595, Las Cruces, 88003, Dona Ana County, (505)646-3219, 45 miles N of El Paso, TX.
Opened: 1962. **Holes:** 18. **Par:** 72/74. **Yards:** 7,040/5,858. **Course rating:** 74.1/70.7.
Slope: 133/120. **Architect:** Floyd Farley. **Green fee:** $17. **Credit cards:** MC,VISA,DISC. **Reduced fees:** Weekdays, twilight. **Caddies:** No. **Golf carts:** $7. **Discount golf packages:** No. **Season:** Year-round. **High:** April-May/Sept.-Oct. **On site lodging:** No. **Rental clubs:** Yes. **Walking policy:** Unrestricted walking. **Metal spikes allowed:** Yes. **Range:** Yes (grass/mats). **To obtain tee times:** Call Friday for upcoming weekdays. Call Wednesday for upcoming weekend.
Notes: 1987 Women's NCAA Championship; 1968 Men's NCAA Championship.
Subscriber comments: Great town, great golf...Tight landing areas, difficult greens...Wind-wind-wind.

★★★NEW MEXICO TECH GOLF COURSE

PU-1 Canyon Rd., Socorro, 87801, Socorro County, (505)835-5335, 75 miles S of Albuquerque.
Opened: 1953. **Holes:** 18. **Par:** 72/73. **Yards:** 6,688/5,887. **Course rating:** 71.2/72.8.
Slope: 126/122. **Architect:** James Voss. **Green fee:** $15/$17. **Credit cards:** MC,VISA,DISC. **Reduced fees:** Twilight, seniors, juniors. **Caddies:** No. **Golf carts:** $18. **Discount golf packages:** Yes. **Season:** Year-round. **High:** April-Oct. **On site

lodging: No. **Rental clubs:** Yes. **Walking policy:** Unrestricted walking. **Metal spikes allowed:** No. **Range:** Yes (grass/mats). **To obtain tee times:** Call 7 days in advance. **Subscriber comments:** A fun old course...Need your whole game, hilly, lots of fun...One of the best.

★★½OCOTILLO PARK GOLF COURSE
PM-N. Lovington Hwy., Hobbs, 88240, Lea County, (505)397-9297, 4 miles N of Hobbs.
Opened: 1955. **Holes:** 18. **Par:** 72/72. **Yards:** 6,716/5,245. **Course rating:** 70.5/69.0.
Slope: 121/108. **Architect:** Warren Cantrell/M. Ferguson. **Green fee:** $8/$8. **Credit cards:** All major. **Reduced fees:** Weekdays, twilight, seniors, juniors. **Caddies:** No.
Golf carts: $8. **Discount golf packages:** Yes. **Season:** Year-round. **High:** April-Aug.
On site lodging: No. **Rental clubs:** Yes. **Walking policy:** Unrestricted walking. **Metal spikes allowed:** Yes. **Range:** Yes (grass/mats). **To obtain tee times:** Call Wednesday 8 a.m.

★★★PARADISE HILLS GOLF CLUB
PU-10035 Country Club Lane, Albuquerque, 87114, Bernalillo County, (505)898-7001.
Opened: 1963. **Holes:** 18. **Par:** 72/74. **Yards:** 6,801/6,090. **Course rating:** 71.7/73.5.
Slope: 125/118. **Architect:** Red Lawrence. **Green fee:** $22/$31. **Credit cards:** All major. **Reduced fees:** Weekdays, low season, twilight, seniors, juniors. **Caddies:** No.
Golf carts: $7. **Discount golf packages:** Yes. **Season:** Year-round. **High:** March-Oct.
On site lodging: Yes. **Rental clubs:** Yes. **Walking policy:** Mandatory cart. **Metal spikes allowed:** No. **Range:** Yes (grass). **To obtain tee times:** Call 7 days in advance with credit card to guarantee.
Subscriber comments: Location over 6,000 feet elevation...A good test, a pleasant surprise...Very nice course with open fairways.

PICACHO HILLS COUNTRY CLUB
6861 Via Campestre, Las Cruces, 88005, Dona Ana County, (505)523-8641.
Opened: 1978. **Holes:** 18. **Par:** 72/72. **Yards:** 6,880/5,214. **Course rating:** 72.9/70.0.
Slope: 134/118. **Architect:** Joe Finger. **Green fee:** $25/$30. **Credit cards:** MC,VISA.
Reduced fees: N/A. **Caddies:** No. **Golf carts:** N/A. **Discount golf packages:** No.
Season: Year-round. **High:** N/A. **On site lodging:** No. **Rental clubs:** Yes. **Walking policy:** Unrestricted walking. **Metal spikes allowed:** No. **Range:** Yes (grass). **To obtain tee times:** Call up to 7 days in advance. Members only play until 11 a.m. daily.

★★★★½PINON HILLS GOLF COURSE
PM-2101 Sunrise Pkwy., Farmington, 87402, San Juan County,
(505)326-6066, 180 miles N of Albuquerque.
Opened: 1989. **Holes:** 18. **Par:** 72/72. **Yards:** 7,249/5,522. **Course rating:** 73.3/71.1. **Slope:** 130/126. **Architect:** Ken Dye. **Green fee:** $12/$15. **Credit cards:** MC,VISA. **Reduced fees:** Weekdays. **Caddies:** No. **Golf carts:** $15. **Discount golf packages:** No. **Season:** Year-round. **High:** May-Oct. **On site lodging:** No. **Rental clubs:** Yes. **Walking policy:** Unrestricted walking. **Metal spikes allowed:** No. **Range:** Yes (grass/mats). **To obtain tee times:** Call 3 days in advance. Out-of-town players may call up to 60 days in advance for $5 reservation fee.
Notes: Ranked 2nd in 1997 Best in State.
Subscriber comments: Must be one of the best muny courses anywhere...The best in New Mexico...Golf Digest made this famous, now you can't get on...Great layout and views...It's almost worth moving to Farmington for this!...Helps to play with a local.

(GREAT VALUE)

★★★PUEBLO DE COCHITI GOLF COURSE
PU-5200 Cochiti Hwy., Cochiti Lake, 87083, Sandoval County, (505)465-2239, 35 miles SW of Santa Fe.
Opened: 1981. **Holes:** 18. **Par:** 72/72. **Yards:** 6,451/5,292. **Course rating:** 71.2/70.6.
Slope: 131/121. **Architect:** Robert Trent Jones Jr. **Green fee:** $20/$25. **Credit cards:** MC,VISA,DISC. **Reduced fees:** Weekdays. **Caddies:** No. **Golf carts:** $20. **Discount golf packages:** No. **Season:** Year-round weather permitting. **High:** March-Sept. **On site lodging:** No. **Rental clubs:** Yes. **Walking policy:** Unrestricted walking. **Metal spikes allowed:** Yes. **Range:** Yes (grass). **To obtain tee times:** Call up to 7 days in advance.
Notes: Ranked 7th in 1997 Best in State.

Subscriber comments: One of the best anywhere...Too many goofy holes...Short, tight course...Very hilly, small greens, fun course...Spectacular location, worth the effort to find it. No clubhouse...A must experience, awesome elevated tees...True championship course...Local knowledge helps.

RIO MIMBRES COUNTRY CLUB

Motel Drive East, Deming, 88030, Luna County, (505)546-9481, 100 miles NW of El Paso.
Opened: 1950. **Holes:** 18. **Par:** 72/72. **Yards:** 3,701/5,454. **Course rating:** 72.0/69.0.
Slope: 125/111. **Architect:** Keith Foster. **Green fee:** $14/$16. **Credit cards:** None.
Reduced fees: Juniors. **Caddies:** No. **Golf carts:** $7. **Discount golf packages:** Yes.
Season: Year-round. **High:** June-Aug. **On site lodging:** No. **Rental clubs:** Yes.
Walking policy: Unrestricted walking. **Metal spikes allowed:** Yes. **Range:** Yes (grass).
To obtain tee times: Tee times for weekends only. Members have priority until Friday morning.

RIO RANCHO GOLF & COUNTRY CLUB

500 Country Club Dr. S.E., Rio Rancho, 87124, Sandoval County, (505)892-8440.
Architect: Desmond Muirhead. **Caddies:** No. **Discount golf packages:** No. **On site lodging:** No. **Rental clubs:** No. **Metal spikes allowed:** Yes. **Range:** Yes.
Call club for further information.
Subscriber comments: Tricky water holes on front nine.

★★★SANTA ANA GOLF CLUB

PU-288 Prairie Star Rd., Bernalillo, 87004, Sandoval County, (505)867-9464, 15 miles N of Albuquerque.
Opened: 1991. **Holes:** 27. **Architect:** Ken Killian. **Green fee:** $25/$32. **Credit cards:** All major. **Reduced fees:** Weekdays, low season, twilight, seniors, juniors. **Caddies:** No. **Golf carts:** $10. **Discount golf packages:** No. **Season:** Year-round. **High:** March-Oct. **On site lodging:** No. **Rental clubs:** Yes. **Walking policy:** Unrestricted walking.
Metal spikes allowed: Yes. **Range:** Yes (grass/mats). **To obtain tee times:** Call 7 days in advance for weekdays and 3 days in advance for weekends.
Notes: Ranked 3rd in 1997 Best in State. 1999 Women's Amateur Public Links Championship; 1993 Nike Tour.
CHEENA/STAR
Par: 71/71. **Yards:** 7,152/5,058. **Course rating:** 72.9/67.3. **Slope:** 134/121.
TAMAYA/CHEENA
Par: 71/71. **Yards:** 7,258/5,044. **Course rating:** 74.1/68.2. **Slope:** 132/122.
TAMAYA/STAR
Par: 72/72. **Yards:** 7,192/4,924. **Course rating:** 73.1/68.3. **Slope:** 133/118.
Subscriber comments: Nice use of natural setting...Can be very windy...Great wind course, fair for all handicaps...Another beauty and challenging...Tough par 3s. Desert course, greens great but slopes severe.
Special Notes: Formerly Valle Grande Golf Club.

★★★TAOS COUNTRY CLUB

Hwy. 570 W., Rancho de Taos, 87557, Taos County, (505)758-7300, (800)758-7375, 58 miles N of Santa Fe.
Opened: 1992. **Holes:** 18. **Par:** 72/72. **Yards:** 7,302/5,310. **Course rating:** 73.6/69.0.
Slope: 129/125. **Architect:** Jep Wille. **Green fee:** $23/$40. **Credit cards:** MC,VISA,AMEX. **Reduced fees:** Weekdays, twilight. **Caddies:** Yes. **Golf carts:** $22.
Discount golf packages: Yes. **Season:** March-Nov. **High:** June-Sept. **On site lodging:** No. **Rental clubs:** Yes. **Walking policy:** Unrestricted walking. **Metal spikes allowed:** No. **Range:** Yes (grass/mats). **To obtain tee times:** Call 7 days in advance.
Notes: Ranked 4th in 1997 Best in State.
Subscriber comments: Ball goes a long way at 7,000 ft. elevation...A jewel in the desert...Go there!

TIERRA DEL SOL GOLF COURSE

1000 Golf Course Rd., Belen, 87002, Valencia County, (505)865-5056, 34 miles S of Albuquerque.
Opened: 1971. **Holes:** 18. **Par:** 72/72. **Yards:** 6,703/5,512. **Course rating:** 71.0/71.2.
Slope: 117/114. **Architect:** N/A. **Green fee:** $15/$19. **Credit cards:** MC,VISA.

Reduced fees: Weekdays, twilight, juniors. **Caddies:** No. **Golf carts:** $9. **Discount golf packages:** No. **Season:** Year-round. **High:** April-Oct. **On site lodging:** No. **Rental clubs:** Yes. **Walking policy:** Walking at certain times. **Metal spikes allowed:** Yes. **Range:** Yes (grass). **To obtain tee times:** Call up to one week in advance. **Special Notes:** Also has an executive course.

★★★★UNIVERSITY OF NEW MEXICO GOLF COURSE

PU-3601 University Blvd., S.E., Albuquerque, 87111, Bernalillo County, (505)277-4546. **Opened:** 1966. **Holes:** 18. **Par:** 72/73. **Yards:** 7,248/6,031. **Course rating:** 74.7/75.1. **Slope:** 138/131. **Architect:** Robert "Red" Lawrence. **Green fee:** $18/$40. **Credit cards:** MC,VISA. **Reduced fees:** Weekdays, twilight, seniors, juniors. **Caddies:** No. **Golf carts:** $20. **Discount golf packages:** No. **Season:** Year-round. **High:** May-Sept. **On site lodging:** No. **Rental clubs:** Yes. **Walking policy:** Unrestricted walking. **Metal spikes allowed:** No. **Range:** Yes (grass). **To obtain tee times:** Call Thursday at 7:30 a.m. for Saturday through Friday tee time.

Notes: Ranked 5th in 1997 Best in State.

Subscriber comments: Not for the weak of heart. Tough layout. Five sets of tees...Always a pleasure to play...A great long course with no gimmicks...Greens too big, but easy to putt, break to the river.

★★★ADIRONDACK GOLF & COUNTRY CLUB
PU-88 Golf Rd., Peru, 12972, Clinton County, (518)643-8403, (800)346-1761, 70 miles S of Montreal.
Opened: 1990. **Holes:** 18. **Par:** 72/72. **Yards:** 6,851/5,069. **Course rating:** 71.9/67.9. **Slope:** 123/115. **Architect:** Geoffrey Cornish and Brian Silva. **Green fee:** $18/$28. **Credit cards:** MC,VISA,DISC. **Reduced fees:** Weekdays, low season, twilight, seniors, juniors. **Caddies:** No. **Golf carts:** N/A. **Discount golf packages:** No. **Season:** March-Dec. **High:** July-Aug. **On site lodging:** No. **Rental clubs:** Yes. **Walking policy:** Unrestricted walking. **Metal spikes allowed:** Yes. **Range:** Yes (grass). **To obtain tee times:** Call Wednesday for upcoming Saturday, Sunday and Monday. Call Sunday for Tuesday through Friday.
Subscriber comments: Hidden treasure, might be best public course in area...Beautiful green fairways, lined with pine trees...Tight and tough course...Florida on front nine, North Carolina on back...Sandy...Very underrated.
Special Notes: Surcharge for metal spike shoes.

★★AFTON GOLF CLUB
PU-Afton Lake Rd., Afton, 13730, Chenago County, (607)639-2454, (800)238-6618, 23 miles E of Binghamton.
Opened: N/A. **Holes:** 18. **Par:** 72/72. **Yards:** 6,268/4,835. **Course rating:** 69.0/65.6. **Slope:** 113/110. **Architect:** Graden Decker. **Green fee:** $13/$16. **Credit cards:** None. **Reduced fees:** Weekdays, seniors, juniors. **Caddies:** No. **Golf carts:** $18. **Discount golf packages:** Yes. **Season:** March-Nov. **High:** Summer. **On site lodging:** No. **Rental clubs:** Yes. **Walking policy:** Unrestricted walking. **Metal spikes allowed:** Yes. **Range:** No. **To obtain tee times:** Call 800 number.

★★½ALBAN HILLS COUNTRY CLUB
PU-129 Alban Hills Dr., Johnstown, 12095, Fulton County, (518)762-3717, 40 miles W of Albany.
Opened: 1980. **Holes:** 18. **Par:** 70/70. **Yards:** 6,005/5,094. **Course rating:** 66.3/67.6. **Slope:** 103/105. **Architect:** Attillio Albanese. **Green fee:** $9/$16. **Credit cards:** None. **Reduced fees:** Weekdays, low season, twilight, seniors, juniors. **Caddies:** No. **Golf carts:** $19. **Discount golf packages:** No. **Season:** April-Nov. **High:** June-Aug. **On site lodging:** No. **Rental clubs:** Yes. **Walking policy:** Unrestricted walking. **Metal spikes allowed:** Yes. **Range:** No. **To obtain tee times:** Call 7 days in advance for weekends.
Subscriber comments: A very short course. Very open greens are kept in incredible shape, just like a pool table...Great views...A few interesting holes, a few losers...First four holes lull you into false sense of security.

★★AMHERST AUDUBON GOLF COURSE
PU-500 Maple Rd., Williamsville, 14221, Erie County, (716)631-7139.
Architect: William Harries. **Caddies:** No. **Discount golf packages:** No. **On site lodging:** No. **Rental clubs:** No. **Metal spikes allowed:** Yes. **Range:** No.
Call club for further information.

★★APALACHIN GOLF COURSE
PU-607 S Apalachin Rd, Apalachin, 13732, Tioga County, (607)625-2682, 20 miles W of Binghamton.
Opened: 1964. **Holes:** 18. **Par:** 71/73. **Yards:** 5,727/5,000. **Course rating:** N/A. **Slope:** N/A. **Architect:** John Martin, Tim Shearer. **Green fee:** $8/$14. **Credit cards:** None. **Reduced fees:** Weekdays, low season, seniors, juniors. **Caddies:** No. **Golf carts:** $18. **Discount golf packages:** Yes. **Season:** April-First snow. **High:** May-Aug. **On site lodging:** No. **Rental clubs:** Yes. **Walking policy:** Unrestricted walking. **Metal spikes allowed:** Yes. **Range:** No. **To obtain tee times:** Call.

★★★APPLE GREEN GOLF COURSE
161 S. St., Highland, 12528, (914)883-5500.
Call club for further information.
Subscriber comments: Built from apple orchard, free apples!...Decisions, decisions, used every club...Very good course...Great layout among apple treelined fairways...Course is unique, only trees on course are apple trees.

★★★ARROWHEAD GOLF COURSE
PU-7185 E. Taft Rd., East Syracuse, 13057, Onondaga County, (315)656-7563.
Opened: 1968. **Holes:** 18. **Par:** 72/73. **Yards:** 6,700/5,156. **Course rating:** 70.9/68.5.
Slope: 113/109. **Architect:** Dick Snyder. **Green fee:** $15/$15. **Credit cards:** None.
Reduced fees: Seniors, juniors. **Caddies:** No. **Golf carts:** $16. **Discount golf packages:** No. **Season:** April-Nov. **High:** May-Sept. **On site lodging:** No. **Rental clubs:** Yes. **Walking policy:** Unrestricted walking. **Metal spikes allowed:** Yes. **Range:** No. **To obtain tee times:** First come, first served.
Subscriber comments: Walkable...No sand but plenty of water, greens in great condition...Boring layout...Mosquito repellent a must...Good course for all players.
Special Notes: Also has 9-hole course.

★★½AUBURN GOLF & COUNTRY CLUB
PU-RD 6, E. Lake Rd., Auburn, 13021, Cayuga County, (315)253-3152.
Architect: Tom Bendelow. **Caddies:** No. **Discount golf packages:** No. **On site lodging:** No. **Rental clubs:** No. **Metal spikes allowed:** Yes. **Range:** No.
Call club for further information.
Subscriber comments: Several short holes...Very nice place to play golf...Course improving year by year.

★★★BALLSTON SPA COUNTRY CLUB
Rte. 67, Ballston Spa, 12020, Saratoga County, (518)885-7935, 20 miles N of Albany.
Opened: 1926. **Holes:** 18. **Par:** 71/74. **Yards:** 6,215/5,757. **Course rating:** 69.3/69.4.
Slope: 124/122. **Architect:** Pete Craig. **Green fee:** $40/$50. **Credit cards:** MC,VISA.
Reduced fees: N/A. **Caddies:** No. **Golf carts:** Included in Green Fee. **Discount golf packages:** No. **Season:** April-Nov. **High:** June-Sept. **On site lodging:** No. **Rental clubs:** Yes. **Walking policy:** Mandatory cart. **Metal spikes allowed:** No. **Range:** Yes (grass). **To obtain tee times:** Call one week in advance. Members only on weekends.
Subscriber comments: Short, tight and challenging...Tall pine trees guard short narrow fairways, lots of hidden water, you need accuracy more than distance...Tough greens...Beautiful use of ponds and streams.

★★★BARKER BROOK GOLF CLUB
PU-6080 Rogers Rd., Oriskany Falls, 13425, Oneida County, (315)821-6438, 13 miles S of Utica.
Opened: 1965. **Holes:** 18. **Par:** 72/72. **Yards:** 6,402/5,501. **Course rating:** 70.6/71.8.
Slope: 120/118. **Architect:** David Keshler. **Green fee:** $15/$18. **Credit cards:** MC,VISA. **Reduced fees:** Weekdays, low season, twilight. **Caddies:** No. **Golf carts:** $20. **Discount golf packages:** No. **Season:** April-Nov. **High:** June-Aug. **On site lodging:** No. **Rental clubs:** Yes. **Walking policy:** Unrestricted walking. **Metal spikes allowed:** Yes. **Range:** Yes (grass/mats). **To obtain tee times:** Call up to 3 days in advance.
Subscriber comments: Greens excellent...A fairly new back nine makes the 18 feel like two different courses...No frills, lots of elevation on front nine...Some tricky holes...New nine is good.

★★½BATAVIA COUNTRY CLUB
7909 Batavia-Byron Rd., Batavia, 14020, Genesee County, (716)343-7600.
Architect: Tyron & Schwartz. **Caddies:** No. **Discount golf packages:** No. **On site lodging:** No. **Rental clubs:** No. **Metal spikes allowed:** Yes. **Range:** No.
Call club for further information.
Subscriber comments: Open in off season months when you can't get on any other course...Long and wide open...Wide open, big, undulating greens...Too many blind approaches...Enjoyed 15th hole the best!

★★★BATTLE ISLAND GOLF COURSE
PU-Rte. 48, Battle Island State Park, Fulton, 13069, Oswego County, (315)592-3361, 21 miles N of Syracuse.
Opened: N/A. **Holes:** 18. **Par:** 72/72. **Yards:** 5,973/5,561. **Course rating:** 67.9/68.7.
Slope: 109. **Architect:** N/A. **Green fee:** $14/$17. **Credit cards:** None. **Reduced fees:** Seniors, juniors. **Caddies:** No. **Golf carts:** $20. **Discount golf packages:** No. **Season:** April-Nov. **High:** Aug.-Sept. **On site lodging:** No. **Rental clubs:** Yes. **Walking policy:**

Unrestricted walking. **Metal spikes allowed:** Yes. **Range:** No. **To obtain tee times:** First come, first served.
Subscriber comments: Very fast, rolling greens...Fun to play, several out-of-bounds on right...Short but challenging...Very scenic...Best public course around.

★★BEAVER ISLAND STATE PARK GOLF COURSE

PU-Beaver Island State Park, Grand Island, 14072, Erie County, (716)773-4668, 8 miles N of Buffalo.
Opened: 1937. **Holes:** 18. **Par:** 72/74. **Yards:** 6,697/6,178. **Course rating:** 69.8/70.0. **Slope:** 108/110. **Architect:** William Harries/A. Russell Tryon. **Green fee:** $14/$17. **Credit cards:** MC,VISA. **Reduced fees:** Weekdays, twilight, seniors, juniors. **Caddies:** No. **Golf carts:** $20. **Discount golf packages:** No. **Season:** April-Nov. **High:** July-Aug. **On site lodging:** No. **Rental clubs:** Yes. **Walking policy:** Unrestricted walking. **Metal spikes allowed:** Yes. **Range:** Yes (grass/mats). **To obtain tee times:** Call up to 4 days in advance between 9 a.m. and 2 p.m. Mon.-Fri.

★★½BEEKMAN COUNTRY CLUB

PU-11 Country Club Rd., Hopewell Junction, 12533, Dutchess County, (914)226-7700, 36 miles N of White Plains.
Opened: 1963. **Holes:** 27. **Architect:** Phillip Shatz/Cortland Fish. **Green fee:** $15/$25. **Credit cards:** MC,VISA. **Reduced fees:** Weekdays, low season, twilight, seniors, juniors. **Caddies:** No. **Golf carts:** $10. **Discount golf packages:** Yes. **Season:** April-Nov. **High:** July-Aug. **On site lodging:** No. **Rental clubs:** Yes. **Walking policy:** Walking at certain times. **Metal spikes allowed:** Yes. **Range:** Yes (grass/mats). **To obtain tee times:** Call.
HIGHLAND/VALLEY
Par: 70/71. **Yards:** 6,213/5,266. **Course rating:** 70.1/71.2. **Slope:** 123/123.
TACONIC/HIGHLAND
Par: 71/72. **Yards:** 6,387/5,507. **Course rating:** 71.4/72.6. **Slope:** 126/118.
TACONIC/VALLEY
Par: 71/71. **Yards:** 6,300/5,385. **Course rating:** 70.4/70.8. **Slope:** 121/121.
Subscriber comments: Nice course which is fairly accessible...Hard to find balls that miss fairway, very pretty course...Fun place but not for a serious match...Highland 4th and 5th are good tests...Clean open setting for golf...Valley nine is very plain.

★★★BELLPORT COUNTRY CLUB

S. Country Rd., Bellport, 11713, Suffolk County, (516)286-7206.
Call club for further information.
Subscriber comments: Beautiful greens, hole that overlooks ocean is worth the trip...Watch out for the wind!...Short course, but a great layout, great course to walk.

★★BERGEN POINT COUNTRY CLUB

PU-69 Bergen Ave., West Babylon, 11704, Suffolk County, (516)661-8282, 30 miles E of New York City.
Opened: 1972. **Holes:** 18. **Par:** 71/71. **Yards:** 6,637/5,707. **Course rating:** 71.4/71.8. **Slope:** 120/122. **Architect:** William F. Mitchell. **Green fee:** $19/$32. **Credit cards:** None. **Reduced fees:** Weekdays, low season, twilight, seniors, juniors. **Caddies:** No. **Golf carts:** $25. **Discount golf packages:** Yes. **Season:** March-Dec. **High:** June-Oct. **On site lodging:** No. **Rental clubs:** Yes. **Walking policy:** Unrestricted walking. **Metal spikes allowed:** No. **Range:** Yes (mats). **To obtain tee times:** Call.

BETHPAGE STATE PARK GOLF COURSES

PU-Farmingdale, 11735, Nassau County, (516)293-8899, 18 miles E of New York City.
Architect: A.W. Tillinghast. **Green fee:** $20/$24. **Credit cards:** None. **Reduced fees:** Weekdays, low season, twilight, seniors. **Caddies:** No. **Season:** Year-round. **High:** May-Sept. **On site lodging:** No. **Rental clubs:** Yes. **Walking policy:** Unrestricted walking. **Metal spikes allowed:** Yes. **Range:** Yes. **To obtain tee times:** Call one week in advance for reservations.

★★★★½BLACK COURSE
Opened: 1935. **Holes:** 18. **Par:** 71/71. **Yards:** 7,065/6,556. **Course rating:** 75.4/78.9. **Slope:** 144/146. **Golf carts:** $24. **Discount golf packages:** Yes.
Notes: Ranked 100th in 1997-98 America's 100 Greatest; 10th in 1997 Best in State; 2002 U.S. Open.
Subscriber comments: Best public facility ever played...Great test for mid to low handicaps...Worth the long wait...Need to keep pace of play up...Where else can you play a US Open course for $20?...More sand than the Sahara...Long waits, come early to play...Fascinating bunker placement, a shotmaker's course...From the tips, the toughest course I've ever played, loved it.

★★★BLUE COURSE
Opened: 1930. **Holes:** 18. **Par:** 72/72. **Yards:** 6,684/6,213. **Course rating:** 72.2/75.5. **Slope:** 126/130. **Golf carts:** Included in Green Fee. **Discount golf packages:** Yes.
Subscriber comments: My favorite course on Long Island...Not as fun as the Black, but not as brutal either...A few tough holes...Front nine very tough, back lightens up...Finishing holes (17th and 18th) are a good test of your golf abilities.

★★★GREEN COURSE
Opened: 1930. **Holes:** 18. **Par:** 71/71. **Yards:** 6,267/5,903. **Course rating:** 69.8/73.3. **Slope:** 121/125. **Golf carts:** $24. **Discount golf packages:** No.
Subscriber comments: Holds up under heavy traffic...Toughest greens at Bethpage...Course has nice elevated tees...Very hilly...Fun, pretty, but slow...Real golf, not gimmicky...Not as easy as some say...If you can't play Black, play Green...My favorite public course...I love that you must walk the course.

★★★½RED COURSE
Opened: 1930. **Holes:** 18. **Par:** 70/70. **Yards:** 6,756/6,198. **Course rating:** 73.0/76.0. **Slope:** 127/131. **Golf carts:** $24. **Discount golf packages:** No.
Subscriber comments: Second best at Bethpage...Prettiest of the Bethpage courses...Hardest first hole around...Hope you like doglegs...First hole should be a par 5...Too many long par 4s...I like this course better than the Black...Course in great shape considering amount of play...As close as you can get to Black course.

★★½YELLOW COURSE
Opened: 1930. **Holes:** 18. **Par:** 71/71. **Yards:** 6,316/5,680. **Course rating:** 70.1/67.2. **Slope:** 121/115. **Golf carts:** $24. **Discount golf packages:** No. **To obtain tee times:** Call one week in advance.
Subscriber comments: Underrated, a terrific course...Course is the easiest at Bethpage...A sound traditional flat course...The worst of the group but still a great day of golf...No bad courses at Bethpage.

★★★BLUE HILL GOLF CLUB
285 Blue Hill Rd., Pearl River, 10965, Rockland County, (914)735-2094, 20 miles N of New York.
Opened: 1924. **Holes:** 18. **Par:** 72/72. **Yards:** 6,471/5,651. **Course rating:** 70.6/70.6. **Slope:** 116/117. **Architect:** Stephen Kay. **Green fee:** $27/$33. **Credit cards:** None. **Reduced fees:** Weekdays, twilight. **Caddies:** No. **Golf carts:** $26. **Discount golf packages:** No. **Season:** March-Dec. **High:** June-Sept. **On site lodging:** Yes. **Rental clubs:** No. **Walking policy:** Unrestricted walking. **Metal spikes allowed:** Yes. **Range:** Yes. **To obtain tee times:** Call one day in advance.
Subscriber comments: Outstanding conditions...Nice views overlooking reservoir, great par 3s...Wide open, large greens...Very short course, new nine holes challenging...Some difficult holes...Ego booster.

★½BLUE STONE GOLF CLUB
PU-44 Scott St., Oxford, 13830, Chenango County, (607)843-8352, 28 miles N of Binghamton.
Opened: 1930. **Holes:** 18. **Par:** 71/72. **Yards:** 6,068/4,290. **Course rating:** 66.1/65.2. **Slope:** 121/100. **Architect:** N/A. **Green fee:** $10/$15. **Credit cards:** None. **Reduced fees:** Weekdays, low season. **Caddies:** No. **Golf carts:** $18. **Discount golf packages:**

Yes. **Season:** March-Nov. **High:** June-Aug. **On site lodging:** No. **Rental clubs:** Yes. **Walking policy:** Unrestricted walking. **Metal spikes allowed:** Yes. **Range:** No. **To obtain tee times:** Call 1 day in advance.
Special Notes: Spikeless shoes encouraged.

★★½BLUFF POINT GOLF & COUNTRY CLUB
75 Bluff Point Dr., Plattsburgh, 12901, Clinton County, (518)563-3420, (800)438-0985, 60 miles S of Montreal.
Opened: 1890. **Holes:** 18. **Par:** 72/74. **Yards:** 6,309/5,295. **Course rating:** 70.6/71.0. **Slope:** 122/121. **Architect:** A.W. Tillinghast. **Green fee:** $30/$35. **Credit cards:** MC,VISA. **Reduced fees:** Low season, twilight. **Caddies:** No. **Golf carts:** $11. **Discount golf packages:** Yes. **Season:** April-Nov. **High:** June-Sept. **On site lodging:** Yes. **Rental clubs:** Yes. **Walking policy:** Unrestricted walking. **Metal spikes allowed:** Yes. **Range:** Yes (grass). **To obtain tee times:** Guests may call 5 days in advance.
Subscriber comments: Third oldest resort course in US on gorgeous Lake Champlain...Wide open, putts break toward lake...Good seniors' course...Delightful course...Every hole different...Beautiful, tricky winds.

★½BRAEMAR COUNTRY CLUB
4704 Ridge Rd. W., Spencerport, 14559, Monroe County, (716)352-1535.
Architect: Morrison & Morrison. **Caddies:** No. **Discount golf packages:** No. **On site lodging:** No. **Rental clubs:** No. **Metal spikes allowed:** Yes. **Range:** No.
Call club for further information.

★★½BRANTINGHAM GOLF CLUB
PU-P.O. Box 151, Brantingham, 13312, Lewis County, (315)348-8218, 55 miles N of Utica.
Opened: N/A. **Holes:** 18. **Par:** 71/74. **Yards:** 5,268/4,886. **Course rating:** 64.5. **Slope:** 97. **Architect:** Fred Rhone. **Green fee:** $14/$14. **Credit cards:** None. **Reduced fees:** Twilight. **Caddies:** No. **Golf carts:** $16. **Discount golf packages:** No. **Season:** April-Oct. **High:** July-Aug. **On site lodging:** No. **Rental clubs:** Yes. **Walking policy:** Unrestricted walking. **Metal spikes allowed:** Yes. **Range:** No. **To obtain tee times:** First come, first served.
Subscriber comments: Just a place to play when you need to...Challenging holes and greens...Nice course...Very picturesque.

★★½BRENTWOOD COUNTRY CLUB
PU-100 Pennsylvania Ave., Brentwood, 11717, Suffolk County, (516)436-6060, 45 miles E of New York City.
Opened: 1920. **Holes:** 18. **Par:** 72/72. **Yards:** 6,173/5,835. **Course rating:** 69.3/68.4. **Slope:** 121/111. **Architect:** Devereux Emmet. **Green fee:** $18/$28. **Credit cards:** None. **Reduced fees:** Weekdays, low season, twilight, seniors, juniors. **Caddies:** No. **Golf carts:** $26. **Discount golf packages:** No. **Season:** March-Dec. **High:** May-July. **On site lodging:** No. **Rental clubs:** Yes. **Walking policy:** Unrestricted walking. **Metal spikes allowed:** Yes. **Range:** No. **To obtain tee times:** Call 3 days in advance for weekends only for a $2 fee per person.
Subscriber comments: Clean and well-kept facility...Fair test, good value, easy to walk...Nice course, no water holes, but classic layout and long...Most holes too wide open and straight...Fun course for high handicapper.

★★BRIAR CREEK GOLF COURSE
PU-Pangburn Rd., Princetown, 12056, Schenectady County, (518)355-6145, 10 miles W of Albany.
Opened: 1963. **Holes:** 18. **Par:** 70/71. **Yards:** 5,667/5,187. **Course rating:** N/A. **Slope:** N/A. **Architect:** P. Greenwood/R.W. Parks. **Green fee:** $17/$20. **Credit cards:** None. **Reduced fees:** Seniors. **Caddies:** No. **Golf carts:** $20. **Discount golf packages:** No. **Season:** April-Nov. **High:** May-Sept. **On site lodging:** No. **Rental clubs:** Yes. **Walking policy:** Unrestricted walking. **Metal spikes allowed:** Yes. **Range:** No. **To obtain tee times:** Call.

★★BRIGHTON PARK GOLF COURSE
PU-Brompton Rd., Town of Tonawanda, 14150, Erie County, (716)695-2580, 5 miles N of Buffalo.
Opened: 1963. **Holes:** 18. **Par:** 72/73. **Yards:** 6,535/5,852. **Course rating:** 70.7/73.5. **Slope:** 108/109. **Architect:** William Harries and A. Russell Tyron. **Green fee:** $16/$19. **Credit cards:** None. **Reduced fees:** Weekdays, low season, twilight, seniors. **Caddies:** No. **Golf carts:** $18. **Discount golf packages:** No. **Season:** April-Nov. **High:** June-Aug. **On site lodging:** No. **Rental clubs:** Yes. **Walking policy:** Unrestricted walking. **Metal spikes allowed:** Yes. **Range:** Yes (grass). **To obtain tee times:** Phone in system 7 days in advance.

★★★½BRISTOL HARBOUR GOLF & RESORT
R-5500 Seneca Point Rd., Canandaigua, 14424, Ontario County, (716)396-2460, (800)288-8248, 30 miles S of Rochester.
Opened: 1972. **Holes:** 18. **Par:** 72/72. **Yards:** 6,700/5,500. **Course rating:** 72.6/73.0. **Slope:** 126/126. **Architect:** Robert Trent Jones. **Green fee:** $30/$45. **Credit cards:** MC,VISA,AMEX. **Reduced fees:** Weekdays, low season, resort guests, twilight, seniors, juniors. **Caddies:** No. **Golf carts:** Included in Green Fee. **Discount golf packages:** Yes. **Season:** April-Nov. **High:** June-Sept. **On site lodging:** Yes. **Rental clubs:** Yes. **Walking policy:** Mandatory cart. **Metal spikes allowed:** Yes. **Range:** Yes (grass/mats). **To obtain tee times:** General public may call up to 7 days in advance. **Subscriber comments:** Superb layout, scenic delight...Very hilly and picturesque...Best time to play is in the fall...Front nine on the lake is the prettiest in New York State...One nine is open, the other carved out of the woods...Has its own Amen Corner (14, 15, 16)...Course is not long, but shots must be placed.

★★★BROCKPORT COUNTRY CLUB
3739 County Line Rd., Brockport, 14420, Monroe County, (716)638-6486, 25 miles W of Rochester.
Opened: 1975. **Holes:** 18. **Par:** 72/72. **Yards:** 6,400/5,000. **Course rating:** 70.1/68.0. **Slope:** 128/112. **Architect:** Joe Basso. **Green fee:** $16/$20. **Credit cards:** None. **Reduced fees:** Weekdays. **Caddies:** No. **Golf carts:** $10. **Discount golf packages:** No. **Season:** April-Nov. **High:** June-Aug. **On site lodging:** No. **Rental clubs:** No. **Walking policy:** Unrestricted walking. **Metal spikes allowed:** Yes. **Range:** No. **To obtain tee times:** Call. **Subscriber comments:** Good layout, easy to post a good score...Not recommended for low handicap...Back nine great...Short course, but very entertaining, very good mix of holes, several risk-reward holes...Flat front nine, rolling back nine.

★★★BYRNCLIFF GOLF CLUB
R-Rte. 20A, Varysburg, 14167, Wyoming County, (716)535-7300, 35 miles SE of Buffalo.
Opened: 1965. **Holes:** 18. **Par:** 72/73. **Yards:** 6,783/5,545. **Course rating:** 73.1/75.1. **Slope:** 115/119. **Architect:** Russ Tryon. **Green fee:** $30/$34. **Credit cards:** All major. **Reduced fees:** Weekdays, low season, resort guests, twilight, seniors. **Caddies:** No. **Golf carts:** Included in Green Fee. **Discount golf packages:** Yes. **Season:** April-Nov. **High:** June-Aug. **On site lodging:** Yes. **Rental clubs:** Yes. **Walking policy:** Unrestricted walking. **Metal spikes allowed:** Yes. **Range:** Yes (grass/mats). **To obtain tee times:** Call. **Subscriber comments:** Carved out of mountain...Cart recommended, hilly...Many different holes, good greens...Very,very challenging...Very few level lies...A fun course, better in spring and fall...Long, if you make a mistake, you pay for it.

★½C-WAY GOLF CLUB
PU-37093 NYS Rte 12, Clayton, 13624, Jefferson County, (315)686-4562, 82 miles N of Syracuse.
Opened: 1964. **Holes:** 18. **Par:** 71/71. **Yards:** 6,120/5,780. **Course rating:** 68.0/68.0. **Slope:** N/A. **Architect:** N/A. **Green fee:** $17. **Credit cards:** MC,VISA. **Reduced fees:** N/A. **Caddies:** No. **Golf carts:** $16. **Discount golf packages:** Yes. **Season:** May-Nov. **High:** Summer. **On site lodging:** No. **Rental clubs:** Yes. **Walking policy:** Unrestricted walking. **Metal spikes allowed:** Yes. **Range:** No. **To obtain tee times:** Call up to 3 days in advance.

★★½CAMILLUS COUNTRY CLUB
5690 Bennetts Corners Rd., Camillus, 13031, Onondaga County, (315)672-3770, 20 miles W of Syracuse.
Opened: 1962. **Holes:** 18. **Par:** 73/73. **Yards:** 6,368/5,573. **Course rating:** 70.1/71.4. **Slope:** 115/110. **Architect:** N/A. **Green fee:** $15/$18. **Credit cards:** MC,VISA. **Reduced fees:** Weekdays, low season, seniors, juniors. **Caddies:** No. **Golf carts:** $9. **Discount golf packages:** Yes. **Season:** April-Nov. **High:** June-Aug. **On site lodging:** No. **Rental clubs:** Yes. **Walking policy:** Unrestricted walking. **Metal spikes allowed:** Yes. **Range:** Yes (grass). **To obtain tee times:** Call up to 7 days in advance. **Subscriber comments:** Very hilly, need a cart...Some blind shots.

★½CANAJOHARIE COUNTRY CLUB
Rte. 163, Canajoharie, 13317, Montgomery County, (518)673-8183, 37 miles SE of Utica.
Opened: 1940. **Holes:** 18. **Par:** 70/71. **Yards:** 5,744/4,833. **Course rating:** 66.4/65.7. **Slope:** 109/105. **Architect:** Scott & John North. **Green fee:** $12/$16. **Credit cards:** MC,VISA. **Reduced fees:** Juniors. **Caddies:** No. **Golf carts:** $19. **Discount golf packages:** No. **Season:** April-Oct. **High:** June-Aug. **On site lodging:** No. **Rental clubs:** Yes. **Walking policy:** Unrestricted walking. **Metal spikes allowed:** Yes. **Range:** Yes (grass). **To obtain tee times:** Call golf shop for weekend starting times.

★★★CANASAWACTA COUNTRY CLUB
Country Club Rd., Norwich, 13815, Chenango County, (607)336-2685, 37 miles NE of Binghamton.
Opened: 1920. **Holes:** 18. **Par:** 70/71. **Yards:** 6,271/5,166. **Course rating:** 69.9/68.8. **Slope:** 120/114. **Architect:** Russell Bailey. **Green fee:** $18/$22. **Credit cards:** None. **Reduced fees:** Low season, twilight, juniors. **Caddies:** No. **Golf carts:** $22. **Discount golf packages:** No. **Season:** April-Oct. **High:** June-Aug. **On site lodging:** No. **Rental clubs:** Yes. **Walking policy:** Unrestricted walking. **Metal spikes allowed:** Yes. **Range:** No. **To obtain tee times:** Call up to 3 days in advance.
Subscriber comments: Hilly, good test...Challenging design, fun to play...Tough par 3s...Very hilly, few level lies...A secluded treasure...Some easy holes and some killer par 4s...Enjoy playing here each year.

★½CARDINAL HILLS GOLF COURSE
PU-Conewango Rd., Randolph, 14772, Chattaraugus County, (716)358-5409.
Call club for further information.

★½CASOLWOOD GOLF COURSE
PU-New Boston Rd., Box 163, Canastota, 13032, Madison County, (315)697-9164, 15 miles E of Syracuse.
Opened: 1969. **Holes:** 18. **Par:** 71/71. **Yards:** 6,100/5,700. **Course rating:** N/A. **Slope:** N/A. **Architect:** Richard L. Quick/Richard A. Quick. **Green fee:** $14. **Credit cards:** MC,VISA. **Reduced fees:** Weekdays, seniors. **Caddies:** No. **Golf carts:** $18. **Discount golf packages:** No. **Season:** March-Dec. **High:** June-Sept. **On site lodging:** No. **Rental clubs:** Yes. **Walking policy:** Unrestricted walking. **Metal spikes allowed:** Yes. **Range:** No. **To obtain tee times:** Call on Wednesday for upcoming weekend. **Special Notes:** Spikeless shoes encouraged.

★★★½CASPERKILL COUNTRY CLUB
575 South Rd., Poughkeepsie, 12601, Dutchess County, (914)433-2222, 70 miles N of New York City.
Opened: 1944. **Holes:** 18. **Par:** 72/72. **Yards:** 6,691/4,868. **Course rating:** 72.4/67.9. **Slope:** 130/117. **Architect:** Robert Trent Jones. **Green fee:** $40/$40. **Credit cards:** All major. **Reduced fees:** Twilight, juniors. **Caddies:** No. **Golf carts:** $24. **Discount golf packages:** No. **Season:** March-Dec. **High:** March-Dec. **On site lodging:** No. **Rental clubs:** Yes. **Walking policy:** Unrestricted walking. **Metal spikes allowed:** No. **Range:** Yes (Mats). **To obtain tee times:** Call 1 day in advance at 6:45 a.m. for weekdays. Call Wednesday at 7:30 p.m. for following weekend.
Subscriber comments: A lot of fun, some challenging holes...Country club-type course...Variety of different holes...Slickest greens I've ever seen...Outstanding. **Special Notes:** Formerly IBM Mid Hudson Valley Golf Course.

CEDAR VIEW GOLF COURSE
PU-Rte. 37C, Rooseveltown, 13683, St. Lawrence County, (315)764-9104, 70 miles N of Syracuse.
Opened: 1986. **Holes:** 18. **Par:** 72/72. **Yards:** 6,027/5,175. **Course rating:** 68.8/69.6. **Slope:** 119/121. **Architect:** N/A. **Green fee:** $13/$16. **Credit cards:** MC,VISA. **Reduced fees:** N/A. **Caddies:** No. **Golf carts:** $18. **Discount golf packages:** No. **Season:** May-Oct. **High:** July-Aug. **On site lodging:** No. **Rental clubs:** Yes. **Walking policy:** Unrestricted walking. **Metal spikes allowed:** Yes. **Range:** No. **To obtain tee times:** Call.

★★★CENTERPOINTE COUNTRY CLUB
2231 Brickyard Rd., Canandaigua, 14424, Ontario County, (716)924-5346, 25 miles SE of Rochester.
Opened: 1963. **Holes:** 18. **Par:** 71/71. **Yards:** 6,717/5,213. **Course rating:** 70.7/68.3. **Slope:** 116/107. **Architect:** John Thornton/Elmer Michaels. **Green fee:** $15/$22. **Credit cards:** MC,VISA. **Reduced fees:** Weekdays, low season, twilight, seniors, juniors. **Caddies:** No. **Golf carts:** $20. **Discount golf packages:** Yes. **Season:** April-Nov. **High:** June-Aug. **On site lodging:** No. **Rental clubs:** Yes. **Walking policy:** Unrestricted walking. **Metal spikes allowed:** Yes. **Range:** Yes (grass). **To obtain tee times:** Public may call up to 3 days in advance.
Subscriber comments: Have to hit all the shots...Tough when it's windy...Greens are very good...Fun to play, plenty of birdies out there...Gently rolling with good greens...Better be straight off the tee...Good course getting better.

★★CENTRAL VALLEY GOLF CLUB
PU-206 Smith Clove Rd., Central Valley, 10917, Orange County, (914)928-6924, 50 miles N of New York City.
Opened: 1922. **Holes:** 18. **Par:** 70/73. **Yards:** 5,644/5,317. **Course rating:** 67.7/70.9. **Slope:** 116/120. **Architect:** Hal Purdy. **Green fee:** $23/$33. **Credit cards:** MC,VISA,AMEX. **Reduced fees:** Weekdays, low season, twilight, seniors, juniors. **Caddies:** No. **Golf carts:** $24. **Discount golf packages:** No. **Season:** April-Nov. **High:** May-Aug. **On site lodging:** No. **Rental clubs:** Yes. **Walking policy:** Unrestricted walking. **Metal spikes allowed:** Yes. **Range:** No. **To obtain tee times:** Call up to 7 days in advance.
Subscriber comments: Tough course...Very hilly...Need hoofs like a goat on some holes...Uphill holes impossible, downhill too easy...Small greens...Take a cart.

CHAUTAUQUA GOLF CLUB
R-Rte. 394, Chautauqua, 14722, Chautauqua County, (716)357-6211, 70 miles S of Buffalo. **Green fee:** $17/$30. **Credit cards:** MC,VISA. **Reduced fees:** Weekdays, low season, twilight. **Caddies:** No. **Golf carts:** $10. **Discount golf packages:** Yes. **Season:** April-Nov. **High:** June-Aug. **On site lodging:** No. **Rental clubs:** Yes. **Walking policy:** Unrestricted walking. **Metal spikes allowed:** Yes. **Range:** Yes (grass/mats). **To obtain tee times:** Call up to 7 days in advance. Large groups may call further in advance.
★★★HILLS COURSE
Opened: 1994. **Holes:** 18. **Par:** 72/72. **Yards:** 6,412/5,076. **Course rating:** 72.1/72.7. **Slope:** 118/110. **Architect:** Xen Hassenplug.
Subscriber comments: Beautiful views...Great place to go to play 36 holes on a weekday...More scenic than Lake Course but many holes too contrived.
★★★LAKE COURSE
Opened: 1913. **Holes:** 18. **Par:** 72/74. **Yards:** 6,462/5,423. **Course rating:** 71.1/71.7. **Slope:** 115/108. **Architect:** Donald Ross.
Subscriber comments: Challenging, thinking golfer's course...Greens much better than Hill Course, 7th hole is a bear...A great view.

★★★CHENANGO VALLEY GOLF COURSE
PU-153 State Park Rd., Chenango Forks, 13746, Broome County, (607)648-9804.
Opened: 1932. **Holes:** 18. **Par:** 72/72. **Yards:** 6,271/5,246. **Course rating:** 70.6/69.5. **Slope:** 124/116. **Architect:** Hal Purdy. **Green fee:** $14/$19. **Credit cards:** MC,VISA. **Reduced fees:** Weekdays, seniors, juniors. **Caddies:** No. **Golf carts:** $20. **Discount golf packages:** No. **Season:** April-Nov. **High:** June-Aug. **On site lodging:** Yes. **Rental clubs:** Yes. **Walking policy:** Unrestricted walking. **Metal spikes allowed:** Yes. **Range:**

No. **To obtain tee times:** Call.
Subscriber comments: Good layout...Beautiful treelined course, hit it straight or be penalized...My favorite for difficulty, fairness and accuracy...Play in the fall when trees are in color (heaven on earth)...Woodsy, lots of gnats!...All par 4s look alike...Enjoyable.

★★½CHESTNUT HILL COUNTRY CLUB
PU-1330 Broadway, Darien Center, 14040, Genesee County, (716)547-9699.
Opened: N/A. **Holes:** 18. **Par:** 72/72. **Yards:** 6,653/5,466. **Course rating:** 72.0/70.6.
Slope: 119/115. **Architect:** N/A. **Green fee:** $15/$30. **Credit cards:** MC,VISA,DISC.
Reduced fees: Weekdays. **Caddies:** No. **Golf carts:** Included in Green Fee. **Discount golf packages:** No. **Season:** April-Nov. **High:** N/A. **On site lodging:** No. **Rental clubs:** Yes. **Walking policy:** N/A. **Metal spikes allowed:** Yes. **Range:** Yes (grass). **To obtain tee times:** Call up to 10 days in advance.
Subscriber comments: Challenging, long with lots of hills...Interesting holes...Placement over distance...Average course...A lot of tournament play...Cart paths too close to fairways and greens...Fastest greens in Western NY.

★½CHILI COUNTRY CLUB
760 Scottsville - Chili Rd., Scottsville, 14546, Monroe County, (716)889-9325, 10 miles S of Rochester.
Opened: 1959. **Holes:** 18. **Par:** 72/72. **Yards:** 6,628/5,498. **Course rating:** 71.7/70.4.
Slope: 117/110. **Architect:** Joe DeMino. **Green fee:** $10/$18. **Credit cards:** MC,VISA,DISC. **Reduced fees:** Weekdays, low season, twilight, seniors, juniors.
Caddies: No. **Golf carts:** $20. **Discount golf packages:** No. **Season:** Year-round.
High: July-Aug. **On site lodging:** No. **Rental clubs:** Yes. **Walking policy:** Unrestricted walking. **Metal spikes allowed:** Yes. **Range:** Yes (grass). **To obtain tee times:** Call.

★★★CITY OF AMSTERDAM MUNICIPAL GOLF COURSE
PM-Upper Van Dyke Ave., Amsterdam, 12010, Montgomery County, (518)842-4265, 15 miles NE of Schenectady.
Opened: 1938. **Holes:** 18. **Par:** 71/74. **Yards:** 6,370/5,352. **Course rating:** 70.2/70.2.
Slope: 120/110. **Architect:** Robert Trent Jones. **Green fee:** $16/$18. **Credit cards:** None. **Reduced fees:** Seniors. **Caddies:** No. **Golf carts:** $20. **Discount golf packages:** No. **Season:** April-Nov. **High:** July-Aug. **On site lodging:** No. **Rental clubs:** Yes. **Walking policy:** Unrestricted walking. **Metal spikes allowed:** Yes. **Range:** Yes (grass/mats). **To obtain tee times:** Call two days in advance for weekends only.
Subscriber comments: Small greens, blind shots, scenic...Needs better paths for people that walk...Great Robert Trent Jones layout, long but fair...Very hilly, tough walk...I love the elevated tees and greens, and the view...Fun course.

★★CLEARVIEW GOLF CLUB
PM-202-12 Willets Point Blvd., Bayside, 11360, Queens County, (718)229-2570, New York City.
Opened: N/A. **Holes:** 18. **Par:** 70/70. **Yards:** 6,473/5,721. **Course rating:** 70.1/70.4.
Slope: 119/115. **Architect:** William H. Tucker. **Green fee:** $24/$26. **Credit cards:** MC,VISA,AMEX. **Reduced fees:** Twilight, seniors, juniors. **Caddies:** No. **Golf carts:** $24. **Discount golf packages:** No. **Season:** Year-round. **High:** May-Sept. **On site lodging:** No. **Rental clubs:** Yes. **Walking policy:** Unrestricted walking. **Metal spikes allowed:** Yes. **Range:** No. **To obtain tee times:** Call.
Special Notes: Spikeless shoes preferred.

★★★★COLGATE UNIVERSITY SEVEN OAKS GOLF CLUB
E. Lake and Payne Sts., Hamilton, 13346, Madison County, (315)824-1432.
Opened: N/A. **Holes:** 18. **Par:** 72/72. **Yards:** 6,915/5,315. **Course rating:** 72.3/71.0.
Slope: 127/128. **Architect:** Robert Trent Jones. **Green fee:** $25/$50. **Credit cards:** MC,VISA. **Reduced fees:** Low season, resort guests, juniors. **Caddies:** Yes. **Golf carts:** $22. **Discount golf packages:** Yes. **Season:** April-Oct. **High:** June-Aug. **On site lodging:** No. **Rental clubs:** Yes. **Walking policy:** Unrestricted walking. **Metal spikes allowed:** Yes. **Range:** Yes (grass). **To obtain tee times:** Call up to 14 days in advance.
Notes: 1990 Ben Hogan Tour host; 1977 NCAA Division I National Championship.
Subscriber comments: Great course, tough test, has it all...Play with a Colgate graduate, save money...US Open rough...Big flat greens...Toughest opening hole upstate...You'll never forget this course...Love that creek, covered bridge.

★★★½COLONIAL SPRINGS GOLF COURSE
PU-1 Long Island Ave., East Farmingdale, 11735, Suffolk County, (516)643-1056, (800)643-0051, 33 miles E of New York City.
Opened: 1995. **Holes:** 27. **Par:** 72/72. **Yards:** 6,800/5,450. **Course rating:** 71.7/70.5. **Slope:** 124/119. **Architect:** Arthur Hills. **Green fee:** $69/$75. **Credit cards:** MC,VISA,AMEX. **Reduced fees:** Weekdays, low season, twilight. **Caddies:** No. **Golf carts:** Included in Green Fee. **Discount golf packages:** No. **Season:** March-Dec. **High:** April-Oct. **On site lodging:** No. **Rental clubs:** Yes. **Walking policy:** Mandatory cart. **Metal spikes allowed:** No. **Range:** Yes (grass/mats). **To obtain tee times:** Call.
Subscriber comments: A daily fee country club, ideal for entertaining clients...Excellent layout...Like North Carolina in Long Island...A good track, needs to mature...Particularly liked Valley nine with its contours...Nice addition to the area.

CONCORD RESORT HOTEL
R-Kiamesha Lake, Kiamesha Lake, 12751, Sullivan County, (914)794-4000, (800)431-3850, 90 miles NW of New York.
Credit cards: All major,Diners Club. **Reduced fees:** Weekdays, resort guests, twilight. **Golf carts:** Included in Green Fee. **Discount golf packages:** Yes. **Season:** April-Nov. **High:** June-Aug. **On site lodging:** Yes. **Rental clubs:** Yes. **Metal spikes allowed:** Yes. **To obtain tee times:** Call anytime in advance with credit card number. 72 hour cancellation policy.

★★★INTERNATIONAL GOLF COURSE
Opened: 1950. **Holes:** 18. **Par:** 71/71. **Yards:** 6,619/5,564. **Course rating:** 72.2/73.6. **Slope:** 127/125. **Architect:** A.H. Tull. **Green fee:** $40/$55. **Caddies:** No. **Walking policy:** Unrestricted walking. **Range:** Yes (grass/mats).
Subscriber comments: Good course design, a couple of unfair greens...Challenging and hilly...Short from white, fun, interesting holes...Nice, challenging mountain course...Cannot compare with the Monster.

★★★★MONSTER GOLF COURSE
Opened: 1963. **Holes:** 18. **Par:** 72/72. **Yards:** 7,654/5,201. **Course rating:** 70.6. **Slope:** 121. **Architect:** Joseph Finger. **Green fee:** $60/$90. **Caddies:** Yes. **Walking policy:** Mandatory cart. **Range:** Yes (grass).
Notes: Ranked 17th in 1997 Best in State.
Subscriber comments: Challenging...Too long, too hard...17th hole is a thinking man hole...World-class course, should be played at least once...Just try to play bogey golf...Some great views...Too long for King Kong!

★★★★CONKLIN PLAYERS CLUB
PU-1520 Conklin Rd., Conklin, 13748, Broome County, (607)775-3042, 70 miles S of Syracuse.
Opened: 1991. **Holes:** 18. **Par:** 72/72. **Yards:** 6,772/4,699. **Course rating:** 72.5/67.8. **Slope:** 127/116. **Architect:** R. Rickard/R. Brown/M. Brown. **Green fee:** $23/$29. **Credit cards:** All major. **Reduced fees:** Weekdays, low season, seniors. **Caddies:** No. **Golf carts:** $10. **Discount golf packages:** No. **Season:** April-Nov. **High:** May-Oct. **On site lodging:** No. **Rental clubs:** Yes. **Walking policy:** Walking at certain times. **Metal spikes allowed:** No. **Range:** Yes (grass). **To obtain tee times:** Call.
Subscriber comments: Much prettier than many private clubs...Interesting holes and elevation changes...Tough holes, definite club-selection course...A little gimmicky, but a lot of fun, scenic...Can be enjoyed by players of all abilities.

★★COPAKE COUNTRY CLUB
PU-Lake Copake, Craryville, 12521, Columbia County, (518)325-4338, 15 miles E of Hudson.
Opened: N/A. **Holes:** 18. **Par:** 72/72. **Yards:** 6,129/5,329. **Course rating:** 68.8/69.6. **Slope:** 113/113. **Architect:** N/A. **Green fee:** $11/$25. **Credit cards:** MC,VISA. **Reduced fees:** Weekdays, seniors, juniors. **Caddies:** No. **Golf carts:** $12. **Discount golf packages:** No. **Season:** April-Nov. **High:** June-Aug. **On site lodging:** No. **Rental clubs:** Yes. **Walking policy:** Unrestricted walking. **Metal spikes allowed:** Yes. **Range:** No. **To obtain tee times:** Call anytime in advance.

★★½CRAB MEADOW GOLF CLUB

PU-Waterside Rd., Northport, 11768, Suffolk County, (516)757-8800, 28 miles E of New York City.
Opened: 1960. **Holes:** 18. **Par:** 72/72. **Yards:** 6,575/5,807. **Course rating:** 70.2/72.6. **Slope:** 116/116. **Architect:** William F. Mitchell. **Green fee:** $30/$30. **Credit cards:** None. **Reduced fees:** Twilight, seniors, juniors. **Caddies:** No. **Golf carts:** $24. **Discount golf packages:** No. **Season:** March-Dec. **High:** April-Sept. **On site lodging:** No. **Rental clubs:** Yes. **Walking policy:** Unrestricted walking. **Metal spikes allowed:** Yes. **Range:** Yes. **To obtain tee times:** Call up to 7 days in advance.
Subscriber comments: Some interesting holes...Control is all-important for good scores...Great views of the sound...Excellent variety of holes...Great town course.

★★CRAGIE BRAE GOLF CLUB

PU-4391 Union St., Scottsville, 14546, Monroe County, (716)889-1440, 10 miles S of Rochester.
Opened: 1963. **Holes:** 18. **Par:** 72/72. **Yards:** 6,400/5,900. **Course rating:** 68.5/68.5. **Slope:** 105/130. **Architect:** James G. Harrison. **Green fee:** $13/$15. **Credit cards:** None. **Reduced fees:** Low season, seniors, juniors. **Caddies:** No. **Golf carts:** $20. **Discount golf packages:** No. **Season:** April-Nov. **High:** May-July. **On site lodging:** No. **Rental clubs:** Yes. **Walking policy:** Walking at certain times. **Metal spikes allowed:** Yes. **Range:** Yes. **To obtain tee times:** Call 2 days before.

★★★CRAIG WOOD GOLF COURSE

PU-Cascade Rd. Rte. 73, Lake Placid, 12946, Essex County, (518)523-9811, (800)421-9811, 135 miles N of Albany.
Opened: 1920. **Holes:** 18. **Par:** 72/72. **Yards:** 6,554/5,500. **Course rating:** 70.6/70.2. **Slope:** 114/118. **Architect:** Seymour Dunn. **Green fee:** $20. **Credit cards:** MC,VISA. **Reduced fees:** Resort guests, twilight. **Caddies:** No. **Golf carts:** $12. **Discount golf packages:** Yes. **Season:** May-Oct. **High:** July-Aug. **On site lodging:** No. **Rental clubs:** Yes. **Walking policy:** Unrestricted walking. **Metal spikes allowed:** Yes. **Range:** Yes (grass/mats). **To obtain tee times:** Call.
Subscriber comments: Up in the Adirondack Mountains...Front nine too open, back nine great...Beautiful views of the mountains...Good test of golf...Best course in Adirondacks, walkable...Incredible views make you forget your troubles.

★★½CRONINS GOLF RESORT

PU-Golf Course Rd., Box 40, Warrensburg, 12885, Warren County, (518)623-9336, 7 miles N of Lake George.
Opened: 1930. **Holes:** 18. **Par:** 70/71. **Yards:** 6,121/5,757. **Course rating:** 68.6/68.3. **Slope:** 119/117. **Architect:** Patrick Cronin. **Green fee:** $16/$18. **Credit cards:** N/A. **Reduced fees:** N/A. **Caddies:** No. **Golf carts:** N/A. **Discount golf packages:** No. **Season:** April-Nov. **High:** July-Aug. **On site lodging:** No. **Rental clubs:** No. **Walking policy:** Unrestricted walking. **Metal spikes allowed:** Yes. **Range:** No. **To obtain tee times:** Call up to 3 days in advance.
Subscriber comments: Beautiful views, some really interesting holes, should be played at least once...Friendly and you won't lose many balls...Short, tricky back nine.

★★½DANDE FARMS COUNTRY CLUB

PU-6883 Cedar St., Akron, 14001, Erie County, (716)542-2027.
Call club for further information.
Subscriber comments: Would be a killer course with sand...Very basic, no traps...Flat, not much trouble...Short course...Good walking course...Easy to score, ego booster...Best kept secret for a public course, seems easy but is deceptive.

★★★½DEERFIELD COUNTRY CLUB

100 Craig Hill Dr., Brockport, 14420, Monroe County, (716)392-8080, 20 miles W of Rochester.
Opened: 1963. **Holes:** 18. **Par:** 72/72. **Yards:** 7,083/5,623. **Course rating:** 73.9/72.4. **Slope:** 138/123. **Architect:** Peter Craig. **Green fee:** $15/$30. **Credit cards:** MC,VISA. **Reduced fees:** Weekdays, low season, twilight, seniors. **Caddies:** No. **Golf carts:** Included in Green Fee. **Discount golf packages:** No. **Season:** April-Dec. **High:** June-Aug. **On site lodging:** No. **Rental clubs:** Yes. **Walking policy:** Unrestricted walking.

Metal spikes allowed: Yes. **Range:** Yes (grass). **To obtain tee times:** Call up to 7 days in advance.
Subscriber comments: Has promise, couple of great holes...The most challenging of any public or semi-private course in area...Huge undulating greens...16 as tough a par 4 as you can get...Good practice area.
Special Notes: Also has 9-hole East Course.

★★★DEERWOOD GOLF COURSE
PM-1818 Sweeney St., North Tonawanda, 14120, Niagara County, (716)695-8525, 12 miles N of Buffalo.
Opened: 1975. **Holes:** 18. **Par:** 72/73. **Yards:** 6,948/6,150. **Course rating:** 73.0/75.0.
Slope: 117/123. **Architect:** Tryon & Schwartz. **Green fee:** $8/$20. **Credit cards:** None.
Reduced fees: Weekdays, twilight. **Caddies:** No. **Golf carts:** $18. **Discount golf packages:** No. **Season:** April-Dec. **High:** June-Aug. **On site lodging:** No. **Rental clubs:** No. **Walking policy:** Unrestricted walking. **Metal spikes allowed:** Yes. **Range:** Yes (grass). **To obtain tee times:** Call.
Subscriber comments: Watch out for deer...Flat layout, some tight holes...Very nice layout, but flat...Will use every club in bag...Best municipal course in western NY.

★★½DOMENICO'S GOLF COURSE
PU-13 Church Rd., Whitesboro, 13492, Oneida County, (315)736-9812, 4 miles W of Utica.
Opened: 1982. **Holes:** 18. **Par:** 72/75. **Yards:** 6,715/5,458. **Course rating:** 70.5/71.5.
Slope: 118/115. **Architect:** Joseph Spinella. **Green fee:** $12/$14. **Credit cards:** None.
Reduced fees: Weekdays, twilight. **Caddies:** No. **Golf carts:** $10. **Discount golf packages:** No. **Season:** March-Nov. **High:** May-Aug. **On site lodging:** No. **Rental clubs:** Yes. **Walking policy:** Unrestricted walking. **Metal spikes allowed:** Yes. **Range:** No. **To obtain tee times:** Call.
Subscriber comments: Good course, challenge for local players...Great walking course...You can play as many holes as you'd like...Young course, needs time.
Special Notes: Spikeless shoes preferred.

★★DOUGLASTON GOLF CLUB
PU-63-20 Marathon Pkwy., Douglaston, 11363, Queens County, (718)224-6566.
Architect: William H. Tucker. **Caddies:** No. **Discount golf packages:** No. **On site lodging:** No. **Rental clubs:** No. **Metal spikes allowed:** Yes. **Range:** No.
Call club for further information.

★★DRUMLINS WEST GOLF CLUB
PU-800 Nottingham Rd., Syracuse, 13224, Onondaga County, (315)446-5580, 5 miles E of Syracuse.
Opened: 1935. **Holes:** 18. **Par:** 70/70. **Yards:** 6,030/4,790. **Course rating:** 68.2/71.0.
Slope: N/A. **Architect:** Leonard MacComber. **Green fee:** $9/$14. **Credit cards:** MC,VISA,DISC. **Reduced fees:** Twilight, seniors, juniors. **Caddies:** No. **Golf carts:** $23. **Discount golf packages:** Yes. **Season:** April-Nov. **High:** May-Aug. **On site lodging:** No. **Rental clubs:** Yes. **Walking policy:** Unrestricted walking. **Metal spikes allowed:** Yes. **Range:** Yes (grass/mats). **To obtain tee times:** Call.

★★½DUNWOODIE GOLF CLUB
PU-Wasylenko Lane, Yonkers, 10701, Westchester County, (914)968-2771, 10 miles N of New York City.
Opened: N/A. **Holes:** 18. **Par:** 70/72. **Yards:** 5,815/4,511. **Course rating:** 68.3/67.8.
Slope: 117/117. **Architect:** N/A. **Green fee:** $37/$42. **Credit cards:** MC,VISA,AMEX.
Reduced fees: Twilight, seniors, juniors. **Caddies:** No. **Golf carts:** $22. **Discount golf packages:** No. **Season:** April-Dec. **High:** April-Nov. **On site lodging:** No. **Rental clubs:** Yes. **Walking policy:** Unrestricted walking. **Metal spikes allowed:** Yes. **Range:** Yes (grass). **To obtain tee times:** Call (914)593-4653.
Subscriber comments: Tight and short, love it...Best of area public courses...Short par 4s tricky...Boring back nine...Five par 3s, four on back nine...Helps if there had been a mountain goat in your family.

★★½DURAND EASTMAN GOLF COURSE

PU-1200 Kings Hwy. N., Rochester, 14617, Monroe County, (716)342-9810.
Opened: 1935. **Holes:** 18. **Par:** 70/72. **Yards:** 6,089/5,727. **Course rating:** 68.8/71.7.
Slope: 112/113. **Architect:** Robert Trent Jones. **Green fee:** $12/$13. **Credit cards:**
None. **Reduced fees:** Weekdays, low season, seniors, juniors. **Caddies:** No. **Golf
carts:** $16. **Discount golf packages:** Yes. **Season:** April-Nov. **High:** June-Aug. **On site
lodging:** No. **Rental clubs:** Yes. **Walking policy:** Unrestricted walking. **Metal spikes
allowed:** Yes. **Range:** Yes (grass). **To obtain tee times:** First come, first served.
Subscriber comments: Deer all over the course make it scenic...Underwent extensive
restructuring in '96...A truly scenic and beautiful course...A lot of elevated tee boxes,
some very tight holes cut into hillsides...Treelined, need to place shots.

★★★DUTCH HOLLOW COUNTRY CLUB

Benson Rd., Owasco, 13130, Cayuga County, (315)784-5052, 19 miles SW of
Syracuse.
Opened: 1925. **Holes:** 18. **Par:** 71/72. **Yards:** 6,460/5,045. **Course rating:** 70.3/70.3.
Slope: 120/113. **Architect:** Willard S. Hall. **Green fee:** $17/$20. **Credit cards:**
MC,VISA. **Reduced fees:** Weekdays, low season, twilight, seniors, juniors. **Caddies:**
No. **Golf carts:** $11. **Discount golf packages:** Yes. **Season:** April-Nov. **High:** May-
Sept. **On site lodging:** No. **Rental clubs:** Yes. **Walking policy:** Unrestricted walking.
Metal spikes allowed: Yes. **Range:** Yes (grass/mats). **To obtain tee times:** Call.
Subscriber comments: Underrated...Always a pleasure, wicked slick
greens...Enjoyable place to be...Good solid course, good fun, some great holes...Many
blind shots...Variety of terrain and hole placement...Nice track along lake...Use every
club in bag...Tricky, hidden water hazards...Great use of creek flowing through course.

★★DYKER BEACH GOLF COURSE

PU-86th St. and 7th Ave., Brooklyn, 11228, Kings County, (718)836-9722, New York
City.
Opened: 1928. **Holes:** 18. **Par:** 71/72. **Yards:** 6,548/5,696. **Course rating:** 68.8.
Slope: 113. **Architect:** John Van Kleek. **Green fee:** $15/$18. **Credit cards:** MC,VISA.
Reduced fees: Weekdays, twilight, seniors, juniors. **Caddies:** No. **Golf carts:** $23.
Discount golf packages: No. **Season:** Year-round. **High:** May-Oct. **On site lodging:**
No. **Rental clubs:** Yes. **Walking policy:** Unrestricted walking. **Metal spikes allowed:**
Yes. **Range:** No. **To obtain tee times:** Call tee time number up to 11 days in advance.

★★½EAGLE CREST GOLF CLUB

PU-1004 Ballston Lake Rd., Rte. 146A, Clifton Park, 12065, Saratoga County,
(518)877-7082, 12 miles S of Saratoga.
Opened: 1962. **Holes:** 18. **Par:** 72/72. **Yards:** 6,814/5,082. **Course rating:** 72.4/68.6.
Slope: 126/117. **Architect:** N/A. **Green fee:** $18/$22. **Credit cards:** N/A. **Reduced
fees:** Weekdays. **Caddies:** No. **Golf carts:** $22. **Discount golf packages:** No.
Season: March-Nov. **High:** May-Sept. **On site lodging:** No. **Rental clubs:** Yes.
Walking policy: Unrestricted walking. **Metal spikes allowed:** No. **Range:** Yes (grass).
To obtain tee times: Foursomes may call up to 3 days in advance. All others call up to
2 days in advance.
Subscriber comments: Good layout, lots of character...Small greens...Course improv-
ing, often unreasonable pin placements...Fast greens with a lot of contour.

★★★EAGLE VALE GOLF COURSE

PU-4344 Nine Mile Point Rd., Fairport, 14450, Monroe County, (716)377-5200, 15
miles SE of Rochester.
Opened: 1987. **Holes:** 18. **Par:** 71/72. **Yards:** 6,584/5,801. **Course rating:** 70.9/73.0.
Slope: 124/121. **Architect:** Bill Brown/Neil Hirsch. **Green fee:** $21/$34. **Credit cards:**
MC,VISA,AMEX. **Reduced fees:** Weekdays, low season, seniors, juniors. **Caddies:** No.
Golf carts: Included in Green Fee. **Discount golf packages:** Yes. **Season:** April-Dec.
High: June-Aug. **On site lodging:** No. **Rental clubs:** Yes. **Walking policy:** Walking at
certain times. **Metal spikes allowed:** Yes. **Range:** Yes. **To obtain tee times:** Call 1 day
in advance for weekdays and 3 days in advance for weekends and holidays.
Subscriber comments: A challenge for all levels...Young course, nice layout, needs 20
years of tree growth...Greens read true...A few tough holes.

EISENHOWER PARK GOLF

PU-Eisenhower Park, East Meadow, 11554, Nassau County, (516)542-0015, 20 miles E of New York City.

Architect: Robert Trent Jones. **Green fee:** $7/$28. **Credit cards:** None. **Reduced fees:** Weekdays, low season, seniors. **Caddies:** No. **Golf carts:** $22. **Discount golf packages:** No. **Season:** Year-round. **High:** May-Oct. **On site lodging:** No. **Rental clubs:** Yes. **Walking policy:** Unrestricted walking. **Metal spikes allowed:** Yes. **To obtain tee times:** Call golf shop.

★★BLUE COURSE

Opened: 1947. **Holes:** 18. **Par:** 72/72. **Yards:** 6,026/5,800. **Course rating:** 68.7/74.1. **Slope:** 112/122. **Range:** Yes.

Subscriber comments: Reachable par 5s...Course is easy...Wide open...My three pre-teens love it...Very little variety, all holes heavily trapped at greens...Too short, great greens...Dual par 3s keep you moving...Slow pace of play, get there early.

★★★RED COURSE

Opened: 1914. **Holes:** 18. **Par:** 72/72. **Yards:** 6,756/5,449. **Course rating:** 71.5/69.8. **Slope:** 119/115. **Range:** No.
Notes: 1926 PGA Championship.

Subscriber comments: Red course is everyone's favorite...The best Eisenhower course...Scenic with a few water holes...Greens are exceptional, best of the three courses...Par-3 13th toughest tee shot on Long Island...Retirees' heaven.

★★WHITE COURSE

Opened: 1947. **Holes:** 18. **Par:** 72/72. **Yards:** 6,269/5,920. **Course rating:** 69.5/71.4. **Slope:** 115/117. **Range:** No.

Subscriber comments: Every hole the same—elevated greens, two bunkers...Challenging, with many elevated greens...Wide open...Holes are too similiar but greens have gotten better...Huge bunkers front every green...Can be a test when the wind blows.

★★ELM TREE GOLF COURSE

PU-283 St. Rte. No.13, Cortland, 13045, Cortland County, (607)753-1341, 30 miles S of Syracuse.

Opened: 1966. **Holes:** 18. **Par:** 70/74. **Yards:** 6,251/5,520. **Course rating:** 66.4/66.3. **Slope:** 100/99. **Architect:** Alder Jones. **Green fee:** $9/$13. **Credit cards:** MC,VISA. **Reduced fees:** Weekdays, low season, resort guests, twilight, seniors, juniors. **Caddies:** No. **Golf carts:** $20. **Discount golf packages:** Yes. **Season:** April-Nov. **High:** June-Aug. **On site lodging:** No. **Rental clubs:** No. **Walking policy:** Unrestricted walking. **Metal spikes allowed:** Yes. **Range:** Yes (grass/mats). **To obtain tee times:** Call 1 day in advance.

★★½ELMA MEADOWS GOLF CLUB

PU-1711 Girdle Rd., Elma, 14059, Erie County, (716)655-3037.

Opened: 1959. **Holes:** 18. **Par:** 70/75. **Yards:** 6,316/6,000. **Course rating:** 69.8/73.8. **Slope:** 107/118. **Architect:** William Harries and A. Russell Tryon. **Green fee:** $11/$13. **Credit cards:** None. **Reduced fees:** Weekdays, seniors, juniors. **Caddies:** No. **Golf carts:** $18. **Discount golf packages:** No. **Season:** Year-round weather permitting. **High:** June-Aug. **On site lodging:** No. **Rental clubs:** Yes. **Walking policy:** Unrestricted walking. **Metal spikes allowed:** No. **Range:** Yes (grass). **To obtain tee times:** First come, first served.

Subscriber comments: With good help could be outstanding...Some very interesting holes, big elevation changes...A very challenging short course...Good public course for the money...Need short iron game.

★★ELY PARK MUNICIPAL GOLF COURSE

PM-67 Ridge Road, Binghamton, 13905, Broome County, (607)772-7231.

Opened: 1932. **Holes:** 18. **Par:** 70. **Yards:** 6,410. **Course rating:** 69.4. **Slope:** 115. **Architect:** Ernest E. Smith. **Green fee:** $12/$13. **Credit cards:** None. **Reduced fees:** Seniors. **Caddies:** No. **Golf carts:** N/A. **Discount golf packages:** No. **Season:** April-Nov. **High:** Summer. **On site lodging:** No. **Rental clubs:** Yes. **Walking policy:** Unrestricted walking. **Metal spikes allowed:** Yes. **Range:** Yes (grass/mats). **To obtain tee times:** Call for weekends and holidays.

★★★½EN-JOIE GOLF CLUB
PU-722 W. Main St., Endicott, 13760, Broome County, (607)785-1661, (888)436-5643, 9 miles W of Binghamton.
Opened: 1927. **Holes:** 18. **Par:** 72/74. **Yards:** 7,016/5,205. **Course rating:** 73.0/69.8. **Slope:** 125/118. **Architect:** Michael Hurdzan. **Green fee:** $20/$20. **Credit cards:** MC,VISA. **Reduced fees:** Seniors, juniors. **Caddies:** No. **Golf carts:** $20. **Discount golf packages:** No. **Season:** March-Dec. **High:** May-Sept. **On site lodging:** No. **Rental clubs:** Yes. **Walking policy:** Unrestricted walking. **Metal spikes allowed:** No. **Range:** Yes (grass/mats). **To obtain tee times:** Call up to 3 days in advance for weekends. Call up to 7 days in advance for weekends.
Notes: Annual B.C. Open on PGA Tour.
Subscriber comments: PGA Tour stop, tough driving course, good test...Some holes dull...Long and flat, tight fairways, sometimes can't play all holes due to upgrading...Simply awesome...Good to match your play hole-by-hole with pros...A great old course, local knowledge helpful...Good walking.

★★★ENDWELL GREENS GOLF CLUB
PU-3675 Sally Piper Rd., Endwell, 13760, Broome County, (607)785-4653, 5 miles W of Binghamton.
Opened: 1968. **Holes:** 18. **Par:** 72/76. **Yards:** 7,104/5,382. **Course rating:** 73.6/70.6. **Slope:** 121/117. **Architect:** Geoffrey Cornish. **Green fee:** $16/$18. **Credit cards:** MC,VISA,DISC. **Reduced fees:** Weekdays, low season, seniors, juniors. **Caddies:** No. **Golf carts:** $11. **Discount golf packages:** No. **Season:** April-Nov. **High:** May-Aug. **On site lodging:** No. **Rental clubs:** Yes. **Walking policy:** Walking at certain times. **Metal spikes allowed:** Yes. **Range:** Yes (grass/mats). **To obtain tee times:** Public may call 2 days in advance. Members may call up to 14 days in advance.
Subscriber comments: Very hilly...Quality golf course, moderately difficult with big greens...Every lie is uphill, downhill or sidehill...Slow greens, scenic, excellent junior program...Hills make it a long course to play...Double greens...Mound in middle of 17th green goofy...Quintessential public course with potential to be better.

★★FILLMORE GOLF CLUB
PU-Tollgate Rd., Locke, 13092, Cayuga County, (315)497-3145.
Architect: Alder Jones. **Caddies:** No. **Discount golf packages:** No. **On site lodging:** No. **Rental clubs:** No. **Metal spikes allowed:** Yes. **Range:** No.
Call club for further information.

FORD HILL COUNTRY CLUB
PU-Rte. 26, Ford Hill Rd., Whitney Point, 13862, Chenango County, (607)692-8938.
Architect: Richard L. Driscoll. **Caddies:** No. **Discount golf packages:** No. **On site lodging:** No. **Rental clubs:** No. **Metal spikes allowed:** Yes. **Range:** No.
Call club for further information.
★½BLUE/ORANGE
Holes: 18.
★½WHITE/BLUE
Holes: 18.

★★FOREST PARK GOLF COURSE
PU-Forest Park Dr., Woodhaven, 11421, Queens County, (718)296-0999.
Opened: 1901. **Holes:** 18. **Par:** 67/67. **Yards:** 5,820/5,431. **Course rating:** 67.5/69.5. **Slope:** 111/116. **Architect:** Tom Bendelow. **Green fee:** $7/$17. **Credit cards:** MC,VISA. **Reduced fees:** Weekdays, low season, twilight, seniors, juniors. **Caddies:** No. **Golf carts:** $23. **Discount golf packages:** No. **Season:** Year-round. **High:** April-Sept. **On site lodging:** No. **Rental clubs:** Yes. **Walking policy:** Unrestricted walking. **Metal spikes allowed:** Yes. **Range:** No. **To obtain tee times:** Call in advance up to seven days.

★★★½FOXFIRE AT VILLAGE GREEN
PU-One Village Blvd., Baldwinsville, 13027, Onondaga County, (315)638-2930, 9 miles NW of Syracuse.
Opened: 1974. **Holes:** 18. **Par:** 72/72. **Yards:** 6,887/5,405. **Course rating:** 72.8/71.5. **Slope:** 127/115. **Architect:** Hal Purdy. **Green fee:** $19/$21. **Credit cards:** All major.

Reduced fees: Seniors, juniors. **Caddies:** No. **Golf carts:** $11. **Discount golf packages:** Yes. **Season:** March-Nov. **High:** June-Aug. **On site lodging:** No. **Rental clubs:** Yes. **Walking policy:** Walking at certain times. **Metal spikes allowed:** Yes. **Range:** Yes (grass/mats). **To obtain tee times:** Call up to 7 days in advance.
Subscriber comments: Good variety, good test of golf...Great greens...Some tight shots, can get demoralized if your game is so-so...Holes 11 through 15 toughest stretch around...Tight fairways, championship-type course...Condo course, good layout...Must hit ball straight to score...Nice course gets too much play.

★★★GARRISON GOLF CLUB
Rte. 9, Garrison, 10524, Putnam County, (914)424-3605, 50 miles N of New York City.
Opened: 1962. **Holes:** 18. **Par:** 72/70. **Yards:** 6,470/5,041. **Course rating:** 71.3/69.3.
Slope: 130/122. **Architect:** Dick Wilson. **Green fee:** $20/$55. **Credit cards:** MC,VISA.
Reduced fees: Weekdays, twilight, seniors. **Caddies:** No. **Golf carts:** $15. **Discount golf packages:** No. **Season:** April-Nov. **High:** June-Aug. **On site lodging:** No. **Rental clubs:** Yes. **Walking policy:** Walking at certain times. **Metal spikes allowed:** Yes. **Range:** Yes (grass). **To obtain tee times:** Call up to one week in advance.
Subscriber comments: Beautiful Hudson River views...Nice layout, mature course...Fine, challenging, downhill lies predominate...Fast greens...Rangers keep you moving...Starting holes best...Narrow fairways, lots of water and small greens challenge even a mid-handicapper...Tough walk...Wonderful in the fall, West Point in view.

GENESEE VALLEY GOLF COURSE
PU-1000 E. River Rd., Rochester, 14623, Monroe County, (716)424-2920.
Architect: Frances Baker. **Green fee:** $12/$13. **Credit cards:** None. **Reduced fees:** Low season, twilight, seniors, juniors. **Caddies:** No. **Golf carts:** $9. **Discount golf packages:** Yes. **Season:** April-Nov. **High:** June-July. **On site lodging:** No. **Rental clubs:** Yes. **Walking policy:** Unrestricted walking. **Metal spikes allowed:** Yes. **Range:** No. **To obtain tee times:** Call for weekends.
★★NEW COURSE
Opened: 1927. **Holes:** 18. **Par:** 67/69. **Yards:** 5,270/5,270. **Course rating:** 67.4.
Slope: 93/100.
★★OLD COURSE
Opened: 1900. **Holes:** 18. **Par:** 71/77. **Yards:** 6,374/6,007. **Course rating:** 69.3/73.2.
Slope: 104/112.

★★★½GLEN OAK GOLF COURSE
PU-711 Smith Rd., East Amherst, 14051, Erie County, (716)688-5454.
Opened: 1969. **Holes:** 18. **Par:** 72/72. **Yards:** 6,730/5,561. **Course rating:** 72.4/71.9.
Slope: 129/118. **Architect:** Robert Trent Jones. **Green fee:** $22/$40. **Credit cards:** MC,VISA. **Reduced fees:** Weekdays, low season, twilight, seniors. **Caddies:** No. **Golf carts:** Included in Green Fee. **Discount golf packages:** No. **Season:** April-Nov. **High:** June-Aug. **On site lodging:** No. **Rental clubs:** Yes. **Walking policy:** Mandatory cart. **Metal spikes allowed:** Yes. **Range:** Yes (grass/mats). **To obtain tee times:** Call up to 3 days in advance.
Subscriber comments: Bring plenty of balls, this one is tough...Great layout, each hole different...Speedy greens...Best course in area (my favorite)...Making dramatic comeback...Could become one of the best around...Shotmaker's course.

★★½GOLDEN OAK GOLF CLUB
PU-Rte. 79 S., Windsor, 13865, Broome County, (607)655-3217, 12 miles SE of Binghamton.
Opened: 1972. **Holes:** 18. **Par:** 69/69. **Yards:** 5,500/4,500. **Course rating:** 67.0/65.0.
Slope: 117/115. **Architect:** Paul Kern. **Green fee:** $10/$13. **Credit cards:** MC,VISA.
Reduced fees: Weekdays. **Caddies:** No. **Golf carts:** $9. **Discount golf packages:** Yes. **Season:** April-Nov. **High:** June-Aug. **On site lodging:** No. **Rental clubs:** Yes. **Walking policy:** Unrestricted walking. **Metal spikes allowed:** Yes. **Range:** No. **To obtain tee times:** Call 2 days in advance.
Subscriber comments: Contrasting nines, front more difficult and back very short...Strange, short layout...Good for ego...Great par 3s on front nine.

★★★½GREEN LAKES STATE PARK GOLF CLUB

PU-7900 Greenlake Rd., Fayetteville, 13066, Onondaga County, (315)637-0258, 7 miles S of Syracuse.
Opened: 1936. **Holes:** 18. **Par:** 71/74. **Yards:** 6,212/5,481. **Course rating:** 68.4/70.6. **Slope:** 113/120. **Architect:** Robert Trent Jones. **Green fee:** $17/$20. **Credit cards:** MC,VISA. **Reduced fees:** Weekdays, seniors, juniors. **Caddies:** No. **Golf carts:** $20. **Discount golf packages:** No. **Season:** April-Nov. **High:** May-Sept. **On site lodging:** Yes. **Rental clubs:** Yes. **Walking policy:** Unrestricted walking. **Metal spikes allowed:** Yes. **Range:** No. **To obtain tee times:** Call 4 days in advance.
Subscriber comments: Very good layout, tough course, good value...Best of state courses, not walkable for seniors...Bad lies but good golf...One of the most enjoyable courses I've played...A hidden gem...Very challenging, hilly, great greens.

★★★★GREYSTONE GOLF CLUB

PU-1400 Atlantic Ave., Walworth, 14568, Wayne County, (315)524-0022, (800)810-2325, 12 miles E of Rochester.
Opened: 1996. **Holes:** 18. **Par:** 72/72. **Yards:** 6,500/5,300. **Course rating:** 70.2/70.7. **Slope:** 121/122. **Architect:** Craig Schreiner. **Green fee:** $28/$37. **Credit cards:** MC,VISA,AMEX. **Reduced fees:** Weekdays, low season, twilight, seniors. **Caddies:** No. **Golf carts:** $33. **Discount golf packages:** No. **Season:** April-Nov. **High:** Summer. **On site lodging:** No. **Rental clubs:** Yes. **Walking policy:** Walking at certain times. **Metal spikes allowed:** Yes. **Range:** Yes (grass). **To obtain tee times:** Call up to 7 days in advance.
Subscriber comments: Great layout, very different...Excellent new course...A great finishing hole...Will be outstanding when it matures...First class, must play...Best public course in area...Numerous tee boxes make course enjoyable for all levels.

★★★½GROSSINGER COUNTRY CLUB

PU-26 Rte. 52 E., Liberty, 12754, Sullivan County, (914)292-9000, 98 miles NW of New York.
Opened: 1965. **Holes:** 27. **Architect:** Joe Finger. **Credit cards:** MC,VISA,AMEX. **Reduced fees:** Weekdays, low season, twilight, seniors, juniors. **Caddies:** No. **Golf carts:** Included in Green Fee. **Discount golf packages:** Yes. **Season:** April-Nov. **High:** June-Sept. **On site lodging:** No. **Rental clubs:** Yes. **Walking policy:** Mandatory cart. **Metal spikes allowed:** No. **Range:** Yes (grass/mats). **To obtain tee times:** Call up to 14 days in advance.
LAKE COURSE
Par: 72/75. **Yards:** 6,839/5,875. **Course rating:** 72.9/73.2. **Slope:** 134. **Green fee:** $40/$75.
VALLEY COURSE
Par: 72/74. **Yards:** 6,750/6,085. **Course rating:** 72.5/74.4. **Slope:** 133. **Green fee:** $40/$75.
VISTA COURSE
Par: 72/73. **Yards:** 6,625/5,840. **Course rating:** 72.1/73.3. **Slope:** 132. **Green fee:** $38/$69.
Subscriber comments: Best in Catskill area...Each hole a challenge...Beautiful setting...Greens like Persian rug...Most of fairways are very narrow...One of the hidden gems in New York State...Afternoon rates wonderful...Small greens.

★½GROVER CLEVELAND GOLF COURSE

PU-3781 Main St., Amherst, 14226, Erie County, (716)862-9470, (716)862-9470, 3 miles N of Buffalo.
Opened: 1912. **Holes:** 18. **Par:** 69. **Yards:** 5,584. **Course rating:** 67.5. **Slope:** 101. **Architect:** N/A. **Green fee:** $9/$10. **Credit cards:** None. **Reduced fees:** Weekdays, seniors, juniors. **Caddies:** No. **Golf carts:** $17. **Discount golf packages:** No. **Season:** April-Nov. **High:** June-Aug. **On site lodging:** No. **Rental clubs:** Yes. **Walking policy:** Unrestricted walking. **Metal spikes allowed:** No. **Range:** Yes. **To obtain tee times:** First come, first served.

★★½HAMLET WIND WATCH GOLF CLUB
PU-1715 Vanderbuilt Motor Pkwy., Hauppauge, 11788, Suffolk County, (516)232-9850, 45 miles E of New York City.
Opened: 1990. **Holes:** 18. **Par:** 71/71. **Yards:** 6,512/5,146. **Course rating:** 71.0/68.6. **Slope:** 128/118. **Architect:** Joe Lee. **Green fee:** $25/$72. **Credit cards:** All major. **Reduced fees:** Low season, resort guests, twilight, juniors. **Caddies:** No. **Golf carts:** Included in Green Fee. **Discount golf packages:** No. **Season:** Year-round. **High:** April-Oct. **On site lodging:** Yes. **Rental clubs:** Yes. **Walking policy:** Mandatory cart. **Metal spikes allowed:** No. **Range:** Yes (grass/mats). **To obtain tee times:** Hotel guests may call 60 days in advance. Nonguests call 3 days in advance.
Subscriber comments: Could be a good test...Narrow fairways, good ball-striking a must...Needs time to fill in...Needs some polish, clean up edges...Nice all-around place to play...Conditions have improved...Great bunkering, tough approaches.

★★★½HANAH COUNTRY INN & GOLF RESORT
R-Rte. 30, Margaretville, 12455, Deleware County, (914)586-4849, (800)752-6494, 42 miles W of Kingston.
Opened: 1992. **Holes:** 18. **Par:** 72/72. **Yards:** 7,033/5,294. **Course rating:** 73.5/69.7. **Slope:** 133/123. **Architect:** Koji Nagasaka. **Green fee:** $40/$55. **Credit cards:** MC,VISA. **Reduced fees:** Weekdays, low season, resort guests, twilight, seniors. **Caddies:** No. **Golf carts:** Included in Green Fee. **Discount golf packages:** Yes. **Season:** April-Oct. **High:** June-July. **On site lodging:** Yes. **Rental clubs:** Yes. **Walking policy:** Mandatory cart. **Metal spikes allowed:** Yes. **Range:** Yes (grass/mats). **To obtain tee times:** Call.
Subscriber comments: Golf rating should be five but play too slow...Superb, actually three different courses: a standard nine, four easy mountain holes, five killer lake holes...Strange layout but challenging...Almost unfair from blue tees.
Special Notes: Spikeless shoes encouraged.

HARBOUR POINTE COUNTRY CLUB
PU-Rte. 18 and 98, Waterport, 14571, Orleans County, (716)798-3010.
Architect: Joe DeMino. **Caddies:** No. **Discount golf packages:** No. **On site lodging:** No. **Rental clubs:** No. **Metal spikes allowed:** Yes. **Range:** No.
Call club for further information.

★★½HAUPPAUGE COUNTRY CLUB
Veterans Memorial Hwy., Hauppauge, 11788, Suffolk County, (516)724-7500, 30 miles E of New York City.
Opened: 1960. **Holes:** 18. **Par:** 72/74. **Yards:** 6,525/5,925. **Course rating:** 71.0/75.5. **Slope:** 122/131. **Architect:** N/A. **Green fee:** $20/$70. **Credit cards:** MC,VISA,AMEX. **Reduced fees:** Weekdays, low season, twilight, seniors. **Caddies:** No. **Golf carts:** $30. **Discount golf packages:** No. **Season:** March-Dec. **High:** May-Oct. **On site lodging:** No. **Rental clubs:** Yes. **Walking policy:** Walking at certain times. **Metal spikes allowed:** Yes. **Range:** Yes (Mats). **To obtain tee times:** Call up to 7 days in advance Monday-Friday.
Subscriber comments: Worth a visit...Wind conditions really affect your game here...Good bunkering near greens...Course should be walked...Wooded with lots of doglegs, some elevated tees...Not long, accuracy a must.

★★★½HILAND GOLF CLUB
195 Haviland Rd., Queensbury, 12804, Warren County, (518)761-4653, 45 miles N of Albany.
Opened: 1988. **Holes:** 18. **Par:** 72/72. **Yards:** 6,632/5,677. **Course rating:** 72.5/72.5. **Slope:** 133/123. **Architect:** Steven Kay. **Green fee:** $33. **Credit cards:** MC,VISA,AMEX. **Reduced fees:** Weekdays, low season, resort guests, twilight. **Caddies:** No. **Golf carts:** $13. **Discount golf packages:** No. **Season:** April-Nov. **High:** June-Sept. **On site lodging:** No. **Rental clubs:** Yes. **Walking policy:** Unrestricted walking. **Metal spikes allowed:** No. **Range:** Yes (grass/mats). **To obtain tee times:** Call. Tee times required.
Subscriber comments: My favorite course...A good challenge...Flat, straight course...Good greens, some strong holes...Some holes too close to others...Good for the free swinger...Good finishing holes on each nine.

★★HILLENDALE GOLF COURSE
PU-218 Applegate Rd., Ithaca, 14850, Tompkins County, (607)273-2363, (800)286-2838, 50 miles S of Syracuse.
Opened: 1912. **Holes:** 18. **Par:** 71/73. **Yards:** 6,002/5,705. **Course rating:** 68.8/69.3. **Slope:** 115/116. **Architect:** Novickas/Sommer. **Green fee:** $13/$14. **Credit cards:** MC,VISA. **Reduced fees:** Weekdays, low season, twilight, seniors, juniors. **Caddies:** No. **Golf carts:** $16. **Discount golf packages:** Yes. **Season:** April-Oct. **High:** June-Aug. **On site lodging:** No. **Rental clubs:** Yes. **Walking policy:** Unrestricted walking. **Metal spikes allowed:** Yes. **Range:** Yes (grass). **To obtain tee times:** Call golf shop up to 7 days in advance.

★★★HOLIDAY VALLEY RESORT
R-Rte. 219, Ellicottville, 14731, Cattaraugus County, (716)699-2346, 48 miles S of Buffalo.
Opened: 1961. **Holes:** 18. **Par:** 72/73. **Yards:** 6,555/5,381. **Course rating:** 71.3/74.0. **Slope:** 125/115. **Architect:** Russ Tryon. **Green fee:** $15/$30. **Credit cards:** All major. **Reduced fees:** Weekdays, low season, twilight. **Caddies:** No. **Golf carts:** $11. **Discount golf packages:** Yes. **Season:** April-Oct. **High:** June-Sept. **On site lodging:** Yes. **Rental clubs:** Yes. **Walking policy:** Walking at certain times. **Metal spikes allowed:** Yes. **Range:** Yes (grass/mats). **To obtain tee times:** Call up to 3 days in advance.
Subscriber comments: Very hilly...Hole no. 11 is a crazy hole...Tight, challenging, fantastic scenery...Very short...Blind shots...Ski resort, several unique holes...Wow, golfing on ski slopes, loved it...Greens are killers.

HYDE PARK GOLF COURSE
PU-4343 Porter Rd., Niagara Falls, 14305, Niagara County, (716)297-2067, 20 miles NW of Buffalo.
Opened: 1920. **Architect:** William Harries. **Green fee:** $15/$20. **Credit cards:** None. **Reduced fees:** Seniors, juniors. **Caddies:** No. **Golf carts:** $20. **Discount golf packages:** No. **Season:** April-Nov. **High:** June-Sept. **On site lodging:** No. **Rental clubs:** Yes. **Walking policy:** Unrestricted walking. **Metal spikes allowed:** Yes. **Range:** Yes (grass). **To obtain tee times:** First come, first served.
★½NORTH COURSE
Holes: 18. **Par:** 70/70. **Yards:** 6,400/5,700. **Course rating:** 70.0/72.0. **Slope:** 110/110.
★½RED/WHITE COURSE
Holes: 18. **Par:** 71/71. **Yards:** 6,850/6,500. **Course rating:** N/A. **Slope:** N/A.

★★½INDIAN ISLAND COUNTRY CLUB
PM-Riverside Dr., Riverhead, 11901, Suffolk County, (516)727-7776, 70 miles E of New York City.
Opened: 1972. **Holes:** 18. **Par:** 72/72. **Yards:** 6,378/5,524. **Course rating:** 71.0/72.8. **Slope:** 122/124. **Architect:** William Mitchell. **Green fee:** $9/$20. **Credit cards:** None. **Reduced fees:** Low season, twilight, seniors, juniors. **Caddies:** No. **Golf carts:** $12. **Discount golf packages:** Yes. **Season:** March-Dec. **High:** May-Sept. **On site lodging:** No. **Rental clubs:** Yes. **Walking policy:** Unrestricted walking. **Metal spikes allowed:** No. **Range:** Yes (Mats). **To obtain tee times:** Available only to Suffolk County green key card holders.
Subscriber comments: Nice views, a little scruffy...Very relaxing place...Pretty and a lot of fun...Always windy, tough short par 5s...Holes on the bay are great...Some memorable holes...Tight fairways...Interesting short course.

★★★ISLAND'S END GOLF & COUNTRY CLUB
Rte. 25, Greenport, 11944, Suffolk County, (516)477-0777.
Architect: Herbert Strong. **Caddies:** No. **Discount golf packages:** No. **On site lodging:** No. **Rental clubs:** No. **Metal spikes allowed:** Yes. **Range:** No.
Call club for further information.
Subscriber comments: Flat, unassuming course except for the par 3 overlooking the sound...Par-3 16th is awesome!...Worth the drive to the end of the earth...Best kept secret on Long Island...Back nine beautiful late in afternoon.

★★½JAMES BAIRD STATE PARK GOLF CLUB

PU-122C Freedom Plains Rd., Pleasant Valley, 12569, Dutchess County, (914)473-1052, 5 miles E of Poughkeepsie.

Opened: N/A. **Holes:** 18. **Par:** 71/74. **Yards:** 6,616/5,541. **Course rating:** 71.3/75.2. **Slope:** 124/131. **Architect:** Robert Trent Jones. **Green fee:** $14/$17. **Credit cards:** None. **Reduced fees:** Low season, twilight, seniors, juniors. **Caddies:** No. **Golf carts:** $20. **Discount golf packages:** No. **Season:** April-Nov. **High:** May-Aug. **On site lodging:** No. **Rental clubs:** Yes. **Walking policy:** Unrestricted walking. **Metal spikes allowed:** Yes. **Range:** Yes. **To obtain tee times:** Call two days in advance.

Subscriber comments: Challenging...Good test of skills...Wide open...Back nine very good...Old-time layout...Best to play in early season.

★½KISSENA PARK GOLF COURSE

PU-164-15 Booth Memorial Ave., Flushing, 11365, Queens County, (718)939-4594, New York City.

Opened: 1937. **Holes:** 18. **Par:** 64/64. **Yards:** 4,727/4,425. **Course rating:** 61.8/65.6. **Slope:** 101/106. **Architect:** John Van Kleek. **Green fee:** $16/$18. **Credit cards:** None. **Reduced fees:** Weekdays, twilight, seniors, juniors. **Caddies:** No. **Golf carts:** N/A. **Discount golf packages:** No. **Season:** Year-round. **High:** N/A. **On site lodging:** No. **Rental clubs:** Yes. **Walking policy:** Unrestricted walking. **Metal spikes allowed:** Yes. **Range:** No. **To obtain tee times:** Call seven days in advance.

★★★KUTSHER'S COUNTRY CLUB

R-Kutsher Rd., Monticello, 12701, Sullivan County, (914)794-6000, 80 miles N of New York City.

Opened: 1962. **Holes:** 18. **Par:** 71/71. **Yards:** 7,001/5,676. **Course rating:** 73.5/72.3. **Slope:** 123/119. **Architect:** William F. Mitchell. **Green fee:** $45. **Credit cards:** None. **Reduced fees:** Weekdays, resort guests, twilight. **Caddies:** No. **Golf carts:** Included in Green Fee. **Discount golf packages:** Yes. **Season:** April-Nov. **High:** July-Aug. **On site lodging:** Yes. **Rental clubs:** Yes. **Walking policy:** Mandatory cart. **Metal spikes allowed:** Yes. **Range:** Yes (grass/mats). **To obtain tee times:** Call 7 days in advance. Hotel guests may call up to 30 days in advance.

Subscriber comments: One of the better secrets of the Catskills, best greens around...Moderate challenge...Front nine very good, always fun...Great old course...Beautiful layout in the country.

★★½LA TOURETTE GOLF CLUB

PU-1001 Richmond Hill Rd., Staten Island, 10306, Richmond County, (718)351-1889, New York City.

Opened: 1930. **Holes:** 18. **Par:** 72/72. **Yards:** 6,692/5,493. **Course rating:** 70.7/70.9. **Slope:** 119/115. **Architect:** John Van Kleek. **Green fee:** $20/$22. **Credit cards:** MC,VISA. **Reduced fees:** Twilight, seniors, juniors. **Caddies:** No. **Golf carts:** $24. **Discount golf packages:** No. **Season:** Year-round. **High:** May-Sept. **On site lodging:** No. **Rental clubs:** Yes. **Walking policy:** Unrestricted walking. **Metal spikes allowed:** Yes. **Range:** No. **To obtain tee times:** Call one week in advance.

Subscriber comments: Wide open course...Enough contour to be interesting...Great holes along bay...Best public course in NYC...Nice views...Nothing fancy, picturesque.

LAKE PLACID RESORT

R-Mirror Lake Dr., Lake Placid, 12946, Essex County, (518)523-4460, (800)874-1980, 20 miles W of Plattsburgh.

Opened: 1895. **Green fee:** $15/$25. **Credit cards:** All major. **Reduced fees:** Weekdays, low season, resort guests, twilight. **Caddies:** No. **Golf carts:** $26. **Discount golf packages:** Yes. **Season:** April-Oct. **High:** July-Aug. **On site lodging:** No. **Rental clubs:** Yes. **Walking policy:** Unrestricted walking. **Metal spikes allowed:** Yes. **Range:** Yes (grass). **To obtain tee times:** Call or come in.

★★★LINKS COURSE

Holes: 18. **Par:** 71/71. **Yards:** 6,759/5,107. **Course rating:** 72.5. **Slope:** 120. **Architect:** Seymour Dunn.

Subscriber comments: Good driving course, wide open, great views...Superb links layout.

Special Notes: Also has 9-hole executive course.

★★½MOUNTAIN COURSE
Holes: 18. **Par:** 70/70. **Yards:** 6,216/4,784. **Course rating:** 70.8. **Slope:** 126.
Architect: Alex Findley.
Subscriber comments: Tough, narrow, wooded fairways...Beautiful views of mountains...Interesting wildlife...Nice view of Olympic ski jumps...Too many blind shots...Most greens slope away from approach shots...Tough to walk.
Special Notes: Also has 9-hole executive course.

★★★LAKE SHORE COUNTRY CLUB
1165 Greenleaf Rd., Rochester, 14612, Monroe County, (716)663-0300, 5 miles N of Rochester.
Opened: 1932. **Holes:** 18. **Par:** 70/73. **Yards:** 6,343/5,561. **Course rating:** 67.2/72.0.
Slope: 116/117. **Architect:** Calvin Black. **Green fee:** $22/$22. **Credit cards:**
MC,VISA,DISC. **Reduced fees:** Twilight. **Caddies:** No. **Golf carts:** $10. **Discount golf packages:** Yes. **Season:** April-Nov. **High:** June-Aug. **On site lodging:** No. **Rental clubs:** No. **Walking policy:** Unrestricted walking. **Metal spikes allowed:** No. **Range:** Yes (grass/mats). **To obtain tee times:** Call same day for weekdays. Call Thursday for upcoming weekend.
Subscriber comments: Great finishing hole...Mountain scenery...Fairly flat and open...A fair layout for mid-handicappers...A little short...Fairways too close together.

★★LE ROY COUNTRY CLUB
7759 E. Main Rd., Le Roy, 14482, Genesee County, (716)768-7330, 20 miles W of Rochester.
Opened: 1930. **Holes:** 18. **Par:** 71/74. **Yards:** 6,382/5,752. **Course rating:** 69.6/71.0.
Slope: 115/117. **Architect:** Don Woodward. **Green fee:** $14/$18. **Credit cards:**
MC,VISA. **Reduced fees:** Weekdays, low season, twilight, seniors, juniors. **Caddies:**
Yes. **Golf carts:** $22. **Discount golf packages:** Yes. **Season:** April-Oct. **High:** June-Aug. **On site lodging:** No. **Rental clubs:** Yes. **Walking policy:** Unrestricted walking.
Metal spikes allowed: Yes. **Range:** Yes (grass/mats). **To obtain tee times:** Call.

★★★½LEATHERSTOCKING GOLF COURSE
R-Nelson Ave., Cooperstown, 13326, Otsego County, (607)547-5275, 50 miles NW of Albany.
Opened: 1909. **Holes:** 18. **Par:** 72/72. **Yards:** 6,324/5,254. **Course rating:** 71.0/69.2.
Slope: 124/116. **Architect:** Devereux Emmet. **Green fee:** $55/$65. **Credit cards:**
MC,VISA,AMEX. **Reduced fees:** Resort guests, twilight. **Caddies:** No. **Golf carts:** $16.
Discount golf packages: No. **Season:** April-Oct. **High:** June-Sept. **On site lodging:**
Yes. **Rental clubs:** Yes. **Walking policy:** Walking at certain times. **Metal spikes allowed:** Yes. **Range:** No. **To obtain tee times:** Call 6 days in advance.
Subscriber comments: Very scenic, very tough course...Short course...A wonderful old course...Very unusual golf course...Elevation changes are a killer...Lakeside beauty, not a level lie on the course...Holes around the lake are memorable.

★★★LIMA GOLF & COUNTRY CLUB
PU-2681 Plank Rd., Lima, 14485, Livingston County, (716)624-1490, 20 miles S of Rochester.
Opened: 1963. **Holes:** 18. **Par:** 72/74. **Yards:** 6,768/5,624. **Course rating:** 72.3/74.0.
Slope: 117. **Architect:** N/A. **Green fee:** $12/$17. **Credit cards:** MC,VISA. **Reduced fees:** Weekdays, low season, seniors. **Caddies:** No. **Golf carts:** $9. **Discount golf packages:** No. **Season:** April-Oct. **High:** June-Sept. **On site lodging:** No. **Rental clubs:** Yes. **Walking policy:** Unrestricted walking. **Metal spikes allowed:** Yes. **Range:** Yes (grass). **To obtain tee times:** Call golf shop up to one week in advance.
Subscriber comments: Improving year to year...Fair layout...Huge greens...Too open, too windy...Not much of a challenge...Long par 4s...Too many parallel fairways.

★★★★THE LINKS AT HIAWATHA LANDING
PU-2350 Marshland Rd., Apalachin, 13732, Tioga County, (607)687-6952, 10 miles W of Binghamton.
Opened: 1994. **Holes:** 18. **Par:** 72/72. **Yards:** 7,067/5,101. **Course rating:** 73.5/68.4.
Slope: 131/113. **Architect:** Brian Silva and Mark Mungeam. **Green fee:** $29/$45.
Credit cards: All major. **Reduced fees:** Weekdays, low season, twilight, juniors.
Caddies: No. **Golf carts:** $10. **Discount golf packages:** Yes. **Season:** April-Nov.

High: June-Sept. **On site lodging:** No. **Rental clubs:** Yes. **Walking policy:** Unrestricted walking. **Metal spikes allowed:** No. **Range:** Yes (grass). **To obtain tee times:** Call 7 days in advance.

Subscriber comments: Interesting holes, especially watery 18th...Very difficult for high handicap...Great links experience, very different...Championship tough from the tips...I think everyone should play this course once...Very tough when wind blows.

★★½LIVERPOOL GOLF & COUNTRY CLUB

PU-7209 Morgan Rd., Liverpool, 13090, Onondaga County, (315)457-7170, 5 miles N of Syracuse.

Opened: 1949. **Holes:** 18. **Par:** 71/69. **Yards:** 6,412/5,487. **Course rating:** 70.7/69.3. **Slope:** 114/113. **Architect:** Archie S. Ajemian and Sons. **Green fee:** $18/$20. **Credit cards:** None. **Reduced fees:** Weekdays, low season, twilight, seniors, juniors. **Caddies:** No. **Golf carts:** $20. **Discount golf packages:** No. **Season:** Year-round. **High:** April-Nov. **On site lodging:** No. **Rental clubs:** Yes. **Walking policy:** Unrestricted walking. **Metal spikes allowed:** Yes. **Range:** No. **To obtain tee times:** Call.

Subscriber comments: Very busy course but in good shape...Close to the city...Nice par 3s...Open year-round even when snow is on the ground...Interesting course.

MALONE GOLF CLUB

Country Club Rd., Malone, 12953, Franklin County, (518)483-2926, 70 miles S of Montreal. **Architect:** Robert T. Jones/W.Wilkinson/A. Murray. **Green fee:** $26/$26. **Credit cards:** MC,VISA,AMEX. **Reduced fees:** Twilight. **Caddies:** No. **Discount golf packages:** Yes. **Season:** April-Oct. **High:** June-Aug. **On site lodging:** No. **Rental clubs:** Yes. **Walking policy:** Unrestricted walking. **Metal spikes allowed:** No. **Range:** No. **To obtain tee times:** Call up to 7 days in advance.

★★★½EAST COURSE

Opened: 1939. **Holes:** 18. **Par:** 72/73. **Yards:** 6,545/5,224. **Course rating:** 71.5/69.9. **Slope:** 123/117. **Golf carts:** $24.

Subscriber comments: Very remote but a good track...Hidden gem in the north country...First nine classic, wonderful par 3s...Excellent mountain challenges and views.

★★★½WEST COURSE

Opened: 1987. **Holes:** 18. **Par:** 71/72. **Yards:** 6,592/5,468. **Course rating:** 71.3/67.5. **Slope:** 126/115. **Golf carts:** $22.

Subscriber comments: Great complex course...Test of golf for seniors...Enjoyable golf but not nearly the easiest layout.

★★MAPLE MOOR GOLF COURSE

PU-1128 N. St., White Plains, 10605, Westchester County, (914)946-1830, 20 miles N of New York City.

Opened: 1923. **Holes:** 18. **Par:** 71/74. **Yards:** 6,226/5,812. **Course rating:** 68.8/71.9. **Slope:** 110/119. **Architect:** Archie Capper. **Green fee:** $15/$40. **Credit cards:** MC,VISA. **Reduced fees:** Twilight, seniors, juniors. **Caddies:** No. **Golf carts:** $22. **Discount golf packages:** No. **Season:** April-Dec. **High:** May-Aug. **On site lodging:** No. **Rental clubs:** Yes. **Walking policy:** Unrestricted walking. **Metal spikes allowed:** Yes. **Range:** No. **To obtain tee times:** Call one week in advance.

★★MARINE PARK GOLF CLUB

PU-2880 Flatbush Ave., Brooklyn, 11234, Kings County, (718)338-7113.

Opened: 1964. **Holes:** 18. **Par:** 72/72. **Yards:** 6,866/5,323. **Course rating:** 70.5. **Slope:** 118. **Architect:** Robert Trent Jones. **Green fee:** $9/$26. **Credit cards:** All major. **Reduced fees:** Weekdays, low season, twilight, seniors, juniors. **Caddies:** No. **Golf carts:** $23. **Discount golf packages:** No. **Season:** Year-round. **High:** May-Aug. **On site lodging:** No. **Rental clubs:** Yes. **Walking policy:** Unrestricted walking. **Metal spikes allowed:** Yes. **Range:** No. **To obtain tee times:** Call 7 days in advance.

★★★½MARK TWAIN GOLF CLUB

PU-Corning Rd., Elmira, 14903, Chemung County, (607)737-5770, 50 miles W of Binghamton.

GOOD VALUE

Opened: 1939. **Holes:** 18. **Par:** 72/76. **Yards:** 6,829/5,571. **Course rating:** 73.6/72.3. **Slope:** 123/121. **Architect:** Donald Ross. **Green fee:** $13/$15. **Credit cards:** None. **Reduced fees:** Weekdays, twilight, seniors, juniors. **Caddies:** No. **Golf carts:** $11. **Discount golf packages:** No. **Season:**

April-Oct. **High:** June-Aug. **On site lodging:** No. **Rental clubs:** Yes. **Walking policy:** Unrestricted walking. **Metal spikes allowed:** Yes. **Range:** Yes (grass). **To obtain tee times:** Call.

Subscriber comments: Interesting course, enjoyable to play...Good test for all...Excellent challenge...Long hitters' course...Big greens with a lot of break on putts...All par 3s to blind mostly uphill greens...Deep bunkers...Super layout!

★★MASSENA COUNTRY CLUB

PU-Rte. 131, Massena, 13662, St. Lawrence County, (315)769-2293, 160 miles N of Syracuse.

Opened: 1958. **Holes:** 18. **Par:** 71/75. **Yards:** 6,602/5,361. **Course rating:** 70.1/70.0. **Slope:** 110/111. **Architect:** Albert Murray. **Green fee:** $22. **Credit cards:** MC,VISA. **Reduced fees:** Low season, twilight. **Caddies:** Yes. **Golf carts:** $20. **Discount golf packages:** No. **Season:** May-Oct. **High:** June-Aug. **On site lodging:** No. **Rental clubs:** Yes. **Walking policy:** Unrestricted walking. **Metal spikes allowed:** No. **Range:** Yes (grass/mats). **To obtain tee times:** Call up to 2 days in advance.

★★★MCCANN MEMORIAL GOLF CLUB

PU-155 Wilbur Blvd., Poughkeepsie, 12603, Dutchess County, (914)471-3917, 65 miles N of New York City.

Opened: 1972. **Holes:** 18. **Par:** 72/72. **Yards:** 6,524/5,354. **Course rating:** 72.0/71.4. **Slope:** 128/123. **Architect:** William F. Mitchell. **Green fee:** $25/$30. **Credit cards:** None. **Reduced fees:** Seniors, juniors. **Caddies:** No. **Golf carts:** $22. **Discount golf packages:** No. **Season:** March-Dec. **High:** April-Oct. **On site lodging:** No. **Rental clubs:** Yes. **Walking policy:** Unrestricted walking. **Metal spikes allowed:** Yes. **Range:** Yes (grass). **To obtain tee times:** Call.

Subscriber comments: Very good course...Big greens, good layout...Best public course around...Nice course but costly to non-residents.

★★★MIDDLE ISLAND COUNTRY CLUB

PU-Yapank Rd., Middle Island, 11953, Suffolk County, (516)924-5100, 75 miles E of New York City.

Opened: 1964. **Holes:** 27. **Architect:** Baier Lustgarten. **Green fee:** $22. **Credit cards:** None. **Reduced fees:** N/A. **Caddies:** No. **Golf carts:** $14. **Discount golf packages:** No. **Season:** Year-round. **High:** April-Oct. **On site lodging:** No. **Rental clubs:** Yes. **Walking policy:** Walking at certain times. **Metal spikes allowed:** Yes. **Range:** No. **To obtain tee times:** Call one week in advance.

DOGWOOD/OAKTREE
Par: 72/74. **Yards:** 6,934/5,809.
DOGWOOD/SPRUCE
Par: 72/74. **Yards:** 7,015/5,909.
OAKTREE/SPRUCE
Par: 72/72. **Yards:** 7,027/5,906.

Subscriber comments: Good variety of holes...Better hit them straight, tough for short or wild hitters...Any combination makes for a good day...Tough with trees lining fairways...Dogwood is a fun nine...Old style course, great bunkers, narrow in spots.

★★★MOHANSIC GOLF CLUB

PU-Baldwin Rd., Yorktown Heights, 10598, Westchester County, (914)962-4049, 37 miles N of New York City.

Opened: 1925. **Holes:** 18. **Par:** 70/75. **Yards:** 6,500/5,594. **Course rating:** 69.9/75.2. **Slope:** 120/127. **Architect:** Tom Winton. **Green fee:** $35/$40. **Credit cards:** None. **Reduced fees:** Weekdays, twilight, seniors, juniors. **Caddies:** No. **Golf carts:** $21. **Discount golf packages:** No. **Season:** April-Dec. **High:** June-Aug. **On site lodging:** No. **Rental clubs:** Yes. **Walking policy:** Unrestricted walking. **Metal spikes allowed:** Yes. **Range:** Yes. **To obtain tee times:** Call computerized tee times (914)962-4065.

Subscriber comments: Nice course, fairways slope too much...A lot of hills...Some fairway bunkers would make it great...Nice greens...Tough to get times, best to play in late summer...Best of the Westchester county courses.

★★★★MONTAUK DOWNS STATE PARK GOLF COURSE

PU-S. Fairview Ave., Montauk, 11954, Suffolk County, (516)668-1100, 110 miles E of New York City.
Opened: 1968. **Holes:** 18. **Par:** 72/72. **Yards:** 6,762/5,797. **Course rating:** 73.3/75.9. **Slope:** 133/135. **Architect:** Robert Trent Jones/Rees Jones. **Green fee:** $25/$30. **Credit cards:** MC,VISA. **Reduced fees:** Twilight, seniors. **Caddies:** No. **Golf carts:** $12. **Discount golf packages:** No. **Season:** Year-round. **High:** July-Sept. **On site lodging:** No. **Rental clubs:** Yes. **Walking policy:** Unrestricted walking. **Metal spikes allowed:** Yes. **Range:** Yes. **To obtain tee times:** Reservation Card: Call up to 7 days in advance. No Reservation Card: Call up to 2 days in advance.
Subscriber comments: Long, interesting, one of nicest I've played...A challenge when windy, a must play...Bring your 'A' game or more balls...A real test on windy days...Absolutely worth the drive to the end of Long Island...Great mix of golf and nature...Too bad it's 75 miles from nowhere...Feels like you're at a private club.

GREAT VALUE

MOORESVILLE MUNICIPAL GOLF COURSE

W. Wilson Ave, Mooresville, 28115, Sullivan County, (704)663-2539.
Call club for further information.

★½MOSHOLU GOLF COURSE

PU-3700 Jerome Ave., Bronx, 10467, Bronx County, (718)655-9164, New York City.
Opened: 1914. **Holes:** 9. **Par: Architect:** Stephen Kay. **Caddies:** No. **Discount golf packages:** No. **On site lodging:** No. **Rental clubs:** No. **Metal spikes allowed:** Yes. **Range:** No.
Call club for further information.

★★★½NEVELE COUNTRY CLUB

R-Rte. 209, Ellenville, 12428, Ulster County, (914)647-6000, (800)647-6000, 90 miles N of New York.
Opened: 1955. **Holes:** 18. **Par:** 70/70. **Yards:** 6,600/4,600. **Course rating:** 71.9/71.1. **Slope:** 128/126. **Architect:** Tom Fazio. **Green fee:** $45/$55. **Credit cards:** MC,VISA,AMEX. **Reduced fees:** Weekdays, resort guests, twilight. **Caddies:** No. **Golf carts:** Included in Green Fee. **Discount golf packages:** Yes. **Season:** April-Dec. **High:** May-Sept. **On site lodging:** Yes. **Rental clubs:** Yes. **Walking policy:** Mandatory cart. **Metal spikes allowed:** Yes. **Range:** Yes (grass/mats). **To obtain tee times:** Hotel guests call 21 days in advance. Nonguests call 14 days in advance.
Subscriber comments: Good challenge for any golfer...Fun course to play, very good greens...A short course...Scenic course in fall...Wind, water, woods and hills make it very interesting and fun...Front side lulls you to sleep, back side wakes you up.

★★½THE NEW COURSE AT ALBANY

PU-65 O'Neil Rd., Albany, 12208, Albany County, (518)489-3526, 3 miles W of Albany.
Opened: 1991. **Holes:** 18. **Par:** 71/71. **Yards:** 6,300/4,990. **Course rating:** 69.4/72.0. **Slope:** 117/113. **Architect:** Bob Smith and Ed Bosse. **Green fee:** $10/$22. **Credit cards:** None. **Reduced fees:** Twilight. **Caddies:** No. **Golf carts:** $10. **Discount golf packages:** No. **Season:** April-Nov. **High:** June-Aug. **On site lodging:** No. **Rental clubs:** Yes. **Walking policy:** Unrestricted walking. **Metal spikes allowed:** Yes. **Range:** Yes (grass/mats). **To obtain tee times:** Call 1 day in advance.
Subscriber comments: Layout fantastic, greens only OK...Challenging...Not much style, two distinct nines...Was terrible, now a delight...Need to be a mountain goat to walk this course.

★★NIAGARA COUNTY GOLF COURSE

PM-314 Davison Rd., Lockport, 14094, Niagara County, (716)439-8738.
Opened: 1964. **Holes:** 18. **Par:** 72/73. **Yards:** 6,464/5,182. **Course rating:** 69.3/74.1. **Slope:** 108. **Architect:** N/A. **Green fee:** $10/$18. **Credit cards:** None. **Reduced fees:** Twilight, seniors, juniors. **Caddies:** No. **Golf carts:** $17. **Discount golf packages:** No. **Season:** April-Nov. **High:** July-Aug. **On site lodging:** No. **Rental clubs:** Yes. **Walking policy:** Unrestricted walking. **Metal spikes allowed:** Yes. **Range:** Yes (grass). **To obtain tee times:** N/A.
Special Notes: Spikeless encouraged.

★★NIAGARA ORLEANS COUNTRY CLUB

PU-Telegraph Rd, Middleport, 14105, Niagara County, (716)735-9000, 7 miles E of Lockport.
Opened: 1931. **Holes:** 18. **Par:** 71/71. **Yards:** 6,018/5,109. **Course rating:** 65.0/65.0. **Slope:** 106/106. **Architect:** N/A. **Green fee:** $14/$17. **Credit cards:** None. **Reduced fees:** Weekdays, low season, twilight, seniors, juniors. **Caddies:** No. **Golf carts:** $20. **Discount golf packages:** No. **Season:** April-Nov. **High:** N/A. **On site lodging:** No. **Rental clubs:** Yes. **Walking policy:** Unrestricted walking. **Metal spikes allowed:** Yes. **Range:** No. **To obtain tee times:** Call.

★★½OLD HICKORY GOLF CLUB

6653 Big Tree Rd., Livonia, 14487, Livingston County, (716)346-2450, 20 miles S of Rochester.
Opened: 1990. **Holes:** 18. **Par:** 72/72. **Yards:** 6,650/5,450. **Course rating:** 70.2/70.7. **Slope:** 109/111. **Architect:** Pete Craig. **Green fee:** $14/$16. **Credit cards:** None. **Reduced fees:** Low season, seniors, juniors. **Caddies:** No. **Golf carts:** $10. **Discount golf packages:** No. **Season:** April-Oct. **High:** May-Sept. **On site lodging:** No. **Rental clubs:** Yes. **Walking policy:** Unrestricted walking. **Metal spikes allowed:** Yes. **Range:** Yes (grass). **To obtain tee times:** Call 7 days in advance.
Subscriber comments: Will be best pubic course in the area when trees have grown...Wide open...Young course but very challenging.

★★★½OYSTER BAY TOWN GOLF COURSE

PU-Southwood Rd., Woodbury, 11797, Nassau County, (516)364-1180, 35 miles E of New York.
Opened: 1989. **Holes:** 18. **Par:** 70/70. **Yards:** 6,351/5,109. **Course rating:** 71.5/70.4. **Slope:** 131/126. **Architect:** Tom Fazio. **Green fee:** $40/$50. **Credit cards:** None. **Reduced fees:** Weekdays, low season, twilight, seniors, juniors. **Caddies:** No. **Golf carts:** N/A. **Discount golf packages:** No. **Season:** Year-round. **High:** April-Oct. **On site lodging:** No. **Rental clubs:** Yes. **Walking policy:** Unrestricted walking. **Metal spikes allowed:** Yes. **Range:** Yes. **To obtain tee times:** First come, first served.
Subscriber comments: Need straight tee shots, beautiful layout...Interesting short course...Need super light touch on the greens...Last four holes outstanding...Narrow fairways...Well laid out considering lack of property.

PEEK'N PEAK RESORT

R-1405 Olde Rd., Clymer, 14724, Chautauqua County, (716)355-4141, 20 miles SE of Erie, PA.
Opened: 1974. **Architect:** Fred Garbin. **Credit cards:** All major. **Reduced fees:** Weekdays, twilight, seniors. **Caddies:** No. **Discount golf packages:** Yes. **Season:** April-Nov. **High:** June-Sept. **On site lodging:** Yes. **Rental clubs:** Yes. **Metal spikes allowed:** Yes. **To obtain tee times:** Call golf shop.

★★★½LOWER COURSE

Holes: 18. **Par:** 72/72. **Yards:** 6,260/5,328. **Course rating:** 69.0/69.5. **Slope:** 115/112. **Green fee:** $25/$30. **Golf carts:** $11. **Walking policy:** Unrestricted walking. **Range:** Yes (grass).
Subscriber comments: This is one ski resort that really knows golf...Need to play if in the area...Lower Course plain vanilla golf...Play the 18 on the hill, awesome...Top course.

UPPER COURSE

Holes: 18. **Par:** N/A. **Yards:** N/A. **Course rating:** N/A. **Slope:** N/A. **Green fee:** $50/$55. **Golf carts:** Included in Green Fee. **Walking policy:** Mandatory cart. **Range:** No.

PELHAM-SPLIT ROCK GOLF COURSE

PU-870 Shore Rd., Bronx, 10464, Bronx County, (718)885-1258.
Architect: John Van Kleek. **Green fee:** $15/$17. **Credit cards:** MC,VISA. **Reduced fees:** Weekdays, twilight, seniors, juniors. **Caddies:** No. **Discount golf packages:** No. **Season:** Year-round. **High:** May-Sept. **On site lodging:** No. **Rental clubs:** Yes. **Walking policy:** Unrestricted walking. **Metal spikes allowed:** Yes. **To obtain tee times:** Call up to 12 days in advance for weekends and up to seven days on weekdays. Credit card is needed to hold reservation for weekend.

★★PELHAM COURSE
Opened: 1932. **Holes:** 18. **Par:** 71/71. **Yards:** 6,991/5,634. **Course rating:** 69.6/69.6.
Slope: 114/115. **Golf carts:** $12. **Range:** No.
★★½SPLIT ROCK COURSE
Opened: 1934. **Holes:** 18. **Par:** 71/71. **Yards:** 6,714/5,509. **Course rating:** 71.9/71.7.
Slope: 125/122. **Golf carts:** $13. **Range:** Yes.
Subscriber comments: Nice layout...Very tough, tight especially first seven holes...Better layout than Pelham...Fun, but not easy.

★★PHILIP J. ROTELLA GOLF COURSE
PU-Thiells and Mt. Ivy Rds., Thiells, 10984, Rockland County, (914)354-1616, 20 miles N of New York City.
Opened: 1985. **Holes:** 18. **Par:** 72/72. **Yards:** 6,502/4,856. **Course rating:** 71.4/68.1.
Slope: 128/117. **Architect:** Hal Purdy. **Green fee:** $24/$31. **Credit cards:** None.
Reduced fees: Twilight, seniors, juniors. **Caddies:** No. **Golf carts:** $22. **Discount golf packages:** Yes. **Season:** March-Dec. **High:** May-July. **On site lodging:** No. **Rental clubs:** Yes. **Walking policy:** Walking at certain times. **Metal spikes allowed:** No.
Range: Yes (Mats). **To obtain tee times:** Call.

★½PINE GROVE COUNTRY CLUB
3185 Milton Ave, Camillus, 13031, Onondaga County, (315)672-9272, 4 miles W of Syracuse.
Opened: 1960. **Holes:** 18. **Par:** 71. **Yards:** 5,326. **Course rating:** N/A. **Slope:** N/A.
Architect: Barry Jordan. **Green fee:** $12/$14. **Credit cards:** All major. **Reduced fees:** Weekdays, low season, twilight, seniors. **Caddies:** No. **Golf carts:** $17. **Discount golf packages:** No. **Season:** March-Dec. **High:** May-Aug. **On site lodging:** No. **Rental clubs:** Yes. **Walking policy:** Unrestricted walking. **Metal spikes allowed:** Yes. **Range:** Yes (grass/mats). **To obtain tee times:** No tee times.

★★★PINE HILLS COUNTRY CLUB
162 Wading River Rd., Manorville, 11949, Suffolk County, (516)878-4343.
Call club for further information.
Subscriber comments: Enjoyable golf...Interesting course...My back hurts just thinking about the 220-yard par 3...Brutal from blues, playable at all levels from whites...Hard to walk...Back nine is better...Wide open but not as easy as you think...Wide fairways...Excellent practice facilities.

★★½PUTNAM COUNTRY CLUB
PU-Hill St., Mahopac, 10541, Putnam County, (914)628-4200, 50 miles N of New York City.
Opened: 1955. **Holes:** 18. **Par:** 71/73. **Yards:** 6,774/5,799. **Course rating:** 72.4/73.7.
Slope: 129/132. **Architect:** William F. Mitchell. **Green fee:** $22/$38. **Credit cards:** MC,VISA,AMEX,ATM Debit cards. **Reduced fees:** Weekdays, twilight, seniors, juniors.
Caddies: No. **Golf carts:** $12. **Discount golf packages:** No. **Season:** March-Dec.
High: June-Sept. **On site lodging:** No. **Rental clubs:** Yes. **Walking policy:** Walking at certain times. **Metal spikes allowed:** No. **Range:** Yes (grass). **To obtain tee times:** Call 7 days in advance.
Subscriber comments: Laid out well...Par-4 9th uphill is very tough...Front nine very good, back nine needs work...Difficult lies are frequent with sloping terrain.

★★★★RADISSON GREENS GOLF CLUB
8055 Potter Rd., Baldwinsville, 13027, Onondaga County, (315)638-0092, 15 miles NW of Syracuse.
Opened: 1977. **Holes:** 18. **Par:** 72/73. **Yards:** 7,010/5,543. **Course rating:** 73.3/70.0.
Slope: 128/124. **Architect:** Robert Trent Jones. **Green fee:** $19/$22. **Credit cards:** None. **Reduced fees:** Seniors. **Caddies:** No. **Golf carts:** $22. **Discount golf packages:** No. **Season:** April-Nov. **High:** May-Sept. **On site lodging:** No. **Rental clubs:** No. **Walking policy:** Walking at certain times. **Metal spikes allowed:** Yes. **Range:** Yes (grass). **To obtain tee times:** Call Monday for upcoming weekend.
Subscriber comments: Very tough, but very enjoyable...Requires good shotmaking...Great greens and fairways...Challenging, every hole different...Great design...Makes you a better player...Always a great day...Par 5s are brutal.

RICCI MEADOWS GOLF COURSE
PU-1939 Oak Orchard Rd. (Rte. 98), Albion, 14411, Orleans County, (716)682-3280, 30 miles W of Rochester.
Opened: N/A. **Holes:** 18. **Par:** 71/72. **Yards:** 5,268/4,597. **Course rating:** 63.0/63.4. **Slope:** 102/100. **Architect:** N/A. **Green fee:** $11/$11. **Credit cards:** None. **Reduced fees:** Seniors. **Caddies:** No. **Golf carts:** $10. **Discount golf packages:** No. **Season:** April-Nov. **High:** June-Aug. **On site lodging:** No. **Rental clubs:** No. **Walking policy:** Unrestricted walking. **Metal spikes allowed:** Yes. **Range:** No. **To obtain tee times:** Tee times not necessary.

★★RIVERVIEW COUNTRY CLUB
PU-847 Riverview Rd, Rexford, 12148, Saratoga County, (518)399-2345, 15 miles N of Albany.
Opened: 1964. **Holes:** 18. **Par:** 73/74. **Yards:** 7,095/5,815. **Course rating:** 73.7/73.4. **Slope:** 128/124. **Architect:** N/A. **Green fee:** $18/$22. **Credit cards:** VISA. **Reduced fees:** Weekdays. **Caddies:** No. **Golf carts:** $20. **Discount golf packages:** No. **Season:** April-Nov. **High:** Summer. **On site lodging:** No. **Rental clubs:** Yes. **Walking policy:** Unrestricted walking. **Metal spikes allowed:** Yes. **Range:** Yes (grass). **To obtain tee times:** Call on Wednesday for upcoming weekend.

★★★ROCK HILL COUNTRY CLUB
PU-105 Clancy Rd., Manorville, 11949, Suffolk County, (516)878-2250, 60 miles E of New York City.
Opened: 1965. **Holes:** 18. **Par:** 71/72. **Yards:** 7,050/5,390. **Course rating:** 73.7/71.4. **Slope:** 128/121. **Architect:** Frank Duane. **Green fee:** $26/$30. **Credit cards:** None. **Reduced fees:** Weekdays, low season, twilight, seniors, juniors. **Caddies:** No. **Golf carts:** $28. **Discount golf packages:** No. **Season:** Year-round. **High:** May-Sept. **On site lodging:** No. **Rental clubs:** Yes. **Walking policy:** Walking at certain times. **Metal spikes allowed:** Yes. **Range:** Yes (grass). **To obtain tee times:** Call 7 days in advance.
Subscriber comments: Great, just great!...Two very different nines...Plays longer than the yardage...Last four holes can ruin you...Good variety of holes...Fun to play...Long tough test, many hilly lies...Some excellent views of Long Island.

★★★ROCKLAND LAKE STATE PARK GOLF CLUB
PU-100 Route 9 W, Congers, 10920, Orange County, (914)268-6250.
Call club for further information.
Subscriber comments: Challenging, great scenery...Hilly course...The best state course, other than Bethpage Black...The course design is beautiful, winding through a wooded state park, lots of wildlife, deer always on 14th...Interesting layout...Long waits.

★★★ROME COUNTRY CLUB
5342 Rte. 69, Rome, 13440, Oneida County, (315)336-6464, 25 miles E of Syracuse.
Opened: 1929. **Holes:** 18. **Par:** 72/75. **Yards:** 6,775/5,505. **Course rating:** 71.8/70.4. **Slope:** 125. **Architect:** N/A. **Green fee:** $16/$22. **Credit cards:** MC,VISA. **Reduced fees:** Weekdays. **Caddies:** No. **Golf carts:** $20. **Discount golf packages:** Yes. **Season:** Year-round. **High:** May-Aug. **On site lodging:** No. **Rental clubs:** Yes. **Walking policy:** Unrestricted walking. **Metal spikes allowed:** Yes. **Range:** Yes (grass/mats). **To obtain tee times:** Call.
Subscriber comments: Challenging...Great greens, very good shotmaker's course...A fun place to play...Lousy design for first three holes, better back nine.

★★★RONDOUT COUNTRY CLUB
PU-Box 194 Whitfield Rd, Accord, 12404, Ulster County, (914)626-2513.
Opened: 1970. **Holes:** 18. **Par:** 72/72. **Yards:** 6,468/4,822. **Course rating:** 72.7/68.4. **Slope:** 128/116. **Architect:** N/A. **Green fee:** $16/$26. **Credit cards:** MC,VISA,DISC. **Reduced fees:** Weekdays, juniors. **Caddies:** No. **Golf carts:** $12. **Discount golf packages:** Yes. **Season:** March-Oct. **High:** May-Sept. **On site lodging:** No. **Rental clubs:** Yes. **Walking policy:** Walking at certain times. **Metal spikes allowed:** Yes. **Range:** Yes (grass/mats). **To obtain tee times:** Call on Monday for upcoming weekend.
Subscriber comments: Tight but nice...Scenic beauty...Two tough par 5s...Deceptively tough, terrific...A mid-Hudson gem, dramatic vistas.

NEW YORK

★★½ROTHLAND GOLF COURSE
PU-12089 Clarence Center Rd., Akron, 14001, Erie County, (716)542-4325, 15 miles
NE of Buffalo.
Opened: 1980. **Holes:** 27. **Architect:** Bill Roth. **Green fee:** $17/$21. **Credit cards:**
MC,VISA,DISC. **Reduced fees:** Weekdays, low season, twilight, seniors. **Caddies:** No.
Golf carts: $19. **Discount golf packages:** No. **Season:** April-Nov. **High:** June-Sept.
On site lodging: No. **Rental clubs:** Yes. **Walking policy:** Unrestricted walking. **Metal
spikes allowed:** Yes. **Range:** Yes (grass/mats). **To obtain tee times:** Call 7 days in
advance.
GOLD/WHITE
Par: 72/72. **Yards:** 6,044/5,513. **Course rating:** 69.0/68.0. **Slope:** 105/103.
RED/GOLD
Par: 72/72. **Yards:** 6,486/5,893. **Course rating:** 70.5/71.3. **Slope:** 113/112.
RED/WHITE
Par: 72/72. **Yards:** 6,216/5,922. **Course rating:** 69.5/69.5. **Slope:** 108/105.
Subscriber comments: Gold nine tight, White open...White finishing holes offer little
challenge...Keeps improving...Red features long par 4s...Red/Gold combo can be
fun...All three fairly well maintained...Holes fun to play.

★★★★THE SAGAMORE GOLF CLUB
R-110 Sagamore Rd., Bolton Landing, 12814, Warren County, (518)644-9400, 60 miles
N of Albany.
Opened: 1928. **Holes:** 18. **Par:** 70/71. **Yards:** 6,890/5,261. **Course rating:** 72.9/73.0.
Slope: 130/122. **Architect:** Donald Ross. **Green fee:** $70/$70. **Credit cards:** All major.
Reduced fees: N/A. **Caddies:** No. **Golf carts:** Included in Green Fee. **Discount golf
packages:** Yes. **Season:** April-Nov. **High:** May-Oct. **On site lodging:** Yes. **Rental
clubs:** Yes. **Walking policy:** Mandatory cart. **Metal spikes allowed:** Yes. **Range:** Yes
(grass). **To obtain tee times:** You can make tee times when you book your reservations with the resort.
Subscriber comments: A scenic layout...Beautiful in the fall...Challenging old
course...View from first tee is awesome...No two holes the same, control is
key...Classically designed course, easy looking holes will humble you...Best resort
course in the state...Typical Donald Ross greens...Very hilly, uneven lies.

★★★ST. LAWRENCE UNIVERSITY GOLF COURSE
PU-Rte. 11, Canton, 13617, St. Lawrence County, (315)386-4600, 68 miles S of
Ottawa, Canada.
Opened: 1936. **Holes:** 18. **Par:** 72/73. **Yards:** 6,694/5,430. **Course rating:** 72.1/73.1.
Slope: 122/120. **Architect:** Devereux Emmet. **Green fee:** $19/$23. **Credit cards:**
MC,VISA. **Reduced fees:** Weekdays, low season, resort guests, twilight, juniors.
Caddies: No. **Golf carts:** $24. **Discount golf packages:** Yes. **Season:** April-Oct. **High:**
June-Aug. **On site lodging:** Yes. **Rental clubs:** Yes. **Walking policy:** Unrestricted walk-
ing. **Metal spikes allowed:** Yes. **Range:** Yes (grass/mats). **To obtain tee times:** Call 2
days in advance.
Subscriber comments: A north country must...Great layout through old white pine
growth...Great greens, flat treelined layout, playable from whites...Marginal but fun.

★★SALMON CREEK COUNTRY CLUB
355 Washington St., Spencerport, 14559, Monroe County, (716)352-4300.
Opened: 1963. **Holes:** 18. **Par:** 72. **Yards:** 6,200. **Course rating:** 69.5. **Slope:** 121.
Architect: Pete Craig. **Green fee:** $18/$21. **Credit cards:** MC,VISA. **Reduced fees:**
Seniors. **Caddies:** No. **Golf carts:** $20. **Discount golf packages:** Yes. **Season:** March-
Dec. **High:** May-Sept. **On site lodging:** No. **Rental clubs:** Yes. **Walking policy:**
Unrestricted walking. **Metal spikes allowed:** Yes. **Range:** Yes (grass/mats). **To obtain
tee times:** Public may call up to 3 days in advance.

★SANCTUARY GOLF CLUB
PU-Rte. 118, Yorktown, 10598, Westchester County, (703)893-3054.
Call club for further information.
Special Notes: Formerly Loch Ledge Golf Club.

★★★½SARATOGA SPA GOLF COURSE

PU-Saratoga Spa State Park, 19 Roosevelt D, Saratoga Springs, 12866, Saratoga County, (518)584-2006, 24 miles N of Albany.
Opened: 1962. **Holes:** 18. **Par:** 72/72. **Yards:** 7,149/5,649. **Course rating:** 73.7/72.5. **Slope:** 130/122. **Architect:** Bill Mitchell. **Green fee:** $17/$20. **Credit cards:** MC,VISA. **Reduced fees:** Seniors, juniors.
Caddies: No. **Golf carts:** $21. **Discount golf packages:** No. **Season:** April-Nov. **High:** June-Aug. **On site lodging:** Yes. **Rental clubs:** Yes. **Walking policy:** Unrestricted walking. **Metal spikes allowed:** Yes. **Range:** Yes (grass). **To obtain tee times:** Call up to 7 days in advance between 9 a.m. and 5 p.m.
Subscriber comments: Best public course in the area...Pure pleasure...Sets standard for government-run facility...Extremely slow play, nice walking course, big greens...Classic old course...Lots of pines...Nice course to play...Tough from tiger tees.
Special Notes: Also has 9-hole, par-29 course.

(GREAT VALUE)

★★SAXON WOODS GOLF COURSE

PU-315 Mamaroneck Ave., Scarsdale, 10583, Westchester County, (914)725-3814, 5 miles N of White Plains.
Opened: 1931. **Holes:** 18. **Par:** 71/73. **Yards:** 6,397/5,617. **Course rating:** 70.2/71.2. **Slope:** 119/120. **Architect:** Tom Winton. **Green fee:** $12/$40. **Credit cards:** None. **Reduced fees:** Weekdays, twilight, seniors, juniors. **Caddies:** No. **Golf carts:** $20. **Discount golf packages:** No. **Season:** April-Dec. **High:** June-Aug. **On site lodging:** No. **Rental clubs:** Yes. **Walking policy:** Unrestricted walking. **Metal spikes allowed:** Yes. **Range:** No. **To obtain tee times:** Call.

★★★SCHENECTADY GOLF COURSE

PM-400 Oregon Ave., Schenectady, 12309, Schenectady County, (518)382-5155, 18 miles E of Albany.
Opened: 1935. **Holes:** 18. **Par:** 72/72. **Yards:** 6,570/5,275. **Course rating:** 71.1/68.1. **Slope:** 123/115. **Architect:** Jim Thomson. **Green fee:** $14/$20. **Credit cards:** None. **Reduced fees:** Seniors, juniors. **Caddies:** No. **Golf carts:** $19. **Discount golf packages:** No. **Season:** April-Nov. **High:** May-Aug. **On site lodging:** No. **Rental clubs:** Yes. **Walking policy:** Unrestricted walking. **Metal spikes allowed:** Yes. **Range:** Yes (grass). **To obtain tee times:** Call 2 days in advance.
Subscriber comments: Great muny...A little work could make it a top notch course...Every hole has interest...Fast greens...Back nine very good test...Well maintained, fun to play...Challenging without being overbearing.

★★★½SEGALLA COUNTRY CLUB

PU-P.O. Box C, Amenia, 12501, Dutchess County, (914)373-9200, 25 miles E of Poughkeepsie.
Opened: 1992. **Holes:** 18. **Par:** 72/72. **Yards:** 6,617/5,601. **Course rating:** 72.0/72.3. **Slope:** 133/129. **Architect:** Albert Zikorus. **Green fee:** $21/$29. **Credit cards:** MC,VISA,AMEX. **Reduced fees:** Weekdays, low season, twilight, seniors, juniors. **Caddies:** No. **Golf carts:** $22. **Discount golf packages:** No. **Season:** April-Nov. **High:** May-Sept. **On site lodging:** No. **Rental clubs:** Yes. **Walking policy:** Walking at certain times. **Metal spikes allowed:** No. **Range:** Yes (mats). **To obtain tee times:** Call 6 days in advance starting at 6:30 a.m.
Subscriber comments: Beautiful course, nicely cut into the hills...Tough and demanding, stay in the short grass...You won't be bored on this one...Wait till young trees grow in...What views...Too bad people found out about it...Can't get into too much trouble.

★★★SHADOW LAKE GOLF & RAQUET CLUB

PU-1850 Five Mile Line Rd., Penfield, 14526, Monroe County, (716)385-2010, 10 miles SE of Rochester.
Opened: 1977. **Holes:** 18. **Par:** 71/72. **Yards:** 6,164/5,498. **Course rating:** 68.5/70.5. **Slope:** 111/112. **Architect:** Pete Craig. **Green fee:** $10/$22. **Credit cards:** MC,VISA,AMEX. **Reduced fees:** Weekdays, low season, twilight, seniors. **Caddies:** No. **Golf carts:** $11. **Discount golf packages:** No. **Season:** March-Dec. **High:** June-Aug. **On site lodging:** No. **Rental clubs:** Yes. **Walking policy:** Walking at certain times. **Metal spikes allowed:** Yes. **Range:** No. **To obtain tee times:** Call one week in advance.

Subscriber comments: Short course, very pretty...Nice front, boring back...Friendly course, playable at all levels...Fairly flat and woodsy...Course getting tougher with age...Numerous hazards, ponds, trees...Enjoyable for beginners.
Special Notes: Also has 9-hole par-31 executive course.

★★★½SHADOW PINES GOLF CLUB
PU-600 Whalen Rd., Penfield, 14526, Monroe County, (716)385-8550.
Opened: 1985. **Holes:** 18. **Par:** 72/72. **Yards:** 6,763/5,292. **Course rating:** 72.4/70.4.
Slope: 124/123. **Architect:** Pete Craig/Gardner Odenbach. **Green fee:** $16/$23. **Credit cards:** MC,VISA,AMEX. **Reduced fees:** Weekdays, low season, twilight, seniors.
Caddies: No. **Golf carts:** $12. **Discount golf packages:** Yes. **Season:** April-Nov.
High: June-Aug. **On site lodging:** No. **Rental clubs:** Yes. **Walking policy:** Mandatory cart. **Metal spikes allowed:** Yes. **Range:** Yes (grass). **To obtain tee times:** Call in advance.
Subscriber comments: Requires good shotmaking...Several great par 4s, beautiful scenery...Makes you think...Very difficult back nine...The front nine is fairly flat and well bunkered while the back nine has hills with fewer bunkers due to the terrain.

★★★SHERIDAN PARK GOLF CLUB
PU-Center Park Dr., Tonawanda, 14150, Erie County, (716)875-1811, 3 miles N of Buffalo.
Opened: 1933. **Holes:** 18. **Par:** 71/74. **Yards:** 6,534/5,656. **Course rating:** 71.3/74.0.
Slope: 116/116. **Architect:** William Harries. **Green fee:** $16/$19. **Credit cards:** None.
Reduced fees: Weekdays, twilight. **Caddies:** No. **Golf carts:** $18. **Discount golf packages:** No. **Season:** April-Nov. **High:** June-Aug. **On site lodging:** No. **Rental clubs:** Yes. **Walking policy:** Unrestricted walking. **Metal spikes allowed:** Yes. **Range:** Yes (mats). **To obtain tee times:** Call 7 days in advance.
Notes: 1962 U.S. Publinx.
Subscriber comments: Water hazards are placed in strategic locations, making for good challenges...Front is boring, but back nine is outstanding...Some of the nicest holes in western NY...Tough course, par 4s will eat you up...Very good layout, not for duffers.

★★SILVER LAKE GOLF COURSE
PU-915 Victory Blvd., Staten Island, 10301, Richmond County, (718)447-5686.
Opened: 1929. **Holes:** 18. **Par:** 69/69. **Yards:** 6,050/5,202. **Course rating:** 67.7/71.2.
Slope: 110/119. **Architect:** John Van Kleek. **Green fee:** $15/$17. **Credit cards:** MC,VISA. **Reduced fees:** Weekdays, low season, twilight, seniors, juniors. **Caddies:** No. **Golf carts:** $23. **Discount golf packages:** Yes. **Season:** Year-round. **High:** May-Sept. **On site lodging:** No. **Rental clubs:** Yes. **Walking policy:** Unrestricted walking. **Metal spikes allowed:** Yes. **Range:** Yes. **To obtain tee times:** Call.

★★SIX-S GOLF COURSE
PU-Transit Bridge Rd., Belfast, 14711, Allegany County, (716)365-2201, 65 miles SE of Buffalo.
Opened: 1965. **Holes:** 18. **Par:** 72/72. **Yards:** 6,210/4,826. **Course rating:** 69.5/69.7.
Slope: 120/115. **Architect:** William F. Short. **Green fee:** $11/$12. **Credit cards:** MC,VISA,AMEX. **Reduced fees:** Weekdays, twilight, seniors, juniors. **Caddies:** No.
Golf carts: $10. **Discount golf packages:** No. **Season:** March-Nov. **High:** July-Aug.
On site lodging: No. **Rental clubs:** No. **Walking policy:** Unrestricted walking. **Metal spikes allowed:** Yes. **Range:** No. **To obtain tee times:** Tee times not required.

★★★SMITHTOWN LANDING GOLF CLUB
PU-495 Landing Ave., Smithtown, 11787, Suffolk County, (516)360-7618, 35 miles E of New York.
Opened: N/A. **Holes:** 18. **Par:** 72/72. **Yards:** 6,114/5,263. **Course rating:** 70.9/69.8.
Slope: 125/122. **Architect:** Stephen Kay. **Green fee:** $18/$27. **Credit cards:** None.
Reduced fees: Weekdays, low season. **Caddies:** No. **Golf carts:** $24. **Discount golf packages:** No. **Season:** Year-round. **High:** May-Sept. **On site lodging:** No. **Rental clubs:** No. **Walking policy:** Unrestricted walking. **Metal spikes allowed:** Yes. **Range:** Yes. **To obtain tee times:** Tee times taken weekends and holidays for residents only.
Subscriber comments: Very hilly, but lots of fun to play...If you don't hit it straight, you're in trouble...Tough par 3s...A 580-yard par 5 which gives nothing back.

★★★½SOARING EAGLES GOLF CLUB
PU-201 Middle Rd., Horseheads, 14845, Chemung County, (607)796-5059, 10 miles N of Elmira.
Opened: 1940. **Holes:** 18. **Par:** 72/72. **Yards:** 6,625/4,930. **Course rating:** 71.6/67.5. **Slope:** 117/108. **Architect:** Fran Cartwright. **Green fee:** $7/$19. **Credit cards:** MC,VISA. **Reduced fees:** Twilight, seniors, juniors. **Caddies:** No. **Golf carts:** $20. **Discount golf packages:** No. **Season:** April-Nov. **High:** June-Sept. **On site lodging:** No. **Rental clubs:** Yes. **Walking policy:** Unrestricted walking. **Metal spikes allowed:** Yes. **Range:** Yes (grass). **To obtain tee times:** Call 7 days in advance.
Subscriber comments: Great greens and layout, needs a touch of finishing...Long, sandy, large and fast greens...Well balanced course, all can enjoy...Excellent state course...Played a round during the week in under four hours...Undulating greens.

★½SOUTH SHORE GOLF COURSE
PU-200 Huguenot Ave., Staten Island, 10312, Richmond County, (718)984-0101.
Opened: 1927. **Holes:** 18. **Par:** 72/72. **Yards:** 6,366/5,435. **Course rating:** N/A/69.8. **Slope:** 113/114. **Architect:** Devereux Emmet and Alfred Tull. **Green fee:** $15/$17. **Credit cards:** MC,VISA. **Reduced fees:** Twilight, seniors, juniors. **Caddies:** No. **Golf carts:** $24. **Discount golf packages:** No. **Season:** March-Dec. **High:** May-Sept. **On site lodging:** No. **Rental clubs:** Yes. **Walking policy:** Unrestricted walking. **Metal spikes allowed:** Yes. **Range:** No. **To obtain tee times:** Call ten days in advance.

★★★½SPOOK ROCK GOLF COURSE
PU-233 Spook Rock Rd., Suffern, 10901, Rockland County, (914)357-3085, 30 miles NW of New York City.
Opened: 1970. **Holes:** 18. **Par:** 72/72. **Yards:** 6,894/4,953. **Course rating:** 73.3/70.9. **Slope:** 129/118. **Architect:** Frank Duane. **Green fee:** $41/$41. **Credit cards:** None. **Reduced fees:** Twilight. **Caddies:** No. **Golf carts:** $25. **Discount golf packages:** No. **Season:** April-Nov. **High:** May-Sept. **On site lodging:** No. **Rental clubs:** Yes. **Walking policy:** Unrestricted walking. **Metal spikes allowed:** No. **Range:** Yes (mats). **To obtain tee times:** Call Sunday after 5 p.m. for weekdays and Thursday after 7 a.m. for weekend play.
Subscriber comments: One of the better public courses in NY...Very tight...Tough to get a tee time but worth waiting...Love the improvements...Layout of course is outstanding...A lot of woods, play can be very slow...Met Lawrence Taylor there...

★★SPRAIN LAKE GOLF CLUB
PU-290 Grassy Sprain Rd., Yonkers, 10710, Westchester County, (914)779-9827.
Opened: 1940. **Holes:** 18. **Par:** 70/71. **Yards:** 6,010/5,500. **Course rating:** 68.6/70.2. **Slope:** 114/115. **Architect:** Tom Winton. **Green fee:** $35/$45. **Credit cards:** None. **Reduced fees:** Weekdays, twilight, seniors, juniors. **Caddies:** No. **Golf carts:** $23. **Discount golf packages:** No. **Season:** April-Dec. **High:** June-Aug. **On site lodging:** No. **Rental clubs:** Yes. **Walking policy:** Unrestricted walking. **Metal spikes allowed:** Yes. **Range:** No. **To obtain tee times:** Call.

★★★½SPRING LAKE GOLF CLUB
PU-30 E. Bartlett Rd., Middle Island, 11953, Suffolk County, (516)924-5115, 45 miles E of New York City.
Opened: 1967. **Holes:** 18. **Par:** 72/72. **Yards:** 7,048/5,732. **Course rating:** 73.2/70.0. **Slope:** 128/120. **Architect:** Jurgens & Company. **Green fee:** $23/$32. **Credit cards:** None. **Reduced fees:** Weekdays, twilight. **Caddies:** No. **Golf carts:** $26. **Discount golf packages:** No. **Season:** Year-round. **High:** April-Oct. **On site lodging:** No. **Rental clubs:** Yes. **Walking policy:** Walking at certain times. **Metal spikes allowed:** Yes. **Range:** Yes (grass/mats). **To obtain tee times:** Call golf shop.
Subscriber comments: Good test of golf, big greens...Lots of play each day...Solid muny off beaten track...Distance is key at this course...Course is straightforward. **Special Notes:** Also has a 9-hole course.

★★½STONY FORD GOLF CLUB

PM-550 Rte. 416, Montgomery, 12549, Orange County, (914)457-1532, 70 miles N of New York City.
Opened: 1968. **Holes:** 18. **Par:** 72/72. **Yards:** 6,550/4,856. **Course rating:** 72.4/72.4.
Slope: 128/128. **Architect:** Hal Purdy. **Green fee:** $10/$28. **Credit cards:** None.
Reduced fees: Weekdays, low season, twilight, seniors. **Caddies:** No. **Golf carts:** $10.
Discount golf packages: No. **Season:** April-Nov. **High:** May-Sept. **On site lodging:**
No. **Rental clubs:** Yes. **Walking policy:** Unrestricted walking. **Metal spikes allowed:**
Yes. **Range:** Yes (grass). **To obtain tee times:** N/A.
Subscriber comments: Doglegs galore...Very enjoyable layout, great variety of holes...Excellent views, interesting shots from elevation changes...Good course playable for all handicaps.

★★½SUNKEN MEADOW STATE PARK GOLF CLUB

PU-Sunken Meadow State Park, Rte. 25A, Kings Park, 11754, Suffolk County, (516)269-3838, 40 miles E of New York City.
Opened: 1964. **Holes:** 27. **Architect:** Alfed Tull. **Green fee:** $19/$22. **Credit cards:**
None. **Reduced fees:** Seniors. **Caddies:** No. **Golf carts:** N/A. **Discount golf packages:** No. **Season:** April-Nov. **High:** April-Sept. **On site lodging:** No. **Rental clubs:**
Yes. **Walking policy:** Unrestricted walking. **Metal spikes allowed:** Yes. **Range:** Yes
(grass). **To obtain tee times:** First come, first served.
BLUE/GREEN
Par: 71/71. **Yards:** 6,185/5,638. **Course rating:** 73.2/77.5. **Slope:** 119/112.
BLUE/RED
Par: 71/71. **Yards:** 6,100/5,627. **Course rating:** 73.2/70.0. **Slope:** 120/112.
RED/GREEN
Par: 72/72. **Yards:** 6,165/5,567. **Course rating:** 73.6/70.3. **Slope:** 120/113.
Subscriber comments: Decent holes...A wonderful combo of doglegs (Blue) with the less challenging (Green)...Three easy nines, good for seniors and high handicappers...The Blue/Red is the best combo...Very flat and boring.

★★★SWAN LAKE GOLF CLUB

PU-373 River Rd., Manorville, 11949, Suffolk County, (516)369-1818, 10 miles W of Riverhead.
Opened: 1979. **Holes:** 18. **Par:** 72/72. **Yards:** 7,011/5,245. **Course rating:** 72.5/69.0.
Slope: 121/112. **Architect:** Don Jurgens. **Green fee:** $27/$30. **Credit cards:** None.
Reduced fees: Twilight. **Caddies:** No. **Golf carts:** $13. **Discount golf packages:** No.
Season: Year-round. **High:** April-Oct. **On site lodging:** No. **Rental clubs:** Yes. **Walking policy:** Walking at certain times. **Metal spikes allowed:** Yes. **Range:** No. **To obtain tee times:** Call up to 7 days in advance.
Subscriber comments: Very large greens...If you can't hit these greens you're awful...Go 18 holes without a three-putt and Brad Faxon had better look out...Long holes from blue tees...Well worth the ride from NYC...Florida-type course up north...Very busy but always well taken care of.

★★★TARRY BRAE GOLF CLUB

PM-Pleasant Valley Rd., South Fallsburg, 12779, Sullivan County, (914)434-2620.
Opened: 1962. **Holes:** 18. **Par:** 72/76. **Yards:** 6,888/5,610. **Course rating:** 73.1/72.1.
Slope: 128/123. **Architect:** William Mitchell. **Green fee:** $18/$25. **Credit cards:** None.
Reduced fees: Weekdays, low season, twilight. **Caddies:** No. **Golf carts:** $13.
Discount golf packages: No. **Season:** April-Nov. **High:** June-Sept. **On site lodging:**
No. **Rental clubs:** Yes. **Walking policy:** Walking at certain times. **Metal spikes allowed:** Yes. **Range:** Yes (grass/mats). **To obtain tee times:** Call Wednesday for upcoming Saturday. Call on Thursday for upcoming Sunday.
Subscriber comments: Pretty course...Good par 3s...Challenging, big greens, aprons tricky, tight fairways...Easy to get on, easy to play...Great views...Mountain course...Interesting sequence of holes...Best kept secret in the Catskills.

★★★½TENNANAH LAKE GOLF & TENNIS CLUB

100 Belle Rd., Suite 2, Roscoe, 12776, Sullivan County, (607)498-5502.
Opened: 1911. **Holes:** 18. **Par:** 72/72. **Yards:** 6,769/5,797. **Course rating:** 73.7/74.7.
Slope: 132/131. **Architect:** Alfred H. Tull. **Green fee:** $28/$32. **Credit cards:**

MC,VISA,AMEX. **Reduced fees:** Weekdays, resort guests, twilight, seniors, juniors. **Caddies:** No. **Golf carts:** $28. **Discount golf packages:** Yes. **Season:** May-Oct. **High:** June-Aug. **On site lodging:** Yes. **Rental clubs:** Yes. **Walking policy:** Walking at certain times. **Metal spikes allowed:** Yes. **Range:** Yes (grass/mats). **To obtain tee times:** Call up to 21 days in advance.
Subscriber comments: Very scenic...Enjoyable, back nine better...Still a hidden gem...Every hole is different...Magnificent scenery...A little difficult to find...Layout is boring in spots...Small greens and high hills.

★★★TERRY HILLS GOLF COURSE
PU-5122 Clinton St. Rd., Batavia, 14020, Genesee County, (716)343-0860, (800)825-8633, 30 miles E of Buffalo.
Opened: 1930. **Holes:** 27. **Architect:** Ed Ault/Mark Mungeam. **Green fee:** $15/$19. **Credit cards:** MC,VISA. **Reduced fees:** Low season, twilight, seniors. **Caddies:** No. **Golf carts:** $10. **Discount golf packages:** Yes. **Season:** March-Nov. **High:** June-Aug. **On site lodging:** No. **Rental clubs:** Yes. **Walking policy:** Walking at certain times. **Metal spikes allowed:** No. **Range:** No. **To obtain tee times:** Call up to one week in advance.
A/B
Par: 72/72. **Yards:** 6,124/5,166. **Course rating:** 69.2/68.4. **Slope:** 110/104.
A/C
Par: 72/72. **Yards:** 6,292/5,245. **Course rating:** 68.4/67.8. **Slope:** 106/98.
B/C
Par: 72/72. **Yards:** 6,354/5,147. **Course rating:** 68.8/68.2. **Slope:** 106/102.
Subscriber comments: Short, but there are some fun holes...Short and tricky course...Like the rolling fairways...Not many flat lies...Should be better now that construction is finished...Beautiful 18th hole...Can't play it enough .

★★★½THENDARA GOLF CLUB
P.O. Box 153, Thendara, 13472, Herkimer County, (315)369-3136, 55 miles N of Utica.
Opened: 1921. **Holes:** 18. **Par:** 72/73. **Yards:** 6,435/5,757. **Course rating:** 70.2/72.8. **Slope:** 124/121. **Architect:** Donald Ross. **Green fee:** $20/$20. **Credit cards:** MC,VISA. **Reduced fees:** Twilight. **Caddies:** No. **Golf carts:** $20. **Discount golf packages:** No. **Season:** May-Oct. **High:** July-Sept. **On site lodging:** No. **Rental clubs:** Yes. **Walking policy:** Walking at certain times. **Metal spikes allowed:** Yes. **Range:** Yes (grass/mats). **To obtain tee times:** Non-members may call 1 day in advance. Some tee times are reserved for members on weekends.
Subscriber comments: Outstanding back nine through the woods...Wait until black flies leave...Front side open, scenery gorgeous especially in fall...Back side is a bowling alley...Must be played in the fall...Adirondack favorite.

★★★THOMAS CARVEL COUNTRY CLUB
PU-Ferris Rd., Pine Plains, 12567, Dutchess County, (518)398-7101, 30 miles NE of Paughkeepsie.
Opened: 1962. **Holes:** 18. **Par:** 73/75. **Yards:** 7,025/5,066. **Course rating:** 73.5/69.0. **Slope:** 127/115. **Architect:** William Mitchell. **Green fee:** $33/$39. **Credit cards:** MC,VISA. **Reduced fees:** Weekdays, low season, twilight, seniors. **Caddies:** No. **Golf carts:** Included in Green Fee. **Discount golf packages:** Yes. **Season:** April-Nov. **High:** May-Sept. **On site lodging:** No. **Rental clubs:** Yes. **Walking policy:** Mandatory cart. **Metal spikes allowed:** Yes. **Range:** Yes (grass). **To obtain tee times:** Call up to 7 days in advance.
Subscriber comments: Long and hilly, enjoy front better than back...Fast greens always a challenge...Underrated course with good greens, opening holes are tough...Variety is good, from wide to narrow...Plenty of blind shots, have to think...Length is a must on the back...Could use more fairway bunkers.

★★½THOUSAND ISLANDS GOLF CLUB
PU-County Rd. 100 Wellesley Island E., Wellesley Island, 13640, Jefferson County, (315)482-9454, 35 miles N of Watertown.
Opened: 1923. **Holes:** 18. **Par:** 72/74. **Yards:** 6,302/5,240. **Course rating:** 69.2/68.5. **Slope:** 118/114. **Architect:** Seth Raynor. **Green fee:** $23/$25. **Credit cards:** MC,VISA,AMEX. **Reduced fees:** Weekdays, low season, resort guests, twilight, juniors. **Caddies:** No. **Golf carts:** $22. **Discount golf packages:** Yes. **Season:** April-Nov.

High: June-Sept. **On site lodging:** Yes. **Rental clubs:** Yes. **Walking policy:** Walking at certain times. **Metal spikes allowed:** Yes. **Range:** Yes (grass). **To obtain tee times:** Call.

Subscriber comments: Unusual terrain...Best public course Thousand Islands has to offer...Some beautiful holes on St. Lawrence River...Great views.

★★TIMBER POINT GOLF COURSE
PU-Great River Rd., Great River, 11739, Suffolk County, (516)581-2401, 50 miles E of New York City.
Opened: 1927. **Holes:** 27. **Architect:** H.S. Colt and C.H. Alison/William Mitchell. **Green fee:** $9/$35. **Credit cards:** None. **Reduced fees:** Weekdays, low season, twilight, seniors, juniors. **Caddies:** No. **Golf carts:** $25. **Discount golf packages:** No. **Season:** Year-round. **High:** June-Aug. **On site lodging:** No. **Rental clubs:** Yes. **Walking policy:** Unrestricted walking. **Metal spikes allowed:** No. **Range:** Yes (mats). **To obtain tee times:** Nonresidents may call golf shop for same day reservations. Residents may call 7 days in advance.
RED/BLUE
Par: 72/72. **Yards:** 6,642/5,455. **Course rating:** 72.9/72.5. **Slope:** 121/119.
RED/WHITE
Par: 72/72. **Yards:** 6,441/5,358. **Course rating:** 70.6/70.5. **Slope:** 116/114.
WHITE/BLUE
Par: 72/72. **Yards:** 6,525/5,367. **Course rating:** 71.9/71.5. **Slope:** 116/115.

★★½TIOGA COUNTRY CLUB
PU-151 Ro-Ki Blvd, Nichols, 13812, Tioga County, (607)699-3881.
Opened: 1967. **Holes:** 18. **Par:** 71/72. **Yards:** 5,848/5,193. **Course rating:** 69.3/70.8. **Slope:** 119/115. **Architect:** Hal Purdy. **Green fee:** $13/$16. **Credit cards:** MC,VISA. **Reduced fees:** Twilight. **Caddies:** No. **Golf carts:** $20. **Discount golf packages:** No. **Season:** April-Nov. **High:** June-Aug. **On site lodging:** No. **Rental clubs:** Yes. **Walking policy:** Unrestricted walking. **Metal spikes allowed:** Yes. **Range:** No. **To obtain tee times:** Call 1 day in advance.
Subscriber comments: Hilly, country layout, some dull holes...Surprisingly pleasant...Fast greens, short course...Should be a billy goat to play here...Top notch greens...The best course nobody plays...A little too cutesy.

★★½TOMASSO'S CHEMUNG GOLF COURSE
PU-County Rd. 60, Waverly, 14892, Chemung County, (607)565-2323.
Opened: 1962. **Holes:** 18. **Par:** 69/69. **Yards:** 6,000/5,525. **Course rating:** 66.3/66.0. **Slope:** N/A. **Architect:** Lou Tomasso. **Green fee:** $11/$13. **Credit cards:** None. **Reduced fees:** Weekdays, low season, twilight, seniors. **Caddies:** No. **Golf carts:** $18. **Discount golf packages:** Yes. **Season:** Year-round. **High:** May-Sept. **On site lodging:** No. **Rental clubs:** No. **Walking policy:** Unrestricted walking. **Metal spikes allowed:** Yes. **Range:** No. **To obtain tee times:** First come, first served.
Subscriber comments: Gets better each year...No sand or rough...Short, sporty course with small greens.

★★★½TOWN OF WALLKILL GOLF CLUB
PU-40 Sands Rd., Middletown, 10940, Orange County, (914)361-1022, 55 miles NW of New York City.
Opened: 1991. **Holes:** 18. **Par:** 72/72. **Yards:** 6,437/5,171. **Course rating:** 70.6/69.7. **Slope:** 128/122. **Architect:** Steve Esposito. **Green fee:** $22/$31. **Credit cards:** None. **Reduced fees:** Weekdays, twilight, seniors. **Caddies:** No. **Golf carts:** $12. **Discount golf packages:** No. **Season:** April-Nov. **High:** June-Aug. **On site lodging:** No. **Rental clubs:** Yes. **Walking policy:** Unrestricted walking. **Metal spikes allowed:** Yes. **Range:** Yes (grass). **To obtain tee times:** Call Saturday for following week.
Subscriber comments: I love this tricky course, C-shaped par 5 is unique...Very nice greens, fairways are challenging...Course carved out of beautiful wetland and forest...Lots of water comes into play...Wonderful, challenging course.

★★★½TRI COUNTY COUNTRY CLUB
Rte. 39, Forestville, 14062, Chautauqua County, (716)965-9723, 50 miles S of Buffalo.
Opened: 1924. **Holes:** 18. **Par:** 71/72. **Yards:** 6,639/5,574. **Course rating:** 70.9/71.0. **Slope:** 118/113. **Architect:** Al Shart. **Green fee:** $24/$27. **Credit cards:** MC,VISA.

Reduced fees: Weekdays. **Caddies:** No. **Golf carts:** $25. **Discount golf packages:** Yes. **Season:** April-Oct. **High:** July-Aug. **On site lodging:** No. **Rental clubs:** No. **Walking policy:** Unrestricted walking. **Metal spikes allowed:** Yes. **Range:** Yes (grass/mats). **To obtain tee times:** Call golf shop.
Subscriber comments: Strategy is a must...Tough scoring on some holes...Nice rural setting, undulating greens are tough.

★★½VALLEY VIEW GOLF CLUB
PU-620 Memorial Pkwy., Utica, 13502, Oneida County, (315)732-8755.
Opened: 1936. **Holes:** 18. **Par:** 71/73. **Yards:** 6,583/5,942. **Course rating:** 69.2/72.6. **Slope:** 118/116. **Architect:** Robert Trent Jones. **Green fee:** $11/$14. **Credit cards:** None. **Reduced fees:** Twilight. **Caddies:** No. **Golf carts:** $10. **Discount golf packages:** No. **Season:** April-Nov. **High:** April-Aug. **On site lodging:** No. **Rental clubs:** Yes. **Walking policy:** Unrestricted walking. **Metal spikes allowed:** Yes. **Range:** No. **To obtain tee times:** First come, first served.

★★VAN CORTLANDT PARK GOLF CLUB
PU-Van Cortlandt Park S. and Bailey Ave., Bronx, 10471, Bronx County, (718)543-4595, 5 miles N of New York.
Opened: 1895. **Holes:** 18. **Par:** 70/70. **Yards:** 6,122/5,421. **Course rating:** 68.9/73.0. **Slope:** 112/120. **Architect:** T. McClure Peters. **Green fee:** $10/$21. **Credit cards:** MC,VISA,AMEX. **Reduced fees:** Twilight, seniors, juniors. **Caddies:** No. **Golf carts:** $23. **Discount golf packages:** Yes. **Season:** Year-round. **High:** April-Oct. **On site lodging:** No. **Rental clubs:** Yes. **Walking policy:** Unrestricted walking. **Metal spikes allowed:** Yes. **Range:** No. **To obtain tee times:** Call 10 days in advance with credit card to guarantee.
Special Notes: Oldest municipal course in the U.S.

VICTOR HILLS GOLF CLUB
PU-1460 Brace Rd., Victor, 14564, Ontario County, (716)924-3480.
Opened: 1973. **Architect:** Pete Craig. **Green fee:** $19/$19. **Credit cards:** MC,VISA. **Reduced fees:** Twilight. **Caddies:** No. **Golf carts:** $20. **Discount golf packages:** No. **Season:** Year-round weather permitting. **High:** May-Sept. **On site lodging:** No. **Rental clubs:** Yes. **Walking policy:** Unrestricted walking. **Metal spikes allowed:** Yes. **Range:** No. **To obtain tee times:** Call up to 7 days in advance.
★★★NORTH COURSE
Holes: 18. **Par:** 72/72. **Yards:** 6,440/6,454. **Course rating:** 71.3/72.6. **Slope:** 119/117.
Subscriber comments: Two courses offer different challenges...A lot of blind shots, good greens...Very hilly and challenging...Exceptional use of land for layout...Tough for the average golfer...Neither 18 is long, but both require good shotmaking.
SOUTH COURSE
Holes: 18. **Par:** 72/72. **Yards:** 6,663/5,670. **Course rating:** 71.5/72.9. **Slope:** 121/119.
Special Notes: Also has a 9-hole executive course.

★★★½VILLA ROMA COUNTRY CLUB
Villa Roma Rd., Callicoon, 12723, Sullivan County, (914)887-5097, (800)727-8455, 100 miles N of New York City.
Opened: 1987. **Holes:** 18. **Par:** 71/72. **Yards:** 6,231/4,791. **Course rating:** 70.6/68.3. **Slope:** 125/117. **Architect:** David Postelwaite. **Green fee:** $35/$48. **Credit cards:** All major. **Reduced fees:** Weekdays, resort guests, twilight, seniors. **Caddies:** No. **Golf carts:** Included in Green Fee. **Discount golf packages:** Yes. **Season:** April-Nov. **High:** May-Sept. **On site lodging:** Yes. **Rental clubs:** Yes. **Walking policy:** Mandatory cart. **Metal spikes allowed:** Yes. **Range:** Yes (grass). **To obtain tee times:** Call golf shop.
Subscriber comments: Pretty views, short, but nice...Excellent layout...Fun course to play...Challenging, tough greens...Greens are very tricky and immense.

★★½WATERTOWN GOLF CLUB
P.O. Box 927, Watertown, 13601, Jefferson County, (315)782-4040.
Opened: 1926. **Holes:** 18. **Par:** 72/73. **Yards:** 6,309/5,492. **Course rating:** 69.4/67.9. **Slope:** 113/114. **Architect:** Geoffrey S. Cornish/James Huber. **Green fee:** $20/$20. **Credit cards:** None. **Reduced fees:** Twilight. **Caddies:** No. **Golf carts:** $9. **Discount golf packages:** Yes. **Season:** April-Oct. **High:** June-Aug. **On site lodging:** No. **Rental**

clubs: Yes. **Walking policy:** Unrestricted walking. **Metal spikes allowed:** Yes. **Range:** Yes (grass/mats). **To obtain tee times:** Call Wednesday for upcoming weekend and call Friday for next Tuesday and Wednesday.

★★★★WAYNE HILLS COUNTRY CLUB
2250 Gannett Rd., Lyons, 14489, Wayne County, (315)946-6944.
Opened: 1959. **Holes:** 18. **Par:** 72/73. **Yards:** 6,854/5,556. **Course rating:** 72.8/72.0. **Slope:** 125/116. **Architect:** Lawrence Packard. **Green fee:** $31/$43. **Credit cards:** MC,VISA. **Reduced fees:** Weekdays, twilight, juniors. **Caddies:** No. **Golf carts:** Included in Green Fee. **Discount golf packages:** No. **Season:** April-Nov. **High:** May-Sept. **On site lodging:** No. **Rental clubs:** No. **Walking policy:** Mandatory cart. **Metal spikes allowed:** Yes. **Range:** Yes (grass). **To obtain tee times:** Call 3 days in advance after 3 p.m.
Subscriber comments: A must play, great walking course...Treelined fairways, small greens...Worth the drive from the city...A well kept secret...Tough to find but worth the effort...Interesting holes from high elevation.

WEBSTER GOLF CLUB
Credit cards: All major. **Caddies:** No. **Discount golf packages:** No. **Season:** April-Nov. **On site lodging:** No. **Rental clubs:** No. **Metal spikes allowed:** Yes. **To obtain tee times:** Call.
★★★EAST COURSE
440 Salt Rd., Webster, 14580, Monroe County, (716)265-1920, 10 miles E of Rochester.
Opened: 1957. **Holes:** 18. **Par:** 71/73. **Yards:** 6,916/5,710. **Course rating:** 73.2/73.0. **Slope:** 128/121. **Architect:** James G. Harrison. **Green fee:** $20/$23. **Reduced fees:** Weekdays. **Golf carts:** $22. **High:** June-Aug. **Walking policy:** Walking at certain times. **Range:** Yes (grass).
Subscriber comments: Tight course, well protected greens...Great greens...Well laid out, long...Good mix of long and short holes, must be accurate to score.
★★WEST COURSE
415 Salt Rd., Webster, 14580, Monroe County, (716)265-1307, 10 miles E of Rochester.
Opened: 1975. **Holes:** 18. **Par:** 70/70. **Yards:** 6,003/5,400. **Course rating:** 66.6/68.5. **Slope:** 106/108. **Architect:** Tom Murphy/Eddie Rieflin. **Green fee:** $15/$18. **Reduced fees:** Seniors, juniors. **Golf carts:** $15. **High:** June-Sept. **Walking policy:** Unrestricted walking. **Range:** No.

★★★½WELLSVILLE COUNTRY CLUB
Riverside Dr, Wellsville, 14895, Allegany County, (716)593-6337, 30 miles E of Orlean.
Opened: 1911. **Holes:** 18. **Par:** 71/72. **Yards:** 6,253/5,527. **Course rating:** 71.5/70.4. **Slope:** 121/113. **Architect:** N/A. **Green fee:** $25/$25. **Credit cards:** MC,VISA,AMEX. **Reduced fees:** N/A. **Caddies:** No. **Golf carts:** N/A. **Discount golf packages:** No. **Season:** April-Nov. **High:** June-Aug. **On site lodging:** No. **Rental clubs:** No. **Walking policy:** Unrestricted walking. **Metal spikes allowed:** Yes. **Range:** Yes (grass). **To obtain tee times:** Public may call in advance for availability.
Subscriber comments: Tough tight course...Good variety of holes...Accuracy is key, greens are fast and a delight.

★★½WEST SAYVILLE GOLF CLUB
PU-Montauk Hwy., West Sayville, 11796, Suffolk County, (516)567-1704.
Opened: 1968. **Holes:** 18. **Par:** 72/72. **Yards:** 6,715/5,387. **Course rating:** 72.5/71.2. **Slope:** 124/119. **Architect:** William Mitchell. **Green fee:** $19/$32. **Credit cards:** DISC. **Reduced fees:** Weekdays, low season, twilight, seniors, juniors. **Caddies:** No. **Golf carts:** $12. **Discount golf packages:** No. **Season:** Year-round. **High:** May-Sept. **On site lodging:** No. **Rental clubs:** Yes. **Walking policy:** Unrestricted walking. **Metal spikes allowed:** Yes. **Range:** Yes (grass/mats). **To obtain tee times:** Nonresidents may call same day for tee times.

★★★½WESTPORT COUNTRY CLUB
PU-Liberty St., Westport, 12993, Essex County, (518)962-4470, (800)600-6655, 90 miles S of Montreal, Canada.
Opened: 1898. **Holes:** 18. **Par:** 72/72. **Yards:** 6,544/5,256. **Course rating:** 71.5/70.5.

Slope: 120/112. **Architect:** Tom Winton. **Green fee:** $10/$25. **Credit cards:** MC,VISA,DISC. **Reduced fees:** Weekdays, low season, resort guests, twilight, juniors. **Caddies:** No. **Golf carts:** $10. **Discount golf packages:** Yes. **Season:** April-Oct. **High:** June-Aug. **On site lodging:** Yes. **Rental clubs:** Yes. **Walking policy:** Walking at certain times. **Metal spikes allowed:** Yes. **Range:** Yes (grass/mats). **To obtain tee times:** Call. **Subscriber comments:** Out of the way but excellent...Overlooks Lake Champlain...Front and back nines totally different...Great views.

★★★WHITEFACE CLUB ON LAKE PLACID

R-P.O. Box 231, Lake Placid, 12946, Essex County, (518)523-2551.
Opened: 1898. **Holes:** 18. **Par:** 72/74. **Yards:** 6,490/5,635. **Course rating:** 70.6/73.9. **Slope:** 123/125. **Architect:** John Van Kleek. **Green fee:** $20/$30. **Credit cards:** All major. **Reduced fees:** Weekdays, low season, resort guests, twilight, juniors. **Caddies:** No. **Golf carts:** $28. **Discount golf packages:** Yes. **Season:** May-Oct. **High:** July-Aug. **On site lodging:** Yes. **Rental clubs:** Yes. **Walking policy:** Unrestricted walking. **Metal spikes allowed:** Yes. **Range:** Yes (grass). **To obtain tee times:** Call any time. **Subscriber comments:** Nice resort course up in the Adirondacks...Good mix of driver holes and narrow wooded fairways...Old fashioned turn-of-the-century course.

★★★WILD WOOD COUNTRY CLUB

1201 W. Rush Rd., Rush, 14543, Monroe County, (716)334-5860.
Opened: 1968. **Holes:** 18. **Par:** 71/72. **Yards:** 6,431/5,368. **Course rating:** 70.2/70.1. **Slope:** 120/116. **Architect:** Pete Craig. **Green fee:** $18/$20. **Credit cards:** MC,VISA. **Reduced fees:** Low season, seniors. **Caddies:** No. **Golf carts:** $20. **Discount golf packages:** Yes. **Season:** April-Oct. **High:** July-Aug. **On site lodging:** No. **Rental clubs:** Yes. **Walking policy:** Unrestricted walking. **Metal spikes allowed:** Yes. **Range:** Yes (grass). **To obtain tee times:** Call golf shop. **Subscriber comments:** Difficult course, long, well conditioned...Many trees and creeks...Very hilly, some blind shots.

★★★WILLOWBROOK COUNTRY CLUB

PU-4200 Lake Ave., Lockport, 14094, Niagara County, (716)434-0111,.
Opened: 1956. **Holes:** 18. **Par:** 71/71. **Yards:** 6,018/5,713. **Course rating:** 68.9/67.7. **Slope:** 112/112. **Architect:** George Graff. **Green fee:** $13/$20. **Credit cards:** MC,VISA. **Reduced fees:** Weekdays, low season, twilight, seniors. **Caddies:** No. **Golf carts:** $9. **Discount golf packages:** Yes. **Season:** April-Nov. **High:** June-Aug. **On site lodging:** No. **Rental clubs:** Yes. **Walking policy:** Unrestricted walking. **Metal spikes allowed:** Yes. **Range:** Yes (grass). **To obtain tee times:** Call 7 days in advance. **Subscriber comments:** Good layout, good greens...Fast greens...Fairly flat, some interesting holes...Short in length...Improving every year, always upgrading course.

★★★WINDHAM COUNTRY CLUB

PU-S. St., Windham, 12496, Greene County, (518)734-9910, 45 miles SW of Albany.
Opened: 1927. **Holes:** 18. **Par:** 71/72. **Yards:** 6,088/4,876. **Course rating:** 69.9/68.4. **Slope:** 127/114. **Architect:** Seth Raynor. **Green fee:** $11/$30. **Credit cards:** MC,VISA. **Reduced fees:** Weekdays, low season, resort guests, twilight, seniors, juniors. **Caddies:** No. **Golf carts:** $24. **Discount golf packages:** Yes. **Season:** April-Oct. **High:** June-Sept. **On site lodging:** No. **Rental clubs:** Yes. **Walking policy:** Walking at certain times. **Metal spikes allowed:** Yes. **Range:** No. **To obtain tee times:** Call 1 day in advance for weekdays. Call on Monday for weekend. **Subscriber comments:** Very nice, tricky, pretty course...Quirky...Very hilly and scenic...Too many blind shots...Relaxed and scenic...Front nine easy to play...Good mountain course...Pretty, plenty of wildlife.

★★½WINGED PHEASANT GOLF LINKS

1475 Sand Hill Rd., Shortsville, 14548, Ontario County, (716)289-8846.
Opened: 1963. **Holes:** 18. **Par:** 70/72. **Yards:** 6,400/5,835. **Course rating:** 69.0/72.0. **Slope:** 118/119. **Architect:** Pete Craig. **Green fee:** $18/$20. **Credit cards:** MC,VISA,AMEX. **Reduced fees:** Weekdays, low season, resort guests, twilight, seniors, juniors. **Caddies:** Yes. **Golf carts:** $20. **Discount golf packages:** No. **Season:** March-Nov. **High:** June-Aug. **On site lodging:** No. **Rental clubs:** Yes. **Walking policy:** Walking at certain times. **Metal spikes allowed:** No. **Range:** Yes (grass/mats). **To obtain tee times:** Call 7 days in advance.

★★★½ANGEL'S TRACE GOLF LINKS
PU-1215 Angel's Club Dr. S.W., Sunset Beach, 28468, Brunswick County, (910)579-2277, 18 miles N of Myrtle Beach, SC.
Opened: 1995. **Holes:** 36. **Par:** 72/72. **Yards:** 6,640/4,524. **Course rating:** 73.6/68.2. **Slope:** 139/118. **Architect:** Clyde Johnston. **Green fee:** $10/$55. **Credit cards:** MC,VISA,AMEX. **Reduced fees:** Low season, juniors. **Caddies:** No. **Golf carts:** $17. **Discount golf packages:** No. **Season:** Year-round. **High:** March-May, Oct.-Nov. **On site lodging:** No. **Rental clubs:** Yes. **Walking policy:** Mandatory cart. **Metal spikes allowed:** Yes. **Range:** Yes (grass). **To obtain tee times:** N/A.
Subscriber comments: Good new course, fast rolling greens (bent)...True greens, nice layout...Very scenic...Well maintained...Great service, especially considering our cart ended up in a pond...Pro shop stands out.

★★★½BALD HEAD ISLAND CLUB
R-P.O. Box 3070, Bald Head Island, 28461, Brunswick County, (910)457-7310, (800)234-1666, 30 miles S of Wilmington.
Opened: 1975. **Holes:** 18. **Par:** 72/72. **Yards:** 6,855/4,810. **Course rating:** 74.2/69.5. **Slope:** 143/121. **Architect:** George Cobb. **Green fee:** $36/$45. **Credit cards:** All major. **Reduced fees:** Low season, resort guests, juniors. **Caddies:** No. **Golf carts:** $14. **Discount golf packages:** Yes. **Season:** Year-round. **High:** May-Sept. **On site lodging:** Yes. **Rental clubs:** Yes. **Walking policy:** Walking at certain times. **Metal spikes allowed:** Yes. **Range:** Yes (grass). **To obtain tee times:** Call golf shop seven days in advance.
Subscriber comments: Great links course...Great atmostphere, ferry to and from course...A great experience!...Best kept secret in NC...Golf course for players...Windy, tight and fair...Challenging course, changes daily, great getaway...Fast greens.

★★★½BAYONET AT PUPPY CREEK GOLF CLUB
PU-349 S. Parker Church Rd., Raeford, 28736, Hoke County, (910)904-1500, (888)229-6638, 8 miles W of Fayetteville.
Opened: 1995. **Holes:** 18. **Par:** 72/72. **Yards:** 7,036/4,453. **Course rating:** 73.2/65.0. **Slope:** 132/112. **Architect:** Willard Byrd. **Green fee:** $17/$24. **Credit cards:** MC,VISA,AMEX. **Reduced fees:** Weekdays, low season, resort guests, twilight, seniors, juniors. **Caddies:** No. **Golf carts:** $13. **Discount golf packages:** No. **Season:** Year-round. **High:** March-May; Sept-Oct. **On site lodging:** No. **Rental clubs:** Yes. **Walking policy:** Walking at certain times. **Metal spikes allowed:** Yes. **Range:** Yes (grass). **To obtain tee times:** N/A.
Subscriber comments: Very interesting holes...Used every club...Tough greens, very demanding...Don't always have to hit driver...One of the best new courses in the area...Excellent layout, good condition, good value...Good practice facility.

★★★BEACON RIDGE GOLF & COUNTRY CLUB
R-6000 Longleaf Dr., West End, 27376, Moore County, (910)673-2950, (800)416-5204, 10 miles W of Pinehurst.
Opened: 1988. **Holes:** 18. **Par:** 72/72. **Yards:** 6,414/4,730. **Course rating:** 70.7/67.1. **Slope:** 125/115. **Architect:** Gene Hamm. **Green fee:** $20/$36. **Credit cards:** MC,VISA,DISC. **Reduced fees:** Weekdays, low season, resort guests, twilight, seniors, juniors. **Caddies:** No. **Golf carts:** $16. **Discount golf packages:** Yes. **Season:** Year-round. **High:** Spring/Fall. **On site lodging:** Yes. **Rental clubs:** Yes. **Walking policy:** Walking at certain times. **Metal spikes allowed:** Yes. **Range:** Yes (grass). **To obtain tee times:** Call anytime.
Subscriber comments: Very pleasant...Hilly and interesting...Fun to play...Good selection of "easy and hard" holes with wide variety of lies possible...Great warm-up for Pinehurst courses...Very tight but fun, lots of trouble...Most greens elevated.

★★½BEAU RIVAGE PLANTATION COUNTRY CLUB
6230 Carolina Beach Rd., Wilmington, 28412, New Hanover County, (910)392-9022, (800)628-7080, 10 miles SE of Wilmington.
Opened: 1988. **Holes:** 18. **Par:** 72/72. **Yards:** 6,709/4,612. **Course rating:** 72.5/67.1. **Slope:** 136/114. **Architect:** Joe Gestner/Eddie Lewis. **Green fee:** $30/$49. **Credit cards:** All major. **Reduced fees:** Low season, resort guests, twilight. **Caddies:** No. **Golf carts:** Included in Green Fee. **Discount golf packages:** Yes. **Season:** Year-round. **High:** March-Sept. **On site lodging:** Yes. **Rental clubs:** Yes. **Walking policy:**

Mandatory cart. **Metal spikes allowed:** Yes. **Range:** Yes (grass). **To obtain tee times:** Call golf shop between 7 a.m. and 7 p.m.

Subscriber comments: A great day of golf, a test for all skill levels...Nice, affordable beach course... No waiting...Fun...Long rides between holes.

★½BEL AIRE GOLF CLUB

1517 Pleasant Ridge Rd., Greensboro, 27409, Guilford County, (919)668-2413.
Architect: R. Brame. **Caddies:** No. **Discount golf packages:** No. **On site lodging:** No. **Rental clubs:** No. **Metal spikes allowed:** Yes. **Range:** Yes.
Call club for further information.

★★★BELVEDERE PLANTATION GOLF & COUNTRY CLUB

2368 Country Club Dr., Hampstead, 28443, Pender County, (910)270-2703, 15 miles NE of Wilmington.
Opened: 1970. **Holes:** 18. **Par:** 71/72. **Yards:** 6,401/4,992. **Course rating:** 71.2/68.5. **Slope:** 128/113. **Architect:** Russell Bruney. **Green fee:** $20/$45. **Credit cards:** MC,VISA. **Reduced fees:** Low season, resort guests, twilight, juniors. **Caddies:** No. **Golf carts:** Included in Green Fee. **Discount golf packages:** Yes. **Season:** Year-round. **High:** March-May. **On site lodging:** Yes. **Rental clubs:** Yes. **Walking policy:** Mandatory cart. **Metal spikes allowed:** Yes. **Range:** Yes (grass). **To obtain tee times:** Call one week in advance.

Subscriber comments: Great golf...Excellent test...Fast, elevated greens...They've done a lot to it...Amateur design...Very clean and neat, great lunch, best in area.

BIRKDALE GOLF CLUB

PU-16500 Birkdale Commons Pkwy., Huntersville, 28078, Mecklenburg County, (704)895-8038, 15 miles N of Charlotte.
Opened: 1997. **Holes:** 18. **Par:** 72/72. **Yards:** 7,013/5,175. **Course rating:** 74.1/69.7. **Slope:** 138/123. **Architect:** Arnold Palmer and Ed Seay. **Green fee:** $46/$71. **Credit cards:** MC,VISA,AMEX. **Reduced fees:** Twilight, juniors. **Caddies:** Yes. **Golf carts:** Included in Green Fee. **Discount golf packages:** No. **Season:** Year-round. **High:** April-June; Sept.-Oct. **On site lodging:** No. **Rental clubs:** Yes. **Walking policy:** Unrestricted walking. **Metal spikes allowed:** No. **Range:** Yes (grass/mats). **To obtain tee times:** Call up to 8 days in advance.

★★½BLACK MOUNTAIN GOLF COURSE

PU-106 Montreat Rd., Black Mountain, 28711, Buncombe County, (704)669-2710, 15 miles E of Asheville.
Opened: 1928. **Holes:** 18. **Par:** 71/71. **Yards:** 6,181/5,780. **Course rating:** 69.5/68.1. **Slope:** 129/113. **Architect:** Ross Taylor. **Green fee:** N/A. **Credit cards:** MC,VISA. **Reduced fees:** N/A. **Caddies:** No. **Golf carts:** N/A. **Discount golf packages:** No. **Season:** Year-round. **High:** May-Oct. **On site lodging:** No. **Rental clubs:** No. **Walking policy:** N/A. **Metal spikes allowed:** Yes. **Range:** No. **To obtain tee times:** N/A.

Subscriber comments: Great people, great layout...Beautiful golf course, fun to play, limited facilities...Gets better every year (course condition)...Challenging course, especially par-6 17th.

★★BLAIR PARK GOLF CLUB

PM-1901 S. Main St., High Point, 27260, Guilford County, (910)883-3497, 18 miles SW of Greensboro.
Opened: 1936. **Holes:** 18. **Par:** 72/72. **Yards:** 6,449/5,171. **Course rating:** 69.4/67.3. **Slope:** 111/107. **Architect:** Rick Briley. **Green fee:** $10/$12. **Credit cards:** None. **Reduced fees:** Twilight, seniors, juniors. **Caddies:** No. **Golf carts:** $9. **Discount golf packages:** No. **Season:** Year-round. **High:** June-Aug. **On site lodging:** No. **Rental clubs:** Yes. **Walking policy:** Walking at certain times. **Metal spikes allowed:** Yes. **Range:** No. **To obtain tee times:** Call one week in advance.

★★★½BLUE RIDGE COUNTRY CLUB

R-Hwy. 221, Linville Falls, 28647, Avery County, (704)756-4013.
Opened: 1995. **Holes:** 18. **Par:** 72/72. **Yards:** 6,862/5,203. **Course rating:** 72.9/70.4. **Slope:** 128/116. **Architect:** Clifton, Ezell and Clifton. **Green fee:** $25/$48. **Credit cards:** All major. **Reduced fees:** Weekdays, low season, twilight, seniors, juniors. **Caddies:** No. **Golf carts:** Included in Green Fee. **Discount golf packages:** No.

Season: Year-round. **High:** June-Oct. **On site lodging:** Yes. **Rental clubs:** Yes.
Walking policy: Unrestricted walking. **Metal spikes allowed:** Yes. **Range:** Yes (grass).
To obtain tee times: Call golf shop.
Subscriber comments: Fun to play but tough, good facilities, great service...Beautiful
layout. Very well kept...Very tight fairways, fast greens...In beautiful NC foothills, shotmaking required...Two totally different nine-hole designs...What a pleasant
surprise...Great mountain course, without the tricks...Great golf! Lodge has nice rooms.

★★ BOGUE BANKS COUNTRY CLUB
152 Oak Leaf Dr. Rte.3, Pine Knoll Shores, 28512, Carteret County, (919)726-1034, 5
miles S of Morehead City.
Opened: N/A. **Holes:** N/A. **Par:** N/A. **Yards:** N/A. **Course rating:** N/A. **Slope:** N/A.
Architect: Maurice Brackett. **Green fee:** N/A. **Credit cards:** N/A. **Reduced fees:** N/A.
Caddies: No. **Golf carts:** N/A. **Discount golf packages:** No. **Season:** Year-round.
High: May-Aug. **On site lodging:** No. **Rental clubs:** No. **Walking policy:** Unrestricted
walking. **Metal spikes allowed:** Yes. **Range:** No. **To obtain tee times:** N/A.

★★★ BOONE GOLF CLUB
PU-Fairway Dr., Boone, 28607, Watauga County, (704)264-8760, 90 miles W of
Winston-Salem.
Opened: 1958. **Holes:** 18. **Par:** 71/75. **Yards:** 6,401/5,172. **Course rating:** 70.1/69.1.
Slope: 120/113. **Architect:** Ellis Maples. **Green fee:** $25/$35. **Credit cards:** MC,VISA.
Reduced fees: Weekdays, low season, twilight. **Caddies:** No. **Golf carts:** $10.
Discount golf packages: Yes. **Season:** April-Nov. **High:** June-Aug. **On site lodging:**
No. **Rental clubs:** Yes. **Walking policy:** Walking at certain times. **Metal spikes
allowed:** Yes. **Range:** No. **To obtain tee times:** Call one week in advance.
Subscriber comments: Great little course, beautiful, easy...Thick rough...Lots of fog,
enjoyable, tricky greens...Fastest greens I ever played...Very playable...Good fairways...Links nine, rolling nine.

★★½ BRANDYWINE BAY GOLF & COUNTRY CLUB
PU-224 Brandywine Blvd., Morehead City, 28557, Carteret County, (919)247-2541, 40
miles E of New Bern.
Opened: 1980. **Holes:** 18. **Par:** 71/71. **Yards:** 6,609/5,191. **Course rating:** 72.2/68.5.
Slope: 119/119. **Architect:** Bruce Devlin. **Green fee:** $18/$23. **Credit cards:** MC,VISA.
Reduced fees: Low season, twilight. **Caddies:** No. **Golf carts:** $15. **Discount golf
packages:** Yes. **Season:** Year-round. **High:** March-Oct. **On site lodging:** No. **Rental
clubs:** No. **Walking policy:** Walking at certain times. **Metal spikes allowed:** Yes.
Range: Yes (grass). **To obtain tee times:** Call anytime.
Subscriber comments: Good place to build a golf course...Need all shots...Lots of
hazards, woods and water...Another great public course...Nice layout. Good
service...Friendly staffers...Short and full of doglegs...One of best in this section.

★½ BRIARCREEK GOLF CLUB
P.O. Box 440, High Shoals, 28077, Gaston County, (704)922-4208.
Call club for further information.

★★★ BRICK LANDING PLANTATION GOLF & COUNTRY CLUB
R-1900 Goose Creek Rd., Ocean Isle Beach, 28469, Brunswick County, (910)754-
5545, (800)438-3006, 15 miles N of N. Myrtle Beach, SC.
Opened: 1988. **Holes:** 18. **Par:** 72/71. **Yards:** 6,752/4,707. **Course rating:** 72.1/67.0.
Slope: 141/116. **Architect:** H.M. Brazeal. **Green fee:** $31/$61. **Credit cards:** MC,VISA.
Reduced fees: Twilight, juniors. **Caddies:** No. **Golf carts:** Included in Green Fee.
Discount golf packages: Yes. **Season:** Year-round. **High:** March-April/Oct. **On site
lodging:** Yes. **Rental clubs:** Yes. **Walking policy:** Mandatory cart. **Metal spikes
allowed:** Yes. **Range:** Yes (grass). **To obtain tee times:** Call golf shop.
Subscriber comments: Pretty setting, very short par 3s... Water on 17 holes...Bring a
lot of balls...Very challenging, great scenery...Target golf, not easy...Very penal but good
greens...Toughest course I've played...Great views of Intracoastal Waterway.

★★½ BRIERWOOD GOLF CLUB
Hwy. 179, Shallotte, 28459, Brunswick County, (910)754-4660, (888)274-3796, 35 miles
SW of Wilmington.

Opened: 1966. **Holes:** 18. **Par:** 72/72. **Yards:** 6,607/4,812. **Course rating:** 71.0/67.0. **Slope:** 129/114. **Architect:** Ben Ward. **Green fee:** $20/$48. **Credit cards:** MC,VISA. **Reduced fees:** Weekdays, low season, twilight, seniors. **Caddies:** No. **Golf carts:** Included in Green Fee. **Discount golf packages:** Yes. **Season:** Year-round. **High:** April-Oct. **On site lodging:** No. **Rental clubs:** Yes. **Walking policy:** Mandatory cart. **Metal spikes allowed:** No. **Range:** No. **To obtain tee times:** Call golf shop.
Notes: Sunbelt Seniors; Jack Frost.
Subscriber comments: Beautiful fairways...Basic but great...Pleasure to play...Nice golf, fun to play, reasonable...Some strong holes, some weak, fun to play, nice people, good value...Good course to play, wide open...Really enjoyed the course.

★★★BRUNSWICK PLANTATION GOLF RESORT
R-Hwy. 17 N., Calabash, 28467, Brunswick County, (910)287-7888, (800)848-0290, 25 miles N of Myrtle Beach, SC.
Opened: 1992. **Holes:** 27. **Par:** 72/72. **Yards:** 6,779/5,210. **Course rating:** 72.7/70.4. **Slope:** 131/115. **Architect:** Willard Byrd. **Green fee:** $25/$75. **Credit cards:** All major. **Reduced fees:** Weekdays, low season, resort guests, twilight, juniors. **Caddies:** No. **Golf carts:** Included in Green Fee. **Discount golf packages:** Yes. **Season:** Year-round. **High:** March-April/Oct. **On site lodging:** Yes. **Rental clubs:** Yes. **Walking policy:** Mandatory cart. **Metal spikes allowed:** Yes. **Range:** Yes (grass). **To obtain tee times:** Obtain tee times through Myrtle Beach packages or call direct.
Subscriber comments: Good, challenging...Deep rough, fast greens, loved it!...Great golf experience all the way around...Fun course, fair for ladies...Excellent pro shop and restaurant...Beautiful layout...Great variety.

★★½BRUSHY MOUNTAIN GOLF CLUB
P.O. Box 457, Taylorsville, 28681, Alexander County, (704)632-4804.
Call club for further information.
Subscriber comments: Nice finishing hole...A real mountain jewel...Long and short...Good greens, average fairways.

BRYAN PARK & GOLF CLUB
PM-6275 Bryan Park Rd., Brown Summit, 27214, Guilford County, (910)375-2200, 10 miles NE of Greensboro. **Credit cards:** MC,VISA,AMEX. **Reduced fees:** Weekdays, low season, twilight, seniors, juniors. **Caddies:** No. **Discount golf packages:** Yes. **Season:** Year-round. **High:** April-Sept. **On site lodging:** No. **Rental clubs:** Yes. **Metal spikes allowed:** Yes. **Range:** Yes (grass).
★★★★CHAMPIONS COURSE
Opened: 1990. **Holes:** 18. **Par:** 72/72. **Yards:** 7,135/5,395. **Course rating:** 74.4/71.0. **Slope:** 130/122. **Architect:** Rees Jones. **Green fee:** $22/$26. **Golf carts:** $12. **Walking policy:** Walking at certain times. **To obtain tee times:** Call up to 30 days in advance for weekdays; 7 days for weekend and holidays.
Notes: Ranked 17th in 1997 Best in State.
Subscriber comments: Good hole variety...Borders lake...Challenging. Immaculate...Long par-4 finishing hole...Too much golf course for high handicapper...Lake breeze provides relief from even midsummer heat...Steady, long and fair. Great use of bunkering.
★★★½PLAYERS COURSE
Opened: 1974. **Holes:** 18. **Par:** 72/72. **Yards:** 7,076/5,260. **Course rating:** 73.0/70.5. **Slope:** 128/120. **Architect:** George Cobb/Rees Jones. **Green fee:** $13/$30. **Golf carts:** $10. **Walking policy:** Unrestricted walking. **To obtain tee times:** Call up to one month in advance for weekdays. Call Wednesday at 8 a.m. for weekend and holidays.
Subscriber comments: Long, very fair...Long walk between holes...1 and 18 probably toughest opening and closing holes in NC...Top 10 on my golf list...Hard to beat.

★★BUNCOMBE COUNTY MUNICIPAL GOLF CLUB
PM-226 Fairway Dr., Asheville, 28805, Buncombe County, (704)298-1867.
Opened: 1927. **Holes:** 18. **Par:** 72/72. **Yards:** 6,356/4,897. **Course rating:** 70.1/68.8. **Slope:** 111/109. **Architect:** Donald Ross. **Green fee:** $15/$15. **Credit cards:** N/A. **Reduced fees:** Weekdays, twilight. **Caddies:** No. **Golf carts:** $12. **Discount golf packages:** No. **Season:** Year-round. **High:** April-Oct. **On site lodging:** No. **Rental clubs:** No. **Walking policy:** Unrestricted walking. **Metal spikes allowed:** Yes. **Range:** No. **To obtain tee times:** Call golf shop for weekends only.

★★CALABASH GOLF LINKS
R-820 Thomasboro Rd., Calabash, 28467, Brunswick County, (910)575-5000, (800)841-5971, 10 miles N of Myrtle Beach, SC.
Opened: 1996. **Holes:** 18. **Par:** 72/72. **Yards:** 6,612/4,850. **Course rating:** 72.0/68.4. **Slope:** 128/108. **Architect:** Willard Byrd. **Green fee:** $25/$54. **Credit cards:** All major. **Reduced fees:** Low season, resort guests, twilight, juniors. **Caddies:** No. **Golf carts:** Included in Green Fee. **Discount golf packages:** Yes. **Season:** Year-round. **High:** Sept.-Nov.; March-May. **On site lodging:** No. **Rental clubs:** Yes. **Walking policy:** Mandatory cart. **Metal spikes allowed:** Yes. **Range:** Yes (grass). **To obtain tee times:** Call golf shop.
Notes: Dupont World Amateur.

★★½CAPE GOLF & RACQUET CLUB
535 The Cape Blvd., Wilmington, 28412, New Hanover County, (910)799-3110, (800)291-9847, 55 miles N of Myrtle Beach, SC.
Opened: 1985. **Holes:** 18. **Par:** 72/72. **Yards:** 6,790/4,948. **Course rating:** 73.1/69.3. **Slope:** 133/118. **Architect:** Gene Hamm. **Green fee:** $25/$45. **Credit cards:** All major. **Reduced fees:** Weekdays, low season, resort guests, twilight, seniors. **Caddies:** No. **Golf carts:** Included in Green Fee. **Discount golf packages:** Yes. **Season:** Year-round. **High:** March-July; Sept. **On site lodging:** Yes. **Rental clubs:** Yes. **Walking policy:** Mandatory cart. **Metal spikes allowed:** Yes. **Range:** Yes (grass). **To obtain tee times:** Call golf shop.
Subscriber comments: Very nice...A little bit of links style...Short, narrow, good greens...Windy days tough...Great layout, challenging holes, alligators.

THE CAROLINA
PU-277 Avenue of the Carolina, Whispering Pines, 28327, Moore County, (910)949-2811, (888)725-6372, 5 miles NE of Pinehurst.
Opened: 1997. **Holes:** 18. **Par:** 72/72. **Yards:** 6,928/4,828. **Course rating:** N/A. **Slope:** N/A. **Architect:** Arnold Palmer and Ed Seay. **Green fee:** $60/$79. **Credit cards:** MC,VISA,DISC. **Reduced fees:** Weekdays, low season, twilight. **Caddies:** No. **Golf carts:** Included in Green Fee. **Discount golf packages:** Yes. **Season:** Year-round. **High:** March-May; Oct. **On site lodging:** No. **Rental clubs:** Yes. **Walking policy:** Unrestricted walking. **Metal spikes allowed:** No. **Range:** Yes (grass). **To obtain tee times:** Call golf shop.

★★★CAROLINA LAKES GOLF CLUB
PU-53 Carolina Lakes Rd., Sanford, 27330, Harnett County, (919)499-5421, (800)942-8633, 18 miles N of Fayetteville.
Opened: 1981. **Holes:** 18. **Par:** 70/70. **Yards:** 6,400/5,010. **Course rating:** 70.7/67.0. **Slope:** 117/110. **Architect:** Roger Rulewich and Jim Hickey. **Green fee:** $10/$15. **Credit cards:** MC,VISA. **Reduced fees:** Weekdays, low season, resort guests, twilight, seniors, juniors. **Caddies:** No. **Golf carts:** $12. **Discount golf packages:** Yes. **Season:** Year-round. **High:** March-May. **On site lodging:** No. **Rental clubs:** Yes. **Walking policy:** Walking at certain times. **Metal spikes allowed:** Yes. **Range:** Yes (grass/mats). **To obtain tee times:** Call up to one week in advance.
Subscriber comments: Great course, very challenging...Greens too fast for high handicapers...Rolling terrain; big greens...Nothing wrong with this course...Reasonable length, fair to ladies...Nice everyday course.

★★★CAROLINA PINES GOLF & COUNTRY CLUB
390 Carolina Pines Blvd., New Bern, 28560, Craven County, (919)444-1000.
Holes: 18. **Par:** 72/72. **Yards:** 6,250/5,900. **Slope:** 115/111. **Architect:** Ron Borsset. **Caddies:** No. **Discount golf packages:** No. **On site lodging:** No. **Rental clubs:** No. **Metal spikes allowed:** Yes. **Range:** No.
Call club for further information.
Subscriber comments: 15th hole one of best in NC...Pleasant place to play...Great marshes...Many houses along fairways. Slice one, you've bought a window.

★★★CAROLINA SHORES GOLF & COUNTRY CLUB
PU-99 Carolina Shores Dr., Calabash, 28467, Brunswick County, (910)579-2181, (800)579-8292, 7 miles N of Myrtle Beach.

Opened: 1974. **Holes:** 18. **Par:** 72/72. **Yards:** 6,783/6,231. **Course rating:** N/A. **Slope:** 128/122. **Architect:** Tom Jackson. **Green fee:** $16/$44. **Credit cards:** MC,VISA,AMEX. **Reduced fees:** Low season. **Caddies:** No. **Golf carts:** $22. **Discount golf packages:** No. **Season:** Year-round. **High:** March-April; Oct.-Nov. **On site lodging:** No. **Rental clubs:** Yes. **Walking policy:** Mandatory cart. **Metal spikes allowed:** Yes. **Range:** Yes (grass). **To obtain tee times:** Call golf shop.
Subscriber comments: Good golf. Lots of room to play...Good test from back tees...Lots of sand and water...Tough course...Tight, tough...Typical beach area course...Over 90 sand traps make shot placement important.

★★½CHARLOTTE GOLF LINKS
PU-11500 Providence Rd., Charlotte, 28277, Mecklenburg County, (704)846-7990.
Opened: 1993. **Holes:** 18. **Par:** 71/72. **Yards:** 6,700/5,279. **Course rating:** 71.5/70.3. **Slope:** 121/117. **Architect:** Tom Doak. **Green fee:** $16/$33. **Credit cards:** MC,VISA,AMEX. **Reduced fees:** Weekdays, low season, twilight, seniors, juniors. **Caddies:** No. **Golf carts:** $13. **Discount golf packages:** Yes. **Season:** Year-round. **High:** April-Nov. **On site lodging:** No. **Rental clubs:** Yes. **Walking policy:** Walking at certain times. **Metal spikes allowed:** Yes. **Range:** Yes (grass). **To obtain tee times:** Call one week in advance.
Subscriber comments: Tough from the tips...Easy if you stay out of the tall grass...Target golf; front and back nines different...Great practice facility...Course maturing nicely...Requires accurate placement of tee shots.

★★½CHARLOTTE NATIONAL GOLF CLUB
6920 Howey Bottoms Rd., Indian Trail, 28079, Union County, (704)882-8282, 15 miles E of Charlotte.
Opened: 1996. **Holes:** 18. **Par:** 72/72. **Yards:** 7,227/5,423. **Course rating:** 74.9/71.3. **Slope:** 129/127. **Architect:** Russell Breeden. **Green fee:** $22/$45. **Credit cards:** All major. **Reduced fees:** N/A. **Caddies:** No. **Golf carts:** Included in Green Fee. **Discount golf packages:** No. **Season:** Year-round. **High:** March-Oct. **On site lodging:** No. **Rental clubs:** Yes. **Walking policy:** Walking at certain times. **Metal spikes allowed:** No. **Range:** Yes (grass/mats). **To obtain tee times:** Call golf shop.
Subscriber comments: All you want to play from back tees...Good course for the stray hitter...Challenging yet fun; will get better with age.

★★★CHATUGE SHORES GOLF COURSE
PU-260 Golf Course Rd., Hayesville, 28904, Clay County, (704)389-8940, 110 miles SW of Asheville.
Opened: 1971. **Holes:** 18. **Par:** 72/72. **Yards:** 6,687/4,950. **Course rating:** 71.3/68.3. **Slope:** 123/120. **Architect:** John V. Townsend. **Green fee:** $18/$18. **Credit cards:** MC,VISA. **Reduced fees:** N/A. **Caddies:** No. **Golf carts:** $6. **Discount golf packages:** No. **Season:** Year-round. **High:** June-Aug. **On site lodging:** No. **Rental clubs:** Yes. **Walking policy:** Unrestricted walking. **Metal spikes allowed:** Yes. **Range:** Yes (grass/mats). **To obtain tee times:** Call up to three days in advance.
Subscriber comments: Inexpensive, well laid out, mountain course, greens always good...Good course but weird layout...Simply a good test of golf...Beautiful setting...Tough greens, great character.

★★CHEROKEE HILLS GOLF & COUNTRY CLUB
R-Harshaw Rd., Murphy, 28906, Cherokee County, (704)837-5853, (800)334-3905, 90 miles N of Altanta.
Opened: 1969. **Holes:** 18. **Par:** 72/72. **Yards:** 6,724/5,172. **Course rating:** 70.0/68.0. **Slope:** 113/117. **Architect:** Wells and West Inc. **Green fee:** $15. **Credit cards:** MC,VISA,AMEX. **Reduced fees:** Resort guests, juniors. **Caddies:** No. **Golf carts:** $11. **Discount golf packages:** Yes. **Season:** Year-round. **High:** May-Nov. **On site lodging:** Yes. **Rental clubs:** Yes. **Walking policy:** Walking at certain times. **Metal spikes allowed:** Yes. **Range:** Yes (grass). **To obtain tee times:** Call 48 hours in advance. Tee times can also be made at the same time as reservation of golf package.

★★½CHEVIOT HILLS GOLF CLUB
PU-7301 Capital Blvd., Raleigh, 27604, Wake County, (919)876-9920.
Opened: 1930. **Holes:** 18. **Par:** 71/71. **Yards:** N/A. **Course rating:** N/A. **Slope:** N/A. **Architect:** Gene Hamm. **Green fee:** $15/$22. **Credit cards:** MC,VISA. **Reduced fees:**

N/A. **Caddies:** No. **Golf carts:** $11. **Discount golf packages:** No. **Season:** Year-round. **High:** Spring-Fall. **On site lodging:** No. **Rental clubs:** No. **Walking policy:** Walking at certain times. **Metal spikes allowed:** Yes. **Range:** No. **To obtain tee times:** Call up to 7 days in advance for weekdays; Tuesday prior for weekends.

Subscriber comments: A old, playable course...Good variety. Good par 3s. Hills and trees...Tougher than it's Slope/rating...Not open Sunday mornings.

Special Notes: Course opens at noon on Sundays.

★★★CLEGHORN PLANTATION GOLF & COUNTRY CLUB

PU-200 Golf Circle, Rutherfordton, 28139, Rutherford County, (704)286-9117, 70 miles W of Charlotte.

Opened: 1969. **Holes:** 18. **Par:** 72/73. **Yards:** 6,903/4,751. **Course rating:** 74.6/68.1. **Slope:** 134/111. **Architect:** George Cobb. **Green fee:** $24/$32. **Credit cards:** MC,VISA. **Reduced fees:** Weekdays, seniors. **Caddies:** No. **Golf carts:** Included in Green Fee. **Discount golf packages:** Yes. **Season:** Year-round. **High:** April-Sept. **On site lodging:** No. **Rental clubs:** Yes. **Walking policy:** Mandatory cart. **Metal spikes allowed:** Yes. **Range:** Yes (grass). **To obtain tee times:** Call in advance.

Subscriber comments: A mountain course that requires total concentration...Hilly, difficult, worth playing...Hit it straight, no room for error here...Fun to play...Stay out of rough...Can play long...Pretty, interesting...Must hit long irons...A real mountain treat, great fun in remote area...Challenging, many hazards...Tough yet fair.

★★★THE CLUB AT LONGLEAF

2001 Midland Rd., Southern Pines, 28387, Moore County, (910)692-6100, (800)889-5323, 60 miles S of Raleigh.

Opened: 1988. **Holes:** 18. **Par:** 71/71. **Yards:** 6,600/4,719. **Course rating:** 69.7/65.7. **Slope:** 117/108. **Architect:** Dan Maples. **Green fee:** $30/$60. **Credit cards:** MC,VISA. **Reduced fees:** Low season, resort guests, twilight, juniors. **Caddies:** No. **Golf carts:** $17. **Discount golf packages:** Yes. **Season:** Year-round. **High:** March-May/Sept.-Oct. **On site lodging:** Yes. **Rental clubs:** Yes. **Walking policy:** Walking at certain times. **Metal spikes allowed:** Yes. **Range:** Yes (grass). **To obtain tee times:** Call the above 800 number.

Subscriber comments: Nice place to play...Great fun...Accommodations excellent...A feel-good course...Unique layout, very fair...Front nine and back two different courses...Second nine more varied...Fun to play...Routing through old horse training ground is gimmicky...Good food...A great course for short hitters.

Special Notes: Cart fee mandatory.

COUNTRY CLUB OF WHISPERING PINES

2 Clubhouse Blvd., Whispering Pines, 28327, Moore County, (910)949-2311, 55 miles SW of Raleigh.

Opened: 1959. **Architect:** Ellis Maples. **Green fee:** $40/$40. **Credit cards:** MC,VISA,AMEX. **Reduced fees:** Low season, resort guests, juniors. **Caddies:** No. **Golf carts:** $15. **Discount golf packages:** Yes. **Season:** Year-round. **High:** March-Oct. **On site lodging:** Yes. **Rental clubs:** Yes. **Walking policy:** Mandatory cart. **Metal spikes allowed:** Yes. **Range:** Yes (grass). **To obtain tee times:** Call two days in advance.

★★★EAST COURSE

Holes: 18. **Par:** 72/72. **Yards:** 7,138/5,542. **Course rating:** 73.9/72.0. **Slope:** 125/123.

Subscriber comments: Good condition, three holes very short (par 4s)...Bring long driver...Just plain nice folks...No clubhouse...Enjoyable...Fair course; over sandhills and pine trees; greens small and fast...A long course, but good to play...Very good greens.

★★★WEST COURSE

Holes: 18. **Par:** 71/71. **Yards:** 6,363/5,135. **Course rating:** 70.3/69.8. **Slope:** 128/121.

Subscriber comments: Fun...Not overseeded...Excellent Bermuda fairways...Nine holes hilly; nine holes level; greens mixed size...Lots of water for the Pinehurst area.

★★★CROOKED CREEK GOLF CLUB

4621 Shady Greens Dr., Fuquay-Varina, 27526, Wake County, (919)557-7529, 12 miles S of Raleigh.

Opened: 1994. **Holes:** 18. **Par:** 71/71. **Yards:** 6,239/4,689. **Course rating:** 68.9/67.3. **Slope:** 121/116. **Architect:** Chuck Smith. **Green fee:** $18/$26. **Credit cards:** MC,VISA. **Reduced fees:** Low season, twilight, seniors, juniors. **Caddies:** No. **Golf carts:** $12. **Discount golf packages:** No. **Season:** Year-round. **High:** April-July; Sept.-Nov. **On site**

lodging: No. **Rental clubs:** Yes. **Walking policy:** Unrestricted walking. **Metal spikes allowed:** Yes. **Range:** Yes (grass). **To obtain tee times:** Call golf shop.
Subscriber comments: A challenge from back tees...Still a young course...Some hokey holes but great scenery on back nine...Know the yardage on holes requiring lay up or pay the price...Another Carolina classic!

★★½CROOKED CREEK GOLF CLUB
764 Crooked Creek Rd., Hendersonville, 28739, Henderson County, (704)692-2011.
Call club for further information.
Subscriber comments: Wide fairways...Great view in the mountains...No food or drink facilities...Good layout. Fun course...A flat Florida course in the NC mountains...Good weekend course, very hilly but walkable...Good for beginners.

★½CRYSTAL SPRINGS GOLF CLUB
P.O. Box 9, Pineville, 28134, Mecklenburg County, (704)588-2640.
Architect: John J. Criscione/Gene Thomas. **Caddies:** No. **Discount golf packages:** No. **On site lodging:** No. **Rental clubs:** No. **Metal spikes allowed:** Yes. **Range:** No.
Call club for further information.

★★★½THE CURRITUCK CLUB
R-Clubhouse Dr. Hwy. 12, Corolla, 27959, Dare County, (919)453-9400, (888)453-9400,
60 miles S of Virginia Beach, VA.
Opened: 1996. **Holes:** 18. **Par:** 72/72. **Yards:** 6,885/4,766. **Course rating:** 74.0/68.5.
Slope: 136/120. **Architect:** Rees Jones. **Green fee:** $45/$85. **Credit cards:** MC,VISA.
Reduced fees: Low season, resort guests, twilight, seniors. **Caddies:** No. **Golf carts:** N/A. **Discount golf packages:** No. **Season:** Year-round. **High:** June-Sept. **On site lodging:** Yes. **Rental clubs:** Yes. **Walking policy:** Unrestricted walking. **Metal spikes allowed:** Yes. **Range:** Yes (grass/mats). **To obtain tee times:** Call up to 1 year in advance.
Subscriber comments: Excellent new course...Wind makes course very difficult...Best on Outer Banks...Located between ocean and sound...Wonderful layout.
Special Notes: Spikeless encouraged.

★★★CYPRESS LAKES GOLF COURSE
PU-Rt. 1, Cypress Lakes Rd., Hope Mills, 28348, Cumberland County, (910)483-0359,
10 miles S of Fayetteville.
Opened: 1968. **Holes:** 18. **Par:** 72/74. **Yards:** 6,943/5,272. **Course rating:** 73.2/69.7.
Slope: 133/118. **Architect:** L.B. Floyd. **Green fee:** $15/$17. **Credit cards:** MC,VISA.
Reduced fees: Weekdays, seniors, juniors. **Caddies:** No. **Golf carts:** $13. **Discount golf packages:** Yes. **Season:** Year-round. **High:** Spring/Fall. **On site lodging:** No.
Rental clubs: Yes. **Walking policy:** Unrestricted walking. **Metal spikes allowed:** Yes.
Range: Yes (grass). **To obtain tee times:** Call anytime.
Subscriber comments: Great value. Good greens...Most courteous and friendly...The Floyds' home course...Super people...This could easily be my #1 of all time, I love it...Could play it every day...Limited trouble course, lots of openess.

★★★★CYPRESS LANDING GOLF CLUB
600 Clubhouse Dr., Chocowinity, 27817, (919)946-7788, 19 miles E of Greenville.
Opened: 1996. **Holes:** 18. **Par:** 72/72. **Yards:** 6,850/4,989. **Course rating:** 72.8/68.8. **Slope:** 130/118. **Architect:** Bill Love. **Green fee:** $30/$36. **Credit cards:** MC,VISA. **Reduced fees:** Weekdays.
Caddies: No. **Golf carts:** Included in Green Fee. **Discount golf packages:** Yes.
Season: Year-round. **High:** April-May; Sept.-Oct. **On site lodging:** No. **Rental clubs:** Yes. **Walking policy:** Mandatory cart. **Metal spikes allowed:** No. **Range:** Yes (grass).
To obtain tee times: Call up to 2 days in advance.
Subscriber comments: Will be one of the best in three years...Great for average golfer...Scenic, super service...New, beautiful and playable. Great 18th hole.

★★★DEERCROFT GOLF CLUB
30000 Deercroft Dr., Wagram, 28396, Scotland County, (910)369-3107, 19 miles S of Pinehurst.
Opened: 1984. **Holes:** 18. **Par:** 72/72. **Yards:** 6,745/5,443. **Course rating:** 72.6/67.0.

Slope: 125/113. **Architect:** Gardner Gildey. **Green fee:** $26/$65. **Credit cards:** MC,VISA,AMEX. **Reduced fees:** Weekdays, low season, twilight, seniors, juniors. **Caddies:** No. **Golf carts:** Included in Green Fee. **Discount golf packages:** Yes. **Season:** Year-round. **High:** Spring/Fall. **On site lodging:** No. **Rental clubs:** Yes. **Walking policy:** Unrestricted walking. **Metal spikes allowed:** Yes. **Range:** Yes (grass). **To obtain tee times:** Call golf shop. Tee times also available through most hotels in the area.

Subscriber comments: Wonderful experience...Should shoot handicap...Carolina beauty at its best...Demands accuracy...Well kept and fun to play...Very challenging, difficult starting hole...A good course with some moderate length...Great test of abilities.

★★★½DEVIL'S RIDGE GOLF CLUB

5107 Linksland Dr., Holly Springs, 27540, Wake County, (919)557-6100, 10 miles SW of Raleigh.

Opened: 1991. **Holes:** 18. **Par:** 72/72. **Yards:** 7,002/5,244. **Course rating:** 73.7/69.8. **Slope:** 138/121. **Architect:** John LaFoy. **Green fee:** $23/$36. **Credit cards:** MC,VISA. **Reduced fees:** Weekdays, low season, twilight, seniors, juniors. **Caddies:** No. **Golf carts:** $13. **Discount golf packages:** Yes. **Season:** Year-round. **High:** April-June. **On site lodging:** No. **Rental clubs:** Yes. **Walking policy:** Walking at certain times. **Metal spikes allowed:** Yes. **Range:** Yes (grass). **To obtain tee times:** Call one week in advance.

Subscriber comments: My favorite course in the area, also a challenge...A fun day...Tight, lots of blind shots...Loved the variety...The name fits, superior experience...Makes you concentrate but not gimicky...Great experience...Lots of character.

★★½THE DIVIDE

PU-6803 Stevens Mill Rd., Matthews, 28105, Mecklenburg/Union County, (704)882-8088, 20 miles SE of Charlotte.

Opened: 1995. **Holes:** 18. **Par:** 72/73. **Yards:** 6,973/5,213. **Course rating:** 74.4/70.3. **Slope:** 137. **Architect:** John Cassell. **Green fee:** $32/$42. **Credit cards:** MC,VISA,AMEX. **Reduced fees:** Low season, seniors, juniors. **Caddies:** No. **Golf carts:** Included in Green Fee. **Discount golf packages:** No. **Season:** Year-round. **High:** April-June; Sept.-Oct. **On site lodging:** No. **Rental clubs:** Yes. **Walking policy:** Mandatory cart. **Metal spikes allowed:** Yes. **Range:** Yes (grass). **To obtain tee times:** Call golf shop.

Subscriber comments: Many great holes...Tough layout, two district nines...Nice track, computer yardage nice...Beautiful, young course...Good variety of holes...No.2 very tough for average golfer, too much marsh area...Very good layout.

★½DUCK HAVEN GOLF CLUB

PU-1202 Eastwood Rd., Wilmington, 28403, New Hanover County, (910)791-7983.
Opened: 1961. **Holes:** 18. **Par:** 71/72. **Yards:** 6,453/5,361. **Course rating:** 71.6/71.8. **Slope:** 125/121. **Architect:** Raiford Trask Sr.. **Green fee:** $15/$20. **Credit cards:** None. **Reduced fees:** Weekdays, twilight, seniors, juniors. **Caddies:** No. **Golf carts:** Included in Green Fee. **Discount golf packages:** Yes. **Season:** Year-round. **High:** March-Oct. **On site lodging:** No. **Rental clubs:** Yes. **Walking policy:** Unrestricted walking. **Metal spikes allowed:** Yes. **Range:** No. **To obtain tee times:** Tee times not required.

★★★DUCK WOODS COUNTRY CLUB

50 S. Dogwood Trail, Kitty Hawk, 27949, Dare County, (919)261-2609, 70 miles S of Norfolk, VA.

Opened: 1968. **Holes:** 18. **Par:** 72/72. **Yards:** 6,650/5,407. **Course rating:** 71.3/70.7. **Slope:** 132/127. **Architect:** Ellis Maples. **Green fee:** $60/$70. **Credit cards:** MC,VISA. **Reduced fees:** N/A. **Caddies:** No. **Golf carts:** Included in Green Fee. **Discount golf packages:** No. **Season:** Year-round. **High:** May-Sept. **On site lodging:** No. **Rental clubs:** Yes. **Walking policy:** Mandatory cart. **Metal spikes allowed:** No. **Range:** Yes (grass). **To obtain tee times:** Call 3 days in advance.

Subscriber comments: My favorite Outer Banks course...Lots of water, a few good holes...Nice views...Fairways very nice...Check wind speed before the round.

★★★½DUKE UNIVERSITY GOLF CLUB

PU-Rte. 751 and Science Dr., Durham, 27708, Durham County, (919)681-2288.
Opened: 1957. **Holes:** 18. **Par:** 72/73. **Yards:** 7,045/5,505. **Course rating:** 73.9/71.2.

Slope: 137/124. **Architect:** Robert Trent Jones/Rees Jones. **Green fee:** $38/$53. **Credit cards:** MC,VISA. **Reduced fees:** Weekdays, twilight, seniors, juniors. **Caddies:** No. **Golf carts:** $17. **Discount golf packages:** Yes. **Season:** Year-round. **High:** March-Sept. **On site lodging:** Yes. **Rental clubs:** Yes. **Walking policy:** Unrestricted walking. **Metal spikes allowed:** Yes. **Range:** Yes (grass). **To obtain tee times:** Call up to seven days in advance.

Notes: Ranked 13th in 1997 Best in State.

Subscriber comments: The most beautiful scenery I have ever seen...Great layout, terrific traps, perfect golf...Tough greens and bunkers, accurate iron shots critical...Magnificent clubhouse...Another well designed course for low handicap player.

★★★½EAGLE CHASE GOLF CLUB

3215 Brantley Rd., Marshville, 28103, Union County, (704)385-9000, 30 miles N of Charlotte.

Caddies: No. **Discount golf packages:** No. **Season:** Year-round. **High:** April-June; Sept.-Nov. **On site lodging:** No. **Rental clubs:** No. **Walking policy:** Unrestricted walking. **Metal spikes allowed:** Yes. **Range:** No.

Call club for further information.

Subscriber comments: Awesome, worth the trip to find...Hole #2 is one of the toughest holes around...Very challenging. Great shape...Hilly...Demanding and interesting, good shape...Lots of elevation changes.

★★EAGLE CREST GOLF COURSE

PU-4400 Auburn Church Rd., Garner, 27529, Wake County, (919)772-6104, 5 miles S of Raleigh.

Opened: 1968. **Holes:** 18. **Par:** 71/71. **Yards:** 6,514/4,875. **Course rating:** 70.5/67.3. **Slope:** 118/113. **Architect:** Baucom & Assoc.. **Green fee:** $15/$21. **Credit cards:** MC,VISA. **Reduced fees:** Weekdays, twilight, seniors, juniors. **Caddies:** No. **Golf carts:** $10. **Discount golf packages:** No. **Season:** Year-round. **High:** April-Sept. **On site lodging:** No. **Rental clubs:** Yes. **Walking policy:** Unrestricted walking. **Metal spikes allowed:** Yes. **Range:** Yes (grass). **To obtain tee times:** Call one week in advance.

★★½ECHO FARMS GOLF & COUNTRY CLUB

4114 Echo Farms Blvd., Wilmington, 28412, New Hanover County, (910)791-9318.

Opened: 1974. **Holes:** 18. **Par:** 72/72. **Yards:** 7,014/5,142. **Course rating:** 74.2/70.7. **Slope:** 132/121. **Architect:** Gene Hamm. **Green fee:** $20/$35. **Credit cards:** All major. **Reduced fees:** Low season, resort guests. **Caddies:** No. **Golf carts:** Included in Green Fee. **Discount golf packages:** Yes. **Season:** Year-round. **High:** April-Oct. **On site lodging:** No. **Rental clubs:** Yes. **Walking policy:** Mandatory cart. **Metal spikes allowed:** Yes. **Range:** Yes (grass). **To obtain tee times:** Call ahead.

Subscriber comments: Big, wide, open, OK condition. Bring your long irons...Nice course...Real par 5s from backs...Good layout, some tight landing zones, fair...Take two sand irons, you'll wear one out...Nice beach course.

★★★½THE EMERALD GOLF CLUB

5000 Clubhouse Dr., New Bern, 28562, Craven County, (919)633-4440.

Opened: 1988. **Holes:** 18. **Par:** 72/72. **Yards:** 6,924/5,287. **Course rating:** 73.8/68.2. **Slope:** 129/114. **Architect:** Rees Jones. **Green fee:** $21/$42. **Credit cards:** MC,VISA. **Reduced fees:** Low season, twilight, juniors. **Caddies:** No. **Golf carts:** Included in Green Fee. **Discount golf packages:** Yes. **Season:** Year-round. **High:** March-May/Oct. **On site lodging:** No. **Rental clubs:** Yes. **Walking policy:** Mandatory cart. **Metal spikes allowed:** No. **Range:** Yes (grass). **To obtain tee times:** Call two days in advance.

Subscriber comments: Super greens, tight fairways...Real challenge...Good coastal course...Best in the area...Short hitters can score...Best of everything...Good test of golf...A good challenge...Long, tough layout. Plenty of marsh, H2O...Excellent shape, best course in area...18th great finishing hole.

★★★½ETOWAH VALLEY COUNTRY CLUB

R-450 Brickyard Rd., Etowah, 28729, Henderson County, (704)891-7141, (800)451-8174, 18 miles SE of Asheville.

Opened: 1967. **Holes:** 27. **Architect:** Edmund Ault. **Green fee:** $29/$29. **Credit cards:**

All major. **Reduced fees:** Low season. **Caddies:** No. **Golf carts:** $15. **Discount golf packages:** Yes. **Season:** Year-round. **High:** April-Oct. **On site lodging:** Yes. **Rental clubs:** Yes. **Walking policy:** Walking at certain times. **Metal spikes allowed:** Yes. **Range:** Yes (grass/mats). **To obtain tee times:** Call two days in advance.

SOUTH/NORTH
Par: 73/73. **Yards:** 6,911/5,391. **Course rating** 72.4/69.9. **Slope:** 125/117.
SOUTH/WEST
Par: 72/72. **Yards:** 7,108/5,524. **Course rating:** 73.7/71.3. **Slope:** 125/119.
WEST/NORTH
Par: 73/73. **Yards:** 7,005/5,363. **Course rating:** 73.1/70.2. **Slope:** 125/117.
Subscriber comments: Three nines, from flat to rolling to hilly. Beautiful scenery...North nine in most challenging, good layout, plenty of trees, food service very good...South is best; West is good; North will mature. West has steep ups and downs.

FAIRFIELD HARBOUR COUNTRY CLUB
1100 Pelican Dr., New Bern, 28560, Craven County, (919)514-0050, 100 miles SE of Raleigh.
Architect: Dominic Palumbo. **Credit cards:** All major. **Reduced fees:** Low season, twilight. **Caddies:** No. **Golf carts:** $10. **Discount golf packages:** Yes. **Season:** Year-round. **High:** Spring/Fall. **On site lodging:** Yes. **Rental clubs:** Yes. **Walking policy:** Walking at certain times. **Metal spikes allowed:** Yes. **Range:** Yes (grass). **To obtain tee times:** Call in advance.

★★★**HARBOUR POINTE COURSE**
Opened: 1989. **Holes:** 18. **Par:** 72/72. **Yards:** 6,650/5,100. **Course rating:** 71.8/68.6. **Slope:** 125/111. **Green fee:** $24.
Subscriber comments: Highly recommend it...Fair layout...Blends in with nature...Loved it...Great golf.

★★★**SHORELINE COURSE**
Opened: 1972. **Holes:** 18. **Par:** 72/72. **Yards:** 6,802/5,200. **Course rating:** 72.1/70.0. **Slope:** 128/118. **Green fee:** $24/$24.
Subscriber comments: On river, access with boat to sound and ocean, condos...Missed fairway means water...Worth the $...Lots of retired Yankees.

FAIRFIELD MOUNTAINS
R- **Green fee:** $25/$39. **Credit cards:** All major,Diners Club. **Reduced fees:** Low season, resort guests, twilight, juniors. **Caddies:** No. **Golf carts:** Included in Green Fee. **Discount golf packages:** Yes. **Season:** Year-round. **High:** April-Oct. **On site lodging:** Yes. **Rental clubs:** Yes. **Metal spikes allowed:** Yes. **Range:** Yes (grass). **To obtain tee times:** Call golf shop up to 14 days in advance.

★★★½**APPLE VALLEY GOLF CLUB**
201 Blvd. of The Mountains, Lake Lure, 28746, Rutherford County, (704)625-2888, 50 miles SE of Asheville.
Opened: 1986. **Holes:** 18. **Par:** 72/72. **Yards:** 6,726/4,661. **Course rating:** 72.5/66.3. **Slope:** 138/114. **Architect:** Dan Maples. **Walking policy:** Mandatory cart.
Subscriber comments: A must play, both courses are nice...Some funky holes. Some beautiful views...Outstanding scenery, great layouts...Awesome back 9! Impressive mountains in distance...Pro shop very accommodating...Narrow.

★★★½**BALD MOUNTAIN GOLF CLUB**
201 Blvd. of The Mountains, Lake Lure, 28746, Rutherford County, (704)625-2626, 50 miles SE of Asheville.
Opened: 1974. **Holes:** 18. **Par:** 72/72. **Yards:** 6,575/4,808. **Course rating:** 72.2/67.1. **Slope:** 125/114. **Architect:** W.B. Lewis. **Walking policy:** Walking at certain times.
Subscriber comments: Bring your iron game, stay out of creek...Beautiful place for golf...Good mountain course, great 18th hole...Superior in service...Friendly staff...Hard to choose between the two...Play Apple Valley first.

★★**FINLEY GOLF CLUB AT UNC**
PU-Finley Golf Club Rd., Chapel Hill, 27515, Orange County, (919)962-2349, 5 miles S of Durham.
Opened: 1949. **Holes:** 18. **Par:** 72/73. **Yards:** 6,580/5,277. **Course rating:** 71.3/69.7. **Slope:** 127/118. **Architect:** George Cobb/John LaFoy. **Green fee:** $9/$24. **Credit cards:** MC,VISA. **Reduced fees:** Weekdays, twilight, seniors, juniors. **Caddies:** No. **Golf carts:** $11. **Discount golf packages:** No. **Season:** Year-round. **High:** April-Oct.

On site lodging: No. Rental clubs: Yes. Walking policy: Unrestricted walking. Metal spikes allowed: Yes. Range: Yes (grass). To obtain tee times: Call Monday prior to weekend or University holiday. Call up to two days in advance for weekdays.

★★FOX SQUIRREL COUNTRY CLUB

591 S. Shore Dr., Boiling Spring Lakes, 28461, Brunswick County, (910)845-2625, 25 miles S of Wilmington.
Opened: 1962. Holes: 18. Par: 72/72. Yards: 6,762/5,349. Course rating: 72.5/70.7. Slope: 125/117. Architect: Ed Ricobboni. Green fee: $15/$20. Credit cards: MC,VISA. Reduced fees: N/A. Caddies: No. Golf carts: $12. Discount golf packages: Yes. Season: Year-round. High: June-Sept. On site lodging: No. Rental clubs: Yes. Walking policy: Unrestricted walking. Metal spikes allowed: Yes. Range: No. To obtain tee times: Call 24 hours in advance.

FOXFIRE RESORT & COUNTRY CLUB

R-9 Foxfire Blvd., Jackson Springs, 27281, Moore County, (910)295-4563, 60 miles S of Raleigh.
Opened: 1968. Architect: Gene Hamm. Green fee: $35/$64. Credit cards: All major. Reduced fees: Low season, resort guests, juniors. Caddies: No. Golf carts: Included in Green Fee. Discount golf packages: Yes. Season: Year-round. High: March-May/Sept.-Oct. On site lodging: Yes. Rental clubs: Yes. Walking policy: Mandatory cart. Metal spikes allowed: Yes. Range: Yes (grass). To obtain tee times: Call anytime.

★★½EAST COURSE

Holes: 18. Par: 72/72. Yards: 6,851/5,256. Course rating: 73.5/70.5. Slope: 131/119. Subscriber comments: Both courses present a fair test...Very good golf course, but average for the sand hills...Just golf. Some days that's enough...Good variety of holes...Wonderful memories...Narrow fairways, high rough.

★★★WEST COURSE

Holes: 18. Par: 72/72. Yards: 6,742/5,273. Course rating: 72.4/70.3. Slope: 129/115. Subscriber comments: Good test of golf, very challenging holes...Very fair to average and upward golfer...Tough No.2 hole...Challenging in the wind...Nice staff.

★★FRENCH BROAD GOLF CENTER

5 French Broad Ave., Fletcher, 28732, Henderson County, (704)687-8545.
Architect: Carl Lidden. Caddies: No. Discount golf packages: No. On site lodging: No. Rental clubs: No. Metal spikes allowed: Yes. Range: No.
Call club for further information.

★½GASTONIA MUNICIPAL GOLF CLUB

PM-530 Niblick Dr., Gastonia, 28052, Gaston County, (704)866-6945, 20 miles S of Charlotte.
Opened: 1931. Holes: 9. Par: 71/71. Yards: 6,474/4,341. Course rating: 71.3/66.1. Slope: 128/110. Architect: N/A. Green fee: $9/$14. Credit cards: MC,VISA. Reduced fees: Twilight. Caddies: No. Golf carts: $9. Discount golf packages: No. Season: Year-round. High: April-Sept. On site lodging: No. Rental clubs: No. Walking policy: Unrestricted walking. Metal spikes allowed: Yes. Range: No. To obtain tee times: Call Monday morning for weekends and holidays; no times for weekdays.

★★★GATES FOUR COUNTRY CLUB

6775 Irongate Dr., Fayetteville, 28306, Cumberland County, (910)425-2176.
Opened: 1971. Holes: 18. Par: 72/72. Yards: 6,865/5,368. Course rating: 73.4/70.5. Slope: 122/115. Architect: Willard Byrd. Green fee: $15/$29. Credit cards: MC,VISA. Reduced fees: Weekdays, low season, resort guests, juniors. Caddies: No. Golf carts: $11. Discount golf packages: Yes. Season: Year-round. High: Spring/Fall. On site lodging: No. Rental clubs: Yes. Walking policy: Walking at certain times. Metal spikes allowed: No. Range: Yes (grass). To obtain tee times: Call one week in advance.
Subscriber comments: Hard, hard and hard...Fun course but still a challenge...Good design, poor restaurant and pro shop...Tee times hard to come by on Sat/Sun...Tight fairways...Enjoyable round...Nice challenge for all handicaps...Rather wide fairways.

★★★½THE GAUNTLET AT ST. JAMES PLANTATION

Hwy. 211., Southport, 28461, Brunswick County, (910)253-3008, (800)247-4806, 28 miles S of Wilmington.

Opened: 1990. **Holes:** 18. **Par:** 72/72. **Yards:** 7,022/5,048. **Course rating:** 75.0/69.7. **Slope:** 142/119. **Architect:** P.B. Dye. **Green fee:** $40/$60. **Credit cards:** MC,VISA,AMEX. **Reduced fees:** Low season, twilight, seniors. **Caddies:** No. **Golf carts:** Included in Green Fee. **Discount golf packages:** Yes. **Season:** Year-round. **High:** March-May. **On site lodging:** No. **Rental clubs:** Yes. **Walking policy:** Mandatory cart. **Metal spikes allowed:** Yes. **Range:** Yes (grass). **To obtain tee times:** Call golf shop.

Subscriber comments: Nice course, hard greens...Wide and excellent fairways, 17th is very difficult...You have to earn it here...Always a wind...Finishing holes tough...Near coast...Golfer needs to be on top of his game!...Great Bermuda greens...Worth the effort to find and play...Has steadily matured/improved...Tough traps.

★★★½GLEN CANNON COUNTRY CLUB

Wilson Rd., Brevard, 28712, Transylvania County, (704)884-9160, 25 miles S of Asheville.

Opened: 1967. **Holes:** 18. **Par:** 72/72. **Yards:** 6,548/5,172. **Course rating:** 71.7/69.1. **Slope:** 124/117. **Architect:** Willie B. Lewis. **Green fee:** $25/$50. **Credit cards:** MC,VISA. **Reduced fees:** Twilight. **Caddies:** No. **Golf carts:** Included in Green Fee. **Discount golf packages:** No. **Season:** Year-round. **High:** April-Oct. **On site lodging:** No. **Rental clubs:** Yes. **Walking policy:** Mandatory cart. **Metal spikes allowed:** Yes. **Range:** Yes (grass). **To obtain tee times:** Call one day in advance.

Subscriber comments: Well kept. Scenic. Water!...Great layout. Good condition...Take a camera for a picture of 2nd...Pretty mountain course. Waterfalls and views...All the golf I want in a day...Premier course.

GRANDOVER RESORT & CONFERENCE CENTER

R-1000 Club Rd., Greensboro, 27407, Guilford County, (910)294-1800, (800)472-6301.

Architect: David Graham/Gary Panks. **Green fee:** $60/$60. **Credit cards:** All major. **Reduced fees:** N/A. **Caddies:** No. **Golf carts:** Included in Green Fee. **Discount golf packages:** No. **Season:** Year-round. **High:** March-Nov. **On site lodging:** No. **Rental clubs:** Yes. **Walking policy:** Walking at certain times. **Metal spikes allowed:** Yes. **Range:** Yes (grass). **To obtain tee times:** Call up to 7 days in advance.

★★★★EAST COURSE

Opened: 1996. **Holes:** 18. **Par:** 72/72. **Yards:** 7,100/5,500. **Course rating:** 74.3/71.7. **Slope:** 140/121.

Subscriber comments: Finest course in 50-mile radius of Greensboro...Beautiful stone work...Simply the best course I have ever played!...Excellent and difficult greens...Great clubhouse...Worth a visit.

WEST COURSE

Opened: 1997. **Holes:** 18. **Par:** 72/72. **Yards:** 6,800/5,050. **Course rating:** 72.5/69.2. **Slope:** 136/116.

★½GREAT SMOKIES RESORT GOLF CLUB

R-One Hilton Dr., Asheville, 28806, Buncombe County, (704)253-5874, (800)733-3211. **Opened:** 1974. **Holes:** 18. **Par:** 70/70. **Yards:** 5,900/4,600. **Course rating:** 69.5/67.0. **Slope:** 118/113. **Architect:** William B. Lewis. **Green fee:** $17/$30. **Credit cards:** All major,Diners Club. **Reduced fees:** Weekdays, low season, resort guests, twilight. **Caddies:** No. **Golf carts:** $13. **Discount golf packages:** Yes. **Season:** Year-round. **High:** April-Oct. **On site lodging:** Yes. **Rental clubs:** Yes. **Walking policy:** Walking at certain times. **Metal spikes allowed:** Yes. **Range:** No. **To obtain tee times:** Hotel guests may call one year in advance; outside play two days in advance.

★★★½GREENSBORO NATIONAL GOLF CLUB

PU-330 Niblick Dr., Summerfield, 27358, Rockingham County, (910)342-1113, 8 miles NW of Greensboro.

Opened: 1995. **Holes:** 18. **Par:** 72/72. **Yards:** 6,922/4,911. **Course rating:** 72.6/67.1. **Slope:** 125/108. **Architect:** N/A. **Green fee:** $35/$40. **Credit cards:** All major.

Reduced fees: Seniors, juniors. **Caddies:** No. **Golf carts:** Included in Green Fee. **Discount golf packages:** No. **Season:** Year-round. **High:** March-Oct. **On site lodging:** No. **Rental clubs:** Yes. **Walking policy:** Walking at certain times. **Metal spikes allowed:** No. **Range:** Yes (grass/mats). **To obtain tee times:** Call up to 7 days in advance.
Subscriber comments: What a pleasure!...Nicest greens in area...Best public in Greensboro...Give resort quality service...Good challenge, pretty...Prepare to three-putt!...Super collection of par 3s...Great bent greens, fun and interesting layout.

★★★THE GROVE PARK INN RESORT
R-290 Macon Ave., Asheville, 28804, Buncombe County, (704)252-2711, (800)438-5800.
Opened: 1894. **Holes:** 18. **Par:** 71/71. **Yards:** 6,520/4,687. **Course rating:** 71.7/68.6. **Slope:** 125/111. **Architect:** Willie Park/Donald Ross. **Green fee:** $20/$44. **Credit cards:** All major,Diners Club. **Reduced fees:** Low season, twilight. **Caddies:** No. **Golf carts:** N/A. **Discount golf packages:** Yes. **Season:** Year-round. **High:** April-Nov. **On site lodging:** Yes. **Rental clubs:** Yes. **Walking policy:** Walking at certain times. **Metal spikes allowed:** Yes. **Range:** No. **To obtain tee times:** Call anytime.
Subscriber comments: Fun short course...Nice for amateurs, good service, beautiful course...Great...Spectacular! Easier than it looks...Historical course, nice layout...Best service ever!...Great views from holes near hotel...Hilly, fun to play...Great staff, attentive to details...On sunny days, atop the Blue Ridge, very nice.

★★★HAWKSNEST GOLF & SKI RESORT
PU-2058 Skyland Dr., Banner Elk, 28607, Watauga County, (704)963-6561, (800)822-4295, 70 miles W of Winston-Salem.
Opened: 1969. **Holes:** 18. **Par:** 72/72. **Yards:** 6,244/4,799. **Course rating:** N/A. **Slope:** 113/110. **Architect:** Property owners. **Green fee:** $22/$38. **Credit cards:** MC,VISA,DISC. **Reduced fees:** Weekdays, low season, twilight. **Caddies:** No. **Golf carts:** Included in Green Fee. **Discount golf packages:** Yes. **Season:** April-Nov. **High:** July-Aug. **On site lodging:** No. **Rental clubs:** No. **Walking policy:** Mandatory cart. **Metal spikes allowed:** Yes. **Range:** No. **To obtain tee times:** N/A.
Subscriber comments: Par 3 signature hole a beauty...Loved it!...Beautiful in the spring...Nice mountain course...Fall scenery awesome. Tight fairways require accuracy. Great, slick-as-a-pickpocket greens...Outstanding views, 4,000+ feet elevation.

★★½HEDINGHAM GOLF CLUB
4801 Harbour Towne Dr., Raleigh, 27604, Wake County, (919)250-3030.
Opened: 1992. **Holes:** 18. **Par:** 72/72. **Yards:** 6,604/4,828. **Course rating:** 72.1/66.8. **Slope:** 124/107. **Architect:** Dave Postlethwait. **Green fee:** $20/$29. **Credit cards:** All major,Debit cards.. **Reduced fees:** Weekdays, twilight, seniors, juniors. **Caddies:** No. **Golf carts:** $13. **Discount golf packages:** No. **Season:** Year-round. **High:** April-May; Sept.-Oct. **On site lodging:** No. **Rental clubs:** Yes. **Walking policy:** Walking at certain times. **Metal spikes allowed:** Yes. **Range:** Yes (grass/mats). **To obtain tee times:** Call up to 7 days in advance.
Subscriber comments: Very fair course for all levels of play...Probably the best public greens in the triangle...Crowded on weekend...Tough to walk...Nice clubhouse, very playable...Great little neighborhood course.

★★½HIGH HAMPTON INN & COUNTRY CLUB
R-Hwy. 107 S., Box 338, Cashiers, 28717, Jackson County, (704)743-2450, (800)334-2551, 65 miles S of Asheville.
Opened: 1923. **Holes:** 18. **Par:** 71. **Yards:** 6,012. **Course rating:** 68.5. **Slope:** 120. **Architect:** George Cobb. **Green fee:** $18/$28. **Credit cards:** All major. **Reduced fees:** Low season, resort guests, twilight. **Caddies:** No. **Golf carts:** $11. **Discount golf packages:** Yes. **Season:** April-Nov. **High:** June-Aug. **On site lodging:** Yes. **Rental clubs:** Yes. **Walking policy:** Unrestricted walking. **Metal spikes allowed:** Yes. **Range:** Yes (grass). **To obtain tee times:** Call golf shop.
Subscriber comments: Incredible scenic old layout...Good for women and super-seniors...8th hole good...Great service...Charming accommodations, good food...A fun course to walk.

★★★½HIGHLAND CREEK GOLF CLUB

PU-7001 Highland Creek Pkwy., Charlotte, 28269, Mecklenburg County, (704)875-9000, 10 miles N of Charlotte.

Opened: 1993. **Holes:** 18. **Par:** 72/72. **Yards:** 7,008/5,005. **Course rating:** 73.3/70.1. **Slope:** 133/128. **Architect:** Clifton, Ezell and Clifton. **Green fee:** $44/$50. **Credit cards:** MC,VISA,AMEX. **Reduced fees:** Weekdays, low season. **Caddies:** No. **Golf carts:** Included in Green Fee. **Discount golf packages:** No. **Season:** Year-round. **High:** April-Sept. **On site lodging:** No. **Rental clubs:** Yes. **Walking policy:** Mandatory cart. **Metal spikes allowed:** Yes. **Range:** Yes (grass). **To obtain tee times:** Call three days in advance.

Subscriber comments: Fair layout, good finishing hole...Well designed, creeks, long...Best public golf in Charlotte!...Lightning fast greens...Homes close to fairways...All you want...Good, fun course, tough from tips, every hole different.

★★HILLCREST GOLF CLUB

PU-2450 S. Stratford Rd., Winston-Salem, 27103, Forsyth County, (910)765-5269.

Opened: 1931. **Holes:** 27. **Architect:** J. T. Jones. **Green fee:** $13/$17. **Credit cards:** MC,VISA,DISC. **Reduced fees:** Weekdays, low season, twilight, seniors, juniors. **Caddies:** No. **Golf carts:** $10. **Discount golf packages:** No. **Season:** Year-round. **High:** March-Sept. **On site lodging:** No. **Rental clubs:** Yes. **Walking policy:** Unrestricted walking. **Metal spikes allowed:** Yes. **Range:** No. **To obtain tee times:** Call Thursday 8 a.m. for upcoming weekend.

CEDARSIDE/HILLSIDE
Par: 72/74. **Yards:** 5,839/5,531. **Course rating:** 66.5. **Slope:** 104.
CEDARSIDE/LAKESIDE
Par: 72. **Yards:** 5,848. **Course rating:** 66.5. **Slope:** 104.
HILLSIDE/LAKESIDE
Par: 72. **Yards:** 5,869. **Course rating:** 66.5. **Slope:** 104.

★★★½HOUND EARS CLUB

P.O. Box 188, Blowing Rock, 28604, Watauga County, (704)963-4321, 90 miles W of Asheville.

Opened: 1963. **Holes:** 18. **Par:** 72/73. **Yards:** 6,165/4,959. **Course rating:** 69.4/66.8. **Slope:** 122/110. **Architect:** George Cobb. **Green fee:** $38/$75. **Credit cards:** MC,VISA,AMEX. **Reduced fees:** N/A. **Caddies:** No. **Golf carts:** $14. **Discount golf packages:** Yes. **Season:** April-Nov. **High:** June-Sept. **On site lodging:** Yes. **Rental clubs:** Yes. **Walking policy:** Walking at certain times. **Metal spikes allowed:** Yes. **Range:** Yes (grass). **To obtain tee times:** Must stay in Lodge to play.

Subscriber comments: Good mountain resort course...A fun golf course...Great layout and scenery. Great condition, super golf...Greens make it a test...Slow play but good value...Great resort, beautiful views, great food...Play it in autumn, great facilities, great service...Partly valley, partly mountains, enjoyed to play.

★★★HYLAND HILLS GOLF CLUB

PU-4100 U.S. No.1 N., Southern Pines, 28387, Moore County, (910)692-3752, 5 miles E of Pinehurst.

Opened: 1974. **Holes:** 18. **Par:** 72/72. **Yards:** 6,726/4,677. **Course rating:** 70.4/66.8. **Slope:** 124/109. **Architect:** Tom Jackson. **Green fee:** $20/$55. **Credit cards:** MC,VISA. **Reduced fees:** N/A. **Caddies:** No. **Golf carts:** $16. **Discount golf packages:** Yes. **Season:** Year-round. **High:** March-May/Oct. **On site lodging:** Yes. **Rental clubs:** Yes. **Walking policy:** Walking at certain times. **Metal spikes allowed:** Yes. **Range:** Yes (grass). **To obtain tee times:** Call in advance.

Subscriber comments: Greens are very true...Long par 5s, hilly, real challenging holes, great service...Great layout, several challenging holes...Every hole different, lots of fun...Good restaurant...Par 3 over water with tricky green, very playable, good conditioning...Interesting, scenic...Creative layout...Hilly terrain.

★★INDIAN VALLEY GOLF COURSE

PU-1005 Indian Valley Dr., Burlington, 27217, Alamance County, (910)584-7871, 20 miles E of Greensboro.

Opened: 1967. **Holes:** 18. **Par:** 70/70. **Yards:** 6,610/5,606. **Course rating:** 71.3/68.4. **Slope:** 115/113. **Architect:** Ellis Maples. **Green fee:** $9/$14. **Credit cards:** MC,VISA.

Reduced fees: Weekdays, low season, resort guests, twilight, seniors, juniors. **Caddies:** No. **Golf carts:** $9. **Discount golf packages:** Yes. **Season:** Year-round. **High:** April-Oct. **On site lodging:** No. **Rental clubs:** No. **Walking policy:** Unrestricted walking. **Metal spikes allowed:** Yes. **Range:** Yes (grass). **To obtain tee times:** Call Monday for weekend tee times at 8 a.m.

★★★JAMESTOWN PARK GOLF CLUB
PM-7014 E. Fork Rd., Jamestown, 27282, Guilford County, (910)454-4912, 3 miles SW of Greensboro.
Opened: 1972. **Holes:** 18. **Par:** 72/72. **Yards:** 6,665/5,298. **Course rating:** 72.6/70.7. **Slope:** 126/118. **Architect:** John Townsend. **Green fee:** $14/$16. **Credit cards:** MC,VISA,DISC. **Reduced fees:** Weekdays, seniors, juniors. **Caddies:** No. **Golf carts:** $9. **Discount golf packages:** No. **Season:** Year-round. **High:** May-Sept. **On site lodging:** No. **Rental clubs:** Yes. **Walking policy:** Walking at certain times. **Metal spikes allowed:** Yes. **Range:** Yes (grass). **To obtain tee times:** Call one week in advance for weekdays. Call Thursday prior to weekend of play.
Subscriber comments: Demanding of low handicaps, pro shop helpful for first timer...Long par 4s. A lot of holes uphill to the green...Many improvements...Fair golf test from blue markers...Just perfect. Good golf, great people.

★★★½JEFFERSON LANDING CLUB
Box 110, Jefferson, 28640, Ashe County, (910)246-5555, 80 miles from Winston Salem.
Opened: N/A. **Holes:** 18. **Par:** 72/72. **Yards:** 7,111/4,960. **Course rating:** N/A. **Slope:** 121/103. **Architect:** Larry Nelson and Dennis Lehmann. **Green fee:** N/A. **Credit cards:** All major,. **Reduced fees:** Weekdays, low season, resort guests, twilight. **Caddies:** No. **Golf carts:** Included in Green Fee. **Discount golf packages:** Yes. **Season:** March-Nov. **High:** June-Sept. **On site lodging:** Yes. **Rental clubs:** No. **Walking policy:** Mandatory cart. **Metal spikes allowed:** Yes. **Range:** Yes (grass/mats). **To obtain tee times:** N/A.
Subscriber comments: Can mountain golf get any better? A must!!!...Not too hilly...Beautiful vistas...Very nice, open...Very flat for a mountain course...Worth finding.

★★★½KEITH HILLS COUNTRY CLUB
Country Club Dr., Buies Creek, 27506, Harnett County, (910)893-5051, (800)334-4111, 30 miles S of Raleigh.
Opened: 1975. **Holes:** 18. **Par:** 72/72. **Yards:** 6,703/5,225. **Course rating:** 71.6/69.6. **Slope:** 129/120. **Architect:** Ellis Maples. **Green fee:** $18/$26. **Credit cards:** MC,VISA. **Reduced fees:** Low season, juniors. **Caddies:** No. **Golf carts:** $14. **Discount golf packages:** Yes. **Season:** Year-round. **High:** March-June. **On site lodging:** No. **Rental clubs:** Yes. **Walking policy:** Walking at certain times. **Metal spikes allowed:** Yes. **Range:** Yes (grass). **To obtain tee times:** Call golf shop.
Subscriber comments: Very demanding tee shots. Beautiful course...Variety of the hole design...Still the best lemonade of any golf course in NC...Good solid course with water on play good mix of holes.

★★★½LANE TREE GOLF COURSE
2317 Salem Church Rd., Goldsboro, 27530, Wayne County, (919)734-1245, 43 miles SE of Raleigh.
Opened: 1992. **Holes:** 18. **Par:** 72/72. **Yards:** 7,016/5,217. **Course rating:** 72.4/68.9. **Slope:** 131/120. **Architect:** John LaFoy. **Green fee:** $10/$25. **Credit cards:** MC,VISA,AMEX. **Reduced fees:** Weekdays, low season, twilight, seniors. **Caddies:** No. **Golf carts:** $14. **Discount golf packages:** No. **Season:** Year-round. **High:** April-Sept. **On site lodging:** No. **Rental clubs:** Yes. **Walking policy:** Walking at certain times. **Metal spikes allowed:** No. **Range:** Yes (grass). **To obtain tee times:** Call three days in advance.
Subscriber comments: Best greens in eastern Carolina. Great clubhouse...Excellent course. Negative: golfers sometimes start on 10th...Championship caliber from the tips; beautiful property...Nice place to play...Excellent facilities, immaculate...Good variety of 4s and 3s...Plays like a much more mature course...Use all clubs in bag.

★★★★LEGACY GOLF LINKS
PU-U.S. Hwy. 15-501 S., Aberdeen, 28315, Moore County, (910)944-8825, (800)344-8825, 2 miles S of Pinehurst.

Opened: 1991. **Holes:** 18. **Par:** 72/72. **Yards:** 6,989/4,948. **Course rating:** 73.2/68.3. **Slope:** 132/120. **Architect:** Jack Nicklaus II. **Green fee:** $39/$85. **Credit cards:** MC,VISA,AMEX. **Reduced fees:** Low season, resort guests, juniors. **Caddies:** No. **Golf carts:** Included in Green Fee. **Discount golf packages:** Yes. **Season:** Year-round. **High:** Spring/Fall. **On site lodging:** No. **Rental clubs:** Yes. **Walking policy:** Mandatory cart. **Metal spikes allowed:** Yes. **Range:** Yes (grass). **To obtain tee times:** Call in advance.
Notes: Host of Women's Amateur U.S. Public Links Championship in 2000.
Subscriber comments: One of the nicest courses in NC. Great course for women...Friendly...Back nine is terrific...Four excellent par 3s...Speaks well for Jack II...Super...Must stay focused...How you play it changes with seasons...The friendliest service imaginable...Great mix of holes. Natural setting.

★★½LINCOLN COUNTRY CLUB
2108 Country Club Rd., Lincolnton, 28092, Lincoln County, (704)735-1382, 20 miles NW of Charlotte.
Opened: 1991. **Holes:** 18. **Par:** 72/72. **Yards:** 6,467/5,011. **Course rating:** 70.4/69.0. **Slope:** 125/118. **Architect:** Peter Tufts. **Green fee:** $22/$28. **Credit cards:** MC,VISA. **Reduced fees:** Weekdays, seniors, juniors. **Caddies:** No. **Golf carts:** Included in Green Fee. **Discount golf packages:** No. **Season:** Year-round. **High:** April-Oct. **On site lodging:** No. **Rental clubs:** No. **Walking policy:** Unrestricted walking. **Metal spikes allowed:** Yes. **Range:** Yes (grass). **To obtain tee times:** Call three days in advance.
Subscriber comments: Great front nine, very nice people...Front nine very tough...Nice layout. Short front side, long back side, not much room for error. Challenging.

★★★½LINVILLE GOLF COURSE
R-Linville Ave., Linville, 28646, Avery County, (704)733-4363, 60 miles NE of Asheville.
Opened: 1924. **Holes:** 18. **Par:** 72/72. **Yards:** 6,780/5,086. **Course rating:** 72.7/69.3. **Slope:** 135/119. **Architect:** Donald Ross. **Green fee:** $41/$41. **Credit cards:** None. **Reduced fees:** N/A. **Caddies:** No. **Golf carts:** $14. **Discount golf packages:** No. **Season:** May-Oct. **High:** May-Oct. **On site lodging:** Yes. **Rental clubs:** Yes. **Walking policy:** Mandatory cart. **Metal spikes allowed:** Yes. **Range:** Yes (grass). **To obtain tee times:** Must be a guest at Eseeola Lodge.
Subscriber comments: Great course...Best "original" course in the NC Mountains...Great scenery, well maintained, trout in streams...Stay at lodge. Excellent!...Classic short course, tough greens.

★★★LITTLE RIVER FARM GOLF LINKS
PU-500 Little River Farm Rd., Carthage, 28374, Moore County, (910)949-4600, 5 miles N of Pinehurst.
Opened: 1996. **Holes:** 18. **Par:** 72/72. **Yards:** 6,909/5,092. **Course rating:** 73.6/69.4. **Slope:** 132/118. **Architect:** Dan Maples. **Green fee:** $40/$70. **Credit cards:** MC,VISA. **Reduced fees:** N/A. **Caddies:** No. **Golf carts:** $17. **Discount golf packages:** Yes. **Season:** Year-round. **High:** April-May; Oct. **On site lodging:** No. **Rental clubs:** Yes. **Walking policy:** Unrestricted walking. **Metal spikes allowed:** Yes. **Range:** Yes (grass). **To obtain tee times:** Call golf shop.
Subscriber comments: Visually pleasing, but better have a forecaddie...Let roughs grow in and this is a tough test of golf...Narrow, tough, water...Several greens severe but superb and fun design...Greens are fast and undulating...Great setting, fun to play.

★★LOCHMERE GOLF CLUB
2511 Kildare Farm Rd., Cary, 27511, Wake County, (919)851-0611, 5 miles W of Raleigh.
Opened: 1986. **Holes:** 18. **Par:** 71/73. **Yards:** 6,627/4,904. **Course rating:** 71.3/67.5. **Slope:** 123/112. **Architect:** Gene Hamm. **Green fee:** $20/$29. **Credit cards:** MC,VISA. **Reduced fees:** Weekdays, twilight, seniors, juniors. **Caddies:** No. **Golf carts:** $13. **Discount golf packages:** No. **Season:** Year-round. **High:** N/A. **On site lodging:** No. **Rental clubs:** Yes. **Walking policy:** Walking at certain times. **Metal spikes allowed:** Yes. **Range:** Yes (grass). **To obtain tee times:** Call one week in advance.

★★★LOCKWOOD FOLLY COUNTRY CLUB
19 Clubhouse Dr. S.W., Holden Beach, 28462, Brunswick County, (910)842-5666, (800)443-7891, 40 miles N of Myrtle Beach, SC.
Opened: 1988. **Holes:** 18. **Par:** 72/72. **Yards:** 6,836/5,524. **Course rating:** 73.8/70.9. **Slope:** 139/122. **Architect:** Willard C. Byrd. **Green fee:** $25/$62. **Credit cards:** MC,VISA. **Reduced fees:** Low season, resort guests, juniors. **Caddies:** No. **Golf carts:** $17. **Discount golf packages:** Yes. **Season:** Year-round. **High:** Spring/Fall. **On site lodging:** Yes. **Rental clubs:** Yes. **Walking policy:** Mandatory cart. **Metal spikes allowed:** Yes. **Range:** Yes (grass). **To obtain tee times:** Call up to one year in advance between 7 a.m. and 5 p.m.
Subscriber comments: Beautiful and difficult, but fair. Very friendly staff...A fun course, good hospitality, hole variety...Played it twice, loved it twice, hit it straight...Sand is definitely present, good course...Watch out for the foxes.

★★THE LODGE GOLF COURSE
PU-Rte. 3, Hwy. 74 E., Laurinburg, 28352, Scotland County, (910)277-0311, 50 miles S of Fayetteville.
Opened: 1982. **Holes:** 18. **Par:** 72/72. **Yards:** 6,570/4,830. **Course rating:** 69.4/65.5. **Slope:** 112/102. **Architect:** Tom Jackson. **Green fee:** $17/$23. **Credit cards:** None. **Reduced fees:** Twilight, seniors. **Caddies:** No. **Golf carts:** N/A. **Discount golf packages:** Yes. **Season:** Year-round. **High:** April-Sept. **On site lodging:** No. **Rental clubs:** Yes. **Walking policy:** Unrestricted walking. **Metal spikes allowed:** Yes. **Range:** Yes (grass). **To obtain tee times:** First come, first served.

★★★½MAGGIE VALLEY RESORT GOLF CLUB
R-340 Country Club Rd., Maggie Valley, 28751, Haywood County, (704)926-6013, 40 miles W of Asheville.
Opened: 1963. **Holes:** 18. **Par:** 72/73. **Yards:** 6,336/5,195. **Course rating:** 69.8/69.4. **Slope:** 121/117. **Architect:** Bill Prevost. **Green fee:** $15/$33. **Credit cards:** All major. **Reduced fees:** Weekdays, low season, twilight, juniors. **Caddies:** No. **Golf carts:** $14. **Discount golf packages:** Yes. **Season:** Year-round. **High:** March-Nov. **On site lodging:** Yes. **Rental clubs:** Yes. **Walking policy:** Walking at certain times. **Metal spikes allowed:** Yes. **Range:** Yes (grass/mats). **To obtain tee times:** Call one day in advance.
Subscriber comments: Fine mountain resort...Beautiful location...Undulating greens, great layout, cordial atmosphere...Majestic, challenging, great views...Don't try to walk back nine...The food and service was superb...Caters to the 65+ crowd...Busy.

★★MAGNOLIA COUNTRY CLUB
171 Magnolia Country Club Lane, Magnolia, 28453, Duplin County, (910)289-2126, 40 miles N of Wilmington.
Opened: 1974. **Holes:** 18. **Par:** 71/71. **Yards:** 6,400/4,600. **Course rating:** 69.8/68.3. **Slope:** 116/109. **Architect:** J.P. Smith/Doug Smith. **Green fee:** $8/$14. **Credit cards:** None. **Reduced fees:** Weekdays, resort guests, twilight, seniors, juniors. **Caddies:** No. **Golf carts:** $9. **Discount golf packages:** No. **Season:** Year-round. **High:** June-Aug. **On site lodging:** No. **Rental clubs:** Yes. **Walking policy:** Unrestricted walking. **Metal spikes allowed:** Yes. **Range:** No. **To obtain tee times:** Call for weekend tee times only.

★★½MALLARD HEAD COUNTRY CLUB
P.O. Box 480, Mooresville, 28115, Iredell County, (704)664-7031, 25 miles N of Charlotte.
Opened: 1979. **Holes:** 18. **Par:** 72/72. **Yards:** 6,904/5,469. **Course rating:** 72.8/70.5. **Slope:** 121/121. **Architect:** J. Porter Gibson. **Green fee:** $15/$20. **Credit cards:** MC,VISA. **Reduced fees:** N/A. **Caddies:** No. **Golf carts:** $9. **Discount golf packages:** No. **Season:** Year-round. **High:** April-Oct. **On site lodging:** No. **Rental clubs:** Yes. **Walking policy:** Walking at certain times. **Metal spikes allowed:** Yes. **Range:** Yes (grass). **To obtain tee times:** Call Thursday morning for weekends and holidays; anytime for weekdays.
Subscriber comments: Excellent local course, fun for all...Fun to play...Great greens...Great people...Tight pin placements.

★★★½MARSH HARBOUR GOLF LINKS
PU-Hwy. 179, Calabash, 28467, Brunswick County, (910)579-3161, (800)377-2315.
Opened: 1980. **Holes:** 18. **Par:** 71/71. **Yards:** 6,690/4,795. **Course rating:** 72.4/67.7.
Slope: 134/115. **Architect:** Dan Maples. **Green fee:** $30/$75. **Credit cards:**
MC,VISA,AMEX. **Reduced fees:** Low season, resort guests. **Caddies:** No. **Golf carts:**
$18. **Discount golf packages:** Yes. **Season:** Year-round. **High:** March-April/Oct. **On
site lodging:** No. **Rental clubs:** Yes. **Walking policy:** Mandatory cart. **Metal spikes
allowed:** Yes. **Range:** Yes (grass). **To obtain tee times:** Call up to nine months in
advance. Deposit required during high season.
Subscriber comments: Take a camera...Very good course...A lot of marsh, tough
course...Fun course, some of the best par 5s I have played...7, 8, 9, 16, 17, 18 some of
the finest holes anywhere...Great service! Fine fun at a beautiful course...Must play.

MEADOWLANDS GOLF CLUB
R-P.O. Box 4159 - Calabash Rd. NW, Calabash, 28467, Brunswick County, (910)287-
7529, (888)287-7529, 21 miles N of Myrtle Beach, SC.
Opened: 1997. **Holes:** 18. **Par:** 72/72. **Yards:** 7,110/4,947. **Course rating:** N/A. **Slope:**
N/A. **Architect:** Willard Byrd. **Green fee:** $29/$75. **Credit cards:** MC,VISA,DISC.
Reduced fees: Low season, resort guests, twilight, juniors. **Caddies:** No. **Golf carts:**
$18. **Discount golf packages:** No. **Season:** Year-round. **High:** March-April; Oct. **On
site lodging:** No. **Rental clubs:** Yes. **Walking policy:** Walking at certain times. **Metal
spikes allowed:** Yes. **Range:** Yes (grass). **To obtain tee times:** Call golf shop.

★★★½MEADOWLANDS GOLF COURSE
PU-582 Motsinger Rd., Winston-Salem, 27107, Davidson County, (910)769-1011.
Opened: 1995. **Holes:** 18. **Par:** 72/72. **Yards:** 6,706/4,745. **Course rating:** 71.8/67.1.
Slope: 123/114. **Architect:** Hale Irwin and Stan Gentry. **Green fee:** $36/$40. **Credit
cards:** MC,VISA,AMEX. **Reduced fees:** Weekdays, seniors, juniors. **Caddies:** No. **Golf
carts:** Included in Green Fee. **Discount golf packages:** No. **Season:** Year-round.
High: April-Oct. **On site lodging:** No. **Rental clubs:** Yes. **Walking policy:** Walking at
certain times. **Metal spikes allowed:** Yes. **Range:** Yes (grass). **To obtain tee times:**
Call golf shop.
Subscriber comments: Very nice experience...Good layout. No expense
spared...Feels like the mountains...Has matured rapidly...Limited play...Loved it. Best
around here...Narrow fairways.

★★★½THE MEMBERS CLUB AT ST. JAMES PLANTATION
PU-3779 Members Club Blvd. #160, Southport, 28461, Brunswick County, (910)253-
9500, (800)474-9277, 28 miles SE of Wilmington.
Opened: 1996. **Holes:** 18. **Par:** 72/72. **Yards:** 6,887/5,206. **Course rating:** 73.5/70.5.
Slope: 127/121. **Architect:** Hale Irwin. **Green fee:** $38/$83. **Credit cards:** MC,VISA.
Reduced fees: Low season, juniors. **Caddies:** No. **Golf carts:** Included in Green Fee.
Discount golf packages: No. **Season:** Year-round. **High:** Feb.-May. **On site lodging:**
No. **Rental clubs:** Yes. **Walking policy:** Mandatory cart. **Metal spikes allowed:** No.
Range: Yes (grass). **To obtain tee times:** Call golf shop.
Subscriber comments: Widest fairways on east coast, large fast greens...Plan your
shots...Irwin was king to high handicappers...Nice layout...Most beautiful mountain
greens, excellent...Should be premier course when mature, challenging for all.

★★★½MID PINES GOLF CLUB
R-1010 Midland Rd., Southern Pines, 28387, Moore County, (910)692-9362, (800)323-
2114, 70 miles S of Raleigh.
Opened: 1921. **Holes:** 18. **Par:** 72/75. **Yards:** 6,515/5,592. **Course rating:** 71.4/72.3.
Slope: 127/128. **Architect:** Donald Ross. **Green fee:** $49/$120. **Credit cards:**
MC,VISA,AMEX. **Reduced fees:** Low season, resort guests, twilight. **Caddies:** No.
Golf carts: Included in Green Fee. **Discount golf packages:** Yes. **Season:** Year-round.
High: March-May; Sept.-Oct. **On site lodging:** Yes. **Rental clubs:** Yes. **Walking policy:**
Unrestricted walking. **Metal spikes allowed:** No. **Range:** Yes (grass). **To obtain tee
times:** Call in advance.
Subscriber comments: Quaint, beautiful...Joy to play...We were made to feel wel-
come, fun...Golf, service and people made my stay outstanding...Stately Carolina pines,
memorable experience...Approach to 18 is a visual joy.

★★★½MILL CREEK GOLF CLUB

PU-1700 St. Andrews Dr., Mebane, 27302, Alamance County, (919)563-4653, 20 miles W of Durham.
Opened: 1995. **Holes:** 18. **Par:** 72/72. **Yards:** 7,004/4,884. **Course rating:** 73.7/67.5. **Slope:** 141/113. **Architect:** Rick Robbins and Gary Koch. **Green fee:** $22/$30. **Credit cards:** All major. **Reduced fees:** Weekdays, low season, twilight, seniors, juniors. **Caddies:** No. **Golf carts:** $12. **Discount golf packages:** No. **Season:** Year-round. **High:** April-Oct. **On site lodging:** No. **Rental clubs:** Yes. **Walking policy:** Unrestricted walking. **Metal spikes allowed:** Yes. **Range:** Yes (grass). **To obtain tee times:** Call up to 7 days in advance.
Notes: Ranked 6th in 1996 Best New Affordable Courses.
Subscriber comments: One of best courses in NC...Friendly staff...Good practice range...Hilly, nice and pretty...Very fine layout. Good shape...US Open rough, scenic...Keep it in fairway!...Another must play on I-85 corridor from Greensboro/Raleigh...Nice layout, long and plays tough from the tips.

★★½MONROE COUNTRY CLUB

PM-Hwy. 601-S., Monroe, 28110, Union County, (704)282-4661, 20 miles SE of Charlotte.
Opened: 1936. **Holes:** 18. **Par:** 72/73. **Yards:** 6,759/4,964. **Course rating:** 71.8/68.6. **Slope:** 118/117. **Architect:** Donald Ross/Tom Jackson. **Green fee:** $13/$18. **Credit cards:** MC,VISA. **Reduced fees:** Weekdays, low season, seniors. **Caddies:** No. **Golf carts:** $10. **Discount golf packages:** No. **Season:** Year-round. **High:** May-Aug. **On site lodging:** No. **Rental clubs:** Yes. **Walking policy:** Walking at certain times. **Metal spikes allowed:** Yes. **Range:** Yes (grass). **To obtain tee times:** Call up to 5 days in advance.
Subscriber comments: Views unbelievable, course fair...Sand traps need work...Caters to seniors...Back nine a little known Donald Ross design.

★★MOORESVILLE GOLF COURSE

PM-W. Wilson Rd., Mooresville, 28115, Iredell County, (704)663-2539, 25 miles N of Charlotte.
Opened: 1963. **Holes:** 18. **Par:** 72/72. **Yards:** 6,528/4,976. **Course rating:** 72.5/68.6. **Slope:** 124/115. **Architect:** Donald Ross/J. Porter Gibson. **Green fee:** $10/$14. **Credit cards:** MC,VISA. **Reduced fees:** Seniors, juniors. **Caddies:** No. **Golf carts:** $11. **Discount golf packages:** No. **Season:** Year-round. **High:** April-Nov. **On site lodging:** No. **Rental clubs:** Yes. **Walking policy:** Walking at certain times. **Metal spikes allowed:** Yes. **Range:** Yes (grass). **To obtain tee times:** Call 24 hours in advance for weekdays and one week in advance for weekends and holidays.

★★½MOREHEAD CITY COUNTRY CLUB

Country Club Rd., Morehead City, 28557, Carteret County, (919)726-4917.
Architect: C.C. McCurston and Philip Ball. **Caddies:** No. **Discount golf packages:** No. **On site lodging:** No. **Rental clubs:** No. **Metal spikes allowed:** Yes. **Range:** No.
Call club for further information.
Subscriber comments: Fun course, excellent tournaments...No frills, no water, open. Don't need course management...Nice old course, liked it so much we purchased a homesite here.

★★★★MOUNT MITCHELL GOLF CLUB

PU-7590 Hwy. 80 S., Burnsville, 28714, Yancey County, (704)675-5454, 55 miles NE of Asheville.
Opened: 1975. **Holes:** 18. **Par:** 72/72. **Yards:** 6,475/5,455. **Course rating:** 70.0/69.5. **Slope:** 121/117. **Architect:** Fred Hawtree. **Green fee:** $30/$49. **Credit cards:** MC,VISA. **Reduced fees:** Weekdays, low season, resort guests. **Caddies:** No. **Golf carts:** Included in Green Fee. **Discount golf packages:** Yes. **Season:** April-Nov. **High:** May-Oct. **On site lodging:** Yes. **Rental clubs:** Yes. **Walking policy:** Walking at certain times. **Metal spikes allowed:** Yes. **Range:** No. **To obtain tee times:** Call two weeks in advance. You must guarantee with credit card during times of heavy play.
Subscriber comments: Belongs in first rank of American public courses...Wonderful setting for golf. First class, a must play...Mixture of flat and hilly holes...Challenging but playable for all.

★★★MOUNTAIN AIRE GOLF CLUB
PU-1104 Golf Course Rd., West Jefferson, 28694, Ashe County, (910)877-4716.
Opened: 1950. **Holes:** 18. **Par:** 71/71. **Yards:** 6,107/4,143. **Course rating:** 68.5/62.3.
Slope: 118/97. **Architect:** N/A. **Green fee:** $12/$20. **Credit cards:** MC,VISA. **Reduced fees:** Weekdays, low season, twilight, juniors. **Caddies:** No. **Golf carts:** $10. **Discount golf packages:** Yes. **Season:** March-Nov. **High:** June-Aug. **On site lodging:** Yes. **Rental clubs:** Yes. **Walking policy:** Unrestricted walking. **Metal spikes allowed:** Yes. **Range:** Yes (grass). **To obtain tee times:** Call golf shop.
Subscriber comments: Beautiful scenery, not one level lie...Good condition, fair, fun course...Great staff...Uncrowded. Changing three holes...Requires all the golf shots, well maintained...Truly mountain golf, nice average course.

★★★½MOUNTAIN GLEN GOLF CLUB
Box 326, Newland, 28657, Avery County, (704)733-5804.
Architect: George W. Cobb. **Caddies:** No. **Discount golf packages:** No. **On site lodging:** No. **Rental clubs:** No. **Metal spikes allowed:** Yes. **Range:** No.
Call club for further information.
Subscriber comments: Great mountain course, very scenic, well groomed...Very nice, course flows well, mature bent greens, friendly staff...Fun course, good views...Too crowded...Beautiful mountain setting, fast greens...Tough back-nine holes, beautiful scenery...Front side/back side two different courses.

★★★½NAGS HEAD GOLF LINKS
R-5615 S. Seachase Dr., Nags Head, 27959, Dare County, (919)441-8073, (800)851-9404, 75 miles S of Virginia Beach, VA.
Opened: 1987. **Holes:** 18. **Par:** 71/71. **Yards:** 6,200/5,800. **Course rating:** 68.8/66.9.
Slope: 130/126. **Architect:** Bob Moore. **Green fee:** $25/$75. **Credit cards:** MC,VISA.
Reduced fees: Low season, resort guests, twilight, seniors, juniors. **Caddies:** No. **Golf carts:** Included in Green Fee. **Discount golf packages:** Yes. **Season:** Year-round.
High: June-Aug. **On site lodging:** Yes. **Rental clubs:** Yes. **Walking policy:** Mandatory cart. **Metal spikes allowed:** Yes. **Range:** Yes (grass/mats). **To obtain tee times:** Call golf shop up to one year in advance.
Subscriber comments: Fun seaside course, a mix of holes...Links-style course, must play if in the Outer Banks...Many blind tee shots, holes on sound are perfect...If wind blows, it will eat your lunch.
Special Notes: Spikeless encouraged.

★★★½THE NEUSE GOLF CLUB
918 Birkdale Dr., Clayton, 27520, Johnston County, (919)550-0550.
Opened: 1993. **Holes:** 18. **Par:** 72/72. **Yards:** 7,010/5,478. **Course rating:** 73.5/72.2.
Slope: 136/126. **Architect:** John LaFoy. **Green fee:** $20/$27. **Credit cards:** MC,VISA.
Reduced fees: Weekdays, low season, twilight, seniors, juniors. **Caddies:** No. **Golf carts:** $13. **Discount golf packages:** No. **Season:** Year-round. **High:** April-Oct. **On site lodging:** No. **Rental clubs:** Yes. **Walking policy:** Walking at certain times. **Metal spikes allowed:** Yes. **Range:** Yes (grass). **To obtain tee times:** Call golf shop.
Subscriber comments: Plays like mountain course...Target course, fun...Unbelievable terrain from a flat state! Great scenery!...Friendliest rangers...Outstanding back nine...Beautiful setting, tight fairways.

★★★★NORTH SHORE COUNTRY CLUB
101 N. Shore Dr., Sneads Ferry, 28460, Onslow County, (910)327-2410, (800)828-5035, 25 miles N of Wilmington.
Opened: 1988. **Holes:** 18. **Par:** 72/72. **Yards:** 6,866/5,039. **Course rating:** 72.8/68.7.
Slope: 134/122. **Architect:** Bob Moore. **Green fee:** $24/$47. **Credit cards:** MC,VISA.
Reduced fees: Weekdays, low season, twilight, juniors. **Caddies:** No. **Golf carts:** Included in Green Fee. **Discount golf packages:** Yes. **Season:** Year-round. **High:** March-Nov. **On site lodging:** No. **Rental clubs:** Yes. **Walking policy:** Mandatory cart. **Metal spikes allowed:** Yes. **Range:** Yes (grass). **To obtain tee times:** Call up to one year in advance.
Subscriber comments: Nice par 3s, watch out for alligators...Favorite course in NC...A challenge with a view...Beautiful course, excellent shape...Not crowded...Waterfowl are abundant, winding fairways, beautiful.

★★★½OAK HOLLOW GOLF COURSE

PM-3400 N. Centennial St., High Point, 27265, Guilford County, (910)883-3260, 8 miles S of Greensboro.
Opened: 1972. **Holes:** 18. **Par:** 72/72. **Yards:** 6,483/4,796. **Course rating:** 71.6/67.4. **Slope:** 124/114. **Architect:** Pete Dye. **Green fee:** $13/$16. **Credit cards:** None. **Reduced fees:** Seniors, juniors. **Caddies:** No. **Golf carts:** $10. **Discount golf packages:** No. **Season:** Year-round. **High:** April-Aug. **On site lodging:** No. **Rental clubs:** Yes. **Walking policy:** Walking at certain times. **Metal spikes allowed:** Yes. **Range:** Yes (grass/mats). **To obtain tee times:** Call 48 hours in advance for weekdays. Call Thursday for upcoming weekend.
Subscriber comments: Long and challenging from back tees, very friendly, post low scores, beautiful lakefront course, greens and fairways excellent...Very fun course, very scenic...You must place your shots!...They don't take credit cards for green fees.

★★½OAK ISLAND GOLF & COUNTRY CLUB

PU-928 Caswell Beach Rd., Oak Island, 28465, Brunswick County, (910)278-5275, 23 miles from Wilmington.
Opened: N/A. **Holes:** 18. **Par:** 72/72. **Yards:** 6,608/5,437. **Course rating:** N/A. **Slope:** 128/121. **Architect:** George Cobb. **Green fee:** N/A. **Credit cards:** MC,VISA. **Reduced fees:** Weekdays, low season. **Caddies:** No. **Golf carts:** N/A. **Discount golf packages:** Yes. **Season:** Year-round. **High:** June-Oct. **On site lodging:** No. **Rental clubs:** No. **Walking policy:** N/A. **Metal spikes allowed:** Yes. **Range:** Yes (grass). **To obtain tee times:** N/A.
Subscriber comments: I learned how to play in a wind tunnel...Off ocean, always windy...Good course, greens are slow...Locals' course. You get your money's worth...Fairly short, sneaky tough.

★★★½OAK VALLEY GOLF CLUB

261 Oak Valley Blvd., Advance, 27006, Davie County, (910)940-2000, 10 miles W of Winston-Salem.
Opened: 1995. **Holes:** 18. **Par:** 72/72. **Yards:** 7,058/5,197. **Course rating:** 74.0/68.0. **Slope:** 134/115. **Architect:** Arnold Palmer and Ed Seay. **Green fee:** $26/$41. **Credit cards:** N/A. **Reduced fees:** N/A. **Caddies:** No. **Golf carts:** N/A. **Discount golf packages:** No. **Season:** N/A. **High:** N/A. **On site lodging:** No. **Rental clubs:** No. **Walking policy:** N/A. **Metal spikes allowed:** Yes. **Range:** No. **To obtain tee times:** N/A.
Subscriber comments: Scenic, hilly, Palmer standards...Tough par 4s...Long from blues, dry county...Will be great course when develops.

★★OAKWOOD HILLS GOLF CLUB

R-U.S. Highway #1 S., Pinebluff, 28373, Moore County, (910)281-3169, 12 miles S of Pinehurst.
Opened: 1972. **Holes:** 18. **Par:** 72/70. **Yards:** 6,583/4,677. **Course rating:** 71.8/66.0. **Slope:** 127/103. **Architect:** Frank Hicks. **Green fee:** $15/$15. **Credit cards:** MC,VISA. **Reduced fees:** Low season, resort guests. **Caddies:** No. **Golf carts:** $20. **Discount golf packages:** Yes. **Season:** Year-round. **High:** March/May-Oct./Dec. **On site lodging:** Yes. **Rental clubs:** Yes. **Walking policy:** Walking at certain times. **Metal spikes allowed:** Yes. **Range:** Yes (grass). **To obtain tee times:** Call golf shop up to five months in advance.

★★★OCEAN HARBOUR GOLF LINKS

PU-Ocean Harbour Golf Dr., Calabash, 28467, Brunswick County, (803)448-8398.
Holes: 18. **Architect:** Clyde Johnston. **Caddies:** No. **Discount golf packages:** No. **On site lodging:** No. **Rental clubs:** No. **Metal spikes allowed:** Yes. **Range:** No. Call club for further information.
Subscriber comments: Many choices on tee boxes...Good course, friendly people, lovely setting and atmosphere...Plenty of water, long par 5s...Tough for beginners...Uncrowded...Challenging, shotmaker's course...Well designed course, tough...Par 3s are similar lengths...Awe-inspiring marsh holes.

★★½OCEAN ISLE BEACH GOLF COURSE
6000 Pro Shop Dr., S.W., Ocean Isle Beach, 28470, Brunswick County, (910)579-2610, 30 miles N of Myrtle Beach, SC.
Opened: 1977. **Holes:** 18. **Par:** 72/72. **Yards:** 6,626/5,075. **Course rating:** 71.8/69.5. **Slope:** 132/111. **Architect:** Russell Breeden and Dan Breeden. **Green fee:** $10/$30. **Credit cards:** All major. **Reduced fees:** Weekdays, low season, twilight, juniors. **Caddies:** No. **Golf carts:** $18. **Discount golf packages:** Yes. **Season:** Year-round. **High:** March/May-Sept./Nov. **On site lodging:** No. **Rental clubs:** Yes. **Walking policy:** Walking at certain times. **Metal spikes allowed:** Yes. **Range:** Yes (grass). **To obtain tee times:** Call golf shop.
Subscriber comments: Great walking beach course...Flat but interesting...Good course for higher handicappers...Nice course moderate skill needed.

OCEAN RIDGE PLANTATION
PU- **Credit cards:** All major. **Reduced fees:** Weekdays, low season, resort guests, juniors. **Caddies:** No. **Golf carts:** $19. **Discount golf packages:** Yes. **Season:** Year-round. **High:** Spring/Fall. **On site lodging:** No. **Rental clubs:** Yes. **Walking policy:** Mandatory cart. **Metal spikes allowed:** Yes. **Range:** Yes (grass). **To obtain tee times:** Golf packages or call golf shop.

★★★½LION'S PAW GOLF LINKS
351 Ocean Ridge Pkwy., Sunset Beach, 28469, Brunswick County, (910)287-1717, (800)233-1801, 9 miles N of North Myrtle Beach, SC.
Opened: 1991. **Holes:** 18. **Par:** 72/72. **Yards:** 7,003/5,363. **Course rating:** 74.6/69.1. **Slope:** 138/118. **Architect:** Willard Byrd. **Green fee:** $20/$50.
Subscriber comments: Front nine conventional, back British...Good course design, good condition...Helpful personnel...Lack of trees replaced with sand and water...Fun course, let it fly. Lots of moguls. You don't need to be a shotmaker.

★★★½PANTHER'S RUN GOLF CLUB
351 Ocean Ridge Pkwy. S.W., Sunset Beach, 28469, Brunswick County, (910)287-1703, (800)233-1801, 9 miles N of North Myrtle Beach, SC.
Opened: 1995. **Holes:** 18. **Par:** 72/73. **Yards:** 7,086/5,023. **Course rating:** 74.8/68.8. **Slope:** 140/116. **Architect:** Tim Cate. **Green fee:** $28/$63.
Subscriber comments: A fun "flatland" course...Would play over and over...Every bit as good as Lion's Paw...Not your typical beach course...Watch out if it's windy.

★★★½OLDE BEAU GOLF CLUB AT ROARING GAP
Hwy. 21, Roaring Gap, 28668, Alleghany County, (910)363-3044, (800)752-1634, 60 miles NW of Winston-Salem.
Opened: 1991. **Holes:** 18. **Par:** 72/75. **Yards:** 6,705/4,912. **Course rating:** 71.2/67.5. **Slope:** 131/118. **Architect:** Billy Satterfield. **Green fee:** $50/$65. **Credit cards:** N/A. **Reduced fees:** N/A. **Caddies:** No. **Golf carts:** $13. **Discount golf packages:** No. **Season:** March-Dec. **High:** July; Oct. **On site lodging:** No. **Rental clubs:** Yes. **Walking policy:** Mandatory cart. **Metal spikes allowed:** Yes. **Range:** Yes (grass). **To obtain tee times:** Call up to 14 days in advance.
Subscriber comments: Excellent mountain course...Awesome, wow...Great views, pack your parachute for 17th...Great view on every hole...Target golf...Some wacky holes but great scenery...Blind shots...Never crowded...Take your camera...Tough.

OLDE FORT GOLF CLUB
PU-3189 River Rd. SE, Winnabow, 28479, Brunswick County, (910)371-9940, 12 miles S of Wilmington.
Opened: 1985. **Holes:** 18. **Par:** 72/72. **Yards:** 6,311/4,580. **Course rating:** N/A. **Slope:** N/A. **Architect:** N/A. **Green fee:** $13/$20. **Credit cards:** N/A. **Reduced fees:** Weekdays, low season, resort guests, twilight, seniors, juniors. **Caddies:** No. **Golf carts:** Included in Green Fee. **Discount golf packages:** No. **Season:** Year-round. **High:** March-Nov. **On site lodging:** No. **Rental clubs:** No. **Walking policy:** Unrestricted walking. **Metal spikes allowed:** No. **Range:** No. **To obtain tee times:** First come, first served.

★★★OLDE POINT COUNTRY CLUB
Country Club Dr. & Hwy. 17, N., Hampstead, 28443, Pender County, (910)270-2403, 18 miles N of Wilmington.

Opened: 1974. **Holes:** 18. **Par:** 72/72. **Yards:** 6,913/5,133. **Course rating:** 72.5/69.0. **Slope:** 136/115. **Architect:** Jerry Turner. **Green fee:** $25/$45. **Credit cards:** MC,VISA,AMEX. **Reduced fees:** Weekdays, low season. **Caddies:** No. **Golf carts:** Included in Green Fee. **Discount golf packages:** Yes. **Season:** Year-round. **High:** March-May. **On site lodging:** Yes. **Rental clubs:** Yes. **Walking policy:** Mandatory cart. **Metal spikes allowed:** Yes. **Range:** Yes (grass). **To obtain tee times:** Call golf shop in advance.
Notes: TPC Tour Players 1987.
Subscriber comments: Challenging course, variable layout...Still the #1 hotdogs in the country...11th one of the hardest par 5s around...Some great holes.

★★★½OYSTER BAY GOLF LINKS
PU-Hwy. 179, Sunset Beach, 28468, Brunswick County, (910)579-7391, (800)377-2315, 18 miles N of Myrtle Beach, SC.
Opened: 1983. **Holes:** 18. **Par:** 71/71. **Yards:** 6,785/4,825. **Course rating:** 74.1/67.7. **Slope:** 137/117. **Architect:** Dan Maples. **Green fee:** $30/$75. **Credit cards:** MC,VISA,AMEX. **Reduced fees:** Low season, resort guests. **Caddies:** No. **Golf carts:** $18. **Discount golf packages:** Yes. **Season:** Year-round. **High:** March/April/Oct. **On site lodging:** No. **Rental clubs:** Yes. **Walking policy:** Mandatory cart. **Metal spikes allowed:** Yes. **Range:** Yes (grass). **To obtain tee times:** Call up to nine months in advance. Deposit required during high season. Reservations available for all six Legends Group courses and Legends Resorts.
Subscriber comments: Another top 5 favorite course. Has it all, views of marshlands, great mix of holes. You won't forget 13!...Great hotdog bar...Combines risk with reward...Great yardage book...Loved all the water, heather, great condition, entrance nice...Wicked first four holes...Par 3s are super...Beautiful view from 18 green.

★★PAWTUCKET GOLF CLUB
1 Pawtucket Rd., Charlotte, 28214, Mecklenburg County, (704)394-5909.
Architect: Russell Breeden. **Caddies:** No. **Discount golf packages:** No. **On site lodging:** No. **Rental clubs:** No. **Metal spikes allowed:** Yes. **Range:** No.
Call club for further information.

PEARL GOLF LINKS
PU-1300 Pearl Blvd. S.W., Sunset Beach, 28468, Brunswick County, (910)579-8132, 10 miles N of Myrtle Beach, S.C.
Opened: 1987. **Architect:** Dan Maples. **Credit cards:** All major. **Reduced fees:** Twilight, juniors. **Caddies:** No. **Golf carts:** Included in Green Fee. **Discount golf packages:** No. **Season:** Year-round. **High:** Spring/Fall. **On site lodging:** No. **Rental clubs:** Yes. **Walking policy:** Mandatory cart. **Metal spikes allowed:** Yes. **Range:** Yes (grass). **To obtain tee times:** Call golf shop.
★★★½EAST COURSE
Holes: 18. **Par:** 72/72. **Yards:** 6,749/5,125. **Course rating:** 73.1/73.9. **Slope:** 135/129. **Green fee:** $35/$69.
Subscriber comments: Excellent finishing holes...Beautiful, great place to play. This is a must!...Scenic course, wildlife aplenty...Great greens, good golf experience...Couple of holes on Intracoastal Waterway...Trees are more mature than most...Several interesting holes...Better condition than sister course.
★★★½WEST COURSE
Holes: 18. **Par:** 72/72. **Yards:** 7,000/5,188. **Course rating:** 73.2/73.4. **Slope:** 132/127. **Green fee:** $31/$69.
Subscriber comments: Tougher than East Course...Better bring your "A" game...Great par 5s...14-18 are tough as any...Fair and challenging for all...Good layout, fun.

★½PINE GROVE GOLF CLUB
PU-1108 Costner Rd., Shelby, 28150, Cleveland County, (704)487-0455,.
Opened: 1960. **Holes:** 18. **Par:** 70/70. **Yards:** 6,238/4,774. **Course rating:** 67.9/63.5. **Slope:** 110/100. **Architect:** P.J. Smith. **Green fee:** $7/$13. **Credit cards:** N/A. **Reduced fees:** Weekdays, seniors. **Caddies:** No. **Golf carts:** $12. **Discount golf packages:** No. **Season:** Year-round. **High:** June-Aug. **On site lodging:** No. **Rental clubs:** No. **Walking policy:** Walking at certain times. **Metal spikes allowed:** Yes. **Range:** No. **To obtain tee times:** Call for weekends and holidays.
Subscriber comments: Not many traps...Small course, good for the beginner.

★★½PINE KNOLLS GOLF CLUB
PU-1100 Quail Hollow Rd., Kernersville, 27284, Forsyth County, (910)993-8300, 9 miles NE of Winston Salem.
Opened: 1969. **Holes:** 18. **Par:** 72/72. **Yards:** 6,287/4,480. **Course rating:** 70.0/65.0. **Slope:** 121/92. **Architect:** Clyde Holder. **Green fee:** $15/$19. **Credit cards:** MC,VISA. **Reduced fees:** Weekdays, low season, twilight, seniors, juniors. **Caddies:** No. **Golf carts:** $12. **Discount golf packages:** Yes. **Season:** Year-round. **High:** May-Oct. **On site lodging:** No. **Rental clubs:** Yes. **Walking policy:** Walking at certain times. **Metal spikes allowed:** Yes. **Range:** Yes (grass/mats). **To obtain tee times:** Call up to 7 days in advance.
Subscriber comments: The layout is bad, conditions OK...Turtle-back greens...Large greens...New owners. Trying to improve design and condition.

★★★★PINE NEEDLES LODGE & GOLF CLUB
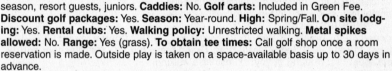

R-1005 Midland Rd, Southern Pines, 28387, Moore County, (910)692-8611, (800)747-7272, 70 miles S of Raleigh.
Opened: 1927. **Holes:** 18. **Par:** 71/71. **Yards:** 6,708/5,039. **Course rating:** 72.2/68.4. **Slope:** 131/118. **Architect:** Donald Ross. **Green fee:** $75/$135. **Credit cards:** MC,VISA,AMEX. **Reduced fees:** Low season, resort guests, juniors. **Caddies:** No. **Golf carts:** Included in Green Fee. **Discount golf packages:** Yes. **Season:** Year-round. **High:** Spring/Fall. **On site lodging:** Yes. **Rental clubs:** Yes. **Walking policy:** Unrestricted walking. **Metal spikes allowed:** No. **Range:** Yes (grass). **To obtain tee times:** Call golf shop once a room reservation is made. Outside play is taken on a space-available basis up to 30 days in advance.
Notes: 1996 U.S. Women's Open Championship.
Subscriber comments: The kind of course you could play every day and not get tired of. Don't overlook this course when you visit Pinehurst...Great food and lodging!!...A classic. Great! Attractive scenery...Peggy Kirk Bell and family are gracious custodians of Donald's treasure...Best practice area for solitude.

★★PINE TREE GOLF CLUB
PU-1680 Pine Tree Lane, Kernersville, 27284, Forsyth County, (910)993-5598, 10 miles W of Greensboro.
Opened: 1970. **Holes:** 18. **Par:** 71/71. **Yards:** 6,604/4,897. **Course rating:** 71.0/67.0. **Slope:** 113/110. **Architect:** Gene Hamm. **Green fee:** $15/$19. **Credit cards:** MC,VISA. **Reduced fees:** Seniors. **Caddies:** No. **Golf carts:** $11. **Discount golf packages:** No. **Season:** Year-round. **High:** April-Oct. **On site lodging:** No. **Rental clubs:** Yes. **Walking policy:** Walking at certain times. **Metal spikes allowed:** Yes. **Range:** Yes (grass). **To obtain tee times:** Call up to 10 days in advance.

★★★½PINEHURST PLANTATION GOLF CLUB
Midland Rd., Pinehurst, 28374, Moore County, (910)695-3193, (800)633-2685, 50 miles SW of Raleigh.
Opened: 1993. **Holes:** 18. **Par:** 72/72. **Yards:** 7,135/5,046. **Course rating:** 74.5/68.8. **Slope:** 140/125. **Architect:** Arnold Palmer and Ed Seay. **Green fee:** $60/$115. **Credit cards:** MC,VISA,AMEX. **Reduced fees:** N/A. **Caddies:** No. **Golf carts:** Included in Green Fee. **Discount golf packages:** No. **Season:** Year-round. **High:** April-May/Oct. **On site lodging:** No. **Rental clubs:** Yes. **Walking policy:** Mandatory cart. **Metal spikes allowed:** Yes. **Range:** Yes (grass). **To obtain tee times:** Have head pro set up a tee time or call golf shop out of season.
Notes: Ranked 19th in 1997 Best in State.
Subscriber comments: Interesting holes, fair to seniors/ladies...Quality Pinehurst course (another)...Best in area for all skill levels...Thoroughly enjoyable!...Great layout, tough finishing holes...My favorite.

PINEHURST RESORT & COUNTRY CLUB

R- (Nos. 1-5) Carolina Vista St., Pinehurst, 28374, Moore County, (910)295-8141, (800)795-4653, 70 miles SW of Raleigh.
Credit cards: All major,Carte Blanche,Diners Club. **Reduced fees:** Low season, twilight. **Golf carts:** Included in Green Fee. **Season:** Year-round. **High:** Spring/Fall. **On site lodging:** Yes. **Rental clubs:** Yes.

Metal spikes allowed: Yes. **Range:** Yes (grass). **To obtain tee times:** Call 1-800-ITS-GOLF. You must be a resort guest to play.

★★★PINEHURST NO. 1

Opened: 1898. **Holes:** 18. **Par:** 70/73. **Yards:** 6,102/5,307. **Course rating:** 68.3/70.1. **Slope:** 117/117. **Architect:** Donald Ross. **Green fee:** $70/$110. **Caddies:** Yes. **Discount golf packages:** Yes. **Walking policy:** Unrestricted walking.

Subscriber comments: The whole facility is great with many things to do...Flat, wide, open...Great facilities, overpriced...Typical vacation golf course...Not difficult. Very historic..Like all Pinehurst courses. Always perfect.

Special Notes: Walking allowed only with a caddy.

★★★★★PINEHURST NO. 2

Opened: 1901. **Holes:** 18. **Par:** 72/74. **Yards:** 7,053/5,863. **Course rating:** 74.1/74.2. **Slope:** 131/135. **Architect:** Donald Ross. **Green fee:** $150/$190. **Caddies:** Yes. **Discount golf packages:** Yes. **Walking policy:** Unrestricted walking..

Notes: Ranked 9th in 1997-98 America's 100 Greatest; 1st in 1997 Best in State; 1991-92 Tour Championship; 1994 U.S. Senior Open; 1999 U.S. Open.

Subscriber comments: Pinehurst No. 2, what else do you need to say?...Too tough for me!...Greens fast and good, swales...As close to perfection as it gets! Play the course and know the condition of the courses on the PGA Tour!...It's golf heaven...Great golf services, excellent condition, pricey...Top of the line.

Special Notes: Walking allowed only with a caddie.

★★★PINEHURST NO. 3

Opened: 1907. **Holes:** 18. **Par:** 70/72. **Yards:** 5,662/5,199. **Course rating:** 67.2/70.1. **Slope:** 112/114. **Architect:** Donald Ross. **Green fee:** $70/$110. Yes. **Discount golf packages:** Yes. **Walking policy:** Unrestricted walking.

Subscriber comments: Tough greens, tight...Really fun...Small greens...Typical vacation golf course...#3 is a great warmup for #2. Very hard to hit greens...Short, but deadly. Crowned greens will get you...How do you describe a masterpiece?

★★★½PINEHURST NO. 4

Opened: 1914. **Holes:** 18. **Par:** 72/73. **Yards:** 6,919/5,696. **Course rating:** 73.3/71.8. **Slope:** 126/119. **Architect:** Donald Ross. **Green fee:** $70/$110. **Caddies:** Yes. **Discount golf packages:** Yes. **Walking policy:** Unrestricted walking.

Subscriber comments: An excellent overall experience, must use a caddie to get the full effect...Good course, fair but tough, last three holes tough...Quality course and amenities...As good as No. 2 for Ross lovers...Great place to go with the "boys"; No. 4 is almost as good as No. 2...A great complement to No. 2...A lot like No. 2.

★★★½PINEHURST NO. 5

Opened: 1961. **Holes:** 18. **Par:** 72/73. **Yards:** 6,827/5,658. **Course rating:** 73.4/74.7. **Slope:** 130/131. **Architect:** Ellis Maples. **Green fee:** $70/$110. **Caddies:** Yes. **Discount golf packages:** Yes. **Walking policy:** Unrestricted walking.

Subscriber comments: Some water...Least challenging of Pinehurst courses...Good course, long, challenge...Many fun shots...Tight course, keep it straight...Service very good, excellent conditions. Never disappointing...Golf at its greatest...Good value.

★★★½PINEHURST NO. 6

U.S. 15-501, Pinehurst, 28374, Moore County, (910)295-8145, (800)795-4653, 70 miles SW of Raleigh.

Opened: 1979. **Holes:** 18. **Par:** 72/72. **Yards:** 7,092/5,436. **Course rating:** 75.6/71.2. **Slope:** 139/125. **Architect:** Tom Fazio and George Fazio. **Green fee:** $70/$110. **Caddies:** No. **Discount golf packages:** Yes. **Walking policy:** Mandatory cart.

Subscriber comments: Holes 6, 7 and 8 are unbelievable...Good course, average conditions...Easier than Pinehurst No. 2 and No. 7 but a worthy track...Good course for average golfer...Probably the toughest track...Wow!...Heaven!...Could play four times a week.

★★★★PINEHURST NO. 7

U.S. 15-501, Pinehurst, 28374, Moore County, (910)295-8540, (800)795-4653, 70 miles SW of Raleigh.

Opened: 1986. **Holes:** 18. **Par:** 72/72. **Yards:** 7,125/4,996. **Course rating:** 75.6/69.4. **Slope:** 145/124. **Architect:** Rees Jones. **Green fee:** $120/$160. **Caddies:** No. **Discount golf packages:** Yes. **Walking policy:** Unrestricted walking.

Notes: Ranked 9th in 1997 Best in State.

Subscriber comments: Enjoyed as much as No. 2, beautiful scenery...Outstanding golf course, great service...Fair but challenging...Good for low handicappers...Pales in comparison to No. 2 and No. 8...Very good for the amount of play...Helps your ego after

#2 hits you...Any of the Pinehurst courses suit me just fine!

★★★★PINEHURST NO. 8
Murdocksville Rd., Pinehurst, 28374, Moore County, (910)295-8760, (800)795-4653.
Opened: 1996. **Holes:** 18. **Par:** 72/72. **Yards:** 7,092/5,177. **Course rating:** 74.0/68.9.
Slope: 135/112. **Architect:** Tom Fazio. **Green fee:** $130/$170. **Caddies:** Yes. **Discount golf packages:** No. **Walking policy:** Unrestricted walking.
Notes: Ranked 5th in 1997 Best in State; 3rd in 1996 Best New Upscale Courses. 1997 PGA Club Professional Championship.
Subscriber comments: Fazio did Pinehurst proud. Very varied design, like three courses in one...Caddies necessary (blind tee shots on front nine)...No. 2 has a twin; it's No. 8...Beautiful new clubhouse and practice area...No. 8 is becoming a much better course than No. 2...Better keep it on the fairway.
Special Notes: Spikeless encouraged at all courses.

★★★½THE PIT GOLF LINKS
PU-Highway 5 (between Pinehurst & Aberdeen), Pinehurst, 28374, Moore County, (910)944-1600, (800)574-4653, 35 miles W of Fayetteville.
Opened: 1985. **Holes:** 18. **Par:** 72/72. **Yards:** 6,600/4,759. **Course rating:** 72.3/68.4.
Slope: 139/121. **Architect:** Dan Maples. **Green fee:** $25/$70. **Credit cards:** MC,VISA.
Reduced fees: Low season, twilight, juniors. **Caddies:** No. **Golf carts:** $17. **Discount golf packages:** Yes. **Season:** Year-round. **High:** March/May-Oct. **On site lodging:** No.
Rental clubs: Yes. **Walking policy:** Unrestricted walking. **Metal spikes allowed:** Yes.
Range: Yes (grass). **To obtain tee times:** Call 800-574-4653.
Subscriber comments: Favorite Pinehurst area course...You either love it or you hate it. I love it...Challenging. Great water holes!...Sand dunes and water to contend with...A lot of potential penalty shots...When you miss a fairway you can forget par.

★★★★PORTERS NECK COUNTRY CLUB
Vintage Club Dr., Wilmington, 28405, New Hanover County, (910)686-1177, (800)947-8177, 3 miles N of Wilmington.
Opened: 1991. **Holes:** 18. **Par:** 72/72. **Yards:** 7,209/5,268. **Course rating:** 75.6/71.2.
Slope: 140/124. **Architect:** Tom Fazio. **Green fee:** $45/$75. **Credit cards:** MC,VISA,AMEX. **Reduced fees:** Weekdays, low season, resort guests, twilight.
Caddies: No. **Golf carts:** Included in Green Fee. **Discount golf packages:** Yes.
Season: Year-round. **High:** Feb.-May; Aug.-Oct. **On site lodging:** No. **Rental clubs:** Yes. **Walking policy:** Mandatory cart. **Metal spikes allowed:** No. **Range:** Yes (grass).
To obtain tee times: Call golf shop in advance.
Notes: Ranked 14th in 1997 Best in State.
Subscriber comments: Best course on coast...Great variety of holes...Worth the effort. Greens small. Tough...Very nicely laid out, a pleasure to play...Great links style course...Excellent course and people...Tough when the wind is up.

★★½QUAIL RIDGE GOLF COURSE
5634 Quail Ridge Dr., Sanford, 27330, Lee County, (919)776-6623, (800)344-6276.
Opened: 1965. **Holes:** 18. **Par:** 72/73. **Yards:** 6,875/5,280. **Course rating:** 73.2/70.8.
Slope: 125/117. **Architect:** Gene Hamm. **Green fee:** $25/$35. **Credit cards:** MC,VISA.
Reduced fees: Weekdays, low season, twilight, seniors, juniors. **Caddies:** No. **Golf carts:** Included in Green Fee. **Discount golf packages:** Yes. **Season:** Year-round.
High: Spring/Fall. **On site lodging:** Yes. **Rental clubs:** Yes. **Walking policy:** Walking at certain times. **Metal spikes allowed:** Yes. **Range:** Yes (grass/mats). **To obtain tee times:** Call golf shop.
Subscriber comments: Really improving...Great layout, somewhat tough...Dries out in summer...Hills are challenging, give course character...Great condition, friendly staff, huge greens.

★½QUAKER MEADOWS GOLF CLUB
PM-826 N. Green St., Morganton, 28655, Burke County, (704)437-2677.
Opened: N/A. **Holes:** N/A. **Par:** 71/71. **Yards:** 6,410/5,002. **Course rating:** 70.0/68.2.
Slope: 117/110. **Architect:** Russell Breeden. **Green fee:** $10/$14. **Credit cards:** N/A.
Reduced fees: N/A. **Caddies:** No. **Golf carts:** $10. **Discount golf packages:** No.
Season: Year-round. **High:** N/A. **On site lodging:** No. **Rental clubs:** No. **Walking policy:** Walking at certain times. **Metal spikes allowed:** Yes. **Range:** Yes (grass). **To obtain tee times:** Call up to 7 days in advance for weekends and holidays.

★★½QUAKER NECK COUNTRY CLUB
299 Country Club Rd., Trenton, 28585, Jones County, (919)224-5736, (800)657-5156, 10 miles S of New Bern.
Opened: 1966. **Holes:** 18. **Par:** 72/73. **Yards:** 6,405/5,080. **Course rating:** 68.0/69.0. **Slope:** 113/106. **Architect:** Russell T. Burney. **Green fee:** $10/$14. **Credit cards:** MC,VISA,DISC. **Reduced fees:** Weekdays, low season. **Caddies:** No. **Golf carts:** $11. **Discount golf packages:** Yes. **Season:** Year-round. **High:** June-Aug. **On site lodging:** No. **Rental clubs:** Yes. **Walking policy:** Unrestricted walking. **Metal spikes allowed:** Yes. **Range:** Yes (grass). **To obtain tee times:** Call golf shop.
Subscriber comments: Must stay on fairway...Nice layout...If you like playing in a natural wooded environment, this nature habitat is ideal. Situated along the edge of the Trent River and surrounded by virgin hardwoods and pines.

★★★QUARRY HILLS COUNTRY CLUB
George Bason Rd., Graham, 27253, Alamance County, (910)578-2602, 20 miles W of Chapel Hill.
Opened: 1970. **Holes:** 18. **Par:** 70/70. **Yards:** 6,617/4,905. **Course rating:** 71.9/68.0. **Slope:** 130/116. **Architect:** Ellis Maples/Ed Seay. **Green fee:** $30/$40. **Credit cards:** N/A. **Reduced fees:** N/A. **Caddies:** No. **Golf carts:** $11. **Discount golf packages:** No. **Season:** Year-round. **High:** March-Nov. **On site lodging:** No. **Rental clubs:** No. **Walking policy:** Unrestricted walking. **Metal spikes allowed:** No. **Range:** Yes (grass/mats). **To obtain tee times:** Call golf shop.
Notes: PGA Tour Qualifying Site.
Subscriber comments: Great par 3s...Hit straight at the quarry hole...Layout is great...13th hole over quarry is fun...Very nice, very challenging.

★★½REEDY CREEK GOLF COURSE
PU-585 Reedy Creek Rd., Four Oaks, 27524, Johnston County, (919)934-7502, (800)331-2572, 20 miles S of Raleigh.
Opened: 1988. **Holes:** 18. **Par:** 72/72. **Yards:** 6,426/5,179. **Course rating:** 70.5/69.0. **Slope:** 117/115. **Architect:** Gene Hamm. **Green fee:** $10/$25. **Credit cards:** MC,VISA. **Reduced fees:** Weekdays, resort guests, twilight, seniors, juniors. **Caddies:** No. **Golf carts:** $10. **Discount golf packages:** Yes. **Season:** Year-round. **High:** April-Sept. **On site lodging:** No. **Rental clubs:** Yes. **Walking policy:** Walking at certain times. **Metal spikes allowed:** Yes. **Range:** Yes (grass). **To obtain tee times:** Call golf shop at least one week in advance for your choice on weekends.
Subscriber comments: Fun course, nice people...Has improved in recent years...Designed for all players...Easy, slow greens...Great for walking and working on swing...Exceptionally friendly staff, quick Bermuda greens.

★★★½REEMS CREEK GOLF CLUB
Pink Fox Cove Rd., Weaverville, 28787, Buncombe County, (704)645-4393, (800)762-8379, 12 miles N of Asheville.
Opened: 1989. **Holes:** 18. **Par:** 72/72. **Yards:** 6,477/4,605. **Course rating:** 71.6/66.9. **Slope:** 133/114. **Architect:** Martin Hawtree. **Green fee:** $39/$44. **Credit cards:** MC,VISA. **Reduced fees:** Weekdays, low season, resort guests, juniors. **Caddies:** No. **Golf carts:** Included in Green Fee. **Discount golf packages:** Yes. **Season:** Year-round. **High:** March-Oct. **On site lodging:** No. **Rental clubs:** Yes. **Walking policy:** Mandatory cart. **Metal spikes allowed:** Yes. **Range:** Yes (grass). **To obtain tee times:** Call up to 30 days in advance. Groups larger than 24 players call six months in advance.
Subscriber comments: Premier course, magnificent views...Great condition, western NC's best...Bent from tee to green, cartpath only but worth it, some breathtaking shots...Most enjoyable after you know where the holes are...Excellent mountain course...Some tough holes...Wonderful service, nice clubhouse.

★★★REYNOLDS PARK GOLF CLUB
PM-2391 Reynolds Park Rd., Winston-Salem, 27107, Forsyth County, (910)650-7660.
Opened: 1939. **Holes:** 18. **Par:** 71/72. **Yards:** 6,350/5,538. **Course rating:** 70.0/70.0. **Slope:** 118/118. **Architect:** Ellis Maples. **Green fee:** $14/$16. **Credit cards:** MC,VISA. **Reduced fees:** Weekdays, low season, twilight, seniors, juniors. **Caddies:** No. **Golf carts:** Included in Green Fee. **Discount golf packages:** No. **Season:** Year-round. **High:** April-Sept. **On site lodging:** No. **Rental clubs:** Yes. **Walking policy:** Walking at

certain times. **Metal spikes allowed:** Yes. **Range:** Yes (grass). **To obtain tee times:** Call seven days in advance.
Subscriber comments: Don't make side bets unless you know your opponent...Condition much improved...A great test from the back tees...Greens excellent...Hit every club in my bag...Nice practice range.

★★RICHMOND PINES COUNTRY CLUB

145 Richmond Pines Dr., Rockingham, 28379, Richmond County, (910)895-3279, 50 miles E of Charlotte.
Opened: 1926. **Holes:** 18. **Par:** 72/72. **Yards:** 6,267/5,051. **Course rating:** 70.5/68.9. **Slope:** 124/119. **Architect:** Donald Ross. **Green fee:** $16/$27. **Credit cards:** MC,VISA. **Reduced fees:** N/A. **Caddies:** No. **Golf carts:** Included in Green Fee. **Discount golf packages:** No. **Season:** April-May; Aug.-Oct. **High:** N/A. **On site lodging:** No. **Rental clubs:** No. **Walking policy:** Unrestricted walking. **Metal spikes allowed:** Yes. **Range:** Yes (grass). **To obtain tee times:** Call up to 7 days in advance.

★★★RIVER BEND GOLF CLUB

PU-3005 Longwood Dr., Shelby, 28150, Cleveland County, (704)482-4286.
Opened: 1965. **Holes:** 18. **Par:** 72/72. **Yards:** 6,691/5,009. **Course rating:** 72.0/68.2. **Slope:** 132/111. **Architect:** Russell Breeden. **Green fee:** $20/$36. **Credit cards:** MC,VISA,DISC. **Reduced fees:** Weekdays, seniors, juniors. **Caddies:** No. **Golf carts:** Included in Green Fee. **Discount golf packages:** Yes. **Season:** Year-round. **High:** May-Oct. **On site lodging:** No. **Rental clubs:** Yes. **Walking policy:** Walking at certain times. **Metal spikes allowed:** Yes. **Range:** Yes (grass). **To obtain tee times:** Call golf shop one day to one week in advance.
Subscriber comments: More Yankees than NYC...Always nice shape and people are very nice...Rolling layout makes a great twilight walking course. Snack bar staff gives free refills with a smile...Fairways like carpet (best course I've played in my area).

RIVERWOOD GOLF CLUB

PU-400 Riverwood Dr., Clayton, 27520, Johnston County, (919)550-1919.
Opened: 1997. **Holes:** 18. **Par:** 72/72. **Yards:** 7,012/4,970. **Course rating:** 73.8/68.8. **Slope:** 130/115. **Architect:** David Postlethwait. **Green fee:** $20/$31. **Credit cards:** All major. **Reduced fees:** Weekdays, twilight, seniors, juniors. **Caddies:** No. **Golf carts:** $13. **Discount golf packages:** No. **Season:** Year-round. **High:** April-Sept. **On site lodging:** No. **Rental clubs:** No. **Walking policy:** Walking at certain times. **Metal spikes allowed:** Yes. **Range:** Yes (grass/mats). **To obtain tee times:** Call golf shop.

★★★ROCK BARN CLUB OF GOLF

3791 Golf Dr., Conover, 28613, Catawba County, (704)459-9279, 60 miles NW of Charlotte.
Opened: 1969. **Holes:** 27. **Par:** 72/72. **Yards:** 6,778/4,812. **Course rating:** 72.2/67.7. **Slope:** 132/117. **Architect:** Tom Jackson. **Green fee:** $31/$36. **Credit cards:** MC,VISA. **Reduced fees:** Weekdays, seniors. **Caddies:** No. **Golf carts:** $11. **Discount golf packages:** No. **Season:** Year-round. **High:** April-Oct. **On site lodging:** No. **Rental clubs:** Yes. **Walking policy:** Unrestricted walking. **Metal spikes allowed:** Yes. **Range:** Yes (grass). **To obtain tee times:** Call three days in advance.
Subscriber comments: Be sure to pull off I-40 and play this one...New nine lots of fun...27 holes, East nine different, tight fairways...Course has good variety of holes...Simple yet ample facilities...Long, hilly, difficult...A lot of fun.

★★★SANDPIPER BAY GOLF & COUNTRY CLUB

PU-800 Sandpiper Bay Dr., Sunset Beach, 28468, Brunswick County, (910)579-9120, (800)356-5827, 25 miles N of Myrtle Beach, SC.
Opened: 1987. **Holes:** 18. **Par:** 71/71. **Yards:** 6,503/4,869. **Course rating:** 71.6/68.3. **Slope:** 119/113. **Architect:** Dan Maples. **Green fee:** $14/$52. **Credit cards:** MC,DISC. **Reduced fees:** Weekdays, low season. **Caddies:** No. **Golf carts:** $18. **Discount golf packages:** Yes. **Season:** Year-round. **High:** Spring/Fall. **On site lodging:** No. **Rental clubs:** Yes. **Walking policy:** Mandatory cart. **Metal spikes allowed:** Yes. **Range:** Yes (grass). **To obtain tee times:** Call golf shop.
Subscriber comments: Real fun par 3s, nice clubhouse...Friendly people, good layout...Great course to score on, friendly staff...Women-friendly...You can score pretty good here. Fair for everyone.

NORTH CAROLINA

★★SANDY RIDGE GOLF COURSE

PU-2025 Sandy Ridge Rd., Colfax, 27235, Guilford County, (910)668-0408, 5 miles W of Greensboro.

Opened: 1970. **Holes:** 18. **Par:** 72/72. **Yards:** 6,025/5,600. **Course rating:** N/A. **Slope:** N/A. **Architect:** Gene Hamm. **Green fee:** $12/$15. **Credit cards:** MC,VISA,DISC. **Reduced fees:** Seniors. **Caddies:** No. **Golf carts:** $8. **Discount golf packages:** No. **Season:** Year-round. **High:** June-Sept. **On site lodging:** No. **Rental clubs:** No. **Walking policy:** Walking at certain times. **Metal spikes allowed:** Yes. **Range:** No. **To obtain tee times:** Call Monday before weekend wanting to play.

★★★SAPPHIRE MOUNTAIN GOLF CLUB

R-50 Slicer's Ave., Sapphire, 28774, Jackson County, (704)743-1174, 60 miles S of Asheville.

Opened: 1981. **Holes:** 18. **Par:** 70/70. **Yards:** 6,185/4,547. **Course rating:** 69.3/65.9. **Slope:** 127/114. **Architect:** Ron Garl. **Green fee:** N/A. **Credit cards:** All major. **Reduced fees:** Low season, resort guests, twilight, juniors. **Caddies:** No. **Golf carts:** Included in Green Fee. **Discount golf packages:** Yes. **Season:** May-Dec. **High:** May-Oct. **On site lodging:** Yes. **Rental clubs:** Yes. **Walking policy:** Unrestricted walking. **Metal spikes allowed:** Yes. **Range:** Yes (grass). **To obtain tee times:** N/A. **Subscriber comments:** Very scenic, challenging, wonderful people...Mountain beauty...Fast greens...Excellent varity of holes; friendly staff.

★★½SCOTHURST GOLF COURSE

Hwy. 20 E. P.O. Box 88, Lumber Bridge, 28357, Robeson County, (910)843-5357, 20 miles S of Fayetteville.

Opened: 1965. **Holes:** 18. **Par:** 72/72. **Yards:** 7,000/5,150. **Course rating:** 72.9/70.0. **Slope:** 118/111. **Architect:** Everett Nash. **Green fee:** $25/$28. **Credit cards:** N/A. **Reduced fees:** Weekdays, low season. **Caddies:** No. **Golf carts:** Included in Green Fee. **Discount golf packages:** Yes. **Season:** Year-round. **High:** March-Sept. **On site lodging:** No. **Rental clubs:** Yes. **Walking policy:** Walking at certain times. **Metal spikes allowed:** Yes. **Range:** Yes (grass). **To obtain tee times:** Call golf shop. **Subscriber comments:** Tight fairways, nice layout, some tough holes...Very good greens...Great course with very friendly people...Plays long, fairly flat.

★★★SEA SCAPE GOLF COURSE

R-300 Eckner St., Kitty Hawk, 27949, Dare County, (919)261-2158, 70 miles NE of Norfolk, VA.

Opened: 1968. **Holes:** 18. **Par:** 72/73. **Yards:** 6,409/5,536. **Course rating:** 70.4/70.9. **Slope:** 120/115. **Architect:** Art Wall. **Green fee:** $35/$60. **Credit cards:** MC,VISA. **Reduced fees:** Low season, resort guests, twilight, juniors. **Caddies:** No. **Golf carts:** Included in Green Fee. **Discount golf packages:** No. **Season:** Year-round. **High:** May-Oct. **On site lodging:** No. **Rental clubs:** Yes. **Walking policy:** Mandatory cart. **Metal spikes allowed:** Yes. **Range:** Yes (grass). **To obtain tee times:** Call anytime between 7 a.m. and 7 p.m. Reservations can be made up to one year in advance. **Subscriber comments:** Sea views, woodland holes...Good mix of holes...More links. Reminded me of Scotland...First encounter with Cayman range balls..."On the beach" can be very literal here...Hit the ball straight, score low...Fun for average golfer, forgiving on most holes...Great layout with many difficult elevations.

SEA TRAIL PLANTATION

R- **Credit cards:** All major. **Caddies:** No. **Discount golf packages:** Yes. **Season:** Year-round. **High:** March-April/Oct. **On site lodging:** Yes. **Rental clubs:** Yes. **Walking policy:** Mandatory cart. **Metal spikes allowed:** Yes. **To obtain tee times:** Call anytime.

★★★½DAN MAPLES COURSE

211 Clubhouse Rd., Sunset Beach, 28468, Brunswick County, (910)287-1125, (800)546-5748, 20 miles N of Myrtle Beach, SC.

Opened: 1985. **Holes:** 18. **Par:** 72/72. **Yards:** 6,751/5,090. **Course rating:** 71.7/68.5. **Slope:** 121/108. **Architect:** Dan Maples. **Green fee:** $22/$62. **Reduced fees:** Resort guests, juniors. **Golf carts:** $18. **Range:** Yes (grass/mats). **Subscriber comments:** Always a pleasure, very fair, no gimmicks. A must...Great pro shop...Enjoyed food and lodgings...Reachable par 5s...Highly organized. Facility is beautiful; people are extremely friendly...Easiest of the three courses but challenging.

★★★½REES JONES COURSE
211 Clubhouse Rd., Sunset Beach, 28468, Brunswick County, (910)287-1122, (800)546-5748, 20 miles N of Myrtle Beach, SC.
Opened: 1989. **Holes:** 18. **Par:** 72/72. **Yards:** 6,761/4,912. **Course rating:** 72.4/68.5. **Slope:** 132/115. **Architect:** Rees Jones. **Green fee:** $28/$67. **Reduced fees:** Low season, resort guests, juniors. **Golf carts:** $16. **Range:** Yes (grass).
Subscriber comments: Best of the three here...Just tee it up and let it rip. Very good, tough...Plays long, very long, great bent greens...Traditional course...Excellent condition and layout...You'll use every club in the bag.

★★★½WILLARD BYRD COURSE
211 Clubhouse Rd., Sunset Beach, 28468, Brunswick County, (910)287-1122, (800)546-5748, 20 miles N of Myrtle Beach, SC.
Opened: 1990. **Holes:** 18. **Par:** 72/72. **Yards:** 6,750/4,697. **Course rating:** 72.1/69.1. **Slope:** 128/121. **Architect:** Willard Byrd. **Green fee:** $22/$62. **Reduced fees:** Resort guests, juniors. **Golf carts:** $18. **Range:** Yes (grass).
Subscriber comments: Good course, but not as challenging as the Jones. Some interesting par 5s that give you some eagle possibilities...Best at Sea Trail...Loved views, water...Stayed on site, three nice courses...Pleasant layout for all skill levels.

★★★SEVEN LAKES COUNTRY CLUB
P.O. Box 686, West End, 27376, Moore County, (910)673-1092, 10 miles W of Pinehurst.
Opened: 1976. **Holes:** 18. **Par:** 72/73. **Yards:** 6,927/5,192. **Course rating:** 74.0/71.0. **Slope:** 139/124. **Architect:** Peter Tufts. **Green fee:** $30/$45. **Credit cards:** None. **Reduced fees:** Low season, juniors. **Caddies:** No. **Golf carts:** $15. **Discount golf packages:** Yes. **Season:** Year-round. **High:** Spring/Fall. **On site lodging:** Yes. **Rental clubs:** Yes. **Walking policy:** Mandatory cart. **Metal spikes allowed:** Yes. **Range:** Yes (grass). **To obtain tee times:** Call golf shop.
Subscriber comments: Outstanding. Each hole very different...Greens were fast...Good layout, good condition...Thanks to Mr. Tufts for making it accessible...Good layout, good greens...Nice, good for all levels.

★½SHAMROCK GOLF CLUB
PU-1722 Shamrock Dr., Burlington, 27215, Alamance County, (910)226-7045, (800)849-0995, 35 miles E of Greensboro.
Opened: 1952. **Holes:** 18. **Par:** 72/72. **Yards:** 6,416/5,017. **Course rating:** 69.0/67.5. **Slope:** 113/113. **Architect:** Calvin Walker. **Green fee:** $5/$8. **Credit cards:** MC,VISA. **Reduced fees:** Weekdays, low season, twilight, seniors, juniors. **Caddies:** No. **Golf carts:** Included in Green Fee. **Discount golf packages:** Yes. **Season:** Year-round. **High:** March-Oct. **On site lodging:** No. **Rental clubs:** Yes. **Walking policy:** Walking at certain times. **Metal spikes allowed:** Yes. **Range:** Yes (grass). **To obtain tee times:** Call up to one month in advance.

★★★SILVER CREEK GOLF CLUB
PU-601 Pelletier Loop Rd., Swansboro, 28584, Carteret County, (919)393-8058, 25 miles N of Jacksonville.
Opened: 1986. **Holes:** 18. **Par:** 72/72. **Yards:** 6,526/5,412. **Course rating:** 71.6/68.1. **Slope:** 117/110. **Architect:** Gene Hamm. **Green fee:** $22/$42. **Credit cards:** MC,VISA. **Reduced fees:** Low season, resort guests, seniors. **Caddies:** No. **Golf carts:** Included in Green Fee. **Discount golf packages:** Yes. **Season:** Year-round. **High:** May-Oct. **On site lodging:** No. **Rental clubs:** Yes. **Walking policy:** Walking at certain times. **Metal spikes allowed:** Yes. **Range:** Yes (grass/mats). **To obtain tee times:** Call in advance.
Subscriber comments: Water, water everywhere. Excellent...Great scenery and great holes...Old style, with elevated greens...Good drives a must.

★★★½THE SOUND GOLF LINKS AT ALBEMARLE PLANTATION
101 Clubhouse Dr., Hertford, 27944, Perquimans County, (919)426-5555, (800)535-0704, 80 miles NE of Norfolk, VA.
Opened: 1990. **Holes:** 18. **Par:** 72/72. **Yards:** 6,500/4,665. **Course rating:** 70.1/66.3. **Slope:** 125/113. **Architect:** Dan Maples. **Green fee:** $30/$35. **Credit cards:** MC,VISA. **Reduced fees:** Weekdays, twilight, juniors. **Caddies:** No. **Golf carts:** Included in Green Fee. **Discount golf packages:** No. **Season:** Year-round. **High:** April-Sept. **On site lodging:** No. **Rental clubs:** Yes. **Walking policy:** Mandatory cart. **Metal spikes**

allowed: No. **Range:** Yes (grass). **To obtain tee times:** Call four months in advance. **Subscriber comments:** One of the nicest I have played. Tough par 3s, great shape and lots of marsh...Lots of layup shots...Carved out of swamp. Usually see deer.

★★½SOURWOOD FOREST GOLF COURSE

PU-8055 Pleasanthill Church Rd., Snow Camp, 27349, Alamance County, (910)376-8166, 15 miles S of Burlington.
Opened: 1990. **Holes:** 18. **Par:** 72/72. **Yards:** 6,862/5,022. **Course rating:** 72.1/68.0. **Slope:** 117/106. **Architect:** Elmo Cobb. **Green fee:** $8/$12. **Credit cards:** N/A. **Reduced fees:** Weekdays, twilight, seniors. **Caddies:** No. **Golf carts:** $10. **Discount golf packages:** No. **Season:** Year-round. **High:** N/A. **On site lodging:** No. **Rental clubs:** No. **Walking policy:** Walking at certain times. **Metal spikes allowed:** Yes. **Range:** No. **To obtain tee times:** N/A.
Subscriber comments: Nice small course with premium on driving the ball...Lots of trees, hit it straight, fast greens...If you can find it, you'll enjoy it...Added additional nine holes...Not the next Pinehurst but challenging and fun to play.

★★★SPRINGDALE COUNTRY CLUB

R-200 Golfwatch Rd., Canton, 28716, Haywood County, (704)235-8451, (800)553-3027, 11 miles S of Waynesville.
Opened: 1968. **Holes:** 18. **Par:** 72/72. **Yards:** 6,812/5,421. **Course rating:** 72.4/72.2. **Slope:** 126/113. **Architect:** Joseph Holmes. **Green fee:** $15/$40. **Credit cards:** MC,VISA,AMEX. **Reduced fees:** Twilight. **Caddies:** No. **Golf carts:** $15. **Discount golf packages:** Yes. **Season:** Year-round. **High:** April-May. **On site lodging:** Yes. **Rental clubs:** No. **Walking policy:** Walking at certain times. **Metal spikes allowed:** Yes. **Range:** Yes (grass). **To obtain tee times:** Call up to 5 days in advance.
Subscriber comments: .Like playing two different courses (front nine and back nine)...Great views...Front nine more varied, back nine flat valley, small clubhouse...Many blind shots.

★★★½STAR HILL GOLF & COUNTRY CLUB

202 Clubhouse Dr., Cape Carteret, 28584, Carteret County, (919)393-8111, 25 miles W of Jacksonville.
Opened: 1967. **Holes:** 27. **Architect:** Russell T. Burney. **Green fee:** $15/$35. **Credit cards:** MC,VISA. **Reduced fees:** Low season, resort guests, twilight. **Caddies:** No. **Golf carts:** $10. **Discount golf packages:** Yes. **Season:** Year-round. **High:** June-Aug. **On site lodging:** No. **Rental clubs:** Yes. **Walking policy:** Walking at certain times. **Metal spikes allowed:** Yes. **Range:** Yes (grass). **To obtain tee times:** Call to reserve time for any month of current year.
PINES/LAKES
Par: 71/72. **Yards:** 6,448/4,897. **Course rating:** 70.2/66.8. **Slope:** 113/103.
SANDS/LAKES
Par: 71/72. **Yards:** 6,361/4,786. **Course rating:** 70.9/73.2. **Slope:** 118/108.
SANDS/PINES
Par: 72/72. **Yards:** 6,301/4,669. **Course rating:** 70.5/73.6. **Slope:** 115/107.
Subscriber comments: Enjoyable course, not overly long...27 holes...Interesting, nice setting, playable...Fun beach layout, great for everyone...One of my favorites...Great vacation spot...Best greens in NC, a pleasure to play...Great vacation spot.

STONEBRIDGE GOLF CLUB

2721 Swilcan Burn, Monroe, 28112, Union County, (704)283-8998, (888)337-2582, 10 miles S of Charlotte.
Opened: 1997. **Holes:** 18. **Par:** 72/72. **Yards:** 6,905/5,145. **Course rating:** N/A. **Slope:** N/A. **Architect:** Richard B. Osborne. **Green fee:** $24/$34. **Credit cards:** MC,VISA,AMEX. **Reduced fees:** Weekdays, twilight, juniors. **Caddies:** No. **Golf carts:** $14. **Discount golf packages:** No. **Season:** Year-round. **High:** N/A. **On site lodging:** No. **Rental clubs:** Yes. **Walking policy:** Walking at certain times. **Metal spikes allowed:** No. **Range:** Yes (grass). **To obtain tee times:** Call up to 4 days in advance.

★★★½STONEY CREEK GOLF CLUB

PU-911 Golf House Rd. E., Stoney Creek, 27377, Guilford County, (910)449-5688, 12 miles E of Greensboro.
Opened: 1992. **Holes:** 18. **Par:** 72/72. **Yards:** 7,063/4,737. **Course rating:** 74.1/69.8.

Slope: 144/123. **Architect:** Tom Jackson. **Green fee:** $21/$26. **Credit cards:** MC,VISA,AMEX. **Reduced fees:** Weekdays, low season, twilight, seniors, juniors. **Caddies:** No. **Golf carts:** $14. **Discount golf packages:** Yes. **Season:** Year-round. **High:** Spring/Fall. **On site lodging:** No. **Rental clubs:** Yes. **Walking policy:** Walking at certain times. **Metal spikes allowed:** Yes. **Range:** Yes (grass). **To obtain tee times:** Call up to 7 days in advance.

Subscriber comments: Nice course...Need to play more than once to score well...Fast greens. 1 and 14 tough. Good par 3s...Good design, challenging...Shotmaker's course. Need "A" game...Good value for seniors.

★★★½TALAMORE RESORT AT PINEHURST

PU-1595 Midland Rd., Southern Pines, 28387, Moore County, (910)692-5884, 2 miles E of Pinehurst.

Opened: 1992. **Holes:** 18. **Par:** 71/72. **Yards:** 7,020/4,945. **Course rating:** 72.9/69.0. **Slope:** 142/125. **Architect:** Rees Jones. **Green fee:** $39/$87. **Credit cards:** MC,VISA. **Reduced fees:** Low season, resort guests, twilight, juniors. **Caddies:** Yes. **Golf carts:** Included in Green Fee. **Discount golf packages:** Yes. **Season:** Year-round. **High:** Spring/Fall. **On site lodging:** Yes. **Rental clubs:** Yes. **Walking policy:** Walking at certain times. **Metal spikes allowed:** Yes. **Range:** Yes (grass). **To obtain tee times:** Call golf shop.

Notes: Ranked 18th in 1997 Best in State.

Subscriber comments: Like playing Pinehurst without Pinehurst prices...Has a big-time golf course feel...Nice layout...Lloved the llamas...No weak holes, elevation changes...Incorporates natural beauty.

TANGLEWOOD PARK

PU-Hwy. 158 W., Clemmons, 27012, Forsyth County, (910)778-6320, 5 miles W of Winston-Salem.

Architect: Robert Trent Jones. **Green fee:** $16/$50. **Credit cards:** MC,VISA,AMEX. **Reduced fees:** Weekdays, low season, resort guests, twilight, seniors, juniors. **Caddies:** No. **Golf carts:** $14. **Discount golf packages:** Yes. **Season:** Year-round. **High:** Spring/Fall. **On site lodging:** Yes. **Rental clubs:** Yes. **Walking policy:** Walking at certain times. **Metal spikes allowed:** No. **Range:** Yes (grass/mats). **To obtain tee times:** Call seven days in advance. Lodge guests may make tee times when booking reservations.

★★★★CHAMPIONSHIP COURSE

Opened: 1957. **Holes:** 18. **Par:** 72/74. **Yards:** 7,022/5,119. **Course rating:** 74.5/70.9. **Slope:** 140/130.

Notes: Ranked 11th in 1997 Best in State; 1974 PGA Championship; Senior Tour Vantage Championship.

Subscriber comments: Very tough, long course, uphill landing areas...Super golf course...Excellent chance to play "big" tournament course...Beautiful rolling terrain...Good facilities, crowded...Well bunkered, timely tee times, great diversity...Elevated greens, sand...Bunkers, bunkers, and more bunkers.

★★★REYNOLDS COURSE

Opened: 1959. **Holes:** 18. **Par:** 72/72. **Yards:** 6,469/5,432. **Course rating:** 71.0/70.2. **Slope:** 125/120.

Subscriber comments: Short and tight...Great layout. Scenic...Tough test...Great sister course, from back. Tough. Great value...Pay the extra money for the PGA course...Tighter, prettier than Championship Course...Good facilities...Not a poor sister to Championship Course.

★★TWIN OAKS GOLF COURSE

PU-320 Twin Oaks Rd., Statesville, 28625, Iredell County, (704)872-3979, 50 miles N of Charlotte.

Opened: 1960. **Holes:** 18. **Par:** 72/72. **Yards:** 6,368/4,632. **Course rating:** 69.2/70.2. **Slope:** 112/114. **Architect:** N/A. **Green fee:** $12/$22. **Credit cards:** MC,VISA,AMEX. **Reduced fees:** Weekdays. **Caddies:** No. **Golf carts:** Included in Green Fee. **Discount golf packages:** No. **Season:** Year-round. **High:** April-Aug. **On site lodging:** No. **Rental clubs:** Yes. **Walking policy:** Walking at certain times. **Metal spikes allowed:** Yes. **Range:** Yes (grass). **To obtain tee times:** Call anytime.

★★½WAKE FOREST COUNTRY CLUB

13239 Capital Blvd., Wake Forest, 27587, Wake County, (919)556-3416, 9 miles N of Raleigh.

Opened: 1961. **Holes:** 18. **Par:** 72/72. **Yards:** 6,952/5,124. **Course rating:** 74.4/70.0. **Slope:** 135/122. **Architect:** Gene Hamm. **Green fee:** $16/$21. **Credit cards:** MC,VISA. **Reduced fees:** Twilight, seniors, juniors. **Caddies:** No. **Golf carts:** $12. **Discount golf packages:** No. **Season:** Year-round. **High:** April-June. **On site lodging:** No. **Rental clubs:** Yes. **Walking policy:** Walking at certain times. **Metal spikes allowed:** Yes. **Range:** Yes (grass). **To obtain tee times:** Weekday tee times are available seven days in advance. Weekend times are available on Thursday at noon. A credit card is required for weekend tee times.

Subscriber comments: Excellent facility, nice course layout, fair...1st hole longest par 5 in golf, 700-plus yards... Top 10 on my list...Bunkers typically contain a mix of gravel and clay...Need good iron play...Good improvement on the greens.

★★½WALNUT WOODS GOLF COURSE

PU-3172 Alamance Church Rd., Julian, 27283, Guilford County, (910)697-8140, 25 miles SE of Greensboro.

Opened: 1978. **Holes:** 18. **Par:** 73/73. **Yards:** 6,409/4,962. **Course rating:** 70.1/68.1. **Slope:** 126/114. **Architect:** Ralph Clendenin. **Green fee:** $18/$23. **Credit cards:** MC,VISA. **Reduced fees:** Seniors. **Caddies:** No. **Golf carts:** Included in Green Fee. **Discount golf packages:** No. **Season:** Year-round. **High:** May-Sept. **On site lodging:** No. **Rental clubs:** Yes. **Walking policy:** Walking at certain times. **Metal spikes allowed:** Yes. **Range:** Yes (grass/mats). **To obtain tee times:** First come, first served.

Subscriber comments: Good condition, hump-backed greens...Good course for afternoon game...Ego builder...Fairly hilly...Interesting holes...Tight fairways.

★★★WAYNESVILLE COUNTRY CLUB INN

R-Ninevah Rd., Waynesville, 28786, Haywood County, (704)452-4617, 25 miles E of Asheville.

GOOD SERVICE

Opened: 1926. **Holes:** 27. **Architect:** Tom Jackson. **Green fee:** $13/$28. **Credit cards:** MC,VISA. **Reduced fees:** Low season, resort guests, twilight, juniors. **Caddies:** No. **Golf carts:** $14. **Discount golf packages:** Yes. **Season:** Year-round. **High:** March-Oct. **On site lodging:** Yes. **Rental clubs:** Yes. **Walking policy:** Walking at certain times. **Metal spikes allowed:** Yes. **Range:** No. **To obtain tee times:** Call one day in advance. Guests at the hotel may make tee times at time of reservation.

CAROLINA/BLUE RIDGE
Par: 70/70. **Yards:** 5,943/5,002. **Course rating:** 66.8/67.0. **Slope:** 104/104.
CAROLINA/DOGWOOD
Par: 70/70. **Yards:** 5,798/4,927. **Course rating:** 66.4/66.6. **Slope:** 103/103.
DOGWOOD/BLUE RIDGE
Par: 70/70. **Yards:** 5,803/4,565. **Course rating:** 66.4/65.0. **Slope:** 105/100.

Subscriber comments: Great golf vacation destination...Beautiful course, staff great...Very relaxing short courses, great for seniors...Food is excellent, service and rooms are very good...Most enjoyable course and atmosphere...Watch for the bull if you hit it in the cow pasture...I love it.

★★WENDELL COUNTRY CLUB

180 Jake May Dr., Wendell, 27591, Wake County, (919)365-7337, 15 miles E of Raleigh.

Opened: N/A. **Holes:** 18. **Par:** 71/71. **Yards:** 6,358/4,891. **Course rating:** 69.5/68.0. **Slope:** 116/113. **Architect:** Ken Dye. **Green fee:** $10/$19. **Credit cards:** MC,VISA. **Reduced fees:** Seniors. **Caddies:** No. **Golf carts:** $10. **Discount golf packages:** No. **Season:** Year-round. **High:** N/A. **On site lodging:** No. **Rental clubs:** No. **Walking policy:** Walking at certain times. **Metal spikes allowed:** Yes. **Range:** No. **To obtain tee times:** Call golf shop.

★★WESTPORT GOLF COURSE

PU-7494 Golf Course Dr. S., Denver, 28037, Lincoln County, (704)483-5604, 25 miles N of Charlotte.

Opened: 1968. **Holes:** 18. **Par:** 72/72. **Yards:** 6,805/5,600. **Course rating:** 72.3/69.5.

Slope: 123/118. **Architect:** Porter Gibson. **Green fee:** $15/$22. **Credit cards:** MC,VISA,DISC. **Reduced fees:** Weekdays, twilight, seniors. **Caddies:** No. **Golf carts:** $11. **Discount golf packages:** No. **Season:** Year-round. **High:** April-Oct. **On site lodging:** No. **Rental clubs:** Yes. **Walking policy:** Walking at certain times. **Metal spikes allowed:** Yes. **Range:** Yes (grass). **To obtain tee times:** Call up to 7 days in advance.

★★½WHISPERING WOODS GOLF CLUB
26 Sandpiper Dr., Whispering Pines, 28327, Moore County, (910)949-4653, (800)224-5061, 6 miles NE of Pinehurst.
Opened: 1975. **Holes:** 18. **Par:** 70/70. **Yards:** 6,334/4,924. **Course rating:** 70.5/68.7. **Slope:** 122/122. **Architect:** Ellis Maples. **Green fee:** $25/$50. **Credit cards:** All major. **Reduced fees:** Low season, twilight, seniors, juniors. **Caddies:** No. **Golf carts:** $15. **Discount golf packages:** Yes. **Season:** Year-round. **High:** Spring/Fall. **On site lodging:** No. **Rental clubs:** Yes. **Walking policy:** Mandatory cart. **Metal spikes allowed:** Yes. **Range:** No. **To obtain tee times:** Call up to one year in advance up to day of play. Credit card required for out of town reservation.
Subscriber comments: Some interesting holes and greens...Congratulations on successful rehab...A relatively short course that can keep you in trouble...Short hilly course, greens excellent, fairways thin and rough...Friendly people.

★★★½WOODBRIDGE GOLF LINKS
PU-1007 New Camp Creek Church Rd., Kings Mountain, 28086, Cleveland County, (704)482-0353, 30 miles W of Charlotte.
Opened: 1976. **Holes:** 18. **Par:** 72/73. **Yards:** 6,743/5,151. **Course rating:** 72.3/70.4. **Slope:** 131/127. **Architect:** Bob Toski and Porter Gibson. **Green fee:** $28/$38. **Credit cards:** MC,VISA. **Reduced fees:** N/A. **Caddies:** No. **Golf carts:** Included in Green Fee. **Discount golf packages:** No. **Season:** Year-round. **High:** April-Oct. **On site lodging:** No. **Rental clubs:** Yes. **Walking policy:** Walking at certain times. **Metal spikes allowed:** Yes. **Range:** Yes (grass). **To obtain tee times:** Call up to one week in advance.
Subscriber comments: Nice setting with views of surrounding Moss Lake and the Blue Ridge Mountains...Always fun, back nine harder than front.

★★★½WOODLAKE COUNTRY CLUB
R-150 Woodlake Blvd., Vass, 28394, Moore County, (910)245-4686, (800)334-1126, 60 miles S of Raleigh.
Opened: 1973. **Holes:** 27. **Architect:** Ellis Maples and Dan Maples. **Green fee:** $30/$70. **Credit cards:** MC,VISA. **Reduced fees:** Weekdays, low season, resort guests, twilight. **Caddies:** No. **Golf carts:** Included in Green Fee. **Discount golf packages:** Yes. **Season:** Year-round. **High:** March-May. **On site lodging:** Yes. **Rental clubs:** No. **Walking policy:** Mandatory cart. **Metal spikes allowed:** Yes. **Range:** Yes (grass). **To obtain tee times:** Call up to one year in advance.
LAKE SHORE/CYPRESS CREEK
Par: 72/72. **Yards:** 7,012/5,255. **Course rating:** 73.4/71.4. **Slope:** 134/128.
CYPRESS CREEK/CRANES COVE
LAKE SHORE/CRANES COVE
Subscriber comments: Beautiful, real challenge...Tougher than a boarding house steak...Great course for hard matches. Lots of water and you must think your way around course...Very good course. Good blend of hill and lakes, open and treed areas plays long.

★★½BOIS DE SIOUX GOLF CLUB

PU-N. 4th St. and 13th Ave., Wahpeton, 58075, Richland County, (701)642-3673, 45 miles S of Fargo.
Opened: 1924. **Holes:** 18. **Par:** 72/72. **Yards:** 6,675/5,500. **Course rating:** 71.3/71.4. **Slope:** 122/119. **Architect:** Robert Bruce Harris. **Green fee:** $17/$19. **Credit cards:** None. **Reduced fees:** Weekdays. **Caddies:** No. **Golf carts:** $18. **Discount golf packages:** No. **Season:** April-Nov. **High:** April-Sept. **On site lodging:** No. **Rental clubs:** Yes. **Walking policy:** Unrestricted walking. **Metal spikes allowed:** Yes. **Range:** Yes (grass/mats). **To obtain tee times:** Call 7 days in advance.
Subscriber comments: Greens especially interesting, plays long...Courteous staff...Always a pleasure to play this course where the front nine is in North Dakota and the back nine in Minnesota...Pick the right season to play here, late summer.

★★★½EDGEWOOD GOLF COURSE

PU-3218 2nd St. N., Fargo, 58102, Cass County, (701)232-2824.
Opened: 1951. **Holes:** 18. **Par:** 71/71. **Yards:** 6,369/5,176. **Course rating:** 68.4/68.9. **Slope:** 122/115. **Architect:** Robert Bruce Harris. **Green fee:** $15/$18. **Credit cards:** MC,VISA. **Reduced fees:** Twilight, seniors, juniors. **Caddies:** No. **Golf carts:** $18. **Discount golf packages:** Yes. **Season:** April-Nov. **High:** July-Aug. **On site lodging:** No. **Rental clubs:** Yes. **Walking policy:** Unrestricted walking. **Metal spikes allowed:** Yes. **Range:** Yes (grass/mats). **To obtain tee times:** Call 3 days in advance.
Notes: Ranked 4th in 1997 Best in State.
Subscriber comments: Mature course...Old-fashion design. Fair test...Fun course, old trees, great value for the money...Wooded, short, very interesting...Well maintained, lots of trees...Best muny I have ever played. Old river course...Enjoy a "cold one" in the 19th hole...Tight course...Play it more than once.

★★★½HEART RIVER MUNICIPAL GOLF COURSE

PM-8th St. S.W., Dickinson, 58601, Stark County, (701)225-9412.
Opened: 1983. **Holes:** 18. **Par:** 72/72. **Yards:** 6,734/4,738. **Course rating:** N/A. **Slope:** N/A. **Architect:** Abe Epinosa/Dick Phelps, Brad Benz and Mike Poellot. **Green fee:** $10/$14. **Credit cards:** MC,VISA. **Reduced fees:** Juniors. **Caddies:** No. **Golf carts:** $15. **Discount golf packages:** No. **Season:** March-Oct. **High:** June-Aug. **On site lodging:** No. **Rental clubs:** Yes. **Walking policy:** Unrestricted walking. **Metal spikes allowed:** No. **Range:** Yes (grass). **To obtain tee times:** Call 3 days in advance.
Subscriber comments: Fun and challenging...Great course. Lots of water in back nine...The course was nice from tee to green.

★★★½JAMESTOWN COUNTRY CLUB

RR1 SE of City, Jamestown, 58401, Stutsman County, (701)252-8448.
Opened: 1963. **Holes:** 18. **Par:** 72/72. **Yards:** 6,567/5,252. **Course rating:** 70.9/69.7. **Slope:** 122/114. **Architect:** N/A. **Green fee:** $20/$25. **Credit cards:** None. **Reduced fees:** N/A. **Caddies:** No. **Golf carts:** $20. **Discount golf packages:** No. **Season:** April-Oct. **High:** June-Aug. **On site lodging:** No. **Rental clubs:** No. **Walking policy:** Unrestricted walking. **Metal spikes allowed:** Yes. **Range:** Yes (grass). **To obtain tee times:** Call up to 7 days in advance.
Subscriber comments: Beautiful James River Valley...Nice track...Newly revitalized, tree planting...Lost a lot of trees last two years...Challenging course.

★★½LINCOLN PARK GOLF COURSE

PU-P.O. Box 12429, Grand Forks, 58208, Grand Forks County, (701)746-2788.
Opened: 1929. **Holes:** 18. **Par:** 71/71. **Yards:** 6,006/5,382. **Course rating:** 67.0/69.7. **Slope:** 108/112. **Architect:** N/A. **Green fee:** $12/$14. **Credit cards:** MC,VISA,DISC. **Reduced fees:** Twilight. **Caddies:** No. **Golf carts:** $15. **Discount golf packages:** No. **Season:** April-Oct. **High:** May-July. **On site lodging:** No. **Rental clubs:** No. **Walking policy:** Unrestricted walking. **Metal spikes allowed:** Yes. **Range:** No. **To obtain tee times:** Call up to 7 days in advance.
Subscriber comments: Very busy. Very basic...Easy course but excellent value and service...Short muny, crowded...Short course made interesting with trees...Nice flat municipal course along the Red River...Nice way to spend a morning.

NORTH DAKOTA

★★★★½ THE LINKS OF NORTH DAKOTA AT RED MIKE RESORT

PU-Hwy. 1804, Ray, 58802, Williams County, (701)568-2600.
Opened: 1995. **Holes:** 18. **Architect:** Stephen Kay. **Caddies:** No.
Discount golf packages: No. **On site lodging:** No. **Rental clubs:** No.
Metal spikes allowed: Yes. **Range:** No.
Call club for further information.

Notes: Ranked 1st in 1997 Best in State; 2nd in 1996 Best New
Affordable Courses.
Subscriber comments: Little earth moved in this natural setting...Gem
in middle of nowhere...Best in the region...Excellent value. Beautiful
views. Wind a factor. Very long from tees...Spectacular scenery...Terrific
layout...The best $25 green fee in the country...Not seen and played bet-
ter course in four states...Very natural surrounding...Outstanding
greens...Choice of tee boxes is great, immaculate fairways.

★★★ MAPLE RIVER GOLF CLUB

I-94 Exit 338, Mapleton, 58059, Cass County, (701)282-5415, 12 miles W of Fargo.
Opened: 1966. **Holes:** 9. **Par:** 36/37. **Yards:** 3,329/2,822. **Course rating:** 71.1/71.1.
Slope: 123/120. **Architect:** N/A. **Green fee:** $15/$17. **Credit cards:** MC,VISA.
Reduced fees: Weekdays, seniors, juniors. **Caddies:** No. **Golf carts:** $17. **Discount
golf packages:** No. **Season:** April-Oct. **High:** N/A. **On site lodging:** No. **Rental clubs:**
Yes. **Walking policy:** Unrestricted walking. **Metal spikes allowed:** Yes. **Range:** Yes
(grass). **To obtain tee times:** Call.
Subscriber comments: Greens excellent, fast, some holes very long...Fun nine holes,
can be windy...Fall is beautiful, maple trees...Best greens in ND. Great secret.

★★★½ MINOT COUNTRY CLUB

Hwy. 15 W., Minot, 58701, Ward County, (701)839-6169.
Opened: 1929. **Holes:** 18. **Par:** 72/72. **Yards:** 6,667/6,217. **Course rating:** N/A. **Slope:**
124/121. **Architect:** Tom Vardon/Robert Bruce Harris. **Green fee:** N/A. **Credit cards:**
MC,VISA. **Reduced fees:** Weekdays. **Caddies:** No. **Golf carts:** N/A. **Discount golf
packages:** No. **Season:** April-Nov. **High:** June-Aug. **On site lodging:** No. **Rental
clubs:** No. **Walking policy:** N/A. **Metal spikes allowed:** Yes. **Range:** Yes (grass). **To
obtain tee times:** N/A.
Notes: Ranked 5th in 1997 Best in State.
Subscriber comments: Best course in ND. Excellent staff...Compares with the North
Country's best...Best course in North Dakota...Nice course, excellent value.

★★½ PLAINSVIEW GOLF COURSE AT GRAND FORKS A.F.B.

641 Alert Ave.,Bldg.811, Grand Forks AFB, Grand Forks, 58205, Grand Forks County,
(701)747-4279, 15 miles W of Grand Forks.
Opened: 1971. **Holes:** 18. **Par:** 72/72. **Yards:** 6,685/5,360. **Course rating:** 69.9/65.9.
Slope: 102/100. **Architect:** N/A. **Green fee:** $6/$11. **Credit cards:** MC,VISA,DISC.
Reduced fees: Juniors. **Caddies:** No. **Golf carts:** $14. **Discount golf packages:** No.
Season: April-Nov. **High:** June-July. **On site lodging:** No. **Rental clubs:** Yes. **Walking
policy:** Unrestricted walking. **Metal spikes allowed:** Yes. **Range:** Yes (grass/mats). **To
obtain tee times:** Call anytime.
Subscriber comments: Wide open with few trees and out-of-bounds...Hacker's paradise. If you like to spray it, you can.

★★★ PRAIRIE WEST GOLF COURSE

PU-2709 Long Spur Trail, Mandan, 58554, Morton County, (701)667-3222, 2 miles SW
of Bismarck.
Opened: 1992. **Holes:** 18. **Par:** 72/72. **Yards:** 6,681/5,452. **Course rating:** 71.6/70.1.
Slope: 127/118. **Architect:** Don Herfort. **Green fee:** $16. **Credit cards:** All major.
Reduced fees: Seniors, juniors. **Caddies:** No. **Golf carts:** $16. **Discount golf pack-
ages:** No. **Season:** April-Oct. **High:** July-Aug. **On site lodging:** No. **Rental clubs:** Yes.
Walking policy: Unrestricted walking. **Metal spikes allowed:** Yes. **Range:** Yes (grass).
To obtain tee times: Call 1 day in advance.
Subscriber comments: Leave your woods in the bag to beat narrow fairways...Nice
track. Needs maturing...Should be top course in ND in a few years...Nice layout, needs
time to mature.

NORTH DAKOTA

★★★½RIVERWOOD GOLF CLUB
PU-725 Bismarck Dr, Bismarck, 58502, Burleigh County, (701)222-6462.
Opened: 1969. **Holes:** 18. **Par:** 72/72. **Yards:** 6,941/5,196. **Course rating:** 70.0/68.6.
Slope: 130/112. **Architect:** N/A. **Green fee:** $16/$16. **Credit cards:** All major.
Reduced fees: Seniors, juniors. **Caddies:** No. **Golf carts:** $17. **Discount golf packages:** No. **Season:** April-Oct. **High:** June-Sept. **On site lodging:** No. **Rental clubs:**
Yes. **Walking policy:** Unrestricted walking. **Metal spikes allowed:** Yes. **Range:** Yes
(grass/mats). **To obtain tee times:** Call 1 day in advance.
Subscriber comments: Lots of mature trees...Need to know all the shots...Excellent
layout. Very busy. Good staff...Trees are biggest hazard...Best course I have played in
the state...Lots of trees making it one of the harder courses in North Dakota...Play at
dusk and enjoy the wildlife...Still the best in Bismarck...Double-dogleg, par 5 15th a
shotmaker's hole.

★★★ROSE CREEK GOLF COURSE
PU-1500 Rose Creek Pkwy., Fargo, 58107, Cass County, (701)235-5100.
Opened: 1993. **Holes:** 18. **Par:** 72/72. **Yards:** 6,616/5,062. **Course rating:** 71.4/68.8.
Slope: 123/114. **Architect:** Dick Phelps. **Green fee:** $15/$18. **Credit cards:** MC,VISA.
Reduced fees: Twilight, seniors, juniors. **Caddies:** No. **Golf carts:** $18. **Discount golf
packages:** Yes. **Season:** April-Nov. **High:** May-Aug. **On site lodging:** No. **Rental
clubs:** Yes. **Walking policy:** Unrestricted walking. **Metal spikes allowed:** Yes. **Range:**
Yes (grass/mats). **To obtain tee times:** Call 7 days in advance.
Subscriber comments: Poor turf; some holes still not mature...New course with potential...Wide open, windy...Fairly new, great clubhouse, open, challenging, fun...Dinner
here is a must...Could be a very good course...Links-type course... Difficult when
windy...Great clubhouse...Should mature to a much better facility.

★★★½SOURIS VALLEY GOLF CLUB
PU-2400 14th Ave. S.W., Minot, 58701, Ward County, (701)838-4112.
Opened: 1967. **Holes:** 18. **Par:** 72/72. **Yards:** 6,815/5,474. **Course rating:** 72.5/71.2. **Slope:** 126/118. **Architect:** William James Spear.
Green fee: $13/$13. **Credit cards:** None. **Reduced fees:** Twilight,
seniors, juniors. **Caddies:** No. **Golf carts:** $15. **Discount golf packages:** No. **Season:** April-Oct. **High:** June-Aug. **On site lodging:** No. **Rental clubs:** Yes.
Walking policy: Unrestricted walking. **Metal spikes allowed:** Yes. **Range:** Yes. **To
obtain tee times:** Call golf shop 24 hours in advance.
Subscriber comments: Nice layout. Very, very busy...Challenging, ample water hazards...Great course in excellent shape...Nice course for the money...Good, tough muny.
Overplayed though...One of my favorites...Outstanding course condition, best course
played in five years...Tough course, water, sand, trees make for a challenge.

★★½TOM O'LEARY GOLF COURSE
PU-1200 N. Washington St., Bismarck, 58501, Burleigh County, (701)222-6531.
Opened: 1987. **Holes:** 18. **Par:** 68/68. **Yards:** 5,800/4,026. **Course rating:** 65.0/62.3.
Slope: 110/97. **Architect:** David Gill and Garrett Gill. **Green fee:** $11/$15. **Credit
cards:** MC,VISA,DISC. **Reduced fees:** Seniors, juniors. **Caddies:** No. **Golf carts:** $17.
Discount golf packages: No. **Season:** April-Oct. **High:** June-Sept. **On site lodging:**
No. **Rental clubs:** Yes. **Walking policy:** Unrestricted walking. **Metal spikes allowed:**
Yes. **Range:** Yes (grass/mats). **To obtain tee times:** Call 1 day in advance.
Subscriber comments: Changes and improvements in past few years make it a fun
challenge...Short holes, small greens...Good learning course...Best cared-for course in
the state. Nice...Hills and hills and more hills.

GOOD VALUE

OHIO

★★AIRPORT GOLF COURSE
PM-900 N. Hamilton Rd., Columbus, 43219, Franklin County, (614)645-3127.
Opened: 1965. **Holes:** 18. **Par:** 70/72. **Yards:** 6,383/5,504. **Course rating:** 68.1.
Slope: 107. **Architect:** Jack Kidwell. **Green fee:** $13/$15. **Credit cards:** MC,VISA.
Reduced fees: Low season, twilight, seniors, juniors. **Caddies:** No. **Golf carts:** $20.
Discount golf packages: No. **Season:** Year-round. **High:** May-Sept. **On site lodging:**
No. **Rental clubs:** Yes. **Walking policy:** Unrestricted walking. **Metal spikes allowed:**
Yes. **Range:** No. **To obtain tee times:** Call.

★★★½APPLE VALLEY GOLF CLUB
PU-433 Clubhouse Dr., Howard, 43028, Knox County, (614)397-7664, (800)359-7664,
6 miles E of Mt. Vernon.
Opened: 1971. **Holes:** 18. **Par:** 72/75. **Yards:** 6,946/6,116. **Course rating:** 72.4/74.9.
Slope: 116/120. **Architect:** William Newcomb. **Green fee:** $16/$20. **Credit cards:**
MC,VISA,DISC. **Reduced fees:** Twilight, seniors. **Caddies:** No. **Golf carts:** $10.
Discount golf packages: No. **Season:** March-Oct. **High:** June-Aug. **On site lodging:**
No. **Rental clubs:** No. **Walking policy:** Walking at certain times. **Metal spikes
allowed:** Yes. **Range:** Yes (grass). **To obtain tee times:** Call as far in advance as possible.
Subscriber comments: One of my favorites...A fine public course...Fun to play...Some
nice long par 4s...Some good water holes...Somewhat open but very challenging...Very
nice scenic views.

★★½ATWOOD RESORT GOLF COURSE
R-2650 Lodge Rd., Dellroy, 44620, Carroll County, (330)735-2211, (800)362-6406, 25
miles S of Canton.
Opened: 1951. **Holes:** 18. **Par:** 70/70. **Yards:** 6,152/4,188. **Course rating:** 65.7/62.0.
Slope: 102/91. **Architect:** Oiler. **Green fee:** $10/$18. **Credit cards:** All major. **Reduced
fees:** Weekdays, low season, resort guests, seniors, juniors. **Caddies:** No. **Golf carts:**
$10. **Discount golf packages:** Yes. **Season:** Year-round. **High:** June-Sept. **On site
lodging:** Yes. **Rental clubs:** Yes. **Walking policy:** Unrestricted walking. **Metal spikes
allowed:** Yes. **Range:** Yes. **To obtain tee times:** Call golf shop.
Subscriber comments: Very scenic course...Very hilly, long par 5s, very short par
3s...Beautiful in the fall, very hilly...Neat little course in a relaxing atmosphere.
Special Notes: Also has lighted 9-hole par-3 course.

★★★★AVALON LAKES GOLF COURSE
R-One American Way, Warren, 44484, Trumbull County, (330)856-8898, 40 miles SE of
Cleveland.
Opened: 1968. **Holes:** 18. **Par:** 71/71. **Yards:** 7,001/5,324. **Course rating:** 74.3/70.1.
Slope: 127/116. **Architect:** Pete Dye. **Green fee:** $55. **Credit cards:** MC,VISA,AMEX.
Reduced fees: Weekdays, low season, twilight. **Caddies:** No. **Golf carts:** Included in
Green Fee. **Discount golf packages:** No. **Season:** April-Oct. **High:** June-Aug. **On site
lodging:** Yes. **Rental clubs:** Yes. **Walking policy:** Mandatory cart. **Metal spikes
allowed:** Yes. **Range:** Yes (grass/mats). **To obtain tee times:** Call.
Notes: 1993-present, Giant Eagle LPGA Classic.
Subscriber comments: Beautiful facility, top to bottom...Great golfing...Beautiful championship course...Good resort course, very good flat layout...Great layout...Lower handicaps will love it...Top notch, championship quality...Tight and lined with trees.

★★AVON FIELD GOLF COURSE
PU-4081 Reading Rd., Cincinnati, 45229, Hamilton County, (513)281-0322, 5 miles N
of Cincinnati.
Opened: 1914. **Holes:** 18. **Par:** 66/66. **Yards:** 5,325/4,618. **Course rating:** 63.9/63.5.
Slope: 99/98. **Architect:** William Langford. **Green fee:** $13/$16. **Credit cards:** None.
Reduced fees: Low season, seniors, juniors. **Caddies:** No. **Golf carts:** $10. **Discount
golf packages:** No. **Season:** Year-round. **High:** May-Aug. **On site lodging:** No. **Rental
clubs:** Yes. **Walking policy:** Unrestricted walking. **Metal spikes allowed:** Yes. **Range:**
Yes (grass/mats). **To obtain tee times:** Call.
Subscriber comments: City course...Short, hilly but good condition...Nothing special
at all, but it beats work...For beginners; short, easy.

OHIO

★★BARBERTON BROOKSIDE COUNTRY CLUB
PU-3727 Golf Course Dr., Barberton, 44203, Summit County, (330)825-4539, 5 miles W of Akron.
Opened: N/A. **Holes:** N/A. **Par:** 72/72. **Yards:** 6,448/5,098. **Course rating:** 72.0/71.8. **Slope:** 104/104. **Architect:** N/A. **Green fee:** $11/$23. **Credit cards:** MC,VISA. **Reduced fees:** Weekdays, low season, seniors, juniors. **Caddies:** No. **Golf carts:** $17. **Discount golf packages:** No. **Season:** Year-round weather permitting. **High:** April-Sept. **On site lodging:** No. **Rental clubs:** No. **Walking policy:** Walking at certain times. **Metal spikes allowed:** No. **Range:** No. **To obtain tee times:** Call golf shop.

★★★BEAVER CREEK MEADOWS GOLF COURSE
PU-12774 St. Rte. 7, Lisbon, 44432, Columbiana County, (330)385-3020, 30 miles S of Youngstown.
Opened: 1984. **Holes:** 18. **Par:** 71/72. **Yards:** 6,500/5,500. **Course rating:** 68.7/68.5. **Slope:** N/A. **Architect:** Bruce Weber. **Green fee:** $12/$16. **Credit cards:** None. **Reduced fees:** Weekdays, low season. **Caddies:** No. **Golf carts:** $18. **Discount golf packages:** No. **Season:** March-Dec. **High:** June-Aug. **On site lodging:** No. **Rental clubs:** No. **Walking policy:** Unrestricted walking. **Metal spikes allowed:** Yes. **Range:** Yes (grass/mats). **To obtain tee times:** Call.
Subscriber comments: Play from blue tees, fun course...Short course, two totally different nines...Short and easy...Good course...Good hotdogs...Excellent value...Wonderful surrounding scenery.

★½BEDFORD TRAILS GOLF COURSE
PU-713 Bedford Rd., Coitsville, 44436-9504, Mahoning County, (330)536-2234, 1 mile E of Youngstown.
Opened: 1962. **Holes:** 18. **Par:** 70/70. **Yards:** 6,160/5,170. **Course rating:** N/A. **Slope:** N/A. **Architect:** Tom Grischow. **Green fee:** $10/$15. **Credit cards:** MC,VISA. **Reduced fees:** Weekdays, low season, seniors, juniors. **Caddies:** No. **Golf carts:** $9. **Discount golf packages:** No. **Season:** Year-round. **High:** May-Sept. **On site lodging:** No. **Rental clubs:** No. **Walking policy:** Unrestricted walking. **Metal spikes allowed:** Yes. **Range:** Yes (grass/mats). **To obtain tee times:** Call golf shop.

★★★½BENT TREE GOLF CLUB
PU-350 Bent Tree Rd., Sunbury, 43074, Delaware County, (614)965-5140, 20 miles N of Columbus.
Opened: 1988. **Holes:** 18. **Par:** 72/72. **Yards:** 6,805/5,280. **Course rating:** 72.1/69.2. **Slope:** 122/113. **Architect:** Denis Griffiths & Assoc.. **Green fee:** $42/$55. **Credit cards:** MC,VISA,AMEX. **Reduced fees:** Weekdays, low season, twilight, seniors. **Caddies:** No. **Golf carts:** Included in Green Fee. **Discount golf packages:** Yes. **Season:** Jan.-Dec. **High:** May-Oct. **On site lodging:** No. **Rental clubs:** Yes. **Walking policy:** Walking at certain times. **Metal spikes allowed:** Yes. **Range:** Yes (grass). **To obtain tee times:** Call up to 7 days in advance with credit card to reserve.
Subscriber comments: Good test of golf...Tough course, fun, lots of sand for central Ohio...Great layout. A must play course...Country club quality.

★★BIG BEAVER CREEK GOLF COURSE
PU-1762 Zahn's Corner Rd., Piketon, 45661, Pike County, (614)289-3643, (800)554-6534, 59 miles S of Columbus.
Opened: 1996. **Holes:** 18. **Par:** N/A. **Yards:** N/A. **Course rating:** N/A. **Slope:** N/A. **Architect:** D.W. Bloomfield. **Green fee:** $17/$20. **Credit cards:** All major. **Reduced fees:** N/A. **Caddies:** No. **Golf carts:** $10. **Discount golf packages:** Yes. **Season:** March-Nov. **High:** July-Sept. **On site lodging:** No. **Rental clubs:** Yes. **Walking policy:** Unrestricted walking. **Metal spikes allowed:** Yes. **Range:** Yes (grass). **To obtain tee times:** Call up to 14 days in advance.

★★½BIG MET GOLF CLUB
PU-4811 Valley Pkwy., Fairview Park, 44126, Cuyahoga County, (216)331-1070, 2 miles W of Cleveland.
Opened: 1926. **Holes:** 18. **Par:** 72/74. **Yards:** 6,125/5,870. **Course rating:** 68.0/72.0. **Slope:** 108/113. **Architect:** Stanley Thompson. **Green fee:** $11/$15. **Credit cards:** MC,VISA. **Reduced fees:** Low season, seniors, juniors. **Caddies:** No. **Golf carts:** $18.

Discount golf packages: Yes. **Season:** March-Dec. **High:** May-Aug. **On site lodging:** No. **Rental clubs:** No. **Walking policy:** Unrestricted walking. **Metal spikes allowed:** Yes. **Range:** No. **To obtain tee times:** Call five days in advance.
Subscriber comments: Very enjoyable at all levels...Park-like setting in the valley...Watch for deer.

★★★BLACKHAWK GOLF CLUB
PU-8830 Dustin Rd., Galena, 43021, Delaware County, (614)965-1042, 20 miles NE of Columbus.
Opened: 1964. **Holes:** 18. **Par:** 71/71. **Yards:** 6,550/4,726. **Course rating:** 70.6/66.0.
Slope: 115/106. **Architect:** Jack Kidwell. **Green fee:** $22. **Credit cards:** MC,VISA,DISC. **Reduced fees:** Low season, twilight, seniors. **Caddies:** No. **Golf carts:** $10. **Discount golf packages:** No. **Season:** March-Dec. **High:** May-Oct. **On site lodging:** No. **Rental clubs:** Yes. **Walking policy:** Unrestricted walking. **Metal spikes allowed:** Yes. **Range:** Yes (grass/mats). **To obtain tee times:** Call 7 days in advance for weekends.
Subscriber comments: Nice course, but a little short...Old course, well groomed...Many great par 4s...Good golf out in the country, nice layout, very playable...#18 is a great finishing hole...Good variety of holes, must play.

★★½BLACKLICK WOODS GOLF COURSE
PU-7309 E. Livingston Ave., Reynoldsburg, 43068, Franklin County, (614)861-3193.
Opened: 1965. **Holes:** 18. **Par:** 72/75. **Yards:** 6,819/5,018. **Course rating:** 71.9/68.0.
Slope: 124/116. **Architect:** Jack Kidwell/Jodie Kinney. **Green fee:** $16/$16. **Credit cards:** MC,VISA. **Reduced fees:** Low season, twilight. **Caddies:** No. **Golf carts:** $18.
Discount golf packages: No. **Season:** Year-round. **High:** May-Aug. **On site lodging:** No. **Rental clubs:** Yes. **Walking policy:** Unrestricted walking. **Metal spikes allowed:** Yes. **Range:** Yes (grass/mats). **To obtain tee times:** Call on Monday for upcoming weekend.
Subscriber comments: Reopened after major renovations, tough, need all your shots...Top notch for a public course.
Special Notes: Also has 18-hole executive Green Course.

★★★½BLACKMOOR GOLF CLUB
PU-2200 Kragel Rd., Richmond, 43844, Jefferson County, (614)765-5502, 50 miles W of Pittsburgh, PA.
Opened: 1995. **Holes:** 18. **Par:** 72/72. **Yards:** 6,500/4,963. **Course rating:** 71.2/68.8.
Slope: 136/124. **Architect:** John Robinson. **Green fee:** $26/$35. **Credit cards:** All major. **Reduced fees:** Weekdays, low season, seniors. **Caddies:** No. **Golf carts:** Included in Green Fee. **Discount golf packages:** No. **Season:** Year-round. **High:** May-Sept. **On site lodging:** No. **Rental clubs:** No. **Walking policy:** Walking at certain times. **Metal spikes allowed:** Yes. **Range:** Yes (grass). **To obtain tee times:** Call golf shop.
Subscriber comments: Great course, makes you think...New course, nice layout...Course hilly and tight...Tight but short; accuracy is key.

★★★½BLUE ASH GOLF COURSE
PU-4040 Cooper Rd., Cincinnati, 45241, Hamilton County, (513)745-8577, 15 miles N of Cincinnati.
Opened: 1979. **Holes:** 18. **Par:** 72/72. **Yards:** 6,643/5,125. **Course rating:** 72.6/70.3.
Slope: 127/124. **Architect:** Kidwell and Hurdzan. **Green fee:** $22/$18. **Credit cards:** None. **Reduced fees:** Low season, seniors, juniors. **Caddies:** No. **Golf carts:** $22.
Discount golf packages: No. **Season:** Year-round. **High:** May-Sept. **On site lodging:** No. **Rental clubs:** Yes. **Walking policy:** Unrestricted walking. **Metal spikes allowed:** Yes. **Range:** No. **To obtain tee times:** Nonresidents call 5 days in advance.
Subscriber comments: Great condition, difficult layout...Must play, great value...Difficult course, a lot of high scores...One of my favorites. Outstanding all around...Good layout, interesting holes, tough undulating greens...First three holes make or break your round.

★½BLUFFTON GOLF CLUB
PU-8575 N. Dixie Hwy., Bluffton, 45817, Allen County, (419)358-6230, 15 miles N of Lima.

Opened: 1941. **Holes:** 18. **Par:** 72/72. **Yards:** 6,633/5,822. **Course rating:** 69.2/69.8. **Slope:** 103/95. **Architect:** Ken Mast. **Green fee:** $12. **Credit cards:** None. **Reduced fees:** Weekdays, low season, seniors, juniors. **Caddies:** No. **Golf carts:** $9. **Discount golf packages:** No. **Season:** March-Nov. **High:** June-Aug. **On site lodging:** No. **Rental clubs:** Yes. **Walking policy:** Unrestricted walking. **Metal spikes allowed:** Yes. **Range:** Yes (grass/mats). **To obtain tee times:** Call 7 days in advance.
Subscriber comments: Wide open...Back and forth over the creek...Course improving.

BOB O'LINK GOLF CLUB

PU-2400 Applegrove St. NW, North Canton, 44720, (330)494-0535.
Holes: 18. **Caddies:** No. **Discount golf packages:** No. **On site lodging:** No. **Rental clubs:** No. **Metal spikes allowed:** No. **Range:** No.
Call club for further inforamtion.

★★BOB-O-LINK GOLF COURSE

PU-4141 Center Rd., Avon, 44011, Lorain County, (216)934-6217, 20 miles W of Cleveland.
Opened: 1969. **Holes:** 27. **Architect:** N/A. **Green fee:** $12/$14. **Credit cards:** None. **Reduced fees:** Weekdays, seniors, juniors. **Caddies:** No. **Golf carts:** $16. **Discount golf packages:** No. **Season:** Year-round. **High:** May-Sept. **On site lodging:** No. **Rental clubs:** Yes. **Walking policy:** Unrestricted walking. **Metal spikes allowed:** Yes. **Range:** Yes (grass/mats). **To obtain tee times:** Call 7 days in advance.
RED/BLUE
Par: 71/71. **Yards:** 6,052/4,808. **Course rating:** 66.6/62.6. **Slope:** 115/112.
RED/WHITE
Par: 71/71. **Yards:** 6,263/5,050. **Course rating:** 66.6/62.6. **Slope:** 108/107.
WHITE/BLUE
Par: 72/72. **Yards:** 6,383/5,103. **Course rating:** 68.4/64.8. **Slope:** 115/115.

★★BOLTON FIELD GOLF COURSE

PU-6005 Alkire Rd., Columbus, 43119, Franklin County, (614)645-3050, 81 miles SW of Columbus.
Opened: 1971. **Holes:** 18. **Par:** 72/72. **Yards:** 7,034/5,204. **Course rating:** 71.9/68.6. **Slope:** 118/113. **Architect:** Jack Kidwell. **Green fee:** $12/$14. **Credit cards:** MC,VISA. **Reduced fees:** Weekdays, low season, twilight, seniors, juniors. **Caddies:** No. **Golf carts:** $20. **Discount golf packages:** Yes. **Season:** Year-round. **High:** May-Sept. **On site lodging:** No. **Rental clubs:** Yes. **Walking policy:** Unrestricted walking. **Metal spikes allowed:** Yes. **Range:** Yes (grass). **To obtain tee times:** Call Sunday night prior to weekend. Call 7 days in advance for weekdays.

★½BOSTON HILLS COUNTRY CLUB

PU-105/124 E. Hines Hill Rd., Boston Heights, 44236, Summit County, (216)656-2438, 30 miles S of Cleveland.
Opened: 1923. **Holes:** 18. **Par:** 71/71. **Yards:** 6,117/4,987. **Course rating:** 68.2/67.4. **Slope:** 110/105. **Architect:** Wink Chadwick. **Green fee:** $15/$19. **Credit cards:** None. **Reduced fees:** Weekdays, low season, seniors, juniors. **Caddies:** No. **Golf carts:** $19. **Discount golf packages:** No. **Season:** Year-round. **High:** June-Aug. **On site lodging:** Yes. **Rental clubs:** Yes. **Walking policy:** Unrestricted walking. **Metal spikes allowed:** Yes. **Range:** Yes (grass). **To obtain tee times:** Call one week in advance.

★★½BRANDYWINE COUNTRY CLUB

PU-5555 Akron Peninsula Rd., Peninsula, 44264, Summit County, (330)657-2525, 10 miles NW of Akron.
Opened: 1962. **Holes:** 18. **Par:** 72/75. **Yards:** 6,470/5,625. **Course rating:** 70.2/70.5. **Slope:** 113/113. **Architect:** Earl Yesberger. **Green fee:** $19/$24. **Credit cards:** None. **Reduced fees:** Weekdays, twilight, seniors. **Caddies:** No. **Golf carts:** $22. **Discount golf packages:** Yes. **Season:** Year-round. **High:** May-Sept. **On site lodging:** No. **Rental clubs:** Yes. **Walking policy:** Unrestricted walking. **Metal spikes allowed:** Yes. **Range:** No. **To obtain tee times:** Call 7 days in advance.

★★BRIARDALE GREENS GOLF COURSE

PM-24131 Briardale Ave., Euclid, 44123, Cuyahoga County, (216)289-8574, 8 miles E of Cleveland.

Opened: 1977. **Holes:** 18. **Par:** 70/70. **Yards:** 6,127/4,977. **Course rating:** 69.1/70.5. **Slope:** 116/118. **Architect:** Dick LaConte. **Green fee:** $16/$18. **Credit cards:** MC,VISA. **Reduced fees:** Weekdays, low season, resort guests, twilight, seniors, juniors. **Caddies:** No. **Golf carts:** $8. **Discount golf packages:** Yes. **Season:** March-Nov. **High:** May-Sept. **On site lodging:** No. **Rental clubs:** Yes. **Walking policy:** Unrestricted walking. **Metal spikes allowed:** Yes. **Range:** Yes (grass/mats). **To obtain tee times:** Call 7 days in advance.

★★½BRIARWOOD GOLF COURSE
PU-2737 Edgerton Rd., Broadview Heights, 44147, Cuyahoga County, (216)237-5271, 22 miles S of Cleveland.
Opened: 1965. **Holes:** 27. **Architect:** Ted McAnlis. **Green fee:** $19/$29. **Credit cards:** MC,VISA,AMEX. **Reduced fees:** Weekdays, low season, twilight, seniors, juniors. **Caddies:** No. **Golf carts:** $11. **Discount golf packages:** No. **Season:** April-Dec. **High:** May-Sept. **On site lodging:** No. **Rental clubs:** Yes. **Walking policy:** Unrestricted walking. **Metal spikes allowed:** Yes. **Range:** Yes (grass/mats). **To obtain tee times:** Call Saturday a.m. for following weekend.
BLUE/RED
Par: 71/71. **Yards:** 6,405/5,355. **Course rating:** 70.1/69.9. **Slope:** 117/110.
BLUE/WHITE
Par: 71/71. **Yards:** 6,500/5,365. **Course rating:** 70.8/68.9. **Slope:** 117/108.
RED/WHITE
Par: 72/72. **Yards:** 6,985/5,860. **Course rating:** 72.8/71.6. **Slope:** 125/115.
Subscriber comments: Nice assortment of holes...Wide open, minimal hazards...Challenging.

★★½BUCKEYE HILLS COUNTRY CLUB
226 Miami Trace Rd., Greenfield, 45123, Highland County, (937)981-4136, 50 miles E of Cincinnati.
Opened: 1970. **Holes:** 18. **Par:** 71/72. **Yards:** 6,393/4,907. **Course rating:** 70.4/67.4. **Slope:** 121/113. **Architect:** X. G. Hassenplug. **Green fee:** $14/$18. **Credit cards:** MC,VISA. **Reduced fees:** N/A. **Caddies:** No. **Golf carts:** $10. **Discount golf packages:** No. **Season:** March-Nov. **High:** N/A. **On site lodging:** No. **Rental clubs:** No. **Walking policy:** Unrestricted walking. **Metal spikes allowed:** No. **Range:** No. **To obtain tee times:** Call up to 7 days in advance.
Subscriber comments: Good layout...Rolling hills leave some blind shots...Tough little course, a lot of fun...Nice layout...Challenging, scenic course.

★★½BUNKER HILL GOLF COURSE
PU-3060 Pearl Rd., Medina, 44256, Medina County, (330)722-4174, 20 miles S of Cleveland.
Opened: 1927. **Holes:** 18. **Par:** 70/72. **Yards:** 6,044/5,481. **Course rating:** 67.1/68.9. **Slope:** 107/110. **Architect:** Mateo and Sons. **Green fee:** $18/$23. **Credit cards:** MC,VISA. **Reduced fees:** Weekdays, low season, seniors, juniors. **Caddies:** No. **Golf carts:** $20. **Discount golf packages:** No. **Season:** March-Nov. **High:** May-Aug. **On site lodging:** No. **Rental clubs:** Yes. **Walking policy:** Walking at certain times. **Metal spikes allowed:** Yes. **Range:** No. **To obtain tee times:** Call for weekends and holidays.
Subscriber comments: Scenic but short...New holes will make course much harder...Standard muny course...Enjoyable, would return...Could become exceptional.

★★CALIFORNIA GOLF COURSE
PU-5920 Kellogg Ave., Cincinnati, 45228, Hamilton County, (513)231-6513.
Opened: 1936. **Holes:** 18. **Par:** 70/71. **Yards:** 6,216/5,626. **Course rating:** 70.0/71.4. **Slope:** 116/113. **Architect:** Wm. H. Diddel. **Green fee:** $16/$17. **Credit cards:** None. **Reduced fees:** Low season, seniors, juniors. **Caddies:** No. **Golf carts:** $19. **Discount golf packages:** No. **Season:** Year-round. **High:** April-Sept. **On site lodging:** No. **Rental clubs:** Yes. **Walking policy:** Unrestricted walking. **Metal spikes allowed:** Yes. **Range:** No. **To obtain tee times:** Call one day in advance.

★★★CARROLL MEADOWS GOLF COURSE
PU-1130 Meadowbrook, Carrollton, 44615, Carroll County, (330)627-2663.
Opened: 1989. **Architect:** John F. Robinson. **Caddies:** No. **Discount golf packages:**

No. **On site lodging:** No. **Rental clubs:** No. **Metal spikes allowed:** Yes. **Range:** No. Call club for further information.

Subscriber comments: I like this course, it is challenging but not impossible...Will be better with age...Nice country golf course.

★★★CASSEL HILLS GOLF COURSE

PU-201 S. Cassel Rd., Vandalia, 45377, Montgomery County, (937)890-1300, 5 miles N of Dayton.

Opened: 1974. **Holes:** 18. **Par:** 71/71. **Yards:** 6,617/5,600. **Course rating:** 72.0/70.8. **Slope:** 139/125. **Architect:** Bruce von Roxburg. **Green fee:** $16/$24. **Credit cards:** MC,VISA. **Reduced fees:** N/A. **Caddies:** No. **Golf carts:** $20. **Discount golf packages:** No. **Season:** Feb.-Dec. **High:** April-Oct. **On site lodging:** No. **Rental clubs:** Yes. **Walking policy:** Unrestricted walking. **Metal spikes allowed:** Yes. **Range:** No. **To obtain tee times:** Call up to 7 days in advance.

Subscriber comments: Recent alterations improved course...Good course, lots of trees, good challenge...Look out for deer!...A few unusual holes.

CASTLE SHANNON GOLF COURSE

PU-105 Castle Shannon Blvd., Hopedale, 43976, Jefferson County, (614)937-2373, 58 miles W of Pittsburgh, PA.

Opened: 1996. **Holes:** 18. **Par:** 71/71. **Yards:** 6,896/4,752. **Course rating:** 72.2/66.7. **Slope:** 129/115. **Architect:** Gary Grandstaff. **Green fee:** $24/$29. **Credit cards:** MC,VISA. **Reduced fees:** Seniors. **Caddies:** No. **Golf carts:** N/A. **Discount golf packages:** No. **Season:** Year-round weather permitting. **High:** N/A. **On site lodging:** No. **Rental clubs:** Yes. **Walking policy:** Mandatory cart. **Range:** Yes (grass). **To obtain tee times:** Call.

★★½CATAWBA WILLOWS GOLF & COUNTRY CLUB

PU-2590 Sand Rd., Port Clinton, 43452, Ottawa County, (419)-734-2524.
Call club for further information.

Subscriber comments: Very short, water on every hole...Very pleasant, short but narrow...Lots of water, challenging, sloped greens.

★★CHAMPION LINKS GOLF CLUB

PU-4891 Clovercrest Dr. N.W., Warren, 44483, Trumbull County, (330)872-5559.
Call club for further information.

★★★½CHAMPIONS GOLF COURSE

PU-3900 Westerville Rd., Columbus, 43224, Franklin County, (614)645-7111.

Opened: 1953. **Holes:** 18. **Par:** 70/72. **Yards:** 6,555/5,427. **Course rating:** 71.2/71.2. **Slope:** 127/127. **Architect:** Robert Trent Jones. **Green fee:** $27/$29. **Credit cards:** MC,VISA. **Reduced fees:** Weekdays, low season, twilight, seniors, juniors. **Caddies:** No. **Golf carts:** $21. **Discount golf packages:** Yes. **Season:** Year-round. **High:** May-Oct. **On site lodging:** No. **Rental clubs:** Yes. **Walking policy:** Walking at certain times. **Metal spikes allowed:** Yes. **Range:** Yes (grass/mats). **To obtain tee times:** Call 7 days in advance.

Subscriber comments: Classic golf course...Have to think your way around...With better care, would be excellent...Great layout...Old course, good layout.

★★★CHAPEL HILL GOLF COURSE

PU-7516 Johnstown Rd., Mount Vernon, 43050, Knox County, (740)393-3999, (800)393-3499, 38 miles NE of Columbus.

Opened: 1996. **Holes:** 18. **Par:** 72/72. **Yards:** 6,900/4,600. **Course rating:** 72.2/69.4. **Slope:** 128/119. **Architect:** Barry Serafin. **Green fee:** $18/$20. **Credit cards:** MC,VISA. **Reduced fees:** Weekdays, low season. **Caddies:** No. **Golf carts:** $11. **Discount golf packages:** No. **Season:** Year-round. **High:** April-Oct. **On site lodging:** No. **Rental clubs:** Yes. **Walking policy:** Unrestricted walking. **Metal spikes allowed:** Yes. **Range:** Yes (grass). **To obtain tee times:** Call anytime for weekday. Call up to 7 days in advance for weekend.

Subscriber comments: New course, hilly, interesting...Some picturesque holes...Will be good course...Needs time to mature, scenic holes, good variety.

OHIO

★★CHAPEL HILLS GOLF COURSE
PU-3381 Austinburg Rd., Ashtabula, 44004, Ashtabula County, (216)997-3791, (800)354-9608, 45 miles E of Cleveland.
Opened: 1957. **Holes:** 18. **Par:** 72/72. **Yards:** 5,971/4,507. **Course rating:** 68.6/65.7. **Slope:** 112/104. **Architect:** Bill Franklin. **Green fee:** $12/$17. **Credit cards:** MC,VISA. **Reduced fees:** Weekdays, seniors, juniors. **Caddies:** No. **Golf carts:** $8. **Discount golf packages:** No. **Season:** April-Nov. **High:** June-Sept. **On site lodging:** No. **Rental clubs:** Yes. **Walking policy:** Unrestricted walking. **Metal spikes allowed:** Yes. **Range:** Yes (grass). **To obtain tee times:** Call.

★★★CHARDON LAKES GOLF COURSE
PU-470 S. St., Chardon, 44024, Geauga County, (440)285-4653, 35 miles NE of Cleveland.
Opened: 1931. **Holes:** 18. **Par:** 71/73. **Yards:** 6,789/5,077. **Course rating:** 73.1/66.6. **Slope:** 135/111. **Architect:** Birdie Way/Don Tincher. **Green fee:** $21/$31. **Credit cards:** All major. **Reduced fees:** Low season, seniors, juniors. **Caddies:** No. **Golf carts:** $10. **Discount golf packages:** No. **Season:** April-Nov. **High:** June-Sept. **On site lodging:** Yes. **Rental clubs:** Yes. **Walking policy:** Unrestricted walking. **Metal spikes allowed:** No. **Range:** Yes (grass). **To obtain tee times:** Call up to 14 days in advance for weekdays. Call Monday after 8 a.m. for upcoming weekend or holiday.
Subscriber comments: Challenging, big tough greens...Lovely course...Mixture of tough and easy holes...Three toughest finishing holes in NE Ohio.

★★CHEROKEE HILLS GOLF CLUB
PU-5740 Center Rd., Valley City, 44280, Medina County, (330)225-6122, 31 miles NW of Akron.
Opened: 1981. **Holes:** 18. **Par:** 70/70. **Yards:** 6,210/5,880. **Course rating:** 68.3/70.3. **Slope:** 109/116. **Architect:** Brian Huntley. **Green fee:** $12/$20. **Credit cards:** MC,VISA. **Reduced fees:** Weekdays, low season, twilight, seniors, juniors. **Caddies:** No. **Golf carts:** $25. **Discount golf packages:** Yes. **Season:** Year-round. **High:** April-Oct. **On site lodging:** No. **Rental clubs:** Yes. **Walking policy:** Unrestricted walking. **Metal spikes allowed:** Yes. **Range:** No. **To obtain tee times:** Call in advance.

★★½CHEROKEE HILLS GOLF COURSE
4622 County Rd. 49 N., Bellefontaine, 43311, Logan County, (937)599-3221, 45 miles NW of Columbus.
Opened: 1970. **Holes:** 18. **Par:** 71/74. **Yards:** 6,448/5,327. **Course rating:** 70.8/70.3. **Slope:** 115/108. **Architect:** Cherster Kurtz. **Green fee:** $14/$17. **Credit cards:** MC,VISA. **Reduced fees:** Weekdays, low season, juniors. **Caddies:** No. **Golf carts:** $10. **Discount golf packages:** Yes. **Season:** March-Dec. **High:** May-Sept. **On site lodging:** No. **Rental clubs:** Yes. **Walking policy:** Unrestricted walking. **Metal spikes allowed:** Yes. **Range:** No. **To obtain tee times:** Call 7 days in advance.

★★★CHIPPEWA GOLF CLUB
PU-12147 Shank Rd., Doylestown, 44230, Wayne County, (330)658-6126, (800)321-1701, 5 miles S of Akron.
Opened: 1962. **Holes:** 18. **Par:** 71/72. **Yards:** 6,273/4,877. **Course rating:** 69.1/67.0. **Slope:** 109/103. **Architect:** Harrison and Garbin. **Green fee:** $11/$18. **Credit cards:** All major. **Reduced fees:** Weekdays, low season, seniors, juniors. **Caddies:** No. **Golf carts:** $19. **Discount golf packages:** No. **Season:** Year-round. **High:** April-Oct. **On site lodging:** No. **Rental clubs:** Yes. **Walking policy:** Unrestricted walking. **Metal spikes allowed:** Yes. **Range:** Yes (grass/mats). **To obtain tee times:** Call.
Subscriber comments: Some great holes...14 through 16 will make or break your day!...Front nine so-so, back nine very challenging...Lots of hills on the back nine, a fair course...Long par 4s with large rolling greens...Tough, hilly course...Best back nine around.

★★CLIFFSIDE GOLF COURSE
PU-100 Cliffside Dr., Gallipolis, 45631, Gallia County, (614)446-4653, 30 miles NE of Huntington.
Opened: 1988. **Holes:** 18. **Par:** 72/72. **Yards:** 6,598/5,268. **Course rating:** 70.5/66.8. **Slope:** 115/109. **Architect:** Jack Kidwell. **Green fee:** $15/$16. **Credit cards:** MC,VISA.

Reduced fees: Weekdays, low season. **Caddies:** No. **Golf carts:** $10. **Discount golf packages:** No. **Season:** Year-round. **High:** April-Oct. **On site lodging:** No. **Rental clubs:** Yes. **Walking policy:** Unrestricted walking. **Metal spikes allowed:** No. **Range:** No. **To obtain tee times:** Call 7 days in advance.

★★★½COLONIAL GOLFERS CLUB

PU-10985 Harding Hwy., Harrod, 45850, Allen County, (419)649-3350, (800)234-7468, 10 miles E of Lima.
Opened: 1973. **Holes:** 18. **Par:** 72/74. **Yards:** 7,000/5,000. **Course rating:** 72.2/68.7. **Slope:** 139/111. **Architect:** Bob Holtosberry/Tom Holtosberry. **Green fee:** $15/$19. **Credit cards:** MC,VISA. **Reduced fees:** Weekdays, low season, twilight, seniors, juniors. **Caddies:** No. **Golf carts:** $10. **Discount golf packages:** No. **Season:** March-Dec. **High:** June-Aug. **On site lodging:** No. **Rental clubs:** Yes. **Walking policy:** Unrestricted walking. **Metal spikes allowed:** Yes. **Range:** Yes (grass). **To obtain tee times:** Call golf shop.
Subscriber comments: Front nine is open, round begins on No. 10...Pretty...An enjoyable course to play, challenging but not punishing, very popular...9 and 18 excellent par 5s...Excellent public course.

★★★★COOKS CREEK GOLF CLUB

PU-16405 U.S. Hwy. 23 S., Ashville, 43103, Pickaway County, (614)983-3636, (800)430-4653, 15 miles S of Columbus.
Opened: 1993. **Holes:** 18. **Par:** 72/72. **Yards:** 7,071/4,995. **Course rating:** 73.7/68.2. **Slope:** 131/120. **Architect:** Michael Hurdzan and John Cook. **Green fee:** $30/$59. **Credit cards:** All major,Diners Club. **Reduced fees:** Low season, twilight. **Caddies:** No. **Golf carts:** Included in Green Fee. **Discount golf packages:** No. **Season:** Year-round. **High:** April-Oct. **On site lodging:** No. **Rental clubs:** Yes. **Walking policy:** Unrestricted walking. **Metal spikes allowed:** Yes. **Range:** Yes (grass). **To obtain tee times:** Call up to 7 days in advance.
Notes: Ranked 9th in 1995 Best New Public Courses.
Subscriber comments: Long course, impossible to walk due to terrain...Fun, interesting routing, variety of holes, water...Needs time to mature...Will be a classic...Very wet on the lower holes...Some unique holes...Excellent layout. Hill and valley course.

★★½COPELAND HILLS GOLF COURSE

PU-41703 Metz Rd., Columbiana, 44408, Columbiana County, (330)482-3221, 20 miles S of Youngstown.
Opened: 1960. **Holes:** 18. **Par:** 72/74. **Yards:** 6,857/5,763. **Course rating:** 72.7/72.7. **Slope:** 121/120. **Architect:** R. Albert Anderson. **Green fee:** $27/$30. **Credit cards:** None. **Reduced fees:** Weekdays, seniors, juniors. **Caddies:** No. **Golf carts:** Included in Green Fee. **Discount golf packages:** No. **Season:** April-Dec. **High:** July-Sept. **On site lodging:** No. **Rental clubs:** Yes. **Walking policy:** Unrestricted walking. **Metal spikes allowed:** Yes. **Range:** Yes (grass). **To obtain tee times:** Call up to 1 year in advance.

★★★COUNTRY ACRES GOLF CLUB

17374 St. Rte. 694, Ottawa, 45875, Putnam County, (419)532-3434, 20 miles N of Lima.
Opened: 1978. **Holes:** 18. **Par:** 72/72. **Yards:** 6,464/4,961. **Course rating:** 69.9/67.9. **Slope:** 126/113. **Architect:** John Simmons. **Green fee:** $16/$19. **Credit cards:** MC,VISA. **Reduced fees:** Seniors, juniors. **Caddies:** No. **Golf carts:** $10. **Discount golf packages:** Yes. **Season:** March-Dec. **High:** June-Sept. **On site lodging:** No. **Rental clubs:** Yes. **Walking policy:** Unrestricted walking. **Metal spikes allowed:** Yes. **Range:** Yes (grass). **To obtain tee times:** Call 7 days in advance.
Subscriber comments: Tough finishing holes...Fair course, enjoyable to play...Short and tricky...Well bunkered...Fairly wide open, often windy...Great par 5 18th hole with fairway bunkers and island green...Demanding par 3s.

★★COUNTRYSIDE GOLF COURSE

PU-1421 Struthers Coit Rd., Lowellville, 44436, Mahoning County, (330)755-0016, 5 miles S of Youngstown.
Opened: 1967. **Holes:** 18. **Par:** 71/71. **Yards:** 6,461/5,399. **Course rating:** 70.5/70.1. **Slope:** N/A. **Architect:** N/A. **Green fee:** $16/$18. **Credit cards:** MC,VISA. **Reduced fees:** Weekdays, low season, seniors, juniors. **Caddies:** No. **Golf carts:** $16. **Discount**

golf packages: No. **Season:** March-Nov. **High:** May-Aug. **On site lodging:** No. **Rental clubs:** No. **Walking policy:** Unrestricted walking. **Metal spikes allowed:** Yes. **Range:** No. **To obtain tee times:** Call.

★★★CROOKED TREE GOLF CLUB

3595 Mason Montgomery Rd., Mason, 45040, Warren County, (513)398-3933.
Architect: Denny Acomb. **Caddies:** No. **Discount golf packages:** No. **On site lodging:** No. **Rental clubs:** No. **Metal spikes allowed:** Yes. **Range:** Yes.
Call club for further information.
Subscriber comments: Tee placement a must, fall golf is beautiful...Nice use of terrain and creeks...Leave driver home...Some exceptional holes.

★★★½DARBY CREEK GOLF COURSE

PU-19300 Orchard Rd., Marysville, 43040, Union County, (937)349-7491, (800)343-2729, 18 miles NW of Columbus.
Opened: 1993. **Holes:** 18. **Par:** 72/72. **Yards:** 7,054/5,245. **Course rating:** 72.7/68.1.
Slope: 124/114. **Architect:** Geoffrey S. Cornish and Brian Silva. **Green fee:** $18/$24.
Credit cards: MC,VISA. **Reduced fees:** Weekdays, twilight, seniors. **Caddies:** No.
Golf carts: $10. **Discount golf packages:** Yes. **Season:** Year-round. **High:** May-Oct.
On site lodging: No. **Rental clubs:** Yes. **Walking policy:** Walking at certain times.
Metal spikes allowed: Yes. **Range:** Yes (grass). **To obtain tee times:** Call 60 days in advance.
Subscriber comments: Jekyll and Hyde front and back: front open, back long and tight...Good mixture of new and old architecture styles...Long course from the back tees, fun to play.

★★½DEER CREEK STATE PARK GOLF COURSE

R-20635 Waterloo Rd., Mount Sterling, 43143, Pickaway County, (740)869-3088.
Opened: 1982. **Holes:** 18. **Par:** 72/72. **Yards:** 7,134/5,611. **Course rating:** 73.7/71.7.
Slope: 113/113. **Architect:** Jack Kidwell and Michael Hurdzan. **Green fee:** $14/$19.
Credit cards: MC,VISA. **Reduced fees:** Weekdays, low season, resort guests, twilight, seniors, juniors. **Caddies:** No. **Golf carts:** $11. **Discount golf packages:** Yes. **Season:** Year-round. **High:** May-Sept. **On site lodging:** Yes. **Rental clubs:** Yes. **Walking policy:** Unrestricted walking. **Metal spikes allowed:** Yes. **Range:** Yes (grass). **To obtain tee times:** Overnight park guests may call anytime for tee times. Others call Monday a.m. on week of play.
Subscriber comments: Nice open layout, course will age well...Good state-run course...Challenging, fun to play.

★★DEER LAKE GOLF CLUB

PU-6300 Lake Rd. W., Geneva, 44041, Ashtabula County, (216)466-8450.
Call club for further information.

DEER TRACK GOLF CLUB

6160 SR 727, Goshen, 45122, Cincinnati County, (513)625-2500.
Opened: 1996. **Holes:** 18. **Par:** 71/72. **Yards:** 6,352/5,425. **Course rating:** 70.7/70.5.
Slope: 127/123. **Architect:** Phillip Buress. **Green fee:** $20/$20. **Credit cards:** MC,VISA,DISC. **Reduced fees:** Seniors, juniors. **Golf carts:** $10. **Season:** Year-round. **High:** April-Nov. **Walking policy:** Unrestricted walking. **Range:** Yes (grass). **To obtain tee times:** Call 7 days in advance.

★★★DEER TRACK GOLF CLUB

PU-9488 Leavitt Rd., Elyria, 44035, Lorain County, (216)986-5881, 30 miles W of Cleveland.
Opened: 1989. **Holes:** 18. **Par:** 71/71. **Yards:** 6,410/5,191. **Course rating:** 70.3/68.7.
Slope: 124/115. **Architect:** Tony Dalio. **Green fee:** $11/$17. **Credit cards:** MC,VISA.
Reduced fees: Low season, seniors. **Caddies:** No. **Golf carts:** $18. **Discount golf packages:** No. **Season:** Year-round. **High:** April-Oct. **On site lodging:** No. **Rental clubs:** No. **Walking policy:** Unrestricted walking. **Metal spikes allowed:** Yes. **Range:** Yes (grass/mats). **To obtain tee times:** Call golf shop.
Subscriber comments: Back nine will keep you on your toes...Good seniors course...Interesting layout...A very nice course to walk...Water, sand and tight fairways, challenging...A good course but can be tough.

OHIO

★★★DETWILER GOLF COURSE
PU-4001 N. Summit St., Toledo, 43611, Lucas County, (419)726-9353, 45 miles S of Detroit.
Opened: 1971. **Holes:** 18. **Par:** 71/71. **Yards:** 6,497/5,137. **Course rating:** 70.2/68.6. **Slope:** 114/108. **Architect:** Arthur Hills. **Green fee:** $7/$24. **Credit cards:** MC,VISA,AMEX. **Reduced fees:** N/A. **Caddies:** No. **Golf carts:** $11. **Discount golf packages:** No. **Season:** Year-round. **High:** April-Oct. **On site lodging:** No. **Rental clubs:** Yes. **Walking policy:** Unrestricted walking. **Metal spikes allowed:** Yes. **Range:** Yes (grass/mats). **To obtain tee times:** Call up to 7 days in advance.
Subscriber comments: Great natural setting, abundant wildlife...Great course...Too many wild geese all over...Interesting holes, challenging, not overly long, fast greens...Early Arthur Hills design, good test of golf.

★★DORLON GOLF CLUB
PU-18000 Station Rd., Columbia Station, 44028, Lorain County, (440)236-8234, 22 miles SW of Cleveland.
Opened: 1970. **Holes:** 18. **Par:** 72/74. **Yards:** 7,154/5,691. **Course rating:** 74.0/67.4. **Slope:** 131/118. **Architect:** William Mitchell. **Green fee:** $18/$18. **Credit cards:** None. **Reduced fees:** Weekdays, low season, seniors, juniors. **Caddies:** No. **Golf carts:** $17. **Discount golf packages:** No. **Season:** April-Nov. **High:** May-Sept. **On site lodging:** No. **Rental clubs:** Yes. **Walking policy:** Unrestricted walking. **Metal spikes allowed:** Yes. **Range:** Yes (grass/mats). **To obtain tee times:** Call.

★★EAGLES NEST GOLF COURSE
PU-1540 St. Rte. No.28, Loveland, 45140, Clermont County, (513)722-1241, 15 miles E of Cincinnati.
Opened: N/A. **Holes:** 18. **Par:** 71/71. **Yards:** 6,145/4,868. **Course rating:** 69.7/66.9. **Slope:** 120/108. **Architect:** Taylor Boyd. **Green fee:** $14/$17. **Credit cards:** MC,VISA,DISC. **Reduced fees:** Seniors, juniors. **Caddies:** No. **Golf carts:** $20. **Discount golf packages:** No. **Season:** Year-round. **High:** April-Sept. **On site lodging:** No. **Rental clubs:** Yes. **Walking policy:** Unrestricted walking. **Metal spikes allowed:** Yes. **Range:** Yes (grass/mats). **To obtain tee times:** Call 7 days in advance.

★★★★EAGLESTICKS GOLF COURSE
PU-2655 Maysville Pike, Zanesville, 43701, Muskingum County, (614)454-4900, (800)782-4493, 60 miles E of Columbus.
Opened: 1990. **Holes:** 18. **Par:** 70/70. **Yards:** 6,412/4,137. **Course rating:** 70.1/63.7. **Slope:** 120/96. **Architect:** Mike Hurdzan. **Green fee:** $25/$35. **Credit cards:** MC,VISA,AMEX. **Reduced fees:** Weekdays, low season, twilight, seniors, juniors. **Caddies:** No. **Golf carts:** $10. **Discount golf packages:** Yes. **Season:** April-Dec. **High:** June-Aug. **On site lodging:** No. **Rental clubs:** Yes. **Walking policy:** Unrestricted walking. **Metal spikes allowed:** Yes. **Range:** Yes (grass). **To obtain tee times:** Call golf shop up to one year in advance.
Notes: Ranked 20th in 1997 Best in State.
Subscriber comments: Water, sand, hills, trees, it has it all...Too hard to walk...Very interesting layout...Outstanding short golf course...Terrific changes in elevation to test you...Fantastic course, moderately difficult but really fun.

★★THE ELMS COUNTRY CLUB
PU-1608 Manchester Rd. S.W., North Lawrence, 44666, Stark County, (330)833-2668, (800)600-3567, 45 miles S of Cleveland.
Opened: 1932. **Holes:** 27. **Par:** 72/74. **Yards:** 6,545/5,034. **Course rating:** 69.9/67.2. **Slope:** 110/101. **Architect:** Ed Rottman. **Green fee:** $17/$20. **Credit cards:** MC,VISA. **Reduced fees:** Weekdays, low season, twilight, seniors, juniors. **Caddies:** No. **Golf carts:** $25. **Discount golf packages:** Yes. **Season:** Feb.-Dec. **High:** May-Sept. **On site lodging:** No. **Rental clubs:** Yes. **Walking policy:** Unrestricted walking. **Metal spikes allowed:** No. **Range:** Yes (grass/mats). **To obtain tee times:** Call golf shop.

EMERALD WOODS
PU-12501 N. Boone Rd., Columbia Station, 44028, Lorain County, (216)236-8940, 14 miles SW of Cleveland.
Opened: 1967. **Architect:** Raymond McClain. **Credit cards:** None. **Caddies:** No. Golf

carts: $19. **Reduced fees:** Weekdays, seniors. **Discount golf packages:** No. **Season:** Year-round weather permitting. **High:** Summer. **On site lodging:** No. **Rental clubs:** Yes. **Walking policy:** Unrestricted walking. **Metal spikes allowed:** No. **Range:** No. **To obtain tee times:** Call up to 7 days in advance for weekends and holidays.

★★**SAINT ANDREWS/PINE VALLEY COURSE**

Holes: 18. **Par:** 72/73. **Yards:** 6,629/5,080. **Course rating:** 72.1/66.4. **Slope:** N/A. **Green fee:** $18/$21.

★½**AUDREY'S/HEATHER STONE COURSE**

Holes: 18. **Par:** 70/71. **Yards:** 6,673/5,295. **Course rating:** 71.1/68.2. **Slope:** N/A. **Green fee:** $17/$19.

Special Notes: Also has a 9-hole course.

★★★**ERIE SHORES GOLF COURSE**

PU-7298 Lake Rd. E., North Madison, 44057, Lake County, (216)428-3164, (800)225-3742, 40 miles E of Cleveland.

Opened: 1957. **Holes:** 18. **Par:** 70/70. **Yards:** 6,000/4,750. **Course rating:** 68.2/67.0. **Slope:** 116/108. **Architect:** Ben W. Zink. **Green fee:** $12/$16. **Credit cards:** MC,VISA,DISC. **Reduced fees:** Weekdays, low season, seniors, juniors. **Caddies:** No. **Golf carts:** $11. **Discount golf packages:** No. **Season:** Year-round. **High:** May-Sept. **On site lodging:** No. **Rental clubs:** Yes. **Walking policy:** Unrestricted walking. **Metal spikes allowed:** Yes. **Range:** Yes (grass/mats). **To obtain tee times:** Call on Monday for upcoming weekend.

Subscriber comments: Short course...Much improved in recent years...Some scenic holes...Makes you think...Built on sand, can play anytime.

★½**ESTATE GOLF CLUB**

PU-3871 Tschopp Rd., Lancaster, 43130, Fairfield County, (614)654-4444, (800)833-8463, 4 miles N of Lancaster.

Opened: 1967. **Holes:** 18. **Par:** 71/72. **Yards:** 6,405/5,680. **Course rating:** 69.9. **Slope:** 113. **Architect:** Donald Arledge. **Green fee:** $13/$16. **Credit cards:** MC,VISA. **Reduced fees:** Weekdays, twilight, seniors, juniors. **Caddies:** No. **Golf carts:** $22. **Discount golf packages:** Yes. **Season:** Year-round. **High:** June-Sept. **On site lodging:** No. **Rental clubs:** Yes. **Walking policy:** Unrestricted walking. **Metal spikes allowed:** Yes. **Range:** Yes (grass). **To obtain tee times:** Call 7 days in advance.

★★½**FAIRFIELD GOLF CLUB**

PU-2200 John Gray Rd., Fairfield, 45014, Butler County, (513)867-5385.

Opened: 1976. **Holes:** 18. **Par:** 70/70. **Yards:** 6,250/4,900. **Course rating:** 69.5/68.8. **Slope:** 123/113. **Architect:** Jack Kidwell and Michael Hurdzan. **Green fee:** $19/$22. **Credit cards:** MC,VISA. **Reduced fees:** Seniors, juniors. **Caddies:** No. **Golf carts:** $11. **Discount golf packages:** No. **Season:** March-Dec. **High:** June-Aug. **On site lodging:** No. **Rental clubs:** Yes. **Walking policy:** Walking at certain times. **Metal spikes allowed:** Yes. **Range:** No. **To obtain tee times:** Call 9 days in advance.

Subscriber comments: Good course...Layout has potential...Fun to play, could be harder...Nice course, pretty easy...Good variety of holes.

★★½**FAIRWAY PINES GOLF COURSE**

PU-1777 Blaise-Nemeth Rd., Painesville, 44077, Lake County, (440)357-7800.

Architect: X.G. Hassenplug. **Caddies:** No. **Discount golf packages:** No. **On site lodging:** No. **Rental clubs:** No. **Metal spikes allowed:** Yes. **Range:** No. Call club for further information.

Subscriber comments: Nice layout...A flat track...Fairly open, yet still enough trees to keep you honest...Very flat, long course from the back tees.

★½**FALLEN TIMBERS FAIRWAYS**

7711 Timbers Blvd., Waterville, 43566, Lucas County, (419)878-4653, 12 miles S of Toledo.

Opened: 1992. **Holes:** 18. **Par:** 71/71. **Yards:** 5,741/4,969. **Course rating:** 66.4/66.4. **Slope:** 103/103. **Architect:** N/A. **Green fee:** $16/$20. **Credit cards:** MC,VISA,AMEX. **Reduced fees:** Weekdays, low season, twilight, seniors, juniors. **Caddies:** No. **Golf carts:** $10. **Discount golf packages:** No. **Season:** April-Oct. **High:** June-Aug. **On site lodging:** No. **Rental clubs:** Yes. **Walking policy:** Unrestricted walking. **Metal spikes allowed:** Yes. **Range:** Yes (grass/mats). **To obtain tee times:** Call 7 days in advance.

★★FLAGSTONE GOLF CLUB

PU-13683 St. Rte. 38, Marysville, 43040, Union County, (937)642-1816, (800)742-0899, 15 miles W of Cloumbus.
Opened: 1925. **Holes:** 18. **Par:** 72/72. **Yards:** 6,323/5,111. **Course rating:** 69.6/68.9.
Slope: 115/113. **Architect:** N/A. **Green fee:** $14/$19. **Credit cards:** MC,VISA.
Reduced fees: Weekdays, low season, twilight, seniors. **Caddies:** No. **Golf carts:** $9.
Discount golf packages: No. **Season:** Year-round. **High:** May-Sept. **On site lodging:**
No. **Rental clubs:** Yes. **Walking policy:** Unrestricted walking. **Metal spikes allowed:**
Yes. **Range:** No. **To obtain tee times:** Call up to one week in advance.

★★½FOREST HILLS GOLF CENTER

PU-41971 Oberlin Rd., Elyria, 44035, Lorain County, (216)323-2632, 30 miles W of Cleveland.
Opened: N/A. **Holes:** 18. **Par:** 70/71. **Yards:** 6,161/5,125. **Course rating:** 69.7/67.6. **Slope:** 117/105. **Architect:** Charlie Smith. **Green fee:** $10/$12. **Credit cards:** None. **Reduced fees:** N/A. **Caddies:** No. **Golf carts:** N/A. **Discount golf packages:** No. **Season:** March-Dec. **High:** N/A. **On site lodging:** No. **Rental clubs:** Yes. **Walking policy:** Unrestricted walking. **Metal spikes allowed:** Yes. **Range:** Yes (grass/mats). **To obtain tee times:** Call up to 7 days in advance for weekends and holidays.
Subscriber comments: A very scenic golf course, with a mix of tough holes and easier holes...Lots of fun...Excellent metro course.

★½FOREST OAKS GOLF COURSE

PU-U.S. Rte. No.422 and St. Rte. No.305, Southington, 44470, Trumbull County, (330)898-2852.
Opened: 1958. **Holes:** 18. **Par:** 72/72. **Yards:** 6,122/5,867. **Course rating:** N/A. **Slope:** N/A. **Architect:** Myron Beechy. **Green fee:** $16/$17. **Credit cards:** MC,VISA,DISC.
Reduced fees: Weekdays, low season, seniors, juniors. **Caddies:** No. **Golf carts:** $16.
Discount golf packages: No. **Season:** March-Nov. **High:** May-Aug. **On site lodging:**
No. **Rental clubs:** Yes. **Walking policy:** Unrestricted walking. **Metal spikes allowed:**
Yes. **Range:** Yes (grass/mats). **To obtain tee times:** Call golf shop.
Special Notes: Also has a 9-hole par 35.

★★★★FOWLER'S MILL GOLF COURSE

PU-13095 Rockhaven Rd., Chesterland, 44026, Geauga County, (440)729-7569, 30 miles E of Cleveland.
Opened: 1972. **Holes:** 27. **Architect:** Pete Dye. **Green fee:** $22/$52. **Credit cards:** MC,VISA,AMEX. **Reduced fees:** Weekdays, low season, twilight, seniors, juniors.
Caddies: No. **Golf carts:** $3. **Discount golf packages:** No. **Season:** March-Oct. **High:** June-Aug. **On site lodging:** No. **Rental clubs:** Yes. **Walking policy:** Unrestricted walking. **Metal spikes allowed:** No. **Range:** Yes (grass). **To obtain tee times:** Call up to 30 days in advance.
RED/BLUE
Par: 72/72. **Yards:** 6,595/5,913. **Course rating:** 72.1/73.6. **Slope:** 128/123.
WHITE/BLUE
Par: 72/72. **Yards:** 7,002/5,950. **Course rating:** 74.7/73.9. **Slope:** 136/122.
RED/WHITE
Par: 72/72. **Yards:** 7,002/5,797. **Course rating:** 74.7/73.0. **Slope:** 136/123.
Subscriber comments: Lots of big old trees...Challenging Pete Dye layout, beautiful...Very challenging, must be good iron player...Great variety of golf holes...The Red nine gets a bad rap...Great layout, will challenge anyone.

★★★FOX DEN GOLF CLUB

PU-2770 Call Rd., Stow, 44224, Summit County, (330)673-3443, (888)231-4693, 8 miles N of Akron.
Opened: 1966. **Holes:** 18. **Par:** 72/72. **Yards:** 6,447/5,473. **Course rating:** 70.4/69.0.
Slope: 115/114. **Architect:** Frank Schmiedel. **Green fee:** $15/$24. **Credit cards:** MC,VISA. **Reduced fees:** Weekdays, low season, seniors, juniors. **Caddies:** No. **Golf carts:** $19. **Discount golf packages:** No. **Season:** March-Nov. **High:** May-Sept. **On site lodging:** No. **Rental clubs:** No. **Walking policy:** Unrestricted walking. **Metal spikes allowed:** Yes. **Range:** Yes (grass/mats). **To obtain tee times:** Call ahead.

Subscriber comments: Great challenging course...Suprisingly tough for short track...Above average...Hope it can stay a secret...Hilly in parts, good length, scenic, sharp doglegs...Average short course...Wide open, par 3s are too easy.

FOXFIRE GOLF CLUB
PU-10799 St. Rte. 104, Lockbourne, 43137, Pickaway County, (614)224-3694, 15 miles S of Columbus.
Credit cards: MC,VISA,AMEX.**Caddies:** No. **Discount golf packages:** No. **Season:** Year-round. **High:** June-Sept. **On site lodging:** No. **Rental clubs:** Yes. **Walking policy:** Unrestricted walking. **Metal spikes allowed:** Yes. **Range:** Yes (grass/mats). **To obtain tee times:** Call up to 14 days in advance.
★★★FOXFIRE COURSE
Opened: 1974. **Holes:** 18. **Par:** 72/72. **Yards:** 6,891/5,175. **Course rating:** 71.1/69.1.
Slope: 118/112. **Architect:** Jack Kidwell. **Green fee:** $18/$20. **Reduced fees:** Low season, seniors, juniors. **Golf carts:** $20.
Subscriber comments: Still enjoyable to play, back nine has more difficult holes...The 17th (629 yards) is amazing...Deceptive, nice layout, par 5s long...Long but fair. Have to hit them straight.
★★★½PLAYERS CLUB AT FOXFIRE
Opened: 1993. **Holes:** 18. **Par:** 72/72. **Yards:** 7,077/5,255. **Course rating:** 74.2/70.3.
Slope: 132/121. **Architect:** Jack Kidwell/Barry Serafin. **Green fee:** $30. **Reduced fees:** Low season. **Golf carts:** $10.
Subscriber comments: Beautiful course, thinker's course...Holes 5 to 14 are magnificent links style...14th is evil...Narrow, long and big trees...Outstanding track, really makes you think your way around...A couple of beautiful holes.

★★½GENEVA ON THE LAKE GOLF CLUB
PU-Golf Ave., Geneva On The Lake, 44041, Ashtabula County, (216)466-8797.
Architect: Stanley Thompson. **Caddies:** No. **Discount golf packages:** No. **On site lodging:** No. **Rental clubs:** No. **Metal spikes allowed:** Yes. **Range:** No.
Call club for further information.

★★½GLENEAGLES GOLF CLUB
PM-2615 Glenwood Dr., Twinsburg, 44087, Summit County, (216)425-3334, 20 miles SE of Cleveland.
Opened: 1990. **Holes:** 18. **Par:** 72/72. **Yards:** 6,545/5,147. **Course rating:** 72.2/69.4.
Slope: 121/115. **Architect:** Ted McAnlis. **Green fee:** $19/$22. **Credit cards:** MC,VISA.
Reduced fees: Weekdays, twilight, seniors, juniors. **Caddies:** No. **Golf carts:** $10.
Discount golf packages: No. **Season:** April-Nov. **High:** June-Aug. **On site lodging:** No. **Rental clubs:** No. **Walking policy:** Unrestricted walking. **Metal spikes allowed:** Yes. **Range:** Yes (grass). **To obtain tee times:** Call up to 14 days in advance.

★★★GLENVIEW GOLF COURSE
PU-10965 Springfield Pike, Cincinnati, 45246, Hamilton County, (513)771-1747.
Opened: 1974. **Holes:** 27. **Par:** 72/72. **Yards:** 6,965/5,091. **Course rating:** 72.3/69.9.
Slope: 132/110. **Architect:** Arthur Hills/Mike Hurdzan. **Green fee:** $20/$20. **Credit cards:** None. **Reduced fees:** Low season, seniors, juniors. **Caddies:** No. **Golf carts:** $20. **Discount golf packages:** No. **Season:** Year-round. **High:** May-Sept. **On site lodging:** No. **Rental clubs:** Yes. **Walking policy:** Unrestricted walking. **Metal spikes allowed:** Yes. **Range:** Yes (grass). **To obtain tee times:** Call golf shop.
Subscriber comments: Could be much better...Good course and range...Great new third nine...Extremely tough from black tees.

THE GOLF CENTER AT KINGS ISLAND
PU-6042 Fairway Dr., Mason, 45040, Warren County, (513)398-7700, 25 miles from Cincinnati.
Credit cards: All major,Diners Club, Carte Blanche. **Caddies:** No. **Golf carts:** $11.
Discount golf packages: No. **Season:** March-Dec. **High:** May-Sept. **On site lodging:** No. **Rental clubs:** Yes. **Metal spikes allowed:** Yes. **Range:** Yes (grass/mats). **To obtain tee times:** Call up to 7 days in advance.
★★★BRUIN COURSE
Opened: 1971. **Holes:** 18. **Par:** 61. **Yards:** 3,428. **Course rating:** N/A. **Slope:** N/A.
Architect: Jack Nicklaus and Desmond Muirhead. **Green fee:** $12/$13. **Reduced fees:**

Weekdays, seniors, juniors. **Walking policy:** Unrestricted walking.
Subscriber comments: Nice track...Excellent course. Good for beginners and to tune up iron play...Great short layout for practice.
Special Notes: Formerly Jack Nicklaus Sports Center.

★★★½GRIZZLY COURSE (NORTH/SOUTH/WEST)
Opened: 1971. **Holes:** 27. **Par:** 71/71 (N/S); 72/72 (N/W); 71/71 (S/W). **Yards:** 6,800/5,143 (N/S); 6,777/5,176 (N/W); 6,660/5,139 (S/W). **Course rating:** 72.3/69.2 (N/S); 72.7/69.4 (N/W); 72.2/69.2 (S/W). **Slope:** 135/114 (N/S); 132/117 (N/W); 130/116 (S/W). **Architect:** Jack Nicklaus and Desmond Muirhead/Jay Morrish. **Green fee:** $27/$65. **Reduced fees:** Weekdays, low season, twilight. **Walking policy:** Walking at certain times.
Notes: Ohio Kings Island Open; LPGA Championship; Kroger Senior Classic.
Subscriber comments: Very nice course, interesting par 3s...Beautiful course, challenge for low-handicappers...18th is memorable.
Special Notes: Formerly The Jack Nicklaus Sports Center.

★★★½THE GOLF CLUB AT YANKEE TRACE
PM-10000 Yankee St., Centerville, 45458, Montgomery County, (937)438-4653, 15 miles S of Dayton.
Opened: 1995. **Holes:** 18. **Par:** 72/72. **Yards:** 7,139/5,204. **Course rating:** 75.5/70.5. **Slope:** 140/124. **Architect:** Gene Bates. **Green fee:** $34/$37. **Credit cards:** All major. **Reduced fees:** Twilight, juniors. **Caddies:** No. **Golf carts:** $12. **Discount golf packages:** No. **Season:** March-Dec. **High:** March-Oct. **On site lodging:** No. **Rental clubs:** Yes. **Walking policy:** Unrestricted walking. **Metal spikes allowed:** No. **Range:** Yes (grass). **To obtain tee times:** Call 7 days in advance.
Subscriber comments: Very nice young course. With time it should get better...Outstanding, great layout...Getting better...Great newer course, good risk/reward challenge...Challenging layout, best four closing holes around.
Special Notes: Also has three practice holes.

★★½THE GOLF COURSES OF WINTON WOODS
PU-1515 W. Sharon Rd., Cincinnati, 45240, Hamilton County, (513)825-3770, 14 miles N of Cincinnati.
Opened: 1993. **Holes:** 18. **Par:** 72/72. **Yards:** 6,376/4,554. **Course rating:** 70.0/66.6. **Slope:** 120/108. **Architect:** Michael Hurdzan. **Green fee:** $17/$17. **Credit cards:** MC,VISA. **Reduced fees:** Seniors, juniors. **Caddies:** No. **Golf carts:** $11. **Discount golf packages:** No. **Season:** March-Dec. **High:** May-Sept. **On site lodging:** No. **Rental clubs:** Yes. **Walking policy:** Unrestricted walking. **Metal spikes allowed:** Yes. **Range:** Yes (grass/mats). **To obtain tee times:** Call 5 days in advance.

★★½GRANDVIEW GOLF CLUB
PU-13404 Old State Rd., Middlefield, 44062, Geauga County, (216)834-1824.
Opened: 1929. **Holes:** 18. **Par:** 70/72. **Yards:** 5,914/5,451. **Course rating:** 68.7/70.2. **Slope:** 114/110. **Architect:** Richard W. LaConte and Ted McAnlis. **Green fee:** $10/$18. **Credit cards:** N/A. **Reduced fees:** Seniors, juniors. **Caddies:** No. **Golf carts:** $20. **Discount golf packages:** No. **Season:** April-Nov. **High:** June-Aug. **On site lodging:** No. **Rental clubs:** No. **Walking policy:** Unrestricted walking. **Metal spikes allowed:** Yes. **Range:** No. **To obtain tee times:** Call.

★★★½GRANVILLE GOLF COURSE
PU-555 Newark Rd., Granville, 43023, Licking County, (614)587-4653.
Opened: 1925. **Holes:** 18. **Par:** 71/72. **Yards:** 6,612/5,413. **Course rating:** 71.3/70.6. **Slope:** 126/121. **Architect:** Donald Ross/Jack Kidwell. **Green fee:** $16/$29. **Credit cards:** MC,VISA,DISC. **Reduced fees:** N/A. **Caddies:** Yes. **Golf carts:** $12. **Discount golf packages:** No. **Season:** Year-round. **High:** April-Nov. **On site lodging:** No. **Rental clubs:** Yes. **Walking policy:** Walking at certain times. **Metal spikes allowed:** Yes. **Range:** Yes (grass/mats). **To obtain tee times:** Call 7 days in advance with credit card to guarantee.
Subscriber comments: One of Ohio's best...Fifteen of the best golf holes, three bad ones...Traditional Donald Ross course...Lot of hills, uphill doglegs, fun!...Wonderful, awesome, great course...Beautiful, especially 16 and 18...Unique combo of an old course with some updated holes...One of the prettiest courses I've played...Lots of hills, great scenery...14-18 just great holes.

★★GREAT TRAIL GOLF COURSE
PU-10154 Great Trail Dr., Minerva, 44657, Carroll County, (330)868-6770.
Opened: 1970. **Holes:** 27. **Par:** N/A. **Yards:** 7. **Course rating:** N/A. **Slope:** N/A.
Architect: Romain Fry. **Green fee:** $12/$14. **Credit cards:** MC,VISA. **Reduced fees:**
Weekdays, resort guests. **Caddies:** No. **Golf carts:** $14. **Discount golf packages:**
Yes. **Season:** Year-round weather permitting. **High:** June-Sept. **On site lodging:** Yes.
Rental clubs: No. **Walking policy:** Unrestricted walking. **Metal spikes allowed:** No.
Range: No. **To obtain tee times:** Call golf shop.

★★GREEN CREST GOLF COURSE
PU-7813 Bethany Rte. 1, Middletown, 45042, Butler County, (513)777-2090.
Call club for further information.

★★★GREEN HILLS GOLF CLUB
PU-1959 S. Main St., Clyde, 43410, Sandusky County, (419)547-7947, (800)234-4766.
Opened: 1958. **Holes:** 18. **Par:** 71/74. **Yards:** 6,172/5,417. **Course rating:** N/A. **Slope:**
100/100. **Architect:** T. Crockett/B. Crockett/M. Fritz. **Green fee:** $13/$18. **Credit cards:**
All major. **Reduced fees:** Weekdays, low season. **Caddies:** No. **Golf carts:** $18.
Discount golf packages: No. **Season:** April-Jan. **High:** June-Aug. **On site lodging:**
No. **Rental clubs:** Yes. **Walking policy:** Unrestricted walking. **Metal spikes allowed:**
Yes. **Range:** Yes (grass). **To obtain tee times:** Call up to 7 days in advance.
Subscriber comments: Interesting layout...Some unfair holes...Back nine is
short...Challenging small course...Enjoyable challenge...Excellent course.

★★GREEN VALLEY GOLF CLUB
2673 Pleasant Valley Rd., N.E., New Philadelphia, 44663, Tuscarawas County,
(330)364-2812, 20 miles S of Canton.
Opened: 1961. **Holes:** 18. **Par:** 72/73. **Yards:** 6,500/5,200. **Course rating:** 71.5/69.5.
Slope: 117/113. **Architect:** N/A. **Green fee:** $11/$11. **Credit cards:** MC,VISA.
Reduced fees: Weekdays, low season, twilight. **Caddies:** No. **Golf carts:** $16.
Discount golf packages: Yes. **Season:** March-Nov. **High:** May-Aug. **On site lodging:**
No. **Rental clubs:** Yes. **Walking policy:** Unrestricted walking. **Metal spikes allowed:**
Yes. **Range:** Yes (grass/mats). **To obtain tee times:** Call 1 day in advance.

★★GROVEBROOK GOLF COURSE
5525 Hoover Rd., Grove City, 43123, Franklin County, (614)875-2497.
Call club for further information.

★★★★HAWKS NEST GOLF CLUB
PU-2800 E. Pleasant Home Rd., Creston, 44691, Wayne County, (330)435-4611, 20
miles S of Akron.
Opened: 1993. **Holes:** 18. **Par:** 72/72. **Yards:** 6,670/4,767. **Course rating:** 71.5/67.9.
Slope: 124/110. **Architect:** Steve Burns. **Green fee:** $20/$25. **Credit cards:** MC,VISA.
Reduced fees: Weekdays, seniors, juniors. **Caddies:** No. **Golf carts:** $10. **Discount
golf packages:** Yes. **Season:** April-Dec. **High:** May-Oct. **On site lodging:** No. **Rental
clubs:** Yes. **Walking policy:** Unrestricted walking. **Metal spikes allowed:** No. **Range:**
Yes (mats). **To obtain tee times:** Call.
Subscriber comments: Maturing and getting better and better...Not bad for a newer
course...Some quirky par 4s, fun course...Interesting combination of holes...New
course, very nice...I love it.

★★★½HAWTHORNE HILLS GOLF CLUB
1000 Fetter Rd., Lima, 45801, Allen County, (419)221-1891, 74 miles N of Dayton.
Opened: 1963. **Holes:** 27. **Par:** 72/72. **Yards:** 6,710/5,695. **Course rating:** 71.6/71.9.
Slope: 119/118. **Architect:** Harold Paddock. **Green fee:** $17/$19. **Credit cards:** None.
Reduced fees: Weekdays. **Caddies:** No. **Golf carts:** $10. **Discount golf packages:**
No. **Season:** March-Nov. **High:** May-Sept. **On site lodging:** No. **Rental clubs:** Yes.
Walking policy: N/A. **Metal spikes allowed:** Yes. **Range:** Yes (grass). **To obtain tee
times:** Call in advance.
Subscriber comments: Nice, playable layout...Slicers beware, good for hookers...Very
few level lies...Great place to play...Nice rolling layout.
Special Notes: Also has a 9-hole executive course.

★★★½HEATHERWOODE GOLF CLUB

PU-88 Heatherwoode Blvd., Springboro, 45066, Warren County, (513)748-3222, 15 miles S of Dayton.

Opened: 1991. **Holes:** 18. **Par:** 71/71. **Yards:** 6,730/5,069. **Course rating:** 72.9/69.8. **Slope:** 138/127. **Architect:** Denis Griffiths. **Green fee:** $42/$52. **Credit cards:** MC,VISA,AMEX. **Reduced fees:** Weekdays, low season, twilight, seniors, juniors. **Caddies:** No. **Golf carts:** $3. **Discount golf packages:** No. **Season:** Year-round. **High:** May-Aug. **On site lodging:** No. **Rental clubs:** Yes. **Walking policy:** Unrestricted walking. **Metal spikes allowed:** Yes. **Range:** Yes (grass/mats). **To obtain tee times:** Call 7 days in advance.

Subscriber comments: An exceptional city course...Beautiful course. Tough par 3s...A few holes remind me of Myrtle Beach...Great test of golf...Requires all the shots.

★★★HEMLOCK SPRINGS GOLF CLUB

PU-4654 Cold Springs Rd., Geneva, 44041, Ashtabula County, (216)466-4044, (800)436-5625, 40 miles E of Cleveland.

Opened: 1961. **Holes:** 18. **Par:** 72/72. **Yards:** 6,812/5,453. **Course rating:** 72.8/73.8. **Slope:** 123/115. **Architect:** Benjamin W. Zink. **Green fee:** $18/$23. **Credit cards:** MC,VISA. **Reduced fees:** Weekdays, low season, twilight, seniors, juniors. **Caddies:** No. **Golf carts:** $10. **Discount golf packages:** Yes. **Season:** April-Nov. **High:** June-Aug. **On site lodging:** No. **Rental clubs:** Yes. **Walking policy:** Unrestricted walking. **Metal spikes allowed:** Yes. **Range:** Yes (grass/mats). **To obtain tee times:** Call anytime.

Subscriber comments: Great course, must be long off tee...Challenging from tips...Good variety of holes, not too difficult...Tough par 3s, some good holes...Rural area...Interesting layout...Pretty layout, some great holes.

★★½HIAWATHA GOLF COURSE

PU-901 Beech St., Mount Vernon, 43050, Knox County, (740)393-2886, 40 miles NE of Columbus.

Opened: 1962. **Holes:** 18. **Par:** 72/74. **Yards:** 6,721/5,100. **Course rating:** 71.5/68.5. **Slope:** N/A. **Architect:** Jack Kidwell. **Green fee:** $11/$13. **Credit cards:** MC,VISA. **Reduced fees:** Weekdays, low season, twilight, seniors, juniors. **Caddies:** No. **Golf carts:** $10. **Discount golf packages:** Yes. **Season:** March-Nov. **High:** July-Aug. **On site lodging:** No. **Rental clubs:** No. **Walking policy:** Unrestricted walking. **Metal spikes allowed:** Yes. **Range:** No. **To obtain tee times:** Call.

Subscriber comments: Good golf for the money...Fun to play!...Great value, hill course, elevated greens, snack bar.

★★½HICKORY FLAT GREENS

PU-54188 Township Rd. 155, West Lafayette, 43845, Coshocton County, (614)545-7796, 25 miles SW of New Philadelphia.

Opened: 1970. **Holes:** 18. **Par:** 72/72. **Yards:** 6,600/5,124. **Course rating:** 70.4/68.3. **Slope:** 109/105. **Architect:** Jack Kidwell. **Green fee:** $14/$14. **Credit cards:** None. **Reduced fees:** Weekdays, low season, twilight, seniors, juniors. **Caddies:** No. **Golf carts:** $11. **Discount golf packages:** Yes. **Season:** Year-round. **High:** May-Sept. **On site lodging:** No. **Rental clubs:** Yes. **Walking policy:** Unrestricted walking. **Metal spikes allowed:** Yes. **Range:** Yes (grass). **To obtain tee times:** Call anytime.

Subscriber comments: Flat course, beautiful layout, wide fairways...Like the name says, a mostly flat course...Rather average.

★★½HICKORY GROVE GOLF CLUB

PU-6302 State Rte. 94, Harpster, 43323, Wyandot County, (614)496-2631, (800)833-6619, 15 miles N of Marion.

Opened: 1963. **Holes:** 18. **Par:** 72/76. **Yards:** 6,874/5,376. **Course rating:** 71.0/69.1. **Slope:** 108/105. **Architect:** J. Craig Bowman. **Green fee:** $10/$12. **Credit cards:** MC,VISA,DISC. **Reduced fees:** Weekdays, twilight. **Caddies:** No. **Golf carts:** $20. **Discount golf packages:** Yes. **Season:** March-Nov. **High:** June-Aug. **On site lodging:** No. **Rental clubs:** Yes. **Walking policy:** Unrestricted walking. **Metal spikes allowed:** Yes. **Range:** Yes (grass/mats). **To obtain tee times:** Call.

★★HICKORY GROVE GOLF COURSE
1490 Fairway Dr., Jefferson, 44047, Ashtabula County, (216)576-3776.
Opened: 1962. **Holes:** 18. **Par:** 72/73. **Yards:** 6,500/5,593. **Course rating:** 70.9/71.5.
Slope: N/A. **Architect:** N/A. **Green fee:** $10/$16. **Credit cards:** MC,VISA. **Reduced fees:** N/A. **Caddies:** No. **Golf carts:** $17. **Discount golf packages:** No. **Season:** April-Oct. **High:** N/A. **On site lodging:** No. **Rental clubs:** Yes. **Walking policy:** Unrestricted walking. **Metal spikes allowed:** Yes. **Range:** Yes (grass). **To obtain tee times:** Call up to 14 days in advance.

★★HICKORY NUT GOLF CLUB
PU-23601 Royalton Rd., Columbia Station, 44028, Lorain County, (440)236-8008, 1 mile W of Strongsville.
Opened: 1968. **Holes:** 18. **Par:** 71/73. **Yards:** 6,424/6,424. **Course rating:** 69.5.
Slope: 124. **Architect:** N/A. **Green fee:** $16/$18. **Credit cards:** None. **Reduced fees:** Seniors. **Caddies:** No. **Golf carts:** $20. **Discount golf packages:** No. **Season:** April-Oct. **High:** April-Oct. **On site lodging:** No. **Rental clubs:** Yes. **Walking policy:** Unrestricted walking. **Metal spikes allowed:** Yes. **Range:** No. **To obtain tee times:** First come, first served.

★★★HICKORY WOODS GOLF COURSE
PU-1240 Hickory Woods Dr., Loveland, 45140, Clermont County, (513)575-3900, 15 miles N of Cincinnati.
Opened: 1983. **Holes:** 18. **Par:** 70/71. **Yards:** 6,105/5,115. **Course rating:** 70.1/69.4.
Slope: 119/113. **Architect:** Dennis Acomb. **Green fee:** $21/$31. **Credit cards:** MC,VISA,AMEX. **Reduced fees:** Low season, seniors, juniors. **Caddies:** No. **Golf carts:** $10. **Discount golf packages:** No. **Season:** Year-round. **High:** April-Aug. **On site lodging:** No. **Rental clubs:** Yes. **Walking policy:** Unrestricted walking. **Metal spikes allowed:** Yes. **Range:** No. **To obtain tee times:** Call 6 days in advance.
Subscriber comments: Very scenic, lots of trees...Open front nine, very tight back...Always fun to play.

★½HIDDEN HILLS GOLF CLUB
PU-4886 County Rd. 16, Woodville, 43469, Sandusky County, (419)849-3693, 20 miles SE of Toledo.
Opened: 1968. **Holes:** 18. **Par:** 71/71. **Yards:** 5,730/5,403. **Course rating:** 66.9/70.2.
Slope: N/A. **Architect:** Elizabeth Piece. **Green fee:** $12/$14. **Credit cards:** None.
Reduced fees: Weekdays, low season, twilight, seniors, juniors. **Caddies:** No. **Golf carts:** $16. **Discount golf packages:** No. **Season:** May-Nov. **High:** June-Aug. **On site lodging:** No. **Rental clubs:** Yes. **Walking policy:** Unrestricted walking. **Metal spikes allowed:** Yes. **Range:** No. **To obtain tee times:** Call.

★½HIDDEN LAKE GOLF COURSE
PU-5370 E. State Rd. 571, Tipp City, 45371, Miami County, (937)667-8880, 12 miles N of Dayton.
Opened: 1988. **Holes:** 18. **Par:** 72/72. **Yards:** 6,562/5,357. **Course rating:** 70.5/69.3.
Slope: 114/111. **Architect:** Don Dick. **Green fee:** $9/$18. **Credit cards:** All major.
Reduced fees: Low season, seniors, juniors. **Caddies:** No. **Golf carts:** $9. **Discount golf packages:** No. **Season:** Year-round. **High:** March-Nov. **On site lodging:** No.
Rental clubs: Yes. **Walking policy:** Unrestricted walking. **Metal spikes allowed:** Yes.
Range: Yes. **To obtain tee times:** Call one week in advance.

★★HIGHLAND PARK GOLF CLUB
PU-3550 Green Rd., Cleveland, 44122, Cuyahoga County, (216)348-7273.
Architect: Sandy Alves. **Caddies:** No. **Discount golf packages:** No. **On site lodging:** No. **Rental clubs:** No. **Metal spikes allowed:** Yes. **Range:** No.
Call club for further information.

★★½HILLCREST GOLF CLUB
800 W. Bigelow, Findlay, 45840, Hancock County, (419)423-7211.
Architect: Ed Rettig/Gene Cleary. **Caddies:** No. **Discount golf packages:** No. **On site lodging:** No. **Rental clubs:** No. **Metal spikes allowed:** Yes. **Range:** No.
Call club for further information.

★★½HILLIARD LAKES GOLF CLUB
PU-31665 Hilliard Rd., Westlake, 44145, Cuyahoga County, (440)871-9578, 15 miles W of Cleveland.
Opened: 1968. **Holes:** 18. **Par:** 72/75. **Yards:** 6,680/5,636. **Course rating:** 70.0/74.0. **Slope:** 124/118. **Architect:** Dick LaConte. **Green fee:** $18/$18. **Credit cards:** MC,VISA. **Reduced fees:** Weekdays, seniors, juniors. **Caddies:** No. **Golf carts:** $24. **Discount golf packages:** No. **Season:** March-Nov. **High:** May-Sept. **On site lodging:** No. **Rental clubs:** No. **Walking policy:** Unrestricted walking. **Metal spikes allowed:** Yes. **Range:** Yes (grass/mats). **To obtain tee times:** Call.

★★★HINCKLEY HILLS GOLF COURSE
PU-300 State Rd., Hinckley, 44233, Medina County, (216)278-4861, 17 miles S of Cleveland.
Opened: 1964. **Holes:** 18. **Par:** 73/72. **Yards:** 6,831/5,465. **Course rating:** 71.6/70.9. **Slope:** 125/118. **Architect:** Harold Paddock Sr. **Green fee:** $24/$24. **Credit cards:** MC,VISA. **Reduced fees:** N/A. **Caddies:** No. **Golf carts:** $24. **Discount golf packages:** Yes. **Season:** April-Nov. **High:** May-Sept. **On site lodging:** No. **Rental clubs:** Yes. **Walking policy:** Walking at certain times. **Metal spikes allowed:** Yes. **Range:** No. **To obtain tee times:** Call golf shop.
Subscriber comments: Killer par 5s...Too hilly to walk...Good up and down course...Nice mix of holes.

★★HOLLY HILLS GOLF CLUB
PU-4699 N. State Hwy. 42, Waynesville, 45068, Warren County, (513)897-4921, 20 miles SE of Dayton.
Opened: 1962. **Holes:** 18. **Par:** 71. **Yards:** 6,785. **Course rating:** 72.3. **Slope:** N/A. **Architect:** William Diddel. **Green fee:** $15/$18. **Credit cards:** MC,VISA. **Reduced fees:** Weekdays, twilight, seniors, juniors. **Caddies:** No. **Golf carts:** $19. **Discount golf packages:** No. **Season:** March-Nov. **High:** N/A. **On site lodging:** No. **Rental clubs:** No. **Walking policy:** Unrestricted walking. **Metal spikes allowed:** Yes. **Range:** Yes (grass). **To obtain tee times:** Call up to 7 days advance.

★★½HOMESTEAD GOLF COURSE
PU-5327 Worley Rd., Tipp City, 45371, Miami County, (937)698-4876.
Architect: Bill Amick. **Caddies:** No. **Discount golf packages:** No. **On site lodging:** No. **Rental clubs:** No. **Metal spikes allowed:** Yes. **Range:** No.
Call club for further information.

★★HOMESTEAD SPRINGS GOLF COURSE
PU-5888 London Lancaster Rd., Groveport, 43125, Franklin County, (614)836-5872, 15 miles SE of Columbus.
Opened: 1972. **Holes:** 18. **Par:** 72/72. **Yards:** 6,463/4,907. **Course rating:** 69.7. **Slope:** 111. **Architect:** Harlan (Bud) Rainier. **Green fee:** $23/$25. **Credit cards:** None. **Reduced fees:** N/A. **Caddies:** No. **Golf carts:** $9. **Discount golf packages:** No. **Season:** Year-round. **High:** April-Oct. **On site lodging:** No. **Rental clubs:** No. **Walking policy:** Unrestricted walking. **Metal spikes allowed:** Yes. **Range:** No. **To obtain tee times:** N/A.

★★½HUBBARD GOLF COURSE
PU-6233 W. Liberty St. S.E., Hubbard, 44425, Trumbull County, (330)534-9026.
Architect: W.J. Powell. **Caddies:** No. **Discount golf packages:** No. **On site lodging:** No. **Rental clubs:** No. **Metal spikes allowed:** Yes. **Range:** No.
Call club for further information.
Subscriber comments: Nice course for the money and fun too...Watch out for par-3 16th...Short, old course, small greens.

★★★½HUESTON WOODS GOLF COURSE
R-6962 Brown Rd., Oxford, 45056, Butler County, (513)523-8081, (800)282-7275, 25 miles N of Cincinnati.
Opened: 1969. **Holes:** 18. **Par:** 72/72. **Yards:** 7,005/5,258. **Course rating:** 73.1/69.1. **Slope:** 132/120. **Architect:** Jack Kidwell. **Green fee:** $16/$22. **Credit cards:** MC,VISA. **Reduced fees:** Weekdays, resort guests, twilight, seniors, juniors. **Caddies:** No. **Golf**

carts: $11. **Discount golf packages:** Yes. **Season:** March-Nov. **High:** June-Sept. **On site lodging:** Yes. **Rental clubs:** Yes. **Walking policy:** Unrestricted walking. **Metal spikes allowed:** Yes. **Range:** Yes (grass/mats). **To obtain tee times:** Call 7 days in advance for weekdays. Call 7:30 a.m. Tuesday for upcoming weekend. Hotel guests may make tee times at any time with reservation number.

Subscriber comments: Good layout...Nice variety...Very nice state park course...I like the trees!...Always play in fall, spectacular!...Scenic and quiet...Tight course! Accuracy a must...Too many doglegs right, longest par 3s you will find.

★★★★INDIAN SPRINGS GOLF CLUB
PU-11111 State Rte. 161, Mechanicsburg, 43044, Champaign County, (937)834-2111, (800)752-7846, 23 miles W of Columbus.
Opened: 1990. **Holes:** 18. **Par:** 72/72. **Yards:** 7,123/5,733. **Course rating:** 73.8/72.6. **Slope:** 126/122. **Architect:** Jack Kidwell. **Green fee:** $26/$35. **Credit cards:** MC,VISA,DISC. **Reduced fees:** Weekdays, low season, twilight. **Caddies:** No. **Golf carts:** $10. **Discount golf packages:** No. **Season:** March-Oct. **High:** June-Aug. **On site lodging:** No. **Rental clubs:** Yes. **Walking policy:** Unrestricted walking. **Metal spikes allowed:** Yes. **Range:** Yes (grass). **To obtain tee times:** Call 7 days in advance.
Subscriber comments: A great shotmaker's course...Good to very good layout, a couple of Mickey Mouse holes...Great design, very tough greens, remote location...Very scenic...Very long from the tips...Plays very long when wet...18 is a beast...633-yard par 5 6th difficult...Pleasant surprise, in the middle of nowhere.

★★½IRISH HILLS GOLF COURSE
PU-7020 Newark Rd., Mount Vernon, 43050, Knox County, (614)397-6252.
Opened: N/A. **Holes:** 18. **Par:** 71/75. **Yards:** 6,503/5,890. **Course rating:** 70.2. **Slope:** N/A. **Architect:** N/A. **Green fee:** $10/$12. **Credit cards:** MC,VISA. **Reduced fees:** N/A. **Caddies:** No. **Golf carts:** $8. **Discount golf packages:** No. **Season:** March-Nov. **High:** June-Aug. **On site lodging:** No. **Rental clubs:** No. **Walking policy:** Unrestricted walking. **Metal spikes allowed:** Yes. **Range:** No. **To obtain tee times:** Call golf shop.

★★★IRONWOOD GOLF CLUB
1015 W. Leggett, Wauseon, 43567, Fulton County, (419)335-0587.
Opened: 1971. **Holes:** 18. **Par:** 72/74. **Yards:** 6,965/5,306. **Course rating:** 72.2/69.2. **Slope:** 112/106. **Architect:** Ben Hadden/Margaret Alan. **Green fee:** $11/$18. **Credit cards:** None. **Reduced fees:** Weekdays. **Caddies:** No. **Golf carts:** $10. **Discount golf packages:** No. **Season:** March-Nov. **High:** June-Aug. **On site lodging:** No. **Rental clubs:** Yes. **Walking policy:** Unrestricted walking. **Metal spikes allowed:** No. **Range:** Yes (grass). **To obtain tee times:** Call 7 days in advance.
Subscriber comments: Nice challenge, flat...Average...Wide open...Small town gem. Good course design.

★★★IRONWOOD GOLF COURSE
445 State Rd., Hinckley, 44233, Medina County, (330)278-7171.
Architect: Harold Paddock. **Caddies:** No. **Discount golf packages:** No. **On site lodging:** No. **Rental clubs:** No. **Metal spikes allowed:** Yes. **Range:** No.
Call club for further information.
Subscriber comments: Course hilly, challenging...Many elevated greens, bring your lob wedge, hilly...Hit 'em long...Some great par 4s...Fair test of skills; scenic...Four good par 3s...Good mix of holes.

★★★½J.E. GOOD PARK GOLF CLUB
PU-530 Nome Ave., Akron, 44320, Summit County, (330)864-0020, 35 miles S of Cleveland.
Opened: 1926. **Holes:** 18. **Par:** 71/71. **Yards:** 6,663/4,926. **Course rating:** 72.0/69.1. **Slope:** 123/115. **Architect:** Bertie Way. **Green fee:** $18/$20. **Credit cards:** None. **Reduced fees:** Low season, seniors, juniors. **Caddies:** No. **Golf carts:** $10. **Discount golf packages:** No. **Season:** March-Dec. **High:** May-Oct. **On site lodging:** No. **Rental clubs:** No. **Walking policy:** Unrestricted walking. **Metal spikes allowed:** Yes. **Range:** Yes. **To obtain tee times:** Call 7 days in advance.
Notes: 1993 National Amateur Qualifier.

Subscriber comments: Good tree-lined public course. Will test all skill levels...Some long par 4s, tight layout with many trees...Very nice city-owned course...A lot of challenging holes...Great old-style golf course...Classic, traditional course.

★★½JAMAICA RUN GOLF CLUB
PU-8781 Jamaica Rd., Germantown, 45327, Montgomery County, (937)866-4333, 15 miles SW of Dayton.
Opened: 1989. **Holes:** 18. **Par:** 72/72. **Yards:** 6,587/5,092. **Course rating:** 71.0/69.2. **Slope:** 121/115. **Architect:** Denny/Mays/Bowman. **Green fee:** $15/$17. **Credit cards:** MC,VISA. **Reduced fees:** Low season, seniors, juniors. **Caddies:** No. **Golf carts:** $10. **Discount golf packages:** No. **Season:** Year-round. **High:** April-Sept. **On site lodging:** No. **Rental clubs:** Yes. **Walking policy:** Unrestricted walking. **Metal spikes allowed:** Yes. **Range:** Yes (grass/mats). **To obtain tee times:** Call 7 days in advance.
Subscriber comments: Improving course; wide open most holes...Short par 5s...Fun "open" golf...Some good holes, very playable...Great for family play.

★★½JAYCEE GOLF COURSE
PU-12100 Pleasant Valley Rd., Chillicothe, 45601, Ross County, (614)775-7659, 60 miles S of Columbus.
Opened: 1957. **Holes:** 18. **Par:** 72/74. **Yards:** 6,893/5,181. **Course rating:** 72.0/69.8. **Slope:** 124/117. **Architect:** Ted Cox/Jack Kidwell. **Green fee:** $10/$12. **Credit cards:** MC,VISA. **Reduced fees:** Weekdays, seniors, juniors. **Caddies:** No. **Golf carts:** $10. **Discount golf packages:** No. **Season:** March-Dec. **High:** June-July. **On site lodging:** No. **Rental clubs:** Yes. **Walking policy:** Unrestricted walking. **Metal spikes allowed:** Yes. **Range:** Yes (grass). **To obtain tee times:** Call 7 days in advance.

★★★JAYCEE PUBLIC GOLF COURSE
PU-2710 Jackson Rd., Zanesville, 43701, Muskingum County, (614)452-1860.
Opened: 1949. **Holes:** 18. **Par:** 71/76. **Yards:** 6,660/6,200. **Course rating:** 67.8/72.3. **Slope:** N/A. **Architect:** Zanesville Jaycees. **Green fee:** $12/$14. **Credit cards:** None. **Reduced fees:** Twilight, seniors, juniors. **Caddies:** No. **Golf carts:** $10. **Discount golf packages:** No. **Season:** Year-round. **High:** May-Sept. **On site lodging:** No. **Rental clubs:** Yes. **Walking policy:** Unrestricted walking. **Metal spikes allowed:** Yes. **Range:** No. **To obtain tee times:** Call 7 days in advance for weekends only.
Subscriber comments: Good all around course...Showing major improvements...Best course for the money.

★★½KINGS MILL GOLF COURSE
2500 Berringer Rd., Waldo, 43356, Marion County, (614)726-2626.
Opened: 1966. **Holes:** 18. **Par:** 70/74. **Yards:** 6,099/5,318. **Course rating:** 68.1/68.8. **Slope:** 106/109. **Architect:** Jack Kidwell. **Green fee:** $16/$17. **Credit cards:** MC,VISA,AMEX. **Reduced fees:** Low season, juniors. **Caddies:** No. **Golf carts:** $18. **Discount golf packages:** Yes. **Season:** March-Dec. **High:** May-Oct. **On site lodging:** No. **Rental clubs:** Yes. **Walking policy:** Unrestricted walking. **Metal spikes allowed:** Yes. **Range:** No. **To obtain tee times:** Call 7 days in advance, or further in advance with a credit card.
Subscriber comments: Friendly, front and back are like two different courses...Country course with trees and hills...Short, must be accurate.

★★KINGSWOOD GOLF COURSE
PU-4188 Irwin Simpson Rd., Mason, 45040, Warren County, (513)398-5252.
Call club for further information.

KITTY HAWK GOLF CLUB
PU-3383 Chuck Wagner Lane, Dayton, 45414, Montgomery County, (937)237-5424.
Opened: 1962. **Architect:** Robert Bruce Harris. **Green fee:** $17/$19. **Credit cards:** MC,VISA. **Reduced fees:** Low season, seniors, juniors. **Caddies:** No. **Golf carts:** $20. **Discount golf packages:** No. **Season:** Year-round. **High:** April-Oct. **On site lodging:** No. **Rental clubs:** Yes. **Walking policy:** Unrestricted walking. **Metal spikes allowed:** Yes. **Range:** Yes (grass/mats).**To obtain tee times:** Call Tuesday at noon for upcoming weekend.

OHIO

★★½EAGLE COURSE
Holes: 18. **Par:** 72/75. **Yards:** 7,115/5,887. **Course rating:** 72.8/74.3. **Slope:** 120/123.
Subscriber comments: Variety of holes gives good challenge...Good local course...Long, flat, large greens...Nice walk.

★★HAWK COURSE
Holes: 18. **Par:** 72/73. **Yards:** 6,766/5,638. **Course rating:** 71.1/73.3. **Slope:** 118/121.
Special Notes: Also has 18-hole par-3 course called the Kitty.

★★★LAKESIDE GOLF COURSE
PU-PO Box 680, St Rt 60, Beverly, 45715, Morgan County, (614)984-4265, 18 miles N of Marietta.
Opened: 1959. **Holes:** 18. **Par:** 70/70. **Yards:** 6,421/4,528. **Course rating:** 71.4/69.1.
Slope: 109/103. **Architect:** N/A. **Green fee:** $25/$28. **Credit cards:** MC,VISA.
Reduced fees: Weekdays, twilight. **Caddies:** No. **Golf carts:** Included in Green Fee.
Discount golf packages: No. **Season:** Year-round. **High:** May-Sept. **On site lodging:** Yes. **Rental clubs:** Yes. **Walking policy:** Unrestricted walking. **Metal spikes allowed:** Yes. **Range:** Yes (grass). **To obtain tee times:** Call for weekends and holidays.
Subscriber comments: Long front nine, tough. Short back nine...Nines play like two different courses...Good course.

★★LAKESIDE GOLF COURSE
2404 S.E. River Rd., Lake Milton, 44429, Mahoning County, (330)547-2797.
Architect: Edmund B. Ault. **Caddies:** No. **Discount golf packages:** No. **On site lodging:** No. **Rental clubs:** No. **Metal spikes allowed:** Yes. **Range:** No.
Call club for further information.

★★LARCH TREE GOLF COURSE
PU-2765 N. Snyder Rd., Trotwood, 45426, Montgomery County, (937)854-1951, 6 miles NW of Dayton.
Opened: 1970. **Holes:** 18. **Par:** 72/74. **Yards:** 6,982/5,912. **Course rating:** 71.5/72.7.
Slope: 107/107. **Architect:** Jack Kidwell. **Green fee:** $16/$16. **Credit cards:** None.
Reduced fees: Low season, twilight, seniors, juniors. **Caddies:** No. **Golf carts:** $10.
Discount golf packages: No. **Season:** Year-round. **High:** May-Oct. **On site lodging:** No. **Rental clubs:** Yes. **Walking policy:** Unrestricted walking. **Metal spikes allowed:** Yes. **Range:** Yes (grass/mats). **To obtain tee times:** Call up to 21 days in advance.
Special Notes: Also has an executive course.

★★★★THE LEGENDS OF MASSILLON
PM-2700 Augusta Dr., Massillon, 44646, Stark County, (330)830-4653, (888)830-7277, 60 miles S of Cleveland.
Opened: 1995. **Holes:** 18. **Par:** 72/72. **Yards:** 7,002/4,696. **Course rating:** 73.7/67.0.
Slope: 121/108. **Architect:** John Robinson. **Green fee:** $22/$32. **Credit cards:** MC,VISA. **Reduced fees:** Low season, twilight, seniors, juniors. **Caddies:** No. **Golf carts:** $10. **Discount golf packages:** No. **Season:** April-Oct. **High:** June-Sept. **On site lodging:** No. **Rental clubs:** No. **Walking policy:** Unrestricted walking. **Metal spikes allowed:** No. **Range:** Yes (grass). **To obtain tee times:** Call.
Subscriber comments: Long course, deep rough, lots of sand...Beautiful layout, great course...Links style...New, should be outstanding in a few years...New, maturing, excellent diversity of holes...Nice combination of water holes and doglegs...Big greens.

★★★LIBERTY HILLS GOLF CLUB
PU-665 Rd. 190 W., Bellefontaine, 43311, Logan County, (937)592-4653, (800)816-2255, 50 miles W of Columbus.
Opened: 1920. **Holes:** 18. **Par:** 70/70. **Yards:** 6,005/4,400. **Course rating:** 68.0/64.0.
Slope: 115/104. **Architect:** Barry Serafin. **Green fee:** $17/$18. **Credit cards:** MC,VISA. **Reduced fees:** Weekdays, seniors, juniors. **Caddies:** No. **Golf carts:** $9.
Discount golf packages: No. **Season:** Feb.-Dec. **High:** May-Oct. **On site lodging:** No. **Rental clubs:** No. **Walking policy:** Unrestricted walking. **Metal spikes allowed:** Yes. **Range:** Yes (grass/mats). **To obtain tee times:** Call anytime.
Subscriber comments: Front nine: old established course built 1920s. Each hole very different, small greens. Back nine: newer, greens bigger...Pleasant atmosphere, decent course.
Special Notes: Formerly Bellefontaine Country Club.

★★½LICKING SPRINGS TROUT & GOLF CLUB

PU-2250 Horns Hill Rd., Newark, 43055, Licking County, (614)366-2770, (800)204-3638, 35 miles E of Columbus.
Opened: 1960. **Holes:** 18. **Par:** 71/71. **Yards:** 6,400/5,035. **Course rating:** 70.0/68.7.
Slope: 116/107. **Architect:** Jack Kidwell. **Green fee:** $14/$15. **Credit cards:** MC,VISA,AMEX. **Reduced fees:** Weekdays, low season, twilight, seniors, juniors.
Caddies: No. **Golf carts:** $10. **Discount golf packages:** No. **Season:** Year-round.
High: May-Sept. **On site lodging:** No. **Rental clubs:** Yes. **Walking policy:** Unrestricted walking. **Metal spikes allowed:** Yes. **Range:** No. **To obtain tee times:** Call. Tee times required for weekends.
Subscriber comments: Very hilly, need to play more than once...Hilly and scenic...Fun course and improving...Great small course...Closing holes are monsters...Beautifully scenic on certain holes...Blind shots...Lots of character.

★★★½THE LINKS AT ECHO SPRINGS

PU-5940 Loudon St., Johnstown, 43031, Licking County, (614)587-1890, (800)597-3240, 30 miles E of Columbus.
Opened: 1996. **Holes:** 18. **Par:** 72/72. **Yards:** 6,900/2,239. **Course rating:** 72.4/65.0.
Slope: 127/108. **Architect:** Barry Serafin. **Green fee:** $16/$20. **Credit cards:** MC,VISA,AMEX. **Reduced fees:** Weekdays. **Caddies:** No. **Golf carts:** $10. **Discount golf packages:** No. **Season:** March-Dec. **High:** May-Sept. **On site lodging:** No.
Rental clubs: Yes. **Walking policy:** Unrestricted walking. **Metal spikes allowed:** Yes.
Range: Yes (grass). **To obtain tee times:** Call up to 7 days in advance.
Subscriber comments: Will be excellent...New course, a few unfair holes...Exciting first six holes...Rolling terrain, very pretty, cut through woods...Memorable.

★★½LOCUST HILLS GOLF CLUB

PU-5575 N. River Rd., Springfield, 45502, Clark County, (937)265-5152.
Call club for further information.
Subscriber comments: Flat and wide open...Nothing memorable...Excellent value for family and juniors...Country setting, some testy holes...Good public course.

★★LOST NATION GOLF COURSE

PU-38890 Hodgson Rd., Willoughby, 44094, Lake County, (440)953-4280, 25 miles E of Cleveland.
Opened: 1928. **Holes:** 18. **Par:** 72/73. **Yards:** 6,400/5,700. **Course rating:** 69.4/70.9.
Slope: 113/112. **Architect:** H.S. Colt and C.H. Allison. **Green fee:** $11/$17. **Credit cards:** None. **Reduced fees:** Weekdays, low season, seniors, juniors. **Caddies:** No.
Golf carts: $10. **Discount golf packages:** Yes. **Season:** Year-round. **High:** May-Oct.
On site lodging: No. **Rental clubs:** No. **Walking policy:** Unrestricted walking. **Metal spikes allowed:** Yes. **Range:** Yes (grass/mats). **To obtain tee times:** Call 7 days in advance.

★★LOYAL OAK GOLF COURSE

PU-2909 S. Cleve-Mass Rd., Norton, 44203, Summit County, (330)825-2904, 10 miles W of Akron.
Opened: 1931. **Holes:** 27. **Architect:** N/A. **Green fee:** $13/$17. **Credit cards:** None.
Reduced fees: Seniors, juniors. **Caddies:** No. **Golf carts:** $17. **Discount golf packages:** No. **Season:** March-Nov. **High:** May-Sept. **On site lodging:** No. **Rental clubs:** Yes. **Walking policy:** Unrestricted walking. **Metal spikes allowed:** Yes. **Range:** No. **To obtain tee times:** Call anytime.

★★LYONS DEN GOLF

PU-Rte. 93 at 21, Canal Fulton, 44614, Stark County, (330)854-9910, (800)801-6007, 14 miles S of Akron.
Opened: 1962. **Holes:** 18. **Par:** 69/69. **Yards:** 5,774/5,228. **Course rating:** 65.0.
Slope: 97/102. **Architect:** Bill Lyons. **Green fee:** $9/$18. **Credit cards:** MC,VISA.
Reduced fees: Weekdays, low season. **Caddies:** No. **Golf carts:** $18. **Discount golf packages:** Yes. **Season:** Year-round. **High:** May-Sept. **On site lodging:** No. **Rental clubs:** Yes. **Walking policy:** Unrestricted walking. **Metal spikes allowed:** No. **Range:** Yes (grass/mats). **To obtain tee times:** Call.

★½MAHONING GOLF COURSE
PU-700 E. Liberty St., Girard, 44420, Trumbull County, (330)545-2517, 45 miles E of Cleveland.
Opened: N/A. **Holes:** 18. **Par:** 70/73. **Yards:** 6,276/5,810. **Course rating:** N/A. **Slope:** N/A. **Architect:** N/A. **Green fee:** $12/$16. **Credit cards:** N/A. **Reduced fees:** Weekdays, low season, seniors, juniors. **Caddies:** No. **Golf carts:** $16. **Discount golf packages:** Yes. **Season:** Year-round weather permitting. **High:** May-Sept. **On site lodging:** No. **Rental clubs:** No. **Walking policy:** Unrestricted walking. **Metal spikes allowed:** Yes. **Range:** No. **To obtain tee times:** Call up to 10 days in advance for weekends.

★★★½MANAKIKI GOLF CLUB
PU-35501 Eddy Rd., Willoughby, 44094, Lake County, (440)942-2500, 18 miles E of Cleveland.
Opened: 1929. **Holes:** 18. **Par:** 72/72. **Yards:** 6,625/5,390. **Course rating:** 71.4/72.8. **Slope:** 128/121. **Architect:** Donald Ross. **Green fee:** $13/$19. **Credit cards:** MC,VISA. **Reduced fees:** Low season, seniors, juniors. **Caddies:** No. **Golf carts:** $10. **Discount golf packages:** No. **Season:** March-Dec. **High:** May-Sept. **On site lodging:** No. **Rental clubs:** Yes. **Walking policy:** Unrestricted walking. **Metal spikes allowed:** Yes. **Range:** No. **To obtain tee times:** Call 5 days in advance beginning at noon.
Subscriber comments: A great old track...A great Donald Ross layout...Beautiful 18 holes, tough....Heavily played...In its heyday a PGA stop, a nice trip down memory lane...Hard to get on...Great 15th hole, par 3.

★★★MAPLE RIDGE GOLF COURSE
PU-Rte. 45, P.O. Box 17, Austinburg, 44010, Ashtabula County, (440)969-1368, (800)922-1368, 50 miles E of Cleveland.
Opened: 1960. **Holes:** 18. **Par:** 70/70. **Yards:** 6,001/5,400. **Course rating:** 68.5/69.0. **Slope:** 118/118. **Architect:** Lawrence Porter. **Green fee:** $13/$16. **Credit cards:** MC,VISA. **Reduced fees:** Seniors, juniors. **Caddies:** No. **Golf carts:** $18. **Discount golf packages:** No. **Season:** March-Nov. **High:** June-Aug. **On site lodging:** No. **Rental clubs:** Yes. **Walking policy:** Unrestricted walking. **Metal spikes allowed:** Yes. **Range:** No. **To obtain tee times:** Call 14 days in advance.
Subscriber comments: Good all around course...Back nine too short...Scenic, good value...It's challenging, lots of trees. Narrow fairways...Easy walking.

★★★MAPLECREST GOLF COURSE
PU-219 Tallmadge Rd., Kent, 44240, Portage County, (330)673-2722, 3 miles E of Akron.
Opened: 1926. **Holes:** 18. **Par:** 71/72. **Yards:** 6,412/5,285. **Course rating:** 69.2/67.8. **Slope:** 108/113. **Architect:** Edward Ashton. **Green fee:** $15/$22. **Credit cards:** None. **Reduced fees:** Weekdays, seniors. **Caddies:** No. **Golf carts:** $18. **Discount golf packages:** No. **Season:** March-Oct. **High:** May-Aug. **On site lodging:** No. **Rental clubs:** No. **Walking policy:** Unrestricted walking. **Metal spikes allowed:** Yes. **Range:** Yes (grass). **To obtain tee times:** Call after preceeding Sunday.
Subscriber comments: Long and challenging...Good mixture of holes...Rolling terrain...Killer par 3s...Old established course...Good straightforward, challenging golf...Mature course, lots of trees...Great landscaping.

★★★★MAUMEE BAY RESORT GOLF COURSE
PU-1750 Park Rd. No.2, Oregon, 43618, Lucas County, (419)836-9009.
Opened: 1990. **Holes:** 18. **Par:** 72/72. **Yards:** 6,941/5,221. **Course rating:** 73.3/70.5. **Slope:** 129/118. **Architect:** Arthur Hills. **Green fee:** $20/$26. **Credit cards:** All major,Diners Club. **Reduced fees:** Weekdays, low season, twilight, seniors, juniors. **Caddies:** No. **Golf carts:** $12. **Discount golf packages:** Yes. **Season:** April-Oct. **High:** May-Aug. **On site lodging:** Yes. **Rental clubs:** Yes. **Walking policy:** Walking at certain times. **Metal spikes allowed:** Yes. **Range:** Yes (grass/mats). **To obtain tee times:** Call 7 days in advance for weekdays. Call on Wednesday at 8 a.m. for upcoming weekend or holiday.
Subscriber comments: Great links layout...Scottish links, wind and all...Tough on windy day...Next to the windy Lake Erie shore. Very challenging...Excellent challenge...Water in play, not one tree on course.

OHIO

MAYFAIR COUNTRY CLUB
2229 Raber Rd., Uniontown, 44685, Summit County, (330)699-2209.
Architect: Edmund B. Ault. **Caddies:** No. **Discount golf packages:** No. **On site lodging:** No. **Rental clubs:** No. **Metal spikes allowed:** Yes. **Range:** No.
Call club for further information.
★★EAST COURSE
Holes: 18.
★★★WEST COURSE
Holes: 18.
Subscriber comments: West much nicer than East...Not long, but plenty of sand...Pleasant surprise...West course above average...Nice layout..Great breakfast/golf special...Challenging holes.

★★MIAMI SHORES GOLF COURSE
PU-Rutherford Dr., Troy, 45373, Miami County, (937)335-4457, 15 miles N of Dayton.
Opened: 1949. **Holes:** 18. **Par:** 72/73. **Yards:** 6,200/5,417. **Course rating:** 67.6/68.5.
Slope: 97/101. **Architect:** Donald Ross. **Green fee:** $19. **Credit cards:** None.
Reduced fees: N/A. **Caddies:** No. **Golf carts:** $10. **Discount golf packages:** No.
Season: March-Dec. **High:** June-Aug. **On site lodging:** No. **Rental clubs:** Yes.
Walking policy: Unrestricted walking. **Metal spikes allowed:** Yes. **Range:** No. **To obtain tee times:** Call up to 8 days in advance.

★★★MIAMI WHITEWATER FOREST GOLF COURSE
PU-8801 Mount Hope Rd., Harrison, 45030, Hamilton County, (513)367-4627, 18 miles NW of Cincinnati.
Opened: 1959. **Holes:** 18. **Par:** 72/72. **Yards:** 6,780/5,093. **Course rating:** 72.1/69.3.
Slope: 125/110. **Architect:** Hamilton County Park District. **Green fee:** $14/$17. **Credit cards:** None. **Reduced fees:** Seniors, juniors. **Caddies:** No. **Golf carts:** $11. **Discount golf packages:** No. **Season:** March-Dec. **High:** June-Aug. **On site lodging:** No. **Rental clubs:** Yes. **Walking policy:** Unrestricted walking. **Metal spikes allowed:** Yes. **Range:** Yes (mats). **To obtain tee times:** Call 5 days in advance starting at 6 p.m.
Subscriber comments: Getting better, good starter course...Good practice course, very wide open...Some very interesting holes...Always a pleasure.

★★½MILL CREEK GOLF CLUB
7259 Penn Rd., Ostrander, 43061, Delaware County, (614)666-7711, (800)695-5175, 10 miles N of Columbus.
Opened: 1973. **Holes:** 18. **Par:** 72/72. **Yards:** 6,300/5,100. **Course rating:** 69.0/70.0.
Slope: 111/111. **Architect:** Bill Black. **Green fee:** $15/$19. **Credit cards:** MC,VISA,DISC. **Reduced fees:** Weekdays, low season, seniors, juniors. **Caddies:** No. **Golf carts:** $9. **Discount golf packages:** Yes. **Season:** March-Dec. **High:** June-Sept. **On site lodging:** No. **Rental clubs:** No. **Walking policy:** Unrestricted walking. **Metal spikes allowed:** Yes. **Range:** Yes (grass/mats). **To obtain tee times:** Call up to 14 days in advance with credit card to guarantee.
Subscriber comments: Nice little course, good confidence builder...Very nice short course...Straightforward rural course...Water makes it interesting...Basic golf, some tricked up holes...Good little course.

MILL CREEK PARK GOLF COURSE
PU-W. Golf Dr., Boardman, 44512, Mahoning County, (330)758-2729.
Architect: Donald Ross. **Green fee:** $15/$20. **Credit cards:** MC,VISA. **Reduced fees:** Low season, seniors, juniors. **Caddies:** No. **Golf carts:** $19. **Discount golf packages:** No. **Season:** April-Nov. **High:** June-Sept. **On site lodging:** No. **Rental clubs:** No. **Walking policy:** Unrestricted walking. **Metal spikes allowed:** Yes. **Range:** No. **To obtain tee times:** Call or come in Wednesday 6 a.m. for upcoming weekend.
★★★½NORTH COURSE
Opened: 1928. **Holes:** 18. **Par:** 70/74. **Yards:** 6,412/5,889. **Course rating:** 71.9/74.4.
Slope: 124/117.
Subscriber comments: Pretty course...Tight and tough...Real nice public course...Beautiful old muny...Halls of oak trees...How can you go wrong with 36 holes by Donald Ross?...Great layout...9 and 18 great closers...Two great layouts.
Special Notes: Also have an 18-hole par-3 course.

OHIO

★★★½SOUTH COURSE
Opened: 1937. **Holes:** 18. **Par:** 70/75. **Yards:** 6,511/6,102. **Course rating:** 71.8/74.9. **Slope:** 129/118.
Subscriber comments: Lots of trees...Level, easy walking. Reminds me of South Carolina course...Small greens, premium on the approach...Tough doglegs, better hit straight...Tighter than the North, hit it straight, use all your clubs.
Special Notes: Also has an 18-hole par-3 course.

★★MINERVA LAKE GOLF CLUB
PU-2955 Minerva Lake Rd., Columbus, 43231, Franklin County, (614)882-9988, 10 miles N of Columbus.
Opened: 1931. **Holes:** 18. **Par:** 69. **Yards:** 5,638. **Course rating:** 67.8. **Slope:** 103.
Architect: Woody Waugh. **Green fee:** $13/$16. **Credit cards:** MC,VISA,DISC.
Reduced fees: Weekdays, low season, twilight, seniors. **Caddies:** No. **Golf carts:** $18.
Discount golf packages: No. **Season:** March-Dec. **High:** May-July. **On site lodging:** No. **Rental clubs:** Yes. **Walking policy:** Unrestricted walking. **Metal spikes allowed:** Yes. **Range:** No. **To obtain tee times:** Call 7 days in advance.

★★★½MOHICAN HILLS GOLF CLUB
PU-25 Ashland County Rd. 1950, Jeromesville, 44840, Ashland County, (419)368-3303, 10 miles E of Wooster.
Opened: 1972. **Holes:** 18. **Par:** 72/72. **Yards:** 6,536/4,976. **Course rating:** 71.1/67.9. **Slope:** 122/112. **Architect:** Jack Kidwell. **Green fee:** $16/$18. **Credit cards:** MC,VISA. **Reduced fees:** Weekdays. **Caddies:** No. **Golf carts:** $10. **Discount golf packages:** No. **Season:** April-Dec. **High:** June-Aug. **On site lodging:** No. **Rental clubs:** Yes. **Walking policy:** Unrestricted walking. **Metal spikes allowed:** Yes. **Range:** Yes (grass). **To obtain tee times:** Call 7 days in advance.
Subscriber comments: Most severe greens I've seen...Great classic layout, rolling terrain, playable...Four difficult holes...Beautiful layout...Very pleasant surprise. Fun to play, lots of variety...Nice course, but a long walk.

★★NEUMANN GOLF COURSE
PM-7215 Bridgetown Rd., Cincinnati, 45248, Hamilton County, (513)574-1320, 15 miles W of Cincinnati.
Opened: 1965. **Holes:** 27. **Architect:** William H. Diddel. **Green fee:** $17/$17. **Credit cards:** None. **Reduced fees:** Low season, seniors, juniors. **Caddies:** No. **Golf carts:** $10. **Discount golf packages:** No. **Season:** Year-round. **High:** March-Nov. **On site lodging:** No. **Rental clubs:** Yes. **Walking policy:** Unrestricted walking. **Metal spikes allowed:** Yes. **Range:** Yes (mats). **To obtain tee times:** Call 2 days in advance for weekends.
RED/BLUE
Par: 70/72. **Yards:** 6,069/4,288. **Course rating:** 67.7/60.3. **Slope:** 105/90.
RED/WHITE
Par: 71/72. **Yards:** 5,957/4,349. **Course rating:** 67.7/60.9. **Slope:** 108/91.
WHITE/BLUE
Par: 71/72. **Yards:** 6,200/4,279. **Course rating:** 68.9/60.9. **Slope:** 111/90.

★★NORTHMOOR GOLF CLUB
8330 State Rte. 703 E., Celina, 45822, Mercer County, (419)394-4896, 40 miles SE of Lima.
Opened: 1923. **Holes:** 18. **Par:** 70/70. **Yards:** 5,802/5,086. **Course rating:** 66.8/68.0. **Slope:** 102/102. **Architect:** Alex "Nipper" Campbell. **Green fee:** $13/$17. **Credit cards:** MC,VISA. **Reduced fees:** Low season. **Caddies:** No. **Golf carts:** $8. **Discount golf packages:** No. **Season:** Year-round. **High:** April-Oct. **On site lodging:** No. **Rental clubs:** Yes. **Walking policy:** Unrestricted walking. **Metal spikes allowed:** Yes. **Range:** Yes (grass/mats). **To obtain tee times:** Call up to 14 days in advance for weekends and holidays.

★★½OAK GROVE GOLF COURSE
PU-14901 German Church Rd., Atwater, 44201, Portage County, (330)823-8823, 4 miles N of Alliance.
Opened: 1928. **Holes:** 18. **Par:** 71/75. **Yards:** 6,570/5,550. **Course rating:** 69.4/70.5.

Slope: N/A. Architect: N/A. Green fee: $11/$13. Credit cards: None. Reduced fees: Weekdays. Caddies: No. Golf carts: $16. Discount golf packages: No. Season: Year-round. High: June-Aug. On site lodging: No. Rental clubs: Yes. Walking policy: Unrestricted walking. Metal spikes allowed: Yes. Range: Yes (grass). To obtain tee times: Call golf shop.

OAK KNOLLS GOLF CLUB
PU-6700 State Rte. 43, Kent, 44240, Portage County, (330)673-6713, 10 miles NE of Akron.
Green fee: $18/$23. Credit cards: MC,VISA,DISC. Reduced fees: Weekdays, low season, twilight, seniors, juniors. Caddies: No. Golf carts: $19. Discount golf packages: No. High: May-Sept. On site lodging: No. Rental clubs: No. Walking policy: Unrestricted walking. Metal spikes allowed: Yes. Range: Yes (grass/mats). To obtain tee times: Call anytime.

★★½EAST COURSE
Opened: 1963. Holes: 18. Par: 71/72. Yards: 6,483/5,279. Course rating: 70.5/69.7. Slope: 111/107. Architect: Howard Morrette. Season: March-Nov.
Subscriber comments: Rolling terrain...Wide open courses...Average course, but open all year round...Better than average...Wide open and flat...Long par 4s, but not much character.

★★½WEST COURSE
Opened: 1970. Holes: 18. Par: 72/72. Yards: 6,373/5,681. Course rating: 69.0/71.3. Slope: 112/112. Architect: Jon Wegenek. Season: April-Sept.
Subscriber comments: Great place to spend a day of golf...Tougher of the two 18s. Prefer West over East...Predominantly open, though some holes offer challenge.

★★★½OAK SHADOWS GOLF CLUB
PU-1797 Hillandale Rd. N.E., New Philadelphia, 44663, Tuscarawas County, (330)343-2426, (888)802-7289, 30 miles S of Canton.
Opened: 1996. Holes: 18. Par: 72. Yards: 7,015. Course rating: 72.0. Slope: 122. Architect: John Robinson. Green fee: $18/$19. Credit cards: MC,VISA,DISC. Reduced fees: Weekdays, low season, twilight, seniors, juniors. Caddies: No. Golf carts: $10. Discount golf packages: No. Season: March-Dec. High: May-Oct. On site lodging: No. Rental clubs: No. Walking policy: Walking at certain times. Metal spikes allowed: Yes. Range: Yes (grass). To obtain tee times: Call.
Subscriber comments: New, needs maturing. If windy, look out, lots of sidehill lies...10th is a downhill roller coaster...For a new course, excellent...Nice layout, will be tough when mature.

★★★½ORCHARD HILLS GOLF & COUNTRY CLUB
11414 Caves Rd., Chesterland, 44026, Geauga County, (216)729-1963, 20 miles E of Cleveland.
Opened: 1962. Holes: 18. Par: 72/72. Yards: 6,409/5,651. Course rating: 71.1/72.6. Slope: 126/122. Architect: Gordon Alves. Green fee: $12/$26. Credit cards: MC,VISA. Reduced fees: Weekdays, seniors, juniors. Caddies: No. Golf carts: $22. Discount golf packages: No. Season: April-Nov. High: May-Sept. On site lodging: No. Rental clubs: Yes. Walking policy: Unrestricted walking. Metal spikes allowed: Yes. Range: No. To obtain tee times: Tee times for members only.
Subscriber comments: Tight, picturesque...Accurate driving needed to score on this course...Picturesque course, rolling hills.

★★★OTTAWA PARK GOLF COURSE
PU-1 Walden Pond, Toledo, 43606, Lucas County, (419)472-2059.
Opened: 1899. Holes: 18. Par: 71/71. Yards: 5,079/4,715. Course rating: 64.2/67.2. Slope: 110/111. Architect: Sylvanus Pierson Jermain. Green fee: $16/$24. Credit cards: MC,VISA,AMEX. Reduced fees: Low season, twilight, seniors, juniors. Caddies: No. Golf carts: $22. Discount golf packages: No. Season: Year-round weather permitting. High: N/A. On site lodging: No. Rental clubs: No. Walking policy: Unrestricted walking. Metal spikes allowed: Yes. Range: No. To obtain tee times: Call.
Notes: Amateur Public Links Championship.
Subscriber comments: Very short but lots of character and just plain fun...Nice course. Short but narrow...Requires accuracy, short par 3s.

OHIO

★★★OXBOW GOLF & COUNTRY CLUB
PU-County Rd. 85, Belpre, 45714, Washington County, (614)423-6771, (800)423-0443, 120 miles SE of Columbus.
Opened: 1974. **Holes:** 18. **Par:** 71/72. **Yards:** 6,558/4,858. **Course rating:** 70.9/68.8. **Slope:** 117/109. **Architect:** Jack Kidwell. **Green fee:** $15/$18. **Credit cards:** MC,VISA,DISC. **Reduced fees:** Seniors, juniors. **Caddies:** No. **Golf carts:** $12. **Discount golf packages:** Yes. **Season:** Year-round. **High:** May-July. **On site lodging:** No. **Rental clubs:** Yes. **Walking policy:** Unrestricted walking. **Metal spikes allowed:** Yes. **Range:** Yes (grass/mats). **To obtain tee times:** Call golf shop.
Subscriber comments: Interesting layout...Toughest course in area...Variety of holes...Long, beautiful, tough...Enjoyable test, out of the way.

★★★½PEBBLE CREEK GOLF CLUB
PU-4300 Algire Rd., Lexington, 44904, Richland County, (419)884-3434, 8 miles S of Mansfield.
Opened: 1971. **Holes:** 18. **Par:** 72/72. **Yards:** 6,554/5,195. **Course rating:** 70.8/69.1. **Slope:** 117/113. **Architect:** Richard LaConte/Jack Kidwell. **Green fee:** $15/$18. **Credit cards:** MC,VISA. **Reduced fees:** Weekdays, seniors, juniors. **Caddies:** No. **Golf carts:** $11. **Discount golf packages:** No. **Season:** March-Oct. **High:** N/A. **On site lodging:** No. **Rental clubs:** Yes. **Walking policy:** Unrestricted walking. **Metal spikes allowed:** Yes. **Range:** Yes (grass). **To obtain tee times:** Call up to 14 days in advance. Groups over 20 may call up to 1 year in advance.
Subscriber comments: Challenging without being a killer...Quite a few tight driving holes...Out of the way...Creeks all over the course...Great par 3s...Nice mature track.

★½PHEASANT RUN GOLF COURSE
PU-711 Pheasant Run Dr., La Grange, 44050, Lorain County, (216)355-5035, 35 miles SW of Cleveland.
Opened: 1964. **Holes:** 18. **Par:** 72/72. **Yards:** 6,345/5,006. **Course rating:** 69.3/67.5. **Slope:** 111/108. **Architect:** Star Builders. **Green fee:** $12/$15. **Credit cards:** None. **Reduced fees:** N/A. **Caddies:** No. **Golf carts:** N/A. **Discount golf packages:** No. **Season:** Year-round. **High:** March-Nov. **On site lodging:** No. **Rental clubs:** No. **Walking policy:** Unrestricted walking. **Metal spikes allowed:** Yes. **Range:** No. **To obtain tee times:** Call or come in.

★★PINE BROOK GOLF COURSE
PU-11043 N. Durkee Rd., Grafton, 44044, Lorain County, (440)748-2939, (800)236-8689, 22 miles SW of Cleveland.
Opened: 1959. **Holes:** 18. **Par:** 70/70. **Yards:** 6,062/5,225. **Course rating:** 66.8/68.9. **Slope:** 110/109. **Architect:** Pete Dye. **Green fee:** $15/$19. **Credit cards:** MC,VISA. **Reduced fees:** Weekdays, seniors, juniors. **Caddies:** No. **Golf carts:** $18. **Discount golf packages:** Yes. **Season:** Year-round. **High:** June-Aug. **On site lodging:** No. **Rental clubs:** Yes. **Walking policy:** Unrestricted walking. **Metal spikes allowed:** Yes. **Range:** Yes (grass/mats). **To obtain tee times:** Call anytime.

★★★PINE HILL GOLF COURSE
4382 Kauffman Rd., Carroll, 43112, Fairfield County, (614)837-3911, 18 miles SE of Columbus.
Opened: 1965. **Holes:** 18. **Par:** 72/72. **Yards:** 6,673/4,927. **Course rating:** 68.9/64.5. **Slope:** 112/102. **Architect:** Jack Kidwell. **Green fee:** $14/$15. **Credit cards:** MC,VISA,DISC. **Reduced fees:** N/A. **Caddies:** No. **Golf carts:** $10. **Discount golf packages:** No. **Season:** Year-round. **High:** May-Aug. **On site lodging:** No. **Rental clubs:** No. **Walking policy:** Unrestricted walking. **Metal spikes allowed:** Yes. **Range:** Yes. **To obtain tee times:** Call for weekend or holiday with credit card to guarantee.
Subscriber comments: Wide open but long...Fun holes...Nice people...Nothing spectacular, but always a good test. Fun to play...A very pleasant course.

★★★★PINE HILLS GOLF CLUB
PU-433 W. 130th St., Hinckley, 44233, Medina County, (330)225-4477, 15 miles S of Cleveland.
Opened: 1957. **Holes:** 18. **Par:** 72/73. **Yards:** 6,482/5,685. **Course rating:** 71.2/74.3. **Slope:** 124/126. **Architect:** Harold Paddock. **Green fee:** $25/$25. **Credit cards:**

MC,VISA. **Reduced fees:** N/A. **Caddies:** No. **Golf carts:** $10. **Discount golf packages:** No. **Season:** April-Dec. **High:** April-Nov. **On site lodging:** No. **Rental clubs:** Yes. **Walking policy:** Unrestricted walking. **Metal spikes allowed:** Yes. **Range:** No. **To obtain tee times:** Call golf shop.
Subscriber comments: Beautiful course...Hilly, very tight, wooded...Some outstanding holes...Interesting layout for shotmakers...A pleasure to golf here...Great course, plush...Interesting terrain.

★★PINE RIDGE COUNTRY CLUB
PU-30601 Ridge Rd., Wickliffe, 44092, Lake County, (216)943-0293, (800)254-7275, 15 miles NE of Cleveland.
Opened: 1924. **Holes:** 18. **Par:** 71/75. **Yards:** 6,137/5,672. **Course rating:** 69.6/73.0. **Slope:** 118/122. **Architect:** Harold Paddock. **Green fee:** $13/$17. **Credit cards:** MC,VISA. **Reduced fees:** Weekdays, low season, twilight, seniors. **Caddies:** Yes. **Golf carts:** $12. **Discount golf packages:** Yes. **Season:** Year-round. **High:** April-Oct. **On site lodging:** No. **Rental clubs:** Yes. **Walking policy:** Mandatory cart. **Metal spikes allowed:** Yes. **Range:** Yes. **To obtain tee times:** Call 7:00 a.m. Monday for upcoming weekend. Call 7 days in advance for weekdays.

★★½PINE VALLEY GOLF CLUB
PU-469 Reimer Rd., Wadsworth, 44281, Medina County, (330)335-3375, 1 mile E of Wadsworth.
Opened: 1962. **Holes:** 18. **Par:** 72/74. **Yards:** 6,097/5,268. **Course rating:** 68.5/67.9. **Slope:** 109/107. **Architect:** Cliff Deming. **Green fee:** $13/$17. **Credit cards:** None. **Reduced fees:** Weekdays, seniors. **Caddies:** No. **Golf carts:** $18. **Discount golf packages:** No. **Season:** March-Nov. **High:** May-Oct. **On site lodging:** No. **Rental clubs:** No. **Walking policy:** Unrestricted walking. **Metal spikes allowed:** Yes. **Range:** Yes (grass). **To obtain tee times:** Call golf shop.
Subscriber comments: Fun course, fun staff, fun day...Not long, wide open on front, trees on back...A fun course...Short course.

★★★PIPESTONE GOLF CLUB
PU-4344 Benner Rd., Miamisburg, 45342, Montgomery County, (937)866-4653, 8 miles S of Dayton.
Opened: 1992. **Holes:** 18. **Par:** 72/72. **Yards:** 6,939/5,207. **Course rating:** 72.1/69.2. **Slope:** 137/121. **Architect:** Arthur Hills. **Green fee:** $23/$29. **Credit cards:** MC,VISA. **Reduced fees:** Twilight. **Caddies:** No. **Golf carts:** $10. **Discount golf packages:** No. **Season:** March-Dec. **High:** June-Aug. **On site lodging:** No. **Rental clubs:** Yes. **Walking policy:** Unrestricted walking. **Metal spikes allowed:** Yes. **Range:** Yes (grass). **To obtain tee times:** Call golf shop seven days in advance.
Subscriber comments: Good solid course; four or five great holes...Some good holes...Arthur Hills rules! 18th is awesome...Picturesque, a good test of golf skill...Fairly open...Gets better each year, not great, good.

★★PLEASANT HILL GOLF CLUB
PU-6487 Hankins Rd., Middletown, 45044, Butler County, (513)539-7220, 20 miles N of Cincinnati.
Opened: 1969. **Holes:** 18. **Par:** 71/71. **Yards:** 6,586/4,723. **Course rating:** 70.9/66.9. **Slope:** 117/107. **Architect:** Jack Kidwell. **Green fee:** $16/$19. **Credit cards:** MC,VISA. **Reduced fees:** Low season, seniors, juniors. **Caddies:** No. **Golf carts:** $11. **Discount golf packages:** No. **Season:** Year-round. **High:** June-July. **On site lodging:** No. **Rental clubs:** Yes. **Walking policy:** Unrestricted walking. **Metal spikes allowed:** Yes. **Range:** Yes (grass). **To obtain tee times:** Call Monday for weekend; call anytime for weekday.

★★½PLEASANT HILL GOLF COURSE
PU-13461 Aquilla Rd., Chardon, 44024, Geauga County, (440)285-2428, 30 miles E of Cleveland.
Opened: 1965. **Holes:** 27. **Architect:** Dalton Pfouts. **Green fee:** $10/$18. **Credit cards:** MC,VISA. **Reduced fees:** Weekdays, low season, seniors. **Caddies:** No. **Golf carts:** $18. **Discount golf packages:** No. **Season:** March-Nov. **High:** May-Nov. **On site lodging:** No. **Rental clubs:** Yes. **Walking policy:** Unrestricted walking. **Metal spikes allowed:** Yes. **Range:** No. **To obtain tee times:** Call golf shop.

OHIO

FRONT/BACK
Par: 71/71. **Yards:** 6,212/5,446. **Course rating:** 67.5. **Slope:** 113.
FRONT/MIDDLE
Par: 70/70. **Yards:** 6,308/5,174. **Course rating:** 67.5. **Slope:** 113.
MIDDLE/BACK
Par: 71/71. **Yards:** 6,351/5,276. **Course rating:** 67.5. **Slope:** 113.
Subscriber comments: Tight tough par 3s...Hilly pasture lands...Open, lacks rough...Nice country course, not many blind shots.

★★★½PLEASANT VALLEY COUNTRY CLUB
PU-3830 Hamilton Rd., Medina, 44256, Medina County, (330)725-5770, 25 miles S of Cleveland.
Opened: 1970. **Holes:** 18. **Par:** 72/72. **Yards:** 6,912/4,984. **Course rating:** 73.4/68.9.
Slope: 123/113. **Architect:** Jack Kidwell. **Green fee:** $19/$24. **Credit cards:** None.
Reduced fees: Weekdays. **Caddies:** No. **Golf carts:** $20. **Discount golf packages:** No. **Season:** April-Nov. **High:** June-Aug. **On site lodging:** No. **Rental clubs:** No.
Walking policy: Unrestricted walking. **Metal spikes allowed:** Yes. **Range:** No. **To obtain tee times:** Call up to 7 days in advance.
Subscriber comments: Long and challenging...Back nine very tight...Excellent course for all golfers...Challenging from back tees...Lots of tall trees...Bring your long irons...Pleasant experience.

★★½POWDERHORN GOLF COURSE
PU-3991 Bates Rd., Madison, 44057, Lake County, (216)428-5951, (800)863-3742, 40 miles NE of Cleveland.
Opened: 1981. **Holes:** 18. **Par:** 70/70. **Yards:** 6,004/4,881. **Course rating:** 68.5/67.6.
Slope: 117/113. **Architect:** Anderson & Lesniak. **Green fee:** $15/$17. **Credit cards:** MC,VISA. **Reduced fees:** Weekdays, low season, seniors, juniors. **Caddies:** No. **Golf carts:** $10. **Discount golf packages:** Yes. **Season:** Year-round. **High:** April-Oct. **On site lodging:** No. **Rental clubs:** Yes. **Walking policy:** Unrestricted walking. **Metal spikes allowed:** Yes. **Range:** No. **To obtain tee times:** Call 7 days in advance.
Subscriber comments: Good challenge for all levels...Interesting layout, toughest first hole around...Very tight, long par 3s.

PRAIRIE VIEW GOLF COURSE
PU-26770 SR 67, Waynesfield, 45896, Auglaize County, (419)568-7888, 12 miles E of Wapakoneta.
Opened: 1991. **Holes:** 18. **Par:** 72/72. **Yards:** 6,348/5,575. **Course rating:** N/A. **Slope:** N/A. **Architect:** Charles Buffenbarger. **Green fee:** $12/$12. **Credit cards:** None.
Reduced fees: N/A. **Caddies:** No. **Golf carts:** $17. **Discount golf packages:** No.
Season: March-Nov. **High:** May-Sept. **On site lodging:** No. **Rental clubs:** Yes.
Walking policy: Unrestricted walking. **Metal spikes allowed:** Yes. **Range:** Yes (grass/mats). **To obtain tee times:** Call 1 day in advance.

★★★½PUNDERSON STATE PARK GOLF COURSE
PU-11755 Kinsman Rd., Newbury, 44065, Geauga County, (440)564-5465, 25 miles E of Cleveland.
Opened: 1969. **Holes:** 18. **Par:** 72/72. **Yards:** 6,815/5,769. **Course rating:** 72.9/72.3.
Slope: 125/122. **Architect:** Jack Kidwell. **Green fee:** $18/$27. **Credit cards:** All major,Diners Club. **Reduced fees:** Weekdays, low season, twilight, seniors. **Caddies:** No. **Golf carts:** $12. **Discount golf packages:** No. **Season:** March-Nov. **High:** N/A. **On site lodging:** Yes. **Rental clubs:** Yes. **Walking policy:** Walking at certain times. **Metal spikes allowed:** Yes. **Range:** No. **To obtain tee times:** Call at 7 a.m. on the Thursday prior to weekend.
Subscriber comments: Beautiful, hard course...7, 8 and 9 great holes...Always a favorite. Challenging due to length, though fair...Long, tough, and enjoyable...Some really good holes...Challenging rolling hills...Beautiful, long, tough greens.

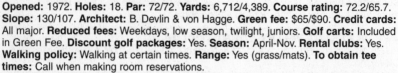

QUAIL HOLLOW RESORT & COUNTRY CLUB

11080 Concord Hambden Rd., Painesville, 44077, Lake County, (216)350-3500, (800)792-0258, 30 miles E of Cleveland.
Caddies: No. **High:** June-Aug. **On site lodging:** Yes. **Metal spikes allowed:** Yes.

★★★★DEVLIN-VON HAGGE COURSE

Opened: 1972. **Holes:** 18. **Par:** 72/72. **Yards:** 6,712/4,389. **Course rating:** 72.2/65.7. **Slope:** 130/107. **Architect:** B. Devlin & von Hagge. **Green fee:** $65/$90. **Credit cards:** All major. **Reduced fees:** Weekdays, low season, twilight, juniors. **Golf carts:** Included in Green Fee. **Discount golf packages:** Yes. **Season:** April-Nov. **Rental clubs:** Yes. **Walking policy:** Walking at certain times. **Range:** Yes (grass/mats). **To obtain tee times:** Call when making room reservations.
Subscriber comments: Great course...Great day even in the rain...Each hole a challenge...Resort golf at its best...Really nice...Super tough rough!...Very challenging, tight, pro atmosphere.

★★★★½WEISKOPF-MORRISH COURSE

Opened: 1996. **Holes:** 18. **Par:** 71/71. **Yards:** 6,872/5,166. **Course rating:** 73.9/70.0. **Slope:** 130/117. **Architect:** Tom Weiskopf and Jay Morrish. **Green fee:** $50/$75. **Credit cards:** MC,VISA,AMEX,Diners Club. **Reduced fees:** Twilight. **Golf carts:** $18. **Discount golf packages:** No. **Season:** March-Oct. **Rental clubs:** No. **Walking policy:** Unrestricted walking. **Range:** No. **To obtain tee times:** Overnight guests or member guests only may call.
Notes: Ranked 15th in 1997 Best in State; 9th in 1996 Best New Upscale Courses.
Subscriber comments: Excellent test of golf...New, but what a layout...Tough course for an intermediate golfer...Beautiful layout, tough...Some great holes...Great new course, classic...Once it fully matures it will be great.

★★★RACCOON HILL GOLF CLUB

PU-485 Judson Rd., Kent, 44240, Portage County, (330)673-2111, 10 miles NE of Akron.
Opened: 1989. **Holes:** 18. **Par:** 71/71. **Yards:** 6,068/4,650. **Course rating:** 69.2/67.0. **Slope:** 115/106. **Architect:** Bill Snetsinger. **Green fee:** $15/$26. **Credit cards:** None. **Reduced fees:** Weekdays, low season, twilight, seniors, juniors. **Caddies:** No. **Golf carts:** $9. **Discount golf packages:** No. **Season:** March-Nov. **High:** May-Sept. **On site lodging:** No. **Rental clubs:** No. **Walking policy:** Unrestricted walking. **Metal spikes allowed:** Yes. **Range:** No. **To obtain tee times:** Call.
Subscriber comments: A little short, but testy...Average layout, too many doglegs...Back nine nice links-style course...Some challenging holes...Good bar...Nice golf course, some easy, some hard...Short but sort of tricky...Has improved greatly.

★★½RACCOON INTERNATIONAL GOLF CLUB

PU-3275 Worthington Rd. S.W., Granville, 43023, Licking County, (614)587-0921, (888)692-7898, 25 miles from Columbus.
Opened: N/A. **Holes:** 18. **Par:** 72/72. **Yards:** 6,586/6,094. **Course rating:** N/A. **Slope:** 125/116. **Architect:** N/A. **Green fee:** N/A. **Credit cards:** MC,VISA. **Reduced fees:** Weekdays, low season, resort guests. **Caddies:** No. **Golf carts:** N/A. **Discount golf packages:** No. **Season:** Year-round. **High:** Mar-Oct. **On site lodging:** No. **Rental clubs:** No. **Walking policy:** N/A. **Metal spikes allowed:** Yes. **Range:** Yes. **To obtain tee times:** Call.
Subscriber comments: It's golf, no frills...Excellent course, tough...Challenging...Much improved...Fair course, good layout...Small tricky greens.

★★★½RAINTREE COUNTRY CLUB

4350 Mayfair Rd., Uniontown, 44685, Summit County, (330)699-3232, (800)371-0017, 5 miles S of Akron.
Opened: 1992. **Holes:** 18. **Par:** 72/72. **Yards:** 6,811/5,030. **Course rating:** 73.0/68.5. **Slope:** 127/114. **Architect:** Brian Huntley. **Green fee:** $20/$27. **Credit cards:** MC,VISA. **Reduced fees:** Weekdays, low season, resort guests, twilight, seniors, juniors. **Caddies:** No. **Golf carts:** $10. **Discount golf packages:** Yes. **Season:** Year-round. **High:** April-Oct. **On site lodging:** No. **Rental clubs:** Yes. **Walking policy:** Walking at certain times. **Metal spikes allowed:** No. **Range:** Yes (grass/mats). **To obtain tee times:** Call or come in up to 1 year in advance.

Subscriber comments: Beautiful course and clubhouse...Wonderful layout, good challenge from tips...Some bland holes, some outstanding holes...Great finishing hole, par 5 with divided fairway...A great track that tests all your skills...Lots of old trees...Maturing fast.

★★½RAYMOND MEMORIAL GOLF CLUB

PU-3860 Trabue Rd., Columbus, Franklin County, (614)275-2025.
Architect: Robert Trent Jones. **Caddies:** No. **Discount golf packages:** No. **On site lodging:** No. **Rental clubs:** No. **Metal spikes allowed:** Yes. **Range:** No.
Call club for further information.

★½REEVES GOLF COURSE

PU-4747 Playfield Lane, Cincinnati, 45226, Hamilton County, (513)321-1433.
Opened: 1965. **Holes:** 18. **Par:** 70/74. **Yards:** 6,200/5,630. **Course rating:** 68.4/70.2.
Slope: 109/102. **Architect:** William H. Diddel. **Green fee:** $17/$17. **Credit cards:** None. **Reduced fees:** Low season, seniors, juniors. **Caddies:** No. **Golf carts:** $10.
Discount golf packages: No. **Season:** Year-round. **High:** May-Sept. **On site lodging:** No. **Rental clubs:** Yes. **Walking policy:** Unrestricted walking. **Metal spikes allowed:** Yes. **Range:** Yes (grass/mats). **To obtain tee times:** Xeta computer system or call 1 day in advance.
Special Notes: Also has a 9-hole par-3 course.

REID PARK MEMORIAL GOLF COURSE

PU-1325 Bird Rd., Springfield, 45505, Clark County, (937)324-7725, 43 miles W of Columbus.
Opened: 1967. **Architect:** Jack Kidwell. **Green fee:** $16/$16. **Credit cards:** None.
Reduced fees: Twilight. **Caddies:** No. **Golf carts:** $20. **Discount golf packages:** No.
Season: Year-round. **High:** May-Oct. **On site lodging:** No. **Rental clubs:** Yes. **Walking policy:** Unrestricted walking. **Metal spikes allowed:** Yes. **Range:** Yes (grass). **To obtain tee times:** Call eight days in advance.

★★★NORTH COURSE

Holes: 18. **Par:** 72/72. **Yards:** 6,760/5,035. **Course rating:** 72.5/69.2. **Slope:** 130/118.
Subscriber comments: Nice layout...Good layout for most part...Easy to walk. Challenging holes...Pretty course but all the holes are predictable...Great course, short, accuracy a premium...Old, tall trees, rolling fairways, very pretty...#15 is a tough hole...Hilly, very forgiving, average sized greens...Positioning is key to your success.

★★½SOUTH COURSE

Holes: 18. **Par:** 72/72. **Yards:** 6,500/4,895. **Course rating:** 69.0/66.5. **Slope:** 110/102.
Subscriber comments: Nice course...South course is not bad, but not impressive...Good snack bar...Big greens, not a lot of trouble, fun for high handicapper...Easier than the North course, fun!...Nice walking course.

★★½RICKENBACKER GOLF CLUB

PU-5600 Airbase Rd., Groveport, 43125, Franklin County, (614)491-5000, 10 miles S of Columbus.
Opened: 1959. **Holes:** 18. **Par:** 72/72. **Yards:** 7,003/5,476. **Course rating:** 72.6/71.2.
Slope: 117/117. **Architect:** N/A. **Green fee:** $10/$19. **Credit cards:** All major.
Reduced fees: Weekdays, low season, twilight, seniors, juniors. **Caddies:** No. **Golf carts:** $10. **Discount golf packages:** Yes. **Season:** Year-round. **High:** June-Aug. **On site lodging:** No. **Rental clubs:** Yes. **Walking policy:** Unrestricted walking. **Metal spikes allowed:** No. **Range:** Yes (grass). **To obtain tee times:** Call up to 5 days in advance.
Special Notes: Formerly Steeplechase Country Club.

★★★RIDGE TOP GOLF COURSE

PU-7441 Tower Rd., Medina, 44256, Medina County, (330)725-5500, (800)679-9839, 20 miles S of Cleveland.
Opened: 1970. **Holes:** 18. **Par:** 71/71. **Yards:** 6,211/4,968. **Course rating:** 70.0/67.9.
Slope: 109/106. **Architect:** Robert Pennington. **Green fee:** $17/$21. **Credit cards:** MC,VISA,DISC. **Reduced fees:** Weekdays, low season, seniors, juniors. **Caddies:** No.
Golf carts: $18. **Discount golf packages:** No. **Season:** March-Nov. **High:** June-Aug.
On site lodging: No. **Rental clubs:** No. **Walking policy:** Unrestricted walking. **Metal spikes allowed:** Yes. **Range:** No. **To obtain tee times:** Call golf shop.

Subscriber comments: A fun place to play...Nice layout...Short; too many blind shots...We keep coming back...Interesting layout...Many unique challenging holes...Scenic...Pleasant to play...18th is a par 3.

★★RIVER BEND GOLF COURSE
PU-5567 Upper River Rd., Miamisburg, 45342, Montgomery County, (937)859-8121, 5 miles S of Dayton.
Opened: 1963. **Holes:** 18. **Par:** 72/75. **Yards:** 7,000/5,980. **Course rating:** 70.8. **Slope:** 112. **Architect:** Robert Bruce Harris. **Green fee:** $12/$19. **Credit cards:** None. **Reduced fees:** Low season, seniors, juniors. **Caddies:** No. **Golf carts:** $9. **Discount golf packages:** No. **Season:** Year-round. **High:** June-Aug. **On site lodging:** No. **Rental clubs:** Yes. **Walking policy:** Unrestricted walking. **Metal spikes allowed:** Yes. **Range:** No. **To obtain tee times:** Call 7 days in advance.

★★★½RIVER GREENS GOLF COURSE
PU-22749 State Rte. 751, West Lafayette, 43845, Coshocton County, (614)545-7817, 25 miles SW of New Philadelphia.
Opened: 1967. **Holes:** 27. **Par:** 72/73. **Yards:** 6,588/5,409. **Course rating:** 70.9/70.2. **Slope:** 114/113. **Architect:** Jack Kidwell. **Green fee:** $16/$18. **Credit cards:** MC,VISA. **Reduced fees:** N/A. **Caddies:** No. **Golf carts:** $10. **Discount golf packages:** Yes. **Season:** March-Dec. **High:** March-Sept. **On site lodging:** No. **Rental clubs:** Yes. **Walking policy:** Unrestricted walking. **Metal spikes allowed:** Yes. **Range:** Yes (grass/mats). **To obtain tee times:** Call 7 day in advance.
Subscriber comments: All around good experience every time...Nice course, especially third nine...Nice little track, little short...Fun course, new nine very playable...Very nice, very professional, nice clubhouse...Great 27 holes...Great walking course...Excellent place to play...Pine trees make accuracy critical. Solid and fun.
Special Notes: Also has 9-hole par-36 Pine Course.

★★★½RIVERBY HILLS GOLF COURSE
PU-16571 W. River Rd., Bowling Green, 43402, Wood County, (419)878-5941.
Architect: Harold Paddock. **Caddies:** No. **Discount golf packages:** No. **On site lodging:** No. **Rental clubs:** No. **Metal spikes allowed:** Yes. **Range:** No.
Call club for further information.
Subscriber comments: Country setting. Good variety...Good course for all around play...Decent course...Great back 9; 12th dogleg left, water on left and in front of green...Two different nines. Front is open and long. Back is narrow and wooded...Good course design...A few interesting holes.

★★ROCKY FORK GOLF & TENNIS CENTER
9965 State Rte. 124, Hillsboro, 45133, Highland County, (937)393-9004.
Call club for further information.

★★ROLLING ACRES GOLF COURSE
63 State Route 511, Nova, 44859, Ashland County, (419)652-3160.
Call club for further information.

★★½ROLLING GREEN GOLF CLUB
PU-15900 Mayfield Rd., Huntsburg, 44046, Geauga County, (216)636-5171, 50 miles E of Cleveland.
Opened: 1970. **Holes:** 18. **Par:** 71/71. **Yards:** 6,551/5,512. **Course rating:** 70.1/69.4. **Slope:** 120/111. **Architect:** N/A. **Green fee:** $11/$18. **Credit cards:** None. **Reduced fees:** Weekdays, seniors, juniors. **Caddies:** No. **Golf carts:** $20. **Discount golf packages:** No. **Season:** April-Oct. **High:** June-Aug. **On site lodging:** No. **Rental clubs:** No. **Walking policy:** Unrestricted walking. **Metal spikes allowed:** Yes. **Range:** Yes (grass). **To obtain tee times:** Call golf shop.

★½ROLLING GREEN GOLF COURSE
7656 Lutz Ave. NW, Massillon, 44646, Stark County, (330)854-3800.
Call club for further information.

★★½ROLLING MEADOWS GOLF CLUB

PU-11233 Industrial Pkwy., Marysville, 43040, Union County, (937)873-4567, 15 miles W of Columbus.
Opened: 1996. **Holes:** 18. **Par:** 71/71. **Yards:** 6,750/5,832. **Course rating:** 71.1/72.0.
Slope: 119/119. **Architect:** David Savic. **Green fee:** $17/$20. **Credit cards:** All major.
Reduced fees: Weekdays, low season, seniors. **Caddies:** No. **Golf carts:** $10.
Discount golf packages: No. **Season:** March-Dec. **High:** May-Sept. **On site lodging:** No. **Rental clubs:** Yes. **Walking policy:** Unrestricted walking. **Metal spikes allowed:** Yes. **Range:** No. **To obtain tee times:** Call up to 7 days in advance.
Subscriber comments: Very new course, needs to mature...Wide open course with some potential as it ages...Fun back nine...Fitting name, very playable.

★★★½ROYAL AMERICAN LINKS GOLF CLUB

3300 Miller Paul Rd., Galena, 43021, Delaware County, (614)965-1215, 17 miles N of Columbus.
Opened: 1992. **Holes:** 18. **Par:** 72/72. **Yards:** 6,839/5,172. **Course rating:** 72.8/70.1.
Slope: 128/111. **Architect:** Michael Hurdzan. **Green fee:** $20/$35. **Credit cards:** MC,VISA,DISC. **Reduced fees:** Weekdays, low season, twilight, seniors, juniors.
Caddies: No. **Golf carts:** $12. **Discount golf packages:** No. **Season:** March-Dec.
High: June-Sept. **On site lodging:** No. **Rental clubs:** Yes. **Walking policy:** Unrestricted walking. **Metal spikes allowed:** Yes. **Range:** Yes (grass). **To obtain tee times:** Call 7 days in advance.
Subscriber comments: Adequate course, great clubhouse...Very tough from back tees...Has several very good holes...Always very windy...Nice out of the way course...Links-style course, can be windy and hard...Worth the drive to play...Calls for a variety of shots...Links style, well bunkered...Not many trees...Good use of water...Challenging.

★★RUNNING FOX GOLF COURSE

PU-310 Sunset, Chillicothe, 45601, Ross County, (614)775-9955, 42 miles S of Columbus.
Opened: 1974. **Holes:** 27. **Architect:** Ted Cox. **Green fee:** $10/$12. **Credit cards:** MC,VISA. **Reduced fees:** Seniors, juniors. **Caddies:** No. **Golf carts:** $19. **Discount golf packages:** Yes. **Season:** Year-round. **High:** June-July. **On site lodging:** No. **Rental clubs:** Yes. **Walking policy:** Unrestricted walking. **Metal spikes allowed:** Yes. **Range:** Yes (grass). **To obtain tee times:** Call anytime.
RED/BLUE
Par: 72. **Yards:** 6,432/5,645. **Course rating:** 70.5. **Slope:** 113.
RED/WHITE
Par: 72. **Yards:** 6,538/5,685. **Course rating:** 70.5. **Slope:** 113.
WHITE/BLUE
Par: 72. **Yards:** 6,568/6,220. **Course rating:** 70.5. **Slope:** 113.

★½SAFARI GOLF CLUB

PU-P.O. Box 400, Powell, 43065, Delaware County, (614)645-3444, 15 miles N of Columbus.
Opened: N/A. **Holes:** 18. **Par:** 72/72. **Yards:** 6,507/4,827. **Course rating:** N/A. **Slope:** 109/110. **Architect:** Jimmy Duros. **Green fee:** N/A. **Credit cards:** MC,VISA,DISC.
Reduced fees: Weekdays, seniors, juniors. **Caddies:** No. **Golf carts:** N/A. **Discount golf packages:** No. **Season:** Year-round. **High:** May-Sept. **On site lodging:** No. **Rental clubs:** Yes. **Walking policy:** Unrestricted walking. **Metal spikes allowed:** Yes. **Range:** Yes (grass). **To obtain tee times:** Call on Monday for upcoming weekend.

★★½ST. ALBANS GOLF CLUB

PU-3833 Northridge Rd. N.W., Alexandria, 43001, Licking County, (614)924-8885, 25 miles E of Columbus.
Opened: 1988. **Holes:** 18. **Par:** 71/71. **Yards:** 6,732/5,513. **Course rating:** 71.6/71.1.
Slope: 112. **Architect:** Tony Price. **Green fee:** $11/$13. **Credit cards:** None. **Reduced fees:** Low season, seniors. **Caddies:** No. **Golf carts:** $23. **Discount golf packages:** No. **Season:** March-Dec. **High:** May-Aug. **On site lodging:** No. **Rental clubs:** No.
Walking policy: Unrestricted walking. **Metal spikes allowed:** Yes. **Range:** No. **To obtain tee times:** Call.

★★★½SAINT DENIS GOLF COURSE

PU-10660 Chardon Rd., Chardon, 44024, Geauga County, (440)285-2183, (800)843-5676, 25 miles NE of Cleveland.
Opened: 1967. **Holes:** 18. **Par:** 72/72. **Yards:** 6,600/5,900. **Course rating:** 72.5/72.0.
Slope: 115/117. **Architect:** N/A. **Green fee:** $18/$23. **Credit cards:** None. **Reduced fees:** Weekdays, seniors. **Caddies:** No. **Golf carts:** $10. **Discount golf packages:** No.
Season: April-Oct. **High:** N/A. **On site lodging:** No. **Rental clubs:** No. **Walking policy:** Unrestricted walking. **Metal spikes allowed:** Yes. **Range:** No. **To obtain tee times:** Call up to 7 days in advance.
Subscriber comments: Improved every year...Excellent course, tough holes...Very scenic, good challenge...Fun front nine...Nice location...Beautiful course, fun to play...Very hilly, challenging...Nice country course.

★★★SALEM HILLS GOLF & COUNTRY CLUB

12688 Salem-Warren Rd., Salem, 44460, Mahoning County, (330)337-8033, 15 miles S of Youngstown.
Opened: 1966. **Holes:** 18. **Par:** 72/72. **Yards:** 7,146/5,597. **Course rating:** 74.3/69.7.
Slope: 126/114. **Architect:** Butch Ross. **Green fee:** $16/$18. **Credit cards:** MC,VISA.
Reduced fees: Weekdays, seniors, juniors. **Caddies:** No. **Golf carts:** $9. **Discount golf packages:** Yes. **Season:** April-Nov. **High:** June-Aug. **On site lodging:** No. **Rental clubs:** No. **Walking policy:** Unrestricted walking. **Metal spikes allowed:** Yes. **Range:** Yes (grass/mats). **To obtain tee times:** Call.
Subscriber comments: Nice course, fun...Older, some variety...Nice #9 hole...Long, great test of all clubs.

★★★SALT FORK STATE PARK GOLF COURSE

PU-14755 Cadiz Rd., Lore City, 43755, Guernsey County, (614)432-7185, 6 miles E of Cambridge.
Opened: 1972. **Holes:** 18. **Par:** 71/71. **Yards:** 6,056/5,241. **Course rating:** 68.3/69.7.
Slope: 110/113. **Architect:** Jack Kidwell. **Green fee:** $13/$13. **Credit cards:** MC,VISA.
Reduced fees: Low season, resort guests, seniors. **Caddies:** No. **Golf carts:** $12.
Discount golf packages: Yes. **Season:** Year-round. **High:** May-Oct. **On site lodging:** Yes. **Rental clubs:** Yes. **Walking policy:** Unrestricted walking. **Metal spikes allowed:** Yes. **Range:** Yes (grass/mats). **To obtain tee times:** Call golf shop.
Subscriber comments: Hilliest course ever played...Very interesting, well laid out, hilly...Scenic, hard to walk...You won't have one flat lie all day...A mountain challenge...Beautiful views in autumn...Awesome #10 tee looking out over course; bring climbing shoes.

★★★½SAWMILL CREEK GOLF & RACQUET CLUB

R-2401 Cleveland Rd. W., Huron, 44839, Erie County, (419)433-3789, 65 miles W of Cleveland.
Opened: 1973. **Holes:** 18. **Par:** 71/74. **Yards:** 6,813/5,416. **Course rating:** 72.3/70.6.
Slope: 128/120. **Architect:** George Fazio and Tom Fazio. **Green fee:** $45. **Credit cards:** All major. **Reduced fees:** Low season. **Caddies:** No. **Golf carts:** $28. **Discount golf packages:** Yes. **Season:** April-Oct. **High:** June-Sept. **On site lodging:** Yes. **Rental clubs:** Yes. **Walking policy:** Unrestricted walking. **Metal spikes allowed:** Yes. **Range:** No. **To obtain tee times:** Call golf shop. Off season call Sawmill Creek Resort at 1-800-SAWMILL.
Subscriber comments: Very challenging course...Huge difficult greens...Difficult; very windy...Decent resort course, four excellent par 3s...When Lake Erie winds whip up, this is a difficult course...Solid Tom Fazio design.

★★★★½SHAKER RUN GOLF CLUB

PU-4361 Greentree Rd., Lebanon, 45036, Warren County, (513)727-0007, 18 miles N of Cincinnati.
Opened: 1979. **Holes:** 18. **Par:** 72/72. **Yards:** 6,965/5,075. **Course rating:** 75.4/68.8. **Slope:** 141/121. **Architect:** Arthur Hills. **Green fee:** $49/$70. **Credit cards:** MC,VISA,AMEX. **Reduced fees:** Low season, twilight, seniors, juniors. **Caddies:** No. **Golf carts:** Included in Green Fee. **Discount golf packages:** Yes. **Season:** March-Dec. **High:** May-Oct. **On site lodging:** No. **Rental clubs:** Yes. **Walking policy:** Walking at certain times. **Metal spikes allowed:** Yes.

Range: Yes (grass). **To obtain tee times:** Call 7 days in advance.
Subscriber comments: Great course, worth traveling to, very tough...Great test of golf...Doesn't get much better than this...Very nice, wish I could clear water on 18...Great par 3s...Challenging course with excellent greens...A great and relatively unknown public-access course...Best kept secret in Ohio...9 and 18 around lake.

★★SHAMROCK GOLF CLUB

PU-4436 Powell Rd., Powell, 43065, Delaware County, (614)792-6630, 12 miles N of Columbus.
Opened: 1988. **Holes:** 18. **Par:** 71/71. **Yards:** 6,300/5,400. **Course rating:** 67.5/68.0.
Slope: 115/110. **Architect:** Jack Kidwell and Michael Hurdzan. **Green fee:** $14/$19.
Credit cards: MC,VISA,DISC. **Reduced fees:** Low season, twilight, seniors, juniors.
Caddies: No. **Golf carts:** $11. **Discount golf packages:** No. **Season:** Year-round.
High: May-Oct. **On site lodging:** No. **Rental clubs:** Yes. **Walking policy:** Walking at certain times. **Metal spikes allowed:** Yes. **Range:** Yes (grass). **To obtain tee times:** Call seven days in advance.

★★★SHARON WOODS GOLF COURSE

PM-11350 Swing Rd., Cincinnati, 45241, Hamilton County, (513)769-4325, 15 miles N of Cincinnati.
Opened: 1938. **Holes:** 18. **Par:** 70/70. **Yards:** 6,652/5,288. **Course rating:** 72.3/65.5.
Slope: 131/117. **Architect:** William Diddle. **Green fee:** $14/$18. **Credit cards:** MC,VISA. **Reduced fees:** Seniors, juniors. **Caddies:** No. **Golf carts:** $11. **Discount golf packages:** No. **Season:** March-Dec. **High:** April-Sept. **On site lodging:** No.
Rental clubs: Yes. **Walking policy:** Unrestricted walking. **Metal spikes allowed:** Yes.
Range: No. **To obtain tee times:** Call up to 5 days in advance starting at 6 p.m.
Subscriber comments: Tough, long and hilly...Trees all around...Very good course. Old-style layout...3rd hole is a dandy...Front nine long, back nine hilly...Hole 18 is unforgettable after a par-3 17th that you'll want to play over and over.

★★★SHAWNEE HILLS GOLF COURSE

PU-18753 Egbert Rd., Bedford, 44146, Cuyahoga County, (440)232-7184, 10 miles SE of Cleveland.
Opened: 1957. **Holes:** 18. **Par:** 71/73. **Yards:** 6,160/6,029. **Course rating:** 68.7/72.5.
Slope: 112/116. **Architect:** Ben Zink. **Green fee:** $11/$15. **Credit cards:** MC,VISA.
Reduced fees: Low season, seniors, juniors. **Caddies:** No. **Golf carts:** $18. **Discount golf packages:** Yes. **Season:** March-Dec. **High:** May-Sept. **On site lodging:** No.
Rental clubs: Yes. **Walking policy:** Unrestricted walking. **Metal spikes allowed:** Yes.
Range: Yes. **To obtain tee times:** Call up to 5 days in advance.
Subscriber comments: Open course, easy to score on...Nice walk-on course...Front nine super...Back a little more difficult...Some memorable holes...Interesting but not provocative.

★★SHAWNEE LOOKOUT GOLF CLUB

PU-2030 Lawrencburg, North Bend, 45052, Hamilton County, (513)941-0120.
Architect: Jack Kidwell and Michael Hurdzan. **Caddies:** No. **Discount golf packages:** No. **On site lodging:** No. **Rental clubs:** No. **Metal spikes allowed:** Yes. **Range:** No.
Call club for further information.

★★★SHAWNEE STATE PARK GOLF COURSE

P.O. Box 148, Friendship, 45630, Scioto County, (614)858-6681.
Architect: Jack Kidwell and Michael Hurdzan. **Caddies:** No. **Discount golf packages:** No. **On site lodging:** No. **Rental clubs:** No. **Metal spikes allowed:** Yes. **Range:** No.
Call club for further information.
Subscriber comments: Beautiful setting...Good test, but nothing spectacular...Very nice course, good for all golfers...Attractive course along Ohio River...Scenic layout.

★★½SHELBY OAKS GOLF CLUB

PU-9900 Sidney Freyburg Rd., Sidney, 45365, Shelby County, (937)492-2883, 31 miles S of Lima.
Opened: 1964. **Holes:** 27. **Architect:** Ken Killian and Dick Nugent. **Green fee:** $17/$19. **Credit cards:** MC,VISA. **Reduced fees:** Twilight. **Caddies:** No. **Golf carts:** $9. **Discount golf packages:** No. **Season:** March-Nov. **High:** May-Oct. **On site lodg-**

ing: No. **Rental clubs:** Yes. **Walking policy:** Unrestricted walking. **Metal spikes allowed:** Yes. **Range:** Yes. **To obtain tee times:** Call 7 days in advance.
SOUTH/NORTH
Par: 72/72. **Yards:** 6,561/5,465. **Course rating:** 70.5/70.5. **Slope:** 115/111.
SOUTH/WEST
Par: 72/72. **Yards:** 6,100/5,700. **Course rating:** N/A. **Slope:** 113/111.
WEST/NORTH
Par: 72/72. **Yards:** 6,650/5,205. **Course rating:** 70.9/70.9. **Slope:** 115/111.
Subscriber comments: Not difficult but fun...Excellent practice area, nice test of golf...Has 27 holes...Wide driving areas...North/South OK, West course is new.

★★SKYLAND GOLF COURSE
PU-2085 Center Rd., Hinckley, 44233, Medina County, (330)225-5698, 20 miles S of Cleveland.
Opened: 1932. **Holes:** 18. **Par:** 72/74. **Yards:** 6,239/5,491. **Course rating:** 68.9/70.7.
Slope: 113/112. **Architect:** N/A. **Green fee:** $17/$20. **Credit cards:** MC,VISA.
Reduced fees: Weekdays, seniors, juniors. **Caddies:** No. **Golf carts:** $20. **Discount golf packages:** No. **Season:** April-Oct. **High:** June-Sept. **On site lodging:** No. **Rental clubs:** No. **Walking policy:** Unrestricted walking. **Metal spikes allowed:** Yes. **Range:** Yes (grass). **To obtain tee times:** Call golf shop.

★★½SKYLAND PINES GOLF CLUB
3550 Columbus Rd. N.E., Canton, 44705, Stark County, (330)454-5131, 5 miles E of Canton.
Opened: N/A. **Holes:** 18. **Par:** 72/72. **Yards:** 6,467/5,279. **Course rating:** 69.6/69.6.
Slope: 113/113. **Architect:** N/A. **Green fee:** $14/$20. **Credit cards:** MC,VISA,DISC.
Reduced fees: Low season. **Caddies:** No. **Golf carts:** $9. **Discount golf packages:** No. **Season:** Feb.-Dec. **High:** April-Nov. **On site lodging:** No. **Rental clubs:** Yes.
Walking policy: Walking at certain times. **Metal spikes allowed:** Yes. **Range:** Yes (grass/mats). **To obtain tee times:** Call golf shop in advance.
Subscriber comments: Nice layout, short...Average...Good course...Nice mixture...Challenging par 5s...Good tune-up, not too tough, flat greens...Small greens, a few good holes...Very enjoyable course to play.

★★★½SLEEPY HOLLOW GOLF COURSE
PM-9445 Brecksville Rd., Brecksville, 44141, Cuyahoga County, (440)526-4285, 15 miles S of Cleveland.
Reduced fees: Weekdays, low season, seniors, juniors. **Caddies:** No. **On site lodging:** No. **Rental clubs:** Yes. **Walking policy:** Unrestricted walking. **Metal spikes allowed:** Yes.
Opened: 1925. **Holes:** 18. **Par:** 71/73. **Yards:** 6,630/5,715. **Course rating:** 71.9/73.5.
Slope: 124/128. **Architect:** Stanley Thompson. **Green fee:** $19/$19. **Credit cards:** MC,VISA. **Golf carts:** $10. **Discount golf packages:** Yes. **Season:** March-Dec. **High:** May-Sept. **Range:** Yes (mats). **To obtain tee times:** Call golf shop at noon 5 days in advance.
Subscriber comments: Beautiful, challenging, lots of trouble...Old country club, now public...Pretty layout, nice for outings...Nice old-style course...Bring only your A-game.

SNOW HILL COUNTRY CLUB
11093 State Rte. 73, New Vienna, 45159, Clinton County, (937)987-2922.
Architect: Dennis Acomb. **Caddies:** No. **Discount golf packages:** No. **On site lodging:** No. **Rental clubs:** No. **Metal spikes allowed:** Yes. **Range:** No.
Call club for further information.

★★★SOUTH TOLEDO GOLF CLUB
PU-3915 Heatherdowns Blvd, Toledo, 43614, Lucas County, (419)385-4678.
Call club for further information.
Subscriber comments: Fun to play. Flat...A fair challenge...Average, improving...Flat, easy to walk course...I especially enjoyed hole #7, the par-3 island green...Last few years getting better...Old-style country club-type course...Good public layout.

★★SPRING HILLS GOLF CLUB
PU-S Rte 43, Box 128, East Springfield, 43925, Jefferson County, (614)543-3270, 13 miles NW of Steubenville.
Opened: 1970. **Holes:** 18. **Par:** 71/71. **Yards:** 6,558/5,560. **Course rating:** 70.9. **Slope:** 119. **Architect:** N/A. **Green fee:** $12/$14. **Credit cards:** MC,VISA. **Reduced fees:** Weekdays, low season, seniors, juniors. **Caddies:** No. **Golf carts:** $11. **Discount golf packages:** No. **Season:** Feb.-Dec. **High:** N/A. **On site lodging:** No. **Rental clubs:** No. **Walking policy:** N/A. **Metal spikes allowed:** Yes. **Range:** Yes (grass). **To obtain tee times:** Call golf shop.

★★★★STONEWATER GOLF CLUB
1 Club Dr., Highland Heights, 44143, Cuyahoga County, (440)461-4653.
Opened: 1996. **Holes:** 18. **Par:** 72/72. **Yards:** 7,100/5,067. **Course rating:** 75.2/70.0. **Slope:** 139/124. **Architect:** Hurdzan/Fry Golf Design. **Green fee:** $45/$68. **Credit cards:** MC,VISA,AMEX. **Reduced fees:** Weekdays, low season, twilight. **Caddies:** Yes. **Golf carts:** $17. **Discount golf packages:** No. **Season:** March-Oct. **High:** May-Oct. **On site lodging:** No. **Rental clubs:** Yes. **Walking policy:** Walking at certain times. **Metal spikes allowed:** No. **Range:** Yes (grass). **To obtain tee times:** Non-members may call up to 4 days in advance.
Notes: Ranked 4th in 1997 Best New Upscale Public Courses.
Subscriber comments: Great potential...New excellent course, great five finishing holes...Finally, excellent, upscale golf in Cleveland.

★★★½SUGAR BUSH GOLF COURSE
11186 N. St., State Rte. 88, Garrettsville, 44231, Portage County, (330)527-4202.
Architect: Harold Paddock. **Caddies:** No. **Discount golf packages:** No. **On site lodging:** No. **Rental clubs:** No. **Metal spikes allowed:** Yes. **Range:** No.
Call club for further information.
Subscriber comments: Beautiful, tough, scenic...Very interesting course...Good variety of holes...Hidden beauty, worth the drive...Great greens, challenging, hilly, a good test.

★★½SUGAR CREEK GOLF COURSE
950 Elmore E. Rd., Elmore, 43416, Ottwa County, (419)862-2551, 20 miles S of Toledo.
Opened: 1963. **Holes:** 18. **Par:** 71/71. **Yards:** 6,331/5,092. **Course rating:** 66.5/64.4. **Slope:** 102/98. **Architect:** Stan Neeb and Leon Neeb. **Green fee:** $12/$14. **Credit cards:** MC,VISA. **Reduced fees:** Weekdays, low season, twilight, seniors, juniors. **Caddies:** No. **Golf carts:** $18. **Discount golf packages:** Yes. **Season:** March-Dec. **High:** June-Sept. **On site lodging:** No. **Rental clubs:** Yes. **Walking policy:** Walking at certain times. **Metal spikes allowed:** Yes. **Range:** Yes (grass/mats). **To obtain tee times:** Call anytime.

★★½SUGAR ISLE GOLF COUNTRY
PU-2469 Dayt-Lakeview Rd., New Carlisle, 45344, Clark County, (937)845-8699.
Opened: 1974. **Holes:** 18. **Par:** 72/72. **Yards:** 6,754/5,636. **Course rating:** 70.2/71.1. **Slope:** 107/110. **Architect:** Jack Kidwell and Michael Hurdzan. **Green fee:** $13/$16. **Credit cards:** MC,VISA. **Reduced fees:** Weekdays, seniors. **Caddies:** No. **Golf carts:** $10. **Discount golf packages:** No. **Season:** Year-round. **High:** June-Sept. **On site lodging:** No. **Rental clubs:** Yes. **Walking policy:** Unrestricted walking. **Metal spikes allowed:** Yes. **Range:** Yes (grass). **To obtain tee times:** Call 7 days in advance. Groups of 20 or more may call further in advance with deposit.

★★SUGARCREEK GOLF COURSE
PU-Winklepleck Rd., Sugarcreek, 44681, Tuscarawas County, (330)852-9989, 8 miles W of New Philadelphia.
Opened: 1929. **Holes:** 18. **Par:** 72/72. **Yards:** 6,200/6,006. **Course rating:** 67.4/66.4. **Slope:** 107/100. **Architect:** Stan Neeb. **Green fee:** N/A. **Credit cards:** None. **Reduced fees:** Weekdays, seniors. **Caddies:** No. **Golf carts:** $10. **Discount golf packages:** No. **Season:** Year-round. **High:** N/A. **On site lodging:** No. **Rental clubs:** Yes. **Walking policy:** Unrestricted walking. **Metal spikes allowed:** No. **Range:** Yes (grass/mats). **To obtain tee times:** Call golf shop.
Notes: 1997 State Army vs. Navy; 1989 State Elks.

★★SUNNYHILL GOLF CLUB
PU-3734 Sunnybrook Rd., Kent, 44240, Portage County, (330)673-1785, 5 miles E of Akron.
Opened: 1921. **Holes:** 27. **Par:** 71/72. **Yards:** 6,289/5,083. **Course rating:** 68.4/68.4. **Slope:** 110/107. **Architect:** Ferdinand Garbin. **Green fee:** $10/$19. **Credit cards:** MC,VISA,DISC. **Reduced fees:** Weekdays, low season, seniors, juniors. **Caddies:** No. **Golf carts:** Included in Green Fee. **Discount golf packages:** No. **Season:** March-Jan. **High:** May-Aug. **On site lodging:** No. **Rental clubs:** No. **Walking policy:** Unrestricted walking. **Metal spikes allowed:** Yes. **Range:** Yes (grass). **To obtain tee times:** Call ahead.
Special Notes: Also has 9-hole par-34 Middle Course.

★★SWEETBRIAR GOLF & PRO SHOP
PU-750 Jaycox Rd., Avon Lake, 44012, Lorain County, (216)933-9001, 20 miles W of Cleveland.
Opened: 1966. **Holes:** 27. **Architect:** Ron Palmer. **Green fee:** $17/$22. **Credit cards:** MC,VISA. **Reduced fees:** Low season, twilight, seniors, juniors. **Caddies:** No. **Golf carts:** $20. **Discount golf packages:** No. **Season:** Year-round. **High:** May-Oct. **On site lodging:** No. **Rental clubs:** Yes. **Walking policy:** Unrestricted walking. **Metal spikes allowed:** Yes. **Range:** Yes (mats). **To obtain tee times:** Call on Wednesday morning for upcoming weekend. No tee times for weekdays.
FIRST/SECOND
Par: 72/74. **Yards:** 6,491/5,521. **Course rating:** 68.7/68.9. **Slope:** 106/105.
FIRST/THIRD
Par: 70/73. **Yards:** 6,075/5,414. **Course rating:** 66.3/68.0. **Slope:** 100/105.
SECOND/THIRD
Par: 72/73. **Yards:** 6,292/5,411. **Course rating:** 67.5/68.3. **Slope:** 104/104.

★★½SYCAMORE HILLS GOLF CLUB
3728 W. Hayes Ave., Fremont, 43420, Sandusky County, (419)332-5716, 35 miles SE of Toledo.
Opened: 1964. **Holes:** 27. **Par:** 70/72. **Yards:** 6,221/5,076. **Course rating:** 67.3/66.3. **Slope:** 110/107. **Architect:** Doug Michael. **Green fee:** $12/$15. **Credit cards:** MC,VISA. **Reduced fees:** Weekdays, low season, seniors, juniors. **Caddies:** No. **Golf carts:** $17. **Discount golf packages:** No. **Season:** March-Dec. **High:** April-Sept. **On site lodging:** No. **Rental clubs:** Yes. **Walking policy:** Unrestricted walking. **Metal spikes allowed:** Yes. **Range:** Yes (grass). **To obtain tee times:** Call in advance for weekends and holidays.
Subscriber comments: Getting better every year...Two tough finishing holes, nice course...Interesting, requires many different shots...27-hole golf course...Nine new holes add variety...Could use some added length.

★★½TABLE ROCK GOLF CLUB
PU-3005 Wilson Rd., Centerburg, 43011, Knox County, (614)625-6859, (800)688-6859, 20 miles N of Columbus.
Opened: 1973. **Holes:** 18. **Par:** 72/72. **Yards:** 6,729/5,303. **Course rating:** 71.4/69.2. **Slope:** 119/115. **Architect:** Jack Kidwell. **Green fee:** $14/$19. **Credit cards:** All major. **Reduced fees:** Weekdays, low season, twilight, seniors, juniors. **Caddies:** No. **Golf carts:** $10. **Discount golf packages:** No. **Season:** Year-round. **High:** May-Sept. **On site lodging:** No. **Rental clubs:** Yes. **Walking policy:** Unrestricted walking. **Metal spikes allowed:** Yes. **Range:** Yes (grass). **To obtain tee times:** Call 14 days in advance.

TAM O'SHANTER GOLF COURSE
PU-5055 Hills and Dales Rd. N.W., Canton, 44708, Stark County, (330)477-5111, (800)462-9964, 50 miles S of Cleveland.
Opened: 1928. **Architect:** Leonard Macomber. **Green fee:** $12/$24. **Credit cards:** MC,VISA. **Reduced fees:** Weekdays, low season, resort guests, seniors, juniors. **Caddies:** No. **Golf carts:** $10. **Discount golf packages:** Yes. **Season:** Year-round. **High:** April-Oct. **On site lodging:** No. **Rental clubs:** Yes. **Walking policy:** Unrestricted walking. **Metal spikes allowed:** Yes. **Range:** Yes (grass). **To obtain tee times:** Call up to 1 year in advance with credit card to guarantee.

★★★DALES COURSE
Holes: 18. **Par:** 70/75. **Yards:** 6,509/5,317. **Course rating:** 70.4/69.7. **Slope:** 110/109.
Subscriber comments: Very challenging, thick rough, usually have a "snowman" or two...Good professional course, hard course for high handicap players...Great for weekend getaway...Championship course...Good challenge.
Special Notes: Spikeless shoes encouraged.

★★★HILLS COURSE
Holes: 18. **Par:** 70/75. **Yards:** 6,385/5,076. **Course rating:** 69.1/67.4. **Slope:** 104/102.
Subscriber comments: Excellent course...Nice layout, small greens...Old course, good test...Strong start, weak finish...Average course, thick rough...Very hilly...Outstanding course...A pleasant experience...Nice challenge...Tough to walk.
Special Notes: Spikeless shoes encouraged.

★★TAMARAC GOLF CLUB
PU-500 Stevick Rd., Lima, 45807, Allen County, (419)331-2951.
Opened: 1950. **Holes:** 18. **Par:** 72/72. **Yards:** 6,109/5,029. **Course rating:** 69.8/67.9.
Slope: N/A. **Architect:** Bob Holopeter. **Green fee:** $12/$15. **Credit cards:** MC,VISA.
Reduced fees: Twilight, seniors. **Caddies:** No. **Golf carts:** $15. **Discount golf packages:** Yes. **Season:** March-Dec. **High:** April-Sept. **On site lodging:** No. **Rental clubs:** Yes. **Walking policy:** Unrestricted walking. **Metal spikes allowed:** Yes. **Range:** Yes (grass). **To obtain tee times:** Call anytime.
Special Notes: Also has 9-hole par-3 course.

★★★TAMER WIN GOLF & COUNTRY CLUB
PU-2940 Niles Cortland Rd. N.E., Cortland, 44410, Trumbull County, (330)637-2881, 20 miles N of Youngstown.
Opened: 1961. **Holes:** 18. **Par:** 71/74. **Yards:** 6,275/5,623. **Course rating:** 70.0/71.6.
Slope: 114/116. **Architect:** Charles E. Winch. **Green fee:** $16/$19. **Credit cards:** All major. **Reduced fees:** Low season, seniors, juniors. **Caddies:** No. **Golf carts:** $8.
Discount golf packages: No. **Season:** April-Dec. **High:** May-Sept. **On site lodging:** No. **Rental clubs:** No. **Walking policy:** Unrestricted walking. **Metal spikes allowed:** Yes. **Range:** No. **To obtain tee times:** Call for weekends and holidays.
Subscriber comments: Good basic golf...Great back nine, friendly front nine...Average course...Lots of trees on back nine...Good community course.

★★TANGLEWOOD GOLF CLUB
PU-1086 Cheshire Rd., Delaware, 43015, Delaware County, (614)548-6715, 10 miles N of Columbus.
Opened: 1967. **Holes:** 18. **Par:** 72/72. **Yards:** 6,950/6,300. **Course rating:** 69.0/69.0.
Slope: 113/113. **Architect:** Jack Kidwell. **Green fee:** $18/$21. **Credit cards:** MC,VISA.
Reduced fees: N/A. **Caddies:** No. **Golf carts:** $10. **Discount golf packages:** No.
Season: March-Nov. **High:** N/A. **On site lodging:** No. **Rental clubs:** No. **Walking policy:** Unrestricted walking. **Metal spikes allowed:** Yes. **Range:** No. **To obtain tee times:** Call up to 7 days in advance.

★★★TANNENHAUF GOLF CLUB
PU-11411 McCallum Ave., Alliance, 44601, Stark County, (330)823-4402, (800)533-5140, 10 miles E of Canton.
Opened: 1959. **Holes:** 18. **Par:** 72/72. **Yards:** 6,666/5,455. **Course rating:** 72.0/70.8.
Slope: 111/109. **Architect:** James G. Harrison and Fred Ganbim. **Green fee:** $18/$20.
Credit cards: MC,VISA. **Reduced fees:** Weekdays, low season, twilight, seniors, juniors. **Caddies:** No. **Golf carts:** $20. **Discount golf packages:** Yes. **Season:** Year-round weather permitting. **High:** June-Aug. **On site lodging:** No. **Rental clubs:** Yes.
Walking policy: Unrestricted walking. **Metal spikes allowed:** Yes. **Range:** Yes (grass).
To obtain tee times: Call.
Subscriber comments: Long, decent mix of holes...A cut above average...Challenging, nice long par 4s...Tight course, lots of trees...Flat playable course...Excellent snack bar...Not too tough, flat greens.
Special Notes: Spikeless shoes preferred.

★★½THORN APPLE COUNTRY CLUB
1051 Alton Darby Creek Rd., Galloway, 43119, Franklin County, (614)878-7703, 10 miles W of Columbus.

Opened: 1966. Holes: 18. Par: 72/74. Yards: 7,037/5,901. Course rating: 72.6/71.7. Slope: 116/115. Architect: Jack Kidwell. Green fee: $16/$17. Credit cards: MC,VISA. Reduced fees: Twilight. Caddies: No. Golf carts: $18. Discount golf packages: No. Season: Year-round. High: April-Oct. On site lodging: No. Rental clubs: Yes. Walking policy: Unrestricted walking. Metal spikes allowed: Yes. Range: No. To obtain tee times: Call 7 days in advance for weekends and holidays.

★★★THUNDER HILL GOLF CLUB

PU-7050 Griswold Rd., Madison, 44057, Geauga County, (216)298-3474.
Opened: 1976. Holes: 18. Par: 72/72. Yards: 7,223/5,524. Course rating: 78.0. Slope: 151/127. Architect: Fred Slagle. Green fee: $25/$30. Credit cards: MC,VISA. Reduced fees: Low season, seniors, juniors. Caddies: No. Golf carts: Included in Green Fee. Discount golf packages: Yes. Season: April-Dec. High: May-Sept. On site lodging: No. Rental clubs: No. Walking policy: Mandatory cart. Metal spikes allowed: Yes. Range: No. To obtain tee times: Call anytime.
Subscriber comments: Lots of water...Bring your fishing rod...Major improvements, lots of sand and water...General layout good...More water than Lake Erie...Don't play medal; match play only...Water, water, water.

THUNDERBIRD HILLS GOLF CLUB

PU-1316 Mudbrook Rd., SR 13, Huron, 44839, Erie County, (419)433-4552.
Architect: Bruce Palmer. Green fee: $18/$21. Credit cards: MC,VISA,DISC. Reduced fees: Weekdays, low season, seniors, juniors. Caddies: No. Golf carts: $11. Discount golf packages: No. High: April-Nov. On site lodging: No. Rental clubs: Yes. Metal spikes allowed: Yes. Range: Yes (grass/mats). To obtain tee times: Call.
★★★NORTH COURSE
Opened: 1960. Holes: 18. Par: 72/74. Yards: 6,464/5,993. Course rating: 70.3/74.0. Slope: 109/121.. Season: Year-round. Walking policy: Unrestricted walking.
Subscriber comments: Classic old layout...Great pro shop...The North course is older, but South course is nice...Great course, exciting 10th across water...Hilly and scenic...Fun course.
★★★SOUTH COURSE
Opened: 1995. Holes: 18. Par: 72/72. Yards: 6,235/4,660. Course rating: N/A. Slope: N/A. Season: April-Oct. Walking policy: Walking at certain times.
Subscriber comments: A young course, could be real good with seasoning...Wide open...Beautiful, beautiful, beautiful...Still young but has potential...Has promise.

★★½TREE LINKS GOLF COURSE

PU-3482 C.R. 10, Bellefontaine, 43311, Logan County, (937)592-7888, (800)215-7888, 35 miles NW of Columbus.
Opened: 1992. Holes: 18. Par: 73/73. Yards: 6,421/4,727. Course rating: 70.1/66.6. Slope: 121/115. Architect: N/A. Green fee: $35/$35. Credit cards: MC,VISA. Reduced fees: Weekdays, low season, seniors, juniors. Caddies: No. Golf carts: Included in Green Fee. Discount golf packages: Yes. Season: Year-round. High: March-Oct. On site lodging: No. Rental clubs: Yes. Walking policy: Unrestricted walking. Metal spikes allowed: Yes. Range: Yes (grass). To obtain tee times: Call 1 day in advance.

★★½TURKEYFOOT LAKE GOLF LINKS

PU-294 W. Turkeyfoot Lake Rd., Akron, 44319, Summit County, (330)644-5971, (800)281-4484, 5 miles S of Akron.
Opened: 1925. Holes: 27. Architect: Harry Smith. Green fee: $15/$22. Credit cards: None. Reduced fees: Weekdays, low season, seniors, juniors. Caddies: No. Golf carts: $22. Discount golf packages: No. Season: Year-round. High: May-Sept. On site lodging: No. Rental clubs: No. Walking policy: Unrestricted walking. Metal spikes allowed: Yes. Range: No. To obtain tee times: Call for weekend tee times.
FIRST/SECOND
Par: 71/72. Yards: 6,168/5,190. Course rating: 70.0/68.4. Slope: 116/111.
FIRST/THIRD
Par: 71/72. Yards: 5,452/4,678. Course rating: 66.8/61.3. Slope: 116/111.
SECOND/THIRD
Par: 70/70. Yards: 5,122/4,322. Course rating: 65.0/65.1. Slope: 116/111.

OHIO

★★★TURNBERRY GOLF COURSE
PU-1145 Clubhouse Rd., Pickerington, 43147, Fairfield County, (614)645-2582, 12 miles E of Columbus.
Opened: 1991. **Holes:** 18. **Par:** 72/73. **Yards:** 6,757/5,440. **Course rating:** 71.1/68.8. **Slope:** 114/110. **Architect:** Arthur Hills. **Green fee:** $16/$24. **Credit cards:** MC,VISA. **Reduced fees:** Weekdays, low season, twilight, seniors, juniors. **Caddies:** No. **Golf carts:** $10. **Discount golf packages:** Yes. **Season:** Year-round. **High:** April-Oct. **On site lodging:** No. **Rental clubs:** Yes. **Walking policy:** Walking at certain times. **Metal spikes allowed:** Yes. **Range:** Yes (grass). **To obtain tee times:** Call 7 days in advance.
Subscriber comments: Large uphill climb to clubhouse...Elevated greens...New course, wide open...Getting better every year...Nice links course...Fairly good test of golf...Good public course, flat...17th will test all but the best golfers.

★★TWIN LAKES GOLF COURSE
PU-2220 Marion Ave. Rd., Mansfield, 44903, Richland County, (419)529-3777.
Architect: Jack Kidwell. **Caddies:** No. **Discount golf packages:** No. **On site lodging:** No. **Rental clubs:** No. **Metal spikes allowed:** Yes. **Range:** No.
Call club for further information.

★★½TWIN RUN GOLF COURSE
PU-2505 Eaton Rd., Hamilton, 45013, Butler County, (513)868-5833, 15 miles NW of Cincinnati.
Opened: 1963. **Holes:** 18. **Par:** 72/74. **Yards:** 6,551/5,391. **Course rating:** 70.8/69.9. **Slope:** 123/112. **Architect:** William Diddel. **Green fee:** $16/$16. **Credit cards:** None. **Reduced fees:** Low season, seniors, juniors. **Caddies:** No. **Golf carts:** $21. **Discount golf packages:** No. **Season:** March-Dec. **High:** March-Oct. **On site lodging:** No. **Rental clubs:** Yes. **Walking policy:** Unrestricted walking. **Metal spikes allowed:** Yes. **Range:** Yes (grass/mats). **To obtain tee times:** Call on Monday for upcoming weekend. Tee times required on weekends; open golf on weekdays.
Subscriber comments: Some good holes...Great first hole...Open, rolling...Several interesting holes.

★★½VALLEY VIEW GOLF COURSE
PU-1401 George Rd, Lancaster, 43130, Fairfield County, (614)687-1112, (800)281-7305, 20 miles SE of Columbus.
Opened: 1956. **Holes:** 18. **Par:** 71. **Yards:** 6,400. **Course rating:** 68.9. **Slope:** 117. **Architect:** Bill George. **Green fee:** $15/$17. **Credit cards:** MC,VISA. **Reduced fees:** N/A. **Caddies:** No. **Golf carts:** $18. **Discount golf packages:** No. **Season:** Year-round. **High:** June-Sept. **On site lodging:** No. **Rental clubs:** No. **Walking policy:** N/A. **Metal spikes allowed:** Yes. **Range:** No. **To obtain tee times:** Call.
Subscriber comments: Not very long...Hilly country course...Hilly, small greens, short but challenging and unique...Lots of rolling hills...Average, fun to play, short course.

★★★½VALLEYWOOD GOLF CLUB
13502 Airport Hwy., Swanton, 43558, Lucas County, (419)826-3991, 15 miles W of Toledo.
Opened: 1929. **Holes:** 18. **Par:** 71/73. **Yards:** 6,364/5,588. **Course rating:** 69.6/71.6. **Slope:** 115/121. **Architect:** Arthur Hill. **Green fee:** $20/$24. **Credit cards:** MC,VISA,DISC. **Reduced fees:** Seniors. **Caddies:** No. **Golf carts:** $11. **Discount golf packages:** No. **Season:** Feb.-Dec. **High:** April-Nov. **On site lodging:** No. **Rental clubs:** Yes. **Walking policy:** Unrestricted walking. **Metal spikes allowed:** Yes. **Range:** No. **To obtain tee times:** Call 7 days in advance.
Subscriber comments: Fun, interesting...Pure golf at its best...Nice operation...Tough first hole, tough finishing holes...Nice layout...Very fair.

★★★★THE VINEYARD GOLF COURSE
PM-600 Nordyke Rd., Cincinnati, 45255, Hamilton County, (513)474-3007, 10 miles E of Cincinnati.
Opened: 1987. **Holes:** 18. **Par:** 71/71. **Yards:** 6,789/4,747. **Course rating:** 73.0/65.7. **Slope:** 129/113. **Architect:** Jack Kidwell and Michael Hurdzan. **Green fee:** $20/$24. **Credit cards:** MC,VISA. **Reduced fees:**

Seniors, juniors. **Caddies:** No. **Golf carts:** $11. **Discount golf packages:** Yes.
Season: March-Nov. **High:** May-Sept. **On site lodging:** No. **Rental clubs:** Yes.
Walking policy: Unrestricted walking. **Metal spikes allowed:** Yes. **Range:** No. **To obtain tee times:** Call 5 days in advance of play at 6 p.m.
Notes: National Minority Junior Championship.
Subscriber comments: Country club atmosphere in a public track! Best in Cincinnati...Getting better, year by year...Back nine harder than front...Overall best public golf in the area...Very popular, hard to obtain tee time...Several challenging holes...Very scenic and beautiful, good attention to detail.

WEATHERWAX GOLF COURSE
PM-5401 Mosiman Rd., Middletown, 45042, Butler County, (513)425-7886, 35 miles N of Cincinnati.
Opened: 1972. **Architect:** Arthur Hills. **Credit cards:** MC,VISA. **Reduced fees:** Seniors, juniors. **Caddies:** No. **Golf carts:** $10. **Discount golf packages:** No. **Season:** Year-round. **High:** April-Nov. **On site lodging:** No. **Rental clubs:** Yes. **Walking policy:** Unrestricted walking. **Metal spikes allowed:** Yes. **Range:** Yes (grass).
★★★½**VALLEYVIEW/HIGHLANDS COURSE**
Holes: 18. **Par:** 72/72. **Yards:** 6,756/5,253. **Course rating:** 72.0/69.8. **Slope:** 120/114.
Green fee: $19. **To obtain tee times:** Call 7 days in advance.
Subscriber comments: Overall fine facility for a city course...Good course...Worth finding, somewhat out of the way...Fun to mix and match nines...Tight, long.
★★★½**WOODSIDE/MEADOWS COURSE**
Holes: 18. **Par:** 72/72. **Yards:** 7,174/5,669. **Course rating:** 73.4/71.5. **Slope:** 116/112.
Green fee: $10/$19. **To obtain tee times:** Call up to 7 days in advance for weekends and holidays.
Subscriber comments: Wider of the two 18s..Long but exciting...Good layout, very natural and quiet...Always fun...Long and lacks character of other 18.

★½WESTERN RESERVE GOLF & COUNTRY CLUB
1543 Fixler Rd., Sharon Center, 44274, Medina County, (330)239-2839, 10 miles S of Cleveland.
Opened: 1964. **Holes:** 18. **Par:** 71/72. **Yards:** 6,239/4,599. **Course rating:** 73.6/72.5.
Slope: 124/109. **Architect:** Timmy Thompson. **Green fee:** $14/$19. **Credit cards:** N/A.
Reduced fees: Weekdays, low season, twilight, seniors, juniors. **Caddies:** No. **Golf carts:** $20. **Discount golf packages:** Yes. **Season:** Year-round. **High:** Aug.-Oct. **On site lodging:** No. **Rental clubs:** Yes. **Walking policy:** Unrestricted walking. **Metal spikes allowed:** Yes. **Range:** No. **To obtain tee times:** Call.

★½WESTERN ROW GOLF COURSE
PU-7392 Mason-Montgomery Rd., Mason, 45040, Warren County, (513)398-8886, 19 miles N of Cincinnati.
Opened: 1963. **Holes:** 18. **Par:** 72/72. **Yards:** 6,746/5,701. **Course rating:** 71.4/71.2.
Slope: 121/120. **Architect:** William Diddel. **Green fee:** $17. **Credit cards:** MC,VISA,DISC. **Reduced fees:** Low season, twilight, seniors, juniors. **Caddies:** No. **Golf carts:** $18. **Discount golf packages:** No. **Season:** Year-round. **High:** April-Oct. **On site lodging:** No. **Rental clubs:** Yes. **Walking policy:** Unrestricted walking. **Metal spikes allowed:** Yes. **Range:** No. **To obtain tee times:** First come, first served.

★★★WHETSTONE GOLF & SWIM CLUB
PU-5211 Marion Mt. Gilead Rd., Caledonia, 43314, Marion County, (740)389-4343, (800)272-3215, 6 miles NE of Marion.
Opened: 1971. **Holes:** 18. **Par:** 72/72. **Yards:** 6,674/5,023. **Course rating:** 71.7/73.6.
Slope: 120/111. **Architect:** Dick LaConte. **Green fee:** $12/$15. **Credit cards:** MC,VISA,AMEX. **Reduced fees:** Weekdays, seniors. **Caddies:** No. **Golf carts:** $21. **Discount golf packages:** No. **Season:** April-Oct. **High:** April-Oct. **On site lodging:** No. **Rental clubs:** No. **Walking policy:** Unrestricted walking. **Metal spikes allowed:** Yes. **Range:** Yes (grass). **To obtain tee times:** Call seven days in advance.
Subscriber comments: Long course, flat...Tough course...Some tough holes...Fun and challenging course.

★★WILLOW CREEK GOLF CLUB
PU-15905 Darrow Rd., Vermilion, 44089, Erie County, (216)967-4101, 40 miles W of Cleveland.
Opened: 1948. **Holes:** 18. **Par:** 72/76. **Yards:** 6,356/5,419. **Course rating:** 68.0/68.0.
Slope: 108/111. **Architect:** Dick Palmer. **Green fee:** $14/$16. **Credit cards:** None.
Reduced fees: Weekdays, low season, seniors. **Caddies:** No. **Golf carts:** $9.
Discount golf packages: Yes. **Season:** March-Dec. **High:** April-Sept. **On site lodging:**
No. **Rental clubs:** Yes. **Walking policy:** Unrestricted walking. **Metal spikes allowed:**
Yes. **Range:** Yes (grass). **To obtain tee times:** Call 7 days in advance for upcoming
weekend.

★★½WILLOW RUN GOLF COURSE
PU-State Rtes. 310 and 161, Pataskala, 43001, Licking County, (614)927-1932.
Architect: Don Price. **Caddies:** No. **Discount golf packages:** No. **On site lodging:**
No. **Rental clubs:** No. **Metal spikes allowed:** Yes. **Range:** No.
Call club for further information.
Subscriber comments: Fun course...OK public course...Always an enjoyable round...A
nice course that the owners constantly improve...Tight course, some narrow fair-
ways...You will use every club in your bag.

★★★★WINDMILL LAKES GOLF CLUB
PU-6544 State Rte. 14, Ravenna, 44266, Portage County, (330)297-0440, 30 miles SE
of Cleveland.
Opened: 1971. **Holes:** 18. **Par:** 70/70. **Yards:** 6,936/5,368. **Course rating:** 73.8/70.4.
Slope: 128/115. **Architect:** Edward Ault. **Green fee:** $16/$35. **Credit cards:** MC,VISA.
Reduced fees: Low season, twilight, seniors, juniors. **Caddies:** No. **Golf carts:** $9.
Discount golf packages: No. **Season:** March-Nov. **High:** May-Sept. **On site lodging:**
No. **Rental clubs:** Yes. **Walking policy:** Unrestricted walking. **Metal spikes allowed:**
Yes. **Range:** Yes (grass/mats). **To obtain tee times:** Call 2 days in advance.
Subscriber comments: A great test of all your shots...This course has all of the chal-
lenges...Long and difficult, challenging. Great course!...Wonderful, awesome, great
course...Better have your long game with you...Superior design...Great layout, beautiful...Everything about the course is enjoyable.

★★★WOODLAND GOLF CLUB
PU-4900 Swisher Rd., Cable, 43009, Champaign County, (937)653-8875, (888)395-
2001, 36 miles NW of Columbus.
Opened: 1972. **Holes:** 18. **Par:** 71/71. **Yards:** 6,473/4,886. **Course rating:** 70.1/67.7.
Slope: 116/110. **Architect:** Jack Kidwell. **Green fee:** $17/$20. **Credit cards:**
MC,VISA,DISC. **Reduced fees:** Weekdays, low season, twilight, seniors, juniors.
Caddies: No. **Golf carts:** $10. **Discount golf packages:** No. **Season:** Year-round.
High: April-Oct. **On site lodging:** No. **Rental clubs:** Yes. **Walking policy:** Unrestricted
walking. **Metal spikes allowed:** Yes. **Range:** Yes (grass). **To obtain tee times:** Call
ahead anytime.
Subscriber comments: Good variety...Challenging layout...Half open, half wooded and
tight. All hilly...Excellent layout. Hilly, but walkable...Worth the drive...Lots of trees, some
very good holes...A very enjoyable course, tight, tough.

★★WOODRIDGE GOLF & SWIM CLUB
PU-1313 S. Main St., Mansfield, 44907, Richland County, (419)756-1026.
Call club for further information.
Special Notes: Formerly Possum Run Golf Club.

★★★THE WOODS GOLF CLUB
PU-12083 U.S. 127 S., Van Wert, 45891, Van Wert County, (419)238-0441, 40 miles E
of Ft. Wayne.
Opened: 1962. **Holes:** 18. **Par:** 72/72. **Yards:** 6,775/5,025. **Course rating:** 70.4/70.4.
Slope: 118/116. **Architect:** William Spear. **Green fee:** $14/$16. **Credit cards:**
MC,VISA. **Reduced fees:** N/A. **Caddies:** No. **Golf carts:** $9. **Discount golf packages:**
No. **Season:** March-Dec. **High:** May-Sept. **On site lodging:** No. **Rental clubs:** Yes.
Walking policy: Unrestricted walking. **Metal spikes allowed:** Yes. **Range:** Yes
(grass/mats). **To obtain tee times:** Call on Monday for upcoming weekend.

OHIO

★★WYANDOT GOLF COURSE
3032 Columbus Rd., Centerburg, 43011, Knox County, (740)625-5370, (800)986-4653, 20 miles N of Columbus.
Opened: 1978. **Holes:** 18. **Par:** 72/72. **Yards:** 6,422/5,486. **Course rating:** 68.4/70.3. **Slope:** 113/115. **Architect:** Noah Salyers. **Green fee:** $11/$14. **Credit cards:** MC,VISA. **Reduced fees:** Weekdays, low season, seniors. **Caddies:** No. **Golf carts:** $9. **Discount golf packages:** No. **Season:** Year-round. **High:** April-Oct. **On site lodging:** No. **Rental clubs:** Yes. **Walking policy:** Unrestricted walking. **Metal spikes allowed:** Yes. **Range:** No. **To obtain tee times:** Call golf shop.

★★★½YANKEE RUN GOLF COURSE
PU-7610 Warren Sharon Rd., Brookfield, 44403, Trumbull County, (330)448-8096, (800)446-5346, 60 miles NW of Pittsburgh, PA.
Opened: 1931. **Holes:** 18. **Par:** 70/73. **Yards:** 6,501/5,140. **Course rating:** 70.7/69.0. **Slope:** 119/109. **Architect:** Bill Jones/Jerry Mathews. **Green fee:** $21/$25. **Credit cards:** All major. **Reduced fees:** Weekdays, low season, seniors, juniors. **Caddies:** No. **Golf carts:** $9. **Discount golf packages:** Yes. **Season:** March-Nov. **High:** May-Sept. **On site lodging:** No. **Rental clubs:** Yes. **Walking policy:** Unrestricted walking. **Metal spikes allowed:** No. **Range:** No. **To obtain tee times:** Call up to 7 days in advance. Call anytime in advance with credit card.
Subscriber comments: Great course...Best kept secret in Ohio, every hole is difficult, no two are alike, beautifully landscaped.
Special Notes: Spikeless shoes encouraged.

★★★½ZOAR VILLAGE GOLF CLUB
PU-P.O. Box 647, Zoar, 44697, Tuscarawas County, (330)874-4653, (888)874-4654, 6 miles N of Dover.
Opened: 1975. **Holes:** 18. **Par:** 72/72. **Yards:** 6,535/5,235. **Course rating:** 70.7/69.7. **Slope:** 117/115. **Architect:** Geoffrey Cornish. **Green fee:** $20/$20. **Credit cards:** None. **Reduced fees:** Weekdays, seniors. **Caddies:** No. **Golf carts:** $20. **Discount golf packages:** Yes. **Season:** March-Dec. **High:** July-Aug. **On site lodging:** No. **Rental clubs:** Yes. **Walking policy:** Walking at certain times. **Metal spikes allowed:** No. **Range:** Yes (grass). **To obtain tee times:** Call up to 10 months in advance.
Subscriber comments: Flat course but challenging...Good short course...Lots of character...Holes are challenging...Mature course, nice mix of water/bunkers...Huge greens, wide open...Another beautiful course.

★★½ADAMS MUNICIPAL GOLF COURSE

PM-5801 E. Tuxedo Blvd., Bartlesville, 74006, Washington County, (918)337-5313, 45 miles N of Tulsa.
Opened: 1963. **Holes:** 18. **Par:** 72/74. **Yards:** 6,819/5,655. **Course rating:** 72.0/71.8. **Slope:** 119/117. **Architect:** Floyd Farley. **Green fee:** $15/$15. **Credit cards:** None. **Reduced fees:** Weekdays, twilight, seniors, juniors. **Caddies:** No. **Golf carts:** $16. **Discount golf packages:** No. **Season:** Year-round. **High:** March-Oct. **On site lodging:** No. **Rental clubs:** Yes. **Walking policy:** Unrestricted walking. **Metal spikes allowed:** Yes. **Range:** Yes (grass). **To obtain tee times:** Come in person one week in advance for weekdays. For weekend play call five days in advance.
Subscriber comments: Nice basic golf...Good layout, challenging...Fun.

★★★ARROWHEAD GOLF COURSE

PU-HC-67, Box 6, Canadian, 74425, Pittsburg County, (918)339-2769, 20 miles N of McAlester.
Opened: 1965. **Holes:** 18. **Par:** 72/75. **Yards:** 6,741/5,342. **Course rating:** 71.4. **Slope:** 119. **Architect:** Floyd Farley. **Green fee:** $9/$11. **Credit cards:** MC,VISA,DISC. **Reduced fees:** Weekdays, low season, twilight, seniors, juniors. **Caddies:** No. **Golf carts:** $8. **Discount golf packages:** Yes. **Season:** Year-round. **High:** April-Sept. **On site lodging:** Yes. **Rental clubs:** Yes. **Walking policy:** Unrestricted walking. **Metal spikes allowed:** Yes. **Range:** Yes (grass). **To obtain tee times:** Call one week in advance.
Subscriber comments: A beautiful course in trees...Nice big greens...Improved dramatically over past 10 years...Long and hilly...#16 outstanding risk/reward hole...Great course for the beginner or average golfer. Great scenery.

★★★½BAILEY GOLF CLUB RANCH

PU-10105 Larkin Bailey Blvd., Owasso, 74055, Tulsa County, (918)272-9339.
Opened: 1993. **Holes:** 18. **Par:** 72/72. **Yards:** 6,753/4,898. **Course rating:** 73.1/68.4. **Slope:** 132/115. **Architect:** Bland Pittman. **Green fee:** $15/$23. **Credit cards:** All major. **Reduced fees:** Weekdays, low season, twilight, seniors, juniors. **Caddies:** No. **Golf carts:** $10. **Discount golf packages:** No. **Season:** Year-round. **High:** April-Oct. **On site lodging:** No. **Rental clubs:** Yes. **Walking policy:** Walking at certain times. **Metal spikes allowed:** No. **Range:** Yes (grass). **To obtain tee times:** Call pro shop 8 days in advance beginning at 11:00 a.m.
Subscriber comments: Scenery changes are interesting...No. 17 is good par 3...Excellent and difficult...New design, played through home development...#2 is very tough playing from the tips...Links style, very good all the way...Fun course, excellent short par 4s...No two holes alike...Back nine very good...Great layout.

★★★BATTLE CREEK GOLF CLUB

PM-3200 N. Battle Creek Dr., Broken Arrow, 74012, Tulsa County, (918)259-8633, 5 miles E of Tulsa.
Opened: 1997. **Holes:** 18. **Par:** 72/72. **Yards:** 7,273/5,580. **Course rating:** 76.4/69.8. **Slope:** 130/118. **Architect:** Bland Pittman. **Green fee:** $17/$46. **Credit cards:** All major. **Reduced fees:** Weekdays, low season, resort guests, twilight, seniors, juniors. **Caddies:** No. **Golf carts:** $11. **Discount golf packages:** No. **Season:** Year-round. **High:** May-Sept. **On site lodging:** No. **Rental clubs:** No. **Walking policy:** Walking at certain times. **Metal spikes allowed:** No. **Range:** Yes (grass). **To obtain tee times:** Call golf shop.
Subscriber comments: Great new course...94 sand traps...Outstanding new course.

★★★½BOILING SPRINGS GOLF CLUB

PU-R.R. 2, Woodward, 73801, Woodward County, (405)256-1206, 83 miles W of Enid.
Opened: 1979. **Holes:** 18. **Par:** 71/75. **Yards:** 6,454/4,944. **Course rating:** 69.6/68.6. **Slope:** 117/117. **Architect:** Don Sechrest. **Green fee:** $8/$13. **Credit cards:** MC,VISA,DISC. **Reduced fees:** Weekdays, seniors, juniors. **Caddies:** No. **Golf carts:** $15. **Discount golf packages:** No. **Season:** Year-round. **High:** April-Oct. **On site lodging:** No. **Rental clubs:** Yes. **Walking policy:** Unrestricted walking. **Metal spikes allowed:** Yes. **Range:** Yes (grass). **To obtain tee times:** No tee times required.

GREAT VALUE

Subscriber comments: Narrow fairways and heavy rough...Back to nature, animals everywhere...Beautiful, you wouldn't believe you're in western Oklahoma...A fun course...Outstanding course...Tight but fun...Augusta on the great plains...Love the elevated tee shots...Oklahoma's best kept secret!...Not long but narrow.

★★★★CEDAR CREEK GOLF COURSE

R-P.O. Box 10, Broken Bow, 74728, McCurtain County, (405)494-6456, 60 miles NE of Paris, TX.

Opened: 1975. **Holes:** 18. **Par:** 72/72. **Yards:** 6,724/5,762. **Course rating:** 72.1. **Slope:** 132. **Architect:** Floyd Farley/Art Proctor. **Green fee:** $9/$12. **Credit cards:** MC,VISA,DISC. **Reduced fees:** Weekdays, low season, resort guests, twilight, seniors, juniors. **Caddies:** No. **Golf carts:** $15. **Discount golf packages:** Yes. **Season:** Year-round. **High:** April-Oct. **On site lodging:** Yes. **Rental clubs:** Yes. **Walking policy:** Unrestricted walking. **Metal spikes allowed:** Yes. **Range:** Yes (grass). **To obtain tee times:** Call at least seven days in advance. **Subscriber comments:** Beautiful course, great greens, one of best in Oklahoma...Great layout, tough track...Tight fairways...Fun to play...Scenic, hidden secret...Beautiful tight course in mountains.

(GOOD VALUE badge)

CEDAR VALLEY GOLF CLUB

PU-210 Par Ave., Guthrie, 73044, Logan County, (405)282-4800, 30 miles N of Oklahoma City.

Opened: 1975. **Architect:** Duffy Martin/Floyd Farley. **Green fee:** $10/$13. **Credit cards:** MC,VISA,AMEX. **Reduced fees:** Weekdays, seniors, juniors. **Caddies:** No. **Golf carts:** $16. **Discount golf packages:** No. **Season:** Year-round. **High:** May-Aug. **On site lodging:** No. **Rental clubs:** Yes. **Walking policy:** Unrestricted walking. **Metal spikes allowed:** Yes. **Range:** Yes (grass). **To obtain tee times:** Call one day in advance for weekdays. Call seven days in advance for weekends.

★★★AUGUSTA COURSE

Holes: 18. **Par:** 70/72. **Yards:** 6,602/5,170. **Course rating:** 70.3/69.1. **Slope:** 108/117. **Subscriber comments:** Very well laid out. Nice landscaping...Mature course; fun for average player...Nice scenery...Easy, short course...Narrow fairways...Has a lot of water...Challenging...Fun to play.

★★★½INTERNATIONAL COURSE

Holes: 18. **Par:** 70/72. **Yards:** 6,520/4,955. **Course rating:** 71.1/68.4. **Slope:** 112/115. **Subscriber comments:** Good beginner course...Wide open, good water holes.

CIMARRON NATIONAL GOLF CLUB

PU-500 Duffy's Way, Guthrie, 73044, Logan County, (405)282-7888, 20 miles N of Oklahoma City.

Opened: 1992. **Architect:** Duffy Martin. **Green fee:** $12/$16. **Credit cards:** All major. **Reduced fees:** Weekdays. **Caddies:** No. **Golf carts:** $18. **Discount golf packages:** No. **Season:** Year-round. **High:** May-Sept. **On site lodging:** No. **Rental clubs:** Yes. **Walking policy:** Walking at certain times. **Metal spikes allowed:** No. **Range:** Yes (grass). **To obtain tee times:** Call one day in advance for weekdays. Call one week in advance for weekends and holidays.

★★★AQUA CANYON COURSE

Holes: 18. **Par:** 70/71. **Yards:** 6,515/5,439. **Course rating:** 69.6/66.4. **Slope:** 114/110. **Subscriber comments:** Enjoyable, but easy...Front and back nines like two different courses...Average...Beautiful course and layout...One of the best courses in Oklahoma...Slowly maturing...Great variation in terrain...Easier than sister course.

★★★CIMARRON COURSE

Holes: 36. **Par:** 70/70. **Yards:** 6,653/5,559. **Course rating:** 68.1/66.1. **Slope:** 120/113. **Subscriber comments:** Lots of water. Take extra sleeve of balls...Good course, four great holes: 12, 13, 14, 15...Many tough par 4s, forced carries...Scary but forgiving...Except for a couple of holes, a good course...Course is a challenge...Young course, some confusing holes.

★★★½COFFEE CREEK GOLF COURSE

PU-4000 N. Kelly, Edmond, 73003, Oklahoma County, (405)340-4653, 15 miles N of Oklahoma City.

Opened: 1991. **Holes:** 18. **Par:** 70/70. **Yards:** 6,700/5,200. **Course rating:** 71.5/70.5. **Slope:** 129/122. **Architect:** N/A. **Green fee:** $17/$23. **Credit cards:** All major.

Reduced fees: Weekdays, twilight, seniors, juniors. **Caddies:** No. **Golf carts:** $9.
Discount golf packages: No. **Season:** Year-round. **High:** May-Sept. **On site lodging:** No. **Rental clubs:** Yes. **Walking policy:** Unrestricted walking. **Metal spikes allowed:** No. **Range:** Yes (grass). **To obtain tee times:** Call seven days in advance.
Subscriber comments: Improving with age...Very tight...One real stupid hole...Excellent course...Housing closing in on course...Quiet surroundings, great hot-dogs...Great neighborhood course...For a new course very well developed, good golf...Really enjoyed the course. Made me think about my shots.

EARLYWINE PARK GOLF COURSE
PU-11500 S. Portland Ave., Oklahoma City, 73170, Oklahoma County, (405)691-1727.
Green fee: $13/$13. **Credit cards:** MC,VISA. **Reduced fees:** Weekdays, low season, twilight, seniors, juniors. **Caddies:** No. **Golf carts:** $16. **Discount golf packages:** No. **Season:** Year-round. **High:** March-Nov. **On site lodging:** No. **Rental clubs:** Yes. **Walking policy:** Unrestricted walking. **Metal spikes allowed:** No. **Range:** Yes (grass). **To obtain tee times:** Call one day in advance for weekdays and for weekends call the previous weekend.

★★★**NORTH COURSE**
Opened: 1993. **Holes:** 18. **Par:** 72/72. **Yards:** 6,721/4,843. **Course rating:** 71.9/70.4. **Slope:** 126/122. **Architect:** Randy Heckenkemper.
Subscriber comments: Excellent public course...Will improve with age...Nice lay-out...Good course design/shot values for muny course...For a city course, very nice...North course better than South, but enjoy both...Picturesque, fun...Excellent large greens...Excellent test of golf from back tees...Several tight narrow fairways.

★★½**SOUTH COURSE**
Opened: 1976. **Holes:** 18. **Par:** 71/71. **Yards:** 6,728/5,388. **Course rating:** 69.5/71.6. **Slope:** 107/117. **Architect:** Floyd Farley.
Subscriber comments: Much easier than North and not as interesting...Tough, tight.

★★★ELK CITY GOLF & COUNTRY CLUB
108 Lakeridge Rd., Elk City, 73644, Beckham County, (405)225-3556.
Opened: 1954. **Holes:** 18. **Par:** 71/71. **Yards:** 6,208/4,678. **Course rating:** 68.9/65.9. **Slope:** 106/98. **Architect:** Bob Dunning/Don Sechrest. **Green fee:** $10/$14. **Credit cards:** None. **Reduced fees:** Weekdays, twilight. **Caddies:** No. **Golf carts:** $17. **Discount golf packages:** No. **Season:** Year-round. **High:** May-Oct. **On site lodging:** No. **Rental clubs:** Yes. **Walking policy:** Unrestricted walking. **Metal spikes allowed:** No. **Range:** Yes (grass). **To obtain tee times:** Call golf shop.
Subscriber comments: Fun couse, not many problems...6th a great golf hole...Two nines completely different...A variety of interesting holes.

★★½FALCONHEAD RESORT & COUNTRY CLUB
605 Falconhead Dr., Burneyville, 73430, Love County, (405)276-9284.
Opened: 1960. **Holes:** 18. **Par:** 72/71. **Yards:** 6,400/5,280. **Course rating:** 69.9/70.3. **Slope:** 118/120. **Architect:** Waco Turner. **Green fee:** $25/$35. **Credit cards:** All major. **Reduced fees:** Resort guests, seniors, juniors. **Caddies:** No. **Golf carts:** Included in Green Fee. **Discount golf packages:** Yes. **Season:** Year-round. **High:** April-Oct. **On site lodging:** Yes. **Rental clubs:** Yes. **Walking policy:** Mandatory cart. **Metal spikes allowed:** No. **Range:** Yes (grass). **To obtain tee times:** Call 1 day in advance.
Subscriber comments: Good golf, great atmosphere, great people...Quiet location.

★★★FIRE LAKE GOLF COURSE
PU-1901 S. Gordon Cooper, Shawnee, 74801, Pottawatomie County, (405)275-4471, 30 miles SE of Oklahoma City.
Opened: 1983. **Holes:** 18. **Par:** 70/71. **Yards:** 6,335/4,992. **Course rating:** 69.6. **Slope:** 121. **Architect:** Don Sechrest. **Green fee:** $7/$13. **Credit cards:** MC,VISA,DISC. **Reduced fees:** Weekdays, twilight, seniors, juniors. **Caddies:** No. **Golf carts:** $17. **Discount golf packages:** No. **Season:** Year-round. **High:** May-July. **On site lodging:** No. **Rental clubs:** Yes. **Walking policy:** Unrestricted walking. **Metal spikes allowed:** Yes. **Range:** Yes (grass/mats). **To obtain tee times:** Call one week in advance.
Subscriber comments: Lots of water, but fun to play. Not too hard...Tight fairways, undulating greens, accuracy course...Very pretty, lots of water...Bring plenty of golf balls...Good use of land.

★★★★FOREST RIDGE GOLF CLUB

PU-7501 E. Kenosha, Broken Arrow, 74014, Wagoner County, (918)357-2282, 12 miles SE of Tulsa.
Opened: 1989. **Holes:** 18. **Par:** 71/72. **Yards:** 7,069/5,341. **Course rating:** 74.0/70.5. **Slope:** 134/112. **Architect:** Randy Heckenkemper. **Green fee:** $30/$60. **Credit cards:** All major. **Reduced fees:** Weekdays, low season, twilight. **Caddies:** No. **Golf carts:** Included in Green Fee. **Discount golf packages:** No. **Season:** Year-round. **High:** March-Oct. **On site lodging:** No. **Rental clubs:** Yes. **Walking policy:** Unrestricted walking. **Metal spikes allowed:** No. **Range:** Yes (grass). **To obtain tee times:** Call four days in advance.
Notes: Ranked 6th in 1997 Best in State.
Subscriber comments: Matches many resort courses...Great course, especially in the fall...Tight but fun, lush fairways...Solid public course, long and tough...Great layout, straight shots a must...First time around is tough.

★★★FORT COBB STATE PARK GOLF COURSE

P.O. Box 497, Fort Cobb, 73038, Caddo County, (405)643-2398.
Architect: Floyd Farley/Don Sechrest. **Caddies:** No. **Discount golf packages:** No. **On site lodging:** No. **Rental clubs:** No. **Metal spikes allowed:** Yes. **Range:** Yes.
Call club for further information.
Subscriber comments: The back nine will eat you up...Open front, tight back...Lots of wildlife. Enjoyable...Very challenging.

★★½FOUNTAINHEAD STATE GOLF COURSE

R-HC60 Box 1350, Checotah, 74426, McIntosh County, (918)689-3209, 60 miles S of Tulsa.
Opened: 1964. **Holes:** 18. **Par:** 72/72. **Yards:** 6,919/4,864. **Course rating:** 71.3/67.3. **Slope:** 116/98. **Architect:** Floyd Farley. **Green fee:** $7/$12. **Credit cards:** All major. **Reduced fees:** Weekdays, twilight, seniors, juniors. **Caddies:** No. **Golf carts:** $17. **Discount golf packages:** Yes. **Season:** Year-round. **High:** March-Oct. **On site lodging:** Yes. **Rental clubs:** Yes. **Walking policy:** Unrestricted walking. **Metal spikes allowed:** Yes. **Range:** Yes (grass). **To obtain tee times:** Call seven days in advance.
Subscriber comments: Demanding...Nice big greens...Beautiful views, hilly, rocky, fun.

★★GLEN EAGLES GOLF COURSE

PU-20239 E. 41st St., Broken Arrow, 74014, Wagoner County, (918)355-4422, 30 miles E of Tulsa.
Opened: 1994. **Holes:** 18. **Par:** 72/72. **Yards:** 6,909/5,257. **Course rating:** 72.2/73.0. **Slope:** 115/116. **Architect:** N/A. **Green fee:** $12/$15. **Credit cards:** N/A. **Reduced fees:** N/A. **Caddies:** No. **Golf carts:** $18. **Discount golf packages:** No. **Season:** Year-round. **High:** May-Sept. **On site lodging:** No. **Rental clubs:** Yes. **Walking policy:** Unrestricted walking. **Metal spikes allowed:** No. **Range:** Yes (grass/mats). **To obtain tee times:** Call golf shop.

★★★THE GOLF CLUB AT CIMARRON TRAILS

PU-1400 Lovers Lane, Perkins, 74059, Payne County, (405)547-5701, 70 miles NE of Oklahoma City.
Opened: 1994. **Holes:** 18. **Par:** 72/72. **Yards:** 6,959/5,128. **Course rating:** 74.0/65.8. **Slope:** 124/106. **Architect:** Kevin Benedict. **Green fee:** $12/$25. **Credit cards:** MC,VISA. **Reduced fees:** Twilight. **Caddies:** No. **Golf carts:** $9. **Discount golf packages:** Yes. **Season:** Year-round. **High:** March-Oct. **On site lodging:** No. **Rental clubs:** Yes. **Walking policy:** Walking at certain times. **Metal spikes allowed:** Yes. **Range:** Yes (grass/mats). **To obtain tee times:** Call seven days in advance.
Subscriber comments: Nice course, open, water, some trees...Fairly new, nice layout...Needs to mature...Great finishing hole...Will get better with age...Great course, well designed...Hilly with good greens, challenging approach shots, fairly open.

★★★HERITAGE HILLS GOLF COURSE

PU-3140 Tee Dr., Claremore, 74017, Rogers County, (918)341-0055, 30 miles N of Tulsa.
Opened: 1977. **Holes:** 18. **Par:** 71/72. **Yards:** 6,760/5,324. **Course rating:** 72.6/71.0. **Slope:** 120. **Architect:** Don Sechrest. **Green fee:** $16/$16. **Credit cards:** None.

OKLAHOMA

Reduced fees: Weekdays, twilight, seniors, juniors. **Caddies:** No. **Golf carts:** $17. **Discount golf packages:** Yes. **Season:** Year-round. **High:** April-Sept. **On site lodging:** No. **Rental clubs:** Yes. **Walking policy:** Unrestricted walking. **Metal spikes allowed:** No. **Range:** Yes (grass). **To obtain tee times:** For weekday tee time call one day in advance or come in two days in advance. For weekend and holidays call Wednesday prior at 7 a.m. by phone or in person.
Subscriber comments: Hilly, sometimes severe...A few nice challenges...Outstanding golf course for the money...Very pretty back nine...Hilly...Trees...Par 5s are all long, three-shot holes...Short from whites, tough from blues.

★★★ JOHN CONRAD REGIONAL GOLF COURSE
PU-711 S. Douglas Blvd., Midwest City, 73130, Oklahoma County, (405)732-2209, 3 miles E of Oklahoma City.
Opened: 1971. **Holes:** 18. **Par:** 72/74. **Yards:** 6,854/5,511. **Course rating:** 72.0/70.8. **Slope:** 115/119. **Architect:** Floyd Farley. **Green fee:** $13/$13. **Credit cards:** None. **Reduced fees:** Twilight, seniors, juniors. **Caddies:** No. **Golf carts:** $17. **Discount golf packages:** Yes. **Season:** Year-round. **High:** April-Oct. **On site lodging:** No. **Rental clubs:** Yes. **Walking policy:** Unrestricted walking. **Metal spikes allowed:** Yes. **Range:** Yes (grass/mats). **To obtain tee times:** Call 24 hours in advance.
Subscriber comments: An excellent experience...Nice course, good mix...Fairly flat course...One of the better courses...17th very tough par 4...Requires all the shots. Tough finish.

★★★★★ KARSTEN CREEK GOLF CLUB
Rte. 5, Box 159, Stillwater, 74074, Payne County, (405)743-1658, 55 miles NE of Oklahoma City.
Opened: 1994. **Holes:** 18. **Par:** 72/72. **Yards:** 7,095/4,906. **Course rating:** 74.8/70.1. **Slope:** 142/127. **Architect:** Tom Fazio. **Green fee:** $125/$125. **Credit cards:** MC,VISA,AMEX. **Reduced fees:** N/A. **Caddies:** Yes. **Golf carts:** Included in Green Fee. **Discount golf packages:** No. **Season:** Year-round. **High:** April-Sept. **On site lodging:** No. **Rental clubs:** No. **Walking policy:** Unrestricted walking. **Metal spikes allowed:** No. **Range:** Yes (grass). **To obtain tee times:** Call two days in advance.
Notes: Ranked 3rd in 1997 Best in State.
Subscriber comments: Very tough from the back tees, great course...Awesome course...Fazio gem...Great golf course, high rates...Zoysia fairways and perfect greens...An absolute gem! This course could host a major...One of the best golf courses in the U.S. Has it all!...Just excellent golf. It can chew you up and spit you out...You can't believe you are in Oklahoma!...Great course...Nicest course in the state...A must...If God played golf, this is where he'd tee it up...Shot placement a must...Incredible golf course. Great challenge...Expensive but worth it, a fantastic course...Bring at least a dozen balls...Outstanding golf course...Tough walk through the woods of Oklahoma...Awesome track, best in state.

★★★ KICKING BIRD GOLF COURSE
PU-1600 E. Danforth Rd., Edmond, 73034, Oklahoma County, (405)341-5350, 10 miles N of Oklahoma City.
Opened: 1971. **Holes:** 18. **Par:** 71/72. **Yards:** 6,816/4,801. **Course rating:** 71.4/68.5. **Slope:** 127/117. **Architect:** Floyd Farley/Mark Hayes. **Green fee:** $15/$20. **Credit cards:** All major. **Reduced fees:** Weekdays, twilight, seniors, juniors. **Caddies:** No. **Golf carts:** $8. **Discount golf packages:** No. **Season:** Year-round. **High:** May-Sept. **On site lodging:** No. **Rental clubs:** Yes. **Walking policy:** Unrestricted walking. **Metal spikes allowed:** No. **Range:** Yes (grass). **To obtain tee times:** Call one day in advance for weekdays and call one week in advance for weekends.
Subscriber comments: Must play course...Tight fairways make it hard to stay out of the woods...Rolling country for Oklahoma...Being redesigned; should be nice...Tight driving holes, good risk/reward, challenging...Busy but fun to play...One of the better munys in the country.

★★½ LAFORTUNE PARK GOLF COURSE
PU-5501 S. Yale Ave., Tulsa, 74135, Tulsa County, (918)596-8627.
Opened: 1960. **Holes:** 18. **Par:** 72/73. **Yards:** 6,970/5,780. **Course rating:** 72.8/72.9. **Slope:** 123/117. **Architect:** Floyd Farley. **Green fee:** $9/$15. **Credit cards:** None. **Reduced fees:** Twilight, seniors, juniors. **Caddies:** No. **Golf carts:** $9. **Discount golf**

packages: No. **Season:** Year-round. **High:** March-Aug. **On site lodging:** No. **Rental clubs:** Yes. **Walking policy:** Unrestricted walking. **Metal spikes allowed:** Yes. **Range:** Yes (grass/mats). **To obtain tee times:** Call golf shop.
Subscriber comments: Long, challenging...Gets a lot of play, still good...Good driving range...4th is great par 4...Always friendly.
Special Notes: Also has 18-hole par 3 course.

LAKE HEFNER GOLF CLUB
PU-4491 S. Lake Hefner Dr., Oklahoma City, 73116, Oklahoma County, (405)843-1565.
Green fee: $8/$13. **Credit cards:** MC,VISA. **Reduced fees:** Twilight, seniors, juniors.
Caddies: No. **Golf carts:** $17. **Discount golf packages:** No. **Season:** Year-round.
High: March-Sept. **On site lodging:** No. **Rental clubs:** Yes. **Walking policy:**
Unrestricted walking. **Metal spikes allowed:** No. **Range:** Yes (grass). **To obtain tee times:** Call 1 day in advance for weekdays and 7 days in advance for weekends and holidays.
★★★NORTH COURSE
Opened: 1994. **Holes:** 18. **Par:** 72/72. **Yards:** 6,970/5,169. **Course rating:** 74.2/69.6.
Slope: 128/117. **Architect:** Randy Heckenkemper.
Subscriber comments: Links-type course, beautiful views...Tough...Flat course with few trees. Nice view of Lake Hefner...Recently redesigned, clever and challenging...Nice redesign of a former mediocre track...Nice 18, fair but tough...One of the best city courses...Much improved...Good food...A good winter course because of overseeding...Some good holes.
★★½SOUTH COURSE
Opened: 1962. **Holes:** 18. **Par:** 70/73. **Yards:** 6,305/5,393. **Course rating:** 68.9/71.2.
Slope: 111/115. **Architect:** Floyd Farley.
Subscriber comments: Not extremely difficult, but fun. Best driving range around...Small greens make them hard to hit...Easier than North.
Special Notes: Also has 3-hole par-9 Academy Course.

★★½LAKE MURRAY RESORT GOLF
R-3310 S. Lake Murray Dr., Ardmore, 73401, Carter County, (405)223-6613, 90 miles N of Dallas.
Opened: 1960. **Holes:** 18. **Par:** 70/71. **Yards:** 6,250/4,800. **Course rating:** 69.2/70.8.
Slope: 122/122. **Architect:** Floyd Farley. **Green fee:** $10/$12. **Credit cards:** All major.
Reduced fees: Twilight, seniors, juniors. **Caddies:** No. **Golf carts:** $17. **Discount golf packages:** No. **Season:** Year-round. **High:** May-Sept. **On site lodging:** Yes. **Rental clubs:** Yes. **Walking policy:** Unrestricted walking. **Metal spikes allowed:** Yes. **Range:** Yes (grass). **To obtain tee times:** Call up to 4 days in advance.
Subscriber comments: Fun course to play, several pretty holes...Short course, new back nine added...Course needs to mature...A lot of different looks. I liked it.

★★LAKE TEXOMA GOLF RESORT
R-P.O. Box 279, Kingston, 73439, Marshall County, (405)564-3333, 65 miles N of Dallas, TX.
Opened: 1958. **Holes:** 18. **Par:** 71/74. **Yards:** 6,523/5,747. **Course rating:** 71.4/68.7.
Slope: 126/111. **Architect:** Floyd Farley. **Green fee:** $10/$12. **Credit cards:** MC,VISA,DISC. **Reduced fees:** Weekdays, low season, resort guests, twilight, seniors, juniors. **Caddies:** No. **Golf carts:** $17. **Discount golf packages:** Yes. **Season:** Year-round. **High:** April-Oct. **On site lodging:** Yes. **Rental clubs:** Yes. **Walking policy:** Unrestricted walking. **Metal spikes allowed:** No. **Range:** Yes (grass). **To obtain tee times:** Call Wednesday at noon for tee times for upcoming weekend and holidays, only.

★★LAKESIDE MEMORIAL GOLF CLUB
Rte. 2, Box 685, Stillwater, 74075, Payne County, (405)372-3399.
Architect: Labron Harris Sr. **Caddies:** No. **Discount golf packages:** No. **On site lodging:** No. **Rental clubs:** No. **Metal spikes allowed:** Yes. **Range:** Yes.
Call club for further information.

★★★LAKEVIEW GOLF COURSE
PU-3905 N. Commerce, Ardmore, 73401, Carter County, (405)223-4260, 88 miles S of Oklahoma City.
Opened: 1971. **Holes:** 18. **Par:** 71/72. **Yards:** 6,881/5,032. **Course rating:** 71.2/67.5.

Slope: 114/113. **Architect:** Fillmore Vaughn. **Green fee:** $9/$11. **Credit cards:** All major. **Reduced fees:** Weekdays, twilight, seniors, juniors. **Caddies:** No. **Golf carts:** $18. **Discount golf packages:** No. **Season:** Year-round. **High:** April-Sept. **On site lodging:** No. **Rental clubs:** Yes. **Walking policy:** Unrestricted walking. **Metal spikes allowed:** No. **Range:** Yes (grass). **To obtain tee times:** Call Wednesday for upcoming weekend.

Subscriber comments: Fun course for the money, pretty along lake...Backside completely different from the front, great views...Great course.

★★★LEW WENTZ MEMORIAL GOLF COURSE

PU-2928 L.A. Cann Dr., Ponca City, 74604, Kay County, (405)767-0433.
Opened: 1940. **Holes:** 18. **Par:** 71/70. **Yards:** 6,400/5,450. **Course rating:** 70.0/71.8. **Slope:** 125/123. **Architect:** Floyd Farley. **Green fee:** $10/$13. **Credit cards:** None. **Reduced fees:** Weekdays, seniors, juniors. **Caddies:** No. **Golf carts:** $16. **Discount golf packages:** No. **Season:** Year-round. **High:** April-Oct. **On site lodging:** No. **Rental clubs:** Yes. **Walking policy:** Unrestricted walking. **Metal spikes allowed:** Yes. **Range:** No. **To obtain tee times:** Call two days in advance.

Subscriber comments: One of the best munys...Can be windy!...Some nice holes on the lake...Very nice course in a small town...Beautiful course, especially the back nine along the lake!.

LINCOLN PARK GOLF COURSE

PM-4001 N.E. Grand Blvd., Oklahoma City, 73111, Oklahoma County, (405)424-1421.
Architect: Arthur Jackson. **Credit cards:** MC,VISA. **Reduced fees:** Twilight, seniors, juniors. **Caddies:** No. **Golf carts:** $17. **Discount golf packages:** No. **Season:** Year-round. **High:** April-Sept. **On site lodging:** No. **Rental clubs:** Yes. **Walking policy:** Unrestricted walking. **Metal spikes allowed:** No. **Range:** Yes (grass). **To obtain tee times:** Call one week in advance for weekends and one day in advance for weekdays.

★★½EAST COURSE

Opened: 1960. **Holes:** 18. **Par:** 70/71. **Yards:** 6,535/5,467. **Course rating:** 70.0/66.2. **Slope:** 120/112. **Green fee:** $8/$13.

Subscriber comments: Enjoyable city course...Open course, tough on a windy day...Average in every respect but nice...Pretty, lots of water and trees.

★★½WEST COURSE

Opened: 1922. **Holes:** 18. **Par:** 70/71. **Yards:** 6,600/5,587. **Course rating:** 70.7/68.4. **Slope:** 121/115. **Green fee:** $6/$11.

Subscriber comments: Good muny golf...A lot of uphill shots...16th, dogleg left to elevated green, tough...A little harder than East...Just like an old pair of shoes.

MOHAWK PARK GOLF CLUB

PM-5223 E. 41st St. N., Tulsa, 74115, Tulsa County, (918)425-6871.
Green fee: $8/$15. **Credit cards:** None. **Reduced fees:** Twilight, seniors, juniors. **Caddies:** No. **Golf carts:** $18. **Discount golf packages:** No. **Season:** Year-round. **High:** June-July. **On site lodging:** No. **Rental clubs:** Yes. **Walking policy:** Unrestricted walking. **Metal spikes allowed:** Yes. **Range:** N/A. **To obtain tee times:** Call golf shop.

★★½PECAN VALLEY COURSE

Opened: 1957. **Holes:** 18. **Par:** 70/70. **Yards:** 6,499/5,130. **Course rating:** 71.6/69.6. **Slope:** 124/119. **Architect:** Floyd Farley.

Subscriber comments: A hard short course...Improved recently...Lots of huge trees, water, large greens...Fun course, not too long, easy to walk.

★★½WOODBINE COURSE

Opened: 1927. **Holes:** 18. **Par:** 72/76. **Yards:** 6,898/6,202. **Course rating:** 71.0/73.9. **Slope:** 115/127. **Architect:** William H. Diddel.

Subscriber comments: The two courses at Mohawk are vastly different, but equally challenging. ..Trees and water, challenging...Good for beginners.

PAGE BELCHER GOLF COURSE

PM-6666 S. Union Ave., Tulsa, 74132, Tulsa County, (918)446-1529.
Green fee: $13/$15. **Credit cards:** All major. **Reduced fees:** Weekdays, twilight, seniors, juniors. **Caddies:** No. **Golf carts:** $18. **Discount golf packages:** No. **Season:** Year-round. **High:** April-Oct. **On site lodging:** No. **Rental clubs:** Yes. **Walking policy:** Unrestricted walking. **Metal spikes allowed:** No. **Range:** Yes (grass). **To obtain tee times:** Call (918)582-6000.

★★★ OLD PAGE COURSE
Opened: 1977. **Holes:** 18. **Par:** 71/71. **Yards:** 6,826/5,532. **Course rating:** 72.0/71.5.
Slope: 121/118. **Architect:** Leon Howard.
Notes: 1988 USGA Women's Public Links.
Subscriber comments: Enjoyable golf...Great Zoysia fairways...Huge greens, excellent fairways, trees...Rolling hills...Average muny...Popular, good layout...Ball placement a must, hard course.

★★★½ STONE CREEK COURSE
Opened: 1987. **Holes:** 18. **Par:** 71/71. **Yards:** 6,539/5,144. **Course rating:** 72.3/69.9.
Slope: 126/127. **Architect:** Don Sechrest.
Notes: Ranked 9th in 1997 Best in State.
Subscriber comments: Best public course in Tulsa...Pretty fun course...Tougher than Old Page, good option for better player...Not for the timid...All the par 3s are tough...Lots of ponds and creeks...Large to medium greens, hills, trees, water...Above average muny...Has its own Amen Corner (6, 7, 8).

★★½ QUARTZ MOUNTAIN GOLF COURSE
R-Rte. 1, Box 35, Lone Wolf, 73655, Kiowa County, (405)563-2520, 70 miles NW of Lawton.
Opened: N/A. **Holes:** 18. **Par:** 71/71. **Yards:** 6,595/5,706. **Course rating:** 70.8. **Slope:** 119. **Architect:** Floyd Farley/Art Proctor. **Green fee:** $9/$12. **Credit cards:** All major.
Reduced fees: Resort guests, twilight, seniors, juniors. **Caddies:** No. **Golf carts:** $17.
Discount golf packages: Yes. **Season:** Year-round. **High:** May-Aug. **On site lodging:** Yes. **Rental clubs:** Yes. **Walking policy:** Unrestricted walking. **Metal spikes allowed:** No. **Range:** Yes (grass). **To obtain tee times:** Call after noon Wednesday for following weekend or holiday.
Subscriber comments: Nice new clubhouse, challenging new nine, hard to walk...Great setting for golf course...Needs work, wide open...Beautiful scenery.

★★ SAND SPRINGS MUNICIPAL GOLF COURSE
PU-1801 N. McKinley, Sand Springs, 74063, Tulsa County, (918)246-2606, 8 miles NW of Tulsa.
Opened: 1956. **Holes:** 18. **Par:** 71/70. **Yards:** 6,113/4,692. **Course rating:** 69.5/68.4.
Slope: 125/118. **Architect:** Floyd Farley. **Green fee:** $7/$16. **Credit cards:** MC,VISA.
Reduced fees: Weekdays, low season, twilight, seniors, juniors. **Caddies:** No. **Golf carts:** $19. **Discount golf packages:** Yes. **Season:** Year-round. **High:** April-Oct. **On site lodging:** No. **Rental clubs:** Yes. **Walking policy:** Unrestricted walking. **Metal spikes allowed:** No. **Range:** Yes (grass). **To obtain tee times:** Call golf shop.

★★ SAPULPA MUNICIPAL GOLF COURSE
PM-Off Highway 66, Sapulpa, 74067, Creek County, (918)224-0237, 12 miles SW of Tulsa.
Opened: 1995. **Holes:** 18. **Par:** 70. **Yards:** 6,523. **Course rating:** 71.3. **Slope:** 123.
Architect: Jerry Slack and Mark Hayes. **Green fee:** $12/$14. **Credit cards:** All major.
Reduced fees: Twilight, seniors, juniors. **Caddies:** No. **Golf carts:** $16. **Discount golf packages:** No. **Season:** Year-round. **High:** June-Aug. **On site lodging:** No. **Rental clubs:** Yes. **Walking policy:** Unrestricted walking. **Metal spikes allowed:** No. **Range:** No. **To obtain tee times:** Call two days in advance.

★★½ SEQUOYAH STATE PARK GOLF CLUB
R-Rte. 1, Box 201, Hulbert, 74441, Cherokee County, (918)772-2297, 45 miles SE of Tulsa.
Opened: 1954. **Holes:** 18. **Par:** 70/73. **Yards:** 5,860/5,555. **Course rating:** 66.7/69.9.
Slope: 109/113. **Architect:** Floyd Farley. **Green fee:** $9/$12. **Credit cards:** All major.
Reduced fees: Weekdays, twilight, seniors, juniors. **Caddies:** No. **Golf carts:** $16.
Discount golf packages: Yes. **Season:** Year-round. **High:** June-Aug. **On site lodging:** Yes. **Rental clubs:** Yes. **Walking policy:** Unrestricted walking. **Metal spikes allowed:** No. **Range:** Yes (grass). **To obtain tee times:** Call seven days in advance for weekends and holidays.
Subscriber comments: State owned...Lots of trees. Hilly...Laid out around a huge body of water...Very beautiful setting.

OKLAHOMA

SHANGRI-LA GOLF RESORT
R-R-R. No.3, Afton, 74331, Delaware County, (918)257-4204, (800)331-4060, 70 miles NE of Tulsa.
Opened: 1970. **Architect:** Don Sechrest. **Green fee:** $50/$70. **Credit cards:** All major. **Reduced fees:** Weekdays, low season, resort guests. **Caddies:** No. **Golf carts:** Included in Green Fee. **Discount golf packages:** Yes. **Season:** Year-round. **High:** April-Oct. **On site lodging:** Yes. **Rental clubs:** Yes. **Walking policy:** Walking at certain times. **Metal spikes allowed:** Yes. **Range:** Yes (grass). **To obtain tee times:** Call two weeks in advance.
★★★½BLUE COURSE
Holes: 18. **Par:** 72/73. **Yards:** 7,012/5,892. **Course rating:** 74.0/74.8. **Slope:** 132/126.
Subscriber comments: Nice track, good greens...Blue: championship quality...Fun layout to play, usually very windy...Fast undulating greens...Long and difficult...If you can putt these greens, you're damn good...Great course...A lot of fun to play...Challenging.
★★★½GOLD COURSE
Holes: 18. **Par:** 70/71. **Yards:** 5,932/4,517. **Course rating:** 66.8/66.8. **Slope:** 123/112.
Subscriber comments: Gold: fun course...Easier of two resort courses...Perfect for scrambles...Prepare to lose some balls in water...Enjoyed playing there...Loved the contrast between front and back nines...Challenging par 3s. Short fun course.

★★★SILVERHORN GOLF CLUB
PU-11411 N. Kelley Ave., Oklahoma City, 73131, Oklahoma County, (405)752-1181, 10 miles N of Oklahoma City.
Opened: 1991. **Holes:** 18. **Par:** 71/71. **Yards:** 6,800/4,943. **Course rating:** 73.4/71.0. **Slope:** 128/113. **Architect:** Randy Heckenkemper. **Green fee:** $24/$28. **Credit cards:** All major. **Reduced fees:** Weekdays, low season, twilight, seniors, juniors. **Caddies:** No. **Golf carts:** $9. **Discount golf packages:** No. **Season:** Year-round. **High:** April-Sept. **On site lodging:** No. **Rental clubs:** Yes. **Walking policy:** Unrestricted walking. **Metal spikes allowed:** Yes. **Range:** Yes (grass). **To obtain tee times:** Call five days in advance.
Subscriber comments: Tight, trees, some water...Best new course in Oklahoma City area, very fair...Super layout; par-5 No. 4 is a wild one...Tough winding course, good fairway bunker placement...Front nine challenging; back nine even more so...Country club atmosphere, challenging layout...Spunky design and fun to play.

★★★SOUTH LAKES GOLF COURSE
PU-9253 S. Elwood, Jenks, 74037, Tulsa County, (918)746-3760, 3 miles SW of Tulsa.
Opened: 1989. **Holes:** 18. **Par:** 71/71. **Yards:** 6,340/5,242. **Course rating:** 68.6/70.4. **Slope:** 113/116. **Architect:** Randy Heckenkemper. **Green fee:** $16/$16. **Credit cards:** None. **Reduced fees:** Twilight, seniors, juniors. **Caddies:** No. **Golf carts:** N/A. **Discount golf packages:** No. **Season:** Year-round. **High:** April-Sept. **On site lodging:** No. **Rental clubs:** Yes. **Walking policy:** Unrestricted walking. **Metal spikes allowed:** No. **Range:** Yes (grass/mats). **To obtain tee times:** Call golf shop.
Subscriber comments: Excellent challenge for short yardage course...A little too easy for an experienced golfer...Good practice facilities...A very tight fun course to play...Short, lots of water...Highly walkable...Large greens.

★★SPUNKY CREEK COUNTRY CLUB
1890 Country Club Dr., Catoosa, 74015, Rogers County, (918)266-2207, 3 miles E of Tulsa.
Opened: 1921. **Holes:** 18. **Par:** 72/73. **Yards:** 6,639/5,748. **Course rating:** 71.5/72.9. **Slope:** 124/127. **Architect:** Perry Maxwell. **Green fee:** $14/$16. **Credit cards:** MC,VISA. **Reduced fees:** Weekdays, low season, twilight, seniors, juniors. **Caddies:** No. **Golf carts:** $9. **Discount golf packages:** No. **Season:** Year-round. **High:** March-Oct. **On site lodging:** No. **Rental clubs:** Yes. **Walking policy:** Unrestricted walking. **Metal spikes allowed:** Yes. **Range:** No. **To obtain tee times:** Call two days in advance beginning at 7 a.m.

★★★SUNSET HILLS GOLF COURSE
PU-Sunset Lane, Guyton, 73942, Texas County, (405)338-7404, 120 miles N of Amarillo, TX.
Opened: 1932. **Holes:** 18. **Par:** 71/74. **Yards:** 6,732/5,780. **Course rating:** 67.5/68.0.

Slope: 108/112. **Architect:** Bob Dunning. **Green fee:** $9/$12. **Credit cards:** None. **Reduced fees:** Twilight. **Caddies:** No. **Golf carts:** $16. **Discount golf packages:** No. **Season:** Year-round. **High:** June-Aug. **On site lodging:** No. **Rental clubs:** Yes. **Walking policy:** Unrestricted walking. **Metal spikes allowed:** Yes. **Range:** Yes (grass). **To obtain tee times:** First come, first served.
Subscriber comments: Great for Oklahoma Panhandle...Wind is always a factor.

★★★THUNDERCREEK GOLF COURSE
2300 W Hwy 270, McAlester, 74502, Pittsburg County, (918)423-5799.
Call club for further information.
Subscriber comments: New and tough...Will be excellent...Improving each year...Lets you make a gambling decision on each hole...Can be very tricky course to play. Nice tight fairways...A lot of different holes.

★★★TROSPER PARK GOLF COURSE
PU-2301 S.E. 29th, Oklahoma City, 73129, Oklahoma County, (405)677-8874.
Opened: N/A. **Holes:** 18. **Par:** 71/71. **Yards:** 6,631/5,067. **Course rating:** 71.5/74.1.
Slope: 125/114. **Architect:** Arthur Jackson. **Green fee:** $8/$13. **Credit cards:** MC,VISA. **Reduced fees:** Twilight, seniors. **Caddies:** No. **Golf carts:** $17.
Discount golf packages: No. **Season:** Year-round. **High:** March-Sept. **On site lodging:** No. **Rental clubs:** No. **Walking policy:** Unrestricted walking. **Metal spikes allowed:** Yes. **Range:** Yes (grass/mats). **To obtain tee times:** Call Saturday morning for following weekend; 1 day in advance for weekdays.
Subscriber comments: An excellent course, nothing great but no deficiencies...One of the toughest finishing holes around...Some water and creeks...City owned...Fun to play. #18 has everybody talking...Getting better...Interesting course, enjoyable to play.

★★★★UNIVERSITY OF OKLAHOMA GOLF COURSE
PU-1 Par Dr., Norman, 73019, Cleveland County, (405)325-6716.
Opened: 1996. **Holes:** 18. **Par:** 72/72. **Yards:** 7,197/5,310. **Course rating:** 74.9/71.6.
Slope: 134/119. **Architect:** Bob Cupp. **Green fee:** $15/$30. **Credit cards:** MC,VISA,AMEX. **Reduced fees:** Weekdays, low season, twilight, seniors, juniors.
Caddies: No. **Golf carts:** $20. **Discount golf packages:** No. **Season:** Year-round. **High:** April-Oct. **On site lodging:** No. **Rental clubs:** Yes. **Walking policy:** Unrestricted walking. **Metal spikes allowed:** No. **Range:** Yes (grass). **To obtain tee times:** Call Wednesday at 7 a.m. for upcoming weekend. Open play on weekdays.
Subscriber comments: Very challenging, but fair, super remodeling...Since redesign, best in the area...Too many changes to original layout (Perry Maxwell)...Maxwell would be proud...Will be a gem...Beautiful and tough...Bring all 14 golf clubs, you will need them...Southern Oklahoma's best public course!.

★★WESTWOOD PARK GOLF COURSE
PU-2400 Westport Dr., Norman, 73069, Cleveland County, (405)321-0433.
Opened: 1967. **Holes:** 18. **Par:** 70/74. **Yards:** 6,015/5,525. **Course rating:** 67.7/71.0.
Slope: 108/120. **Architect:** Floyd Farley. **Green fee:** $6/$14. **Credit cards:** None.
Reduced fees: Weekdays, twilight, seniors. **Caddies:** No. **Golf carts:** $18. **Discount golf packages:** No. **Season:** Year-round. **High:** April-Sept. **On site lodging:** No. **Rental clubs:** Yes. **Walking policy:** Unrestricted walking. **Metal spikes allowed:** No. **Range:** Yes (grass). **To obtain tee times:** Weekend tee times only. Call as early as Saturday for following weekend.

★★★WHITE HAWK GOLF CLUB
14515 S. Yale Ave., Bixby, 74008, Tulsa County, (918)366-4653, 10 miles S of Tulsa.
Opened: 1994. **Holes:** 18. **Par:** 72/72. **Yards:** 6,982/5,148. **Course rating:** 74.1.
Slope: 134. **Architect:** Randy Heckenkemper. **Green fee:** $22/$27. **Credit cards:** MC,VISA,AMEX. **Reduced fees:** Weekdays, low season, twilight, seniors, juniors.
Caddies: No. **Golf carts:** $10. **Discount golf packages:** Yes. **Season:** Year-round. **High:** May-Oct. **On site lodging:** No. **Rental clubs:** Yes. **Walking policy:** Unrestricted walking. **Metal spikes allowed:** No. **Range:** Yes (grass). **To obtain tee times:** Nonmembers call 7 days in advance.
Subscriber comments: Will be even better when it matures...Wonderful course...Young course, interesting layout...Front nine bites, back nine fun...Tests all of the shots in your bag...Great par 3s...Nice varity of holes...Good course.

★★★½AWBREY GLEN GOLF CLUB

2500 N.W. Awbrey Glen Dr., Bend, 97701, Deschutes County, (541)388-8526, 150 miles SE of Portland.
Opened: 1993. **Holes:** 18. **Par:** 72/72. **Yards:** 7,007/5,459. **Course rating:** 72.8/69.6. **Slope:** 130/119. **Architect:** Gene "Bunny" Mason. **Green fee:** $45/$45. **Credit cards:** MC,VISA. **Reduced fees:** Low season, juniors. **Caddies:** No. **Golf carts:** $13. **Discount golf packages:** Yes. **Season:** March-Oct. **High:** May-Sept. **On site lodging:** No. **Rental clubs:** Yes. **Walking policy:** Unrestricted walking. **Metal spikes allowed:** Yes. **Range:** Yes (grass). **To obtain tee times:** Call 7 days in advance.
Subscriber comments: The views are worth it!...Very scenic—interesting holes—well groomed...This is a great course, lot of long shots...Beautiful course. Large flat greens. Excellent service...Long and hilly...Too tricked up.

BLACK BUTTE RANCH

R-Hwy. 20, Black Butte Ranch, 97759, Deschutes County, (503)595-1500, (800)399-2322, 25 miles NE of Bend.
Green fee: $39/$55. **Credit cards:** All major. **Reduced fees:** Weekdays, low season, twilight, juniors. **Caddies:** No. **Golf carts:** $28. **Discount golf packages:** Yes. **Season:** March-Nov. **High:** June-Sept. **On site lodging:** Yes. **Rental clubs:** Yes. **Walking policy:** Unrestricted walking. **Metal spikes allowed:** No. **Range:** Yes (grass/mats). **To obtain tee times:** Guests may call up to 14 days in advance, non-guests 7 days.

★★★½BIG MEADOW COURSE

Opened: 1971. **Holes:** 18. **Par:** 72/72. **Yards:** 6,870/5,716. **Course rating:** 72.0/70.5. **Slope:** 127/115. **Architect:** Robert Muir Graves.
Subscriber comments: Excellent course, pristine environment...Beautiful scenery—nicely groomed...The views on this course belong on calendars...Older type resort course...Best of the two at Black Butte...Big greens...Back nine is awesome, huge pines and aspens tower over fairway...Must be straight hitter.

★★★½GLAZE MEADOW COURSE

Opened: 1982. **Holes:** 18. **Par:** 72/72. **Yards:** 6,560/5,616. **Course rating:** 71.5/72.1. **Slope:** 128/120. **Architect:** Gene "Bunny" Mason.
Notes: Ranked 12th in 1997 Best in State.
Subscriber comments: Scenic, quality golf experience...You will use every club in your bag...Most peaceful and quiet of courses...Summer and fall best time to play...Great scenery, course in top shape...Most beautiful location to be found anywhere!...A little tougher than Big Meadow.

★★½BROADMOOR GOLF COURSE

PU-3509 N.E. Columbia Blvd., Portland, 97211, Multnomah County, (503)281-1337, 4 miles NE of Portland.
Opened: 1931. **Holes:** 18. **Par:** 72/74. **Yards:** 6,498/5,384. **Course rating:** 70.3/69.9. **Slope:** 118/110. **Architect:** George Junor. **Green fee:** $18/$20. **Credit cards:** MC,VISA. **Reduced fees:** Weekdays, low season. **Caddies:** No. **Golf carts:** $10. **Discount golf packages:** No. **Season:** Year-round. **High:** May-Sept. **On site lodging:** No. **Rental clubs:** Yes. **Walking policy:** Unrestricted walking. **Metal spikes allowed:** Yes. **Range:** Yes (grass). **To obtain tee times:** Call golf shop one week in advance.
Subscriber comments: Cute, public 18 holes, challenging drives (long holes)...Lots of water...Bad drainage when wet. Plays long...Lots of trees, water, very hilly...Lovely course, good mix of holes.

★★CEDAR LINKS GOLF CLUB

PU-3155 Cedar Links Dr., Medford, 97504, Jackson County, (541)773-4373, (800)853-2754.
Opened: 1972. **Holes:** 18. **Par:** 70/71. **Yards:** 6,215/5,145. **Course rating:** 68.9/68.7. **Slope:** 114/112. **Architect:** Coverstone/Graves. **Green fee:** $20/$22. **Credit cards:** MC,VISA,DISC. **Reduced fees:** Seniors, juniors. **Caddies:** No. **Golf carts:** $9. **Discount golf packages:** No. **Season:** Year-round. **High:** May-Sept. **On site lodging:** No. **Rental clubs:** Yes. **Walking policy:** Unrestricted walking. **Metal spikes allowed:** Yes. **Range:** Yes (mats). **To obtain tee times:** Call golf shop up to 7 days in advance.

★★COLWOOD NATIONAL GOLF CLUB
PU-7313 N.E. Columbia Blvd., Portland, 97218, Multnomah County, (503)254-5515.
Opened: 1930. **Holes:** 18. **Par:** 70/74. **Yards:** 6,200/5,800. **Course rating:** 69.1/71.0.
Slope: 115/111. **Architect:** A. Vernon Macan. **Green fee:** $16/$18. **Credit cards:**
None. **Reduced fees:** Juniors. **Caddies:** No. **Golf carts:** $28. **Discount golf packages:** No. **Season:** Year-round. **High:** April-Oct. **On site lodging:** No. **Rental clubs:**
Yes. **Walking policy:** Unrestricted walking. **Metal spikes allowed:** Yes. **Range:** No. **To
obtain tee times:** Call seven days in advance.

EAGLE CREST RESORT
R-1522 Cline Falls Rd., Redmond, 97756, Deschutes County, (541)923-4653, 7 miles E
of Redmond.
Green fee: $37. **Credit cards:** All major. **Reduced fees:** Low season, resort guests,
juniors. **Caddies:** No. **Golf carts:** $25. **Discount golf packages:** Yes. **Season:** Year-round. **High:** April-Oct. **On site lodging:** Yes. **Rental clubs:** Yes. **Walking policy:**
Walking at certain times. **Metal spikes allowed:** Yes. **Range:** Yes (grass). **To obtain
tee times:** Public may call two weeks in advance but must guarantee with a credit card.
Owners one month in advance; tournaments six months in advance with credit card
guarantee.

★★★EAGLE CREST COURSE
Opened: 1986. **Holes:** 18. **Par:** 72/72. **Yards:** 6,673/5,395. **Course rating:** 71.5/69.8.
Slope: 123/109. **Architect:** Gene "Bunny" Mason.
Subscriber comments: Dynamite greens. Fast...Nice place, a real challenge...In great
shape for winter play...Great layout and scenery...Good resort facility with both easy
and difficult holes...Never boring—must keep ball in play...Greens in perfect shape,
great views...Very fair and interesting, resort course...Excellent fairways and greens.

★★★RESORT COURSE
Opened: N/A. **Holes:** 18. **Par:** 72/72. **Yards:** 6,673/5,395. **Course rating:** N/A. **Slope:**
123/109. **Architect:** N/A.
Subscriber comments: Great layout and scenery...Can be a real challenge with
winds...Lots of wildlife...Fun course, beautiful scenery...Excellent course, you use all
your clubs...High desert. It's a challenge from start to finish...Accommodations are outstanding.

★★★½RIDGE COURSE
Opened: 1993. **Holes:** 18. **Par:** 72/72. **Yards:** 6,477/4,773. **Course rating:** 70.8.
Slope: 123. **Architect:** John Thronson.
Subscriber comments: Scenic—well developed, challenging...Not overly long but fun
layout...Requires all shots...Excellent hard fast greens...Very challenging, especially
putting...Lots of variety. Lightning fast greens.

★★★★EAGLE POINT GOLF COURSE
PU-100 Eagle Point Dr., Eagle Point, 97524, Jackson County, (541)826-8225, 9 miles NE of Medford.
Opened: 1996. **Holes:** 18. **Par:** 72/72. **Yards:** 7,099/5,071. **Course rating:** 74.3/68.9. **Slope:** 131/113. **Architect:** Robert Trent Jones Jr.
Green fee: $35/$40. **Credit cards:** MC,VISA,AMEX. **Reduced fees:**
Weekdays, low season, twilight, juniors. **Caddies:** No. **Golf carts:** $20. **Discount golf
packages:** No. **Season:** Year-round. **High:** May-Sept. **On site lodging:** No. **Rental
clubs:** Yes. **Walking policy:** Unrestricted walking. **Metal spikes allowed:** Yes. **Range:**
Yes (grass). **To obtain tee times:** Call up to 7 days in advance. Additional fees for
bookings prior to 7 days.
Notes: Ranked 3rd in 1997 Best New Affordable Public Courses.
Subscriber comments: Lots of sand...Best course in southern Oregon!...Gorgeous,
beautiful, difficult, fun...Nice driving range...A beautifully conditioned course...A quality
course, especially for low handicappers...A jewel—pretty difficult.

(GOOD VALUE)

★★★EASTMORELAND GOLF COURSE
PU-2425 S.E. Bybee Blvd., Portland, 97202, Multnomah County, (503)775-2900.
Opened: 1921. **Holes:** 18. **Par:** 72/74. **Yards:** 6,529/5,646. **Course rating:** 71.7/71.4.
Slope: 123/117. **Architect:** H. Chandler Egan. **Green fee:** $18/$20. **Credit cards:**
MC,VISA. **Reduced fees:** Seniors, juniors. **Caddies:** No. **Golf carts:** $24. **Discount
golf packages:** No. **Season:** Year-round. **High:** June-Sept. **On site lodging:** No.

OREGON

Rental clubs: Yes. Walking policy: Unrestricted walking. Metal spikes allowed: Yes.
Range: Yes. To obtain tee times: Call six days in advance.
Notes: Ranked 13th in 1997 Best in State; 1990 USGA Public Links.
Subscriber comments: Good layout, some tough holes, nice pro-shop...Good old
course but shows the wear of lots of play...Scenic, good driving, putting challenge, back
nine beautiful...Well used, well maintained...Good relaxer course...Excellent when in
good shape...Mostly flat, lot of beautiful trees.

★★★★ELKHORN VALLEY GOLF CLUB

PU-32295 N. Fork Rd., Lyons, 97358, Marion County, (503)897-3368,
36 miles E of Salem.
Opened: 1996. Holes: 9. Par: 36. Yards: 3,169. Course rating: 71.4.
Slope: 136. Architect: Don Cutler. Green fee: $24/$24. Credit cards:
MC,VISA. Reduced fees: Juniors. Caddies: No. Golf carts: $20.
Discount golf packages: No. Season: March-Oct. High: June-Sept. On site lodging:
No. Rental clubs: Yes. Walking policy: Unrestricted walking. Metal spikes allowed:
Yes. Range: No. To obtain tee times: Call golf shop.
Subscriber comments: A slice of heaven...Laid out in a circle, beautiful, challenging,
nine holes but who cares?...In my opinion the best course in Western Oregon. Those
who like the outdoors, scenery, an occasional elk or deer grazing in the rough of sec-
ond fairway will agree...Beautiful new (tiny) clubhouse.

(GOOD VALUE)

★★★EMERALD VALLEY GOLF CLUB

83301 Dale Kuni Rd., Creswell, 97426, Lane County, (541)895-2174, 10 miles S of
Eugene.
Opened: 1964. Holes: 18. Par: 72/73. Yards: 6,873/5,371. Course rating: 73.0/70.8.
Slope: 126/122. Architect: Bob Baldock. Green fee: $26/$29. Credit cards:
MC,VISA,AMEX. Reduced fees: Weekdays, low season, twilight, seniors, juniors.
Caddies: No. Golf carts: $20. Discount golf packages: No. Season: Year-round.
High: June-Sept. On site lodging: No. Rental clubs: Yes. Walking policy:
Unrestricted walking. Metal spikes allowed: No. Range: Yes (grass/mats). To obtain
tee times: Call up to one week in advance.
Subscriber comments: Nice holes along Willamette River...Challenging, scenic...Long
from blues, flat, many trees, tough grass...This is a fun course...Tough course—good
food...A true Northwest golf course.

★★★FOREST HILLS GOLF COURSE

36260 S.W. Tongue Lane, Cornelius, 97113, Washington County, (503)357-3347, 25
miles SW of Portland.
Opened: 1927. Holes: 18. Par: 72/74. Yards: 6,173/5,673. Course rating: 69.7/71.7.
Slope: 122/114. Architect: Don Bell. Green fee: $28/$28. Credit cards:
MC,VISA,AMEX. Reduced fees: Juniors. Caddies: No. Golf carts: $20. Discount golf
packages: No. Season: Year-round. High: May-Sept. On site lodging: No. Rental
clubs: Yes. Walking policy: Unrestricted walking. Metal spikes allowed: Yes. Range:
Yes (grass/mats). To obtain tee times: Call golf shop seven days in advance.
Saturday, Sunday and holidays no 9-hole play or twosomes before 1 p.m.
Subscriber comments: Fun course, mature course...Short, sharp doglegs, excellent,
fast greens...Good public course...A nice course, very nice practice area...Short course
with some good holes...Hasn't changed—always fun.

★★GEARHART GOLF LINKS

PU-N. Marion St., Gearhart, 97138, Clatsop County, (503)738-3538, 90 miles NW of
Portland.
Opened: 1892. Holes: 18. Par: 72/74. Yards: 6,089/5,882. Course rating: 68.7/70.5.
Slope: 114/112. Architect: N/A. Green fee: $25/$25. Credit cards: MC,VISA.
Reduced fees: N/A. Caddies: No. Golf carts: $25. Discount golf packages: No.
Season: Year-round. High: April-Oct. On site lodging: Yes. Rental clubs: Yes.
Walking policy: Unrestricted walking. Metal spikes allowed: Yes. Range: Yes (grass).
To obtain tee times: Call anytime.

GLENDOVEER GOLF COURSE

PU-14015 N.E. Glisan, Portland, 97230, Multnomah County, (503)253-7507.
Opened: 1926. Green fee: $18/$19. Credit cards: None. Reduced fees: Seniors,

juniors. **Caddies:** No. **Golf carts:** $24. **Discount golf packages:** No. **Season:** Year-round. **High:** May-Sept. **On site lodging:** No. **Rental clubs:** Yes. **Walking policy:** Unrestricted walking. **Metal spikes allowed:** Yes. **Range:** Yes (mats). **To obtain tee times:** Call tee time number (292-8570) six days in advance.

★★½EAST COURSE
Holes: 18. **Par:** 73/75. **Yards:** 6,296/5,142. **Course rating:** 69.3/73.5. **Slope:** 119/120. **Architect:** John Junor.
Subscriber comments: Challenging and fun...Lots of big trees, kinda tight fairways...Nice fairways, big and open course...Lots and lots of trees. Well kept...Fast greens, big tall fir trees not found on newer courses...Beautiful mature course.

★★WEST COURSE
Holes: 18. **Par:** 71/75. **Yards:** 5,922/5,117. **Course rating:** 67.5/70.8. **Slope:** 111/110. **Architect:** Frank Stenzel.

★★½THE GOLF CLUB OF OREGON
PU-905 NW Spring Hill Dr., Albany, 97321, Benton County, (541)928-8338, 20 miles S of Salem.
Opened: 1930. **Holes:** 18. **Par:** 70/71. **Yards:** 5,836/5,089. **Course rating:** 67.8/68.9. **Slope:** 111/117. **Architect:** N/A. **Green fee:** $20/$20. **Credit cards:** N/A. **Reduced fees:** Low season, seniors, juniors. **Caddies:** No. **Golf carts:** $20. **Discount golf packages:** No. **Season:** Year-round. **High:** May-Sept. **On site lodging:** No. **Rental clubs:** Yes. **Walking policy:** Unrestricted walking. **Metal spikes allowed:** Yes. **Range:** Yes (mats). **To obtain tee times:** Call up to 7 days in advance.
Subscriber comments: Nice everyday course, well maintained...Rather short, OK...Fun track...Wonderful front nine, back nine needs maturing...Improving.

★★★GRANTS PASS COUNTRY CLUB
230 Espey Rd., Grants Pass, 97527, Josephine County, (541)476-0849.
Architect: Bob Baldock and Robert L. Baldock. **Caddies:** No. **Discount golf packages:** No. **On site lodging:** No. **Rental clubs:** No. **Metal spikes allowed:** Yes. **Range:** Yes.
Call club for further information.
Subscriber comments: Tough back nine, lots of trees...Very nice and challenging...Good course, quite a challenge.

★★½GRESHAM GOLF COURSE
2155 N.E. Division St., Gresham, 97030, Multnomah County, (503)665-3352, 15 miles E of Portland.
Opened: 1965. **Holes:** 18. **Par:** 72/72. **Yards:** 6,008/5,284. **Course rating:** 68.1/69.0. **Slope:** 109/107. **Architect:** N/A. **Green fee:** $19/$22. **Credit cards:** MC,VISA. **Reduced fees:** N/A. **Caddies:** No. **Golf carts:** $24. **Discount golf packages:** No. **Season:** Year-round. **High:** June-Sept. **On site lodging:** No. **Rental clubs:** Yes. **Walking policy:** Walking at certain times. **Metal spikes allowed:** Yes. **Range:** Yes (grass/mats). **To obtain tee times:** N/A.
Subscriber comments: Not bad...Good for intermediates...Creative use of space.

★★½HARBOR LINKS GOLF COURSE
PU-601 Harbor Isles Blvd., Klamath Falls, 97601, Klamath County, (541)882-0609, 280 miles SE of Portland.
Opened: 1986. **Holes:** 18. **Par:** 72/72. **Yards:** 6,272/5,709. **Course rating:** 69.3/71.2. **Slope:** 117/119. **Architect:** Ken Black. **Green fee:** $23/$25. **Credit cards:** MC,VISA. **Reduced fees:** Weekdays, low season, twilight, seniors, juniors. **Caddies:** No. **Golf carts:** $20. **Discount golf packages:** No. **Season:** Year-round. **High:** June-Sept. **On site lodging:** No. **Rental clubs:** Yes. **Walking policy:** Unrestricted walking. **Metal spikes allowed:** Yes. **Range:** Yes. **To obtain tee times:** Call anytime one week in advance.
Subscriber comments: Water all over, some awkward layouts...Well-groomed, fun course...Old nine short and simple, new nine good test—excellent condition.

HERON LAKES GOLF COURSE
PU-3500 N. Victory Blvd., Portland, 97217, Multnomah County, (503)289-1818.
Credit cards: MC,VISA,DISC. **Caddies:** No. **Golf carts:** $24. **Discount golf packages:** No. **Season:** Year-round. **High:** March-Oct. **On site lodging:** No. **Rental clubs:**

Yes. **Walking policy:** Unrestricted walking. **Metal spikes allowed:** Yes. **Range:** Yes (grass/mats). **To obtain tee times:** Call golf shop.

★★★½ GREAT BLUE COURSE

Opened: 1971. **Holes:** 18. **Par:** 72/72. **Yards:** 6,916/5,285. **Course rating:** 73.6/69.8. **Slope:** 132/120. **Architect:** Robert Trent Jones/Robert Trent Jones Jr. **Green fee:** $20/$29. **Reduced fees:** Weekdays, low season, seniors, juniors.

Subscriber comments: Good links layout. Lots of water. Hard fast greens...Well-maintained public course...A lot of water and sand, bring extra balls...Great challenge for a public course...Not for high handicappers.

★★★ GREENBACK COURSE

Opened: 1970. **Holes:** 18. **Par:** 72/72. **Yards:** 6,595/5,224. **Course rating:** 71.4/69.4. **Slope:** 124/113. **Architect:** Robert Trent Jones Jr. **Green fee:** $18/$20. **Reduced fees:** Low season, seniors, juniors.

Subscriber comments: Water makes it interesting...Nice older course, good pro shop and driving range...Easier than Blue...Lots of water!

★★★ INDIAN CREEK GOLF CLUB

PU-3605 Brookside Dr., Hood River, 97031, Hood River County, (541)386-7770, 60 miles E of Portland.
Opened: 1990. **Holes:** 18. **Par:** 72/72. **Yards:** 6,118/4,547. **Course rating:** 70.2/67.7. **Slope:** 124/116. **Architect:** Carl Martin/Dave Martin. **Green fee:** $12/$29. **Credit cards:** MC,VISA,DISC. **Reduced fees:** Twilight, seniors. **Caddies:** No. **Golf carts:** $25. **Discount golf packages:** No. **Season:** Year-round. **High:** April-Oct. **On site lodging:** No. **Rental clubs:** No. **Walking policy:** Unrestricted walking. **Metal spikes allowed:** Yes. **Range:** Yes (grass). **To obtain tee times:** Call up to 7 days in advance.

Subscriber comments: Quirky course in an apple orchard...Great Columbia Gorge setting...Great course, but very hilly. Ride...Great view of Mt. Hood, better not be in a hurry...Excellent greens...Fun course, great scenery, good condition...Excellent staff.

★★½ JUNIPER GOLF CLUB

139 S.E. Sisters Ave., Redmond, 97756, Deschutes County, (541)548-3121, (800)600-3121, 125 miles SE of Portland.
Opened: 1953. **Holes:** 18. **Par:** 72/72. **Yards:** 6,525/5,598. **Course rating:** 71.3/70.9. **Slope:** 124/115. **Architect:** Tim Berg. **Green fee:** $25/$25. **Credit cards:** MC,VISA. **Reduced fees:** Low season, juniors. **Caddies:** No. **Golf carts:** $20. **Discount golf packages:** No. **Season:** Year-round. **High:** May-Oct. **On site lodging:** No. **Rental clubs:** Yes. **Walking policy:** Unrestricted walking. **Metal spikes allowed:** Yes. **Range:** Yes (grass/mats). **To obtain tee times:** Call one month in advance.

Subscriber comments: Very good course, greens well maintained...Very playable...Muny course, condition better every year...Good greens. Million-dollar mountain views...A pleasure and challenging.

★★½ KAH-NEE-TA RESORT GOLF CLUB

R-P.O. Box K, Warm Springs, 97761, Wasco County, (541)553-1112, (800)831-0100, 115 miles SE of Portland.
Opened: 1972. **Holes:** 18. **Par:** 72/73. **Yards:** 6,352/5,195. **Course rating:** 73.1/70.0. **Slope:** 123/116. **Architect:** William Bell/Bunny Mason. **Green fee:** $30/$35. **Credit cards:** All major,Diners Club. **Reduced fees:** Weekdays, low season, resort guests, seniors, juniors. **Caddies:** No. **Golf carts:** $26. **Discount golf packages:** Yes. **Season:** Year-round. **High:** March-Oct. **On site lodging:** Yes. **Rental clubs:** Yes. **Walking policy:** Unrestricted walking. **Metal spikes allowed:** Yes. **Range:** Yes (grass). **To obtain tee times:** Call up to 14 days in advance.

Subscriber comments: Above average. Easy par 5s...Good shape, bring all your shots...Great summer course...Great place to practice in the wind. Great layout...Good public course...Jewel in the desert, 17th among toughest...Great greens.

★½ KENTUCK GOLF COURSE

675 Golf Course Lane, North Bend, 97459, Coos County, (541)756-4464.
Call club for further information.

★★ THE KNOLLS GOLF CLUB

PU-1919 Recreation Lane, Sutherlin, 97479, Douglas County, (541)459-4422, 50 miles S of Eugene.

Opened: 1970. Holes: 18. Par: 72/73. Yards: 6,346/5,427. Course rating: 70.3/71.5. Slope: 121/122. Architect: Mike Deprez. Green fee: $18/$18. Credit cards: MC,VISA. Reduced fees: Twilight. Caddies: No. Golf carts: $18. Discount golf packages: No. Season: Year-round. High: June-Aug. On site lodging: No. Rental clubs: Yes. Walking policy: Unrestricted walking. Metal spikes allowed: Yes. Range: Yes (grass). To obtain tee times: Call one week in advance.

★★LAKESIDE GOLF CLUB

3245 Club House Dr., Lincoln City, 97367, Lincoln County, (541)994-8442, 50 miles W of Salem.
Opened: 1925. Holes: 18. Par: 66/71. Yards: 5,007/4,318. Course rating: 64.9/66.2. Slope: 109/104. Architect: N/A. Green fee: $22/$30. Credit cards: All major. Reduced fees: Twilight, seniors, juniors. Caddies: No. Golf carts: $25. Discount golf packages: No. Season: Year-round. High: May-Sept. On site lodging: No. Rental clubs: Yes. Walking policy: Unrestricted walking. Metal spikes allowed: Yes. Range: Yes (grass). To obtain tee times: Call golf shop.

★★★½LANGDON FARMS GOLF CLUB

PU-24377 N.E. Airport Rd., Aurora, 97002, Marion County, (503)678-4653.
Opened: 1995. Holes: 18. Par: 71/71. Yards: 6,950/5,249. Course rating: 73.3/69.4. Slope: 125/114. Architect: John Fought and Robert Cupp. Green fee: $45/$50. Credit cards: All major. Reduced fees: Twilight. Caddies: No. Golf carts: $10. Discount golf packages: Yes. Season: Year-round. High: April-Oct. On site lodging: No. Rental clubs: Yes. Walking policy: Unrestricted walking. Metal spikes allowed: Yes. Range: Yes (grass/mats). To obtain tee times: Call up to 60 days in advance.
Subscriber comments: Great place. Charming...Depressed fairways make excellent course more playable..Staff treats you like a welcome guest.

★★★LOST TRACKS GOLF CLUB

PU-60205 Sunset View Dr., Bend, 97702, Deschutes County, (541)385-1818.
Opened: 1996. Holes: 18. Architect: Brian Whitcomb. Caddies: No. Discount golf packages: No. On site lodging: No. Rental clubs: No. Metal spikes allowed: Yes. Range: Yes.
Call club for further information.
Subscriber comments: Nice course, very challenging, friendly...New course, needs some seasoning...You've got to work to score.

★★½MCNARY GOLF CLUB

6255 River Rd. North, Salem, 97303, Marion County, (503)393-4653, 45 miles S of Portland.
Opened: 1962. Holes: 18. Par: 71/71. Yards: 6,178/5,370. Course rating: 69.2/71.2. Slope: 121/116. Architect: N/A. Green fee: $20/$28. Credit cards: MC,VISA. Reduced fees: Weekdays, low season, twilight, juniors. Caddies: No. Golf carts: $20. Discount golf packages: No. Season: Year-round. High: April-Oct. On site lodging: No. Rental clubs: No. Walking policy: Unrestricted walking. Metal spikes allowed: Yes. Range: No. To obtain tee times: Call golf club.
Subscriber comments: Fun to play. Greens are always nice...OK course and layout...A great tight course—requires precise shotmaking!

★★★½MEADOW LAKES GOLF COURSE

PU-300 Meadow Lakes Dr., Prineville, 97754, Crook County, (541)447-7113, (800)577-2797, 38 miles NE of Bend.
Opened: 1993. Holes: 18. Par: 72/72. Yards: 6,731/5,155. Course rating: 73.1/69.0. Slope: 131/121. Architect: William Robinson. Green fee: $12/$29. Credit cards: MC,VISA. Reduced fees: Low season. Caddies: No. Golf carts: $11. Discount golf packages: Yes. Season: Year-round. High: June-Sept. On site lodging: No. Rental clubs: Yes. Walking policy: Unrestricted walking. Metal spikes allowed: Yes. Range: Yes (grass/mats). To obtain tee times: Call up to one year in advance guaranteed with credit card, otherwise six days without credit card.
Notes: 1996 Golf Digest's Environmental Leaders in Golf Award.
Subscriber comments: Great layout concept for reclaimed land...Public course with lots of water, great condition, no trees, flat...Often windy in afternoon.

★★ MERIWETHER NATIONAL GOLF CLUB

PU-5200 S.W. Rood Bridge Rd., Hillsboro, 97123, Washington County, (503)648-4143, 25 miles W of Portland.
Opened: 1960. **Holes:** 27. **Par:** 72/73. **Yards:** 6,719/5,766. **Course rating:** 71.3/67.2. **Slope:** 121/112. **Architect:** Fred Federsfield. **Green fee:** $18/$20. **Credit cards:** MC,VISA. **Reduced fees:** Juniors. **Caddies:** No. **Golf carts:** $20. **Discount golf packages:** No. **Season:** Year-round. **High:** April-Oct. **On site lodging:** No. **Rental clubs:** Yes. **Walking policy:** Walking at certain times. **Metal spikes allowed:** Yes. **Range:** Yes (grass). **To obtain tee times:** Call up to 7 days in advance.

★★★ MOUNTAIN HIGH GOLF COURSE

PU-60650 China Hat Rd., Bend, 97702, Deschutes County, (541)382-1111, 180 miles SE of Portland.
Opened: 1986. **Holes:** 18. **Par:** 72/72. **Yards:** 6,656/5,268. **Course rating:** 72.0/69.2. **Slope:** 131/120. **Architect:** N/A. **Green fee:** $28/$40. **Credit cards:** MC,VISA. **Reduced fees:** Low season, twilight. **Caddies:** No. **Golf carts:** Included in Green Fee. **Discount golf packages:** No. **Season:** April-Nov. **High:** June-Sept. **On site lodging:** No. **Rental clubs:** Yes. **Walking policy:** Unrestricted walking. **Metal spikes allowed:** Yes. **Range:** Yes (mats). **To obtain tee times:** Call golf shop.

★★ MOUNTAIN VIEW GOLF CLUB

PU-27195 S.E. Kelso Rd., Boring, 97009, Clackamas County, (503)663-4869, 20 miles SE of Portland.
Opened: 1963. **Holes:** 18. **Par:** 71/73. **Yards:** 6,056/5,294. **Course rating:** 69.2/69.2. **Slope:** 122/111. **Architect:** Jack Waltmeyer. **Green fee:** $18/$20. **Credit cards:** MC,VISA. **Reduced fees:** Weekdays, seniors, juniors. **Caddies:** No. **Golf carts:** $20. **Discount golf packages:** No. **Season:** Year-round. **High:** April-Oct. **On site lodging:** No. **Rental clubs:** Yes. **Walking policy:** Unrestricted walking. **Metal spikes allowed:** Yes. **Range:** Yes (grass). **To obtain tee times:** Call golf shop.

NINE PEAKS MADRAS GOLF & COUNTRY CLUB

1152 NW Golf Course Lane, Madras, 97741, Jefferson County, (541)475-3511. Call club for further information.

★★ OAK KNOLL GOLF COURSE

PU-6335 Hwy. 22, Independence, 97351, Polk County, (503)378-0344, 6 miles W of Salem.
Opened: 1926. **Holes:** 18. **Par:** 72/72. **Yards:** 6,208/5,239. **Course rating:** 68.6/69.2. **Slope:** 113/113. **Architect:** Bill Ashby. **Green fee:** $20/$25. **Credit cards:** MC,VISA. **Reduced fees:** Weekdays, low season, seniors, juniors. **Caddies:** No. **Golf carts:** $20. **Discount golf packages:** Yes. **Season:** Year-round. **High:** June-Oct. **On site lodging:** No. **Rental clubs:** Yes. **Walking policy:** Unrestricted walking. **Metal spikes allowed:** Yes. **Range:** Yes (grass). **To obtain tee times:** Call golf shop.

★★½ OCEAN DUNES GOLF LINKS

PU-3345 Munsel Lake Rd., Florence, 97439, Lane County, (541)997-3232, (800)468-4833, 60 miles W of Eugene.
Opened: 1963. **Holes:** 18. **Par:** 71/72. **Yards:** 6,018/5,044. **Course rating:** 70.0/70.6. **Slope:** 124/128. **Architect:** William G. Robinson. **Green fee:** $24/$28. **Credit cards:** MC,VISA,DISC. **Reduced fees:** Twilight, seniors, juniors. **Caddies:** No. **Golf carts:** $24. **Discount golf packages:** No. **Season:** Year-round. **High:** April-Nov. **On site lodging:** No. **Rental clubs:** No. **Walking policy:** Unrestricted walking. **Metal spikes allowed:** Yes. **Range:** Yes (grass/mats). **To obtain tee times:** Call golf shop.
Subscriber comments: Tremendous layout. Trees, water and sand...Keep it straight, dunes (waste areas) eat up strokes.

★★½ OREGON CITY GOLF CLUB

PU-20124 S. Beavercreek Rd., Oregon City, 97045, Clackamas County, (503)656-2846, 15 miles S of Portland.
Opened: 1922. **Holes:** 9. **Par:** 71/75. **Yards:** 5,964/5,259. **Course rating:** 67.9/69.4. **Slope:** 116/113. **Architect:** H. Beals/R. Seon/J. Herberger. **Green fee:** $15/$25. **Credit cards:** MC,VISA. **Reduced fees:** Weekdays, seniors, juniors. **Caddies:** No. **Golf carts:**

$25. **Discount golf packages:** No. **Season:** Year-round. **High:** June-Sept. **On site lodging:** No. **Rental clubs:** Yes. **Walking policy:** Unrestricted walking. **Metal spikes allowed:** Yes. **Range:** No. **To obtain tee times:** Call up to 14 days in advance. **Subscriber comments:** Nice, but narrow, old clubhouse, shorter course...Test your skills...Flat, classic...New clubhouse being built...They are improving it....Nice muny...Very nice course, good mix of holes.

★★★½OREGON GOLF ASSOCIATION MEMBERS COURSE AT TUKWILA
PU-2990 Boonesferry Rd., Woodburn, 97071, Marion County, (503)981-6105.
Opened: 1996. **Holes:** 18. **Par:** 72/72. **Yards:** 6,650/5,498. **Course rating:** 72.1/72.2. **Slope:** 132/125. **Architect:** Bill Robinson. **Green fee:** $24/$40. **Credit cards:** MC,VISA. **Reduced fees:** Juniors. **Caddies:** No. **Golf carts:** $20. **Discount golf packages:** No. **Season:** Year-round. **High:** May-Oct. **On site lodging:** No. **Rental clubs:** Yes. **Walking policy:** Unrestricted walking. **Metal spikes allowed:** Yes. **Range:** Yes (grass/mats). **To obtain tee times:** Call up to 5 days in advance.
Notes: Ranked tied for 8th in 1996 Best New Affordable Courses.
Subscriber comments: New course—great condition, very fair!...Great course, driving range. A challenge...Has both easy and hard holes. Lots of bunkers. Great par 3s...Excellent varietyl...Par 5 4th hole is a killer...Short but challenging.

★★★½PERSIMMON COUNTRY CLUB
500 S.E. Butler Rd., Gresham, 97080, Multnomah County, (503)661-1800.
Opened: 1993. **Holes:** 18. **Par:** 72/72. **Yards:** 6,678/4,852. **Course rating:** 71.2/66.1. **Slope:** 125/112. **Architect:** Gene "Bunny" Mason. **Green fee:** $45/$75. **Credit cards:** MC,VISA,AMEX. **Reduced fees:** Low season, twilight. **Caddies:** No. **Golf carts:** Included in Green Fee. **Discount golf packages:** No. **Season:** Year-round. **High:** N/A. **On site lodging:** No. **Rental clubs:** Yes. **Walking policy:** Unrestricted walking. **Metal spikes allowed:** Yes. **Range:** Yes (grass/mats). **To obtain tee times:** Call up to 3 days in advance.
Subscriber comments: Very young course, could be tough when trees grow...Good quality course. Fast greens...Beautiful setting but too many hilly holes. #9 and #18 were nice...Very difficult from back tees...Outstanding views.

★★PROGRESS DOWNS GOLF COURSE
PU-8200 S.W. Scholls Ferry Rd., Beaverton, 97005, Washington County, (503)646-5166, 4 miles S of Portland.
Opened: 1966. **Holes:** 18. **Par:** 71/73. **Yards:** 6,426/5,626. **Course rating:** 69.8/71.7. **Slope:** 112/115. **Architect:** City of Portland. **Green fee:** $18/$20. **Credit cards:** All major. **Reduced fees:** Weekdays, seniors, juniors. **Caddies:** Yes. **Golf carts:** N/A. **Discount golf packages:** No. **Season:** Year-round. **High:** April-Oct. **On site lodging:** No. **Rental clubs:** Yes. **Walking policy:** Unrestricted walking. **Metal spikes allowed:** Yes. **Range:** Yes (mats). **To obtain tee times:** In person seven days in advance or phone in six days in advance.

★★★★½PUMPKIN RIDGE GOLF CLUB (GHOST CREEK COURSE)
PU-12930 Old Pumpkin Ridge Rd., North Plains, 97133, Washington County, (503)647-9977, 20 miles W of Portland.
Opened: 1992. **Holes:** 18. **Par:** 71/71. **Yards:** 6,839/5,206. **Course rating:** 73.6/70.4. **Slope:** 135/117. **Architect:** Bob Cupp. **Green fee:** $52/$90. **Credit cards:** All major. **Reduced fees:** Weekdays, low season, twilight. **Caddies:** Yes. **Golf carts:** $25. **Discount golf packages:** No. **Season:** Year-round. **High:** April-Oct. **On site lodging:** No. **Rental clubs:** Yes. **Walking policy:** Unrestricted walking. **Metal spikes allowed:** No. **Range:** Yes (grass/mats). **To obtain tee times:** Eight days with frequent player card; six days in person; seven days by phone.
Notes: Ranked 81st in 1997-98 America's 100 Greatest; 2nd in 1997 Best in State. Nike Tour Championship 1993-94; 1996 US Amateur Championship.
Subscriber comments: One of the best public courses in the U.S...Great fairways and greens...Has to be good to host U.S. Amateur!...World-class course! Best in Northwest...Great pro shop/dining room...The best in Oregon! Greens fast, fairways long...Has a "major" feel—worth every penny!...Very fair yet very difficult, great condition, as good as it gets...Tiger loves it.

★★★QUAIL RUN GOLF COURSE
PU-16725 Northridge Dr., La Pine, 97739, Deschutes County, (541)536-1303, (800)895-4653, 22 miles S of Bend.
Opened: 1991. **Holes:** 9. **Par:** 72/72. **Yards:** 7,024/5,414. **Course rating:** 72.2/69.6. **Slope:** 126/116. **Architect:** Jim Ramey. **Green fee:** $24/$24. **Credit cards:** MC,VISA,DISC. **Reduced fees:** Low season, twilight, juniors. **Caddies:** No. **Golf carts:** $20. **Discount golf packages:** No. **Season:** March-Nov. **High:** June-Sept. **On site lodging:** No. **Rental clubs:** Yes. **Walking policy:** Unrestricted walking. **Metal spikes allowed:** Yes. **Range:** Yes (grass). **To obtain tee times:** Call up to 30 days in advance.
Subscriber comments: Great little course...Bring the kids in the afternoon for great twilight value...Surprising course—nine holes but all very good, could be tough from the back...Lots of wildlife, beautiful views, challenge in wind...Nice people...Only nine holes but a great nine holes.

★★★QUAIL VALLEY GOLF COURSE
PU-12565 N.W. Aerts Rd., Banks, 97106, Washington County, (503)324-4444, 20 miles W of Portland.
Opened: 1994. **Holes:** 18. **Par:** 72/72. **Yards:** 6,603/5,519. **Course rating:** 71.6/71.5. **Slope:** 122/117. **Architect:** John Zoller Jr.. **Green fee:** $25/$25. **Credit cards:** MC,VISA,AMEX. **Reduced fees:** N/A. **Caddies:** No. **Golf carts:** $22. **Discount golf packages:** No. **Season:** Year-round. **High:** June-Sept. **On site lodging:** No. **Rental clubs:** Yes. **Walking policy:** Unrestricted walking. **Metal spikes allowed:** Yes. **Range:** Yes (grass/mats). **To obtain tee times:** Call up to 7 days in advance.
Subscriber comments: Great course, gets windy...Nice new course, driving range. Good facility...Wide open, wind provides the challenge...Nice greens...Fun.

THE RESERVE VINEYARDS & GOLF CLUB
4805 SW 229th Ave., Aloha, 97007, Washington County, (503)649-8191, 20 miles W of Portland.
Credit cards: All major. **Reduced fees:** Weekdays, low season, twilight. **Caddies:** No. **Golf carts:** Included in Green Fee. **Discount golf packages:** No. **Season:** Year-round. **High:** April-Oct. **On site lodging:** No. **Rental clubs:** Yes. **Walking policy:** Unrestricted walking. **Metal spikes allowed:** No. **Range:** Yes (grass). **To obtain tee times:** Call up to 30 days in advance.
Notes: Fred Meyer Challenge.
CUPP COURSE
Opened: 1998. **Holes:** 18. **Par:** 72/72. **Yards:** 6,895/5,735. **Course rating:** N/A. **Slope:** N/A. **Architect:** Bob Cupp. **Green fee:** $80/$80.
FOUGHT COURSE
Opened: 1997. **Holes:** 18. **Par:** 72/72. **Yards:** 7,196/5,189. **Course rating:** 74.3/70.1. **Slope:** 134/121. **Architect:** John Fought. **Green fee:** $60/$80.

★★★RESORT AT THE MOUNTAIN
R-68010 E. Fairway Ave., Welches, 97067, Clackamas County, (503)622-3151, (800)669-4653, 45 miles from Portland.
Opened: 1928. **Holes:** 27. **Architect:** N/A. **Green fee:** $20/$33. **Credit cards:** All major, Diners Club, Carte Blanche. **Reduced fees:** Weekdays, low season, resort guests, twilight, juniors. **Caddies:** No. **Golf carts:** $25. **Discount golf packages:** Yes. **Season:** Year-round. **High:** May-Oct. **On site lodging:** Yes. **Rental clubs:** Yes. **Walking policy:** Unrestricted walking. **Metal spikes allowed:** Yes. **Range:** No. **To obtain tee times:** Call up to 14 days in advance.
FOXGLOVE/PINECONE
Par: 70/71. **Yards:** 5,776/5,031. **Course rating:** 68.0/70.0. **Slope:** 116/116.
FOXGLOVE/THISTLE
Par: 72/74. **Yards:** 6,443/5,693. **Course rating:** 70.0/74.0. **Slope:** 119/123.
PINECONE/THISTLE
Par: 70/71. **Yards:** 6,032/5,246. **Course rating:** 68.0/70.0. **Slope:** 116/115.
Subscriber comments: Breathtaking views—fun...Great layout, tight fairways...Thistle is long and flat; Pine short, tricky...Great layout, tight fairways...Gorgeous setting over-all—some truly beautiful holes and some good challenges.

★★★ RIVER'S EDGE GOLF RESORT
R-400 NW Pro Shop Dr., Bend, 97701, Deschutes County, (541)389-2828.
Opened: 1988. **Holes:** 18. **Par:** 72/73. **Yards:** 6,683/5,381. **Course rating:** 72.6/71.8.
Slope: 137/135. **Architect:** Robert Muir Graves. **Green fee:** $18/$36. **Credit cards:**
MC,VISA. **Reduced fees:** Weekdays, low season, resort guests, twilight, juniors.
Caddies: No. **Golf carts:** $12. **Discount golf packages:** Yes. **Season:** Year-round.
High: May-Sept. **On site lodging:** Yes. **Rental clubs:** Yes. **Walking policy:**
Unrestricted walking. **Metal spikes allowed:** Yes. **Range:** Yes (grass/mats). **To obtain**
tee times: Call. Credit card will hold reservation more than one week.
Subscriber comments: Tough! Hilly, excellent course...Very tough for average
golfer...Friendly staff...Improved a lot in last year...Not for the faint of heart...Wow,
Indiana Jones golf. What an adventure!

★★½ RIVERIDGE GOLF COURSE
PU-3800 N. Delta, Eugene, 97408, Lane County, (541)345-9160.
Opened: 1990. **Holes:** 18. **Par:** 71/71. **Yards:** 6,256/5,146. **Course rating:** 68.6/67.7.
Slope: 116/112. **Architect:** Ric Jeffries. **Green fee:** $24/$30. **Credit cards:** MC,VISA.
Reduced fees: Low season, seniors, juniors. **Caddies:** No. **Golf carts:** $20. **Discount**
golf packages: Yes. **Season:** Year-round. **High:** May-Sept. **On site lodging:** No.
Rental clubs: Yes. **Walking policy:** Unrestricted walking. **Metal spikes allowed:** Yes.
Range: Yes (grass/mats). **To obtain tee times:** Call seven days in advance.
Subscriber comments: Enjoyable, worth the stop if travelling through area...A bit tight
to fit the area. Good range and instruction...Nice, short, well-maintained, easy course.
Special Notes: Offers a green fee discount if using spikeless shoes.

★★½ ROSE CITY MUNICIPAL GOLF CLUB
PU-2200 NE 71st, Portland, 97213, Multnomah County, (503)253-4744.
Opened: N/A. **Holes:** 18. **Par:** 72/72. **Yards:** 6,455/5,619. **Course rating:** N/A. **Slope:**
118/117. **Architect:** George Otten. **Green fee:** N/A. **Credit cards:** MC,VISA,DISC.
Reduced fees: Weekdays. **Caddies:** No. **Golf carts:** $24. **Discount golf packages:**
No. **Season:** Year-round. **High:** June-Aug. **On site lodging:** No. **Rental clubs:** No.
Walking policy: Unrestricted walking. **Metal spikes allowed:** Yes. **Range:** No. **To**
obtain tee times: Call up to 6 days in advance.
Subscriber comments: Well maintained for large amount of traffic...Nice older course,
no range—a challenge, lots of trees...Good old course. Stays dry in winter.

★★★ SALEM GOLF CLUB
2025 Golf Course Rd., Salem, 97302, Marion County, (503)363-6652.
Opened: 1928. **Holes:** 18. **Par:** 72/72. **Yards:** 6,200/5,163. **Course rating:** 69.6/70.0.
Slope: 118. **Architect:** Ercel Kay. **Green fee:** $30/$35. **Credit cards:** MC,VISA.
Reduced fees: Low season, twilight, juniors. **Caddies:** Yes. **Golf carts:** $20. **Discount**
golf packages: No. **Season:** Year-round. **High:** July-Sept. **On site lodging:** No. **Rental**
clubs: Yes. **Walking policy:** Unrestricted walking. **Metal spikes allowed:** Yes. **Range:**
Yes (grass/mats). **To obtain tee times:** Call two days in advance for weekdays or on
Monday for the upcoming weekend.
Subscriber comments: Great short 18...Semi-private. Beautiful clubhouse. Short, narrow, beautiful...Good quality. Old, classic feel to the course...Nice course with good
people...Narrow fairways...Stately, tall trees give country club feel.

★★★½ SALISHAN GOLF LINKS
R-Hwy. 101, Gleneden Beach, 97388, Lincoln County, (541)764-3632, (888)725-4742,
58 miles W of Salem.
Opened: 1965. **Holes:** 18. **Par:** 72/72. **Yards:** 6,453/5,689. **Course rating:** 72.1/73.6.
Slope: 128/127. **Architect:** Fred Federspiel. **Green fee:** $30/$60. **Credit cards:** All
major,Diners Club. **Reduced fees:** Low season, resort guests, juniors. **Caddies:** No.
Golf carts: $26. **Discount golf packages:** Yes. **Season:** Year-round. **High:** May-Oct.
On site lodging: Yes. **Rental clubs:** Yes. **Walking policy:** Unrestricted walking. **Metal**
spikes allowed: Yes. **Range:** Yes (grass). **To obtain tee times:** Call two weeks in
advance.
Notes: Ranked 14th in 1997 Best in State.
Subscriber comments: Excellent condition, small greens, beautiful, treelined...Tight
and scenic...Up into trees front nine, back nine seaside, very nice.

★½SANDELIE GOLF COURSE
28333 SW Mountain Rd., West Linn, 97068, Clackamas County, (503)655-1461.
Call club for further information.

★★★★SANDPINES GOLF LINKS
PU-1201 35th St., Florence, 97439, Lane County, (541)997-1940, 60 miles W of Eugene.
Opened: 1993. **Holes:** 18. **Par:** 72/72. **Yards:** 6,954/5,346. **Course rating:** 74.0/65.8.
Slope: 129/111. **Architect:** Rees Jones. **Green fee:** $25/$45. **Credit cards:** MC,VISA.
Reduced fees: Twilight. **Caddies:** Yes. **Golf carts:** $26. **Discount golf packages:** Yes.
Season: Year-round. **High:** June-Oct. **On site lodging:** No. **Rental clubs:** Yes.
Walking policy: Unrestricted walking. **Metal spikes allowed:** Yes. **Range:** Yes
(grass/mats). **To obtain tee times:** Call two weeks in advance or sign up for golf pack-
age (800)422-5091.
Notes: Ranked 6th in 1997 Best in State.
Subscriber comments: Lots of sand—lots of pines...Outstanding course, tough when
wind blows...Beautiful dunes course—can be very windy and wet...Lots of wind in afternoon but good layout...Maybe Oregon's finest. Breathtaking scenery. Big-time
golf...Beautiful, uncrowded, superb condition...Great coastal course with trees.

★★½SANTIAM GOLF CLUB
PU-8724 Golf Club Rd. S.E., Aumsville, 97325, Marion County, (503)769-3485, 15
miles SE of Salem.
Opened: 1958. **Holes:** 18. **Par:** 72/72. **Yards:** 6,392/5,469. **Course rating:** 69.9/70.7.
Slope: 123/119. **Architect:** Fred Federspiel. **Green fee:** $20/$20. **Credit cards:** None.
Reduced fees: Seniors, juniors. **Caddies:** No. **Golf carts:** $20. **Discount golf pack-
ages:** No. **Season:** Year-round. **High:** July-Sept. **On site lodging:** No. **Rental clubs:**
Yes. **Walking policy:** Unrestricted walking. **Metal spikes allowed:** Yes. **Range:** Yes
(grass). **To obtain tee times:** Call one week in advance for Friday through Monday.
Subscriber comments: Nice layout...Several creeks run through course...Easy but
nice course...Steadily improving course.

SHADOW BUTTE GOLF CLUB
PM-1345 Golf Course Rd., Ontario, 97914, Malheur County, (541)889-9022, (888)303-
4653, 60 miles NW of Boise.
Opened: 1968. **Holes:** 18. **Par:** 72/74. **Yards:** 6,795/5,742. **Course rating:** 70.4/73.3.
Slope: 116/120. **Architect:** N/A. **Green fee:** $10/$11. **Credit cards:** MC,VISA.
Reduced fees: Juniors. **Caddies:** No. **Golf carts:** $16. **Discount golf packages:** No.
Season: Feb.-Nov. **High:** March-June. **On site lodging:** No. **Rental clubs:** Yes.
Walking policy: Unrestricted walking. **Metal spikes allowed:** Yes. **Range:** Yes (grass).
To obtain tee times: Call golf shop up to 7 days in advance.
Special Notes: Formerly Edisto-Butte Municipal Golf Course.

★★½SHIELD CREST GOLF COURSE
3151 Shield Crest Dr., Klamath Falls, 97603, Klamath County, (541)884-5305.
Call club for further information.
Subscriber comments: Nice course...Still a young course, fairly simple layout. Great
greens...Long, wide fairways, tight doglegs, good golf.

★★★½STONERIDGE GOLF COURSE
PU-500 E. Antelope Rd., Eagle Point, 97524, Jackson County, (541)830-4653, 8 miles
NE of Medford.
Opened: 1995. **Holes:** 18. **Par:** 72/72. **Yards:** 6,738/4,986. **Course rating:** 72.6/72.6.
Slope: 132/118. **Architect:** James Cochran. **Green fee:** $20/$24. **Credit cards:**
MC,VISA. **Reduced fees:** Low season. **Caddies:** No. **Golf carts:** N/A. **Discount golf
packages:** No. **Season:** Year-round. **High:** March-Nov. **On site lodging:** No. **Rental
clubs:** Yes. **Walking policy:** Unrestricted walking. **Metal spikes allowed:** Yes. **Range:**
Yes (grass/mats). **To obtain tee times:** Call up to 7 days in advance.
Subscriber comments: Interesting young course, will improve with age...Interesting
variety of holes, awesome views...The course has a good layout, needs a little time for
maturity...Beautiful setting and friendly...A gem—bring your long irons.

SUNRIVER LODGE & RESORT

R- **Credit cards:** All major. **Caddies:** No. **Discount golf packages:** Yes.
Season: April-Oct. **High:** June-Aug. **On site lodging:** Yes. **Rental clubs:** Yes. **Walking policy:** Unrestricted walking. **Metal spikes allowed:** Yes. **Range:** Yes (grass/mats). **To obtain tee times:** Lodge guests at time of reservation. Public call 30 days in advance.

★★★★½CROSSWATER CLUB

P.O. Box 4818, Sunriver, 97707, Deschutes County, (541)593-6196, (800)547-3922, 20 miles S of Bend.
Opened: 1995. **Holes:** 18. **Par:** 72/72. **Yards:** 7,683/5,359. **Course rating:** 76.9/69.8.
Slope: 150/125. **Architect:** Robert Cupp/John Fought. **Green fee:** $95/$115. **Reduced fees:** N/A. **Golf carts:** Included in Green Fee.
Notes: Golf Digest School site. Ranked 4th in 1997 Best in State; 1st in 1995 Best New Resort Courses.
Subscriber comments: Difficult for 30-handicap but beautiful and a fun challenge...Pick the right tees for play...A real test; fun to play...Will dominate any level of golfer...Great facility!...Scenery outstanding, pleasant staff...Breathtaking...Tee shots to clear wetlands...Outstanding...Great test, lots of water, fast greens.

★★★½NORTH WOODLANDS COURSE

P.O. Box 3609, Sunriver, 97707, Deschutes County, (541)593-3703, 12 miles S of Bend.
Opened: 1981. **Holes:** 18. **Par:** 72/72. **Yards:** 6,880/5,446. **Course rating:** 73.0/70.3.
Slope: 131/118. **Architect:** Robert Trent Jones Jr. **Green fee:** $30/$65. **Reduced fees:** Low season, resort guests, twilight, juniors. **Golf carts:** $25.
Notes: Golf Digest School site. Ranked 5th in 1997 Best in State.
Subscriber comments: Outstanding views...Interesting, challenging, tough greens...Well-maintained course. Beautiful holes...Great course condition and practice area...Beautiful woods layout.

★★★SOUTH MEADOWS COURSE

P.O. Box 3609, Sunriver, 97707, Deschutes County, (541)593-3750, 12 miles S of Bend.
Opened: 1968. **Holes:** 18. **Par:** 72/72. **Yards:** 6,960/5,847. **Course rating:** 72.9/71.7.
Slope: 130/116. **Architect:** Fred Federspiel. **Green fee:** $25/$50. **Reduced fees:** Low season, resort guests, twilight, juniors. **Golf carts:** $25.
Notes: Golf Digest School site.
Subscriber comments: Great view of Mt. Batchelor...Very nice place to play...Oldest course at Sunriver. Very nice feel to it...More wide open than sister course...Not as exciting as Woodlands...A relatively forgiving course that still presents a challenge.

SUTHERLIN KNOLLS GOLF COURSE

1919 Recreation Lane, Sutherlin, 97479, Douglas County, (541)459-4422.
Call club for further information.

★★★★TOKATEE GOLF CLUB

PU-54947 McKenzie Hwy., Blue River, 97413, Lane County, (541)822-3220, (800)452-6376, 47 miles E of Eugene.
Opened: 1966. **Holes:** 18. **Par:** 72/72. **Yards:** 6,842/5,651. **Course rating:** 72.0/71.2. **Slope:** 126/115. **Architect:** Ted Robinson. **Green fee:** $32/$32. **Credit cards:** MC,VISA. **Reduced fees:** Juniors. **Caddies:** No.
Golf carts: $24. **Discount golf packages:** No. **Season:** Feb.-Nov. **High:** June-Sept. **On site lodging:** No. **Rental clubs:** Yes. **Walking policy:** Unrestricted walking. **Metal spikes allowed:** Yes. **Range:** Yes (grass). **To obtain tee times:** Call in advance.
Notes: Ranked 8th in 1997 Best in State.
Subscriber comments: Great course right in the timber...One of the best, no homes, wilderness setting...Great view and setting...Beautiful course in the mountains—yet flat...Dream golf...Picturesque, some very tight holes...Great, nothing like it for pure golf...Strict pace of play enforced...Course has one drawback: it's too far out of town.

★½TOP O SCOTT GOLF COURSE

PU-12000 S.E. Stevens Rd., Portland, 97266, Clackamas County, (503)654-5050, 6 miles SE of Portland.
Opened: 1926. **Holes:** 18. **Par:** 67/67. **Yards:** 4,826/3,670. **Course rating:** 64.5/65.4.

Slope: 100/101. **Architect:** N/A. **Green fee:** $16/$18. **Credit cards:** MC,VISA. **Reduced fees:** N/A. **Caddies:** No. **Golf carts:** $22. **Discount golf packages:** No. **Season:** Year-round. **High:** May-Oct. **On site lodging:** No. **Rental clubs:** Yes. **Walking policy:** Unrestricted walking. **Metal spikes allowed:** Yes. **Range:** Yes (mats). **To obtain tee times:** Call golf shop.

★★★TRYSTING TREE GOLF CLUB

PU-34028 Electric Rd., Corvallis, 97333, Benton County, (541)752-3332, 34 miles SW of Salem.

Opened: 1988. **Holes:** 18. **Par:** 72/72. **Yards:** 7,014/5,516. **Course rating:** 73.9/71.3. **Slope:** 129/118. **Architect:** Ted Robinson. **Green fee:** $27/$27. **Credit cards:** MC,VISA,DISC. **Reduced fees:** Juniors. **Caddies:** No. **Golf carts:** $22. **Discount golf packages:** No. **Season:** Year-round. **High:** May-Oct. **On site lodging:** No. **Rental clubs:** Yes. **Walking policy:** Unrestricted walking. **Metal spikes allowed:** Yes. **Range:** Yes (grass/mats). **To obtain tee times:** Call 7 days in advance.

Subscriber comments: University course—well maintained...Flat, wide-open but long with tough greens...Very nice pro...Plays better than it looks...Sneaky...Lush fairways, fast greens, good design—open...A nice test of golf...Two great nines. Front is open and rolling, back treelined and tight...Very windy but playable...Still new—will get tougher when trees mature...Tough par 5s.

★½UMATILLA GOLF COURSE

PU-705 Willamette, Umatilla, 97882, Umatilla County, (541)922-3006, 54 miles SW of Walla Walla, WA.

Opened: 1968. **Holes:** 18. **Par:** 70/72. **Yards:** 6,000/5,700. **Course rating:** 68.9/74.0. **Slope:** 119/113. **Architect:** N/A. **Green fee:** $10/$16. **Credit cards:** MC,VISA,DISC. **Reduced fees:** Low season, juniors. **Caddies:** No. **Golf carts:** $24. **Discount golf packages:** Yes. **Season:** Year-round. **High:** March-Oct. **On site lodging:** Yes. **Rental clubs:** Yes. **Walking policy:** Unrestricted walking. **Metal spikes allowed:** Yes. **Range:** Yes (grass). **To obtain tee times:** Show up or call within half an hour.

★★★½WIDGI CREEK GOLF CLUB

18707 Century Dr., Bend, 97709, Deschutes County, (541)382-4449, 160 miles S of Portland.

Opened: 1991. **Holes:** 18. **Par:** 72/72. **Yards:** 6,879/5,070. **Course rating:** 72.5/69.2. **Slope:** 137/124. **Architect:** Robert Muir Graves. **Green fee:** $29/$75. **Credit cards:** MC,VISA. **Reduced fees:** Weekdays, low season, juniors. **Caddies:** Yes. **Golf carts:** $26. **Discount golf packages:** No. **Season:** March-Nov. **High:** May-Sept. **On site lodging:** No. **Rental clubs:** Yes. **Walking policy:** Unrestricted walking. **Metal spikes allowed:** Yes. **Range:** Yes (grass). **To obtain tee times:** Call up to 1 month in advance.

Subscriber comments: Beautiful scenery—many different looks—took a lot of thought...Great little muny...Tight, but fun, well groomed...Easy to walk, difficult and undulating greens, tight fairways...Nice variety of holes.

PENNSYLVANIA

★★ALLENTOWN MUNICIPAL GOLF COURSE
PM-3400 Tilghman St., Allentown, 18104, Lehigh County, (610)395-9926, 65 miles S of Philadelphia.
Opened: 1955. **Holes:** 18. **Par:** 73/73. **Yards:** 7,085/5,635. **Course rating:** 72.0/71.3. **Slope:** 127/123. **Architect:** A.L. Weisenberger Assoc.. **Green fee:** $12/$16. **Credit cards:** None. **Reduced fees:** Low season, twilight, seniors, juniors. **Caddies:** No. **Golf carts:** $20. **Discount golf packages:** No. **Season:** Year-round. **High:** May-Sept. **On site lodging:** No. **Rental clubs:** Yes. **Walking policy:** Unrestricted walking. **Metal spikes allowed:** Yes. **Range:** Yes (grass). **To obtain tee times:** In person seven days in advance.

★★APPLEWOOD GOLF COURSE
Mt. Zion Rd., West Pittson, (717)388-2500.
Call club for further information.

★★½ARMITAGE GOLF COURSE
PM-800 Orres Bridge Rd., Mechanicsburg, 17055, Cumberland County, (717)737-5344, 5 miles W of Harrisburg.
Opened: 1962. **Holes:** 18. **Par:** 70/70. **Yards:** 6,000/5,200. **Course rating:** 66.9. **Slope:** 112. **Architect:** Ed Ault. **Green fee:** $14/$18. **Credit cards:** MC,VISA. **Reduced fees:** Twilight, seniors, juniors. **Caddies:** No. **Golf carts:** $10. **Discount golf packages:** No. **Season:** March-Dec. **High:** May-Sept. **On site lodging:** No. **Rental clubs:** No. **Walking policy:** Unrestricted walking. **Metal spikes allowed:** Yes. **Range:** Yes (grass/mats). **To obtain tee times:** Call up to 7 days in advance.
Subscriber comments: Busy, but fun local course; 17th is great!...Great course for the money...Short par 4s...Short but good target golf.

★★ARNOLD'S GOLF CLUB
PU-R.D. No.2, Nescopeck, 18635, Luzerne County, (717)752-7022.
Call club for further information.

★★★ARROWHEAD GOLF COURSE
PU-1539 Weavertown Rd., Douglassville, 19518, Berks County, (610)582-4258, 9 miles E of Reading.
Opened: 1954. **Holes:** 18. **Par:** 71/71. **Yards:** 6,002/6,002. **Course rating:** 68.9/73.4. **Slope:** 116/124. **Architect:** John McLean. **Green fee:** $14/$17. **Credit cards:** None. **Reduced fees:** Weekdays, low season, twilight. **Caddies:** No. **Golf carts:** $17. **Discount golf packages:** No. **Season:** Year-round. **High:** N/A. **On site lodging:** No. **Rental clubs:** Yes. **Walking policy:** Unrestricted walking. **Metal spikes allowed:** Yes. **Range:** Yes (grass/mats). **To obtain tee times:** Call or come in.
Subscriber comments: Very wide fairways...Fine playing condition...Tough little course, 245-yard par 3...Wait until you get to 16 and 17!...Long, narrow.
Special Notes: Also has 9-hole par-34 Blue Course.

★★½ASHBOURNE COUNTRY CLUB
SP-Ashbourne & Oak Lane Rds, Cheltenham, 19012, Montgomery County, (215)635-3090.
Call club for further information.
Subscriber comments: Private club service, great golf holes and condition...Liked back nine better...Expensive, but country club setting, very pretty...A little too short but well maintained...Crowded.

★★½AUBREYS GOLF CLUB
PU-Mercer Rd., Butler, 16001, Butler County, (412)287-4832.
Call club for further information.
Subscriber comments: Open front, tight back...Front nine's a cakewalk, back rates among the most difficult in western Pa...Very hilly, narrow back nine.

★★★½BAVARIAN HILLS GOLF COURSE
PU-Mulligan Rd., St. Mary's, 15857, Elk County, (814)834-3602, 135 miles N of Pittsburgh.
Opened: 1990. **Holes:** 18. **Par:** 71/73. **Yards:** 6,290/4,845. **Course rating:** 68.8/67.2.

Slope: 126/115. **Architect:** Bill Love and Brian Ault. **Green fee:** $17. **Credit cards:** None. **Reduced fees:** Twilight, juniors. **Caddies:** No. **Golf carts:** $18. **Discount golf packages:** No. **Season:** April-Nov. **High:** June-Aug. **On site lodging:** No. **Rental clubs:** Yes. **Walking policy:** Unrestricted walking. **Metal spikes allowed:** Yes. **Range:** Yes (mats). **To obtain tee times:** Call Monday for upcoming weekend.
Subscriber comments: Nice mountain course...Tricky greens...Course was very good, the facilities good...Outstanding course, little traffic...Narrow and short course but good...Good condition, great views, no flat lies here.

★★★ BEDFORD SPRINGS GOLF COURSE
R-Business Rte. 220 S., Bedford, 15522, Bedford County, (814)623-8999, 80 miles E of Pittsburgh.
Opened: 1924. **Holes:** 18. **Par:** 74/74. **Yards:** 7,000/5,535. **Course rating:** N/A. **Slope:** N/A. **Architect:** Donald Ross. **Green fee:** N/A. **Credit cards:** All major. **Reduced fees:** N/A. **Caddies:** No. **Golf carts:** N/A. **Discount golf packages:** No. **Season:** May-Oct. **High:** June-Sept. **On site lodging:** No. **Rental clubs:** Yes. **Walking policy:** Mandatory cart. **Metal spikes allowed:** Yes. **Range:** Yes (grass). **To obtain tee times:** Call up to 12 hours in advance.
Subscriber comments: Great for long ball hitters...Scenic, playable for all golfers...Course is designed well, needs more maintenance.

★★½ BETHLEHEM MUNICIPAL GOLF CLUB
PM-400 Illicks Mills Rd., Bethlehem, 18017, Northampton County, (610)691-9393.
Opened: 1956. **Holes:** 18. **Par:** 71/71. **Yards:** 6,830/5,119. **Course rating:** N/A. **Slope:** N/A. **Architect:** William Gordon and David Gordon. **Green fee:** $10/$20. **Credit cards:** None. **Reduced fees:** Weekdays, twilight, seniors, juniors. **Caddies:** No. **Golf carts:** $10. **Discount golf packages:** No. **Season:** Year-round. **High:** March-Oct. **On site lodging:** No. **Rental clubs:** Yes. **Walking policy:** Unrestricted walking. **Metal spikes allowed:** Yes. **Range:** Yes (grass). **To obtain tee times:** Residents sign up Thursday, others sign up Friday for $1 fee.
Subscriber comments: Some challenging holes...Easy to walk, was treated well..Birdies are hard to come by...Older course, very good...Hilly, greens good...Tough muny...A real good test.
Special Notes: Also has a 9-hole executive course.

BLACK HAWK GOLF COURSE
PU-644 Blackhawk Rd., Beaver Falls, 15010, Beaver County, (412)843-2542, 35 miles NW of Pittsburgh.
Opened: 1927. **Architect:** Paul Frable. **Green fee:** $10/$19. **Credit cards:** All major. **Reduced fees:** Weekdays, low season, seniors. **Caddies:** No. **Golf carts:** $10. **Discount golf packages:** No. **Season:** Year-round. **High:** June-Aug. **On site lodging:** No. **Rental clubs:** Yes. **Walking policy:** Unrestricted walking. **Metal spikes allowed:** Yes. **Range:** Yes (grass/mats).
★★½ FIRST COURSE
Holes: 18. **Par:** 72/72. **Yards:** 6,114/5,365. **Course rating:** 67.7/68.6. **Slope:** 112/113.
To obtain tee times: Call 7 days in advance for weekends and holidays only.
Subscriber comments: Good walking course...Wide open...Great people, nice greens...Mature, very hilly.
★★½ SECOND COURSE
Holes: 18. **Par:** 72/72. **Yards:** 6,285/5,552. **Course rating:** 67.7/68.6. **Slope:** 112/113.
To obtain tee times: Call 7 days in advance.
Subscriber comments: Old, tight, well kept...Long, hilly...Front side has strong holes, back nine is squeezed into the pines...Sloping, rolling fairways.

★★½ BLACKWOOD GOLF COURSE
PU-510 Red Corner Rd., Douglassville, 19518, Berks County, (610)385-6200, 12 miles E of Reading.
Opened: 1970. **Holes:** 18. **Par:** 70/70. **Yards:** 6,403/4,826. **Course rating:** 68.6/62.0. **Slope:** 115/95. **Architect:** William Gordon. **Green fee:** $12/$23. **Credit cards:** None. **Reduced fees:** Weekdays, low season, twilight, seniors. **Caddies:** No. **Golf carts:** N/A. **Discount golf packages:** No. **Season:** Year-round. **High:** May-Sept. **On site lodging:** No. **Rental clubs:** Yes. **Walking policy:** Unrestricted walking. **Metal spikes allowed:** Yes. **Range:** Yes (grass/mats). **To obtain tee times:** Call 2 weeks in advance.

Subscriber comments: Wide open, my type of course...Get to hit every club in the bag...Course pretty much open...Nice scenery...Has really improved...Basic golf but always in real good shape.

★★½BLUE MOUNTAIN VIEW GOLF COURSE
PU-Blue Mt. Dr., R.D. 1, Box 106, Fredericksburg, 17026, Lebanon County, (717)865-4401, 23 miles E of Harrisburg.
Opened: 1963. **Holes:** 18. **Par:** 71/73. **Yards:** 6,010/4,520. **Course rating:** 68.2/64.9. **Slope:** 110/101. **Architect:** William and David Gordon. **Green fee:** $11/$20. **Credit cards:** None. **Reduced fees:** Weekdays, low season, seniors, juniors. **Caddies:** No. **Golf carts:** $9. **Discount golf packages:** No. **Season:** Year-round. **High:** April-Sept. **On site lodging:** No. **Rental clubs:** No. **Walking policy:** Unrestricted walking. **Metal spikes allowed:** Yes. **Range:** Yes. **To obtain tee times:** Call golf shop.
Subscriber comments: Fast greens, hills...Nice course for average golfer...Pleasant mountain course.

★½BON-AIR GOLF CLUB
PU-505 McCormick Rd., Coraopolis, 15108, Allegheny County, (412)262-2992, 10 miles W of Pittsburgh.
Opened: 1932. **Holes:** 18. **Par:** 71/73. **Yards:** 5,821/4,809. **Course rating:** 68.5/69.5. **Slope:** 117/120. **Architect:** N/A. **Green fee:** $11/$18. **Credit cards:** MC,VISA. **Reduced fees:** Weekdays, low season, seniors. **Caddies:** No. **Golf carts:** $11. **Discount golf packages:** Yes. **Season:** Year-round. **High:** April-Sept. **On site lodging:** No. **Rental clubs:** Yes. **Walking policy:** Walking at certain times. **Metal spikes allowed:** Yes. **Range:** No. **To obtain tee times:** Call 24 hours in advance.

BRIARWOOD GOLF CLUB
PU-4775 W. Market St., York, 17404, York County, (717)792-9776, (800)432-1555, 40 miles N of Baltimore, MD.
Green fee: $18/$25. **Credit cards:** MC,VISA,MAC/Cirrus. **Reduced fees:** Weekdays, low season, resort guests, twilight, seniors. **Caddies:** No. **Golf carts:** $12. **Discount golf packages:** Yes. **Season:** Year-round. **High:** March-Oct. **On site lodging:** No. **Rental clubs:** Yes. **Walking policy:** Unrestricted walking. **Metal spikes allowed:** Yes. **To obtain tee times:** Call.
★★½EAST COURSE
Opened: 1955. **Holes:** 18. **Par:** 72/72. **Yards:** 6,550/5,120. **Course rating:** 69.7/67.8. **Slope:** 116/112. **Architect:** Charles Klingensmith. **Range:** Yes (grass/mats).
Subscriber comments: Great greens...Old course, wide open, big greens, okay conditions...Wide open, can let it rip...Medium difficulty...Always well groomed...Good greens.
★★½WEST COURSE
Opened: 1990. **Holes:** 18. **Par:** 70/70. **Yards:** 6,350/4,820. **Course rating:** 69.7/67.3. **Slope:** 119/112. **Architect:** Ault and Clark. **Range:** No.
Subscriber comments: Scenic course, helpful people...Nice layout but too short from whites...Good but crowded...Walk anytime, some great holes.

★★★★THE BRIDGES GOLF CLUB
PU-6729 York Rd, Abbottstown, 17301, Adams County, (717)624-9551, 17 miles W of York.
Opened: 1995. **Holes:** 18. **Par:** 72/72. **Yards:** 6,713/5,104. **Course rating:** 71.7/69.6. **Slope:** 132/113. **Architect:** Altland Brothers. **Green fee:** $26/$37. **Credit cards:** All major. **Reduced fees:** Weekdays, resort guests, seniors, juniors. **Caddies:** No. **Golf carts:** $12. **Discount golf packages:** Yes. **Season:** March-Dec. **High:** N/A. **On site lodging:** Yes. **Rental clubs:** Yes. **Walking policy:** Unrestricted walking. **Metal spikes allowed:** No. **Range:** Yes (grass). **To obtain tee times:** Call 14 days in advance.
Subscriber comments: Exceptional layout, beautiful course, covered bridges...Excellent conditions, bent fairways and greens, hidden gem...Championship golf course, best in area...Carved out of the woods...Best new course in area...Great condition for new course, too expensive...Nice variety of holes. Use every club.

★★★BUCK HILL GOLF CLUB
Golf Dr., Buck Hill Falls, 18323, Monroe County, (717)595-7730, 50 miles N of Allentown.
Opened: 1901. **Holes:** 27. **Architect:** Donald Ross. **Green fee:** $30/$45. **Credit cards:**

MC,VISA. **Reduced fees:** Twilight. **Caddies:** No. **Golf carts:** $14. **Discount golf packages:** No. **Season:** April-Nov. **High:** June-Sept. **On site lodging:** No. **Rental clubs:** Yes. **Walking policy:** Mandatory cart. **Metal spikes allowed:** Yes. **Range:** Yes (grass). **To obtain tee times:** Call 7 days in advance. Groups of 12 or more may call farther in advance.

RED/BLUE
Par: 70/72. **Yards:** 6,150/5,370. **Course rating:** 69.8/70.2. **Slope:** 120/121.
RED/WHITE
Par: 70/72. **Yards:** 6,300/5,620. **Course rating:** 70.4/71.2. **Slope:** 122/124.
WHITE/BLUE
Par: 72/72. **Yards:** 6,450/5,550. **Course rating:** 71.0/72.8. **Slope:** 126/126.
Subscriber comments: Nice course, a little expensive...Red Course is a hidden gem. No houses...Old Donald Ross style...Tough course, very well maintained...Plenty of uphill, downhill, sidehill lies.

★★★½BUCKNELL GOLF CLUB
Rte. No.1, Lewisburg, 17837, Union County, (717)523-8193, 60 miles N of Harrisburg.
Opened: 1930. **Holes:** 18. **Par:** 70/71. **Yards:** 6,268/5,387. **Course rating:** 70.3/71.2. **Slope:** 128/122. **Architect:** Edmund B. Ault. **Green fee:** $25/$32. **Credit cards:** All major. **Reduced fees:** Weekdays. **Caddies:** No. **Golf carts:** $13. **Discount golf packages:** No. **Season:** March-Nov. **High:** June-Aug. **On site lodging:** No. **Rental clubs:** Yes. **Walking policy:** Unrestricted walking. **Metal spikes allowed:** Yes. **Range:** Yes (grass). **To obtain tee times:** Call 7 days in advance.
Subscriber comments: Very enjoyable, easy to get on...Great course in sleepy college town...A hidden gem, excellent overall value...Narrow and treelined, a challenge for most...Beautiful course, no gimmicks.
Special Notes: Spikeless encouraged.

(GOOD VALUE)

★★★BUTLER'S GOLF COURSE
PU-800 Rock Run Rd., Elizabeth, 15037, Allegheny County, (412)751-9121, 15 miles SE of Pittsburgh.
Opened: 1928. **Holes:** 18. **Par:** 72/73. **Yards:** 6,606/5,560. **Course rating:** 68.9/70.8. **Slope:** 117/119. **Architect:** John Butler. **Green fee:** $18/$28. **Credit cards:** All major,Diner's Club. **Reduced fees:** Weekdays, low season, twilight, seniors, juniors. **Caddies:** No. **Golf carts:** $20. **Discount golf packages:** No. **Season:** Year-round. **High:** April-Oct. **On site lodging:** Yes. **Rental clubs:** Yes. **Walking policy:** Walking at certain times. **Metal spikes allowed:** Yes. **Range:** Yes (grass). **To obtain tee times:** Call 7 days in advance for weekday. Call Tuesday 10 a.m. for weekend play.
Subscriber comments: Best four closing holes in western Pa....Lots of play, good shape...Nice course with tough holes...Good greens and fairways, easy walking, very good layout...One of best around Pittsburgh.

★★½CABLE HOLLOW GOLF CLUB
PU-RD #2, Norberg Rd, Russell, 16345, Warren County, (814)757-4765, 150 miles N of Pittsburgh.
Opened: 1968. **Holes:** 18. **Par:** 72/73. **Yards:** 6,300/5,200. **Course rating:** 68.7/69.0. **Slope:** 108/109. **Architect:** N/A. **Green fee:** $8/$17. **Credit cards:** All major. **Reduced fees:** Weekdays, low season, twilight, seniors. **Caddies:** No. **Golf carts:** $18. **Discount golf packages:** No. **Season:** March-Nov. **High:** June-Aug. **On site lodging:** No. **Rental clubs:** Yes. **Walking policy:** Unrestricted walking. **Metal spikes allowed:** Yes. **Range:** No. **To obtain tee times:** Call anytime in advance.
Subscriber comments: A true gem, beautiful to play in the fall...Great value with even better scenery!

CARROLL VALLEY GOLF RESORT
R- **Architect:** Ed Ault. **Credit cards:** MC,VISA,DISC. **Reduced fees:** Weekdays, low season, resort guests, twilight, seniors. **Caddies:** No. **Golf carts:** $12. **Discount golf packages:** Yes. **High:** April-Oct. **Rental clubs:** Yes. **Metal spikes allowed:** Yes.
★★★½CARROLL VALLEY COURSE
121 Sanders Rd., Fairfield, 17320, Adams County, (717)642-8252, (800)548-8504, 10 miles W of Gettysburg.

Opened: 1965. **Holes:** 18. **Par:** 71/72. **Yards:** 6,633/5,005. **Course rating:** 71.2/67.6. **Slope:** 120/114. **Green fee:** $22/$29. **Season:** Year-round. **On site lodging:** Yes. **Walking policy:** Walking at certain times. **Range:** No. **To obtain tee times:** Call Friday for following Monday-Sunday tee times. Groups and packages may call farther in advance.
Subscriber comments: Truly a mountain resort course. A shotmakers course...Great course, scenic...Long par 3s, scenic, good solid golf...Six par 3s, six par 4s and six par 5s...Some tough par 3s for average golfer.

★★★MOUNTAIN VIEW COURSE
Bullfrog Rd., Fairfield, 17320, Adams County, (717)642-5848, 8 miles W of Gettysburg.
Opened: 1979. **Holes:** 18. **Par:** 71/70. **Yards:** 6,343/5,024. **Course rating:** 70.2/68.2. **Slope:** 122/113. **Green fee:** $19/$23. **Season:** March-Nov. **On site lodging:** No. **Walking policy:** Unrestricted walking. **Range:** Yes (grass/mats). **To obtain tee times:** Call Friday the following Monday-Sunday tee times. Groups and golf packages may call any time.
Subscriber comments: Front easy, back tight. Nice greens...Hills, water and bunkers...Wide open mostly, long course, scenic...Relative easy, good for a mid-handicap...Open layout, finishing holes tighter...Very flat...Beautiful view of mountains.

★★½CASTLE HILLS GOLF COURSE
PU-110 W. Oakwood Way, New Castle, 16105, Lawrence County, (412)652-8122, 50 miles N of Pittsburgh.
Opened: 1930. **Holes:** 18. **Par:** 72/73. **Yards:** 6,415/5,784. **Course rating:** 69.7/73.3. **Slope:** 118/113. **Architect:** N/A. **Green fee:** $16/$17. **Credit cards:** None. **Reduced fees:** Low season, seniors, juniors. **Caddies:** No. **Golf carts:** $9. **Discount golf packages:** No. **Season:** March-Dec. **High:** May-Sept. **On site lodging:** No. **Rental clubs:** No. **Walking policy:** Unrestricted walking. **Metal spikes allowed:** Yes. **Range:** Yes (grass). **To obtain tee times:** Call.
Subscriber comments: Well kept...Old but nice, short yardage...Scenic course...Good western Pa. public course.

★★CEDAR RIDGE GOLF COURSE
PU-1225 Barlow Two Taverns Rd., Gettysburg, 17325, Adams County, (717)359-4480, 43 miles S of Harrisburg.
Opened: 1987. **Holes:** 18. **Par:** 72/72. **Yards:** 6,132/5,546. **Course rating:** 69.5/69.3. **Slope:** 114/114. **Architect:** Roger Weaver. **Green fee:** $12/$17. **Credit cards:** VISA,AMEX,DISC. **Reduced fees:** Weekdays, low season, twilight, seniors. **Caddies:** No. **Golf carts:** $9. **Discount golf packages:** No. **Season:** Year-round. **High:** April-Nov. **On site lodging:** No. **Rental clubs:** Yes. **Walking policy:** Unrestricted walking. **Metal spikes allowed:** Yes. **Range:** No. **To obtain tee times:** Call.

CEDARBROOK GOLF COURSE
PU-R.D. No.3, Belle Vernon, 15012, Westmoreland County, (412)929-8300, 25 miles SW of Pittsburgh.
Opened: N/A. **Architect:** Michael Hurdzan. **Green fee:** $18/$27. **Credit cards:** All major. **Reduced fees:** Low season, seniors, juniors. **Caddies:** No. **Golf carts:** $10. **Discount golf packages:** No. **Season:** Year-round. **High:** April-Sept. **On site lodging:** No. **Rental clubs:** Yes. **Metal spikes allowed:** Yes. **Range:** Yes (grass/mats). **To obtain tee times:** Call 7 days in advance.

★★★GOLD COURSE
Holes: 18. **Par:** 72/70. **Yards:** 6,710/5,211. **Course rating:** 72.4/70.2. **Slope:** 135/121. **Walking policy:** Walking at certain times.
Subscriber comments: Play it from the tips and it will test you...True championship track, tight fairways, tough doglegs, medium greens...Very tough par 3s. Four sets of tees. Long back nine.

★★★RED COURSE
Holes: 18. **Par:** 71/71. **Yards:** 6,154/4,577. **Course rating:** 68.3/65.3. **Slope:** 120/111. **Walking policy:** Unrestricted walking.
Subscriber comments: Not real long but requires accuracy...The owners took one excellent 18 hole challenge and tried to make two courses. They were better off leaving one alone...Short course, well maintained, challenging bunkers.

★★★CENTER SQUARE GOLF CLUB

PU-Rte. 73 and Whitehall Rd., Center Square, 19422, Montgomery County, (610)584-5700, 20 miles W of Philadelphia.

Opened: 1963. **Holes:** 18. **Par:** 71/73. **Yards:** 6,296/5,598. **Course rating:** 69.3/70.6. **Slope:** 119/114. **Architect:** Edward Ault. **Green fee:** $17/$26. **Credit cards:** MC,VISA. **Reduced fees:** Twilight, seniors. **Caddies:** No. **Golf carts:** $36. **Discount golf packages:** No. **Season:** Year-round. **High:** April-Oct. **On site lodging:** No. **Rental clubs:** Yes. **Walking policy:** Walking at certain times. **Metal spikes allowed:** Yes. **Range:** Yes (grass). **To obtain tee times:** Call eight days in advance for weekdays. Call Wednesday a.m. for weekend.
Notes: 1997, 1980 U.S. Women's Amateur Public Links.
Subscriber comments: Greens kept well, good fairways...Wide open, fun...Fair to all golfers...Nice short course with good variety of holes. Play from tips...Front nine wide open, back nine a little tighter.

★★★½CENTER VALLEY CLUB

PU-3300 Center Valley Pky., Center Valley, 18034, Lehigh County, (610)791-5580, 3 miles S of Allentown/Bethlehem.

Opened: 1992. **Holes:** 18. **Par:** 72/72. **Yards:** 6,904/4,932. **Course rating:** 74.1/70.6. **Slope:** 135/123. **Architect:** Geoffrey Cornish. **Green fee:** $29/$58. **Credit cards:** All major. **Reduced fees:** Twilight. **Caddies:** No. **Golf carts:** Included in Green Fee. **Discount golf packages:** No. **Season:** Year-round. **High:** May-Oct. **On site lodging:** No. **Rental clubs:** Yes. **Walking policy:** Walking at certain times. **Metal spikes allowed:** Yes. **Range:** Yes (grass/mats). **To obtain tee times:** Call up to 7 days in advance with credit card.
Subscriber comments: Nine holes links, nine holes American, received a bucket of balls free with playing...Good test, range of tees...Class course, tough, well-designed...One of the best in eastern Pa....Upscale course, challenging for average golfer...Sixteen super holes.

★★★½CHAMPION LAKES GOLF COURSE

PU-R.D. 1, Box 285, Bolivar, 15923, Westmoreland County, (412)238-5440, 50 miles E of Pittsburgh.

Opened: 1968. **Holes:** 18. **Par:** 71/74. **Yards:** 6,608/5,556. **Course rating:** 69.0/72.1. **Slope:** 128/127. **Architect:** Paul Erath. **Green fee:** $22/$27. **Credit cards:** None. **Reduced fees:** Weekdays, low season. **Caddies:** No. **Golf carts:** $10. **Discount golf packages:** No. **Season:** April-Dec. **High:** May-Sept. **On site lodging:** Yes. **Rental clubs:** Yes. **Walking policy:** Unrestricted walking. **Metal spikes allowed:** Yes. **Range:** Yes (grass/mats). **To obtain tee times:** Call.
Subscriber comments: Take your "A" game. Long, narrow, tough. I love it...One of the best in Pa. Beautiful layout...You better be a straight hitter to score on this course....Nice area of Pennsylvania...Western Pa.'s best kept secret, outstanding.

★★CHEROKEE GOLF COURSE

PU-217 Elysburg Rd., Danville, 17821, North Umberland County, (717)275-2005, 50 miles N of Harrisburg.

Opened: 1973. **Holes:** 18. **Par:** 72/72. **Yards:** 6,037/4,524. **Course rating:** 68.4/65.1. **Slope:** 114/102. **Architect:** Brouse Family. **Green fee:** $14/$17. **Credit cards:** All major. **Reduced fees:** Weekdays. **Caddies:** No. **Golf carts:** $9. **Discount golf packages:** No. **Season:** Year-round. **High:** May-Aug. **On site lodging:** No. **Rental clubs:** Yes. **Walking policy:** Unrestricted walking. **Metal spikes allowed:** Yes. **Range:** No. **To obtain tee times:** Call anytime.

CHERRY WOOD GOLF COURSE

PU-204 Truxall Rd., Apollo, 15613-9005, Westmoreland County, (412)727-2546, 35 miles NE of Pittsburgh.

Opened: 1997. **Holes:** 9. **Par:** 70/70. **Yards:** 6,230/3,970. **Course rating:** N/A. **Slope:** N/A. **Architect:** John S. Chernega. **Green fee:** $16/$18. **Credit cards:** MC,VISA. **Reduced fees:** Weekdays, seniors. **Caddies:** No. **Golf carts:** $20. **Discount golf packages:** No. **Season:** April-Oct. **High:** N/A. **On site lodging:** No. **Rental clubs:** Yes. **Walking policy:** Unrestricted walking. **Metal spikes allowed:** Yes. **Range:** Yes (grass). **To obtain tee times:** Call.

★★★★CHESTNUT RIDGE GOLF CLUB

PU-R.D. 1, Box 578, Blairsville, 15717, Indiana County, (412)459-7188, (800)770-0000, 35 miles E of Pittsburgh.
Opened: 1993. **Holes:** 18. **Par:** 72/72. **Yards:** 6,812/5,363. **Course rating:** 73.0/71.2. **Slope:** 134/126. **Architect:** Bill Love and Ault and Clark.
Green fee: $40/$49. **Credit cards:** MC,VISA,AMEX. **Reduced fees:** Weekdays, twilight. **Caddies:** No. **Golf carts:** $10. **Discount golf packages:** Yes. **Season:** April-Nov. **High:** April-Nov. **On site lodging:** No. **Rental clubs:** No. **Walking policy:** Unrestricted walking. **Metal spikes allowed:** Yes. **Range:** Yes (grass). **To obtain tee times:** Call 7 days in advance.
Subscriber comments: Front nine placement golf, back nine open and longer...Country club quality, holes 3, 4 and 5 beautiful...Easy to play for ladies. Pretty level...First class operation with a good price/value...First six holes laid out as well as any in country...Beautiful clubhouse.

★★COBB'S CREEK GOLF CLUB

PU-72 Lansdowne Ave., Philadelphia, 19151, Philadelphia County, (215)877-8707.
Opened: 1916. **Holes:** 18. **Par:** 71/71. **Yards:** 6,660/6,130. **Course rating:** 68.6/68.1. **Slope:** 117/114. **Architect:** Hugh Wilson. **Green fee:** $22/$26. **Credit cards:** All major. **Reduced fees:** Weekdays, twilight, seniors, juniors. **Caddies:** No. **Golf carts:** $26. **Discount golf packages:** No. **Season:** Year-round. **High:** April-Oct. **On site lodging:** No. **Rental clubs:** Yes. **Walking policy:** Unrestricted walking. **Metal spikes allowed:** Yes. **Range:** Yes (grass/mats). **To obtain tee times:** Call 7 days in advance.
Special Notes: Also has 18-hole Karakung Course.

★★CONLEY'S RESORT INN

R-740 Pittsburgh Rd., Butler, 16001, Butler County, (412)586-7711, (800)344-7303, 30 miles N of Pittsburgh.
Opened: 1963. **Holes:** 18. **Par:** 72/72. **Yards:** 6,200/5,625. **Course rating:** 69.0/69.0. **Slope:** 110/110. **Architect:** Nicholas Innotti. **Green fee:** $19/$28. **Credit cards:** All major. **Reduced fees:** Weekdays, low season, resort guests, twilight, seniors. **Caddies:** No. **Golf carts:** $11. **Discount golf packages:** Yes. **Season:** Year-round. **High:** April-Oct. **On site lodging:** Yes. **Rental clubs:** Yes. **Walking policy:** Walking at certain times. **Metal spikes allowed:** Yes. **Range:** No. **To obtain tee times:** Call up to one year in advance.

★★½COOL CREEK COUNTRY CLUB

PU-Cool Creek Rd., Wrightsville, 17368, York County, (717)252-3691, (800)942-2444, 10 miles W of Lancaster.
Opened: 1948. **Holes:** 18. **Par:** 71/70. **Yards:** 6,521/5,703. **Course rating:** 71.1/72.6. **Slope:** 118/118. **Architect:** Chester Ruby. **Green fee:** $22/$30. **Credit cards:** MC,VISA,AMEX. **Reduced fees:** Weekdays, low season, resort guests, twilight, seniors, juniors. **Caddies:** No. **Golf carts:** $12. **Discount golf packages:** Yes. **Season:** Year-round. **High:** April-Oct. **On site lodging:** No. **Rental clubs:** Yes. **Walking policy:** Walking at certain times. **Metal spikes allowed:** Yes. **Range:** Yes (mats). **To obtain tee times:** Call. Credit cards required to reserve tee times during high season on weekends.
Subscriber comments: Nice tight course with rolling hills...No.13 tough driving hole.

★★½COREY CREEK GOLF CLUB

U.S. Rte. No.6 E., Mansfield, 16933, Tioga County, (717)662-3520, 35 miles SW of Elmira, NY.
Opened: 1927. **Holes:** 18. **Par:** 72/72. **Yards:** 6,571/4,920. **Course rating:** 71.1/66.0. **Slope:** 120/110. **Architect:** Herb Peterson/Jack Marsh. **Green fee:** $10/$20. **Credit cards:** MC,VISA. **Reduced fees:** Weekdays, low season, twilight. **Caddies:** No. **Golf carts:** $12. **Discount golf packages:** Yes. **Season:** April-Nov. **High:** May-Oct. **On site lodging:** No. **Rental clubs:** Yes. **Walking policy:** Walking at certain times. **Metal spikes allowed:** Yes. **Range:** No. **To obtain tee times:** Call anytime in advance.
Subscriber comments: Good value...Difficult greens...Undulating greens are the character of this course...Scenic views, good service.

PENNSYLVANIA

★★★★COUNTRY CLUB AT WOODLOCH SPRINGS
R-Woodloch Dr., Hawley, 18428, Wayne County, (717)685-2100, 50 miles E of Scranton.
Opened: 1992. **Holes:** 18. **Par:** 72/72. **Yards:** 6,579/4,973. **Course rating:** 72.3/71.6. **Slope:** 143/130. **Architect:** Rocky Roquemore. **Green fee:** $46/$70. **Credit cards:** MC,VISA,AMEX. **Reduced fees:** Weekdays. **Caddies:** No. **Golf carts:** Included in Green Fee. **Discount golf packages:** No. **Season:** May-Oct. **High:** June-Aug. **On site lodging:** Yes. **Rental clubs:** Yes. **Walking policy:** Walking at certain times. **Metal spikes allowed:** No. **Range:** Yes (grass/mats). **To obtain tee times:** Call 7 days in advance.
Subscriber comments: Want to go back, tough but fun...Nice mountain course, many carries over wetlands, chasms...Challenge for every golfer, great greens...Magnificent.

COUNTRY CLUB OF HERSHEY
R-1000 E. Derry Rd., Hershey, 17033, Dauphin County, (717)533-2464, (800)900-4653, 12 miles E of Harrisburg.
Credit cards: MC,VISA,AMEX. **Reduced fees:** Weekdays, low season, twilight. **Caddies:** No. **Golf carts:** Included in Green Fee. **Discount golf packages:** Yes. **Season:** Year-round. **High:** May-Oct. **On site lodging:** Yes. **Rental clubs:** Yes. **Metal spikes allowed:** Yes. **Range:** Yes (grass). **To obtain tee times:** Call golf shop.
★★★½EAST COURSE
Opened: 1970. **Holes:** 18. **Par:** 71/71. **Yards:** 7,061/5,645. **Course rating:** 73.6/71.6. **Slope:** 128/127. **Architect:** George Fazio. **Green fee:** $64/$82. **Walking policy:** Mandatory cart.
Notes: 1997 Nike Hershey Open.
Subscriber comments: Excellent conditioned course...Many elevated greens...Fast greens, long and tough, good challenge...Tight and tricky, unique par 3s...Strong aroma of chocolate...Long, hard, immaculate, must play...Good test of golf.
★★★★WEST COURSE
Opened: 1930. **Holes:** 18. **Par:** 73/76. **Yards:** 6,860/5,908. **Course rating:** 73.1/74.7. **Slope:** 131/127. **Architect:** Maurice McCarthy. **Green fee:** $84/$107. **Walking policy:** Mandatory cart.
Notes: 1940 PGA Championship; 1975-94 LPGA Keystone Open.
Subscriber comments: Belongs in the top 50...Great par 3s...Nice traditional course...Some unique holes, good conditioning...Good course and service, good shape...Classic. A "must play" course.
Special Notes: Formerly Hershey Country Club.
★★★½SOUTH COURSE
PU-600 W Derry Rd, Hershey, 17033, Dauphin County, (717)534-3450, (800)900-4653, 12 miles E of Harrisburg.
Opened: 1927. **Holes:** 18. **Par:** 70/71. **Yards:** 6,103/4,817. **Course rating:** 69.8/69.6. **Slope:** 121/107. **Architect:** Maurice McCarthy. **Green fee:** $35/$43. **Golf carts:** N/A. **Walking policy:** Walking at certain times.
Subscriber comments: Nice short course, great condition...Loved it, more like the old-time courses...Great track. Tough...9th and 10th are awesome...A pleasure to play, should not be considered the poor Hershey stepchild.
Special Notes: Formerly Hershey Parkview Golf Course.

★★★CROSS CREEK RESORT
PU-P.O. Box 432, Titusville, 16354, Crawford County, (814)827-9611, 56 miles S of Erie.
Opened: 1959. **Holes:** 18. **Par:** 70/70. **Yards:** 6,495/5,285. **Course rating:** 68.6/68.4. **Slope:** 112/108. **Architect:** Ferdinand Garbin. **Green fee:** $28. **Credit cards:** All major. **Reduced fees:** Low season. **Caddies:** No. **Golf carts:** $13. **Discount golf packages:** Yes. **Season:** April-Oct. **High:** June-Aug. **On site lodging:** Yes. **Rental clubs:** No. **Walking policy:** Walking at certain times. **Metal spikes allowed:** Yes. **Range:** No. **To obtain tee times:** Call.
Subscriber comments: Challenging course layout, keeps you coming back...Great resort, golf and food great...Golf packages are the best...Outstanding course, facilities and service...Course nice, you can score...Absolutely the best outing course in the northeast...Great, fair for all golfers.

★★★ CULBERTSON HILLS GOLF RESORT
R-Rte. 6N W., Edinboro, 16412, Erie County, (814)734-3114, 15 miles S of Erie.
Opened: 1931. **Holes:** 18. **Par:** 72/73. **Yards:** 7,012/5,815. **Course rating:** 71.7/72.9.
Slope: 123/123. **Architect:** Thomas Bendelow. **Green fee:** $22/$25. **Credit cards:**
MC,VISA. **Reduced fees:** Weekdays, low season, resort guests, twilight, seniors,
juniors. **Caddies:** No. **Golf carts:** $12. **Discount golf packages:** Yes. **Season:** April-
Nov. **High:** June-Aug. **On site lodging:** Yes. **Rental clubs:** Yes. **Walking policy:**
Walking at certain times. **Metal spikes allowed:** Yes. **Range:** No. **To obtain tee times:**
Call.
Subscriber comments: Only 18 of the toughest, longest holes I've played...Good
course with a lot of potential. No sand traps...Near Edinboro Lake, beautiful course.
Large greens...Good size greens, need to be long and straight.

★★½ CUMBERLAND GOLF CLUB
2395 Ritner Hwy., Carlisle, 17013, Cumberland County, (717)249-5538, 5 miles S of
Carlisle.
Opened: 1962. **Holes:** 18. **Par:** 72. **Yards:** 6,900. **Course rating:** 70.4. **Slope:** 121.
Architect: James Gilmore Harrison and Ferdinand Garbin. **Green fee:** $13/$18. **Credit
cards:** All major. **Reduced fees:** N/A. **Caddies:** No. **Golf carts:** $18. **Discount golf
packages:** No. **Season:** March-Dec. **High:** April-Sept. **On site lodging:** No. **Rental
clubs:** Yes. **Walking policy:** N/A. **Metal spikes allowed:** Yes. **Range:** Yes (grass/mats).
To obtain tee times: Call in advance.
Subscriber comments: Basic public course, good mix of long and short holes...Price
makes this course as attractive as any...Mature trees, greens always in good
shape...Beautiful greens...Course has potential...Long and short par 4s, straightaway
par 5s, long par 3s.

★★★½ DAUPHIN HIGHLANDS GOLF COURSE
PU-650 S. Harrisburg St., Harrisburg, 17113, Dauphin County, (717)986-1984, 5 miles
E of Harrisburg.
Opened: 1995. **Holes:** 18. **Par:** 72/72. **Yards:** 7,035/5,327. **Course rating:** 73.4/70.1.
Slope: 125/114. **Architect:** Bill Love and Dan Schnegal. **Green fee:** $19/$28. **Credit
cards:** MC,VISA. **Reduced fees:** Weekdays, low season, twilight, seniors, juniors.
Caddies: No. **Golf carts:** $12. **Discount golf packages:** No. **Season:** Year-round.
High: April-Oct. **On site lodging:** No. **Rental clubs:** Yes. **Walking policy:** Unrestricted
walking. **Metal spikes allowed:** No. **Range:** Yes (grass/mats). **To obtain tee times:**
Call 6 days in advance.
Subscriber comments: Great new course, challenging...Some very interesting
holes...Hard to find, nice layout...A golfing pleasure...First class...Challenging holes, will
get even better as it matures...Good new track, fairly open, fair course...Excellent
course and driving range...Nice layout for a new course, very hilly.

★★ DEEP VALLEY GOLF COURSE
PU-169 Hartmann Rd., Harmony, 16037, Butler County, (412)452-8021, 25 miles NE of
Pittsburgh.
Opened: 1958. **Holes:** 18. **Par:** 72. **Yards:** 6,310. **Course rating:** N/A. **Slope:** N/A.
Architect: N/A. **Green fee:** $11/$16. **Credit cards:** None. **Reduced fees:** Low season,
seniors. **Caddies:** No. **Golf carts:** $21. **Discount golf packages:** No. **Season:** Year-
round. **High:** March-Oct. **On site lodging:** No. **Rental clubs:** Yes. **Walking policy:**
Unrestricted walking. **Metal spikes allowed:** Yes. **Range:** No. **To obtain tee times:**
First come, first served.

★★★½ DEER RUN GOLF CLUB
4321 Monier Rd., Gibsonia, 15044, Allegheny County, (412)265-4800.
Opened: 1994. **Holes:** 18. **Par:** 72/73. **Yards:** 7,018/5,238. **Course rating:** 74.2/71.2.
Slope: 134/128. **Architect:** Ron Forse. **Green fee:** N/A. **Credit cards:** MC,VISA.
Reduced fees: N/A. **Caddies:** No. **Golf carts:** $12. **Discount golf packages:** No.
Season: Year-round. **High:** N/A. **On site lodging:** No. **Rental clubs:** No. **Walking poli-
cy:** N/A. **Metal spikes allowed:** Yes. **Range:** No. **To obtain tee times:** Call.
Subscriber comments: At 7,000 yards, as difficult as any championship course...Nice
track, interesting...Western Pa. needs more courses like this...Great wooded setting,
some great holes, great terrain.

PENNSYLVANIA

★★★DONEGAL HIGHLANDS GOLF CLUB
PU-R.D. No.1, Donegal, 15628, Westmoreland County, (412)423-7888, 35 miles SE of Pittsburgh.
Opened: 1991. **Holes:** 18. **Par:** 72/72. **Yards:** 6,130/4,520. **Course rating:** 69.6/65.7. **Slope:** 121/113. **Architect:** James Gayton/Ron Forse. **Green fee:** $16/$26. **Credit cards:** MC,VISA. **Reduced fees:** Weekdays, low season, seniors, juniors. **Caddies:** No. **Golf carts:** $12. **Discount golf packages:** Yes. **Season:** March-Nov. **High:** June-Aug. **On site lodging:** No. **Rental clubs:** Yes. **Walking policy:** Unrestricted walking. **Metal spikes allowed:** Yes. **Range:** Yes (grass). **To obtain tee times:** Call 7 days in advance.
Subscriber comments: Front nine/back nine altogether different. Some memorable holes....Most of course is short and wide open...Nice practice area...Demanding, No. 17 a great hole.

★★★DOWN RIVER GOLF CLUB
PU-R.D. No.2, P.O. Box 628, Everett, 15537, Bedford County, (814)652-5193, 40 miles S of Altoona.
Opened: 1967. **Holes:** 18. **Par:** 72/73. **Yards:** 6,855/5,513. **Course rating:** 70.5/71.6. **Slope:** 115/118. **Architect:** Xen Hassenplug. **Green fee:** $13/$15. **Credit cards:** All major. **Reduced fees:** Weekdays, twilight, juniors. **Caddies:** No. **Golf carts:** $10. **Discount golf packages:** Yes. **Season:** April-Nov. **High:** June-Sept. **On site lodging:** No. **Rental clubs:** No. **Walking policy:** Unrestricted walking. **Metal spikes allowed:** Yes. **Range:** Yes (grass). **To obtain tee times:** Call up to one week in advance.
Subscriber comments: All around great...Wide open, nice golf...Long and open, easy for walking...Long course, challenging, fast greens...Wide open, greens nice, tough to putt when fast...It gets nicer every year, great staff.

★★★DOWNING GOLF COURSE
PU-Troupe Rd., Harborcreek, 16421, Erie County, (814)899-5827, 6 miles E of Erie.
Opened: 1962. **Holes:** 18. **Par:** 72/74. **Yards:** 7,175/6,259. **Course rating:** 73.0/74.4. **Slope:** 114/115. **Architect:** Garbin and Harrison. **Green fee:** $12/$15. **Credit cards:** None. **Reduced fees:** Low season, twilight. **Caddies:** No. **Golf carts:** $15. **Discount golf packages:** No. **Season:** Year-round. **High:** March-Nov. **On site lodging:** No. **Rental clubs:** No. **Walking policy:** Unrestricted walking. **Metal spikes allowed:** Yes. **Range:** Yes (grass). **To obtain tee times:** For Saturday call on Wednesday; call any-time for other days.
Subscriber comments: Long, easy holes...Long and windy, big, quick, undulating greens...Good length, but wide open and plain. Tough in wind...Beautiful muny. Challenging, yet fair. Staff goes out of their way to help...Very nice municipal course, challenging...Not much trouble, long and open.

★★★½DOWNINGTOWN COUNTRY CLUB
PU-P.O. Box 408, Rte. 30, Downingtown, 19335, Chester County, (610)269-2000, 25 miles W of Philadelphia.
Opened: N/A. **Holes:** 18. **Par:** 72/72. **Yards:** 6,619/5,092. **Course rating:** 72.9/69.4. **Slope:** 132/119. **Architect:** George Fazio. **Green fee:** $38/$49. **Credit cards:** MC,VISA. **Reduced fees:** Weekdays, low season, twilight, seniors. **Caddies:** No. **Golf carts:** $20. **Discount golf packages:** Yes. **Season:** Year-round. **High:** May-Sept. **On site lodging:** No. **Rental clubs:** Yes. **Walking policy:** Unrestricted walking. **Metal spikes allowed:** Yes. **Range:** No. **To obtain tee times:** Call up to 7 days in advance.
Subscriber comments: Nice layout; money well spent on renovations...Good service...Difficult, a short game test...Tough, but fair. Love it...Good golf and at a four-hour pace...Rough pretty deep...Par 3s back to back...Nice layout. Good condition...Nicest public course in Chester County...A thinker's course...Fast, firm greens, walking encouraged...Tremendous resurrection of old public facility...Comeback course of the decade.

★★★DUCK HOLLOW GOLF CLUB
PU-347 Duck Hollow Rd., Uniontown, 15401, Fayette County, (412)439-3150, 40 miles S of Pittsburgh.
Opened: 1975. **Holes:** 18. **Par:** 72/74. **Yards:** 6,538/6,112. **Course rating:** 69.0. **Slope:** N/A. **Architect:** N/A. **Green fee:** $17/$22. **Credit cards:** MC,VISA. **Reduced fees:** Weekdays, low season, seniors, juniors. **Caddies:** No. **Golf carts:** $11. **Discount**

golf packages: Yes. **Season:** Year-round. **High:** June-Aug. **On site lodging:** No. **Rental clubs:** Yes. **Walking policy:** Walking at certain times. **Metal spikes allowed:** No. **Range:** Yes (grass). **To obtain tee times:** Call 7 days in advance.
Subscriber comments: Nice course, make sure to lay up on 15th...Great junior rates...Has changed ownership and is in best shape since constructed.
Special Notes: Formerly Colonial Golf Club.

★★★½EAGLE LODGE COUNTRY CLUB
R-Ridge Pike and Manor Rd., Lafayette Hill, 19444, Montgomery County, (610)940-4787, (800)523-3000, 10 miles W of Philadelphia.
Opened: 1983. **Holes:** 18. **Par:** 71/71. **Yards:** 6,759/5,260. **Course rating:** 72.8/70.4. **Slope:** 130/123. **Architect:** Rees Jones. **Green fee:** $80/$90. **Credit cards:** All major,Diners Club. **Reduced fees:** Low season, resort guests. **Caddies:** No. **Golf carts:** Included in Green Fee. **Discount golf packages:** Yes. **Season:** Year-round. **High:** April-Oct. **On site lodging:** Yes. **Rental clubs:** Yes. **Walking policy:** Mandatory cart. **Metal spikes allowed:** No. **Range:** Yes (grass). **To obtain tee times:** Call with credit card to hold reservation.
Subscriber comments: Feels like a private club; traditional, hilly course...Nice, but demanding...A number of interesting holes...Greens are testers...Tough, classic layout, well-maintained.

★★★EDGEWOOD IN THE PINES GOLF COURSE
PU-Edgewood Rd., Drums, 18201, Luzerne County, (717)788-1101, 25 miles S of Wilkes-Barre.
Opened: 1980. **Holes:** 18. **Par:** 72/72. **Yards:** 6,721/5,184. **Course rating:** 71.9/69.9. **Slope:** N/A. **Architect:** David Gordon. **Green fee:** $15/$17. **Credit cards:** None. **Reduced fees:** Weekdays, low season, twilight. **Caddies:** No. **Golf carts:** $12. **Discount golf packages:** No. **Season:** April-Nov. **High:** May-Aug. **On site lodging:** No. **Rental clubs:** Yes. **Walking policy:** Walking at certain times. **Metal spikes allowed:** Yes. **Range:** No. **To obtain tee times:** Call 7 days in advance.
Subscriber comments: Fairways and greens in good shape, food fair...Back nine enjoyable...Well groomed with lots of traps...One of the best courses in the area, well managed...Short course with some nasty surprises.

★★★½EMPORIUM COUNTRY CLUB
Cameron Rd., Star Rte., Emporium, 15834, Cameron County, (814)486-7715.
Opened: 1954. **Holes:** 18. **Par:** 72/72. **Yards:** 6,032/5,233. **Course rating:** 68.5/69.0. **Slope:** 118/115. **Architect:** Members. **Green fee:** $17/$20. **Credit cards:** None. **Reduced fees:** Weekdays, juniors. **Caddies:** No. **Golf carts:** $9. **Discount golf packages:** Yes. **Season:** March-Nov. **High:** April-Sept. **On site lodging:** No. **Rental clubs:** Yes. **Walking policy:** Mandatory cart. **Metal spikes allowed:** Yes. **Range:** Yes (grass). **To obtain tee times:** Call.
Subscriber comments: Very memorable. Beautifully cut out of a side of a mountain. Very woodsy, fall is a challenging time to find your shot among the leaves...Best within 100 miles...Hilly, well maintained, challenging course.

★½ERIE GOLF CLUB
PU-6050 Old Zuck Rd., Erie, 16506, Erie County, (814)866-0641.
Opened: 1964. **Holes:** 18. **Par:** 69/72. **Yards:** 5,682/4,977. **Course rating:** 67.2/68.2. **Slope:** 111/109. **Architect:** James Gilmore Harrison. **Green fee:** $11/$14. **Credit cards:** None. **Reduced fees:** Twilight, seniors, juniors. **Caddies:** No. **Golf carts:** $15. **Discount golf packages:** No. **Season:** March-Nov. **High:** April-Oct. **On site lodging:** No. **Rental clubs:** Yes. **Walking policy:** Unrestricted walking. **Metal spikes allowed:** Yes. **Range:** No. **To obtain tee times:** Call golf shop.

★½EXETER GOLF CLUB
PU-811 Shelbourne Rd., Reading, 19606, Berks County, (610)779-1211.
Opened: 1957. **Holes:** 9. **Par:** 35/35. **Yards:** 3,000/2,555. **Course rating:** N/A. **Slope:** N/A. **Architect:** Enrico Filippini. **Green fee:** $12/$18. **Credit cards:** MC,VISA. **Reduced fees:** Weekdays, twilight, seniors. **Caddies:** No. **Golf carts:** $20. **Discount golf packages:** No. **Season:** Year-round. **High:** April-Nov. **On site lodging:** No. **Rental clubs:** Yes. **Walking policy:** Unrestricted walking. **Metal spikes allowed:** Yes. **Range:** No. **To obtain tee times:** Call anytime, no restrictions.

★★★FAIRVIEW GOLF COURSE
PU-Rte. 72 South, Quentin, 17083, Lebanon County, (717)273-3411, (800)621-6557, 5 miles S of Lebanon.
Opened: 1959. **Holes:** 18. **Par:** 71/73. **Yards:** 6,227/5,221. **Course rating:** 69.2/72.9. **Slope:** 106/115. **Architect:** Frank Murray and Russell Roberts. **Green fee:** $11/$24. **Credit cards:** MC,VISA. **Reduced fees:** Weekdays, low season, twilight, seniors, juniors. **Caddies:** No. **Golf carts:** $12. **Discount golf packages:** No. **Season:** Year-round. **High:** May-Sept. **On site lodging:** No. **Rental clubs:** Yes. **Walking policy:** Unrestricted walking. **Metal spikes allowed:** Yes. **Range:** Yes. **To obtain tee times:** Call up to 14 days in advance.
Subscriber comments: Good course, easy, good value...Near country club conditions....Has some interesting par 3s...Rolling hills, nice greens.

★★FERNWOOD RESORT & COUNTRY CLUB
R-Rte. 209, Bushkill, 18324, Monroe County, (717)588-9500, (800)233-8103, 42 miles SE of Scranton.
Opened: 1968. **Holes:** 18. **Par:** 72/72. **Yards:** 6,100/4,800. **Course rating:** 68.8/63.3. **Slope:** 125/115. **Architect:** Nicholas Psiahas. **Green fee:** $40/$50. **Credit cards:** MC,VISA,AMEX. **Reduced fees:** Low season, resort guests, twilight. **Caddies:** No. **Golf carts:** Included in Green Fee. **Discount golf packages:** Yes. **Season:** April-Nov. **High:** July-Sept. **On site lodging:** Yes. **Rental clubs:** Yes. **Walking policy:** Mandatory cart. **Metal spikes allowed:** Yes. **Range:** Yes (grass). **To obtain tee times:** Call anytime.

★★½FIVE PONDS GOLF CLUB
PU-1225 W. St. Rd., Warminster, 18974, Bucks County, (215)956-9727, 14 miles N of Philadelphia.
Opened: 1988. **Holes:** 18. **Par:** 71/71. **Yards:** 6,760/5,430. **Course rating:** 71.0/70.1. **Slope:** 121/117. **Architect:** X.G. Hassenplug. **Green fee:** $21/$25. **Credit cards:** MC,VISA,MAC. **Reduced fees:** Weekdays, low season, twilight, seniors. **Caddies:** No. **Golf carts:** $12. **Discount golf packages:** No. **Season:** Year-round. **High:** April-Sept. **On site lodging:** No. **Rental clubs:** Yes. **Walking policy:** Walking at certain times. **Metal spikes allowed:** Yes. **Range:** Yes (grass). **To obtain tee times:** Call 7 days in advance.
Subscriber comments: Excellent for senior golfers...Good design keeps play moving...Fun golf, nice greens, not too easy...Back nine has some very tough holes, a good public course...Takes a heavy traffic load.

★★FLATBUSH GOLF COURSE
PU-940 Littlestown Rd., Littletown, 17340, Adams County, (717)359-7125, 40 miles S of Harrisburg.
Opened: 1989. **Holes:** 18. **Par:** 71/71. **Yards:** 6,717/5,401. **Course rating:** 72.4/72.2. **Slope:** 122/120. **Architect:** Ault & Clark. **Green fee:** $16/$20. **Credit cards:** MC,VISA. **Reduced fees:** Low season, twilight, seniors. **Caddies:** No. **Golf carts:** $10. **Discount golf packages:** No. **Season:** Year-round. **High:** May-Sept. **On site lodging:** No. **Rental clubs:** Yes. **Walking policy:** Unrestricted walking. **Metal spikes allowed:** Yes. **Range:** Yes (grass). **To obtain tee times:** Call 7-10 days in advance, especially for weekends.

★★★FLYING HILLS GOLF COURSE
PU-10 Village Center Dr., Reading, 19607, Berks County, (610)775-4063.
Opened: 1971. **Holes:** 18. **Par:** 70/70. **Yards:** 6,023/5,176. **Course rating:** 68.2/68.8. **Slope:** 118/118. **Architect:** Mr. Rahenkamp. **Green fee:** $14/$17. **Credit cards:** None. **Reduced fees:** Weekdays, low season. **Caddies:** No. **Golf carts:** $10. **Discount golf packages:** No. **Season:** Year-round. **High:** March-Sept. **On site lodging:** No. **Rental clubs:** Yes. **Walking policy:** Unrestricted walking. **Metal spikes allowed:** Yes. **Range:** No. **To obtain tee times:** Call golf shop.
Subscriber comments: Good greens, walking allowed...A bit tight (houses)...Tough track...There are quite a few gut-tightening tee shots here...Hit it straight, fast greens.

★★FOUR SEASONS GOLF CLUB
PU-750 Slocum Ave., Exeter, 18643-1030, Luzerne County, (717)655-8869, 6 miles N of Wilkes-Barre.

PENNSYLVANIA

Opened: 1960. Holes: 18. Par: 70/70. Yards: 5,748/4,306. Course rating: 68.0/66.0. Slope: N/A. Architect: Ferdinand Garbin. Green fee: $12/$14. Credit cards: None. Reduced fees: Weekdays, twilight. Caddies: No. Golf carts: $9. Discount golf packages: No. Season: Year-round. High: May-Sept. On site lodging: No. Rental clubs: Yes. Walking policy: Unrestricted walking. Metal spikes allowed: Yes. Range: Yes (grass). To obtain tee times: Call Monday for weekend or holiday.

★★½FOX HOLLOW GOLF CLUB
PU-2020 Trumbauersville Rd., Quakertown, 18951, Bucks County, (215)538-1920. Opened: 1957. Holes: 18. Par: 71/71. Yards: 6,613/4,984. Course rating: 70.2/67.1. Slope: 123/120. Architect: Dave Gordon. Green fee: $16/$25. Credit cards: MC,VISA. Reduced fees: Weekdays, low season, twilight, seniors, juniors. Caddies: No. Golf carts: $11. Discount golf packages: No. Season: Year-round. High: May-Sept. On site lodging: No. Rental clubs: Yes. Walking policy: Walking at certain times. Metal spikes allowed: Yes. Range: Yes (grass). To obtain tee times: Call anytime in advance.
Subscriber comments: Nice layout, good conditions...Lots of variety, different holes...Short but fun...Scenic back nine...An average course, no big negatives.

★★FOX RUN GOLF COURSE
PU-R.D. No. 2 River Rd., Beaver Falls, 15010, Beaver County, (412)847-3568, 30 miles NW of Pittsburgh.
Opened: 1962. Holes: 18. Par: 72/72. Yards: 6,510/5,337. Course rating: 69.6/72.2. Slope: 113/117. Architect: Max Mesing. Green fee: $14/$17. Credit cards: None. Reduced fees: Low season, seniors, juniors. Caddies: No. Golf carts: $20. Discount golf packages: No. Season: Year-round. High: May-Sept. On site lodging: No. Rental clubs: No. Walking policy: Unrestricted walking. Metal spikes allowed: Yes. Range: Yes (grass/mats). To obtain tee times: Call.

★★★FOXCHASE GOLF CLUB
PU-300 Stevens Rd., Stevens, 17578, Lancaster County, (717)336-3673, 50 miles NW of Philadelphia.
Opened: 1991. Holes: 18. Par: 72/72. Yards: 6,689/4,690. Course rating: 72.7/66.9. Slope: 124/116. Architect: John Thompson. Green fee: $15.50/$38. Credit cards: MC,VISA,DISC. Reduced fees: Weekdays, low season, twilight, seniors, juniors. Caddies: No. Golf carts: Included in Green Fee. Discount golf packages: No. Season: Year-round. High: April-Oct. On site lodging: No. Rental clubs: Yes. Walking policy: Walking at certain times. Metal spikes allowed: Yes. Range: Yes (grass/mats). To obtain tee times: Call pro shop 8 days prior to day of play or use credit card to obtain tee times prior to 8 days.
Subscriber comments: Fairly short course but difficult in wind...Very well kept, short course, open...Large greens...Wide fairways.

★FRANKLIN D. ROOSEVELT GOLF CLUB
PM-20th & Pattison Ave., Philadelphia, 19145, Philadelphia County, (215)462-8997. Opened: N/A. Holes: 18. Par: 69/69. Yards: 5,894/5,413. Course rating: 68.7/68.7. Slope: 113/113. Architect: N/A. Green fee: $17/$21. Credit cards: All major. Reduced fees: Weekdays, twilight, seniors, juniors. Caddies: No. Golf carts: $24. Discount golf packages: No. Season: Year-round. High: N/A. On site lodging: No. Rental clubs: No. Walking policy: Unrestricted walking. Metal spikes allowed: Yes. Range: Yes (grass). To obtain tee times: Call 7 days in advance.

★★★GALEN HALL COUNTRY CLUB
PU-Galen Hall Rd., P.O. Box 129, Wernersville, 19565, Berks County, (610)678-9535. Opened: 1907. Holes: 9. Par: 72/73. Yards: 6,271/5,117. Course rating: 70.2/68.8. Slope: 113/113. Architect: Alex Findlay. Green fee: $16/$20. Credit cards: MC,VISA,DISC. Reduced fees: N/A. Caddies: No. Golf carts: $10. Discount golf packages: No. Season: Year-round. High: May-Oct. On site lodging: Yes. Rental clubs: Yes. Walking policy: Walking at certain times. Metal spikes allowed: Yes. Range: Yes (grass). To obtain tee times: Call anytime.
Subscriber comments: Tough old course, small greens...A lot of sidehill lies...Very hilly, but good views...Blind holes...Greens are like I-95...No. 15 tough test from blues...Nice island green.

★★GENERAL WASHINGTON GOLF COURSE
PU-2750 Egypt Rd., Audubon, 19407, Montgomery County, (610)666-7602, 4 miles W of Philadelphia.
Opened: 1945. **Holes:** 18. **Par:** 70/72. **Yards:** 6,300/5,300. **Course rating:** 67.5/67.4. **Slope:** N/A. **Architect:** William F. Mitchell. **Green fee:** $16/$20. **Credit cards:** None. **Reduced fees:** Low season, twilight, seniors, juniors. **Caddies:** No. **Golf carts:** $22. **Discount golf packages:** Yes. **Season:** Year-round. **High:** April-Oct. **On site lodging:** No. **Rental clubs:** Yes. **Walking policy:** Unrestricted walking. **Metal spikes allowed:** Yes. **Range:** No. **To obtain tee times:** 7 days in advance.

★★½GLEN BROOK COUNTRY CLUB
PU-Glenbrook Rd., Stroudsburg, 18360, Monroe County, (717)421-3680, 75 miles W of New York.
Opened: 1924. **Holes:** 18. **Par:** 72/72. **Yards:** 6,536/5,234. **Course rating:** 71.4/69.4. **Slope:** 123/117. **Architect:** Robert White. **Green fee:** $33/$37. **Credit cards:** None. **Reduced fees:** Weekdays, low season, resort guests, twilight, seniors. **Caddies:** No. **Golf carts:** Included in Green Fee. **Discount golf packages:** Yes. **Season:** April-Nov. **High:** May-Oct. **On site lodging:** Yes. **Rental clubs:** Yes. **Walking policy:** Walking at certain times. **Metal spikes allowed:** Yes. **Range:** No. **To obtain tee times:** Call golf shop.
Subscriber comments: Good golfing, nice day...Short course, charming restaurant...Hilly, tight...Good challenge.

★★THE GOLF CLUB AT SHEPHERD HILLS
PU-1160 S. Krocks Rd., Wescosville, 18106, Lehigh County, (610)391-0644.
Opened: 1964. **Holes:** 18. **Par:** 70/73. **Yards:** 6,500/5,842. **Course rating:** 69.5/70.8. **Slope:** 116/115. **Architect:** N/A. **Green fee:** N/A. **Credit cards:** N/A. **Reduced fees:** N/A. **Caddies:** No. **Golf carts:** N/A. **Discount golf packages:** No. **Season:** Year-round. **High:** May-Sept. **On site lodging:** No. **Rental clubs:** No. **Walking policy:** Unrestricted walking. **Metal spikes allowed:** Yes. **Range:** No. **To obtain tee times:** Call club.

★★½GRAND VIEW GOLF CLUB
PU-1000 Clubhouse Dr., North Braddock, 15104, Allegheny County, (412)351-5390, 8 miles E of Pittsburgh.
Opened: N/A. **Holes:** 18. **Par:** 71/71. **Yards:** 6,111/4,817. **Course rating:** 71.9/69.4. **Slope:** 132/122. **Architect:** N/A. **Green fee:** $32/$42. **Credit cards:** MC,VISA,AMEX. **Reduced fees:** Twilight, seniors, juniors. **Caddies:** No. **Golf carts:** Included in Green Fee. **Discount golf packages:** No. **Season:** Year-round. **High:** April-Sept. **On site lodging:** No. **Rental clubs:** No. **Walking policy:** Walking at certain times. **Metal spikes allowed:** Yes. **Range:** Yes (grass/mats). **To obtain tee times:** Call 7 days in advance.
Subscriber comments: Narrow, go left or right ball is lost...Good golfers can play with all irons...Everyone should play at least once...A fun course but don't keep score.

★★GRANDVIEW GOLF CLUB
PU-2779 Carlisle Rd., York, 17404, York County, (717)764-2674, 4 miles N of York.
Opened: 1924. **Holes:** 18. **Par:** 72/73. **Yards:** 6,639/5,578. **Course rating:** 70.5/71.1. **Slope:** 119/120. **Architect:** N/A. **Green fee:** $17/$23. **Credit cards:** MC,VISA,DISC. **Reduced fees:** Weekdays, low season, resort guests, twilight, seniors, juniors. **Caddies:** No. **Golf carts:** $10. **Discount golf packages:** Yes. **Season:** Year-round. **High:** April-Oct. **On site lodging:** No. **Rental clubs:** Yes. **Walking policy:** Unrestricted walking. **Metal spikes allowed:** Yes. **Range:** No. **To obtain tee times:** Call.

★★½GREEN ACRES GOLF CLUB
PU-RD No.4, Rte. 408, Titusville, 16354, Crawford County, (814)827-3589.
Call club for further information.
Subscriber comments: Cheap golf, some challenging holes...Best buy in basic golf in Pennsylvania...Course is short, but service is great...Well kept.

★★GREEN MEADOWS GOLF COURSE
PU-2451 N Brickyard Rd., North East, 16428, Erie County, (814)725-5009, 15 miles E of Erie.

Caddies: No. **On site lodging:** No. **Walking policy:** Unrestricted walking. **Metal spikes allowed:** Yes.
Opened: 1975. **Holes:** 18. **Par:** 72/71. **Yards:** 5,988/5,144. **Course rating:** 67.1/68.0.
Slope: 102/102. **Architect:** Bob Boyd. **Green fee:** $12/$14. **Credit cards:** N/A.
Reduced fees: Seniors. **Golf carts:** $18. **Discount golf packages:** No. **Season:** April-Oct. **High:** June-Aug. **Rental clubs:** No. **Range:** Yes (grass). **To obtain tee times:** First come, first served.

★★★GREEN MEADOWS GOLF COURSE
R.D. 2, Box 224 Rte. 19, Volant, 16156, Lawrence County, (412)530-7330, 45 miles N of Pittsburgh.
Opened: 1964. **Holes:** 18. **Par:** 72/72. **Yards:** 6,196/5,220. **Course rating:** 68.4.
Slope: 108. **Architect:** N/A. **Green fee:** $15/$18. **Credit cards:** MC,VISA. **Reduced fees:** Weekdays, low season, seniors, juniors. **Golf carts:** $9. **Discount golf packages:** Yes. **Season:** March-Dec. **High:** April-Sept. **Rental clubs:** Yes. **Range:** Yes (grass/mats). **To obtain tee times:** Call golf shop anytime.
Subscriber comments: A little flat, but not a bad layout...Wide open, nice greens...Some nice challenges.

★★GREEN POND COUNTRY CLUB
PU-3604 Farmersville Rd., Bethlehem, 18017, Northampton County, (610)691-9453.
Opened: 1931. **Holes:** 18. **Par:** 71/74. **Yards:** 6,521/5,541. **Course rating:** 69.4/69.7.
Slope: 126/112. **Architect:** Alex Findlay. **Green fee:** $18/$24. **Credit cards:** None.
Reduced fees: Weekdays, twilight, seniors, juniors. **Caddies:** No. **Golf carts:** $12.
Discount golf packages: No. **Season:** Year-round. **High:** April-Nov. **On site lodging:** No. **Rental clubs:** Yes. **Walking policy:** Unrestricted walking. **Metal spikes allowed:** Yes. **Range:** Yes (grass). **To obtain tee times:** Tee times only on weekends, call the Monday before.

★★★GREENCASTLE GREENS GOLF CLUB
2000 Castlegreen Dr., Greencastle, 17225, Franklin County, (717)597-1188, (717)593-9192, 75 miles NW of Baltimore.
Opened: 1991. **Holes:** 18. **Par:** 72/74. **Yards:** 6,908/5,315. **Course rating:** 72.6/70.3.
Slope: 129/124. **Architect:** Robert L. Elder. **Green fee:** $17/$28. **Credit cards:** MC,VISA. **Reduced fees:** Weekdays, low season, twilight, seniors, juniors. **Caddies:** No. **Golf carts:** $11. **Discount golf packages:** Yes. **Season:** Year-round. **High:** April-Oct. **On site lodging:** No. **Rental clubs:** Yes. **Walking policy:** Walking at certain times. **Metal spikes allowed:** Yes. **Range:** Yes (grass/mats). **To obtain tee times:** Call up to 7 days in advance.
Subscriber comments: Super course, friendly clubhouse...Good test for amateur golfers...Par 3s are fun-filled, waterfalls, an island green...One tough customer; especially 10th, water, long course.

★★½HARRISBURG NORTH GOLF COURSE
PU-1724 Rte. 25, Millersburg, 17061, Dauphin County, (717)692-3664, 24 miles NE of Harrisburg.
Opened: 1963. **Holes:** 18. **Par:** 71/71. **Yards:** 6,960/6,600. **Course rating:** 68.8/69.2.
Slope: 115/117. **Architect:** N/A. **Green fee:** $10/$17. **Credit cards:** MC,VISA.
Reduced fees: N/A. **Caddies:** No. **Golf carts:** $25. **Discount golf packages:** No.
Season: Year-round. **High:** June-Aug. **On site lodging:** No. **Rental clubs:** No. **Walking policy:** Unrestricted walking. **Metal spikes allowed:** Yes. **Range:** Yes (grass). **To obtain tee times:** Call anytime.
Subscriber comments: Worth the drive. Varied layout...Front and back nines like two different courses...Back nine very tight...No flat greens...Four of five par 3s are in the 200-yard range...No. 10 very tough, uphill 200-plus over water.
Special Notes: Spikeless shoes preferred.

★★★★½HARTEFELD NATIONAL GOLF CLUB
PU-1 Hartefeld Dr., Avondale, 19311, Chester County, (610)268-8800, (800)240-7373, 35 miles S of Philadelphia.
Opened: 1995. **Holes:** 18. **Par:** 71/71. **Yards:** 6,969/5,065. **Course rating:** 73.2/69.8. **Slope:** 131/123. **Architect:** Tom Fazio. **Green fee:** $50/$95. **Credit cards:** All major. **Reduced fees:** Low season, twilight.

Caddies: No. **Golf carts:** Included in Green Fee. **Discount golf packages:** No. **Season:** Year-round. **High:** May-Oct. **On site lodging:** No. **Rental clubs:** Yes. **Walking policy:** N/A. **Metal spikes allowed:** No. **Range:** Yes (grass/mats). **To obtain tee times:** Call 7 days in advance.
Notes: Ranked 15th in 1997 Best in State; 6th in 1996 Best New Upscale Courses.
Subscriber comments: Beautiful golf course, great views, bit pricey...Long and tough...Better service than most private clubs...Wow! Tom Fazio has outdone himself, tough to get a time...Worthy of a major championship.

★★★HAWK VALLEY GOLF CLUB
PU-1319 Crestview Dr., Denver, 17517, Lancaster County, (717)445-5445, (800)522-4295, 25 miles NE of Lancaster.
Opened: 1971. **Holes:** 18. **Par:** 72/72. **Yards:** 6,628/5,661. **Course rating:** 70.3/70.2. **Slope:** 132/119. **Architect:** William Gordon. **Green fee:** $18/$21. **Credit cards:** MC,VISA,AMEX. **Reduced fees:** Juniors. **Caddies:** No. **Golf carts:** $14. **Discount golf packages:** Yes. **Season:** Year-round. **High:** April-Nov. **On site lodging:** No. **Rental clubs:** Yes. **Walking policy:** Walking at certain times. **Metal spikes allowed:** Yes. **Range:** No. **To obtain tee times:** Weekday call 8 days in advance; weekend and holidays call anytime in advance.
Subscriber comments: Fine course, fast greens...A hidden pleasure!...Fast greens, very picturesque...Even in March course was immaculate.

★★★HERITAGE HILLS GOLF RESORT & CONFERENCE CENTER
R-2700 Mt. Rose Ave., York, 17402, York County, (717)755-4653, (800)942-2444, 25 miles S of Harrisburg.
Opened: 1989. **Holes:** 18. **Par:** 71/71. **Yards:** 6,330/5,075. **Course rating:** 70.6/69.5. **Slope:** 120/116. **Architect:** Russell Roberts. **Green fee:** $25/$32. **Credit cards:** All major. **Reduced fees:** Weekdays, low season, twilight, seniors. **Caddies:** No. **Golf carts:** $12. **Discount golf packages:** No. **Season:** Year-round. **High:** April-Sept. **On site lodging:** Yes. **Rental clubs:** Yes. **Walking policy:** Walking at certain times. **Metal spikes allowed:** Yes. **Range:** Yes (mats). **To obtain tee times:** Call.
Subscriber comments: One of the best in the area. Some very tough, tricky holes...Huge greens...You'll need every club for this one...Very hilly...Good mix of hole layouts...Very good bunkers...Pace of play can be slow...Great five closing holes...Always in great condition.

★★½HICKORY HEIGHTS GOLF CLUB
PU-116 Hickory Heights Dr., Bridgeville, 15017, Allegheny County, (412)257-0300, 12 miles NE of Pittsburgh.
Opened: 1992. **Holes:** 18. **Par:** 72/72. **Yards:** 6,531/5,002. **Course rating:** 71.6/69.6. **Slope:** 131/125. **Architect:** Michael Hurdzan. **Green fee:** $22/$38. **Credit cards:** MC,VISA. **Reduced fees:** Weekdays, low season, twilight, seniors, juniors. **Caddies:** No. **Golf carts:** $3. **Discount golf packages:** No. **Season:** Year-round. **High:** April-Oct. **On site lodging:** No. **Rental clubs:** Yes. **Walking policy:** Walking at certain times. **Metal spikes allowed:** Yes. **Range:** Yes (grass). **To obtain tee times:** Call 5 days in advance.
Subscriber comments: Hilly, plenty of blind shots, don't need to hit driver often...Can be really tough if it's windy...Tough, brutal if your game is marginal.

HICKORY VALLEY GOLF CLUB
PU-1921 Ludwig Rd., Gilbertsville, 19525, Montgomery County, (610)754-9862, 25 miles NW of Philadelphia.
Opened: 1968. **Architect:** Ron Pritchard. **Credit cards:** MC,VISA,DISC. **Reduced fees:** Low season, twilight, seniors, juniors. **Caddies:** No. **Golf carts:** $10. **Discount golf packages:** No. **Season:** Year-round. **High:** April-Oct. **On site lodging:** No. **Rental clubs:** Yes. **Walking policy:** Walking at certain times. **Metal spikes allowed:** Yes. **Range:** Yes (mats).

★★★AMBASSADOR GOLF COURSE
Holes: 18. **Par:** 72/72. **Yards:** 6,442/5,058. **Course rating:** 70.3/69.0. **Slope:** 116/116. **Green fee:** $19/$28. **To obtain tee times:** Call.
Subscriber comments: A lot of water and tree hazards...Small greens...Tough par 3s, worth the stop...New course. Outstanding, great shape. Left-to-right holes a theme...Snakelike creek comes in play all day.

PENNSYLVANIA

PRESIDENTIAL GOLF COURSE
Holes: 18. **Par:** 72/72. **Yards:** 6,676/5,271. **Course rating:** 72.8/71.2. **Slope:** 133/128.
Green fee: $18/$38. **To obtain tee times:** Call 7 days in advance.

★★★½HIDDEN VALLEY FOUR SEASONS RESORT
R-One Craighead Dr., Hidden Valley, 15502, Somerset County, (814)443-8444,
(800)946-5348, 60 miles SE of Pittsburgh.
Opened: 1987. **Holes:** 18. **Par:** 72/72. **Yards:** 6,589/5,027. **Course rating:** 73.5/69.2.
Slope: 142/129. **Architect:** Russell Roberts. **Green fee:** $25/$43. **Credit cards:** All
major,Diners Club. **Reduced fees:** Weekdays, low season, resort guests, twilight.
Caddies: No. **Golf carts:** $16. **Discount golf packages:** Yes. **Season:** April-Nov.
High: June-Aug. **On site lodging:** Yes. **Rental clubs:** Yes. **Walking policy:** Mandatory
cart. **Metal spikes allowed:** Yes. **Range:** Yes (grass/mats). **To obtain tee times:** Call
800 number. Weekday tee times taken 14 days in advance.
Subscriber comments: Short but tight, beautiful views, challenging...A tough test on
the greens....Hell to find, but worth it.
Special Notes: Formerly Golf Club at Hidden Valley. Spikeless shoes encouraged.

★★★½HIDEAWAY HILLS GOLF CLUB
PU-P.O. Box 158, Kresgville, 18333, Monroe County, (610)681-6000, 60 miles N of
Philadelphia.
Opened: 1994. **Holes:** 18. **Par:** 72/72. **Yards:** 6,933/5,047. **Course rating:** 72.7/68.4.
Slope: 127/116. **Architect:** N/A. **Green fee:** $22/$32. **Credit cards:** All major.
Reduced fees: Weekdays, low season, resort guests, twilight. **Caddies:** No. **Golf
carts:** $15. **Discount golf packages:** No. **Season:** March-Dec. **High:** April-Oct. **On
site lodging:** Yes. **Rental clubs:** Yes. **Walking policy:** Mandatory cart. **Metal spikes
allowed:** Yes. **Range:** Yes (mats). **To obtain tee times:** Call golf shop.
Subscriber comments: Very nice; many slope and elevation changes...Great
views...No.10 beautiful driving hole...Nos. 7 and 10 great...Spectacular par 3s...A must
play, words cannot do enough, bring your camera, especially in the fall.

★★★HONEY RUN GOLF & COUNTRY CLUB
3131 S. Salem Church Rd., York, 17404, York County, (717)792-9771, (800)475-4657, 3
miles W of York.
Opened: 1971. **Holes:** 18. **Par:** 72/72. **Yards:** 6,797/5,948. **Course rating:** 72.4/74.0.
Slope: 123/125. **Architect:** Edmund B. Ault. **Green fee:** $20/$29. **Credit cards:**
MC,VISA. **Reduced fees:** Weekdays, low season, resort guests, twilight, seniors,
juniors. **Caddies:** No. **Golf carts:** $9. **Discount golf packages:** Yes. **Season:** Year-
round. **High:** May-Aug. **On site lodging:** No. **Rental clubs:** Yes. **Walking policy:**
Walking at certain times. **Metal spikes allowed:** Yes. **Range:** Yes (grass). **To obtain
tee times:** Call golf shop as far in advance as needed.
Subscriber comments: Big greens...Fun course, one of the best values in South
Central Pa...Tough. Not many flat lies...Outstanding greens, tough course.

★★HORSHAM VALLEY GOLF CLUB
PU-500 Babylon Rd., Ambler, 19002, Montgomery County, (215)646-4707, 15 miles
NW of Philadelphia.
Opened: 1957. **Holes:** 18. **Par:** 66/66. **Yards:** 5,115/4,430. **Course rating:** 62.4/60.8.
Slope: 102/96. **Architect:** Jack Melville/Doug Melville. **Green fee:** $19/$26. **Credit
cards:** All major. **Reduced fees:** Weekdays, low season, twilight, seniors, juniors.
Caddies: No. **Golf carts:** $24. **Discount golf packages:** Yes. **Season:** Year-round.
High: April-Oct. **On site lodging:** No. **Rental clubs:** Yes. **Walking policy:** Unrestricted
walking. **Metal spikes allowed:** Yes. **Range:** Yes (grass). **To obtain tee times:**
Weekdays 1 day in advance; weekends 7 days in advance.

INDIAN RUN GOLF CLUB
PU-24 Penny Lane, Avelia, 15312, Washington County, (412)587-0140.
Opened: 1998. **Holes:** 18. **Par:** 72/72. **Yards:** 6,600/5,050. **Course rating:** 71.2/68.8.
Slope: 136/124. **Architect:** David Black. **Green fee:** $26/$3. **Credit cards:** All major.
Reduced fees: Weekdays, low season, seniors. **Caddies:** No. **Golf carts:** Included in
Green Fee. **Discount golf packages:** No. **Season:** Year-round. **High:** May-Sept. **On
site lodging:** No. **Rental clubs:** No. **Walking policy:** Walking at certain times. **Metal
spikes allowed:** No. **Range:** Yes (grass). **To obtain tee times:** Call.

PENNSYLVANIA

★½INDIAN RUN GOLF COURSE
RD No. 2, Mc Clure, 17841, Snyder County, (717)658-3516.
Call club for further information.

★½INGLESIDE GOLF CLUB
PU-300 N. Bailey Rd., Thorndale, 19372, Chester County, (610)384-9128, 45 miles W of Philadelphia.
Opened: 1964. **Holes:** 18. **Par:** N/A. **Yards:** N/A. **Course rating:** N/A. **Slope:** N/A. **Architect:** N/A. **Green fee:** $18/$25. **Credit cards:** MC,VISA. **Reduced fees:** Twilight, seniors, juniors. **Caddies:** No. **Golf carts:** $13. **Discount golf packages:** No. **Season:** Year-round. **High:** April-Oct. **On site lodging:** No. **Rental clubs:** Yes. **Walking policy:** Unrestricted walking. **Metal spikes allowed:** Yes. **Range:** Yes (grass/mats). **To obtain tee times:** Call 7 days in advance.

★★★½IRON MASTERS COUNTRY CLUB
RD No. 1, Roaring Spring, 16673, Bedford County, (814)224-2915, 15 miles S of Altoona.
Opened: 1962. **Holes:** 18. **Par:** 72/75. **Yards:** 6,644/5,683. **Course rating:** 72.2/73.6. **Slope:** 130/119. **Architect:** Edmund B. Ault. **Green fee:** $31/$31. **Credit cards:** MC,VISA. **Reduced fees:** Weekdays. **Caddies:** No. **Golf carts:** $14. **Discount golf packages:** Yes. **Season:** April-Dec. **High:** June-Aug. **On site lodging:** No. **Rental clubs:** Yes. **Walking policy:** Unrestricted walking. **Metal spikes allowed:** Yes. **Range:** Yes. **To obtain tee times:** Call 14 days in advance.
Subscriber comments: Best in spring and fall....Very tight, iron course only...Blind tee shots, fast greens, interesting, hilly, wooded...You'll need every shot in the bag...Few slants on fairway. Decent shape.

★½JOHN F. BYRNE GOLF COURSE
PU-9500 Leon St., Philadelphia, 19114, Philadelphia County, (215)632-8666.
Opened: N/A. **Holes:** 18. **Par:** 67/67. **Yards:** 5,200/4,662. **Course rating:** 65.0/61.4. **Slope:** 107/98. **Architect:** N/A. **Green fee:** $16/$20. **Credit cards:** All major. **Reduced fees:** Weekdays, low season, twilight, seniors, juniors. **Caddies:** No. **Golf carts:** $25. **Discount golf packages:** Yes. **Season:** Year-round. **High:** May-Oct. **On site lodging:** No. **Rental clubs:** Yes. **Walking policy:** Unrestricted walking. **Metal spikes allowed:** Yes. **Range:** No. **To obtain tee times:** Call 7 days in advance.

★★KIMBERTON GOLF CLUB
PU-Rte. 23, Kimberton, 19442, Chester County, (610)933-8836, 30 miles W of Philadelphia.
Opened: 1962. **Holes:** 18. **Par:** 70/71. **Yards:** 6,304/5,010. **Course rating:** 69.4/67.4. **Slope:** 123/112. **Architect:** George Fazio. **Green fee:** $13/$25. **Credit cards:** MC,VISA. **Reduced fees:** Weekdays, low season, twilight, seniors, juniors. **Caddies:** No. **Golf carts:** $20. **Discount golf packages:** No. **Season:** Year-round. **High:** May-Sept. **On site lodging:** No. **Rental clubs:** Yes. **Walking policy:** Unrestricted walking. **Metal spikes allowed:** Yes. **Range:** No. **To obtain tee times:** Call 7 days in advance.

★★★LENAPE HEIGHTS GOLF COURSE
PU-950 Golf Course Rd., Ford City, 16226, Armstrong County, (412)763-2201, 40 miles NE of Pittsburgh.
Opened: 1967. **Holes:** 18. **Par:** 71/71. **Yards:** 6,145/4,869. **Course rating:** 69.0/67.4. **Slope:** 120/114. **Architect:** Ferdinand Garbin. **Green fee:** $12/$15. **Credit cards:** MC,VISA. **Reduced fees:** Weekdays. **Caddies:** No. **Golf carts:** $9. **Discount golf packages:** No. **Season:** March-Nov. **High:** April-Sept. **On site lodging:** No. **Rental clubs:** Yes. **Walking policy:** Unrestricted walking. **Metal spikes allowed:** Yes. **Range:** No. **To obtain tee times:** Call Tuesday for upcoming weekend.
Subscriber comments: Fair to middling front; improving new back...Par 5 moat hole is great...A new back nine, a hilly front, you'll hit every club in the bag...Blue collar course...Well kept.

★★½LIMEKILN GOLF CLUB
PU-1176 Limekiln Pike, Ambler, 19002, Montgomery County, (215)643-0643, 10 miles NW of Philadelphia.

Opened: 1966. **Holes:** 27. **Architect:** Wrenn/Janis. **Green fee:** $22/$28. **Credit cards:** MC,VISA. **Reduced fees:** Low season, twilight, seniors. **Caddies:** No. **Golf carts:** $12. **Discount golf packages:** No. **Season:** Year-round. **High:** April-Oct. **On site lodging:** No. **Rental clubs:** Yes. **Walking policy:** Walking at certain times. **Metal spikes allowed:** Yes. **Range:** Yes (grass/mats). **To obtain tee times:** Call Monday for upcoming weekend. Tee times required for weekends and holidays.

BLUE/RED
Par: 70/72. **Yards:** 6,200/5,282. **Course rating:** 67.5/67.5. **Slope:** 114/114.
RED/WHITE
Par: 70/71. **Yards:** 6,240/5,227. **Course rating:** 67.8/67.8. **Slope:** 114/114.
WHITE/BLUE
Par: 70/71. **Yards:** 6,415/5,848. **Course rating:** 68.7/68.7. **Slope:** 114/114.
Subscriber comments: Blue nine toughest...Holes range from easy to very difficult...Course is always in good shape...White/Blue best combo.

★★★**LINDEN HALL GOLF CLUB**
R-R.D. No. 1, Dawson, 15428, Fayette County, (412)529-2366, (800)944-3238, 37 miles S of Pittsburgh.
Opened: 1950. **Holes:** 18. **Par:** 72/77. **Yards:** 6,675/5,900. **Course rating:** 71.2/73.6. **Slope:** 122/123. **Architect:** N/A. **Green fee:** $18/$25. **Credit cards:** All major. **Reduced fees:** Weekdays, low season, resort guests, seniors, juniors. **Caddies:** No. **Golf carts:** $22. **Discount golf packages:** Yes. **Season:** Year-round. **High:** March-Nov. **On site lodging:** Yes. **Rental clubs:** Yes. **Walking policy:** Unrestricted walking. **Metal spikes allowed:** Yes. **Range:** Yes. **To obtain tee times:** Call.
Subscriber comments: Great surroundings and view...Long, but wide open. Huge greens...Great par 3s...Good length, walkable, No. 6 a great par 4.

★★**LOCH NAIRN GOLF CLUB**
PU-RR No. 1, McCue Rd., Avondale, 19311, Chester County, (610)268-2234.
Call club for further information.

★★★**LOCUST VALLEY GOLF CLUB**
PU-5525 Locust Valley Rd., Coopersburg, 18036, Lehigh County, (610)282-4711, 45 miles N of Philadelphia.
Opened: 1954. **Holes:** 18. **Par:** 72/74. **Yards:** 6,451/5,444. **Course rating:** 71.0/71.3. **Slope:** 132/121. **Architect:** William Gordon & Son. **Green fee:** $19/$27. **Credit cards:** MC,VISA. **Reduced fees:** Low season, twilight, seniors. **Caddies:** No. **Golf carts:** $11. **Discount golf packages:** No. **Season:** March-Dec. **High:** May-Sept. **On site lodging:** No. **Rental clubs:** Yes. **Walking policy:** Walking at certain times. **Metal spikes allowed:** Yes. **Range:** No. **To obtain tee times:** Call 7 days in advance.
Subscriber comments: Good from back tees...Firm, fast greens. Tight...Narrow, tree-lined fairways...Challenging course, especially for women.

★★★**LOST CREEK GOLF CLUB**
PU-Rte. No. 35, Oakland Mills, 17076, Juniata County, (717)463-2450.
Call club for further information.
Subscriber comments: Very nice course at a very good price...Worth trying, some real challenging holes...Long and open. You'll use every club in the bag...Nice public course, conditions have improved, fun course to play.

★★½**MACOBY RUN GOLF COURSE**
PU-5275 McLeans Station Rd., Green Lane, 18054, Montgomery County, (215)541-0161, 20 miles SE of Allentown.
Opened: 1991. **Holes:** 18. **Par:** 72. **Yards:** 6,319. **Course rating:** 69.5. **Slope:** 118. **Architect:** David Horn. **Green fee:** $15/$19. **Credit cards:** MC,VISA. **Reduced fees:** Low season, seniors, juniors. **Caddies:** No. **Golf carts:** $9. **Discount golf packages:** No. **Season:** Year-round. **High:** May-Sept. **On site lodging:** No. **Rental clubs:** Yes. **Walking policy:** Unrestricted walking. **Metal spikes allowed:** Yes. **Range:** Yes (grass/mats). **To obtain tee times:** Call 7 days in advance.
Subscriber comments: Excellent value. Fun...Forgiving course...Many elevation changes, get a cart! Great...Wide open, variable speed greens...Neat little course.

★★★MAJESTIC RIDGE GOLF CLUB

PU-2437 Adin Lane, Chambersburg, 17201, Franklin County, (717)267-3444, (888)743-4346, 50 miles S of Harrisburg.
Opened: 1992. **Holes:** 18. **Par:** 72/70. **Yards:** 6,481/4,349. **Course rating:** 72.3/64.4. **Slope:** 132/112. **Architect:** N/A. **Green fee:** $16/$24. **Credit cards:** MC,VISA. **Reduced fees:** Twilight, seniors. **Caddies:** No. **Golf carts:** $12. **Discount golf packages:** Yes. **Season:** Year-round. **High:** May-Sept. **On site lodging:** No. **Rental clubs:** Yes. **Walking policy:** Walking at certain times. **Metal spikes allowed:** Yes. **Range:** Yes (grass). **To obtain tee times:** Call.
Subscriber comments: A lot of blind shots...Great course, friendly clubhouse...Good variety of holes...Condition of course gets better every year...Very challenging! Lots of hidden hazards!...Quite hilly, variety of tees, placement golf.

★★MANADA GOLF CLUB

PU-609 Golf Lane, Grantville, 17028, Dauphin County, (717)469-2400, 15 miles N of Harrisburg.
Opened: 1963. **Holes:** 18. **Par:** 72/72. **Yards:** 6,705/5,276. **Course rating:** 70.7/68.8. **Slope:** 117/111. **Architect:** William Gordon. **Green fee:** $14/$22. **Credit cards:** MC,VISA. **Reduced fees:** Weekdays, low season, twilight, seniors, juniors. **Caddies:** No. **Golf carts:** $11. **Discount golf packages:** No. **Season:** Year-round. **High:** April-Sept. **On site lodging:** No. **Rental clubs:** Yes. **Walking policy:** Unrestricted walking. **Metal spikes allowed:** Yes. **Range:** Yes. **To obtain tee times:** Weekends phone early.

★★½MANOR GOLF CLUB

PU-R.D. 8, Bran Rd., Sinking Spring, 19608, Berks County, (610)678-9597, 75 miles W of Philadelphia.
Opened: 1923. **Holes:** 18. **Par:** 70/70. **Yards:** 5,425/4,660. **Course rating:** 65.7/62.2. **Slope:** 108/101. **Architect:** Alex Findley. **Green fee:** $15/$19. **Credit cards:** N/A. **Reduced fees:** Weekdays, low season, twilight, juniors. **Caddies:** No. **Golf carts:** $10. **Discount golf packages:** No. **Season:** Year-round. **High:** April-Oct. **On site lodging:** No. **Rental clubs:** Yes. **Walking policy:** Unrestricted walking. **Metal spikes allowed:** Yes. **Range:** Yes (grass). **To obtain tee times:** Call golf shop.
Subscriber comments: A lot of hills, fast greens...Short, hilly, hidden greens...Some tight wooded holes...Nice family golf course...Interesting holes, very hilly.

★½MANOR VALLEY GOLF CLUB

PU-2095 Denmark Manor Rd., Export, 15632, Westmoreland County, (412)744-4242, 28 miles E of Pittsburgh.
Opened: 1963. **Holes:** 18. **Par:** 72/79. **Yards:** 6,327/6,327. **Course rating:** 69.9/71.7. **Slope:** N/A. **Architect:** Frye Brothers. **Green fee:** $10/$16. **Credit cards:** None. **Reduced fees:** Seniors. **Caddies:** No. **Golf carts:** $10. **Discount golf packages:** No. **Season:** March-Dec. **High:** April-Oct. **On site lodging:** No. **Rental clubs:** Yes. **Walking policy:** Unrestricted walking. **Metal spikes allowed:** Yes. **Range:** Yes. **To obtain tee times:** Call anytime.

★★½MAYAPPLE GOLF LINKS

PU-1 Mayapple Dr., Carlisle, 17013, Cumberland County, (717)258-4088, 15 miles SW of Harrisburg.
Opened: 1992. **Holes:** 18. **Par:** 71/72. **Yards:** 6,541/5,595. **Course rating:** 71.3/69.6. **Slope:** 116/114. **Architect:** Ron Garl. **Green fee:** $12/$19. **Credit cards:** MC,VISA,AMEX. **Reduced fees:** Weekdays, low season, resort guests, twilight, seniors. **Caddies:** No. **Golf carts:** $29. **Discount golf packages:** No. **Season:** Year-round. **High:** May-Sept. **On site lodging:** No. **Rental clubs:** No. **Walking policy:** Unrestricted walking. **Metal spikes allowed:** Yes. **Range:** Yes (grass). **To obtain tee times:** Call up to one week in advance.
Subscriber comments: Only links-style course in area, very nice...The 17th is a tough hole, don't hit onto mounds...Flat, long, not overly difficult but challenging.

★★★MAYFIELD GOLF CLUB

PU-I-80 Exit 9N Pa. Rte. 68, Clarion, 16214, Clarion County, (814)226-8888, 90 miles NE of Pittsburgh.
Opened: 1974. **Holes:** 18. **Par:** 72/72. **Yards:** 6,990/5,439. **Course rating:** 73.0/71.0.

Slope: 117/118. **Architect:** X.G. Hassenplug. **Green fee:** $12/$22. **Credit cards:** None. **Reduced fees:** Weekdays. **Caddies:** No. **Golf carts:** $10. **Discount golf packages:** Yes. **Season:** April-Oct. **High:** June-Aug. **On site lodging:** Yes. **Rental clubs:** No. **Walking policy:** Walking at certain times. **Metal spikes allowed:** Yes. **Range:** Yes (grass). **To obtain tee times:** Call.

Subscriber comments: Greens are fast and tough...Excellent course...Greens were very sloped...Great back nine...Long, windy, open front nine...Severe slopes on some greens...Well maintained, good greens, challenging.

★★½MEADOWINK GOLF CLUB

PU-4076 Bulltown Rd., Murrysville, 15668, Westmoreland County, (412)327-8243, 20 miles E of Pittsburgh.

Opened: 1970. **Holes:** 18. **Par:** 72/72. **Yards:** 6,139/5,103. **Course rating:** 68.2/66.9. **Slope:** 125/118. **Architect:** Ferdinand Garbin. **Green fee:** $18/$23. **Credit cards:** MC,VISA. **Reduced fees:** Weekdays, low season, seniors. **Caddies:** No. **Golf carts:** $11. **Discount golf packages:** Yes. **Season:** Year-round. **High:** April-Sept. **On site lodging:** No. **Rental clubs:** Yes. **Walking policy:** Unrestricted walking. **Metal spikes allowed:** Yes. **Range:** No. **To obtain tee times:** Call 7 days in advance. One year in advance for group outings over 16 people.

Subscriber comments: Class organization, especially for outings...Local favorite, well conditioned, not long but tricky...No. 11 a great par 3.

★★MERCER PUBLIC GOLF COURSE

PU-Rte. No. 58 and Golf Rd., Mercer, 16137, Mercer County, (412)662-9951, 60 miles N of Pittsburgh.

Opened: 1959. **Holes:** 18. **Par:** 72/72. **Yards:** 6,194/5,366. **Course rating:** 70.4/69.9. **Slope:** 111/111. **Architect:** Mike Maneini. **Green fee:** $12/$15. **Credit cards:** None. **Reduced fees:** Low season, seniors. **Caddies:** No. **Golf carts:** $8. **Discount golf packages:** No. **Season:** Year-round. **High:** May-Sept. **On site lodging:** No. **Rental clubs:** Yes. **Walking policy:** Walking at certain times. **Metal spikes allowed:** Yes. **Range:** Yes (grass). **To obtain tee times:** Call golf club.

★★MIDDLETOWN COUNTRY CLUB

PU-420 N. Bellevue Ave., Langhorne, 19047, Bucks County, (215)757-6953, 14 miles N of Philadelphia.

Opened: 1918. **Holes:** 18. **Par:** 69/69. **Yards:** 5,930/5,675. **Course rating:** N/A. **Slope:** N/A. **Architect:** N/A. **Green fee:** $16/$27. **Credit cards:** All major. **Reduced fees:** Weekdays, low season, twilight, seniors, juniors. **Caddies:** No. **Golf carts:** $13. **Discount golf packages:** Yes. **Season:** Year-round. **High:** May-Oct. **On site lodging:** No. **Rental clubs:** Yes. **Walking policy:** Unrestricted walking. **Metal spikes allowed:** Yes. **Range:** No. **To obtain tee times:** Call 7 days in advance.

★★★MILL RACE GOLF COURSE

R-RR No. 2, Benton, 17814, Columbia County, (717)925-2040.

Opened: 1970. **Holes:** 18. **Par:** 70/71. **Yards:** 6,096/4,791. **Course rating:** 68.6/68.3. **Slope:** 126/122. **Architect:** Geoffrey Cornish. **Green fee:** $14/$18. **Credit cards:** MC,VISA. **Reduced fees:** Weekdays, seniors, juniors. **Caddies:** No. **Golf carts:** $10. **Discount golf packages:** No. **Season:** March-Nov. **High:** May-Aug. **On site lodging:** No. **Rental clubs:** Yes. **Walking policy:** Walking at certain times. **Metal spikes allowed:** Yes. **Range:** Yes (grass). **To obtain tee times:** Call one week in advance.

Subscriber comments: Short course, great for handicaps of all kinds...Lots of water, 10 holes...Offers enough of a challenge but is not overly tough on average golfer...Wide open...Good course to walk...Weekday specials, good course, enjoyable.

★★MOCCASIN RUN GOLF COURSE

PU-Box 402, Schoff Rd., Atglen, 19310, Chester County, (610)593-7322.

Opened: 1988. **Holes:** 18. **Par:** 72/72. **Yards:** 6,400/5,275. **Course rating:** 69.0/69.2. **Slope:** 121/120. **Architect:** John Thompson. **Green fee:** $19/$28. **Credit cards:** MC,VISA. **Reduced fees:** Weekdays, low season, twilight, seniors, juniors. **Caddies:** No. **Golf carts:** $10. **Discount golf packages:** Yes. **Season:** Year-round. **High:** April-Oct. **On site lodging:** No. **Rental clubs:** Yes. **Walking policy:** Unrestricted walking. **Metal spikes allowed:** Yes. **Range:** Yes (grass). **To obtain tee times:** Call 7 days in advance.

★★½MOHAWK TRAILS GOLF COURSE
PU-RD No. 7, Box 243, New Castle, 16102, Lawrence County, (412)667-8570, 50 miles N of Pittsburgh.
Opened: 1965. **Holes:** 18. **Par:** 72. **Yards:** 6,324. **Course rating:** 70.3. **Slope:** 108. **Architect:** Eichenlaub family. **Green fee:** $13/$15. **Credit cards:** None. **Reduced fees:** Weekdays, low season, seniors. **Caddies:** No. **Golf carts:** N/A. **Discount golf packages:** No. **Season:** March-Dec. **High:** May-Sept. **On site lodging:** No. **Rental clubs:** Yes. **Walking policy:** Unrestricted walking. **Metal spikes allowed:** Yes. **Range:** No. **To obtain tee times:** Call 7 days in advance. Weekday tee times for 8 or more.
Subscriber comments: Lots of hills...Some tough holes...A very tight course, challenging!...Early wide open, nice clubhouse, good cheap food...Front and back nines like two different courses.

★★★MONROE VALLEY GOLF CLUB
PU-RD No. 1, Jonestown, 17038, Lebanon County, (717)865-2375.
Opened: 1968. **Holes:** 18. **Par:** 72/72. **Yards:** 6,884/5,254. **Course rating:** 71.9/65.0. **Slope:** 115/108. **Architect:** Edmund B. Ault. **Green fee:** $15/$24. **Credit cards:** MC,VISA,AMEX. **Reduced fees:** Weekdays, low season, twilight, seniors, juniors. **Caddies:** No. **Golf carts:** $10. **Discount golf packages:** No. **Season:** Year-round. **High:** May-Sept. **On site lodging:** No. **Rental clubs:** Yes. **Walking policy:** Unrestricted walking. **Metal spikes allowed:** No. **Range:** Yes (grass/mats). **To obtain tee times:** Call 7 days in advance.
Subscriber comments: Plays long, also large greens, enjoyed...A few forced carries, a little flat...Open, beautiful course between mountains...13 and 16 great holes.

★★★MOUNT AIRY LODGE GOLF COURSE
R-42 Woodland Rd., Mount Pocono, 18344, Monroe County, (717)839-8811, (800)441-4410, 30 miles E of Scranton.
Opened: 1980. **Holes:** 18. **Par:** 72/73. **Yards:** 7,123/5,771. **Course rating:** 74.3/73.3. **Slope:** 138/122. **Architect:** Hal Purdy. **Green fee:** $40/$50. **Credit cards:** All major. **Reduced fees:** Weekdays, resort guests, twilight. **Caddies:** No. **Golf carts:** $15. **Discount golf packages:** Yes. **Season:** April-Nov. **High:** May-Sept. **On site lodging:** Yes. **Rental clubs:** Yes. **Walking policy:** Mandatory cart. **Metal spikes allowed:** Yes. **Range:** Yes. **To obtain tee times:** Call any time of year, but at least 7 days in advance.
Subscriber comments: Great views...18 toughest hole that pros won't play...Very tough, sometimes unfair...Beautiful resort course. Many blind shots, long...Very scenic. Shotmaker's course...No two holes alike...Long and difficult.

★★MOUNT ODIN PARK GOLF CLUB
PU-Mt. Odin Park Dr., Greensburg, 15601, Westmoreland County, (412)834-2640, 30 miles SE of Pittsburgh.
Opened: 1935. **Holes:** 18. **Par:** 70/72. **Yards:** 5,395/4,733. **Course rating:** 65.0/68.0. **Slope:** 108/104. **Architect:** X.G. Hassenplug. **Green fee:** $13/$15. **Credit cards:** None. **Reduced fees:** N/A. **Caddies:** No. **Golf carts:** $8. **Discount golf packages:** Yes. **Season:** Year-round. **High:** April-Sept. **On site lodging:** No. **Rental clubs:** Yes. **Walking policy:** Unrestricted walking. **Metal spikes allowed:** Yes. **Range:** Yes (grass). **To obtain tee times:** Come in person weekend prior or call on Monday for upcoming weekend.

★★★MOUNTAIN LAUREL RESORT HOTEL & GOLF CLUB
R-Rte. 534 and I80, White Haven, 18661, Luzerne County, (717)443-7424, (800)458-5921, 80 miles NW of Philadelphia.
Opened: 1969. **Holes:** 18. **Par:** 72/72. **Yards:** 6,798/5,631. **Course rating:** 72.3/71.9. **Slope:** 113/113. **Architect:** Geoffrey Cornish. **Green fee:** $40/$47. **Credit cards:** All major. **Reduced fees:** Weekdays, low season, resort guests, twilight, seniors. **Caddies:** No. **Golf carts:** Included in Green Fee. **Discount golf packages:** Yes. **Season:** April-Nov. **High:** June-Aug. **On site lodging:** Yes. **Rental clubs:** Yes. **Walking policy:** Walking at certain times. **Metal spikes allowed:** Yes. **Range:** Yes (grass). **To obtain tee times:** Tee times are required with a credit card to guarantee.
Subscriber comments: Nice layout, lots of water...Very scenic...Well worth the trip...Large greens...Play it in the fall...First 5 or 6 holes tame, then course gets very tough...Good course for beginners, nice course to walk, great greens.

PENNSYLVANIA

MOUNTAIN MANOR INN & GOLF CLUB
Creek Rd., Marshall's Creek, 18335, Monroe County, (717)223-1290, 100 miles N of Philadelphia.
Opened: 1945. **Architect:** Russell Scott. **Green fee:** $18/$28. **Credit cards:** None. **Reduced fees:** Weekdays, low season, resort guests, twilight. **Caddies:** No. **Golf carts:** $27. **Discount golf packages:** Yes. **Season:** April-Nov. **High:** April-Oct. **On site lodging:** Yes. **Rental clubs:** Yes. **Walking policy:** Unrestricted walking. **Metal spikes allowed:** Yes. **Range:** Yes (grass). **To obtain tee times:** No tee times.

★★½BLUE/YELLOW COURSE
Holes: 18. **Par:** 71/71. **Yards:** 6,233/5,079. **Course rating:** 68.5/68.5. **Slope:** 115/115.
Subscriber comments: Fun, nice views, great value...Not very easy to get tee times...Flat wide open...Always a pleasure to visit...Fun course.

★★★½ORANGE/SILVER COURSE
Holes: 18. **Par:** 73/73. **Yards:** 6,426/5,146. **Course rating:** 71.0/71.5. **Slope:** 132/124.
Subscriber comments: Difficult layout, challenging (especially par-6 hole)...Some holes somewhat unfair...Very hilly...Some really neat holes...Fun mountain course, fast play, well managed.

★★½MOUNTAIN VALLEY GOLF COURSE
PU-Burma Rd., Mahanoy City, 17948, Schuylkill County, (717)467-2242.
Call club for further information.
Subscriber comments: Hard to walk (hills). If you hit it straight, the course is fun...Variety of holes, drive straight.

★★MURRYSVILLE GOLF CLUB
PU-3804 Sardis Rd., Murrysville, 15668, Westmoreland County, (412)327-0726, 20 miles E of Pittsburgh.
Opened: 1938. **Holes:** 18. **Par:** 70/74. **Yards:** 5,575/5,250. **Course rating:** 64.4/67.2.
Slope: 99/107. **Architect:** James Noble & Son. **Green fee:** $15/$17. **Credit cards:** None. **Reduced fees:** Seniors. **Caddies:** No. **Golf carts:** $9. **Discount golf packages:** No. **Season:** April-Nov. **High:** June-Aug. **On site lodging:** No. **Rental clubs:** Yes. **Walking policy:** Unrestricted walking. **Metal spikes allowed:** Yes. **Range:** No. **To obtain tee times:** N/A.

NEMACOLIN WOODLANDS RESORT & SPA
R-Rte. 40 E., Farmington, 15437, Fayette County, (412)329-6111, (800)422-2736, 65 miles SE of Pittsburgh.
Credit cards: MC,VISA,AMEX. **Caddies:** No. **Golf carts:** Included in Green Fee. **Discount golf packages:** Yes. **Season:** April-Nov. **On site lodging:** Yes. **Rental clubs:** Yes. **Walking policy:** Mandatory cart. **Metal spikes allowed:** Yes. **To obtain tee times:** Resort guests call 60 days in advance. Daily fee call 7 days in advance.

(GOOD SERVICE)

★★★★½MYSTIC ROCK GOLF COURSE
Opened: 1995. **Holes:** 18. **Par:** 72/72. **Yards:** 6,832/4,800. **Course rating:** 75.0/68.8.
Slope: 146/125. **Architect:** Pete Dye. **Green fee:** $109/$119. **Reduced fees:** Low season, resort guests, twilight. **High:** May-Oct. **Range:** Yes (grass/mats).
Notes: Ranked 4th in 1995 Best New Resort Courses.
Subscriber comments: Expensive, worth it...Excellent new course...Sets a new standard for greatness...Good off-season rate in spring...New Pete Dye gem! $100 fee is tough to swallow...Pete Dye special, greens hard, great course otherwise...Could be most beautiful course ever built.

★★★½WOODLANDS LINKS GOLF CLUB
Opened: 1976. **Holes:** 18. **Par:** 71/71. **Yards:** 6,814/4,825. **Course rating:** 73.0/67.3.
Slope: 131/115. **Architect:** Joe Hardy/Willard Rockwell. **Green fee:** $38/$69. **Reduced fees:** Low season, twilight. **High:** May-Sept. **Range:** Yes (grass).
Subscriber comments: Orchids to Joe Hardy and his idea for a resort...Expensive, worth it...Fair test of golf skills. Beautiful facility...Lots of sand...Nice course, excellent service...Tough but fair...Immaculate...A beautiful mountain course.

★★½NORTH FORK GOLF & TENNIS CLUB
RD No. 4, Box 218, Johnstown, 15905, Cambria County, (814)288-2822, 65 miles SE of Pittsburgh.

Opened: 1934. **Holes:** 18. **Par:** 72/72. **Yards:** 6,470/5,762. **Course rating:** 71.1/72.0.
Slope: 124/114. **Architect:** Fred Garbin. **Green fee:** $16/$18. **Credit cards:** All major.
Reduced fees: Juniors. **Caddies:** No. **Golf carts:** $12. **Discount golf packages:** No.
Season: April-Oct. **High:** June-Aug. **On site lodging:** No. **Rental clubs:** No. **Walking policy:** Unrestricted walking. **Metal spikes allowed:** No. **Range:** No. **To obtain tee times:** Call up to 7 days in advance. Open to the public Monday, Wednesday and Friday after 2 p.m.
Subscriber comments: Average course...So-so layout, hard to walk...Good greens, half of course is on side of hill.

★★★½NORTH HILLS GOLF CLUB
PU-1450 N. Center St., Corry, 16407, Erie County, (814)664-4477, 24 miles SE of Erie.
Opened: 1967. **Holes:** 18. **Par:** 71/72. **Yards:** 6,800/5,146. **Course rating:** 71.0/71.4. **Slope:** 115/119. **Architect:** Edmond Ault. **Green fee:** $11/$28. **Credit cards:** MC,VISA. **Reduced fees:** Weekdays, low season, twilight. **Caddies:** No. **Golf carts:** $20. **Discount golf packages:** No. **Season:** April-Oct. **High:** July-Aug. **On site lodging:** No. **Rental clubs:** Yes. **Walking policy:** Unrestricted walking. **Metal spikes allowed:** Yes. **Range:** Yes (grass). **To obtain tee times:** First come, first served.
Subscriber comments: Beautiful course, excellent value, would play every day...Long, nice layout well maintained...Best muny course I've played, always in nice shape, price is good...Nice scenery.

★★½NORTH PARK GOLF COURSE
PU-Kummer Rd., Allison Park, 15101, Allegheny County, (412)935-1967.
Call club for further information.
Subscriber comments: Beautiful, tough layout. No. 8 par-4 one of toughest in area...Very wide fairways, long course...Public golf, decent course, priced fair.

★★½NORTHAMPTON VALLEY COUNTRY CLUB
Rte. 332, Richboro, 18954, Bucks County, (215)355-2234, 15 miles NE of Philadelphia.
Opened: 1964. **Holes:** 18. **Par:** 70/71. **Yards:** 6,377/5,586. **Course rating:** 69.2/70.0.
Slope: 123/118. **Architect:** Ed Ault. **Green fee:** $16/$30. **Credit cards:** MC,VISA,AMEX. **Reduced fees:** Weekdays, twilight, seniors. **Caddies:** No. **Golf carts:** $12. **Discount golf packages:** No. **Season:** Year-round. **High:** April-Oct. **On site lodging:** No. **Rental clubs:** Yes. **Walking policy:** Walking at certain times. **Metal spikes allowed:** Yes. **Range:** No. **To obtain tee times:** Call.
Subscriber comments: Short but a challenge, No.18 is a sucker hole...Tight course, good service...Short, big greens, a lot of play...Tight fairways.

NORTHWIND GOLF LODGE
PU-700 S. Shore Trail, Indian Lake, 15926, (814)754-4975, 15 miles E of Johnstown.
Opened: N/A. **Holes:** 18. **Par:** 72/72. **Yards:** 6,199/5,244. **Course rating:** 70.2/72.0.
Slope: 128/124. **Architect:** Musser Engineering Inc.. **Green fee:** $16/$18. **Credit cards:** All major. **Reduced fees:** Weekdays, low season, resort guests, twilight. **Caddies:** No. **Golf carts:** $12. **Discount golf packages:** Yes. **Season:** March-Nov. **High:** June-Aug. **On site lodging:** Yes. **Rental clubs:** Yes. **Walking policy:** Unrestricted walking. **Metal spikes allowed:** Yes. **Range:** Yes (grass/mats). **To obtain tee times:** Call.

★★½OAKBROOK GOLF COURSE
PU-251 Golf Course Rd, Stoystown, 15563, Somerset County, (814)629-5892, 60 miles E of Pittsburgh.
Opened: 1965. **Holes:** 18. **Par:** 71/73. **Yards:** 5,935/5,530. **Course rating:** 67.4/70.4.
Slope: 109/113. **Architect:** H.J. Hillegas. **Green fee:** $16/$18. **Credit cards:** None.
Reduced fees: N/A. **Caddies:** No. **Golf carts:** $20. **Discount golf packages:** No.
Season: April-Nov. **High:** June-Aug. **On site lodging:** No. **Rental clubs:** Yes. **Walking policy:** Unrestricted walking. **Metal spikes allowed:** Yes. **Range:** Yes (grass). **To obtain tee times:** Ball rack system.
Subscriber comments: Challenging...Nice course in mountain setting. Very easy to walk...Love this place!...Several fairways side by side.

★★★½OLDE HOMESTEAD GOLF CLUB
PU-6598 Rte. 309, New Tripoli, 18066, Lehigh County, (610)298-4653, 15 miles NW of Allentown.
Opened: 1995. **Holes:** 18. **Par:** 72/72. **Yards:** 6,900/5,013. **Course rating:** 73.8/68.5.
Slope: 132/115. **Architect:** Jim Blaukovitch. **Green fee:** $28/$38. **Credit cards:**
MC,VISA,AMEX. **Reduced fees:** Weekdays, low season, twilight, seniors, juniors.
Caddies: No. **Golf carts:** $10. **Discount golf packages:** No. **Season:** March-Dec.
High: May-Oct. **On site lodging:** No. **Rental clubs:** Yes. **Walking policy:** Walking at certain times. **Metal spikes allowed:** Yes. **Range:** Yes (grass/mats). **To obtain tee times:** Call 6 days in advance.
Subscriber comments: Upscale public course at fairly reasonable fee...Nice scenic course...Golf in the country, no distractions, good design.

★★½OVERLOOK GOLF COURSE
PU-2040 Lititz Pike, Lancaster, 17601, Lancaster County, (717)569-9551, 60 miles W of Philadelphia.
Opened: 1930. **Holes:** 18. **Par:** 70/71. **Yards:** 6,100/4,962. **Course rating:** 69.2/68.4.
Slope: 110/113. **Architect:** Abe Domback. **Green fee:** $14/$21. **Credit cards:**
MC,VISA. **Reduced fees:** Low season, seniors. **Caddies:** No. **Golf carts:** $10.
Discount golf packages: No. **Season:** Year-round. **High:** May-Aug. **On site lodging:**
No. **Rental clubs:** Yes. **Walking policy:** Unrestricted walking. **Metal spikes allowed:**
Yes. **Range:** No. **To obtain tee times:** Call 7 days in advance for weekends only.
Subscriber comments: Many parallel fairways. Very good condition...Small greens...Short but in good shape. Always a quick round here.

★★½PANORAMA GOLF COURSE
PU-Rte. 1, Forest City, 18421, Susquehanna County, (717)222-3525, 2 miles W of Forest City.
Opened: 1964. **Holes:** 18. **Par:** 72. **Yards:** 7,256/5,345. **Course rating:** 73.0. **Slope:**
122/122. **Architect:** N/A. **Green fee:** $14/$18. **Credit cards:** MC,VISA. **Reduced fees:**
N/A. **Caddies:** No. **Golf carts:** $22. **Discount golf packages:** No. **Season:** April-Nov.
High: July-Aug. **On site lodging:** No. **Rental clubs:** No. **Walking policy:** Unrestricted walking. **Metal spikes allowed:** Yes. **Range:** Yes (grass). **To obtain tee times:** Call 7 days in advance.
Subscriber comments: Great facility in middle of nowhere. Play blues if you dare...A well kept secret, great scenery as the name suggests.

★★PARK GOLF COURSE
PU-RD 4, Conneaut Lake, 16316, Crawford County, (814)382-9974.
Call club for further information.

★★★PARK HILLS COUNTRY CLUB
Highland Ave., Altoona, 16602, Blair County, (814)944-2631.
Opened: 1927. **Holes:** 18. **Par:** 71/70. **Yards:** 6,004/4,843. **Course rating:** 69.3/69.3.
Slope: 126/122. **Architect:** James Gilmore Harrison. **Green fee:** $22/$44. **Credit cards:** N/A. **Reduced fees:** N/A. **Caddies:** No. **Golf carts:** N/A. **Discount golf packages:** No. **Season:** April-Nov. **High:** July. **On site lodging:** No. **Rental clubs:** No.
Walking policy: N/A. **Metal spikes allowed:** Yes. **Range:** No. **To obtain tee times:**
Call.
Subscriber comments: Great greens, nice country setting...Small greens, high rough...Tight, short, fast greens, hilly challenging.

★★★PAXON HOLLOW COUNTRY CLUB
850 Paxon Hollow Rd., Media, 19063, Delaware County, (610)353-0220.
Call club for further information.
Subscriber comments: Short, hilly course with neat finishing hole...Gets a lot of play, avoid weekends...Killer par-5 18th. Well managed...Short, but challenging.

PENN NATIONAL GOLF CLUB & INN
PU-3720 Clubhouse Dr., Fayetteville, 17222, Franklin County, (717)352-3000, (800)221-7366, 39 miles SW of Harrisburg.
Green fee: $17/$32. **Credit cards:** MC,VISA,AMEX. **Reduced fees:** Weekdays, low

season, twilight, seniors, juniors. **Caddies:** No. **Golf carts:** $13. **Discount golf packages:** Yes. **Season:** Year-round. **High:** April-Oct. **On site lodging:** Yes. **Rental clubs:** Yes. **Walking policy:** Unrestricted walking. **Metal spikes allowed:** Yes. **Range:** Yes (grass). **To obtain tee times:** Call golf club up to 30 days in advance.

★★★½**FOUNDERS COURSE**

Opened: 1968. **Holes:** 18. **Par:** 72/72. **Yards:** 6,958/5,367. **Course rating:** 73.2/70.1. **Slope:** 129/116. **Architect:** Ed Ault.

Subscriber comments: Great golf at the original, new 18 just as good...Traditional, old, cut-in-the-trees course...Scenic view of mountains...People are fantastic...Easily walkable, playable...Super, every hole is interesting...Nice course, long, well maintained. President Clinton played here a few years ago.

IRON FORGE COURSE

Opened: 1996. **Holes:** 18. **Par:** 72/72. **Yards:** 6,980/5,350. **Course rating:** 72.9/69.5. **Slope:** 123/114. **Architect:** William R. Love.

PENNSYLVANIA STATE UNIVERSITY GOLF COURSE

PU-1523 W. College Ave., State College, 16802, Centre County, (814)865-4653, 90 miles SE of Harrisburg.

Credit cards: All major. **Caddies:** No. **Golf carts:** N/A. **Discount golf packages:** Yes. **Season:** March-Nov. **High:** June-Sept. **On site lodging:** Yes. **Rental clubs:** Yes. **Metal spikes allowed:** Yes. **To obtain tee times:** Call up to 7 days in advance.

★★★½**BLUE COURSE**

Opened: 1970. **Holes:** 18. **Par:** 72/72. **Yards:** 6,525/5,128. **Course rating:** 72.0/69.8. **Slope:** 128/118. **Architect:** Harrison and Garbin/Tom Clark. **Green fee:** $26/$26. **Reduced fees:** Twilight. **Walking policy:** Unrestricted walking. **Range:** Yes.

Subscriber comments: Big, tough greens...Short but demanding, especially on prettier back nine. Inexpensive during week...Lush fairways great service, one of the best public courses I have played...Skip football game and play instead.

★★½**WHITE COURSE**

Opened: 1994. **Holes:** 18. **Par:** 70/70. **Yards:** 6,008/5,212. **Course rating:** 68.2/69.4. **Slope:** 115/116. **Architect:** Tom Clark. **Green fee:** $20/$20. **Reduced fees:** N/A. **Walking policy:** Walking at certain times. **Range:** Yes (mats).

Subscriber comments: Huge bunkers...Fairly forgiving track. Good for ego. Great prices...Good practice...Challenging with variety of conditions, hills, trees, doglegs, sand and water...Easier of two PSU courses.

★★PERRY GOLF COURSE

PU-220 Zion's Church Rd., Shoemakersville, 19555, Berks County, (610)562-3510, 12 miles N of Reading.

Opened: 1964. **Holes:** 18. **Par:** 70. **Yards:** 6,000. **Course rating:** 68.1. **Slope:** 112. **Architect:** N/A. **Green fee:** $11/$15. **Credit cards:** N/A. **Reduced fees:** N/A. **Caddies:** No. **Golf carts:** N/A. **Discount golf packages:** No. **Season:** Year-round. **High:** May-Sept. **On site lodging:** No. **Rental clubs:** No. **Walking policy:** Unrestricted walking. **Metal spikes allowed:** Yes. **Range:** No. **To obtain tee times:** Call.

★★½PICKERING VALLEY GOLF CLUB

PU-S. White Horse Rd., Phoenixville, 19460, Chester County, (610)933-2223, 20 miles W of Philadelphia.

Opened: 1985. **Holes:** 18. **Par:** 72/72. **Yards:** 6,530/5,235. **Course rating:** 70.3/64.5. **Slope:** 122/111. **Architect:** John Thompson. **Green fee:** $20/$27. **Credit cards:** None. **Reduced fees:** Weekdays, twilight, seniors. **Caddies:** No. **Golf carts:** $20. **Discount golf packages:** No. **Season:** Year-round. **High:** April-Oct. **On site lodging:** No. **Rental clubs:** Yes. **Walking policy:** Walking at certain times. **Metal spikes allowed:** Yes. **Range:** Yes (grass). **To obtain tee times:** Call 7 days in advance on weekends.

Subscriber comments: Very hilly, huge greens...Very hard to score; know your uneven lies...Three fairly long downhill par 3s make the course...Very challenging and tight with fast greens.

★★★★PILGRIM'S OAK GOLF COURSE

PU-1107 Pilgrim's Pathway, Peach Bottom, 17563, Lancaster County, (717)548-3011, 24 miles S of Lancaster.
Opened: 1996. **Holes:** 18. **Par:** 72/71. **Yards:** 7,043/5,064. **Course rating:** 73.4/70.7. **Slope:** 138/129. **Architect:** Michael Hurdzan. **Green fee:** $20/$36. **Credit cards:** MC,VISA,Debit Card. **Reduced fees:** Weekdays, low season, twilight, seniors. **Caddies:** Yes. **Golf carts:** $12. **Discount golf packages:** No. **Season:** Year-round. **High:** May-Oct. **On site lodging:** No. **Rental clubs:** No. **Walking policy:** Unrestricted walking. **Metal spikes allowed:** No. **Range:** Yes (grass). **To obtain tee times:** Call up to 14 days in advance.
Subscriber comments: Young, worth the drive...Hidden gem. A lot of walking, excellent design...Challenging, clean, lovely setting...Excellent blend of holes...Each hole has a unique feature that makes it memorable. Super value...The most caring staff I have ever experienced; as this course matures, it will only get better...Fun course.

★★★½PINE ACRES COUNTRY CLUB

1401 W. Warren Rd., Bradford, 16701, McKean County, (814)362-2005, 80 miles S of Buffalo, NY.
Opened: 1965. **Holes:** 18. **Par:** 72/72. **Yards:** 6,700/5,600. **Course rating:** 70.3/72.3. **Slope:** 120/120. **Architect:** James G. Harrison. **Green fee:** $22/$22. **Credit cards:** MC,VISA. **Reduced fees:** N/A. **Caddies:** No. **Golf carts:** $20. **Discount golf packages:** No. **Season:** April-Oct. **High:** June-Aug. **On site lodging:** No. **Rental clubs:** Yes. **Walking policy:** Unrestricted walking. **Metal spikes allowed:** Yes. **Range:** Yes (grass). **To obtain tee times:** Call 7 days in advance for weekends and holidays only.
Subscriber comments: Course was good, facility was good...Beautiful course, well taken care of, greens are very fast in summer...Very challenging on some holes, easy to walk...Contoured very nice throughout the mountainside.

★★★PINE CREST GOLF CLUB

PU-101 Country Club Dr., Lansdale, 19446, Montgomery County, (215)855-6112.
Opened: 1990. **Holes:** 18. **Par:** 70/70. **Yards:** 6,331/5,284. **Course rating:** 69.3/68.1. **Slope:** 122/118. **Architect:** Ron Prichard. **Green fee:** N/A. **Credit cards:** N/A. **Reduced fees:** N/A. **Caddies:** No. **Golf carts:** N/A. **Discount golf packages:** No. **Season:** N/A. **High:** N/A. **On site lodging:** No. **Rental clubs:** No. **Walking policy:** N/A. **Metal spikes allowed:** Yes. **Range:** No. **To obtain tee times:** Call.
Subscriber comments: Good course, tight, well groomed, great greens...Links style...Winds through housing development...Gets lots of play...Very tight, very plush, slicers/duck hookers stay away, too many windows.

★★★PINE GROVE GOLF COURSE

PU-401 Diamond Rd., Grove City, 16127, Mercer County, (412)458-9942.
Call club for further information.
Subscriber comments: Nice place to scramble...Very well maintained, pleasant staff...Short, senior friendly layout, busy on weekends...Easy to walk...Small greens.

★★PINE HILL GOLF COURSE

PU-263 Leech Rd., Greenville, 16125, Mercer County, (412)588-8053.
Opened: 1967. **Holes:** 18. **Par:** 72/72. **Yards:** 6,013/5,430. **Course rating:** N/A. **Slope:** N/A. **Architect:** Charles Loreno. **Green fee:** $12/$13. **Credit cards:** N/A. **Reduced fees:** N/A. **Caddies:** No. **Golf carts:** $17. **Discount golf packages:** No. **Season:** April-Nov. **High:** June-Aug. **On site lodging:** No. **Rental clubs:** No. **Walking policy:** N/A. **Metal spikes allowed:** Yes. **Range:** No. **To obtain tee times:** Call.

★½PINE HILLS GOLF COURSE

PU-140 S. Keyser Ave., Taylor, 18517, Lackawanna County, (717)562-0138.
Opened: 1967. **Holes:** 18. **Par:** 71. **Yards:** 6,011. **Course rating:** N/A. **Slope:** N/A. **Architect:** Andrew Evanish. **Green fee:** $9/$10. **Credit cards:** N/A. **Reduced fees:** Weekdays, seniors. **Caddies:** No. **Golf carts:** $16. **Discount golf packages:** No. **Season:** Year-round. **High:** N/A. **On site lodging:** No. **Rental clubs:** No. **Walking policy:** Unrestricted walking. **Metal spikes allowed:** Yes. **Range:** No. **To obtain tee times:** N/A.

PENNSYLVANIA

★★PITTSBURGH NORTH GOLF CLUB
PU-3800 Bakerstown Rd., Bakerstown, 15007, Allegheny County, (412)443-3800.
Opened: 1950. **Holes:** 27. **Par:** 72/73. **Yards:** 7,021/5,075. **Course rating:** 68.8/68.3.
Slope: 128/114. **Architect:** O.J. Price. **Green fee:** $15/$21. **Credit cards:**
MC,VISA,DISC. **Reduced fees:** Low season, seniors, juniors. **Caddies:** No. **Golf carts:**
$20. **Discount golf packages:** No. **Season:** Year-round. **High:** June-Aug. **On site**
lodging: No. **Rental clubs:** Yes. **Walking policy:** Walking at certain times. **Metal**
spikes allowed: Yes. **Range:** Yes (grass/mats). **To obtain tee times:** Call 7 days in
advance.

★★½PLEASANT VALLEY GOLF CLUB
PU-Stewartstown, 17363, York County, (717)993-2184, 22 miles N of Towson, MD.
Opened: 1964. **Holes:** 18. **Par:** 72/74. **Yards:** 6,540/5,250. **Course rating:** 69.4/70.5.
Slope: 119/117. **Architect:** Charles Shirey. **Green fee:** $15/$19. **Credit cards:** All
major. **Reduced fees:** Weekdays, low season, twilight, seniors, juniors. **Caddies:** No.
Golf carts: $11. **Discount golf packages:** Yes. **Season:** Year-round. **High:** March-Oct.
On site lodging: No. **Rental clubs:** Yes. **Walking policy:** Unrestricted walking. **Metal**
spikes allowed: Yes. **Range:** No. **To obtain tee times:** Call. Credit card needed to
hold reservation.
Subscriber comments: Acceptable golf, priced right...Long, but fair...Short, open
course, hard greens and fairways...Good mix of holes...Can't beat the weekday bargains...Get the weekday breakfast and lunch and all the golf you want...Short.

★★PLEASANT VALLEY GOLF COURSE
PU-R.R. No. 1, Box 58, Vintondale, 15961, Indiana County, (814)446-6244, 10 miles N
of Johnstown.
Opened: 1966. **Holes:** 18. **Par:** 71/72. **Yards:** 6,498/5,361. **Course rating:** 69.8/70.3.
Slope: 124/115. **Architect:** Telford M. Dixon. **Green fee:** $13/$15. **Credit cards:**
MC,VISA,DISC. **Reduced fees:** Weekdays, low season, juniors. **Caddies:** No. **Golf**
carts: $11. **Discount golf packages:** Yes. **Season:** March-Dec. **High:** May-Oct. **On**
site lodging: No. **Rental clubs:** Yes. **Walking policy:** Walking at certain times. **Metal**
spikes allowed: Yes. **Range:** Yes (grass). **To obtain tee times:** Call golf shop.

POCONO MANOR INN & GOLF CLUB
R-P.O. Box 7, Pocono Manor, 18349, Monroe County, (717)839-7111, (800)233-8150,
20 miles from Scranton.
Green fee: N/A. **Credit cards:** MC,VISA,AMEX. **Reduced fees:** Weekdays, resort
guests, twilight. **Caddies:** No. **Golf carts:** $30. **Discount golf packages:** Yes. **Season:**
April-Nov. **High:** May-Oct. **On site lodging:** Yes. **Rental clubs:** No. **Walking policy:**
Mandatory cart. **Metal spikes allowed:** Yes. **Range:** Yes (grass). **To obtain tee times:**
Call golf shop.
★★½EAST COURSE
Opened: 1919. **Holes:** 18. **Par:** 72/72. **Yards:** 6,480/6,113. **Course rating:** N/A. **Slope:**
N/A. **Architect:** Donald Ross.
Subscriber comments: Enjoyed the funnel hole, need to play twice...New tees, cart
paths, upgrades done well to old Ross design...In the woods very nice.
★★WEST COURSE
Opened: 1960. **Holes:** 18. **Par:** 72/72. **Yards:** 6,857/5,706. **Course rating:** N/A. **Slope:**
N/A. **Architect:** George Fazio.

★★★QUAIL VALLEY GOLF CLUB
901 Teeter Rd., Littletown, 17340, Adams County, (717)359-8453.
Opened: 1993. **Holes:** 18. **Par:** 72/72. **Yards:** 7,042/5,218. **Course rating:** 72.9/69.5.
Slope: 123/113. **Architect:** Paul Hicks. **Green fee:** $15/$25. **Credit cards:** MC,VISA.
Reduced fees: Weekdays, low season, twilight, seniors, juniors. **Caddies:** No. **Golf**
carts: $10. **Discount golf packages:** No. **Season:** Year-round. **High:** March-Oct. **On**
site lodging: No. **Rental clubs:** No. **Walking policy:** Unrestricted walking. **Metal**
spikes allowed: Yes. **Range:** Yes (grass/mats). **To obtain tee times:** Call 7 days in
advance.
Subscriber comments: Long course, good value...No. 3 is the tightest fairway I ever
played...A strong layout, tight and open both...Fun course...Always windy, tough layout...If you like bump and run, this course is for you...Wonderful service.

★★★½QUICKSILVER GOLF CLUB
PU-2000 Quicksilver Rd., Midway, 15060, Washington County, (412)796-1811, 18 miles SW of Pittsburgh.
Opened: 1990. **Holes:** 18. **Par:** 72/74. **Yards:** 7,120/5,067. **Course rating:** 75.7/68.6. **Slope:** 145/115. **Architect:** Don Nagode. **Green fee:** $50/$65. **Credit cards:** All major. **Reduced fees:** Low season, twilight, seniors, juniors. **Caddies:** No. **Golf carts:** $15. **Discount golf packages:** Yes. **Season:** March-Dec. **High:** May-Oct. **On site lodging:** No. **Rental clubs:** Yes. **Walking policy:** Walking at certain times. **Metal spikes allowed:** Yes. **Range:** Yes (grass/mats). **To obtain tee times:** Call or come in 6 days in advance.
Notes: 1993-97 Pittsburgh Senior Classic.
Subscriber comments: Senior Tour stop...Senior Tour's toughest, penal rough, sloping greens, hills and wind tough...Good scoring layout...Fun to play, fast greens...Some blind tee shots...Great clubhouse.

★★½RICH MAIDEN GOLF COURSE
PU-R.D. No. 2, Box 2099, Fleetwood, 19522, Berks County, (610)926-1606, (800)905-9555, 10 miles N of Reading.
Opened: 1932. **Holes:** 18. **Par:** 69/70. **Yards:** 5,635/5,145. **Course rating:** 63.7/65.1. **Slope:** 97/99. **Architect:** Jake Merkel. **Green fee:** $14/$19. **Credit cards:** None. **Reduced fees:** Weekdays, low season, twilight, seniors, juniors. **Caddies:** No. **Golf carts:** $19. **Discount golf packages:** Yes. **Season:** Year-round. **High:** April-Sept. **On site lodging:** No. **Rental clubs:** Yes. **Walking policy:** Unrestricted walking. **Metal spikes allowed:** Yes. **Range:** No. **To obtain tee times:** Call or come in.
Subscriber comments: Short, easy course with tough greens; good for short game...Nice restaurant, fun golf day...Short, but still challenging.

★★RIVER VALLEY COUNTRY CLUB
SP-RD 4, Box 582, Westfield, 16950, Tioga County, (814)367-2202, 30 miles S of Corning.
Opened: 1964. **Holes:** 18. **Par:** 72/72. **Yards:** 6,258/5,625. **Course rating:** 70.2/67.1. **Slope:** 116/111. **Architect:** Geoffrey Cornish. **Green fee:** $15/$18. **Credit cards:** All major. **Reduced fees:** Weekdays, low season. **Caddies:** No. **Golf carts:** $24. **Discount golf packages:** Yes. **Season:** April-Nov. **High:** June-Aug. **On site lodging:** No. **Rental clubs:** No. **Walking policy:** Unrestricted walking. **Metal spikes allowed:** No. **Range:** No. **To obtain tee times:** Call in advance.

★★★½RIVERSIDE GOLF CLUB
PU-24527 Hwy. 19, Cambridge Springs, 16403, Crawford County, (814)398-4537, 18 miles S of Erie.
Opened: 1915. **Holes:** 18. **Par:** 71/72. **Yards:** 6,334/5,287. **Course rating:** 69.7/69.5. **Slope:** 119/116. **Architect:** N/A. **Green fee:** $17/$26. **Credit cards:** All major. **Reduced fees:** Weekdays, low season, twilight, seniors, juniors. **Caddies:** No. **Golf carts:** $12. **Discount golf packages:** Yes. **Season:** March-Oct. **High:** June-Sept. **On site lodging:** No. **Rental clubs:** Yes. **Walking policy:** Walking at certain times. **Metal spikes allowed:** Yes. **Range:** Yes (grass). **To obtain tee times:** Call 30 days in advance for local and up to a year in advance for out-of-area travelers.
Subscriber comments: Fine course to walk, always in great shape...Very green, true test...Great condition, lots of sand in right places...Best-kept secret in NW Pa....Large greens...Good par 3s, good shape...Very good clubhouse.

★½ROLLING FIELDS GOLF COURSE
PU-Hankey Church Rd., Murraysville, 15668, Westmoreland County, (412)335-7522, 15 miles E of Pittsburgh.
Opened: 1955. **Holes:** N/A. **Par:** 70/72. **Yards:** 6,085/5,025. **Course rating:** 68.9. **Slope:** 105/110. **Architect:** John Chernega. **Green fee:** $12/$16. **Credit cards:** N/A. **Reduced fees:** Weekdays, seniors, juniors. **Caddies:** No. **Golf carts:** $19. **Discount golf packages:** No. **Season:** Year-round. **High:** April-Oct. **On site lodging:** No. **Rental clubs:** Yes. **Walking policy:** Unrestricted walking. **Metal spikes allowed:** Yes. **Range:** No. **To obtain tee times:** Call 7 days in advance.

PENNSYLVANIA

★★½ROLLING GREEN GOLF CLUB
PU-Rt. 136, Eighty-four, 15301, Washington County, (412)222-9671.
Opened: 1957. **Holes:** 18. **Par:** 71/71. **Yards:** 6,000/4,500. **Course rating:** N/A. **Slope:** N/A. **Architect:** N/A. **Green fee:** $15/$17. **Credit cards:** MC,VISA. **Reduced fees:** Weekdays, low season, seniors, juniors. **Caddies:** No. **Golf carts:** $18. **Discount golf packages:** No. **Season:** March-Oct. **High:** May-July. **On site lodging:** No. **Rental clubs:** No. **Walking policy:** Walking at certain times. **Metal spikes allowed:** Yes. **Range:** Yes. **To obtain tee times:** Call up to 5 days in advance for weekends.
Subscriber comments: Good greens...Great course, very difficult...Good course for practice..Pleasant playing, well maintained, many marshy areas.

★★ROLLING HILLS GOLF COURSE
PU-RD No. 1, Rte. 208, Pulaski, 16143, Lawrence County, (412)964-8201, 10 miles E of Youngstown, OH.
Opened: 1967. **Holes:** 18. **Par:** 71/76. **Yards:** 6,000/5,552. **Course rating:** N/A. **Slope:** N/A. **Architect:** Frank Kwolsek. **Green fee:** $9/$14. **Credit cards:** MC,VISA. **Reduced fees:** Weekdays, low season, seniors, juniors. **Caddies:** No. **Golf carts:** $9. **Discount golf packages:** Yes. **Season:** Year-round. **High:** June-Aug. **On site lodging:** No. **Rental clubs:** Yes. **Walking policy:** Unrestricted walking. **Metal spikes allowed:** Yes. **Range:** No. **To obtain tee times:** Call in advance. Required on weekends.

★★ROLLING MEADOWS GOLF CLUB
23 Rolling Meadows Rd., Ashland, 17921, Schuylkill County, (717)875-1204, 12 miles N of Pottsville.
Opened: 1964. **Holes:** 18. **Par:** 68/69. **Yards:** 5,200/5,200. **Course rating:** N/A. **Slope:** N/A. **Architect:** N/A. **Green fee:** $14/$15. **Credit cards:** N/A. **Reduced fees:** Weekdays, low season, twilight. **Caddies:** No. **Golf carts:** $12. **Discount golf packages:** No. **Season:** Year-round. **High:** June-Aug. **On site lodging:** No. **Rental clubs:** Yes. **Walking policy:** Unrestricted walking. **Metal spikes allowed:** Yes. **Range:** Yes. **To obtain tee times:** Call.

★★★★ROYAL OAKS GOLF COURSE
PU-3350 W. Oak St., Lebanon, 17042, Lebanon County, (717)274-2212, 15 miles NE of Hershey.
Opened: 1992. **Holes:** 18. **Par:** 71/71. **Yards:** 6,486/4,695. **Course rating:** 71.4/66.9. **Slope:** 121/109. **Architect:** Ron Forse. **Green fee:** $15/$32. **Credit cards:** All major. **Reduced fees:** Weekdays, low season, twilight, seniors, juniors. **Caddies:** No. **Golf carts:** $8. **Discount golf packages:** No. **Season:** Year-round. **High:** April-Nov. **On site lodging:** No. **Rental clubs:** Yes. **Walking policy:** Unrestricted walking. **Metal spikes allowed:** Yes. **Range:** Yes (grass). **To obtain tee times:** Available 7 days in advance unless credit card number or deposit is taken. Tee times required 7 days a week.
Subscriber comments: Good shape, well bunkered...A must play...A little too flat for me, but great fairways and greens and lots of sand...Long, well kept course...Fine practice area..Lack of trees allows winds to make play tricky.
Special Notes: Spikeless encouraged.

★★★SAXON GOLF COURSE
PU-839 Ekastown Rd., Sarver, 16055, Butler County, (412)353-2130.
Call club for further information.
Subscriber comments: Level and easy walking. No bunkers, some tight holes...Back nine very beautiful to play...The flattest course in southwestern Pa.

★★★SCRANTON MUNICIPAL GOLF COURSE
PU-RD 4, Lake Ariel, 18436, Wayne County, (717)689-2686.
Opened: 1960. **Holes:** 18. **Par:** 72/73. **Yards:** 6,638/5,763. **Course rating:** 69.9/70.6. **Slope:** 113/112. **Architect:** N/A. **Green fee:** $11/$20. **Credit cards:** N/A. **Reduced fees:** N/A. **Caddies:** No. **Golf carts:** $20. **Discount golf packages:** No. **Season:** April-Nov. **High:** June-Aug. **On site lodging:** No. **Rental clubs:** Yes. **Walking policy:** Unrestricted walking. **Metal spikes allowed:** Yes. **Range:** Yes (grass/mats). **To obtain tee times:** Call.
Subscriber comments: Best muny greens you have ever seen...Well designed, very challenging...Price, conditions, staff are first rate...Play it from the blues for a challenge.

★★½SEVEN SPRINGS COUNTRY CLUB
357 Pineview Dr., Elizabeth, 15037, Allegheny County, (412)384-7730.
Call club for further information.
Subscriber comments: Great value on very well maintained course...Good course for lazy Sunday, relaxing day...Hilly, large elevation change tee to green.

★★★½SEVEN SPRINGS MOUNTAIN RESORT GOLF COURSE
R-RD No. 1, Champion, 15622, Westmoreland County, (814)352-7777, 60 miles SE of Pittsburgh.
Opened: 1969. **Holes:** 18. **Par:** 71/72. **Yards:** 6,360/4,934. **Course rating:** 70.6/68.3. **Slope:** 116/111. **Architect:** Xen Hassenplug. **Green fee:** $55/$60. **Credit cards:** MC,VISA,DISC. **Reduced fees:** Weekdays, low season, resort guests, twilight. **Caddies:** No. **Golf carts:** Included in Green Fee. **Discount golf packages:** Yes. **Season:** April-Oct. **High:** July-Aug. **On site lodging:** Yes. **Rental clubs:** Yes. **Walking policy:** Walking at certain times. **Metal spikes allowed:** Yes. **Range:** Yes (grass). **To obtain tee times:** Call 48 hours in advance unless a guest at the resort then tee times can be made same time as reservation.
Subscriber comments: Spectacular views...Nice mountain course, great scenery...Cannot get home in two at No.17.

★★½SHADOW BROOK GOLF COURSE
RD 6, Tunkhannock, 18657, Wyoming County, (717)836-5417.
Call club for further information.
Subscriber comments: A tight course on a small property...Very hilly, and must think carefully of where to put the ball...Back nine on side of hill...Small hard greens.

★★★SHAWNEE INN GOLF RESORT
R-River Rd., Shawnee-on-Delaware, 18356, Monroe County, (717)421-1500, (800)742-9633, 90 miles W of New York City.
Opened: 1904. **Holes:** 27. **Architect:** A.W. Tillinghast/William Diddel. **Green fee:** $35/$70. **Credit cards:** All major,Diners Club. **Reduced fees:** Weekdays, low season, resort guests, twilight, seniors. **Caddies:** No. **Golf carts:** Included in Green Fee. **Discount golf packages:** Yes. **Season:** April-Nov. **High:** May-Aug. **On site lodging:** Yes. **Rental clubs:** Yes. **Walking policy:** Mandatory cart. **Metal spikes allowed:** Yes. **Range:** Yes (mats). **To obtain tee times:** Confirm tee times with credit card. Cancellation policy is 24 hours.
Notes: 1938 PGA Championship; 1967 NCAA Championship.
RED/BLUE
Par: 72/74. **Yards:** 6,800/5,650. **Course rating:** 72.2/71.4. **Slope:** 132/121.
RED/WHITE
Par: 72/74. **Yards:** 6,589/5,424. **Course rating:** 72.4/71.1. **Slope:** 131/121.
WHITE/BLUE
Par: 72/74. **Yards:** 6,665/5,398. **Course rating:** 72.8/72.5. **Slope:** 129/123.
Subscriber comments: Nice course...Flat open course...Plays slow. Small greens...Many years of golf history...Nice hotel, excellent layout...Good food, good course, value...No food service on course. Very average course.

★★SILVER SPRINGS GOLF CLUB
PU-136 Sample Bridge Rd., Mechanicsburg, 17055, Cumberland County, (717)766-0462, 10 miles NW of Harrisburg.
Opened: N/A. **Holes:** 18. **Par:** 70/70. **Yards:** 6,000/5,500. **Course rating:** 68.0/66.0. **Slope:** 114/109. **Architect:** George Fazio. **Green fee:** $14/$18. **Credit cards:** MC,VISA. **Reduced fees:** Weekdays, low season, twilight. **Caddies:** No. **Golf carts:** $20. **Discount golf packages:** No. **Season:** Year-round. **High:** March-Nov. **On site lodging:** No. **Rental clubs:** Yes. **Walking policy:** Unrestricted walking. **Metal spikes allowed:** Yes. **Range:** Yes (grass/mats). **To obtain tee times:** Call.

★★★SINKING VALLEY COUNTRY CLUB
Cape Cod Rd., Altoona, 16601, Blair County, (814)684-0662.
Call club for further information.
Subscriber comments: Very scenic course...Nice local course, sloping greens...Excellent care, interesting greens...Beautifully manicured grounds.

★★SKYLINE GOLF COURSE

PU-Rte. 247, R.D. No. 1, Carbondale, 18407, Lackawanna County, (717)282-5993.
Opened: 1959. **Holes:** 18. **Par:** 66/66. **Yards:** 4,719/3,866. **Course rating:** N/A. **Slope:** N/A. **Architect:** Carl Weinschenk/Andrew Petrilak. **Green fee:** N/A. **Credit cards:** N/A. **Reduced fees:** N/A. **Caddies:** No. **Golf carts:** N/A. **Discount golf packages:** No. **Season:** April-Nov. **High:** June-Aug. **On site lodging:** No. **Rental clubs:** Yes. **Walking policy:** Unrestricted walking. **Metal spikes allowed:** Yes. **Range:** No. **To obtain tee times:** N/A.

★★★SKYTOP LODGE

R-Skytop, 18357, Monroe County, (717)595-8910, (800)345-7759.
Opened: 1928. **Holes:** 18. **Par:** 71/75. **Yards:** 6,256/5,683. **Course rating:** 70.2/72.8. **Slope:** 121/122. **Architect:** Robert White. **Green fee:** $25/$40. **Credit cards:** MC,VISA,AMEX. **Reduced fees:** N/A. **Caddies:** No. **Golf carts:** $17. **Discount golf packages:** Yes. **Season:** April-Oct. **High:** June-Sept. **On site lodging:** Yes. **Rental clubs:** Yes. **Walking policy:** Walking at certain times. **Metal spikes allowed:** Yes. **Range:** Yes (mats). **To obtain tee times:** Tee times required. Call golf shop.
Subscriber comments: Set in an above average, traditional resort...Well-conditioned course. Outstanding people in pro shop...Better than average conditions.

★★★SOUTH HILLS GOLF CLUB

PU-925 Westminster Ave., Hanover, 17331, York County, (717)637-7500, 35 miles N of Baltimore.
Opened: 1959. **Holes:** 27. **Architect:** William and David Gordon. **Green fee:** $10/$23. **Credit cards:** None. **Reduced fees:** Weekdays, low season, seniors, juniors. **Caddies:** No. **Golf carts:** $11. **Discount golf packages:** No. **Season:** Year-round. **High:** May-Oct. **On site lodging:** No. **Rental clubs:** Yes. **Walking policy:** Walking at certain times. **Metal spikes allowed:** Yes. **Range:** Yes (grass). **To obtain tee times:** Call golf shop.
NORTH/SOUTH
Par: 71/71. **Yards:** 6,575/5,704. **Course rating:** N/A. **Slope:** N/A.
NORTH/WEST
Par: 72/72. **Yards:** 6,709/5,196. **Course rating:** N/A. **Slope:** N/A.
SOUTH/WEST
Par: 71/71. **Yards:** 6,478/5,076. **Course rating:** N/A. **Slope:** N/A.
Subscriber comments: Lots of hills, tough...Very playable course for average player...Traditional golf course, with best prices on food and drink...Old course, mature trees, nice setting, great course.

★★SOUTH PARK GOLF COURSE

PU-E. Park Dr., Library, 15129, Allegheny County, (412)835-3545, 8 miles S of Pittsburgh.
Opened: 1928. **Holes:** 27. **Par:** 72/73. **Yards:** 6,584/5,580. **Course rating:** 70.9/70.6. **Slope:** 123/114. **Architect:** N/A. **Green fee:** $14/$17. **Credit cards:** N/A. **Reduced fees:** Juniors. **Caddies:** No. **Golf carts:** $17. **Discount golf packages:** No. **Season:** Year-round. **High:** June-Aug. **On site lodging:** No. **Rental clubs:** Yes. **Walking policy:** Unrestricted walking. **Metal spikes allowed:** Yes. **Range:** No. **To obtain tee times:** No tee times.
Notes: 1934 Amateur Public Links.
Special Notes: Also has 9-hole course.

★★★SOUTHMOORE GOLF COURSE

PU-235 Moorestown Dr., Bath, 18014, Northampton County, (610)837-7200, 15 miles E of Allentown.
Opened: 1994. **Holes:** 18. **Par:** 71/71. **Yards:** 6,183/4,955. **Course rating:** 71.2/65.0. **Slope:** 126/112. **Architect:** Jim Blaukovich. **Green fee:** $22/$45. **Credit cards:** MC,VISA. **Reduced fees:** N/A. **Caddies:** No. **Golf carts:** N/A. **Discount golf packages:** No. **Season:** Year-round. **High:** May-Oct. **On site lodging:** No. **Rental clubs:** No. **Walking policy:** N/A. **Metal spikes allowed:** Yes. **Range:** No. **To obtain tee times:** Call 5 days in advance.
Subscriber comments: Interesting par 3s, long par 5s...Nice newer course, fun to play, scenic and hilly layout...Good mix short and long holes. No. 5 par 3 a wild green...Breathtaking scenery...Great course, large greens, beautiful all around.

★★SPORTSMANS GOLF CLUB
3800 Linglestown Rd., Harrisburg, 17110, Dauphin County, (717)545-0023.
Call club for further information.

★★SPRING HOLLOW GOLF COURSE
PU-3350 Schulkill Rd., Spring City, 19475, Chester County, (610)948-5566, 20 miles E
of Reading.
Opened: 1994. **Holes:** 18. **Par:** 70/70. **Yards:** 6,218/5,075. **Course rating:** 69.1/67.7.
Slope: 113/113. **Architect:** John Thompson. **Green fee:** $15/$22. **Credit cards:** N/A.
Reduced fees: N/A. **Caddies:** No. **Golf carts:** $13. **Discount golf packages:** No.
Season: Year-round. **High:** April-Oct. **On site lodging:** No. **Rental clubs:** Yes. **Walking
policy:** Unrestricted walking. **Metal spikes allowed:** No. **Range:** No. **To obtain tee
times:** Call up to 14 days in advance.

★★SPRINGDALE GOLF CLUB
PU-R.D. No. 3, Box 40C, Uniontown, 15401, Fayette County, (412)439-4400, 50 miles S
of Pittsburgh.
Opened: N/A. **Holes:** 18. **Par:** 70/71. **Yards:** 6,100/5,350. **Course rating:** 67.5/68.5.
Slope: 115/115. **Architect:** N/A. **Green fee:** $12/$15. **Credit cards:** None. **Reduced
fees:** Weekdays, low season, seniors. **Caddies:** No. **Golf carts:** $20. **Discount golf
packages:** No. **Season:** April-Nov. **High:** June-Aug. **On site lodging:** No. **Rental
clubs:** Yes. **Walking policy:** Unrestricted walking. **Metal spikes allowed:** Yes. **Range:**
No. **To obtain tee times:** First come, first served.

★★½STANDING STONE GOLF CLUB
PU-Rte. 26 N., Huntingdon, 16652, Huntingdon County, (814)643-4800.
Opened: 1973. **Holes:** 18. **Par:** 70/70. **Yards:** 6,593/5,528. **Course rating:** 71.4/71.1.
Slope: 120/120. **Architect:** Geoffrey Cornish. **Green fee:** $20/$25. **Credit cards:**
None. **Reduced fees:** Twilight. **Caddies:** No. **Golf carts:** Included in Green Fee.
Discount golf packages: No. **Season:** March-Nov. **High:** March-Sept. **On site lodg-
ing:** No. **Rental clubs:** Yes. **Walking policy:** Mandatory cart. **Metal spikes allowed:**
Yes. **Range:** Yes (grass). **To obtain tee times:** Call seven days in advance.
Subscriber comments: Wide open and long...Quality course, also very
affordable...Lots of water, cheap...Excellent service.

★★★½STATE COLLEGE ELKS COUNTRY CLUB
Rte. 322 Box 8, Boalsburg, 16827, Centre County, (814)466-6451, 5 miles E of State
College.
Opened: 1964. **Holes:** 18. **Par:** 71/72. **Yards:** 6,358/5,125. **Course rating:** 70.9/70.2.
Slope: 123/119. **Architect:** Erdman. **Green fee:** $30/$30. **Credit cards:** All major.
Reduced fees: N/A. **Caddies:** No. **Golf carts:** $12. **Discount golf packages:** No.
Season: April-Nov. **High:** May-Sept. **On site lodging:** No. **Rental clubs:** Yes. **Walking
policy:** Unrestricted walking. **Metal spikes allowed:** Yes. **Range:** Yes (grass). **To
obtain tee times:** Call 3 days in advance.
Subscriber comments: Excellent...The greens are very fast...Nothing tricky, attentive
staff, best greens...Great course, long par 3s...Short but enjoyable...Super course,
windy...Challenging, some water, some length, 18 fast greens...Very hilly.

★★★½STONE HEDGE COUNTRY CLUB
PU-R.D. No. 4, Tunkhannock, 18657, Wyoming County, (717)836-5108, 22 miles W of
Scranton.
Opened: 1991. **Holes:** 18. **Par:** 71/71. **Yards:** 6,644/5,046. **Course rating:** 71.9/69.7.
Slope: 124/122. **Architect:** Jim Blaukovitch. **Green fee:** $20/$28. **Credit cards:**
MC,VISA. **Reduced fees:** Weekdays, low season, twilight, seniors. **Caddies:** No. **Golf
carts:** $9. **Discount golf packages:** No. **Season:** April-Dec. **High:** May-Sept. **On site
lodging:** No. **Rental clubs:** No. **Walking policy:** Mandatory cart. **Metal spikes
allowed:** No. **Range:** Yes (grass). **To obtain tee times:** Call three days in advance or
earlier if out of town.
Subscriber comments: Best value in northeast Pa. No. 2 an impossible par 4...Good
test of golf, back side requires good shots...Very good specials, great mountain
course...Very scenic and well groomed...Mountainside course. Great holes.

★★★½ STOUGHTON ACRES GOLF CLUB

PU-904 Sunset Dr., Butler, 16001, Butler County,
(412)285-3633.
Call club for further information.
Subscriber comments: Service outstanding along with
the golf...Tough for public Pa. course, good people, low
price, nice sand....Great value, very cheap, so cheap always
busy, nice people...No.11 one of best par 4s around.

★★★ SUGARLOAF GOLF CLUB

PU-R.D. No. 2, Sugarloaf, 18249, Luzerne County, (717)384-4097, (888)342-5784, 6
miles W of Hazleton.
Opened: 1967. **Holes:** 18. **Par:** 72/72. **Yards:** 6,845/5,620. **Course rating:** 73.0/72.8.
Slope: 122/120. **Architect:** Geoffrey Cornish. **Green fee:** $15/$15. **Credit cards:**
MC,VISA,MAC. **Reduced fees:** Twilight. **Caddies:** No. **Golf carts:** $25. **Discount golf
packages:** No. **Season:** March-Nov. **High:** July-Aug. **On site lodging:** No. **Rental
clubs:** Yes. **Walking policy:** Walking at certain times. **Metal spikes allowed:** Yes.
Range: Yes (grass). **To obtain tee times:** Call.
Subscriber comments: Excellent greens...Very good mountain course, interesting layout...Front nine wide open, back is tight with water, trees...Large greens, mature
course, plenty of hazards...Very hilly. Lots of risk, reward shots.

★★ SUNSET GOLF COURSE

PU-Geyer's Church Rd. & Sunset Dr., Middletown, 17057, Dauphin County, (717)944-
5415, 12 miles E of Harrisburg.
Opened: N/A. **Holes:** 18. **Par:** 70/71. **Yards:** 6,328/5,255. **Course rating:** 69.1/69.9.
Slope: 113/113. **Architect:** Air Force. **Green fee:** $10/$20. **Credit cards:** MC,VISA.
Reduced fees: Low season, seniors, juniors. **Caddies:** No. **Golf carts:** $11. **Discount
golf packages:** No. **Season:** Year-round. **High:** May-Sept. **On site lodging:** No. **Rental
clubs:** Yes. **Walking policy:** Unrestricted walking. **Metal spikes allowed:** Yes. **Range:**
Yes (mats). **To obtain tee times:** Call golf shop.

★★ SYLVAN HEIGHTS GOLF COURSE

PU-Rte. 65, Ellwood - New Castle Rd., New Castle, 16101, Lawrence County,
(412)658-8021, 50 miles N of Pittsburgh.
Opened: N/A. **Holes:** 18. **Par:** 71/71. **Yards:** 6,081/6,781. **Course rating:** N/A. **Slope:**
N/A. **Architect:** N/A. **Green fee:** $9/$9. **Credit cards:** None. **Reduced fees:** Seniors.
Caddies: No. **Golf carts:** $15. **Discount golf packages:** No. **Season:** Year-round.
High: April-Oct. **On site lodging:** No. **Rental clubs:** No. **Walking policy:** Unrestricted
walking. **Metal spikes allowed:** Yes. **Range:** No. **To obtain tee times:** Call anytime.

★★★½ TAM O'SHANTER GOLF CLUB

PU-I-80 And Rte. 18 N., Hermitage, 16159, Mercer County, (412)981-3552, 40 miles
NW of Pittsburgh.
Opened: 1931. **Holes:** 18. **Par:** 72/76. **Yards:** 6,537/5,385. **Course rating:** 69.4/70.2.
Slope: 121/113. **Architect:** Emil Loeffler. **Green fee:** $19/$23. **Credit cards:**
MC,VISA,DISC. **Reduced fees:** Weekdays, low season, resort guests, seniors, juniors.
Caddies: Yes. **Golf carts:** $9. **Discount golf packages:** Yes. **Season:** March-Nov.
High: June-Sept. **On site lodging:** Yes. **Rental clubs:** Yes. **Walking policy:**
Unrestricted walking. **Metal spikes allowed:** Yes. **Range:** Yes (grass/mats). **To obtain
tee times:** Call. Tee times available daily.
Subscriber comments: Thinking man's course, one of Pa.'s finest...Not too tough, not
too easy. The green on last par 3 can kill you...No. 3 a great par 5...Old, beautiful, traditional golf course..Great course for the buck.

★★★ TAMIMENT RESORT & CONFERENCE CENTER GOLF CLUB

R-Bushkill Falls Rd., Tamiment, 18371, Pike County, (717)588-6652, (800)233-8105, 75
miles W of New York.
Opened: 1951. **Holes:** 18. **Par:** 72/72. **Yards:** 6,858/5,598. **Course rating:** 72.7/71.9.

Slope: 130/124. **Architect:** Robert Trent Jones. **Green fee:** $22/$35. **Credit cards:** All major. **Reduced fees:** Weekdays, low season, resort guests, twilight, juniors. **Caddies:** No. **Golf carts:** $17. **Discount golf packages:** Yes. **Season:** April-Nov. **High:** May-Sept. **On site lodging:** Yes. **Rental clubs:** Yes. **Walking policy:** Walking at certain times. **Metal spikes allowed:** Yes. **Range:** No. **To obtain tee times:** Hotel guests at time room reservations are made. Nonguests may call up to 30 days in advance.
Subscriber comments: Long course great for weekend getaways...Very enjoyable...Great Pocono Mountain course...Great shape. Fast greens...Trent Jones course, enough said...Fun, beautiful scenery...Needs shorter women's tees.

★★½TANGLEWOOD MANOR GOLF CLUB & LEARNING CENTER
PU-Scotland Rd., Quarryville, 17566, Lancaster County, (717)786-2220, 10 miles S of Lancaster.
Opened: 1969. **Holes:** 18. **Par:** 72/74. **Yards:** 6,400/5,200. **Course rating:** 70.7/70.7. **Slope:** 118/118. **Architect:** Chester Ruby. **Green fee:** $15/$24. **Credit cards:** MC,VISA. **Reduced fees:** Weekdays, low season, resort guests, twilight, seniors, juniors. **Caddies:** No. **Golf carts:** $12. **Discount golf packages:** Yes. **Season:** March-Dec. **High:** May-Oct. **On site lodging:** No. **Rental clubs:** Yes. **Walking policy:** Walking at certain times. **Metal spikes allowed:** No. **Range:** Yes (grass/mats). **To obtain tee times:** Call.
Subscriber comments: Thinking person's course, challenging both mind and skills...Great family owned course...Very nice track all-around.

★½TIMBER RIDGE GOLF CLUB
PU-RD No. 6, Box 2057, Mount Pleasant, 15666, Westmoreland County, (412)547-1909, 17 miles SE of Pittsburgh.
Opened: 1983. **Holes:** 18. **Par:** 72/72. **Yards:** 6,600/5,277. **Course rating:** 69.9/68.9. **Slope:** 126/112. **Architect:** Fred Garbin. **Green fee:** $15/$20. **Credit cards:** All major. **Reduced fees:** Weekdays, low season, seniors, juniors. **Caddies:** No. **Golf carts:** $10. **Discount golf packages:** No. **Season:** Year-round. **High:** April-Oct. **On site lodging:** No. **Rental clubs:** Yes. **Walking policy:** Unrestricted walking. **Metal spikes allowed:** Yes. **Range:** No. **Tee times:** First come, first served. Call 7a.m.-9a.m.

★★★★TOFTREES RESORT
R-1 Country Club Lane, State College, 16803, Centre County, (814)238-7600, (800)452-3602, 90 miles NW of Harrisburg.
Opened: 1968. **Holes:** 18. **Par:** 72/72. **Yards:** 7,018/5,555. **Course rating:** 74.3/71.8. **Slope:** 134/126. **Architect:** Ed Ault. **Green fee:** $34/$47. **Credit cards:** All major,Diners Club, Carte Blanche. **Reduced fees:** Weekdays, low season, twilight, seniors. **Caddies:** No. **Golf carts:** $15. **Discount golf packages:** Yes. **Season:** April-Nov. **High:** June-Sept. **On site lodging:** Yes. **Rental clubs:** Yes. **Walking policy:** Walking at certain times. **Metal spikes allowed:** Yes. **Range:** Yes (grass). **To obtain tee times:** Public, 14 days in advance; Resort guests, 30 days in advance.
Subscriber comments: Kudos, fantastic, it doesn't get any better...Long; challenging; outstanding accommodations/food...Holes cut out of woods...Fairly long, fast greens...Very hilly and long from the back tees...Fantastic for fall, excellent condition...Incredible conditions and layout. Worth playing over and over again.

★★★TOWANDA COUNTRY CLUB
RR 06, Box 6180, Towanda, 18848, Bradford County, (717)265-6939, 100 miles N of Harrisburg.
Opened: 1927. **Holes:** 18. **Par:** 71/76. **Yards:** 6,100/5,600. **Course rating:** 68.0/67.0. **Slope:** 119/102. **Architect:** Bill Glenn/Warner Burger. **Green fee:** $14/$17. **Credit cards:** MC,VISA. **Reduced fees:** Seniors. **Caddies:** No. **Golf carts:** $20. **Discount golf packages:** Yes. **Season:** April-Dec. **High:** May-Sept. **On site lodging:** No. **Rental clubs:** Yes. **Walking policy:** Mandatory cart. **Metal spikes allowed:** No. **Range:** No. **To obtain tee times:** Call golf shop.
Subscriber comments: Short, challenging; small, fast greens...Good test, best deal in northeast Pa...Fun golf course, good greens...Good greens, short and hilly. Friendly.

★★★½TREASURE LAKE GOLF CLUB
R-13 Treasure Lake, Dubois, 15801, Clearfield County, (814)375-1807, 110 miles NE of Pittsburgh.

Opened: N/A. **Holes:** 18. **Par:** 72/74. **Yards:** 6,278/5,283. **Course rating:** 71.4/72.7. **Slope:** 135. **Architect:** Dominic Palombo. **Green fee:** $23/$36. **Credit cards:** MC,AMEX,DISC. **Reduced fees:** N/A. **Caddies:** No. **Golf carts:** $12. **Discount golf packages:** No. **Season:** May-Oct. **High:** June-Aug. **On site lodging:** No. **Rental clubs:** No. **Walking policy:** Unrestricted walking. **Metal spikes allowed:** Yes. **Range:** No. **To obtain tee times:** Call up to 14 days in advance.
Subscriber comments: Cut out of the forest...Plush conditions, trying to hit down a tunnel on every shot. Very tight...Difficult course due to sloping fairways, but beautifully maintained...Good mountain scenery, must have all golf shots.

★★½TURBOT HILLS GOLF COURSE
PU-RR No. 2, Milton, 17847, North Umberland County, (717)742-9852.
Call club for further information.
Subscriber comments: Nice older, course...Very long course...Great course for the money...Challenging par 4s and par 3s. Several blind shots...Hilly.

★★½TWIN PONDS GOLF COURSE
PU-700 Gilbertsville Rd., Gilbertsville, 19525, Montgomery County, (610)369-1901.
Opened: 1963. **Holes:** 18. **Par:** 70/70. **Yards:** 5,588/4,747. **Course rating:** 65.5/67.7. **Slope:** 111/119. **Architect:** N/A. **Green fee:** N/A. **Credit cards:** None. **Reduced fees:** Weekdays, twilight, seniors. **Caddies:** No. **Golf carts:** $20. **Discount golf packages:** No. **Season:** Year-round. **High:** March-Nov. **On site lodging:** No. **Rental clubs:** Yes. **Walking policy:** Walking at certain times. **Metal spikes allowed:** Yes. **Range:** Yes (grass). **To obtain tee times:** Call.
Subscriber comments: Short course, great for beginners...Short course, hard to par, great greens...Nice mix of short and long par 3s, 4s, and 5s. Great 19th hole.

★½TWINING VALLEY GOLF CLUB
PU-1400 Twining Rd., Dresher, 19025, Montgomery County, (215)659-9917, 5 miles N of Philadelphia.
Opened: 1931. **Holes:** 18. **Par:** 71/72. **Yards:** 6,513/5,300. **Course rating:** 65.9. **Slope:** 114. **Architect:** Jock Mellville. **Green fee:** $20/$24. **Credit cards:** All major. **Reduced fees:** N/A. **Caddies:** No. **Golf carts:** $24. **Discount golf packages:** No. **Season:** Year-round. **High:** April-Oct. **On site lodging:** No. **Rental clubs:** Yes. **Walking policy:** Walking at certain times. **Metal spikes allowed:** Yes. **Range:** Yes (grass/mats). **To obtain tee times:** Call 7 days in advance.
Subscriber comments: Good municipal course with some challenging holes...Very short. A number of par 4s are driveable.

★★★★TYOGA COUNTRY CLUB
RR 6, Wellsboro, 16901, Tioga County, (717)724-1653, 50 miles S of Corning, NY.
Opened: 1923. **Holes:** 18. **Par:** 71/73. **Yards:** 6,335/5,227. **Course rating:** 71.3/70.8. **Slope:** 135/128. **Architect:** Edmund B. Ault. **Green fee:** $45/$45. **Credit cards:** MC,VISA. **Reduced fees:** N/A. **Caddies:** No. **Golf carts:** Included in Green Fee. **Discount golf packages:** Yes. **Season:** April-Nov. **High:** June-Sept. **On site lodging:** No. **Rental clubs:** Yes. **Walking policy:** Mandatory cart. **Metal spikes allowed:** No. **Range:** Yes. **To obtain tee times:** Call golf shop.
Subscriber comments: Beautiful, traditional old course...Excellent mountain course, employees very friendly.

★★★UPPER PERK GOLF COURSE
PU-Rte. 663 & Ott Rd., Pennsburg, 18073, Montgomery County, (215)679-5594, 50 miles NE of Philadelphia.
Opened: 1977. **Holes:** 18. **Par:** 71/71. **Yards:** 6,381/5,249. **Course rating:** 70.0/69.6. **Slope:** 117/113. **Architect:** Bob Hendricks. **Green fee:** $16/$26. **Credit cards:** MC,VISA. **Reduced fees:** Weekdays, low season, twilight, seniors, juniors. **Caddies:** No. **Golf carts:** $20. **Discount golf packages:** No. **Season:** March-Dec. **High:** May-Sept. **On site lodging:** No. **Rental clubs:** No. **Walking policy:** Walking at certain times. **Metal spikes allowed:** Yes. **Range:** No. **To obtain tee times:** Call up to 14 days in advance.
Subscriber comments: Wide open, greens hold very well...Good track usually in extra good shape...Great golf for the price...Easy back nine...Tougher when windy...A nice Sunday afternoon course...Large greens.

★½VALLEY FORGE GOLF CLUB

PU-401 N. Gulf Rd., King Of Prussia, 19406, Montgomery County, (610)337-1776, 25 miles W of Philadelphia.
Opened: 1929. **Holes:** 18. **Par:** 71/73. **Yards:** 6,200/5,668. **Course rating:** 68.9/71.1. **Slope:** 113. **Architect:** Alex Findlay. **Green fee:** $18/$23. **Credit cards:** None. **Reduced fees:** N/A. **Caddies:** No. **Golf carts:** $26. **Discount golf packages:** No. **Season:** March-Nov. **High:** June-July. **On site lodging:** No. **Rental clubs:** Yes. **Walking policy:** Unrestricted walking. **Metal spikes allowed:** Yes. **Range:** No. **To obtain tee times:** Call seven days in advance.

★★VALLEY GREEN GOLF & COUNTRY CLUB

PU-RD No. 2, Box 449F, Greensburg, 15601, Westmoreland County, (412)837-6366, 40 miles SE of Pittsburgh.
Opened: 1965. **Holes:** 18. **Par:** 72/72. **Yards:** 6,345/5,450. **Course rating:** 67.5/67.5. **Slope:** 104/104. **Architect:** X.G. Hassenplug. **Green fee:** $15/$17. **Credit cards:** None. **Reduced fees:** Seniors. **Caddies:** No. **Golf carts:** $18. **Discount golf packages:** No. **Season:** Year-round. **High:** April-Sept. **On site lodging:** No. **Rental clubs:** Yes. **Walking policy:** Unrestricted walking. **Metal spikes allowed:** Yes. **Range:** No. **To obtain tee times:** Call golf shop.

★★½VALLEY GREEN GOLF COURSE

PU-1227 Valley Green Rd., Etters, 17319, York County, (717)938-4200, 15 miles S of Harrisburg.
Opened: 1964. **Holes:** 18. **Par:** 71/71. **Yards:** 6,000/5,500. **Course rating:** 67.0/67.0. **Slope:** 110/109. **Architect:** Short/Leggett. **Green fee:** $11/$17. **Credit cards:** MC,VISA. **Reduced fees:** Weekdays, low season, twilight, seniors, juniors. **Caddies:** No. **Golf carts:** $10. **Discount golf packages:** No. **Season:** March-Nov. **High:** April-Oct. **On site lodging:** No. **Rental clubs:** Yes. **Walking policy:** Unrestricted walking. **Metal spikes allowed:** Yes. **Range:** No. **To obtain tee times:** Call golf shop 7 days in advance.
Subscriber comments: Good shape, front nine short. Back nine OK...Short, small greens...No flat lies here, small tough greens.

★½VENANGO TRAIL GOLF COURSE

970 Freeport Rd., Mars, 16046, Butler County, (412)776-4400, 18 miles N of Pittsburgh.
Opened: 1954. **Holes:** 18. **Par:** 72/72. **Yards:** 6,200/5,518. **Course rating:** 69.9/74.0. **Slope:** 120/117. **Architect:** James Gilmore Harrison. **Green fee:** $11/$20. **Credit cards:** All major. **Reduced fees:** Weekdays, low season, seniors, juniors. **Caddies:** No. **Golf carts:** $10. **Discount golf packages:** Yes. **Season:** Year-round. **High:** April-Oct. **On site lodging:** No. **Rental clubs:** No. **Walking policy:** Walking at certain times. **Metal spikes allowed:** Yes. **Range:** No. **To obtain tee times:** Call 48 hours in advance.

★★VENANGO VALLEY INN & GOLF CLUB

PU-Rte. 19, Venango, 16440, Crawford County, (814)398-4330, 30 miles S of Erie.
Opened: 1972. **Holes:** 18. **Par:** 71/71. **Yards:** 6,202/4,769. **Course rating:** 69.9/69.0. **Slope:** 101/101. **Architect:** Paul E. Erath. **Green fee:** $9/$16. **Credit cards:** N/A. **Reduced fees:** Weekdays, seniors. **Caddies:** No. **Golf carts:** $8. **Discount golf packages:** Yes. **Season:** Year-round. **High:** N/A. **On site lodging:** No. **Rental clubs:** Yes. **Walking policy:** Unrestricted walking. **Metal spikes allowed:** Yes. **Range:** No. **To obtain tee times:** Call.
Subscriber comments: New owners doing great job, much potential...Good luck putting No.14...Staff is good, food excellent...Fairly open course with not much trouble.

★★½WATER GAP COUNTRY CLUB

P.O. Box 188, Mountain Rd., Delaware Water Gap, 18327, Monroe County, (717)476-0300, 70 miles W of New York City.
Opened: 1921. **Holes:** 18. **Par:** 72/74. **Yards:** 6,237/5,199. **Course rating:** 69.0/69.0. **Slope:** 125/114. **Architect:** Robert White. **Green fee:** $33/$42. **Credit cards:** All major. **Reduced fees:** Weekdays, seniors. **Caddies:** No. **Golf carts:** Included in Green Fee. **Discount golf packages:** Yes. **Season:** March-Nov. **High:** July-Sept. **On site lodging:**

Yes. **Rental clubs:** Yes. **Walking policy:** Walking at certain times. **Metal spikes allowed:** Yes. **Range:** No. **To obtain tee times:** Call 5 days in advance. **Notes:** 1927-28 Eastern Open.
Subscriber comments: Very enjoyable...Time warp golf and resort...Nice place for overnight outing...Hilly. Elevated greens and tees. Usually nice shape...The food is the best part...Excellent for average hitter...Hilly, tight, beautiful.

★★½WEDGEWOOD GOLF CLUB
PU-4875 Limeport Pike, Coopersburg, 18036, Lehigh County, (610)797-4551.
Opened: 1963. **Holes:** 18. **Par:** 71/72. **Yards:** 6,162/5,622. **Course rating:** 68.8/65.8. **Slope:** 122/108. **Architect:** William and David Gordon. **Green fee:** $17/$35. **Credit cards:** MC,VISA. **Reduced fees:** Weekdays, low season, twilight, seniors. **Caddies:** No. **Golf carts:** $22. **Discount golf packages:** No. **Season:** Year-round. **High:** April-Sept. **On site lodging:** No. **Rental clubs:** Yes. **Walking policy:** Walking at certain times. **Metal spikes allowed:** Yes. **Range:** Yes (grass). **To obtain tee times:** Call golf shop.
Subscriber comments: Short, tight and fun...For the amount of play in great condition...Accommodating staff...Short, well kept, walkable.

WHITE DEER PARK & GOLF COURSE
PU-R.R. No. 1, P.O. Box 183, Montgomery, 17752, Lycoming County, (717)547-2186, 8 miles S of Williamsport.
Green fee: $12/$19. **Credit cards:** MC,VISA,DISC. **Reduced fees:** Weekdays, low season, twilight, seniors, juniors. **Caddies:** No. **Golf carts:** $10. **Discount golf packages:** No. **Season:** Year-round. **High:** May-Sept. **On site lodging:** No. **Rental clubs:** Yes. **Walking policy:** Unrestricted walking. **Metal spikes allowed:** Yes. **Range:** Yes (grass). **To obtain tee times:** Call Monday after 6 p.m. for upcoming weekend. For weekdays call 3 days in advance.
★★★CHALLENGE
Opened: 1989. **Holes:** 18. **Par:** 72/72. **Yards:** 6,605/4,742. **Course rating:** 71.6/68.4. **Slope:** 133/125. **Architect:** Lindsay Ervin and Assoc.
Subscriber comments: Hard, long, true test of golf, woodsy, beautiful in fall...Outstanding variety. Heavily bunkered.
★★½VINTAGE
Opened: 1965. **Holes:** 18. **Par:** 72/72. **Yards:** 6,405/4,843. **Course rating:** 69.7/68.5. **Slope:** 122/120. **Architect:** Kenneth J. Polakowski.
Subscriber comments: Good for the beginning golfer. Wide open but still challenging on some holes...Plenty of sand, trees and water.

★★★½WHITETAIL GOLF CLUB
PU-2679 Klein Rd., Bath, 18014, Northampton County, (610)837-9626, 7 miles N of Allentown.
Opened: 1993. **Holes:** 18. **Par:** 72/72. **Yards:** 6,432/5,152. **Course rating:** 70.6/65.3. **Slope:** 128/113. **Architect:** Jim Blaukovitch. **Green fee:** $33/$45. **Credit cards:** MC,VISA,AMEX. **Reduced fees:** Weekdays, low season, twilight, seniors, juniors. **Caddies:** No. **Golf carts:** Included in Green Fee. **Discount golf packages:** Yes. **Season:** March-Dec. **High:** May-Sept. **On site lodging:** No. **Rental clubs:** Yes. **Walking policy:** Walking at certain times. **Metal spikes allowed:** No. **Range:** Yes (grass). **To obtain tee times:** Call 7 days in advance, 7 days a week.
Subscriber comments: Great greens, rolling hills...Good maintenance, varied holes...Nice views, good layout, fun and difficult to play...Good course, good service areas...Country club condition, fast greens...Great course, hilly.

★★★½WILKES-BARRE GOLF CLUB
PU-1001 Fairway Dr., Wilkes-Barre, 18702, Luzerne County, (717)472-3590, 25 miles N of Scranton.
Opened: 1968. **Holes:** 18. **Par:** 72/74. **Yards:** 6,912/5,690. **Course rating:** 72.8/73.2. **Slope:** 125/115. **Architect:** Geoffrey Cornish. **Green fee:** $20/$20. **Credit cards:** MC,VISA,AMEX. **Reduced fees:** Weekdays, low season, twilight, seniors, juniors. **Caddies:** No. **Golf carts:** $11. **Discount golf packages:** Yes. **Season:** April-Nov. **High:** June-Aug. **On site lodging:** No. **Rental clubs:** Yes. **Walking policy:** Walking at certain times. **Metal spikes allowed:** Yes. **Range:** Yes (grass). **To obtain tee times:** Call one week in advance.

Subscriber comments: Fantastic Pocono layout, long par 3s...Nice, long and open...Exceptional condition, challenging, fair. Better than most private courses...Golf course is hard, I like it...Best municipal course in eastern Pa....Great condition for amount of traffic. Friendly staff.

★★½WILLOW HOLLOW GOLF COURSE

PU-RD No. 1, Box 1366, Prison Rd., Leesport, 19533, Berks County, (610)373-1505, 6 miles N of Reading.
Opened: 1959. **Holes:** 18. **Par:** 70/70. **Yards:** 5,810/4,435. **Course rating:** 67.1.
Slope: 105/99. **Architect:** Harvey Haupt. **Green fee:** $10/$20. **Credit cards:** MC,VISA.
Reduced fees: Weekdays, twilight, seniors. **Caddies:** No. **Golf carts:** $10. **Discount golf packages:** Yes. **Season:** Year-round. **High:** May-Sept. **On site lodging:** No.
Rental clubs: Yes. **Walking policy:** Walking at certain times. **Metal spikes allowed:** Yes. **Range:** No. **To obtain tee times:** Call up to 30 days in advance for weekends. For weekdays call up to 14 days in advance.
Subscriber comments: Fast greens and good playing...Short but interesting holes, always in good shape...Nice walking course.

★★½WOODLAND HILLS COUNTRY CLUB

Lower Saucon Rd., Hellertown, 18055, Northampton County, (610)838-7192.
Opened: 1968. **Holes:** 18. **Par:** 72/72. **Yards:** 6,761/5,965. **Course rating:** 70.3/68.1.
Slope: 121/110. **Architect:** N/A. **Green fee:** $20/$25. **Credit cards:** MC,VISA.
Reduced fees: Weekdays, low season, seniors, juniors. **Caddies:** No. **Golf carts:** $13.
Discount golf packages: No. **Season:** Year-round. **High:** April-Sept. **On site lodging:** No. **Rental clubs:** Yes. **Walking policy:** Walking at certain times. **Metal spikes allowed:** Yes. **Range:** Yes (grass). **To obtain tee times:** Call 14 days in advance.
Subscriber comments: Getting better condition-wise every year...Nos. 16, 17, 18 very tough finish...Short but challenging; mature course.

★★★★WYNCOTE GOLF CLUB

50 Wyncote Dr., Oxford, 19363, Chester County, (610)932-8900, 50 miles SW of Philadelphia.
Opened: 1993. **Holes:** 18. **Par:** 72/72. **Yards:** 7,012/5,454. **Course rating:** 73.8/71.6.
Slope: 128/126. **Architect:** Brian Ault. **Green fee:** $30/$57. **Credit cards:** All major.
Reduced fees: Weekdays, twilight, seniors, juniors. **Caddies:** Yes. **Golf carts:** $12.
Discount golf packages: No. **Season:** March-Dec. **High:** May-Oct. **On site lodging:** No. **Rental clubs:** Yes. **Walking policy:** Walking at certain times. **Metal spikes allowed:** Yes. **Range:** Yes (grass). **To obtain tee times:** Call one week in advance. Credit card must be used to reserve weekend tee times.
Subscriber comments: Authentic links layout, beautifully maintained, my favorite course in the state...The windiest place in America, forget par...Wind always a factor. Great course, great value...Brutal! Savage! Loved it!

★★½BOULDER HILLS GOLF & COUNTRY CLUB

PU-87 Kingston Rd., Richmond, 02898, Washington County, (401)539-4653.
Opened: 1995. **Holes:** 18. **Par: Architect:** Tripp Davis III. **Caddies:** No. **Discount golf packages:** No. **On site lodging:** No. **Rental clubs:** No. **Metal spikes allowed:** Yes. **Range:** No.
Call club for further information.
Subscriber comments: Very hilly, pretty views...Love this course, shotmaker's course...Steep hills make this a bear!

★★★COUNTRY VIEW GOLF CLUB

PU-49 Club Lane, Harrisville, 02830, Providence County, (401)568-7157, 15 miles N of Providence.
Opened: 1965. **Holes:** 18. **Par:** 70/70. **Yards:** 6,067/4,755. **Course rating:** 69.2/67.0. **Slope:** 119/105. **Architect:** Carl Dexter. **Green fee:** $16/$25. **Credit cards:** None. **Reduced fees:** Weekdays, low season, twilight, seniors. **Caddies:** No. **Golf carts:** $22. **Discount golf packages:** Yes. **Season:** March-Nov. **High:** June-Sept. **On site lodging:** No. **Rental clubs:** Yes. **Walking policy:** Unrestricted walking. **Metal spikes allowed:** Yes. **Range:** No. **To obtain tee times:** Call up to seven days in advance for weekdays. For weekends call Monday.
Subscriber comments: Front nine hilly. Back nine flat. Wide open...Small greens, good challenge. Snack bar on the 15th...Demanding par 3s, challenging front nine.

★★★CRANSTON COUNTRY CLUB

PU-69 Burlingame Rd., Cranston, 02921, Providence County, (401)826-1683, 7 miles S of Providence.
Opened: 1970. **Holes:** 18. **Par:** 71/72. **Yards:** 6,750/5,499. **Course rating:** 72.4. **Slope:** 124. **Architect:** Geoffrey Cornish. **Green fee:** $22/$30. **Credit cards:** MC,VISA,DISC. **Reduced fees:** Weekdays, low season, twilight, seniors. **Caddies:** No. **Golf carts:** $11. **Discount golf packages:** No. **Season:** March-Dec. **High:** May-Sept. **On site lodging:** No. **Rental clubs:** Yes. **Walking policy:** Unrestricted walking. **Metal spikes allowed:** Yes. **Range:** Yes (grass/mats). **To obtain tee times:** Call Tuesday for upcoming weekend. For weekdays call three days in advance.
Subscriber comments: Good golf...Very wet after rain storms...Usually windy there which can make it play long...Excellent large undulating greens...Has improved in recent years...Challenging track for all levels.

★★★½EXETER COUNTRY CLUB

PU-320 Ten Rod Rd., Exeter, 02822, Washington County, (401)295-1178, 15 miles S of Warwick.
Opened: N/A. **Holes:** 18. **Par:** 72/72. **Yards:** 6,919/5,733. **Course rating:** N/A. **Slope:** 123/115. **Architect:** Geoffrey S. Cornish. **Green fee:** N/A. **Credit cards:** MC,VISA. **Reduced fees:** Low season, twilight. **Caddies:** No. **Golf carts:** N/A. **Discount golf packages:** No. **Season:** March-Nov. **High:** June-Sept. **On site lodging:** Yes. **Rental clubs:** No. **Walking policy:** N/A. **Metal spikes allowed:** Yes. **Range:** Yes (grass). **To obtain tee times:** N/A.
Subscriber comments: Outstanding course, very scenic, well groomed...Long course from back tees, great upkeep!...Features beverage wagon around course.

★★★FOSTER COUNTRY CLUB

67 Johnson Rd., Foster, 02825, Providence County, (401)397-7750, 32 miles W of Providence.
Opened: 1964. **Holes:** 18. **Par:** 72/74. **Yards:** 6,200/5,500. **Course rating:** 69.5/70.0. **Slope:** 114/112. **Architect:** N/A. **Green fee:** $20/$22. **Credit cards:** MC,VISA. **Reduced fees:** Twilight. **Caddies:** No. **Golf carts:** $20. **Discount golf packages:** Yes. **Season:** April-Dec. **High:** May-Sept. **On site lodging:** No. **Rental clubs:** Yes. **Walking policy:** Unrestricted walking. **Metal spikes allowed:** Yes. **Range:** No. **To obtain tee times:** Call 7 days in advance.
Subscriber comments: Lots of different holes, use every club...Keeps getting better but desperately needs traps...Good layout, hit the big dog...Unexpected pleasure, very playable and scenic.

★★★GREEN VALLEY COUNTRY CLUB

371 Union St., Portsmouth, 02871, Newport County, (401)849-2162, 5 miles N of Newport.

Opened: 1957. **Holes:** 18. **Par:** 71/71. **Yards:** 6,830/5,459. **Course rating:** 72.0/69.5. **Slope:** 126/120. **Architect:** Manuel Raposa. **Green fee:** $20/$30. **Credit cards:** All major. **Reduced fees:** Weekdays, low season, twilight. **Caddies:** No. **Golf carts:** $22. **Discount golf packages:** No. **Season:** March-Dec. **High:** May-Oct. **On site lodging:** No. **Rental clubs:** Yes. **Walking policy:** Walking at certain times. **Metal spikes allowed:** Yes. **Range:** Yes (grass). **To obtain tee times:** Call three days in advance.

Subscriber comments: Long and windy, good test...Well kept fairways and greens...Great clubhouse.

★★½LAUREL LANE GOLF CLUB

309 Laurel Lane, West Kingston, 02892, Washington County, (401)783-3844, 25 miles S of Providence.

Opened: 1961. **Holes:** 18. **Par:** 71/70. **Yards:** 6,031/5,381. **Course rating:** 68.1/70.8. **Slope:** 113/115. **Architect:** Richard Holly Sr./John Thoren/John Bota. **Green fee:** $20/$25. **Credit cards:** MC,VISA,DISC. **Reduced fees:** Weekdays, low season, twilight, juniors. **Caddies:** No. **Golf carts:** $20. **Discount golf packages:** No. **Season:** March-Dec. **High:** June-Sept. **On site lodging:** No. **Rental clubs:** Yes. **Walking policy:** Unrestricted walking. **Metal spikes allowed:** Yes. **Range:** Yes (grass/mats). **To obtain tee times:** Call golf shop.

Subscriber comments: Demanding back nine...Don't let this one fool you. Plays tough...Nice place, will go back.

★½MEADOW BROOK GOLF CLUB

PU-163 Kingstown Rd., Wyoming, 02898, Washington County, (401)539-8491, 32 miles N of Providence.

Opened: 1929. **Holes:** 18. **Par:** 71/73. **Yards:** 6,075/5,605. **Course rating:** N/A. **Slope:** N/A. **Architect:** Rob Roy Rawlings. **Green fee:** $12/$15. **Credit cards:** None. **Reduced fees:** Weekdays, low season, twilight. **Caddies:** No. **Golf carts:** $15. **Discount golf packages:** No. **Season:** April-Feb. **High:** July-Aug. **On site lodging:** No. **Rental clubs:** No. **Walking policy:** Unrestricted walking. **Metal spikes allowed:** Yes. **Range:** Yes (grass). **To obtain tee times:** First come, first served.

★★MELODY HILL GOLF COURSE

PU-Off Saw Mill Rd., Harmony, 02829, Providence County, (401)949-9851, 15 miles S of Providence.

Opened: 1967. **Holes:** 18. **Par:** 71. **Yards:** 6,185. **Course rating:** 69.0. **Slope:** 113. **Architect:** Samuel Mitchell. **Green fee:** $18/$21. **Credit cards:** N/A. **Reduced fees:** Seniors. **Caddies:** No. **Golf carts:** N/A. **Discount golf packages:** No. **Season:** April-Nov. **High:** May-Aug. **On site lodging:** No. **Rental clubs:** No. **Walking policy:** Unrestricted walking. **Metal spikes allowed:** Yes. **Range:** No. **To obtain tee times:** First come, first served.

★★★½MONTAUP COUNTRY CLUB

500 Anthony Rd., Portsmouth, 02871, Providence County, (401)683-9882, 15 miles S of Providence.

Opened: 1923. **Holes:** 18. **Par:** 71/73. **Yards:** 6,429/5,430. **Course rating:** 71.4/72.3. **Slope:** 123/120. **Architect:** Geoffrey S. Cornish. **Green fee:** $35/$35. **Credit cards:** N/A. **Reduced fees:** N/A. **Caddies:** No. **Golf carts:** $26. **Discount golf packages:** No. **Season:** Year-round. **High:** May-Oct. **On site lodging:** No. **Rental clubs:** No. **Walking policy:** Unrestricted walking. **Metal spikes allowed:** Yes. **Range:** No. **To obtain tee times:** Call golf shop.

Subscriber comments: Good front nine, back nine like a huge open pit...Great winter course...Toughest first hole anywhere...Nice water views on the back nine.

★★★NORTH KINGSTOWN MUNICIPAL GOLF COURSE

PM-1 Callahan Rd., North Kingstown, 02852, Washington County, (401)294-4051, 15 miles S of Providence.

Opened: 1943. **Holes:** 18. **Par:** 70/70. **Yards:** 6,161/5,227. **Course rating:** 69.7/69.5. **Slope:** 119/115. **Architect:** Unknown. **Green fee:** $15/$26. **Credit cards:** None.

Reduced fees: Weekdays, low season, twilight. **Caddies:** No. **Golf carts:** $22. **Discount golf packages:** No. **Season:** March-Dec. **High:** May-Oct. **On site lodging:** No. **Rental clubs:** Yes. **Walking policy:** Unrestricted walking. **Metal spikes allowed:** Yes. **Range:** Yes (grass). **To obtain tee times:** Call 2 days in advance beginning at 8 a.m. during regular season.

Subscriber comments: Lots of play, good shape and variety...Good for high handicappers...Too many geese...A seaside links located on Narragansett Bay.

★★★½RICHMOND COUNTRY CLUB

PU-74 Sandy Pond Rd., Richmond, 02832, Washington County, (401)364-9200, 30 miles S of Providence.

Opened: 1993. **Holes:** 18. **Par:** 71/71. **Yards:** 6,826/4,974. **Course rating:** 72.1. **Slope:** 121. **Architect:** Cornish & Silva. **Green fee:** $25/$30. **Credit cards:** None. **Reduced fees:** Weekdays, twilight. **Caddies:** No. **Golf carts:** $20. **Discount golf packages:** No. **Season:** April-Nov. **High:** June-Sept. **On site lodging:** No. **Rental clubs:** Yes. **Walking policy:** Unrestricted walking. **Metal spikes allowed:** Yes. **Range:** No. **To obtain tee times:** Call one day in advance beginning at 7 a.m.

Subscriber comments: Thought I was in Carolinas!...Enjoyable to play, tight fairways...Make sure you stay for dinner after this easily walkable and most playable bentgrass layout..Tall pines border most fairways.

★★★TRIGGS MEMORIAL GOLF COURSE

PU-1533 Chalkstone Ave., Providence, 02909, Providence County, (401)521-8460.

Opened: 1933. **Holes:** 18. **Par:** 72/73. **Yards:** 6,596/5,598. **Course rating:** 71.9. **Slope:** 126. **Architect:** Donald Ross. **Green fee:** $21/$25. **Credit cards:** None. **Reduced fees:** Low season, seniors. **Caddies:** No. **Golf carts:** $23. **Discount golf packages:** No. **Season:** Year-round. **High:** June-Aug. **On site lodging:** No. **Rental clubs:** Yes. **Walking policy:** Unrestricted walking. **Metal spikes allowed:** Yes. **Range:** No. **To obtain tee times:** Call.

Subscriber comments: Worth a look!...I fell in love with this worn Ross design the first time I played it...Difficult par 3s...Fast greens...Difficult for novice...Oasis in the city, but the high rough is killer if you miss the fairway...Classic old course, on the comeback.

★★★WINNAPAUG COUNTRY CLUB

184 Shore Rd., Westerly, 02891, Washington County, (401)596-1237, 30 miles S of Providence.

Opened: 1922. **Holes:** 18. **Par:** 72/72. **Yards:** 6,337/5,113. **Course rating:** 68.9/69.0. **Slope:** 113/110. **Architect:** Donald Ross. **Green fee:** $22/$28. **Credit cards:** MC,VISA,AMEX. **Reduced fees:** Twilight. **Caddies:** No. **Golf carts:** $11. **Discount golf packages:** Yes. **Season:** Year-round. **High:** June-Sept. **On site lodging:** Yes. **Rental clubs:** Yes. **Walking policy:** Unrestricted walking. **Metal spikes allowed:** Yes. **Range:** Yes (grass/mats). **To obtain tee times:** Call seven days in advance.

Subscriber comments: Some very interesting holes, good views of ocean...Weird layout...I make it a point to play here at least once a year...Considering that one of our foursome put a ball through the clubhouse window we were treated with the utmost service...Could use directional signs to some tees.

★★★ARCADIAN SHORES GOLF CLUB

PU-701 Hilton Rd., Myrtle Beach, 29577, Horry County, (803)449-5217, (800)249-9228.
Opened: 1974. **Holes:** 18. **Par:** 72/72. **Yards:** 6,938/5,229. **Course rating:** 73.2/69.9.
Slope: 136/117. **Architect:** Rees Jones. **Green fee:** $43/$90. **Credit cards:** All major.
Reduced fees: Low season, resort guests, juniors. **Caddies:** No. **Golf carts:** Included
in Green Fee. **Discount golf packages:** Yes. **Season:** Year-round. **High:** March-
May/Oct. **On site lodging:** Yes. **Rental clubs:** Yes. **Walking policy:** Mandatory cart.
Metal spikes allowed: Yes. **Range:** Yes (grass/mats). **To obtain tee times:** Call up to
1 year in advance or book a golf package through Myrtle Beach Hilton.
Subscriber comments: Classic layout...2nd hole a great par 3 over water...Well
designed, beauty stays with you when it's over...Excellent "old style" easy Rees Jones
layout (watch for gators!)...Enjoyed the layout.

★★★½ARROWHEAD COUNTRY CLUB

PU-1201 Burcal Rd., Myrtle Beach, 29577, Horry County, (803)236-3243, (800)236-
3243, 3 miles W of Myrtle Beach.
Opened: 1994. **Holes:** 18. **Par:** 72/72. **Yards:** 6,666/4,812. **Course rating:** 71.1/71.2.
Slope: 130/116. **Architect:** Tom Jackson and Ray Floyd. **Green fee:** $41/$90. **Credit
cards:** MC,VISA,AMEX. **Reduced fees:** Juniors. **Caddies:** No. **Golf carts:** Included in
Green Fee. **Discount golf packages:** No. **Season:** Year-round. **High:** Spring/Fall. **On
site lodging:** No. **Rental clubs:** Yes. **Walking policy:** Mandatory cart. **Metal spikes
allowed:** Yes. **Range:** Yes (grass). **To obtain tee times:** Book through accommodations host or call golf shop.
Subscriber comments: Exceptional course...Good variety of tees...Too much water. A
penal golfing experience...Every hole a postcard...New nine by waterway
exciting!...Close to the airport.

★★½AZALEA SANDS GOLF CLUB

PU-2100 Hwy. 17 S., North Myrtle Beach, 29582, Horry County, (803)272-6191,
(800)252-2312, 10 miles N of Myrtle Beach.
Opened: 1972. **Holes:** 18. **Par:** 72/72. **Yards:** 6,902/5,172. **Course rating:** 72.5/70.2.
Slope: 123/119. **Architect:** Gene Hamm. **Green fee:** $26/$60. **Credit cards:** MC,VISA.
Reduced fees: Low season, resort guests, twilight, juniors. **Caddies:** No. **Golf carts:**
Included in Green Fee. **Discount golf packages:** Yes. **Season:** Year-round. **High:**
Spring/Fall. **On site lodging:** No. **Rental clubs:** Yes. **Walking policy:** Walking at cer-
tain times. **Metal spikes allowed:** Yes. **Range:** No. **To obtain tee times:** Call golf
shop.
Subscriber comments: A decent, fairly open course...Picturesque! Easy layout...Flat
as a pool table...Nice course on the Strand...Fine course for the average golfer.

BAY TREE GOLF PLANTATION

PU-P.O. Box 240, North Myrtle Beach, 29597, Horry County, (803)249-1487, (800)845-
6191, 8 miles N of Myrtle Beach.
Opened: 1972. **Architect:** George Fazio/Russell Breedon. **Green fee:** $19/$42. **Credit
cards:** All major. **Reduced fees:** Low season, juniors. **Caddies:** No. **Golf carts:** $18.
Discount golf packages: Yes. **Season:** Year-round. **High:** March-April. **On site lodging:** Yes. **Rental clubs:** Yes. **Walking policy:** Walking at certain times. **Metal spikes
allowed:** Yes. **Range:** Yes (grass). **To obtain tee times:** Call anytime.
★★½GOLD COURSE
Holes: 18. **Par:** 72/72. **Yards:** 6,942/5,264. **Course rating:** 72.0/69.7. **Slope:** 135/117.
Notes: 1977 LPGA Tour Championship.
Subscriber comments: Basic golf...OK beach course...Interesting challenging lay-
out...Hard to stay in the fairways for slicers...Wide open...Good fair course.
★★½GREEN COURSE
Holes: 18. **Par:** 72/72. **Yards:** 7,044/5,362. **Course rating:** 72.5/69.0. **Slope:** 135/118.
Notes: PGA Tour Qualifying School.
Subscriber comments: Long but fair-good test of skills...Very busy place. Nice
course...Sees too much play...Par 3 course is more interesting than regular course.
★★½SILVER COURSE
Holes: 18. **Par:** 72/72. **Yards:** 6,871/5,417. **Course rating:** 70.5/69.0. **Slope:** 131/116.
Subscriber comments: Not even close to Green or Gold...Slowish greens, open fair-
ways...Every green well bunkered.

SOUTH CAROLINA

★★★BEACHWOOD GOLF CLUB
PU-1520 Hwy. 17 S., North Myrtle Beach, 29582, Horry County, (803)272-6168, (800)526-4889, 12 miles N of Myrtle Beach.
Opened: 1968. **Holes:** 18. **Par:** 72/72. **Yards:** 6,825/6,344. **Course rating:** N/A. **Slope:** 121/117. **Architect:** Gene Hamm. **Green fee:** $12/$46. **Credit cards:** MC,VISA,AMEX. **Reduced fees:** Low season, twilight, juniors. **Caddies:** No. **Golf carts:** $17. **Discount golf packages:** No. **Season:** Year-round. **High:** March-Oct. **On site lodging:** No. **Rental clubs:** Yes. **Walking policy:** Mandatory cart. **Metal spikes allowed:** Yes. **Range:** Yes (grass). **To obtain tee times:** Call.
Subscriber comments: Nice, big trees. Park-like setting...Basic course but worth playing...Very wide fairways, greens large...Played almost 70 courses on the Strand and I always come back to this one...Just great...Good warm-up for Myrtle.

BELLE TERRE GOLF COURSE
R-4073 U.S. Hwy. 501, Myrtle Beach, 29579, Horry County, (803)236-8888, (800)340-0072, 3 miles NW of Myrtle Beach.
Opened: 1995. **Architect:** Rees Jones. **Credit cards:** All major. **Reduced fees:** Low season, resort guests, juniors. **Caddies:** No. **Season:** Year-round. **High:** Spring/Fall. **On site lodging:** No. **Rental clubs:** Yes. **Metal spikes allowed:** Yes. **Range:** Yes (grass). **To obtain tee times:** Call.
★★★½CHAMPIONSHIP COURSE
Holes: 18. **Par:** 72/72. **Yards:** 7,013/5,049. **Course rating:** 74.0. **Slope:** 134/126. **Green fee:** $20/$70. **Golf carts:** $18. **Discount golf packages:** No. **Walking policy:** Mandatory cart.
Notes: 1996-97 Dupont World Amateur Handicap Championship.
Subscriber comments: A must at Myrtle Beach...Great course, nice clubhouse, friendly...Too many holes look similiar...Will be top 10 in Myrtle Beach...A lot of testy drives over water...Holes 1, 2, 3, 18 stand out...Water comes into play a lot.
PAR 58 COURSE
Holes: 18. **Par:** 58/58. **Yards:** 3,201/2,802. **Course rating:** 57.8. **Slope:** 93. **Green fee:** $15/$30. **Golf carts:** $15. **Discount golf packages:** Yes. **Walking policy:** Unrestricted walking.

★★½BERKELEY COUNTRY CLUB
Old Hwy. 52, Moncks Corner, 29461, Berkeley County, (803)761-4880, 20 miles N of Charleston.
Opened: 1959. **Holes:** 18. **Par:** 72/72. **Yards:** 6,696/5,100. **Course rating:** 71.2/67.9. **Slope:** 114/106. **Architect:** George Cobb. **Green fee:** $15/$19. **Credit cards:** MC,VISA,DISC. **Reduced fees:** Low season, seniors. **Caddies:** No. **Golf carts:** $11. **Discount golf packages:** No. **Season:** Year-round. **High:** April-Aug. **On site lodging:** No. **Rental clubs:** Yes. **Walking policy:** N/A. **Metal spikes allowed:** Yes. **Range:** Yes (grass/mats). **To obtain tee times:** Call 2 days in advance.
Subscriber comments: Nice public course. Reasonable...Excellent course, very long...Never too busy, nice rural setting...Long, but fair-great for high handicappers...Not much of a challenge.

★★★½BLACKMOOR GOLF CLUB
R-6100 Longwood Rd., Hwy. 707, Murrells Inlet, 29576, Horry County, (803)650-5555, 12 miles S of Myrtle Beach.
Opened: 1990. **Holes:** 18. **Par:** 72/72. **Yards:** 6,614/4,807. **Course rating:** 71.1/67.9. **Slope:** 126/115. **Architect:** Gary Player. **Green fee:** $23/$70. **Credit cards:** MC,VISA. **Reduced fees:** Low season, resort guests, juniors. **Caddies:** No. **Golf carts:** $17. **Discount golf packages:** Yes. **Season:** Year-round. **High:** Spring/Fall. **On site lodging:** No. **Rental clubs:** Yes. **Walking policy:** Mandatory cart. **Metal spikes allowed:** Yes. **Range:** Yes (grass). **To obtain tee times:** Call golf shop.
Subscriber comments: Challenging layout, but enjoyable...Gary Player at his best...Some blind shots. Lots of wildlife...18th hole the best...Friendliest in Myrtle...Gary Player must love doglegs...Very good layout...Four or five contrived holes.

★★½BONNIE BRAE GOLF COURSE
1316 Fork Shoals Rd., Greenville, 29605, Greenville County, (864)277-4178.
Call club for further information.
Subscriber comments: Hard greens, a lot of bunkers...One of my personal
favorites...Good solid public course...Not bad for the price...Needs new clubhouse.

★★★BOSCOBEL GOLF CLUB
Hwy. 76, Pendleton, 29670, Anderson County, (803)646-3991, 28 miles SW of
Greenville.
Opened: 1932. **Holes:** 18. **Par:** 71/72. **Yards:** 6,400/5,023. **Course rating:** 69.8/67.8.
Slope: 115/114. **Architect:** Fred Bolton. **Green fee:** $13/$17. **Credit cards:** MC,VISA.
Reduced fees: N/A. **Caddies:** No. **Golf carts:** $18. **Discount golf packages:** Yes.
Season: Year-round. **High:** March-Aug. **On site lodging:** No. **Rental clubs:** No.
Walking policy: Unrestricted walking. **Metal spikes allowed:** Yes. **Range:** No. **To
obtain tee times:** Call 1 day in advance.
Subscriber comments: Very fast greens...Has several weird holes...Good all around
course, good for all levels...Watch out for the gators...Just an average course, fast
greens.

★★★½BUCK CREEK GOLF CLUB
PU-701 Bucks Trail, Hwy. 9, Longs, 29568, Horry County, (803)399-
2660, (800)344-0982, 6 miles NE of North Myrtle Beach.
Opened: 1990. **Holes:** 27. **Architect:** Tom Jackson. **Green fee:**
$22/$66. **Credit cards:** MC,VISA. **Reduced fees:** Weekdays, low
season, resort guests, twilight, seniors, juniors. **Caddies:** No. **Golf
carts:** $18. **Discount golf packages:** Yes. **Season:** Year-round. **High:** Spring/Fall. **On
site lodging:** No. **Rental clubs:** Yes. **Walking policy:** Mandatory cart. **Metal spikes
allowed:** Yes. **Range:** Yes (grass). **To obtain tee times:** Call.
CYPRESS/TUPELO
Par: 72/72. **Yards:** 6,865/4,956. **Course rating:** 72.4/68.4.
Slope: 132/124.
MEADOW/CYPRESS
Par: 72/72. **Yards:** 6,751/4,972. **Course rating:** 71.1/67.5. **Slope:**
126/117.
MEADOW/TUPELO
Par: 72/72. **Yards:** 6,729/4,972. **Course rating:** 71.6/67.5. **Slope:** 126/117.
Notes: Annual Dupont World Amateur.
Subscriber comments: Had a great time...Fun, challenging, shotmaker's
layout...Carved out of a wildlife preserve...Tough finishing hole...Tupelo nine is most
unforgiving I have ever played...Have to be long and accurate on most
holes...Friendly...Long but fair. Need best game, have to think.

BURNING RIDGE GOLF CLUB
R-Hwy. 501 W., Conway, 29577, Horry County, (803)347-0538, (800)833-6337, 5 miles
E of Myrtle Beach.
Architect: Gene Hamm. **Green fee:** $29/$65. **Credit cards:** MC,VISA. **Reduced fees:**
Weekdays, low season, twilight. **Caddies:** No. **Golf carts:** Included in Green Fee.
Discount golf packages: Yes. **Season:** Year-round. **High:** Spring/Fall. **On site lodg-
ing:** No. **Rental clubs:** Yes. **Walking policy:** Mandatory cart. **Metal spikes allowed:**
Yes. **Range:** Yes (grass). **To obtain tee times:** Call 2 days in advance.
★★★EAST COURSE
Opened: 1985. **Holes:** 18. **Par:** 72/72. **Yards:** 6,780/4,524. **Course rating:** 73.1/65.4.
Slope: 132/111.
Subscriber comments: Nice course, older, mature...Lots of sand...Can play tough on
windy day...Lots of water and sand, challenging...Makes you play a "thinking
game"...Quaint, beautiful par 3s...You need to be a shotmaker on this course.
★★★WEST COURSE
Opened: 1980. **Holes:** 18. **Par:** 72/72. **Yards:** 6,714/4,831. **Course rating:** 73.0/66.2.
Slope: 128/112.
Subscriber comments: Very playable...One of many good Myrtle courses...Much bet-
ter than East course...A lot of fun...A factory...Fair layout...Testing course, must play.

★★★★½CALEDONIA GOLF & FISH CLUB

PU-369 Caledonia Dr., Pawleys Island, 29585, Georgetown County, (803)237-3675, (800)483-6800, 15 miles S of Myrtle Beach.
Opened: 1994. **Holes:** 18. **Par:** 70/70. **Yards:** 6,526/4,957. **Course rating:** 70.9/68.2. **Slope:** 132/113. **Architect:** Mike Strantz. **Green fee:** $108. **Credit cards:** All major. **Reduced fees:** N/A. **Caddies:** No. **Golf carts:** Included in Green Fee. **Discount golf packages:** Yes. **Season:** Year-round. **High:** Spring/Fall. **On site lodging:** No. **Rental clubs:** Yes. **Walking policy:** Mandatory cart. **Metal spikes allowed:** Yes. **Range:** No. **To obtain tee times:** Call golf shop or hotel golf director for tee times.
Notes: Ranked 15th in 1997 Best in State.
Subscriber comments: Beautiful course, setting and clubhouse...A work of art...18th hole, second shot over water. What a finish...Short course, but immaculate...Great course; No.9 is a questionable par 3 (too short)...Awesome, too good to be called a public course...First class facility, mint conditions, what an experience...If you can't get on Augusta this will do just fine...Don't go there and don't tell your friends.

★★★CALHOUN COUNTRY CLUB

Rte. 3 Country Club Rd., St. Matthews, 29135, Calhoun County, (803)823-2465, 30 miles S of Columbia.
Opened: 1957. **Holes:** 18. **Par:** 71/71. **Yards:** 6,339/4,812. **Course rating:** 70.9/66.4. **Slope:** 119/110. **Architect:** Ellis Maples. **Green fee:** $10/$25. **Credit cards:** MC,VISA. **Reduced fees:** Weekdays, twilight, seniors, juniors. **Caddies:** No. **Golf carts:** Included in Green Fee. **Discount golf packages:** No. **Season:** Year-round. **High:** March-April. **On site lodging:** No. **Rental clubs:** No. **Walking policy:** Walking at certain times. **Metal spikes allowed:** Yes. **Range:** Yes (grass). **To obtain tee times:** Call golf shop.
Subscriber comments: Good course...Outstanding hotdogs...Too difficult from tips with any wind...Many elevation changes. Pretty par 3s. Jewel in th middle of nowhere...A hidden treasure.

★½CAROLINA DOWNS COUNTRY CLUB

PU-294 Shiloh Rd., York, 29745, York County, (803)684-5878, 18 miles S of Charlotte, NC.
Opened: 1984. **Holes:** 18. **Par:** 72/72. **Yards:** 6,335/4,624. **Course rating:** 69.5/67.4. **Slope:** 133/123. **Architect:** Boony Harper. **Green fee:** $20/$25. **Credit cards:** All major. **Reduced fees:** Weekdays, low season, seniors, juniors. **Caddies:** No. **Golf carts:** Included in Green Fee. **Discount golf packages:** Yes. **Season:** Year-round. **High:** May-Oct. **On site lodging:** No. **Rental clubs:** No. **Walking policy:** Walking at certain times. **Metal spikes allowed:** Yes. **Range:** Yes (grass). **To obtain tee times:** No starting times.

★★½CAROLINA SPRINGS GOLF CLUB

1680 Scuffletown Rd., Fountain Inn, 29644, Greenville County, (864)862-3551, 8 miles S of Greenville.
Opened: 1968. **Holes:** 27. **Architect:** Russell Breeden. **Green fee:** $30/$40. **Credit cards:** All major. **Reduced fees:** Weekdays, low season, twilight, seniors, juniors. **Caddies:** No. **Golf carts:** Included in Green Fee. **Discount golf packages:** Yes. **Season:** Year-round. **High:** April-Sept. **On site lodging:** No. **Rental clubs:** Yes. **Walking policy:** Walking at certain times. **Metal spikes allowed:** Yes. **Range:** Yes (grass/mats). **To obtain tee times:** Call up to 5 days in advance.
PINES/CEDAR
Par: 72/72. **Yards:** 6,676/5,084. **Course rating:** 72.6/68.9. **Slope:** 132/116.
WILLOWS/CEDAR
Par: 72/72. **Yards:** 6,643/5,135. **Course rating:** 72.0/68.5. **Slope:** 126/113.
WILLOWS/PINES
Par: 72/72. **Yards:** 6,815/5,223. **Course rating:** 72.8/69.3. **Slope:** 130/119.
Subscriber comments: Super course, 27 holes, bent grass, greens fast...Wide open golf...Fair design...Two mature nines. Fair test of accuracy...Good public course, playable for all golfers.

★★★½CEDAR CREEK GOLF CLUB

2475 Club Dr., Aiken, 29803, Aiken County, (803)648-4206, 25 miles E of Augusta, GA.
Opened: 1991. **Holes:** 18. **Par:** 72/72. **Yards:** 7,206/5,231. **Course rating:** 73.3/69.1.
Slope: 125/115. **Architect:** Arthur Hills. **Green fee:** $36/$36. **Credit cards:**
MC,VISA,AMEX. **Reduced fees:** Low season, resort guests, twilight, seniors. **Caddies:**
No. **Golf carts:** Included in Green Fee. **Discount golf packages:** Yes. **Season:** Year-round. **High:** April-Sept. **On site lodging:** No. **Rental clubs:** Yes. **Walking policy:**
Walking at certain times. **Metal spikes allowed:** Yes. **Range:** Yes (grass). **To obtain tee times:** Call 7 days in advance.
Subscriber comments: Several great holes...Rolling course so don't expect many level lies...A real test...Challenging course...Will only get better with maturity...No.2 very tough Par 5. Tough course.

★★CHARLESTON MUNICIPAL GOLF COURSE

PM-2110 Maybank Hwy., Charleston, 29412, Charleston County, (803)795-6517.
Opened: 1927. **Holes:** 18. **Par:** 72/72. **Yards:** 6,411/5,202. **Course rating:** 70.2/69.2.
Slope: 112/114. **Architect:** John E. Adams. **Green fee:** $10/$15. **Credit cards:**
MC,VISA. **Reduced fees:** Twilight, seniors, juniors. **Caddies:** No. **Golf carts:** $20.
Discount golf packages: No. **Season:** Year-round. **High:** Spring/Fall. **On site lodging:**
No. **Rental clubs:** Yes. **Walking policy:** Unrestricted walking. **Metal spikes allowed:**
Yes. **Range:** Yes (grass/mats). **To obtain tee times:** Call or come in 7 days in advance for threesomes and foursomes.

★★★½CHARLESTON NATIONAL COUNTRY CLUB

1360 National Dr., Mount Pleasant, 29464, Charleston County, (803)884-7799, 10 miles
E of Charleston.
Opened: 1989. **Holes:** 18. **Par:** 72/72. **Yards:** 6,975/5,103. **Course rating:** 74.0/70.8.
Slope: 140/126. **Architect:** Rees Jones. **Green fee:** $32/$64. **Credit cards:**
MC,VISA,DISC. **Reduced fees:** Weekdays, low season, resort guests, twilight, seniors,
juniors. **Caddies:** Yes. **Golf carts:** Included in Green Fee. **Discount golf packages:**
Yes. **Season:** Year-round. **High:** Spring/Fall. **On site lodging:** No. **Rental clubs:** Yes.
Walking policy: Mandatory cart. **Metal spikes allowed:** Yes. **Range:** Yes (grass/mats).
To obtain tee times: Call.
Subscriber comments: A sparkling jewel in the marsh, super...Lost ball potential at every hole...Fun to play but tough...Target golf through the wetlands...When the wind blows, conditions are really tough...Nice scenery, some holes unfair.

★★★½CHERAW STATE PARK GOLF COURSE

PU-100 State Park Rd., Cheraw, 29520, Chesterfield County, (803)537-2215, (800)868-9630, 40 miles from Florence.
Opened: N/A. **Holes:** 18. **Par:** 72/72. **Yards:** 6,900/5,408. **Course rating:** 73.4/70.8. **Slope:** 130/120. **Architect:** Tom Jackson. **Green fee:**
$13/$18. **Credit cards:** MC,VISA. **Reduced fees:** Weekdays. **Caddies:**
No. **Golf carts:** $12. **Discount golf packages:** Yes. **Season:** Year-round. **High:** March-June. **On site lodging:** Yes. **Rental clubs:** No. **Walking policy:** N/A. **Metal spikes allowed:** Yes. **Range:** Yes (grass/mats). **To obtain tee times:** Call.
Subscriber comments: Cheap price, great course...Very nice layout, #13 is a great hole...Played on a cold, rainy day and loved it...A hidden gem!...Tough back nine...Shh! Don't tell anyone! Worth the drive from Myrtle.

★★CHESTER GOLF CLUB

770 Old Richburg Rd., Chester, 29706, Chester County, (803)581-5733, 45 miles S of
Charlotte.
Opened: 1971. **Holes:** 18. **Par:** 72/72. **Yards:** 6,811/5,347. **Course rating:** 72.0/70.1.
Slope: 124/116. **Architect:** Russell Breeden. **Green fee:** $18/$21. **Credit cards:** None.
Reduced fees: N/A. **Caddies:** No. **Golf carts:** $13. **Discount golf packages:** No.
Season: Year-round. **High:** April-Oct. **On site lodging:** No. **Rental clubs:** No. **Walking policy:** Walking at certain times. **Metal spikes allowed:** No. **Range:** Yes (grass). **To obtain tee times:** Call.
Subscriber comments: Well kept. Fun to play...Kind of bland...Good golf, seldom crowded...Friendly folks, not very challenging...Course OK, wide open.

SOUTH CAROLINA

★★CHICKASAW POINT COUNTRY CLUB
500 Hogan Dr., Westminster, 29693, Oconee County, (864)972-9623.
Call club for further information.

THE CLUB AT SEABROOK ISLAND
R-1002 Landfall Way, Seabrook Island, 29455, Charleston County,
(803)768-1000, 20 miles S of Charleston.
Green fee: $50/$120. **Credit cards:** All major. **Reduced fees:** N/A.
Caddies: No. **Golf carts:** Included in Green Fee. **Discount golf packages:** Yes. **Season:** Year-round. **High:** Feb.-Aug. **On site lodging:** Yes.
Rental clubs: Yes. **Walking policy:** Mandatory cart. **Metal spikes allowed:** No.
Range: Yes (grass). **To obtain tee times:** Must be a resort guest to play. Tee times
may be reserved with golf package.

★★★½CROOKED OAKS COURSE
Opened: 1982. **Holes:** 18. **Par:** 72/72. **Yards:** 6,832/5,250. **Course rating:** 73.2/70.1.
Slope: 126/119. **Architect:** Robert T. Jones.
Subscriber comments: Great play, would recommend...Good resort course...Nothing
special...Big oaks, nice course, I'll go back...Narrow landing areas and compact greens,
tough...More target golf...Tight but fair with the driver...Resort is as nice as Kiawah, but
golf is only decent.

★★★½OCEAN WINDS COURSE
Opened: 1976. **Holes:** 18. **Par:** 72/72. **Yards:** 6,805/5,524. **Course rating:** 73.5/73.1.
Slope: 130/127. **Architect:** Willard Byrd.
Subscriber comments: Good test, nice greens...The best of the Seabrook courses,
interesting...Nice layout, above average clubhouse...Very tight, scenic, nice
people...Fun to play, good par 3s...Ocean type course, tight fairways...Ocean views
from 14th tee.

★★COBB'S GLEN COUNTRY CLUB
2201 Cobb's Way, Anderson, 29621, Anderson County, (864)226-7688, (800)624-7688,
28 miles S of Greenville.
Opened: 1975. **Holes:** 18. **Par:** 72/72. **Yards:** 7,002/5,312. **Course rating:** 72.3/72.0.
Slope: 129/121. **Architect:** George Cobb. **Green fee:** $20/$25. **Credit cards:**
MC,VISA,AMEX. **Reduced fees:** Weekdays, seniors, juniors. **Caddies:** No. **Golf carts:**
$10. **Discount golf packages:** Yes. **Season:** Year-round. **High:** April-Oct. **On site
lodging:** Yes. **Rental clubs:** Yes. **Walking policy:** Walking at certain times. **Metal
spikes allowed:** Yes. **Range:** Yes (grass/mats). **To obtain tee times:** Call 2 days in
advance.
Subscriber comments: Long course from back markers...Challenging, you get use of
all your clubs...Traditional layout...Excellent big fast greens, tough from tips.

★½COLDSTREAM COUNTRY CLUB
Hwy. 60, Irmo, 29063, Lexington County, (803)781-0114, 14 miles NW of Columbia.
Opened: 1974. **Holes:** 18. **Par:** 71/71. **Yards:** 6,155/5,097. **Course rating:** 70.1/68.7.
Slope: 122. **Architect:** Michael Mungo. **Green fee:** $22/$28. **Credit cards:** MC,VISA.
Reduced fees: Weekdays, low season, resort guests, twilight, seniors, juniors.
Caddies: No. **Golf carts:** Included in Green Fee. **Discount golf packages:** No.
Season: Year-round. **High:** April-Oct. **On site lodging:** No. **Rental clubs:** Yes. **Walking
policy:** Mandatory cart. **Metal spikes allowed:** Yes. **Range:** No. **To obtain tee times:**
Call 48 hours in advance. Members have priority tee times on weekends.

★★COLONIAL CHARTERS GOLF CLUB
PU-301 Charter Dr., Longs, 29301, Horry County, (803)399-4653, (800)833-6337, 3
miles from N. Myrtle Beach.
Opened: 1988. **Holes:** 18. **Par:** 72/72. **Yards:** 6,769/5,079. **Course rating:** 73.0/70.2.
Slope: 131/120. **Architect:** John Simpson. **Green fee:** $29/$65. **Credit cards:** All
major. **Reduced fees:** Low season, twilight. **Caddies:** No. **Golf carts:** Included in
Green Fee. **Discount golf packages:** Yes. **Season:** Year-round. **High:** Spring/Fall. **On
site lodging:** Yes. **Rental clubs:** Yes. **Walking policy:** Mandatory cart. **Metal spikes
allowed:** Yes. **Range:** Yes (grass). **To obtain tee times:** Call.
Subscriber comments: Fun to play, some hard holes...Very nice...Needs better
drainage...Good course...Some very challenging holes.

SOUTH CAROLINA

★★★½COOSAW CREEK COUNTRY CLUB
4210 Club Course Dr., North Charleston, 29420, Dorchester County, (803)767-9000, 10 miles NW of Charleston.
Opened: 1993. **Holes:** 18. **Par:** 71/71. **Yards:** 6,593/5,064. **Course rating:** 71.3/69.1. **Slope:** 129/117. **Architect:** Arthur Hills. **Green fee:** $18/$37. **Credit cards:** MC,VISA,AMEX. **Reduced fees:** Weekdays, low season, juniors. **Caddies:** No. **Golf carts:** $15. **Discount golf packages:** Yes. **Season:** Year-round. **High:** Spring/Fall. **On site lodging:** No. **Rental clubs:** Yes. **Walking policy:** Walking at certain times. **Metal spikes allowed:** Yes. **Range:** Yes (grass). **To obtain tee times:** Call up to 7 days in advance.
Subscriber comments: Fun course, good condition...First nine scenic and fun. Back nine really difficult...A lot of fun but tight fairways.

★★½COUNTRY CLUB OF BEAUFORT
8 Barnwell Dr., Beaufort, 29902, Beaufort County, (803)522-1605, (800)869-1617, 45 miles N of Savannah, GA.
Opened: 1973. **Holes:** 18. **Par:** 72/72. **Yards:** 6,506/4,880. **Course rating:** 71.2/67.8. **Slope:** 118/120. **Architect:** Russell Breedon. **Green fee:** $40/$40. **Credit cards:** MC,VISA. **Reduced fees:** Twilight, juniors. **Caddies:** No. **Golf carts:** Included in Green Fee. **Discount golf packages:** Yes. **Season:** Year-round. **High:** Spring/Fall. **On site lodging:** No. **Rental clubs:** Yes. **Walking policy:** Unrestricted walking. **Metal spikes allowed:** Yes. **Range:** Yes (grass). **To obtain tee times:** Call up to 7 days in advance.
Subscriber comments: A guaranteed fun round for a very reasonable price. Take a camera to photo the gators and scenery...Not a great course, low fees, great welcome, good food.

★★★½COUNTRY CLUB OF HILTON HEAD
70 Skull Creek Dr., Hilton Head Island, 29926, Beaufort County, (803)681-4653, 35 miles NE of Savannah, GA.
Opened: 1987. **Holes:** 18. **Par:** 72/72. **Yards:** 6,919/5,373. **Course rating:** 73.6/71.3. **Slope:** 132/123. **Architect:** Rees Jones. **Green fee:** $52/$79. **Credit cards:** All major,Diners Club. **Reduced fees:** Low season, twilight. **Caddies:** No. **Golf carts:** Included in Green Fee. **Discount golf packages:** No. **Season:** Year-round. **High:** Spring/Fall. **On site lodging:** No. **Rental clubs:** Yes. **Walking policy:** Mandatory cart. **Metal spikes allowed:** Yes. **Range:** Yes (grass/mats). **To obtain tee times:** Call up to 90 days in advance.
Subscriber comments: Another very good Hilton Head course...Top quality facility...Fun track, a lot of doglegs...Very enjoyable golf course.

★★★½CROWFIELD GOLF & COUNTRY CLUB
300 Hamlet Circle, Goose Creek, 29445, Berkeley County, (803)764-4618, 20 miles NW of Charleston.
Opened: 1990. **Holes:** 18. **Par:** 72/72. **Yards:** 7,003/5,682. **Course rating:** 73.7/67.3. **Slope:** 134. **Architect:** Bob Spence. **Green fee:** $30/$69. **Credit cards:** All major. **Reduced fees:** Weekdays, low season, twilight. **Caddies:** No. **Golf carts:** Included in Green Fee. **Discount golf packages:** Yes. **Season:** Year-round. **High:** Spring. **On site lodging:** No. **Rental clubs:** Yes. **Walking policy:** Walking at certain times. **Metal spikes allowed:** Yes. **Range:** Yes (grass). **To obtain tee times:** Call anytime in advance with credit card to guarantee.
Subscriber comments: Very nice course, hard to find...A challenge, lot of bunkers and hills, wonderful course...Demanding par 5s, a fair test with plenty of mounds, water and trees...Scenic inland course.

★★★CYPRESS BAY GOLF CLUB
R-Hwy 17, North Myrtle Beach, 29566, Horry County, (803)249-1017, (800)833-5638, 7 miles N of Myrtle Beach.
Opened: 1972. **Holes:** 18. **Par:** 72/72. **Yards:** 6,502/4,920. **Course rating:** 71.2/69.0. **Slope:** 122/113. **Architect:** Russell Breeden. **Green fee:** $28/$59. **Credit cards:** None. **Reduced fees:** Low season, twilight. **Caddies:** No. **Golf carts:** $19. **Discount golf packages:** No. **Season:** Year-round. **High:** Spring/Fall. **On site lodging:** No. **Rental clubs:** Yes. **Walking policy:** Walking at certain times. **Metal spikes allowed:** Yes. **Range:** No. **To obtain tee times:** Call.

Subscriber comments: Very fun to play, nice layout...Nice golf course, a good golf test...I broke a window on a condo...Great par 3s...Winding fairways...Some good holes, beach golf...Three great finishing holes...Lots of water.

DAUFUSKIE ISLAND CLUB & RESORT

Green fee: $80/$145. **Credit cards:** All major. **Reduced fees:** Resort guests. **Caddies:** No. **Golf carts:** Included in Green Fee. **Discount golf packages:** No. **Season:** Year-round. **High:** March-June/Sept.-Nov. **Rental clubs:** No. **Walking policy:** Unrestricted walking. **Metal spikes allowed:** Yes. **Range:** Yes (grass). **To obtain tee times:** Call golf club.

BLOODY POINT

P.O. Box 23671, Hilton Head Island, 29925, Beaufort County, (803)842-2000, (800)648-6778.
Opened: 1991. **Holes:** 18. **Par:** 72/72. **Yards:** 6,900/5,220. **Course rating:** 73.2/69.7. **Slope:** 135/126. **Architect:** Tom Weiskopf/Jay Morrish. **On site lodging:** No.

MELROSE COURSE

P.O. Box 23285, Hilton Head Island, 29925, Beaufort County, (803)341-4810, (800)648-6778.
Opened: 1987. **Holes:** 18. **Par:** 72/72. **Yards:** 7,081/5,575. **Course rating:** 74.2/72.3. **Slope:** 138/126. **Architect:** Jack Nicklaus. **On site lodging:** Yes.

DEER TRACK GOLF RESORT

R-1705 Platt Blvd., Surfside Beach, 29587, Horry County, (803)650-2146, (800)548-9186, 8 miles S of Myrtle Beach.
Opened: 1974. **Architect:** Bob Toski and Porter Gibson. **Green fee:** $8/$42. **Credit cards:** MC,VISA. **Reduced fees:** Weekdays, low season, resort guests, twilight, juniors. **Caddies:** No. **Golf carts:** $19. **Discount golf packages:** Yes. **Season:** Year-round. **High:** Spring/Fall. **On site lodging:** Yes. **Rental clubs:** Yes. **Walking policy:** Walking at certain times. **Metal spikes allowed:** Yes. **Range:** Yes (grass/mats). **To obtain tee times:** Call golf shop.

★★½SOUTH COURSE

Holes: 18. **Par:** 71/71. **Yards:** 6,916/5,226. **Course rating:** 72.9/70.6. **Slope:** 119/120.
Subscriber comments: Course great. Did not like condo houses right on top of holes...Supposed to be the worse of the two courses, but I like it better...OK course, good price, nothing super, just OK...A nice course...Lots of water, must place shots.

★★★TOSKI LINKS

Holes: 18. **Par:** 72/72. **Yards:** 7,203/5,353. **Course rating:** 73.5/69.6. **Slope:** 121/119.
Subscriber comments: Basic course...Plenty of doglegs, slicer delight, large greens...Course excellent. North has less water than South...Typical South Carolina course...Good layout; heads above South course...Nice course...Long par 3s surrounded by bunkers.

★★★★THE DUNES GOLF & BEACH CLUB

9000 N. Ocean Blvd., Myrtle Beach, 29572, Horry County, (803)449-5914.
Opened: N/A. **Holes:** 18. **Par:** 72/72. **Yards:** 7,165/5,390. **Course rating:** 72.1/72.3. **Slope:** 141/132. **Architect:** Robert Trent Jones. **Green fee:** $80/$133. **Credit cards:** MC,VISA. **Reduced fees:** Low season. **Caddies:** No. **Golf carts:** Included in Green Fee. **Discount golf packages:** Yes. **Season:** Year-round. **High:** Spring/Fall. **On site lodging:** No. **Rental clubs:** Yes. **Walking policy:** Mandatory cart. **Metal spikes allowed:** No. **Range:** Yes (grass/mats). **To obtain tee times:** Call in advance.
Notes: 1994-98 Senior Tour Championship; 1962 Women's U.S. Open.
Subscriber comments: Like playing on tour; excellent from tee to green...Fun course, outstanding greens, tough par 4s...A shrine, always challenging...Snobby, overrated...Old style course, magnificent tees, some outstanding holes, fun to play...Great test on a windy day.

★★★½THE DUNES WEST GOLF CLUB

3535 Wando Plantation Way, Mount Pleasant, 29464, Charleston County, (803)856-9000, 10 miles E of Charleston.
Opened: 1991. **Holes:** 18. **Par:** 72/72. **Yards:** 6,871/5,278. **Course rating:** 73.4/69.2. **Slope:** 131/118. **Architect:** Arthur Hills. **Green fee:** $30/$60. **Credit cards:** MC,VISA,AMEX. **Reduced fees:** Weekdays, low season, resort guests, twilight, juniors. **Caddies:** No. **Golf carts:** Included in Green Fee. **Discount golf packages:** Yes.

Season: Year-round. **High:** March-May/Oct. **On site lodging:** No. **Rental clubs:** Yes. **Walking policy:** Mandatory cart. **Metal spikes allowed:** Yes. **Range:** Yes (grass). **To obtain tee times:** Call. Credit card required for reserving more than 14 days in advance.

Subscriber comments: Beautiful Low Country design, could play it everyday...Tough finishing five holes...Probably the best course in Charleston area...Typical of Old South, beautiful course, scenic oak drive.

★DUSTY HILLS COUNTRY CLUB

Country Club Rd., Marion, 29571, Marion County, (803)423-2721, 20 miles E of Florence.

Opened: 1928. **Holes:** 18. **Par:** 72/74. **Yards:** 6,120/4,995. **Course rating:** 69.0/68.0. **Slope:** 114/114. **Architect:** N/A. **Green fee:** $12/$12. **Credit cards:** None. **Reduced fees:** Resort guests. **Caddies:** No. **Golf carts:** $12. **Discount golf packages:** Yes. **Season:** Year-round. **High:** Sept.-Nov. **On site lodging:** No. **Rental clubs:** Yes. **Walking policy:** Unrestricted walking. **Metal spikes allowed:** Yes. **Range:** Yes (grass). **To obtain tee times:** Call golf shop 1 day in advance.

★★★EAGLE NEST GOLF CLUB

R-Hwy. 17 N., North Myrtle Beach, 29597, Horry County, (803)249-1449, (800)543-3113, 1 mile N of North Myrtle Beach.

Opened: 1971. **Holes:** 18. **Par:** 72/72. **Yards:** 6,901/5,105. **Course rating:** 73.0/69.8. **Slope:** 120/116. **Architect:** Gene Hamm. **Green fee:** $12/$43. **Credit cards:** MC,VISA,AMEX. **Reduced fees:** Resort guests, twilight. **Caddies:** No. **Golf carts:** $18. **Discount golf packages:** Yes. **Season:** Year-round. **High:** March-April/Oct. **On site lodging:** No. **Rental clubs:** Yes. **Walking policy:** Walking at certain times. **Metal spikes allowed:** Yes. **Range:** Yes (grass/mats). **To obtain tee times:** Call up to 1 year in advance.

Subscriber comments: Vintage course...Friendliest place at beach...Very playable for average golfer, good husband and wife course...Interesting course with three tough holes to finish...No driving range, small course...Pretty old course with some tough holes...Good course, great 18th hole.

★★½EASTPORT GOLF CLUB

PU-Hwy. 17, North Myrtle Beach, 29597, Horry County, (803)249-3997, (800)334-9035, 2 miles N of N. Myrtle Beach.

Opened: 1988. **Holes:** 18. **Par:** 70/70. **Yards:** 6,202/4,698. **Course rating:** 69.1/65.7. **Slope:** 116/114. **Architect:** Denis Griffiths. **Green fee:** $6/$33. **Credit cards:** MC,VISA. **Reduced fees:** Weekdays. **Caddies:** No. **Golf carts:** $16. **Discount golf packages:** No. **Season:** Year-round. **High:** March-May. **On site lodging:** No. **Rental clubs:** Yes. **Walking policy:** Mandatory cart. **Metal spikes allowed:** Yes. **Range:** No. **To obtain tee times:** Call 2 days in advance.

Subscriber comments: Fun short course with tricky water hazards. #18 very hard...Short and tight course, 18th is amazing hole...Short but challenging course...Well designed water holes...Good course to work out the winter kinks...Cute, easy course. Fun 18th...Good course to start a Myrtle Beach vacation, enjoyable.

★★★EDISTO BEACH GOLF CLUB

R-24 Fairway Dr., Edisto Island, 29438, Colleton County, (803)869-1111, 45 miles S of Charleston.

Opened: 1973. **Holes:** 18. **Par:** 71/72. **Yards:** 6,212/5,306. **Course rating:** 69.5/70.3. **Slope:** 118/120. **Architect:** Tom Jackson. **Green fee:** $29/$44. **Credit cards:** MC,VISA,DISC. **Reduced fees:** Weekdays, low season, resort guests, juniors. **Caddies:** No. **Golf carts:** Included in Green Fee. **Discount golf packages:** Yes. **Season:** Year-round. **High:** April-Nov. **On site lodging:** Yes. **Rental clubs:** Yes. **Walking policy:** Walking at certain times. **Metal spikes allowed:** Yes. **Range:** No. **To obtain tee times:** Call golf shop.

Subscriber comments: Short and fun. Tight fairways...Beautiful golf course...Layout OK. Enjoyed a lot, spent honeymoon there...Nice layout. Very Scenic...Tough course...Water, water everywhere...Fun layout, no range.

Special Notes: Formerly Country Club at Edisto.

★★½FALCON'S LAIR GOLF COURSE
1308 Falcon's Dr., Walhalla, 29691, Oconee County, (803)638-0000, 40 miles SW of Greenville.
Opened: 1991. **Holes:** 18. **Par:** 72/74. **Yards:** 6,955/5,238. **Course rating:** 72.1/70.6. **Slope:** 124/123. **Architect:** Harry Bowers. **Green fee:** $22/$26. **Credit cards:** MC,VISA. **Reduced fees:** Weekdays, low season, twilight, seniors, juniors. **Caddies:** No. **Golf carts:** $10. **Discount golf packages:** Yes. **Season:** Year-round. **High:** March-Oct. **On site lodging:** No. **Rental clubs:** Yes. **Walking policy:** Walking at certain times. **Metal spikes allowed:** Yes. **Range:** Yes (grass/mats). **To obtain tee times:** First come, first served.
Subscriber comments: Shotmaker's course...Uncrowded. Trouble around greens...Good course.

★★★FORT MILL GOLF CLUB
101 Country Club Dr., Fort Mill, 29716, York County, (803)547-2044.
Opened: 1948. **Holes:** 18. **Par:** 72/72. **Yards:** 6,865/5,448. **Course rating:** 72.5/70.0. **Slope:** 123/123. **Architect:** Donald Ross/George Cobb. **Green fee:** $18/$22. **Credit cards:** MC,VISA. **Reduced fees:** N/A. **Caddies:** No. **Golf carts:** $35. **Discount golf packages:** No. **Season:** Year-round. **High:** April-Sept. **On site lodging:** No. **Rental clubs:** No. **Walking policy:** Mandatory cart. **Metal spikes allowed:** Yes. **Range:** No. **To obtain tee times:** Call on Wednesday for upcoming weekend. Weekdays call up to 2 days in advance.
Subscriber comments: Good, challenging course...Needs driving range...A challenge...OK, but not great...Mature, challenging...Nice test of golf.

★★★FOX CREEK GOLF CLUB
Hwy. 15 S., Lydia, 29079, Darlington County, (803)332-0613, 20 miles W of Florence.
Opened: 1988. **Holes:** 18. **Par:** 72/72. **Yards:** 6,903/5,271. **Course rating:** 72.7/67.9. **Slope:** 128/106. **Architect:** Ernest Wallace. **Green fee:** $13/$18. **Credit cards:** MC,VISA. **Reduced fees:** Weekdays, resort guests, seniors, juniors. **Caddies:** No. **Golf carts:** $10. **Discount golf packages:** Yes. **Season:** Year-round. **High:** Feb.-May/Sept.-Nov. **On site lodging:** No. **Rental clubs:** Yes. **Walking policy:** Walking at certain times. **Metal spikes allowed:** Yes. **Range:** Yes (grass). **To obtain tee times:** Call.
Subscriber comments: Worth playing anytime, staff very friendly...Great course for the money...Slowly maturing...Good small town course.

★★★FOXBORO GOLF CLUB
R-1438 Wash Davis Rd., Summerton, 29148, Clarendon County, (803)478-7000, (800)468-7061, 75 miles NE of Charleston.
Opened: 1988. **Holes:** 18. **Par:** 72/72. **Yards:** 6,889/5,386. **Course rating:** 71.1/68.4. **Slope:** 117/114. **Architect:** Porter Gibson. **Green fee:** $15/$29. **Credit cards:** MC,VISA. **Reduced fees:** Low season. **Caddies:** No. **Golf carts:** Included in Green Fee. **Discount golf packages:** Yes. **Season:** Year-round. **High:** Spring/Fall. **On site lodging:** No. **Rental clubs:** Yes. **Walking policy:** Mandatory cart. **Metal spikes allowed:** Yes. **Range:** No. **To obtain tee times:** Call golf shop.
Subscriber comments: Flat course, great greens...Making improvements...Very accommodating...Lots of OB stakes...Good cheap golf!...Fun public course, easy play...Wide-open course, out in the boonies...Course has changed much for the better.

★★★GATOR HOLE GOLF COURSE
PU-700 Hwy. 17., North Myrtle Beach, 29582, Horry County, (803)249-3543, (800)447-2668.
Opened: 1980. **Holes:** 18. **Par:** 70/70. **Yards:** 6,000/4,685. **Course rating:** 69.8/65.9. **Slope:** 116/112. **Architect:** Rees Jones. **Green fee:** $32/$56. **Credit cards:** MC,VISA. **Reduced fees:** Twilight, juniors. **Caddies:** No. **Golf carts:** $17. **Discount golf packages:** No. **Season:** Year-round. **High:** March-May. **On site lodging:** No. **Rental clubs:** Yes. **Walking policy:** Mandatory cart. **Metal spikes allowed:** Yes. **Range:** Yes (grass). **To obtain tee times:** Call up to 1 year in advance.
Subscriber comments: Fun course, take one extra club at #18...7th hole among Myrtle's prettiest...Short course, six par 3s, fun to play...Everything about Myrtle Beach is great...Low cost, great 18th hole...Not too bad...Real sleeper.

SOUTH CAROLINA

★★★THE GAUNTLET AT LAUREL VALLEY
253 Chinquapin Rd., Tigerville, 29688, Greenville County, (864)895-6758.
Opened: 1993. **Holes:** 18. **Par:** 72/72. **Yards:** 6,713/4,545. **Course rating:** 72.1/69.7.
Slope: 135/119. **Architect:** P.B. Dye. **Green fee:** $25/$39. **Credit cards:**
MC,VISA,AMEX. **Reduced fees:** Weekdays, low season, twilight, seniors, juniors.
Caddies: No. **Golf carts:** Included in Green Fee. **Discount golf packages:** Yes.
Season: Year-round. **High:** March-Oct. **On site lodging:** No. **Rental clubs:** Yes.
Walking policy: Walking at certain times. **Metal spikes allowed:** Yes. **Range:** Yes
(grass/mats). **To obtain tee times:** Call up to 5 days in advance.
Subscriber comments: Nice course; tough holes...Tough course, very hilly...Unfair
course...Too many blind holes and forced carries...Great challenge, fun to play...Narrow,
short but not to be missed.

★★★½GLEN DORNOCH WATERWAY GOLF LINKS
PU-P.O. Box 390, North Myrtle Beach, 29597, Horry County,
(803)249-2541, (800)717-8784, 15 miles N of Myrtle Beach.
Opened: 1996. **Holes:** 18. **Par:** 72/72. **Yards:** 6,850/5,002. **Course rat-**
ing: 73.2/69.8. **Slope:** 141/129. **Architect:** Clyde Johnston. **Green fee:**
$61/$106. **Credit cards:** MC,VISA,AMEX. **Reduced fees:** Low season.
Caddies: No. **Golf carts:** N/A. **Discount golf packages:** No. **Season:** Year-round.
High: Spring/Fall. **On site lodging:** No. **Rental clubs:** Yes. **Walking policy:** Mandatory
cart. **Metal spikes allowed:** Yes. **Range:** Yes (grass). **To obtain tee times:** Call up to 1
year in advance.
Subscriber comments: Great shape for a new course...Tough test. Last three holes
like a coral snake: beautiful and deadly...Absolutely fantastic...Outstanding 16th, 17th
and 18th holes...The last three holes will leave you breathless.

★★★½GOLDEN BEAR GOLF CLUB
72 Golden Bear Way, Hilton Head, 29926, Beaufort County, (803)689-2200, 42 miles
SE of Savannah, GA.
Opened: 1992. **Holes:** 18. **Par:** 72/72. **Yards:** 7,014/4,974. **Course rating:** 73.7/69.3.
Slope: 132/120. **Architect:** Bruce Borland. **Green fee:** $35/$62. **Credit cards:**
MC,VISA,AMEX. **Reduced fees:** Low season, resort guests, twilight, juniors. **Caddies:**
No. **Golf carts:** $19. **Discount golf packages:** Yes. **Season:** Year-round. **High:**
Spring/Fall. **On site lodging:** No. **Rental clubs:** Yes. **Walking policy:** Mandatory cart.
Metal spikes allowed: Yes. **Range:** Yes (grass). **To obtain tee times:** Call golf shop
between 6:30 a.m.-6:30 p.m.
Subscriber comments: A pleasant surprise...Fun course...emanding layout for 20
handicapper...Traditional layout, not too interesting...Very interesting variety of holes.

★★★GOLDEN HILLS GOLF & COUNTRY CLUB
100 Scotland Dr., Lexington, 29072, Lexington County, (803)957-3355, 15 miles W of
Columbia.
Opened: 1988. **Holes:** 18. **Par:** 71/71. **Yards:** 6,561/4,951. **Course rating:** 71.2/68.0.
Slope: 134/113. **Architect:** Ron Garl. **Green fee:** $19/$38. **Credit cards:** MC,VISA.
Reduced fees: Weekdays, low season. **Caddies:** No. **Golf carts:** $10. **Discount golf**
packages: No. **Season:** Year-round. **High:** Spring. **On site lodging:** No. **Rental clubs:**
Yes. **Walking policy:** Unrestricted walking. **Metal spikes allowed:** Yes. **Range:** No. **To**
obtain tee times: Call 2 days in advance.
Subscriber comments: Fun, hilly course, several holes along small river, great setting.

★★★½THE GOLF CLUB OF SOUTH CAROLINA AT CRICKENTREE
1084 Langford Rd., Blythewood, 29016, Richland County, (803)754-8600, 12 miles NE
of Columbia.
Opened: 1987. **Holes:** 18. **Par:** 72/72. **Yards:** 7,002/4,791. **Course rating:** 74.2/71.3.
Slope: 140/130. **Architect:** Ken Killian. **Green fee:** $29/$39. **Credit cards:** MC,VISA.
Reduced fees: Weekdays, twilight, seniors. **Caddies:** No. **Golf carts:** Included in
Green Fee. **Discount golf packages:** No. **Season:** Year-round. **High:** Spring/Fall. **On**
site lodging: No. **Rental clubs:** Yes. **Walking policy:** Mandatory cart. **Metal spikes**
allowed: Yes. **Range:** Yes (grass). **To obtain tee times:** Call golf shop.
Subscriber comments: Target golf...Many elevation changes...Very nice...Tough, hilly
layout...The course has really improved.

THE GOLF PROFESSIONALS CLUB

139 Frances Marion Circle, Beaufort, 29902, Beaufort County, (843)524-3635, 7 miles E of Beaufort.
Opened: 1971. **Architect:** N/A. **Green fee:** $30/$30. **Credit cards:** All major. **Reduced fees:** N/A. **Caddies:** No. **Golf carts:** Included in Green Fee. **Discount golf packages:** No. **Season:** Year-round. **High:** Spring/Fall. **On site lodging:** No. **Rental clubs:** Yes. **Walking policy:** Walking at certain times. **Metal spikes allowed:** No. **Range:** Yes (grass). **To obtain tee times:** Call in advance.
★½**CHAMPIONS COURSE**
Holes: 18. **Par:** 72/72. **Yards:** 6,811/5,241. **Course rating:** 73.4/70.8. **Slope:** 124/121.
PLAYERS COURSE
Holes: 18. **Par:** 72/72. **Yards:** 6,000/5,192. **Course rating:** 67.4/68.4. **Slope:** 104/107.

★★★★**HARBOUR TOWN GOLF LINKS**
R-11 Lighthouse Lane, Hilton Head Island, 29928, Beaufort County, (803)363-4485, (800)955-8337, 45 miles N of Savannah, GA.
Opened: 1969. **Holes:** 18. **Par:** 71/71. **Yards:** 6,916/5,019. **Course rating:** 74.0/69.0. **Slope:** 136/117. **Architect:** Pete Dye. **Green fee:** $105/$175. **Credit cards:** All major. **Reduced fees:** Low season, resort guests, juniors. **Caddies:** No. **Golf carts:** Included in Green Fee. **Discount golf packages:** Yes. **Season:** Year-round. **High:** Spring/Fall. **On site lodging:** Yes. **Rental clubs:** Yes. **Walking policy:** Walking at certain times. **Metal spikes allowed:** Yes. **Range:** Yes (grass). **To obtain tee times:** Call with credit card to guarantee.
Notes: Ranked 60th in 1997-98 America's 100 Greatest; 3rd in 1997 Best in State. MCI Classic/Heritage Classic venue since 1969.
Subscriber comments: Expensive, must play once, great finishing holes...Tight fairways, small greens, wind...Played from tips, can appreciate touring pros...Maybe Pete's best, 17 and 18 are awesome...Overrated; overpriced...Smallest greens I have ever played...What a layout! A must play...Enjoyed walking it.

★★★★**HEATHER GLEN GOLF LINKS**
PU-Hwy. 17 N., Little River, 29566, Horry County, (803)249-9000, (800)868-4536, 12 miles N of Myrtle Beach.
Opened: 1987. **Holes:** 27. **Architect:** Willard Byrd/Clyde Johnston.
Green fee: $30/$81. **Credit cards:** MC,VISA,AMEX. **Reduced fees:** N/A. **Caddies:** No. **Golf carts:** $18. **Discount golf packages:** Yes.
Season: Year-round. **High:** March-May/Oct. **On site lodging:** No. **Rental clubs:** Yes. **Walking policy:** Mandatory cart. **Metal spikes allowed:** Yes. **Range:** Yes (grass). **To obtain tee times:** Call anytime.
RED/BLUE
Par: 72/72. **Yards:** 6,771/5,053. **Course rating:** 72.4/69.3. **Slope:** 127/117.
RED/WHITE
Par: 72/72. **Yards:** 6,783/5,101. **Course rating:** 72.4/69.3. **Slope:** 130/117.
WHITE/BLUE
Par: 72/72. **Yards:** 6,822/5,127. **Course rating:** 72.4/69.3. **Slope:** 130/117.
Notes: Dupont World Amateur.
Subscriber comments: As good as you can find in Myrtle...Very good design and condition, tough when windy!...Many interesting holes, beautiful course...One of the best...Course management is a must, go with a good sand game...Beautiful course. A pleasure to play...Not typical Myrtle Beach...Many memorable holes.

★★★★**HERITAGE CLUB**
PU-Hwy. 17 S., Pawleys Island, 29585, Georgetown County, (803)237-3424, (800)377-2315, 20 miles S of Myrtle Beach.
Opened: 1986. **Holes:** 18. **Par:** 71/71. **Yards:** 7,100/5,325. **Course rating:** 74.2/71.0. **Slope:** 137/125. **Architect:** Dan Maples. **Green fee:** $30/$75. **Credit cards:** MC,VISA,AMEX. **Reduced fees:** Low season, resort guests. **Caddies:** No. **Golf carts:** $18. **Discount golf packages:** Yes. **Season:** Year-round. **High:** March/April/Oct. **On site lodging:** No. **Rental clubs:** Yes. **Walking policy:** Mandatory cart. **Metal spikes allowed:** Yes. **Range:** Yes (grass/mats). **To obtain tee times:** Call up to 9 months in advance. Deposit required during high season.
Notes: Ranked 20th in 1997 Best in State.

Subscriber comments: Beautiful setting, great clubhouse...A great enjoyable course to play...Long par 4s...Greens too severe...Treelined entrance, like Augusta...#18 is a gut check par 5...Stay away from back tees in the wind...My favorite Myrtle Beach course (I've played 50+).

★★★HERON POINT GOLF CLUB

R-6980 Blue Heron Blvd., Myrtle Beach, 29575, Horry County, (803)650-6664, (800)786-7671, 60 miles N of Charleston.
Opened: 1989. **Holes:** 18. **Par:** 72/72. **Yards:** 6,477/4,734. **Course rating:** 71.0/69.2. **Slope:** 120/121. **Architect:** Willard Byrd. **Green fee:** $35/$49. **Credit cards:** MC,VISA,DISC. **Reduced fees:** Weekdays, low season, resort guests, twilight, seniors, juniors. **Caddies:** No. **Golf carts:** Included in Green Fee. **Discount golf packages:** Yes. **Season:** Year-round. **High:** Spring/Fall. **On site lodging:** No. **Rental clubs:** Yes. **Walking policy:** Walking at certain times. **Metal spikes allowed:** Yes. **Range:** Yes (grass/mats). **To obtain tee times:** Call 7 days in advance.
Notes: 1993-97 Dupont World Amateur.
Subscriber comments: Interesting layout through woods and houses, 9 and 18 great par 5s...Lots of fun...Short from the whites...Tight, finesse course, must keep it in fairway...Condo golf...A lot of water!...It's OK, not the most challenging.

★★★HICKORY KNOB GOLF CLUB

R-off Hwy. 378, McCormick, 29835, McCormick County, (864)391-2450, (800)491-1764, 38 miles N of Augusta, GA.
Opened: N/A. **Holes:** 18. **Par:** 72/72. **Yards:** 6,560/4,905. **Course rating:** 72.1/67.3. **Slope:** 119/120. **Architect:** Tom Jackson. **Green fee:** $13/$18. **Credit cards:** MC,VISA. **Reduced fees:** Weekdays, twilight, seniors, juniors. **Caddies:** No. **Golf carts:** $12. **Discount golf packages:** Yes. **Season:** Year-round. **High:** April-Oct. **On site lodging:** Yes. **Rental clubs:** Yes. **Walking policy:** Unrestricted walking. **Metal spikes allowed:** Yes. **Range:** Yes (grass). **To obtain tee times:** Call.
Subscriber comments: A great stay and play, state park facilities...Tough, tough course. You need every shot...Great forest/lake setting. Too bad it's so far off the beaten path...Lots of wildlife. Good price...Very scenic along the lake...Ducks everywhere!...Delightful experience; beautiful course...Distracting scenery...Long drive, but nice course.

★½HIGHLAND PARK COUNTRY CLUB

555 Highland Park Dr., Aiken, 29801, Aiken County, (803)649-6029, 20 miles N of Augusta, GA.
Opened: 1912. **Holes:** 18. **Par:** 70/70. **Yards:** 6,200/5,400. **Course rating:** 68.0. **Slope:** 115. **Architect:** J.R. Inglis. **Green fee:** $9/$9. **Credit cards:** None. **Reduced fees:** N/A. **Caddies:** No. **Golf carts:** $9. **Discount golf packages:** No. **Season:** Year-round. **High:** Spring. **On site lodging:** No. **Rental clubs:** No. **Walking policy:** Unrestricted walking. **Metal spikes allowed:** Yes. **Range:** No. **To obtain tee times:** Tee times are not required.

★HILLANDALE GOLF COURSE

105 S. Parker Rd., Greenville, 29609, Greenville County, (864)232-0011.
Call club for further information.

★★½HILLCREST GOLF CLUB

PU-1099 Old St. Matthews Rd., Orangeburg, 29116, Orangeburg County, (803)533-6030, 35 miles SE of Columbia.
Opened: 1972. **Holes:** 18. **Par:** 72/72. **Yards:** 6,722/5,208. **Course rating:** 70.5/67.8. **Slope:** 119/107. **Architect:** Russell Breeden. **Green fee:** $12/$14. **Credit cards:** All major. **Reduced fees:** Low season. **Caddies:** No. **Golf carts:** $9. **Discount golf packages:** Yes. **Season:** Year-round. **High:** March-May. **On site lodging:** No. **Rental clubs:** Yes. **Walking policy:** Unrestricted walking. **Metal spikes allowed:** Yes. **Range:** Yes (grass/mats). **To obtain tee times:** Call golf shop.
Subscriber comments: Good course...Excellent public course. Really improved...Good small town golf course, usually uncrowded.

SOUTH CAROLINA

★★★½HILTON HEAD NATIONAL GOLF CLUB
PU-60 Hilton Head National Dr., Bluffton, 29910, Beaufort County, (803)842-5900, (888)955-1234, 30 miles from Savannah.
Opened: 1989. **Holes:** 18. **Par:** 72/72. **Yards:** 6,779/5,589. **Course rating:** N/A. **Slope:** 124/115. **Architect:** Gary Player. **Green fee:** $40/$95. **Credit cards:** MC,VISA,AMEX. **Reduced fees:** Weekdays, low season, resort guests, twilight. **Caddies:** No. **Golf carts:** Included in Green Fee. **Discount golf packages:** Yes. **Season:** Year-round. **High:** Spring/Fall. **On site lodging:** No. **Rental clubs:** Yes. **Walking policy:** Mandatory cart. **Metal spikes allowed:** Yes. **Range:** Yes (grass/mats). **To obtain tee times:** Call.
Subscriber comments: Absolutely beautiful course...Nice place, a real favorite...A unique experience...Picturesque, well groomed...Great double green at 9/18, beautiful layout, fun...Short, but fun...Thinking man's course! Must plan shot placement...Great resort course with all the trimmings...Nice layout, just tough enough...Very well kept.

★★★½HUNTER'S CREEK PLANTATION GOLF CLUB
702 Hunter's Creek Blvd., Greenwood, 29649, Greenwood County, (864)223-9286, 47 miles SW of Greenville.
Opened: 1994. **Holes:** 18. **Par:** 72/72. **Yards:** 6,999/4,977. **Course rating:** 73.6/67.5. **Slope:** 133/119. **Architect:** Tom Jackson. **Green fee:** $26/$35. **Credit cards:** MC,VISA. **Reduced fees:** Weekdays, low season, juniors. **Caddies:** No. **Golf carts:** Included in Green Fee. **Discount golf packages:** No. **Season:** Year-round. **High:** April-June. **On site lodging:** No. **Rental clubs:** Yes. **Walking policy:** Unrestricted walking. **Metal spikes allowed:** Yes. **Range:** Yes (grass). **To obtain tee times:** Call seven days in advance.
Subscriber comments: Has it all. Beautiful course...Young but very nice...One of the best courses around...Fun course, need to play from back tees...Nice facility...Very new course, will get better in time...Good test from back tees. Good variety of holes.

★★★½INDIAN RIVER GOLF CLUB
200 Congaree Hunt Dr., West Columbia, 29170, Lexington County, (803)955-0080, 15 miles W of Columbia.
Opened: 1992. **Holes:** 18. **Par:** 71/71. **Yards:** 6,507/4,643. **Course rating:** 71.7/66.9. **Slope:** 133/113. **Architect:** Lyndell Young. **Green fee:** N/A. **Credit cards:** MC,VISA,AMEX. **Reduced fees:** Weekdays, low season, resort guests, twilight, seniors, juniors. **Caddies:** No. **Golf carts:** Included in Green Fee. **Discount golf packages:** Yes. **Season:** Year-round. **High:** March-May. **On site lodging:** No. **Rental clubs:** Yes. **Walking policy:** Walking at certain times. **Metal spikes allowed:** Yes. **Range:** Yes (grass). **To obtain tee times:** Call up to 14 days in advance.
Subscriber comments: Good course...Best in Columbia in my opinion, beautiful all summer...Fast roller coaster greens. No fun...Great elevation changes, greens are exceptional...Nice lakeside course...Greens like warped 33 records...Get used to some long putts, greens are enormous...Easy par 5s...Best in Columbia.

★★½INDIAN WELLS GOLF CLUB
PU-100 Woodlake Dr., Garden City, 29576, Horry County, (803)651-1505, (800)833-6337, 10 miles S of Myrtle Beach.
Opened: 1984. **Holes:** 18. **Par:** 72/72. **Yards:** 6,624/4,872. **Course rating:** 71.9/68.2. **Slope:** 125/118. **Architect:** Gene Hamm. **Green fee:** $5/$40. **Credit cards:** MC,VISA,DISC. **Reduced fees:** Low season, resort guests, twilight, juniors. **Caddies:** No. **Golf carts:** $18. **Discount golf packages:** Yes. **Season:** Year-round. **High:** Spring/Fall. **On site lodging:** No. **Rental clubs:** Yes. **Walking policy:** Walking at certain times. **Metal spikes allowed:** Yes. **Range:** Yes (grass). **To obtain tee times:** Call up to 1 year in advance.
Subscriber comments: Very nice course, high difficulty from back tees...Tough water holes...Water everywhere, bring golf balls...Nice layout.

★★★INDIGO CREEK GOLF PLANTATION
PU-P.O. Box 15437, Surfside Beach, 29587, Horry County, (803)650-0381, (800)833-6337, 10 miles S of Myrtle Beach.
Opened: 1990. **Holes:** 18. **Par:** 72/72. **Yards:** 6,750/4,921. **Course rating:** 72.4/69.7. **Slope:** 134/126. **Architect:** Willard Byrd. **Green fee:** $26/$60. **Credit cards:**

MC,VISA,DISC. **Reduced fees:** Low season, twilight. **Caddies:** No. **Golf carts:** Included in Green Fee. **Discount golf packages:** Yes. **Season:** Year-round. **High:** Spring/Fall. **On site lodging:** No. **Rental clubs:** Yes. **Walking policy:** Mandatory cart. **Metal spikes allowed:** Yes. **Range:** Yes (grass). **To obtain tee times:** Call 800 number 2 days in advance.
Subscriber comments: Lots of water and wildlife...Nice par 3s, fair test of golf, not incredible...Tougher than it looks; don't use driver on all par 4s or 5s, water every-where...Average Myrtle Beach course...Sleeper course, pretty decent, lots of doglegs.

★★½ISLAND GREEN GOLF CLUB - DOGWOOD/HOLLY/TALL OAKS
455 Sunehanna Dr., Unit STE-1, Myrtle Beach, 29587, Horry County, (803)650-2186.
Holes: 27. **Architect:**William Mooney.
Call club for further information.
Subscriber comments: Good shape, lots of challenges...Tight fairways, saw an alliga-tor...Not the best in Myrtle Beach, but not the worst...Look out for gators...Nice course, did not like playing among condos...Good layout.

★★½ISLAND WEST GOLF CLUB
R-U.S. Hwy. 278, Bluffton, 29910, Beaufort County, (803)689-6660, 25 miles NE of Savannah, GA.
Opened: 1991. **Holes:** 18. **Par:** 72/72. **Yards:** 6,803/4,938. **Course rating:** 72.1/66.5. **Slope:** 129/116. **Architect:** Fuzzy Zoeller and Clyde Johnston. **Green fee:** $39/$65. **Credit cards:** MC,VISA,AMEX. **Reduced fees:** Low season, resort guests, twilight, juniors. **Caddies:** No. **Golf carts:** Included in Green Fee. **Discount golf packages:** Yes. **Season:** Year-round. **High:** Spring/Fall. **On site lodging:** No. **Rental clubs:** Yes. **Walking policy:** Walking at certain times. **Metal spikes allowed:** Yes. **Range:** Yes (grass). **To obtain tee times:** Call up to 1 year in advance. Reservations for 8 or more players require credit card.
Subscriber comments: Wide open, flat...Solid but nothing special...Nice course...Not too long, a good placement course...Let it rip! Thanks Fuzzy...Fair course, no outstand-ing holes.

KIAWAH ISLAND RESORT
R- **Credit cards:** All major,Diners Club. **Golf carts:** Included in Green Fee. **Discount golf packages:** Yes. **Season:** Year-round. **High:** Spring/Fall. **On site lodging:** Yes. **Rental clubs:** Yes. **Walking policy:** Walking at certain times. **Metal spikes allowed:** Yes. **Range:** Yes (grass). **To obtain tee times:** Call up to 5 days in advance with credit card to guarantee.

★★★½COUGAR POINT COURSE
12 Kiawah Beach Dr., Kiawah Island, 29455, Charleston County, (803)768-2121, (800)654-2924, 21 miles S of Charleston.
Opened: 1997. **Holes:** 18. **Par:** 72/72. **Yards:** 6,861/4,776. **Course rating:** 73.0/66.3. **Slope:** 134/112. **Architect:** Gary Player. **Green fee:** $99/$119. **Reduced fees:** Low season, resort guests, twilight, juniors. **Caddies:** Yes.
Subscriber comments: Great course...Enjoyable and great service...Another Player gem!...Gary Player never was a long hitter. Short course. Leave driver at home...I lost a ball to a gator...Fun resort course...Beautiful, redone in 1996, excellent course...Compared to Ocean Course, it is easy.
Special Notes: Formerly Marsh Point Course.
★★★OAK POINT GOLF COURSE
4255 Bohicket Rd., Johns Island, 29455, Charleston County, (803)768-7431, 20 miles S of Charleston.
Opened: 1989. **Holes:** 18. **Par:** 72/72. **Yards:** 6,759/4,671. **Course rating:** 73.3/69.8. **Slope:** 137/121. **Architect:** Clyde Johnston. **Green fee:** $40/$60. **Credit cards:** MC,VISA. **Reduced fees:** Low season, juniors. **Caddies:** No. **High:** April-Oct. **On site lodging:** No.
Subscriber comments: Affordable, enjoyable, near Kiawah...Some blind shots, but you will like it...Only two bad holes...Easy from the front tees. Fair test from the back tees...Must play when in Charleston...Watch for bald eagles.
★★★★½OCEAN COURSE
1000 Ocean Course Dr., Kiawah Island, 29455, Charleston County, (803)768-2121, 21 miles S of Charleston.

Opened: 1991. **Holes:** 18. **Par:** 72/72. **Yards:** 7,371/5,327. **Course rating:** 76.7/72.9. **Slope:** 145/133. **Architect:** Pete Dye. **Green fee:** $109/$155. **Reduced fees:** Low season, resort guests, juniors. **Caddies:** No.
Notes: Ranked 41st in 1997-98 America's 100 Greatest; 1st in 1997 Best in State. 1997 World Cup; 1991 Ryder Cup.
Subscriber comments: Beautiful, tough, expensive. Not for high handicaps...One of the best in the world, super tough...Dye's ultimate test. Play 17 from the tips!...Worth every penny...Utterly spectacular views, spectacular golf...Very difficult if you aren't driving really good...Too hard for a 2-handicap...Beat yourself in the head with a hammer: it's cheaper...Ultimate seaside golf. Play the white tees...Impossible in wind!

★★★★ OSPREY POINT COURSE
Governors Dr., Kiawah Island, 29455, Charleston County, (803)768-2121, 21 miles S of Charleston.
Opened: 1988. **Holes:** 18. **Par:** 72/72. **Yards:** 6,678/5,122. **Course rating:** 71.8/69.6. **Slope:** 124/120. **Architect:** Tom Fazio. **Green fee:** $119. **Reduced fees:** Low season, resort guests, twilight, juniors. **Caddies:** No.
Subscriber comments: Water and sand everywhere...Nice Fazio course...Most playable Kiawah course. Locals' favorite...Generous landing areas...Love the new clubhouse...Enjoyable layout, plush new clubhouse...Memorable 18th hole, stratightforward test of golf...Great views of tidal marsh.

★★★½ TURTLE POINT COURSE
Turtle Point Lane, Kiawah Island, 29455, Charleston County, (803)768-2121, (800)845-2471, 21 miles S of Charleston.
Opened: 1981. **Holes:** 18. **Par:** 72/72. **Yards:** 6,925/5,247. **Course rating:** 74.0/71.1. **Slope:** 142/126. **Architect:** Jack Nicklaus. **Green fee:** $60/$119. **Reduced fees:** Low season, resort guests, juniors. **Caddies:** No.
Notes: 1990 PGA Cup Matches.
Subscriber comments: Three holes on the ocean are toughies...Stay clear of gators...Don't even play if don't have long iron game...Not the Ocean Course, but a good Nicklaus design, tight with small greens...Reputation based on three holes.

★★★ LAKE MARION GOLF CLUB
PM-P.O. Box 160, Santee, 29142, Orangeburg County, (803)854-2554, (800)344-6534, 50 miles S of Columbia.
Opened: 1979. **Holes:** 18. **Par:** 72/72. **Yards:** 6,670/5,254. **Course rating:** 71.6/69.8. **Slope:** 117/112. **Architect:** Eddie Riccoboni. **Green fee:** $25/$40. **Credit cards:** MC,VISA,AMEX. **Reduced fees:** Juniors. **Caddies:** No. **Golf carts:** Included in Green Fee. **Discount golf packages:** Yes. **Season:** Year-round. **High:** March-May. **On site lodging:** No. **Rental clubs:** Yes. **Walking policy:** Mandatory cart. **Metal spikes allowed:** Yes. **Range:** Yes (grass/mats). **To obtain tee times:** Call.
Subscriber comments: Sporty course...Fun to play...Big greens, good test...Very enjoyable, great variety...Fun course, hilly, fair layout...Love the 1st hole...A pleasant surprise. Golf is not difficult but course is lovely...Not over difficult, good for all players...Older course with character and appeal...Good stop on way to Florida.

★★★½ LAKEWOOD LINKS
3600 Greenview Pkwy., Sumter, 29150, Sumter County, (803)481-5700, 43 miles S of Columbia.
Opened: 1989. **Holes:** 18. **Par:** N/A. **Yards:** N/A. **Course rating:** N/A. **Slope:** N/A. **Architect:** J. Porter Gibson. **Green fee:** $11/$22. **Credit cards:** None. **Reduced fees:** N/A. **Caddies:** No. **Golf carts:** N/A. **Discount golf packages:** No. **Season:** Year-round. **High:** Feb.-April. **On site lodging:** No. **Rental clubs:** No. **Walking policy:** Mandatory cart. **Metal spikes allowed:** Yes. **Range:** No. **To obtain tee times:** Call up to 2 days in advance.
Subscriber comments: Greens very good, water comes with play...Great people...One of the better courses in area, will return...Very enjoyable. Good placement of shots required...You have to look to find it, but well worth the look.

★★★½ LEGEND OAK'S PLANTATION GOLF CLUB
PU-118 Legend Oaks Way, Summerville, 29485, Dorchester County, (803)821-4077, 19 miles N of Charleston.
Opened: 1994. **Holes:** 18. **Par:** 72/72. **Yards:** 6,974/4,945. **Course rating:** 72.3/69.4. **Slope:** 124/116. **Architect:** Scott Pool. **Green fee:** $38/$38. **Credit cards:** MC,VISA.

Reduced fees: Low season, twilight. **Caddies:** No. **Golf carts:** $12. **Discount golf packages:** Yes. **Season:** Year-round. **High:** March-Nov. **On site lodging:** No. **Rental clubs:** Yes. **Walking policy:** Unrestricted walking. **Metal spikes allowed:** Yes. **Range:** Yes (grass). **To obtain tee times:** Call 7 days in advance.

Subscriber comments: Nice course, requires accurate irons...Best all around for beauty, value and playability...Wide fairways lined with trees, big greens, homes, beautiful clubhouse, challenging 8th and 17th over water...Good layout, good golf, needs more time to become a very good course...A hidden gem, best deal in the low country.

THE LEGENDS
R-Hwy. 501, Myrtle Beach, 29577, Horry County, (803)236-9318, (800)377-2315.
Green fee: $30/$75. **Credit cards:** MC,VISA,AMEX. **Reduced fees:** Low season, resort guests. **Caddies:** No. **Golf carts:** $18. **Discount golf packages:** Yes. **Season:** Year-round. **High:** March-April/Oct. **On site lodging:** Yes. **Rental clubs:** Yes. **Walking policy:** Mandatory cart. **Metal spikes allowed:** Yes. **Range:** Yes (grass/mats). **To obtain tee times:** Call up to 9 months in advance.

★★★½HEATHLAND COURSE
Opened: 1990. **Holes:** 18. **Par:** 71/71. **Yards:** 6,785/5,115. **Course rating:** 74.5/71.0. **Slope:** 127/121. **Architect:** Tom Doak.
Subscriber comments: Scottish-like course...Nice links layout...A great Scottish imitation. Authentic and fun...St. Andrews meets Disney World...Some nice, short par 4s...A real links experience...Favorite of three Legends on site, British Open wind...No trees. Deep bunkers. Windy...All three courses great, this is what golf is about...Great practice facility.

★★★½MOORLAND COURSE
Opened: 1990. **Holes:** 18. **Par:** 72/72. **Yards:** 6,799/4,905. **Course rating:** 76.8/72.8. **Slope:** 140/127. **Architect:** P.B. Dye.
Subscriber comments: No trees but still hard to score, some excellent holes...Too tough for 7-handicaper...Scariest bunkers ever...Unique layout, I love it!...Looks like the moon in some places...Too synthetic, too many mounds...Unlike anything else you've ever played, fun...Great course...What a challenge.

★★★½PARKLAND COURSE
Opened: 1992. **Holes:** 18. **Par:** 72/72. **Yards:** 7,170/5,570. **Course rating:** 74.3/72.9. **Slope:** 131/127. **Architect:** Legends Group Design.
Subscriber comments: Great course, super long from tips...Enjoyable layout, nice mix of holes...Natural scenic beauty, pure golf...Huge greens.

★★½THE LINKS AT STONO FERRY
PU-5365 Forest Oaks Dr., Hollywood, 29449, Charleston County, (803)763-1817, 12 miles S of Charleston.
Opened: 1989. **Holes:** 18. **Par:** 72/72. **Yards:** 6,606/4,928. **Course rating:** 68.3/69.2. **Slope:** 115/119. **Architect:** Ron Garl. **Green fee:** $12/$30. **Credit cards:** MC,VISA. **Reduced fees:** Weekdays, low season, twilight, seniors. **Caddies:** No. **Golf carts:** Included in Green Fee. **Discount golf packages:** Yes. **Season:** Year-round. **High:** March-May/Oct. **On site lodging:** No. **Rental clubs:** Yes. **Walking policy:** Walking at certain times. **Metal spikes allowed:** Yes. **Range:** Yes (grass/mats). **To obtain tee times:** Call up to 7 days in advance.
Subscriber comments: Holes on Stono River scenic...Beautiful back nine...Some great water holes...SNice setting and layout, challenging but fair.

★★★LINKS O'TRYON
11250 New Cut Rd., Campobello, 29322, Spartanburg County, (864)473-1728, (888)525-4657, 20 miles N of Greenville.
Opened: 1988. **Holes:** 18. **Par:** 72/72. **Yards:** 7,100/5,011. **Course rating:** 72.1/67.4. **Slope:** 130/113. **Architect:** Tom Jackson. **Green fee:** $30/$55. **Credit cards:** All major. **Reduced fees:** Weekdays, twilight. **Caddies:** No. **Golf carts:** Included in Green Fee. **Discount golf packages:** No. **Season:** Year-round. **High:** March-Nov. **On site lodging:** No. **Rental clubs:** Yes. **Walking policy:** Walking at certain times. **Metal spikes allowed:** Yes. **Range:** Yes (grass). **To obtain tee times:** Call.
Subscriber comments: Short, interesting course...Good track, playable...Scenic mountain views, on old peach orchard...Easy to walk...Nice course, some tough doglegs...Nice track in the foothills. Enough hills to make it interesting...Scenic, challenging...One of my favorites.

★★★LINRICK GOLF COURSE
PM-356 Campground Rd., Columbia, 29203, Richland County, (803)754-6331, 7 miles N of Columbia.

Opened: 1972. **Holes:** 18. **Par:** 73/73. **Yards:** 6,919/5,243. **Course rating:** 72.8/69.4. **Slope:** 125. **Architect:** Russell Breeden. **Green fee:** $10/$12. **Credit cards:** None. **Reduced fees:** Seniors, juniors.
Caddies: No. **Golf carts:** $7. **Discount golf packages:** No. **Season:** Year-round. **High:** March-Sept. **On site lodging:** No. **Rental clubs:** Yes. **Walking policy:** Unrestricted walking. **Metal spikes allowed:** Yes. **Range:** Yes (grass). **To obtain tee times:** Tuesday through Friday available Monday morning after 9:00 a.m.; Saturday through Monday available on Thursday morning after 9:00 a.m. Daily times available open to close of business.
Subscriber comments: Excellent course, cost is very low...Harder than you would think...Wide open, easy...Great for municipal course. Challenging design...Lots of water and trees...Tough test of golf at extremely reasonable price...No easy holes after #1.

LITCHFIELD BEACH & GOLF RESORT
R-Hwy 17S, Pawleys Island, 29585, Georgetown County, (800)344-5590, 20 miles S of Myrtle Beach.

Green fee: $35/$77. **Credit cards:** All major. **Reduced fees:** Low season, resort guests, juniors. **Caddies:** No. **Golf carts:** $18. **Discount golf packages:** Yes. **Season:** Year-round. **High:** March-April/Oct.-Nov. **On site lodging:** Yes. **Rental clubs:** Yes. **Walking policy:** Mandatory cart. **Metal spikes allowed:** Yes. **Range:** Yes (grass/mats). **To obtain tee times:** Call golf club.

★★★LITCHFIELD COUNTRY CLUB
(803)237-3411.

Opened: 1966. **Holes:** 18. **Par:** 72/72. **Yards:** 6,752/5,264. **Course rating:** 72.6/69.9. **Slope:** 130/119. **Architect:** Willard Byrd.
Notes: Dupont World Amateur.
Subscriber comments: Nice course, not tricked up...A truly enjoyable experience...Great old style course...Classic Myrtle-type course...A very scenic golf course...Nice course, fun from white tees, gold tees much tougher.

★★★½WILLBROOK PLANTATION GOLF CLUB
(803)237-4900.

Opened: 1988. **Holes:** 18. **Par:** 72/72. **Yards:** 6,704/4,963. **Course rating:** 71.8/67.7. **Slope:** 125/118. **Architect:** Dan Maples.
Subscriber comments: Excellent course...Good beach course for us hackers...Picturesque. Older track with character...Average course. Above average atmosphere...Some dull holes...Beautiful course...Friendly staff...Beautiful closing hole...Very enjoyable course, wife loved it...Beautiful, quiet.

★★★½RIVER COURSE
(803)237-8755.

Opened: 1986. **Holes:** 18. **Par:** 72/72. **Yards:** 6,677/5,084. **Course rating:** 72.2/66.5. **Slope:** 125/110. **Architect:** Tom Jackson.
Subscriber comments: 18th is gorgeous...Pretty course. Lush fairways...Several interesting holes...A wonderful plantation style course with water hazards and an island green...Some holes too close to houses...Great par 3s.

★★★½THE LONG BAY CLUB
R-350 Foxtail Dr., Longs, 29568, Horry County, (803)399-2222, (800)344-5590, 15 miles NW of North Myrtle Beach.

Opened: 1988. **Holes:** 18. **Par:** 72/72. **Yards:** 7,021/5,598. **Course rating:** 74.3/72.1. **Slope:** 137/127. **Architect:** Jack Nicklaus. **Green fee:** $42/$87. **Credit cards:** All major,Diners Club. **Reduced fees:** Low season, resort guests, juniors. **Caddies:** No. **Golf carts:** $18. **Discount golf packages:** Yes. **Season:** Year-round. **High:** Spring/Fall. **On site lodging:** No. **Rental clubs:** Yes. **Walking policy:** Mandatory cart. **Metal spikes allowed:** Yes. **Range:** Yes (grass/mats). **To obtain tee times:** Contact your hotel golf director or tee time central up to 1 year in advance.
Subscriber comments: Tough Nicklaus layout; target shots to well bunkered greens; 10th hole the best...Sometimes three-tiered greens, thanks Jack...Very good, challenging, fun course...Very long for average golfer, waste areas are fun...From the tips, could be a tour stop...Come on Jack, give us a chance.

★★★½MAN O' WAR GOLF
R-5601 Leeshire Blvd., Myrtle Beach, 29579, Horry County, (803)236-8000,.
Opened: 1996. **Holes:** 18. **Par:** 72/72. **Yards:** 6,967/4,965. **Course rating:** 72.9/71.2.
Slope: 133/121. **Architect:** Dan Maples. **Green fee:** $43/$87. **Credit cards:** MC,VISA.
Reduced fees: N/A. **Caddies:** No. **Golf carts:** Included in Green Fee. **Discount golf**
packages: No. **Season:** Year-round. **High:** March-April, Oct. **On site lodging:** No.
Rental clubs: Yes. **Walking policy:** Mandatory cart. **Metal spikes allowed:** Yes.
Range: Yes (grass). **To obtain tee times:** Call up to 1 year in advance.
Subscriber comments: Large greens, wide fairways...Nice new track. Water not in play
as much as it looks...Can't remember any holes...Great new course. Excellent greens.
Needs more trees...Good track, interesting par 3s...Will get nicer as it
matures...Risk/reward par 5s and back-to-back island greens a hoot!

★★★½MIDLAND VALLEY COUNTRY CLUB
151 Midland Dr., Aiken, 29829, Aiken County, (803)663-7332, (800)486-0240, 10 miles
N of Augusta, GA.
Opened: 1961. **Holes:** 18. **Par:** 71/74. **Yards:** 6,849/5,542. **Course rating:** 72.1/71.8.
Slope: 127/125. **Architect:** Ellis Maples. **Green fee:** $13/$23. **Credit cards:** MC,VISA.
Reduced fees: Low season, seniors. **Caddies:** No. **Golf carts:** $12. **Discount golf**
packages: No. **Season:** Year-round. **High:** March-June. **On site lodging:** No. **Rental**
clubs: Yes. **Walking policy:** Mandatory cart. **Metal spikes allowed:** Yes. **Range:** Yes
(grass). **To obtain tee times:** Call.
Subscriber comments: A must play...Improvements have made it a good place to
play...Good course, challenging greens.

★½MILER COUNTRY CLUB
400 Country Club Blvd., Summerville, 29483, Dorchester County, (803)873-2210, 20
miles W of Charleston.
Opened: 1925. **Holes:** 18. **Par:** 71/71. **Yards:** 6,001/5,400. **Course rating:** 68.8/68.9.
Slope: 114/110. **Architect:** Ricciboni/Kemp. **Green fee:** $17/$31. **Credit cards:** None.
Reduced fees: Weekdays, low season, twilight. **Caddies:** No. **Golf carts:** $12.
Discount golf packages: No. **Season:** Year-round. **High:** Spring/Fall. **On site lodging:**
No. **Rental clubs:** No. **Walking policy:** Unrestricted walking. **Metal spikes allowed:**
Yes. **Range:** No. **To obtain tee times:** Call.

MYRTLE BEACH NATIONAL GOLF CLUB
R-4900 National Dr., Myrtle Beach, 29579, Horry County, (803)448-2308, (800)344-
5590, 8 miles W of Myrtle Beach.
Architect: Arnold Palmer and Francis Duane. **Credit cards:** All major,Diners Club.
Caddies: No. **Golf carts:** $18. **Discount golf packages:** Yes. **Season:** Year-round.
High: Spring/Fall. **On site lodging:** No. **Rental clubs:** Yes. **Walking policy:** Walking at
certain times. **Metal spikes allowed:** Yes. **Range:** Yes (grass/mats). **To obtain tee**
times: Contact your hotel golf director or call tee time central up to 1 year in advance.
★★★½KINGS NORTH COURSE
Opened: 1973. **Holes:** 18. **Par:** 72/72. **Yards:** 7,017/4,816. **Course rating:** 72.6/67.0.
Slope: 136/122. **Green fee:** $100/$112. **Reduced fees:** Low season, resort guests,
juniors.
Notes: Ranked 10th in 1997 Best New Upscale Public Courses.
Subscriber comments: Top of the line public courses...Most memorable hole: par 5
with island fairway...Arnie did a fantastic job...Course much tougher after redesign,
some tricked up holes.
★★★SOUTHCREEK COURSE
Opened: 1975. **Holes:** 18. **Par:** 72/72. **Yards:** 6,416/4,723. **Course rating:** 70.5/66.5.
Slope: 123/109. **Green fee:** $23/$58. **Reduced fees:** Weekdays, low season, resort
guests, twilight, juniors.
Subscriber comments: Good course...Houses too close to course...Winding layout but
fair...Nothing remarkable...Fun, good place to tune up...Too short, boring layout...Good
place to play...Great, moderately priced golf.
★★★½WEST COURSE
Opened: 1973. **Holes:** 18. **Par:** 72/72. **Yards:** 6,866/5,307. **Course rating:** 73.0/69.0.
Slope: 119/109. **Green fee:** $23/$58. **Reduced fees:** Low season, resort guests,
juniors.

Notes: Dupont World Amateur site.
Subscriber comments: Nice layout through the pines. No underbrush in woods...Wide open, easy to score on...A middle of the road course, many holes seem the same...Beautiful scenery, worth playing...No "wow" holes...Some good holes, lots of doglegs...Very enjoyable.

★★★MYRTLE WEST GOLF CLUB
PU-Hwy. 9 W., North Myrtle Beach, 29582, Horry County, (803)249-1478, (800)842-8390, 11 miles W of Myrtle Beach.
Opened: 1989. **Holes:** 18. **Par:** 72/72. **Yards:** 6,787/4,859. **Course rating:** 72.7/67.9. **Slope:** 132/113. **Architect:** Tom Jackson. **Green fee:** $25/$63. **Credit cards:** MC,VISA,AMEX. **Reduced fees:** Low season. **Caddies:** No. **Golf carts:** Included in Green Fee. **Discount golf packages:** Yes. **Season:** Year-round. **High:** Spring/Fall. **On site lodging:** No. **Rental clubs:** Yes. **Walking policy:** Mandatory cart. **Metal spikes allowed:** Yes. **Range:** Yes (grass). **To obtain tee times:** Call up to 9 months in advance. Call up to 2 days in advance with golf card or coupon.
Subscriber comments: Worth the drive out of town. Tough but fun to play...Nothing outstanding, nothing bad...Variety of holes, fun course...Not a lot of trees...This course has come a long way!...17 and 18 are great finishing holes.

MYRTLEWOOD GOLF CLUB
Hwy. 17 at 48th Ave. N., Myrtle Beach, 29577, Horry County, (803)449-5134, (800)283-3633.
Credit cards: All major. **Caddies:** No. **Golf carts:** $18. **Discount golf packages:** Yes. **Season:** Year-round. **High:** Spring/Fall. **On site lodging:** No. **Rental clubs:** Yes. **Walking policy:** Mandatory cart. **Metal spikes allowed:** No. **Range:** Yes (grass). **To obtain tee times:** Call in advance. Deposit or credit card required in high season. Or, contact your hotel golf director to reserve times.
★★★½PALMETTO COURSE
Opened: 1973. **Holes:** 18. **Par:** 72/72. **Yards:** 6,957/5,305. **Course rating:** 72.7/70.1. **Slope:** 121/117. **Architect:** Edmund Ault. **Green fee:** $24/$57. **Reduced fees:** Low season, resort guests, juniors.
Subscriber comments: Fun from start to finish...Typical Myrtle Beach course...Take dead aim on 18 and stay out of the Intracoastal...Front nine fairly easy, but back nine much tougher...Played bad but still had a good time.
★★★½PINEHILLS COURSE
Opened: 1993. **Holes:** 18. **Par:** 72/72. **Yards:** 6,640/4,906. **Course rating:** 72.0/67.4. **Slope:** 125/113. **Architect:** Arthur Hills. **Green fee:** $28/$60. **Reduced fees:** Low season, resort guests, seniors.
Subscriber comments: Good golf experience at Myrtle Beach, a bit short, but nice par 5s and par 3s...Tough driving course...Nice variety of holes...Free golf on Christmas Day...Redesign is a success...Rolling course, reminds one of Cape Cod.

★★★NORTHWOODS GOLF CLUB
PU-201 Powell Rd., Columbia, 29203, Richland County, (803)786-9242, 4 miles S of Columbia.
Opened: 1990. **Holes:** 18. **Par:** 72/72. **Yards:** 6,800/5,000. **Course rating:** 71.9/67.8. **Slope:** 122/116. **Architect:** P.B. Dye. **Green fee:** $19/$28. **Credit cards:** MC,VISA,AMEX. **Reduced fees:** Weekdays, low season, twilight, seniors, juniors. **Caddies:** No. **Golf carts:** $11. **Discount golf packages:** Yes. **Season:** Year-round. **High:** May-Oct. **On site lodging:** No. **Rental clubs:** Yes. **Walking policy:** Walking at certain times. **Metal spikes allowed:** Yes. **Range:** Yes (grass/mats). **To obtain tee times:** Call 7 days in advance. Out of state players may call up to 30 days in advance.
Subscriber comments: Good layout...Favorite course in Columbia...Very fair to all levels. No tricks...Awesome design except 1st and 10th identical...Nice course, getting better with age...Back nine especially interesting...Back nine is a killer.

★★★OAK HILLS GOLF CLUB
PU-7629 Fairfield Rd., Columbia, 29203, Richland County, (803)735-9830, (800)263-5218.
Opened: 1990. **Holes:** 18. **Par:** 72/72. **Yards:** 6,894/4,574. **Course rating:** 72.4/65.8. **Slope:** 122/110. **Architect:** Steve Melnyk. **Green fee:** $23/$37. **Credit cards:** MC,VISA,AMEX. **Reduced fees:** Weekdays, low season, twilight, seniors, juniors.

Caddies: No. Golf carts: Included in Green Fee. Discount golf packages: Yes.
Season: Year-round. High: Spring/Fall. On site lodging: No. Rental clubs: Yes.
Walking policy: Unrestricted walking. Metal spikes allowed: Yes. Range: Yes
(grass/mats). To obtain tee times: Call up to 3 days in advance.
Subscriber comments: Nice waterfall on back nine, tough course...Fairly new course,
finally maturing...Rolling hills, tiered/sloped greens, excellent trap positions, lots of
mounds...Fun course...Good track...Continues to impove.

★★OAKDALE COUNTRY CLUB

3700 W. Lake Dr., Florence, 29501, Florence County, (803)662-0368.
Opened: 1964. Holes: 18. Par: 72/73. Yards: 6,300/5,000. Course rating: 70.0/67.1.
Slope: 117/109. Architect: Roland "Robby" Robertson. Green fee: $15/$20. Credit
cards: None. Reduced fees: N/A. Caddies: No. Golf carts: $10. Discount golf pack-
ages: No. Season: Year-round. High: March-April. On site lodging: No. Rental clubs:
Yes. Walking policy: Walking at certain times. Metal spikes allowed: Yes. Range: Yes
(grass/mats). To obtain tee times: Call.

★★★½OCEAN CREEK GOLF COURSE

R-90B Ocean Creek Blvd., Fripp Island, 29920, Beaufort County,
(803)838-1576, (800)933-0050, 30 miles N of Hilton Head.
Opened: 1995. Holes: 18. Par: 71/71. Yards: 6,510/4,824. Course rating: 71.4/69.5. Slope: 131/121. Architect: Davis Love III and Bob
Spence. Green fee: $49/$69. Credit cards: MC,VISA,AMEX. Reduced
fees: Low season, resort guests, twilight, juniors. Caddies: No. Golf carts: Included in
Green Fee. Discount golf packages: No. Season: Year-round. High: Spring/Fall. On
site lodging: Yes. Rental clubs: Yes. Walking policy: Unrestricted walking. Metal
spikes allowed: No. Range: Yes (grass). To obtain tee times: Call 800 number.
Subscriber comments: Good course, best score in years. Fun...Davis Love did himself proud. Marsh, woods, water...Marsh holes are spectacular...Great setting for golf,
would do it again...Shotmaker's course, like Harbour Town but cheaper.

★★★½OCEAN POINT GOLF LINKS

R-250 Ocean Point Dr., Fripp Island, 29920, Beaufort County, (803)838-
2309, (800)845-4100, 20 miles SE of Beaufort.
Opened: 1964. Holes: 18. Par: 72/72. Yards: 6,590/4,951. Course rating: 72.2/69.5. Slope: 129/113. Architect: George Cobb. Green fee:
$44/$59. Credit cards: All major. Reduced fees: Weekdays, low season, resort guests, juniors. Caddies: No. Golf carts: Included in Green Fee. Discount
golf packages: Yes. Season: Year-round. High: Spring/Fall. On site lodging: Yes.
Rental clubs: Yes. Walking policy: Walking at certain times. Metal spikes allowed:
Yes. Range: Yes (grass/mats). To obtain tee times: Call golf shop or make reservation
through resort.
Subscriber comments: Oceanside golf, windy...Tough on windy days, beautiful
views...Nice views on 9 and 18...Lots of water...Alligators everywhere...Good course,
fun to play...Great facilities...Some very good holes, some so-so holes.

OLD CAROLINA GOLF CLUB

PU-90 Buck Island Rd., Bluffton, 29910, Beaufort County, (803)785-6363, (888)785-
7274, 6 miles W of Hilton Head.
Opened: 1996. Holes: 18. Par: 72/71. Yards: 6,805/4,475. Course rating: 73.1/67.0.
Slope: 142/121. Architect: Clyde Johnston. Green fee: $46/$79. Credit cards:
MC,VISA. Reduced fees: Low season, resort guests, twilight, juniors. Caddies: No.
Golf carts: Included in Green Fee. Discount golf packages: No. Season: Year-round.
High: Spring/Fall. On site lodging: No. Rental clubs: Yes. Walking policy:
Unrestricted walking. Metal spikes allowed: No. Range: Yes (grass). To obtain tee
times: Call up to 4 months in advance with credit card to guarantee.

★★★½OLD SOUTH GOLF LINKS

R-50 Buckingham Plantation Dr., Bluffton, 29910, Beaufort County, (803)785-5353,
(800)257-8997, 25 miles N of Hilton Head.
Opened: 1991. Holes: 18. Par: 72/71. Yards: 6,772/4,776. Course rating: 72.4/69.6.
Slope: 129/123. Architect: Clyde Johnston. Green fee: $49/$83. Credit cards:
MC,VISA,AMEX. Reduced fees: Low season, resort guests, twilight, juniors. Caddies:

No. **Golf carts:** Included in Green Fee. **Discount golf packages:** Yes. **Season:** Year-round. **High:** March-April. **On site lodging:** No. **Rental clubs:** Yes. **Walking policy:** Unrestricted walking. **Metal spikes allowed:** Yes. **Range:** Yes (grass). **To obtain tee times:** Call golf shop.

Subscriber comments: Interesting with tidal areas, marsh...Lots of water. Back nine a killer...Fabulous course, links style, very tough with wind...Play it when the tide is in, better aesthetics...Knockout views...Wonderful holes designed through marshes.

★★★½OYSTER REEF GOLF CLUB

155 High Bluff Rd., Hilton Head Island, 29925, Beaufort County, (803)681-7717, 35 miles NE of Savannah, GA.

Opened: 1982. **Holes:** 18. **Par:** 72/72. **Yards:** 7,027/5,288. **Course rating:** 73.7/69.8. **Slope:** 131/118. **Architect:** Rees Jones. **Green fee:** $48/$79. **Credit cards:** All major. **Reduced fees:** Low season, resort guests, juniors. **Caddies:** No. **Golf carts:** Included in Green Fee. **Discount golf packages:** Yes. **Season:** Year-round. **High:** Spring/Fall. **On site lodging:** No. **Rental clubs:** Yes. **Walking policy:** Mandatory cart. **Metal spikes allowed:** No. **Range:** Yes (grass). **To obtain tee times:** Call up to 90 days in advance.

Subscriber comments: Excellent course, beautiful scenery, very tough...Par 3 6th is a gem...A sleeper, fun to play...There are no boring holes, some are tough and scenic...Nice layout, very fair...Good course for "straight shooters"...Traditional type design offering good test for all skill levels...Great views of marsh, wildlife.

PALMETTO DUNES RESORT

R- **Credit cards:** MC,VISA,AMEX. **Caddies:** No. **Golf carts:** Included in Green Fee. **Discount golf packages:** Yes. **Season:** Year-round. **High:** April/Oct. **On site lodging:** Yes. **Rental clubs:** Yes. **Metal spikes allowed:** Yes. **To obtain tee times:** Resort guests call up to 90 in advance. Others call up to 60 days in advance.

★★★★ARTHUR HILLS COURSE

P.O. Box 5849, Hilton Head, 29938, Beaufort County, (803)785-1140, (800)827-3006, 50 miles NE of Savannah, GA.

Opened: 1986. **Holes:** 18. **Par:** 72/72. **Yards:** 6,651/4,999. **Course rating:** 71.4/68.5. **Slope:** 127/118. **Architect:** Arthur Hills. **Green fee:** $75/$110. **Reduced fees:** Resort guests. **Walking policy:** Unrestricted walking. **Range:** Yes (grass).

Notes: 1990 Women's NCAA Division I; Annual Golf World/Palmetto Dunes Collegiate.

Subscriber comments: Wow! Not your typical low country links. Rolling fairways, quick greens, tees for all skills...Save up for at least one run at it...My favorite course on Hilton Head, great par 5s...Lots of wildlife. Deer on cart path...Really fun to play...Challenging, great greens...Good, tough course, one of the best on Hilton Head.

★★★½GEORGE FAZIO COURSE

P.O. Box 5849, Hilton Head, 29928, Beaufort County, (803)785-1130, (800)827-3006, 50 miles NE of Savannah, GA.

Opened: 1974. **Holes:** 18. **Par:** 70/70. **Yards:** 6,875/5,273. **Course rating:** 74.2/70.8. **Slope:** 132/127. **Architect:** George Fazio. **Green fee:** $50/$81. **Reduced fees:** Resort guests, juniors. **Walking policy:** Walking at certain times. **Range:** No.

Subscriber comments: Narrow fairways, too much water...Best for long hitters...Great finishing holes...Tons of bunkers; very tough finishing holes...Very tough if played from back tees.

★★★½ROBERT TRENT JONES COURSE

P.O. Box 5849, Hilton Head, 29938, Beaufort County, (803)785-1136, (800)827-3006, 50 miles NE of Savannah, GA.

Opened: 1969. **Holes:** 18. **Par:** 72/72. **Yards:** 6,710/5,425. **Course rating:** 72.2/70.3. **Slope:** 123/123. **Architect:** Robert Trent Jones. **Green fee:** $55/$81. **Reduced fees:** Low season, resort guests, juniors. **Walking policy:** Mandatory cart. **Range:** Yes (grass/mats).

Subscriber comments: I like it, an easy course with the wind calm...Very playable. Not too hard. Great course to relax on...#10 par 5 spectacular signature hole...User friendly...Fun resort course.

PALMETTO HALL PLANTATION

R-108 Fort Howell Dr., Hilton Head Island, 29926, Beaufort County, (803)689-4100, (800)827-3006, 30 miles N of Savannah, GA.

Green fee: $55/$90. **Credit cards:** MC,VISA,AMEX. **Reduced fees:** Resort guests, juniors. **Caddies:** No. **Golf carts:** Included in Green Fee. **Discount golf packages:** Yes. **Season:** Year-round. **High:** Spring/Fall. **On site lodging:** No. **Rental clubs:** Yes. **Metal spikes allowed:** Yes. **Range:** Yes (grass). **To obtain tee times:** Call.

★★★½ARTHUR HILLS COURSE
Opened: 1991. **Holes:** 18. **Par:** 72/72. **Yards:** 6,918/4,956. **Course rating:** 72.2/68.6. **Slope:** 132/119. **Architect:** Arthur Hills. **Walking policy:** Mandatory cart.
Subscriber comments: One of the better courses on Hilton Head...Best of two Hall courses, lots of wildlife....Nice course, long par 4s...Nice course that will only get better with age...Tough course, length a problem for high handicaps.

★★★½ROBERT CUPP COURSE
Opened: 1993. **Holes:** 18. **Par:** 72/72. **Yards:** 7,079/5,220. **Course rating:** 74.8/71.1. **Slope:** 141/126. **Architect:** Robert Cupp. **Walking policy:** Unrestricted walking.
Subscriber comments: Amazing use of geometric architecture...Hit out of square bunkers, off of pyramid rough...Weird layout...Unique design. Not too wacky if you stay in the fairway...Emphasis on geometric shapes more gimmicky than anything else.

★★★PARKLAND GOLF CLUB
295 E. Deadfall Rd., Greenwood, 29649, Greenwood County, (864)229-5086.
Opened: 1985. **Holes:** 18. **Par:** 72/72. **Yards:** 6,520/5,130. **Course rating:** 70.8/68.3. **Slope:** 124/115. **Architect:** John Park. **Green fee:** $15/$20. **Credit cards:** MC,VISA. **Reduced fees:** Weekdays, seniors, juniors. **Caddies:** No. **Golf carts:** $11. **Discount golf packages:** Yes. **Season:** Year-round. **High:** March-Nov. **On site lodging:** No. **Rental clubs:** No. **Walking policy:** Unrestricted walking. **Metal spikes allowed:** Yes. **Range:** Yes (grass). **To obtain tee times:** Call for weekends and holidays.
Subscriber comments: Traditional golf...A very tight public course, demands good shotmaking, some very challenging par 4s over water...Excellent but difficult.

★★PATRIOTS POINT LINKS
PU-1 Patriots Point Rd., Mount Pleasant, 29464, Charleston County, (803)881-0042, (800)221-2424, 2 miles N of Charleston.
Opened: 1981. **Holes:** 18. **Par:** 72/72. **Yards:** 6,838/5,562. **Course rating:** 72.1/71.0. **Slope:** 118/115. **Architect:** Willard Byrd. **Green fee:** $30/$50. **Credit cards:** MC,VISA,AMEX. **Reduced fees:** Weekdays, low season, resort guests, twilight, juniors. **Caddies:** No. **Golf carts:** Included in Green Fee. **Discount golf packages:** Yes. **Season:** Year-round. **High:** Spring/Fall. **On site lodging:** Yes. **Rental clubs:** Yes. **Walking policy:** Walking at certain times. **Metal spikes allowed:** Yes. **Range:** Yes (grass/mats). **To obtain tee times:** Call.

★★★½PAWLEYS PLANTATION GOLF CLUB
R-Hwy. 17, Pawleys Island, 29585, Georgetown County, (803)237-6200, (800)367-9959, 30 miles S of Myrtle Beach.
Opened: 1988. **Holes:** 18. **Par:** 72/72. **Yards:** 7,026/4,979. **Course rating:** 74.8/70.1. **Slope:** 140/126. **Architect:** Jack Nicklaus. **Green fee:** N/A. **Credit cards:** All major. **Reduced fees:** Low season, resort guests. **Caddies:** No. **Golf carts:** N/A. **Discount golf packages:** No. **Season:** Year-round. **High:** Spring/Fall. **On site lodging:** No. **Rental clubs:** Yes. **Walking policy:** Mandatory cart. **Metal spikes allowed:** No. **Range:** Yes (grass). **To obtain tee times:** Call.
Notes: Ranked 14th in 1997 Best in State.
Subscriber comments: Great all around...Jack's lesson is that golf can be a humbling game....Nasty if it's windy. Some weird holes...True test of golf, if wind blows bring an extra dozen balls.

★★½PAWPAW COUNTRY CLUB
600 George St., Bamberg, 29003, Bamberg County, (803)245-4171.
Opened: N/A. **Holes:** 18. **Par:** N/A. **Yards:** N/A. **Course rating:** N/A. **Slope:** N/A. **Architect:** Russell Breeden. **Green fee:** $7/$13. **Credit cards:** MC,VISA. **Reduced fees:** Juniors. **Caddies:** No. **Golf carts:** $8. **Discount golf packages:** No. **Season:** Year-round. **High:** N/A. **On site lodging:** Yes. **Rental clubs:** Yes. **Walking policy:** Unrestricted walking. **Metal spikes allowed:** Yes. **Range:** Yes (grass). **To obtain tee times:** Call golf shop.
Subscriber comments: Getting better every day!...Easy course...Good course for rural area, good layout.

SOUTH CAROLINA

★★★½PERSIMMON HILL GOLF CLUB
PU-Rt. 3, Box 364, Saluda, 29138, Saluda County, (803)275-3522, 35 miles NE of Augusta, GA.
Opened: 1962. **Holes:** 18. **Par:** 72/73. **Yards:** 6,925/5,449. **Course rating:** 72.3/71.1. **Slope:** 122/121. **Architect:** Russell Breeden. **Green fee:** $10/$18. **Credit cards:** MC,VISA,AMEX. **Reduced fees:** Weekdays, low season, twilight. **Caddies:** No. **Golf carts:** $12. **Discount golf packages:** Yes. **Season:** Year-round. **High:** March-May. **On site lodging:** No. **Rental clubs:** Yes. **Walking policy:** Walking at certain times. **Metal spikes allowed:** Yes. **Range:** Yes (grass/mats). **To obtain tee times:** Call 7 days in advance.
Subscriber comments: Very good course, especially last couple of years...Terrific golf course...Augusta National's cousin...Fun to play...Another good one...#18 a 600-yard par 5..Straightforward traditional course...Long course for average player.

★★★½PINE FOREST COUNTRY CLUB
1000 Congressional Blvd., Summerville, 29483, Dorchester County, (803)851-1193, 20 miles W of Charleston.
Opened: 1992. **Holes:** 18. **Par:** 72/72. **Yards:** 6,905/5,007. **Course rating:** 73.6/67.7. **Slope:** 140/120. **Architect:** Bob Spence. **Green fee:** $25/$40. **Credit cards:** MC,VISA. **Reduced fees:** Weekdays, low season, twilight, juniors. **Caddies:** No. **Golf carts:** Included in Green Fee. **Discount golf packages:** Yes. **Season:** Year-round. **High:** March-May. **On site lodging:** No. **Rental clubs:** Yes. **Walking policy:** Unrestricted walking. **Metal spikes allowed:** Yes. **Range:** Yes (grass). **To obtain tee times:** Call.
Subscriber comments: Tough course, very undulating greens...Must think...Will wear you out...Lot of water, real challenge for all play.

★★★½PINE LAKES INTERNATIONAL COUNTRY CLUB
5603 Woodside Ave., Myrtle Beach, 29577, Horry County, (803)449-6459, (800)446-6817.
Opened: 1927. **Holes:** 18. **Par:** 71/71. **Yards:** 6,609/5,376. **Course rating:** 71.5/71.6. **Slope:** 125/129. **Architect:** Robert White. **Green fee:** $45/$95. **Credit cards:** MC,VISA,AMEX. **Reduced fees:** Resort guests. **Caddies:** No. **Golf carts:** $20. **Discount golf packages:** Yes. **Season:** Year-round. **High:** March-April. **On site lodging:** No. **Rental clubs:** Yes. **Walking policy:** Mandatory cart. **Metal spikes allowed:** Yes. **Range:** Yes (grass/mats). **To obtain tee times:** Call up to 1 year in advance with deposit.
Subscriber comments: This is the way golf should be...Great tradition, try the chowder on a cool day...Basic golf made nice...Service first, OK golf...First course in Myrtle Beach...First class treatment from the moment you arrive...Nice being pampered...I love everything about this course...Classic design.

★★½PINELAND PLANTATION GOLF CLUB
7305 Myrtle Beach Hwy., Sumter, 29051, Sumter County, (803)495-3550, (800)746-3843, 20 miles S of Florence.
Opened: 1974. **Holes:** 18. **Par:** 72/72. **Yards:** 7,000/5,344. **Course rating:** 73.0/70.2. **Slope:** 127/119. **Architect:** Russell Breeden. **Green fee:** $20/$38. **Credit cards:** MC,VISA. **Reduced fees:** Weekdays, low season, resort guests, twilight, seniors, juniors. **Caddies:** No. **Golf carts:** Included in Green Fee. **Discount golf packages:** Yes. **Season:** Year-round. **High:** March-April. **On site lodging:** No. **Rental clubs:** Yes. **Walking policy:** Walking at certain times. **Metal spikes allowed:** Yes. **Range:** Yes (grass). **To obtain tee times:** Call.
Subscriber comments: Trying to improve...Nice layout.

★★PINETUCK GOLF CLUB
2578 Tuckaway Rd., Rock Hill, 29730, York County, (803)327-1141.
Opened: 1971. **Holes:** 18. **Par:** 71/74. **Yards:** 6,567/4,870. **Course rating:** 71.7/68.2. **Slope:** 127/111. **Architect:** George Dunlap. **Green fee:** $17/$23. **Credit cards:** MC,VISA. **Reduced fees:** Weekdays, twilight, seniors, juniors. **Caddies:** No. **Golf carts:** $12. **Discount golf packages:** Yes. **Season:** Year-round. **High:** March-Oct. **On site lodging:** No. **Rental clubs:** Yes. **Walking policy:** Walking at certain times. **Metal spikes allowed:** Yes. **Range:** Yes (grass/mats). **To obtain tee times:** Call anytime for weekends and holidays.

★½POCALLA SPRINGS COUNTRY CLUB

1700 Hwy. 15 S., Sumter, 29150, Sumter County, (803)481-8322.
Opened: 1920. **Holes:** 18. **Par:** 71/71. **Yards:** 6,350/5,500. **Course rating:** 68.0/65.0.
Slope: 115/111. **Architect:** Ed Riccoboni. **Green fee:** $7/$10. **Credit cards:** MC,VISA.
Reduced fees: Weekdays, low season, resort guests, twilight, seniors, juniors.
Caddies: No. **Golf carts:** $8. **Discount golf packages:** Yes. **Season:** Year-round.
High: April-Sept. **On site lodging:** No. **Rental clubs:** Yes. **Walking policy:** Unrestricted walking. **Metal spikes allowed:** Yes. **Range:** Yes (grass). **To obtain tee times:** Call golf shop.

PORT ROYAL GOLF CLUB

R- **Credit cards:** MC,VISA,AMEX. **Reduced fees:** Low season, resort guests, twilight, juniors. **Caddies:** No. **Golf carts:** Included in Green Fee. **Discount golf packages:** Yes. **Season:** Year-round. **High:** March-May/Sept. **On site lodging:** No. **Rental clubs:** Yes. **Walking policy:** Mandatory cart. **Metal spikes allowed:** Yes. **Range:** Yes (grass/mats). **To obtain tee times:** Call 800 number.

★★★BARONY COURSE

10A Grasslawn Ave., Hilton Head, 29928, Beaufort County, (803)681-1760, (800)234-6318, 40 miles NE of Savannah, Ga.
Opened: 1968. **Holes:** 18. **Par:** 72/72. **Yards:** 6,530/5,253. **Course rating:** 71.6/70.1.
Slope: 129/115. **Architect:** Willard Byrd. **Green fee:** $49/$80.
Subscriber comments: A very nice layout...Not very long. Some good holes...Good spot for higher handicappers. Short...OK as a warm-up; neither fish nor fowl, strictly routine...User friendly, picturesque, views of ocean are great.

★★★PLANTER'S ROW COURSE

10-A Grasslawn Ave., Hilton Head, 29928, Beaufort County, (803)686-8801, (800)234-6318, 40 miles NE of Savannah, GA.
Opened: 1983. **Holes:** 18. **Par:** 72/72. **Yards:** 6,520/5,126. **Course rating:** 71.7/68.9.
Slope: 133/116. **Architect:** George Cobb/Willard Byrd. **Green fee:** $49/$80.
Subscriber comments: Great 19th hole...Nice layout. Beautiful clubhouse...Course OK, good design...Enjoyable course, had to play a lot of different shots...Easiest but still a fair golf course...Average for Hilton Head...Tight, must play target golf.

★★★½ROBBER'S ROW COURSE

10A Grasslawn Ave., Hilton Head, 29928, Beaufort County, (803)681-1760, (800)234-6318, 40 miles NE of Savannah, Ga.
Opened: 1968. **Holes:** 18. **Par:** 72/72. **Yards:** 6,642/5,000. **Course rating:** 72.6/70.4.
Slope: 134/115. **Architect:** Willard Byrd/Pete Dye. **Green fee:** $54/$80.
Subscriber comments: Resort golf...This course might be the best in Port Royal. A nice variety of holes, tricky greens...Typical resort course; easy to score on...Water.

★★★POSSUM TROT GOLF CLUB

R-Possum Trot Rd., North Myrtle Beach, 29582, Horry County, (803)272-5341, (800)626-8768.
Opened: 1968. **Holes:** 18. **Par:** 72/72. **Yards:** 6,966/5,160. **Course rating:** 73.0/69.6.
Slope: 118/111. **Architect:** Russell Breeden. **Green fee:** $32/$64. **Credit cards:** All major. **Reduced fees:** Twilight, juniors. **Caddies:** No. **Golf carts:** Included in Green Fee. **Discount golf packages:** Yes. **Season:** Year-round. **High:** Spring/Fall. **On site lodging:** No. **Rental clubs:** Yes. **Walking policy:** Walking at certain times. **Metal spikes allowed:** Yes. **Range:** Yes (grass/mats). **To obtain tee times:** Call anytime.
Subscriber comments: Hidden treasure...Myrtle Beach basic...My wife loves it..Has some real par 4s, diamond in the rough...Nice finishing holes...Like the last hole a lot.

★★★QUAIL CREEK GOLF CLUB

PU-Hwy. 501 W., Myrtle Beach, 29578, Horry County, (800)833-6337, (800)833-6337.
Opened: N/A. **Holes:** 18. **Par:** 72/72. **Yards:** 6,812/5,287. **Course rating:** 72.8/70.2.
Slope: 119/112. **Architect:** Gene Hamm. **Green fee:** $4/$41. **Credit cards:** MC,VISA,DISC. **Reduced fees:** Low season, twilight, juniors. **Caddies:** No. **Golf carts:** $19. **Discount golf packages:** No. **Season:** Year-round. **High:** Spring/Fall. **On site lodging:** No. **Rental clubs:** No. **Walking policy:** Walking at certain times. **Metal spikes allowed:** Yes. **Range:** Yes (grass). **To obtain tee times:** Call golf shop.
Subscriber comments: Nice wood setting...Wide fairways, fun to play...Nice layout, not very hard, like it...A good course to play after three-month layoff...I loved the wildlife...Off the beaten track, but worth the trip...Fun for all levels.

★½RACCOON RUN GOLF CLUB
PU-8950 Hwy. 707, Myrtle Beach, 29575, Horry County, (803)650-2644, 10 miles S of Myrtle Beach.
Opened: 1977. **Holes:** 18. **Par:** 73/73. **Yards:** 7,349/5,535. **Course rating:** 74.0/69.5. **Slope:** 120/109. **Architect:** Gene Hamm. **Green fee:** $18/$35. **Credit cards:** MC,VISA. **Reduced fees:** Low season, juniors. **Caddies:** No. **Golf carts:** $17. **Discount golf packages:** No. **Season:** Year-round. **High:** Feb.-April. **On site lodging:** No. **Rental clubs:** No. **Walking policy:** Walking at certain times. **Metal spikes allowed:** Yes. **Range:** No. **To obtain tee times:** Call up to 6 months in advance.

★★★½REGENT PARK GOLF CLUB
PU-6000 Regent Pkwy., Fort Mill, 29715, York County, (803)547-1300, 16 miles S of Charlotte, NC.
Opened: 1994. **Holes:** 18. **Par:** 72/72. **Yards:** 6,848/5,245. **Course rating:** 72.6/69.5. **Slope:** 132/123. **Architect:** Ron Garl. **Green fee:** $43/$52. **Credit cards:** All major. **Reduced fees:** Resort guests, twilight, seniors, juniors. **Caddies:** No. **Golf carts:** Included in Green Fee. **Discount golf packages:** No. **Season:** Year-round. **High:** April-Oct. **On site lodging:** Yes. **Rental clubs:** Yes. **Walking policy:** Mandatory cart. **Metal spikes allowed:** Yes. **Range:** Yes (grass/mats). **To obtain tee times:** Call 3 days in advance starting at 8 a.m.
Subscriber comments: Beautiful course...Great practice facility. Beautiful layout. Play from the tips...Good layout, 8th hole is tough...Way too many three and four-tiered greens...No.8 too long for most golfers.

★½RIVER CLUB ON THE ASHLEY
222 Fairington Dr., Summerville, 29485, Dorchester County, (803)873-7110, 20 miles NE of Charleston.
Opened: 1971. **Holes:** 18. **Par:** 72/72. **Yards:** 6,712/5,025. **Course rating:** 70.5/68.5. **Slope:** 115/115. **Architect:** Russell Breeden. **Green fee:** $30/$40. **Credit cards:** MC,VISA. **Reduced fees:** Weekdays, low season. **Caddies:** No. **Golf carts:** $15. **Discount golf packages:** No. **Season:** Year-round. **High:** April-Aug. **On site lodging:** No. **Rental clubs:** Yes. **Walking policy:** Walking at certain times. **Metal spikes allowed:** Yes. **Range:** Yes (grass). **To obtain tee times:** Call.

★★★½RIVER FALLS PLANTATION
PU-100 Player Blvd., Duncan, 29334, Spartanburg County, (864)433-9192, 10 miles N of Greenville.
Opened: 1990. **Holes:** 18. **Par:** 72/72. **Yards:** 6,734/4,928. **Course rating:** 72.1/68.2. **Slope:** 127/125. **Architect:** Gary Player. **Green fee:** $32/$41. **Credit cards:** All major. **Reduced fees:** Low season, resort guests, seniors, juniors. **Caddies:** No. **Golf carts:** Included in Green Fee. **Discount golf packages:** Yes. **Season:** Year-round. **High:** April-Aug. **On site lodging:** No. **Rental clubs:** Yes. **Walking policy:** Walking at certain times. **Metal spikes allowed:** Yes. **Range:** Yes (grass). **To obtain tee times:** Call.
Subscriber comments: Nice course, need all the shots, several hazards near greens...Can't overpower the course...Good layout...Thinker's course...A fun course with some exciting holes...Tight, good challenge of golf.

★★★RIVER HILLS GOLF & COUNTRY CLUB
PU-3670 Ceder Creek Run, Little River, 29566, Horry County, (803)399-2100, (800)264-3810, 10 miles N of Myrtle Beach.
Opened: 1989. **Holes:** 18. **Par:** 72/72. **Yards:** 7,006/4,932. **Course rating:** 73.3/67.7. **Slope:** 136/120. **Architect:** Tom Jackson. **Green fee:** $22/$47. **Credit cards:** All major. **Reduced fees:** Twilight. **Caddies:** No. **Golf carts:** $18. **Discount golf packages:** Yes. **Season:** Year-round. **High:** Spring/Fall. **On site lodging:** No. **Rental clubs:** Yes. **Walking policy:** Mandatory cart. **Metal spikes allowed:** Yes. **Range:** Yes (grass). **To obtain tee times:** Call up to 1 year in advance.
Subscriber comments: A gem in North Myrtle, finishing hole great...Target course, tight fairways, 16,17 and 18 are murder...Too much home construction...I took out a window...Worth the money, fun, above average Myrtle Beach area course.

★★★RIVER OAKS GOLF PLANTATION
R-831 River Oaks Dr., Myrtle Beach, 29577, Horry County, (803)236-2222, (800)762-8813.
Opened: 1987. **Holes:** 27. **Architect:** Gene Hamm. **Green fee:** $25/$60. **Credit cards:** MC,VISA,AMEX. **Reduced fees:** Low season, resort guests, twilight, juniors. **Caddies:** No. **Golf carts:** Included in Green Fee. **Discount golf packages:** Yes. **Season:** Year-round. **High:** Spring/Fall. **On site lodging:** No. **Rental clubs:** Yes. **Walking policy:** Mandatory cart. **Metal spikes allowed:** Yes. **Range:** Yes (grass). **To obtain tee times:** Call golf shop or book through hotel.
BEAR/FOX
Par: 72/72. **Yards:** 6,778/5,133. **Course rating:** 72.0/69.7. **Slope:** 126/116.
OTTER/BEAR
Par: 72/72. **Yards:** 6,877/5,188. **Course rating:** 72.5/69.7. **Slope:** 125/118.
OTTER/FOX
Par: 72/72. **Yards:** 6,791/5,043. **Course rating:** 71.7/69.7. **Slope:** 125/118.
Subscriber comments: Very nice course...27 holes played, lots of variety...Good solid challenge...Best kept secret in Myrtle Beach...No outstanding holes, nice course...Three interesting and different nines...Great warm-up...Great layout, some water.

★★½ROBBERS ROOST GOLF COURSE
PU-Hwy. 17 N., North Myrtle Beach, 29597, Horry County, (803)249-1471, (800)352-2384.
Opened: 1968. **Holes:** 18. **Par:** 70/72. **Yards:** 7,148/5,387. **Course rating:** 74.4/70.2. **Slope:** 137/116. **Architect:** Russell Breeden. **Green fee:** $29/$56. **Credit cards:** MC,VISA,AMEX. **Reduced fees:** Low season, twilight. **Caddies:** No. **Golf carts:** Included in Green Fee. **Discount golf packages:** No. **Season:** Year-round. **High:** March-April. **On site lodging:** No. **Rental clubs:** Yes. **Walking policy:** Mandatory cart. **Metal spikes allowed:** Yes. **Range:** Yes (grass). **To obtain tee times:** Call up to one year in advance.
Subscriber comments: Typical Myrtle Beach golf course...Solid golf course...Course is very flat...Needs help...I like it so well I played two straight days.

★★½ROLLING HILLS GOLF CLUB
PU-1790 Hwy. 501, Galavants Ferry, 29544, Horry County, (803)358-4653, (800)633-2380, 25 miles W of Myrtle Beach.
Opened: 1988. **Holes:** 18. **Par:** 72/72. **Yards:** 6,749/5,141. **Course rating:** 72.1/68.3. **Slope:** 124/109. **Architect:** Gene Hamm. **Green fee:** $10/$27. **Credit cards:** MC,VISA,DISC. **Reduced fees:** Weekdays, low season, resort guests, twilight, seniors, juniors. **Caddies:** No. **Golf carts:** $16. **Discount golf packages:** Yes. **Season:** Year-round. **High:** Spring/Fall. **On site lodging:** No. **Rental clubs:** Yes. **Walking policy:** Walking at certain times. **Metal spikes allowed:** Yes. **Range:** Yes (grass/mats). **To obtain tee times:** Call 800 number.
Subscriber comments: Basic golf course...Good tune-up for the Beach...Wide open...Improving by leaps and bounds.

★★★ROSE HILL COUNTRY CLUB
One Clubhouse Dr., Bluffton, 29910, Beaufort County, (803)757-2160.
Holes: 27. **Architect:**Gene Hamm.
Call club for further information.
EAST/SOUTH/WEST
Subscriber comments: Nice course, fun to play...Good Low Country golf, very tight, senic...West nine as hard as it gets...I enjoy Rose Hill more each time I play...Lots of traps...West most interesting.

★★½SALUDA VALLEY COUNTRY CLUB
598 Beaver Dam Rd., Williamston, 29697, Anderson County, (803)847-7102, 20 miles N of Greenville.
Opened: 1964. **Holes:** 18. **Par:** 72/72. **Yards:** 6,430/5,126. **Course rating:** 70.8/69.4. **Slope:** 119/114. **Architect:** William B. Lewis. **Green fee:** $10/$15. **Credit cards:** None. **Reduced fees:** Weekdays. **Caddies:** No. **Golf carts:** $8. **Discount golf packages:** No. **Season:** Year-round. **High:** April-Sept. **On site lodging:** No. **Rental clubs:** No.

Walking policy: Unrestricted walking. **Metal spikes allowed:** Yes. **Range:** Yes (grass/mats). **To obtain tee times:** Call 3 days in advance.
Subscriber comments: Plenty of trees...Nice course, but short...Nice old layout, super value...Short course, good for all.

★★★SANTEE NATIONAL GOLF CLUB
R-Hwy. 6 W., Santee, 29142, Orangeburg County, (803)854-3531, (800)448-0152, 60 miles N of Charleston.
Opened: 1989. **Holes:** 18. **Par:** 72/72. **Yards:** 6,858/4,748. **Course rating:** 72.1/68.2. **Slope:** 120/116. **Architect:** Porter Gibson. **Green fee:** $25/$40. **Credit cards:** All major. **Reduced fees:** Weekdays, low season, resort guests, seniors, juniors. **Caddies:** No. **Golf carts:** Included in Green Fee. **Discount golf packages:** Yes. **Season:** Year-round. **High:** Spring/Fall. **On site lodging:** Yes. **Rental clubs:** Yes. **Walking policy:** Mandatory cart. **Metal spikes allowed:** Yes. **Range:** Yes (grass). **To obtain tee times:** Call 800 number.
Subscriber comments: Back nine excellent...Very good in every respect...Beautiful hole designs, especially on back nine...Open front, wooded back...Nice setting...Great stop on way South...Easy and pleasant...Greens don't break much, enjoyable.

★★★SEA GULL GOLF CLUB
PU-P.O. Box 2607, Pawleys Island, 29585, Georgetown County, (803)448-5931, 20 miles S of Myrtle Beach.
Opened: N/A. **Holes:** 18. **Par:** 72/72. **Yards:** 6,910/5,250. **Course rating:** N/A. **Slope:** 128/115. **Architect:** Gene Hamm. **Green fee:** N/A. **Credit cards:** MC,VISA. **Reduced fees:** Low season. **Caddies:** No. **Golf carts:** N/A. **Discount golf packages:** No. **Season:** Year-round. **High:** Spring/Fall. **On site lodging:** Yes. **Rental clubs:** No. **Walking policy:** N/A. **Metal spikes allowed:** Yes. **Range:** No. **To obtain tee times:** Call golf shop.
Subscriber comments: Very playable, open...Old design has some nice holes...Motel on course with great breakfast...Quiet setting...Unpretentious.

SEA PINES PLANTATION CLUB
R-100 N. Sea Pines Dr., Hilton Head, 29928, Beaufort County, (803)842-1894, (800)955-8337, 30 miles E of Savannah, GA.
Architect: George Cobb. **Credit cards:** All major,Diners Club. **Reduced fees:** Low season, resort guests, twilight, juniors. **Caddies:** No. **Golf carts:** Included in Green Fee. **Discount golf packages:** Yes. **Season:** Year-round. **High:** Spring/Fall. **On site lodging:** Yes. **Rental clubs:** Yes. **Walking policy:** Walking at certain times. **Metal spikes allowed:** Yes. **Range:** Yes (grass). **To obtain tee times:** Call 800 number.
★★★½OCEAN COURSE
Opened: 1960. **Holes:** 18. **Par:** 72/72. **Yards:** 6,906/5,325. **Course rating:** 72.8/71.1. **Slope:** 133/124. **Green fee:** $78/$90.
Subscriber comments: Scenic, don't forget to look around...Par 3 into ocean fun...Too tough for a resort course...Good solid tough layout...Lots of water makes this course interesting...Great new design, fair for women.
★★★SEA MARSH COURSE
Opened: 1964. **Holes:** 18. **Par:** 72/72. **Yards:** 6,515/5,054. **Course rating:** 70.0/69.8. **Slope:** 120/123. **Green fee:** $70/$80.
Subscriber comments: Enjoyable, fair and forgiving...A good fair test of golf...Nice course to get your game in shape...User friendly fairways.

★★½SHADOWMOSS PLANTATION GOLF CLUB
20 Dunvegan Dr., Charleston, 29414, Charleston County, (803)556-8251, (800)338-4971.
Opened: 1971. **Holes:** 18. **Par:** 72/72. **Yards:** 6,700/5,200. **Course rating:** 72.4/70.2. **Slope:** 123/120. **Architect:** Russell Breeden. **Green fee:** $22/$45. **Credit cards:** MC,VISA,AMEX. **Reduced fees:** Weekdays, low season, resort guests, twilight, juniors. **Caddies:** No. **Golf carts:** Included in Green Fee. **Discount golf packages:** Yes. **Season:** Year-round. **High:** March-May. **On site lodging:** No. **Rental clubs:** Yes. **Walking policy:** Walking at certain times. **Metal spikes allowed:** Yes. **Range:** Yes (grass). **To obtain tee times:** Call up to 6 months in advance.
Subscriber comments: Average challenge...Good enjoyable course...Too many homes too close to course...18 was a very nice hole.

SOUTH CAROLINA

★★★SHIPYARD GOLF CLUB
R-P.O. Drawer 7229, Hilton Head Island, 29938, Beaufort County, (803)686-8802.
Opened: N/A. **Holes:** 27. **Architect:** George W. Cobb. **Green fee:** $59/$88. **Credit cards:** MC,VISA,AMEX. **Reduced fees:** Twilight. **Caddies:** N/A. **Golf carts:** Included in Green Fee. **Discount golf packages:** Yes. **Season:** Year-round. **High:** Spring/Fall. **On site lodging:** Yes. **Rental clubs:** Yes. **Walking policy:** Mandatory cart. **Metal spikes allowed:** Yes. **Range:** Yes (grass/mats). **To obtain tee times:** Call reservations.
Notes: 1982-84 Senior Tour host.
BRIGANTINE/CLIPPER
Par: 72/72. **Yards:** 6,818/5,190. **Course rating:** 73.0/69.3. **Slope:** 128/116.**CLIPPER/GALLEON**
Par: 72/72. **Yards:** 6,830/5,391. **Course rating:** 73.0/70.5. **Slope:** 129/119. **Caddies:** No.
GALLEON/BRIGANTINE
Par: 72/72. **Yards:** 6,716/5,115. **Course rating:** 72.6/68.8. **Slope:** 128/114. **Caddies:** Yes.
Subscriber comments: Resort golf...Ho-hum...Incredible number of alligators...Nice old Hilton Head course but the holes tend to look alike...A most pleasurable experience. Gators let us play through.

★★★½SOUTH CAROLINA NATIONAL GOLF CLUB
8 Waveland Ave., Beaufort, 29902, Beaufort County, (803)524-0300, (800)221-9582, 40 miles N of Savannah, GA.
Opened: 1985. **Holes:** 18. **Par:** 71/71. **Yards:** 6,625/4,933. **Course rating:** 71.0/67.4. **Slope:** 127/116. **Architect:** George Cobb. **Green fee:** $35/$49. **Credit cards:** All major. **Reduced fees:** Low season, resort guests, twilight, juniors. **Caddies:** No. **Golf carts:** N/A. **Discount golf packages:** Yes. **Season:** Year-round. **High:** Year-round. **On site lodging:** No. **Rental clubs:** Yes. **Walking policy:** Walking at certain times. **Metal spikes allowed:** Yes. **Range:** Yes (grass). **To obtain tee times:** Call up to 1 year in advance.
Subscriber comments: Short track...Nice layout...Recent improvements to an already great Cobb layout...A real bargain, don't miss it!...Much improved...Fair test of golf in an Old South setting...A beautiful course with lots of water and marshes.
Special Notes: Formerly Cat Island Golf Club.

★★★SPRING LAKE COUNTRY CLUB
1375 Spring Lake Rd., York, 29745, York County, (803)684-4898, 20 miles S of Charlotte, NC.
Opened: 1960. **Holes:** 18. **Par:** 72/72. **Yards:** 6,748/4,975. **Course rating:** 72.8/67.3. **Slope:** 126/108. **Architect:** Fred Bolton/Bob Renaud. **Green fee:** $15/$21. **Credit cards:** MC,VISA. **Reduced fees:** Weekdays, juniors. **Caddies:** No. **Golf carts:** $11. **Discount golf packages:** No. **Season:** Year-round. **High:** May-Oct. **On site lodging:** No. **Rental clubs:** Yes. **Walking policy:** Walking at certain times. **Metal spikes allowed:** Yes. **Range:** Yes (grass). **To obtain tee times:** Call for Fridays, weekends and holidays.
Subscriber comments: Nice variety of holes. Fun to play...Good average course, fun to play, good value... Good value for the money.

★★★½STONEY POINT GOLF CLUB
709 Swing About Dr., Greenwood, 29648, Greenwood County, (864)942-0900, 35 miles S of Greenville.
Opened: 1990. **Holes:** 18. **Par:** 72/72. **Yards:** 6,760/5,060. **Course rating:** 72.1/70.3. **Slope:** 125/120. **Architect:** Tom Jackson. **Green fee:** $15/$22. **Credit cards:** MC,VISA. **Reduced fees:** Twilight, seniors, juniors. **Caddies:** No. **Golf carts:** $13. **Discount golf packages:** No. **Season:** Year-round. **High:** Spring/Fall. **On site lodging:** No. **Rental clubs:** Yes. **Walking policy:** Walking at certain times. **Metal spikes allowed:** No. **Range:** Yes (grass). **To obtain tee times:** Call 7 days in advance.
Subscriber comments: A course that requires each club in bag...Beautiful lakeside setting...Good golf!...Nice layout, interesting holes, greens too severe...Some great holes...A hidden jewel, need to try it to find out why...#18 a perfect finishing hole when money is on the line...Good variety of holes, tough from tips for average golfer.

★★½SUMMERSETT GOLF CLUB
111 Pilot Rd., Greenville, 29609, Greenville County, (803)834-4781, 5 miles N of Greenville.
Opened: 1938. **Holes:** 18. **Par:** 72/72. **Yards:** 6,025/4,910. **Course rating:** 68.3/67.6. **Slope:** 114/119. **Architect:** Tom Jackson. **Green fee:** $12/$19. **Credit cards:** MC,VISA. **Reduced fees:** Seniors. **Caddies:** No. **Golf carts:** $11. **Discount golf packages:** Yes. **Season:** Year-round. **High:** April-Aug. **On site lodging:** No. **Rental clubs:** Yes. **Walking policy:** Walking at certain times. **Metal spikes allowed:** Yes. **Range:** No. **To obtain tee times:** Call 7 days in advance.
Subscriber comments: Nice course for the buck, mountain view...Small greens, tight fairways...Short but fun.

★★★½SURF GOLF & BEACH CLUB
1701 Springland Lane, North Myrtle Beach, 29597, Horry County, (803)249-1524, (800)765-7873, 60 miles S of Wilmington.
Opened: 1960. **Holes:** 18. **Par:** 72/72. **Yards:** 6,842/5,178. **Course rating:** 72.6/68.2. **Slope:** 126/111. **Architect:** George Cobb. **Green fee:** $27/$69. **Credit cards:** MC,VISA. **Reduced fees:** Low season. **Caddies:** No. **Golf carts:** $18. **Discount golf packages:** Yes. **Season:** Year-round. **High:** Spring/Fall. **On site lodging:** No. **Rental clubs:** Yes. **Walking policy:** Mandatory cart. **Metal spikes allowed:** No. **Range:** Yes (grass/mats). **To obtain tee times:** Contact golf shop or have hotel make tee times.
Subscriber comments: Traditional style course, lunch buffet a must...One of the best finishing holes...Beautiful live oaks and moss.

★★★★½TIDEWATER GOLF CLUB
PU-4901 Little River Neck Rd., North Myrtle Beach, 29582, Horry County, (803)249-3829, (800)446-5363, 10 miles N of Myrtle Beach.
Opened: 1990. **Holes:** 18. **Par:** 72/72. **Yards:** 7,150/4,665. **Course rating:** 74.9/68.6. **Slope:** 140/126. **Architect:** Ken Tomlinson. **Green fee:** $42/$87. **Credit cards:** MC,VISA,AMEX. **Reduced fees:** Juniors. **Caddies:** No. **Golf carts:** $18. **Discount golf packages:** No. **Season:** Year-round. **High:** Year-round. **On site lodging:** Yes. **Rental clubs:** Yes. **Walking policy:** Walking at certain times. **Metal spikes allowed:** Yes. **Range:** Yes (grass). **To obtain tee times:** Call golf shop in advance, send deposit, time is then reconfirmed.
Notes: Ranked 10th in 1997 Best in State.
Subscriber comments: If it's breezy, be humble in tee selection...Best course in Myrtle Beach area...One great hole after another...Great par 3 holes...Extremely challenging, especially along the ocean...Great transition from forest to sea...Thinking is required to score well....Myrtle Beach golf at its finest.

★★★½TIMBERLAKE PLANTATION GOLF CLUB
284 Club Dr., Chapin, 29036, Lexington County, (803)345-9909, 30 miles NW of Columbia.
Opened: 1986. **Holes:** 18. **Par:** 72/72. **Yards:** 6,703/5,111. **Course rating:** 73.2/69.8. **Slope:** 132/118. **Architect:** Willard Byrd. **Green fee:** $16/$22. **Credit cards:** MC,VISA,AMEX. **Reduced fees:** Weekdays, low season, resort guests, seniors, juniors. **Caddies:** No. **Golf carts:** $12. **Discount golf packages:** Yes. **Season:** Year-round. **High:** April-May/Aug.-Nov. **On site lodging:** No. **Rental clubs:** Yes. **Walking policy:** Unrestricted walking. **Metal spikes allowed:** Yes. **Range:** Yes (grass). **To obtain tee times:** Call 7 days in advance.
Subscriber comments: Enjoyable, traditional...Long, lots of carries over marsh-lands...Hole 18 is a great risk/reward...A gem that is ready to be polished...Good course around Lake Murray, lots of carry on par 3s...Well worth drive to play.

★★★½TRADITION GOLF CLUB
PU-1027 Willbrook Blvd., Pawleys Island, 29585, Georgetown County, (803)237-5041, (800)833-6337, 20 miles S of Myrtle Beach.
Opened: 1995. **Holes:** 18. **Par:** 72/72. **Yards:** 6,919/5,111. **Course rating:** 72.0/68.4. **Slope:** 129/113. **Architect:** Ron Garl. **Green fee:** $31/$79. **Credit cards:** MC,VISA. **Reduced fees:** Low season, twilight. **Caddies:** No. **Golf carts:** $19. **Discount golf packages:** Yes. **Season:** Year-round. **High:** Spring/Fall. **On site lodging:** No. **Rental clubs:** Yes. **Walking policy:** Walking at certain times. **Metal spikes allowed:** Yes.

Range: Yes (grass). **To obtain tee times:** Call with credit card to reserve.
Subscriber comments: Some very interesting holes...Beautiful course and facilities...Solid, typical Carolina course...Young course that will improve.

TRUE BLUE
PU-900 Blue Stem Dr., Pawleys Island, 29585, Georgetown County, (803)235-0900, (888)483-6800, 20 miles S of Myrtle Beach.
Opened: 1998. **Holes:** 18. **Par:** 72/72. **Yards:** 6,980/5,880. **Course rating:** N/A. **Slope:** N/A. **Architect:** Mike Strantz. **Green fee:** $45/$88. **Credit cards:** All major. **Reduced fees:** N/A. **Caddies:** No. **Golf carts:** $18. **Discount golf packages:** No. **Season:** Year-round. **High:** Spring/Fall. **On site lodging:** No. **Rental clubs:** Yes. **Walking policy:** Mandatory cart. **Metal spikes allowed:** No. **Range:** Yes (grass/mats). **To obtain tee times:** Call.

★★★½VERDAE GREENS GOLF CLUB
R-650 Verdae Blvd., Greenville, 29607, Greenville County, (864)676-1500, 90 miles SW of Charlotte, NC.
Opened: 1989. **Holes:** 18. **Par:** 72/72. **Yards:** 6,773/5,012. **Course rating:** 72.6/68.1. **Slope:** 133/116. **Architect:** Willard Byrd. **Green fee:** $35/$49. **Credit cards:** MC,VISA,AMEX. **Reduced fees:** Weekdays, low season, resort guests, twilight, seniors, juniors. **Caddies:** No. **Golf carts:** Included in Green Fee. **Discount golf packages:** Yes. **Season:** Year-round. **High:** March-Nov. **On site lodging:** Yes. **Rental clubs:** Yes. **Walking policy:** Walking at certain times. **Metal spikes allowed:** Yes. **Range:** Yes (grass/mats). **To obtain tee times:** Call 7 days in advance.
Notes: 1992-97 Nike Tour Upstate Classic.
Subscriber comments: Outstanding, shotmaker's course...Tough par 3s...A wonderful course in the heart of Greenville...Good layout with nice variety of holes from the tips...Blind tee shots, hard to play first time...Nike Tour course.

★★★VILLAGE GREEN GOLF CLUB
Hwy. 176, Gramling, 29348, Spartanburg County, (864)472-2411, 14 miles NW of Spartanburg.
Opened: 1969. **Holes:** 18. **Par:** 72/74. **Yards:** 6,372/5,280. **Course rating:** 71.0/70.0. **Slope:** 122/123. **Architect:** Russell Breeden and Dan Breeden. **Green fee:** $13/$18. **Credit cards:** None. **Reduced fees:** N/A. **Caddies:** No. **Golf carts:** N/A. **Discount golf packages:** No. **Season:** Year-round. **High:** April-Sept. **On site lodging:** No. **Rental clubs:** Yes. **Walking policy:** Unrestricted walking. **Metal spikes allowed:** Yes. **Range:** Yes (grass). **To obtain tee times:** Call on Thursday for upcoming weekend.
Subscriber comments: Tight course but fair...Back nine more traditional.

★★★★WACHESAW PLANTATION EAST
911 Riverwood Dr., Murrells Inlet, 29576, Georgetown County, (803)357-2090, (888)922-0027, 90 miles N of Charleston.
Opened: 1996. **Holes:** 18. **Par:** 72/72. **Yards:** 6,993/4,995. **Course rating:** 73.6/68.8. **Slope:** 135/117. **Architect:** Clyde Johnston. **Green fee:** $55/$107. **Credit cards:** MC,VISA,AMEX. **Reduced fees:** Low season, resort guests, juniors. **Caddies:** No. **Golf carts:** Included in Green Fee. **Discount golf packages:** Yes. **Season:** Year-round. **High:** Spring/Fall. **On site lodging:** No. **Rental clubs:** Yes. **Walking policy:** Walking at certain times. **Metal spikes allowed:** No. **Range:** Yes (grass/mats). **To obtain tee times:** Call golf shop or book through hotel.
Notes: 1997 LPGA Susan G. Komen International.
Subscriber comments: Not a poor hole on the course...One of the best new layouts in area...God's country (back nine)...Beautiful live oaks, nice layout, friendly folks...Beautiful, must play!

GREAT SERVICE

★★★½THE WALKER COURSE AT CLEMSON UNIVERSITY
110 Madren Center Dr., Clemson, 29634, Pickens County, (864)656-0236, 35 miles S of Greenville.
Opened: 1995. **Holes:** 18. **Par:** 72/72. **Yards:** 6,911/4,667. **Course rating:** 72.8/65.7. **Slope:** 137/107. **Architect:** D.J. DeVictor. **Green fee:** $26/$46. **Credit cards:** MC,VISA. **Reduced fees:** Weekdays, low season, twilight, seniors, juniors. **Caddies:** No. **Golf carts:** Included in Green Fee. **Discount golf packages:** No. **Season:** Year-round. **High:** March-Oct. **On site lodging:** Yes. **Rental clubs:** Yes. **Walking policy:**

Unrestricted walking. **Metal spikes allowed:** Yes. **Range:** Yes (grass). **To obtain tee times:** Call up to 3 days in advance.
Subscriber comments: First nine challenging, be warmed up and ready to play...Totally different front and back...Classic setting...9th hole a bear...Great new track...Will be an excellent course in a few more years.

★★★WATERWAY HILLS GOLF CLUB

R-9731 Hwy. 17N, Restaurant Row, Myrtle Beach, 29578, Horry County, (803)449-6488, (800)344-5590.
Opened: 1975. **Holes:** 27. **Architect:** Robert Trent Jones/Rees Jones. **Green fee:** $23/$58. **Credit cards:** All major,Diners Club,Carte Blanche. **Reduced fees:** Low season, resort guests. **Caddies:** No. **Golf carts:** $18. **Discount golf packages:** Yes. **Season:** Year-round. **High:** March-April/Oct. **On site lodging:** No. **Rental clubs:** Yes. **Walking policy:** Walking at certain times. **Metal spikes allowed:** No. **Range:** Yes (grass/mats). **To obtain tee times:** Call your hotel golf director or Tee Time Central 800 number up to 1 year in advance.
LAKES/RAVINES
Par: 72/72. **Yards:** 6,339/4,825. **Course rating:** 70.6/67.3. **Slope:** 123/110.
OAKS/LAKES
Par: 72/72. **Yards:** 6,461/5,069. **Course rating:** 71.0/68.7. **Slope:** 119/113.
RAVINES/OAKS
Par: 72/72. **Yards:** 6,420/4,914. **Course rating:** 70.8/67.6. **Slope:** 121/113.
Subscriber comments: Good family course...Short course, driver not a necessity...Ravines course very difficult...Tee off in a real wilderness, what fun!

★★½WEDGEFIELD PLANTATION GOLF CLUB

Hwy 701 N., Georgetown, 29440, Georgetown County, (803)546-8587, 20 miles S of Myrtle Beach.
Opened: 1974. **Holes:** 18. **Par:** 72/73. **Yards:** 6,705/5,249. **Course rating:** 72.2/69.9. **Slope:** 123/119. **Architect:** Porter Gibson. **Green fee:** $35/$55. **Credit cards:** MC,VISA. **Reduced fees:** Low season, twilight. **Caddies:** No. **Golf carts:** Included in Green Fee. **Discount golf packages:** Yes. **Season:** Year-round. **High:** Spring/Fall. **On site lodging:** Yes. **Rental clubs:** Yes. **Walking policy:** Mandatory cart. **Metal spikes allowed:** Yes. **Range:** Yes (grass). **To obtain tee times:** Call golf shop.
Subscriber comments: Water and sand on almost all holes...A real challenge...Beautiful plantation course...Far enough from Myrtle Beach, not busy...Another old plantation, great back nine with live alligators...Super layout.

★★★½THE WELLMAN CLUB

Hwy. 41-51 S., 328 Country Club Dr., Johnsonville, 29555, Florence County, (803)386-2521, (800)258-2935, 42 miles W of Myrtle Beach.
Opened: 1966. **Holes:** 18. **Par:** 72/72. **Yards:** 7,018/5,281. **Course rating:** 73.9/69.5. **Slope:** 129/105. **Architect:** Ellis Maples. **Green fee:** $16/$28. **Credit cards:** MC,VISA,AMEX. **Reduced fees:** Weekdays, low season, resort guests, seniors, juniors. **Caddies:** No. **Golf carts:** $12. **Discount golf packages:** Yes. **Season:** Year-round. **High:** Feb.-May. **On site lodging:** No. **Rental clubs:** Yes. **Walking policy:** Walking at certain times. **Metal spikes allowed:** No. **Range:** Yes (grass). **To obtain tee times:** Call at least 2 days in advance.
Subscriber comments: Off beaten track, worth the drive...A good casual golf course...I could play here every day...Hidden gem. Solid design. Joy to play.

★½WHITE PINES GOLF CLUB

PU-614 Mary Lane, Camden, 29020, Kershaw County, (803)432-7442, 20 miles NE of Columbia.
Opened: 1989. **Holes:** 18. **Par:** 72/72. **Yards:** 6,800/4,806. **Course rating:** 71.3/66.9. **Slope:** 125/112. **Architect:** Claude Weathers. **Green fee:** $15/$15. **Credit cards:** None. **Reduced fees:** Weekdays, low season, resort guests, twilight, seniors, juniors. **Caddies:** No. **Golf carts:** Included in Green Fee. **Discount golf packages:** Yes. **Season:** Year-round. **High:** April-Oct. **On site lodging:** No. **Rental clubs:** Yes. **Walking policy:** Mandatory cart. **Metal spikes allowed:** Yes. **Range:** Yes (grass). **To obtain tee times:** First come, first served.

★★½WICKED STICK GOLF LINKS
PU-1051 Coventry Rd., Myrtle Beach, 29575, Horry County, (803)215-2500, (800)797-8425.
Opened: 1995. **Holes:** 18. **Par:** 72/72. **Yards:** 7,001/4,911. **Course rating:** 72.2/70.1. **Slope:** 129/123. **Architect:** Clyde Johnston and John Daly. **Green fee:** $22/$47. **Credit cards:** MC,VISA. **Reduced fees:** Low season, resort guests, twilight, juniors. **Caddies:** No. **Golf carts:** $18. **Discount golf packages:** Yes. **Season:** Year-round. **High:** March-Oct. **On site lodging:** No. **Rental clubs:** Yes. **Walking policy:** Walking at certain times. **Metal spikes allowed:** Yes. **Range:** Yes (grass/mats). **To obtain tee times:** Call up to 13 months in advance. Advance tee times must be secured by credit card.
Subscriber comments: An average Myrtle Beach Course...Long course, generous landing areas...Wide open, fun...Course uninspired, except for #16...Front nine nothing special, back better...Too damn long, 265-yard par 3!...Great name.

WILD DUNES RESORT
R- **Architect:** Tom Fazio. **Credit cards:** All major,Diners Club. **Golf carts:** Included in Green Fee. **Discount golf packages:** Yes. **Season:** Year-round. **High:** Spring/Fall. **On site lodging:** Yes. **Rental clubs:** Yes. **Metal spikes allowed:** Yes.

★★★½HARBOR COURSE
5881 Palmetto Dr., Isle of Palms, 29451, Charleston County, (803)886-2301, (800)845-8880, 12 miles SW of Charleston.
Opened: 1986. **Holes:** 18. **Par:** 70/70. **Yards:** 6,446/4,774. **Course rating:** 70.9/68.1. **Slope:** 124/117. **Green fee:** $35/$85. **Reduced fees:** Low season, resort guests, twilight, juniors. **Caddies:** No. **Walking policy:** Mandatory cart. **Range:** No. **To obtain tee times:** Call golf shop.
Subscriber comments: Fun ocean course...Narrow fairways, lots of water...Fun layout, last three holes great...Short course but very challenging...17 and 18 great holes...Great buffet breakfast, lots of bacon...Wind is a killer.

★★★★LINKS COURSE
5757 Palm Blvd., Isle of Palms, 29451, Charleston County, (803)886-2180, (800)845-8880, 12 miles NE of Charleston.
Opened: 1980. **Holes:** 18. **Par:** 72/72. **Yards:** 6,722/4,849. **Course rating:** 72.7/69.1. **Slope:** 131/121. **Green fee:** $50/$145. **Reduced fees:** Low season, resort guests, juniors. **Caddies:** Yes. **Walking policy:** Unrestricted walking. **Range:** Yes (grass/mats). **To obtain tee times:** Call golf shop.
Notes: Ranked 8th in 1997 Best in State. 1985 U.S. Senior Amateur Championship.
Subscriber comments: Good test, if windy can be brutal...The nicer of two courses...Final three holes great...Condos everywhere...Great course...Holes along the ocean are beautiful...Ready to go back!

WILD WING PLANTATION
R-1000 Wild Wing Blvd., Conway, 29526, Horry County, (803)347-9464, (800)736-9464, 7 miles N of Myrtle Beach.
Credit cards: All major. **Reduced fees:** Weekdays, low season, resort guests, twilight. **Caddies:** No. **Golf carts:** $19. **Discount golf packages:** Yes. **Season:** Year-round. **High:** April/Oct. **On site lodging:** Yes. **Rental clubs:** Yes. **Metal spikes allowed:** Yes. **Range:** Yes (grass). **To obtain tee times:** Call tee time operations by phone or in person. Times must be guaranteed with a credit card or pre-paid. If booking on a golf package, the hotel will be responsible for the tee time.

★★★★AVOCET COURSE
Opened: 1993. **Holes:** 18. **Par:** 72/72. **Yards:** 7,127/5,298. **Course rating:** 74.2/70.4. **Slope:** 128/118. **Architect:** Larry Nelson and Jeff Brauer. **Green fee:** N/A. **Walking policy:** Mandatory cart.
Subscriber comments: Best of four Wild Wing courses...Best golf complex in Myrtle Beach...Course very sculptured...Red carpet extended...Enjoy all the Wild Wing flock!...Worth every penny...Great par 3s...Excellent variety of holes...Nice layout, excellent condition.

★★★½FALCON COURSE
Opened: 1994. **Holes:** 18. **Par:** 72/72. **Yards:** 7,082/5,190. **Course rating:** 74.4/70.4. **Slope:** 134/118. **Architect:** Rees Jones. **Green fee:** N/A. **Walking policy:** Walking at certain times.
Notes: Ranked 18th in 1997 Best in State.
Subscriber comments: Good course with some great lake holes...All the Wild Wing courses are terrific. Play them every year on Myrtle Beach pilgrimage. Always in great shape...12 and 16 are terrific golf experiences...Bring your "A" game.

★★★½HUMMINGBIRD COURSE
Opened: 1992. **Holes:** 18. **Par:** 72/72. **Yards:** 6,853/5,168. **Course rating:** 73.6/69.5. **Slope:** 135/123. **Architect:** Willard Byrd. **Green fee:** $17/$70. **Walking policy:** Mandatory cart.
Subscriber comments: Very pleasing course to play...Looks scary (water) but plenty of room to land...Worth including in your Myrtle Beach agenda, well maintained...Very playable and enjoyable.

★★★★WOOD STORK COURSE
Opened: 1991. **Holes:** 18. **Par:** 72/72. **Yards:** 7,044/5,409. **Course rating:** 74.1/70.7. **Slope:** 130/121. **Architect:** Willard Byrd. **Green fee:** N/A. **Walking policy:** Mandatory cart.
Subscriber comments: Traditional course, excellent greens and fairways...Very nice resort layout...Great clubhouse, carts and conditions...Challenging course...Good challenge, holes fair for all.

★★★½THE WITCH
R-1900 Hwy. 544, Conway, 29526, Horry County, (803)448-1300, 8 miles N of Myrtle Beach.
Opened: 1989. **Holes:** 18. **Par:** 71/71. **Yards:** 6,702/4,812. **Course rating:** 71.2/69.0. **Slope:** 133/109. **Architect:** Dan Maples. **Green fee:** $44/$93. **Credit cards:** MC,VISA. **Reduced fees:** Low season, juniors. **Caddies:** No. **Golf carts:** Included in Green Fee. **Discount golf packages:** Yes. **Season:** Year-round. **High:** Feb.-May/Sept.-Nov. **On site lodging:** No. **Rental clubs:** Yes. **Walking policy:** Mandatory cart. **Metal spikes allowed:** Yes. **Range:** Yes (grass). **To obtain tee times:** Call golf shop. Deposit required during peak season.
Subscriber comments: You will never forget it...All nature and wetland preserved...Love the tee markers (look like witch hats)...Many tight driving holes...Don't go to Myrtle Beach and not play here...Funkier than Snoop Doggy Dog!

★★★½THE WIZARD GOLF COURSE
PU-4601 Leeshore Blvd., Myrtle Beach, 29579, Horry County, (803)236-9393, 8 miles W of Myrtle Beach.
Opened: 1996. **Holes:** 18. **Par:** 71/71. **Yards:** 6,721/4,972. **Course rating:** 71.9/70.2. **Slope:** 128/119. **Architect:** Dan Maples. **Green fee:** $26/$69. **Credit cards:** MC,VISA. **Reduced fees:** Juniors. **Caddies:** No. **Golf carts:** $18. **Discount golf packages:** No. **Season:** Year-round. **High:** Feb.-May/Sept.-Nov. **On site lodging:** No. **Rental clubs:** Yes. **Walking policy:** Mandatory cart. **Metal spikes allowed:** Yes. **Range:** Yes (grass). **To obtain tee times:** Call up to 1 year in advance.
Subscriber comments: Totally enjoyable...Great golf, beautiful golf course...Too wide open for me...Tricky greens.

THE BLUFFS
PU-2021 E. Main St., Vermillion, 57069, Clay County, (605)677-7058, 60 miles S of Sioux Falls.
Opened: 1996. **Holes:** 18. **Par:** 72/72. **Yards:** 6,684/4,926. **Course rating:** 72.4/63.9. **Slope:** 123/100. **Architect:** Pat Wyss. **Green fee:** $13/$16. **Credit cards:** MC,VISA. **Reduced fees:** N/A. **Caddies:** No. **Golf carts:** $15. **Discount golf packages:** No. **Season:** April-Oct. **High:** June-Aug. **On site lodging:** No. **Rental clubs:** Yes. **Walking policy:** Unrestricted walking. **Metal spikes allowed:** No. **Range:** Yes (grass). **To obtain tee times:** Call up to 7 days in advance.

★★½CENTRAL VALLEY GOLF CLUB
Highway 38, Hartford, 57033, Minnehaha County, (605)528-3971.
Call club for further information.
Subscriber comments: Not a walker's course, too long from green to next tee box...Great value...Open course, some good holes...Few hazards, small greens, rather short...Reachable par 4s...Best greens in the state...Short and easy but very nice greens.

★★½EDGEBROOK GOLF COURSE
PM-Rte. #1 Box 1A, Brookings, 57006, Brookings County, (605)692-6995, 1 mile S of Brookings.
Opened: 1974. **Holes:** 18. **Par:** 70/70. **Yards:** 6,078/5,041. **Course rating:** N/A. **Slope:** 113/111. **Architect:** Patrick H. Wyss. **Green fee:** $12/$15. **Credit cards:** N/A. **Reduced fees:** N/A. **Caddies:** No. **Golf carts:** N/A. **Discount golf packages:** No. **Season:** April-Oct. **High:** May-July. **On site lodging:** No. **Rental clubs:** Yes. **Walking policy:** N/A. **Metal spikes allowed:** Yes. **Range:** Yes (grass). **To obtain tee times:** Call.
Subscriber comments: Fast, fast greens, not overly long...Few hazards on back nine, good maintenance...Greens hold incredibly well and roll fairly true and quick...Not the toughest course but you will use most clubs in your bag.

★★½ELMWOOD GOLF COURSE
PU-2604 W. Russell, Sioux Falls, 57104, Minnehaha County, (605)367-7092.
Opened: 1923. **Holes:** 18. **Par:** 72/72. **Yards:** 6,850/5,750. **Course rating:** 72.1/72.0. **Slope:** 129/125. **Architect:** Lawrence Packard. **Green fee:** $13/$15. **Credit cards:** MC,VISA,DISC. **Reduced fees:** N/A. **Caddies:** No. **Golf carts:** $9. **Discount golf packages:** No. **Season:** April-Oct. **High:** May-Aug. **On site lodging:** No. **Rental clubs:** Yes. **Walking policy:** Unrestricted walking. **Metal spikes allowed:** No. **Range:** Yes (grass/mats). **To obtain tee times:** Come in 7 days in advance or call 6 days in advance.
Subscriber comments: Better course for big hitters...Old course with lots of timber. Noise from airport...Good track; too much play, though...Standard muny, airport adjacent can be distracting...27 holes, diversified for every level of play.
Special Notes: Also 9-hole par-36 East Course.

★★★FOX RUN GOLF COURSE
PU-600 W. 27th St., Yankton, 57078, Yankton County, (605)665-8456, 75 miles SW of Sioux Falls.
Opened: 1993. **Holes:** 18. **Par:** 72/72. **Yards:** 6,731/5,209. **Course rating:** 70.8/68.6. **Slope:** 122/115. **Architect:** Patrick Wyss. **Green fee:** $13/$15. **Credit cards:** MC,VISA. **Reduced fees:** Weekdays. **Caddies:** No. **Golf carts:** $15. **Discount golf packages:** No. **Season:** March-Oct. **High:** May-Aug. **On site lodging:** No. **Rental clubs:** Yes. **Walking policy:** Unrestricted walking. **Metal spikes allowed:** No. **Range:** Yes (grass/mats). **To obtain tee times:** Call golf shop 7 days in advance.
Subscriber comments: Excellent condition for young course...Nos. 9 and 18 are great holes...Prairie course, long and wide, 18th hole is spectacular risk/reward hole...Good design calls for good shotmaking, will improve with age.

★★★½HART RANCH GOLF COURSE
PU-Spring Creek Rd., Rapid City, 57701, Pennington County, (605)341-5703, 8 miles S of Rapid City.
Opened: 1985. **Holes:** 18. **Par:** 72/72. **Yards:** 6,841/4,999. **Course rating:** 72.5/70.1. **Slope:** 127/124. **Architect:** Patrick Wyss. **Green fee:** $16/$25. **Credit cards:** All major.

SOUTH DAKOTA

Reduced fees: N/A. **Caddies:** No. **Golf carts:** $20. **Discount golf packages:** No. **Season:** April-Oct. **High:** June-Aug. **On site lodging:** No. **Rental clubs:** Yes. **Walking policy:** Unrestricted walking. **Metal spikes allowed:** Yes. **Range:** Yes (grass). **To obtain tee times:** Call up to 7 days in advance.
Subscriber comments: Awesome scenery. The 16th is like the Valley of Death...Great variety, makes you think and use the whole bag and a beautiful setting to boot...A real enjoyable experience...There are some surprises it you don't know the course.

★★★★HILLCREST GOLF & COUNTRY CLUB
2206 Mulberry, Yankton, 57078, Yankton County, (605)665-4621, 51 miles SW of Sioux City, IA.
Opened: 1953. **Holes:** 18. **Par:** 72/73. **Yards:** 6,874/5,726. **Course rating:** 72.2/72.2. **Slope:** 130/126. **Architect:** Chick Adams. **Green fee:** $30/$36. **Credit cards:** MC,VISA. **Reduced fees:** Weekdays. **Caddies:** Yes. **Golf carts:** $18. **Discount golf packages:** No. **Season:** April-Nov. **High:** June-Aug. **On site lodging:** No. **Rental clubs:** Yes. **Walking policy:** Unrestricted walking. **Metal spikes allowed:** No. **Range:** Yes (grass). **To obtain tee times:** Call 7 days in advance.
Subscriber comments: It's been nice for 20+ years...Really tough championship course. Half the greens are small derby hat greens. Tough to stay on and tougher for short chip shots. Very beautiful...Great golf course, maybe the best in S.D.

★★HILLSVIEW GOLF CLUB
PU-4201 SD Hwy. 34, Pierre, 57501, Hughes County, (605)224-6191, 180 miles NE of Rapid City.
Opened: 1965. **Holes:** 18. **Par:** 72/73. **Yards:** 6,828/5,470. **Course rating:** 71.4/73.9. **Slope:** 122/119. **Architect:** Charles Maddox. **Green fee:** $16/$16. **Credit cards:** MC,VISA. **Reduced fees:** Juniors. **Caddies:** No. **Golf carts:** $18. **Discount golf packages:** No. **Season:** April-Oct. **High:** June-Aug. **On site lodging:** No. **Rental clubs:** Yes. **Walking policy:** Unrestricted walking. **Metal spikes allowed:** Yes. **Range:** Yes (grass/mats). **To obtain tee times:** Call golf shop.

KUEHN PARK GOLF COURSE
PU-2904 Kuehn Park Rd., Sioux Falls, 57106, Minnehaha County, (605)367-7162.
Opened: 1976. **Holes:** 9. **Par:** 30/30. **Yards:** 2,076/1,704. **Course rating:** 72.1/72.0. **Slope:** 129/125. **Architect:** Don Herfort. **Green fee:** $11/$14. **Credit cards:** MC,VISA. **Reduced fees:** Weekdays, seniors, juniors. **Caddies:** No. **Golf carts:** $8. **Discount golf packages:** No. **Season:** April-Oct. **High:** May-Aug. **On site lodging:** No. **Rental clubs:** Yes. **Walking policy:** Unrestricted walking. **Metal spikes allowed:** No. **Range:** Yes (grass/mats). **To obtain tee times:** Come in up to 7 days in advance or call up to 6 days in advance.

★★★½LAKEVIEW GOLF COURSE
PM-3300 N. Ohlman, Mitchell, 57301, Davison County, (605)995-4060, 60 miles W of Sioux Falls.
Opened: 1978. **Holes:** 18. **Par:** 72/73. **Yards:** 6,670/5,808. **Course rating:** 71.3/72.6. **Slope:** 124/125. **Architect:** Richard Watson. **Green fee:** $16/$16. **Credit cards:** MC,VISA. **Reduced fees:** N/A. **Caddies:** No. **Golf carts:** $16. **Discount golf packages:** No. **Season:** April-Oct. **High:** June-Aug. **On site lodging:** No. **Rental clubs:** Yes. **Walking policy:** Unrestricted walking. **Metal spikes allowed:** Yes. **Range:** Yes (grass). **To obtain tee times:** Call or stop by anytime.
Subscriber comments: Excellent course, challenging...Older course, lots of trees...Mix of old treelined holes, with new holes with water...Wonderful but difficult greens...Great course, excellent condition, good value.

★★LEE PARK GOLF COURSE
PM-8th Ave. N.W., Aberdeen, 57401, Brown County, (605)626-7092, 230 miles NW of Sioux Falls.
Opened: 1933. **Holes:** 18. **Par:** 72/72. **Yards:** 6,346/5,138. **Course rating:** 69.6/68.3. **Slope:** 128/122. **Architect:** N/A. **Green fee:** $13/$14. **Credit cards:** MC,VISA. **Reduced fees:** Weekdays, twilight. **Caddies:** No. **Golf carts:** $14. **Discount golf packages:** No. **Season:** April-Nov. **High:** June-Aug. **On site lodging:** No. **Rental clubs:** Yes. **Walking policy:** Walking at certain times. **Metal spikes allowed:** Yes. **Range:** Yes (grass). **To obtain tee times:** Call for weekend play.

★★★½MEADOWBROOK GOLF COURSE
PU-3625 Jackson Blvd., Rapid City, 57702, Pennington County, (605)394-4191.
Opened: 1976. **Holes:** 18. **Par:** 72/72. **Yards:** 7,054/5,603. **Course rating:** 73.0/71.1.
Slope: 138/130. **Architect:** David Gill. **Green fee:** $18/$26. **Credit cards:** None.
Reduced fees: Weekdays, low season, seniors, juniors. **Caddies:** No. **Golf carts:** $18.
Discount golf packages: No. **Season:** Year-round. **High:** April-Oct. **On site lodging:**
No. **Rental clubs:** Yes. **Walking policy:** Unrestricted walking. **Metal spikes allowed:**
Yes. **Range:** Yes (grass/mats). **To obtain tee times:** Call up to 1 day in advance or
through advance booking for an additional $4 per player.
Notes: Ranked 3rd in 1997 Best in State. 1984 Women's Public Links.
Subscriber comments: New water system, should be good again...Many strategic
holes...Challenging muny, most should play the white tees...Every hole gets better, slow
on weekends...Was being worked on...Creek makes it interesting.

★★★★MOCCASIN CREEK COUNTRY CLUB
SP-39084 130th St., Aberdeen, 57401, Brown County, (605)226-0989.
Opened: 1971. **Holes:** 18. **Par:** 72/73. **Yards:** 7,125/5,416. **Course rating:** 72.5/69.4.
Slope: 138/127. **Architect:** Charles Maddox. **Green fee:** $35/$35. **Credit cards:** None.
Reduced fees: No. **Caddies:** No. **Golf carts:** $18. **Discount golf packages:** No.
Season: April-Nov. **High:** June-Aug. **On site lodging:** No. **Rental clubs:** Yes. **Walking
policy:** Unrestricted walking. **Metal spikes allowed:** No. **Range:** Yes (grass/mats). **To
obtain tee times:** Call 2 days in advance for weekday play. Members only on weekends and holidays.
Notes: Ranked 5th in 1997 Best in State.
Subscriber comments: Excellent fairways and greens, timbered, tight tee shots...Best
kept golf secret in Dakotas..A lot of holes pretty nondescript...Great course; back side is
fabulous...The rough, fairways and greens all fine tuned...Championship caliber course,
great conditions...Great staff, long challenging course.

★★★PRAIRIE GREEN GOLF COURSE
PU-600 E. 69th St., Sioux Falls, 57108, Minnehaha County, (605)367-6076, (800)585-
6076.
Opened: 1995. **Holes:** 18. **Par:** 72/72. **Yards:** 7,179/5,250. **Course rating:** 74.2/70.2.
Slope: 134/122. **Architect:** Dick Nugent. **Green fee:** $18/$21. **Credit cards:** MC,VISA.
Reduced fees: Weekdays, twilight, seniors, juniors. **Caddies:** No. **Golf carts:** $9.
Discount golf packages: Yes. **Season:** April-Oct. **High:** May-Sept. **On site lodging:**
No. **Rental clubs:** Yes. **Walking policy:** Unrestricted walking. **Metal spikes allowed:**
No. **Range:** Yes (grass). **To obtain tee times:** Call 7 days in advance.
Notes: Ranked 2nd in 1997 Best in State; 5th in 1996 Best New Affordable Courses.
Subscriber comments: WOW! Scotland in South Dakota! Nice links course...Good
newer course, usually windy...Water, water everywhere. Will mature nicely, good
test...Too long between tees...Walkers at a disadvantage...Tough and long...Bring the
sand wedge...Bring your driver and hit it well, otherwise you'll shoot big numbers.

★★★★SOUTHERN HILLS GOLF COURSE
PM-W Hwy. 18, Hot Springs, 57747, Fall River County, (605)745-
6400, 45 miles N of Rapid City.
Opened: 1979. **Holes:** 9. **Par:** 35/35. **Yards:** 2,969/2,620. **Course
rating:** 33.8/36.3. **Slope:** 128/133. **Architect:** Dick Phelps and Brad
Benz. **Green fee:** $18/$18. **Credit cards:** None. **Reduced fees:** N/A.
Caddies: No. **Golf carts:** $18. **Discount golf packages:** No. **Season:** March-Oct.
High: June-Aug. **On site lodging:** No. **Rental clubs:** Yes. **Walking policy:** Unrestricted
walking. **Metal spikes allowed:** Yes. **Range:** Yes. **To obtain tee times:** Call.
Subscriber comments: Best nine-hole course in Midwest...Walking this course is like
hiking in the Alps...Only nine holes but the best anywhere...Set in Black Hills. Lots of
fairly extreme elevation changes and steeply graded greens...Sidehill/downhill putts can
be a real adventure...Located 50 miles from Mt. Rushmore National Park.

(GOOD VALUE)

★★½TWO RIVERS GOLF CLUB
PU-150 S. Oak Tree Lane, Dakota Dunes, 57049, Union County, (605)232-3241, 6
miles N of Sioux City, IA.
Opened: 1921. **Holes:** 18. **Par:** 72/73. **Yards:** 6,181/5,603. **Course rating:** 69.0/71.0.

SOUTH DAKOTA

Slope: 120/112. **Architect:** N/A. **Green fee:** $13/$16. **Credit cards:** All major. **Reduced fees:** Low season. **Caddies:** No. **Golf carts:** $10. **Discount golf packages:** No. **Season:** April-Oct. **High:** June-Sept. **On site lodging:** No. **Rental clubs:** Yes. **Walking policy:** Unrestricted walking. **Metal spikes allowed:** Yes. **Range:** Yes (grass/mats). **To obtain tee times:** May call 7 days in advance.
Subscriber comments: Greens are as good as Dakota Dunes...Very little room for error...Country club course turned public, newer replacement holes need maturity...Old course with lots of trees. Pretty short.

★★★WATERTOWN MUNICIPAL GOLF COURSE
PM-351 S. Lake Dr., Watertown, 57201, Codington County, (605)882-6262.
Opened: N/A. **Holes:** 18. **Par:** 72/78. **Yards:** 5,220/5,858. **Course rating:** 67.4/71.3. **Slope:** 106/114. **Architect:** Phil Wigton. **Green fee:** $13/$15. **Credit cards:** None. **Reduced fees:** Twilight. **Caddies:** No. **Golf carts:** $17. **Discount golf packages:** No. **Season:** April-Oct. **High:** May-Sept. **On site lodging:** No. **Rental clubs:** Yes. **Walking policy:** Unrestricted walking. **Metal spikes allowed:** Yes. **Range:** Yes (grass/mats). **To obtain tee times:** Call 7 days in advance for weekends. Call up to same day for weekday.
Subscriber comments: Good shape for a muny...Good test of golf...Fun course to play...Well maintained. Too easy.

★★★½WILLOW RUN GOLF COURSE
PU-E. Hwy. 38/42, Sioux Falls, 57103, Minnehaha County, (605)335-5900.
Opened: 1988. **Holes:** 18. **Par:** 71/71. **Yards:** 6,505/4,855. **Course rating:** 71.1/68.7. **Slope:** 127/119. **Architect:** Joel Goldstrand. **Green fee:** $14/$16. **Credit cards:** MC,VISA. **Reduced fees:** Weekdays, twilight, seniors, juniors. **Caddies:** No. **Golf carts:** $9. **Discount golf packages:** Yes. **Season:** March-Nov. **High:** May-Oct. **On site lodging:** No. **Rental clubs:** Yes. **Walking policy:** Unrestricted walking. **Metal spikes allowed:** Yes. **Range:** Yes (grass). **To obtain tee times:** Call seven days in advance.
Subscriber comments: Excellent course, memorable holes...Water comes into play. Beautiful layout...Target golf, leave driver at home...Some holes very good and challenging...One of the best munys I've played.

★½AUDUBON PARK GOLF COURSE

PM-4160 Park Ave., Memphis, 38117, Shelby County, (901)683-6941.
Opened: 1952. **Holes:** 18. **Par:** N/A. **Yards:** 6,418/5,615. **Course rating:** N/A. **Slope:** N/A. **Architect:** N/A. **Green fee:** N/A. **Credit cards:** N/A. **Reduced fees:** N/A.
Caddies: No. **Golf carts:** $18. **Discount golf packages:** No. **Season:** Year-round.
High: N/A. **On site lodging:** No. **Rental clubs:** No. **Walking policy:** Unrestricted walking. **Metal spikes allowed:** Yes. **Range:** Yes (grass). **To obtain tee times:** Call.

★★½BANEBERRY GOLF & RESORT

PU-704 Harrison Ferry Rd., Baneberry, 37890, Jefferson County, (423)674-2500, (800)951-4653, 35 miles E of Knoxville.
Opened: 1972. **Holes:** 18. **Par:** 71/72. **Yards:** 6,694/4,829. **Course rating:** 72.6/68.5.
Slope: 125/117. **Architect:** Bob Thompson. **Green fee:** $12/$15. **Credit cards:** All major. **Reduced fees:** N/A. **Caddies:** No. **Golf carts:** $11. **Discount golf packages:** Yes. **Season:** Year-round. **High:** April-May/Oct. **On site lodging:** Yes. **Rental clubs:** Yes. **Walking policy:** Unrestricted walking. **Metal spikes allowed:** Yes. **Range:** Yes (grass). **To obtain tee times:** Call golf shop.
Subscriber comments: Made welcome, service great...Nice course, worth playing, very friendly...Good accommodations...Houses close to some fairways.

★★½BENT CREEK GOLF RESORT

R-3919 E. Pkwy., Gatlinburg, 37738, Sevier County, (423)436-3947, (800)251-9336, 40 miles SW of Knoxville.
Opened: 1972. **Holes:** 18. **Par:** 72/73. **Yards:** 6,182/5,111. **Course rating:** 70.3/69.2.
Slope: 127/117. **Architect:** Gary Player. **Green fee:** $20/$35. **Credit cards:** MC,VISA.
Reduced fees: Low season, resort guests, twilight. **Caddies:** No. **Golf carts:** $14.
Discount golf packages: Yes. **Season:** Year-round. **High:** March-Nov. **On site lodging:** Yes. **Rental clubs:** Yes. **Walking policy:** Walking at certain times. **Metal spikes allowed:** Yes. **Range:** Yes (grass/mats). **To obtain tee times:** Tee times may be made up to a year in advance and must be guaranteed with a major credit card.
Subscriber comments: Great place, open front, hilly back...Great fairways and greens...Back nine short and blind...Mountain views...Tricky layout.

★★★BIG CREEK GOLF CLUB

6195 Woodstock-Cuba Rd., Millington, 38053, Shelby County, (901)353-1654, 12 miles N of Memphis.
Opened: 1977. **Holes:** 18. **Par:** 72/72. **Yards:** 7,052/5,086. **Course rating:** 72.8/69.6.
Slope: 121/111. **Architect:** G.S. Mitchell. **Green fee:** $18/$28. **Credit cards:** MC,VISA,AMEX. **Reduced fees:** Weekdays, low season, twilight, seniors, juniors.
Caddies: No. **Golf carts:** $10. **Discount golf packages:** No. **Season:** Year-round.
High: April-Sept. **On site lodging:** No. **Rental clubs:** Yes. **Walking policy:** Unrestricted walking. **Metal spikes allowed:** Yes. **Range:** Yes (grass). **To obtain tee times:** Public may call 4 days in advance.
Subscriber comments: Two nines very different, fun...Excellent staff, course is long and challenging—sand, water and hills...Fast bent greens, long course, pretty forest setting, challenging...Good layout. Good greens, difficult back nine.

★★½BRAINERD GOLF COURSE

PU-5203 Old Mission Rd., Chattanooga, 37411, Hamilton County, (423)855-2692.
Opened: 1926. **Holes:** 18. **Par:** 72/72. **Yards:** 6,468/5,403. **Course rating:** 69.8/69.9.
Slope: 119/118. **Architect:** Donald Ross. **Green fee:** $13/$16. **Credit cards:** MC,VISA.
Reduced fees: Weekdays, seniors, juniors. **Caddies:** No. **Golf carts:** $9. **Discount golf packages:** No. **Season:** Year-round. **High:** April-Sept. **On site lodging:** No.
Rental clubs: No. **Walking policy:** Walking at certain times. **Metal spikes allowed:** Yes. **Range:** No. **To obtain tee times:** Call two days in advance.
Subscriber comments: Easy course, straight fairways...Homey...Very old course needs some revamping, but nice place...Very solid 3s—nice old course.

★★★BROWN ACRES GOLF COURSE

PU-406 Brown Rd., Chattanooga, 37421, Hamilton County, (423)855-2680.
Opened: 1975. **Holes:** 18. **Par:** 71/71. **Yards:** 6,774/4,923. **Course rating:** 72.5/66.1.
Slope: 122/110. **Architect:** Grant Wencel. **Green fee:** $13/$16. **Credit cards:**

MC,VISA. **Reduced fees:** Seniors, juniors. **Caddies:** No. **Golf carts:** N/A. **Discount golf packages:** No. **Season:** Year-round. **High:** N/A. **On site lodging:** No. **Rental clubs:** Yes. **Walking policy:** Walking at certain times. **Metal spikes allowed:** No. **Range:** Yes (grass/mats). **To obtain tee times:** Call 2 days in advance.
Subscriber comments: Since redo it has improved greatly...I-75 noise distracts...Fast greens, long course. Hard to walk. Very good facilities...Sneaky long, improving...Good course, very good condition, I-75 runs throught the middle of course.

★★½BUFFALO VALLEY GOLF COURSE
PU-90 Country Club Dr., Unicoi, 37692, Unicoi County, (423)928-1022, 3 miles SE of Johnson City.
Opened: N/A. **Holes:** 18. **Par:** 71/72. **Yards:** 6,624/4,968. **Course rating:** 71.7/69.6.
Slope: 119/111. **Architect:** N/A. **Green fee:** $17/$19. **Credit cards:** MC,VISA.
Reduced fees: Weekdays. **Caddies:** No. **Golf carts:** $29. **Discount golf packages:** Yes. **Season:** Year-round. **High:** April-Sept. **On site lodging:** Yes. **Rental clubs:** Yes.
Walking policy: Unrestricted walking. **Metal spikes allowed:** Yes. **Range:** Yes (grass).
To obtain tee times: Call 48 hours in advance for weekends and holidays only.
Subscriber comments: A good test, great layout...Very good, a pleasure to play.

★½CAMELOT GOLF COURSE
PU-908 Pressman's Home Rd., Rogersville, 37857, Hawkins County, (423)272-7499, (800)764-7499, 27 miles SW of Kingsport.
Opened: 1987. **Holes:** 18. **Par:** 73/73. **Yards:** 6,844/5,035. **Course rating:** 72.3/68.2.
Slope: 119/110. **Architect:** Robert Thomason. **Green fee:** $9/$11. **Credit cards:** MC,VISA. **Reduced fees:** N/A. **Caddies:** No. **Golf carts:** $85. **Discount golf packages:** No. **Season:** Year-round. **High:** June-Aug. **On site lodging:** No. **Rental clubs:** No. **Walking policy:** Unrestricted walking. **Metal spikes allowed:** Yes. **Range:** No. **To obtain tee times:** Call.

★½CARROLL LAKE GOLF CLUB
1305 Carroll Lake Rd., McKenzie, 38201, Carroll County, (901)352-5998, 45 miles N of Jackson.
Opened: 1961. **Holes:** 18. **Par:** 71/71. **Yards:** 5,517/4,868. **Course rating:** 68.0/68.0.
Slope: 123/120. **Architect:** R. Albert Anderson. **Green fee:** $14/$14. **Credit cards:** MC,VISA,AMEX. **Reduced fees:** Weekdays, low season, seniors, juniors. **Caddies:** No. **Golf carts:** $18. **Discount golf packages:** No. **Season:** Year-round. **High:** April-Nov. **On site lodging:** No. **Rental clubs:** Yes. **Walking policy:** Unrestricted walking. **Metal spikes allowed:** Yes. **Range:** No. **To obtain tee times:** Call golf shop.

★★½COUNTRY HILLS GOLF COURSE
PU-1501 Saundersville Rd., Hendersonville, 37075, Sumner County, (615)824-1100, 10 miles N of Nashville.
Opened: 1990. **Holes:** 18. **Par:** 70/70. **Yards:** 6,100/4,800. **Course rating:** 71.2/67.8.
Slope: 119/114. **Architect:** Leon Howard. **Green fee:** $13/$20. **Credit cards:** MC,VISA,AMEX. **Reduced fees:** Weekdays, low season, twilight, seniors, juniors.
Caddies: No. **Golf carts:** $10. **Discount golf packages:** Yes. **Season:** Year-round.
High: March-Oct. **On site lodging:** No. **Rental clubs:** Yes. **Walking policy:** Unrestricted walking. **Metal spikes allowed:** Yes. **Range:** Yes (grass). **To obtain tee times:** Call 7 days in advance.
Subscriber comments: Very nice and slick greens...Has a couple of funky holes, not fair...Continuous improvement...Very hilly—lots of trees...Too many blind shots.

★★★THE CROSSINGS GOLF CLUB
2585 Hwy. 81 N., Jonesboro, 37659, Washington County, (423)348-8844, 75 miles N of Knoxville.
Opened: 1994. **Holes:** 18. **Par:** 72/72. **Yards:** 6,366/5,072. **Course rating:** 70.1/68.2.
Slope: 118/112. **Architect:** Gary Roger Baird. **Green fee:** $25/$25. **Credit cards:** MC,VISA. **Reduced fees:** N/A. **Caddies:** No. **Golf carts:** $8. **Discount golf packages:** No. **Season:** Year-round. **High:** March-Oct. **On site lodging:** No. **Rental clubs:** Yes. **Walking policy:** Unrestricted walking. **Metal spikes allowed:** Yes. **Range:** Yes (grass/mats). **To obtain tee times:** Call 5 days in advance.
Subscriber comments: Maturing slowly....Good service...Extremely playable, yet very challenging...Fun to play, a lot of potential.

★★★½CUMBERLAND GARDENS RESORT

PU-Hwy. 70 East, Crab Orchard, 37723, Cumberland County, (615)484-5285, 45 miles W of Knoxville.

Opened: 1988. **Holes:** 18. **Par:** 72/72. **Yards:** 6,689/5,021. **Course rating:** 74.2/70.9. **Slope:** 132/123. **Architect:** Robert Renaud. **Green fee:** $25/$36. **Credit cards:** All major. **Reduced fees:** Weekdays, low season. **Caddies:** No. **Golf carts:** Included in Green Fee. **Discount golf packages:** Yes. **Season:** Year-round. **High:** April-Oct. **On site lodging:** Yes. **Rental clubs:** Yes. **Walking policy:** Mandatory cart. **Metal spikes allowed:** Yes. **Range:** Yes (grass). **To obtain tee times:** Call weekdays at 8 a.m. and weekends at 7 a.m.

Subscriber comments: Spectacular holes and views....Fairways cut through mountain caverns...Breathtaking views! Little room for error...Mountain golf on old ski runs—what fun and beauty...Long, strong and great views.

Special Notes: Formerly Briarwood Golf Course.

★★DAVY CROCKETT GOLF COURSE

PM-4380 Rangeline, Memphis, 38127, Shelby County, (901)358-3375.

Opened: 1961. **Holes:** 18. **Par:** 72/72. **Yards:** 6,200/5,900. **Course rating:** 68.5/67.2. **Slope:** 118/114. **Architect:** Harry Isabelle. **Green fee:** $10/$12. **Credit cards:** MC,VISA. **Reduced fees:** Weekdays. **Caddies:** No. **Golf carts:** $18. **Discount golf packages:** No. **Season:** Year-round. **High:** April-Oct. **On site lodging:** No. **Rental clubs:** Yes. **Walking policy:** Unrestricted walking. **Metal spikes allowed:** Yes. **Range:** No. **To obtain tee times:** Call.

★½DEAD HORSE LAKE GOLF COURSE

PU-9700 Sherrill Lane, Knoxville, 37932, Knox County, (423)693-5270, 10 miles W of Knoxville.

Opened: 1973. **Holes:** 18. **Par:** 71/73. **Yards:** 6,225/5,132. **Course rating:** 69.1. **Slope:** 116. **Architect:** Joe Parker/Pete Parker. **Green fee:** $15/$20. **Credit cards:** MC,VISA. **Reduced fees:** Seniors. **Caddies:** No. **Golf carts:** $10. **Discount golf packages:** No. **Season:** Year-round. **High:** March-Aug. **On site lodging:** No. **Rental clubs:** No. **Walking policy:** Unrestricted walking. **Metal spikes allowed:** Yes. **Range:** Yes (grass/mats). **To obtain tee times:** Call 7 days in advance.

★★★DEER CREEK GOLF CLUB

1055 Deer Creek Dr., Crossville, 38558, Cumberland County, (615)456-0178, 60 miles W of Knoxville.

Opened: 1989. **Holes:** 18. **Par:** 72/72. **Yards:** 6,251/4,917. **Course rating:** 69.6/67.2. **Slope:** 122/114. **Architect:** Robert Renaud. **Green fee:** $15/$23. **Credit cards:** MC,VISA. **Reduced fees:** N/A. **Caddies:** No. **Golf carts:** $12. **Discount golf packages:** Yes. **Season:** Year-round. **High:** April-Oct. **On site lodging:** No. **Rental clubs:** Yes. **Walking policy:** Walking at certain times. **Metal spikes allowed:** No. **Range:** Yes (grass). **To obtain tee times:** Call 3 days in advance.

Subscriber comments: Great fun course. Good design...Short course, but very good...Beautiful scenery, nice course...Demands accuracy. Great service...Streams, trees, mountains—unhurried golf...Quiet as a tomb, pretty, well kept.

★★½DYERSBURG MUNICIPAL GOLF COURSE

PM-Golf Course Rd., Dyersburg, 38024, Dyer County, (901)286-7620.

Opened: N/A. **Holes:** N/A. **Par:** 71/71. **Yards:** 3,180/2,637. **Course rating:** 69.7/71.0. **Slope:** 117/118. **Architect:** Scott Nall. **Green fee:** $8/$8. **Credit cards:** N/A. **Reduced fees:** N/A. **Caddies:** No. **Golf carts:** $14. **Discount golf packages:** No. **Season:** Year-round. **High:** May-Sept. **On site lodging:** No. **Rental clubs:** No. **Walking policy:** Unrestricted walking. **Metal spikes allowed:** Yes. **Range:** No. **To obtain tee times:** Call.

Subscriber comments: Open, Bermuda greens, back is hillier—fun course...Excellent public course, attractive...Excellent shape for muny.

★★★EAGLE'S LANDING GOLF CLUB

PU-1556 Old Knox Hwy, Sevierville, 37876, Sevier County, (423)429-4223, 20 miles E of Knoxville.

Opened: 1994. **Holes:** 18. **Par:** 72/72. **Yards:** 6,919/4,591. **Course rating:** 73.5/68.8.

Slope: 134/120. **Architect:** D.J. DeVictor. **Green fee:** $29/$46. **Credit cards:** MC,VISA. **Reduced fees:** Weekdays, low season, twilight, juniors. **Caddies:** No. **Golf carts:** Included in Green Fee. **Discount golf packages:** No. **Season:** Year-round. **High:** May-Oct. **On site lodging:** No. **Rental clubs:** Yes. **Walking policy:** Mandatory cart. **Metal spikes allowed:** Yes. **Range:** Yes (grass). **To obtain tee times:** Call up to 30 days in advance for tee times.

Subscriber comments: Extremely difficult for average amateur...A great course, tight, scenic, long...Beautiful view of the mountains, interesting layout...Par 3s long from back tees. Spectacular view of Smokies...Beautiful course.

★★★½EASTLAND GREEN GOLF COURSE

PU-550 Club House Lane, Clarksville, 37043, Montgomery County, (615)358-9051, 45 miles NW of Nashville.

Opened: 1990. **Holes:** 18. **Par:** 72/72. **Yards:** 6,437/4,790. **Course rating:** 71.5/68.4. **Slope:** 123/116. **Architect:** East Green Development Corp.. **Green fee:** $16/$21. **Credit cards:** All major. **Reduced fees:** Twilight, seniors, juniors. **Caddies:** No. **Golf carts:** $16. **Discount golf packages:** No. **Season:** Year-round. **High:** April-Aug. **On site lodging:** No. **Rental clubs:** Yes. **Walking policy:** Unrestricted walking. **Metal spikes allowed:** Yes. **Range:** Yes (grass). **To obtain tee times:** Call 5 days in advance.

Subscriber comments: Good public course—very interesting layout...Great course, maturing nicely...Greens excellent...Staff always nice. Good course that will be better when trees mature...Short course, no real trouble, wide open.

Special Notes: Also has 9-hole Eastland Green South Course.

★★★½EGWANI FARMS GOLF COURSE

PU-3920 Singleton Station Rd., Rockford, 37853, Blount County, (423)970-7132, 8 miles S of Knoxville.

Opened: 1991. **Holes:** 18. **Par:** 72/72. **Yards:** 6,708/4,680. **Course rating:** 71.9/66.1. **Slope:** 126/113. **Architect:** D.J. DeVictor. **Green fee:** $40/$50. **Credit cards:** MC,VISA. **Reduced fees:** N/A. **Caddies:** No. **Golf carts:** Included in Green Fee. **Discount golf packages:** No. **Season:** Year-round. **High:** April-Oct. **On site lodging:** No. **Rental clubs:** Yes. **Walking policy:** Mandatory cart. **Metal spikes allowed:** Yes. **Range:** Yes (grass). **To obtain tee times:** Call 7 days in advance.

Subscriber comments: Simple layout. But the best greens...Very nice people...Know how to treat golfers...A must play, everything says class. Fair test of golf...Customer comes first...Very nice course, difficult and challenging...Good greens.

★★½ELIZABETHTON MUNICIPAL GOLF CLUB

PM-Golf Club Rd., Elizabethton, 37643, Carter County, (423)542-8051, 9 miles W of Johnson City.

Opened: 1934. **Holes:** 18. **Par:** 72/72. **Yards:** 6,339/4,335. **Course rating:** 71.2/67.7. **Slope:** 129/118. **Architect:** D.J. DeVictor. **Green fee:** $17/$30. **Credit cards:** MC,VISA. **Reduced fees:** Low season. **Caddies:** No. **Golf carts:** Included in Green Fee. **Discount golf packages:** No. **Season:** Year-round. **High:** April-Sept. **On site lodging:** No. **Rental clubs:** Yes. **Walking policy:** Unrestricted walking. **Metal spikes allowed:** Yes. **Range:** Yes (grass). **To obtain tee times:** Call 7 days in advance.

Subscriber comments: Good course for a muny...A lot of blind shots...Excellent rebuilt greens...Keeps your attention, fast greens...Redesign a bit funky, but greens make it a challenge...Short course—tough to putt greens.

★★★½FALL CREEK FALLS STATE PARK GOLF COURSE

PU-Rte. 3, Pikeville, 37367, Bledsoe County, (423)881-5706, (800)250-8611, 70 miles N of Chattanooga.

Opened: 1972. **Holes:** 18. **Par:** 72/72. **Yards:** 6,669/6,051. **Course rating:** 71.6/74.8. **Slope:** 127/126. **Architect:** Joe Lee. **Green fee:** $19/$19. **Credit cards:** All major. **Reduced fees:** Seniors, juniors. **Caddies:** No. **Golf carts:** $10. **Discount golf packages:** Yes. **Season:** Year-round. **High:** May-Oct. **On site lodging:** Yes. **Rental clubs:** Yes. **Walking policy:** Unrestricted walking. **Metal spikes allowed:** Yes. **Range:** Yes (grass). **To obtain tee times:** Call at least two weeks in advance.

Subscriber comments: State park gem. Need a guide to find it...Beautiful course, blends in well with environment...State park golf at its best...Wilderness golf—deer everywhere...Great course, lots of sand, made welcome...Very tough course.

FOREST HILL GOLF COURSE

PU-200 Kubo Rd., Drummonds, 38023-0157, Tipton County, (901)835-2152, 20 miles N of Memphis.
Opened: 1993. **Holes:** 18. **Par:** 72/72. **Yards:** 6,609/5,220. **Course rating:** N/A. **Slope:** N/A. **Architect:** Hiroshi Kubo. **Green fee:** $15/$20. **Credit cards:** MC,VISA,AMEX. **Reduced fees:** Weekdays, low season, twilight, seniors, juniors. **Caddies:** No. **Golf carts:** $10. **Discount golf packages:** Yes. **Season:** Year-round. **High:** March-Oct. **On site lodging:** Yes. **Rental clubs:** No. **Walking policy:** Walking at certain times. **Metal spikes allowed:** Yes. **Range:** Yes (grass). **To obtain tee times:** Call 7 days in advance.

★★½ FORREST CROSSING GOLF COURSE

PU-750 Riverview Dr., Franklin, 37064, Williamson County, (615)794-9400, 15 miles S of Nashville.
Opened: 1988. **Holes:** 18. **Par:** 72/72. **Yards:** 6,968/5,011. **Course rating:** 73.6/69.1. **Slope:** 125/114. **Architect:** Gary Roger Baird. **Green fee:** $23/$33. **Credit cards:** All major. **Reduced fees:** Weekdays, low season, twilight. **Caddies:** No. **Golf carts:** $10. **Discount golf packages:** No. **Season:** Year-round. **High:** April-Oct. **On site lodging:** No. **Rental clubs:** Yes. **Walking policy:** Walking at certain times. **Metal spikes allowed:** Yes. **Range:** Yes (grass). **To obtain tee times:** Call 8 days in advance.
Subscriber comments: 16th, across the river, is challenging...Challenging holes. River holes. Scenic...Fun course with huge greens...Lots of water; well laid out.

★★ FOX MEADOWS GOLF COURSE

PM-3064 Clarke Rd., Memphis, 38115, Shelby County, (901)362-0232.
Opened: 1960. **Holes:** 18. **Par:** 71/72. **Yards:** 6,545/5,095. **Course rating:** 69.9/66.7. **Slope:** 108/102. **Architect:** Chic Adams. **Green fee:** $13/$15. **Credit cards:** None. **Reduced fees:** Seniors, juniors. **Caddies:** No. **Golf carts:** $16. **Discount golf packages:** No. **Season:** Year-round. **High:** May-Sept. **On site lodging:** No. **Rental clubs:** Yes. **Walking policy:** Unrestricted walking. **Metal spikes allowed:** Yes. **Range:** No. **To obtain tee times:** Call anytime.

★½ GALLOWAY GOLF COURSE

PU-3815 Walnut Grove Rd., Memphis, 38111, Shelby County, (901)685-7805.
Opened: 1926. **Holes:** 18. **Par:** 71/73. **Yards:** 5,844/5,472. **Course rating:** 67.4/71.3. **Slope:** 109/117. **Architect:** N/A. **Green fee:** $13/$15. **Credit cards:** None. **Reduced fees:** Juniors. **Caddies:** No. **Golf carts:** $19. **Discount golf packages:** No. **Season:** Year-round. **High:** Apr.-Oct. **On site lodging:** No. **Rental clubs:** Yes. **Walking policy:** Unrestricted walking. **Metal spikes allowed:** Yes. **Range:** No. **To obtain tee times:** Call 7 days in advance.

★★½ GATLINBURG GOLF COURSE

PU-520 Dollywood Lane, Pigeon Forge, 37868, Sevier County, (423)453-3912, 34 miles SW of Knoxville.
Opened: 1955. **Holes:** 18. **Par:** 71/72. **Yards:** 6,281/4,718. **Course rating:** 72.3/68.9. **Slope:** 125/117. **Architect:** William B. Langford/Bob Cupp. **Green fee:** $25/$35. **Credit cards:** MC,VISA. **Reduced fees:** Twilight, juniors. **Caddies:** No. **Golf carts:** $15. **Discount golf packages:** Yes. **Season:** Year-round. **High:** May-Oct. **On site lodging:** No. **Rental clubs:** Yes. **Walking policy:** Walking at certain times. **Metal spikes allowed:** Yes. **Range:** No. **To obtain tee times:** Call 7 days in advance.
Notes: 1957-58 LPGA site.
Subscriber comments: Very challenging. A lot of hills...A gem in the middle of the Pigeon Forge Zoo...Beautiful views, course in good shape...Very good mountain golf...Mountain golf, scenic, course improved...You must be physically fit.

★★★½ GRAYSBURG HILLS GOLF COURSE

PU-910 Graysburg Hills Rd., Chuckey, 37641, Greene County, (423)234-8061, 12 miles NE of Greenville.
Opened: 1978. **Holes:** 27. **Architect:** Rees Jones/Roger Packard. **Green fee:** $20/$25. **Credit cards:** MC,VISA,AMEX. **Reduced fees:** N/A. **Caddies:** No. **Golf carts:** $10. **Discount golf packages:** Yes. **Season:** Year-round. **High:** April-Oct. **On site lodging:** No. **Rental clubs:** Yes. **Metal spikes allowed:** Yes. **Range:** Yes (grass).

Walking policy: Walking at certain times. **To obtain tee times:** Call up to 1 year in advance.

FODDERSTACK/CHIMNEYTOP
Par: 72/72. **Yards:** 6,875/5,362. **Course rating:** 73.0/70.5. **Slope:** 134/123.
KNOBS/CHIMNEYTOP
Par: 72/72. **Yards:** 6,743/5,474. **Course rating:** 72.2/71.3. **Slope:** 133/125.
KNOBS/FODDERSTACK
Par: 72/72. **Yards:** 6,834/5,562. **Course rating:** 72.8/71.2. **Slope:** 128/122.
Subscriber comments: Excellent course in remote area...Contrasting nines...Great course in beautiful farm country!...A real gem, great undulating greens...One of the best public courses, where you are made to feel like family.

★★★ THE GREENS AT DEERFIELD
R-1001 The Clubhouse Dr., LaFollette, 37766, Campbell County, (423)566-0040, (800)325-2788, 45 miles N of Knoxville.
Opened: N/A. **Holes:** 18. **Par:** 71/71. **Yards:** 6,716/4,776. **Course rating:** 72.8/69.8. **Slope:** 131/125. **Architect:** Bobby Clampett. **Green fee:** $29/$35. **Credit cards:** MC,VISA,DISC. **Reduced fees:** N/A. **Caddies:** No. **Golf carts:** Included in Green Fee. **Discount golf packages:** Yes. **Season:** March-Dec. **High:** March-Oct. **On site lodging:** Yes. **Rental clubs:** Yes. **Walking policy:** Mandatory cart. **Metal spikes allowed:** Yes. **Range:** Yes (mats). **To obtain tee times:** Call 7 days in advance.
Subscriber comments: New course. Great greens. Beautiful scenery...Extremely hilly course, very difficult...Remote, but tee shot at 3rd worth trip...Very tough course. Good condition, but very tight...Very quiet setting—great holes...Hilly terrain.

★★½ HARPETH HILLS GOLF COURSE
PM-2424 Old Hickory Blvd., Nashville, 37221, Davidson County, (615)862-8493.
Opened: 1968. **Holes:** 18. **Par:** 72/72. **Yards:** 6,900/5,200. **Course rating:** 73.1/71.2. **Slope:** 126/124. **Architect:** N/A. **Green fee:** $14/$14. **Credit cards:** None. **Reduced fees:** N/A. **Caddies:** No. **Golf carts:** $16. **Discount golf packages:** No. **Season:** Year-round. **High:** May-Sept. **On site lodging:** No. **Rental clubs:** Yes. **Walking policy:** Unrestricted walking. **Metal spikes allowed:** Yes. **Range:** Yes (grass). **To obtain tee times:** Call seven days in advance.
Subscriber comments: Largest greens in Nashville—good track...Requires some length off tee...Difficult to get tee time, nice views...Not much water.

★★★½ HEATHERHURST GOLF CLUB
R-P.O. Box 2000, Fairfield Glade, 38558, Cumberland County, (615)484-3799, 6 miles W of Crossfield.
Opened: 1988. **Holes:** 27. **Architect:** Gary Roger Baird. **Green fee:** $15/$38. **Credit cards:** All major. **Reduced fees:** N/A. **Caddies:** No. **Golf carts:** $9. **Discount golf packages:** Yes. **Season:** Year-round. **High:** April-Oct. **On site lodging:** Yes. **Rental clubs:** Yes. **Walking policy:** Walking at certain times. **Metal spikes allowed:** Yes. **Range:** Yes (grass). **To obtain tee times:** Call 5 days in advance.
CREEK/MOUNTAIN
Par: 72/72. **Yards:** 6,800/4,789. **Course rating:** 70.2/66.9. **Slope:** 123/112.
PINE/CREEK
Par: 72/72. **Yards:** 6,700/4,630. **Course rating:** 69.2/66.8. **Slope:** 119/111.
PINE/MOUNTAIN
Par: 72/72. **Yards:** 6,650/4,637. **Course rating:** 69.4/66.1. **Slope:** 120/110.
Subscriber comments: Outstanding staff, scenic, wide fairways...Nicely kept. A little wet...Great for shorter hitters. Creek has toughest par 5 in East Tennessee. Always great condition!...Excellent scenery. Witnessed deer on course with fog as a backdrop...Beautiful scenery—mountain golf...Excellent, maintained but crowded.
Special Notes: Formerly known as Fairfield Glade Resort.

★★★½ HENRY HORTON STATE PARK GOLF COURSE
PU-4358 Nashville Hwy., Chapel Hill, 37034, Marshall County, (615)364-2319, 30 miles S of Nashville.
Opened: 1963. **Holes:** 18. **Par:** 72/73. **Yards:** 7,060/5,625. **Course rating:** 74.3/72.1. **Slope:** 128/117. **Architect:** N/A. **Green fee:** $16/$16. **Credit cards:** MC,VISA,AMEX. **Reduced fees:** Seniors, juniors. **Caddies:** No. **Golf carts:** $18. **Discount golf pack-**

ages: No. **Season:** Year-round. **High:** May-June. **On site lodging:** Yes. **Rental clubs:** Yes. **Walking policy:** Unrestricted walking. **Metal spikes allowed:** Yes. **Range:** Yes (grass). **To obtain tee times:** Call Tuesday for upcoming weekend.
Subscriber comments: Long, big greens, wide fairways, nice state park...Wooded. Good fairways...Elevated greens...Proves state can run a good course...Open course, good for free swingers...Finishing hole par 5 almost 600 yards.

★★★★HERMITAGE GOLF COURSE
PU-3939 Old Hickory Blvd., Old Hickory, 37138, Davidson County, (615)847-4001, 10 miles NE of Nashville.
Opened: 1986. **Holes:** 18. **Par:** 72/72. **Yards:** 6,775/5,475. **Course rating:** 71.9/70.8. **Slope:** 122/120. **Architect:** Gary Roger Baird. **Green fee:** $25/$29. **Credit cards:** All major. **Reduced fees:** Twilight. **Caddies:** No. **Golf carts:** $12. **Discount golf packages:** No. **Season:** Year-round. **High:** April-Oct. **On site lodging:** No. **Rental clubs:** Yes. **Walking policy:** Walking at certain times. **Metal spikes allowed:** No. **Range:** Yes (grass/mats). **To obtain tee times:** Call 5 days in advance. May make tee times up to one year in advance with credit card.
Notes: LPGA Sara Lee Classic since 1988.
Subscriber comments: Best in Nashville area, fast greens, good practice...Good shape, challenge...A true championship layout, challenging, narrow fairways, soft greens, good people, pro shop has good selection...Great course and range—deep bluegrass rough...Great scenic view, great golf...Back nine plays longer.

★★★HOLIDAY LINKS GOLF RESORT
R-815 Tennessee Ave., Crossville, 38555, Cumberland County, (931)456-4060, 60 miles W of Knoxville.
Opened: 1983. **Holes:** 18. **Par:** 72/72. **Yards:** 6,411/4,844. **Course rating:** 71.9/70.0. **Slope:** 124/121. **Architect:** Ron Garl. **Green fee:** $21/$26. **Credit cards:** MC,VISA. **Reduced fees:** N/A. **Caddies:** No. **Golf carts:** Included in Green Fee. **Discount golf packages:** Yes. **Season:** Year-round. **High:** April-Sept. **On site lodging:** Yes. **Rental clubs:** Yes. **Walking policy:** Walking at certain times. **Metal spikes allowed:** Yes. **Range:** Yes (grass). **To obtain tee times:** Call.
Subscriber comments: Mountain course, island green par 3, wildlife a must...Good course if taken care of. Back nine tough. 15th unbelivable!...Not crowded—beautiful scenery...Front nine OK, back very nice...A fun day of golf—very serene.
Special Notes: Formerly Thunder Hollow Golf Club.

★½HUNTERS POINT GOLF CLUB
PU-1500 Hunters Point Pike, Lebanon, 37087, Wilson County, (615)444-7521, 25 miles E of Nashville.
Opened: 1966. **Holes:** 18. **Par:** 72/73. **Yards:** 6,573/5,600. **Course rating:** 69.6/71.5. **Slope:** 108/111. **Architect:** Robert Renaud. **Green fee:** $10/$15. **Credit cards:** MC,VISA. **Reduced fees:** Weekdays, low season, seniors, juniors. **Caddies:** No. **Golf carts:** $10. **Discount golf packages:** Yes. **Season:** Year-round. **High:** May-Oct. **On site lodging:** No. **Rental clubs:** Yes. **Walking policy:** Unrestricted walking. **Metal spikes allowed:** Yes. **Range:** Yes (grass). **To obtain tee times:** First come, first served.

★★★INDIAN HILLS GOLF CLUB
PU-405 Calumet Trace, Murfreesboro, 37130, Rutherford County, (615)895-3642, 25 miles SE of Nashville.
Opened: 1988. **Holes:** 18. **Par:** 71/71. **Yards:** 6,495/5,686. **Course rating:** 72.8/70.3. **Slope:** 125/118. **Architect:** N/A. **Green fee:** $10/$21. **Credit cards:** MC,VISA. **Reduced fees:** Weekdays, low season, twilight, seniors, juniors. **Caddies:** No. **Golf carts:** $9. **Discount golf packages:** Yes. **Season:** Year-round. **High:** April-Oct. **On site lodging:** No. **Rental clubs:** Yes. **Walking policy:** Walking at certain times. **Metal spikes allowed:** Yes. **Range:** Yes (grass). **To obtain tee times:** Call three days in advance.
Subscriber comments: Short holes with nice fairways...Tight, OBs...Bent greens. Interesting holes...Nice layout course creates interesting shot making...Back nine not quite as challenging...Nice clubhouse, shop...Extra nice fairways.

TENNESSEE

★★IRONWOOD GOLF COURSE
PU-3801 Ironwood Rd., Cookeville, 38501, Putnam County, (615)528-2331, 80 miles W of Nashville.
Opened: 1971. **Holes:** 18. **Par:** 72/72. **Yards:** 6,311/5,023. **Course rating:** 70.7/68.5. **Slope:** 123/112. **Architect:** Bobby Nichols. **Green fee:** $11. **Credit cards:** MC,VISA,DISC. **Reduced fees:** Weekdays, low season, seniors, juniors. **Caddies:** No. **Golf carts:** $9. **Discount golf packages:** No. **Season:** Year-round. **High:** April-Sept. **On site lodging:** No. **Rental clubs:** Yes. **Walking policy:** Unrestricted walking. **Metal spikes allowed:** Yes. **Range:** Yes (grass). **To obtain tee times:** First come, first served.

★★KNOXVILLE GOLF COURSE
PM-3925 Schaad Rd., Knoxville, 37912, Knox County, (423)691-7143.
Opened: 1984. **Holes:** 18. **Par:** 72/72. **Yards:** 6,528/5,325. **Course rating:** 71.5/69.7. **Slope:** 119/110. **Architect:** D.J. DeVictor. **Green fee:** $10/$14. **Credit cards:** MC,VISA. **Reduced fees:** Weekdays, twilight, seniors, juniors. **Caddies:** No. **Golf carts:** $10. **Discount golf packages:** No. **Season:** Year-round. **High:** April-Nov. **On site lodging:** No. **Rental clubs:** Yes. **Walking policy:** Unrestricted walking. **Metal spikes allowed:** Yes. **Range:** No. **To obtain tee times:** Call one week in advance.

★★½LAMBERT ACRES GOLF CLUB
3402 Tuckaleechee Park, Maryville, 37803, Blount County, (423)982-9838, 18 miles S of Knoxville.
Opened: 1965. **Holes:** 27. **Architect:** Don Charles. **Green fee:** $17/$17. **Credit cards:** None. **Reduced fees:** N/A. **Caddies:** No. **Golf carts:** $8. **Discount golf packages:** No. **Season:** Year-round. **High:** May-Oct. **On site lodging:** No. **Rental clubs:** Yes. **Walking policy:** Unrestricted walking. **Metal spikes allowed:** Yes. **Range:** No. **To obtain tee times:** First come, first served.
RED/ORANGE
Par: 72/72. **Yards:** 6,282/4,753. **Course rating:** 70.1/68.3. **Slope:** 121/105.
RED/WHITE
Par: 72/72. **Yards:** 6,480/4,511. **Course rating:** 70.8/66.2. **Slope:** 118/102.
WHITE/ORANGE
Par: 72/72. **Yards:** 6,292/4,704. **Course rating:** 69.6/66.4. **Slope:** 119/105.
Subscriber comments: Beautiful course with mountain backdrop...Old course—not many hazards such as traps or water...Tops for high handicapper...Golf is good, scenery is magnificent...Fun course...Beautiful setting, challenging...Orange course is very hilly and hard to walk...Beautiful setting in foothills of Smoky mountains...The scenery is breathtaking. Mountains and more mountains...Nice fairways in summer, but heavy play.

★★½THE LEGACY GOLF CLUB
PU-100 Ray Floyd Dr., Springfield, 37172, Robertson County, (615)384-4653, 20 miles N of Nashville.
Opened: 1996. **Holes:** 18. **Par:** 72/72. **Yards:** 6,755/4,860. **Course rating:** 73.3/68.2. **Slope:** 131/118. **Architect:** Ray Floyd/Augusta Golf, Inc.. **Green fee:** $12/$21. **Credit cards:** All major. **Reduced fees:** Low season, seniors, juniors. **Caddies:** No. **Golf carts:** $11. **Discount golf packages:** No. **Season:** Year-round. **High:** June-Sept. **On site lodging:** No. **Rental clubs:** Yes. **Walking policy:** Unrestricted walking. **Metal spikes allowed:** No. **Range:** Yes (grass). **To obtain tee times:** May call up to 5 days in advance.
Subscriber comments: New Ray Floyd course—still needs to mature...No let up. Every hole a challenge...Best new course I've seen...Treat you like they want you back, course a bit young...Very challenging course.
Special Notes: Spikeless encouraged.

★★★★LEGENDS CLUB OF TENNESSEE - ROPER'S KNOB COURSE
1500 Legends Club Lane, Franklin, 37068, Williamson County, (615)790-1300, 15 miles S of Nashville.
Opened: 1992. **Holes:** 36. **Par:** 71/71. **Yards:** 7,113/5,290. **Course rating:** 74.7/71.4. **Slope:** 129/121. **Architect:** Tom Kite and Bob Cupp. **Green fee:** $63/$69. **Credit cards:** All major. **Reduced fees:**

Weekdays, twilight. **Caddies:** No. **Golf carts:** Included in Green Fee. **Discount golf packages:** Yes. **Season:** Year-round. **High:** April-Oct. **On site lodging:** No. **Rental clubs:** Yes. **Walking policy:** Mandatory cart. **Metal spikes allowed:** Yes. **Range:** Yes (grass). **To obtain tee times:** Call up to 3 days in advance.
Subscriber comments: Outstanding all-around facility and course...Beautiful fairways!...Wonderful golf course...Zoysia fairways. Bent greens...A challenge for any golfer...Outstanding condition—always a challenge...Wonderful practice range.
Special notes: Also has 18-hole private Ironhorse Course.

★★LONG HOLLOW GOLF COURSE
PU-1080 Long Hollow Pike, Gallatin, 37066, Sumner County, (615)451-3120.
Opened: 1983. **Holes:** 18. **Par:** 70/70. **Yards:** 6,000/4,952. **Course rating:** 66.7/66.6.
Slope: 109/101. **Architect:** Kevin Tucker. **Green fee:** $18/$18. **Credit cards:** N/A.
Reduced fees: N/A. **Caddies:** No. **Golf carts:** $15. **Discount golf packages:** No.
Season: Year-round. **High:** May-Sept. **On site lodging:** No. **Rental clubs:** Yes.
Walking policy: Unrestricted walking. **Metal spikes allowed:** Yes. **Range:** Yes (grass/mats). **To obtain tee times:** Call.

★★★★MARRIOTT'S GOLF CLUB AT SHILOH FALLS
P.O. Box 11, Pickwick Dam, 38365, Hardin County, (901)689-5050, 100 miles E of Memphis.
Opened: 1993. **Holes:** 18. **Par:** 72/72. **Yards:** 6,713/5,156. **Course rating:** 73.1/71.3.
Slope: 136/128. **Architect:** Jerry Pate. **Green fee:** $32/$49. **Credit cards:** All major.
Reduced fees: Weekdays, low season, resort guests, juniors. **Caddies:** No. **Golf carts:** Included in Green Fee. **Discount golf packages:** Yes. **Season:** Year-round.
High: April-Oct. **On site lodging:** Yes. **Rental clubs:** Yes. **Walking policy:** Walking at certain times. **Metal spikes allowed:** Yes. **Range:** Yes (grass). **To obtain tee times:** Call up to 14 days in advance.
Subscriber comments: Pretty holes and fairly challenging...This is a very interesting and fun course...Fun elevator ride...Good practice facilities...Very scenic layout...Great signature hole—Island Green! Friendly service...Very manicured. Great layout.

★★MCCABE FIELD GOLF COURSE
PU-46th Ave. & Murphy Rd., Nashville, 37209, Davidson County, (615)862-8491.
Opened: 1939. **Holes:** 27. **Architect:** N/A. **Green fee:** $16/$16. **Credit cards:** MC,VISA. **Reduced fees:** Seniors, juniors. **Caddies:** No. **Golf carts:** $16. **Discount golf packages:** No. **Season:** Year-round. **High:** April-Sept. **On site lodging:** No.
Rental clubs: Yes. **Walking policy:** Unrestricted walking. **Metal spikes allowed:** Yes.
Range: No. **To obtain tee times:** Call seven days in advance.
MIDDLE/NORTH
Par: 71/71. **Yards:** 6,481/5,876. **Course rating:** 69.6/69.6. **Slope:** 112/112.
MIDDLE/SOUTH
Par: 70/70. **Yards:** 6,023/5,590. **Course rating:** 68.6/68.6. **Slope:** 110/110.
NORTH/SOUTH
Par: 71/71. **Yards:** 6,522/5,866. **Course rating:** 69.7/69.7. **Slope:** 111/111.

★★MEADOWVIEW GOLF CLUB
17085 Wilcox Dr., Kingsport, 37662, Sullivan County, (423)245-3521.
Call club for further information.

★★½MEMPHIS OAKS GOLF CLUB
4143 E Holmes Rd, Memphis, 38118, Shelby County, (901)363-4001.
Opened: N/A. **Holes:** 18. **Par:** 71/71. **Yards:** 6,271/5,212. **Course rating:** 70.8. **Slope:** 119. **Architect:** John Frazier. **Green fee:** $18/$38. **Credit cards:** MC,VISA,AMEX.
Reduced fees: Weekdays, low season, twilight. **Caddies:** No. **Golf carts:** N/A.
Discount golf packages: No. **Season:** Year-round. **High:** June-Sept. **On site lodging:** No. **Rental clubs:** Yes. **Walking policy:** Mandatory cart. **Metal spikes allowed:** Yes.
Range: Yes (grass). **To obtain tee times:** Call up to 7 days in advance.
Subscriber comments: Very tight course. Narrow. Doglegs left and right. Hard to play with my natural slice off the tee...Good practice putting green.

TENNESSEE

★★MOCCASIN BEND GOLF CLUB
PU-381 Moccasin Bend Rd., Chattanooga, 37405, Hamilton County, (423)267-3585, 3 miles N of Chattanooga.
Opened: 1966. **Holes:** 18. **Par:** 72/72. **Yards:** 6,469/5,290. **Course rating:** 69.6/69.0. **Slope:** 111/109. **Architect:** Alex McKay. **Green fee:** $14/$17. **Credit cards:** MC,VISA. **Reduced fees:** Seniors, juniors. **Caddies:** No. **Golf carts:** $10. **Discount golf packages:** Yes. **Season:** Year-round. **High:** April-Oct. **On site lodging:** No. **Rental clubs:** Yes. **Walking policy:** Walking at certain times. **Metal spikes allowed:** Yes. **Range:** Yes (grass). **To obtain tee times:** Call for weekends and holidays.

★★★MONTGOMERY BELL STATE PARK GOLF COURSE
PU-800 Hotel Ave., Burns, 37029, Dickson County, (615)797-2578, 35 miles W of Nashville.
Opened: 1970. **Holes:** 18. **Par:** 71/72. **Yards:** 6,091/4,961. **Course rating:** 69.3/68.8. **Slope:** 121/116. **Architect:** Gary Roger Baird. **Green fee:** $19/$19. **Credit cards:** MC,VISA,AMEX. **Reduced fees:** Seniors, juniors. **Caddies:** No. **Golf carts:** $20. **Discount golf packages:** Yes. **Season:** Year-round. **High:** April-Nov. **On site lodging:** Yes. **Rental clubs:** No. **Walking policy:** Unrestricted walking. **Metal spikes allowed:** Yes. **Range:** Yes (grass). **To obtain tee times:** Call 6 days in advance.
Subscriber comments: State Park course—great greens...Fun time for all...Great course. Narrow fairways test skills...Well-designed holes and beautiful scenery...Nice to play. Best grass fairways in South...Nice people...Hilly, tight, lots of pine trees. Scenic...Abundant wildlife, deer on course...Great for high handicappers...Good course, excellent scenery, isolated from hole to hole...Short course, requires precision; scenic, fun course; usually crowded; par 5s reachable; much improved; on some holes best to leave driver in bag.

★★★NASHBORO GOLF CLUB
PU-1101 Nashboro Blvd., Nashville, 37217, Davidson County, (615)367-2311.
Opened: 1974. **Holes:** 18. **Par:** 72/75. **Yards:** 6,887/5,485. **Course rating:** 73.5/72.3. **Slope:** 134/121. **Architect:** B.J. Wihry. **Green fee:** $36/$42. **Credit cards:** All major. **Reduced fees:** Weekdays, low season, twilight. **Caddies:** No. **Golf carts:** Included in Green Fee. **Discount golf packages:** Yes. **Season:** Year-round. **High:** April-Sept. **On site lodging:** No. **Rental clubs:** Yes. **Walking policy:** Walking at certain times. **Metal spikes allowed:** Yes. **Range:** Yes (grass). **To obtain tee times:** Weekend tee times may be made beginning the Tuesday prior to the weekend. Weekday tee times amy be made up to 14 days in advance.
Subscriber comments: Excellent and challenging course. Well groomed...Fun to play...Good course—tough to score well...Difficult for average golfer. Tight. Greens quick. Pretty...One of the most challenging in Nashville...Lots of good holes.

★★★ORGILL PARK GOLF COURSE
PU-9080 Bethuel Rd., Millington, 38053, Shelby County, (901)872-3610, 10 miles N of Memphis.
Opened: 1972. **Holes:** 18. **Par:** 70/71. **Yards:** 6,284/4,574. **Course rating:** 68.6/68.3. **Slope:** 113/108. **Architect:** Press Maxwell. **Green fee:** $13/$14. **Credit cards:** All major. **Reduced fees:** Weekdays, low season, seniors, juniors. **Caddies:** No. **Golf carts:** $9. **Discount golf packages:** No. **Season:** Year-round. **High:** April-Sept. **On site lodging:** No. **Rental clubs:** Yes. **Walking policy:** Unrestricted walking. **Metal spikes allowed:** Yes. **Range:** Yes (grass). **To obtain tee times:** Call 1 day in advance for weekdays and 2 days in advance for weekends.
Subscriber comments: Good course—well kept...Good course, water, no sand. It does make you think about shots...Bermuda greens, pine trees, water, challenging but fair...Best muny in Memphis—fun and challenging.

★★½PARIS LANDING GOLF COURSE
PU-16055 Hwy.79 N., Buchanan, 38222, Henry County, (901)644-1332, 40 miles S of Clarksville.
Opened: 1971. **Holes:** 18. **Par:** 72/72. **Yards:** 6,612/6,408. **Course rating:** N/A. **Slope:** 126/124. **Architect:** Benjamin Wihry. **Green fee:** $15/$19. **Credit cards:** MC,VISA,AMEX. **Reduced fees:** N/A. **Caddies:** No. **Golf carts:** N/A. **Discount golf packages:** Yes. **Season:** Year-round. **High:** April-June/Sept.-Oct. **On site lodging:** Yes.

Rental clubs: No. **Walking policy:** Unrestricted walking. **Metal spikes allowed:** Yes. **Range:** Yes (grass). **To obtain tee times:** Call.
Subscriber comments: Beautiful river views/steep hills...Next to modern inn and cabins in woods. Have to hit straight...Great scenery and nature.

★★★PICKWICK LANDING STATE PARK GOLF COURSE
PU-Hwy. No.57 P.O. Box 15, Pickwick Dam, 38365, Hardin County, (901)689-3149, 120 miles E of Memphis.
Opened: 1973. **Holes:** 18. **Par:** 72/72. **Yards:** 6,478/5,229. **Course rating:** 70.2/68.7. **Slope:** 118/115. **Architect:** Benjamin Whiry. **Green fee:** $19/$19. **Credit cards:** All major. **Reduced fees:** Weekdays, low season, juniors. **Caddies:** No. **Golf carts:** $20. **Discount golf packages:** Yes. **Season:** Year-round. **High:** March-Sept. **On site lodging:** No. **Rental clubs:** Yes. **Walking policy:** Unrestricted walking. **Metal spikes allowed:** No. **Range:** Yes (grass). **To obtain tee times:** Call.
Subscriber comments: Great shape, best greens of all state parks, long for ladies...Long, hard and very playable...Many improvements always being made...Tight and hilly, nice greens, worth a visit...Must be able to work your shots.

★★PINE HILL GOLF COURSE
PM-1005 Alice Ave., Memphis, 38106, Shelby County, (901)775-9434.
Opened: N/A. **Holes:** 18. **Par:** 72/73. **Yards:** 5,908/5,014. **Course rating:** 65.9/66.7. **Slope:** 114/116. **Architect:** N/A. **Green fee:** $9/$11. **Credit cards:** MC,VISA,AMEX. **Reduced fees:** Seniors, juniors. **Caddies:** No. **Golf carts:** N/A. **Discount golf packages:** No. **Season:** Year-round. **High:** May-Sept. **On site lodging:** No. **Rental clubs:** Yes. **Walking policy:** Unrestricted walking. **Metal spikes allowed:** Yes. **Range:** Yes (grass). **To obtain tee times:** First come, first served.

★★★½QUAIL RIDGE GOLF COURSE
PU-4055 Altruria Rd., Bartlett, 38135, Shelby County, (901)386-6951, 5 miles N of Memphis.
Opened: 1994. **Holes:** 18. **Par:** 71/70. **Yards:** 6,600/5,206. **Course rating:** 71.8. **Slope:** 128. **Architect:** David Pfaff. **Green fee:** $21/$31. **Credit cards:** All major. **Reduced fees:** Twilight, seniors, juniors. **Caddies:** No. **Golf carts:** $10. **Discount golf packages:** No. **Season:** Year-round. **High:** April-Oct. **On site lodging:** No. **Rental clubs:** No. **Walking policy:** Walking at certain times. **Metal spikes allowed:** No. **Range:** Yes (grass/mats). **To obtain tee times:** Call 5 days in advance.
Subscriber comments: One of Memphis' best-kept secrets. Great course...Fair, not too long, backside pretty in fall...Best in Memphis, slow play...Great course, great layout, great fun...Good challenge, free range balls...Reachable par 5s.

★★½THE QUARRY GOLF CLUB
1001 Reads Lake Rd., Chattanooga, 37415, Hamilton County, (423)875-8888.
Call club for further information.

★★★½RIVER ISLANDS GOLF CLUB
PU-9610 Kodak Rd., Kodak, 37764, Knox County, (423)933-0100, (800)347-4837, 15 miles E of Knoxville.
Opened: 1990. **Holes:** 18. **Par:** 72/72. **Yards:** 7,001/4,973. **Course rating:** 75.4/69.4. **Slope:** 133/118. **Architect:** Arthur Hills. **Green fee:** $29/$49. **Credit cards:** MC,VISA,AMEX. **Reduced fees:** Weekdays, low season, twilight. **Caddies:** No. **Golf carts:** Included in Green Fee. **Discount golf packages:** Yes. **Season:** Year-round. **High:** April-Oct. **On site lodging:** No. **Rental clubs:** Yes. **Walking policy:** Mandatory cart. **Metal spikes allowed:** Yes. **Range:** Yes (grass). **To obtain tee times:** Call golf shop.
Notes: Ranked 9th in 1997 Best in State.
Subscriber comments: Beauty along river. Challenging holes...From the tips this is a test of Smoky Mountain golf...Great island greens...Beautiful, challenging. Great course maintenance...Beautiful, challenging par 3s...A hidden gem.

★★★½ROAN VALLEY GOLF ESTATES

Hwy. 421 S., Mountain City, 37683, Johnson County, (423)727-7931, 20 miles N of Boone, NC.

Opened: 1982. **Holes:** 18. **Par:** 72/72. **Yards:** 6,736/4,370. **Course rating:** 71.8/68.9. **Slope:** 120/107. **Architect:** Dan Maples. **Green fee:** $32/$40. **Credit cards:** MC,VISA. **Reduced fees:** Weekdays, low season, juniors. **Caddies:** No. **Golf carts:** Included in Green Fee. **Discount golf packages:** No. **Season:** April-Nov. **High:** May-Oct. **On site lodging:** Yes. **Rental clubs:** Yes. **Walking policy:** Walking at certain times. **Metal spikes allowed:** Yes. **Range:** No. **To obtain tee times:** Call anytime.

Subscriber comments: Great mountain course...Interesting layout, some flat, some hilly...Very scenic...Beautiful scenery, greens smooth and fast...Course always in good shape...Long and wide...True mountain golf; scenic, enjoyable, remote.

★★★½SADDLE CREEK GOLF CLUB

PU-1435 Finley Beech Rd., Lewisburg, 37091, Marshall County, (615)270-7280.

Opened: 1995. **Holes:** 18. **Par:** 72/72. **Yards:** 6,700/4,999. **Course rating:** 71.9/67.9. **Slope:** 127/120. **Architect:** Gene Bates. **Green fee:** $17/$22. **Credit cards:** VISA,AMEX. **Reduced fees:** Twilight. **Caddies:** No. **Golf carts:** $10. **Discount golf packages:** No. **Season:** Year-round. **High:** N/A. **On site lodging:** No. **Rental clubs:** No. **Walking policy:** Unrestricted walking. **Metal spikes allowed:** Yes. **Range:** Yes (grass). **To obtain tee times:** Call 5 days in advance.

Subscriber comments: Front nine tight, water, sand, good practice area...Hardest starting hole I've ever played!...Best new course in mid TN.; front nine conventional, back side links-like...Very good course for no trees...A lot of water—fast greens.

★½SOUTHWEST POINT GOLF COURSE

PU-Decatur Highway S., Kingston, 37763, Roane County, (423)376-5282.

Opened: 1964. **Holes:** 18. **Par:** 72/74. **Yards:** 6,673/6,086. **Course rating:** 70.3/70.0. **Slope:** N/A. **Architect:** Alex McKay. **Green fee:** $12/$22. **Credit cards:** MC,VISA. **Reduced fees:** Weekdays, low season, twilight, seniors. **Caddies:** No. **Golf carts:** $10. **Discount golf packages:** No. **Season:** Year-round. **High:** March-Aug. **On site lodging:** No. **Rental clubs:** Yes. **Walking policy:** Unrestricted walking. **Metal spikes allowed:** Yes. **Range:** No. **To obtain tee times:** Tee times not required.

Special Notes: Spikeless encouraged.

★★★SPRINGHOUSE GOLF CLUB

R-18 Springhouse Lane, Nashville, 37214, Davidson County, (615)871-7759.

Opened: 1990. **Holes:** 18. **Par:** 72/72. **Yards:** 7,007/5,126. **Course rating:** 74.0/70.2. **Slope:** 133/118. **Architect:** Larry Nelson and Jeff Brauer. **Green fee:** $65/$80. **Credit cards:** All major. **Reduced fees:** Low season, seniors. **Caddies:** No. **Golf carts:** Included in Green Fee. **Discount golf packages:** No. **Season:** Year-round. **High:** April-Oct. **On site lodging:** Yes. **Rental clubs:** Yes. **Walking policy:** Mandatory cart. **Metal spikes allowed:** No. **Range:** Yes (grass/mats). **To obtain tee times:** Tee times are required and are taken up to 7 days in advance. Opryland hotel guests call 30 days in advance.

Notes: 1994-present, BellSouth Senior Classic.

Subscriber comments: Mounds beside fairways, links style...Needs to mature, good layout...Links along river. Groomed. Excellent clubhouse...Long from back tees...Wonderful experience in every way, best run, best staff.

★★★STONEBRIDGE GOLF COURSE

PU-3049 Davies Plantation Rd. S., Memphis, 38133, Shelby County, (901)382-1886.

Opened: 1972. **Holes:** 18. **Par:** 71/71. **Yards:** 6,788/5,012. **Course rating:** 73.3/66.8. **Slope:** 133/113. **Architect:** George W. Cobb. **Green fee:** $20/$30. **Credit cards:** All major. **Reduced fees:** Weekdays, low season. **Caddies:** No. **Golf carts:** $12. **Discount golf packages:** No. **Season:** Year-round. **High:** April-Sept. **On site lodging:** No. **Rental clubs:** Yes. **Walking policy:** Walking at certain times. **Metal spikes allowed:** No. **Range:** Yes (grass/mats). **To obtain tee times:** Call 5 days in advance.

Subscriber comments: Fairly tight—good length...Good course, well maintained, some houses too close to course...Challenging course, bent greens, a few 90-degree doglegs, water, fun...Good test for all the clubs and skills you have.

★★★½STONEHENGE GOLF CLUB
PU-222 Fairfield Blvd., Fairfield Glade, 38558, Cumberland County, (615)484-3731, (800)624-8755, 60 miles W of Knoxville.
Opened: 1984. **Holes:** 18. **Par:** 72/72. **Yards:** 6,549/5,000. **Course rating:** 71.5/70.2. **Slope:** 131/124. **Architect:** Joe Lee and Rocky Roquemore. **Green fee:** $35/$60. **Credit cards:** All major. **Reduced fees:** Low season, resort guests, twilight, juniors. **Caddies:** No. **Golf carts:** Included in Green Fee. **Discount golf packages:** Yes. **Season:** Year-round. **High:** April-Oct. **On site lodging:** Yes. **Rental clubs:** Yes. **Walking policy:** Mandatory cart. **Metal spikes allowed:** Yes. **Range:** Yes (grass). **To obtain tee times:** Written, 30 days in advance to Central Tee Times, P.O. Box 2000, Fairfield Glade, TN 38558. Call 5 days in advance.
Notes: Ranked 5th in 1997 Best in State.
Subscriber comments: Mountain course. Beautiful. Challenging...Bent grass fairways, soft course...The views! great course...Good layout, nice people, but the course is always wet...Shorter, tighter than most...Incredible, beautiful, 14th is breathtaking.

★★★SWAN LAKE GOLF COURSE
PM-581 Dunbar Cave Rd., Clarksville, 37043, Montgomery County, (615)648-0479, 40 miles NW of Nashville.
Opened: N/A. **Holes:** 18. **Par:** 71/72. **Yards:** 6,419/5,155. **Course rating:** 70.5/69.0. **Slope:** 116/112. **Architect:** Benjamin Wihry. **Green fee:** $14/$14. **Credit cards:** MC,VISA. **Reduced fees:** Seniors. **Caddies:** No. **Golf carts:** $16. **Discount golf packages:** No. **Season:** Year-round. **High:** March-Oct. **On site lodging:** No. **Rental clubs:** No. **Walking policy:** Unrestricted walking. **Metal spikes allowed:** Yes. **Range:** No. **To obtain tee times:** Call Wednesday for Saturday tee times. Call Thursday for Sunday.
Subscriber comments: Nice people, few hold-ups, greens excellent, tight fairways, good pro, nice established course, can get soggy after rain...Good personnel, course needs work...Fast greens—lots of elevation—long and narrow...Good test of golf.

★★T.O. FULLER GOLF COURSE
PM-1400 Pavillion Dr., Memphis, 38109, Shelby County, (901)543-7771.
Opened: 1956. **Holes:** 18. **Par:** 72/73. **Yards:** 6,000/5,656. **Course rating:** 71.0/72.0. **Slope:** 117/110. **Architect:** City of Memphis. **Green fee:** $12/$15. **Credit cards:** MC,VISA,AMEX. **Reduced fees:** Weekdays, low season, seniors, juniors. **Caddies:** No. **Golf carts:** $20. **Discount golf packages:** No. **Season:** Year-round. **High:** May-Dec. **On site lodging:** No. **Rental clubs:** Yes. **Walking policy:** Unrestricted walking. **Metal spikes allowed:** Yes. **Range:** No. **To obtain tee times:** Call 5 days in advance.

★★½TED RHODES GOLF COURSE
PU-1901 Ed Temple Blvd., Nashville, 37208, Davidson County, (615)862-8463.
Opened: 1994. **Holes:** 18. **Par:** 72/72. **Yards:** 6,660/5,732. **Course rating:** 71.8/68.3. **Slope:** 120/115. **Architect:** Gary Roger Baird. **Green fee:** $8/$16. **Credit cards:** None. **Reduced fees:** Seniors, juniors. **Caddies:** No. **Golf carts:** $14. **Discount golf packages:** No. **Season:** Year-round. **High:** May-Sept. **On site lodging:** No. **Rental clubs:** Yes. **Walking policy:** Unrestricted walking. **Metal spikes allowed:** Yes. **Range:** Yes (grass). **To obtain tee times:** Call 7 days in advance.
Subscriber comments: Nice for a new course...Excellent greens and plenty of hazards. Makes for an interesting round...Fairly good municipal course, well kept but needs some work. Back nine is best...Excellent course for all caliber players.

★★★THREE RIDGES GOLF COURSE
PU-6101 Wise Springs Rd., Knoxville, 37918, Knox County, (423)687-4797.
Opened: 1991. **Holes:** 18. **Par:** 72/72. **Yards:** 6,825/5,225. **Course rating:** 73.2/70.7. **Slope:** 128/121. **Architect:** Ault, Clark & Assoc.. **Green fee:** $8/$19. **Credit cards:** All major. **Reduced fees:** Weekdays, twilight, seniors, juniors. **Caddies:** No. **Golf carts:** $10. **Discount golf packages:** No. **Season:** Year-round. **High:** April-Oct. **On site lodging:** No. **Rental clubs:** Yes. **Walking policy:** Unrestricted walking. **Metal spikes allowed:** Yes. **Range:** Yes (grass). **To obtain tee times:** Call seven days in advance.
Subscriber comments: Challenging, well-kept. Keep it in the fairway!...Good challenge—course in great shape...Much improved—great for a county owned course...Always friendly staff...Tough but fair. Will test you...Very hilly. Don't walk unless you're in good shape...Good greens—plenty of length.

★★★TWO RIVERS GOLF COURSE
PM-3140 McGavock Pike, Nashville, 37214, Davidson County, (615)889-2675, 10 miles E of Nashville.
Opened: 1968. **Holes:** 18. **Par:** 72/72. **Yards:** 6,595/5,336. **Course rating:** 71.5/70.4.
Slope: 120/116. **Architect:** Dave Bennett and Leon Howard. **Green fee:** $16/$16.
Credit cards: None. **Reduced fees:** N/A. **Caddies:** No. **Golf carts:** $16. **Discount golf packages:** No. **Season:** Year-round. **High:** April-Sept. **On site lodging:** No. **Rental clubs:** Yes. **Walking policy:** Unrestricted walking. **Metal spikes allowed:** No. **Range:** No. **To obtain tee times:** Call up to seven days in advance, seven days a week.
Subscriber comments: Good public course—wide open on most holes...Best metro course around; little bit of everything...Top-notch instruction...Good shape—not a tough course...Gets heavy play...Short but good greens...Fun course—fair.

★★½WARRIOR'S PATH STATE PARK
PU-P.O. Box 5026, Kingsport, 37663, Sullivan County, (423)323-4990, 90 miles E of Knoxville.
Opened: 1972. **Holes:** 18. **Par:** 72/72. **Yards:** 6,581/5,328. **Course rating:** 71.2/72.4.
Slope: 115/117. **Architect:** George Cobb. **Green fee:** $16/$19. **Credit cards:** MC,VISA. **Reduced fees:** Weekdays, low season, seniors, juniors. **Caddies:** No. **Golf carts:** $10. **Discount golf packages:** Yes. **Season:** Year-round. **High:** March-Aug. **On site lodging:** No. **Rental clubs:** No. **Walking policy:** Unrestricted walking. **Metal spikes allowed:** Yes. **Range:** Yes (grass). **To obtain tee times:** Call 7 days in advance.
Subscriber comments: Very pretty, crowded on weekend...Fairways and greens very nice...Excellent staff, average layout...Very hilly course...Course is getting better.

★★WHITTLE SPRINGS GOLF COURSE
PU-3113 Valley View Dr., Knoxville, 37917, Knox County, (423)525-1022.
Opened: N/A. **Holes:** 18. **Par:** 70/70. **Yards:** 6,000/4,884. **Course rating:** N/A. **Slope:** 110/106. **Architect:** N/A. **Green fee:** N/A. **Credit cards:** N/A. **Reduced fees:** N/A.
Caddies: No. **Golf carts:** N/A. **Discount golf packages:** No. **Season:** Year-round.
High: Jan-Sept. **On site lodging:** No. **Rental clubs:** No. **Walking policy:** N/A. **Metal spikes allowed:** Yes. **Range:** Yes (grass). **To obtain tee times:** N/A.
Subscriber comments: Great basic golf at a fair price...Short, high-handicapper course...Tight course...Old course could use some work...Good for average golfer...Good confidence builder.

★★★½WILLOW CREEK GOLF CLUB
12003 Kingston Pike, Knoxville, 37922, Knox County, (423)675-0100, 12 miles W of Knoxville.
Opened: 1988. **Holes:** 18. **Par:** 72/74. **Yards:** 7,266/5,557. **Course rating:** 73.5/71.9.
Slope: 130/119. **Architect:** Bill Oliphant. **Green fee:** $24/$31. **Credit cards:** MC,VISA,AMEX. **Reduced fees:** Low season, juniors. **Caddies:** No. **Golf carts:** $14. **Discount golf packages:** No. **Season:** Year-round. **High:** April-Oct. **On site lodging:** No. **Rental clubs:** Yes. **Walking policy:** Walking at certain times. **Metal spikes allowed:** Yes. **Range:** Yes (grass). **To obtain tee times:** Call 7 days in advance.
Subscriber comments: Good greens/fairways, tough hill shots, real challenge...Great design. Beautiful layout. Hackers beware...Great staff—open—long putts!...Excellent golf course, tests all levels of players. Very good service and attention, excellent practice facilities. Good to walk...A joy to play, greens hold...A couple of trick holes.

★★★WINDTREE GOLF COURSE
PU-810 Nonaville Rd., Mount Juliet, 37122, Wilson County, (615)754-4653, 15 miles NE of Nashville.
Opened: 1991. **Holes:** 18. **Par:** 72/72. **Yards:** 6,557/5,126. **Course rating:** 71.1/69.6.
Slope: 124/117. **Architect:** John LaFoy. **Green fee:** $19/$23. **Credit cards:** MC,VISA,AMEX. **Reduced fees:** Twilight. **Caddies:** No. **Golf carts:** N/A. **Discount golf packages:** No. **Season:** Year-round. **High:** April-Sept. **On site lodging:** No. **Rental clubs:** Yes. **Walking policy:** Walking at certain times. **Metal spikes allowed:** Yes. **Range:** Yes (grass). **To obtain tee times:** Call Mondays for upcoming weekend.
Subscriber comments: Fun course. Not too long yet a joy to play. Big, well-maintained greens...Many types of shots required during your round...Front nine flat, back hilly. Good track. Nice staff...Nice elevation changes.

★★ALICE MUNICIPAL GOLF COURSE
PM-Texas Blvd., Alice, 78332, Jim Wells County, (512)664-7033, 40 miles W of Corpus Christi.
Opened: N/A. **Holes:** 18. **Par:** 71/72. **Yards:** 5,991/4,853. **Course rating:** 67.8/65.6.
Slope: 100/100. **Architect:** Ralph Plummer. **Green fee:** $6/$7. **Credit cards:** MC,VISA.
Reduced fees: Twilight, seniors. **Caddies:** No. **Golf carts:** $14. **Discount golf packages:** No. **Season:** Year-round. **High:** April-Aug. **On site lodging:** No. **Rental clubs:** No. **Walking policy:** Unrestricted walking. **Metal spikes allowed:** Yes. **Range:** No. **To obtain tee times:** Call Wednesday for upcoming weekend.

★★ALPINE GOLF CLUB
PU-2385 Smelley Rd., Longview, 75605, Gregg County, (903)753-4515, 45 miles N of Shreveport, LA.
Opened: 1955. **Holes:** 18. **Par:** 70/70. **Yards:** 5,435/4,795. **Course rating:** 67.4/67.4.
Slope: 108/108. **Architect:** W.L. Benningfield. **Green fee:** $17/$17. **Credit cards:** MC,DISC. **Reduced fees:** N/A. **Caddies:** No. **Golf carts:** $8. **Discount golf packages:** No. **Season:** Year-round. **High:** March-July. **On site lodging:** No. **Rental clubs:** Yes. **Walking policy:** Unrestricted walking. **Metal spikes allowed:** Yes. **Range:** Yes (mats). **To obtain tee times:** Call.

★★★ANDREWS COUNTY GOLF COURSE
PU-P.O. Box 348, Andrews, 79714, Andrews County, (915)524-1462, 36 miles NW of Odessa.
Opened: N/A. **Holes:** 18. **Par:** 70/72. **Yards:** 6,300/5,331. **Course rating:** 68.9/69.7.
Slope: 116/110. **Architect:** Warren Cantrell. **Green fee:** $12/$17. **Credit cards:** MC,VISA. **Reduced fees:** N/A. **Caddies:** No. **Golf carts:** N/A. **Discount golf packages:** No. **Season:** Year-round. **High:** May-July. **On site lodging:** No. **Rental clubs:** No. **Walking policy:** Unrestricted walking. **Metal spikes allowed:** Yes. **Range:** Yes (grass/mats). **To obtain tee times:** Call golf shop.
Subscriber comments: Very nice West Texas course...Country club course at muny price...Soft, grassy fairways...Keeping ball in fairways a must...Much improved, course great fun...Narrow fairways, greens are excellent.

★½ASCARATE PARK GOLF COURSE
PU-6900 Delta Dr., El Paso, 79905, El Paso County, (915)772-7381.
Opened: 1958. **Holes:** 18. **Par:** 71/72. **Yards:** 6,505/5,650. **Course rating:** 69.4/66.2.
Slope: 114/107. **Architect:** George Hoffman. **Green fee:** $5/$10. **Credit cards:** None. **Reduced fees:** Weekdays, twilight, seniors, juniors. **Caddies:** No. **Golf carts:** $16. **Discount golf packages:** No. **Season:** Year-round. **High:** Year-round. **On site lodging:** No. **Rental clubs:** Yes. **Walking policy:** Unrestricted walking. **Metal spikes allowed:** Yes. **Range:** Yes (grass). **To obtain tee times:** Call one week in advance for weekends.
Special Notes: Also has 9-hole course.

BARTON CREEK RESORT & COUNTRY CLUB
R- **Credit cards:** MC,VISA,AMEX. **Reduced fees:** N/A. **Caddies:** No.
Golf carts: Included in Green Fee. **Discount golf packages:** Yes.
Season: Year-round. **High:** Spring/Fall. **On site lodging:** Yes. **Rental clubs:** Yes. **Walking policy:** Unrestricted walking. **Metal spikes allowed:** Yes. **Range:** Yes (grass/mats). **To obtain tee times:** Must be an overnight resort guest, club member or conference guest to obtain a tee time.

★★★½CRENSHAW AND COORE COURSE
8212 Barton Club Dr., Austin, 78735, Travis County, (512)329-4608, (800)336-6158, 12 miles W of Austin.
Opened: 1991. **Holes:** 18. **Par:** 71/71. **Yards:** 6,678/4,843. **Course rating:** 71.0/67.2.
Slope: 124/110. **Architect:** Ben Crenshaw and Bill Coore. **Green fee:** $95/$95.
Subscriber comments: The best and most enjoyable place I've ever taken any divots from...Mid to high handicappers should enjoy...Short course, fast greens...Back to back par 5s great...Bring your short game...Weakest of the three.

★★★★½FAZIO COURSE
8212 Barton Club Dr., Austin, 78735, Travis County, (512)329-4001, (800)336-6158, 12 miles W of Austin.

Opened: 1986. **Holes:** 18. **Par:** 72/72. **Yards:** 6,956/5,207. **Course rating:** 74.0/69.4. **Slope:** 135/120. **Architect:** Tom Fazio. **Green fee:** $135.
Notes: Ranked 2nd in 1997 Best in State. 1990-94 Liberty Mutual Legends of Golf.
Subscriber comments: Spectacularly scenic, too hard from tips...Hilly course with lots of blind tee shots...Buy yardage book...Well placed tee shots a plus for scoring...I expected more challenge and diversity...Tough design without water holes...Very difficult for average golfer...Has character, play once and you can remember holes.

★★★★PALMER-LAKESIDE COURSE
1800 Clubhouse Hill Dr., Spicewood, 78669, Travis County, (830)693-4589, (800)888-2257, 25 miles W of Austin.
Opened: 1986. **Holes:** 18. **Par:** 71/71. **Yards:** 6,657/5,067. **Course rating:** 71.0/71.0. **Slope:** 124/124. **Architect:** Arnold Palmer and Ed Seay. **Green fee:** $95/$95.
Subscriber comments: Long drive to get there but worth it...Great views from tee boxes...Good practice area...Hidden in the hills...Bring your A game...Always very windy...The golf wonderful even on a bad day...Didn't like lay-up par 4s, a few gimmicky holes...Fair from any set of tees...Just a notch below Fazio.

★★½BATTLE LAKE GOLF COURSE
PU-Rte. 1, Mart, 76664, McLennan County, (254)876-2837, 15 miles SE of Waco.
Opened: N/A. **Holes:** 18. **Par:** 72/74. **Yards:** 6,608/5,254. **Course rating:** 70.7/69.3. **Slope:** 116/112. **Architect:** N/A. **Green fee:** $6/$12. **Credit cards:** All major. **Reduced fees:** Weekdays, low season, twilight, seniors, juniors. **Caddies:** No. **Golf carts:** $9. **Discount golf packages:** No. **Season:** Year-round. **High:** March-Oct. **On site lodging:** No. **Rental clubs:** Yes. **Walking policy:** Unrestricted walking. **Metal spikes allowed:** Yes. **Range:** Yes (grass/mats). **To obtain tee times:** Call 7 days in advance for weekends and holidays.
Subscriber comments: Good place to play...Getting better, new range opening...Some strange holes...Back nine is a neat layout, front nine poor...It will be a very good course in time.

★★★½THE BATTLEGROUND AT DEER PARK GOLF COURSE
PU-1600 Georgia Ave., Deer Park, 77536, Harris County, (281)478-4653, 20 miles SE of Houston.
Opened: 1996. **Holes:** 18. **Par:** 72/72. **Yards:** 6,942/5,526. **Course rating:** 73.6/73.1. **Slope:** 130/134. **Architect:** Tom Knickerbocker and Charlie Epps. **Green fee:** $22/$30. **Credit cards:** MC,VISA,AMEX. **Reduced fees:** Weekdays, twilight, seniors, juniors. **Caddies:** No. **Golf carts:** $30. **Discount golf packages:** No. **Season:** Year-round. **High:** N/A. **On site lodging:** No. **Rental clubs:** Yes. **Walking policy:** Unrestricted walking. **Metal spikes allowed:** Yes. **Range:** Yes (grass/mats). **To obtain tee times:** Call up to 7 days in advance.
Subscriber comments: Very demanding off the tee...Could be great when course matures...Classic public course...Off the beaten path, really tough when windy...Tight fairways, expensive for muny course...Easy to lose lots of balls due to water.

★★★BAY FOREST GOLF COURSE
PU-201 Bay Forest Dr., LaPorte, 77571, Harris County, (281)471-4653, 20 miles SE of Houston.
Opened: 1988. **Holes:** 18. **Par:** 72/72. **Yards:** 6,756/5,094. **Course rating:** 72.4/69.0. **Slope:** 126/113. **Architect:** Riviere and Marr. **Green fee:** $12/$18. **Credit cards:** All major. **Reduced fees:** Twilight, seniors. **Caddies:** No. **Golf carts:** $18. **Discount golf packages:** No. **Season:** Year-round. **High:** April-Oct. **On site lodging:** No. **Rental clubs:** Yes. **Walking policy:** Unrestricted walking. **Metal spikes allowed:** Yes. **Range:** Yes (grass). **To obtain tee times:** Call Monday for the following 7 days.
Subscriber comments: Lots of water, tough when windy...Back nine gets a little boring...Tough but fair, very good value...Very long from greens to tees...Good variety in layout...Good all year long...Greens very average.

★★★BAYOU DIN GOLF CLUB
PU-8537 LaBelle Rd., Beaumont, 77705, Jefferson County, (409)796-1327, 85 miles E of Houston. **Green fee:** $11/$16.
Opened: 1959. **Holes:** 27. **Architect:** Jimmy Witcher. **Credit cards:** MC,VISA. **Reduced fees:** Twilight, seniors, juniors. **Caddies:** No. **Golf carts:** $8. **Discount golf packages:** No. **Season:** Year-round. **High:** March-Aug. **On site lodging:** No. **Rental**

clubs: Yes. **Walking policy:** Unrestricted walking. **Metal spikes allowed:** Yes. **Range:** Yes (grass/mats). **To obtain tee times:** Call golf shop.

BAYOU BACK/LINKS 9
Par: 71/71. **Yards:** 6,495/5,233. **Course rating:** 70.6/64.7. **Slope:** 118/105.

BAYOU FRONT/BAYOU BACK
Par: 71/71. **Yards:** 6,285/5,339. **Course rating:** 68.5/64.4. **Slope:** 108/98.

BAYOU FRONT/LINKS 9
Par: 72/72. **Yards:** 7,020/5,672. **Course rating:** 72.1/66.1. **Slope:** 116/103.

Subscriber comments: Like the new nine the best...The links nine is great...Short course, medium green speed...The new nine is the best in Beaumont...Links style, hit it far and watch it run...Only complaint, floods too easily, fun course.

★★½**BAYOU GOLF CLUB**
PU-2800 Ted Dudley Dr., Texas City, 77590, Galveston County, (409)643-5850, 30 miles SE of Houston.
Opened: 1974. **Holes:** 18. **Par:** 72/73. **Yards:** 6,665/5,448. **Course rating:** 71.0/73.0. **Slope:** 114/118. **Architect:** Joe Finger. **Green fee:** $10/$14. **Credit cards:** None. **Reduced fees:** Twilight, seniors. **Caddies:** No. **Golf carts:** $16. **Discount golf packages:** No. **Season:** Year-round. **High:** N/A. **On site lodging:** No. **Rental clubs:** Yes. **Walking policy:** Unrestricted walking. **Metal spikes allowed:** Yes. **Range:** Yes (grass). **To obtain tee times:** Call Wednesday for weekend times. Open play weekdays.
Subscriber comments: Good course, lots of water...Windy as hell, not a bad layout...If you like wind and water this is the place to play...Augusta greens...Wide open.

BEAR CREEK GOLF WORLD
PU-16001 Clay Rd., Houston, 77084, Harris County, (281)855-4720.
Green fee: $17/$56. **Credit cards:** MC,VISA,AMEX. **Reduced fees:** Weekdays, low season, twilight, seniors, juniors. **Caddies:** No. **Golf carts:** $11. **Discount golf packages:** No. **Season:** Year-round. **High:** April-Oct. **On site lodging:** No. **Rental clubs:** Yes. **Walking policy:** Walking at certain times. **Metal spikes allowed:** Yes. **Range:** Yes (grass). **To obtain tee times:** Call 3 days in advance. Members may call 14 days in advance.

★★**CHALLENGER COURSE**
Opened: 1968. **Holes:** 18. **Par:** 66/66. **Yards:** 5,295/4,432. **Course rating:** 64.2/64.7. **Slope:** 103/103. **Architect:** Bruce Littell.

★★★**MASTERS COURSE**
Opened: 1972. **Holes:** 18. **Par:** 72/72. **Yards:** 7,131/5,544. **Course rating:** 74.1/72.1. **Slope:** 133/125. **Architect:** Jay Riviere.
Notes: Ranked 14th in 1997 Best in State.
Subscriber comments: Played with Emmitt Smith...Front nine better than back nine...Traditional golf at its best, lots of sand...Needs a little attention...Fairly straightforward layout...Play sometimes slow due to volume...Great finishing hole...This one will test your patience and skills...Excellent for an urban layout...Resting on reputation...A real test from the tips...Slightly overrated but a solid course.

★★**PRESIDENTS COURSE**
Opened: 1968. **Holes:** 18. **Par:** 72/72. **Yards:** 6,562/5,728. **Course rating:** 69.1/70.6. **Slope:** 110/111. **Architect:** Jay Riviere.

★★½**BLACKHAWK GOLF CLUB**
PU-2714 Kelly Lane, Pflugerville, 78660, Travis County, (512)251-9000, 15 miles NE of Austin.
Opened: 1991. **Holes:** 18. **Par:** 72/72. **Yards:** 7,103/5,538. **Course rating:** 73.5/71.1. **Slope:** 123/121. **Architect:** Hollis Stacy and Charles Howard. **Green fee:** $21/$32. **Credit cards:** MC,VISA,AMEX. **Reduced fees:** Weekdays, low season, twilight, seniors, juniors. **Caddies:** No. **Golf carts:** $11. **Discount golf packages:** No. **Season:** Year-round. **High:** April-Sept. **On site lodging:** No. **Rental clubs:** Yes. **Walking policy:** Walking at certain times. **Metal spikes allowed:** Yes. **Range:** Yes (grass/mats). **To obtain tee times:** Call up to 5 days in advance.
Subscriber comments: Young course, open, will get better as it matures...Needs some trees...Always improving...Tough when it's windy—which is always.

★★BLUEBONNET COUNTRY GOLF COURSE

Rte. 2, Box 3471, Navasota, 77868, Grimes County, (409)894-2207.
Opened: 1972. **Holes:** 18. **Par:** 72/72. **Yards:** 6,495/5,159. **Course rating:** 71.0/70.4.
Slope: 129/129. **Architect:** Jay Riviere. **Green fee:** $5/$18. **Credit cards:** All major.
Reduced fees: Weekdays, twilight, seniors, juniors. **Caddies:** No. **Golf carts:** $18.
Discount golf packages: No. **Season:** Year-round. **High:** Spring/Fall. **On site lodging:**
No. **Rental clubs:** No. **Walking policy:** Walking at certain times. **Metal spikes
allowed:** Yes. **Range:** No. **To obtain tee times:** Call on Monday for upcoming week-
end. Call up to 7 days in advance for holiday.

★★½BLUEBONNET HILL GOLF CLUB

PU-9100 Decker Lane, Austin, 78724, Travis County, (512)272-4228.
Opened: 1991. **Holes:** 18. **Par:** 72/72. **Yards:** 6,503/5,241. **Course rating:** 70.0/68.2.
Slope: 113/107. **Architect:** Jeff Brauer. **Green fee:** $9/$19. **Credit cards:** MC,VISA.
Reduced fees: Weekdays, twilight, seniors, juniors. **Caddies:** No. **Golf carts:** $17.
Discount golf packages: Yes. **Season:** Year-round. **High:** March-Aug. **On site lodging:** No. **Rental clubs:** Yes. **Walking policy:** Unrestricted walking. **Metal spikes
allowed:** Yes. **Range:** Yes (grass). **To obtain tee times:** Call 5 days in advance for
weekdays. Call on Thursday at 7:30 a.m. for upcoming weekend.
Subscriber comments: Short but enjoyable, good greens...Has some interesting
holes...Public golf as it was meant to be...A bit of a links course...Wind makes the
course feel longer...Just hard enough to be interesting.

★★½BRACKENRIDGE PARK MUNICIPAL GOLF COURSE

PU-2315 Ave. B, San Antonio, 78215, Bexar County, (210)226-5612.
Opened: 1922. **Holes:** 18. **Par:** 72/72. **Yards:** 6,185/5,216. **Course rating:** 67.0/69.2.
Slope: 122/112. **Architect:** A.W. Tillinghast. **Green fee:** $11/$16. **Credit cards:**
MC,VISA. **Reduced fees:** Weekdays, low season, twilight, seniors, juniors. **Caddies:**
No. **Golf carts:** $15. **Discount golf packages:** Yes. **Season:** Year-round. **High:** March-
Nov. **On site lodging:** No. **Rental clubs:** Yes. **Walking policy:** Unrestricted walking.
Metal spikes allowed: Yes. **Range:** No. **To obtain tee times:** Call golf shop.
Notes: 1923-65 Texas Open.
Subscriber comments: Makes you want to move to Texas...Historic course allowed to
run down...Big trees on front nine, open back nine.

★★½BRIARWOOD GOLF CLUB

4511 Briarwood Dr., Tyler, 75709, Smith County, (903)593-7741, 84 miles SE of Dallas.
Opened: 1955. **Holes:** 18. **Par:** 71/71. **Yards:** 6,512/4,735. **Course rating:** 70.6/66.1.
Slope: 118/111. **Architect:** N/A. **Green fee:** $19/$27. **Credit cards:** MC,VISA.
Reduced fees: N/A. **Caddies:** No. **Golf carts:** $10. **Discount golf packages:** No.
Season: Year-round. **High:** May-June. **On site lodging:** No. **Rental clubs:** Yes.
Walking policy: Unrestricted walking. **Metal spikes allowed:** Yes. **Range:** Yes (grass).
To obtain tee times: Call golf shop.
Subscriber comments: Very fun layout...Greens are slick...Long course, nice set-
ting...Good course from back tees, others just average...Interesting par 3s.

★★★½BRIDLEWOOD GOLF CLUB

PU-4000 West Windsor, Flower Mound, 75028, Tarrant County,
(972)355-4800, 20 miles NW of Dallas.
Opened: 1997. **Holes:** 18. **Par:** 72/72. **Yards:** 7,036/5,278. **Course rating:** 73.6/70.7. **Slope:** 130/120. **Architect:** D.A. Weibring. **Green fee:**
$55/$65. **Credit cards:** All major. **Reduced fees:** Weekdays, low sea-
son, twilight, seniors, juniors. **Caddies:** No. **Golf carts:** Included in Green Fee.
Discount golf packages: No. **Season:** Year-round. **High:** N/A. **On site lodging:** No.
Rental clubs: No. **Walking policy:** Unrestricted walking. **Metal spikes allowed:** No.
Range: Yes (grass). **To obtain tee times:** Call up to 6 days in advance.
Subscriber comments: New, will improve with age...Best new course in North
Texas...Generous fairways and greens.

★★½BROCK PARK GOLF COURSE
PM-8201 John Ralston Rd., Houston, 77044, Harris County, (281)458-1350.
Opened: 1952. **Holes:** 18. **Par:** 72/74. **Yards:** 6,487/5,650. **Course rating:** 70.7.
Slope: 114. **Architect:** A.C. Ray. **Green fee:** $3/$11. **Credit cards:** None. **Reduced fees:** Weekdays, twilight. **Caddies:** No. **Golf carts:** $17. **Discount golf packages:** No.
Season: Year-round. **High:** N/A. **On site lodging:** No. **Rental clubs:** Yes. **Walking policy:** Unrestricted walking. **Metal spikes allowed:** Yes. **Range:** Yes (grass). **To obtain tee times:** Call on Wednesday starting at 6:35 for upcoming weekend. First come, first served weekdays.
Subscriber comments: Good layout, position course...Good winter course, fairways hard in summer...Plain golf...Better greens would make it great...Favorite muny course.

★★BROWNSVILLE COUNTRY CLUB
PM-1800 W. San Marcelo, Brownsville, 78521, Cameron County, (956)541-2582.
Opened: 1972. **Holes:** 18. **Par:** 70/70. **Yards:** 6,066/4,846. **Course rating:** 69.5/65.5.
Slope: 107/113. **Architect:** Don Sechrest. **Green fee:** $4/$8. **Credit cards:** None.
Reduced fees: N/A. **Caddies:** No. **Golf carts:** $7. **Discount golf packages:** No.
Season: Year-round. **High:** Dec.-April. **On site lodging:** No. **Rental clubs:** No.
Walking policy: Unrestricted walking. **Metal spikes allowed:** Yes. **Range:** No. **To obtain tee times:** Call.

★½BRYAN GOLF COURSE
PU-206 W. Villa Maria, Bryan, 77801, Brazos County, (409)823-0126, 84 miles NW of Houston.
Opened: 1925. **Holes:** 18. **Par:** 70/70. **Yards:** 6,280/4,576. **Course rating:** 69.7/65.5.
Slope: 110/103. **Architect:** Fred Marbury. **Green fee:** $10/$13. **Credit cards:** MC,VISA,AMEX. **Reduced fees:** Weekdays, low season, twilight, seniors, juniors.
Caddies: No. **Golf carts:** $8. **Discount golf packages:** No. **Season:** Year-round. **High:** April-Aug. **On site lodging:** No. **Rental clubs:** Yes. **Walking policy:** Unrestricted walking. **Metal spikes allowed:** Yes. **Range:** No. **To obtain tee times:** Call.

★★★★BUFFALO CREEK GOLF CLUB
PU-624 Country Club Dr., Rockwall, 75087, Rockwall County, (972)771-4003, 15 miles E of Dallas.
Opened: 1992. **Holes:** 18. **Par:** 71/71. **Yards:** 7,012/5,209. **Course rating:** 73.8/67.0.
Slope: 135/113. **Architect:** Weiskopf and Morrish. **Green fee:** $40/$75. **Credit cards:** MC,VISA,AMEX. **Reduced fees:** Weekdays, low season, twilight, seniors, juniors.
Caddies: No. **Golf carts:** Included in Green Fee. **Discount golf packages:** Yes.
Season: Year-round. **High:** April-Oct. **On site lodging:** No. **Rental clubs:** Yes. **Walking policy:** Unrestricted walking. **Metal spikes allowed:** No. **Range:** Yes (grass). **To obtain tee times:** Call 5 days in advance.
Subscriber comments: Terrific experience in daily fee golf...Great layout, top five public in Texas...Very fast greens...Each set of tees presents different challenges...Could do without computer in cart...Links style course with trees...Every hole different...Monster in the wind...Toughest course ever played...Lots of terrain for North Texas...One of my favorite courses in the Dallas area.

★★½CANYON LAKE GOLF & COUNTRY CLUB
405 Watts Ln, Canyon Lake, 78133, Comal County, (830)899-3372, 25 miles N of San Antonio.
Opened: 1980. **Holes:** 18. **Par:** 72/72. **Yards:** 6,168/4,726. **Course rating:** 70.1/68.1.
Slope: 122/119. **Architect:** N/A. **Green fee:** $26/$32. **Credit cards:** All major.
Reduced fees: Weekdays, resort guests, twilight, seniors, juniors. **Caddies:** No. **Golf carts:** Included in Green Fee. **Discount golf packages:** No. **Season:** Year-round.
High: Nov.-May. **On site lodging:** No. **Rental clubs:** Yes. **Walking policy:** Unrestricted walking. **Metal spikes allowed:** No. **Range:** Yes (grass). **To obtain tee times:** Call up to 7 days in advance.
Subscriber comments: Beautiful scenery, deer everywhere...Unexpected pleasure...Short, but interesting...Nice Texas Hill Country scenery.

★★★CAPE ROYALE GOLF COURSE
Lake Livingstone, Coldspring, 77331, San Jacinto County, (409)653-2388.
Architect: Bruce Littell. **Caddies:** No. **Discount golf packages:** No. **On site lodging:** No. **Rental clubs:** No. **Metal spikes allowed:** Yes. **Range:** No.
Call club for further information.
Subscriber comments: Toughest greens in the state, my favorite...Premium on good shotmaking...Beautiful scenery...Hilly, north of Houston, great change...Funky...Great view of adjoining lake...Short course but fast tricky greens.

★½CASA BLANCA GOLF COURSE
PU-3900 Casa Blanca, Laredo, 78041, Webb County, (956)791-7262.
Opened: 1922. **Holes:** 18. **Par:** 72/72. **Yards:** 6,390/5,631. **Course rating:** 71.0/68.9. **Slope:** 115/115. **Architect:** Carter Morrish and Roy Becthol. **Green fee:** $8/$10. **Credit cards:** All major. **Reduced fees:** Weekdays, seniors, juniors. **Caddies:** No. **Golf carts:** $14. **Discount golf packages:** Yes. **Season:** Year-round. **High:** Feb.-Oct. **On site lodging:** No. **Rental clubs:** Yes. **Walking policy:** Unrestricted walking. **Metal spikes allowed:** Yes. **Range:** Yes (grass). **To obtain tee times:** Call on Wednesday for upcoming weekend.

★★★★CEDAR CREEK GOLF COURSE
PU-8250 Vista Colina, San Antonio, 78255, Bexar County, (210)695-5050.
Opened: 1989. **Holes:** 18. **Par:** 72/72. **Yards:** 7,103/5,535. **Course rating:** 73.4/70.8. **Slope:** 132/113. **Architect:** Finger, Dye and Spann. **Green fee:** $30/$44. **Credit cards:** All major. **Reduced fees:** Weekdays, low season, twilight, seniors, juniors. **Caddies:** No. **Golf carts:** Included in Green Fee. **Discount golf packages:** No. **Season:** Year-round. **High:** Year-round. **On site lodging:** No. **Rental clubs:** Yes. **Walking policy:** Unrestricted walking. **Metal spikes allowed:** Yes. **Range:** Yes (grass/mats). **To obtain tee times:** Call golf shop.
Subscriber comments: One of best in Texas, need all shots...Lots of elevated tee boxes and greens...You'd better play this one if visiting San Antonio...Most beautiful public course I've ever seen...100-foot drop off first tee, many hills...Unique setting in ravines in Texas Hill Country...Be straight.

GOOD VALUE

★★★CEDAR CREST GOLF COURSE
PU-1800 Southerland, Dallas, 75223, Dallas County, (214)670-7615.
Opened: 1923. **Holes:** 18. **Par:** 71/75. **Yards:** 6,550/5,594. **Course rating:** 71.0/76.0. **Slope:** 121/116. **Architect:** A.W. Tillinghast. **Green fee:** $11/$14. **Credit cards:** All major. **Reduced fees:** Twilight, seniors, juniors. **Caddies:** Yes. **Golf carts:** $18. **Discount golf packages:** No. **Season:** Year-round. **High:** April-Sept. **On site lodging:** No. **Rental clubs:** Yes. **Walking policy:** Unrestricted walking. **Metal spikes allowed:** Yes. **Range:** Yes (grass). **To obtain tee times:** Call two days in advance.
Subscriber comments: A "classique," small greens, tough but fair....Great old layout...Fairways very hard...Small bowled greens...Dallas' best old course, 600-yard 1st hole quite a start, five long par 3s.

★★THE CEDARS ON BERGSTROM
PU-Bldg 3711, Old Bergstrom AFB, Austin, 78753, Travis County, (512)385-4653, 10 miles SE of Austin.
Opened: 1954. **Holes:** 18. **Par:** 71/72. **Yards:** 6,576/5,300. **Course rating:** 69.5/70.5. **Slope:** 115/116. **Architect:** Curly Tice. **Green fee:** $10/$13. **Credit cards:** MC,VISA,AMEX. **Reduced fees:** Weekdays, twilight, seniors, juniors. **Caddies:** No. **Golf carts:** $8. **Discount golf packages:** No. **Season:** Year-round. **High:** May-Oct. **On site lodging:** No. **Rental clubs:** Yes. **Walking policy:** Unrestricted walking. **Metal spikes allowed:** Yes. **Range:** Yes (grass). **To obtain tee times:** Call up to 7 days in advance.

★★½CHAMBERS COUNTY GOLF COURSE
PU-1 Pinchback Dr., Anahuac, 77514, Chambers County, (409)267-8235, 43 miles W of Beaumont.
Opened: 1975. **Holes:** 18. **Par:** 72/73. **Yards:** 6,909/5,014. **Course rating:** 71.5/67.5. **Slope:** 116/106. **Architect:** Leon Howard/R.T. Pinch. **Green fee:** $9/$11. **Credit cards:**

MC,VISA,AMEX,DISC,Pulse Pay. **Reduced fees:** Weekdays, twilight. **Caddies:** No. **Golf carts:** $7. **Discount golf packages:** No. **Season:** Year-round. **High:** June-Aug. **On site lodging:** No. **Rental clubs:** Yes. **Walking policy:** Unrestricted walking. **Metal spikes allowed:** Yes. **Range:** Yes (grass/mats). **To obtain tee times:** Call golf shop Thursday 7 a.m.
Subscriber comments: Neat course, hard to finish...Challenging from the back tees...Add 40 bunkers, then call me...Greens have tough reads...Water strategically located...Lots of trees, tight fairways.

★★★½CHASE OAKS GOLF CLUB
PU-7201 Chase Oaks Blvd., Plano, 75025, Collin County, (972)517-7777.
Opened: 1986. **Holes:** 18. **Par:** 72/72. **Yards:** 6,762/5,105. **Course rating:** 74.4/70.0. **Slope:** 139/128. **Architect:** Von Hagge and Devlin. **Green fee:** $37/$47. **Credit cards:** MC,VISA,AMEX,DISC,Diners Club. **Reduced fees:** Weekdays, low season, twilight, seniors, juniors. **Caddies:** No. **Golf carts:** $12. **Discount golf packages:** No. **Season:** Year-round. **High:** April-Nov. **On site lodging:** No. **Rental clubs:** Yes. **Walking policy:** Walking at certain times. **Metal spikes allowed:** Yes. **Range:** Yes (grass/mats). **To obtain tee times:** Call 3 days in advance at 8 a.m.
Subscriber comments: Very challenging and tight...Requires knowledge of course for each shot...Very tricky, almost unfair for average golfer...Must bring "A" driving game...Toughest in the Metroplex...Too easy from the whites.
Special Notes: Also has 9-hole course.

★★CHEROKEE COUNTRY CLUB
Henderson Highway, Jacksonville, 75766, Cherokee County, (903)586-2141.
Call club for further information.

★★½CHESTER W. DITTO GOLF CLUB
PM-801 Brown Blvd., Arlington, 76011, Tarrant County, (817)275-5941.
Opened: 1982. **Holes:** 18. **Par:** 72/72. **Yards:** 6,727/5,555. **Course rating:** 70.8/71.2. **Slope:** 117/116. **Architect:** Killian and Nugent. **Green fee:** $10/$12. **Credit cards:** MC,VISA,DISC. **Reduced fees:** Weekdays, twilight, seniors, juniors. **Caddies:** No. **Golf carts:** $8. **Discount golf packages:** No. **Season:** Year-round. **High:** April-Sept. **On site lodging:** No. **Rental clubs:** Yes. **Walking policy:** Unrestricted walking. **Metal spikes allowed:** Yes. **Range:** Yes (grass). **To obtain tee times:** Call Tuesday at 6 a.m. for Wednesday through the next Tuesday.
Subscriber comments: Typical muny...Always crowded...Tight back nine...Lots of hard pars...Unique few holes...Good mix of holes to challenge all levels of golfers.

★★★CIELO VISTA GOLF COURSE
PU-1510 Hawkins, El Paso, 79925, El Paso County, (915)591-4927.
Opened: 1977. **Holes:** 18. **Par:** 71/71. **Yards:** 6,411/5,421. **Course rating:** 69.4/69.4. **Slope:** 122/113. **Architect:** Marvin Ferguson. **Green fee:** $14/$18. **Credit cards:** MC,VISA. **Reduced fees:** Weekdays, twilight. **Caddies:** No. **Golf carts:** $16. **Discount golf packages:** Yes. **Season:** Year-round. **High:** April-Oct. **On site lodging:** No. **Rental clubs:** Yes. **Walking policy:** Unrestricted walking. **Metal spikes allowed:** Yes. **Range:** Yes (grass/mats). **To obtain tee times:** Call on Tuesday at 7 a.m. for upcoming week-end.
Subscriber comments: Great small course...Fun to play, great for seniors...Gives you your money's worth...Winter grass allows good playability in winter...Very tight fairways.

★★★½CIRCLE C GOLF CLUB
PU-7401 Hwy. 45, Austin, 78739, Travis County, (512)288-4297.
Opened: 1992. **Holes:** 18. **Par:** 72/72. **Yards:** 6,859/5,236. **Course rating:** 72.7/69.9. **Slope:** 122/120. **Architect:** Jay Morrish. **Green fee:** $29/$51. **Credit cards:** MC,VISA,AMEX. **Reduced fees:** Weekdays, low season, twilight, juniors. **Caddies:** No. **Golf carts:** Included in Green Fee. **Discount golf packages:** Yes. **Season:** Year-round. **High:** Spring/Fall. **On site lodging:** No. **Rental clubs:** Yes. **Walking policy:** Walking at certain times. **Metal spikes allowed:** Yes. **Range:** Yes (grass). **To obtain tee times:** Call 10 days in advance, or further in advance for groups of 12 or more.
Subscriber comments: The best hidden treasure in Austin...Fun, not too difficult...Good greens...Good pace...One of the best courses in Hill Country including private clubs...Tight, lots of rocks, miss a fairway—bad news.

★★½CLEAR LAKE GOLF CLUB
PU-1202 Reseda Dr., Houston, 77062, Harris County, (281)488-0252, 15 miles S of Houston.
Opened: 1964. **Holes:** 18. **Par:** 72/72. **Yards:** 6,757/5,924. **Course rating:** 71.7/71.1. **Slope:** 113/111. **Architect:** George Fazio. **Green fee:** $18/$34. **Credit cards:** All major. **Reduced fees:** Twilight. **Caddies:** No. **Golf carts:** Included in Green Fee. **Discount golf packages:** No. **Season:** Year-round. **High:** N/A. **On site lodging:** No. **Rental clubs:** No. **Walking policy:** Walking at certain times. **Metal spikes allowed:** Yes. **Range:** Yes (grass). **To obtain tee times:** Call up to 7 days in advance.
Subscriber comments: Faux links style, very playable...Good length with small greens...Same hole over and over...Open, fun to play, good mature trees.

★★CLEBURNE MUNI GOLF COURSE
Country Club Rd., Cleburne, 76031, Johnson County, (817)641-4501.
Call club for further information.

★★★★THE CLIFFS GOLF CLUB
R-Star Rte. Box 19, Graford, 76449, Palo Pinto County, (940)779-3926, (888)843-2543, 75 miles NW of Fort Worth.
Opened: 1988. **Holes:** 18. **Par:** 71/71. **Yards:** 6,808/4,876. **Course rating:** 73.9/68.4. **Slope:** 143/124. **Architect:** Bruce Devlin and Robert von Hagge. **Green fee:** $42/$65. **Credit cards:** All major. **Reduced fees:** Weekdays, low season, twilight, seniors, juniors. **Caddies:** No. **Golf carts:** Included in Green Fee. **Discount golf packages:** Yes. **Season:** Year-round. **High:** April-Sept. **On site lodging:** Yes. **Rental clubs:** Yes. **Walking policy:** Mandatory cart. **Metal spikes allowed:** Yes. **Range:** Yes (grass). **To obtain tee times:** Call 7 days in advance.
Subscriber comments: Hardest course I've ever played...Poor layout for retirement area, too many long carries...Well worth the drive...Beautiful but not designed for average golfer...Four-sleeve course...Too many blind views...Gimmicky course...Spectacular view from 9th hole...Unusual lakeview holes.

★★½THE CLUB AT RUNAWAY BAY
400 Half Moon Way, Runaway Bay, 76426, Wise County, (940)575-2228, 45 miles NW of Fort Worth.
Opened: 1968. **Holes:** 18. **Par:** 71/71. **Yards:** 6,650/5,197. **Course rating:** 70.9/68.2. **Slope:** 116/108. **Architect:** Leon Howard. **Green fee:** $20/$40. **Credit cards:** MC,VISA,DISC. **Reduced fees:** Low season, resort guests, twilight, juniors. **Caddies:** No. **Golf carts:** $10. **Discount golf packages:** Yes. **Season:** Year-round. **High:** April-June/Oct. **On site lodging:** No. **Rental clubs:** Yes. **Walking policy:** Walking at certain times. **Metal spikes allowed:** No. **Range:** Yes (grass/mats). **To obtain tee times:** Call up to seven days in advance.
Subscriber comments: Should improve when new greens mature...Great layout.

★★★½COLUMBIA LAKES
R-188 Freeman Blvd., West Columbia, 77486, Brazoria County, (409)345-5455, (800)231-1030, 50 miles SE of Houston.
Opened: 1972. **Holes:** 18. **Par:** 72/72. **Yards:** 6,967/5,280. **Course rating:** 75.7/71.7. **Slope:** 131/122. **Architect:** Jack Miller/Tom Fazio. **Green fee:** $50/$65. **Credit cards:** MC,VISA,AMEX,DISC,Diners Club. **Reduced fees:** Weekdays, low season, resort guests. **Caddies:** No. **Golf carts:** Included in Green Fee. **Discount golf packages:** Yes. **Season:** Year-round. **High:** April-June. **On site lodging:** Yes. **Rental clubs:** Yes. **Walking policy:** Unrestricted walking. **Metal spikes allowed:** Yes. **Range:** Yes (grass/mats). **To obtain tee times:** Call.
Subscriber comments: Good course to practice shot strategy...Plenty of water and well laid out...Tight driving...OB too close...Stay out of bunkers...Terrific layout, great greens, dries slowly when it rains...5th hole is a slicer's nightmare.

★★½COMANCHE TRAIL GOLF CLUB
PM-4200 S. Grand, Amarillo, 79103, Randall County, (806)378-4281.
Opened: 1990. **Holes:** 18. **Par:** 72/72. **Yards:** 7,180/5,524. **Course rating:** 72.9/70.0. **Slope:** 117/108. **Architect:** Charles Howard. **Green fee:** $9/$11. **Credit cards:** None. **Reduced fees:** Twilight, seniors, juniors. **Caddies:** No. **Golf carts:** $18. **Discount golf**

packages: No. **Season:** Year-round. **High:** March-Sept. **On site lodging:** No. **Rental clubs:** Yes. **Walking policy:** Unrestricted walking. **Metal spikes allowed:** Yes. **Range:** Yes (grass). **To obtain tee times:** Call on Thursday morning at 7:00 a.m. for upcoming weekend. Call 1 day in advance for weekdays.
Subscriber comments: Wide open, windy, fair layout...Bad rough, otherwise fair...Good layout, drainage problems...Will get better with age.

★★COMANCHE TRAIL GOLF CLUB
800 Comanche Park Rd., Big Spring, 79720, Howard County, (915)264-2366.
Opened: 1934. **Holes:** 18. **Par:** 71/72. **Yards:** 6,327/5,098. **Course rating:** 68.9/66.1.
Slope: 113/98. **Architect:** William Cantrell. **Green fee:** $9/$14. **Credit cards:** All major.
Reduced fees: Seniors, juniors. **Caddies:** No. **Golf carts:** $17. **Discount golf packages:** No. **Season:** Year-round. **High:** March-Nov. **On site lodging:** No. **Rental clubs:** No. **Walking policy:** Unrestricted walking. **Metal spikes allowed:** Yes. **Range:** No. **To obtain tee times:** Call on Wednesday for upcoming weekend. Walk-ins welcome weekdays.

★★½CONNALLY GOLF COURSE
PU-7900 Concord Rd., Waco, 76705, McLennan County, (254)799-6561.
Opened: 1959. **Holes:** 18. **Par:** 72/73. **Yards:** 6,975/5,950. **Course rating:** 72.5/73.8.
Slope: 116/120. **Architect:** Ralph Plummer. **Green fee:** $8/$12. **Credit cards:** MC,VISA. **Reduced fees:** Twilight, seniors, juniors. **Caddies:** No. **Golf carts:** $10.
Discount golf packages: No. **Season:** Year-round. **High:** April-Sept. **On site lodging:** No. **Rental clubs:** Yes. **Walking policy:** Unrestricted walking. **Metal spikes allowed:** Yes. **Range:** Yes (grass/mats). **To obtain tee times:** Call 7 days in advance for weekends and holidays only.
Subscriber comments: Really enjoy it, especially the back nine...Back nine has more character...Course has water problem after rain...Greens are top notch...Few bunkers.

★★½COTTONWOOD CREEK GOLF COURSE
PU-5200 Bagby Dr., Waco, 76711, McLennan County, (254)752-2474.
Opened: 1983. **Holes:** 18. **Par:** 72/72. **Yards:** 7,123/5,724. **Course rating:** 73.3/71.9.
Slope: 129/120. **Architect:** Joe Finger. **Green fee:** $9/$12. **Credit cards:** MC,VISA.
Reduced fees: Weekdays, low season, seniors, juniors. **Caddies:** No. **Golf carts:** $8.
Discount golf packages: No. **Season:** Year-round. **High:** March-Oct. **On site lodging:** No. **Rental clubs:** Yes. **Walking policy:** Unrestricted walking. **Metal spikes allowed:** Yes. **Range:** Yes (grass). **To obtain tee times:** Call three to five days in advance.
Subscriber comments: Enjoy the course very much...More difficult than it looks...Could be super course...New greens; they need to let the rough grow out...Long windy course...Needs work, getting better.

★★COUNTRY VIEW GOLF CLUB
PU-240 W. Beltline Rd., Lancaster, 75146, Dallas County, (972)227-0995.
Opened: 1989. **Holes:** 18. **Par:** 71/71. **Yards:** 6,609/5,048. **Course rating:** 71.0/68.2.
Slope: 120/114. **Architect:** Ron Garl. **Green fee:** $12/$17. **Credit cards:** MC,VISA,DISC. **Reduced fees:** Low season, twilight, seniors, juniors. **Caddies:** No.
Golf carts: $20. **Discount golf packages:** No. **Season:** Year-round. **High:** April-Oct.
On site lodging: No. **Rental clubs:** Yes. **Walking policy:** Unrestricted walking. **Metal spikes allowed:** Yes. **Range:** Yes (grass). **To obtain tee times:** Call three days prior to play.

★★★CREEKVIEW GOLF CLUB
PU-1602 E. Hwy. 175, Crandall, 75114, Kaufman County, (972)427-3811, 25 miles SE of Dallas.
Opened: 1995. **Holes:** 18. **Par:** 72/72. **Yards:** 7,238/5,459. **Course rating:** 74.1/71.2.
Slope: 119/115. **Architect:** Dick Phelps. **Green fee:** $31/$43. **Credit cards:** All major.
Reduced fees: N/A. **Caddies:** No. **Golf carts:** Included in Green Fee. **Discount golf packages:** No. **Season:** Year-round. **High:** Spring/Fall. **On site lodging:** No. **Rental clubs:** Yes. **Walking policy:** Unrestricted walking. **Metal spikes allowed:** Yes. **Range:** Yes. **To obtain tee times:** Call up to 7 days in advance for weekdays. Call on Wednesday for upcoming weekend.
Subscriber comments: Bent-grass greens are best in this area...Fun and challenging course, thought-provoking...Par 3s too long...Enjoyable new public fee layout.

★CROSS CREEK GOLF CLUB
800 Bellwood Golf Rd., Tyler, 75709, Smith County, (903)597-4871.
Call club for further information.

★★★½CROSS TIMBERS GOLF COURSE
PU-1181 S. Stewart, Azle, 76020, Polker County, (817)444-4940, 14 miles NW of Fort Worth.
Opened: 1995. **Holes:** 18. **Par:** 72/72. **Yards:** 6,734/5,051. **Course rating:** 71.5/68.2.
Slope: 128/113. **Architect:** Jeff Brauer. **Green fee:** $18/$22. **Credit cards:** MC,VISA,AMEX. **Reduced fees:** Weekdays, twilight, seniors, juniors. **Caddies:** No. **Golf carts:** $10. **Discount golf packages:** No. **Season:** Year-round. **High:** March-Oct. **On site lodging:** No. **Rental clubs:** Yes. **Walking policy:** Unrestricted walking. **Metal spikes allowed:** Yes. **Range:** Yes (grass). **To obtain tee times:** Call 3 days prior to play.
Subscriber comments: Great new course...Needs to mature...Requires thought to play...Mean starting holes, excellent greens...Windy, windy, windy...Must score on front nine...Good course but 1st hole is too difficult to start...Tight.

★★CRYSTAL FALLS GOLF COURSE
PU-3400 Crystal Falls Pkwy., Leander, 78641, Travis County, (512)259-5855, 14 miles N of Austin.
Opened: 1990. **Holes:** 18. **Par:** 72/72. **Yards:** 6,654/5,194. **Course rating:** 72.3/70.0.
Slope: 126/123. **Architect:** Charles Howard and Jack Miller. **Green fee:** $18/$25.
Credit cards: MC,VISA. **Reduced fees:** Weekdays, low season, twilight, juniors. **Caddies:** No. **Golf carts:** $8. **Discount golf packages:** Yes. **Season:** Year-round. **High:** April-Oct. **On site lodging:** No. **Rental clubs:** Yes. **Walking policy:** Unrestricted walking. **Metal spikes allowed:** Yes. **Range:** Yes (grass). **To obtain tee times:** Call three days in advance.

CYPRESSWOOD GOLF CLUB
PU-21602 Cypresswood Dr., Spring, 77373, Harris County, (281)821-6300.
Architect: Rick Forester. **Green fee:** $31/$38. **Credit cards:** MC,VISA,AMEX.
Reduced fees: Weekdays, twilight, seniors, juniors. **Caddies:** No. **Golf carts:** $24.
Discount golf packages: No. **Season:** Year-round. **High:** March-Oct. **On site lodging:** No. **Rental clubs:** Yes. **Walking policy:** Unrestricted walking. **Metal spikes allowed:** Yes. **Range:** Yes (grass/mats). **To obtain tee times:** Call up to 3 days in advance.
★★★½CREEK COURSE
Opened: 1988. **Holes:** 18. **Par:** 72/72. **Yards:** 6,937/5,549. **Course rating:** 72.0/69.1.
Slope: 124/113.
Subscriber comments: Each hole isolated...Excellent greens...Both courses very good...Tighter than Cypress course...Lots of pine trees...Very challenging course...Beautiful layout...Great scenery, worth the trip.
★★★½CYPRESS COURSE
Opened: 1987. **Holes:** 18. **Par:** 72/72. **Yards:** 6,906/5,599. **Course rating:** 71.8/67.6.
Slope: 123/111.
Subscriber comments: Better maintained than Creek Course...You need to play it...Picturesque...Both courses are excellent, fair layouts...Good shot values...Outstanding terrain...Course demands precise drives.

★★★DEL LAGO GOLF RESORT
R-600 La Costa Blvd., Montgomery, 77356-5349, Montgomery County, (409)582-6100, (800)335-2446, 50 miles N of Houston.
Opened: 1985. **Holes:** 18. **Par:** 72/72. **Yards:** 7,007/5,854. **Course rating:** 72.6/71.7.
Slope: 131/122. **Architect:** Dave Marr and Jay Riviere. **Green fee:** $50/$65. **Credit cards:** All major. **Reduced fees:** Weekdays, resort guests, twilight, seniors, juniors.
Caddies: No. **Golf carts:** Included in Green Fee. **Discount golf packages:** Yes.
Season: Year-round. **High:** May-Oct. **On site lodging:** Yes. **Rental clubs:** Yes. **Walking policy:** Walking at certain times. **Metal spikes allowed:** Yes. **Range:** Yes (grass/mats).
To obtain tee times: Call.
Subscriber comments: Very nice track...Long, challenging layout, but needs more money on greens and fairways...Beautiful course on Lake Conroe...No short par 4s...I drive 144 miles to play this course...Difficult but fair...A whole lot of fun.

★★★½DELAWARE SPRINGS GOLF COURSE
PU-Hwy. 281 S., Burnet, 78611, Burnet County, (512)756-8951, 50 miles NW of Austin.
Opened: 1992. **Holes:** 18. **Par:** 72/71. **Yards:** 6,819/5,770. **Course rating:** 72.0/66.5.
Slope: 121/107. **Architect:** Dave Axland and Don Proctor. **Green fee:** $15/$25. **Credit cards:** All major. **Reduced fees:** Twilight, seniors, juniors. **Caddies:** No. **Golf carts:** $9.
Discount golf packages: No. **Season:** Year-round. **High:** March-Sept. **On site lodging:** No. **Rental clubs:** Yes. **Walking policy:** Walking at certain times. **Metal spikes allowed:** Yes. **Range:** Yes (grass/mats). **To obtain tee times:** Call up to 14 days in advance.
Subscriber comments: A gem in the Hill Country, a lot of character...I enjoyed it completely...Would love to play every day...Multiple tees allows you to to pick your own poison...Tight course with good bunkering...Minimalist architecture makes it great fun.

★★½DEVINE GOLF COURSE
PU-116 Malone Dr., Devine, 78016, Medina County, (830)665-9943.
Architect: Built by members. **Caddies:** No. **Discount golf packages:** No. **On site lodging:** No. **Rental clubs:** No. **Metal spikes allowed:** Yes. **Range:** No.
Call club for further information.
Subscriber comments: Two different nines, fun course...Some holes are laid out funny...Like playing two different courses.

★★½ECHO CREEK COUNTRY CLUB
FM 317, Athens, 75778, Henderson County, (903)852-7094, 22 miles SW of Tyler.
Opened: 1989. **Holes:** 18. **Par:** 71/73. **Yards:** 6,200/5,000. **Course rating:** 69.2/69.2.
Slope: 120/118. **Architect:** Rusty Lambert. **Green fee:** $12/$18. **Credit cards:** None.
Reduced fees: Resort guests, seniors. **Caddies:** No. **Golf carts:** $18. **Discount golf packages:** No. **Season:** Year-round. **High:** March-Aug. **On site lodging:** No. **Rental clubs:** Yes. **Walking policy:** Unrestricted walking. **Metal spikes allowed:** Yes. **Range:** Yes (grass). **To obtain tee times:** Call golf shop.
Subscriber comments: Nice challange...Hidden gem with small town...Very good par 5s, water, elevated greens...Very good layout.

★½ELM GROVE GOLF COURSE
PU-3202 Milwaukee, Lubbock, 79407, Lubbock County, 806-799-7801.
Opened: N/A. **Holes:** 18. **Par:** 71/72. **Yards:** 6,401/5,480. **Course rating:** N/A. **Slope:** N/A. **Architect:** N/A. **Green fee:** $8/$13. **Credit cards:** All major. **Reduced fees:** Twilight, seniors, juniors. **Caddies:** No. **Golf carts:** $9. **Discount golf packages:** No.
Season: Year-round. **High:** N/A. **On site lodging:** No. **Rental clubs:** Yes. **Walking policy:** Unrestricted walking. **Metal spikes allowed:** Yes. **Range:** Yes (grass/mats). **To obtain tee times:** Call up to 3 days in advance.
Special Notes: Spikeless shoes preferred.

★★★★EVERGREEN POINT GOLF CLUB
PU-1530 Evergreen Point Rd., Baytown, 77520, Harris County,
(281)837-9000, 20 miles SE of Houston.
Opened: 1996. **Holes:** 18. **Par:** 72/72. **Yards:** 7,000/5,298. **Course rating:** 73.0/72.2. **Slope:** 129/130. **Architect:** Jay Riviere and Dave Marr. **Green fee:** $20/$27. **Credit cards:** All major. **Reduced fees:** Twilight, seniors, juniors. **Caddies:** No. **Golf carts:** $18. **Discount golf packages:** No.
Season: Year-round. **High:** June-Nov. **On site lodging:** No. **Rental clubs:** Yes.
Walking policy: Unrestricted walking. **Metal spikes allowed:** Yes. **Range:** Yes (grass).
To obtain tee times: Call up to 7 days in advance.
Subscriber comments: Will be one of best in Houston area...Outstanding new layout that will improve with time...No tricks, just golf (and a lot of it from the back)...Tight, fair and very scenic...Heavily wooded...The driving range is the finest I've seen, a major addition for golfers of southeast Texas.

(GOOD VALUE)

★★★★THE FALLS RESORT & COUNTRY CLUB
1001 N. Falls Dr., New Ulm, 78950, Colorado County, (409)992-3123, 60 miles W of Houston.
Opened: 1985. **Holes:** 18. **Par:** 72/73. **Yards:** 6,757/5,326. **Course rating:** 72.3/70.0.
Slope: 135/125. **Architect:** Jay Riviere and Dave Marr. **Green fee:** $47/$62. **Credit**

cards: MC,VISA,AMEX. **Reduced fees:** Weekdays, resort guests. **Caddies:** No. **Golf carts:** Included in Green Fee. **Discount golf packages:** No. **Season:** Year-round. **High:** March-Aug. **On site lodging:** Yes. **Rental clubs:** Yes. **Walking policy:** Walking at certain times. **Metal spikes allowed:** Yes. **Range:** Yes (grass/mats). **To obtain tee times:** Call 4 days in advance.
Subscriber comments: Nice layout, middle of nowhere...Has something for everyone...Golf at its best, too bad it's hidden away...A real find, take food, no place to eat...Deer are in the gallery...Tough, memorable round of golf...Greens are fast. Accuracy a must, lots of trees...Liked the old greens better...Wow, what a track!

FIREWHEEL GOLF PARK
PU-600 W. Blackburn Rd., Garland, 75044, Dallas County, (972)205-2795, 10 miles N of Dallas.
Architect: Dick Phelps. **Green fee:** $18/$26. **Credit cards:** MC,VISA,AMEX. **Reduced fees:** Twilight, seniors. **Caddies:** No. **Golf carts:** $10. **Discount golf packages:** No. **Season:** Year-round. **High:** April-Sept. **On site lodging:** No. **Rental clubs:** Yes. **Walking policy:** Unrestricted walking. **Metal spikes allowed:** Yes. **Range:** Yes (grass/mats). **To obtain tee times:** Call on Thursday at 8:00 a.m. for Friday through Thursday.
★★★**LAKES COURSE**
Opened: 1987. **Holes:** 18. **Par:** 71/71. **Yards:** 6,625/5,215. **Course rating:** 72.0/69.1. **Slope:** 126/110.
Subscriber comments: Narrow with lots of water...Take plenty of balls...No easy hole, makes you play every club...Has some tricky holes...Great Bermuda greens...Challenging par 5s, plays long from the tips...Hard golf course, but fun to play.
★★★**OLD COURSE**
Opened: 1983. **Holes:** 18. **Par:** 72/72. **Yards:** 7,054/5,692. **Course rating:** 74.1/71.7. **Slope:** 129/117.
Subscriber comments: Doesn't look too tough, but score tends to be high...Good for long hitters...Great 9th hole, condition suspect...Not as challenging as the Lakes Course...Layout a little boring...Wide open, fun to play...Nice views, good terrain.

★★½**FLYING L RANCH GOLF COURSE**
R-P.O. Box 1959, Bandera, 78003, Bandera County, (830)796-8466, (800)646-5407, 40 miles NW of San Antonio.
Opened: 1975. **Holes:** 18. **Par:** 72/72. **Yards:** 6,646/5,442. **Course rating:** 71.0/69.9. **Slope:** 123/109. **Architect:** N/A. **Green fee:** $17/$18. **Credit cards:** All major. **Reduced fees:** Weekdays, resort guests, twilight, seniors, juniors. **Caddies:** No. **Golf carts:** $10. **Discount golf packages:** Yes. **Season:** Year-round. **High:** April-Sept. **On site lodging:** Yes. **Rental clubs:** Yes. **Walking policy:** Unrestricted walking. **Metal spikes allowed:** Yes. **Range:** Yes (grass). **To obtain tee times:** Call in advance.
Subscriber comments: Excellent country setting...OK for a dude ranch layout...Trees in fairway, not fair...Wide open, few hazards.

★★★½**FOREST CREEK GOLF CLUB**
PU-99 Twin Ridge Pkwy., Round Rock, 78664, Williamson County, (512)388-2874, 10 miles N of Austin.
Opened: 1989. **Holes:** 18. **Par:** 72/72. **Yards:** 7,084/5,601. **Course rating:** 72.8/71.9. **Slope:** 130/124. **Architect:** Dick Phelps. **Green fee:** $39/$50. **Credit cards:** All major. **Reduced fees:** Weekdays, low season, twilight, seniors, juniors. **Caddies:** No. **Golf carts:** Included in Green Fee. **Discount golf packages:** No. **Season:** Year-round. **High:** March-Oct. **On site lodging:** No. **Rental clubs:** Yes. **Walking policy:** Walking at certain times. **Metal spikes allowed:** Yes. **Range:** Yes (grass/mats). **To obtain tee times:** Call 7 days in advance.
Subscriber comments: Fun place to play...You should try it...Some tight holes...Wind comes into play...Real challenge from the back tees...Good long course with an intimidating name...Country club feel at muny prices...Need local knowledge.

★★**FORT BROWN MUNICIPAL GOLF COURSE**
PM-300 River Levee Rd., Brownsville, 78520, Cameron County, (956)541-0394, (956)685-7202.
Opened: 1958. **Holes:** 18. **Par:** 72/72. **Yards:** 6,172/4,803. **Course rating:** 67.0/67.0. **Slope:** 108/108. **Architect:** N/A. **Green fee:** $6/$7. **Credit cards:** MC,VISA,AMEX.

Reduced fees: Twilight, juniors. **Caddies:** No. **Golf carts:** $8. **Discount golf packages:** No. **Season:** Year-round. **High:** Jan.-March. **On site lodging:** No. **Rental clubs:** Yes. **Walking policy:** Unrestricted walking. **Metal spikes allowed:** Yes. **Range:** Yes (grass). **To obtain tee times:** Call up to 1 day in advance.

FOUR SEASONS RESORT & CLUB

4150 N. MacArthur Blvd., Irving, 75038, Dallas County, (972)717-2530, (800)332-3442, 10 miles NW of Dallas.
Green fee: $135/$150. **Credit cards:** MC,VISA,AMEX,Diners Club.
Reduced fees: Low season, resort guests, twilight. **Caddies:** No. **Golf carts:** Included in Green Fee. **Discount golf packages:** Yes. **Season:** Year-round. **High:** Feb.-Oct. **On site lodging:** Yes. **Rental clubs:** Yes. **Walking policy:** Mandatory cart. **Metal spikes allowed:** No. **Range:** Yes (grass). **To obtain tee times:** Hotel guests may call up to 45 days in advance.
Notes: 1983-present, GTE Byron Nelson Classic.

(GREAT SERVICE)

★★★★COTTONWOOD VALLEY COURSE
Opened: 1983. **Holes:** 18. **Par:** 71/72. **Yards:** 6,862/5,320. **Course rating:** 73.4/70.6. **Slope:** 133/116. **Architect:** Robert Trent Jones/Jay Morrish.
Subscriber comments: Fair challenge, bent greens...More fun than the TPC Course...Cottonwood is great sister course...Wide open...Just as good as TPC Course now...Greens outstanding...Better layout than TPC...Magnificent course, 1st hole is stunning surprise, green is shaped like Texas, bunker like Oklahoma.

★★★★TPC COURSE
Opened: 1986. **Holes:** 18. **Par:** 70/70. **Yards:** 6,899/5,340. **Course rating:** 73.5/70.6. **Slope:** 135/116. **Architect:** Jay Morrish, Byron Nelson and Ben Crenshaw.
Subscriber comments: I want to play again...OK but still needs more trees to block office buildings...Home of the Byron Nelson, who wouldn't want to play here?...Awesome, long but fair...Long not overly tough...Keep it in fairway, great greens...Great conditions, not a stiff challenge...Fun to play where pros play...Nice to say you played it once...Play there on business.

★½FOX CREEK GOLF COURSE

PU-Rte. 3, Hempstead, 77445, Waller County, (409)826-2131, 40 miles NW of Houston.
Opened: N/A. **Holes:** 18. **Par:** 70/70. **Yards:** 5,750/4,680. **Course rating:** N/A. **Slope:** N/A. **Architect:** N/A. **Green fee:** N/A. **Credit cards:** MC,VISA. **Reduced fees:** Weekdays, twilight. **Caddies:** No. **Golf carts:** N/A. **Discount golf packages:** No. **Season:** Year-round. **High:** March-Sept. **On site lodging:** No. **Rental clubs:** No. **Walking policy:** N/A. **Metal spikes allowed:** Yes. **Range:** Yes (grass). **To obtain tee times:** N/A.

FREEPORT GOLF COURSE

830 Slaughter Rd., Freeport, 77541, Brazoria County, (409)233-8311.
Call club for further information.

★★GABE LOZANO SR. GOLF CENTER

PM-4401 Old Brownsville Rd., Corpus Christi, 78405, Nueces County, (512)883-3696.
Opened: 1962. **Holes:** 27. **Par:** 72/72. **Yards:** 6,953/5,149. **Course rating:** 72.6/68.8. **Slope:** 128/112. **Architect:** Leon Howard. **Green fee:** $9/$13. **Credit cards:** MC,VISA. **Reduced fees:** Weekdays, twilight, seniors, juniors. **Caddies:** No. **Golf carts:** $7. **Discount golf packages:** Yes. **Season:** Year-round. **High:** N/A. **On site lodging:** No. **Rental clubs:** Yes. **Walking policy:** Unrestricted walking. **Metal spikes allowed:** Yes. **Range:** Yes (grass). **To obtain tee times:** Call on Wednesday at 8 a.m. for upcoming weekend. Call up to 1 day in advance for weekdays.
Special Notes: Also has a 9-hole Executive Course.

★½GAINESVILLE MUNICIPAL GOLF CLUB

PM-200 S. Rusk, Gainesville, 76240, Cooke County, (940)668-4560, (940)665-2161.
Call club for further information.

TEXAS

★★½GALVESTON ISLAND MUNICIPAL GOLF COURSE
PU-1700 Sydnor Lane, Galveston, 77554, Galveston County, (409)744-2366, 50 miles SE of Houston.
Opened: 1989. **Holes:** 18. **Par:** 72/73. **Yards:** 6,969/5,407. **Course rating:** 73.0/71.4. **Slope:** 131/121. **Architect:** Carlton Gipson. **Green fee:** $13/$25. **Credit cards:** All major. **Reduced fees:** Weekdays, resort guests, twilight, seniors, juniors. **Caddies:** No. **Golf carts:** $10. **Discount golf packages:** Yes. **Season:** Year-round. **High:** April-Oct. **On site lodging:** No. **Rental clubs:** Yes. **Walking policy:** Unrestricted walking. **Metal spikes allowed:** Yes. **Range:** Yes (grass/mats). **To obtain tee times:** Call Tuesday at 8 a.m. Call 4 days in advance for holiday.
Subscriber comments: Good muny course, challenging and more interesting after 5th hole...If you don't three-putt at least once, you're Ben Crenshaw.

GARDEN VALLEY GOLF RESORT
R-22049 FM 1995, Lindale, 75771, Smith County, (903)882-6107, (800)443-8577, 80 miles E of Dallas.
Credit cards: MC,VISA,AMEX. **Caddies:** No. **Golf carts:** $12. **Discount golf packages:** Yes. **Season:** Year-round. **High:** April-Oct. **On site lodging:** No. **Rental clubs:** Yes. **Metal spikes allowed:** No. **Range:** Yes (grass). **To obtain tee times:** Call 800 number. If local call golf shop number.
★★★★DOGWOOD COURSE
Opened: 1992. **Holes:** 18. **Par:** 72/72. **Yards:** 6,754/5,532. **Course rating:** 72.4/72.5. **Slope:** 132/130. **Architect:** John Sanford. **Green fee:** $44/$52. **Reduced fees:** Weekdays, low season, resort guests, twilight. **Walking policy:** Mandatory cart.
Subscriber comments: Could be the best experience next to Augusta...Best course in East Texas...Very tough from tips...Out of the way...Outstanding in every way...Must play if you're in the area...Small greens...Paradise, let's keep this one a secret...Great layout and setting...Unique course...Beautiful, lovely with flowers.
★★½HUMMINGBIRD COURSE
Opened: N/A. **Holes:** 18. **Par:** 71/71. **Yards:** 6,446/5,131. **Course rating:** 71.0/69.0. **Slope:** N/A. **Architect:** Leon Howard. **Green fee:** $21/$21. **Reduced fees:** Weekdays, low season, twilight, seniors. **Walking policy:** Unrestricted walking.
Subscriber comments: OK course...Short, fun, easy, some trouble...No comparison to Dogwood...A nice old course...Challenging course, keeps you guessing...Small greens, leaves are problem in fall, needs sand.

★★½GLENBROOK GOLF COURSE
PU-8205 N. Bayou Dr., Houston, 77017, Harris County, (713)649-8089, 15 miles S of Houston.
Opened: 1924. **Holes:** 18. **Par:** 71/71. **Yards:** 6,427/5,258. **Course rating:** 70.7/70.7. **Slope:** 120/117. **Architect:** Robert McKinney. **Green fee:** $11/$14. **Credit cards:** MC,VISA. **Reduced fees:** Weekdays, low season, twilight, seniors, juniors. **Caddies:** No. **Golf carts:** $9. **Discount golf packages:** Yes. **Season:** Year-round. **High:** April-Oct. **On site lodging:** No. **Rental clubs:** Yes. **Walking policy:** Unrestricted walking. **Metal spikes allowed:** Yes. **Range:** No. **To obtain tee times:** Call or stop by anytime after 7 a.m. Thursday.
Subscriber comments: Very good all around golf...Interesting course, multiple shots over large bayou...Long carries over water...Short course but difficult.

★★★½THE GOLF CLUB AT CINCO RANCH
PU-23030 Cinco Ranch Blvd., Katy, 77450, Fort Bend County, (281)395-4653, 20 miles W of Houston.
Opened: 1994. **Holes:** 18. **Par:** 72/72. **Yards:** 7,044/5,263. **Course rating:** 73.7/70.3. **Slope:** 132/118. **Architect:** Carlton Gipson. **Green fee:** $40/$50. **Credit cards:** All major. **Reduced fees:** Weekdays, twilight, seniors, juniors. **Caddies:** No. **Golf carts:** Included in Green Fee. **Discount golf packages:** No. **Season:** Year-round. **High:** April-June. **On site lodging:** No. **Rental clubs:** Yes. **Walking policy:** Mandatory cart. **Metal spikes allowed:** Yes. **Range:** Yes (grass). **To obtain tee times:** Nonresidents may call up to 7 days in advance. Residents may call up to 9 days in advance.
Subscriber comments: Great layout that will only get better as course matures...Planned community course...Links style course, can get windy...New course, no shade (tough in August in Texas)...Good finishing holes.

★★½GRAND PRAIRIE MUNICIPAL GOLF COURSE
PM-3202 S.E. 14th St., Grand Prairie, 75052, Dallas County, (972)263-0661.
Opened: 1964. **Holes:** 27. **Architect:** Ralph Plummer. **Green fee:** $14/$16. **Credit cards:** MC,VISA. **Reduced fees:** Twilight, seniors, juniors. **Caddies:** No. **Golf carts:** $21. **Discount golf packages:** No. **Season:** Year-round. **High:** May-Sept. **On site lodging:** No. **Rental clubs:** Yes. **Walking policy:** Unrestricted walking. **Metal spikes allowed:** Yes. **Range:** Yes (grass/mats). **To obtain tee times:** 7 a.m. in person or 8 a.m. by phone on Thursdays for weekends and holidays only.
RED/BLUE
Par: 72/72. **Yards:** 6,500/5,465. **Course rating:** 71.0/65.3. **Slope:** 118/102.
RED/WHITE
Par: 71/71. **Yards:** 6,219/5,176. **Course rating:** 69.5/64.2. **Slope:** 94/98.
WHITE/BLUE
HPar: 71/71. **Yards:** 6,309/5,275. **Course rating:** 69.5/64.3. **Slope:** 112/98.
Subscriber comments: Lots of water...No sand, but some excellent holes...Fun to play short holes...Red/Blue is best golf challenge on this 27-hole layout...Fair golf with no gimmicks...Toughest par 3s in Dallas from back tees.

★★★GRAPEVINE GOLF COURSE
PU-3800 Fairway Dr., Grapevine, 76051, Tarrant County, (817)481-0421.
Opened: 1979. **Holes:** 18. **Par:** 72/72. **Yards:** 6,953/5,786. **Course rating:** 72.0/72.5. **Slope:** 128/113. **Architect:** Joe Finger and Byron Nelson. **Green fee:** $14/$16. **Credit cards:** MC,VISA,AMEX. **Reduced fees:** Twilight, seniors, juniors. **Caddies:** No. **Golf carts:** $18. **Discount golf packages:** No. **Season:** Year-round. **High:** April-Sept. **On site lodging:** No. **Rental clubs:** Yes. **Walking policy:** Unrestricted walking. **Metal spikes allowed:** Yes. **Range:** Yes (grass/mats). **To obtain tee times:** Call 3 days in advance, 7 a.m. in person or 1 p.m. by phone.
Subscriber comments: Long course, fair, interesting...Bring all your shots, must play to appreciate...Very large greens, go for a fun round...Has some good holes, pretty flat...Too hard to get tee times...Good test, maintenance spotty...Not memorable.

★½GRAYSON COUNTY COLLEGE GOLF COURSE
PU-7109 Dinn, Denison, 75020, Grayson County, (903)786-9719, 70 miles N of Dallas.
Opened: 1961. **Holes:** 18. **Par:** 72/72. **Yards:** 6,452/4,876. **Course rating:** 70.0. **Slope:** 114. **Architect:** Joe Finger. **Green fee:** $8/$13. **Credit cards:** MC,VISA. **Reduced fees:** Weekdays, twilight. **Caddies:** No. **Golf carts:** $17. **Discount golf packages:** No. **Season:** Year-round. **High:** May-June. **On site lodging:** No. **Rental clubs:** Yes. **Walking policy:** Unrestricted walking. **Metal spikes allowed:** Yes. **Range:** Yes (grass/mats). **To obtain tee times:** Call 7 a.m. Thursday for upcoming weekend.

★★★½GREATWOOD GOLF CLUB
PU-6767 Greatwood Pkwy., Sugar Land, 77479, Fort Bend County, (281)343-9999, (888)343-4001, 20 miles SW of Houston.
Opened: 1990. **Holes:** 18. **Par:** 72/72. **Yards:** 6,836/5,220. **Course rating:** 72.6/70.0. **Slope:** 130/125. **Architect:** Carlton Gipson. **Green fee:** $44/$58. **Credit cards:** All major. **Reduced fees:** Twilight, seniors, juniors. **Caddies:** No. **Golf carts:** Included in Green Fee. **Discount golf packages:** No. **Season:** Year-round. **High:** March-Oct. **On site lodging:** No. **Rental clubs:** Yes. **Walking policy:** Mandatory cart. **Metal spikes allowed:** Yes. **Range:** Yes (grass/mats). **To obtain tee times:** Call 3 days in advance of the day you wish to play, starting at 8 a.m.
Subscriber comments: Awesome course, worth a visit...Beautiful setting near Brazos River...Great new course...The two finishing holes will rattle your teeth...Lots of blind shots and hilly lies...Super course, but a little long for the average golfer.

★★GREEN MEADOWS GOLF CLUB
PU-6138 Franz Rd., Katy, 77493, Harris County, (281)391-3670, 8 miles W of Houston.
Opened: 1965. **Holes:** 18. **Par:** 70/70. **Yards:** 5,440/4,949. **Course rating:** 66.3/70.5. **Slope:** 104/110. **Architect:** Jay Riviere. **Green fee:** $9/$20. **Credit cards:** All major. **Reduced fees:** Twilight, seniors. **Caddies:** No. **Golf carts:** $9. **Discount golf packages:** No. **Season:** Year-round. **High:** Jan.-Aug. **On site lodging:** No. **Rental clubs:** No. **Walking policy:** Unrestricted walking. **Metal spikes allowed:** Yes. **Range:** No. **To obtain tee times:** Foursomes call on Thursday starting at 8 a.m. for weekends.

★★½ GROVER C. KEATON GOLF COURSE
PM-2323 Jim Miller Rd., Dallas, 75227, Dallas County, (214)670-8784.
Opened: 1978. **Holes:** 18. **Par:** 72/72. **Yards:** 6,511/5,054. **Course rating:** 70.6/68.1.
Slope: 113/113. **Architect:** Dave Bennett. **Green fee:** $11/$14. **Credit cards:**
MC,VISA,AMEX. **Reduced fees:** Weekdays, low season, twilight, seniors, juniors.
Caddies: No. **Golf carts:** $17. **Discount golf packages:** No. **Season:** Year-round.
High: March-Aug. **On site lodging:** No. **Rental clubs:** Yes. **Walking policy:**
Unrestricted walking. **Metal spikes allowed:** Yes. **Range:** Yes (grass). **To obtain tee times:** Call two days in advance.
Subscriber comments: A lot of water and large trees...Front nine nice, back marginal...Nice layout, but built in flood plain...First five holes the toughest.

★★ GUS WORTHAM PARK GOLF COURSE
PU-7000 Capitol, Houston, 77011, Harris County, (713)921-3227.
Opened: N/A. **Holes:** 18. **Par:** 72/74. **Yards:** 6,400/6,000. **Course rating:** 69.5/74.2.
Slope: 113/118. **Architect:** N/A. **Green fee:** $10/$14. **Credit cards:** MC,VISA,AMEX.
Reduced fees: Weekdays, twilight, seniors, juniors. **Caddies:** No. **Golf carts:** $18.
Discount golf packages: No. **Season:** Year-round. **High:** April-May. **On site lodging:**
No. **Rental clubs:** Yes. **Walking policy:** Unrestricted walking. **Metal spikes allowed:**
Yes. **Range:** Yes (grass). **To obtain tee times:** Call one day in advance.

★★ HEATHER RUN GOLF & FISH CLUB
1600 Western Oaks Dr., Waco, 76712, McLennan County, (254)772-8100.
Opened: 1969. **Holes:** 18. **Par:** 70/70. **Yards:** 6,400/5,040. **Course rating:** 70.7/68.7.
Slope: 122/120. **Architect:** Greg Juster. **Green fee:** $10/$13. **Credit cards:** All major.
Reduced fees: Weekdays, low season, resort guests, twilight, seniors, juniors.
Caddies: No. **Golf carts:** $9. **Discount golf packages:** Yes. **Season:** Year-round.
High: April-Nov. **On site lodging:** No. **Rental clubs:** Yes. **Walking policy:** Unrestricted
walking. **Metal spikes allowed:** Yes. **Range:** Yes (grass/mats). **To obtain tee times:**
Call up to 7 days in advance. Call up to 60 days in advance for large groups.
Special Notes: Formerly Western Oaks Country Club.

★★½ HENRY HOMBERG MUNICIPAL GOLF COURSE
PU-5940 Babe Zaharias Dr., Beaumont, 77705, Jefferson County, (409)842-3220, 75
miles E of Houston.
Opened: 1930. **Holes:** 18. **Par:** 72/73. **Yards:** 6,786/5,660. **Course rating:** 71.2/70.0.
Slope: 116/116. **Architect:** Ralph Plummer. **Green fee:** $8/$9. **Credit cards:**
MC,VISA,AMEX. **Reduced fees:** Weekdays, twilight, seniors, juniors. **Caddies:** No.
Golf carts: $15. **Discount golf packages:** No. **Season:** Year-round. **High:** March-June. **On site lodging:** No. **Rental clubs:** Yes. **Walking policy:** Unrestricted walking.
Metal spikes allowed: Yes. **Range:** Yes (grass/mats). **To obtain tee times:** Call 2 days
in advance for weekends or holidays at 9 a.m.
Subscriber comments: Get there early to beat the crowd...Fun to walk...Back nine
really good...Heavily wooded...Old muny course, if you can get on, go for it.

★★ HERMANN PARK GOLF COURSE
PU-6201 Golf Course Dr., Houston, 77030, Harris County, (713)526-0077.
Opened: 1922. **Holes:** 18. **Par:** 71/72. **Yards:** 5,966/5,369. **Course rating:** 68.1/64.5.
Slope: 103/97. **Architect:** John Bredemus. **Green fee:** $15. **Credit cards:**
MC,VISA,AMEX. **Reduced fees:** Twilight, seniors, juniors. **Caddies:** No. **Golf carts:**
$18. **Discount golf packages:** No. **Season:** Year-round. **High:** April-Sept. **On site
lodging:** No. **Rental clubs:** Yes. **Walking policy:** Walking at certain times. **Metal
spikes allowed:** Yes. **Range:** Yes (grass/mats). **To obtain tee times:** First come, first
served.

★★★ HIDDEN HILLS PUBLIC GOLF COURSE
PU-N. Hwy. 70, Pampa, 79066, Gray County, (806)669-5866, 56 miles NE of Amarillo.
Opened: 1990. **Holes:** 18. **Par:** 71/71. **Yards:** 6,463/5,196. **Course rating:** 69.4/68.0.
Slope: 122/116. **Architect:** Ray Hardy. **Green fee:** $6/$12. **Credit cards:** MC,VISA.
Reduced fees: Weekdays, twilight, seniors, juniors. **Caddies:** No. **Golf carts:** $16.
Discount golf packages: No. **Season:** Year-round. **High:** May-Sept. **On site lodging:**
No. **Rental clubs:** Yes. **Walking policy:** Unrestricted walking. **Metal spikes allowed:**

Yes. **Range:** Yes (grass). **To obtain tee times:** Call for tee times on Saturday, Sunday, and Holidays.

Subscriber comments: Very good course for fairly new layout...Tough to play in wind...Good challenge, uphill, downhill or sidehill lies...Great fairways, tough small greens...Fairways are really wider than they look...Hard to hit greens, like an anthill.

★★★½HILL COUNTRY GOLF CLUB

R-9800 Hyatt Resort Dr., San Antonio, 78251, Bexar County, (210)520-4040, (888)901-4653, 15 miles W of San Antonio.
Opened: 1993. **Holes:** 18. **Par:** 72/72. **Yards:** 6,913/4,781. **Course rating:** 73.9/67.8. **Slope:** 136/114. **Architect:** Arthur Hills. **Green fee:** $60/$100. **Credit cards:** MC,VISA,AMEX,DISC,Diners Club. **Reduced fees:** Weekdays, low season, twilight, juniors. **Caddies:** No. **Golf carts:** Included in Green Fee. **Discount golf packages:** Yes. **Season:** Year-round. **High:** Spring/Fall. **On site lodging:** Yes. **Rental clubs:** Yes. **Walking policy:** Unrestricted walking. **Metal spikes allowed:** Yes. **Range:** Yes (grass/mats). **To obtain tee times:** Hotel guests can make tee times with room reservations. Others call 7 days in advance.

(GOOD SERVICE)

Subscriber comments: Better than most resort courses...Top notch, super golf and picture perfect views...A must play if you visit San Antonio...Challenging Hill Country track could use more driving area on a few holes...Keep it in the fairway.

★★HOGAN PARK GOLF COURSE

PU-3600 N. Fairground Rd., Midland, 79705, Midland County, (915)685-7360, 300 miles W of Fort Worth.
Opened: 1959. **Holes:** 27. **Par:** 70/72. **Yards:** 6,615/5,775. **Course rating:** 68.5/69.0. **Slope:** 110/103. **Architect:** Charles Campbell/Jimmy Gamewell. **Green fee:** $9/$13. **Credit cards:** MC,VISA. **Reduced fees:** Weekdays, low season, twilight, seniors, juniors. **Caddies:** No. **Golf carts:** $17. **Discount golf packages:** No. **Season:** Year-round. **High:** May-Oct. **On site lodging:** No. **Rental clubs:** Yes. **Walking policy:** Unrestricted walking. **Metal spikes allowed:** Yes. **Range:** Yes (grass/mats). **To obtain tee times:** Call golf shop.

HORSESHOE BAY RESORT

R-Bay W. Blvd., Horseshoe Bay, 78657, Burnet County, (830)598-6561.
Green fee: $60/$85. **Credit cards:** All major. **Reduced fees:** Weekdays, low season, resort guests, juniors. **Caddies:** No. **Golf carts:** $10. **Discount golf packages:** Yes. **Season:** Year-round. **High:** March-Nov. **On site lodging:** Yes. **Rental clubs:** Yes. **Walking policy:** Mandatory cart. **Metal spikes allowed:** Yes. **Range:** Yes (grass). **To obtain tee times:** Call seven days in advance.

★★★★APPLEROCK COURSE

Opened: 1986. **Holes:** 18. **Par:** 72/72. **Yards:** 6,999/5,509. **Course rating:** 73.9/71.6. **Slope:** 134/117. **Architect:** Robert Trent Jones.
Subscriber comments: Two great courses, long and hard but enjoyable, well kept, occasional difficult to play time...All Horseshoe courses are great...Weakest of the three...Hilly with interesting variety...Golfers' heaven in 54 holes...Play Apple to warm up...The most beautiful spring flowers in Texas.

★★★★½RAM ROCK COURSE

Opened: 1981. **Holes:** 18. **Par:** 71/71. **Yards:** 6,946/5,306. **Course rating:** 73.9/71.4. **Slope:** 137/121. **Architect:** Robert Trent Jones/Roger Rulewich.
Notes: Ranked 11th in 1997 Best in State.
Subscriber comments: Hard course...Difficult but fair, better than any daily fee course that I have ever played...One of my top 10 courses ever...Open course tough with wind...Best greens in Texas, par-5 9th is unbelievable...This course will kill you, but what a way to die...Don't keep score, just enjoy...Incredible golf experience.

★★★½SLICK ROCK

Rte. Big Spur, Horseshoe Bay, 78657, Burnet County, (830)598-2561, 52 miles W of Austin.
Opened: 1972. **Holes:** 18. **Par:** 72/72. **Yards:** 6,834/5,832. **Course rating:** 72.6/70.2. **Slope:** 125/115. **Architect:** Robert Trent Jones.
Subscriber comments: Easy course, fun to play...Front nine OK, back very good, deer, wild turkey...Greens are slick...Best of three for average golfer...Waterfall hole best tee box in US...Pales in comparison to Ram Rock.

HYATT BEAR CREEK GOLF & RACQUET CLUB

PU-3500 Bear Creek Court, DFW Airport, 75261, Dallas County, (972)615-6800, 25 miles W of Dallas.

Opened: 1981. **Architect:** Ted Robinson. **Green fee:** $65/$75. **Credit cards:** All major. **Reduced fees:** Weekdays, low season, twilight, seniors, juniors. **Caddies:** No. **Discount golf packages:** Yes. **Season:** Year-round. **High:** April-Nov. **On site lodging:** No. **Rental clubs:** Yes. **Walking policy:** Unrestricted walking. **Metal spikes allowed:** No. **Range:** Yes (grass). **To obtain tee times:** Call 5 days in advance.

★★★½EAST COURSE

Holes: 18. **Par:** 72/72. **Yards:** 6,670/5,620. **Course rating:** 72.5/72.4. **Slope:** 127/124. **Golf carts:** $12.

Subscriber comments: Not as long as West but what a layout...Don't hit any 9-irons when the planes are landing...Need to play with course management in mind...Great course if the planes don't bother you...Tricked up and too narrow.

★★★½WEST COURSE

Holes: 18. **Par:** 72/72. **Yards:** 6,675/5,570. **Course rating:** 72.7/72.5. **Slope:** 130/122. **Golf carts:** Included in Green Fee.

Subscriber comments: Hard course and planes drive you nuts...The better of the two Bear Creek courses...Tight fairways with lots of trees, bring lots of balls...Both excellent considering the rounds played...Requires "A" game to score well...Certain fairways have too much slope, lie of ball more affected by terrain than skill of golfer.

INDIAN CREEK GOLF CLUB

PM-1650 W. Frankford, Carrollton, 75007, Denton County, (972)492-3620, (800)369-4137, 10 miles N of Dallas.

Architect: Dick Phelps. **Credit cards:** MC,VISA,DISC. **Reduced fees:** Weekdays, twilight, seniors, juniors. **Caddies:** No. **Golf carts:** $9. **Discount golf packages:** No. **Season:** Year-round. **High:** March-Oct. **On site lodging:** No. **Rental clubs:** Yes. **Walking policy:** Unrestricted walking. **Metal spikes allowed:** Yes. **Range:** Yes (grass/mats). **To obtain tee times:** Call 3 days in advance.

★★★CREEKS COURSE

Opened: 1984. **Holes:** 18. **Par:** 72/72. **Yards:** 7,218/4,967. **Course rating:** 74.7/68.2. **Slope:** 136/114. **Green fee:** $23.

Subscriber comments: Could be excellent with better care...Creek comes in play on some holes, harder of the two...Demanding and long from back, must play smart, good Bermuda greens...Too crowded...Fantastic last three holes...Easily reachable par 5s.

★★★LAKES COURSE

Opened: 1987. **Holes:** 18. **Par:** 72/72. **Yards:** 7,060/5,367. **Course rating:** 72.9/69.9. **Slope:** 135/114. **Green fee:** $26.

Subscriber comments: Tight course, challenging...Long from the tips...Good layout, 9th and 18th are killers...Not fun...Lined with lakes and trees...Just another course...Afterthought to Creeks Course...All holes much the same...Lots of doglegs.

★★★¼IRON HORSE GOLF COURSE

PM-6200 Skylark Circle, North Richland Hill, 76180, Tarrant County, (817)485-6666, 20 miles SW of Fort Worth.

Opened: 1990. **Holes:** 18. **Par:** 70/70. **Yards:** 6,690/5,083. **Course rating:** 71.8/69.6. **Slope:** 130/119. **Architect:** Richard Phelps. **Green fee:** $27/$38. **Credit cards:** MC,VISA,AMEX. **Reduced fees:** Weekdays, twilight, seniors, juniors. **Caddies:** No. **Golf carts:** $12. **Discount golf packages:** No. **Season:** Year-round. **High:** March-Oct. **On site lodging:** No. **Rental clubs:** Yes. **Walking policy:** Unrestricted walking. **Metal spikes allowed:** Yes. **Range:** Yes (grass/mats). **To obtain tee times:** Call 3 days in advance.

Subscriber comments: Shotmaker's course, love it except for slow play...Leave your driver at home...Excellent greens...Very nice layout, good use of natural terrain...Target golf, pleasing to the eye...Take a lot of balls.

★★★J.F. SAMMONS PARK GOLF COURSE

PM-2220 W. Ave. D, Temple, 76504, Bell County, (254)778-8282, 50 miles N of Austin.

Opened: 1987. **Holes:** 18. **Par:** 70/70. **Yards:** 6,100/4,450. **Course rating:** 69.8/65.8. **Slope:** 129/110. **Architect:** N/A. **Green fee:** $6/$13. **Credit cards:** MC,VISA. **Reduced fees:** Weekdays, low season, twilight, seniors, juniors. **Caddies:** No. **Golf carts:** N/A.

Discount golf packages: No. **Season:** Year-round. **High:** Spring/Fall. **On site lodging:** No. **Rental clubs:** Yes. **Walking policy:** Unrestricted walking. **Metal spikes allowed:** Yes. **Range:** Yes (grass). **To obtain tee times:** Call 7 days in advance. Deposit required for goups of 16 or more.
Subscriber comments: Get ready for the water...Nice layout...Excellent fairways, marginal greens...Very interesting short course...Water on eight of first nine holes, need to select right iron...Fun for a beginner, some unique water holes to contend with.

★★★ JERSEY MEADOW GOLF COURSE
PU-8502 Rio Grande, Houston, 77040, Harris County, (713)896-0900.
Opened: 1956. **Holes:** 27. **Architect:** Carlton Gibson. **Green fee:** $27/$36. **Credit cards:** MC,VISA,AMEX. **Reduced fees:** Weekdays, low season, twilight, seniors, juniors. **Caddies:** No. **Golf carts:** Included in Green Fee. **Discount golf packages:** No. **Season:** Year-round. **High:** April-Oct. **On site lodging:** No. **Rental clubs:** Yes. **Walking policy:** Walking at certain times. **Metal spikes allowed:** Yes. **Range:** Yes (grass). **To obtain tee times:** Call Wednesday a.m. for weekend tee times. Call one week in advance for weekdays.
RED/BLUE
Par: 72/72. **Yards:** 6,400/5,098. **Course rating:** 68.9/64.2. **Slope:** 118/107.
RED/WHITE
Par: 72/72. **Yards:** 6,583/5,383. **Course rating:** 70.5/69.9. **Slope:** 120/103.
WHITE/BLUE
Par: 72/72. **Yards:** 6,383/5,215. **Course rating:** 70.4/65.8. **Slope:** 118/108.
Subscriber comments: Short layout, requires finesse...Blue simple...Good average course, open...Three nines, always at wait a the turn...Medium difficulty with some tight fairways...The three courses are being physically upgraded.

★★★ JIMMY CLAY GOLF COURSE
PM-5400 Jimmy Clay Dr., Austin, 78744, Travis County, (512)444-0999.
Opened: 1974. **Holes:** 18. **Par:** 72/72. **Yards:** 6,857/5,036. **Course rating:** 72.4/68.5. **Slope:** 124/110. **Architect:** Joseph Finger. **Green fee:** $12/$13. **Credit cards:** None. **Reduced fees:** Weekdays, twilight, seniors, juniors. **Caddies:** No. **Golf carts:** $8. **Discount golf packages:** No. **Season:** Year-round. **High:** Aug. **On site lodging:** No. **Rental clubs:** Yes. **Walking policy:** Unrestricted walking. **Metal spikes allowed:** Yes. **Range:** Yes (grass). **To obtain tee times:** Call 1 day in advance. Call on Friday for weekend.
Subscriber comments: Good challenging course...Slightly boring course, long...Greens are great...Plays long from the blues...Good muny, front nine open, back nine tight...Best Austin muny.

★★½ JOHN PITMAN MUNICIPAL GOLF COURSE
PM-S. Main St., Hereford, 79045, Deaf Smith County, (806)363-7139.
Call club for further information.
Subscriber comments: Like the wide open...Front nine and back nine play like two separate courses, some tough holes on windy days...Simple, short but has a couple of challenging holes...Well laid out and maintained.

★★½ KILLEEN MUNICIPAL GOLF COURSE
PM-406 Roy Reynolds Dr., Killeen, 76543, Bell County, (254)699-6034, 50 miles N of Austin.
Opened: 1969. **Holes:** 18. **Par:** 72/72. **Yards:** 6,700/5,109. **Course rating:** 69.5/68.3. **Slope:** 107/109. **Architect:** Jay Riviere. **Green fee:** $8/$9. **Credit cards:** MC,VISA. **Reduced fees:** Twilight, seniors, juniors. **Caddies:** No. **Golf carts:** $16. **Discount golf packages:** No. **Season:** Year-round. **High:** March-Oct. **On site lodging:** No. **Rental clubs:** Yes. **Walking policy:** Unrestricted walking. **Metal spikes allowed:** Yes. **Range:** Yes (grass). **To obtain tee times:** Call Wednesday for upcoming weekend.
Subscriber comments: Excellent low-budget operation...Not a tough challenge, but a good change of pace...Best holes are on the back nine.

★★★ KINGWOOD COVE GOLF CLUB
PU-805 Hamblen Rd., Kingwood, 77339, Harris County, (281)358-1155, 20 miles N of Houston.
Opened: N/A. **Holes:** 18. **Par:** 71/71. **Yards:** 6,722/5,601. **Course rating:** 71.9/73.2.

Slope: 118/114. Architect: N/A. Green fee: $25/$35. Credit cards: MC,VISA,AMEX,DISC,Diners Club. Reduced fees: Weekdays, low season, twilight, seniors, juniors. Caddies: No. Golf carts: $12. Discount golf packages: Yes. Season: Year-round. High: Spring/Fall. On site lodging: No. Rental clubs: Yes. Walking policy: Unrestricted walking. Metal spikes allowed: Yes. Range: Yes (grass/mats). To obtain tee times: Call up to 7 days in advance.
Subscriber comments: Good when dry terrible when wet...Nothing special, just a nice golf course...Fun course...Nice layout...Greens needed work...Good course all around...Good challenge from tips.

★★L.B. HOUSTON PARK GOLF COURSE
11223 Luna Rd., Dallas, 75229, Dallas County, (214)670-6322.
Call club for further information.

★½L.E. RAMEY GOLF COURSE
PU-FM 3320, Kingsville, 78363, Kleberg County, (512)592-1101, 30 miles S of Corpus Christi.
Opened: 1974. Holes: 18. Par: 72/72. Yards: 6,995/5,540. Course rating: 72.5/71.3. Slope: 128/107. Architect: N/A. Green fee: $8/$10. Credit cards: All major. Reduced fees: Weekdays, twilight. Caddies: No. Golf carts: $15. Discount golf packages: No. Season: Year-round. High: March-June. On site lodging: No. Rental clubs: No. Walking policy: Unrestricted walking. Metal spikes allowed: Yes. Range: Yes (grass). To obtain tee times: N/A.

★★★★½LA CANTERA GOLF CLUB
R-16641 La Cantera Pkwy., San Antonio, 78256, Bexar County, (210)558-4653, (800)446-5387.
Opened: 1994. Holes: 18. Par: 72/72. Yards: 7,001/4,953. Course rating: 72.5/67.1. Slope: 134/108. Architect: Weiskopf and Morrish.
Green fee: $50/$105. Credit cards: All major. Reduced fees: N/A.
Caddies: No. Golf carts: Included in Green Fee. Discount golf packages: No. Season: Year-round. High: March-Oct. On site lodging: No. Rental clubs: Yes. Walking policy: Mandatory cart. Metal spikes allowed: Yes. Range: Yes (grass). To obtain tee times: Call up to 6 days in advance. Call 7-30 days in advance with an additional $10 per person charge.
Notes: Ranked 5th in 1997 Best in State; 1st in 1995 Best New Public Courses. La Cantera Texas Open.
Subscriber comments: Every hole is scenic, great golf...Course landscaping a work of art including sculptured markers...Diverse holes and topography, big fast undulating greens...It's got everything, newer course will keep getting better and better...Nice view of San Antonio...Absolutely beautiful course...The signature hole is one of the best in golf, teeing it up off a 100-foot cliff...Too many short par 4s.

(GREAT SERVICE)

★★★LADY BIRD JOHNSON MUNICIPAL GOLF COURSE
PM-Hwy. 16 S., Fredericksburg, 78624, Gillespie County, (830)997-4010, (800)950-8147, 70 miles N of San Antonio.
Opened: 1969. Holes: 18. Par: 72/72. Yards: 6,432/5,092. Course rating: 70.3/68.0. Slope: 125/112. Architect: Jeffrey Brauer. Green fee: $11/$17. Credit cards: MC,VISA. Reduced fees: Weekdays.
Caddies: No. Golf carts: $17. Discount golf packages: No. Season: Year-round. High: March-Nov. On site lodging: No. Rental clubs: Yes. Walking policy: Unrestricted walking. Metal spikes allowed: Yes. Range: Yes (grass/mats). To obtain tee times: Call golf shop.
Subscriber comments: Great layout...Fun course, tow different nines...Shhh! Keep it a secret...Very scenic, some fairways are tight while others are wide open, not very much sand...Weird but fun...Unique tee shots over gullies...Crowded by snow birds.

(GOOD VALUE)

★★LAKE ARLINGTON GOLF COURSE
PU-1516 Green Oaks Blvd. W., Arlington, 76013, Tarrant County, (817)451-6101, 25 miles W of Dallas.
Opened: 1963. Holes: 18. Par: 71/71. Yards: 6,637/5,485. Course rating: 70.7/71.0. Slope: 117/114. Architect: Ralph Plummer. Green fee: $10/$12. Credit cards: MC,VISA,DISC. Reduced fees: Twilight, seniors, juniors. Caddies: No. Golf carts: $8.

Discount golf packages: No. Season: Year-round. High: April-Aug. On site lodging: No. Rental clubs: Yes. Walking policy: Unrestricted walking. Metal spikes allowed: Yes. Range: Yes (grass). To obtain tee times: Call on Tuesday starting 6 a.m. for Wednesday through next Tuesday.

★★★LAKE HOUSTON GOLF CLUB

PU-27350 Afton Way, Huffman, 77336, Harris County, (281)324-1841.
Opened: 1971. Holes: 18. Par: 72/72. Yards: 6,940/5,553. Course rating: 74.2/73.3. Slope: 131/130. Architect: Jay Riviere. Green fee: $19/$32. Credit cards: MC,VISA,AMEX. Reduced fees: Weekdays, twilight, seniors, juniors. Caddies: No. Golf carts: Included in Green Fee. Discount golf packages: Yes. Season: Year-round. High: Spring/Fall. On site lodging: No. Rental clubs: Yes. Walking policy: Walking at certain times. Metal spikes allowed: Yes. Range: Yes (grass). To obtain tee times: Call up to 7 days in advance.
Subscriber comments: Great finishing holes...A lot of trees...Houston's best kept secret...Up and down, several doglegs, fast greens...No holes side by side, cut through woods...No frills, but some good and tough holes.

★★½LAKE PARK GOLF COURSE

PU-6 Lake Park Rd., Lewisville, 75067, Denton County, (972)436-5332, 25 miles N of Dallas.
Opened: 1996. Holes: 18. Par: 70/70. Yards: 6,135/4,960. Course rating: 68.3. Slope: 108. Architect: Richard Watson/Jeffrey Brauer. Green fee: $10/$24. Credit cards: MC,VISA,AMEX. Reduced fees: Weekdays, twilight, seniors, juniors. Caddies: No. Golf carts: $11. Discount golf packages: No. Season: Year-round. High: April-Oct. On site lodging: No. Rental clubs: Yes. Walking policy: Unrestricted walking. Metal spikes allowed: Yes. Range: Yes (grass). To obtain tee times: Call up to 3 days in advance. Call on Wednesday at 8 a.m. for upcoming weekend.
Subscriber comments: Holes too close to each other...Improving...Just redesigned, links style, wide open...Good beginner's course...Easy...Needs more bunkers...Short and easy course...Good improvements.

★★LAKE WHITNEY COUNTRY CLUB

Rte. 1, Box 2075, Whitney, 76692, Hill County, (254)694-2313, 55 miles S of Dallas.
Opened: 1968. Holes: 18. Par: 70/71. Yards: 6,296/5,020. Course rating: 67.6/69.8. Slope: N/A. Architect: Leon Howard. Green fee: $15/$15. Credit cards: None. Reduced fees: Weekdays, low season, twilight, seniors, juniors. Caddies: No. Golf carts: N/A. Discount golf packages: Yes. Season: Year-round. High: March-Nov. On site lodging: Yes. Rental clubs: Yes. Walking policy: Unrestricted walking. Metal spikes allowed: Yes. Range: Yes. To obtain tee times: Call.

LAKEWAY RESORT

R-602 Lakeway Dr., Austin, 78734, Travis County, (512)261-7173, 12 miles SW of Austin.
Opened: N/A. Architect: Leon Howard. Green fee: $38/$46. Credit cards: MC,VISA,AMEX. Reduced fees: Weekdays. Caddies: No. Golf carts: $12. Discount golf packages: Yes. Season: Year-round. High: Spring/Fall. On site lodging: Yes. Rental clubs: No. Walking policy: Unrestricted walking. Metal spikes allowed: Yes. Range: Yes (grass/mats). To obtain tee times: Call.

★★★LIVE OAK COURSE

Holes: 18. Par: 72/72. Yards: 6,643/5,472. Course rating: N/A. Slope: 121/122.
Subscriber comments: Good layout...Nice, quiet place to play, no bunkers yet...Take lots of balls...New watering system in fairways will make it a gem...OK, but not great golf, beautiful scenery...Be accurate...Hilly terrain.

★★★YAUPON COURSE

Holes: 18. Par: 72/72. Yards: 6,565/5,032. Course rating: N/A. Slope: 123/119.
Subscriber comments: Good resort course, lots of deer...Fun, killer uphill long par 5 into the wind...Course in good shape but lacks interest...Not for the golfer who shoots 100-plus, difficult course...Challenging course, lots of blind shots.

★★½LANDA PARK MUNICIPAL GOLF COURSE

PM-310 Golf Course Dr., New Braunfels, 78130, Comal County, (210)608-2174, 30 miles N of San Antonio.

Opened: 1932. **Holes:** 18. **Par:** 72/72. **Yards:** 6,103/4,919. **Course rating:** 68.9/67.4. **Slope:** 112/106. **Architect:** David Bennett and Leon Howard. **Green fee:** $15/$15. **Credit cards:** None. **Reduced fees:** N/A. **Caddies:** No. **Golf carts:** $18. **Discount golf packages:** No. **Season:** Year-round. **High:** Jan.-Aug. **On site lodging:** No. **Rental clubs:** Yes. **Walking policy:** Unrestricted walking. **Metal spikes allowed:** Yes. **Range:** No. **To obtain tee times:** Call up to 2 days in advance. Call at 9 a.m. on Thursday for upcoming weekend.

Subscriber comments: Nice little course, not real crowded...First few hole picturesque...Course is fun, but needs work...Not well marked from green to next tee...Short holes easy to score on...Pleasant test, water will grab you.

★★LEON VALLEY GOLF COURSE

PU-709 E. 24th Ave., Belton, 76513, Bell County, (254)939-5271, 6 miles W of Temple. **Opened:** 1962. **Holes:** 18. **Par:** 72/73. **Yards:** 6,610/5,412. **Course rating:** 67.8/66.7. **Slope:** N/A. **Architect:** Dick Norman. **Green fee:** $9/$12. **Credit cards:** MC,VISA. **Reduced fees:** Twilight, seniors, juniors. **Caddies:** No. **Golf carts:** $10. **Discount golf packages:** No. **Season:** Year-round. **High:** June-Aug. **On site lodging:** No. **Rental clubs:** Yes. **Walking policy:** Unrestricted walking. **Metal spikes allowed:** Yes. **Range:** No. **To obtain tee times:** Call on Thursday for Saturday and Sunday only.

★★★THE LINKS AT TENNWOOD

PU-22602 Hegar Rd., Hockley, 77447, Harris County, (713)757-5465, (800)865-4657. **Opened:** 1993. **Holes:** 18. **Par:** 72/73. **Yards:** 6,880/5,238. **Course rating:** 70.8/68.3. **Slope:** 120/109. **Architect:** Tom Fazio. **Green fee:** $10/$25. **Credit cards:** MC,VISA,AMEX. **Reduced fees:** Weekdays, twilight, seniors, juniors. **Caddies:** No. **Golf carts:** $9. **Discount golf packages:** Yes. **Season:** Year-round. **High:** Spring/Fall. **On site lodging:** No. **Rental clubs:** Yes. **Walking policy:** Walking at certain times. **Metal spikes allowed:** Yes. **Range:** Yes (grass). **To obtain tee times:** Call 1 day in advance for weekdays and Thursday at 9 a.m. for upcoming weekend.

Subscriber comments: Good confidence builder, fun to play...Combination links and parkland...Still a favorite municipal...Super tight front nine, open back but hard to figure out first time...Front nine has oaks...No.17 fun short par 4 (256 yards) that just kills me...19th hole cheeseburgers worth 18 holes to get.

★★★LIONS MUNICIPAL GOLF COURSE

PM-2901 Enfield Rd., Austin, 78703, Travis County, (512)477-6963. **Opened:** N/A. **Holes:** 18. **Par:** 71/71. **Yards:** 6,001/4,931. **Course rating:** N/A. **Slope:** 118. **Architect:** Leon Howard. **Green fee:** N/A. **Credit cards:** N/A. **Reduced fees:** Twilight. **Caddies:** No. **Golf carts:** N/A. **Discount golf packages:** No. **Season:** Year-round. **High:** June-Aug. **On site lodging:** No. **Rental clubs:** No. **Walking policy:** N/A. **Metal spikes allowed:** Yes. **Range:** Yes. **To obtain tee times:** N/A.

Subscriber comments: Short, lots trees...One of my favorite places to play...Wonderful old, short course...Greens are very grainy...Has famous 16th. "Hogan's Hole"...A little gem from old times...A fun course for both beginners and scratch golfers...16th is a great hole...I've never played in under five hours...Lots of Texas golf history.

★★★★LONGWOOD GOLF CLUB

PU-13300 Longwood Trace, Cypress, 77429, Harris County, (281)373-4100. **Opened:** 1995. **Holes:** 27. **Architect:** Keith Fergus and Harry Yewens. **Green fee:** $44/$55. **Credit cards:** MC,VISA,AMEX. **Reduced fees:** Weekdays, twilight, seniors, juniors. **Caddies:** No. **Golf carts:** Included in Green Fee. **Discount golf packages:** No. **Season:** Year-round. **High:** Spring/Fall. **On site lodging:** No. **Rental clubs:** No. **Walking policy:** Mandatory cart. **Metal spikes allowed:** Yes. **Range:** Yes (grass). **To obtain tee times:** Call up to 4 days in advance.

PALMETTO/POST OAK
Par: 72/72. **Yards:** 6,647/4,872. **Course rating:** 72.2/72.2. **Slope:** 133/133.

PINE/PALMETTO
Par: 72/72. **Yards:** 6,758/4,860. **Course rating:** 72.8/68.9. **Slope:** 136/123.

POST OAK/PINE
Par: 72/72. **Yards:** 6,925/5,094. **Course rating:** 73.6/69.9. **Slope:** 139/124.

Subscriber comments: Great layout, good shotmaker's course...Have to hit long to play well...New course that will soon be very nice...Beautiful setting, fun to play...Challenging yet fair, rolling terrain.

LOST VALLEY GOLF SHOP
R-P.O. Box 2170, Bandera, 78003, Bandera County, (830)460-7958, (800)378-8681, 30 miles N of San Antonio.
Opened: 1955. **Holes:** 18. **Par:** 72. **Yards:** 6,210. **Course rating:** 69.2. **Slope:** 116. **Architect:** N/A. **Green fee:** $10/$15. **Credit cards:** MC,VISA,AMEX. **Reduced fees:** Resort guests, twilight, seniors, juniors. **Caddies:** No. **Golf carts:** $9. **Discount golf packages:** Yes. **Season:** Year-round. **High:** April-Aug. **On site lodging:** Yes. **Rental clubs:** Yes. **Walking policy:** Walking at certain times. **Metal spikes allowed:** Yes. **Range:** No. **To obtain tee times:** Call.

★★★½MARRIOTT'S GOLF CLUB AT FOSSIL CREEK
PU-3401 Clubgate Dr., Fort Worth, 76137, Tarrant County, (817)847-1900.
Opened: 1987. **Holes:** 18. **Par:** 72/72. **Yards:** 6,865/5,066. **Course rating:** 73.6/68.5. **Slope:** 131/111. **Architect:** Arnold Palmer and Ed Seay. **Green fee:** $46/$72. **Credit cards:** MC,VISA,AMEX. **Reduced fees:** Weekdays, twilight. **Caddies:** No. **Golf carts:** Included in Green Fee. **Discount golf packages:** No. **Season:** Year-round. **High:** March-June/Sept. **On site lodging:** No. **Rental clubs:** Yes. **Walking policy:** Mandatory cart. **Metal spikes allowed:** No. **Range:** Yes (grass). **To obtain tee times:** Call 5 days in advance.
Subscriber comments: Great design, incredibly fun from the tips...Many blind shots to greens...Some scenic holes...Fun, challenging course, but needs some maturing...Good par 3s...Tough course in 20mph winds...Awesome risk/reward...Most enjoyable public course in Ft. Worth...Better have a hot putter.

★★MAXWELL GOLF CLUB
PM-1002 S. 32nd St., Abilene, 79602, Taylor County, (915)692-2737, 160 miles W of Dallas.
Opened: 1930. **Holes:** 18. **Par:** 71/71. **Yards:** 6,125/5,031. **Course rating:** 68.1/66.5. **Slope:** 111/105. **Architect:** N/A. **Green fee:** $11/$15. **Credit cards:** MC,VISA. **Reduced fees:** Twilight, seniors, juniors. **Caddies:** No. **Golf carts:** $16. **Discount golf packages:** No. **Season:** Year-round. **High:** July-Aug. **On site lodging:** No. **Rental clubs:** Yes. **Walking policy:** Unrestricted walking. **Metal spikes allowed:** Yes. **Range:** Yes (grass). **To obtain tee times:** Call 7 days in advance.

★★★MEADOWBROOK GOLF COURSE
PM-1815 Jenson Rd., Fort Worth, 76112, Tarrant County, (817)457-4616, 5 miles E of Fort Worth.
Opened: 1924. **Holes:** 18. **Par:** 71/71. **Yards:** 6,363/5,000. **Course rating:** 70.2/68.4. **Slope:** 126/116. **Architect:** N/A. **Green fee:** $6/$20. **Credit cards:** All major. **Reduced fees:** Twilight, seniors, juniors. **Caddies:** No. **Golf carts:** $18. **Discount golf packages:** No. **Season:** Year-round. **High:** April-Oct. **On site lodging:** No. **Rental clubs:** Yes. **Walking policy:** Unrestricted walking. **Metal spikes allowed:** Yes. **Range:** No. **To obtain tee times:** Call up to 7 days in advance.
Subscriber comments: Old but lots of shots needed...Great layout...Rolling terrain...Challenges iron play...Interesting from the tips...My favorite Ft. Worth course...Long par 5 to start makes it challenging...Very good muny.

MEADOWBROOK MUNICIPAL GOLF COMPLEX
PU-601 Municipal Dr., Lubbock, 79403, Lubbock County, (806)765-6679.
Opened: 1934. **Architect:** Warren Cantrell. **Credit cards:** MC,VISA,DISC. **Reduced fees:** Weekdays, twilight, seniors, juniors. **Caddies:** No. **Golf carts:** $9. **Discount golf packages:** No. **Season:** Year-round. **On site lodging:** No. **Rental clubs:** Yes. **Walking policy:** Unrestricted walking. **Metal spikes allowed:** No. **Range:** Yes (grass/mats). **To obtain tee times:** Call 5 days in advance.
★★CANYON
Holes: 18. **Par:** 71/72. **Yards:** 6,450/5,686. **Course rating:** 71.6/74.3. **Slope:** 118. **Green fee:** $14/$18. **High:** April-Sept.
★★CREEK
Holes: 18. **Par:** 70/70. **Yards:** 6,200/5,055. **Course rating:** 69.0/70.5. **Slope:** 113. **Green fee:** $10/$14. **High:** June-Oct.

★★★½MEMORIAL PARK GOLF COURSE
PU-1001 Memorial Loop Park E., Houston, 77007, Harris County, (713)862-4033.
Opened: 1936. **Holes:** 18. **Par:** 72/72. **Yards:** 7,164/5,459. **Course rating:** 73.0/67.7.
Slope: 122/114. **Architect:** John Bredemus/Baxter Spann. **Green fee:** N/A. **Credit cards:** None. **Reduced fees:** Weekdays, twilight. **Caddies:** No. **Golf carts:** $20.
Discount golf packages: No. **Season:** Year-round. **High:** April-Aug. **On site lodging:** No. **Rental clubs:** Yes. **Walking policy:** Unrestricted walking. **Metal spikes allowed:** Yes. **Range:** Yes (grass/mats). **To obtain tee times:** Call up to 3 days in advance.
Notes: 1947, 1951-63 Houston Open.
Subscriber comments: Classic course, fun and fair...Always busy...A must play since they redesigned last year...Big greens, big fairways, big trees, let out the shaft...Fun course for any golfer's ability...If you don't play it, you lose...Best Houston city course...A successful course restoration.

★½MESQUITE GOLF COURSE
PU-825 N. Hwy. 67, Mesquite, 75150, Dallas County, (972)270-7457, 15 miles E of Dallas.
Opened: 1963. **Holes:** 18. **Par:** 71/72. **Yards:** 6,280/5,028. **Course rating:** 69.1/70.2.
Slope: 116/113. **Architect:** Marvin Ferguson. **Green fee:** $5/$16. **Credit cards:** MC,VISA. **Reduced fees:** Weekdays, low season, twilight, seniors, juniors. **Caddies:** No. **Golf carts:** N/A. **Discount golf packages:** No. **Season:** Year-round. **High:** March-Oct. **On site lodging:** No. **Rental clubs:** Yes. **Walking policy:** Unrestricted walking.
Metal spikes allowed: Yes. **Range:** Yes (grass). **To obtain tee times:** Call Thursday for Saturday, Sunday and holidays. Weekdays call two days in advance.

★★★½MILL CREEK GOLF & COUNTRY CLUB
R-1610 Club Circle, Salado, 76571, Bell County, (254)947-5698, (800)736-3441, 50 miles N of Austin.
Opened: 1981. **Holes:** 18. **Par:** 71/73. **Yards:** 6,486/5,250. **Course rating:** 72.1/69.6.
Slope: 128/114. **Architect:** Robert Trent Jones Jr. **Green fee:** $55/$65. **Credit cards:** MC,VISA. **Reduced fees:** Weekdays, resort guests. **Caddies:** No. **Golf carts:** Included in Green Fee. **Discount golf packages:** Yes. **Season:** Year-round. **High:** March-Oct.
On site lodging: Yes. **Rental clubs:** Yes. **Walking policy:** Mandatory cart. **Metal spikes allowed:** Yes. **Range:** Yes (grass). **To obtain tee times:** Call up to 2 days in advance.
Subscriber comments: Good, could play it every day...Challenging course...Great course in winter...Great layout, fun test...Several memorable holes, good variety, all clubs needed...A fun place to relax, play golf and enjoy.

★★★½MISSION DEL LAGO GOLF COURSE
PU-1250 Mission Grande, San Antonio, 78214, Bexar County, (210)627-2522, 2 miles S of San Antonio.
Opened: 1989. **Holes:** 18. **Par:** 72/72. **Yards:** 7,200/5,601. **Course rating:** 73.6/70.2.
Slope: 130/121. **Architect:** Denis Griffiths. **Green fee:** $21/$40. **Credit cards:** All major. **Reduced fees:** Weekdays, low season, resort guests, twilight, seniors, juniors.
Caddies: No. **Golf carts:** Included in Green Fee. **Discount golf packages:** Yes.
Season: Year-round. **High:** Spring/Fall. **On site lodging:** No. **Rental clubs:** Yes.
Walking policy: Unrestricted walking. **Metal spikes allowed:** Yes. **Range:** Yes (grass).
To obtain tee times: Call up to 90 days in advance.
Subscriber comments: Go off the gold tees, great time...Good test of golf, use all the clubs...A real pleasure to play...Need middle tees...Lot of bunkers...Out of the way location, but worth the search...Look out for wild animals, bobcats, snakes, etc.

★★MORRIS WILLIAMS GOLF CLUB
PM-4305 Manor Rd., Austin, 78723, Travis County, (512)926-1298.
Opened: 1964. **Holes:** 18. **Par:** 72/72. **Yards:** 6,636/5,273. **Course rating:** 71.5/70.4.
Slope: 121/117. **Architect:** Leon Howard. **Green fee:** $12/$13. **Credit cards:** None.
Reduced fees: Weekdays, twilight, seniors, juniors. **Caddies:** No. **Golf carts:** $17.
Discount golf packages: Yes. **Season:** Year-round. **High:** March-Nov. **On site lodging:** No. **Rental clubs:** Yes. **Walking policy:** Unrestricted walking. **Metal spikes allowed:** Yes. **Range:** Yes (grass). **To obtain tee times:** Call 1 day in advance for weekdays and Friday a.m. for weekends and holidays.

★★NOCONA HILLS GOLF COURSE
179 Country Club Dr., Nocona, 76255, Montague County, (940)825-3444, 58 miles E of Wichita Falls.
Opened: 1973. **Holes:** 18. **Par:** 72/72. **Yards:** 6,155/4,971. **Course rating:** 71.3/64.1. **Slope:** 111/103. **Architect:** Leon Howard and Charles Howard. **Green fee:** $10/$15. **Credit cards:** MC,VISA. **Reduced fees:** Seniors, juniors. **Caddies:** No. **Golf carts:** N/A. **Discount golf packages:** No. **Season:** Year-round. **High:** April-Nov. **On site lodging:** Yes. **Rental clubs:** Yes. **Walking policy:** Walking at certain times. **Metal spikes allowed:** Yes. **Range:** Yes (grass). **To obtain tee times:** Call up to 7 days in advance.

★★★½OLD ORCHARD GOLF CLUB
PU-13134 FM 1464, Richmond, 77469, Fort Bend County, (281)277-3300, 15 miles SW of Houston.
Opened: 1990. **Holes:** 27. **Architect:** C. Gibson, H. Yewens and K. Forgus. **Green fee:** $30/$55. **Credit cards:** MC,VISA,AMEX,Pulse Pay. **Reduced fees:** Twilight, seniors, juniors. **Caddies:** No. **Golf carts:** Included in Green Fee. **Discount golf packages:** No. **Season:** Year-round. **High:** Spring/Fall. **On site lodging:** No. **Rental clubs:** Yes. **Walking policy:** Unrestricted walking. **Metal spikes allowed:** Yes. **Range:** Yes (grass/mats). **To obtain tee times:** Call or come in up to 6 days in advance.
BARN/RANGE
Par: 72/72. **Yards:** 6,927/5,166. **Course rating:** 73.6/69.4. **Slope:** 127/114.
STABLES/BARN
Par: 72/72. **Yards:** 6,888/5,035. **Course rating:** 73.5/69.0. **Slope:** 130/113.
STABLES/RANGE
Par: 72/72. **Yards:** 6,687/5,010. **Course rating:** 71.7/68.1. **Slope:** 124/111.
Subscriber comments: Fun course, a great setting for golf...Range nine is least interesting, wide open...All three nines are good, fun...Barn course tight...Range tough in wind...All of the courses at Old Orchard are simply great...Always windy, makes you think...Get BBQ at turn...Lots of old pecan trees.

★★½OLMOS BASIN GOLF CLUB
7022 N. McCullough, San Antonio, 78216, Bexar County, (210)826-4041. Call club for further information.
Subscriber comments: Long, tough, challenging, bring your "wind cheater"...Flat...Much improved...Pretty good golf course, nothing spectacular...Good muny...Slow play, fivesomes allowed...Open course, good for beginners.

★★½OSO BEACH MUNICIPAL GOLF COURSE
PU-5601 S. Alameda, Corpus Christi, 78412, Nueces County, (512)991-5351.
Opened: 1938. **Holes:** 18. **Par:** 70/70. **Yards:** 6,223/4,994. **Course rating:** 69.9/68.8. **Slope:** 119/118. **Architect:** John Bredemus. **Green fee:** $10/$12. **Credit cards:** MC,VISA. **Reduced fees:** Twilight, seniors, juniors. **Caddies:** No. **Golf carts:** $8. **Discount golf packages:** No. **Season:** Year-round. **High:** Jan.-April. **On site lodging:** No. **Rental clubs:** Yes. **Walking policy:** Walking at certain times. **Metal spikes allowed:** Yes. **Range:** No. **To obtain tee times:** Call Wednesday for Saturday and Sunday.
Subscriber comments: Must have a good wind game...Fun course, good greens...Watch out for the alligator...Local favorite, improving...Small greens.

★★★★PAINTED DUNES DESERT GOLF COURSE
PU-12000 McCombs, El Paso, 79934, El Paso County, (915)821-2122.
Opened: 1991. **Holes:** 18. **Par:** 72/72. **Yards:** 6,925/5,717. **Course rating:** 74.0/74.5. **Slope:** 137/123. **Architect:** Ken Dye. **Green fee:** $19/$23. **Credit cards:** MC,VISA,AMEX. **Reduced fees:** Twilight, seniors, juniors. **Caddies:** No. **Golf carts:** $18. **Discount golf packages:** No. **Season:** Year-round. **High:** April/May/Sept. **On site lodging:** No. **Rental clubs:** Yes. **Walking policy:** Unrestricted walking. **Metal spikes allowed:** Yes. **Range:** Yes (grass/mats). **To obtain tee times:** Call 7 days in advance for weekdays. Call Monday starting at 7 a.m. for upcoming weekend.
Notes: Ranked 9th in 1997 Best in State.
Subscriber comments: The desert setting is awesome...Better be a straight hitter...

A true test...Everyone should play, slick greens, select proper tee box for enjoyment...This is truly what every public course should be...Excellent layout, can use all your clubs...Incredible greens, quick and undulating...Bring your lob wedge...Never know direction of bounce off dunes...One of the best I've ever played.

★★PALACIO REAL COUNTRY CLUB
Monte Cristo Rd., Edinburg, 78539, Hidalgo County, (956)381-0964.
Call club for further information.
Special Notes: Formerly Monte Cristo Golf Course.

★★★PALO DURO CREEK GOLF CLUB
50 Country Club Dr., Canyon, 79015, Randall County, (806)655-1106, 12 miles S of Amarillo.
Opened: N/A. **Holes:** 18. **Par:** 72/74. **Yards:** 6,865/5,120. **Course rating:** 72.1/66.9. **Slope:** 117/105. **Architect:** Henry Hughes. **Green fee:** $10/$15. **Credit cards:** MC,VISA. **Reduced fees:** Twilight, seniors, juniors. **Caddies:** No. **Golf carts:** $16. **Discount golf packages:** No. **Season:** Year-round. **High:** April-Sept. **On site lodging:** No. **Rental clubs:** Yes. **Walking policy:** Unrestricted walking. **Metal spikes allowed:** No. **Range:** Yes (grass). **To obtain tee times:** Call.
Subscriber comments: Greens are cut to perfection...Nice with plenty of trees...Good placement of water hazards...Good layout, challenging...Lots of water, yardage a factor, lots of layups.

★½PASADENA MUNICIPAL GOLF COURSE
PM-1000 Duffer, Houston, 77034, Harris County, (281)481-0834.
Opened: 1978. **Holes:** 18. **Par:** 72/72. **Yards:** 6,750/4,910. **Course rating:** 72.2/67.9. **Slope:** 118/108. **Architect:** Jay Riviere. **Green fee:** $9/$13. **Credit cards:** MC,VISA,AMEX,DISC,Diners Club. **Reduced fees:** Weekdays, twilight, seniors, juniors. **Caddies:** No. **Golf carts:** $19. **Discount golf packages:** No. **Season:** Year-round. **High:** March-Aug. **On site lodging:** No. **Rental clubs:** Yes. **Walking policy:** Unrestricted walking. **Metal spikes allowed:** Yes. **Range:** Yes (grass). **To obtain tee times:** Call on Wednesday 7:30 a.m. for weekend/holiday tee times.

PEACH TREE GOLF CLUB
6212 CR 152 W., Bullard, 75757, Smith County, (903)894-7079, 9 miles S of Tyler.
Credit cards: MC,VISA,DISC. **Reduced fees:** Weekdays, twilight, seniors, juniors. **Caddies:** No. **Golf carts:** $10. **Discount golf packages:** No. **Season:** Year-round. **High:** April-Sept. **On site lodging:** No. **Rental clubs:** Yes. **Walking policy:** Unrestricted walking. **Metal spikes allowed:** Yes. **Range:** Yes (grass).
★★★OAKHURST COURSE
Opened: 1993. **Holes:** 18. **Par:** 72/72. **Yards:** 6,813/5,086. **Course rating:** 72.1/68.4. **Slope:** 126/118. **Architect:** Carlton Gibson. **Green fee:** $18/$26. **To obtain tee times:** Call 6 days in advance.
Subscriber comments: My favorite course...Enjoyed course...New course, will be very good in a few years...Great course...Nice course, average fairways and greens.
★½PEACH TREE COURSE
Opened: 1986. **Holes:** 18. **Par:** 70/71. **Yards:** 5,556/4,467. **Course rating:** 65.7/65.5. **Slope:** 109/111. **Architect:** Dan Hurst. **Green fee:** $10/$14. **To obtain tee times:** First come, first served.
Subscriber comments: Poor second cousin...Flat and basic.

★★★½PECAN VALLEY GOLF CLUB
PU-4700 Pecan Valley Dr., San Antonio, 78223, Bexar County, (210)333-9018, (800)336-3418, 6 miles S of San Antonio.
Opened: 1963. **Holes:** 18. **Par:** 71/72. **Yards:** 7,071/5,621. **Course rating:** 74.5/73.0. **Slope:** 136/126. **Architect:** J. Press Maxwell. **Green fee:** $30/$57. **Credit cards:** MC,VISA,AMEX. **Reduced fees:** Weekdays, low season, twilight, seniors, juniors. **Caddies:** No. **Golf carts:** Included in Green Fee. **Discount golf packages:** No. **Season:** Year-round. **High:** Spring/Fall. **On site lodging:** No. **Rental clubs:** Yes. **Walking policy:** Mandatory cart. **Metal spikes allowed:** Yes. **Range:** Yes (grass). **To obtain tee times:** Call 14 days in advance with credit card.
Notes: 1968-70 Texas Open; 1968 PGA Championship.

Subscriber comments: Good test of golf, tough holes...Historical markers around course...Tough par 4s, narrow fairways...Course conditions improving...Don't be above any flag...Trees, water, calls for shotmaking...Past its prime...A favorite to play in San Antonio...Still a great course.

PECAN VALLEY GOLF COURSE

PM-6400 Pecan Dr., Fort Worth, 76126, Tarrant County, (817)249-1845, 35 miles W of Dallas.
Opened: N/A. **Architect:** Ralph Plummer/Bland Pittman. **Green fee:** $12/$15. **Credit cards:** All major. **Reduced fees:** Weekdays, low season, twilight, seniors, juniors.
Caddies: No. **Golf carts:** $16. **Discount golf packages:** Yes. **Season:** Year-round.
High: April-Nov. **On site lodging:** No. **Rental clubs:** Yes. **Walking policy:** Unrestricted walking. **Metal spikes allowed:** Yes. **Range:** Yes (grass/mats).
★★**HILLS COURSE**
Holes: 18. **Par:** 72/72. **Yards:** 6,577/5,275. **Course rating:** 71.4/69.7. **Slope:** 128/115.
To obtain tee times: Call tee time number up to 5 days in advance.
★★★**RIVER COURSE**
Holes: 18. **Par:** 71/72. **Yards:** 6,562/5,419. **Course rating:** 71.3/69.6. **Slope:** 124/109.
To obtain tee times: Call Monday at noon for that week.
Subscriber comments: River Course more difficult...Very challenging, great greens...Good layout...Better than its sister course...Tight fairways...Possibly best muny in Ft. Worth...Course has been in better shape...Front nine a little boring, love the back nine...Heavily played...Many holes can be deceptive...Neat finishing par 5.

PERRYTON MUNICIPAL GOLF COURSE

402 SE 24th. St., Perryton, 79070, Ochiltree County, (806)435-5381.
Call club for further information.

★★★PHEASANT TRAILS GOLF COURSE

PU-Hwy. 119, Dumas, 79029, Moore County, (806)935-7375, 45 miles N of Amarillo.
Opened: 1945. **Holes:** 18. **Par:** 71/71. **Yards:** 6,481/5,292. **Course rating:** 69.5/70.5.
Slope: 111/117. **Architect:** N/A. **Green fee:** $8/$11. **Credit cards:** MC,VISA. **Reduced fees:** Twilight, juniors. **Caddies:** No. **Golf carts:** $17. **Discount golf packages:** No.
Season: Year-round. **High:** March-Nov. **On site lodging:** No. **Rental clubs:** Yes.
Walking policy: Unrestricted walking. **Metal spikes allowed:** Yes. **Range:** Yes (grass).
To obtain tee times: Call Friday for weekend.
Subscriber comments: For a little town I think they do a great job...Two different nines, new nine longer and challenging, old nine fun...Best fairways on a municipal course in Texas panhandle...Can play ball down all year.

★★½PHILLIPS COUNTRY CLUB

Sterling Rd., Borger, 79007, Hutchinson County, (806)274-6812.
Call club for further information.
Subscriber comments: Good fairways and great greens...Easy to score, easy to get in trouble...Leave the driver at home, water, and OB.

★★★PINE FOREST GOLF CLUB

2509 Riverside Dr., Bastrop, 78602, Bastrop County, (512)321-1181.
Call club for further information.
Subscriber comments: Beautiful course, could play every day...A sleeper on the river...Back nine better, worth a stop...Hilly, blind shots...Best-kept secret in Texas, unique...Target golf...Please don't publish, it's a secret, great landscape.

PINE RIDGE GOLF COURSE

PU-Pine Mill Rd., Paris, 75462, Lamar County, (903)785-8076, 100 miles NE of Dallas.
Opened: 1987. **Holes:** 18. **Par:** 72/72. **Yards:** 5,855/4,462. **Course rating:** N/A. **Slope:** N/A. **Architect:** Raney/Exum. **Green fee:** $9/$11. **Credit cards:** MC,VISA,DISC.
Reduced fees: Weekdays, twilight. **Caddies:** No. **Golf carts:** $16. **Discount golf packages:** No. **Season:** Year-round. **High:** April-Oct. **On site lodging:** No. **Rental clubs:** Yes. **Walking policy:** Unrestricted walking. **Metal spikes allowed:** Yes. **Range:** Yes (grass/mats). **To obtain tee times:** Call for weekends.

★★★½ PINNACLE COUNTRY CLUB

200 Pinnacle Club Dr., Mabank, 75147, Henderson County, (903)451-9797, 60 miles SE of Dallas.
Opened: 1988. **Holes:** 18. **Par:** 71/71. **Yards:** 6,641/5,222. **Course rating:** 72.9/70.8. **Slope:** 135/129. **Architect:** Don January. **Green fee:** $16/$28. **Credit cards:** MC,VISA,AMEX. **Reduced fees:** Weekdays, twilight, seniors. **Caddies:** No. **Golf carts:** $9. **Discount golf packages:** Yes. **Season:** Year-round. **High:** March-Aug. **On site lodging:** No. **Rental clubs:** Yes. **Walking policy:** Walking at certain times. **Metal spikes allowed:** Yes. **Range:** Yes (grass/mats). **To obtain tee times:** Call 3 days in advance.
Subscriber comments: Trees, trees, water and more trees...Toughest course I've played, very tight...OB on most holes, trees on all holes...Leave driver at home...Tight course, challenging...Beautiful trip through the woods, have to hit the fairway.

★★½ PLANO MUNICIPAL GOLF COURSE

4501 E. 14th St., Plano, 75074, Collin County, (972)423-5444.
Architect: Don January and Billy Martindale. **Caddies:** No. **Discount golf packages:** No. **On site lodging:** No. **Rental clubs:** No. **Metal spikes allowed:** Yes. **Range:** No.
Subscriber comments: Good muny...No-frills muny that gets too much play...Lots of water...Wide open for the most part...Not really a difficult course, but fun...Tough finishing holes...Could be great, long...Easy to get tee times...Has a few great holes.

★★½ PLANTATION GOLF CLUB

PU-4701 Plantation Lane, Frisco, 75035, Collin County, (972)335-4653, 20 miles N of Dallas.
Opened: 1988. **Holes:** 18. **Par:** 72/72. **Yards:** 6,382/5,945. **Course rating:** 70.9/70.4. **Slope:** 122/117. **Architect:** Richard Ellis. **Green fee:** $40/$55. **Credit cards:** MC,VISA,AMEX. **Reduced fees:** Weekdays, low season, twilight. **Caddies:** No. **Golf carts:** Included in Green Fee. **Discount golf packages:** Yes. **Season:** Year-round. **High:** Year-round. **On site lodging:** No. **Rental clubs:** Yes. **Walking policy:** Mandatory cart. **Metal spikes allowed:** No. **Range:** Yes (grass). **To obtain tee times:** Call up to 7 days in advance.
Subscriber comments: Too short, many lay-ups...Has some interesting holes...Too many houses too close to the course.

★★½ QUAIL CREEK COUNTRY CLUB

Bastrop Highway, San Marcos, 78666, Hays County, (512)353-1665.
Call club for further information.
Subscriber comments: Play under four hours...Very dry course...Above average public course...Some tiny greens...Not crowded...Short course, but must be precise...Greens are too small...Getting better.

★★★★ THE QUARRY GOLF CLUB

PU-444 E. Basse Rd., San Antonio, 78209, Bexar County, (210)824-4500, (800)347-7759.
Opened: 1993. **Holes:** 18. **Par:** 71/71. **Yards:** 6,740/4,897. **Course rating:** 72.4/67.4. **Slope:** 128/115. **Architect:** Keith Foster. **Green fee:** $75/$85. **Credit cards:** All major. **Reduced fees:** Twilight. **Caddies:** No. **Golf carts:** Included in Green Fee. **Discount golf packages:** No. **Season:** Year-round. **High:** March-Nov. **On site lodging:** No. **Rental clubs:** Yes. **Walking policy:** Unrestricted walking. **Metal spikes allowed:** Yes. **Range:** Yes (grass). **To obtain tee times:** Call 30 days in advance with credit card.
Notes: Ranked 7th in 1997 Best in State.
Subscriber comments: Unbelievable back nine, breathtaking...Still talking about this round...Front nine is links style, every hole on back nine is a thriller...Golf in a bowl...Truly unique layout in a quarry...Some long carries...Most original layout in Texas, very challenging...Play at least once.

★★½RABBIT RUN GOLF CLUB

Beaumont, Jefferson County, (409)866-7545.
Call club for further information.
Subscriber comments: The last three holes are good finishing holes...18th green is an elevated killer...Good practice course...Young course needs to mature, several hidden water hazards, fast greens...Still has way to go...Punished for decent shots.

RANCHO VIEJO RESORT & COUNTRY CLUB

R-No.1 Rancho Viejo Dr., Rancho Viejo, 78575, Cameron County, (956)350-4000, (800)531-7400, 3 miles N of Brownsville.
Opened: 1971. **Architect:** Dennis W. Arp. **Green fee:** $35/$40. **Credit cards:** MC,VISA,AMEX. **Reduced fees:** Resort guests. **Caddies:** No. **Golf carts:** $12. **Discount golf packages:** Yes. **Season:** Year-round. **High:** Oct.-May. **On site lodging:** Yes. **Rental clubs:** Yes. **Walking policy:** Walking at certain times. **Metal spikes allowed:** Yes. **Range:** Yes (grass). **To obtain tee times:** Hotel guests 30 days in advance.

★★★EL ANGEL COURSE

Holes: 18. **Par:** 71/72. **Yards:** 6,318/5,087. **Course rating:** 71.5/67.6. **Slope:** 120/113.
Subscriber comments: Front and back nines entirely different, back nine in quarry is a good experience...Easier than the Diablo course...A big Texas welcome...Wide open...Very forgiving course, setting is great.

★★★EL DIABLO COURSE

Holes: 18. **Par:** 70/73. **Yards:** 6,847/5,556. **Course rating:** 73.7/70.7. **Slope:** 129/122.
Subscriber comments: The course is great...A real test when the wind blows...Very challenging, best greens in area...Country club setting.

★★½RATLIFF RANCH GOLF LINKS

PU-7500 N. Grandview, Odessa, 79768, Ector County, (915)550-8181, 3 miles N of Odessa.
Opened: 1988. **Holes:** 18. **Par:** 72/72. **Yards:** 6,800/4,900. **Course rating:** 73.0/68.9. **Slope:** 122/110. **Architect:** Jeff Brauer. **Green fee:** $12/$17. **Credit cards:** MC,VISA,DISC. **Reduced fees:** Weekdays, twilight, seniors, juniors. **Caddies:** No. **Golf carts:** $8. **Discount golf packages:** No. **Season:** Year-round. **High:** March-Sept. **On site lodging:** No. **Rental clubs:** Yes. **Walking policy:** Unrestricted walking. **Metal spikes allowed:** Yes. **Range:** Yes (grass/mats). **To obtain tee times:** Call Thursday for upcoming weekend or holiday.
Subscriber comments: Very challenging layout...Greens good, fairways poor...12th hole is the best par 3 in West Texas...Links style...Long and traditional, nice big greens.

★★★½RAYBURN COUNTRY CLUB & RESORT

R-1000 Wingate Blvd., Sam Rayburn, 75951, Jasper County, (409)698-2958, (800)882-1442, 82 miles N of Beaumont.

Opened: 1967. **Holes:** 27. **Architect:** Riviere/Von Hagge and Devlin/R. Trent Jones. **Green fee:** $28/$35. **Credit cards:** All major. **Reduced fees:** Weekdays, low season, twilight, juniors. **Caddies:** No. **Golf carts:** $20. **Discount golf packages:** Yes. **Season:** Year-round. **High:** Spring/Fall. **On site lodging:** Yes. **Rental clubs:** Yes. **Walking policy:** Walking at certain times. **Metal spikes allowed:** Yes. **Range:** Yes (grass/mats). **To obtain tee times:** Call golf shop.

BLUE/GOLD
Par: 72/72. **Yards:** 6,731/5,824. **Course rating:** 71.3/72.2. **Slope:** 116/126.
BLUE/GREEN
Par: 72/72. **Yards:** 6,719/5,237. **Course rating:** 72.5/71.0. **Slope:** 129/123.
GOLD/GREEN
Par: 72/72. **Yards:** 6,728/5,301. **Course rating:** 72.2/71.0. **Slope:** 124/118.
Subscriber comments: Good test of golf in East Texas...No.1 is a hole you will remember...Gold is the best of the nines...Lots of elevation changes, fairways tight in places...Hit it straight or watch your ball roll into the ravines...Green nine hilly and tight, almost unplayable...Hill Country golf in East Texas, great layout.

REEVES COUNTY GOLF COURSE

88 Starley Dr., Pecos, 79772, Reeves County, (915)447-2858.
Opened: N/A. **Holes:** N/A. **Par:** N/A. **Yards:** N/A. **Course rating:** N/A. **Slope:** N/A.
Architect: N/A. **Green fee:** $17/$24. **Credit cards:** MC,VISA,AMEX. **Reduced fees:**
Low season, twilight, seniors, juniors. **Caddies:** No. **Golf carts:** $10. **Discount golf**
packages: Yes. **Season:** N/A. **High:** N/A. **On site lodging:** No. **Rental clubs:** No.
Walking policy: N/A. **Metal spikes allowed:** Yes. **Range:** No. **To obtain tee times:**
Call 2 days in advance at 8 a.m. for weekends and holidays.

★★★★RIDGEVIEW RANCH GOLF CLUB

2501 Ridgeview Dr., Plano, 75025, Collin County, (972)390-1039.
Call club for further information.
Subscriber comments: Great new muny, need more of these...Incredible for a brand
new course...Will get better...Great course for long hitters...Good challenge for all levels...Best new course in DFW in years...Long par 4s into prevailing wind...Incredible
natural use of land...Best new course around.

★★★½RIO COLORADO GOLF COURSE

PM-FM 2668 and Riverside Park, Bay City, 77414, Matagorda County, (409)244-2955,
80 miles S of Houston.
Opened: 1993. **Holes:** 18. **Par:** 72/72. **Yards:** 6,824/5,020. **Course rating:** 73.1/69.1.
Slope: 127/116. **Architect:** Gary Player Design Company. **Green fee:** $17/$24. **Credit**
cards: MC,VISA,AMEX. **Reduced fees:** Low season, twilight, seniors, juniors.
Caddies: No. **Golf carts:** $10. **Discount golf packages:** Yes. **Season:** Year-round.
High: April-Oct. **On site lodging:** No. **Rental clubs:** Yes. **Walking policy:** Unrestricted
walking. **Metal spikes allowed:** Yes. **Range:** Yes (grass/mats). **To obtain tee times:**
Call 2 days in advance at 8 a.m. for weekends and holidays.
Subscriber comments: Out of the way, links style...Good mix of traditional and links in
one...A good country course...Open front, tight back...Flat course, long par 5s, plenty of
bunkers, nice course.

★★★RIVER BEND RESORT

R-Rte. 8, Box 649, Brownsville, 78520, Cameron County, (956)548-0192, 3 miles W of
Brownsville.
Opened: 1985. **Holes:** 18. **Par:** 72/72. **Yards:** 6,828/5,126. **Course rating:** 72.6/71.6.
Slope: 119/119. **Architect:** Mike Ingram. **Green fee:** $17/$17. **Credit cards:** MC,VISA.
Reduced fees: N/A. **Caddies:** No. **Golf carts:** $9. **Discount golf packages:** Yes.
Season: Year-round. **High:** Nov.-March. **On site lodging:** Yes. **Rental clubs:** Yes.
Walking policy: Unrestricted walking. **Metal spikes allowed:** No. **Range:** Yes (grass).
To obtain tee times: Call up to 3 days in advance.
Subscriber comments: Long, tough par 3s...Nice green fairways and greens for
Texas...Hilly but nice...Small greens...Par 4s a little short.

★★RIVER CREEK PARK GOLF COURSE

PU-1177 Farmarket Rd., Burkburnett, 76354, Wichita County, (940)855-3361.
Opened: N/A. **Holes:** 18. **Par:** 71/73. **Yards:** 6,800/5,100. **Course rating:** 69.0/69.1.
Slope: 104/104. **Architect:** Buddy Pierson/Richard Boyd. **Green fee:** $7/$8. **Credit**
cards: MC,VISA. **Reduced fees:** Twilight, seniors, juniors. **Caddies:** No. **Golf carts:**
$10. **Discount golf packages:** No. **Season:** Year-round. **High:** May-July. **On site lodg-**
ing: No. **Rental clubs:** Yes. **Walking policy:** Unrestricted walking. **Metal spikes**
allowed: Yes. **Range:** Yes (grass). **To obtain tee times:** Call up to one week in
advance.

★★★½RIVER PLACE GOLF CLUB

4207 River Place Blvd., Austin, 78730, Travis County, (512)346-6784.
Opened: 1984. **Holes:** 18. **Par:** 71/71. **Yards:** 6,611/4,720. **Course rating:** 72.0/65.5.
Slope: 128/113. **Architect:** Tom Kite and Roy Bechtol. **Green fee:** $50/$65. **Credit**
cards: MC,VISA,AMEX. **Reduced fees:** Twilight, seniors, juniors. **Caddies:** No. **Golf**
carts: Included in Green Fee. **Discount golf packages:** No. **Season:** Year-round.
High: March-Oct. **On site lodging:** No. **Rental clubs:** Yes. **Walking policy:** Mandatory
cart. **Metal spikes allowed:** Yes. **Range:** Yes (grass/mats). **To obtain tee times:** Call 7
days in advance.

Subscriber comments: A great "eat you alive" course, give me a second try...Hit it straight...Beautiful natural setting, especially at sunrise and sunset, still some goofy golf...A must play, before it goes private...Just a few holes from being outstanding...This course is simply too difficult.

★★½RIVERCHASE GOLF CLUB
PU-700 Riverchase Dr., Coppell, 75019, Dallas County, (972)462-8281.
Opened: 1988. **Holes:** 18. **Par:** 71/71. **Yards:** 6,593/6,041. **Course rating:** 72.0/69.3.
Slope: 124/119. **Architect:** George Fazio. **Green fee:** $25/$65. **Credit cards:**
MC,VISA,AMEX. **Reduced fees:** Weekdays, low season, twilight, seniors, juniors.
Caddies: No. **Golf carts:** Included in Green Fee. **Discount golf packages:** Yes.
Season: Year-round. **High:** April-Oct. **On site lodging:** No. **Rental clubs:** Yes. **Walking policy:** Walking at certain times. **Metal spikes allowed:** No. **Range:** Yes (grass/mats).
To obtain tee times: Call up to 3 days in advance.
Subscriber comments: Had fun trying to hit Barry Switzer's house...Like playing in a wind tunnel...Only play when it is not windy...Good place to see Dallas Cowboys...Stay away if you fade the ball.

★★★RIVERSIDE GOLF CLUB
PU-3000 Riverside Pkwy., Grand Prairie, 75050, Dallas County, (817)640-7800, 20 miles SW of Dallas.
Opened: 1984. **Holes:** 18. **Par:** 72/72. **Yards:** 7,025/5,175. **Course rating:** 74.4/69.5.
Slope: 132/113. **Architect:** Roger Packard. **Green fee:** $48/$58. **Credit cards:**
MC,VISA,AMEX. **Reduced fees:** Weekdays, twilight, seniors, juniors. **Caddies:** No.
Golf carts: Included in Green Fee. **Discount golf packages:** Yes. **Season:** Year-round.
High: Spring/Fall. **On site lodging:** No. **Rental clubs:** Yes. **Walking policy:** Walking at certain times. **Metal spikes allowed:** Yes. **Range:** Yes (grass). **To obtain tee times:** Call 5 days in advance. Credit card required for weekend reservation. Times are available farther out with prepayment of full amount.
Subscriber comments: Challenging course...Good layout except after rain...Several difficult holes...Tough, not for beginners...Water, rough can be devastating...Great 18th hole...Too many fairway bunkers...First hole lulls you into false security.

★½RIVERSIDE GOLF CLUB
900 W. 29th, San Angelo, 76903, Tom Green County, (915)653-6130.
Opened: 1965. **Holes:** 18. **Par:** 72. **Yards:** 6,499. **Course rating:** 70.5. **Slope:** 113.
Architect: John Dublin. **Green fee:** $9/$12. **Credit cards:** MC,VISA,DISC. **Reduced fees:** N/A. **Golf carts:** N/A. **Discount golf packages:** No. **High:** N/A. **Walking policy:** Unrestricted walking. **Range:** Yes (grass/mats). **To obtain tee times:** Call.

★★RIVERSIDE GOLF COURSE
PU-1020 Grove Blvd., Austin, 78741, Travis County, (512)386-7077, 2 miles E of Austin.
Opened: 1948. **Holes:** 18. **Par:** 71/71. **Yards:** 6,562/5,334. **Course rating:** 70.3/69.6.
Slope: 122/112. **Architect:** Perry Maxwell. **Green fee:** $15/$20. **Credit cards:**
MC,VISA,AMEX. **Reduced fees:** Weekdays, twilight, seniors, juniors. **Caddies:** No.
Golf carts: $10. **Discount golf packages:** No. **Season:** Year-round. **High:** May-Aug.
On site lodging: No. **Rental clubs:** Yes. **Walking policy:** Unrestricted walking. **Metal spikes allowed:** Yes. **Range:** No.**To obtain tee times:** Call 3 days in advance.

★★★RIVERSIDE GOLF COURSE
302 McWright Rd., Victoria, 77901, Victoria County, (512)573-4521.
Opened: 1953. **Holes:** 27. **Architect:** Ralph Plummer/Jay Riviere. **Green fee:** $10/$12.
Credit cards: N/A. **Reduced fees:** Weekdays, juniors. **Golf carts:** $12. **High:** May-Sept. **Rental clubs:** No. **To obtain tee times:** First come, first served.
RED/WHITE
Par: 72/72. **Yards:** 6,488/5,121. **Course rating:** 71.4/70.4. **Slope:** 122/117.
RED/WHITE
Par: 72/72. **Yards:** 6,606/5,497. **Course rating:** 71.4/70.4. **Slope:** 122/117.
WHITE/BLUE
Par: 72/72. **Yards:** 6,430/5,150. **Course rating:** 70.8/70.4. **Slope:** 121/117.
Subscriber comments: Always in excellent shape...I would rate this one of the best municipal golf courses around, that goes for all 27 holes...Huge pecan trees line fairways. Good test...A challenge, makes you think about your iron shots.

★★½RIVERSIDE MUNICIPAL GOLF COURSE
PM-203 McDonald, San Antonio, 78210, Bexar County, (210)533-8371.
Opened: 1929. **Holes:** 18. **Par:** 72/72. **Yards:** 6,729/5,730. **Course rating:** 72.0/72.0.
Slope: 128/121. **Architect:** Vern Schmidt. **Green fee:** $6/$16. **Credit cards:** All major.
Reduced fees: Weekdays, low season, resort guests, twilight, seniors, juniors.
Caddies: No. **Golf carts:** $15. **Discount golf packages:** Yes. **Season:** Year-round.
High: April-Sept. **On site lodging:** No. **Rental clubs:** Yes. **Walking policy:**
Unrestricted walking. **Metal spikes allowed:** Yes. **Range:** No. **To obtain tee times:**
May call up to a week in advance.
Subscriber comments: Play this course and learn something...Just your average
muny...Challenging...Greens and fairways are poorly kept...Tough par 5s...Back nine is
better than front...Lots of trouble for a flat course.
Special Notes: Also 9-hole par-3 course.

RIVERWOOD GOLF COURSE
Highway 105, Vidor, 77662, Orange County, (409)768-1710.
Call club for further information.

★★ROCKWOOD GOLF COURSE
PM-1851 Jacksboro Hwy., Fort Worth, 76114, Tarrant County, (817)624-1771.
Opened: 1940. **Holes:** 27. **Architect:** John Bredemus. **Green fee:** $12/$14. **Credit
cards:** MC,VISA,AMEX. **Reduced fees:** Weekdays, twilight, seniors, juniors. **Caddies:**
No. **Golf carts:** $17. **Discount golf packages:** No. **Season:** Year-round. **High:** March-
Oct. **On site lodging:** No. **Rental clubs:** Yes. **Walking policy:** Unrestricted walking.
Metal spikes allowed: Yes. **Range:** Yes (grass/mats). **To obtain tee times:** Call 7 days
in advance.
NORTH/RIVER
Par: 72/76. **Yards:** 6,994/5,778. **Course rating:** 67.5/69.5. **Slope:** 115/115.
SOUTH/NORTH
Par: 71/73. **Yards:** 6,340/5,556. **Course rating:** 72.0. **Slope:** 115.
SOUTH/RIVER
Par: 71/73. **Yards:** 6,660/5,704. **Course rating:** 72.6/69.0. **Slope:** 115/115.

★★½ROLLING HILLS GOLF CLUB
R-P.O. Box 1242, Hilltop Lakes, 77871, Leon County, (409)855-2100, 38 miles NE of
Bryan-College Station.
Opened: 1958. **Holes:** 18. **Par:** 72/73. **Yards:** 6,330/5,635. **Course rating:** 70.1/71.5.
Slope: 111/117. **Architect:** C.M. Mimms. **Green fee:** $14/$17. **Credit cards:**
MC,VISA,AMEX. **Reduced fees:** N/A. **Caddies:** No. **Golf carts:** $16. **Discount golf
packages:** No. **Season:** Year-round. **High:** May-Aug. **On site lodging:** Yes. **Rental
clubs:** Yes. **Walking policy:** Unrestricted walking. **Metal spikes allowed:** Yes. **Range:**
Yes (grass). **To obtain tee times:** Call golf shop.
Subscriber comments: Isolated but worth the trip...Long course, very little traffic.

ROSS ROGERS GOLF CLUB
PM-722 N.W. 24th St., Amarillo, 79107, Potter County, (806)378-3086. **Architect:**
James Rettenberry. **Green fee:** $9/$13. **Credit cards:** MC,VISA,DISC. **Reduced fees:**
Weekdays, seniors, juniors. **Caddies:** No. **Golf carts:** $18. **Discount golf packages:**
No. **Season:** Year-round. **High:** May-Oct. **On site lodging:** No. **Rental clubs:** Yes.
Walking policy: Unrestricted walking. **Range:** Yes (grass/mats). **To obtain tee times:**
Call or walk in.
★★½EAST COURSE
Opened: 1977. **Holes:** 18. **Par:** 72/72. **Yards:** 6,858/5,575. **Course rating:** 70.8/69.5.
Slope: 112/111. **Metal spikes allowed:** Yes.
Subscriber comments: Wind, wind, wind...Good place to play...Greens as fast as
linoleum...Old course, nice layout...More challenging layout than West Course...Basic
golf...You need long irons and fairway woods here.
★★★WEST COURSE
Opened: 1940. **Holes:** 18. **Par:** 72/72. **Yards:** 6,602/5,392. **Course rating:** 69.2/68.2.
Slope: 110/108. **Metal spikes allowed:** No.
Subscriber comments: Extra large greens...Not bad...Links course...Shorter than East
Course...Long with southwest wind...A little easier than the East, but not much.

★★★½ROY KIZER GOLF COURSE
PU-5400 Jimmy Clay Dr., Austin, 78744, Travis County, (512)444-0999.
Opened: 1994. **Holes:** 18. **Par:** 71/71. **Yards:** 6,749/5,018. **Course rating:** 71.6.
Slope: 125. **Architect:** Randolph Russell. **Green fee:** $17/$23. **Credit cards:** All major.
Reduced fees: Weekdays, twilight, seniors, juniors. **Caddies:** No. **Golf carts:** $8.
Discount golf packages: No. **Season:** Year-round. **High:** N/A. **On site lodging:** No.
Rental clubs: Yes. **Walking policy:** Unrestricted walking. **Metal spikes allowed:** Yes.
Range: Yes (grass). **To obtain tee times:** Call Tuesday for Friday, Saturday and
Sunday. Call 3 days in advance for weekdays.
Subscriber comments: No trees, very windy...Fake mounding and no trees do not a
links course make...Best muny in Austin...Exact yardage markers in fairway...Great
practice area...Wind makes all the difference...Great links course...Fun layout.

★★★SAN SABA MUNICIPAL GOLF COURSE
PM-Golf Course Rd., San Saba, 76877, San Saba County,
(915)372-3212, 90 miles NW of Austin.
Opened: 1972. **Holes:** 18. **Par:** 72/72. **Yards:** 6,904/5,246. **Course
rating:** 72.5/69.0. **Slope:** 119/113. **Architect:** Sorrell Smith. **Green
fee:** $9/$13. **Credit cards:** MC,VISA,AMEX. **Reduced fees:** N/A.
Caddies: No. **Golf carts:** $9. **Discount golf packages:** No. **Season:** Year-round. **High:**
March-Oct. **On site lodging:** No. **Rental clubs:** Yes. **Walking policy:** Unrestricted
walking. **Metal spikes allowed:** Yes. **Range:** Yes (grass). **To obtain tee times:** First
come, first served.
Subscriber comments: Really fun to play...A sleeper in the Hill Country...Play the back
nine twice, forget the front...The river along the side is a bear for us that hook...Back
nine has lots of large trees...Get off the interstate and play it...Great finishing hole.

★½SCOTT SCHREINER MUNICIPAL GOLF COURSE
PM-1 Country Club Dr., Kerrville, 78028, Kerr County, (830)257-4982.
Opened: 1921. **Holes:** 18. **Par:** 72/72. **Yards:** 6,554/5,285. **Course rating:** 70.5/69.2.
Slope: 118/117. **Architect:** John Bredemus/R.D. Kaiser. **Green fee:** $8/$11. **Credit
cards:** None. **Reduced fees:** Juniors. **Caddies:** No. **Golf carts:** $13. **Discount golf
packages:** No. **Season:** Year-round. **High:** April-Oct. **On site lodging:** No. **Rental
clubs:** Yes. **Walking policy:** Unrestricted walking. **Metal spikes allowed:** Yes. **Range:**
Yes (grass). **To obtain tee times:** Call 3 days in advance.

★★½SEVEN OAKS RESORT & COUNTRY CLUB
1300 Circle Dr., Mission, 78572, Hidalgo County, (956)581-6267, 7 miles W of McAllen.
Opened: 1983. **Holes:** 18. **Par:** 70/70. **Yards:** 6,089/4,867. **Course rating:** 69.2/66.8.
Slope: 108/98. **Architect:** Unknown. **Green fee:** $14. **Credit cards:** All major.
Reduced fees: Low season, juniors. **Caddies:** No. **Golf carts:** $17. **Discount golf
packages:** No. **Season:** Year-round. **High:** Nov.-March. **On site lodging:** No. **Rental
clubs:** Yes. **Walking policy:** Unrestricted walking. **Metal spikes allowed:** Yes. **Range:**
Yes (grass/mats). **To obtain tee times:** Call 1 day in advance.
Subscriber comments: Hard fairways and greens, bump and run it...Most improved
course in the valley...Front nine is tight, back longer and more open.

★★½SHADOW HILLS GOLF COURSE
6002 3rd St., Lubbock, 79499, Lubbock County, (806)793-9700.Call club for further information.
Subscriber comments: Pretty flat, windy...Manicured flatland...Trees needs more time
to grow...Unique layout, very tough at times...Perfect West Texas course.

★★SHARPSTOWN MUNICIPAL GOLF COURSE
PM-6600 Harbor Town Dr., Houston, 77036, Harris County, (713)988-2099.
Opened: 1957. **Holes:** 18. **Par:** 70/72. **Yards:** 6,660/5,883. **Course rating:** 69.7/72.0.
Slope: 113/113. **Architect:** Ralph Plummer. **Green fee:** $4/$13. **Credit cards:**
MC,VISA,ATM Debit. **Reduced fees:** Weekdays, twilight, seniors, juniors. **Caddies:** No.
Golf carts: $16. **Discount golf packages:** No. **Season:** Year-round. **High:** N/A. **On
site lodging:** No. **Rental clubs:** Yes. **Walking policy:** Unrestricted walking. **Metal
spikes allowed:** Yes. **Range:** No. **To obtain tee times:** Call up to 3 days in advance
for weekends and holidays.
Notes: 1966 Texas State Open; 1964-65 Houston Open.

★★½SHARY MUNICIPAL GOLF COURSE
PM-2201 Mayberry, Mission, 78572, Hidalgo County, (956)580-8770, 6 miles W of McAllen.
Opened: 1929. **Holes:** 27. **Par:** 71/71. **Yards:** 6,025/4,893. **Course rating:** 68.9/68.8. **Slope:** 105/105. **Architect:** George Williams. **Green fee:** $9/$10. **Credit cards:** None. **Reduced fees:** Juniors. **Caddies:** No. **Golf carts:** $8. **Discount golf packages:** No. **Season:** Year-round. **High:** Jan.-March. **On site lodging:** No. **Rental clubs:** Yes. **Walking policy:** Unrestricted walking. **Metal spikes allowed:** Yes. **Range:** Yes (grass). **To obtain tee times:** Call one day in advance.
Subscriber comments: Great course, lots of fun...Too many internal OB, good hazards...A new back nine has really helped...Very tight fairways...Good for straight short hitters.

SHERRILL PARK GOLF COURSE
PM-2001 E. Lookout Dr., Richardson, 75080, Collin County, (972)234-1416, 10 miles N of Dallas.
Opened: 1971. **Architect:** Leon Howard. **Green fee:** $14/$17. **Credit cards:** None. **Reduced fees:** Weekdays, low season, twilight, seniors, juniors. **Caddies:** No. **Golf carts:** $8. **Discount golf packages:** Yes. **Season:** Year-round. **High:** May-Nov. **On site lodging:** No. **Rental clubs:** Yes. **Walking policy:** Unrestricted walking. **Metal spikes allowed:** Yes. **Range:** Yes (grass).**To obtain tee times:** Weekdays call one week in advance. Weekends call the Friday before.
★★½COURSE NO.1
Holes: 18. **Par:** 72/72. **Yards:** 6,800/5,455. **Course rating:** 72.6/72.0. **Slope:** 126/118.
Subscriber comments: Drainage was problem, but they're fixing that...Good fun, short but difficult...Lovely treelined golf course...Par 5s are killers...When in shape a good track...Course No. 1 is quite a bit better than Course No. 2.
★★COURSE NO.2
Holes: 18. **Par:** 70/70. **Yards:** 6,083/5,476. **Course rating:** 66.0/68.0. **Slope:** 113/113.

★★★½SILVERHORN GOLF CLUB OF TEXAS
PU-1100 W. Bitters Rd., San Antonio, 78216, Bexar County, (210)545-5300, 12 miles NW of San Antonio.
Opened: 1995. **Holes:** 18. **Par:** 72/72. **Yards:** 6,922/5,271. **Course rating:** 73.1/66.4. **Slope:** 129/109. **Architect:** Randy Heckenkemper. **Green fee:** $65/$65. **Credit cards:** MC,VISA,AMEX. **Reduced fees:** Twilight, seniors, juniors. **Caddies:** No. **Golf carts:** Included in Green Fee. **Discount golf packages:** Yes. **Season:** Year-round. **High:** N/A. **On site lodging:** No. **Rental clubs:** Yes. **Walking policy:** Unrestricted walking. **Metal spikes allowed:** Yes. **Range:** Yes (grass). **To obtain tee times:** Call up to 7 days in advance. Call up to 30 days in advance for additional $10 per person.
Subscriber comments: I like it but can't tell you why...Recommend to any golfer...New course that looks and plays like it's more mature...Very playable...Great new public course in San Antonio...Course opened too early, expect much improvement...Hit ball in fairway to score.

★★½SINTON MUNICIPAL GOLF COURSE
Robert Welder Park Hwy.#181, Sinton, 78387, San Patricio County, (512)364-9013. Call club for further information.
Subscriber comments: Basic golf...The greens are a little smaller than most...Good course for a small town...Lots of oak trees and wildlife, good greens...No bunkers, boring...They do a lot with very little.

★★½SLEEPY HOLLOW GOLF & COUNTRY CLUB
4747 S. Loop 12, Dallas, 75216, Dallas County, (214)371-3433, 7 miles S of Dallas.
Opened: 1961. **Holes:** 18. **Par:** 71/71. **Yards:** 7,031/5,878. **Course rating:** 73.4/74.1. **Slope:** 125/123. **Architect:** Press Maxwell. **Green fee:** $20/$30. **Credit cards:** All major. **Reduced fees:** Twilight. **Caddies:** No. **Golf carts:** $11. **Discount golf packages:** No. **Season:** Year-round. **High:** March-Oct. **On site lodging:** No. **Rental clubs:** Yes. **Walking policy:** Unrestricted walking. **Metal spikes allowed:** Yes. **Range:** Yes (grass). **To obtain tee times:** Call after 8 a.m. on Tuesdays for the following week.
Subscriber comments: Could be outstanding, par 3s tough...Long par 5s, lots of water...Long, use every club...18th is a neat hole.

★SOUTHWEST GOLF CENTER
PU-Hollywood & Coulter, Amarillo, 79119, Potter County, (806)355-7161, 1 mile SW of Amarillo.
Opened: 1967. **Holes:** 18. **Par:** 72/74. **Yards:** 7,018/5,700. **Course rating:** 69.7/73.0. **Slope:** 100/104. **Architect:** Bobby Westfall. **Green fee:** $8/$12. **Credit cards:** MC,VISA,DISC. **Reduced fees:** Weekdays, low season, seniors, juniors. **Caddies:** No. **Golf carts:** $18. **Discount golf packages:** Yes. **Season:** Year-round. **High:** April-Oct. **On site lodging:** No. **Rental clubs:** Yes. **Walking policy:** Unrestricted walking. **Metal spikes allowed:** Yes. **Range:** Yes (grass). **To obtain tee times:** Call up to 10 days in advance.

★★★½SOUTHWYCK GOLF CLUB
PU-2901 Clubhouse Dr., Pearland, 77584, Brazoria County, (713)436-9999, 10 miles S of Houston.
Opened: 1988. **Holes:** 18. **Par:** 72/72. **Yards:** 7,015/5,211. **Course rating:** 72.9/68.9. **Slope:** 123/112. **Architect:** Ken Kavanaugh. **Green fee:** $25/$45. **Credit cards:** MC,VISA,AMEX. **Reduced fees:** Weekdays, low season, twilight, seniors, juniors. **Caddies:** No. **Golf carts:** Included in Green Fee. **Discount golf packages:** Yes. **Season:** Year-round. **High:** Spring/Fall. **On site lodging:** No. **Rental clubs:** Yes. **Walking policy:** Walking at certain times. **Metal spikes allowed:** Yes. **Range:** Yes (grass). **To obtain tee times:** Call (713)777-1100.
Subscriber comments: Great short par 4s...Challenging links style, tough when windy...Stay in the fairway or bye-bye ball...Short, many options from tee...Fun course to play, good variety, well maintained, one of my favorites in Houston...Pot bunkers and deep rough make this course memorable...Different for Houston area...Must play appropriate tees...Lots of water.

★★★★SQUAW VALLEY GOLF COURSE
PU-HCR 51-45B Hwy. 67, Glen Rose, 76043, Somervell County, (817)897-7956, (800)831-8259, 60 miles SW of Fort Worth.
Opened: 1992. **Holes:** 18. **Par:** 72/72. **Yards:** 7,062/5,014. **Course rating:** 73.6/70.0. **Slope:** 130/117. **Architect:** Jeff Brauer. **Green fee:** $19/$23. **Credit cards:** MC,VISA,DISC. **Reduced fees:** Weekdays, twilight, seniors. **Caddies:** No. **Golf carts:** $33. **Discount golf packages:** No. **Season:** Year-round. **High:** April-Oct. **On site lodging:** No. **Rental clubs:** Yes. **Walking policy:** Walking at certain times. **Metal spikes allowed:** Yes. **Range:** Yes (grass/mats). **To obtain tee times:** Call or come in 5 days in advance.
Subscriber comments: I'd drive 10 hours to play this every weekend...Please keep it a secret...Two completly different nines...Links style for 12 holes...Enjoyable, tough but fair...A great design for any golfer...Excellent in every way...The wind can be demonic on the front nine, the back nine has beautiful, huge native trees.

★★½STEPHEN F. AUSTIN GOLF COURSE
Park Rd. 38, San Felipe, 77473, Austin County, (409)885-2811, 40 miles W of Houston.
Opened: 1953. **Holes:** 9. **Par:** 70/70. **Yards:** 5,813/5,137. **Course rating:** 67.3/69.7. **Slope:** 120/111. **Architect:** N/A. **Green fee:** N/A. **Credit cards:** MC,VISA,AMEX. **Reduced fees:** N/A. **Caddies:** No. **Golf carts:** $18. **Discount golf packages:** No. **Season:** Year-round. **High:** N/A. **On site lodging:** No. **Rental clubs:** Yes. **Walking policy:** Unrestricted walking. **Metal spikes allowed:** Yes. **Range:** No. **To obtain tee times:** Call on Thursday at 8 a.m. for upcoming weekend.
Subscriber comments: Basic golf with a couple of good holes...A little off the beaten path, but some of the most difficult holes around...Short, tight and worth drive from Houston...Beautiful oak trees and rolling hills.

★★½STEVENS PARK GOLF COURSE
PM-1005 N. Montclair, Dallas, 75208, Dallas County, (214)670-7506.
Opened: 1922. **Holes:** 18. **Par:** 71/71. **Yards:** 6,005/5,000. **Course rating:** 65.0/68.0. **Slope:** 124/118. **Architect:** Arthur Davis. **Green fee:** N/A. **Credit cards:** MC,VISA. **Reduced fees:** Weekdays, low season, twilight, seniors, juniors. **Caddies:** No. **Golf carts:** $18. **Discount golf packages:** Yes. **Season:** Year-round. **High:** April-Dec. **On site lodging:** No. **Rental clubs:** Yes. **Walking policy:** Unrestricted walking. **Metal spikes allowed:** Yes. **Range:** No. **To obtain tee times:** Call 2 days in advance for

weekdays. Come in Thursday at 6 a.m. or call by noon.
Subscriber comments: Short but fun...Good course, requires variety of shots...Small greens...Very wooded and hilly...Short but sneaky, going for big shot can bring trouble into play...Driveable par 4s...Some classic memorable holes.

★★★★SUGARTREE GOLF CLUB

Hwy. 1189, P.O. Box 98, Dennis, 76439, Parker County, (817)596-4991, 35 miles W of Fort Worth.
Opened: 1987. **Holes:** 18. **Par:** 71/71. **Yards:** 6,775/5,254. **Course rating:** 72.8/71.0. **Slope:** 138/125. **Architect:** Phil Lumsden. **Green fee:** $21/$31. **Credit cards:** All major. **Reduced fees:** Weekdays, low season, twilight, seniors, juniors. **Caddies:** No. **Golf carts:** $9. **Discount golf packages:** No. **Season:** Year-round. **High:** March-Oct. **On site lodging:** No. **Rental clubs:** Yes. **Walking policy:** Unrestricted walking. **Metal spikes allowed:** No. **Range:** Yes (grass). **To obtain tee times:** Call up to 7 days in advance.
Subscriber comments: Toughest, tightest course nobody has heard of...Hope you can hit a 2-iron real straight...Treelined with lots of wildlife...Shotmaker's course...Too many blind shots...Leave driver at home...Humbling, add 20 to your handicap...Very tricky, never a chance to catch breath...Great course in the middle of nowhere...Hangman's tree, great par 3s...Small, good greens.

(GOOD VALUE)

★★★½SWEETWATER COUNTRY CLUB

1900 Country Club Lane, Sweetwater, 79556, Nolan County, (915)235-8093, 45 miles E of Abilene.
Opened: 1957. **Holes:** 18. **Par:** 71/72. **Yards:** 6,362/5,316. **Course rating:** 70.0. **Slope:** 118. **Architect:** M.C. Alston. **Green fee:** $15/$20. **Credit cards:** None. **Reduced fees:** N/A. **Caddies:** No. **Golf carts:** $13. **Discount golf packages:** No. **Season:** Year-round. **High:** April-Aug. **On site lodging:** No. **Rental clubs:** Yes. **Walking policy:** Unrestricted walking. **Metal spikes allowed:** Yes. **Range:** Yes (grass/mats). **To obtain tee times:** Call.
Subscriber comments: Another quiet course...Great layout...Typical West Texas golf course...Bent grass greens...Narrow treelined fairways...Excellent course, maybe too much OB...Fairways are so plush I feel guilty when I take a divot.

★★★½TANGLERIDGE GOLF CLUB

PU-818 TangleRidge Dr., Grand Prairie, 75052, Dallas County, (972)299-6837, 30 miles SW of Dallas.
Opened: 1995. **Holes:** 18. **Par:** 72/72. **Yards:** 6,835/5,187. **Course rating:** 72.2/70.2. **Slope:** 129/117. **Architect:** Jeff Brauer. **Green fee:** $35/$45. **Credit cards:** MC,VISA,AMEX. **Reduced fees:** Twilight, seniors, juniors. **Caddies:** No. **Golf carts:** $11. **Discount golf packages:** No. **Season:** Year-round. **High:** May-Sept. **On site lodging:** No. **Rental clubs:** Yes. **Walking policy:** Unrestricted walking. **Metal spikes allowed:** Yes. **Range:** Yes (grass). **To obtain tee times:** Call up to 3 days in advance at 8 a.m.
Notes: Ranked 8th in 1997 Best in State.
Subscriber comments: Closest thing Dallas has to "Hill Country" golf...Great fun, will go back...Needs to mature...Need to overseed fairways in winter...Tough greens to read...A lot of different looks...There is no par 5 in Dallas area harder than No.8.

★★★TANGLEWOOD RESORT

R-Hwy. 120 N., Pottsboro, 75076, Grayson County, (903)786-4140, (800)833-6569, 68 miles N of Dallas.
Opened: 1971. **Holes:** 18. **Par:** 72/72. **Yards:** 6,993/4,925. **Course rating:** 73.7/67.5. **Slope:** 128/104. **Architect:** Ralph Plummer and Arnold Palmer. **Green fee:** $27/$38. **Credit cards:** All major. **Reduced fees:** Twilight. **Caddies:** No. **Golf carts:** $12. **Discount golf packages:** Yes. **Season:** Year-round. **High:** Spring/Fall. **On site lodging:** Yes. **Rental clubs:** Yes. **Walking policy:** Walking at certain times. **Metal spikes allowed:** Yes. **Range:** Yes (grass). **To obtain tee times:** Call golf shop up to 30 days in advance.
Subscriber comments: Great variety of holes...Have seen great improvements from year to year...Lovely course on Lake Texoma, plays quite long...Some holes too long for average golfer...Beautiful scenery.

★★★½ TAPATIO SPRINGS RESORT & CONFERENCE CENTER

R-W. Johns Rd., Boerne, 78006, Kendall County, (830)537-4197, (800)999-3299, 25 miles N of San Antonio.

Opened: 1980. **Holes:** 18. **Par:** 72/72. **Yards:** 6,472/5,179. **Course rating:** 70.9/69.5. **Slope:** 122/118. **Architect:** Billy Johnston. **Green fee:** $65/$75. **Credit cards:** All major. **Reduced fees:** Resort guests, juniors. **Caddies:** No. **Golf carts:** Included in Green Fee. **Discount golf packages:** Yes. **Season:** Year-round. **High:** Spring/Fall. **On site lodging:** Yes. **Rental clubs:** Yes. **Walking policy:** Mandatory cart. **Metal spikes allowed:** Yes. **Range:** Yes (grass/mats). **To obtain tee times:** Call 7 days in advance. Resort guest 30 days in advance with hotel confirmation.

Subscriber comments: Fun course, keep coming back...Great place to visit, deer abound, pretty Hill Country course...Incredible views, lots of challenges...Very hilly...You can shoot low scores if the wind is low...Great place for a weekend.

Special Notes: Also 9-hole executive course.

TENISON PARK GOLF COURSE

PM-3501 Samuell, Dallas, 75223, Dallas County, (214)670-1402, 3 miles E of Dallas.

Opened: 1927. **Architect:** Ralph Plummer. **Green fee:** $5/$16. **Credit cards:** MC,VISA,AMEX. **Reduced fees:** Weekdays, twilight, seniors, juniors. **Caddies:** No. **Golf carts:** $17. **Discount golf packages:** No. **Season:** Year-round. **High:** April-Oct. **On site lodging:** No. **Rental clubs:** Yes. **Walking policy:** Unrestricted walking. **Metal spikes allowed:** Yes. **Range:** No. **To obtain tee times:** For weekend times come in person on Thursday at 6 a.m. or phone in at noon.

★★½ EAST COURSE

Holes: 18. **Par:** 72/75. **Yards:** 6,772/5,392. **Course rating:** 72.0/70.2. **Slope:** 123/113. **Notes:** 1968 National Publinks Championship.

Subscriber comments: Hard to play, shots must be on line..Long par 4s...Hard to get weekend tee times...Could be in better condition...Lee Trevino hustled here...Play only in spring and fall...Long and flat, except first and 18th.

★★½ WEST COURSE

Holes: 18. **Par:** 72/75. **Yards:** 6,822/5,648. **Course rating:** 72.0/72.2. **Slope:** 121/118.

Subscriber comments: Great layout, dry...Not as hard as East, but well set up...Great character...Enjoyed the up and down terrain and interesting layout...Fun, scenic, relatively tough course...Can be challenging, especially if you're in the trees.

★★ TEXAS A&M UNIVERSITY GOLF COURSE

PU-Bizzell St., College Station, 77843, Brazos County, (409)845-1723, 100 miles SE of Houston.

Opened: 1951. **Holes:** 18. **Par:** 70/73. **Yards:** 6,513/5,238. **Course rating:** 71.0/68.3. **Slope:** 122/109. **Architect:** Ralph Plummer. **Green fee:** $8/$16. **Credit cards:** All major. **Reduced fees:** Weekdays, twilight. **Caddies:** No. **Golf carts:** $8. **Discount golf packages:** No. **Season:** Year-round. **High:** April-Oct. **On site lodging:** No. **Rental clubs:** Yes. **Walking policy:** Unrestricted walking. **Metal spikes allowed:** Yes. **Range:** No. **To obtain tee times:** Only one week in advance available on Friday, Saturday, Sunday.

TIERRA SANTA GOLF CLUB

PM-1901 Club de Amistad, Weslaco, 78596, Hidalgo County, (956)973-1811, (800)838-5769, 20 miles E of McAllen.

Opened: 1997. **Holes:** 18. **Par:** 72/72. **Yards:** 7,101/5,283. **Course rating:** 74.5/72.5. **Slope:** 140/125. **Architect:** Jeff Brauer. **Green fee:** $20/$23. **Credit cards:** All major. **Reduced fees:** Weekdays, low season, resort guests, twilight, seniors, juniors. **Caddies:** No. **Golf carts:** $9. **Discount golf packages:** Yes. **Season:** Year-round. **High:** Nov.-March. **On site lodging:** No. **Rental clubs:** Yes. **Walking policy:** Unrestricted walking. **Metal spikes allowed:** Yes. **Range:** Yes (grass/mats). **To obtain tee times:** Call up to 2 days in advance.

★★★½ TIMARRON GOLF & COUNTRY CLUB

PU-14000 Byron Nelson Pkwy., Southlake, 76092, Tarrant County, (817)481-7529, 20 miles E of Fort Worth.

Opened: 1994. **Holes:** 18. **Par:** 72/72. **Yards:** 7,100/5,330. **Course rating:** 74.2/71.3. **Slope:** 137/120. **Architect:** Byron Nelson and Baxter Spann. **Green fee:** $45/$60.

Credit cards: MC,VISA,AMEX. **Reduced fees:** Weekdays. **Caddies:** No. **Golf carts:** Included in Green Fee. **Discount golf packages:** No. **Season:** Year-round. **High:** March-April. **On site lodging:** No. **Rental clubs:** Yes. **Walking policy:** Mandatory cart. **Metal spikes allowed:** Yes. **Range:** Yes (grass). **To obtain tee times:** Call three days in advance.
Notes: Ranked 7th in 1995 Best New Public Courses.
Subscriber comments: Great layout, play it before it goes private...Could be best in area...Lots of water and sand...Stay in fairways...Still growing up...Nice course which will improve with age.

★ TIMBER-VIEW GOLF COURSE
PU-4508 E. Enon, Fort Worth, 76140, Tarrant County, (817)478-3601, 10 miles S of Fort Worth.
Opened: 1963. **Holes:** 18. **Par:** 72/72. **Yards:** 6,486/5,406. **Course rating:** 70.4/70.0. **Slope:** N/A. **Architect:** Thomas Fouts. **Green fee:** $7/$10. **Credit cards:** None. **Reduced fees:** Weekdays, seniors. **Caddies:** No. **Golf carts:** $16. **Discount golf packages:** Yes. **Season:** Year-round. **High:** March-Sept. **On site lodging:** No. **Rental clubs:** Yes. **Walking policy:** Unrestricted walking. **Metal spikes allowed:** Yes. **Range:** No. **To obtain tee times:** First come, first served 7 days a week.

★★½ TONY BUTLER GOLF COURSE
PU-2640 S. M St., Harlingen, 78550, Cameron County, (956)430-6685, 120 miles S of Corpus Christi.
Opened: 1927. **Holes:** 27. **Par:** 71/71. **Yards:** 6,320/5,680. **Course rating:** 69.1/69.1. **Slope:** 113/112. **Architect:** Dennis W. Arp. **Green fee:** $10/$10. **Credit cards:** MC,VISA. **Reduced fees:** Juniors. **Caddies:** No. **Golf carts:** $9. **Discount golf packages:** No. **Season:** Year-round. **High:** Oct.-March. **On site lodging:** No. **Rental clubs:** Yes. **Walking policy:** Unrestricted walking. **Metal spikes allowed:** Yes. **Range:** Yes (grass). **To obtain tee times:** Call one day in advance starting at 6:30 a.m.
Subscriber comments: Basic muny with good variety...Let's keep this our secret...Good course, not easy for a high handicapper...Needs water and it would be a good course...Contoured greens, can be tough if windy.

★★★½ TOUR 18
PU-3102 FM 1960 E., Humble, 77338, Harris County, (281)540-1818, (800)856-8687, 22 miles NE of Houston.
Opened: 1992. **Holes:** 18. **Par:** 72/72. **Yards:** 6,807/5,583. **Course rating:** 72.2/66.6. **Slope:** 126/113. **Architect:** Dennis Wilkerson. **Green fee:** $65/$75. **Credit cards:** All major. **Reduced fees:** Twilight, juniors. **Caddies:** No. **Golf carts:** Included in Green Fee. **Discount golf packages:** Yes. **Season:** Year-round. **High:** April-May/Sept.-Nov. **On site lodging:** No. **Rental clubs:** Yes. **Walking policy:** Mandatory cart. **Metal spikes allowed:** Yes. **Range:** Yes (grass). **To obtain tee times:** Call seven days in advance begining at 7:15 a.m.
Subscriber comments: If you can't play the real thing this is really nice...Good job of making a copy...It's as close as I'll get to playing Amen Corner...Somewhat of a novelty, but worth playing...A poor man's golf vacation...A unique way to spend a day, all the holes are fun...Too much play, too long of a round.

★★★★ TOUR 18 GOLF CLUB
PU-8718 Amen Corner, Flower Mound, 75028, Tarrant County, (817)430-2000, 10 miles NW of Dallas.
Opened: 1995. **Holes:** 18. **Par:** 72/72. **Yards:** 7,033/5,493. **Course rating:** 74.3/66.3. **Slope:** 138/119. **Architect:** D. Wilkerson/B. Jacobsen/J. Williams. **Green fee:** $75/$85. **Credit cards:** N/A. **Reduced fees:** N/A. **Caddies:** No. **Golf carts:** Included in Green Fee. **Discount golf packages:** No. **Season:** Year-round. **High:** Spring/Fall. **On site lodging:** No. **Rental clubs:** No. **Walking policy:** Mandatory cart. **Metal spikes allowed:** Yes. **Range:** No. **To obtain tee times:** Call up to 7 days in advance with credit card; up to 30 days prepaid non-refundable.
Subscriber comments: Better if you know golf history before playing...Killer course...Greens need maturity...Tourist trap...More fun than other Tour 18...No real sense of flow...Slow play a problem...Great course, but hard to duplicate Amen Corner in North Texas...No easy holes...It's like going to Disneyland.

★★TREELINE GOLF CLUB
17505 N. Eldridge Pkwy., Tomball, 77375, Harris County, (281)376-1542.
Call club for further information.

★★★TURTLE HILL GOLF COURSE
PU-Rte. 373 N., P.O. Box 660, Muenster, 76252, Cook County, (940)759-4896, 15 miles
W of Gainsville.
Opened: 1993. **Holes:** 18. **Par:** 72/72. **Yards:** 6,510/4,821. **Course rating:** 72.2/69.5.
Slope: 123/116. **Architect:** Dick Murphy. **Green fee:** $24/$32. **Credit cards:** MC,VISA.
Reduced fees: Weekdays, juniors. **Caddies:** No. **Golf carts:** Included in Green Fee.
Discount golf packages: Yes. **Season:** Year-round. **High:** April-Sept. **On site lodging:**
No. **Rental clubs:** Yes. **Walking policy:** Unrestricted walking. **Metal spikes allowed:**
Yes. **Range:** Yes (grass/mats). **To obtain tee times:** Call 7 days in advance.
Subscriber comments: Best greens north of Dallas...Great par 3s...Different, has a
wild quality, fun to play, will improve as it matures...Hard to believe it was built by two
guys and one bulldozer (no kidding)...Wonderful little course...Look forward to playing
again.

★★★½TWIN CREEKS GOLF CLUB
PU-501 Twin Creeks Dr., Allen, 75013, Collin County, (972)390-8888.
Opened: 1995. **Holes:** 18. **Par:** 72/72. **Yards:** 6,924/4,790. **Course rating:** N/A. **Slope:**
N/A. **Architect:** Palmer Course Design Co.. **Green fee:** $38/$65. **Credit cards:**
MC,VISA,AMEX. **Reduced fees:** Weekdays, twilight, juniors. **Caddies:** No. **Golf carts:**
Included in Green Fee. **Discount golf packages:** No. **Season:** Year-round. **High:** April-
Oct. **On site lodging:** No. **Rental clubs:** Yes. **Walking policy:** Unrestricted walking.
Metal spikes allowed: No. **Range:** Yes (grass/mats). **To obtain tee times:** Call 5 days
in advance.
Subscriber comments: Great layout, always windy...Good, sloping, gigantic
greens...Short course, must play the golds...Tough yet fair...Best auto yardage system,
good course...If you par 17th you've played well.

★★TWIN WELLS GOLF COURSE
PU-2000 E. Shady Grove Rd., Irving, 75060, Dallas County, (972)438-4340, 5 miles W
of Dallas.
Opened: 1988. **Holes:** 18. **Par:** 72/72. **Yards:** 6,636/6,239. **Course rating:** 70.9/69.3.
Slope: 117/113. **Architect:** Brian Ault and Bill Love. **Green fee:** $16/$24. **Credit cards:**
MC,VISA,AMEX. **Reduced fees:** Weekdays, low season, twilight, juniors. **Caddies:** No. **Golf carts:** $22. **Discount golf packages:** Yes. **Season:** Year-round.
High: March-Dec. **On site lodging:** No. **Rental clubs:** Yes. **Walking policy:**
Unrestricted walking. **Metal spikes allowed:** Yes. **Range:** Yes (grass/mats). **To obtain
tee times:** Call up to 3 days in advance.

UNDERWOOD GOLF COMPLEX
3200 Coe Ave., El Paso, 79904, El Paso County, (915)562-2066.
Opened: 1945. **Architect:** N/A. **Green fee:** $8/$18. **Credit cards:** MC,VISA. **Reduced
fees:** Weekdays, twilight. **Caddies:** No. **Golf carts:** $16. **Discount golf packages:** No.
Season: Year-round. **High:** April-Nov. **On site lodging:** No. **Rental clubs:** Yes.
Walking policy: Unrestricted walking. **Metal spikes allowed:** Yes. **Range:** Yes (grass).
To obtain tee times: Call for weekday tee times only. Lottery system for weekends.
SUNRISE COURSE
Holes: 18. **Par:** 72/72. **Yards:** 6,642/5,498. **Course rating:** 73.1/71.1. **Slope:** 126/124.
★★★★SUNSET COURSE
Holes: 18. **Par:** 72/72. **Yards:** 6,629/5,531. **Course rating:** 70.1/70.4.
Slope: 116/109.
Subscriber comments: This is an army course, well kept...Narrow
fairways with lots of rough.

GREAT VALUE

★★½VALLEY INN & COUNTRY CLUB
FM Rd. 802 and Central Blvd., Brownsville, 78520, Cameron County, (956)546-5331.
Call club for further information.
Subscriber comments: Long but fair...Greens too grainy...Too much
water...Uneventful.

TEXAS

★★★½WATERWOOD NATIONAL RESORT & COUNTRY CLUB
R-One Waterwood, Huntsville, 77340, San Jacinto County, (409)891-5050, (800)441-5211, 75 miles N of Houston.
Opened: 1975. **Holes:** 18. **Par:** 71/73. **Yards:** 6,872/5,029. **Course rating:** 73.7/68.0.
Slope: 142/117. **Architect:** Roy Dye. **Green fee:** $30/$50. **Credit cards:** MC,VISA,AMEX,DISC,Diners Club. **Reduced fees:** Low season, twilight, seniors, juniors. **Caddies:** No. **Golf carts:** $20. **Discount golf packages:** Yes. **Season:** Year-round. **High:** April-June. **On site lodging:** Yes. **Rental clubs:** Yes. **Walking policy:** Unrestricted walking. **Metal spikes allowed:** Yes. **Range:** Yes (grass). **To obtain tee times:** Call up to 7 days in advance.
Notes: Ranked 4th in 1997 Best in State.
Subscriber comments: Outstanding golf, I will return...Unbelievably tough from gold tees...13 and 14 as pretty and difficult as it gets...A challenge, worth the drive...Muny conditions but layout is tour caliber...Most challenging in Southern Texas.

★★★WEDGEWOOD GOLF CLUB
PU-5454 Hwy. 105 W., Conroe, 77304, Montgomery County, (409)441-4653, 50 miles N of Houston.
Opened: 1988. **Holes:** 18. **Par:** 72/72. **Yards:** 6,817/5,071. **Course rating:** 73.7/69.6.
Slope: 134/128. **Architect:** Ron Prichard. **Green fee:** $20/$40. **Credit cards:** MC,VISA,AMEX. **Reduced fees:** Weekdays, twilight, seniors, juniors. **Caddies:** No.
Golf carts: $10. **Discount golf packages:** No. **Season:** Year-round. **High:** Spring/Fall.
On site lodging: No. **Rental clubs:** Yes. **Walking policy:** Unrestricted walking. **Metal spikes allowed:** Yes. **Range:** Yes (grass/mats). **To obtain tee times:** Call 7 days in advance for weekdays. Call on Wednesday for upcoming weekend.
Subscriber comments: Tight fairways, treelined, hilly...Very brutal, not a course for the driver...Do not like a course where you can't see greens from tees...Doglegs, drops, uneven lies...Fantastic shotmaker's course...A great course when kept up...Too difficult for average player...Must know course...The right mix of sand, water, hills.

★★WEEKS PARK MUNICIPAL GOLF COURSE
PM-4400 Lake Park Dr., Wichita Falls, 76302, Wichita County, (940)767-6107.
Opened: N/A. **Holes:** 18. **Par:** 72/73. **Yards:** 6,470/4,915. **Course rating:** 70.0/67.8.
Slope: 117/109. **Architect:** Jeff Brauer. **Green fee:** $10/$12. **Credit cards:** MC,VISA.
Reduced fees: Weekdays, twilight, seniors, juniors. **Caddies:** No. **Golf carts:** $8.
Discount golf packages: No. **Season:** Year-round. **High:** N/A. **On site lodging:** No.
Rental clubs: Yes. **Walking policy:** Unrestricted walking. **Metal spikes allowed:** Yes.
Range: No. **To obtain tee times:** Call.

★★★★WHITE BLUFFS GOLF CLUB
Golf Dr. 1, Whitney, 76692, Hill County, (254)694-3656, (888)944-8325.
Opened: 1992. **Holes:** 18. **Par:** 72/72. **Yards:** 6,845/5,292. **Course rating:** 73.3/72.4.
Slope: 132/128. **Architect:** Lee Singletary/Bruce Lietzke. **Green fee:** $38/$62. **Credit cards:** All major. **Reduced fees:** Resort guests, twilight, juniors. **Caddies:** No. **Golf carts:** Included in Green Fee. **Discount golf packages:** No. **Season:** Year-round.
High: April-Oct. **On site lodging:** Yes. **Rental clubs:** Yes. **Walking policy:** Unrestricted walking. **Metal spikes allowed:** No. **Range:** Yes (grass). **To obtain tee times:** Call up to 7 days in advance.
Subscriber comments: Several challenging holes...When greens are in good condition this is a great track...Excellent test of golf...Don't ever get above the hole, three-putt for sure...Back nine is as hard as can be...Lake Whitney is an awesome background, holes play through canyons.

★★★½WILLOW SPRINGS GOLF CLUB
PM-202 Coliseum Rd., San Antonio, 78219, Bexar County, (210)226-6721.
Opened: 1923. **Holes:** 18. **Par:** 72/72. **Yards:** 7,221/5,631. **Course rating:** 73.9/72.5.
Slope: 134/120. **Architect:** Emil Loeffler and John McGlynn. **Green fee:** $14/$16.
Credit cards: All major. **Reduced fees:** Weekdays, twilight, seniors, juniors. **Caddies:** No. **Golf carts:** $16. **Discount golf packages:** No. **Season:** Year-round. **High:** Nov.-Aug. **On site lodging:** No. **Rental clubs:** Yes. **Walking policy:** Unrestricted walking.
Metal spikes allowed: Yes. **Range:** No. **To obtain tee times:** Call in advance.
Notes: 1941-49 Texas Open.

Subscriber comments: Long, grip it and rip it...Solid golf challenge, good muny...Must play for tourists...Enjoyable course, interesting layout...Tough holes, par-5 2nd hole is a great start...Lots of draw shots needed.

★★WOODLAKE COUNTRY CLUB
SP-6500 Woodlake Pkwy, San Antonio, 78244, Bexar County, (210)661-6124.
Architect: Desmond Muirhead. **Caddies:** No. **Discount golf packages:** No. **On site lodging:** No. **Rental clubs:** No. **Metal spikes allowed:** Yes. **Range:** No.
Call club for further information.
Subscriber comments: Always great to play...Use all your clubs...Fairways thin...Fun time...Small greens, don't miss them...Wide course, short holes allow you to make up for mistakes...Very interesting layout, greens are small and fast, good wedge play a must, however fairways allow for monster drives.

★★½WOODLAND HILLS GOLF COURSE
PU-319 Woodland Hills Dr., Nacogdoches, 75961, Polk County, (409)564-2762, 120 miles NE of Houston.
Opened: N/A. **Holes:** 18. **Par:** 72/72. **Yards:** 6,672/6,218. **Course rating:** N/A. **Slope:** 123/114. **Architect:** Don January and Bill Martindale. **Green fee:** N/A. **Credit cards:** MC,VISA. **Reduced fees:** Weekdays, twilight. **Caddies:** No. **Golf carts:** N/A. **Discount golf packages:** No. **Season:** Year-round. **High:** April-Aug. **On site lodging:** No. **Rental clubs:** No. **Walking policy:** N/A. **Metal spikes allowed:** Yes. **Range:** Yes (grass). **To obtain tee times:** N/A.
Subscriber comments: Hilly course but enjoyable, good greens...Very hilly...A very fun course...Interesting variety of holes...Tight fairways, requires all your clubs...Some very difficult holes.

THE WOODLANDS RESORT & COUNTRY CLUB
R- **Caddies:** No. **Discount golf packages:** Yes. **Season:** Year-round.
On site lodging: Yes. **Walking policy:** Unrestricted walking. **Metal spikes allowed:** Yes. **Range:** Yes (grass/mats).

★★★½NORTH COURSE
2301 N. Millbend Dr., The Woodlands, 77380, Montgomery County, (281)367-1100, 22 miles N of Houston.
Opened: 1976. **Holes:** 18. **Par:** 72/72. **Yards:** 6,881/5,245. **Course rating:** 72.2/72.1. **Slope:** 126/120. **Architect:** Joe Lee. **Green fee:** $57/$65. **Credit cards:** MC,VISA,AMEX,DISC,. **Reduced fees:** Weekdays, low season, twilight. **Golf carts:** $12. **High:** Spring/Fall. **Rental clubs:** No. **To obtain tee times:** Call.
Subscriber comments: Bring lots of balls or your "A" game...Super course, great layout, greens could be better...Pleasure to play...Sand, sand, sand...Tough par 4s...You work for your score...One of the best in Houston area.
Special Notes: Spikeless shoes encouraged.

★★★★TPC COURSE
1730 S. Millbend Dr., The Woodlands, 77380, Montgomery County, (281)367-7285, 25 miles N of Houston.
Opened: 1985. **Holes:** 18. **Par:** 72/72. **Yards:** 7,018/5,326. **Course rating:** 73.7/72.1. **Slope:** 136/128. **Architect:** Von Hagge and Devlin. **Green fee:** $85/$105. **Credit cards:** All major. **Reduced fees:** Weekdays, twilight, juniors. **Golf carts:** Included in Green Fee. **High:** April-Oct. **Rental clubs:** Yes. **To obtain tee times:** Call up to 7 days in advance.
Notes: Shell Houston Open.
Subscriber comments: Totally different course from behind white tees...17th will eat your lunch...Fun to play courses pros play...Suffers a little from volume of play...Tour quality...Be a pro for a day...Worth a return visit...Good as it gets...It makes you appreciate how good the pros are...Great if you like target courses...Island green tough...Plays through tall pine trees...Hard for average players.

★★WORLD HOUSTON GOLF CLUB
PU-4000 Greens Rd., Houston, 77032, Harris County, (281)449-8384.
Opened: N/A. **Holes:** 18. **Par:** 72/72. **Yards:** 6,642/5,204. **Course rating:** 71.2/71.4. **Slope:** 119/123. **Architect:** Garrett Gill and George B. Williams. **Green fee:** $19/$29. **Credit cards:** MC,VISA,AMEX. **Reduced fees:** Low season, twilight, seniors, juniors. **Caddies:** No. **Golf carts:** Included in Green Fee. **Discount golf packages:** Yes.

TEXAS

Season: Year-round. **High:** March-Oct. **On site lodging:** No. **Rental clubs:** Yes. **Walking policy:** Unrestricted walking. **Metal spikes allowed:** Yes. **Range:** Yes (grass). **To obtain tee times:** Call golf shop.

★½ Z BOAZ GOLF COURSE
PM-3240 Lackland Rd., Fort Worth, 76116, Tarrant County, (817)738-6287.
Opened: 1937. **Holes:** 18. **Par:** 70/70. **Yards:** 6,033/4,782. **Course rating:** 69.6/68.0. **Slope:** 124/107. **Architect:** Ralph Plummer. **Green fee:** $11/$13. **Credit cards:** MC,VISA. **Reduced fees:** Weekdays, twilight, seniors, juniors. **Caddies:** No. **Golf carts:** $8. **Discount golf packages:** No. **Season:** Year-round. **High:** N/A. **On site lodging:** No. **Rental clubs:** Yes. **Walking policy:** Unrestricted walking. **Metal spikes allowed:** Yes. **Range:** No. **To obtain tee times:** Call Mondays after noon for the following week.

UTAH

★★BEN LOMOND GOLF COURSE
PU-1800 N. Hwy. #89, Ogden, 84404, Weber County, (801)782-7754, 5 miles N of
Ogden.
Opened: 1956. **Holes:** 18. **Par:** 72/72. **Yards:** 6,176/5,445. **Course rating:** 67.2/68.6.
Slope: 104/107. **Architect:** N/A. **Green fee:** $8/$16. **Credit cards:** N/A. **Reduced
fees:** Seniors, juniors. **Caddies:** No. **Golf carts:** $16. **Discount golf packages:** No.
Season: March-Dec. **High:** May-Sept. **On site lodging:** No. **Rental clubs:** No.
Walking policy: Unrestricted walking. **Metal spikes allowed:** Yes. **Range:** No. **To
obtain tee times:** Call Thursday for weekends and holidays. For weekdays call 1 day in
advance.

★★★½BIRCH CREEK GOLF CLUB
PU-600 E. Center St., Smithfield, 84335, Cache County, (801)563-6825.
Call club for further information.
Subscriber comments: Best kept secret in Northern Utah...Remote
location; excellent layout and condition; use all clubs...Well taken care of.
Love it...Layout is so good, greens are tough, grass is excellent...Plenty
of trees, gullies, and water to make every challenging. Great place, not crowded, could
this be our secret?...Management makes you feel good about playing.

★★★BONNEVILLE GOLF COURSE
PU-954 Connor St., Salt Lake City, 84108, Salt Lake County, (801)583-9513, 4 miles
SE of Salt Lake City.
Opened: 1929. **Holes:** 18. **Par:** 72/74. **Yards:** 6,824/5,860. **Course rating:** 71.0/71.6.
Slope: 120/119. **Architect:** William F. Bell. **Green fee:** $20/$20. **Credit cards:**
MC,VISA. **Reduced fees:** Seniors, juniors. **Caddies:** No. **Golf carts:** $20. **Discount
golf packages:** No. **Season:** March-Nov. **High:** April-Sept. **On site lodging:** No.
Rental clubs: Yes. **Walking policy:** Unrestricted walking. **Metal spikes allowed:** Yes.
Range: Yes (grass/mats). **To obtain tee times:** Call tee-time number 7 days in
advance or course 48 hours prior to day of play.
Subscriber comments: Good course. One of the oldest in Salt Lake...Lots of elevation
changes...Course in great shape ...One of the best public courses in state...Good variety of holes. Beautiful scenery...Hasn't changed in 30 years.

★★★½BOUNTIFUL RIDGE GOLF COURSE
PU-2430 S. Bountiful Blvd., Bountiful, 84010, Davis County,
(801)298-6040, 5 miles N of Salt Lake City.
Opened: 1975. **Holes:** 18. **Par:** 71/72. **Yards:** 6,523/5,098. **Course
rating:** 70.2/67.6. **Slope:** 122/116. **Architect:** William H. Neff. **Green
fee:** $16/$16. **Credit cards:** MC,VISA. **Reduced fees:** Seniors,
juniors. **Caddies:** No. **Golf carts:** $8. **Discount golf packages:** Yes. **Season:** March-
Nov. **High:** May-Aug. **On site lodging:** No. **Rental clubs:** Yes. **Walking policy:**
Unrestricted walking. **Metal spikes allowed:** No. **Range:** No. **To obtain tee times:** Call
day before for weekdays. Call Thursday prior to weekends and holidays.
Subscriber comments: Many improvements...Best bunkers in Utah...Tremendous
older course, best greens in the west!...Beautiful vistas...Public courses are regulated
by the state, thus values are unbelievable. Mountainside golf, views of great Salt
Lake...Everything breaks to the lake.

★★½CEDAR RIDGE GOLF COURSE
PU-200 East 900 North, Cedar City, 84720, Iron County, (435)586-2970, 170 miles N of
Las Vegas.
Opened: 1962. **Holes:** 18. **Par:** 71/71. **Yards:** 6,635/5,076. **Course rating:** 69.7/68.5.
Slope: 118/113. **Architect:** N/A. **Green fee:** $18/$18. **Credit cards:** MC,VISA.
Reduced fees: Seniors. **Caddies:** No. **Golf carts:** $16. **Discount golf packages:** No.
Season: Feb.-Dec. **High:** May-Sept. **On site lodging:** No. **Rental clubs:** Yes. **Walking
policy:** Unrestricted walking. **Metal spikes allowed:** Yes. **Range:** Yes (grass). **To
obtain tee times:** First come, first served.
Subscriber comments: Great mountain course. Always good condition...Fast greens,
great location, good challenge...Excellent layout...Short course with a few neat holes.

★★★DAVIS PARK GOLF COURSE
PU-1074 E. Nicholls Rd., Fruit Heights, 84037, Davis County, (801)546-4154, 17 miles N of Salt Lake City.
Opened: 1964. **Holes:** 18. **Par:** 71/71. **Yards:** 6,481/5,295. **Course rating:** 69.3/68.7. **Slope:** 117/114. **Architect:** Pierre Hualde/Ernie Schnieter. **Green fee:** $17/$18. **Credit cards:** MC,VISA. **Reduced fees:** Weekdays, seniors, juniors. **Caddies:** No. **Golf carts:** $9. **Discount golf packages:** No. **Season:** March-Nov. **High:** May-Aug. **On site lodging:** No. **Rental clubs:** Yes. **Walking policy:** Unrestricted walking. **Metal spikes allowed:** No. **Range:** Yes (grass). **To obtain tee times:** Call 1 day in advance for weekdays and Thursday for upcoming weekend.
Subscriber comments: Very good short 18...Well kept...Good variety of shots required...Great views, better walking course...In great shape despite heavy play...Very busy, tough to get weekend times.

★★★DIXIE RED HILLS GOLF CLUB
PU-1000 N. 700 W., St. George, 84770, Washington County, (435)634-5852, 100 miles N of Las Vegas.
Opened: 1965. **Holes:** 9. **Par:** 34. **Yards:** 2,564. **Course rating:** 65.9. **Slope:** 119. **Architect:** N/A. **Green fee:** $25/$25. **Credit cards:** MC,VISA. **Reduced fees:** Low season. **Caddies:** No. **Golf carts:** $20. **Discount golf packages:** No. **Season:** Year-round. **High:** Oct.-May. **On site lodging:** No. **Rental clubs:** Yes. **Walking policy:** Unrestricted walking. **Metal spikes allowed:** No. **Range:** Yes (grass/mats). **To obtain tee times:** Call.
Subscriber comments: Fun course...Nice nine holes...Love the Red Rocks...Tougher than it looks...Beautiful, too bad not enough room for 18...Challenging.

★★★EAGLE MOUNTAIN GOLF COURSE
PU-960 E. 700 S., Brigham City, 84302, Box Elder County, (801)723-3212, 55 miles N of Salt Lake City.
Opened: 1989. **Holes:** 18. **Par:** 71/71. **Yards:** 6,769/4,767. **Course rating:** 71.4/65.4. **Slope:** 119/101. **Architect:** Bill Neff. **Green fee:** $15/$15. **Credit cards:** None. **Reduced fees:** N/A. **Caddies:** No. **Golf carts:** $8. **Discount golf packages:** No. **Season:** March-Nov. **High:** April-Sept. **On site lodging:** No. **Rental clubs:** Yes. **Walking policy:** Unrestricted walking. **Metal spikes allowed:** Yes. **Range:** Yes (grass). **To obtain tee times:** Call one day in advance for weekdays and two days in advance for weekends and holidays.
Subscriber comments: Local course, well kept, hilly, lots of trouble...Good service, friendly...Need trees to mature...Front nine is a challenging walk...Extremely popular course...Back nine interesting...Carry your bag and be in shape.

★★★EAGLEWOOD GOLF COURSE
PU-1110 E. Eaglewood Dr., North Salt Lake City, 84054, Davis County, (801)299-0088.
Opened: 1994. **Holes:** 18. **Par:** 71/71. **Yards:** 6,800/5,200. **Course rating:** 71.1/68.8. **Slope:** 121/112. **Architect:** Keith Foster. **Green fee:** $16/$17. **Credit cards:** MC,VISA. **Reduced fees:** Weekdays, low season, juniors. **Caddies:** No. **Golf carts:** $9. **Discount golf packages:** Yes. **Season:** March-Nov. **High:** June-July. **On site lodging:** No. **Rental clubs:** Yes. **Walking policy:** Unrestricted walking. **Metal spikes allowed:** Yes. **Range:** Yes (grass). **To obtain tee times:** Call two days in advance.
Subscriber comments: Fun mountain course...Beautiful setting, long, lots of water and hazards...Lies high above Salt Lake Flats. Interesting layout...Hard to walk, still new, future looks good....Great view, nice clubhouse...Great views of Great Salt Lake...Tough course...Too many houses too close, many blind shots.

★★½EAST BAY GOLF COURSE
PU-1860 S. E. Bay Blvd., Provo, 84601, Utah County, (801)373-6262.
Opened: 1986. **Holes:** 27. **Par:** 71/72. **Yards:** 6,932/5,125. **Course rating:** 67.6/66.6. **Slope:** 116/106. **Architect:** William H. Neff. **Green fee:** $17/$17. **Credit cards:** MC,VISA. **Reduced fees:** N/A. **Caddies:** No. **Golf carts:** $17. **Discount golf packages:** No. **Season:** March-Nov. **High:** May-Sept. **On site lodging:** No. **Rental clubs:** Yes. **Walking policy:** Unrestricted walking. **Metal spikes allowed:** Yes. **Range:** Yes (grass). **To obtain tee times:** Call 1 day in advance. May call Thursday for weekend reservations.

Subscriber comments: Recent improvements make course more playable...The water hazards!...Need marshals and better maintenance...Greens are challenging.
Special Notes: Also has 9-hole junior course.

★★★ENTRADA AT SNOW CANYON

R-2511 W. Entrada Trail, St. George, 84770, Washington County, (801)674-7500, 110 miles E of Las Vegas.
Opened: 1996. **Holes:** 18. **Par:** 72/72. **Yards:** 7,262/5,454. **Course rating:** 74.4/70.8. **Slope:** 127/121. **Architect:** Johnny Miller and Fred Bliss. **Green fee:** $40/$60. **Credit cards:** N/A. **Reduced fees:** Low season, twilight. **Caddies:** No. **Golf carts:** Included in Green Fee. **Discount golf packages:** Yes. **Season:** Year-round. **High:** Oct.-May. **On site lodging:** No. **Rental clubs:** Yes. **Walking policy:** Mandatory cart. **Metal spikes allowed:** No. **Range:** Yes (grass). **To obtain tee times:** Call 30 days in advance.
Notes: Ranked 9th in 1997 Best New Upscale Public Courses.
Subscriber comments: Fun, but difficult Johnny Miller design...A great challenge for any golfer...Tough holes running through lava...Too hard for high handicaps...Lava beds will eat balls...Toughest course in Utah...Unbelievable holes...Beautiful setting.

★★★GLADSTAN GOLF CLUB

PU-One Gladstan Dr., Payson, 84651, Utah County, (801)465-2549, (800)634-3009.
Opened: 1988. **Holes:** 18. **Par:** 71/71. **Yards:** 6,509/4,782. **Course rating:** 70.7/67.4. **Slope:** 121/111. **Architect:** Bill Neff. **Green fee:** $16/$17. **Credit cards:** MC,VISA. **Reduced fees:** Seniors, juniors. **Caddies:** No. **Golf carts:** $15. **Discount golf packages:** Yes. **Season:** March-Nov. **High:** May-Aug. **On site lodging:** No. **Rental clubs:** Yes. **Walking policy:** Unrestricted walking. **Metal spikes allowed:** Yes. **Range:** Yes (grass/mats). **To obtain tee times:** Call Monday for the following week.
Subscriber comments: Two completly different nines...A lot of memorable holes...A fine mountain course...Beautiful mountain setting...Never crowded, exciting back nine...Lots of scrub oak! Bring extra balls!...Good staff...Short, tight.

★★GLENDALE GOLF COURSE

PU-1630 W. 2100 S., Salt Lake City, 84119, Salt Lake County, (801)974-2403.
Opened: 1973. **Holes:** 18. **Par:** 72/73. **Yards:** 7,000/5,930. **Course rating:** 70.9/72.5. **Slope:** 117/120. **Architect:** William F. Bell. **Green fee:** $18/$18. **Credit cards:** MC,VISA,DISC. **Reduced fees:** Weekdays, seniors, juniors. **Caddies:** No. **Golf carts:** $20. **Discount golf packages:** No. **Season:** March-Nov. **High:** May-Aug. **On site lodging:** No. **Rental clubs:** Yes. **Walking policy:** Unrestricted walking. **Metal spikes allowed:** Yes. **Range:** Yes (grass). **To obtain tee times:** Call tee-time number 7 days in advance or golf shop 1 day in advance.

★★GLENMOOR GOLF & COUNTRY CLUB

PU-9800 S. 4800 W., South Jordon, 84065, Salt Lake County, (801)280-1742, 12 miles S of Salt Lake City.
Opened: 1965. **Holes:** 18. **Par:** 72/72. **Yards:** 6,900/5,800. **Course rating:** 70.9/72.0. **Slope:** 117/118. **Architect:** William H. Neff. **Green fee:** $17/$18. **Credit cards:** MC,VISA. **Reduced fees:** Weekdays, seniors. **Caddies:** No. **Golf carts:** $18. **Discount golf packages:** No. **Season:** Year-round. **High:** May-Sept. **On site lodging:** No. **Rental clubs:** Yes. **Walking policy:** Unrestricted walking. **Metal spikes allowed:** Yes. **Range:** Yes (grass). **To obtain tee times:** Call 7 days in advance. Call Monday for weekdays and Thursday for weekends.

★★★½GREEN SPRING GOLF COURSE

PU-588 N. Green Spring Dr., Washington, 84780, Washington County, (801)673-7888.
Opened: 1989. **Holes:** 18. **Par:** 71/71. **Yards:** 6,717/5,042. **Course rating:** 72.6/69.8. **Slope:** 131/119. **Architect:** Gene Bates. **Green fee:** $20/$30. **Credit cards:** MC,VISA. **Reduced fees:** Weekdays, low season, twilight, juniors. **Caddies:** No. **Golf carts:** $9. **Discount golf packages:** Yes. **Season:** Year-round. **High:** Oct.-May. **On site lodging:** No. **Rental clubs:** Yes. **Walking policy:** Unrestricted walking. **Metal spikes allowed:** No. **Range:** Yes (grass/mats). **To obtain tee times:** Call 30 to 60 days in advance.
Subscriber comments: Nice desert course...One of the best in state...Bring lots of balls, plays longer than you think...Spectacular scenery...Course in great shape...Excellent...The two ravine holes are extreme, beautiful...Very challenging natural terrain...Superb greens.

★★★½HOBBLE CREEK GOLF CLUB

PU-E. Hobble Creek Canyon Rd., Springville, 84663, Utah County, (801)489-6297, 15 miles S of Provo.
Opened: 1966. **Holes:** 18. **Par:** 71/73. **Yards:** 6,315/5,435. **Course rating:** 69.4/69.5. **Slope:** 120/117. **Architect:** William Bell. **Green fee:** $15/$17. **Credit cards:** None. **Reduced fees:** Seniors, juniors.
Caddies: No. **Golf carts:** $16. **Discount golf packages:** No. **Season:** March-Nov.
High: July-Sept. **On site lodging:** No. **Rental clubs:** Yes. **Walking policy:** Unrestricted walking. **Metal spikes allowed:** Yes. **Range:** Yes (grass). **To obtain tee times:** Call Monday for Tuesday through the following Monday.

Subscriber comments: One of the best mountain courses in Utah...Great canyon course...One of my favorite courses. Creeks and trees make it tough...Wonderful variety of holes...A jewel in the canyon...Great mountain golf, watch for frost...Fun, fun, fun...Scenic, challenging, reasonable...Best golf value in Utah year-after-year...Especially gorgeous in the fall.

★★★½HOMESTEAD GOLF CLUB

R-700 N. Homestead Dr., Midway, 84049, Wasatch County, (435)654-5588, (800)327-7220, 30 miles SE of Salt Lake City.
Opened: 1990. **Holes:** 18. **Par:** 72/72. **Yards:** 7,017/5,091. **Course rating:** 73.0/68.8. **Slope:** 135/118. **Architect:** Bruce Summerhays. **Green fee:** $15/$40. **Credit cards:** MC,VISA,AMEX,DISC,Diners Club. **Reduced fees:** Weekdays, low season, resort guests, twilight, seniors. **Caddies:** No. **Golf carts:** $10. **Discount golf packages:** Yes.
Season: April-Oct. **High:** June-Sept. **On site lodging:** Yes. **Rental clubs:** Yes. **Walking policy:** Unrestricted walking. **Metal spikes allowed:** Yes. **Range:** Yes (grass). **To obtain tee times:** Hotel guests call 14 days in advance, others call one week in advance.
Notes: Ranked 8th in 1997 Best in State.
Subscriber comments: Beautiful and difficult layout in a mountain valley...Fun course to play, setting is very peaceful...Romantic getaway to the mountains...Great vacation spot...Challenging...Golf staff go out of their way to make you feel welcome.

★★★½JEREMY RANCH COUNTRY CLUB

8770 N. Jeremy Rd., Park City, 84060, Summit County, (801)531-9000.
Call club for further information.
Notes: Ranked 2nd in 1997 Best in State.
Subscriber comments: Bring lots of balls, demands planning...Now a private course...Golf in the mountains changes one's perspective...Target golf...Nice setting...Previous home to Senior Tour stop...Much improved since it went private...Love this course.

★★½LAKESIDE GOLF COURSE

PU-1201 N. 1100 W., West Bountiful, 84087, Davis County, (801)295-1019, 10 miles N of Salt Lake City.
Opened: 1966. **Holes:** 18. **Par:** 71/71. **Yards:** 6,030/4,895. **Course rating:** 67.2/66.5. **Slope:** 113/115. **Architect:** William H. Neff. **Green fee:** $16/$16. **Credit cards:** MC,VISA,DISC. **Reduced fees:** Seniors, juniors. **Caddies:** No. **Golf carts:** $9.
Discount golf packages: No. **Season:** March-Oct. **High:** June-Aug. **On site lodging:** No. **Rental clubs:** Yes. **Walking policy:** Unrestricted walking. **Metal spikes allowed:** No. **Range:** Yes (grass/mats). **To obtain tee times:** Call Mondays for Tuesday-Friday. Call Thursday for Saturday, Sunday and Monday.
Subscriber comments: Wide open...Short easy holes....Nice course, great for practice rounds. Lots of diverse shots.
Special Notes: Formerly West Bountiful City Golf Course.

★★★½OGAN RIVER GOLF COURSE

PU-550 W. 1000 S., Logan, 84321, Cache County, (435)750-0123, 80 miles N of Salt Lake City.
Opened: 1993. **Holes:** 18. **Par:** 71/71. **Yards:** 6,502/5,048. **Course rating:** 70.5/78.9. **Slope:** 124/117. **Architect:** Robert Muir Graves.
Green fee: $15/$15. **Credit cards:** MC,VISA. **Reduced fees:** Seniors, juniors. **Caddies:** No. **Golf carts:** $9. **Discount golf packages:** No. **Season:**

March-Oct. **High:** June-Sept. **On site lodging:** No. **Rental clubs:** Yes. **Walking policy:** Unrestricted walking. **Metal spikes allowed:** Yes. **Range:** Yes (grass). **To obtain tee times:** Call 7 days in advance.

Subscriber comments: Target golf course, need driver a few times...Ask for a cheat sheet at the pro shop to shave five strokes...Use all your clubs, makes you think...Lots of water, lots of challenges, but fun to play...Great layout amongst the marshes...A very pleasant place to play...Watch out for the river running through it.

★★MEADOW BROOK GOLF COURSE

PU-4197 S. 1300 W., Taylorsville, 84123, Salt Lake County, (801)266-0971.
Opened: 1953. **Holes:** 18. **Par:** 72/72. **Yards:** 6,800/5,605. **Course rating:** 70.0/67.9.
Slope: 110/104. **Architect:** Mick Riley. **Green fee:** $17/$18. **Credit cards:** None.
Reduced fees: Weekdays, seniors, juniors. **Caddies:** Yes. **Golf carts:** $17. **Discount golf packages:** No. **Season:** March-Dec. **High:** May-Oct. **On site lodging:** No. **Rental clubs:** Yes. **Walking policy:** Unrestricted walking. **Metal spikes allowed:** Yes. **Range:** Yes (grass). **To obtain tee times:** Call golf shop.
Notes: 1955 Utah Open.

★★★½MOAB GOLF CLUB

PU-2705 S.E. Bench Rd., Moab, 84532, Grand County, (801)259-6488, 220 miles E of Salt Lake City.
Opened: 1960. **Holes:** 18. **Par:** 72/72. **Yards:** 6,819/4,725. **Course rating:** 72.2/69.6. **Slope:** 125/110. **Architect:** N/A. **Green fee:** $18/$18.
Credit cards: MC,VISA. **Reduced fees:** Juniors. **Caddies:** No. **Golf carts:** $8. **Discount golf packages:** Yes. **Season:** Year-round. **High:** Spring/Fall. **On site lodging:** No. **Rental clubs:** Yes. **Walking policy:** Unrestricted walking. **Metal spikes allowed:** Yes. **Range:** Yes (grass). **To obtain tee times:** Call 30 days in advance with credit card.

GREAT VALUE

Subscriber comments: A beautiful layout in the Red Rock hills... New back nine great...Great course, great views, great people...Blend of old and new nines...Red Rocks and green grass, most beautiful course in the state.

★★★MOUNT OGDEN GOLF COURSE

PU-1787 Constitution Way, Ogden, 84403, Weber County, (801)629-8700.
Opened: 1985. **Holes:** 18. **Par:** 71/72. **Yards:** 6,300/4,980. **Course rating:** 70.5/69.5.
Slope: 121/111. **Architect:** Bill Neff. **Green fee:** $15/$15. **Credit cards:** MC,VISA.
Reduced fees: N/A. **Caddies:** No. **Golf carts:** $8. **Discount golf packages:** No.
Season: March-Nov. **High:** April-Oct. **On site lodging:** No. **Rental clubs:** Yes. **Walking policy:** Unrestricted walking. **Metal spikes allowed:** Yes. **Range:** Yes (grass). **To obtain tee times:** Call on Wednesday for weekend tee times. Weekdays, call one day in advance.
Subscriber comments: Short, tough, narrow mountain course, a challenge for most...Tight driving areas...Don't walk, ride! Lots of scrub oak...Maintenance is very good...Must hit great shots to be good on some holes...Hit it straight, lots of blind shots.

MOUNTAIN DELL GOLF CLUB

PU-Parleys Canyon, Salt Lake City, 84109, Salt Lake County, (801)582-3812.
Opened: 1962. **Architect:** Bill Neff. **Green fee:** $20/$20. **Credit cards:** MC,VISA.
Reduced fees: Weekdays, twilight, seniors, juniors. **Caddies:** No. **Golf carts:** $10.
Discount golf packages: No. **Season:** April-Nov. **High:** June-Aug. **On site lodging:** No. **Rental clubs:** Yes. **Walking policy:** Unrestricted walking. **Metal spikes allowed:** No. **Range:** Yes (grass). **To obtain tee times:** Call golf shop.

★★★½CANYON COURSE

Holes: 18. **Par:** 72/73. **Yards:** 6,787/5,447. **Course rating:** 71.3/71.1. **Slope:** 126/112.
Subscriber comments: Most improved old course in Utah...A mix of old and new holes...Good challenge for even low handicapers...Canyon makes putting tough...Nice setting...Well maintained...Ball carries a long way in high altitude...Challenging course, seldom hot...Mountain setting...My favorite two courses, long walk but worth it.

★★★½LAKE COURSE

Holes: 18. **Par:** 71/71. **Yards:** 6,709/5,066. **Course rating:** 72.2/67.6. **Slope:** 129/109.
Subscriber comments: Almost as tough as the Canyon Course...Too far between greens and tee boxes. Little room for mistakes...Must be able to hit long drives over canyons...Beautiful setting, excellent public course.

★★MOUNTAIN VIEW GOLF CLUB
PU-2400 W. 8660 S., West Jordan, 84084, Salt Lake County, (801)255-9211, 20 miles S of Salt Lake City.
Opened: 1968. **Holes:** 18. **Par:** 72/72. **Yards:** 6,764/5,827. **Course rating:** 70.2/69.9. **Slope:** 112/118. **Architect:** William H. Neff. **Green fee:** $17/$18. **Credit cards:** N/A. **Reduced fees:** N/A. **Caddies:** No. **Golf carts:** $19. **Discount golf packages:** No. **Season:** March-Nov. **High:** June-Aug. **On site lodging:** No. **Rental clubs:** Yes. **Walking policy:** Unrestricted walking. **Metal spikes allowed:** No. **Range:** Yes (grass). **To obtain tee times:** Call Monday for Tuesday and Wednesday. Call Wednesday for Thursday and Friday. Call Thurdsay for Saturday, Sunday and Monday.

★★½MURRAY PARKWAY GOLF CLUB
PU-6345 S. Murray Pkwy. Ave., Murray, 84123, Salt Lake County, (801)262-4653, 8 miles S of Salt Lake City.
Opened: 1986. **Holes:** 18. **Par:** 72/72. **Yards:** 6,800/5,800. **Course rating:** 71.3/71.0. **Slope:** 120/118. **Architect:** Robert Muir Graves. **Green fee:** $19/$19. **Credit cards:** MC,VISA,DISC. **Reduced fees:** Juniors. **Caddies:** No. **Golf carts:** $9. **Discount golf packages:** No. **Season:** March-Nov. **High:** June-Aug. **On site lodging:** No. **Rental clubs:** Yes. **Walking policy:** Unrestricted walking. **Metal spikes allowed:** No. **Range:** Yes (grass). **To obtain tee times:** Call Monday for Tuesday and Wednesday tee times. Call Wednesday for Thursday and Friday and call Thursday for Saturday, Sunday and Monday.
Subscriber comments: Good mixture of long and narrow. Hard to get on...Short yardage, fun and popular, nice hilly contours...Holes close to one another, listen for fore...Great view of surrounding mountains. Great pullcarts...Wide open.

★★★PARK CITY GOLF COURSE
PU-Lower Park Ave., Park City, 84060, Summit County, (801)649-8701, 25 miles SE of Salt Lake City.
Opened: 1963. **Holes:** 18. **Par:** 72/72. **Yards:** 6,754/5,600. **Course rating:** 71.7/71.4. **Slope:** 127/123. **Architect:** Bill Neff. **Green fee:** $20/$25. **Credit cards:** MC,VISA. **Reduced fees:** Low season. **Caddies:** No. **Golf carts:** $10. **Discount golf packages:** No. **Season:** April-Oct. **High:** May-Sept. **On site lodging:** No. **Rental clubs:** Yes. **Walking policy:** Unrestricted walking. **Metal spikes allowed:** Yes. **Range:** Yes (grass). **To obtain tee times:** Call seven days in advance. Two or more tee times require a credit card.
Subscriber comments: Look out for moose...Park city's best course, scenery great...Golfed and skied the same day! Ball goes long way.

★★★½PARK MEADOWS COUNTRY CLUB
2000 Meadows Dr., Park City, 84068, Summit County, (801)649-2460, 30 miles SE of Salt Lake City.
Opened: 1983. **Holes:** 18. **Par:** 72/73. **Yards:** 7,400/5,816. **Course rating:** 74.4/72.2. **Slope:** 129/125. **Architect:** Jack Nicklaus. **Green fee:** $55/$95. **Credit cards:** MC,VISA,AMEX. **Reduced fees:** N/A. **Caddies:** No. **Golf carts:** $13. **Discount golf packages:** Yes. **Season:** April-Oct. **High:** June-Aug. **On site lodging:** No. **Rental clubs:** Yes. **Walking policy:** Mandatory cart. **Metal spikes allowed:** Yes. **Range:** Yes (grass). **To obtain tee times:** Non-members call 7 days in advance.
Notes: Ranked 6th in 1997 Best in State; Senior Tour Franklin Quest Championship since 1993.
Subscriber comments: Course will be private...Super course, great service...Tough course for me...Nice fairways...Windy...Tooo looong...Windy, links, lots of sand, challenging...Only Jack can play this course...A wonderful links-style course.

★★★RIVERBEND GOLF COURSE
PU-12800 S. 1040 W., Riverton, 84065, Salt Lake County, (801)253-3673, 15 miles S of Salt Lake City.
Opened: 1995. **Holes:** 18. **Par:** 72/72. **Yards:** 6,876/5,081. **Course rating:** 69.9/68.7. **Slope:** 118/111. **Architect:** Gene Bates. **Green fee:** $18/$20. **Credit cards:** MC,VISA. **Reduced fees:** Seniors, juniors. **Caddies:** No. **Golf carts:** $9. **Discount golf packages:** No. **Season:** Year-round. **High:** April-Oct. **On site lodging:** No. **Rental clubs:** Yes. **Walking policy:** Unrestricted walking. **Metal spikes allowed:** No. **Range:** Yes

(grass). **To obtain tee times:** Call Thursday for upcoming weekend.
Notes: Ranked 7th in 1997 Best in State.
Subscriber comments: New course, good layout...Makes me feel as if I'm playing the PGA...Many elevation changes...Great setting...Use all your clubs....Great for a new course...Great cheeseburger!!...Excellent course, fair greens...Always very windy...Two distict nines, nice public course.

★★ROSE PARK GOLF CLUB
PU-1386 N. Redwood Rd., Salt Lake City, 84116, Salt Lake County, (801)596-5030.
Opened: 1960. **Holes:** 18. **Par:** 72/75. **Yards:** 6,696/5,816. **Course rating:** 69.6/70.8.
Slope: 109/112. **Architect:** Mick Riley/William F. Bell. **Green fee:** $17/$18. **Credit cards:** MC,VISA. **Reduced fees:** Seniors, juniors. **Caddies:** No. **Golf carts:** $20.
Discount golf packages: No. **Season:** Feb.-Dec. **High:** May-Sept. **On site lodging:** No. **Rental clubs:** Yes. **Walking policy:** Unrestricted walking. **Metal spikes allowed:** No. **Range:** Yes (grass). **To obtain tee times:** Call 7 days in advance.

★★½ROUND VALLEY COUNTRY CLUB
1875 E Round Valley Rd., Morgan, 84050, Morgan County, (801)829-3796.
Call club for further information.
Subscriber comments: Nice country course...Water in play on nearly every hole. Good views...Has an on-course campground...Several tight holes along river, new back nine...Lots of water on front nine.

★★½ST. GEORGE GOLF CLUB
PU-2190 S. 1400 E., St. George, 84770, Washington County, (801)634-5854, 110 miles NE of Las Vegas.
Opened: 1975. **Holes:** 18. **Par:** 73/73. **Yards:** 7,213/5,197. **Course rating:** 71.7/68.9.
Slope: 123/114. **Architect:** David Bingaman. **Green fee:** $35/$35. **Credit cards:** MC,VISA. **Reduced fees:** Low season. **Caddies:** No. **Golf carts:** $20. **Discount golf packages:** No. **Season:** Year-round. **High:** Oct.-May. **On site lodging:** No. **Rental clubs:** Yes. **Walking policy:** Unrestricted walking. **Metal spikes allowed:** No. **Range:** No. **To obtain tee times:** Call 14 days in advance.
Subscriber comments: Accuracy a must. Great for seniors...Much improved over past years...Excellent greens...Great winter getaway...Great walking course...Basic golf...Like the new waste (sand) areas...Best golf for price in St. George.

★★★SCHNEITER'S BLUFF AT WEST POINT
PU-300 N. 3500 W., West Point, 84015, Davis County, (801)773-0731, 20 miles N of Salt Lake City.
Opened: 1995. **Holes:** 18. **Par:** 72/72. **Yards:** 6,833/5,419. **Course rating:** 70.2.
Slope: 115. **Architect:** E. Schneiter/B. Schneiter/J. Schneiter. **Green fee:** $17/$17.
Credit cards: MC,VISA,DISC. **Reduced fees:** Seniors, juniors. **Caddies:** No. **Golf carts:** $16. **Discount golf packages:** Yes. **Season:** Feb.-Nov. **High:** June-Sept. **On site lodging:** No. **Rental clubs:** Yes. **Walking policy:** Unrestricted walking. **Metal spikes allowed:** No. **Range:** Yes (grass). **To obtain tee times:** Call Thursday for upcoming weekend. Call 1 day in advance for weekday.
Subscriber comments: Nice conditions for a new course...Needs to mature...Great winter golf...Well maintained. Fun course. Good staff...A flat course, wide fairways, a few bunkers...Still growing, better with age...Short but difficult layout.

★½SCHNEITER'S PEBBLE BROOK LINKS
PU-8968 South 1300 E., Sandy, 84094, Salt Lake County, (801)566-2181, 7 miles SE of Salt Lake City.
Opened: 1974. **Holes:** 18. **Par:** N/A. **Yards:** N/A. **Course rating:** N/A. **Slope:** N/A.
Architect: Schneiter Golf. **Green fee:** $13/$19. **Credit cards:** All major. **Reduced fees:** Seniors, juniors. **Caddies:** No. **Golf carts:** $18. **Discount golf packages:** No. **Season:** Year-round. **High:** April-Dec. **On site lodging:** No. **Rental clubs:** Yes. **Walking policy:** Unrestricted walking. **Metal spikes allowed:** Yes. **Range:** Yes (grass/mats). **To obtain tee times:** Call golf shop.

★★★SCHNEITER'S RIVERSIDE GOLF COURSE
PU-5460 S. Weber Dr., Ogden, 84405, Weber County, (801)399-4636, 30 miles N of Salt Lake City.

Opened: 1961. **Holes:** 18. **Par:** 71/71. **Yards:** 6,177/5,217. **Course rating:** 68.4/68.5. **Slope:** 114/113. **Architect:** Schneiter. **Green fee:** $17/$17. **Credit cards:** All major. **Reduced fees:** Seniors, juniors. **Caddies:** No. **Golf carts:** $16. **Discount golf packages:** No. **Season:** March-Nov. **High:** May-Aug. **On site lodging:** No. **Rental clubs:** Yes. **Walking policy:** Walking at certain times. **Metal spikes allowed:** Yes. **Range:** Yes (grass). **To obtain tee times:** Call Thursday for upcoming weekend. For weekday call one day in advance.
Subscriber comments: Nice little course...Course is always in excellent shape...Fun place to play, but crowded...Making great improvements...Short, tight, treelined.

★★½SHERWOOD HILLS RESORT GOLF COURSE
R-Highway 89-91, Wellsville, 84339, Cache County, (801)245-6055, 6 miles S of Logan.
Opened: 1973. **Holes:** 9. **Par:** 36/37. **Yards:** 3,315/2,830. **Course rating:** N/A. **Slope:** N/A. **Architect:** Mark Dixon Ballif. **Green fee:** $18/$18. **Credit cards:** MC,VISA.
Reduced fees: Weekdays, resort guests, seniors. **Caddies:** No. **Golf carts:** $18.
Discount golf packages: Yes. **Season:** April-Nov. **High:** June-Aug. **On site lodging:** Yes. **Rental clubs:** Yes. **Walking policy:** Unrestricted walking. **Metal spikes allowed:** Yes. **Range:** Yes (grass). **To obtain tee times:** Call anytime in advance.
Subscriber comments: Very short par 5s, great view in the fall... A great walking course...Comfy little course, seldom crowded...Nice mountain area, some narrow holes...Fun course for a vacation spot...A fun place to play...Service is great.

★★½SOUTHGATE GOLF CLUB
PU-1975 S. Tonaquint Dr., St. George, 84770, Washington County, (801)628-0000, 100 miles N of Las Vegas.
Opened: 1984. **Holes:** 18. **Par:** 70/70. **Yards:** 6,038/5,504. **Course rating:** 70.3/68.2. **Slope:** 121/118. **Architect:** Bill Neff. **Green fee:** $25/$25. **Credit cards:** MC,VISA. **Reduced fees:** Low season, twilight, juniors. **Caddies:** No. **Golf carts:** $20. **Discount golf packages:** No. **Season:** Year-round. **High:** Oct.-May. **On site lodging:** No. **Rental clubs:** Yes. **Walking policy:** Unrestricted walking. **Metal spikes allowed:** No. **Range:** Yes (grass/mats). **To obtain tee times:** Call 14 days in advance.
Subscriber comments: Front nine needs work. Back nine is new, has potential...Tough course, well laid out...Very accommodating...Back nine best part of course...Super golf pro instructor...Fairly flat, open fairways.

★★½SPANISH OAKS GOLF CLUB
PU-2300 E. Powerhouse Rd., Spanish Fork, 84660, Utah County, (801)798-9816, 7 miles N of Provo.
Opened: 1983. **Holes:** 18. **Par:** 72/73. **Yards:** 6,358/5,319. **Course rating:** 68.7/68.9. **Slope:** 116/113. **Architect:** Billy Casper and Gary Darling. **Green fee:** $15/$15. **Credit cards:** All major. **Reduced fees:** Twilight, seniors, juniors. **Caddies:** No. **Golf carts:** $15. **Discount golf packages:** No. **Season:** March-Oct. **High:** May-Sept. **On site lodging:** No. **Rental clubs:** Yes. **Walking policy:** Unrestricted walking. **Metal spikes allowed:** Yes. **Range:** Yes (grass). **To obtain tee times:** Call one week in advance.
Subscriber comments: Short and open...Good greens...Little bit of everything...Always windy...Very short back nine. Fairly easy course...Super challenge for high handicap...Wide fairways...Plays longer than listed.

★★½STANSBURY PARK GOLF CLUB
PU-#1 Country Club Dr., Tooele, 84074, Tooele County, (801)328-1483, 25 miles SE of Salt Lake City.
Opened: 1972. **Holes:** 18. **Par:** 72/72. **Yards:** 6,831/5,722. **Course rating:** 71.6/71.5. **Slope:** 125/121. **Architect:** Bill Neff. **Green fee:** $13/$15. **Credit cards:** None. **Reduced fees:** Weekdays, low season. **Caddies:** No. **Golf carts:** $7. **Discount golf packages:** No. **Season:** Feb.-Nov. **High:** June-Aug. **On site lodging:** No. **Rental clubs:** Yes. **Walking policy:** Unrestricted walking. **Metal spikes allowed:** Yes. **Range:** Yes (grass). **To obtain tee times:** Call Thursday for weekends. Call Saturday or Sunday for following weekdays.
Subscriber comments: Water on 16 holes...Beautiful terrain... A challenge for all...Good price.

★★★★SUNBROOK GOLF CLUB

PU-2240 Sunbrook Dr., St. George, 84770, Washington County, (801)634-5866, 120 miles N of Las Vegas.

Opened: 1990. **Holes:** 27. **Architect:** Ted G. Robinson/John Harbottle. **Green fee:** $36/$36. **Credit cards:** MC,VISA. **Reduced fees:** Low season. **Caddies:** No. **Golf carts:** $20. **Discount golf packages:** No. **Season:** Year-round. **High:** Oct.-May. **On site lodging:** No. **Rental clubs:** Yes. **Walking policy:** Unrestricted walking. **Metal spikes allowed:** No. **Range:** Yes (grass/mats). **To obtain tee times:** Call Mondays for the following week.

POINTE/BLACKROCK
Par: 72/72. **Yards:** 6,758/5,155. **Course rating:** 73.8/71.4. **Slope:** 133/125.
POINTE/WOODBRIDGE
Par: 72/72. **Yards:** 6,818/5,286. **Course rating:** 73.0/71.1. **Slope:** 129/121.
WOODBRIDGE/BLACKROCK
Par: 72/72. **Yards:** 6,828/5,233. **Course rating:** 74.0/74.1. **Slope:** 134/126.
Notes: Ranked 1st in 1997 Best in State.
Subscriber comments: One of the best courses in Utah...Tough but fair, worth playing again and again...Hands down the best in Southern Utah!...Good Ted Robinson design, excellent shape...Bring your "A" putting game...Target golf...The best public course in the state!...Sporty, fair golf course...Beautiful and exciting.

★★★TRI-CITY GOLF COURSE

PU-1400 N. 200 E., American Fork, 84003, Utah County, (801)756-3594, 30 miles S of Salt Lake City.

Opened: 1972. **Holes:** 18. **Par:** 72/73. **Yards:** 7,077/6,304. **Course rating:** 73.0/73.0. **Slope:** 125/124. **Architect:** Joe Williams. **Green fee:** $18/$18. **Credit cards:** MC,VISA. **Reduced fees:** Seniors, juniors. **Caddies:** No. **Golf carts:** $14. **Discount golf packages:** No. **Season:** March-Oct. **High:** May-Aug. **On site lodging:** No. **Rental clubs:** Yes. **Walking policy:** Unrestricted walking. **Metal spikes allowed:** No. **Range:** Yes (grass). **To obtain tee times:** Call up to 10 days in advance.
Subscriber comments: Long, narrow, tough, old course...Elevation is 5,000 feet... Golfing in a heavy forest. Gnarly old trees everywhere...Tight driving holes. Nice greens...Long track with a couple of unfair holes.

★★★★VALLEY VIEW GOLF COURSE

PU-2501 E. Gentile, Layton, 84040, Davis County, (801)546-1630, 15 miles N of Salt Lake City.

Opened: 1974. **Holes:** 18. **Par:** 72/74. **Yards:** 6,652/5,755. **Course rating:** 71.0/73.2. **Slope:** 123/125. **Architect:** William Hull. **Green fee:** $17/$18. **Credit cards:** All major. **Reduced fees:** Seniors, juniors. **Caddies:** No. **Golf carts:** $18. **Discount golf packages:** No. **Season:** March-Nov. **High:** May-Sept. **On site lodging:** No. **Rental clubs:** Yes. **Walking policy:** Unrestricted walking. **Metal spikes allowed:** No. **Range:** Yes (grass). **To obtain tee times:** Call Thursday 7 a.m. for Friday, Saturday, Sunday and Monday holidays. One day in advance for weekdays.
Notes: Ranked 9th in 1997 Best in State.
Subscriber comments: Good, fun course...One of Utah's best...On caliber with private courses. Great views. Elevation changes tops...Fun to play...Slick fast greens...Public golf course that looks like country club...Superb public course, great scenery, tough finishing...Always in great condition, continually improving.

★★★½WASATCH STATE PARK GOLF CLUB

PU-P.O. Box 10, Midway, 84049, Wasatch County, (435)654-0532, 35 miles E of Salt Lake City.

Holes: 27. **Architect:** Bill Neff. **Green fee:** $17/$19. **Credit cards:** MC,VISA. **Reduced fees:** N/A. **Caddies:** No. **Golf carts:** N/A. **Discount golf packages:** No. **Season:** April-Nov. **High:** July-Aug. **On site lodging:** No. **Rental clubs:** No. **Walking policy:** Unrestricted walking. **Metal spikes allowed:** No. **Range:** Yes (grass/mats). **To obtain tee times:** Call 7 a.m. Monday for weekends. Call 7 a.m. Thursday for following weekdays.

CANYON/LAKE
Par: 72/72. **Yards:** 6,942/5,573. **Course rating:** N/A. **Slope:** N/A.

UTAH

CANYON/MOUNTAIN
Par: 72. **Yards:** 6,808/5,627. **Course rating:** 72.0. **Slope:** N/A.
LAKE/MOUNTAIN
Par: 72/72. **Yards:** 6,712/5,368. **Course rating:** N/A. **Slope:** N/A.
Subscriber comments: One of the most beautiful courses in Utah...Challenge for all players. Best fall scenery ever...All three nines offer a different twist...Allow the resident moose to "play through"!...Prettiest setting in state...Great burgers...Mother Nature at her finest...Great family courses. Camp and play golf...Forget scoring, enjoy just being there...Looks just like Switzerland.

★★½WEST RIDGE GOLF COURSE
PU-5055 S. W. Ridge Blvd., West Valley City, 84118, Salt Lake County, (801)966-4653, 10 miles SW of Salt Lake City.
Opened: 1991. **Holes:** 18. **Par:** 71/71. **Yards:** 6,734/5,027. **Course rating:** 72.2/68.1.
Slope: 125/118. **Architect:** William H. Neff. **Green fee:** $16/$18. **Credit cards:** All major. **Reduced fees:** Weekdays, low season, seniors, juniors. **Caddies:** No. **Golf carts:** $9. **Discount golf packages:** Yes. **Season:** March-Nov. **High:** April-Aug. **On site lodging:** No. **Rental clubs:** Yes. **Walking policy:** Unrestricted walking. **Metal spikes allowed:** No. **Range:** Yes (grass). **To obtain tee times:** Call 7 days in advance.
Subscriber comments: Short but tight. Greens very undulating...Usually windy...Wonderfully laid out course for area...Hilly. New course. Good value...New nine holes are nice...Harder than it looks, great views, excellent upkeep.

★★★½WINGPOINTE GOLF COURSE
PU-3602 W. 100 N., Salt Lake City, 84122, Salt Lake County, (801)575-2345.
Opened: 1990. **Holes:** 18. **Par:** 72/72. **Yards:** 7,101/5,228. **Course rating:** 73.3/72.0. **Slope:** 131/125. **Architect:** Arthur Hills. **Green fee:** $16/$18. **Credit cards:** MC,VISA. **Reduced fees:** Weekdays, low season, seniors, juniors. **Caddies:** No. **Golf carts:** $16. **Discount golf packages:** No. **Season:** Year-round. **High:** May-Oct. **On site lodging:** No. **Rental clubs:** Yes. **Walking policy:** Walking at certain times. **Metal spikes allowed:** Yes. **Range:** Yes (grass). **To obtain tee times:** Call tee-time number up to 7 days in advance.
Notes: Ranked 10th in 1997 Best in State.
Subscriber comments: A great course located right next to the airport...Lots of variety from different tee boxes. Noise from airplanes a distraction...Very challenging links-type course. Great pro...737s play through...Pretty flat...Good layout...Wonderful variety, a good change for a Utah course...Right at the end of the runway.

(GOOD VALUE)

★★★½WOLF CREEK RESORT RESORT
3900 N. Wolf Creek Dr., Eden, 84310, Weber County, (801)745-3365, 14 miles N of Ogden.
Opened: N/A. **Holes:** 18. **Par:** 72/72. **Yards:** 6,845/5,332. **Course rating:** N/A. **Slope:** 134/127. **Architect:** Mark Dixon Ballif. **Green fee:** N/A. **Credit cards:** MC,VISA,AMEX. **Reduced fees:** Weekdays, low season, resort guests, twilight, seniors, juniors. **Caddies:** No. **Golf carts:** N/A. **Discount golf packages:** Yes. **Season:** March-Nov. **High:** May-Sept. **On site lodging:** Yes. **Rental clubs:** No. **Walking policy:** Unrestricted walking. **Metal spikes allowed:** No. **Range:** No. **To obtain tee times:** N/A.
Subscriber comments: Fine mountain course with great scenery...My favorite course in Utah!...Greens are like putting on ice...Fantastic mountain scenery...Links-type course. Great way to spend the day...Beautiful view!...What a contrast! 18 holes, two courses, old and new...You'll love it, cooler in the summer than the valley.

★★ALBURG COUNTRY CLUB

Rte. 129, South Alburg, 05440, Grand Isle County, (802)796-3586, 40 miles N of Burlington.
Opened: 1967. **Holes:** 18. **Par:** 72/75. **Yards:** 6,391/5,536. **Course rating:** 70.2/71.2.
Slope: 119/120. **Architect:** Dick Ellison. **Green fee:** $12/$25. **Credit cards:** None.
Reduced fees: Weekdays, low season, twilight, juniors. **Caddies:** No. **Golf carts:** $20.
Discount golf packages: Yes. **Season:** May-Oct. **High:** July-Aug. **On site lodging:**
No. **Rental clubs:** Yes. **Walking policy:** Unrestricted walking. **Metal spikes allowed:**
Yes. **Range:** Yes (grass/mats). **To obtain tee times:** Call on Wednesday for upcoming weekend.

★★BASIN HARBOR GOLF CLUB

R-Basin Harbor Rd., Vergennes, 05491, Addison County, (802)475-2309, 30 miles S of Burlington.
Opened: 1927. **Holes:** 18. **Par:** 72/72. **Yards:** 6,511/5,700. **Course rating:** 70.7/67.1.
Slope: 120/113. **Architect:** A. Campbell/R. Mitchell/G. Cornish. **Green fee:** $37/$42.
Credit cards: MC,VISA. **Reduced fees:** Low season, resort guests, twilight, juniors.
Caddies: No. **Golf carts:** $25. **Discount golf packages:** Yes. **Season:** May-Oct. **High:**
July-Aug. **On site lodging:** Yes. **Rental clubs:** Yes. **Walking policy:** Unrestricted walking. **Metal spikes allowed:** Yes. **Range:** Yes (grass). **To obtain tee times:** Public may call 2 days in advance. Resort guests may call anytime in advance.
Subscriber comments: Easy layout—can be windy on the lake holes...Beautiful...Scenic views of Lake Champlain...Great place, great setting, great atmosphere...Fast greens, great vacation spot!...Wide open.

★★½CHAMPLAIN COUNTRY CLUB

Rte. 7 North, Swanton, 05488, Franklin County, (802)527-1187, 3 miles N of St. Albans.
Opened: 1915. **Holes:** 18. **Par:** 70/70. **Yards:** 6,252/5,209. **Course rating:** 69.9/65.0.
Slope: 123/115. **Architect:** Duer Irving Sewall. **Green fee:** $21/$24. **Credit cards:**
MC,VISA,DISC. **Reduced fees:** Weekdays, low season, twilight. **Caddies:** Yes. **Golf carts:** $22. **Discount golf packages:** Yes. **Season:** April-Oct. **High:** July-Aug. **On site lodging:** No. **Rental clubs:** Yes. **Walking policy:** Unrestricted walking. **Metal spikes allowed:** No. **Range:** No. **To obtain tee times:** June-Oct. call 3 days in advance for weekends and holidays.
Subscriber comments: Challenging small greens...Good layout.

★★★½COUNTRY CLUB OF BARRE

PU-Plainfield Rd., Barre, 05641, Washington County, (802)476-7658, 4 miles E of Barre.
Opened: 1924. **Holes:** 18. **Par:** 71/71. **Yards:** 6,191/5,515. **Course rating:** 70.2/72.0.
Slope: 123/116. **Architect:** Wayne Stiles. **Green fee:** $30/$30. **Credit cards:** MC,VISA.
Reduced fees: N/A. **Caddies:** No. **Golf carts:** $14. **Discount golf packages:** No.
Season: April-Oct. **High:** June-Aug. **On site lodging:** No. **Rental clubs:** No. **Walking policy:** Unrestricted walking. **Metal spikes allowed:** No. **Range:** Yes (grass/mats). **To obtain tee times:** Call up to 7 days in advance.
Subscriber comments: Challenging course in the middle of nowhere...Several blind holes—tough but nice...Very scenic...Demanding layout...Tight and fairly long.

★★★CROWN POINT COUNTRY CLUB

Weathersfield Center Rd., Springfield, 05156, Windsor County, (802)885-1010, 100 miles N of Hartford, CT.
Opened: 1953. **Holes:** 18. **Par:** 72/72. **Yards:** 6,602/5,542. **Course rating:** 71.2/71.3.
Slope: 123/117. **Architect:** William Mitchell. **Green fee:** $34/$43. **Credit cards:**
MC,VISA. **Reduced fees:** Weekdays, twilight, juniors. **Caddies:** No. **Golf carts:** $28.
Discount golf packages: No. **Season:** April-Oct. **High:** N/A. **On site lodging:** No.
Rental clubs: Yes. **Walking policy:** Unrestricted walking. **Metal spikes allowed:** Yes.
Range: Yes (grass). **To obtain tee times:** Call up to 3 days in advance.
Subscriber comments: Too many hills and blind spots!...Best clubhouse views of the course I've ever seen...Good, fun course; par 3s are terrific...No houses, just great golf...Great in the fall, always something to look at...Intimidating 18th caps the round...Big carry on 6 and 9...Quite open, easy to score well.

★½ESSEX COUNTRY CLUB
PU-332 Old Stage Rd., Essex Junction, 05452, Chittenden County, (802)879-3232, 10 miles NE of Burlington.
Opened: 1988. **Holes:** 18. **Par:** 72/72. **Yards:** 6,500/5,700. **Course rating:** 70.4/69.0. **Slope:** 117/112. **Architect:** Graham Cooke. **Green fee:** $19/$20. **Credit cards:** MC,VISA. **Reduced fees:** Twilight. **Caddies:** No. **Golf carts:** $20. **Discount golf packages:** No. **Season:** April-Nov. **High:** N/A. **On site lodging:** No. **Rental clubs:** Yes. **Walking policy:** N/A. **Metal spikes allowed:** Yes. **Range:** Yes (grass/mats). **To obtain tee times:** Call.

★★★½GLENEAGLES GOLF COURSE AT THE EQUINOX
R-Historic Rte. 7-A., Manchester Village, 05254, Bennington County, (802)362-3223, 70 miles SE of Albany, NY.
Opened: 1926. **Holes:** 18. **Par:** 71/71. **Yards:** 6,423/5,082. **Course rating:** 71.3/65.2. **Slope:** 129/117. **Architect:** Walter Travis/Rees Jones. **Green fee:** $70/$80. **Credit cards:** All major. **Reduced fees:** Twilight. **Caddies:** Yes. **Golf carts:** $18. **Discount golf packages:** Yes. **Season:** May-Nov. **High:** May-Sept. **On site lodging:** Yes. **Rental clubs:** Yes. **Walking policy:** Walking at certain times. **Metal spikes allowed:** Yes. **Range:** No. **To obtain tee times:** Call up to 7 days in advance.
Notes: Ranked 3rd in 1997 Best in State.
Subscriber comments: Tops in New England—God plays here...Beautiful vistas...Play it at least once...Old course, recently upgraded. Some excellent holes...Worth the trip...One weird hole—hitting over road...A favorite...The fairways are like greens, I was afraid to make divots...Interesting holes—particularly back nine.

★★★½GREEN MOUNTAIN NATIONAL GOLF COURSE
PM-Rte. 100 - Barrows Town Rd., Sherburne, 05751, Chittenden County, (802)422-4653.
Opened: 1996. **Holes:** 18. **Par:** 71/71. **Yards:** 6,589/4,740. **Course rating:** 72.6/68.3. **Slope:** 139/118. **Architect:** Gene Bates. **Green fee:** $38/$42. **Credit cards:** MC,VISA,AMEX. **Reduced fees:** Weekdays, resort guests, twilight, juniors. **Caddies:** No. **Golf carts:** $15. **Discount golf packages:** Yes. **Season:** May-Nov. **High:** June-Oct. **On site lodging:** No. **Rental clubs:** Yes. **Walking policy:** Walking at certain times. **Metal spikes allowed:** Yes. **Range:** Yes (grass/mats). **To obtain tee times:** Call up to 7 days in advance.
Notes: Ranked 5th in 1997 Best New Upscale Public Courses.
Subscriber comments: Lost ball if you stray off fairways, very tough...New course will get even better, great golf...A must in the fall.

★★★HAYSTACK GOLF CLUB
Mann Rd., Wilmington, 05363, Windham County, (802)464-8301.
Opened: 1972. **Holes:** 18. **Par:** 72/74. **Yards:** 6,549/5,396. **Course rating:** 71.5/71.4. **Slope:** 128/120. **Architect:** Desmond Muirhead. **Green fee:** $30/$45. **Credit cards:** All major. **Reduced fees:** Weekdays, low season, resort guests, juniors. **Caddies:** No. **Golf carts:** $14. **Discount golf packages:** Yes. **Season:** May-Nov. **High:** July-Aug. **On site lodging:** No. **Rental clubs:** Yes. **Walking policy:** Walking at certain times. **Metal spikes allowed:** Yes. **Range:** Yes (grass/mats). **To obtain tee times:** Call in advance.
Subscriber comments: A must play mountain course—watch the weather...Pat Bradley's brother is the pro...Challenging course—close fairways can be dangerous...Very tough greens...Great views...I left an expensive watch there and it was returned!...Lots of fun.

★★★KILLINGTON GOLF RESORT
R-Killington Rd., Killington, 05751, Rutland County, (802)422-6700, 16 miles E of Rutland.
Opened: 1984. **Holes:** 18. **Par:** 72/72. **Yards:** 6,326/5,108. **Course rating:** 70.6/71.2. **Slope:** 126/123. **Architect:** Geoffrey Cornish. **Green fee:** $45/$45. **Credit cards:** All major. **Reduced fees:** Low season, twilight, juniors. **Caddies:** No. **Golf carts:** $15. **Discount golf packages:** Yes. **Season:** May-Oct. **High:** July-Aug. **On site lodging:** Yes. **Rental clubs:** Yes. **Walking policy:** Unrestricted walking. **Metal spikes allowed:** Yes. **Range:** Yes. **To obtain tee times:** Call up to 5 days in advance. Golf packages may be reserved when hotel reservations are made.

Subscriber comments: Tough course. Good challenges. Walking is tiring...A typical ski resort golf course...Challenging but fair...Beautiful scenery...Prepare to lose balls...Hilly and lots of blind shots...Very wet early spring when I played...Like playing a roller coaster...Target golf, some wild elevation changes...Wonderful views.

★★★KWINIASKA GOLF CLUB

Spear St., Shelburne, 05482, Chittenden County, (802)985-3672,.
Opened: 1964. **Holes:** 18. **Par:** 72/72. **Yards:** 7,067/5,670. **Course rating:** 72.5/72.6. **Slope:** 128/119. **Architect:** Bradford Caldwell. **Green fee:** $25/$25. **Credit cards:** MC,VISA. **Reduced fees:** Twilight. **Caddies:** No. **Golf carts:** $22. **Discount golf packages:** No. **Season:** April-Nov. **High:** June-Aug. **On site lodging:** No. **Rental clubs:** Yes. **Walking policy:** Unrestricted walking. **Metal spikes allowed:** Yes. **Range:** Yes (grass). **To obtain tee times:** Call 1 day in advance.
Subscriber comments: The course looks easy, but the layout is more than bargained for...Tough to gauge yardages...Over 7,000 yards, but plays shorter, #5 impossible into wind...I'd return...A definite must in Vermont...Very nice course. Should never lose a ball here...Long when wind is blowing.

★★★LAKE MOREY COUNTRY CLUB

R-Lake Morey Rd., Fairlee, 05045, Orange County, (802)333-4800, (800)423-1227, 167 miles N of Boston.
Opened: 1910. **Holes:** 18. **Par:** 70/70. **Yards:** 6,024/4,942. **Course rating:** 68.4/68.0. **Slope:** 118/116. **Architect:** Geoffrey Cornish. **Green fee:** $27/$34. **Credit cards:** MC,VISA. **Reduced fees:** Low season, resort guests, twilight, seniors. **Caddies:** No. **Golf carts:** $26. **Discount golf packages:** No. **Season:** April-Nov. **High:** July-Aug. **On site lodging:** Yes. **Rental clubs:** Yes. **Walking policy:** Unrestricted walking. **Metal spikes allowed:** No. **Range:** Yes (grass/mats). **To obtain tee times:** Public may call up to 4 days in advance. Members may call up to 7 days in advance. Resort guests may book when room reservation is made.
Subscriber comments: Good course complements excellent inn and surroundings...Some lovely holes...Nice course, beautiful colors, tough ravines!...Back nine tougher than front...Poor man's resort...Crowded...Too easy from whites.

★★LAKE ST. CATHERINE COUNTRY CLUB

Rte. 30 Lake Rd., Poultney, 05764, Rutland County, (802)287-9341, 23 miles SW of Rutland.
Opened: 1986. **Holes:** 18. **Par:** 72/72. **Yards:** 6,293/4,940. **Course rating:** 70.9/68.2. **Slope:** 127/116. **Architect:** N/A. **Green fee:** $18/$25. **Credit cards:** MC,VISA. **Reduced fees:** Low season. **Caddies:** No. **Golf carts:** $25. **Discount golf packages:** Yes. **Season:** April-Oct. **High:** July-Aug. **On site lodging:** No. **Rental clubs:** Yes. **Walking policy:** Unrestricted walking. **Metal spikes allowed:** Yes. **Range:** No. **To obtain tee times:** Call up to 7 days in advance.

★★½MONTAGUE GOLF CLUB

2 Golf Lane, Randolph, 05060, Orange County, (802)728-3806.
Opened: 1925. **Holes:** 18. **Par:** 70/71. **Yards:** 5,910/5,064. **Course rating:** 68.6/68.7. **Slope:** 120/111. **Architect:** Geoffrey S. Cornish. **Green fee:** $21/$27. **Credit cards:** MC,VISA. **Reduced fees:** Weekdays, low season, twilight. **Caddies:** No. **Golf carts:** $23. **Discount golf packages:** Yes. **Season:** April-Oct. **High:** June-Aug. **On site lodging:** No. **Rental clubs:** Yes. **Walking policy:** Unrestricted walking. **Metal spikes allowed:** Yes. **Range:** Yes (grass). **To obtain tee times:** Call 2 days in advance.
Subscriber comments: Easy course, walkable...Very interesting holes on first nine...Beautiful views, great test of skills...Uncrowded.

★★MOUNT ANTHONY GOLF & TENNIS CENTER

PU-943 Bank St., Bennington, 05201, Bennington County, (802)447-7079, 30 miles E of Albany, NY.
Opened: 1897. **Holes:** 18. **Par:** 71/71. **Yards:** 6,146/4,942. **Course rating:** 70.5/67.7. **Slope:** 125/106. **Architect:** Jay Jerome. **Green fee:** $25/$30. **Credit cards:** None. **Reduced fees:** N/A. **Caddies:** No. **Golf carts:** $11. **Discount golf packages:** No. **Season:** April-Oct. **High:** July-Sept. **On site lodging:** No. **Rental clubs:** No. **Walking policy:** Unrestricted walking. **Metal spikes allowed:** Yes. **Range:** Yes. **To obtain tee times:** Call up to 7 days in advance.

VERMONT

★★★MOUNT SNOW GOLF CLUB
R-Country Club Rd., West Dover, 05356, Windham County, (802)464-5642, (800)451-4211, 70 miles E of Albany, NY.
Opened: 1964. **Holes:** 18. **Par:** 72/74. **Yards:** 6,894/5,839. **Course rating:** 72.4/72.5. **Slope:** 130/118. **Architect:** Geoffrey Cornish. **Green fee:** $46. **Credit cards:** MC,VISA,AMEX. **Reduced fees:** Weekdays, low season, resort guests, twilight, juniors. **Caddies:** No. **Golf carts:** $15. **Discount golf packages:** Yes. **Season:** May-Oct. **High:** July-Aug. **On site lodging:** Yes. **Rental clubs:** Yes. **Walking policy:** Unrestricted walking. **Metal spikes allowed:** Yes. **Range:** Yes (grass/mats). **To obtain tee times:** Call.
Subscriber comments: Great course, great scenery...Love playing in the mountains...Fast true greens...Good holes. But several blind shots...Very wet and soggy in spring...Beautiful in fall, use every club in the bag...Watch out for deer...Picturesque, hilly. Good tee boxes. Good golf school.

NESHOBE GOLF CLUB
Town Farm Rd., Brandon, 05733, Rutland County, (802)247-3611, 15 miles N of Rutland.
Opened: 1959. **Holes:** 18. **Par:** 72/71. **Yards:** 6,362/5,042. **Course rating:** 71.6/64.9. **Slope:** 15/115. **Architect:** Steve Durkee. **Green fee:** $30/$35. **Credit cards:** MC,VISA. **Reduced fees:** Twilight, juniors. **Caddies:** No. **Golf carts:** $28. **Discount golf packages:** No. **Season:** April-Oct. **High:** June-Aug. **On site lodging:** No. **Rental clubs:** Yes. **Walking policy:** Unrestricted walking. **Metal spikes allowed:** No. **Range:** Yes (grass). **To obtain tee times:** Call or come in up to 5 days in advance.

★★★NEWPORT COUNTRY CLUB
Pine Hill Rd., Newport, 05855, Orleans County, (802)334-2391, 80 miles NE of Burlington.
Opened: N/A. **Holes:** 18. **Par:** 72/72. **Yards:** 6,453/5,312. **Course rating:** 69.4/69.3. **Slope:** 109/111. **Architect:** Ralph Barton. **Green fee:** $21/$21. **Credit cards:** MC,VISA. **Reduced fees:** Twilight. **Caddies:** No. **Golf carts:** $21. **Discount golf packages:** No. **Season:** April-Oct. **High:** July-Aug. **On site lodging:** No. **Rental clubs:** Yes. **Walking policy:** Unrestricted walking. **Metal spikes allowed:** Yes. **Range:** Yes (grass). **To obtain tee times:** Call up to 2 days in advance.
Subscriber comments: Challenging course...Wide fairways...Unbelievable views, interesting layout, good golf...Very scenic finishing hole...New clubhouse...Restaurant great.

★★★ORLEANS COUNTRY CLUB
Rte. 58, P.O. Box 217, Orleans, 05860, Orleans County, (802)754-2333.
Opened: 1929. **Holes:** 18. **Par:** 72/72. **Yards:** 6,200/5,595. **Course rating:** 69.3. **Slope:** 121. **Architect:** Alex Reid. **Green fee:** $21/$21. **Credit cards:** MC,VISA. **Reduced fees:** N/A. **Caddies:** No. **Golf carts:** $22. **Discount golf packages:** Yes. **Season:** April-Oct. **High:** June-Sept. **On site lodging:** No. **Rental clubs:** No. **Walking policy:** Unrestricted walking. **Metal spikes allowed:** Yes. **Range:** Yes (grass). **To obtain tee times:** Call up to 1 day in advance after 9 a.m.
Subscriber comments: Flat. Very walkable. Great food...Fun little course...Friendly atmosphere, good golf...Great restaurant.

★★★PROCTOR-PITTSFORD COUNTRY CLUB
PU-Corn Hill Rd., Proctor, 05763, Rutland County, (802)483-9379, 3 miles N of Rutland.
Opened: N/A. **Holes:** 18. **Par:** 70/72. **Yards:** 6,052/5,446. **Course rating:** 69.4/66.1. **Slope:** 121/115. **Architect:** Henry Collin/Ray Keyser. **Green fee:** $27/$27. **Credit cards:** MC,VISA. **Reduced fees:** Twilight, juniors. **Caddies:** No. **Golf carts:** $11. **Discount golf packages:** No. **Season:** April-Nov. **High:** July-Aug. **On site lodging:** No. **Rental clubs:** Yes. **Walking policy:** Unrestricted walking. **Metal spikes allowed:** No. **Range:** Yes (grass). **To obtain tee times:** Call 2 days in advance.
Subscriber comments: Nine new holes wonderful, mountain views...Very interesting, keep driver in bag on most holes...Pretty in fall, golf for everyone.

★★½RALPH MYHRE COUNTRY CLUB OF MIDDLEBURY COLLEGE
Rte. 1, Middlebury, 05753, Addison County, (802)443-5125, 35 miles S of Burlington.
Opened: N/A. **Holes:** 18. **Par:** 71/71. **Yards:** 6,379/5,337. **Course rating:** 71.3/66.9.

Slope: 129/120. **Architect:** Ralph Myhre. **Green fee:** $29/$18. **Credit cards:** MC,VISA. **Reduced fees:** Twilight, juniors. **Caddies:** No. **Golf carts:** $28. **Discount golf packages:** No. **Season:** April-Oct. **High:** July-Aug. **On site lodging:** No. **Rental clubs:** Yes. **Walking policy:** Unrestricted walking. **Metal spikes allowed:** Yes. **Range:** Yes (grass). **To obtain tee times:** Call.

Subscriber comments: Very challenging par 3s...Wide fairways. Tough but fair...College course...Beautiful scenery, average golf...Lots of bunkers...Nice place to play.

★★½ROCKY RIDGE GOLF CLUB

68 Ledge Rd., Burlington, 05401, Chittenden County, (802)482-2191, 12 miles S of Burlington.

Opened: 1963. **Holes:** 18. **Par:** 72/72. **Yards:** 6,000/5,230. **Course rating:** 69.1/68.7. **Slope:** 124/110. **Architect:** Ernest Farrington. **Green fee:** $22/$22. **Credit cards:** MC,VISA. **Reduced fees:** Twilight. **Caddies:** No. **Golf carts:** $22. **Discount golf packages:** No. **Season:** April-Nov. **High:** July-Aug. **On site lodging:** No. **Rental clubs:** Yes. **Walking policy:** Unrestricted walking. **Metal spikes allowed:** Yes. **Range:** Yes (grass). **To obtain tee times:** Call Thursday at 7 a.m. for upcoming weekend.

Subscriber comments: A great course. A thorough challenge for all...Good assortment of holes...Relatively short, but some tight holes...A couple of holes the devil designed...Challenging walk, 13th an uphill nightmare.

★★★½RUTLAND COUNTRY CLUB

N. Grove St., Rutland, 05701, Rutland County, (802)773-3254.

Opened: 1902. **Holes:** 18. **Par:** 70/71. **Yards:** 6,100/5,446. **Course rating:** 69.7/71.6. **Slope:** 125/125. **Architect:** George Low. **Green fee:** $50/$50. **Credit cards:** MC,VISA. **Reduced fees:** N/A. **Caddies:** No. **Golf carts:** $27. **Discount golf packages:** No. **Season:** April-Oct. **High:** June-Aug. **On site lodging:** No. **Rental clubs:** Yes. **Walking policy:** Mandatory cart. **Metal spikes allowed:** Yes. **Range:** Yes. **To obtain tee times:** Call one day in advance.

Notes: Ranked 4th in 1997 Best in State.

Subscriber comments: Hilly course...Great fairways, nice layout, almost 100 years old...I had a great time...Aged to perfection. Worth playing...Need your putting game.

★★★½ST. JOHNSBURY COUNTRY CLUB

Rte. 5 Memorial Dr., St. Johnsbury, 05819, Caledonia County, (802)748-9894, (800)748-8899, 175 miles N of Boston.

Opened: 1923. **Holes:** 18. **Par:** 70/70. **Yards:** 6,323/4,685. **Course rating:** 70.4/65.8. **Slope:** 129/104. **Architect:** Willie Park/Mungo Park. **Green fee:** $28/$32. **Credit cards:** MC,VISA,AMEX. **Reduced fees:** Resort guests, twilight. **Caddies:** No. **Golf carts:** $13. **Discount golf packages:** No. **Season:** April-Oct. **High:** July-Aug. **On site lodging:** No. **Rental clubs:** Yes. **Walking policy:** Unrestricted walking. **Metal spikes allowed:** Yes. **Range:** Yes (grass/mats). **To obtain tee times:** Call up to 3 days in advance.

GOOD VALUE

Subscriber comments: New nine exquisite...Built in mountain, every hole is a picture hole...Too hilly, 10th hole straight up and left like a ski slope...Greatest par 3s in Vermont...True test of golf, tight back...One cannot say all the good things about this course...Two different nines.

★★★STOWE COUNTRY CLUB

R-Cape Cod Rd., Stowe, 05672, Lamoille County, (802)253-4893, (800)253-4754, 37 miles E of Burlington.

Opened: 1950. **Holes:** 18. **Par:** 72/74. **Yards:** 6,206/5,346. **Course rating:** 70.4/66.5. **Slope:** 122/115. **Architect:** Walter Barcomb/William Mitchell. **Green fee:** $35/$65. **Credit cards:** MC,VISA,AMEX,DISC,Diners Club. **Reduced fees:** Weekdays, low season, twilight. **Caddies:** No. **Golf carts:** $16. **Discount golf packages:** Yes. **Season:** May-Oct. **High:** July-Sept. **On site lodging:** Yes. **Rental clubs:** Yes. **Walking policy:** Unrestricted walking. **Metal spikes allowed:** No. **Range:** Yes (grass/mats). **To obtain tee times:** Call anytime. Credit card required to reserve weekends and holidays.

Subscriber comments: Play here and you'll yodel too...Beautiful views, short course should be made more difficult...Nice scenery, tough greens...No.5 is first par 4...Watch out for black flies...Beautiful course, many blind shots due to the terrain, a great work out if you walk the course.

★★★½STRATTON MOUNTAIN COUNTRY CLUB

R-R.R. 1 Box 145, Stratton Mountain, 05155, Windham County, (802)297-4114, (800)787-2886, 40 miles S of Rutland.

Opened: 1965. **Holes:** 27. **Architect:** Geoffrey Cornish. **Green fee:** $56/$69. **Credit cards:** All major. **Reduced fees:** Weekdays, low season, resort guests, twilight, juniors. **Caddies:** No. **Golf carts:** $16. **Discount golf packages:** Yes. **Season:** May-Oct. **High:** July-Aug. **On site lodging:** Yes. **Rental clubs:** Yes. **Walking policy:** Walking at certain times. **Metal spikes allowed:** Yes. **Range:** Yes (grass/mats). **To obtain tee times:** Call up to 14 days in advance.

Notes: 1990-95 McCall's LPGA Classic.

LAKE/FOREST
Par: 72/74. **Yards:** 6,526/5,153. **Course rating:** 71.2/69.8. **Slope:** 125/123.
LAKE/MOUNTAIN
Par: 72/74. **Yards:** 6,602/5,410. **Course rating:** 72.0/71.1. **Slope:** 125/124.
MOUNTAIN/FOREST
Par: 72/74. **Yards:** 6,478/5,163. **Course rating:** 71.2/69.9. **Slope:** 126/123.

Subscriber comments: All three nines are equally great...Wonderful getaway of golf...Great school, course was quite wet in spring...Love the facility...Forest nine not as good as other nines...Enjoyable variety...Spectacular views...Mountain is best nine by far...Can be real windy in fall...What a view!...Difficult to obtain tee time.

★★★½SUGARBUSH GOLF COURSE

R-Golf Course Rd., Warren, 05674, Washington County, (802)583-6725, (800)537-8427, 45 miles SE of Burlington.

Opened: 1962. **Holes:** 18. **Par:** 72/72. **Yards:** 6,524/5,187. **Course rating:** 71.7/70.4. **Slope:** 128/119. **Architect:** Robert Trent Jones. **Green fee:** $38/$49. **Credit cards:** All major. **Reduced fees:** Weekdays, low season, resort guests, twilight, juniors. **Caddies:** No. **Golf carts:** $16. **Discount golf packages:** Yes. **Season:** May-Oct. **High:** July-Oct. **On site lodging:** Yes. **Rental clubs:** Yes. **Walking policy:** Walking at certain times. **Metal spikes allowed:** Yes. **Range:** Yes (grass/mats). **To obtain tee times:** Public may call 1 day in advance; preferred tee times can be made through golf packages.

Subscriber comments: Fun golf course, expensive food...Great layout, good stay and play package, superb scenery...Hard to keep your mind on your game...7th hole calls for second shot aiming at a condo on distant mountainside...Difficult but fun. Worth the money...Fly rod optional. Owned the course on a fall day...Too many blind drives, local knowledge important...One of my favorites in Vermont.

★★★TATER HILL COUNTRY CLUB

Popple Dungeon Rd., Windham, 05143, Windsor County, (802)875-2517, 20 miles E of Manchester.

Opened: 1964. **Holes:** 18. **Par:** 72/72. **Yards:** 6,801/4,979. **Course rating:** 72.3/64.7. **Slope:** 129/113. **Architect:** Mike Higuera. **Green fee:** $25/$66. **Credit cards:** MC,VISA,AMEX. **Reduced fees:** Weekdays, low season, resort guests, twilight, juniors. **Caddies:** No. **Golf carts:** Included in Green Fee. **Discount golf packages:** Yes. **Season:** May-Oct. **High:** July-Aug. **On site lodging:** No. **Rental clubs:** Yes. **Walking policy:** Unrestricted walking. **Metal spikes allowed:** Yes. **Range:** Yes (grass). **To obtain tee times:** Call up to 7 days in advance.

Subscriber comments: Finest flower displays ever seen...Rolling hills, great vistas...Only the strong can walk this course, hilly, tough to hold greens...Golf course difficult and some holes a bit strange...One nine is too easy, the other too difficult.

★★½WEST BOLTON GOLF CLUB

PU-RD 1 Box 305, W. Bolton Rd., Jericho, 05465, Chittenden County, (802)434-4321, 23 miles NE of Burlington.

Opened: 1983. **Holes:** 18. **Par:** 70/71. **Yards:** 5,880/5,094. **Course rating:** 66.3/65.7. **Slope:** 109/103. **Architect:** Xen Wheeler. **Green fee:** $15/$17. **Credit cards:** MC,VISA. **Reduced fees:** Twilight, seniors, juniors. **Caddies:** No. **Golf carts:** $18. **Discount golf packages:** No. **Season:** May-Oct. **High:** June-Aug. **On site lodging:** No. **Rental clubs:** Yes. **Walking policy:** Unrestricted walking. **Metal spikes allowed:** Yes. **Range:** No. **To obtain tee times:** Call 7 days in advance.

Subscriber comments: Short course, but very small greens...Beautiful mountain valley...Great fall colors...A gem of a golf course in a beautiful spot.

★★★WILLISTON GOLF CLUB

PU-P.O. Box 541, Williston, 05495, Chittenden County, (802)878-3747, 7 miles E of Burlington.

Opened: 1926. **Holes:** 18. **Par:** 69/72. **Yards:** 5,685/4,753. **Course rating:** 68.0/64.1. **Slope:** 118/106. **Architect:** Ben Murray. **Green fee:** $20/$20. **Credit cards:** None. **Reduced fees:** Twilight. **Caddies:** No. **Golf carts:** $21. **Discount golf packages:** No. **Season:** May-Nov. **High:** July-Aug. **On site lodging:** No. **Rental clubs:** Yes. **Walking policy:** Unrestricted walking. **Metal spikes allowed:** Yes. **Range:** No. **To obtain tee times:** Call Thursday at 7 a.m. for upcoming weekend. Come in and register for weekdays.

Subscriber comments: Very nice layout...Too bad so short...Tricky. Beautiful flowers. Easy to score well...Must hit wedge well and drives straight to score...Water can be difficult...Fine all around course...Every hole was something different...Deceiving.

★★★WOODSTOCK COUNTRY CLUB

R-Fourteen The Green, Woodstock, 05091, Windsor County, (802)457-6674, 30 miles E of Rutland.

Opened: 1895. **Holes:** 18. **Par:** 69/71. **Yards:** 6,001/4,924. **Course rating:** 69.0/67.0. **Slope:** 121/113. **Architect:** Robert T. Jones. **Green fee:** $49/$63. **Credit cards:** MC,VISA,AMEX. **Reduced fees:** Weekdays, low season, resort guests, twilight. **Caddies:** No. **Golf carts:** $16. **Discount golf packages:** Yes. **Season:** May-Nov. **High:** July-Aug. **On site lodging:** Yes. **Rental clubs:** Yes. **Walking policy:** Unrestricted walking. **Metal spikes allowed:** Yes. **Range:** Yes (grass/mats). **To obtain tee times:** Call day of play.

Subscriber comments: Beautiful holes set in a valley...An enjoyable course...Lots of water...Too many iron tee shots on par 4s...Shotmaker's course...Short and tricky...What golf used to be....Very tight...Takes a couple of rounds to get the hang of this classic course...Doglegsl...Like the movie: A River Runs Through It...Must play if in area, beautiful especially in fall.

★★½ALGONKIAN REGIONAL PARK GOLF COURSE
PU-47001 Fairway Dr., Sterling, 20165, Loudoun County, (703)450-4655, 20 miles W of Washington DC.
Opened: 1972. **Holes:** 18. **Par:** 72/72. **Yards:** 7,015/5,795. **Course rating:** 73.5/74.0.
Slope: 125/113. **Architect:** Ed Ault. **Green fee:** $22/$26. **Credit cards:** MC,VISA,ATM Debit. **Reduced fees:** Weekdays, resort guests, seniors, juniors. **Caddies:** No. **Golf carts:** $24. **Discount golf packages:** No. **Season:** Year-round. **High:** May-Dec. **On site lodging:** Yes. **Rental clubs:** Yes. **Walking policy:** Unrestricted walking. **Metal spikes allowed:** Yes. **Range:** No. **To obtain tee times:** Call or come in Tuesdays at 6:30 a.m. for upcoming weekend or holiday.
Subscriber comments: Wears your fairwood woods out...Narrow fairways make it more challenging than it looks...Above average course, friendly clubhouse...Good walking course.

★★★★AUGUSTINE GOLF CLUB
PU-76 Monument Dr., Stafford, 22554, Stafford County, (540)720-7374, 30 miles S of Washington, DC.
Opened: 1995. **Holes:** 18. **Par:** 71/71. **Yards:** 6,850/4,838. **Course rating:** 71.9/68.2.
Slope: 130/119. **Architect:** Rick Jacobson. **Green fee:** N/A. **Credit cards:** All major.
Reduced fees: N/A. **Caddies:** No. **Golf carts:** N/A. **Discount golf packages:** No.
Season: Year-round. **High:** April-Nov. **On site lodging:** No. **Rental clubs:** Yes.
Walking policy: N/A. **Metal spikes allowed:** Yes. **Range:** Yes (grass/mats). **To obtain tee times:** Call up to 7 days in advance. **Notes:** Ranked 9th in 1997 Best in State; 5th in 1996 Best New Upscale Courses.
Subscriber comments: At the first tee you know it's special...Always in top condition...Lightning fast greens...No.2 hole very striking...Many elevated tees, one of best in area...Expensive, but the conditioning of the course is as good as you will find anywhere...Toughest three starting holes in all of golf!

★★½BELMONT GOLF COURSE
PU-1600 Hilliard Rd., Richmond, 23228, Henrico County, (804)266-4929, 10 miles N of Richmond.
Opened: 1903. **Holes:** 18. **Par:** 71/73. **Yards:** 6,350/5,418. **Course rating:** 70.6/72.6.
Slope: 126/130. **Architect:** A.W. Tillinghast. **Green fee:** $17/$20. **Credit cards:** None.
Reduced fees: Seniors, juniors. **Caddies:** No. **Golf carts:** $11. **Discount golf packages:** No. **Season:** Year-round. **High:** April-Oct. **On site lodging:** No. **Rental clubs:** Yes. **Walking policy:** Unrestricted walking. **Metal spikes allowed:** Yes. **Range:** No. **To obtain tee times:** Call up to 7 days in advance for Weekdays. Call Monday morning for upcoming weekend.
Notes: 1949 PGA Championship.
Subscriber comments: Maintained well, good greens, well managed...Front nine holes are close together...Toughest first hole in Richmond...Very good fairways and large, demanding greens...A lot of beginners...Fun, old, scenic course. A very fun day.

★½BIDE-A-WEE GOLF CLUB
PU-1 Bide-A-Wee Lane, Portsmouth, 23455, Portsmouth City County, (757)393-5269, 5 miles S of Norfolk.
Opened: 1955. **Holes:** 18. **Par:** 72/74. **Yards:** 7,069/5,518. **Course rating:** 72.2/66.4.
Slope: 121/113. **Architect:** Fred Findlay and R.F. Loving, Sr. **Green fee:** $8/$10. **Credit cards:** None. **Reduced fees:** Weekdays, juniors. **Caddies:** No. **Golf carts:** $14.
Discount golf packages: No. **Season:** Year-round. **High:** April-Sept. **On site lodging:** No. **Rental clubs:** Yes. **Walking policy:** Unrestricted walking. **Metal spikes allowed:** Yes. **Range:** Yes (grass/mats). **To obtain tee times:** Call 1 day in advance.

★★★½BIRDWOOD GOLF COURSE
Rte. 250 W., Charlottesville, 22905, Albemarle County, (804)293-4653, 1 mile W of Charlottesville.
Opened: 1984. **Holes:** 18. **Par:** 72/72. **Yards:** 6,820/5,041. **Course rating:** 72.8/65.2.
Slope: 132/116. **Architect:** Lindsey Ervin. **Green fee:** $18/$65. **Credit cards:** MC,VISA. **Reduced fees:** Weekdays, low season, resort guests. **Caddies:** No. **Golf carts:** $15. **Discount golf packages:** Yes. **Season:** Year-round. **High:** April-Oct. **On site lodging:** Yes. **Rental clubs:** Yes. **Walking policy:** Walking at certain times. **Metal

spikes allowed: Yes. **Range:** Yes (grass/mats). **To obtain tee times:** Call up to 7 days in advance.
Notes: U.S. Women's Public Links.
Subscriber comments: Course is challenging and well managed...Don't use up all your good shots on the front nine. The back is tighter and harder...Very good course with diverse holes; very hilly...Great test of golf for the value...Nice contrast of holes. Short/long par 4s...Wonderful vistas, fast greens.

★★½BIRKDALE GOLF & COUNTRY CLUB
8511 Royal Birkdale Dr., Chesterfield, 23832, Chesterfield County, (804)739-8800, 15 miles SW of Richmond.
Opened: 1990. **Holes:** 18. **Par:** 71/71. **Yards:** 6,544/4,459. **Course rating:** 71.1. **Slope:** 122. **Architect:** Dan Maples. **Green fee:** $32/$38. **Credit cards:** MC,VISA,AMEX. **Reduced fees:** Weekdays, low season, resort guests, twilight, seniors, juniors. **Caddies:** No. **Golf carts:** Included in Green Fee. **Discount golf packages:** Yes. **Season:** Year-round. **High:** May-Oct. **On site lodging:** No. **Rental clubs:** Yes. **Walking policy:** Mandatory cart. **Metal spikes allowed:** Yes. **Range:** Yes (grass/mats). **To obtain tee times:** Call 7 days in advance.
Subscriber comments: A well-maintained and well-run golf course...Great layout, great par 3s...Overpriced!...Very short, a few interesting holes...Good design. Nos. 9 and 18 are great holes...Easy from the white tees...Great greens, easy layout.

★★BOW CREEK GOLF COURSE
PU-3425 Clubhouse Rd., Virginia Beach, 23452, Virginia Beach City County, (757)431-3763, 10 miles W of Norfolk.
Opened: 1960. **Holes:** 18. **Par:** 70/70. **Yards:** 5,917/5,181. **Course rating:** 70.4/68.4. **Slope:** 114/104. **Architect:** John Aragona/Fred Sappenfield. **Green fee:** $17. **Credit cards:** DISC. **Reduced fees:** Low season, twilight, seniors, juniors. **Caddies:** No. **Golf carts:** $16. **Discount golf packages:** No. **Season:** Year-round. **High:** April-Sept. **On site lodging:** Yes. **Rental clubs:** Yes. **Walking policy:** Unrestricted walking. **Metal spikes allowed:** Yes. **Range:** Yes (grass). **To obtain tee times:** Call by 8 a.m. on Friday for weekend. First come, first served on weekdays.

★★★½BRISTOW MANOR GOLF CLUB
PU-11507 Valley View Dr., Bristow, 20136, Prince William County, (703)368-3558, 25 miles SW of Washington, D.C.
Opened: 1993. **Holes:** 18. **Par:** 72/74. **Yards:** 7,102/5,527. **Course rating:** 72.9/73.4. **Slope:** 129/128. **Architect:** Ken Killian. **Green fee:** $15/$47. **Credit cards:** MC,VISA,AMEX. **Reduced fees:** Weekdays, low season, twilight, seniors, juniors. **Caddies:** No. **Golf carts:** $13. **Discount golf packages:** No. **Season:** Year-round. **High:** March-Nov. **On site lodging:** No. **Rental clubs:** Yes. **Walking policy:** Walking at certain times. **Metal spikes allowed:** No. **Range:** Yes (grass). **To obtain tee times:** Call anytime in advance.
Subscriber comments: Great links course, better from blue tees...Generally good condition...Hitting every shot in bag. Great condition year round...Fairways like carpets, rough like hay...Well maintained, great greens...New course, fairly hard...One easy and average nine, and one tough nine.

★★½THE BROOKWOODS GOLF CLUB
PU-7325 Club Dr., Quinton, 23141, New Kent County, (804)932-3737, 15 miles E of Richmond.
Opened: 1974. **Holes:** 18. **Par:** 72/72. **Yards:** 6,557/4,897. **Course rating:** 71.2/69.5. **Slope:** 123/119. **Architect:** Algie Pulley. **Green fee:** $14/$19. **Credit cards:** MC,VISA. **Reduced fees:** Twilight, seniors, juniors. **Caddies:** No. **Golf carts:** $11. **Discount golf packages:** Yes. **Season:** Year-round. **High:** April-Oct. **On site lodging:** No. **Rental clubs:** Yes. **Walking policy:** Walking at certain times. **Metal spikes allowed:** Yes. **Range:** Yes (grass/mats). **To obtain tee times:** Call anytime in advance.
Subscriber comments: Good 18 holes for the average golfer...A good deal, but bring your insect repellent...Good buy for money (fun course).

★★★BRYCE RESORT GOLF COURSE
R-P.O. Box 3, Basye, 22810, Shenandoah County, (540)856-2124, 100 miles SW of Washington, D.C.

Opened: 1968. **Holes:** 18. **Par:** 71/71. **Yards:** 6,261/5,240. **Course rating:** 68.8/70.1.
Slope: 122/120. **Architect:** Ed Ault. **Green fee:** $10/$26. **Credit cards:**
MC,VISA,AMEX. **Reduced fees:** Weekdays, low season, resort guests, twilight.
Caddies: No. **Golf carts:** $13. **Discount golf packages:** Yes. **Season:** March-Dec.
High: May-Aug. **On site lodging:** Yes. **Rental clubs:** Yes. **Walking policy:** Mandatory
cart. **Metal spikes allowed:** Yes. **Range:** Yes (grass). **To obtain tee times:** Up to three
days in advance for nonmembers.
Subscriber comments: Beautiful mountain views surrounding course...Nice small
resort. A little out of the way...Tough in fall...Good front nine, back hilly and 18 is a par
3...Beautiful, great course, peaceful and fun.

★★½CARPER'S VALLEY GOLF CLUB
PU-1400 Millwood Pike, Winchester, 22602, Frederick County, (540)662-4319, 65 miles
NW of Washington, D.C.
Opened: 1962. **Holes:** 18. **Par:** 70/71. **Yards:** 6,125/4,930. **Course rating:** 69.5/67.5.
Slope: 118/107. **Architect:** Ed Ault. **Green fee:** $10/$22. **Credit cards:** MC,VISA.
Reduced fees: Weekdays, low season, twilight. **Caddies:** No. **Golf carts:** $12.
Discount golf packages: No. **Season:** Year-round. **High:** April-Oct. **On site lodging:**
No. **Rental clubs:** Yes. **Walking policy:** Walking at certain times. **Metal spikes**
allowed: Yes. **Range:** Yes (grass). **To obtain tee times:** Call or come in up to 5 days in
advance.
Subscriber comments: Not bad, not great but worth the trip...New holes are very
good, easy layout...Good small community course...Back nine very tight.

★★★CAVERNS COUNTRY CLUB RESORT
R-Airport Rd., Luray, 22835, Page County, (540)743-7111, 80 miles W of Washington,
D.C.
Opened: 1976. **Holes:** 18. **Par:** 72/72. **Yards:** 6,499/5,499. **Course rating:** 71.2/72.4.
Slope: 117/120. **Architect:** Hal Purdy. **Green fee:** $19/$29. **Credit cards:** All major.
Reduced fees: Weekdays. **Caddies:** No. **Golf carts:** $11. **Discount golf packages:**
Yes. **Season:** Year-round. **High:** April-June/Sept.-Oct. **On site lodging:** No. **Rental**
clubs: No. **Walking policy:** Unrestricted walking. **Metal spikes allowed:** Yes. **Range:**
No. **To obtain tee times:** Call up to 7 days in advance.
Subscriber comments: Tough course, but fun...Great views, nice elevation
changes...Gorgeous canyon/mountain views, quiet and peaceful...Very scenic layout,
very friendly folks...For the money, great golf, experience.

CEDAR HILLS COUNTRY CLUB
RR No. 1 Box 598, Jonesville, 24263, Lee County, (540)346-1535, 85 miles N of
Knoxville, TN.
Opened: 1967. **Holes:** 18. **Par:** 71/71. **Yards:** 6,466/5,057. **Course rating:** 69.3/65.2.
Slope: 111/101. **Architect:** Horace Smith. **Green fee:** $10/$15. **Credit cards:**
MC,VISA. **Reduced fees:** Weekdays, juniors. **Caddies:** No. **Golf carts:** $9. **Discount**
golf packages: No. **Season:** Year-round. **High:** April-Oct. **On site lodging:** No. **Rental**
clubs: Yes. **Walking policy:** Unrestricted walking. **Metal spikes allowed:** Yes. **Range:**
Yes (grass/mats). **To obtain tee times:** Call anytime.

★★★THE COLONIAL GOLF COURSE
PU-8285 Diascund Rd., James City County, 23089, (757)566-1600, 22 miles from
Richmond.
Opened: 1995. **Holes:** 18. **Par:** 72/72. **Yards:** 6,809/4,568. **Course rating:** 73.1/66.3.
Slope: 132/109. **Architect:** Lester George. **Green fee:** $60/$70. **Credit cards:**
MC,VISA. **Reduced fees:** Low season, twilight, seniors, juniors. **Caddies:** No. **Golf**
carts: Included in Green Fee. **Discount golf packages:** No. **Season:** Year-round.
High: April-Oct. **On site lodging:** No. **Rental clubs:** Yes. **Walking policy:** Unrestricted
walking. **Metal spikes allowed:** Yes. **Range:** Yes (grass/mats). **To obtain tee times:**
Call anytime.
Subscriber comments: Just a great place to play, will have to use your head to play
here...A new course with outstanding everything...Great course with fantastic
wildlife...Narrow fairways, fast greens...Very hilly...Very penal...Scenic woods layout.

★★★THE CROSSINGS GOLF CLUB
PU-800 Virginia Center Pkwy., Glen Allen, 23060, Henrico County, (804)261-0000, 9 miles N of Richmond.
Opened: 1979. **Holes:** 18. **Par:** 72/72. **Yards:** 6,619/5,625. **Course rating:** 70.7/73.2. **Slope:** 126/128. **Architect:** Joe Lee. **Green fee:** $27/$45. **Credit cards:** MC,VISA. **Reduced fees:** Weekdays, low season, seniors, juniors. **Caddies:** No. **Golf carts:** Included in Green Fee. **Discount golf packages:** No. **Season:** Year-round. **High:** March-Nov. **On site lodging:** No. **Rental clubs:** Yes. **Walking policy:** Walking at certain times. **Metal spikes allowed:** Yes. **Range:** Yes (grass). **To obtain tee times:** Call seven days in advance.
Subscriber comments: Nicely manicured course...All around challenging course with great variety in holes, plus convenient practice area and capable staff...Very challenging, fun to play...A very good course, must think on several key holes.

★★★CYPRESS POINT COUNTRY CLUB
5340 Club Head Rd., Virginia Beach, 23455, Virginia Beach City County, (757)490-8822.
Opened: 1987. **Holes:** 18. **Par:** 72/72. **Yards:** 6,680/5,440. **Course rating:** 71.5/70.8. **Slope:** 124/114. **Architect:** Tom Clark and Brian Ault. **Green fee:** $33/$39. **Credit cards:** MC,VISA,AMEX. **Reduced fees:** N/A. **Caddies:** No. **Golf carts:** Included in Green Fee. **Discount golf packages:** No. **Season:** Year-round. **High:** April-Oct. **On site lodging:** No. **Rental clubs:** Yes. **Walking policy:** Mandatory cart. **Metal spikes allowed:** No. **Range:** Yes (grass). **To obtain tee times:** Call up to 7 days in advance for weekdays. Call on Wednesday for upcoming weekend.
Subscriber comments: Straightforward...Challenging, uses every club in the bag. Great staff...Wish the whole course could be more like the 16th and 17th holes.

★★★½DRAPER VALLEY GOLF CLUB
PU-Rte. 1, Box 104, Draper, 24324, Pulaski County, (540)980-4653, 60 miles S of Roanoke.
Opened: 1992. **Holes:** 18. **Par:** 72/72. **Yards:** 7,046/4,793. **Course rating:** 73.3/65.6. **Slope:** 125/113. **Architect:** Harold Louthen. **Green fee:** $16/$25. **Credit cards:** MC,VISA. **Reduced fees:** Weekdays, low season. **Caddies:** No. **Golf carts:** $10. **Discount golf packages:** Yes. **Season:** Year-round. **High:** March-Nov. **On site lodging:** No. **Rental clubs:** Yes. **Walking policy:** Walking at certain times. **Metal spikes allowed:** Yes. **Range:** Yes (grass). **To obtain tee times:** Call 7 days in advance.
Subscriber comments: Wonderful course! People there the most wonderful and friendly; best kept secret...Windy, long from back tees...Best hamburgers in state.

★★FAMILY GOLF CENTER AT OWL'S CREEK
PU-411 S. Birdneck Rd., Virginia Beach, 23451, Virginia Beach City County, (757)428-2800, 15 miles E of Norfolk.
Opened: 1988. **Holes:** 18. **Par:** 62/62. **Yards:** 3,779/2,575. **Course rating:** 59.2/59.9. **Slope:** 77/86. **Architect:** N/A. **Green fee:** $10/$16. **Credit cards:** MC,VISA,AMEX. **Reduced fees:** Low season, twilight, seniors, juniors. **Caddies:** No. **Golf carts:** $8. **Discount golf packages:** No. **Season:** Year-round. **High:** May-Oct. **On site lodging:** No. **Rental clubs:** Yes. **Walking policy:** Walking at certain times. **Metal spikes allowed:** Yes. **Range:** Yes (grass/mats). **To obtain tee times:** Call.

FORD'S COLONY COUNTRY CLUB
R-240 Ford's Colony Dr., Williamsburg, 23188, Williamsburg City County, (757)258-4130, 40 miles SW of Richmond.
Architect: Dan Maples. **Green fee:** $45/$100. **Credit cards:** MC,VISA,AMEX. **Reduced fees:** Weekdays, low season, resort guests, twilight. **Caddies:** No. **Golf carts:** Included in Green Fee. **Discount golf packages:** Yes. **Season:** Year-round. **High:** April-Oct. **On site lodging:** Yes. **Rental clubs:** Yes. **Walking policy:** Mandatory cart. **Metal spikes allowed:** Yes. **Range:** Yes (grass/mats). **To obtain tee times:** Call up to 7 days in advance.
★★★½BLUE/GOLD COURSE
Opened: 1987. **Holes:** 18. **Par:** 71/71. **Yards:** 6,769/5,424. **Course rating:** 72.3. **Slope:** 124/109.
Subscriber comments: Great customer service, top quality golf...Difficult layout but

fun, well organized staff...Great lunch...Very challenging. Nice scenery...Typical Dan Maples risk/reward layout, great views, subtle green contours...Excellent layout, every hole is different...Several long par 4s make scoring tough.

★★★½RED/WHITE COURSE

Opened: 1985. **Holes:** 18. **Par:** 72/72. **Yards:** 6,755/5,614. **Course rating:** 72.3/73.2. **Slope:** 126/132.

Subscriber comments: Great condition and a step better course...Contoured fairways and greens...Enjoyable and beautiful...Challenging shots, good greens, watch the ducks...Course plays left to right, tough on right to left hitters...Original 18, good challenge for all levels...White course par 4s are long, tough.

★★½FOREST GREENS GOLF CLUB

PU-4500 Poa Annua Lane, Triangle, 22172, Prince William County, (703)221-0123, 32 miles S of Washington, DC.

Opened: 1996. **Holes:** 18. **Par:** 72/72. **Yards:** 6,839/5,007. **Course rating:** 71.8/68.7. **Slope:** 129/119. **Architect:** Clyde Johnston. **Green fee:** $20/$38. **Credit cards:** MC,VISA. **Reduced fees:** Weekdays, low season, twilight, seniors, juniors. **Caddies:** No. **Golf carts:** $11. **Discount golf packages:** No. **Season:** Year-round. **High:** April-Oct. **On site lodging:** No. **Rental clubs:** No. **Walking policy:** Walking at certain times. **Metal spikes allowed:** Yes. **Range:** Yes (grass). **To obtain tee times:** Call up to 3 days in advance.

Subscriber comments: The people are great...New course, nice design...Good new course. Greens very good. Needs time...Plays great from whites...New, with great future; design great...Back nine makes the trip worth it.

★★★½THE GAUNTLET GOLF CLUB AT CURTIS PARK

18 Fairway Dr., Fredericksburg, 22406, Stafford County, (540)752-0963, (888)755-7888, 30 miles S of Washington, DC.

Opened: 1995. **Holes:** 18. **Par:** 72/72. **Yards:** 6,857/4,955. **Course rating:** 72.8/69.8. **Slope:** 137/126. **Architect:** P.B. Dye. **Green fee:** $35/$49. **Credit cards:** N/A. **Reduced fees:** Weekdays, low season, twilight, seniors. **Caddies:** No. **Golf carts:** Included in Green Fee. **Discount golf packages:** Yes. **Season:** Year-round weather permitting. **High:** March-Oct. **On site lodging:** No. **Rental clubs:** Yes. **Walking policy:** Walking at certain times. **Metal spikes allowed:** Yes. **Range:** Yes (grass/mats). **To obtain tee times:** Call up to 7 days in advance. Credit card required to reserve weekends and holidays.

Notes: Ranked 10th in 1996 Best New Affordable Courses.

Subscriber comments: Some of the most memorable holes around, wonderful!...Picturesque but challenging...Forces you to think of risk/reward!...Well kept greens and fairways. Majestic feeling...Opening holes a little wild and wooly.

★★½GLENWOOD GOLF CLUB

PU-3100 Creighton Rd., Richmond, 23223, Henrico County, (804)226-1793.

Opened: 1927. **Holes:** 18. **Par:** 71/75. **Yards:** 6,464/5,197. **Course rating:** 70.0/72.1. **Slope:** 114/120. **Architect:** Fred Findlay. **Green fee:** $12/$21. **Credit cards:** MC,VISA. **Reduced fees:** Weekdays, twilight, seniors, juniors. **Caddies:** No. **Golf carts:** $12. **Discount golf packages:** No. **Season:** Year-round. **High:** May-Oct. **On site lodging:** No. **Rental clubs:** Yes. **Walking policy:** Walking at certain times. **Metal spikes allowed:** Yes. **Range:** No. **To obtain tee times:** Call up to 7 days in advance. **Subscriber comments:** Very forgiving, wide fairways...A fair, straightforward old course...Easy for better players.

GOLDEN HORSESHOE GOLF CLUB

R-401 S. England St., Williamsburg, 23185, Williamsburg City County, (757)220-7696, (800)447-8679, 45 miles SW of Richmond.

Green fee: $85/$100. **Credit cards:** All major. **Reduced fees:** Low season, resort guests, twilight. **Caddies:** No. **Golf carts:** Included in Green Fee. **Discount golf packages:** No. **Season:** Year-round. **High:** April-Oct. **On site lodging:** Yes. **Rental clubs:** Yes. **Walking policy:** Unrestricted walking. **Metal spikes allowed:** Yes. **Range:** Yes (grass/mats). **To obtain tee times:** Public may call up to 14 days in advance. Guests may book tee times with room reservation.

Notes: Golf Digest School site. Ranked 8th in 1997 Best in State. 1998 USGA Senior Women's Amateur Championship.

★★★★**GOLD COURSE**
Opened: 1963. **Holes:** 18. **Par:** 71/71. **Yards:** 6,700/5,159. **Course rating:** 73.1/66.2.
Slope: 137/120. **Architect:** Robert Trent Jones.
Notes: Golf Digest School site. Ranked 5th in 1997 Best in State.
Subscriber comments: Hard course...The best in Williamsburg...I never get tired of playing this course...Fantastic par 3s. Expensive but worth it...Hilly...Longest 6,700-yard course imaginable, no weak holes...Spectacular elevations to some holes...Great greens. Must bust it from the tips. Beautiful setting carved out of woods.

★★★★**GREEN COURSE**
Opened: 1992. **Holes:** 18. **Par:** 72/72. **Yards:** 7,120/5,348. **Course rating:** 73.4/69.3.
Slope: 134/109. **Architect:** Rees Jones.
Subscriber comments: Great conditions on superb layout...Nice track, nice employees...Mounding on sides of fairway brings balls to middle...Much easier than Gold...Good value; hard, adventurous, lots of fun...Challenging but playable...Everything about this experience is first class...Excellent conditioning—the best hotdogs on a golf course...Has really become an excellent course.
Special Notes: Also 9-hole executive course.

★★**GOOSE CREEK GOLF CLUB**
43001 Golf Club Rd., Leesburg, 22075, Loudoun County, (703)729-2500, 35 miles W of Washington, D.C.
Opened: 1952. **Holes:** 18. **Par:** 72/72. **Yards:** 6,400/5,235. **Course rating:** 70.3/71.3.
Slope: 121/120. **Architect:** Bill Gordon. **Green fee:** $22/$42. **Credit cards:** MC,VISA,AMEX. **Reduced fees:** Weekdays, low season, twilight, seniors, juniors.
Caddies: No. **Golf carts:** Included in Green Fee. **Discount golf packages:** No.
Season: Year-round. **High:** April-Sept. **On site lodging:** No. **Rental clubs:** Yes.
Walking policy: Mandatory cart. **Metal spikes allowed:** Yes. **Range:** No. **To obtain tee times:** Call up to 4 days in advance.
Special Notes: Spikeless shoes encouraged.

GORDEN TRENT GOLF COURSE
PU-Rd. No. 632, Stuart, 24171, Patrick County, (540)694-3805.
Call club for further information.

GREEN'S FOLLY GOLF COURSE
PU-1085 Green's Folly Rd., South Boston, 24592, Halifax County, (804)572-4998, 60 miles N of Raleigh.
Opened: N/A. **Holes:** N/A. **Par:** 71/75. **Yards:** 6,800/5,600. **Course rating:** 72.0/68.0.
Slope: 121/120. **Architect:** Fred Findlay. **Green fee:** $8/$13. **Credit cards:** None.
Reduced fees: Weekdays, low season, twilight, seniors, juniors. **Caddies:** No. **Golf carts:** $7. **Discount golf packages:** No. **Season:** Year-round. **High:** April-Sept. **On site lodging:** No. **Rental clubs:** Yes. **Walking policy:** Unrestricted walking. **Metal spikes allowed:** Yes. **Range:** Yes (grass/mats). **To obtain tee times:** Call.
Subscriber comments: Nice layout. Best hole is No.18, a long par 5...Not well manicured but a decent price.

★★½**THE HAMPTONS GOLF COURSE**
PU-320 Butler Farm Rd., Hampton, 23666, Hampton City County, (757)766-9148.
Opened: 1989. **Holes:** 27. **Architect:** Michael Hurdzan. **Green fee:** $14/$17. **Credit cards:** MC,VISA,AMEX. **Reduced fees:** Weekdays, low season, seniors, juniors.
Caddies: No. **Golf carts:** $9. **Discount golf packages:** No. **Season:** Year-round. **High:** March-Sept. **On site lodging:** No. **Rental clubs:** Yes. **Walking policy:** Walking at certain times. **Metal spikes allowed:** Yes. **Range:** Yes (grass). **To obtain tee times:** Call 48 hours in advance.
LAKES/LINKS
Par: 71/71. **Yards:** 6,283/4,965. **Course rating:** 69.4/67.2. **Slope:** 110/103.
WOODS/LAKES
Par: 71/71. **Yards:** 6,401/5,398. **Course rating:** 69.9/70.0. **Slope:** 110/111.
WOODS/LINKS
Par: 70/70. **Yards:** 5,940/4,853. **Course rating:** 67.8/66.4. **Slope:** 106/101.
Subscriber comments: Tough layout, good test, lots of water...Lakes nine is a real challange...Lakes difficult for average golfer...Lakes one of the prettiest around...Long carries over water; Links course is short...A lot of irons off the tee. Well groomed.

★★★½HANGING ROCK GOLF CLUB

PU-1500 Red Lane, Salem, 24135, Salem City County, (540)389-7275, (800)277-7497.
Opened: 1991. **Holes:** 18. **Par:** 73/72. **Yards:** 6,828/4,463. **Course rating:** 72.3/92.6.
Slope: 125/106. **Architect:** Russell Breeden. **Green fee:** $20/$25. **Credit cards:**
MC,VISA. **Reduced fees:** Weekdays, low season, resort guests, twilight, seniors,
juniors. **Caddies:** No. **Golf carts:** $12. **Discount golf packages:** Yes. **Season:** Year-
round. **High:** April-Oct. **On site lodging:** No. **Rental clubs:** Yes. **Walking policy:**
Walking at certain times. **Metal spikes allowed:** Yes. **Range:** Yes (grass/mats). **To
obtain tee times:** Call 1 day in advance for weekday. Call Wednesday at 9 a.m. for
upcoming weekend or holiday.
Subscriber comments: Nice mountain course...Super staff, play the white tees, very
difficult from blue tees...Best kept secret in Virginia...Challenging fairways. Demanding
greens...Good use of elevation changes.

★★★½HELL'S POINT GOLF COURSE

PU-2700 Atwoodtown Rd., Virginia Beach, 23456, Virginia Beach City County,
(757)721-3400, 15 miles E of Norfolk.
Opened: 1982. **Holes:** 18. **Par:** 72/72. **Yards:** 6,966/5,003. **Course rating:** 73.3/71.2.
Slope: 130/116. **Architect:** Rees Jones. **Green fee:** $29/$52. **Credit cards:** All major.
Reduced fees: Weekdays, low season, resort guests, twilight. **Caddies:** No. **Golf
carts:** Included in Green Fee. **Discount golf packages:** Yes. **Season:** Year-round.
High: April-Oct. **On site lodging:** No. **Rental clubs:** Yes. **Walking policy:** Unrestricted
walking. **Metal spikes allowed:** No. **Range:** Yes (grass/mats). **To obtain tee times:**
Call up to 7 days in advance or book through hotel golf package up to 1 year in
advance.
Subscriber comments: Still the best in Va. Beach...Good test of golf...Major mosquito
problem, otherwise top-notch course...Championship course, very
challenging...Outstanding value, a must play, long, scenic...Trees...A well-groomed
course with good scoring opportunities...Big fast greens. Beautiful course.

★★½HERNDON CENTENNIAL GOLF CLUB

PU-909 Ferndale Ave., Herndon, 20170, Fairfax County, (703)471-5769.
Opened: 1979. **Holes:** 18. **Par:** 71/71. **Yards:** 6,445/5,025. **Course rating:** 68.7/69.0.
Slope: 116/121. **Architect:** Edmond Ault. **Green fee:** $24/$29. **Credit cards:**
MC,VISA,DISC. **Reduced fees:** Weekdays, low season, twilight, seniors, juniors.
Caddies: No. **Golf carts:** $24. **Discount golf packages:** No. **Season:** Year-round.
High: May-Sept. **On site lodging:** No. **Rental clubs:** Yes. **Walking policy:** Unrestricted
walking. **Metal spikes allowed:** Yes. **Range:** Yes (grass). **To obtain tee times:** Call 1
day in advance for weekdays. Come in up to 7 days in advance for weekends.
Subscriber comments: Good condition despite very heavy play...Great for average
golfer, short course...Trees planted a dozen years ago have now grown up...Well maintained under heavy traffic...Wide open fairways and greens.

★★★HIDDEN CREEK GOLF CLUB

11599 N. Shore Dr., Reston, 22090, Fairfax County, (703)437-4222.
Call club for further information.
Subscriber comments: Rolling hills, tough from back tees, good shape...Blind tee
shots and hazards...Great service, clubhouse, and tough greens...Challenging for all
levels, great layout...No.13 is strange hole...Good test of golf, outstanding par 4s.

★★★½HIGHLAND GOLFERS' CLUB

PU-8135 Highland Glen Dr., Chesterfield, 23838, Chesterfield County, (804)796-4800,
15 miles S of Richmond.
Opened: 1995. **Holes:** 18. **Par:** 72/72. **Yards:** 6,711/5,019. **Course rating:** 72.1/68.7.
Slope: 133/120. **Architect:** Barton Tuck. **Green fee:** $28/$47. **Credit cards:** MC,VISA.
Reduced fees: Low season, twilight, seniors, juniors. **Caddies:** No. **Golf carts:**
Included in Green Fee. **Discount golf packages:** No. **Season:** Year-round. **High:** April-
Oct. **On site lodging:** No. **Rental clubs:** Yes. **Walking policy:** Mandatory cart. **Metal
spikes allowed:** Yes. **Range:** Yes (grass). **To obtain tee times:** Call golf shop.
Subscriber comments: Probably best public track in central Virginia with dramatic ele-
vation changes. A real test of shotmaking...Too many dangerous blind tee shots...Tough
pin placements always.

★★½HOLLOWS GOLF COURSE
14501 Greenwood Church Rd., Montpelier, 23192, Hanover County, (804)798-2949, 10 miles NW of Richmond.
Opened: 1984. **Holes:** 27. **Architect:** Brian Ault and Tom Clark. **Green fee:** $16/$22. **Credit cards:** MC,VISA. **Reduced fees:** Weekdays, low season, twilight, seniors, juniors. **Caddies:** No. **Golf carts:** $11. **Discount golf packages:** No. **Season:** Year-round. **High:** April-Oct. **On site lodging:** No. **Rental clubs:** Yes. **Walking policy:** Unrestricted walking. **Metal spikes allowed:** Yes. **Range:** Yes (grass/mats). **To obtain tee times:** Call 7 days in advance.
COTTAGE/ROAD
Par: 70/70. **Yards:** 5,969/4,642. **Course rating:** 67.9/63.3. **Slope:** 112/103.
LAKE/COTTAGE
Par: 70/70. **Yards:** 5,829/4,662. **Course rating:** 67.7/63.6. **Slope:** 115/106.
LAKE/ROAD
Par: 70/70. **Yards:** 5,966/4,750. **Course rating:** 68.0/67.1. **Slope:** 112/109.
Subscriber comments: Level course, good greens...Average to good layout, acceptable conditon...A friendly, fun course for middle-handicap golfers...Forgiving course. Don't let up on the 18th hole. Green is built up and hard to hit.

HOLSTON HILLS GOLF CLUB
Country Club Rd., Marion, 24354, Smyth County, (540)783-7484, 165 miles NW of Charlotte, NC.
Opened: 1946. **Holes:** 18. **Par:** 72/75. **Yards:** 6,536/5,171. **Course rating:** 70.8/70.6. **Slope:** 126/119. **Architect:** Edmund B. Ault. **Green fee:** $22/$28. **Credit cards:** None. **Reduced fees:** Weekdays. **Caddies:** No. **Golf carts:** N/A. **Discount golf packages:** No. **Season:** Year-round. **High:** June-Aug. **On site lodging:** No. **Rental clubs:** No. **Walking policy:** Unrestricted walking. **Metal spikes allowed:** Yes. **Range:** No. **To obtain tee times:** Tee times not required.

THE HOMESTEAD RESORT
R- **Credit cards:** MC,VISA,AMEX,DISC,Diners Club. **Reduced fees:** Low season, resort guests, twilight, juniors. **Caddies:** Yes. **Golf carts:** Included in Green Fee. **Discount golf packages:** Yes. **Season:** April-Oct. **High:** April-Oct. **On site lodging:** Yes. **Rental clubs:** Yes. **Walking policy:** Walking at certain times. **Metal spikes allowed:** Yes. **Range:** Yes (grass). **To obtain tee times:** Call.

★★★★★CASCADES COURSE
P.O. Box 2000, Hot Springs, 24445, Bath County, (540)839-3083, (800)838-1766, 150 miles NW of Richmond.
Opened: 1923. **Holes:** 18. **Par:** 70/71. **Yards:** 6,566/5,448. **Course rating:** 72.9/72.9. **Slope:** 136/137. **Architect:** William Flynn. **Green fee:** $75/$125.
Notes: Ranked 42nd in 1997-98 America's 100 Greatest; 1st in 1997 Best in State. 1994 USGA Women's Amateur; 1988 USGA Men's Amateur; 1967 U.S. Women's Open; Curtis Cup; U.S. Men's Senior Amateur.
Subscriber comments: Like St. Andrews and Pebble Beach, play it at least once in your life...The best...Great course, great vacation spot in town...Unique; hotel is outstanding...One of the most beautiful areas I've ever played...Fabulous, challenging, slick, subtle greens...Best course I've seen. Memorable holes. Fast greens...Long from back tees...A must...The best in mountain golf. Can play with caddie...Great test of your golf skills...Classic old course where Sam Snead learned to play—enough said.

★★★★LOWER CASCADES COURSE
P.O. Box 2000, Hot Springs, 24445, Bath County, (540)839-7995, (800)838-1766, 150 miles NW of Richmond.
Opened: 1962. **Holes:** 18. **Par:** 72/70. **Yards:** 6,619/4,726. **Course rating:** 72.2/65.5. **Slope:** 127/116. **Architect:** Robert Trent Jones. **Green fee:** $45/$90.
Subscriber comments: Great, great course condition, perfect staff...Great for middle handicappers...Beauty! Absolutely perfect conditions...Wish I could afford to play there more...Excellent layout and greens...Good resort course. Valley course in mountain setting...Played three times—saw Sam Snead there each time.

★★★½THE OLD COURSE
P.O. Box 2000, Hot Springs, 24445, Bath County, (540)839-7740, (800)838-1766, 150 miles NW of Richmond.

VIRGINIA

Opened: 1892. Holes: 18. Par: 71/72. Yards: 6,200/5,150. Course rating: 70.1/70.0. Slope: 121/117. Architect: Donald Ross. Green fee: $45/$90.
Subscriber comments: Great course, great vacation spot, nice town...Still lots of fun—easy but always in great condition...Great fun...Homestead is great, course historic...First four or five holes all uphill, fast greens...Great elevated tees...Great service...Interesting course—six par 3s, six par 4s, six par 5s.

★★★HONEY BEE GOLF CLUB
PU-5016 S. Independence Blvd., Virginia Beach, 23456, Virginia Beach City County, (757)471-2768.
Opened: 1988. Holes: 18. Par: 70/70. Yards: 6,075/4,929. Course rating: 69.6/67.0. Slope: 123/104. Architect: Rees Jones. Green fee: $27/$44. Credit cards: MC,VISA,AMEX. Reduced fees: Weekdays, low season, twilight, seniors, juniors. Caddies: No. Golf carts: Included in Green Fee. Discount golf packages: Yes. Season: Year-round. High: March-Oct. On site lodging: No. Rental clubs: Yes. Walking policy: Unrestricted walking. Metal spikes allowed: No. Range: Yes (grass). To obtain tee times: Call Wednesday for upcoming weekend. Otherwise call 7 days in advance.
Subscriber comments: Outstanding layout. Nice course to play...Very playable resort type course...Rees Jones! Fun to play...Houses too close...Stay in the fairway! Rough is rough...Lots of water...Excellent range...Great greens, short course.

★★★IVY HILL GOLF CLUB
PU-Rte. 2, Forrest, 24551, Bedford County, (804)525-2680.Call club for further information.
Subscriber comments: Excellent design and greens. A lot of improvements...Much better shape; very hilly; good for the money...Tough layout...Hilly...Old building for clubhouse...Long course with a few blind shots...Front nine in relaxing rural setting. Back nine in beautiful residential area...Pretty course.

★★JORDAN POINT GOLF CLUB
Jordan Point Rd., Hopewell, 23860, Prince George County, (804)458-0141.
Opened: N/A. Holes: 18. Par: 72/72. Yards: 6,510/4,944. Course rating: 70.7/68.6. Slope: 129/113. Architect: Russell Breeden. Green fee: $16. Credit cards: All major. Reduced fees: Seniors. Caddies: No. Golf carts: $11. Discount golf packages: No. Season: Year-round. High: April-Oct. On site lodging: No. Rental clubs: Yes. Walking policy: Walking at certain times. Metal spikes allowed: Yes. Range: No. To obtain tee times: Call up to 7 days in advance.

★★KEMPSVILLE GREENS GOLF CLUB
PU-4840 Princess Anne Rd., Virginia Beach, 23462, Virginia Beach City County, (757)474-8441.
Opened: 1954. Holes: 18. Par: 70/70. Yards: 5,849/4,538. Course rating: 67.8/63.8. Slope: 114/94. Architect: Ellis Maples. Green fee: $10/$18. Credit cards: None. Reduced fees: Twilight, seniors, juniors. Caddies: No. Golf carts: $9. Discount golf packages: No. Season: Year-round. High: June-Aug. On site lodging: No. Rental clubs: Yes. Walking policy: Unrestricted walking. Metal spikes allowed: Yes. Range: Yes (grass/mats). To obtain tee times: Call Friday after 8 a.m. for upcoming weekend and holiday. Open play during the week.

★★★KILN CREEK GOLF & COUNTRY CLUB
1003 Brick Kiln Blvd., Newport News, 23602, Newport News City County, (757)988-3220, 30 miles W of Norfolk.
Opened: 1989. Holes: 18. Par: 72/72. Yards: 6,889/5,313. Course rating: 73.4/69.5. Slope: 130/119. Architect: Tom Clark. Green fee: $35/$50. Credit cards: MC,VISA,AMEX. Reduced fees: Weekdays, low season. Caddies: No. Golf carts: Included in Green Fee. Discount golf packages: No. Season: Year-round. High: April-Oct. On site lodging: Yes. Rental clubs: Yes. Walking policy: Mandatory cart. Metal spikes allowed: Yes. Range: Yes (grass). To obtain tee times: Call one week in advance.
Subscriber comments: Huge bunkers...Premium on driving accuracy...Long layout with buffer along sides of fairways...Lots of sand; new nine not as good...Lots of sand, great challenge...Great service, fast fairways a fun and challenging track, 18th hole is awesome...Good use of mounds and bunkers...Weird layout but fun.

KINGSMILL RESORT & CLUB

R- **Credit cards:** All major. **Reduced fees:** Low season, resort guests, twilight. **Caddies:** No. **Golf carts:** Included in Green Fee. **Discount golf packages:** Yes. **Season:** Year-round. **High:** April-Oct. **On site lodging:** Yes. **Rental clubs:** Yes. **Walking policy:** Mandatory cart. **Metal spikes allowed:** Yes. **Range:** Yes (grass/mats). **To obtain tee times:** Resort guests may make tee times with room reservation. Others may call 1 day in advance.

★★★½PLANTATION COURSE

1010 Kingsmill Rd., Williamsburg, 23185, Williamsburg City County, (757)253-3906, (800)832-5665, 50 miles E of Richmond.
Opened: 1986. **Holes:** 18. **Par:** 72/72. **Yards:** 6,605/4,880. **Course rating:** 72.1/69.2. **Slope:** 126/122. **Architect:** Arnold Palmer/Ed Seay. **Green fee:** $68/$100.
Subscriber comments: Excellent course, hard but fair, great facility...Great greens. A pinch below the Woods...A bit pricey, but an excellent course...Course in good condition and hard...Houses close, many white stakes...Fair...Definitely a playable course...Nice course, great resort...Very good for all abilities.

★★★RIVER COURSE

1010 Kingsmill Rd., Williamsburg, 23185, Williamsburg City County, (757)253-3906, (800)832-5665, 50 miles W of Richmond.
Opened: 1975. **Holes:** 18. **Par:** 71/71. **Yards:** 6,797/4,606. **Course rating:** 73.3/67.4. **Slope:** 137/109. **Architect:** Pete Dye. **Green fee:** $60/$125.
Notes: Ranked 12th in 1997 Best in State. PGA Tour's annual Michelob Championship at Kingsmill.
Subscriber comments: Playable Pete Dye layout...Go every year! The best...Tough course, fun to play, expensive...Good course, slow play...Good challenge...Placement type course, typical Pete Dye greens...A solid challenge, especially from back tees...Very good closing holes...Another great layout. The four finishing holes are a special treat. Great greens bring all your shots...Breathtaking.

★★★WOODS COURSE

1010 Kingsmill Rd., Williamsburg, 23185, Williamsburg City County, (757)253-5960, (800)832-5665, 50 miles W of Richmond.
Opened: 1994. **Holes:** 18. **Par:** 72/72. **Yards:** 6,784/5,140. **Course rating:** 72.7/68.7. **Slope:** 125/120. **Architect:** Tom Clark/Curtis Strange. **Green fee:** $60/$100.
Notes: Ranked 13th in 1997 Best in State.
Subscriber comments: Outstanding holes and beauty...The new one and the whole family will love it...Thank you Curtis. Probably best of three...Great holes. Need all facets of a good gome to break 80...Outstanding everything...Difficult course. Beautifully kept...Lots of ravines...Outstanding layout...Back nine really memorable...Beautiful course, give it six stars on views alone.
Special Notes: Also 9-hole par-3 Bray Links course.

★★LAKE WRIGHT GOLF COURSE

6282 N. Hampton Blvd., Norfolk, 23502, Norfolk City County, (757)459-2255.
Opened: 1969. **Holes:** 18. **Par:** 70/70. **Yards:** 6,174/5,297. **Course rating:** 68.8/68.2. **Slope:** 116/105. **Architect:** Al Jamison. **Green fee:** $18/$20. **Credit cards:** None. **Reduced fees:** Weekdays, low season, seniors. **Caddies:** No. **Golf carts:** $20. **Discount golf packages:** No. **Season:** Year-round. **High:** April-Nov. **On site lodging:** Yes. **Rental clubs:** Yes. **Walking policy:** Walking at certain times. **Metal spikes allowed:** No. **Range:** Yes (grass/mats). **To obtain tee times:** Call 1 day in advance for weekends only.

★★★LAKEVIEW GOLF COURSE

Rte. 11, Harrisonburg, 22801, Rockingham County, (540)434-8937.
Opened: 1962. **Holes:** 27. **Architect:** Ed Ault. **Green fee:** $18/$18. **Credit cards:** None. **Reduced fees:** Twilight. **Caddies:** No. **Golf carts:** $10. **Discount golf packages:** No. **Season:** Year-round. **High:** April-Oct. **On site lodging:** No. **Rental clubs:** Yes. **Walking policy:** Unrestricted walking. **Metal spikes allowed:** Yes. **Range:** Yes. **To obtain tee times:** Call up to seven days in advance.
LAKE/PEAK
Par: 72/72. **Yards:** 6,517/5,637. **Course rating:** 71.0/71.8. **Slope:** 119/113.

LAKE/SPRING
Par: 72/72. **Yards:** 6,303/5,383. **Course rating:** 70.9/70.1. **Slope:** 120/115.
PEAK/SPRING
Par: 72/72. **Yards:** 6,640/5,410. **Course rating:** 71.3/70.1. **Slope:** 121/116.
Subscriber comments: The Lake 9th hole is challenging par 4, requiring a long blind drive and a long iron to a green guarded in front by a pond...A nice walkable layout in central Va...Par 5s reachable in two; several wide fairways...Friendly to visitors.

★★★½LANSDOWNE GOLF CLUB
R-44050 Woodridge Pkwy., Lansdowne, 22075, Loudoun County, (703)729-4071, (800)541-4801, 35 miles W of Washington, D.C.
Opened: 1991. **Holes:** 18. **Par:** 72/72. **Yards:** 7,057/5,213. **Course rating:** 74.0/75.0. **Slope:** 130/134. **Architect:** Robert Trent Jones Jr.. **Green fee:** $80/$90. **Credit cards:** MC,VISA,AMEX. **Reduced fees:** Low season, resort guests, twilight. **Caddies:** No. **Golf carts:** Included in Green Fee. **Discount golf packages:** Yes. **Season:** Year-round. **High:** April-Nov. **On site lodging:** Yes. **Rental clubs:** Yes. **Walking policy:** Mandatory cart. **Metal spikes allowed:** No. **Range:** Yes (grass/mats). **To obtain tee times:** Call 2 days in advance.
Subscriber comments: Everything you could want...Holes 11-16 are as good as any stretch...Too expensive for me but if I were rich...Tees, fairways, greens immaculate...Open front, great back nine...Excellent back nine, terrain rolling with some severe slopes...Bugs were unbearable.

★★LEE PARK GOLF COURSE
PU-3108 Homestead Dr., Petersburg, 23805, Petersburg City County, (804)733-5667, 25 miles N of Richmond.
Opened: 1945. **Holes:** 18. **Par:** 70/70. **Yards:** 6,037/4,946. **Course rating:** 68.0/62.2. **Slope:** 108/96. **Architect:** Fred Findley. **Green fee:** $20/$25. **Credit cards:** None. **Reduced fees:** Weekdays, twilight, seniors, juniors. **Caddies:** No. **Golf carts:** Included in Green Fee. **Discount golf packages:** No. **Season:** Year-round. **High:** June-Aug. **On site lodging:** No. **Rental clubs:** Yes. **Walking policy:** Unrestricted walking. **Metal spikes allowed:** Yes. **Range:** Yes (grass/mats). **To obtain tee times:** None taken.

★★★½LEE'S HILL GOLFERS' CLUB
PU-10200 Old Dominion Pkwy., Fredericksburg, 22408, Spotsylvania County, (540)891-0111, (800)930-3636, 50 miles N of Richmond.
Opened: 1993. **Holes:** 18. **Par:** 72/72. **Yards:** 6,805/5,064. **Course rating:** 72.4/69.2. **Slope:** 128/115. **Architect:** Bill Love. **Green fee:** $13/$33. **Credit cards:** MC,VISA. **Reduced fees:** Weekdays, low season, twilight, seniors, juniors. **Caddies:** No. **Golf carts:** $12. **Discount golf packages:** Yes. **Season:** Year-round. **High:** April-Oct. **On site lodging:** No. **Rental clubs:** Yes. **Walking policy:** Mandatory cart. **Metal spikes allowed:** Yes. **Range:** Yes (grass/mats). **To obtain tee times:** Call 1 day in advance.
Subscriber comments: A great stop off for all going south...Excellent layout even for high handicapper...Fun course. Very good par 3s...Very picturesque, tees fairways, and greens in good shape...One of the best kept and most challenging courses around...Good new course with reasonable rates.

★★★★½THE LEGENDS OF STONEHOUSE
PU-9540 Old Stage Rd., Toano, 23168, James City County, (757)566-1138, (888)825-3436, 40 miles SE of Richmond.
Opened: 1996. **Holes:** 18. **Par:** 71/71. **Yards:** 6,963/5,085. **Course rating:** 75.0/69.1. **Slope:** 140/121. **Architect:** Mike Stranz. **Green fee:** $60/$95. **Credit cards:** MC,VISA,AMEX. **Reduced fees:** N/A. **Caddies:** No. **Golf carts:** Included in Green Fee. **Discount golf packages:** Yes. **Season:** Year-round. **High:** March-Nov. **On site lodging:** No. **Rental clubs:** Yes. **Walking policy:** Unrestricted walking. **Metal spikes allowed:** No. **Range:** Yes (grass). **To obtain tee times:** Call up to 1 year in advance.
Notes: Ranked 3rd in 1997 Best in State; 1st in 1996 Best New Upscale Courses.
Subscriber comments: A real winner...Friendly staff...Played Pine Valley this year and I don't know which is better...Most beautiful in the east...Outstanding beauty...It's a great challenge from any set of tees...Each hole is wonderful and thrilling...A must play...Each hole more beautiful than the last.

VIRGINIA

★★MANASSAS PARK PUBLIC GOLF COURSE
PU-9701 Manassas Dr., Manassas Park, 20111, Price William County, (703)335-0777, 20 miles SW of Washington, DC.
Opened: 1996. **Holes:** 18. **Par:** 72/72. **Yards:** 6,651/4,747. **Course rating:** 72.5/68.1. **Slope:** 133/118. **Architect:** Jerry Slack. **Green fee:** $15/$30. **Credit cards:** MC,VISA. **Reduced fees:** Weekdays, low season, twilight, seniors, juniors. **Caddies:** No. **Golf carts:** $11. **Discount golf packages:** No. **Season:** Year-round. **High:** April-Oct. **On site lodging:** No. **Rental clubs:** Yes. **Walking policy:** Walking at certain times. **Metal spikes allowed:** Yes. **Range:** Yes (grass). **To obtain tee times:** Call up to 3 days in advance.

★★½MARINERS LANDING GOLF & COUNTRY CLUB
Rt. 1, Box 119, Huddleston, 24104, Bedford County, (540)297-7888, 35 miles SE of Roanoke.
Opened: 1994. **Holes:** 18. **Par:** 72/72. **Yards:** 6,902/5,118. **Course rating:** 73.5/70.0. **Slope:** 125/113. **Architect:** Robert Trent Jones. **Green fee:** $25/$35. **Credit cards:** MC,VISA. **Reduced fees:** Weekdays, low season, twilight, juniors. **Caddies:** No. **Golf carts:** Included in Green Fee. **Discount golf packages:** No. **Season:** Year-round. **High:** April-Sept. **On site lodging:** No. **Rental clubs:** Yes. **Walking policy:** Walking at certain times. **Metal spikes allowed:** Yes. **Range:** Yes (grass). **To obtain tee times:** Call golf shop.
Subscriber comments: Outstanding design. Excellent greens. Fairways rough...Long way to go but will be very good; good for the money...Huge greens on par 3s.

★★½MASSANUTTEN RESORT GOLF COURSE
R-P.O. Box 1227, Harrisonburg, 22801, Rockingham County, (540)289-4941, 100 miles S of Washington DC.
Opened: 1975. **Holes:** 18. **Par:** 72/73. **Yards:** 6,408/5,117. **Course rating:** 70.5/69.8. **Slope:** 123/128. **Architect:** Frank Duane/Richard Watson. **Green fee:** $40/$50. **Credit cards:** All major. **Reduced fees:** Resort guests, juniors. **Caddies:** No. **Golf carts:** Included in Green Fee. **Discount golf packages:** No. **Season:** Year-round weather permitting. **High:** April-Oct. **On site lodging:** Yes. **Rental clubs:** Yes. **Walking policy:** Unrestricted walking. **Metal spikes allowed:** Yes. **Range:** Yes (mats). **To obtain tee times:** Call up to 14 days in advance.
Subscriber comments: Massanutten requires very accurate shots as rough is usually high...Very hilly, cart needed to get from greens to tees.

★★½MEADOWCREEK GOLF COURSE
PU-1400 Pen Park Rd., Charlottesville, 22901, Albemarle County, (804)977-0615, 65 miles W of Richmond.
Opened: 1973. **Holes:** 18. **Par:** 71/71. **Yards:** 6,030/4,628. **Course rating:** 68.5/62.0. **Slope:** 118/105. **Architect:** Buddy Loving/Bill Love. **Green fee:** $21/$23. **Credit cards:** MC,VISA. **Reduced fees:** Weekdays, twilight, seniors, juniors. **Caddies:** No. **Golf carts:** $12. **Discount golf packages:** No. **Season:** Year-round. **High:** April-Sept. **On site lodging:** No. **Rental clubs:** Yes. **Walking policy:** Unrestricted walking. **Metal spikes allowed:** Yes. **Range:** Yes (grass/mats). **To obtain tee times:** Call 2 days in advance.
Subscriber comments: Open fairways. Lots of hills. Fun...Best value in Charlottesville...Great course, better back nine than front.

★★★MEADOWS FARMS GOLF COURSE
PU-4300 Flat Run Rd., Locust Grove, 22508, Orange County, (540)854-9890, 14 miles NW of Fredericksburg.
Opened: 1993. **Holes:** 27. **Architect:** Bill Ward. **Green fee:** $24/$34. **Credit cards:** MC,VISA. **Reduced fees:** Weekdays, low season, twilight, seniors, juniors. **Caddies:** No. **Golf carts:** Included in Green Fee. **Discount golf packages:** No. **Season:** Year-round. **High:** April-Oct. **On site lodging:** No. **Rental clubs:** Yes. **Walking policy:** Walking at certain times. **Metal spikes allowed:** No. **Range:** Yes (grass/mats). **To obtain tee times:** Call at least 7 days in advance.
ISLAND GREEN/LONGEST HOLE
Par: 72/72. **Yards:** 7,005/4,541. **Course rating:** 73.2/65.2. **Slope:** 129/110.

ISLAND GREEN/WATERFALL
Par: 70/70. **Yards:** 6,058/4,075. **Course rating:** 68.9/62.8. **Slope:** 123/100.
LONGEST HOLE/WATERFALL
Par: 72/72. **Yards:** 6,871/4,424. **Course rating:** 72.7/65.1. **Slope:** 123/105.
Subscriber comments: Gimmicky but fun. 19 holes—first one's a warmup—great!...A unique and well-kept course, a real treat!...Super staff! Some great shaped holes...Really great par 3s on Waterfall nine...Fits wide range of players.

★★½MILL QUARTER PLANTATION GOLF COURSE
1525 Mill Quarter Dr., Powhatan, 23139, Powhatan County, (804)598-4221, 22 miles W of Richmond.
Opened: 1973. **Holes:** 18. **Par:** 72/72. **Yards:** 6,970/5,280. **Course rating:** 72.2/73.6.
Slope: 118/123. **Architect:** Ed Ault. **Green fee:** $16/$28. **Credit cards:**
MC,VISA,AMEX. **Reduced fees:** Weekdays, low season, resort guests, twilight,
seniors. **Caddies:** No. **Golf carts:** N/A. **Discount golf packages:** Yes. **Season:** Year-round. **High:** April-Sept. **On site lodging:** No. **Rental clubs:** Yes. **Walking policy:**
Unrestricted walking. **Metal spikes allowed:** Yes. **Range:** Yes (grass/mats). **To obtain tee times:** Call 7 days in advance.
Subscriber comments: Need to be a big hitter, rolling and wooded fairways...No.2 is always trouble...Typical Ed Ault course—big greens and lots of room.

NEWPORT NEWS GOLF CLUB AT DEER RUN
PU-901 Clubhouse Way, Newport News, 23608, Newport News City County, (757)886-7925, 30 miles W of Norfolk.
Opened: 1966. **Architect:** Ed Ault. **Credit cards:** MC,VISA. **Caddies:** No. **Discount golf packages:** No. **Season:** Year-round. **High:** April-Nov. **On site lodging:** No. **Rental clubs:** Yes. **Metal spikes allowed:** No. **Range:** Yes (grass/mats). **To obtain tee times:**
Call 7 days in advance for weekdays. Call Thursday beginning at 7 a.m. for weekends and holidays.

★★★CARDINAL COURSE
Holes: 18. **Par:** 72/72. **Yards:** 6,624/4,789. **Course rating:** 70.9/62.8.
Slope: 118/102. **Green fee:** $27/$27. **Reduced fees:** Low season.
Golf carts: $18. **Walking policy:** Unrestricted walking.
Subscriber comments: Excellent muny—better than most
Williamsburg tourist courses...Very well kept. Some good holes...Very
long with big greens...Nice day on course, pleasantly long...Beautiful course; rolling terrain. Up and downhill shots...Good course for the beginning golfer...A gem; enjoy the deer!

(GOOD VALUE)

★★★½DEER RUN COURSE
Holes: 18. **Par:** 72/72. **Yards:** 7,209/5,295. **Course rating:** 73.7/70.0.
Slope: 133/113. **Reduced fees:** N/A. **Golf carts:** Included in Green
Fee. **Walking policy:** Mandatory cart.
Subscriber comments: How can this be a municipal course!
Excellent!...Long, demanding, good greens...Best overall course in area
if not rich...Excellent test—long and demanding—wears you down...A real
bargain...Long and open, big greens...A true test of golf, super great par 3s and
4s...Excellent test of golf skills for all levels.

(GOOD VALUE)

★★OCEAN VIEW GOLF COURSE
PU-9610 Norfolk Ave., Norfolk, 23503, Norfolk City County, (757)480-2094.
Opened: 1929. **Holes:** 18. **Par:** 70/70. **Yards:** 6,200/5,642. **Course rating:** 69.5/69.0.
Slope: 117/116. **Architect:** N/A. **Green fee:** $15/$15. **Credit cards:** MC,VISA.
Reduced fees: Weekdays, low season, twilight, seniors, juniors. **Caddies:** No. **Golf carts:** Included in Green Fee. **Discount golf packages:** Yes. **Season:** Year-round.
High: April-Oct. **On site lodging:** No. **Rental clubs:** Yes. **Walking policy:** Walking at certain times. **Metal spikes allowed:** Yes. **Range:** No. **To obtain tee times:** Call one week in advance.

★★★★OLDE MILL GOLF RESORT
R-Rte. 1, Box 84, Laurel Fork, 24352, Carroll County, (540)398-2211, (800)753-5005,
55 miles N of Winston-Salem, NC.
Opened: 1973. **Holes:** 18. **Par:** 72/72. **Yards:** 6,833/4,876. **Course rating:** 72.7/70.4.
Slope: 127/134. **Architect:** Ellis Maples. **Green fee:** $26/$36. **Credit cards:** All major.

Reduced fees: Weekdays, low season, resort guests, twilight, seniors. **Caddies:** No. **Golf carts:** $13. **Discount golf packages:** Yes. **Season:** Year-round. **High:** April-Oct. **On site lodging:** Yes. **Rental clubs:** Yes. **Walking policy:** Walking at certain times. **Metal spikes allowed:** Yes. **Range:** Yes (grass). **To obtain tee times:** Call between 8 a.m. and 6 p.m. anytime.

Subscriber comments: Awesome, very tough, beautiful course...Virginia's best-kept golf secret...My favorite. Out of the way but worth the trip...Great if you like water and blind shots...Gem in mountains. Bring your straight driver...One of the best and toughest...Hidden jewel, well worth finding, good staff...Excellent cabins for golf package...Premium mountain golf, scenic, small, fast greens...Beautiful, what an adventure...Great variety in hole design...Tough course—high handicappe,r come prepared.

★★OLE MONTEREY GOLF CLUB

PU-1112 Tinker Creek Lane, Roanoke, 24019, Roanoke City County, (540)563-0400. **Opened:** N/A. **Holes:** 18. **Par:** 71/71. **Yards:** 6,712/6,287. **Course rating:** N/A. **Slope:** 116/112. **Architect:** Fred Findlay. **Green fee:** N/A. **Credit cards:** N/A. **Reduced fees:** Weekdays. **Caddies:** No. **Golf carts:** N/A. **Discount golf packages:** No. **Season:** Year-round. **High:** April-Oct. **On site lodging:** No. **Rental clubs:** No. **Walking policy:** N/A. **Metal spikes allowed:** Yes. **Range:** No. **To obtain tee times:** N/A.

★★½PENDERBROOK GOLF CLUB

3700 Golf Trail Lane, Fairfax, 22033, Fairfax County, (703)385-3700, 14 miles W of Washington, DC.
Opened: 1979. **Holes:** 18. **Par:** 71/72. **Yards:** 6,152/5,042. **Course rating:** 71.2/69.1. **Slope:** 130/121. **Architect:** Edmund B. Ault. **Green fee:** $27/$35. **Credit cards:** MC,VISA. **Reduced fees:** Weekdays, low season, seniors, juniors. **Caddies:** No. **Golf carts:** $13. **Discount golf packages:** No. **Season:** Year-round. **High:** March-Oct. **On site lodging:** No. **Rental clubs:** Yes. **Walking policy:** Unrestricted walking. **Metal spikes allowed:** Yes. **Range:** No. **To obtain tee times:** Call 3 days in advance starting at 8 a.m.

Subscriber comments: Nice mix of long, short, uphill and downhill...Target holes aplenty...Hate those houses along the fairways...Very tough, short course, good par 5s...Short, tight, lots of water; always in good shape...Holes 9-12 test your coverage...No. 8 is best on course, No.12 a killer!

★★★PIANKATANK RIVER GOLF CLUB

P.O. Box 424, Rte. 708, Hartfield, 23071, Middlesex County, (804)776-6516, (800)303-3384, 60 miles E of Richmond.
Opened: 1996. **Holes:** 18. **Par:** 72/72. **Yards:** 6,751/4,894. **Course rating:** 73.6/70.0. **Slope:** 130/113. **Architect:** Algie Pulley. **Green fee:** $18/$38. **Credit cards:** MC,VISA. **Reduced fees:** Weekdays, low season, resort guests, twilight, seniors, juniors. **Caddies:** No. **Golf carts:** Included in Green Fee. **Discount golf packages:** Yes. **Season:** Year-round. **High:** April-Nov. **On site lodging:** No. **Rental clubs:** Yes. **Walking policy:** Walking at certain times. **Metal spikes allowed:** Yes. **Range:** Yes (grass). **To obtain tee times:** Call up to 7 days in advance.

Subscriber comments: Great potential...Northern neck's best secret...Good condition, design and challenge...Tough course, good holes.

★★½POHICK BAY REGIONAL GOLF COURSE

PU-10301 Gunston Rd., Lorton, 22079, Fairfax County, (703)339-8585, 15 miles from Washington, DC.
Opened: 1982. **Holes:** 18. **Par:** 72/72. **Yards:** 6,405/4,948. **Course rating:** 71.7/68.9. **Slope:** 131/121. **Architect:** George W. Cobb and John LaFoy. **Green fee:** $16/$26. **Credit cards:** MC,VISA. **Reduced fees:** Weekdays, low season, twilight, seniors, juniors. **Caddies:** No. **Golf carts:** $25. **Discount golf packages:** No. **Season:** Year-round. **High:** April-Nov. **On site lodging:** No. **Rental clubs:** No. **Walking policy:** Unrestricted walking. **Metal spikes allowed:** No. **Range:** Yes (mats). **To obtain tee times:** Call or come in starting at 6:30 a.m. on Tuesday for upcoming weekend or holiday.

Subscriber comments: Short, hilly, tight, take extra balls...Quiet, hit in woods forget it....Lots of up and down...One bad shot equals 2- or 3-over per hole.

★★PRINCE WILLIAM GOLF COURSE
PU-14631 Vint Hill Rd, Nokesville, 20181, Prince William County, (703)754-7111, (800)218-8463, 8 miles SW of Manassas.
Opened: N/A. **Holes:** 18. **Par:** 70/72. **Yards:** 6,606/5,455. **Course rating:** 70.1/71.6.
Slope: 119/119. **Architect:** N/A. **Green fee:** $23/$38. **Credit cards:** MC,VISA,AMEX.
Reduced fees: Twilight, seniors. **Caddies:** No. **Golf carts:** N/A. **Discount golf packages:** No. **Season:** Year-round. **High:** April-Oct. **On site lodging:** No. **Rental clubs:** Yes. **Walking policy:** Walking at certain times. **Metal spikes allowed:** Yes. **Range:** Yes (mats). **To obtain tee times:** Call up to 7 days in advance.

★★★★RASPBERRY FALLS GOLF & HUNT CLUB
PU-41601 Raspberry Dr., Leesburg, 20176, Loudoun County, (703)779-2555, 30 miles NW of Washington, DC.
Opened: 1996. **Holes:** 18. **Par:** 72/72. **Yards:** 7,191/4,854. **Course rating:** 74.3/68.0. **Slope:** 134/115. **Architect:** Gary Player. **Green fee:** $40/$50. **Credit cards:** MC,VISA. **Reduced fees:** Weekdays, low season, twilight. **Caddies:** No. **Golf carts:** $15. **Discount golf packages:** No. **Season:** Year-round. **High:** April-Oct. **On site lodging:** No. **Rental clubs:** Yes. **Walking policy:** Unrestricted walking. **Metal spikes allowed:** No. **Range:** Yes (grass). **To obtain tee times:** Call up to 8 days in advance.
Subscriber comments: Mentally very stimulating, beautiful...Love the sod-faced bunkers and links style...Tees, greens, and fairways. Excellent shape...Excellent new course, bunkers are tough...Best Gary Player course I've played; scenic...Fabulous design. Very fair challenge...Great course. Somewhat expensive.

★★★RED WING LAKE GOLF COURSE
PU-1080 Prosperity Rd., Virginia Beach, 23451, Virginia Beach City County, (757)437-4845.
Opened: 1971. **Holes:** 18. **Par:** 72/72. **Yards:** 7,080/5,285. **Course rating:** 73.7/68.1. **Slope:** 125/102. **Architect:** George Cobb. **Green fee:** $18/$25. **Credit cards:** MC,VISA. **Reduced fees:** Twilight, seniors, juniors. **Caddies:** No. **Golf carts:** $9. **Discount golf packages:** Yes. **Season:** Year-round. **High:** April-Oct. **On site lodging:** No. **Rental clubs:** Yes. **Walking policy:** Walking at certain times. **Metal spikes allowed:** Yes. **Range:** Yes (grass). **To obtain tee times:** Call 1 day in advance.
Subscriber comments: Long and wide open. Allows mistakes...Good challenging layout...Great finishing holes. Both nines can be swampy...Scenic...Very slow play on weekends...Real good greens...A good public course, great potential.

★★★RESTON NATIONAL GOLF COURSE
PU-11875 Sunrise Valley Dr., Reston, 22091, Fairfax County, (703)620-9333.
Opened: 1967. **Holes:** 18. **Par:** 71/72. **Yards:** 6,871/5,936. **Course rating:** 72.9/74.3. **Slope:** 126/132. **Architect:** Edmund Ault. **Green fee:** $32/$60. **Credit cards:** MC,VISA,AMEX. **Reduced fees:** Weekdays, low season, twilight, seniors, juniors. **Caddies:** Yes. **Golf carts:** Included in Green Fee. **Discount golf packages:** Yes. **Season:** Year-round. **High:** April-Oct. **On site lodging:** No. **Rental clubs:** Yes. **Walking policy:** Walking at certain times. **Metal spikes allowed:** Yes. **Range:** Yes. **To obtain tee times:** Call Monday at 8 a.m. for weekdays. Call Wednesday at 8 a.m. for upcoming weekend.
Subscriber comments: Mature, well designed and maintained...Makes you use all clubs...Good course, but too crowded...Pricey, but can't beat location. Solid course. Hard...Good one to walk...Beautiful rolling hills and undulating greens...Have special rates that include lunch.

★★RINGGOLD GOLF CLUB
PU-1493 Ringgold Rd., Ringgold, 24586, Pittsylvania County, (804)822-8728.
Opened: 1962. **Holes:** 18. **Par:** 72/72. **Yards:** 6,588/4,816. **Course rating:** 72.3/64.2. **Slope:** 124/107. **Architect:** Gene Hamm. **Green fee:** $17/$20. **Credit cards:** MC,VISA. **Reduced fees:** Weekdays, low season, seniors. **Caddies:** No. **Golf carts:** $8. **Discount golf packages:** No. **Season:** Year-round. **High:** April-Sept. **On site lodging:** No. **Rental clubs:** Yes. **Walking policy:** Unrestricted walking. **Metal spikes allowed:** Yes. **Range:** Yes. **To obtain tee times:** Call after Wednesday for threesomes and foursomes. Less than three on Blue only.

★★★RIVER'S BEND GOLF COURSE

PU-11700 Hogans Alley, Chester, 23836, Chesterfield County, (804)530-1000, (800)354-2363, 10 miles S of Richmond.

Opened: 1990. **Holes:** 18. **Par:** 71/71. **Yards:** 6,671/4,932. **Course rating:** 71.9/67.8. **Slope:** 132/117. **Architect:** Steve Smyers. **Green fee:** $10/$35. **Credit cards:** MC,VISA,AMEX. **Reduced fees:** Weekdays, low season, twilight, seniors, juniors. **Caddies:** No. **Golf carts:** $12. **Discount golf packages:** Yes. **Season:** Year-round. **High:** April-Oct. **On site lodging:** No. **Rental clubs:** Yes. **Walking policy:** Walking at certain times. **Metal spikes allowed:** Yes. **Range:** Yes (grass). **To obtain tee times:** Call 7 days in advance.

Subscriber comments: Super fast greens, worth the drive, breathtaking 18th...Awesome, beautiful...Some blind tee shots, some goofy holes...Tough, fair...Some great holes, some gimmicks...Good layout except for 16 and 17...Some very difficult holes, especially 18th...Layout for good golfers, difficult approach shots.

★★★★ROYAL NEW KENT GOLF CLUB

PU-P.O. Box 3508, Williamsburg, 23187, Williamsburg City County, (804)966-7023, (888)253-4363, 30 miles E of Richmond.

Opened: 1996. **Holes:** 18. **Par:** 72/72. **Yards:** 7,291/5,231. **Course rating:** 76.5/72.0. **Slope:** 147/130. **Architect:** Mike Strantz. **Green fee:** $60/$85. **Credit cards:** MC,VISA,AMEX. **Reduced fees:** N/A. **Caddies:** No. **Golf carts:** $20. **Discount golf packages:** Yes. **Season:** Year-round. **High:** March-Nov. **On site lodging:** No. **Rental clubs:** Yes. **Walking policy:** Unrestricted walking. **Metal spikes allowed:** No. **Range:** Yes (grass). **To obtain tee times:** Call up to 9 months in advance.

Notes: Ranked 1st in 1997 Best New Upscale Courses.

Subscriber comments: Unbelievable bunkers and scenery, greens were like glass. Best course I've ever played...Very tough...True links style...Great layout, great par 3s...Great greens, long and hard...Be on the right part of green...From back you must be long, great course...Best test, most beautiful and conditioned new course in world...Fascinating, tough, incredible...Memories of Irish links.

★★★½ROYAL VIRGINIA GOLF CLUB

PU-3181 Dukes Rd., Hadensville, 23067, Goochland County, (804)457-2041, 31 miles SE of Charlottesville.

Opened: 1993. **Holes:** 18. **Par:** 72. **Yards:** 7,106. **Course rating:** 73.4. **Slope:** 131. **Architect:** Algie Pulley. **Green fee:** $15/$24. **Credit cards:** MC,VISA. **Reduced fees:** Weekdays, low season, twilight, seniors. **Caddies:** No. **Golf carts:** $11. **Discount golf packages:** No. **Season:** Year-round. **High:** Dec.-Feb. **On site lodging:** No. **Rental clubs:** No. **Walking policy:** Walking at certain times. **Metal spikes allowed:** Yes. **Range:** No. **To obtain tee times:** Call seven days in advance.

Subscriber comments: Great course, greatly kept, great service...Great country course, saw a bobcat and deer...A very challenging course...Extremely long for average golfer...What a secret, great greens...Long par 4s—fast greens with lots of slopes...Long and beautiful course.

★★★SHENANDOAH CROSSING RESORT & COUNTRY CLUB

R-10 Shenandoah Crossing Rd., Gordonsville, 22942, Louisa County, (540)832-9543, (800)467-0592, 30 miles NW of Charlottesville.

Opened: 1991. **Holes:** 18. **Par:** 72/72. **Yards:** 6,192/4,713. **Course rating:** 69.8/66.5. **Slope:** 119/111. **Architect:** Buddy Loving. **Green fee:** $30/$35. **Credit cards:** All major. **Reduced fees:** Weekdays, low season, twilight, seniors, juniors. **Caddies:** No. **Golf carts:** Included in Green Fee. **Discount golf packages:** Yes. **Season:** Year-round. **High:** April-Oct. **On site lodging:** Yes. **Rental clubs:** Yes. **Walking policy:** Walking at certain times. **Metal spikes allowed:** Yes. **Range:** Yes (grass). **To obtain tee times:** Call up to 5 days in advance.

Subscriber comments: Carved out of mature woods. Tight, not overly demanding but still challenging...Decent holes in a spectacular setting...Narrow fairways in forest setting...Great course for mid-handicaps.

★★★SHENANDOAH VALLEY GOLF CLUB

134 Golf Club Circle, Front Royal, 22630, Warren County, (540)636-4653, 15 miles S of Winchester.

Opened: 1966. **Holes:** 27. **Architect:** Buddy Loving. **Green fee:** $10/$31. **Credit cards:** All major. **Reduced fees:** Weekdays, low season, twilight, juniors. **Caddies:** No. **Golf carts:** $13. **Discount golf packages:** Yes. **Season:** Year-round. **High:** March-Oct. **On site lodging:** Yes. **Rental clubs:** Yes. **Walking policy:** Unrestricted walking. **Metal spikes allowed:** Yes. **Range:** Yes (grass/mats). **To obtain tee times:** Weekly tee sheets come out Monday morning.

BLUE/RED
Par: 72/73. **Yards:** 6,399/5,000. **Course rating:** 71.1/67.8. **Slope:** 126/116.
RED/WHITE
Par: 71/71. **Yards:** 6,121/4,700. **Course rating:** 69.6/66.3. **Slope:** 122/114.
WHITE/BLUE
Par: 71/71. **Yards:** 6,330/4,900. **Course rating:** 70.7/66.2. **Slope:** 122/113.

Subscriber comments: A true test of skills on a great trio of nines...Best value...Nice mountain views. Great staff, friendly...Play all day for one low price...Red easy, Blue tough...Tight fairways...Great for mid-level players.

★★★SHENVALEE GOLF CLUB
R-P.O. Box 930, New Market, 22844, Shenandoah County, (540)740-9930, 95 miles W of Washington, DC.

Opened: 1924. **Holes:** 27. **Architect:** Edmund B. Ault. **Green fee:** $22/$25. **Credit cards:** All major. **Caddies:** No. **Golf carts:** $13. **Discount golf packages:** Yes. **Season:** Year-round. **High:** April-Oct. **On site lodging:** Yes. **Rental clubs:** Yes. **Metal spikes allowed:** Yes. **Range:** Yes (grass/mats). **To obtain tee times:** Call.

CREEK/MILLER
Par: 71/71. **Yards:** 6,595/4,757. **Course rating:** 71.1/65.0. **Slope:** 120/102. **Reduced fees:** Weekdays, low season, resort guests, twilight. **Walking policy:** Mandatory cart.
OLDE/CREEK
Par: 71/72. **Yards:** 6,358/4,821. **Course rating:** 70.1/65.2. **Slope:** 117/103. **Reduced fees:** Weekdays, low season, resort guests, twilight. **Walking policy:** Walking at certain times.
OLDE/MILLER
Par: 71/71. **Yards:** 6,297/4,738. **Course rating:** 70.1/65.1. **Slope:** 119/104. **Reduced fees:** Low season, resort guests, twilight. **Walking policy:** Walking at certain times.

Subscriber comments: The scenery is unforgettable...Excellent, staff most accommodating...Senior players paradise...Another course with great Blue Ridge mountain views!...Move back for a challenge...Old course, fairly short, small hard greens.

★★SKYLAND LAKES GOLF COURSE
PU-Mile Post 202.2 Blue Ridge Parkway, Fancy Gap, 24328, Carroll County, (540)728-4923, 50 miles NW of Winston-Salem.

Opened: 1990. **Holes:** 18. **Par:** 71/71. **Yards:** 6,500/5,955. **Course rating:** 70.0/69.0. **Slope:** 119/118. **Architect:** Welch DeBoard. **Green fee:** $17/$25. **Credit cards:** MC,VISA. **Reduced fees:** Weekdays, twilight, seniors. **Caddies:** No. **Golf carts:** Included in Green Fee. **Discount golf packages:** No. **Season:** Year-round. **High:** April-Sept. **On site lodging:** Yes. **Rental clubs:** No. **Walking policy:** Mandatory cart. **Metal spikes allowed:** Yes. **Range:** No. **To obtain tee times:** Call in advance.

★★★SLEEPY HOLE GOLF COURSE
PU-4700 Sleepy Hole Rd., Suffolk, 23435, Suffolk City County, (757)538-4100, 12 miles SW of Norfolk.

Opened: 1972. **Holes:** 18. **Par:** 72/72. **Yards:** 6,813/5,121. **Course rating:** 72.6/64.8. **Slope:** 124/108. **Architect:** Russell Breeden. **Green fee:** $24/$36. **Credit cards:** MC,VISA,AMEX. **Reduced fees:** Weekdays, seniors, juniors. **Caddies:** No. **Golf carts:** Included in Green Fee. **Discount golf packages:** No. **Season:** Year-round. **High:** April-Oct. **On site lodging:** No. **Rental clubs:** Yes. **Walking policy:** Walking at certain times. **Metal spikes allowed:** No. **Range:** Yes (grass/mats). **To obtain tee times:** Call up to 7 days in advance.

Subscriber comments: Long, demanding, makes you like it...A love/hate with the tough No.18....Best public golf course in all Tidewater.

SOMERSET GOLF CLUB
PU-35055 Somerset Ridge Rd., Locust Grove, 22508, Orange County, (540)423-1500, 16 miles W of Fredericksburg.

Opened: 1997. Holes: 18. Par: 72/72. Yards: 6,832/5,262. Course rating: N/A. Slope: N/A. Architect: Jerry Slack. Green fee: N/A. Credit cards: N/A. Reduced fees: N/A. Caddies: No. Golf carts: N/A. Discount golf packages: No. Season: Year-round. High: March-Oct. On site lodging: No. Rental clubs: Yes. Walking policy: Mandatory cart. Metal spikes allowed: No. Range: Yes (grass/mats). To obtain tee times: Call up to 7 days in advance.

★★½SOUTH WALES GOLF COURSE
PU-18363 Golf Lane, Jeffersonton, 22724, Culpeper County, (540)937-3250, 50 miles N of Washington, DC.
Opened: 1960. Holes: 18. Par: 71/73. Yards: 7,077/5,020. Course rating: 73.2/68.5. Slope: 123/104. Architect: Edmund B. Ault. Green fee: $10/$23. Credit cards: MC,VISA,DISC. Reduced fees: Weekdays, low season, twilight, seniors, juniors. Caddies: No. Golf carts: $22. Discount golf packages: No. Season: Year-round. High: April-Oct. On site lodging: No. Rental clubs: Yes. Walking policy: Unrestricted walking. Metal spikes allowed: Yes. Range: Yes (mats). To obtain tee times: Call up to 14 days in advance.
Subscriber comments: A great layout, greens are some of the best around...A long course, very wide fairways...Great course, a hidden jewel...Some long par 4s...Front nine, short and tight, back nine long and open.

★★½STONELEIGH GOLF CLUB
35271 Prestwick Court, Round Hill, 20141, Loudoun County, (703)589-1402, 40 miles W of Washington, DC.
Opened: 1992. Holes: 18. Par: 72/71. Yards: 6,903/5,014. Course rating: 73.4/69.8. Slope: 132/119. Architect: Lisa Maki. Green fee: $48/$58. Credit cards: MC,VISA. Reduced fees: Low season. Caddies: No. Golf carts: Included in Green Fee. Discount golf packages: Yes. Season: Year-round. High: March-Nov. On site lodging: No. Rental clubs: Yes. Walking policy: Walking at certain times. Metal spikes allowed: No. Range: Yes (grass/mats). To obtain tee times: Call.
Subscriber comments: Target golf. Holes 2 and 3 are killers...Wacky design but fun; eclectic...A lot of blind shots—love it or hate it...Great view on No. 2.

★★½STUMPY LAKE GOLF CLUB
PU-4797 E. Indian River Rd., Virginia Beach, 23456, Virginia Beach City County, (757)467-6119.
Opened: 1944. Holes: 18. Par: 72/72. Yards: 6,800/5,200. Course rating: 72.2/67.1. Slope: 119/97. Architect: Robert Trent Jones. Green fee: $18/$20. Credit cards: All major. Reduced fees: Weekdays, low season, twilight, seniors, juniors. Caddies: No. Golf carts: $10. Discount golf packages: No. Season: Year-round. High: April-Oct. On site lodging: No. Rental clubs: Yes. Walking policy: Walking at certain times. Metal spikes allowed: No. Range: Yes (grass/mats). To obtain tee times: Call on Wednesday before noon for upcoming weekend. First come, first served on weekdays.
Subscriber comments: Nice views on lake, wet, new greens...A lot of wildlife, wet a lot, beautiful area, average greens.

★★★SUFFOLK GOLF COURSE
PU-1227 Holland Rd., Suffolk, 23434, Suffolk City County, (757)539-6298, 2 miles W of Suffolk.
Opened: 1950. Holes: 18. Par: 72/72. Yards: 6,340/5,561. Course rating: 70.3/71.1. Slope: 121/112. Architect: Dick Wilson. Green fee: $13/$14. Credit cards: None. Reduced fees: Weekdays, seniors, juniors. Caddies: No. Golf carts: $8. Discount golf packages: No. Season: Year-round. High: May-Sept. On site lodging: No. Rental clubs: Yes. Walking policy: Walking at certain times. Metal spikes allowed: Yes. Range: Yes (mats). To obtain tee times: Call up to 7 days in advance for weekdays. Call at 8 a.m. Wednesday for upcoming weekend.
Subscriber comments: One of the best values you'll ever find...Challenging all aspects of game, rolling back nine...Quirky muny—might not use a driver from 11-17, good closing par 5...Great old layout.

★★★SYCAMORE CREEK GOLF COURSE
PU-1991 Manakin Rd., Manakin Sabot, 23103, Goochland County, (804)784-3544, 15 miles E of Richmond.

VIRGINIA

Opened: 1992. **Holes:** 18. **Par:** 70/70. **Yards:** 6,256/5,149. **Course rating:** 69.7/64.6.
Slope: 124/114. **Architect:** Mike Hurzdan. **Green fee:** $30/$39. **Credit cards:** All
major. **Reduced fees:** Weekdays, low season, twilight, seniors, juniors. **Caddies:** No.
Golf carts: Included in Green Fee. **Discount golf packages:** No. **Season:** Year-round.
High: April-Oct. **On site lodging:** No. **Rental clubs:** Yes. **Walking policy:** Mandatory
cart. **Metal spikes allowed:** No. **Range:** Yes (grass). **To obtain tee times:** Call 3 days
in advance. Call on Wednesday for upcoming weekend or holiday.
Subscriber comments: Beautiful fairways and greens...Fairly short, but scenic and
fun...Hilly and swampy...Some great short par 4s, short but fun layout...Nice layout,
pretty good shape...Fun to play...Short, wet, soft greens, leave driver home...Nice layout, hills and moguls, placement key.

★★★★THE TIDES INN (GOLDEN EAGLE GOLF COURSE)

R-Golden Eagle Dr., Irvington, 22480, Lancaster County, (804)438-5501,
(800)843-3746, 70 miles E of Richmond.
Opened: 1976. **Holes:** 18. **Par:** 72/72. **Yards:** 6,963/5,384. **Course rat-**
ing: 74.3/70.9. **Slope:** 134/126. **Architect:** George Cobb. **Green fee:**
$40/$70. **Credit cards:** MC,VISA,AMEX. **Reduced fees:** Weekdays, low
season, resort guests. **Caddies:** No. **Golf carts:** $15. **Discount golf packages:** Yes.
Season: March-Dec. **High:** April-Oct. **On site lodging:** Yes. **Rental clubs:** Yes.
Walking policy: Walking at certain times. **Metal spikes allowed:** Yes. **Range:** Yes
(grass/mats). **To obtain tee times:** Call golf shop. Hotel guests may reserve tee times
anytime in advance.
Notes: Ranked 14th in 1997 Best in State.
Subscriber comments: Worth the trip...Great condition, nice lunch. Nos. 6,9 and 18
quite good...Expensive, but worth every penny...Get the crab cake sandwich...Eye
appealing, tight...Great...Pricey but worth it. Great course...Always fun to play, always in
good condition...Championship course, No.5 is intimidating, lots of water.

★★★½TIDES LODGE (TARTAN COURSE)

R-1 St. Andrews Lane, Irvington, 22480, Lancaster County,
(804)438-6200, (800)248-4337, 65 miles E of Richmond.
Opened: 1959. **Holes:** 18. **Par:** 72/72. **Yards:** 6,586/5,121. **Course**
rating: 71.5/69.2. **Slope:** 124/116. **Architect:** Sir Guy
Campbell/George Cobb. **Green fee:** $25/$53. **Credit cards:**
MC,VISA,AMEX. **Reduced fees:** Weekdays, low season, resort guests, twilight.
Caddies: Yes. **Golf carts:** $15. **Discount golf packages:** Yes. **Season:** March-Dec.
High: May-Oct. **On site lodging:** Yes. **Rental clubs:** Yes. **Walking policy:** Unrestricted
walking. **Metal spikes allowed:** Yes. **Range:** Yes (grass). **To obtain tee times:** Call at
least one week in advance to get desired time.
Subscriber comments: A great place for two couples for 3/4-day getaway...Great
course, great place...An unknown gem...Sneaky tough...This is the way all golf resorts
should be!...Good course, great all day play...Almost as good as Golden Eagle...A
sleeper, can jump up at you, small greens...Nice course, well maintained.

★★TWIN LAKES GOLF COURSE

PU-6100 Clifton Rd., Clifton, 22024, Fairfax County, (703)631-9099, 20 miles W of
Washington DC.
Opened: 1967. **Holes:** 18. **Par:** 73/73. **Yards:** 7,010/5,935. **Course rating:** 73.0/72.6.
Slope: 121/118. **Architect:** Charles Schalestock. **Green fee:** $19/$23. **Credit cards:**
MC,VISA. **Reduced fees:** Weekdays, seniors, juniors. **Caddies:** No. **Golf carts:** $20.
Discount golf packages: No. **Season:** Year-round. **High:** May-Sept. **On site lodging:**
No. **Rental clubs:** Yes. **Walking policy:** Unrestricted walking. **Metal spikes allowed:**
Yes. **Range:** No. **To obtain tee times:** Call (703)758-1800 for advance times, golf shop
number for day of play/walk-on times (if available). Tee time strongly recommended.

★★★½VIRGINIA OAKS GOLF & COUNTRY CLUB

8101 Virginia Oaks Dr., Gainesville, 22065, Prince William County, (703)754-7977, 25
miles W of Washington, DC.
Opened: 1995. **Holes:** 18. **Par:** 72/72. **Yards:** 6,925/4,852. **Course rating:** 73.5.
Slope: 133. **Architect:** P.B. Dye. **Green fee:** $35/$51. **Credit cards:** MC,VISA,AMEX.
Reduced fees: Twilight, seniors, juniors. **Caddies:** No. **Golf carts:** $14. **Discount golf**
packages: Yes. **Season:** Year-round. **High:** April-Oct. **On site lodging:** No. **Rental**

clubs: Yes. **Walking policy:** Walking at certain times. **Metal spikes allowed:** No.
Range: Yes (grass/mats). **To obtain tee times:** Call up to 7 days in advance.
Subscriber comments: You must play this course, it's great!...A great golfing experi-
ence, some very tough holes...Good test of all shots. Beautiful setting on Lake
Manassas...Good variety of holes, huge greens for most holes, fun to play.

★★½WESTLAKE GOLF & COUNTRY CLUB

360 Chestnut Creek Dr., Hardy, 24101, Franklin County, (540)721-4214, (800)296-
7277, 20 miles SE of Roanoke.
Opened: 1989. **Holes:** 18. **Par:** 72/72. **Yards:** 6,540/4,582. **Course rating:** 71.7/65.6.
Slope: 128/114. **Architect:** Russell Breeden. **Green fee:** $19/$24. **Credit cards:**
MC,VISA. **Reduced fees:** Twilight, juniors. **Caddies:** No. **Golf carts:** $10. **Discount
golf packages:** No. **Season:** Year-round. **High:** May-Sept. **On site lodging:** No. **Rental
clubs:** Yes. **Walking policy:** Walking at certain times. **Metal spikes allowed:** Yes.
Range: Yes (grass). **To obtain tee times:** Call up to 3 days in advance.
Subscriber comments: Good condition, good views, not crowded...Many challenging
holes...Hidden jewel near Smith Mountain Lake...Roller coaster greens.
Special Notes: Formerly Chestnut Creek Golf Club.

★★½WESTPARK GOLF CLUB

R-59 Clubhouse Dr. S.W., Leesburg, 20175, Loudoun County, (703)777-7023, 20 miles
W of Fairfax.
Opened: 1968. **Holes:** 18. **Par:** 71/71. **Yards:** 6,521/5,027. **Course rating:** 71.1/69.0.
Slope: 121/111. **Architect:** Edmund Ault. **Green fee:** $19/$27. **Credit cards:**
MC,VISA,AMEX. **Reduced fees:** Weekdays, low season, twilight, seniors. **Caddies:**
No. **Golf carts:** $13. **Discount golf packages:** No. **Season:** Year-round weather per-
mitting. **High:** April-Oct. **On site lodging:** No. **Rental clubs:** Yes. **Walking policy:**
Walking at certain times. **Metal spikes allowed:** Yes. **Range:** Yes (mats). **To obtain tee
times:** Call on Tuesday for upcoming weekend.
Subscriber comments: Some easy holes make this a morale booster...Cheap; accessible, striving to better itself...Wide fairways kept in fairly good shape...You must position to score...A fairly standard type course. Good greens...A fun and deceptive layout.

★★★½WILLIAMSBURG NATIONAL GOLF CLUB

PU-3700 Centerville Rd., Williamsburg, 23188, Williamsburg City County, (757)258-
9642, 40 miles E of Richmond.
Opened: 1995. **Holes:** 18. **Par:** 72/72. **Yards:** 6,950/5,200. **Course rating:** 72.9/69.7.
Slope: 130/127. **Architect:** Jim Lipe. **Green fee:** $30/$50. **Credit cards:**
MC,VISA,AMEX. **Reduced fees:** Weekdays, low season, resort guests. **Caddies:** No.
Golf carts: $16. **Discount golf packages:** No. **Season:** Year-round. **High:** N/A. **On
site lodging:** No. **Rental clubs:** Yes. **Walking policy:** Walking at certain times. **Metal
spikes allowed:** Yes. **Range:** Yes (grass). **To obtain tee times:** Call anytime in
advance with credit card to reserve.
Subscriber comments: Well maintained, great greens...Very nice condition, tourist
course with good greens, nice layout...Worth trying to find...Excellent greens...Mounds
and bunkers...Super round of golf...Good shape, good design, good value.

WINTERGREEN RESORT

R-P.O. Box 706, Wintergreen, 22958, Nelson County, (804)325-8240, (804)325-8250,
(800)325-2200, 43 miles W of Charlottesville.
Credit cards: All major. **Reduced fees:** Weekdays, low season, resort guests.
Caddies: No. **Golf carts:** $16. **Discount golf packages:** Yes. **High:** May-Oct. **On site
lodging:** Yes. **Rental clubs:** Yes. **Metal spikes allowed:** Yes. **To obtain tee times:** Call
up to 90 days in advance.

★★★½DEVIL'S KNOB GOLF CLUB

Opened: 1976. **Holes:** 18. **Par:** 70/70. **Yards:** 6,576/5,101. **Course rating:** 72.4/68.6.
Slope: 126/118. **Architect:** Ellis Maples. **Green fee:** $48/$72. **Season:** April-Oct.
Walking policy: Walking at certain times. **Range:** Yes (grass/mats).
Subscriber comments: Breathtaking mountain course...Narrow fairways...Spectacular
mountain views...Great place to spend the weekend...Very scenic when not foggy; slick
greens...Novel, interesting, steep...Mountainside greens hard to read; lots of shots up
and down; treelined fairways.

VIRGINIA

★★★★**STONEY CREEK AT WINTERGREEN**
Opened: 1988. **Holes:** 18. **Par:** 72/72. **Yards:** 7,003/5,500. **Course rating:** 74.0/71.0.
Slope: 132/125. **Architect:** Rees Jones. **Green fee:** $45/$65. **Season:** Year-round.
Walking policy: Mandatory cart. **Range:** Yes (grass).
Notes: Ranked 6th in 1997 Best in State.
Subscriber comments: One of the best in Va., immaculate fairways...Very scenic in
fall, enjoyable...A truly demanding, beautiful course...Delightful, no bad
holes...Risk/reward decisions on may holes; creek comes into play on many holes;
Immaculate conditions...Good challenge for many abilities. Friendly staff.

★★**WOLF CREEK GOLF & COUNTRY CLUB**
Rte. 1 Box 421, Bastian, 24314, Bland County, (540)688-4610, 20 miles NW of
Wytheville.
Opened: 1982. **Holes:** 18. **Par:** 71/71. **Yards:** 6,215/4,788. **Course rating:** 68.7/71.0.
Slope: 107/128. **Architect:** Maurice Brackett. **Green fee:** $13/$18. **Credit cards:**
MC,VISA. **Reduced fees:** Weekdays, low season, seniors, juniors. **Caddies:** No. **Golf
carts:** $10. **Discount golf packages:** Yes. **Season:** Year-round. **High:** April-Oct. **On
site lodging:** No. **Rental clubs:** Yes. **Walking policy:** Walking at certain times. **Metal
spikes allowed:** Yes. **Range:** Yes (grass). **To obtain tee times:** Call 7 days in advance
for weekends; 2 days in advance for weekdays.

★★½**WOODLANDS GOLF COURSE**
PU-9 Woodland Rd., Hampton, 23663, Hampton City County,
(757)727-1195.
Opened: 1927. **Holes:** 18. **Par:** 69/69. **Yards:** 5,391/4,154. **Course rat-
ing:** 65.6/62.9. **Slope:** 113/106. **Architect:** Donald Ross. **Green fee:**
$10/$14. **Credit cards:** MC,VISA. **Reduced fees:** Seniors, juniors.
Caddies: No. **Golf carts:** $14. **Discount golf packages:** No. **Season:** Year-round.
High: April-Sept. **On site lodging:** No. **Rental clubs:** Yes. **Walking policy:**
Unrestricted walking. **Metal spikes allowed:** Yes. **Range:** No. **To obtain tee times:**
Call 3 days in advance after noon.
Subscriber comments: Short, cheap, fun to play...A super city-owned course...Tough,
short course...Great price for seniors, very good greens.

★★★ALDERBROOK GOLF & YACHT CLUB

R-300 Country Club Dr. E., Union, 98592, Mason County, (360)898-2560, (888)898-2560, 35 miles NW of Olympia.
Opened: 1966. **Holes:** 18. **Par:** 72/73. **Yards:** 6,326/5,500. **Course rating:** 70.9/72.2.
Slope: 122/125. **Architect:** Ray Coleman. **Green fee:** $27/$32. **Credit cards:** MC,VISA. **Reduced fees:** Weekdays, low season, resort guests, seniors. **Caddies:** No.
Golf carts: $24. **Discount golf packages:** Yes. **Season:** Year-round. **High:** April-Oct.
On site lodging: Yes. **Rental clubs:** Yes. **Walking policy:** Unrestricted walking. **Metal spikes allowed:** Yes. **Range:** Yes (grass). **To obtain tee times:** Call Monday prior to weekend or holiday.
Subscriber comments: A jewel off the beaten path...Beautiful mountain views...Tight course...Good conditions...Best to play in July/August.

★★★½APPLE TREE GOLF COURSE

PU-8804 Occidental Ave., Yakima, 98908, Yakima County, (509)966-5877, 140 miles NW of Seattle.
Opened: 1992. **Holes:** 18. **Par:** 72/72. **Yards:** 6,892/5,428. **Course rating:** 73.3/72.0.
Slope: 129/124. **Architect:** John Steidel/Apple Tree Partnership. **Green fee:** $25/$50.
Credit cards: MC,VISA. **Reduced fees:** Weekdays, low season, twilight, seniors, juniors. **Caddies:** No. **Golf carts:** $24. **Discount golf packages:** No. **Season:** Year-round. **High:** March-Oct. **On site lodging:** No. **Rental clubs:** Yes. **Walking policy:** Unrestricted walking. **Metal spikes allowed:** Yes. **Range:** Yes (grass/mats). **To obtain tee times:** Call up to 30 days in advance when calling from outside the Yakima area. Call 7 days in advance in the Yakima area. Groups of 16 or more may book up to 1 year in advance.
Notes: Ranked 10th in 1997 Best in State.
Subscriber comments: Well-named course routed through apple orchards...One of the best public courses I've ever played...Worth the drive from Seattle...Enjoyed an apple fresh from the tree...Lushest lawn east of the mountains...Great island green.

★★AUBURN GOLF COURSE

PU-29630 Green River Rd., Auburn, 98002, King County, (253)833-2350.
Opened: 1969. **Holes:** 18. **Par:** 71/71. **Yards:** 6,350/6,004. **Course rating:** 69.5/68.4.
Slope: 116/109. **Architect:** Milton Bauman/Glenn Proctor. **Green fee:** $19/$21. **Credit cards:** None. **Reduced fees:** N/A. **Caddies:** No. **Golf carts:** $10. **Discount golf packages:** No. **Season:** Year-round. **High:** June-Sept. **On site lodging:** No. **Rental clubs:** No. **Walking policy:** Unrestricted walking. **Metal spikes allowed:** Yes. **Range:** No. **To obtain tee times:** Call up to 7 days in advance.

★★★AVALON GOLF CLUB

PU-1717 Kelleher Rd., Burlington, 98233, Skagit County, (360)757-1900, (800)624-0202, 55 miles N of Seattle.
Opened: 1991. **Holes:** 27. **Architect:** Robert Muir Graves. **Green fee:** $22/$37. **Credit cards:** MC,VISA. **Reduced fees:** Weekdays, low season, twilight, seniors, juniors.
Caddies: Yes. **Golf carts:** $23. **Discount golf packages:** Yes. **Season:** Year-round.
High: May-Sept. **On site lodging:** No. **Rental clubs:** Yes. **Walking policy:** Unrestricted walking. **Metal spikes allowed:** Yes. **Range:** Yes (grass/mats). **To obtain tee times:** Call up to 5 days in advance, or up to 1 year in advance pre-paid.
NORTH/SOUTH
Par: 72/72. **Yards:** 6,771/5,534. **Course rating:** 73.3/72.7. **Slope:** 129/125.
NORTH/WEST
Par: 72/72. **Yards:** 6,597/5,236. **Course rating:** 72.5/70.7. **Slope:** 127/121.
WEST/SOUTH
Par: 72/72. **Yards:** 6,576/5,318. **Course rating:** 72.3/71.2. **Slope:** 129/122.
Subscriber comments: Outstanding staff...Wonderful, tough course...Makes you play all clubs in bag...Great bargain...All three nines have a different character and style. Great doglegs...A beautiful course, not particularly long, but challenging.

★★BATTLE CREEK GOLF COURSE

PU-6006 Meridian Ave. N., Marysville, 98271, Snohomish County, (360)659-7931, (800)655-7931, 30 miles N of Seattle.
Opened: 1990. **Holes:** 18. **Par:** 73/73. **Yards:** 6,575/5,391. **Course rating:** 71.4/70.9.

Slope: 125/124. **Architect:** Fred Jacobson. **Green fee:** $20/$25. **Credit cards:** MC,VISA. **Reduced fees:** Weekdays, low season, twilight, seniors, juniors. **Caddies:** No. **Golf carts:** $21. **Discount golf packages:** Yes. **Season:** Year-round. **High:** May-Aug. **On site lodging:** No. **Rental clubs:** Yes. **Walking policy:** Unrestricted walking. **Metal spikes allowed:** Yes. **Range:** Yes (grass). **To obtain tee times:** Call up to 7 days in advance.

★★BELLEVUE MUNICIPAL GOLF COURSE
PM-5500 140th N.E., Bellevue, 98005, King County, (425)451-7250.
Opened: 1969. **Holes:** 18. **Par:** 71/71. **Yards:** 5,800/5,100. **Course rating:** 66.5/68.6.
Slope: 110/111. **Architect:** N/A. **Green fee:** $20/$20. **Credit cards:** None. **Reduced fees:** Low season, twilight, seniors, juniors. **Caddies:** No. **Golf carts:** $23. **Discount golf packages:** No. **Season:** Year-round. **High:** May-Aug. **On site lodging:** No. **Rental clubs:** Yes. **Walking policy:** Unrestricted walking. **Metal spikes allowed:** Yes. **Range:** Yes (mats). **To obtain tee times:** Call Monday after 9 a.m. for the following 7 days.

★★BROOKDALE GOLF COURSE
PU-1802 Brookdale Rd. E., Tacoma, 98445, Pierce County, (253)537-4400, (800)281-2428, 35 miles S of Seattle.
Opened: 1931. **Holes:** 18. **Par:** 71/71. **Yards:** 6,425/5,440. **Course rating:** 69.6/70.0.
Slope: 112/111. **Architect:** Al Smith. **Green fee:** $7/$20. **Credit cards:** MC,VISA.
Reduced fees: Weekdays, low season, twilight, seniors, juniors. **Caddies:** No. **Golf carts:** $20. **Discount golf packages:** Yes. **Season:** Year-round. **High:** April-Oct. **On site lodging:** No. **Rental clubs:** Yes. **Walking policy:** Unrestricted walking. **Metal spikes allowed:** Yes. **Range:** Yes. **To obtain tee times:** Call or stop by up to 7 days in advance.

★★½CAMALOCH GOLF COURSE
PU-326 N. E. Camano Dr., Camano Island, 98292, Island County, (360)387-3084, (800)628-0469, 45 miles N of Seattle.
Opened: 1990. **Holes:** 18. **Par:** 71/71. **Yards:** 6,144/5,192. **Course rating:** 70.0/70.9.
Slope: 125/122. **Architect:** N/A. **Green fee:** $14/$23. **Credit cards:** MC,VISA,DISC.
Reduced fees: Weekdays, low season, twilight, seniors, juniors. **Caddies:** No. **Golf carts:** $20. **Discount golf packages:** No. **Season:** Year-round. **High:** May-Sept. **On site lodging:** No. **Rental clubs:** Yes. **Walking policy:** Unrestricted walking. **Metal spikes allowed:** Yes. **Range:** Yes (grass). **To obtain tee times:** Call in advance. Walk-ons welcome.
Subscriber comments: Great potential...Narrow fairways but playable...Poor drainage...Nice course, but overpriced...Good pro...Redesigned holes excellent.

★★★½CANYON LAKES GOLF COURSE
PU-3700 Canyon Lakes Dr., Kennewick, 99337, Benton County, (509)582-3736, 210 miles SE of Seattle.
Opened: 1981. **Holes:** 18. **Par:** 72/72. **Yards:** 6,973/5,543. **Course rating:** 73.4/72.0.
Slope: 127/124. **Architect:** John Steidel. **Green fee:** $18/$25. **Credit cards:** MC,VISA.
Reduced fees: Weekdays, resort guests, twilight, juniors. **Caddies:** No. **Golf carts:** $12. **Discount golf packages:** Yes. **Season:** Year-round. **High:** March-Nov. **On site lodging:** No. **Rental clubs:** Yes. **Walking policy:** Unrestricted walking. **Metal spikes allowed:** Yes. **Range:** Yes (grass/mats). **To obtain tee times:** Call 7 days in advance.
Subscriber comments: Fine course, lots of wind, good value...Marshals keep play moving...Huge greens, lots of three-putt possibilites...Great condition...Challenging course, interesting holes...Friendliest employees.

★★½CAPITOL CITY GOLF CLUB
PU-5225 Yelm Hwy. S.E., Olympia, 98513, Thurston County, (360)491-5111, (800)994-2582.
Opened: 1961. **Holes:** 18. **Par:** 72/72. **Yards:** 6,536/5,510. **Course rating:** 70.9/71.7.
Slope: 123/122. **Architect:** Donald Hogan. **Green fee:** $17/$22. **Credit cards:** MC,VISA. **Reduced fees:** Weekdays, low season, twilight, seniors, juniors. **Caddies:** No. **Golf carts:** $13. **Discount golf packages:** No. **Season:** Year-round. **High:** June-Aug. **On site lodging:** No. **Rental clubs:** Yes. **Walking policy:** Unrestricted walking. **Metal spikes allowed:** Yes. **Range:** Yes (grass). **To obtain tee times:** Call seven days ahead.

Subscriber comments: Great greens...Best wet weather course I've putted any-where!...Surrounding homes detract...Good test. Some narrow holes, others wide, plenty of sand...Have to hit it straight. Nice staff.

★½CARNATION GOLF COURSE
1810 W Snoqualmie River Rd. N.E., Carnation, 98014, King County, (206)583-0314.
Opened: 1967. Holes: 18. Par: 71/68. Yards: 6,004/4,623. Course rating: 67.6/65.0.
Slope: 113/103. Architect: Bob Tachell. Green fee: $22/$25. Credit cards: MC,VISA.
Reduced fees: Weekdays, low season, twilight, seniors, juniors. Caddies: No. Golf
carts: $20. Discount golf packages: No. Season: Year-round. High: May-Oct. On site
lodging: No. Rental clubs: Yes. Walking policy: Unrestricted walking. Metal spikes
allowed: Yes. Range: Yes (grass/mats). To obtain tee times: Call up to 14 days in
advance.

★★CEDARCREST GOLF CLUB
PU-6810 84th St. N.E., Marysville, 98270, Snohomish County, (360)659-3566, 35 miles
N of Seattle.
Opened: 1927. Holes: 18. Par: 70/70. Yards: 5,811/4,846. Course rating: 67.0/66.6.
Slope: 114/112. Architect: Thomson, Wolveridge, Fream and Steidel. Green fee: $21.
Credit cards: MC,VISA,DISC. Reduced fees: Seniors, juniors. Caddies: No. Golf
carts: $20. Discount golf packages: No. Season: Year-round. High: June-Aug. On
site lodging: No. Rental clubs: Yes. Walking policy: Unrestricted walking. Metal
spikes allowed: Yes. Range: Yes (grass). To obtain tee times: Call 7 days in advance.

★★½CEDARS GOLF CLUB
PU-15001 N.E. 181st St., Brush Prairie, 98606, Clark County, (360)687-4233, 20 miles
N of Portland, OR.
Opened: 1975. Holes: 18. Par: 72/73. Yards: 6,423/5,216. Course rating: 71.2/71.1.
Slope: 129/117. Architect: Jerry James. Green fee: $16/$18. Credit cards: None.
Reduced fees: Juniors. Caddies: No. Golf carts: $20. Discount golf packages: No.
Season: Year-round. High: May-Oct. On site lodging: No. Rental clubs: Yes. Walking
policy: Walking at certain times. Metal spikes allowed: Yes. Range: Yes (grass/mats).
To obtain tee times: Call up to 7 days in advance.
Subscriber comments: Target golf...Wet in winter, but fun course...Fine when not
wet...Short, but plenty of trouble...Wetlands everywhere.

★★★CHEWELAH GOLF & COUNTRY CLUB
2537 Sand Canyon Rd., Chewelah, 99109, Stevens County, (509)935-6807, 60 miles N
of Spokane.
Opened: 1976. Holes: 18. Par: 72/74. Yards: 6,511/5,672. Course rating: 70.9/72.2.
Slope: 125/124. Architect: Keith Hellstrom. Green fee: $8/$16. Credit cards: None.
Reduced fees: Seniors, juniors. Caddies: No. Golf carts: $22. Discount golf pack-
ages: No. Season: April-Oct. High: May-Sept. On site lodging: No. Rental clubs:
Yes. Walking policy: Unrestricted walking. Metal spikes allowed: No. Range: Yes
(mats). To obtain tee times: Call 30 days in advance.
Subscriber comments: Tight, narrow and challenging...Fun and reasonably
priced...Set in trees, demanding course...Nice small town course.

★★★½CLASSIC COUNTRY CLUB
PU-4908 208th St. E., Spanaway, 98387, Pierce County, (253)847-4440, (800)924-
9557, 60 miles S of Seattle.
Opened: 1991. Holes: 18. Par: 72/72. Yards: 6,793/5,580. Course rating: 73.6/73.3.
Slope: 133/128. Architect: Bill Overdorf. Green fee: $20/$45. Credit cards:
MC,VISA,AMEX,JCB. Reduced fees: Weekdays, low season, twilight, seniors, juniors.
Caddies: No. Golf carts: $23. Discount golf packages: Yes. Season: Year-round.
High: May-Oct. On site lodging: No. Rental clubs: Yes. Walking policy: Unrestricted
walking. Metal spikes allowed: Yes. Range: Yes (grass/mats). To obtain tee times:
Call or come in up to 7 days in advance.
Subscriber comments: Easy to walk...Good greens, good design...Grounds well maintained...Big greens...Busy but friendly course...Excellent course for good golfers...Long,
narrow. Nice course but hit a straight drive...Come prepared to play your "A"
game...Tight landing areas...Fast greens, narrow fairways...Bunkers everywhere, a
good test of golf.

★CLOVER VALLEY GOLF COURSE
PU-5180 Country Club Way SE, Port Orchard, 98366, Kitsap County, (360)871-2236.
Opened: 1966. **Holes:** 18. **Par:** 69/70. **Yards:** 5,370/4,799. **Course rating:** 65.0/67.0.
Slope: 102/107. **Architect:** N/A. **Green fee:** $6/$16. **Credit cards:** None. **Reduced fees:** N/A. **Caddies:** No. **Golf carts:** $18. **Discount golf packages:** No. **Season:** Year-round. **High:** May-Sept. **On site lodging:** No. **Rental clubs:** No. **Walking policy:** N/A.
Metal spikes allowed: Yes. **Range:** No. **To obtain tee times:** Call.

★★★½THE CREEK AT QUALCHAN GOLF COURSE
PU-301 E. Meadowlane Rd., Spokane, 99204, Spokane County, (509)448-9317.
Opened: 1993. **Holes:** 18. **Par:** 72/72. **Yards:** 6,599/5,538. **Course rating:** 71.6/72.3. **Slope:** 127/126. **Architect:** William Robinson. **Green fee:** $16/$22. **Credit cards:** MC,VISA. **Reduced fees:** Juniors.
Caddies: No. **Golf carts:** $22. **Discount golf packages:** Yes. **Season:** March-Oct. **High:** May-Sept. **On site lodging:** No. **Rental clubs:** Yes. **Walking policy:** Unrestricted walking. **Metal spikes allowed:** Yes. **Range:** Yes (grass). **To obtain tee times:** Nonresidents may call anytime with credit card to guarantee.
Subscriber comments: Tight course...Excellent service...Tough holes and funky holes...Spokane is the best golf town in the country!...Tough driving holes...Scenic...Tight, different, good condition...Very well laid out...Accuracy a must, another Spokane muny gem...Great positional golf course...Get a cart...Great course...Rather new, tough back nine.

(GOOD VALUE)

★★½DESERT AIRE GOLF COURSE
505 Club House Way W., Desert Aire, 99349, Grant County, (509)932-4439.
Opened: 1975. **Holes:** 18. **Par:** 72/73. **Yards:** 6,501/5,786. **Course rating:** 70.5/72.6.
Slope: 115/120. **Architect:** Jim Krause. **Green fee:** $16/$18. **Credit cards:** MC,VISA.
Reduced fees: N/A. **Caddies:** No. **Golf carts:** $15. **Discount golf packages:** Yes.
Season: Year-round. **High:** June-Oct. **On site lodging:** Yes. **Rental clubs:** Yes.
Walking policy: Unrestricted walking. **Metal spikes allowed:** Yes. **Range:** Yes (grass).
To obtain tee times: Call one week in advance.
Subscriber comments: Well maintained, nice greens, good views...Fun but somewhat tricky...Scenic along Columbia River...Back nine plays tough into wind.

★★★★½DESERT CANYON GOLF RESORT
R-1201 Desert Canyon Blvd., Orondo, 98843, Douglas County, (509)784-1111, (509)258-4173, 25 miles N of Wenatchee.
Opened: 1993. **Holes:** 18. **Par:** 72/72. **Yards:** 7,293/4,899. **Course rating:** 74.0/67.5.
Slope: 127/104. **Architect:** Jack Frei. **Green fee:** $38/$70. **Credit cards:** MC,VISA,AMEX. **Reduced fees:** Weekdays, low season, twilight, seniors, juniors.
Caddies: No. **Golf carts:** Included in Green Fee. **Discount golf packages:** Yes.
Season: March-Nov. **High:** July-Aug. **On site lodging:** Yes. **Rental clubs:** Yes.
Walking policy: Mandatory cart. **Metal spikes allowed:** Yes. **Range:** Yes (grass). **To obtain tee times:** Call 7 days in advance, or prepay up to 30 days in advance.
Notes: Ranked 2nd in 1997 Best in State.
Subscriber comments: Best layout in tri-state area!...The best golf course I've ever played...The views are majestic, best shape. Fairways like carpet, huge greens...Tough when wind comes up...Satellites on carts neat...Excellent pro shop/lunch facility...Fabulous 18-hole putting course...Courteous staff.

★★★DOWNRIVER GOLF CLUB
PU-N. 3225 Columbia Circle, Spokane, 99205, Spokane County, (509)327-5269.
Opened: 1927. **Holes:** 18. **Par:** 71/73. **Yards:** 6,130/5,592. **Course rating:** 68.8/70.9.
Slope: 115/114. **Architect:** Local Citizens Committee. **Green fee:** $18/$18. **Credit cards:** MC,VISA. **Reduced fees:** N/A. **Caddies:** No. **Golf carts:** $22. **Discount golf packages:** No. **Season:** Feb.-.Nov. **High:** May-Sept. **On site lodging:** No. **Rental clubs:** Yes. **Walking policy:** Unrestricted walking. **Metal spikes allowed:** Yes. **Range:** No. **To obtain tee times:** Call anytime.
Subscriber comments: Country-club course with muny rates...Treelined and well taken care of...Another Spokane course, built in the '20s...Tight, narrow, short...Good value, nice course...Old and still good.

DRUIDS GLEN GOLF CLUB

PU-29925 207th Ave. S.E., Kent, 98042, King County, (253)638-1200.
Opened: 1997. **Holes:** 18. **Par:** 72/72. **Yards:** 7,146/5,354. **Course rating:** 74.8/70.6. **Slope:** 137/121. **Architect:** Keith Foster. **Green fee:** $29/$53. **Credit cards:** MC,VISA. **Reduced fees:** Weekdays, low season, twilight, seniors, juniors. **Caddies:** No. **Golf carts:** $28. **Discount golf packages:** No. **Season:** Year-round. **High:** March-Oct. **On site lodging:** No. **Rental clubs:** Yes. **Walking policy:** Unrestricted walking. **Metal spikes allowed:** No. **Range:** Yes (grass). **To obtain tee times:** Call up to 14 days in advance.

★★★DUNGENESS GOLF & COUNTRY CLUB

1965 Woodcock Rd., Sequim, 98382, Clallam County, (360)683-6344, (800)447-6826, 105 miles NW of Tacoma.
Opened: 1964. **Holes:** 18. **Par:** 72/72. **Yards:** 6,372/5,344. **Course rating:** 70.4/70.1. **Slope:** 121/119. **Architect:** Ray Coleman. **Green fee:** $15/$25. **Credit cards:** MC,VISA. **Reduced fees:** Weekdays, twilight, juniors. **Caddies:** No. **Golf carts:** $20. **Discount golf packages:** Yes. **Season:** Year-round. **High:** April-Oct. **On site lodging:** No. **Rental clubs:** Yes. **Walking policy:** Unrestricted walking. **Metal spikes allowed:** Yes. **Range:** Yes (grass). **To obtain tee times:** Call anytime.
Subscriber comments: Good walking course...Weather nice most of the time...Great course for the money...Clubhouse food excellent...Sporty, good test, not too hard...Very nice layout.

★★★½EAGLEMONT GOLF CLUB

4127 Eaglemont Dr., Mount Vernon, 98274, Skagit County, (360)424-0800, (800)368-8876, 23 miles S of Bellingham.
Opened: 1994. **Holes:** 18. **Par:** 72/72. **Yards:** 7,006/5,307. **Course rating:** 73.4/70.7. **Slope:** 134/124. **Architect:** John Steidel. **Green fee:** $37/$47. **Credit cards:** MC,VISA,AMEX. **Reduced fees:** Weekdays, low season, twilight, seniors, juniors. **Caddies:** No. **Golf carts:** Included in Green Fee. **Discount golf packages:** No. **Season:** Year-round. **High:** June-Aug. **On site lodging:** No. **Rental clubs:** Yes. **Walking policy:** Mandatory cart. **Metal spikes allowed:** Yes. **Range:** Yes (grass). **To obtain tee times:** Call 7 days in advance.
Subscriber comments: Well laid out, good bargain on weekdays...Well kept...Good greens...Priced right, good service...The views are worth paying for...Target golf at its best...Stay in fairway or forget it...Can't get enough of this one.

★★½ECHO FALLS PUBLIC COUNTRY CLUB

PU-20414 121 First Ave. S.E., Snohomish, 98290, Snohomish County, (360)668-3030, 10 miles NE of Bellevue.
Opened: 1992. **Holes:** 18. **Par:** 70/71. **Yards:** 6,123/4,357. **Course rating:** 68.9/64.6. **Slope:** 126/115. **Architect:** Jack Frei. **Green fee:** $23/$40. **Credit cards:** MC,VISA,AMEX. **Reduced fees:** Weekdays, low season, resort guests, twilight, seniors, juniors. **Caddies:** No. **Golf carts:** $13. **Discount golf packages:** Yes. **Season:** Year-round. **High:** April-Sept. **On site lodging:** No. **Rental clubs:** Yes. **Walking policy:** Unrestricted walking. **Metal spikes allowed:** Yes. **Range:** Yes. **To obtain tee times:** Call 5 days in advance.
Subscriber comments: Nos. 17 and 18 great finishing holes...Good maintenance, improving each year...Island green at 18.

★★½ELK RUN GOLF CLUB

PU-22500 S.E. 275th Place, Maple Valley, 98038, King County, (425)432-8800, 35 miles S of Seattle.
Opened: 1989. **Holes:** 18. **Par:** 71/71. **Yards:** 5,847/5,400. **Course rating:** 68.7/70.4. **Slope:** 118/115. **Architect:** Pete Peterson. **Green fee:** $20/$27. **Credit cards:** MC,VISA. **Reduced fees:** Weekdays, low season, seniors, juniors. **Caddies:** No. **Golf carts:** Included in Green Fee. **Discount golf packages:** Yes. **Season:** Year-round. **High:** May-Aug. **On site lodging:** No. **Rental clubs:** Yes. **Walking policy:** Unrestricted walking. **Metal spikes allowed:** Yes. **Range:** Yes (mats). **To obtain tee times:** Call up to 5 days in advance.
Subscriber comments: New front nine is impressive...Fixed up, becoming good little course...Wide open spaces...Greens great.

★★ENUMCLAW GOLF CLUB
PM-45220 288 Ave. S.E., Enumclaw, 98022, King County, (360)825-2827.
Opened: N/A. **Holes:** 18. **Par:** 70/71. **Yards:** 5,561/5,211. **Course rating:** 66.0/68.8.
Slope: 106/110. **Architect:** N/A. **Green fee:** $17/$17. **Credit cards:** MC,VISA.
Reduced fees: Seniors, juniors. **Caddies:** No. **Golf carts:** $20. **Discount golf packages:** No. **Season:** Year-round. **High:** July-Aug. **On site lodging:** No. **Rental clubs:** Yes. **Walking policy:** Unrestricted walking. **Metal spikes allowed:** Yes. **Range:** No. **To obtain tee times:** Call up to 10 days in advance.

★★ESMERALDA GOLF COURSE
PU-3933 E. Courtland, Spokane, 99207, Spokane County, (509)487-6291.
Opened: 1956. **Holes:** 18. **Par:** 70/72. **Yards:** 6,249/5,594. **Course rating:** 69.2/70.8.
Slope: 114/117. **Architect:** Francis James. **Green fee:** $14/$18. **Credit cards:** MC,VISA. **Reduced fees:** Twilight, seniors. **Caddies:** No. **Golf carts:** $20. **Discount golf packages:** No. **Season:** Feb.-Nov. **High:** May-Aug. **On site lodging:** No. **Rental clubs:** Yes. **Walking policy:** Unrestricted walking. **Metal spikes allowed:** Yes. **Range:** Yes (grass/mats). **To obtain tee times:** Call 1 day in advance for weekdays or 7 days in advance for weekends.

★★THE FAIRWAYS AT WEST TERRACE
PU-9810 W. Melville Rd, Cheney, 99004, Spokane County, (509)747-8418, 10 miles W of Spokane.
Opened: 1987. **Holes:** 18. **Par:** 72/72. **Yards:** 6,398/5,152. **Course rating:** 69.9/69.0.
Slope: 114/113. **Architect:** N/A. **Green fee:** $12/$18. **Credit cards:** MC,VISA,DISC.
Reduced fees: Weekdays, low season, twilight, seniors, juniors. **Caddies:** No. **Golf carts:** $20. **Discount golf packages:** No. **Season:** Year-round. **High:** June-Sept. **On site lodging:** No. **Rental clubs:** Yes. **Walking policy:** Unrestricted walking. **Metal spikes allowed:** Yes. **Range:** Yes (grass). **To obtain tee times:** Call golf shop. Tee times open Saturday for the following week.

★½FOSTER GOLF LINKS
PU-13500 Interuban Ave. S., Tukwila, 98168, King County, (206)242-4221.
Opened: 1925. **Holes:** 18. **Par:** 69/70. **Yards:** 4,930/4,695. **Course rating:** 62.3/65.1.
Slope: 94/98. **Architect:** George Eddie. **Green fee:** $17/$17. **Credit cards:** MC,VISA.
Reduced fees: Twilight, seniors, juniors. **Caddies:** No. **Golf carts:** $18. **Discount golf packages:** No. **Season:** Year-round. **High:** May-Sept. **On site lodging:** No. **Rental clubs:** Yes. **Walking policy:** Unrestricted walking. **Metal spikes allowed:** Yes. **Range:** No. **To obtain tee times:** Call 7 days in advance.

★★½GALLERY GOLF COURSE
PU-3065 N. Cowpens Rd., Whidbey Island, Oak Harbor, 98277, Island County, (360)257-2178, 60 miles N of Seattle.
Opened: N/A. **Holes:** 18. **Par:** 72/74. **Yards:** 6,351/5,454. **Course rating:** 76.1/66.0.
Slope: 128/113. **Architect:** U.S. Navy. **Green fee:** $20/$22. **Credit cards:** MC,VISA.
Reduced fees: Low season, twilight, juniors. **Caddies:** No. **Golf carts:** $14. **Discount golf packages:** No. **Season:** Year-round. **High:** June-Sept. **On site lodging:** No.
Rental clubs: Yes. **Walking policy:** Unrestricted walking. **Metal spikes allowed:** Yes.
Range: Yes (grass). **To obtain tee times:** Call.
Subscriber comments: Got caught in rain but still enjoyed the round...Tame 18-hole course, good in wet weather...Terrific views of Puget Sound.

★★½GLENEAGLES GOLF COURSE
PU-7619 Country Club Dr., Arlington, 98223, Snohomish County, (360)435-6713, (888)232-4653, 42 miles NE of Seattle.
Opened: 1995. **Holes:** 18. **Par:** 70/70. **Yards:** 6,002/4,937. **Course rating:** 69.8/69.9.
Slope: 129/125. **Architect:** William Teufel. **Green fee:** $21/$26. **Credit cards:** MC,VISA,AMEX. **Reduced fees:** Twilight, seniors, juniors. **Caddies:** No. **Golf carts:** $10. **Discount golf packages:** No. **Season:** Year-round. **High:** April-Sept. **On site lodging:** No. **Rental clubs:** Yes. **Walking policy:** Unrestricted walking. **Metal spikes allowed:** Yes. **Range:** Yes (grass). **To obtain tee times:** Call 7 days in advance.
Subscriber comments: Short but don't let that fool you...Easy, enjoyable course at regular tees...Tight, tough, practice your irons!...Stay out of the woods.

GOLD MOUNTAIN GOLF COMPLEX

PU-7263 W. Belfair Valley Rd., Bremerton, 98312, Kitsap County, (360)415-5432, (800)249-2363, 25 miles SW of Seattle.
Opened: 1996. **Credit cards:** MC,VISA. **Reduced fees:** Weekdays, twilight, seniors, juniors. **Caddies:** No. **Golf carts:** $22. **Discount golf packages:** No. **Season:** Year-round. **High:** April-Sept. **On site lodging:** No. **Rental clubs:** Yes. **Walking policy:** Unrestricted walking. **Metal spikes allowed:** Yes. **Range:** Yes (grass). **To obtain tee times:** Call 7 days in advance at 11 a.m. Groups of 12-27 may book 30 days in advance, and groups of 28 or more may book up to 1 year in advance.

CASCADE COURSE

Holes: 18. **Par:** 71/74. **Yards:** 6,707/5,306. **Course rating:** 71.3/69.9. **Slope:** 120/116. **Architect:** Ken Tyson. **Green fee:** $20/$24.

★★★½OLYMPIC COURSE

Holes: 18. **Par:** 72/72. **Yards:** 7,003/5,220. **Course rating:** 73.1/69.2. **Slope:** 128/115. **Architect:** John Harbottle. **Green fee:** $25/$29.
Notes: Ranked 2nd in 1997 Best New Affordable Public Courses.
Subscriber comments: Wonderful experience, like a country club...Could be best municipal value in Puget Sound area...Super course design...Excellent course...36 holes of natural beauty...Two excellent 18- hole tracks...Old 18 was good, new 18 is excellent...Great practice area.

GREAT VALUE

★★GRANDVIEW GOLF COURSE

PU-7738 Portal Way, Custer, 98240, Whatcom County, (360)366-3947.
Opened: N/A. **Holes:** 18. **Par:** 72/72. **Yards:** 6,514/5,673. **Course rating:** 70.8/71.2. **Slope:** 118/120. **Architect:** N/A. **Green fee:** $18/$21. **Credit cards:** MC,VISA,DISC. **Reduced fees:** Weekdays, low season, twilight, seniors, juniors. **Caddies:** No. **Golf carts:** $22. **Discount golf packages:** No. **Season:** Year-round. **High:** May-Sept. **On site lodging:** No. **Rental clubs:** No. **Walking policy:** Unrestricted walking. **Metal spikes allowed:** Yes. **Range:** No. **To obtain tee times:** Call.

★★★½HANGMAN VALLEY GOLF COURSE

PU-E. 2210 Hangman Valley Rd., Spokane, 99223, Spokane County, (509)448-1212.
Opened: 1969. **Holes:** 18. **Par:** 72/71. **Yards:** 6,904/5,699. **Course rating:** 71.9/71.8. **Slope:** 126/125. **Architect:** Bob Baldock. **Green fee:** $14/$19. **Credit cards:** None. **Reduced fees:** Seniors, juniors. **Caddies:** No. **Golf carts:** $22. **Discount golf packages:** No. **Season:** March-Oct. **High:** May-Sept. **On site lodging:** No. **Rental clubs:** Yes. **Walking policy:** Unrestricted walking. **Metal spikes allowed:** Yes. **Range:** Yes. **To obtain tee times:** Call Tuesday at 7 a.m. for the next 7 days.
Subscriber comments: Good course for walking, pretty setting...Toughest course in Spokane...A good hilly course with water and fast greens...Excellent staff...Most challenging par 5s I've seen on one course...Excellent value...Nice course and nice people.

GREAT VALUE

★★★½HARBOUR POINTE GOLF CLUB

PU-11817 Harbour Pointe Blvd., Mukilteo, 98275, Snohomish County, (425)355-6060, (800)233-3128, 15 miles N of Seattle.
Opened: 1990. **Holes:** 18. **Par:** 72/72. **Yards:** 6,862/4,842. **Course rating:** 72.8/68.8. **Slope:** 135/117. **Architect:** Arthur Hills. **Green fee:** $25/$45. **Credit cards:** MC,VISA. **Reduced fees:** Weekdays, low season, twilight, seniors, juniors. **Caddies:** No. **Golf carts:** $13. **Discount golf packages:** No. **Season:** Year-round. **High:** May-Oct. **On site lodging:** No. **Rental clubs:** Yes. **Walking policy:** Unrestricted walking. **Metal spikes allowed:** Yes. **Range:** Yes (grass/mats). **To obtain tee times:** Call 7 days in advance.
Subscriber comments: Great course, good operation...Too many houses...Great layout...Great variety, front nine water, back nine trees...Always getting better...Greens improved a ton.

★★★HIGH CEDARS GOLF CLUB

PU-14604 149th St. Court E., Orting, 98360, Pierce County, (360)893-3171, 14 miles SE of Tacoma.
Opened: 1971. **Holes:** 27. **Par:** 71/71. **Yards:** 6,303/5,409. **Course rating:** 69.7/70.7. **Slope:** 114/115. **Architect:** N/A. **Green fee:** $22/$30. **Credit cards:** MC,VISA.

Reduced fees: Weekdays, twilight, seniors, juniors. **Caddies:** No. **Golf carts:** $22. **Discount golf packages:** Yes. **Season:** Year-round. **High:** April-Nov. **On site lodging:** No. **Rental clubs:** Yes. **Walking policy:** Unrestricted walking. **Metal spikes allowed:** Yes. **Range:** Yes (mats). **To obtain tee times:** Call 7 days in advance.
Subscriber comments: Beautiful layout...Outstanding course, best Mt. Rainier view...Excellent service...Daffodils in spring...Great greens, fun to play, a fair test of skill...Nice little course...Nice putting course.
Special Notes: Also has 9-hole executive course.

★★★½HOMESTEAD GOLF & COUNTRY CLUB
115 E. Homestead Blvd., Lynden, 98264, Whatcom County, (360)354-1196, (800)354-1196, 15 miles N of Bellingham.
Opened: 1995. **Holes:** 18. **Par:** 72/72. **Yards:** 6,927/5,570. **Course rating:** 73.2/72.0. **Slope:** 129/124. **Architect:** Bill Overdorf. **Green fee:** $14/$30. **Credit cards:** MC,VISA,AMEX. **Reduced fees:** Weekdays, low season, resort guests, twilight, seniors, juniors. **Caddies:** No. **Golf carts:** $10. **Discount golf packages:** No. **Season:** Year-round. **High:** April-Oct. **On site lodging:** No. **Rental clubs:** Yes. **Walking policy:** Unrestricted walking. **Metal spikes allowed:** Yes. **Range:** Yes (grass). **To obtain tee times:** Call 7 days in advance.
Subscriber comments: No.18 island green, interesting hole...Flat farmland course, but very tough from blues or greens...New course, new clubhouse being built, high quality...Lots of room but lots of trouble.

★★★HORSESHOE LAKE GOLF CLUB
PU-1250 S.W. Clubhouse Ct., Port Orchard, 98367, Kitsap County, (253)857-3326, (800)843-1564, 10 miles W of Tacoma.
Opened: 1992. **Holes:** 18. **Par:** 71/71. **Yards:** 6,105/5,115. **Course rating:** 68.0/68.0. **Slope:** 116/112. **Architect:** Jim Richardson. **Green fee:** $21/$31. **Credit cards:** All major. **Reduced fees:** Weekdays, low season, twilight, seniors, juniors. **Caddies:** No. **Golf carts:** Included in Green Fee. **Discount golf packages:** Yes. **Season:** Year-round. **High:** N/A. **On site lodging:** No. **Rental clubs:** No. **Walking policy:** Mandatory cart. **Metal spikes allowed:** Yes. **Range:** Yes (grass). **To obtain tee times:** Call up to 7 days in advance.
Subscriber comments: Great course...Good course for 18+ handicapper...Tight fairways, better hit it straight...Don't like mandatory cart rule...Quiet, peaceful atmosphere.

HOT SPRINGS GOLF COURSE
PU-One St. Martin Rd., Carson, 98610, Skamania County, (509)427-5150, (800)755-5661, 45 miles E of Portland, OR.
Opened: 1991. **Holes:** 18. **Par:** 73/73. **Yards:** 6,559/5,365. **Course rating:** 72.1/68.9. **Slope:** 125/116. **Architect:** Rudy Hegewald/Bob Hendrickson. **Green fee:** $10/$16. **Credit cards:** MC,VISA. **Reduced fees:** Low season, seniors. **Caddies:** No. **Golf carts:** $16. **Discount golf packages:** Yes. **Season:** Year-round. **High:** May-Sept. **On site lodging:** No. **Rental clubs:** Yes. **Walking policy:** Unrestricted walking. **Metal spikes allowed:** Yes. **Range:** Yes (grass). **To obtain tee times:** Call golf shop.

★★★★INDIAN CANYON GOLF COURSE
PU-W. 4304 W. Dr., Spokane, 99204, Spokane County, (509)747-5353.
Opened: 1935. **Holes:** 18. **Par:** 72/72. **Yards:** 6,255/5,943. **Course rating:** 70.7/65.9. **Slope:** 126/115. **Architect:** H. Chandler Egan. **Green fee:** $22/$22. **Credit cards:** MC,VISA. **Reduced fees:** Twilight, juniors. **Caddies:** No. **Golf carts:** $22. **Discount golf packages:** No. **Season:** March-Oct. **High:** May-Sept. **On site lodging:** Yes. **Rental clubs:** Yes. **Walking policy:** Unrestricted walking. **Metal spikes allowed:** Yes. **Range:** Yes (grass/mats). **To obtain tee times:** Call anytime in advance.
Notes: 1985 USGA Women's Public Links; 1941, 1984 USGA Men's Public Links.
Subscriber comments: Great price for championship golf...Terrific traditional course...Hilly, not long but good test of golf...Fun, some great elevation changes...Tight fairways, lots of trees. Great finishing hole.

GREAT VALUE

★★JACKSON PARK GOLF COURSE
1000 NE 135th St., Seattle, 98125, King County, (206)363-4747.
Call club for further information.

★★JEFFERSON PARK GOLF COURSE
PU-4101 Beacon Ave., Seattle, 98108, King County, (206)762-4513.
Opened: 1917. **Holes:** 18. **Par:** 70/70. **Yards:** 6,019/5,449. **Course rating:** N/A. **Slope:** 115/112. **Architect:** Robert Johnstone and Jim Barnes. **Green fee:** N/A. **Credit cards:** MC,VISA. **Reduced fees:** Twilight. **Caddies:** No. **Golf carts:** N/A. **Discount golf packages:** No. **Season:** Year-round. **High:** March-Oct. **On site lodging:** No. **Rental clubs:** No. **Walking policy:** N/A. **Metal spikes allowed:** Yes. **Range:** Yes. **To obtain tee times:** N/A.

★★★½KAYAK POINT GOLF COURSE
PU-15711 Marine Dr., Stanwood, 98292, Snohomish County, (360)652-9676, (800)562-3094, 45 miles N of Seattle.
Opened: 1977. **Holes:** 18. **Par:** 72/72. **Yards:** 6,719/5,346. **Course rating:** 72.7/72.8. **Slope:** 133/129. **Architect:** Ron Fream. **Green fee:** $20/$30. **Credit cards:** MC,VISA,DISC. **Reduced fees:** Weekdays, low season, twilight, seniors, juniors. **Caddies:** No. **Golf carts:** $25. **Discount golf packages:** No. **Season:** Year-round. **High:** May-Sept. **On site lodging:** No. **Rental clubs:** Yes. **Walking policy:** Unrestricted walking. **Metal spikes allowed:** Yes. **Range:** Yes (grass/mats). **To obtain tee times:** Call 7 days in advance for weekdays. Call Monday a.m. for upcoming weekend. Call anytime in advance with prepayment.
Subscriber comments: Great walk with Mother Nature...Tough course, but one of the best..The most challenging course I've played...This one will make you play better.

★½KENWANDA GOLF COURSE
PU-14030 Kenwanda Dr., Snohomish, 98290, Snohomish County, (360)668-1166.
Opened: 1962. **Holes:** 18. **Par:** 69/72. **Yards:** 5,336/5,336. **Course rating:** 65.3/70.4. **Slope:** 119/126. **Architect:** Dr. Roy Goss. **Green fee:** $18/$18. **Credit cards:** MC,VISA. **Reduced fees:** N/A. **Caddies:** No. **Golf carts:** N/A. **Discount golf packages:** Yes. **Season:** Year-round. **High:** June-Aug. **On site lodging:** No. **Rental clubs:** Yes. **Walking policy:** Unrestricted walking. **Metal spikes allowed:** Yes. **Range:** No. **To obtain tee times:** Call up to 7 days in advance.

★★½LAKE CHELAN GOLF COURSE
PU-1501 Golf Course Dr., Chelan, 98816, Chelan County, (509)682-8026, (800)246-5361, 45 miles N of Wenatchee.
Opened: 1971. **Holes:** 18. **Par:** 72/72. **Yards:** 6,440/5,501. **Course rating:** 70.3/70.9. **Slope:** 119/113. **Architect:** Ron Sloan. **Green fee:** $25/$25. **Credit cards:** MC,VISA. **Reduced fees:** Twilight, seniors, juniors. **Caddies:** No. **Golf carts:** $22. **Discount golf packages:** Yes. **Season:** March-Nov. **High:** June-Aug. **On site lodging:** No. **Rental clubs:** Yes. **Walking policy:** Unrestricted walking. **Metal spikes allowed:** Yes. **Range:** Yes (grass). **To obtain tee times:** Call up to 7 days in advance.
Subscriber comments: Great views...Greens are much improved...Elevated tees and small greens make it tough...Easy walk.

★★★LAKE PADDEN GOLF COURSE
PU-4882 Samish Way, Bellingham, 98226, Whatcom County, (360)738-7400, 80 miles N of Seattle.
Opened: 1970. **Holes:** 18. **Par:** 72/72. **Yards:** 6,675/5,496. **Course rating:** 71.3/71.9. **Slope:** 122/126. **Architect:** Proctor & Goss. **Green fee:** $15/$20. **Credit cards:** MC,VISA. **Reduced fees:** Seniors, juniors. **Caddies:** No. **Golf carts:** $20. **Discount golf packages:** No. **Season:** Year-round. **High:** May-Sept. **On site lodging:** No. **Rental clubs:** Yes. **Walking policy:** Unrestricted walking. **Metal spikes allowed:** Yes. **Range:** Yes (grass/mats). **To obtain tee times:** Call 7 days in advance.

(GOOD VALUE)

Subscriber comments: Great test of golf, best muny I've ever played...Tough, but fair...Some challenging holes, good greens...Course takes a long time to dry out after rains...Great challenge for a public course...A nice surprise...One of the best bargains in the Puget Sound area.

★★★½LAKE SPANAWAY GOLF COURSE
PU-15602 Pacific Ave., Tacoma, 98444, Pierce County, (253)531-3660, 30 miles S of Seattle.

WASHINGTON

Opened: 1967. **Holes:** 18. **Par:** 72/74. **Yards:** 6,810/5,935. **Course rating:** 71.8/73.4. **Slope:** 121/123. **Architect:** AV Macan and Ken Tyson. **Green fee:** $13/$19. **Credit cards:** MC,VISA,DISC. **Reduced fees:** Weekdays, seniors, juniors. **Caddies:** No. **Golf carts:** $20. **Discount golf packages:** No. **Season:** Year-round. **High:** May-Oct. **On site lodging:** No. **Rental clubs:** Yes. **Walking policy:** Unrestricted walking. **Metal spikes allowed:** Yes. **Range:** Yes (grass/mats). **To obtain tee times:** Call 5 days in advance. **Subscriber comments:** Old muny, plays long, good shape...A good municipal course...Some good long 4 pars...Great layout with huge trees. Area jewel...Nice winter course, good people, good value...Nice long course. Good greens...Great pro staff.

★★LAKE WILDERNESS GOLF COURSE
PU-25400 Witte Rd. S.E., Maple Valley, 98038, King County, (425)432-9405, 30 miles SE of Seattle.
Opened: N/A. **Holes:** 18. **Par:** 70/70. **Yards:** 5,218/4,544. **Course rating:** 66.1/66.6. **Slope:** 118/117. **Architect:** Ray Coleman. **Green fee:** $5/$22. **Credit cards:** MC,VISA,AMEX. **Reduced fees:** Weekdays, low season, twilight, seniors, juniors. **Caddies:** No. **Golf carts:** $20. **Discount golf packages:** Yes. **Season:** Year-round. **High:** June-Aug. **On site lodging:** No. **Rental clubs:** Yes. **Walking policy:** Unrestricted walking. **Metal spikes allowed:** Yes. **Range:** No. **To obtain tee times:** Call or come in up to 14 days in advance.

★★★LAKELAND VILLAGE GOLF COURSE
Old Ranch Rd., Allyn, 98524, Mason County, (360)275-6100, 40 miles W of Olympia.
Opened: 1972. **Holes:** 27. **Architect:** Bunny Mason. **Green fee:** $18/$22. **Credit cards:** MC,VISA. **Reduced fees:** Weekdays, low season, twilight, seniors, juniors. **Caddies:** No. **Golf carts:** $21. **Discount golf packages:** No. **Season:** Year-round. **High:** Summer. **On site lodging:** No. **Rental clubs:** Yes. **Walking policy:** Unrestricted walking. **Metal spikes allowed:** Yes. **Range:** Yes (grass). **To obtain tee times:** Call up to 7 days in advance.
GENERATION 1/GENERATION 2
Par: 71/72. **Yards:** 5,724/4,925. **Course rating:** 68.5/69.9. **Slope:** 117/119.
GENERATION 2/GENERATION 3
Par: 72/72. **Yards:** 6,471/5,334. **Course rating:** 71.5/71.0. **Slope:** 122/121.
GENERATION 3/GENERATION 1
Par: 72/72. **Yards:** 5,915/5,081. **Course rating:** 68.8/69.2. **Slope:** 114/117.
Subscriber comments: Great golf community, not an easy course...Head pro friendly and helpful. Keep it in play and you can score well...Every hole is different...Good course with different terrain.

★★½LEAVENWORTH GOLF CLUB
9101 Icicle Rd., Leavenworth, 98826, Chelan County, (509)548-7267, 110 miles E of Seattle.
Opened: 1927. **Holes:** 18. **Par:** 71/71. **Yards:** 5,711/5,343. **Course rating:** 67.0/69.6. **Slope:** 110/112. **Architect:** N/A. **Green fee:** $20/$20. **Credit cards:** MC,VISA. **Reduced fees:** N/A. **Caddies:** No. **Golf carts:** $20. **Discount golf packages:** No. **Season:** April-Nov. **High:** April-Oct. **On site lodging:** No. **Rental clubs:** Yes. **Walking policy:** Unrestricted walking. **Metal spikes allowed:** Yes. **Range:** No. **To obtain tee times:** Call on Monday prior to play.
Subscriber comments: Beautiful course in the mountains...Fun course next to river...Short course, but fun.

★★LEGION MEMORIAL GOLF COURSE
PM-144 W Marine View Dr., Everett, 98201, Snohomish County, (425)259-4653, 30 miles N of Seattle.
Opened: 1934. **Holes:** 18. **Par:** 72. **Yards:** 6,800. **Course rating:** N/A. **Slope:** N/A. **Architect:** N/A. **Green fee:** $18. **Credit cards:** None. **Reduced fees:** N/A. **Caddies:** No. **Golf carts:** $20. **Discount golf packages:** No. **Season:** Year-round. **High:** May-Sept. **On site lodging:** No. **Rental clubs:** No. **Walking policy:** Unrestricted walking. **Metal spikes allowed:** Yes. **Range:** No. **To obtain tee times:** Call up to 7 days in advance for weekdays. Call on Monday for upcoming weekend.

★★★½LEWIS RIVER GOLF COURSE

PU-3209 Lewis River Rd., Woodland, 98674, Cowlitz County, (360)225-8254, (800)341-9426, 30 miles N of Portland, OR.

Opened: 1968. **Holes:** 18. **Par:** 72/73. **Yards:** 6,352/5,260. **Course rating:** 69.5/68.9. **Slope:** 124/118. **Architect:** N/A. **Green fee:** $25/$31. **Credit cards:** MC,VISA. **Reduced fees:** Twilight, seniors, juniors. **Caddies:** No. **Golf carts:** $24. **Discount golf packages:** No. **Season:** Year-round. **High:** June-Sept. **On site lodging:** No. **Rental clubs:** Yes. **Walking policy:** Unrestricted walking. **Metal spikes allowed:** Yes. **Range:** Yes (grass). **To obtain tee times:** Call up to 7 days in advance.
Subscriber comments: Excellent year-round course...Short front nine. Long back...Terrific course, good shape, pleasant people...Great improvements after flood of '96. Fun...Great restaurant.

★★½LIBERTY LAKE GOLF CLUB

PU-E. 24403 Sprague, Liberty Lake, 99019, Spokane County, (509)255-6233, 20 miles W of Spokane.

Opened: 1959. **Holes:** 18. **Par:** 70/74. **Yards:** 6,398/5,886. **Course rating:** 69.8/75.7. **Slope:** 121/134. **Architect:** Curly Houston. **Green fee:** $14/$19. **Credit cards:** None. **Reduced fees:** Seniors, juniors. **Caddies:** No. **Golf carts:** $20. **Discount golf packages:** No. **Season:** Year-round. **High:** June-Sept. **On site lodging:** No. **Rental clubs:** Yes. **Walking policy:** Unrestricted walking. **Metal spikes allowed:** Yes. **Range:** Yes (grass/mats). **To obtain tee times:** Call on Tuesday for following week.
Subscriber comments: Nice course for weekend golf, flat. Easy to walk...Back nine is great...Excellent early and late season course...Front nine great...Long par 4s...Looks easy, but difficult.

★★½LIPOMA FIRS GOLF COURSE

PU-18615 110th Ave. E., Puyallup, 98374, Pierce County, (253)841-4396, (800)649-4396, 10 miles SE of Tacoma.

Opened: 1989. **Holes:** 27. **Architect:** Bill Stowe. **Green fee:** $17/$22. **Credit cards:** None. **Reduced fees:** Weekdays, low season, twilight, seniors, juniors. **Caddies:** No. **Golf carts:** $20. **Discount golf packages:** No. **Season:** Year-round. **High:** April-Oct. **On site lodging:** No. **Rental clubs:** Yes. **Walking policy:** Unrestricted walking. **Metal spikes allowed:** Yes. **Range:** Yes (grass/mats). **To obtain tee times:** Call 7 days in advance.

GOLD/BLUE
Par: 72/72. **Yards:** 6,805/5,517. **Course rating:** 72.2/70.8. **Slope:** 122/116.
GREEN/BLUE
Par: 72/72. **Yards:** 6,687/5,473. **Course rating:** 70.0/70.6. **Slope:** 122/117.
GREEN/GOLD
Par: 72/72. **Yards:** 6,722/5,476. **Course rating:** 72.1/70.4. **Slope:** 122/117.

Subscriber comments: Great winter course, drains well...Maturing into a good course...Fairly flat course...Very accommodating.

★★½MADRONA LINKS GOLF COURSE

PU-3604 22nd Ave. N.W., Gig Harbor, 98335, Pierce County, (253)851-5193, 2 miles NW of Tacoma.

Opened: 1978. **Holes:** 18. **Par:** 71/73. **Yards:** 5,602/4,737. **Course rating:** 65.5/65.6. **Slope:** 110/110. **Architect:** Ken Tyson. **Green fee:** $20/$22. **Credit cards:** MC,VISA. **Reduced fees:** Twilight, seniors, juniors. **Caddies:** No. **Golf carts:** $20. **Discount golf packages:** No. **Season:** Year-round. **High:** March-Oct. **On site lodging:** No. **Rental clubs:** Yes. **Walking policy:** Unrestricted walking. **Metal spikes allowed:** Yes. **Range:** Yes (grass/mats). **To obtain tee times:** Call or come in 7 days in advance.
Subscriber comments: Nice local course...Great restaurant...Sweet and short, but don't hit a Madrona tree...Links? Hills and valleys more like it.

★★½MAPLEWOOD GOLF CLUB

PU-4000 Maple Valley Hwy., Renton, 98055, King County, (425)255-3194, 15 miles SE of Seattle.

Opened: 1928. **Holes:** 18. **Par:** 71/72. **Yards:** 5,712/5,040. **Course rating:** 67.4/68.7. **Slope:** 112/114. **Architect:** Al Smith. **Green fee:** $14/$22. **Credit cards:** MC,VISA.

Reduced fees: Seniors, juniors. **Caddies:** No. **Golf carts:** $20. **Discount golf packages:** No. **Season:** Year-round. **High:** March-Nov. **On site lodging:** No. **Rental clubs:** Yes. **Walking policy:** Unrestricted walking. **Metal spikes allowed:** Yes. **Range:** Yes (mats). **To obtain tee times:** Call 7 days in advance for weekdays. Call Monday for upcoming weekend.

Subscriber comments: Nice public clubhouse, a couple of good par 3s...Great with new clubhouse and restaurant...A great mix of styles, tough track.

★★★★MCCORMICK WOODS GOLF COURSE

PU-5155 McCormick Woods Dr. S.W., Port Orchard, 98367, Kitsap County, (360)895-0130, (800)373-0130, 20 miles NW of Tacoma.
Opened: 1988. **Holes:** 18. **Par:** 72/72. **Yards:** 7,040/5,299. **Course rating:** 74.1/71.1. **Slope:** 135/122. **Architect:** Jack Frei. **Green fee:** $22/$52. **Credit cards:** All major. **Reduced fees:** Weekdays, low season, twilight, seniors. **Caddies:** No. **Golf carts:** $22. **Discount golf packages:** No. **Season:** Year-round. **High:** June-Sept. **On site lodging:** No. **Rental clubs:** Yes. **Walking policy:** Unrestricted walking. **Metal spikes allowed:** Yes. **Range:** Yes (grass/mats). **To obtain tee times:** From out of state, call 30 days in advance. State residents call 5 days in advance after 9 a.m. Weekends and holidays require credit card to reserve.
Notes: Ranked 5th in 1997 Best in State.
Subscriber comments: Good one. Very pretty...Interesting course, good winter prices...Bend it right, bend it left...Beautiful setting, well maintained...Tough and gorgeous...Best course in Washington state!...Fairways and greens are immaculate.

★★½MEADOW PARK GOLF COURSE

PU-7108 Lakewood Dr. W., Tacoma, 98467, Pierce County, (253)473-3033, 27 miles S of Seattle.
Opened: 1917. **Holes:** 18. **Par:** 71/73. **Yards:** 6,093/5,262. **Course rating:** 68.9/70.2. **Slope:** 116/115. **Architect:** John Steidel. **Green fee:** $16/$24. **Credit cards:** MC,VISA. **Reduced fees:** Weekdays, seniors, juniors. **Caddies:** No. **Golf carts:** $18. **Discount golf packages:** Yes. **Season:** Year-round. **High:** May-Sept. **On site lodging:** No. **Rental clubs:** Yes. **Walking policy:** Unrestricted walking. **Metal spikes allowed:** Yes. **Range:** Yes. **To obtain tee times:** Call 7 days in advance.
Subscriber comments: Super muny. Nice greens. Fun design...Unique layout, back nine very different from front...Tough muny. Friendly people, nice public course...Never know it's in the middle of Tacoma.

★★★½MEADOWWOOD GOLF COURSE

PU-E. 24501 Valley Way, Liberty Lake, 99019, Spokane County, (509)255-9539, 12 miles E of Spokane.
Opened: 1988. **Holes:** 18. **Par:** 72/72. **Yards:** 6,846/5,880. **Course rating:** 72.1/73.5. **Slope:** 126/131. **Architect:** Robert Muir Graves. **Green fee:** $18/$18. **Credit cards:** None. **Reduced fees:** Seniors, juniors. **Caddies:** No. **Golf carts:** $22. **Discount golf packages:** No. **Season:** March-Nov. **High:** May-Aug. **On site lodging:** No. **Rental clubs:** Yes. **Walking policy:** Walking at certain times. **Metal spikes allowed:** Yes. **Range:** Yes. **To obtain tee times:** Nonresidents may call 10 days in advance.
Subscriber comments: Well kept secret...Good challenging course...Be in shape to walk...Lush and open...Watch out when wind blows...Well conditioned.

★★★½MERIWOOD GOLF COURSE

PU-4550 Meriwood Dr., Lacey, 98516, Thurston County, (360)412-0495, (800)706-1881, 10 miles S of Olympia.
Opened: 1995. **Holes:** 18. **Par:** 72/72. **Yards:** 7,170/5,600. **Course rating:** 74.6/72.8. **Slope:** 128/123. **Architect:** Bill Overdorf. **Green fee:** $30/$47. **Credit cards:** MC,VISA,AMEX. **Reduced fees:** Weekdays, low season, twilight, seniors, juniors. **Caddies:** No. **Golf carts:** Included in Green Fee. **Discount golf packages:** Yes. **Season:** Year-round. **High:** April-Sept. **On site lodging:** No. **Rental clubs:** Yes. **Walking policy:** Mandatory cart. **Metal spikes allowed:** Yes. **Range:** Yes (grass/mats). **To obtain tee times:** Call 30 days in advance.
Subscriber comments: Quiet, peaceful...Tough but fair...Excellent public course...My favorite Puget Sound course.

★★★MINT VALLEY GOLF CLUB

PU-4002 Pennsylvania St., Longview, 98632, Cowlitz County, (360)577-3395, (800)928-8929, 38 miles N of Portland, OR.
Opened: 1976. **Holes:** 18. **Par:** 71/71. **Yards:** 6,379/5,231. **Course rating:** 69.4/69.0. **Slope:** 114/109. **Architect:** Ronald Fream. **Green fee:** $15/$20. **Credit cards:** None. **Reduced fees:** Weekdays, low season, twilight, seniors, juniors. **Caddies:** No. **Golf carts:** $24. **Discount golf packages:** No. **Season:** Year-round. **High:** May-Sept. **On site lodging:** Yes. **Rental clubs:** Yes. **Walking policy:** Unrestricted walking. **Metal spikes allowed:** Yes. **Range:** Yes (grass/mats). **To obtain tee times:** Call up to 7 days in advance.
Subscriber comments: Great people...A high risk/reward course...Flat, fairly wide open, wet in winter...Prettiest course in Washington from June to September.

★★½MOUNT ADAMS COUNTRY CLUB

1250 Rockyford, Toppenish, 98448, Yakima County, (509)865-4440.
Call club for further information.
Subscriber comments: Flat but challenging...Small, fast greens...Working on fairways...Not much variety...Great people!

★★MOUNT SI GOLF COURSE

PU-9010 Boalch Ave. S.E., Snoqualmie, 98065, King County, (425)881-1541, 27 miles SE of Seattle.
Opened: 1927. **Holes:** 18. **Par:** 72/72. **Yards:** 6,304/5,439. **Course rating:** 68.5/68.8. **Slope:** 116/108. **Architect:** Gary Barter. **Green fee:** $23/$28. **Credit cards:** MC,VISA. **Reduced fees:** Low season, twilight, seniors, juniors. **Caddies:** No. **Golf carts:** $22. **Discount golf packages:** No. **Season:** Year-round. **High:** April-Sept. **On site lodging:** No. **Rental clubs:** Yes. **Walking policy:** Unrestricted walking. **Metal spikes allowed:** Yes. **Range:** Yes (grass). **To obtain tee times:** Call anytime.

MOUNTAIN VIEW GOLF COURSE

340 Orchard Dr., North Bend, 98045, King County, (425)888-1817.
Call club for further information.

★★NEWAUKUM VALLEY GOLF COURSE

PU-153 Newaukum Golf Dr., Chehalis, 98532, Lewis County, (360)748-0461, 85 miles SE of Seattle.
Opened: 1979. **Holes:** 27. **Architect:** H.M. Date/J.H. Date. **Green fee:** $10/$20. **Credit cards:** MC,VISA. **Reduced fees:** Weekdays, low season, twilight, seniors, juniors. **Caddies:** No. **Golf carts:** $16. **Discount golf packages:** Yes. **Season:** Year-round. **High:** May-Sept. **On site lodging:** No. **Rental clubs:** Yes. **Walking policy:** Unrestricted walking. **Metal spikes allowed:** Yes. **Range:** No. **To obtain tee times:** Call anytime.
EAST/WEST
Par: 72/72. **Yards:** 6,213/5,287. **Course rating:** 68.4/68.9. **Slope:** 109/110.
SOUTH/EAST
Par: 72/72. **Yards:** 6,168/5,102. **Course rating:** 68.5/68.3. **Slope:** 109/108.
SOUTH/WEST
Par: 72/72. **Yards:** 6,491/5,519. **Course rating:** 69.9/70.6. **Slope:** 113/112.

★★NILE GOLF CLUB

6601 244th S.W., Mountlake Terrace, 98043, Snohomish County, (425)776-5154, 5 miles N of Seattle.
Opened: 1969. **Holes:** 18. **Par:** 68/69. **Yards:** 5,000/4,617. **Course rating:** 64.5/66.0. **Slope:** 105/106. **Architect:** Norman Woods. **Green fee:** $25/$25. **Credit cards:** MC,VISA. **Reduced fees:** Juniors. **Caddies:** No. **Golf carts:** $21. **Discount golf packages:** No. **Season:** Year-round. **High:** June-Aug. **On site lodging:** No. **Rental clubs:** Yes. **Walking policy:** Unrestricted walking. **Metal spikes allowed:** Yes. **Range:** No. **To obtain tee times:** Call.

★★NISQUALLY VALLEY GOLF CLUB

15425 Mosman St. NE, Yelm, 98597, Thurston County, (360)458-3332.
Call club for further information.

WASHINGTON

★★★NORTH BELLINGHAM GOLF COURSE
PU-205 W. Smith Rd., Bellingham, 98226, Whatcom County, (360)398-8300, (888)322-6224.
Opened: 1995. **Holes:** 18. **Par:** 72/72. **Yards:** 6,816/5,160. **Course rating:** 72.1/68.7.
Slope: 124/112. **Architect:** Ted Locke. **Green fee:** $20/$27. **Credit cards:**
MC,VISA,AMEX,DISC,JCB. **Reduced fees:** Weekdays, low season, twilight, seniors,
juniors. **Caddies:** No. **Golf carts:** $11. **Discount golf packages:** Yes. **Season:** Year-round. **High:** May-Sept. **On site lodging:** No. **Rental clubs:** Yes. **Walking policy:**
Unrestricted walking. **Metal spikes allowed:** Yes. **Range:** Yes (grass/mats). **To obtain
tee times:** Call up to 7 days in advance.
Subscriber comments: True links-style course...A bit of old Scotland
transformed...Good winter course, long...Solid gold, I liked it...Drains really
well...Greens greased lightning...Good condition, enjoyable course with reasonable
prices...A great links course. Wind is only problem.

★★★NORTH SHORE GOLF & COUNTRY CLUB
PU-4101 N. Shore Blvd. N.E., Tacoma, 98422, Pierce County, (253)927-1375,
(800)447-1375.
Opened: 1961. **Holes:** 18. **Par:** 71/73. **Yards:** 6,305/5,442. **Course rating:** 69.9/70.7.
Slope: 120/118. **Architect:** Glen Proctor and Roy Goss. **Green fee:** $18/$28. **Credit
cards:** MC,VISA,AMEX. **Reduced fees:** Weekdays, low season, twilight, juniors.
Caddies: No. **Golf carts:** $20. **Discount golf packages:** No. **Season:** Year-round.
High: May-Sept. **On site lodging:** No. **Rental clubs:** Yes. **Walking policy:** Unrestricted
walking. **Metal spikes allowed:** Yes. **Range:** Yes (grass/mats). **To obtain tee times:**
Call 7 days in advance.
Subscriber comments: Excellent design...Nice, fast greens...Challenging and narrow
in spots...A few great holes...Friendly staff...Great pro shop.

★★OAKSRIDGE GOLF COURSE
PU-1052 Monte-Elma Rd., Elma, 98541, Grays Harbor County, (360)482-3511, 80
miles SW of Seattle.
Opened: 1935. **Holes:** 18. **Par:** 70/72. **Yards:** 5,643/5,423. **Course rating:** 65.3/68.9.
Slope: 100/108. **Architect:** N/A. **Green fee:** $12/$14. **Credit cards:** MC,VISA.
Reduced fees: Low season, seniors, juniors. **Caddies:** No. **Golf carts:** $16. **Discount
golf packages:** No. **Season:** Year-round. **High:** June-Sept. **On site lodging:** No.
Rental clubs: Yes. **Walking policy:** Unrestricted walking. **Metal spikes allowed:** Yes.
Range: Yes (mats). **To obtain tee times:** Call up to 1 day in advance.

★★OCEAN SHORES GOLF COURSE
R-500 Canal Dr. N.E., Ocean Shores, 98569, Grays Harbor County, (360)289-3357,
130 miles SW of Seattle.
Opened: 1965. **Holes:** 18. **Par:** 71/72. **Yards:** 6,252/5,173. **Course rating:** 70.2/69.6.
Slope: 115/115. **Architect:** Ray Coleman. **Green fee:** $15/$25. **Credit cards:**
MC,VISA. **Reduced fees:** Low season, seniors, juniors. **Caddies:** No. **Golf carts:** $22.
Discount golf packages: Yes. **Season:** Year-round. **High:** May-Sept. **On site lodging:**
No. **Rental clubs:** Yes. **Walking policy:** Unrestricted walking. **Metal spikes allowed:**
Yes. **Range:** No. **To obtain tee times:** Call up to 1 year in advance; at least 7 days in
advance.

★★★★PORT LUDLOW GOLF COURSE
R-751 Highland Dr., Port Ludlow, 98365, Jefferson County, (360)437-0272, (800)732-1239, 20 miles NW of Seattle.
Opened: 1975. **Holes:** 27. **Architect:** Robert Muir Graves. **Green fee:** $29/$55. **Credit
cards:** MC,VISA,AMEX. **Reduced fees:** Weekdays, low season, resort guests, twilight.
Caddies: No. **Golf carts:** $14. **Discount golf packages:** Yes. **Season:** Year-round.
High: May-Sept. **On site lodging:** Yes. **Rental clubs:** Yes. **Walking policy:**
Unrestricted walking. **Metal spikes allowed:** Yes. **Range:** Yes (grass/mats). **To obtain
tee times:** Resort guests may make tee times up to 6 months in advance. Public may
call up to 7 days in advance.
TIDE/TIMBER
Par: 72/72. **Yards:** 6,787/5,598. **Course rating:** 72.7/72.9. **Slope:** 131/126.

TIMBER/TRAIL
Par: 72/72. **Yards:** 6,746/5,112. **Course rating:** 73.6/70.8. **Slope:** 138/124.
TRAIL/TIDE
Par: 72/72. **Yards:** 6,683/5,192. **Course rating:** 73.1/71.3. **Slope:** 138/124.
Subscriber comments: Fast greens...Great area and natural settings...I love the new nine but boy it is tough...Beautiful! Supreme conditions...No bail out areas. Tough course...One of Washington's best...The original 18 (Tide/Timber) is best.

★★★QUAIL RIDGE GOLF COURSE
PU-3600 Swallows Nest Dr., Clarkston, 99403, Asotin County, (509)758-8501, 100 miles S of Spokane.
Opened: 1966. **Holes:** 18. **Par:** 71/71. **Yards:** 5,861/4,720. **Course rating:** 68.1/66.2. **Slope:** 114/107. **Architect:** Mark Poe. **Green fee:** $13/$15. **Credit cards:** MC,VISA,DISC. **Reduced fees:** Juniors. **Caddies:** No. **Golf carts:** $20. **Discount golf packages:** No. **Season:** Year-round. **High:** April-Sept. **On site lodging:** No. **Rental clubs:** Yes. **Walking policy:** Unrestricted walking. **Metal spikes allowed:** Yes. **Range:** Yes (grass/mats). **To obtain tee times:** Call 7 days in advance.
Subscriber comments: Course has some fun holes...Very nice since the addition of the new nine holes...Get a cart, all holes on a hill...Great layout, accuracy and length needed to score...Rolling terrain, busy but fun course...Nice pro shop and clubhouse.

★★½RIVERBEND GOLF COMPLEX
PU-2019 W. Meeker St., Kent, 98032, King County, (253)854-3673, 18 miles S of Seattle.
Opened: 1989. **Holes:** 18. **Par:** 72/72. **Yards:** 6,633/5,538. **Course rating:** 70.1/70.1. **Slope:** 119/114. **Architect:** John Steidel. **Green fee:** $19/$23. **Credit cards:** MC,VISA. **Reduced fees:** Weekdays, low season, twilight, seniors, juniors. **Caddies:** Yes. **Golf carts:** $20. **Discount golf packages:** No. **Season:** Year-round. **High:** April-Sept. **On site lodging:** Yes. **Rental clubs:** Yes. **Walking policy:** Unrestricted walking. **Metal spikes allowed:** Yes. **Range:** Yes (mats). **To obtain tee times:** Call.
ubscriber comments: Links style...Good track, price is fair, tough...Plays long, lots of water and sand.

★★★RIVERSIDE COUNTRY CLUB
PU-1451 N.W. Airport Rd., Chehalis, 98532, Lewis County, (360)748-8182, (800)242-9486, 27 miles S of Olympia.
Opened: 1945. **Holes:** 18. **Par:** 71/72. **Yards:** 6,155/5,456. **Course rating:** 69.3/71.2. **Slope:** 118/116. **Architect:** Roy Goss and Glen Proctor. **Green fee:** $10/$22. **Credit cards:** MC,VISA,DISC. **Reduced fees:** Weekdays, low season, twilight, seniors, juniors. **Caddies:** No. **Golf carts:** $20. **Discount golf packages:** No. **Season:** Year-round. **High:** April-Sept. **On site lodging:** No. **Rental clubs:** Yes. **Walking policy:** Unrestricted walking. **Metal spikes allowed:** Yes. **Range:** Yes (grass/mats). **To obtain tee times:** Call.
Subscriber comments: Well maintained, super greens...Nice rural course...Floods every year, still great shape...Quiet in the countryside...Never crowded.

★★ROLLING HILLS GOLF COURSE
PU-2485 N.E. McWilliams Rd., Bremerton, 98311, Kitsap County, (360)479-1212.
Opened: 1972. **Holes:** 18. **Par:** 70/70. **Yards:** 5,910/5,465. **Course rating:** 67.9/71.0. **Slope:** 115/117. **Architect:** Don Hogan. **Green fee:** $20/$22. **Credit cards:** All major. **Reduced fees:** Low season, seniors, juniors. **Caddies:** No. **Golf carts:** $20. **Discount golf packages:** No. **Season:** Year-round. **High:** April-Sept. **On site lodging:** No. **Rental clubs:** Yes. **Walking policy:** Unrestricted walking. **Metal spikes allowed:** Yes. **Range:** No. **To obtain tee times:** Call up to 7 days in advance.

★★½SAGE HILLS GOLF CLUB
10400 Sagehill Rd. SE, Warden, 98857, Grant County, (509)349-2603.
Call club for further information.
Subscriber comments: Interesting, some different blind flat holes...Long uphill finishing hole...Greens true and consistent.
Special Notes: Formerly Warden Golf Course.

★★★★ SEMIAHMOO GOLF & COUNTRY CLUB

R-8720 Semiahmoo Pkwy., Blaine, 98230, Whatcom County, (206)371-7005, (800)770-7992, 40 miles S of Vancouver BC.
Opened: 1986. **Holes:** 18. **Par:** 72/72. **Yards:** 7,005/5,288. **Course rating:** 74.5/71.6. **Slope:** 130/126. **Architect:** Arnold Palmer and Ed Seay. **Green fee:** $34/$75. **Credit cards:** MC,VISA,AMEX. **Reduced fees:** Weekdays, low season, resort guests, twilight. **Caddies:** Yes. **Golf carts:** $15. **Discount golf packages:** Yes. **Season:** Year-round. **High:** July-Sept. **On site lodging:** Yes. **Rental clubs:** Yes. **Walking policy:** Unrestricted walking. **Metal spikes allowed:** Yes. **Range:** Yes (grass/mats). **To obtain tee times:** Call 3 days in advance for week-days; 1 day in advance for Saturday and 2 days in advance for Sunday. Hotel guests may book up to 90 days in advance.
Notes: Ranked 7th in 1997 Best in State.
Subscriber comments: Course continues to improve...Nice Palmer design...Friendly and helpful people...Many holes surrounded by trees...Best resort course in Northwest...Great course to walk.

★★★½ SHUKSAN GOLF CLUB

PU-1500 E. Axton Rd., Bellingham, 98226, Whatcom County, (360)398-8888, (800)801-8897, 45 miles S of Vancouver BC.
Opened: 1994. **Holes:** 18. **Par:** 72/72. **Yards:** 6,706/5,253. **Course rating:** 70.3/68.5. **Slope:** 128/118. **Architect:** Rick Dvorak. **Green fee:** $19/$33. **Credit cards:** MC,VISA. **Reduced fees:** Weekdays, low season, twilight, seniors, juniors. **Caddies:** No. **Golf carts:** $11. **Discount golf packages:** Yes. **Season:** Year-round. **High:** April-Oct. **On site lodging:** No. **Rental clubs:** Yes. **Walking policy:** Unrestricted walking. **Metal spikes allowed:** Yes. **Range:** Yes (grass/mats). **To obtain tee times:** Call 7 days in advance.
Subscriber comments: Great clubhouse...The most enjoyable course to play...A great new course. Stunning views on a clear day...Memorable holes...Outstanding public...Great interesting course. I could play this one everyday. Fun-fun-fun.

★★ SIMILK BEACH GOLF COURSE

PU-1250 Christiansen Rd., Anacortes, 98221, Skagit County, (360)293-3444, 31 miles S of Bellingham.
Opened: 1955. **Holes:** 18. **Par:** 72/76. **Yards:** 6,205/5,934. **Course rating:** 68.9/73.3. **Slope:** 111/121. **Architect:** Bill Overdorf. **Green fee:** $18/$20. **Credit cards:** MC,VISA. **Reduced fees:** Weekdays, low season, juniors. **Caddies:** No. **Golf carts:** $20. **Discount golf packages:** No. **Season:** Year-round. **High:** March-Sept. **On site lodging:** No. **Rental clubs:** Yes. **Walking policy:** Unrestricted walking. **Metal spikes allowed:** Yes. **Range:** Yes (grass). **To obtain tee times:** Call anytime in advance.

★★★½ SKAMANIA LODGE GOLF COURSE

R-1131 Skamania Lodge Way, Stevenson, 98671, Skamania County, (509)427-2541, (800)293-0418, 45 miles E of Portland, OR.
Opened: 1993. **Holes:** 18. **Par:** 70/69. **Yards:** 5,776/4,362. **Course rating:** 68.9/65.2. **Slope:** 127/115. **Architect:** Bunny Mason. **Green fee:** $18/$35. **Credit cards:** MC,VISA,AMEX,DISC,Diners Club. **Reduced fees:** Low season, resort guests, twilight, juniors. **Caddies:** No. **Golf carts:** $26. **Discount golf packages:** Yes. **Season:** Year-round. **High:** June-Oct. **On site lodging:** Yes. **Rental clubs:** Yes. **Walking policy:** Unrestricted walking. **Metal spikes allowed:** Yes. **Range:** Yes (grass/mats). **To obtain tee times:** Lodge guests may call upon confirmation of reservations. Others call up to 14 days in advance.

★★★ SNOHOMISH GOLF COURSE

PU-7806 147th Ave. S.E., Snohomish, 98290, Snohomish County, (360)568-2676, 20 miles NE of Seattle.
Opened: 1967. **Holes:** 18. **Par:** 72/74. **Yards:** 6,858/5,980. **Course rating:** 72.7/74.1. **Slope:** 126/129. **Architect:** Roy Goss. **Green fee:** $20/$25. **Credit cards:** MC,VISA. **Reduced fees:** Weekdays, twilight, seniors, juniors. **Caddies:** No. **Golf carts:** $21. **Discount golf packages:** Yes. **Season:** Year-round. **High:** May-Sept. **On site lodging:** No. **Rental clubs:** Yes. **Walking policy:** Unrestricted walking. **Metal spikes allowed:**

Yes. **Range:** Yes (grass/mats). **To obtain tee times:** Call 7 days in advance.
Subscriber comments: Another great course with good value...Great course all
year...Played it last fall for first time. Will now be yearly trip...Nice old treelined course.

★★SNOQUALMIE FALLS GOLF COURSE
PU-35109 Fish Hatchery Rd. SE, Fall City, 98024, King County, (425)222-5244, 25
miles E of Seattle.
Opened: 1963. **Holes:** 18. **Par:** 71/71. **Yards:** 5,413/5,175. **Course rating:** 65.3/68.9.
Slope: 105/114. **Architect:** N/A. **Green fee:** $17/$25. **Credit cards:** MC,VISA.
Reduced fees: Weekdays, low season, seniors, juniors. **Caddies:** No. **Golf carts:** $22.
Discount golf packages: No. **Season:** Year-round. **High:** May-Sept. **On site lodging:**
No. **Rental clubs:** Yes. **Walking policy:** Unrestricted walking. **Metal spikes allowed:**
Yes. **Range:** Yes (grass). **To obtain tee times:** Call up to 6 days in advance.

★★SUDDEN VALLEY GOLF & COUNTRY CLUB
2145 Lake Whatcom Blvd., Bellingham, 98226, Whatcom County, (360)734-6435, 8
miles E of Bellingham.
Opened: 1970. **Holes:** 18. **Par:** 72/72. **Yards:** 6,553/5,627. **Course rating:** 71.8/72.8.
Slope: 126/124. **Architect:** Ted Robinson. **Green fee:** $20/$35. **Credit cards:**
MC,VISA,AMEX. **Reduced fees:** Weekdays, low season, twilight, juniors. **Caddies:** No.
Golf carts: $23. **Discount golf packages:** Yes. **Season:** Year-round. **High:** July-Sept.
On site lodging: No. **Rental clubs:** Yes. **Walking policy:** Unrestricted walking. **Metal
spikes allowed:** Yes. **Range:** Yes (grass/mats). **To obtain tee times:** Call up to 7 days
in advance.
Subscriber comments: Flat front, on lake, very hilly back...Lots of different looks,
great location...Beautiful course, wish it was more inexpensive.

★★SUMNER MEADOWS GOLF LINKS
PU-14802 8th St. E., Sumner, 98390, Pierce County, (253)863-8198, (888)258-3348,
15 miles N of Tacoma.
Opened: 1995. **Holes:** 18. **Par:** 72/72. **Yards:** 6,753/3,564. **Course rating:** 72.2/71.3.
Slope: 128/125. **Architect:** Lynn William Horn. **Green fee:** $16/$26. **Credit cards:**
MC,VISA,AMEX. **Reduced fees:** Weekdays, low season, twilight, seniors, juniors.
Caddies: No. **Golf carts:** $20. **Discount golf packages:** No. **Season:** Year-round.
High: May-Sept. **On site lodging:** No. **Rental clubs:** Yes. **Walking policy:** Unrestricted
walking. **Metal spikes allowed:** Yes. **Range:** Yes (grass/mats). **To obtain tee times:**
Call up to 30 days in advance.
Subscriber comments: Water everywhere! Bring your scuba gear...Good
drainage...Mental challenge from any tee box, must play smart...Best links-style course
in Washington...Nice staff...Short, but water and wind can make challenging.

★★SUN DANCE GOLF COURSE
PU-9725 N. 9 Mile Rd., Nine Mile Falls, 99026, Spokane County, (509)466-4040, 9
miles NW of Spokane.
Opened: 1963. **Holes:** 18. **Par:** 70/72. **Yards:** 6,200/5,910. **Course rating:** 68.0/72.6.
Slope: 112/119. **Architect:** Dale Knott. **Green fee:** $14/$15. **Credit cards:** MC,VISA.
Reduced fees: Weekdays, seniors, juniors. **Caddies:** No. **Golf carts:** $20. **Discount
golf packages:** No. **Season:** March-Nov. **High:** N/A. **On site lodging:** No. **Rental
clubs:** Yes. **Walking policy:** Unrestricted walking. **Metal spikes allowed:** Yes. **Range:**
Yes (mats). **To obtain tee times:** Call up to 7 days in advance.

★★SUN WILLOWS GOLF CLUB
PU-2035 N. 20th St., Pasco, 99301, Franklin County, (509)545-3440, 110 miles N of
Spokane.
Opened: 1959. **Holes:** 18. **Par:** 72/72. **Yards:** 6,800/5,600. **Course rating:** 70.1/68.2.
Slope: 119/119. **Architect:** Robert Muir Graves. **Green fee:** $18/$18. **Credit cards:**
MC,VISA. **Reduced fees:** N/A. **Caddies:** No. **Golf carts:** $24. **Discount golf pack-
ages:** No. **Season:** Year-round. **High:** March-Sept. **On site lodging:** No. **Rental clubs:**
Yes. **Walking policy:** Unrestricted walking. **Metal spikes allowed:** Yes. **Range:** Yes
(grass). **To obtain tee times:** Call up to 7 days in advance.
Subscriber comments: Good cheap golf, little crowded...Fun course, fairly easy.

WASHINGTON

★★★SUNLAND GOLF & COUNTRY CLUB
109 Hilltop Dr., Sequim, 98382, Clallam County, (360)683-8365, 100 miles NE of Seattle.
Opened: 1971. **Holes:** 18. **Par:** 72/73. **Yards:** 6,319/5,557. **Course rating:** 70.4/71.5. **Slope:** 120/120. **Architect:** A. Vernon Macan. **Green fee:** $28/$33. **Credit cards:** MC,VISA. **Reduced fees:** Juniors. **Caddies:** No. **Golf carts:** $22. **Discount golf packages:** No. **Season:** Year-round. **High:** April-Sept. **On site lodging:** No. **Rental clubs:** Yes. **Walking policy:** Unrestricted walking. **Metal spikes allowed:** Yes. **Range:** Yes (grass). **To obtain tee times:** Call seven days in advance.
Subscriber comments: Plays well in winter...Narrow fairways, fast greens, pleasant...Curves to right, slicer's delight.

★★½SUNTIDES GOLF COURSE
PU-231 Pence Rd., Yakima, 98908, Yakima County, (509)966-9065.
Opened: 1963. **Holes:** 18. **Par:** 70/71. **Yards:** 6,015/5,509. **Course rating:** 67.8/70.6. **Slope:** 110/116. **Architect:** Joe Grier. **Green fee:** $18/$18. **Credit cards:** MC,VISA. **Reduced fees:** Juniors. **Caddies:** No. **Golf carts:** $20. **Discount golf packages:** No. **Season:** Feb.-Nov. **High:** May-June. **On site lodging:** No. **Rental clubs:** Yes. **Walking policy:** Unrestricted walking. **Metal spikes allowed:** Yes. **Range:** Yes (mats). **To obtain tee times:** Call 3 days in advance.
Subscriber comments: Good short public course...Crowded...Pleasant course, fast greens...Wide open, condition improving.

★★TALL CHIEF GOLF COURSE
PU-1313 Snoqualmie River Rd. S.E., Fall City, 98024, King County, (425)222-5911, 21 miles SE of Seattle.
Opened: 1965. **Holes:** 18. **Par:** 70/71. **Yards:** 5,422/4,867. **Course rating:** 66.0/66.5. **Slope:** 119/117. **Architect:** Frank Avant. **Green fee:** $20/$23. **Credit cards:** MC,VISA. **Reduced fees:** Weekdays, low season, twilight, seniors, juniors. **Caddies:** No. **Golf carts:** $20. **Discount golf packages:** Yes. **Season:** Year-round. **High:** June-Sept. **On site lodging:** No. **Rental clubs:** Yes. **Walking policy:** Unrestricted walking. **Metal spikes allowed:** Yes. **Range:** No. **To obtain tee times:** Call 6 days in advance.

★★½THREE LAKES GOLF CLUB
2695 Golf Dr., Malaga, 98828, Chelan County, (509)663-5448.
Call club for further information.
Subscriber comments: Tight, fun...Short but tough around greens.

★★½THREE RIVERS GOLF COURSE
PU-2222 S. River Rd., Kelso, 98626, Cowlitz County, (360)423-4653, (800)286-7765, 40 miles N of Portland, OR.
Opened: 1982. **Holes:** 18. **Par:** 72/72. **Yards:** 6,846/5,455. **Course rating:** 72.1/68.5. **Slope:** 127/120. **Architect:** Robert Muir Graves. **Green fee:** $12/$19. **Credit cards:** None. **Reduced fees:** Low season, twilight, seniors, juniors. **Caddies:** No. **Golf carts:** $22. **Discount golf packages:** No. **Season:** Year-round. **High:** May-Sept. **On site lodging:** No. **Rental clubs:** Yes. **Walking policy:** Unrestricted walking. **Metal spikes allowed:** Yes. **Range:** Yes (grass/mats). **To obtain tee times:** Call or come in up to 7 days in advance.
Subscriber comments: Great for beginners, flat wide open...Driest course in Northwest...Outstanding winter course in both condition and price.

★★★TRI-CITY COUNTRY CLUB
314 N. Underwood, Kennewick, 99336, Benton County, (509)783-6014, 120 miles SW of Spokane.
Opened: 1938. **Holes:** 18. **Par:** 65/65. **Yards:** 4,700/4,400. **Course rating:** 62.5/65.2. **Slope:** 112/115. **Architect:** Bert Lesley. **Green fee:** $20/$25. **Credit cards:** None. **Reduced fees:** Juniors. **Caddies:** No. **Golf carts:** $24. **Discount golf packages:** No. **Season:** Year-round. **High:** May-Sept. **On site lodging:** No. **Rental clubs:** Yes. **Walking policy:** Unrestricted walking. **Metal spikes allowed:** Yes. **Range:** No. **To obtain tee times:** Nonmembers may call 2 days in advance.
Subscriber comments: Great short course...Short, par 65, lots of trees...Deceptively tight...Good for short game...Accuracy a must...Made to feel welcome.

★★★TRI-MOUNTAIN GOLF COURSE

PU-1701 N.W. 299th St., Ridgefield, 98642, Clark County, (360)887-3004, 15 miles N of Vancouver, BC.

Opened: 1994. **Holes:** 18. **Par:** 72/72. **Yards:** 6,580/5,284. **Course rating:** 71.1/69.8. **Slope:** 120/117. **Architect:** Bill Robinson. **Green fee:** $23/$29. **Credit cards:** MC,VISA. **Reduced fees:** Weekdays, low season, twilight, seniors, juniors. **Caddies:** No. **Golf carts:** $22. **Discount golf packages:** Yes. **Season:** Year-round. **High:** April-Oct. **On site lodging:** No. **Rental clubs:** Yes. **Walking policy:** Unrestricted walking. **Metal spikes allowed:** Yes. **Range:** Yes (mats). **To obtain tee times:** Call 7 days in advance at 7 a.m.

Subscriber comments: Windy, best public greens in the Northwest...Lots of sand and water...Makes me think...Can't wait for trees to mature...Remote with rustic facilities, but links-style course is top-notch.

★★½TUMWATER VALLEY GOLF CLUB

PU-4611 Tumwater Valley Dr., Tumwater, 98501, Thurston County, (360)943-9500, 60 miles S of Seattle.

Opened: 1970. **Holes:** 18. **Par:** 72/72. **Yards:** 7,154/5,504. **Course rating:** 73.1/70.4. **Slope:** 120/114. **Architect:** Procter and Goss. **Green fee:** $17/$24. **Credit cards:** MC,VISA. **Reduced fees:** Weekdays, low season, twilight, seniors, juniors. **Caddies:** No. **Golf carts:** $20. **Discount golf packages:** No. **Season:** Year-round. **High:** May-Oct. **On site lodging:** No. **Rental clubs:** Yes. **Walking policy:** Unrestricted walking. **Metal spikes allowed:** Yes. **Range:** Yes (grass). **To obtain tee times:** Call up to eight days in advance.

Subscriber comments: Wide fairways most holes, nice walking course...Good summer course...New ownership making good changes!...Good muny...Long from tips...Good test of golf; favorite.

★½TYEE VALLEY GOLF COURSE

PU-2401 S. 192nd, Seattle, 98188, King County, (206)878-3540.
Call club for further information.

★★½VETERANS MEMORIAL GOLF COURSE

PU-201 E. Rees, Walla Walla, 99362, Walla Walla County, (509)527-4507.

Opened: N/A. **Holes:** 18. **Par:** 72/72. **Yards:** 6,311/5,732. **Course rating:** N/A. **Slope:** 114/121. **Architect:** Frank James. **Green fee:** $16/$16. **Credit cards:** None. **Reduced fees:** Seniors, juniors. **Caddies:** No. **Golf carts:** $24. **Discount golf packages:** No. **Season:** Year-round. **High:** April-Sept. **On site lodging:** No. **Rental clubs:** Yes. **Walking policy:** Unrestricted walking. **Metal spikes allowed:** Yes. **Range:** Yes (grass/mats). **To obtain tee times:** Call golf shop.

Subscriber comments: Mature course. Takes advantage of terrain...Friendly pro and staff...Good course...The more you play this course the more you like it.

★★WALTER E. HALL MEMORIAL GOLF COURSE

PM-1226 W. Casino Rd., Everett, 98204, Snohomish County, (425)353-4653, 25 miles N of Seattle.

Opened: 1972. **Holes:** 18. **Par:** 72/73. **Yards:** 6,450/5,657. **Course rating:** 69.6/71.6. **Slope:** 117/118. **Architect:** John Steidel. **Green fee:** $12/$18. **Credit cards:** None. **Reduced fees:** Seniors, juniors. **Caddies:** No. **Golf carts:** N/A. **Discount golf packages:** No. **Season:** Year-round. **High:** April-Oct. **On site lodging:** No. **Rental clubs:** Yes. **Walking policy:** Unrestricted walking. **Metal spikes allowed:** Yes. **Range:** No. **To obtain tee times:** Call 7 days in advance for weekdays. Call on Monday at 9 a.m. for upcoming weekend.

★★½WANDERMERE GOLF COURSE

PU-N. 13700 Division St., Spokane, 99208, Spokane County, (509)466-8023, 10 miles N of Spokane.

Opened: 1929. **Holes:** 18. **Par:** 70/71. **Yards:** 6,115/5,420. **Course rating:** 68.9/70.7. **Slope:** 109/111. **Architect:** Lee Wayne Ross. **Green fee:** $16/$17. **Credit cards:** MC,VISA. **Reduced fees:** Seniors, juniors. **Caddies:** No. **Golf carts:** $22. **Discount golf packages:** No. **Season:** March-Nov. **High:** June-Sept. **On site lodging:** No. **Rental clubs:** Yes. **Walking policy:** Unrestricted walking. **Metal spikes allowed:** Yes.

Range: Yes (grass/mats). **To obtain tee times:** Call up to 1 day in advance for weekdays; up to 7 days in advance for weekends beginning at 6:30 a.m.
Subscriber comments: It's fun...Wide open...You play up the hill and down the valley...Well run...Nice place to spend an afternoon.

★½WEST RICHLAND MUNICIPAL GOLF COURSE

PM-4000 Fallon Dr., West Richland, 99352, Benton County, (509)967-2165, 200 miles E of Seattle.
Opened: 1950. **Holes:** 18. **Par:** 70/70. **Yards:** 6,103/5,516. **Course rating:** 67.7/70.3. **Slope:** 114/114. **Architect:** N/A. **Green fee:** $13/$13. **Credit cards:** N/A. **Reduced fees:** N/A. **Caddies:** No. **Golf carts:** $20. **Discount golf packages:** No. **Season:** Year-round. **High:** March-Oct. **On site lodging:** No. **Rental clubs:** Yes. **Walking policy:** Unrestricted walking. **Metal spikes allowed:** Yes. **Range:** Yes (grass). **To obtain tee times:** Call.

★★½WEST SEATTLE GOLF COURSE

PU-4470 35th Ave. S.W., Seattle, 98126, King County, (206)935-5187, 5 miles S of Seattle.
Opened: 1939. **Holes:** 18. **Par:** 72/72. **Yards:** 6,600/5,700. **Course rating:** 70.9/72.6. **Slope:** 119/123. **Architect:** HC Egan. **Green fee:** $18/$18. **Credit cards:** MC,VISA. **Reduced fees:** Twilight, seniors, juniors. **Caddies:** No. **Golf carts:** $20. **Discount golf packages:** No. **Season:** Year-round. **High:** May-Sept. **On site lodging:** No. **Rental clubs:** Yes. **Walking policy:** Unrestricted walking. **Metal spikes allowed:** Yes. **Range:** No. **To obtain tee times:** Call up to 6 days in advance.
Subscriber comments: Best of the Seattle munys...Great value, getting better.

★★★WILLOWS RUN GOLF CLUB

PU-10402 Willows Rd. N.E., Redmond, 98052, King County, (425)883-1200, 7 miles N of Bellevue.
Opened: 1994. **Holes:** 18. **Par:** 72/72. **Yards:** 6,806/5,633. **Course rating:** 71.6/71.4. **Slope:** 119/121. **Architect:** Lisa Maki. **Green fee:** $29/$42. **Credit cards:** MC,VISA. **Reduced fees:** Weekdays, low season, twilight, seniors, juniors. **Caddies:** Yes. **Golf carts:** $22. **Discount golf packages:** Yes. **Season:** Year-round. **High:** March-Oct. **On site lodging:** No. **Rental clubs:** Yes. **Walking policy:** Unrestricted walking. **Metal spikes allowed:** Yes. **Range:** Yes (grass/mats). **To obtain tee times:** Call 7 days in advance.
Subscriber comments: Super golf course...Links course, good test...Good staff...New course withinin wetlands, no trees...First nine and second nine are similar.

★★½BEL MEADOW COUNTRY CLUB
Rte. 1 Box 450, Mount Clare, 26408, Harrison County, (304)623-3701, 5 miles S of Clarksburg.
Opened: 1965. **Holes:** 18. **Par:** 72/72. **Yards:** 6,938/5,517. **Course rating:** 73.0/71.5.
Slope: 126/122. **Architect:** Robert Trent Jones. **Green fee:** $17/$20. **Credit cards:**
MC,VISA,DISC. **Reduced fees:** Weekdays, low season, twilight, seniors. **Caddies:** No.
Golf carts: $11. **Discount golf packages:** No. **Season:** Year-round. **High:** May-Sept.
On site lodging: No. **Rental clubs:** Yes. **Walking policy:** Walking at certain times.
Metal spikes allowed: Yes. **Range:** Yes (grass/mats). **To obtain tee times:** Call 7 days in advance during season (April-Oct.) for weekends and holidays.
Subscriber comments: Challenging and very fun to play!...Nice folks, making a commitment to restore...Tough for high handicaps.

★★BIG BEND GOLF CLUB
PU-P.O. Box 329, Tornado, 25202, Kanawha County, (304)341-8023, 15 miles SW of Charleston.
Opened: 1964. **Holes:** 18. **Par:** 71/72. **Yards:** 6,327/5,762. **Course rating:** 69.6.
Slope: 116. **Architect:** Evans Family. **Green fee:** $12/$14. **Credit cards:** None.
Reduced fees: N/A. **Caddies:** No. **Golf carts:** $19. **Discount golf packages:** No.
Season: Year-round. **High:** May-Oct. **On site lodging:** No. **Rental clubs:** No. **Walking policy:** Unrestricted walking. **Metal spikes allowed:** Yes. **Range:** No. **To obtain tee times:** Call up to 7 days in advance.

★★★½CACAPON RESORT
R-Rt. 1, Box 304, Berkeley Springs, 25411, Morgan County, (304)258-1022, (800)225-5982, 25 miles N of Winchester, VA.
Opened: 1974. **Holes:** 18. **Par:** 72/72. **Yards:** 6,940/5,510. **Course rating:** 72.3/70.8.
Slope: 126/118. **Architect:** Robert Trent Jones. **Green fee:** $19/$22. **Credit cards:**
MC,VISA. **Reduced fees:** Low season, seniors. **Caddies:** No. **Golf carts:** $19.
Discount golf packages: Yes. **Season:** Year-round weather permitting. **High:** April-Oct.
On site lodging: Yes. **Rental clubs:** Yes. **Walking policy:** Unrestricted walking. **Metal spikes allowed:** Yes. **Range:** Yes (grass). **To obtain tee times:** Resort guests with lodging deposit; all others call 7 days in advance.
Subscriber comments: West Virginia gem, unique par 3s...Mid-October is the best time to go—unforgettable...Eastern US's best kept secret...Very nice for state-run course, has nice variety...Golf, value and scenery are outstanding.

★★★½CANAAN VALLEY RESORT GOLF COURSE
R-Rte. 1, Box 330, Davis, 26260, Tucker County, (304)866-4121x2632, (800)622-4121, 80 miles W of Harrisonburg, VA.
Opened: 1968. **Holes:** 18. **Par:** 72/72. **Yards:** 6,982/5,820. **Course rating:** 73.4/71.8.
Slope: 125/115. **Architect:** Geoffrey Cornish. **Green fee:** $24/$24. **Credit cards:**
MC,VISA,AMEX,DISC,Diners Club. **Reduced fees:** Seniors. **Caddies:** No. **Golf carts:**
$30. **Discount golf packages:** Yes. **Season:** April-Nov. **High:** June-Aug. **On site lodging:** Yes. **Rental clubs:** Yes. **Walking policy:** Unrestricted walking. **Metal spikes allowed:** Yes. **Range:** Yes (grass/mats). **To obtain tee times:** Resort guests may book tee times with room reservations.
Subscriber comments: Wonderful scenery—watch out for the deer!...Beautiful layout, great views...Very good condition...Shotmaker's course.

1884 OAKHURST LINKS
PU-1 Montague Lane, White Sulpher Springs, 24986, (304)536-1884.
Opened: 1884. **Holes:** 9. **Par:** N/A. **Yards:** 2,235. **Course rating:** N/A. **Slope:** N/A.
Architect: Russel Montague/Bob Cupp. **Green fee:** $65/$65. **Credit cards:**
MC,VISA,DISC. **Reduced fees:** N/A. **Caddies:** No. **Golf carts:** N/A. **Discount golf packages:** No. **Season:** May-Nov. **High:** Sept. **On site lodging:** No. **Rental clubs:** No.
Walking policy: Unrestricted walking. **Metal spikes allowed:** Yes. **Range:** No. **To obtain tee times:** Call anytime in advance.
Special Notes: Unique antique course. One of the oldest golf courses in the US. Equipment included with green fees.

★★★ESQUIRE COUNTRY CLUB

PU-Esquire Dr., Barboursville, 25504, Cabell County, (304)736-1476.
Opened: N/A. **Holes:** 18. **Par:** 72/72. **Yards:** 6,905/5,250. **Course rating:** 72.2/69.2.
Slope: 116/104. **Architect:** X.G. Hassenplug. **Green fee:** $27/$29. **Credit cards:**
None. **Reduced fees:** N/A. **Caddies:** No. **Golf carts:** Included in Green Fee. **Discount golf packages:** No. **Season:** Year-round. **High:** April-Oct. **On site lodging:** No. **Rental clubs:** Yes. **Walking policy:** Walking at certain times. **Metal spikes allowed:** Yes.
Range: No. **To obtain tee times:** Call up to 7 days in advance.
Subscriber comments: Long course, mostly wide open...Well-kept, hard to find...A good course made better by the staff...No sand on course, grass bunkers tough...Three beautiful finishing holes...Decent public course with good length.

★★★★GLADE SPRINGS RESORT

R-200 Lake Dr., Daniels, 25832, Raleigh County, (304)763-2050, (800)634-5233, 8 miles S of Beckley.
Opened: 1973. **Holes:** 18. **Par:** 72/72. **Yards:** 6,941/4,884. **Course rating:** 73.5/67.6.
Slope: 135/118. **Architect:** George Cobb. **Green fee:** $40/$65. **Credit cards:**
MC,VISA,AMEX. **Reduced fees:** Weekdays, low season, resort guests, twilight, juniors.
Caddies: No. **Golf carts:** Included in Green Fee. **Discount golf packages:** Yes.
Season: Year-round. **High:** May-Oct. **On site lodging:** Yes. **Rental clubs:** Yes. **Walking policy:** Unrestricted walking. **Metal spikes allowed:** Yes. **Range:** Yes (grass). **To obtain tee times:** Resort guests may book tee times with confirmed room reservation. Public may call 7 days in advance.
Notes: Ranked 5th in 1997 Best in State.
Subscriber comments: Beautiful resort...Wonderful layout, great experience...Beautiful, challenging course, nice practice area...Great layout in woods of W.Va....One of the nicest in state, a high price for me but fair for facility.

★★½GOLF CLUB OF WEST VIRGINIA

PU-Box 199, Rte. 1, Waverly, 26184, Wood County, (304)464-4420, 10 miles NE of Parkersburg.
Opened: 1950. **Holes:** 18. **Par:** 70/71. **Yards:** 6,018/5,011. **Course rating:** 68.9/67.9.
Slope: 116/109. **Architect:** Lauren Parish. **Green fee:** $20/$25. **Credit cards:**
MC,VISA,DISC. **Reduced fees:** Weekdays, low season, twilight, seniors, juniors.
Caddies: No. **Golf carts:** N/A. **Discount golf packages:** Yes. **Season:** Year-round.
High: April-Sept. **On site lodging:** No. **Rental clubs:** Yes. **Walking policy:**
Unrestricted walking. **Metal spikes allowed:** Yes. **Range:** No. **To obtain tee times:**
Call anytime.
Subscriber comments: Rolling hills...Fun course—not long...Decent muny...Hilly course, nice layout, take a cart...Quaint, good for high handicap.

★★★GRANDVIEW COUNTRY CLUB

PU-1500 Scottridge Dr., Beaver, 25813, Raleigh County, (304)763-2520, 8 miles S of Beckley.
Opened: 1973. **Holes:** 18. **Par:** 72/72. **Yards:** 6,834/4,910. **Course rating:** 70.2/67.3.
Slope: 112/107. **Architect:** Randy Scott/Glenn Scott. **Green fee:** $13/$17. **Credit cards:** None. **Reduced fees:** N/A. **Caddies:** No. **Golf carts:** $18. **Discount golf packages:** No. **Season:** May-Nov. **High:** June-Aug. **On site lodging:** No. **Rental clubs:** No.
Walking policy: Walking at certain times. **Metal spikes allowed:** Yes. **Range:** Yes (grass). **To obtain tee times:** Call.
Subscriber comments: Great experiences...Easy, fun...Interesting back nine...Best course in W.Va. Par-3 No.15 most beautiful hole...Well kept, scenic, very affordable.

THE GREENBRIER

R-300 W. Main St., White Sulphur Springs, 24986, Greenbrier County, (304)536-1110, (800)624-6070, 250 miles SW of Washington, DC.
Credit cards: MC,VISA,AMEX,Diners Club. **Caddies:** Yes. **Golf carts:** Included in Green Fee. **Discount golf packages:** Yes. **High:** April-Oct.
On site lodging: Yes. **Rental clubs:** Yes. **Walking policy:** Unrestricted walking; caddies in the morning. **Metal spikes allowed:** No. **Range:** Yes (grass/mats).
To obtain tee times: Resort guests call up to 4 months in advance. Public may call up to 3 days in advance.

GREAT SERVICE

WEST VIRGINIA

★★★★½GREENBRIER COURSE
Opened: 1925. **Holes:** 18. **Par:** 72/72. **Yards:** 6,681/5,150. **Course rating:** 73.1/70.1.
Slope: 135/119. **Architect:** Seth Raynor/Jack Nicklaus. **Green fee:** $80/$225.
Reduced fees: Resort guests, juniors. **Season:** April-Nov.
Notes: Ranked 2nd in 1997 Best in State. 1994 Solheim Cup; 1979 Ryder Cup.
Subscriber comments: Very comfortable place...Great course, great service...May be best resort course in US. Little slice of heaven...All that you would expect at Greenbrier...Classic golf—as it should be!...Long and difficult; placement shots...Great course but hard, bunkers placed where I hit it.

★★★★LAKESIDE COURSE
Opened: 1963. **Holes:** 18. **Par:** 70/70. **Yards:** 6,336/5,020. **Course rating:** 69.8/68.3.
Slope: 122/113. **Architect:** Dick Wilson. **Green fee:** $42/$225. **Reduced fees:** Low season. **Season:** Year-round.
Subscriber comments: Fantastic...Challenging and peaceful...A special place...Wide open...Not long, but tough, well kept...Excellent golf course.

★★★★OLD WHITE COURSE
Opened: 1913. **Holes:** 18. **Par:** 70/70. **Yards:** 6,640/5,658. **Course rating:** 72.1/69.9.
Slope: 130/119. **Architect:** C.B. Macdonald and S.J. Raynor. **Green fee:** $80/$225.
Reduced fees: Low season, juniors. **Season:** Year-round.
Notes: Ranked 3rd in 1997 Best in State.
Subscriber comments: Super Macdonald layout. Love it...Great course, expensive and great staff...Fantastic...A special place...Superb and difficult greens...A primer in classic design, one of my favorites in the world...Beautiful setting, great fairway turf...Wonderful old course.

GREENBRIER VALLEY COUNTRY CLUB
Rte. 219 N., Lewisburg, 24901, Greenbrier County, (304)645-3660.
Call club for further information.

★★GREENHILLS COUNTRY CLUB
Rte. 56, Ravenswood, 26164, Jackson County, (304)273-3396.
Opened: 1960. **Holes:** 18. **Par:** 72/74. **Yards:** 6,056/5,018. **Course rating:** 68.6/69.0.
Slope: 119/108. **Architect:** Paul Lemon. **Green fee:** $15/$22. **Credit cards:**
MC,VISA,DISC. **Reduced fees:** Weekdays, low season, resort guests. **Caddies:** No.
Golf carts: $8. **Discount golf packages:** Yes. **Season:** Year-round. **High:** April-Oct.
On site lodging: Yes. **Rental clubs:** No. **Walking policy:** Unrestricted walking. **Metal spikes allowed:** Yes. **Range:** Yes (grass/mats). **To obtain tee times:** Call up to 6 days in advance.
Subscriber comments: Some tight holes due to evergreens...Short, good greens...Excellent all-around course.

★★★★HAWTHORNE VALLEY GOLF COURSE
R-10 Snowshoe Dr., Snowshoe, 26209, Slatyfork County, (304)572-1000.
Opened: 1994. **Holes:** 18. **Par:** 72/72. **Yards:** 7,045/4,363. **Course rating:** 72.1/64.3.
Slope: 130/103. **Architect:** Gary Player. **Green fee:** $43/$58. **Credit cards:**
MC,VISA,AMEX. **Reduced fees:** Weekdays, low season, resort guests. **Caddies:** No.
Golf carts: Included in Green Fee. **Discount golf packages:** Yes. **Season:** May-Nov.
High: July-Sept. **On site lodging:** Yes. **Rental clubs:** Yes. **Walking policy:** Mandatory cart. **Metal spikes allowed:** Yes. **Range:** Yes (grass). **To obtain tee times:** Call.
Notes: Ranked 4th in 1997 Best in State.
Subscriber comments: Beautiful, challenging course...Incredible! Breathtaking, a must play!...Staff was courteous, respectful, efficient and even sympathetic.

★★½HIGHLAND SPRINGS GOLF COURSE
PU-1600 Washington Pike, Wellsburg, 26070, Brooke County, (304)737-2201.
Opened: 1963. **Holes:** 18. **Par:** 72/75. **Yards:** 6,853/5,739. **Course rating:** 72.4/72.1.
Slope: 118/113. **Architect:** James Gilmore Harrison. **Green fee:** $7/$18. **Credit cards:**
MC,VISA. **Reduced fees:** Weekdays, seniors, juniors. **Caddies:** No. **Golf carts:** N/A.
Discount golf packages: No. **Season:** March-Dec. **High:** June-Aug. **On site lodging:**
No. **Rental clubs:** No. **Walking policy:** Unrestricted walking. **Metal spikes allowed:**
Yes. **Range:** No. **To obtain tee times:** Call in advance for weekends and holidays.
Subscriber comments: Good local...Good layout and greens, marginal fairways and tees...Open course, not easy, clubhouse adequate...Great in spring...No frills golf.

LAKEVIEW RESORT & CONFERENCE CENTER

R-Rte. 6 Box 88A, Morgantown, 26505, Monongalia County, (304)594-2011, (800)624-8300, 60 miles S of Pittsburgh.
Credit cards: MC,VISA,AMEX,DISC,Diners Club. **Reduced fees:** Weekdays, low season, resort guests, juniors. **Caddies:** No. **Golf carts:** $15. **Discount golf packages:** Yes. **High:** June-Sept. **On site lodging:** Yes. **Rental clubs:** Yes. **Walking policy:** Mandatory cart. **Metal spikes allowed:** Yes. **Range:** Yes (grass/mats). **To obtain tee times:** Hotel guests may call up to 14 days in advance. Public may call 10 days in advance.

★★★★LAKEVIEW COURSE

Opened: 1953. **Holes:** 18. **Par:** 72/72. **Yards:** 6,800/5,432. **Course rating:** 72.8/71.8. **Slope:** 130/118. **Architect:** Jim Harrison. **Green fee:** $25/$45. **Season:** Year-round.
Subscriber comments: Great surroundings and view—excellent in every way...Very good resort package. Hilly...Soft terrain, plays long, treelined, elevation changes are tough...Scenic, lots of water, challenging greens.

★★★MOUNTAINVIEW COURSE

Opened: 1984. **Holes:** 18. **Par:** 72/72. **Yards:** 6,447/5,242. **Course rating:** 70.7/69.4. **Slope:** 119/122. **Architect:** Brian Ault. **Green fee:** $22/$27. **Season:** April-Oct.
Subscriber comments: Well-named...Getting better each year, hilly, fun...Magnificent views...Difficult, hilly course...Sidehill lies abound...Some long par 5s. Great accommodations...If you play both courses on a package you can't beat price, food and service!.

★★★LAVELETTE GOLF CLUB

PU-Lynn Oak Dr., Lavalette, 25535, Wayne County, (304)525-7405, 5 miles S of Huntington.
Opened: 1991. **Holes:** 18. **Par:** 71/71. **Yards:** 6,262/5,257. **Course rating:** 69.5/72.6. **Slope:** 118/120. **Architect:** Bill Ward Jr. **Green fee:** $15/$17. **Credit cards:** All major. **Reduced fees:** Weekdays. **Caddies:** No. **Golf carts:** $11. **Discount golf packages:** No. **Season:** Year-round. **High:** May-Sept. **On site lodging:** No. **Rental clubs:** Yes. **Walking policy:** Unrestricted walking. **Metal spikes allowed:** Yes. **Range:** Yes (grass/mats). **To obtain tee times:** Call 6 days in advance.
Subscriber comments: Great condition...Very hilly—some interesting holes...Has a par-6 hole...Always well kept.

★★½LEWISBURG ELKS COUNTRY CLUB

PU-Rte. 219 N., Lewisburg, 24901, Greenbrier County, (304)645-3660, 70 miles S of Roanoke.
Opened: 1940. **Holes:** 18. **Par:** 70/70. **Yards:** 5,609/4,373. **Course rating:** 65.0/65.5. **Slope:** 108/110. **Architect:** Ray Vaughan. **Green fee:** $14/$17. **Credit cards:** MC,VISA. **Reduced fees:** Weekdays, low season. **Caddies:** No. **Golf carts:** $9. **Discount golf packages:** Yes. **Season:** Year-round. **High:** April-Nov. **On site lodging:** No. **Rental clubs:** Yes. **Walking policy:** Unrestricted walking. **Metal spikes allowed:** Yes. **Range:** No. **To obtain tee times:** Call.
Subscriber comments: Fun course, well maintained...Great little course...Short, tight course—postage stamp green.

★★★½LOCUST HILL GOLF COURSE

1 St. Andrews Dr., Charles Town, 25414, Jefferson County, (304)728-7300, 60 miles W of Washington, D.C.
Opened: 1991. **Holes:** 18. **Par:** 72/72. **Yards:** 7,005/5,112. **Course rating:** 73.5/72.0. **Slope:** 128/120. **Architect:** Edmund Ault/Guy Rando. **Green fee:** $15/$28. **Credit cards:** MC,VISA. **Reduced fees:** Weekdays, low season, twilight, seniors. **Caddies:** No. **Golf carts:** $12. **Discount golf packages:** Yes. **Season:** Year-round. **High:** May-Oct. **On site lodging:** No. **Rental clubs:** Yes. **Walking policy:** Walking at certain times. **Metal spikes allowed:** Yes. **Range:** Yes (grass). **To obtain tee times:** Call Monday after 7 a.m. for upcoming weekend. Call up to 7 days in advance for weekdays.
Subscriber comments: Good course for reasonable fees. Test all the shots...Tough but fair—if you score well here, you've played well...Challenging water holes, especially 15th and 18th...A great gem hidden away but convenient for Washington DC players.

MEADOW PONDS GOLF COURSE
PU-Rte. 7 W., Cassville, 26527, Monongalia County, (304)328-5570.
Opened: 1963. **Holes:** 18. **Par:** 69/69. **Yards:** 5,328/5,026. **Course rating:** 64.9/63.9.
Slope: 102/100. **Architect:** Bob Holt. **Green fee:** $10/$12. **Credit cards:** All major.
Reduced fees: Weekdays. **Caddies:** No. **Golf carts:** N/A. **Discount golf packages:**
No. **Season:** Year-round. **High:** N/A. **On site lodging:** No. **Rental clubs:** Yes. **Walking policy:** Unrestricted walking. **Metal spikes allowed:** Yes. **Range:** Yes (grass). **To obtain tee times:** Call Mondays.

OGLEBAY RESORT & CONFERENCE CENTER
PU-Oglebay Park, Rte. 88N., Wheeling, 26003, Ohio County, (304)243-4050, (800)624-6988, 55 miles SW of Pittsburgh.
Credit cards: All major. **Reduced fees:** Weekdays, resort guests. **Caddies:** Yes.
Discount golf packages: Yes. **On site lodging:** Yes. **Rental clubs:** Yes. **Walking policy:** Unrestricted walking. **Metal spikes allowed:** Yes. **Range:** No. **To obtain tee times:** Resort guests may call up to 1 year in advance with reservation. Public may call up to 60 days in advance.
★★CRISPIN COURSE
Opened: 1933. **Holes:** 18. **Par:** 71/71. **Yards:** 5,627/5,100. **Course rating:** 66.6/68.4.
Slope: 109/103. **Architect:** Robert Biery. **Green fee:** $18/$18. **Golf carts:** $11.
Season: Year-round. **High:** May-Aug.
★★★½SPEIDEL COURSE
Opened: 1971. **Holes:** 18. **Par:** 71/71. **Yards:** 7,000/5,241. **Course rating:** 73.5/69.7.
Slope: 137/120. **Architect:** Robert Trent Jones. **Green fee:** $30/$35. **Golf carts:** $12.
Season: March-Nov. **High:** May-Aug.
Subscriber comments: Very scenic, excellent...Caters to locals, but when you can get in, great golf...Well worth the drive from Cleveland.

★★★½PIPESTEM GOLF CLUB
PU-Pipestem State Park, Pipestem, 25979, Summers County, (304)466-1800, (800)225-5982.
Opened: 1970. **Holes:** 18. **Par:** 72/72. **Yards:** 6,884/5,623. **Course rating:** 72.4/72.0.
Slope: 124/117. **Architect:** Geoffrey Cornish. **Green fee:** $17/$22. **Credit cards:**
MC,VISA,AMEX. **Reduced fees:** Weekdays, low season, seniors. **Caddies:** No. **Golf carts:** $19. **Discount golf packages:** Yes. **Season:** Year-round. **High:** May-Sept. **On site lodging:** Yes. **Rental clubs:** Yes. **Walking policy:** Unrestricted walking. **Metal spikes allowed:** Yes. **Range:** Yes (grass). **To obtain tee times:** Guests may book tee times with room reservation. Public may call 7 days in advance.
Subscriber comments: Several exceptional holes...Easy to play...Nice greens, great setting...Good mountain course, long from blues. Lodge views beautiful...Good golf package...Fun to play, great scenery.

★★½RIVERSIDE GOLF CLUB
PU-Rte. 1, Mason, 25260, Mason County, (304)773-5354, (800)261-3031.
Opened: 1975. **Holes:** 18. **Par:** 70/72. **Yards:** 6,198/4,842. **Course rating:** 69.2/72.0.
Slope: 118/117. **Architect:** Kidwell and Hurdzan. **Green fee:** $12/$14. **Credit cards:**
MC,VISA. **Reduced fees:** Weekdays. **Caddies:** No. **Golf carts:** $8. **Discount golf packages:** No. **Season:** Year-round. **High:** April-Sept. **On site lodging:** No. **Rental clubs:** Yes. **Walking policy:** Unrestricted walking. **Metal spikes allowed:** Yes. **Range:** No. **To obtain tee times:** Call.
Subscriber comments: Nice middle-of-the-road public course...Flat course—easy to walk...Good for a change.

★★SANDY BRAE GOLF COURSE
PU-19 Osborne Mills Rd., Clendenin, 25045, Kanawha County, (304)341-8004, 25 miles N of Charleston.
Opened: 1965. **Holes:** 18. **Par:** 69/74. **Yards:** 5,648/5,312. **Course rating:** 66.7.
Slope: 101/98. **Architect:** Edmund B. Ault. **Green fee:** $11/$14. **Credit cards:**
MC,VISA. **Reduced fees:** Weekdays, low season, twilight, seniors. **Caddies:** No. **Golf carts:** $8. **Discount golf packages:** No. **Season:** Year-round. **High:** April-Oct. **On site lodging:** No. **Rental clubs:** Yes. **Walking policy:** Unrestricted walking. **Metal spikes allowed:** Yes. **Range:** No. **To obtain tee times:** Call 7 days in advance.

★★½SCARLET OAKS COUNTRY CLUB

2 Dairy Rd., Poca, 25159, Putnam County, (304)755-8079, 15 miles NW of Charleston.
Opened: 1980. **Holes:** 18. **Par:** 72/72. **Yards:** 6,700/5,036. **Course rating:** 72.3/69.3.
Slope: 129/109. **Architect:** McDavid family. **Green fee:** $27/$30. **Credit cards:**
MC,VISA,AMEX,DISC,Diners Club. **Reduced fees:** N/A. **Caddies:** No. **Golf carts:**
Included in Green Fee. **Discount golf packages:** No. **Season:** March-Dec. **High:**
June-July. **On site lodging:** No. **Rental clubs:** Yes. **Walking policy:** Mandatory cart.
Metal spikes allowed: Yes. **Range:** Yes (grass). **To obtain tee times:** Call 7 days in
advance.
Subscriber comments: Very tight, well kept, nice people here...Target course...Tight
course—good course for all-round player...Short, narrow, shotmaker's course.

★½SLEEPY HOLLOW GOLF & COUNTRY CLUB

Golf Course Rd., Charles Town, 25414, Jefferson County, (304)725-5210.
Opened: 1962. **Holes:** 18. **Par:** 72/72. **Yards:** 6,600/5,766. **Course rating:** 70.6/72.3.
Slope: 115/104. **Architect:** L.L. Love. **Green fee:** $10/$17. **Credit cards:** None.
Reduced fees: Weekdays, low season, twilight, seniors. **Caddies:** No. **Golf carts:** $12.
Discount golf packages: No. **Season:** Year-round. **High:** May-Aug. **On site lodging:**
No. **Rental clubs:** Yes. **Walking policy:** Unrestricted walking. **Metal spikes allowed:**
Yes. **Range:** Yes (grass). **To obtain tee times:** Call anytime.

★★SOUTH HILLS GOLF CLUB

PU-1253 Gihon Rd., Parkersburg, 26101, Wood County, (304)422-8381, 70 miles N of
Charleston.
Opened: 1953. **Holes:** 18. **Par:** 71/71. **Yards:** 6,467/4,842. **Course rating:** 71.2/70.3.
Slope: 129/115. **Architect:** Gary Grandstaff. **Green fee:** $13/$15. **Credit cards:** All
major. **Reduced fees:** Low season. **Caddies:** No. **Golf carts:** $9. **Discount golf packages:** Yes. **Season:** Year-round. **High:** May-Sept. **On site lodging:** No. **Rental clubs:**
Yes. **Walking policy:** Unrestricted walking. **Metal spikes allowed:** Yes. **Range:** Yes
(grass). **To obtain tee times:** Call.

★★½STONEBRIDGE GOLF CLUB

Burke St. Ext., Rte. 5, Martinsburg, 25401, Berkeley County, (304)263-4653, 60 miles
W of Washington, DC.
Opened: 1922. **Holes:** 18. **Par:** 71/72. **Yards:** 6,161/4,996. **Course rating:** 69.7/67.9.
Slope: 119/108. **Architect:** Bob Elder. **Green fee:** $16/$25. **Credit cards:** All major.
Reduced fees: Weekdays, low season, resort guests, twilight. **Caddies:** No. **Golf
carts:** $11. **Discount golf packages:** Yes. **Season:** Year-round weather permitting.
High: May-Sept. **On site lodging:** No. **Rental clubs:** Yes. **Walking policy:** Walking at
certain times. **Metal spikes allowed:** Yes. **Range:** Yes (grass/mats). **To obtain tee
times:** Call 7 days in advance.
Subscriber comments: A classic front nine, with a newly designed back nine, make
for a fun and memorable 18 holes...Play it in the fall of the year.

★★SUGARWOOD GOLF CLUB

PU-Sugarwood Rd., Lavalette, 25535, Wayne County, (304)523-6500, 6 miles S of
Huntington.
Opened: 1965. **Holes:** 18. **Par:** 69. **Yards:** 6,000. **Course rating:** 66.7. **Slope:** 102.
Architect: Dave Whechel. **Green fee:** $15/$17. **Credit cards:** MC,VISA. **Reduced
fees:** N/A. **Caddies:** No. **Golf carts:** $10. **Discount golf packages:** No. **Season:** Year-round. **High:** May-Sept. **On site lodging:** No. **Rental clubs:** Yes. **Walking policy:**
Unrestricted walking. **Metal spikes allowed:** Yes. **Range:** Yes (grass). **To obtain tee
times:** Call.

★★★TWIN FALLS STATE PARK GOLF COURSE

PU-P.O. Box 1023, Mullens, 25882, Wyoming County, (304)294-4044, (800)225-5982,
28 miles SW of Beckley.
Opened: 1968. **Holes:** 18. **Par:** 71/71. **Yards:** 6,382/5,202. **Course rating:** 70.1/69.5.
Slope: 122/112. **Architect:** Geoffrey Cornish/George Cobb. **Green fee:** $19/$22.
Credit cards: MC,VISA,AMEX,Diners Club. **Reduced fees:** Weekdays, low season,
seniors. **Caddies:** No. **Golf carts:** $19. **Discount golf packages:** Yes. **Season:** Year-

round. **High:** June-Oct. **On site lodging:** Yes. **Rental clubs:** Yes. **Walking policy:** Unrestricted walking. **Metal spikes allowed:** Yes. **Range:** No. **To obtain tee times:** Call.

Subscriber comments: Hard to find but a true gem. You need all your clubs here...Well kept secret. Can't wait to go back.

★★★TYGART LAKE COUNTRY CLUB

PU-Rte.1 Knottsville Rd., Grafton, 26354, Taylor County, (304)265-3100, 4 miles E of Grafton.

Opened: 1969. **Holes:** 18. **Par:** 72/75. **Yards:** 6,257/5,420. **Course rating:** 70.0/71.0. **Slope:** 115/113. **Architect:** James Gilmore Harrison and Ferdinand Garbin. **Green fee:** $13/$18. **Credit cards:** None. **Reduced fees:** N/A. **Caddies:** No. **Golf carts:** $12. **Discount golf packages:** No. **Season:** March-Oct. **High:** June-Aug. **On site lodging:** No. **Rental clubs:** Yes. **Walking policy:** Unrestricted walking. **Metal spikes allowed:** Yes. **Range:** Yes (grass/mats). **To obtain tee times:** Call up to 14 days in advance.

Subscriber comments: Beautiful, a great addition to this little community...Oustanding variety of holes, good conditioning and begins and ends with tough holes...Wide open, good for handicap.

★★½VALLEY VIEW GOLF COURSE

PU-Rte. #220 South, Moorefield, 26836, Hardy County, (304)538-6564, 145 miles W of Washington, DC.

Opened: 1969. **Holes:** 18. **Par:** 71/72. **Yards:** 6,129/4,928. **Course rating:** 68.0/65.4. **Slope:** 108/110. **Architect:** Russell Roberts. **Green fee:** $16/$19. **Credit cards:** None. **Reduced fees:** Twilight. **Caddies:** No. **Golf carts:** $15. **Discount golf packages:** No. **Season:** Year-round. **High:** May-Aug. **On site lodging:** No. **Rental clubs:** Yes. **Walking policy:** Unrestricted walking. **Metal spikes allowed:** Yes. **Range:** Yes (grass). **To obtain tee times:** First come, first served.

★★★½WOODRIDGE PLANTATION GOLF CLUB

R-301 Woodridge Dr., Mineral Wells, 26150, Wood County, (304)489-1800, (800)869-1001, 6 miles S of Parkersburg.

Opened: 1993. **Holes:** 18. **Par:** 71/71. **Yards:** 6,830/5,031. **Course rating:** 72.7/70.5. **Slope:** 128/116. **Architect:** John Salyers. **Green fee:** $18/$35. **Credit cards:** MC,VISA. **Reduced fees:** N/A. **Caddies:** No. **Golf carts:** Included in Green Fee. **Discount golf packages:** No. **Season:** Year-round. **High:** March-Nov. **On site lodging:** No. **Rental clubs:** Yes. **Walking policy:** Mandatory cart. **Metal spikes allowed:** No. **Range:** Yes (grass). **To obtain tee times:** Call.

Subscriber comments: Superior greens, great links design, tricky; friendly staff...Well kept. Tough holes. Super-nice people...Challenging from the tips...Good course for hookers...The years ahead will make it better.

★★★½THE WOODS RESORT

R-Mountain Lake Rd., Hedgesville, 25427, Berkeley County, (304)754-7222, (800)248-2222, 90 miles W of Washington, DC.

Opened: 1989. **Holes:** 27. **Par:** 72/71. **Yards:** 6,608/4,900. **Course rating:** 72.2/68.5. **Slope:** 121/107. **Architect:** Ray Johnston. **Green fee:** $22/$32. **Credit cards:** MC,VISA,AMEX. **Reduced fees:** Weekdays, low season, twilight, seniors, juniors. **Caddies:** No. **Golf carts:** $11. **Discount golf packages:** Yes. **Season:** Year-round. **High:** April-Sept. **On site lodging:** Yes. **Rental clubs:** Yes. **Walking policy:** Walking at certain times. **Metal spikes allowed:** No. **Range:** Yes (grass/mats). **To obtain tee times:** Call 5 days in advance.

Subscriber comments: Improves each year...Spectacular 16th hole...Worth the ride from DC...Good blend of new course with old...Beautiful scenery, great layout...Good mountain views.

★★★½ABBEY SPRINGS GOLF COURSE
R-Country Club Dr., Fontana on Geneva Lake, 53125, Walworth County, (414)275-6111, 50 miles SW of Milwaukee.
Opened: 1971. **Holes:** 18. **Par:** 72/72. **Yards:** 6,466/5,439. **Course rating:** 71.4/72.4. **Slope:** 133/129. **Architect:** Ken Killian and Dick Nugent. **Green fee:** $70/$70. **Credit cards:** All major. **Reduced fees:** Weekdays, low season, juniors. **Caddies:** No. **Golf carts:** Included in Green Fee. **Discount golf packages:** Yes. **Season:** April-Nov. **High:** June-Sept. **On site lodging:** No. **Rental clubs:** Yes. **Walking policy:** Walking at certain times. **Metal spikes allowed:** No. **Range:** Yes (grass). **To obtain tee times:** Call up to 30 days in advance.
Subscriber comments: A must play in late September....Spectacular views—several driveable holes...A great golf course, top 10 in Wisconsin...Beautiful, well-designed, extremely challenging...Better hit it straight...Hilly and forested with occasional water...Nice resort course. Good variety...Excellent course condition—great setting for golf...Take a camera—scenic views...Beautiful views of Lake Geneva.

★★ALPINE RESORT GOLF COURSE
R-P.O. Box 200, Egg Harbor, 54209, Door County, (920)868-3232, 60 miles from Green Bay.
Opened: 1926. **Holes:** 27. **Architect:** Francis H. Schaller. **Green fee:** $21/$25. **Credit cards:** MC,VISA. **Reduced fees:** Resort guests, twilight. **Caddies:** No. **Golf carts:** $22. **Discount golf packages:** Yes. **Season:** May-Oct. **High:** July-Aug. **On site lodging:** Yes. **Rental clubs:** No. **Walking policy:** N/A. **Metal spikes allowed:** Yes. **Range:** No. **To obtain tee times:** Call.
RED/BLUE
Par: 70/70. **Yards:** 5,850/5,440. **Course rating:** 67.7. **Slope:** 109.
RED/WHITE
Par: 70/73. **Yards:** 6,000/5,879. **Course rating:** 67.6. **Slope:** 117.
WHITE/BLUE
Par: 71/73. **Yards:** 6,200/5,837. **Course rating:** 69.4. **Slope:** 122.
Subscriber comments: Excellent scenic views from "top nine"...Bring an easel and paint brush...9th best par 4 in golf!...Pretty lake vistas and ledges...Great views on Blue nine...Beautiful countryside, no rough...Short, easy, fun...A couple of interesting holes. The rest fairly mundane...Scenic...Very challenging shotmaker's course.

★★★ANTIGO BASS LAKE COUNTRY CLUB
P.O. Box 268, Antigo, 54409, Langlade County, (715)623-6196.
Call club for further information.
Subscriber comments: Great little course. Best 19th hole in Wisconsin...Lakes, wooded fairways—short...User-friendly, good for seniors...Very well groomed, new water system...Good for grandma...Requires good iron play. It's a challenging 18 holes...Beautiful holes, short but challenging, fun, friendly members.

★★½BARABOO COUNTRY CLUB
1010 Lake St., Baraboo, 53913, Sauk County, (608)356-8195, (800)657-4981, 35 miles N of Madison.
Opened: 1962. **Holes:** 18. **Par:** 72/72. **Yards:** 6,570/5,681. **Course rating:** 71.3/72.5. **Slope:** 124/122. **Architect:** Edward Lawrence Packard. **Green fee:** $17/$30. **Credit cards:** MC,VISA. **Reduced fees:** Weekdays, low season, twilight. **Caddies:** No. **Golf carts:** $26. **Discount golf packages:** Yes. **Season:** April-Oct. **High:** June-Aug. **On site lodging:** No. **Rental clubs:** Yes. **Walking policy:** Unrestricted walking. **Metal spikes allowed:** Yes. **Range:** Yes (grass). **To obtain tee times:** Call or come in up to 7 days in advance.
Subscriber comments: Lots of diversity. Use many different clubs...Could be more challenging...Hilly, nice views, hole routing strange...Fun to play...Steep hills...One of the more underrated courses in south-central WI.

★★½BEAVER DAM COUNTRY CLUB
PU-Highway 33 NW-W8884 Sunset Dr., Beaver Dam, 53916, Dodge County, (920)885-4106.
Opened: 1969. **Holes:** 18. **Par:** 72/70. **Yards:** 5,976/5,219. **Course rating:** N/A. **Slope:** 112/104. **Architect:** N/A. **Green fee:** $20/$21. **Credit cards:** MC,VISA,AMEX.

Reduced fees: Twilight. **Caddies:** No. **Golf carts:** $22. **Discount golf packages:** No. **Season:** April-Oct. **High:** June-July. **On site lodging:** No. **Rental clubs:** Yes. **Walking policy:** Walking at certain times. **Metal spikes allowed:** No. **Range:** No. **To obtain tee times:** Call.

Subscriber comments: Good course...Several risk/reward decisions on short holes...Course layout good...Wide open, tougher in the wind...Course needs work, long rough.

★½BIG OAKS GOLF COURSE
6117 123rd St., Kenosha, 53140, Kenosha County, (414)694-4200.
Call club for further information.

BLACKWOLF RUN GOLF CLUB
R-1111 W. Riverside Dr., Kohler, 53044, Sheboygan County, (920)457-4446, (800)344-2838, 55 miles N of Milwaukee.
Opened: 1988. **Architect:** Pete Dye. **Green fee:** $124/$124. **Credit cards:** All major. **Reduced fees:** Low season, twilight. **Caddies:** Yes. **Golf carts:** $16. **Discount golf packages:** No. **Season:** April-Oct. **High:** June-Sept. **On site lodging:** Yes. **Rental clubs:** Yes. **Walking policy:** Unrestricted walking. **Metal spikes allowed:** No. **Range:** Yes (grass/mats). **To obtain tee times:** Call up to 14 days in advance. Guests may book anytime in advance with confirmed hotel reservation.

★★★★½MEADOW VALLEYS COURSE
Holes: 18. **Par:** 72/72. **Yards:** 7,142/5,065. **Course rating:** 74.7/69.5. **Slope:** 143/125. **Notes:** Ranked 5th in 1997 Best in State. 1998 U.S. Women's Open; 1995-97 Andersen Consulting World Championship.
Subscriber comments: Thought it as good as River Course...Excellent shape...Fall color is spectacular...Toughest back nine I've ever played. Relentless...World-class...A lot more fun than its popular "sister course"...Spectacular and spikeless only...Love it. Got engaged on 7th tee box...Outstanding, very penal...Pay the price—worth it!...Very challenging on a windy day.

★★★★★RIVER COURSE
Holes: 18. **Par:** 72/72. **Yards:** 6,991/5,115. **Course rating:** 74.9/70.7. **Slope:** 151/128. **Notes:** Ranked 50th in 1997-98 America's 100 Greatest; 1st in 1997 Best in State. 1998 U.S. Women's Open; 1995-97 Andersen Consulting World Championship.
Subscriber comments: Incredible beauty. Challenging golf. Great condition. Playing in the fall is as good as golf gets...Beautiful monster...Excellent foward, middle tees...A piece of heaven, worth a six-hour drive...Target golf at its best. Extremely penal to wayward shots...Good medicine for inflated egos...Nice clubhouse and pro shop...Playable for us mid-handicappers—torture from the tips.

★★★THE BLUFFS GOLF CLUB
PU-600 Losey Blvd. N., La Crosse, 54601, La Crosse County, (608)784-0567.
Opened: N/A. **Holes:** 18. **Par:** 71/72. **Yards:** 6,061/5,375. **Course rating:** 68.5/70.4. **Slope:** 120/118. **Architect:** N/A. **Green fee:** $14/$21. **Credit cards:** MC,VISA. **Reduced fees:** Weekdays, low season, twilight, seniors, juniors. **Caddies:** No. **Golf carts:** $18. **Discount golf packages:** No. **Season:** April-Dec. **High:** May-Sept. **On site lodging:** No. **Rental clubs:** Yes. **Walking policy:** Unrestricted walking. **Metal spikes allowed:** Yes. **Range:** No. **To obtain tee times:** Call up to 5 days in advance.
Subscriber comments: Older course with mature trees takes course management...Narrow fairways, some water, good greens, fun...Wooded holes were beautiful, others bland...Tight, short course...Very tight front nine. No7 a killer par-3.

★★★★THE BOG GOLF CLUB
PU-3121 County Hwy. I, Saukville, 53080, Ozaukee County, (414)284-7075, (800)484-3264, 28 miles N of Milwaukee.
Opened: 1995. **Holes:** 18. **Par:** 72/72. **Yards:** 7,110/5,110. **Course rating:** 74.9/70.3. **Slope:** 142/124. **Architect:** Arnold Palmer and Ed Seay. **Green fee:** $108. **Credit cards:** MC,VISA,AMEX. **Reduced fees:** Low season, twilight. **Caddies:** No. **Golf carts:** Included in Green Fee. **Discount golf packages:** No. **Season:** April-Nov. **High:** June-Oct. **On site lodging:** No. **Rental clubs:** Yes. **Walking policy:** Unrestricted walking. **Metal spikes allowed:** No. **Range:** Yes (grass). **To obtain tee times:** Call.

WISCONSIN

Notes: Ranked 6th in 1997 Best in State.
Subscriber comments: Some great holes, local knowledge needed...Best practice range in Wisconsin...Lots of blind shots; tricky greens...Maybe the best golf course in Wisconsin...A difficult back nine—requires precise tee shots. Hard to play first time. Blind shots. Need to play twice...Don't be too proud—from the tips it's only for single digits!...A real challenge with beautiful scenery.

★½BRIDGEWOOD GOLF COURSE
PU-1040 Bridgewood Dr., Neenah, 54956, Winnebago County, (920)722-9819.
Opened: 1949. **Holes:** 18. **Par:** 71/71. **Yards:** 6,015/5,907. **Course rating:** N/A. **Slope:** N/A. **Architect:** Jack Taylor. **Green fee:** $12/$14. **Credit cards:** None. **Reduced fees:** Seniors, juniors. **Caddies:** No. **Golf carts:** $10. **Discount golf packages:** No. **Season:** April-Nov. **High:** May-Aug. **On site lodging:** No. **Rental clubs:** Yes. **Walking policy:** Unrestricted walking. **Metal spikes allowed:** Yes. **Range:** No. **To obtain tee times:** No tee times given.

BRIGHTON DALE GOLF CLUB
PU-830-248th Ave., Kansasville, 53139, Kenosha County, (414)878-1440, 21 miles SW of Racine.
Opened: 1992. **Architect:** David Gill. **Green fee:** $18/$21. **Credit cards:** MC,VISA.
Caddies: No. **Golf carts:** $19. **Discount golf packages:** No. **Season:** April-Nov. **High:** May-Sept. **On site lodging:** No. **Rental clubs:** Yes. **Walking policy:** N/A. **Metal spikes allowed:** Yes. **Range:** Yes (mats). **To obtain tee times:** Call 12 days in advance.

★★★BLUE SPRUCE COURSE
Holes: 18. **Par:** 72/72. **Yards:** 6,687/5,988. **Course rating:** 72.0/72.1.
Slope: 129/125. **Reduced fees:** Weekdays, low season.
Subscriber comments: Very nice for a state-owned golf course...Can walk on on weekends...Very wooded and sometimes tight—well groomed...Nice distance between holes. Interesting elevation changes...Beautiful scenery...Tough course, well maintained.

★★★½WHITE BIRCH COURSE
Holes: 18. **Par:** 72/72. **Yards:** 6,977/6,206. **Course rating:** 73.3/73.2.
Slope: 130/126. **Reduced fees:** N/A.
Subscriber comments: Great variety, gets better with time...Good shape...Long, tough course...5th hole toughest par 4 in Wisconsin...Tough small greens...A gem—hills, valleys, sand, challenge, well-maintained, true greens...Trees and hills.
Special Notes: Also has a 9-hole course.

★★★★BRISTLECONE PINES GOLF CLUB
1500 E. Arlene Dr., Hartland, 53029, Waukesha County, (414)367-7880, 20 miles W of Milwaukee.
Opened: 1996. **Holes:** 18. **Par:** 71/71. **Yards:** 6,857/4,867. **Course rating:** 73.2/68.2. **Slope:** 131/116. **Architect:** Scott Miller. **Green fee:** $65/$65. **Credit cards:** MC,VISA,AMEX. **Reduced fees:** N/A. **Caddies:** Yes. **Golf carts:** Included in Green Fee. **Discount golf packages:** No. **Season:** April-Nov. **High:** June-Aug. **On site lodging:** No. **Rental clubs:** Yes. **Walking policy:** Unrestricted walking. **Metal spikes allowed:** No. **Range:** Yes (grass). **To obtain tee times:** Call up to 2 days in advance.
Subscriber comments: Course has great potential...Very good conditions for newer course...Target course...A real up and comer...An unexpected surprise—new, but maintained, great layout, country club service...Best new course in state...Very good design—fabulous clubhouse.

★★BRISTOL OAKS COUNTRY CLUB
16801 - 75th St., Bristol, 53104, Kenosha County, (414)857-2302, 25 miles S of Milwaukee.
Opened: 1964. **Holes:** 18. **Par:** 72/72. **Yards:** 6,187/5,655. **Course rating:** 69.2/66.5. **Slope:** 117/110. **Architect:** Edward Lockie. **Green fee:** $16/$22. **Credit cards:** MC,VISA,AMEX. **Reduced fees:** Twilight, seniors. **Caddies:** No. **Golf carts:** $22. **Discount golf packages:** Yes. **Season:** Year-round. **High:** May-Oct. **On site lodging:** No. **Rental clubs:** Yes. **Walking policy:** Walking at certain times. **Metal spikes allowed:** Yes. **Range:** Yes (grass/mats). **To obtain tee times:** Call.

★★★★BROWN COUNTY GOLF COURSE
PU-897 Riverdale Dr., Oneida, 54155, Brown County, (920)497-1731, 7 miles W of Green Bay.
Opened: 1957. **Holes:** 18. **Par:** 72/73. **Yards:** 6,729/5,801. **Course rating:** 72.1/72.7. **Slope:** 133/127. **Architect:** Edward Lawrence Packard. **Green fee:** $21/$27. **Credit cards:** None. **Reduced fees:** Seniors, juniors. **Caddies:** No. **Golf carts:** $25. **Discount golf packages:** No. **Season:** April-Oct. **High:** June-Aug. **On site lodging:** No. **Rental clubs:** Yes. **Walking policy:** Unrestricted walking. **Metal spikes allowed:** Yes. **Range:** Yes (grass/mats). **To obtain tee times:** Call 1 day in advance for weekdays. Call Monday at 6 p.m. for upcoming weekend or holiday.
Subscriber comments: Beautiful, challenging...Tough back nine! Tight fairways, wooded...Excellent shape for public course...Beautiful mature course—each hole a different challenge...Elevation changes severe on most holes...Best forest preserve course you'll play...Course is well laid out, wooded setting with hills and water hazards make for a challenging round of golf...Forgiving off tee. Good test of golf for bogey golfer.

GREAT VALUE

★★★★BROWN DEER PARK GOLF COURSE
PU-7835 N. Green Bay Rd., Milwaukee, 53209, Milwaukee County, (414)352-8080.
Opened: 1929. **Holes:** 18. **Par:** 71/71. **Yards:** 6,716/5,927. **Course rating:** 72.6/68.7. **Slope:** 132/125. **Architect:** George Hansen/Roger Packard and Andy North. **Green fee:** $25/$61. **Credit cards:** MC,VISA. **Reduced fees:** Weekdays, low season, seniors, juniors. **Caddies:** No. **Golf carts:** $24. **Discount golf packages:** No. **Season:** April-Oct. **High:** June-Sept. **On site lodging:** No. **Rental clubs:** Yes. **Walking policy:** Unrestricted walking. **Metal spikes allowed:** Yes. **Range:** Yes (grass/mats). **To obtain tee times:** Call or come in.
Notes: Ranked 8th in 1997 Best in State. 1994-present, Greater Milwaukee Open; 1977, 1966, 1951 U.S. Public Links.
Subscriber comments: Must hit the shot straight or in woods...Challenging, very fair...Super traditional...The rough is brutal...Superb test from back tees—all you want!...Getting back to one of best public courses...Usually great conditions...Keep it in the fairway!...Excellent traditional course—no tricks...Beautiful fairways and greens...Tight lush fairways—excellent fast greens.

★★½BROWNS LAKE GOLF COURSE
PU-3110 S. Browns Lake Dr., Burlington, 53105, Racine County, (414)878-3714.
Opened: 1923. **Holes:** 18. **Par:** 72/73. **Yards:** 6,449/5,706. **Course rating:** 70.2/70.4. **Slope:** 122/121. **Architect:** David Gill. **Green fee:** $20/$20. **Credit cards:** None. **Reduced fees:** Seniors, juniors. **Caddies:** No. **Golf carts:** $24. **Discount golf packages:** No. **Season:** April-Oct. **High:** June-Sept. **On site lodging:** No. **Rental clubs:** Yes. **Walking policy:** Unrestricted walking. **Metal spikes allowed:** Yes. **Range:** Yes (grass). **To obtain tee times:** Call 7 days in advance for a $4 charge.
Subscriber comments: Nice variety of holes, good greens...County owned—good condition...Hilly...For all abilities...Long par 5s....A fun, sporty course, some long par 4s.
Special Notes: Spikeless shoes encouraged.

BUTTERNUT HILLS GOLF COURSE
off Cty. B, Sarona, 54870, Washburn County, (715)635-8563.
Call club for further information.

★★★CAMELOT COUNTRY CLUB
PU-W192 Highway 67, Lomira, 53048, Dodge County, (920)269-4949, (800)510-4949.
Opened: 1966. **Holes:** 18. **Par:** 70/72. **Yards:** 6,046/5,338. **Course rating:** 68.8/70.2. **Slope:** 124/123. **Architect:** Homer Fieldhouse. **Green fee:** $20/$23. **Credit cards:** MC,VISA. **Reduced fees:** Weekdays, low season, resort guests, twilight, seniors, juniors. **Caddies:** No. **Golf carts:** $24. **Discount golf packages:** Yes. **Season:** March-Nov. **High:** July-Aug. **On site lodging:** No. **Rental clubs:** Yes. **Walking policy:** Unrestricted walking. **Metal spikes allowed:** Yes. **Range:** Yes (grass/mats). **To obtain tee times:** Call up to 7 days in advance.
Subscriber comments: A very challenging layout...Sloping fairways, lots of water...Well kept. Great scenery...Smaller course that's challenging...I like the par 3s (elevated tees)...Fun tract, remote from metro areas...Nice public facility.

WISCONSIN

★★CASTLE ROCK GOLF COURSE
PU-W. 6285 Welch Prairie Rd., Mauston, 53948, Junea County, (608)847-4658, (800)851-4853, 2 miles NW of Wisconsin Dells.
Opened: 1991. **Holes:** 18. **Par:** 72/71. **Yards:** 6,160/5,318. **Course rating:** 70.1/70.6. **Slope:** 126/122. **Architect:** Art Johnson/Jim Van Pee and Gary Van Pee. **Green fee:** $16/$22. **Credit cards:** MC,VISA. **Reduced fees:** Weekdays, twilight, seniors, juniors. **Caddies:** No. **Golf carts:** $20. **Discount golf packages:** Yes. **Season:** April-Oct. **High:** June-Aug. **On site lodging:** No. **Rental clubs:** Yes. **Walking policy:** Unrestricted walking. **Metal spikes allowed:** Yes. **Range:** Yes (grass). **To obtain tee times:** Call.

★★★CHASKA GOLF COURSE
PU-Wisconsin Ave. Hwy. 10 West, Appleton, 54912, Outagamie County, (920)757-5757, 90 miles NW of Milwaukee.
Opened: 1975. **Holes:** 18. **Par:** 72/72. **Yards:** 6,912/5,864. **Course rating:** 72.8/73.2. **Slope:** 129/126. **Architect:** Lawrence Packard. **Green fee:** $18/$21. **Credit cards:** MC,VISA. **Reduced fees:** Twilight, seniors, juniors. **Caddies:** No. **Golf carts:** $22. **Discount golf packages:** No. **Season:** April-Nov. **High:** May-Aug. **On site lodging:** No. **Rental clubs:** Yes. **Walking policy:** Unrestricted walking. **Metal spikes allowed:** No. **Range:** Yes (grass). **To obtain tee times:** Call 5 days in advance.
Subscriber comments: Pretty little course—nicely kept up yet gets lots of beginners...Lots of sand—wide open fairways...Some good par 4s...Holes over water—good greens, nice clubhouse...Great bar and bartenders...Plays long but well groomed...From easy to difficult...Accurate approach shots a must.

★★★CHERRY HILLS LODGE & GOLF COURSE
R-5905 Dunn Rd., Sturgeon Bay, 54235, Door County, (920)743-3240, (800)545-2307, 40 miles NE of Green Bay.
Opened: 1977. **Holes:** 18. **Par:** 72/72. **Yards:** 6,163/5,432. **Course rating:** 69.2/71.0. **Slope:** 121/122. **Architect:** N/A. **Green fee:** $17/$26. **Credit cards:** All major. **Reduced fees:** Weekdays, low season, twilight, seniors, juniors. **Caddies:** No. **Golf carts:** $12. **Discount golf packages:** Yes. **Season:** April-Oct. **High:** June-Aug. **On site lodging:** Yes. **Rental clubs:** Yes. **Walking policy:** Unrestricted walking. **Metal spikes allowed:** Yes. **Range:** Yes (grass). **To obtain tee times:** Call anytime.
Subscriber comments: Wife's favorite—nice course...Hilly—small greens...Nice semiprivate resort course...Beautiful course, friendly employees, loved it...They let us bring our two-year-old on course with us...Great facilities, hotel, resturant and golf...Open front, hilly back...Tough but playable—tough greens.

★★½CHRISTMAS MOUNTAIN VILLAGE GOLF CLUB
R-S. 944 Christmas Mountain Rd., Wisconsin Dells, 53965, Sauk County, (608)254-3971, 40 miles NW of Madison.
Opened: 1970. **Holes:** 18. **Par:** 71/71. **Yards:** 6,589/5,479. **Course rating:** 72.1/72.1. **Slope:** 129/126. **Architect:** Art Johnson. **Green fee:** $40/$44. **Credit cards:** All major. **Reduced fees:** Low season, twilight, seniors. **Caddies:** No. **Golf carts:** Included in Green Fee. **Discount golf packages:** Yes. **Season:** March-Nov. **High:** May-Sept. **On site lodging:** Yes. **Rental clubs:** Yes. **Walking policy:** Walking at certain times. **Metal spikes allowed:** Yes. **Range:** Yes (grass). **To obtain tee times:** Call up to 14 days in advance or book a golf package anytime.
Subscriber comments: Mature pines, very good layout...Traps in the middle of fairways on several holes...Typical resort course with lots of play...Rolling, work your way past cabins and condos with care...Beautiful 18 holes, they run the gamut...Combine play with a stay at one of the villas and you have a great getaway.

★★★CLIFTON HIGHLANDS GOLF COURSE
Cty. Rds. MM & F, Prescott, 54021, Pierce County, (715)262-5141.
Call club for further information.
Subscriber comments: Always in great shape, variety of shots needed, never a straight putt...Very tough course from tips, scenic, enjoyable...Beautiful course, something for all levels of golfers, beautiful back nine...Good staff...Excellent greens, fast, nice variety of holes...Fun to play.

★★½CLIFTON HOLLOW GOLF CLUB
PU-12166 W. 820th. Ave., River Falls, 54022, Pierce County, (715)425-9781, (800)487-8879, 30 miles E of St. Paul, MN.
Opened: 1973. **Holes:** 18. **Par:** 71/72. **Yards:** 6,381/5,117. **Course rating:** 69.6/68.6.
Slope: 118/114. **Architect:** Gordon Emerson. **Green fee:** $20/$25. **Credit cards:**
MC,VISA. **Reduced fees:** Weekdays, seniors, juniors. **Caddies:** No. **Golf carts:** $24.
Discount golf packages: No. **Season:** April-Nov. **High:** June-Aug. **On site lodging:**
No. **Rental clubs:** Yes. **Walking policy:** Unrestricted walking. **Metal spikes allowed:**
No. **Range:** Yes (grass). **To obtain tee times:** Call 7 days in advance.
Subscriber comments: Nice course, beautiful setting...Open and forgiving for duffers
like me. Yet enough challenge to avoid boredom...Two very short par 4 holes...Good
layout, good variety of holes. Good greens...Friendly...Always groomed well.
Special Notes: Also a 9-hole par-3 course.

★★COACHMAN'S GOLF RESORT
R-984 County Hwy. A, Edgerton, 53534, Dane County, (608)884-8484.
Call club for further information.

★★★½COUNTRY CLUB OF WISCONSIN
PU-2241 Highway. W., Grafton, 53024, Ozaukee County, (414)375-2444, 20 miles N of
Milwaukee.
Opened: 1994. **Holes:** 18. **Par:** 72/72. **Yards:** 7,108/5,499. **Course rating:** 74.7/67.4.
Slope: 137/119. **Architect:** Mattingly and Kuehn. **Green fee:** $25/$55. **Credit cards:**
MC,VISA,AMEX. **Reduced fees:** Weekdays, low season, twilight, juniors. **Caddies:** No.
Golf carts: $13. **Discount golf packages:** Yes. **Season:** April-Nov. **High:** May-Sept.
On site lodging: No. **Rental clubs:** Yes. **Walking policy:** Walking at certain times.
Metal spikes allowed: No. **Range:** Yes (grass/mats). **To obtain tee times:** Call 5 days
in advance.
Subscriber comments: Scenic. Big. Wide (held my slices)...Great greens—make you
think...Quick greens, great staff...Very good service...Very interesting new layout. Great
greens...Young course. Needs maturing...Very challenging—very well maintained...10th
hole is great gamble par 5...Great all-around layout for all handicaps...Links golf...Great
scenery and conditions...People/staff extemely friendly, helpful.

★★COUNTRYSIDE GOLF CLUB
PU-W. 726 Weiler Rd., Kaukauna, 54130, Outagamie County, (920)766-2219, 15 miles
S of Green Bay.
Opened: 1964. **Holes:** 18. **Par:** 71/71. **Yards:** 6,183/5,187. **Course rating:** 68.9/73.2.
Slope: 114/122. **Architect:** N/A. **Green fee:** $16/$17. **Credit cards:** None. **Reduced
fees:** Weekdays, low season, seniors, juniors. **Caddies:** No. **Golf carts:** $22. **Discount
golf packages:** Yes. **Season:** April-Oct. **High:** June-Aug. **On site lodging:** No. **Rental
clubs:** Yes. **Walking policy:** Unrestricted walking. **Metal spikes allowed:** Yes. **Range:**
Yes (grass/mats). **To obtain tee times:** Call in advance.

★★½CRYSTAL SPRINGS GOLF CLUB
PU-N. 8055 French Rd., Seymour, 54165, Outagamie County, (920)833-6348,
(800)686-2984, 17 miles W of Green Bay.
Opened: 1967. **Holes:** 18. **Par:** 72/73. **Yards:** 6,596/5,497. **Course rating:** 70.7/74.5.
Slope: 120/124. **Architect:** Edward Lockie. **Green fee:** $16/$18. **Credit cards:**
MC,VISA. **Reduced fees:** Twilight, seniors, juniors. **Caddies:** No. **Golf carts:** $21.
Discount golf packages: No. **Season:** April-Nov. **High:** June-Aug. **On site lodging:**
No. **Rental clubs:** Yes. **Walking policy:** Walking at certain times. **Metal spikes
allowed:** Yes. **Range:** Yes (grass/mats). **To obtain tee times:** Call golf shop.
Subscriber comments: 9 and 18 are the best finishing holes in the state...Greens well
maintained...Finishing holes are murder. Very nice clubhouse...Making good improvements, can be fun, can be slow...Some weak holes on back nine...A testy country
course—hills, water, small fast greens...Nice course. Short back nine.

★★★CUMBERLAND GOLF CLUB
PM-2400 5th St., Cumberland, 54829, Barron County, (715)822-4333, 2 miles W of
Cumberland.
Opened: 1991. **Holes:** 18. **Par:** 72/71. **Yards:** 6,272/5,004. **Course rating:** 70.7/70.1.

Slope: 129/116. **Architect:** Don Herfort. **Green fee:** $19/$21. **Credit cards:** MC,VISA. **Reduced fees:** Low season. **Caddies:** No. **Golf carts:** $21. **Discount golf packages:** No. **Season:** April-Oct. **High:** June-Aug. **On site lodging:** No. **Rental clubs:** Yes. **Walking policy:** Unrestricted walking. **Metal spikes allowed:** Yes. **Range:** Yes (grass). **To obtain tee times:** Call up to 5 days in advance.
Subscriber comments: Challenging, with lots of water and very scenic...Clubhouse is nice, with lots of flowers...Pretty land, rolling hills...Friendly, nice small-town course...Through woods, old nine and new nine.

★★CURRIE PARK GOLF COURSE
PM-3535 N. Mayfair Rd., Wauwatosa, 53226, Milwaukee County, (414)453-7030, 5 miles W of Milwaukee.
Opened: N/A. **Holes:** 18. **Par:** 71/72. **Yards:** 6,420/5,811. **Course rating:** 68.6/72.4. **Slope:** 115/120. **Architect:** George Hansen. **Green fee:** $8/$18. **Credit cards:** MC,VISA. **Reduced fees:** Weekdays, low season, twilight, seniors, juniors. **Caddies:** No. **Golf carts:** $24. **Discount golf packages:** No. **Season:** April-Oct. **High:** June-Sept. **On site lodging:** No. **Rental clubs:** Yes. **Walking policy:** Unrestricted walking. **Metal spikes allowed:** Yes. **Range:** No. **To obtain tee times:** Call or walk on.

★★★DEERTRAK GOLF COURSE
PU-W. 930 Hwy. O, Oconomowoc, 53066, Dodge County, (920)474-4444, 25 miles NW of Milwaukee.
Opened: 1986. **Holes:** 18. **Par:** 72/72. **Yards:** 6,313/5,114. **Course rating:** 70.2/69.2. **Slope:** 120/116. **Architect:** Don Chapman. **Green fee:** N/A. **Credit cards:** MC,VISA. **Reduced fees:** Seniors. **Caddies:** No. **Golf carts:** N/A. **Discount golf packages:** No. **Season:** March-Nov. **High:** N/A. **On site lodging:** No. **Rental clubs:** No. **Walking policy:** Unrestricted walking. **Metal spikes allowed:** No. **Range:** No. **To obtain tee times:** Call.
Subscriber comments: Beautiful, scenic, fun...Scenic par 3s...Good test, requires all the clubs...Enjoyable—well kept...A shorter, but interesting layout. Rewards good shots...Short but nice back nine...Short but kept up very well. Always improving course...The 16th is as challenging as any in the country...Interesting layout for finishing holes...Short shotmaker's course.

★★DELBROOK GOLF COURSE
PM-700 S. 2nd St., Delavan, 53115, Walworth County, (414)728-3966, 45 miles SW of Milwaukee.
Opened: 1928. **Holes:** 18. **Par:** 72/72. **Yards:** 6,519/5,599. **Course rating:** 70.8/71.3. **Slope:** 123/121. **Architect:** James Foulis. **Green fee:** $11/$24. **Credit cards:** None. **Reduced fees:** Weekdays, low season, twilight. **Caddies:** No. **Golf carts:** $10. **Discount golf packages:** No. **Season:** March-Nov. **High:** June-Aug. **On site lodging:** No. **Rental clubs:** No. **Walking policy:** Unrestricted walking. **Metal spikes allowed:** No. **Range:** Yes (grass). **To obtain tee times:** Call up to 7 days in advance.

★★★DEVIL'S HEAD RESORT & CONVENTION CENTER
R-S. 6330 Bluff Rd., Merrimac, 53561, Sauk County, (608)493-2251, (800)472-6670, 35 miles N of Madison.
Opened: 1973. **Holes:** 18. **Par:** 73/73. **Yards:** 6,861/5,141. **Course rating:** 72.4/64.4. **Slope:** 129/113. **Architect:** Art Johnson/Willis Stack. **Green fee:** $26/$46. **Credit cards:** MC,VISA. **Reduced fees:** Low season, twilight. **Caddies:** No. **Golf carts:** Included in Green Fee. **Discount golf packages:** Yes. **Season:** April-Oct. **High:** June-Aug. **On site lodging:** Yes. **Rental clubs:** Yes. **Walking policy:** Walking at certain times. **Metal spikes allowed:** Yes. **Range:** No. **To obtain tee times:** Nonguests call 14 days in advance for weekdays or 2 days in advance for weekends.
Subscriber comments: Very scenic...This course has it all: interesting golf, good food and lodging...I love the stone fences on the back nine!...Peaceful walk through nature...Beautiful, inexpensive, comfortable...Terrific track...Holes #2, 6, 11, 18 make the course challenging...Fun course, interesting layout...Upper course very beautiful and challenging...Hidden jewel. Very picturesque.

★★½DOOR CREEK GOLF COURSE
PU-4321 Vilas, Cottage Grove, 53527, Dane County, (608)839-5656, 3 miles E of Madison.

WISCONSIN

Opened: 1990. Holes: 27. Par: 71/71. Yards: 6,475/5,189. Course rating: 70.5/69.7. Slope: 119/111. Architect: Bradt family. Green fee: $22/$24. Credit cards: MC,VISA,DISC. Reduced fees: Weekdays, low season, seniors, juniors. Caddies: No. Golf carts: $10. Discount golf packages: No. Season: Year-round. High: May-Sept. On site lodging: No. Rental clubs: Yes. Walking policy: Unrestricted walking. Metal spikes allowed: Yes. Range: Yes (grass/mats). To obtain tee times: Call up to 7 days in advance.

Subscriber comments: Growing up into a nice course...They treat you super...Short but nice—they want you to come back...A very nice blue collar course...Great par 3s, well maintained...Fairly new, excellent conditioning...New course, will be great when it matures...Challenges the average golfer. Not long but high in quality....Great clubhouse.

★★★DRETZKA PARK GOLF COURSE
PU-12020 W. Bradley Rd., Milwaukee, 53224, Milwaukee County, (414)354-7300.
Opened: 1967. Holes: 18. Par: 72/72. Yards: 6,832/5,680. Course rating: 70.8/74.6. Slope: 124/123. Architect: Evert Kincaid. Green fee: $13/$17. Credit cards: MC,VISA. Reduced fees: Twilight, seniors, juniors. Caddies: No. Golf carts: $10. Discount golf packages: No. Season: March-Nov. High: May-Sept. On site lodging: No. Rental clubs: Yes. Walking policy: Unrestricted walking. Metal spikes allowed: Yes. Range: Yes (grass/mats). To obtain tee times: Call.

Subscriber comments: Tough county golf—challenging...Good condition; fantastic large greens. Tough...18th is neat...Sometimes an effort to walk...Rough very difficult...No tricks—all out in front, pretty, few traps...Plays to lower handicap. Could use more sand...The hill at 17 is killer...Good elevation changes throughout...Be long and fairly straight!...Steep climbs on 9 and 18 holes...Fairly difficult, lots of creeks.

★★★½DRUGAN'S CASTLE MOUND
PU-W 7665 Sylvester Rd., Holmen, 54636, La Crosse County, (608)526-3225.
Opened: 1970. Holes: 18. Par: 72/72. Yards: 6,492/4,852. Course rating: 70.7/67.5. Slope: 120/110. Architect: N/A. Green fee: $20/$23. Credit cards: MC,VISA,DISC. Reduced fees: N/A. Caddies: No. Golf carts: $23. Discount golf packages: No. Season: April-Nov. High: July-Aug. On site lodging: No. Rental clubs: Yes. Walking policy: Unrestricted walking. Metal spikes allowed: No. Range: No. To obtain tee times: Call or come in up to 14 days in advance.

Subscriber comments: Great bluffs course—kept well...Great challenge when with the guys, very playable with the wife and family....Polite and helpful staff—nice greens...Good mix of holes...Great scenery...Very nice fairways and greens, good course layout, some fairways are pretty tight...Great greens...Friendly people. Excellent restaurant!...Not too long of a course.

EAGLE BLUFF GOLF COURSE
Route 1 County Trunk, Hurley, 54534, Iron County, (715)561-3552.
Call club for further information.

★★★EAGLE RIVER GOLF COURSE
PU-527 McKinley Blvd., Eagle River, 54521, Vilas County, (715)479-8111, 70 miles N of Wausau.
Opened: 1923. Holes: 18. Par: 71/72. Yards: 6,103/5,167. Course rating: 69.3/67.8. Slope: 121/119. Architect: Don Herfort. Green fee: $22/$28. Credit cards: MC,VISA. Reduced fees: Low season, resort guests, twilight, juniors. Caddies: No. Golf carts: $11. Discount golf packages: Yes. Season: May-Oct. High: July-Aug. On site lodging: No. Rental clubs: Yes. Walking policy: Unrestricted walking. Metal spikes allowed: Yes. Range: Yes (grass). To obtain tee times: Threesomes and foursomes call 7 days in advance. Twosomes and singles call 2 days in advance.

Subscriber comments: Tough course...Greens like glass...Great scenic beauty, excellent...Some tough, tight holes...A bit crowded...Hidden treasure of Wisconsin...Nice hills...Different look at each hole. Tight...Facilities very good, hospitable people...Front nine great, small greens, short course...Back nine very tight, #11 a great water hole...Tough putting...Well maintained...I actually saw deer on course.

★★★EDGEWOOD GOLF COURSE
W240, S10050 Castle Rd., Big Bend, 53103, Waukesha County, (414)662-3110, 20 miles SW of Milwaukee.

Opened: 1969. **Holes:** 27. **Architect:** N/A. **Green fee:** $20/$31. **Credit cards:** MC,VISA. **Reduced fees:** Low season, seniors, juniors. **Caddies:** No. **Golf carts:** $12. **Discount golf packages:** No. **Season:** April-Oct. **High:** June-Aug. **On site lodging:** No. **Rental clubs:** Yes. **Walking policy:** Unrestricted walking. **Metal spikes allowed:** Yes. **Range:** Yes (grass). **To obtain tee times:** Call up to 7 days in advance.

RED/GOLD
Par: 72/72. **Yards:** 6,492/5,889. **Course rating:** N/A. **Slope:** N/A.

RED/WHITE
Par: 72/73. **Yards:** 6,613/5,507. **Course rating:** N/A. **Slope:** N/A.

WHITE/GOLD
Par: 72/71. **Yards:** 6,551/5,386. **Course rating:** N/A. **Slope:** N/A.

Subscriber comments: Challenging, scenic...Original 18 are best. Water and trees. Very scenic...27 holes, choice of types of nines...Red and White good tests...Really nice greens!...Often soggy. Watch out for bugs and goose guano...Good variety par 3, 4, 5s. A thinking man's golf course.

Special Notes: Adding 9 holes in 1998. Spikeless encouraged.

★★★EVANSVILLE COUNTRY CLUB

PU-8501 Cemetery Rd., Evansville, 53536, Rock County, (608)882-6524.
Opened: 1964. **Holes:** 18. **Par:** 72/72. **Yards:** 6,559/5,366. **Course rating:** 71.0/70.3. **Slope:** 127/122. **Architect:** Built by members. **Green fee:** $20/$22. **Credit cards:** MC,VISA. **Reduced fees:** Low season, juniors. **Caddies:** No. **Golf carts:** $20. **Discount golf packages:** No. **Season:** April-Oct. **High:** June-Aug. **On site lodging:** No. **Rental clubs:** Yes. **Walking policy:** Unrestricted walking. **Metal spikes allowed:** Yes. **Range:** Yes (grass). **To obtain tee times:** Call up to 7 days in advance.
Subscriber comments: Kind of short but nice—some holes too easy...Older country club, newer back nine holes...Have to think through your shots...People are always friendly...Hilly, lots of trees. Challenging course, well kept...New holes need to mature a little, nice rolling hills...Super greens—undulating.

★★★EVERGREEN GOLF CLUB

PU-Hwys. No.12 and 67N., Elkhorn, 53121, Walworth County, (414)723-5722, (800)868-8618, 40 miles SW of Milwaukee.
Opened: 1973. **Holes:** 27. **Architect:** Dick Nugent/Gary Welsh. **Green fee:** $25/$32. **Credit cards:** MC,VISA,DISC. **Reduced fees:** Weekdays, low season. **Caddies:** No. **Golf carts:** $13. **Discount golf packages:** Yes. **Season:** March-Dec. **High:** May-Sept. **On site lodging:** No. **Rental clubs:** Yes. **Walking policy:** Walking at certain times. **Metal spikes allowed:** Yes. **Range:** Yes (grass). **To obtain tee times:** Call in advance. 2 day cancellation required.

EAST/SOUTH
Par: 72/72. **Yards:** 6,501/5,357. **Course rating:** 71.7/71.0. **Slope:** 127/121.

NORTH/EAST
Par: 72/72. **Yards:** 6,280/5,347. **Course rating:** 70.8/71.3. **Slope:** 125/121.

NORTH/SOUTH
Par: 72/72. **Yards:** 6,431/5,522. **Course rating:** 71.7/71.9. **Slope:** 128/124.

Subscriber comments: Pretty and sporty...Well maintained but plays very short. Little challenge...Great par 5s...Scenic course, fairways lined with homes, must hit fairway...Course was in fantastic shape challenging but fair...Well maintained greens, great employees...Allows all shots, friendly...Best value in fall...Short but lots of doglegs...They do all the little things well...Local knowledge a must, blind shots.

★½FAR VU GOLF COURSE

PU-4985 State Rd. 175, Oshkosh, 54901, Winnebago County, (920)231-2631.
Opened: 1964. **Holes:** 18. **Par:** 72/74. **Yards:** 6,192/5,381. **Course rating:** 69.3/71.1. **Slope:** N/A. **Architect:** Norman Pfeiffer. **Green fee:** $13/$15. **Credit cards:** MC,VISA. **Reduced fees:** Seniors, juniors. **Caddies:** No. **Golf carts:** $20. **Discount golf packages:** No. **Season:** April-Oct. **High:** June-Aug. **On site lodging:** No. **Rental clubs:** Yes. **Walking policy:** Unrestricted walking. **Metal spikes allowed:** Yes. **Range:** No. **To obtain tee times:** Call 7 days in advance.

FOX HILLS RESORT

R-250 W. Chruch St., Mishicot, 54228, Manitowoc County, (414)755-2831, (800)950-7615, 30 miles SE of Green Bay.

Opened: 1961. **Architect:** Edward Lockie. **Green fee:** $12/$28. **Credit cards:** All major. **Reduced fees:** Weekdays, low season, twilight, seniors. **Caddies:** No. **Golf carts:** $12. **Discount golf packages:** Yes. **Season:** April-Nov. **High:** June-Aug. **On site lodging:** Yes. **Rental clubs:** Yes. **Walking policy:** Unrestricted walking. **Metal spikes allowed:** Yes. **Range:** Yes (grass). **To obtain tee times:** Call, no requirements.

★★½CLASSIC COURSE

BACK/BLUE
Holes: 27. **Par:** N/A. **Yards:** N/A. **Course rating:** N/A. **Slope:** N/A.
FRONT/BACK
Holes: 27. **Par:** 72/72. **Yards:** 6,374/5,788. **Course rating:** 70.5/67.5. **Slope:** 123/117.
FRONT/BLUE
Holes: 27. **Par:** 71/73. **Yards:** 6,410/5,721. **Course rating:** 70.0/67.1. **Slope:** 122/116.
Subscriber comments: Challenging—well kept, and the restaurant is recognized all through state and Midwest for its cuisine and charm...Short...Great views...Needs work to improve the course...Late summer, fairways dry/hard. Greens good.

★★★FOX HILLS NATIONAL GOLF CLUB

Opened: 1988. **Holes:** 18. **Architect:** Bob Lohmann. **Par:** 72/72. **Yards:** 7,017/5,366. **Course rating:** 73.8/71.0. **Slope:** 136/124.
Subscriber comments: Needs a little more maturing, links type...Challenging course—very interesting...A gimmicky course...Dunes, dunes and more dunes...Good links lay-out. Wide open...Tough course to score on...Always windy—nice layout—good test...Good when wind is tough...Hope you can play out of sand—great layout...A fun links course...Full-length bunkers and mounds.

★★★½FOXFIRE GOLF CLUB

PU-Hwy. 54 & Hwy. 10, Waupaca, 54981, Waupaca County, (715)256-1700.
Opened: 1996. **Holes:** 18. **Par:** 70/70. **Yards:** 6,528/5,022. **Course rating:** 70.9/69.4. **Slope:** 124/115. **Architect:** David Truttman. **Green fee:** $21/$29. **Credit cards:** MC,VISA. **Reduced fees:** Weekdays, low season, twilight, seniors, juniors. **Caddies:** No. **Golf carts:** $10. **Discount golf packages:** No. **Season:** April-Nov. **High:** June-Aug. **On site lodging:** No. **Rental clubs:** Yes. **Walking policy:** Unrestricted walking. **Metal spikes allowed:** Yes. **Range:** Yes (grass). **To obtain tee times:** Call up to 10 days in advance or anytime in advance with credit card to guarantee.
Subscriber comments: Excellent new course, challenging, well kept...Excellent people, service...Good course and a fair amount of trees/water...Needs a couple years to mature...Good middle-handicap course. Great condition.

GENEVA NATIONAL GOLF CLUB

R-1221 Geneva National Ave. S., Lake Geneva, 53147, Walworth County, (414)245-7000, 45 miles SW of Milwaukee.
Opened: 1991. **Green fee:** $90/$100. **Credit cards:** MC,VISA,AMEX. **Reduced fees:** Weekdays, low season, resort guests, twilight. **Caddies:** No. **Golf carts:** Included in Green Fee. **Discount golf packages:** Yes. **Season:** March-Oct. **On site lodging:** Yes. **Rental clubs:** Yes. **Walking policy:** Mandatory cart. **Metal spikes allowed:** No. **Range:** Yes (grass). **To obtain tee times:** Call 14 days in advance.

(GOOD SERVICE seal)

★★★★PALMER COURSE

Holes: 18. **Par:** 72/72. **Yards:** 7,171/4,904. **Course rating:** 74.8/68.7. **Slope:** 140/122. **Architect:** Arnold Palmer and Ed Seay. **High:** June-Sept.
Notes: Ranked 10th in 1997 Best in State.
Subscriber comments: Great practice facilities—the closing three are killers...Rolling fairways, well maintained, picturesque...A real gem. Great condition. Great views...Spectacular course! Tough slopes...Go early, have the place to yourself. Golf you will remember...Beautiful course; tough; challenging; 17th memorable...Beautiful wooded setting...Service as if you were at a private club.

★★★★TREVINO COURSE

Holes: 18. **Par:** 72/72. **Yards:** 7,120/5,193. **Course rating:** 74.5/70.1. **Slope:** 137/124. **Architect:** Lee Trevino/Wm. Graves Design Co.. **High:** May-Oct.
Subscriber comments: Short, but challenging greens...Great practice facities—great course...Love those left to right holes...Good layout and fair...Nice view—lots of hills...Newer course with older feeling...Winning design, superb holes in woods...Pick the right tees...A young course, but really good potential. Challenging, especially for higher handicappers, but a good time.

★½GEORGE WILLIAMS COLLEGE GOLF CLUB

PU-350 N. Lake Shore, Williams Bay, 53191, Walworth County, (414)245-9507, 40 miles SW of Milwaukee.

Opened: 1906. **Holes:** 18. **Par:** 67/68. **Yards:** 5,066/4,721. **Course rating:** 63.4/65.5. **Slope:** 102/106. **Architect:** James Naismith. **Green fee:** $9/$20. **Credit cards:** MC,VISA. **Reduced fees:** Weekdays, twilight, seniors, juniors. **Caddies:** No. **Golf carts:** $20. **Discount golf packages:** No. **Season:** April-Nov. **High:** July-Aug. **On site lodging:** Yes. **Rental clubs:** Yes. **Walking policy:** N/A. **Metal spikes allowed:** Yes. **Range:** No. **To obtain tee times:** Call.

★★GOLDEN SANDS GOLF COMMUNITY

300 Naber Rd., Cecil, 54111, Shawano County, (715)745-2189, 35 miles NW of Green Bay.

Opened: 1970. **Holes:** 18. **Par:** 70/73. **Yards:** 6,115/5,945. **Course rating:** N/A. **Slope:** 112/117. **Architect:** N/A. **Green fee:** $18/$23. **Credit cards:** All major. **Reduced fees:** N/A. **Caddies:** No. **Golf carts:** $23. **Discount golf packages:** No. **Season:** May-Oct. **High:** June-Aug. **On site lodging:** No. **Rental clubs:** Yes. **Walking policy:** Unrestricted walking. **Metal spikes allowed:** Yes. **Range:** Yes (grass). **To obtain tee times:** Call in advance.

THE GOLF COURSES OF LAWSONIA

R-W2615 S. Valley View Dr., Green Lake, 54941, Green Lake County, (920)294-3320, (800)529-4453, 35 miles SW of Oshkosh.

Credit cards: All major. **Reduced fees:** Low season, resort guests, twilight. **Caddies:** No. **Golf carts:** Included in Green Fee. **Discount golf packages:** Yes. **Season:** April-Nov. **High:** June-Sept. **On site lodging:** Yes. **Rental clubs:** Yes. **Walking policy:** Walking at certain times. **Metal spikes allowed:** Yes. **Range:** Yes (grass/mats). **To obtain tee times:** Call anytime 8 months in advance.

★★★★LINKS COURSE

Opened: 1930. **Holes:** 18. **Par:** 72/71. **Yards:** 6,764/5,078. **Course rating:** 72.8/68.9. **Slope:** 130/114. **Architect:** William Langford. **Green fee:** $37/$49.

Subscriber comments: Old-style. Heavy mounding. Elevated greens...Elevated greens make some holes really tough...A great experience—challenging, well cared for...A Wisconsin course with no beer?...A must stop for any level golfer. ...Great old course...Tough greens. Must be long and hit fades into elevated greens...Good staff...Byron Nelson used to hold course record...1930 design still excites me!

★★★★WOODLANDS COURSE

Opened: 1982. **Holes:** 18. **Par:** 72/72. **Yards:** 6,618/5,106. **Course rating:** 71.5/69.1. **Slope:** 129/120. **Architect:** Rocky Roquemore. **Green fee:** $43/$64.

Subscriber comments: Beautiful and challenging, lots of fairway, grass bunkers...Beautiful and scenic...Newest of two outstanding layouts. Very scenic...Tight, wooded and tough...Still no beer. Great layout...Deer everywhere...Breathtaking scenery and great golf...Heavy woods...A must play in the fall; play stops to allow a deer family to cross the fairway...Well maintained...Excellent test. Beautiful surroundings...All types of terrain...Excellant course layout...Wildlife everywhere...Better than links sister. Will teach you to hit straight.

GRAND GENEVA RESORT & SPA

R-7036 Grand Geneva Way, Lake Geneva, 53147, Walworth County, (414)248-2556, (800)558-3417, 40 miles SW of Milwaukee.

Opened: 1969. **Green fee:** $65/$95. **Credit cards:** MC,VISA,AMEX,DISC,Diners Club. **Caddies:** No. **Golf carts:** Included in Green Fee. **Discount golf packages:** Yes. **Season:** April-Nov. **High:** May-Sept. **On site lodging:** Yes. **Rental clubs:** Yes. **Walking policy:** Mandatory cart. **Metal spikes allowed:** No. **Range:** Yes (grass/mats). **To obtain tee times:** Guests may call 30 days in advance. Public may call up to 14 days with credit card to reserve.

★★★★BRUTE COURSE

Holes: 18. **Par:** 72/72. **Yards:** 6,997/5,244. **Course rating:** 71.5/70.0. **Slope:** 136/129. **Architect:** Robert Bruce Harris. **Reduced fees:** Weekdays, low season, resort guests, twilight.

Subscriber comments: Very tough. Great conditioning...Outstanding views—high greens...Intimidating but fun to play...Long, challenging, great shape...Great greens!...Majestic views of Wisconsin countryside, fast greens, big bunkers...Too tough for average golfer, hilly...Both courses wide open lots of water and sand.

★★★½HIGHLANDS COURSE

Holes: 18. **Par:** 71/71. **Yards:** 6,633/5,038. **Course rating:** 71.5/68.3. **Slope:** 125/115. **Architect:** Pete Dye and Jack Nicklaus/Bob Cupp. **Reduced fees:** Weekdays, low season, twilight.

Subscriber comments: Good layout, fun to play, just tough enough...Nice environment, beautiful course, well managed...Feels like you're on course by yourself in wooded setting...Some blind shots, not too long, challenging...Great condition, super service...Testy course, very interesting...Tight and tough, great finishing hole, soft in spring...Really picks up after first few holes.

★★½GRANT PARK GOLF COURSE

PU-100 Hawthorne Ave., South Milwaukee, 53172, Milwaukee County, (414)762-4646, 12 miles S of Milwaukee.

Opened: 1920. **Holes:** 18. **Par:** 67/71. **Yards:** 5,174/5,147. **Course rating:** 64.1/68.4. **Slope:** 110/103. **Architect:** George Hansen. **Green fee:** $8/$18. **Credit cards:** MC,VISA. **Reduced fees:** Weekdays, low season, twilight, seniors, juniors. **Caddies:** No. **Golf carts:** $24. **Discount golf packages:** No. **Season:** Year-round. **High:** June-Aug. **On site lodging:** No. **Rental clubs:** Yes. **Walking policy:** Unrestricted walking. **Metal spikes allowed:** Yes. **Range:** Yes. **To obtain tee times:** Walk-ons accepted. Members of automated system may call up to 7 days in advance.

Subscriber comments: An emerald jewel on the lake...Nice short public course, well used....Nice park-like atmoshere near lake...Not very long but tricky, beautiful setting...A great iron course that requires a degree of acuracy...Very enjoyable and good layout...Great beginner's course. Be ready for a slow round...Short but sweet. Nice layout...Lots of trees, big rolling greens, fun.

★★GREENFIELD PARK GOLF COURSE

PU-2028 S. 124th. St., West Allis, 53227, Milwaukee County, (414)453-1750. Call club for further information.

★★HALLIE GOLF CLUB

3798 Golfview Dr., Chippewa Falls, 54729, Chippewa County, (715)723-8524. Call club for further information.

★★½HARTFORD GOLF CLUB

7072 Lee Rd., Hartford, 53027, Washington County, (414)673-2710, 30 miles NW of Milwaukee.

Opened: 1933. **Holes:** 18. **Par:** 72/74. **Yards:** 6,406/5,850. **Course rating:** 69.8/72.3. **Slope:** 114/119. **Architect:** Killian and Nugent. **Green fee:** $23/$25. **Credit cards:** MC,VISA. **Reduced fees:** Twilight. **Caddies:** Yes. **Golf carts:** $11. **Discount golf packages:** No. **Season:** April-Dec. **High:** May-Sept. **On site lodging:** No. **Rental clubs:** Yes. **Walking policy:** Unrestricted walking. **Metal spikes allowed:** Yes. **Range:** Yes (grass). **To obtain tee times:** Call 7 days in advance.

Subscriber comments: Not a real tough course, but you're always treated well...Nice fun tract...Good facilities...Good conditions. Beautiful greens. Fun to play...Really nice layout, well manicured, great people!...Tight—nice mix of holes...Lots of sand and no water...April golf, good shape for early season, nice course.

★★★HAWTHORNE HILLS GOLF CLUB

PU-4720 County Hwy. I, Saukville, 53080, Ozaukee County, (414)692-2151, 25 miles N of Milwaukee.

Opened: 1965. **Holes:** 18. **Par:** 72/72. **Yards:** 6,595/5,307. **Course rating:** 70.5/69.1. **Slope:** 118/114. **Architect:** Bob Lohmann. **Green fee:** $14/$22. **Credit cards:** MC,VISA. **Reduced fees:** Low season, seniors, juniors. **Caddies:** No. **Golf carts:** $22. **Discount golf packages:** No. **Season:** April-Oct. **High:** April-Oct. **On site lodging:** No. **Rental clubs:** Yes. **Walking policy:** Unrestricted walking. **Metal spikes allowed:** No. **Range:** No. **To obtain tee times:** Residents up to 7 days in advance. Nonresidents up to 3 days in advance.

Subscriber comments: Better grade muny...Beautiful layout...Improvements have helped substantially...Nice country course—very good shape!...Very forgiving...Hilly, good variety...Nice muny layout...Great deal for county residents.

★★★½HAYWARD GOLF & TENNIS CENTER
R.R. No.10 Wittwer St., Hayward, 54843, Sawyer County, (715)634-2760.
Call club for further information.
Subscriber comments: Good layout and well maintained...Always improving their course...Absolutely manicured, enjoyable, perfect greens, tee boxes...Has character...Very nice clubhouse...Greens always nice; straight and long...Nice course and friendly.

★½HICKORY HILLS COUNTRY CLUB
PU-W 3095 Hickory Hills Rd., Chilton, 53014, Calumet County, (920)849-2912, (888)849-2912, 25 miles SE of Appleton.
Opened: N/A. **Holes:** 18. **Par:** 71/72. **Yards:** 6,130/5,916. **Course rating:** N/A. **Slope:** 121/117. **Architect:** N/A. **Green fee:** $12/$12. **Credit cards:** MC. **Reduced fees:** Weekdays. **Caddies:** No. **Golf carts:** N/A. **Discount golf packages:** Yes. **Season:** May-Nov. **High:** June-Aug. **On site lodging:** No. **Rental clubs:** Yes. **Walking policy:** Unrestricted walking. **Metal spikes allowed:** Yes. **Range:** Yes (mats). **To obtain tee times:** Call.

★★½HIGH CLIFF GOLF COURSE
PU-W 5055 Golf Course Rd., Sherwood, 54169, Calumet County, (920)734-1162, 12 miles E of Appleton.
Opened: 1968. **Holes:** 18. **Par:** 71/71. **Yards:** 6,106/4,932. **Course rating:** 67.1/62.7. **Slope:** 113/104. **Architect:** N/A. **Green fee:** $16/$20. **Credit cards:** MC,VISA,DISC. **Reduced fees:** Seniors, juniors. **Caddies:** No. **Golf carts:** $22. **Discount golf packages:** No. **Season:** April-Oct. **High:** N/A. **On site lodging:** Yes. **Rental clubs:** No. **Walking policy:** Unrestricted walking. **Metal spikes allowed:** No. **Range:** Yes (grass). **To obtain tee times:** Call 7 days in advance.
Subscriber comments: Nice park course—easy to play...Nicely laid out. Good conditions...Some blind shots...Cliff holes make the course...Scenic...Good parking, fair conditions, scenic...Scenic course w/some great golf holes, especially along the escarpment...Very good. Front nine excellent...Back nine needs work.

★★½HILLMOOR GOLF CLUB
Hwy. 50 E., Box 186, Lake Geneva, 53147, Walworth County, (414)248-4570, 50 miles N of Chicago.
Opened: 1924. **Holes:** 18. **Par:** 72/72. **Yards:** 6,350/5,360. **Course rating:** 71.0/65.3. **Slope:** 123/113. **Architect:** James Foulis. **Green fee:** $24/$34. **Credit cards:** MC,VISA. **Reduced fees:** Weekdays, low season, resort guests, twilight, seniors, juniors. **Caddies:** No. **Golf carts:** $13. **Discount golf packages:** Yes. **Season:** March-Dec. **High:** May-Oct. **On site lodging:** Yes. **Rental clubs:** Yes. **Walking policy:** Walking at certain times. **Metal spikes allowed:** Yes. **Range:** Yes (grass/mats). **To obtain tee times:** Call in advance.
Subscriber comments: Very challenging holes...Good muny course...Needs some grooming, but good greens...Tougher than it looks, good use of small footprint of land...Fun course to play...Sneaky—two distinct nines. Very nice staff.

★★½HON-E-KOR COUNTRY CLUB
1141 Riverview Dr., Box 439, Kewaskum, 53040, Washington County, (414)626-2520, 5 miles N of West Bend.
Opened: 1962. **Holes:** 27. **Architect:** Jim Korth. **Green fee:** $20/$25. **Credit cards:** MC,VISA. **Reduced fees:** Weekdays, low season, seniors, juniors. **Caddies:** No. **Golf carts:** $22. **Discount golf packages:** No. **Season:** April-Nov. **High:** May-Sept. **On site lodging:** No. **Rental clubs:** Yes. **Walking policy:** Unrestricted walking. **Metal spikes allowed:** No. **Range:** Yes (grass/mats). **To obtain tee times:** Call 2 days in advance.
RED/BLUE
Par: 70/71. **Yards:** 6,011/5,164. **Course rating:** 68.7/70.3. **Slope:** 118/122.
RED/WHITE
Par: 70/71. **Yards:** 5,959/5,145. **Course rating:** 66.0/70.3. **Slope:** 116/122.
WHITE/BLUE
Par: 70/70. **Yards:** 6,033/5,161. **Course rating:** 67.6/70.3. **Slope:** 120/122.
Subscriber comments: Very short—great greens...Good course. Expansion matured well. Pretty...Very good course...White nine is the only challenging side.

★★★½ HUDSON GOLF CLUB
378 Frontage Rd., Hudson, 54016, St. Croix County, (715)386-6515.
Call club for further information.
Subscriber comments: Being redone, six new holes, new clubhouse...Tough par 3s on the front, good condition, will need to see how new changes will come out...Good greens...Sporty course. Like the new par 5 18th...Fast greens.

★★★ IDLEWILD GOLF COURSE
PU-4146 Golf Valley Dr., Sturgeon Bay, 54235, Door County, (920)743-3334, 40 miles NE of Green Bay.
Opened: 1978. **Holes:** 18. **Par:** 72/73. **Yards:** 6,889/5,886. **Course rating:** 72.7/73.4. **Slope:** 130/128. **Architect:** N/A. **Green fee:** $20/$30. **Credit cards:** MC,VISA. **Reduced fees:** Twilight, seniors, juniors. **Caddies:** No. **Golf carts:** $12. **Discount golf packages:** Yes. **Season:** April-Oct. **High:** June-Sept. **On site lodging:** No. **Rental clubs:** Yes. **Walking policy:** Unrestricted walking. **Metal spikes allowed:** No. **Range:** Yes (grass). **To obtain tee times:** Call anytime in advance during season.
Subscriber comments: A sleeper; excellent, tough layout. 9 and 18 memorable...Good test of golf—good variety in par 5s...Course was in good shape, easy to get on...Great water holes...Always windy, tons of hills...Improved, friendly, pleasant, pretty, quiet...Interesting, challenging, excellent condition....Will be great when mature...Greens are living proof that spikeless works...Great greens.
Special Notes: Formerly known as Lost Creek Golf Course.

★★ INSHALLA COUNTRY CLUB
R-N 11060 Clear Lake Rd., Tomahawk, 54487, Lincoln County, (715)453-3130, 39 miles N of Wausau.
Opened: 1964. **Holes:** 18. **Par:** 70/70. **Yards:** 5,659/5,269. **Course rating:** 66.6/65.5. **Slope:** 109/104. **Architect:** John Hein/John F. Hein. **Green fee:** $20/$24. **Credit cards:** All major. **Reduced fees:** Low season, twilight, juniors. **Caddies:** No. **Golf carts:** $24. **Discount golf packages:** No. **Season:** April-Nov. **High:** June-Aug. **On site lodging:** No. **Rental clubs:** Yes. **Walking policy:** N/A. **Metal spikes allowed:** Yes. **Range:** No. **To obtain tee times:** Call up to 7 days in advance.

★★★ IVES GROVE GOLF LINKS
PU-14101 Washington Ave., Sturtevant, 53177, Racine County, (414)878-3714, 6 miles SW of Racine.
Opened: 1971. **Holes:** 27. **Architect:** David Gill. **Green fee:** $18/$20. **Credit cards:** None. **Reduced fees:** Seniors, juniors. **Caddies:** No. **Golf carts:** $23. **Discount golf packages:** No. **Season:** March-Nov. **High:** May-Sept. **On site lodging:** No. **Rental clubs:** No. **Walking policy:** Unrestricted walking. **Metal spikes allowed:** Yes. **Range:** Yes (grass/mats). **To obtain tee times:** Call 7 days in advance.
RED/WHITE
Par: 72/72. **Yards:** 6,965/5,440. **Course rating:** 72.8. **Slope:** 130.
BLUE/RED
Par: 72/72. **Yards:** 7,000/5,370. **Course rating:** 73.0. **Slope:** 131.
WHITE/BLUE
Par: 72/72. **Yards:** 6,985/5,380. **Course rating:** 73.0. **Slope:** 131.
Subscriber comments: New nine is great...Nicely kept. Good service...Always windy...Errant shots are not heavily penalized...Wide open but fun...Strategy a premium; can penalize sloppy play...Kept in excellent shape, excellent greens...Decent design, challenging enough...Will get better with age...Windiest layout in Wisconsin, but worth it...Fun, open-feel golf course...Nice public facility.

★★★ JOHNSON PARK GOLF COURSE
PU-6200 Northwestern Ave., Racine, 53406, Racine County, (414)637-2840.
Opened: 1931. **Holes:** 18. **Par:** 72/74. **Yards:** 6,683/5,732. **Course rating:** 70.8/73.0. **Slope:** 117/120. **Architect:** Todd Sloan. **Green fee:** $13/$20. **Credit cards:** MC,VISA,DISC. **Reduced fees:** Weekdays, low season, seniors, juniors. **Caddies:** No. **Golf carts:** $22. **Discount golf packages:** No. **Season:** April-Nov. **High:** June-Aug. **On site lodging:** No. **Rental clubs:** Yes. **Walking policy:** Unrestricted walking. **Metal spikes allowed:** Yes. **Range:** Yes (grass/mats). **To obtain tee times:** Call 7 days in advance with credit card to guarantee.

Subscriber comments: Old established muny course. Nice...Strict with time limits...Interesting muny...Usually in decent shape, nice layout...You will finish in four hours!...Nice public facility...Fun track to play...Good muny course, big trees and a good layout...Marshals were very helpful and effective...Good muny, fast play, nice design, woods.

KETTLE HILLS GOLF COURSE

PU-3375 State Hwy. 167 W., Richfield, 53076, Washington County, (414)255-2200, 20 miles NW of Milwaukee.

Architect: Don Zimmermann. **Credit cards:** MC,VISA. **Caddies:** No. **Golf carts:** $11. **Discount golf packages:** No. **Season:** April-Nov. **High:** May-Sept. **On site lodging:** No. **Rental clubs:** Yes. **Walking policy:** Unrestricted walking. **Metal spikes allowed:** No. **Range:** Yes (grass/mats). **To obtain tee times:** Call up to 9 days in advance.

★★★PONDS/WOODS COURSE

Opened: 1987. **Holes:** 18. **Par:** 72/72. **Yards:** 6,787/5,171. **Course rating:** 72.5/69.6. **Slope:** 128/123. **Green fee:** $21/$25. **Reduced fees:** Weekdays, low season, twilight, juniors.

Subscriber comments: Keeps getting better...Very challenging—good condition—nice clubhouse...Good test...Always in great shape, well marshalled. Beautiful color in the fall...Good course with variety...Scenic—tough finishing holes...Beautiful scenery—good specials when available...Challenging with variety of holes—mix of water and sand...Thinking man's golf...Woods nine is quite enjoyable...Lives up to the name—plenty of hills, ponds and woods.

★★½VALLEY COURSE

Opened: 1990. **Holes:** 18. **Par:** 72/72. **Yards:** 6,455/5,088. **Course rating:** 70.9/69.2. **Slope:** 122/116. **Green fee:** $18/$25. **Reduced fees:** Weekdays, low season, twilight, seniors, juniors.

Subscriber comments: Course layout not conventional but good...Interesting track...Very scenic...More wide open than the ponds/woods course...Not a bad design, needs to mature...Links style—scoreable...Nice facilities. Challenging holes...Open course, but good variety...Newer course, good condition, challenging, excellent views...Not long, but fun.

★★½KETTLE MORAINE GOLF CLUB

PU-4299 Highway 67, Dousman, 53118, Waukesha County, (414)965-6200, 35 miles W of Milwaukee.

Opened: 1969. **Holes:** 18. **Par:** 72/72. **Yards:** 6,406/5,203. **Course rating:** 70.3/69.5. **Slope:** 118/116. **Architect:** Dwayne Dewey Laak. **Green fee:** $25/$28. **Credit cards:** N/A. **Reduced fees:** Low season, twilight. **Caddies:** No. **Golf carts:** $12. **Discount golf packages:** No. **Season:** April-Nov. **High:** June-Sept. **On site lodging:** No. **Rental clubs:** Yes. **Walking policy:** Unrestricted walking. **Metal spikes allowed:** Yes. **Range:** Yes (grass). **To obtain tee times:** Call up to 21 days in advance.

Subscriber comments: Challenging. Fun to play...Very good test of golf, pretty views. Mix of hills and flat holes...Helpful staff—some rough fairways...Nice layout...Lots of water, great scenery...Fun course; each hole is very different...Challenging doglegs...Target golf due to trees, fun...Clubhouse nice...Very mature trees...Small greens make average length course tough but fun...Tight, woods, water, hills.

★★KILLARNEY HILLS GOLF COURSE

PU-163 Radio Rd, River Falls, 54022, Pierce County, (715)425-8501, (800)466-7999, 23 miles E of St. Paul, MN.

Opened: 1994. **Holes:** 18. **Par:** 72/73. **Yards:** 6,434/5,055. **Course rating:** 70.8/64.4. **Slope:** 120/107. **Architect:** Gordon Emerson. **Green fee:** $15/$19. **Credit cards:** MC,VISA. **Reduced fees:** Twilight, seniors, juniors. **Caddies:** No. **Golf carts:** $18. **Discount golf packages:** No. **Season:** April-Nov. **High:** May-Aug. **On site lodging:** No. **Rental clubs:** Yes. **Walking policy:** Unrestricted walking. **Metal spikes allowed:** Yes. **Range:** Yes (grass). **To obtain tee times:** Call.

★★½KOSHKONONG MOUNDS COUNTRY CLUB

W 7670 Koshkonong Mounds Rd., Fort Atkinson, 53538, Jefferson County, (920)563-2823, 40 miles S of Madison.

Opened: 1944. **Holes:** 18. **Par:** 71/72. **Yards:** 6,432/5,813. **Course rating:** 70.0/72.1. **Slope:** 121/121. **Architect:** Art Johnson. **Green fee:** $19/$23. **Credit cards:** MC,VISA.

Reduced fees: N/A. **Caddies:** No. **Golf carts:** $22. **Discount golf packages:** No. **Season:** April-Oct. **High:** May-Aug. **On site lodging:** No. **Rental clubs:** No. **Walking policy:** Walking at certain times. **Metal spikes allowed:** No. **Range:** No. **To obtain tee times:** Call 2 days in advance.

Subscriber comments: Very hilly but challenging...Rolling course, #18 beautiful view...Excellent service...Several holes picture-postcard view...Several areas under construction, should be better...A sporty course, fair assessment for weekender.

★★½KRUEGER MUNICIPAL GOLF CLUB

PM-1611 Hackett St., Beloit, 53511, Rock County, (608)362-6503, 65 miles E of Milwaukee.

Opened: 1917. **Holes:** 9. **Par:** 70/71. **Yards:** 6,103/5,550. **Course rating:** 69.0/71.5. **Slope:** 121. **Architect:** Stanley Pelchar. **Green fee:** N/A. **Credit cards:** None. **Reduced fees:** Twilight, seniors, juniors. **Caddies:** No. **Golf carts:** $20. **Discount golf packages:** No. **Season:** March-Nov. **High:** May-Aug. **On site lodging:** No. **Rental clubs:** No. **Walking policy:** Unrestricted walking. **Metal spikes allowed:** Yes. **Range:** No. **To obtain tee times:** Call.

Subscriber comments: Just a nice course to play—bring all your shots...It has very good par 3s. The course is well maintained but too many holes run in the same direction....Nice little muny course...Looks easy, plays harder...Treat you very well.

★★★★LAKE ARROWHEAD GOLF COURSE

PU-1195 Apache Lane, Nekoosa, 54457, Adams County, (715)325-2929, 13 miles S of Wisconsin Rapids.

Opened: 1983. **Holes:** 18. **Par:** 72/72. **Yards:** 6,624/5,213. **Course rating:** 72.3/70.2. **Slope:** 135/125. **Architect:** Killian and Nugent. **Green fee:** $29/$40. **Credit cards:** MC,VISA. **Reduced fees:** Low season, twilight. **Caddies:** No. **Golf carts:** $12. **Discount golf packages:** Yes. **Season:** April-Oct. **High:** May-Sept. **On site lodging:** Yes. **Rental clubs:** Yes. **Walking policy:** Unrestricted walking. **Metal spikes allowed:** No. **Range:** Yes (grass). **To obtain tee times:** Call up to 30 days in advance. Groups of 16 or more call anytime in advance.

Subscriber comments: Lots of sand, beautiful course...Excellent fairways, woods all around...Long course to walk, lots of sand...Beautiful setting—well manicured...Touch course—but pleasant to play...Fun, just the right amount of challenge...Keep it straight or you're in trouble! Well groomed...Bent-grass fairways, very difficult approach shots...Wonderful sense of isolation on each hole...Each hole different from the last. **Special Notes:** Opening a new 18 in August 1998.

★½LAKE BEULAH COUNTRY CLUB

N9430 E. Shore Drive, Mukwonago, 53149, Walworth County, (414)363-8147, 20 miles W of Milwaukee.

Opened: N/A. **Holes:** 18. **Par:** 68/69. **Yards:** 5,715/4,891. **Course rating:** 66.7/69.8. **Slope:** 108/113. **Architect:** Roy & James Jacobs. **Green fee:** $17/$20. **Credit cards:** MC,VISA. **Reduced fees:** Low season, seniors, juniors. **Caddies:** No. **Golf carts:** $22. **Discount golf packages:** No. **Season:** April-Nov. **High:** July-Aug. **On site lodging:** No. **Rental clubs:** Yes. **Walking policy:** Unrestricted walking. **Metal spikes allowed:** Yes. **Range:** No. **To obtain tee times:** Call up to 7 days in advance.

Special Notes: Also have a 9-hole course.

★★½LAKE BREEZE GOLF CLUB

PU-6333 Highway 110, Winneconne, 54986, Winnebago County, (920)582-7585, (800)330-9189, 10 miles NW of Oshkosh.

Opened: 1991. **Holes:** 18. **Par:** 72/72. **Yards:** 6,896/5,748. **Course rating:** 72.2/71.9. **Slope:** 121/118. **Architect:** Homer Fieldhouse. **Green fee:** $12/$17. **Credit cards:** MC,VISA. **Reduced fees:** Low season, twilight, seniors, juniors. **Caddies:** No. **Golf carts:** $11. **Discount golf packages:** Yes. **Season:** April-Oct. **High:** June-Aug. **On site lodging:** No. **Rental clubs:** Yes. **Walking policy:** Unrestricted walking. **Metal spikes allowed:** Yes. **Range:** Yes (grass). **To obtain tee times:** Call 1 day in advance.

Subscriber comments: Will be a better course when trees are full...Nice people...A new course getting better...Some holes too close, nice for new course...Needs 20 years to mature...Kind of plain, some interesting holes...Back nine better.

WISCONSIN

★★½LAKE LAWN GOLF COURSE

R-Highway 50 E., Delavan, 53115, Walworth County, (414)728-7950, (800)338-5253.
Opened: 1928. **Holes:** 18. **Par:** 70/70. **Yards:** 6,418/5,215. **Course rating:** 69.2/64.1.
Slope: 120/107. **Architect:** Dick Nugent. **Green fee:** $48/$56. **Credit cards:**
MC,VISA,AMEX,DISC,Diners Club. **Reduced fees:** Weekdays, low season, resort
guests, twilight, seniors, juniors. **Caddies:** No. **Golf carts:** Included in Green Fee.
Discount golf packages: Yes. **Season:** April-Oct. **High:** June-Aug. **On site lodging:**
Yes. **Rental clubs:** Yes. **Walking policy:** Walking at certain times. **Metal spikes
allowed:** Yes. **Range:** Yes (grass/mats). **To obtain tee times:** Resort guests may book
anytime in advance with room reservation. Public may call 2 days in advance.
Subscriber comments: Lake holes very scenic...Well maintained...Good resort
course...Narrow fairways...Hard fast greens....Beautiful course. Challenging in the
wind...Very nice resort course...Average...Fairly open, excellent greens...Good layout,
well kept.

★★LAKE PARK GOLF COURSE

PU-N. 112 W. 17300 Mequon Rd., Germantown, 53022, Washington County, (414)255-
4200, 15 miles N of Milwaukee.
Opened: 1974. **Holes:** 27. **Architect:** Lloyd B. Robinson. **Green fee:** $9/$23. **Credit
cards:** MC,VISA. **Reduced fees:** Weekdays, low season, twilight, seniors. **Caddies:**
No. **Golf carts:** $11. **Discount golf packages:** No. **Season:** April-Oct. **High:** May-Sept.
On site lodging: No. **Rental clubs:** No. **Walking policy:** Unrestricted walking. **Metal
spikes allowed:** Yes. **Range:** No. **To obtain tee times:** Call.
RED/BLUE
Par: 72/73. **Yards:** 6,642/5,875. **Course rating:** 71.9/76.0. **Slope:** 126/129.
RED/WHITE
Par: 72/75. **Yards:** 7,010/6,069. **Course rating:** 73.6/77.2. **Slope:** 131/134.
WHITE/BLUE
Par: 72/76. **Yards:** 6,812/6,068. **Course rating:** 72.9/77.0. **Slope:** 126/131.

★★LAKE SHORE GOLF COURSE

PU-2175 Punhoqua St., Oshkosh, 54901, Winnebago County, (920)235-6200,.
Opened: 1920. **Holes:** 18. **Par:** 70/71. **Yards:** 6,030/5,162. **Course rating:** 68.2/69.4.
Slope: 120/119. **Architect:** N/A. **Green fee:** $13/$13. **Credit cards:** MC,VISA.
Reduced fees: Seniors, juniors. **Caddies:** No. **Golf carts:** $18. **Discount golf pack-
ages:** No. **Season:** April-Nov. **High:** June-Aug. **On site lodging:** No. **Rental clubs:**
Yes. **Walking policy:** Unrestricted walking. **Metal spikes allowed:** Yes. **Range:** Yes
(grass/mats). **To obtain tee times:** Call 7 days in advance for weekends and holidays.

★★LAKE WINDSOR GOLF CLUB

PU-4628 Golf Rd., Windsor, 53598, Dane County, (608)255-6100, 5 miles N of
Madison.
Opened: 1963. **Holes:** 27. **Architect:** N/A. **Green fee:** $10/$20. **Credit cards:**
MC,VISA. **Reduced fees:** Weekdays, low season, twilight, seniors, juniors. **Caddies:**
No. **Golf carts:** $9. **Discount golf packages:** No. **Season:** March-Nov. **High:** June-
Aug. **On site lodging:** No. **Rental clubs:** Yes. **Walking policy:** Unrestricted walking.
Metal spikes allowed: Yes. **Range:** No. **To obtain tee times:** Call one week in
advance.
RED/BLUE
Par: 71/71. **Yards:** 5,983/5,143. **Course rating:** 68.0/72.0. **Slope:** 115/122.
RED/WHITE
Par: 72/72. **Yards:** 6,228/5,348. **Course rating:** 69.2/73.0. **Slope:** 118/127.
WHITE/BLUE
Par: 71/71. **Yards:** 6,157/5,215. **Course rating:** 68.5/73.0. **Slope:** 118/127.

★★½LAKE WISCONSIN COUNTRY CLUB

N1076 Golf Rd., Prairie Du Sac, 53578, Columbia County, (608)643-2405.
Call club for further information.
Subscriber comments: Short, mediocre—good condition...The four par 3s on back
nine are fun!...Course in great condition...Not crowded—enjoyable...Two totally different
courses, front and back...Good vacation golf...Front nine challenging, back nine no
problem...Short, fast greens, tight.

★★★LAKEWOODS FOREST RIDGES GOLF COURSE

R-H.C. 73, Cable, 54821, Bayfield County, (715)794-2698, (800)255-5937, 80 miles SE of Duluth.

Opened: 1995. **Holes:** 18. **Par:** 71/71. **Yards:** 6,270/4,442. **Course rating:** 70.9/66.9. **Slope:** 137/123. **Architect:** Joel Goldstrand. **Green fee:** $45/$45. **Credit cards:** MC,VISA,DISC. **Reduced fees:** Low season, resort guests, twilight. **Caddies:** No. **Golf carts:** Included in Green Fee. **Discount golf packages:** Yes. **Season:** May-Oct. **High:** June-Sept. **On site lodging:** Yes. **Rental clubs:** Yes. **Walking policy:** Mandatory cart. **Metal spikes allowed:** Yes. **Range:** Yes (grass/mats). **To obtain tee times:** Call 7 days in advance.

Subscriber comments: Great layout. Outstanding resort. Needs to grow in...Much too difficult for average resort player, too penal, scenic...Nice newer course—will get better.

★★LITTLE RIVER COUNTRY CLUB

N2235 Shore Dr., Marinette, 54143, Marinette County, (715)732-2221, 2 miles S of Marinette.

Opened: 1927. **Holes:** 18. **Par:** 70/71. **Yards:** 5,749/5,083. **Course rating:** 65.7/68.0. **Slope:** 108/111. **Architect:** N/A. **Green fee:** $18/$21. **Credit cards:** MC,VISA. **Reduced fees:** Weekdays. **Caddies:** No. **Golf carts:** N/A. **Discount golf packages:** No. **Season:** April-Oct. **High:** N/A. **On site lodging:** No. **Rental clubs:** No. **Walking policy:** Unrestricted walking. **Metal spikes allowed:** No. **Range:** Yes (grass). **To obtain tee times:** Call up to 7 days in advance.

★★★LUCK GOLF COURSE

PM-1520 S. Shore Dr., Luck, 54853, Polk County, (715)472-2939, 65 miles NE of St. Paul, MN.

Opened: 1938. **Holes:** 18. **Par:** 71/72. **Yards:** 6,122/5,198. **Course rating:** 70.0/70.4. **Slope:** 122/119. **Architect:** N/A. **Green fee:** $20. **Credit cards:** MC,VISA. **Reduced fees:** Weekdays, twilight, juniors. **Caddies:** No. **Golf carts:** $10. **Discount golf packages:** No. **Season:** April-Nov. **High:** June-Aug. **On site lodging:** No. **Rental clubs:** Yes. **Walking policy:** Unrestricted walking. **Metal spikes allowed:** Yes. **Range:** Yes (grass). **To obtain tee times:** Call up to 4 days in advance.

Subscriber comments: Esthetically beautiful...Newer nine holes make it a challenge...Very fun to play. Tough undulating greens...Nice little out-of-way, lodge-type course...Great all-day rate...Nice small-town layout...Beautiful, mature course...New holes will mature nicely...Very old, but always green when dry weather comes.

★★★½MADELINE ISLAND GOLF CLUB

P.O. Box 83, La Pointe, 54850, Ashland County, (715)747-3212, 25 miles N of Ashland. **Opened:** 1966. **Holes:** 18. **Par:** 71/72. **Yards:** 6,366/5,506. **Course rating:** 71.0/71.7. **Slope:** 131/127. **Architect:** Robert Trent Jones. **Green fee:** $36/$45. **Credit cards:** MC,VISA. **Reduced fees:** Low season, twilight, juniors. **Caddies:** No. **Golf carts:** $25. **Discount golf packages:** No. **Season:** May-Oct. **High:** June-Sept. **On site lodging:** No. **Rental clubs:** Yes. **Walking policy:** Unrestricted walking. **Metal spikes allowed:** Yes. **Range:** Yes (grass). **To obtain tee times:** Call anytime.

Subscriber comments: Nice course—worth the ferry trip...Excellent golf course, but the highlight is the island, just off shore of Bayfield, in Lake Superior.

★★½MAPLE GROVE COUNTRY CLUB

W. 4142 County B, West Salem, 54669, La Crosse County, (608)786-0340, 10 miles NW of LaCrosse.

Opened: 1929. **Holes:** 18. **Par:** 71/71. **Yards:** 6,485/5,578. **Course rating:** 70.1/70.9. **Slope:** 122/121. **Architect:** Leland Thompson. **Green fee:** $18/$20. **Credit cards:** MC,VISA. **Reduced fees:** Weekdays, low season, twilight, seniors. **Caddies:** No. **Golf carts:** $20. **Discount golf packages:** Yes. **Season:** April-Nov. **High:** June-Aug. **On site lodging:** No. **Rental clubs:** Yes. **Walking policy:** Unrestricted walking. **Metal spikes allowed:** Yes. **Range:** Yes (grass/mats). **To obtain tee times:** Call 7 days in advance. Groups of 30 or more call anytime.

Subscriber comments: Lots of potential...Front and back different, just enjoyable...Long back nine, course has potential but needs better care...Nice hilly course.

WISCONSIN

★★★MAPLECREST COUNTRY CLUB
9401 18th St., Kenosha, 53144, Kenosha County, (414)859-2887, 20 miles S of Milwaukee.
Opened: 1929. **Holes:** 18. **Par:** 70/70. **Yards:** 6,396/5,056. **Course rating:** 70.9/71.0. **Slope:** 121/124. **Architect:** Leonard Macomber. **Green fee:** $14/$20. **Credit cards:** None. **Reduced fees:** Low season, twilight, seniors. **Caddies:** No. **Golf carts:** N/A. **Discount golf packages:** No. **Season:** March-Nov. **High:** May-Sept. **On site lodging:** No. **Rental clubs:** Yes. **Walking policy:** Unrestricted walking. **Metal spikes allowed:** Yes. **Range:** Yes (grass/mats). **To obtain tee times:** Call 7 days in advance.
Subscriber comments: Excellent condition...Slick greens...Very flat...Long course, fun for free swingers...Open and nicely groomed...No sand and no water. Basic golf...Nice design, great greens and many memorable holes...Long par 4s...Great layout, short and long, fast greens on hills...Sloping greens, tough course.

★½MARSHFIELD COUNTRY CLUB
PU-11426 Wren Rd., Marshfield, 54449, Wood County, (715)384-4409, (800)690-4409, 1 mile W of Marshfield.
Opened: N/A. **Holes:** 18. **Par:** 70/70. **Yards:** 6,004/5,376. **Course rating:** N/A. **Slope:** 115/111. **Architect:** N/A. **Green fee:** $17/$18. **Credit cards:** All major. **Reduced fees:** Weekdays, low season, twilight, seniors, juniors. **Caddies:** No. **Golf carts:** $20. **Discount golf packages:** No. **Season:** April-Nov. **High:** May-Sept. **On site lodging:** No. **Rental clubs:** Yes. **Walking policy:** Unrestricted walking. **Metal spikes allowed:** Yes. **Range:** Yes (grass/mats). **To obtain tee times:** Call.

★★★½MASCOUTIN GOLF CLUB
PU-W1635 County Trunk A, Berlin, 54923, Green Lake County, (920)361-2360, 20 miles W of Oshkosh.
Opened: 1975. **Holes:** 18. **Par:** 72/73. **Yards:** 6,821/5,133. **Course rating:** 72.8/69.9. **Slope:** 130/122. **Architect:** Larry Packard. **Green fee:** $20/$38. **Credit cards:** MC,VISA. **Reduced fees:** Weekdays, low season, twilight, juniors. **Caddies:** No. **Golf carts:** $12. **Discount golf packages:** Yes. **Season:** April-Oct. **High:** May-Sept. **On site lodging:** No. **Rental clubs:** Yes. **Walking policy:** Walking at certain times. **Metal spikes allowed:** No. **Range:** Yes (grass). **To obtain tee times:** Call anytime.
Subscriber comments: Always a great round. Open, but has its penalties...Flat, young in places, huge greens...Great views, especially in the fall...Very good golf without any tricks...Fun course to play, not too hard...Good course, good shape...Difficult course from back tees, wonderful greens...Nice layout. Condition only good...Lovely, great greens...Fast small greens. Nice course.
Special Notes: Additional 9 holes opening in 1999.

★★MAXWELTON BRAES GOLF RESORT
7200 Hwy. 57, Baileys Harbor, 54202, Door County, (920)839-2321.
Call club for further information.

★★MAYVILLE GOLF CLUB
PU-325 S. German St., Mayville, 53050, Dodge County, (920)387-2999, 25 miles S of Fond du Lac.
Opened: 1931. **Holes:** 18. **Par:** 71/72. **Yards:** 6,173/5,235. **Course rating:** 69.5/70.0. **Slope:** 119/115. **Architect:** Bob Lohmann. **Green fee:** $17/$22. **Credit cards:** MC,VISA. **Reduced fees:** Weekdays, low season, twilight, seniors, juniors. **Caddies:** No. **Golf carts:** $11. **Discount golf packages:** No. **Season:** April-Oct. **High:** June-Aug. **On site lodging:** No. **Rental clubs:** Yes. **Walking policy:** Unrestricted walking. **Metal spikes allowed:** Yes. **Range:** No. **To obtain tee times:** Call 7 days in advance.

★★★MCGAUSLIN BROOK GOLF & COUNTRY CLUB
17067 Clubhouse Lane, Lakewood, 54138, Oconto County, (715)276-7623.
Opened: 1965. **Holes:** 18. **Par:** 70/70. **Yards:** 5,926/4,886. **Course rating:** 67.1/62.5. **Slope:** 115/105. **Architect:** N/A. **Green fee:** $16/$21. **Credit cards:** MC,VISA,DISC. **Reduced fees:** Weekdays, low season. **Caddies:** No. **Golf carts:** $18. **Discount golf packages:** No. **Season:** April-Oct. **High:** July-Aug. **On site lodging:** No. **Rental clubs:** No. **Walking policy:** Unrestricted walking. **Metal spikes allowed:** Yes. **Range:** No. **To obtain tee times:** Call up to 3 days in advance.

Subscriber comments: Fun course to play, interesting layout...Excellent northern Wisconsin course, tight back nine...This course is well maintained...Course better than most, gets a lot of play...Very nice course, greens rolling (tough]...Great greens...Very nice short course. Watch for crossover golfers on back...Hitting across the creek three times on the back nine. People are friendly.

★★MEADOW LINKS GOLF COURSE

PU-1540 Johnston Dr., Manitowoc, 54220, Manitowoc County, (920)682-6842, 35 miles SE of Green Bay.
Opened: 1929. **Holes:** 18. **Par:** 72/72. **Yards:** 5,934/5,254. **Course rating:** 67.8/69.2.
Slope: 114/114. **Architect:** N/A. **Green fee:** $10/$16. **Credit cards:** MC,VISA.
Reduced fees: Seniors, juniors. **Caddies:** No. **Golf carts:** $18. **Discount golf packages:** No. **Season:** April-Oct. **High:** June-Aug. **On site lodging:** No. **Rental clubs:** Yes.
Walking policy: Unrestricted walking. **Metal spikes allowed:** Yes. **Range:** No. **To obtain tee times:** Call.

★★MEEK-KWON PARK GOLF COURSE

PM-6333 W Bonniwell Rd 136nth, Mequon, 53092, Ozaukee County, (414)242-1310, 25 miles N of Milwaukee.
Opened: 1974. **Holes:** 18. **Par:** 70/70. **Yards:** 6,465/5,472. **Course rating:** 70.5/70.8.
Slope: 120/118. **Architect:** N/A. **Green fee:** $11/$22. **Credit cards:** MC,VISA.
Reduced fees: Seniors. **Caddies:** No. **Golf carts:** $22. **Discount golf packages:** No.
Season: April-Oct. **High:** June-Aug. **On site lodging:** No. **Rental clubs:** No. **Walking policy:** Unrestricted walking. **Metal spikes allowed:** No. **Range:** No. **To obtain tee times:** Call 3 days in advance.

★★½MERRILL GOLF CLUB

PU-1604 O'Day St., Merrill, 54452, Lincoln County, (715)536-2529, 20 miles N of Wausaw.
Opened: 1932. **Holes:** 18. **Par:** 72/72. **Yards:** 6,456/5,432. **Course rating:** 70.2/70.0.
Slope: 120/111. **Architect:** Tom Vardon. **Green fee:** $12/$20. **Credit cards:** All major.
Reduced fees: Weekdays, twilight, seniors, juniors. **Caddies:** No. **Golf carts:** $20.
Discount golf packages: No. **Season:** April-Oct. **High:** June-Aug. **On site lodging:** No. **Rental clubs:** Yes. **Walking policy:** Unrestricted walking. **Metal spikes allowed:** Yes. **Range:** Yes (mats). **To obtain tee times:** Call 7 days in advance.
Subscriber comments: Several blind second shots...Muny—easy...Sleeper, pleasant surprise. Interesting and challenging...Nice course, tough greens.

★★MID-VALLEE GOLF COURSE

PU-3134 Apple Creek Rd., De Pere, 54115, Brown County, (920)532-6674, 10 miles S of Green Bay.
Opened: 1963. **Holes:** 27. **Par:** 70/72. **Yards:** 6,400/5,624. **Course rating:** 69.1.
Slope: 122/120. **Architect:** Edward Lockie. **Green fee:** $17/$22. **Credit cards:** MC,VISA. **Reduced fees:** N/A. **Caddies:** No. **Golf carts:** $20. **Discount golf packages:** No. **Season:** April-Oct. **High:** June-Aug. **On site lodging:** No. **Rental clubs:** No.
Walking policy: N/A. **Metal spikes allowed:** Yes. **Range:** Yes (grass/mats). **To obtain tee times:** Call up to 7 days in advance.

★★★MILL RUN GOLF COURSE

PU-3905 Kane Rd., Eau Claire, 54703, Eau Claire County, (715)834-1766, (800)241-1766, 65 miles E of Minneapolis/St. Paul, MN.
Opened: 1981. **Holes:** 18. **Par:** 70/71. **Yards:** 6,078/4,744. **Course rating:** 68.7/66.6.
Slope: 116/109. **Architect:** Gordon Emerson. **Green fee:** $19/$20. **Credit cards:** All major. **Reduced fees:** Weekdays, seniors, juniors. **Caddies:** No. **Golf carts:** $10.
Discount golf packages: Yes. **Season:** April-Oct. **High:** April-Oct. **On site lodging:** No. **Rental clubs:** Yes. **Walking policy:** Unrestricted walking. **Metal spikes allowed:** Yes. **Range:** Yes (grass). **To obtain tee times:** Call anytime.
Subscriber comments: Nice except for power lines...As course matures it will improve. Always in great condition...Many short holes....Short, nice course, well maintained...Open but challenging—great flower scenery...Short from white tees, outstanding landscaping, professional staff...Shorter course, but beautifully maintained, good practice facilities.

WISCONSIN

★★MUSKEGO LAKES COUNTRY CLUB
S. 100 W. 14020 Loomis Rd., Muskego, 53150, Waukesha County, (414)425-6500, 13 miles SW of Milwaukee.
Opened: 1969. **Holes:** 18. **Par:** 71/72. **Yards:** 6,498/5,493. **Course rating:** 71.5/71.7. **Slope:** 126/123. **Architect:** Larry Packard. **Green fee:** $18/$26. **Credit cards:** MC,VISA. **Reduced fees:** Weekdays, low season, seniors, juniors. **Caddies:** No. **Golf carts:** $13. **Discount golf packages:** No. **Season:** April-Nov. **High:** May-Sept. **On site lodging:** No. **Rental clubs:** Yes. **Walking policy:** Unrestricted walking. **Metal spikes allowed:** Yes. **Range:** Yes (grass/mats). **To obtain tee times:** Call up to 4 days in advance. Foursomes required on weekends before 1 p.m.

★★½MYSTERY HILLS GOLF CLUB
PU-3149 Dickinson Rd., De Pere, 54115, Brown County, (920)336-6077, 2 miles SE of Green Bay.
Opened: 1963. **Holes:** 18. **Par:** 72/72. **Yards:** 6,254/5,569. **Course rating:** 70.1/72.2. **Slope:** 120/120. **Architect:** N/A. **Green fee:** $16/$18. **Credit cards:** All major. **Reduced fees:** Weekdays. **Caddies:** No. **Golf carts:** $22. **Discount golf packages:** No. **Season:** Year-round. **High:** May-Aug. **On site lodging:** No. **Rental clubs:** Yes. **Walking policy:** Unrestricted walking. **Metal spikes allowed:** Yes. **Range:** Yes (grass/mats). **To obtain tee times:** Call up to 6 months in advance.
Subscriber comments: Very nice course—beautiful setting...Nice layout...Nice site for a golf course...Some good holes and some very easy holes...Has potential to be a great course...Nice plush fairways. Good layout...Course was well maintained, great practice facilities and pro shop. Previous construction makes course fun and challenging...Improved course 100 percent...First to open in spring.
Special Notes: Also has a 9-hole course.

★★★★NAGA-WAUKEE GOLF COURSE
PU-1897 Maple Ave., Pewaukee, 53072, Waukesha County, (414)367-2153, 20 miles W of Milwaukee.
Opened: 1966. **Holes:** 18. **Par:** 72/72. **Yards:** 6,780/5,796. **Course rating:** 71.8/72.6. **Slope:** 125/125. **Architect:** Lawrence Packard. **Green fee:** $17/$29. **Credit cards:** MC,VISA. **Reduced fees:** Weekdays, low season, twilight, seniors, juniors. **Caddies:** No. **Golf carts:** $11. **Discount golf packages:** No. **Season:** April-Dec. **High:** May-Sept. **On site lodging:** No. **Rental clubs:** Yes. **Walking policy:** Unrestricted walking. **Metal spikes allowed:** Yes. **Range:** Yes (grass/mats). **To obtain tee times:** Call 4 days in advance.
Subscriber comments: Long, interesting, hills, wooded, excellent pro and staff, not to be missed...One of the best public courses anywhere...Beautiful, scenic, new-conditioned course. Long enough...Good place to buy used golf balls...Tough to walk...Greens and fairways in excellent condition...A terrific public course...Fantastic views; tough...Hard to get tee time.

NEMADJI GOLF COURSE
PU-5 N. 58th St. E., Superior, 54880, Douglas County, (715)394-9022.
Green fee: $12/$20. **Credit cards:** All major. **Reduced fees:** Low season, twilight, juniors. **Caddies:** Yes. **Golf carts:** $18. **Discount golf packages:** No. **Season:** April-Oct. **High:** June-Aug. **On site lodging:** No. **Rental clubs:** Yes. **Walking policy:** Unrestricted walking. **Metal spikes allowed:** Yes. **Range:** Yes (grass/mats). **To obtain tee times:** Call up to 14 days in advance.

★★★½EAST/WEST COURSE
Opened: 1981. **Holes:** 18. **Par:** 72/72. **Yards:** 6,701/5,252. **Course rating:** 72.7/70.7. **Slope:** 133/124. **Architect:** D.W. Herfort.
Subscriber comments: Well-run and well-maintained municipal courses...Well-equipped pro shop, fast greens and friendly...Greens are tremendous...East/West most fun...Best service in area...Excellent greens, variety of shots...Friendliest staff around, best greens, keep it straight...The par 5 7th is the best of a superb new nine.

★★★½NORTH/SOUTH COURSE
Opened: 1932. **Holes:** 18. **Par:** 71/71. **Yards:** 6,362/4,983. **Course rating:** 69.7/67.8. **Slope:** 120/114. **Architect:** Stanley Pelchar.

WISCONSIN

Subscriber comments: Well-run and well-maintained municipal courses...Fun to play, great shape, great par 3s...Nice practice area...Pretty flat—not much trouble...North/South OK but not as much fun as East/West...Greens decent, course boring...Short but challenging, well maintained...Some very good holes, average greens.

★★½NEW BERLIN HILLS GOLF COURSE

PM-13175 W. Graham St., New Berlin, 53151, Waukesha County, (414)780-5200.
Opened: 1908. **Holes:** 18. **Par:** 71/71. **Yards:** 6,517/5,346. **Course rating:** 71.7/70.8.
Slope: 127/123. **Architect:** Art Johnson. **Green fee:** $16/$25. **Credit cards:** MC,VISA.
Reduced fees: Weekdays, seniors, juniors. **Caddies:** No. **Golf carts:** $12. **Discount golf packages:** No. **Season:** April-Nov. **High:** June-Sept. **On site lodging:** No. **Rental clubs:** Yes. **Walking policy:** Unrestricted walking. **Metal spikes allowed:** Yes. **Range:** No. **To obtain tee times:** Call up to 7 days in advance.
Subscriber comments: Great course for scoring...Best condition in 35 years...Not bad, if you can ignore the freeway and condos...Course condition good and improving...Plays to average golfer...Challenging greens. A nice area secret...Greens too fast for being slanty...Making a great comeback after much neglect.

★★★★NEW RICHMOND GOLF CLUB

1226 180th Ave., New Richmond, 54017, St. Croix County, (715)246-6724, 30 miles NE of St. Paul, MN.
Opened: 1923. **Holes:** 18. **Par:** 72/73. **Yards:** 6,716/5,547. **Course rating:** 72.5/71.7. **Slope:** 136/129. **Architect:** Bill Kidd Sr./Don Herfort.
Green fee: $25/$30. **Credit cards:** MC,VISA. **Reduced fees:** Weekdays, low season, seniors, juniors. **Caddies:** No. **Golf carts:** $11. **Discount golf packages:** No. **Season:** April-Oct. **High:** June-Aug. **On site lodging:** No. **Rental clubs:** Yes.
Walking policy: Unrestricted walking. **Metal spikes allowed:** Yes. **Range:** Yes (grass/mats). **To obtain tee times:** Call 2 days in advance.
Subscriber comments: Uses the natural beauty of area well...One of the best public courses in Wisconsin...3 to 18 are great. Cool course...Challenging course, always in great shape...A well kept secret, lots of fun and never too crowded...Championship course in the pines...A nice small-town course.

★★½NICOLET COUNTRY CLUB

PU-Hwy. 8, Laona, 54541, Forest County, (715)674-4780, 35 miles SE of Rhinelander.
Opened: 1960. **Holes:** 18. **Par:** 67/67. **Yards:** 4,713/4,093. **Course rating:** 62.2/62.3.
Slope: 104/100. **Architect:** N/A. **Green fee:** $15/$17. **Credit cards:** MC,VISA.
Reduced fees: N/A. **Caddies:** No. **Golf carts:** $19. **Discount golf packages:** No.
Season: April-Oct. **High:** June-Sept. **On site lodging:** No. **Rental clubs:** Yes. **Walking policy:** N/A. **Metal spikes allowed:** Yes. **Range:** Yes (grass). **To obtain tee times:** Call up to 7 days in advance.
Subscriber comments: Short but difficult, excellent condition...Short, woody, leave driver in bag...Very enjoyable course...90-degree doglegs...Fun golf course...Funny course, needs work, but fun playing...Short course but very affordable and friendly.

★½NIPPERSINK COUNTRY CLUB

N1055 Tombeau Rd., Genoa City, 53128, Walworth County, (414)279-6311.
Call club for further information.

★★★½NORTHBROOK COUNTRY CLUB

407 NorthBrook Dr., Luxemburg, 54217, Kewaunee County, (920)845-2383.
Opened: 1971. **Holes:** 18. **Par:** 71/72. **Yards:** 6,223/5,495. **Course rating:** 69.2/70.9.
Slope: 121/116. **Architect:** Ed Langert. **Green fee:** $13/$23. **Credit cards:** MC,VISA.
Reduced fees: Weekdays, low season, seniors, juniors. **Caddies:** Yes. **Golf carts:** $23.
Discount golf packages: No. **Season:** April-Oct. **High:** June-Aug. **On site lodging:** No. **Rental clubs:** Yes. **Walking policy:** Unrestricted walking. **Metal spikes allowed:** No. **Range:** Yes (grass). **To obtain tee times:** Call 7 days in advance.
Subscriber comments: Enjoyable course...Challenging 18 holes...Course in excellent shape...Nice variety of holes...Well maintained—challenging fast greens...Very difficult—lots of trees...Super 18 holes for small town...Need to be short on all approach shots...Great appearance, plays well...Local knowledge required, softspikes only, difficult greens...Excellent dining, friendly people.

WISCONSIN

★★★★NORTHWOOD GOLF COURSE
PU-6301 Hwy. 8 W., Rhinelander, 54501, Oneida County, (715)282-6565, 50 miles N of Wausau.
Opened: 1989. **Holes:** 18. **Par:** 72/72. **Yards:** 6,724/5,338. **Course rating:** 73.1/71.3. **Slope:** 140/129. **Architect:** Don Herfort. **Green fee:** $29/$29. **Credit cards:** MC,VISA. **Reduced fees:** Juniors. **Caddies:** No. **Golf carts:** $22. **Discount golf packages:** Yes. **Season:** April-Oct. **High:** June-Sept. **On site lodging:** No. **Rental clubs:** Yes. **Walking policy:** Unrestricted walking. **Metal spikes allowed:** Yes. **Range:** Yes (grass). **To obtain tee times:** Call up to 14 days in advance.
Subscriber comments: Great course. Very good layout...Most challenging course in the state...Very tight fairways, scenic...Wonderful! Thoroughly enjoyed...Too many trees, fun for occasional play...Beautiful course...Narrow fairways, island green, fun course...Best of the northern WI courses...Not too forgiving!...Very pretty woodland course, interesting layout, always fun.

OAK RIDGE GOLF COURSE
Bowers Lake Rd., Milton, 53563, Rock County, (608)868-4353, 4 miles N of Janesville.
Opened: 1975. **Holes:** 27. **Par:** 71/72. **Yards:** 5,949/5,519. **Course rating:** 69.9/69.5. **Slope:** 117/111. **Architect:** N/A. **Green fee:** $18/$20. **Credit cards:** MC,VISA,DISC. **Reduced fees:** N/A. **Caddies:** No. **Golf carts:** $20. **Discount golf packages:** No. **Season:** March-Nov. **High:** June-Aug. **On site lodging:** No. **Rental clubs:** Yes. **Walking policy:** Unrestricted walking. **Metal spikes allowed:** No. **Range:** Yes (grass). **To obtain tee times:** Call.

★★★OAKWOOD PARK GOLF COURSE
PU-3600 W. Oakwood Rd., Franklin, 53132, Milwaukee County, (414)281-6700, 8 miles S of Milwaukee.
Opened: 1971. **Holes:** 18. **Par:** 72/72. **Yards:** 7,008/6,179. **Course rating:** 72.5/74.4. **Slope:** 121/123. **Architect:** Edward Lawrence Packard. **Green fee:** $10/$22. **Credit cards:** MC,VISA. **Reduced fees:** Weekdays, seniors, juniors. **Caddies:** No. **Golf carts:** $24. **Discount golf packages:** No. **Season:** April-Oct. **High:** June-Aug. **On site lodging:** No. **Rental clubs:** Yes. **Walking policy:** Walking at certain times. **Metal spikes allowed:** Yes. **Range:** Yes (grass/mats). **To obtain tee times:** Call anytime.
Subscriber comments: Muny course—great shape...7,000 yards of pure fun...Well maintained for county course...Strategic golf a plus...Good course to let it fly...The new clubhouse will be greatly appreciated...Great county course, nice and long, get your money's worth...Wide fairways...Long, tough, flat, good shape.

★★½ODANA HILLS GOLF COURSE
4635 Odana Rd., Madison, 53711, Dane County, (608)266-4078.
Call club for further information.
Subscriber comments: One of the better public fee courses...Fun course—well maintained...Conditions are fair, greens are slowly being rebuilt...Short holes and long holes. Good test for amateurs...Easier muny, great for my kids...Crowded. good municipal course...Mature trees. Good muny...Great layout with lots of pines...Good course—particularly the final five holes...Always busy, good but nothing special.

★★★½OLD HICKORY GOLF CLUB
Hwy. 33 E., Beaver Dam, 53916, Dodge County, (920)887-7577, 30 miles NE of Madison.
Opened: 1920. **Holes:** 18. **Par:** 72/73. **Yards:** 6,688/5,644. **Course rating:** 72.5/72.8. **Slope:** 129/127. **Architect:** Tom Bendelow. **Green fee:** $40/$50. **Credit cards:** MC,VISA. **Reduced fees:** Low season. **Caddies:** No. **Golf carts:** $12. **Discount golf packages:** No. **Season:** April-Oct. **High:** June-Aug. **On site lodging:** No. **Rental clubs:** Yes. **Walking policy:** Walking at certain times. **Metal spikes allowed:** No. **Range:** Yes (grass/mats). **To obtain tee times:** Call 7 days in advance.
Subscriber comments: Fun course to play; small greens...Well maintained/blind shots/challenging...Very challenging, fast greens, requires accuracy...Beautiful old course, very well kept...A real treat; super layout; watch out for #14; beautiful...Lots of large trees...Not excessively long, but a very mature, hilly course and very well maintained...Enjoyable old design...Quaint, small-town atmosphere.

WISCONSIN

★★½OLDE HIGHLANDER GOLF CLUB AT OLYMPIA RESORT
R-1350 Royale Mile Rd., Oconomowoc, 53066, Waukesha County, (414)567-6048, 30 miles W of Milwaukee.
Opened: 1971. **Holes:** 18. **Par:** 72/71. **Yards:** 6,458/5,688. **Course rating:** 70.5/72.4.
Slope: 118/119. **Architect:** Randy Warobick. **Green fee:** $24/$28. **Credit cards:** All major. **Reduced fees:** Weekdays, low season, twilight, seniors, juniors. **Caddies:** No.
Golf carts: $12. **Discount golf packages:** Yes. **Season:** April-Nov. **High:** June-Sept.
On site lodging: Yes. **Rental clubs:** Yes. **Walking policy:** Walking at certain times.
Metal spikes allowed: Yes. **Range:** Yes (grass). **To obtain tee times:** Call.
Subscriber comments: Good course, great potential...Condition better than past years...Wide variety of holes.

★½PAGANICA GOLF COURSE
PU-3850 Silverlake, Oconomowoc, 53066, Waukesha County, (414)567-0171.
Opened: 1965. **Holes:** 18. **Par:** 72/74. **Yards:** 6,576/5,663. **Course rating:** 70.7/71.5.
Slope: 116/116. **Architect:** Luke Frye. **Green fee:** $22/$24. **Credit cards:** None.
Reduced fees: Low season, seniors. **Caddies:** No. **Golf carts:** $11. **Discount golf packages:** No. **Season:** March-Dec. **High:** June-Aug. **On site lodging:** No. **Rental clubs:** Yes. **Walking policy:** Unrestricted walking. **Metal spikes allowed:** Yes. **Range:** Yes (grass/mats). **To obtain tee times:** Call 7 days in advance.

★★½PECKS WILDWOOD GOLF COURSE
PU-10080 Highway 70 W., Minocqua, 54548, Oneida County, (715)356-3477, 70 miles N of Wausau.
Opened: 1983. **Holes:** 18. **Par:** 71/71. **Yards:** 5,869/5,483. **Course rating:** 68.6/71.0.
Slope: 115/118. **Architect:** N/A. **Green fee:** $25/$25. **Credit cards:** MC,VISA.
Reduced fees: Low season. **Caddies:** No. **Golf carts:** $20. **Discount golf packages:** Yes. **Season:** April-Oct. **High:** N/A. **On site lodging:** No. **Rental clubs:** Yes. **Walking policy:** Unrestricted walking. **Metal spikes allowed:** No. **Range:** Yes (mats). **To obtain tee times:** Call.
Subscriber comments: Great vacation golf with kids along, nice people...Several very challenging holes, slow greens, narrow fairways...OK all around...Very tight course, fun to play.

★★★½PENINSULA STATE PARK GOLF COURSE
PU-Hwy. 42, Ephraim, 54211, Door County, (920)854-5791, 70 miles NE of Green Bay.
Opened: 1921. **Holes:** 18. **Par:** 71/72. **Yards:** 6,261/5,083. **Course rating:** 69.8/70.3.
Slope: 124/121. **Architect:** Edward Lawrence Packard. **Green fee:** $20/$24. **Credit cards:** None. **Reduced fees:** Twilight, juniors. **Caddies:** No. **Golf carts:** $20. **Discount golf packages:** No. **Season:** May-Oct. **High:** June-Sept. **On site lodging:** No. **Rental clubs:** Yes. **Walking policy:** Unrestricted walking. **Metal spikes allowed:** Yes. **Range:** Yes (grass). **To obtain tee times:** Call up to 30 days in advance, or come in during season.
Subscriber comments: Excellent course—beautiful setting, very challenging...Very busy in summer...Made our camping trip more enjoyable...A lot of fun, many changes in elevation...Gorgeous scenery. 12th memorable...Very scenic—best to play in fall...Breathtaking views...The course takes a back seat to the scenery...Better to play after Labor Day or before Memorial Day...Heavy play...Short course—small greens.

★★★PETRIFYING SPRINGS GOLF COURSE
PU-4909 7th St., Kenosha, 53144, Kenosha County, (414)552-9052, 30 miles S of Milwaukee.
Opened: 1922. **Holes:** 18. **Par:** 71/72. **Yards:** 5,979/5,588. **Course rating:** 67.8/70.9.
Slope: 119/122. **Architect:** Joseph A. Roseman. **Green fee:** $18/$21. **Credit cards:** MC,VISA. **Reduced fees:** N/A. **Caddies:** No. **Golf carts:** $18. **Discount golf packages:** No. **Season:** April-Nov. **High:** June-Aug. **On site lodging:** No. **Rental clubs:** Yes. **Walking policy:** Unrestricted walking. **Metal spikes allowed:** No. **Range:** No. **To obtain tee times:** Call 12 days in advance for a fee of $4.
Subscriber comments: Good muny course...Beautiful in the fall...Beautiful park, well kept up...Back nine is fun...Hilly, well kept, enjoyable...Nice older course. A lot of golfers...Last three holes on back a real test...No driving range, but they have a green to pitch to...Course too short...Nice woodsy course.

WISCONSIN

★★PINEWOOD COUNTRY CLUB
PU-4660 Lakewood Rd., Harshaw, 54529, Oneida County, (715)282-5500, (800)746-3963, 13 miles S of Minocqua.
Opened: 1962. **Holes:** 18. **Par:** 70/70. **Yards:** 6,245/4,854. **Course rating:** 69.8/67.7. **Slope:** 123/115. **Architect:** N/A. **Green fee:** $22/$24. **Credit cards:** MC,VISA,DISC. **Reduced fees:** Low season, twilight, juniors. **Caddies:** No. **Golf carts:** $24. **Discount golf packages:** No. **Season:** April-Oct. **High:** June-Aug. **On site lodging:** Yes. **Rental clubs:** Yes. **Walking policy:** Unrestricted walking. **Metal spikes allowed:** No. **Range:** Yes (grass/mats). **To obtain tee times:** Call.

★★★PLEASANT VIEW GOLF CLUB
PM-1322 Pleasant View Dr., Middleton, 53562, Dane County, (608)831-6666, 1 mile N of Madison.
Opened: 1957. **Holes:** 18. **Par:** 92/72. **Yards:** 6,436/5,514. **Course rating:** 70.0/17.5. **Slope:** 122/116. **Architect:** Art Johnson. **Green fee:** $23/$26. **Credit cards:** MC,VISA. **Reduced fees:** Weekdays, low season, twilight, seniors, juniors. **Golf carts:** $24. **Discount golf packages:** Yes. **Season:** April-Oct. **High:** June-Aug. **On site lodging:** No. **Rental clubs:** Yes. **Walking policy:** Unrestricted walking. **Metal spikes allowed:** Yes. **Range:** Yes (grass/mats). **To obtain tee times:** Call.
Subscriber comments: Improved much last couple years...Use every club, smart play rewarded...A sleeper, great scoring, go out of way to please...Good condition—peaceful...Beautiful scenery with challenging course...Rolling—long—nice...Beautiful setting...Gorgeous in fall...Front nine too many blind shots, back nine outstanding layout, tough 18th.
Special Notes: Also has a par-3 course.

★★★PORTAGE COUNTRY CLUB
E. Hwy. No. 33, Portage, 53901, Columbia County, (608)742-5121, 20 miles S of Wisconsin Dells.
Opened: N/A. **Holes:** 18. **Par:** 72/74. **Yards:** 6,356/4,946. **Course rating:** 70.4/68.0. **Slope:** 127/119. **Architect:** Art Johnson. **Green fee:** $27/$32. **Credit cards:** None. **Reduced fees:** Weekdays. **Caddies:** No. **Golf carts:** $14. **Discount golf packages:** No. **Season:** April-Nov. **High:** N/A. **On site lodging:** No. **Rental clubs:** Yes. **Walking policy:** Unrestricted walking. **Metal spikes allowed:** No. **Range:** Yes (grass). **To obtain tee times:** Call up to 7 days in advance.
Subscriber comments: A very hard course, but well-staffed and maintained...Tight, but short, 3rd great par 3...Lots of trees—challenging...Tough, tight, fast greens...Some very difficult holes...Some holes very tight, small greens, need to think here...Great course, good test of skills...Fun, tight, scenic and not too busy!...Blends old and new course design—interesting holes.

★★★QUIT-QUI-OC GOLF CLUB
PU-500 Quit-Qui-Oc Lane, Elkhart Lake, 53020, Sheboygan County, (920)876-2833, 50 miles N of Milwaukee.
Opened: 1925. **Holes:** 18. **Par:** 70/71. **Yards:** 6,178/5,134. **Course rating:** 69.6/64.9. **Slope:** 119/109. **Architect:** Bendelow/Wiese. **Green fee:** $18/$25. **Credit cards:** MC,VISA. **Reduced fees:** Weekdays, low season, twilight, seniors, juniors. **Caddies:** No. **Golf carts:** $12. **Discount golf packages:** No. **Season:** April-Nov. **High:** May-Sept. **On site lodging:** No. **Rental clubs:** Yes. **Walking policy:** Unrestricted walking. **Metal spikes allowed:** Yes. **Range:** Yes (grass). **To obtain tee times:** Call 4 days in advance.
Subscriber comments: Scenic...This course is excellent...Excellent old-fashioned, traditional course, small excellent greens...Gets better every year...Narrow...Staff makes you feel like family!...Some great par 3s. No.15 great challenge...Great greens, never a flat lie...Fun course, old layout, scenic views, nice people...Hilly and undulating fairways...Nice little course, great setting.

★★★RAINBOW SPRINGS GOLF CLUB
PU-S103 W33599 Hwy. 99, Mukwonago, 53149, Waukesha County, (414)363-4550, (800)465-3631, 30 miles SW of Milwaukee.
Opened: 1964. **Holes:** 18. **Par:** 72/72. **Yards:** 6,914/5,135. **Course rating:** 73.4/69.8. **Slope:** 132/120. **Architect:** Francis Schroedel. **Green fee:** $22/$26. **Credit cards:**

MC,VISA. **Reduced fees:** Weekdays, low season, twilight, seniors, juniors. **Caddies:** No. **Golf carts:** $13. **Discount golf packages:** Yes. **Season:** April-Nov. **High:** June-Sept. **On site lodging:** No. **Rental clubs:** Yes. **Walking policy:** Walking at certain times. **Metal spikes allowed:** Yes. **Range:** Yes (grass). **To obtain tee times:** Call up to 14 days in advance with credit card to guarantee. 48-hour cancellation policy.
Subscriber comments: Very tough. Water everywhere...Flat but very tight...Nice condition. Lots of trouble...No bunkers, no hills, but it is always a challenge for all levels to shoot a good round and without losing golf balls...Crowned greens, hard to hold...Very woody with swamps and bugs, bring repellant.
Special Notes: Also 18-hole executive course.

★★★½REEDSBURG COUNTRY CLUB
Hwy. 33, Reedsburg, 53959, Sauk County, (608)524-6000, 14 miles SW of Wisconsin Dells.
Opened: 1924. **Holes:** 18. **Par:** 72/73. **Yards:** 6,300/5,324. **Course rating:** 70.5/70.3. **Slope:** 129/124. **Architect:** Ken Killian and Dick Nugent. **Green fee:** $38. **Credit cards:** MC,VISA. **Reduced fees:** Weekdays, low season, twilight. **Caddies:** No. **Golf carts:** $13. **Discount golf packages:** No. **Season:** March-Nov. **High:** June-Aug. **On site lodging:** No. **Rental clubs:** Yes. **Walking policy:** Unrestricted walking. **Metal spikes allowed:** No. **Range:** Yes (grass). **To obtain tee times:** Call up to 30 days in advance.
Subscriber comments: Short but a good track...Tough, tight, fast...Lightning greens...Good variety, greens excellent...Slick greens. Excellent fairways. Fun...Quiet small-town atmosphere...Excellent facility, good restaurant...Small-town country club, fun layout, nice people, pretty...Excellent greens, with some very tough and interesting holes...Great staff and service, best greens around.

★★½REID GOLF COURSE
PM-1100 E. Fremont, Appleton, 54915, Outagamie County, (920)832-5926.
Opened: 1941. **Holes:** 18. **Par:** 71/72. **Yards:** 5,968/5,296. **Course rating:** 67.6/69.1. **Slope:** 114/115. **Architect:** Miller Cohenen. **Green fee:** $14/$16. **Credit cards:** None. **Reduced fees:** Twilight, seniors, juniors. **Caddies:** No. **Golf carts:** $16. **Discount golf packages:** No. **Season:** April-Oct. **High:** June-Aug. **On site lodging:** No. **Rental clubs:** Yes. **Walking policy:** Unrestricted walking. **Metal spikes allowed:** Yes. **Range:** Yes (grass). **To obtain tee times:** Call 3 days in advance.
Subscriber comments: Good, clean, friendly public course...Excellent teaching pro...Basic muny, some back nine holes have character, otherwise pretty simple, decent shape...Very challenging, trees...Short and easy to score low...Good muny course. Some poor greens...Conditioning improving...Nice municipal, not spectaclar.

★★★THE RIDGES GOLF COURSE
2311 Griffith Ave., Wisconsin Rapids, 54494, Wood County, (715)424-3204, 100 miles N of Madison.
Opened: 1963. **Holes:** 18. **Par:** 72/72. **Yards:** 6,289/5,018. **Course rating:** 71.3/69.9. **Slope:** 129/122. **Architect:** N/A. **Green fee:** $35/$35. **Credit cards:** MC,VISA. **Reduced fees:** Low season, twilight. **Caddies:** No. **Golf carts:** $22. **Discount golf packages:** Yes. **Season:** April-Oct. **High:** June-Aug. **On site lodging:** No. **Rental clubs:** Yes. **Walking policy:** Unrestricted walking. **Metal spikes allowed:** Yes. **Range:** Yes (grass/mats). **To obtain tee times:** Call anytime.
Subscriber comments: Back nine great—challenging—new clubhouse...Boring front, great back...Challenging but fun...Must see this back nine...New owners. On its way up!...Very nice people...Front wide open, back tight.

★★★½RIVER FALLS GOLF CLUB
1011 E. Division St., River Falls, 54022, Pierce County, (715)425-0032, (800)688-1511, 25 miles E of St. Paul, MN.
Opened: 1929. **Holes:** 18. **Par:** 72/72. **Yards:** 6,471/5,166. **Course rating:** 71.0/69.5. **Slope:** 123/116. **Architect:** N/A. **Green fee:** $17/$26. **Credit cards:** MC,VISA,AMEX. **Reduced fees:** Seniors, juniors. **Caddies:** No. **Golf carts:** $20. **Discount golf packages:** No. **Season:** April-Oct. **High:** May-Sept. **On site lodging:** No. **Rental clubs:** Yes. **Walking policy:** Unrestricted walking. **Metal spikes allowed:** Yes. **Range:** Yes (grass). **To obtain tee times:** Call 3 days in advance.
Subscriber comments: Tough par 4s—well maintained—staff is very good...Very chal-

lenging, beautiful mature course...Hilly, beautiful, fast greens...Beautiful holes in gently rolling countryside...Nice quiet course...One escalator hole...Some of the best greens in the area. Outstanding maintenance...Scenic, fun...Very nice thinking golf!

★★½RIVERDALE COUNTRY CLUB

PU-5008 South 12th St., Sheboygan, 53081, Sheboygan County, (920)458-2561, 50 miles N of Milwaukee.

Opened: 1929. **Holes:** 18. **Par:** 70/72. **Yards:** 5,875/5,651. **Course rating:** 67.4/71.3. **Slope:** 109/116. **Architect:** N/A. **Green fee:** $12/$20. **Credit cards:** MC,VISA. **Reduced fees:** N/A. **Caddies:** No. **Golf carts:** $20. **Discount golf packages:** No. **Season:** April-Oct. **High:** June-Aug. **On site lodging:** No. **Rental clubs:** Yes. **Walking policy:** Unrestricted walking. **Metal spikes allowed:** Yes. **Range:** Yes (grass). **To obtain tee times:** Call on Wednesday for upcoming weekend.

Subscriber comments: Very friendly people...Average course, but worth playing...Old course, rolling fairways increase challenge...Nice back nine...Short—very sloped greens...Very nice place for children/juniors—excellent atmosphere towards them.

★★½RIVERMOOR COUNTRY CLUB

30802 Waterford Dr., Waterford, 53185, Racine County, (414)534-2500.

Opened: 1929. **Holes:** 18. **Par:** 70/72. **Yards:** 6,256/5,839. **Course rating:** 68.7/72.7. **Slope:** 121/125. **Architect:** Billy Sixty Jr.. **Green fee:** $22/$28. **Credit cards:** MC,VISA,DISC. **Reduced fees:** Low season, twilight, seniors. **Caddies:** No. **Golf carts:** $12. **Discount golf packages:** No. **Season:** March-Nov. **High:** June-Aug. **On site lodging:** No. **Rental clubs:** Yes. **Walking policy:** Unrestricted walking. **Metal spikes allowed:** Yes. **Range:** No. **To obtain tee times:** Call 7 days in advance.

Subscriber comments: Hit your ball straight and you'll enjoy. Tough course but good...Fun little golf course...Good greens, nice variety...Great golf—dinner specials...Only balata will sit on these tiny greens...Fun course with treelined fairways, good greens...Very narrow course, nice layout, challenge to spray hitters...Serious test, narrow fairways, heavily wooded.

★★★RIVERSIDE GOLF COURSE

PU-2100 Golf Course Rd., Janesville, 53545, Rock County, (608)757-3080, 35 miles SE of Madison.

Opened: 1924. **Holes:** 18. **Par:** 72/72. **Yards:** 6,508/5,147. **Course rating:** 70.7/68.9. **Slope:** 123/116. **Architect:** Robert Bruce Harris. **Green fee:** $19/$22. **Credit cards:** MC,VISA. **Reduced fees:** Weekdays, seniors, juniors. **Caddies:** No. **Golf carts:** $11. **Discount golf packages:** No. **Season:** April-Nov. **High:** June-Aug. **On site lodging:** No. **Rental clubs:** Yes. **Walking policy:** Unrestricted walking. **Metal spikes allowed:** Yes. **Range:** Yes (grass). **To obtain tee times:** Call up to 10 days in advance.

Subscriber comments: Very good city-owned course...Great old mature course...Never need reservations. Well-kept secret...Fun course to play. Good shape...Lots of trees lining fairways, great scenery, train can slow down a round...No crowds, great 20-handicapper course...All putts break toward the river...Challenging, scenic, relaxed atmosphere.

★★★½ROCK RIVER HILLS GOLF COURSE

Main St. Rd., Horicon, 53032, Dodge County, (920)485-4990, 45 miles N of Milwaukee.

Opened: 1969. **Holes:** 18. **Par:** 70/70. **Yards:** 6,243/5,160. **Course rating:** 70.5/70.0. **Slope:** 127/121. **Architect:** Homer Fieldhouse/Bob Lohmann. **Green fee:** $18/$24. **Credit cards:** MC,VISA. **Reduced fees:** Seniors, juniors. **Caddies:** No. **Golf carts:** $20. **Discount golf packages:** No. **Season:** April-Oct. **High:** June. **On site lodging:** No. **Rental clubs:** Yes. **Walking policy:** Unrestricted walking. **Metal spikes allowed:** Yes. **Range:** Yes (grass). **To obtain tee times:** Call up to 7 days in advance.

Subscriber comments: Nice course. Greens can be a bit hard to hold in summer heat...Well maintained—friendly staff...Well maintained—lovely setting in marshland—geese...Beautiful river course...Challenging layout with good conditons...Back nine is tough, friendly staff...The wildlife and birds were wonderful...Nice, hidden gem, must play when dry.

★★★ROLLING MEADOWS GOLF COURSE

PM-560 W. Rolling Meadows Dr., Fond Du Lac, 54935, Fond Du Lac County, (920)929-3735, 55 miles N of Milwaukee.

Opened: 1973. **Holes:** 27. **Par:** 72/72. **Yards:** 7,000/5,100. **Course rating:** 73.5/69.5. **Slope:** 131/121. **Architect:** Nugent & Associates. **Green fee:** $25/$27. **Credit cards:** MC,VISA. **Reduced fees:** N/A. **Caddies:** No. **Golf carts:** $24. **Discount golf packages:** No. **Season:** April-First Snow. **High:** May-Aug. **On site lodging:** No. **Rental clubs:** Yes. **Walking policy:** Unrestricted walking. **Metal spikes allowed:** Yes. **Range:** Yes (grass/mats). **To obtain tee times:** Call 1 day in advance for weekdays or Thursday at 7 a.m. for upcoming weekend or holiday.

Subscriber comments: Much improved since reconstruction...Very playable, good public layout...New nine needs some time to mature...Good muny course...Good conditions, but too open, some hills...Open, good variety...Has large greens. Good 27-hole course.

★★½ROYAL SCOT GOLF COURSE & SUPPER CLUB

PU-4831 Church Rd., New Franken, 54229, Brown County, (920)866-2356, 5 miles N of Green Bay.

Opened: 1971. **Holes:** 18. **Par:** 72/72. **Yards:** 6,572/5,474. **Course rating:** 70.7/70.7. **Slope:** 122/118. **Architect:** Don Herfort. **Green fee:** $17/$20. **Credit cards:** MC,VISA,DISC. **Reduced fees:** Seniors, juniors. **Caddies:** No. **Golf carts:** $22. **Discount golf packages:** No. **Season:** April-Oct. **High:** June-Aug. **On site lodging:** No. **Rental clubs:** Yes. **Walking policy:** Unrestricted walking. **Metal spikes allowed:** Yes. **Range:** Yes (grass). **To obtain tee times:** Call up to 5 days in advance.

Subscriber comments: Interesting layout. Boggy. Great greens. Excellent food...Not much trouble...Wet in spring. Well maintained...Not a great course but fun to play...Nice facility. Crowded on weekends.

ST. CROIX NATIONAL GOLF CLUB

PU-1603 County Rd. V, Somerset, 54025, (612)888-5988, 25 miles NE of St. Paul, MN.

Opened: 1996. **Holes:** 18. **Par:** 72/72. **Yards:** 6,909/5,251. **Course rating:** 73.9/66.3. **Slope:** 138/119. **Architect:** Joel Goldstrand. **Green fee:** $28/$38. **Credit cards:** MC,VISA,AMEX. **Reduced fees:** Twilight, seniors. **Caddies:** No. **Golf carts:** $24. **Discount golf packages:** No. **Season:** April-Oct. **High:** June-Aug. **On site lodging:** No. **Rental clubs:** Yes. **Walking policy:** Unrestricted walking. **Metal spikes allowed:** No. **Range:** Yes (grass). **To obtain tee times:** Call up to 7 days in advance.

★★★½ST. GERMAIN MUNICIPAL GOLF CLUB

PU-9041 Hwy. 70 W., St. Germain, 54558, Vilas County, (715)542-2614, 80 miles N of Wausau.

Opened: 1993. **Holes:** 18. **Par:** 72/72. **Yards:** 6,651/5,233. **Course rating:** 72.2/70.3. **Slope:** 130/121. **Architect:** Don Stepanik Jr.. **Green fee:** $18/$28. **Credit cards:** All major. **Reduced fees:** Low season, twilight. **Caddies:** No. **Golf carts:** $12. **Discount golf packages:** Yes. **Season:** April-Oct. **High:** June-Sept. **On site lodging:** Yes. **Rental clubs:** Yes. **Walking policy:** Unrestricted walking. **Metal spikes allowed:** No. **Range:** Yes (grass). **To obtain tee times:** Call up to 7 days in advance.

Subscriber comments: Fairways are narrow, but beautiful and well groomed...A gem of a course. Treelined...Spent too much time in woods, too narrow!...Don't need driver, must be straight...Best clubhouse in the state next to Blackwolf Run...New course—golf may be outstanding when mature...Pro shop, bar, restaurant are tops!

★★SANDALWOOD COUNTRY CLUB

2954 Sandlewood Rd., Abrams, 54101, Oconto County, (920)826-7770. Call club for further information.

★★SCENIC VIEW COUNTRY CLUB

PU-4415 Club Dr., Slinger, 53086, Washington County, (414)644-5661, 20 miles NW of Milwaukee.

Opened: 1961. **Holes:** 18. **Par:** 72/71. **Yards:** 6,296/5,358. **Course rating:** 68.6/70.1. **Slope:** 115/115. **Architect:** Robert Raasch. **Green fee:** $16/$19. **Credit cards:** MC,VISA. **Reduced fees:** Weekdays, low season, seniors. **Caddies:** No. **Golf carts:** $22. **Discount golf packages:** No. **Season:** March-Nov. **High:** June-Aug. **On site lodging:** No. **Rental clubs:** Yes. **Walking policy:** Unrestricted walking. **Metal spikes allowed:** Yes. **Range:** Yes (grass). **To obtain tee times:** Call up to seven days in advance.

★★★★SENTRYWORLD GOLF COURSE

PU-601 N. Michigan Ave., Stevens Point, 54481, Portage County, (715)345-1600, 90 miles N of Madison.

Opened: 1981. **Holes:** 18. **Par:** 72/72. **Yards:** 7,055/5,197. **Course rating:** 74.5/71.6. **Slope:** 144/130. **Architect:** Robert Trent Jones Jr. **Green fee:** $40/$65. **Credit cards:** MC,VISA,AMEX. **Reduced fees:** Low season, twilight, juniors. **Caddies:** No. **Golf carts:** Included in Green Fee. **Discount golf packages:** Yes. **Season:** April-Oct. **High:** June-Aug. **On site lodging:** No. **Rental clubs:** Yes. **Walking policy:** Unrestricted walking. **Metal spikes allowed:** No. **Range:** Yes (grass). **To obtain tee times:** Call.

Notes: Ranked 4th in 1997 Best in State.

Subscriber comments: Short but beautiful—well manicured...16th flower hole is worth the admission...Coming back to original condition...Good service all around the course...Beautiful course requires all the shots. 18th hole is classic...A lot of sand....Absolutely outstanding...Immaculate conditions, even in the woods. Every shot a unique challenge...About as close as we get to the magnolias of Augusta.

★★½SHAWANO LAKE GOLF CLUB

PU-W5714 Lake Dr., Shawano, 54166, Shawano County, (715)524-4890, 25 miles NW of Green Bay.

Opened: 1922. **Holes:** 18. **Par:** 71/71. **Yards:** 6,231/5,496. **Course rating:** 72.9/70.4. **Slope:** 128/128. **Architect:** Marty Garrity. **Green fee:** $12/$19. **Credit cards:** MC,VISA. **Reduced fees:** Weekdays, low season, resort guests, twilight, seniors, juniors. **Caddies:** No. **Golf carts:** $11. **Discount golf packages:** Yes. **Season:** April-Nov. **High:** June-Sept. **On site lodging:** No. **Rental clubs:** Yes. **Walking policy:** Unrestricted walking. **Metal spikes allowed:** No. **Range:** Yes (grass/mats). **To obtain tee times:** Call up to 14 days in advance.

Subscriber comments: Great potential. Will be great course once improvements completed...Very good back nine...Greens small...Excellent/challenging...Nice old course on its way back!

★★½SHEBOYGAN TOWN & COUNTRY CLUB

PU-W1945 County Highway J, Sheboygan, 53083, Sheboygan County, (920)467-2509, 5 miles W of Sheboygan.

Opened: 1962. **Holes:** 18. **Par:** 71/73. **Yards:** 5,913/5,221. **Course rating:** 67.8/64.6. **Slope:** 113/106. **Architect:** N/A. **Green fee:** $11/$20. **Credit cards:** None. **Reduced fees:** Weekdays, juniors. **Caddies:** No. **Golf carts:** $20. **Discount golf packages:** No. **Season:** April-Nov. **High:** July. **On site lodging:** No. **Rental clubs:** Yes. **Walking policy:** Unrestricted walking. **Metal spikes allowed:** Yes. **Range:** Yes (grass). **To obtain tee times:** Call on Thursday for upcoming weekend.

Subscriber comments: Huge pro shop—fun course...Not much trouble...Largest selection of equipment in Midwest, including stores...Generally good condition...Nice course. Slow play. Good food at clubhouse...Service-orientated pro shop...Fun course, challenging...Could be outstanding 27 holes.

Special Notes: Also 9-hole course.

★★★SILVER SPRING GOLF COURSE

N.56 W.21318 Silver Spring Rd., Menomonee Falls, 53051, Waukesha County, (414)252-4666.

Call club for further information.

Subscriber comments: A lot of fun. #9 is a dandy, very tough to putt. Great facility...A real challenge course—nice greens—friendly staff...Long from tips, fair greens, fairly wide open...Great condition—scenic. Two 18s now. Fun course...Gimmicky holes...Nice variety...New course maturing nicely...Tough roughs, fast greens; #8 and #9 are great.

★★★½SKYLINE GOLF CLUB

11th and Golf Rd., Black River Falls, 54615, Jackson County, (715)284-2613, 125 miles NW of Madison.

Opened: 1957. **Holes:** 18. **Par:** 72/72. **Yards:** 6,371/5,122. **Course rating:** 70.6/69.4. **Slope:** 123/112. **Architect:** Edward L. Packard and Brent Wadsworth. **Green fee:** $21/$23. **Credit cards:** MC,VISA. **Reduced fees:** Low season, resort guests. **Caddies:** No. **Golf carts:** $21. **Discount golf packages:** No. **Season:** April-Nov. **High:** May-Aug. **On site lodging:** No. **Rental clubs:** Yes. **Walking policy:** Unrestricted walking. **Metal

spikes allowed: No. **Range:** Yes (grass). **To obtain tee times:** Call.
Subscriber comments: Facility is great...A hidden treasure. nice people. Great course...Back side—watch out for the trees...Great golf, great people...Scenic and rolling, excellent golf for the cost...Large new clubhouse!...Great muny, rolling course...Hilly course, good shape, fun day, hard to walk.

★★½SONGBIRD HILLS GOLF CLUB

PU-W259 N8700 Hwy. J, Hartland, 53029, Waukesha County, (414)246-7050, 15 miles W of Milwaukee.
Opened: 1992. **Holes:** 18. **Par:** 70/70. **Yards:** 5,556/5,074. **Course rating:** 66.2/64.0. **Slope:** 110/105. **Architect:** Harold E. Hoffman. **Green fee:** $20/$24. **Credit cards:** MC,VISA. **Reduced fees:** Weekdays, low season, twilight, seniors, juniors. **Caddies:** No. **Golf carts:** $22. **Discount golf packages:** No. **Season:** April-Nov. **High:** June-Aug. **On site lodging:** No. **Rental clubs:** Yes. **Walking policy:** Unrestricted walking. **Metal spikes allowed:** Yes. **Range:** Yes (grass). **To obtain tee times:** Call.
Subscriber comments: Love this tricky little course...Beautifully maintained course—great fairways—a challenge...Fairly nice course for a new one. Excellent new clubhouse that can be used for parties...Weird and different.
Special Notes: Spikeless shoes encouraged.

★½SOUTH HILLS COUNTRY CLUB

PU-3047 Hwy 41, Franksville, 53126, Racine County, (414)835-4441, (800)736-4766, 15 miles S of Milwaukee.
Opened: 1927. **Holes:** 18. **Par:** 72/76. **Yards:** 6,403/6,107. **Course rating:** 69.4/75.0. **Slope:** 118/125. **Architect:** N/A. **Green fee:** $18/$22. **Credit cards:** MC,VISA,AMEX. **Reduced fees:** Weekdays, low season. **Caddies:** No. **Golf carts:** $24. **Discount golf packages:** Yes. **Season:** Year-round weather permitting. **High:** May-Oct. **On site lodging:** No. **Rental clubs:** Yes. **Walking policy:** Unrestricted walking. **Metal spikes allowed:** Yes. **Range:** Yes (grass/mats). **To obtain tee times:** Call 7 days in advance.

★★★½SPARTA MUNICIPAL GOLF COURSE

PM-1210 E Montgomery St., Sparta, 54656, Monroe County, (608)269-3022, 25 miles E of La Crosse.
Opened: 1984. **Holes:** 18. **Par:** 72/72. **Yards:** 6,544/5,648. **Course rating:** 70.8/71.6. **Slope:** 127/125. **Architect:** Art Johnson. **Green fee:** $16/$19. **Credit cards:** None. **Reduced fees:** Low season, seniors, juniors. **Caddies:** No. **Golf carts:** N/A. **Discount golf packages:** No. **Season:** April-Oct. **High:** May-July. **On site lodging:** No. **Rental clubs:** No. **Walking policy:** Unrestricted walking. **Metal spikes allowed:** No. **Range:** No. **To obtain tee times:** Call up to 2 days in advance.
Subscriber comments: Nice muny course, but crowded...Friendly/surprisingly challenging/good food...Excellent greens...Pine tree holes very pretty...Nice new nine, front average...Well maintained for busy course...Beautiful course. Challenging enough to be a lot of fun...Good small town course, nice place to spend a day...A great layout on a limited amount of land...Very undulating, quick greens.

★★★½SPOONER GOLF CLUB

County Trunk H N., Spooner, 54801, Washburn County, (715)635-3580, 85 miles N of Eau Claire.
Opened: 1930. **Holes:** 18. **Par:** 71/72. **Yards:** 6,417/5,084. **Course rating:** 70.9/68.8. **Slope:** 128/117. **Architect:** Tom Vardon/G. Emerson. **Green fee:** $20/$22. **Credit cards:** MC,VISA. **Reduced fees:** Weekdays, twilight. **Caddies:** No. **Golf carts:** $22. **Discount golf packages:** No. **Season:** April-Oct. **High:** June-Aug. **On site lodging:** No. **Rental clubs:** Yes. **Walking policy:** Unrestricted walking. **Metal spikes allowed:** Yes. **Range:** Yes (grass). **To obtain tee times:** Call 30 days in advance starting on the 25th of the preceeding month.
Subscriber comments: Very good condition...Great greens...Excellent shape, beautiful, well maintained...Excellent fairways and with tough par 4s...Plan your vacation around this one...A beautiful, coniditioned course...Greens hold and putt true...Tough, long finishing par 4!...Lot of different holes, lot of trees.

★★½SPRING VALLEY COUNTRY CLUB

PU-23913 Wilmot Rd., Salem, 53168, Kenosha County, (414)862-2626, 9 miles W of Kenosha.

Opened: 1924. **Holes:** 18. **Par:** 70/70. **Yards:** 6,354/5,968. **Course rating:** 70.1/68.9. **Slope:** 119/113. **Architect:** William B. Langford and Theodore J. Moreau. **Green fee:** $19. **Credit cards:** MC,VISA. **Reduced fees:** Weekdays, low season, twilight, seniors. **Caddies:** No. **Golf carts:** $10. **Discount golf packages:** No. **Season:** Year-round. **High:** April-Nov. **On site lodging:** No. **Rental clubs:** No. **Walking policy:** Unrestricted walking. **Metal spikes allowed:** Yes. **Range:** Yes (grass). **To obtain tee times:** Call anytime.
Subscriber comments: Fast greens...Best during spring and fall, interesting layout...No sand traps...Deceptively difficult greens, no sand traps...Good husband and wife course...Nice rolling hills...Offers some very interesting holes...Hilly, fun course, nothing fancy...With traps and roughs, this could be real interesting, tough greens.

★★½SPRING VALLEY GOLF CLUB
Van Buren Rd., Spring Valley, 54767, Pierce County, (715)778-5513, (800)236-0009, 50 miles E of St. Paul, MN.
Opened: 1974. **Holes:** 18. **Par:** 71/72. **Yards:** 6,114/4,735. **Course rating:** 68.5/68.0. **Slope:** 124/116. **Architect:** Gordy Emmerson. **Green fee:** $15/$18. **Credit cards:** MC,VISA,DISC. **Reduced fees:** Seniors. **Caddies:** No. **Golf carts:** $17. **Discount golf packages:** No. **Season:** March-Nov. **High:** May-Sept. **On site lodging:** No. **Rental clubs:** No. **Walking policy:** Unrestricted walking. **Metal spikes allowed:** Yes. **Range:** No. **To obtain tee times:** Call.
Subscriber comments: Good course, well-kept secret...Tight fairway—interesting lay-out...Fast, elevated greens make for a fun round.

★★★★THE SPRINGS GOLF CLUB RESORT
R-400 Springs Dr., Spring Green, 53588, Sauk County, (608)588-7707, (800)822-7774, 35 miles NW of Madison.
Opened: 1969. **Holes:** 27. **Architect:** Robert T. Jones. **Green fee:** $55/$55. **Credit cards:** All major. **Reduced fees:** Low season, twilight. **Caddies:** No. **Golf carts:** $13. **Discount golf packages:** Yes. **Season:** Year-round. **High:** April-Oct. **On site lodging:** Yes. **Rental clubs:** Yes. **Walking policy:** Walking at certain times. **Metal spikes allowed:** Yes. **Range:** Yes (grass/mats). **To obtain tee times:** Resort guests and members call 7 days in advance. Public call 6 days in advance.
BACK/NORTH
Par: 72/72. **Yards:** 6,534/5,285. **Course rating:** 71.9/70.6. **Slope:** 134/125..
FRONT/BACK
Par: 72/72. **Yards:** 6,554/5,640. **Course rating:** 71.5/70.3. **Slope:** 132/123.
FRONT/NORTH
Par: 72/72. **Yards:** 6,544/5,673. **Course rating:** 71.6/70.7. **Slope:** 130/124.
Subscriber comments: The new nine is great...Professional course, people are real pros...Great course...Some tricky greens...North course is beautiful...Open layout, nice views, North is interesting...Very pretty....Great service. Great maintenance...Good challenge, nice upgrade...Original 18 a real gem...Nice variety of holes...Tight fairways.

★★½SQUIRES COUNTRY CLUB
PU-4970 Country Club Rd., Port Washington, 53074, Ozaukee County, (414)285-3402, 25 miles N of Milwaukee.
Opened: 1927. **Holes:** 18. **Par:** 70/70. **Yards:** 5,800/5,067. **Course rating:** 67.3/68.2. **Slope:** 112/112. **Architect:** N/A. **Green fee:** $23. **Credit cards:** MC,VISA,DISC. **Reduced fees:** Weekdays, twilight, seniors, juniors. **Caddies:** No. **Golf carts:** $12. **Discount golf packages:** No. **Season:** April-Oct. **High:** May-Oct. **On site lodging:** No. **Rental clubs:** Yes. **Walking policy:** Unrestricted walking. **Metal spikes allowed:** No. **Range:** Yes (grass/mats). **To obtain tee times:** Call 7 days in advance.
Subscriber comments: Love those greens...Fun course—good fairways—some challenging holes...Beautiful views of Lake Michigan...Scenic course...Contoured course—ravine par 5...Being on the bluffs on Lake Michigan makes the wind a challenge as well as the course. Bring a sweater anytime...Many improvements made in the last 14 yrs...Very interesting holes, staff is very accommodating...Short but tricky.

★★SUN PRAIRIE GOLF COURSE
Happy Valley Rd., Sun Prairie, 53590, Dane County, (608)837-6211.
Call club for further information.

TEAL WING GOLF CLUB

R-Rte. 7, Ross Rd., Hayward, 54843, Sawyer County, (715)462-9051, 20 miles NE of Hayward.
Opened: 1995. **Holes:** 18. **Par:** 72/72. **Yards:** 6,379/5,218. **Course rating:** 72.1/71.2. **Slope:** 139/127. **Architect:** N/A. **Green fee:** $30/$40. **Credit cards:** MC,VISA. **Reduced fees:** Low season, resort guests, twilight. **Caddies:** No. **Golf carts:** $20. **Discount golf packages:** No. **Season:** May-Oct. **High:** July-Aug. **On site lodging:** Yes. **Rental clubs:** Yes. **Walking policy:** Unrestricted walking. **Metal spikes allowed:** Yes. **Range:** Yes (grass). **To obtain tee times:** Call.
Special Notes: Spikeless shoes encouraged.

★★★TELEMARK GOLF CLUB

R-Telemark Rd., Cable, 54821, Bayfield County, (715)798-3104, 150 miles NE of Minneapolis, MN.
Opened: 1970. **Holes:** 18. **Par:** 72/72. **Yards:** 6,403/5,691. **Course rating:** 70.6/67.0. **Slope:** 128/119. **Architect:** N/A. **Green fee:** $25/$25. **Credit cards:** MC,VISA. **Reduced fees:** Resort guests. **Caddies:** No. **Golf carts:** $24. **Discount golf packages:** No. **Season:** May-Oct. **High:** N/A. **On site lodging:** Yes. **Rental clubs:** Yes. **Walking policy:** Walking at certain times. **Metal spikes allowed:** Yes. **Range:** Yes (grass). **To obtain tee times:** Call anytime in advance.
Subscriber comments: Very woodsy, very pretty. Deer and bear...Nice setting for golf...Very scenic, you'll need all the shots...Beautiful layout—very scenic course with the many hills and trees...Great layout and area—super variety of golf.

★★THAL ACRES LINKS & LANES

PU-N6109 CTHM, Westfield, 53964, Marquette County, (608)296-2850, 50 miles N of Madison.
Opened: 1963. **Holes:** 18. **Par:** 70/72. **Yards:** 5,672/5,211. **Course rating:** 66.5/69.3. **Slope:** 114/118. **Architect:** N/A. **Green fee:** $20. **Credit cards:** MC,VISA. **Reduced fees:** N/A. **Caddies:** No. **Golf carts:** $24. **Discount golf packages:** No. **Season:** April-Oct. **High:** June-Aug. **On site lodging:** No. **Rental clubs:** Yes. **Walking policy:** Unrestricted walking. **Metal spikes allowed:** Yes. **Range:** Yes (grass). **To obtain tee times:** Call anytime.

★★½TRAPP RIVER GOLF CLUB

PU-Hwy. WW, Wausau, 54403, Marathon County, (715)675-3044.
Opened: N/A. **Holes:** 18. **Par:** 72/72. **Yards:** 6,335/4,935. **Course rating:** 69.3/67.3. **Slope:** 116/109. **Architect:** N/A. **Green fee:** $14/$20. **Credit cards:** All major. **Reduced fees:** Low season, twilight, seniors, juniors. **Caddies:** No. **Golf carts:** $10. **Discount golf packages:** No. **Season:** April-Nov. **High:** June-Aug. **On site lodging:** No. **Rental clubs:** Yes. **Walking policy:** Unrestricted walking. **Metal spikes allowed:** Yes. **Range:** Yes (grass/mats). **To obtain tee times:** Call up to 7 days in advance.
Subscriber comments: Working to improve blind shots...Wide open...Well maintained. Wish it was a little longer...Much improved over previous years...8th hole needs work—elevated sloped green...Needs more maturing.

★★★★TRAPPERS TURN GOLF CLUB

PU-652 Trappers Turn Dr., Wisconsin Dells, 53965, Sauk County, (608)253-7000, (800)221-8876, 50 miles N of Madison.
Opened: 1991. **Holes:** 18. **Par:** 72/72. **Yards:** 6,550/5,013. **Course rating:** 72.0/69.5. **Slope:** 131/122. **Architect:** Andy North and Roger Packard. **Green fee:** $39/$62. **Credit cards:** All major. **Reduced fees:** Weekdays, low season, resort guests, twilight. **Caddies:** No. **Golf carts:** Included in Green Fee. **Discount golf packages:** Yes. **Season:** April-Oct. **High:** July-Aug. **On site lodging:** Yes. **Rental clubs:** Yes. **Walking policy:** Walking at certain times. **Metal spikes allowed:** Yes. **Range:** Yes (grass). **To obtain tee times:** Call up to 30 days in advance. Resort guests and outings call anytime in advance.
Subscriber comments: Loved the par 3 into the canyon...Championship style—sometimes crowded but worth the wait...Outstanding! Great finishing hole...Great layout—fine service!...Handy to interstate...Sporty, fun, manageable; great test of golf...Not long but can be tough...Always in great shape, nice design, a blast to play...Beautiful, hills, valleys, nonstop fun—first class service...Tight, hilly; good views, fast greens.

★★★TREE ACRES GOLF COURSE
PU-5254 Pleasant Dr, Plover, 54467, Portage County, (715)341-4530.
Call club for further information.
Subscriber comments: Hidden gem—well kept—enjoyable...Very nice short course...Rather easy course...Good family course. Good condition. Friendly...Short course, don't overclub...Nice way to spend a Sunday morning...Wide open—swing away!

★★★½TROUT LAKE GOLF & COUNTRY CLUB
PU-3800 Hwy. 51 N., Arbor Vitae, 54568, Vilas County, (715)385-2189, 80 miles N of Wausau.
Opened: 1926. **Holes:** 18. **Par:** 72/71. **Yards:** 6,175/5,263. **Course rating:** 69.9/70.3. **Slope:** 124/122. **Architect:** Charles Maddox and Frank P. MacDonald. **Green fee:** $21/$31. **Credit cards:** MC,VISA. **Reduced fees:** Low season. **Caddies:** No. **Golf carts:** $12. **Discount golf packages:** No. **Season:** April-Oct. **High:** June-Sept. **On site lodging:** No. **Rental clubs:** Yes. **Walking policy:** Unrestricted walking. **Metal spikes allowed:** Yes. **Range:** No. **To obtain tee times:** Call 14 days in advance.
Subscriber comments: Turning into a great 18 holes...Pretty country in Northern Wisconsin...Very nice shape—narrow...Excellent greens...Bald eagles fly up and down Trout River and over the course. Tough par 3s...Isolated—beautiful!...Pretty course. Excellent condition...Wonderful, great greens...Typical Northwoods course, some tight and pretty holes.

★★★TURTLEBACK GOLF & CONFERENCE CENTER
PU-W. Allen Rd., Rice Lake, 54868, Barron County, (715)234-7641, 1 mile W of Rice Lake.
Opened: 1982. **Holes:** 18. **Par:** 71/71. **Yards:** 6,604/5,291. **Course rating:** 72.0/70.6. **Slope:** 129/120. **Architect:** Todd Severud. **Green fee:** $22/$25. **Credit cards:** All major. **Reduced fees:** Weekdays. **Caddies:** No. **Golf carts:** $22. **Discount golf packages:** No. **Season:** April-Oct. **High:** June-Aug. **On site lodging:** No. **Rental clubs:** Yes. **Walking policy:** Unrestricted walking. **Metal spikes allowed:** No. **Range:** Yes (grass/mats). **To obtain tee times:** Call up to 14 days in advance.
Subscriber comments: Short challenging course, great condition...Very well maintained. Excellent facility...Very good condition—good challenge and fun...OK course, pleasant staff...Nice greens, overall great condition, low traffic...New holes with bentgrass fairways.

★★½TUSCUMBIA GOLF CLUB
Illinois Ave., Green Lake, 54941, Green Lake County, (920)294-3240, (800)294-3381, 65 miles N of Milwaukee.
Opened: 1896. **Holes:** 18. **Par:** 71/71. **Yards:** 6,301/5,619. **Course rating:** 70.1/73.2. **Slope:** 122/123. **Architect:** Tom Bendelow. **Green fee:** $24/$36. **Credit cards:** MC,VISA,DISC. **Reduced fees:** Low season, twilight, seniors, juniors. **Caddies:** No. **Golf carts:** $24. **Discount golf packages:** Yes. **Season:** April-Oct. **High:** June-Sept. **On site lodging:** No. **Rental clubs:** Yes. **Walking policy:** Unrestricted walking. **Metal spikes allowed:** Yes. **Range:** Yes (grass/mats). **To obtain tee times:** Call.
Subscriber comments: Very good greens, outstanding staff...Very small greens...Good condition...Good old course...Local course that improves every year...Treelined, oldest course in state...Old-style traditional golf course...Back and forth front nine, good conditions...A fair test...Mature trees add to the history...Tight and fun! A certain "sameness" to many holes.

★½TWIN LAKES COUNTRY CLUB
1230 Legion Dr., Twin Lakes, 53181, Kenosha County, (920)877-2500, 50 miles SW of Milwaukee.
Opened: 1912. **Holes:** 18. **Par:** 70/71. **Yards:** 5,930/4,946. **Course rating:** 67.2/67.3. **Slope:** 115/113. **Architect:** Leonard Macomber. **Green fee:** $18/$24. **Credit cards:** MC,VISA. **Reduced fees:** Weekdays, twilight, seniors. **Caddies:** No. **Golf carts:** $11. **Discount golf packages:** No. **Season:** March-Nov. **High:** June-Aug. **On site lodging:** No. **Rental clubs:** Yes. **Walking policy:** Unrestricted walking. **Metal spikes allowed:** Yes. **Range:** Yes (grass/mats). **To obtain tee times:** Call 7 days in advance.

★★TWIN OAKS COUNTRY CLUB
PU-4871 County Hwy. R, Denmark, 54208, Brown County, (920)863-2716, 5 miles S of Green Bay.
Opened: 1968. **Holes:** 18. **Par:** 72/72. **Yards:** 6,468/5,214. **Course rating:** 69.6/68.3. **Slope:** 116/103. **Architect:** N/A. **Green fee:** $13/$17. **Credit cards:** None. **Reduced fees:** Weekdays, low season, twilight, seniors, juniors. **Caddies:** No. **Golf carts:** $9. **Discount golf packages:** No. **Season:** March-Nov. **High:** June-Aug. **On site lodging:** No. **Rental clubs:** Yes. **Walking policy:** Unrestricted walking. **Metal spikes allowed:** Yes. **Range:** Yes (grass/mats). **To obtain tee times:** Call up to 7 days in advance.

★★★TWO OAKS NORTH GOLF CLUB
PU-Cty. Hwy. F, Wautoma, 54982, Waushara County, (920)787-7132, (800)236-6257, 35 miles W of Oshkosh.
Opened: 1995. **Holes:** 18. **Par:** 72/72. **Yards:** 6,552/5,034. **Course rating:** 70.7/68.3. **Slope:** 120/111. **Architect:** Robert Lohmann/John Houdek. **Green fee:** $16/$23. **Credit cards:** MC,VISA. **Reduced fees:** Weekdays, low season, twilight, seniors. **Caddies:** No. **Golf carts:** $22. **Discount golf packages:** No. **Season:** April-Oct. **High:** June-Aug. **On site lodging:** No. **Rental clubs:** Yes. **Walking policy:** Unrestricted walking. **Metal spikes allowed:** No. **Range:** Yes (grass/mats). **To obtain tee times:** Call up to 7 days in advance.
Subscriber comments: Well maintained. Good greens. Very good staff...Many trees on both sides of fairways...Good golf course, nice condition...Interesting layout, scenic...Built on sand, takes water very well...Fun layout...New course—needs to mature.

★★★★½UNIVERSITY RIDGE GOLF COURSE
PU-7120 County Trunk PD, Verona, 53593, Dane County, (608)845-7700, (800)897-4343, 8 miles SW of Madison.
Opened: 1991. **Holes:** 18. **Par:** 72/72. **Yards:** 6,888/5,005. **Course rating:** 73.2/68.9. **Slope:** 142/121. **Architect:** Robert Trent Jones Jr. **Green fee:** $34/$49. **Credit cards:** MC,VISA,AMEX. **Reduced fees:** Low season, twilight, juniors. **Caddies:** No. **Golf carts:** $15. **Discount golf packages:** No. **Season:** April-Oct. **High:** May-Sept. **On site lodging:** No. **Rental clubs:** Yes. **Walking policy:** Unrestricted walking. **Metal spikes allowed:** Yes. **Range:** Yes (grass/mats). **To obtain tee times:** Call up to 6 days in advance. Groups of 8 or more may book anytime in advance.
Notes: Ranked 7th in 1997 Best in State. 1998 NCAA Women's Championship.
Subscriber comments: Great variety and imagination—tough!...Students are truly spoiled...Had to take a step back and just look at each hole...Wonderful course—beautifully groomed...One nine though woods, other nine holes hilly...Spectacular layout. Excellent conditioning. Great pro shop. Creme de la creme...#2 a real test of positioning...Quality facility in every respect...Wall-to-wall championship layout...Hard to get tee time...Makes you want to go back to college...Great course—never quite sure of club selection...Excellent design with great risk...Top notch course, treated like royalty.

★★¼UTICA HILLS GOLF COURSE
PU-3350 Knott Rd., Oshkosh, 54903, Winnebago County, (920)233-4446, 50 miles S of Green Bay.
Opened: 1974. **Holes:** 18. **Par:** 72/72. **Yards:** 6,081/5,404. **Course rating:** 68.3/70.1. **Slope:** 116/117. **Architect:** N/A. **Green fee:** $15/$18. **Credit cards:** None. **Reduced fees:** Seniors, juniors. **Caddies:** No. **Golf carts:** $20. **Discount golf packages:** No. **Season:** April-Dec. **High:** June-Aug. **On site lodging:** No. **Rental clubs:** Yes. **Walking policy:** Unrestricted walking. **Metal spikes allowed:** No. **Range:** Yes (grass). **To obtain tee times:** Call.
Subscriber comments: Nice little "hidden" course. Easy access. Low scores possible...Flat and open spaces, nice greens...Nice greens—fairways need work—good practice facilities...Good local course...Fair, nothing to note but 18th hole.

★★★½VOYAGER VILLAGE COUNTRY CLUB
28851 Kilkare Rd., Danbury, 54830, Burnett County, (715)259-3911, (800)782-0329, 55 miles S of Duluth, MN.
Opened: 1970. **Holes:** 18. **Par:** 72/72. **Yards:** 6,638/5,711. **Course rating:** 71.6/72.4.

Slope: 123/122. **Architect:** William James Spear. **Green fee:** $21/$25. **Credit cards:** MC,VISA. **Reduced fees:** Weekdays. **Caddies:** No. **Golf carts:** $24. **Discount golf packages:** Yes. **Season:** April-Oct. **High:** June-Aug. **On site lodging:** No. **Rental clubs:** Yes. **Walking policy:** Unrestricted walking. **Metal spikes allowed:** Yes. **Range:** Yes (grass). **To obtain tee times:** Call 5 days in advance.
Subscriber comments: A gem in the middle of nowhere...Course design and play excellent...You get to use every club in your bag...Excellent shape...Good...Woodsy layout. Good vacation course...Great meals, nice course cut into woods...Challenging layout...Tough, very tired after walking 18 holes...Good fall colors.
Special Notes: Also have a 9-hole par-3 course.

★★★WANAKI GOLF COURSE
20830 W. Libson Rd., Menomonee Falls, 53051, Waukesha County, (414)252-3480.
Call club for further information.
Subscriber comments: County course better every year...Good course—mostly flat...Long layout through the woods...Nice blue-collar course...Sleeper...Easy to walk...Nice greens—back nine has long holes...Very tough public course.

★★½WESTERN LAKES GOLF CLUB
W287 N1963 Oakton Rd., Pewaukee, 53072, Waukesha County, (414)691-1181,
Opened: 1988. **Holes:** 18. **Par:** 72/72. **Yards:** 6,587/5,662. **Course rating:** 71.0/71.8.
Slope: 122/122. **Architect:** Lawrence Packard. **Green fee:** $26/$32. **Credit cards:** MC,VISA,AMEX. **Reduced fees:** Low season, twilight. **Caddies:** No. **Golf carts:** $25.
Discount golf packages: No. **Season:** April-Nov. **High:** June-Sept. **On site lodging:** No. **Rental clubs:** Yes. **Walking policy:** Unrestricted walking. **Metal spikes allowed:** Yes. **Range:** Yes (grass/mats). **To obtain tee times:** Call up to 7 days in advance.
Subscriber comments: Gets better every year/fun to play...Nice fairways—nice greens—well-managed play (no waiting)...Excellent greens, low terrain sometimes boggy...Good layout. Some holes play very difficult...Every hole has one penal side, one bail-out option...Course continues to improve every year...Water on most holes, good fairways.

★★WESTHAVEN GOLF CLUB
PU-1400 Westhaven St., Oshkosh, 54904, Winnebago County, (920)233-4640.
Opened: 1969. **Holes:** 18. **Par:** 70/70. **Yards:** 5,877/5,175. **Course rating:** 67.6/71.6.
Slope: 115/118. **Architect:** Homer Fieldhouse. **Green fee:** $17/$19. **Credit cards:** MC,VISA. **Reduced fees:** Seniors, juniors. **Caddies:** No. **Golf carts:** $22. **Discount golf packages:** No. **Season:** April-Nov. **High:** N/A. **On site lodging:** No. **Rental clubs:** Yes. **Walking policy:** Unrestricted walking. **Metal spikes allowed:** Yes. **Range:** Yes (grass). **To obtain tee times:** Call.

★★★WHITNALL PARK GOLF CLUB
PU-5879 S. 92nd St., Hales Corners, 53130, Milwaukee County, (414)425-7931.
Opened: 1932. **Holes:** 18. **Par:** 71/74. **Yards:** 6,216/5,778. **Course rating:** 69.9/72.1.
Slope: 117/119. **Architect:** George Hansen. **Green fee:** $22. **Credit cards:** MC,VISA.
Reduced fees: Low season, twilight, seniors, juniors. **Caddies:** No. **Golf carts:** $24.
Discount golf packages: No. **Season:** April-Nov. **High:** June-Sept. **On site lodging:** No. **Rental clubs:** Yes. **Walking policy:** Unrestricted walking. **Metal spikes allowed:** Yes. **Range:** No. **To obtain tee times:** Call same day.
Subscriber comments: County course jewel...Very good—tough...Mature, hilly, treelined...Views from some holes outstanding...The ideal muny?...Pleasant park setting, fun layout, fairly short test...Sporty—some hills.

★★WILDERNESS RESORT & GOLF COURSE
R-511 E. Adams St., Wisconsin Dells, 53965, Adams County, (608)253-4653, (800)867-9453, 35 miles NW of Madison.
Opened: 1997. **Holes:** 18. **Par:** 71/71. **Yards:** 6,512/5,489. **Course rating:** 70.8/68.9.
Slope: 131/122. **Architect:** Art Johnson. **Green fee:** $55/$65. **Credit cards:** MC,VISA.
Reduced fees: Weekdays, low season, resort guests, twilight. **Caddies:** No. **Golf carts:** $20. **Discount golf packages:** Yes. **Season:** April-Oct. **High:** June-Aug. **On site lodging:** No. **Rental clubs:** Yes. **Walking policy:** Unrestricted walking. **Metal spikes allowed:** Yes. **Range:** Yes (grass/mats). **To obtain tee times:** Call up to 30 days in advance.

WISCONSIN

★★WILLOW RUN GOLF CLUB
N12 W26506 Golf Rd., Pewaukee, 53072, Waukesha County, (414)544-8585, 15 miles W of Milwaukee.
Opened: 1960. **Holes:** 18. **Par:** 71/71. **Yards:** 6,521/5,233. **Course rating:** 70.0/69.1. **Slope:** 115/112. **Architect:** Dewey Solcum. **Green fee:** $22/$27. **Credit cards:** MC,VISA,AMEX. **Reduced fees:** Weekdays, twilight, seniors, juniors. **Caddies:** No. **Golf carts:** $24. **Discount golf packages:** Yes. **Season:** March-Dec. **High:** June-Sept. **On site lodging:** Yes. **Rental clubs:** Yes. **Walking policy:** Unrestricted walking. **Metal spikes allowed:** Yes. **Range:** Yes (grass/mats). **To obtain tee times:** Call up to 7 days in advance.

★★WINAGAMIE GOLF COURSE
3501 Winagamie Dr., Neenah, 54956, Winnebago County, (920)757-5453.
Opened: 1963. **Holes:** 18. **Par:** 73/73. **Yards:** 6,355/5,422. **Course rating:** 69.5/69.9. **Slope:** 115/115. **Architect:** Julius Jacobson. **Green fee:** $12/$15. **Credit cards:** None. **Reduced fees:** Weekdays, low season, twilight, seniors, juniors. **Caddies:** No. **Golf carts:** $20. **Discount golf packages:** Yes. **Season:** April-Oct. **High:** May-Aug. **On site lodging:** No. **Rental clubs:** Yes. **Walking policy:** Unrestricted walking. **Metal spikes allowed:** Yes. **Range:** Yes (grass). **To obtain tee times:** Call.

★★WISCONSIN RIVER GOLF CLUB
PU-705 W. River Dr., Stevens Point, 54481, Portage County, (715)344-9152, 232 miles N of Chicago.
Opened: 1961. **Holes:** 18. **Par:** 72/72. **Yards:** 6,695/4,805. **Course rating:** 71.6/68.5. **Slope:** 124/116. **Architect:** Larry Roberts. **Green fee:** $18/$21. **Credit cards:** MC,VISA,DISC. **Reduced fees:** Low season, seniors, juniors. **Caddies:** No. **Golf carts:** $10. **Discount golf packages:** No. **Season:** April-Nov. **High:** June-Aug. **On site lodging:** No. **Rental clubs:** Yes. **Walking policy:** Unrestricted walking. **Metal spikes allowed:** Yes. **Range:** Yes (grass). **To obtain tee times:** Call anytime.

★★WOODSIDE COUNTRY CLUB
PU-530 Erie Rd., Green Bay, 54301, Brown County, (920)468-5729.
Opened: N/A. **Holes:** 18. **Par:** 71. **Yards:** 5,417. **Course rating:** 67.6. **Slope:** 115. **Architect:** N/A. **Green fee:** $14/$17. **Credit cards:** MC,VISA. **Reduced fees:** Weekdays, seniors. **Caddies:** No. **Golf carts:** $18. **Discount golf packages:** No. **Season:** April-Oct. **High:** N/A. **On site lodging:** No. **Rental clubs:** Yes. **Walking policy:** Unrestricted walking. **Metal spikes allowed:** Yes. **Range:** No. **To obtain tee times:** Call up to 7 days in advance.

YAHARA HILLS GOLF COURSE
PU-6701 E. Broadway, Madison, 53718, Dane County, (608)838-3126.
Opened: 1967. **Architect:** Art Johnson. **Green fee:** $14/$20. **Credit cards:** MC,VISA. **Reduced fees:** Low season, seniors, juniors. **Caddies:** No. **Golf carts:** $22. **Discount golf packages:** No. **Season:** April-Nov. **High:** April-Aug. **On site lodging:** No. **Rental clubs:** Yes. **Walking policy:** Unrestricted walking. **Metal spikes allowed:** Yes. **7**Yes (grass). **To obtain tee times:** Call 7 days in advance.
★★½EAST COURSE
Holes: 18. **Par:** 72/72. **Yards:** 7,200/6,115. **Course rating:** 71.9/73.4. **Slope:** 116/118. **Subscriber comments:** Good staff. Very large greens...Not great but OK, nice head pro...Too many holes look alike...Usually windy. Large greens...Fair test of golf...Nice muny, open, easy access...Decent well-run public course...Very long...Good muny, nothing spectacular but tougher than Slope indicates.
★★½WEST COURSE
Holes: 18. **Par:** 72/73. **Yards:** 7,000/5,705. **Course rating:** 71.6/71.4. **Slope:** 118/116. **Subscriber comments:** Good low-budget course. More fun than East...Very nice muny...Great for my kids...Lots of traffic...Long...Reachable par 5s, long par 4s...Big greens, good condition, lot of holes look the same...Open, prairie-type course with hills...Let it rip. Long and open, huge tees and greens...Rather monotonous course—long and open.

★★½AIRPORT GOLF CLUB

PU-4801 Central, Cheyenne, 82009, Laramie County, (307)637-6418, 100 miles N of Denver, CO.

Opened: 1927. **Holes:** 18. **Par:** 70/74. **Yards:** 6,121/5,661. **Course rating:** 67.1/69.5. **Slope:** 99/112. **Architect:** N/A. **Green fee:** $14/$14. **Credit cards:** MC,VISA. **Reduced fees:** Twilight. **Caddies:** No. **Golf carts:** $16. **Discount golf packages:** No. **Season:** Year-round. **High:** May-Oct. **On site lodging:** No. **Rental clubs:** Yes. **Walking policy:** Unrestricted walking. **Metal spikes allowed:** No. **Range:** Yes (grass). **To obtain tee times:** Call on Friday for upcoming weekend.

Subscriber comments: Very dissimilar nines: one trees/water; the other flat open...Played well on this course, enjoyed low flying aircraft...Seven holes on front nine, very picturesque...Acceptable track, good practical course.

★★★BELL NOB GOLF CLUB

PU-4600 Overdale Dr., Gillette, 82718, Campbell County, (307)686-7069, 140 miles W of Rapid City, SD.

Opened: 1981. **Holes:** 18. **Par:** 72/72. **Yards:** 7,024/5,555. **Course rating:** 70.8/70.6. **Slope:** 119/116. **Architect:** Frank Hummel. **Green fee:** $18/$18. **Credit cards:** MC,VISA. **Reduced fees:** N/A. **Caddies:** No. **Golf carts:** $9. **Discount golf packages:** No. **Season:** April-Oct. **High:** May-Aug. **On site lodging:** No. **Rental clubs:** Yes. **Walking policy:** Unrestricted walking. **Metal spikes allowed:** No. **Range:** Yes (grass). **To obtain tee times:** Call up to 7 days in advance.

Subscriber comments: Some pin positions can be overly difficult...Nice course...Home course, it's wide open. The wind makes it tough...Antelope, sage grouse and wildlife galore.

★★★½BUFFALO GOLF CLUB

PU-P.O. Box 759, Buffalo, 82834, Johnson County, (307)684-5266, 110 miles N of Casper.

Opened: 1928. **Holes:** 18. **Par:** 71/72. **Yards:** 6,684/5,512. **Course rating:** 70.9/69.8. **Slope:** 116/115. **Architect:** Bill Poirot/Frank Hummel. **Green fee:** $18/$18. **Credit cards:** MC,VISA. **Reduced fees:** N/A. **Caddies:** No. **Golf carts:** $18. **Discount golf packages:** No. **Season:** March-Nov. **High:** May-Sept. **On site lodging:** No. **Rental clubs:** Yes. **Walking policy:** Unrestricted walking. **Metal spikes allowed:** Yes. **Range:** Yes (grass/mats). **To obtain tee times:** Call anytime.

Subscriber comments: Great!...Mountain view, up and downhill holes, beautiful old cottonwood trees...Front nine fun, back routine...Good experience, very good value...Never a level lie, not much trouble, large greens...Best buy in the state.

★★★CASPER MUNICIPAL GOLF COURSE

PM-2120 Allendale, Casper, 82601, Natrona County, (307)234-2405, 300 miles N of Denver.

Opened: 1929. **Holes:** 27. **Architect:** Robert Muir Graves. **Green fee:** $15/$15. **Credit cards:** None. **Reduced fees:** N/A. **Caddies:** No. **Golf carts:** $8. **Discount golf packages:** No. **Season:** March-Oct. **High:** May-Aug. **On site lodging:** No. **Rental clubs:** Yes. **Walking policy:** Unrestricted walking. **Metal spikes allowed:** Yes. **Range:** Yes (grass/mats). **To obtain tee times:** Call 1 day in advance beginning 7 a.m.

HIGHLANDS/LINKS
Par: 71/73. **Yards:** 6,562/5,500. **Course rating:** 69.7/69.7. **Slope:** 113/118.
HIGHLANDS/PARK
Par: 70/72. **Yards:** 6,253/5,492. **Course rating:** 68.1/69.3. **Slope:** 108/113.
PARK/LINKS
Par: 71/71. **Yards:** 6,317/5,384. **Course rating:** 68.4/68.8. **Slope:** 108/112.

Subscriber comments: Too crowded, but is well taken care of...Surprisingly nice in the middle of a nice valley, some rough areas...Very good golf with nine new holes.

★★★DOUGLAS COMMUNITY CLUB

PU-64 Golf Course Rd., Douglas, 82633, Converse County, (307)358-5099, 50 miles E of Casper.

Opened: 1974. **Holes:** 18. **Par:** 71/72. **Yards:** 6,253/5,323. **Course rating:** 68.4/68.5. **Slope:** 107/103. **Architect:** Vern Knisley. **Green fee:** $13/$16. **Credit cards:** None. **Reduced fees:** Weekdays. **Caddies:** No. **Golf carts:** $8. **Discount golf packages:** No.

Season: April-Oct. **High:** June-Aug. **On site lodging:** No. **Rental clubs:** Yes. **Walking policy:** Unrestricted walking. **Metal spikes allowed:** Yes. **Range:** Yes (grass/mats). **To obtain tee times:** Call.

Subscriber comments: Super shape. Variety: Water, trees, sand...Beautiful...Plays short, sponge-like soft greens...A nice surprise in the middle of nowhere...Another great Wyoming course.

★★★FRANCIS E. WARREN AFB GOLF COURSE

PU-7103 Randall Ave., F.E. Warren AFB, 82005, Laramie County, (307)775-3556, 1 mile NW of Cheyenne.

Opened: 1949. **Holes:** 18. **Par:** 71/75. **Yards:** 6,585/5,186. **Course rating:** 68.2/67.0. **Slope:** 105/102. **Architect:** U.S. Government. **Green fee:** $8/$16. **Credit cards:** MC,VISA. **Reduced fees:** Twilight. **Caddies:** No. **Golf carts:** $16. **Discount golf packages:** Yes. **Season:** Year-round. **High:** April-Oct. **On site lodging:** Yes. **Rental clubs:** Yes. **Walking policy:** Unrestricted walking. **Metal spikes allowed:** No. **Range:** Yes (grass). **To obtain tee times:** Call 2 days in advance.

Subscriber comments: Fun course, well maintained...Goose droppings make course slippery...18th a good challenge, finishing hole—love the antelope on the course...Relaxing, never rushed...Few hazards, open fairways, easier to play.

★★½GLENN "RED" JACOBY GOLF CLUB

PU-University of Wyoming, Laramie, 82070, Albany County, (307)745-3111, 120 miles N of Denver, CO.

Opened: 1932. **Holes:** 18. **Par:** 70/72. **Yards:** 6,540/5,395. **Course rating:** 67.3/68.1. **Slope:** 108/109. **Architect:** N/A. **Green fee:** $13/$19. **Credit cards:** MC,VISA. **Reduced fees:** Juniors. **Caddies:** No. **Golf carts:** $10. **Discount golf packages:** No. **Season:** March-Nov. **High:** June-Aug. **On site lodging:** No. **Rental clubs:** Yes. **Walking policy:** Unrestricted walking. **Metal spikes allowed:** Yes. **Range:** Yes (grass). **To obtain tee times:** Call 1 day in advance.

Subscriber comments: OK, straight, rates going up each year...Nice course...Fairways cut too short, greens in good shape and fairly quick and true.

★★★GREEN HILLS MUNICIPAL GOLF COURSE

PM-1455 Airport Rd., Worland, 82401, Washakie County, (307)347-8972, 180 miles S of Billings, MT.

Opened: 1954. **Holes:** 18. **Par:** 72/72. **Yards:** 6,444/5,104. **Course rating:** 69.3/68.0. **Slope:** 113/113. **Architect:** Dennis Smith/Dennis Bower. **Green fee:** $16/$18. **Credit cards:** None. **Reduced fees:** Juniors. **Caddies:** No. **Golf carts:** $16. **Discount golf packages:** No. **Season:** April-Oct. **High:** June-Aug. **On site lodging:** No. **Rental clubs:** Yes. **Walking policy:** Unrestricted walking. **Metal spikes allowed:** No. **Range:** Yes (grass). **To obtain tee times:** Call anytime.

Subscriber comments: Great shape, easy to score, friendly...Nice course...Old, established and great fun...Older front nine hilly with trees, new back nine wide open, small greens...A true secret, once back nine matures, watch out.

★★★★JACKSON HOLE GOLF & TENNIS CLUB

R-5000 Spring Gulch Rd., Jackson, 83001, Teton County, (307)733-3111.

Opened: 1967. **Holes:** 18. **Par:** 72/73. **Yards:** 7,168/6,036. **Course rating:** 72.3/73.2. **Slope:** 133/125. **Architect:** Bob Baldock/Robert Trent Jones. **Green fee:** $60/$100. **Credit cards:** MC,VISA,AMEX. **Reduced fees:** Low season, twilight. **Caddies:** No. **Golf carts:** Included in Green Fee. **Discount golf packages:** No. **Season:** April-Oct. **High:** June-Aug. **On site lodging:** No. **Rental clubs:** Yes. **Walking policy:** Walking at certain times. **Metal spikes allowed:** No. **Range:** Yes (grass). **To obtain tee times:** Call anytime with credit card.

Notes: Ranked 1st in 1997 Best in State. 1993 U.S. Women's Public Links; 1988 U.S. Men's Public Links.

Subscriber comments: Some very difficult holes for high handicapper...Beautiful setting...Played behind President Clinton (way behind)...Outstanding—what a view!...Excellent golf; a bit snobbish...Too expensive for a working stiff...Without a doubt, the ultimate experience...Now too many people know about this course!

WYOMING

★★KENDRICK GOLF COURSE
PU-Big Goose Rd., Sheridan, 82801, Sheridan County, (307)674-8148, 125 miles SE of Billings, MT.
Opened: 1940. **Holes:** 18. **Par:** 72/73. **Yards:** 6,800/5,549. **Course rating:** 71.3/70.8. **Slope:** 116/113. **Architect:** Edward A. Hunnicutt/Frank Hummel. **Green fee:** $15/$15. **Credit cards:** None. **Reduced fees:** Juniors. **Caddies:** No. **Golf carts:** N/A. **Discount golf packages:** No. **Season:** April-Oct. **High:** May-July. **On site lodging:** No. **Rental clubs:** Yes. **Walking policy:** Unrestricted walking. **Metal spikes allowed:** Yes. **Range:** Yes (grass). **To obtain tee times:** Call one week in advance.

★★★½OLIVE GLENN GOLF & COUNTRY CLUB
802 Meadow Lane, Cody, 82414, Park County, (307)587-5551, 102 miles S of Billings, MT.
Opened: 1970. **Holes:** 18. **Par:** 72/72. **Yards:** 6,880/5,654. **Course rating:** 71.6/71.2. **Slope:** 124/120. **Architect:** Bob Baldock. **Green fee:** $28/$28. **Credit cards:** MC,VISA. **Reduced fees:** Juniors. **Caddies:** No. **Golf carts:** $10. **Discount golf packages:** Yes. **Season:** April-Oct. **High:** June-Aug. **On site lodging:** No. **Rental clubs:** Yes. **Walking policy:** Unrestricted walking. **Metal spikes allowed:** Yes. **Range:** Yes (grass). **To obtain tee times:** Call up to 7 days in advance.
Notes: Ranked 5th in 1997 Best in State.
Subscriber comments: Condition excellent. Very good value. Service and people good...Well maintained, windy...Needs more watering, very dry.

★★★POWELL COUNTRY CLUB
600 Highway 114, Powell, 82435, Park County, (307)754-7259.
Call club for further information.
Subscriber comments: Back nine hard, front nine narrow...New back nine made this a very good course...Some interesting holes.

PURPLE SAGE GOLF CLUB
P.O. Box 755, Evanston, 82930, Uinta County, (307)789-2383, 75 miles E of Salt Lake City, UT.
Opened: N/A. **Holes:** 9. **Par:** N/A. **Yards:** N/A. **Course rating:** N/A. **Slope:** N/A. **Architect:** N/A. **Green fee:** $18/$18. **Credit cards:** MC,VISA. **Reduced fees:** N/A. **Caddies:** No. **Golf carts:** $16. **Discount golf packages:** No. **Season:** N/A. **High:** N/A. **On site lodging:** No. **Rental clubs:** Yes. **Walking policy:** Unrestricted walking. **Metal spikes allowed:** No. **Range:** Yes (grass/mats). **To obtain tee times:** Call.

★★★RENDEZVOUS MEADOWS GOLF CLUB
PU-1 Clubhouse Rd., Pinedale, 82941, Sublette County, (307)367-4252, 78 miles S of Jackson.
Opened: 1985. **Holes:** 9. **Par:** 36/36. **Yards:** 3,255/2,760. **Course rating:** 69.8/70.3. **Slope:** 118/118. **Architect:** William Hull. **Green fee:** $12/$15. **Credit cards:** None. **Reduced fees:** Weekdays. **Caddies:** No. **Golf carts:** $15. **Discount golf packages:** No. **Season:** April-Oct. **High:** July-Aug. **On site lodging:** No. **Rental clubs:** Yes. **Walking policy:** Unrestricted walking. **Metal spikes allowed:** No. **Range:** Yes (grass). **To obtain tee times:** Call in advance for weekends.
Subscriber comments: Very good course for beginners...Course in great shape, great views of mountains, very enjoyable.

★★★½RIVERTON COUNTRY CLUB
4275 Country Club Dr., Riverton, 82501, Fremont County, (307)856-4779, 117 miles W of Casper.
Opened: 1970. **Holes:** 18. **Par:** 72/72. **Yards:** 7,064/5,549. **Course rating:** 72.2/71.0. **Slope:** 128/119. **Architect:** Richard Watson. **Green fee:** $20/$30. **Credit cards:** MC,VISA. **Reduced fees:** N/A. **Caddies:** No. **Golf carts:** $10. **Discount golf packages:** No. **Season:** March-Oct. **High:** June-Aug. **On site lodging:** No. **Rental clubs:** Yes. **Walking policy:** Unrestricted walking. **Metal spikes allowed:** Yes. **Range:** Yes (grass). **To obtain tee times:** Call up to 7 days in advance.
Subscriber comments: Needs work...Home course, great!...Underrated.

WYOMING

★★½ SARATOGA GOLF CLUB
P.O. Box 1214, Saratoga, 82331, Carbon County, (307)326-5261.
Call club for further information.
Subscriber comments: Somewhat overpriced...This nine-hole course is a pleasant delight. It was a lot of fun...Needs work...Climate makes it tough on the course.

★★★ STAR VALLEY RANCH COUNTRY CLUB
P.O. Box 159, Thayne, 83127, Lincoln County, (307)883-2230, 50 miles from Jackson.
Opened: 1970. **Holes:** 27. **Par:** N/A. **Yards:** N/A. **Course rating:** N/A. **Slope:** N/A.
Architect: N/A. **Green fee:** $16/$37. **Credit cards:** MC,VISA. **Reduced fees:** Weekdays. **Caddies:** No. **Golf carts:** $17. **Discount golf packages:** No. **Season:** April-Oct. **High:** June-Aug. **On site lodging:** No. **Rental clubs:** Yes. **Walking policy:** Unrestricted walking. **Metal spikes allowed:** No. **Range:** Yes (grass). **To obtain tee times:** Call or come in 4 days in advance.
Subscriber comments: Beautiful setting...4th hole on original nine as tough as it gets...Houses too close to fairways...Nice mountain course, needs some grooming.

★★★★ TETON PINES RESORT & COUNTRY CLUB
R-3450 Clubhouse Dr., Jackson, 83001, Teton County, (307)733-1733, (800)238-2223, 150 miles N of Salt Lake City, UT.
Opened: 1987. **Holes:** 18. **Par:** 72/72. **Yards:** 7,412/5,486. **Course rating:** 74.2/70.8.
Slope: 137/117. **Architect:** Arnold Palmer and Ed Seay. **Green fee:** $50/$140. **Credit cards:** MC,VISA,AMEX,Diners Club. **Reduced fees:** Weekdays, low season, resort guests, juniors. **Caddies:** Yes. **Golf carts:** Included in Green Fee. **Discount golf packages:** Yes. **Season:** May-Oct. **High:** June-Sept. **On site lodging:** Yes. **Rental clubs:** Yes. **Walking policy:** Mandatory cart. **Metal spikes allowed:** No. **Range:** Yes (grass/mats). **To obtain tee times:** Call anytime.
Notes: Ranked 3rd in 1997 Best in State.
Subscriber comments: Great resort course with fantastic views of Tetons...Too expensive...Amazing views. The best I've played...Great four finishing holes...Very nice course, spikeless, greens in great condition...Wonderful vacation course, nice challenge, beautiful spot...Very stylish...After Yellowstone, you have to treat yourself.

★★★ TORRINGTON MUNICIPAL GOLF COURSE
PM-W. 15th. St., Torrington, 82240, Goshen County, (307)532-3868.
Opened: N/A. **Holes:** 18. **Par:** 72/73. **Yards:** 6,298/5,344. **Course rating:** 67.7/69.2.
Slope: 112/112. **Architect:** N/A. **Green fee:** $15/$16. **Credit cards:** None. **Reduced fees:** Weekdays. **Caddies:** No. **Golf carts:** $12. **Discount golf packages:** No.
Season: Year-round. **High:** June-Aug. **On site lodging:** No. **Rental clubs:** Yes.
Walking policy: Unrestricted walking. **Metal spikes allowed:** No. **Range:** Yes (grass).
To obtain tee times: Call in advance for weekends only.
Subscriber comments: Very good back nine...New nine great, riverside...Good pro shop, tight back nine...Open front, treed back.
Special Notes: Formerly Cottonwood Country Club.

★★★ WHITE MOUNTAIN GOLF COURSE
PU-1501 Clubhouse Dr., Rock Springs, 82901, Sweetwater County, (307)352-1415.
Opened: 1979. **Holes:** 18. **Par:** 72/73. **Yards:** 7,000/5,666. **Course rating:** 72.4/73.1.
Slope: 122/115. **Architect:** Dick Phelps/Donald G. Brauer. **Green fee:** $15/$15. **Credit cards:** None. **Reduced fees:** Juniors. **Caddies:** No. **Golf carts:** $15. **Discount golf packages:** No. **Season:** April-Oct. **High:** June-Sept. **On site lodging:** No. **Rental clubs:** Yes. **Walking policy:** Unrestricted walking. **Metal spikes allowed:** No. **Range:** Yes (grass/mats). **To obtain tee times:** Call one week in advance.
Subscriber comments: Nice course...Very windy course...Great course given what they had to work with...Not overplayed—hope not many find it!...Watch out for the wind.

Part II

Canada

ALBERTA

★★★½ BANFF SPRINGS GOLF COURSE
R-One Golf Course Rd., Banff, T0L 0C0, (403)762-6833, 70 miles NW of Calgary.
Opened: 1928. **Holes:** 27. **Architect:** Stanley Thompson/William G. Robinson. **Green fee:** $65/$90. **Credit cards:** MC,VISA,AMEX,DISC,Diners, JCB. **Reduced fees:** Low season. **Caddies:** No. **Golf carts:** Included in Green Fee. **Discount golf packages:** Yes. **Season:** May-Oct. **High:** June-Sept. **On site lodging:** Yes. **Rental clubs:** Yes. **Walking policy:** Walking at certain times. **Metal spikes allowed:** Yes. **Range:** Yes (mats). **To obtain tee times:** Call or fax with a credit card to guarantee.
RUNDLE/SULPHER
Par: 71/71. **Yards:** 6,626/5,964. **Course rating:** 72.0. **Slope:** 124.
RUNDLE/TUNNEL
Par: 71/71. **Yards:** 6,443/5,652. **Course rating:** 71.5. **Slope:** 124.
TUNNEL/SULPHER
Par: N/A. **Yards:** N/A. **Course rating:** N/A. **Slope:** N/A.
Subscriber comments: Scenic wonder and fine challenges...Expect to see elk...Who can play with such views?...Terrific course and atmosphere...A joy to behold! Excellent facilities...Some awesome holes...Beautiful backdrop.

★★★½ BARRHEAD GOLF CLUB
PU-P.O. Box 4090, Barrhead, T7N 1A1, (403)674-3053, 60 miles NW of Edmonton.
Opened: 1991. **Holes:** 18. **Par:** 72/72. **Yards:** 6,593/5,351. **Course rating:** 72.0/71.0. **Slope:** 127/120. **Architect:** Les Furber. **Green fee:** $15/$24. **Credit cards:** MC,VISA. **Reduced fees:** Low season, twilight. **Caddies:** No. **Golf carts:** $23. **Discount golf packages:** Yes. **Season:** April-Oct. **High:** N/A. **On site lodging:** No. **Rental clubs:** Yes. **Walking policy:** Unrestricted walking. **Metal spikes allowed:** Yes. **Range:** Yes (grass/mats). **To obtain tee times:** Call 7 days in advance.
Subscriber comments: Fun course, friendly people...Nice river course...This course is awesome!...Excellent back nine.

★★ BROADMOOR PUBLIC GOLF COURSE
PU-2025 Oak St., Sherwood Park, T8A 0W9, (403)467-7373, 10 miles E of Edmonton.
Opened: 1960. **Holes:** 18. **Par:** 71/71. **Yards:** 6,345/5,517. **Course rating:** 69.5/70.4. **Slope:** 122/120. **Architect:** Norman H. Woods. **Green fee:** $23/$25. **Credit cards:** MC,VISA,AMEX,ATM Debit Cards. **Reduced fees:** Weekdays, twilight, seniors, juniors. **Caddies:** No. **Golf carts:** $24. **Discount golf packages:** No. **Season:** April-Oct. **High:** May-June. **On site lodging:** No. **Rental clubs:** Yes. **Walking policy:** Unrestricted walking. **Metal spikes allowed:** Yes. **Range:** Yes (grass/mats). **To obtain tee times:** Call 3 days in advance.

★★★ CANMORE GOLF & CURLING CLUB
2000 8th Ave., Canmore, TIW 142, (403)678-4785, 55 miles W of Calgary.
Opened: 1961. **Holes:** 18. **Par:** 71/72. **Yards:** 6,309/5,258. **Course rating:** 69.1/70.3. **Slope:** 122/125. **Architect:** Bill Newis. **Green fee:** $38/$38. **Credit cards:** MC,VISA,AMEX. **Reduced fees:** Low season, resort guests, juniors. **Caddies:** No. **Golf carts:** $25. **Discount golf packages:** No. **Season:** April-Oct. **High:** June-Aug. **On site lodging:** No. **Rental clubs:** Yes. **Walking policy:** Unrestricted walking. **Metal spikes allowed:** Yes. **Range:** Yes (mats). **To obtain tee times:** Resort guests and golf packages book up to 60 days in advance. Public call 3 days in advance.
Subscriber comments: Great small-town course in mountain setting...Very scenic and reasonably priced...Easy walk...Heavy play.

★★★½ COLONIALE GOLF & COUNTRY CLUB
10 Country Club Dr., Beaumont, T4X 1M1, (403)929-4653, 2 miles S of Edmonton.
Opened: 1993. **Holes:** 18. **Par:** 72/72. **Yards:** 7,020/5,344. **Course rating:** 73.8/72.1. **Slope:** 145/126. **Architect:** Bill Newis. **Green fee:** $30/$48. **Credit cards:** MC,VISA. **Reduced fees:** Weekdays, low season, twilight, seniors, juniors. **Caddies:** No. **Golf**

carts: Included in Green Fee. **Discount golf packages:** Yes. **Season:** April-Oct. **High:** May-Sept. **On site lodging:** No. **Rental clubs:** Yes. **Walking policy:** Mandatory cart. **Metal spikes allowed:** Yes. **Range:** Yes (grass/mats). **To obtain tee times:** Call 2 days in advance, or anytime in advance with credit card to guarantee and 24-hour cancellation.

Subscriber comments: Great variety, great people...Bring your "A" game...Interesting and challenging layout. Worth playing...No goofy surprises.

★★★ CONNAUGHT GOLF CLUB

2802 13th Ave. S.E., Medicine Hat, T1A 3P9, (403)526-0737, 185 miles E of Calgary.
Opened: N/A. **Holes:** 18. **Par:** 72/73. **Yards:** 6,993/5,800. **Course rating:** 74.0/73.5. **Slope:** 128/126. **Architect:** A.L. (Ron) Ehlert. **Green fee:** $30/$30. **Credit cards:** MC,VISA. **Reduced fees:** Low season, juniors. **Caddies:** No. **Golf carts:** $24. **Discount golf packages:** No. **Season:** April-Oct. **High:** June-Aug. **On site lodging:** No. **Rental clubs:** Yes. **Walking policy:** Unrestricted walking. **Metal spikes allowed:** Yes. **Range:** Yes (mats). **To obtain tee times:** Non-members may call 1 day in advance for weekdays, and Thursdays for upcoming weekend.
Subscriber comments: If there were a most-improved category, this one would win...Very unforgiving if you make mistakes, lots of hazards...Wide open.
Special Notes: Spikeless shoes encouraged.

★★★½ COTTONWOOD GOLF & COUNTRY CLUB

Box 28, Site 2, RR #1, DeWinton, TOL OXO, (403)938-7200, 10 miles SE of Calgary.
Opened: 1990. **Holes:** 18. **Par:** 72/72. **Yards:** 6,747/5,054. **Course rating:** 72.5/67.5. **Slope:** 129/118. **Architect:** Bill Newis. **Green fee:** $50. **Credit cards:** MC,VISA,AMEX. **Reduced fees:** Twilight, juniors. **Caddies:** No. **Golf carts:** $25. **Discount golf packages:** No. **Season:** April-Oct. **High:** June-July. **On site lodging:** No. **Rental clubs:** Yes. **Walking policy:** Unrestricted walking. **Metal spikes allowed:** No. **Range:** Yes (grass/mats). **To obtain tee times:** Call 4 days in advance starting at noon.
Subscriber comments: Nice family course...Great layout, great practice area...Island green...Service is good.

COUNTRYSIDE GOLF COURSE

PU-51466 Range Rd. 232, Sherwood Park, T8B 1L1, (403)467-9254, 6 miles SE of Edmonton.
Opened: 1986. **Holes:** 18. **Par:** 72. **Yards:** 6,025/5,600. **Course rating:** 68.5. **Slope:** 113. **Architect:** Solomon. **Green fee:** $16/$20. **Credit cards:** MC,VISA,AMEX. **Reduced fees:** Weekdays, seniors. **Caddies:** No. **Golf carts:** $22. **Discount golf packages:** Yes. **Season:** April-Oct. **High:** N/A. **On site lodging:** No. **Rental clubs:** Yes. **Walking policy:** Unrestricted walking. **Metal spikes allowed:** No. **Range:** Yes (grass/mats). **To obtain tee times:** Call 2 days in advance for weekdays. Call on Monday for upcoming weekend or holiday.

★★★½ D'ARCY RANCH GOLF CLUB

PU-Hwy. 29 and Milligan Dr., Okotoks, TOL 1T0, (403)938-4455, (800)803-8810, 14 miles S of Calgary.
Opened: 1991. **Holes:** 18. **Par:** 72/73. **Yards:** 6,919/5,529. **Course rating:** 72.3/71.3. **Slope:** 126/122. **Architect:** Finger, Dye and Spann. **Green fee:** $45/$45. **Credit cards:** MC,VISA,AMEX. **Reduced fees:** Twilight. **Caddies:** No. **Golf carts:** $26. **Discount golf packages:** No. **Season:** April-Oct. **High:** May-Sept. **On site lodging:** No. **Rental clubs:** Yes. **Walking policy:** Unrestricted walking. **Metal spikes allowed:** Yes. **Range:** Yes (grass/mats). **To obtain tee times:** Outside of province, call 7 days in advance. Local, call 2 days in advance. Call Thursday at 7 a.m. for weekends and holidays.
Subscriber comments: Every hole is unique. Excellent par 3s...Nice layout, rolling hills...Challenging, scenic, valleys and cliffs...Ravine setting.

★★★ DINOSAUR TRAIL GOLF & COUNTRY CLUB

PU-P.O. Box 1511, Drumheller, T0J 0Y0, (403)823-5622, 110 miles NE of Calgary.
Opened: 1995. **Holes:** 18. **Par:** 72/73. **Yards:** 6,401/5,093. **Course rating:** 71.2/68.4. **Slope:** 135/110. **Architect:** Sid Puddicombe. **Green fee:** $27/$27. **Credit cards:** MC,VISA. **Reduced fees:** Seniors, juniors. **Caddies:** No. **Golf carts:** $24. **Discount golf packages:** No. **Season:** May-Oct. **High:** June-Aug. **On site lodging:** No. **Rental clubs:** Yes. **Walking policy:** Unrestricted walking. **Metal spikes allowed:** Yes. **Range:**

Yes (grass/mats). **To obtain tee times:** Call up to 14 days in advance. Credit card required for 3 or more players.
Subscriber comments: Continously upgrading and improving...Courteous staff...First nine is so-so, back nine is wild! Amongst badlands.

★★★THE DUNES GOLF & WINTER CLUB
PU-RR #1, Site 4, Box 1, Grande Prairie, T8V 5N3, (403)538-4333.
Opened: 1992. **Holes:** 18. **Par:** 71/72. **Yards:** 6,418/5,274. **Course rating:** 69.3/70.1.
Slope: 124/123. **Architect:** Mel Watchhorn. **Green fee:** $20/$28. **Credit cards:**
MC,VISA,AMEX. **Reduced fees:** Low season, seniors. **Caddies:** No. **Golf carts:** $24.
Discount golf packages: Yes. **Season:** March-Oct. **High:** April-Sept. **On site lodging:**
No. **Rental clubs:** Yes. **Walking policy:** Unrestricted walking. **Metal spikes allowed:**
Yes. **Range:** Yes (grass/mats). **To obtain tee times:** Call up to 14 days in advance with credit card. Call 1 day in advance for weekdays. Call Friday for upcoming weekend or holiday.
Subscriber comments: Tight, well maintained, lots of trees and water.

★½EAGLE ROCK GOLF COURSE
PU-TWP 510, RR 234, South Edmonton, T6H 4N6, (403)464-4653, 5 miles SE of Edmonton.
Opened: 1990. **Holes:** 18. **Par:** 71/71. **Yards:** 6,587/5,429. **Course rating:** 72.0/71.1.
Slope: 120/120. **Architect:** Sid Puddicome. **Green fee:** $12/$24. **Credit cards:**
MC,VISA. **Reduced fees:** Weekdays, seniors. **Caddies:** No. **Golf carts:** $22. **Discount golf packages:** No. **Season:** April-Nov. **High:** June-Aug. **On site lodging:** No. **Rental clubs:** Yes. **Walking policy:** Unrestricted walking. **Metal spikes allowed:** Yes. **Range:** Yes (grass). **To obtain tee times:** Call 7 days in advance.

★★★GOOSE HUMMOCK GOLF CLUB
PU-P.O. Box 1221, Gibbons, T0A 1N0, (403)921-2444, 20 miles N of Edmonton.
Opened: 1989. **Holes:** 18. **Par:** 71/71. **Yards:** 6,604/5,408. **Course rating:** 74.0/71.5.
Slope: 141/121. **Architect:** Bill Robinson. **Green fee:** $24/$29. **Credit cards:**
MC,VISA,AMEX,Debit Card. **Reduced fees:** Twilight, seniors, juniors. **Caddies:** No.
Golf carts: $22. **Discount golf packages:** No. **Season:** April-Oct. **High:** June-Aug. **On site lodging:** No. **Rental clubs:** Yes. **Walking policy:** Unrestricted walking. **Metal spikes allowed:** Yes. **Range:** Yes (grass/mats). **To obtain tee times:** Call 14 days in advance with credit card, or 2 days in advance without credit card.
Subscriber comments: Tough holes, lots of water...Plays long...Bring extra balls...Interesting terrain...Beautiful in September!

★★½HENDERSON LAKE GOLF CLUB
PU-S. Parkside Dr., Lethbridge, T1J 4A2, (403)329-6767, 120 miles S of Calgary.
Opened: 1917. **Holes:** 18. **Par:** 70/75. **Yards:** 6,512/5,976. **Course rating:** 70.5/73.1.
Slope: 120/123. **Architect:** Norman H. Woods. **Green fee:** $25/$25. **Credit cards:**
MC,VISA. **Reduced fees:** Low season, twilight, juniors. **Caddies:** No. **Golf carts:** $22.
Discount golf packages: Yes. **Season:** April-Oct. **High:** May-Aug. **On site lodging:**
No. **Rental clubs:** Yes. **Walking policy:** Unrestricted walking. **Metal spikes allowed:**
Yes. **Range:** No. **To obtain tee times:** Call two days in advance.
Subscriber comments: Good old muny track...Tight...Decent layout, flat, interesting when wind blows...Difficult to score well...Good for all levels.

★★★★HERITAGE POINTE GOLF & COUNTRY CLUB
R-R.R. No.1, Heritage Pointe Dr., De Winton, T0L 0X0, (403)256-2002, 6 miles S of Calgary.
Opened: 1992. **Holes:** 27. **Architect:** Ron Garl. **Green fee:** $43/$70.
Credit cards: MC,VISA,AMEX. **Reduced fees:** Twilight, seniors, juniors.
Caddies: No. **Golf carts:** Included in Green Fee. **Discount golf packages:** Yes. **Season:** April-Oct. **High:** June-Aug. **On site lodging:** No. **Rental clubs:** Yes. **Walking policy:** Walking at certain times. **Metal spikes allowed:** Yes. **Range:** Yes (grass). **To obtain tee times:** Call 7 days in advance with credit cart.
DESERT/HERITAGE
Par: 72/73. **Yards:** 7,044/4,967. **Course rating:** 74.0/68.0. **Slope:** 128/129.
POINTE/DESERT
Par: 72/72. **Yards:** 6,936/4,944. **Course rating:** 73.0/67.0. **Slope:** 131/125.

POINTE/HERITAGE
Par: 72/73. **Yards:** 6,904/4,773. **Course rating:** 73.0/66.0. **Slope:** 137/128.
Subscriber comments: Outstanding service, gorgeous views, tough holes...Natural setting...A must play when in Calgary...Very challenging...Pointe/Heritage best combo...Some gimmicky holes.

HINTON GOLF CLUB
PU-Hwy. 16 W., Hinton, T7V 1Y2, (403)865-2904, 175 miles W of Edmonton.
Opened: 1964. **Holes:** 18. **Par:** 72/72. **Yards:** 6,729/5,700. **Course rating:** 72.0/70.0.
Slope: 125. **Architect:** N/A. **Green fee:** $27/$27. **Credit cards:** MC,VISA,AMEX.
Reduced fees: Twilight, juniors. **Caddies:** No. **Golf carts:** $24. **Discount golf packages:** Yes. **Season:** April-Oct. **High:** May-Aug. **On site lodging:** No. **Rental clubs:** Yes.
Walking policy: Unrestricted walking. **Metal spikes allowed:** Yes. **Range:** Yes (grass/mats). **To obtain tee times:** Call anytime.

★★½INDIAN LAKES GOLF CLUB
PU-Site 2, R.R. No.1, Enoch, T7X 343, (403)470-5475, 6 miles N of Edmonton.
Opened: 1989. **Holes:** 18. **Par:** 71/71. **Yards:** 6,650/5,600. **Course rating:** 69.5/67.0.
Slope: 128/128. **Architect:** William G. Robinson. **Green fee:** $20/$26. **Credit cards:** MC,VISA,AMEX. **Reduced fees:** N/A. **Caddies:** No. **Golf carts:** $22. **Discount golf packages:** No. **Season:** April-Oct. **High:** June-Aug. **On site lodging:** No. **Rental clubs:** Yes. **Walking policy:** Unrestricted walking. **Metal spikes allowed:** Yes. **Range:** Yes (grass). **To obtain tee times:** Call 2 days in advance.
Subscriber comments: Very natural layout, great variety...Good layout.

★★½IRONHEAD GOLF & COUNTRY CLUB
P.O. Box 69, Wabamun, T0E 2K0, (403)892-4653.
Call club for further information.
Subscriber comments: Beautiful course...Tee boxes are so good, they could be the greens on some courses! Fantastic.

★★★★JASPER PARK LODGE GOLF COURSE
R-Box 40, Jasper, T0E 1E0, (403)852-6089, 210 miles W of Edmonton.
Opened: 1925. **Holes:** 18. **Par:** 71/75. **Yards:** 6,663/5,935. **Course rating:** 70.5/73.5.
Slope: 121/122. **Architect:** Stanley Thompson. **Green fee:** $40/$69. **Credit cards:** MC,VISA,AMEX,DISC,Diners Club, JCB. **Reduced fees:** Low season, twilight, juniors.
Caddies: No. **Golf carts:** $15. **Discount golf packages:** Yes. **Season:** April-Oct. **High:** June-Sept. **On site lodging:** Yes. **Rental clubs:** Yes. **Walking policy:** Unrestricted walking. **Metal spikes allowed:** Yes. **Range:** Yes (grass/mats). **To obtain tee times:** Call anytime.
Subscriber comments: Wonderful resort, the views are outstanding. Greens fast...Friendly staff...Lot of wildlife...Excellent service, excellent golf...Fabulous setting...Great fun...Manicured greens and fairways.

KANANASKIS COUNTRY GOLF CLUB
R-P.O. Box 1710, Kananaskis Village, T0L 2H0, (403)591-7070, 50 miles SW of Calgary.
Opened: 1983. **Architect:** Robert Trent Jones Sr. **Green fee:** $45/$45.
Credit cards: MC,VISA,AMEX. **Reduced fees:** Twilight, seniors, juniors.
Caddies: No. **Golf carts:** $13. **Discount golf packages:** No. **Season:** May-Oct. **High:** June-Sept. **On site lodging:** Yes. **Rental clubs:** Yes. **Walking policy:** Unrestricted walking. **Metal spikes allowed:** Yes. **Range:** Yes (grass/mats). **To obtain tee times:** Call up to 60 days in advance with credit card.

★★★★½MT. KIDD COURSE
Holes: 18. **Par:** 72/72. **Yards:** 7,083/5,539. **Course rating:** 72.8/71.5.
Slope: 134/127.
Subscriber comments: Great golf, even better scenery...Lots of sand...The most fun golf you can play...Country club excellence...Great experience...Well groomed, very good pace for resort course...You can't find any better mountain golf courses in Canada...Take a camera.

★★★★½ MT. LORETTE COURSE
Holes: 18. **Par:** 72/72. **Yards:** 7,102/5,429. **Course rating:** 74.1/72.0. **Slope:** 137.
Subscriber comments: Better of the two, water, sand everything...Spectacular/challenging...Excellent views from all holes...Can be very windy...Best all-round course I've played.

★★½ LAKESIDE GREENS GOLF & COUNTRY CLUB
555 Lakeside Greens Dr., Chestermere, T1X 1O5, (403)569-9111, 4 miles E of Calgary.
Opened: 1992. **Holes:** 18. **Par:** 71/71. **Yards:** 6,804/5,063. **Course rating:** 72.5/68.8. **Slope:** 134/118. **Architect:** Bill Newis. **Green fee:** $30/$37. **Credit cards:** MC,VISA,AMEX,Debit Card. **Reduced fees:** Weekdays, twilight, seniors, juniors. **Caddies:** No. **Golf carts:** $24. **Discount golf packages:** No. **Season:** April-Oct. **High:** June-Aug. **On site lodging:** No. **Rental clubs:** No. **Walking policy:** N/A. **Metal spikes allowed:** Yes. **Range:** Yes (mats). **To obtain tee times:** Call 5 days in advance for weekdays. Call on Thursday at 7 a.m. for upcoming weekend.
Subscriber comments: Fairly easy and open. Lots of water. Beautiful clubhouse...Houses close to the course...Great scenery...Easy walking.

★★½ LAND-O-LAKES GOLF CLUB
102 Fairway Dr., Coaldale, T1M 1H1, (403)345-2582, 6 miles E of Lethbridge.
Opened: 1987. **Holes:** 18. **Par:** 71/72. **Yards:** 6,459/5,634. **Course rating:** 72.0/73.0. **Slope:** 119/126. **Architect:** Les Furber. **Green fee:** $20/$25. **Credit cards:** MC,VISA. **Reduced fees:** Weekdays, juniors. **Caddies:** No. **Golf carts:** $20. **Discount golf packages:** Yes. **Season:** April-Oct. **High:** May-Sept. **On site lodging:** No. **Rental clubs:** Yes. **Walking policy:** Unrestricted walking. **Metal spikes allowed:** Yes. **Range:** Yes (grass/mats). **To obtain tee times:** Call 2 days in advance.
Subscriber comments: Sand, sand, sand...Many houses bordering, dogleg par 5s...Lots of H2O, flat.

★★★ THE LINKS AT SPRUCE GROVE
PU-Calahoo Rd., Spruce Grove, T7X 3B4, (403)962-4653, 10 miles E of Edmonton.
Opened: 1983. **Holes:** 18. **Par:** 72/72. **Yards:** 6,767/5,748. **Course rating:** 71.0/72.0. **Slope:** 125/126. **Architect:** Bill Robinson. **Green fee:** $20/$29. **Credit cards:** MC,VISA. **Reduced fees:** Weekdays, low season, twilight, seniors, juniors. **Caddies:** No. **Golf carts:** $24. **Discount golf packages:** No. **Season:** April-Oct. **High:** June-Aug. **On site lodging:** No. **Rental clubs:** Yes. **Walking policy:** Unrestricted walking. **Metal spikes allowed:** Yes. **Range:** Yes (grass/mats). **To obtain tee times:** Call 2 days in advance.
Subscriber comments: Plays different every day...Fast greens...Architecturally challenging, close to houses...Very good prairie course.

★★★ MAPLE RIDGE GOLF COURSE
1240 Mapleglade Dr. S.E., Calgary, (403)974-1825. Call club for further information.
Subscriber comments: Pleasant and reasonable...Challenging for lower handicaps yet easy enough for a beginner to enjoy...Nice mixture of water, trees, bush...Elevation changes affect club selection...13th awesome.

★★ MCCALL LAKE GOLF COURSE
2108 23rd Ave., S.W., Calgary, T2T 0W1, (403)974-1805. Call club for further information.

★★½ MCKENZIE MEADOWS GOLF CLUB
PU-17215 McKenzie Meadows Dr. SE, Calgary, T2H 0J9, (403)257-2255.
Opened: 1996. **Holes:** 18. **Par:** 72/72. **Yards:** 6,508/5,132. **Course rating:** 70.5/67.8. **Slope:** 124/116. **Architect:** Gary Browning & Associates. **Green fee:** $32/$35. **Credit cards:** None. **Reduced fees:** Weekdays, twilight, seniors. **Caddies:** No. **Golf carts:** $25. **Discount golf packages:** No. **Season:** April-Oct. **High:** June-Sept. **On site lodging:** No. **Rental clubs:** No. **Walking policy:** Unrestricted walking. **Metal spikes allowed:** Yes. **Range:** No. **To obtain tee times:** Call up to 3 days in advance.
Subscriber comments: Good course, need to toughen up rough...Short and pretty...Wide open, fun course...Very playable.

★★½ MEDICINE HAT GOLF & COUNTRY CLUB
P.O. Box 232, Medicine Hat, T1A 7E9, (403)527-8086, 180 miles SW of Calgary.
Opened: 1933. **Holes:** 18. **Par:** 72/72. **Yards:** 6,612/5,606. **Course rating:** 72.5/72.5.
Slope: 131/123. **Architect:** Tom Bendelow. **Green fee:** $30/$30. **Credit cards:** All
major. **Reduced fees:** Low season, twilight. **Caddies:** No. **Golf carts:** $25. **Discount
golf packages:** No. **Season:** April-Oct. **High:** N/A. **On site lodging:** No. **Rental clubs:**
Yes. **Walking policy:** Unrestricted walking. **Metal spikes allowed:** No. **Range:** Yes
(mats). **To obtain tee times:** Call 2 days in advance.
Subscriber comments: Six really good holes...Fun...Challenging...Treelined fairways
and large greens...Can't get into a lot of trouble...Very picturesque.

★★ OLDS GOLF CLUB
PU-R.R. #1, Site 2, Box 13, Olds, T4H 1P2, (403)556-8008, 45 miles N of Calgary.
Opened: 1982. **Holes:** 18. **Par:** 72/73. **Yards:** 6,662/5,886. **Course rating:** 70.4/72.5.
Slope: 121/121. **Architect:** N/A. **Green fee:** $21/$24. **Credit cards:** MC,VISA,Debit
Cards. **Reduced fees:** Weekdays, juniors. **Caddies:** No. **Golf carts:** $24. **Discount
golf packages:** No. **Season:** May-Oct. **High:** June-Aug. **On site lodging:** No. **Rental
clubs:** Yes. **Walking policy:** Unrestricted walking. **Metal spikes allowed:** Yes. **Range:**
Yes (grass). **To obtain tee times:** Call on Wednesday for upcoming weekend or holiday. Call on Sunday for following week.

★★★★ PARADISE CANYON GOLF & COUNTRY CLUB
185 Canyon Blvd., Lethbridge, T1K 6V1, (403)381-7500, 120 miles S
of Calgary.
Opened: 1992. **Holes:** 18. **Par:** 71/71. **Yards:** 6,810/5,282. **Course
rating:** 73.1/70.6. **Slope:** 132/127. **Architect:** Bill Newis. **Green fee:**
$30/$35. **Credit cards:** MC,VISA. **Reduced fees:** Weekdays, twilight.
Caddies: No. **Golf carts:** $25. **Discount golf packages:** No. **Season:** April-Nov. **High:**
May-Aug. **On site lodging:** No. **Rental clubs:** Yes. **Walking policy:** Unrestricted walking. **Metal spikes allowed:** Yes. **Range:** Yes (grass/mats). **To obtain tee times:** Call 3
days in advance.
Subscriber comments: Diamond in the desert, 12th hole memorable...Not a flat green
anywhere...Wind makes club selection challenging...Links-style course, keep it in the
fairway!...Not for beginners, plays long, excellent greens.

★★★ PHEASANTBACK GOLF & COUNTRY CLUB
PU-P.O. Box 1621, Stettler, T0C 2L0, (403)742-4653.
Opened: 1995. **Holes:** 18. **Par:** 71/71. **Yards:** 6,104/4,631. **Course rating:** N/A. **Slope:**
N/A. **Architect:** Bill Robinson. **Green fee:** $20/$20. **Credit cards:** MC,VISA. **Reduced
fees:** Low season, resort guests, twilight, seniors, juniors. **Caddies:** No. **Golf carts:**
$10. **Discount golf packages:** Yes. **Season:** April-Oct. **High:** May-June. **On site lodg-
ing:** No. **Rental clubs:** Yes. **Walking policy:** Unrestricted walking. **Metal spikes
allowed:** Yes. **Range:** Yes (grass). **To obtain tee times:** Call one week in advance.
Subscriber comments: Hidden jewel, will be tremendous course when it
matures...Tricky the first time around, water!...Very surprising.

★★½ PICTURE BUTTE GOLF & WINTER CLUB
P.O. Box 359, Picture Butte, T0K 1V0, (403)732-4157, 20 miles N of Lethbridge.
Opened: 1963. **Holes:** 18. **Par:** 72/73. **Yards:** 6,390/5,127. **Course rating:** 70.5/71.5.
Slope: N/A. **Architect:** Les Furber and Jim Eremko. **Green fee:** $19/$23. **Credit cards:**
MC,VISA. **Reduced fees:** Low season, twilight, seniors, juniors. **Caddies:** No. **Golf
carts:** $25. **Discount golf packages:** No. **Season:** March-Oct. **High:** May-Sept. **On
site lodging:** No. **Rental clubs:** Yes. **Walking policy:** Unrestricted walking. **Metal
spikes allowed:** Yes. **Range:** Yes (grass). **To obtain tee times:** Call 2 days in
advance.
Subscriber comments: Challenging, usually windy!....Par 4s on the back are too long.

★★★ PONOKA COMMUNITY GOLF COURSE
PU-P.O. Box 4145, Ponoka, T4J 1R5, (403)783-4626, 60 miles S of Edmonton.
Opened: 1987. **Holes:** 18. **Par:** 72/72. **Yards:** 6,500/5,800. **Course rating:** 69.9/72.4.
Slope: 121/131. **Architect:** William G. Robinson. **Green fee:** $23/$27. **Credit cards:**
MC,VISA,AMEX. **Reduced fees:** N/A. **Caddies:** No. **Golf carts:** $25. **Discount golf

packages: No. **Season:** April-Oct. **High:** June-Aug. **On site lodging:** No. **Rental clubs:** No. **Walking policy:** Unrestricted walking. **Metal spikes allowed:** Yes. **Range:** Yes. **To obtain tee times:** Call 2 days in advance for weekdays. Call Thursday for upcoming weekend. Call anytime in advance with credit card.

Subscriber comments: Great golf, back nine fantastic...Tougher than it looks...Friendly staff...Worth the stop.

★★★THE RANCH GOLF & COUNTRY CLUB

52516 Range Rd. 262, Spruce Grove, T7Y 1A5, (403)470-4700, 3 miles W of Edmonton.

Opened: 1989. **Holes:** 18. **Par:** 71/71. **Yards:** 6,526/5,082. **Course rating:** 70.4/70.7. **Slope:** 129/124. **Architect:** Western Golf. **Green fee:** $26/$31. **Credit cards:** MC,VISA,AMEX. **Reduced fees:** Weekdays, low season, twilight, seniors, juniors. **Caddies:** No. **Golf carts:** $24. **Discount golf packages:** No. **Season:** April-Oct. **High:** May-Sept. **On site lodging:** No. **Rental clubs:** Yes. **Walking policy:** Unrestricted walking. **Metal spikes allowed:** Yes. **Range:** Yes (mats). **To obtain tee times:** Call 2 days in advance.

Subscriber comments: Lots of trees, some water, good test...Variety of holes, challenging for everyone...Some quirky holes, but always interesting.

★★★½REDWOOD MEADOWS GOLF & COUNTRY CLUB

Box 1 Site 7 R.R.No.1, Calgary, T2P 2G4, (403)949-3663.

Opened: 1976. **Holes:** 18. **Par:** 72/73. **Yards:** 7,000/6,108. **Course rating:** 72.7/74.0. **Slope:** 129/134. **Architect:** Stan Leonard. **Green fee:** $35/$35. **Credit cards:** MC,VISA,AMEX. **Reduced fees:** Juniors. **Caddies:** No. **Golf carts:** $24. **Discount golf packages:** No. **Season:** April-Oct. **High:** May-Sept. **On site lodging:** No. **Rental clubs:** Yes. **Walking policy:** Unrestricted walking. **Metal spikes allowed:** Yes. **Range:** Yes (grass). **To obtain tee times:** Call three days in advance for weekdays only.

Subscriber comments: You better have a good long game!...Narrow fairways, well treed, a marksman's course...Solid design cut out of the evergreens...Great natural beauty.

★★★RIVER BEND GOLF COURSE

PU-P.O. Box 157, Red Deer, T4N 5E8, (403)343-8311, 100 miles N of Calgary.

Opened: 1986. **Holes:** 18. **Par:** 72/72. **Yards:** 6,516/5,514. **Course rating:** 71.5/70.5. **Slope:** 113. **Architect:** Bill Robinson. **Green fee:** $25/$31. **Credit cards:** MC,VISA. **Reduced fees:** Weekdays, twilight. **Caddies:** No. **Golf carts:** $22. **Discount golf packages:** No. **Season:** April-Oct. **High:** June-Aug. **On site lodging:** No. **Rental clubs:** Yes. **Walking policy:** Unrestricted walking. **Metal spikes allowed:** Yes. **Range:** Yes (grass/mats). **To obtain tee times:** Out-of-state visitors may call anytime in advance. Locally, call 2 days in advance.

Subscriber comments: Not many trouble spots...Good variety of golf holes...Wide fairways, large greens, several holes water comes into play.

★★½RIVERSIDE GOLF COURSE

PU-8630 Rowland Rd., Edmonton, T6A 3X1, (403)496-8702.

Opened: 1951. **Holes:** 18. **Par:** 71/75. **Yards:** 6,306/5,984. **Course rating:** 71.0/74.0. **Slope:** 114. **Architect:** N/A. **Green fee:** $20/$23. **Credit cards:** MC,VISA. **Reduced fees:** Low season. **Caddies:** No. **Golf carts:** $20. **Discount golf packages:** No. **Season:** April-Oct. **High:** May-Aug. **On site lodging:** No. **Rental clubs:** Yes. **Walking policy:** Unrestricted walking. **Metal spikes allowed:** Yes. **Range:** No. **To obtain tee times:** Call two days in advance.

Subscriber comments: Old-style golf, very mature, well treed...Scenic river valley...In river valley, tougher than it looks...Strong finish.

★★SHAGANAPPI POINT GOLF COURSE

PM-P.O. Box 2100, Station M, Calgary, T2P 2M5, (403)974-1810.

Opened: 1917. **Holes:** 18. **Par:** 68. **Yards:** 5,195. **Course rating:** 66.1. **Slope:** 112. **Architect:** Neil Little. **Green fee:** $20/$22. **Credit cards:** None. **Reduced fees:** N/A. **Caddies:** No. **Golf carts:** $24. **Discount golf packages:** No. **Season:** April-Oct. **High:** May-July. **On site lodging:** No. **Rental clubs:** Yes. **Walking policy:** Unrestricted walking. **Metal spikes allowed:** Yes. **Range:** Yes (grass). **To obtain tee times:** Call 4 days in advance.

★★½SHAW-NEE SLOPES GOLF COURSE
820 146 Ave. S.W., Calgary, T2X 3C0, (403)256-1444.
Opened: 1965. **Holes:** 18. **Par:** 72/73. **Yards:** 6,478/5,691. **Course rating:** 70.5/72.1. **Slope:** 122/130. **Architect:** Peter Olynyk and Ernie Tate. **Green fee:** $32/$35. **Credit cards:** MC,VISA. **Reduced fees:** Weekdays, twilight, seniors. **Caddies:** No. **Golf carts:** $24. **Discount golf packages:** No. **Season:** April-Nov. **High:** June-Aug. **On site lodging:** No. **Rental clubs:** Yes. **Walking policy:** Unrestricted walking. **Metal spikes allowed:** No. **Range:** Yes. **To obtain tee times:** Call up to 4 days in advance.
Subscriber comments: Fun to play...Not too difficult...Course surrounded by residential development.

★½SHERWOOD PARK GOLF COURSE
PU-52321 Range Rd. 233, Sherwood Park, T8B 1C8, (403)467-5060, 5 miles E of Edmonton.
Opened: 1960. **Holes:** 18. **Par:** 72/70. **Yards:** 6,045/5,859. **Course rating:** 67.3/69.0. **Slope:** 112. **Architect:** William Brinkworth. **Green fee:** $22/$24. **Credit cards:** MC,VISA. **Reduced fees:** Weekdays, low season. **Golf carts:** $24. **Discount golf packages:** No. **Season:** April-Oct. **High:** May-Sept. **On site lodging:** No. **Rental clubs:** Yes. **Walking policy:** Unrestricted walking. **Metal spikes allowed:** No. **Range:** Yes (grass/mats). **To obtain tee times:** Call Wednesday for upcoming weekend. Call 2 days in advance for weekdays.

SPRUCE MEADOWS GOLF & COUNTRY CLUB
PU-P.O. Box 548, Sexsmith, TOH 3C0, (403)568-4653, 12 miles N of Grand Prairie.
Opened: 1982. **Holes:** 18. **Par:** 71/72. **Yards:** 6,527/5,909. **Course rating:** 73.0/73.0. **Slope:** 117. **Architect:** Ed Sodergren. **Green fee:** $18/$20. **Credit cards:** MC,VISA,Debit Cards. **Reduced fees:** Weekdays, low season, resort guests. **Caddies:** No. **Golf carts:** $20. **Discount golf packages:** Yes. **Season:** April-Oct. **High:** N/A. **On site lodging:** No. **Rental clubs:** Yes. **Walking policy:** Unrestricted walking. **Metal spikes allowed:** Yes. **Range:** Yes (grass/mats). **To obtain tee times:** Call anytime.

★★VICTORIA GOLF COURSE
PU-12130 River Rd., Edmonton, (403)496-4710.
Opened: 1907. **Holes:** 18. **Par:** 71/74. **Yards:** 6,081/6,081. **Course rating:** 67.9/71.4. **Slope:** 99/116. **Architect:** City of Edmonton. **Green fee:** $23/$23. **Credit cards:** MC,VISA,AMEX. **Reduced fees:** Weekdays, low season, twilight, seniors, juniors. **Caddies:** No. **Golf carts:** $20. **Discount golf packages:** Yes. **Season:** April-Oct. **High:** June-Sept. **On site lodging:** No. **Rental clubs:** Yes. **Walking policy:** N/A. **Metal spikes allowed:** Yes. **Range:** Yes (mats). **To obtain tee times:** Call up to 2 days in advance.

★★★WINTERGREEN GOLF & COUNTRY CLUB
P.O. Bag No.2, Bragg Creek, T0L 0K0, (403)949-3333, 29 miles SW of Calgary.
Opened: 1991. **Holes:** 18. **Par:** 71/71. **Yards:** 6,595/5,047. **Course rating:** 72.0/69.9. **Slope:** 137/128. **Architect:** Bill Newis. **Green fee:** $38/$40. **Credit cards:** MC,VISA. **Reduced fees:** Weekdays, low season, twilight, seniors, juniors. **Caddies:** No. **Golf carts:** $25. **Discount golf packages:** No. **Season:** April-Oct. **High:** June-Sept. **On site lodging:** No. **Rental clubs:** Yes. **Walking policy:** Unrestricted walking. **Metal spikes allowed:** Yes. **Range:** Yes (grass/mats). **To obtain tee times:** Call 4 days in advance.
Subscriber comments: Tough course, water and trees will test skills...Scenic, some very nice holes, difficult finish.

★★★★WOLF CREEK GOLF RESORT
R-R.R. No.3 Site 10, Ponoka, T4J 1R3, (403)783-6050, 70 miles S of Edmonton.
Opened: 1984. **Holes:** 27. **Architect:** Rod Whitman. **Green fee:** $40/$40. **Credit cards:** MC,VISA,AMEX. **Reduced fees:** Twilight, seniors, juniors. **Caddies:** Yes. **Golf carts:** $25. **Discount golf packages:** Yes. **Season:** April-Oct. **High:** June-Sept. **On site lodging:** No. **Rental clubs:** Yes. **Walking policy:** Unrestricted walking. **Metal spikes allowed:** Yes. **Range:** Yes (grass). **To obtain tee times:** Call anytime with credit card.

CANADA

EAST/SOUTH
Par: 70/70. **Yards:** 6,818/5,144. **Course rating:** 74.2/69.0. **Slope:** 135/117.
SOUTH/WEST
Par: 70/70. **Yards:** 6,730/4,990. **Course rating:** 74.5/69.0. **Slope:** 135/117.
WEST/EAST
Par: 70/70. **Yards:** 6,516/4,880. **Course rating:** 72.3/69.0. **Slope:** 138/117.
Subscriber comments: Nature at its best...Great design, very challenging, brain strain...Great driving holes, love the bunkers...Worth the drive from Calgary or Edmonton...Rugged, unforgiving terrain.

BRITISH COLUMBIA

★★½ARBUTUS RIDGE GOLF & COUNTRY CLUB
3515 Telegraph Rd., Cobble Hill, V0R 1L1, (250)743-5000, 18 miles N of Victoria.
Opened: 1988. **Holes:** 18. **Par:** 72/72. **Yards:** 6,478/5,241. **Course rating:** 72.3/70.2. **Slope:** 131/122. **Architect:** William Robinson. **Green fee:** $30/$37. **Credit cards:** MC,VISA,AMEX. **Reduced fees:** Low season, twilight, juniors. **Caddies:** No. **Golf carts:** $27. **Discount golf packages:** Yes. **Season:** Year-round. **High:** May-Sept. **On site lodging:** No. **Rental clubs:** Yes. **Walking policy:** Unrestricted walking. **Metal spikes allowed:** Yes. **Range:** Yes (grass/mats). **To obtain tee times:** Call 4 days in advance.
Subscriber comments: Great views of ocean...Hilly, good condition, can walk...Good resort community course/facility.

★★BELMONT GOLF COURSE
22555 Telegraph Trail, Langley, V3A 6X5, (604)888-9898, 20 miles SE of Vancouver.
Opened: 1993. **Holes:** 18. **Par:** 70/70. **Yards:** 6,416/4,951. **Course rating:** 70.5/68.1. **Slope:** 122/114. **Architect:** Les Furber. **Green fee:** $25/$36. **Credit cards:** MC,VISA. **Reduced fees:** Weekdays, low season, twilight, seniors, juniors. **Caddies:** No. **Golf carts:** $24. **Discount golf packages:** No. **Season:** Year-round. **High:** July-Aug. **On site lodging:** No. **Rental clubs:** Yes. **Walking policy:** Unrestricted walking. **Metal spikes allowed:** Yes. **Range:** No. **To obtain tee times:** Call three days in advance at 9 a.m.

★★★★BIG SKY GOLF & COUNTRY CLUB
R-1690 Airport Rd., Pemberton, V0N 2L0, (604)894-6106, (800)668-7900, 85 miles N of Vancouver.
Opened: 1994. **Holes:** 18. **Par:** 72/72. **Yards:** 7,001/5,208. **Course rating:** 73.5/70.5. **Slope:** 133/120. **Architect:** Bob Cupp. **Green fee:** $70/$85. **Credit cards:** MC,VISA,AMEX. **Reduced fees:** Weekdays, low season, twilight, juniors. **Caddies:** Yes. **Golf carts:** $25. **Discount golf packages:** Yes. **Season:** April-Oct. **High:** June-Sept. **On site lodging:** No. **Rental clubs:** Yes. **Walking policy:** Unrestricted walking. **Metal spikes allowed:** No. **Range:** Yes (grass/mats). **To obtain tee times:** Call.
Notes: Ranked 2nd in 1994 Best New Canadian Courses.
Subscriber comments: Like playing on carpet...Lots of water, impeccable greens...Breathtaking...Everyone very friendly...Great golf academy...Mountain backdrops are the best in the Whistler area.

★★BURNABY MOUNTAIN GOLF COURSE
PU-7600 Halifax St., Burnaby, V5A 4M8, (604)280-7355, 10 miles E of Vancouver.
Opened: 1969. **Holes:** 18. **Par:** 71. **Yards:** 6,301. **Course rating:** N/A. **Slope:** N/A. **Architect:** N/A. **Green fee:** $29/$29. **Credit cards:** MC,VISA. **Reduced fees:** Twilight, seniors, juniors. **Caddies:** No. **Golf carts:** $25. **Discount golf packages:** No. **Season:** Year-round. **High:** June-Aug. **On site lodging:** No. **Rental clubs:** Yes. **Walking policy:** Unrestricted walking. **Metal spikes allowed:** Yes. **Range:** Yes (mats). **To obtain tee times:** Call 1 day in advance at noon for weekdays. Call 2 days in advance at 8 a.m. for weekends.

CANADA

★★★½CASTLEGAR GOLF CLUB
PU-P.O. Box 3430, Castlegar, V1N 3N8, (250)365-5006, (800)666-0324, 180 miles N of Spokane, WA.
Opened: 1966. **Holes:** 18. **Par:** 72/76. **Yards:** 6,677/6,178. **Course rating:** 72.6/75.9. **Slope:** 127/133. **Architect:** Designed by members.
Green fee: $24/$27. **Credit cards:** N/A. **Reduced fees:** Twilight.
Caddies: No. **Golf carts:** $25. **Discount golf packages:** Yes. **Season:** April-Oct. **High:** July-Sept. **On site lodging:** No. **Rental clubs:** Yes. **Walking policy:** Unrestricted walking. **Metal spikes allowed:** Yes. **Range:** Yes. **To obtain tee times:** Outside 60 miles may call anytime within reason.
Subscriber comments: A jewel in a mountain setting...Mountainous, rocky, no hooks or slices, beautiful!...Very friendly staff, excellent course.

★★★★CHATEAU WHISTLER GOLF CLUB
R-4612 Blackcomb Way, Whistler, V0N 1B4, (604)938-2095, 75 miles N of Vancouver.
Opened: 1993. **Holes:** 18. **Par:** 72/72. **Yards:** 6,635/5,157. **Course rating:** 73.0/70.0. **Slope:** 142/124. **Architect:** Robert Trent Jones Jr.
Green fee: $70/$114. **Credit cards:** MC,VISA,AMEX,DISC,Diners Club, En Route. **Reduced fees:** Weekdays, low season, resort guests, twilight.
Caddies: No. **Golf carts:** Included in Green Fee. **Discount golf packages:** Yes.
Season: May-Oct. **High:** June-Sept. **On site lodging:** Yes. **Rental clubs:** Yes. **Walking policy:** Mandatory cart. **Metal spikes allowed:** Yes. **Range:** No. **To obtain tee times:** Call 7 days a week. Resort guests may book within same calendar year.
Notes: Ranked 1st in 1993 Best New Canadian Courses.
Subscriber comments: Beautiful, challenging...Exciting elevation changes...Magnificent scenery and wildlife...Very challenging for average golfer...One tough course, every hole feels uphill.

★★★CHRISTINA LAKE GOLF CLUB
339 2nd Ave., Christina Lake, V0H 1H0, (250)447-9313, 12 miles E of Grand Forks.
Opened: 1963. **Holes:** 18. **Par:** 72/73. **Yards:** 6,615/5,725. **Course rating:** 71.5/71.3. **Slope:** 125/123. **Architect:** Les Furber. **Green fee:** $21/$32. **Credit cards:** MC,VISA,Direct Debit. **Reduced fees:** Twilight, juniors. **Caddies:** No. **Golf carts:** $25. **Discount golf packages:** Yes. **Season:** April-Oct. **High:** July-Sept. **On site lodging:** No. **Rental clubs:** Yes. **Walking policy:** Unrestricted walking. **Metal spikes allowed:** Yes. **Range:** Yes (grass). **To obtain tee times:** Out of town may book tee times in advance.
Subscriber comments: Easy long walk, good for all levels...New nine good, old nine ho-hum, three great par 3s...Very good layout.

★★★½CORDOVA BAY GOLF COURSE
PU-5333 Cordova Bay Rd., Victoria, V8Y 2L3, (250)658-4075, 15 miles N of Downtown Victoria.
Opened: 1991. **Holes:** 18. **Par:** 72/72. **Yards:** 6,642/5,269. **Course rating:** 72.0/72.0. **Slope:** 122/119. **Architect:** Bill Robinson. **Green fee:** $42/$45. **Credit cards:** MC,VISA,AMEX. **Reduced fees:** Weekdays, low season, twilight, juniors. **Caddies:** No. **Golf carts:** $27. **Discount golf packages:** No. **Season:** Year-round. **High:** May-Sept. **On site lodging:** No. **Rental clubs:** Yes. **Walking policy:** Unrestricted walking. **Metal spikes allowed:** Yes. **Range:** Yes (mats). **To obtain tee times:** Prepay up to 1 year in advance.
Subscriber comments: Picturesque golf course, nice condition...Nice practice range and restaurant. Good winter play...Staff was very accommodating...Good placement of moguls to increase difficulty.

★★★½CROWN ISLE GOLF CLUB
399 Clubhouse Dr., Courtenay, V9N 6Z8, (250)338-6811, (800)668-3244, 100 miles NW of Vancouver.
Opened: 1993. **Holes:** 18. **Par:** 72/72. **Yards:** 7,024/5,169. **Course rating:** 74.2/68.5. **Slope:** 133/114. **Architect:** Graham Cooke & Assoc.. **Green fee:** $30/$43. **Credit cards:** MC,VISA,Interac. **Reduced fees:** Weekdays, low season, twilight, juniors. **Caddies:** No. **Golf carts:** $25. **Discount golf packages:** Yes. **Season:** Year-round.

High: April-Oct. **On site lodging:** Yes. **Rental clubs:** Yes. **Walking policy:** Unrestricted walking. **Metal spikes allowed:** Yes. **Range:** Yes (grass/mats). **To obtain tee times:** Call.
Subscriber comments: Best course on Vancouver Island...First par 3 eats balls...Excellent layout...Nice stonework on course...Doglegs, water and sand. Tight in places. Easy walk...Tough but forgiving.

★★DUNCAN MEADOWS GOLF COURSE
Highway 18 & North Rd., Duncan, V9L 1N9, (250)746-8993, 35 miles N of Victoria.
Opened: 1993. **Holes:** 18. **Par:** 72/72. **Yards:** 6,616/5,356. **Course rating:** 72.6/66.6. **Slope:** 128/114. **Architect:** Claude Muret. **Green fee:** $22/$30. **Credit cards:** MC,VISA. **Reduced fees:** Low season, twilight, seniors, juniors. **Caddies:** No. **Golf carts:** $25. **Discount golf packages:** No. **Season:** Year-round. **High:** June-Aug. **On site lodging:** No. **Rental clubs:** Yes. **Walking policy:** Unrestricted walking. **Metal spikes allowed:** Yes. **Range:** Yes (grass/mats). **To obtain tee times:** Call up to 4 days in advance.

DUNES AT KAMLOOPS
SP-652 Dunes Dr., Kamloops, V2B 8M8, (250)579-3300, (888)881-4653
Opened: 1997. **Holes:** 18. **Architect:** Graham Cooke.
Call club for further information.
Notes: Ranked 2nd in 1997 Best New Canadian Courses.

★★★EAGLE POINT GOLF & COUNTRY CLUB
PU-8888 Barnhartvale Rd., Kamloops, V2C 2J3, (250)573-2453, (888)863-2453, 225 miles NE of Vancouver.
Opened: 1991. **Holes:** 18. **Par:** 72/72. **Yards:** 6,762/5,315. **Course rating:** 73.4/70.6. **Slope:** 137/126. **Architect:** Robert Heaslip. **Green fee:** $36/$40. **Credit cards:** MC,VISA,AMEX,Interac. **Reduced fees:** Weekdays, low season, resort guests, twilight, seniors, juniors. **Caddies:** No. **Golf carts:** $28. **Discount golf packages:** Yes. **Season:** March-Oct. **High:** April-Sept. **On site lodging:** No. **Rental clubs:** Yes. **Walking policy:** Unrestricted walking. **Metal spikes allowed:** Yes. **Range:** Yes (grass/mats). **To obtain tee times:** Call.
Subscriber comments: A ramble through the woods! First timers need a map...Quite hilly, must be accurate...A beautiful setting...Dogleg after dogleg.

★★EAGLECREST GOLF CLUB
2035 Island Hwy. W., Qualicum Beach, V9K 1G1, (250)752-6311, (800)567-1320, 25 miles N of Nanaimo.
Opened: 1971. **Holes:** 18. **Par:** 71/71. **Yards:** 6,813/5,430. **Course rating:** 70.6/71.0. **Slope:** 122/123. **Architect:** Warren Radomski. **Green fee:** $25/$33. **Credit cards:** MC,VISA. **Reduced fees:** Low season, resort guests, twilight, juniors. **Caddies:** No. **Golf carts:** $25. **Discount golf packages:** Yes. **Season:** Year-round. **High:** May-Oct. **On site lodging:** No. **Rental clubs:** Yes. **Walking policy:** Unrestricted walking. **Metal spikes allowed:** Yes. **Range:** Yes (grass). **To obtain tee times:** Call anytime or book through hotel with credit card to guarantee.

★★★FAIRMONT HOT SPRINGS RESORT
R-P.O. Box 10, Fairmont Hot Springs, V0B 1L0, (250)345-6514, (800)663-4979, 200 miles SW of Calgary.
Opened: 1963. **Holes:** 18. **Par:** 72/72. **Yards:** 6,522/5,513. **Course rating:** 71.3/70.8. **Slope:** 126/121. **Architect:** Lloyd Wilder. **Green fee:** $35/$42. **Credit cards:** All major. **Reduced fees:** Weekdays, low season, resort guests, twilight, juniors. **Caddies:** No. **Golf carts:** $23. **Discount golf packages:** Yes. **Season:** March-Oct. **High:** May-Sept. **On site lodging:** Yes. **Rental clubs:** Yes. **Walking policy:** Unrestricted walking. **Metal spikes allowed:** Yes. **Range:** No. **To obtain tee times:** Call.
Subscriber comments: Beautiful scenery, always a pleasure to play...Everything breaks to the valley...Well planned. Makes you work...Always a treat, tough but fair, great shape...Good mountain golf...Good restaurant.

★★★FAIRMONT RIVERSIDE GOLF RESORT
5099 Riverview Dr., Fairmont Hot Springs, V0B 1L0, (250)345-6346, (800)665-2112, 180 miles W of Calgary.

Opened: 1988. **Holes:** 18. **Par:** 71/71. **Yards:** 6,507/5,349. **Course rating:** 71.1/71.3. **Slope:** 128/126. **Architect:** Bill Newis. **Green fee:** $35/$45. **Credit cards:** MC,VISA,AMEX. **Reduced fees:** Weekdays, resort guests, twilight, juniors. **Caddies:** Yes. **Golf carts:** $24. **Discount golf packages:** Yes. **Season:** March-Nov. **High:** June-Sept. **On site lodging:** No. **Rental clubs:** Yes. **Walking policy:** Unrestricted walking. **Metal spikes allowed:** Yes. **Range:** Yes (grass/mats). **To obtain tee times:** Call in advance, credit card required.

Subscriber comments: Great course, great scenery...Long, flat but challenging...Play across Columbia River...After your round, head to the hot springs.

★★★★ FAIRVIEW MOUNTAIN GOLF CLUB

Old Golf Course Rd., Oliver, V0H 1T0, (250)498-3521, 70 miles S of Kelowna.

GOOD VALUE

Opened: 1991. **Holes:** 18. **Par:** 72/73. **Yards:** 6,557/5,382. **Course rating:** 71.5/73.5. **Slope:** 130/127. **Architect:** Les Furber. **Green fee:** $27/$35. **Credit cards:** MC,VISA,AMEX. **Reduced fees:** Low season, twilight, juniors. **Caddies:** No. **Golf carts:** $14. **Discount golf packages:** Yes. **Season:** March-Oct. **High:** June-Sept. **On site lodging:** No. **Rental clubs:** Yes. **Walking policy:** Unrestricted walking. **Metal spikes allowed:** Yes. **Range:** Yes (mats). **To obtain tee times:** Call 5 days in advance.

Subscriber comments: Keep going back, seeing new challenges...Outstanding golf. Outstanding views...Lots of uphill, downhill lies...Golf and nature at its best.

★★★ FAIRWINDS GOLF & COUNTRY CLUB

R-3730 Fairwinds Dr., Nanoose Bay, V0R 2R0, (250)468-7666, 6 miles N of Nanaimo. **Opened:** 1988. **Holes:** 18. **Par:** 71/71. **Yards:** 6,141/5,173. **Course rating:** 70.6/70.7. **Slope:** 123/129. **Architect:** Les Furber and Jim Eremko. **Green fee:** $25/$40. **Credit cards:** MC,VISA,AMEX. **Reduced fees:** Weekdays, low season, twilight, juniors. **Caddies:** No. **Golf carts:** $24. **Discount golf packages:** No. **Season:** Year-round. **High:** May-Oct. **On site lodging:** Yes. **Rental clubs:** Yes. **Walking policy:** Unrestricted walking. **Metal spikes allowed:** Yes. **Range:** Yes (grass/mats). **To obtain tee times:** Resort guests may book anytime with confirmed room reservation. Public may call 3 days in advance.

Subscriber comments: Just excellent...Good tight short course...Beautiful scenery, target golf at its best...Great food...Very good facilities.

★★★½ THE FALLS GOLF & COUNTRY CLUB

8341 Nixon Rd., Rosedale, V0X 1X0, (604)794-3380, 60 miles E of Vancouver. **Opened:** 1996. **Holes:** 18. **Par:** 71. **Yards:** 6,767. **Course rating:** N/A. **Slope:** 133. **Architect:** Ted Locke. **Green fee:** $30/$59. **Credit cards:** MC,VISA,Interac. **Reduced fees:** Weekdays, low season, resort guests, twilight, seniors, juniors. **Caddies:** No. **Golf carts:** Included in Green Fee. **Discount golf packages:** No. **Season:** Feb.-Nov. **High:** June-Sept. **On site lodging:** No. **Rental clubs:** Yes. **Walking policy:** Mandatory cart. **Metal spikes allowed:** No. **Range:** Yes (grass). **To obtain tee times:** Call up to 5 days in advance.

Subscriber comments: Multi tee boxes for every level. Spectacular views. Best new course in BC...Spectacular elevation, well maintained, tricky greens...Target golf...Nice area and personnel...Extreme elevation changes.

★½ FORT LANGLEY GOLF COURSE

9782 McKinnon Crescent, Fort Langley, V1M 2R5, (604)888-5911, 14 miles NW of Langley.

Opened: 1968. **Holes:** 18. **Par:** 70/75. **Yards:** 6,428/5,681. **Course rating:** 70.0/71.5. **Slope:** 115/126. **Architect:** James Bryce & Tony Turney. **Green fee:** $30/$35. **Credit cards:** MC,VISA,AMEX,Diners Club. **Reduced fees:** Weekdays, low season, twilight, seniors, juniors. **Caddies:** No. **Golf carts:** $26. **Discount golf packages:** Yes. **Season:** Year-round. **High:** May-Sept. **On site lodging:** No. **Rental clubs:** Yes. **Walking policy:** Unrestricted walking. **Metal spikes allowed:** Yes. **Range:** Yes (grass). **To obtain tee times:** Call 7 days in advance for weekdays. Call Thursday at 7 a.m. for weekends.

★★ FRASERVIEW GOLF COURSE

PU-7800 Vivian St., Vancouver, V5S 2V7, (604)280-8633.
Opened: 1960. **Holes:** 18. **Par:** 71/74. **Yards:** 6,346/6,058. **Course rating:** 69.8/72.0.

Slope: 118/121. **Architect:** Howard Norman/Tom McBroom. **Green fee:** $30/$30.
Credit cards: MC,VISA. **Reduced fees:** Twilight, seniors, juniors. **Caddies:** No. **Golf carts:** $24. **Discount golf packages:** No. **Season:** Year-round. **High:** April-Oct. **On site lodging:** No. **Rental clubs:** Yes. **Walking policy:** Unrestricted walking. **Metal spikes allowed:** Yes. **Range:** Yes. **To obtain tee times:** Call 2 days in advance at noon for weekdays. Call Thursdays at noon for weekends.

★★½FURRY CREEK GOLF & COUNTRY CLUB
R-Highway 99, P.O. Box 1000, Lions Bay, VON 2E0, (604)922-9461, 27 miles N of Vancouver.
Opened: 1993. **Holes:** 18. **Par:** 72/70. **Yards:** 6,184/4,525. **Course rating:** 72.1.
Slope: 136. **Architect:** Robert Muir Graves. **Green fee:** $60/$80. **Credit cards:** MC,VISA,AMEX,Diners, JCB. **Reduced fees:** Weekdays, low season, resort guests, twilight, seniors, juniors. **Caddies:** No. **Golf carts:** Included in Green Fee. **Discount golf packages:** Yes. **Season:** March-Nov. **High:** July-Sept. **On site lodging:** No.
Rental clubs: Yes. **Walking policy:** Mandatory cart. **Metal spikes allowed:** Yes.
Range: Yes (grass). **To obtain tee times:** Call up to 30 days in advance.
Subscriber comments: Views rival Hawaii...Great setting, tough. Not for everyone...Goofy layout...Fantastic views overcome a few hokey holes.

★★★½GALLAGHER'S CANYON GOLF & COUNTRY CLUB
4320 Gallagher's Dr. W., Kelowna, V1W 3Z9, (250)861-4240, 250 miles NE of Vancouver.
Opened: 1980. **Holes:** 18. **Par:** 72/73. **Yards:** 6,890/5,505. **Course rating:** 73.5/73.8.
Slope: 136/131. **Architect:** Bill Robinson. **Green fee:** $35/$65. **Credit cards:** MC,VISA,AMEX. **Reduced fees:** Low season, twilight, juniors. **Caddies:** Yes. **Golf carts:** $30. **Discount golf packages:** Yes. **Season:** April-Oct. **High:** May-Sept. **On site lodging:** No. **Rental clubs:** Yes. **Walking policy:** Unrestricted walking. **Metal spikes allowed:** Yes. **Range:** Yes (grass). **To obtain tee times:** Call anytime in advance within same calendar year.
Subscriber comments: Great use of canyon and well treed locations, very good test, very hilly...Don't play this with a hangover...Scenery, course and golf beautiful...Bring your best game.
Special Notes: Also 9-hole par-32 course.

★★★½GOLDEN GOLF & COUNTRY CLUB
576 Dogtooth Rd., Golden, V0A 1H0, (250)344-2700, 150 miles W of Calgary.
Opened: 1985. **Holes:** 18. **Par:** 72/72. **Yards:** 6,818/5,380. **Course rating:** 72.8/70.5. **Slope:** 134/130. **Architect:** Les Furber. **Green fee:** $22/$37. **Credit cards:** MC,VISA,Debit Cards. **Reduced fees:** Twilight, seniors, juniors. **Caddies:** No. **Golf carts:** $25. **Discount golf packages:** Yes. **Season:** April-Oct. **High:** June-Sept. **On site lodging:** No. **Rental clubs:** Yes. **Walking policy:** Unrestricted walking. **Metal spikes allowed:** Yes. **Range:** Yes (grass). **To obtain tee times:** Call anytime.
Subscriber comments: A treasure in the Rockies! You gotta love it!...Breathtaking scenery and good holes...Take time to enjoy the deer, moose and eagles that live on the course...Picturesque...Distinctly different nines.

★★★GORGE VALE GOLF CLUB
1005 Craigflower Rd., Victoria, V9A 2X9, (250)386-3401.
Opened: 1930. **Holes:** 18. **Par:** 72/75. **Yards:** 6,382/5,998. **Course rating:** 70.8/74.9.
Slope: 131/136. **Architect:** A.V. Macan. **Green fee:** $33/$48. **Credit cards:** MC,VISA.
Reduced fees: N/A. **Caddies:** No. **Golf carts:** $26. **Discount golf packages:** No.
Season: Year-round. **High:** N/A. **On site lodging:** No. **Rental clubs:** Yes. **Walking policy:** Unrestricted walking. **Metal spikes allowed:** Yes. **Range:** Yes (grass). **To obtain tee times:** Call 2 days in advance.
Subscriber comments: Lots of interesting holes...A fun course...Very good layout for hilly terrain...Great men's night...A good test but playable...Busy, old, hilly.

CANADA

★★★½HARVEST GOLF CLUB
R-2725 KLO Rd., Kelowna, V0H 1G0, (250)862-3103, (800)257-8577, 200 miles NE of Vancouver.
Opened: 1994. **Holes:** 18. **Par:** 72/72. **Yards:** 7,104/5,454. **Course rating:** 73.0/61.1. **Slope:** 126. **Architect:** Graham Cooke. **Green fee:** $48/$65. **Credit cards:** MC,VISA,AMEX. **Reduced fees:** Low season, resort guests, twilight, juniors. **Caddies:** No. **Golf carts:** $55. **Discount golf packages:** Yes. **Season:** March-Oct. **High:** May-Sept. **On site lodging:** No. **Rental clubs:** Yes. **Walking policy:** Unrestricted walking. **Metal spikes allowed:** No. **Range:** Yes (grass/mats). **To obtain tee times:** Call from Nov. 1 for entire following season. **Subscriber comments:** Great course, wonderful stuff...Great for beginners, nice scenery, wide open...Beautiful, lush, in an apple orchard...Nice soft greens...Friendliest staff, well manicured, interesting doglegs.

★★½KELOWNA SPRINGS GOLF COURSE
480 Penno Rd., Kelowna, V1X 6S3, (250)765-4653.
Opened: 1990. **Holes:** 18. **Par:** 71/71. **Yards:** 6,156/5,225. **Course rating:** 69.6/70.0. **Slope:** 117/118. **Architect:** Les Furber. **Green fee:** $25/$35. **Credit cards:** MC,VISA,AMEX,Debit Cards. **Reduced fees:** Weekdays, low season, twilight, juniors. **Caddies:** No. **Golf carts:** $27. **Discount golf packages:** Yes. **Season:** March-Nov. **High:** April-Oct. **On site lodging:** Yes. **Rental clubs:** Yes. **Walking policy:** Unrestricted walking. **Metal spikes allowed:** No. **Range:** Yes (mats). **To obtain tee times:** Call. **Subscriber comments:** Very good walking course...Surprise course, with lots of water, challenging...Popular with seniors...Great setting in the valley...Friendly staff.

★★★★KOKANEE SPRINGS GOLF RESORT
R-Box 96, Crawford Bay, V0B 1E0, (250)227-9362, (800)979-7999, 120 miles N of Spokane, WA.
Opened: 1967. **Holes:** 18. **Par:** 71/74. **Yards:** 6,537/5,747. **Course rating:** 72.8/74.6. **Slope:** 143/138. **Architect:** Norman Woods. **Green fee:** $41/$41. **Credit cards:** MC,VISA,AMEX. **Reduced fees:** Resort guests, twilight, juniors. **Caddies:** No. **Golf carts:** $26. **Discount golf packages:** Yes. **Season:** April-Oct. **High:** July-Sept. **On site lodging:** Yes. **Rental clubs:** Yes. **Walking policy:** Unrestricted walking. **Metal spikes allowed:** Yes. **Range:** Yes (grass/mats). **To obtain tee times:** Call 800 number. **Subscriber comments:** Massive greens, great course in middle of nowhere...Beautiful rockies setting...Great forested mountain course...Make the trip, worthwhile...Fabulous elevated first tee, view of Kokanee Glacier.

THE LONE WOLF GOLF CLUB
PU-P.O. Box 300, Taylor, V0C 2K0, (250)789-3711, 12 miles from Fort St. John.
Opened: 1995. **Holes:** 18. **Par:** 72/73. **Yards:** 6,817/5,968. **Course rating:** 72.5/68.5. **Slope:** 128/118. **Architect:** Albers Bros. **Green fee:** $22/$25. **Credit cards:** MC,VISA,AMEX,Debit Card. **Reduced fees:** Weekdays, seniors, juniors. **Caddies:** No. **Golf carts:** $25. **Discount golf packages:** Yes. **Season:** April-Oct. **High:** June-Aug. **On site lodging:** No. **Rental clubs:** Yes. **Walking policy:** Unrestricted walking. **Metal spikes allowed:** Yes. **Range:** Yes (grass/mats). **To obtain tee times:** Call 1 day in advance. Advance booking for groups available. **Special Notes:** Formerly Taylor Golf & Country Club.

★★★MAYFAIR LAKES GOLF & COUNTRY CLUB
5460 N. 7 Rd., Richmond, V6V 1R7, (604)276-0505, 7 miles S of Vancouver.
Opened: 1989. **Holes:** 18. **Par:** 71/72. **Yards:** 6,641/5,277. **Course rating:** 73.0/71.0. **Slope:** 123/123. **Architect:** Les Furber. **Green fee:** $40/$45. **Credit cards:** MC,VISA,AMEX. **Reduced fees:** Weekdays, low season, twilight, seniors, juniors. **Caddies:** No. **Golf carts:** $28. **Discount golf packages:** No. **Season:** Year-round. **High:** April-Oct. **On site lodging:** No. **Rental clubs:** Yes. **Walking policy:** Unrestricted walking. **Metal spikes allowed:** Yes. **Range:** Yes (grass/mats). **To obtain tee times:** Call 2 days in advance at 9 a.m. for weekdays and Friday 9 a.m. for weekends. **Subscriber comments:** Grooming is immaculate, lots of water...Have to play it a few times...Nice facility, well maintained, good food...No trees...Good risk reward par 5s...Windy most of the time.

★★★MCCLEERY GOLF COURSE
PM-7188 MacDonald St., Vancouver, V6N 1G2, (604)257-8191.
Opened: 1959. **Holes:** 18. **Par:** 71/71. **Yards:** 6,265/5,010. **Course rating:** 69.6/67.1.
Slope: 126/110. **Architect:** Ted Baker & Associates. **Green fee:** $16/$32. **Credit cards:** MC,VISA. **Reduced fees:** Low season, twilight, seniors, juniors. **Caddies:** No.
Golf carts: $24. **Discount golf packages:** No. **Season:** Year-round. **High:** April-Oct.
On site lodging: No. **Rental clubs:** Yes. **Walking policy:** Unrestricted walking. **Metal spikes allowed:** Yes. **Range:** Yes (mats). **To obtain tee times:** Call up to 5 days in advance.
Subscriber comments: Interesting, fair challenge...Renovation completed '97, good job...Nice layout.

★★★½MEADOW GARDENS GOLF COURSE
19675 Meadow Gardens Way, Pitt Meadows, V3Y 1Z2, (604)465-5474, 12 miles E of Vancouver.
Opened: 1994. **Holes:** 18. **Par:** 72/72. **Yards:** 7,041/5,519. **Course rating:** 74.7/72.8.
Slope: 134/130. **Architect:** Les Furber and Jim Eremko. **Green fee:** $45/$65. **Credit cards:** MC,VISA,AMEX. **Reduced fees:** Weekdays, low season, twilight, seniors, juniors. **Caddies:** Yes. **Golf carts:** $25. **Discount golf packages:** No. **Season:** Year-round. **High:** April-Oct. **On site lodging:** No. **Rental clubs:** Yes. **Walking policy:** Unrestricted walking. **Metal spikes allowed:** Yes. **Range:** Yes (grass/mats). **To obtain tee times:** Call 7 days in advance.
Subscriber comments: Unique design, good test of golf...Magnificent clubhouse...Tough, well designed layout on flattish land, greens/bunkers very good...Don't miss this one, best layout in the area.

★★★½MORNINGSTAR GOLF CLUB
PU-525 Lowry's Rd., Parksville, V9P 2R8, (250)248-8161, 30 miles N of Nanaimo.
Opened: 1991. **Holes:** 18. **Par:** 72/72. **Yards:** 7,018/5,313. **Course rating:** 75.2/71.2.
Slope: 144/135. **Architect:** Les Furber and Jim Eremko. **Green fee:** $20/$40. **Credit cards:** MC,VISA. **Reduced fees:** Low season, twilight, seniors, juniors. **Caddies:** No.
Golf carts: $30. **Discount golf packages:** Yes. **Season:** Year-round. **High:** March-Nov.
On site lodging: No. **Rental clubs:** Yes. **Walking policy:** Unrestricted walking. **Metal spikes allowed:** Yes. **Range:** Yes (grass). **To obtain tee times:** Call 7 days in advance.
Subscriber comments: Water and trees. Good walking course despite distance between some holes...Several key tee shots...A real challenge from blues...Tough mix of links and wooded holes...Strong design.

★★★NANAIMO GOLF CLUB
2800 Highland Blvd., Nanaimo, V95 3N8, (250)758-6332, 70 miles N of Victoria.
Opened: 1962. **Holes:** 18. **Par:** 72/72. **Yards:** 6,667/5,648. **Course rating:** 73.2/68.5.
Slope: 129/119. **Architect:** N/A. **Green fee:** $43. **Credit cards:** MC,VISA. **Reduced fees:** N/A. **Caddies:** No. **Golf carts:** $26. **Discount golf packages:** No. **Season:** Year-round. **High:** April-Sept. **On site lodging:** No. **Rental clubs:** Yes. **Walking policy:** Unrestricted walking. **Metal spikes allowed:** Yes. **Range:** Yes (mats). **To obtain tee times:** Call 2 days in advance.
Subscriber comments: Beautiful scenery, everything slopes to water...Worth playing...Established course. Nice greens. Can get windy...Classic, long, challenging course, great views.

★★★★NICKLAUS NORTH GOLF COURSE
R-8080 Nicklaus North Blvd., Whistler, V0N 1B0, (604)938-9898, (800)386-9898, 90 miles N of Vancouver.
Opened: 1995. **Holes:** 18. **Par:** 71/71. **Yards:** 6,908/4,730. **Course rating:** 73.8/66.3.
Slope: 138/113. **Architect:** Jack Nicklaus. **Green fee:** $65/$108. **Credit cards:** MC,VISA,AMEX. **Reduced fees:** Weekdays, low season, twilight. **Caddies:** No. **Golf carts:** $25. **Discount golf packages:** Yes. **Season:** May-Oct. **High:** June-Sept. **On site lodging:** Yes. **Rental clubs:** Yes. **Walking policy:** Unrestricted walking. **Metal spikes allowed:** Yes. **Range:** Yes (grass). **To obtain tee times:** Call anytime within season. Groups may book up to 2 years in advance.
Notes: Ranked 1st in 1996 Best New Canadian Courses.

Subscriber comments: The best. Friendly service...Most water on the left making it perfect for a slicer...Allows walking...A monster, toughest set of par 3s I've ever played...A black bear ran across fairway behind us.

NORTHVIEW GOLF & COUNTRY CLUB

PU-6857 168th St., Surrey, V3S 8E7, (604)576-4653, (888)574-2211, 18 miles SE of Vancouver.
Architect: Arnold Palmer. **Credit cards:** MC,VISA,AMEX,Diners Club, En Route. **Reduced fees:** Weekdays, low season, twilight, seniors, juniors. **Caddies:** No. **Golf carts:** $28. **Discount golf packages:** No. **Season:** Year-round. **High:** April-Sept. **On site lodging:** No. **Rental clubs:** Yes. **Walking policy:** Unrestricted walking. **Metal spikes allowed:** Yes. **Range:** Yes (grass/mats). **To obtain tee times:** Call 7 days in advance at 9 a.m.

★★★½CANAL COURSE

Opened: 1995. **Holes:** 18. **Par:** 72/72. **Yards:** 7,191/5,394. **Course rating:** 74.4/70.1. **Slope:** 137/108. **Green fee:** $40/$45.
Subscriber comments: Easier than the Ridge Course...Lots of water...Wide open, good conditions, good facilities...Bring lots of balls.

★★★½RIDGE COURSE

Opened: 1994. **Holes:** 18. **Par:** 72/72. **Yards:** 6,900/5,131. **Course rating:** 73.4. **Slope:** 139. **Green fee:** $55/$65.
Notes: 1996-98 Greater Vancouver Open.
Subscriber comments: Demanding, PGA Tour venue...A great walking course...Good variety of holes...Good course for walking...Views...The first four holes can kill you....#8 great.

★★★½OLYMPIC VIEW GOLF CLUB

PU-643 Latoria Rd., Victoria, V9C 3A3, (250)474-3671.
Opened: 1990. **Holes:** 18. **Par:** 72/71. **Yards:** 6,513/5,220. **Course rating:** 73.1/70.5. **Slope:** 142/124. **Architect:** Bill Robinson. **Green fee:** $32/$48. **Credit cards:** MC,VISA,AMEX. **Reduced fees:** Weekdays, low season, twilight, juniors. **Caddies:** No. **Golf carts:** $25. **Discount golf packages:** Yes. **Season:** Year-round. **High:** April-Oct. **On site lodging:** No. **Rental clubs:** Yes. **Walking policy:** Unrestricted walking. **Metal spikes allowed:** Yes. **Range:** Yes (grass). **To obtain tee times:** Call 3 days in advance or up to 90 days in advance with a credit card.
Subscriber comments: Excellent layout, service and facilities...Quite hilly...Bring a dozen balls...Great clubhouse, challenging course, target golf...Nature at its best...Nicely treed.

★★★OSOYOOS GOLF & COUNTRY CLUB

12300 46th Ave., Osoyoos, V0H 1V0, (250)495-7003, 81 miles S of Kelowna.
Opened: 1971. **Holes:** 27. **Architect:** Boyd Barr. **Green fee:** $22/$34. **Credit cards:** MC,VISA. **Reduced fees:** Low season, twilight. **Caddies:** No. **Golf carts:** $34. **Discount golf packages:** Yes. **Season:** March-Dec. **High:** July-Aug. **On site lodging:** No. **Rental clubs:** Yes. **Walking policy:** Unrestricted walking. **Metal spikes allowed:** Yes. **Range:** Yes (grass). **To obtain tee times:** Call.
DESERT/MEADOWS
Par: 72/72. **Yards:** 6,318/5,303. **Course rating:** 70.6/71.8. **Slope:** 116/123.
PARK/DESERT
Par: 72/72. **Yards:** 6,223/5,109. **Course rating:** 69.5/70.5. **Slope:** 119/119.
PARK/MEADOWS
Par: 72/72. **Yards:** 6,323/5,214. **Course rating:** 70.6/71.7. **Slope:** 123/121.
Subscriber comments: Course may be short, but you must be very accurate...Good for all handicaps...Great par 3s on Desert...All around great experience...Good layout. Good for all handicaps.

★★★PEACE PORTAL GOLF COURSE

16900 4th Ave., South Surrey, V4A 9N3, (604)538-4818, (800)354-7544, 30 miles S of Vancouver.
Opened: 1928. **Holes:** 18. **Par:** 72/73. **Yards:** 6,363/5,621. **Course rating:** 70.7/73.5. **Slope:** 127/133. **Architect:** Francis L. James. **Green fee:** $41/$45. **Credit cards:** MC,VISA,AMEX,Interac Debit Card. **Reduced fees:** Low season, twilight, juniors. **Caddies:** No. **Golf carts:** $27. **Discount golf packages:** No. **Season:** Year-round.

High: April-Sept. **On site lodging:** No. **Rental clubs:** Yes. **Walking policy:** Unrestricted walking. **Metal spikes allowed:** Yes. **Range:** Yes (grass/mats). **To obtain tee times:** Call 7 days in advance at 8 a.m. Call Thursday at 8 a.m. for upcoming weekend.
Subscriber comments: Very hilly, flat lies rare...Fine old venue...Has character...Lynx, geese, deer, moose, crow, raven, fox, coyote and wolf.

★★½PENTICTON GOLF & COUNTRY CLUB
Eckhardt Ave. W., Penticton, V2A 6K3, (250)492-8727, 27 miles S of Kelowna.
Opened: 1920. **Holes:** 18. **Par:** 70/72. **Yards:** 6,131/5,609. **Course rating:** 70.0/73.0. **Slope:** 127/130. **Architect:** Les Furber. **Green fee:** $35/$35. **Credit cards:** MC,VISA. **Reduced fees:** Low season, resort guests, twilight, juniors. **Caddies:** No. **Golf carts:** $23. **Discount golf packages:** Yes. **Season:** Feb.-Nov. **High:** April-Oct. **On site lodging:** No. **Rental clubs:** Yes. **Walking policy:** Unrestricted walking. **Metal spikes allowed:** Yes. **Range:** No. **To obtain tee times:** Call 1 day in advance.
Subscriber comments: Put the big stick away, think before hitting...Walking delight...Flat and wide open...Great for beginners.

★★★PITT MEADOWS GOLF CLUB
P.O. Box 29, 13615 Harris Rd., Pitt Meadows, V3Y 2E5, (604)465-4711.
Opened: 1963. **Holes:** 18. **Par:** 72/74. **Yards:** 6,516/5,927. **Course rating:** 71.4/74.0. **Slope:** 126/129. **Architect:** Built by members. **Green fee:** $35/$50. **Credit cards:** MC,VISA,Interac. **Reduced fees:** Low season, juniors. **Caddies:** No. **Golf carts:** $25. **Discount golf packages:** No. **Season:** Year-round. **High:** May-Oct. **On site lodging:** No. **Rental clubs:** No. **Walking policy:** Unrestricted walking. **Metal spikes allowed:** Yes. **Range:** Yes (grass/mats). **To obtain tee times:** Call 1 day in advance.
Subscriber comments: Fun for shotmakers...Nicely reshaped flattish course, good everyday course.

★★★PREDATOR RIDGE GOLF RESORT
R-360 Commonage Rd., Vernon, V1T 6M8, (250)542-3436, 36 miles N of Kelowna.
Opened: 1991. **Holes:** 18. **Par:** 73/73. **Yards:** 7,156/5,475. **Course rating:** 76.0/72.9. **Slope:** 131/131. **Architect:** Les Furber. **Green fee:** $45/$60. **Credit cards:** MC,VISA,AMEX. **Reduced fees:** Low season, resort guests, twilight, juniors. **Caddies:** No. **Golf carts:** $30. **Discount golf packages:** Yes. **Season:** April-Oct. **High:** June-Sept. **On site lodging:** No. **Rental clubs:** Yes. **Walking policy:** Unrestricted walking. **Metal spikes allowed:** Yes. **Range:** Yes (grass). **To obtain tee times:** Call up to 1 year in advance with credit card.
Subscriber comments: Magnificent challenge...Wonderful layout, very difficult from the blues...No. 4 is tops!...Each hole a thrill. Great setting.

★★★½THE REDWOODS
PU-22011 88th Ave., Langley, V1M 2M3, (604)882-5132, (604)882-5153.
Opened: 1994. **Holes:** 18. **Par:** 71/71. **Yards:** 6,616/5,452. **Course rating:** 71.8/67.0. **Slope:** 129/120. **Architect:** Ted Locke. **Green fee:** $12/$47. **Credit cards:** MC,VISA. **Reduced fees:** Weekdays, low season, twilight, seniors, juniors. **Caddies:** No. **Golf carts:** $27. **Discount golf packages:** No. **Season:** Year-round. **High:** April-Oct. **On site lodging:** No. **Rental clubs:** Yes. **Walking policy:** Unrestricted walking. **Metal spikes allowed:** Yes. **Range:** Yes (mats). **To obtain tee times:** Call 2 days in advance from 9 a.m.
Subscriber comments: A lot of big trees and variety of creeks...Rewarded for playing smart...Mixed elevations, great walk, good practice facilities...Great for all levels...Some odd holes, but enjoyable setting.

★★★RIVERSHORE GOLF CLUB
Comp 1 Site 13 R.R. No.2, Kamloops, V2C 2J3, (250)573-4622.
Opened: 1982. **Holes:** 18. **Par:** 72/72. **Yards:** 7,007/5,445. **Course rating:** 74.4/71.3. **Slope:** 131/122. **Architect:** Robert Trent Jones Sr. **Green fee:** $35/$45. **Credit cards:** MC,VISA,AMEX. **Reduced fees:** Weekdays, low season, resort guests, twilight, juniors. **Caddies:** No. **Golf carts:** $25. **Discount golf packages:** Yes. **Season:** March-Oct. **High:** April-Sept. **On site lodging:** Yes. **Rental clubs:** Yes. **Walking policy:** Unrestricted walking. **Metal spikes allowed:** Yes. **Range:** Yes (grass/mats). **To obtain tee times:** Call golf shop.

Subscriber comments: Feels like Scotland...Excellent condition...Keep ball on short grass...Course always perfect. Fairways and green like carpet. Wind makes it tough...Deceptive, difficult.

★★½RIVERWAY PUBLIC GOLF COURSE
PM-9001 Riverway Place, Burnaby, V5J 5J3, (604)280-4653, 2 miles E of Vancouver.
Opened: 1995. **Holes:** 18. **Par:** 72/72. **Yards:** 7,004/5,437. **Course rating:** 73.4/72.0.
Slope: 132/125. **Architect:** Les Furber. **Green fee:** $38/$38. **Credit cards:**
MC,VISA,Debit Cards. **Reduced fees:** Low season, twilight, seniors, juniors. **Caddies:**
No. **Golf carts:** $25. **Discount golf packages:** No. **Season:** Year-round. **High:** N/A. **On site lodging:** No. **Rental clubs:** Yes. **Walking policy:** Mandatory cart. **Metal spikes allowed:** Yes. **Range:** Yes (mats). **To obtain tee times:** Call 2 days in advance at noon.
Subscriber comments: Polite staff, fair challenge...Scotland comes to BC, a real links-style course...Landscaped well...Built on a dump!.

★★½ROSSLAND TRAIL COUNTRY CLUB
P.O. Box 250, Trail, V1R 4L5, (250)693-2255, 100 miles N of Spokane, WA.
Opened: 1963. **Holes:** 18. **Par:** 71/72. **Yards:** 6,489/5,786. **Course rating:** 69.8/73.5.
Slope: 121/129. **Architect:** Reg Stone and Roy Stone. **Green fee:** $32/$32. **Credit cards:** MC,VISA. **Reduced fees:** Twilight, juniors. **Caddies:** No. **Golf carts:** $25.
Discount golf packages: Yes. **Season:** March-Oct. **High:** June-Aug. **On site lodging:** No. **Rental clubs:** Yes. **Walking policy:** Unrestricted walking. **Metal spikes allowed:** Yes. **Range:** Yes (grass/mats). **To obtain tee times:** Call golf shop or book through hotel.
Subscriber comments: Well groomed, nicely reworked holes, rounds almost always four hours, good everyday course.
Special Notes: Also has 9-hole par-36 Rossland Course.

★★½SHADOW RIDGE GOLF CLUB
3770 Bulman, Kelowna, V1Y 7P7, (250)765-7777.
Opened: 1988. **Holes:** 18. **Par:** 71/72. **Yards:** 6,475/5,777. **Course rating:** 70.3/74.0.
Slope: 123/130. **Architect:** N/A. **Green fee:** $24/$33. **Credit cards:** MC,VISA,AMEX.
Reduced fees: Weekdays, resort guests, twilight, juniors. **Caddies:** No. **Golf carts:** $24. **Discount golf packages:** No. **Season:** March-Nov. **High:** April-Sept. **On site lodging:** No. **Rental clubs:** Yes. **Walking policy:** Unrestricted walking. **Metal spikes allowed:** Yes. **Range:** Yes (mats). **To obtain tee times:** Call anytime.
Subscriber comments: Nice layout, needs some maturing...Great pro shop, good service...A nice family course, not too tough...Easy to walk.

★★½SHANNON LAKE GOLF COURSE
PU-2649 Shannon Lake Rd., Westbank, V4T 1V6, (250)768-4577.
Opened: 1985. **Holes:** 18. **Par:** 72/72. **Yards:** 6,151/5,075. **Course rating:** 69.9/70.1.
Slope: 122/126. **Architect:** John Moore. **Green fee:** $25/$30. **Credit cards:** MC,VISA.
Reduced fees: Low season, resort guests, twilight, juniors. **Caddies:** No. **Golf carts:** $24. **Discount golf packages:** Yes. **Season:** March-Nov. **High:** June-Aug. **On site lodging:** No. **Rental clubs:** Yes. **Walking policy:** Unrestricted walking. **Metal spikes allowed:** Yes. **Range:** Yes (grass/mats). **To obtain tee times:** Call.
Subscriber comments: Sporty, gimmicky course, OK for fun...Nice course...In the Ponderosas.

★★★SPALLUMCHEEN GOLF & COUNTRY CLUB
PU-P.O. Box 218, Vernon, V1T 6M2, (250)545-5824.
Opened: 1972. **Holes:** 18. **Par:** 71/71. **Yards:** 6,423/5,294. **Course rating:** 71.4/70.6.
Slope: 130/123. **Architect:** Bill Simms/Cyril Foster. **Green fee:** $32/$38. **Credit cards:** MC,VISA,AMEX. **Reduced fees:** Twilight. **Caddies:** No. **Golf carts:** $26. **Discount golf packages:** No. **Season:** April-Oct. **High:** June-Aug. **On site lodging:** No. **Rental clubs:** Yes. **Walking policy:** Unrestricted walking. **Metal spikes allowed:** Yes. **Range:** Yes (grass/mats). **To obtain tee times:** Call up to 2 days in advance.
Subscriber comments: Well laid out...Good greens, easy walk...Pro shop staff outstanding...Most holes good.
Special Notes: Also have a 9-hole par 35 executive course.

★★★★SPRINGS AT RADIUM GOLF COURSE
PU-Stanley St. and Columbia Ave., Radium Hot Springs, V0A 1M0, (250)347-6200, (800)667-6444, 90 miles NE of Banff, Alberta.
Opened: 1988. **Holes:** 18. **Par:** 72/72. **Yards:** 6,801/5,163. **Course rating:** 74.0/70.8. **Slope:** 143/126. **Architect:** Les Furber. **Green fee:** $40/$45. **Credit cards:** MC,VISA,AMEX. **Reduced fees:** Weekdays, twilight, juniors. **Caddies:** No. **Golf carts:** $27. **Discount golf packages:** Yes. **Season:** March-Oct. **High:** June-Sept. **On site lodging:** No. **Rental clubs:** Yes. **Walking policy:** Unrestricted walking. **Metal spikes allowed:** Yes. **Range:** Yes (grass). **To obtain tee times:** Call from Jan. 9th for the upcoming year with credit card to reserve.
Subscriber comments: Awesome!...Lost partner in deep trap on par 3...World class. Carry your big stick...Great scenery...Best course in the valley...Lots of wildlife...Decent, no gimmicks...Very interesting holes.

★★★SQUAMISH VALLEY GOLF & COUNTRY CLUB
2458 Mamquam Rd., Squamish, V0N 3G0, (604)898-9691, 50 miles N of Vancouver.
Opened: 1971. **Holes:** 18. **Par:** 72/72. **Yards:** 6,495/5,148. **Course rating:** 71.8/69.9. **Slope:** 132/113. **Architect:** Gordon McKay/Robert Muir Graves. **Green fee:** $28/$40. **Credit cards:** MC,VISA. **Reduced fees:** Low season, twilight, seniors, juniors. **Caddies:** No. **Golf carts:** $30. **Discount golf packages:** No. **Season:** March-Nov. **High:** May-Sept. **On site lodging:** No. **Rental clubs:** Yes. **Walking policy:** Unrestricted walking. **Metal spikes allowed:** Yes. **Range:** Yes (grass/mats). **To obtain tee times:** Call up to 7 days in advance.
Subscriber comments: Good bang for buck...Nice mountain views and good combination of hazards...Reworked and getting better...Picturesque...Long, scenic, good walking course.

★★★★STOREY CREEK GOLF CLUB
McGimpsey Rd., Campbell River, V9W 6J3, (250)923-3673, 90 miles N of Nanaimo.
Opened: 1989. **Holes:** 18. **Par:** 72/72. **Yards:** 6,657/5,434. **Course rating:** 73.1/72.0. **Slope:** 138/129. **Architect:** Les Furber. **Green fee:** $24/$36. **Credit cards:** MC,VISA. **Reduced fees:** Low season, resort guests, twilight, juniors. **Caddies:** No. **Golf carts:** $23. **Discount golf packages:** Yes. **Season:** Year-round. **High:** April-Oct. **On site lodging:** No. **Rental clubs:** Yes. **Walking policy:** Unrestricted walking. **Metal spikes allowed:** Yes. **Range:** Yes (grass/mats). **To obtain tee times:** Call 2 days in advance.
Subscriber comments: You won't forget your round...Fun to play...Lots of trees, narrow fairways...Solid driving is the key...Every hole isolated...Walk through nature...Long and interesting. No houses...Lose a lot of balls.

★★SUMMERLAND GOLF & COUNTRY CLUB
2405 Mountain Ave., Summerland, V0H 1Z0, (250)494-9554, 36 miles S of Kelowna.
Opened: 1980. **Holes:** 18. **Par:** 72/72. **Yards:** 6,535/5,655. **Course rating:** 70.7/73.4. **Slope:** 121/128. **Architect:** Jim McIntyre. **Green fee:** $30/$30. **Credit cards:** MC,VISA. **Reduced fees:** Low season, resort guests, twilight, juniors. **Caddies:** No. **Golf carts:** $25. **Discount golf packages:** Yes. **Season:** March-Oct. **High:** June-Sept. **On site lodging:** No. **Rental clubs:** Yes. **Walking policy:** Unrestricted walking. **Metal spikes allowed:** Yes. **Range:** Yes (grass). **To obtain tee times:** Call up to 4 days in advance.

★★★SUNSET RANCH GOLF & COUNTRY CLUB
4001 Anderson Rd., Kelowna, V1Y 7V8, (250)765-7700.
Opened: 1991. **Holes:** 18. **Par:** 72/72. **Yards:** 6,558/5,752. **Course rating:** 71.2/73.3. **Slope:** 128/125. **Architect:** J. Bruce Carr. **Green fee:** $27/$39. **Credit cards:** MC,VISA,AMEX. **Reduced fees:** Twilight, juniors. **Caddies:** No. **Golf carts:** $25. **Discount golf packages:** No. **Season:** March-Oct. **High:** N/A. **On site lodging:** No. **Rental clubs:** Yes. **Walking policy:** Unrestricted walking. **Metal spikes allowed:** Yes. **Range:** Yes (grass). **To obtain tee times:** Call.
Subscriber comments: It's a tight one, better keep ball on fairway...Good par 3s, but some goofy holes...Keep it straight. Pay attention.

★★★SWAN-E-SET BAY RESORT & COUNTRY CLUB
PU-16651 Rennie Rd., Pitt Meadows, V3Y 1Z1, (604)465-3888, (800)235-8188, 27 miles E of Vancouver.

Opened: 1993. **Holes:** 18. **Par:** 72/72. **Yards:** 7,000/5,632. **Course rating:** 73.8/71.5. **Slope:** 130/120. **Architect:** Lee Trevino. **Green fee:** $25/$60. **Credit cards:** MC,VISA,AMEX,Diners Club. **Reduced fees:** Weekdays, low season, twilight, seniors. **Caddies:** No. **Golf carts:** $25. **Discount golf packages:** No. **Season:** Year-round. **High:** April-Oct. **On site lodging:** No. **Rental clubs:** Yes. **Walking policy:** Unrestricted walking. **Metal spikes allowed:** Yes. **Range:** Yes (grass/mats). **To obtain tee times:** Call 7 days in advance.
Subscriber comments: Wide fairways, very good greens...Hilly, fun course, variety of holes...Great setting...Rewards are available if you play strategically...Lot of potential, great setting and clubhouse.

★★★★½TRICKLE CREEK GOLF RESORT
R-P.O. Box 190, Kimberley, V1A 2Y6, (250)427-3389, (888)874-2553, 200 miles SW of Calgary.
Opened: 1993. **Holes:** 18. **Par:** 72/72. **Yards:** 6,896/5,080. **Course rating:** 74.8/71.1. **Slope:** 143/131. **Architect:** Les Furber. **Green fee:** $37/$37. **Credit cards:** MC,VISA,AMEX. **Reduced fees:** Weekdays, twilight. **Caddies:** No. **Golf carts:** $24. **Discount golf packages:** Yes. **Season:** May-Oct. **High:** May-Sept. **On site lodging:** No. **Rental clubs:** Yes. **Walking policy:** Unrestricted walking. **Metal spikes allowed:** Yes. **Range:** Yes (grass). **To obtain tee times:** Call anytime starting Jan. 1st for the upcoming year.
Subscriber comments: Lives up to reputation...They don't get much better than this...Signature hole and number 10 intimidating...Par-3 11th must see...The kind of course that has rainbows you play through.

★★½UNIVERSITY GOLF CLUB
PU-5185 University Blvd., Vancouver, V6T 1X5, (604)224-1818.
Opened: 1929. **Holes:** 18. **Par:** 72/72. **Yards:** 6,584/5,653. **Course rating:** 71.5/71.9. **Slope:** 122/122. **Architect:** Davey Black. **Green fee:** $28/$48. **Credit cards:** MC,VISA,AMEX. **Reduced fees:** Low season, twilight. **Caddies:** No. **Golf carts:** $32. **Discount golf packages:** No. **Season:** Year-round. **High:** April-Oct. **On site lodging:** No. **Rental clubs:** Yes. **Walking policy:** Unrestricted walking. **Metal spikes allowed:** Yes. **Range:** Yes (grass/mats). **To obtain tee times:** Call 7 days in advance with credit card.
Subscriber comments: Good redesign of an old public course...Good location close to downtown...Great trees...Wide open, some nice par 3s.

★★★½VERNON GOLF & COUNTRY CLUB
800 Kalamalka Lake Rd., Vernon, V1T 6V2, (250)542-9126, 20 miles N of Kelowana.
Opened: 1913. **Holes:** 18. **Par:** 72/74. **Yards:** 6,597/5,666. **Course rating:** 71.1/71.4. **Slope:** 123/118. **Architect:** Ernie Brown. **Green fee:** $25/$40. **Credit cards:** MC,VISA. **Reduced fees:** Low season, twilight. **Caddies:** No. **Golf carts:** $26. **Discount golf packages:** Yes. **Season:** March-Oct. **High:** May-Aug. **On site lodging:** No. **Rental clubs:** Yes. **Walking policy:** Unrestricted walking. **Metal spikes allowed:** Yes. **Range:** Yes (mats). **To obtain tee times:** Call Thursday. after 2 p.m. for play on Saturday, Sunday and Monday Call Sunday after 2 p.m. for Tuesday-Friday.
Subscriber comments: Hilly, can walk...Fun course...Excellent greens, well laid out, friendly atmosphere...Good pro shop, excellent food, good sevice...Always a good choice, a pleasure and challenge to play.

★★★★WESTWOOD PLATEAU GOLF & COUNTRY CLUB
PU-3251 Plateau Blvd., Coquitlam, V3E 2B8, (604)941-4236.
Opened: 1995. **Holes:** 18. **Par:** 72/72. **Yards:** 6,770/5,014. **Course rating:** 71.9. **Slope:** 154. **Architect:** Michael Hurdzan. **Green fee:** N/A. **Credit cards:** MC,VISA,AMEX,Diners Club. **Reduced fees:** Weekdays, low season, twilight, juniors. **Caddies:** No. **Golf carts:** N/A. **Discount golf packages:** No. **Season:** March-Oct. **High:** May-Sept. **On site lodging:** No. **Rental clubs:** Yes. **Walking policy:** Unrestricted walking. **Metal spikes allowed:** Yes. **Range:** Yes (grass/mats). **To obtain tee times:** Call.

GOOD SERVICE

Notes: Ranked 2nd in 1995 Best New Canadian Courses.
Subscriber comments: Can't believe you're only 30 minutes from city...Best to keep driver in bag...Great views...Cut right out of forest on side of mountain, spectacular...Simply the best...Lots of elevation changes.
Special Notes: Also has 9-hole par-31 course.

★★★WHISTLER GOLF CLUB
R-4001 Whistler Way, Whistler, V0N 1B4, (800)376-1777, 100 miles N of Vancouver.
Opened: 1982. **Holes:** 18. **Par:** 72/72. **Yards:** 6,400/5,434. **Course rating:** 71.3/70.5.
Slope: 128/120. **Architect:** Arnold Palmer. **Green fee:** $50/$85. **Credit cards:**
MC,VISA,AMEX. **Reduced fees:** Low season, twilight. **Caddies:** No. **Golf carts:** $28.
Discount golf packages: Yes. **Season:** May-Oct. **High:** June-Sept. **On site lodging:**
Yes. **Rental clubs:** Yes. **Walking policy:** Unrestricted walking. **Metal spikes allowed:**
Yes. **Range:** Yes (grass/mats). **To obtain tee times:** Call within 30 days of play. Hotel
guests may call anytime.
Subscriber comments: Beautiful setting, fun course...Straightforward...Fun course for
shotmakers...Easy to walk...Thoroughly enjoyable, tough! Great scenery...Beauty of
mountains, target golf.

MANITOBA

★★★★CLEAR LAKE GOLF COURSE
PU-Box 328, Onanole, R0J 1N0, (204)848-4653, 150 miles NW of
Winnipeg.
Opened: 1933. **Holes:** 18. **Par:** 72/72. **Yards:** 6,070/6,070. **Course rat-
ing:** 69.3/72.7. **Slope:** 120/130. **Architect:** Stanley Thompson. **Green
fee:** $24/$28. **Credit cards:** MC,VISA. **Reduced fees:** Low season,
twilight, juniors. **Caddies:** No. **Golf carts:** $13. **Discount golf packages:** No. **Season:**
May-Oct. **High:** June-Aug. **On site lodging:** No. **Rental clubs:** Yes. **Walking policy:**
Unrestricted walking. **Metal spikes allowed:** Yes. **Range:** No. **To obtain tee times:**
Call up to 7 days in advance.
Subscriber comments: Beautiful setting, located in hilly area of mostly flat
Manitoba...Three-hour drive west of Winnipeg...Fine old course...Rolling, nice views in
a national park, along lake...Just relax and enjoy surroundings.

(GOOD VALUE)

★★★½FALCON LAKE GOLF COURSE
PU-Falcon Lake, R0E 0N0, (204)349-2554, 85 miles E of Winnipeg.
Opened: 1958. **Holes:** 18. **Par:** 72/73. **Yards:** 6,937/5,978. **Course rating:** 72.6/72.0. **Slope:** 121/115. **Architect:** Norman Woods. **Green fee:**
$25/$28. **Credit cards:** MC,VISA,AMEX. **Reduced fees:** Weekdays,
twilight, seniors, juniors. **Caddies:** No. **Golf carts:** $23. **Discount golf**
packages: No. **Season:** April-Oct. **High:** July-Aug. **On site lodging:** Yes. **Rental
clubs:** Yes. **Walking policy:** Unrestricted walking. **Metal spikes allowed:** Yes. **Range:**
Yes (grass/mats). **To obtain tee times:** Call up to 14 days in advance beginning at 7
p.m.
Subscriber comments: Very long, scenic. Good mixture of holes, wide, treelined fairways...A good challenge...Wildlife: bears, fox, deer, geese.
Special Notes: Formerly Falcon Beach.

(GOOD VALUE)

★★★½HECLA GOLF COURSE AT GULL HARBOR RESORT
R-P.O. Box 1000, Riverton, R0C 2R0, (204)279-2072, (800)267-6700,
110 miles N of Winnipeg.
Opened: 1975. **Holes:** 18. **Par:** 72/72. **Yards:** 6,678/5,535. **Course rating:** 71.7/70.7. **Slope:** 122/118. **Architect:** Jack Thompson. **Green fee:**
$23/$27. **Credit cards:** MC,VISA,AMEX. **Reduced fees:** Twilight,
seniors, juniors. **Caddies:** No. **Golf carts:** $23. **Discount golf packages:** Yes. **Season:**
May-Oct. **High:** June-Aug. **On site lodging:** Yes. **Rental clubs:** Yes. **Walking policy:**
Unrestricted walking. **Metal spikes allowed:** Yes. **Range:** Yes (grass). **To obtain tee
times:** Public may call 14 days in advance. Resort guests may call anytime.
Subscriber comments: Lovely layout...Wide fairways and big soft greens (lots of
fun)...Manitoba's Pebble Beach, lake comes into play, isolated area...Can't stray off fairways or ball is lost in woods.

(GREAT VALUE)

★★JOHN BLUMBERG GOLF COURSE
PU-4540 Portage Ave., Headingley, R4H IC8, (204)986-3490, 1 mile W of Winnipeg.
Opened: 1969. **Holes:** 27. **Par:** 71/71. **Yards:** 6,343/5,844. **Course rating:** 70.2/68.0.

Slope: 116/111. **Architect:** Robbie Robinson. **Green fee:** $18/$18. **Credit cards:** MC,VISA,AMEX. **Reduced fees:** Twilight, seniors, juniors. **Caddies:** No. **Golf carts:** $22. **Discount golf packages:** No. **Season:** April-Nov. **High:** May-Sept. **On site lodging:** No. **Rental clubs:** Yes. **Walking policy:** Unrestricted walking. **Metal spikes allowed:** Yes. **Range:** Yes (grass/mats). **To obtain tee times:** Call 3 days in advance. **Special Notes:** Also 9-hole par-34 course.

★★★LARTERS AT ST. ANDREWS GOLF & COUNTRY CLUB
30 River Rd., St. Andrews, R1A 2V1, (204)334-2107, 5 miles N of Winnipeg.
Opened: 1990. **Holes:** 18. **Par:** 71/71. **Yards:** 6,526/5,374. **Course rating:** 71.0/69.7. **Slope:** 122/113. **Architect:** David Wagner. **Green fee:** $27/$30. **Credit cards:** MC,VISA,AMEX,Diners Club. **Reduced fees:** Twilight, juniors. **Caddies:** No. **Golf carts:** $27. **Discount golf packages:** Yes. **Season:** April-Oct. **High:** May-Sept. **On site lodging:** No. **Rental clubs:** Yes. **Walking policy:** Unrestricted walking. **Metal spikes allowed:** Yes. **Range:** Yes (grass/mats). **To obtain tee times:** Non-members call 7 days in advance.
Subscriber comments: Well groomed...Very nice. Beautiful clubhouse. Good golf...Moves at good pace...A treat to play...Exceptional golf staff.

★★★★THE LINKS AT QUARRY OAKS
PU-Box 3629, Hwy. 311 E., Steinbach, R0A 2A0, (204)326-4653, 35 miles SE of Winnipeg.
Opened: 1992. **Holes:** 18. **Par:** 72/72. **Yards:** 7,009/5,422. **Course rating:** 73.0/70.0. **Slope:** 133/121. **Architect:** Les Furber. **Green fee:** $30/$45. **Credit cards:** MC,VISA,AMEX. **Reduced fees:** Weekdays, low season, twilight, seniors, juniors. **Caddies:** No. **Golf carts:** Included in Green Fee. **Discount golf packages:** Yes. **Season:** April-Oct. **High:** July-Aug. **On site lodging:** No. **Rental clubs:** Yes. **Walking policy:** Unrestricted walking. **Metal spikes allowed:** Yes. **Range:** Yes (grass). **To obtain tee times:** Call 14 days in advance with credit card.
Subscriber comments: Great course to play regardless of skill...Good playing 15th hole, island green...Memorable...A very challenging course, great.
Special Notes: Expanding to 27 holes in summer 1998.

★★½SELKIRK GOLF & COUNTRY CLUB
P.O. Box 15, Selkirk, R1A 21B, (204)482-2050.
Call club for further information.
Subscriber comments: Nice rural course...Good variety of holes, challenging, inexpensive...Good all around...Prone to spring flooding.

★★½STEINBACH FLY-IN GOLF COURSE
P.O. Box 3716, Steinbach, R0A 2A0, (204)326-6813.
Opened: 1970. **Holes:** 18. **Par:** 72/72. **Yards:** 6,500/5,488. **Course rating:** 70.9/66.6. **Slope:** 119/110. **Architect:** Clinton E. Robinson. **Green fee:** $12/$24. **Credit cards:** MC,VISA. **Reduced fees:** Weekdays, low season, twilight, seniors, juniors. **Caddies:** No. **Golf carts:** $22. **Discount golf packages:** No. **Season:** April-Oct. **High:** May-Sept. **On site lodging:** No. **Rental clubs:** No. **Walking policy:** N/A. **Metal spikes allowed:** Yes. **Range:** Yes (grass). **To obtain tee times:** Call 2 days in advance.
Subscriber comments: Owners make improvements every year...Nice way to spend four hours, not too crowded...Open layout and good value makes it popular with high handicappers...Challenging.

★★★TEULON GOLF & COUNTRY CLUB
PU-Hwy. 7 N., Teulon, R0C 3B0, (204)886-4653, 30 miles N of Winnipeg.
Opened: 1961. **Holes:** 18. **Par:** 72/71. **Yards:** 6,426/5,256. **Course rating:** 71.0/69.0. **Slope:** 115/111. **Architect:** Robert Heaslip. **Green fee:** $12/$24. **Credit cards:** MC,VISA,AMEX. **Reduced fees:** Weekdays, low season, twilight, seniors, juniors. **Caddies:** No. **Golf carts:** $22. **Discount golf packages:** Yes. **Season:** April-Oct. **High:** June-Aug. **On site lodging:** No. **Rental clubs:** Yes. **Walking policy:** Unrestricted walking. **Metal spikes allowed:** Yes. **Range:** Yes (grass/mats). **To obtain tee times:** Call 2 days in advance. Walk-ons welcome in off-peak season.
Subscriber comments: Quiet country course, gets better every year...Fairways are really good and layout is challenging...Go for it on #11.

NEW BRUNSWICK

★★½THE ALGONQUIN GOLF COURSE
R-151 Reed Ave., St. Andrews, E0G 2X0, (506)529-7142, 60 miles SW of Saint John.
Opened: 1894. **Holes:** 18. **Par:** 72/73. **Yards:** 6,474/5,949. **Course rating:** 69.3/73.0.
Slope: 114/127. **Architect:** Donald Ross. **Green fee:** $25/$39. **Credit cards:**
MC,VISA,AMEX,DISC,Diners Club, En Route. **Reduced fees:** Low season, twilight.
Caddies: No. **Golf carts:** $30. **Discount golf packages:** Yes. **Season:** April-Oct. **High:**
July-Aug. **On site lodging:** Yes. **Rental clubs:** Yes. **Walking policy:** Unrestricted walking. **Metal spikes allowed:** Yes. **Range:** Yes (grass). **To obtain tee times:** Call anytime throughout season. During off season tee times can be obtained when booking accommodation (506)529-8823.
Subscriber comments: Great traditional course...6th tee is pretty overlooking water...Short course, great seaside holes...Some nice holes on ocean; many ho-hum holes; overrated...Early century layout, needs better care.
Special Notes: Also has 9-hole par-31 executive course called Woodland.

★★★AROOSTOOK VALLEY COUNTRY CLUB
Box 448, Perth Andover, E0J 1VO, (207)476-8083.
Call club for further information.
Subscriber comments: Great variety of holes...Tough walk, some blind shots, club selection very hard...Scenic plus. Friendly, par 5s outstanding.

★½COUNTRY MEADOWS GOLF CLUB
149 Catamount Rd., Moncton, E1G 1B4, (506)858-8909, 8 miles N of Moncton.
Opened: 1973. **Holes:** 18. **Par:** 72/72. **Yards:** 6,314/5,363. **Course rating:** 69.1/71.1.
Slope: 116/119. **Architect:** Doug Sullivan. **Green fee:** $20/$20. **Credit cards:**
MC,VISA. **Reduced fees:** N/A. **Caddies:** No. **Golf carts:** $22. **Discount golf packages:** No. **Season:** April-Oct. **High:** N/A. **On site lodging:** No. **Rental clubs:** Yes.
Walking policy: Unrestricted walking. **Metal spikes allowed:** Yes. **Range:** Yes (grass).
To obtain tee times: First come, first served.

★★★COVERED BRIDGE GOLF & COUNTRY CLUB
PU-Trans Canada Highway, Hartland, E0J 1N0, Carleton County, (506)375-1112, 65 miles N of Fredericton.
Opened: 1992. **Holes:** 18. **Par:** 72/72. **Yards:** 6,609/5,412. **Course rating:** 71.3.
Slope: 132/111. **Architect:** John Robinson. **Green fee:** $27/$27. **Credit cards:**
MC,VISA. **Reduced fees:** N/A. **Caddies:** No. **Golf carts:** $24. **Discount golf packages:** Yes. **Season:** May-Oct. **High:** June-Aug. **On site lodging:** Yes. **Rental clubs:**
Yes. **Walking policy:** N/A. **Metal spikes allowed:** Yes. **Range:** Yes (grass). **To obtain tee times:** Call 4 days in advance.
Subscriber comments: Young course, good potential, scenic...A good test of golf now—as it matures it will get even better...Par-3 7th worth the trip.

★★★★EDMUNDSTON GOLF CLUB
PU-570 Victoria St., C.P. 263, Edmundston, E3V 3K9, Madawaska County, (506)735-3086.
Opened: N/A. **Holes:** 18. **Par:** 73/73. **Yards:** 6,815/6,514. **Course rating:** 69.4/69.7.
Slope: 113/118. **Architect:** N/A. **Green fee:** $25/$36. **Credit cards:** MC,VISA.
Reduced fees: Weekdays. **Caddies:** Yes. **Golf carts:** $26. **Discount golf packages:**
Yes. **Season:** May-Oct. **High:** June-Aug. **On site lodging:** No. **Rental clubs:** No.
Walking policy: N/A. **Metal spikes allowed:** Yes. **Range:** Yes (grass). **To obtain tee times:** Call (506) 735-4831.
Subscriber comments: Old course, beautifuly taken care of...Lots of large oak trees...Challenging...Tough par 73, treelined and tight. Hills and meadows.

★★½FREDERICTON GOLF & CURLING CLUB
331 Golf Club Rd., Fredericton, E3B 429, (506)458-1003.
Opened: 1917. **Holes:** 18. **Par:** 70/72. **Yards:** 6,285/5,450. **Course rating:** N/A. **Slope:**
120/122. **Architect:** C. Robinson/G. Cornish and W. Robinson. **Green fee:** $35/$35.
Credit cards: MC,VISA. **Reduced fees:** N/A. **Caddies:** No. **Golf carts:** $30. **Discount golf packages:** No. **Season:** April-Nov. **High:** July-Sept. **On site lodging:** No. **Rental

clubs: Yes. **Walking policy:** N/A. **Metal spikes allowed:** Yes. **Range:** Yes (grass). **To obtain tee times:** Walk-ons welcome.
Subscriber comments: Very short...A few holes too close to road...Three-hour rounds routine. Tough par 3s...Short but challenging, road divides course.

GAGE GOLF & CURLING ASSOCIATION
13 Waterville Rd. R.R. 3, Oromocto, E2V 2G3, (506)357-9343.
Call club for further information.

GOLF BOUCTOUCHE
Case Postale 568, Bouctouche, E0A 1G0, (506)743-5251.
Call club for further information.
Subscriber comments: Very tough on high handicapper, lots of hills...Fairly flat, good challenge.

GOWAN BRAE GOLF & COUNTRY CLUB
150 Youghall Dr., Bathurst, E2A 321, Gloucester County, (506)546-2707.
Opened: 1958. **Holes:** 18. **Par:** 72/74. **Yards:** 6,577/5,979. **Course rating:** 71.3/73.0.
Slope: 129/125. **Architect:** Robbie Robinson. **Green fee:** $36/$36. **Credit cards:**
MC,VISA. **Reduced fees:** Twilight. **Caddies:** No. **Golf carts:** $30. **Discount golf packages:** No. **Season:** May-Nov. **High:** July-Aug. **On site lodging:** No. **Rental clubs:** Yes.
Walking policy: Unrestricted walking. **Metal spikes allowed:** Yes. **Range:** Yes
(grass/mats). **To obtain tee times:** Call 2 days in advance.
Subscriber comments: Tough when windy. Great waterside scenery...Fantastic condition...Well worth a stop, great back nine.

GRAND FALLS GOLF CLUB
Main St., Grand-Sault, E3Y 1A7, (506)475-6008, 120 miles N of Fredericton.
Opened: 1990. **Holes:** 18. **Par:** 72/72. **Yards:** 6,650/5,000. **Course rating:** 71.5/71.5.
Slope: 122/124. **Architect:** Bob Moote. **Green fee:** $25/$25. **Credit cards:** MC,VISA.
Reduced fees: Low season. **Caddies:** No. **Golf carts:** $25. **Discount golf packages:**
Yes. **Season:** May 1-Oct. 31. **High:** June 1-Sept.15. **On site lodging:** No. **Rental
clubs:** Yes. **Walking policy:** Unrestricted walking. **Metal spikes allowed:** Yes. **Range:**
Yes (grass). **To obtain tee times:** Call golf shop.
Subscriber comments: Crushed white seashells used in place of sand in traps is beautiful...Redesigned front nine, maturing will be outstanding...Hilly. Good greens. Fun round. Left to right shot a help.

★★★HAMPTON COUNTRY CLUB
PU-William Bell Dr., Rte. 100, Hampton, E0G 1Z0, Kings County, (506)832-3407, 10 miles E of Saint John.
Opened: 1972. **Holes:** 18. **Par:** 72/73. **Yards:** 6,291/5,430. **Course rating:** 69.9/72.0.
Slope: 118/132. **Architect:** Cecil Manuge. **Green fee:** $20/$28. **Credit cards:**
MC,VISA. **Reduced fees:** Low season, twilight. **Caddies:** No. **Golf carts:** $25.
Discount golf packages: Yes. **Season:** N/A. **High:** July-Aug. **On site lodging:** No.
Rental clubs: Yes. **Walking policy:** Unrestricted walking. Metal spikes allowed: Yes.
Range: Yes (grass). **To obtain tee times:** Call 2 days in advance.
Subscriber comments: Severe elevation changes, par 6: 666 yards...Hilly in spots.
Nice views. Busy on weekends...Views of Saint John River.

★★LAKESIDE GOLF CLUB
1896 Rte. 134, Lakeville, E1H 1A7, Westmorland County, (506)861-9441, 3 miles E of Moncton.
Opened: 1926. **Holes:** 18. **Par:** 70/71. **Yards:** 5,880/5,612. **Course rating:** 67.3/68.3.
Slope: 110/117. **Architect:** N/A. **Green fee:** $25/$25. **Credit cards:** MC,VISA.
Reduced fees: N/A. **Caddies:** No. **Golf carts:** $25. **Discount golf packages:** No.
Season: May-Nov. **High:** July-Aug. **On site lodging:** No. **Rental clubs:** Yes. **Walking
policy:** Unrestricted walking. **Metal spikes allowed:** Yes. **Range:** Yes (grass/mats). **To
obtain tee times:** Call 20 days in advance.

LE CLUB DE GOLF DE ST. IGNACE
R.R. H1, Site 1, Box 11, St. Ignace, E0A 2Z0, Kent County, (506)876-3737, 55 miles N of Moncton.

Opened: 1984. **Holes:** 18. **Par:** 72. **Yards:** 6,325. **Course rating:** 70.2. **Slope:** 125. **Architect:** N/A. **Green fee:** $20/$25. **Credit cards:** MC,VISA. **Reduced fees:** N/A. **Caddies:** No. **Golf carts:** $25. **Discount golf packages:** No. **Season:** May-Oct. **High:** July-Aug. **On site lodging:** No. **Rental clubs:** Yes. **Walking policy:** Unrestricted walking. **Metal spikes allowed:** Yes. **Range:** Yes (grass/mats). **To obtain tee times:** Call. **Subscriber comments:** Very hilly, some tough holes...A real test, stay in the fairway. Has one of the most challenging par 3s in region.

★★★½MACTAQUAC PROVINCIAL PARK GOLF CLUB
PU-Mouth of Keswick, Keswick, E0H 1N0, (506)363-4925, 15 miles N of Fredericton.
Opened: 1970. **Holes:** 18. **Par:** 72/72. **Yards:** 7,030/5,756. **Course rating:** 74.0/71.0. **Slope:** 131/117. **Architect:** William Mitchell. **Green fee:** $30/$35. **Credit cards:** MC,VISA. **Reduced fees:** Low season, twilight. **Caddies:** No. **Golf carts:** $24. **Discount golf packages:** No. **Season:** May-Oct. **High:** May-Oct. **On site lodging:** No. **Rental clubs:** Yes. **Walking policy:** Unrestricted walking. **Metal spikes allowed:** Yes. **Range:** Yes (grass). **To obtain tee times:** Call 2 days in advance for locals, anytime for nonresidents.
Subscriber comments: In a wooded setting...Championship course, huge greens...Tough, long course with deep rough and wildlife...Well bunkered...Too much sameness to all holes...Good practice area.

★★½MAGNETIC HILL GOLF & COUNTRY CLUB
PU-1 Tee Time Dr., Moncton, E1G 3T7, Westmorland County, (506)858-1611.
Opened: 1967. **Holes:** 18. **Par:** 70/70. **Yards:** 5,692/5,292. **Course rating:** 66.4/69.2. **Slope:** 112/115. **Architect:** N/A. **Green fee:** $26/$26. **Credit cards:** MC,VISA. **Reduced fees:** N/A. **Caddies:** No. **Golf carts:** $27. **Discount golf packages:** No. **Season:** May-Oct. **High:** June-Aug. **On site lodging:** No. **Rental clubs:** No. **Walking policy:** Unrestricted walking. **Metal spikes allowed:** Yes. **Range:** No. **To obtain tee times:** Call.
Subscriber comments: Very good...Short par 4s...Too long walk between holes, hilly, enjoy playing there...Challenging, interesting blend of holes.

MAPLEWOOD GOLF & COUNTRY CLUB
PU-R.R. 4 D-424, Moncton, E1C 868, (506)858-7840, 6 miles N of Moncton.
Opened: 1983. **Holes:** 18. **Par:** 71/71. **Yards:** 6,152/5,026. **Course rating:** 69.3/67.2. **Slope:** 118/111. **Architect:** N/A. **Green fee:** $22/$22. **Credit cards:** VISA. **Reduced fees:** N/A. **Caddies:** No. **Golf carts:** $24. **Discount golf packages:** No. **Season:** May-Oct. **High:** July-Aug. **On site lodging:** No. **Rental clubs:** No. **Walking policy:** Unrestricted walking. **Metal spikes allowed:** Yes. **Range:** No. **To obtain tee times:** Call Thursday or after for Saturday and Sunday tee times.
Subscriber comments: 18 nice finishing hole...Young course, family owned, long par 3s, short par 5s...New nine holes more interesting than old nine.

MIRAMICHI GOLF & COUNTRY CLUB
930 Water St., Miramichi, E1X 3M5, Northhumberland County, (506)622-2068.
Opened: 1925. **Holes:** 18. **Par:** 71/71. **Yards:** 6,212/5,371. **Course rating:** 69.3/73.0. **Slope:** 116/127. **Architect:** John Robinson. **Green fee:** $30/$30. **Credit cards:** MC,VISA. **Reduced fees:** N/A. **Caddies:** Yes. **Golf carts:** $24. **Discount golf packages:** Yes. **Season:** May-Oct. **High:** June-Sept. **On site lodging:** No. **Rental clubs:** Yes. **Walking policy:** Unrestricted walking. **Metal spikes allowed:** Yes. **Range:** Yes (grass). **To obtain tee times:** Call two days in advance.
Subscriber comments: Has been improved a lot, small greens...Older, traditional course, fun to play, clubhouse is a heritage site—150+ years old.

★★★MONCTON GOLF AND COUNTRY CLUB
212 Coverdale Rd., Riverview, E1B 4T9, Moroland County, (506)387-3855.
Opened: 1929. **Holes:** 18. **Par:** N/A. **Yards:** N/A. **Course rating:** N/A. **Slope:** N/A. **Architect:** Stanley Thompson. **Green fee:** N/A. **Credit cards:** MC,VISA,AMEX. **Reduced fees:** N/A. **Caddies:** Yes. **Golf carts:** N/A. **Discount golf packages:** No. **Season:** May-Oct. **High:** N/A. **On site lodging:** No. **Rental clubs:** Yes. **Walking policy:** Unrestricted walking. **Metal spikes allowed:** No. **Range:** Yes (grass). **To obtain tee times:** Call up to 2 days in advance.
Subscriber comments: Short uninteresting holes...Good layout, some good holes...No real drama, but good test...Tough par 3s...Well wooded; challenging.

CANADA

★★½PETITCODIAC VALLEY GOLF & COUNTRY CLUB
Golf Course Rd., Petitcodiac, E0A 2H0, (506)756-8129, 25 miles W of Moncton.
Opened: N/A. **Holes:** 18. **Par:** 71/71. **Yards:** 5,932/5,581. **Course rating:** 66.7/71.1.
Slope: 114/119. **Architect:** N/A. **Green fee:** $24/$24. **Credit cards:** MC. **Reduced fees:** Resort guests, seniors, juniors. **Caddies:** No. **Golf carts:** $20. **Discount golf packages:** Yes. **Season:** April-Oct. **High:** July-Sept. **On site lodging:** No. **Rental clubs:** Yes. **Walking policy:** Unrestricted walking. **Metal spikes allowed:** Yes. **Range:** Yes (grass). **To obtain tee times:** Call.
Subscriber comments: Expansion is maturing nicely...Mountain setting...Fun, unassuming but tough...Interesting holes.

★★★½PINE NEEDLES GOLF & COUNTRY CLUB
PU-R.R. No.1, P.O. Box 1, Shediac, E0A 3G0, (506)532-4634, 20 miles NE of Moncton.
Opened: 1973. **Holes:** 27. **Architect:** N/A. **Green fee:** $25/$25. **Golf carts:** $23.
Credit cards: MC,VISA,Interac. **Reduced fees:** Twilight. **Caddies:** No. **Discount golf packages:** No. **Season:** May-Oct. **High:** July-Aug. **On site lodging:** No. **Rental clubs:** Yes. **Walking policy:** Unrestricted walking. **Metal spikes allowed:** Yes. **Range:** No. **To obtain tee times:** Call 2 days in advance for weekends and holidays.
ORCHARD/RIVER
Par: 72/73. **Yards:** 6,091/5,354. **Course rating:** 67.6/69.8. **Slope:** 112/123.
PINE/ORCHARD
Par: 71/72. **Yards:** 5,919/5,280. **Course rating:** 66.2/69.4. **Slope:** 106/119.
RIVER/PINE
Par: 73/73. **Yards:** 6,430/5,338. **Course rating:** 69.7/71.4. **Slope:** 119/127.
Subscriber comments: Beautiful course. Many long carries off tees...River nine great, Orchard nine good for warm-up. Avoid weekends...Friendly staff...River nine great, Pine OK.

RESTIGOUCHE GOLF & COUNTRY CLUB
PU-Box 8 Site 11 R.R. 2, Campbellton, E3N 3E8, (506)789-7628.
Opened: 1923. **Holes:** 18. **Par:** 70/73. **Yards:** 5,652/4,989. **Course rating:** 69.1/69.0.
Slope: 126/119. **Architect:** N/A. **Green fee:** $19/$27. **Credit cards:** MC,VISA.
Reduced fees: Low season. **Caddies:** No. **Golf carts:** $21. **Discount golf packages:** No. **Season:** May-Oct. **High:** July-Aug. **On site lodging:** No. **Rental clubs:** Yes.
Walking policy: Unrestricted walking. **Metal spikes allowed:** Yes. **Range:** No. **To obtain tee times:** Call 1 day in advance.
Subscriber comments: Pretty in fall, reasonable course, not challenging...Has great possibilities, needs improvement.

★★½RIVERBEND GOLF & FISHING CLUB
PU-R.R. 9, Nashwauk Village, Fredericton, E3B 4X9, York County, (506)452-7277, 15 miles N of Fredericton.
Opened: 1992. **Holes:** 18. **Par:** 72/72. **Yards:** 6,436/5,466. **Course rating:** 71.0/71.1.
Slope: 121/114. **Architect:** N/A. **Green fee:** $24/$24. **Credit cards:** MC,VISA.
Reduced fees: N/A. **Caddies:** No. **Golf carts:** $20. **Discount golf packages:** Yes.
Season: April-Oct. **High:** May-Sept. **On site lodging:** No. **Rental clubs:** Yes. **Walking policy:** Unrestricted walking. **Metal spikes allowed:** Yes. **Range:** Yes (grass). **To obtain tee times:** Call.
Subscriber comments: Very tough, long marsh, grass and trees, improving yearly...No room for errors, narrow fairways...1 and 10 too similar.

★★★ROCKWOOD PARK GOLF COURSE
PU-784 Sandy Pt. Rd., St. John, E2L 4B3, St. John County, (506)634-0090.
Opened: 1973. **Holes:** 18. **Par:** 70/69. **Yards:** 6,017/5,023. **Course rating:** 68.0/69.0.
Slope: 117/113. **Architect:** N/A. **Green fee:** $20/$25. **Credit cards:** MC,VISA.
Reduced fees: Weekdays, low season, twilight, seniors, juniors. **Caddies:** No. **Golf carts:** $25. **Discount golf packages:** No. **Season:** May-Oct. **High:** June-Sept. **On site lodging:** No. **Rental clubs:** Yes. **Walking policy:** Unrestricted walking. **Metal spikes allowed:** Yes. **Range:** Yes (mats). **To obtain tee times:** Call 1 day in advance.
Subscriber comments: Wide variety of style on holes, elevation changes...Excellent municipal course, big greens...Challenging and exceptionally picturesque...Must stay in play or ball lost, heavy woods.

CANADA

ST. STEPHEN GOLF CLUB
R.R. 6 Tower Hill, St. Stephen, E3L 2Y3 (506)466-5336.
Call club for further information.

★★½SUSSEX GOLF & CURLING CLUB
Piccadilly Rd., Sussex, E0E 1P0, (506)433-6493, 40 miles E of St. John.
Opened: 1973. **Holes:** 18. **Par:** 72/73. **Yards:** 6,287/5,752. **Course rating:** 69.7/72.0.
Slope: 117/119. **Architect:** N/A. **Green fee:** $22/$26. **Credit cards:** MC,VISA.
Reduced fees: N/A. **Caddies:** No. **Golf carts:** $23. **Discount golf packages:** No.
Season: May-Oct. **High:** July-Sept. **On site lodging:** No. **Rental clubs:** Yes. **Walking policy:** Unrestricted walking. **Metal spikes allowed:** Yes. **Range:** Yes (grass). **To obtain tee times:** Call 2 days in advance.
Subscriber comments: Interesting course, good mix of golf holes...Fun course, scenic, a little hilly...Mosquitos are incredible..Two tough finishing holes, 17 and 18...Course in valley setting, friendly staff.

★★½WESTFIELD GOLF & COUNTRY CLUB
8 Golf Club Rd., Westfield, E0G 3J0, (506)757-2907, 20 miles N of St. John.
Opened: 1917. **Holes:** 18. **Par:** 69/72. **Yards:** 5,799/5,710. **Course rating:** 66.8/70.0.
Slope: 113/114. **Architect:** N/A. **Green fee:** $35/$35. **Credit cards:** VISA. **Reduced fees:** N/A. **Caddies:** No. **Golf carts:** $25. **Discount golf packages:** No. **Season:** May-Oct. **High:** July-Aug. **On site lodging:** No. **Rental clubs:** Yes. **Walking policy:** Unrestricted walking. **Metal spikes allowed:** Yes. **Range:** No. **To obtain tee times:** Call 2 days in advance.
Subscriber comments: Short old course...Very mature. Bit short, nice views. Good mix of holes...An older, well-maintained course, great dining area and 19th hole...Lots of blind tee shots...Well-wooded and challenging.

NEWFOUNDLAND

BLOMIDON GOLF & COUNTRY CLUB
Wess Valley Rd., Corner Brook, A2H 2X9, (709)634-2523.
Opened: 1952. **Holes:** 18. **Par:** 69/72. **Yards:** 5,500/5,400. **Course rating:** 67.0/70.0.
Slope: 116/121. **Architect:** Alfred H. Tull. **Green fee:** $25/$25. **Credit cards:** MC,VISA.
Reduced fees: N/A. **Caddies:** No. **Golf carts:** $22. **Discount golf packages:** No.
Season: May-Oct. **High:** June-Aug. **On site lodging:** No. **Rental clubs:** Yes. **Walking policy:** Unrestricted walking. **Metal spikes allowed:** Yes. **Range:** No. **To obtain tee times:** Call or come in up to 3 days in advance.

★★★½TERA NOVA PARK LODGE & GOLF COURSE
R-General Delivery, Port Blandford, A0C 2G0, (709)543-2626.
Opened: 1984. **Holes:** 18. **Par:** 71/71. **Yards:** 6,546/5,433. **Course rating:** 71.9/72.5.
Slope: 128/129. **Architect:** Robbie Robinson/Doug Carrick. **Green fee:** $35/$37.
Credit cards: MC,VISA,AMEX,DISC,En Route. **Reduced fees:** Weekdays, low season, resort guests, twilight, juniors. **Caddies:** Yes. **Golf carts:** $28. **Discount golf packages:** Yes. **Season:** May-Oct. **High:** July-Sept. **On site lodging:** Yes. **Rental clubs:** Yes. **Walking policy:** Unrestricted walking. **Metal spikes allowed:** Yes. **Range:** Yes (grass/mats). **To obtain tee times:** Call anytime during the season with credit card to guarantee.
Subscriber comments: Breathtaking...Fantastic course in tune with nature. Wildlife abundant...Several holes over water.
Special Notes: Formerly Twin Rivers Golf Course.

NOVA SCOTIA

★★★ABERCROMBIE GOLF CLUB
P.O. Box 516, New Glasgow, B2H 5E7, (902)752-6249, 90 miles W of Halifax.
Opened: 1918. **Holes:** 18. **Par:** 72. **Yards:** 6,300. **Course rating:** 71.0. **Slope:** 124.

Architect: Clinton E. Robinson. **Green fee:** $35/$35. **Credit cards:** VISA. **Reduced fees:** Twilight. **Caddies:** No. **Golf carts:** $18. **Discount golf packages:** No. **Season:** May-Sept. **High:** July-Aug. **On site lodging:** No. **Rental clubs:** Yes. **Walking policy:** Unrestricted walking. **Metal spikes allowed:** Yes. **Range:** Yes (grass/mats). **To obtain tee times:** Call 10 days in advance.
Subscriber comments: Good all around...Nothing fancy, good solid golf...Challenging narrow fairways...An excellent test of golf.

★★★AMHERST GOLF CLUB
P.O. Box 26, Amherst, B4H 3Z6, (902)667-8730, 140 miles W of Halifax.
Opened: 1912. **Holes:** 18. **Par:** 71/71. **Yards:** 6,367/5,439. **Course rating:** 71.0/71.0.
Slope: 122/115. **Architect:** Clinton E. Robinson. **Green fee:** $35/$35. **Credit cards:** VISA. **Reduced fees:** Twilight. **Caddies:** No. **Golf carts:** N/A. **Discount golf packages:** No. **Season:** May-Oct. **High:** N/A. **On site lodging:** No. **Rental clubs:** No. **Walking policy:** Unrestricted walking. **Metal spikes allowed:** Yes. **Range:** Yes (grass). **To obtain tee times:** Call.
Subscriber comments: A secret gem, tough course, tricky greens, great finishing hole...Carved out of rolling farmland, scenic marsh vistas, windy...Long course, well kept and interesting, friendly staff.

★★½ANTIGONISH GOLF & COUNTRY CLUB
P.O. Box 1341, Antigonish, B2G 2L7, (902)863-4749.
Opened: 1926. **Holes:** 18. **Par:** 72/72. **Yards:** 6,605/5,109. **Course rating:** 73.0/69.0.
Slope: 130/118. **Architect:** N/A. **Green fee:** $30/$30. **Credit cards:** MC,VISA,AMEX.
Reduced fees: Twilight. **Caddies:** No. **Golf carts:** $25. **Discount golf packages:** Yes.
Season: May-Oct. **High:** July-Aug. **On site lodging:** No. **Rental clubs:** Yes. **Walking policy:** Unrestricted walking. **Metal spikes allowed:** Yes. **Range:** Yes (grass). **To obtain tee times:** Call.
Subscriber comments: Some very challenging holes...Hospitality excellent!...Vista of town seen from hillside. Elevation, trees close to greens.

★★★½ASHBURN GOLF CLUB
P.O. Box 22038, Halifax, B3L 4T7, (902)861-4013.
Call club for further information.
Subscriber comments: All around good golf, expensive...Honest, hilly layout, challenging green shapes...Wooded, good test, vast greens...Wonderful course, well kept in all areas and interesting.

BELL BAY GOLF CLUB
PU-Baddeck, (902)295-1333.
Opened: N/A. **Holes:** N/A. **Par:** N/A. **Yards:** N/A. **Course rating:** N/A. **Slope:** N/A.
Architect: N/A. **Green fee:** $45/$45. **Credit cards:** N/A. **Reduced fees:** N/A. **Caddies:** No. **Golf carts:** N/A. **Discount golf packages:** No. **Season:** N/A. **High:** N/A. **On site lodging:** No. **Rental clubs:** No. **Walking policy:** Unrestricted walking. **Metal spikes allowed:** No. **Range:** No. **To obtain tee times:** N/A.

★★½BRIGHTWOOD GOLF & COUNTRY CLUB
227 School St., Dartmouth, B3A 2Y5, (902)469-7879.
Opened: N/A. **Holes:** 18. **Par:** 68/71. **Yards:** 5,579/5,276. **Course rating:** 66.6/90.6.
Slope: 116/122. **Architect:** W. Parks Jr./D. Ross/Robert Moote. **Green fee:** N/A. **Credit cards:** VISA,AMEX. **Reduced fees:** N/A. **Caddies:** No. **Golf carts:** N/A. **Discount golf packages:** No. **Season:** April-Oct. **High:** N/A. **On site lodging:** No. **Rental clubs:** No. **Walking policy:** Unrestricted walking. **Metal spikes allowed:** Yes. **Range:** No. **To obtain tee times:** Call 1 day in advance.
Subscriber comments: Most hilly course I've ever played. Tough...Short, deep rough...Scenic vistas of Halifax Harbour, well-wooded, hilly, good test.

★★★DUNDEE RESORT GOLF COURSE
R-R-R. 2, West Bay, B0E 3K0, Richmond County, (902)345-0420, (800)565-1774, 155 miles E of Halifax.
Opened: 1977. **Holes:** 18. **Par:** 72/72. **Yards:** 6,475/5,236. **Course rating:** 71.9/71.7.
Slope: 135/131. **Architect:** Bob Moote. **Green fee:** $30/$33. **Credit cards:** MC,VISA,AMEX,DISC,Diners Club, Enroute. **Reduced fees:** Weekdays, resort guests,

twilight. **Caddies:** No. **Golf carts:** $30. **Discount golf packages:** Yes. **Season:** May-Oct. **High:** June-Sept. **On site lodging:** Yes. **Rental clubs:** Yes. **Walking policy:** Unrestricted walking. **Metal spikes allowed:** Yes. **Range:** No. **To obtain tee times:** Call 1 day in advance.

Subscriber comments: Lots of hills, great view of lake...Very hilly, fair test of golf...Hit the fairways or shoot high scores...Nice facilities and good value...Impossible to get out of rough!...Fantastic highland golf.

★★★★½ HIGHLANDS LINKS GOLF COURSE

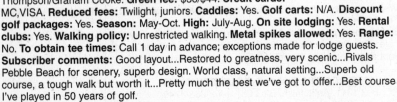

PU-Cape Breton Highlands Nt'l Pk., Ingonish Beach, B0C 1L0, (902)285-2600, (800)441-1118, 70 miles S of Sydney.
Opened: 1942. **Holes:** 18. **Par:** 72/72. **Yards:** 6,596/5,243. **Course rating:** 73.9/73.3. **Slope:** 139/131. **Architect:** Stanley Thompson/Graham Cooke. **Green fee:** $36/$44. **Credit cards:** MC,VISA. **Reduced fees:** Twilight, juniors. **Caddies:** Yes. **Golf carts:** N/A. **Discount golf packages:** Yes. **Season:** May-Oct. **High:** July-Aug. **On site lodging:** Yes. **Rental clubs:** Yes. **Walking policy:** Unrestricted walking. **Metal spikes allowed:** Yes. **Range:** No. **To obtain tee times:** Call 1 day in advance; exceptions made for lodge guests.
Subscriber comments: Good layout...Restored to greatness, very scenic...Rivals Pebble Beach for scenery, superb design. World class, natural setting...Superb old course, a tough walk but worth it...Pretty much the best we've got to offer...Best course I've played in 50 years of golf.

★★★ KEN-WO COUNTRY CLUB

9514 Commercial St., New Minas, B7N 3E9, (902)681-5388, 60 miles NW of Halifax.
Opened: 1921. **Holes:** 18. **Par:** 70/73. **Yards:** 6,308/5,915. **Course rating:** 69.2/72.0. **Slope:** 120/122. **Architect:** N/A. **Green fee:** $28/$35. **Credit cards:** MC,VISA. **Reduced fees:** Twilight. **Caddies:** No. **Golf carts:** $24. **Discount golf packages:** Yes. **Season:** April-Nov. **High:** June-Aug. **On site lodging:** Yes. **Rental clubs:** Yes. **Walking policy:** Unrestricted walking. **Metal spikes allowed:** Yes. **Range:** Yes (grass). **To obtain tee times:** Call 2 days in advance.
Subscriber comments: Good test of golf...Need a variety of shots here...Nice course, solid back nine...Nice place, mix of farmland and woods.

LINGAN COUNTRY CLUB

P.O. Box 1252, 1225 Grand Lake Rd., Sydney, B1P 6J9, (902)562-1112, 260 miles N of Halifax.
Opened: 1908. **Holes:** 18. **Par:** 72/74. **Yards:** 6,620/5,834. **Course rating:** 71.4/73.5. **Slope:** 125/129. **Architect:** Stanley Thompson. **Green fee:** $20/$40. **Credit cards:** MC,VISA. **Reduced fees:** N/A. **Caddies:** No. **Golf carts:** $27. **Discount golf packages:** No. **Season:** May-Oct. **High:** July-Aug. **On site lodging:** No. **Rental clubs:** No. **Walking policy:** Unrestricted walking. **Metal spikes allowed:** Yes. **Range:** Yes (grass). **To obtain tee times:** Call.

★★★ PARAGON GOLF & COUNTRY CLUB

368 Brookside Dr., Kingston, B0P 1R0, (902)765-2554, 100 miles NW of Halifax.
Opened: 1964. **Holes:** 18. **Par:** 72/72. **Yards:** 6,245/5,580. **Course rating:** 69.5/72.1. **Slope:** 123/123. **Architect:** Gordie Shaw. **Green fee:** $29/$32. **Credit cards:** VISA. **Reduced fees:** Twilight. **Caddies:** No. **Golf carts:** $20. **Discount golf packages:** No. **Season:** April-Nov. **High:** May-Aug. **On site lodging:** No. **Rental clubs:** Yes. **Walking policy:** Unrestricted walking. **Metal spikes allowed:** Yes. **Range:** No. **To obtain tee times:** Non-members call 1 day in advance.
Subscriber comments: Excellent test of golf...The course is always in good shape!...Tough par 3s, easy par 5s.

★★★½ THE PINES RESORT HOTEL GOLF COURSE

R-P.O. Box 70, Digby, B0V 1A0, (902)245-4104, (800)667-4637, 150 miles SW of Halifax.
Opened: 1932. **Holes:** 18. **Par:** 71/75. **Yards:** 6,204/5,865. **Course rating:** 70.0/73.0. **Slope:** 121/131. **Architect:** Stanley Thompson. **Green fee:** $35/$35. **Credit cards:** MC,VISA,AMEX,DISC,En Route. **Reduced fees:** N/A. **Caddies:** No. **Golf carts:** $28. **Discount golf packages:** Yes. **Season:** May-Oct. **High:** July-Sept. **On site lodging:** Yes. **Rental clubs:** Yes. **Walking policy:** Unrestricted walking. **Metal spikes allowed:**

Yes. **Range:** No. **To obtain tee times:** Call. No restrictions.
Subscriber comments: If you like par 3s this is the course for you, especially hole #2...Superb Inn...Interesting hilly course, good layout...Babe Ruth loved this place!...Like walking into a piece of the past; woods and rolling hills.

★★★THE TRURO GOLF CLUB
Golf St., Truro, B2N 6L1, (902)893-4650, 50 miles NW of Halifax.
Opened: 1903. **Holes:** 18. **Par:** 71/72. **Yards:** 6,500/5,636. **Course rating:** 70.9/72.4. **Slope:** 123/125. **Architect:** Robbie Robinson/Stanley Thompson. **Green fee:** $20/$36. **Credit cards:** MC,VISA,AMEX. **Reduced fees:** Low season, twilight. **Caddies:** No. **Golf carts:** $26. **Discount golf packages:** No. **Season:** April-Nov. **High:** May-Sept. **On site lodging:** No. **Rental clubs:** Yes. **Walking policy:** Unrestricted walking. **Metal spikes allowed:** Yes. **Range:** Yes (grass). **To obtain tee times:** Call 1 day in advance.
Subscriber comments: Very pleasant atmosphere...Very wide open fairways (you can let it rip)...Excellent walking course...Farmland; can be very windswept; well maintained, good test.

ONTARIO

AGUASABON GOLF COURSE
PU-Beach Rd., Terrace Bay, P0T 2W0, (807)825-3844, 130 miles E of Thunder Bay.
Opened: 1964. **Holes:** 9. **Par:** 36/37. **Yards:** 3,200/2,900. **Course rating:** N/A. **Slope:** N/A. **Architect:** N/A. **Green fee:** N/A. **Credit cards:** MC,VISA. **Reduced fees:** Low season, twilight, seniors, juniors. **Caddies:** No. **Golf carts:** $20. **Discount golf packages:** No. **Season:** May-Oct. **High:** June-Aug. **On site lodging:** No. **Rental clubs:** Yes. **Walking policy:** N/A. **Metal spikes allowed:** Yes. **Range:** Yes (grass). **To obtain tee times:** First come, first served.
Subscriber comments: Beautiful scenic golf course on Lake Superior...Nice course for small community.

★★★★½ANGUS GLEN GOLF CLUB
PU-10080 Kennedy Rd., Markham, L6C 1N9, (905)887-5157, 25 miles N of Toronto.
Opened: 1994. **Holes:** 18. **Par:** 72/72. **Yards:** 7,376/5,721. **Course rating:** 76.0/73.3. **Slope:** 143/129. **Architect:** Doug Carrick. **Green fee:** $85/$110. **Credit cards:** MC,VISA,AMEX. **Reduced fees:** Low season. **Caddies:** No. **Golf carts:** Included in Green Fee. **Discount golf packages:** No. **Season:** April-Nov. **High:** May-Oct. **On site lodging:** No. **Rental clubs:** Yes. **Walking policy:** Mandatory cart. **Metal spikes allowed:** Yes. **Range:** Yes (grass/mats). **To obtain tee times:** Call 60 days in advance.
Notes: Ranked 1st in 1995 Best New Canadian Courses.
Subscriber comments: Nicest, most demanding course in Ontario...One of the top 5 I have ever played. Beautiful...Excellent design and a treat to play...Good pro shop...The staff makes you feel like a king for the day, the locker room is fantastic, food is great at a good price.

★★★BAY OF QUINTE COUNTRY CLUB
R.R. No.2 Trent Rd., Belleville, K8N 4Z9, (613)968-7063, 115 miles E of Toronto.
Opened: 1921. **Holes:** 18. **Par:** 72/73. **Yards:** 6,840/5,701. **Course rating:** 72.4/71.4. **Slope:** 125/113. **Architect:** Howard Watson. **Green fee:** $27/$38. **Credit cards:** MC,VISA. **Reduced fees:** Low season, twilight, juniors. **Caddies:** No. **Golf carts:** $30. **Discount golf packages:** No. **Season:** April-Nov. **High:** May-Sept. **On site lodging:** No. **Rental clubs:** Yes. **Walking policy:** Unrestricted walking. **Metal spikes allowed:** Yes. **Range:** Yes (grass/mats). **To obtain tee times:** Call 5 days in advance for weekdays. Call Thursday at noon for upcoming weekend or holiday.
Subscriber comments: Typical county course in Southern Ottawa...Nice layout...Long par 4s, friendly staff...Relatively flat...Subtle greens.

★★★BEECHWOOD GOLF & COUNTRY CLUB
4680 Thorold Townline Rd., Niagara Falls, L2E 6S4, (905)680-4653.
Opened: 1960. **Holes:** 18. **Par:** 72/72. **Yards:** 6,700/5,400. **Course rating:** 73.0/69.8.

Slope: 126/116. Architect: R. Moote/B. Antonsen. Green fee: $28/$32. Credit cards: MC,VISA,AMEX. Reduced fees: Weekdays, low season, twilight. Caddies: No. Golf carts: $28. Discount golf packages: Yes. Season: April-Nov. High: April-Sept. On site lodging: No. Rental clubs: No. Walking policy: Unrestricted walking. Metal spikes allowed: Yes. Range: Yes (grass/mats). To obtain tee times: Local non-members call 4 days in advance. Visitors may reserve in advance without restrictions.
Subscriber comments: Interesting layout, fast greens...Great back nine...Fun to play...Holes close together...Very friendly service.

★★★½BLUE SPRINGS GOLF CLUB
170 York St., Acton, L7J 1M4, (519)853-0904.
Call club for further information.
Subscriber comments: Many elevated tees. Spectacular views...Lots of water and lots of fun...Hidden gem; a few Augusta-like holes...Scenic, challenging, and well groomed...Difficult course; beautiful setting..

★★★BROCKVILLE COUNTRY CLUB
P.O. Box 42, Brockville, K6V 5T7, (613)342-2468.
Call club for further information.
Subscriber comments: Too bad No. 2 wasn't downhill instead of uphill...Interesting par 3s, many elevation changes.

★★★BROOKLEA GOLF & COUNTRY CLUB
751 Yonge St., Midland, L4R 2E1, (705)526-7532, (800)257-0428, 90 miles N of Toronto.
Opened: 1959. Holes: 18. Par: 72/72. Yards: 6,645/5,585. Course rating: 71.2/71.4. Slope: 126/126. Architect: Rene Muylaert. Green fee: $34/$38. Credit cards: MC,VISA,AMEX. Reduced fees: Weekdays, resort guests, twilight. Caddies: No. Golf carts: $13. Discount golf packages: Yes. Season: Year-round. High: June-Sept. On site lodging: No. Rental clubs: Yes. Walking policy: Unrestricted walking. Metal spikes allowed: Yes. Range: Yes (grass/mats). To obtain tee times: Call up to 4 days in advance.
Subscriber comments: Part links, part park, nice experience...Great course, good value, friendly staff, fair to all golfers...Well groomed, easy access.
Special Notes: Also has 9-hole executive West Course.

★★CALABOGIE HIGHLANDS RESORT & GOLF CLUB
PU-1234 Barryvale Rd., Calabogie, K0J 1H0, Renfrew County, (613)752-2171, 55 miles SW of Ottawa.
Opened: 1983. Holes: 18. Par: 72/72. Yards: 6,735/5,632. Course rating: 71.4/72.0. Slope: 126/129. Architect: Dolgos & Assoc.. Green fee: $15/$25. Credit cards: MC,VISA,AMEX,Interac. Reduced fees: Weekdays, low season, resort guests, twilight, juniors. Caddies: No. Golf carts: $25. Discount golf packages: Yes. Season: April-Nov. High: June-Aug. On site lodging: Yes. Rental clubs: Yes. Walking policy: Unrestricted walking. Metal spikes allowed: Yes. Range: Yes (grass/mats). To obtain tee times: Call 7 days in advance.
Subscriber comments: Friendly staff; memorable holes...Play this course in the fall when the leaves are turning color.
Special Notes: Also has 9-hole par-35 course.

★★½CALEDON COUNTRY CLUB
PU-2121 Old Baseline Rd., R.R. No.1, Inglewood, L0N 1K0, Peel County, (905)838-0121, 10 miles N of Brampton.
Opened: 1961. Holes: 18. Par: 71/71. Yards: 6,140/5,414. Course rating: 71.5/69.9. Slope: 132/129. Architect: Rene Muylaert. Green fee: $38/$43. Credit cards: MC,VISA,AMEX,En Route. Reduced fees: Weekdays, low season, twilight, seniors, juniors. Caddies: No. Golf carts: N/A. Discount golf packages: No. Season: April-Nov. High: June-Aug. On site lodging: No. Rental clubs: No. Walking policy: Unrestricted walking. Metal spikes allowed: Yes. Range: Yes (grass/mats). To obtain tee times: Call up to 7 days in advance.
Subscriber comments: Course is straightforward...Not long but good variety, picturesque, hilly so walking is a workout...Short, scenic and enjoyable golf.

★★CARDINAL GOLF CLUB

PU-2740 Hwy. 9, R.R. No.1, Kettleby, L0G 1J0, (905)841-2195, 20 miles N of Toronto.
Opened: 1989. **Holes:** 54. **Par:** 72/72. **Yards:** 6,450/5,750. **Course rating:** 71.5/64.9.
Slope: 114/104. **Architect:** Dan Lavis. **Green fee:** $10/$38. **Credit cards:**
MC,VISA,AMEX. **Reduced fees:** Weekdays, low season, twilight, seniors, juniors.
Caddies: No. **Golf carts:** $14. **Discount golf packages:** No. **Season:** April-Nov. **High:**
June-Aug. **On site lodging:** No. **Rental clubs:** Yes. **Walking policy:** Unrestricted walking. **Metal spikes allowed:** Yes. **Range:** Yes (grass/mats). **To obtain tee times:** Call up
to 14 days in advance.
Special Notes: Also has 18-hole par-58 short course.

★★★CARLISLE GOLF & COUNTRY CLUB

PU-523 Carlisle Rd., Carlisle, L0R 1H0, (905)689-8820, (800)661-4343, 10 miles N of
Burlington.
Opened: 1991. **Holes:** 18. **Par:** 72/72. **Yards:** 6,557/5,232. **Course rating:** 70.6/72.9.
Slope: 119/104. **Architect:** Ted Baker. **Green fee:** $45/$50. **Credit cards:**
MC,VISA,AMEX. **Reduced fees:** Weekdays, low season, seniors, juniors. **Caddies:** No.
Golf carts: $30. **Discount golf packages:** Yes. **Season:** April-Nov. **High:** June-Aug.
On site lodging: No. **Rental clubs:** Yes. **Walking policy:** Unrestricted walking. **Metal
spikes allowed:** Yes. **Range:** Yes (grass/mats). **To obtain tee times:** Call up to 7 days
in advance.
Subscriber comments: Some of the nicest greens around...Challenge!...Very nice layout, good atmosphere...Great for scoring.

★★½CHAPPLES GOLF COURSE

530 Chapples Dr., Thunder Bay, (807)623-7070.
Call club for further information.
Subscriber comments: My home course gets better and better!...Central location.
Good shape...Very special in the fall.

★★½CHIPPEWA GOLF & COUNTRY CLUB

Hwy. 21 N., Southampton, N0H 2L0, (519)797-3684, 23 miles W of Owen Sound.
Opened: 1964. **Holes:** 18. **Par:** 72/72. **Yards:** 6,420/5,392. **Course rating:** 69.5/70.0.
Slope: 116/109. **Architect:** S. Thompson. **Green fee:** $22/$28. **Credit cards:**
MC,VISA. **Reduced fees:** Low season, twilight. **Caddies:** No. **Golf carts:** $24.
Discount golf packages: Yes. **Season:** April-Nov. **High:** May-Sept. **On site lodging:**
No. **Rental clubs:** Yes. **Walking policy:** Unrestricted walking. **Metal spikes allowed:**
Yes. **Range:** Yes (grass). **To obtain tee times:** Call Sunday for the upcoming week.
Subscriber comments: Average course...Flat, but challenging.

★★½DEER RUN GOLF CLUB

PU-Bloomfield Rd. No.3, Blenheim, N08 1A0, (519)676-1566, 11 miles S of Chothom.
Opened: 1993. **Holes:** 18. **Par:** 72/72. **Yards:** 6,386/5,303. **Course rating:** 70.4/65.0.
Slope: N/A. **Architect:** Bill Dickie Assoc. **Green fee:** $12/$18. **Credit cards:**
MC,VISA,AMEX. **Reduced fees:** Weekdays, low season, twilight. **Caddies:** No. **Golf
carts:** $12. **Discount golf packages:** Yes. **Season:** April-Nov. **High:** June-July. **On site
lodging:** No. **Rental clubs:** Yes. **Walking policy:** Unrestricted walking. **Metal spikes
allowed:** Yes. **Range:** Yes (grass). **To obtain tee times:** Call golf shop.
Subscriber comments: Challenging yet fair...Very nice greens, clubhouse is
great...Good shape for a new layout.

DEERHURST RESORT

R- **Caddies:** No. **Golf carts:** Included in Green Fee. **Discount golf packages:** Yes. **On
site lodging:** Yes. **Rental clubs:** Yes. **Metal spikes allowed:** Yes. **Range:** Yes
(grass/mats).

★★★★½DEERHURST HIGHLANDS GOLF COURSE

R.R. No. 4, Huntsville, P0A 1K0, (705)789-2381, 120 miles N of Toronto.
Opened: 1990. **Holes:** 18. **Par:** 72/73. **Yards:** 7,011/5,393. **Course rating:** 74.5/71.2.
Slope: 140/125. **Architect:** Robert Cupp and Tom McBroom. **Green fee:** $79/$84.
Credit cards: MC,VISA,AMEX. **Reduced fees:** Weekdays, low season, resort guests,
twilight. **Season:** May-Oct. **High:** June-Aug. **Walking policy:** Mandatory cart. **To
obtain tee times:** Call 7 days in advance.

Subscriber comments: Blues are a real test, whites make the course more enjoyable for average player...True "Canadian" experience...Gorgeous setting, many good holes...In the fall you feel like you are golfing in a painting...Very tough, very pretty, good condition...Best golf in Ontario...An excellent test and top resort...Superb in all aspects.

★★★**DEERHURST LAKESIDE GOLF COURSE**
1235 Deerhurst Dr., Huntsville, P1H 2E8, (705)789-7878, 120 miles N of Toronto.
Opened: 1972. **Holes:** 18. **Par:** 65/65. **Yards:** 4,500/3,800. **Course rating:** 62.4/63.0.
Slope: 101/104. **Architect:** C.E. Robinson. **Green fee:** $26/$49. **Credit cards:** All major. **Reduced fees:** Low season, resort guests, twilight, juniors. **Season:** April-Oct.
High: July-Sept. **Walking policy:** Walking at certain times. **To obtain tee times:** Call.
Subscriber comments: Beautifully sculpted from Ontario wilderness into a clean, scenic and challenging course...Everyone very accommodating.

DELHI GOLF & COUNTRY CLUB
905 James St., Delhi, N4B 2E2, (519)582-1621, 40 miles SE of London.
Opened: 1960. **Holes:** 18. **Par:** 71/72. **Yards:** 6,400/5,200. **Course rating:** 71.3/69.4.
Slope: 114/121. **Architect:** George Coreno. **Green fee:** $22/$25. **Credit cards:**
MC,VISA,AMEX. **Reduced fees:** Weekdays, twilight, seniors, juniors. **Caddies:** No.
Golf carts: $26. **Discount golf packages:** Yes. **Season:** March-Dec. **High:** May-Sept.
On site lodging: No. **Rental clubs:** Yes. **Walking policy:** Unrestricted walking. **Metal spikes allowed:** Yes. **Range:** Yes (grass/mats). **To obtain tee times:** Call.

★★½**DON VALLEY GOLF COURSE**
PM-4200 Yonge St., Toronto, M2P 1N9, (416)392-2465.
Opened: 1956. **Holes:** 18. **Par:** 71/71. **Yards:** 6,109/5,040. **Course rating:** 70.0/67.5.
Slope: 124/121. **Architect:** Howard Watson/David Moote. **Green fee:** $29/$33. **Credit cards:** MC,VISA,AMEX. **Reduced fees:** Twilight. **Caddies:** Yes. **Golf carts:** $25.
Discount golf packages: No. **Season:** April-Nov. **High:** July-Aug. **On site lodging:**
No. **Rental clubs:** Yes. **Walking policy:** Unrestricted walking. **Metal spikes allowed:**
Yes. **Range:** Yes (grass). **To obtain tee times:** Call up to 7 days in advance.
Subscriber comments: Great municipal course in traditional up and down layout...Lots of hills...Challenging public track, very busy, rolling...Narrow.

★★★**DOON VALLEY GOLF CLUB**
PU-500 Doon Valley Dr., Kitchener, N2P 1B4, (519)741-2939, 60 miles W of Toronto.
Opened: 1955. **Holes:** 18. **Par:** 72/73. **Yards:** 6,193/5,507. **Course rating:** 68.1.
Slope: 115/106. **Architect:** Clinton E. Robinson. **Green fee:** $23/$27. **Credit cards:**
MC,VISA,AMEX,Debit Cards. **Reduced fees:** Weekdays, twilight, juniors. **Caddies:** No.
Golf carts: $25. **Discount golf packages:** Yes. **Season:** April-Nov. **High:** May-Oct. **On site lodging:** No. **Rental clubs:** Yes. **Walking policy:** Unrestricted walking. **Metal spikes allowed:** Yes. **Range:** Yes (grass). **To obtain tee times:** Call Saturday a.m. for following weekend. Call up to 7 days in advance at 7 p.m. for weekdays.
Subscriber comments: Very nice layout...Flattish, relaxing, higher handicps will enjoy...Nice course. Moves well.

★★★★**EAGLE CREEK GOLF COURSE**
PU-109 Royal Troon Lane, Dunrobin, K0A 1T0, (613)832-0728, 18 miles W of Ottawa.
Opened: 1991. **Holes:** 18. **Par:** 72/72. **Yards:** 7,067/5,413. **Course rating:** 74.3/71.5.
Slope: N/A. **Architect:** Ken Venturi and Ken Skodacek. **Green fee:** $48/$48. **Credit cards:** MC,VISA,AMEX. **Reduced fees:** Twilight. **Caddies:** No. **Golf carts:** $30.
Discount golf packages: No. **Season:** April-Oct. **High:** June-Aug. **On site lodging:**
No. **Rental clubs:** Yes. **Walking policy:** Unrestricted walking. **Metal spikes allowed:**
Yes. **Range:** Yes (grass). **To obtain tee times:** Call 7 days in advance. Out of town reservations anytime with credit card.
Subscriber comments: Very tough and demanding...A must play, brilliant routing, every hole gives you options...Beautiful layout, lots of water...Subway just a par 3 away...Variety of holes, good finishing hole.

★★**FANSHAWE GOLF CLUB**
2835 Sunningdale Rd. East, London, N5X 3Y7, (519)455-2770, 120 miles W of Toronto.
Opened: 1950. **Holes:** 27. **Par:** 71/70. **Yards:** 6,528/5,518. **Course rating:** 70.5/71.8.
Slope: 113/116. **Architect:** John Moffatt Sr. **Green fee:** $23/$23. **Credit cards:**

MC,VISA,Debit Card. **Reduced fees:** Twilight. **Caddies:** No. **Golf carts:** $26. **Discount golf packages:** No. **Season:** April-Nov. **High:** May-Sept. **On site lodging:** No. **Rental clubs:** No. **Walking policy:** Unrestricted walking. **Metal spikes allowed:** Yes. **Range:** Yes (grass). **To obtain tee times:** Call.
Subscriber comments: Decent muny...Red/White nines better than Blue.

FIRE FIGHTERS GORMLEY GREEN GOLF CLUB
PU-P.O. Box 278, Gormley, L0H 1G0, (905)888-1219, 12 miles N of Toronto. **Green fee:** $30/$44. **Credit cards:** VISA,AMEX. **Reduced fees:** Weekdays, twilight, seniors. **Caddies:** No. **Golf carts:** $25. **Discount golf packages:** No. **Season:** April-Nov. **High:** June-Sept. **On site lodging:** No. **Rental clubs:** Yes. **Walking policy:** Unrestricted walking. **Metal spikes allowed:** Yes. **Range:** Yes (grass/mats). **To obtain tee times:** Call.
★★CIRCLE COURSE
Opened: 1978. **Holes:** 18. **Par:** 70/70. **Yards:** 6,618/5,658. **Course rating:** 72.0. **Slope:** 115. **Architect:** Rene Muylaert and Charles Muylaert.
Subscriber comments: Wide forgiving fairways, excellent for high handicappers...Clubhouse facilities need upgrading.
★★★CREEK COURSE
Opened: N/A. **Holes:** 18. **Par:** 72/72. **Yards:** 6,948/5,958. **Course rating:** 73.1. **Slope:** 128. **Architect:** Rene Muylaert.
Subscriber comments: A good test, over water and valleys, tough 18th hole...Excellent condition for busy course. Very organized.

FIRE FIGHTERS ROLLING HILLS GOLF CLUB
PU-P.O. Box 519, Gormley, LOH 1G0, (905)888-1955, 12 miles N of Toronto.
Opened: N/A. **Architect:** N/A. **Credit cards:** MC,VISA,AMEX. **Reduced fees:** Weekdays, twilight, seniors. **Caddies:** No. **Golf carts:** $25. **Discount golf packages:** No. **Season:** April-Nov. **High:** June-Sept. **On site lodging:** No. **Rental clubs:** Yes. **Walking policy:** Unrestricted walking. **Metal spikes allowed:** Yes. **Range:** No. **To obtain tee times:** Call.
★★BLUE
Holes: 18. **Par:** 72/75. **Yards:** 6,340/5,664. **Course rating:** 68.5. **Slope:** 112. **Green fee:** $26/$38.
Subscriber comments: OK for group play...Good complex.
★★GOLD
Holes: 18. **Par:** 62/62. **Yards:** 4,010/3,681. **Course rating:** N/A. **Slope:** N/A. **Green fee:** $18/$30.
Subscriber comments: Too easy, not challenging...Good hole placements.
★★½RED
Holes: 18. **Par:** 70. **Yards:** 4,894. **Course rating:** 61.3. **Slope:** 95. **Green fee:** $22/$34.
Subscriber comments: Course plays well...Great upkeep of greens.

★★½FLAMBOROUGH HILLS GOLF CLUB
P.O. Box 9, Copetown, L0R 1J0, (905)627-1743, 15 miles W of Hamilton.
Opened: 1960. **Holes:** 27. **Architect:** N/A. **Green fee:** $20/$32. **Credit cards:** MC,VISA,Interac. **Reduced fees:** Weekdays, seniors. **Caddies:** No. **Golf carts:** $14. **Discount golf packages:** No. **Season:** March-Oct. **High:** N/A. **On site lodging:** No. **Rental clubs:** Yes. **Walking policy:** N/A. **Metal spikes allowed:** Yes. **Range:** Yes. **To obtain tee times:** Call 10 days in advance for weekdays. Call on Tuesday for upcoming weekend.
HILLS/LAKES
Par: 73/73. **Yards:** 6,580/5,269. **Course rating:** 69.5/69.2. **Slope:** 114.
HILLS/WOODS
Par: 73/73. **Yards:** 6,331/5,451. **Course rating:** 68.5/70.9. **Slope:** 116.
WOODS/LAKES
Par: 72/72. **Yards:** 6,259/5,288. **Course rating:** 69.0/70.0. **Slope:** 114.
Subscriber comments: Fair layout for all abilities...Undulating course, well placed water on Lakes...Hilly...Newest nine (Lakes) is the best.

★★★★FOREST CITY NATIONAL GOLF CLUB
PU-16540 Robin's Hill Rd., London, N6A 4C1, (519)451-0994.
Opened: 1993. **Holes:** 18. **Par:** 72/72. **Yards:** 6,850/5,119. **Course rating:** 73.6/69.4.

Slope: 132/116. **Architect:** Craig Schreiner. **Green fee:** $40/$45. **Credit cards:** MC,VISA. **Reduced fees:** Weekdays, low season, twilight. **Caddies:** No. **Golf carts:** Included in Green Fee. **Discount golf packages:** No. **Season:** April-Nov. **High:** June-Aug. **On site lodging:** No. **Rental clubs:** Yes. **Walking policy:** Unrestricted walking. **Metal spikes allowed:** Yes. **Range:** Yes (grass/mats). **To obtain tee times:** Call up to 7 days in advance.

Subscriber comments: One of the nicest courses around...Outstanding staff and facility...Tough, but fair for women, beautiful scenery, excellent practice facility...Fun to play...Fast, hard greens, penal rough.

FORT WILLIAM COUNTRY CLUB
R.R. 4, 1350 Mountain Rd., Thunder Bay, P7C 4Z2, (807)475-8925.
Opened: 1923. **Holes:** 18. **Par:** 72/74. **Yards:** 6,500/5,795. **Course rating:** 69.0/71.0. **Slope:** 127/123. **Architect:** N/A. **Green fee:** $32/$40. **Credit cards:** MC,VISA. **Reduced fees:** Juniors. **Caddies:** No. **Golf carts:** $22. **Discount golf packages:** No. **Season:** April-Nov. **High:** May-Sept. **On site lodging:** No. **Rental clubs:** Yes. **Walking policy:** Unrestricted walking. **Metal spikes allowed:** Yes. **Range:** Yes (grass). **To obtain tee times:** Call.

Subscriber comments: Good golf course. A little pricey...Top of the line in our fair (cold) city...Expensive, but very good...Very scenic.

★★★★½GLEN ABBEY GOLF CLUB
PU-1333 Dorval Dr., Oakville, L6J 4Z3, (905)844-1811, 20 miles W of Toronto.
Opened: 1977. **Holes:** 18. **Par:** 73/74. **Yards:** 7,112/5,520. **Course rating:** 75.5/71.4. **Slope:** 140/117. **Architect:** Jack Nicklaus. **Green fee:** $90/$145. **Credit cards:** MC,VISA,AMEX. **Reduced fees:** Low season. **Caddies:** No. **Golf carts:** Included in Green Fee. **Discount golf packages:** No. **Season:** April-Oct. **High:** May-Oct. **On site lodging:** No. **Rental clubs:** Yes. **Walking policy:** Unrestricted walking. **Metal spikes allowed:** Yes. **Range:** Yes (grass/mats). **To obtain tee times:** Call from March 1 for upcoming season with credit card to reserve. No changes or cancellations accepted. **Notes:** 1977-96 Bell Canadian Open.

Subscriber comments: Very picturesque, fantastic clubhouse, great design...Not cheap, but have to play where the pros play...A truly great experience...Bring your "A" game or weep...Great finishing hole...Canada's best public course...Play from the blues on 11 and 14...Treat you like a king.

★★★½HAWK RIDGE GOLF CLUB
PU-P.O. Box 874, Orillia, L3V 6K8, (705)329-4653, 60 miles N of Toronto.
Opened: 1991. **Holes:** 27. **Par:** 72. **Yards:** 6,933. **Course rating:** 73.2. **Slope:** 120. **Architect:** Rene Muylaert/Bruce Dodson. **Green fee:** $25/$40. **Credit cards:** MC,VISA,AMEX. **Reduced fees:** Resort guests, twilight, seniors, juniors. **Caddies:** No. **Golf carts:** $30. **Discount golf packages:** Yes. **Season:** April-Nov. **High:** June-Sept. **On site lodging:** No. **Rental clubs:** Yes. **Walking policy:** Unrestricted walking. **Metal spikes allowed:** Yes. **Range:** Yes (grass/mats). **To obtain tee times:** Call golf shop.

Subscriber comments: Beautiful links-style course...Nice resort course, area hotel a good value...Manage your game and you will score well.

HIDDEN LAKE GOLF & COUNTRY CLUB
1137 #1 Side Rd., Burlington, L7R 3X4, Halton County, (905)336-3660, 35 miles W of Toronto.
Opened: 1963. **Architect:** N/A. **Green fee:** $25/$42. **Credit cards:** MC,VISA. **Reduced fees:** Weekdays, low season, twilight, seniors, juniors. **Caddies:** No. **Golf carts:** $30. **Discount golf packages:** No. **Season:** March-Nov. **High:** May-Sept. **On site lodging:** No. **Rental clubs:** Yes. **Walking policy:** Unrestricted walking. **Metal spikes allowed:** No. **Range:** Yes (grass). **To obtain tee times:** Call up to 6 days in advance.
★★½NEW COURSE
Holes: 18. **Par:** 72/71. **Yards:** 6,645/5,217. **Course rating:** 72.1/68.9. **Slope:** 124/111.
Subscriber comments: Old course allows bump and run, new course demands wedges...Bland scenery...Should be great.
OLD COURSE
Holes: 18. **Par:** 71/70. **Yards:** 6,559/5,369. **Course rating:** 71.0/69.1. **Slope:** 122/110.

★★★HOCKLEY VALLEY RESORT
R-R.R. No.1, Orangeville, L9W 2Y8, (519)942-0754, 30 miles NW of Toronto.
Opened: 1989. **Holes:** 18. **Par:** 70/70. **Yards:** 6,403/4,646. **Course rating:** 71.0/71.0.
Slope: 130/126. **Architect:** Thomas McBroom. **Green fee:** $46/$75. **Credit cards:** All major. **Reduced fees:** Weekdays, low season, resort guests, twilight. **Caddies:** No.
Golf carts: Included in Green Fee. **Discount golf packages:** Yes. **Season:** April-Nov.
High: June-Sept. **On site lodging:** Yes. **Rental clubs:** Yes. **Walking policy:** Mandatory cart. **Metal spikes allowed:** No. **Range:** Yes (grass/mats). **To obtain tee times:** Hotel guests can book anytime. Others call 7 days in advance.
Subscriber comments: Wonderful vistas. Lots of elevation changes...Beautiful setting, good golf...Super people...Swirling winds across valleys, great...Love this golf course..OK golf, nothing unique or special.

★★HORNBY TOWER GOLF CLUB
PU-Hornby Rd., Hornby, L0P 1E0, (905)878-3421.
Call club for further information.

★★★½HORSESHOE VALLEY RESORT
R-R.R. No.1, Barrie, L4M 4Y8, (705)835-2790, 60 miles N of Toronto.
Opened: 1974. **Holes:** 18. **Par:** 72/72. **Yards:** 6,167/5,232. **Course rating:** 71.0/67.0.
Slope: 131/122. **Architect:** Rene Muylaert. **Green fee:** $45/$55. **Credit cards:**
MC,VISA,AMEX,Diners Club. **Reduced fees:** Weekdays, low season, resort guests, twilight. **Caddies:** No. **Golf carts:** $30. **Discount golf packages:** No. **Season:** April-Oct. **High:** June-Sept. **On site lodging:** Yes. **Rental clubs:** Yes. **Walking policy:** Walking at certain times. **Metal spikes allowed:** Yes. **Range:** Yes (grass/mats). **To obtain tee times:** Resort guests may make book with room reservation. Others call 7 days in advance.
Subscriber comments: Makes you think...Pleasure to play...Very picturesque layout...Good layout, nice people...1st hole conflicts with ski lifts, otherwise OK...Excellent...Scenic and tough, has all resort facilities.
Special Notes: Also 9-hole par-36 Highlands Course.

★★½HUMBER VALLEY GOLF COURSE
Toronto, (416)392-2488.
Call club for further information.
Subscriber comments: Shortish yet enjoyable, established, small greens...Great shape...Nice layout. Avoid weekends...Narrow fairways with trees and a river runs through it...City course, many hackers...No driving range.

★★INDIAN CREEK GOLF & COUNTRY CLUB
120 Indian Creek Rd. W., Chatham, N7M 5L6, Kent County, (519)354-7666.
Opened: 1956. **Holes:** 18. **Par:** 71/73. **Yards:** 6,200/5,471. **Course rating:** 68.6/71.4.
Slope: 113/119. **Architect:** Paul Sironen. **Green fee:** $15/$18. **Credit cards:** MC,VISA.
Reduced fees: Low season, twilight, seniors, juniors. **Caddies:** No. **Golf carts:** $22.
Discount golf packages: Yes. **Season:** March-Dec. **High:** May-Oct. **On site lodging:** No. **Rental clubs:** Yes. **Walking policy:** Unrestricted walking. **Metal spikes allowed:** Yes. **Range:** No. **To obtain tee times:** Call up to 7 days in advance.

★★★KANATA LAKES GOLF & COUNTRY CLUB
7000 Campeau Dr., Kanata, K2K 1X5, (613)592-1631, 10 miles W of Ottawa.
Opened: 1991. **Holes:** 18. **Par:** 70/70. **Yards:** 6,730/5,328. **Course rating:** 73.0/70.0.
Slope: N/A. **Architect:** Thomas McBroom. **Green fee:** $42/$46. **Credit cards:**
MC,VISA. **Reduced fees:** N/A. **Caddies:** No. **Golf carts:** $15. **Discount golf packages:** No. **Season:** April-Oct. **High:** July-Aug. **On site lodging:** No. **Rental clubs:** Yes.
Walking policy: Unrestricted walking. **Metal spikes allowed:** Yes. **Range:** Yes. **To obtain tee times:** Call two days in advance after 8 a.m.
Subscriber comments: Tight, challenging course in middle of surburban development...Tough par 4s...Excellent design, variety, challenging front nine...Smiling service...Long hikes through real estate, but good golf.

KENOGAMISIS GOLF COURSE
P.O. Box 790, Geraldton, P0T 1M0, (807)854-1029, 180 miles NE of Thunder Bay.
Opened: 1937. **Holes:** 9. **Par:** 72/74. **Yards:** 6,558/5,982. **Course rating:** 72.2/72.6.
Slope: 134/116. **Architect:** Stanley Thompson. **Green fee:** $20/$22. **Credit cards:**
MC,VISA. **Reduced fees:** Weekdays, juniors. **Caddies:** No. **Golf carts:** N/A. **Discount golf packages:** No. **Season:** May-Sept. **High:** N/A. **On site lodging:** No. **Rental clubs:** Yes. **Walking policy:** Unrestricted walking. **Metal spikes allowed:** Yes. **Range:**
No. **To obtain tee times:** Not required.
Subscriber comments: Only 9 holes but a nice course...Friendly club.

★★★½KINGSVILLE GOLF CLUB
Hwy. 18 W., Kingsville, N9Y 2E9, Essex County, (519)733-6585, 35 miles SE of Detroit, MI.
Opened: 1925. **Holes:** 27. **Architect:** N/A. **Green fee:** $36. **Credit cards:** MC,VISA.
Reduced fees: Low season, twilight, juniors. **Caddies:** No. **Golf carts:** $14. **Discount golf packages:** No. **Season:** March-Nov. **High:** June-Aug. **On site lodging:** No. **Rental clubs:** No. **Walking policy:** Unrestricted walking. **Range:** Yes (grass). **To obtain tee times:** Call 2 days in advance.
RED/GOLD
Par: 27/73. **Yards:** 6,622/5,545. **Course rating:** 72.9/71.3. **Slope:** 134/120. **Metal spikes allowed:** No.
RED/WHITE
Par: 72/73. **Yards:** 6,364/5,808. **Course rating:** 70.9/72.7. **Slope:** 126/120. **Metal spikes allowed:** Yes.
WHITE/GOLD
Par: 72/72. **Yards:** 6,394/5,288. **Course rating:** 71.1/70.0. **Slope:** 132/119. **Metal spikes allowed:** Yes.
Subscriber comments: Gold nine is outstanding test of golf...Excellent elevations...Stanley Thompson nine excellent...Red/White the easiest...Big trees, very flat...Good par 3s...White/Gold good test of short and long game.

LAKE JOSEPH CLUB
RR 2, Port Carling, P0B 1J0, (705)765-3115, (800)291-9899.
Opened: 1996. **Holes:** 18. **Architect:** Tom McBroom. **On site lodging:** Yes. **To obtain tee times:** Must be resort guest.
Call club for further information.
Notes: Ranked 1st in 1997 Best New Canadian Courses.

★★½THE LINKS OF ROCKWAY GLEN
3290 9th St. Louth, St. Catharines, L2R 6P7, (905)641-4536.
Opened: 1991. **Holes:** 18. **Par:** 72/72. **Yards:** 6,914/5,033. **Course rating:** 72.0/68.9.
Slope: 124/118. **Architect:** Robert Moote. **Green fee:** $36/$36. **Credit cards:**
MC,VISA. **Reduced fees:** No. **Caddies:** No. **Golf carts:** No. **Discount golf packages:** No. **Season:** April-Oct. **High:** May-Sept. **On site lodging:** No. **Rental clubs:**
Yes. **Walking policy:** Unrestricted walking. **Metal spikes allowed:** Yes. **Range:** Yes (grass). **To obtain tee times:** Call golf shop.
Subscriber comments: Getting better every year...Great potential...Short, wide open...Challenging greens; fairways.

LIONHEAD GOLF & COUNTRY CLUB
PU-8525 Mississauga Rd., Brampton, L6V 3N2, (905)455-4900, 10 miles W of Toronto.
Opened: 1991. **Architect:** Ted Baker. **Credit cards:** MC,VISA,AMEX.
Reduced fees: Low season. **Caddies:** No. **Golf carts:** Included in Green Fee. **Discount golf packages:** No. **Season:** April-Nov. **High:** May-Oct.
On site lodging: No. **Rental clubs:** Yes. **Walking policy:** Mandatory cart. **Metal spikes allowed:** Yes. **Range:** Yes (grass). **To obtain tee times:** Book with credit card one to 60 days in advance.
★★★★½LEGENDS COURSE
Holes: 18. **Par:** 72/72. **Yards:** 7,198/5,730. **Course rating:** 77.0/74.0. **Slope:** 151/137.
Green fee: $75/$125.
Subscriber comments: Enjoyed it so much I didn't care about my score. You're treated

CANADA

like royalty for the day...Play it from the back and enjoy the view...Very difficult but stunningly beautiful...As good as golf gets.

★★★★MASTERS COURSE
Holes: 18. **Par:** 72/72. **Yards:** 7,035/5,553. **Course rating:** 75.0/72.5. **Slope:** 146/131. **Green fee:** $75/$110.
Subscriber comments: Premier courses in Ontario...Fabulous challenge, tough to score well...Fast greens, nice course layout, well maintained...Manicured, tough, strategy play...Links, tough in the wind.

★★★½LOCH MARCH GOLF & COUNTRY CLUB
PU-1755 Old Carp Rd., Kanata, K2K 1X7, (613)839-5885, 28 miles W of Ottawa.
Opened: 1987. **Holes:** 18. **Par:** 72/72. **Yards:** 6,750/5,178. **Course rating:** 72.0/65.0. **Slope:** 129/113. **Architect:** Mark Fuller. **Green fee:** $40/$40. **Credit cards:** MC,VISA,AMEX,Interac. **Reduced fees:** N/A. **Caddies:** No. **Golf carts:** $25. **Discount golf packages:** Yes. **Season:** May-Nov. **High:** June-Aug. **On site lodging:** No. **Rental clubs:** Yes. **Walking policy:** Unrestricted walking. **Metal spikes allowed:** Yes. **Range:** Yes (grass/mats). **To obtain tee times:** Call 2 days in advance.
Subscriber comments: A real treat but demanding...A thoroughly enjoyable experience. Beautiful scenery,challenging target golf, lots of water.

LOMBARD GLEN GOLF CLUB
R.R. No.1, Lombardy, K0G 1L0, (613)283-5318, 5 miles SW of Smith Falls.
Opened: 1967. **Holes:** 18. **Par:** 70/70. **Yards:** 6,061/4,890. **Course rating:** 68.1/62.4. **Slope:** 113/109. **Architect:** David Moote. **Green fee:** $25/$26. **Credit cards:** MC,VISA. **Reduced fees:** Twilight. **Caddies:** No. **Golf carts:** $25. **Discount golf packages:** No. **Season:** April-Nov. **High:** July-Sept. **On site lodging:** No. **Rental clubs:** No. **Walking policy:** Unrestricted walking. **Metal spikes allowed:** Yes. **Range:** Yes (grass). **To obtain tee times:** Call up to 7 days in advance.

★★MANDERLEY ON THE GREEN
R.R. No.3, North Gower, K0A 2T0, (613)489-2066, 6 miles S of Ottawa.
Opened: 1964. **Holes:** 18. **Par:** 71/71. **Yards:** 6,414/5,668. **Course rating:** 70.0/72.0. **Slope:** 123/126. **Architect:** Howard Watson. **Green fee:** $15/$32. **Credit cards:** MC,VISA,AMEX. **Reduced fees:** Weekdays, low season, twilight. **Caddies:** No. **Golf carts:** $14. **Discount golf packages:** Yes. **Season:** April-Oct. **High:** June-Sept. **On site lodging:** No. **Rental clubs:** Yes. **Walking policy:** Unrestricted walking. **Metal spikes allowed:** Yes. **Range:** Yes (grass/mats). **To obtain tee times:** Call 2 days in advance.

MANITOUWADGE GOLF COURSE
PU-P.O. Box 3097, Manitouwadge, P0T 2C0, (807)826-4265, 250 miles E of Thunder Bay.
Opened: 1971. **Holes:** 9. **Par:** 36. **Yards:** 3,250. **Course rating:** 72.2. **Slope:** 129. **Architect:** N/A. **Green fee:** N/A. **Credit cards:** MC,VISA. **Reduced fees:** Seniors, juniors. **Caddies:** No. **Golf carts:** N/A. **Discount golf packages:** Yes. **Season:** May-Sept. **High:** July-Aug. **On site lodging:** No. **Rental clubs:** Yes. **Walking policy:** Unrestricted walking. **Metal spikes allowed:** Yes. **Range:** No. **To obtain tee times:** Not required.

★★MAPLES OF BALLANTRAE LODGE & GOLF CLUB
R-R.R. No.4, Stouffville, L4A 7X5, (905)640-6077, (800)344-5527, 30 miles NE of Toronto.
Opened: 1982. **Holes:** 18. **Par:** 72/73. **Yards:** 6,715/5,250. **Course rating:** 70.0/69.5. **Slope:** 126/116. **Architect:** R.F. Bob Moote & Assoc. **Green fee:** $30/$38. **Credit cards:** MC,VISA,AMEX. **Reduced fees:** Weekdays, low season, resort guests, twilight, seniors, juniors. **Caddies:** No. **Golf carts:** $26. **Discount golf packages:** Yes. **Season:** April-Nov. **High:** June-Aug. **On site lodging:** Yes. **Rental clubs:** Yes. **Walking policy:** Unrestricted walking. **Metal spikes allowed:** Yes. **Range:** Yes (grass). **To obtain tee times:** Call 1 day in advance for weekdays. Call Thursday at 8 a.m. for upcoming weekend or holiday.

★★½MILL RUN GOLF & COUNTRY CLUB
269 Durham Rd. #8, Uxbridge, L9P 1R1, (905)852-6212, (800)465-8633, 7 miles W of Toronto.
Opened: 1985. **Holes:** 18. **Par:** 72/72. **Yards:** 6,800/5,385. **Course rating:** 72.8/70.5. **Slope:** 131/117. **Architect:** Rene Muylaert. **Green fee:** $24/$37. **Credit cards:** MC,VISA,AMEX,Interac. **Reduced fees:** Weekdays, low season, twilight, seniors, juniors. **Caddies:** No. **Golf carts:** $25. **Discount golf packages:** Yes. **Season:** April-Oct. **High:** June-Aug. **On site lodging:** No. **Rental clubs:** Yes. **Walking policy:** Unrestricted walking. **Metal spikes allowed:** Yes. **Range:** Yes (grass). **To obtain tee times:** Call up to 5 days in advance.
Subscriber comments: High ground, great views, 10th hole simply great...A course that teases you. A wide open front nine followed by tight back nine...Terrifying in spots...A pleasant pace...Good service and food.

★★★★MONTERRA GOLF COURSE
R-R.R. No.3, Collingwood, L9Y 3Z2, (705)445-0231x407, 100 miles N of Toronto.
Opened: 1989. **Holes:** 18. **Par:** 72/72. **Yards:** 6,581/5,139. **Course rating:** 71.8/69.5. **Slope:** 129/116. **Architect:** Thomas McBroom. **Green fee:** $26/$54. **Credit cards:** MC,VISA,AMEX. **Reduced fees:** Low season, resort guests, twilight. **Caddies:** No. **Golf carts:** $15. **Discount golf packages:** Yes. **Season:** May-Nov. **High:** May-Oct. **On site lodging:** Yes. **Rental clubs:** Yes. **Walking policy:** Unrestricted walking. **Metal spikes allowed:** No. **Range:** Yes (grass/mats). **To obtain tee times:** Resort guest when confirming reservation. General public call 3 days in advance.
Subscriber comments: All around very good golf...Resort, excellent in every way...Gorgeous...Remembered every hole after first round.

★★★½NOBLETON LAKES GOLF CLUB
PU-125 Nobleton Lakes Dr., Nobelton, L0G 1N0, (905)859-4070, 20 miles NW of Toronto.
Opened: 1975. **Holes:** 18. **Par:** 72/72. **Yards:** 7,089/5,819. **Course rating:** 75.3/72.8. **Slope:** 145. **Architect:** Rene & Charlie Muylaert. **Green fee:** $63/$68. **Credit cards:** MC,VISA,AMEX. **Reduced fees:** Low season, twilight. **Caddies:** No. **Golf carts:** Included in Green Fee. **Discount golf packages:** No. **Season:** April-Nov. **High:** May-Oct. **On site lodging:** No. **Rental clubs:** Yes. **Walking policy:** Mandatory cart. **Metal spikes allowed:** Yes. **Range:** Yes (grass). **To obtain tee times:** Call 5 days in advance.
Subscriber comments: Fabulous design, tough track, great test...Long hitters track, a must play...Course knowledge is appreciated...Beautiful track through mature woods...Some blind tee shots.

★★NORTHRIDGE PUBLIC GOLF COURSE
PM-320 Balmoral Dr., Brantford, N3R 7S2, (519)753-6112, 15 miles W of Hamilton.
Opened: 1957. **Holes:** 18. **Par:** 72/74. **Yards:** 6,300/5,830. **Course rating:** 68.5/72.1. **Slope:** 110/114. **Architect:** N/A. **Green fee:** $24/$24. **Credit cards:** MC,VISA. **Reduced fees:** Twilight. **Caddies:** No. **Golf carts:** $24. **Discount golf packages:** Yes. **Season:** April-Nov. **High:** June-Sept. **On site lodging:** No. **Rental clubs:** Yes. **Walking policy:** Unrestricted walking. **Metal spikes allowed:** Yes. **Range:** Yes (grass). **To obtain tee times:** Call up to 7 days in advance.

★★★THE OAKS OF ST. GEORGE GOLF CLUB
269 German School Rd., R.R. No.1, Paris, N3L 3E1, (519)448-3673, 2 miles NW of Brantford.
Opened: 1992. **Holes:** 18. **Par:** 72/72. **Yards:** 6,328/5,628. **Course rating:** 71.1/67.9. **Slope:** 123/115. **Architect:** David Moote and R.F. Moote. **Green fee:** $30/$35. **Credit cards:** MC,VISA. **Reduced fees:** Twilight, seniors, juniors. **Caddies:** No. **Golf carts:** $26. **Discount golf packages:** Yes. **Season:** May-Oct. **High:** June-Sept. **On site lodging:** No. **Rental clubs:** Yes. **Walking policy:** Unrestricted walking. **Metal spikes allowed:** Yes. **Range:** Yes (grass/mats). **To obtain tee times:** Call.
Subscriber comments: Interesting holes...Beautiful...Real gem. Short but fair. Excellent layout...If playing for first time be warned—lots of blind shots...Challenging, with a great back nine.

OLIVER'S NEST GOLF & COUNTRY CLUB

PU-P.O. Box 75, Lindsay, K9V 4R8, Victoria County, (705)953-2093, (888)953-6378.
Opened: 1997. **Holes:** 18. **Par:** 71/72. **Yards:** 6,625/5,185. **Course rating:** 72.2/65.2.
Slope: 127/111. **Architect:** Graham Cooke. **Green fee:** $32/$40. **Credit cards:**
MC,VISA,Debit cards. **Reduced fees:** Weekdays, low season, twilight, seniors, juniors.
Caddies: No. **Golf carts:** $26. **Discount golf packages:** Yes. **Season:** April-Nov.
High: June-Aug. **On site lodging:** No. **Rental clubs:** Yes. **Walking policy:** Unrestricted
walking. **Metal spikes allowed:** No. **Range:** Yes (grass). **To obtain tee times:** Call
888-953-6378.

★★★★OSPREY VALLEY RESORT

PU-R.R. No.2, Alton, L0N 1A0, (519)927-9034, (800)833-1561, 20 miles NW of Toronto.
Opened: 1992. **Holes:** 18. **Par:** 71/71. **Yards:** 6,810/5,248. **Course rating:** 72.6/69.0.
Slope: 128/118. **Architect:** Douglas Carrick. **Green fee:** $49/$59. **Credit cards:**
MC,VISA,AMEX. **Reduced fees:** Twilight, seniors, juniors. **Caddies:** No. **Golf carts:**
$30. **Discount golf packages:** No. **Season:** April-Dec. **High:** May-Sept. **On site lodging:** No. **Rental clubs:** Yes. **Walking policy:** Unrestricted walking. **Metal spikes
allowed:** Yes. **Range:** No. **To obtain tee times:** Call with credit card to reserve.
Subscriber comments: The best links course in Ontario that no one knows
about...Gorgeous...Few amenities, but course is absolutely fabulous...Don't miss. You'll
think you're in Scotland.

★★PAKENHAM HIGHLANDS GOLF CLUB

PU-Hwy. 15 at McWatty Rd., Pakenham, K0A 2X0, (613)624-5550, 25 miles W of
Ottawa.
Opened: 1994. **Holes:** 18. **Par:** 72/72. **Yards:** 6,561/5,360. **Course rating:** 70.2/70.0.
Slope: 122/113. **Architect:** Rick Fleming. **Green fee:** $24/$28. **Credit cards:**
MC,VISA,AMEX,Interac. **Reduced fees:** Weekdays, twilight. **Caddies:** No. **Golf carts:**
$25. **Discount golf packages:** Yes. **Season:** April-Oct. **High:** June-Aug. **On site lodging:** No. **Rental clubs:** Yes. **Walking policy:** Unrestricted walking. **Metal spikes
allowed:** Yes. **Range:** Yes (grass/mats). **To obtain tee times:** Call 5 days in advance.

PENINSULA GOLF CLUB

PM-P.O. Bag TM Peninsula Rd, Marathon, P0T 2E0, (807)229-1392, 180 miles NE of
Thunder Bay.
Opened: 1948. **Holes:** 9. **Par:** 72/71. **Yards:** 6,032/5,352. **Course rating:** 68.0/69.0.
Slope: 128/111. **Architect:** N/A. **Green fee:** $12/$19. **Credit cards:** None. **Reduced
fees:** Seniors, juniors. **Caddies:** No. **Golf carts:** $12. **Discount golf packages:** No.
Season: May-Sept. **High:** N/A. **On site lodging:** No. **Rental clubs:** Yes. **Walking policy:** Unrestricted walking. **Metal spikes allowed:** Yes. **Range:** No. **To obtain tee times:**
Call in advance.
Subscriber comments: Nice place to play...Inexpensive and challenging.

★★★★PENINSULA LAKES GOLF CLUB

569 Hwy. 20 W., Fenwick, L0S 1C0, (905)892-8844.
Opened: 1980. **Holes:** 18. **Par:** 72/73. **Yards:** 6,500/5,523. **Course rating:** 72.5/71.3.
Slope: 131/121. **Architect:** Rene Muylaert. **Green fee:** $23/$45. **Credit cards:**
MC,VISA. **Reduced fees:** N/A. **Caddies:** No. **Golf carts:** $28. **Discount golf packages:** No. **Season:** April-Nov. **High:** June-Aug. **On site lodging:** No. **Rental clubs:** No.
Walking policy: Unrestricted walking. **Metal spikes allowed:** Yes. **Range:** Yes
(grass/mats). **To obtain tee times:** Call Wednesday for weekend times; 2 days in
advance for weekday times.
Subscriber comments: One the nicest between Buffalo and Toronto...Beautiful course,
new clubhouse...From old quarry...A real jewel, one of the area's best...Great use of
previously unusable land.

★★★PHEASANT RUN GOLF CLUB

18033 Con. 5 R.R. No.1, Sharon, L0G 1V0, (905)898-3917, 30 miles N of Toronto.
Opened: 1980. **Holes:** 27. **Architect:** Rene Muylaert and Charles Muylaert. **Green
fee:** $50/$60. **Credit cards:** MC,VISA,AMEX. **Reduced fees:** Weekdays, low season,
twilight, seniors, juniors. **Caddies:** No. **Golf carts:** $32. **Discount golf packages:** No.
Season: April-Nov. **High:** April-Nov. **On site lodging:** No. **Rental clubs:** Yes. **Walking

policy: Unrestricted walking. **Metal spikes allowed:** Yes. **Range:** Yes (grass/mats). **To obtain tee times:** Call up to 7 days in advance.

MIDLANDS/HIGHLANDS
Par: 73/73. **Yards:** 6,460/5,205. **Course rating:** 72.8/67.0. **Slope:** 136/127.

SOUTHERN UPLAND/HIGHLANDS
Par: 72/72. **Yards:** 6,254/5,041. **Course rating:** 71.0/65.3. **Slope:** 135/124.

SOUTHERN UPLAND/MIDLANDS
Par: 71/71. **Yards:** 6,058/4,880. **Course rating:** 70.9/65.0. **Slope:** 133/120.

Subscriber comments: Somewhat short, very scenic and narrow...Great to walk...Good golf...Highlands only one worth playing.

★★½PINE KNOT GOLF & COUNTRY CLUB
5421 Hamilton Rd., Dorchester, N0L 1G6, (519)268-3352, 7 miles E of London.
Opened: 1992. **Holes:** 18. **Par:** 71/71. **Yards:** 6,500/5,003. **Course rating:** 71.7/69.0.
Slope: 127/115. **Architect:** John Robinson. **Green fee:** $26/$32. **Credit cards:** MC,VISA,AMEX. **Reduced fees:** Low season. **Caddies:** No. **Golf carts:** $25. **Discount golf packages:** Yes. **Season:** April-Nov. **High:** June-Aug. **On site lodging:** No. **Rental clubs:** Yes. **Walking policy:** Unrestricted walking. **Metal spikes allowed:** Yes. **Range:** Yes (grass/mats). **To obtain tee times:** Call up to 7 days in advance.
Subscriber comments: Friendly people. Tricky course...Wide open, but enjoyable course...Plays easier than rating...Short par 4s...Formerly farmland.

PINES OF GEORGINA GOLF CLUB
P.O. Box 44, Hwy. 48, Pefferlaw, L0E 1N0, (705)437-1669, 50 miles NE of Toronto.
Opened: 1992. **Holes:** 18. **Par:** 70/70. **Yards:** 6,012/5,457. **Course rating:** 67.8/65.7.
Slope: 112/107. **Architect:** R.F. Bob Moote & Assoc. **Green fee:** $20/$26. **Credit cards:** MC,VISA. **Reduced fees:** Weekdays, low season, twilight. **Caddies:** No. **Golf carts:** $13. **Discount golf packages:** Yes. **Season:** April-Nov. **High:** June-Aug. **On site lodging:** No. **Rental clubs:** Yes. **Walking policy:** Unrestricted walking. **Metal spikes allowed:** Yes. **Range:** Yes (grass/mats). **To obtain tee times:** Call 7 days in advance.
Subscriber comments: What a test, back nine is as tight as it gets, a gem. Leave driver in the bag.

★★★PINESTONE RESORT & CONFERENCE CENTER
P.O. Box 809, Haliburton, K0M 1S0, (705)457-3444, (800)461-0357, 120 miles NE of Toronto.
Opened: 1976. **Holes:** 18. **Par:** 71/73. **Yards:** 6,023/5,533. **Course rating:** 69.0/70.0.
Slope: 128/130. **Architect:** J. Elstone/J. Davidson. **Green fee:** $45. **Credit cards:** MC,VISA,AMEX. **Reduced fees:** Weekdays, low season, resort guests. **Caddies:** No. **Golf carts:** $30. **Discount golf packages:** Yes. **Season:** May-Oct. **High:** July-Sept. **On site lodging:** Yes. **Rental clubs:** Yes. **Walking policy:** Unrestricted walking. **Metal spikes allowed:** Yes. **Range:** Yes (grass). **To obtain tee times:** Call 6 a.m. to 6 p.m. daily.
Subscriber comments: A reasonable resort course...Not long but tight and fair. Interesting short par 4s...Target golf, beautiful...Good midweek dinner deals.

★★★½RENFREW GOLF CLUB
P.O. Box 276, Renfrew, K7V 4A4, (613)432-7729, (888)805-3739.
Opened: 1929. **Holes:** 18. **Par:** 71/74. **Yards:** 6,440/5,650. **Course rating:** 71.1/72.7. **Slope:** 127/125. **Architect:** George Cumming.
Green fee: $27/$29. **Credit cards:** N/A. **Reduced fees:** Low season, juniors. **Caddies:** No. **Golf carts:** $25. **Discount golf packages:** No.
Season: May-Oct. **High:** June-Sept. **On site lodging:** No. **Rental clubs:** Yes. **Walking policy:** Unrestricted walking. **Metal spikes allowed:** Yes. **Range:** Yes (grass). **To obtain tee times:** N/A.
Subscriber comments: Very scenic wooded hills...Always in great condition...Mature...Links course...Nice finishing hole.

GREAT VALUE

★★★RICHMOND HILL GOLF CLUB
PU-8755 Bathurst St., Richmond Hill, L4C 0H4, (905)889-4653, 5 miles N of Toronto.
Opened: 1992. **Holes:** 18. **Par:** 70/70. **Yards:** 6,004/4,935. **Course rating:** 67.8/64.0.
Slope: 120. **Architect:** Rene Muylaert. **Green fee:** $24/$49. **Credit cards:** MC,VISA,AMEX. **Reduced fees:** Weekdays, low season, twilight, seniors. **Caddies:**

No. **Golf carts:** $29. **Discount golf packages:** Yes. **Season:** April-Nov. **High:** June-Aug. **On site lodging:** No. **Rental clubs:** Yes. **Walking policy:** Unrestricted walking. **Metal spikes allowed:** Yes. **Range:** Yes. **To obtain tee times:** Call 2 days in advance with credit card. Purchase a green fee package for 4 day advance booking. **Subscriber comments:** Wonderful layout...Still maturing. Master finishing hole...#10, #11, #18 will test your accuracy.

★★RICHVIEW GOLF & COUNTRY CLUB
2406 Bronty Rd., Oakville, L6J 4Z5, (905)827-1211.
Call club for further information.

RIVENDELL GOLF CLUB
R.R. No.1, Verona, KOH 2WO, (613)374-3404, 18 miles N of Kingston.
Opened: 1980. **Holes:** 18. **Par:** 71/71. **Yards:** 6,070/5,127. **Course rating:** 68.5/68.9. **Slope:** 116/116. **Architect:** Robert Heaslip. **Green fee:** $21/$25. **Credit cards:** MC,VISA. **Reduced fees:** Low season, resort guests, twilight. **Caddies:** No. **Golf carts:** $20. **Discount golf packages:** No. **Season:** May-Oct. **High:** April-Sept. **On site lodging:** No. **Rental clubs:** Yes. **Walking policy:** Unrestricted walking. **Metal spikes allowed:** Yes. **Range:** No. **To obtain tee times:** Call golf shop.

★★½RIVER ROAD GOLF COURSE
PM-2115 River Rd., London, N6A 4C3, (519)452-1822, 100 miles SW of Toronto.
Opened: 1992. **Holes:** 18. **Par:** 72/72. **Yards:** 6,480/5,386. **Course rating:** 72.6/70.0. **Slope:** 130/126. **Architect:** Bill Fox Sr. **Green fee:** $22/$22. **Credit cards:** MC,VISA. **Reduced fees:** Twilight. **Caddies:** No. **Golf carts:** $26. **Discount golf packages:** No. **Season:** March-Dec. **High:** June-Aug. **On site lodging:** No. **Rental clubs:** Yes. **Walking policy:** Unrestricted walking. **Metal spikes allowed:** Yes. **Range:** No. **To obtain tee times:** Call 2 days in advance.
Subscriber comments: Nicely laid out, lots of sand...Very tight, good test of golf...A very nice layout...Best greens in London.

★★★ROSELAND GOLF & CURLING CLUB
PU-455 Kennedy Dr. W., Windsor, N9G 1S8, (519)969-3810, 5 miles S of Detroit.
Opened: 1928. **Holes:** 18. **Par:** 72/74. **Yards:** 6,588/5,914. **Course rating:** 70.6/73.1. **Slope:** 119/123. **Architect:** Doanld Ross. **Green fee:** $22/$28. **Credit cards:** MC,VISA. **Reduced fees:** Weekdays, low season, twilight, seniors. **Caddies:** No. **Golf carts:** $28. **Discount golf packages:** No. **Season:** April-Oct. **High:** June-Aug. **On site lodging:** No. **Rental clubs:** Yes. **Walking policy:** Unrestricted walking. **Metal spikes allowed:** Yes. **Range:** No. **To obtain tee times:** Call Wednesday 9 a.m. for Saturday and Thursday 9 a.m. for Sunday and Monday holidays.
Subscriber comments: Very good for city-owned course...Classic layout.

★★★½ROYAL WOODBINE GOLF CLUB
195 Galaxy Blvd., Etobicoke, M9W 6R7, (416)674-4653, 1 mile W of Toronto.
Opened: 1992. **Holes:** 18. **Par:** 71/71. **Yards:** 6,446/5,102. **Course rating:** 74.1/71.2. **Slope:** 139/120. **Architect:** Michael Hurdzan. **Green fee:** $100/$100. **Credit cards:** MC,VISA,AMEX,Enroute. **Reduced fees:** Low season, twilight. **Caddies:** No. **Golf carts:** Included in Green Fee. **Discount golf packages:** No. **Season:** April-Nov. **High:** May-Sept. **On site lodging:** No. **Rental clubs:** Yes. **Walking policy:** Walking at certain times. **Metal spikes allowed:** Yes. **Range:** Yes (grass/mats). **To obtain tee times:** Call with credit card.
Notes: Infinniti Tour Ch.
Subscriber comments: Shotmaker's course. Leave the driver at home...Great staff...Tough for average player...Target golf defined, jet traffic overhead...Vary narrow and short...Great use of available land.

★★★½ST. ANDREWS VALLEY GOLF CLUB
PU-368 St. John Sideroad E., Aurora, L4G 3G8, (905)727-7888, 20 miles N of Toronto.
Opened: 1993. **Holes:** 18. **Par:** 72/72. **Yards:** 7,304/5,536. **Course rating:** 77.4/68.5. **Slope:** N/A. **Architect:** Rene Muylaert. **Green fee:** $49/$69. **Credit cards:** MC,VISA,AMEX,Diner's Club. **Reduced fees:** Weekdays, twilight. **Caddies:** No. **Golf carts:** $14. **Discount golf packages:** Yes. **Season:** April-Nov. **High:** June-Aug. **On site lodging:** No. **Rental clubs:** Yes. **Walking policy:** Unrestricted walking. **Metal spikes**

allowed: Yes. **Range:** Yes (grass/mats). **To obtain tee times:** Call up to 14 days in advance.

Subscriber comments: Well designed with subtle difficulties. Very accommodating to public...Superb, challenging, a joy, par on 18 feels like birdie...Challenging with good variety...Very long from back...Tests every club.

★★★ST. CLAIR PARKWAY GOLF COURSE
PU-Moore Rd. 6, Mooretown, N0N 1M0, (519)867-2810, 12 miles S of Sarnia.
Opened: 1971. **Holes:** 18. **Par:** 71/72. **Yards:** 6,720/5,731. **Course rating:** 70.5/71.0. **Slope:** 118/122. **Architect:** William Aimers. **Green fee:** $20/$30. **Credit cards:** MC,VISA. **Reduced fees:** Low season, twilight. **Caddies:** No. **Golf carts:** $27. **Discount golf packages:** No. **Season:** April-Nov. **High:** July-Aug. **On site lodging:** No. **Rental clubs:** Yes. **Walking policy:** Unrestricted walking. **Metal spikes allowed:** Yes. **Range:** No. **To obtain tee times:** Call up to 7 days in advance.
Subscriber comments: Extremely long, fairly easy...A real pleasure.

★★★½SAUGEEN GOLF CLUB
PU-R.R. #2, Port Elgin, N0H 2C6, (519)389-4031, 25 miles W of Owen Sound.
Opened: 1925. **Holes:** 27. **Par:** N/A. **Yards:** N/A. **Course rating:** N/A. **Slope:** N/A. **Architect:** N/A. **Green fee:** $30. **Credit cards:** N/A. **Reduced fees:** Weekdays, resort guests. **Caddies:** No. **Golf carts:** $25. **Discount golf packages:** No. **Season:** April-Oct. **High:** July-Aug. **On site lodging:** No. **Rental clubs:** Yes. **Walking policy:** Unrestricted walking. **Metal spikes allowed:** Yes. **Range:** Yes (grass). **To obtain tee times:** Call 3 days in advance after 1 p.m.
Subscriber comments: Beautiful course...New nine fantastic, now 27 holes...Have incorporated new with old...Playable for all golfers...Excellent.

★★★½SILVER LAKES GOLF & COUNTRY CLUB
21114 Yonge St., R.R. No.1, Newmarket, L3Y 4V8, (905)836-8070, 20 miles N of Toronto.
Opened: 1994. **Holes:** 18. **Par:** 72/74. **Yards:** 6,910/5,210. **Course rating:** 74.5/73.5. **Slope:** 135/121. **Architect:** David Moote. **Green fee:** $48/$58. **Credit cards:** MC,VISA,AMEX. **Reduced fees:** Weekdays, low season, twilight, seniors, juniors. **Caddies:** No. **Golf carts:** $28. **Discount golf packages:** No. **Season:** April-Nov. **High:** June-Aug. **On site lodging:** No. **Rental clubs:** Yes. **Walking policy:** Unrestricted walking. **Metal spikes allowed:** Yes. **Range:** Yes (grass/mats). **To obtain tee times:** Call 5 days in advance.
Subscriber comments: Excellent design, fairways narrow. Have to plan each shot...As close to Myrtle Beach-type course that you will get in Canada...Unique driving range (all water)...Interesting layout.

SUMMERHEIGHTS GOLF LINKS
PU-1160 S. Branch Rd., Cornwall, K6H 5R6, (613)938-8009, 70 miles S of Ottawa.
Opened: 1962. **Holes:** 27. **Architect:** Robert Heaslip. **Green fee:** $23/$26. **Credit cards:** MC,VISA,AMEX. **Reduced fees:** Low season, twilight. **Caddies:** No. **Golf carts:** $25. **Discount golf packages:** No. **Season:** May-Oct. **High:** June-Aug. **On site lodging:** No. **Rental clubs:** Yes. **Walking policy:** Unrestricted walking. **Metal spikes allowed:** Yes. **Range:** Yes (grass). **To obtain tee times:** Call 2 days in advance.
SOUTH/NORTH
Par: 72/72. **Yards:** 6,345/5,372. **Course rating:** 69.8/71.1. **Slope:** 120/123.
SOUTH/WEST
Par: 72/72. **Yards:** 6,450/5,681. **Course rating:** 70.0. **Slope:** 123.
WEST/NORTH
Par: 72/72. **Yards:** 6,236/5,301. **Course rating:** 69.5/65.5. **Slope:** 118/109.

★★½SUTTON CREEK GOLF & COUNTRY CLUB
R.R. No.2, Walker and Guesto, Essex, N8M 2X6, (519)726-6179, 10 miles S of Windsor.
Opened: 1988. **Holes:** 18. **Par:** 72/73. **Yards:** 6,856/5,286. **Course rating:** 72.5/70.5. **Slope:** 132/118. **Architect:** Robert Heaslip. **Green fee:** $20/$35. **Credit cards:** MC,VISA. **Reduced fees:** Weekdays, seniors, juniors. **Caddies:** No. **Golf carts:** $14. **Discount golf packages:** No. **Season:** April-Nov. **High:** June-Sept. **On site lodging:** No. **Rental clubs:** No. **Walking policy:** Unrestricted walking. **Metal spikes allowed:**

Yes. **Range:** Yes (grass). **To obtain tee times:** Call golf shop in advance.
Subscriber comments: Improved dramatically...Has great potential...Very good course and facilities.

★★TAM O'SHANTER GOLF COURSE

PU-2481 Birchmount Rd., Toronto, M1T 2M6, (416)392-2547.
Opened: N/A. **Holes:** 18. **Par:** 71/70. **Yards:** 6,043/4,958. **Course rating:** 68.4. **Slope:** 120. **Architect:** N/A. **Green fee:** $15/$28. **Credit cards:** MC,VISA,AMEX. **Reduced fees:** N/A. **Caddies:** No. **Golf carts:** $27. **Discount golf packages:** No. **Season:** April-Dec. **High:** N/A. **On site lodging:** No. **Rental clubs:** Yes. **Walking policy:** N/A. **Metal spikes allowed:** Yes. **Range:** No. **To obtain tee times:** Call up to 7 days in advance.

★★THAMES VALLEY GOLF COURSE

PU-850 Sunninghill Ave., London, N6H 2L9, (519)471-5750.
Opened: 1924. **Holes:** 27. **Par:** 71/75. **Yards:** 6,314/5,759. **Course rating:** 70.5/72.9. **Slope:** 122/126. **Architect:** E.V. Buchanan. **Green fee:** $22. **Credit cards:** MC,VISA. **Reduced fees:** N/A. **Caddies:** No. **Golf carts:** $26. **Discount golf packages:** No. **Season:** April-Nov. **High:** May-Sept. **On site lodging:** No. **Rental clubs:** Yes. **Walking policy:** Unrestricted walking. **Metal spikes allowed:** Yes. **Range:** No. **To obtain tee times:** Call up to 2 days in advance.

★★★½THUNDERBIRD GOLF & COUNTRY CLUB

995 Myrtle Rd. W., Ashburn, L0B 1A0, (905)686-1121, 18 miles NE of Toronto.
Opened: 1959. **Holes:** 18. **Par:** 72/72. **Yards:** 6,819/5,828. **Course rating:** 72.9/71.0. **Slope:** 127. **Architect:** Bill Ogle/Wilson Paterson. **Green fee:** $20/$45. **Credit cards:** MC,VISA,AMEX. **Reduced fees:** Weekdays, low season, twilight. **Caddies:** No. **Golf carts:** $28. **Discount golf packages:** Yes. **Season:** April-Nov. **High:** June-Aug. **On site lodging:** No. **Rental clubs:** Yes. **Walking policy:** Unrestricted walking. **Metal spikes allowed:** Yes. **Range:** Yes (grass). **To obtain tee times:** Call 7 days in advance with credit card to reserve.
Subscriber comments: Must manage your game well to score, check your ego at the door...Many hazards...Great layout...Wind often a factor, always a good test...Great old-style course...Busy on weekends...Tight fairways.

★★★½UPPER CANADA GOLF COURSE

PU-R.R. No.1, Morrisburg, K0C 1X0, (613)543-2003, (800)437-2233, 50 miles S of Ottawa.
Opened: 1966. **Holes:** 18. **Par:** 72/73. **Yards:** 6,900/6,008. **Course rating:** 71.8/74.2. **Slope:** 121/130. **Architect:** Robbie Robinson. **Green fee:** $30/$35. **Credit cards:** MC,VISA,AMEX. **Reduced fees:** Low season, twilight, seniors, juniors. **Caddies:** No. **Golf carts:** $30. **Discount golf packages:** Yes. **Season:** April-Nov. **High:** June-Aug. **On site lodging:** No. **Rental clubs:** Yes. **Walking policy:** Unrestricted walking. **Metal spikes allowed:** Yes. **Range:** Yes (grass). **To obtain tee times:** Call 3 days in advance.
Subscriber comments: Play from the back tees for the true course difficulty...Nice layout; standard clubhouse...One of the best and toughest courses in this area...Fantastic back nine...Very long course for women...Lots of geese.

★★★½WHIRLPOOL GOLF COURSE

PU-Niagara Pkwy., Niagara Falls, L2E 6T2, (905)356-1140, 25 miles N of Buffalo, NY.
Opened: 1951. **Holes:** 18. **Par:** 72/71. **Yards:** 6,994/5,929. **Course rating:** 73.5/73.0. **Slope:** 130/124. **Architect:** Stanley Thompson/David Moote. **Green fee:** $23/$36. **Credit cards:** MC,VISA,AMEX. **Reduced fees:** Low season, twilight. **Caddies:** No. **Golf carts:** $28. **Discount golf packages:** Yes. **Season:** March-Nov. **High:** June-Sept. **On site lodging:** No. **Rental clubs:** Yes. **Walking policy:** Unrestricted walking. **Metal spikes allowed:** Yes. **Range:** No. **To obtain tee times:** Call anytime in advance with credit card.
Subscriber comments: Exceptional beauty...Superior service, great food!...Rolling fairways...Great views, beside the Niagara Gorge...Great par 3s...Great mix of 3s, 4s and 5s...Fun if you ignore the tourist helicopters.

CANADA

★★½WILLO-DELL COUNTRY CLUB
10325 Willo-Dell Rd., Port Robinson, L0S 1K0, (905)295-8181, (800)790-0912.
Opened: 1964. **Holes:** 18. **Par:** 72/73. **Yards:** 6,407/5,752. **Course rating:** 70.0/71.0.
Slope: 123/144. **Architect:** Nicol Thompson. **Green fee:** $28/$35. **Credit cards:**
MC,VISA. **Reduced fees:** Low season, twilight. **Caddies:** No. **Golf carts:** $30.
Discount golf packages: Yes. **Season:** April-Oct. **High:** June-Aug. **On site lodging:**
No. **Rental clubs:** Yes. **Walking policy:** Unrestricted walking. **Metal spikes allowed:**
Yes. **Range:** Yes (grass). **To obtain tee times:** Call 7 days in advance.
Subscriber comments: Good greens, interesting front nine...Nice track, flat...All ser-
vices...Treated like a member...Good course.

PRINCE EDWARD ISLAND

★★½BELVEDERE GOLF & WINTER CLUB
P.O. Box 253, Charlottetown, C1A 1E3, (902)892-7838.
Opened: 1906. **Holes:** 18. **Par:** 72/74. **Yards:** 6,425/5,380. **Course rating:** 69.8/73.2.
Slope: 121/123. **Architect:** N/A. **Green fee:** $35/$45. **Credit cards:** MC,VISA,AMEX.
Reduced fees: Low season. **Caddies:** No. **Golf carts:** $25. **Discount golf packages:**
No. **Season:** May-Oct. **High:** June-Aug. **On site lodging:** No. **Rental clubs:** No.
Walking policy: Unrestricted walking. **Metal spikes allowed:** No. **Range:** Yes. **To
obtain tee times:** Call (902)892-7383 in summer; (902)566-5542 in winter.
Subscriber comments: Old city course...Good facilities, tee boxes good...No
denim...Fast greens...Front nine fairways open, back nine, treelined.

★★★½BRUDENELL RIVER GOLF COURSE
PU-Roseneath, C0A 1R0, (902)652-8965, (800)377-8336, 30 miles SE of
Charlottetown.
Opened: 1969. **Holes:** 18. **Par:** 72/69. **Yards:** 6,542/5,052. **Course rating:** 72.0/70.5.
Slope: 131/129. **Architect:** Robbie Robinson. **Green fee:** $33/$41. **Credit cards:**
MC,VISA,AMEX. **Reduced fees:** Low season, resort guests, twilight, seniors. **Caddies:**
Yes. **Golf carts:** $26. **Discount golf packages:** Yes. **Season:** May-Nov. **High:** June-
Sept. **On site lodging:** Yes. **Rental clubs:** Yes. **Walking policy:** Unrestricted walking.
Metal spikes allowed: Yes. **Range:** Yes (grass). **To obtain tee times:** Call or fax in
advance. Confirmation provided with credit card reference.
Notes: Canadian Tour.
Subscriber comments: Fast, readable greens, excellent facilities, tight
course...Memorable holes...Long par 5s...Nice variety, scenic vistas, beautiful
resort...Ocean views, open, Nos. 5 and 10 best.

★½GLEN AFTON GOLF CLUB
PU-Nine Mile Creek R.R. 2, Cornwall, C0A 1H0, (902)675-3000, 15 miles from
Charlottetown.
Opened: 1973. **Holes:** 18. **Par:** 70/70. **Yards:** 5,736/5,490. **Course rating:** 67.5/70.1.
Slope: 111/115. **Architect:** William Robinson. **Green fee:** $15/$21. **Credit cards:**
VISA. **Reduced fees:** Low season. **Caddies:** No. **Golf carts:** $20. **Discount golf pack-
ages:** No. **Season:** May-Nov. **High:** July-Sept. **On site lodging:** No. **Rental clubs:** Yes.
Walking policy: Unrestricted walking. **Metal spikes allowed:** Yes. **Range:** No. **To
obtain tee times:** Call golf shop.

★★★GREEN GABLES GOLF COURSE
PU-Rte. No.6, Cavendish, C0A 1N0, (902)963-2488, 25 miles NW of Charlottetown.
Opened: 1939. **Holes:** 18. **Par:** 72/74. **Yards:** 6,459/5,589. **Course rating:** 71.5/72.0.
Slope: 122/124. **Architect:** Stanley Thompson. **Green fee:** $18/$33. **Credit cards:**
MC,VISA. **Reduced fees:** Weekdays, low season, twilight. **Caddies:** No. **Golf carts:**
$26. **Discount golf packages:** No. **Season:** May-Oct. **High:** July-Aug. **On site lodg-
ing:** No. **Rental clubs:** Yes. **Walking policy:** Unrestricted walking. **Metal spikes
allowed:** Yes. **Range:** Yes (grass). **To obtain tee times:** Call.
Subscriber comments: Historical site...Magnificent ocean views...Beautiful course,
with many water holes...Play around Anne's house...Good variety of open and wooded
holes.

★★★★★THE LINKS AT CROWBUSH COVE

PU-P.O. Box 204, Morell, C0A 1S0, (902)961-73000, (800)377-8337, 20 miles E of Charlottetown.

Opened: 1993. **Holes:** 18. **Par:** 72/72. **Yards:** 6,936/5,490. **Course rating:** 75.0/68.0. **Slope:** 134/114. **Architect:** Thomas McBroom. **Green fee:** $40/$47. **Credit cards:** MC,VISA,AMEX. **Reduced fees:** Low season, resort guests, seniors. **Caddies:** No. **Golf carts:** $26. **Discount golf packages:** Yes. **Season:** May-Oct. **High:** July-Aug. **On site lodging:** No. **Rental clubs:** Yes. **Walking policy:** Unrestricted walking. **Metal spikes allowed:** Yes. **Range:** Yes (grass).

To obtain tee times: Call ten days in advance with credit card number.

Notes: Ranked 1st in 1994 Best New Canadian Courses.

Subscriber comments: Spectacular views, great condition...Pebble Beach of the Maritimes...Wind conditions change often...Excellent test for the low handicapper...Indescribable, come see for yourself!...Immaculate, spectacular, not for beginners...Target golf, use all your clubs...Risk/reward on every hole.

★★★½MILL RIVER GOLF COURSE

R-P.O. Box 13, O'Leary, C0B 1K0, (902)859-8873, (800)377-8337, 35 miles NW of Summerside.

Opened: 1971. **Holes:** 18. **Par:** 72/72. **Yards:** 6,827/5,983. **Course rating:** 75.0/70.5. **Slope:** 132/127. **Architect:** C.E. (Robbie) Robinson. **Green fee:** $28/$35. **Credit cards:** MC,VISA,AMEX. **Reduced fees:** Low season, twilight, seniors. **Caddies:** No. **Golf carts:** $26. **Discount golf packages:** Yes. **Season:** May-Oct. **High:** June-Sept. **On site lodging:** Yes. **Rental clubs:** Yes. **Walking policy:** Unrestricted walking. **Metal spikes allowed:** Yes. **Range:** Yes (grass). **To obtain tee times:** Call up to 10 days in advance.

Subscriber comments: Several rebuilt holes...Challenging and scenic...Very good design...Up and down terrain, converted farm...Treelined, along river...Par 5s excellent...Interesting mix of woods, farm, orchard.

★½RUSTICO RESORT GOLF & COUNTRY CLUB

R-R.R. No.3, South Rustico, C0A 1N0, (902)963-2357, (800)465-3734, 12 miles N of Charlottetown.

Opened: 1980. **Holes:** 18. **Par:** 73/73. **Yards:** 6,675/5,550. **Course rating:** N/A. **Slope:** N/A. **Architect:** John Langdale. **Green fee:** $15/$26. **Credit cards:** MC,VISA. **Reduced fees:** Weekdays, low season, resort guests, twilight, seniors, juniors. **Caddies:** No. **Golf carts:** $22. **Discount golf packages:** Yes. **Season:** April-Oct. **High:** July-Aug. **On site lodging:** Yes. **Rental clubs:** Yes. **Walking policy:** Unrestricted walking. **Metal spikes allowed:** Yes. **Range:** Yes (grass). **To obtain tee times:** Call golf shop.

★★★STANHOPE GOLF & COUNTRY CLUB

PU-York R.R. No.1, Stanhope, C0A 1P0, (902)672-2842, 15 miles N of Charlottetown.

Opened: 1970. **Holes:** 18. **Par:** 72/74. **Yards:** 6,439/5,785. **Course rating:** 71.0/72.0. **Slope:** 118. **Architect:** Robbie Robinson. **Green fee:** $20/$35. **Credit cards:** MC,VISA,Interac. **Reduced fees:** Weekdays, low season, resort guests. **Caddies:** Yes. **Golf carts:** $29. **Discount golf packages:** Yes. **Season:** May-Oct. **High:** July-Aug. **On site lodging:** No. **Rental clubs:** No. **Walking policy:** Unrestricted walking. **Metal spikes allowed:** Yes. **Range:** Yes (grass). **To obtain tee times:** Call anytime.

Subscriber comments: Ocean views, windy, tough back nine...Difficult greens, many water holes, long par 4s...Back nine worth it....Friendly staff.

★★★SUMMERSIDE GOLF CLUB

PU-Bayview Dr., Summerside, C1N 1A9, (902)436-2505, 30 miles SE of Charlottetown.

Opened: 1926. **Holes:** 18. **Par:** 72/72. **Yards:** 6,428/6,106. **Course rating:** N/A. **Slope:** 122/119. **Architect:** John Watson. **Green fee:** $27/$32. **Credit cards:** MC,VISA,AMEX. **Reduced fees:** Low season, twilight. **Caddies:** No. **Golf carts:** $26. **Discount golf packages:** Yes. **Season:** May-Oct. **High:** July-Aug. **On site lodging:** No. **Rental clubs:** Yes. **Walking policy:** Unrestricted walking. **Metal spikes allowed:** Yes. **Range:** Yes (grass/mats). **To obtain tee times:** Call.

Subscriber comments: Very good, grounds well kept...Nice course, easy walking...Flat parkland course, fairly wide open. Friendly service, fast greens.

QUEBEC

BAIE MISSISQUOI GOLF CLUB
PU-321 Ave. Venise W., Venise-en-Quebec, J0J 2K0, (514)244-5932, 40 miles SE of Montreal.
Opened: 1962. **Holes:** 18. **Par:** 72/73. **Yards:** 6,357/5,664. **Course rating:** N/A. **Slope:** 114/113. **Architect:** Gerry Huot. **Green fee:** $15/$29. **Credit cards:** MC,VISA. **Reduced fees:** Weekdays, low season, twilight, juniors. **Caddies:** No. **Golf carts:** $23. **Discount golf packages:** No. **Season:** April-Oct. **High:** June-Aug. **On site lodging:** Yes. **Rental clubs:** Yes. **Walking policy:** Unrestricted walking. **Metal spikes allowed:** Yes. **Range:** Yes (grass/mats). **To obtain tee times:** Call 3 days in advance.

★★½DORVAL GOLF CLUB
PU-2000 Ave. Revechon, Dorval, 89P 2S7, (514)631-6624.
Call club for further information.
Subscriber comments: Great golf course, good shape, good service...Crowded, but close to town.

GOLF LE MIRAGE GOLF CLUB
3737 Chemin Martin, Terrebonne, J6W 5C7, (514)477-4854, 15 miles NE of Montreal.
Opened: 1993. **Architect:** Graham Cooke. **Green fee:** $35/$45. **Credit cards:** MC,VISA,AMEX,A.T.M., Enroute, Diners. **Reduced fees:** Weekdays. **Caddies:** Yes. **Golf carts:** $24. **Discount golf packages:** Yes. **Season:** May-Nov. **High:** July-Aug. **On site lodging:** No. **Rental clubs:** Yes. **Walking policy:** Unrestricted walking. **Metal spikes allowed:** Yes. **Range:** Yes (grass). **To obtain tee times:** Call up to five days in advance for weekdays and two days in advance for weekends.
★★★ARIZONA COURSE
Holes: 18. **Par:** 71/72. **Yards:** 6,210/5,217. **Course rating:** 70.5/70.8. **Slope:** 129/131.
Subscriber comments: Waste bunkers galore!...Pretty good imitation of a desert course...Short but very interesting, best near Montreal.
★★★★CAROLINA COURSE
Holes: 18. **Par:** 71/71. **Yards:** 6,708/5,701. **Course rating:** 71.5/71.9. **Slope:** 125/123.
Subscriber comments: One of Montreal's best golf experiences...Closest thing to Myrtle Beach in Quebec...Longer than Arizona, good condition.

★★★GRAY ROCKS GOLF CLUB
525 Rue Principale, Mont Tremblant, J0T 1Z0, (819)425-2771x7604, (800)567-6744, 78 miles NW of Montreal.
Opened: N/A. **Holes:** 18. **Par:** 72/72. **Yards:** 6,330/5,623. **Course rating:** 70.0/72.0. **Slope:** 119/118. **Architect:** N/A. **Green fee:** $30/$42. **Credit cards:** MC,VISA,AMEX. **Reduced fees:** Weekdays, low season, resort guests, twilight. **Caddies:** Yes. **Golf carts:** $32. **Discount golf packages:** Yes. **Season:** May-Oct. **High:** July-Aug. **On site lodging:** Yes. **Rental clubs:** Yes. **Walking policy:** Unrestricted walking. **Metal spikes allowed:** Yes. **Range:** Yes (grass/mats). **To obtain tee times:** Call 7 days in advance for weekdays and 2 days in advance for weekends.
Subscriber comments: Beautiful...Nose-bleeding downhill lies!...Nice greens.

★★★½LE CHATEAU MONTEBELLO
R-392 Rue Notre Dame, Montebello, J0V 1L0, (819)423-4653, 60 miles E of Ottawa.
Opened: 1929. **Holes:** 18. **Par:** 70/72. **Yards:** 6,235/4,998. **Course rating:** 70.0/72.0. **Slope:** 129/128. **Architect:** Stanley Thompson. **Green fee:** $55/$55. **Credit cards:** MC,VISA,AMEX,DISC,Diners Club.
Reduced fees: Weekdays, low season, twilight. **Caddies:** No. **Golf carts:** Included in Green Fee. **Discount golf packages:** Yes. **Season:** May-Oct. **High:** June-Sept. **On site lodging:** Yes. **Rental clubs:** Yes. **Walking policy:** Mandatory cart. **Metal spikes allowed:** Yes. **Range:** Yes (grass/mats). **To obtain tee times:** Call 7 days in advance.
Subscriber comments: Excellent, challenging course, cut out of mountains and trees, great condition...Spectacular autumn colors...Glorious scenery, one hole tees off a cliff to a fairway some 100 feet below, sensational!...Classic design.

GREAT SERVICE

CANADA

★★★½LE CLUB DE GOLF CARLING LAKE
R-Rte. 327 N., Pine Hill, J0V 1A0, (514)476-1212, 60 miles N of
Montreal.
Opened: 1961. **Holes:** 18. **Par:** 72/72. **Yards:** 6,691/5,352. **Course
rating:** 72.0/71.0. **Slope:** 126/123. **Architect:** Howard Watson. **Green
fee:** $37/$42. **Credit cards:** MC,VISA,AMEX. **Reduced fees:**
Weekdays, low season, twilight. **Caddies:** No. **Golf carts:** $21. **Discount golf packages:** No. **Season:** May-Oct. **High:** June-Sept. **On site lodging:** Yes. **Rental clubs:**
Yes. **Walking policy:** Mandatory cart. **Metal spikes allowed:** Yes.
Range: No. **To obtain tee times:** Call with credit card number to
reserve.
Subscriber comments: Hidden jewel, very seldom busy...Must play
in fall, scenery is truly spectacular...Very hilly and deceiving...Front
short but tight, back long and open.

★★½LE GOLF CHANTECLER
PU-Box 165, Ste. Adele, J0R 1L0, (514)229-3742, 30 miles N of Montreal.
Opened: N/A. **Holes:** 18. **Par:** 70/70. **Yards:** 6,280/6,110. **Course rating:** N/A. **Slope:**
N/A. **Architect:** N/A. **Green fee:** N/A. **Credit cards:** MC,AMEX. **Reduced fees:**
Weekdays, low season. **Caddies:** No. **Golf carts:** Included in Green Fee. **Discount
golf packages:** Yes. **Season:** May-Oct. **High:** June-Sept. **On site lodging:** Yes. **Rental
clubs:** No. **Walking policy:** N/A. **Metal spikes allowed:** Yes. **Range:** No. **To obtain
tee times:** N/A.
Call club for further information.

★★★LE ROYAL BROMONT GOLF CLUB
400 Chemin Compton, Bromont, J2L 1E9, (514)534-5582, 45 miles SE of Montreal.
Opened: 1993. **Holes:** 18. **Par:** 72/72. **Yards:** 6,611/5,181. **Course rating:** 72.2/70.3.
Slope: 127/123. **Architect:** Graham Cooke. **Green fee:** $30/$50. **Credit cards:**
MC,VISA,Interac. **Reduced fees:** Twilight. **Caddies:** No. **Golf carts:** Included in Green
Fee. **Discount golf packages:** No. **Season:** April-Nov. **High:** June-Sept. **On site lodging:** No. **Rental clubs:** Yes. **Walking policy:** Unrestricted walking. **Metal spikes
allowed:** Yes. **Range:** Yes (mats). **To obtain tee times:** Call up to 3 days in advance.
Subscriber comments: Front nine in a field, back nine in woods, very nice...Pee-wee
driving range, decent track...Best condition in Quebec, best greens.

MANOIR RICHELIEU
R-19 Ran Terrebonne, P.O. Box 338, Point-au-Pic, G0T 1M0, (418)665-3925, (800)665-
8082, 90 miles from Quebec.
Opened: 1921. **Holes:** 18. **Par:** 71/72. **Yards:** 6,220/5,205. **Course rating:** 70.0/72.0.
Slope: 131/115. **Architect:** Herbert Strong. **Green fee:** $58/$58. **Credit cards:**
MC,VISA,AMEX,. **Reduced fees:** Resort guests. **Caddies:** No. **Golf carts:** Included in
Green Fee. **Discount golf packages:** Yes. **Season:** May-Oct. **High:** June-Sept. **On site
lodging:** No. **Rental clubs:** No. **Walking policy:** Mandatory cart. **Metal spikes
allowed:** Yes. **Range:** No. **To obtain tee times:** Call up to 7 days in advance.
Subscriber comments: Views...Some tricked-up holes, challenging...Hold your cap.

MONTREAL MUNICIPAL GOLF COURSE
PM-4235 Viau St., Montreal, H2A 1M1, (514)872-4653.
Opened: 1923. **Holes:** 9. **Par:** N/A. **Yards:** 1,800/1,400. **Course rating:** N/A. **Slope:**
N/A. **Architect:** Albert Murray. **Green fee:** N/A. **Credit cards:** None. **Reduced fees:**
N/A. **Caddies:** No. **Golf carts:** N/A. **Discount golf packages:** No. **Season:** April-Oct.
High: June-July. **On site lodging:** No. **Rental clubs:** Yes. **Walking policy:** N/A. **Metal
spikes allowed:** Yes. **Range:** Yes (grass). **To obtain tee times:** Call 1 day in advance.
Call club for further information.

★★★½OWL'S HEAD
R-181 Chemin Owl's Head, Mansonville, J0E 1X0, (514)292-3666, 75 miles SE of
Montreal.
Opened: 1992. **Holes:** 18. **Par:** 72/72. **Yards:** 6,705/5,295. **Course rating:** 72.0/69.0.
Slope: N/A. **Architect:** Graham Cooke. **Green fee:** $33/$40. **Credit cards:**
MC,VISA,AMEX. **Reduced fees:** Weekdays, low season, twilight. **Caddies:** No. **Golf**

carts: $13. **Discount golf packages:** Yes. **Season:** May-Oct. **High:** June-Aug. **On site lodging:** Yes. **Rental clubs:** Yes. **Walking policy:** Unrestricted walking. **Metal spikes allowed:** Yes. **Range:** Yes (grass/mats). **To obtain tee times:** Hotel guests can reserve anytime. Public may call up to 5 days in advance.

Subscriber comments: Lovely, well maintained and challenging...Lots of bunkers...Wonderful country setting...Great layout, not busy...The most scenic course in Eastern Canada...Good risk/reward holes, white granite sand, use all the clubs.

★★★★½TREMBLANT GOLF RESORT

R-3005 Chemin Principal, Mont Tremblant, J0T 1Z0, (819)681-4653, 90 miles N of Montreal.

Opened: 1995. **Holes:** 18. **Par:** 72/72. **Yards:** 6,826/5,115. **Course rating:** 73.0/69.0. **Slope:** 131/113. **Architect:** Thomas McBroom. **Green fee:** $39/$100. **Credit cards:** MC,VISA,AMEX. **Reduced fees:** Weekdays, low season, resort guests, twilight. **Caddies:** No. **Golf carts:** Included in Green Fee. **Discount golf packages:** Yes. **Season:** May-Oct. **High:** June-Sept. **On site lodging:** Yes. **Rental clubs:** Yes. **Walking policy:** Mandatory cart. **Metal spikes allowed:** Yes. **Range:** Yes (grass). **To obtain tee times:** Resort guests may book with room reservation. Public may call up to 3 days in advance.

Notes: Ranked 2nd in 1996 Best New Canadian Courses.

Subscriber comments: Beautiful holes, spectacular views...All holes different...Great mountain golf! Many forced carries from tips...Reminds one of Banff and Jasper...What a course—what a sight—what an experience!

SASKATCHEWAN

★★★COOKE MUNICIPAL GOLF COURSE

PU-900 22nd St. E., Prince Albert, S6V 1P1, (306)763-2502, 93 miles NE of Saskatoon.

Opened: 1935. **Holes:** 18. **Par:** 71/72. **Yards:** 6,319/5,719. **Course rating:** 69.4/72.6. **Slope:** 118/124. **Architect:** Hubert Cooke/Danny Jutras. **Green fee:** $15. **Credit cards:** MC,VISA,AMEX. **Reduced fees:** Low season, twilight, juniors. **Caddies:** No. **Golf carts:** $20. **Discount golf packages:** Yes. **Season:** April-Oct. **High:** June-Aug. **On site lodging:** No. **Rental clubs:** Yes. **Walking policy:** Unrestricted walking. **Metal spikes allowed:** Yes. **Range:** Yes (grass/mats). **To obtain tee times:** Call one day in advance at 8 a.m. Call Friday a.m. for Saturday and Sunday and holidays.

Subscriber comments: Lovely course, set amongst large firs, very challenging...Good bang for your buck...Traditional style...Great improvements—fun.

★★★ELMWOOD GOLF CLUB

P.O. Box 373, Swift Current, S9H 3V8, (306)773-2722, 165 miles W of Regina.

Opened: 1924. **Holes:** 18. **Par:** 71/74. **Yards:** 6,380/5,610. **Course rating:** 70.2/72.0. **Slope:** 120/119. **Architect:** William Brinkworth. **Green fee:** $13/$24. **Credit cards:** MC,VISA. **Reduced fees:** N/A. **Caddies:** No. **Golf carts:** $24. **Discount golf packages:** No. **Season:** April-Oct. **High:** May-Sept. **On site lodging:** No. **Rental clubs:** Yes. **Walking policy:** Unrestricted walking. **Metal spikes allowed:** Yes. **Range:** Yes (grass). **To obtain tee times:** Call one day in advance.

Subscriber comments: Challenging, nice layout...Best-kept secret in Saskatchewan...Excellent course, very well groomed.

★★★ESTEVAN WOODLAWN GOLF CLUB

PU-P.O. Box 203, Estevan, S4A 2A3, (306)634-2017, 120 miles SE of Regina.

Opened: 1945. **Holes:** 18. **Par:** 71/72. **Yards:** 6,320/5,409. **Course rating:** 70.0/73.0. **Slope:** 123/118. **Architect:** Les Furber. **Green fee:** $22/$22. **Credit cards:** MC,VISA. **Reduced fees:** Juniors. **Caddies:** No. **Golf carts:** $22. **Discount golf packages:** No. **Season:** May-Oct. **High:** June-Aug. **On site lodging:** No. **Rental clubs:** Yes. **Walking policy:** Unrestricted walking. **Metal spikes allowed:** Yes. **Range:** Yes (grass). **To obtain tee times:** Call 24 hours in advance.

Subscriber comments: Great condition, a bit flat...Mature condition of course for early season visit...Home course, forgiving front, water on back.

★★★MAINPRIZE REGIONAL PARK & GOLF COURSE
PU-Box 488, Midale, S0C 1S0, (306)458-2452.
Opened: 1994. **Holes:** 18. **Par:** 72/72. **Yards:** 7,022/5,672. **Course rating:** 74.7/72.2.
Slope: 128/118. **Architect:** John Robinson. **Green fee:** $14/$19. **Credit cards:**
MC,VISA. **Reduced fees:** N/A. **Caddies:** No. **Golf carts:** $21. **Discount golf packages:** No. **Season:** May-Oct. **High:** June-Aug. **On site lodging:** No. **Rental clubs:** Yes.
Walking policy: Unrestricted walking. **Metal spikes allowed:** Yes. **Range:** Yes (grass).
To obtain tee times: Call golf shop seven days in advance.
Subscriber comments: Long par 4s, excellent prairie course...Rarely see other
golfers...If the wind blows, difficult. Not a tree in sight.

★★★½NORTH BATTLEFORD GOLF & COUNTRY CLUB
P.O. Box 372, North Battleford, S9A 2Y3, (306)937-5659.
Opened: 1969. **Holes:** 18. **Par:** 72/74. **Yards:** 6,638/5,609. **Course rating:** 71.6/66.4.
Slope: 119/112. **Architect:** Ray Buffel. **Green fee:** $15/$22. **Credit cards:** MC,VISA.
Reduced fees: Twilight, seniors, juniors. **Caddies:** No. **Golf carts:** $22. **Discount golf
packages:** Yes. **Season:** April-Oct. **High:** June-Aug. **On site lodging:** No. **Rental
clubs:** Yes. **Walking policy:** Unrestricted walking. **Metal spikes allowed:** Yes. **Range:**
Yes (mats). **To obtain tee times:** Call golf shop.
Subscriber comments: Has good version of Amen Corner, very good course and
facilities...Very nice. Very tricky greens...Long course, lots of elevation changes!...Slick
greens, getting better as it matures.

★★★★WASKESIU GOLF COURSE
PU-P.O. Box 234, Waskesiu Lake, S0J 2Y0, (306)663-5302, 50 miles
N of Prince Albert.
Opened: 1936. **Holes:** 18. **Par:** 70/71. **Yards:** 6,051/5,710. **Course
rating:** 67.5/71.0. **Slope:** 111/111. **Architect:** Stanley Thompson.
Green fee: $16/$23. **Credit cards:** MC,VISA,AMEX. **Reduced fees:**
Twilight, juniors. **Caddies:** No. **Golf carts:** $22. **Discount golf packages:** No. **Season:**
May-Sept. **High:** July-Aug. **On site lodging:** No. **Rental clubs:** Yes. **Walking policy:**
Unrestricted walking. **Metal spikes allowed:** Yes. **Range:** Yes (mats). **To obtain tee
times:** Call one day in advance at 9 a.m. or when the golf shop opens.
Subscriber comments: A walker's delight...It is pristine, mature, the type of course
you want to play in your bare feet. Gorgeous!...Trees, but lots of playing
room...Challenging and beautiful. There is wildlife viewed.

(GREAT VALUE)

THE WILLOWS GOLF & COUNTRY CLUB
PU-382 Cartwright Rd., Saskatoon, S7K 3J8, (306)956-1100.
Opened: 1991. **Architect:** Bill Newis. **Green fee:** $28/$33. **Credit cards:**
MC,VISA,AMEX. **Reduced fees:** Weekdays, twilight, seniors, juniors. **Caddies:** No.
Golf carts: $12. **Discount golf packages:** No. **Season:** April-Oct. **High:** May-Aug. **On
site lodging:** No. **Rental clubs:** Yes. **Walking policy:** Unrestricted walking. **Metal
spikes allowed:** Yes. **Range:** Yes (grass/mats). **To obtain tee times:** Call or come in
three days in advance.
★★½BRIDGES/XENA COURSE
Holes: 18. **Par:** 72/72. **Yards:** 7,070/5,564. **Course rating:** 73.1/71.8. **Slope:** 130/128.
Subscriber comments: Both courses offer a links-style treat. Effective challenges and
interesting play...Very fair...Good variety of obstacles.
★★½LAKES/ISLAND COURSE
Holes: 18. **Par:** 71/71. **Yards:** 6,839/5,137. **Course rating:** 72.5/69.4. **Slope:** 125/121.
Subscriber comments: Typical prairie course, well bunkered...Huge mounds along
fairways, very enjoyable, massive clubhouse...Some tough, mostly easy.

Part III

Mexico

BAJA NORTE

★★BAJA COUNTRY CLUB
Canon San Carlos, KM. 15.25 S/N, Ensenada, B.C. Mexico, (011-52)(526)173-0303, 8 miles S of Ensenada.
Opened: 1991. **Holes:** 18. **Par:** 72/72. **Yards:** 6,834/5,203. **Course rating:** 73.1/69.5. **Slope:** 137/117. **Architect:** Enrique Valenzuela. **Green fee:** $28/$34. **Credit cards:** MC,VISA. **Reduced fees:** Weekdays. **Caddies:** No. **Golf carts:** Included in Green Fee. **Discount golf packages:** Yes. **Season:** Year-round. **High:** Jan.-Oct. **On site lodging:** No. **Rental clubs:** Yes. **Walking policy:** Mandatory cart. **Metal spikes allowed:** Yes. **Range:** Yes. **To obtain tee times:** Call anytime.

★★★½BAJAMAR OCEAN FRONT GOLF RESORT
R-KM 77.5 Carrectora Esenica Tijuana, Ensenada, (011-52)(615)501-61, (800)225-2418, 20 miles S of Ensenada.
Opened: 1975. **Holes:** 27. **Architect:** Percy Clifford/David Fleming. **Green fee:** $50/$70. **Credit cards:** MC,VISA,AMEX. **Reduced fees:** Weekdays, resort guests, twilight, seniors. **Caddies:** No. **Golf carts:** Included in Green Fee. **Discount golf packages:** Yes. **Season:** Year-round. **High:** May-Sept. **On site lodging:** Yes. **Rental clubs:** Yes. **Walking policy:** Mandatory cart. **Metal spikes allowed:** No. **Range:** Yes (grass). **To obtain tee times:** Call golf shop.

GOOD VALUE

LAGOS/VISTA
Par: 71/71. **Yards:** 6,968/4,696. **Course rating:** 74.9/66.6. **Slope:** 143/113.
OCEANO/LAGOS
Par: 71/71. **Yards:** 6,903/5,103. **Course rating:** 73.6. **Slope:** 135.
Special Notes: Phone prefix 011-52.
VISTA/OCEANO
Par: 72/72. **Yards:** 7,145/5,175. **Course rating:** 74.7. **Slope:** 138.
Subscriber comments: Ocean views that rival Pebble Beach or Hawaii...The Oceano nine is a must play...Too gimmicky...Spectacular new ocean nine with four holes right on the coast...Terrific, watch out for whales!...Fantastic.

★★★½REAL DEL MAR GOLF CLUB
R-19 1/2 KM Ensenada, Toll Rd., Tijuana, (011-52)(663)134-06, (800)803-6038, 16 miles S of San Diego, CA.
Opened: 1993. **Holes:** 18. **Par:** 72/72. **Yards:** 6,403/5,033. **Course rating:** 70.5/68.5. **Slope:** 131/119. **Architect:** Pedro Guerreca. **Green fee:** $43/$49. **Credit cards:** MC,VISA,AMEX. **Reduced fees:** Weekdays, low season, resort guests, twilight, juniors. **Caddies:** Yes. **Golf carts:** Included in Green Fee. **Discount golf packages:** No. **Season:** Year-round. **High:** June-Sept. **On site lodging:** Yes. **Rental clubs:** Yes. **Walking policy:** Walking at certain times. **Metal spikes allowed:** Yes. **Range:** Yes (grass/mats). **To obtain tee times:** Call 7 days in advance.
Subscriber comments: New course that will please once the many plantings become mature...Very pretty course, too narrow in places, can get really windy...Small landing areas...Challenging course, very inexpensive, scenic.

★★★TIJUANA COUNTRY CLUB
Blvd. Agua Caliente No. 11311, Col. Avia, Tijuana, (011-52)(668)178-55, 20 miles S of San Diego, CA.
Opened: 1927. **Holes:** 18. **Par:** 72/72. **Yards:** 6,869/5,517. **Course rating:** 73.0/72.0. **Slope:** 129/127. **Architect:** N/A. **Green fee:** $22/$27. **Credit cards:** MC,VISA. **Reduced fees:** Twilight, seniors, juniors. **Caddies:** Yes. **Golf carts:** $20. **Discount golf packages:** Yes. **Season:** Year-round. **High:** N/A. **On site lodging:** No. **Rental clubs:** Yes. **Walking policy:** Unrestricted walking. **Metal spikes allowed:** Yes. **Range:** Yes (grass). **To obtain tee times:** Call up to 30 days in advance.
Subscriber comments: Beautiful old course...Tough 213-yard par 3.

MEXICO

BAJA SUR

★★★★★CABO DEL SOL GOLF CLUB
R-KM-175 Carraterra Transpeninsular Hwy., Los Cabos, 23410, (011-52)(114)582-00, (800)386-2465, 4 miles NE of Cabo San Lucas.
Opened: 1994. **Holes:** 18. **Par:** 72/72. **Yards:** 7,037/4,696. **Course rating:** N/A. **Slope:** N/A. **Architect:** Jack Nicklaus. **Green fee:** $203. **Credit cards:** MC,VISA,AMEX. **Reduced fees:** Weekdays, low season, resort guests. **Caddies:** No. **Golf carts:** Included in Green Fee. **Discount golf packages:** Yes. **Season:** Year-round. **High:** Oct.-June. **On site lodging:** Yes. **Rental clubs:** Yes. **Walking policy:** Walking at certain times. **Metal spikes allowed:** Yes. **Range:** Yes (grass). **To obtain tee times:** Call 800 number for prepaid advance tee times. Locally call up to 7 days in advance.
Subscriber comments: The best 18th hole anywhere!...Many memorable holes. Challenging and fun...Golf heaven!...Back nine very tough...Spectacular, world class...17th from championship tee worth the green fee...Pebble Beach in Spanish...Jack, you've done it again...Many forced carries, choose tees carefully...One of the very best in the world.

★★★★CABO REAL GOLF CLUB
KM 19.5 Carraterra, Transpeninsular, San Jose Del Cabo, 23410, (011-52)(114)400-40, (800)227-1212.
Opened: N/A. **Holes:** 18. **Par:** N/A. **Yards:** N/A. **Course rating:** N/A. **Slope:** N/A. **Architect:** Robert Trent Jones Jr. **Green fee:** $110/$165. **Credit cards:** N/A. **Reduced fees:** N/A. **Caddies:** No. **Golf carts:** Included in Green Fee. **Discount golf packages:** No. **Season:** N/A. **High:** N/A. **On site lodging:** No. **Rental clubs:** No. **Walking policy:** Mandatory cart. **Metal spikes allowed:** Yes. **Range:** No. **To obtain tee times:** N/A.
Subscriber comments: Target golf, fast greens...A lot of variety, very tough course...Most reasonable of courses in area, beautiful views...Great golf course, but very pricey...Very good layout...Superb views throughout, a treat!...What ocean holes.

★★★CABO SAN LUCAS COUNTRY CLUB
Carretera Transpeninsular KM 3.6, Cabo San Lucas, 23410, (011-52)(114)346-53, (800)280-6998.
Opened: 1994. **Holes:** 18. **Par:** 72/72. **Yards:** 7,136/5,100. **Course rating:** 75.7/70.3. **Slope:** 137/122. **Architect:** Roy Dye. **Green fee:** $88/$132. **Credit cards:** MC,VISA,AMEX. **Reduced fees:** Low season. **Caddies:** No. **Golf carts:** Included in Green Fee. **Discount golf packages:** Yes. **Season:** Year-round. **High:** Nov.-May. **On site lodging:** Yes. **Rental clubs:** Yes. **Walking policy:** Mandatory cart. **Metal spikes allowed:** Yes. **Range:** Yes (grass/mats). **To obtain tee times:** Call.
Subscriber comments: Resort style course, desert views, good value for the area...Bought golf balls from children on the course and ate oranges from a fairway tree...Less interesting than other local courses.

★★½CAMPO DE GOLF SAN JOSE
PU-Paseo Finisterra #1, San Jose del Cabo, 23400, (011-52)(114)209-05, 150 miles S of La Paz.
Opened: 1988. **Holes:** 9. **Par:** 35/35. **Yards:** 3,111/2,443. **Course rating:** N/A. **Slope:** N/A. **Architect:** Mario Schjtanan/Joe Finger. **Green fee:** $40/$40. **Credit cards:** MC,VISA,AMEX. **Reduced fees:** N/A. **Caddies:** No. **Golf carts:** $40. **Discount golf packages:** No. **Season:** Year-round. **High:** Nov.-Feb. **On site lodging:** No. **Rental clubs:** Yes. **Walking policy:** Walking at certain times. **Metal spikes allowed:** Yes. **Range:** No. **To obtain tee times:** Call.
Subscriber comments: Nice quick-to-play course...Good nine-hole warm-up on way to Cabo area...The views of the Sea of Cortez was great.

★★★★½PALMILLA GOLF CLUB
Carretera Transpeninsular KM 27, San Jose del Cabo, (011-52)(114)452-50, (800)386-2465, 27 miles N of San Jose del Cabo.
Opened: 1992. **Holes:** 27. **Architect:** Jack Nicklaus. **Green fee:** $75/$180. **Credit cards:** MC,VISA,AMEX. **Reduced fees:** Weekdays, low season, resort guests. **Caddies:** No. **Golf carts:** Included in Green Fee. **Discount golf packages:** Yes. **Season:** Year-round. **High:** Oct.-May. **On site lodging:** Yes. **Rental clubs:** Yes.

Walking policy: Mandatory cart. **Metal spikes allowed:** Yes. **Range:** Yes (grass). **To obtain tee times:** Hotel Palmilla guests may call up to 1 year in advance. Public may call 7 days in advance.

ARROYO/OCEAN
Par: 72/72. **Yards:** 6,849/5,029. **Course rating:** 73.4/62.8. **Slope:** 136/106.

MOUNTAIN/ARROYO
Par: 72/72. **Yards:** 6,939/5,858. **Course rating:** 74.3/67.1. **Slope:** 144/109.

MOUNTAIN/OCEAN
Par: 72/72. **Yards:** 7,114/5,219. **Course rating:** 74.9/68.8. **Slope:** 139/109.

Subscriber comments: Magnificent!...Desert golf the way it was meant to be, splendid...All three nines are exceptional, some holes you will never forget...Desert course with ocean views...No. 8 great par 3...Get to Cabo before the tourists spoil it...Interesting holes, especially 14 and 15...Worth playing once.

COLIMA

★★★★ISLA NAVIDAD GOLF CLUB
R-Manzanillo, (011-52)(335)555-56.
Green fee: $80/$80. **Caddies:** Yes. **Golf carts:** Included in Green Fee. Call club for further information

Subscriber comments: Has anyone else played here? I go twice a year and we are the only people on this beautiful, manicured, rewarding course...Fabulous experience!...Wow! Oasis in the middle of nowhere! Gorgeous!...Some nice holes.

★★LAS HADAS RESORT
R-Manzanillo, (011-52)(333)400-00.
Opened: 1974. **Holes:** 18. **Par:** 71/71. **Yards:** 6,492/5,535. **Course rating:** 73.7/69.1.
Slope: 132/126. **Architect:** Roy Dye. **Green fee:** $40/$56. **Credit cards:**
MC,VISA,AMEX. **Reduced fees:** N/A. **Caddies:** Yes. **Golf carts:** N/A. **Discount golf packages:** Yes. **Season:** Year-round. **High:** Year-round. **On site lodging:** Yes. **Rental clubs:** Yes. **Walking policy:** Cart or caddie mandatory. **Metal spikes allowed:** Yes. **Range:** Yes (grass). **To obtain tee times:** N/A.

ESTADO DE MEXICO

RANCHO AVANDARO COUNTRY CLUB
Valle de Bravo, (011-52)(726)601-22.
Call club for further information.

GUERRERO

★★★ACAPULCO PRINCESS CLUB DE GOLF
R-A.P. 1351, Acapulco, 39300, (011-52)(746)910-00, 7 miles E of Acapulco.
Opened: 1971. **Holes:** 18. **Par:** 72/72. **Yards:** 6,355/5,400. **Course rating:** 69.4/69.6.
Slope: 117/115. **Architect:** Ted Robinson. **Green fee:** $60/$80. **Credit cards:**
MC,VISA,AMEX,Diners. **Reduced fees:** Resort guests, twilight. **Caddies:** No. **Golf carts:** Included in Green Fee. **Discount golf packages:** No. **Season:** Year-round.
High: Nov.-April. **On site lodging:** Yes. **Rental clubs:** Yes. **Walking policy:** Mandatory cart. **Metal spikes allowed:** Yes. **Range:** Yes (grass). **To obtain tee times:** Guests of hotel may call up to 2 days in advance. Non-guests call 1 day in advance.
Subscriber comments: Beautiful. Fair for all levels...Back nine more fun...Resort golf...Good course.

★★★CAMPO DE GOLF IXTAPA GOLF COURSE
PU-Blvd. Ixtapa S/N, Ixtapa, (011-52)(755)311-63, 3 miles S of Zihuantanejo.
Opened: 1975. **Holes:** 18. **Par:** 72/72. **Yards:** 6,868/5,801. **Course rating:** 70.0.
Slope: N/A. **Architect:** Robert Trent Jones Jr. **Green fee:** $50/$50. **Credit cards:**

MC,VISA,AMEX. **Reduced fees:** Twilight, seniors, juniors. **Caddies:** Yes. **Golf carts:** $25. **Discount golf packages:** No. **Season:** Year-round. **High:** Nov.-April. **On site lodging:** No. **Rental clubs:** Yes. **Walking policy:** Cart or caddie mandatory. **Metal spikes allowed:** Yes. **Range:** Yes (grass/mats). **To obtain tee times:** First come, first served.

Subscriber comments: Beautiful with jungle, gators and ocean views...Decent course.

★★★MARINA IXTAPA CLUB DE GOLF

R-Calle De La Darsena s/n Lote 8 Final de, Ixtapa, 40880, (011-52)(755)314-10, 130 miles NW of Acapulco.

Opened: 1994. **Holes:** 18. **Par:** 72/72. **Yards:** 6,800/5,197. **Course rating:** 74.1/73.2. **Slope:** 138/128. **Architect:** Robert von Hagge. **Green fee:** $65/$85. **Credit cards:** MC,VISA,AMEX. **Reduced fees:** Weekdays, low season, resort guests, twilight, seniors, juniors. **Caddies:** Yes. **Golf carts:** Included in Green Fee. **Discount golf packages:** Yes. **Season:** Year-round. **High:** Dec.-April. **On site lodging:** Yes. **Rental clubs:** Yes. **Walking policy:** Cart or caddie mandatory. **Metal spikes allowed:** Yes. **Range:** Yes (grass/mats). **To obtain tee times:** Call golf shop.

Subscriber comments: Straightforward front nine, more interesting back...Location idyllic...Water on 16 holes!...Newly developed track, some oustanding holes, especially the 18th.

★★★½PIERRE MARQUES GOLF CLUB

R-Playa Revolcadero, Acapulco, 39300, (011-52)(746)610-00, 7 miles E of Acapulco.
Opened: 1967. **Holes:** 18. **Par:** 72/73. **Yards:** 6,557/5,197. **Course rating:** 71.5/69.8. **Slope:** 127/116. **Architect:** Percy Clifford. **Green fee:** $63/$84. **Credit cards:** MC,VISA,AMEX,Diners Club. **Reduced fees:** Resort guests, twilight. **Caddies:** No. **Golf carts:** Included in Green Fee. **Discount golf packages:** No. **Season:** Year-round. **High:** Nov.-March. **On site lodging:** Yes. **Rental clubs:** Yes. **Walking policy:** Mandatory cart. **Metal spikes allowed:** Yes. **Range:** Yes (grass). **To obtain tee times:** Guests may call up to 2 days in advance. Non-guests may call up to 1 day in advance.
Subscriber comments: Very short resort course but I enjoyed it.

TRES VIDAS ACAPULCO GOLF COURSE

Carret, A Barra Vieja KM 7, Apartado Postal No. 105, Acapulco, (011-52)(746)210-10. Call club for further information.

JALISCO

EL TAMARINDO GOLF CLUB

Careyes, (011-52)(335)150-31.
Call club for further information.

★★★MARINA VALLARTA CLUB DE GOLF

Puerto Vallarta, (011-52)(322)105-45.
Opened: N/A. **Holes:** N/A. **Par:** N/A. **Yards:** N/A. **Course rating:** N/A. **Slope:** N/A. **Architect:** N/A. **Green fee:** $80/$100. **Credit cards:** N/A. **Reduced fees:** N/A. **Caddies:** Yes. **Golf carts:** Included in Green Fee. **Discount golf packages:** No. **Season:** N/A. **High:** N/A. **On site lodging:** No. **Rental clubs:** No. **Walking policy:** Mandatory cart. **Metal spikes allowed:** Yes. **Range:** Yes. **To obtain tee times:** N/A.
Subscriber comments: The place to play in Puerto Vallarta...Great caddies...Great practice facility...Lots of fun, fairly easy. Alligators in the water hazards...Nearby airport distracting...View on back nine is the best...Good fun.

MORELOS

COUNTRY CLUB COCOYOC

R-Circuito Del Hombre S/N, Cocoyoc, 62738, (011-52)(735)611-88, 65 miles S of Mexico City.
Opened: 1977. **Holes:** 18. **Par:** 72/72. **Yards:** 6,287/5,250. **Course rating:** 69.7/68.1.

Slope: 127/116. **Architect:** Mario Schjetnan. **Green fee:** $65/$65. **Credit cards:** MC,VISA,AMEX. **Reduced fees:** Weekdays, resort guests. **Caddies:** Yes. **Golf carts:** $15. **Discount golf packages:** Yes. **Season:** Year-round. **High:** N/A. **On site lodging:** Yes. **Rental clubs:** Yes. **Walking policy:** Unrestricted walking. **Metal spikes allowed:** Yes. **Range:** Yes (grass). **To obtain tee times:** N/A.

OAXACA

TANGOLUNDA GOLF COURSE

Conocido Huatulco, Huatulco, 70989, (011-91)(958)100-37, 150 miles SW of Oaxaca.
Opened: 1991. **Holes:** 18. **Par:** 72/72. **Yards:** 6,870/5,605. **Course rating:** 74.6/73.8.
Slope: 131/126. **Architect:** Mario Schjetnandantan. **Green fee:** $40/$50. **Credit cards:** MC,VISA,AMEX. **Reduced fees:** Juniors. **Caddies:** Yes. **Golf carts:** $33. **Discount golf packages:** Yes. **Season:** Year-round. **High:** Dec.-April. **On site lodging:** Yes. **Rental clubs:** Yes. **Walking policy:** N/A. **Metal spikes allowed:** Yes. **Range:** Yes (grass). **To obtain tee times:** Call.

QUINTANA ROO

★★½POK-TA-POK CLUB DE GOLF CANCUN

R-KM 7.5 Blvd. Kukulcan, Hotel Zone, Cancun, (011-52)(988)312-30, (011-52)(988)312-77.
Opened: N/A. **Holes:** 18. **Par:** 72/72. **Yards:** 6,602/5,244. **Course rating:** 71.9/71.0.
Slope: 121/120. **Architect:** Robert Trent Jones Jr. **Green fee:** $80/$100. **Credit cards:** MC,VISA,AMEX. **Reduced fees:** Low season, resort guests, twilight. **Caddies:** Yes.
Golf carts: Included in Green Fee. **Discount golf packages:** No. **Season:** Year-round.
High: Dec.-April. **On site lodging:** No. **Rental clubs:** Yes. **Walking policy:** Walking at certain times. **Metal spikes allowed:** Yes. **Range:** Yes (grass). **To obtain tee times:** Call.
Subscriber comments: Windy, interesting layout, some real nice views...Not bad for Cancun...Beautiful views: bay and Mayan ruins...Lot of fun.

SINALOA

★★★EL CID GOLF & COUNTRY CLUB

R-Mazatlan, (011-52)(691)333-33.
Opened: 1973. **Holes:** 27. **Par:** 72/72. **Yards:** 6,729/5,752. **Course rating:** 73.2/72.0.
Slope: 132/127. **Architect:** Lee Trevino. **Green fee:** $50/$50. **Credit cards:** MC,VISA,AMEX. **Reduced fees:** Resort guests. **Caddies:** Yes. **Golf carts:** N/A.
Discount golf packages: No. **Season:** Year-round. **High:** Feb.-March. **On site lodging:** No. **Rental clubs:** Yes. **Walking policy:** Walking at certain times with caddie.
Metal spikes allowed: Yes. **Range:** Yes (grass). **To obtain tee times:** N/A.
Subscriber comments: Narrow fairways. Greens difficult to read...Very demanding and long...Great old course, caddies are great.

ESTRELLA DEL MAR GOLF CLUB

Mazatlan, (011-52)(698)233-00.
Call club for further information.

MEXICO

SONORA

★★★½**MARINA SAN CARLOS CAMPO DE GOLF**
San Carlos, (011-52)(622)611-02.
Opened: 1977. **Holes:** 18. **Par:** 72/73. **Yards:** 6,542/5,072. **Course rating:** 71.0/63.9.
Slope: 118/104. **Architect:** Roy Dye. **Green fee:** $30/$40. **Credit cards:** MC,VISA.
Reduced fees: Low season, juniors. **Caddies:** No. **Golf carts:** Included in Green Fee.
Discount golf packages: Yes. **Season:** Year-round. **High:** Oct.-April. **On site lodging:**
Yes. **Rental clubs:** No. **Walking policy:** Mandatory cart. **Metal spikes allowed:** Yes.
Range: Yes (grass). **To obtain tee times:** Call golf shop.
Subscriber comments: Great course...Since the greens were redone, a super course.

Part IV

The Islands

ABACO

★★★★**TREASURE CAY GOLF CLUB**
R-Treasure Cay, (242)365-8045, (800)327-1584,
Opened: 1965. **Holes:** 18. **Par:** 72/73. **Yards:** 6,985/5,690. **Course rating:** N/A. **Slope:** N/A. **Architect:** Dick Wilson. **Green fee:** $50/$50. **Credit cards:** MC,VISA,AMEX. **Reduced fees:** Resort guests. **Caddies:** No. **Golf carts:** $25. **Discount golf packages:** Yes. **Season:** Year-round. **High:** Nov.-April. **On site lodging:** Yes. **Rental clubs:** Yes. **Walking policy:** Walking at certain times. **Metal spikes allowed:** Yes. **Range:** Yes (grass). **To obtain tee times:** Not required.
Subscriber comments: Scenic, desert-type course, windy...Generally very tight...Great quiet location.

ARUBA

★★★★**TIERRA DEL SOL COUNTRY CLUB**
R-Malmokweg 2/N, (011)(297)860-978, 10 miles N of Oranjestad.
Opened: 1995. **Holes:** 18. **Par:** 71/71. **Yards:** 6,811/5,002. **Course rating:** 74.2/70.6. **Slope:** 132/121. **Architect:** Robert Trent Jones Jr. **Green fee:** $85/$120. **Credit cards:** MC,VISA,AMEX. **Reduced fees:** Weekdays, low season, resort guests, twilight, juniors. **Caddies:** No. **Golf carts:** Included in Green Fee. **Discount golf packages:** Yes. **Season:** Year-round. **High:** Nov.-April. **On site lodging:** Yes. **Rental clubs:** Yes. **Walking policy:** Mandatory cart. **Metal spikes allowed:** Yes. **Range:** Yes (grass). **To obtain tee times:** Call or book through hotel.
Subscriber comments: Great island course...Much too windy...Five-club wind...Designed to incorporate prevailing winds...An experience in playing a desert course by the ocean...Friendly and attentive staff...A lot of fun when the wind howls...Beautiful course cut into barren terrain...Friendly and courteous...Honeymooners bring your clubs.

BARBADOS

★★★★½**ROYAL WESTMORELAND GOLF & COUNTRY CLUB**
St. James, (246)422-4653, 5 miles N of Bridgeton.
Opened: 1984. **Holes:** 18. **Par:** 72/72. **Yards:** 6,870/5,333. **Course rating:** 74.4/72.5. **Slope:** 130/124. **Architect:** Robert Trent Jones Jr. **Green fee:** $60/$170. **Credit cards:** MC,VISA,AMEX. **Reduced fees:** Low season, resort guests. **Caddies:** Yes. **Golf carts:** Included in Green Fee. **Discount golf packages:** Yes. **Season:** Year-round. **High:** Dec.-April. **On site lodging:** Yes. **Rental clubs:** Yes. **Walking policy:** Mandatory cart. **Metal spikes allowed:** No. **Range:** Yes (grass). **To obtain tee times:** Call or book through hotel.
Subscriber comments: Didn't expect to find such a nice course in the islands...Paradise...Fantastic views and design...Wow. Putts break to ocean!

★★**SANDY LANE GOLF CLUB**
R-Sandy Lane, St. James, (246)432-1311.
Opened: 1961. **Holes:** 18. **Par:** 72/72. **Yards:** 6,553/5,520. **Course rating:** 70.2/70.8. **Slope:** 122/120. **Architect:** Robertson Ward. **Green fee:** $55/$85. **Credit cards:** MC,VISA,AMEX. **Reduced fees:** Low season, resort guests, twilight. **Caddies:** Yes. **Golf carts:** N/A. **Discount golf packages:** No. **Season:** Year-round. **High:** Dec.-April. **On site lodging:** Yes. **Rental clubs:** Yes. **Walking policy:** Unrestricted walking. **Metal spikes allowed:** Yes. **Range:** Yes (grass). **To obtain tee times:** Call 48 hours in advance. Resort guests may book tee times at time of room reservation.
Subscriber comments: Good, playable course...Some nice views of Caribbean sea.

BERMUDA

★★BELMONT GOLF & COUNTRY CLUB
R-P.O. Box WK 251, Warwick, WKBX, (441)236-6400, 5 miles W of Hamilton.
Opened: 1928. **Holes:** 18. **Par:** 70/72. **Yards:** 5,800/4,900. **Course rating:** 68.6/67.7. **Slope:** 128/116. **Architect:** Deveraux Emmet. **Green fee:** $65/$65. **Credit cards:** MC,VISA,AMEX. **Reduced fees:** Resort guests, twilight, juniors. **Caddies:** No. **Golf carts:** $20. **Discount golf packages:** No. **Season:** Year-round. **High:** Oct.-May. **On site lodging:** Yes. **Rental clubs:** Yes. **Walking policy:** Walking at certain times. **Metal spikes allowed:** Yes. **Range:** Yes (mats). **To obtain tee times:** Resort Guests may call up to 60 days in advance. Others may call 2 days in advance.
Subscriber comments: Short, quirky course...Lots of scenic views...Nice resort course, not difficult but fun...Basic, not memorable...Blind holes, elevated greens. Very challenging for the average duffer...Great vacation course.

★★★½CASTLE HARBOUR GOLF CLUB
R-6 Paynters Rd., Hamilton Parish, (441)293-2040x6670, 5 miles E of Hamilton.
Opened: 1930. **Holes:** 18. **Par:** 71/71. **Yards:** 6,440/4,995. **Course rating:** 71.3/69.2. **Slope:** 128/116. **Architect:** Charles H. Banks. **Green fee:** $70/$110. **Credit cards:** MC,VISA,AMEX,Bermuda. **Reduced fees:** Low season, resort guests, twilight, juniors. **Caddies:** No. **Golf carts:** N/A. **Discount golf packages:** Yes. **Season:** Year-round. **High:** April-June/Sept.-Nov. **On site lodging:** Yes. **Rental clubs:** Yes. **Walking policy:** Mandatory cart. **Metal spikes allowed:** Yes. **Range:** No. **To obtain tee times:** Resort guests may call 30 days in advance. Others may call 2 days in advance.
Subscriber comments: Marvelous hilly test...Very hilly course, great scenery...Downhill lies to uphill greens...Outstanding scenic location...Great course...Blind holes...Stay on second floor rooms above 1st tee...Good resort golf.

THE MID OCEAN CLUB
1 Mid Ocean Club Dr., St. George's, GE 02, (441)293-0330, 7 miles E of Hamilton.
Opened: 1922. **Holes:** 18. **Par:** 71/71. **Yards:** 6,512/5,042. **Course rating:** 72.0/69.5. **Slope:** 138/121. **Architect:** Charles Blair Macdonald. **Green fee:** $140/$140. **Credit cards:** MC,VISA,AMEX. **Reduced fees:** N/A. **Caddies:** Yes. **Golf carts:** $40. **Discount golf packages:** No. **Season:** Year-round. **High:** Oct.-June. **On site lodging:** Yes. **Rental clubs:** Yes. **Walking policy:** Unrestricted walking. **Metal spikes allowed:** Yes. **Range:** Yes (grass/mats). **To obtain tee times:** Local resort guests may play Monday, Wednesday and Friday only. Book through hotel.

OCEAN VIEW GOLF COURSE
PU-2 Barkers Hill Rd, Devonshire, DV05, (441)295-9077, 3 miles E of Hamilton.
Opened: N/A. **Holes:** 9. **Par:** 35/36. **Yards:** 2,940/2,450. **Course rating:** 67.3/67.3. **Slope:** 122/119. **Architect:** N/A. **Green fee:** $32/$32. **Credit cards:** MC,VISA,AMEX. **Reduced fees:** Twilight, juniors. **Caddies:** No. **Golf carts:** $17. **Discount golf packages:** No. **Season:** Year-round. **High:** Sept.-May. **On site lodging:** No. **Rental clubs:** Yes. **Walking policy:** Walking at certain times. **Metal spikes allowed:** Yes. **Range:** Yes (mats). **To obtain tee times:** Call (441)295-6500.

★★★★PORT ROYAL GOLF COURSE
PU-Middle Rd., Southampton, SNBX, (441)234-0972.
Opened: 1970. **Holes:** 18. **Par:** 71/72. **Yards:** 6,561/5,577. **Course rating:** 72.0/72.5. **Slope:** 134/127. **Architect:** Robert Trent Jones. **Green fee:** $50/$70. **Credit cards:** MC,VISA,AMEX. **Reduced fees:** Twilight, seniors, juniors. **Caddies:** No. **Golf carts:** $50. **Discount golf packages:** Yes. **Season:** Year-round. **High:** April-Dec. **On site lodging:** No. **Rental clubs:** Yes. **Walking policy:** Walking at certain times. **Metal spikes allowed:** Yes. **Range:** Yes (grass/mats). **To obtain tee times:** Call (441)295-6500 up to 4 days in advance.
Subscriber comments: Beautiful views along the ocean...Trent Jones delight...Just as good as Mid-Ocean!...Probably the only thing not overpriced in Bermuda...Breathtaking par 3s...A few great holes...16th hole unforgettable...Playable and challenging.

THE ISLANDS

RIDDELL'S BAY GOLF & COUNTRY CLUB
Riddell's Bay Rd., Warwick, WK 236 (WK BX), (441)238-1060.
Opened: 1922. **Holes:** 18. **Par:** 70/72. **Yards:** 5,668/5,324. **Course rating:** 66.6/69.7.
Slope: 118/114. **Architect:** Devereux Emmett. **Green fee:** $60/$80. **Credit cards:**
MC,VISA,AMEX. **Reduced fees:** Weekdays. **Caddies:** No. **Golf carts:** $40. **Discount
golf packages:** Yes. **Season:** Year-round. **High:** N/A. **On site lodging:** No. **Rental
clubs:** Yes. **Walking policy:** Unrestricted walking. **Metal spikes allowed:** No. **Range:**
No. **To obtain tee times:** Must be staying at a local hotel to play. Call up to 1 day in
advance.

ST. GEORGE'S GOLF CLUB
PU-1 Park Rd., St. George's, GE03, (441)297-8353.
Opened: 1985. **Holes:** 18. **Par:** 62/62. **Yards:** 4,043/3,344. **Course rating:** 62.8/62.8.
Slope: 103/100. **Architect:** Robert Trent Jones. **Green fee:** $43/$43. **Credit cards:**
MC,VISA,AMEX. **Reduced fees:** N/A. **Caddies:** No. **Golf carts:** $17. **Discount golf
packages:** No. **Season:** Year-round. **High:** May, Nov. **On site lodging:** No. **Rental
clubs:** Yes. **Walking policy:** Walking at certain times. **Metal spikes allowed:** Yes.
Range: No. **To obtain tee times:** Call up to 30 days in advance, or fax up to 6 months
in advance.

SOUTHAMPTON PRINCESS GOLF COURSE
R-101 South Shore Rd., Southampton, SN 02, (441)239-6952.
Opened: 1971. **Holes:** 18. **Par:** 54/54. **Yards:** 2,737/2,229. **Course rating:** 53.7/53.2.
Slope: 81/77. **Architect:** Theodore G. Robinson. **Green fee:** $52/$57. **Credit cards:**
MC,VISA,AMEX. **Reduced fees:** Resort guests, twilight, juniors. **Caddies:** No. **Golf
carts:** Included in Green Fee. **Discount golf packages:** Yes. **Season:** Year-round.
High: April-Nov. **On site lodging:** Yes. **Rental clubs:** Yes. **Walking policy:** Walking at
certain times. **Metal spikes allowed:** Yes. **Range:** No. **To obtain tee times:** Call or fax
in advance.

CAYMAN ISLANDS

★★★½THE LINKS AT SAFE HAVEN
Grand Cayman, (345)949-5988.
Opened: 1994. **Holes:** 18. **Par:** 71/71. **Yards:** 6,606/4,765. **Course rating:** N/A. **Slope:**
N/A. **Architect:** Roy Case. **Green fee:** $90. **Credit cards:** MC,VISA,AMEX. **Reduced
fees:** N/A. **Caddies:** No. **Golf carts:** Included in Green Fee. **Discount golf packages:**
Yes. **Season:** Year-round. **High:** Dec.-May. **On site lodging:** No. **Rental clubs:** Yes.
Walking policy: Walking at certain times. **Metal spikes allowed:** Yes. **Range:** Yes
(grass). **To obtain tee times:** Non-members call one day in advance.
Subscriber comments: New course but could be outstanding in future. Wind is a big
factor...Neighboring construction...Several great holes, will be great course when
mature...Links, windy and plenty of sand.

DOMINICAN REPUBLIC

CASA DE CAMPO RESORT & COUNTRY CLUB
R-La Romana, (809)523-3187x3158, 45 miles NW of Santo Domingo.
Architect: Pete Dye. **Credit cards:** MC,VISA,AMEX. **Reduced fees:**
Resort guests, twilight, juniors. **Caddies:** Yes. **Golf carts:** Included in
Green Fee. **Discount golf packages:** Yes. **Season:** Year-round. **High:**
Dec.-April. **On site lodging:** Yes. **Rental clubs:** Yes. **Walking policy:**
Walking at certain times. **Metal spikes allowed:** Yes. **To obtain tee times:** Fax golf
office at (809)523-8800.
★★★½LINKS COURSE
Opened: 1976. **Holes:** 18. **Par:** 71/71. **Yards:** 6,461/4,521. **Course rating:** 70.0/65.7.
Slope: 124/113. **Green fee:** $60/$85. **Range:** Yes (grass/mats).
Subscriber comments: Nice links course...Not as spectacular as the Teeth but still a

great course...Good resort course...Great vacation course...Hard from back tees...Almost as good!

★★★★★**TEETH OF THE DOG**
Opened: 1970. **Holes:** 18. **Par:** 72/72. **Yards:** 6,888/5,571. **Course rating:** 74.1/72.9. **Slope:** 140/130. **Green fee:** $60/$125. **Range:** Yes (grass).
Subscriber comments: The best in the world...Short par 3 on ocean is beautiful...Spectacular!...This must be what Pebble Beach was like 30 years ago...Go to the juice bar, best caddies anywhere...Beautiful holes by water...Worth the trip just to hear your heart pound...Breathtaking scenery...A jewel.

(GOOD VALUE)

★★★**RADISSON PUERTO PLATA GOLF RESORT**
Playa Dorado Dr., Puerto Plata, (809)586-5360.
Call club for further information.
Subscriber comments: Nice layout. Interesting holes...Better than expected...Flat course, tough when wind blows, lots of water.

GRAND BAHAMA ISLAND

BAHAMAS PRINCESS RESORT & CASINO
R-P.O. Box F-40207, Freeport, (242)352-6721, 52 miles SE of Palm Beach, FL.
Opened: 1964. **Architect:** Dick Wilson/Joe Lee. **Green fee:** $49/$63. **Credit cards:** All major. **Reduced fees:** Resort guests, juniors. **Caddies:** No. **Golf carts:** Included in Green Fee. **Discount golf packages:** Yes. **Season:** Year-round. **High:** Nov.-April. **On site lodging:** Yes. **Rental clubs:** Yes. **Walking policy:** Mandatory cart. **Metal spikes allowed:** Yes. **Range:** Yes (grass/mats). **To obtain tee times:** Call. Tee times required Nov.-April.

★★★½**EMERALD COURSE**
Holes: 18. **Par:** 72/75. **Yards:** 6,679/5,722. **Course rating:** 72.3/73.1. **Slope:** 121/121.
Subscriber comments: Super course...Nice courses but they see a lot of use...Typical resort club...Both courses a pleasant surprise...Good for Bahamas, hilly and green...Very good, enjoyable.

★★★**RUBY COURSE**
Holes: 18. **Par:** 72/74. **Yards:** 6,750/5,622. **Course rating:** 72.4/72.4. **Slope:** 122/120.
Subscriber comments: Few memorable holes...Both courses are comparable and a challenge...Pretty course...Good resort course, small greens offer challenge.

FORTUNE HILLS GOLF & COUNTRY CLUB
R-P.O. Box 5-42619, Freeport, (242)373-4500.
Opened: 1971. **Holes:** 9. **Par:** 72/74. **Yards:** 6,916/6,164. **Course rating:** N/A. **Slope:** N/A. **Architect:** N/A. **Green fee:** $30/$30. **Credit cards:** N/A. **Reduced fees:** N/A. **Caddies:** No. **Golf carts:** $32. **Discount golf packages:** No. **Season:** N/A. **High:** N/A. **On site lodging:** No. **Rental clubs:** Yes. **Walking policy:** Walking at certain times. **Metal spikes allowed:** Yes. **Range:** Yes. **To obtain tee times:** Call.

★★★½**LUCAYA GOLF & COUNTRY CLUB**
R-P.O. Box F42500, Freeport, (242)373-1066.
Opened: 1962. **Holes:** 18. **Par:** 72/75. **Yards:** 6,824/5,978. **Course rating:** 72.1/74.5. **Slope:** 128/129. **Architect:** Dick Wilson. **Green fee:** $75/$75. **Credit cards:** MC,VISA,AMEX. **Reduced fees:** Low season, resort guests, juniors. **Caddies:** No. **Golf carts:** Included in Green Fee. **Discount golf packages:** Yes. **Season:** Year-round. **High:** Oct.-March. **On site lodging:** No. **Rental clubs:** Yes. **Walking policy:** Mandatory cart. **Metal spikes allowed:** Yes. **Range:** Yes (grass). **To obtain tee times:** Call one day in advance.
Subscriber comments: Beautiful course...A cut above...Best course on the island...Challenging test...Tough but fair, friendly folks...Nice course for Bahamas.

JAMAICA

CAYMANAS GOLF COURSE
Spanish Town, St. Catherine, (876)922-3388, 10 miles E of Kingston.
Opened: 1958. **Holes:** 18. **Par:** 72/72. **Yards:** 6,570/6,130. **Course rating:** 71.0/70.0.
Slope: 70/72. **Architect:** Howard Watson. **Green fee:** $35/$50. **Credit cards:**
MC,VISA,AMEX. **Reduced fees:** Resort guests, juniors. **Caddies:** Yes. **Golf carts:** $20.
Discount golf packages: Yes (through the Jamaica Pegasus Hotel). **Season:** Year-round. **High:** May-Sept. **On site lodging:** No. **Rental clubs:** Yes. **Walking policy:**
Unrestricted walking. **Metal spikes allowed:** Yes. **Range:** Yes (grass). **To obtain tee times:** Call.
Subscriber comments: Nice old course.

CONSTANT SPRING GOLF CLUB
Kingston, (876)924-1610.
Call club for further information.

★★★HALF MOON GOLF, TENNIS & BEACH CLUB
R-Rose Hall, Montego Bay, (876)953-2560, (800)626-0592, 7 miles W of Montego Bay.
Opened: 1961. **Holes:** 18. **Par:** 72/72. **Yards:** 7,119/5,148. **Course rating:** 73.7/68.9.
Slope: 127/115. **Architect:** Robert Trent Jones. **Green fee:** $95. **Credit cards:**
MC,VISA,AMEX. **Reduced fees:** Resort guests. **Caddies:** Yes. **Golf carts:** $30.
Discount golf packages: Yes. **Season:** Year-round. **High:** Dec.-April. **On site lodging:**
Yes. **Rental clubs:** Yes. **Walking policy:** Unrestricted walking (caddies are mandatory).
Metal spikes allowed: Yes. **Range:** Yes (grass). **To obtain tee times:** Call or come in.
Subscriber comments: Super, a pleasure to play. Great holes...Flat, windy and
nice...Not a great layout...Too much money...Very nice, great hotel...Nice mix of long
open front nine, target back nine; wonderful caddies.

★★½IRONSHORE GOLF & COUNTRY CLUB
R-P.O. Box 531, Montego Bay No.2, St. James, (876)953-2800.
Opened: 1971. **Holes:** 18. **Par:** 72/73. **Yards:** 6,600/5,400. **Course rating:** 72.0/73.0.
Slope: N/A. **Architect:** Robert Moote. **Green fee:** $34/$45. **Credit cards:**
MC,VISA,AMEX. **Reduced fees:** Low season, resort guests, juniors. **Caddies:** Yes.
Golf carts: $29. **Discount golf packages:** Yes. **Season:** Year-round. **High:** Dec.-April.
On site lodging: No. **Rental clubs:** Yes. **Walking policy:** Unrestricted walking. **Metal spikes allowed:** Yes. **Range:** Yes (grass). **To obtain tee times:** Call.
Subscriber comments: Nice course, OK to play...The people are wonderful.

★★★NEGRIL HILLS GOLF CLUB
(876)957-4638.
Call club for further information.
Subscriber comments: Beautiful course in the Jamaican mountains. Very tough...If
you have to play while you're in Jamaica, this is your best value...Excellent caddies.

★★½SANDALS GOLF & COUNTRY CLUB
Upton, Ocho Rios, (876)975-0119, (800)726-3257.
Opened: 1954. **Holes:** 18. **Par:** 71/72. **Yards:** 6,424/5,080. **Course rating:** N/A. **Slope:**
N/A. **Architect:** Howard Watson. **Green fee:** N/A. **Credit cards:** MC,VISA,AMEX.
Reduced fees: Resort guests. **Caddies:** Yes. **Golf carts:** N/A. **Discount golf packages:** Yes. **Season:** Year-round. **High:** Dec.-March. **On site lodging:** No. **Rental clubs:**
Yes. **Walking policy:** Unrestricted walking. **Metal spikes allowed:** Yes. **Range:** No. **To
obtain tee times:** Call 7 days in advance.
Subscriber comments: Excellent resort course...Golfing in paradise...Caddies very
helpful; make that essential. Ask for Herman...Great views...Not a tough track...Fun,
demanding course, small greens. Rapidly improving.

★★★½SUPER CLUBS GOLF CLUB AT RUNAWAY BAY
R-Runaway Bay P.O. Box 58, St. Ann, (876)973-2561, 15 miles W of Ocho Rios.
Opened: 1960. **Holes:** 18. **Par:** 72/72. **Yards:** 6,871/5,389. **Course rating:** 72.4/70.3.
Slope: 124/117. **Architect:** John Harris. **Green fee:** $50/$50. **Credit cards:**
MC,VISA,AMEX. **Reduced fees:** Low season, resort guests. **Caddies:** Yes. **Golf carts:**

THE ISLANDS

$25. **Discount golf packages:** Yes. **Season:** Year-round. **High:** Jan.-March. **On site lodging:** Yes. **Rental clubs:** Yes. **Walking policy:** Unrestricted walking. **Metal spikes allowed:** Yes. **Range:** Yes (grass/mats). **To obtain tee times:** First come, first served.
Subscriber comments: Good if you like wind...Played four times in one week and enjoyed each outing...Good design and great views. Excellent caddies! Ask for Cliff...Several very good and scenic holes...Course is great fun.

★★★★THE TRYALL CLUB, RESORT & VILLAS
R-Sandy Bay Main Rd., Hanover, (876)956-5681, 15 miles W of Montego Bay.
Opened: 1959. **Holes:** 18. **Par:** 71/73. **Yards:** 6,920/5,669. **Course rating:** 72.5/72.5. **Slope:** 133/122. **Architect:** Ralph Plummer. **Green fee:** $40/$125. **Credit cards:** MC,VISA,AMEX,Diners Club. **Reduced fees:** Low season, resort guests. **Caddies:** Yes. **Golf carts:** $27. **Discount golf packages:** Yes. **Season:** Year-round. **High:** Dec.-April. **On site lodging:** Yes. **Rental clubs:** Yes. **Walking policy:** Unrestricted walking. **Metal spikes allowed:** Yes. **Range:** Yes (grass). **To obtain tee times:** Call 1 day in advance.
Notes: Johnnie Walker World Championship of Golf.
Subscriber comments: Gorgeous course. Wind can be interesting...World-class golf, superb dining...Best vacation I've ever had...Great caddies...Very challenging...As good as it gets in the Caribbean.

GOOD SERVICE

★★★WYNDHAM ROSE HALL GOLF & BEACH RESORT
R-Montego Bay, (876)953-2650x89, 10 miles NE of Montego Bay.
Opened: 1973. **Holes:** 18. **Par:** 72/73. **Yards:** 6,991/5,309. **Course rating:** 71.8/73.5. **Slope:** 130/118. **Architect:** Hank Smedley. **Green fee:** $50/$60. **Credit cards:** MC,VISA,AMEX. **Reduced fees:** Low season, resort guests. **Caddies:** Yes. **Golf carts:** $33. **Discount golf packages:** Yes. **Season:** Year-round. **High:** Nov.-May. **On site lodging:** Yes. **Rental clubs:** Yes. **Walking policy:** Mandatory cart. **Metal spikes allowed:** Yes. **Range:** Yes (grass). **To obtain tee times:** Contact golf shop (ext. 89) in advance.
Subscriber comments: Lovely scenic back nine...Average...A monster: long, narrow, mountains, jungle, oceanfront. What a mix, very humbling...Nice layout, outstanding views, bring your camera...Some crazy holes in the hills.

NEVIS

★★★★FOUR SEASONS RESORT NEVIS
R-Pinney's Beach, (869)469-1111.
Opened: 1991. **Holes:** 18. **Par:** 71/71. **Yards:** 6,766/5,153. **Course rating:** 71.7/69.3. **Slope:** 125/117. **Architect:** Robert Trent Jones Jr. **Green fee:** $110/$135. **Credit cards:** All major. **Reduced fees:** Juniors. **Caddies:** No. **Golf carts:** Included in Green Fee. **Discount golf packages:** Yes. **Season:** Year-round. **High:** Dec.-April. **On site lodging:** Yes. **Rental clubs:** Yes. **Walking policy:** Mandatory cart. **Metal spikes allowed:** Yes. **Range:** Yes (grass). **To obtain tee times:** Call in advance with resort reservations or make them daily.
Subscriber comments: Unbelievable setting, golf in never-never land...Course so good I almost got divorced on my honeymoon...Gentle trade winds make tough shot selections...Breathtaking vistas...Great views, 10 uphill, hard holes. Great staff...Great views, fun holes. Very good for resort course...15th is a roller coaster.

GREAT SERVICE

NEW PROVIDENCE

★★½CABLE BEACH GOLF CLUB
R-W. Bay St., Nassau, (242)327-6000x6746, (800)432-0221.
Opened: 1929. **Holes:** 18. **Par:** 72/72. **Yards:** 7,040/6,114. **Course rating:** 72.0/72.0. **Slope:** N/A. **Architect:** Deveraux Emmet. **Green fee:** $50/$60. **Credit cards:** MC,VISA,AMEX. **Reduced fees:** Low season, resort guests, twilight, seniors, juniors. **Caddies:** No. **Golf carts:** $60. **Discount golf packages:** Yes. **Season:** Year-round.

High: Dec.-April. **On site lodging:** Yes. **Rental clubs:** Yes. **Walking policy:** Walking at certain times. **Metal spikes allowed:** Yes. **Range:** Yes (grass/mats). **To obtain tee times:** Call club.
Subscriber comments: Needs work...Better hit it straight, lots of water, true greens...Some challenging holes...Expensive for what you get...Impossible rough.

★★★PARADISE ISLAND GOLF CLUB
R-P.O. Box N-4777, Nassau, (242)363-3925.
Opened: 1961. **Holes:** 18. **Par:** 72/73. **Yards:** 6,770/6,003. **Course rating:** 71.6/71.4.
Slope: 114/124. **Architect:** Dick Wilson. **Green fee:** $55/$135. **Credit cards:**
MC,VISA,AMEX. **Reduced fees:** Weekdays, low season, resort guests, juniors.
Caddies: No. **Golf carts:** Included in Green Fee. **Discount golf packages:** Yes.
Season: Year-round. **High:** Nov.-April. **On site lodging:** Yes. **Rental clubs:** Yes.
Walking policy: Mandatory cart. **Metal spikes allowed:** Yes. **Range:** Yes (grass/mats).
To obtain tee times: Call in advance.
Subscriber comments: Courteous, scenic, well maintained...Just a beautiful course...Surprising ocean course, great views, nice test with wind blowing...Picturesque conditions, just OK for the money...Beautiful vistas...Nice par 3 along ocean.

★★SOUTH OCEAN GOLF & BEACH RESORT
R-S. Ocean Dr., Nassau, (242)362-4391x23.
Opened: 1972. **Holes:** 18. **Par:** 72/72. **Yards:** 6,707/5,908. **Course rating:** 72.5/75.0.
Slope: 128/130. **Architect:** Joe Lee. **Green fee:** $45/$45. **Credit cards:**
MC,VISA,AMEX,DISC,Diners Club. **Reduced fees:** Low season, resort guests, juniors.
Caddies: No. **Golf carts:** $25. **Discount golf packages:** Yes. **Season:** Year-round.
High: Nov.-April. **On site lodging:** Yes. **Rental clubs:** Yes. **Walking policy:** Mandatory cart. **Metal spikes allowed:** Yes. **Range:** Yes (grass). **To obtain tee times:** Call 24 hours in advance.
Subscriber comments: Great layout, outstanding potential...A little run down...Away from it all...Not difficult...Nice staff. Weak course.

PUERTO RICO

★★½BAHIA BEACH PLANTATION
PU-Rte. 187 Km. 4.2, Rio Grande, 00745, (787)256-5600, 16 miles E of San Juan.
Opened: 1991. **Holes:** 18. **Par:** 72/72. **Yards:** 6,695/5,648. **Course rating:** 71.5/72.5.
Slope: 124/124. **Architect:** J.B. Gold. **Green fee:** $30/$75. **Credit cards:**
MC,VISA,AMEX,Diners Club. **Reduced fees:** Weekdays, low season, twilight, seniors, juniors. **Caddies:** No. **Golf carts:** Included in Green Fee. **Discount golf packages:** No.
Season: Year-round. **High:** Nov.-April. **On site lodging:** No. **Rental clubs:** Yes.
Walking policy: Mandatory cart. **Metal spikes allowed:** Yes. **Range:** Yes (grass/mats).
To obtain tee times: Call 7 days in advance or reserve through e-mail
www.golfbahia.com.
Subscriber comments: Course needs water, but beautiful...Good variety...Tight fairways, a challenge...Watch out if it's windy!...Not plush but has a raw beauty...Last three holes finish along the beach, spectacular...Most difficult in Puerto Rico.

★★½BERWIND COUNTRY CLUB
Rte. 187 KM 4.7, Rio Grande, 00745, (787)876-3056, 15 miles E of San Juan.
Opened: 1962. **Holes:** 18. **Par:** 72/72. **Yards:** 7,011/5,772. **Course rating:** 72.6/72.1.
Slope: 127/123. **Architect:** Frank Murray. **Green fee:** $35/$45. **Credit cards:**
MC,VISA,AMEX. **Reduced fees:** Juniors. **Caddies:** No. **Golf carts:** Included in Green Fee. **Discount golf packages:** No. **Season:** Year-round. **High:** Oct.-April. **On site lodging:** No. **Rental clubs:** Yes. **Walking policy:** Mandatory cart. **Metal spikes allowed:** Yes. **Range:** Yes (grass/mats). **To obtain tee times:** Call. Club is open to non-members weekdays before 11:00 a.m only.
Subscriber comments: Nice private course open to public certain days...Small greens, plays long...Improving considerably.

★★★½THE GOLF CLUB AT EL CONQUISTADOR

R-Rd. 987, K.M. 3.4, Las Croabas, 00738, (787)863-6784, 31 miles E of San Juan.

Opened: 1992. **Holes:** 18. **Par:** 72/72. **Yards:** 6,662/5,131. **Course rating:** 70.6/67.2. **Slope:** 122/113. **Architect:** Arthur Hills. **Green fee:** $75/$140. **Credit cards:** All major. **Reduced fees:** Low season, twilight, juniors. **Caddies:** No. **Golf carts:** Included in Green Fee. **Discount golf packages:** Yes. **Season:** Year-round. **High:** Dec.-March. **On site lodging:** Yes. **Rental clubs:** Yes. **Walking policy:** Mandatory cart. **Metal spikes allowed:** Yes. **Range:** Yes (grass). **To obtain tee times:** Call.

Subscriber comments: Beautiful, exciting course. Great elevation changes...Constant wind makes course unfair...Beautiful scenery, too hilly...Best course in Puerto Rico. Outstanding vistas...Putting a real challenge...Too many goofy holes.

HYATT DORADO BEACH RESORT

R-Carr. 693, Dorado, 00646, (787)796-8961, 22 miles W of San Juan.

Opened: 1958. **Architect:** Robert Trent Jones. **Green fee:** $60/$100. **Credit cards:** All major. **Caddies:** No. **Golf carts:** $40. **Discount golf packages:** Yes. **Season:** Year-round. **High:** Dec.-March. **On site lodging:** Yes. **Rental clubs:** Yes. **Walking policy:** Mandatory cart. **Metal spikes allowed:** Yes. **Range:** Yes (grass). **To obtain tee times:** Resort guests call in advance. Others call day of play.

★★★★EAST COURSE

Holes: 18. **Par:** 72/74. **Yards:** 6,985/5,883. **Course rating:** 72.8/72.6. **Slope:** 127/124. **Reduced fees:** Resort guests, twilight, juniors.

Subscriber comments: Best of the four layouts at resort...Love holes 1l-18 on ocean, great course...This is the place for a golf vacation...Awesome course, best in Caribbean...A few great holes. A few average holes...Putts always break toward ocean...Marvelous tropical golf...Super course, plush, although 13th always gets me.

★★★½WEST COURSE

Holes: 18. **Par:** 72/74. **Yards:** 6,913/5,883. **Course rating:** 72.6/73.1. **Slope:** 127/125. **Reduced fees:** Weekdays, low season, resort guests, twilight, juniors.

Subscriber comments: Very nice course, love the long par-5 10th...An absolute delight...Great course, few weak holes...Considered the lesser of the two; not in my book. Very challenging layout...Good resort course...Great course, but it's not the East.

HYATT REGENCY CERROMAR BEACH

R-Rte. 693, Dorado, 00646, (787)796-8915x3213, 26 miles W of San Juan.

Opened: 1971. **Architect:** Robert Trent Jones. **Green fee:** $30/$100. **Credit cards:** MC,VISA,AMEX,DISC,Diners Club. **Reduced fees:** Weekdays, low season, resort guests, twilight, juniors. **Caddies:** No. **Golf carts:** $20. **Discount golf packages:** Yes. **Season:** Year-round. **High:** Dec.-March. **On site lodging:** Yes. **Rental clubs:** Yes. **Walking policy:** Mandatory cart. **Metal spikes allowed:** Yes. **Range:** Yes (grass). **To obtain tee times:** Resort guests may call anytime during stay. Nonguests call day of play.

★★★NORTH COURSE

Holes: 18. **Par:** 72/72. **Yards:** 6,843/5,547. **Course rating:** 72.2/71.1. **Slope:** 125/121. **Subscriber comments:** Good resort course. No. 9 a beautiful par 3...Good but not spectacular...Nice scenery...Terrific ocean views...Better than South Course.

★★★SOUTH COURSE

Holes: 18. **Par:** 72/72. **Yards:** 7,047/5,486. **Course rating:** 73.1/70.8. **Slope:** 127/120. **Subscriber comments:** Several challenging holes...Great golf...More open than Dorado courses...Tough wind.

★★★½PALMAS DEL MAR RESORT

R-175 Candelero Dr., Humacao, 00792, (787)852-6000x54, (787)725-6270, 35 miles S of San Juan.

Opened: 1974. **Holes:** 18. **Par:** 72/72. **Yards:** 6,803/5,432. **Course rating:** 72.8/71.5. **Slope:** 127/122. **Architect:** Gary Player. **Green fee:** $57/$135. **Credit cards:** MC,VISA,AMEX. **Reduced fees:** Weekdays, low season, resort guests, twilight. **Caddies:** No. **Golf carts:** Included in Green Fee. **Discount golf packages:** Yes. **Season:** Year-round. **High:** Dec.-April. **On site lodging:** Yes. **Rental clubs:** Yes. **Walking policy:** Mandatory cart. **Metal spikes allowed:** Yes. **Range:** Yes (grass). **To**

obtain tee times: Resort guests with golf package may call upon confirmation. Guests w/o package call 3 days in advance. Others call same day.
Subscriber comments: Short front nine but tricky, long back nine but beautiful...Some stunning holes...18 is a par 5, great finishing hole...Front nine and back nine are two different golf courses...Excellent resort course.

★★PUNTA BORINQUEN GOLF & COUNTRY CLUB

PU-Golf St., Ramey, Aguadilla, 00604, (787)890-2987, 25 miles NE of Mayaguez.
Opened: N/A. **Holes:** 18. **Par:** 72/71. **Yards:** 6,869/4,908. **Course rating:** 71.5/71.0.
Slope: 128/118. **Architect:** Fred Garbin. **Green fee:** $18/$20. **Credit cards:**
MC,VISA,AMEX,Debit Cards. **Reduced fees:** Weekdays, twilight. **Caddies:** No. **Golf carts:** $24. **Discount golf packages:** No. **Season:** Year-round. **High:** Sept.-Feb. **On site lodging:** No. **Rental clubs:** Yes. **Walking policy:** Walking at certain times. **Metal spikes allowed:** Yes. **Range:** Yes (grass). **To obtain tee times:** Call after 7 a.m. on Thursday for upcoming weekend.
Subscriber comments: Wide open, overlooks the ocean, amazing wind almost always...Nice ocean vistas...Basic golf.

RIO MAR COUNTRY CLUB

R-Call Box 2888, Palmer, 00721, Rio Grande County, (787)888-8811, 25 miles E of San Juan.
Opened: 1975. **Green fee:** $75/$125. **Credit cards:** MC,VISA,AMEX. **Reduced fees:**
Low season, resort guests, twilight, juniors. **Caddies:** No. **Golf carts:** Included in Green Fee. **Discount golf packages:** No. **Season:** Year-round. **High:** Dec.-May. **On site lodging:** Yes. **Rental clubs:** Yes. **Walking policy:** Mandatory cart. **Metal spikes allowed:** Yes. **Range:** Yes (grass). **To obtain tee times:** Call.
★★★½OCEAN COURSE
Holes: 18. **Par:** 72/72. **Yards:** 6,845/5,510. **Course rating:** 70.7/69.0. **Slope:** 126/124.
Architect: George Fazio/Tom Fazio.
Subscriber comments: Typical resort course, watch out for beach on 16!...Nice course on ocean...Condos everywhere; still a few nice ocean holes...New clubhouse is a wonder...My favorite on Puerto Rico.
RIVER COURSE
Holes: 18. **Par:** 72/72. **Yards:** 6,945/5,119. **Course rating:** 74.5/69.8. **Slope:** 135/120.

ST. CROIX

★★½BUCCANEER HOTEL GOLF COURSE

R-P.O. Box 218, 00820, (340)773-2100, 3 miles from Christiansted.
Opened: 1973. **Holes:** 18. **Par:** 70/70. **Yards:** 5,810/4,499. **Course rating:** 67.0/64.0.
Slope: 116/108. **Architect:** Robert Joyce. **Green fee:** $25/$50. **Credit cards:**
MC,VISA,AMEX,DISC. **Reduced fees:** Low season, resort guests. **Caddies:** No. **Golf carts:** $14. **Discount golf packages:** Yes. **Season:** Year-round. **High:** Dec.-April. **On site lodging:** Yes. **Rental clubs:** No. **Walking policy:** Unrestricted walking. **Metal spikes allowed:** Yes. **Range:** No. **To obtain tee times:** Call.
Subscriber comments: Gorgeous views, interesting holes...Lack of water makes upkeep difficult. Fun course...Super views, too bad it's so short, but fun to play...Nice and hilly...Great island vistas.

★★★½CARAMBOLA GOLF CLUB

72 Estate River, Kingshill, 00851, (340)778-5638.
Opened: 1966. **Holes:** 18. **Par:** 72/73. **Yards:** 6,843/5,424. **Course rating:** 72.7/71.0.
Slope: 131/123. **Architect:** Robert Trent Jones. **Green fee:** $35/$55. **Credit cards:**
MC,VISA,AMEX. **Reduced fees:** Low season, resort guests, twilight. **Caddies:** No.
Golf carts: Included in Green Fee. **Discount golf packages:** No. **Season:** Year-round.
High: Dec.-April. **On site lodging:** Yes. **Rental clubs:** Yes. **Walking policy:** Mandatory cart. **Metal spikes allowed:** Yes. **Range:** Yes (grass). **To obtain tee times:** Resort guests by mail or phone up to 30 days in advance. Nonguests call 24 hours in advance.
Subscriber comments: Hilly terrain, breezy...Great island course. Pleasantly surprising...Good restaurant and bar...Excellent resort, secluded part of island...Beautiful, tough, need to play several times to understand it.

THE ISLANDS

ST. KITTS

★★½ROYAL ST. KITTS GOLF CLUB
PU-P.O. Box 315, Frigate Bay, (869)465-8339, 2 miles N of Basseterre.
Opened: 1976. **Holes:** 18. **Par:** 72/72. **Yards:** 6,918/5,349. **Course rating:** 73.0/69.0.
Slope: 125. **Architect:** Harris/Thompson/Wolveridge/Fream. **Green fee:** $31/$35.
Credit cards: All major. **Reduced fees:** Resort guests, seniors, juniors. **Caddies:** No.
Golf carts: $40. **Discount golf packages:** Yes. **Season:** Year-round. **High:** Dec-May.
On site lodging: No. **Rental clubs:** Yes. **Walking policy:** Mandatory cart. **Metal
spikes allowed:** Yes. **Range:** Yes (grass). **To obtain tee times:** Call.
Subscriber comments: Beautiful area, fun course...Constant breeze off the Atlantic
makes this a challenge...Basic golf...Flat, dry and firm. Not a bad course though...Very
enjoyable...Some tough holes. Very windy...Favorite course in the islands.

ST. MAARTEN

★★MULLET BAY GOLF CLUB
P.O. Box 309, Phillipsburg, (011)(599)552-801 1, 10 miles from Phillipsburg.
Opened: 1971. **Holes:** 18. **Par:** 70/71. **Yards:** 6,300/5,700. **Course rating:** 69.0/68.0.
Slope: 115/111. **Architect:** Joe Lee. **Green fee:** $65/$125. **Credit cards:**
MC,VISA,AMEX. **Reduced fees:** Resort guests. **Caddies:** No. **Golf carts:** Included in
Green Fee. **Discount golf packages:** Yes. **Season:** Year-round. **High:** Nov.-May. **On
site lodging:** Yes. **Rental clubs:** Yes. **Walking policy:** Mandatory cart. **Metal spikes
allowed:** Yes. **Range:** Yes (grass). **To obtain tee times:** Call golf professional.
Subscriber comments: First hole by water is fun...Only island course, beautiful...Great
location. Absolutely beautiful...Plenty of water and wind...Just a fair Caribbean
course...A fun course...Some very nice, scenic golf holes.

ST. THOMAS

★★½MAHOGANY RUN GOLF COURSE
PU-No.1 Mahogany Run Rd. N., 00801, (340)777-6006, (800)253-7103.
Opened: 1980. **Holes:** 18. **Par:** 70/70. **Yards:** 6,022/4,873. **Course rating:** 70.1/72.6.
Slope: 123/111. **Architect:** George Fazio/Tom Fazio. **Green fee:** $85. **Credit cards:** All
major. **Reduced fees:** Low season, twilight. **Caddies:** No. **Golf carts:** $15. **Discount
golf packages:** Yes. **Season:** Year-round. **High:** Oct.-April. **On site lodging:** No.
Rental clubs: Yes. **Walking policy:** Mandatory cart. **Metal spikes allowed:** Yes.
Range: Yes (grass/mats). **To obtain tee times:** Call up to 3 days in advance with golf
package. Others call 2 days in advance.
Subscriber comments: Three good holes...Devil's Triangle is memorable...Love teeing
off next to iguanas...Fun course, up and down, scenic and spectacular...Needs
water...Great ocean holes...Tight, short, condition improving...Some breathtaking holes.

TOBAGO

MOUNT IRVING BAY GOLF CLUB
Scarborough, (868)539-8871.
Call club for further information.

TURKS & CAICOS

★★★½PROVO GOLF CLUB

R-Grace Bay Rd., Providenciales, (649)946-5991.
Opened: 1992. **Holes:** 18. **Par:** 72/72. **Yards:** 6,560/4,979. **Course rating:** 71.2/68.5. **Slope:** 124/116. **Architect:** Karl Litten. **Green fee:** $70/$95. **Credit cards:** MC,VISA,AMEX. **Reduced fees:** Resort guests. **Caddies:** No. **Golf carts:** Included in Green Fee. **Discount golf packages:** Yes. **Season:** Year-round. **High:** Dec.-April. **On site lodging:** No. **Rental clubs:** Yes. **Walking policy:** Mandatory cart. **Metal spikes allowed:** Yes. **Range:** Yes (grass/mats). **To obtain tee times:** Call.
Subscriber comments: Remarkably good course, not crowded, interesting holes...A very windy island...Excellent Caribbean resort course; wind always in play; bring lots of balls...Hidden jem...Nice layout, need wind for challenge, only course on island.

Geographical Directory
by Town/City

A

Abbottstown, Pa., The Bridges Golf Club, *734*
Aberdeen, N.C., Legacy Golf Links, *642*
Aberdeen, S.Dak.
Lee Park Golf Course, *809*
Moccasin Creek Country Club, *810*
Abilene, Texas, Maxwell Golf Club, *848*
Abrams, Wis., Sandalwood Country Club, *960*
Absecon, N.J., Marriott's Seaview Resort, *577*
Acapulco, Guerrero
Acapulco Princess Club de Golf, *1028*
Pierre Marques Golf Club, *1029*
Tres Vidas Acapulco Golf Course, *1029*
Accord, N.Y., Rondout Country Club, *616*
Acme, Mich., Grand Traverse Resort, *439*
Acton, Ontario, Blue Springs Golf Club, *1004*
Acworth, Ga.
Centennial Golf Club, *242*
Cobblestone Golf Course, *245*
Adams, Minn., Cedar River Country Club, *495*
Addison, Ill., Oak Meadows Golf Club, *308*
Adel, Iowa, River Valley Golf Course, *356*
Adrian, Mich.
Center View Golf Course, *423*
Woodlawn Golf Club, *491*
Advance, N.C., Oak Valley Golf Club, *648*
Afton, N.Y., Afton Golf Club, *590*
Afton, Okla., Shangri-La Golf Resort, *717*
Aguadilla, Puerto Rico, Punta Borinquen Golf & Country Club, *1042*
Aiea (Oahu), Hawaii, Pearl Country Club, *269*
Aiken, S.C.
Cedar Creek Golf Club, *778*
Highland Park Country Club, *786*
Midland Valley Country Club, *792*
Akron, N.Y.
Dande Farms Country Club, *600*
Rothland Golf Course, *617*
Akron, Ohio
J.E. Good Park Golf Club, *683*
Turkeyfoot Lake Golf Links, *704*
Alachua, Fla., Heritage Links Country Club at Turkey Creek, *198*
Alameda, Calif., Chuck Corica Golf Complex, *83*
Alamosa, Colo., Cattails Golf Club, *143*
Albany, Minn., Albany Golf Course, *492*
Albany, N.Y., The New Course at Albany, *613*

Albany, Oreg., The Golf Club of Oregon, *722*
Albert Lea, Minn., Green Lea Golf Course, *501*
Albion, Mich., Tomac Woods Golf Course, *483*
Albion, N.Y., Ricci Meadows Golf Course, *616*
Albuquerque, N.Mex.
Arroyo del Oso Municipal Golf Course, *585*
Ladera Golf Course, *585*
Los Altos Golf Course, *586*
Paradise Hills Golf Club, *587*
University of New Mexico Golf Course, *589*
Aledo, Ill., Hawthorn Ridge Golf Club, *295*
Alexandria, Ky., A.J. Jolly Golf Course, *366*
Alexandria, Minn., Alexandria Golf Club, *492*
Alexandria, Ohio, St. Albans Golf Club, *697*
Algonquin, Ill., Golf Club of Illinois, *294*
Alhambra, Calif., Alhambra Municipal Golf Course, *75*
Alice, Texas, Alice Municipal Golf Course, *826*
Allegan, Mich., Cheshire Hills Golf Course, *424*
Allen, Texas, Twin Creeks Golf Club, *864*
Allendale, Mich., The Meadows Golf Club, *458*
Allentown, Pa., Allentown Municipal Golf Course, *732*
Alliance, Nebr., Skyview Golf Course, *549*
Alliance, Ohio, Tannenhauf Golf Club, *703*
Allison Park, Pa., North Park Golf Course, *755*
Alloway, N.J., Holly Hills Golf Club, *575*
Allyn, Wash., Lakeland Village Golf Course, *915*
Aloha, Oreg., The Reserve Vineyards & Golf Club, *727*
Alpena, Mich., Alpena Golf Club, *413*
Alpharetta, Ga.
The Champions Club of Atlanta, *243*
Crooked Creek Golf Club, *245*
Riverpines Golf Club, *257*
White Columns Golf Club, *261*
Alpine, Ala., Alpine Bay Golf & Country Club, *26*
Alto, Mich.
Saskatoon Golf Club, *475*
Tyler Creek Recreation Area, *485*
Alton, Ill., Spencer T. Olin Community Golf Course, *320*

Alton, Ontario, Osprey Valley Resort, *1013*

Altoona, Iowa, Terrace Hills Golf Course, *357*

Altoona, Pa.
Park Hills Country Club, *756*
Sinking Valley Country Club, *762*

Amana, Iowa, Amana Colonies Golf Course, *348*

Amarillo, Texas
Comanche Trail Golf Club, *833*
Ross Rogers Golf Club, *857*
Southwest Golf Center, *860*

Ambier, Pa., Horsham Valley Golf Club, *748*

Ambler, Pa., Limekiln Golf Club, *749*

Amelia Island, Fla.
Amelia Island Plantation, *172*
The Golf Club at Amelia Island, *194*

Amenia, N.Y., Segalla Country Club, *618*

American Fork, Utah, Tri-City Golf Course, *876*

Americus, Ga., Brickyard Plantation Golf Club, *241*

Ames, Iowa, Veenker Memorial Golf Course, *358*

Amherst, Mass., Hickory Ridge Country Club, *403*

Amherst, N.H.
Amherst Country Club, *560*
Souhegan Woods Golf Club, *566*

Amherst, Nova Scotia, Amherst Golf Club, *1001*

Amherst, N.Y., Grover Cleveland Golf Course, *606*

Amsterdam, N.Y., City of Amsterdam Municipal Golf Course, *598*

Anaconda, Mont., Fairmont Hot Springs Resort, *541*

Anacortes, Wash., Similk Beach Golf Course, *921*

Anaheim, Calif.
Anaheim Hills Golf Course, *75*
Dad Miller Golf Course, *85*

Anahuac, Texas, Chambers County Golf Course, *831*

Anchorage, Alaska
Anchorage Golf Course, *41*
Eagleglen Golf Course, *41*

Anchorage, Ky., Long Run Golf Club, *372*

Anderson, S.C., Cobb's Glen Country Club, *779*

Andover, Kans., Terradyne Resort Hotel & Country Club, *364*

Andrews, Ind., Etna Acres Golf Course, *331*

Andrews, Texas, Andrews County Golf Course, *826*

Angel Fire, N.Mex., Angel Fire Country Club, *585*

Angels Camp, Calif., Greenhorn Creek Golf Club, *93*

Angola, Ind.
Lake James Golf Club, *336*
Zollner Golf Course, *347*

Ankeny, Iowa
Briarwood Golf Course, *349*
Otter Creek Golf Club, *354*

Ann Arbor, Mich.
Huron Hills Golf Course, *447*
Leslie Park Golf Course, *453*
Stonebridge Golf Club, *478*

Annadale, Minn., Albion Ridges Golf Course, *492*

Anoka, Minn.
Greenhaven Country Club, *501*
Rum River Hills Golf Club, *515*

Anthony, N.Mex., Dos Lagos Golf Club, *585*

Antigo, Wis., Antigo Bass Lake Country Club, *933*

Antigonish, Nova Scotia, Antigonish Golf & Country Club, *1001*

Antioch, Ill., Antioch Golf Club, *280*

Apache Junction, Ariz., Apache Creek Golf Club, *43*

Apalachin, N.Y.
Apalachin Golf Course, *590*
The Links at Hiawatha Landing, *610*

Apollo Beach, Fla., Apollo Beach Golf & Sea Club, *172*

Apollo, Pa., Cherry Wood Golf Course, *737*

Apple Valley, Minn., Valleywood Golf Course, *519*

Appleton, Wis.
Chaska Golf Course, *937*
Reid Golf Course, *958*

Aptos, Calif., Aptos Seascape Golf Course, *76*

Arab, Ala., Twin Lakes Golf Course, *40*

Arbor Vitae, Wisc., Trout Lake Golf & Country Club, *965*

Arcadia, Calif., Santa Ana Golf Course, *126*

Arcadia, Fla., Sunnybreeze Golf Course, *230*

Ardmore, Okla.
Lake Murray Resort Golf, *714*
Lakeview Golf Course, *714*

Arlington, Texas
Chester W. Ditto Golf Club, *832*
Lake Arlington Golf Course, *845*

Arlington, Wash., Gleneagles Golf Course, *911*

Arnold, Md., Bay Hills Golf Club, *386*

Arnolds Park, Iowa, Emerald Hills Golf Club, *351*

Arundel, Maine, Dutch Elm Golf Club, *381*

Arvada, Colo.
Indian Tree Golf Club, *149*
Lake Arbor Golf Course, *150*
West Woods Golf Club, *158*

Arvin, Calif., Sycamore Canyon Golf Club, *133*

Ashburn, Ontario, Thunderbird Golf & Country Club, *1017*

Asheville, N.C.
Buncombe County Municipal Golf Club, *630*

Great Smokies Resort Golf Club, *639*
The Grove Park Inn Resort, *640*
Ashland, Nebr.
Ashland Country Club, *544*
Quarry Oaks Golf Club, *548*
Ashland, N.H., White Mountain Country Club, *567*
Ashland, Pa., Rolling Meadows Golf Club, *761*
Ashtabula, Ohio, Chapel Hills Golf Course, *671*
Ashville, Ohio, Cooks Creek Golf Club, *672*
Aspen, Colo., Aspen Golf Course, *140*
Atascadero, Calif., Chalk Mountain Golf Club, *82*
Atglen, Pa., Moccasin Run Golf Course, *752*
Athens, Ala., Chriswood Golf Course, *27*
Athens, Ga., University of Georgia Golf Club, *260*
Athens, Texas, Echo Creek Country Club., *836*
Atlanta, Ga.
Bobby Jones Golf Club, *241*
Browns Mill Golf Course, *241*
Lakeside Country Club, *251*
North Fulton Golf Course, *254*
Atlanta, Mich., Elk Ridge Golf Club, *430*
Atlantis, Fla., Atlantis Country Club & Inn, *173*
Attica, Ind., Harrison Hills Golf & Country Club, *334*
Atwater, Calif., Rancho del Ray Golf Club, *118*
Atwater, Ohio, Oak Grove Golf Course, *689*
Au Gres, Mich., Huron Breeze Golf & Country Club, *447*
Auburn, Ala.
Auburn Links at Mill Creek, *26*
Indian Pines Golf Club, *32*
Auburn, Ill., Edgewood Golf Course, *290*
Auburn, Maine, Prospect Hill Golf Course, *383*
Auburn, N.Y., Auburn Golf & Country Club, *591*
Auburn, Wash., Auburn Golf Course, *906*
Audubon, Pa., General Washington Golf Course, *745*
Augusta, Ga.
Forest Hills Golf Club, *246*
Goshen Plantation Country Club, *248*
Augusta, Mich.
Gull Lake View Golf Club, *442*
Stonehedge Golf Course, *479*
Aumsville, Oreg., Santiam Golf Club, *729*
Aurora, Colo.
Aurora Hills Golf Course, *141*
John F. Kennedy Golf Club, *149*
Meadow Hills Golf Course, *151*
Aurora, Ill.
Fox Valley Golf Club, *292*
Orchard Valley Golf Club, *310*
Phillips Park Golf Course, *311*

Aurora, Mo., Honey Creek Golf Club, *532*
Aurora, Ontario, St. Andrews Valley Golf Club, *1015*
Aurora, Oreg., Langdon Farms Golf Club, *724*
Austin, Minn., Ramsey Golf Club, *513*
Austin, Texas
Barton Creek Resort & Country Club, *826*
Bluebonnet Hill Golf Club, *829*
The Cedars on Bergstrom, *831*
Circle Golf Club, *832*
Jimmy Clay Golf Course, *844*
Lakeway Resort, *846*
Lions Municipal Golf Course, *847*
Morris Williams Golf Club, *849*
River Place Golf Club, *855*
Riverside Golf Course, *856*
Roy Kizer Golf Course, *858*
Austinburg, Ohio, Maple Ridge Golf Course, *687*
Avelia, Pa., Indian Run Golf Club, *748*
Aventura, Fla., Turnberry Isle Resort & Club, *233*
Avila Beach, Calif., Avila Beach Resort Golf Course, *76*
Avon, Colo.
Beaver Creek Golf Club, *141*
Eagle Vail Golf Club, *145*
Avon, Conn., Blue Fox Run Golf Club, *159*
Avon Lake, Ohio, Sweetbriar Golf & Pro Shop, *702*
Avon, Ohio, Bob-O-Link Golf Course, *668*
Avondale, Pa.
Hartefeld National Golf Club, *746*
Loch Nairn Golf Club, *750*
Azle, Texas, Cross Timbers Golf Course, *835*
Azusa, Calif., Azusa Greens Golf Course, *76*

B

Bad Axe, Mich., Verona Hills Golf Club, *486*
Baddeck, Nova Scotia, Bell Bay Golf Club, *1001*
Baileys Harbor, Wis., Maxwelton Braes Golf Resort, *951*
Bakersfield, Calif.
Kern River Golf Course, *98*
Rio Bravo Country Club, *121*
Valle Grande Golf Course, *137*
Bakerstown, Pa., Pittsburgh North Golf Club, *759*
Bald Head Island, N.C., Bald Head Island Club, *627*
Baldwin, Mich., Marquette Trails Country Club, *456*
Baldwinsville, N.Y.
Foxfire at Village Green, *604*
Radisson Greens Golf Club, *615*
Ballston Spa, N.Y., Ballston Spa Country Club, *591*

Belding, Mich., Candlestone Golf Club, *421*

Belen, N.Mex., Tierra del Sol Golf Course, *588*

Belfast, N.Y., Six-S Golf Course, *619*

Bellaire, Mich., Shanty Creek, *477*

Belle Plane, Minn., Valley View Golf Club, *518*

Belle Vernon, Pa., Cedarbrook Golf Course, *736*

Belleair, Fla., Belleview Biltmore Resort & Golf Club, *174*

Bellefontaine, Ohio
Cherokee Hills Golf Course, *671*
Liberty Hills Golf Club, *685*
Tree Links Golf Course, *704*

Belleville, Ill.
Clinton Hill Country Club, *286*
The Orchards Golf Club, *310*

Belleville, N.J., Hendricks Field Golf Course, *575*

Belleville, Ontario, Bay of Quinte Country Club, *1003*

Bellevue, Nebr., Willow Lakes Golf Course, *549*

Bellevue, Wash., Bellevue Municipal Golf Course, *907*

Bellingham, Mass.
Maplegate Country Club, *405*
New England Country Club, *405*

Bellingham, Wash.
Lake Padden Golf Course, *914*
North Bellingham Golf Course, *919*
Shuksan Golf Club, *921*
Sudden Valley Golf & Country Club, *922*

Bellport, N.Y., Bellport Country Club, *592*

Beloit, Wis., Krueger Municipal Golf Club, *948*

Belpre, Ohio, Oxbow Golf & Country Club, *691*

Belton, Mo.
Belton Municipal Golf Course, *528*
Southview Golf Club, *538*

Belton, Texas, Leon Valley Golf Course, *847*

Belvidere, N.J., Apple Mountain Golf Club, *568*

Bemidji, Minn.
Bemidji Town & Country Club, *493*
Castle Highlands Golf Course, *495*

Bend, Oreg.
Awbrey Glen Golf Club, *719*
Lost Tracks Golf Club, *724*
Mountain High Golf Course, *725*
River's Edge Golf Resort, *728*
Widgi Creek Golf Club, *731*

Bennington, Vt., Mount Anthony Golf & Tennis Center, *880*

Bensenville, Ill., White Pines Golf Club, *325*

Benton, Ark., Longhills Golf Club, *72*

Benton Harbor, Mich.
Blossom Trails Golf Course, *417*
Lake Michigan Hills Golf Club, *451*

Benton, Pa., Mill Race Golf Course, *752*

Berkeley, Calif., Tilden Park Golf Course, *135*

Berkeley Springs, W.Va., Cacapon Resort, *926*

Berlin, Md.
The Bay Club, *386*
The Beach Club Golf Links, *386*
Eagle's Landing Golf Club, *388*
Ocean City Golf & Yacht Club, *393*
Rum Pointe Seaside Golf Links, *395*

Berlin, Wis., Mascoutin Golf Club, *951*

Bermuda Dunes, Calif., Sun City Palm Desert Golf Club, *132*

Bernalillo, N.Mex., Santa Ana Golf Club, *588*

Bernardston, Mass., Crumpin-Fox Club, *401*

Bessemer, Ala.
Bent Brook Golf Course, *26*
Frank House Municipal Golf Club, *29*

Bethany, Conn., Woodhaven Country Club, *169*

Bethel Island, Calif., Bethel Island Golf Course, *78*

Bethel, Maine, The Bethel Inn & Country Club, *380*

Bethlehem, N.H.
Bethlehem Country Club, *560*
Maplewood Country Club, *563*

Bethlehem, Pa.
Bethlehem Municipal Golf Club, *733*
Green Pond Country Club, *746*

Bettendorf, Iowa
Hidden Hills Golf Course, *352*
Palmer Hills Municipal Golf Course, *355*

Beulah, Mich.
Crystal Lake Golf Club, *426*
Pinecroft Golf Club, *467*

Beverly Hills, Fla., Twisted Oaks Golf Club, *233*

Beverly, Ohio, Lakeside Golf Course, *685*

Big Bend, Wis., Edgewood Golf Course, *940*

Big Canoe, Ga., Big Canoe Golf Club, *240*

Big Rapids, Mich.
Katke Golf Course FSU, *449*
Meceola Country Club, *458*
Winters Creek Golf Club, *490*

Big Sky, Mont., Big Sky Golf Club, *540*

Big Spring, Texas, Comanche Trail Golf Club, *834*

Bigfort, Mont., Eagle Bend Golf Club, *540*

Billings, Mont.
Lake Hills Golf Course, *541*
Peter Yegen Jr. Golf Club, *542*

Biloxi, Miss.
Blackjack Bay Golf Links, *522*
Broadwater Resort, *522*
Dogwood Hills Golf Club, *523*
Edgewater Bay Golf Course, *524*
Sunkist Country Club, *526*

Binghamton, N.Y., Ely Park Municipal Golf Course, *603*

Bragg Creek, Alberta, Wintergreen Golf & Country Club, *981*

Brainerd, Minn.
Madden's on Gull Lake, *505*
Pine Meadows Golf Course, *512*

Brampton, Ontario, Lionhead Golf & Country Club, *1010*

Brandenburg, Ky., Doe Valley Golf Club, *367*

Brandon, Miss., Bay Pointe Resort & Golf Club, *522*

Brandon, Vt., Neshobe Golf Club, *881*

Branson, Mo.
Pointe Royale Golf Club, *536*
Thousand Hills Golf Club, *539*

Brantford, Ontario, Northridge Public Golf Course, *1012*

Brantingham, N.Y., Brantingham Golf Club, *594*

Braselton, Ga., Chateau Elan Resort, *243*

Brazil, Ind., Forest Park Golf Course, *332*

Brea, Calif., Imperial Golf Club, *97*

Breckenridge, Colo., Breckenridge Golf Club, *141*

Brecksville, Ohio, Sleepy Hollow Golf Course, *700*

Breezy Point, Minn., Breezy Point Resort, *494*

Bremen, Ga., Maple Creek Golf Course, *253*

Bremerton, Wash.
Gold Mountain Golf Complex, *912*
Rolling Hills Golf Course, *920*

Brentwood, N.Y., Brentwood Country Club, *594*

Bretton Woods, N.H., Mount Washington Hotel & Resort, *563*

Brevard, N.C., Glen Cannon Country Club, *639*

Brewster, Mass.
Captains Golf Course, *400*
Ocean Edge Golf Club, *407*

Bridgeport, Mich., Green Acres Golf Course, *440*

Bridgeville, Pa., Hickory Heights Golf Club, *747*

Bridgewater, N.J., Green Knoll Golf Course, *574*

Bridgman, Mich., Pebblewood Country Club, *464*

Brigantine, N.J., Brigantine Golf Links, *569*

Brigham City, Utah, Eagle Mountain Golf Course, *869*

Brighton, Colo., Riverdale Golf Club, *154*

Brighton, Mich.
Huron Meadows Golf Course, *447*
Oak Pointe, *462*

Bristol, Ill., Blackberry Oaks Golf Course, *282*

Bristol, Ind., Raber Golf Course, *341*

Bristol, Wis., Bristol Oaks Country Club, *935*

Bristow, Va., Bristow Manor Golf Club, *886*

Broadview Heights, Ohio, Briarwood Golf Course (Broadview Heights, *669*

Brockport, N.Y.
Brockport Country Club, *595*
Deerfield Country Club, *600*

Brockton, Mass., D.W. Field Golf Club, *401*

Brockville, Ontario, Brockville Country Club, *1004*

Broken Arrow, Okla.
Battle Creek Golf Club, *709*
Forest Ridge Golf Club, *712*
Glen Eagles Golf Course, *712*

Broken Bow, Okla., Cedar Creek Golf Course, *710*

Bromont, Quebec, Le Royal Bromont Golf Club, *1021*

Bronston, Ky., Woodson Bend Resort, *375*

Bronx, N.Y.
Mosholu Golf Course, *613*
Pelham-Split Rock Golf Course, *614*
Van Cortlandt Park Golf Club, *624*

Brookfield, Ohio, Yankee Run Golf Course, *708*

Brookings, S.Dak., Edgebrook Golf Course, *808*

Brooklyn, Mich.
Clark Lake Golf Club, *424*
Greenbrier Golf Course, *441*
Hills Heart of the Lakes Golf Club, *446*

Brooklyn, N.Y.
Dyker Beach Golf Course, *602*
Marine Park Golf Club, *611*

Brooklyn Park, Minn., Edinburgh USA Golf Club, *499*

Brooksville, Fla.
The Dunes Golf Club at Seville, *189*
Sherman Hills Golf Club, *228*
World Woods Golf Club, *238*

Brookville, Ind., Brook Hill Golf Club, *328*

Broomfield, Colo., Eagle Golf Club, *144*

Brown Summit, N.C., Bryan Park & Golf Club, *630*

Brownsburg, Ind., Westchase Golf Club, *346*

Brownsville, Texas
Brownsville Country Club, *830*
Fort Brown Municipal Golf Course, *837*
River Bend Resort, *855*
Valley Inn & Country Club, *864*

Brunswick, Ga., Oak Grove Island Golf Club, *254*

Brunswick, Maine, Brunswick Golf Club, *381*

Brush Prairie, Wash., Cedars Golf Club, *908*

Brutus, Mich., Pine Hill Golf Club, *465*

Bryan, Texas, Bryan Golf Course, *830*

Buchanan, Tenn., Paris Landing Golf Course, *821*

Buck Hill Falls, Pa., Buck Hill Golf Club, *734*

Buena, N.J., Buena Vista Country Club, *569*

Chicago, Ill.
Edgebrook Golf Club, *290*
Evergreen Golf & Country Club, *290*
Harborside International Golf Center, *295*
Indian Boundary Golf Course, *298*
Jackson Park Golf Course, *299*
Chico, Calif., Bidwell Park Golf Course, *78*
Chicopee, Mass., Chicopee Golf Club, *400*
Chillicothe, Ohio
Jaycee Golf Course, *684*
Running Fox Golf Course, *697*
Chilton, Wis., Hickory Hills Country Club, *945*
China Lake, Calif., China Lake Golf Club, *83*
Chino, Calif., El Prado Golf Course, *89*
Chino Hills, Calif., Los Serranos Lakes Golf & Country Club, *103*
Chippewa Falls, Wis., Hallie Golf Club, *944*
Chocowinity, N.C., Cypress Landing Golf Club, *634*
Christina Lake, British Columbia, Christina Lake Golf Club, *983*
Chuckey, Tenn., Graysburg Hills Golf Course, *816*
Chula Vista, Calif., Eastlake Country Club, *88*
Cicero, Ind., Bear Slide Golf Club, *327*
Cincinnati, Ohio
Avon Field Golf Course, *665*
Blue Ash Golf Course, *667*
California Golf Course, *669*
Glenview Golf Course, *677*
The Golf Courses of Winton Woods, *678*
Neumann Golf Course, *689*
Reeves Golf Course, *695*
Sharon Woods Golf Course, *699*
The Vineyard Golf Course, *705*
Citronelle, Ala., Citronelle Municipal Golf Course, *27*
Citrus Springs, Fla., Citrus Springs Country Club, *180*
City of Industry, Calif., Industry Hills Sheraton Resort & Conference Center, *97.*
Clare, Mich., Firefly Golf Links, *432*
Claremore, Okla., Heritage Hills Golf Course, *712*
Clarion, Pa., Mayfield Golf Club, *751*
Clark, N.J., Oak Ridge Golf Course, *578*
Clarkston, Mich.
Clarkston Creek Golf Club, *425*
Pine Knob Golf Club, *465*
Clarkston, Wash., Quail Ridge Golf Course, *920*
Clarksville, Ind., Wooded View Golf Club, *347*
Clarksville, Tenn.
Eastland Green Golf Course, *815*
Swan Lake Golf Course, *824*
Clayton, Calif., Oakhurst Country Club, *111*
Clayton, Ind., Deer Creek Golf Club, *330*

Clayton, N.C.
The Neuse Golf Club, *647*
Riverwood Golf Club, *655*
Clayton, N.Y., C-Way Golf Club, *595*
Clearwater, Fla.
Chi Chi Rodriguez Golf Club, *179*
Clearwater Country Club, *180*
Cleburne, Texas, Cleburne Muni Golf Course, *833*
Clemmons, N.C., Tanglewood Park, *659*
Clemson, S.C., The Walker Course at Clemson University, *804*
Clendenin, W.Va., Sandy Brae Golf Course, *930*
Clermont, Fla.
Clerbrook Resort, *181*
Palisades Golf Club, *213*
Cleveland, Ohio, Highland Park Golf Club, *681*
Clever, Mo., Hidden Valley Golf Links, *532*
Clewiston, Fla., Clewiston Golf Course, *181*
Clifton Park, N.Y., Eagle Crest Golf Club, *602*
Clifton, Va., Twin Lakes Golf Course, *903*
Clinton, Ind., Geneva Hills Golf Club, *333*
Clinton, Iowa, Valley Oaks Golf Club, *357*
Clinton, N.J., Beaver Brook Country Club, *568*
Clinton Township, Mich.
Fern Hill Golf & Country Club, *432*
Partridge Creek Golf Club, *464*
Clio, Calif., The Golf Club at Whitehawk Ranch, *92*
Clio, Mich., Vienna Greens Golf Course, *486*
Cloudcroft, N.Mex., The Lodge Golf Club, *586*
Clyde, Ohio, Green Hills Golf Club, *679*
Clymer, N.Y., Peek'n Peak Resort, *614*
Coaldale, Alberta, Land-o-Lakes Golf Club, *978*
Cobble Hill, British Columbia, Arbutus Ridge Golf & Country Club, *982*
Cochiti Lake, N.Mex., Pueblo De Cochiti Golf Course, *587*
Cocoa Beach, Fla., Cocoa Beach Golf Course, *182*
Cocoyoc, Morelos, Country Club Cocoyoc, *1029*
Cody, Wyo., Olive Glenn Golf & Country Club, *971*
Coeur D'Alene, Idaho, Coeur D'Alene Resort Golf Course, *275*
Cohutta, Ga., Nob North Golf Course, *254*
Coitsville, Ohio, Bedford Trails Golf Course, *666*
Cold Spring, Minn., Rich Spring Golf Course, *514*
Coldspring, Texas, Cape Royale Golf Course, *831*
Coleraine, Minn., Eagle Ridge Golf Course, *498*
Colfax, N.C., Sandy Ridge Golf Course, *656*

Davison, Mich., Sugarbush Golf Club, *480*

Dawson, Pa., Linden Hall Golf Club, *750*

Dawsonville, Ga., Gold Creek Golf Club, *248*

Dayton, Minn., Daytona Country Club, *497*

Dayton, Nev., Dayton Valley Country Club, *552*

Dayton, Ohio, Kitty Hawk Golf Club, *684*

Daytona Beach, Fla.

Daytona Beach Golf Course, *185*

Indigo Lakes Golf Club, *200*

LPGA International, *203*

Pelican Bay Country Club, *215*

Spruce Creek Country Club, *229*

De Motte, Ind., Sandy Pines Golf Course, *342*

De Pere, Wis.

Mid-Vallee Golf Course, *952*

Mystery Hills Golf Club, *953*

De Winton, Alberta

Cottonwood Golf & Country Club, *975*

Heritage Pointe Golf & Country Club, *976*

De Witt, Mich.

Highland Hills Golf Course, *446*

Prairie Creek Golf Course, *469*

Dearborn Heights, Mich., Warren Valley Golf Course, *486*

Dearborn, Mich., Dearborn Hills Golf Club, *427*

Death Valley, Calif., Furnace Creek Golf Course, *92*

DeBary, Fla., Debary Golf & Country Club, *185*

Decatur, Ala., Point Mallard Golf Course, *37*

Decatur, Ill.

Faries Park Golf Course, *290*

Hickory Point Golf Club, *296*

Nelson Park Golf Course, *306*

Scovill Golf Club, *318*

Deer Park, Texas, The Battleground at Deer Park Golf Course, *827*

Deerfield Beach, Fla., Deer Creek Golf Club, *186*

Deerwood, Minn.

Cuyuna Country Club, *497*

Ruttger's Bay Lake Lodge, *515*

Delavan, Wis.

Delbrook Golf Course, *939*

Lake Lawn Golf Course, *949*

Delaware, Ohio, Tanglewood Golf Club, *703*

Delaware Water Gap, Pa., Water Gap Country Club, *768*

Delhi, Ontario, Delhi Golf & Country Club, *1006*

Dellroy, Ohio, Atwood Resort Golf Course, *665*

Delray Beach, Fla.

Delray Beach Golf Club, *186*

The Links at Polo Trace, *204*

Delton, Mich., Mullenhurst Golf Course, *460*

Deltona, Fla., Deltona Hills Golf & Country Club, *187*

Deming, N.Mex., Rio Mimbres Country Club, *588*

Denison, Texas, Grayson County College Golf Course, *840*

Denmark, Wis., Twin Oaks Country Club, *966*

Dennis, Mass.

Dennis Highlands Golf Course, *401*

Dennis Pines Golf Course, *402*

Dennis, Texas, Sugartree Golf Club, *861*

Denver, Colo.

City Park Golf Club, *143*

Foothills Golf Course, *146*

Overland Park Golf Course, *152*

Park Hill Golf Club, *152*

Wellshire Golf Course, *158*

Willis Case Golf Course, *158*

Denver, N.C., Westport Golf Course, *660*

Denver, Pa., Hawk Valley Golf Club, *747*

Derby, Kans., Hidden Lakes Golf Course, *361*

Derwood, Md., Needwood Golf Course, *392*

Des Moines, Iowa

A.H. Blank Golf Course, *348*

Grandview Golf Course, *352*

Waveland Golf Course, *358*

Desert Aire, Wash., Desert Aire Golf Course, *909*

Desert Hot Springs, Calif.

Desert Dunes Golf Club, *86*

Missions Lakes Country Club, *107*

Destin, Fla.

Emerald Bay Golf Course, *190*

Indian Bayou Golf & Country Club, *199*

Sandestin Resort, *224*

Seascape Resort, *226*

Detroit Lakes, Minn.

Detroit Country Club, *498*

Wildflower at Fair Hills, *520*

Detroit, Mich.

Palmer Park Golf Course, *464*

Rogell Golf Course, *473*

Rouge Park Golf Club, *474*

Devine, Texas, Devine Golf Course, *836*

Devonshire, Bermuda, Ocean View Golf Course, *1035*

Dewey, Ariz., Prescott Country Club, *59*

Dexter, Mich., Hudson Mills Metro Park Golf Course, *446*

Diamond Bar, Calif., Diamond Bar Golf Club, *87*

Diamond City, Ark., Diamond Hills Golf Course, *70*

Diamondhead, Miss., Diamondhead Country Club, *523*

Dickinson, N.Dak., Heart River Municipal Golf Course, *662*

Digby, Nova Scotia, The Pines Resort Hotel Golf Course, *1002*

Dixon, Ill., Lost Nation Golf Club, *304*

Dixville Notch, N.H., The Balsams Grand Resort Hotel, *560*

Enoch, Alberta, Indian Lakes Golf Club, *977*

Ensenada, Baja Norte
Baja Country Club, *1026*
Bajamar Ocean Front Golf Resort, *1026*
Enumclaw, Wash., Enumclaw Golf Club, *911*
Ephraim, Wis., Peninsula State Park Golf Course, *956*
Erie, Pa., Erie Golf Club, *742*
Escanaba, Mich., Highland Golf Club, *446*
Escondido, Calif.
Castle Creek Country Club, *81*
Eagle Crest Golf Club, *88*
Meadow Lake Golf Course, *105*
The Vineyard at Escondido, *138*
Welk Resort Center, *138*
Essex Junction, Vt., Essex Country Club, *879*
Essex, Md., Rocky Point Golf Club, *395*
Essex, Ontario, Sutton Creek Golf & Country Club, *1016*
Essexville, Mich., Bay County Golf Course, *414*
Estes Park, Colo., Estes Park Golf Course, *145*
Estevan, Saskatchewan, Estevan Woodlawn Golf Club, *1022*
Etobicoke, Ontario, Royal Woodbine Golf Club, *1015*
Etowah, N.C., Etowah Valley Country Club, *636*
Etters, Pa., Valley Green Golf Course, *768*
Euclid, Ohio, Briardale Greens Golf Course, *668*
Eufaula, Ala., Lakepoint Resort Golf Course, *33*
Eugene, Oreg., Riveridge Golf Course, *728*
Eustis, Fla., Black Bear Golf Club, *175*
Evans, Ga., Jones Creek Golf Club, *251*
Evanston, Wyo., Purple Sage Golf Club, *971*
Evansville, Ind.
Fendrich Golf Course, *331*
Helfrich Golf Course, *334*
Evansville, Wis., Evansville Country Club, *941*
Everett, Pa., Down River Golf Club, *741*
Everett, Wash.
Legion Memorial Golf Course, *915*
Walter E. Hall Memorial Golf Course, *924*
Evergreen, Colo., Evergreen Golf Course, *145*
Ewa Beach (Oahu), Hawaii
Hawaii Prince Golf Club, *263*
New Ewa Beach Golf Club, *268*
West Loch Golf Course, *273*
Excelsior Springs, Mo., Excelsior Springs Golf Club, *531*
Exeter, Pa., Four Seasons Golf Club, *743*
Exeter, R.I., Exeter Country Club, *771*
Export, Pa., Manor Valley Golf Club, *751*

F

Fairbanks, Alaska
Fairbanks Golf & Country Club, *41*
North Star Golf Course, *42*
Fairfax, Va., Penderbrook Golf Club, *898*
Fairfield Bay, Ark., Mountain Ranch Golf Club, *72*
Fairfield, Calif.
Paradise Valley Golf Course, *114*
Rancho Solano Golf Course, *120*
Fairfield, Conn.
D. Fairchild-Wheeler Golf Course, *161*
H. Smith Richardson Golf Course, *162*
Fairfield Glade, Tenn.
Heatherhurst Golf Club, *817*
Stonehenge Golf Club, *824*
Fairfield, Ohio, Fairfield Golf Club, *675*
Fairfield, Pa., Carroll Valley Golf Resort, *735*
Fairhope, Ala.
Quail Creek Golf Course, *37*
Rock Creek Golf Club, *38*
Fairlee, Vt., Lake Morey Country Club, *880*
Fairmont Hot Springs, British Columbia
Fairmont Hot Springs Resort, *984*
Fairmont Riverside Golf Resort, *984*
Fairmont, Minn., Rose Lake Golf Course, *514*
Fairport, N.Y., Eagle Vale Golf Course, *602*
Fairton, N.J., Cohanzick Country Club, *570*
Fairview Heights, Ill., Stonewolf Golf Club, *321*
Fairview Park, Ohio, Big Met Golf Club, *666*
Falcon Lake, Manitoba, Falcon Lake Golf Course, *994*
Fall City, Wash.
Snoqualmie Falls Golf Course, *922*
Tall Chief Golf Course, *923*
Fall River Mills, Calif., Fall River Valley Golf & Country Club, *90*
Fallbrook, Calif.
Fallbrook Golf Club, *90*
Pala Mesa Resort, *113*
Fancy Gap, Va., Skyland Lakes Golf Course, *901*
Fargo, N.Dak.
Edgewood Golf Course, *662*
Rose Creek Golf Course, *664*
Farmingdale, Maine, Kennebec Heights Golf Club, *382*
Farmingdale, N.J.
Howell Park Golf Course, *576*
Spring Meadow Golf Course, *583*
Farmingdale, N.Y., Bethpage State Park Golf Courses, *592*
Farmington, Conn.
Tunxis Plantation Country Club, *168*
Westwoods Golf Club, *169*
Farmington Hills, Mich., Glen Oaks Golf & Country Club, *436*

Goldsboro, N.C., Lane Tree Golf Course, *642*

Goleta, Calif., Sandpiper Golf Course, *126*

Gonic, N.H., Rochester Country Club, *565*

Goodrich, Mich., Goodrich Country Club, *437*

Goodyear, Ariz.
Eagle's Nest Country Club at Pebble Creek, *47*
Estrella Mountain Golf Course, *48*
Palm Valley Golf Club, *57*

Goose Creek, S.C., Crowfield Golf & Country Club, *780*

Gordonsville, Va., Shenandoah Crossing Resort & Country Club, *900*

Gorham, Maine, Gorham Golf Club, *382*

Gormley, Ontario
Fire Fighters Gormley Green Golf Club, *1007*
Fire Fighters Rolling Hills Golf Club, *1007*

Goshen, Ind., Black Squirrel Golf Club, *327*

Goshen, Ohio, Deer Track Golf Club, *673*

Graeagle, Calif., Graeagle Meadows Golf Course, *93*

Graford, Texas, The Cliffs Golf Club, *833*

Grafton, Ohio, Pine Brook Golf Course, *691*

Grafton, Wis., Country Club of Wisconsin, *938*

Grafton, W.Va., Tygart Lake Country Club, *932*

Graham, N.C., Quarry Hills Country Club, *654*

Grain Valley, Mo., Valley Hills Golf Club, *539*

Gramling, S.C., Village Green Golf Club, *804*

Granby, Mass., Westover Golf Course, *412*

Grand Blanc, Mich.
Grand Blanc Golf & Country Club, *438*
Woodfield Golf & Country Club, *491*

Grand Cayman, The Links at Safe Haven, *1036*

Grand Forks, N.Dak.
Lincoln Park Golf Course, *662*
Plainsview Golf Course at Grand Forks A.F.B., *663*

Grand Haven, Mich., Grand Haven Golf Club, *438*

Grand Island, Nebr.
Grand Island Municipal Golf Course, *545*
Indianhead Golf Club, *546*

Grand Island, N.Y., Beaver Island State Park Golf Course, *592*

Grand Junction, Colo., Tiara Rado Golf Course, *156*

Grand Lake, Colo., Grand Lake Golf Course, *147*

Grand Ledge, Mich.
Grand Ledge Country Club, *439*
Ledge Meadows Golf Course, *453*

Grand Prairie, Texas
Grand Prairie Municipal Golf Course, *840*
Riverside Golf Club, *856*
Tangleridge Golf Club, *861*

Grand Rapids, Mich.
English Hills Golf Course, *431*
The Golf Club at Thornapple Pointe, *437*
Gracewil Country Club, *437*
Grand Rapids Golf Club, *439*
Indian Trails Golf Course, *448*
Lincoln Country Club, *453*
Meadow Lane Golf Course, *458*

Grand Rapids, Minn.
Pokegama Golf Club, *512*
Sugarbrooke Golf Club, *517*
Wendigo Golf Course, *520*

Grand-Sault, New Brunswick, Grand Falls Golf Club, *997*

Grande Prairie, Alberta, The Dunes Golf & Winter Club, *976*

Grandview, Mo., River Oaks Golf Club, *537*

Grandville, Mich., Maple Hill Golf Course, *455*

Granger, Ind., Juday Creek Golf Course, *336*

Granger, Iowa, Jester Park Golf Course, *353*

Granite City, Ill., Legacy Golf Club, *302*

Grant, Mich., Brigadoon Golf Club, *420*

Grant, Minn., Sawmill Golf Club, *516*

Grant Park, Ill., Minne Monesse Golf Club, *306*

Grantham, N.H., Eastman Golf Links, *562*

Grants Pass, Oreg., Grants Pass Country Club, *722*

Grantville, Pa., Manada Golf Club, *751*

Granville, Ohio
Granville Golf Course, *678*
Raccoon International Golf Club, *694*

Grapevine, Texas, Grapevine Golf Course, *840*

Grass Valley, Calif., Alta Sierra Golf & Country Club, *75*

Grayling, Mich.
Fox Run Country Club, *434*
Grayling Country Club, *440*

Grayslake, Ill., Brae Loch Country Club, *283*

Graysville, Ala., Mountain View Golf Club, *35*

Great Falls, Mont., R.O. Speck Municipal Golf Course, *542*

Great River, N.Y., Timber Point Golf Course, *623*

Greeley, Colo.
Boomerang Links, *141*
Highland Hills Golf Course, *148*

Green Bay, Wis., Woodside Country Club, *968*

Green Lake, Wis.
The Golf Courses of Lawsonia, *943*
Tuscumbia Golf Club, *965*

Green Lane, Pa., Macoby Run Golf Course, *750*

Hampton, New Brunswick, Hampton
Country Club, *997*
Hampton, Va.
The Hampton's Golf Course, *890*
Woodlands Golf Course, *905*
Hanceville, Ala., Cullman Golf Course,
28
Hanover, Ill., Storybrook Country Club,
321
Hanover, Jamaica, The Tryall Club,
Resort & Villas, *1039*
Hanover, N.H., Hanover Country Club,
562
Hanover, Pa., South Hills Golf Club, *763*
Harbor Springs, Mich.
Boyne Highlands Resort, *417*
Chestnut Valley Golf Course, *424*
Harbor Point Golf Course, *443*
Little Traverse Bay Golf Club, *454*
Harborcreek, Pa., Downing Golf Course,
741
Hardy, Va., Westlake Golf & Country
Club, *904*
Harlingen, Texas, Tony Butler Golf
Course, *863*
Harmony, Pa., Deep Valley Golf Course,
740
Harmony, R.I., Melody Hill Golf Course,
772
Harpersville, Ala., Meadows Golf
Course, *35*
Harpster, Ohio, Hickory Grove Golf Club,
680
Harrisburg, Pa.
Dauphin Highlands Golf Course, *740*
Sportmans Golf Club, *764*
Harrison, Ark., Harrison Country Club,
71
Harrison, Mich.
Snow Snake Ski & Golf Club, *477*
The Tamaracks, *481*
Harrison , Ohio, Miami Whitewater
Forest Golf Course, *688*
Harrisonburg, Va.
Lakeview Golf Course, *894*
Massanutten Resort Golf Course, *896*
Harrisville, R.I., Country View Golf Club,
771
Harrod, Ohio, Colonial Golfers Club,
672
Harrodsburg, Ky., Bright Leaf Golf
Resort, *366*
Harsens Island, Mich., Middle Channel
Golf & Country Club, *458*
Harshaw, Wis., Pinewood Country Club,
957
Hartfield, Va., Piankatank River Golf
Club, *898*
Hartford City, Ind., Laurel Lakes Golf
Course, *337*
Hartford, Conn.
Goodwin Park Golf Course, *162*
Keney Golf Course, *162*
Hartford, S.Dak., Central Valley Golf
Club, *808*
Hartford, Wis., Hartford Golf Club, *944*

Hartland, Mich.
Dunham Hills Golf & Country Club, *428*
Hartland Glen Golf & Country Club, *443*
The Majestic at Lake Walden, *455*
Hartland, New Brunswick, Covered
Bridge Golf & Country Club, *996*
Hartland, Wis.
Bristlecone Pines Golf Club, *935*
Songbird Hills Golf Club, *962*
Hartsburg, Mo., Eagle Knoll Golf Club, *530*
Harvard, Ill., Plum Tree National Golf
Club, *312*
Harvard, Mass., Shaker Hills Golf Club,
409
Harwich, Mass., Cranberry Valley Golf
Course, *400*
Haslett, Mich., Pine Lake Golf Course,
466
Hastings, Mich.
Hastings Country Club, *443*
River Bend Golf Course, *471*
Hastings, Minn.
Afton Alps Golf Course, *492*
Bellwood Oaks Golf Course, *493*
Hidden Greens Golf Club, *502*
Hastings, Nebr., Southern Hills Golf
Course, *549*
Hattiesburg, Miss.
Timberton Golf Club, *527*
USM's Van Hook Golf Course, *527*
Hauppauge, N.Y.
Hamlet Wind Watch Golf Club, *607*
Hauppauge Country Club, *607*
Haverhill, Mass., Crystal Springs Golf
Club, *401*
Hawley, Minn., Hawley Golf & Country
Club, *501*
Hawley, Pa., Country Club at Woodloch
Springs, *739*
Hayden Lake, Idaho, Avondale Golf
Club, *274*
Hayesville, N.C., Chatuge Shores Golf
Course, *632*
Hayfield, Minn., Oaks Country Club, *510*
Hayward, Calif., Skywest Golf Course,
130
Hayward, Wis.
Hayward Golf & Tennis Center, *945*
Teal Wing Golf Club, *964*
Headingley, Manitoba, John Blumberg
Golf Course, *994*
Heber Springs, Ark., The Red Apple Inn
& Country Club, *73*
Hebron, Conn.
Blackledge Country Club, *159*
Tallwood Country Club, *167*
Hedgesville, W.Va., The Woods Resort,
932
Helen, Ga., Innsbruck Resort & Golf
Club, *250*
Helena, Mont., Bill Roberts Municipal
Golf Course, *540*
Hellertown, Pa., Woodland Hills Country
Club, *770*
Hemet, Calif., Seven Hills Golf Course,
128

Hempstead, Texas, Fox Creek Golf
Course, *838*

Henderson, Nev.
Black Mountain Golf & Country Club, *551*
The Legacy Golf Club, *555*
The Links at Montelago, *556*
Wild Horse Golf Club, *558*

Hendersonville, N.C., Crooked Creek
Golf Club, *634*

Hendersonville, Tenn., Country Hills Golf
Course, *813*

Hercules, Calif., Franklin Canyon Golf
Course, *91*

Hereford, Texas, John Pitman Municipal
Golf Course, *844*

Hermitage, Pa., Tam O'Shanter Golf
Club, *765*

Hernando, Fla., Citrus Hills Golf &
Country Club, *180*

Herndon, Va., Herndon Centennial Golf
Club, *891*

Herrin, Ill., Green Acres Golf Course, *294*

Hersey, Mich., Spring Valley Golf Course,
478

Hershey, Pa., Country Club of Hershey,
739

Hertford, N.C., The Sound Golf Links at
Albemarle Plantation, *657*

Hesperia, Calif., Hesperia Golf & Country
Club, *95*

Hesston, Kans., Hesston Municipal Golf
Park, *361*

Hibbing, Minn., Mesaba Country Club,
507

Hickory Hills, Ill., Hickory Hills Country
Club, *295*

Hidden Valley, Pa., Hidden Valley Four
Seasons Resort, *748*

High Point, N.C.
Blair Park Golf Club, *628*
Oak Hollow Golf Course, *648*

High Shoals, N.C., Briarcreek Golf Club,
629

Highland Heights, Ohio, Stonewater
Golf Club, *701*

Highland, Ind., Wicker Memorial Park
Golf Course, *346*

Highland, N.Y., Apple Green Golf
Course, *590*

Highland Park, Ill.
Highland Park Country Club, *296*
Sunset Valley Golf Club, *321*

Hillman, Mich., Thunder Bay Golf Resort,
482

Hillsboro, Mo., Raintree Country Club,
537

Hillsboro, Ohio, Rocky Fork Golf &
Tennis Center, *696*

Hillsboro, Oreg., Meriwether National
Golf Club, *725*

Hillside, Ill., Fresh Meadows Golf
Course, *292*

Hilltop Lakes, Texas, Rolling Hills Golf
Club, *857*

Hilo, Hawaii, Hilo Municipal Golf Course,
263

Hilton Head Island, S.C.
Country Club of Hilton Head, *780*
Daufuskie Island Club & Resort, *781*
Golden Bear Golf Club, *784*
Harbour Town Golf Links, *785*
Oyster Reef Golf Club, *795*
Palmetto Dunes Resort, *795*
Palmetto Hall Plantation, *795*
Port Royal Golf Club, *798*
Sea Pines Plantation Club, *801*
Shipyard Golf Club, *802*

Hinckley, Minn., Grand National Golf
Club, *500*

Hinckley, Ohio
Hinckley Hills Golf Course, *682*
Ironwood Golf Course, *683*
Pine Hills Golf Club, *691*
Skyland Golf Course, *700*

Hingham, Mass., South Shore Country
Club, *410*

Hinton, Alberta, Hinton Golf Club, *977*

Hobbs, N.Mex., Ocotillo Park Golf
Course, *587*

Hobe Sound, Fla., Lost Lake Golf Club,
205

Hockley, Texas, The Links at Tennwood,
847

Hoffman Estates, Ill.
Highland Woods Golf Course, *297*
Hilldale Golf Club, *297*
Poplar Creek Country Club, *313*

Holden Beach, N.C., Lockwood Folly
Country Club, *644*

Holland, Mich.
West Ottawa Golf Club, *487*
Winding Creek Golf Course, *490*

Hollis, N.H., Overlook Country Club,
564

Hollister, Calif.
Ridgemark Golf & Country Club, *121*
San Juan Oaks Golf Club, *125*

Holly, Mich.
Bramblewood Golf Course, *418*
Heather Highlands Golf Club, *443*

Holly Springs, Miss., Kirkwood National
Golf Club, *524*

Holly Springs, N.C., Devil's Ridge Golf
Club, *635*

Hollywood, Fla., The Club at Emerald
Hills, *181*

Hollywood, S.C., The Links at Stono
Ferry, *790*

Holmen, Wis., Drugan's Castle Mound,
940

Homestead, Fla., Redland Golf &
Country Club, *219*

Honolulu (Oahu), Hawaii
Ala Wai Golf Course, *262*
Hawaii Kai Golf Course, *263*
Royal Kunia Country Club, *270*

Hood River, Oreg., Indian Creek Golf
Club, *723*

Hope Mills, N.C., Cypress Lakes Golf
Course, *634*

Hopedale, Ohio, Castle Shannon Golf
Course, *670*

Hopewell Junction, N.Y., Beekman Country Club, *592*

Hopewell, Va., Jordan Point Golf Club, *893*

Hopkins, Minn., Meadowbrook Golf Course, *507*

Hopkinsville, Ky., Western Hills Golf Course, *375*

Hopkinton, Mass., Saddle Hill Country Club, *409*

Horicon, Wis., Rock River Hills Golf Course, *959*

Hornby, Ontario, Hornby Tower Golf Club, *1009*

Horseheads, N.Y., Soaring Eagles Golf Club, *620*

Horseshoe Bay, Texas, Horseshoe Bay Resort, *842*

Horseshoe Bend, Ark., Cedar Glade Golf Course, *69*

Hot Springs, Ark., Hot Springs Country Club, *71*

Hot Springs, S.Dak., Southern Hills Golf Course, *810*

Hot Springs, Va., The Homestead Resort, *892*

Houghton Lake, Mich., The Quest Golf Club, *469*

Houghton, Mich., Portage Lake Golf Course, *469*

Houston, Minn., Valley High Country Club, *518*

Houston, Texas
Bear Creek Golf World, *828*
Brock Park Golf Course, *830*
Clear Lake Golf Club, *833*
Glenbrook Golf Course, *839*
Gus Wortham Park Golf Course, *841*
Hermann Park Golf Course, *841*
Jersey Meadow Golf Course, *844*
Memorial Park Golf Course, *849*
Pasadena Municipal Golf Course, *851*
Sharpstown Municipal Golf Course, *858*

Howard, Ohio, Apple Valley Golf Club, *665*

Howell, Mich.
Dama Farms Golf Course, *427*
Faulkwood Shores Golf Club, *431*
Hunter's Ridge Golf Club, *446*
Ironwood Golf Club, *449*
Marion Oaks Golf Club, *456*

Howey-in-the-Hills, Fla.
Bella Vista Golf & Yacht Club, *174*
Mission Inn Golf & Tennis Resort, *209*

Huatulco, Oaxaca, Tangolunda Golf Course, *1030*

Hubbard, Ohio, Hubbard Golf Course, *682*

Huddleston, Va., Mariners Landing Golf & Country Club, *896*

Hudson, N.H., Green Meadow Golf Club, *562*

Hudson, Wis., Hudson Golf Club, *946*

Hudsonville, Mich.
Gleneagle Golf Club., *436*
Rolling Hills Golf Course, *473*

Huffman, Texas, Lake Houston Golf Club, *846*

Hulbert, Okla., Sequoyah State Park Golf Club, *716*

Humacao, Puerto Rico, Palmas del Mar Resort, *1041*

Humble, Texas, Tour 18, *863*

Huntersville, N.C., Birkdale Golf Club, *628*

Huntingdon, Pa., Standing Stone Golf Club, *764*

Huntington Woods, Mich., Rackham Golf Club, *469*

Huntley, Ill., Pinecrest Golf & Country Club, *312*

Huntsburg, Ohio, Rolling Green Golf Club, *696*

Huntsville, Ala.
Colonial Golf Club, *27*
Hampton Cove Golf Club, *31*
Huntsville Municipal Golf Course, *32*

Huntsville, Ontario, Deerhurst Resort, *1005*

Huntsville, Texas, Waterwood National Resort & Country Club, *865*

Hurley, Wis., Eagle Bluff Golf Course, *940*

Huron, Ohio
Sawmill Creek Golf & Racquet Club, *698*
Thunderbird Hills Golf Club, *704*

Hutchinson, Kans., Carey Park Golf Club, *359*

Hyannis, Mass.
Hyannis Golf Club at Iyanough Hills, *404*
Tara Hyannis Golf Course, *411*

Hyde Park, Mass., George Wright Golf Course, *403*

I

Idaho Falls, Idaho
Pinecrest Municipal Golf Course, *276*
Sage Lakes Municipal Golf, *277*
Sand Creek Golf Club, *277*

Ignace, New Brunswick, Le Club de Golf de St. Ignace, *997*

Incline Village, Nebr., Incline Village Golf Resort, *554*

Independence, Ky., The Golf Courses at Kenton County, *369*

Independence, Mo., Crackerneck Golf Course, *529*

Independence, Oreg. Oak Knoll Golf Course, *725*

Indian Lake Estates, Fla., Indian Lake Estates Golf & Country Club, *200*

Indian Lake, Pa., Northwind Golf Lodge, *755*

Indian River, Mich., Indian River Golf Club, *448*

Indian Trail, N.C., Charlotte National Golf Club, *632*

Indian Wells, Calif., Golf Resort at Indian Wells, *92*

Indianapolis, Ind.
Brickyard Crossing Golf Club, *328*
Coffin Golf Club, *329*

Lindstrom, Minn., Chisago Lakes Golf Course, *496*
Lino Lakes, Minn., Chomonix Golf Course, *496*
Linville Falls, N.C., Blue Ridge Country Club, *628*
Linville, N.C., Linville Golf Course, *643*
Linwood, Mich., Maple Leaf Golf Course, *455*
Lions Bay, British Columbia, Furry Creek Golf & Country Club, *986*
Lisbon, Ohio, Beaver Creek Meadows Golf Course, *666*
Litchfield, Minn., Litchfield Golf Course, *504*
Litchfield, N.H., Passaconaway Country Club, *564*
Litchfield Park, Ariz., The Wigwam Golf & Country Club, *67*
Lithonia, Ga.
Metropolitan Golf Club, *253*
Mystery Valley Golf Course, *253*
Little Falls, Minn., Little Falls Country Club, *505*
Little River, S.C.
Heather Glen Golf Links, *785*
River Hills Golf & Country Club, *799*
Little Rock, Ark.
Hindman Park Golf Course, *71*
Rebsamen Park Golf Course, *73*
War Memorial Golf Course, *74*
Littleton, Colo.
Arrowhead Golf Club, *140*
Lone Tree Golf Club, *150*
The Meadows Golf Club, *151*
Raccoon Creek Golf Club, *154*
South Suburban Golf Course, *155*
Littletown, Pa.
Flatbush Golf Course, *743*
Quail Valley Golf Club, *759*
Livermore, Calif.
Las Positas Golf Course, *101*
Poppy Ridge Golf Course, *116*
Liverpool, N.Y., Liverpool Golf & Country Club, *611*
Livonia, Mich.
Fox Creek Golf Course, *433*
Idle Wyld Country Club, *447*
Whispering Willows Golf Course, *488*
Livonia, N.Y., Old Hickory Golf Club, *614*
Lockbourne, Ohio), Foxfire Golf Club, *677*
Locke, N.Y., Fillmore Golf Club, *604*
Lockport, Ill.
Big Run Golf Club, *281*
Broken Arrow Golf Club, *283*
Old Oak Country Club, *309*
Woodbine Golf Course, *326*
Lockport, N.Y.
Niagara County Golf Course, *613*
Willowbrook Country Club, *626*
Locust Grove, Va.
Meadow Farms Golf Course, *896*
Somerset Golf Club, *901*
Lodi, Calif.
Lockeford Springs Golf Course, *102*
Micke Grove Golf Links, *106*

Logan, Utah, Ogan River Golf Course, *871*
Logansport, Ind.
Dykeman Park Golf Course, *330*
Ironhorse Golf Club, *335*
Lombardy, Ontario, Lombard Glen Golf Club, *1011*
Lomira, Wis., Camelot Country Club, *936*
Lompoc, Calif., La Purisima Golf Course, *99*
London, Ky., Crooked Creek Golf Club, *367*
London, Ontario
Fanshawe Golf Club, *1006*
Forest City National Golf Club, *1007*
River Road Golf Course, *1015*
Thames Valley Golf Course, *1017*
Lone Wolf, Okla., Quartz Mountain Golf Course, *716*
Long Beach, Calif.
El Dorado Park Golf Club, *88*
Recreation Park Golf Course, *120*
Skylinks Golf Club, *130*
Long Grove, Ill., Kemper Lakes Golf Course, *300*
Long Grove, Iowa, Glynns Creek Golf Course, *352*
Longboat Key, Fla., Longboat Key Club (Islandside Course), *205*
Longmont, Colo.
Lake Valley Golf Club, *150*
Twin Peaks Golf Course, *157*
Longs, S.C.
Buck Creek Golf Club, *776*
Colonial Charters Golf Club, *779*
The Long Bay Club, *791*
Longview, Texas, Alpine Golf Club, *826*
Longview, Wash., Mint Valley Golf Club, *918*
Longville, Minn., Ridgewood Golf Course, *514*
Longwood, Fla.
Sabal Point Country Club, *223*
Wekiva Golf Club, *237*
Lore City, Ohio, Salt Fork State Park Golf Course, *698*
Lorton, Va., Pohick Bay Regional Golf Course, *898*
Los Alamitos, Calif., Cypress Golf Club, *85*
Los Alamos, N.Mex., Los Alamos Golf Club, *586*
Los Angeles, Calif.
Chester Washington Golf Course, *83*
Griffith Park, *94*
Rancho Park Golf Course, *119*
Los Cabos, Baja Sur, Cabo del Sol Golf Club, *1027*
Louisville, Colo., Coal Creek Golf Course, *143*
Louisville, Ky.
Indian Springs Golf Club, *370*
Iroquois Golf Course, *370*
Quail Chase Golf Club, *374*
Seneca Golf Course, *374*
Shawnee Golf Course, *374*

Loveland, Colo.
Mariana Butte Golf Course, *151*
The Olde Course at Loveland, *152*
Loveland, Ohio
Eagles Nest Golf Course, *674*
Hickory Woods Golf Course, *681*
Lowell, Mich., Deer Run Golf Club, *428*
Lowellville, Ohio, Countryside Golf
Course, *672*
Lubbock, Texas
Elm Grove Golf Course, *836*
Meadowbrook Municipal Golf Complex,
848
Shadow Hills Golf Course, *858*
Lucas, Ky., Barren River State Park Golf
Course, *366*
Luck, Wis., Luck Golf Course, *950*
Ludington, Mich.
Lakeside Links, *452*
Lincoln Hills Golf Club, *453*
Lum, Mich., Lum International Golf Club,
454
Lumber Bridge, N.C., Scothurst Golf
Course, *656*
Luray, Va., Caverns Country Club Resort,
887
Lutherville, Md., Pine Ridge Golf
Course, *393*
Lutsen, Minn., Superior National Golf
Course, *517*
Lutz, Fla., Tournament Players Club of
Tampa Bay, *233*
Luxemburg, Wis., Northbrook Country
Club, *954*
Lydia, S.C., Fox Creek Golf Club, *783*
Lynden, Wash., Homestead Golf &
Country Club, *913*
Lynn, Mass., Larry Gannon Golf Club, *405*
Lynnfield, Mass., Sagamore Spring Golf
Club, *409*
Lyons, N.Y., Wayne Hills Country Club,
625
Lyons, Oreg., Elkhorn Valley Golf Club,
721

M

Mabank, Texas, Pinnacle Country Club,
312
McAfee, N.J., Great Gorge Country Club,
574
McAlester, Okla., Thundercreek Golf
Course, *718*
McCall, Idaho, McCall Municipal Golf
Course, *276*
McCalla, Ala., Tannehill National Golf
Course, *39*
McClure, Pa., Indian Run Golf Course, *749*
McComb, Miss., Quail Hollow Golf
Course, *526*
McCook, Nebr., Heritage Hills Golf
Course, *545*
McCormick, S.C., Hickory Knob Golf
Club, *786*
McDonough, Ga., Georgia National Golf
Club, *247*

McHenry, Ill., Chapel Hill Country Club,
285
McHenry, Md., The Golf Club at Wisp, *390*
McKee City, N.J., May's Landing Country
Club, *577*
McKenzie Meadows, Alberta, McKenzie
Meadows Golf Club, *978*
McKenzie, Tenn., Carroll Lake Golf Club,
813
Mackinac Island, Mich.
Grand Hotel Golf Club, *438*
Wawashkamo Golf Club, *486*
McKinleyville, Calif., Beau Pre Golf
Club, *77*
Macomb, Mich.
Bello Woods Golf Club, *415*
Hickory Hollow Golf Course, *444*
Sycamore Hills Golf Club, *480*
Wolverine Golf Club, *490*
Macon, Ga.
Barrington Hall Golf Club, *240*
Bowden Golf Course, *241*
McPherson, Kans., Turkey Creek Golf
Course, *365*
McRae, Ga., Wallace Adams Golf
Course, *260*
Madera, Calif., Madera Municipal Golf
Course, *104*
Madison, Ohio
Powderhorn Golf Course, *693*
Thunder Hill Golf Club, *704*
Madison, Wis.
Odana Hills Golf Course, *955*
Yahara Hills Golf Course, *968*
Madras, Oreg., Nine Peaks Madras Golf
& Country Club, *725*
Magazine, Ark., Lil'Bit A Heaven Golf
Club, *72*
Maggie Valley, N.C., Maggie Valley
Resort Golf Club, *644*
Magnolia, N.C., Magnolia Country Club,
644
Mahanoy City, Pa., Mountain Valley Golf
Course, *754*
Mahomet, Ill., Lake of the Woods Golf
Club, *301*
Mahopac, N.Y., Putnam Country Club,
615
Mahwah, N.J., Darlington Golf Course,
571
Malaga, Wash., Three Lakes Golf Club,
923
Malibu, Calif., Malibu Country Club, *104*
Malmokweg, Aruba, Tierra del Sol
Country Club, *1034*
Malone, N.Y., Malone Golf Club, *611*
Manahawkin, N.J., Ocean Acres Country
Club, *578*
Manakin Sabot, Va., Sycamore Creek
Golf Course, *902*
Manassas, Va., Manassas Park Public
Golf Course, *896*
Mancelona, Mich., Lakes of the North
Deer Run, *451*
Manchester, N.H., Derryfield Country
Club, *561*

Manchester Village, Vt., Gleaneagles Golf Course at the Equinox, *879*
Mandan, N.Dak., Prairie West Golf Course, *663*
Manhattan, Kans., Stagg Hill Golf Club, *364*
Manistee, Mich., Manistee Golf & Country Club, *455*
Manitouwadge, Ontario, *1011*
Manitowoc, Wis., Meadow Links Golf Course, *952*
Manorville, N.Y.
Pine Hills Country Club, *615*
Rock Hill Country Club, *616*
Swan Lake Golf Club, *621*
Mansfield, Ohio
Twin Lakes Golf Course, *705*
Woodridge Golf & Swim Club, *707*
Mansfield, Pa., Corey Creek Golf Club, *738*
Mansonville, Quebec, Owl's Head, *1021*
Manteno, Ill., Manteno Golf Club, *304*
Manzanillo, Colima
Isla Navidad Golf Club, *1028*
Las Hadas Resort, *1028*
Maple Grove, Minn.
Rush Creek Golf Club, *515*
Sundance Golf Club, *517*
Maple Valley, Wash.
Elk Run Golf Club, *910*
Lake Wilderness Golf Course, *915*
Mapleton, N.Dak., Maple River Golf Club, *663*
Maplewood, Minn., Goodrich Golf Course, *500*
Marana, Ariz., Heritage Highlands Golf & Country Club, *51*
Marathon, Ontario, Peninsula Golf Club, *1013*
Marengo, Ill., Marengo Ridge Golf Club, *304*
Margaretville, N.Y., Hanah Country Inn & Golf Resort, *607*
Margate, Fla., Oriole Golf & Tennis Club of Margate, *212*
Marietta, Ga., City Club Marietta, *244*
Marinette, Wis., Little River Country Club, *950*
Marion, Ill., Kokopelli Golf Club, *300*
Marion, Ind.
Hart Golf Course, *334*
Shady Hills Golf Course, *343*
Walnut Creek Golf Course, *346*
Marion, Iowa, Squaw Creek Golf Course, *357*
Marion, S.C., Dusty Hills Country Club, *782*
Marion, Va., Holston Hills Golf Club, *892*
Markham, Ontario, Angus Glen Golf Club, *1003*
Marne, Mich., Western Greens Golf Course, *487*
Marquette, Mich.
Chocolay Downs Golf Course, *424*
Marquette Golf & Country Club, *456*

Marshall, Minn.
Marshall Golf Club, *506*
Marshall High School Golf Club, *506*
Marshall's Creek, Pa., Mountain Manor Inn & Golf Club, *754*
Marshfield, Mass., Green Harbor Golf Club, *403*
Marshfield, Wis., Marshfield Country Club, *951*
Marshville, N.C., Eagle Chase Golf Club, *636*
Marstons Mills, Mass., Olde Barnstable Fairgrounds Golf Course, *407*
Mart, Texas, Battle Lake Golf Course, *827*
Martinsburg, W.Va., Stonebridge Golf Club, *931*
Marysville, Calif., Plumas Lake Golf & Country Club, *116*
Marysville, Mich., Marysville Golf Course, *457*
Marysville, Ohio
Darby Creek Golf Course, *673*
Flagstone Golf Club, *676*
Rolling Meadows Golf Club, *697*
Marysville, Wash.
Battle Creek Golf Course, *906*
Cedarcrest Golf Club, *908*
Maryville, Mo., Mozingo Lake Golf Course, *535*
Maryville, Tenn., Lambert Acres Golf Club, *819*
Mashpee, Mass.
New Seabury Country Club, *406*
Quashnet Valley Country Club, *408*
Mason City, Iowa, Highland Park Golf Course, *352*
Mason, Mich.
Branson Bay Golf Course, *419*
El Dorado Golf Course, *430*
Mason Hills Golf Course, *457*
Mason, Ohio
Crooked Tree Golf Club, *673*
The Golf Center at Kings Island, *677*
Kingswood Golf Course, *684*
Western Row Golf Course, *706*
Mason, W.Va., Riverside Golf Club, *930*
Massena, N.Y., Massena Country Club, *612*
Massillon, Ohio
The Legends of Massillon, *685*
Rolling Green Golf Course, *696*
Mather, Calif., Mather Golf Course, *105*
Matthews, N.C., The Divide, *635*
Mattoon, Ill., Meadowview Golf Course, *305*
Maunaloa (Molokai), Hawaii, Kaluakoi Golf Course, *264*
Mauston, Wis., Castle Rock Golf Course, *937*
Mayville, Mich., Greenbriar Golf Course, *441*
Mayville, Wis., Mayville Golf Club, *951*
Mazatlan, Sinaloa
El Cid Golf & Country Club, *1030*
Estrella del Mar Golf Club, *1030*

Midland, Texas, Hogan Park Golf
Course, *842*
Midway, Pa., Quicksilver Golf Club, *760*
Midway, Utah
Homestead Golf Club, *871*
Wasatch State Park Golf Club, *876*
Midwest City, Okla., John Conrad
Regional Golf Course, *713*
Milan, Ill.
Indian Bluff Golf Course, *297*
Pinnacle Country Club, *312*
Milford, Kans., Rolling Meadows Golf
Course, *363*
Milford, Mich.
Kensington Metro Park Golf Club, *450*
Mystic Creek Golf Club, *460*
Mililani (Oahu), Hawaii, Mililani Golf
Club, *268*
Milledgeville, Ga., Little Fishing Creek
Golf Club, *252*
Millersburg, Pa., Harrisburg North Golf
Course, *746*
Milliken, Colo., Mad Russian Golf
Course, *151*
Millington, Tenn.
Big Creek Golf Club, *812*
Orgill Park Golf Course, *821*
Millstadt, Ill., Triple Lakes Golf Course,
323
Milpitas, Calif.
Spring Valley Golf Club, *131*
Summit Pointe Golf Club, *132*
Milton, Fla.
The Moors Golf Club, *209*
Tanglewood Golf & Country Club, *230*
Milton, N.J., Bowling Green Golf Club, *569*
Milton, Pa., Turbot Hills Golf Course, *767*
Milton, Wis., Oak Ridge Golf Course, *955*
Milwaukee, Wis.
Brown Deer Park Golf Course, *936*
Dretzka Park Golf Course, *940*
Mineral Wells, W.Va., Woodridge
Plantation Golf Club, *932*
Minerva, Ohio, Great Trail Golf Course,
679
Minneapolis, Minn.
Columbia Golf Course, *496*
Francis A. Gross Golf Course, *500*
Hiawatha Golf Course, *502*
Minocqua, Wis., Pecks Wildwood Golf
Course, *956*
Minot, N.Dak.
Minot Country Club, *663*
Souris Valley Golf Club, *664*
Miramichi, New Brunswick, Miramichi
Golf & Country Club, *998*
Mishicot, Wis., Fox Hills Resort, *941*
Mission, Texas
Seven Oaks Resort & Country Club, *858*
Shary Municipal Golf Course, *859*
Missoula, Mont., Larchmont Golf Course,
541
Mitchell, S.Dak., Lakeview Golf Course,
809
Mitchellville, Md., Enterprise Golf
Course, *389*

Moab, Utah, Moab Golf Club, *872*
Mobile, Ala.
Azalea City Golf Club, *26*
Linksman Golf Club, *34*
Modesto, Calif.
Creekside Golf Course, *84*
Dryden Park Golf Course, *88*
Momence, Ill., South Shore Golf Course,
319
Moncks Corner, S.C., Berkeley Country
Club, *775*
Moncton, New Brunswick
Country Meadows Golf Club, *996*
Magnetic Hill Golf & Country Club, *998*
Maplewood Golf & Country Club, *998*
Monmouth, Ill., Gibson Woods Golf
Course, *292*
Monroe, Conn., Whitney Farms Golf
Course, *169*
Monroe, La., Chennault Park Golf
Course, *376*
Monroe, Mich.
Green Meadows Golf Course, *441*
Raisin River Country Club, *470*
Monroe, N.C.
Monroe Country Club, *646*
Stonebridge Golf Club, *658*
Mont Tremblant, Quebec
Gray Rocks Golf Club, *1020*
Tremblant Golf Resort, *1022*
Montague, Mich.
Hickory Knoll Golf Course, *445*
Old Channel Trail Golf Club, *463*
Montague, N.J., High Point Country Club,
575
Montauk, N.Y., Montauk Downs State
Park Golf Course, *613*
Montebello, Calif., Montebello Golf Club,
107
Montebello, Quebec, Le Chateau
Montebello, *1020*
Montego Bay, Jamaica
Half Moon Golf, Tennis & Beach Club,
1038
Ironshore Golf & Country Club, *1038*
The Wyndham Rose Hall Golf & Beach
Resort, *1039*
Monterey, Calif.
Laguna Seca Golf Club, *100*
Old Del Monte Golf Course, *112*
Montevallo, Ala., Montevallo Golf Club, *35*
Montgomery, Ala.
Lagoon Park Golf Course, *33*
River Run Golf Course, *37*
Montgomery, N.Y., Stony Ford Golf Club,
621
Montgomery, Pa., White Deer Park &
Golf Course, *769*
Montgomery, Texas, Del Lago Golf
Resort, *835*
Monticello, Minn.
Monticello Country Club, *508*
Silver Springs Golf Course, *516*
Monticello, N.Y., Kutsher's Country Club,
609
Montpelier, Va., Hollows Golf Course, *892*

Murrysville, Pa.
Meadowink Golf Club, *752*
Murraysville Golf Club, *754*
Rolling Fields Golf Course, *760*
Muscatine, Iowa, Muscatine Municipal
  Golf Course, *354*
Muscle Shoals, Ala., Cypress Lakes Golf
  & Country Club, *28*
Muskego, Wis., Muskego Lakes Country
  Club, *953*
Muskegon, Mich.
Chase Hammond Golf Course, *423*
Fruitport Golf Club, *434*
Lincoln Golf Club, *453*
Oak Ridge Golf Club, *462*
Myrtle Beach, S.C.
Arcadian Shores Golf Club, *774*
Arrowhead Country Club, *774*
Belle Terre Golf Course, *775*
The Dunes Golf & Beach Club, *781*
Heron Point Golf Club, *786*
Island Green Golf Club, *788*
The Legends, *790*
Man O' War Golf, *792*
Myrtle Beach National Golf Club, *792*
Pine Lakes International Country Club, *797*
Quail Creek Golf Club, *798*
Raccoon Run Golf Club, *799*
River Oaks Golf Plantation, *800*
Waterway Hills Golf Club, *805*
Wicked Stick Golf Links, *806*
The Wizard Golf Course, *807*

N

Naalehu, Hawaii, Discovery Harbour Golf
  & Country Club, *262*
Nacogdoches, Texas, Woodland Hills
  Golf Course, *866*
Nags Head, N.C., Nags Head Golf Links,
  647
Nampa, Idaho
Centennial Golf Club, *274*
Ridgecrest Golf Club, *277*
Nanaimo, British Columbia, Nanaimo
  Golf Club, *988*
Nanoose Bay, British Columbia,
  Fairwinds Golf & Country Club, *985*
Napa, Calif.
The Chardonnay Golf Club, *82*
Chimney Rock Golf Course, *83*
Napa Municipal Golf Club, *109*
Silverado Country Club & Resort, *129*
Naperville, Ill.
Country Lakes Village Golf Club, *287*
Springbrook Golf Course, *321*
Tamarack Golf Club, *322*
Naples, Fla.
Lely Resort & Country Club, *203*
Marco Shores Country Club, *206*
Marriott's Golf Club at Marco, *207*
Naples Beach Hotel & Golf Club, *210*
Palm River Country Club, *215*
Quality Inn & Suites Golf Resort, *219*
Nashua, N.H., Sky Meadow Country
  Club, *566*

Nashville, Ind., Salt Creek Golf Club,
  342
Nashville, Mich., Mulberry Fore Golf
  Course, *459*
Nashville, Tenn.
Harpeth Hills Golf Course, *817*
McCabe Field Golf Course, *820*
Nashboro Golf Club, *821*
Springhouse Golf Club, *823*
Two Rivers Golf Course, *825*
Nashville, Tenn..Ted Rhodes Golf
  Course, *824*
Nassau, New Providence
Cable Beach Golf Club, *1039*
Paradise Island Golf Club, *1040*
South Ocean Golf & Beach Resort, *1040*
Navarre, Fla., The Club at Hidden Creek,
  181
Navasota, Texas, Bluebonnet Country
  Golf Course, *829*
Needles, Calif., Needles Municipal Golf
  Course, *110*
Neenah, Wis.
Bridgewood Golf Course, *935*
Winagamie Golf Course, *968*
Nekoosa, Wis., Lake Arrowhead Golf
  Course, *948*
Nellis AFB, Nev., Sunrise Vista Golf
  Club, *558*
Neptune, N.J.
Jumping Brook Country Club, *576*
Shark River Golf Course, *582*
Nescopeck, Pa., Arnold's Golf Club, *732*
Neshanic, N.J., Hillsborough Country
  Club, *575*
Nevada, Mo., Frank E. Peters Municipal
  Golf Course, *531*
New Baltimore, Mich.
Cedar Glen Golf Club, *422*
Salt River Country Club, *475*
New Berlin, Wis., New Berlin Hills Golf
  Course, *954*
New Bern, N.C.
Carolina Pines Golf & Country Club, *631*
The Emerald Club, *636*
Fairfield Harbour Country Club, *637*
New Boston, Mich., Willow Metropark
  Golf Course, *490*
New Braunfels, Texas, Landa Park
  Municipal Golf Course, *846*
New Britain, Conn., Stanley Golf Club,
  167
New Buffalo, Mich., Whittaker Woods
  Golf Club, *489*
New Carlisle, Ohio, Sugar Isle Golf
  Country, *701*
New Castle, Pa.
Castle Hills Golf Course, *736*
Mohawk Trails Golf Course, *753*
Sylvan Heights Golf Course, *765*
New Era, Mich., Grand View Golf Course,
  440
New Franken, Wis., Royal Scot Golf
  Course & Supper Club, *960*
New Glasgow, Nova Scotia,
  Abercrombie Golf Club, *1000*

Ocho Rios, Jamaica, Sandals Golf & Country Club, *1038*
Ocoee, Fla., Forest Lake Golf Club of Ocoee, *192*
Oconomowoc, Wis.
Deertrak Golf Course, *939*
Olde Highlander Golf Club at Olympia Resort, *956*
Paganica Golf Course, *956*
Odessa, Fla., The Eagles Golf Club, *189*
Odessa, Texas, Ratliff Ranch Golf Links, *854*
O'Fallon, Ill., Tamarack Country Club, *322*
O'Fallon, Mo., The Falls Golf Club, *531*
Ogden, Utah
Ben Lomond Golf Course, *868*
Mount Ogden Golf Course, *872*
Schneiter's Riverside Golf Course, *874*
Ojai, Calif.
Ojai Valley Inn, *111*
Soule Park Golf Course, *131*
Oklahoma City, Okla.
Earlywine Park Golf Course, *711*
Lake Hefner Golf Club, *714*
Lincoln Park Golf Course, *715*
Silverhorn Golf Club, *717*
Trosper Park Golf Course, *718*
Okoboji, Iowa, Brooks Golf Club, *349*
Okotoks, Alberta, D'Arcy Ranch Golf Club, *975*
Olathe, Kans., Heritage Park Golf Course, *360*
Old Hickory, Tenn., Hermitage Golf Course, *818*
Olds, Alberta, Olds Golf Club, *979*
O'Leary, P.E.I., Mill River Golf Course, *1019*
Olive Branch, Miss.
Cherokee Valley Golf Club, *523*
Holiday Golf Club, *524*
Plantation Golf Club, *526*
Wedgewood Golf Course, *527*
Oliver, British Columbia, Fairview Mountain Golf Club, *985*
Olney, Md., Trotters Glen Golf Course, *396*
Olympia, Wash., Capitol City Golf Club, *907*
Olympic Valley, Calif., Resort at Squaw Creek, *121*
Omaha, Nebr.
Applewood Golf Course, *544*
Benson Park Golf Course, *544*
Elmwood Park Golf Course, *544*
The Knolls Golf Course, *547*
Miracle Hill Golf & Tennis Center, *547*
Tiburon Golf Club, *549*
Onamia, Minn., Izaty's Golf & Yacht Club, *503*
Onanole, Manitoba, Clear Lake Golf Course, *994*
Oneida, Wis., Brown County Golf Course, *936*
Onset, Mass., Bay Pointe Country Club, *398*

Ontario, Calif., Whispering Lakes Golf Course, *139*
Ontario, Oreg., Shadow Butte Golf Club, *729*
Opelika, Ala., Grand National Golf Club, *30*
Orange City, Fla., Monastery Golf & Country Club, *209*
Orange City, Iowa, Landsmeer Golf Club, *353*
Orange, Conn.
Grassy Hill Country Club, *162*
Orange Hills Country Club, *164*
Orange Park, Fla., Eagle Harbor Golf Club, *189*
Orangeburg, S.C., Hillcrest Golf Club, *786*
Orangeville, Ontario, Hockley Valley Resort, *1009*
Oregon City, Oreg., Oregon City Golf Club, *725*
Oregon, Ill., Silver Ridge Golf Course, *319*
Oregon, Ohio, Maumee Bay Resort Golf Course, *687*
Orilla, Ontario, Hawk Ridge Golf Club, *1008*
Oriskany Falls, N.Y., Barker Brook Golf Club, *591*
Orland Park, Ill., Silver Lake Country Club, *319*
Orlando, Fla.
Arnold Palmer's Bay Hill Club & Lodge, *173*
Eastwood Golf Club, *190*
Grand Cypress Golf Club, *196*
Hunter's Creek Golf Club, *198*
International Golf Club, *201*
Metrowest Country Club, *208*
Orlando World center-Marriott, *212*
Rosemont Golf & Country Club, *222*
Ventura Country Club, *234*
Wedgefield Golf & Country Club, *236*
Orleans, Vt., Orleans Country Club, *881*
Ormond Beach, Fla.
Halifax Plantation Golf Club, *197*
Ridgewood Lakes Golf Club, *220*
River Bend Golf Club, *220*
Riviera Country Club, *221*
Tomoka Oaks Golf & Country Club, *232*
Oromocto, New Brunswick, Gage Golf & Curling Association, *997*
Orondo, Wash., Desert Canyon Golf Resort, *909*
Orono, Maine, Penobscot Valley Country Club, *383*
Oroville, Calif., Table Mountain Golf Course, *134*
Orting, Wash., High Cedars Golf Club, *912*
Ortonville, Minn., Ortonville Municipal Golf Course, *510*
Osage Beach, Mo.
Dogwood Hills Golf Club, *530*
Marriott's Tan-Tar-A Resort, *534*
Oscoda, Mich., Lakewood Shores Resort, *452*

Oshkosh, Wis.
Far Vu Golf Course, *941*
Lake Shore Golf Course, *949*
Utica Hills Golf Course, *966*
Westhaven Golf Club, *967*
Oskaloosa, Iowa, Edmundson Golf Course, *350*
Osoyoos, British Columbia, Osoyoos Golf & Country Club, *989*
Ostego, Mich., Prairiewood Golf Course, *469*
Ostrander, Ohio, Mill Creek Golf Club, *688*
Oswego, Ill., Fox Bend Golf Course., *291*
Ottawa Lake, Mich., Whiteford Valley Golf Club, *489*
Ottawa, Ohio, Country Acres Golf Club, *672*
Ottumwa, Iowa, Ottumwa Municipal Golf Course, *355*
Overland Park, Kans.
Deer Creek Golf Club, *360*
Overland Park Golf Club, *362*
St. Andrews Golf Course, *363*
Oviedo, Fla., Ekana Golf Club, *190*
Owasco, N.Y., Dutch Hollow Country Club, *602*
Owasso, Okla., Bailey Golf Club Ranch, *709*
Owatonna, Minn., Brooktree Municipal Golf Course, *494*
Owings Mills, Md., Worthington Valley Country Club, *397*
Oxford, Ind., Oak Grove Country Club, *338*
Oxford, Mich.
Devil's Ridge Golf Club, *428*
Mulberry Hills Golf Course, *460*
Oxford Hills Golf Club, *463*
Oxford, Miss.
Grand Oaks Resort, *524*
Ole Miss Golf Club, *525*
Oxford, N.Y., Blue Stone Golf Club, *593*
Oxford, Ohio, Hueston Woods Golf Course, *682*
Oxford, Pa., Wyncote Golf Club, *770*
Oxnard, Calif., River Ridge Golf Club, *122*
Ozark, Ala., Willow Oaks Golf Club, *40*
Ozawkie, Kans., Village Greens Golf Club, *365*

P

Pacific Grove, Calif., Pacific Grove Municipal Golf Links, *113*
Pacifica, Calif., Sharp Park Golf Course, *128*
Pacolma, Calif., Hansen Dam Golf Course, *95*
Paducah, Ky., Paxton Park Golf Club, *373*
Page, Ariz., Lake Powell National Golf Club, *53*
Pagosa Springs, Colo., Pagosa Springs Golf Club, *152*

Pahrump, Nev., Calvada Valley Golf & Country Club, *551*
Painesville, Ohio
Fairway Pines Golf Course, *675*
Quail Hollow Resort & Country Club, *694*
Palatine, Ill., Palatine Hills Golf Course, *310*
Palm Beach, Fla., The Breakers Club, *178*
Palm Beach Gardens, Fla.
Palm Beach Gardens Municipal Golf Coursem, *214*
PGA National Golf Club, *213*
Palm City, Fla., Golden Bear Golf Club at Hammock Creek, *194*
Palm Coast, Fla.
Matanzas Woods Golf Club, *207*
Palm Coast Resort, *215*
Palm Harbor Golf Club, *215*
Pine Lakes Country Club, *216*
Palm Desert, Calif.
Desert Falls Country Club, *86*
Desert Willow Golf Resort, *87*
Marriott's Desert Springs Resort & Spa, *104*
Palm Desert Resort Country Club, *113*
Palm Harbor, Fla.
Innisbrook Hilton Resort, *200*
Lansbrook Golf Course, *203*
Tarpon Woods Golf & Country Club, *231*
Palm Springs, Calif.
Canyon South Golf Course, *81*
Palm Springs Country Club, *113*
Tahquitz Creek Resort, *134*
Palmer, Alaska, Palmer Golf Course, *42*
Palmer, Puerto Rico, Rio Mar Country Club, *1042*
Palmetto, Fla., Imperial Lakewoods Golf Club, *199*
Palos Heights, Ill., Westgate Valley Golf Club, *325*
Palos Park, Ill., Palos Country Club, *310*
Palos Verdes Estates, Calif., Palos Verdes Golf Club, *114*
Pampa, Texas, Hidden Hills Public Golf Course, *841*
Pana, Ill., Oak Terrace Golf Course, *308*
Panama City Beach, Fla.
Hombre Golf Club, *198*
Marriott's Bay Point Resort, *206*
Signal Hill Golf & Country Club, *228*
Panora, Iowa, Lake Panorama National Golf Course, *353*
Paradise Valley, Ariz., Stonecreek, The Golf Club, *63*
Paramus, N.J., Paramus Golf Club, *579*
Paris, Ill., Sycamore Hills Golf Club, *322*
Paris, Ky., Houston Oaks Golf Course, *370*
Paris, Ontario, The Oaks of St. George Golf Club, *1012*
Paris, Texas, Pine Ridge Golf Course, *852*
Park City, Ky., Park Mammoth Golf Club, *373*

Petersburg, Mich., Deme Acres Golf Course, 428

Petitcodiac, New Brunswick, Petitcodiac Valley Golf & Country Club, 999

Petoskey, Mich., Crooked Tree Golf Club, 426

Pewaukee, Wis.
Naga-Waukee Golf Course, 953
Western Lakes Golf Club, 967
Willow Run Golf Club, 968

Pflugerville, Texas, Blackhawk Golf Club, 828

Philadelphia, Pa.
Cobb's Creek Golf Club, 738
Franklin D. Roosevelt Golf Club, 744
John F. Byrne Golf Course, 749

Phillipsburg, St. Maarten, Mullet Bay Golf Club, 1043

Phoenix, Ariz.
Ahwatukee Country Club, 43
Arizona Biltmore Country Club, 44
Cave Creek Golf Club, 45
Club West Golf Club, 45
Encanto Golf Course, 48
The Foothills Golf Club, 48
Maryvale Golf Club, 55
Mountain View Golf Club, 56
Papago Golf Course, 57
The Pointe Hilton Resort at South Mountain, 58
The Pointe Hilton Resort at Tapatio Cliffs, 59
The Raven Golf Club at South Mountain, 60

Phoenixville, Pa., Pickering Valley Golf Club, 757

Pickerington, Ohio, Turnberry Golf Course, 705

Pickwick Dam, Tenn.
Marriott's Golf Club at Shiloh Falls, 820
Pickwick Landing State Park Golf Course, 822

Picture Butte, Alberta, Picture Butte Golf & Winter Club, 979

Pierre, S.Dak., Hillsview Golf Club, 809

Pigeon Forge, Tenn., Gatlinburg Golf Course, 816

Pigeon, Mich., Scenic Country Club, 476

Piketon, Ohio, Big Beaver Creek Golf Course, 666

Pikeville, Tenn., Fall Creek Falls State Park Golf Course, 815

Pinckney, Mich.
Rush Lake Hills Golf Club, 474
Whispering Pines Golf Club, 488

Pinconning, Mich., Green Hills Golf Club, 440

Pine Hill, Quebec, Le Club de Golf Carling Lake, 1021

Pine Knoll Shores, N.C., Bogue Banks Country Club, 629

Pine Mountain, Ga., Callaway Gardens Resort, 242

Pine Plains, N.Y., Thomas Carvel Country Club, 622

Pinebluff, N.C., Oakwood Hills Golf Club, 648

Pinedale, Wyo., Rendezvous Meadows Golf Club, 971

Pinehurst, N.C.
Pinehurst Plantation Golf Club, 651
Pinehurst Resort & Country Club, 651
The Pit Golf Links, 653

Pineville, N.C., Crystal Springs Golf Club, 634

Pinney's Beach, Nevis, Four Seasons Resort Nevis, 1039

Pioneer, Calif., Mace Meadows Golf & Country Club, 103

Pipestem, W.Va., Pipestem Golf Club, 930

Piscataway, N.J., Rutgers University Golf Club, 582

Pitt Meadows, British Columbia
Meadow Gardens Golf Course, 988
Pitt Meadows Golf Club, 990
Swan-E-Set Bay Resort & Country Club, 992

Pittsburg, Calif., Pittsburg Delta View Golf Course, 116

Plainfield, Ill.
Carillon Golf Club, 284
Naperbrook Golf Course, 306

Plainville, Mass., Heather Hill Country Club, 403

Plainwell, Mich., Lake Doster Golf Club, 450

Plano, Texas
Chase Oaks Golf Club, 832
Plano Municipal Golf Course, 853

Plant City, Fla.
Plant City Golf Club, 217
Walden Lakes Golf & Country Club, 235

Plantation, Fla., Jacaranda Golf Club, 201

Plattsburgh, N.Y., Bluff Point Golf & Country Club, 594

Pleasant Valley, N.Y., James Baird State Park Golf Club, 609

Plover, Wis., Three Acres Golf Course, 965

Plymouth, Ind.
Plymouth Rock Golf Course, 340
Swan Lake Golf Club, 344
Tri-Way Golf Club, 345

Plymouth, Mass.
Atlantic Country Club, 398
Squirrel Run Golf & Country Club, 410

Plymouth, Mich.
Brae Burn Golf Course, 418
Fox Hills Golf & Conference Center, 433
Hilltop Golf Course, 446
St. John's Golf Club, 475

Plymouth, Minn.
Elm Creek Golf Links of Plymouth, 499
Hampton Hills Golf Course, 501
Hollydale Golf Course, 502

Poca, W.Va., Scarlett Oaks Country Club, 931

Pocatello, Idaho
Highland Golf Course, 276
Riverside Golf Course, 277

Providence, R.I., Triggs Memorial Golf Course, *773*

Providenciales, Turks & Caicos Islands, Provo Golf Club, *1044*

Provo, Utah, East Bay Golf Course, *869*

Prudenville, Mich., White Deer Country Club, *488*

Pueblo, Colo.
Pueblo City Park Golf Course, *154*
Walking Stick Golf Course, *157*

Pueblo West, Colo., Pueblo West Golf Course, *154*

Puerto Plata, Dominican Republic, Radisson Puerto Plata Golf Resort, *1037*

Puerto Vallarta, Jalisco, Marina Vallarta Club de Golf, *1029*

Pukalani (Maui), Hawaii, Pukalani Country Club, *270*

Pulaski, Pa., Rolling Hills Golf Course, *761*

Punaluu, Hawaii, Seamountain Golf Course, *270*

Puyallup, Wash., Lipoma Firs Golf Course, *916*

Q

Quakertown, Pa., Fox Hollow Golf Club, *744*

Qualicum Beach, British Columbia, Eaglecrest Golf Club, *984*

Quantico, Md., Green Hill Yacht & Country Club, *390*

Quarryville, Pa., Tanglewood Manor Golf Club & Learning Center, *766*

Queen Creek, Ariz., The Links at Queen Creek, *54*

Queensbury, N.Y., Hiland Golf Club, *607*

Queenstown, Md., Queenstown Harbor Golf Links, *394*

Quentin, Pa., Fairview Golf Course, *743*

Quincy, Fla., Golf Club of Quincy, *195*

Quincy, Ill., Westview Golf Course, *325*

Quinton, Va., The Brookwoods Golf Club, *886*

R

Racine, Wis., Johnson Park Golf Course, *946*

Radium Hot Springs, British Columbia, Springs at Radium Golf Course, *992*

Raeford, N.C., Bayonet at Puppy Creek Golf Club, *627*

Raleigh, N.C.
Cheviot Hills Golf Club, *632*
Hedingham Golf Club, *640*

Ramona, Calif.
Mount Woodson Country Club, *108*
San Vicente Inn & Golf Club, *125*

Ramsey, Minn., The Links at Northfork, *504*

Rancho Cucamonga, Calif., Empire Lakes Golf Course, *90*

Rancho de Taos, N.Mex., Taos Country Club, *588*

Rancho Mirage, Calif.
Marriott's Rancho Las Palmas Resort & Country Club, *104*
Mission Hills North Golf Course, *106*
The Westin Mission Hills Resort, *138*

Rancho Murieta, Calif., Rancho Murieta Country Club, *119*

Rancho Palos Verdes, Calif., Los Verdes Golf Course, *103*

Rancho Santa Fe, Calif., Morgan Run Resort & Club, *108*

Rancho Santa Margarita, Calif., Tijeras Creek Golf Club, *135*

Rancho Viejo, Texas, Rancho Viejo Resort & Country Club, *854*

Randolph, N.Y., Cardinal Hills Golf Course, *596*

Randolph, Vt., Montague Golf Club, *880*

Rangeley, Maine, Mingo Springs Golf Course, *382*

Rantoul, Ill., Willow Pond Golf Course, *325*

Rapid City, S.Dak.
Hart Ranch Golf Course, *808*
Meadowbrook Golf Course, *810*

Rathdrum, Idaho, Twin Falls Village Golf Course, *279*

Ravenna, Mich., Ravenna Golf Course, *471*

Ravenna, Ohio, Windmill Lakes Golf Club, *707*

Ravenswood, W.Va., Greenhills Country Club, *928*

Ray, Mich., Pine Valley Golf Club, *466*

Ray, N.Dak., The Links of North Dakota at Red Mike Resort, *663*

Ray Township, Mich., Northbrook Golf Club, *461*

Raymond, Miss., Eagle Ridge Golf Course, *523*

Reading, Pa.
Exeter Golf Club, *742*
Flying Hills Golf Course, *743*

Red Deer, Alberta, River Bend Golf Course, *980*

Red Lodge, Mont., Red Lodge Mountain Resort Golf Course, *543*

Red Wing, Minn., Mississippi Dunes Golf Links, *508*

Redding, Calif., Gold Hills Country Club, *92*

Redford, Mich., Glenhurst Golf Course, *437*

Redmond, Oreg.
Eagle Crest Resort, *720*
Juniper Golf Club, *723*

Redmond, Wash., Willows Run Golf Club, *925*

Reedsburg, Wis., Reedsburg Country Club, *958*

Rehoboth Beach, Del., Old Landing Golf Club, *170*

Rehoboth, Mass., Rehoboth Country Club, *408*

Rock Island, Ill.
Highland Springs Golf Course, *296*
Saukie Municipal Golf Course, *317*
Rock Springs, Wyo., White Mountain
Golf Course, *972*
Rockford, Ill.
Aldeen Golf Club, *280*
Elliott Golf Course, *290*
Ingersoll Memorial Golf Club, *298*
Sandy Hollow Golf Course, *317*
Rockford, Mich.
Braeside Golf Course, *418*
North Kent Golf Course, *460*
Rockford, Tenn., Egwani Farms Golf
Course, *815*
Rockingham, N.C., Richmond Pines
Country Club, *655*
Rockland, Maine, Rockland Golf Club,
384
Rockledge, Fla., Turtle Creek Golf Club,
233
Rockleigh, N.J., Rockleigh Golf Course,
581
Rockport, Maine, Samoset Resort Golf
Club, *384*
Rockton, Ill., Macktown Golf Course,
304
Rockville, Md., Redgate Municipal Golf
Course, *394*
Rockwall, Texas, Buffalo Creek Golf
Club, *830*
Rogers, Ark., Prairie Creek Country
Club, *72*
Rogers, Minn.
Fox Hollow Golf Club, *500*
Pheasant Run Golf Club, *511*
Rogersville, Ala., Joe Wheeler State
Park Golf Course, *32*
Rogersville, Tenn., Camelot Golf Course,
813
Rohnert Park, Calif., Mountain Shadows
Golf Course, *109*
Rome City, Ind., Limberlost Golf Club,
337
Rome, Ga., Stonebridge Golf Club, *260*
Rome, N.Y., Rome Country Club, *616*
Romeo, Mich.
Greystone Golf Club, *441*
Heather Hills Golf Course, *444*
Romulus, Mich., Shady Hollow Golf
Course, *476*
Ronan, Mont., Mission Mountain Country
Club, *542*
Rooseveltown, N.Y., Cedar View Golf
Course, *597*
Roscoe, Ill., The Ledges Golf Club, *302*
Roscoe, N.Y., Tennanah Lake Golf &
Tennis Club, *621*
Roscommon, Mich., Burning Oak
Country Club, *420*
Rosedale, British Columbia, The Falls
Golf & Country Club, *985*
Rosemead, Calif., Whittier Narrows Golf
Course, *139*
Rosemount, Minn., Rich Valley Golf
Club, *514*

Roseneath, P.E.I., Brudenell River Golf
Course, *1018*
Roseville, Calif.
Roseville Diamond Oaks Municipal Golf
Course, *123*
Woodcreek Golf Club, *139*
Rothbury, Mich., Thoroughbred Golf
Club at Double JJ Resort, *482*
Rotonda, Fla., Rotonda Golf & Country
Club, *222*
Round Hill, Va., Stoneleigh Golf Club,
902
Round Lake Beach, Ill., Renwood
Country Club, *316*
Round Rock, Texas, Forest Creek Golf
Club, *837*
Royal Palm Beach, Fla., The Village Golf
Club, *235*
Ruidoso, N.Mex., The Links at Sierra
Blanca, *585*
Runaway Bay, Jamaica, Super Clubs
Golf Club at Runaway Bay, *1038*
Runaway Bay, Texas, The Club at
Runaway Bay, *833*
Runnells, Iowa, Toad Valley Public Golf
Course, *357*
Rush, N.Y., Wild Wood Country Club, *626*
Ruskin, Fla., The Golf Club at Cypress
Creek, *194*
Russell, Pa., Cable Hollow Golf Club,
735
Rutherfordton, N.C., Cleghorn Plantation
Golf & Country Club, *633*
Rutland, Vt., Rutland Country Club, *882*
Rutledge, Ga., Hard Labor Creek State
Park Golf Course, *249*

S

Saco, Maine, Biddeford Saco Country
Club, *381*
Sacramento, Calif.
Bartley W. Cavanaugh Golf Course, *77*
Bing Maloney Golf Course, *78*
Cordova Golf Course, *83*
Haggin Oaks Golf Course, *94*
Safford, Ariz., Mount Graham Municipal
Golf Course, *55*
Saginaw, Mich.
Crooked Creek Golf Club, *426*
Swan Valley Golf Course, *480*
Valley View Farm Golf Course, *485*
St. Andrews, Manitoba, Larters at St.
Andrews Golf & Country Club, *995*
St. Andrews, New Brunswick, The
Algonquin Golf Course, *996*
St. Anne, Ill.
Kankakee Elks Country Club, *299*
Oak Springs Golf Course, *308*
St. Augustine, Fla.
Marsh Creek Country Club, *207*
Radisson Ponce de Leon Golf &
Conference Resort, *219*
St. Augustine Shores Golf Club, *224*
St. Catharines, Ontario, The Links of
Rockway Glen, *1010*

St. Catherine, Jamaica, Caymanas Golf
  Course, *1038*
St. Charles, Ill.
Blackhawk Golf Club, *282*
Pheasant Run Resort Golf Course, *311*
Pottawatomie Park Golf Course, *313*
St. Charles, Mich., Kimberley Oaks Golf
  Club, *450*
St. Charles, Minn., St. Charles Golf Club,
  515
St. Charles, Mo., Missouri Bluffs Golf
  Club, *535*
St. Clair, Mich., Rattle Run Golf Course,
  470
St. Clair Shores, Mich., St. Clair Shores
  Country Club, *474*
St. George, Utah
Dixie Red Hills Golf Club, *869*
Entrada at Snow Canyon, *870*
St. George Golf Club, *874*
Southgate Golf Club, *875*
Sunbrook Golf Club, *876*
St. George's, Bermuda
The Mid Ocean Club, *1035*
St. George's Golf Club, *1036*
St. Germain, Wis., St. Germain Municipal
  Golf Club, *960*
St. Helena, Calif., Meadowood Resort
  Golf Course, *105*
St. James, Barbados
Royal Westmoreland Golf & Country Club,
  1034
Sandy Lane Golf Club, *1034*
St. John, Ind.
Lake Hills Golf Club, *336*
Palmira Golf & Country Club, *339*
St. John, New Brunswick, Rockwood
  Park Golf Course, *999*
St. Johns, Mich., The Emerald at Maple
  Creek Golf Course, *431*
St. Johnsbury, Vt., St. Johnsbury
  Country Club, *882*
St. Joseph, Mich., The Oaks Country
  Club, *462*
St. Joseph, Mo., Fairview Golf Course,
  531
St. Louis, Mo.
Cherry Hills Golf Club, *529*
Eagle Springs Golf Course, *531*
Forest Park Golf Course, *531*
Hawk Ridge Golf Club, *532*
Normandie Golf Club, *535*
Quail Creek Golf Club, *536*
Tapawingo National Golf Club, *539*
St. Marys, Ga., Osprey Cove Golf Club,
  255
St. Mary's, Pa., Bavarian Hills Golf
  Course, *732*
St. Matthews, S.C., Calhoun Country
  Club, *777*
St. Michaels, Md., Harbourtowne Golf
  Resort & Country Club, *390*
St. Paul, Minn.
Como Golf Course, *496*
Highland Park Golf Course, *502*
Keller Golf Course, *503*

Les Bolstad Univ. of Minnesota Golf Club,
  504
Park Golf Course, *511*
St. Peter, Minn., Shoreland Golf & Tennis
  Club, *516*
St. Petersburg, Fla.
Mangrove Bay Golf Course, *206*
Renaissance Vinoy Resort, *220*
St. Simons Island, Ga.
Hampton Club, *248*
St. Simons Island Club, *257*
Sea Island Golf Club, *258*
Sea Palms Resort, *258*
St. Stephen, New Brunswick, St.
  Stephen Golf Club, *1000*
Salado, Texas, Mill Creek Golf & Country
  Club, *849*
Salem, N.H., Campbell's Scottish
  Highlands Golf Course, *561*
Salem, Ohio, Salem Hills Golf & Country
  Club, *698*
Salem, Oreg.
McNary Golf Club, *724*
Salem Golf Club, *728*
Salem, Va., Hanging Rock Golf Club,
  891
Salem, Wis., Spring Valley Country Club,
  962
Salina, Kans., Salina Municipal Golf
  Course, *363*
Salinas, Calif., Salinas Fairways Golf
  Course, *123*
Salisbury, Md., Nutters Crossing Golf
  Club, *392*
Salt Lake City, Utah
Bonneville Golf Course, *868*
Glendale Golf Course, *870*
Mountain Dell Golf Club, *872*
Rose Park Golf Club, *874*
Wingpointe Golf Course, *877*
Saltillo, Miss.
Big Oaks Golf Club, *522*
Natchez Trace Golf Club, *525*
Saluda, S.C., Persimmon Hill Golf Club,
  797
Sam Rayburn, Texas, Rayburn Counry
  Club & Resort, *854*
San Angelo, Texas, Riverside Golf Club,
  856
San Antonio, Texas
Brackenridge Park Municipal Golf Course,
  829
Cedar Creek Golf Course, *831*
Hill Country Golf Club, *842*
La Cantera Golf Club, *845*
Mission del Lago Golf Course, *849*
Olmos Basin Golf Club, *850*
Pecan Valley Golf Club, *851*
Silverhorn Golf Club of Texas, *859*
Willow Springs Golf Club, *865*
Woodlake Country Club, *866*
San Bernardino, Calif.
San Bernardino Golf Club, *123*
Shandin Hills Golf Club, *128*
San Carlos, Sonora, Marina San Carlos
  Campo de Golf, *1031*

Schaumburg, Ill., Schaumburg Golf Club, *318*

Schenectady, N.Y., Schenectady Golf Course, *618*

Schererville, Ind., Scherwood Golf Course, *342*

Schoolcraft, Mich., Olde Mill Golf Club, *463*

Scotch Plains, N.J., Ash Brook Golf Course, *568*

Scotts, Mich., Indian Run Golf Club, *448*

Scottsbluff, Nebr., Riverview Golf Club, *548*

Scottsboro, Ala., Goose Pond Colony Golf Course, *29*

Scottsdale, Ariz.
Gainey Ranch Golf Club, *49*
Grayhawk Golf Club, *50*
Kierland Golf Club, *52*
Legend Trail Golf Club, *53*
McCormick Ranch Golf Club, *55*
Marriott's Camelback Golf Club, *54*
Mountain Shadows, *55*
Orange Tree Golf Club, *57*
Pavilion Lakes Golf Club, *58*
The Phoenician Golf Club, *58*
Scottsdale Country Club, *61*
Talking Stick Golf Club, *64*
Tournament Players Club at Scottsdale, *65*
Troon North Golf Club, *66*

Scottsville, N.Y.
Chili Country Club, *598*
Cragie Brae Golf Club, *600*

The Sea Ranch, Calif., The Sea Ranch Golf Links, *127*

Seabrook Island, S.C., The Club at Seabrook Island, *779*

Seaside, Calif., Bayonet Golf Course, *77*

Seattle, Wash.
Jackson Park Golf Course, *913*
Jefferson Park Golf Course, *914*
Tyee Valley Golf Course, *924*
West Seattle Golf Course, *925*

Sebastian, Fla., Sebastian Municipal Golf Course, *227*

Sebring, Fla.
Country Club of Sebring, *184*
Golf Hammock Country Club, *195*
Harder Hall Country Club, *198*
Spring Lake Golf & Tennis Resort, *229*

Secor, Ill., Fairlakes Golf Course, *290*

Sedona, Ariz.
Oakcreek Country Club, *56*
Sedona Golf Resort, *62*

Sellersburg, Ind.
Covered Bridge Golf Club, *329*
Hidden Creek Golf Club, *334*

Selma, Calif., Selma Valley Golf Course, *127*

Semmes, Ala., Magnolia Grove Golf Club, *34*

Sequim, Wash.
Dungeness Golf & Country Club, *910*
Sunland Golf & Country Club, *923*

Sevierville, Tenn., Eagle's Landing Golf Club, *814*

Sewell, N.J., Ron Jaworski's Eagles' Nest Country Club, *582*

Sexsmith, Alberta, Spruce Meadows Golf & Country Club, *981*

Seymour, Ind., Shadowood Golf Course, *343*

Seymour, Wis., Crystal Springs Golf Club, *938*

Shakopee, Minn.
Lone Pines Country Club, *505*
Stonebrooke Golf Club, *517*

Shalimar, Fla., Shalimar Pointe Golf & Country Club, *227*

Shallotte, N.C., Brierwood Golf Club, *629*

Sharon Center, Ohio, Western Reserve Golf & Country Club, *706*

Sharon, Ontario, Pheasant Run Golf Club, *1013*

Shawano, Wis., Shawano Lake Golf Club, *961*

Shawnee, Kans., Tomahawk Hills Golf Club, *364*

Shawnee, Okla., Fire Lake Golf Course, *711*

Shawnee-on-Delaware, Pa., Shawnee Inn Golf Resort, *762*

Sheboygan, Wis.
Riverdale Country Club, *959*
Sheboygan Town & Country Club, *961*

Shediac, New Brunswick, Pine Needles Golf & Country Club, *999*

Shelburne, Vt., Kwiniaska Golf Club, *880*

Shelby, Mich., Oceana Country Club, *462*

Shelby, N.C.
Pine Grove Golf Club, *650*
River Bend Golf Club, *655*

Shelby Township, Mich.
Cherry Creek Golf Club, *423*
Stony Creek Golf Course, *479*

Shelbyville, Ky., Weissinger Hills Golf Course, *375*

Shelbyville, Mich., Orchard Hills Golf Course, *463*

Shenandoah, Iowa, American Legion Country Club, *348*

Shepherd, Mich., Winding Brook Golf Club, *490*

Sherburne, Vt., Green Mountain National Golf Course, *879*

Sheridan, Wyo., Kendrick Golf Course, *971*

Sherwood Park, Alberta
Broadmoor Public Golf Course, *974*
Countryside Golf Course, *975*
Sherwood Park Golf Course, *981*

Sherwood, Wis., High Cliff Golf Course, *945*

Shoemakersville, Pa., Perry Golf Course, *757*

Short Hills, N.J., East Orange Golf Course, *572*

Shortsville, N.Y., Winged Pheasant Golf Links, *626*

Show Low, Ariz., Silver Creek Golf Club, *63*

Swansboro, N.C., Silver Creek Golf Club, *657*

Swansea, Mass., Swansea Country Club, *410*

Swanton, Ohio, Valleywood Golf Club, *705*

Swanton, Vt., Champlain Country Club, *878*

Swartz Creek, Mich., Genesee Valley Meadows, *435*

Swedesboro, N.J., Beckett Golf Club, *568*

Sweetwater, Texas, Sweetwater Country Club, *861*

Swift Current, Saskatchewan, Elmwood Golf Club, *1022*

Sycamore, Ill., Sycamore Community Golf Course, *322*

Sydney, Nova Scotia, Lingan Country Club, *1002*

Syracuse, Ind.
Maxwelton Golf Club, *338*
South Shore Golf Club, *343*

Syracuse, N.Y., Drumlins West Golf Club, *601*

T

Tacoma, Wash.
Brookdale Golf Course, *907*
Lake Spanaway Golf Course, *914*
Meadow Park Golf Course, *917*
North Shore Golf & Country Club, *919*

Talladega, Ala., Timber Ridge Golf Club, *39*

Tallahassee, Fla.
Hilaman Park Municipal Golf Course, *198*
Killearn Country Club & Inn, *202*
Seminole Golf Club, *227*

Tamarac, Fla., Colony West Country Club, *183*

Tamaroa, Ill., Red Hawk Country Club, *315*

Tamiment, Pa., Tamiment Resort & Conference Center Golf Club, *765*

Tampa, Fla.
Babe Zaharias Golf Course, *173*
Hall of Fame Golf Course, *198*
Northdale Golf Club, *211*
Rocky Point Golf Course, *221*
Rogers Park Golf Course, *221*
University of South Florida Golf Course, *234*
Westchase Golf Club, *237*

Tarpon Springs, Fla., Tarpon Springs Golf Club, *231*

Tavares, Fla., Deer Island Golf Club, *186*

Tawas City, Mich., Tawas Creek Golf Club, *481*

Taylor, British Columbia, The Lone Wolf Golf Club, *987*

Taylor, Mich.
Lakes of Taylor Golf Club, *451*
Taylor Meadows Golf Club, *481*

Taylor, Pa., Pine Hills Golf Course, *758*

Taylorsville, Ill., Lake Shore Golf Course, *301*

Taylorsville, Ky., Tanglewood Golf Course, *375*

Taylorsville, N.C., Brushy Mountain Golf Club, *630*

Taylorsville, Utah, Meadow Brook Golf Course, *872*

Teaneck, N.J., Overpeck County Golf Course, *579*

Tecumseh, Mich., Raisin Valley Golf Club, *470*

Tehachapi, Calif., Horse Thief Country Club, *96*

Telluride, Colo., Telluride Ski & Golf Club, *156*

Temecula, Calif.
Redhawk Golf Club, *120*
Temecula Creek Inn, *135*
Temeku Hills Golf & Country Club, *135*

Tempe, Ariz.
Asu Karsten Golf Course, *43*
Ken McDonald Golf Club, *52*

Temperance, Mich.
Bedford Falls Golf Club, *414*
Giant Oaks Golf Course, *435*

Temple, Texas, J.F. Sammons Park Golf Course, *843*

Terrace Bay, Ontario, Aguasabon Golf Course, *1003*

Terre Haute, Ind.
Hulman Links Golf Course, *335*
William S. Rea Golf Club, *347*

Terrebonne, Quebec, Golf Le Mirage Golf Club, *1020*

Teulon, Manitoba, Teulon Golf & Country Club, *995*

Tewksbury, Mass., Trull Brook Golf Course, *411*

Texarkana, Ark., South Haven Golf Club, *73*

Texas City, Texas, Bayou Golf Club, *828*

Thayne, Wyo., Star Valley Ranch Country Club, *972*

Thendara, N.Y., Thendara Golf Club, *622*

Thiells, N.Y., Philip J. Rotella Golf Course, *615*

Thompson, Conn., Raceway Golf Club, *165*

Thompsonville, Mich., Crystal Mountain Resort, *427*

Thomson, Ga., Belle Meade Country Club, *240*

Thorndale, Pa., Ingleside Golf Club, *749*

Thornton, Colo., Thorncreek Golf Club, *156*

Thousand Oaks, Calif., Los Robles Golf Course, *103*

Three Rivers, Mich., Sauganash Country Club, *476*

Thunder Bay, Ontario
Chapples Golf Course, *1005*
Fort William Country Club, *1008*

Thurmont, Md., Maple Run Golf Course, *391*

Tigerville, S.C., The Gauntlet at Laurel Valley, *784*

W

Wabamun, Alberta, Ironhead Golf & Country Club, *977*
Wabash, Ind., Honeywell Golf Course, *335*
Waco, Texas
Connally Golf Course, *834*
Cottonwood Creek Golf Course, *834*
Heather Run Golf & Fish Club, *841*
Waconia, Minn., Island View Golf Course, *503*
Wadsworth, Ill., Midlane Country Club, *305*
Wadsworth, Ohio, Pine Valley Golf Club, *692*
Wagram, N.C., Deercroft Golf Club, *634*
Wahpeton, N.Dak., Bois De Sioux Golf Club, *662*
Waianae (Oahu), Hawaii
Makaha Valley Country Club, *267*
Sheraton Makaha Golf Club, *270*
Waikoloa, Hawaii
Waikoloa Beach Resort, *271*
Waikoloa Village Golf Club, *272*
Wailea (Maui), Hawaii, Wailea Golf Club, *272*
Wailuku (Maui), Hawaii
Grand Waikapu Resort, Golf & Spa, *262*
Waiehu Golf Course, *271*
Waimanalo (Oahu), Hawaii, Olomana Golf Links, *269*
Waipahu (Oahu), Hawaii, Waikele Golf Club, *271*
Wake Forest, N.C., Wake Forest Country Club, *660*
Wakefield, Mass., Colonial Country Club, *400*
Waldo, Ohio, Kings Mill Golf Course, *684*
Waldorf, Md., Southview Golf Course, *395*
Waleska, Ga., Lake Arrowhead Country Club, *251*
Walhalla, S.C., Falcon's Lair Golf Course, *783*
Walker, Minn., Tianna Country Club, *518*
Walla Walla, Wash., Veterans Memorial Golf Course, *924*
Walled Lake, Mich.
El Dorado Country Club, *429*
The Links at Pinewood, *454*
Wallingford, Conn., Pilgrim's Harbor Country Club, *165*
Walloon Lake, Mich., Springbrook Golf Course, *478*
Walnut, Calif., Los Angeles Royal Vista Golf Course, *102*
Walnut Creek, Calif., Boundary Oaks Country Club, *79*
Walpole, N.H., Hooper Golf Club, *562*
Walworth, N.Y., Greystone Golf Club, *606*
Warden, Wash., Sage Hills Golf Club, *920*
Wareham, Mass., Little Harbor Country Club, *405*
Warm Springs, Oreg., Kah-Nee-Ta resort Golf Club, *723*

Warminster, Pa., Five Ponds Golf Club, *743*
Warner Robins, Ga.
International City Municipal Golf Course, *250*
Landings Golf Club, *252*
Warren, N.J., Warrenbrook Golf Course, *583*
Warren, Ohio
Avalon Lakes Golf Course, *665*
Champion Links Golf Club, *670*
Warren, Vt., Sugarbush Golf Course, *883*
Warrensburg, N.Y., Conins Golf Resort, *600*
Warroad, Minn., Warroad Estates Golf Course, *519*
Warwick, Bermuda
Belmont Golf & Country Club, *1035*
Riddell's Bay Golf & Country Club, *1036*
Wasco, Calif., Wasco Valley Rose Golf Course, *138*
Waseca, Minn., Lakeside Golf Club, *503*
Washburn, Ill., Snag Creek Golf Course, *319*
Washington, D.C.
East Potomac Park Golf Course, *171*
Langston Golf Course, *171*
Rock Creek Park Golf Course, *171*
Washington, Ill.
Pine Lakes Golf Club, *311*
Quail Meadows Golf Course, *314*
Washington, Mich.
Glacier Club, *435*
The Orchards Golf Club, *463*
Romeo Golf & Country Club, *473*
Washington, Utah, Green Spring Golf Course, *870*
Wasilla, Alaska
Settlers Bay Golf Club, *42*
Sleepy Hollow Golf Club, *42*
Waskesiu Lake, Saskatchewan, Waskesiu Golf Course, *1023*
Waterbury, Conn.
East Mountain Golf Club, *161*
Western Hills Golf Club, *168*
Waterford, Mich., Pontiac Country Club, *468*
Waterford, Wis., Rivermoor Country Club, *959*
Waterloo, Ill., Annbriar Golf Course, *280*
Waterloo, Iowa
Byrnes Park Golf Course, *350*
Gates Park Golf Course, *352*
Red Carpet Golf Club, *355*
South Hills Golf Course, *356*
Waterport, N.Y., Harbour Pointe Country Club, *607*
Watertown, Conn., Crestbrook Park Golf Club, *160*
Watertown, Minn., Timber Creek Golf Course, *518*
Watertown, N.Y., Watertown Golf Club, *624*
Watertown, S.Dak., Watertown Municipal Golf Course, *811*

Waterville, Ohio, Fallen Timbers Fairways, *675*

Watervliet, Mich., Paw Paw Lake Golf Course, *464*

Watsonville, Calif., Pajaro Valley Golf Club, *113*

Waukegan, Ill.
Bonnie Brook Golf Club, *282*
Orchard Hills Country Club, *309*

Waupaca, Wis., Foxfire Golf Club, *942*

Wausau, Wis., Trapp River Golf Club, *964*

Wauseon, Ohio, Ironwood Golf Club, *683*

Wautoma, Wis., Two Oaks North Golf Club, *966*

Wauwatosa, Wis., Currie Park Golf Course, *939*

Waveland, Ind., Turkey Run Golf Course, *345*

Waverly, Iowa, Waverly Golf Course, *358*

Waverly, N.Y., Tomasso's Chemung Golf Course, *623*

Waverly, W.Va., Golf Club of West Virginia, *927*

Waycross, Ga., Laura Walker Golf Course, *252*

Wayland, Mass., Sandy Burr Country Club, *409*

Wayne, Nebr., Wayne Country Club, *549*

Wayne, N.J., Passaic County Golf Course, *580*

Waynesfield, Ohio, Prairie View Golf Course, *693*

Waynesville, N.C., Waynesville Country Club Inn, *660*

Waynesville, Ohio, Holly Hills Golf Club, *682*

Weaverville, N.C., Reems Creek Golf Club, *654*

Webberville, Mich., Oak Lane Golf Course, *461*

Webster City, Iowa, Briggs Woods Golf Course, *349*

Webster, N.Y., Webster Golf Club, *625*

Weed, Calif., Lake Shastina Golf Resort, *100*

Weidman, Mich., The Pines at Lake Isabella Golf Club, *467*

Welches, Oreg., Resort Inn at the Mountain, *727*

Wellesley Island, N.Y., Thousand Islands Golf Club, *622*

Wellfleet, Mass., Chequessett Yacht & Country Club, *400*

Wellington, Fla., Binks Forest Golf Course, *175*

Wellington, Kans., Wellington Golf Club, *365*

Wellsboro, Pa., Tyoga Country Club, *767*

Wellsburg, W.Va., Highland Springs Golf Course, *928*

Wellsville, N.Y., Wellsville Country Club, *625*

Wellsville, Utah, Sherwood Hills Resort Golf Course, *875*

Wendell, N.C., Wendell Country Club, *660*

Wendover, Nev., Toana Vista Golf Course, *558*

Wernersville, Pa., Galen Hall Country Club, *744*

Wescosville, Pa., The Golf Club at Shepherd Hills, *745*

Weslaco, Texas, Tierra Santa Golf Club, *862*

Wesley Chapel, Fla., Saddlebrook Resort, *223*

West Allis, Wis., Greenfield Park Golf Course, *944*

West Babylon, N.Y., Bergen Point Country Club, *592*

West Bay, Nova Scotia, Dundee Resort Golf Course, *1001*

West Bloomfield, Mich., Shenandoah Golf & Country Club, *477*

West Bountiful, Utah, Lakeside Golf Course, *871*

West Boxford, Mass., Far Corner Golf Club, *402*

West Boylston, Mass., Wachusett Country Club, *412*

West Branch, Mich., West Branch Country Club, *487*

West Chicago, Ill.
Prairie Landing Golf Club, *313*
St. Andrews Golf & Country Club, *317*

West Columbia, S.C., Indian River Golf Club, *787*

West Columbia, Texas, Columbia Lakes, *833*

West Des Moines, Iowa, Willow Creek Golf Course, *358*

West Dover, Vt., Mount Snow Golf Club, *881*

West End, N.C.
Beacon Ridge Golf & Country Club, *627*
Seven Lakes Country Club, *657*

West Glacier, Mont., Glacier View Golf Course, *541*

West Harrison, Ind., Grand Oak Golf Club, *333*

West Hartford, Conn., Rockledge Country Club, *166*

West Jefferson, N.C., Mountain Aire Golf Club, *647*

West Jordan, Utah, Mountain View Golf Club, *873*

West Kingston, R.I., Laurel Lane Golf Club, *772*

West Lafayette, Ind., Purdue University Golf Course, *341*

West Lafayette, Ohio
Hickory Flat Greens, *680*
River Greens Golf Course, *696*

West Linn, Oreg., Sandelie Golf Course, *729*

West Orange, N.J., Francis A. Byrne Golf Club, *573*

West Palm Beach, Fla.
Breakers West Country Club, *178*
Emerald Dunes Golf Course, *190*

Okeeheelee Golf Course, *211*
Palm Beach Polo & Country Club, *214*
West Palm Beach Municipal Country
    Club, *237*
West Pittson, Pa., Applewood Golf
    Course, *732*
West Point, Utah, Schneiter's Bluff at
    West Point, *874*
West Salem, Wis., Maple Grove Country
    Club, *950*
West Sayville, N.Y., West Sayville Golf
    Club, *625*
West Simsbury, Conn., Simsbury Farms
    Golf Club, *166*
West Suffield, Conn., Airways Golf Club,
    159
West Trenton, N.J., Mountain View Golf
    Course, *578*
West Valley City, Utah, West Ridge Golf
    Course, *877*
West Yarmouth, Mass., Bayberry Hills
    Golf Course, *398*
Westbank, British Columbia, Shannon
    Lake Golf Course, *991*
Westerly, R.I., Winnapaug Country Club,
    773
Westfield, Ind., Hanging Tree Golf Club,
    334
Westfield, New Brunswick, Westfield
    Golf & Country Club, *1000*
Westfield, Pa., River Valley Country Club,
    760
Westfield, Wis., Thal Acres Links &
    Lanes, *964*
Westhampton, N.J., Deerwood Golf
    Club, *571*
Westlake, Ohio, Hilliard Lakes Golf Club,
    682
Westminster, Colo.
Hyland Hills Golf Course-Gold Course,
    148
Legacy Ridge Golf Course, *150*
Westminster, Mass., Westminster
    Country Club, *412*
Westminster, Md., Wakefield Valley Golf
    & Conference Center, *397*
Westminster, S.C., Chickasaw Point
    Country Club, *779*
Weston, Fla., Bonaventure Country Club,
    176
Westover, Md., Great Hope Golf Course,
    390
Westport, Conn., Longshore Club Park,
    163
Westport, N.Y., Westport Country Club,
    625
Wheatley, Ky., Fairway Golf Course, *368*
Wheaton, Ill.
Arrowhead Golf Club, *280*
Cantigny Golf, *284*
Wheaton, Md., Northwest Park Golf
    Course, *392*
Wheeling, Ill., Chevy Chase Golf Club,
    285
Wheeling, W.Va., Oglebay Resort &
    Conference Center, *930*

Whidbey Island, Wash., Gallery Golf
    Course, *911*
Whispering Pines, N.C.
The Carolina, *631*
Country Club of Whispering Pines, *633*
Whispering Woods Golf Club, *661*
Whistler, British Columbia
Chateau Whistler Golf Club, *983*
Nicklaus North Golf Course, *988*
Whistler Golf Club, *994*
White Bear Lake, Minn.
Manitou Ridge Golf Course, *506*
Oneka Ridge Golf Course, *510*
White Haven, Pa., Mountain Laurel
    Resort Hotel & Golf Club, *753*
White Lake, Mich.
Bogie Lake Golf Club, *417*
Indian Springs Metro Park Golf Course,
    448
White Lake Oaks Golf Course, *488*
White Plains, Md., White Plains Regional
    Park Golf Club, *397*
White Plains, N.Y., Maple Moor Golf
    Course, *611*
White Sulphur Springs, W.Va.
1884 Oakhurst Links, *926*
The Greenbrier, *927*
Whitefish, Mo., Whitefish Lake Golf Club,
    543
Whitehall, Mich., Bent Pine Golf Club, *416*
Whitesboro, N.Y., Domenico's Golf
    Course, *601*
Whitman, Mass., Ridder Golf Club, *408*
Whitmore Lake, Mich., Rolling Meadows
    Golf Course, *473*
Whitney Point, N.Y., Ford Hill Country
    Club, *604*
Whitney, Texas
Lake Whitney Country Club, *846*
White Bluffs Golf Club, *865*
Whittington, Ill., Rend Lake Golf Course,
    316
Wichita Falls, Texas, Weeks Park
    Municipal Golf Course, *865*
Wichita, Kans.
Arthur B. Sim Park Golf Course, *359*
Braeburn Golf Club at Wichita State
    University, *359*
L.W. Clapp Golf Course, *361*
MacDonald Golf Course, *362*
Pawnee Prairie Golf Course, *363*
Willow Bend Golf Club, *365*
Wickenburg, Ariz., Los Caballeros Golf
    Club, *54*
Wickliffe, Ohio, Pine Ridge Country
    Club, *692*
Wiggins, Miss., Pine Burr Country Club,
    525
Wildwood, Fla., Continental Country
    Club, *183*
Wilkes-Barre, Pa., Wilkes-Barre Golf
    Club, *769*
Williams, Ariz., Elephant Rocks Golf
    Club, *47*
Williams Bay, Wis., George Williams
    College Golf Club, *943*

Worthington, Minn., Prairie View Golf Course, *512*
Wright City, Mo., Innsbrook Resort Golf Course, *533*
Wrightstown, N.J., Hanover Country Club, *574*
Wrightsville, Pa., Cool Creek Country Club, *738*
Wyoming, Mich.
L.E. Kaufman Golf Club, *450*
The Pines Golf Course, *467*
Wyoming, Minn., Greenwood Golf Links, *501*
Wyoming, R.I., Meadow Brook Golf Club, *772*

Y

Yakima, Wash.
Apple Tree Golf Course, *906*
Suntides Golf Course, *923*
Yankton, S.Dak.
Fox Run Golf Course, *808*
Hillcrest Golf & Country Club, *809*
Yarmouth Port, Mass., Kings Way Golf Club, *404*
Yelm, Wash., Nisqually Valley Golf Club, *918*
Yonkers, N.Y.
Dunwoodie Golf Club, *601*
Sprain Lake Golf Club, *620*
York, Pa.
Briarwood Golf Club, *734*
Grandview Golf Club, *745*

Heritage Hills Golf Resort & Conference Center, *747*
Honey Run Golf & Country Club, *748*
York, S.C.
Carolina Downs Country Club, *777*
Spring Lake Country Club, *802*
Yorktown Heights, N.Y., Mohansic Golf Club, *612*
Yorktown, Ind., The Players Club at Woodland Trails, *339*
Yorktown, N.Y., Sanctuary Golf Club, *617*
Young Harris, Ga., Brasstown Valley Golf Club, *241*
Youngsville, La., Les Vieux Chenes Golf Club, *378*
Ypsilanti, Mich.
Eagle Crest Golf Club, *429*
Green Oaks Golf Course, *441*
Pine View Golf Club, *467*
Yucca Valley, Calif., Blue Skies Country Club, *79*
Yuma, Ariz., Desert Hills Golf Course, *46*

Z

Zanesville, Ohio
Eaglesticks Golf Course, *674*
Jaycee Public Golf Course, *684*
Zellwood, Fla., Zellwood Station Country Club, *239*
Zephyrhills, Fla.
The Links of Lake Bernadette, *204*
Silver Oaks Golf & Country Club, *228*
Zoar, Ohio, Zoar Village Golf Club, *708*

Alphabetical Directory by Course

A

A-Ga-Ming Golf Club, *413*
Abbey Springs Golf Course, *933*
Abercrombie Golf Club, *1000*
Acapulco Princess Club de Golf, *1028*
Adams Municipal Golf Course, *709*
Adirondack Golf & Country Club, *590*
Admiral Lehigh Golf Resort, *172*
Adobe Creek Golf Club, *75*
Adobe Creek National Golf Course, *140*
Afton Alps Golf Course, *492*
Afton Golf Club, *590*
Aguasabon Golf Course, *1003*
A.H. Blank Golf Course, *348*
Ahwatukee Country Club, *43*
Airport Golf Club, *969*
Airport Golf Course, *665*
Airport National Golf, *348*
Airways Golf Club, *159*
A.J. Jolly Golf Course, *366*
Ala Wai Golf Course, *262*
Alban Hills Country Club, *590*
Albany Golf Course, *492*
Albion Ridges Golf Course, *492*
Alburg Country Club, *878*
Aldeen Golf Club, *280*
Alderbrook Golf & Yacht Club, *906*
Alexandria Golf Club, *492*
Algonkian Regional Park Golf Course, *885*
The Algonquin Golf Course, *996*
Alhambra Municipal Golf Course, *75*
Alice Municipal Golf Course, *826*
The Alisal Ranch Golf Course, *75*
Allentown Municipal Golf Course, *732*
Alling Memorial Golf Course, *159*
Alpena Golf Club, *413*
Alpine Bay Golf & Country Club, *26*
Alpine Golf Club, *826*
Alpine Meadows Golf Club, *376*
Alpine Resort Golf Course, *933*
Alta Sierra Golf & Country Club, *75*
Alvamar Golf Club, *359*
Amana Colonies Golf Course, *348*
Amelia Island Plantation, *172*
American Legion Country Club, *348*
Amherst Audubon Golf Course, *590*
Amherst Country Club, *560*
Amherst Golf Club, *1001*
Anaheim Hills Golf Course, *75*
Anchorage Golf Course, *41*
Ancil Hoffman Golf Course, *76*
Andrews County Golf Course, *826*
Angel Fire Country Club, *585*
Angel Park Golf Club, *551*
Angel's Trace Golf Links, *627*
Angus Glen Golf Club, *1003*
Annbriar Golf Course, *280*
Antelope Hills Golf Course, *43*

Antigo Bass Lake Country Club, *933*
Antigonish Golf & Country Club, *1001*
Antioch Golf Club, *280*
Antrim Dells Golf Club, *413*
Apache Creek Golf Club, *43*
Apalachin Golf Course, *590*
Apollo Beach Golf & Sea Club, *172*
Apple Green Golf Course, *590*
Apple Mountain Golf Club, *568*
Apple Tree Golf Course, *906*
Apple Valley Golf Club, *665*
Appletree Golf Course, *140*
Applewood Golf Course (Golden, Colo.), *140*
Applewood Golf Course (Omaha, Nebr.), *544*
Applewood Golf Course (West Pittson, Pa.), *732*
Aptos Seascape Golf Course, *76*
Arboretum Golf Club, *280*
Arbutus Ridge Golf & Country Club, *982*
Arcadian Shores Golf Club, *774*
Arizona Biltmore Country Club, *44*
The Arizona Golf Resort & Conference Center, *44*
Armitage Golf Course, *732*
Arnold Palmer's Bay Hill Club & Lodge, *173*
Arnold's Golf Club, *732*
Aroostook Valley Country Club (Fort Fairfield, Maine), *380*
Aroostook Valley Country Club (Perth Andover, New Brunswick), *996*
Arrowhead Country Club, *774*
Arrowhead Golf Club (Littleton, Colo.), *140*
Arrowhead Golf Club (Wheaton, Ill.), *280*
Arrowhead Golf Course (Canadian, Okla.), *709*
Arrowhead Golf Course (Douglassville, Pa.), *732*
Arrowhead Golf Course (East Syracuse, N.Y.), *591*
Arrowhead Golf Course (Fort Lauderdale, Fla.), *173*
Arroyo del Oso Municipal Golf Course, *585*
Arthur B. Sim Park Golf Course, *359*
Arthur Pack Desert Golf Club, *44*
Ascarate Park Golf Course, *826*
Ash Brook Golf Course, *568*
Ashbourne Country Club, *732*
Ashburn Golf Club, *1001*
Ashland Country Club, *544*
Aspen Golf Course, *140*
The Asu Karsten Golf Course, *43*
Atlantic Country Club, *398*
Atlantis Country Club & Inn, *173*
Atwood Resort Golf Course, *665*
Aubrey's Golf Club, *732*

Auburn Golf & Country Club, *591*
Auburn Golf Course, *906*
Auburn Links at Mill Creek, *26*
Audubon Park Golf Course, *812*
Augustine Golf Club, *885*
Aurora Hills Golf Course, *141*
Autumn Ridge Golf Club, *327*
Avalon Country Club, *568*
Avalon Golf Club, *906*
Avalon Lakes Golf Course, *665*
Avila Beach Resort Golf Course, *76*
Avon Field Golf Course, *665*
Avondale Golf Club, *274*
Awbrey Glen Golf Club, *719*
Azalea City Golf Club, *26*
Azalea Sands Golf Club, *774*
Azusa Greens Golf Course, *76*

B

Babe Zaharias Golf Course, *173*
Bacon Park Golf Course, *240*
The Badlands Golf Club, *551*
Bahamas Princess Resort & Casino,
  1037
Bahia Beach Plantation, *1040*
Baie Missisquoi Golf Club, *1020*
Bailey Golf Club Ranch, *709*
Baja Country Club, *1026*
Bajamar Ocean Front Golf Resort, *1026*
Baker National Golf Course, *492*
Balboa Park Golf Club, *77*
Bald Head Island Club, *627*
Bald Mountain Golf Course, *413*
Ballston Spa Country Club, *591*
Ballymeade Country Club, *398*
Balmoral Golf Course, *492*
Balmoral Woods Country Club, *281*
The Balsams Grand Resort Hotel, *560*
Baneberry Golf & Resort, *812*
Banff Springs Golf Course, *974*
Bangor Municipal Golf Course, *380*
Banner Resort & Country Club, *159*
Bar Harbor Golf Club, *380*
Baraboo Country Club, *933*
Barberton Brookside Country Club, *666*
Bardmoor North Golf Club, *173*
Barker Brook Golf Club, *591*
Barren River State Park Golf Course, *366*
Barrhead Golf Club, *974*
Barrington Hall Golf Club, *240*
Bartlett Hills Golf Course, *281*
Bartley W. Cavanaugh Golf Course, *77*
Barton Creek Resort & Country Club, *826*
Basin Harbor Golf Club, *878*
Bass River Golf Course, *398*
Batavia Country Club, *591*
Bath Country Club, *380*
Battle Creek Golf Club, *709*
Battle Creek Golf Course, *906*
Battle Island Golf Course, *591*
Battle Lake Golf Course, *827*
The Battleground at Deer Park Golf
  Course, *827*
Battlement Mesa Golf Club, *141*
Bavarian Hills Golf Course, *732*

The Bay Club, *386*
Bay County Golf Course, *414*
Bay Forest Golf Course, *827*
Bay Harbor Golf Club, *414*
Bay Hills Golf Club, *386*
Bay Oaks Golf Club, *26*
Bay Pointe Country Club, *398*
Bay Pointe Resort & Golf Club, *522*
Bay of Quinte Country Club, *1003*
Bay Tree Golf Plantation, *774*
Bay Valley Golf Club, *414*
Bayberry Hills Golf Course, *398*
Baymeadows Golf Club, *174*
Bayonet at Puppy Creek Golf Club, *627*
Bayonet Golf Course, *77*
Bayou Din Golf Club, *827*
Bayou Golf Club, *828*
Bayou Oaks Golf Courses, *376*
Bayshore Golf Course, *174*
Baytree National Golf Links, *174*
The Beach Club Golf Links, *386*
Beachwood Golf Club, *775*
Beacon Ridge Golf & Country Club, *627*
Bear Creek Golf World, *828*
Bear Slide Golf Club, *327*
Beau Pre Golf Club, *77*
Beau Rivage Plantation Country Club,
  627
Beaver Brook Country Club, *568*
Beaver Creek Country Club, *386*
Beaver Creek Golf Club, *141*
Beaver Creek Links, *414*
Beaver Creek Meadows Golf Course, *666*
Beaver Dam Country Club, *933*
Beaver Island State Park Golf Course,
  592
Beaver Kreek Golf Club, *240*
Beaver Meadow Golf Club, *560*
Beaver Run Golf Course, *348*
Beckett Golf Club, *568*
Bedford Falls Golf Club, *414*
Bedford Springs Golf Course, *733*
Bedford Trails Golf Course, *666*
Bedford Valley Golf Course, *415*
Beech Hollow Golf Course, *415*
Beechwood Golf & Country Club, *1003*
Beekman Country Club, *592*
Bel Aire Golf Club, *628*
Bel Meadow Country Club, *926*
Belk Park Golf Club, *281*
Bell Bay Golf Club, *1001*
Bell Nob Golf Club, *969*
Bella Vista Golf & Yacht Club, *174*
Belle Meade Country Club, *240*
Belle River Golf & Country Club, *415*
Belle Terre Country Club, *376*
Belle Terre Golf Course, *775*
Belleview Biltmore Resort & Golf Club,
  174
Bellevue Municipal Golf Course, *907*
Bello Woods Golf Club, *415*
Bellport Country Club, *592*
Bellwood Oaks Golf Course, *493*
Belmont Golf & Country Club, *1035*
Belmont Golf Course (Langley, British
  Columbia), *982*

Belmont Golf Course (Richmond, Va.), 885
Belton Municipal Golf Course, 528
Belvedere Golf & Winter Club, 1018
Belvedere Golf Club, 415
Belvedere Plantation Golf & Country Club, 628
Bemidji Town & Country Club, 493
Ben Geren Regional Park Golf Course, 69
Ben Lomond Golf Course, 868
Bennett Valley Golf Course, 77
Benson Park Golf Course, 544
Bent Brook Golf Course, 26
Bent Creek Golf Course, 528
Bent Creek Golf Resort, 812
Bent Oak Golf Club, 528
Bent Pine Golf Club, 416
Bent Tree Golf Club, 666
Bergen Point Country Club, 592
Berkeley Country Club, 775
Berwind Country Club, 1040
The Bethel Inn & Country Club, 380
Bethel Island Golf Course, 78
Bethlehem Country Club, 560
Bethlehem Municipal Golf Club, 733
Bethpage State Park Golf Courses, 592
Bey Lea Golf Club, 568
Biddeford Saco Country Club, 381
Bide-a-Wee Golf Club, 885
Bidwell Park Golf Course, 78
Big Beaver Creek Golf Course, 666
Big Bend Golf Club, 926
Big Canoe Golf Club, 240
Big Creek Golf Club, 812
Big Met Golf Club, 666
Big Oaks Golf Club, 522
Big Oaks Golf Course, 934
Big Run Golf Club, 281
Big Sky Golf & Country Club, 982
Big Sky Golf Club, 540
Bill & Payne Stewart Golf Course, 528
Bill Roberts Municipal Golf Course, 540
The Biltmore Golf Course, 175
Binder Park Golf Course, 416
Bing Maloney Golf Course, 78
Binks Forest Golf Course, 175
Birch Creek Golf Club, 868
Birch Ridge Golf Club, 41
Birdwood Golf Course, 885
Birkdale Golf & Country Club, 886
Birkdale Golf Club, 628
Bittersweet Golf Club, 281
Black Bear Golf & Country Club, 569
Black Bear Golf Club, 175
Black Bear Golf Resort, 416
Black Butte Ranch, 719
Black Creek Golf Club, 241
Black Forest & Wilderness Valley Golf Resort, 416
Black Hawk Golf Course, 733
Black Lake Golf Resort, 78
Black Mountain Golf & Country Club, 551
Black Mountain Golf Course, 628
Black Rock Golf Course, 386
Black Squirrel Golf Club, 327

Blackberry Oaks Golf Course, 282
Blackfoot Municipal Golf Course, 274
Blackhawk Golf Club (Galena, Ohio), 667
Blackhawk Golf Club (Pflugerville, Texas), 828
Blackhawk Golf Club (St. Charles, Ill.), 282
Blackjack Bay Golf Links, 522
Blackledge Country Club, 159
Blacklick Woods Golf Course, 667
Blackmoor Golf Club (Murrells Inlet, S.C.), 775
Blackmoor Golf Club (Richmond, Ohio), 667
Blackthorn Golf Club, 327
Blackwolf Run Golf Club, 934
Blackwood Golf Course, 733
Blair Park Golf Club, 628
Blissful Meadows Golf Club, 399
Blomidon Golf & Country Club, 1000
Bloomingdale Golf Club, 282
Bloomingdale Golfer's Club, 175
Blossom Trails Golf Course, 417
Blue Ash Golf Course, 667
Blue Fox Run Golf Club, 159
Blue Heron Pines Golf Club, 569
Blue Hill Golf Club, 593
Blue Mountain View Golf Course, 734
Blue Ridge Country Club, 628
Blue Rock Golf Course, 399
Blue Skies Country Club, 79
Blue Springs Golf Club, 1004
Blue Stone Golf Club, 593
Blueberry Pines Golf Club, 493
Bluebonnet Country Golf Course, 829
Bluebonnet Hill Golf Club, 829
Bluewater Bay Resort, 176
Bluff Creek Golf Course, 493
Bluff Point Golf & Country Club, 594
The Bluffs, 808
The Bluffs Golf Club, 934
Bluffton Golf Club, 667
Blythe Golf Club, 79
Bob O'Link Golf Club, 668
Bob-O-Link Golf Course (Avon, Ohio), 668
Bob-O-Link Golf Course (Lawrenceburg, Ky.), 366
Bobby Jones Golf Club, 241
Bobby Jones Golf Complex, 176
Boca Raton Resort & Club, 176
Bodega Harbour Golf Links, 79
The Bog Golf Club, 934
Bogie Lake Golf Club, 417
Bogue Banks Country Club, 629
Boiling Springs Golf Club, 709
Bois De Sioux Golf Club, 662
Bolton Field Golf Course, 668
Bon Vivant Country Club, 282
Bon-Air Golf Club, 734
Bonaventure Country Club, 176
Bonifay Country Club, 177
Bonita Springs Golf Club, 177
Bonneville Golf Course, 868
Bonnie Brae Golf Course, 776
Bonnie Brook Golf Club, 282

Buffalo Dunes Golf Course, *359*
Buffalo Golf Club, *969*
Buffalo Grove Golf Club, *283*
Buffalo Hill Golf Course, *540*
Buffalo Run Golf Course, *142*
Buffalo Valley Golf Course, *813*
Bull Creek Golf Course, *242*
Buncombe County Municipal Golf Club, *630*
Bunker Hill Golf Course (Dubuque, Iowa), *350*
Bunker Hill Golf Course (Medina, Ohio), *669*
Bunker Hill Golf Course (Somerset, N.J.), *570*
Bunker Hills Golf Course (Coon Rapids, Minn.), *495*
Bunker Links Municipal Golf Course, *284*
Bunn Golf Course, *284*
Burnaby Mountain Golf Course, *982*
Burning Oak Country Club, *420*
Burning Ridge Golf Club, *776*
Burns Park Golf Course, *69*
Burr Oak Golf Club, *420*
Butler's Golf Course, *735*
Butternut Brook Golf Course, *420*
Butternut Hills Golf Course, *936*
Byrncliff Golf Club, *595*
Byrnes Park Golf Course, *350*
Byron Hills Golf Club, *421*

C

C-Way Golf Club, *595*
Caberfae Peaks Ski & Golf Resort, *421*
Cabin Brook Golf Club, *367*
Cable Beach Golf Club, *1039*
Cable Hollow Golf Club, *735*
Cabo del Sol Golf Club, *1027*
Cabo Real Golf Club, *1027*
Cabo San Lucas Country Club, *1027*
Cacapon Resort, *926*
Cahaba Valley Golf & Country Club, *27*
Calabash Golf Links, *631*
Calabogie Highlands Resort & Golf Club, *1004*
Caledon Country Club, *1004*
Caledonia Golf & Fish Club, *777*
Calhoun Country Club, *777*
California Club, *178*
California Golf Course, *669*
Calimesa Country Club, *80*
Callaway Gardens Resort, *242*
Calusa Lakes Golf Course, *178*
Calvada Valley Golf & Country Club, *551*
Camaloch Golf Course, *907*
Camarillo Springs Golf Course, *80*
Cambrian Ridge Golf Club, *27*
Cambridge Country Club, *387*
Camelot Country Club, *936*
Camelot Golf Course, *813*
Camillus Country Club, *596*
Campbell's Scottish Highlands Golf Course, *561*
Campo de Golf Ixtapa Golf Course, *1028*
Campo de Golf San Jose *1027*

Canaan Valley Resort Golf Course, *926*
Canajoharie Country Club, *596*
Canasawacta Country Club, *596*
Candia Woods Golf Links, *561*
Candlestone Golf Club, *421*
Candlewood Valley Country Club, *160*
Canmore Golf & Curling Club, *974*
Cannon Golf Club, *495*
Canoa Hills Golf Course, *45*
Canterberry Golf Course, *142*
Cantigny Golf, *284*
Canton Public Golf Course, *160*
Canyon Lake Golf & Country Club, *830*
Canyon Lakes Country Club, *80*
Canyon Lakes Golf Course, *907*
Canyon South Golf Course, *81*
Canyon Springs Golf Course, *274*
Cape Arundel Golf Club, *381*
Cape Cod Country Club, *399*
Cape Coral Golf & Tennis Resort, *178*
Cape Golf & Racquet Club, *631*
Cape May National Golf Club, *570*
Cape Royale Golf Course, *831*
Capitol City Golf Club, *907*
Capri Isles Golf Club, *179*
Captains Golf Course, *400*
Carambola Golf Club, *1042*
Cardinal Golf Club, *1005*
Cardinal Golf Course, *284*
Cardinal Hills Golf Course, *596*
Carey Park Golf Club, *359*
Carillon Golf Club, *284*
Carleton Glen Golf Club, *421*
Carlisle Golf & Country Club, *1005*
Carlton Oaks Country Club, *81*
Carmel Mountain Ranch Country Club, *81*
Carmel Valley Ranch Golf Club, *81*
Carnation Golf Course, *908*
The Carolina, *631*
Carolina Downs Country Club, *777*
Carolina Lakes Golf Club, *631*
Carolina Pines Golf & Country Club, *631*
Carolina Shores Golf & Country Club, *631*
Carolina Springs Golf Club, *777*
Carper's Valley Golf Club, *887*
Carriage Greens Country Club, *285*
Carriage Hills Country Club, *495*
Carroll Lake Golf Club, *813*
Carroll Meadows Golf Course, *669*
Carroll Park Golf Course, *387*
Carroll Valley Golf Resort, *735*
Carthage Municipal Golf Course, *529*
Cary Country Club, *285*
Casa Blanca Golf Course, *831*
Casa de Campo Resort & Country Club, *1036*
Casa Grande Municipal Golf Course, *45*
Cascades Golf Course, *422*
Casolwood Golf Course, *596*
Casper Municipal Golf Course, *969*
Casperkill Country Club, *596*
Cassel Hills Golf Course, *670*
Cassville Golf Club, *529*
Castle Creek Country Club, *81*
Castle Harbour Golf Club, *1035*
Castle Highlands Golf Course, *495*

Chippewa Golf & Country Club, *1005*
Chippewa Golf Club, *671*
Chisago Lakes Golf Course, *496*
Chisholm Hills Country Club, *424*
Chocolay Downs Golf Course, *424*
Chomonix Golf Course, *496*
Christina Lake Golf Club, *983*
Christmas Lake Golf Club, *329*
Christmas Mountain Village Golf Club, *937*
Chriswood Golf Course, *27*
Chuck Corica Golf Complex, *83*
Chula Vista Municipal Golf Course, *83*
Cielo Vista Golf Course, *832*
Cimarron National Golf Club, *710*
Cimarrone Golf & Country Club, *180*
Cinder Ridge Golf Links, *286*
Circle Golf Club, *832*
Citronelle Municipal Golf Course, *27*
Citrus Hills Golf & Country Club, *180*
Citrus Springs Country Club, *180*
City of Amsterdam Municipal Golf Course, *598*
City Club Marietta, *244*
City Park Golf Club, *143*
City of San Mateo Golf Course, *83*
Clark Lake Golf Club, *424*
Clarkston Creek Golf Club, *425*
Classic Country Club, *908*
Claycrest Golf Club, *529*
Clear Lake Country Club, *274*
Clear Lake Golf Club, *833*
Clear Lake Golf Course, *994*
Clearbrook Golf Club, *425*
Clearview Golf Club, *598*
Clearwater Country Club, *180*
Cleburne Muni Golf Course, *833*
Cleghorn Plantation Golf & Country Club, *633*
Clerbrook Resort, *181*
Cleveland Heights Golf & Country Club, *181*
Clewiston Golf Course, *181*
The Cliffs Golf Club, *833*
Cliffside Golf Course, *671*
Clifton Highlands Golf Course, *937*
Clifton Hollow Golf Club, *938*
Clinton Hill Country Club, *286*
Clover Valley Golf Course, *909*
The Club at Cordillera, *143*
The Club at Eaglebrooke, *181*
The Club at Emerald Hills, *181*
The Club at Hidden Creek, *181*
The Club at Longleaf, *633*
The Club at Oak Ford, *182*
The Club at Runaway Bay, *833*
The Club at Seabrook Island, *779*
The Club at Winston Trails, *182*
The Club and Lodge at the Bluffs on Thompson Creek, *377*
Club Med Sandpiper, *182*
Club West Golf Club, *45*
Clustered Spires Golf Course, *388*
Coachman's Golf Resort, *938*
Coal Creek Golf Course, *143*
Cobblestone Golf Course, *245*
Cobb's Creek Golf Club, *738*

Cobb's Glen Country Club, *779*
Cocoa Beach Golf Course, *182*
Coeur D'Alene Resort Golf Course, *275*
Coffee Creek Golf Course, *710*
Coffin Golf Club, *329*
Cog Hill Golf Club, *286*
Cohanzick Country Club, *570*
Coldstream Country Club, *779*
Colgate University Seven Oaks Golf Club, *598*
Collindale Golf Club, *143*
Colonial Charters Golf Club, *779*
Colonial Country Club, *400*
Colonial Golf Club, *27*
Colonial Golf Course, *287*
Colonial Golfers Club, *672*
Colonial Springs Golf Course, *599*
Coloniale Golf & Country Club, *974*
Colony West Country Club, *183*
Colton Golf Club, *83*
Columbia Golf Club, *287*
Columbia Golf Course, *496*
Columbia Lakes, *833*
Colwood National Golf Club, *720*
Comanche Trail Golf Club (Amarillo, Texas), *833*
Comanche Trail Golf Club (Big Spring, Texas), *834*
Como Golf Course, *496*
Concho Valley Country Club, *46*
Concord Hills Golf Course, *425*
Concord Resort Hotel, *599*
Conins Golf Resort, *600*
Conklin Players Club, *599*
Conley's Resort Inn, *738*
Connally Golf Course, *834*
Connaught Golf Club, *975*
Connemara Golf Links, *367*
Conquistador Golf Course, *144*
Constant Spring Golf Club, *1038*
Continental Country Club, *183*
Continental Golf Club at Coral Springs, *183*
Cooke Municipal Golf Course, *1022*
Cooks Creek Golf Club, *672*
Cool Creek Country Club, *738*
Cool Lake Golf Club, *329*
Coosaw Creek Country Club, *780*
Copake Country Club, *599*
Copeland Hills Golf Course, *672*
Copper Mountain Resort, *144*
Coral Oaks Golf Course, *183*
Cordova Bay Golf Course, *983*
Cordova Golf Course, *83*
Corey Creek Golf Club, *738*
Coronado Golf Course, *84*
Costa del Sol Golf & Country Club, *183*
Costa Mesa Country Club, *84*
Cottonwood Creek Golf Course, *834*
Cottonwood Golf & Country Club, *975*
Country Acres Golf Club, *672*
The Country Club at Silver Springs Shores, *184*
Country Club at Woodloch Springs, *739*
Country Club of Barre, *878*
Country Club of Beaufort, *780*

Hawthorne Hills Golf Club (Saukville, Wis.), *944*
Hawthorne Valley Golf Course, *928*
Haystack Golf Club, *879*
Hayward Golf & Tennis Center, *945*
Headwaters Country Club, *502*
Heart River Municipal Golf Course, *662*
Heather Glen Golf Links, *785*
Heather Highlands Golf Club, *443*
Heather Hill Country Club, *403*
Heather Hills Golf Course, *444*
Heather Run Golf & Fish Club, *841*
Heatherhurst Golf Club, *817*
Heatherwoode Golf Club, *680*
Hecla Golf Course at Gull Harbor Resort, *994*
Hedingham Golf Club, *640*
Helfrich Golf Course, *334*
Hell's Point Golf Course, *891*
Hemlock Springs Golf Center, *680*
Henderson Golf Club, *249*
Henderson Lake Golf Club, *976*
Hendricks Field Golf Course, *575*
Henry Homberg Municipal Golf Course, *841*
Henry Horton State Park Golf Course, *817*
Heritage Bluffs Golf Club, *295*
Heritage Club, *785*
Heritage Glen Golf Club, *444*
The Heritage Golf Club, *249*
Heritage Highlands Golf & Country Club, *51*
Heritage Hills Golf Course (Claremore, Okla.), *712*
Heritage Hills Golf Course (McCook, Nebr.), *545*
Heritage Hills Golf Resort & Conference Center, *747*
Heritage Links Country Club at Turkey Creek, *198*
Heritage Palms Golf Club, *95*
Heritage Park Golf Course, *360*
Heritage Pointe Golf & Country Club, *976*
Hermann Park Golf Course, *841*
Hermitage Golf Course, *818*
Hermon Meadow Golf Club, *382*
Herndon Centennial Golf Club, *891*
Heron Lakes Golf Course, *722*
Heron Point Golf Club, *786*
Hesperia Golf & Country Club, *95*
Hesston Municipal Golf Park, *361*
Hiawatha Golf Course (Minneapolis, Minn.), *502*
Hiawatha Golf Course (Mount Vernon, Ohio), *680*
Hickory Flat Greens, *680*
Hickory Grove Golf Club, *680*
Hickory Grove Golf Course, *681*
Hickory Heights Golf Club, *747*
Hickory Hills Country Club (Chilton, Wis.), *945*
Hickory Hills Country Club (Hickory Hills, Ill.), *295*
Hickory Hills Golf Club, *444*
Hickory Hollow Golf Course, *444*

Hickory Knob Golf Club, *786*
Hickory Knoll Golf Course, *445*
Hickory Nut Golf Club, *681*
Hickory Point Golf Club, *296*
Hickory Ridge Country Club, *403*
Hickory Ridge Golf Center, *296*
Hickory Valley Golf Club, *747*
Hickory Woods Golf Course, *681*
Hidden Creek Golf Club (Reston, Va.), *891*
Hidden Creek Golf Club (Sellersburg, Ind.), *334*
Hidden Greens Golf Club, *502*
Hidden Hills Golf Club, *681*
Hidden Hills Golf Course, *352*
Hidden Hills Public Golf Course, *841*
Hidden Lake Golf & Country Club, *1008*
Hidden Lake Golf Course (Tipp City, Ohio), *681*
Hidden Lakes Golf Course (Derby, Kans.), *361*
Hidden Lakes Golf Resort, *275*
Hidden Valley Collection of Great Golf, *445*
Hidden Valley Four Seasons Resort, *748*
Hidden Valley Golf Club, *95*
Hidden Valley Golf Course, *545*
Hidden Valley Golf Links, *532*
Hidden Valley Lake Golf & Country Club, *96*
Hiddenbrooke Country Club, *96*
Hideaway Hills Golf Club, *748*
High Cedars Golf Club, *912*
High Cliff Golf Course, *945*
High Hampton Inn & Country Club, *640*
High Mountain Golf Club, *575*
High Point Country Club, *575*
High Pointe Golf Club, *445*
Highland Creek Golf Club, *641*
Highland Golf Club (Conyers, Ga.), *249*
Highland Golf Club (Escanaba, Mich), *446*
Highland Golf Course, *276*
Highland Golf Links, *403*
Highland Golfer's Club, *891*
Highland Hills Golf Course (De Witt, Mich.), *446*
Highland Hills Golf Course (Greeley, Colo.), *148*
Highland Oaks Golf Club, *31*
Highland Park Country Club (Aiken, S.C.), *786*
Highland Park Country Club (Highland Park, Ill.), *296*
Highland Park Golf Club, *681*
Highland Park Golf Course (Bloomington, Ind.), *296*
Highland Park Golf Course (Mason City, Iowa), *352*
Highland Park Golf Course (St. Paul, Minn.), *502*
Highland Springs Golf Course (Rock Island, Ill.), *296*
Highland Springs Golf Course (Wellsburg, W.Va.), *928*
Highland Woods Golf Course, *297*
The Highlands Golf & Country Club, *276*

Los Robles Golf Course, *103*
Los Serranos Lakes Golf & Country Club, *103*
Los Verdes Golf Course, *103*
Lost Creek Golf Club, *750*
Lost Key Golf Club, *205*
Lost Lake Golf Club, *205*
Lost Nation Golf Club, *304*
Lost Nation Golf Course, *686*
Lost Tracks Golf Club, *724*
Lost Valley Golf Shop, *848*
Loyal Oak Golf Course, *686*
LPGA International, *203*
Lucaya Golf & Country Club, *1037*
Luck Golf Course, *950*
Lum International Golf Club, *454*
L.W. Clapp Golf Course, *361*
Lyman Orchards Golf Club, *163*
Lyons Den Golf, *686*

M

McCabe Field Golf Course, *820*
McCall Lake Golf Course, *978*
McCall Municipal Golf Course, *276*
McCann Memorial Golf Club, *612*
McCleery Golf Course, *988*
McCormick Ranch Golf Club, *55*
McCormick Woods Golf Course, *917*
MacDonald Golf Course, *362*
Mace Meadows Golf & Country Club, *103*
McFarland Park Golf Course, *35*
McGauslin Brook Golf & Country Club, *951*
McGuire's Resort, *457*
McKenzie Meadows Golf Club, *978*
Macktown Golf Course, *304*
McNary Golf Club, *724*
Macoby Run Golf Course, *750*
Mactaquac Provincial Park Golf Club, *998*
Mad Russian Golf Course, *151*
Madden's on Gull Lake, *505*
Madeline Island Golf Club, *950*
Madera Municipal Golf Course, *104*
Madison Park Golf Course, *304*
Madrona Links Golf Course, *916*
Maggie Valley Resort Golf Club, *644*
Magnetic Hill Golf & Country Club, *998*
Magnolia Country Club, *644*
Magnolia Grove Golf Club, *34*
Magnolia Valley Golf Club, *205*
Mahogany Run Golf Course, *1043*
Mahoney Golf Course, *547*
Mahoning Golf Course, *687*
Mainprize Regional Park & Golf Course, *1023*
The Majestic at Lake Walden, *455*
Majestic Oaks Golf Club, *505*
Majestic Ridge Golf Club, *751*
Makaha Valley Country Club, *267*
Makalei Hawaii Country Club, *267*
Makena Resort Golf Course, *267*
Malibu Country Club, *104*
Mallard Cove Golf Course, *378*
Mallard Head Country Club, *644*
Malone Golf Club, *611*

Man O' War Golf, *792*
Manada Golf Club, *751*
Manakiki Golf Club, *687*
Manassas Park Public Golf Course, *896*
Manatee County Golf Club, *205*
Manderley on the Green, *1011*
Mangrove Bay Golf Course, *206*
Manistee Golf & Country Club, *455*
Manitou Ridge Golf Course, *506*
Manitouwadge Golf Course, *1011*
Manoir Richelieu, *1021*
Manor Golf Club, *751*
Manor Valley Golf Club, *751*
Manteno Golf Club, *304*
Maple Creek Golf Course, *253*
Maple Grove Country Club, *950*
Maple Grove Golf Course, *455*
Maple Hill Golf Course, *455*
Maple Lane Golf Course, *455*
Maple Leaf Golf Course, *455*
Maple Meadows Golf Course, *304*
Maple Moor Golf Course, *611*
Maple Ridge Golf Club, *253*
Maple Ridge Golf Course (Austinburg, Ohio), *687*
Maple Ridge Golf Course (Calgary, Alberta), *978*
Maple River Golf Club, *663*
Maple Run Golf Course, *391*
Maple Valley Golf & Country Club, *506*
Maplecrest Country Club, *951*
Maplecrest Golf Course, *687*
Maplegate Country Club, *405*
Maples of Ballantrae Lodge & Golf Club, *1011*
Maplewood Country Club, *563*
Maplewood Golf & Country Club, *998*
Maplewood Golf Club (Muncie, Ind.), *337*
Maplewood Golf Club (Renton, Wash.), *916*
Marborough Country Club, *391*
Marco Shores Country Club, *206*
Marcus Pointe Golf Club, *206*
Marengo Ridge Golf Club, *304*
Mariah Hills Golf Course, *362*
Mariana Butte Golf Course, *151*
Marina Ixtapa Club de Golf, *1029*
Marina San Carlos Campo de Golf, *1031*
Marina Vallarta Club de Golf, *1029*
Marine Park Golf Club, *611*
Mariners Landing Golf & Country Club, *896*
Marion Oaks Golf Club, *456*
Mark Twain Golf Club, *611*
Marquette Golf & Country Club, *456*
Marquette Trails Country Club, *456*
Marriott at Sawgrass Resort, *206*
Marriott's Bay Point Resort, *206*
Marriott's Camelback Golf Club, *54*
Marriott's Desert Springs Resort & Spa, *104*
Marriott's Golf Club at Fossil Creek, *848*
Marriott's Golf Club at Marco, *207*
Marriott's Golf Club at Shiloh Falls, *820*
Marriott's Griffin Gate Resort Golf Club, *372*

Marriott's Lake Wood Golf Club, *34*
Marriott's Lincolnshire Resort, *305*
Marriott's Rancho Las Palmas Resort & Country Club, *104*
Marriott's Seaview Resort, *577*
Marriott's Tan-Tar-A Resort, *534*
Marsh Creek Country Club, *207*
Marsh Harbour Golf Links, *645*
Marsh Ridge Resort, *456*
Marshall Golf Club, *506*
Marshall High School Golf Club, *506*
Marshfield Country Club, *951*
Martin County Golf & Country Club, *207*
Marysville Golf Course, *457*
Maryvale Golf Club, *55*
Marywood Golf Club, *457*
Mascoutin Golf Club, *951*
Mason Hills Golf Course, *457*
Massanutten Resort Golf Course, *896*
Massena Country Club, *612*
Matanzas Woods Golf Club, *207*
Mather Golf Course, *105*
Matheson Greens Golf Course, *457*
Maumee Bay Resort Golf Course, *687*
Mauna Kea Beach Golf Course, *268*
Mauna Lani Resort, *268*
Maxwell Golf Club, *848*
Maxwelton Braes Golf Resort, *951*
Maxwelton Golf Club, *338*
Mayapple Golf Links, *751*
Mayfair Country Club (Sanford, Fla.), *208*
Mayfair Country Club (Uniontown, Ohio), *688*
Mayfair Lakes Golf & Country Club, *987*
Mayfield Golf Club, *751*
May's Landing Country Club, *577*
Mayville Golf Club, *951*
Maywood Golf Club, *372*
Meadow Brook Golf Club, *772*
Meadow Brook Golf Course, *872*
Meadow Farms Golf Course, *896*
Meadow Gardens Golf Course, *988*
Meadow Hills Golf Course, *151*
Meadow Lake Golf Course, *105*
Meadow Lake Golf Resort, *541*
Meadow Lakes Golf Course, *724*
Meadow Lane Golf Course, *458*
Meadow Links Golf Course, *952*
Meadow Park Golf Course, *917*
Meadow Ponds Golf Course, *930*
Meadowbrook Golf Club, *208*
Meadowbrook Golf Course (Fort Worth, Texas), *848*
Meadowbrook Golf Course (Hopkins, Minn.), *507*
Meadowbrook Golf Course (Rapid City, S.Dak.), *810*
Meadowbrook Municipal Golf Complex, *848*
Meadowcreek Golf Course, *896*
Meadowink Golf Club, *752*
Meadowlands Golf Club, *645*
Meadowlands Golf Course, *645*
Meadowlark Hills Golf Course, *547*
Meadowood Resort Golf Course, *105*

The Meadows Golf Club (Allendale, Mich.), *458*
The Meadows Golf Club of Blue Island, *305*
The Meadows Golf Club (Dubuque, Iowa), *354*
Meadows Golf Club (Lincoln Park, N.J.), *577*
The Meadows Golf Club (Littleton, Colo.), *151*
The Meadows Golf Course (Harpersville, Ala.), *35*
The Meadows Golf Course (Moorhead, Minn.), *507*
Meadowview Golf Club, *820*
Meadowview Golf Course, *305*
Meadowwood Golf Course, *917*
Meceola Country Club, *458*
Medicine Hat Golf & Country Club, *979*
Meek-Kwon Park Golf Course, *952*
Melody Hill Golf Course, *772*
The Members Club at St. James Plantation, *645*
Memorial Park Golf Course, *849*
Memphis Oaks Golf Club, *820*
Menifee Lakes Country Club, *105*
Merced Hills Golf Club, *106*
Mercer Oaks Golf Club, *577*
Mercer Public Golf Course, *752*
Meriwether National Golf Club, *725*
Meriwood Golf Course, *917*
Merrill Golf Club, *952*
Mesaba Country Club, *507*
Mesquite Golf & Country Club, *106*
Mesquite Golf Course, *849*
Metropolitan Golf Club, *253*
Metrowest Country Club, *208*
Miami National Golf Club, *208*
Miami Shores Country Club, *208*
Miami Shores Golf Course, *688*
Miami Whitewater Forest Golf Course, *688*
Michaywe Hills Resort, *458*
Michigan City Municipal Course, *338*
Micke Grove Golf Links, *106*
The Mid Ocean Club, *1035*
Mid Pines Golf Club, *645*
Mid-Vallee Golf Course, *952*
Middle Channel Golf & Country Club, *458*
Middle Island Country Club, *612*
Middletown Country Club, *752*
Midland Valley Country Club, *792*
Midlane Country Club, *305*
Mile Square Golf Course, *106*
Miler Country Club, *792*
Milham Park Municipal Golf Club, *459*
Mililani Golf Club, *268*
Mill Cove Golf Club, *209*
Mill Creek Golf & Country Club, *849*
Mill Creek Golf Club (Geneva, Ill.), *305*
Mill Creek Golf Club (Mebane, N.C.), *646*
Mill Creek Golf Club (Ostrander, Ohio), *688*
Mill Creek Park Golf Course, *688*
Mill Quarter Plantation Golf Course, *897*
Mill Race Golf Course, *752*
Mill River Golf Course, *1019*

N

Naga-Waukee Golf Course, *953*
Nags Head Golf Links, *647*
Nanaimo Golf Club, *988*
Napa Municipal Golf Club, *109*
Naperbrook Golf Course, *306*
Naples Beach Hotel & Golf Club, *210*
Nashboro Golf Club, *821*
Nassawango Country Club, *392*
Natanis Golf Club, *383*
Natchez Trace Golf Club, *525*
The Natural at Beaver Creek Resort, *460*
Needles Municipal Golf Course, *110*
Needwood Golf Course, *392*
Negril Hills Golf Club, *1038*
Nelson Park Golf Course, *306*
Nemacolin Woodlands Resort & Spa, *754*
Nemadji Golf Course, *953*
Neshobe Golf Club, *881*
Nettle Creek Golf Club, *307*
Neumann Golf Course, *689*
The Neuse Golf Club, *647*
Nevel Meade Golf Course, *373*
Nevele Country Club, *613*
New Berlin Hills Golf Course, *954*
The New Course at Albany, *613*
New England Country Club, *405*
New Ewa Beach Golf Club, *268*
New Melle Lakes Golf Club, *535*
New Mexico State University Golf Course, *586*
New Mexico Tech Golf Course, *586*
New Prague Golf Club, *509*
New Richmond Golf Club, *954*
New Seabury Country Club, *406*
Newaukum Valley Golf Course, *918*
Newman Golf Course, *307*
Newport Country Club, *881*
Newport News Golf Club at Deer Run, *897*
Newton Commonwealth Golf Course, *406*
Niagara County Golf Course, *613*
Niagara Orleans Country Club, *614*
Nicklaus North Golf Course, *988*
Nicolet Country Club, *954*
Nile Golf Club, *918*
Nine Peaks Madras Golf & Country Club, *725*
Nippersink Country Club, *954*
Nisqually Valley Golf Club, *918*
Nob North Golf Course, *254*
Nobleton Lakes Golf Club, *1012*
Nocona Hills Golf Course, *850*
Nordic Hills Resort, *307*
Normandie Golf Club, *535*
Normandy Shores Golf Course, *210*
North Battleford Golf & Country Club, *1023*
North Bellingham Golf Course, *919*
North Conway Country Club, *564*
North Fork Golf & Tennis Club, *754*
North Fulton Golf Course, *254*
North Hills Golf Club, *755*
North Kent Golf Course, *460*
North Kingstown Municipal Golf Course, *772*

North Links Golf Course, *509*
North Palm Beach Country Club, *210*
North Park Golf Course, *755*
North Platte Country Club, *548*
North Port National Golf Club, *535*
North Shore Country Club, *647*
North Shore Golf & Country Club, *919*
North Shore Golf Club, *461*
North Star Golf & Country Club, *461*
North Star Golf Course, *42*
Northampton Valley Country Club, *755*
Northbrook Country Club, *954*
Northbrook Golf Club, *461*
Northdale Golf Club, *211*
Northern Hills Golf Course, *509*
Northern Pines Golf Club, *542*
Northfield Golf Club, *509*
Northgate Golf Course, *556*
Northmoor Golf Club, *689*
Northridge Public Golf Course, *1012*
Northstar-at-Tahoe Resort Golf Course, *110*
Northview Golf & Country Club, *989*
Northwest Park Golf Course, *392*
Northwind Golf Lodge, *755*
Northwood Golf Course (Fremont, Mich.), *461*
Northwood Golf Course (Rhinelander, Wis.), *955*
Northwoods Golf Club, *793*
Norwich Golf Course, *163*
Norwood Country Club, *406*
Nutters Crossing Golf Club, *392*

O

Oak Brook Golf Club, *307*
Oak Brook Golf Course, *307*
Oak Brook Hills Hotel & Resort, *307*
The Oak Club of Genoa, *308*
Oak Creek Golf Club, *110*
Oak Crest Golf Course, *461*
Oak Glen Golf Club, *509*
Oak Glen Golf Course, *308*
Oak Grove Country Club, *338*
Oak Grove Golf Course, *689*
Oak Grove Island Golf Club, *254*
Oak Harbor Golf Club, *378*
Oak Hills Golf Club (Columbia, S.C.)., *793*
Oak Hills Golf Club (Norwalk, Conn.), *164*
Oak Hills Golf Club (Spring Hill, Fla.), *211*
Oak Hollow Golf Course, *648*
Oak Island Golf & Country Club, *648*
Oak Knoll Golf Course (Crown Point, Ind.), *338*
Oak Knoll Golf Course (Independence, Oreg.), *725*
Oak Knolls Golf Club, *690*
Oak Lane Golf Course, *461*
Oak Meadows Golf Club, *308*
Oak Mountain State Park Golf Course, *36*
Oak Pointe, *462*
Oak Ridge Golf Club (Feeding Hills, Mass.), *406*
Oak Ridge Golf Club (Muskegon, Mich.), *462*

Reeves County Golf Course, *855*
Reeves Golf Course, *695*
Regent Park Golf Club, *799*
Rehoboth Country Club, *408*
Reid Golf Course, *958*
Reid Park Memorial Golf Course, *695*
Remington Golf Club, *220*
Renaissance Pineisle Resort, *256*
Renaissance Vinoy Resort, *220*
Rend Lake Golf Course, *316*
Rendezvous Meadows Golf Club, *971*
Renfrew Golf Club, *1014*
Renwood Country Club, *316*
The Reserve Vineyards & Golf Club, *727*
Resort at Squaw Creek, *121*
Resort Inn at the Mountain, *727*
Restigouche Golf & Country Club, *999*
Reston National Golf Course, *899*
Reynolds Park Golf Club, *654*
Reynolds Plantation, *256*
Ricci Meadows Golf Course, *616*
Rich Acres Golf Course, *514*
Rich Maiden Golf Course, *760*
Rich Spring Golf Course, *514*
Rich Valley Golf Club, *514*
Richmond Country Club, *773*
Richmond Forest Golf Club, *471*
Richmond Hill Golf Club, *1014*
Richmond Pines Country Club, *655*
Richter Park Golf Club, *165*
Richview Golf & Country Club, *1015*
Rickenbacker Golf Club, *695*
Riddell's Bay Golf & Country Club, *1036*
Ridder Golf Club, *408*
Ridge Top Golf Course, *695*
Ridgecrest Golf Club, *277*
Ridgefield Golf Course, *165*
Ridgemark Golf & Country Club, *121*
The Ridges Golf Course, *958*
Ridgeview Golf Course, *471*
Ridgeview Ranch Golf Club, *855*
Ridgewood Golf Course, *514*
Ridgewood Lakes Golf Club, *220*
Rifle Creek Golf Course, *154*
Ringgold Golf Club, *899*
Rio Bravo Country Club, *121*
Rio Colorado Golf Course, *855*
Rio Hondo Golf Club, *121*
Rio Mar Country Club, *1042*
Rio Mimbres Country Club, *588*
Rio Rancho Golf & Country Club, *588*
Rio Rico Resort & Country Club, *61*
Rivendell Golf Club, *1015*
River Bend Golf Club (Ormond Beach, Fla.), *220*
River Bend Golf Club (Shelby, N.C.), *655*
River Bend Golf Course (Hastings, Mich.), *471*
River Bend Golf Course (Miamisburg, Ohio), *696*
River Bend Golf Course (Red Deer, Alberta), *980*
River Bend Resort, *855*
The River Club, *220*
River Club on the Ashley, *799*
River Course at the Alisal, *122*

River Creek Park Golf Course, *855*
River Downs Golfers' Club, *394*
River Falls Golf Club, *958*
River Falls Plantation, *799*
River Greens Golf Course, *696*
River Hills Country Club, *221*
River Hills Golf & Country Club, *799*
River Islands Golf Club, *822*
River Oaks Golf Club, *537*
River Oaks Golf Course, *316*
River Oaks Golf Plantation, *800*
River Oaks Municipal Golf Club, *514*
River Park Golf Club, *537*
River Place Golf Club, *855*
River Ridge Golf Club, *122*
River Road Golf Course, *1015*
River Run Golf Club, *394*
River Run Golf Course, *37*
River Run Golf Links, *221*
River Vale Country Club, *581*
River Valley Country Club, *760*
River Valley Golf Course, *356*
River View Golf Course, *122*
Riverbend Golf & Fishing Club, *999*
Riverbend Golf Complex, *920*
Riverbend Golf Course (Fort Wayne, Ind.), *341*
Riverbend Golf Course (Riverton, Utah), *873*
Riverby Hills Golf Course, *696*
Riverchase Golf Club, *856*
Riverdale Country Club, *959*
Riverdale Golf Club, *154*
Riveridge Golf Course, *728*
Rivermoor Country Club, *959*
Riverpines Golf Club, *257*
River's Bend Golf Course, *900*
River's Edge Golf Club, *38*
River's Edge Golf Course, *256*
River's Edge Golf Resort, *728*
Rivershore Golf Club, *990*
Riverside Country Club, *920*
Riverside Golf Club (Cambridge Springs, Pa.), *760*
Riverside Golf Club (Fresno, Calif.), *122*
Riverside Golf Club (Grand Prairie, Texas), *856*
Riverside Golf Club (Mason, W.Va.), *930*
Riverside Golf Club (San Angelo, Texas), *856*
Riverside Golf Course (Austin, Texas), *856*
Riverside Golf Course (Edmonton, Alberta), *980*
Riverside Golf Course (Fenton, Mo.), *537*
Riverside Golf Course (Fresno, Calif,), *122*
Riverside Golf Course (Indianapolis, Ind.), *341*
Riverside Golf Course (Janesville, Wis.), *959*
Riverside Golf Course (Pocatello, Idaho), *277*
Riverside Golf Course (Victoria, Texas), *856*
Riverside Municipal Golf Course (Portland, Maine), *384*

Riverside Municipal Golf Course (San Antonio, Texas), *857*
Riverton Country Club, *971*
Riverview Country Club, *616*
Riverview Golf Club, *548*
Riverview Highlands Golf Club, *472*
Riverway Public Golf Course, *991*
Riverwood Golf Club (Bismarck, N.Dak.), *664*
Riverwood Golf Club (Clayton, N.C.), *655*
Riverwood Golf Club (Port Charlotte, Fla.), *221*
Riverwood Golf Course, *857*
Riverwood Resort, *472*
Riviera Country Club, *221*
R.O. Speck Municipal Golf Course, *542*
Roan Valley Golf Estates, *823*
Robbers Roost Golf Course, *800*
Rochester Country Club, *565*
Rochester Hills Golf & Country Club, *472*
The Rock at Drummond Island, *472*
Rock Barn Club of Golf, *655*
Rock Creek Golf Club, *38*
Rock Creek Park Golf Course, *171*
Rock Hill Country Club, *616*
Rock Hollow Golf Club, *341*
Rock River Hills Golf Course, *959*
Rockland Golf Club, *384*
Rockland Lake State Park Golf Club, *616*
Rockledge Country Club, *166*
Rockleigh Golf Course, *581*
Rockwood Golf Course, *857*
Rockwood Park Golf Course, *999*
Rocky Fork Golf & Tennis Center, *696*
Rocky Point Golf Club, *395*
Rocky Point Golf Course, *221*
Rocky Ridge Golf Club, *882*
Rogell Golf Course, *473*
Rogers Park Golf Course, *221*
Rogue River Golf Course, *473*
Rolling Acres Golf Course, *696*
Rolling Fields Golf Course, *760*
Rolling Green Golf Club (Eighty-Four, Pa.), *761*
Rolling Green Golf Club (Huntsburg, Ohio), *696*
Rolling Green Golf Club (Sarasota, Fla.), *222*
Rolling Green Golf Course, *696*
Rolling Greens Golf Club, *581*
Rolling Hills Golf Club (Galavants Ferry, S.C.), *800*
Rolling Hills Golf Club (Hilltop Lakes, Texas), *857*
Rolling Hills Golf Club (Hudsonville, Mich.), *473*
Rolling Hills Golf Course (Bremerton, Wash.), *920*
Rolling Hills Golf Course (Godfrey, Ill.), *316*
Rolling Hills Golf Course (Hudsonville, Mich.), *473*
Rolling Hills Golf Course (Pulaski, Pa.), *761*
Rolling Hills Hotel & Golf Resort, *222*

Rolling Meadows Golf Club (Ashland, Pa.), *761*
Rolling Meadows Golf Club (Marysville, Ohio), *697*
Rolling Meadows Golf Course (Fond Du Lac, Wis.), *959*
Rolling Meadows Golf Course (Milford, Kans.), *363*
Rolling Meadows Golf Course (Whitmore Lake, Mich.), *473*
Rome Country Club, *616*
Romeo Golf & Country Club, *473*
Ron Jaworski's Eagles' Nest Country Club, *582*
Ron Jaworski's Garrisons Lake Country Club, *170*
Rondout Country Club, *616*
Rose City Municipal Golf Club, *728*
Rose Creek Golf Course, *664*
Rose Hill Country Club, *800*
Rose Lake Golf Course, *514*
Rose Park Golf Club, *874*
Rosedale Golf & Country Club, *222*
Roseland Golf & Curling Club, *1015*
Rosemont Golf & Country Club, *222*
Roseville Diamond Oaks Municipal Golf Course, *123*
Rosewood Lakes Golf Course, *557*
Ross Rogers Golf Club, *857*
Rossland Trail Country Club, *991*
Rothland Golf Course, *617*
Rotonda Golf & Country Club, *222*
Rouge Park Golf Club, *474*
Round Hill Country Club, *408*
Round Valley Country Club, *874*
Roy Kizer Golf Course, *858*
Royak Oaks Golf Course, *761*
Royal American Links Golf Club, *697*
Royal Hylands Golf Club, *341*
Royal Kunia Country Club, *270*
Royal Lakes & Country Club, *257*
Royal Meadows Golf Course, *537*
Royal New Kent Golf Club, *900*
Royal Oak Golf Club (Titusville, Fla.), *223*
Royal Oaks Golf Club (Cartersville, Ga.), *257*
Royal St. Kitts Golf Club, *1043*
Royal Scot Golf Course, *474*
Royal Scot Golf Course & Supper Club, *960*
Royal Tee Country Club, *223*
Royal Virginia Golf Club, *900*
Royal Westmoreland Golf & Country Club, *1034*
Royal Woodbine Golf Club, *1015*
Ruby View Golf Course, *557*
Ruffled Feathers Golf Club, *316*
Rum Pointe Seaside Golf Links, *395*
Rum River Hills Golf Club, *515*
Running Fox Golf Course, *697*
Rush Creek Golf Club, *515*
Rush Lake Hills Golf Club, *474*
Rustico Resort Golf & Country Club, *1019*
Rutgers University Golf Club, *582*
Rutland Country Club, *882*
Ruttger's Bay Lake Lodge, *515*

S

Sabal Point Country Club, *223*
Sable Oaks Golf Club, *384*
Saddle Creek Golf Club (Copperopolis, Calif.), *123*
Saddle Creek Golf Club (Lewisburg, Tenn.), *823*
Saddle Hill Country Club, *409*
Saddlebrook Golf Club, *342*
Saddlebrook Resort, *223*
Safari Golf Club, *697*
The Sagamore Golf Club, *617*
Sagamore Spring Golf Club, *409*
Sagamore-Hampton Golf Club, *565*
Sage Hills Golf Club, *920*
Sage Lakes Municipal Golf, *277*
St. Albans Golf Club, *697*
St. Andrews Golf & Country Club, *317*
St. Andrews Golf Club (Cedar Rapids, Iowa), *356*
St. Andrews Golf Club (Ocean Springs, Miss.), *526*
St. Andrews Golf Course, *363*
St. Andrews Valley Golf Club, *1015*
St. Anne Country Club, *409*
St. Augustine Shores Golf Club, *224*
St. Charles Golf Club, *515*
St. Clair Parkway Golf Course, *1016*
St. Clair Shores Country Club, *474*
St. Croix National Golf Club, *960*
Saint Denis Golf Course, *698*
St. George Golf Club, *874*
St. George's Golf Club, *1036*
St. Germain Municipal Golf Club, *960*
St. Ives Golf Club, *474*
Saint Joe Valley Golf Club, *475*
St. Johns County Golf Club, *224*
St. John's Golf Club, *475*
St. Johnsbury Country Club, *882*
St. Lawrence University Golf Course, *617*
St. Lucie West Country Club, *224*
St. Marlo Country Club, *257*
St. Simons Island Club, *257*
St. Stephen Golf Club, *1000*
Salem Golf Club, *728*
Salem Hills Golf & Country Club, *698*
Salem Hills Golf Club, *475*
Salina Municipal Golf Course, *363*
Salinas Fairways Golf Course, *123*
Salishan Golf Links, *728*
Salmon Creek Country Club, *617*
Salt Creek Golf Club, *342*
Salt Fork State Park Golf Course, *698*
Salt River Country Club, *475*
Saluda Valley Country Club, *800*
Samoset Resort Golf Club, *384*
San Bernardino Golf Club, *123*
San Clemente Municipal Golf Club, *124*
San Dimas Canyon Golf Club, *124*
San Geronimo Golf Course, *124*
San Ignacio Golf Club, *61*
San Jose Municipal Golf Course, *124*
San Juan Hills Country Club, *124*
San Juan Oaks Golf Club, *125*
San Luis Rey Downs Country Club, *125*

San Ramon Royal Vista Golf Club, *125*
San Saba Municipal Golf Course, *858*
San Vicente Inn & Golf Club, *125*
Sanctuary Golf Club, *617*
The Sanctuary Golf Course, *317*
Sand Barrens Golf Club, *582*
Sand Creek Golf Club, *277*
Sand Springs Municipal Golf Course, *716*
Sandals Golf & Country Club, *1038*
Sandalwood Country Club, *960*
Sandelie Golf Course, *729*
Sandestin Resort, *224*
Sandpines Golf Links, *729*
Sandpiper Bay Golf & Country Club, *655*
Sandpiper Golf & Country Club, *225*
Sandpiper Golf Course, *126*
Sandridge Golf Club, *225*
Sandy Brae Golf Course, *930*
Sandy Burr Country Club, *409*
Sandy Hollow Golf Course, *317*
Sandy Lane Golf Club, *1034*
Sandy Pines Golf Course, *342*
Sandy Ridge Golf Course (Colfax, N.C.), *656*
Sandy Ridge Golf Course (Midland, Mich.), *475*
Santa Ana Golf Club, *588*
Santa Ana Golf Course, *126*
Santa Barbara Golf Club, *126*
Santa Clara Golf & Tennis Club, *126*
Santa Maria Golf Course, *379*
Santa Rita Golf Club, *61*
Santa Rosa Golf & Beach Club, *225*
Santa Teresa Golf Club, *127*
Santee National Golf Club, *801*
Santiam Golf Club, *729*
Sapphire Mountain Golf Club, *656*
Sapulpa Municipal Golf Course, *716*
Sarah Shank Golf Course, *342*
Sarasota Golf Club, *226*
Saratoga Golf Club, *972*
Saratoga Spa Golf Course, *618*
Sartell Golf Club, *515*
Saskatoon Golf Club, *475*
Sauganash Country Club, *476*
Saugeen Golf Club, *1016*
Saukie Municipal Golf Course, *317*
Sault Ste. Marie Country Club, *476*
Savannahs at Sykes Creek Golf Club, *226*
Sawgrass Country Club, *226*
Sawmill Creek Golf & Racquet Club, *698*
Sawmill Golf Club, *516*
Saxon Golf Course, *761*
Saxton Woods Golf Course, *618*
Scarlett Oaks Country Club, *931*
Scenic Country Club, *476*
Scenic Hills Country Club, *226*
Scenic Valley Country Club, *960*
The SCGA Members' Club at Rancho California, *123*
Schalamar Creek Golf & Country Club, *226*
Schaumburg Golf Club, *318*
Schenectady Golf Course, *618*
Scherwood Golf Course, *342*

Springbrook Public Golf Club, 259
Springdale Country Club, 658
Springdale Golf Club, 764
Springfield Oaks Golf Course, 478
Springhouse Golf Club, 823
Springs at Radium Golf Course, 992
The Springs Golf Club Resort, 963
Spruce Creek Country Club, 229
Spruce Meadows Golf & Country Club, 981
Spunky Creek Country Club, 717
Spyglass Hill Golf Course, 131
Squamish Valley Golf & Country Club, 992
Squaw Creek Golf Course, 357
Squaw Valley Golf Course, 860
Squires Country Club, 963
Squirrel Run Golf & Country Club, 410
Stagg Hill Golf Club, 364
Standing Stone Golf Club, 764
Stanhope Golf & Country Club, 1019
Stanley Golf Club, 167
Stansbury Park Golf Club, 875
Star Hill Golf & Country Club, 658
Star Valley Ranch Country Club, 972
Starr Pass Golf Club, 63
State College Elks Country Club, 764
States Golf Course, 478
Steele Canyon Golf Club, 132
Steeple Chase Golf Club, 321
Steinbach Fly-In Golf Course, 995
Stephen F. Austin Golf Course, 860
Sterling Farms Golf Club, 167
Stevens Park Golf Course, 860
Stevinson Ranch Golf Club, 132
Stillwaters Resort Golf Course, 38
Stone Creek Golf Club, 259
Stone Hedge Country Club, 764
Stone Mountain Park Golf Course, 259
Stonebridge Golf Club (Ann Arbor, Mich.), 478
Stonebridge Golf Club (Martinsburg, W.Va.), 931
Stonebridge Golf Club (Monroe, N.C.), 658
Stonebridge Golf Club (Rome, Ga.), 260
Stonebridge Golf Course, 823
Stonebrooke Golf Club, 517
Stonecreek, The Golf Club, 63
Stonehedge Golf Course, 479
Stonehenge Golf Club, 824
Stoneleigh Golf Club, 902
Stoneridge Golf Club & Resort, 278
Stoneridge Golf Course, 729
Stonewater Golf Club, 701
Stonewolf Golf Club, 321
Stoney Creek Golf Club, 658
Stoney Mountain Golf Course, 39
Stoney Point Golf Club, 802
Stony Creek Golf Course, 479
Stony Ford Golf Club, 621
Storey Creek Golf Club, 992
Storybrook Country Club, 321
Stoughton Acres Golf Club, 765
Stow Acres Country Club, 410
Stowe Country Club, 882

Stratton Mountain Country Club, 883
Stumpy Lake Golf Club, 902
Sudden Valley Golf & Country Club, 922
Suffolk Golf Course, 902
Sugar Bush Golf Course, 701
Sugar Creek Golf Course, 701
Sugar Hill Country Club, 229
Sugar Hill Golf Club, 260
Sugar Isle Golf Country, 701
Sugar Loaf Resort Golf Club, 479
Sugar Ridge Golf Club, 343
Sugar Springs Country Club, 479
Sugarbrooke Golf Club, 517
Sugarbush Golf Club, 480
Sugarbush Golf Course, 883
Sugarcreek Golf Course, 701
Sugarloaf Golf Club (Carrabassett Valley, Maine), 384
Sugarloaf Golf Club (Sugarloaf, Pa.), 765
Sugartree Golf Club, 861
Sugarwood Golf Club, 931
Sultan's Run Golf Course, 344
Summerfield Golf Club, 230
Summerheights Golf Links, 1016
Summerland Golf & Country Club, 992
Summersett Golf Club, 803
Summerside Golf Club, 1019
Summertree Golf Club, 344
Summit Pointe Golf Club, 132
Sumner Meadows Golf Links, 922
Sun City Las Vegas Golf Club, 557
Sun City Palm Desert Golf Club, 132
Sun City Vistoso Golf Club, 63
Sun Dance Golf Course, 922
Sun Lakes Country Club, 133
Sun Prairie Golf Course, 963
Sun Valley Golf Course, 538
Sun Valley Resort Golf Course, 278
Sun Willows Golf Club, 922
Sunbrook Golf Club, 876
Sundance Golf Club, 517
Sunflower Hills Golf Club, 364
Sunken Meadow State Park Golf Club, 621
Sunkist Country Club, 526
Sunland Golf & Country Club, 923
Sunnybreeze Golf Course, 230
Sunnybrook Golf Club, 480
Sunnyhill Golf Club, 702
Sunnyvale Golf Course, 133
Sunol Valley Golf Course, 133
Sunridge Canyon Golf Club, 64
Sunrise Country Club, 230
Sunrise Golf Club, 230
Sunrise Vista Golf Club, 558
Sunriver Lodge & Resort, 730
Sunset Golf Course, 765
Sunset Hills Golf Course, 717
Sunset Ranch Golf & Country Club, 992
Sunset Valley Golf Club, 321
Sunset Valley Golf Course, 583
Suntides Golf Course, 923
Super Clubs Golf Club at Runaway Bay, 1038
Superior National Golf Course, 517
Superstition Springs Golf Club, 64

Tiara Rado Golf Course, *156*
Tiburon Golf Club, *549*
The Tides Inn, *903*
Tides Lodge, *903*
Tidewater Golf Club, *803*
Tierra del Sol Country Club, *1034*
Tierra del Sol Golf Club (California City, Calif.), *135*
Tierra del Sol Golf Club (Lady Lake, Fla.), *231*
Tierra del Sol Golf Course, *588*
Tierra Santa Golf Club, *862*
Tiger Point Golf & Country Club, *231*
Tijeras Creek Golf Club, *135*
Tijuana Country Club, *1026*
Tilden Park Golf Course, *135*
Timacuan Golf & Country Club, *232*
Timarron Golf & Country Club, *862*
Timber Creek Golf Course, *518*
Timber Point Golf Course, *623*
Timber Ridge Golf Club (Mount Pleasant, Pa.), *766*
Timber Ridge Golf Club (Talladega, Ala.), *39*
Timber Ridge Golf Course, *483*
Timber Trails Country Club, *322*
Timber-View Golf Course, *863*
Timbercreek Golf Club, *39*
Timberlake Plantation Golf Club, *803*
Timberlin Golf Club, *168*
Timberline Golf Course, *357*
The Timbers Golf Club, *483*
The Timbers of Troy, *396*
Timberton Golf Club, *527*
Tioga Country Club, *623*
Tipsinah Mounds Golf Course, *518*
Tipton Municipal Golf Course, *345*
T.O. Fuller Golf Course, *824*
Toad Valley Public Golf Course, *357*
Toana Vista Golf Course, *558*
Toftrees Resort, *766*
Tokatee Golf Club, *730*
Tom O'Leary Golf Course, *664*
Tomac Woods Golf Course, *483*
Tomahawk Hills Golf Club, *364*
Tomasso's Chemung Golf Course, *623*
Tomoka Oaks Golf & Country Club, *232*
Tonto Verde Golf Club, *65*
Tony Butler Golf Course, *863*
Tony Lema Golf Course, *136*
Top O Scott Golf Course, *730*
Topeka Public Golf Club, *365*
Torres Blancas Golf Club, *65*
Torrey Pines Golf Course, *136*
Torrington Municipal Golf Course, *972*
Tour 18, *863*
Tour 18 Golf Club, *863*
Tournament Players Club at the Canyons, *558*
Tournament Players Club at Heron Bay, *232*
Tournament Players Club at Sawgrass, *232*
Tournament Players Club of Scottsdale, *65*
Tournament Players Club of Tampa Bay, *233*

Towanda Country Club, *766*
Town of Wallkill Golf Club, *623*
Towne Lake Hills Golf Club, *260*
Tracy Golf & Country Club, *136*
Tradition Golf Club, *803*
Tramark Golf Course, *527*
Trapp River Golf Club, *964*
Trappers Turn Golf Club, *964*
Treasure Cay Golf Club, *1034*
Treasure Lake Golf Club, *766*
Tree Links Golf Course, *704*
Treeline Golf Club, *864*
Treetops Sylvan Resort, *483*
Tremblant Golf Resort, *1022*
Tres Vidas Acapulco Golf Course, *1029*
Tri County Country Club, *623*
Tri County Golf Club, *345*
Tri-City Country Club, *923*
Tri-City Golf Course, *876*
Tri-Mountain Golf Course, *924*
Tri-Way Golf Club, *345*
Trickle Creek Golf Resort, *993*
Triggs Memorial Golf Course, *773*
Trini Alvarez El Rio Municipal Golf Course, *66*
Triple Lakes Golf Course, *323*
Troon North Golf Club, *66*
Trosper Park Golf Course, *718*
Trotters Glen Golf Course, *396*
Trout Lake Golf & Country Club, *965*
True Blue, *804*
Trull Brook Golf Course, *411*
The Truro Golf Club, *1003*
The Tryall Club, Resort & Villas, *1039*
Trysting Tree Golf Club, *731*
Tubac Golf Resort, *66*
Tuckaway Golf Course, *323*
Tumwater Valley Golf Club, *924*
Tunxis Plantation Country Club, *168*
Turbot Hills Golf Course, *767*
Turf Valley Hotel & Country Club, *396*
Turkey Creek Country Club, *345*
Turkey Creek Golf Course, *365*
Turkey Run Golf Course, *345*
Turkeyfoot Lake Golf Links, *704*
Turnberry Golf Course, *705*
Turnberry Isle Resort & Club, *233*
Turnbull Bay Golf Course, *233*
Turtle Creek Golf Club (Burlington, Mich.), *484*
Turtle Creek Golf Club (Rockledge, Fla.), *233*
Turtle Hill Golf Course, *864*
Turtleback Golf & Conference Center, *965*
Tuscumbia Golf Club, *965*
Tustin Ranch Golf Club, *136*
Twelve Bridges Golf Club, *137*
Twin Birch Golf Course, *484*
Twin Brooks Golf Club, *484*
Twin Creeks Golf Club, *864*
Twin Falls Municipal Golf Course, *279*
Twin Falls State Park Golf Course, *931*
Twin Falls Village Golf Course, *279*
Twin Hills Country Club, *168*
Twin Lakes Country Club, *965*

W

Notes

Notes

Notes

Notes